Personalities

Of The South

Eleventh Edition

published by:

the **American Biographical Institute**

a division of
Historical Preservations of America, Inc.
205 West Martin Street, Post Office Box 226, Raleigh, North Carolina 27602 USA

Library of Congress Catalog Card Number
73-4535

International Standard Book Number
0-934544-04-2

Printed and bound in the United States of America
by
Kingsport Press, Inc., Kingsport, Tennessee, USA

Table of Contents

Preface

The American Biographical Institute presents the Eleventh Edition of *PERSONALITIES OF THE SOUTH*. This volume continues the tradition of recognizing efforts and documenting valuable biographical facts within the South. All entries reflect essential contributions of the individual to all levels of Southern effort and reflect the leadership of this region in fields of professional, civic, cultural, religious, governmental, personal, scientific and educational endeavor.

A new State-Locator Index of all listed biographees is a specialized feature of this volume. There is also a Roster of Honorary Editorial Advisory Board Consultants, ABI Fellows, the American Biographical Institute Research Association Roster, along with deliniative information regarding this series.

Recommendations for *PERSONALITIES OF THE SOUTH* are received from our own Media Research Department, Governing Board of Editors, Board of Directors and nationwide advisors. Nominations are also filed from national universities and colleges; national, state and local professional organizations; service, civic and social organizations; individuals; businesses; and biographees themselves. Nominees are contacted and personal submissions are reviewed by the Governing Board of Editors. Editorial evaluation is the ultimate determinant of publication selection; there is no listing fee. All personal materials are handled with utmost professionality and all files of the Institute are kept in strictest confidence and security in the ABI Library and Record Center.

The Eleventh Edition of *PERSONALITIES OF THE SOUTH* will be an authoritative guide for historians, genealogists, press reporters, biographers, librarians, students, professional and general researchers, scholars, business consultants and general inquirers. Expertise from a fourteen year reputation of quality in producing several national publications qualifies the Institute with the ability and provides it with the overall scope to be knowledgeable, objective and selective in the achievements of the South. Our editors endeavored to compile a balanced, professional and inclusive representation of the South, including approximately 6000 individuals in editorial content.

I express appreciation to all individuals who contributed to the development and production of this volume. The Governing Board of Editors congratulates those individuals selected for the following pages.

J. S. Thomson
Editor-in-Chief
Chairman, Governing Board of Editors
The American Biographical Institute

ABI Biographical Titles

Community Leaders of America
Notable Americans
Personalities of America
Personalities of the South
Personalities of the West and Midwest
The Book of Honor
The American Registry Series
International Youth in Achievement
The Directory of Distinguished Americans

Delineative Information

Individual biographical entries are arranged according to standard alphabetical practice and information for publication is consistently and uniformly presented in the categorical order as below. Coding symbols are clarified below as well.

Editors of the Institute make all attempts to edit accurately the information furnished by each biographee. In the rare event of an error by the publisher, the sole responsibility of the publisher will be to correct such in the subsequent edition of the publication.

Editorial evaluation is the ultimate determinant of publication selection. Admission in this series is based on the value of achievement or recognized outreach of endeavor.

All submissions and files at the Institute are maintained in confidence and adequate security.

Biographical Codes

oc/	Occupation		ed/	Education
b/	Birth		mil/	Military Service
h/	Home Address		pa/	Professional Activities
ba/	Business Address		cp/	Civic & Political Activities
m/	Married-Wife or Husband		r/	Religious Activities
c/	Children		hon/	Other Honors & Activities, etc.
p/	Parents			

Table of Abbreviations

The Following Abbreviations and Symbols Are Frequently Used in This Compilation

AA	Associate of Arts	Am	American, America
AAAS	American Association for the Advancement of Science	AM	Master of Arts
		AMA	American Medical Association
AAC	Army Air Corps	AME	African Methodist Episcopal
AAF	Army Air Force		
AAHE	American Association of Higher Ed	Am Inst EE	American Institute of Electrical Engineers
AAHPER	American Association of Health, Physical Education and Recreation	Am Soc CE	American Society of Civil Engineers
		Am Soc ME	Am Soc of Mechanical Engineers
AART	American Academy of Radiology Technicians	Anal	Analysis, Analyst
AASA	American Academy of School Administrators	Anesth	Anesthesiologist
		ANG	Army National Guard
AAUA	American Association of University Administrators	Anniv	Anniversary
		AP	Associated Press
		APGA	American Personnel and Guidance Association
AAUP	American Association of University Professors	Apr	April
AAUW	American Association of University Women	Apprec	Appreciate, Appreciation
		Approp	Appropriations
AB	Bachelor of Arts	Appt	Appointment
ABA	American Bar Association	Appt'd	Appointed
Acad	Academy, Academic	Apt	Apartment
Acct	Accountant	ARC	American Red Cross
Acctg	Accounting	Arch	Architect, Architecture
Achmt	Achievement	Ariz	Arizona
ACLU	American Civil Liberties Union	ArM	Master of Architecture
		Ark	Arkansas
Activs	Activities	Art	Article, Artillery
Addit	Additional	ASAS	American Society for the Advancement of Science
Adj	Adjunct		
Adm	Administration, Administrative	ASCAP	American Society of Composers, Authors, and Publishers
Admr	Administrator		
Adv	Advisory	ASHA	American Speech and Hearing Association
Advmt	Advancement		
Advr	Advisor	Assessmt	Assessment
Advtg	Advertising	Assn	Association
Aeronaut	Aeronautical	Assoc	Associate
AESP	Association of Elementary School Principals	ASSP	Associaton of Secondary School Principals
AF	Air Force	Asst	Assistant, Assistance
AFB	Air Force Base	Astronom	Astronomy, Astronomical
AFCW	American Federation of Colored Women	Ath	Athlete, Athletic
		Atl	Atlantic
Affil	Affiliate, Affiliation	Att'd, Att'g	Attended, Attending
Agri	Agriculture	Atty	Attorney
Agst	Against	Aug	August
Agt	Agent	AUS	United States Army
Agy	Agency	Auth	Authority
AIA	American Institute of Architects	Aux	Auxiliary
		A-V	Audio-Visual
Ala	Alabama	Ave	Avenue
Alt	Alternate	AWC	American Women Composers

TABLE OF ABBREVIATIONS

The Following Abbreviations and Symbols Are Frequently Used in This Compilation

Awd	Award	Cand	Candidate
Awd'd	Awarded	Capt	Captain
		Cardiovas	Cardiovascular
BA	Bachelor of Arts	Cath	Catholic
Bach	Bachelor	Cav	Cavalry
Balto	Baltimore	CB	Bachelor of Surgery,
Bapt	Baptist		Citizen Band
B Agr	Bachelor of Agriculture	CC	Country Clb
B Arch	Bachelor of Architecture	CDA	Catholic Daughters of
Bat	Batallion		America
BBA	Bachelor of Business	CE	Chemical Engineer
	Administration	CEC	Council for Exceptional
BBB	Better Business Bureau		Children
BC	Bachelor of Chemistry	Cert	Certificate, Certification
BCE	Bachelor of Chemical	Ch	Church
	Engineering	Champ(s)	Champion(s)
Bch	Beach	Chapt	Chapter
BCL	Bachelor of Civil Law	Chatta	Chattanooga
Bd	Board	ChD	Doctor of Chemistry
BD	Bachelor of Divinity	Chd	Children
BDS	Bachelor of Dental Surgery	ChE	Chemical Engineer
BE	Bachelor of Education,	Chem	Chemical, Chemist
	Engineering	Chiro	Chiropractic
BEE	Bachelor of Electrical	Chm	Chairman
	Engineering	Chperson	Chairperson
BF	Bachelor of Finance	CIA	Central Intelligence
B'ham	Birmingham		Agency
Bibliog	Bibliography,	Cinc	Cincinnati
	Bibliographical	Cir	Circle
Bicent	Bicentennial	Cit	Citation
Biog	Biography	Clb	Club
Biol	Biology, Biological	Clin	Clinic, Clinical
Bk, Bkg, Bkr	Bank, Banking, Banker	Clk	Clerk
Bkkpg	Bookkeeping	Cmdr	Commander
Bkkpr	Bookkeeper	Cnslg	Counseling
Bklyn	Brooklyn	Cnslr	Counselor
Bldg	Building	Co	County
Bldr	Builder	CO	Commanding Officer
BLit	Bachelor of Literature	CoChm	Co-Chairman
BLS	Bachelor of Library	C of C	Chamber of Commerce
	Science	Col	College, Collegiate,
Blvd	Boulevard		Colonel
BM	Bachelor of Medicine	Com	Committee
BMus	Bachelor of Music	Comdg	Commanding
BPd, BPe	Bachelor of Physical	Comm	Commission
	Education	Com-man	Committeeman
BPW	Business and Professional	Commend	Commendation
	Women	Commr	Commissioner
Br	Branch	Commun	Community
Brit	Britain, British	Communs	Communications
BS	Bachelor of Science	Com-wom	Committeewoman
BSA	Boy Scouts of America	Conf	Conference
BSc	Bachelor of Science	Cong	Congress
BSED	Bachelor of Science in	Congl	Congressional
	Education	Cong of P's	Congress of Parents and
BT, BTh	Bachelor of Theology	& T's	Teachers
Bultn	Bulletin	Congreg	Congregational
Bur	Bureau	Conserv	Conservation
Bus	Business	Conslt	Consultant
		Consltg	Consulting
Cal	California	Consol	Consolidated

TABLE OF ABBREVIATIONS

The Following Abbreviations and Symbols Are Frequently Used in This Compilation

Constit	Constitution
Constrn	Construction
Cont'd, Cont'g	Continued, Continuing
Contbr	Contributor
Contbtg	Contributing
Conv	Convention
Coop	Cooperation
Coor	Coordinator, Coordinating
Corp	Corporation
Corr	Corresponding, Correspondence
Cosmetol	Cosmetology, Cosmetologist
Coun	Council
Creat & Success Person-alities	Creative and Successful Personalities of the World
CPA	Certified Public Accountant
Cpl	Corporal
CPR	Cardio-Pulmonary Resuscitation
Crim	Criminal
CSB	Bachelor of Christian Science
Ct	Court
Ctl	Central
Ctr	Center
Cult	Cultural
Curric	Curriculum
DAC	Daughters of the American Colonists
DAR	Daughters of the American Revolution
Daugh	Daughter
DAV	Disabled American Veterans
DC	District of Columbia
DCL	Doctor of Canon Law
DD	Doctor of Divinity
DDS	Doctor of Dental Surgery
Dec	December
dec	Deceased
Def	Defense
Deg	Degree
Del	Delegate
Dem	Democrat
Denom	Denomination, Denominational
Dept	Department
Delinq	Delinquent, Delinquency
Dermatol	Dermatology, Dermatologist
Desc	Descendant
Devel	Development
DIB	Dictionary of International Biography
Dic	Dictionary
Dipl	Diploma
Dir	Director, Directory
Dis	Disease

Dist	District
Dist'd	Distinguished
Distn	Distinction
Div	Division, Divinity
DLit, DLitt	Doctor of Literature, Letters
DLS	Doctor of Library Science
DMD	Doctor of Dental Medicine
DMus	Doctor of Music
DO	Doctor of Osteopathy
Doct	Doctoral
Dr	Drive, Doctor
DS, DSc	Doctor of Science
DTh, DTheol	Doctor of Theology
DVM	Doctor of Veterinary Medicine
E	East
Ec	Economics
Ecol	Ecology
Ed	Education
EdB	Bachelor of Education
EdD	Doctor of Education
Edit	Editorial
EdM	Master of Education
Ednl	Educational
Edr	Educator
EE	Electrical Engineer
Elect	Electrical, Electric Electronics
Elem	Elementary
Emer	Emergency
Employmt	Employment
EMR	Educable Mentally Retarded
EMT	Emergency Medical Technician
Ency	Encyclopedia
Eng	English
EngD	Doctor of Engineering
Engr	Engineer
Engrg	Engineering
Entomol	Entomology
Envir	Environment, Environmental
Epis	Episcopal
Equipmt	Equipment
Est	Establish
Establishmt	Establishment
ETO	European Theater of Operations
Eval	Evaluation
Evang	Evangelical
Exam	Examination
Examr	Examiner
Exc	Exchange
Exec	Executive
Ext	Extension
FAA	Federal Aviation Agency
Fac	Faculty

TABLE OF ABBREVIATIONS

The Following Abbreviations and Symbols Are Frequently Used in This Compilation

Fam	Family	Ia	Ia
F&AM	Free and Accepted Mason	IBM	International Business Machines
FBI	Federal Bureau of Investigation	IEEE	Institute of Electrical and Electronic Engineers
FCC	Federal Communications Commission	Ill	Illinois
FDA	Federal Drug Administration	Inc	Incorporated
		incl	Include
Fdg	Founding	incl'g	Including
Fdn	Federation	Indep	Independent, Independence
Fdr	Founder	Indiv	Individual
Feb	February	Indpls	Indianapolis
Fed	Federal	Indust	Industry
Fest	Festival	Inf	Infantry
FFA	Future Farmers of America	Info	Information
		Ins	Insurance
FHA	Future Homemakers of America	Insp	Inspector
		Inst	Institute
Fin	Finance	Instn	Institution
Foun	Foundation	Instnl	Institutional
Frat	Fraternity	Instr	Instructor
Ft	Fort	Instrn	Instruction
Ftball	Football	Intell	Intelligence
FTC	Federal Trade Commission	Intells	Intellectuals
Furn	Furniture	Intl	International
FWB	Free Will Baptist	Intercont	Intercontinental
		Intergovtl	Intergovernmental
		Interpret	Interpretation
Ga	Georgia	Invest	Investigation
GA's	Girls' Auxiliary	Investmt	Investment
GE	General Electric	IOOF	Independent Order of ODD FELLOWS
Gen	General		
Geneal	Genealogy, Genealogical	IPA	International Platform Association
Geo	George		
Geog	Geography, Geographical	IRA	International Reading Association
Geol	Geological		
Gov	Governor	IRS	Internal Revenue Service
Govt	Government	Isl	Island
Govtl	Governmental		
Grad	Graduate, Graduated		
GSA	Girl Scouts of America	Jan	January
Gtr	Greater	JCD	Doctor of Canon Law
Guid	Guidance	JD	Doctor of Law
Gyn	Gynecology	jg	Junior Grade
		Jour	Journal, Journalism
Hd	Head	Jr	Junior
Hdqtrs	Headquarters	Jt	Joint
Hgts	Heights	Jud	Judicial, Judiciary
Hi	Hawaii	Judic	Judicature
Hist	History	Jul	July
Histn	Historian	Jun	June
Hlth	Health	Jurisd	Jurisdiction
Hon	Honor, Honorable	Jurisp	Jurisprudence
Hort	Horticulture	J of P	Justice of the Peace
Hosp	Hospital	Juv	Juvenile
HPER	Health, Physical Education and Recreation	Juv Delinq	Juvenile Delinquent
HS	High School	K	Knights
HUD	Housing and Urban Development	Kgn	Kindergarten
		K of C	Knights of Columbus
Hwy	Highway	K of G	Knights of the Garter
		K of P	Knights of Pythias

TABLE OF ABBREVIATIONS

The Following Abbreviations and Symbols Are Frequently Used in This Compilation

Ks	Kansas	Me	Maine
Ky	Kentucky	Mech	Mechanical
		Med	Medical, Medicine
La	Louisiana	MEd	Master of Education
LA	Los Angeles	Mem	Member
Lab	Laboratory	Meml	Memorial
Lang	Language	MENC	Music Educators National
Laryngol	Laryngological		Conference
LB	Bachelor of Letters	Merch	Merchant
LCA	Lutheran Church of	Metall	Metallurgical
	America	Meth	Methodist
LD	Learning Disabilities	Metro	Metropolitan
Ldg	Leading	Mfg	Manufacturing
Ldr	Leader	Mfr	Manufacturer
Ldrship	Leadership	Mgmt	Management
LDS	Latter Day Saints	Mgr	Manager
Leag	League	Mil	Military
Lectr	Lecturer	Min	Minister, Ministry
Legis	Legislative, Legislature,	Minn	Minnesota
	Legislator, Legislation	Misc	Miscellaneous
LHD	Doctor of Humanities	Miss	Mississippi
LI	Long Island	Mkt	Market
Lib	Library	Mktg	Marketing
Libn	Librarian	Mng	Managing
Lic	License	Mo	Missouri
Lic'd	Licensed	mo, mos	Month, Months
Lit	Literary, Literature	Mod	Modern
Lit(t)B	Bachelor of Literature,	Mont	Montana
	Letters	MPd	Master of Pedagogy
Lit(t)D	Doctor of Literature,	MPE	Master of Physical
	Letters		Education
LLB	Bachelor of Laws	MS, MSc	Master of Science
LLD	Doctor of Laws	MS	Multiple Sclerosis
Ln	Lane, Loan	Mt	Mount
Lng	Learning	Mtl	Mental
Lt	Lieutenant	Mtly	Mentally
Ltd	Limited	Mtn	Mountain
Lttrs	Letters	Mun	Municipal
Luth	Lutheran	Mus	Museum
LWC	League of Women Composers	MusB	Bachelor of Music
LWV	League of Women Voters	Mut	Mutual
Lwyr	Lawyer	Mvt	Movement
MA	Master of Arts	N	North
Mag	Magazine	NAACP	National Association for
MAgr	Master of Agriculture		the Advancement of
Maj	Major		Colored People
Mar	March	NAHPER	National Association of
MArch	Master of Architecture		Health, Physical Educa-
Mat(s)	Material(s)		tion and Recreation
Math	Mathematics	NAm	North America
MB	Bachelor of Medicine	NASA	National Aeronautical and
MBA	Master of Business		Space Administration
	Administrator	Nat	National
Mbrship	Membership	N Atl	North Atlantic
MC	Master of Ceremonies	Nat Reg Prom Ams	National Register of
MCL	Master of Civil Law		Prominent Americans
Md	Maryland	Nav	Naval
MDiv	Master of Divinity	NBC	National Broadcasting
MDS	Master of Dental Surgery		Company
Mdse	Merchandise	NC	North Carolina

TABLE OF ABBREVIATIONS

The Following Abbreviations and Symbols Are Frequently Used in This Compilation

NCNW	National Council of Negro Women	PdB	Bachelor of Pedagogy
NCPGA	North Carolina Personnel and Guidance Association	PDM	Master of Pedagogy
		PE	Physical Education
NCTE, NCTM	National Council of Teachers of English, Math	PeD	Doctor of Pedagogy
		Perf	Performance
ND	North Dakota	Period	Periodical
NE	Northeast	Perm	Permanent
NEA	National Education Association	Pers	Personnel
		Pgh	Pittsburgh
Neb	Nebraska	PharB	Bachelor of Pharmacy
Neurol	Neurology, Neurological	PharD	Doctor of Pharmacy
NG	National Guard	Pharm	Pharmacy, Pharmacist, Pharmacology
NH	New Hampshire		
NJ	New Jersey	PharmM	Master of Pharmacy
NIH	National Institute of Health	PhB	Bachelor of Philosophy
No	Northern	PhD	Doctor of Philosophy
NO	New Orleans	Phil	Philosophy
Nom	Nominee	Phila	Philadelphia
Nom'd, Nom'g	Nominated, Nominating	Philharm	Philharmonic
NM	New Mexico	Photo	Photography
NSA	National Security Agency	Photog	Photographer
NSAC	National Society for Autistic Children	Phy	Physical
		Phys	Physician
Nsg	Nursing	Physiol	Physiologist
NSF	National Science Foundation	Pk	Park
		Pkwy	Parkway
Num	Numerous	Pl	Place
NW	Northwest	Placemt	Placement
NY	New York	PO	Post Office
NYC	New York City	PodD	Doctor of Podiatry
		Polit	Political, Politics
		Pop	Population
OAS	Organization of American States	PR	Puerto Rico
Ob	Obstetrics, Obstetrician	Pract	Practice
Occup	Occupation, Occupational	Precnt	Precinct
OCS	Officer Candidate School	Predoct	Predoctoral
Oct	October	Premed	Premedical
OD	Doctor of Optometry	Pres	President, Presidential
OES	Order of Eastern Star	Presb	Presbyterian
Ofc	Office	Presby	Presbytery
Ofcl	Official	Preven	Prevention
Ofcr	Officer	Prin	Principal
OLC	Oak Leaf Cluster	Prob	Problem
Opports	Opportunities	Prod	Product
Opthal	Opthalmology	Prodn	Production
Optom	Optometry, Optometrist	Prodr	Producer
Orch	Orchestra	Prof	Professor
Org	Organization	Profl	Professional
Org'd	Organized	Prog	Program, Progress
Orgnl	Organizational	Proj	Project
Orgr	Organizer	Prom	Prominent
Orient	Orientation	Prot	Protestant
Orig	Original	Protem	Pro tempore
Ornithol	Ornithology	Psycho	Psychology, Psychologist
Ortho	Orthopedic, Orthopedist	Psychi	Psychiatry, Psychiatrist
Outstg	Outstanding	PTA	Parents and Teachers Association
Pa	Pennsylvania	PTO	Pacific Theater of Operations, Parents and Teachers Organization
Parliamentn	Parliamentarian		
Path	Pathology, Pathologist	Pt-time	Parttime

TABLE OF ABBREVIATIONS

The Following Abbreviations and Symbols Are Frequently Used in This Compilation

Pub	Publish, Publication	Ser	Service
Pub'd	Published	Sev	Several
Pubr	Publisher	Sgt	Sergeant
Pvt	Private	SI	Staten Island
		SJD	Doctor of Judicial Science
QMC	Quartermaster Corps	SM	Master of Science
Qtr(s)	Quarter(s)	So	Southern
Qtrly	Quarterly	Soc	Society
Que	Quebec	Sociol	Sociology
		Spch	Speech
Radiol	Radiology	Spec	Special, Specialist
RAF	Royal Air Force	Spkg	Speaking
RCAF	Royal Canadian Air Force	Spkr	Speaker
Rd	Road	Sprgs	Springs
Rdg	Reading	Sq	Square
Real Est	Real Estate	Sqdrn	Squadron
Rec	Recreation	Sr	Senior
Rec'd	Received	SS	Sunday School
Recog	Recognition	S/Sgt	Staff Sergeant
Reg	Regional, Region	St	State, Street, Saint
Reg'd	Registered	Sta	Station
Rehab	Rehabilitation	Stab	Stabilization
Rel	Religion	Stat	Statistic, Statistician
Relats	Relations	STB	Bachelor of Sacred Theology
Rep	Representative		
Repub	Republican	STD	Doctor of Sacred Theology
Res	Research		
Reschr	Researcher	Subcom	Subcommittee
Resv	Reserve	Subst	Substitute
Retard	Retarded, Retardation	Sum	Summer
Ret'd	Retired	Supr Ct	Supreme Court
Rev	Reverend	Supt	Superintendent
RN	Registered Nurse	Supvn	Supervision
RR	Rural Route, Railroad	Supvr	Supervisor
Rt	Route	Surg	Surgeon, Surgery
Rts	Rights	Symp	Symposium
Rwy	Railway	Symph	Symphony
		Sys	System
S	South		
SF	San Francisco	TB	Tuberculosis
SAR	Sons of the American Revolution	Tchg	Teaching
		Tchr	Teacher
Sask	Saskatchewan	Tech	Technicial, Technician
Savs	Savings	Technol	Technology, Technologist
Savs & Ln	Savings and Loan	Temp	Temporary
SB	Bachelor of Science	Terr	Terrace
SCA	Speech Communication Association	ThD	Doctor of Theology
		Theol	Theology
ScD, SD	Doctor of Science	TMR	Trainable Mentally Retarded
Sch	School		
Sci	DScience	Tnd	Trained
Scis	Sciences	Tng	Training
Scist(s)	Scientist(s)	Tnr	Trainer
ScM	Master of Science	Tour	Tournament
SDA	Seventh-Day Adventist	Trans	Transportation
Sec'dy	Secondary	Treas	Treasurer
Sect	Section	T&T	Telephone & Telegraph
Secy	Secretary	TV	Television
Sel	Selective	Twp	Township
Sem	Seminar, Seminary		
Sept	September	U	United

TABLE OF ABBREVIATIONS

The Following Abbreviations and Symbols Are Frequently Used in This Compilation

UDC	United Daughters of the Confederacy	VFW	Veterans of Foreign Wars
UF	United Fund	VI	Virgin Islands
UN	United Nations	VMD	Doctor of Veterinary Medicine
UNESCO	United Nations Educational, Science and Cultural Organization	Voc	Vocational
		Vol	Volunteer
		VP	Vice President
UNICEF	United Nations International Childrens Emergency Fund	Vt	Vermont
		W	West
UMW	United Methodist Women	w	With
Univ	University	WAC	Women's Army Corps
UPI	United Press International	Wash	Washington
US	United States	WAVES	Women's United States Naval Reserves
USA	United States Army		
USAAC	United States Army Air Corps	Wed	Wednesday
		Wel	Welfare
USAAF	United States Army Air Force	WHO	World Health Organization
		Wis	Wisconsin
USAF	United States Air Force	Wk	Week
USAFR	United States Air Force Reserve	Wkr	Worker
		Wkly	Weekly
USAR	United States Army Reserve	Wkshop	Workshop
		Wm	William
USASC	United States Army Signal Corps	WOW	Woodmen of the World
		WSCS	Women's Society of Christian Service
USCG	United States Coast Guard		
USMC	United States Marine Corps	WVa	West Virginia
USMM	United States Merchant Marine	W/W	Who's Who
		W/W Fin & Indust	Who's Who in Finance and Industry
USN	United States Navy		
USNR	United States Naval Reserve	W/W MW	Who's Who in the Midwest
		Wyo	Wyoming
USPHS	United States Public Health Service		
		Yg	Young
USS	United States Ship	Ygst	Youngest
USSR	Union of Soviet Socialist Republic	YMCA	Young Men's Christian Association
		YMHA	Young Men's Hebrew Association
VA	Veterans Administration		
Va	Virginia	Yr	Year
Val	Valley	Yth	Youth
Var	Various	YWCA	Young Women's Christian Association
VBS	Vacation Bible School		
VChm	Vice Chairman	Zool	Zoology, Zoologist, Zoological
Vet	Veteran, Veterinarian		

Personalities
of the
South

A selected regional series covering
the fifteen states of

Alabama, Arkansas, Florida,
Georgia, Kentucky, Louisiana,
Maryland, Mississippi, North
Carolina, Oklahoma, South
Carolina, Tennessee, Texas,
Virginia, West Virginia

and

District of Columbia, Puerto Rico,
Virgin Islands

PERSONALITIES OF THE SOUTH

A

ABADIE, CHARLES F JR oc/Businessman; b/Sept 9, 1927; h/3405 Tiltree Rd, Hattiesburg, MS 39401; ba/H'burg, MS; m/Verla Mae; c/Charles III (Chuck), Susan Elizabeth, Madeline, Walter Charles, John Charles, Gregory Charles; p/Charles F Sr (dec) and Elsie Abadie, New Orleans, LA; mil/US Nav AF, 4 yrs; pa/Owner Charlie Abadie Loan Co; Bd Mbr, H'burg Loan Exc; cp/Pres, H'burg Lions Club; r/Cath; hon/Lion of Yr 1977-78; Knight of Yr 1977.

ABBOTT, GARY LOUIS SR oc/Clergyman; b/Sept 26, 1947; h/PO Box 790, Harlem, GA 30814; ba/Same; m/Billie Avalie Uselton; c/Gary Louis Jr, Russell Wilson; p/A Louis and Viola K Abbott, Waynesboro, GA; ed/AB Mercer Univ 1969; MDiv SWn Bapt Theol Sem 1972; pa/Clergyman, So Bapt Conv; Chm Exec Com Wn Bapt Assn 1974-75; Bd Trustees Rockridge Bapt Assem 1977; Exec Com Ga Bapt Conv 1977-78; cp/Bd Dirs Kidney Found of Ga; Harlem Rotary Clb; r/So Bapt; hon/W/W Am Rel; DIB; Men of Achmt.

ABBOTT, LESTER B oc/Executive Director; b/Oct 3, 1932; m/Fay D; c/Kenton, Karen, Gordon; p/Mr and Mrs Ed Abbott, Monticello, KY; ed/BA Berea Col 1954; MS Ohio Univ 1960; mil/AUS 1954-56; pa/Tchr-Coach 12 Yrs; Exec Dir Somerset Pulaski Co C of C & Pulaski Co Indust Foun Inc; Ky C of C Execs Assn, Pres 1979-80; cp/Rotary Clb; r/Bapt.

ABBOTT, LYNNE CLARK oc/Clinical Social Worker, Medical Educator; b/Apr 21, 1943; h/708 Versailles Dr, Huntsville, AL 35803; ba/H'ville, m/Brent Johnston Morris; c/Lance, Darren, Wendy, Brendan; p/Ernest D Clark (dec); Hazel Martyn, Orlando, FL; ed/Att'd Meml Hosp Sch of Nsg 1961-63; BA Sangamon St Univ 1974; MSSW Univ Tenn 1976; Att'g Univ Ala 1981-; pa/Fam Sers Ctr, Springfield, Ill 1974-75; Dede Wallace Mtl Hlth Ctr, Nashville, Tenn 1976; Instr Psychi, Univ Ala-H'ville, Sch of Primary Med Care 1976-; NASW, VP Ala Chapt; Soc of Tchrs of Fam Med; Ala Soc Clin Social Wkrs; Ala Soc Hosp Social Wkrs; Acad of Cert'd Social Wkrs; cp/Polit Action for Cand Elect, Treas 1978-80; hon/Social Wkr of Yr, H'ville NASW 1979; Social Wkr of Yr, Tenn Val NASW 1980.

ABEL, FLORINE oc/Retired Teacher, Principal, Supervisor, Administrator; b/Sept 9, 1906; h/1303 64th St NW, Bradenton, FL 33505; c/Yvonne Abel Matt; p/Hamp Jones (dec) and Eliza Worsham Jones Moore (dec); ed/BS Savannah State 1940; MEd Atlanta Univ 1948; EdD Univ of Fla 1966; pa/Elem Tchr; Elem Prin; HS Tchr; Supvr of Black Schs in Manatee Co, Fla; Adv Spec Manatee Co, Fla; Summer Sch Tchr, Spelman Col Nursery Sch, Atlanta, Ga; Cnslr of Girls, Savannah State Col; pa/Sec Fla State Negro Supvrs Assn; Vice Pres Manatee Co Chapt Ret'd Tchrs; Vice Pres Dist Bd of Trustee of Manatee Jr Col; Pres St Petersburg-Tampa Chapt Links Inc; Vice Pres Delta Sigma Theta; cp/LWV; AAUW; Manatee Co Mtl Hlth Assn Vice Pres; hon/Rosenwald Schlr 1940; Wom of the Yr Manatee Co Chapt Zeta Phi Beta 1956; Wom of the Yr St Petersburg-Tampa Chapt Links Inc; Dist'd Ser Awd, Nat Girls Club of Am 1978; Silver Medallion Awd, Sarasota-Manatee Co Chapt of Nat Conf of Christians & Jews 1978; Ser Awds from the Manatee Co Chapt NAACP 1970 & 1978; Elem Sch named for her by Manatee Co Sch Bd 1980; Sorority Edr of 1980, Bradenton Alumnae Chapt Delta Sigma Theta.

ABERCROMBIE, BETTY WEBBER oc/Assistant Director and Coordinator Graduate Studies; b/June 26, 1920; h/126 SW #4B 47th Ave, Miami, FL; ba/Stillwater; c/Kay Titmas, Mary Anneler; p/I I Webber (dec); Faye Webber, Enid, OK; ed/BS 1941, EdD 1972 Okla St Univ; MEd Phillips Univ 1955; pa/Asst Dir & Coor Grad Studies, Sch of Hlth, Phys Ed & Leisure, Okla St Univ; OAHPER; AAHPER; So Nat Assn PE Col Wom; Okla Rec Pk Soc; OEA; NEA; Tchr 6 Yrs Enid Okla; Tchr 19 Yrs, Chm Wom's Hlth, PE, Rec Prog Phillips Univ; r/Pesb; hon/W/W Am Wom; Author Num Profl Articles Incl'g "Curriculum Innovation" *Jour of Phys Ed & Rec* 1979 & "Philosophical Musings" *The Phys Edr.*

ABERNATHY, JAMES RALPH oc/Professor; b/Jan 8, 1926; h/Chapel Hill, NC; ba/Dept Biostatistics, Sch of Public Hlth, Univ NC, Chapel Hill, NC 27514; m/Cherye W; c/David, Cherye, Linda, Bradley; p/Grady L (dec) and Mary P Abernathy, Alexander City, AL; ed/BS Samford Univ 1951; MSPH 1953, PhD 1965 UNC-CH; mil/AUS 1946-47; pa/Statistician, NC St Hlth Dept; Prof Biostats, UNC-CH; Am Statis Assn; Am Public Hlth Assn; Population Assn of Am; Intl Union for Sci Study of Population; r/Prot; hon/Fellow Am Public Hlth Assn; Fellow Am Statis Assn; Author 48 Pubs.

ABERNATHY, RALPH DAVID oc/Minister, Civil Rights Leader, World Peace Leader; b/Mar 11, 1926; ba/Atlanta, GA; m/Juanita Odessa Jones; c/Juandalyn, Donzaleigh, Ralph III, Kwame; p/Will (dec) and Louivory Abernathy (dec); ed/BA Ala St Univ 1950; MA Atlanta Univ; mil/AUS; pa/Pastor W Hunter St Bapt Ch; Pres Emeritus So Christian Ldrship Conf; Adv Bd of Cong of Racial Equality; Presideum, World Peace Coun; World Comm on Hunger; Nat Coun of Chm; Bapt World Alliance; Kappa Alpha; Kappa Alpha Mu; Hon Mem Am Sociol Assn; r/Bapt; hon/Peace Medallion, German Dem Repub; Dr Martin Luther King Awd; 4 Hon Degs; Over 300 Hons & Awds.

ABERNETHY, DONALD DOUGLAS oc/Administrative Assistant to Congressman Stephen L Neal; b/Aug 8, 1931; h/RFD 3, Box 721, Lincolnton, NC 28091; ba/Washington, DC; m/Iris G; c/Douglas, Jeffrey, Jonathan, Beth, Robert; p/Ernest G Abernethy (dec); Lottie E Abernethy, Newton, NC; ed/BA; MEd; mil/AUS 2 yrs; pa/Mem: Adm Assts Assn, NC Dem Clb, Congnl Staff Clb; cp/Dem Party; Past Pres Raeford, NC Kiwanis Clb; r/Bapt; hon/Gideons VIP Bible.

ABLES, CLYDE RAYFORD oc/Pastor; b/Dec 3, 1942; h/Rt 5, Yazoo City, MS; m/Geraldine Rivers; c/Vickie Lynn, Paula Rae; p/Edward Eugene and Ada Lucille Hawk Ables, Yazoo City, MS; ed/Att'd Liberty Bible Col 1974-77; pa/Farmer 13 Yrs; Pastor New Life Fellowship; r/Interdenom.

ABNER, ORVILLE oc/Developmental Engineer, Manager Type Manufacturing Engineering; b/Apr 8, 1940; h/One-Olde Towne Tr. 2, Richmond, KY 40475; ba/Lexington, KY; m/Joan Davidson c/James Paul; p/James William and Sallie Marie Abner, London, Ky; ed/AA 1967, BS Industrial, Vocational & Technical Ed 1969 Eastern Ky Univ; completed 6400 hour tool & die apprenticeship w IBM 1966; mil/Ky ANG 1962-68, 6 mos active duty 1962; pa/IBM Corp 1959-: Tool & Die Maker 1962-69, Mfg Engr 1969-74, Proj Engr 1974-76, 2nd Level Mgr as Proj Mgr over Tool & Model Shop Ser 1976-78, Mgr Type Mfg Engrg; Charter Mem Iota Lambda Sigma (Ind Ed Frat); Mem Masonic Lodge 25, Richmond, Ky; Mem Lexington Scottish Rite (32° Deg Mason) & Oleika Shrine, Lex; cp/Mem Indust Technol Adv (Com at EKU); Mem Madison Co Bd Ed (8 yrs), Chm 1 yr; Mem Steering Com of Madison Co Vocational Sch (8 yrs); r/First Bapt Ch, Richmond.

ABRAHAM, GEORGE ELLIS II oc/Physician; b/Sept 8, 1942; h/Vicksburg, MS; ba/1907 Mission 66, Vicksburg, MS 39180; m/Mary Virginia; c/Emily, Mary Frances, George III, Virginia Helen; p/George E and Mabel E Abraham, Vicksburg, MS; ed/BS 1964, MS 1966, MD 1969 Univ Miss; MD Univ Miss Med Sch 1975; Residency Fam Med, Univ Miss Med Ctr 1975-78; mil/AUS 1969-71; pa/Fam Phys, Pvt Pract; Miss Acad Fam Phys; Am Acad Fam Phys; Miss St Med Assn; Alpha Omega Alpha; diplomate Am Bd of Fam Pract; FAAFP; cp/Rotary Intl; r/En Orthodox; hon/AOA 1974; Med Student of Yr 1974, Univ Miss; Grad magna cum laude Med Sch.

ABRAHAMSON, BERGLJOT oc/Retired School Teacher; b/Mar 27, 1909; h/Star Route, Cossayuna, NY 12823; ba/Clewiston, FL; p/Hans Tobias (dec) and Louise Tomine Abrahamson (dec); ed/PhD (Hon); EdB; pa/Life Mem NEA; Ariz Ret'd Tchrs Assn; cp/Securtiy Coun; Repub Party Crane for Pres; r/Pentecostal; hon/5 yr & 10 yr 4-H Ldrship Certs & Pins; 10 yr Plaque for mbrship in Ariz Ed Assn.

ABRAHAMSON, CAROL A oc/Executive; b/Aug 19, 1950; h/3023-F Cottage Pl, Greensboro, NC 27405; ba/G'boro; p/Roland and Lois Abrahamson, Wilmette, TN; ed/BA Ohio Wesleyan Univ; MBA NYU; pa/VP, Investor Relats, Veritas Assocs Inc 1979-; Dir Public & Fin Affairs, PCA Intl 1978-79; Mgr Investor Relats, McGraw-Hill Inc 1976-78; Assoc, Corp Fin, Donaldson, Lufkin & Jenrette Inc 1974-76; Security Analyst, Alliance Capital Mgmt 1973-74; Portfolio Mgr, Ohio Sch Employees Retirement Sys 1972-73; Fac Logan Elm HS 1971-72; Fin Communs Soc; Fin Wom's Assn of NY; Dir 1977-78, Chm Com to Ed Corp & Non-Profit Bd Dirs 1978, Chm Edn Com 1977-78; Intl Platform Assn; Nat Assn Female Execs; Nat Investor Relats Inst; NOW; NYU Bus Forum; Public Relats Soc of Am; U Commun Sers, Public Info Bd; Wom Execs; Wom for NY; Wom's Ec Round Table; cp/Bd Dirs Natalie Kerr Designs 1978-79; Fac Advr, NYU Grad Sch of Bus 1975-76; hon/Book of Hon; Commun Ldrs & Noteworthy Ams; DIB; Intl Register of Profiles; Intl W/W: Commun Ser, Intells; Men & Wom Dist; Personalities of Am; Notable Ams; W/W: Fin & Indust, E, Am Wom; World W/W Wom; Author *Managing Investor Relations for Results.*

ABRAMS, BOBBY oc/Patrolman; b/Mar 4, 1957; h/Lindale, GA; m/Robbie L; c/Mindy Renee; p/Jeanette Abrams, Armwchee, GA; ed/HS Grad; mil/USN 1975-79; pa/Patrolman, City of Rome Police Dept; r/Bapt.

ABRAMS, LOYD GLENN oc/Branch Manager; b/July 3, 1947; ba/PO Box 190, Midland, TX 79702; m/Pam; c/Julie Rene, Kyle Travis; p/Loyd H (dec) and Mozelle Abrams (dec); ed/BBA TX A & M Univ 1969; pa/Br Mgr of Leasing Assocs Inc; r/Meth.

1

PERSONALITIES OF THE SOUTH

ACERRA, ANDREW JERI oc/President, Chairman of the Board; b/Sept 28, 1916; h/Phillippee Pkwy, Safety Harbor, FL; ba/Oldsmar, FL; m/Maria; c/Andrea, Andrew Jr; p/Salvatore Acerra (dec); Josephine Acerra, NY, NY; ed/BA, MA, PhD; pa/Pres, Chm of Bd Andrew Jeri Co, Inc; Physicist; Conslg Engr 1952; Hillyer Instr Corp, Conslg Engr 1959; Curtis Wright Corp; Contbn in Mil Tng Devices 1960; Radar Devices 1963; Pres Acerra Graphic Arts Labs; cp/Oldsmar C of C; r/Christian; hon/US Patents, Digital Systems, Microminiaturization Techs.

ACEVEDO-AKIN, ANGELA ROSA oc/Visual Information Specialist; b/May 21, 1934; h/601 Cedar Dr, Enterprise, AL 36330; ba/Ft Rucker, Al; m/Robert Floyd; p/(dec); ed/Univ Puerto Rico 1953; Exec Secy Sci, So Bus Univ 1958; BS Troy St Univ 1972; pa/Sr Visual Info Spec, Pubs Prod Br, Directorate of Tng Devel, Ft Rucker; Soc for Tech Communs; Nat Art Ed Assn; Intl Soc Artists; r/Unity; hon/Grad summa cum laude Troy St Univ 1972; Outstg Toastmaster, Prop & Rotor Clb 1979; Toastmaster of Yr; Art Pub'd in *Aviation Digest*.

ACKER, LOUISE IDA oc/Nurse, Administrator (Retired); b/May 19, 1905; h/4525 Tortoise Rd, S Venice, FL; p/Martin and Minnie Acker (dec); ed/WA Foote Meml Hosp 1928; Postgrad Tng Pediatrics, Chd's Hosp; pa/Dir Nsg Sers: Meth Hosp, Ky; Beckley Hosp, WV; Meml Hosp, Fairfield, Ill; Murphy Med Ctr, Warsaw, Ind -1971 (Ret'd); Opened New Hosp, Olney, Ill 1953; Dir Nurses, Ctrville Twp Hosp, St Clair Co, Ill; ANA; Pres Ill Dist #12 Nurses Assn; Treas Fla Nurses Assn Dist #44; Co-Chm Instl Nsg Ser Adm Sect of Ill; Secy Dist #10 E St Louis Nurses Dist Assn; cp/Ser Chm Am Cancer Soc; Charter Mem Beta Sigma Phi; r/Grace U Meth Ch: Choir Mem, Chm Mus Com, Secy, Libn, Mem Ch Bds; hon/Recip Sev Hons & Awds in Recog of Contbns to Nsg Profesion & Commun; Nurse of Yr, Ill Nurses Assn Dist #12; Cert of Apprec 1959, Wom's Aux of St Clair Co Med Soc; Ky Col; Pub'd Author; Listed in Commun Ldrs & Noteworthy Ams; Intl W/W Wom.

ACKER, W L (LOU) oc/Certified Protection Professional, Certified Texas Peace Officer; b/Mar 24, 1937; h/3502 Palm Dr, Mesquite, TX 75150; ba/Irving; m/Peggy Ann; ed/BS Sam Houston St Univ 1975; mil/AUS; Tex St NG Capt Mil Police; pa/Dir N Lake Campus Police Dept; Am Soc Indust Security; Intl Police Assn; Tex Police Assn; US Mil Intell Assn; cp/Dem Cand for Sheriff 1980; Confed Alliance; SCV; Confed Legion of Army of Tenn; Hon Order of Ky Cols; Civil War Round Table of Tex; r/Luth.

ACKERLER, LOIS oc/Executive; b/Aug 17, 1934; h/1715 Marina Terrace N, Ft Myers, FL 33903; m/Lawrence Volk (dec); 2nd Sidney Ackerman; c/Pamela Volk, David Volk, Valerie Volk, (Stepchd:) Mitchell, Eve, Joel, Alan, Stephen; p/Louis and Sara Greenberger, Cape Coral, Fla; ed/BBA magna cum laude Univ of Pgh 1955; pa/Pres Star Gifts Inc, Star Pharm Inc; Secy, Star Gifts of Fla Inc & Star Gifts of G'ville Inc; Beta Gamma Sigma; Gifts & Decorative Accessories Assn; Jewelers Indust Coun; Assoc Nat Assn of Retail Druggists; cp/Rotary Ann; r/Jewish; hon/W/W of South & SE.

ACRES, NORMAN CLIFTON oc/Landman; b/June 4, 1926; h/PO Box 114, Helenwood, TN 37755; m/Pauline Sexton; c/Auther, Paula, Linda, Tammie; p/Audney and Thelma Delna Acres, Oneida, TN; ed/Draughons Bus Col 1947-49; Assoc Deg Louisiana State Univ Sch Bkg 1967-69; Cert Univ of Tenn Mgmt Sch 1976; mil/AUS 1944-47, Bronze Star, Purple Heart; pa/Landman Tenn Land & Exploration Co; Dir Tenn EMT Assn; Dir Tenn Oil & Gas Assn; Bd Dirs Tenn EMT Assn; Bd Dirs Easter Seals; cp/Dir Indust Devel Bd, Scott Co, Tenn; Capt Scott Co Resque Squads; Mem Scott Co Election Comm; Am Legion; VFW; r/Bapt.

ACTON, WILLIAM CARROLL oc/Physician, Radiologist; b/Feb 14 1945; h/Rt 2, Millen, GA 30442; ba/Macon, GA; p/Willam D (dec) and Elizabeth Carroll Acton, Millen, GA; ed/BS Chem; MD; mil/USAR; pa/AMA, Ga Rad Soc; Ga Med Assn; RSNA; cp/Am Cancer Soc; Am Heart Assn; United Way; r/Prot; hon/Phi Beta Kappa; Phi Kappa Phi; Resident of the Yr, Med Col Ga.

ADAIR, LILLIAN DUFFEE oc/Corporate Secretary; b/May 14, 1921; h/Duffee's Hill, Dadeville, AL 36853; ba/D'ville; m/Charles R Jr; p/Cecil Gravlee Sr (dec) and Nell DeVine Duffee (dec); ed/AB Univ Ala 1942; Grad Work: Univ Ala, Auburn Univ; pa/Dir Still Waters Inc; Dir, Secy D'ville Lumber Co; Tchr Tallapoosa Co Bd Ed; Secy-Treas Tallapoosa Co Tchrs Assn; Dir ECARPDCOM; Trustee, Kate Duncan Smith DAR Sch; cp/Pres Worth While Clb, Philomathic Clb, Delphic Clb, Wom of Ch; VP Pta; Chm Am Legion Aux; Regent & Dist IX Dir ASDAR; r/Presb; hon/Wom of Yr 1973; 10 Best Dressed 1976; Williams Conserv Awd 1979.

ADAMS, DAVID oc/Contractor, Attorney; b/Oct 6, 1948; ba/PO Box 2320, Pikeville, KY 41501; m/Annette; c/Davin; p/Stuart H Adams, Pikeville, KY; Geneva Adams, Lexington, KY; ed/BS Pikeville Col; JD Univ of Louisville; pa/Shriners; Kiwanis; Ky Bar Assn; Pike Co Bar Assn;

Am Bar Assn; Delta Theta Phi Law Frat.

ADAMS, GEORGE DOUGLAS oc/Minister; b/Mar 1, 1948; h/218 Evening Side Dr, Chattanooga, TN 37404; ba/1800 Mulberry St, Chattanooga, TN 37404; m/Jan Ferguson; c/Elizabeth Gail, William Douglas, Steven Carlyle; p/George L and Lila L Adams, Chattanooga, TN; ed/Ext Work, Carson-Newman Col, Jefferson City, Tenn 1972-73; Dipl in Theol, The Boyce Bible Col of So Bapt Theol Sem, Louisville, Ky 1975-77; pa/Pastor, Port Royal Bapt Ch, Port Royal, Ky 1975-77, Oak Grove Bapt Ch, Chattanooga, Tenn 1977-; Exec Bd Mem-Chm Nom'g Com Seovatchee Valley Bapt Assn, Whitwell, Tenn 1970-75; Chm Missions Com, Dir SS Work, Henry Co Bapt Ch, New Castle, Ky 1975-77; Music Dir-Chm Nom'g Com Pastor's Conf, Hamilton Co Bapt Assn, Chattanooga, TN 1978-80; r/So Bapt; hon/Billy Graham Sch of Evangelism Awd 1977.

ADAMS, GEORGE EMERY oc/Mathematics Professor; b/Mar 9, 1942; h/211 Chapel Rd, Black Mountain, NC 28711; ba/PO Box 846, Montreat, NC 28757; m/E Elizabeth Bene; c/Robert Edward Lee, Kelly Elizabeth; p/John Emery and Katherine Ellen Adams, Hendersonville, TN; ed/BA in Math (Distn) Manchester Col 1960-63; MA in Math Univ of Ill 1966-67; Fla State Univ 1969-71; pa/Math Tchr, Cleveland, Ohio 1963-66; Asst Prof of Math, Manchester Col 1967-72; Prof and Chm Dept of Math Montreat-Anderson Col 1972; Math Assn of Am 1967-; Am Math Assn of Two Yr Cols 1979-; cp/US Nav Inst 1977-; r/Deacon, Montreat Presb Ch 1976-; hon/Kappa Mu Epsilon, Indiana Alpha Chapter; W/W Among Students in Am Univs and Cols (1963); Nat Sci Foun F'ship (1966); Montreat-Anderson Col Teacher of the Yr 1976, 1978; Outstg Young Men of Am 1978; W/W in the S&SW 1980.

ADAMS, GEORGE RANDALL oc/Assistant Executive Director; b/May 10, 1952; h/898 Twin Lakes Dr, Sumter, SC 29150; m/Marilyn T; c/Heather R; p/Paul Francis Sr and Oveda Carr Adams, Roxboro, NC; ed/BS E Carolina Univ 1974; grad study Univ SC, Dept Govt & Intl Studies 1978-; pa/Regional Planner w Santee-Lynches Coun for Govts 1975-76, Dir of Commun Devel 1977, Dir of Planning 1979, Asst to Dir 1980; Charter Mem, Am Planning Assn; SC Chapt Am Planning Assn; SC Commun Devel Assn; Am Soc for Public Adm; Nat Assn on Rural Devel; cp/Clemson Univ Ext Commun Devel Com; YMCA; Gov's Com on Rural Devel; r/Meth; hon/Author of local govt documents: "Agricultural Land Survey and Analysis" (1977), "Comprehensive Plan for Kershaw, SC" (1976), "Comprehensive Plan for Summerton, SC" (1979), co-authored multi-family housing site survey and analysis 1980.

ADAMS, HELENA BRADLEY (JODY) oc/Teacher; b/Oct 8, 1955; m/Dennis; p/Glenn J Bradley, Cherokee, NC; Charlotte A Bradley, Cherokee, NC; ed/BS Wn Carolina Univ 1977; pa/Tchr Home Ec, Cherokee HS; cp/NC Fed Wom's Clb, Dist Arts Chm; Bryson City Jr Wom's Clb: 1st Vp, 2nd VP, Dist Arts Chm; AHEA, VP 1977; r/Bapt; hon/Clbwom of Yr, Dist I.

ADAMS, HERBERT HALL oc/Minister; b/Feb 27, 1942; h/101 Dogwood Cove, Corbin, KY 40701; ba/Corbin; m/Anne Bennett Broadbent; c/Christopher Herbert; p/Weldon Herbert and Eunice Catherine Adams; ed/BME Murray St Univ 1967; MDiv Louisville Presb Theol Sem 1977; Cert for Pastoral Ed 1975; Cert for Tchg Skills, Nat Tchrs Ed Proj 1976; pa/Min, Corbin Presb Ch; Pres Corbin Min Assn; Nat Tchrs Assn; Ky Ed Assn; St Rep for Gideon, Mo to St Tchrs Assn; cp/Kiwanis Intl; Bd Mem & Secy Big Bros/Big Sis of Am; r/Presb; hon/Tiger Tail Awd, Hall of Dist'd Duck Hunters 1976; Sev Awds in Mus.

ADAMS, JAMES CARLIE II oc/Engineering Executive; b/Aug 25 1941; ba/Hobbs Adams Engineering Co, 1100 Holland Rd, Suffolk, VA 23434; m/Dana Heard; c/James Carlie III, Shannon Dana; p/James Carlie and Julia H Adams, Willow Springs, NC; ed/Staunton Mil Acad 1957-59; NC State Univ 1959-63; mil/AUS 1964; pa/Vice Pres Hobbs Adams Engineering Co 1963-; Pres Pioneer Processors Inc 1967-; JC Adams Inc 1970-; Bd Dirs U Va Bk; Bd Dirs Nat Bark Prodrs Assn, Pres 1978, 79, 80; Nat Peanut Coun.

ADAMS, JOHN MELVIN JR oc/Pastor, Teacher; b/Sept 8, 1950; h/Rt 5 Box 505, Laurel, Miss 39440; ba/Same; m/Darla Kaye Fuller; c/John M III, Trinity Kaye; p/Melvin and Gladys Adams, Bentonia, Miss; ed/AA; BA; MDiv, Luther Rice Sem, Jacksonville, Fla; pa/Dir Dept of Youth, Bapt Assn of Miss; r/Lebanon Bapt Ch; hon/Outstg Young Men of Am 1979; Personalities of Am 1979; Am Registry Series 1979.

ADAMS, LARRY EDWARD oc/Professor; b/Sept 2, 1945; h/204 Clarence Ray Dr, Hattiesburg, MS 39401; ba/H'burg; m/Carroll M; p/Jamie Pruitt, Sheridan, AR; ed/BS; PhD; pa/Prof, Univ So Miss; Am Speech & Hearing Assn; Miss Speech & Hearing Assn; hon/Hon Grad; Excell in Tchg Awd USM.

PERSONALITIES OF THE SOUTH

ADAMS, LEONARD W (BILL) oc/Rancher, Farmer; b/July 20, 1927; h/Rt 1, Pawnee, OK 74058; m/Leanna Adams; c/Rhonda Brien, Sandra Kay Beagle, Billie Lynn Nelson, Robert; p/Leonard H and Rena Adams, Pawnee, OK; mil/AUS 1945; pa/Wheat Farmer; Feeder Cattle Rancher; Indian Elec Coop: Pres, VP, Bd Mem; Black Bear Conservatory Water Dist: Pres, Chm Bd; cp/Hon FFA; r/First Christian Ch; hon/Goodyear Conserv Awd 1980.

ADAMS, LILLIAN LOYCE oc/Professor Emeritus; b/Jan 10, 1912; h/216 Elmwood, Huntsville, TX 77340; ed/BBA, MBA Tex A&I; PhD Univ Tex; mil/DAC; pa/Prof Emeritus Bus Adm; Exec Secy, VP, Pres 1961-62 Tex Bus Ed Assn; Chm SW Region ABCA 1955; Pres H'ville BR AAUW 1947-50; Pres Walker Co, Tex St Tchrs Assn; hon/Alpha Chi; Pi Omega Pi; Sigma Iota Epsilon; Beta Gamma Sigma; Delta Pi Epsilon; Phi Chi Theta; So F'ship Fund Grant 1957-58; Intl Authors & Writers W/W, 7th, 8th, 9th Eds.

ADAMS, LUCY NEELY oc/Homemaker; b/Apr 24, 1934; m/Woodward Jr; c/Joy, John David, Scott, Ben; p/Wadsworth B (dec) and Louise B Neeley, Durham, NC; ed/BA Scarritt Col; Att'd Wesleyan Col; cp/Chp Multiple Sclerosis Dr, Henry Co 1980; r/U Meth; hon/Pres Ch Wom U, Lawrenceburg, TN & Winchester, TN; Contbr to *Upper Room Meditations* & *United Methodist Curriculum*.

ADAMS, RAYTHELL GREENE oc/Farmer; b/Feb 17 1928; h/Rt 2 Box 44-A, Angier, NC 27501; ba/Same; m/Emily Blanchard c/Joseph Ronald, June Michele; p/Silas Greene (dec) and Ila Dupree Adams (dec); ed/Campbell Univ; mil/USN; pa/Chm Black River Twp, Harnett Co ASC Com; Adv Com Farm Home Adm; Bd Dir First Citizens Bk of Angier; Mem Landrace Assn; Past Dir NC Landrace Assn; Past Nat VP Landrace Assn; Past Dir Harnett Farm Bur; Past Bd of Dir Rural Black River Fire Dept.

ADAMS, TERRY WAYNE oc/Student; b/Apr 18, 1957; h/Rt 4 Box 74-B2, Elba, AL 36323; m/Melissa; p/Oscar Willard and Sarah Evelyn Adams, Elba, AL; ed/Att'g Ala Aviation & Tech Col; pa/Tng to be an Aircraft Mechanic; Profl Assn of Diving Instrs: Asst Instr #A-10285; r/Bapt; hon/Dean's List; S'ship from Petro Helicopters Inc 1981.

ADAMS, TROY oc/Criminal Investigator; b/Apr 16, 1921; h/PO Box 248, Tom Bean, TX; ba/Van Alstyne, TX; m/Wilma L; c/Judy Carol Adams Hamilton; p/Richard Fields (dec) and Berta Adams (dec); ed/Assoc Deg in Law Enforcement 1975; Law Enforcement Adv'd Cert 1976; mil/USAF 1941-67, Ret'd Master Sergeant; pa/City Marshall, Tom Bean; r/Bapt; hon/Commend Medal 1967; USAF Loyal Exemplary Serv Awd 1977; Outstg Ldrship 1967; Kiwanis Club, Panama City, Fla; Outstg Ldrship Awd, Grayson Co Sheriff's Dept, Sherman, Fla 1976.

ADAMSON, ANN LENHARDT oc/Assistant Secretary of State; b/Sept 18, 1934; h/2160 East Lake Road, NE, Atlanta, GA 30307; ba/Atlanta; m/Charles L; c/Lisa Ann, Alis Carol; p/Edwin Bernard Lenhardt (dec); Adeline Henderson Lenhardt Foster, Atlanta, GA; cp/Asst Secy of St, Ga; Dem Party; Mem: Hist Oakland Cemetary Assn; Atlanta Zoological Soc; r/Meth.

ADAMSON, N A (ART) oc/Manager; b/Jan 20, 1922; h/Orange, TX; ba/PO Box 1269, Orange, TX 77630; m/Irene B; c/Kathy A Wicoff, Margaret, Bruce, David; p/Norman (dec) and Marion Adamson (dec); ed/BS Bucknell Univ 1944; mil/AUS 1944-46 Corps of Engrs; pa/Mgr, Petrochem Plant, Firestone Tire & Rubber Co 1944-; Tex Chem Coun, Bd Dirs; cp/Orange Meml Hosp Corp: Secy, Bd Dirs; Orange Rotary Clb, Past Pres; r/Presb; hon/Ser Awds: Rotary Clb, U Fund, YMCA.

ADAMSON, WILLIAM E (DUKE) oc/Executive; b/June 9, 1942; h/Sanford, FL; ba/PO Drawer G, Sanford, FL 32771; m/Donna; c/Brent, Brian, Aaron; p/Vivian Porteous, Round Lake, IL; ed/Att'd Univ Ill, Fin Plan'g Inst; pa/18 Yrs Life Ins Profl; Pres U Homes Sers of Fla; Dir Intl Frozen Food Coun; Dir Rich Plan Corp; r/Prot; hon/Mem Million Dollar Round Table.

ADCOX, JAMES MURRAY II oc/Minister; b/Feb 23, 1952; h/2507 Cottonwood, Jonesboro, Ark 72401; ba/Jonesboro; m/Ann Grimmitt; c/James Murray III; Jonathan Murray; Julie Cathey; p/James M (dec) and Theo Lester Adcox, Hohenwald, Tenn; ed/AA Freed-Hardeman Col; BA David Lipscomb Col; MAR Harding Grad Sch of Rel; pa/Minister Southwest Ch of Christ; Frequent spkr at chs and lectrships; Radio Spkr for "A Better Life" Spots; cp/Mem Kiwanis Club Intl; r/Ch of Christ; hon/Outstg Yng Men of Am 1975 & 1979; Outstg Yng Alumnus of Freed-Hardeman Col 1977.

ADDINGTON, WILLIAM HUBERT oc/Rancher; b/Mar 8, 1924; h/3418 Henry Dr, Ft Worth, TX 76118; ba/Same; m/Donna Lorene McCalla; c/Mark Wayne; p/Emory and Lucy Latham Addington; ed/AB 1948 Univ Kan; mil/USAAF 1943-48; pa/Rancher; Former Granary Exec; Oper'g Grain Elevators: Kan, Tex, NM; Ranches: Tex, Wyo, NM, Nev; cp/Repub Cand for Gov of Kan 1960; Mem Kan Ho of Reps 1958-61; St Hwy Commr for Kan 1955-57; Involved in Campaign to Clean up Govt; Filed 35 Impeachmt Memls w US Ho of Reps; Pres Am Dairy Cow Co 1977-.

ADERHOLD, JOSEPHINE ELIZABETH (JODY) oc/Homemaker, Volunteer Worker; b/May 4, 1928; h/Edinburg, TX; m/Samuel Thomas; c/Joseph Cullen, Robin, Thomas Nelson; p/Joseph Cullen (dec) and Mignon M Powell, Edinburg, TX; ed/BA Univ Tex 1948; cp/Edinburg Jr Ser Leag, Sustaining Life Mem; E'burg Gen Hosp Aux: Publicity Chm, Hospitality Cart Chm, Pres; E'burg Chapt Am Field Ser, Pres; r/Presb; hon/Hon Life Mem Preb Wom of Ch 1975; E'burg Wom of Yr 1980.

ADKINS, BOBBY JOE oc/Businessman; b/Nov 19, 1931; h/Rt 1 Bells Hwy, Jackson, TN 38301; ba/Jackson; m/Geraldine Holt; c/Pamela Joe, Deborah Kay, Kimberley Dean; p/Jodie Adkins and Alemda Adkins Longfellow, Dyersburg, TN; pa/Woodmen of the World Life Ins Co; r/Meth; hon/FIC Awd 1975 & 1978; 3rd in Nat for Woodman of the World 1978, 2nd 1977.

ADKISON, CHARLA FRANCES SPEARS oc/Teacher; b/Nov 4, 1950; h/Kinston, AL; ba/Kinston; m/Rodney; p/Charlie and Frances Spears, Opp, AL; ed/BS Univ Montevallo; Master Sec'dy Ed & Biol Auburn Univ-Montgomery 1977; pa/Tchr Kinston HS; AEA; NEA; Ala Acad Sci; Nat & Intl Wildlife Fed; cp/Cent Clb: Secy-Treas; r/Bapt; hon/Outstg Sci Tchr: St of Al 1980, S Region Al Jr Acad of Sci 1980.

ADRIAN, JOHN L oc/Research and Teaching; b/Oct 14, 1947; h/Auburn, AL; m/Wanda Kaye; c/John L III, James Adam; p/John L Sr and Lucille R Adrian; ed/BS 1969, MS 1971 Auburn Univ; PhD Univ Tenn 1974; pa/Assoc Prof, Dept Agric Ecs & Rural Sociol, Auburn Univ; Am Agric Ecs Assn; So Agric Ecs Assn; Am Soc Farm Mgrs & Rural Appraisers; Ala Soc Farm Mgrs & Rural Appraisers; cp/Auburn Lions Clb: Asst Treas, Treas, VP, Pres; r/Bapt; hon/Phi Kappa Phi; Sigma Xi; Gamma Sigma Delta; Author Sev Jour Articles & Bulletins.

AFFELDT, HARLEY PAUL oc/College President; b/Mar 31, 1926; h/Winston-Salem, NC; ba/Forsyth Tech Inst, 2100 Silas Creek Pkwy, Winston-Salem, NC 27103; m/Virginia F; c/James K; p/Harley A (dec) and Lydia S Affeldt, Portsmouth, VA; ed/BS 1950, MEd 1958 VPI & SU; EdD Prog, Nova Univ 1976; mil/USAF 1944-46; pa/Pres Forsyth Tech Inst 1971-; Dir Richmond (Va) Tech Ctr 1966-71; Dir of Student Sers, Forsyth Tech Inst 1960-66; Indust Arts Tchr & Indust Coop Coor, Portsmouth, Va 1950-52 & 1958-60; Life Mem Am Voc Assn; NC Voc Assn; Am Tech Ed Assn; NC Adult Ed Assn; NC Com Col Pres Assn; Phi Delta Kappa; NC St Employees; cp/Stratford Rotary; Ardmore Commun Clb; VPI Alumni Assn; Shrine; Democrat; Bd Dirs Goodwill Rehab Ctr; W-S Indust for Blind; Hospice; Exp in Self Reliance; r/Meth.

AGAN, VERLON OTHO oc/Pastor, Supervisor; b/July 12, 1923; ba/PO Box 523, Pell City, AL 35125; m/Ruby Mae Davis; c/Verlon O Jr, Ruby Janan A Miller, Regina Ruth A Stetler; p/Luther M Agan Sr, Bremen, GA; ed/ThB, God's Bible Sch-Col, Cinci 1945; Att'd Univ Cinci 1946; pa/HS Tchr 1946-51; Pastor 1946-55; Conf Pres, Ala Conf Wesleyan Meth Connection of Chs 1955-64; Pastor 1964-68; Conf Pres, Bible Meth Connection of Chs 1968-; Chm of Bd, Evangelical Bible Mission; cp/PTA, Past Pres; r/Meth; hon/Sev Citations for Services Rendered w Ch; Author Num Articles on Rel & Current Issues.

AGEE, NELL oc/Real Estate Agent; b/Jan 27, 1936; h/Walnut Hill Dr, Deacon Hills, Richmond, KY; ba/Richmond; m/Harold; c/Bruce Coy, Steven Vaughn, Harold Alan; p/Lester and Frances Vaughn, Richmond, KY; ed/Grad Ky Bus Col 1962; Att'd En Ky Univ; pa/Self-Employed Real Est Agt, Brandenburg Real Est; r/First Christian Ch; hon/Chief Scout of Ft Boonesborough 1974; Acctg Awd, Best Acct Ky Bus Col 1962.

AHALT, MARY J oc/Secretary, Consultant; b/Oct 11, 1914; h/7007 Rhode Island Ave, College Park, MD 20740; ba/Same; m/Arthur M (dec); c/Arthur M, Mary Jane A Barker; p/George L (dec) and Grace Eva Cooper Zeigler (dec); pa/Weaver Shirt Co 1928-36; Carty's Furniture Co 1938-39; Tchr Calvert Nursery Sch, 1943-45; Off-Campus Housemother, Univ of Md 1939-43; Typist, Univ Md, Dept Entomology 1951-58; Exec Secy/Bookkeeper, Entomology Soc of Am 1951-53; Univ Md: Prin Steno for Home Demo Agt, Col of Agric 1958-59, Secy Col of Ed 1959-72, Secy to Dean, Col of Ed 1972-; Md Fed BPW Clb: Past Pres, Com Chm, Contbr to Newslttr & Pubs; Mem to Org Co Wom's Action Coalition; Nat Fed BPW Career Advmt Schlr Com 1975-76; Girl Scout Ldr 1951-54; Prince George's Co Intl Wom's Yr Task Force 1975; r/Luth: SS Tchr, Pres Ch Wom 1952 & 74, Mem Ch Coun & Secy 1956-61 & 69-74, Del to LCW Triennial Conv 1974; hon/25 yr Ser awd, Univ Md; BPW Wom of Yr, Col

Park Clb 1978 & Md Fed 1975-76; Cert of Ser, City of Col Park 1;978; Recog'd as Commun Ldr UN Day, Col Park 1975; DIB; World W/W Wom; W/W Am Wom; Other Hons.

AHMAD, NASIHA oc/Physician; b/Mar 15, 1947; h/Chapel Hill, NC; ba/Intl Fertility Res Prog, RTP, NC 27709; m/Syed Husain; c/Syed Mehdi, Zehra; p/Syed A Hamid (dec); Nasima Khatun, Bangladesh; ed/MD Univ Dacca, Bangladesh 1970; pa/Obstetrics & Gyn; Fertility Res; APHA; Jr Hosp Dr's Assn; UK, Pakistan Med Assn, Bangladesh Med Assn; r/Islam; hon/Author *Contraception - A Clinical Trial of Neo Sampoon Vaginal Contraceptive Tablets.*

AHRENS, SANDRA G oc/Deputy Sheriff, Jailer; b/Sept 15, 1959; h/San Marcos, TX; ba/Hays Co Courthouse, San Marcos, TX 78666; p/Kenton S and Lina Ann Ahrens, Kerrville, TX; ed/Att'g SW Tex St Univ; pa/Law Enforcement: Kerr Co Sheriff's Dept, Hays Co Sheriff's Dept; r/Luth; hon/Basic Law Enforcement Cert 1980; Jailer's Cert, Hays Co 1979.

AHUJA, VIJAY oc/Computer Scientist; b/Nov 21, 1942; h/6216 Lakerun Ct, Raleigh, NC 27612; ba/RTP, NC; m/Neeta; c/Vinita, Anant, Devesh; p/Yog Dhyan and Shakuntla Ahuja, Denver, CO; ed/BS, India 1963; MS 1970, PhD 1976 UNC; pa/IBM Corp 1970-; ACM; Sigma Xi; hon/Author Sev Papers & a Book on Computer Commun Networks.

AIKEN, BRUCE TANSILL oc/School Administrator, Management Consultant; b/Sept 5, 1921; h/Brownsville, TX; ba/PO Box 1749, Brownsville, TX 78520; m/Irma Santoscoy; c/Eric Gerard, Corinthia Ann Tansill; p/James Riley Aiken (dec); Olga Overton Tansill Aiken, Brownsville, TX; ed/BBA 1949; MEd 1956; MBA Cand; mil/WWII Major; Tex St Guard, Lt Col; pa/Sch Admr, B'ville Indep Sch Dist; Mgmt Conslt for Pers & Human Resources, Bruce Aiken Assocs; B'ville Ed Assn, Pres; Tex Elem Prins & Suprvs, Dist III Pres; Tex Assn of Sch Pers Admrs; Am Assn Sch Pers Admrs; Intl Pers Mgrs Assn; Tex Pers & Guid Assn; Rio Grande Val Admrs Assn; Lower Rio Grande Val Tchr Ed Ctr, Hon Life Bd of Dirs; Tchrs Profl Practices Comm of Tex, Appt'd by Gov Dolph Briscoe; cp/Cameron Co Hist Comm, Chm; Bicent Comm of B'ville, Chm; Civil War Centennial Comm of B'ville, Co-Chm; B'ville C of C, Dir; Intl Good Neighbor Coun; Tex Southmost Col Alumni Assn, Orgl Pres, B'ville Hist Assn, Pres; Rio Grande Val Museum Assn, Hon Mem; S Cameron Am Heart Assn, Chm; Tip-O-Tex Dist BSA, Pres; Mr Amigo Assn, VP; Charro Days Inc, VP; Assn of AUS, St Dir; Coun on Abandoned Mil Posts; Resv Ofcrs Assn of US, Chapt 29, Secy; Am Legion; B'ville JCs, Hon Life Mem; Kiwanis Intl, Lt Gov Tex-Okla Div 11; Parish Coun Bd, Christ the King Cath Ch; Immaculate Conception Cathedral Restoration Com, Secy; r/Cath.

AINSLIE, MICHAEL LEWIS oc/Executive; b/Dec 5, 1943; h/3021 Q St NC, Wash DC 20007; ba/Wash DC; m/Lucy Scardino; c/Katherine Waring Oxnard, Robbie Ann Scardino Oxnard, Faith Elixabeth Oxnard, Michael Loren; p/George L and Jean Waddell, Ainslie, Kingsport, TN; ed/BA Vanderbilt Univ 1965; MBA Harvard Bus Sch, J Spencer Love Fellow 1968; pa/Pres Nat Trust for Hist Preserv; Sr VP & Chief Operating Ofcr, N-ReN Corp 1975-80; Pres Palmas del Mar Co, Subsidiary Sea Pines Co 1971-75; Assoc, McKinsey Co 1968-71; Former Pres Harvard Bus Sch Clb of Cinci; cp/Chm Corning Fellows Assn; Former Chm Vanderbilt Univ Living Endowment Campaign; Former Fund Raising Chm, Sch for Creative & Performing Arts; r/Epis.

AKERS, DAVID JACKSON oc/Research Scientist; b/Dec 19, 1944; h/504 Overhill St, Morgantown, WV 26505; ba/M'town; m/Peggy; c/Paige, David, Megan; p/Jack and Gladys Akers, Morgantown, WV; ed/BS Geol, MS Geochem; mil/AUS 2 Yrs; pa/Res Sci, WVU; AIME; WV Coal Mining Inst; cp/Scoutmaster; r/Presb.

AKERS, JAMES E (BUTCH) oc/Art Therapist; b/Nov 2, 1949; h/109 Stephens Dr, Dublin, VA 24084; m/Sue Marlowe; c/Christopher Thomas; p/Walter R (dec) and Elverta Ward Akers, Dublin, VA; ed/Assoc Deg, New River Commun Col 1972; BS 1974, MS 1976 Radford Univ; ba/Reg'd Art Therapist, St Albans Pvt Psychi Hosp; Am Art Therapy Assn; Potomac Art Therapy Assn; r/Luth; hon/Good Citizenship Awd 1968; Phi Kappa Phi; Num Awds for Water Color Paintings in Local & St Art Shows.

AKIN, TED MARTIN oc/Associate Justice, Court of Civil Appeals, Fifth Supreme Judicial District; b/Jan 5, 1932; h/5323 N Dentwood Drive, Dallas, TX 75220; ba/Dallas; m/Gloria Lille Dahl; c/Laurel Sheffield, George Leighton-Dahl, Adrienne Lillian, Ashley Griffin-Jones; p/Ted and Lillian Jones Akin, LaFeria, TX; ed/BA So Meth Univ; JD SMU; mil/USAF, 1/Lt, Asst Staff Judge Advocate; pa/Assoc Justice, Ct of Civil Appeals; Phi Alpha Delta; cp/Past Mem Lasso; Dallas C of C; Past Pres Big D Toastmasters; Rotary Clb; Adv Coun Dallas Commun; Chest Trust Fund; Tex Kennel Clb: English Springer Spaniel; Field Trial Assn;

Brookhollow Golf Clb; City Clb; Cipango Clb; Dem Forum; r/St Michael's & All Angels Epis Ch.

AKINS, CLINTON MILES oc/Foreign Missionary; b/Nov 2, 1952; h/1004 Vandalia, Collinsville, IL 62234; ba/Wheaton, IL; m/Kathy Ann Piquard; c/Jennifer Lea, Kimberly Ann, Heather Ruth; p/K C and Fay Stevens Akins, Ft Walton Bch, FL; ed/BA Tenn Temple Univ 1977; MDiv Mid-Am Bapt Theol Sem 1980; mil/AUS 1970-73; pa/Bapt Min: Rainsville Bapt Mission Ch 1975 (Helped Start), Bethel Bapt Ch (Ringgold, Ga) 1976-77, First Bapt Ch Leachville (Ark) 1977, First Bapt Ch Cardwell (Mo) 1977-80; Fgn Missionary to Madagascar; cp/Leo Clb (Lions Intl) Choctawhatchee HS 1970, Treas; r/Bapt; hon/Ser Awd, Yth in Rel.

ALBIN, MARCY B oc/Public Administrator; b/Jan 22, 1952; h/5800 Quantrell Ave, Alexandria, VA 22312; p/Norman and June Albin, Highland Park, IL; ed/BA Univ Wis-Madison 1973; MEd Boston Univ 1975; Master Public Adm 1979 Univ So Cal; pa/Ofc of Secy, HEW; Rep on Sev White House Policy Task Forces incl'g Methadone Diversion Study Group, Sedative-Hypnotic Task Force; Conslt: CONSAD Inc 1976, Staff Assoc US Conf Mayors-Nat Leag Cities Alcohol Staff 1976; Boston Mayor's Ofc Coor'g Coun on Drug Abuse 1976; Treatmt Alternative to Street Crime Prog 1975, Drug Awareness Sems of Am Assn Indust Mgmt 1975; Staff Mem Drug Info Ctr, Madison, Wis 1971; Underground Switchboard, Milwaukee 1971; Asst Dir TV Series on Drug Probs Milwaukee 1971; Alexandria Substance Abuse Coun; hon/Pub'd Author; Univ Wis Alumni Awds: 1 of 6 Most Outstg Sr Wom 1973, 1 of 3 Most Outstg Jr Wom 1972; NSF Grant for Primatae Res 1973; Mem, Pres Mortar Bd 1973.

ALBRECHT, MARVIN JR oc/Florist, Instructor and Department Head; b/June 8, 1937; m/Iris; c/Lisa, Troy, Kristin; p/Marvin and Evelyn Albrecht, Rosenberg, TX; ed/MME Univ Houston 1959; pa/Floirst 29 Yrs; Instr, Dept Hd Floral Dept, Wharton Co Jr Col 8 Yrs; Houston Allied Florist Assn: Dir, VP; Mid-Coast Allied Florist Assn: Pres, VP, Dir; Tex St Florist Assn: VP, Dir; Am Acad Florist; Am Inst Floral Designers; cp/Wharton C of C: Dir, VP, Bicent Chm; Wharton City Charter Comm, Secy; Wharton JCs: Dir, Treas, VP; Pres Wharton Girls Softball Leag; Wharton Yth Fair: Life Mem, Dir; r/Meth; hon/Key Man Awd, JCs 1964; In Process of Writing New Floral Textbook.

ALDERMAN, JAMES E oc/Supreme Court Justice; b/Nov 1, 1936; h/Tallahassee, FL; ba/Supreme Ct of Fla, Supreme Ct Bldg, Tallahassee, FL 32304; m/Jean; c/James Allen; p/B E and Frances Alderman, Ft Pierce, FL; ed/BA 1958, LLB 1961 Univ Fla; pa/Justice, Supreme Ct of Fla 1978-; Judge, 4th Dist Ct Appeal 1976-78; Circuit Judge, 19th Judicial Circuit Ct 1972-76; Co Judge, St Lucie Co, Fla 1971-72; St Lucie Co Bar Assn, Pres; cp/Ft Pierce-St Lucie Co C of C, Pres; St Lucie Co Fair Assn, Pres; Ft Pierce Mutual Concert Assn, Pres; r/Epis; hon/Univ Fla Hall of Fame; Fla Blue Key.

ALDERMAN, JOYCE ANN SPIVEY oc/Associate Real Estate Broker; b/Nov 15, 1941; h/500 8th St, Radford, VA 24141; ba/Radford; m/Robert N; c/Robert Jr, Katrina Jo, Natasha Lois; p/John and Beatrice L Spivey, Austinville, VA; ed/Att'd: Radford Univ, New River Commun Col; Grad Rltrs Inst, Univ Va; pa/Assoc Broker, Giesen-Caldwell Agcy Inc (Oldest Firm in Radford); Nat Assn Real Est Bds; Va Assn Real Est Bds; New River Val Bd Rltrs, Secy 1978; Assoc Mem Soc of Real Est Appraisers; Farm & Land Inst; r/Presb; hon/CRS 1979; Million Dollar Clb 1978, 79.

ALDERMAN, LOUIS CLEVELAND JR oc/College President; b/Aug 12; h/Old Chester Rd, Cochran, GA 31014; ba/Cochran; m/Anne W; c/Amelia Anne, Louis C III, Fielding D, Jonathan A; p/Louis Cleveland Sr (dec) and Minnis Amelia Wooten Alderman (dec); ed/AA So Ga Col 1942; AB Emory Univ 1946; MS Univ Ga 1949; EdD Auburn Univ 1959; mil/AUS WWII; pa/Univ Ga: Instr Biol Rome Ctr 1949-50, Dir Savannah Ctr 1950-51, Dir Rome Ctr 1951-56, Dir Columbus Ctr 1956-59; Dir Henderson Col, Univ Ky 1959-64; Pres Mid Ga Col 1964-; Pres Ga Assn Jr Cols; Ga Col Assn; So Assn Jr Col; So Assn Cols & Schs; Phi Delta Kappa; cp/Dist Gov Rotary Intl Dist 692; Pres & Dir Cochran Rotary Clb; Org'g Pres Mid Ga Chapt SAR; SAR, Nat Com-man Signers of Declaration; r/Bapt: Deacon & Former Chm; hon/Civitan Awd 1955; Clb Ser Awd, Rotary 1959; Outstg Rotarian Awd 1976; Nat Awd SAR 1980; Ford Foun Fellow 1959; Public Hlth Ser Grant 1948-49; Phi Delta Kappa; Phi Beta Lambda; Phi Theta Kappa; Gamma Beta Phi; Author for Profl Jours.

ALDERMAN, LOUIS CLEVELAND III oc/Electrical Engineer, Computer Systems Customer Engineer; b/Oct 7, 1955; h/8910 Brookwulf Dr, Houston, TX 77099; ba/Houston; m/Susanna Marie Egger; c/Louis Cleveland Jr and Anne Augusta Whipple Alderman, Cochran, GA; ed/AS Mid Ga Col 1975; BEE Ga Inst Technol 1977; pa/Hewlett Packard Co, Computer Ser Div: Assoc Computer Sys Customer Engr 1977-78, Computer Sys Customer Engr 1979-; St of Ga Engr-in-Tng; Nat Assn Profl Engrs, Student Mem 1974-75; cp/CAR, Uchee Trails Soc, Charter Pres;

Engrs, Student Mem 1974-75; cp/CAR, Uchee Trails Soc, Charter Pres; SAR; Nat Assn Eagle Scouts; Magna Charta Barons, Somerset Chapt; r/Bapt; hon/St of Ga Gov's Hons Prog, Math 1972; St of Ga & Univ Ga Cert of Merit 1972; Cochran HS Salutatorian & Hon Grad 1973; Nat BETA Clb 1972-73; STAR Student 1973; Dean's List, Mid Ga Col 1973-75; W/W Am Jr Cols 1974-75; Phi Theta Kappa, Kappa Rho Chapt; Wallace Harris Meml S'ship, Mid Ga Col 1973-75; Burgoyne Gibson Moores Meml S'ship, Mid Ga Col 1973; Dean's List, Ga Inst Technol 1975-77; Eagle Scout.

ALDREDGE, JAMES HENRY JR oc/Vocational Guidance Counselor; b/May 8, 1917; h/144 Clarendon Cir, Danville, VA 24541; ba/Petersburg, VA; p/James Henry and Bessie Wagner Aldredge; ed/BBA 1941, MEd 1971 VPI; mil/2nd Lt Coast Artillery Corps 1941; 14th Anti-Aircraft Command in SW Pacific; Maj and Detailed Insp Gen of 14th AA Command; pa/Danville Industs Inc 1947-65, Asst Secy-Treas 1953, Secy-Treas 1968; Petersburg Ed Assn; Dist D Ed Assn; Va Ed Assn; Nat Ed Assn; Trade & Indust Ed Assn; Va Voc Assn; Am Voc Assn; Am Voc Assn; Va Pers & Guid Assn; Am Pers & Guid Assn; cp/Former Secy-Treas Danville JCs; Mem Danville Am Legion Post 325; Danville Golf Club; Mem Euclid Royal Arch Chapt 15; Dove Commandery No 7; Knight Templar; Danville Scottish Rite Bodies & Acca Temple of the Shrine; Past Mem Roman Eagle Lodge No 122; AF & AM; Former Mem Exec Com of Roman Eagle Meml Home Inc of Danville; Former Mem Danville (Host) Lions Club & Mem of Petersburg Lions Club; Mem & Former Bd Mem Calvary Meth Ch of Danville; Affil Mem & Mem Ofcl Bd Wash St Meth Ch, Petersburg; Silver Mem VPI Alumni Assn; Past Pres Danville Area Alumni Assn.

ALDRICH, BETTY B McWHINNY oc/Violinist, String Teacher; b/Apr 4, 1925; h/Rt 6 Box 623, Cleveland, TN, 37311; ba/Collegedale, TN; m/William T Sr; c/William T Jr, Nancy E, Sylvia A Enright, Jeanne M, John M; p/Forest McWhinny (dec) and Edith Tyrrel, C'land, TN; ed/Studies at: San Diego Jr Col, 1943; Pacific Union Col 1944; US Intl Univ 1959-60; Univ of Calif Ext 1961; San Diego St Univ 1969, 74; Southwestern Jr Col 1970-73; Loma Linda Univ (Intl Inst of Conduct'g) 1971; C'land St Commun Col 1978-80; Univ Tenn 1978, 79; So Missionary Col 1976-81; Bayerisches Staats Konsavatorium, Wurzburg, Germany 1949-50; San Diego Acad 1966-72; Studied Cello w Paul Anderson; Studied Violin w William Benner; pa/Violinist; String Teacher; Mus Tchrs Nat Assn Inc; Suzuki Assn of Ams; Am String Tchrs' Assn; cp/C'land Mus Club; r/Seventh-day Adventist; hon/Students Winners Elem String Div Tenn Mus Tchrs' Assn 1979 (violin) & 1980 (cello).

ALDRIDGE, MARVIN WARREN oc/Dentist; b/Apr 27, 1923; h/3301 Tucker Dr, Greenville, NC 27834; ba/G'ville; ed/Med Col Va; UNC; ECU; pa/Am Dental Assn; NC Dental Soc; Past Pres 5th Dist Dental Soc; E Ctrl Dental Soc; Am Acad Periodontology; So Acad Periodontology; Periodontal Study Clb of Carolinas; Past Pres NC Soc for Preventive Dentistry; Past Pres Loblloly Dental Study Clb; Carolina Preventive Study Clb; Past Advr NC Public Hlth, Dental Div; Past Dir Dental Foun NC; Past Regional Chm NC Doctor Dial Prog; cp/G'ville City Coun 4 Yrs, 2 Yrs Mayor Pro-Tem; Past Pres: ECU Alumni Clb, G'ville C of C, Jr C of C, ECU Pirate's Clb, Pitt Med Assocs, G'ville Boys' Clb, G'ville Lions Clb, G'ville Little Leag; Rotary Clb; Dir NC Nat Bank; Past Advr NC Public Hlth Dental Div; r/Meth: Chm Bd of Stewards; hon/Intl Col of Dentists; Pierre Fauchard Acad; Royal Soc Hlth; Delta Sigma Delta, Grad Chapt; Dist'd Ser Awd, Jr C of C; Consltg Staff Pitt Co Meml Hosp; Clin Instr, Dept Surg, Div Dentistry, ECU Sch Med; Att'g Fac, Dentistry, Dept Fam Pract, ECU Sch Med; Author "Muco-gingival Surgery" 1964 & "Practical Preventive Dentistry" 1970 *Journal of NC Dental Soc.*

ALEXANDER, ELLIS TURNER oc/General Manager; b/Nov 26, 1952; h/1 Forest Run, Asheville, NC 28803; ba/Fletcher, NC; m/Nancy Smith; p/Jake F and Doris T Alexander, Salisbury, NC; ed/UNC Chapel Hill, 1975; Young Execs Inst; UNC Chapel Hill 1981; pa/Pilot Freight Carriers Inc 1975-80; Gen Mgr Youngblood Truck Lines Inc 1980-; hon/John Motley Morehead S'ship 1971-75.

ALEXANDER, JOSEPH VANCE oc/Teacher; b/May 25, 1934; h/819 W Union St, Morganton, NC 29655; m/Mary Boggs; c/Mary, Louise; p/William Theodore (dec) and Eloise McDowell Alexander, Lenior, NC; ed/BS 1959, MA 1973 Appalachian St Univ; Att'd Canadian Studies Sem, Royal Mil Col, Kingston, Ontario; Laval Univ 1979; Duke Univ; 1978-79; mil/USMC 1952-55; pa/Elem Sch Tchr, Burke Co Public Schs; NCAE; NEA; ACT; Phi Delta Kappa; Pres Burke Co Unit NCAE; Pres Burke Co Unit ACT; cp/Life Mem DAV, Chapt 43; Scoutmaster Troop 180; VP Burke Co Hist Soc; St Andrews Soc; NCHSAOA; N St Fball Ofcls Assn; Catawba Val Lodge #217, 32° Scottish Rite Mason, Val of Orient; Oasis Temple, AAONMS; Pres Burke Co Shrine Clb; r/Epis; hon/Mens "A" Clb ASTC 1958; Scouter's Key 1967; NC HS Ath Ofcl's Awd 1980; Outstg Student Polit Sci Class, ASU 1972.

ALEXANDER, LAMAR oc/Governor of Tennessee; b/July 3, 1940;

h/Executive Residence, Curtiswood Ln, Nashville, TN 37204; ba/Nashville; m/Honey; c/Drew, Leslee, Kathryn, Will; p/Andy and FloAlexander, Maryville, TN; ed/BA Vanderbilt Univ 1962; JD NYU Sch Law 1965; pa/Gov Tenn 1979-; St Co-Chm Appalachian Regional Comm; Nat Gov's Assn Task Force on Revenue Sharing, Co-Chm; Commentator, Polit Analyst, WSM-TV 1975-77; Advr to Sen Howard H Baker 1977; Tenn Repub Gubernatorial Nom 1974; Ptnr Dearborn & Ewing Attys 1973-78; Chief of Transition between Dunn & Ellington Adms 1970-71; Campaign Mgr, Gov Winfield Dunn 1970; Exec Asst, White Ho Cong Relats Ofc 1969; Leg Asst, US Senator Baker 1967-69; Campaign Coor for Sen Baker 1967-69; Law Clk to Hon John Minor Wisdom, Judge, US Circuit Ct of Appeals, 5th Dist, New Orleans; Assoc, Fowler, Rowntree, Fowler & Robertson, Attys; Reporter, *The Knoxville News Sentinel, Nashville Banner & Maryville-Alcoa Daily Times*; cp/Bd Dirs Maryville Col; Fdr & 1st Chm Tenn Coun on Crime & Delinquency 1973-74; Fdr & Co-Chm Tenn Citizens Com for Revenue Sharing 1971-72; r/Presb: Deacon.

ALEXANDER, LOUIS oc/Writer, Teacher; b/Mar 16, 1917; h/PO Box 158, Bellaire, TX 77401; ba/Houston; m/M C; c/Kathryn, Marjory Lynn, Catherine Ann Chapman, Thomas Chapman III, Suellen Ruggles, Joseph Chapman, Christopher Chapman; p/Louis I Sr (dec) and Gertrude Alexander, Miami Bch, FL; ed/BS Univ Newark; ML Univ Houston; mil/USAFR Lt Col Ret'd; pa/Writer; Tchr Univ Houston; Mem: Nat Conf Editorial Writers, Aviation & Space Writers Assn, Assn for Ed in Jour, Press Clb of Houston; cp/Dist 21 Rep, Citizens Adv Bd for Metro Transit 1980-83; Bellarie NE Civic Clb; hon/Mil DFC, Air Medal w 3 Clusters, Dist Unit Cit w Cluster; AWA Best Documentary, Space, Radio 1973, Ctl Reg.

ALEXANDER, RANDALL LEE oc/Executive Director, Sports Information Director; b/Mar 15, 1954; h/812 Charles Rd, Shelby, NC 28150; m/Melanie Williams; p/Walter Ken and Betty Rierson Alexander, Gastonia, NC; ed/BS Gardner-Webb Col 1976; pa/Exec Dir Gardner-Webb Col Ath Fund Raising; Sports Info Writer Gardner-Webb Col; W Carolina Tennis Assn, VP 1979, Pres 1980; Mem Nat Assn Intercol Aths; Sports Info Dirs Assn; hon/Best Football Prog in Nat (7 eds), Nat Assn of Intercol Aths 1979; 10th Best Football Brochure in Nat, Nat Assn of Intercol Aths 1979; Outstg Yng Men in Am 1979; Most Valuable Tennis Player Gardner-Webb Col 1976; W/W in Am Cols & Univs.

ALEXANDER, ROBERT WILLIAM oc/Chief of Police; b/Oct 13, 1948; h/City Hall, Crab Orchard, KY 40419; ba/Same; m/JoAnn; c/Bruce, Anthony, Jack, Danny; p/Robert L Jr and Alice Junita Gerlack Alexander (dec), Smith Grove, Ky; ed/BA EKU, Richmond, Ky; mil/USMC Maj 7 yrs 7 mos; r/Bapt; hons/3 Purple Hearts; Silver Star; Navy Cross.

ALEXANDER, ROY L oc/Director of Client Services, Marriage and Family Therapist; b/Dec 10, 1947; h/2607 Holly St, Stephenville, TX 76401; m/Judy; c/Bryan; p/Mr and Mrs Mack Alexander, Levelland, TX; ed/BS 1971, MEd 1972 En NM Univ; pa/Prog Develr & Marriage-Fam Therapist, Commun Mtl Hlth Ctr Employment; Instr Psych: Amarillo Col 1972-73, Pt-Time S Plains Jr Col 1973-77; Clin Mem Am Assn Marriage-Fam Therapists; cp/C of C Stephenville, Bd Mem; U Way S'ville, Bd Mem; Optimist Clb; r/Ch of Christ; hon/Outstg Yng Men in Am 1977; Original Pres, Cross Timbers Photo Clb.

ALFORD, LEE S oc/Attorney-at-Law; b/May 16, 1942; h/14 Brookwood Drive, York, SC 29745; ba/York; m/Terri Baker; c/Matthew Lee; p/Lee S Alford Sr (dec); Mary G Bowers, Rock Hill, SC; ed/AB Hist Univ of SC; JD Univ of SC Law Sch; mil/USAF 1960-64; pa/Atty; Mem: York Co, SC Bar Assns, York Co Yg Lwyrs Assn (Past Pres); Admitted to Pract Law: SC St Cts, Fed Dist Ct for SC, 4th Circuit Ct of Appeals, US Supreme Ct; cp/Dem Nom for Probate Judge, York Co 1978; Orgr, Bd Dirs SC JC Fdn Inc; Chm York Red Cross Chapt; Pres Camp Arc Coun; Gen Fund Drive Chm, Pres, VP, Trustee: Wn York Co U Fund; Chm Heart Fund Drive; Cmdr Catawba Power Squadron; Commun Action VP of SC JCs; Hearing Ofcr York School Dist; Others; r/Mem Trinity U Meth Ch, York; hon/JCs: JC of Yr, Key Man, Proj of Yr; Outstg St VP Awd, SC JCs; Sr Mem Awd, Catawba Power Squadron; York Area Dist'd Ser Awd 1977; 1 of 3 Outstg Yg Men in SC 1977; JC Intl Senator 1977.

ALLAIRE, PAUL E oc/Professor; b/Sept 23, 1941; h/208 Westminster Rd, Charlottesville, VA 22901; ba/Ch'ville; m/Janet A; c/Timothy, Benjamin; p/Orien J and Josephine M Allaíre; ed/BE 1963, ME 1964 Yale Univ; PhD Northwestern 1972; pa/Lectr Ethiopian Telecommuns Inst 1964-66; Asst Prof Meml Univ Nfld 1971-72; Asst Prof Univ Va 1972-77; Assoc Prof Univ Va 1977-; Pres VIBCO Res Inc 1979-; Dir Rotat'g Machinery & Controls Industl Res Prog, Univ Va 1980-; Acoustical Soc Am; Am Soc Mech Engrg; Am Soc Engrg Ed; Sigma Xi; Tau Beta Pi; Ed Chm Am Soc Lubrication Engrs; hon/NASA Cert Recog Significant New Technol 1980; Publ'd: "Dynamics of Short Eccentric Plain Seals with High Axial Reynolds Number," "Analysis of Step Journal Bearings-Infinite

PERSONALITIES OF THE SOUTH

Length, Inertia Effects," others.

ALLEN, ELBERT E oc/Dentist; b/Sept 19, 1921; h/2119 Carver Pl, Shreveport, LA 71103; ba/Sh'port; m/Carolyn Sims; ed/BS Wiley Col 1942; DDS Meharry Med Col 1945; FAGD Acad Gen Dentistry 1969; mil/2nd Lt Resv Corps 1941; Capt USAF 1951; USAFR 1953-58; pa/Fdg Mem & Secy 1953-72 N La Dent Soc; Fdg Mem & Past Pres Pelican St Dent Assn; Past Ed NAA Jour La Nat Dent Assn; Past Mem VA Com Nat Dent Assn; Assoc Mem Chgo Dent Soc; NW La Dent Assn; La St Dent Assn; Am Dent Assn; Past Parliamentn & Mem By-Laws & Constit Com Acad Gen Dent; Fdn Denatire Intl; cp/Am Legion Jones Hollinsworth Post 525: Past Comdr; Fin Ofcr 1952-62, Pres Am Legion Improvmt Co Inc; Past Procuremt Chm Bayou Boy's St; Past Post Chm Bayou Boy's St; Past Mem Nat Com Am Legion for Law & Order; Vice Chm Nat Com Am Legion on Americanism; Alpha Chi Chap Kappa Alpha Psi: Past Polemarch; Brother of Yr 1957; Past Provincial Polemarch La, Ark, Tex, Miss; Past Sr Grand Vice Polemarch (Nat VP); Past Grand Polemarch (Nat Pres); Grand Bd Dirs 1964-76; Mem Am Woodmen Sh'port Camp 2; Past Chm LOTA Dist; Supreme Cmdr, Supreme Camp Am Woodmen; Past Exec Secy & Pres Sh'port C of C; Past Mem Geo W Carver Br YMCA; Past Chm Com of Mgmt Carver YMCA; Past Fin Chm Pioneer Div BSA; Past Mem Bd Dirs Sh'port Men Hlth Ctr; Past Mem Bd Dirs, Fdg Mem & Past Mem By-Laws & Constit Com David Raines Rec Org; Past Mem Bd Dirs Am Cancer Soc; Past Mem Bd Dirs Am Red Cross Sh'port Chap; Past Mem Bd Dirs Sh'port Blind Assn; Past Mem Bd Dirs Sh'port Yth Opp Ctr; Bd Trustees Wiley Col; Fdg Mem Mt Moriah Day Care Ctr & Nursery; Past Mem Nat Bd Dirs Nat Coun Christians & Jews; Bd Dirs Salvation Army; Commr Housing Auth City Sh'port; Bd Dirs Wiley Col; r/Meth; hon/W/W in S&SW 1963-65; W/W in Am 1976-77; Notable Am Awd 1976-77; Notable Am of Bicent Era 1976; First Negro Elect'd to any Elective Ofc since Reconstruction Days; Liberty Bell Awd from Sh'port Bar Assn 1970; Silver Beaver Awd 1972; Pierre Fuchared Awd for Outstg Ser to Country for Mil Ser 1952.

ALLEN, ETHELENE M oc/Homemaker; b/Sept 10, 1934; h/Rt 3 Box 236, Four Oaks, NC 27524; m/Leonard R; c/Ransom, Patricia Susan, Barbara Carol, Kevin Miles; p/Beulah B McCabe, Clayton, NC; ed/Att'g Johnston Tech Inst; r/Mission Bapt; hon/Articles Pub's in Num Newspapers.

ALLEN, FRANCES oc/Nurse; b/May 12, 1916; h/PO Box 1551, Hickory, NC 28603; p/Joseph Samuel (dec) and Deliliah H Allen (dec); ed/BS UNC 1952; Master Public Hlth 1961; pa/Conslt Public Hlth Nsg, Div Hlth Ser, Raleigh, NC; Conslt ALCOR, Alice Lloyd Col, Pippa Passe, Ky; Prof Nsg, Berea Col; Prof Nsg, Wn Carolina Univ; Pres Dist Nurses; Fellow APHA; ANA; NLN; cp/VP Hickory Altrusa Clb; Adv Coun Fam Guid Ctr; Coun of So Mtns; Adv Coun C J Harris Hosp; r/Presb; hon/Ky Col 1967; W/W Am Wom 1972; Maternal & Child Hlth Awd 1979; Immunization Survey 1965.

ALLEN, GEORGE CALVIN oc/Athletic Academic Counselor; Assistant Football Coach; b/May 22, 1955; h/2614 Univ Dr 76, Nacogdoches, TX 75961; ba/Nacogdoches; p/Grace Allen, Bay City, TX; ed/BSEd; MSEd; pa/Ath Acad Coun; Asst Fball Coach; Tex St Tchrs Assn; Tex HS Coaches Assn; r/Bapt; hon/W/W Among Students in Cols & Univs.

ALLEN, HAZEL oc/Artist, Homemaker; b/Feb 24, 1909; m/(dec); c/John F; p/Frank Jr (dec) and Luvena B Pickens (dec); ed/Charleston Bus Col; Art Sch; pa/U Fuel Gas Co 20 yrs; Newspaper Reporter: *Town Crier*, Lake City, Tenn & *Anderson County Reporter*, Clinton, Tenn; Artist; cp/Norris Wom's Club; Oak Ridge Art Ctr; Dulin Art Gal; r/Bapt; hon/1st Prize on Art; 2nd Prize on Art; Honorable Mention on Art.

ALLEN, JAMES E oc/Associate Professor; b/May 11, 1935; h/706 Greenwood Rd, Chapel Hill, NC 27514; ba/Chapel Hill; m/Janet; c/Gregory; p/Marguerite Allen, Chapel Hill, NC; ed/BA w Hons Univ Ariz 1957; STB 1960, PhD 1964 Boston Univ; MSPH UNC-CH 1969; pa/Assoc Prof Hlth Adm, Sch of Public Hlth, UNC-CH; Am Public Hlth Assn: Maternal Hlth Care & Fam Plan'g Com, Chm Sub-Com on Standards of Care in Adolescence & Teenage Pregnancy; Population Assn Am; Am Soc Public Adm; Soc for Sci Study of Rel: Reviewer for Manuscripts on Population; Res Assoc, Inst for Res in Social Sci; Past Mem: Am Sociol Assn, Am Soc of Christian Ethics, Nat Coun of Chs; cp/Rotary; r/Meth; hon/Phi Beta Kappa; Delta Sigma Rho; Nat Hon Soc; Baker Grad Awd 1960; Ortho Marriage Cnslg Awd 1961 & 62; US Public Hlth Ser Awd for Adv'd Res, Study in Population 1969; Contbr to *Approaches to the Human Fertility Problem* 1968; Author *The Early Years of Marriage* 1973 & *Managing Teenage Pregnancy: Access to Abortion, Contraception and Sex* 1980.

ALLEN, JERRY ARTHUR oc/Minister; b/Feb 12, 1942; h/617 N Ch St, Mt Olive, NC 28365; m/Ruth Barefoot; c/Jerry Arthur Jr, Jamie Scott;

p/George W and Olive Jean Allen, Four Oaks, NC; ed/Durham Inst Barber'g 1961; NC St Univ Truck Driver Train'g Sch 1973; Cert of Ordination Free Will Bapt Min 1980; Cand BS Mt Olive Col; pa/Min Bethel Free Will Bapt Ch; NC Min Assn; W Conf Orig Free Will Bapts; r/Free Will Bapt; hon/Driver of the Yr Miss Truck'g Co 1974-75; Ministerial S'ship 1980.

ALLEN, JERRY YOUNG oc/Minister; b/Oct 21, 1948; h/PO Box 37, Patterson, NC 28661; m/Virginia Kaye Stampley; c/Bradley Young; p/Ralph Young and Mae Von Tutor Allen; ed/BA Miss Col; MDiv SW Bapt Theol Sem; Post-grad Studies Princton Theol Sem; pa/Bapt Min; Admr; Rotary Intl; Pres Bolivar Co Pastors' Conf; Chm Christian Actions Comm for Bolivar Assn; cp/Prog Chm Rotary; Precnt Chm Repub Party; r/So Bapt; hon/Only Student Elected to 2 Consecutive Terms Student Body Pres SW Bapt Theol Sem.

ALLEN, JOAN SHELLEY oc/Broadcasting; b/Jan 20, 1939; h/305 Edgewood Road, Shelby, NC 28150; ba/Shelby; m/James Platt; c/Kevin Kirk, Virginia Blanche, Sandy Skipper, Randy Shelley, Altman Ann; p/Daniel Burn and Blanche Altman Shelley (dec); pa/Broadcasting; Adm Asst to Pres; Mem: Nat Secys Assn, Secys Guild of Am; cp/Past Treas Shelby Jr Wom's Clb; Former Mem Shelby C of C Tour of Homes Com; Dem Party; r/Adm Bd Ctl U Meth Ch, Shelby; Altar Guild; Chancel Choir; Wk Area on Evangelism; Former VChm of Coun on Ministries; Former Pianist for Yth Choirs; hon/Spec White House Recog for Vol Activities 1977; Nom'd by Ofcls of Wn NC for Vol of Yr for Work w Retarded Chd.

ALLEN, JOHN DAVID oc/Director of Washington Operations, Financial Consultant; IPCO Inc; b/Aug 20, 1944; h/8412 Huerta Court, Alexandria, VA 22309; ba/Same; m/Mary Mullins E; p/Woodrow W and Veronica Ann Allen, Rochester, NY; ed/BA, MBA Univ of Rochester; JD Catholic Univ, Wash, DC; mil/AUS Capt, Awds: DSC, Silver Star, Bronze Star, Purple Heart; pa/Assn MBA Exec; Reg'd Lobbiest, Wash, DC; cp/Alexandria Bus-man Clb; 3rd Degree Mason; r/Roman Cath; hon/W/W in S&SW.

ALLEN, JOHN ELDRIDGE oc/Historian, Former Official US Government; b/Sept 11, 1911; h/(Sum/Fall) 1001 N Main St, Kernersville, NC 27284; (Winter/Sprg) 7339 SW 82nd St, S Miami, FL 33143; m/Mary Edwards; c/Mark Edwards; p/Arthur Vincent and Annie Willis Allen (dec); ed/BBA Univ Miami 1934; MA Geo Wash Univ 1937; mil/USN Ofcr 1942-46, Res Status 1946-55, Lt Cmdr; pa/Fed Civilian Employee & Ofcl 1935-42, 48-59; Mem Ceremonies Group Freedom Train Wash DC 1947; Dedication Group Statue of Nathan Hale, Wash 1948; Jt Com Hon Plaques Wash Homes 9 Former Chief Justices of US 1948-49; Adv Panel Great Lawgivers Sculptored Portraits, House Chamber Wash 1949-50; Lafayette Park Wash Reception Com 200th Anniv Birth of Marquis de Lafayette 1957; Spec Guest Dedication Hist Mus So Fla & Caribbean, Miami 1962; Fdr Mem Patriotic Ed Inc; Renaissance Soc of Am, US Capitol Hist Soc, US Supr Ct Hist Soc (Charter) US Olympic Soc; Chm Thomas Jefferson Meml Wash DC Prog Apr 1952 (Pres Harry Truman Participated); cp/Dem; r/Meth; hon/Pub'd Author.

ALLEN, L CALHOUN JR oc/Mayor, City of Shreveport; b/Feb 8, 1921; h/65 Tealwood, Shreveport, TN 71104; ba/Shreveport; m/Jacqueline Schober; pa/Former Assoc Allen Constrn Co; cp/Elected Shreveport Mayor 1970, Re-elected to 4 Yr Term 1974; Elected Shreveport Public Utilities Commr 1962; Re-elected 1966; Past Pres: Shreveport Coun Navy Leag of US, Southland Dixie Promenade of Forty & Eight, Holiday in Dixie; Past Dist VP, Naval Resv Assn; Exec Bd & Bd Dirs, La St Fair Assn; Chm: La St Fair Comm, Shreve Area Coun Govt; Exec Bd: Shreveport Symph, Shreveport Beautification Foun; VP, Red River Val Assn; Downtown Devel Auth; Shreveport Airport Auth; Past Pres & Exec Bd, Norwela Coun BSA; Past VP & Exec Bd, La Mun Assn; Past Commr, La Stadium & Exposition Dist; Forty & Eight: Past Chef de Gare Voiture 137, Grand Chef de Gare La; Past Cmdr, Am Legion; ARC; Kiwanis; Elks; Others; r/1st Presb Ch, Shreveport: Mem, Elder; hon/Cert of Appreic Shreveport Bossier Voc-Tech Ctr 1976, Dept Vet Affairs 1975, Nat Safe Boating Com 1972; Cert of Merit: Disabled Am Vets 1971, 2nd Air Force; Hon'd by: NAIA, Non-Comm'd Ofcrs Assn, AUS Recruiting Command, USCG Aux, Am Legion, BSA, OES, FFA, Others; Hon Atty Gen, St of La 1960; Hon Col & Aide-de-Camp, Staff of Gov John J McKeithan 1964; W/W: Govt, Am, La, S&SW, Am Polits; DIB; Others.

ALLEN, PAULINE VIRGINIA oc/Retired Accountant; Consultant; b/Feb 7, 1909; h/Box 96, Tunica, MS 38676; ba/Tunica; p/Henry James (dec) and Madia Kennedy Allen (dec); ed/AB Duke Univ 1935; pa/Ret'd Acct; Conslt Fiscal Sers; Ret'd Mem Hosp Fin Mgrs Assn; cp/SS Tchr Sr Citizens Grp; Democrat; r/Meth; hon/W/W Am Wom 1979.

ALLEN-JONES, PAMELA oc/Executive Director; b/Apr 14, 1946; ba/201 S Tuttle Ave, Sarasota, FL 33578; m/R Earle; c/Ty Palmer, Joshua

6

PERSONALITIES OF THE SOUTH

Jon; ed/BEd Univ of London, UK; Grad Studies Univ Colo; pa/Exec Dir Girls Clubs of Sarasota Co Inc; Girls Clubs of Am Inc; cp/Hon Chm Guild Chd's Diabetes Foun Denver; Jr League Sarasota; Exec Bd Chd's Diabetes Foun Denver; Symph Guild Denver; C of C Sarasota; Sarasota Yth Relat'd Ser Assn; hon/High Hopes Awd Chd's Diabetes Foun Denver 1979.

ALLEY, FAYE GREENE oc/Child Care, Wife, Mother; b/Apr 18, 1929; h/212 Cedar Val Rd, Hudson, NC 28638; c/Janice, Ted, Tonna, Chris, Pat, Tim, Bunky; p/Nina B Greene, Hudson, NC; ed/Cleveagus Col 1962; Doll Technol 1980; pa/Dent Asst 9 Yrs; r/Bapt; hon/Home Decorations.

ALLISON, WILLIAM W oc/Executive; b/Oct 9, 1933; h/Atlanta, GA; ba/Coca-Cola Co, PO Drawer 1734, Atlanta, GA 30301; c/Tracey M; p/Andrew T (dec) and Thelma W Allison (dec); ed/BA De Pauw Univ 1954; MA Univ Philippines 1961; MPA Univ Pgh 1966; mil/AUS 1954-56 Spec 3rd Cl; pa/VP, Dir, Commun Relats & Contbns, Coca-Cola Co 1981-; Dpty Dir, Commun Sers Adm, Wash DC 1977-81; Ec Opport: Exec Admr 1969-77, Dpty Admr 1968-69, Assoc Admr for Prog Devel & Plan'g 1966-68; Commun Involvement Coor, Peace Corps Tng Prog, Morehouse-Spelman Cols 1966; Dir Prog Devel, Commun Coun of Atlanta Area 1965; Assoc Dir, Employment on Merit Prog, Am Friends Ser Com 1964-65; Res Asst, Coun of Ec & Cultural Affairs Inc, Univ Philippines 1961-63; Instr & Chm, Dept Social Scis, Am Sch Inc, Makati Rizal, Philippines 1958-61; Jr Exec Prog, Carson, Pirie, Scott & Co 1957; Bd Govs Woodward Acad; Adv Coun Sch of Bus Adm, Atlanta Univ; Past Mem & Past Pres Ga Commun Action Assn; Past Mem Bd Dirs The Coca-Cola Co; Past Secy Bd of Trustees, Big Bros Assn, Atlanta; cp/Past Mem: Bd Dirs N Ctrl Ga Hlth Sys, Bd Dirs Sadie G Mays Meml Nsg Home, Bd Trustees Wesley Homes Inc, Bd Dirs Ga Easter Seal Soc, Bd Trustees Atlanta Arts Alliance, Bd Sponsors The High Museum of Art, Bd Dirs Ga Conservancy Inc, Exec Com Resurgens Atlanta, Ga Chapt Am Soc for Public Adm, Ga St Manpwr Sers Coun, Bd Dirs UNICEF SE Region; Mayor's Task Force on City Reorg 1973; Gov's Comm on Govtl Reform, City of Atlanta & Fulton Co 1977; Adv Com, Sch of Bus Adm, Ga St Univ 1975-79; r/Bahai; hon/Outstg Bus Indiv of Yr, Interracial Coun for Bus Opport 1975; Ivan Allen Jr Human Relats Awd, Morris Brown Col Nat Alumni Assn 1974; Yng Man of Yr, Atlanta Jr C of C 1969; Yng Man of Yr in Public Ser, Y's Men Intl, Omega Chapt 1968; Urban Ser Awd, Ofc of Ec Opport 1967; Outstg Yng Man of Yr; Ldrship Ga 1971; Author Num Articles Inclg "The West, The East and Research" 1963 & "Southeast Asia in Perspective" 1969.

ALLMAN, MARTHA KINZER oc/Operating Room Supervisor; b/May 24, 1938; h/942 Kendrick Creek Rd, Kingsport, TN 37663; ba/K'port; c/Nancy, Bane, Laura, Gray; p/Henry Brinson and Louise Ratcliffe Kinzer, Dublin, VA; ed/LPN Haywood Co Tech 1966; AS E Tenn St Univ 1972; pa/Supervisor Indian Path Hosp: Operat'g Rm, Recovery Rm, Emer Rm; LPN: Haywood Co Hosp, Holston Val Commun Hosp; Coor'g Nurse Holston Val Hosp; Tenn Nurses Assn; Tenn Soc Nsg Ser Dir; Operat'g Rm Res Inst; Bd Dirs Assn Operat'g Rm Nurses; r/Jehovah Witness; hon/W/W SW 1980.

ALLRED, JUDY ANNE ALLEN oc/Underwriter; b/Jan 30, 1949; h/520 Penn Ave, McComb, MS 39648; ba/Same; m/Kenneth B; p/Billie W Allen, McComb, MS; ed/Liberty Nat New Agt Sch 1980; Liberty Nat Tng Course 1980; pa/Life Underwriter; cp/McComb Bus & Profl Wom's Club, Pres Miss Life Underwriters Assn; r/Bapt; hon/Yng Career Wom 1977.

ALLRED, PHILLIP LANCE oc/Assistant Professor; b/Dec 15, 1937; h/PO Box 6073, Huntsville, TX 77340; m/Lenna Hodnett; c/Eric Joseph, Mark Edward, Alysia, Shannon, Christie Lyn, Gary Thomas, Sherry LaRae; p/Everett Lance Allred; Helen Almira Duke; ed/BS 1969, MS 1973 Brigham Young Univ; PhD Univ Utah 1980; mil/USN 1956-60; pa/Asst Prof Audiology Sam Houston St Univ 1976-81; Audiologist Pvt Prac; Am Spch & Hear'g Assn; Tex Spch & Hear'g Assn; Dir Tex Univ Tng Progs in Spch & Audiology; Coun of Univ Supvrs of Practicum in Spch Path; Acad Dispensing Audiologists; cp/Pres Yng Repubs Univ Nevada 1964; hons/W/W in S&SW 1980-81; Author: "Tympanometry and Emergence of Acoustic Reflex in Infants," "A Better Way to Diagnose Middle Ear Problems."

ALLRED, WILLIAM DAVID oc/State Representative; b/Nov 27; h/PO Box 5066, Wichita Falls, TX 76307; m/Patricia Moyer; c/Rebecca Lee, Stephen David, James Moyer; p/James V Allred (dec); Joe Betsy Allred, Wichita Falls; ed/BA TCU 1955; MS Columbia Univ 1961; mil/2 yrs Active, Maj in Army Resv; Grad US Army Command & Gen Staff Col 1977; cp/Mem Tex Ho of Reps.

ALLUISI, EARL ARTHUR oc/Psychologist; b/June 11, 1927; h/15211 Sandia, San Antonio, TX 78232; ba/Brooks AFB, TX; m/Mary Jane Boyle; c/John Carroll, Jean Elizabeth, Paul David Julian, Janet Ann;

p/Humbert Peter (dec) and Elizabeth Mary Dini Alluisi; ed/BS William & Mary; MA, PhD Ohio St Univ; mi/AUS WWII, USAR Ret'd; pa/Psych, AF Human Resources Lab; Fellow: AAAS, APA; Mem Num Profl Socs; cp/Num Vol Orgs; r/Cath; hon/Jerome Eli Awd, Human Factors Soc 1970; Franklin V Taylor Awd, Soc of Engrg Psychs 1971; Phi Beta Kappa.

ALMARAZ, FELIX D JR oc/Professor, Writer; b/Dec 2, 1933; h/5907 Forest Cove, San Antonio, TX 78240; ba/San Antonio; m/Maria O; c/Antonio O; p/Felix D Sr (dec) and Antonia R Almaraz, San Antonio, TX; ed/BA, MA Hist St Mary's Univ, San Antonio; PhD Hist Univ NM, Albuquerque; mil/AUS Corp, Artillery 1953-56; pa/Prof Hist; Spkr-Part in Tex St Hist Assn, Wn Hist Assn; cp/Chm Bexar Co Hist Comm; r/Rom Cath; Mem Mission San Jose Parish, San Antonio; hon/Presidio La Bahia Awd, Sons of Repub of Tex; Awd of Merit, Am Assn for St & Local Hist.

ALMON, RENEAU PEARSON oc/Justice, Supreme Court of Alabama; b/Jul 8, 1937; h/3524 Lancaster Lane, Montgomery, AL 36106; ba/Montgomery; m/Deborah Pearson; c/Jonathan, Jason, Nathaniel, (Stepson:) Tommy Preer; p/Nathaniel L and Mary Johnson Almon, Moulton, AL; ed/BS 1959 Univ of Ala; LLB 1964 Samford Univ, Cumberland Sch of Law; mil/AUS; pa/Justice, Supr Ct of Ala; cp/Former JC, Kiwanian; r/Meth; hon/ODK; Outstg Yg Men in Am 1971; W/W in Am Cols & Univs.

ALMOND, JAMES LINDSAY JR oc/Senior Judge, US Court of Customs & Patent Appeals; b/June 15, 1898; h/208 Wexleigh Dr, Richmond, VA 23229; ba/Wash DC; m/Josephine Minter; p/James Lindsay and Edmonia Burgess Almond (dec); ed/LLB Univ Va; LLD Col of William & Mary; mil/SATC Univ VA 1917-78; pa/Asst Commonwlth Atty, Roanoke,Va 1930-32; Judge Hustings Ct, Roanoke, Va 1933-45; US Cong 1946-48; Atty Gen of Va 1948-57; Gov Va 1958-62; Assoc Judge US Ct of Customs & Patent Appeals 1962-73, Sr Judge 1973-; r/Luth Ch in Am.

ALMOND, JOSEPH C JR oc/Director of Pharmacy Services; b/Feb 29, 1924; h/70 Raleigh Rd, Newport News, VA 23601; m/Helen C; p/(dec); ed/BS Chem Bio 1949; BS Pharm 1951; DPharm 1976; MS Hlth Care Adm 1980; pa/Hosp Pharm (Dir); Lic'd Nsg Home Admr, Tenn & Ala; Am Col Nsg Home Adm; Va Soc Hosp Pharm; Va Pharm Assn (Life Mem); Am Pharm Assn; Peninsula Pharm Assn; r/Bapt; hon/Awd for Highest Average Pharm Chem 1951.

ALSOP, MARGIE ANNE oc/Interpreter for the Deaf; Social Worker; Teacher; Paraprofessional Counselor; b/Jun 9, 1950; h/333 W 1st, El Dorado, AR 71730; ba/El Dorado; p/J F and Catherine C Alsop, Corpus Christi, TX; ed/Sweet Briar Col 1967-69; BA Univ of Tex-Austin 1971; Yg Life Inst, Summer Sem 1971, 72; Para-profl Cnslg Prog; Sec'dy Tchg Cert Univ of Tex 1973; Grad Work in Ed; Sign Lang Classes; Nat Interpreter Tng Consortium Univ of Tenn 1978; Interpreter Workshops 1977-79; Nat Interpreter Tng Consortium Symposium Univ of Ariz 1979; pa/Para-profl Cnslr 1971-72; Patient Care Worker, Austin St Hosp 1973; Set Up Proj New Start, Austin 1974; Dorm Cnslr, Tex Sch for Deaf 1975; UN Conf on Habitat 1976; Set Up, Dir'd Broken Kettle Mtn Sch 1976-78; Tutor of Deaf Students, Ctl Piedmont Commun Col, Charlotte, NC 1978; Interpreter Caseworker 1979; Treas of Bd, Ark Registry of Interpreters for the Deaf 1979; cp/Supporter of Consumer Advocacy Agcies; Work for Environmtl Protection; Other Activities; hon/Delta Sigma.

ALSTON, McCARROLL oc/Transportation; b/Mar 1, 1909; h/426 W Franklin St, Warrenton, NC; m/Annie Mae Omohundro; p/Jack (dec) and Maud K Alston, Warrenton, NC; pa/Drive People to Hosp, Dentist, Meetings, etc; cp/Warrenton Vol Fire Dept; NC St Credit Union; Capital Hlth Sys Agcy Bd; r/Oak Chapel AME Ch; hon/Firemen of Yr Trophy 1968; NC Regional Hamptonian of Yr Awd 1977; John R Hawkins Alumni & Friends Inc Awd 1979.

ALSUP, REBA oc/Businesswoman; b/Aug 21, 1904; h/Owensville Rd, Calvert, TX 77837; m/(dec); p/Mrs. C T Rushing Sr, Bremond, TX; ed/Rice Inst 1922-23; SWn Univ 1923; BA 1927, MA 1930 Baylor; Columbia Univ 1929; La St Univ 1941; Colo Univ 1956; Univ Houston 1956, 57, 58; mil/Corporal WAC; pa/Owner & Mgr Calvert Arts & Crafts; Tchr HS Eng & Span; HS Libn; Archbishop Rummel HS; NRTP; Tex RTA; cp/VP Calvert C of C 1980; r/Meth; hon/Wom of the Yr 1980, Calvert C of C.

ALTAMURA, MICHAEL VICTOR oc/Family Physician; b/Sept 28, 1923; h/500 E Remington Dr, Sunnyvale, CA 94037; ba/Sunnyvale; m/Emily Wandell; c/Michael V Jr, Robert F; p/Frank (dec) and Theresa Altamura, Tustin, CA; ed/BS LI Univ 1949; MA Columbia Univ 1951; DO Kirksville Col of Osteo Med 1961; MD Cal Col of Med 1962; mil/AUS 1942-45, 51-53 1/Lt; pa/Clin Asst Prof Fam & Commun Med Stanford Sch Med 1974-81; Clin Coor Foothill/Stanford Phys Asst Prog 1976-77; Clin Asst Prof Fam & Commun Med Stanford Univ 1974-75; Pres Am Acad

7

PERSONALITIES OF THE SOUTH

Fam Phys Santa Clara Co Chapt; Chief Fam Pract Dept El Camino Hosp 1972-73; cp/Vol Phys Free Clins; r/Luth; hon/Fellow: Royal Soc Hlth, Am Acad Fam Phys, Am Geriatrics Soc; Diplomate Am Bd Fam Pract; Order of the Golden Sword; Am Cancer Soc; Co-Author *Aging Patient - A Guide for Their Care* 1976.

ALTCHULER, STEVEN IRA oc/Nutritional Physiologist; b/Aug 1, 1951; h/535 NASA Rd 1, #403A, Webster, TX 77598; ba/Houston; p/Murray and Lyn Atkins Altchuler, Pt Wash, NY; ed/SB 1973, PhD 1979 MIT; pa/Tchg Asst, MIT 1975-77; Res Asst, MIT 1977-78; Nutritional Physiologist, Biomed Labs, NASA/Johnson Space Ctr 1978-; Reviewer, Sci Books & Films 1980-; Adj Asst Prof of Nutrition, Dept of Human Devel & Consumer Scis, Univ of Houston, Ctrl Campus 1980-; AAAS; Am Col Nutrition, Affil Fellow; Am Statis Assn; Houston-Area Calcium Metabolism Soc, Fdg Mem; Nat Assn EMTs/Paramedics; NY Acad Sci; Nutrition Today Soc; Sigma Xi; Tex Assn EMTs; cp/Alpha Phi Omega, Alpha Chi Chapt 1971-75; Am Red Cross: Water Safety Instr 1969-, CPR Instr 1974-, First Aid Instr 1975-, Asst Capt Emer Aid Stations 1975-77, Capt Emer Aid Stations 1977-78, Disaster Sers Casewkr 1977-78, Disaster Action Team Vol 1977-, Shelter Mgr 1978-; Am Heart Assn: CPR Instr 1974-79, CPR Instr-Tnr 1979-; BSA, Merit Badge Cnslr 1969-74; Clear Lake Emer Med Corps: Paramedic 1978-, Tng Ofcr 1980-, Bd Dirs 1979-80; Forest Bend Civil Defense, Dir Shelter Opers 1979-; hon/Rensselaer Polytech Inst Awd 1969; Grumman Aerospace Corp Schlr 1969; Num Red Cross Ser Awds 1969-; Frederick Gardiner Fassett Jr Awd 1973; Vicks Fellow 1977; Author Num Tech Articles & Presentations.

ALTMAN, JEAN DRENNON oc/Curriculum Co-ordinator; b/June 9, 1928; h/502 Chinquapin Rd, Greenwood, SC 29646; m/Rufus U Jr; c/Janet Elizabeth; p/Oscar Francis (dec) and Elizabeth Ray Drennon, Anderson, SC; ed/AA Anderson Col 1959; Ed Spec Clemson Univ 1980; pa/Curric Coor Jr HS in Sch Dist 50, Greenwood, SC; Elem Ed; Eng Tchr; Eng & Joun Tchr; Guid Cnslr; Asst Prin; NEA; SCEA; Past Pres & Past Bd Dirs, Relations Chm Greenwood Co Ed Assn; Past Public Relations Chm Greenwood Intl Soc of Tchrs; Phi Theta Kappa; cp/Past Mem & Secy Pilot Clb; Mem & Past Treas Am Assn Univ Wom; Mem John A Walker Chap U Daughs of the Confederacy; Vol Work w Yth of Connie Maxwell Bapt Chd's Home; r/Bapt; hon/St Awd Jour Advr 1969.

ALTMAN, STEVEN oc/Associate Vice President, Associate Professor; b/Oct 24, 1945; ba/Fla Intl Univ, Miami, FL 33199; m/Judy Ellen; p/Harold and Estelle Altman, Culver City, CA; ed/BA UCLA 1967; MBA 1969, DBA 1975 So Calif; mil/USAR 1968-74; pa/Asst Dean Univ So Calif 1969-72; Fla Intl Univ: Chm Div Mgmt 1972-77, VP Univ Outreach & Sers 1977-78, Assoc Prof Mgmt 1976-; Acad Mgmt; Intl Pers Mgmt Assn; Indust Relations Res Assn; Soc Profls in Dispute Resolution; Am Arbitration Assn; Am Soc Public Adm; cp/Adv Bd Assn for Retard Citizens; hon/W/W in S&SW 1980; Freedom Foun Gold Medal for Ec 1971; Outstg Fac Mem Fla Intl Univ 1975; Outstg Yng Men of Am 1979; Author 6 Books, 18 Articles, Book Chaps, Res Reports.

ALVARADO, JUANITA oc/Highway Patrol; b/Nov 20, 1954; h/Austin, TX; p/Vicente and Emma G Alvarado, Eagle Pass, TX; pa/Exec Security Detachment, Hwy Patrol; r/Cath; hon/Federal Fed of Martial Arts, 1st Dan Black Belt 1979; DPS Recruit Olympics Medal Winner 1976: 1st Pl Wom's Shot-Put, 2nd Pl Running Long Jump.

ALVERSON, JEWELL REEVE oc/Homemaker, Retired Music Teacher; b/Feb 19, 1897; h/510 Woodlawn Ave, Calhoun, GA 30701; m/(dec); c/Elizabeth Reeve Dreyer, Lawrence Reeve, Charley Phillips Reeve Jr, Elsie Reeve Haynes; p/WB Bridges (dec) and Cora Abbott (dec); pa/Ret'd Mus Tchr; Author; cp/PTA; Pres, Secy, Chm, Wom's Clb; Ofcr in Ch Orgs; r/Meth; hon/Guy Maier Mus Assn; 2 Life Mbrships Calhoun Kiwanis Clb; Exemplary Com Ser Meth Wom.

ALVEY, EDWARD JR oc/Retired Professor and Former Dean; b/June 13, 1902; h/1104 College Ave, Fredericksburg, VA 22401; m/Frances Ellen McClinton; c/Ellen A Montllor; p/Edward (dec) and Ida Floyd Huffman Alvey (dec); ed/BA, MA, PhD Univ Va; LHD Mary Washington Col; pa/Ret'd Prof & Former Dean, Mary Washington Col; Past Pres So Assn of Acad Deans; Past Pres Assn of Va Cols; cp/Past Pres Hist Fredericksbuirg; Gov Jamestown Soc; r/Presb Ch of F'burg: Elder & Chm of Bd Trustees; hon/Phi Beta Kappa; Raven Soc; Phi Delta Kappa; Dist'd Alumnus Awd, Univ Va Sch of Ed; US Treasury Dept Minute Man Awd.

AMIR-MOEZ, ALI REZA oc/Professor; b/Apr 7, 1919; h/Tex Tech Univ, Lubbock, TX 79409; ba/Same; p/Mohammad and Fatema Amir-Moez; ed/BA Univ Teheran 1943; MA 1951, PhD 1955 Univ Calif-LA; pa/Prof Math Tex Tech Univ; Math Res; Mem: Am Math Soc, Math Assn Am, Soc Am Sci & NY Acad Sci; Fellow Tex Acad Sci; hon/Recip Medal "Pro Mundi Beneficio" Academia Brasileira De Ciencias Humanas 1975.

AMJAD, HASSAN oc/Physician, Clinical Researcher, Administrator; b/Nov 27, 1947; ba/200 Veterans Ave, Beckley, WV 25801; m/Lolita Quezon; c/Urooj, Quartel-Ayne, Shabnaum; p/Jafar Hussain and Anwer Fatima Jaffary, Pakistan; ed/MB King Edward Med Col, Pakistan 1970; Postgrad Studies St Univ of NY-Buffalo & Wayne St Univ Sch Med; pa/Instr Med Wayne St Univ, Detroit; Asst Clin Prof Med, Marshall Univ; Chief Med Ser; VA Hosp Beckley, WVa; Fellow, Am Col of Phys; Fellow, Intl Soc of Hematology; Mem NY Acad Scis; Am Soc of Hematology; Am Soc of Clin Oncology; Am Assn for Advmnt of Sci; Am Med Writer Assn; Am Soc Tropical Med & Hygiene; Am Fdn for Clin Res; Raleigh Co Med Soc; Mem SEn Oncology Grp; cp/Bd Dirs Am Heart Assn Raleigh Co; Hospice in So WVa; r/Muslim; hon/Fellowship Am Col of Phys 1978; Intl Soc of Hematology 1980; Marquis W/W in S&SW; Personalities of the South; Approved Cancer Chemotherapy Investigator NIH for Phase 11 Drugs; Author & Co-Author: "Sickle Cell Pain and Season," "Kartagener Syndrome," Others.

AMODIO, JOSEPH JOHN oc/Certified Public Accountant, Controller, Consultant; b/Sept 9, 1947; h/365-2-114th Ave N, St. Petersburg, FL 33702; ba/Clearwater, FL; p/Joseph J Sr and Lillian Barricelli Amodio, Trenton, NJ; ed/BS Univ Nevada; mil/AUS 1966-68; pa/CPA; Controller Mills Div of Airtron Inc; Consultant DP Systems; FICPA, ARCPA, NAA; r/Cath; hon/CPA; W/W in Am Indust & Fin 1979-80.

ANDERS, DAN RANEY oc/Administrative Judge, United States Government; b/Aug 22, 1933; h/11561 North Shore Drive, Reston, VA 22090; ba/Washington, DC; m/Barbara Lynne Gainey; c/Laurie Nan, Melissa Lynne; p/Charles Boatner Anders (dec); Ruth Raney Anders, Gautier, MS; ed/BS; LLB; JD; mil/Adj Gen Ofc, Hq 7th Inf Div Korea; pa/Adm Judge, US Govt; Mem: Am Bar Assn, Fed Bar Assn, Miss Bar Assn, Am Judicature Soc, Nat Conf Bd of Contract Appeals, Nat Lwyrs Clb.

ANDERSEN, MARGARET LOUISE oc/Professor; b/Aug 24, 1948; h/Elkton, MA; ba/Dept of Sociol, Univ Delaware, Newark, DE 19711; p/Milton Lawrence Andersen (dec); Emma Louise Johnson, Rome, GA; ed/BA Ga St Univ 1970; MA 1973, PhD 1976 Univ Mass-Amherst; pa/Prof, Dept Sociol, Univ Del 1974-; Am Sociol Assn; En Sociol Assn; Sociol for Wom in Soc, Pres Del Chapt; Intl Sociol Assn; hon/Excell in Tchg Awd, Univ Del 1980; Outstg Yng Schlr Awd, AAUW, St of Del; Author Num Profl Articles Incl'g "Race and Social Change in the New South" & "Rape Crisis Counseling and the Cult of Individualism" 1980; Book *Thinking About Women: Sociology and the Feminist Imagination* (in press).

ANDERSON, CLYDE oc/Pastor; b/July 26, 1955; h/116 Cheraw St, Bennettsville, SC 29512; m/Loretta Martino; p/George Sr and Sarah Jane Anderson, Mayesville, SC; ed/BA Claflin Col 1977; MDiv Interdenominational Theol Ctr & Gammon Theol Sem 1980; pa/Pastor: St Michael, Smyrna & Shiloh U Meth Chs; Rdg Conslt for the Martin Luther King Jr Ctr for Social Change; cp/Bd Dirs Marlboro Co Mtl Hlth Assn; Marlboro Co Min Alliance; NAACP; Coor Marlboro Co Claflin Col Alumni Assn; Black Meth Ch Renewal; SC Conf U Meth Ch; Chaplain, Ga Retard Ctr 1979; Phi Beta Sigma; Marion Dist Pension Crusade Com; Advr B'ville Parish Sr Citizens Clb; Dir B'ville-Cheraw Area Grp Min; Former Pres Gammon Theol Sem Fellowship; r/Meth; hon/W/W Among Students in Am Univ & Cols 1975-76, 1976-77; SC St Awd Phi Beta Sigma Frat 1977; Outstg Yng Man of Am 1978; The I Dare You Awd 1973; Cert of Recog for Dedicated and Outstg Sers Rendered to the Student Christian League from ITC 1978; Honored by Prospect & Central U Meth Ch for 4 Yrs Ser as Pastor 1980.

ANDERSON, DOLORES FEMER oc/Corporate Secretary; b/May 12, 1928; h/181 Inglewood Way, Greenville, SC 29615; ba/Clinton, SC; m/Robert William; c/Susan A Smith, Nancy A Finkell, Judith, Randi; ed/AA Greenville Tech Col; pa/Corporate Secy; cp/Mem Nat Bd GSA 1969-72; Pres Old Ninety-Six Girl Scout Coun 1966-69; r/Luth; hon/Thanks Badge, Girl Scouts.

ANDERSON, DORIS EHLINGER oc/Attorney; b/Dec 1, 1926; h/5556 Cranbrook, Houston, TX 77056; ba/Houston; m/Wiley N Jr; c/Wiley N III, Joe Ehlinger; p/J O and Cornelia Pagel Ehlinger (dec); ed/BA Rice Univ 1946; LLB 1950, JD Univ Tex; pa/Tex Bar Assn; Am Bar Assn; Wom Aux Houston Bar; Kappa Beta Pi; cp/Harris Co Flood Control Task Force; Fdr & Dir Liberty Belles & Beaux; hon/Outstg Wom of Yr 1977, 81 YWCA; Dosent Bayou Bend; Admiral in Tex Navy; Co-Author *Houston: City of Destiny.*

ANDERSON, EDWIN GLENN oc/Manager; b/June 23, 1956; c/Jesse James; p/Jesse Rhea (dec) and Willene Anderson, Sparta, TN; pa/Mgr of Freds; r/Ch of Christ; hon/Boss of the Yr 1980, Wilson Co; Placed 4th in Top Ten Stores in Baddour Inc 1979.

PERSONALITIES OF THE SOUTH

ANDERSON, EVELYN PEARL CARPENTER oc/Registered Nurse; b/Nov 1, 1938; h/401 Lebanon Ave, Campbellsville, KY 42718; m/Carlos B; c/David Sabin, Lisa Michele, Steven Andrew; p/Orvile J (dec) and Nola M Carpenter, Flemingsburg, KY; ed/RN St. Joseph Hosp Sch of Nsg 1961; BS C'ville Col 1977; Cand MSW/Gerontology Univ Ky; pa/Gerontology Field, Grad Sch Practicum w Region XIV Commun Mtl Hlth 1980; RN: Hayswood Hosp, Maysville, Ky 1961-62; Bapt Hosp, Louisville, Ky; Drs Loveman & Fliegleman, Dermatologists, Louisville; Oneida Bapt Inst, Oneida, Ky 1964-65; Oneida Mntn Hosp, Oneida; Geo Dimmitt Meml Hosp, Humansville, Mi; Pleasant View Nsg Home, Bolivar, Mi; Western Bapt Hosp (ICU), Paducah, Ky 1969-71; Wash Univ Hlth Ser, St Louis, Mi; Centreville Twp Hosp, Centreville, Ill (ICU); Metzmeier Nsg Home (ICU), Campbellsville, Ky, 1980; Hlth Care Coor; Long Term Care Coor Ky Peer Review Org, Louisville, Ky 1977-79; Nat Assn Christians in SW; AAUW; Ky Soc on Aging Inc; Spkr Jamestown Nutrition Site on Drugs & Elderly; Mem Nat Task Force on Drugs & Elderly; Tchr Title IV Tng Workshop on Aging (LCADD); cp/Taylor Co Coun on Aging; Pleasant Val Bapt Ch; r/So Bapt; hon/Recip of a Rural Aging Grant Through the Nat Inst of Mtl Hlth to Attend Grad Sch; Co-Author: "A Survey of Drug Interactions."

ANDERSON, FRANK JAMES oc/Branch Chief, Environmental Impact Analysis; b/Mar 22, 1941; h/11526 Hearthstone Ct, Reston, VA 22091; pa/Washington, DC; m/Diana Rydell; c/James Rydell, Brendan Keeley; p/Robert J and Maxine D Heggie, Wilmette, IL; ed/BS Colo Sch of Mines; MS Univ of Ariz; pa/Br Chief Environmtl Impact Analysis, Ofc of Surface Mining, Dept of Interior; Fdr Profl Soc for earth scientists & land use planners, San Jose, Cal; cp/Soccer coach; hon/3 Yr NDEA Grant for Grad Studies 1966-69; Winner AIME Nat Prize Paper Contest in Mining 1968.

ANDERSON, HAROLD A oc/Pastor; b/June 29, 1935; h/Aberdeen, MS; c/Cindy Lee, Terri Meggs, Karen; p/Connie Anderson Sr, Jacksonville, FL; ed/Att'd Bapt Bible Inst 2 Yrs; BA Mobile Col 1971; MDiv New Orleans Bapt Theol Sem 1974; Work'g on DD in Theol; pa/Wn Auto Supply 15 Yrs; Min So Bapt Chs 14 Yrs; Modr, Franklin Co Bapt Assn 2 Yrs; Pres SW Miss Pastors Conf 1 Yr; Pres Franklin Co Pastor's Conf 3 Yrs; Chm Evangelism Franklin Co Bapt Assn 1 Yr; Chm Temperance Com, Franklin Co Bapt Assn 1 Yr; Chm Missions, Monroe Co Bapt Assn 1 Yr; hon/Outstg Modr, Franklin Bapt Assn 1973-74; S'ship New Orleans Bapt Theol Sem 1973.

ANDERSON, HERBERT R oc/Professional Soldier; b/Mar 5, 1943; h/Summit, MS; m/Jennifer P; c/Timothy S; p/Kelly L and Frances V Anderson, Summit, MS; ed/HS Grad; mil/AUS 1961-81 Sgt 1st Class; r/Bapt.

ANDERSON, HOWARD PALMER oc/United States Senator; b/May 25, 1915; h/1080 Mt Road, Halifax, VA 24558; ba/Washington, DC; m/Mildred Graham Webb; ed/BA Col of William & Mary; LLB Univ of Richmond Law Sch; mil/WWII Vet, Lt (sg); USNR; pa/Lwyr; Former FBI Agent; Mem: Va, Halifax Co Bar Assns, Va St Bar, Va Farm Bur Assn, Univ of Richmond Law Sch Assn; cp/18th Senatorial Dist, Dem 1972-; Mem of House 1958-71; Mason; Lions Clb; Am Legion; Vets of Fgn Wars; Halifax Co C of C; Wilson Meml Ruritan Clb; Former Mem Halifax Co Sch Bd; r/Bapt; hon/Sigma Pi; Delta Theta Phi.

ANDERSON, JAMES OTIS oc/Farmer; b/Apr 15, 1906; h/Rt 2 Hwy 24, Statesboro, LA; m/Martha Bowie Hodges; c/Gene (dec), Donald H; p/Julian Jasper Emerald (dec) and Janie Arsula Williams Anderson (dec); pa/Chief Registrar Bullock Co; Farmer; cp/Bullock Co Histl Soc; 25 Yr Mem Ogeeche Lodge 213 F & A M; r/Primitive Bapt.

ANDERSON, JIM oc/Executive, Author; b/July 29, 1927; p/James William (dec) and Cecelia Bertels Anderson (dec); ed/Hon Grad St Louis Univ (Degs in Mktg, Law, Acctg, & Philosophy); mil/USN Ensign; pa/Real Est Investor; Fdr Quad-Plex Owners of Am (To Help New & Future Small Commercial Property Owners); Fdr Organized Proud Property Owners of Am; Pubr & Owner Brun Press; Sales Exec, Am Broadcasting Co 1960-63; Pioneer TV Exec (Responsible for Turning 7 Failing TV Stations into Profit, Incl'g WTTG, now Am's Most Profitable TV Sta); hon/Author Nat Bestseller *Jim Anderson's How to Live Rent Free in the 1980's*.

ANDERSON, JOE LASHLEE oc/Retired; b/July 27, 1910; h/Rt 1 Box 154, Springville, TN 38256; m/Cassandra; mil/NG 6 Yrs; USN 3 Yrs; r/Meth.

ANDERSON, MARGARET ANNA oc/Registered Nurse; b/Aug 29, 1937; h/Rt 9 Box 429, Elizabethton, TN 47643; ba/Elizabethton; pa/RN; Dir of Nsg Ser; Am Nurse Assn; BPW (local); Am Heart Assn; Assn of Phys Asst; Vol Red Cross; Vol Cancer Soc; r/Roman Cath; hon/Assoc Month Plantation Gen Hosp.

ANDERSON, OPAL HAYNES oc/Train Dispatcher; b/Jan 30, 1930; h/529 Kanawha Ave, Rainelle, WV 25962; m/E B; c/Robert; p/Clarence Lualzo (dec) and Dona Cox Haynes, Russellville, WV; ed/Undergrad Marshall Col 1945; pa/Train Dispatcher, Chessie Sys RR Co; Past 1st VP Rwy Bus Wom's; cp/Mem & Past Worthy Matron OES; Past Grand Rep to Grand Chapt Okla OES; Mem & Past Pres BPW Clb; Past Pres Rainelle GFWC Wom's Clb; Pres So Dist WV Fed Wom's Clbs; 1st VP Lookout Gdn Clb; Past SS Supt, Class Tchr & Mem Choir; Past Den Mother of Cub Scout Troup; Past PTA Pres; Homemaker & Farm Wom's Clb; Writer for Wkly Newspaper 15 Yrs; Aircraft Owner's & Pilots Assn (Pvt Pilot's Lic 32 Yrs); WV Dem Exec Com; Town Coun; r/Meth; hon/Author Book in the Writing of Fam Hist.

ANDERSON, OWANAH PICKENS oc/Project Director; b/Feb 18, 1926; h/2206 Berekeley, Wichita Falls, TX 76308; ba/Wichita Falls; m/Henry J; c/Steve Shelton; p/J Boyt (dec) and Samantha Jones Pickens (dec); ed/Univ Okla; pa/Proj Dir Am Indian Visibility Pub; Pres Appt Nat Adv Com on Wom; HEW Secy Adv Com on Wom; Nat Pol Caucus Adv Bd; cp/Democrat; r/Epis; hon/Wichita Co Bar Assn Liberty Bell Awd 1979.

ANDERSON, PATRICIA E oc/Assistant Executive Director; b/Jan 18, 1942; h/230 Goldendays Dr, Casselberry, FL 32707; ba/Orlando, FL; p/Thomas A and Martha L Crigger Anderson, Filbert, WV; ed/AA Brevard Commun Coll 1975; BS Univ Ctl Fla 1979; mil/USN 1961-64, Jrnlist 3rd Class; pa/Asst Exec Dir Fla Lumber & Bldg Mat Dealers Assn Inc; Advtg Dir Cody Pub Inc; Mng Ed *Beachcomber* Newspaper; Nat Assn Female Execs; Ctl Fla Soc Assn Execs; cp/Democrat; r/Meth.

ANDERSON, RONNIE (RON) J oc/Physician, Educator, Researcher; b/Sept 6, 1946; m/Sue Ann; c/Sarah Elizabeth, Daniel Jerrod; p/Ted J Anderson (dec); Ruby Alice Benjamin; ed/BS Univ Okla SWn 1969; MD Univ Okla Hlth Sci Ctr 1973; pa/Internship: Univ Tex Affiliated Hosps (Parkland Meml & Dallas VA Hosps) 1973-74; Internal Med Residency 1974-75; Chief Med Resident 1976-; Asst Prof Internal Med, Univ Tex Hlth Sci Ctr, Dallas; Asst Dean Clin Affairs, Parkland Meml Hosp; Med Dir Ambulatory Care-Emer Sers; Am Coll Phys; Tex Med Assn; Dall Co Med Soc; Soc for Res & Ed in Primary Care Internal Med; Kappa Psi; Pharm Frat; Adv for Tex Acad of Phys Assts; cp/Advocate Am Med Student Assn for Indian Hlth Ser; Nat Hlth Ser Corps & Bur Hlth Sers; Preceptor for Dallas Indep Sch Dist Talented & Gifted Prog; Bd Dirs Farmer's Br Chapt of Am Heart Assn; Conslt Am Heart Assn for Statewide Hypertension Screening Prog 1980; r/Bapt; hon/Rho Chi Hon Soc 1969; W/W in Am Cols & Univs 1969; Alpha Omega Alpha Med Hon Soc 1973; W/W in S&SW 1979-80; Diplomate of Am Bd of Internal Med 1976; Am Bd Med Examrs 1973; Author & Co-author articles, abstracts, manuscripts incling: "Mucor Mediastinitis," "Alterations in Left Ventricular Mass and Improvements in Patients Treated Effectively for Thyrotoxicosis: A Comparative Echocardiographic Study."

ANDERSON, ROY LEONARD JR oc/Corporate Purchasing Manager; b/Mar 3, 1948; ba/6201 S Freeway, Ft Worth, TX 76101; m/Elaine; c/Jeff Springfield; p/Roy Leonard Sr and Georgia Patheal Anderson, Arlington, TX; ed/BS Univ of Tex Arlington 1971; pa/Alcon Labs: Purchasing Agt, Mgr Ft Worth Purchasing Opers, Corporate Purchasing Mgr; Buyer Toys & Sporting Goods, Titches Dept Stores, Dallas 1971-74; Ft Worth Purchasing Coun; cp/Arlington Optimist Clb; BSA; Chapt Adv Phi Delta Theta Frat r/Presb; hon/W/W in S&SW.

ANDERSON, THOMAS WAYNE oc/Engineer; b/Dec 10, 1946; h/637 Wilderness Rd, Pelham, AL 35124; ba/Birmingham; m/Catherine Lee; c/Melissa Joy; Heather Lee; p/Orville Lynn and Ann Leona Anderson, Jacksonville, FL; ed/Univ Fla 1964-70; Grad Study 1974-75; mil/USNR 1966-72, 2nd Class Petty Ofcr-Ordnance; pa/Hosp Mgmt Sys Indust Engr; Hlth Care Conslt; Dir Sys Devel, Univ Ala Hosp & Clin, Birmingham, Ala; Dir Mgmt Sys Engrg, Bapt Med Ctrs, B'ham; Dir Mgmt Engrg, Sarasota Meml Hosp, Sarasota, Fla; Dir, Mgmt Sys Engrg, Univ Fla Med Ctr, Gainesville; Chapt Pres 1975 & Chapt VP 1974 Am Inst of Indust Engrs; Hosp Mgmt Sys Soc 1972-; cp/Cahaba Val JCs; r/Bapt; hon/W/W in S&SW 1980; LJ Turvaville Achmt Awd 1970; Univ Fla Engrg Ser Key 1970; Co-Author: "A Study of Components of Nursing Job Satisfaction," "Changing Patterns of Psychiatric Inpatients in a University General Hospital."

ANDERSON, VICTORIA ELAINE oc/Executive; b/Sept 4, 1946; c/Kimberly Ann Miley; p/William Brigham and Helen Louise East Anderson, Belleair, FL; ed/AA w Hons Hillsborough Commun Coll 1976; BA Univ S Fla 1978; pa/Regional Condominium Dir, First Property 1980-; Pres Regency Property Mgmt 1978-80; Property Mgr, Flagship Bank of Tampa 1976-78; Property Mgr, First Property Mgmt 1974-76; CAI; Am Bus Wom's Assn; NAFE; Contractors & Bldrs Assn; r/Meth.

ANDERSON, VIVIAN M oc/Teacher; b/Oct 4, 1926; h/Oakland Ave

9

S, Box 303, Mt Juliet, TN 37122; ba/Mt Juliet; m/Crobett W; c/Lawrence O, Randy G, Regina; p/Ira and Elora LaBarreare Mitchell (dec), Falkner, Miss; ed/BS, MEd Middle Tenn St Univ; pa/Bus Ed Tchr & Girls Coach, Ashland HS 1946-47; Bus Ed Tchr, Prentiss Co Sch Sys 1949-60; Elem Tchr, Wilson Co Sch Sys 1960-; Math Textbook Com 1977; Rdg Textbook Com 1965; Curric Guide Com; Pres (1959), Treas (1958); 2nd VP (1968-73), Fin Fac Rep (1974) PTA; Area Rep (1973-74), Bldg Rep (1975), Sr Bldg Rep (1978-79), Tchr Wel (1979-80), Entertainment Com (1978-79), Com for Improving Elem Ed (1974-75) WCEA; TEA; NEA; Grp Guid Conslt Com Chm; Consortium Bd for Middle Tenn; cp/11th Dist Co Comm for Wilson Co Ct 1978-82, Minutes Com 1979-80, Planning & Zoning Com 1979-80; Mt Juliet City Beautiful Comm Bd Mbr 1979-87; r/First Mt Juliet Bapt Ch; Wom's Missionary Soc; Chm Wom's Missionary Prog; Pres & Homemission Chm Fgn Mission; GA Dir; SS Dept Hd 1960-65; SS Tchr 1950-60, 1966-79; Secy of Dept; Tng Union Yth Dir; Bible Sch Dept Hd; hon/Cand for Outstg Tchr of Am 1957-76; Cand for Outstg Tchr of Wilson Co 1976-77.

ANDERSON, WILLIAM STERLING oc/Businessman; b/Mar 3, 1942; h/705 Penarth Road, Spartanburg, SC 29301; ba/Spartanburg; m/Ida Jane Bishop; c/Cheryl Marie, Julie Marie, William Sterling II; p/Jeff William and Agnes Armenia Anderson; ed/AB Ec; mil/AUS Field Artillery 1964-66; SC Nat Guard, Maj; pa/Mem SC Ho of Reps; cp/Mem Gov's Task Force to Study Autombile Rates; Sertoma Clb Pres 1969; Gov Upper Piedmont Dist, Sertoma Intl 2 terms; Mason; Eagle Scout; Previous Ser in House 1977; r/Mem 2nd Presb Ch; hon/Sertoma of Yr 1969; Dist'd Gov Awd, Upper Piedmont Dist of Sertoma Intl; Dist'd Mil Grad, *Chicago Tribune* Awd for Meritorious Ldrship; W/W in Am Cols & Univs.

ANDERSSON, NINA ROMBERG oc/Novelist (Pseudonym: Jane Archer); b/Dec 4, 1945; h/PO Box 30261, Flagstaff, AZ 86001; ba/Same; m/C Dean; p/G S Romberg, Kilgore, TX; Thelma Dennis Romberg, Tyler, TX; ed/BA Advertising Design N Tex St Univ; AA Kilgore Col; pa/Mem: Authors Guild Inc, Authors Leag of Am; cp/Mem Mary Tyler Chapt, Nat Soc DAR; r/Meth; hon/W/W in Pubs: Gaston HS, Kilgore Col.

ANDREW, RONNIE DALE oc/Minister; b/May 22, 1954; ba/Norwood, OH; m/Della Royalty; c/Sarah Brooke; p/George B and JoAnn Andrew, Cincinnati, OH; ed/Assoc Deg Cinc Tech Col 1974; BA Cumberland Col 1976; SWn Bapt Theol Sem 1977-78; MDiv 1980; pa/Pastor, English Bapt Ch, English, Ind; Assoc. Pastor, New Bethel Bapt Ch, Norwood, Ohio; Chm Crawford Co Min Assn; r/So Bapt; hon/Recognized for Leading English Bapt Ch to One of Indiana Bapt Top 13 Chs in Baptisms 1978-79; Outstg Ldrship Awd by Red Cross & St of Ind for Work during English Flood Tragedy 1978.

ANDREWS, DALE oc/Arts & Crafts Director; h/PO Box 128, Daleville, AL 36322; ba/Fort Rucker, AL; ed/Univ of Tex-El Paso; Post Grad Study; mil/USAR; pa/Elem Sch Tchr; Arts & Crafts Dir, McGreggor Range, NM 1972; Supvr of 3 McGreggor Shops 1973; Ft Davis Arts & Crafts Dir 1974; Atlantic Area Arts & Crafts Dir in Canal Zone 1975; Pacific Area Arts & Crafts Dir, Ft Clayton, CZ 1977; Post Arts & Crafts Dir, Ft Rucker, Ala 1978; Currently producing Photo/Graphic designs which are being distributed thru USAAF Exchgs; hon/80 Awds in Local, Nat & Intl Art, Graphic, Arts & Crafts & Photo Shows; Completed 75± Limited Editions of Etchings, Block Prints, Lithos.

ANDREWS, DAVID KIRKLAND oc/Dentist; b/Jan 10, 1954; ba/Lafayette, AL; m/Cynthia Talley; c/David K II, Michelle; p/James H and Eloise M, Nashville, TN; ed/BS Tenn St Univ 1976; DDS Meharry Med Col 1980; mil/Capt Nat Hlth Ser Corp 1981; pa/Dentist: Fam Prac Ctr, Huntsboro, Ala; Lafayette Dental Clin, Lafayette; Am Dental Assn; Nat Dental Assn; Nat Dental Student Assn; Omicron Kappa Upsilon Dental Hons Frat; Beta Kappa Chi Nat Sci Hon Soc; cp/Civitan Clb; r/Ch of Christ; hon/John R Cuff Awd in Gen Pathology 1978; CU Mosby S'ship Awd 1978; Chi Delta Mu Frat Awd 1978; Am Acad Oral Med Awd 1980; Am Acad of Oral Pathology Awd 1980; Valedictorian.

ANDREWS, HAZEL P oc/Accountant; b/July 9, 1923; ba/Lincolnton, NC; m/Andy M; c/Alfred Marion Jr, Cynthia Rebekah, Melissa Ann; p/Robert Pearson (dec) and Nancy Crowe Patterson (dec); ed/Draughans Bus Col 1944; Adv'd Assoc Deg in ProflStandards Prog of NC Assn of Ed Ofc Pers; pa/Acctng & Payroll, Lincoln Co Bd Ed; Local, Dist & St Mem NCAEOP; Area VP NC Fdn Bus & Profl Wom's Clb; cp/Corres Secy Lincoln Co Democrat Wom; Mem Lincoln Co Arts Coun; NC Symph; Apple Festival Com Chm; r/Bapt; hon/Dinner Bell Awd for Gov James B Hunt Jr 1980; Plaque of Appreciation from Lincolnton BPW 1979; Cert of Appreciation from NC Fdn of Bus & Profl Wom 1980.

ANDREWS, IKE F oc/Congressman; b/Sept 2, 1925; ba/2446 Rayburn House Ofc Bldgs, Wash DC 20515; m/Pat Goodwin; c/Alice, Nina Patricia; p/Ina Andres, Bonlee, NC; ed/Att'd Ft Union Mil Acad & Mars Hill Col; BS 1950, LLD 1952 UNC-Chapel Hill; mil/AUS WWII; pa/Admitted to NC Bar 1952; Assoc'd w Law Firm Andrews & Stone Until Elected; NC Gen Assem: Sen 1959, Ho of Reps 1961, 67, 69, 71: Chm Ho Com on Constitutional Amends 1969 & 71, Elected House Majority Ldr & Spkr Pro-Tem 1971; Elected US Ho of Reps 1972: Ho Com on Ed & Labor, Select Com on Aging, Subcoms: Ec Opport Chm & Elem, Sec'dy & Voc Ed; cp/Past Master, Masonic Lodge; Siler City C of C; Am Legion, Rotary Clb; UNC Bd Trustees 1959-, Exec Com 1971-; Chm Chancellor Selection Com UNC-CH; Mem Gov's Comm on Restructuring of Higher Ed; Bd Govs UNC; r/Bapt; hon/Siler City's Yng Man of Yr; 2 Combat Battle Stars; Bronze Star; Purple Heart; First Rep Ever Elected Both Ho Majority Ldr & Spkr Pro-Tem.

ANDREWS, JAMES DAVID oc/Medical Editor, Educator, Author; h/PO Box 4641, Baltimore, MD 21212; ed/Grad: Univ NC, UNC Med Sch, Duke Univ; Student Pendle Hill Ctr; pa/World Affairs Edr, Am Friends Seer Com; Tchr in Ohio; Wesley Foun Dir, Appalachian St Col & Morgan St Univ; Current Med Editor, Johns Hopkins Univ Med Ctr 1964-; Md St Poetry Soc; Haiku Soc of Am; Am Poetry Leag; Goldwayne Writers Guild; Am Med Writers Assn; Wn World Haiku Soc; Spkr, Tar Heel Writers Roundtable 1979; hon/Pub'd Books of Poetry: *Five-Seven-Five,* 1974; *Six Hundred Ships,* 1975; *Full Moon is Rising* 1977; *New Sonnets from Shakespeare: 30 Famous Passages and 30 Companion Sonnets from Shakespeare's Best-Loved Plays* 1979; *Oh, My Comet, Shine!: "Found" Haiku and Senryu, Based on Thought-Forms by Mirtala Bentov* 1979; *Choosing the Best Form for Your Poem: An Illustrated Guide to 15 Noteworthy Verse Forms* 1979; 1st Pl, Nat Writers Clb Poetry Contest 1976; 2 1st Prizes, NC Poetry Soc 1976; 2 2nd Prizes, Md St Poetry Soc 1976; Contemp Authors; DIB; W/W E.

ANDREWS, M DEWAYNE oc/Physician, Assistant Professor; b/May 24, 1944; h/Okla City, OK; ba/Dept Med, PO Box 26901, Okla City, OK 73190; p/Mitchell S and Truel E Andrews, Okla City, OK; ed/BS Baylor Univ 1966; MD Univ Okla Col of Med 1972-74; mil/EIS Ofcr, Ctr for Disease Control, USPHS 1972-74; pa/Intern in Internal Med, Johns Hopkins Hosp 1970-71; Resident in Internal Med, Univ Okla Hlth Scis Ctr 1971-72, 74-75; Fellow Nephrology, Univ Okla Hlth Sci Ctr 1975-76; Asst Prof Med, Univ Okla Col Med 1976-; Dir House Staff Prog, Dept Med, Univ Okla Hlth Sci Ctr 1978-; Am Col Phys; Assn Prog Dirs in Internal Med; AMA; r/Epis; hon/Alpha Omega Alpha 1969; Tchg & Res Schlr, Am Col Phys 1976-79; Author 13 Articles in Var Jours.

ANDREWS, VERA J oc/General Manager; b/Jan 1, 1941; p/Burt M Andrews; Ersie S Stewart; ed/Clemson Univ 1962; Fashion Inst Technol 1964; Univ SC 1967, 68, 69; Num CEU Courses; cp/Skyline Mfg Co: Supvsr; Asst Hd Pattern Maker; Dept Hd; Dir Mfg; Gen Mgr; Mem Nat Ed Com of the AAMA; Mem Adv Bd Kershaw Co Voc Sch; Chm Indust Apparel Com Co Tech Sch; Mem SC Needle Trade Assn; Am Mgmt Assn; cp/Com Chm 1966, Vice Pres 1967, Pres 1969 Local Chapt Bus & Profl Wom's Clb; BPW St Stg Com Chm 1968; Mem Kershaw Co C of C; hon/Recip Dist'd Ser Awd City of Camden 1963; Dist'd Ser Cert Kershaw Co Voc Sch 1978; Yng Career Wom of the Yr City of Camden 1968; State Runner Up; Biographee W/W 1980-81; Co-Author: "Handbook for the Cutting Room."

ANGELL, EAKIN SUE oc/Nurse; b/Apr 11, 1917; h/1335 N Alleghany Ave, Covington, VA; m/(dec); c/Glenden E, Richard Eugene; p/Margaret L Eakin, Covington, VA; ed/Dip Nsg Sch Hinton Hosp; pa/LPN New Born Nursery; cp/Secy & Treas, Grad Nurses Clb; r/Bapt.

ANTHONY, CHRISTINE HOLLAND oc/Civic Leader; b/Dec 18, 1916; h/6707 NW Grand Blvd, Okla City, OK; m/Guy M; c/Charles Ross III, Guy M Jr, Robert H, Roy Jay, Jack H, Tom; p/Albert Houston (dec) and Mable Gordon Holland (dec); ed/BS Univ Okla; pa/Chm Red Resv Bd of Okla City Br of Kan City, Bd of Okla Gas & Elect; cp/Life Mem Symph Bd; World Neighbors Bd; Allied Arts; U Appeal Bd Trustees, Mercy Hosp Bd Advrs; hon/Hon Doct, Okla City Univ.

ANTHONY, ROBERT HOLLAND oc/Business Executive; b/May 15, 1948; h/Oklahoma City, OK; ba/PO Box 25725, Okla City, OK 73125; m/Nancy Bargo; c/Elizabeth Bargo, Christine Holland; p/Guy Mauldin and Christine Elizabeth Holland Anthony, Okla City, OK; ed/BS Univ Penn, Wharton Sch of Ecs 1970, BSc Univ London, London Sch of Ecs 1971; MA Yale Univ Grad Sch 1973; MPA Harvard Univ, Kennedy Sch of Govt 1977; mil/USAR Air Defense Artillery Capt; pa/Pres C R Anthony Co (310 Retail Jr Dept Stores in 21 Sts); Ec Clb of Okla City; cp/Former City Coun-man & Vice-Mayor of Okla City; Dir Okla Sci & Arts Foun; Former Pres Okla Co Coun for Mtlly Retard'd Chd; Former Commr, Okla City Conv & Tourism; r/Crown Hgts U Meth Ch: Mem Bd; hon/Beta Gamma Sigma; Author *Energy "Demand" Studies: An Analysis and Appraisal* 1972.

ANTHONY, SIR YANCEY LAMAR oc/Minister; Ambassador in Exile; b/Feb 13, 1922; h/PO Box 4241 No Ft Myers, FL 33903; p/Cliford

Elmo Anthony; ed/AB Samford Univ 1944; ThB So Bapt Theol Sem 1947; ThD Pioneer Theol Sem 1956; DD Min Tng Col, England; PhD Accademia Universitaria Internazionale (Roma) 1957; PhD Great China Arts Col, World Univ (Hong Kong); Others; pa/Titles (Hereditary): Duke (Prince) of Danzig, Count of San Miguel, Baron von Burg, Baron of Rijeka; Ambassador, Govt of Danzig (Exile); Pastor Bapt Chs: Valley Grove, Tuscumbia, Ala 1942-44, Walnut Grove, Lodiburg, Ky 1944-47, 1st, Ft Walton Bch, Fla 1947-53, Harsh Chapel, Nashville, Tenn 1953-56, Ctl Collegiate, Ft Walton Bch 1956-57; Pres Ft Walton Bch Min Assn; Moderator Okaloosa Co Bapt Assn; Exec Bd Fla Bapt Conv; Pres So Univ 1957-71; Dir: Ch Missions Fund Foun, Ch Devel Foun; Prof, Chair of Diplomatic Sci, Leonardo di Vinci Univ, Italy; Prof Polit Sci Danzig Univ; cp/Pres Better Govt Leag, Okaloosa Co, Fla; Apptd by Govs Collins & Bryant to Bd of Social Wel of Fla, 10 Yrs, Chm 2 Terms; hon/K of Malta; Gold Medal of Labor, Netherlands; Acad of Sci, Rome; Intl Order of Legion of Hon of the Immaculate; Royal Order of St Gereon; Royal Acad Golden Lttrs; Great Chivalry Orders Assn; Nobility Order of Kaspis; Order of Hereditary Nobility; Accademia Gentium Pro Pace; Accademia Gentium Populorum Progressie; Mozart Soc; Der Orden Signum Fidei, Ordre du Merite Africain; Academia de Ciencias Humanisticas y Relaciones; Institut des Relats Diplomatiques; Col & Aide de Camp, Gov Miss; Lt Col & Aide de Camp, Gov Ala; Spec Cit, Senate of W LA (Cal) Col; Num Biogl Listings.

ANTONIO, ANTHOHY oc/Artist; b/Nov 1940; h/905 45th St, Belview, Birmingham, AL 35208; ed/AB Painting & Drawing Birmingham-So Col 1964; MA Painting & Drawing Univ of Ala-Tuscaloosa 1966; Grad Study Univ of Ga 1967; pa/Asst Prof of Art, Univ of Ala-B'ham 1974-75; Wkshops; Conslt; One-man Exhibs incl'g: Univ of Ala-B'ham 1975, The Montgomery Mus of Fine Art 1976; Group Exhibs incl'g: Daniel Bldg Gallery, B'ham 1970, Centre Intl de Paris, France 1975-76; Tchg in: Painting, Sculpture, Ceramics, Drawing, Design, Art Appreciation, Art Ed, Art Hist, Art Criticism; Mem: B'ham Mus of Art, B'ham Art Assn, Ala Art Ed Assn, Metropolitan Mus of Art, MOMA, Smithsonian Art Inst, Guggenheim Art Mus, Col Art Assn of Am; hon/Num Hons & Awds incl'g: Hon'd Artist of the 60's, A Decade of Effective Painting 1970, Daniel Bldg Gall, Recog'd as Outstg Ala Artist, Gov George Wallace 1971, Kelley Fitzpatrick Awd 1972, Montgomery Mus of Fine Art, Painters in Paris, French-Am Celebration of Am's Bicent, Centre Intl de Paris.

ANTONOVA, ELIZABETH oc/Writer, Poet; h/1800 NE 114 St, Miami, FL 33181; m/Martin H Feinman; c/Olga, Tania, Natasha; p/(dec); ed/Att'd Univs in Russia & France; pa/Poetry Soc Am; Nat Leag Am Pen Wom; Rader Poetry Grp; Poetry Socs of Ga, Va & NH; r/Greek Orthodox; hon/Pub'd in *The Independent Woman, Hartford Times, Different, Florida Magazine of Verse, The Garret Notebook, Modern Bard, Southland,* and Other Pubs.

APPLING, RAYMOND NEIL oc/Purchasing Manager; b/July 3, 1936; h/PO Box 582, Idabel, OK 74745; ba/Valliant, OK; m/Pat L; c/Keith, Clayton, Standley, Daniel, Jonathan, Kellyanne; p/Linton A and Aulsa O Appling, Oakman, AL; mil/AUS; pa/Purchasing Mgmt Assn; Paper Indust Mgmt Assn; cp/32° Scottish Rite Mason; r/Bapt.

ARANDA, JUAN M oc/Physician; b/Feb 3, 1942; h/GPO Box 4867, VAH, San Jaun, PR 00936; m/Carmen; c/Juan, Robert, Mary, Elizabeth, David; p/Juan M and Eva Aranda, Ponce, PR; ed/BS; MD; mil/AUS Med Corps 1971-73, Maj; pa/Chief, Cardiol Sect, VAH, San Juan; Assoc Prof Med, Univ PR Sch of Med; r/Cath; hon/Editor, Bulletin PR Med Assn; Clin Assoc Prof Med, Univ Miami Sch Med; Pres PR Soc of Cardiol 1981; FACC 1979.

ARANGO, ABELARDO de JESUS oc/General and Vascular Surgery; b/July 6, 1944; ba/Miami, FL; m/Jeanette Lynn; c/Julia Christina, Jeanette Lynn, Abelardo; p/Abelardo and Julia Restrepo Arango (dec); ed/BS 1960, MD 1967, Univ Antioquia, Medellin, Colombia; pa/Clin Asst Prof, Dept Surg, Sch Med, Univ Miami; FACS; Am Trauma Soc; Assn for Acad Surg; Fla Assn of Gen Surg; Fla Med Assn; So Med Assn; NIH Res Fellow in Liver Diseases 1968; NIH Res Fellow in Trauma, Dade Co Med Assn; AMA; r/Cath; hon/BS summa cum laude; MD summa cum laude; Manuel Uribe Awd, Univ Antioquia 1967; Cont'd Ed Awd, AMA 1970-72; Author-Co-Author Num Profl Pubs.

ARCE, RAUL oc/Building Official; b/Aug 29, 1955; h/Rt 1 Box 339, Weslaco, TX 78596; ba/Weslaco; m/Lucilla Elodia; c/Aimee, Arlissa; p/Raul Sr and Rosa Maria Arce, Weslaco, TX; ed/AAS TSTI 1976; pa/Bldg Ofcl; Val Bldg Ofcls Assn; Bldg Ofcls Assn of Tex (Boat) So Bldg Code Cong; r/Cath; hon/Plumbing Inspectors Lic 1979; Master Elec Inspectors Lic 1979; Bldg Codes Cert, Bldg Ofcls Assn Tex 1980.

ARCHER, BILL oc/United States Congressman; Lawyer; b/March 22, 1928; ba/1024 Longworth Bldg, Washington, DC 20515; m/Patricia

Moore; c/Reyn, Rick, Sharon, Lisa, Barbara; ed/BBA, LLB Univ of Tex-Austin; mil/USAF, Korean War; USAFR Capt 1953-64; pa/Pres Uncle Johnny Mills Inc 1953-61; Dir Hgts St Bank, Houston 1967-70; Atty, Harris, Archer, Parks & Graul 1968-71; cp/Tex Ho of Reps 1966-70; Elected to US Cong, 7th Dist of Tex 1970; Mem: Repub Task Force on Energy & Resources, Repub Chowder & Marching Clb, House Com on Ways & Means, Others; Re-elected to Cong 1972, 74, 76; Dir Houston SPCA; Life Mem Houston Livestock Show & Rodeo; Pres Tex St Soc of Wash, DC 1974-75; Chm Congl Adv Bd, Distributive Ed Clbs of Am; r/Mem St Anne's Ch, Houston; hon/Outstg Intramural Athlete 1951; B'nai B'rith Dist 7 Man of Yr Awd; Spring Branch-Meml C of C Most Representative Citizen Awd; Am Fdn of Small Bus Honor Roll; Nat Associated Bus-men Watchdog of the Treasury Awd; Others.

ARMSTRONG, ANITA GAY oc/Assistant Director; b/Sept 14, 1953; h/Montgomery, AL; ba/73 Washington Ave, Suite 501, Montgomery, AL 36104; p/Frances Rea Armstrong, Mont, AL; ed/BS Univ Ala 1975; MS Troy St Univ 1977; pa/Cnslr, Mont Area Mtl Hlth Auth; Asst Dir Pre-Trial Diversion Prog; Fdr, Advr & Current Bd Mem Friends of Epilepsy 1976-80; Pres, Domestic Abuse Shelter Inc, Bd Dirs 1979-80; Chp DA's Adv Comm on Fam Violence; r/Unitarian; hon/Nom'd for Lotus Awd (Awd'd to persons who have helped the handicapped).

ARMSTRONG, ANNE LEGENDRE oc/Businesswoman; Educator; b/Dec 27, 1927; h/Armstrong Ranch, Armstrong, TX 78338; ba/Kingsville, TX; m/Tobin; c/John Barclay, Katharine Armant, Sarita Storey, James Legendre and Tobin Jr; p/Armant Legendre (dec); Olive Martindale Legendre, New Orleans, LA; ed/BA 1949 Vassar; pa/Appt'd Cnslr to Pres Nixon 1972, Ser'd Under Pres Nixon & Ford; Bd Dirs: Boise Cascade, Braniff Intl, First City Bancorporation of Tex Inc, General Foods, General Motors, Halliburton; Mem Visiting Com for JFK Sch of Govt, Harvard Univ; Former Ambassador to GB; cp/Elected Trustee of Kenedy Co Sch Bd 1968-74; Repub Nat Com-Wom from Tex 1968-73; Co-Chm Repub Nat Com 1971, 72; Mem Policy Bd of Coun on Nat Security & Intl Affairs, Repub Nat Com; r/Epis; hon/Hon LLD's: Bristol Univ, England 1976, Washington & Lee Univ 1976, Williams Col 1977, Mt Vernon Col 1978; Mrs South Tex 1973; Recip Gold Medal Awd, Nat Inst of Social Scis 1977.

ARMSTRONG, CLARIS MARIE oc/Assistant Professor of Math; b/Jul 31, 1919; h/PO Box 577, Miss St, MS 39762; ba/Miss St; p/George Milton Armstrong (dec); ed/BA Union Univ 1955; MA Univ Miss 1963; pa/Math Assn of Am; Sci of Am; Kappa Mu Epsilon: Corr Secy Miss Beta Chapt 8 Yrs, Nat Com to Select Nat Conv Papers for Presentation; AAUW: Bltn Editor Miss Div, St Topic Chm, St Bd, St Chm for St Conv, Reg Chm of Art; Starkville, Miss Br AAUW: Pres, VP, Prog VP, Parliamentn, Topic Chm, Bd & Var Coms; MEA; Miss Woms Cabinet of Public Affairs; Miss Math Progs of Univs & Cols; cp/Gen Advr 4 Yrs, Fac Advr 10 Yrs Gamma Zeta Chapt of Zeta Tau Alpha; Pres, VP, Chm Zeta Tau Alpha; Wkr: Cerebral Palsy Prog, S'ville Travelers Aid Prog, S'ville Civic Symph Orch; Contbr Bks & Mags to MSU & S'ville Lib; Advr Gamma Theta Chapt Pi Kappa Alpha; Delta Kappa Gamma; Est'd Student S'ship, Mid-S Bible Col, Memphis in Hon & Memory of Mother (Eronia Tiner Armstrong S'ship); Wkly Phone Calls & Visits to Shut-ins; Repub, Support Leg Day Sponsored by AAUW, Participant Local Group which Studies Bills, Talks to Senators & Cong-man; r/S'ville 1st Bapt Ch: Mem; Asst & Dir Intermed SS Dept, Asst Dir Intermed Tng Union Dept, Asst & Dir Col Single Tng Union Dept; SS Tch 26 Yrs S'ville & Mempis, Tenn; Bapt Student Union: Fac Advr 10 Yrs, Adult Adv Com 11 Yrs; Tchr: Study Courses in Chs (Miss & Memphis), Yg Peoples Bible Study Group, Memphis, Jr Bible Study Group, Memphis; St of Miss Com to plan Tng Union Progs for Yr; Num Groups in Planning Ch Social Functions; Cnslr; hon/Outstg Fac Mem MSU 1972; Claris Marie Armstrong S'ship Awd, Gamma Theta Chapt Pi Kappa Alpha; Zeta Tau Alpha Alumnae Cert of Merit Awd; DIB; W/W Am Univs & Cols; Eternal Dream Girl of Gamma Theta Chapt of PKA; World W/W Wom; Intl W/W Commun Ser; Intl Register of Profiles.

ARMSTRONG, ERNEST W SR oc/Real Estate Broker, Marriage and Family Counselor; b/May 1, 1915; h/7603 Mason St, N Forestville, MD 20028; c/Earl M, Everett W, Helen A Burch; p/Vinie A Johnson, Soper, OK; ed/AB Dillard Univ 1942; MDiv 1946; Okla-N 1969; PhD Lawrence Univ 1974; AA Real Est 1979, AA Acctg 1981, Prince Georges Commun Col; mil/AUS 20 yrs, Chaplain, Ret'd Col 1969-; pa/Real Est Broker, Armstrong & Burch Rltrs; Former Real Est Conslt, Colquitt-Carruthers Rltrs Inc; Cnslr, Howard Univ Sch of Rel; Edr, Cnslr Annapolis Sr HS 1973-77; Clergyman; Lic'd Marriage Cnslr; Asst Pastor, Enon Bapt Ch, Balto, Md 1970-71; Cnslr, Instr in Social Scis, Triton Commun Col, River Grove, Ill 1969-70; Col Chaplain, Asst Prof Social Scis, Savannah St Col 1948-49; cp/PC Co Mtl Hlth Assn; Md Psychol Assn; Nat Assn Blk Psych; Am Sch Coun Assn; r/Bapt; hon/Pub'd Author; Omega Man of Yr 1963; Okla Mason of Yr 1962.

PERSONALITIES OF THE SOUTH

ARMSTRONG, LUCILE W oc/Textile Quality Control Manager; b/Sept 3, 1924; ba/Opelika, AL; m/Robert N; c/Barbara Hazel; p/Mrs O R Moon, Union Springs, AL; ed/HS Grad; pa/Textile QC Mgr, Opelika Mfg Corp; cp/Pilot Clb of Lee Co: Rec'g Secy, Dir, Pres 1978; Inter-Clb Coun of Civic Clbs, City of Opelika, Pres 1978; r/Meth; hon/Pilot of Yr 1976.

ARNDT, PAULINE B oc/Occupational Specialist; b/Sept 15, 1920; h/Oviedo, FL; ba/601 King St, Oviedo, FL 32765; m/Robert Jerry; c/Margaret, Arden, Ronda, Marsha p/Margaret Brenner, Shelbyville, MI; ed/Co Normal Tchg Cert; pa/Job Placement & Career Cnslg in Sr HS; Seminole Voc Assn; Fla Voc Assn; Am Voc Assn; Seminole Ed Assn; FTP-NEA; Occup Sepc & Guid Assn; FPGA; cp/St Lukes Missionary Guild; Luth Wom's Misisonary Leag; PTA; r/Luth; hon/Outstg Supvr, CETA Prog; Certs of Apprec for Bus Classes.

ARNETT, JERRY LORRIS oc/New Equipment Training Specialist; b/Sept 2, 1948; h/106 Oakhurst Dr, N Augusta, SC 29841; ba/Ft Gordon, GA; m/Penelope Pratt; c/Andrea, Jay Bryan; p/Earnest C Arnett, Hampton, GA; Lucille Lay, Jacksonville Bch, FL; ed/AS DeKalb Commun Col 1979; BBA Cand, Univ SC; mil/AUS 1969-72 SP/5; pa/Elec Estimator, Miller Elec Corp, Jacksonville, Fla 1968-69; Owner & Oper, Arnett Elec 1971-75; AUS Civilian, Ft Gordon 1972-; cp/Our Lady of Peace PTO; Our Lady of Peace Sch Bd, Pres; r/Bapt.

ARNETT, PENELOPE SUSAN PRATT oc/Assistant Professor; b/Apr 3, 1948; h/106 Oakhurst Dr, N Augusta, SC 29841; ba/Aiken, SC; m/Jerry L; c/Andrea Felicia, Jay Bryan; p/Raymond H and Nancy M Pratt, N Augusta, SC; ed/Dip Fairview Gen Hosp Sch of Nsg; BSN 1974, MSN 1975 Med Col of Ga; mil/USANC 1969-71 1/Lt; pa/Staff Nurse, St Joseph Hosp 1971-75; Staff Nurse Med Col Ga 1975; Instr, Col of Nsg, Clemson Univ 1975-76; Asst Prof Nsg, Univ SC Aiken 1976-; ANA; 10th Dist Ga Nurses Assn; Sigma Theta Tau; cp/Am Cancer Soc, N Augusta Unit, Bd Dirs; Our Lady of Peace Sch PTA Pres; r/Cath.

ARRINGTON, CHRISTINE oc/Teacher; b/Oct 2, 1924; h/PO Box 141, Warrenton, NC 27589; m/James T; c/Gayle Denise Newsome; p/James Leonard (dec) and Absilla Parker Newsome; ed/BS Fayetteville St Univ 1949; Further Study Newark St Univ, E Carolina Univ; pa/Warren Co Bd Ed 30 Yrs: Tchr, Prin, Lead Rdg Tchr; Warren Co Unit of NC Assn of Edrs; ACT; NEA Polit Action Com for Edrs; PTA; cp/Pres Warren Co 4-H Ldrs Assn; Activ Ldr, Best Better 4-H Clb; Treas Ladies Aux, Warrenton Vol Fireman Assn; Secy 27 Yrs Warren Co Ushers Conv; Corresp Secy 26 Yrs NC St Ushers Conv; r/Bapt: Supvr of Jr Missionary Dept, Dir Yng Adult Missionary, Chm Usher Bd, Sr Choir, Asst Supvr DVBS; hon/Cert, Warren Co 4-H 1978, 79, 80; Cert of Ldrship from Gov of NC James B Hunt 1980; Plaque for 25 Yrs Ser, NC Bapt Ushers Conv.

ARSEN, LEO oc/Insurance Executive; b/Mar 22, 1933; h/Union Bankers Inc Co, 2551 Elm, Dallas, TX 75226; m/Barbara; c/Steve, Stephanie, John, Aron; p/(dec); ed/HS Grad; mil/USAF 1951-55l pa/VP Mktg, Union Bankers Ins Co; Mktg Planners Intl; Nat Assn of Life Underwriters; Tex Assn Life Underwriters; LIMRA; cp/Alderman, City of Frisco.

ARTEMEL, ENGIN MEHMET oc/Director of Planning & Community Development; b/Jul 31, 1938; h/6727 Pine Creek Ct, McLean, VA 22101; ba/Alexandria, VA; m/Janice Gwen Artemel; c/Suzan, Deniz, Sibel; p/Mehmet Ali Artemel (dec); Fatma Belkis Artemel, Istanbul, Turkey; ed/BArch; BSCE; MA Urban Planning; mil/USN Lt, Oceanographer; pa/Dir of Planning & Commun Devel, City of Alexandria; Mem: Am Inst of Planners; cp/Rotary; r/Moslem; hon/AIP Nat Capitol Area Chapt Excell Awd.

ARTHUR, BRADLEY oc/Sculptor; b/July 20, 1953; ba/Tampa, FL; p/Donald M and Sandra C Arthur; ed/Coconut Grove Sch of Art 1970; Apprentice Hugh Dumont Metal Sculptor 1970-71; BA Univ S Fla 1971-75; Sarah Lawarence Col, So France 1977; Apprentice Yasoo Mizui, Paris, France 1977; Studio Silveio Padli, Pietrasanta, Italy 1979 & 80; pa/Fdr The Art Co; Conslt and Art Dir for Num Cos; Exhbns US & Abroad; hon/Beau Arts Gal, Fla 1972; Tampa Bay Art Ctr, Fla 1977; Lincoln Ctr, NYC 1978; (Big & Yng of Today) Grand-Palais, Paris, France 1980.

ARTHUR, JEFFREY MICHAEL oc/Singer, Musician; b/Aug 1, 1951; ba/Tampa, FL; m/Jane K Whitelaw; p/Donald M Arthur, St Petersburg, FL; Sandra Arthur, Miami Beach, FL; ed/Univ S Fla 1969-73; pa/Mus Prodn; Profl Singer & Musician; Am Advtg Fdn; hon/Clio Awd 1980; Golden Pyramid Awd 1980; Monitor Awd 1980; Two Albums as Artist: Columbia Records 1973; A&M Records (Picked as One of the Seven Best Albums of 1975 by *Time* Magazine Feb 17, 1975).

ARUNAKUL, PUNYA oc/Physician, Otolaryngologist; b/Nov 13, 1944; h/3324 SW Arrowhead, Topeka, KS 66604; m/Srichuntra;

c/Methapan; p/Jim and Chaikoa Arunakul, Bangkok, Thailand; ed/Chulalongkorn Univ, Bangkok, Thailand 1961-65; MD Mahidhol Univ, Bangkok 1965-69; mil/Resvs; pa/Phys; Otolaryngologist; r/Budhism.

ASH, MARY KAY oc/Chairman of Board, Mary Kay Cosmetics Inc; b/May 12; h/7246 Lupton Cir, Dallas, TX 75225; ba/Dallas; m/Melville Jerome; c/Marylyn A Reed (Mrs Gene), Ben Rogers, Richard Rogers; p/Edward Alexander and Lula Vember Wagner (dec); pa/Chm of Bd, Mary Kay Cosmetics Inc; r/Bapt; hon/Cosmetic Career Wom of Yr 1978; Bus Wom of Yr Awd, Assn for Corporate Growth; Humanitarian Awd, Am Cancer Resch Ctr; DSA Hall of Fame Awd; Top 100 Corporate Wom, *Business Week* Mag 1976; TV Appearances; Contest Judge; Others; Listed in W/W Am Wom.

ASH, THOMAS GREY oc/Bank Vice President; b/July 7, 1939; ba/Columbia, SC; m/Arlayne Marie; c/Christopher Joseph, Timothy Kenneth; p/Kenneth (dec) and Marian Ash, Dale City, CA; ed/BA Stanford Univ 1962; MBA Univ SC 1975; mil/USAF 1962-63, Capt; pa/Sr Sys Analyst, Sys Devel Corp 1965-67; Asst Div Mgr, Mkt Planning Div Wilbur Smith & Assoc 1967-70; VP, Dir Data Processing, First Nat Bk SC 1970-; Ed Com Am Bkrs Assn; Chm Opers Com SC Bkrs Assn; Stonier Grad Sch Bkg Exam Bd; Adj Prof USC Grad Sch Bus; Data Processing Mgmt Assn; Assn Sys Mgrs; cp/VP E Columbia Dixie Yth Baseball Comm; Chm Cardinal Newman HS Adv Bd; St Mbrship Chm Alston Wilkes Soc; Pres Providence Home Assn; Pres Hunting Creek Swim & Racquet Clb; Wildewood Country Clb; r/Roman Cath; hon/USAF Commend Medal 1965.

ASHBY, BARBARA B oc/Assistant Director; b/May 1, 1941; h/PO Box 15, Crofton, KY 42217; ba/Greenville, KY; m/Robert L; c/Teresa, Don, Rhonda, Philip, Roy; p/Roy E Sr (dec) and Eula Back, Nortonville, KY; ed/Assoc Deg Nsg; BSN; pa/Asst Dir Nsg & Ed; ANA; NLN; cp/En Star; Mother Advr Rainbow Assembly; r/Bapt; hon/Phi Theta Kappa; Phi Kappa Phi; W/W Am Wom.

ASHCRAFT, CHARLES H oc/Executive Secretary, Treasurer Arkansas Baptist State Convention; b/Dec 19, 1916; h/2010 Grist Mill Rd, Little Rock, AR 72207; ba/Little Rock; m/Sarah Bell; c/Charles II, Quin, Sam; p/Henry Harrison and Ida Mathews Ashcraft (dec); ed/ThM; Hon Doctorate; mil/AUS 1943-46 Chaplain, Maj; Bronze Star; pa/Lic'd to Preach 1934; Mem Fgn Missions Bd, SBC 1952-55; Com on Bds of SBC 1954; Trustee SWBTS 8 Yrs; Taught Sem Ext Courses, Las Vegas 1957-65; Elected 1st Exec Secy Utah-Idaho So Bapt Conv 1965, Ser'd to 1969; Exec Secy Exec Bd Ark Bapt St Conv 1969-; r/So Bapt; hon/W/W: W, S.

ASHER, VERNON oc/Justice of Peace; b/Feb 10, 1915; h/1519 N Robinson, Cleburne, TX 76031; ba/Cleburne; m/Dovie King; p/James Washington Sr and Pattie Stratton Asher (dec); mil/AUS 1942-46 Pvt 1/C; cp/VFW Histn; Jr VCmdr DAV; 1/VCmdr Am Legion; Cleburne Rebbecca Lodge #231; IOOF Noble Grand & Dist Dept Grand Patriarch; K of P; Chem Coun; Cmdr DAV 1981; r/1st Bapt Ch: Past Pres, Secy SS Class; hon/Purple Heart; Good Conduct Medal; Am Theatre Medal; Bronze Star WWII; 10 Yrs 100 Mem Clb, Am Legion; DIB; W/W in Tex; Notable Ams of Bicent Era; Commun Ldrs & Noteworthy Ams; Man Achmt; Others.

ASHWORTH, CHARLES CLAYTON oc/Broadcast Executive; Song Writer; b/Nov 12, 1927; h/760 Lakeshore Dr, El Paso, TX 79932; ba/El Paso; m/Maria Luisa; c/Denise Jean, Clayton Charles; p/Faye McMahan, Mobile, AL; ed/La Salle Univ 1958; mil/US Maritime; USMM; pa/Acct Exec WABB, Mobile, AL; Sr Acct Exec WSGN, Birmingham, AL; Gen Sales Mgr WRBC, Jackson, MS; Gen Sales Mgr WYOL, Nashville, TN; Broadcast Sales Conslt, Ed Sys, NYC; Gen Sales Mgr WMCV-TV, Nashville, TN; Exec VP Taber Ambassadorial, El Paso; Mem Tex Assn Broadcasters; El Paso C of C; cp/Downtown Lions; hon/Outstg Lion 1976 & 77; Dist'd Salesman's Awd of B'ham 1964 & 69; W/W in S&SW 1980-81; Created, Wrote & Dir'd over 180 Orig Radio Promos 1962-80; Author.

ASKEW, REUBIN O'DONOVAN oc/Trade Representative; b/Sept 11, 1928; h/Miami, FL; ba/US Trade Rep, Wash DC 20506; m/Donna Lou Harper; c/Angela Adair, Kevin O'Donovan; p/Leo Goldberg (dec) and Alberta O'Donovan Askew; ed/BS Fla St Univ 1951; Grad Work Denver Univ 1952; LLB Univ Fla 1956; Num Hon Degs; mil/AUS 1946-48; USAF 1951-53; pa/Escambia Co Solicitor, Fla 1956-58; Ptnr Law Firm Levin, Askew, Warfield, Graff & Mabie 1958-79; Mem Fla Ho of Reps 1958-62; Fla Senate, 1962-70, Pres Pro-Tem 1970; Gov Fla 1971-79; Ptnr Law Firm Greenberg, Traurig, Askew, Hoffman, Lipoff, Quentel & Wolff 1979; US Trade Rep 1979-; Am, Fla & Dade Co Bar Assns; Bd Dirs Am Judicature Soc; cp/Chm Select Com on Immigration & Refugee Policy 1979; Chm, Pres Adv Bd on Ambassadorial Appts 1977-79; Chm Ed Comm of Sts; V-Chm & Chm So Gov's Assn; Visiting Chubb Fellow, Yale Univ; Chm Nat Dem Gov's Conf; Chm Nat Gov's Assn; Chm So Growth Policies Bd; Bd Trustees Inst of Art, Dade Co; Chm Dade Co Public Safety

Dir Selection Com; Chm Mildred & Claude Pepper Lib; 1972 Keynote Address, Dem Nat Conv; Bd Dirs Chd's Home Soc; Wn Div Pres Chd's Home Soc; Nat Bd Dirs City of Hope; Delta Tau Delta; Am Legion; Am Assn Museums; Fla Coun of 100; Knights of Red Cross of Constantine; Mason; Shrine; Scottish Rite and York Rite; Rotary; Phi Alpha Delta; r/Presb; hon/ROTC Hon Grad, Fla St Univ 1951; Top Freshman Mem Ho of Reps 1959; Mem Most Outstg Del in Fla 1965; 1 of 5 Outstg Yng Men Fla 1960; 1 of 4 Outstg Sens 1965-67; Most Valuable Senator 1965-67; Outstg Lwyr, Leg, Gov 1971; Profiles in Courage Awd, John F Kennedy Chapt, B'nai B'rith of Wash 1971; Spec Conserv Awd, Nat Wildlife Fed 1972; Gen William Booth Awd, Salvation Army 1973; John F Kennedy Awd, Nat Coun of Jewish Wom 1973; Herbert H Lehman Ethics Medal, Jewish Theol Sem of Am 1973; Alumnus of Yr, Univ Fla Law Review 1973; Fla Engrg Soc Protector of Environment Awd 1973; Leonard L Abess Human Relats Awd, Anti-Defamation Leag 1974; Theodore Roosevelt Awd, Intl Platform Assn 1975; Hubert Harley Awd, Am Judicature Soc 1975; Humanitarian Awd, Fla Comm on Human Relats 1976; Collier Co Conservancy Silver Medal 1978; Cumberland Order Jurisprudence Cumberland Law Sch 1978; Fla Soc of Newspaper Editors Awd 1978; Ldrship Hon Awd, Am Inst of Planners 1978; Outstg Govt Ofcl of Yr, S Fla Coor'g Coun 1979; Medal of Hon, Fla Far Foun 1979; Champ of Higher Indep Ed in Fla Awd 1979; Visiting Fellow, Inst Polits, Harvard Univ 1979; Dist'd Commun Ser Awd, Brandeis Univ 1979; Ethics in Govt Awd, Common Cause 1980.

ATCHLEY, BILL L oc/University President; b/Feb 16, 1932; h/Clemson, SC; ba/Clemson Univ; PO Box 992; Clemson, SC 29631; m/Pat; c/Julie, Pam, David; p/Cecil and Mary Atchley; ed/BS 1957, MS 1959 Univ of Mo; PhD Tex A & M Univ 1965; mil/AUS MP; pa/Asst, Assoc, Prof Engrg Mechs, Univ of Mo; Dean, Col Engrg WVa Univ; Pres Clemson Univ; Am Soc Engrg Ed; Am Soc of Civil Engrs; Newcomen Soc of N Am; Mid-Am St Univs Assn; Nat Soc of Prof Engrs; St Bd of Registration for Profl Engrs, WVa; Sigma Xi; cp/Chm Gov's Com on Energy, Ec & Envir (WVa); Sci & Technol Advr to Senate & House of Delegates of St of WVa; Rotary Clb; Bd Dirs Morgantown C 0 C; Bd Rolla Lions Clb; Mo C of C; Coun-man City of Rolla; r/Meth; hon/Chi Epsilon; Blue Key; Sigma Xi; Men of Sci; Tau Beta Pi; Alumni Merit Awd for Outstg Ldrship & Serv; W/W in Engrg Ed; Outstg Yng Man of Am 1967; Personalities of W&MW; Ford Foun Fellowship; Boss of Yr Awd; Outstg Ser Awd; Commun Ldr of Am 1968; Mem, Acad Sci; W/W in Midwest; Mem Outstg Edrs Am; Knighted Hon St Patrick 1971; Selected as One of 12 Engrg Edrs from Across US to Participate in Special Conf Conducted by Continental Oil Co 1971; Dist'd Ser Awd for Contributions to City of Rolla as Chm Rolla Bicent Com; Author: "Energy Crisis and The Private Enterprise," "Project Independence," Others.

ATCHLEY, BOBBIE JOYCE oc/Registered Nurse; b/June 20, 1935; h/1104 Key St NW, Cleveland, TN 37311; ba/C'land; m/William Leon Sr; c/Richard S, William L Jr; p/JB and Mazie Woody, C'land, TN; ed/LPN Sch 1960; RN C'land St Commun Col 1976; pa/RN; Mid-South Regional Med Prog; r/So Bapt.

ATCHLEY, VIVIAN MARION oc/Teacher; b/Aug 19, 1910; h/ROWE, Rt 2 Box 13, Denton, TX 76201; ba/Denton; c/Linda, Susan, Robert (Bob), Nancy; p/JD (dec) and Maggie Williams Marion (dec); pa/Works w Mtlly Retard'd at Denton St Sch, Denton, TX; r/Bapt.

ATKINS, CYNTHIA oc/Nurse; b/Aug 22, 1951; h/302 E Kennedy Cir, Benson, NC 27504; m/Ernest Sterling Peacock; c/Casandra Yvonne, Sterling Jr; p/Thurman Bridgers, Durham, NC; Frances Ledora Allen, Balto, MD; ed/Att'd Durham Tech Inst: Grad & Lic'd 1970; Clin Exp, Duke Univ Med Ctr; pa/Staff Nurse (LPN) Good Hope Hosp, Erwin, NC; Lectr throughout state on "Parents Rights and Responsibilities Toward Their Children's Education"; cp/Vol for Cancer Soc; Vol Parent 4-H Clb, Benson Primary 1979-80; PTA 1976–; Secy, Local Title 1 PAC, Benson Primary & Elem Schs 1978; Chp Title I PAC, Nom'd Dist Chp for Johnston Co 1979; r/Holiness; hon/Del Nat Coalition for Title 1 Parents, Detroit, Mich 1979 & Louisville, Ky 1980.

ATKINS, HANNAH DIGGS oc/Member Oklahoma House of Representatives; b/1923; h/Route #4, Box 799, Oklahoma City, OK 73111; ba/Oklahoma City; m/Charles Nathaniel; c/Edmund Earl, Charles N, Valerie Ann; p/James Thackeray and Mabel Kennedy Diggs, Winston-Salem, NC; ed/BS St Augustine's Col; BLS Grad Lib Sch of Univ of Chgo; Addit Studies Okla City Univ Sch of Law; MA Studies Univ of Okla; pa/Law Libn, Instr of Law, Instr of Lib Sci 1962-68; Public Spkr; cp/Serving 5th Term as St Rep for Dist 97, Okla St Legislature, Chwom Mtl Hlth & Retardation Com; Mem Coms: Appropriations & Budget, Public Hlth, Higher Ed, Equal Employmt Opportunities 1968–; Nat Com-Wom Dem Nat Com 1976–; Chwom Nat Assn of Black Wom Legislators 1976–; Comm on Presl Nom & Party Structure of Dem Nat Com 1977–; Nat Bd Am Civil Liberties Union; Nat Bd Black Child Devel Inst 1974–; Others; Alpha Kappa Alpha, Past Basileus Beta Sigma Omega Chapt; Okla Comm

on Ed; Urban Leag; Exec Bd Commun Action Prog; Others; r/Mem Ch of the Redeemer Epis Ch; Lic'd Lay Reader, Diocese of Okla; Mem Ch Wom United, Redeemer Ch Wom; Former Mem of Vestry; Former Ch Sch Tchr; hon/Phi Beta Kappa; Nat Public Citizen of Yr, Nat Assn Social Wkrs 1975; Dist'd Ser Awd, Nat Link Inc 1972; Hon Mem Eta Phi Beta; Outstg Wom of Yr: Okla Soroptimist Intl 1965, Theta Sigma Phi 1968, Shawnee Chapt NOW 1976; Outstg Commun Ser, So Region Phi Delta Kappa 1976; W/W: Am Polits, Am Wom, Govt, Black Ams.

ATKINS, MITTIE oc/Retired Postmaster; b/Dec 7, 1913; h/Michie, TN; m/Roy L; p/Wylie Terry (dec) and Glen Dera Latta Gooch (dec); pa/Clerk in Father's Store; Postal Clerk; Postmaster; r/Primitive Bapt.

ATKINSON, CARL P oc/Expediter; b/Dec 26, 1922; h/Paris, TN; p/Joe W (dec) and Rohama Dent Atkinson (dec); ed/Toler's Bus Col, Paris, Tenn 1950; mil/AUS 1942-45; pa/Colt Industs, Paris, Tenn: Qual Control Prod, Expiditer; Paris-Henry Co C of C; cp/Pres Paris Civic League; Am Legion Post 164; Adj VFW Post 4805; Voter League; hon/Civic League Man of Yr 1980.

ATTAYEK, JOSEPH EDWARD JR oc/Parks and Recreation Director; b/Apr 5, 1955; h/PO Box 298, Selma, NC 27576; ba/Selma; p/Joseph E and Margaret D Attayek, Greensboro, NC; ed/BS UNC-Greensboro 1979; pa/Dir Town of Selma Pks & Rec Dept; Asst Dir City of Henderson Pks & Rec Dept; Nat Rec & Pks Assn; NC Rec & Pk Soc; r/Cath.

AULTMAN, LARRY L oc/Minister; b/Feb 14, 1947; h/PO Box 7, Little Elm, TX 75068; ba/Little Elm; m/Donna C; c/Jessica Lauren, Joel Andrew; ed/BA William Carey Col 1969; MDiv 1974, DD 1979 SWn Bapt Theol Sem; pa/Missionary in Africa; Min of Yth, Okla & Tex; Min Ed; Min Outreach; Pastor: Miss, Tex & presently First Bapt Ch, Little Elm; Denton Bapt Assn; Bapt Gen Convention of Tex; cp/Lions Club; r/So Bapt; hon/Outstg Yng Men of Am 1977 & 1980.

AURISPA, EDDIE oc/Executive Director; b/Sept 18, 1949; h/11603 Santa Cruz Dr, Austin, TX 78759; ba/Austin; m/Cheryl Salinas; c/Kristina, Carlos; p/Rafael and Paulina Y Aurispa, Laredo, TX; ed/BA Laredo Jr Col 1971; pa/Good Neighbor Comm of Tex: Exec Dir 1977–, Acting Exec Dir, Dpty Dir, Migrant Labor Coor; Yth Prog Coor, Ec Opport Advmt Corp; Fac Mem Upward Bound Prog Baylor Univ & Paul Quin Col; cp/Bd Dirs Intl Good Neighbor Coun 1977–; Bd Dirs Hermanos de la Frontera Inc 1979–; Baylor Univ Alumni Assn 1971–; League of U Latin Am Citizens 1976–; Bapt Gen Convention of Tex 1959–; First Mexican Bapt Ch 1977–; r/Bapt; hon/Outstg Yng Man of Am 1980; Favorite Son of Jalostotilan 1979; Dedicated to Brotherhood of Man 1978; Latin Am S'ship 1969-71; VP Tex Bapt Yth Congress 1969-71; Outstg ROTC Cadet; Others.

AUSTAD, ARNOLD DAVID oc/Sculptor; b/May 2, 1947; h/92D6 Cynthia Lane, Middletown, CT 06457; ba/Same; m/Carol; p/Ralph (dec) and Pearl Austad (dec); pa/Sculptor.

AUSTIN, JO ANNE oc/Detective; b/May 25; ba/PO Box 388, Dunn, NC; c/Darryl Bruce Henderson, Christopher Dale Henderson, Daniel Odell Henderson, Jerry Donald Jr; p/Martha Denton Prince, Raleigh, NC; ed/Sampson Tech Col 1979; pa/Law Enforcement, Detective, Dunn Police Dept; r/Free Will Bapt.

AUSTIN, JUDIE PIKE MILLER oc/Librarian; b/Nov 17, 1940; h/1509 Delk Dr, High Point, NC 27260; ba/Kernersville; m/Neal F; c/Jennifer Lynn DeJonge, William Michael DeJonge; p/Edgar R and Jeannette Pike Miller, Reading, PA; ed/BA Albright Col 1961; AMLS Univ Mich 1963; pa/Chd's Libn, Jackson Co Lib (Mich); Subj Libn, Rochester Public Lib (NY); Hd Adult Sers, High Point Public Lib (NC); Hd Tech Sers; Asst to Dir; Area Libn, Forsyth Co Public Lib (NC); ALA; NCLA, Chm Intell Freedom Com 1973-77; SELA; cp/High Point Jr Wom's Clb; Altrusa Clb of High Point, Pres 1979-81; r/Prot.

AUTREY, C E oc/Pastor, Professor; b/Sept 17, 1904; h/Sandy, UT; ba/Salt Lake City, UT; m/Aline H; c/Carrol H, Janny; p/E A Autry Sr (dec) and Rose Lee Yates (dec); ed/BA La Col 1930; ThM 1932, ThD 1934 New Orleans Bapt Theol Sem; DD La Col 1961; pa/Pastor: Temple Bapt Ch, Ruston, La 1934; Union City, Tenn 1936-39; First Bapt Ch, W Monroe, La 1939-48; Assoc Dir Evangelism, So Bapt Convention 1948-55; Prof SWn Theol Sem 1955-60; Dir Evangelism, So Bapt Convention 1960-70; Prof New Orleans Sem 1970-72; Pastor Univ Bapt Ch, Salt Lake City, UT 1975–; Dir Sem Ctr, Golden Gate Theol Sem 1978–; hon/VP La So Bapt Convention 1942; Author: Basic Evangelism, 1959; You Can Win Souls, 1961; Others.

AVERY, MARY PAGE oc/Supervisor; b/Mar 2, 1939; h/Rt 1 Box 127, Erwin, NC 28339; m/Wayne G; c/Rickey W, Glenn J; p/Lee Roy and Eva Turner Page, Erwin, NC; ed/HS Grad; pa/Social Sers Eligibility Supvr II, Harnett Co Dept Social Sers; NC Social Sers Assn; cp/Cub Scout

PERSONALITIES OF THE SOUTH

Den Mother; Boy Scout Com Mem; Harnett Co Schs Adv Com; r/Free Will Bapt; hon/Valedictorian 1957; Typing Awd 1957; Shorthand Awd 1957; E R Thomas Scholastic Awd 1957; Lions Clb Scholastic Awd 1957; Am Hist Awd 1956; NCSSA Ctrl Dist Employee of Yr 1981.

AXTON, ARAMINTA ELIZABETH AKIN oc/Teacher, Social Worker; b/Sept 13, 1912; h/1666 Westchester Ave, Winter Pk, FL 32789; ba/Orlando, FL; m/Howard Nelson (dec); c/Kathryn E Burgher (dec), Howard Nelson II, Pamela E, Janice Erin; p/Elisha Gunter Sr and Montine Jones Akin (dec); ed/BS Chem; Certs Genealogy, Parliamentary Law, Law Enforcement; pa/Tchr; Nurse; Fla Social Wkr; Geneal Resr; cp/DAR; DAC; UDC; Nat Soc Sn Dames of Am; Nat Def Activs; r/Bapt; hon/Nat Public Relations Awds from NS DAC 1977, 78, 79; Hon Pres Fla Div UDC; Won 5 Jefferson Davis Medals for Hist Achmts; Am Security Coun Bicent Medal.

AYERS, JAMES LEE oc/Administrator; b/Feb 1, 1945; h/AS Ofc; ba/Miami, FL; m/Mary Jeanette Davis; c/Aaron Keith, Wendy Renee; p/James Samuel and Ethel Le Wester Ayers, Greenville, SC; ed/AS Tidewater Commun Col 1973; BS Geo Wash Univ 1975; mil/USN; pa/Naval Ofcr; Hlth Care Admnstr; Assn of Mil Surgs of US; Am Hosp Assn; Am Soc Mil Comptrollers; Nat Jr Col Scholastic Soc; Phi Theta Kappa; Fed Exec Assn of Puerto Rico; cp/Pres, Bd Dirs & Past Treas Navy Flying Clb; Roosevelt Roads, Puerto Rico: Bd Dirs; Pres Prot Chapel Com; Cub Master Pack 355; Boy Scout Com; Aircraft Owners and Pilots Assn; r/Christian & Missionary Alliance; hon/Mil Decoration: Navy Commend Medal w Combat V; Navy Achmt Medal w Combat V; Purple Heart; Navy Good Conduct Medal; Combat Action Ribbon; Other Unit Citations & Commends to Equal 15 Decorations; W/W in S&SW.

AYERS, STEPHEN CURTIS oc/Communications Executive; b/Aug 28, 1954; h/806 Airport Rd, Blacksburg, VA 24060; ba/Roanoke, VA; m/Karen Ann Van Krey; c/April Ann; p/Herbert and Nancy Jean Kanode Curtis; ed/Assoc Applied Sci Va Western Col 1972-74; New River Col 1974-76; Inst Engrg Techs 1976; pa/Freelance Elecs Sales; Photog; Sports Ed, Circulation Mgr *Blacksburg Sun*; Communications Dispatcher; Co-Owner Profl. Communications Inc; Regional Sales Mgr Universal Communications Sys Inc; Pres B'burg Answering Ser; VP B'burg Vol Fire Dept and First Aid Crew; Bd Dirs Wn Va Emer Med Serv Coun; Mem Assoc Public Safety Communications Ofcrs; Assoc Telephone Answering Exchanges; r/Ch of God.

AYSCUE, ALFRED THOMAS oc/Minister; b/Sept 9, 1933; h/203 Forestview Dr, Mt Airy, NC 17030; ba/Mt Airy; m/Hazel Buchanan; c/Deborah, Lori; p/Robert Thomas (dec) and Minerva Overton Ayscue, Henderson, NC; ed/BA Wake Forest Univ 1956; SEn Bapt Theol Sem 1967; mil/USAF; pa/Pastor Calvary Bapt Ch Mt Airy; Pres Gtr Mt Airy Min Assn; Mem of Com on Coms, Nominating Com and Task Force on Heritage and Polity of NC Bapt St Convention; VChm Bd Dirs of *Biblical Recorder*, Joun of NC Bapt St Convention; cp/Pres Franklin Optimist Clb; r/So Bapt; hons/Articles in *Proclaim, The Baptist Recorder, The Biblical Recorder.*

B

BABETTE, ANITA oc/Commercial Photographer; Photographic Company President; b/Aug 27, 1939; ba/3614 SW Third Ave, Miami, FL 33145; p/Alfred and Mae Klein Greenstein, Miami; ed/Cert in Photo & Silversmithing Centro Superior de Artes Aplicadas 1961; BA 1962, Grad Studies 1965 Wayne St Univ; Cont'd Studies Univ Miami 1967-76; pa/Contbg Writer/Illustrator to Profl Jours 1976-; Ofcl Photog Fla Furniture Mart 1974-75; Conslt in A-V Prodn Fla Intl Univ 1972; Comml Photog & Pres Ad/Photographics, Inc, Miami 1971-; Lectr Comml Photo Miami Photo Col 1971; Photog Post Cards & Guide Books Dukane Press, Hollywood, Fla 1969-70; Other Profl Positions; Spkr Wilson Hicks Intl Conf on Visual Communs, Univ Miami 1976; Nat Assn Wom Bus Owners; Fla Profl Photogs; SEn Profl Photogs Assn; Profl Photogs Am; Intl Ctr Photo; Yg Profls; Nat Home Fashions Leag; cp/Guest Spkr Rotary Clb, Miami 1977; Wayne St Univ Alumni Assn; hon/1st & 2nd Pl Awds, Nat Photographic Competition, Clb Fotografico de Mexico 1960; Cert Merit, Fla Profl Photogs; W/W S&SW; Winner "Why didn't I think of that?" Competition, Industrial Photo.

BABINEAUX, LINDA RANDALL oc/Administrative Assistant; b/Sept 10, 1942; h/115 Blaine Lane, Lafayette, LA 70507; ba/Lafayette; c/Randall James; Russell Blaine; Renee Louise; p/Randall James Wesley and Landry Eugenia Marie Babineaux; ed/Cert PLS by Nat Assn Legal Secys; pa/Admin Asst To Exec Com; Past Pres La Assn Legal Secys; Desk & Derrick; Nat Assn Legal Asst; Acadiana Pers Mgrs; cp/Ragin Rouge; Am Cancer Soc Vol; r/Cath; hon/Legal Secy of Yr, La Assn Legal Secys 1976-77; Ofcr of Yr LALS 1976-77; W/W in Am Wom 1977-78.

BACHI, NAOMI MABEL oc/Student Advisor; b/Mar 26, 1916; h/3700 Mason Hills Dr; Edmond, OK 73034; ba/Edmond; m/Michael Mario; p/Albert James and Maybell Rebecca Patton Baker (dec); ed/Okla Univ 1947-48; Rio Grande Col 1956-57; Chadron St Tchrs Col 1961-62; Ctl St Univ 1965; pa/Records Asst, Ctl St Univ; Admissions & Records Coun; Admissions Coun for Fgn Students; Assoc Intl Student Advr; Nat Assoc Fgn Student Affairs; Ctl St Univ Dames; Edmond Dem Wom's Clb; hon/W/W of Am Wom 1979-80.

BAGBY, WILLIAM WOODROW oc/Minister; b/Nov 11, 1912; h/PO Box 127, Tuskegee, AL 36083; ba/Same; m/Mary Elizabeth Alexander; c/Mary Elizabeth (Mrs O'Farrell Shoemaker); p/Frank Ellis (dec) and Lucy O'Shellie Stokes Bagby (dec); ed/AB Millsaps Col; MDiv Columbia Theol Sem; pa/Permanent Clerk S Miss Presby 1956-66; Stated Clerk E Ala Presby; Pastor; cp/Mem Bd Am Red Cross; BSA; Lion's Clb; Adv Bd Mtl Hlth; r/Presby; hon/Rural Min of Yr, St of Miss 1963.

BAGEN, SARA JACOBS oc/Homemaker; b/Jan 24, 1929; h/1471 Moores Mill Rd NW, Atlanta, GA 30327; m/Leonard; c/Renee Bagen Rinzler, Robyn G, Andrea Bagen Holbrook, Marilyn Bagen Ogden; p/Hyman S (dec) and Sadye S Jacobs, Atlanta, GA; pa/Pres Leo N Levi Nat Arthritis Hosp, Hot Springs, Ark; Pres Hyman S & Sadye Jacobs Foun; cp/Mem SE Bd Anti-Defamation League; Jewish Nat Fund; hon/ODK Ldrship Frat; Ga St B Brith Hillel Awd 1975; W/W of World Jewry.

BAGGETT, AGNES BEAHN oc/State Official; b/Apr 9; h/3202 Montezuma Rd, Montgomery, AL 36106; ba/Montgomery; m/G Lamar (dec); p/John R and Leila T Beahn (dec); ed/Courses Jones Law Sch; pa/L&N RR 1925-27; Num Positions Secy of St Ofc 1927-46; Asst Clk Supr Ct 1946-50; Secy of St 1975-; St Auditor 1955-58; St Treas 1971-75; cp/Am Legion Aux; St Leg Chm; Chm Girls St Ala; hon/Career Wom; 1 of Top Wom in Montgomery.

BAGLEY, BOBBY RAY oc/Military Colonel; b/Feb 10, 1933; h/13130 Hunters Brook, San Antonio, TX 78230; ba/Kelly AFB, TX; m/Edna M; c/Vicki Ann; p/Ralph B and Pauline N Bagley, Suwanee, GA; ed/BGE; MA; Grad Indust Col Armed Forces; mil/USAF Col; Dep for Support to Mil Opers, Hdqtrs USAF Security Ser; Command Pilot; Num Former Mil Positions incl'g: Cmdr TUSLOG Detachmt 94 Karamursel Common Def Installation (Turkey); Dep Cmdr for Opers & Asst Dep Cmdr (363rd TRW), Shaw AFB, Reconnaissance Pilot RF-101 Udorn Royal Thai AFB, Thailand, Others; pa/Air Force Assn; DAEDALIAN; r/Bapt; hon/Hon HHD, Piedmont Col; Silver Star w Oak Leaf Cluster; Legion of Merit w Oak Leaf Cluster; Bronze Star Medal w Valor Device & Oak Leaf Cluster; Air Medal w 3 Oak Leaf Clusters; Air Force Commend Medal w Oak Leaf Cluster; Purple Heart w Oak Leaf Cluster.

BAGWELL, GERALD E oc/Pastor; b/Feb 20, 1936; h/Lakeland, FL; ba/301 N Fla Ave, Lakeland, FL 33801; m/Betty T; c/Greg, Jeff, Phil; p/Cecil and Ola Bagwell, Winder, GA; ed/BS Piedmont Col 1963; MDiv SEn Bapt Theol Sem 1967; ThM 1968, ThD 1969 Luther Rice Sem; pa/Dir Public Relations and Alumni Affairs, Piedmont Col; Pastor: First Bapt Ch, Loganville, GA; First Bapt Ch, Waynesboro, GA; Mtn Pk First Bapt Ch, Stone Mtn, GA; First Bapt Ch, L'land; Pres Lawrenceville Pastor's Conf; Evangelism Chm Lawrenceville Bapt Assn; Evangelism Chm S Fla Bapt Assn; r/Bapt; hon/W/W in GA 1975; Outstg Yng Men of Am 1970; Outstg Grad of Piedmont Col 1967; Selected by Brotherhood Comm to Tour Sn Bapt Mission Work in Mexico 1971; Tchr Nat-wide Sem on Ch Growth, S Korea 1978; Wrote Column for *The True Citizen*, *The TuckerStar*, *Lakeland Ledger*; Article in *Outreach*.

BAHARLOO, CARLA RUZIC oc/Society Editor; h/246 Apt Ct Dr, Apt 113, Baton Rouge, LA 70806; m/Koorosh; p/Joseph P Ruzic Sr, Hattiesburg, MS; Joyce Richardson, Thorndale, TX; ed/USM; pa/Soc Ed, *Daily Star*, Hammond, La; cp/Choreographer, La Touring Chd's Theatre; hon/Sweetheart Hammond Sr Citizens; La Press Awd, 2nd Place Best Wom's Coverage.

BAILEY, BOB G oc/Funeral Director; b/Oct 27, 1950; h/620 S Monta Visa, Ada, OK 74820; ba/Ada; m/Billie L; c/Matthew Brent; p/Riley William Bailey (dec) and Edith Mae Bailey Fish, Ada, OK; ed/BS Ctl St Univ 1973; pa/Funeral Dir; Profl Embalmer; Okla Funeral Dir Assn; Nat Funeral Dir Assn; Comml Travelers of Am; Preceptor Ctl St Univ; Tchr Embalming Ctl St Funeral Dept; cp/Pres Kiwanis Clb Ada; Pres Ada Area Yth Shelter; Ada Masonic Lodge #119; 32° Mason, Scottish Rite, McAlester Consistory; Ada Shrine Clb; Bedouin Shrine Temple; Indep Order Odd Fellows; Ancient Beneficent Order Red Red Rose; E Ctl Chapt Scottish Rite Soc Okla; Bd Dirs Am Red Cross; Okla Heart Assn; Bd Dirs Okla Tourism; Ada C of C; Adv Bd City Ada; Past Pres Ada Commun Theater; Vol Fireman; EMT; Others; r/First Christian Ch of Ada.

BAILEY, DONALD LINCOLN oc/Police Chief; b/Jan 11, 1928; h/13 Leland St, Great Falls, SC 29055; ba/Gt Falls; m/Maggie L; c/Donald L Jr, Charles D, Mark E, Victoria A Bailey Brown; p/Charles E (dec) and Roxie Hazel Bailey (dec); mil/USMC Ret'd; r/Bapt.

BAILEY, KAY oc/Attorney; State Representative; b/Jul 22, 1943; h/3435 Westheimer, Houston, TX 77027; p/Alan and Kathryn Bailey, LaMarque, TX; ed/Univ Tex-Austin; Univ Tex Sch of Law; pa/Admitted St Bar Tex 1967; 1st Wom News Reporter for TV in Houston (Polit Corresp KPRC-TV); Law Pract w Houston Firm of Reynolds, White, Allen & Cook; 1st Wom Elected Bd Dirs Houston St Bar Assn; Nat Order Wom Legs; Chm St Bar Com on Improvemt & Advmt of Bar; St Bar Com on Public Affairs; Appt'd VChm Nat Trans Safety Bd 1976, Acting Chm 1977; cp/Elected Tex Ho of Reps 1972 (1st Repub Wom Elected); Mem Num House Coms; Re-elected 1974; Del Tex Constitutional Conv 1974; Bd Dirs Tex Bill of Rts Foun; VChm Citizens Improvemt Com for Mass Transit Auth; Bd Dirs Tex Rape Preven & Control Proj; Others; hon/Houston Bar Assn Annual Awd for Best TV Reporter in field of Jurisprudence 1970; Only Tex Rep chosen to White House Summit Conf on Inflation, St & Local Govt Sect 1974; Outstg Yg Wom Tex; 1 of 10 Outstg Yg Wom Am; Featured in *Glamour Mag* as 1 of 10 Outstg Working Wom in Am; Wom of Yr, Houston Bapt Univ; Outstg Yg Lwyr in Houston, Houston Jr Bar.

BAILEY, MALCOLM LEE JR oc/Paramedic; b/May 9, 1938; h/222 Nance Cr, Paris, TN 38242; ba/Paris, TN; m/Glenda Joy; c/Malcolm Lee III, Candy Lynn; p/Malcolm Lee Bailey Sr (dec); Eva Louise Atkins (dec); ed/Nashville Auto-Diesel Col 1957; Red Cross First Aid; EMC Course; EMT Course; UT-Nashville; mil/AUS 3 Yrs; USNG 1½ Yrs; pa/Gas & Diesel Mech 22 Yrs; Paramedic Henry Co Ambulance Ser 3 Yrs; Capt Paris-Henry Co Resque Squad; r/Meth; hon/Post Soldier of Month, Feb 1964; GM Only the Best Clb 1965.

BAILEY, MARGARET W oc/Homemaker, Quail Farmer, Artist; b/Nov 12, 1927; h/136 Lowry Ln, Apt 5, Lexington, KY 40503; ba/Same; m/Wade H; c/Vicky B Wall, Teresa B Wolford, Kim M, Jesse L, Julie R; p/James A (dec) and Anna O Wethington, Liberty, KY; pa/Quail Farmer; Egg Shell Artist; r/Christian Ch; hon/1st & 2nd Places Arts & Crafts 4 Times; Newspaper Articles; 2 TV Progs on Quail Farming.

BAINES, DONALD DEAN oc/Lecturer, Management Consultant; b/May 28, 1938; h/202 Poplar St, Prattville, AL 36067; ba/Montgomery, AL; m/Jacque Lee Snyder; c/Treavor Dean, Troy Douglas, Trent Darrin, Ty Dustin, Torrey Dana; ed/BS Colo St Univ 1960; MS Troy St Univ 1974; PhD Columbia Pacific Univ 1980; mil/USAF Lt Col; pa/Fdr & Dir Profl Devel Inc; Former Dir USAF Profl Pers Mgmt Course; Profl Lectr & USAF Spec in Exec Stress; Am Mgmt Assn; Fac Mem: Troy St Univ, Columbia Pacific Univ, Video Univ; r/Bapt; hon/Author: *Nine Steps Toward Beating Executive Stress*, 1979; Articles Pub'd in *Denver Post* & Other Newspapers & Profl Jouns.

BAIRD, DAVID C oc/Evangelist; b/Mar 31, 1957; h/Ebony, VA; ba/PO Box 3, Ebony, VA 23845; p/Lonnie W and Etta L Baird, Ebony, VA; ed/BA Old Dom Univ; Assemblies of God Grad Sch; pa/Fdr & Spkr

"Choice Assemblies;" Spkr Conventions & Crusades; r/Assemblies of God; hon/Winner 2 All-Expense Pd Trips to Mid-East for Scripture Memorization; Outstg Yng Rel Ldr Yr 1980; Author 2 Articles Pub'd in *Tidewater Chronicle.*

BAKER, ALMA JEANNE WATKINS oc/Assistant Dean; b/July 10, 1932; h/Lexington, KY; m/Robert M; p/George Boyd (dec) and Ida Mae Watkins (dec); ed/Univ Louisville 1949-51; BSN, Med Col Va 1955; HSNE Indiana Univ 1965; PhD Univ Mich 1976; pa/Coor & Asst Prof of Psychi/Mtl Hlth Nsg; Estab & Dir Assoc Deg Nsg Prg Ken St Univ; Coor Minority Student Affairs Univ Mich; Tchr Psychi Nsg Butler Jr Commun Col; ANA; KNA; Bd Dirs Nat Black Nurses Assn; Ed-in-Chief Nat Black Nurses Assn; cp/Secy Toastmaster Intl #3054; Zeta Phi Beta; r/Bapt; hon/AA Williams S'ship Awd 1955; Nat Inst Mtl Hlth Fellowship 1964-65; Horace H Rackham Oppor Grant 1972-76; Author & Co-Author: *Nursing Students' Cultural Knowledge and Attitudes Toward Patients,* "Psychiatric Nursing - Outline for Textbook," Others.

BAKER, CHARLES FRANKLIN oc/Police Psychologist; Investigator; b/Feb 15, 1938; h/2216 Spring Hill, Dallas, TX 75228; ba/Dallas; m/Judith Gail; c/Jennifer Eden, Valerie Leigh, Nathan Hugh; p/Ney Hamilton (dec) and Ruby Louise Baker, Dallas, TX; ed/BS Abilene Christian Col; MA So Meth Univ; mil/USAF 1961; USAFR 1961-67; pa/Dallas Police Dept: Investigator; Psychol; Psychol Sers; Dallas Police Assn; Am Psychol Assn; r/Ch of Christ; hon/Ad'd Cert Tex Comm on Law Enforcement Ofcr Standards & Ed; Instr's Cert; Nat Hon Soc in Psychol (Psi Chi); Cert of Merit, Dallas Police Dept; EMT, Parkland Meml Hosp, Dallas.

BAKER, EARL B oc/Social Service Director; b/Dec 3, 1946; h/Rt 2, Box 888, Grand Ridge, FL 32442; ba/Marianna, FL; p/Frank Sr and Daisy Baker, Grand Ridge; ed/AA Chipola Jr Col 1969; BS Fla A&M Univ 1971; Cert Parent Effective Tng Lavern Col 1975; MS NOVA Univ 1979; mil/AUS 1965-67; pa/Dozier Sch, Marianna: Social Ser Dir 1978-, Clin Social Wkr 1975, Social Ser Wkr 1971-74; Coor Title XX Sampling 1978; Charge Aide Fla St Hosp, Chattahoochee, Fla 1968-71; Casework Asst Bur of Prisons, Fed Correction Inst, Tallahassee, Fla 1971; Bd Mem: NW Fla Mtl Hlth Ctr, Fla Assn for Hlth & Social Sers; Pres Chipola Ser Assn; Am Soc Criminology; Pi Gamma Nu; hon/Outstg Trainee Awd, AUS; Hons Awd for High Scholastic Achmt, FAMU; Outstg Vol Ser Awd, Dist II HRS; Outstg Com Awd (2), Chipola Ser Assn.

BAKER, ERIC WHITE oc/Social Worker; b/July 27, 1947; p/Dallard G and Dora E Baker, Lou, KY; ed/AB Bellarmine Col 1970; MSSW Kent Sch Social Work 1974; ACSW 1976; Clin Mem AAMFT 1980; pa/Dist Prog Mgr, Dept Human Resources; Pvt Prac Marriage, Fam, Indiv & Grp Therapy; Lic'd Clin Social Wkr; Bd Mem Sn Reg Inst Intl Assn of Transactional Analysis CPM; cp/Ky Col 1978; r/Roman Cath; hon/W/W 1980; Ky Col 1978.

BAKER, GARLAND RAY oc/Executive; b/Apr 8, 1934; h/Rt 2 Box 72, Russellville, AR 72801; ba/R'ville; m/Glenna Ruth; c/Mary Ann, Cynthia Ruth, Garland Ray Jr; p/R J and Vada Baker, Hattieville, AR; mil/Army Med Corps, Korean Conflict; pa/Pres: G Ray Baker Trucking Inc & Raymar Sound Prodn; Poultry Broker; Co Fair Bd; cp/C of C & R'ville C of C; Bd Mem Ark St; Bd Mem R'ville Public Sch; Justice of Peace Dist 6; UCT; Ark Farm Bur Fed; Quarum Ct; Others; r/1st Assem of God: SS Supt; hon/Father of Yr 1973; Menis Min Light for the Lost; Sponsor Good Life Clb for Elderly.

BAKER, GILBERT RAY oc/Instructor; b/Sept 5, 1956; h/29 Woodlawn, Conway, AR 72032; ba/Conway; p/GJ and Shirley Baker, Wiggins, MS; ed/BFA; MM; pa/Instr of Percussion; Percussive Arts Soc; Ark Symph; cp/Active Mem Ark Repub Party; r/Bapt; Min of Mus.

BAKER, GLADYS MELISSA oc/Retired; b/Sept 26, 1908; h/612 W Hardy, Altus, OK 73521; m/Otis W; c/James L McFadin, Onieta Ruth Dorman, Roy Joe McFadin, Mary Ann Teague, Brittie Emma Chrisman; p/Robert Lee (dec) and Bertha Emma Cooper (dec); pa/Okla Lung Assn; cp/Altus Rebikah Lodge #75; r/So Bapt; hon/Wonder Wkr 1974-79; Wonder Wkr of Yr 1976.

BAKER, HELEN VAUGHAN BURDIN oc/Educator, Historian; b/May 20, 1937; h/734 Alonda Dr, Lafayette, LA 70503; ba/Lafayette; m/Amos E Simpson; c/Larry Eugene, Elizabeth Vaughan, David Scott; p/John Joseph and Helen Rose Broussard, Lafayette, LA; ed/Acad of Sacred Heart 1955; BA Newcomb Col 1959; MS 1970, PhD 1975 SWn Univ; pa/Dept Hist Univ SWn La; Dir Wom in La Collection, Ctr for La Studies; Am Hist Assn; So Hist Assn; Ed *European History Newsletter;* La Hist Assn; SW Social Scis Assn; So Conf Brit Studies; Wn Assn German Studies; cp/Exec Com Lafayette Mayor's Comm on Needs of Wom; hon/So Hist Assn John Snell Prize 1971; Phi Kappa Phi; Phi Alpha Theta; Author: *Death of an Old World: Europe 1914-45;*

Genesis of a New World: Europe 1945-Present; Articles in *Louisiana History, Red River Valley Journal of World History.*

BAKER, JAMES ESTES oc/Diplomat; b/Jan 21, 1935; h/4 E 8th St, New York, NY 10603; ba/NYC; p/Perch H Sr and Mary Baker, Baltimore, MD; ed/BA Haverford Col; MA, MALD Tufts Univ; mil/AUS 1957-59; pa/Dep US Rep to Ec & Social Coun, UN; On Leave as Sr Assoc Intl Fact Finding Ctr, Carnegie Endowmt; cp/NAACP; Coun on Fgn Relats; Am Fgn Ser Assn.

BAKER, KATHRYN TAYLOR oc/Associate Professor; Clinic Program Coordinator; b/Jan 5, 1925; h/1818 Mignon Ave, Memphis, TN 38107; ba/Memphis; m/John; p/John Andrew Taylor (dec); Alma Lou Wharey Taylor, Trenton, TN; ed/BS; MSSW; pa/Assoc Prof Social Work; Coor Reg Clin Prog; Mem Admissions Bd, Arlington Devel Ctr; Secy-Treas AAUP, Univ Tenn Ctr for Hlth Scis Chapt; Hon Bd Mem Memphis Div Am Cancer Soc; Bd Mem: Memphis Heart Assn, Nom'g Com Goodwill Industs, Policy & Public Relats Coms W Tenn Agape; Mem Social Policy & Action Com, Nat Assn Social Wkrs, Memphis; Mem Budget & Admissions Com for Child Care Agys, U Way; Other Profl Positions; Intl Conf on Social Wel; Nat Assn Social Wkrs; Nat Conf on Social Wel; Tenn Conf Social Wel; Am Assn Mtl Deficiency; Memphis Social Wkrs Clb; Tenn Hosp Assn; Tenn Soc Hlth Care Social Wkrs; Univ Tenn Fac Clb; cp/Local Commun Action Assn; Var Polit Activs; r/Ch of Christ: Mem; hon/Fellow, Am Assn Mtl Deficiency; Life Mem Sigma Kappa; Var Edit Activs; Nat Registry of Clin Social Wkrs.

BAKER, LINDA FAYE oc/Seamstress, Taxidermist; b/Oct 3, 1944; h/Rt 7 Box 424, Dunn, NC 28334; m/Claude E Jr; c/Theresa Faye; p/Clarence and Mabel G Turnage, Erwin, NC; ed/Taxidermy Courses; pa/Bonders Inc, Dunn.

BAKER, WILLIAM DUNCAN oc/Senior Engineer; b/Sept 27, 19450; h/3612 Thurman, Amarillo, TX 79109; ba/Amarillo; c/Gray Duncan, Ryan Patrick; p/Alfred S and Koma Jo Johnson Baker, Amarillo; ed/BS Aerospace Engrg Tex A&M Univ; pa/Pres Baker Enterprises; Sr Engr, Bell 1977-; Safety Engr, US Govt 1976-77; Liaison Engr, Bell 1975-76; Boeing: Sys Safety Engr 1974-75, Programming Analyst 1972-74, Sys Safety Engr 1971-72; TSPE; NSPE; Expmtl Aircraft Assn; r/Bapt; hon/Tau Beta Pi; Sigma Gamma Tau; Alpha Phi Omega; Personalities of Am; W/W: S&SW, Technol Today; DIB; Dir of Dist'd Ams; Intl Register of Profiles; Book of Hon.

BAKER, WILLIE GASKIN (Mrs F L) oc/Retired; b/Apr 24, 1897; h/405 Forest Glen Rd, Albany, GA 31707; c/Elsie, Carolyn, Frances (dec), Emma Edith (dec), Joseph Henry (dec), Billie, Robin, F L Jr (dec); p/David E (dec) and Martha Latt Gaskin (dec); ed/Music, Voice, Typing; pa/Farmer until Ret'd; Mus Tchr; Poet; Dir Sch Pageants; Worked w Retard Chd; cp/Played Piano for Silent Movies; r/Meth; hon/Golden Deed Awd From Civic Clbs; Mother of Yr from Albany Wom's Clb; Awds as Student in Jr Col & Col.

BALCOLM, KAREN SUZANNE oc/Information System Specialist/Librarian; b/Feb 15, 1949; ba/San Antonio Col Lib, 1001 Howard St, San Antonio, TX 78284; p/George Sheldon and Marian Dyer Balcolm, San Antonio; ed/AA San Antonio Col 1969; BA 1971, MLS 1972 Univ Tex-Austin; pa/Tex Lib Assn; Spec Libs Assn; Tex Jr Col Tchrs Assn; AAUP; Am Soc Info Ser; Bexar Lib Assn; Am Lib Assn; cp/Life Mem Ex-Students Assn, Univ Tex; Alumni Assn Grad Sch of Lib, Univ Tex; San Antonio Mus Assn; Arts Coun San Antonio; r/So Bapt; hon/Outstg Yng Wom Am; W/W Am Wom.

BALDREE, MARY ONEIDA oc/Executive Housekeeper; b/July 25, 1914; h/Rt 1, Dyersburg, TN 38024; ba/D'burg; m/Cornelius Kelly; c/Bryan Kelly; p/Thomas Frank and Cora Ella Gurley, Fowlkes, TN; ed/Assoc Christian Ed & Bus Admin; pa/Exec Hskp Parkview Hosp; OES #164; Tenn Hosp Hskps Assn; Tenn Hosp Assn; Org'd So Hospitality Chapt of Nat Exec Hskps Assn Inc; SE Dist NEHA: Gov 1967-71; Ed Chm 1973-79; 2nd VP 1979-81; r/Bapt; SS Tchr; Tng Union Dir; Ch Clerk 25 Yrs; Inter & Yng People's Ldr; hon/Dist Hon Awd in Spec Ed 1970 & 72; Fdrs Day Plaque 10 Yrs; Cert for Dept in Hiring Handicapped; St's Dist'd Employer Awd, Hskp Dept.

BALENTINE, ROBERT CHAPMAN oc/Electronics Engineer; b/Dec 29, 1934; h/336 Jack Coleman Dr, NW, Huntsville, AL 35805; ba/Marshall Space Flight Ctr, AL; c/David Michael, Timothy Charles; p/Fred R Balentine, Wister, OK; Eula Chapman Balentine (dec); ed/BS Baylor Univ; pa/Mgr Space Telescope Software, Marshall Space Flight Ctr; Former Mgr Computer Sys & Software for Elements of Space Shuttle; Formerly Assoc'd w Automatic Test Control; r/So Bapt; hon/W/W.

BALES, HAZEL oc/Tire Dealer; b/May 18, 1923; h/1515 Charlestown Jeff Rd, Jeffersonville, IN 47130; ba/Louisville, KY; m/Walter T; p/Alvie J (dec) and Bertie Wilson Albro, L'ville; pa/Tire Dealer Retail; Tire Distributor Wholesale; Pres Bales Firestone #1 Inc & Parkland Supply Co Inc, L'ville; cp/Past Pres Pilot Clb of J'ville r/Prot; hon/W/W of Am Bus Wom; W/W in KY.

BALIN, HOWARD oc/Physician; b/Jan 22, 1927; h/5940 Bahia Honda Way N, St Petersburg Bch, FL; m/Doris; c/Marianne, Susan R, Jane C, Robert D; p/Michael and Esther R Balin, Jenkintown, PA; ed/BA, MD, MSc; Internship; Residencies; Grad Courses; pa/MD, Ob-Gyn; Hosp Staff Appts: Palms of Pasadena Hosp, Lake Seminole Hosp, Bay Front Med Ctr, St Petersburg Gen; Hahnemann Med Col & Hosp: Former Chm Dept Ob-Gyn, Former Prof; Others; Num Other Profl Appts; Num Profl Assns; Reschr; Author or Editor Profl Pubs; Contbr to Textbooks; Sci Exhbns, Motion Pictures, Tchr Video Tapes, Audio Ed Tapes; r/Hebrew; hon/Diplomate, Am Bd Ob-Gyn; Fullbright-Hayes Am Specialist Awd 1967, 69; USAID Sponsored Tour, US St Dept; Hon Socs.

BALL, LOUIS OLIVER JR oc/Professor; b/May 15, 1929; h/405 E Ellis St, Jefferson City, TN 37760; ba/Carson-Newman Col, Jefferson City; m/Mary Charlotte; c/David Louis, Mark Swann; p/Louis and Bonnie Ball, Knoxville, TN; ed/BA 1951, MS 1953 Univ Tenn; MSM 1957, DMA 1962 So Bapt Theol Sem; mil/AUS 1954-56; pa/Prof of Mus & Chief Admin Mus Dept, Carson-Newman Col 1961-; VP So Bapt Ch Mus Conf; Former Pres Tenn Assn Mus Execs in Cols & Univs; Province Gov Phi Mu Alpha Sinfonia 1979; Pi Kappa Lambda; Pres 1975-76 Knoxville Mus Tchrs Assn; Nat Guild Piano Tchrs; r/So Bapt; hon/Patron Delta Omicron Mus Frat; Tchr of Yr, Knoxville Mus Tchrs Assn 1975-76; Author & Arranger: *Hymn Playing*, 1979; *The Heavens Are Telling*, 1979; Others.

BALLADARES, MARIO PEREZ oc/Consul General; b/Sept 29, 1949; h/6625 Pine Tree Ln, Miami Bch, FL 33141; ba/Miami; m/Marilyn E; c/Ana Patricia, Mario Ernesto; p/Ernesto and Maria E de Perez Balladares; ed/BA St Louis Univ & Lindenwood Col; pa/Consul Gen, Repub of Panama; r/Cath.

BALLARD, BETTY RUTH WESLEY oc/Executive; b/Nov 11, 1924; h/Montevallo, AL; m/Douglas Hayden; c/Douglas Hayden Jr; p/Henry Gaston Wesley, B'ham, AL; Ruth Lorine Whitfield Wesley (dec); ed/Att'd Glenn Tech Inst; mil/USO 4th Spec Forces Grp Auxilians; pa/Pres Ballard X-Ray Co & X-Ray Ser & Sales Co Inc; Ala Soc Radiology Technols; Ala Hosp Assn; Inst Hosp Auxilians of Ala; Ala Cattlemen's Assn; Cow Belles; cp/Dem Party; Elect Law Commr, St of Ala; Hon Dpty Sheriff Shelby Co; r/Meth: Adm Bd, Choir Mem; hon/W/W Am Wom.

BALLARD, JOHN WAYNE oc/Gas Executive; b/Aug 26, 1914; ba/Rt 1 Box 60, Oil City, LA 71061; m/Annie Lee Bickham: c/John R, Milton R; p/John William and Nora Wynn Ballard; ed/Centenary Col 1941-45; pa/La Bar 1952; Lab Tech, Shoreline Oil Co 1934-37; Talco Asphalt 0 Refinery 1937-41; Stanolind Oil & Gas Co 1941-42; Chief Chem Princeton Refining Co 1942-45; Asst Chief Engr, Asst Chief Chem Bayou St Oil Co 1946-55; Asst Supt 1948-55, VP Plant Supvsr Caddo Pine Island Corp 1955-68, Pres Gen Mgr 1968-; Dir Caddo Trust & Savs Bk; Pvt Prac Law, Oil City, La 1952-; cp/Democrat, Rotary; Masons; r/Bapt.

BALLOU, LEONARD ROSS oc/Archivist, Organist, Director; b/May 19, 1926; h/Box 19, ECSU, Elizabeth City, NC; c/Joyce, Leonard Jr, Howard, Vicki; p/John J and Edna Deh Ballou, Norfolk, VA; ed/BA Fisk Univ 1949; MA Va St Univ 1964; Assoc of Am Guild Organists 1951; pa/Fla A & M Univ; St Augustine's Col; Ala St Univ; Va St Univ; Elizabeth City St Univ; Dir, Instl Res; Archivist; Organist; NCAIR; AIR; Former Mem SCUP; cp/Democrat; r/Epis; hon/W/W in S&SW; Awds from Alpha Phi Alpha; Boss of Yr 1980-81; Num unpub'd manuscripts.

BALMAT, CORA SUITS oc/Professor; ba/Natchez, MS; m/(dec); c/Sharon Elain Milton; p/Clarissa A Suits, Vernon, NY; ed/Dip Utica St Hosp Sch Nsg 1949; BSN La St Univ 1965; MS Univ Calif 1966; PhD 1977; pa/Prof Nsg; Univ So Miss, Alcorn St Univ; ANA; Nat League Nsg; So Sociol Assn; Applied Anthropol Assn; Delta Kappa Gamma; AAUW; r/Cath; hon/Outstg Edr in Am 1971; Excellence in Tchg Awd 1973; W/W in Am Wom; W/W in Hlth Care; Personalities of South; Co-Author: "Concept in Nursing: Process & Product."

BALSAM, DENNIS M oc/Health Consultant, Physician Assistant; b/May 14, 1945; h/1505 Basswood Ct, Lilburn, GA 30247; ba/Atlanta; m/Marilyn; p/Mildred Balsam, Dallas, TX; ed/BS Tex Tech Univ 1969; BHCSc 1974, PA Cert, SWn Med Sch; Post-Grad Med Tng, Md Inst Emer Med; MCH Emory Univ Sch Med; mil/AUS; pa/Conslt, Medicus Sys Corp 1978-; Clin Coor, Phys Asst Prog, Emory Univ Sch Med 1976-78; Clin Coor, Phys Asst Prog, Med Col Ga 1975-76; Phys Asst, Md Inst Emer Med 1974-75; Num Other Past Positions; AAAS; Electron Microscope Soc Am; Tex Soc Electron Microscopy; Nat Comm on Cert of Phys Assts; Am Acad Phys Assts: Fellow, Ho of Dels, Sargent-at-Arms of Ho of Dels,

Mbrship Com; Ga Assn Phys Assts: Fellow, Bd Dirs; Ga Soc Allied Hlth Professions; Am Public Hlth Assn; Alpha Eta; Assn of Phys Asst Progs, Basic Sci Curric Com; Nat Rural Primary Care Assn; hon/Alpha Eta 1976.

BALTIMORE, CARROLL A SR oc/Pastor; b/May 16, 1943; h/12826 Kettering Dr, Herndon, VA 22070; m/Shirley; c/Vanessa, Carroll, Gregory; p/Helen Baltimore, Hume, VA; ed/Wash Bapt Sem 1967-70; AA Luther Rice Col 1975-76; BIS Geo Mason Univ 1978; ThD Intl Bible Inst & Sem 1980; pa/Pastor: Chestnut Grove Bapt Ch, Brightwood, Va; Shiloh Bapt Ch, Woodville, Va; Mt Pleasant Bapt Ch, Alexandria, Va; Exec Bd Mem No Va Bapt Assn Inc; Exec Bd Mem Lott Carey Fgn Mission Convention Inc; Keynote Spkr Instl Ch of God in Christ Convention 1979; Ed Bd No Va Bapt Assn Inc 1976-80; Auditor Va Fellowship Progressive Nat Bapt Convention Inc 1978-79; Ordination Comm Mt Vernon Bapt Assn Inc 1975-78; Com for Pastoral Awareness 1976-77; Bapt Ctr Bd No Va Bapt Assn 1973-76; No Va Bapt Min Conf; Alexandria Bapt Min Conf; Mt Vernon Min Conf; cp/NAACP; Fairfax Hosp Assn; Bronze Mem Alumni Assn Geo Mason Univ; Foxmill Home Owners Assn; King Tyree Masonic Lodge #292; Citizens Adv Com; Proj Adv Com; Bd Dirs Crossroads Ctr Inc; Bd Dirs Social Ctr Inc; Steering Com for Pres Carter's Elec; hon/Author: "Black Evangelism."

BAMMAN, BETTY MAE oc/Homemaker; b/Nov 1, 1935; h/Rt 3 Box 31, Blountville, TN 37617; m/Otis Dean; c/Jane Casteel, Laura Lunsford, Dean, Susie, Jackie; p/Elgin David (dec) and Lily Juanita Wise (dec); cp/Chm Cystic Fibrosis Foun.

BANDY, EDNA BRASHEARS oc/Appraiser, Deputy Assessor; b/Apr 19, 1934; h/Kingston, TN; ba/Roane Co Cthouse, Kingston, TN 37763; m/Ross O Jr; c/Freida, Steven; p/Clayton L and Martha Eblen Brashears, Kingston, TN; ed/Knoxville Bus Col 1954; Roane St Commun Col 1978; pa/Appraiser for Roane Co 4½ Yrs; Appraiser of Record Sers 15 Yrs; Legal Secy w Roberts & Deatherage 7 Yrs; Secy Accts Payable, Union Carbide 4 Yrs; Intl Assn Assessing Ofcrs; Nat Assn Review Appraisers; Tenn Assn Assessing Ofcrs; E Tenn Assn Assessing Ofcrs; Intl Org Real Estate Appraisers; cp/Recording Secy Roane Co Vol Democratic Clb; Roane Co Legal Secys; Kingston Bus Boosters Clb; r/Meth; hon/First Wom in Tenn and 2nd in Intl Assn of Assessing Ofcrs to Receive Residential Evaluator Spec, Intl Assn Assessing Ofcrs; Cert Review Appraiser, Sr Mem, Nat Assn Review Appraisers.

BANDY, HERMAN MOSBY oc/Retired; b/Apr 5, 1928; h/Rt 4 Box 175, Christiansburg, VA 24073; p/Mosby Fayette Bandy, Blacksburg, VA; Beatrice Jones Bandy (dec); ed/Grad Dale Carnegie Course 1969; Med Asst Courses; mil/AUS 1946-47; pa/Ret'd Justice of Peace, Psychic Weather Forecaster; Writer; cp/VFW, Past Jr Chm; Am Legion; Life Mem DAV, Pub Dir; Life Mem Moose; UCT 30 Yrs; r/Ch of Christ; hon/Predicted Path Hurricane Hazel; Story "Last Court Martial of Civil War."

BANKIT, JUDITH IRENE oc/Nurse; b/May 29, 1947; h/100 E Windsor Castle Dr, Newport News, VA 23602; ba/Newport News; m/Eric Joseph; p/Dona Armand and Dorothy Gertrude LeMay, Nashua, NH; ed/Dip Concord Hosp; BSPA St Joseph's Col; pa/RN; Nsg Supvr; NLN; Va Nurses Assn; r/Luth; hon/W/W of Am Wom 1979-80.

BANKS, DAVID SYLVESTER SR oc/Employment Supervisor; b/Dec 21, 1928; h/837 N Morgan St, Shelby, NC 28150; ba/Shelby; m/Julia Tucker; c/Cheryl, David Jr, Darryl; p/Ceasar Banks (dec); ba/Little Rock Winnsboro, SC; ed/Grad A&T St Univ; mil/AUS 2 Yrs; pa/Former Tchr Shelby Public Schs 9 Yrs; Employmt Supvr PPG Industs; Pres Piedmont Indust Relats Assn; cp/Bd Dirs Cleveland Co Tech Inst; VP NC St Parents' Assn; Chm Cleveland Co U Negro Col Fund; 32nd Deg Prince Hall Mason; Bd Dirs Cleveland Co Boys' Clb; Mem Cleveland Co Alcoholism Task Force; SWATTO; NAACP; Mem Shelby Commun Sch Adv Bd; Num Former Activs; r/Wardell Chapel AMEZ Ch: Trustee, Supt SS; hon/Cleveland Co Mtl Hlth Vol Outstg Ser Awd; PPG Corporate Citizen-of-Yr Awd; Wardell Chapel AMEZ Outstg Ser Awd; Human Relats Awd; Human Relats Coun; PPG Commun Achmt Awd; Others.

BANKS, MARLON CHANDLER oc/Commander USAF; b/Nov 10, 1934, h/100 Arizona Ave, Little Rock AFB, AR 72076; ba/Little Rock AFB; m/Gypsy Scofield; c/Marlon C III; Laura E, Michael S; p/Marlon C (dec) and Opal O Banks, McCrory, AR; ed/BA Bus Admin; mil/Career Ofcr USAF; Squadron Ofcr Sch; Air Command & Staff Col, Industl Col of Armed Forces; pa/Order of Daedalians, Air Force Assn; Omicron Delta Epsilon; cp/Mil Affairs Com; C of C; r/Bapt; hon/Pres Schlr; Hons in Ec/Bus Admin.

BARBER, MELBA MAYLENE oc/Cafe Manager, Waitress; b/Dec 15, 1938; p/Murry F and Bonnie Barber, Stantonville, TN; pa/Waitress & Mgr Same Restaurant 20 Yrs; Former Mem Adamsville Chapt Bus & Profl Wom Assn; cp/Active Mem OES; r/Bapt.

17

BARBER, NANCY BUNDY oc/Social Worker, Therapist; b/May 4, 1934; m/Edward L; p/Merton R and Mabel Sigworth Bundy (dec), Brownsville, TX; ed/BS magna cum laude E Carolina Univ 1974; MSSW Univ Tenn 1980; pa/Social Wkr-Therapist; Fam & Marital Therapy; Hlth Care Corp, Substance Abuse Treatment Unit, Bradley Meml Hosp, Cleveland, Tenn; Nat Assn Social Wkrs; r/Prot; hon/Social Work & Correctional Sers S'ship Awd 1974-75.

BARBER, RICHARD DEAN oc/Art Teacher; b/Feb 5, 1935; h/435 Louise Ave, Charlotte, NC 28204; ba/Charlotte; p/W J and Christine Barber, Mt Holly, NC; ed/BS Wn Carolina Univ; Att'd: UNC-Chapel Hill, UNC-Greensboro, Penland Sch Handicrafts, Appalachian St Univ; pa/Art Tchr Myers Pk HS, Charlotte; Former Tchg Positions: NC Gov's Sch, Gaston Col, UNC-CH, UNC-C, Queens Col; Past Pres Guild Charlotte Artists; NCAE; Originated "Art in the Sky" Sidewalk Show, Govtl Plaza Walkway; Works incl: Watercolors, Pen-and-ink Sketches, Graphics; Featured in 14 One-Man Shows; Rep'd in Perm Collections inclg: Spring Mills, City of Southport, Gaston Co Lib, Mt Holly Lib, Charlotte Mayor's Ofc, Heddon Realty; Rep'd Var Pvt Collections Throughout Country; Lectr; Judge Art Shows; hon/Outstg Yg Edr NC; Finalist Outstg Sec'dy Edr Am; Winner Num Purchase Awds in Southport & Charlotte; 1st Pl, Rel Art Show (2); 1st Pl, Charlotte Guild Artists (4); Elliot O'Hara Water Color Awd; Others; W/W NC.

BARBO, ANITA GAIL oc/Art Studio Manager; b/Dec 1, 1948; h/202 Pinetree Ct, Milton, FL 32570; ba/Pensacola, FL; p/Agdur Andrew and Helen Roena Barbo, Milton, FL; pa/Mgr Art Studio, Instrnl Media Ctr; r/Luth; hon/W/W in Am Wom 1979-80.

BARBOUR, MARY CECIL M oc/Teacher; b/Sept 18, 1915; h/Rt 1 Box 290, Selma, NC 27576; m/James Garland; c/Don Garland; p/Cecil Glenn (dec) and Era Parks Barbour; ed/BS cum laude Appalachian St Tchrs Col 1939; pa/Tchr Primary Ed (32 Yrs Wilson's Mills Sch); Mem Local, St & Fed Ednl Assns; r/Bapt; hon/Twice Tchr of Yr for Wilson's Mills Elem Sch, Yr Book Dedicated to Her 1965.

BARDEN, CHARLES III oc/Accountant, Photographer; b/Oct 9, 1950; 264 Johnson Dr, Clayton, NC 27520, ba/Clayton; m/Betty Carroll; c/Charles Clayton, Jacob Matthew; p/Charles (dec) and Betty Jo Watkins Barden, Clayton, NC; ed/BS Applachian St Univ; pa/Acct; Photog; Photo Clb; Photo Classes & Wkshops; cp/Civitan Clb; Exchange Clb; SGA, ASU; r/Meth SS Tchr.

BARFIELD, EDDIE E oc/Farmer; b/Oct 5, 1945; h/Cottondale, FL; m/Margaret Legatha; c/Lora Leigh, Clinton; p/Bose and Ruby Barfield, C'dale, FL; mil/USAF; pa/Farmer; cp/Farm Bur Bd Dirs; r/Assembly of God.

BARFIELD, KENNY DALE oc/Minister, Educator; b/Nov 17, 1947; h/2030 Saxton Dr, Florence, AL 35630; ba/Florence; m/Nancy Ann Cordray; c/Amber Elizabeth, Lora Allyn; p/Henry Perry and Bernice Olive Barfield, Florence, AL; ed/BA David Lipscomb Col 1969; MA 1972, PhD Cand, Univ Ala; pa/Edr, Dir T B Larimore Forensic Soc, Mars Hill Bible Sch 1969-; Min: Highland Pk Ch of Christ (Muscle Shoals, Ala) 1969-74, Jackson Hgts Ch of Christ (Florence) 1974-78, Sherrod Ave Ch of Christ (Florence) 1978-; Nat Forensic Leag, Double Diamond Coach 1980, Chm Deep S Dist 1977-79; Ala Forensic Edrs Assn, Pres 1976; Am Forensic Assn; So Speech Assn; Ala Speech Commun Assn; Columbia Scholastic Press Advr's Assn; Ala Jour Edrs Assn; r/Ch of Christ; hon/Ala Speech Tchr of Yr 1977; Outstg Yng Rel Ldr, Ala JCs 1976; Author *50 Golden Years: The NFL Nationals* 1980; "Go to the B-1 Subpoint" *The NFL Rostrum* Jan 1979; "Agreeable Surprise" *Photolith* Jan 1970.

BARFIELD, RUFUS LENRO oc/College President; b/Nov 14, 1929; h/11801 Chantilly Ln, Mitchellville, MD 20716; ba/Bowie St Col, Bowie, MD; m/Emma Jean Crawford; c/Rufus Lenro II; Sheila Gail, Joselyn Yvette; p/Cas Low and Katie Marie Upshaw Barfield; ed/BA Ky St Coll 1952; MA Univ Ky 1956; MEd Univ Cinc 1966; Grad Work Ohio St Univ 1967; PhD Miami Univ 1972; Postdoct Study Univ Wis-Madison 1973; mil/Non-Com'd Ofcr, Co Clerk, Unit Supvr & Admin First Sgt; pa/Pres Bowie State Col; VChancellor Acad Affairs & Prof Ed & Psychol Univ Ark; VP Acad Affairs, Dean Acad Sers, Prof Ed & Psychol Ky St Univ; Prin; Elem Tchr; Ohio Dept Elem Sch Prins Profl Growth Com; Cinc Schs Commun Assn Task Force; Cinc Human Relations Aux Com; Exec Coun SWn Ohio Ed Assn; Com for Devel'g Comprehensive Plan for Higher Ed in Ky; Com on Voc Ed for Higher Ed; Com on Chd's Sers; Bd Mem Ky Rural S'ship of Ky Med Assn; NEA; Nat Org on Legal Probs in Ed; Soc Res Admins; Am Assn Sch Admins; Phi Delta Kappa; Am Assn Higher Ed; Coun on Res Policy & Grad Ed; Assn Acad Deans of South; Nat Assn Col Deans, Registrars & Admissions Ofcrs; So Conf Deans of Facs & Acad VP; cp/VP Frankfort's Red Cross Chapt Bd Trustees; Frankfort Chapt Salvation Army Bd Trustees; Franklin Co C of C; Optimist Clb; NAACP; Bd Dirs Prince Geo's C of C; Bd Dirs Md Soc Crippled Chd & Adults; r/Ch

of Christ; hon/Outstg Edr of Am 1973; Dist'g Ser Achmt Awd - Metro Chapts of Phi Beta Sigma 1979; Cert of Awd for Outstg Ser in Corryville Commun Coun of Cinc; Citizen of Day by Cinc Radio WCYN, July 22, 1967; Awd Meritorious Ser as Exec Secy of Walnut Hill's YMCA 1964; Outstg Ser to Univ from Ky St Univ Basketball Team 1975-76; Comm'd Ky Col by Gov of St 1975; Gov to the Comm on Higher Ed 1975; W/W: Among Black Ams, in Ky, in SE; Outstg Personalities in South 1977.

BARFIELD, VIRGINIA GRANT oc/Executive Director; b/Jan 2, 1918; h/PO Box 26, Richland, GA 31825; ba/Columbus, GA; m/William H; p/J D (dec) and Ina M Grant (dec); ed/BS Murray Col; pa/Exec Dir Enrichment Sers Prog Inc; Mgr; Bookkeeper; Muscogee Co Ed Assn; Bd Mem Title I Emer Asst Prog; Muscogee Co Sch Dist Policy Adv Bd; Pres Fed Exec Assn; Other; cp/Muscogee Day Care Bd; Lower Chattahoochee Area Planning and Devel Comm; VP Fed Exec Assn; Bd Dirs Muscogee Co Sr Citizens; Lower Chattahoochee Val Area Manpower Coun; Chmn Richland Planning Comm; Coun Girls Camp; Scout Work; Garden Clb; Hd Red Cross Dr; Nat Rehab Assn; Nat Coun Aging; Nat Coun Trans Disadvantaged; 3rd VP Nat Assn Commun Devel; Chm Nat Net Work Legislative Forum; Nat CAA Exec Dirs Assn; Bd Mem SEn Assn Commun Action Agencies; Past Secy SEn Assn Commun Action Agencies; Past VP SEn CAA; Past Pres SEn CAA; Past Secy-Treas Westvile Histl Handicrafts Inc; Charter Mem Stewart Co Histl Assn; Other; r/Bapt; hon/Urban Ser Awd by Sargent Shriver 1957; Ofc Ec Oppor Ser Awd 1967; Rural Ser Awd 1968; TAP Com Orgnl Awd; Citizenship Awd 1975; CFC Awd 1973; Nat Civil Ser League 1972; Ga Rehab Assn 1972; NACD 1975; Commun Ser Admin 1976; W/W Child Devel Profls 1976.

BARHAM, BETTY HAYS oc/Nurse; b/May 20, 1937; h/251 Joy Dr, McKenzie, TN 38201; ba/Jackson, TN; m/John E; c/Pamela Diane Wolfers; (Foster Chd:) Beverly F Thomas, Sharon T Traywick, Ron Thomas, Danny Thomas, Mary Ann Carter; p/Bob (dec) and Belle Hays, Darden, TN; ed/AA; BSN Univ TN 1979; pa/RN; Nsg Ser Supvr; ANA; Tenn Nurses Assn; cp/Work w Hlth Related Grps; r/Prot; hon/W/W of Am Wom 1978-79; I Dare You; Good Citizenship Awd.

BARHAM, MACK ELWIN oc/Counsel; b/Jun 18, 1924; h/5837 Bellaire Dr, New Orleans, LA 70124; ba/New Orleans; m/Ann LeVois; c/Cret L Megan B (Mrs Thomas Richard); p/Henry A and Lockie Barham (dec); ed/Att'd Univ Colo; LLD; JD La St Univ 1946; pa/Counsel, Lemle, Kelleher, Kohlmeyer & Matthews; Prof Law Tulane Univ Sch of Law; Elected Assoc Justice Supreme Ct La 1968, Re-elected 1973; Ret'd from Supreme Ct 1975; Other Former Positions; Past Pres: La Juv Ct Judges Assn, 4th Dist Bar Assn; Former Mem: Bd Govs La St Bar Assn, La Judicial Coun; Mem La St Law Inst Coms on Revision of Constitution & Civil Code; ABA; Am Judic Soc; Coun La St Law Inst; Nat Appellate Judges Conf; Am Soc Writers on Legal Subjects; Intl Acad Est & Trust Law; Fac Mem Am Acad Judic Ed, Univ Ala; Vsg Prof La St Univ Law Sch; Participant Var Sems, Univ Tex & Univ Ala; Others; cp/Lt Gov Kiwanis Intl; Bastrop Kiwanis Clb: Mem, Past Pres; Chm Ouachita Val Coun; BSA; Former VP S Ctl Reg Ed Lab; r/Prot; hon/Author Num Law Review Articles & Other Pubs; Am Civil Liberty Union Awd for Outstg Sr; Am Foun Sci Creative Intell Awd for Contbn to Natural Law; Awd Recipient, Freedoms Foun at Val Forge; Num Biogl Listings.

BARKDOLL, GERALD L oc/Government Executive; b/Feb 14, 1934; h/1728 Shilling Ln, Silver Spring, MD 20906; ba/Rockville, MD; p/Paul and Myrtle Patterson Barkdoll, Waynesboro, PA; ed/BS 1957, MBA 1963 Drexel Univ; mil/Army Corps Engrs 1957-59; pa/Asst Commr for Planning & Evaluation, Food & Drug Adm; Former Ctl Reg Mgr On-Line Decisions, Inc, Chgo; Former Controller & Corporate Ofcr Englander Co; Reg'd Engr, Ohio; Chi Epsilon; Am Inst Indust Engrs; Wash DC Chapt Planning Execs Inst; Var Other Profl Activs; cp/Mem Vis Com Col of Bus Adm, Drexel Univ; hon/FDA Awd of Merit; HEW Hon "A" Awd.

BARKER, FRANK MOREHEAD JR oc/Senior Minister; b/Jan 31, 1932; h/3181 Dolly Ridge Dr, Birmingham, AL 35243; ba/B'ham; m/Barbara; c/Anita, Frank, Margaret Ann; p/Mrs Frank M Barker; ed/BSTE Auburn Univ 1953; BD, ThM 1960 Columbia Sem; mil/USN 1953-57 Jet Pilot, Lt; pa/Sr Min, Briarwood Presb Ch; r/Presb; hon/Author *The Gospel of John for Group Study* 1977; *Study Guide to First Peter* 1970.

BARKER, J BYRON oc/Minister; b/Dec 18, 1948; h/Bristol, TN; ba/Bristol; m/Kathy R; c/Tara Nicole; p/Louise M Barker, Jonesboro, TN; ed/BB Tenn Temple Univ 1970; Cand Masters Deg; pa/Min in So Bapt Convention; Sr Min Va Ave Bapt Ch, Bristol, Tenn; Min Assn; Bapt Pastors Assn; cp/Masons; r/Bapt; hon/Outstg Citizen Bristol 1979; Pastor of 4th Fastest Growing Ch in Tenn; Ldr in E Tenn Area in SS Growth.

BARKER, SANDRA SUE CASE oc/Teacher; b/Jan 21, 1943; h/Rtr 2 Box 134, Levelland, TX 79336; ba/Levelland; m/Frank; c/Frank, Matt;

p/C H Case, Dallas, TX; Mildred Lewis, Miniola, TX; ed/BS Tex Technol Col 1965; MEd Tex Tech Univ 1979; pa/Elem Tchr Levelland Public Schs 10 Yrs; TSTA, Fac Rep 1981; TCTA; NEA; Levelland Edrs; cp/Beta Sigma Phi, Pres 1971-72, Recording Secy, Corresp Secy; W Tex Running Clb; r/Bapt; hon/Beta Sigma Phi: 6 Yrs Perfect Attendance, Girl of Yr 1974-75, Sweetheart 1975-76; W Tex Running Clb: 1st Feb Clb Race 1981, 6th Palo Duro 4 Mile 1980, 4th Palo Duro 4 Mile 1981, 2nd 5 km & 3rd 3 Mile 1980.

BARKER, THELMA AYN CREWS oc/Consultant; b/Dec 3, 1934; h/Rt 4 Ashport Rd, Jackson, TN 38301; c/Pete Jr, Dilowe, Tommy, Johayna, BB; p/Barney Sr and Thelma Wright Crews, Jackson, TN; ed/BA Union Univ; MEd Memphis St; Additional Hours at Memphis St, UT, LaVerne Col; pa/Conslt, Behavl Mgmt; Mem Educl Orgs; Tenn Guid Assn; Alpha Delta Kappa; Zeta Tau Alpha; r/Bapt; hon/Nominated for Freedom Awds 1973, 74.

BARKLEY, PAUL HUBBARD oc/Minister; b/Oct 1, 1945; h/Dyer, TN; ba/Dyer; m/Rhonda Hodge; c/Karis, Kathryn, Kirk; p/(Mrs) Roy Barkley, Linden, AL; ed/AD Okla St Univ 1966; BA Union Univ 1971; Attending SWn Bapt Theol Sem; pa/Min First Bapt Ch of Dyer (Pastor So Bapt Chs 1971-); Fire Insp; Exec Dir Jackson, Tenn Boys' Clb; Psych Social Wkr; Pres Fayette Bapt Pastor's Conf; Pres Chaplain's Assn McNairy Co Gen Hosp; Bd Trustees Union Univ; cp/Bd Dirs Optimist Clb; Vol Fire Dept; r/So Bapt; hon/On Prog Tenn Bapt Pastor's Conf 1972; 1st Place Soil Stewardship Sermon in Tenn 1980; Outreach 1978.

BARLOW, JIM oc/Judge; h/2903 Lake Shore #306, Waco, TX 76708; c/Kris, Jennifer; ed/BA Tex A&M Univ 1966; JD Baylor Law Sch 1968; pa/Judge, Co Ct at Law #2, 1978-; Pt-time Instr Crim Justice Interm Prog, Baylor Univ Law Sch 1973-77; Pt-time Instr Crim Law, Procedure & Evidence, McLennan Commun Col 1971, 72; McLennan Co Dist Ct 1971-78; Asst Dist Atty McLennan Co 1969-70; Pvt Pract Tyner & Bain, Tyler (Tex) 1968-69; Past Pres Waco-McLennan Co Jr Bar Assn; Waco-McLennan Co Bar Assn; St Bar Tex; Bars of En & Wn Dist Tex, US Dist Ct; Dir Tex Co & Dist Clerks Assn; Assoc Mem Tex Co & Dist Attys Assn; Chm Dist Com on Admissions, St Bar Tex; cp/Waco C of C; Waco JCs: Former Mem, Past Dir; Waco Lodge 92; Scottish Rite; Ks of Pythias; Past Pres Waco-McLennan Co A&M Clb; Past Dir Waco Fdr Lions Clb; Baylor/Waco Foun; Div Chm U Way; Multiple Sclerosis Foun; Citizens Adv Com, Waco Indep Sch Dist; Tex Coun for Input on Crime, Rehab & Preven; r/1st U Meth Ch; hon/1975 Dist'd Ser Awd, Waco JCs; BSA: Eagle Scout, Order of Arrow; Others.

BARNES, ANNETTE CASEY oc/Psychiatrist; b/Dec 18, 1945; h/850 Mann Rd, Bartow, FL 33830; ba/Bartow; m/Raymond F; c/Michelle Annette, Diane Katharine, Casey David, Heather Rose; p/Adkins B (dec) and Helen Morse Casey, Libertyville, IL; ed/BA Lake Forest Col 1968; MD Univ Ill Med Ctr 1972; pa/Psychi; Asst Prof 1975-76; Fla Med Assn; Polk Co Med Assn; Am Psychi Assn; Fla Psychi Soc; cp/Flautist Winter Haven Symph; r/Presb; hon/Alpha Lambda Delta 1965; Beta Beta Beta 1968; Phi Beta Kappa 1968; Bd Cert Am Bd of Psychi & Neuro Inc 1979.

BARNES, BERNARD oc/Editor, Publisher; b/July 11, 1949; h/Moss Point, MS; ba/PO Box 456, Moss Point, MS 39563; m/Toni; c/Nicole; p/Sam Barnes, McComb, MS; Hazel L Woods, Moss Pt, MS; ed/Jackson Co Jr Coll 1967-69; BA Miss St Univ 1969-72; pa/Past Proj Dir; Sys Tng & Redevel Cost Analyst; Mgmt Asst; Ingalls Shipbuilding Corp; Conslt; Editor; Pubr; Phi Beta Sigma Frat; Pres M&M Pub & Adv Inc; Pres Pas-Point Local Devel Co; Pres Commun Devel Foun; Chm Kimberly Dr Block Clb; Mem Nat Press; cp/NAACP; Chm Publicity & Press Com; Bd Mem Jack Co SCLC; r/Bapt; hon/SCLC Outstg Mem Awd 1979; JAC's Commun Ser Awd 1974; Star Outstg Dir Awd 1973; Invited to White House 1979 by Pres Carter; Invited to US Dept of St Fgn Policy Conv 1979-80; Pubr: The Loop Magazine, March; The SW Times 1979; The Pas-Point Journal 1976-.

BARNES, LAVONIA JENKINS oc/Homemaker; b/Apr 16, 1907; h/3217 Robin Rd, Waco, TX 76708; m/Maurice; c/Warner Jenkins; p/Ichem Warner and Della Williamson Jenkins; ed/So Meth Univ 1924-26; BA Baylor Univ 1927; Grad Studies Columbia Univ Sch of Jour 1927-28; pa/Pres Champe Carter McCullock House Mus; Pres Earle Nappier-Kinnarij House Mus; Pres of Bds of Ft House Mus & East Terrace Mus; cp/Pres Waco Heritage Soc 1958; Pres Epis Ch Wom of TX 1958-61; Pres Aux to Am Col of Allergists 1960-62; Served on Many Civic Orgs Bds; r/Epis; hon/Waco Fed'd Clbs Wom of Yr 1954; Altrusa Clb of Waco Wom of Yr 1972; Mortar Bds of Baylor Univ; Comm on Envir Qual Awd 1979; Beautify TX Awd of Commend 1978; Cit Hist Waco Foun 1970 (for Restoration of Earle Harrison House); Ruth Lester Awds - St of TX Awd for Meretorious Ser in Restoration 1979; TX Senate Resolution #489; Mem Friends of Gov's Mansion Bd.

BARNES, LINWARD IRVIN oc/Teacher, Real Estate Salesman; b/May 15, 1952; h/515 Maine Ave, Panama, FL 32401; ba/Same;

m/Barbara A; c/Linward I Jr, Lincherria I; p/J T Sr and Corine H Barnes, Panama City, FL; ed/BS Fla A&M Univ; mil/AUS; pa/Sch Tchr; FTP WEA Human Relats Com; cp/Fla Yng Dem; r/Bapt.

BARNES, MARY W oc/Teacher, Librarian; b/Oct 29, 1934; h/Rt 2Box 56, Goldsboro, NC 27530; m/Alfred B; c/Jacqueline and Jacquenette, Jeannette, Jeri Alfreda, Alfred Jr; p/Albert and Annie Lewis Whitfield (dec), Goldsboro, NC; ed/Chd Devel Assoc 1976; pa/Hd Start Tchr; Resource Libn; Chm NC Chd Devel Assn; NC Hd Start Staff Rep to Nat Conv 1976-77; Mem NC Day Care Assn; NCAEYC; cp/Democrat; Farm Bur; OES; Pres, Sec, Treas Ext Homemaker; 4-H Ldr 1965-74.

BARNES, MARYLOU RIDDLEBERGER oc/Educator; b/Feb 27, 1930; ha/3127 W Roxboro Rd, Atlanta, GA 30324; b/Atlanta; c/Tenley Elizabeth, Rachel Patricia Taylor; p/Hensel Dorsey Riddleberger; Ruby Elizabeth Heltzel; ed/BS Madison Col 1952; BSPT Med Col of Va 1957; MA Madison Col 1968; EdD WVa Univ 1975; pa/Phy Therapist; Prof, Dir & Fdr Div Phy Therapy, WV Univ Med Ctr; Prof & Chm Dept Phy Therapy, Ga St Univ; First Wom Chm of Intercol Ath Coun, WV Univ; Nat Survey Pool of Accred Phy Therapy Schs; Am Phy Therapy Assn; Patient Ser Comm Kidney Foun of WV; Am Soc Allied Hlth Professions; cp/Soroptimist Intl & Chm, Ways & Means Com; hon/Phi Delta Kappa Hon Soc; Kappa Delta Pi Hon Soc; W/W in Hlth Care; W/W in Am Wom; Dist'd Ldrs in Hlth Care; Full Mbrship of Grad Fac at WV Univ; Dist'd Alumni Achmt Awd James Madison Univ; Cert Apprec WV Chapt Am Phy Therapy Assn; Author: The Patient at Home, 1971; The Neurophysiological Basis of Patient Treatment; Others.

BARNES, MELVER RAYMOND oc/Scientific Research; b/Nov 15, 1917; h/Rt 1 Box 424, Linwood, NC 27299; p/Oscar Lester (dec) and Sarah Albertine Rowe Barnes (dec); ed/AB Univ NC 1947; Cont'g Ed Courses 1947-; mil/AUS 1942-45; pa/Chemist Pgh Testing Labs, Greensboro, NC Ofc 1948-49; Chemist NC St Hwy & Public Works Comm 1949-51; US Civil Ser, Dept of Army 1951-70; Indiv Sci Res & Pvt Corresp 1970-; Am Chem Soc; Am Phys Soc; AAAS; r/Christian; hon/W/W S&SW; DIB.

BARNES, NELDA oc/Teacher; Coordinator; b/May 24, 1927; m/J W; c/Marsha Barnes Schwartz, James R; p/Henry J and Opal E Brooks (dec), El Dorado, AR; ed/BA Baylor Univ 1947; MEd Univ Ark 1967; Further Studies E Tex St Univ 1970-80; pa/Crime Preven Coor; Profl Resource Facilitator, SS Tchr; TCSS Profl Resources Com; Assn Tex Edrs; Assn Supvn & Curric Devel; Nat Coun for SS; Tex Coun for SS; Pres E Tex Coun for SS; cp/Alpha Delta Kappa; Junto (Hands Up Chm); 2nd VP Key Dist, Tex Fed'd Wom's Clbs; r/Bapt; hon/PTA Life Mbrship 1978; W/W in Tex Ed 1975-76; Nom Tchr of Yr for Pine St Jr HS 1978 & 1980

BARNES, VELMA ARDELL oc/Realtor; b/Aug 20, 1910; h/2602 Walnut Rd, Norman, OK 73069; ba/Norman; m/Dewey Lloyd (dec); c/Jay T Bailey, (Stepch:) Richard L, Charles W; p/John Paul Miller (dec); Lula Fern Bruce (dec); ed/BA SWn Col; MA Univ Okla; pa/Artist; Tchr; Pres-Owner Velma A Barnes Real Est Inc; Nat Roster of Rltrs; cp/C of C; BPW; Bus Wives; DAR; r/Prot; hon/World W/W Wom; IBC; Tchr of Yr, Lawton, Okla; Rltrs Awd, Norman.

BARNETT, LUTHER ZEDIC oc/Life Insurance Consultant; b/Feb 28, 1924; h/PO Box 3785, Charleston, SC 29407; ba/C'ton; m/Stella Cockerill; c/Julia Ann, James William, Luther Z Jr; p/Mays Miton and Vannie James Barnett (dec); ed/AB Furman Univ; mil/USAAF 1943-45, Dist'd Flying Cross; pa/CLU, Indep Life Ins Conslt, C'ton; Var Positions w Pilot Life Ins Co 1955-71; Lic'd Real Est Broker; Others; cp/JCs: All Local Ofcs, St Com Chm, Nat Dir, Others; Boy Scouts: Var Ofcs & Chmships; Optimist Clb, W Ashley 4 Yrs; Exec Clb of C'ton; Trident C of C; SC Mtl Hlth Assn; Past Pres C'ton Sales & Mktg Clb; Mem Tech Ed Comm for Berkeley-C'ton-Dorchester Trident Tech Col; Bd Dirs CC C'ton; Pres Clb of Pilot Life; r/Bapt; hon/Clint Dunagan Awd; Silver Beaver, BSA; Air Medal; Others.

BARNETT, RONALD HAROLD oc/Pastor; b/Mar 21, 1945; h/Meta, KY; ba/Meta Bapt Ch, Meta, KY 41501; m/Mary Ann; c/Paul, Darik; p/James and Marie Barnett, Waynesburg, KY; ed/Clear Creek Bible Inst 1975; pa/Pastor: Turkey Creek Mission, Knox Co, KY; Liberty Bapt Ch, Scioto Co, OH; Meta Bapt Ch, Pike Co, KY; Exec Bd Pike Assn So Bapt; Messenger So Bapt Conv; Messenger KY Bapt Conv; cp/Mem & Trustee Johns Creek Fish & Game Clb; r/So Bapt; hon/Ordained 1974.

BARNETT, ROSEMARIE LONG oc/Nurse; b/June 19, 1928; h/PO Box 299, Prairieville, LA 70769; ba/Carville, LA; m/John Wesley; c/William, May Frances, John Wesley, Victoria, Edwardanne; p/Thomas Joseph and Francesca Schmidt Long, Webb, MS; ed/Assoc Deg Nsg Miss Delta Jr Col; pa/RN; Am Red Cross Vol; Nat League Nsg; cp/BPW Clb; TB Assn; J of P 1970-74; Com for Re-Elec of Nixon 1972; Repub; r/Cath; hon/Miss Gov's Panel of Wom Ldrs 1973; W/W Am Wom 1979-80; Phi Theta Kappa Hon Soc.

PERSONALITIES OF THE SOUTH

BARON, MARK oc/Scarecrow Artist; b/Nov 24, 1949; h/Columbia, SC; p/Irving and Helen Baron, Silver Spring, MD; ed/Att'd Univ SC 1981, Antioch Col, Columbia Visual Arts Sch 1977; BA Univ Md 1974; pa/Cultural Dir, Harbison Devel Foun; Only Scarecrow Artist in World, Tours US Ldg Scarecrow Design/Construction Wkshops; SC Crafts Guild Bd Dirs; SC Pk & Rec Soc.

BARRETT, BARBARA TAYLOR oc/Civic Worker, Volunteer; b/Dec 5, 1930; h/Oak Ridge, TN; m/John H; c/Deirdre Leigh; p/Luther (dec) and Henrietta Ross Taylor, Houston, TX; ed/Att'd Rice Univ 1949-52, Boston Univ 1952-53; cp/Pres LWV; Treas Clinch Val Campfire Assn; Publicity, Oak Ridge Civic Mus Assn Guild; Public Relats Oak Ridge Art Ctr; r/Epis.

BARRISS, KATHLEEN COLELIA oc/Administrator; b/Feb 14, 1947; h/931 E Austin, Kermit, TX 79745; ba/Jal, NM; m/Leo W; c/Lori Jean; p/George J and Sophia S Parker, Brownsville, PA; ed/RN Westmoreland Sch of Nsg 1968; pa/RN; Supvr; Nsg Admr; In-Ser Ed Coor; Created Basic Critical Care Course; Tchr Self-Created Nurse's Aides Course; Mem AACN; cp/Asst Girl Scout Ldr; R/Prot; hon/W/W Am Wom 1979-80.

BARRON, BOBBY CURTIS oc/Educator; b/Jan 19, 1932; h/Rt 5 Box 141, Canton, GA 30114; ba/Woodstock, GA; m/Yvonne Irene Salladay; c/Katherine Yvonne, Debra Anne, Linda Elaine, Bobbie Jean; p/Thomas Terry and Evelyn Morris Barron; ed/AS Kennesaw Col 1970; BS 1970, MEd 1972, EdS 1976 Univ Ga; mil/USAF 1953-61; pa/Hd Dept Elec: Dekalb Commun Col 1961-66, Iowa Ctrl Commun Col 1966-68; Nat Dir Ed Inc 1968; Evening Dir Pickens Area Tech Sch 1969-76; Dir Voc Ed Etowah HS 1976-; Cons Voc Ed Expansion & Bldg Progs; Am Voc Assn; Ga Voc Assn; NEA; Ga Ed Assn; Navy Res Assn; cp/Mem Adm Bd Hickory Flat Meth Ch; r/Meth; hon/NSF Grantee 1965; Sr Engrg Techn.

BARROW, ALLEN EDWARD oc/Judge; b/Jan 22, 1914; h/2142 E 25th Pl, Tulsa, OK 74114; ba/Tulsa; ed/Att'd Okla A&M Col 1935-36; BA Univ Okla 1936; Postgrad Studies Univ Tulsa; LLB SEn St Col 1942; pa/w FBI 1940-42; Admitted to Okla Bar 1942, Also Supreme Ct US; Pvt Pract, Tulsa 1946-50, 54-62; Counsel SWn Power Adm, Dept Interior, Tulsa 1950-54; Chief Judge US Dist Ct No Dist Okla 1962-; Am Okla Bar Assns; Delta Theta Phi; Phi Eta Sigma; Sigma Chi; cp/Adv Bd Tulsa Salvation Army; Bd Dirs ARC; hon/Outstg Ser Awd, Okla Bar Assn; Significant Sig Awd, Sigma Chi.

BARROWMAN, KINO SAKUMA oc/Executive Director; b/Nov 28, 1943; h/7441 SW 176 St, Miami, FL 33157; ba/Miami; m/John Richard; p/Goro Sakuma, Miami; Mary Ann Drobny Sakuma (dec); ed/AA Miami Dade Commun Col; BS Fla Atlantic Univ; MA Fla Intl Univ; Doct Work; pa/Exec Dir Dade Tchrs Assn; U Tchrs of Dade: Dir Curric & Res, Former Adm Asst to Exec VP; Am Assn for Higher Ed; Smithsonian Assn; Fla Intl Univ Steering Com on Curric; Other Profl Assns; cp/Reg'd Lobbyist, House & Senate; LVW; Dem Com Wom, Dist 38; Former Commr on Dade Co Comm on Status of Wom; Dade Co Pers Bd; Num Others; r/Cath; hon/Speech & Debate S'ship Awd; Outstg Cath of Yr 1962; Kappa Omega; Featured in *Miami Mag* as Outstg Wom in Dade Co.

BARTLETT, DORSEY JOE oc/House of Representatives Staff Official; b/Aug 7, 1926; h/6128 Long Meadow Rd, McLean, VA 22101; ba/Wash DC; m/Virginia Bender; c/Linda Hobgood (Mrs James L), Laura; p/Flavius Dorsey Bartlett (dec); Blanche Hacker Bartlett; ed/Hon LLD Atlanta Law Sch 1970, Salem Col 1971; mil/USMC & USMCR 1944-78, Brigadier Gen; pa/Clerk to the Minority, US Ho of Reps (Serving 5th Term); 37 Yrs w Congress; 1st Congl Rep to Fed Exec Inst, Charlottesville, Va; Bd Dirs FEI Alumni Assn; Spkr Var Public Events; Bd Govs Nat Repub Clb Capitol Hill; Mem Num Profl Orgs; r/Prot; hon/Dist'd Ser Awd, US JCs; George Wash Hon Medal, Freedoms Foun; Legion of Merit.

BARTON, ALEXANDER JAMES oc/Zoologist, Educator; b/May 9, 1924; h/3818 N Vernon St, Arlington, VA 22207; ba/Wash DC; m/Arlene Florence Arment; c/Sandra, Lynne, Alexander James III; p/Paul Carnahan and Barbara Eggers Barton (dec); ed/BS Franklin & Marshall Col 1945; MS Univ Pgh 1956; mil/Capt USNR (Active Duty 1943-45); pa/Prog Dir, Devel, Sci Ed Devel & Res, Nat Sci Foun, Wash DC; Adj Asst Prof Biol, C W Post Col; Dir Savannah Natural Hist Mus; Dir Admissions & Fin Aid, Stony Brook Sch; AAAS; Ecol Soc Am; Herpetologists Leag; Fellow Explorers Clb; Brit Herp Soc; Chm US Preparatory Com & Mem US Delegation to UN Conf on Envir Ed, Tbilisi, Ga, USSR, Oct 1977; Chm Intl Envir Ed Subcom on Fed Interagy Com on Ed 1976-; cp/Potomac Rose Soc: Dir, Past Pres; Past Pres Arlington Rose Foun; Gen Chm Ann NH Mtg Am Rose Soc 1981; r/Presb Ch: Lay Preacher, Deacon; hon/Eagle Scout; Valedictorian; Rhetor, Diagnothian Soc.

BARTON, NELDA ANN LAMBERT oc/Political Leader; b/May 12; h/1311 Seventh St Rd, Corbin, KY 70701; m/Harold Bryan (dec); c/William Grant (dec), Barbara Lynn, Harold Bryan Jr, Stephen Lambert, Suzanne; ed/Att'd Wn Ky Univ 1947-49; Grad Norton Meml Infirmary Sch of Med Technol 1950; Reg'd Med Technologist, Am Soc Clin Pathologists 1951; cp/Repub Nat Com-wom for Ky; Repub Nat Com: Exec Com 1976-, Adv Coun on Gen Govt 1977-, Mem & Subcom Chm Rules Review Com 1976-; KFRW: 2/VP, Exec Com, Former Chm St Conv; Mem Adv Com Repub St Ctl Com; Other Polit Activs; Pres, Bd Dirs: Hillcrest Nsg Home, Corbin, Hazard Nsg Home, Hazard, Ky, Williamsburg Nsg Home, W'burg, Ky; Chm Adv Com to Cumberland Col Assoc Deg Nsg Prog; CoChm Corbin Urban Renewal & Commun Devel Agy; Chm Hlth Ed Com Ky Med Assn Aux; Charter Mem SEn Ky Fine Arts Assn; Others; r/1st Christian Ch: Chm Cir #2**, Yth F'ship, Stewardship Property; hon/Valedictorian, Providence HS; Acad S'ship to Wn Ky Univ; PTA Life Mbrship Awd; Ky Repub Wom of Yr 1969; Bluegrass Coun Boy Scouts Thank You Awd; Ky Col; Ind Sagamore; Dwight David Eisenhower Awd; Hon PhD, Colo Christian Col; "Nelda Barton Day in Corbin", Proclaimed by Corbin Mayor, Oct 22, 1973.

BASS, EUNICE oc/Insurance Agent; b/Sept 15, 1920; m/Maxton; c/Puett, Judith Barnes; p/Clegg (dec) and Julia Williamson; ed/Cert Bus 1963; pa/NC Grange Mutual Ins Agt; cp/Master, Sampson Pomona Grange #47; Master Westbrook Grange #1016; Chm Bd Sampson Tech Col; Pres Sampson Co Dem Wom's Clb; Sampson Co Dem Party: Chm, V-Chm, Secy; Pres Carolina-Va Telephone Mbrship Wom's Org; Secy & Proj Ldr, Westbrook Home Ext Homemkrs Clb; Secy-Treas, Bd of Trustees, Westbrook Commun Bldg; r/U Meth; hon/Life Mem Hopewell U Meth Wom 1968; NC Granger of Yr 1969; Bd Trustee Sampson Tech Inst By Gov Robert W Scott 1971; Re-Appt'd to Sampson Tech Col by Sampson Co Commrs 1979; NC Wom of Yr 1979; NC Contractor's Wife of Yr 1980.

BASS, WILLIAM MICHAEL oc/General Manager, Vice President; b/May 25, 1949; h/2912 Glasgow Dr, Arlington, TX 76015; ba/A'ton; m/Susan; c/Lindsay Nicole; p/William Woodrow (dec) and Wilda A Bass, A'ton, TX; ed/BA Univ Tex-A'ton 1973; pa/Timber Tech Inc: Draftsman 1974, Engrg 1975, Plant Mgr 1978, VP & Gen Mgr 1979; r/Bapt; Pres Sanctuary Choir, Mem Fin Com Fielder Rd Bapt Ch; hon/W/W 1980.

BATES, JOHN PAUL JR oc/Attorney; b/Sept 7, 1955; h/Midland, TX; ba/711 W Indiana, Midland, TX 79701; m/Anne Freitag; p/Mr and Mrs John P Bates, Midland, TX; ed/BA Baylor Univ 1977; JD Baylor Sch Law 1980; pa/Atty at Law, Gen Prac, Corp & Diland Gas; St Bar of Tex; Tex Bar Assn; Midland Co Bar Assn; Permian Basin Landman's Assn; Am Bar Assn.

BATES, LINDA oc/Business/Personnel Management; b/Dec 25, 1939; h/Dallas, TX; ba/Dallas; c/Glenda Ann, Roy Glen, Monty Lee; p/James Fuller Chandler (dec); Linda Lydia Donaldson, Tuscola, TX; ed/Att'd Ridgecrest Bapt Assem 1970-71; Adult Ed, Greenville (Tex) HS 1973; Home Study Courses 1976-80; pa/Unemployment Tax Specialist/Pers Mgmt Spec, Automatic Data Processing 1979-81; Adm Asst to Pers Admr & Plant Mgr, NL Industs Inc 1978-79; Acctg Stock Control & Kardex, Exec Aircraft Ser 1976-78; Adm Asst, Whites Stores Inc 1976; Secy, Receptionist, Stock Control Clk, Asst Purchasing Agt, E Tex Distbrs Inc 1973-75; Tchr's Aide, Greenville HS 1972-73; Yth Cnslr, Greenville/Hunt Co, Tex 1969-75; Nat Assn Female Execs; Tex Assn Pers Conslts; r/So Bapt; hon/Coor OEO, Commun Action for Taylor Co 1969; Chm to By-Laws Com, Abilene, Taylor Co, Tex Chapt OEO Exec Com 1969; Play Pub'd by SBC for Use in St Missions 1970; Instrumental in Securing Unemployment Ins Overpayment for Pengo Inc 1980; W/W Am Wom 1980.

BATSON, BLANCHE DESMOND oc/Printmaker; b/Oct 15, 1929; h/1417 Poplar Blvd, Jackson, MS 39202; ba/Same; m/Blair E; c/John Michael Desmond, Russell Desmond, Margaret Desmond; p/Enos Franklin (dec) and Maggie Russell, Magnolia, MS; ed/BS SEn; MS Univ Tenn; MFA LSU; pa/Printmaker; Former Asst Prof Art, SEn La Univ; Vol Curator Miss Gal, Miss Mus Art; Bd of Miss Art Colony; cp/Friends of Lib; r/Cath; hon/First Prize: St Tammany Art Assn; Miss Art Colony; Many More.

BATTEN, JAMES WILLIAM oc/Professor, Chairman of Department; ba/Greenville, NC; m/Sara Storey; pa/Prof of Res & Chm Dept Sec Ed, ECU, Greenville, NC.

BATTLE, FRANK JR oc/Management Specialist; b/July 15, 1929; h/8132 Cloverland Dr, Nashville, TN 37211; ba/N'ville; m/Ethel Beatrice Hines; p/Frank Sr (dec) and Hattie Mae Taylor Battle, Indianola, MS; ed/BS So Univ 1958; Dip NW Inst Med Technol 1958; MBA Univ 1975, MPA 1977 Fairleigh Dickinson Univ; Cert Occupl Safety Act, Middlesex Co Col 1977; AUS Command & Gen Staff Col 1969; Air War Col, Sr Ser Col 1973; mil/AUS 1962-68 Lt Col; pa/Mgmt Spec, Tenn St Univ; Res Asst, Sch Med, Vanderbilt Univ 1958-62; Master of Public Adm Internship

20

w City Govt of Long Branch, NJ; Soc of Logistics Engrs; Am Soc Public Adm; Assn MBA Execs; Am Acad Polit & Social Sci; Am Med Technols; Nat Defense Transp Assn; Assn AUS; AUS Transp Corps Mus Foun; VFW; cp/Alpha Phi Alpha; Zeta Epsilon Lambda, Chm Budget Com 1975-77; Fairleigh Dickinson Univ Century Clb; Fairleigh Dickinson Alumni Assn; Meth Men's Clb; Fin Com Gordon Meml U Meth Ch; Indep Party; r/U Meth; hon/Recip Merit Cert Meth Bishop of Korea; Recip Num Lttrs/Plaques in Recog of Civil Contbns & Part; Recog'd Nat in Fin & Indust Field; 2 Merit Ser Medals; Bronze Star; 4 Army Commend Medals for Merit Ser; Nat Defense Ser Medal; Armed Forces Reserve Medal w/20 Yr Device; Korean Ser Medal; Vietnam Ser Medal; Repub of Korea Pres Unit Cit; Armed Forces Expedition Medal; Vietnam Campaign Ribbon; Vietnam Unit Cit; UN Ser Medal; Contbr Articles to Profl Jour.

BATTLE, MINNIE oc/Teacher; b/Mar 4, 1944; h/Utica, MS; ba/Utica; p/Glover (dec) and Harriett Battle (dec); ed/AS Coahoma Jr Col 1965; MS Alcorn St Univ 1967; MEd Delta St Univ 1974; Ed Spec Jackson St Univ 1979; pa/Secy Sci Tchr; Secy HS; Secy Utica Jr Col; AVA; MBOEA; MBEA; NBEA; MAVE; CEBOE; NATEBOE; r/Bapt.

BATTLES, WILFRED CLAY oc/Paramedic; b/July 1, 1952; h/Rt 7 Box 328C, Oxford, AL 36203; ba/Talladega, AL; p/W A and Dymple E Battles (dec), Oxford, AL; ed/Paramedic Cert; Cand Assoc Sci Deg; mil/ AUS Chem Corps Spec 4th Class; pa/Paramedic; Mem Oxford Rescue Squad; Fdg Mem E Ala EMT Assn; r/Bapt; hon/Rep for Talladega Co EMT Assn.

BATTS, LANA RICHARDS oc/Economist; b/Feb 17, 1947; h/11116 Saffold Way, Reston, VA 22090; ba/Wash DC; m/Joseph R; p/Lloyd and Laura Nielsen Richards, Oakdale, CA; ed/BA Univ Mont 1968; MA Univ Miami 1976; pa/Economist; Pres Nat Trans Res Bd; Trans Res Forum; Hwy Users Fed; Trans Assn of Am; r/Mormon; hon/W/W Am Wom.

BAUER, KATHY KIRK oc/Real Estate Associate, Student; b/Apr 15, 1959; ha/104 E Elles Dr, Athens, AL 35611; m/Steve; p/Floyd S and Vergie M Kirk, Athens, AL; pa/Col Student; Real Est Assoc; r/Bapt; hon/Sigma Tau Delta; Nat Eng Hon Soc.

BAUGH, JIMMY DALE oc/Minister; b/Apr 3, 1943; ha/PO Box 183, Tanner, AL 35671; m/Gwen Louise; c/Jania LaDawn, Loris Kevin, Rebecca Lynn, Dana Susan, Johnathan Rea, Paul Daniel; p/Loris W and Geneva Baugh, Caraway, AR; ed/US Fgn Ser Inst 1964; Def Lang Inst 1968; BA Intl Bible Col 1976; MA Ala Christian Grad Schol of Rel 1980; mil/AUS 1960-73; pa/Minister, Tanner Ch of Christ; cp/Tanner HS Ath Assn; Nat Hon Soc; Pres HS Band Boosters; Am Legion; VFW; hon/Bronze Star 1960; Jt Sers Commend Medal.

BAUTSCH, VIRGINIA BELLE oc/Secretary; b/Dec 9, 1923; h/1834 Euclid St, Dallas, TX 75206; ba/Dallas; c/Robert Hilton; p/Harry Clay (dec) and Sarah Adelle Slaughter Coleman (dec); mil/USNR 1950-54; pa/Secy, Psychol Sers Dallas Police Dept; Tex Notary Public Assn; Am Bus Wom's Assn; cp/Assoc Mem Nat Trust; r/Bapt; hon/USNR Hon Discharge; W/W Am Wom 1979-80.

BAXLEY, EUGENE L oc/Minister; b/Feb 13, 1930; h/PO Box 37, Hephzibah, GA 30815; ba/Hephzibah; m/Dorothy; c/Kenneth, Kirk; p/L L (dec) and Mae Baxley, Slocomb, AL; ed/AA; BA; mil/Ret'd USMC; pa/Min; Bd of Regents Landmark Bapt Col; cp/Hephzibah Commun Spirit Assn; Co-Chm COSA; Chm Hephzibah Cystic Fibrosis Campgn; r/Bapt; Prin Berean Bapt Sch.

BAXTER, CHERYL HARBIN oc/Nurse; b/Oct 2, 1947; h/901 W David Langan, Mobile, AL 36608; ba/Mobile; m/Jack A Harbin (dec) and Joyce H Dreaden, Mobile, AL; ed/Assoc Deg Nsg; Baccalaureate Deg in Nsg; pa/RN; ANA; Wkg on Masters Deg; cp/Repub; r/Bapt; hon/Alpha Chi Hon Soc, Presidents List; Divl Awd for Nsg, Mobile Col; Ldrship Awd of Sr Class Mobile Col.

BAY, CHARLES HOWARD oc/Salesman; b/Feb 17, 1938; h/PO Box 312, Mt Juliet, TN; ba/Lebanon, TN; m/Peggy Cleibron; c/Kevin Daryl, Richard Kerry; p/Edna Bay, Lebanon, TN; ed/Univ Tenn-Nashville; Num Sales Sems; mil/NG 10 Yrs; pa/Salesman: K O Lester Co, Sears; cp/Mt Juliet Ch Christ: Youth Ldr, Adult Bible Sch Tchr, Song Ldr, Deacon; VP W Elem PTA; Cubmaster BSA; Pres Friendship Christian Cmdr's Clb; Bd Dirs Friendship Christian Sch; r/Ch of Christ.

BAYLESS, DAN J oc/Publications Manager; b/Nov 6, 1939; h/7480 Johnson St, Hollywood, FL 33024; p/Milburn R and Pauline Flannery Bayless (dec); ed/ABA Ft Lauderdale Univ; pa/Pubs Mgr, Modular Computer Sys 1975-; Printing Plant Mgr, Presstime Printing Co 1973-75; Printing Supt, New World Book Mfg Co 1970-73; cp/Broward Co Reproduction Adv Com; IPMA; hon/Men & Wom Dist 1980; Directory of Dist'd Ams 1980; W/W: Intells 1979, S 1978.

BAYNARD, MILDRED MOYER oc/Retired Teacher and Bank Vice President; b/May 10, 1902; h/627 Brightwaters Blvd NE, St Petersburg, FL 33704; m/Robert S (dec); c/Lester Beaumont; p/Charles C and Flora Harter Moyer (dec); ed/BA Univ Neb; cp/Fdg Pres Fla Soc to Prevent Blindness; r/Epis; hon/Shield & Cable Awd, Delta Gamma; Outstg Citizens Awd, Pinellas Co Comm.

BAYS, HATTIE oc/Lecturer; b/Apr 1, 1914; h/309 Chestnut St, Deennellon, FL 32630; m/Charles; c/Eugene Jimmy, Charles Anthony; p/Mose Bentley (dec); Armedia Bryant (dec); pa/Lectr on Behavioral Disability; Real Est Sales; r/Presb; hon/W/W: Am, World of Wom; Friendship Awd.

BEALL, ROY BURNS SR oc/Public Relations; b/Dec 17, 1897; h/300 Broad St, Marianna, FL 32446; ba/Marianna; m/Kitty Howard (dec); c/R B Jr, Kitty Ruth (dec), Jean Beall Neel, William Wallace (dec); p/William Wallace and Mary Alice Rouse Beall (dec); ed/AA; mil/Marion Mil Inst; pa/Owner R B Beall & Co 1916-45; Dir Bank of Malone 1938-42; Owner: Beall Hardward, Beall Implement Co, Beall Tire Co 1945-74; Public Relats Beall Tire Co 1974-; Chm Chipola Col Bd; cp/Mem Jackson Co Sch Bd; SS Tchr; Mason; Lions Clb; Kiwanis Clb; r/Mission Bapt; hon/Silver Beaver Awd; 1st Person Admitted to Chipola Col Ath Hall of Fame; Outstg Citizen of Marianna 1948; Coach of Yr 15 of 27 Yrs Coaching; Oldest Mason in Yrs of Ser, Jackson Co.

BEAMAN, MARGARINE G oc/Executive, Businesswoman; b/Feb 26, 1941; h/1406 Wilshire Blvd, Austin, TX 78722; m/Robert W; c/Ronald and Richard; p/Ryland and Margaret Lena Geistweidt, Mason, TX; pa/Owner Acctg & Conslt Bus; VP & Co-Owner Beaman Metal Co Inc; Florist; BPW Clb, Dist Dir; Austin Jr Wom's Fed; cp/Secy-Treas Tex Assn Pvt Schs; Var Civic & Polit Clbs; r/Luth; hon/Nom'd Most Worthy Citizen of Austin; Exec Pen, Gov of Tex for Activs w Braille Directories & Signs & for Contbs to Handicapped of Tex.

BEARD, GARY ALAN oc/Director of Music; b/Apr 28, 1953; ba/40 E Pkwy S, Memphis, TN 38104; p/Hal P Jr and Jean Lence Beard, Memphis, TN; ed/BMus Memphis St Univ 1975; MMus MSU; DD Universal Bible Inst 1977; pa/Dir Mus & Lindenwood Concerts, Lindenwood Ch; Accompanist, Hurok, Inc 1975-77; Accomp Commun Concerts 1975-77; Treas, Am Guild Organists; Am Choral Dirs Assn; Nat Assn Tchrs of Singing; r/Christian Ch, Disciples of Christ; hon/Sev Acad Jour Articles; Sev Mus Comps.

BEARD, OLAN EUGENE oc/Executive; b/Dec 14, 1953; m/Debbie; c/Jason, Ricky; p/Ulys and Irene Beard, Coleman, TX; ed/Att'd Commercial Col 1973-74; pa/VP Certs of Deposit & New Accts; cp/Former Mem Abilene JCs; r/Bapt; hon/S'ship Cisco Jr Col 1972; Num HS Hons.

BEASLEY, EDWIN LEE oc/Life Underwriter, Teacher, Freelance Writer; b/July 17, 1935; h/961 Plum Hollow Ct, Palm Bay, FL 32905; m/Caryl McGee; c/Caryl Lee, Sara Ann, Ronald F, Jacqueline; p/Marion O and Sara Beasley, Wallingford, PA; ed/BA; MA; mil/Cmdr; Line Ofcr; Intell Subspec; pa/Life Underwriter; Tchr; Freelance Writer; Pub'd Hist of City of Palm Bay; cp/Bd Dirs C of C; Lions Clb; r/Roman Cath; hon/Meritorious Ser Medal; Secy Navy Commend; Navy Achmt Medal; Armed Force Exped Medal; Nat Def; Viet-Nam Ser Medal.

BEASLEY, HERMAN oc/Department Head; h/3801 W Hamilton Rd, Nashville, TN 37218; ba/N'ville; p/Dock and Ella Beasley, New Albany, MS; ed/BA Jackson St Univ 1965; MA Geo Peabody Col 1972; EdD Ill St Univ 1977; pa/Dept Hd, Art Dept, Tenn St Univ; Art Instr: Tenn St Univ, Fisk Univ, New Albany Sch Sys, Union Co Sch Sys; Fam Coun; Coun Boy's Camp; Local, St & Nat Ed Assns; Profl Art Assns; cp/Mason.

BEASLEY, TONY EUGENE oc/Electrician, Student; b/Dec 19, 1960; h/606 S First St, Smithfield, NC 27577; ba/Smithfield; p/Robert and Maybelle Beasley, Smithfield, NC; ed/Elec Deg; pa/Nat Hon Soc; Art Clb; French Clb; Monogram Clb; ICT-VICA; FFA; REACT; cp/Johnston Co Elec League; Rotary; Cerebal Palsy; r/Bapt; hon/Outstg Sr Boy; St & Dist Medals for Elec Comp; Commencement Marshall; Yngest Person to Pass Exam for NC Elec Contractors.

BEATTY, CAROLYN ANN oc/Teacher, Chairman; b/Apr 17, 1942; h/9018 Silver Spring Ln, Houston, TX 77025; ba/Houston, TX; p/Charles A (dec) and Manualla S Beatty, Houston, TX; ed/BA Univ Houston; MA Houston Bapt Univ; pa/Tchr; Chm Eng Dept; Houston Area Coun Tchrs Eng; Nat Coun Tchrs Eng; Tex Coun Tchrs Eng; Nat Assn Sec Sch Dept Chm; Houston Tchrs Assn; Tex St Tchrs Assn; NEA Houston Coun Ed; Congress Houston Tchrs; Delta Kappa Gamma; Beta Sigma Phi; Univ Houston Alumni Assn; Univ Tex Alumni Assn; Smithsonian Assocs; Wom's Ser Corps; Col Wom's Clbs; Mus Fine Arts; cp/Vol Channel 8 Tele-auction; Vol Ser Exhib, Mus Fine Arts; Vol Meth Hosp; Vol Sel'd

PERSONALITIES OF THE SOUTH

Repub Party Cands; r/Meth; hon/Beta Sigma Phi Girl of Yr; Outstg Yng Wom Am; Outstg Sec Edrs; Outstg Yng Edr in Houston Indep Sch Dist 1977.

BEAUBE, ALBERT VARDAMAN oc/Pastor Emeritus; b/Aug 2, 1903; m/Laura Allen; c/Allen, Valeria, James, George, Gwendolyn, Laura, Harry, Robert, Thomas; p/(dec); ed/Lee Col; pa/Pastor Emeritus, Ala City Ch of God; Bd of Dirs Lee Col 4 Yrs; Chm Editorial Com Lee Col 2 yrs; Dist Overseer 12 Yrs; Asst Gen Overseer 1 Yr; Pastor 18 Yrs; Evangelist 7 Yrs; Exec Coun 8 Yrs; St Overseer: SC 1933-39, Ga 1940-44 & 1946-49, Tenn 1948-52, La 1960-64, Ret'd 1966; r/Ch of God; hon/Author "By His Grace" 1966.

BECK, JAMES KEITH oc/Minister; b/Sept 26, 1942; h/PO Box 125, Soso, MS; m/Marcia; c/Kris, Stacy, Jamie; p/Dennis and Ruth Beck, Mooringsport, LA; ed/BA William Carey Col 1973; MRE New Orleans Bapt Theol Sem 1975; pa/Min First Bapt Ch; cp/Coach Soso JC's Girls Softball; r/So Bapt; hon/Citizenship Awd, William Carey Col 1972; Outstg Yng Men Am 1976; W/W in Rel 1977; Pres Pastor's Conf, Pearl River Bapt Assn 1976; Modr, Lamar Bapt Assn 1978-79.

BECK, JAMES PIERCE oc/Pastor; b/Feb 18, 1937; h/Mangum, OK: m/Bobbie Helen; c/James M, David A, Alicia May; p/Marvin E and Reba Beck, Shawnee, OK: ed/BA OBU 1970; At'd Luther Rice Univ; mil/82nd Airborne; pa/Pastor First Bapt Ch; cp/Kiwanis; r/Bapt; hon/W/W 1975.

BECK, LEE RANDOLPH oc/Biologist; b/Mar 7 1942; m/Marjorie C; c/John, Jessica; p/Beverly D Kolner, Oregon City, OR; ed/BA 1965; MS 1966; PhD 1970; pa/Assoc Prof, Univ Ala-Birmingham Sch Med; Phi Kappa Phi; Soc Sigma Xi; Am Fertitlity Soc; Soc Study Reprod; hon/Author & Co-Author.

BECKHAM, WILLIAM BRADLEY oc/Geologist; b/Mar 3, 1954; h/14004 Lake View Dr, Austin, TX 78732; ba/Giddings, TX; m/Jeanie Vowell; p/John A and Eydthe O Beckham, Kilgore, TX; ed/BS Stephen F Austin St Univ; pa/Petro Conslt Geologist, Champlin Explor Inc; E Tex Geological Soc; AAPG; cp/Nat Rifle Assn; Am Mus Natural Hist; Contbr: Tex Mus Natural Hist; r/Christian.

BECKSTROM, HARRIETT PERRY oc/Physician, Surgeon; b/Mar 10, 1925; h/8443 Banquo Dr, Dallas, TX 75228; c/Martin Elmer II, Perry Kent; p/Benjamin H and Trena Elizabeth Perry, Dallas; ed/Att'd Flint Jr Col; DO Kan City Col of Osteopathy & Surg; pa/Staff Mem Dept Anesthesia, Dallas Osteopathic Hosp 1952-73; Staff Mem Dept Anesthesia, E Town Hosp 1973-77; Staff Mem Steven's Pk Hosp 1976-77; Am Osteopathic Col of Anesthesiologists; Nat Am Osteopathic Assn; Tex Osteopathic Med Assn; Dist 5 Osteopathic Med Assn; Intl Anesthesia Res Soc; cp/Am Bus Wom's Assn; Grand Chapt Delta Omega; Lucinda Conner Chapt #1006, OES; r/Zion Luth Ch; hon/Notable Ams 1976-77; Nat Register Prominent Ams & Intl Notables; DIB; Book of Hon 1978.

BECKWORTH, DEBORAH JEAN STUARD oc/Military Officer; b/Feb 17, 1956; h/Box 84 USAFS Augsburg, APO, NY 09458; m/Tim K; p/James Dennis and Dale Sandra Patton Stuard, Dayton, TN; ed/BS Univ Tenn 1979; mil/AUS 1978; MIOBC 1979; Strategic Signals Intell Course 1979; Plt Ldr 1979-80; Com Exec Ofcr 1980-81; pa/AUS Mil Ofcr; Delta Omicrom, Gamma Delta Chapt, Secy 1976-78; cp/Tenn Val Theater; Augsburg (W Germany) Commun Theater; r/Epis; hon/Grad magna cum laude Univ Tenn 1979; Dist'd Mil Grad 1978; Am Legion Scholastic Achmt Awd 1976-78; Acad S'ship Univ Tenn 1974; Miss Congeniality, Tenn Strawberry Fest 1974; Rhea Co Jr Miss 1974.

BECQUART, BETTY LOUISE oc/Writer; b/Oct 20, 1945; h/4300 NW 48, Oklahoma City, OK 73112; ba/Okla City; m/Benjamin F Sanders Jr; p/Victor and Alice Louise Rutledge Becquart, Okla City; ed/BA Okla City Col 1968; MA Cand; pa/Free-lance Writer; C&B Pump, Inc; Mem & Secy-Treas Bd Dirs, Ofc Mgr; Sole Propriator Second Harvest Book Co; Former Spec Ed Tchr Var Public & Pvt Schs 1968-71; Contemp Arts Foud; Cottonwood Arts Foun-Renegade New Arts Theater; Treas Poetry Soc Okla; Okla Writers Fdn; Nat Fdn St Poetry Socs; Am Acad Poets; cp/Okla Wom's Coalition for Equal Rts; Civic Mus Assn; Classical Guitar Soc; Friends of Earth Fdn; Nat Hlth Fdn; Friends of OETA; Am Inst Discussion: Moderator & Discussent; r/Unitarian; hon/Var Awds for Pub *Shadow Garden*; Winner "McBurney Awd" for Poem "Weep Guitar"; Winner "Bennett Awd" for Poem "The Dance"; Intl W/W: Poetry, Intells; Contemp Authors.

BECTON, CHARLES L oc/Attorney at Law; b/Apr 5, 1944; h/3610 Suffolk St, Durham, NC 27707; ba/Chapel Hill; m/Brenda Brown; c/Nicole, Kevin, Michelle; ed/BA Howard Univ 1966; JD Duke Univ Sch of Law 1969; pa/Admitted to Pract: NC St Cts, Fed Dist Cts for En, Mid & Wn Dists of NC, US Ct of Appeals for 4th Circuit, US Supreme Ct; Atty NAACP Legal Defense & Ednl Fund 1969-70; Atty Chambers, Stein,

Ferguson & Becton 1970-; NC Ct of Appeals 1981; Visiting Lectr UNC Sch of Law 1976-; Lectr in Law, Duke Univ Sch of Law 1980; Co-Tchg Team Ldr, Nat Inst of Trial Adv, SE Regionals 1978, 79, 80; Tchg Atty, Harvard Law Sch, Trial Adv Course 1978; Other Tchg Positions; Lectr: Nat Inst Trial Adv, NC Acad Trial Lwyrs, NC Assn Black Lwyrs, NC Public Defenders Assn, NC Assn Wom Attys; cp/Local Advr, NC Fellows Prog 1974-75; Bd Dirs Chapel Hill Drug Action Com 1975-76; Chm Bd of Law Examrs Bar Cand Com 1976; Pres NC Assn Black Lwyrs 1980; Leg Res Study Com to Study the Laws of Evidence & Comparative Negligence 1979-80; NC Ctrs Comm 1980; Judicial Plan'g Com 1980; Bd Govs NC Acad Trial Lwyrs 1978-81; VP Orange Co Bar Assn 1979; Mbrship Chm NC Assn Black Lwyrs 1979; hon/Author Num Profl Mats.

BEGAYE, ANDREW F oc/Evangelist Missionary Pastor; b/June 19, 1950; h/Farmington, NM; ba/501 W Broadway, Farmington, NM 87401; m/Eunice J; c/Quataunya Happy; p/Ambrose (dec) and Mary Woods Begaye, Shiprock, NM; ed/Att'd Contra Costa Col 1971, Jefferson Davis Jr Col 1972, Howard Pane Univ 1972-75; pa/Navajo Agric Prod Indust, Mgr Trainee; Dir Mission Apprentice; DJ KNMI FM 89; Pastor First Indian Bapt Ch; San Juan Bapt Assn; Apprentice So Bapt Assn; cp/Dem Party; r/So Bapt; hon/Sem Ext 1978; Outstg Person, Inlow 1979; Contbr *Home Mission Magazine* 1977.

BEHESHTI, HOOSHANG M oc/Assistant Professor; b/Nov 6, 1948; h/3123 Harmony Ln SW, Roanoke, VA; ba/Radford, VA; m/Pamela; p/Morteza and Fatema Beheshti; ed/BS Tehran Univ 1970; MSc Univ NY 1974; PhD Okla St Univ 1977; pa/Instr Okla St Univ; Asst Prof Tehran Univ; Asst Prof Radford Univ; Nat Soc Profl Engrs; Am Inst Industl Engrs; Ops Res Soc Am; hon/Monetary Awd St Michael Col 1972; S'ship St Univ NY 1973; Tchng Asstship Okla St Univ 1974; Author: *Management Science Applications: Computing and Systems Analysis*, 1981.

BEKURS, WILLIAM McDONOUGH JR oc/Executive Assistant; b/Aug 3, 1942; h/Montgomery, AL; ba/Atty Gen's Office, 250 Adm Bldg, Montgomery, AL 36130; m/Mary Jenson; c/Mary E, Patricia A, Willaim H, Katherine S, James A; p/William McDonough (dec) and Katherine Gray Bekurs, Mobile, AL; ed/McGill Inst 1956-60; BA Univ S Ala 1969-73; mil/USAR Capt; pa/Exec Asst to Atty Gen of Ala; Crim Invest; Crim Jus Adm; Nat Attys Gen Assn; Nat ANA Ala Dist Atty Assn; Nat & Ala Frat Order Police; Ala Peace Ofcrs Assn; Resv Ofcrs Assn of USA; cp/Univ S Ala Alumni Assn; hon/Alpha Phi Sigma; Nat Crim Jus Hon 1972; Psi Chi Nat Psych Hon Soc 1972; Outstg Yng Men of Am 1979; Contbr to Qtrly Jour of Am Crim Jus Assn Fall 1972 & Spring 1973.

BELCHER, EDITH FAYE oc/Associate Director; b/Feb 29, 1932; h/310 Tippett Ave, Apt 2, Morehead, KY 40351; ba/M'head; p/William Kerry (dec) and Josephine Bingham Belcher, Elkhorn City, KY; ed/BA, MA Univ Ky; EdD Geo Peabody Col; pa/Assoc Dir Libs Morehead St Univ 1971-; Tchr 1950-60; Libn Pike Co, Ky Schs 1960-62; Rdg Fest Coor 1955-60; Libn Lexington Schs 1962-64; Chm E Ky Libn's Assn 1961; Tchr Lib Sci Morehead St Univ 1965-70; Conslt 1965; Libn Pike Co Schs 1965; Morehead St Univ: Asst Libn 1965-70, Asst Dir of Libs & Asst Prof Lib Sci 1970-71; Assoc Prof Lib Sci Morehead St Univ 1972; Public Lib Wkshop Co-Dir of Ky 1972, 73, 74, 75, 76, 77, 78, 79; ALA; Manpower Com, SELA; SEn Lib Assn; SELA Prog Devel Com; Ky Lib Assn; BPW Clb; AAUW; Phi Delta Kappa; Alpha Beta Alpha; Ky Hist Soc; KLA Col & Res Sec; KLA Ed Sec; Phi Kappa Phi Hon Soc; AAUW Ky St Div Treas; St Asst Acad Lib Coun of Ky; cp/MSU Univ Senate, Student Disciplinary Bd, Wom's Clb Continuing Ed; Morehead Book Clb; Alpha Beta Alpha; Univ Senate Ad Hoc Parking Com; Lib Com Secy; Feasibility Study for Installation of Solinet; hon/Pub'd Work: "The Instructional Materials Center", 1967.

BELCHER, JULIE ANNE MUNDIE oc/Artist; Instructor; Trainer; b/July 29, 1937; h/Radford, VA; c/Elizabeth Grey; p/George West Mundie; Minnie Rader Mundie Morrow, Radford, VA; ed/Sullins Col 1958; pa/Artist; Equitation Instr; Horse Tnr; Horse Show Exhbr; Equitation Judge; Med Transcriptionist; r/Epis; hon/Painting "Black Jack" Presented to Stable at Ft Myer, Va & is Hanging in Caissoon Rm.

BELCHER, WILLIAM OYD oc/Band Director; b/Dec 11, 1943; h/Rt 6 Fox Hills, Tifton, GA 31794; m/Donna Lyn; c/Ginger Lee, Lyn Dupree; p/Loyd and Mattie Lou Belcher, Eufaula, AL; ed/Troy St Univ 1969; pa/Band Dir, Tift Co HS, Tifton, Ga; Chm Mus Dept, Tift Co HS; Ga Mus Edrs Assn; Mus Ed Nat Conf; NEA; Ga Assn Edrs; Nat Bandmasters Assn; Phi Mu Alpha; Hon Mbrship Kappa Kappa Psi; cp/Springhill Co Clb; r/Meth; hon/Outstg Yng Men Am 1974; Star Tchr Tift Co Schs 1979.

BELL, BILLIE JEAN oc/Associate Professor; b/Jan 23, 1937; h/5215 Newkirk Ln, Houston, TX 77021; ba/Houston; m/William H Jr; c/Elaine Marie, Janet Louise; p/Verlie Knighton, Pineland, TX; ed/BS; MS; pa/Assoc Prof Prairie View A&M Univ, Col Nsg; Houston, Tex & Nat Leags for Nsg; Tex & Am Nurses Assns; Tex Nurses Assn Blue Ribbon Adv

Com on Nurse Manpwr Shortage 1980; cp/YWCA; PTA; Vol Houston Indep Sch Dist; Bd Mem Lanier Jr HS PTA 1980-81; GSA; r/U Meth; hon/Sigma Theta Tau; Outstg Edrs Am; Piper Prof Num 1978; World W/W Wom; Outstg Alumnus Awd, Prairie View A&M Univ 1979; Cert of Apprec, Tex St Bd Nurse Examiners 1981.

BELL, BLANCHE KELLY oc/Executive Director; b/Aug 23, 1923; h/Sanford, FL; m/Thomas Weaver; c/Sylvia Drake, Jasan, Leroy Lockett; p/William (dec) and Thelma Sims Kelly (dec); pa/Exec Dir Rescue Child Care Ctrs Inc; Child Devel Assn, Bd Lectr; Monitor Advocate, Dept HRS-Food & Nutrition; cp/Seminole Commun Col Adv Bd; r/Pastor & Fdr Resue Ch of God; hon/Jefferson Awd 1977; HRS Foster Child Awd 1978; Child Devel Assn Awd 197; Seminole Commun Col Awd 1976; Commun Ser Awd 1980.

BELL, BOB J oc/Professor; b/June 1, 1933; h/2610 Weaver Pl, Texarkana, TX 75501; m/Joyce; c/Beth, Joe; p/Mrs Joe R Bell, Ft Smith, AR; ed/BS Henderson St Univ; MEd Univ Ark; EdD N Tex St Univ; pa/Prof Psych Texarkana Col 1969-; HS Cnslr: San Antonio & Texarkana; SS Tchr: N Little Rock, Ark & Galveston, Tex; Texarkana Psych Assn; Tex Jr Col Tchrs Assn; Phi Delta Kappa; cp/Dir Call Anon (Hot Line Ser) 1972-75; Chm Bd Hardy Meml Meth Ch 1974; r/Meth.

BELL, FRANKLIN ARTHUR JR oc/County Administrator; b/June 12, 1947; ba/135 W Cameron St, Culpepper, VA 22701; m/Diana W; c/Andrea Lynn, Kimberly Opal; p/Franklin A Sr and Pauline E Bell, Hagerstown, MD; ed/BA Shepherd Col; MS Frostburg St Col; pa/Co Amdr, Culpepper Co, Va; Dir Budget, Pers & Adm Functions; Past Pres Nat Assn Accts, Mason-Dixon Chapt; Pres Delta Sigma Pi; cp/Past Mem: Hagerstown Md JCs; Maugansville Ruritan Clb; Coun Mem St Paul's Luth Ch; r/Luth; hon/Man of Yr 1978 (Mason-Dixon Chapt Nat Assn Accts).

BELL, GETHA GINA oc/Writer; b/Sept 23, 1913 (Corpus Christi, TX); h/2980 Holiday Cir, Buford, GA 30518; c/James Paul Harris Jr; p/E Robert Bell (dec); Emma Ann Clark (dec); ed/Att'd Tex A&I; pa/Newspaper Writer: Houston Chronicle, Bay City Daily Tribune, Midland Reporter, San Francisco Chronicle; cp/Lectr & Spkr at Fam Reunions; DAR; Others; r/Epis; hon/Fam Hist in Burke's Peerage; Publr Bells in USA and Allied Families.

BELL, JULIAN AUGUSTUS oc/Plant Manager; b/Oct 30, 1921; h/325 Forrest Ln, Corsicana, TX 75110; ba/Corsicana; m/Barbara Inez; c/Judith L Humphries, John Charles, (Stepchd:) Paul M Humphries, Alan D Humphries, Lisa N Ward, Dana W Humphries; p/Julian Carlisle (dec) and Maebelle Carroll Bell (dec); ed/BS NC St Col 1938-42; Tex Christian Univ 1953-54; Doct Work N Tex St Univ 1958-59; mil/Inf Resv 1942-46; Resv Ofcr 1946-51; USAF 1951-52; Resv Ofcr 1952-67; Ret'd Res Lt Col; pa/Pres & Plant Mgr Universal-Rundle Corp FRP Bathtub & Shower Units 1970-; Assoc Prof Engrg & Hd Engrg Dept Arlington St Col 1949-59; Ready-Hung Door Corp 1959-63; Indust Engr & Salesmgr Loma Corp 1963-68, Plant Mgr 1965-68; Mosites Rubber Co 1968-69; Modern Plastics Mgmt Adv Panel 197; Bd Tax Equalization, City of Corsicana 1971-; cp/Arlington Masonic Lodge 438; Arlington Chapt Coun; Dallas Scottish Rite Bodies; Corsicana Salvation Army Adv Bd; Corsicana C of C; r/Bapt; hon/BS w High Hons.

BELL, MARTHA oc/Cosmetologist; b/Oct 20, 1945; h/Fayetteville, NC; c/Wilfred, Henry, Gwendolyn, Daniel; p/Otha James Bell; Earlean Williams; ed/N Capital Beauty Inst; Harris Barber Col; Nat Assn Cosmetology Sch; Dr Deg Nat Beauty League; pa/Cosmetologist Instr; Hair Dresser; VP Fayetteville Chapt 6 NHCA; Mem C of C; Mem NC Beauticians; cp/NAACP; rel/Bapt; hon/W/W 1980; Fayettville Bus League Achmt Awd 1980; Concerned Wom of Justice 1980; 1st Place Hairweaving 1976.

BELL, SHIRLEY KAY oc/Professor; b/Nov 24, 1941; h/3616 Collins Ferry Rd, Morgantown, WV 26505; ba/M'ton; p/Robert C and Eleanore Marie Hall Bell (dec), Cumberland, OH; ed/BSN Univ Cinc; MSN Wayne St Univ; pa/Univ Prof; ANA; Nat League Nsg; AAUP; APHA; AACN; cp/Am Heart Assn; r/Meth; hon/Sigma Theta Tau; Hon Mem WV S of Nsg Alumni Assn.

BELL, WILLIAM oc/Community Worker; b/June 20, 1926; h/122 Harris St, Jackson, TN 38301; m/Marvelyne; c/Wallace, Gwen, Naomi; p/Kitty Mae Bills; r/Calvary Bapt Ch: Maintenance & Operations for 36 Yrs; hon/William Bells' Day, Calvary Bapt Ch.

BELLO, JAN R oc/Social Worker; b/Mar 19, 1943; h/1520 S Chateau Cr, Lake Charles, LA 70605; ba/Lake Charles; c/Kimberly Kaye; p/Guy W (dec) and Helen J Reynolds (dec); ed/BS, MSW; pa/Bd Cert Social Wkr; NASW; ACSW; r/Cath; hon/Outstg Yng Wom Am 1970; W/W Am Wom 1979.

BELTZ, LAVERNA LOUISE oc/Nurse; b/July 5, 1938; h/10020 Brookmill Ct, Okla City, OK 73159; ba/Okla City; m/Harold E Jr; p/Albert (dec) and Lillie Riffel, Carrier, Okla; ed/BSN; pa/RN; Past Pres & Pres Elect Okla City Chapt Assn of Seventh Day Adventist Nurses; Charter Mem Am Acad Ambulatory Nsg Dir; r/Seventh Day Adventist; hon/W/W Am Wom 1978.

BEMLEY, JESSE L oc/Computer Specialist; b/Apr 17, 1944; h/2316 Naylor Rd SE, Wash DC 20020; ba/Wash DC; p/Timothy Dozie; Paralee Lewis (dec); ed/BS; MS; mil/AUS 1966-68; pa/Computer Spec, Dept Justice 1974-; Asst Chm Data Processing Dept, Strayer Col 1980-; AASPA; SMIS; cp/Dir Afro Am Datanamics Inc 1975-76; r/Bapt; hon/W/W Fin & Indust; Outstg Yng Men Am.

BENDELL, LEONARD oc/Businessman; b/Aug 22, 1941; h/Ocala, FL; ba/PO Drawer 1750, Ocala, FL 32670; m/Roberta; c/Howard A, Teri I; p/David and Hilda Bendell, Miami, FL; ed/Cert Consumer Credit Exec; Accredited Voice Stress Analyst; mil/USAF; pa/Pres Asset Investigation & Disc Inc; Ptnr Video Tape Records; Fla Collectors Assn; VP Am Col Assn; Nat Com Intl Consumer Credit Assn; cp/Rotary Clb; Forest High Booster Clb; Demo Exec Com; r/Jewish; hon/Optomist Pres's Coun Jim Yancey Civic Awd 1964; Author: Effective Collections 1979; Data Processing 1980.

BENDER, MARGARET KRIVONAK oc/Teacher; b/May 2, 1934; h/1107 Vincent Dr, Mt Pleasant, SC 29464; ba/Mt Pleasant; m/Roger Stillman; c/Michele Eve, Christopher Stillman; p/Joseph Krivonak, Central City, PA; Eva Compel (dec); ed/BS Univ Pgh 1952; MAT Citadel 1975; pa/SS Tchr; Bd Dirs SCEA; Pres Charleston Co Ed Assn.

BENEFIELD, LARRY DAVID oc/Associate Professor; b/Oct 15, 1942; h/334 Wilson Ln, Auburn, AL 36830; ba/Auburn; m/Mary L; c/Brynna Layne; p/Doyle L and Dorthy M Benefield, Tucker, GA; ed/BSCE Auburn Univ 1966; MSCE 1972 Auburn Univ; PhD VPI & St Univ 1975; mil/USAF 1967-70 Capt; pa/Assoc Prof Auburn Univ 1979-; Asst Prof Univ Colo 1976-79; Asst Prof Miss St Univ 1975-76; Am Soc Civil Engrs; Water Pollution Control Fed; Am Water Works Assn; Assn Envir Engrg Profs; Nat Soc Profl Engrs; r/Meth; hon/Va Tech Chapter Sigma Xi Outstg Res Awd 1974; Author: Biological Process Design for Wastewater Treatment 1980.

BENGTSON, EDYTHE BEAUNITA oc/Homemaker, Teacher; b/Nov 30, 1915; h/320 Gresham, Baytown, TX 77520; m/Floyd Keith Sr; c/Floyd Keith Jr, Charm Bengtson Cowart; p/Frank Simpson (dec); Edna Stallman, Pgh, TX; cp/Bible Tchr; Past Pres Wom's Clb Baytown; Tex Fed Wom's Clbs; San Jacinto Dist Ofcr Home Life Ch; r/Bapt; 44 Yr Tchr & SS Supt.

BENN, HERMAN THOMAS oc/Attorney; b/Dec 7, 1911; h/128 Wellon St, Suffolk, VA 23434; ba/Suffolk; m/Marian W; p/Mack Sr and Mamie S Benn (dec); ed/BA Va Union Univ; LLB Terrell Law Sch; mil/USAF WWII Tech Sgt; pa/Asst Commonwlth Atty, City of Suffolk; Suffolk, Norfolk, Portsmouth & Am Bars; cp/Bd Dirs Suffolk C of C; r/Epis: Vestryman, Bd Missions; hon/Man of Yr, Suffolk NAACP.

BENNETT, CHARLES E oc/US Congressman; h/400 W Bay St, Jacksonville, FL; ba/Wash DC; m/Dorothy Jean; c/Bruce, James, Lucinda; p/Walter J and Roberta B Bennett (dec); ed/BA, JD Univ Fla; mil/Capt Inf WWII; pa/Lwyr 1934-48; cp/Cong-man 1949-; Past Pres J'ville JCs; Pres Fla Alumni Assn; r/Disciples of Christ; hon/Silver Star; Philippine & French Legions of Hon; Hon Degs.

BENNETT, DONALD GARRY oc/Professor; b/Sept 12, 1952; h/Rt 2 Box 360, Eagle Dr, Cleveland, TN 37311; ba/C'land; m/Vicky Vaught; p/John A and Lena Bennett, Plant City, FL; ed/BA Lee Col; MDiv SWn Bapt Theol Sem; pa/Prof Lee Col; Soc Pentecostal Studies; r/Ch of God; hon/W/W Am Univs & Cols 1973-74; Chaplian Upsilon Xi 1973-74; Pres Pi Delta Omicron 1973-74; Outstg Yng Men Am 1978; Pres Pioneers for Christ 1973-74; VP Theol Fellowship 1976-77.

BENNETT, E RAY oc/Manager; b/Nov 19, 1944; h/3930 W Beach Bv Apt J-5, Biloxi, MS 39351; ba/Gulfport, MS; c/Stephanie Rae; p/Sarah Cooper, Coats, NC; ed/WW Holding Tech Inst 1968; mil/USAF 1963-67; pa/Mgr Biloxi-Gulfport Credit Reporting Ctr, Credit Bur Inc 1974-; Mgr Jewel Box Stores Corp 1968-74; VP Henderson, NC JCs 1971; Broward Co Credit Execs, Ft Lauderdale, Fla 1979; r/Bapt; hon/Hon Discharge USAF.

BENNETT, JAMES PAUL oc/Plant Administrator; b/Dec 31, 1927; h/Rt 5 Box 392G, Staunton, VA 24401; m/Ella Callison; c/Sharon Lorraine Smith, Teresa Ann; p/Oliver E Bennett (dec) and Ada Bennett Proffitt (dec); ed/US Maritime Ser; Upper Iowa Univ; mil/USMM/Maritime Ser 1944-49; AUS 1954-56; pa/Wn St Hosp, Commonwlth Va: Maintenance, Power Plant Ops, Trans, Security; Mem & Past Pres Va Chapt 3 Nat Assn Power Engrs; Former Mem Bd Dirs Blue

PERSONALITIES OF THE SOUTH

Ridge Indust Assn; Pres Shenandoah Val Chapt Va Gov Employees Assn; r/Ordained Deacon & Elder, Presb Ch; hon/Spec Commend Awd AUS 1956; Employee of Yr Awd, Mtl Hlth & Mtl Retard, Commonwlth Va 1980.

BENNETT, WILLIAM N JR oc/Executive; b/Sept 18, 1950; h/2318 Cascade Ln, Albany, GA 31707; ba/Albany, GA; m/Elaine Evans; c/Cory Evan, Bethany Elaine; p/William N Sr and Faye Hoyle Bennett; ed/BBA 1972, MBA 1973 Univ Ga; pa/Pres Data Sys Inc; r/Meth.

BENSON, A D JR oc/Insurance Agent; b/May 9, 1947; h/Rt 1, Erwin, NC 28339; m/Ann M; p/Archie D (dec) and Evelyn Benson, Kenansville, NC; ed/Att'd ECU; mil/USN 1968-72; pa/Ins Agt; NC Life Underwriters Assn; Life Underwriters Polit Action Com; cp/NC Sheriff's Assn; r/Free Will Bapt; hon/HS Fball Team Capt 1965; Mr So Life 1979; #1 Agt in Dist 1979; So Life Hall of Fame 1979; Co Hon Man in Navy Basic Tng 1968.

BENSON, JOHN BERNARD oc/Professor; b/May 25, 1926; h/2022 Ash, Texarkana, AR 75503; ba/Texarkana; m/Marie; c/Michael Louis, Elizabeth Ruth; p/Louis V (dec) and Elsie Benson (dec); ed/BA Berea Col 1949; MSE Henderson St Univ 1962; Dip Adv'd Study Univ Ark 1964; mil/AUS 1954-56; pa/Prof Psych & Sociol 1968-; Lake Charles, La Welfare Dept Case Worker 1949-51; Secy YMCA 1952-54; Phi Delta Kappa; AAUP; Tex Jr Col Tchr Assn; cp/Mem Bd First Meth Ch Texarkana; Ldr Local Boy Scout Troup & Cub Scout Troup; r/Meth; hon/1st Place Danforth Contest Berea Col 1946; Co-Editor *Marriage and the Family*.

BENSON, MELBA WOOSLEY oc/Educational Consultant; b/Apr 14, 1947; h/1007 Bucknell, Arlington, TX 76012; ba/Same; m/Sammy F Countryman; p/Arvel Woosley, Seymour, TX; Vera Tison, Lubbock, TX; ed/BS magna cum laude, MBEd; pa/Ednl Conslt; Nat Bus Ed Assn; Delta Pi Epsilon; Am Mgmt Assn; r/Bapt; hon/W/W Am Wom 1979-80.

BENTLEY, FRANK H oc/Proprietor; b/Apr 18, 1917; ba/Tuskegee, AL; m/Willie D; c/Donald G, Hal E; p/Willie (dec) and Fannie Bentley (dec); ed/Dip St Tchrs Col 1939; Dip Atlanta Col Mortuary Sci 1947; BS Tuskegee Inst 1952; mil/AUS WWII; pa/Propr The Peoples Funeral Home; City Coun-man, Tuskegee; Chm Utility Bd Tuskegee; cp/Tuskegee Civic Assn; NAACP; Nat Funeral Dirs Assn; League of Municipalities; Commun Relats Bd, Ala St Funeral Dirs Assn; E Ala Funeral Dirs Assn; r/Meth; hon/Tuskegee Inst Tigers for Outstg Ser 1978; Dist'd Ser Awd, City of Tuskegee 1979; Pres Assoc Tuskegee Inst 1977; Outstg Ser Awd, Ala Funeral Dirs Awd 1974; Proclamation, City of Tuskegee Recog upon Opening of New Funeral Home 1980.

BENTLEY, SALLYE F oc/Retired Teacher; b/Feb 1, 1910; p/Attaway A and Henrietta Fields (dec); ed/BS 1953; pa/Elem Tchr, Seminole Co 39½ Yrs; Rec'g Secy, Seminole Co Ret'd Tchrs Assn; r/Bapt; hon/Ldrship Cert, St Paul Missionary Bapt Ch 1979; Awd Cert, St James AME Ch 1970; Cert Apprec, 1st Shiloh Missionary Bapt Ch 1965; Seminole Co Sch Bd Resolution of Apprec 1970; Cert of Awd of Ser, St John Missionary Bapt Ch 1962; Cert of Apprec, St Dept of Ed, Tallahassee, Fla 1970; Cit for Dist'd Ser, Am Cancer Soc, Fla Div 1953; Fla A&M Univ 25th Yr Alumni Awd 1978; Apprec Awd, Former Students & Commun 1979; Cert Apprec, St James AME CH 1979; Cert Apprec, New Mt Calvary Missionary Bapt Ch 1971; Cert of Recog, Allen Chapel AME Ch 1967.

BENTON, ANDREW KEITH oc/Assistant to President; h/777 SE 15, Edmond, OK 73034; ba/Okla City, OK; m/Deborah Sue Strickland; p/Darwin K and Nelda L Benton, Lawrence, KS; ed/BS Okla Christian Col 1974; JD Okla City Univ 1979; pa/Asst to Pres Okla Christian Col; Law Student Div Am Bar Assn; r/Ch of Christ; hon/W/W Am Cols & Univs 1972-73 & 73-74; Outstg Yng Men Am 1977.

BENTON, DELMUS CECIL oc/Salesman; b/Dec 30, 1935; m/Bonnell Edmunds; c/Dennis Curtiss and Effie Clements Benton, Claxton, GA; ed/Grad Pt I & II & Hlth Courses of Life Underwriter Trg Coun of Wash DC 1964; 2 Pts Chartered Life Underwriter Courses 1965; Estate Planning Sem 1978; mil/NG Artillery & Armoured Divs Commun Chief; pa/Ins Salesman; Owner Safeway Ins Agcy; Ins Conslt; Estate Planner; Fin Advr; Former Secy, Former Treas & Past Pres Statesboro, Ga Assn Life Underwriters; Instr 5 Yrs Life Underwriter Trg Courses; cp/Polit Minuteman for Statesboro Assn Life Underwriters; Voc Guid Chm Statesboro Kiwanis Clb; Former Treas Citizens Surcharge Com of Savannah; r/Prim Bapt; Past Pres Men's Brotherhood; hon/Winner of Two Merit Awds from Time Ins Co; Winner 15 Pres Clb Convs Inc Trips to England, Mexico, Bermuda, Others; Mem Life Ldrs of Ga.

BERGER, GARY STERLING oc/Specialist in Obstetrics and Gynecology; b/Oct 19, 1942; h/Chapel Hill, NC; ba/Chapel Hill Fertility Sers, Suite 2104, 109 Conner Dr, Chapel Hill, NC 27514; m/Barbara Jean Mackenzie; c/Gregory Sterling, John Pennington; ed/Milton Robert and

Helen Knopf Berger, Miami, FL; ed/AB cum laude Harvard Col 1960-65; MD Univ of Rochester Sch Med & Dent 1965-69; Intern Duke Univ Hosp 1969-70; Asst Resident Johns Hopkins Hosp 1970-71; Resident NC Meml Hosp 1973-76; MS UNC Chapel Hill 1976; mil/Epidemic Intell Ser Ofcr, Ctr for Disease Control; pa/Spec Ob & Gyn; Pres Chapel Hill Fert Sers; Clin Asst Prof, Dept Ob & Gyn & Adj Assoc Prof, Dept Maternal & Child Hlth, UNC; Med Dir Raleigh Wom's Hlth Org, Raleigh, NC; Am Assn Gyn Laparoscopists; Am Col Ob & Gyn; Am Col Preven Med; Am Fert Soc; AMA; Am Public Hlth Assn; Intl Col Surgs; NC Med Assn; Royal Soc Med; Soc Adolescent Med; cp/Dir Charles Fields Med Foun Ltd; Author: *Intrauterine Devices and Their Complications*; *The Safety of Fertility Control*; *Vaginal Contraception*; Num Contbns to Jours.

BERGER, GEORGE DONALD oc/Minister; b/Apr 2, 1942; h/1618 Maple St, Plaquemine, LA 70764; ba/P'mine; m/Jo Ann Patton; c/Pamela Donise, Kimberly Dawn; p/Beverly Benjamin (dec) and Florence Dunn Berger (dec); ed/BS William Carey Col 1964; ThM New Orleans Bapt Theol Sem 1969; ThD Clinton Theol Sem 1977; Other Grad Study SEn La Univ, LSU, Univ So Miss, Nicholls St Univ; mi/AUS Capt; pa/Pastor: First Bapt Ch, P'mine, La 1973-; First Bapt Ch, Sumrall, Miss 1969-73; First Bapt Ch, Springfield, La 1965-69; Gulf Coast Mil Acad 1964-65; Indian Hill Bapt Ch, Miss 1963-64; Treas Baton Rouge Area Min Assn; Pres Baton Rouge Bapt Min Fellowship; VP P'mine Min Assn; cp/Hon Mem Staff Gov Dave Treen, La & Gov Bill Waller, Miss; Pres Sumrall JCs; VP Sumrall Lions Clb; Dir P'mine Rotary Clb; Chm Substance Abuse Coun; Mtl Hlth Bd; r/So Bapt; hon/Editor *Lance* 1964; Contbr *Sermons on Stewardship* 1980.

BERGERON, MAURICE L oc/Director; b/Apr 12, 1940; h/Richmond, KY; ba/Madison Co Ambulance Ser, Eastern By-Pass, Richmond, KY 40475; p/Mr & Mrs Alexander Bergeron, Lewiston, ME; ed/Am·Motel Sch 1973; En Ky Univ; Nav Tactical Data Sys Op Sch 1968; mil/USAF 1959-63; USN 1964-79; pa/Dir Madison Co Ambulance Ser; Bach Enlisted Qtrs Mgr Sch; Pers Mgmt Trg Sch; r/Cath.

BERKEY, MAURICE EDWARD JR oc/Accountant; Manager; b/Feb 17, 1922; h/San Antonio, TX; ba/The Roegelein Co, 1700 S Brazos St, San Antonio, TX 78207; c/Suzanne Manske; p/Maurice E Sr, Salem, IN and Ida Mae Bush Berkey (dec); ed/Ind Ctrl Bus Col 1940-41; Wash Sch Art; mil/AUS WWII under Gen Patton; Sgt Major; pa/Acct; Secy, Treas, Mgr Roegelein Fed Credit Union; Fin Exec; cp/US Senatorial Clb; Am Hist Foun; Am Forestry Assn; Scottish Rite 32° Mason; Smithsonian Assoc Wash Co Hist Soc, Salem, Ind; Nat Hist Soc; Nat Trust for Hist Preserv; Nat Geographic; Art Coun San Antonio; r/Disciples of Christ; hon/Deacon in Ch; Cert & Plaques in Apprec of Work with Credit Union; W/W in Bus & Fin; W/W S&SW.

BERNAL, JESUS R oc/Bilingual Education Director; b/Dec 7, 1953; h/515 S Bernal St, Pearsall, TX 78061; ba/Pearsall; p/Jose B Jr and San Juana R Bernal, Pearsall, TX; ed/BA St Mary's Univ 1976; MA Univ Tex 1977; PhD Cand 1981; pa/Bilingual Ed Dir 1978-; Sch Libn & Media Coor 1978; Instr Acctg; Tech Staff Asst Univ Tex; Coor Manpower Yth Employ Prog; Libn Asst; Phi Delta Kappa; NEA; Tex St Tchrs Assn; Pearsall Edrs Assn; Delta Epsilon Sigma Nat Hon Soc; Mexican Am Hispanic Caucus, Tex St Tchrs Assn; PTA Mem: Pearsall, Tex & Nat; ASCD; AAUP; Nat Assn Bilingual Ed; Tex Assn Bilingual Ed; San Antonio Area Assn Bilingual Ed; Tex Bus Ed Assn; Delta Pi Epsilon Hon Grad Bus Ed Frat; Am Soc Pers Adm; cp/LULAC; Past Pres & Former Secy Cath Ch Parish Coun Pearsall; r/Cath; hon/W/W: S&SW, Among Students in Am Univs & Cols; Outstg Yng Men Am 1980; Hispanic W/W Am; Intl Yth in Achmt Awd 1979; Nat Hispanic Schlr 1977 & 78; Pearsall Edrs Assn Spec Friend Awd; TSTA Dist XX Public Relats Awd; Henderson Foun Fund S'ship; PEA S'ship; Delta Epsilon Sigma Life Mem; Phi Delta Kappa; Delta Pi Epsilon; Rec'd Highest Score on Candidacy Qualifying Exam for MA Deg in Ed at UT-San Antonio 1977.

BERNARD, DELMAR GEORGE oc/Administrative/Clinical Director; b/July 14, 1922; h/512 Apache Dr, Hopkinsville, KY; ba/H'ville; m/Margaret J; c/Sharon, Darrell, Terry, Ronnie, Phillip; p/Della Gary, Caneyville, KY; ed/AS 1972; AA 1975; pa/Adm/Clin Dir, Alcohol Treatment Ctr (Volta House); RN; Ky Alcoholism Coun; Ky Assn Alcohol-Drug Abuse Profls, Treas; r/Luth; hon/Outstg Nurse Student 1972; Outstg Ser in Alcohol Ed, Murray St Univ 1978; Manette Cupp Awd 1980.

BERRY, CHARLES ALLEN oc/Administrator; b/Sept 17, 1923; h/10814 Riverview Dr, Houston, TX 77042; ba/Houston; m/Addella Nance; c/Michael, Charlene B Forrester (Mrs David), Janice B Dudley (Mrs Jay); p/George and Vera Berry, Riverside, CA; ed/BA Univ Cal-B 1945; MD Univ Cal Med Sch-SF 1947; MPH cum laude Harvard Sch of Public Hlth-B 1956; Cert'd in Preventive Med (Aerospace Med) 1957; pa/Pres Univ Tex Hlth Sci Ctr at Houston 1974-; Dir Life Scis, Nat Aeronautics & Space Adm, Wash DC 1971-74; Dir Med Res & Opers,

24

PERSONALITIES OF THE SOUTH

NASA Manned Spacecraft Ctr, Houston 1966-71; Num Other Past Positions; Lic'd in Cal & Tex; Num Acad Appts; Mem Var Edit Bds incl'g "Aerospace Med", Jour of Aerospace Med Assn & "Space Life Scis", Intl Jour of Biol & Med; Num Profl Assns; cp/Bd Dirs: SmithKline Corp, Nassau Bay Nat Bk, SWn Savs & Ln Assn; r/Meth; hon/Aerospace Med Assn: Arnold D Tuttle Awd, Louis H Bauer Fdrs Awd; USAF Cert of Achmt by Surg Gen; Spec Aerospace Med Hon Cit, AMA; Hoyt S Vanderberg Trophy, Arnold Air Soc; Melbourne W Boynton Awd, Am Astronautical Soc; Gold Medal: Am Col of Chest Phys, Czechoslovakian Acad of Med, Prague; John Jeffries Awd, Acad of Nat Scis; AMA Cit; Phys Mission Awd, Carlo Erba Foun, Milan, Italy; Silver Medal for Dist'd Ser, Min of Hlth & Wel, Portugal; Daniel & Florence Guggenheim Intl Astronautics Awd; NASA Exceptl Sci Achmt Medal; Annual Awd for Extraordinary Perf, Am Col of Surgs; NASA Dist'd Ser Medal; Hermann Oberth Awd, Salzburg, 23rd Space Cong; Cmdr Order of Cedars from Pres of Lebanon; Hon Fellow, Am Soc Clin Cardiologists.

BERRY, JULIA ELIZABETH oc/Secretary, Receptionist; b/Feb 14, 1923; h/726 Old Scout Rd, Dadeville, AL 36853; ba/D'ville; m/Douglas E; c/William N, David L, Robert D; p/Charles Homer (dec) and Epsy Beatrice Henderson (dec); ed/Young Bus Col; pa/Secy; Recpt; East Tallapoosa BP&W; Co-Dir Region III PBW Clb; cp/Pleasant Ridge Bapt Ch: Yng Adult SS Tchr; Ch Treas; Pres Wom's Missionary Soc; Tallapoosa Bapt Assn; St Hist for Am Legion of Ala; Treas E Tallapoosa Am Legion; Pres Tallapoosa Co Cowbells 1978-79; Past Pres E Tallapoosa BPW; Past Pres Delphic Clb; Past Pres Dadeville PTA; Chm Tallapoosa Co Ext Coun; Dir Tallapoosa Co Farm Bur; Co-Dir Region III BPW Clb; Co-Chm Tallapoosa Co Cancer Foun; Bd Dirs Camp ASCCA; Op Santa Claus; r/Bapt; hon/Ldrship Awd from Ala Farm Bur Fed 1970; Ldrship Awd from Auburn Univ 1968; Tallapoosa Co Farm Bur Cooking Contest Winner 1979.

BERRY, KATHRLYN BALLARD oc/Teacher; b/Jan 15, 1926; c/Donald Greg, Van Clayton, Joeirthel Almenia, Edryie Joe; p/Elisha (dec) and Florence Smith Ballard, New Orleans, LA; ed/BA Leland Col 1957; MEd So Univ 1971; pa/Elem Tchr, Bains Elem Sch, W Feliciana Parish; LEA; NEA; W Feliciana Parish LEA; cp/BSA Coun; GSA Coun; OES, Recording Secy; Amarhant; Elks; PCR Coun; Cts of Calanthe; Anniv & Flower Dept Nat Elks; Nat Cong of Christian Ed; 4th Dist Assn; r/Bapt; hon/Wom of Yr 1976, Macedonia Bapt Ch; Tchr of Yr 1978, Happi Llanders Civic Clb.

BERRY, LOU H oc/Secretary; b/July 1, 1943; h/2 Kershaw Pl, Belvedere, SC 29841; ba/Belvedere; m/James S; c/Dennis, Susan; p/Milton (dec) and Sudie Holloway, Lincolnton, GA; pa/Legal Secy to Thomas E Huff, Atty & SC St Rep; Recording Secy N Augusta Chapt Nat Secys Assn & Chm Yr Book; Mem of Mbrship, Scrapbook, CPS/Ed, Sem & Secys Week Coms; cp/Den Ldr for Cub Scouts; Org'd Brownie Troop; Team Mother Belvedere Dixie Yth Baseball League; Actively Worked w 1978 Elec of Tom Huff; r/Meth; hon/Secy of Yr 1979, Nat Secys Assn.

BERTRAND, RUSSELL EARL oc/Manager; b/Aug 4, 1948; h/Porter, TX; ba/PO Box 1309, Houston, TX 77001; m/Katherine Ann Feuge; p/Charles Joseph and Nancy Hanks Bertrand, Spring, TX; ed/BSEd Howard Payne Univ 1973; Sch Mil Scis 1973; Houston Fire Acad 1967; mil/USAF 1973-76 1st Lt; pa/Kroger Co: Mgmt Trainee & Pers Asst 1976, Sr Pers Asst 1977-78, Pers Mgr Dist Ctr 1979, Mgr Trans 1980; Am Soc Trg & Devel; Am Soc Pers Adms; cp/Nat Rifle Assn; Alpha Phi Omega; r/Bapt; hon/W/W S&SW.

BEST, MADELINE oc/Guidance Counselor, Teacher; b/May 23, 1908; h/1010 E Side Dr, Greensboro, NC 27406; m/Edward J Sr; c/Marie Gibbs, Edward J Jr, Roma Obephe; p/George H (dec) and Maggie Bridges (dec); ed/BA Bennett Col 1931; MA Tchrs Col Columbia Univ 1943; pa/Guid Cnslr NC Public Schs; Eng Tchr; NEA; Am Pers & Guid Assn; NCET; Nat Coun Deans of Wom; NCTA; NC Pers & Guid Assn; cp/Bennett Col Alumnae Assn; VP Wom in Commun Ser; YWCA; Scout Ldr GSA; VP BPW of Am; r/Meth; Pres UMW; hon/W/W Am Wom 1966-67, 1968-69; Delta Sigma Theta.

BETTERTON, ROBERT JERRY oc/Assistant Vice President; b/May 26, 1949; h/Rt 1 Box 675A, Florence, MS 39073; ba/Jackson, MS; m/Deboria L; c/Brandi Leigh; p/Robert L and Wyneas J Betterton, Bruce, MS; ed/BS Millsaps Col 1971; pa/Asst VP & Mgr Loan Ser Dept, Credit Dept & Microfilm Ops, Unifirst Fed Savings & Loan 1974-; Dir Field Ops Geo Labs Inc 1971-73; Credit Mgr Mobile Homes Bankers Trust Savings & Loan 1973-74; Mem Inst Fin Ed; Assoc of Records Mgrs & Admrs; cp/Republican Party; r/Meth; hon/W/W S&SW 1980.

BETTS, ERNEST C JR oc/Retired Federal Official; b/Aug 27, 1914; h/2040 World Pkwy Blvd, Apt 14, Clearwater, FL 33515; m/Gwendolyn E; c/Ernest C III, Keith W, Willis L; p/Ernest C and Cora L Steffen Betts (dec); pa/Ret'd Asst Secy of Treasury; Am Soc Public Adm; Soc Pers Adm; cp/Past Pres Epping Forest Commun, Annapolis (Md); Past Mem Arlington Co (Va) Sch Bd; r/U Meth: Dist Lay Ldr, Pres Conf Comm on Equitable Salaries; hon/US Treasury: Meritorious & Exceptl Ser Awds, Alexander Hamilton Awd.

BEUTLER, RANDY LEON oc/Cattle Rancher, Student; b/Jan 5, 1961; h/Rt 2, Canute, OK 73626; p/H L (dec) and Faye Graybill, Canute, OK; ed/Student SWn Okla St Univ; pa/Cattle Rnchr; Okla Cattlemen's Assn; cp/Pres Canute Yng Men's Clb; Pres Canute JCs; VP Custer Co Hist Soc; St Del to Okla Dem Conv; Pres's Clb Dem Party; r/Meth; hon/Pres Canute FFA Chap 1978-79; Del Okla Am Legion Boys St 1978; Del Pres Classrom for Yng Ams; Canute FFA Star Chapt Farmer Awd 1978-79; Student of Today Awd 1979; Appt'd by Gov to Gov's Adv Com on Chd, Yth & Fams.

BEVERLY, W RONALD oc/Coordinator of Community Organization; b/July 20, 1948; h/Atlanta, GA; c/Rhonda V; p/Margaret Beverly, Montgomery, AL; ed/BA Morehouse Col 1971; MSW Atlanta Univ 1977; mil/USAF 1971-75 Acctg & Fin Ofc; pa/Coor Commun Org, EOA; Fulton Co Elections Dept; Lemoyne-Owne Col, Memphis; Neighborhood Plan'g Unit-M; r/Bapt; hon/Lemoyne-Owen Col Staff Rep to Black Schlrs Conf, Ohio St Univ 1976.

BEVILL, TOM oc/Member of Congress; b/Mar 27, 1921; h/1600 Alabama Ave, Jasper, AL 35501; ba/Wash DC; m/Lou; c/Susan B, Donald H, Patricia L; p/Herman and Fannie Lou Fike Bevill (dec); ed/BS Univ Ala; LLB Univ Ala Law Sch; mil/AUS 1943-46 Capt; pa/Gen Pract Law, Jasper 1949-67; cp/Mem Ho of Reps 1967-; Former Mem Ala St Leg; Mason; Shriner; r/Bapt.

BEVINS, THOMAS PETER II oc/Chief Operating Officer; b/June 26, 1936; h/PO Box 4845, Shreveport, LA 71104; ba/Shreveport; m/Joyce Ann; c/Thomas Peter, Kelly Elizabeth, Kimberly Ann, Martin Joseph, Julibeth Stapleton, Mary Kathleen; p/Thomas Peter and Louise Stapleton Bevins, Seneca Falls, NY; ed/BA 1962; MA 1975; mil/USN 1954-57; pa/Pres, Chief Operating Ofcr, W L Somner Co, Inc; Am Mgmt Assn; Am Nuclear Soc; Nat Ocean Indust Anns; cp/C of C; r/Cath; hon/W/W Fin & Indust; Bus & Indust Mgmt Awd 1975.

BHAJAN, WILLIAM RUDOLPH oc/Environmental Scientist; b/Jan 16, 1937; h/610 Dos Marinas, Fajardo, PR 00648; ba/Rio Piedras, PR; c/William Roshan, Indira Lymari; p/William Oswald and Lilian Irene Baijnauth Bhajan, Guyana, SAm; ed/BA Intl Am Univ 1962; MS Mich St Univ 1966; PhD Univ Waterloo (Ontario) 1970; pa/Envir Scist Ctr for Energy & Envir Res, Univ PR; PR Water Pollution Control Fdn; Intl Water Resources Assn; Beta Beta Beta; r/Anglican; hon/Intl Scholar 1960-62; Tchg & Res Fellow: Mich St Univ, Univ Waterloo; W/W S&SW.

BHATIA, DIL MOHAN SINGH oc/Geologist, Geochemist; b/Oct 19, 1939; h/Clarksville, TN; ba/C'ville; m/Rajinder; p/G S and Jagjit Bhatia, Bombay, India; ed/BS Jabalpur Univ 1959; MTech Saugar Univ 1962; MS Univ New Brunswick 1970; PhD Univ Mo 1976; pa/UN Advr to Govt of Somali Dem Repub 1981-; Assoc Prof Geol, Austin Peay St Univ 1977-; Geochemist, Mo Geol Land Survey 1973-77; Geol-Geochem New Ungava Iron Ore Co 1970-72; Geol Brunswick Exploration 1968-69; Geol New Brunswick Dept Nat Resources 1967; Conslt: Phillips Petro Co, Intl Oil & Gas, Union Carbide Corp; Soc Mining & Metall Engrs; Sigma Xi; Tenn Acad Scis; r/Sikh; hon/F'ship Nat Res Coun of Can & Geol Survey of Canada 1966-70; US Geol Survey Res Grant 1975-76; Author 1 Book, 25 Pub-Presentations to Nat & Intl Jours & Profl Socs.

BHUGRA, SATNAM SINGH oc/Teacher; b/Sept 1, 1933; h/1311 Red Leaf Ln, E Lansing, MI 48823; ba/Lansing, MI; m/Narinder; c/Maninder, Rupinder, Amritpaul, Amritpreet, Karanueer; p/Harnam Singh (dec) and Ranjit Kaur Sethi Bhugra, India; ed/Ed D; pa/Col Tchr & Resr; NEA; MEA; MAHE; PDK; cp/India-Am Clb; CACS; r/Sikhism; hon/Best Tchr Awd; 1st Pos in MA Exam Among Pvt Cands.

BIBEE, DAVID CHESTER oc/Coach; b/May 31, 1954; m/Lisa Carter; p/H R Bibee; Mary Lynn Bibee, Bristol, TN; ed/BS UT-Knoxville 1977; pa/Col Fball Coach; r/Bapt; hon/S'ship to UT; Liberty Bowl 1974; Gator Bowl 1973; All St Qtrback 1972-73; 4-Sport Letterman.

BICEK, JEANETTE L oc/School Psychologist; b/Aug 6, 1950; h/Okla City, OK; ba/Okla City; p/Lee A (dec) and Violet M Bicek, Okla City, OK; ed/BA cum laude Okla City Univ 1972; MS Trinity Univ, Univ Tex Med Sch 1973; Cert'd Guid Cnslr, Ctrl St Univ; Equal Opport Mgmt Inst; pa/Asst to Chm, Dept Psych, Okla City Univ 1969-71; Coor Study, Okla City Univ 1969; Vol Fam Cnslr, U Appeal 1970; Asst Libn, Dept Libs, St of Okla 1971-72; Vol Probation Ofcr, Municipal Ct Okla City 1971-72; Grad Asst to Dir Clin Psych, Trinity Univ & Tex Univ Med Sch-San Antonio 1972-73; Adm'd Psych Tests for Alcohol Safety Action Prog 1972; Staff Tech Asst III, Robert B Green Hosp 1973; Psychodiagnostician, Commun

25

PERSONALITIES OF THE SOUTH

Guid Ctr, Robert B Green Hosp; Psychometrist & Cnslr, Sacred Heart Sch, Pt-Time 1973-75, Full Time 1975-79; Jr High Yth Dir Pt-time, Sacred Heart Ch 1975-79; Tchr SS Pt-Time St Philip Neri Sch, Midwest City, Okla 1974-75; Cnslr Pt-time Mt St Mary's HS, Okla City 1975-76; Philosophy & Rules & Regulations Bds, Mt St Mary's HS 1975; Archdiocesan Testing Com 1975-; Race Relats/Equal Opport Cnlsr & Tng Ofcr, Okla Mil Dept 1976-; Mem Evaluation Com Cath Sch Ofc, Okla 1978; Gen's Aide 1978; Appt'd to Promotion Bd for Enlisted Pers for Enlisted Pers Being Considered for Promotion within Ranks of E-7 to E-9 1978-; Asst Wom's Basketball Coach, Mt St Mary's HS 1978-; Pers Ofcr, Okla Army NG 1979; Vol Psychometrist, Our Lady of Fatima Sch, Nicoma Pk, Okla 1979-; Asst to Advr for Wom in Okla Army Nat Guard 1979-; Psychmetrist & Conslt, Sacred Heart Sch, Okla City 1979-; Sch Psych Christ the King Sch, Okla City 1979-; Appt'd to Bd to Determine Cands for Ofcr Cand Sch, Okla Army Nat Guard; Appt'd to Enlisted Reclassification Bd 1978; Psych Clb, Okla City Univ; Okla St Psych Assn; APGA; Am Sch Cnslr Assn; Okla Sch Psych Assn; NG Assn; Okla NG Assn; cp/Okla Czechs Inc; Wn Fraternal Bohemian Org; r/Cath; hon/W/W Students in Am Cols & Univs, S&SW; Cardinal Key; Psi Chi; Nat Sorority Hall of Fame.

BICH, NGUYEN NGOC oc/Writer, Translator, Education Specialist; b/July 26, 1937; h/Springfield, VA; ba/Wakefield HS; 4901 S Chesterfield Rd, Arlington, VA 22206; m/Dao Thi Hoi; p/Nguyen Trong Tan (dec) and Nguyen Thi Suu, Springfield, VA; ed/BA Princeton Univ 1958; PhD Cand Columbia Univ 1959-62; pa/Writer, Translr; Ed Spec; Dir Info, Embassy Vietnam 1967-72; VRector Mekong Univ 1972-75; Dir Gen for Overseas Info 1972-75; Vietnamese Resource Spec 1978-; Va Rep NAVAE; cp/Pres Vietnam Refugee Fund Inc; Secy-Gen Buddhist Congreg Ch of Am; r/Buddhist; hon/Fulbright S'ship 1956-58; Columbia Univ Pres's Fellowship 1962-63; Author: *A Thousand Years of Vietnamese Poetry* 1975, Others.

BICKERSTAFF, WANNA RUTH oc/Homemaker, Counselor; b/May 31, 1922; h/2013 Princeton, Midland, TX 79701; ba/Midland; m/(dec); c/Robert S Jr, Bette Angeley; pa/Wayman Kirk (dec) and Alma Scallorn Beal (dec); ed/Hardin-Simmons Univ 1938-39; Tex Tech Univ 1939-40; pa/Lay Cnslr; Indep Investor; Midland Coun on Alcoholism; Regional Bd Alcoholism; Vol in All Commun Drs; Fdg Mem Boys Clb; Ptnrship in Auto Dlrship; r/Presb.

BIDEWELL, CHARLES ROBERT (BOB) oc/Band and Choral Director; b/July 16, 1954; h/3200 Reynolds Pk Rd, Paragould, AR 72450; p/Carl Ben and Martha Mitchell Bidewell, Poplar Bluff, MO; ed/BMus Ark St Univ 1976; MMus 1977; pa/Band & Choral Mus Dir, Paragould Mid Sch; 3 Yrs Manila, Ark Public Schs; Past Pres Manila Ed Assn; Paragould Clrm Tchrs Assn; Ark Ed Assn; NEA; Ark Sch Band & Orchestra Assn; Ark Bandmasters Assn; cp/Chrm Mus Div Greene Co Fine Arts Coun; Part in Following Musicals w Jonesboro Fine Arts Coun & Greene Co Fine Arts Coun: "Hello Dolly", "The King & I"; "1776", "Fiddler on the Roof", Others; r/Organist: Huntington Ave U Meth Ch, First Bapt Ch Blytheville; Choir Dir 1st U Meth Ch Manila; Presently Singing in Chancel Choir 1st Meth Ch Paragould & Dir Jr Handbell Choirs.

BIENEN, KAY G oc/Legislator; b/Jan 1, 1938; h/12411 Radnor Ln, Laurel, MD 20811; ba/Annapolis, MD; m/Sanford M; c/Laura, Janet; p/Paul G Gumbinner, NY, NY; Ruth G Coben; ed/BA Skidmore Col 1959; Grad Study Univ Md-Col Pk; pa/Leg Aide to Del Arthur Dorman 1972-74; cp/Elected Md Gen Assembly 1974, Var Com Activs; Other Polit Activs; Bd Dirs Mtl Hlth Assn Prince George's Co; LWV; Montpelier PTA; Oakland's Citizen's Assn; Laurel Art Guild; Gtr Laurel Hosp Auth, Citizen's Adv Com; Exec Com Nat Conf Christians & Jews; Eisenhower Jr HS PTA.

BIGGERS, JANE RICHARDSON oc/Director Public Relations; b/May 12, 1926; h/1101-1 River Rd, Greenwood, MS 38930; ba/G'wood; m/William M; c/William M Jr, Robert Allen Biggers; p/W S Richardson (dec) and Marion Merritt; ed/AA Stephens Col; BS Tobe-Coburn Sch Fashion Careers; Adv'd Studies NY St Univ, Univ Mo Sch Jour, Univ Va Sch Jour; pa/Buyer for 5 Depts in Ready-to-Wear for McLeans Dept Store 1946-48; Wom's Editor, Feature Fash Editor, News Columnist & Editorial Writer for *Greenwood Commonwealth* 1948-76; Fash Editor *State Times* Fash Reporter on WLBT TV 1955-61; Fash Reporter WJDX Radio 1955-66; Miss Park Comm Asst Dir of Florewood River Plantation in Charge Public Relats, Publicity & Spec Projs 1976-; Dir Public Relats Miss Park Comm 1978-; Pres G'wood-Leflore Bicent Comm; Corres for UPI, AP, *Clarion-Ledger* & *Jackson Daily News*; Miss & Nat Fed Press Wom; Am Assn Pen Wom; Wom in Communication; cp/Greenwood BPW; Greenwood Garden Clb; Past Pres Town & Country Garden Clb; cp/Mem Miss Fed Garden Clbs Inc; Bd Dirs Gtr G'wood Foun of Arts; Bd Dirs Wom's Com of Delta Coun; Fdr G'wood-Leflore Tree Meml Comm; Mem G'wood-Leflore C of C; Bd Mem Am Cancer & Heart Assns; Altrusa Clb; Former

VP Jr Aux; Fdr Cotton Ball; r/Epis; hon/Outstg Bus Wom of Month 1979; Sigma Delta Chi; Listed in 3 Editions of W/W; Miss Press Wom's Outstg Woman of Achmt 1976 (The Highest Hon Accorded a News Profl); Received over 300 Awds for Articles, Photos, etc; Outstg Wom of Yr by BPW Clb; Leflore Co's Outstg Wom of Achmt; First Wom to Chair Com For G'wood-Leflore C of C; 1 of 200 Outstg Wom in US by San Antonio, TX AAUW.

BILBREY, STAN C oc/Manager; b/Oct 28, 1949; h/1807 Ave C, Del Rio, TX 78840; ba/Del Rio; m/Barbara Lyn; c/Charles Monroe II; p/Charles Monroe (dec) and Effie M Bilbrey, San Angelo, TX; pa/Mgr Western Mattress Co; cp/Bd Mem Del Rio Lion's Clb; Coach Babe Ruth Baseball; r/Bapt.

BILL, CAROL E oc/System Engineer; b/June 7, 1946; h/4012 Ronson Dr, Alexandria, VA 22310; ba/Bethesda, MD; p/Frank R and Lillian F Bill, Springfield, MA; ed/BA Am Intl Col; pa/Sys Engr IBM; Mem Bd Wash DC Chapt Data Processing Mgmt Assn 1979; cp/Va Hills Citizen Assn; Polish Jr Leag 1970-76; r/Roman Cath; hon/W/W Am Wom.

BILLEITER, DAVID JOHN JR oc/Pastor, Teacher; b/Nov 18, 1945; h/PO Box 73, Fulton, TX 78358; ba/Fulton; m/Nancy E; c/Kevin, Todd, Brent; p/David J and Betty Jo Billeiter, Kerrville, TX; ed/Dip Pastoral Mins 1974; BRE 1980; pa/Pastor Fulton Bapt Ch; Prin Fulton Christian Acad; Tchr Corpus Christi Christian Inst; Intl Fellowship of Christian Cnslrs; r/Interdenom; hon/Pub'd Articles in Newspapers & Rel Periods.

BILLIONS, NOVELLA STAFFORD oc/Retired Research Physicist; b/Nov 30, 1930; h/707 Owens Dr, SE, Huntsville, AL 35801; m/James Calvin; p/Charlie Elmer Stafford (dec); Beatrice Wolaver Stafford, H'ville; ed/BS Athens St Univ; Postgrad Work Univ Ala-H'ville; mil/USAF (WAF) 1950-53; pa/Res Physicist Army Missile Res & Devel Command, Redstone Arsenal, Ret'd 1977; Am Meteorological Soc; AUSA; FEW; r/Prot; hon/Dept of Army Cert of Achmt 1968; 1st Wom to Launch Missile, Cape Canaveral; W/W Am Wom; World W/W Wom.

BING, RICHARD McPHAIL oc/Attorney; b/Aug 23, 1950; h/12315 Ridgefield Pkwy, Richmond, VA 23233; ba/Richmond; m/Valerie W; c/Jennifer L; p/Ellen J Bing, Williamsburg, VA; ed/BA 1972, JD 1978 Univ Richmond; pa/Atty at Law; Gen Coun Va Gas Retailers Assn; Va St Bar; Am Bar Assn; Va Trial Lawyers Assn; Phi Delta Phi Legal Frat; Soc Ins Res; Staff Assoc Univ Richmond Law Review; Metro Richmond Chapt Univ Richmond Alumni Assn; TC Williams Sch Law Alumni Assn; Lambda Chi Alpha Frat; Kappa Delta Pi; cp/Bd Dirs Tuckahoe Vil Civic Assn; Richmond Area Interclb Coun; Bd Dirs Va St JCs; Legal Counsel Tuckahoe JCs Richmond; Univ Richmond Spider Clb; r/Epis; hon/Staff Mem Univ Richmond Law Review.

BINGHAM, HANNAH TOLBERT REID oc/Teacher; b/Feb 5, 1908; m/A B; c/William Lee Reid Jr; p/John G and Hannah Lites Tolbert (dec); ed/AB Atlanta Univ 1930; MA Columbia Univ 1951; pa/Eng Tchr, Kannapolis City Sys, Kannapolis, NC 40 Yrs; HS Eng Tchr; NCEA; Nat Ret'd Tchrs Assn; Secy Local Ret'd Tchrs Assn; Salisbury City Bd Ed; cp/Ch Wom's U, Secy; Rep to Rowan Christian Min; Dem Party, Judge Local Precnt; r/Meth; hon/Plaques: Dedicated Tchr 1972, Merit Ednl Sers 1962, Ednl Sers & Class Advr 1979.

BINNS, FLOYD THOMAS oc/Minister, Teacher; b/Oct 11, 1905; h/Culpeper, VA; ba/Same; m/Avis Frances (dec); 2nd Cancis; p/Lawrence Dabney (dec) and Bertha Lee Binns (dec); ed/BA Univ Rich 1932; BD Colgate Rochester Div Sch 1934; pa/Min 3 Bapt Chs 1935-81; Public Sch Tchr 1937-73; Pres Culpeper Co Ednl Assn; Pres Va Coun SS; Pres Culpeper Co Ret'd Tchrs Assn; Mem Dept Ed Profl Com on Citizenship Ed; cp/Pres Culpeper Lions Clb; Pres Mitchells Ruritan Clb; Culpeper Co Vol Rescue Squad & Fire Dept; Chaplain Am Assn Ret'd Persons; Pres Mitchells PTA; Pres Culpeper Co PTA; Pres Culpeper Co Chapt Am Red Cross; Pres Culpeper Co Min Assn; Pres Culpeper Co Ret'd Tchrs Assn; Com on Aging, Rappahannock-Rapidan Plan'g Dist; r/Bapt; Modr Shiloh Bapt Assn; hon/Lions Intl for Designing Lions Achmt Plaque 1948; Appeared in Ripley's Believe It or Not 1958; Awd'd 4-H Alumni Pin 1957; Co Sch Bd Named Sch Floyd T Binns 1977; Awd'd Plaque by Ladies Aux to VFW 2524 for Loyalty, Ldrship & Patriotism to Culpeper's People.

BIRCH, ROBERT LOUIS oc/Librarian, Editor, Lecturer; b/Aug 9, 1925; h/3108 Dashiell Rd, Falls Ch, VA 22042; m/Grace Kay; c/John, David, Paul, Mary, Joseph, Rose, Eve, Daisy; p/William Ekin and Anita Elizabeth Bowles Birch (dec); ed/AB, MSLS; pa/Libn Nat Agric Lib, USDA, Wash DC; Lectr; Editor *Pun Banner & Bibliomania*; Linguist; Memory Spec, Application of Memory Sys to Math; Lectr to Handicapped; Lincoln Studies; Res on Alphabet Hist; r/Cath; hon/Spokesman of Yr 1974; Polish Vets Medal; Mem Intl Soc for Philosophical Enquiry 1979; Contbr to *Telicom*.

PERSONALITIES OF THE SOUTH

BIRD, RONALD C oc/State Legislator; Attorney; b/Dec 10, 1936; h/1011 Kayton, San Antonio, TX 78210; ba/San Antonio; m/Barbara; c/Mark, Mauri, Bart; p/Charles Bird (dec); Lillian Bird, San Antonio; ed/BS Wash Univ; LLB St Mary's Univ; mil/AUS & USAF 8 Yrs Active & Resv Duty; pa/St Bar Tex; San Antonio Bar Assn; cp/Mem Tex Ho of Reps; Lions Clb; Cancer Soc; Ks of C; r/Cath; hon/Num Awds as Mem of Leg.

BIRDSONG, GLORIA J oc/Nurse; b/Jan 28, 1930; h/Rt 2 Box 134, Tavares, FL 32778; ba/Leesburg, FL; m/(dec); c/Donald C Wright, William B Wright II; p/Charles W Hill, Tampa, FL; ed/Cand RN Deg; pa/LPN; r/Unitarian; hon/Pres Nsg Class; Outstg Student Yr.

BISHOP, JAMES EDWARD oc/Pastor; b/July 25, 1929; h/511 Kenors Dr, Millersville, MD 21108; b/Glen Burnie, MD; m/Ila Jo; c/Reita Jane, James Leonard, John David; p/Carrie L Baird, Mt Pleasant, TX; ed/BA Howard Col 1958; MDiv SWBTS 1973; Chap Ofcr Orientation 1967; Dip Chap Ofcr Adv Course 1974; MA LIU 1974; mil/USAAF 1946-53; AUS 1966-80 Chap; pa/Pastor Glen Burnie Bapt Ch; Phi Alpha Theta, Hon Hist Frat; cp/Rotarians Intl; Am Yth Activiteis Bd of Govs, Germany; Exec Coun PTSA Old Mill HS; Adv Coun, Guid & Cnslg Dept, Severna Pk Sr HS; r/So Bapt; hon/Nat Hon Soc 1946; Army Commend Medal 1967; Bronze Star 1968; WWII Victory Medal 1946; Cert Achmt 1968; Cert Apprec 1973; Cert Apprec Commend Awd 1973; Cert Appr HMB, SBC 1970; MSM 1980 AUS.

BISHOP, KATHERINE ELIZABETH oc/Artist; b/May 9, 1927; h/Sanford, FL; m/George Donald Jr; c/Katherine Weckerle, Cynthia Brooks, Susan, Carol, Euginia, Marian; p/Marion and Alva Gordon; ed/AA Seminole Commun Col; Att'd Univ Ctrl Fla; cp/Hist Soc Bd of Seminole Co; r/Epis; hon/Phi Theta Kappa; W/W Am Jr Cols; Author History of Sanford.

BISHOP, MINNIE SLADE oc/Retired Librarian; h/2413 Ridge Rd, Mobile, AL 36617; m/Sanford D; c/Sanford D Jr; p/John R and Lossie J Slade (dec); ed/AB Shaw Univ; BSLS Hampton Inst; pa/Ret'd Libn; Am Lib Assn; Ala Lib Assn; NEA; cp/LWV; Bd Mem Cult in Black & White; r/Bapt; hon/Mayor's Awd, City of Prichard, Ala; Hampton Inst Lib Awd; Cit, Ala Ho of Reps.

BISHOP, PHYLLIS ELAINE oc/School Administrator; b/Apr 2, 1941; h/PO Box 72, Pulaski, VA 24301; ba/Pulaski; p/Roy T Bishop (dec); Edrie Barton Bishop, Pulaski; ed/BS; MS; pa/Asst Supt for Instrn, Pulaski Co Schs; Pres Pulaski Co Ed Assn 1972-73; Va Ed Assn; NEA; Assn for Supvn & Curri Devel; Appalachian Reg Supvrs: VP 1977-78, Pres 1978-79; Nu Chapt Delta Kappa Gamma: Pres 1976-80, CoChm Iota St Profl Affairs Com 1975-77; Former Mem Stwide Com of Tchr Eval 1972; Pulaski BPW Clb: Fin Chm 1977-78, Parliamentn 1978-79; cp/Pulaski Music Clb; Bd Dirs New River Val Fine Arts Ctr; r/1st Christian Ch: Mem, Adult Choir Dir, Tchr Adult SS Class, Bd Deacons 1973-76, Bd Elders 1976-79, Secy of Bd, Parliamentn 1977-79; hon/Ldrs in Elem Ed; Outstg Yg Wom Am; Outstg Yg Edr; W/W Sch Dist Ofcls.

BISHOP, SANFORD DIXON JR oc/Attorney; State Representative; b/Feb 4, 1947; h/4129 Roman Dr, Columbus, GA 31907; ba/Columbus; p/Sanford Dixon Sr and Minnie S Bishop, Mobile, AL; ed/BA Morehouse Col 1968; JD Emory Univ 1971; mil/AUS; pa/St Bar Ga; Ala St Bar; ABA; NBA; Am Judic Soc; cp/St Rep; 32nd Deg Mason; Shriner; Ga Assn Black Elected Ofcls; Ga Leg Black Caucus; Dem Party Ga; US Senator Sam Nunn Involvemt Com; r/4th St Bapt Ch, Columbus; hon/Man of Yr 1977, Columbus; W/W Am Polits.

BISHOP, SIDNEY L JR oc/Executive; b/Apr 30, 1930; h/Corpus Christi, TX; ba/1122 S Pardre Isl Dr, Corpus Christi, TX 78416; m/Amelia Faye; c/Donald Craig, Dennis Rodney; p/Sidney L Sr and Clara Bell Bishop, Corpus Christi, TX; pa/Pres Bishop Mobile Ctr Inc; Ranch Investments, Cattle & Qtr Horses; cp/Masonic Lodge; Scottish Rite; Shriner; r/Meth; hon/Sales Dlr Awds; Top Ten Dlrs.

BISHOP, VIRGIL MERRELL oc/Retired Colonel; b/Apr 22, 1926; h/Colonia El Naranjal, La Ceiba, Honduras CAm; m/Dorothy S; c/Stepchd: Kathi B Greene, Michael S Bevet; p/I W and Bernice C Bishop (dec), Alexander City, AL; ed/BS Auburn Univ; mil/Ret'd Col Ala NG; pa/Ret'd Col; r/Bapt; hon/Dist'd Ser Medal of Ala; WWII Silver Star & Bronze Star.

BISHOP, WILLIAM LEE oc/Retired Teacher; b/Nov 5, 1926; h/625 N Main St, Enterprise, AL 35330; p/Dewey Hobson (dec) and Mabel Adams Bishop; Enterprise, AL; ed/BS 1950, MS 1972 Troy St Univ; mil/Ala NG 1944; USN 1944-46; pa/Ret'd HS SS Tchr & Basketball Coach; Phi Delta Kappa; NEA; Fla Tchrs Profession; Holmes Co Tchrs Assn; NCET; Fla Coun Eng Tchrs; Fla Coun SS Tchrs; Pres Holmes Co Tchrs Assn; cp/Enterprise C of C; Am Legion Post #73; Disabled Am Vets, Enterprise

Chapt #9; VP Pea River Hist & Geneal Soc; r/Bapt; hon/Plaque Presented by Poplar Springs HS 1979 in Apprec for 30 Yrs Ser; Plaque Presented 1979 by Holmes Co Tchrs Assn; Cert Merit from VFW of US for Outstg Spokesman for Freedom.

BISKAMP, MONA SPENCER oc/Realtor; b/Apr 4, 1930; h/4831 S Lindhurst, Dallas, TX 75229; ba/Dallas; m/William Taylor Sr; c/William Taylor Jr, Mark S, Brett K, Eric E, Carol E; p/Edgar R Spencer (dec); Myrtle S Burns, Gonzales, TX; ed/GRI, CRS Azusa Col; pa/Realtor; Guest Lectr Univs, Convs, & Profl Grps; Trustee Dallas Symph; Bd Dirs Dallas Civic Opera; Dallas Bd Rltrs; Wom's Coun Rltrs; Rltrs Nat Mktg Inst; Dallas Coun World Affairs; Former Mem The 500 Inc; Dallas Geol & Geophy Aux; r/Epis; hon/Top Prodr Listings & Sales fro Henry S Miller Rltrs 1971-79; Multi-Million $ Clb.

BLACK, BARBARA JOYCE oc/Instructor; b/Sept 20, 1948; h/The Lodge Apts #U102, Jackson, MS 39204; ba/Cleveland, MS; p/G H and Lutie H Black, Columbia, MS; pa/Instr Delta St Univ; Coor Fash Mdsg, Delta St Univ; Dir Delta Models Fash Tm; Lectr & Retail Bus Conslt; AAUW; BPW Clb; So Mktg Assn; r/Bapt; hon/Outstg Yng Wom Am; Finalist Miss St Chicken Cooking Contest 1979; Omicron Delta Kappa Ldrship & S'ship Frat.

BLACKBURN, JAMES ROSS JR oc/Corporation President, Pilot; b/Feb 28, 1930; h/Miami, FL; ba/PO Box 59-2032 AMF, Miami, FL 33159; m/Joyce Gaynelle; c/Linda Marie; Lisa Joyce; p/James Ross (dec) and Esther Louise Blackburn, Tampa, FL; ed/Davidson Col 1948-49; BBA 1953, Post Grad Study 1968-69 Univ Miami; mil/USAF 1953-57 Pilot; pa/Pilot En Airlines 1957-; Mktg Conslt Comrex Corp 1967-73; Pres J R Blackburn & Assoc 1974-76; Pres Blackburn Assoc Inc 1977-; ALPA; Chmn Mil Airlift Command Flight Safety 1967-69; Chm Pilots Communications Com 1973; AMS/OIL Dlrs Assn; Order of Quiet Birdmen; cp/Soc So Fams; Am Sec Coun; US Sen Bus Adv Bd; Steering Com Mem; Mil Order Stars & Bars; r/Bapt; hon/W/W Aviation 1973, S&SW 1980; Editor: *The MPG News* 1980.

BLACKBURN, LAURA BETH oc/Architectural-Interior Designer, Construction Company Executive; b/Feb 19, 1942; h/2315 Pk Ave, Richmond, VA 23220; ba/Same; p/Cecil Clyde Blackburn; Margaret Thelma Kreisheimer; ed/BS Westhampton Col of Univ Richmond 1961, MBA Wash Univ 1963; pa/Archl/Interior Design; Constr Co Exec; Home Bldrs Assn; Local & St Bd Rltrs; Lectr; cp/Big Sister Prog; Va Mtl Htl Prog; r/Prot; hon/W/W Am Wom; Phi Beta Kappa; Bus Wom Yr 1967; Mtl Hlth Vol Yr 1963; Contbr Articles to Var Jouns.

BLACKMAN, BETTY LOU oc/Director Social Services; b/Oct 2, 1930; h/1323 Karen Dr, Venice, FL 33595; ba/Venice, FL; m/Frank Ogilvie Blackman (dec); c/Katherine Lynn, Brenda Sue; p/Jim (dec) and Ola Vastiah Fowler (dec); ed/Columbia Bible Col 1948-51; So Bapt Theol Sem 1964-65; BA 1968, MSSW 1970 Univ Louisville; pa/Dir Social Sers Venice Hosp; Clin Social Wkr Sarasota Palms Psychi Hosp; Sr Psychi Social Wkr River Region Mtl Hlth Agcy; Psychi Social Wkr Fam Relats Ctr, Louisville, Ky; Mgr Fowler's Toddler's Inn Child Care Nsry; Rec Dir Perrine Bapt Ch; Nat Assn Social Wkrs; Nat Assn Social Wkrs Fla Chapt; Am Assn Marriage & Fam Cnslrs; Ky Soc Clin Social Wkrs; Nat Soc Hosp Social Work Dirs of Am Hosp Assn; Fla Chapt Soc Hosp Social Work Dirs; cp/Chm Ctr United Appeal 1974 & 75; Gtr Louisville Area Mtl Retard Com; Pres Elect Venice Area Commun Coun; Chm Ad Hoc Com Regarding Facilities for Plment of Fin Needy Sr Citizens; Venice Hosp Patient Risk Com; Venice Hosp Patient Ed Com; Bd Mem Venice Area Widow to Widow Prog; Adv Com Ctr for Cnslg and Human Devel; Lectr & Wkshop Presenter for Venice Hosp Staff Devel; Hon Crew Mem McHappy Day for Kids; Prog & Sers Eval Com SW Fla Retirement Ctr; Venice Hosp Employee of Month Com; r/So Bapt; hon/W/W S&SW 1980; One of Sarasota Co's 10 Most Eligible Bachelorettes 1980-81.

BLACKMON, DANNY ROBERT oc/Manager and Assistant Vice President; b/Jan 29, 1952; h/2503 Downing St Apt A-6, Wilson, NC 278093; ba/Wilson; p/Hallie Robert and Thelma Taylor Blackmon, Selma, NC; ed/AAS Johnston Tech Col 1973; BS BA Atlantic Christian Col 1980; Courses Am Inst Bnkrs; pa/Asst VP, Mgr Installment Loan Dept, First Citizens Bank & Trust Co; Am Inst Bnkrs; cp/Dem Clb; Fundraising Cystic Fibrosis, Heart Fund, Others; r/Free Will Bapt.

BLACKMON, JO ANN oc/Social Service Coordinator; b/Oct 22, 1953; h/522 Pride Ave, Auburn, AL 35830; ba/Auburn; m/Cody Douglas; p/Leo Burton; Josephine Edwards; ed/BA; pa/Social Sers Coor; cp/Social Concern Com; Elder Ser Provider; r/Meth; hon/Alpha Kappa Alpha; Jr Achmt.

BLAIR, BOBBY CHARLES oc/Project Director; b/Sept 21, 1941; h/4200 Beacon Ct, Bartlesville, OK 74003; ba/B'ville; p/Charles Warren and Hazel Louise Blair, Shawnee, OK; ed/BS Okla St Univ 1964; MBA

27

Univ Tulsa 1969; pa/Mining Chems Proj Dir; Phillips Petro Co 1964-; Soc Plastics Engrs; cp/Republican; r/Disciples of Christ; hon/Co-Inventor & Patentee "High Speed Fibrillation Process"; Phi Theta Kappa; Sons of Am Revol AFROTC Medal 1961; Sigma Tau; Wentz Ser Schlr 1962; Author: "Odorization of LPG and Natural Gas."

BLAIR, MAJOR ELLIOT oc/Businessman; b/Nov 16, 1929; h/2000 Stone, Killeen, TX 76541; m/Mary Patricia; c/Major Elliot Jr, Randall Scott, Kellie Ann; p/John W and Agnes R Blair, Andalusia, AL; ed/Univ Ala 1948-50; mil/AUS 1950-53; pa/Owner Southtown Auto Parts; Universal CIT Credit Corp 1954-59; cp/Mayor Killeen 1976-80; Dir Tex Mun Leag; Pres Regional TML; Pres Ctrl Tex Coun of Gov; Many Others; r/Meth; hon/Many.

BLAISE, PHYNYE LOBUE GARB oc/Artist; b/Nov 26; h/106 N Magnolia St, Hammond, LA 70401; m/Harris K Garb (dec); 2nd John Mervin; c/Carol Diane Garb Alack; p/Angelo (dec) and Francesca Paula Plescia Lobue (dec); ed/SEn La Univ 1938-41; pa/Artist; Co-Fdr "Town & Country Art Leag of Tangipahoa Parish", now the Hammond Art Guild; Life Mem New Orleans Art Assn; Charter Mem France-La Fest; Charter Mem Intl Soc Artists in NY; r/Roman Cath; hon/Paintings Accepted to Hang at Annual La Art Exhib in Old St Capital at Baton Rouge; 1st Place Winner Zemurray Commun Ctr 1969; 1st Place Agridustrial Futurama at SEn La Univ 1964-70; Hon Mention for Still Life; Many Others.

BLAKE, JOHN EVERETT JR oc/Life Underwriter; b/Dec 1, 1950; h/600 N 8th St, Opelika, AL 36801; ba/Auburn; m/Charlsie Taylor; c/Charlsie Denise, John Everett III; p/John E Sr and Ruth Lechner Blake; ed/BS Auburn Univ 1975; pa/Underwriter, NY Life Ins Co; Lee Co Assn of Life Underwriters, Pres 1980; cp/Kiwanis Clb; r/Bapt; hon/Nat Sales Achmt Awd 1978, 79, 80; Star Clb 1976, 77, 78, 79.

BLAKELEY, POLLY FIGG oc/Civic Leader; b/June 24, 1924; h/12 Lagomar Rd, Palm Bch, FL 33480; ba/Brookline, MA; m/Gerald W; c/Jacqueline Tagle Ralson, Terry Tagle Taylor, Amanda Churchill; p/Howard and Edith Figg (dec); cp/Repub Clb Fla; Leukemia Soc Palm Bch, Fla; Bd Metro Ctr, Boston; Bd Sidney Farber Cancer Ctr, Boston; Bd Lesley Col, Cambridge (Mass); VP: Boston Ballet, Buddy Dog (Boston), Farm & Gdn; Bd Dirs French Lib, Boston; Bd Friends of Symph; Ofcr Boston Cir for Charity; V-Chm: Boston Ballet, NE Farm & Gdn Bd, Buddy Dog Humane Soc Bd; r/Prot.

BLAKENEY, ROGER NEAL oc/Professor; b/Sept 19, 1939; h/2220 Bering Dr #7, Houston, TX 77057; ba/Houston; c/Christopher Allan, Benjamin Garrett; ed/BS Tex A&M Univ 1964; MA 1967, PhD 1969 Univ Houston; mil/AUS 1960-62; pa/Univ Houston, Col of Bus Adm: Assoc Prof Orgnl Behavior & Mgmt 1974-, Assoc Prof Behavioral Mgmt Sci 1972-74, Coor Indust Relats Res, Human Resources Ctr 1971-72, Dir Masters Prog 1972, Asst Prof Behavioral Mgmt Sci 1969-72, Instr Mgmt 1968-69, Mem Tchg Staff of Mgmt Devel Ctr for Var Progs 1969-, Mem Staff of Interviewing Inst, Pers Psychol Sers Ctr 1966-; Intl Transactional Analysis Assn; Am Psychol Assn; Acad of Mgmt; Editor: "The Indiu & the Org", "Contemp Pers Mgmt", "Current Issues in Transactional Analysis"; Editorial Bd Transactional Analysis Journal; Pres Blakeney Assocs; hon/Pub'd Author; Sigma Xi; Beta Gamma Sigma; Sigma Iota Epsilon; Psi Chi; Alpha Kappa Delta; Alpha Zeta; Fellow ABI; ABIRA Mem.

BLANCHARD, DANNY EDWARD oc/Professor, Management Consultant; b/Nov 4, 1949; m/Debra; c/Lashanice; ed/BA Oakwood Col 1971; MA Loma-Linda Univ 1973; EdS Vanderbilt 1976; PhD 1979; pa/Prof Psych Oakwood Col; Mgmt Conslt; APA; APGA; Assn Adventist Ser Assn; cp/Pres Bd Rural Sr Sers; r/Seventh Day Adventist; hon/AUS Letter Commend 1977; 13 Pubs in Var Jours.

BLANCHARD, PATRICK G oc/Bank President; Farmer; b/May 15, 1943; h/8109 Sir Galahad Dr, Evans, GA 30809; ba/Martinez, GA; m/Gwen B; c/Mary Brannen; p/John Pierce Sr and Mildred Pollard Blanchard, Appling, GA; ed/BBA Ga So Col; Grad Study, NWn Univ; pa/Pres Ga St Bank, Martinez; Bank Adm Inst; Ga Bkrs Assn; cp/Exc Clb; r/Bapt; hon/Asst St Treas Ga.

BLANKENSHIP, RODNEY WAYNE oc/Assistant Corporate Controller; Executive; b/July 4, 1948; h/3566 Edyefield Dr, Montgomery, AL 36111; ba/Mont; m/Kathryn B; c/Gina G, Benjamin H; p/Lewis and A France Blankenship, Alexander City, AL; ed/BS Auburn Univ 1970; pa/Vulcan Mats Corp 1970-72; Asst Corp Controller, Blount Inc 1972-; VP Indow Indust & Mobile Home Mfr; Nat Assn Accts; cp/Cloverdale Commun Ctr Coun; Fball, Baseball Coach YMCA; U Meth Lay Spkr; Chm Coun on Mins; Adm Bd & Fin Com, Pastor Parish Relats Com, Whitfield Meml U Meth Ch; r/Meth.

BLANTON, ERNESTINE MYNARD oc/Teacher, Painter; b/Nov 6, 1926; h/Rt 6 Box 273A, Bristol, TN 37620; m/Lawson H; c/Lem, Julie;

p/John Noah (dec) and Ruby Crumpler Mynard (dec); ed/Auburn Univ 1948-51; BS Athens Col 1965; Univ Ala 1970-71; MS A & M Univ 1971; pa/Art Tchr Bristol Public Sch Sys; Watercolorist; cp/Pres, Publicity Chm, Bd Dirs Bristol Art Guild & Mus; Tenn Watercolor Soc; r/Meth; hon/Best in Show for Watercolor, Jr Wom's Leag Art Show 1978; Best in Show for Watercolor Jr Wom's Leag Art Show 1980; Awd of Dist for Watercolor 1977, 1980, Va Highlands Fine Arts Fest; Best in Show by Visitor Vote 1980, Va Highlands Fine Arts Fest; Other Awds in Local Shows.

BLANTON, FRED JR oc/Lawyer; b/July 2, 1919; h/1912 K C Dement Ave, Fultondale, AL 35068; ba/Birmingham, AL; m/Mercer P McAvoy; p/Fred Sr (dec) and Mary Covington Blanton (dec); ed/AB cum laude Birmingham-So Col 1935-39; LLB 1942, JD 1970 Univ Va Law Sch; ML 1979 Univ Ala Law Sch; Cook Fellowship Univ Mich Law Sch 1951; mil/USNR 1942; Adm Ofcr 10 Yrs; Comdr; pa/Lawyer Pvt Gen Prac, Birmingham; Supreme Ct of US 1963; US Ct Appeals DC 1968; US Ct Claims 1970; US Tax Ct 1948; US Dist Cts - No, Mid & So Dists of Ala 1946; Ala St Bar; Com Code Revision; Adv Com Continuing Legal Ed 1979-81; Am Soc EEG Technol; cp/Gen Gorgas Post #1; Am Legion; Kelly Ingram Post #668 VFW; Jefferson Co Republican Exec Com 1979-; r/Epis; hon/Cand Chief Just Supreme Ct Ala 1976; Pubs: "The Federal Tort Claims Act in Action"; "EEG - A Trial Aid"; Others.

BLASIUS, JACK MICHAEL oc/Executive; b/Feb 29, 1932; h/1017 W O Ezell Blvd, Spartanburg, SC 29304; m/Sybil Claire; c/Michael Stribling, Kimberly Anne; p/Arthur George (dec) and Jessie Pate Blasius, Tuscaloosa, AL; ed/BS 1954, MBA 1957 Univ Ala; pa/9 Yrs Indust Salesman; Kaiser Aluminum Corp: Area Sales Mgr, Nat Mgr Foundry Prods; Presently Pres & Gen.Mgr Batchelder-Blasius Inc; Past Dir Evelyn Woods Rdg Dynamics; Past Dir Consumer Am Risk Mgmt; Dir Charles Batchelder Co; Dir Statewide Waste Oil & Chem Corp; Bd Dirs First Nat Bank S'burg; Dir & Secy Aluminum Recycle Assn; Dir C of C S'burg, Bd Dirs S'burg Girls' Home; Bd Dirs Jr Achmt S'burg; Pres's Clb Wofford Col; Clemson Ipta S'ship Donor; Fdrs Clb Univ Ala; Thousand Clb Ga Int Technol; Soc Die Casting Engrs; Am Foundryman Soc; Inst Scrap Iron & Steel; Alum Recycling Assn; S'burg Devel Assn; cp/Exec Dirs Clb S'burg YMCA; Rotary Clb; S'burg Country Clb; Piedmont Clb; Atlanta Ath Clb; Ansley Golf Clb; hon/W/W SC; Personalities of South; Outstg Am in South; Dic Intl Biog for Dist'd Achmt; W/W Fin & Indust.

BLAYTON, DORIS ADA oc/Lawyer, Teacher, Accountant; b/Oct 19, 1922; h/1235 Martin Luther King Jr Dr SW, Atlanta, GA 30314; ba/Same; ed/AB; MBA; JD; MA; p/Jesse B Sr (dec) and Willa M Daniels Blayton, Atlanta, GA; pa/St Bar of Ga; Nat Bar, Corp Law Sect; Gate City Bar Assn; Black Lwyrs Conf; NEA; UTA; NCNW; Delta Sigma Theta; cp/YWCA; r/Bapt; hon/Personalities of Atlanta; Nom to Book of Hon.

BLEVINS, DALLAS RAY oc/Assistant Professor; b/Dec 22, 1938; h/6663 Diane Rd, Jacksonville, FL 32211; ba/Jacksonville; m/Lois Eunice; c/Deborah Lynn, Teresa Lee, Jennifer Kay; p/Virgil James and Mary Birtha Blevins, St Mesa, AZ; ed/MBA Univ Omaha 1965; MBA Univ S Fla 1968; DBA Fla St Univ 1976; mil/USAF 1958-69; pa/Asst Prof Fin: Valdosta St Col 1970-74; Univ Ala-Birmingham 1976-79; Univ N Fla 1979-; Am Soc Mil Comptrollers; Adv Nat Ed Com; cp/Mem 2 Fin Coms B'ham Regional Hosp Coun 1978-79; Bd Dirs Regional Hlth Sys Agcy 1979-; r/Preacher & Tchr w Var Congress of Ch of Christ; hon/Acad S'ship 1956; Commend for High Grade Pt 1968; Outstg Contbns Awd 1965; 1 of 5 Outstg Yng Men 1971.

BLEVINS, E EDWARD oc/Corporation President; b/Dec 15, 1942; h/Irving, TX; ba/Am Bank Bldg Sch 301, 800 W Airport Fwy, Irving, TX 75062; c/Eddie, Robby, Tina, Scott, Melinda; p/Mable Carr, Middletown, OH; ed/BS Miami Univ 1968; MBA Univ Dallas 1976; pa/Pres WARM-EE Corp; Prin Blevins & Assocs; Am Mgmt Assn; Sales & Mktg Execs; Dallas Ad Leag; Intl Word Processing Assn; cp/Instr N Lake Col; r/Prot; hon/Dist Awd SBA 1977; W/W 1980; Sigma Iota Epsilon 1976; Articles to: Jour of Bus Harvard Univ Press.

BLEVINS, MARY FRANCES DOBBS oc/Banker; Assistant Vice President Paint and Wallpaper Store; b/Nov 22, 1914; h/312 Hickory Hill Rd, Nicholasville, KY 40356; ba/N'ville; m/James Clarence; p/Charles Alvin and Rose Bishop Dobbs; ed/Bank Adm Inst; pa/Asst VP & Former Bkkpr Blevins Paint & Wallpaper Store; Banker; Former Mem Lena Madison Phillips BPW Clb; cp/Treas Withers Meml Lib; Former Treas Jessamine Co Bd Ed; Former Treas Salvation Army; Solicitor Am Red Cross & Arthritis Dr; r/Disciples of Christ; Former Chm of Deaconesses; hon/W/W Am Wom; Ky Col 1963; Rec'd 20 Yr, 30 Yr & 35 Yr Ser Awds w the First Nat Bank & Trust Co.

BLEVINS, MELVIN EUGENE oc/School Principal; b/Feb 7, 1949; h/Rt 2 Box 300, Morristown, TN 37814; p/Levi C Sr and Julia B Blevins,

Russellville, TN; ed/AA Morristown Col 1969; MS Carson Newman Col 1971; MEd Union Col 1974; pa/Prin Lincoln Hgts Elem Sch; M'town Ed Assn; TEA; NEA; Intl Rdg Assn; cp/Bd Dirs U Way, Progressive Day Care Ctr; Minority Affairs Com, TEA; Tchr Sponsor Red Cross; M'town City Schs Red Cross Rep; hon/Outstg Yng Man Am 1972.

BLEVINS, PHILLIP K oc/Plastic Surgeon; b/Mar 30, 1942; h/Lexington, KY; m/Mary Jo McDaniel; p/Guy Kimble and Marie Guffey Blevins, Monticello, KY; ed/AB 1963, MD 1967 Univ Ky; Gen Surg Residency Harvard 1968-75; Plastic Surg Residency Univ Miss 1975-77; mil/USN Med Corp pa/Plastic & Reconstructive Surg; AMA, KMA; Fayette Co Med Soc; Am Soc Plastic & Reconstructive Surg; SESPRS; Am Cleft Palate Assn; Am Burn Assn; Lexintgon Surg Soc; cp/Civil War Round Table; Order of Ky Cols; r/Epis; hon/Navy Commend Medal 1970.

BLICKSILVER, EDITH oc/Associate Professor; b/Jan 6, 1926; h/1800 Timothy Dr NE, Atlanta, GA 30329; ba/Atlanta; m/Jack; c/Paul, Diane, Robert; p/Simon and Fanny Stettner (dec); ed/BA, MA Smith Col; pa/Assoc Prof Eng, Ga Inst Technol 1963-, NEn Univ 1962-63; Instr Ga Inst Technol Night Sch 1961-62 & 63-65; MLA; Soc for Studies of Multi-Ethnic Lit of US; Col Eng Assn; AAUW; hon/Author *The Ethnic American Wom: Problems, Protests, Lifestyle,* 1979; *Literature as Social Criticism* and *Women's Ethnic Studies* anthology collection.

BLIESENER, ADA MICHELMANN oc/Retired College Teacher and Symphony Cellist; b/Oct 9, 1909; h/Box 119, Brownsboro, AL 35741; c/Betty B Ayers, Carl Jr; p/Henry Ludig (dec) and Ida Meyer Michelman (dec); ed/BMus; MMus; pa/Ret'd Col Tchr; Ret'd Symph Cellist; Pvt Tchg & Mus Comp; r/Prot; hon/Soc Am Mus 1933; Chgo & 5th Intl Competitions for Wom Comprs 1966.

BLISS, MARY ANN oc/Marriage, Family and Child Therapist; b/June 28, 1947; ba/Faith Counseling Center, Faith Presb Ch, John Knox Rd, Tallahassee, FL; c/Elizabeth Manning; p/Mary E Campbell, Palm Bch Gdns, FL; ed/AA Palm Bch Jr Col 1967; BA Univ RI 1969; MA US Intl Univ 1976; pa/Marriage & Fam Therapist; Dir Rehab Sers, Goodwill Industs; Voc Rehab Cnslr; Assoc Mem Am Psych Assn; Clin Mem Am Assn Marriage & Fam Therapists; Nat Rehab Assn; cp/Pres Tallahassee Chapt Fla Rehab Assn; Secy-Treas Tallahassee Convocation; r/Epis; hon/Profl Vol of Yr, Fam Sers Assn, San Diego, Calif 1975.

BLOMSTEDT, ROBERT KENT oc/Associate Professor; b/Feb 17, 1931; h/901 S 23rd St; Kingsville, TX 78363; m/Dona Linder; c/J Kirby, Russell D, Tarin Kay; p/Carl Gus Blomstedt (dec) and Laura Blomstedt Cederblom, Kenedy, TX; ed/BS Tex Luth Col 1952; MEd 1967, PhD 1974 Univ Tex; pa/Tex A&I Univ: Assoc Prof Ed, Undergrad Elem Tchr Ed Fac, Undergrad Second Tchr Ed Fac, Grad Fac, Doct Fac; 12 Public Sch Elem, Jr High, HS Tchr; 2 Yrs Dean Admissions Tex Luth Coll; 12 Yrs Tchr Ed Tex A&I Univ; Intl Platform Assn; Phi Delta Kappa; NEA; Tex Assn Col Tchrs; Tex St Tchrs Assn; Tex Assn Tchr Edrs; Tex Coun Tchrs Maths; Tex Soc Col Tchrs Ed; SW Ednl Res Assn; St Tchr Ctr Com; Tex; A&I Univ Tchr Ctr Orgr/Dir; Tex A&I Univ Fringe Benefits Com; Chm NCATE Study Elem Curric Com; Chm So Assn Dept Ed Self Study Com; Chm-Secy Dept Ed Adv Coun; Chm Dept Ed CBTE Study Com; Chm Eng Proficiency Study Com; Chm Dept Ed Curric Ctr Com; Mem Dept Ed Grad Screening Com; Kingsville Rotary Clb; r/Bapt; hon/Summer Nat Sci Foun Stipend Awd 1962 & 65; Academic Yr NSF Stipend Awd 1966-67; Title IV Experienced Tchr Stipend Awd 1968-69; Gov's Whitehouse Com on Chd & Yth 1972-73; Tex A&I Univ Cap & Gown Soc Top Ten Tchrs 1972-73, 1973-74; Bapt Student Ctr Fav Prof Awd 1973-74, 1975-76; Outstg Edrs Am 1974-75; Intl Platform Assn Selection 1978; W/W S&SW 1979; Intl W/W Intells 1980.

BLOOD, GORDON W oc/Speech Pathologist; b/Aug 25, 1951; h/5 Beachpoint Dr, Oxford, OH 45056; m/Ingrid M; c/Ryan Thomas; p/Gordon Patrick and Cathleen Donovan Blood; ed/BS St Univ Col-Buffalo 1974; MA 1976, PhD 1978, Bowling Green St Univ; pa/Asst Prof Dept Commun Disorders, Radford Univ; Clin Sers Bd, St of Va; Am Speech-Lang-Hearing Assn; Va Speech & Hearing Assn; r/Rom Cath; hon/S'ship to Study in Africa 1973; NSF Grant 1974; Tchg Fellow 1976-78; W/W S&SW 1980; Author Over 15 Articles & 12 Presentations for St, Nat & Intl Convs & Jours.

BLOOD, INGRID MARIA oc/Assistant Professor, Audiologist; b/Mar 30; m/Gordon W; c/Ryan Thomas; p/Rudolph and Hildagarde Unczowsky, Clifton, NJ; ed/BS Montclair St Col 1974; MA 1976, PhD 1978 Bowling Green St Univ; pa/Audiologist; Am Speech & Hearing Assn; Va Speech & Hearing Assn; Acoustical Soc of Am; Am Audiology Soc, Clin/Res Bd & Coun Mem; r/Rom Cath; hon/W/W S&SW 1980; Mass Communicators Awd 1978; Over 15 Presentations to Convs & 11 Articles to St, Nat & Intl Jours.

BLOOM, HAROLD EDWARD oc/Market Research; b/Apr 5, 1946; h/159 SW 101 Way, Coral Springs, FL 33065; ba/Ft Lauderdale, FL; m/Ellen T Friedman; c/Allison, Robert; p/Sidney and Rose Bloom, Lauder Hill, FL; ed/BBA Univ Miami 1968; MBA City Univ NY 1971; pa/Munar Mkt Plan'g Proj Dir 1968-71; Grey Ad Asst, Tech Dir 1971-73; ITT Contl Baking, Mkt Res Mgr 1973-74; Coca-Cola Mgr Consumer Res 1974-78; Pillsbury Co Dir Mkt Res 1978-79; STP Corp Dir Mkt Res 1979-; Am Mktg Assn; Am Mgmt Assn; r/Jewish; hon/W/W S&SW 1980; Article in *Advertising Research* 1977.

BLUMBERG, MICHAEL Z oc/Physician, Assistant Professor; b/July 29, 1945; h/1602 Swansburg Dr, Richmond, VA 23233; ba/Richmond; m/Barbara; c/Jessica, Jason; p/Jerome Blumberg, Margate, FL; Vivian Sterger, Wyncote, PA; ed/BS Brandeis Univ 1963-67; MD Jefferson Med Col 1967-71; mil/USAF 1975-77 Major; pa/Phy; Asst Prof Pediatrics, Med Col of Va; Assoc Va Allergy & Pulmonary; Fellow Am Acad Pediatrics; Richmond Acad Med; Va Med Soc; SE Allergy Soc; Fellow Am Col Allergists; Mem Acad Allergy & Immun; AMA; Va Lung Assn; r/Jewish; hon/Author Many Pubs; Clemens von Pirquet Awd 1974, Am Col Allergy.

BLYTHE, LENAMAE oc/Retired Teacher; b/Jan 16, 1906; h/8 Blythe Ct, Berea, KY 40403; m/Robert H (dec); p/James (dec) and Cornelia Coleman (dec); ed/AB Ky St Col 1933; MA Ind Univ 1941; pa/Ret'd HS Tchr Eng & Hist; Nat Ret'd Tchrs Assn; 2nd VP Berea Br AAUW; cp/Bd Dirs Berea Hosp; Pres Berea Hosp Aux; KET Regional Coun; r/Bapt; hon/Poem Pub'd By the Tenn & Ky Soc of Poets 1976.

BOARD, SALLY ANN oc/Retired Dietitian; b/Apr 2, 1910; h/902 S E St, Culpeper, VA 22701; m/John S; c/John Walfred Ellison; p/Harvey Wilhelm (dec) and Emma Sue Linkous (dec); ed/BS VPI & SU 1930; Cert Dietitian Med Col Va 1932; pa/Ret'd Home Ec Tchr, SC & Va; Dietitian Jefferson Josp, Roanoke & Catawba Sanatorium; 1st Red Cross Nutritionist in Va, Roanoke Chapt; 1st Nutritionist Va Hlth Dept; Exec Dir Richmond Area Heart Assn; Nutritionist & Exec Dir Richmond Area Dairy Coun; Pres Va Dietetic Assn; Am Dietetic Assn; Dist Dietetic Assn; Former Mem Soc for Nutrition Ed; Nutrition Today Soc; cp/Pres Culpeper UDC; Pres Culpeper Garden Clb; Bd of Commun Concert Assn; Served on Bd Co-Hope; Served on Bd FORE; Culpeper Chapt Va Mus; Culpeper Hist Com; Others; r/Presb; hon/Kolbe Awd for Outstg Dietitian 1963; Commun Ser Awd 1973; W/W Am Wom & S&SW; Intl Biog; Va Lives; Intl W/W Intells; Commun Ldrs Va.

BOBO, EUGENIA ANNETTE oc/Assistant Head Resident; b/June 18, 1960; h/118 Alfalfa Ave, Osceola, AR 72370; ba/Fayetteville, AR; p/Garland and Ora L Bobo, Osceola, AR; ed/Att'd Univ Ark; pa/Adm & Pers Mgmt; Asst Hd Resident, Reid Hall, Univ Ark; r/Bapt; hon/Outstg SMILE Student 1980; Campus Ldrship Awd 1980; Delta Sigma Theta, 2nd VP; Phi Eta Sigma 1979.

BOCHMAN, WILLIAM CHARLES JR oc/Evangelist; b/Aug 14, 1946; h/3322-S S Semoran Blvd; Orlando, FL 32807; ba/Orlando; m/Julie Hodge; c/William C III; p/W C Bochman, Sumter, SC; ed/BS Univ SC 1976; Columbia Grad Sch of Bible & Missions 1976-77; Cand Master's Deg Luther Rice Sem; mil/USMC; pa/Evangelist, Jim Wilson Evangelistic Assn; Assoc Pastor First Bapt Ch, Sumter; Prog Dir WDXY Inc, Sumter; cp/Former Song Ldr & Mem Lions Clb; r/So Bapt; hon/Broadcasting Excellence Awd 1971; Author: *Ingredients to Faithful Christian Living* 1980; Article on Personal Life.

BODEN, LILY WRIGHT oc/Homemaker; b/May 26, 1937; m/David Robert; c/David Michael, Deborah Anne; ed/Business Col; pa/Disher Steel Pers Dept, Toronto, Can 1960; cp/Chm Mail Delivery in Gaston Co Hosp NC 1973-74; Pres Gaston Gators Swim Tm 1973-74; Howard Co Ark Crusade Ch Am Can 1978-79; Pres Am Cancer Howard Co 1980; Pres U Meth Wom, Nashville, Ark 1980; hon/Broke Goal for 1978 & 1979 Crusade Dr for Am Cancer Soc.

BODNAR, DONALD GEORGE oc/Research Electrical Engineer; b/Apr 30, 1941; h/Atlanta, GA; ba/Ga Inst Technol, Atlanta, GA 30332; m/Judith Anne Boring; c/David Stephen, Donald George Jr; p/Steve and Daisy Bodnar, Ft Lauderdale, FL; ed/BEE magna cum laude Ga Inst Technol 1963; MSEE Mass Inst Technol 1964; PhD Ga Inst Technol 1969; pa/Ga Inst Technol: Res Engr 1970-73, Sr Res Engr 1973-, Mgr Electromagnetics Ofc 1973-75, Sr Scist Antennas & Countermeasures Div 1977-; Engrg Staff Conslt, Sperry Rand 1969-70; Sr Mem IEEE, Assoc Editor IEEE AP-S Newsletter; Mem IEEE AP-S Adm Com; r/Unitarian Universalist; hon/Alfred P Sloan Fellow 1959-63; Outstg Elec Engrg Grad 1963; Nat Aero & Space Adm Fellow 1963-66; Nat Sci Foun Fellow 166-67; Author Many Major Reports & Pubs inclg "A Lightweight HWL Radar Antenna"; "Frequency Scanned Antenna Study"; Others.

BOE, GERARD PATRICK oc/Health Care Administrator, Scientist; b/Jan 20, 1936; h/3601 Bimini Ct, Augusta, GA 30909; ba/Ft Gordon, GA; m/Irene Margaret; c/Steven Alan; Christine Ann; p/Harold D Boe, Miami, FL; ed/BS W Va Wesleyan Col 1954-58; Univ Miami 1958-59; MS Ohio St Univ 1967-69; PhD Tex A&M Univ 1974-76; mil/USMC 1960-63 Air Intell Ofcr; AUS 1963-81 Clin Lab Ofcr, Hlth Care Admr; pa/Hlth Care Admr; Med Lab Scist; Beta Beta Beta Hon Biol Soc; Intl Soc Clin Lab Technol; Am Soc Allied Hlth Professions; Fdg Mem Soc Air Force Med Lab Scists; Soc Armed Forces Med Lab Scists; Affil Mem Am Soc Clin Path; cp/Chm Brazos Co Blood Prog; Chm Hlth Careers Adv Com; Med Lab Asst Adv Com; r/Meth; hon/Mil: 2 Awds Army Commend Medal 1965 & 74; Bronze Star Medal 1971; Civic: Cert Apprec from Am Red Cross 1976; Journalistic: ISCLT - Ortho Diagnostic Sci Paper Awd 1972; MLO Writing Contest Hon Mention 1980; Author & Co-Author Num Pubs inclg "Military Blood Programs in a US Army Hospital Overseas'; "Some Characteristics of Blood Donor Reactions."

BOECKMAN, CHARLES oc/Author; b/Nov 9, 1920; ba/322 Del Mar Blvd, Corpus Christi, TX 78404; m/Patricia Ellen; c/Sharla Tricia; p/Charles (dec) and Elizabeth von Boeckmann (dec); ed/Att'd Tex Luth Col 1938-39; pa/Am Soc Jours & Authors; r/Luth; hon/Contemporary Authors; DIB; Something About the Author; Papers in Archives at Univ of Oregon; More Than 1000 Short Stories & Articles Pub'd in US & Abroad; Books incl *Surviving Your Parents Divorce* 1980; *And the Beat Goes On* 1972; *Unsolved Riddles of the Ages* 1965.

BOGGS, CORINNE CLAIBORNE (LINDY) oc/Member of Congress; h/623 Bourbon St, New Orleans, LA 70130; ba/Wash DC; m/Hale (dec); c/Thomas H Jr, Barbara B Sigmund, Corinne B Roberts; p/Roland Claiborne (dec); Corinne Morrison Jacobs (dec); ed/BA Sophie Newcomb Col, Tulane Univ 1935; pa/Precnt Capt 5th Precnt, 12th Ward of New Orleans 1939; Elected to Ho of Reps 1973; Ch-wom Dem Nat Conv 1976; House Appropriations Com 1977-; Subcom Energy & Water Devel; Subcom Housing & Urban Devel; Smithsonian Bd of Regents 1977-78; Cong Shipyard Coalition: Co-Chm, Fdg Mem, Port Caucus & Cong-wom's Caucus; Exec Com Dem Cong Campaign Com; Dem Nat Campaign Steering Com 1976; cp/Dem Nat Com; La St Nat Party; Co-Chm Johnson-Humphrey Inaugural Ball 1965; Co-Chm Dem Cong Campaign Dinner 1965; Co-Chm "4 for 64" Registration Campaign; Co-Chm "Lady Bird Spec"; Co-Chm Kennedy-Johnson Inaugural Ball 1961 & Kennedy First Anniversary Gala 1962; Chm Oper Crossroads 1950's; Wom's Nat Dem Clb; Fdr-Pres Dem Cong Wives Forum; Pres Cong Clb 1971-72; r/Rom Cath; hon/Hon LLD Tulane Univ 1978; Salute to Wom, Nat Daughs of Penelope; Hon LLD 1977 Loyola Univ; Hon DLitt, St Mary of the Woods Col 1977; Eleanor Roosevelt Humanities Awd, St of Israel Bonds 1977; Torch of Liberty, Anti-Defamation Leag of B'nai B'rith 1976; Rec'd 1st AMVETS Aux for Humanitarian Endeavors; Recip Dist'd Ser Medal, St Mary's Dominican Col 1976; 1 of 10 Outstg Persons 1976, New Orleans Inst for Human Understanding; Fellow Tulane Univ Coun; Hon DPS Trinity Col 1975; Weiss Meml Awd, Nat Conf of Christians & Jews 1974; Mother Gerard Phelan Gold Medal, Virginia's Marymount Col; BBC Documentary Film "Woman of Action" 1965; Hon Life Mbrships Sev Nat Orgs.

BOGIE, NORA A BROCK oc/Nurse; b/Mar 26, 1920; h/Rt 2, Hustonville, KY 40437; m/William Henry; c/Barbara Bogie Spalding, William Foster; Debra Bogie Williams; p/Elga and Myrtie Brock (dec), Stanford, KY; pa/LPN Ky Sch for the Deaf; cp/Helped w Org of Moreland Bapt Ch, Moreland, Ky; r/Bapt.

BOHLER, GENIE R oc/Executive Manager; b/Nov 10, 1915; h/114 N Anderson St, Morganton, NC 28655; m/Clarence H; p/James F (dec) and Clara Walton Rucker (dec); ed/Athens Bus Sch 1933; Dip SEn Inst Org Exec UNC-Chapel Hill 1950, Adv'd Study 1951-53; pa/Org Mgmt, Exec Mgr Burke Co, NC C of C; 2 3-Yr Terms on Bd Dirs NC Assn C of C Execs; St Del for Am C of C Execs; So Assn C of C Execs; cp/Mem & Former Pres Pilot Clb of Morganton, NC; Charter Mem BPO Does; Charter Mem OES; Charter Mem & Dir of Morganton Lioness Clb; Adv Bd for Burke Co Secys Assn; Mem Co's Nsg Home Adv Com; Adv Bd Parents without Partners; r/Bapt; hon/W/W Am Wom 1967; Burke Co's Wom of Yr 1980.

BOLE, ROBERT H oc/Minister; b/Aug 4, 1944; h/230 Tennyson Cove, Picayune, MS 39466; ba/Picayune; m/Sandy; c/Andrea, J J; p/Glenn R (dec) and Kathleen Bole, Birmingham, AL; ed/ThB, ThM Berean Christian Col; mil/USMCR 6 Yrs; pa/Missionary Trinidad 3 Yrs; Tchr Trinidad Sch Preaching; Radio Spkr; Min 9 Yrs; Mem Speakeasy Toastmasters Intl; r/Ch of Christ; hon/Selected to Speak in 10 Annual Carribbean Lectrships, Port of Spain, Trinidad.

BOLEN, WILLIAM HAROLD oc/Professor, Administrator, Author, Consultant; b/Feb 24, 1943; h/18 Forest Pines Dr, Country Club Ests, Statesboro, GA 30458; ba/S'boro; m/Sheron Lee Smith; c/William Harold Jr, Charles Henry; p/Harold Jean and Lucy Huggins Bolen, Savannah,

GA; ed/BS Ga So Col 1964; MBA 1966, PhD 1972 Univ Ark; pa/Ga So Col: Prof Mktg 1979-, Hd Dept Grad Fac 1973-, Assoc Prof Mktg 1973-79, Asst Prof Mktg 1966-73; Am Acad Advtg; Am Col Retailing Assn, Am Mktg Assn, Delta Sigma Pi, Ga Assn Mktg Edrs, Mid-Atlantic Mktg Assn, Pi Sigma Epsilon, So Mktg Assn, SW Mktg Assn, S'boro-Bulloch Co C of C; hon/"Very Important Prof", Specialty Advtg Assn 1979; 1 of 15 Top Profs, Ga So Col Student Body 1978; Recip Kiplinger F'ship 1978; Free Enterprise Fellow 1975; Omicron Delta Epsilon 1970, Cert'd Advtg Spec 1968; Beta Gamma Sigma 1960; Community Leaders and Noteworthy Americans; DIB; Men of Achmt; Outstg Edrs Am; Num Other Biog Listings; W/W: Am Ed, S&SW; Author *Contemporary Retailing & Advertising*; Articles for Num Pubs.

BOLER, DANNY oc/Pastor; b/Aug 1, 1950; h/PO Box 253, Trinidad, TX 75163; ba/Trinidad; c/Keri Ann, Melissa LeeAnn; p/Otha and Ina Boler, Winnsboro, TX; ed/AA Tyler Jr Col 1968; BS Univ Tex-Tyler 1977; MRE SWn Bapt Theol Sem 1979; mil/USAF 1969-73; pa/Pastor First Bapt Ch Trinidad; r/So Bapt.

BOLESKY, KAREN LUISE oc/Executive; b/Mar 9, 1941; h/1441 Jungle Ave N, St Petersburg, FL 33710; ba/St Petersburg; c/Jesse Phillipe; p/Harold F and Lillian A Bolesky, Mansfield, OH; ed/AA Palm Bch Jr Col 1966; BA 1971, MA 1975 Univ So Fla; pa/Pvt Pract Fam Cnslr 1975-79; Pres-Owner K G Real Food Co 1975-; Nat Rehab Cnslg Assn; Nat Nutritional Food Assn; Nat Hlth Fed; So Hlth Org; cp/Nat Audubon Soc; Nat Assn Female Execs; Hunger Proj; Wilderness Soc; World Runners; r/Prot; hon/W/W Am Wom 1981-82; Art Piece, Univ So Fla Permanent Gal Collection 1971.

BOLNER, CLIFTON JOSEPH oc/Executive; b/July 30, 1928; h/426 Menchaca St, San Antonio, TX 78207; c/Tim, Mike, Deb, Cindy, Bev, Chris, Mary Beth; pa/Pres Bolner's Fiesta Prods Inc; Mem Admissions Com Am Spice Trade Assn; Consumer Div Produce Mktg Assn; cp/The Aggie Clb; Tex ATM Century Clb; San Antonio Symph Soc; San Antonio Mus Assn; Opera Superman; San Antonio Muscular Dystrophy Assn; hon/Recip Dist'd Alumni Awd Ctrl Cath HS 1979; Archbishop Furey Outstg Awd Medal 1969.

BOLTON, EURI BELLE oc/Retired Professor; b/Feb 22, 1895; h/715 N Pelham Rd, Jacksonville, AL 36265; pa/Robert Lee (dec) and Mary Lee Culpepper Bolton (dec); ed/BS 1923, MA 1924, PhD 1931 Geo Peabody Col for Tchrs; pa/Ret'd Prof Psych Ga Col; Prin Rural HS 1915-18; Extension Wkr Ga St Col Women 1918-22; Gen Ed Bd Fellow 1922-15; Ga St Col for Wom: Prof Psych 1925-28, Prof Ed & Psych 1928-49, Prof Psych 1949-58; Prof Psych Emeritus 1958-; Guid Coor NE Houston Indep Sch Dist 1961-66; Conslt St Wel Dept Ga 1943-58; Mem AAAS; Ga, SE & Am Psych Assns; Delta Kappa Gamma; r/Meth; hon/W/W Ala; Am Men Sci; Notable Wom; APA; Pub'd Author.

BOLTON, RHONDA JOANNE c/Radiologic Technologist; b/Nov 3, 1957; h/1427 Kings Cir, Shelby, NC 28150; ba/Kings Mtn; p/Don Bolton, Shelby, NC; Joanne Bolton, Shelby, NC; ed/Gaston Meml Hosp Sch of Radiol Technol 1978; pa/Radiol Technol, Kings Mtn Hosp 3 Yrs; NC Soc Radiol Technol; Am Soc Radiol Technol; cp/Advr Med Explorer Post 412; r/Bapt; hon/Advr of Yr, Med Explorers, Piedmont Coun 1980; Valedictorian Twelve Oaks Acad 1976.

BOLTON, SYNIA CHRISTIAN oc/Secretary; b/July 5, 1915; h/422 Denison, Muskogee, OK 74401; ba/Muskogee; m/A A; p/Arkley (dec) and Effie Christian (dec); ed/BS; BRE; MRE; pa/Ret'd Edr; Secy Ragsdale Mortuary; cp/Dem Clb; Homemakers Clb; Fed Clb; r/Bapt; hon/Rel Tchr of Yr 1974, Okla Sch Rel.

BOLTON, WILLIAM B oc/Lawyer, Banker; h/1103 Princess Anne St, Fredericksburg, VA 22401; p/James W and Molly Newton Bolton; ed/Berea Acad; Nat Bus Col of Roanoke; Lenior Rhyne Col; Bach Deg Col William & Mary 1928; LLB, JD, TC Williams Sch of Law of Univ Richmond 1954; pa/Lawyer; Banker; Chm of Bd of Dirs of U Va Bank of Spotsylvania; Class Agt for Class of 1928 of Col of William & Mary; Perm Pres Class of 27 of Lenior Rhyne Col; Pres Alumni Assn Fries HS; Mem Va St Bar; 15th Judicial Curcuit Bar Assn; F'burg Area Bar Assn; 9 Yrs Prin & Coach Falmouth HS, Stafford Co, Va; 5 Yrs Prin & Coach Stafford Ct House HS; Clerk of House of Del 1954; 2 Terms as Mem 8th Dist Com; Secy of 15th Judicial Circuit Bar Assn; Former Pres F'burg Area Bar Assn; Former Chm Bd of Zoning Appeals for City of F'burg; Served on Bd of Trustees of Chd's Home Soc Va; Served on Bd Trustees F'burg Area Commun Fund; Past Pres Old Dominion Invest Clb; Former Dir Hist F'burg; Former Dir & Legal Ofcr Peoples Bank of Stafford; Fdr Peoples Bank of Spotsylvania (now U Va Bank); Sigma Pi; Omicron Delta Kappa; Nat Ldrship Soc; Delta Theta Phi; Phi Delta Gamma; Tau Kappa Alpha; Kappa Pi Kappa; Kappa Delta Pi; Others; cp/Fdr Stafford Sportsman Clb; Life Mem Falmouth Fire Dept; Fdr White Oak Fire Dept; Fdr & Mem Falmouth HS Alumni Assn; Mary Wash Hosp Assn; F'burg Gal of Mod

Art; Rappahannock Val Coun Retard Chd; Past Dir & Present Mem Hist Falmouth Towne & Stafford Co Inc; Life Mem Nat Ret'd Ofcrs Assn; Mem & Parliamentarian Rappahannock Ret'd Ofcrs Assn; Friends of Library; Hist F'burg Foun; Dixie Lodge #202; AF & AM, Fries, Va; Fdr & Charter Mem Stafford Ruritan Clb; Former Legal Ofcr for F'burg Rescue Squad; Former Chm Mar of Dimes; Fdr & Dir of Frank C Pratt Chapt Va Assn Mtl Hlth; Others; hon/Alumni Plaque for Outstg Sers to Class of 1928, Col of William & Mary.

BOLTZ, CLARA BELLE oc/Homemaker; b/Sept 10, 1918; h/Killeen, TX; m/Delton N; p/Wilson Harris (dec) and Clara M Everett, Gatesville, TX; ed/Durham-Draughon Bus Col 1938; BS N Tex St Univ 1942; 5 Flower Show Schs & 6 Symposiums 1958-80; Flower Show Judging Master Cert 1971; cp/Treas DAR, Ensign Thomas Huling Chapt; Ret'd Ofcrs Wives Clb; Killeen Garden Clb; Ctrl Tex Coun Nat Accred'd Flower Show Judges; Dist V Tex Garden Clbs Inc; Bd Dirs Tex Garden Clbs Inc; r/Bapt; hon/Tex Garden Clbs Pres Citation 1965; Dist V Tex Garden Clbs Dir's Citation 1979; Life Mem Tex Garden Clb 1965; Nat Coun St Garden Clbs Cert of Commend; Asst in Recording Ft Hood Cemeteries in Two Volumes 1979.

BOMAR, RILEY NATHANIEL oc/Minister; b/Apr 16, 1928; h/Rt 1 Box 299A, Union Pt, GA 30669; ba/Same; m/Mary Lou Davis; c/Ricky Harold, Nathan Stanley, Melinda Gail; p/George F (dec) and Rose Bud Bomar, Lafayette, GA; ed/Diploma La Carolina Col 1965; Dip Theol, New Orleans Bapt Theol Sem 1970; mil/USMC 1946-48 Master Sgt; pa/USMC Air Craft Hydraulic Mech & Hydraulic Instr; Pastor Bethesda Bapt Ch, Union Pt; r/So Bapt; hon/Naval Unit Cit; Good Conduct 5 Stars; WWII Victory Medal; Nat Defense 1 Star; UN Ribbon 3 Stars; Korean Pres Medal; Others.

BOND, H JULIAN oc/State Senator; b/Jan 14, 1940; ba/361 W View Dr, SW, Atlanta, GA 30310; ed/BA Morehouse Col 1971; pa/Fdr, Exec Secy, COAHR 1960; Co-Fdr SNCC 1960; Staff Atlanta Inquirer 1960; Communs Dir SNCC 1961-66; cp/Ga Ho of Reps 1965 (Barred from Taking Ofc in Jan 1966); Re-Elect'd Feb 1966 (Again Barred from Taking Ofc); Re-Elect'd Nov 1966, Took Oath of Ofc Jan 1977; Elect'd to Ga St Sen 1974–; Coms: Consumer Affairs, Govtl Opers, V-Chm Human Resources Com; Co-Chm Ga Loyal Nat Dem Del 1968; Bd Dirs: Afro-Am Inst, Delta Min Proj of Nat Coun of Chs, Robert F Kennedy Meml Fund, Martin Luther King Jr Ctr for Social Change, Ctr for Commun Change, Highlander Res & Ed Ctr, Nat Sharecropper's Fund, So Regional Coun, New Dem Coalition, Voter Ed Proj, Nat Adv Coun of Am Civil Liberties Union; Pres So Poverty Law Ctr; Pres Atlanta Br NAACP; Pres Inst So Studies; hon/Hon Degs: Dalhousie Univ, Univ Bridgeport, Wesleyan Univ, Univ Oregon, Syracuse Univ, En Mich Univ, Lincoln Univ, Tuskegee Inst, Howard Univ, Morgan St Univ, Wilberforce Univ, Patterson St Col, NH Col, Detroit Inst Technol; 200 Leader's List, Time; Res Assoc, Voter Ed Proj; Visiting Fellow Inst Applied Polits; IPFU; SCRREW; Speeches Pub'd A Time to Speak; Poems & Articles Appeared in Negro Digest, Motive, Rigts and Reviews, Life, Freedomways, Beyond the Blues, New Negro Poets, American Negro Poetry, The Book of Negro Humor and Others; Acted in Movie Greased Lightning.

BONDS, JOHN BLEDSOE oc/Naval Officer; b/Dec 16, 1939; h/145 Hobcaw Dr, Charleston, SC; ba/FPO, NY, NY; m/Elizabeth Rollins; c/John Jr, Margaret Lynn; p/Fay and Virginia Bledsoe Bonds, Conway, AR; ed/BA Rice Univ 1962; MSIA Geo Wash Univ 1973; MA Brown Univ 1975; mil/Active Duty 1962–; pa/USN Ofcr; Mem Naval Inst; NYYC; Am Sail Trg Assn; Author Mil Articles; cp/Yachtsman, Mem Am Cup Com 1977; r/Epis; hon/Bronze Star; Jt Ser Commend; Navy Achmt Medals.

BONDS, VIRGINIA W oc/Homemaker; b/Oct 18, 1937; h/207 E Rosehill, Deland, FL 32720; m/Charles L; c/Rebecca Lane, Charla Linn; p/E Raymond and Mattye Mae Norwood Warren; ed/Studies in Real Est, Probate Work Univ Tenn; pa/Paralegal Work; Mid-South Title Res; cp/2nd VP Pilot Clb; Pres Wom's Clb; 1st VP Garden Clb; Pres Miss Softball Am; hon/S'ship for Speed & Accurate Typing; S'ship for Clarinet; Won Ribbons in Flower Shows.

BONICK, DOROTHY LOUISE oc/Nurse; b/Oct 21, 1919; h/117 N Houston, Comanche, TX 76442; ba/DeLeon, TX; m/Leonard Edmond; c/James, Lynnette, Faith Long, Bruce, Leonard Jr, Donna; p/Edwin Judson (dec) and Luna Ruth Payne Rice, Comanche, TX; pa/RN; Dir Nsg Sers; ANA; TNA; cp/Repub; r/Cath.

BOOHER, CHARLES B (CHUCK) oc/Machine Repairman; b/Aug 19, 1946; h/Rt 5 Box 426A, Bluff City, TN 47618; ba/Bristol, VA; m/Early L; c/Melisia Dawn; p/Virgil and Ruth Booher, Jonesboro, TN; ed/Va Highland Commun Col 1976; mil/USAF 1964-68; pa/Machine Repairman, Electrolux; cp/Vol Bluff City Rescue Squad (EMT); Am Heart Assn; Regional Hypertension Com Chm; Regional Vehicle Rescue Coor Tenn Assn Rescue Squad; r/Meth; hon/Outstg Yng Man of Yr, Bristol, Va & Tenn JCs 1980.

BOOK, JOHN KENNETH (KENNY) oc/Store Owner; b/June 26, 1950; h/Apt 6, 114 Vil Ct, Winchester, KY 40391; ba/Winchester; p/Vern R Book, Winchester; Pearl I Alford, Winchester; ed/Assoc Deg Acctg; pa/Owner Kenny's Tax Ser; Owner Kenny's Signs Unltd; cp/Cand for City Commissioner 1981; Clark Co Yg Dems; r/Christian; hon/Perf Awd, Nat Press; Ky Col.

BOOKER, DORIS EDWINIA WOODARD oc/Assistant Professor; b/Dec 13, 1936; h/8637 Aldershot Dr, Richmond, VA 23229; ba/Petersburg; c/Angela Denise; p/Edward D Sr and Clarine Jones Woodard, Portsmouth, VA; ed/BA 1959, MA 1970 Va St Col; Further Study: Norfolk St Col 1965, 1971, Bowie St Col 1971, Univ Va 1975; pa/Asst Prof Eng, Va St Univ; Va Assn Tchrs of Eng; Conf of Eng Edrs; NCTE; VEA 1961-70; Pres Northumberland Co Tchrs Assn 1965-67; r/Bapt; hon/Phi Delta Kappa; Delta Sigma Theta; Asst'ship & F'ship, Sch of Ed, Univ Va 1973-75, 1979; Provost's S'ship, Norfolk Div of Va St Col 1955-57; Weaver Awd 1955; Portsmouth Tchrs Assn S'ship 1955; W/W S&SW 1980-81; Author "Women in the Romances of Nathaniel Hawthorne" 1970; "Students Will Read and Like It" 1973.

BOOKHARDT, EDWARD LEE oc/Artist; b/Mar 15, 1930; h/114 Oaks Ct, Sanford, FL 32771; m/Jacqueline C; c/Gregory W, Gary L, Debra A Snyder; pa/E L Bookhardt, Denton, GA; ed/BS; MS; Naval Post Grad Sch; mil/USN 30 Yrs Ser Ret'd Comdr; pa/Cert Sr Engrg Tech; Artist; Fla & Sanford-Seminole Art Assns; cp/Mem Lock Haven Art Ctr; Maitland Art Ctr; r/Prot; hon/Merit Ser Medal; Navy Commend Medal; Naval Achmt Medal; Combat Action Awd; 14 Other Mil Awds; Best of Show, Homosassa Springs Art Show; 1st Place Leesburg Art Fair; 1st Place Sanford-Seminole Art Show; Other Art Awds.

BOONE, EMILY CLARK KIDWELL LINDER oc/Social Worker; b/July 20, 1943; h/9206 Walhampton Dr, Louisville, KY 40222; ba/L'ville; m/Edward W; c/Susan Rebecca Linder; p/Edgar Clark (dec) and Emily Florence Scruggs Kidwell, Cinci, OH; ed/BA Univ Cinci 1964; MSW Wash Univ 1970; pa/Conslt Pvt Prac 1977–; Social Wkr Our Lady of Peace Hosp; Mem NASW; VP NASW Ky Chapt; AAUW; Nat Conf Social Work; Social Work Voc Bur; Ky Assn Spec in Grp Work; Am Soc Trg & Devel; cp/LWV; Mose Green Dem Clb; Nat Wom's Polit Grp; Ky Pro-ERA Alliance; Intl Wom's Yr; NOW; L'ville & Jefferson Co's Human Relats Comm; Ky Regional Plan'g & Devel Agy's Bicycle Trans Com; L'ville Wheelmen; ACLU; Common Cause; Parkview Heights Housing Corp; Block Ptnrship Prog; Acid Rescue; r/Luth; hon/L'ville YWCA 1978 Outstg Wom in SS; W/W Am Wom; Ky Chapt Del to Nat Invitl Forum on Clin Social Work.

BOONE, HARRY LINDSAY JR oc/Snackfood Wholesale Distributor; b/Feb 5, 1950; h/Rt 1 Box 426, Carrollton, VA 23314; ba/Portsmouth, VA; m/Ann Candler Carowell; c/Lynn; pa/Harry L Sr (dec) and Martha R Boone, Portsmouth, VA; ed/AAS Tidewater Commun Col; mil/USMCR 1969-74 Corporal; pa/VP Boone Dist Co Inc; VP Pet Supplies Inc; Owner Dirty Harry's Gun Shop; Snackfood Wholesale Dist; Va Food Dlrs Assn; Tidewater Food Dlrs Assn; Wise Food Dlrs Assn; Nat Assn Fed Licensed Firearms Dlrs; cp/Past VChancellor Tidewater Lodge #16 Knights of Pythias; Cmdr Stonewall Jackson #380 Sons of Confed Vets; Cmdr Capt Cary F Grimes Chapt Mil Order of Stars & Bars; Cmdr Capt Maj John Pelham Alliance #3 Resv Ofcrs Confed Alliance; Cmdr 1st Brigade Va Div SCV; Sgt Major Wash Grays, N-S Skirmish Assn; 1st Lt Co A 5th Va Cav Army of Tenn; Endowment Mem Nat Rifle Assn; Life Mem Am Pistol & Rifle Assn; Capt Friends of the Confed Soc; Corres Civil War Press Corps; Confed Meml Lit Soc; So Nat Party; r/Epis; hon/Cert Apprec Va Div SCV 1979; Dixie Clb Gen HQ SCV 1979; Order of Battleflag Cmdr Class RVCA 1980; Portsmouth Clean Commun Comm Awd 1979-80; Cert Rifle & Pistol Instr; Wash Grays Topshooter Awd 1978 & 79.

BOOTH, MARY JEAN YOUNG oc/Speech Pathologist; b/Jan 27, 1942; h/3533 La Nell, Bossier City, LA 71112; ba/Bossier City; c/Chrsitopher Lee, Virginia Elizabeth, Mary Catherine; p/Marion Albert (dec) and Charlotte Brandau Young, Abbeville, LA; ed/BS Univ Miss for Wom 64; MCD La St Univ Med Ctr 1978; pa/Speech-Lang Pathol for St Residential Facility for Mtl Retard; Mem Shreve-Bossier Speech & Hearing Assn; La Speech-Lang-Hearing Assn; Intl Assn Logopedics & Phoniatrics; cp/Den Ldr Cub Scout Den 3 Pack 205; BSA; Bellaire PTA; LSW Alumni Assn; r/Epis; hon/W/W S&SW 1980-81.

BOOZER, JOHN ELBERT oc/Minister of Music; b/May 2, 1948; 3225 Jenks Ave, Panama City, FL 32405; ba/Panama City; m/Patricia Patterson; c/John Britt, Carol Jo Beth; p/Goldee and Mary Lou Boozer; ed/BCM Samford Univ 1972; MCM So Bapt Sem 1977; pa/Min of Mus; Mem So Bapt Ch Mus Conf; ACDA; MENC; Fla Singing Men; cp/Bd Dirs Boy's Clbs; Mem YMCA; Bd Dirs Panama City Mus Assn; r/Bapt; Ordained Min.

BOREN, DAVID L oc/Governor; b/Apr 21, 1941; m/Molly W Shi;

c/Carrie, Dan; p/Mr & Mrs Lyle H Boren; ed/Hons Grad Yale Univ; Masters in Govt w hon Oxford Univ (England); Grad Okla Univ Col Law; mil/Okla NG 6 Yrs, Capt; pa/Pract Law Seminole; Former Chm Det Govt, Okla Bapt Univ, Shawnee; cp/Elected Gov Okla 1974; Nat Gov's Assn: Mem Natural Resources & Envir Mgmt Com, VChm Human Resources Com; So Gov's Conf: VChm, Chm Energy Com; Mem Steering Com Ed Comm of Sts; Chm Ozarks Reg Comm; Former Chm Interst Oil Compact Comm; Past Chm So Growth Policies Bd; Former Mem Okla Ho of Reps; hon/Elected Most Intell Mem, Okla Ho of Reps; Rhodes Scholar; Outstg Grad in Class, Okla Univ Col Law Fac; Named 1 of 10 Outstg Yg Men, US JCs.

BOREN, MOLLY SARVER oc/Realtor; b/Nov 9, 1939; h/13519 Indian Cr, Houston, TX 77079; ba/Houston; m/William M; c/Susan, Patricia, Janet, Jenny, Burton, Cliff; p/Joseph B and Molly Brasfield Sarver, Auburn, AL; ed/AB Auburn Univ; pa/Realtor; Houston Bd of Rltrs; Tex Assn of Rltrs; cp/Bd Houston Symph Leag; Symph Annual Fund Dr; Symph Subscription Dr; Woms Inst; Yng Wom of Arts; Pres Kappa Delta Alumnae Assn of Houston; Past Pres Houston Auburn Alumnae Assn; r/Presb; hon/Pi Kappa Phi; Mortar Bd; W/W Am Wom 1979-80.

BORKAN, WILLIAM NOAH oc/Electrical Engineer; Inventor; b/Apr 29, 1956; h/3031 Prairie Ave, Miami Bch, Fl 33140; ba/Miami Bch; p/Martin Soloman and Annabelle Borkan, Miami Bch; ed/BSEE; pa/ASHRAE; AAEE; ISES; SAE; hon/W/W S&SW; Energy Monitor & Control Sys Patent; Method & Device for Estimating Fuel Consumption Patent; Home Energy Control Sys Patent; Neurostimulator Sys Patents Pending.

BOROWSKY, JANE BARROW oc/Assistant Professor; b/July 18, 1937; h/Statesboro, GA; ba/Dept of Foreign Langs-LB8081, Ga So Col, Statesboro, GA 30458; m/Anton G; c/Anton G Jr, (Stepchd:) Richard, Ann; /Cecil C and Katherine Sawyer Barrow, Coolidge, GA; ed/AB N Ga Col 1959; MA Emory Univ 1961; Cert d'Études Francais, Universite de Grenoble 1965; pa/Asst Prof Modern Langs, Ga So Col; AAUP, Local Chapt VP 1979-80, Pres 1980-81; Am Assn Tchrs French; S Atlantic MLA; Mtn Interstate Fgn Lang Conf; Fac Senate, Com to Search for Dean of Students, Com on Coms, Chm Fgn Students Com 1978-79; Dir Rotary Foun Summer Lang Inst 1977-82; cp/ABWA, Chm Ed Com, Chm Spring Enrollment; r/Bapt; hon/Siler S'ship Awd 1958; S'ship for Summer Study at Universite de Laval, Quebec, Canada 1958; Woodrow Wilson F'ship 1959-60; W/W Students in Am Univs & Cols.

BOSIER, BETTY BROWN oc/Businesswoman; b/Feb 14, 1947; ba/Sumter, SC; c/Albertus Bosier Jr; Kelvin Bosier; p/Buster and Lear Holliday Brown, Paxville, SC; ed/Sumter Area Tech Col; pa/Campbell Soup Co; cp/Paxville Town Coun-wom; r/Bapt; hon/Awd for Wkg w Multiple Schlerosis Soc; Perfect Attendence Campbell Soup Co; NAACP Awd.

BOTTS, MERCEDES BLOW oc/Management Specialist; b/June 18, 1923; h/12004 Edgepark Ct, Potomac, MD 20854; ba/Alexandria, VA; m/Samuel Douglas; c/Ronald Anthony, Samuel York, John Myron, Sidney Vincent; p/Beverly York Sr (dec) and Laura Mae Wright Blow, Phila, PA; pa/Indust Prop Mgmt Spec; Mem Tri-St Nat Prop Mgmt Assn; cp/VP Montgomery Co Wom's Comm; Potomac Woms Repub Clb; Rock Creek Wom's Repub Clb; r/Cath; hon/UN Assn CAD Human Righs; Cosmo BPW Clb Outstg Wom of Yr 1972.

BOUCHER, BETTY JANE oc/Corporate Secretary-Bookkeeper; b/Oct 16, 1944; h/3008 Joyce Ln, Memphis, Tn 38116; ba/Memphis; p/Mr and Mrs C R Boucher, Memphis, TN; ed/Draughon's Bus Sch 1962; Acctg Deg 1964; pa/Philco Fin Co 1964-65; Wonder Snack Food 1965; Corp Secy-Bkkpr C R Boucher Constrn Co Inc 1965-; Memphis Chapt #13 Nat Assn Wom in Constrn: Pres 1975-76 & 78-79, VP 1974-75, Treas 1980-81, Bd Dirs 1976-77, 77-78, 79-80; Region V Com Mem NAWIC Mbrship Promtion Com 1978-79; Region V Com Mem on NAWIC Occup Res & Referral Com 1979-80 & 80-81; cp/Bd Dirs WAGES Inc 1978-, Treas 1980-; Quota Clb of Memphis: Pres 1980-81 & 81-82, Recording Secy 1979-80, 1st VP 1978-79, Treas 1975-76, 76-77, 77-78; Wom's Exec Coun of Memphis; Public Affairs Coun of Memphis; Bethel Grove Chapt OES of Tenn; r/Bapt; hon/Jessie Ramsey Awd for Ser, Quota Clb of Memphis 1979; W/W Am Wom 1981.

BOUCHER, CARTER oc/Artist; b/Aug 8, 1954; h/4302 N Main St, Anderson, SC 29621; p/George H and Annie Laurie Keaton Boucher; ed/BA Univ SC 1977; Att'd Furman Univ, E Tenn St Univ; pa/Asst Prog Dir Salvation Army Boys Clb, July-Aug 1978; Art Dir Creative Media Prods Inc, 1977-78; Public Relats Conslt, Univ SC Writing Lab 1977-78; Originator of ID-Art; Charter Mem; hon/Shows & Awds: Greenwood Fest of Flowers 1977, USC Juried Sr Show 1977, Anderson Co Arts Coun Fac Show 1976, Spring Mills 1976, Arts & Crafts Fair of Trenton 1976, USC

Juried Art Auction 1975, Ltd Eds of 5 Ink Drawings Pub'd Under "Original Compromise Co" 1975, E Tenn St Univ Hons Show 1972; Pub'd Poetry: "A Trip to Nowhere" 1971, "Psyche Out in Eden, Love, in Eden Tonight Breathe in Blood" 1972, "Death Stuck a Cold Finger in My Ear" 1976.

BOUCHER, FREDERICK CARLYLE oc/State Senator; Attorney at Law; b/Aug 1, 1946; h/279 B E Main St, Abingdon, VA 24210; ba/Abingdon; ed/BA Roanoke Col 1968; JD Univ Va Law Sch 1971; pa/Var Bar Assns; Am Judic Soc; cp/Mem Va Sen 1975-; Va St Crime Comm; Va Coal & Energy Com; Com on Interst Coop; Bd Dirs Bank of Damascus; Bd Dirs Client Centered Legal Sers of SW Va; Chm Va Sen Dem Caucus Policy Com; r/Meth; hon/Outstg Bus Man, A'don JCs 1975; Outstg Yng Men Am 1980.

BOUNDS, IDUMA oc/Retired Teacher; b/Aug 4, 1906; h/Rt 3 Box 109, Picayune, MS 39466; m/(dec); c/Margaret Walline Stewart, Carol Sue Sonier; ed/BS; pa/Ret'd Sch Tchr; OES Chapt 89; Ret'd Tchrs Assn; Exec Com AAPP; cp/Home Dem Clb Prs; Parliamentarian of Co Dem Coun; Tchr of WMA 10 Yrs; Hist Mus Coun; r/Bapt; hon/25 Yr Pin OES & Home Dem Work; 1st Place Nat Awd for Hlth Prog in USA; Many Other 1st Place Hon in St.

BOUNDS, SARAH ETHELINE oc/Educator, Historian; b/Nov 5, 1942; h/1100 Bob Wallace Ave SE, Huntsville, AL 35801; p/Leo D (dec) and Alice Etheline Bounds (dec); ed/AB Birmingham-So Col 1963; MA 1965, EdS 1971, PhD 1977 Univ Ala; pa/Asst Prof Ed, Supvr Student Tchrs U of N Ala, 1978; Hist Instr Univ Ala 1978-; Alpha Delta Kappa; Kappa Delta Pi; Phi Alpha Theta; Huntsville Hist Soc; Ala Assn Hists; Ala Hist Assn; Assn Tchr Edrs; Ala Pers & Guid Assn; Nat Coun Tchrs SS; AAUW; cp/Pilot Clb; Vol Leukemia Soc of Am; Am Heart Assn; r/Meth; hon/Outstg Yng Wom of Am 1976; W/W S&SW 1980; Contbr to *Huntsville Historical Review* Oct 1973, Apr 1974, Jan 1976.

BOURGEOIS, LINDA ROSS ROBERTSON oc/Executive Director; b/Jan 19, 1938; h/817 Farley Dr, Huntsville, AL 35802; ba/H'ville; c/Frederick Joseph III, Jacqueline Marie; p/Wilton Durward and Gertrude Hemming Robertson, Sallis, MS; ed/MA; MS; pa/Exec Dir N Ala Capt Epilepsy Foun of Am Inc; Am Soc Assn Execs; Nat Assn Epilepsy Execs; Forum of Agcy Dirs; cp/H'ville Coun Human Relats; H'ville Ballet Assn VP; H'ville Madison Co Dance Coun VP; r/Cath; hon/W/W: Wom, Intells; Valedictorian HS; Alpha Psi Omega; Kappa Delta Pi; World W/W Wom; Outstg Achmt Awd Tenn Val Chapt EMT Assn; Outstg Serv Awd Cnslg & Growth Ctr, H'ville 1975 & 76.

BOURLAND, VERGAL H oc/General Manager; b/Oct 28, 1915; h/2621 Colonial Pkwy, Ft Worth, TX 76109; ba/Ft Worth; m/Margaret; c/Michael, Richard, Mary, Martha; ed/Cert Clb Mgr of Clb Mgrs Assn of Am 1969; Adv'd Mgmt Tech of CMAA 1972; Communs Skills for Clb Mgr of CMAA 1977; Adv'd Tech of Conslts 1979; mil/AUS 1942; pa/Gen Mgr Colonial Country Clb; Tex Lone Star Chapt Clb Mgrs Assn of Am; Nat Pres Appliance, Radio & TV Assn; cp/Pres Univ Bapt Ch Brotherhood; Rotary Clb of Ft Worth; r/Bapt; hon/RCA Music City 1973.

BOURQUE, ROBERT MARTIN oc/Educator, Electronics Technician; b/June 1, 1953; h/PO Box 148, Kenbridge, VA 23944; ba/Alberta, VA; m/Dixie Higdon; p/Robert J Bourque, CT; Mae M Hudson, VA; ed/AAS Southside Va Comm Col 1973; BS VPI & St Univ 1978; pa/Asst Prof Elec Ser, Southside Va Comm Col 1973-; Elec Tech: Smiths TV, Bill May TV, Hamner Elec 1968-; Phi Kappa Phi; hon/1st Class FCC Radio-Telephone License 1975; Cert Elec Tech ISCET 1977; W/W S&SW 1980-81; Co-Author: *The Theory and Servicing of AM-FM and FM Stereo Receivers* 1980.

BOUTWELL, CLOYCE DALE oc/Retired; b/May 20, 1918; m/Teruko Topa; mil/20 Yrs; pa/Ret'd Ins Agt; r/Prot; hon/Var Awds as Cmdr of Am Legion.

BOWEN, MATILDA R oc/Homemaker, Fashion Consultant; b/Mar 24, 1919; h/Hillwinds, Greeneville, TN 37743; ba/Same; m/Elba W; c/Matilda B Green; p/John N (dec) and Elizabeth Wagner Rasar, Greeneville, TN; pa/Fashion Conslt; cp/Pres Garden Coun; Pres Westside Garden Clb; Past Pres Andrew Johnson Clb; Yth Bldrs of G'ville; Arts Guild; Poak House; Mem Heritage Trust; 1st VP Humane Soc; Commun Comcert; Little Theater; r/Bapt; hon/Nominated 3 Yrs & 1980 Named Outstg Wom of Yr.

BOWEN, RICHARD DALE oc/Pastor; b/Jan 18, 1936; h/PO Box 267, Dewar, OK 74431; m/Sandra Kaye Adams; c/Jeffrey Alan, Mark Adam; p/Arthur Iverson (dec) and Norma Belle Bowen (dec); ed/Dip Theol, SWn Bapt Sem 1970; MDiv 1972, ThD 1975 Luther Rice Sem; mil/USN; pa/Pastor First Bapt Ch Dewar; So Bapt Pastorates in Tex, Ark, Mich, Ga & Okla 1958-; Dir Bapt Student Work, En OSC 1966-69; N Am Assn Ventriloquists; Author: "Tongues of Corinth - Genuine or Counterfeit?" 1976.

32

BOWERS, CAROL ANN ROBERTS oc/Music Teacher, Pianist; b/Sept 10, 1944; h/1005 W Eufaula, Norman, OK 73069; ba/Norman; c/Elisabeth Kristine; p/Sarah Louise Roberts, Norman, OK; ed/BMus William Carey Col 1966; MMus Univ Okla 1976; pa/Vocal Mus Tchr; Pianist; Mem NEA; OEA; Profl Edrs of Norman; Perf'd for Local Mus Clbs & St Convs; cp/Assists Girl Scout Troop; Worked in Local Polit Campaigns; Involved in City Coun Activiteis; r/Bapt; hon/Miss Mus Tchrs Assn Winner 1963-65 (Piano Concerto & Sol Contests); W/W Am Cols & Univs; World W/W: Mus 1974, Wom 1976.

BOWERS, JANETTE oc/Division Director; b/Nov 13, 1933; m/Richard Edwin; c/Connie, Clay, Cole, Kelly, Casey, George; p/Tot and Leslie Mae Lawhon, Alpine, TX; ed/BS Sam Houston St Univ 1954; MA Sul Ross St Univ 1970; pa/Dir of Div of Adult & Cont'g Ed, Sul Ross St Univ; Tex Assn for Commun Ser & Cont'g Ed, Immediate Past Pres; cp/Pilot Clb of Alpine: Pres, 1st VP, 2nd VP, Chm Every Com; Pilot Intl; Gov Tex Dist; Delta Kappa Gamma, Constitutional Com Chm; Am Legion Aux, Girls St Chm; Am Cancer Soc, Pres; Am Assn Ret'd Persons, Chapt 2100, Hon Sr Citizens Clb of Alpine; Chm Bd of Sunshine House; Alpine Indep Sch Dist Bd of Trustees, Secy; Alpine C of C, Tourism Com; Alpine Buck Boosters; Alpine Band Boosters; Sul Ross Wom's Org; Daughs of Repub of Tex; r/Presb; hon/W/W Am Wom 1977, 80; Outstg Vol in Tex; World W/W Win 1978-81; Finalist Nat Vol Activist Awd 1977; World W/W Commun Ser 1978 & 79; Outstg Citizen of Alpine 1976; Personalities of the S 1978-81; Notable Ams 1978-79; Commun Ldrs Am 1978-79; Men & Wom Dist 1980; W/W Am 1971; Personalities Am 1972; World W/W Wom 1981; Contemporary Personages 1981.

BOWERS, LINDA KAY oc/Teacher; b/Feb 13, 1951; ba/N Hgts Sch, Rome, GA 30161; m/Stephen R; p/Horace Thomas and Eva Jean Beavers, Etowah, TN; ed/Att'd Carson Newman Col 1969-70; BS Tenn Wesleyan Col 1973; MEd Berry Col 1978; pa/Tchr Rome City Schs; GAE; RAE; BCAE, Bldg Rep; NEA; cp/Berry Wom's Clb; Floyd Co Yng Repubs; Glenwood Precinct Com Mem, Alternate to Co Repub Conv; r/Bapt; hon/Tchr of Yr, N Hgts Sch 1980-81.

BOWLES, JAY CLYDE oc/Deputy Director; b/Apr 25, 1942; h/Rt 6 Box 630, Mooresville, NC 28115; ba/NY, NY; m/Mary Kathryn; c/Regina Lynn, Jason Christopher; p/Junius Clyde (dec) and Eloise Donaldson Bowles; ed/BS Univ Tenn; pa/Dpty Dir Broadcast Sers, The Associated Press; Sigma Delta Chi; Radio-TV News Dirs Assn; Nat Radio Broadcasters Assn; Nat & Overseas Press Clbs; r/Presb.

BOWLING, LOWELL O oc/Electrolux Salesman; b/Aug 25, 1947; h/Rt 2 Box 117, Nancy, KY 42544; ba/Somerset; m/Phyllis; c/Cynthia, Oreida Faye; p/Altro (dec) and Faye Huff Bowling (dec); ed/HS Grad; pa/Salesman 12 Yrs; cp/Mason; r/Bapt; hon/Electrolux Sales Hall of Fame 1978, 79; Awd Electrolux Nat Record Earnings Wk 1979; Expense Paid Vacation to London in Sales Victory w Electrolux 1979; 3 Certs for Earning of $1000.00 a Wk Clb w Electrolux; Expense Paid Vacation to NY in Sales Contest w Electrolux 1978; Electrolux Cert of Accomp for Outstg Sales Perf 1979; Won 2 Mopeds for Being #1 Salesman in Bluegrass Div w Electrolux; Gold Medal Winner w Electrolux, Picture Appeared on Cover of TV Guide 1980; Trip to Wash DC in Sales Contest 1980; Awarded 1979 Sedan Seville Cadillac in Sales Contest 1980; Trip to Puerto Rice in Sales Contest 1979; Trip to Hawaii 1976; Trip to Mexico 1977.

BOWMAN, ROBERT D oc/Architect; b/May 30, 1947; h/1750 Seminole Dr, Sarasota, FL 33579; p/Avery E (dec) and Ruby M Bowman, Mt Sterling, OH; ed/BArch Ohio St Univ 1970; pa/Arch; Pt-time Opera Singer; Mem Am Inst Archs; cp/Advr to Plan'g Comm; Artistic Selection Advr; r/Presb; hon/Aluminum Assn Awd for Lightweight Playground Equip.

BOWMAN, THELMA SHANKS oc/Homemaker, Politician; b/Apr 30, 1928; h/209 S Lynn Ave, Elizabethton, TN 37643; m/Hoyle E (dec); c/Elizabeth Carolyn Thomas, Hoyle E Jr; Suzanne Chambers; Barbara J, John E; p/Ruble Shanks, Chuckey, TN; ed/ETSU; Geo Wash Univ; Grad of Steed Col (formerly Johnson City Bus Col); pa/Ofc Mgmt; Cand 4th Dist Seat in Tenn Ho of Rep1980; cp/St Div Bd Mem Am Cancer Soc; VChm Repub Party Tenn; r/Prot; hon/Most Outstg Female Citizen of Carter Co.

BOYCE, JEDDIAH MONROE oc/Retired; b/June 28, 1924; h/285 SW Roc Rosa Dr, Palm Bay, FL 32905; m/Edna K; c/Clintin Wayne (dec); Eugene Francis, Sandra Anne, Stepchd: Virginia Quackenbush, Elaine Wood, George Burger, Clarence Covert; p/Nelson (dec) and Clarabelle Emmons, Neptune, NJ; mil/USN 1942-45; USCG 1947-50; USAF 1954-55; cp/Past Cmdr Chapt 77 Dav Jackson, NJ; Past Nat Dept Chief of BAP; hon/Many Awds from the Disabled Am Chapts & Nat Chapts; Nominated for Man of Yr in Jackson, NJ.

BOYD, FAY MERRILL oc/Postmaster; b/Mar 29, 1935; h/Rt 1 Box 71, Porterville, MS 39352; ba/P'ville; m/Claiborne Kinard II; 2nd C K; c/Kim Merrill, Claiborne Kinard III (dec); p/Ellis Phillip (dec) and Erlean Zachry Merrill (dec); pa/Postmaster; Nat Assn Postmasters of US; Am Postal Wkrs Union; cp/Active in Local Activites, Commun Clbs, Fund Drives; r/P'ville Meth Ch: Editor Ch Paper, Secy-Treas SS, Yth Ldr.

BOYD, JIMMY WAYNE oc/Manager; b/Jan 21, 1948; h/PO Box 149, Fritch, TX 79036; ba/Borger; m/Sandra; c/Lisa, Jimmy, Steven; p/C A and Maxine Boyd, Lubbock, TX; ed/BSCE Tex Tech Univ 1970; pa/Mgr Power Generation, J M Huber Corp; Reg'd Profl Engr, Tex; ASPE; cp/Fritch C of C; Tex Public Utilities Comm, Task Force on Cogeneration; Fritch City Coun, Spec Com; r/Bapt; Chm of Deacons.

BOYD, LILLIE A oc/Retired Librarian; b/Jan 31, 1927; h/Rt 3 Box 60, Hanceville, AL 35077; ba/H'ville; m/William Matthew; c/Jo Anna Minnitt, Robbin Leeth; p/Andrew and Cora Ayers, H'ville, AL; pa/Ret'd Libn; Bd of Pension & Security; cp/Repub Wkr in Commun; r/Meth; hon/Hons from Tchrs & Students.

BOYD, OTIS oc/Store Owner; b/Sept 1, 1914; h/130 Hillsboro Rd, Morton, MS 39117; ba/Same; m/Omega; p/James (dec) and Alice Morton (dec); mil/AUS WWII Qtrmaster; pa/Owner Grocery Store; cp/Chm Day Care Ctr; r/Bapt; hon/Cancer Dr Hons; Hond'd by Gov Finch, Hon'd by City of Morton; Civil Ser Hons.

BOYD, TOM W oc/Associate Professor; b/July 4, 1933; h/1111 24th Ave SW, Norman, OK 73069; ba/Norman; c/Timothy Charles, Katrina Gay; p/Kathleen West, Lufkin, TX; pa/Assoc Prof Univ OK 1969-; r/Presb Ordained Min; hon/AMACO Foun Good Tchg Awd 1975; Baldwin Tchg Awd 1979.

BOYDSTON, CAROL ANN oc/President Advertising Agency; b/Dec 21, 1939; h/Tallahassee, FL; ba/211 Delta Ct, Tallahassee, FL 32303; m/William Cliff; c/Susie Cliff, Cynthia Ann, David Alan, Christopher William; p/Cecil James Colwell, Tampa, FL; Barbara Helen Edwards (dec); ed/Fla St Univ 1957-59; Jacksonville Jr Col 1966-67; pa/Pres Boydston Ad & Creative Sers 1977-; Tallahassee Ad Fed; Am Soc Profl & Exec Wom; cp/St Leg Liason for Am Ad Fed; Com Mem Mayor's Adv Com 1977; Tallahassee C of C; Fla Small Bus Assn; r/Presb; hon/2 Addy Awds 1977; 14 Addy Awds 1978; 21 Addy Awds 1979.

BOYER, VIOLA LILLIE oc/Teacher; b/Oct 5, 1927; h/1207 E Lamar, Ranger, TX 76470; b/Gorman, TX; m/Carl; c/Cheri Wesley; p/Sam and Gladys Seay, Ranger, TX; ed/BS; MR; pa/Tchr Spec Ed; NEA, TSTA; cp/SS Tchr; Dir Yng Married Dept; r/Bapt; hon/W/W Am Wom 1979-80.

BOYLES, MARY LOU MASSEY oc/Homemaker; b/Jan 22, 1929; h/108 Sgt Prentiss Dr, Natchez, MS 39120; m/Barney Lewis; c/Jeanette Byars, Frances Byars King; p/James Allen and Edna Brannan Massey, Woodville, MS; ed/BS Miss Univ for Wom 1951; pa/Sigma Alpha Iota; Kappa Delta Epsilon; Pres AAUW 1953; cp/VP Mus Arts Leag Natchez 1979; Pres Natchez Garden Clb 1980-82; r/VP Wom of Ch 1977.

BRACEWELL, MERVELL WINZER oc/Professor and Coordinator; b/Oct 21, 1927; h/1337 Rapides Dr, New Orleans, LA 70122; ba/New Orleans; m/Pohlmann J Jr; c/Jennifer Coleman Parker; p/Charlie and Elvia Major Winzer, Homer, LA; ed/RN; BSN; MSN; MPH; DPH; Cert in Gerontological Nsg; mil/USAF Nurses Corps; pa/Staff Nurse Freedmen's Hosp 1956-57; Nsg Instr Freedmen's Hosp Sch Nsg, Howard Univ 1957-61; Dir Sch Nsg Firestone Med Ctr, Harbel, Liberia 1962-68; Nsg Inst Los Angeles Co Med Ctr Sch Nsg 1969-70; NIH Fellow Johns Hopkins Univ Sch Public Hlth 1970-73; Chm Div Nsg Dillard Univ, New Orleans 1973-78; Prof & Coor Psychi & Commun Mtl Hlth Nsg, La St Univ Med Ctr Sch of Nsg Grad Prog 1978-; Ed Adm Cons & Tchrs Sec, Nat Leag for Nsg; ANA; Bd Dirs S La Leag for Nsg; Adv Bd Cont Ed New Orleans Public Schs, Zonta Intl; Chi Eta Pi; Pop Assn Am; World Pop Soc; APHA; Nat Assn for Wom Deans, Adm & Cnslrs; cp/Gov's Comm, Comp Stwide Plan'g for Nsg; Steering Com 1st Gov's Conf for La Wom; Steering Com Gov's Sec Annual Conf on Aging; Trustee Miss Indust Col, Holly Springs; r/CME; hon/Recog of Ser to Intl Nsg, Freedmen's Hosp Nurses Alumni Clbs Inc; USAF Awd; W/W: Hlth Care, S&SW.

BRACEWELL, THOMAS FREDERICK oc/Psychologist; b/Aug 19, 1944; h/Apt 109, Fiewerest Apts, Dothan, AL; ba/Dothan; c/Paul Wesley Jeremy Sean; p/Walter Jefferson (dec) and Francis Bracewell, Dothan, AL; ed/BS Troy St Univ 1969; ThM Emory Univ 1973; MS, PhD Geo Wash Univ 1980; mil/AUS; pa/Cnslg Psych; Pastoral Cnslr; Mtl Hlth Clin Dir; Min; Army Resvs Ofcrs Assn; Armed Forces Chap Assn; Assn AUS; Assn of Rel Cnslrs; Am Pers & Guid Assn; cp/JCs; Elks; Olympia Spa & Country Clb; r/Meth.

BRACKS, OSCAR JR oc/Podiatrist; b/Oct 21, 1947; ba/1153 Evans Ave, Ft Worth, TX 76104; m/Sylvia Robinson; p/Oscar Sr and Vivian

Bracks, Texas City, TX; ed/AS Morehouse Col 1969; BS Ga St Univ 1973; DPM Ohio Col Podiatric 1978; pa/Phys-Podiatrist; Am Podiatry Assn; Nat Podiatry Assn; Nat Med Assn; Tex Podiatry Assn; Tarrant Co Podiatry Assn; Nom'g Com, Region VII, Tarrant Co Podiatry Assn; cp/NAACP; CNR Plann; Interdenom Mins Alliance; F&AM Lodge #75; Ft Worth Consistory #1562; Ft Worth Mins Union; Bd Dirs, VP, Sickle Cell Anemia Assn Tex; Concerned Voters Coun Inc, Treas; Tarrant Co Heart Assn; Neighborhood Devel Corp; Aging Ser Com III; r/Bapt, Ordained Min 1975; hon/Outstg Yng Man Am 1980; Outstg Role Model 1980; Martin Luther King Awd 1980; Outstg Part in Commun Projs 1981.

BRADBURY, ROSANNE B oc/Speech Pathologist; b/Jan 10, 1944; h/606 David St, Winter Springs, FL 32708; ba/Orlando; m/Luke L; c/Steven James Bunker Jr, Amy Elizabeth Bunker; p/Melvin D and Mattye Cox Brown, Athens, GA; ed/BS 1968, MEd 1971 Univ Ga; pa/Speech Pathol; Barrow Co Schs, Winder, Ga 1968-69; Madison Co Schs, Danielsville, Ga 1969-70; Hall Co Schs, Gainesville, Ga 1971-72; Hope Haven Sch for Retard'd Chd, Athens, Ga 1972-73, Buford City Schs 1973-75; Duval Co Bd of Public Instrn, Jacksonville, Fla 1975-79; Orange Co Public Schs, Orlando, Fla 1979-; Am Speech-Lang-Hearing Assn, Cert of Clin Comp; Zeta Phi Eta, Pres 1967-68, Alumni Advr 1968-69; Duval Tchrs U, Fac Rep 1977-79; cp/OES, Assoc Conductress 1979; Bahia Shrine Temple Legionette; USS Yosemite Wives, Pres 1977; Sarsfield Wives, Pres 1975; CPO Wives Clb, RTC, Orlando; Repub Party; r/Disciples of Christ; hon/Sallie Maude Jones Schlr, Univ Ga 1966-68; US Public Hlth Grad Fellow 1970-71; Kappa Delta Pi; Phi Kappa Phi; W/W S&SW 1980-81; Delta Zeta.

BRADDOCK, PAUL FRANK oc/Judge; b/Oct 5, 1946; h/Rt 2 Box 268, Rienzi, MS 38864; ba/Corinth, MS; m/Peggy; c/Junior, Wallace; p/Paul Sr and Bernice Braddock, Rienzi, MS; mil/AUS Vietnam; pa/Supvr & Just Ct Judge; Dpty Sheriff; cp/Master Mason; 32° Scottish Rite; Life Vet; r/Bapt; hon/Cert Achmt AUS Vietnam.

BRADDY, JOHNNY ELL oc/Veterinarian; b/Aug 8, 1949; h/530 NW Dr, Silver Spring, MD 20901; ba/Silver Spring; m/Ever; c/Brandon; p/Charlie and Evelyn Braddy, Barlow, FL; ed/BS; DVM; pa/Vet; Mem Am Vet Med Assn; DC Acad Vet Med; cp/VP PTA; Master Mason; Redemption Lodge #24; r/Prot; hon/W/W Fin & Indust.

BRADLEY, JOHN D oc/Band Director; b/Apr 18, 1936; h/469 Kenney Rd, Augusta, GA 30906; ba/Augusta; m/Winnette; c/John Jr, Trinita Denise; p/Calvin Bradley (dec); Willie Mae Clark, Houston, TX; ed/BMus Tex So Univ 1958; MMus Vander Cook Col Mus 1966; Further Studies Ga So Col 1964, Univ SC 1975; pa/Band Dir; NBA; MENC; GMEA; NEA; GAE; NAJE; GAJE; Richmond Co Band Dirs Assn; 10th Dist Band Assn; Richmond Co Assn Edrs; Phi Beta Sigma; Kappa Kappa Psi; cp/JCs; CSRA Plan'g & Devel Com; YWCA; PTA Coun; C of C; Black Arts Fest; Sr Citizens of Augusta; Miss Augusta Pageant; Augusta Exchange Clb; Augusta Annual Arts Fest; Augusta Players; Gov George Busbee's Election Affair; Ga Regional Hosp; Ground Break'g Ceremony for Augusta Civic Ctr; Redevel Auth; r/Bapt; hon/Ga St C of C Regional Tchr of Yr 1969; GTEA Awd 1969; Apprec Trophy Westside Band Boosters Clb 1977-78; Apprec Trophy Sr High All-Co Concert Band; Augusta Col Cert of Aprec & Recog for Profl Ser in Tchr Prep Prog; Phi Beta Sigma Crescent of Yr 1956; Jenkins Co Tchr of Yr 1969; Outstg Jazz Edr Awd from Nat Band Assn 1979.

BRADLEY, JOSEPH EDWARD oc/Priest, Principal; b/Apr 24, 1943; ba/Owensboro Cath HS, 1524 Parrish Ave, Owensboro, KY 42301; p/Martin W and Anna Bradley, Leitchfield, KY; ed/BBA, BSEd Loyola Univ 1968; MEd Xavier Univ; MDiv Pontifical Col Josephinum; pa/Roman Cath Priest; Prin Owensboro Cath HS; r/Roman Cath.

BRADLEY, LEON oc/Artist; b/Nov 20, 1931; m/Betty Lee; c/Sandra Lee, Vicky E M; p/Wallace P and Oletta May Bradley, Corn, OK; pa/Artist; hon/Art Shows: 4th Place 1974; 4th Place 1975; 3rd Place 1979; 1st Place 1980; Others.

BRADLEY, STEVEN RUSSELL oc/Pastor; b/May 19, 1947; h/206 Caldwell St, Clinton, SC 29325; ba/Clinton; m/Harriet Campbell; c/Joseph Steven, Brian Richard; p/Fred Franklin and Naomi Russell Bradley, Pelzer, SC; ed/AA Anderson Jr Col 1968; BA Furman Univ 1971; MDiv SEn Bapt Theol Sem 1974; pa/Pastor, Davidson St Bapt Ch; Mem Hopewell Area Min Assn; Petersburg Bapt Pastors Conf; Laurens Bapt Pastors Conf Pres Elect; Clinton Area Min Assn; Past Mem Va Bapt Hist Assn; Mem SC, So & Petersburg Bapt Hist Assn; Anderson Col Alumni Assn; Furman Univ Alumni Assn; SEBTS Alumni Assn; cp/Yng Dems for Kennedy, Pelzer-Williamston Chapt; Hopewell, Va, Sr Citizens Adv Coun; r/So Bapt; hon/Cert Ordination 1971; Cert of License to Preach the Gospel 1965.

BRADSHAW, CHARLES HOWARD oc/Purchasing Manager; b/Mar 23, 1926; h/Rt 1 Box 823, Camden, AR 71701; m/Otabel; c/Michael Howard, Susan Charla Suttle; p/Charles Richard (dec) and Hattie Mae Bradshaw (dec); mil/USN; pa/Purchasing Mgr Intl Paper Co; St & Nat Purchas'g Mgrs Assn; cp/Dem Com-man; Adv Bd Camden Area Voc Sch; Pres Camden Lions Clb; Pres Camden Boys Clb; Pres Camden U Fund; VP Camden C of C; 32° Mason; Shriner; r/Meth; hon/Plaque Camden Lions Clb 1976; Plaque Camden U Fund 1976.

BRADSHAW, HARRY W oc/Pilot; b/Apr 9, 1934; h/Roanoke, VA; m/Wanda P; c/LeeAnna Kay, Joe Peyton, Robert Carlton; p/Joseph (dec) and Lucille Bradshaw (dec); ed/HS Grad; mil/AUS 1953-55; pa/Pilot, Piedmont Airlines; cp/Masonic Lodge; Quietbirdmen of Am; r/Prot.

BRADY, BRYAN VIRGIL oc/Farmer, Retired Teacher; b/July 29, 1906; h/RR 1, Sweetwater, OK 73666; c/Albryn Evel, D'jiela Rae, Berylene Vee, Clarnell, Bryan Virgil II; ed/BS 1930, MS 1938 Okla St Univ; pa/Tchr Sci & Agric in Cols & HS 41 Yrs; Owns 640-Acre Organic Farm; NEA; Okla St Tchrs Assn; Tex St Tchrs Assn; Tex Clrm Tchrs Assn; Bd Dirs Beckham Co Farm & Home Adm; cp/Lions Clb Intl; r/Ch of Christ; hon/First Conservation Demonstration Farm in US; Catcher St Louis Cardinals.

BRADY, LAURA E oc/Land Manager; b/June 17, 1947; h/Midland, Tx; ba/Gibraltar Savings Ctr, Suite 360, Midland, TX 79701; m/Jack L; c/Scott Lee, Jacqueline Renae, Phillip Edward; p/Wesley Allen (dec) and Ora Arlie Edwards (dec); pa/Land Mgr, Gibraltar Savings; Am Assn Petro Landmen; Desk & Derrick Clb of N Am; r/Meth.

BRAIMAN, DALE EDWARD oc/Youth Program Director; b/Apr 15, 1952; m/Marihelen; p/Martin Braiman, Pompano Beach, FL; Gaye Smolin, Jacksonville, FL; ed/BA Berea Col 1977; Cand MAR Yale Univ 1982; pa/Assoc Dir Presb Child Wel Agcy; Res Dir Madison ABC Prog; Ky Grp Child Care Asn; Settlement Insts of Appalachia; cp/Chm Perry Co Sch Adv Bd; r/Jewish; hon/Phi Kappa Phi; Beekman Bible Schlr.

BRANCH, JOE L oc/Retired; b/Nov 19, 1899; h/Rt 2 Box 268, Smithdale, MS 39664; m/Georgina McNair; c/Anne Branch Walker; p/Jefferson J and Mabel Burris Branch; ed/Miss St Univ 1918-20; mil/USNR 1918-21; pa/Mktg Spec & Insp Poultry & Beef Indust, Dept Agri & Commerce 1956-65; Mgr 2000 Acre Cattle & Cotton Plantation 1943-54 (Operated 1st Cotton Picker in Area); MPIA cp/Amile Co Miss Elec Comm 1968-76; r/Bapt.

BRANDT, EDWARD WILLIAM III oc/Minister, Psychologist; b/Sept 20, 1945; h/12605; King Arthur Ct, Glenn Dale, MD 20869; ba/New Carrollton, MD; m/Janice Cosbey; c/Derek Edward, Danielle Jacqueline; p/Edward Wm Jr and Betty Harmon Brandt, Staunton, VA; ed/BA Trinity Col 1968; MDiv Wesley Theol Sem 1971; M T H S Harvard Div Sch 1975; PhD Harvard Univ 1978; pa/Pastor First Bapt Ch of New Carrollton; Clin Psychol; APA; NPA; Am Assn Christian Cnslrs; Nat Assn Evangelicals; r/Bapt; hon/Phi Beta Kappa 1974; Valedictorian Trinity Col 1968.

BRANTLEY, SYLVIA LUZETTE oc/4-H Youth Agent; b/Oct 9, 1949; h/526 N 26th Apt A105, Hattiesburg, MS 39401; ba/H'burg; p/Lindsey and Teretha Brantley, Eupora, MS; ed/BS; MA; pa/4-H Yth Agt Forret Co; Alcorn Alumni Clb; Phi Delta Kappa; Am Home Ec Assn; MS Assn of Extens; cp/Vol Vork for Retard Ctr; Sewing Tchr to Girls in Detention Ctr; r/Meth; hon/Assistantship to Univ Miss Grad Sch.

BRASFIELD, CAROLYN ALLEN oc/Secretary; b/Oct 13, 1923; h/3103 N Hancock Ave, Odessa, TX 79762; ba/Odessa; m/Otis E; c/Otis E Jr; p/Edward L (dec) and Lucille Bonner Allen (dec); ed/Grad Harrison Bus Col 1943; pa/Home Savings Assn: Asst Secy 1967-70, Sr Savings Ofcr & Asst VP 1970-78; Secy Meister Industs Inc 1978-; cp/BSA; PTA; DeMolay Mothers Cir 1954-64; DAR: Regent 1975-77, V Regent 1979-81; Permian Basin Geneal Soc; UDC, Pres 1961-62, 77-80; Magna Charta Dames; OES; r/Bapt; hon/Tex Wom of Dist, McAdams; W/W Am Wom 1981-82.

BRASSELL, CARL STEVE oc/Minister; b/Feb 15, 1956; h/3095 Baronne St, Pensacola, FL 32506; m/Gale Arlene; p/Paul F Brassell, Atlanta, GA; Jean S Brassell, Pensacola, FL; ed/BA Union Univ 1981; AA Clarke Col 1979; pa/Ordained Bapt Min; Pastor Calvary Bapt Ch, Humboldt, Tenn 1979-80; Supply Min: Area Chs in Tenn 1979, Sandridge Bapt Ch (Lake, Miss) 1978; Area Chs in Miss 1978; Pastor New Good Hope Bapt Ch, Pulaski, Miss 1977-78; Staff Evangelist Shalimar Bapt Ch Summer 1975; Radio Evangelist 1974-75; hon/Pi Gamma Mu; Frank Fair S'ship, Min Achmt, Clarke Col 1978; Dean's List, Clarke Col 1977; W/W Am HS Students 1974.

BRASWELL, ETHEL LANIER oc/Retired Teacher, Realtor; b/July 18, 1906; h/602 Canal St, Decatur, AL 35001; m/John Olan; c/Shirley B Coleman; John Braswell Jr; p/Wiley Matthew (dec) and Neppie Buchanan

Till Lanier (dec); ed/2 Yrs Col; Spec Voice & Dance Trg; pa/Ret'd Tchr Mus & Drama; Rltr; cp/UDC Mus Clb; Arts Coun; OES; r/Bapt.

BRATCHER, MARGIE NAN HOLBROOK oc/Teacher; b/Nov 14, 1938; h/3337 Sharpview Lane, Dallas, TX 75228; m/James C; c/Belinda; p/W M and Minnie Holbrook, Denton, TX; ed/BS N Tex St Univ 1960; MS E Tex St Univ 1970; pa/Kindergarten & 1st Grade Tchr in Dallas Indep Sch Dist 1960-; r/Bapt; hon/Life Mbrship PTA 1979; Ross Perot Excell in Tchg Awd 1980.

BRATT, JAMES HOWARD oc/Counselor; Coordinator, Teacher; b/Aug 27, 1944; h/8717 78th Ave N, Seminole, FL 33542; ba/Seminole; m/Carol Ann Scheibler; c/Michael J, Patrick J, Kevin J, Maureen; p/Joseph Frederick Bratt, Park Ridge, NJ; Martha Krower Bratt, Indian Rocks Beach, FL; ed/AS St Pete Jr Col; BA 1978, MEd 1979 Univ Tampa; PhD Cand SEn Univ; mil/USAF; USAR; pa/Dir Comprehensive Cnslg Ctr; Coor Ped Psychi Horizon Hosp; Instr Tampa Col; Cnslr Morton Plant Hosp; Cnslr Medfield Ctr; Am Pers & Guid Assn; Mtl Hlth Assn; cp/Golden Rule Lodge 90; r/Prot; hon/W/W S&SW; Nom'd W/W Am Cols & Univs; Spec Sr Hons Univ Tampa 1978; Outstg First-Term Reenlistee 1605 Wing MAC USAF 1979.

BRATTON, SAM I JR oc/Special Assistant to Governor; b/Jan 28, 1945; h/511 E 7th St, Little Rock, AR 72202; ba/Little Rock; p/Sam I Sr and Pauline K Bratton, Earle, AR; ed/BA Hendrix Col; JD Univ Ark Sch Law; pa/Spec Asst to Gov Bill Clinton of Ark; Am & Ark Bar Assns; Former Asst Atty Gen; Editor 1975 Edition "Sch Laws of Ark"; cp/Quapaw Qtr Assn; hon/Outstg Yg Men Am, Ark Law Review.

BRATTON, THOMAS WILLIAM oc/Supervisor; b/July 21, 1936; h/Rt 2 Box 69A, Henry, TN 38231; ba/Paris, TN; m/Janice Marie Olive; c/Felicia Lynne, Nerissa Leigh, William Timothy; p/Robert B (dec) and Myrtle M McClure Bratton, Paris, TN; ed/BBA 1957; mil/Tenn NG 15 Yrs; pa/Rd Supvr Henry Co; Tenn Sers Assn 2nd VP 1977; Region IV Rd Ofcls 1st VP 1980; Tennesseans for Better Transp; cp/Pres Woodmen of World 1972-; Civitan VP 1974; Elks Lodge 1980; r/Ch of Christ; hon/Mr Woodman Awd 1974; Trustee Woodman of World 1979.

BRAZDA, FREDERICK WICKS oc/Physician; b/Dec 17, 1945; h/6525 Argonne Blvd, New Orleans, LA 70124; ba/New Orleans; m/Margaret Mary Hubbell; c/Geoffrey Frederick; p/Fred George and Helen Josephine Wicks Brazda, Metairie, LA; ed/BS cum laude Tulane Univ 1966; MD LSU Med Ctr 1970; Intern 1970-71, Resident 1971-75 Charity Hosp, New Orleans; mil/USAR 1971-77 Major; pa/Staff Pathol Hotel Dieu Hosp, New Orleans 1975-; Dir Sch of Med Tech, Hotel Dieu 1976-; Cnslt Pathol St Tammany Parish Hosp, Covington, La & Riverside Hosp, Franklinton, La 1975-; Asst Clin Prof Pathol & Med Tech LSU Med Ctr, New Orleans 1976-; AMA; Am Soc Clin Pathols; Diplomate Am Bd of Pathol; Col Am Pathols; Am Assn for Clin Chem; La Path Soc; Gtr New Orleans Path Soc; So Med Assn; Orleans Parish Med Soc; La St Med Soc; Phi Beta Pi Med Frat; cp/La Civil Ser Leag; Friends of City Pk; Friends of Audobon Zoo; Mem New Orleans Mus Art; WYES-TV; r/Roman Cath; hon/Phi Beta Kappa 1966; Alpha Omega Alpha 1969; W/W S&SW; Contbr to Chest Feb 1980.

BREAZEALE, MARVIN E oc/Sheriff; b/Sept 18, 1938; h/PO Box 39, Purvis, MS 39475; ba/Same; m/Betty Rose; c/Stacy, Matthew; p/Lester W and Edith M Breazeale, Purvis, MS; ed/BS Univ So Miss; Grad of Miss Law Enforcement Acad; pa/Sheriff Lamar Co, Miss; Former Lamar Co Farm Bur Ins Agt; Mem Univ So Miss: Alumni Assn, Big Gold Clb, Hardwood Clb, Inter-Alumni Coun, M Clb, cp/Past Pres Purvis Lions Clb; Pres Lamar Co Heart Assn; Lambda Alpha Epsilon; Former Fin Chm BSA; Shriner Hamasa Temple; Mason Purvis Lodge 434; hon/Recip L V Murray Outstg Lion 1974; Recip JC Outstg Yng Man of Lamar Co 1974.

BRECHEEN, DORIS WILKINSON oc/Revenue Supervisor; b/Jan 2, 1927; h/8017 Sholar Dr, Baton Rouge, LA 70809; ba/Baton Rouge; m/(dec); c/Latitia Brabham, Bonness Arland Brabham, Leslie Doris, William E; p/Horace Eugene and Nora Foreman Wilkinson, Liberty, MS; ed/Dip Spencer Bus Col 1946; Cert La St Univ 1981; pa/Revenue Supvr, Ofc Audit & Taxpayer; Asst, La Dept Revenue & Taxation 1959-; Intl Am Soc Profl & Exec Wom; Nat Assn Female Execs; r/Bapt; hon/Outstg Employee of Yr 1977, Dept Revenue & Taxation; Hon Mention of Charles Dunbar Awd; Career Ser Awd Prog, La Civil Ser Leag; W/W Am Wom.

BRECKENRIDGE, HOWARD JR oc/Contractor, President Construction Company; b/Oct 20, 1941; h/713 S 36th St, Louisville, KY 40211; m/Alice; c/Leslie L, William E; p/Mary C Breckenridge, Louisville, KY; ed/Jefferson Communn Col 1968-69; pa/Pres & Contractor H-B Construction Co; NAMC; Minority Contractors of Ky; cp/Shawnee Neighborhood Clb Pres; Bd Mem Jefferson Co Housing Auth; r/Bapt; hon/Shawnnee Neighborhood Assn 1975; BSA 1971.

BRECKENRIDGE, MARILYN GRACE oc/Librarian, Journalist; b/Jan 20, 1931; h/Paragould, AR; m/Rayo Franklin; c/Joey Franklin; p/Virgil Taylor, Beech Grove, AR; Essie Taylor (dec); ed/BSE Ark St Univ; MLS Univ Miss-Oxford; pa/HS Libn 23 Yrs, Jour Tchr 5 Yrs, Greene Co Tech HS; Secy-Treas Wkly Fishing Show "The Rayo Breckenridge Show"; AEA; NEA, Pres; Delta Kappa Gamma, Pres; Ark Lib Assn; Greene Co Tchrs Assn; St Beta Clb Sponsor; cp/Mthly Vis to Nsg Home; SS Tchr; Pianist; r/Meth; hon/Recip Ark St Univ Student of Dist 1964; Ark St Beta Sponsor; Delta Kappa Gamma S'ship 1960; Wkly Column "From the Pro's Mouth" in Jonesboro Sun.

BREECE, SHIRLEY LOOPER oc/Realtor Broker Associate; b/July 21, 1935; h/Blackwell, OK; ba/206 W Blackwell Ave, Blackwell, OK 74631; m/Robert W; c/Jeanne R Young; p/Travis G and Ethel Glenora Looper, Blackwell, OK; ed/ABA No Okla Col 1968; BS NWn Okla St Univ 1970; MEd Ctrl St Univ 1975; Sapp Inst Real Est 1976; Okla Sch of Real Est 1979; Grad Rltrs Inst 1978; Cert'd Residential Spec Inst 1979; pa/Rltr Broker Assoc, Mng Broker, Breece Agcy; VP Credit Bur of Blackwell; Nat Assn Rltrs; Okla Assn Rltrs; Blackwell Bd of Rltrs, Pres 1980 & 81, VP 1980; Grad Rltr Inst; Okla Chapt Cert'd Residential Spec, Charter Mem 1979; Kappa Delta Pi; cp/Blackwell Camp Fire Bd of Dirs, Secy; Top of Okla Hist Soc; BPW Clb, Yth Ed Chm; Meth Wom's Soc of Christian Ser, Cir Chm; Kay Co Dem Party; r/Meth; hon/Rltr of Yr 1980; Ser Awd, Life Mem Wom's Soc of Christian Ser 1969; Pres's Hons 1968; Million Dollar Prodr Clb 1979 & 80.

BREEZE, EDWIN CARTER oc/Minister of Music and Education; b/Apr 22, 1930; h/1101 16th Ave, Conway, SC 29526; m/Patricia Ann; c/Mark, Scott, Sidney Ann; p/S W (dec) and Ruth Breeze, Benton, IL; ed/BMus So Ill Univ 1966; Master Sacred Mus Wittenberg Univ 1972; mil/Ret'd USAF Sr Master Sgt; pa/USAF 1951-71; Deaconal Min Mus & Ed, First U Meth Ch 1972-; Pt-time Instr Coastal Carolina Col 1972-; Am Guild Organist; Christian Guild; Organ Hist Soc; Mus Tchrs Nat Assn; SC Mus Tchrs Assn; Am Guild Eng Handbell Ringers; F'ship of U Meths in Mus; Worship & Other Arts; Pres SC F'ship 1977-78; Non Comm'd Ofcrs Assn; Bd of Deaconal Min & Worship Com, SC Conf U Meth Ch; cp/Conway Kiwanis Clb 1972-; Coastal Commun Concert Assn; Am Legion Post 111; r/Meth; hon/Sacred Solo "God the Architect" 1972.

BRENNER, JO ANN FISHMAN oc/Speech and Language Pathologist; Center Director; b/Apr 17, 1953; h/2306 Thousand Oaks Dr, Richmond, VA 23229; ba/Ashland; m/Theodore I; p/Herman and Nina R Fishman, Atlanta, GA; ed/AA Univ Fla 1973; BS 1974, MEd 1977 Univ Va; pa/Ctr Dir, Summer Rec for the Mtlly Retard'd, Henrico Co 1978-; Speech & Lang Pathol, Hanover Co Schs 1977-; RJCC Camps Unit Hd Summer 1977; Am Speech-Lang-Hearing Assn; Speech & Hearing Assn of Va; Alpha Lambda Delta, VP 1972-73; Sigma Tau Sigma; cp/Accent, Univ Fla; Pres Master Plan Com, Univ Va; hon/W/W S&SW 1980-81; Cert of Clin Comp, ASLHA 1978; Univ Va's Z Soc Shannon Schlr Awd, Thomas Jefferson Cup (Top 4th-Yr Student); Dean's List, Univ Fla & Univ Va 1971-77; Pres's Hon Roll, Univ Fla 1971-73; Cert Merit, Univ Ga 1970; H O Smith Schlr, Kiwanis Clb of N-side Atlanta 1971; W/W in HS 1971; Num Awds & Hons in HS.

BRERETON, THOMAS FRANCIS oc/Associate Professor; b/May 21, 1945; h/San Antonio, TX; ba/Dept Urban Studies, Trinity Univ, San Antonio, TX 78284; m/Maritza Beato; c/Alejandro, David; p/John T and Lucy G Brereton, San Antonio, TX; ed/BSFA Georgetown Univ 1967; MRP 1970, PhD 1973 Syracuse Univ; pa/Assoc Prof 1972-78, Assoc Prof of Urban Studies, Trinity Univ 1978-; Cnslt Nat Capital Plan'g Comm, Wash DC 1971-72; Am Inst Cert'd Planners; hon/Outstg Ser Awd, Tex Chapt Am Inst Planners 1975; Author "The Problems of Race and Sex in Public Agency Staffs" Public Administration Review 1977; Other.

BRESKO, EDNA RUTH M oc/Educational Research & Program Specialist; b/Mar 24, 1915; h/1638 Mt Vernon Ave, Petersburg, VA 23803; m/Edward Philip; ed/BS Social Sci Wm & Mary; MEd Supvn & Adm Univ Va; pa/Life Mem, Past Pres, Capitol Dist Nat Fdn Music Clbs; Bd Mem, Va Fdn Music Clbs; Past Pres, P'burg Music Clb; cp/Orgr, Pres, Southside Va Commun Concert Assn; Bd Mem, Va Christian Endeavor U; Past Pres, Am Legion Aux; r/Congreg: Dist SS Supt; hon/Pub'd Author: Articles Hist Pageant for Ch Golden Jubilee, Booklet Ch Hist; W/W Am Wom; Cert: Sem Fin Mgmt, Christian Studies.

BRETTO, CHARLOTTE CHRISTINE oc/Psychotherapist; b/Feb 16, 1953; h/Raleigh, NC; ba/4915 Waters Edge Dr, Suite 100, Raleigh, NC 27606; p/Thomas J (dec) and Sarah L Bretto, Coal City, IL; ed/BGS Univ Miami 1973; MS Biscayne Col 1975; pa/Prog Cnslr, Here's Help Proj, Dasein Drug Abuse Preven Prog 1973-74; Marriage & Fam Therapist, Fam Life Ctr, Miami 1974-76; Coor US Ofc of Ed Alcohol & Drug Abuse Cluster Grant, Wake Co Public Sch Sys 1976-77; Pvt Pract, Marriage & Fam Therapist, Raleigh Guid Ctr 1976-79; Pvt Pract Ptnrship, Indiv, Marital, Fam & Grp Therapy, Tng & Supvn, Fam Therapy Lng Ctr 1979-;

NC Assn Drug Abuse Preven; Nat Coun Fam Relats; Clin Mem Am Assn Marriage & Fam Therapy; Secy-Treas NC Assn Marriage & Fam Theapy; NC Grp Behavior Soc; Mtl Hlth Assn Wake Co; cp/NC LWV; NC Assn Marriage & Fam Therapy, Coor 1980 White House Conf on Fams; NC Del to White House Conf on Fams; hon/NC Cert'd Marital & Fam Therapist 1980; Gov's Awd for Dist'd Merit Ser to People of NC 1980; NC St Coor for the Carolinas Primary Preven Conf 1980; Author "Substance Abuse is a Family Problem" 1979 & "American Families in the 1980's - Implications for Marriage and Family Therapist" 1979.

BREWER, BETTY ANN oc/Executive Secretary; b/Dec 23, 1950; h/3236 Cloverwood Dr, Nashville, TN 37214; ba/Columbus, MS; m/Phil C; c/Teresa Dawn, Mark Curtis; p/Walter W and Mary S House, Columbus, MS; ed/Univ Miss; pa/Exec Secy So Elec Supply; cp/Xi Alpha Epsilon; Beta Sigma Phi; GTR Med Ctr Softball Tm; FCCB Clb; r/Ch of Christ; hon/Employee of Yr Awd 1976; W/W Am Wom 1979-80; Rotary Girl 1968; Lib Awd 1968; Band Awd 1968.

BREWER, DAVID CURTIS oc/Minister of Music; b/Nov 5, 1954; h/3851 Pelzer Ave, Montgomery, AL 36109; ba/Montgomery; m/Marilyn M; p/Mr & Mrs L R Brewer, McComb, MS; ed/AA SW Jr Col 1974; BMEd 1976, MMus 1977 Mis Col; pa/Min Mus Dalraida Bapt Ch; 17 Mus Orgs; Dir Largest Adult Choir in Ala; Conductor Full Orch from Birmingham Symph w Adult Choir in Montgomery Civic Ctr Each Christmas; Asst Dir for Chm of Fine Arts at Miss Col 1976-77; cp/St & Assnl Evangelism Bd; r/Bapt; hon/Hall of Fame; Outstg Teenager of Am 1976; Phi Theta Kappa.

BREWER, EULA WITHROW oc/Teacher; b/Apr 2, 1917; h/Rt 5, Shelby, NC 28150; m/Charles Woodrow; c/Barbara Ann; p/Charlie E (dec) and Mattie Canipe Withrow (dec); ed/BS; pa/NEA; NCAE; ACT; cp/Polkville Wom's Clb; Former Scout Ldr; r/Bapt.

BREWER, ORPHA ROSETA oc/Artist; b/Mar 12, 1923; h/Rt 2, Rector, AR 72451; m/Leon F; c/Eddie, Gail McDonald, Dale; p/(dec); ed/Art Courses; pa/Artist; Tchr; cp/Fairview Ext Homemkrs Clb; Rector Wom's Clb; r/Ch of Christ; hon/Awds & Ribbons from Co & St Fairs & Art Shows; Artist of Mo, June 1981, Fine Arts Coun Parogould, Ark.

BREWINGTON, DAVID ROSS oc/Chaplain; b/Mar 1, 1927; h/Rt 2 Box 71, Jacksonville, NC 28540; ba/Kinston, NC; m/Emma; c/David Jr, Jerylone, Shermon, Frank, Matthew, Mike, Melanie and Melissa; p/John D and Caromal Brewington, Pembroke, NC; ed/BA Pembroke St Univ 1963; DMin U Theol Sem 1980; mil/AUS 1945-46; pa/Chap NC Dept Human Resources 1980-; Prot Chaps Assn; Correctional Chaps Assn; cp/DAV Lions; Sudan Shrine; r/So Bapt.

BRIAN, ALEXIS MORGAN JR oc/Lawyer; h/1738 S Carrollton Ave, New Orleans, LA 70118; m/Elizabeth Louise Graham; c/Robert Morgan, Ellen Graham; ed/BS 1949; MS Trinity Univ 1954; JD LSU Law Ctr 1956; mil/USAF 1951-55; pa/Gen Civil Law Pract; Assoc Ptnr 1961-79 Deutsch, Kerrigan & Stiles; Sr Ptnr 1979- Brian, Simon, Peragine, Smith & Redfern; Am Bar Assn: Ins Sect Fidelity & Surety Com 1977-, Constrn Indust Forum Com 1977-; La St Bar Assn: Com on Bar Admission Asst Examiner 1968-, Cont'g Legal Ed Sem Spkr 1972-; New Orleans Bar Assn: Cont'g Legal Ed Sem Spkr 1971-, Law Day Spkr 1959-, US Naturalization Ceremony Spkr 1971-; Intl Assn Ins Counsel, Fidelity & Surety Com 1972-; La Assn Defense Counsel, Sem Spkr 1967-; Defense Res Inst 1972-; Am Arbitration Assn, Arbitrator 1970-; Inst of Cont'g Legal Ed, LSU Law Ctr, Sem Spkr 1972-; cp/Goodwill Industs of New Orleans: Bd Dirs 1969-, VP & Exec Com 1975-77, Adv Bd 1978; LSU Foun 1976-; La Civil Ser Leag 1975-; Intl House 1975-; Life Mem LSU Alumni Fed; Trinity Univ Alumni Assn 1954-; Life Mem LSU Law Ctr Alumni Assn; WYES-TV Sponsor Clb 1974-; BSA, Local Merit Badge Cnslr 1963-; Upper Carrollton Neighborhood Assn, ACORN Affil 1976-, VP 1976; Past Mem Yng Men's Bus Clb; Past Asst Scoutmaster Local Troops 99 & 48, BSA; New Orleans Bapt Theol Sem Foun, Bd Dirs 1972-; Inter-Varsity Christian F'ship, Bd Dirs 1974-; Ams U for Separation of Ch & St, Nat Legal Adv Coun 1977-; Christian Legal Soc 1977-; r/Bapt; hon/W/W: Am Law, Rel, S&SW; Personalities of Am; Personalities of S; DIB; Notable Ams of Bicent Era; Commun Ldrs & Noteworthy Ams; Men of Achmt; New Orleans Legal Secys Assn Boss of Yr Awd 1966.

BRICE, LAURIE SIMONTON SR oc/Superintendent of Institution for Children (State Agency), (Education); b/Apr 18, 1916; h/Rt 1, McCormick, SC 29835; m/Margaret Mae Hemminger; c/Laurie S Jr Wylie; James Douglas, Carolyn Ann; p/Eugene Douglas Brice (dec); Laura Lee Jamison (dec); ed/AB Erskine Col 1937; MEd Univ os SC 1948; Cert in Psychology, Univ Pittsburgh 1943; mil/AUS 1942-46; pa/Mem, Piedmont Technical Col Comm, Greenwood, SC; Life Mem, NEA; Mem, Am Assn of Sch Admrs; cp/Lions Clb; SC Historical Soc; Am Legion; McCormick Co Devel Bd, Secy-Treas 1964-68; r/Presb: Elder; hon/New School Facility Dedicated 1976, LS Brice School & Activs Bldg.

BRIDGES, HOWARD SNEED oc/Minister, Teacher; b/July 21, 1921; m/Eula Mae; c/Helen Marie, Daniel Blane, Mary Sue, (Stepchd:) Larry Scott, Russell Wayne, Dona Kay; p/Truett J and Grace Bridges, Vernon, TX; ed/BA Hardin Simmons Univ 1946; BD Golden Gate Bapt Theol Sem 1960; pa/Bapt Min 40 Yrs; Public Sch Tchr 21 yrs; Bapt Assn: Secy-Treas, Modr; Life Mem, Tex St Tchrs Assn, Treas; NEA; TCTA; cp/Woodman of World Lodge; BSA Scoutmaster; Kiwanis Clb; r/So Bapt; hon/Hardin-Simmons Campus Beast 1943.

BRIDGES, LEON oc/Company Principal; b/Aug 18, 1932; ba/Baltimore, MD; m/Eloise Avonne; c/Vanessa Joy, Elise Gay, Leon Jr, Elliott Reynolds; p/Agnes Goodall, Los Angeles, CA; ed/BArch Univ Wash 1959; Post Grad Study; pa/Prin Leon Bridges Co 1972-; AIA; NOMA; Md Soc Archs; Balto Chapt AIA; Vis Prof So Univ, Baton Rouge, La 1970; Guild for Rel Arch; Mtl Hlth Confs on Commun Mtl Hlth Ctr Design; cp/Black Exec Exc Prog 1970-73; Wash St Coun on Higher Ed; Exec Com Planned Parenthood/World Pop; Metro YMCA Balto; African-Am Devel Corp; City Balto Archl & Engrg Awds Com 1978-; Kappa Alpha Psi Frat; White House Conf on Small Bus; Commun Chest of Balto; Ctr for Metro Plan'g & Res, Johns Hopkins Univ; Planned Parenthood of Md; Ctr Clb; Balto Urban Leag; hon/Balto JC Victor Frenkil Achmt Awd 1973; King Co Plan'g Com Recog for Outstg Contbn 1966-69; Nat Endowment for the Arts 1975; Home of the Yr 1968; Nat Cit for Design Excell in Commun Arch 1971; Man of Yr Nat Assn Negro BPW Clbs 1978.

BRIDGES, RONALD CLAYTON oc/Horse Shoer & Trainer; b/Nov 23, 1948; h/Rt 1, Barry, TX 75102; ba/Same; m/Becky; c/Clayton; Lloyd; p/O C and Alma Bridges, Barry, TX; ed/2 Degs in Horseshoeing Brazosport Col; pa/Shoeing & Trg Horses; cp/F'ship of Christian Aths Cowboy Chapt; r/Bapt; hon/Written About by Houston Post, Brazosport Facts, Dailey Sun.

BRIDGES, S EVELYN oc/Teacher, Librarian; b/Aug 20, 1920; h/Box 27, Boiling Springs, NC 28017; m/Gail; c/Martha; p/LD (dec) and Nettie Welborn Bridges (dec); ed/Att'd Wn Carolina Univ; BA Limestone; LS Appalachian St Univ; pa/Clrm Tchr 13 yrs; Libn 14 Yrs; NCAE; NEA; ACT; ALA; NCLA; SELA; Alpha Epsilon, Delta Kappa Gamma, Chapt Pres; r/Bapt.

BRIGHTWELL, JUANITA S oc/Librarian; b/Jan 4, 1918; h/1307 Hancock Dr, Americus, GA 31709; ba/Americus; m/Louie; c/Claire Shaeffer; p/Robert Beauregard (dec) and Lottie Davis Sumner, Americus, GA; ed/BSEd Ga Col at Milledgeville 1938; MLib Emory Univ 1965; pa/Libn; ALA; SEn Lib Assn; Ga Lib Assn; AAUW; BPW; cp/Am Camellian; Azalea Garden Clb; Past Pres Alpha Chi Omega; DAR; UDC; Delta Kappa Gamma; r/Bapt; hon/Tchr Merit S'ship 1962-65; Wom of Yr; Americus Civitan Clb Outstg Public Servant Awd 1973; W/W: Am, Am Wom, Am Ed, Lib Sci, Intl, S&SW, Am & Europe, US, Ga; World W/W Wom; DIB; Personalities of South; Nat Social Dir; Foremost Women in Communs; Creative & Successful Personalities of World; 2000 Wom of Achmt; Nat Register of Prom Ams & Intl Notables; Men & Wom of Dist.

BRINKHAUS, ARMAND JOSEPH oc/State Legislator; b/Nov 7, 1935; h/80 Drawer E, Sunset, LA 70584; m/Margaret Bellemin; c/Michelle, Armand Joseph, Celeste, Julia, Andre, Renee, Margeurite; p/Armand L and Julia E Thom Brinkhaus; ed/Springhill Col 1954; Univ So La 1954-56; JD Loyola Law Sch 1960; pa/Admitted La Bar 1960; Law Clk 3rd Circuit Ct Appeals, Lake Charles, La 1960; Law Pract in Lafayette, La 1961-62, Sunset, La 1962-; Partner Firm of Olivier & Brinkhaus, Sunset 1962-; Mem La Ho of Reps 1968-75; Mem La Senate 1976-; Del Fgn Policy Conf St Dept 1970; Am, La, St Landry Parish Bar Assns; Am Judic Soc; Am Trial Lwyrs Assn; cp/Yg Mens Bus Clb; WOW; Lion; Elk; K of C (4th Deg).

BRINKLEY, MARK KENTON oc/Landscape Architect and Graphic Designer; b/Mar 21, 1952; h/1406 Sweetbriar Ave, Norfolk, VA 23509; ba/Norfolk; p/John Trotman and Shirley Joyce McLean Brinkley, Franklin, VA; ed/Atlantic Christian Col 1970-71; Old Dominion Univ 1979-; mil/AUS ROTC Ranger Platoon; pa/Landscape Arch; Graphic Designer; VP & Assoc Edward G Carson & Assocs Inc; Assoc Mem Am Soc Landscape Archs; Secy Va Chapt ASLA; cp/Sigma Phi Epsilon; Past Treas Dismal Swamp Rangers, N-S Skirmish Assn; Charter Mem & Past Secy Stonewall Jackson Camp 380, SCV; Charter Mem & Secy Capt Carey F Grimes Chapt Mil Order Stars & Bars; Friends of Confederacy Soc of London, England; Confed Meml Lit Soc; Trustee Confed Mus, Richmond, Va; St Andrews Soc, Williamsburg, Va; Clan McLean Soc USA; Life Mem Kempsville Chapt Order of De Molay; Nat Hist Soc; Nat Trust for Hist Preservation; Archaeol Inst Am; Smithsonian Inst; Va Hist Soc; Suffolk-Nansmond Hist Soc; Suffolk Civil War Roundtable; 41st Regiment of Va Volunteer Infantry (Re-enactment Grp); r/Presb; hon/John Phillip Sousa Band Awd 1969-70; Master Councilor of Kempsville Chapt Order of De Molay 1970; Illustrious Knight Cmdr of Ocean View Priory, Order of Knighthood 1973-74; St Sr Councilor for Va St De Molay Assn 1972-73;

PERSONALITIES OF THE SOUTH

Nat Rep De Molay Awd 1971; Awd'd En Va Region Rep De Molay Awd & Va St Runner-Up Awds 1970-71; Green Hon Key 1972; Winner Va St De Molay Assn Dist'd Ser Awd 1973; Life Mem & Holder Deg of Chevalier for Outstg Merit & Unusual Ser to Order of De Molay 1973; Winner 7th Am Song Fest for Orig Comp "What's the Use?" 1980; Winner Coveted Old Dominion Univ Army ROTC Ranger Tab for Outstg Profiency in Rappelling, Phy Condition'g & Mil Skills 1980.

BRINSON, DAVIE GRAY oc/Clergyman; b/Aug 22, 1945; h/110 Bryan Circle, Greenville, NC 27834; ba/G'ville; m/Jean B; c/Jeanie Lynn, David Alan, Michael Todd; p/Linister Thomas (dec) and Thesse Ora B Brinson (dec); ed/BA; ThG; Hon DD; pa/Min & Chap for G'ville City & Police Dept; cp/Mason Crown Pt Lodge; York Rite Mason; Editor York Rite Paper for G'ville; r/Orig Free Will Bapt; hon/Recip Min S'ship Mt Olive Col; Recip Hon DD from Universal Bible Col; Kappa Pi Chi; Appt'd G'ville City & G'ville Police Chaplain; Appt'd Public Relats Dir Camp Vandemere Inc; Appt'd Dir Rel Life at Free Will Bapt Chd's Home.

BRINSON, VALERA oc/Teacher; b/Nov 26, 1937; h/Rt 1, Uvalda, GA 30473; ba/Columbus, GA; p/George W Brinson, Lyons, GA; Myrtle J Brinson, Auburn, AL; ed/BS; MA; pa/Tchr Phy Sci; Sci Res; cp/Defeated Cand for Co Sch Supt; r/Meth hon/Star Tchr Awd 1973.

BRISARD, YVONNE STEPHANIE oc/Assistant Professor; b/Nov 13, 1935; h/1111 N St Charles #7, Okla City, OK 73127; ba/Edmond, OK; m/Thurdell Wickliff; c/Kevin Erwin, Adrienne Denise; p/Heinrich J Brisard (dec); Nellie Brisard Williamson (dec); ed/BA, MA Univ Chgo; PhD Univ Wis-Madison; pa/Asst Prof, Ctrl St Univ; Intl Rdg Assn; AAUW; cp/Orgr Neighborhood Tutoring Ctr; Work w Parent Grps; r/Prot.

BRISTER, MARK A oc/Minister; b/Aug 8, 1951; h/Bolivar, MO; ba/PO Box 358, Bolivar, MO 65613; m/Rhonda Rhee Evatt; p/C W and Gloria N Brister, Ft Worth, TX; ed/BA Baylor Univ 1973; MDiv 1976, PhD 1980, SWn Bapt Theol Sem; pa/Pastor First Bapt Ch, Bolivar, Mo 1980-; Prof SWn Bapt Theol Sem, 1977-80; Phi Eta Sigma; cp/Rotary Intl; r/So Bapt; hon/W/W Am Cols & Univs 1974, 75, 76, 78, 79; Outstg Yng Men Am 1978, 79; Outstg Grad in Sch of Theol, SWn Bapt Theol Sem, Albert Venting Jr Meml Awd 1976; Am Bible Soc Awd in Preaching.

BRITTAIN, KATHY H oc/Instructor; b/Aug 5, 1949; h/220 E Cherry St, Jonesboro, AR 72401; m/Eddie; c/Wesley, Shann; p/Evelyn Osborn, Memphis, TN; ed/BSE 1977, MSE 1978 Ark St Univ; EdD Memphis St Univ 1981; pa/Instr; Devel'd Ceta Data Processing Prog; Devel'd Curric to Tch Data Processing Classes for Jonesboro Area Voc Tech; Tchr Bus Communs Memphis St Univ; Phi Kappa Phi; Delta Pi Epsilon; Am Bus Communs Assn; Nat Bus Ed Assn; Prog Chm DPMA; hon/Outstg Yng Wom in Am 1979; W/W Am Univs & Cols 1978-79; Phi Beta Lambda Awd for Outstg Grad Student 1978; Author: "Top-Row Proficiency in Typewriting" 1979; "Face the Future with Adaptability to Change" 1980; Others.

BRITTON, BARBARA ANN oc/Secretary; b/May 7, 1930; h/Box 206, 224 W Choctaw, Savanna, OK 74565; ba/McAlester, OK; m/Johnie J Sr; c/Susan Diane Lyles Oldham, Jon Brian Lyles, Patricia Kathleen, Johnie J Jr; p/Claude Howard Tiger, Weleetka, OK; Della Inez Stowers, Savanna, OK; pa/Secy to Commun Sers Dir for City McAlester; cp/Rebekah Lodge; OES; Indian Nation CBers; Mil Wives Clb; VFW Aux; r/Bapt; hon/Soloist for: St Rebekah Assem; Intl Rebekah Assem; St Rebekah Choir.

BRITTON, JACKIE PEELE oc/Farmer; b/Feb 5, 1948; h/RFD 2 Box 113C, Williamston, NC 27892; ba/Same; m/Patricia Keel; c/Kristi Elizabeth; p/William C and Susan D Britton, Williamston, NC; ed/AAS Pitt Tech Inst; mil/USN; pa/Farmer; Farm Bur; Peanut Commodity Comm; cp/Ruritan Nat; r/Christian; hon/NC St Seed Champ 1976 & 77.

BRITTON, MICHAEL LINN oc/Minister, Lieutenant US Army, Student; b/Sept 27, 1956; h/Box 15, Covington, OK 73730; ba/Same; m/Cassandra L; c/Mandy; p/M Robert and Shirley D Britton, Terre Haute, IN; ed/BA cum laude Johnson Bible Col 1978; Cand MDiv Philips Univ; Further Studies Oxford Univ 1981; mil/AUS Lt, Chaplain, Staff Spec; pa/Sr Min Covington Ch; Lt AUS; Student Phillips Univ; Assoc Prodr & Editor Christian Rel TV Show "By the Way"; Hosp Chaplain; Sr Assc & Yth Min; Promo Pers of Christian Chd's Home; Min Assn Ill & Okla; Nat Rifle Assn; cp/Min Assn Covington; Little Leag & Babe Ruth Baseball Coack; YMCA; BSA; Scout Ldr; Grad Sem Senator; Sojourners; r/Christian Ch Indep; hon/Nat Hon Soc 1974; Nat Stran Steel Awd 1974; YMCA Ser Awd 1975, 79; Nat Rifle Assn Awd 1974; Ordain'd into Min 1976; Nat Deans List Cols & Univs 1977-78; Weekly Columnist *The Covington Record*.

BROADHURST, NORMAN NEIL oc/Executive; b/Dec 17, 1946;

h/5714 Council Grove, Houston, TX 77088; ba/Houston; m/Victoria Rose Thomson; c/Scott Andrew; p/Frank Spencer and Dorothy Mae Broadhurst, Fair Oaks, CA; ed/BS Calif St Univ 1975; MBA Golden Gate Univ 1975; mil/USAFR 1966-73; pa/Del Monte Corp 1969-76; Colgate Palmolive 1976-78; Coca-Cola Co: New Prods Brand Devel Mgr 1978-79, Brand Mgr 1979-; Am Mktg Assn; Toastmasters Intl 1974-76; hon/W/W S&SW.

BROADWAY, BENJAMIN FAYETTE oc/Minister; b/Aug 9, 1915; h/PO Box 408, Gibson, NC 28343; ba/Gibson; m/Alice Lanier; c/Benjamin Fayette Jr, John William, Alice Jane; p/George Lafayette (dec) and Bertha Louise Finch Broadway (dec); ed/AB Furman Univ 1938; ThM So Bapt Theol Sem 1943; mil/USNR WWII Chap; pa/Semi-Ret'd Bapt Min; cp/Past Mem Civitan Intl; Lions Intl; r/So Bapt; hon/W/W S&SW.

BROADWAY, CHRISTIANA RUTH JOHNSON oc/Teacher; b/Aug 22, 1953; h/Rt 1 Box 185A, Kinston, NC 28501; ba/Kinston; m/Charles A III; c/Christiana Laura; p/R E L Jr and Anna Ruth Hill Johnson, Kinston, NC; ed/BS 1974; MS 1978; pa/Tchr Sci Ed Woodington Jr HS 6 Yrs; Tchr Chem Bethel Christian Acad 1 Yr; NCAE; Pres NC Student Home Ecs Assn 1973; cp/OES; r/Bapt; hon/Most Outstg Sr Awd E Carolina Univ 1974; Most Outstg Tchr Awd Woodington Jr HS 1980.

BROADWAY, RONALD REX oc/Insurance Broker; b/Sept 14, 1956; h/1933 W 10th St, Apt B1, Laurel, MS 39440; ba/Laurel; p/Rex R and Dorothy J Broadway, Laurel, MS; ed/ALA; ABA; mil/USN; pa/Ins Broker; Conslt; cp/Miss Yng Dems; Laurel JCs; r/Bapt; hon/Ldg So Div Agt 1979.

BROBST, WILLIAM A oc/Director of Transportation Safety; b/Jan 31, 1930; h/SR 285, Kitty Hawk, NC 27949; ba/Wash DC; m/Lucy Anne; c/Linda, Gail, Kathy, Diana, David, Dennis, Dannette; p/William E and Doris I Brobst (dec); ed/BS NWn Univ; mil/USNR Cmdr; pa/Dir Trans Safety, US Dept Energy; Pres Transport Envir Inc 1978-; Formerly Assoc'd w: Energy Res & Devel Adm 1975-77, Atomic Energy Comm 1970-74, Interst Commerce Comm/Dept Trans 1966-70; Am Nuclear Soc; Nat Acad Scis; Hlth Physics Soc; Nat Def Trans Assn; cp/Am Heart Assn; Red Cross; Sierra Clb; Nat Wildlife Foun; Am Bonanza Soc; Nat Assn Watch & Clock Collectors; Nat Rifle Assn; Am Motorcycle Assn; r/Prot; hon/Spec Achmt Awd, ERDA; Commend for Public Ser, DOT; Public Ser Awd, ICC; Nav Resv Commend Medal, USN; Spec Achmt Commend, AEC; Chief of Nav Pers Awd, USN; Silver Lifesaving Medal, US Treasury; Pub'd Author.

BROCHU, ROBERT HENRY SR oc/USAF; b/June 9, 1939; h/405 S Ash, Altus AFB, OK 73521; ba/Altus; m/Eloise Mary; c/Robert Henry Jr, Raymond Joseph, Mary Florence; p/Henry Joseph (dec) and Florence Hattie Brochu (dec); mil/USAF 18 Yrs; r/Salvation Army; hon/Salvation Army Corps and Div Man of Yr.

BROCKMAN, PAUL ROBERT oc/Public Administrator; Civic Leader; Organization & Management Advisor; b/May 5, 1934; h/200 Forest Dr, Falls Ch, VA 22046; ba/Wash DC; m/Nancy Tilghman Edward; c/Lauren Tilghman, Rebecca Fortner; p/H C Brockman, Topeka, KS; Naomi Fortner Brockman (dec); ed/BA Baker Univ 1959; MA Am Univ 1968; Grad Study, Univ Va; mil/AUS 1956-58; pa/Hist Falls Ch, Inc (Hist Restoration Co): Fdr 1975-, Dir & Pres 1975-78; NASA St & Local Relats Ofcr 1978-; Spec Asst, NASA Technol Utilization Ofc 1977-78; Sr Mgmt Analyst, NASA HQs 1969-77; Chief, Res & Handicapped Progs, Budget & Manpower Div, US Ofc of Ed 1967-69; Other Past Positions; Am Soc for Public Adm, Coun Mem Nat Capitol Area Chapt; cp/Mem Var Rec & Cult Assns; Past Mem Bd Mgrs, Va Scottish Games Assn; Patron & Orgr Mod Renewal of Scottish Fiddling in US; VA Commr, Clan Donald-USA; Elected City Coun-man, Falls Ch 1971-76; Metro Wash Coun of Govs: Past Mem Bd Dirs, Past VP, Former Chm & Mem Num Coms incl'g Chm Bicent Com & Cong of Bicent Comms of Metro Wash; Others; r/The Falls Ch (Epis): Mem, Lay Ldr; hon/Fellow, Nat Inst of Public Affairs; Outstg Yg Men Am; W/W in Govt; NASA Space Ship Earth.

BROHARD, ELLEN B oc/Professor; b/Aug 11, 1942; h/Rt 2 Box 218F, Leesburg, VA 22075; ba/Sterling, VA; m/Thomas L; c/Bill, Mark; pa/Patrick L and Effie B Brady, Ashland, VA; ed/BS Longwood Col 1963; MS VPI & St Univ 1975; pa/Secretarial Sci Asst Prof & Prog Coor, No Va Commun Col; Chm Fac Concerns Com; BPW Clb; cp/Longwood Col Alumni; Soccer Assn; Asst Coach; Cub Scout Secy; Phi Mu; r/Bapt; hon/W/W S&SW.

BROKAW, MARVIN J JR oc/Banker; b/Nov 14, 1938; h/3010 Merrimac Dr, Montgomery, AL 36111; ba/Mont; m/Charlotte Carpenter; c/Leslie Diane; p/Eleanor Brokaw, Beulah, MI; ed/BA Mich St Univ 1960; mil/AUS Security Agcy; pa/Mktg Ofcr, First Ala Bank of Mont; Bank Mktg Assn; Am Inst Bnkg; Mont Advtg Clb: Past Pres, Mem Bd Dirs; cp/Kiwanis Clb; Bd Dirs YWCO; Adv Bd Public TV; Gov's Conf on Libs; r/Meth; hon/Silver Medal Awd, Mont Advt Clb 1978.

BROOKS, FREDERIC LENOX oc/News Anchorman; b/June 10, 1935; h/Juban Rd, Denham Springs, LA; ba/Baton Rouge, LA; m/C Darnanne Herron; c/Frederic Glenn, Freida Dawn; p/Roy Lenox and Mable Mullis Brooks, Lavinia, TN; ed/Grad Pathfinder Broadcasting Sch, Wash DC; pa/FBI 1953-54; KWFT TV 1959-64; KPRC TV & Radio 1964-66; WBRZ TV: News Dir 1972-74, Special Proj Dir & News Anchorman 1974-; Radio-TV News Dir's Assn; r/Bapt; hon/UPI Best Newsfilm Story 1964; Assoc Press Best On-Scene Newsfilm 1970; Am Bar Assn Media Awd for Ct Reporting 1971; Chgo Film Fest Creative Excell Awd 1979; Contbr Articles to: RTNDA Bulletin; *American History Illustrated; Civil War Times Illustrated; State Times-Morning Advocate* Newspaper.

BROOKS, GARLAND ODELL oc/Carpenter; b/Mar 26, 1938; h/Rt 1 Box 474, Stuarts Draft, VA 24477; m/Helen Conner; c/Sheila, Lisa; p/Isaac Martin and Alice Ruth Chandler Brooks, Stuarts Draft, VA; ed/Maintenance Sch, E I DuPont 4 Yrs; mil/Va NG 6 Yrs; pa/Maintenance-Carpenter E I DuPont; cp/Greenville Ruritan Clb; Coach Little Leag & Babe Ruth Baseball; Stuarts Draft Rescue Squad; r/Bapt; hon/Key Person Awd, Ridgeview Christian Sch 1977-78; Helping Hand Awd, Stuarts Draft Rescue Squad, 1978; Sr Squad Mem of Yr, Stuarts Draft Rescue Squad 1980.

BROOKS, JAMES L oc/Psychologist; b/Mar 5, 1933; h/5618 Grce Pt Ln, Houston, TX 77048; ba/Houston; m/Marva; c/Sheila, Henrietta, Jeannetta; p/James Brooks; Henrietta Bridges, Orange, TX; ed/BS; MEd; MA; mil/Armored Calvary & Transp Corp; pa/Psych; cp/Local Civic Grps; St Philip Sch Bd; Houston Urban Leag; Citizens Adv Coun for Non-Public Schs; Active in St & Local Govt; r/Cath; hon/Num Civic & Ser Awds; Listed in Notable Ams of Bicent Era.

BROOKS, JAMES (JIM) WRIGHT oc/Minister; b/Sept 17, 1942; h/Shreveport, LA; ba/1220 N Hearne Ave, S'port, LA 71107; m/Kathy; c/Jan, Jimbo; p/A Q and Estelle Johns Brooks, S'port, LA; ed/BA La Col 1972; MDiv SWn Bapt Theol Sem 1974; mil/AUS 1960-63 Security Agcy; pa/Min Cherokee Pk Bapt Ch; NW La Epilepsy Assn; Common Bd Inc; cp/Civil Air Patrol; r/So Bapt; hon/Dist'd Ldrship Grad 1962; 7th Army NCO Acad Cert of Esteem 1963; Blue L 1969; Outstg SGA Mem 1967-68; Beginning Swimming Instr Am Red Cross 1969-.

BROOKS, JOHN D (PETE) oc/Construction Supervisor; b/Mar 13, 1927; h/Mineola, TX; ba/Mineola; m/Bonnie June Haynes; c/Delmer Huel, Sharron June; p/Charlie F (dec) and Mae E Brooks, Henderson, TX; mil/AUS 1945-46; pa/32 Yrs Tex Hwy Dept Maintenance; r/Bapt; hon/Lady Bird Hwy Beautification Awd 1980.

BROOKS, JUNE oc/Oil and Gas Company President; b/Jun 24, 1924; ba/915 Stanley Ave, Ardmore, OK 73401; c/Claudia B Chappell, Rebecca Susan, William Ben; p/Major M and Lillian Berry Brooks, Ardmore; pa/Pres & Fdr June Brooks Oil & Gas Co; Am Petrol Inst; Bd Dirs Indep Petrol Assn; Am Assn Petrol Landmen; Okla City Landmen's Assn; Okla Petrol Coun; Okla Indep Petrol Assn; Tex Indep Prodrs & Royalty Owners Assn; SPE-AIME; API Spkr's Bur, Wash DC; IPAA Spkr's Bur, Wash DC; AAPL Com on Land Use Bills; Energy Res Assocs, Dallas, TX; API On-Shore Exploration Com, Public Info Subcom; AAUW; r/Presb; hon/Spec Ser Awd for Dist'd Ser, AAPL; Spkr's Awd, Okla Petrol Coun; Cert of Apprec, Univ Ks.

BROOKS, OWEN WAYNE oc/Minister, Counselor; b/July 6, 1933; h/7098 Greystone Dr, Riverdale, GA 30274; ba/Riverdale; m/Ruth Mowell; c/Carlton Wayne, Bonnie; p/Owen King and Geraldine Garrison Brooks (dec), Miami, FL; ed/BA Mercer Univ 1957; BD, ThM New Orleans Bapt Theol Sem 1960; DMin Luther Rice Sem 1980; mil/USN 1952 Lt Cmdr; pa/Sr Min First Bapt Ch Riverdale; Am Assn Marriage & Family Cnslrs; Chaplain Clayton Co Police & Sheriffs Dept; cp/Lions Intl; Regional Dir BSA; Bd Dirs YWCA; Intl Assn Police Chiefs & Chaplains, St Pres; Mason; r/So Bapt; hon/Blue Key Hon Soc 1956; JC Outstg Yng Man of Yr 1972; Sidney Sullivan Awd, Mercer Univ 1957; Author: "The Law Enforcement Chaplain" 1980; "Restless Pews" 1978.

BROOKS, VELMA LOTRICE oc/Cosmetologist; b/Jan 7, 1931; h/3434 S R L Thornton Fwy, Dallas, TX 75224; c/Sandra, Terry, Daryl; ed/Bethume Cookeman Col; El Centro Jr Col; Prairie View A&M Univ; Mme C J Walker Beauty Col; pa/Dir Velma B's Beauty Acad; Instr Mme C J Walker Beauty Col; Beauty Opr Velma B's Coiffures; Beauty Opr Neighborhood Beauty Salon; Tech C J Walker Mfg Co & Simpson Labs; Owner Pretty Girl Fash Boutique; YWCA; NAACP Chapt of Cedar Crest; NHCA; First Black Wom to Become Mem OHFC; Alpha Chi Omega Sorority; Bd Dirs Simpson Labs; Fdr Nat Hairweavers Assn; r/Christian; hon/Bus Wom of Yr Psi Lambda 1979; W/W Black Am 197-78; Bus Wom of Yr Pylon N B L 1976; Bus Wom of Yr S Dallas BPW 1975; Trail Blazers Awd 1974; Dedicated Wom Awd 1973; Bus Wom of Yr Theta Nu Sigma 1971; Won Over 100 Awds & Trophies for Outstg Work in Field of Cosmetology; 1st Place Paris Festival, Awd'd Golden Rose (Highest Awd Given for Indiv Hairstyling).

BROOME, DOUGLAS RAY oc/Minister of Music and Youth; b/Oct 4, 1956; p/Hollis R and Laverna L Broome, Terry, MS; ed/AA Clarke Col 1979; BA Miss Col 1980; pa/Min; r/Bapt; hon/Jr Col Achmt S'ship; Laird-Morrison S'ship (Twice); H M King Meml S'ship; Dean's List, Miss Col; John C and Alma Cowley S'ship; W O Students in Am Jr Cols; Pres Student Body, Dean's & Pres's List Clarke Col.

BROOME, SADIE ALLRAN oc/Teacher; b/June 2, 1954; h/300 S Elm St, Cherryville, NC 28021; ba/Belmont, NC; c/Stephanie Lynn Arthurs; p/W J and Sadie A Allran, C'ville, NC; ed/BS; MEd; pa/Non-Categorical Tchr of Resource Students w Specific Learning or Behavior Disabilities; Chm Sch Com for Placement of Excepl Chd; Sch Evaluator of Chd w Spec Needs; cp/Secy C'ville Little Theater; r/Luth; hon/Phi Kappa Phi; William Danforth Good Citizen Awd; Nat Hon Soc; Co-Ed CHENOCA.

BROTHERS, CASSIE MARIE CAMPBELL oc/Library Administrator; b/Oct 20, 1928; h/123 Summit Dr, Helena, AR 72342; ba/Helena; m/William John Jr; c/William John III, Brooke Ann B Tappan; p/John Calvin Sr and Marie Parker Campbell (dec); ed/BSE Univ Ark; MLS Univ Miss; pa/Dir Lib Media Sers, W Helena Sch Dist; Pres Ark Lib Assn; Am Lib Assn; Helena Lib Assn; AECT; Ark AV Assn; Exec Bd Mem SWn Lib Assn; Ark Lib Comm; Ark Assn Ed Profl Edrs; Ark Assn Ednl Admrs; cp/Sec'dy Curric Comm for Ednl TV; Phillips Co Hist Assn; r/Meth; hon/Delta Kappa Gamma; Sigma Alpha Iota; Zeta Tau Alpha.

BROWDER, JOHNIE MAE GOMILLION oc/School Principal; b/Oct 2, 1919; h/Rt 1, McKenzie, AL 36456; ba/Greenville, AL; m/Ralph J; c/Ralph Thaddeus, Tempie Leah Mutschler; p/Thad J (dec) and Irene Lee Gomillion, McKenzie, AL; ed/BS Troy St Univ 19459; MEd Auburn Univ 1956; AA Cert 1959-60; pa/Tchr McKenzie HS 21 Yrs; Supvr of Guid, Butler Co Public Schs 6 Yrs; Prin W O Parmer Elem Sch 1971-; Butler Co Ed Assn: Secy, Treas, VP, Pres; AEA; NEA; NAESP; ACSAS; AAESA; ASCD; r/Bapt; hon/Delta Kappa Gamma; Kappa Delta Pi; Intl Platform Com.

BROWDER, MILFORD O oc/Businessman; b/Sept 24, 1936; h/1620 Shiloh Rd, Corinth, MS 38834; ba/Corinth; m/Shirley Ann; c/Tony O, Teri Lynn; p/Oshie (dec) and Mary Browder, Corinth, MS; ed/Sr Exec Acctg & Floral Design & Mgmt; pa/Interior Decorator; Floral Designer; cp/City Beautification Chm 2 Yrs; hon/Pres N Miss Florist Assn; Am Inst Floral Designers.

BROWN, ALFRED WILLIAM oc/Reading Teacher; b/June 19, 1932; h/Box 505, Talihina, OK 74952; m/Margie Nell; c/Winifred Nell; p/Arthur Wille (dec) and Lela Mae Brown, Muse, OK; ed/LLB La Salle; MS OSU; BS E Ctrl; mil/USN 1951-59; pa/Rdg Tchr; NEA; cp/Dem Party; hon/Recog of Masters Prog in Nat Security.

BROWN, AMANDA J oc/Human Resource Development Specialist; b/July 28, 1930; m/Julius J; c/Kayre LeVelle; p/Richard and Emmaline Jones, Coosada, AL; ed/BS Tuskegee Inst 1950; MA NYU 1958; PhD Fla St Univ 1979; pa/Univ Ga Coop Ext Ser; Ga Home Ec Assn, Chm Res & Reporting; Ga Assn Ext Home Ec, St Staff Rep; Am Home Ec Assn, V-Chm Ext Sects; cp/Camp Relitso Inc, Secy; Housing Task Force, Chm Housing Rehab; r/Meth; hon/Perfect Attendance in HS; Tchr of Yr; Dist'd Ser Awd.

BROWN, BILLIE GORDON oc/Minister; b/Oct 4, 1934; h/Oct 4, 1934; h/Williamsburg, KY; m/Patricia N; c/Jeffrey A, Brian D; p/Sterling and Nora Brown, Williamsburg, KY; ed/AB Clear Creek Bible Col 1959; BA Cumberland Col 1961; BD So Bapt Theol Sem 1965; MA Am Mgmt Sch, Wn Reserve; ml/USN Ret'd; pa/Missionary/Pastor, Home Missions Bd, So Bapt Conv; Am Assn Marraige Cnslrs; cp/BSA: Chm Exec Bd, Lake Cumberland Dist 1976-82; Hon Order of Ky Cols, Dpty Sheriff, Whitley City, Chaplain 1980-82; r/Bapt; hon/W/W: S 1968, Ky 1969.

BROWN, BILLY GUNN oc/Justice Court Judge; b/May 21, 1932; h/4805 37th Ave, Meridian, MS 39301; ba/Meridian; m/Brenda; c/Melissa, Holly; p/William Preston (dec) and Catherine Gunn Brown, Meridian, MS; ed/BBA; mil/AUS Ret'd; pa/Just Ct Judge Dist 1; Acctg & Auditing; cp/Just Ct Ofcrs Assn; Am Legion; VFW; DAV; r/Presb.

BROWN, BILLY JOE oc/Minister, Insurance Broker; b/Sept 15, 1934; h/Rt 6, Val Grove Rd, Cedartown, GA 30125; ba/Marietta, GA; m/Mattie L Pierle; c/Sharan Ann Burgdurf; Billy Joe Jr, Peggy Lynn Camp, Rebecca Lynn Hooper; p/Lillian Edith Brown, Rune, GA; ed/BBA Calif Wn Univ 1978; Bible Inst 1976-79; Cand for Masters 1981; mil/AUS 1950-53; pa/Bapt Min; Inst Broker; cp/Congressional Adv Com Ga 7th Dist; r/Bapt; hon/Cert of Apprec from Dept of Defense S Korea 1976; Cert of Apprec Jon Ju Korea 1978; Cert of Apprec Polk Co Bapt Assn 1979.

BROWN, BINA RUTH oc/Businesswoman; b/Mar 13, 1921; h/906 Branton Ave, Columbia, MS 39429; ba/Same; p/Rufus (dec) and Nebraska Welborn Brown (dec); ed/AA Jones Co Jr Col 1940; BA Maryville Col 1942; Dip Intl Accts Soc 1954; pa/Owner Brown Enterprises (Acctg, Import'g, Piano Tuning, Income Tax Work); Violist Jackson Symph Orch 1947-77; Miss Fed BPW Clbs; r/Worldwide Ch of God; hon/BPW S'ship to Col; Best Sr Thesis 1938; 1st Place Meadl in Spanish 1939.

BROWN, BUTLER MALLOY oc/Artist; b/Dec 17, 1937; h/Rt 3, Hawkinsville, GA 31036; m/Laverne T; c/Anthony Allen, Julie Rene; p/Bunk D and Mary Magdalene Brown, H'ville; pa/Participant "Art in the Embassies Prog"; Painting on Loan to Ambassador Schwartz, Bahamas; r/Bapt; hon/Work in Collections of: Pres Carter, King Khalid of Saudi Arabia, Huang Chen, Min Cult, Peoples Repub of China.

BROWN, CAROL WYNN oc/Civic Worker; b/Aug 17, 1937; h/2711 Park Hill Dr, Ft Worth, TX 76109; m/C Harold; c/Tracey, Terry, Allison, Harold; p/Sproesser (dec) and Mildred Patton Wynn, Ft Worth, TX; ed/BS magna cum laude Tex Christian Univ 1957; cp/Camp Carter YMCA, Bd Dirs 1974-81; Ft Worth Jr Leag: Bd Dirs 1964-68, Sustaining Mem 1978-; Ft Worth Opera Board 1970-74; Ft Worth Lib Bd 1973-79; Vol Ctr Com of Tarrant Co U Way 1972-79, Chm 1976; Plan'g & Res Coun of Tarrant U Way 1975-81; Steering Coun 1979-81, Camping Com Chm 1978-81; Chm Ch Cir Univ Christian Ch 1975-77, Study Chm 1975-77, Worship Chm of Wom of Univ Christian Ch 1978-80, Publicity Chm 1981-, Mem of Choir; City Camping Chm, First Tex Coun of Camp Fire Girls 1968, Vol Day Camp Councellor 1966-72, Ldr 1965-72; Tex Hist Survey Com 196973; Vol Planned Parenthood 1966-68; Vol Blind Chd's Ser Ctr 1964-66; Ft Worth C of C, Ladies Div; Zi Eta Pi; Kappa Kappa Gamma, Pres Ft Worth Alumni 1965, Pres Epsilon Alpha House Bd 1967, Chapt Advr 1968-72; Pi Beta Phi Mother's Clb, Pres 1980; Repub Clb; r/Univ Christian Ch; hon/Columnist *The American Brittany*; Recip Carnegie Hero Cert 1972; Distaff Handlers Awd, Am Brittany Clb 1977; Charlotte Joy Farnsworth Awd, First Tex Coun of Camp Fire Girls 1970.

BROWN, CHARLES HOWARD oc/Marketing Specialist; h/PO Box 952, Forrest City, AR 72335; ba/Forrest City; m/Claudia Hughes; c/Charles H Jr, Cedric Lynn, Carleton Hughes; p/Arthur J Sr (dec) and Bessie Griffin Brown, Wilmot, AR; ed/BS; Grad Studies; pa/Mktg Spec E Ark Produce Mktg Assn; Former Mem AEA; NEA; AEATA; Conserv Soc Am; cp/NAACP; Ambassador Civic Clb; Omega Psi Phi; r/St Luke AME Ch; hon/Dist'd Ser Awd Omega Psi Phi 1973.

BROWN, CLETA JEAN oc/Nursing Administration, Clinical Specialist; b/July 28, 1948; h/Rt 5 Box 820; Burleson, TX 76028; m/Fred H; c/Shane Justin; p/Cleo and Anita Cogburn, Burleson, TX; ed/BSN TCU 1970; MSN U Tex Austin 1977; pa/Nsg Adm, Harris Hosp-Meth; Clin Spec; RN; Am Heart Assn; ANA; TNA; TNA#3; AACN; Nat Hon Soc Nsg; Sigma Theta Tau; cp/Nat Paraplegic Assn; United Way of Tarrant Co; r/Meth; hon/W/W Am Wom 1979-80; Spec Care Assn Hall of Fame Awd 1978-79; CCRN Critical Care RN.

BROWN, CONGER E oc/Administrator; b/Sept 19, 1931; h/Rt 1, Box 279-M, Duncan, OK 73533; ba/Duncan; m/Sandra; c/Eugene Scott, Randall Stacey, Vernon Conger, Steven Dean; p/Conger Brown (dec); Evelyn R Brown, Kingston, OK; ed/BS; MEd; Adm Certn; mil/AUS 1954-56, Capt 2nd Inf; pa/Dir Duncan-Stephens City Civil Def, Civil Def Preparedness Agy 1977-; Dist Supt Schs Temple Public Schs, Temple, Okla 1975-77; Mun Judge, Temple 1975-77; Dist Supt Schs, Bokchito (Okla) Schs 1973-75; Okla City Public Schs 1967-73: Classroom Tchr, Sch Cnslr, Asst Admr; Other Previous Positions: Am & Okla Assns Sch Admrs; Cooperative Coun Sch Admrs; AAUP; VP SW Area Okla Assn Civil Def Dirs; Okla Assn Sch Bus Ofcls; Nat Resv Ofcrs Assn; Okla Chapt Mil Order World Wars; cp/Past Pres Lions Clb, Bokchito; Former Secy Kiwanis, Temple; Elks Lodge; Others; r/Meth.

BROWN, DAVID MICHAEL oc/Superintendent of Schools; b/Apr 3, 1950; h/Rt 1 Box 220, North, SC 29112; ba/North; m/Mary Green Brush; p/Reginald C and Margaret Louvenia Thames Brown, Florence, SC; ed/BA Newberry Col; MA SC Univ; pa/Supt; SCEA; NEA; AASA; IRA; Phi Delta Kappa; cp/United Way; BSA; Chm Lib Bd O'burg Co; DSS Chd House Review Bd Chm; r/Epis; hon/Human Relats Awd 1976; SC Supt of Yr 1978.

BROWN, EARLE PORTER oc/Electronic Engineer; b/Nov 29, 1929; h/Salisbury, NC; p/Jesse Oscar and Ola Sue Brown, Salisbury, NC; ed/Att'd MIT 1962, Univ Alaska 1959, Air Univ 1958; mil/USAF 1956-61; pa/Sales, Res, Engrg; cp/Knights Comdr of Ct of Hon; Master of Fulton AF&AM; Master of Lodge of Perfection; Past Comdr Knights Templor; Past Master RSM; Past Comdr Coun of Kodish; Past High Priest RAM; Past Pres AMD; Past Pres Rowan Shrine Clb; Knighted to Royal Order of Scotland, Knight Masons of USA St Patricks; r/Bapt.

BROWN, FRANK THOMAS oc/Instructor; Sculptor; Graphic Artist; b/Jan 20, 1936; h/220 W Madison, Baltimore, MD 20201; ba/Same; m/Sylvia Martha; c/Alleanore, Sharrone, Mercia; p/Frank Charles Sr and Emily Christina Brown; ed/BS 1976, MA 1978 Morgan St Univ; pa/Instr Mech Engrg; Instr Sculpture, Graphics, Art Hist; Contbr to Sev S AfricanMags incl'g: *Contrast, Cape Times, Drum*; Num One-man Exhibits incl'g: Sea Point Pavilion, Cape Town, S Africa 1971-73, New Martin Luther King Ctr, Pa 1974, Capital Hill, Wash DC 1978, Howard Law Sch 1978, Shell S Africa 1978, USA Info Ctr, S Africa 1978; Sev Group Shows incl'g: Black Arts Calenda 1977, Morgan St Univ 1976, Univ Balto 1974; Alpha Kappa Mu; r/Ch of England; hon/Sev S'ships & Bursaries; 8 Gold Dips.

BROWN, GWENDOLYN RUTH oc/Music Specialist; b/May 17, 1942; h/1222 Carolina St, Graham, TX 76046; ba/Abilene, TX; p/Earle Robert and Alice Jewell Washburn Brown, Graham, TX; ed/BME; ME; pa/Mus Spec; NEA; Tex Mus Edrs Assn; Tex St Chrts Assn; cp/Chatauqua Lit & Sci Clb; Abilene Chorale Inc; Abilene Evening Lions Clb; r/Ch of Christ; hon/Mu Phi Epsilon; Kappa Delta Pi.

BROWN, J BILLY oc/Pastor; b/Aug 10, 1934; h/Dalton, GA; m/Edna C; c/Timothy J; p/W O (dec) and Zula Brown, Cedartown, GA; ed/N Ga Bible Inst 1975; New Orleans Bapt Theol Sem 1978; mil/Ga NG 1953-62; pa/Pastor Carolyn Bapt Ch; Cost Acct Aragon Mills 1956-70; Past Chm: Am Bible Soc; Evangelism Com; Com on Coms; Ch Trg Dir for N Ga Bapt Assn; VP & Prog Chm Pastors Conf for N Ga & Murray Co; cp/Ruritan Clb; r/Bapt.

BROWN, J CURTISS oc/Chief Justice; b/Oct 4, 1921; h/523 Bolton Pl, Houston, TX 77024; ba/Houston; m/Lovice; c/Curtiss Jr, William A, Catherine Ann; p/Aubrey Murphy and Eva Thate Brown, Lovington, NM; ed/AS Tarleton St Univ 1940; LLB Univ Tex Sch Law 1943; pa/Chief Justice 14th Supreme Judicial Dist Tex, Houston 1976-; Assoc Justice 14th Supreme Judicial Dist 1973-76; St Bar Tex: Bd Dirs 1966-70, Chm Bd Dirs 1969-70; Editor in Chief Tex Law Review; Chancellors, Am Col Trial Lwyrs; r/Prot.

BROWN, JAMES HENRY oc/Assistant State Soil Scientist; b/Oct 18, 1946; h/1245 Pene Lane, Auburn, AL 36830; ba/Auburn; m/Joyanne Burrow; c/Tracy Joy, Christina Lane; p/Doc Felix and Mary Louise Brown, Augusta, AR; ed/BSA Ark St Univ 1969; Grad Credit, Iowa St Univ 1977; mil/Ark ANG 1968-75 1st Lt; pa/Soil Scist, Soil Conser Ser, USDA, Ark & Ala 14 Yrs; US Agcy of Intl Devel, Senegal, Africa May & June 1980; Profl Soil Classifiers of Ala, Secy-Treas; Profl Soil Classifiers Assn of Ark; Soil Conserv Soc Am; Ala Soil Fertility Soc; Am Soc of Agronomy; Soil Sci Soc Am; Nat Assn Conserv Dist; Nat Geog Soc; cp/F&AM; Scottish Rite Bodies, 32° Mason; Jr C of C, Bd Dirs; r/Bapt; hon/Cert of Merit, Soil Conserv Ser 1976, 72; Prin Author "Soil Survey of Randolph Co, Ark" 1980.

BROWN, JETHER LEE WALKER oc/Principal; b/June 13, 1928; h/5161 Gault St, Jackson, MS 39209; ba/Jackson; m/R Jess Sr; c/Jacqualy B Roberts, Richard Jess Jr; p/Emanuel B and Johnnie Coleman Walker; ed/Spec Deg Jackson St Univ 1976; MEd Ind Univ 1962; BS Tougaloo Col 1950; pa/Elem Sch Prin 1976-; Elem Sch Tchr 1965-76; Second Sch Tchr 1950-65; Delta Sigma Theta; Christ the King PTA Treas 1960-63; cp/W Jackson Garden Clb 1956-; r/Meth; hon/Phi Kappa Phi Hon Soc 1976.

BROWN, JOHN W oc/Chief Executive Officer; b/Sept 15, 1934; h/6535 Evergreen, Kalamazoo, MI 49002; ba/Kalamazoo; m/Rosemary K; c/Sarah Beth, Janine; p/Albert T (dec) and Treva Moody Brown, Paris, TN; ed/BS Auburn Univ 1957; pa/Pres & Chief Exec Ofcr; Dir Am Nat Bank & Trust of Mich; Dir Clausing Corp; cp/Dir Jr Achmt; r/Prot.

BROWN, KENNETH ALDEN oc/Minister; b/Feb 6, 1941; h/1408 Piedmont Dr, Paducah, KY 42001; ba/Paducah; m/Marianne Reed; c/Cheryl Anne, James Alden; p/David Alden Brown (dec); Lillian M Ward, Paducah, KY; ed/AB Murray St Univ 1963; ThB 1976, MMin magna cum laude 1979 Mid-Continent Bapt Bible Col; Cand DMin Luther Rice Sem; Wn Bapt Hosp Paducah Clin Pastoral Ed; mil/Army ROTC; pa/Pastor Bapt Tabernacle Ch; W Union Bapt Assn; Chm Prog Com Assnl Min's Conf; Exec Bd Mem Ky Bapt Conv; Secy Missions Com Ky Bapt Conv; cp/Hon Order Ky Cols; Hon Capt Belle of Louisville; Jackson Purchase Hist Soc; Mkt House Mus; r/So Bapt; hon/W/W Ky 1974; Outstg Am in South 1975; Ky's Bicent Register 1976.

BROWN, KENNETH NEIL oc/Minister; b/July 24, 1948; h/317 Bonnahurst Dr, Hermitage, TN 37076; ba/Nashville, TN; m/Cynthia Hautman; c/Kara Margaret, Joel David, Dorothy Erin; p/Raymond Arthur and Margaret Dowdy Brown, Dickson, TN; ed/BS Shorter Col 1975; MDiv SEn Bapt Theol Sem 1978; mil/USAF 1966-70; Chaplain USAR; pa/Min, Lakewood Bapt Ch, Nashville; Christian Cnslrs Assn; cp/Lions Intl; Free & Accepted Mason; r/So Bapt; hon/Soc of Dist'd Am HS Students Nat Apprec Awd 1980.

39

PERSONALITIES OF THE SOUTH

BROWN, LEE ELLIOTT oc/Academic Administrator; b/Apr 15, 1938; h/2829 Timmons Ln #162, Houston, TX 77027; ba/Houston; c/Gerald, Kirsten; p/Helen Holmes; ed/BA Col of New Rochelle 1973; MPA LI Univ 1976; pa/Dir, Div Enrollmnt Sers, Univ Houston, Ctrl Campus; Am Pers & Guid Assn; Assn of Non-White Concerns; Am Col Pers Assn; Am Soc for Public Adm; Conf of Minority Public Adms; Com for Human Resource Devel; AAUW; Nat Assn Black Sch Edrs; CASE; Tex Assn Wom Deans, Admrs & Cnslrs; Am Assn Col Registrars & Admissions Ofcrs; cp/Spec Projs Cnslt, Operation Breadbasket; Bd Dirs Houston Area Wom's Ctr; Bd Trustees Riverside Gen Hosp, Houston; Black Dems of Westchester Co 1976-77; Former Mem Many Others.

BROWN, LINDA JO oc/Coordinator; b/Nov 14, 1949; h/Rt 1, Anderson, SC 29621; m/Paul M; c/Kelly, Shaun; pa/Coor, Spec Sr Adult Prog, Sch Dist 5.

BROWN, MABEL LOUISE BAKER oc/Data Processing; b/Nov 27, 1943; h/East Gadsden, AL; m/Hubert; c/Derrick Lynn, Daryn Eugene, Dante Eric; p/Willie Ardie (dec) and Maudie Louise Banks Brown (dec); ed/Dip Garfield Voc Sch 1968; Gadsden St Jr Col 1978-79; pa/Data Processing, Anniston Army Depot; cp/Grad of Trg for Ser Biblical Class, Mt Moriah Bapt Ch; SS Tchr of Bible Class, Mt Gilead Bapt Ch; r/Bapt; Pres Yng Matrons #2 Org, Advr Yng Adult & Jr Choirs; hon/Woman of Yr, Macedonia Bapt Ch 1980.

BROWN, MARIAN LEE oc/Circuit Clerk; b/Oct 26, 1929; h/206 S 14th Ave, Hattiesburg, MS 39401; ba/H'burg; m/Donald E; c/Donna Gail Brown Mooney, Kenneth, Wesley, Wayne, Debra, Diane; pa/Arthur (dec) and Anna Carley O'Briant (dec); pa/Circuit Clerk; Legal Secys Assn; ABWA; r/Bapt.

BROWN, MILDRED JOHNSON oc/Psychologist; b/Dec 27, 1933; h/2330 Good Hope Rd SE 804, Wash DC 20020; ba/Wash DC; p/Nicholas O (dec) and Irene D Johnson, Mobile, AL; ed/BS; MEd; PhD; pa/Sch Psych; Phi Delta Kappa; Nat Assn Sch Psych; Am Alliance for Hlth, PE & Rec; cp/Vol Ser to Aged & Infirm; Ser to Yths in Need of Placemnt Assistance; Alpha Kappa Alpha; r/Cath; hon/Pres's Awd for Acad Achmt; Recip Var Acad Relat'd Fin Awds inclg Nat Inst Mtl Hlth F'ship, Terminal F'ship Awd for Doctoral Investigation.

BROWN, PATSY SUE oc/Salesperson; b/Nov 10, 1941; h/PO Box 25, Liberty, MS 39645; ba/Centreville; m/Herbert J; p/Mr and Mrs R C Jones, Liberty, MS; ed/Draughon's Bus Col 1960; Pvt Pilot's Lic 1965; Commercial Pilot's Lic 1968; Att'd SLU 1975; pa/Salesperson, Hardwood Lumber; cp/BPW; Charter Mem Baton Rouge 99s (Wom's Flyers Clb); Amite Chapt DAR; r/Meth.

BROWN, RANDALL ALLEN oc/Executive Director; b/June 17, 1952; h/Athens, TX; ba/404 Carroll St, Athens, TX 75751; m/Lorraine; c/Lorrie; p/Jack D Brown, New Orleans, LA; Mary Lou Carlile, Dallas, TX; ed/BA Paris Jr Col 1972; BS McNeese St Univ 1976; pa/Profl Baseball Player, San Diego Padres 1974-76; Exec Dir Henderson Co YMCA; r/Bapt.

BROWN, RAY oc/Retail Sales and Fleet Manager; b/Aug 7, 1921; h/2700 San Diego Ave, El Paso, TX 79930; ba/El Paso; m/Mary Alyce; c/Ray III, Mary Alyce Tynan, James, Patrick M, Arlene E; p/Ray (dec) and Amy J Brown, El Paso, TX; ed/TCM NM Mil Inst 1943; mil/AUS COE Capt; pa/Caterpillar Tractor Dlr 1948-52; Mexico Mine Op 1952-60; Ford Sales & Mgmt 1960-, Kemp Motor Co, El Paso; Ford Soc Master Sales Cnslrs; cp/AIME; Social, Profl Sales, 1st Chm Adv Bd; r/Cath; hon/Top Hatter Ford Awd; 18th Consec Yr Ford Profl Sales Cnslr.

BROWN, RICHARD oc/ABC Investigator; b/Dec 16, 1951; h/7 Sandhurst Circle, Little Rock, AR 72209; b/Little Rock; m/Patricia Nunn; c/Shawnrick Malik, Brandi Charmane; p/Richard Brown, Chgo, IL; Marie Brown, Camden, AR; pa/ABC Invest; cp/PTA; Elks; NAACP; r/Bapt; hon/Letter from Gov Clinton on Wonderful Job Perf.

BROWN, RICHARD JESS SR oc/Attorney; b/Sept 12, 1912; h/5161 Gault St, Jackson, MS 39209; ba/Jackson; m/Jether W; c/Jacqulyn Brown Roberts, Richard Jess Jr; p/Jess Brown (dec); Ernestine Love (dec); ed/BEd Ill St Univ 1935; MS Ed Ind Univ 1942; LLB LaSalle Univ; TX So Univ Law Sch; pa/Prac Law w Brown, Alexander & Sanders; Miss St Bar Assn; Nat Bar Assn; Magnolia Bar Assn; Nat Judicure Soc; Am Bar Assn; cp/Masons; Elks Lodge; Phi Beta Sigma; Jackson Progressive Voters Leag; r/Prot; hon/Hon Doc Laws, Natchez Col 1973; Legal Defense Lawyer of Yr 1964; C Francis Straton Awd of NBA 1965; Lawyer Guild Awd 1965; Jack Young Lawyer Awd 1976.

BROWN, RICKEY oc/Clerk; b/June 12, 1959; h/Box 19 Adams St, Selmer, TN 38375; p/Evan Jr and Nona Jean Brown, Selmer, TN; pa/Supvr Warehouse Ops, ITT Grinnell Corp, Henderson, TN; Woodmen of World; Tenn Constable's Assn; cp/Selmer Vol Fire Dept; McNairy Co Civil Defense Unit; r/Bapt; hon/Nat Yth Bd of Dirs 1979; Mem Editorial Bd *Westagram Jour*, Bolivar, Tenn.

BROWN, ROBERT JOSEPH oc/Under Secretary of Labor; b/Sept 10, 1929; h/9311 Holly Oak Ct, Bethesda, MD 20034; ba/Wash DC; m/Iolene Cecilia Gau; c/Joseph, Mary, Timothy, Patrick, Barbara, Susan, Thomas, Brenda; p/George R Brown, Pasadena, CA; Eileen Marie Bagley (dec); ed/AA Univ Minn 1951; pa/Under Secy of Labor; cp/Dem Party; r/Rom Cath; hon/Awd for Outstg Career Achmt, Dept Labor.

BROWN, ROSCOE DELANO oc/Teacher; State Legislator; b/Feb 23, 1915; h/1107 Holly St, Jonesboro, AR 72401; ba/J'boro; m/L Belle Morris; c/Al Tripp, Charlotte Ann, Ramona Kay; p/John Madison and Mary Pate Brown, W Plains, MO; ed/BSE Ark St Univ 1949; MSE Geo Peabody for Tchr 1952; mil/AUS 1940-45, 153 Inf Alaska; pa/Tchr 1952-55, 1959-75; NEA; AEA; cp/Ark Leg 1963-75; Employee US Senate 1955-59; Mason; Am Legion; DAV; Pi Kappa Alpha; r/1st U Meth Ch: Adm Bd; hon/Ed Commr of Sts; PKA Hall of Fame.

BROWN, SANDRA (SANDI) LOY oc/Financial and Estate Planner; h/1663 Hillcrest Rd #241, Mobile, AL; ba/Mobile; p/Loy and Maridean Sigman Brown, Bogue Chitto, MS; ed/AA SW Jr Col; BA Mis Col; MRE New Orleans Bapt Sem; pa/Fin & Est Planner, Loy Brown Co; Life Underwriters; Ldrs Round Table Clb; cp/Jr Wom's Clb; Art Assns; r/Bapt; hon/Rookie of Yr 1978; Paul Revere Ldrs Round Table Mem; Writer Var Articles & Manuscripts for So Bapt Conv.

BROWN, VIRGINIA MAE oc/Commissioner; b/Nov 13, 1923; ed/AB WVa Univ 1945; LLB, JD 1947 WVa Col Law; pa/Admitted to Pract Law Before Sev Cts; Commr Interst Commerce Comm 1964-77; Public Ser Comm 1962; Ins Commr WVa 1961; Legal Counsel to Gov of WVa 1961; Asst Atty Gen 1952; Exec Secy WVa Judic Coun 1949; Law Clerk to Atty Gen WVa 1947; Sch Tchr Winfield HS, Winfield, WVa 1944.

BROWN, WILLEX JR oc/Composer, Trumpeter, Producer; b/Sept 19, 1955; h/1101 E Caswell St, Kinston, NC 28501; ba/New York, NY; p/Willex Sr (dec) and Helen Louise Brown, Kinston, NC; ed/Att'd ECU Summer 1973, Berklee Col Mus 1973-75, Boston Sch of Electronic Mus 1974, Juilliard Sch 1975-78; BS NYU 1979; pa/Co-Owner & Exec Bd Mem Unisphere Pub'g Records & Tapes Inc; Trumpeter in Var Chs & Bands in NYC; Tech Dir Bhasker Dances of India 1979; Co-Producer Barbara Watts & Friends Dance Concert 1980; Conductor Our Lady of Atonement Choir 1980; Production Staff Universal Jazz Coalition 1976-78; Black Artists Guild; Universal Jazz Coalition; Musician's Local 802; cp/Bldg Co-Chp Cystic Fibrosis Assn 1980; r/Cath; hon/Dean's List NYU 1979; Nat Endowment of the Arts F'ship Grant in Jazz Comp 1980.

BROWN, WILLIAM RAY oc/City Administrator; b/July 2, 1948; h/611 Major Dr, Manning, SC 29102; ba/Manning; p/Ernest and Kate Ray McKenzie, Dillon, SC; ed/BA 1972, MPA 1974 USC; mil/USNR 1965-66, 1974-76; USMCR 1971-72, 1979-80; pa/City Adm 1978-; Co Adm 1977-78; Region Coun Govt 1975-76; Intl City Mgmt Assn; Am Soc Public Adm; Acad Polit Sci; cp/Masons; Am Legion; Rotary; r/Presb; hon/Pres Cert to Viet Nam Vets 1979; Outstg Yng Men Am 1978; W/W S&SW 1980; Navy Achmt Awd w Combat V Device; Combat Action Ribbon; Navy Unit Citation Ribbon; Viet Nam Campaign Ribbon; Viet Nam Ser Ribbon w 8 Stars; Navy Expert Pistol; Nat Defense Medal; Marine Corp Expert Rifle Badge.

BROWNE, WILLIAM JOSEPH oc/Bank Vice President; b/May 27, 1921; h/3525 Norbourne Blvd, Louisville, KY 40201; ba/L'ville; m/Rita Tong; c/William Joseph III, Paul Burnell; p/William Joseph Browne (dec); Marie Anna Young (dec); ed/BA Providence Col; Grad Studies Columbia Univ; Univ L'ville Sch Law; mil/AUS WWII; pa/Sr VP Citizens Fidelity Bank & Trust Co; Am Bnkrs; Consumer Bnkrs; Sales & Mktg Execs; Ky Bnkrs; Dir Accept Inc; Soc Cert'd Consumer Credit Execs; cp/Ky Hist Soc; Ky Cols; r/Roman Cath; Archdiscesean Fund; hon/W/W Fin & Indust.

BROWNING, WILLIAM C oc/Director of Personnel; b/Jan 9, 1956; h/308 N 40th Ave, Hattiesburg, MS 39401; ba/H'burg; m/Teresa Green; p/Joseph Edward and Elizabeth Hamilton Browning, Mobile, AL; ed/BA William Carey Col; pa/Dir Pers, S Miss Elec Power Assn; Am Soc Pers Adm; So Miss Pers Assn; cp/United Way; Carey Showcase Adv Bd; r/Bapt; hon/Citizen of Yr 1976; Outstg Yng Men of Am 1979; Special Pres Com on Campus Devel, Wm Carey Col.

BROWNLEE, MARY CATHERINE (CATHY) oc/Parts Manager, Mechanic; b/Apr 23, 1949; h/1433 Marigold, Borger, TX; ba/Borger; m/Thomas Ray; c/Brian Thomas, Tracey Anne; p/Charles D (dec) and Muriel Gilbert, Borger, TX; pa/Parts Mgr, Mech, Bob Cooper Buick-Pontiac Inc; r/Bapt.

BRUCE, YALE BENJAMIN oc/Director of Community Services; Minister; b/Feb 26, 1936; h/320 N Lincoln, Daytona Bch, FL 32014; ba/Daytona Bch; m/Gloria Sykes; c/Yale Benjamin III, Clifton, Derek, Yolanda; p/Ephraim and Floril (dec); ed/AA; BDiv; Degs Received at Morris Brown Col, Fla A&M Univ; pa/Dir Commun Sers, Volusia Co, Fla; Min Allen Chapel AME Ch, Daytona Bch; Nat Coun Chs; Former Dir Commun Action Agy; cp/C of C, Daytona Bch; NAACP; Masons; r/Allen Chapel AME Ch: Min.

BRUCK, CHARLOTTE MARIE oc/Counselor/Consultant; b/Sept 30, 1917; h/2100 S Conway Rd, #I-5, Orlando, FL 32806; ba/Orlando; p/Nick and Laura Bruck (dec); ed/MEd; BA; pa/Writer; Lectr; Artist; Co-Fdr & Former Dir of REACH Prog (Sister of Providence); Co-Fdr Guid Coun; Author *Discovery Through Guidance Series* (10 Books); r/Cath; hon/Ser Awds: Nat Cath Guid Conf, Diocese of Orlando, Silva Mind Control.

BRUFF, BEVERLY OLIVE oc/Public Relations Director; b/Dec 15, 1926; h/508 Tomahawk Trail, San Antonio, TX 78232; ba/San Antonio; p/Albert Griffith (dec) and Hazel Smith Bruff, San Antonio, TX; ed/BA Sophie Newcomb; pa/Assn of Girl Scout Exec Staff; Tex Public Relats Assn; Tex Press Wom; Wom in Communs; Am Wom in Radio & TV; Alamo Bus Communicators; Nat Fdn Press Wom; Coun of Pres; Coun of Intl Relats; Zoning Comm, Hill Country Village; Soc Fundraising Execs; hon/1974 Silver Spur Awd; Tex Press Wom Writing Awds 1970-73.

BRUMBELOE, THOMAS EZRA oc/Financial & Administrative Executive; b/Feb 28, 1927; h/PO Box 726, Canton, GA 30114; ba/Same; m/Gladys L; c/Thomas L, Robert A; p/Edna Cosper Brumbeloe, Roanoke, AL; ed/BS, BS Auburn Univ; mil/US Navy, WWII; pa/Fin & Adm Exec; Var Trade Assns; cp/Lions; Aide de Camp, Gov's Staff, St of Ga; r/Meth; hon/W/W: Ga, Bus & Fin.

BRUMFIELD, DON oc/Clerk; b/Jan 21, 1934; h/Rt 6, Richmond, KY 40475; m/Mayme S; c/Tim, April; pa/Line Clerk; r/Bapt; hon/Author: *Expressions of Love* 1980.

BRUMFIELD, ROBERT EDSEL oc/Banker; b/May 28, 1943; h/Rt 1 Box 11, Bogue Chitto, MS 39629; ba/Brookhaven, MS; p/Sandy Bickham (dec) and Mildred Seab Brumfield (dec); ed/Cert Draughon's Bus Col; Basic & Standard Certs Am Inst Bnkng; mil/Miss Air NG; pa/VP St Bank & Trust Co; Past Pres SW Miss Chapt Bank Adm Inst; cp/Dir Brookhaven Noon Lions Clb; Dir C of C; Mem Lincoln Co Repub Exec Com; r/Bapt; hon/Contact Clb Awd Presented by Brookhaven-Lincoln Co C of C.

BRUMFIELD, SHANNON MAUREEN oc/Speech and Language Pathologist; b/Sept 14, 1946; h/2314 Calhoun St, New Orleans, LA 70118; ba/Metairie, LA; p/Fred Orlan and Mary Kathleen Maloney Brumfield, New Orleans, LA; ed/BA La St Univ 1968; MA Temple Univ 1970; PhD Univ Fla 1978; pa/Pvt Prac Speech & Lang Pathol; Am Speech Lang Hearing Assn, Cert Clin Competence-Speech; La Speech & Hearing Assn, License in Speech Pathol; Am Edrs of Deaf; Cert by Nat Coun Ed of Deaf; Intl Assn Logopedics & Phoniatrics; cp/Alliance for Good Govt, Jeunesse d'Orleans; La Coun Performing Arts; Jr Com of Wom's Opera Guild; Kappa Kappa Gamma Alumnae; Orleans Clb; Les Amies Ensembles; hon/Pub'd in *Journal of Speech and Hearing Disorders; American Annals of the Deaf*; Papers Presented at Wkshops & Nat Am Speech, Lang & Hearing Convs.

BRYAN, JACOB FRANKLIN III oc/Chief Executive Officer and Chairman of the Board; b/Feb 26, 1908; h/4255 Yacht Clb Rd, Jacksonville, FL 32210; ba/J'ville; m/Josephine Christian Hendley; c/Jacob Franklin IV, Carter Byrd, Kendall Gibson; p/Jacob Franklin II (dec) and Olive Julia Gibson Bryan (dec); ed/Hon LLD Bethune-Cookeman Col 1965; pa/Chm Bd Dirs & Chief Exec Ofcr Indep Life & Accident Ins Co & Herald Life Ins Co; Bd Dirs: Fla First Nat Bank of J'ville, Fla Nat Banks of Fla, Fla Federal Savings & Loan Assn; Num Others; cp/Fla Hist Soc; J'ville Hist Soc; Nat Trust for Hist Preserv; Fla Soc SAR; J'ville Chapt SAR; Dirby-Smith Camp SCV; Order of Stars & Bars; Fla Heart Assn; Am Cancer Soc; Indust Am Corp; Fl St C of C; Jr Achmt; Mar of Dimes; Chd's Mus; Child Guid Clin; Chd's Home Soc of Fla; US Indust Coun; Commun Plan'g Coun of J'ville Area; Chm Citizens Com of Juvenile Ct; Charter Mem 200 Clb of J'ville; Bold New J'ville Prog Com; Meninak Clb of J'ville; Newcomen Soc Fla; Public Affairs Com & Ednl Com of Nat Assn Mfcs; Bapt Meml Hosp Bd Trustees; J'ville Univ Bd Trustees; Fla Yacht Clb; Timuquana Country Clb; River Clb; Seminole Clb; Ye Mystic Revellers; Others; hon/Hon Life Mem Alpha Kappa Psi; Boss of Yr, Arlington Jr C of C 1960; Man of Yr, Fla St Assn Life Underwriters 1960; Boss of Yr, Am Bus Wom's Assn 1965; Spec Awd of Apprec, Fla Cancer Soc 1959; Ted Arnold Awd for Outstg Ser & Civic Accomplishments from J'ville Jr C of C; Recip of Top Mgmt Awd in Commerce & Indust 1968; Elected to Jean Ribault at 400th Celeb; Trail Blazers Awd, J'ville Assn Life Underwriters 1969; Appt'd Chief of J'ville Fire Div 1976.

BRYANT, ANITA JANE oc/Entertainer, Executive; b/Mar 25, 1940; ba/Selma, AL; c/Robert Einar Green Jr, Gloria Lynn Green, William Bryant Green and Barbara Elisabet Green; p/Warren Gene Bryant, Sasakwa, OK; Anniece Lenora Cate, Terlton, OK; ed/Att'd NWn Univ 1959; DLitt Am Christian Col 1978; pa/Miss Okla and Runner-Up Miss Am Contest 1959; Guest Star Bob Hope's Christmas Tours 1960-67; Sang Star Spangled Banner for Dem & Repub Convs 1968; Num White House Perfs 1964-69; Num Billy Graham Evangelistic Crusades 1965-; Perf'd at Orange Bowl & Super Bowl Games 1970-71; TV, Recording Artist, Author 1971-; Chm Bd Protect Am's Chd Inc; Spokeswom for Coca-Cola Co 1963-67, St of Fla Citrus Indust 1968-80, Friedrich Air Conditioning Co 1969-; USO Nat Coun 1961-66; Bd Mem Wom's USO of NY 1965-; Hon Chm Freedoms Foun at Val Forge 1969-70; First Foun for One Nation Under God 1969-; Am Orchid Soc 1970-; Friends of Art Soc 1970-; Com Mem Proj Survival 1970-; Film Narrator *Drugs Are Like That* 1970; Hon Chm Mtl Hlth Assn Fla 1970-; Pres Save Our Chd Inc; cp/Univ Tampa Alumni Assn; Fla Future Bus Ldrs of Am; hon/Recip USO 25th Anniv Silver Medallion Awd 1966; VFW Gold Medal & Cit Awd 1966; Ldrship Awd, Freedoms Foun at Val Forge 1969; Wom of Yr Awd 1970; VFW Citizenship Gold Medal & Cit 1978; Named #1 Most Admired Wom in Am, Good Housekeeping Poll 1978-80; Named to Gallup Poll Most Admired Wom List 1978; Listed on 25 Most Influential Wom in Am List 1978-79; Nom'd for Grammy Awd for Best Rel Recording of *How Great Thou Art* 1968; Named to Okla Hall of Fame 1966; Hon Dr Deg William Carey Col; Author: *Mine Eyes Have Seen the Glory* 1970, *Amazing Grace* 1971, *Bless This House* 1972, *Fishers of Men* 1973, *Light My Candle* 1974, Bless This Food - The Anita Bryant Family Cookbook 1975, *Running the Good Race* 1976, *The Anita Bryant Story* 1977, *Raising God's Children, At Any Cost*; Most Recent Records: *Anita Bryant's Greatest Sacred Hits & Singing a New Song*.

BRYANT, ELIZABETH NOE oc/Nurse; b/Apr 29, 1940; h/1127 Rutledge Ave, Florence, SC 29501; ba/Florence; c/Kimberly Haws, Pure Leeds; p/William L Jr and Dorothy R Noe, Daytona Bch, FL; ed/BSN Boston Univ; MEd Francis Marion Col 1979; pa/RN; ANA; SCNA; NLN; SCLN; Num Coms; cp/Bd Dirs SC Heart Assn; Num Coms; r/Prot; hon/W/W Am Wom.

BRYANT, HOWELL DEE oc/Businessman; b/July 10, 1915; h/2621 Division St, Texarkana, AR 75501; ba/Texarkana; m/Anita Louise; c/Howell Wayne, Donna Jayne, Linda Anita Moilen; p/Willie B (dec) and Nettie Collins Bryant (dec); mil/AUS 4 Yrs; pa/Owner & Oper Mattress & Upholstery Shop; cp/Bd Public Affairs Texarkana 2 Yrs; Citizen Com Texarkana; Quorum Ct; r/Meth; hon/Four Battle Stars; Unit Cit.

BRYANT, JIMMY CARL oc/Minister; b/July 14, 1940; h/Rt 1 Box 171, Summerville, GA 30747; ba/S'ville; m/Esther Timbes; c/Michael Carl, James Alan; p/Carl Bryant (dec); Jewel Martin, Tupelo, MS; ed/Att'd NE Miss Jr Col; BA Blue Mtn Col; Grad Work Univ N Ala; In-Ser Tng Wn Mtl Hlth Inst; mil/USN 19757-61; pa/Pastor: First Bapt Ch (Counce, Tenn), Walnut Bapt Ch (Walnut, Miss), N Corinth Bapt Ch (Corinth, Miss), Highland Bapt Ch (Tishomingo, Miss), New Liberty Bapt Ch (Glen, Miss) & S Summerville Bapt Ch (S'ville, Ga); Radio Announcer WVOM (Iuka, Miss) & WBIP (Booneville, Miss); Former: Assnl SS Dir, Jt Missions Com Chm, Stewardship & Evangelism Com Chm, Pastor-Advr Ch Tng Dept SW Tenn Region, Ofcr in Min Assn & Local Pastors Conf; Work'd w Bill Penley Evangelistic Assn: Area Crusade Dir, Cnslr Tng; cp/Little Leag/YMCA Sports Activs; Vol Fireman; Spec Dpty, Courtesy Involvement; r/So Bapt; hon/Author "When the Shoe Is On the Other Foot" *Church Administration* May 1981.

BRYANT, LeEARL ANN oc/Corporate Engineer; b/Oct 3, 1942; h/416 N Taylor Ave, Pgh, PA 15212; ba/Pgh; ed/BSEE; MSEE; pa/Corp Engrg Staff, Rockwell Intl; Tex Soc Profl Engrs; Inst Elec Engrs; Penn Acad Sci; Am Soc for Engrg Ed; Soc Wom Engrg; hon/Outstg Yng Wom Am 1971; Yng Engr of Tex 1975; Bus Wom of Yr 1970.

BRYANT, R KELLY JR oc/Assistant Secretary; h/618 Bernice St, Durham, NC 27703; m/Artelia Tennessee; ed/BS Hampton Inst 1940; Att'd NC Col 1941-42, Courses Life Ofc Mgmt Assn; pa/Bkkpr Peoples Bldg & Loan Assn, Hampton, Va 1940; Bkkpr Mutual Saving & Loan Assn, Durham, NC 1941-44; NC Mutual Life Ins Co: Chief Clerk, Ordinary Dept 1944-56, Mgr Ordinary Dept 1956-60, Asst Secy-Mgr, Ordinary Dept 1960-65, Asst Secy 1965-; Secy Durham Bus & Profl Chain 1943-; Secy Chain Investment Corp; cp/Trustee White Rock Bapt Ch, Chm Auditing Com; First Worshipful Master & Secy A S Hunter Lodge #825 F&A Masons; Secy Durham Bus & Profl Chain 1943-; Secy Durham Outboard Boating Clb 1966-; Chm Audit & Budget Com, Most Worshipful Prince Hall Grand Lodge F&A Masons of Jurisdiction of NC, Investment Com; Nat & Durham Chapts, Nat Hampton Alumni Assn, Treas NC Region; Ed Com Durham Com on Black Affairs; Adv Com Local OMBE Proj; Bd Dirs Vol Sers Bur: Inc'd Chm, Nom'g Com; Durham C of C; Adv Com Durham City Bd of Ed; Chm Sch Improvement Com, Burton Sch

PERSONALITIES OF THE SOUTH

PTA; Scoutmaster Boy Scout Troop 187, Burton Sch 1951-; Registrar Burton Sch Voting Precnt #13 1951-; Former Mem & Ofcr Num Civic Orgs; r/Bapt; hon/Silver Beaver Awd, BSA 1953; NC Hamptonian of Yr 1957; Man of Yr, Durham Housewives Leag 1958; Alumni Merit Awd, Nat Hampton Alumni Assn 1969; Apprec for Ser Awd, A S Hunter Lodge #825 1974; Most Outstg Secy, A S Hunter Lodge 1976; Recip Spec Cert, Durham City Coun 1977; Man of Yr, Durham Outboard Boating Clb 1978; Apprec for Ser Awd, Nat Hampton Alumni Assn 1979.

BRYANT, SUE MEDLIN oc/Legal Secretary; b/Mar 30, 1955; h/606 Third Ave, Selma, NC 27576; ba/Smithfield; m/Cecil Ray; c/Meredith Leigha Nicole, Hannah Meghan Suzanne; p/Ernest Bernard and Frances Hughes Medlin, Selma, NC; ed/EMT Deg Johnston Tech Inst 1974; pa/Legal Secy 1973-; Future Bus Ldrs Am 1970-73, Secy 1972-73; r/Free Will Bapt; hon/1st Pl Awd, NC St Clerical Div, Bus Ldrs Am 1973; Poem "I Heard You Crying" Pub'd *Grass Roots Poetry of Johnston County* July 1980.

BRYANT, SYLVIA LEIGH oc/Editor-Publisher, Poet; b/May 8, 1947; h/Rt 5 Bos 498A, Madison Hgts, VA 24572; p/Mr and Mrs Hundley Bryant, Madison Hgts, VA; pa/Editor-Pubr *The Anthology Society*; Poet; Pres The Anthology Soc; Area Publicity Chm, Dr Stella Woodall Poetry Soc; r/Bapt; hon/Gold Medal, Accademia Leonardo da Vinci 1980; Poet Laureate, Dr Stella Woodall Poetry Soc Intl; Cert of Merit, Accadamia Leonardo da Vinci 1980; Rep St of Va in Mar 1981 Issue *Poet*; Cert Apprec ABI; Author Num Poems & Editor Num Anthols.

BRYE, BRUCE A oc/Environmental Engineer; b/Oct 28, 1937; h/1002 Arden Way, Signal Mountain, TN 37377; ba/Chattanooga, TN; m/Jean R; p/M O Brye, Waverly, IA; Lydia E Brye (dec); ed/BS, MS Univ Ia; pa/Envir Engr Water Quality & Ecology Br, Div Envir Planning, Tenn Val Auth; Reg'd Profl Engr: Ia, Tenn; NSPE; TSPE; AWWA; WPCF; ASCE; r/Bapt: Deacon, SS Tchr, Usher, Assoc Treas, Counting & Fin Coms; hon/Chi Epsilon; Charter Mem Order of Engr, Chatta Chapt.

BRZEZICKI, MICHAEL JOSEPH oc/Hospital Management Consultant; h/Murfreesboro, TN; ba/Health Concepts Inc, 3332 Powell Ave, Nashville, TN 37204; m/Anne Mather; p/Stanley Walter and Elizabeth Neidzwicki Brzezicki, Bristol, CT; ed/AA NWn Conn Com Col 1969; Ctrl Conn St Col 1969-70; Queens Col 1972-73; Moheghan Commun Col 1973-74; mil/USN 1971-74; pa/VP Health Concepts; Hosp Mgmt Conslt; Tenn Soc Ctrl Ser Pers; Intl Matls Mgmt Soc; Am Soc Hosp Ctrl Ser Pers; Am Hosp Assn; Intl Assn Hosp Ctrl Serv Mgmt; Tenn Hosp Assn; r/Cath; hon/Sailor of the Quarter 1969; Cert Operating Room Tech 1973; W/W S&SW 1980-81; Cert Profl Hlth Care Matls Mgr 1980; Author Num Articles incl'g "You May Be Hazardous to Your Health"; "But My Hospital is Too Old."

BUCHANAN, GWENDOLYN ANN JONES oc/Nurse; b/June 17, 1927; h/5301 Listen Cir, Spencer, OK 73084; ba/Okla City, OK; m/Jim Charles Sr; c/Linda S Laakman, Cynthia D Patterson, Thomas B, Jim Charles Jr; p/Thomas B (dec) and Gwendolyn Jones, Spencer, OK; ed/Dip Col of Nsg, Univ Cinci 1945; BSN Univ Okla 1967; MSN Col Nsg Univ Okla 1978; pa/RN, Clin Supvr, Nurse Practitioner, VA Med Ctr, Okla City; Sigma Theta Tau; ANA; ONA; Nat Leag Nsg; Okla Leag Nsg; Emer Dept Nurses Assn; Okla Home Hlth Care Assn; cp/OES; ONCAP; r/Lutheran; hon/Recog of Excell by Univ Okla Col of Nsg for Except Acad Achmt, Clin Nsg, Cummun Ser.

BUCHANAN, SUE B oc/Executive Secretary and Office Manager; b/Mar 11, 1921; h/PO Box 93, Morehead, KY 40351; ba/Owingsville, KY; m/Reuel H; c/John, Emily, Susan; p/Jesse McAfee (dec) and Laura Cornelia Bryant Broadrick (dec); ed/Assoc Deg; pa/Exec Secy & Ofc Mgr Gateway Area Devel Dist; Owner, Mgr Sue's Secretarial Sers; cp/Martha R Jones Foun, Asbury Theol Sem; Past Pres Jr Wom's Clb; r/Meth; hon/W/W Am Wom 1979-80; Cert Recog from Ky Comm on Wom.

BUCHER, FRANCOIS oc/Professor; b/June 11, 1927; h/1601 Groveland Hills Dr, Tallahassee, FL 32301; ba/Fla St Univ, Tallahassee; c/Claudia, Bernard; ed/PhD Bern, Switz 1955; pa/SUNY-Binghamton 1970-77, Princeton Univ 1963-69, Brown Univ 1960-62, Yale Univ 1954-60, Univ Minn 1952-53; Prof Medieval Art & Architecture, SUNY-Binghamton 1970-; Chm, Grad Com: SUNY-Binghamton 1970-; Co-Dir Ctr for Medieval & Early Renaissance Studies, SUNY-Binghamton 1973-75, Sr Fellow of Ctr 1975-; Pres Intl Ctr of Medieval Art 1966-70; Dir Soc of Architectural Histns 1964-67; Exec Coun Arts, St of NJ 1965-70; Chm Plan'g Bd, Millstone, NJ 1964-70; Trustee, Interfuture 1968-; Fellow: Inst for Adv'd Study 1962-63, SEn Inst for Medieval & Renaissance Studies 1967, Ctr for Medieval & Early Renaissance Studies 1969-, Intl Ctr of Medieval Art, Guggenheim 1956, 66-67; Dist'd Schlr, SC Cols 1968-69; Vis'g Prof, Centre d'Etudes Superieures Medievales, Poitiers 1968; Editor *Gesta*, Jour of Intl Ctr of Medieval Art 1961-70; Fac Exch Schlr, St Univ NY 1976-; hon/Author Num Books Incl'g *Notre-Dame de Bonmont und*

die ersten Zisterzienser-abteien der Schweiz 1957 & *Principles of Medieval Architecture* 1979; Num Articles & Profl Papers.

BUCK, CAROLYN FELTER oc/Executive; b/Sept 17, 1941; h/Tomball, TX; ba/PO Drawer 38271, Houston, TX 77088; p/John Vincent Felter, Houston, TX; May Louise Robinson Felter, Austin, TX; ed/BA Parson Col 1964; pa/Tchr 9 Yrs; VP Mktg 8 Yrs; Nat Assn Female Execs; cp/Tex Wom Polit Causus; r/Prot; hon/W/W Am Wom.

BUCK, EDGAR ALTON oc/Executive; b/July 23, 1941; h/Tennent, Charleston, SC 29412; m/Margaret B; c/Susanne Tennent, Edgar A; p/Mr and Mrs Alton Buck, Charleston, SC; ed/BS ECU 1964; mil/USCG; pa/Pres & Owner Rhodes-Buck Bldg Supply Inc & Charleston Wood Industs; Bd Dirs So Bank & Trust Co; Carolina Lumber & Bldrs Mats Assn, Bd Dirs 1976-79; cp/C'ton Co Coun 1974-78, V-Chm 1976; Pres Co Clb of C'ton 1975; r/Epis; hon/Outstg Yng Men Am 1973.

BUCK, VIVIAN LOUISE oc/Businesswoman; b/Sept 30, 1926; h/1413 Park Ave, Sanford, FL 32771; ba/Sanford; m/Richard W; c/Frederick W Nimon, Murray E Nimon, Barbara Luth; p/Hassel (dec) and Lena Black, Titusville, FL; pa/Restaurant Owner; Fla Restaurant Assn; cp/Sanford BPW Clb; SISTER Inc VP; Wom's Clb Sanford; Sanford Bus Assn; Sanford C of C; BPO Does Drive #86 Winter Park; Ctrl Fla Chorale; Sr Citizens; Kiwanis Clb of Sanford; Mutual Concert Assn; Ballet Guild; Dem Wom's Clb; Winter Park Elks; PESO; Am Bus Wom; Good Samaritan Home; Jr Wom's Clb; r/Presb; hon/Kiwanis Roberta Gatchel Awd; Seminole Co Fed Wom's Clbs Wom of Yr.

BUCKINS, HATTIE M FREEMAN oc/Teacher; h/Atlanta, GA; p/Mary Freeman, Atlanta, GA; ed/AB Clark Col 1941; MS Hampton Inst; Cert Elem Ed, Atlanta Univ 1949; Cert Adm 1969, Cert Elem Ed 1976; pa/Tchr Home Ec, Washington HS 1941-58; Home Ec Tchr Price HS 1958-59; Intermediate Level Tchr, C F Harper Elem Sch 1959-; Atlanta Assn Edrs; GAE; NAE; cp/Treas Carolina F Harper PTSA, Grade Parents Advr; PTA Exec Bd; r/Bapt; hon/Wilkes Co Tchr of Yr 1975 & 76; Nom to WSB Tchr Hall of Fame; C F Harper Tchr of Yr 1980-81.

BUCKNER, JAMES RUSSELL oc/Instructor; b/Nov 26, 1951; h/Cullowhee; ba/Mus Dept, Western Carolina Univ, Cullowhee, NC 29723; m/Suzanne Cheryl Negus; p/Russell L and Arlene J Buckner, Charles City, IA; ed/BMus Iowa St Univ 1975; MMus Univ Mich 1976; pa/Instr Trumpet & Mus Theory, WCU 1980-; WN Mo St Univ, Quincy Col 1977-80, West HS, Waterloo, Ia 1976-77; Intl Trumpet Guild; Nat Assn Wind & Percussion Instrs; r/Meth; hon/Pi Kappa Lambda.

BUCKNER, ROBERT oc/Social Worker; b/July 27, 1938; h/PO Box 235, Boley, OK 74829; ba/Boley; m/Darnell; c/Sharon D, Sheryl D, Sherry D, Stephanie D, Shanna D; p/Robert Sr (dec) and Mary Buckner, Okla City, OK; ed/BA; MSW; mil/AUS 1961-63; pa/Social Wkr; Nat Assn Blacks in Crim Jus; NASW; APWA; cp/Kiwanis Clb; Boley C of C; Kappa Alpha Psi; r/Bapt; hon/W/W Am Col & Univs; Gatesville St Sch Outstg Social Ser Awd; Outstg Work Tex Yth Coun.

BUEGLER, BRIAN JOSEPH oc/Deputy Sheriff, Prison Supervisor; b/June 18, 1950; h/1530 Swafford Cir SW, Cullman, AL 35055; ba/Cullman; m/Madalyn B; p/Joseph A and Eileen M Buegler, Lincroft, NJ; ed/BS; pa/Sgt Dpty Sheriff, Prison & Ct Supvr; Ala Sheriff's Assn; Past Chief of Reserve; Past Secy & VP St Res Assn; cp/K of C; Am Red Cross Bd Mem; Civil Defense; r/Roman Cath; hon/Nat Hon Soc; W/W Am Cols & Univs; Hon Mem Sheriff's Boys & Girls Ranches.

BUEHRING, MARY ELLEN ROST oc/Legal Assistant; b/May 8, 1936; h/1051 Black Acre Trail, Casselberry, FL 32708; ba/Winter Park; m/Charles A; c/Chad, Christopher; p/Fred Arthur and Mary Madeline Hensley Rost (dec); ed/Grad w Hons Orange Bus Col 1954; Nat Certs PLS, CPS, CLA; Pre-Law S Tex 1955-57; BS w Hons Rollins Col 1980; Grad Student Raines Reporting Sch, Orlando; pa/Legal Asst, Winderweedle, Haines, Ward & Woodman, PA; Owner Num Bus's: Antique Shop, Interior Decorating Bus, Landscaping Co, Fla Inst Legal Assts; Fla Legal Assts Inc: Pres 1980-81, VP 1979-80, Initial Bd Dirs 1976-79; Nat Assn Legal Assts: 2nd VP 1978-79, Secy 1977-78, Dir 1977, Public Relats Dir, Histn & Resolutions Com 1975-77, Lwyr/Legal Asst Referral Spec Com 1977; Fla Soc Cert'd Profl Secys; Nat Assn Legal Secys; cp/Adv Bd: Univ Ctrl Fla Legal Asst Prog, Valencia Commun Col Legal Asst & Legal Secy Prog, Seminole Jr Col Bus Dept; Owner & Tchr, Fla Inst Legal Assts; Spkr for Cols, Schs & Profl Orgs on Legal Asst Profession & Cert; Modr & Session Ldr for Sems & Wkshops, Nat Assn Legal Assts Inc; Standards Com, Fla Legal Assts Inc 1976-80; hon/Nom'd to Serve as Lay Person, Fla Bar's Unauthorized Pract of Law Com; Valedictorian, Palm Bch HS 1953; Author "Setting Standards for Legal Assistants" *Florida Bar Journal* Jan 1979; Textbooks for Fla Inst Legal Assts 1981; Num Chapts for Textbook Mats; "Introduction" to Manual for Legal Assts 1979; Others.

BUEKER, KATHLEEN ANN oc/Consultant; b/May 10, 1930; h/Box 339, Deltaville, VA 23043; p/John W and Margaret Hoff Bueker, Saginaw, MI; ed/RN 1951; BS 1957; MS 1962; PhD 1969; pa/St Elizabeths Hosp 1951-69; Nat Inst Mtl Hlth 1969-77; Pvt Pract 1977-; Am Sociol Assn; Am Public Hlth Assn; cp/Nat Audubon Soc; Nat Wildlife Fed; r/Meth; hon/W/W: Am Wom, Hlth Care, Commun Ser, Wom of World; Dist'd Men & Wom of World; Contbr to Jours & Articles Reproduced in Books.

BUGG, CHARLES oc/Pastor; b/Dec 25, 1942; h/130 W Pennsylvania Ave, DeLand, FL 32720; ba/DeLand; m/Diane; c/Laura Beth, David; p/Mr and Mrs B E Bugg, Clearwater, FL; ed/BA Stetson Univ 1965; MDiv 1969, PhD 1972 So Bapt Theol Sem; pa/Pastor: First Bapt Ch of Eau Gallie 1972-74, Powers Dr Bapt Ch 1974-76, First Bapt Ch DeLand 1976-; Pres Fla Bapt Hist Soc; Chm Stetson Trustee Nominat'g Com; Moderator Seminole Bapt Assn; Mem Com on Nominations of Fla Bapt Conv; cp/Pres Gtr DeLand Min Assn; Bd Dirs DeLand Rotary Clb; Tchr Stetson Univ Extension; Field Supvr So Bapt Sem; Bd Dirs So Brevard YMCA; r/Bapt; hon/5 Outstg Yng Men of Fla 1976; Outstg Yng Men of Am 1975; Borden Prize 1962; W/W Am Cols 1965; Algernon Sydney Sullivan Awd 1965.

BUICE, PATTERSON N oc/Counselor, Teacher; b/Feb 3, 1934; h/Box 2076 WW, 785 Will Scarlet, Macon, GA 31210; ba/Macon; m/B Carl; c/Merrianne Buice Dyer, Shannon Warwick, Samuel Walton, William Daniel (dec), Christopher Carl; p/Andrew Walton and Elizabeth Merritt Nall; ed/Peabody Col 1953-55; AB Oglethorpe Univ 1956; MEd Ga St Univ; EdS Univ Notre Dame; Emory Univ Advanced Studies PhD Cand 1979-; pa/Atlanta Public Sch Tchr 1956-68; Instr Brenau Col 1970; Instr Tom Gordon's Parent Effectiveness Trg 1972-78; Cnslr Holy Trinity Cnslg Ctr 1976-78; Cnslr Pvt Prac 1979-; Clin Mem Am Marriage & Fam Therapist; Ga Marriage & Fam Therapist; Am Pers & Guid Assn; r/Epis; hon/WW: Am Cols & Univs 1954-55, S&SW 1981; Wom of Yr, Gainesville, Ga 1970; Algernon Sidney Sullivan Awd 1955; Outstg Yng Wom Am 1968.

BUIST, SAM IZLAR oc/Retired Educator; b/June 24, 1924; h/Rt 4 Box 86, Greenwood, SC; m/Doris Miller; c/Mary Elizabeth Eubanks, Charles Samuel, Deborah Brock, James Miller, Michael Earl p/Samuel I (dec) and Mary Louise Buist, Newberry, SC; ed/BS Erskine Col 1952; MEd Univ SC 1955; mil/USAAF WWII 1943-46; pa/Ret'd Public Sch Edr: Cross, SC 1952-53; Bamberg, SC 1953-55; Elem Prin & HS Coach Blackville, SC 1955-61; Elem Prin Greenwood, SC 1961-80; Mem Co Ed Assn in Each Co Wrkd; Pres Greenwood Co Ed Assn 1969-70; Served on Constitutional Com that Wrote Former Black & White Constitution for SC Ed Assn; Exec Bd 1976-80 SC Elem Prin Assn; Served on Sev Accreditation Tms as Evaluator for Schs for So Sch Assn; cp/York Rite Order of Masonic Org; Master Mason in Good Standing; Past Mem Kiwanis, Moose; Am Legion; r/Meth; hon/Winner Sev Oratorical Contests.

BULLOCK, MARION WYVETTA RATLEDGE oc/Former Secretary; b/July 24, 1951; h/5316 Wakefield St, Phila, PA 19144; p/Thomas E (dec) and Carrie Ratledge, Phila, TN; ed/AS Cleveland St Commun Col 1972; Cert Nat Secys Assn 1977; pa/Former Secy for Dept Hd of Mech Engrg, Union Carbide Corp-Nuclear Div, Oak Ridge Gaseous Diffusion Plant 1973-81; Conduct Sems & Trg Progs; Oak Ridge Chapt Nat Secys Assn Intl: Corresp Secy 1979-80, VP 1980-81; Oak Ridge Chapt NSA Spkrs Bur; r/Faith F'ship Ch & Outreach; Evangelist; Assoc Min; hon/Mem of Yr, Oak Ridge Chapt NSA 1980; Outstg Yng Wom Am 1980; Cert Apprec Oak Ridge Kiwanis Clb 1979.

BULLOCK, ROBERT EDWARD oc/Insurance Agent; b/Feb 21, 1941; h/Meridian, MS; ba/PO Box 1729, Meridian, MS 39301; m/Margene Ann Dement; c/Robert E Jr, Jamie H; p/Edward Nelson (dec) and Axeth Hodge Bullock, Meridian, MS; ed/BS Miss St Univ 1963; pa/Life Agt, Gtr Miss Life Ins Co 1963-66; VP & Major Stockholder Meyer & Rosenbaum Inc, Gen & Life Ins, 1966-; Past Secy, Treas, VP & Pres Meridian, Miss Assn Life Underwriters; cp/Charter & Century Clb Mem Miss Life Underwriters Polit Action Com; Chm of Law & Leg Activities, Phi Kappa Nat Frat; r/Cath; hon/Ben F Cameron Awd for Outstg Ath 1959; Col Grant; Miss St Univ Col Fball S'ship; Outstg Assn Achmt Awd as Pres Meridian Assn Life Underwriters 1967-68; Agt of Yr, Aetna Life & Casualty 1972; Chartered Life Underwriter 1972; Nat Qual Awd, Nat Assn Life Underwriters; Nat Sales Achmt Awd 1978; 1976 Qualifying Mem Million Dollar Round Table; Aetna Life Corp of Regionaires Awd; Aetna Life Ldr Clb Awd 1972; Aetna Life Outstg Prod Awd 1975; Aetna Life Top Prodr Awd 1972; W/W: S&SW 1980, Am, Fin & Indust 1980-81; Nominated for Men of Achmt 1981.

BUMPERS, DALE oc/US Senator; b/Aug 12, 1925; m/Betty Flanagan; c/Brent, Bill, Brook; mil/USMC WWII S/Sgt; pa/Owner Charleston Hardware & Furniture Co 1951-66; Owner Angus Breeding Farm 1966-70; City Atty, Charleston & Law Pract 1951-70; Sworn into US Senate, Jan 1975; Mem Energy & Nat Resources Com: Chm Pks, Rec & Renewable Resources Subcom, Mem Res & Devel Subcom, Mem Energy Regulation Subcom; Mem Appropriations Com: Defense Subcom, DC Subcom, Leg Br Subcom, St, Justice & Commerce, the Judiciary & Related Agcys Subcom, Treasury, Postal Ser & Gen Govt Subcom; Mem Small Bus Com: Chm Fin, Investment & Tax Subcom, Ec Devel, Mktg & Fam Farmer Subcom; Mem Dem Policy Com; cp/Gov Ark 1971-75; Pres C'ton Sch Bd; r/U Meth; hon/Author Regulatory Reform Act.

BUNCE, LOUISE LONGNECKER oc/Supervisor; b/Nov 19, 1930; h/205 Vivian Dr, Fayetteville, NC 28301; ba/F'ville; m/Leon Warren Sr; c/Gwendolyn Louise, Leon Warren Jr, David Michael; p/Albert Franklin Sr (dec) and Sara E Longnecker, F'ville, NC; ed/HS Grad; pa/Customer Ser Supvr, Carolina Telephone Co; AFCEA 1981; Nat Trust for Hist Preserv 1980-81; cp/Dem; Woodhaven Gdn Clb, Secy 1980; Epsilon Sigma Alpha, Chm Philanthropic Com 1968; Guid Coun, Pine Forest HS 1969-70.

BUNTING, JOHN JAMES oc/Doctor; h/6307 S Rice, Bellaire, TX 77401; ba/Houston, TX; m/Katharyne Denton; c/Beverly Sue Moor, John James Jr, William D; p/James Henry and Dora Smith Bunting; ed/BS Lafayette Col 1934; MD Univ Md Sch Med 1938; Internship Univ Hosp, Baltimore, Md 1938-40; Var Residencies; Further Study; pa/Clin Assoc Prof Med Univ Tex Med Sch-Houston 1972-; Ben Taub Clin: Assoc Prof Med 1963-, Asst Clin Prof Med 1948-63; Baylor Univ: Assoc Clin Prof Med 1965-, Asst Clin Prof 1949-65; Instr Diseases of Chest, Jersey City Med Ctr 1940-41; Other Acad Positions; Conslt Staff Mem Meml Bapt Hosp 1946-; Active Staff Mem: Hermann Hosp 1947-, Ben Taub Hosp 1948-; Courtesy Staff Mem: Jefferson Davis Hosp 1947-, Meth Hosp 1948-, Twelve Oaks Hosp 1966-, St Anthony Ctr 1967-, Rosewood Gen Hosp 1969-, Diagnostic Ctr Hosp 1970-, Ctr Pavilion Hosp 1971-, Med Ctr Del Oro Hosp 1975-; Diplomate Am Bd Internal Med; Fellow: Am Col Chest Phys, Am Col Angiology, Royal Soc Hlth; Tex Assn Disability Examrs; Am Heart Assn; Tex Diabetes Assn; Am Cancer Soc; Am Diabetes Assn; AAAS; Am Geriatrics Soc; Am Thoracic Soc; Am Soc Tropical Med & Hygiene; NY Acad Scis; Am Soc Internal Med; Num Others; hon/Author Num Sci Articles; Contbr & Edit Bd Mem *Book of Health*, 3rd Edition, 1973.

BURCHFIELD, JEWEL CALVIN oc/Security Director; b/Sept 10, 1932; h/Rt 1 Box 138A, Crandell, GA 30711; ba/Eton, GA; m/Mary Mozelle Phillips; c/James Eugene, Melissa Ann, David Calvin, Mary Teresa, Nancy Lynne; p/Burdon Eugene (dec) and Eunice Mae Griffin Burchfield, Tuleta, TX; pa/USAF 22½ Yrs, SMSgt, Security Police Supt, Ret'd; USAF Master Instr Cert; pa/Security Dir; Former Saftey Ofcr, Dalton; Ga Assn Security Pers; Peace Ofcrs Assn Ga; Am Soc Pers Adm; cp/BSA; PTA; r/Bapt; hon/Bronze Star Medal; 4 AF Commend Medal; Trophy for Outstg Markmanship, Cobb Co Police Acad.

BURDETTE, THEODORE ALLEN oc/Locomotive Engineer; b/Mar 7, 1913; h/Rt 11, Sevierville, TN 37862; ba/Pigeon Forge, TN; m/Blanch Pearl; c/Cody Allen, Viola Maude Riordan, Rita Louise Hamrick, Anita Marie; p/Louis (dec) and Maude Burdette, Bomont, WV; pa/Locomotive Engr; US Mail Carrier by Horseback 1930-32; r/Meth.

BURES, PAUL LESLIE JR oc/Television Executive; b/Apr 19, 1933; h/1010 Idlebrook St, Houston, TX 77070; ba/Houston; m/Felicia M Visconti; c/Kristen Lee, Heather Elizabeth; p/Paul Leslie and Margaret Elizabeth Bures; ed/BS Miami Univ, Ohio; mil/USCG 1952-55; pa/Gen Sales Mgr KTRK-TV 1971-; Exec Chm TVB Sales Adv Com 1977-; Nat Acad TV Arts & Scis; cp/Houston C of C; r/Epis; hon/Script Editor: *Your Competitive Medium* 1979; *The Sum of the Alternatives* 1978; *Television: The Persuasive Medium* 1980.

BURGE, JERRY C oc/Insurance Agent, Realtor; b/Aug 8, 1925; h/PO Box 73, Poplarville, MS 39470; ba/P'ville; m/Virgil O; c/George C, Bruce, Scott, Dana Ferguson; p/Ernest E (dec) and Serena Speed Clark (dec); ed/Jr Col; pa/Ins Agt; Rltr GRI; Pearl River Co Bd Rltrs; cp/Pres Miss Ext Homemakers Coun 1980-81; r/Bapt.

BURGESS, BLAIR DAVIS SR oc/Senior Enlisted Logistician; b/Nov 29, 1942; h/Rt 3, Box 211, Baxter, TN 39544; m/Helen Y Hayes; c/Blair Davis Jr, Brian Hayes; p/Bernice E and Gladys L Davidson Burgess, Bloomington Springs, TN; ed/AA Ctrl Tex Col 1980; mil/Tenn Army NG 1958-64; AUS 1964-; pa/Sr Enlisted Logistician, AUS; cp/Free & Accepted Mason Cookville Lodge #266; Chapter 132, Coun 122 & Commandery 29 Royal Arch Masons Union City, Tenn; Sharon Temple Masonic Shrine; Ky HS Ath Assn; r/Bapt; hon/Nat Defense Ser Medal 1964; Armed Forces Expeditionary Medal 1968; Good Conduct Medal 1st Awd 1968; Bronze Star Medal 1969; Good Conduct Medal 2nd Awd 1971; Army Accommodation Medal 1st Awd 1972; Army Accommodation Medal 2nd Awd 1974; Merit Ser Medal 1st Awd 1977; Merit Ser Medal 2nd Awd 1979.

BURKE, ARNOLD LEE oc/Research Engineer; b/412 S 31st, Temple,

TX 76501; p/Arnold V Burke, McKinney, TX; pa/Former Plant Supt in Memphis; Supt & Plant Engr in 3 Mfg Firms in Abilene 12 Yrs; Ret'd in Temple to Build the Recently Opened Res & Devel Ctr, Temple (Develop Electric Pump Unit); 16 Yrs Res Spent in Building Gasless, Exhaustless Engine, that runs on Nitrogen & Oxygen & Recycles its Gas for Later Use; Has Begun Work on Developing Engine for Indust Prodn; Continues Res on Other Projs, incl'g 14 New Gas Compounds to be used for Fuel; hon/Featured in *Temple Daily Telegram;* Articles: *The Dairymen Mag & The Farm Show Mag.*

BURKE, MAXINE CALDWELL oc/Director Career Planning and Placement; b/July 6, 1936; ba/Career Placement/Plan'g, So Univ Shreveport, 3050 Cooper Rd, Shreveport, LA; c/Michelyn; p/Mittie Fields; ed/BA So Univ 1957; MFA Howard Univ 1972; MEd Prairie View A&M Univ 1981; pa/Dir Career Plan'g & Placement; Alpha Kappa Alpha; cp/YWCA; Urban Leag; NAACP; r/Cath; hon/Art Tchr of Yr 1979-80; Cert of Achmt, SUSBO's Art Clb 1980-81.

BURKHARDT, MARY ELIZABETH oc/Marketing Executive; b/Feb 21, 1945; h/3147 Golden Oak, Dallas, TX 75234; ba/Irving, TX; m/Doug Hellman; p/Elizabeth Mary Osborne Mitchell Hiza, Pompano Beach, FL; ed/BA Trenton St Col 1966; MA Montclaire St Col 1969; MBA Univ Dallas 1979; pa/Thomas J Lyston Inc 1969-73; Assoc Prof Fairleigh Dickinson Univ 1969-73; Coca-Cola USA 1974-75; Frito-Lay Inc 1975-78; The Drawing Bd 1978-79; Mktg Exec GTE Ser Corp 1979-; Mkt Res Assn Nat Secy; Am Mktg Assn Nat Dir; Soc for Advmt of Mgmt; Am Mgmt Assn; cp/Am Cancer Crusade; United Fund; GSA; hon/W/W S&SW; Author Mktg Articles.

BURKS, GILBERT DENSON oc/Businessman; b/Aug 19, 1901; h/Drawer C, Hanceville, AL 35077; ba/H'ville; m/A D; c/Grover C; p/Albert Stephen (dec) and Florence Virginia Kent Burks (dec); pa/Owner & Attendant Filling Station; r/Bapt; hon/Truck Driving Safety Awds.

BURKS, JIMMY L oc/Minister; b/Feb 18, 1930; h/Camden, AR; m/Barbara Q; c/Jodie C, Judy K, Jimmy L Jr; p/Cecil R (dec) and Jewel Burks (dec); ed/BA Baylor Univ 1951; BD SWn Theol Sem 1955; DMin Luther Rice Sem 1978; pa/Min, Cullendale First Bapt Ch, Camden; Mem Exec Bd Ark Bapt Gen Conv; cp/Exec Bd Ovachita Co Hlth Unit; Past Pres S Ark Commun Action Ser; Past Mem Rotary Clb; r/Bapt; hon/Hon'd for Help to Commun in Disaster of 1979, May 1980; Author, *So Now You Are a Deacon* 1979.

BURLESON, NOYCE M oc/Teacher, Director; b/Oct 15, 1930; h/Box 246, Meadow, TX 79345; ba/Meadow; m/Joe A; c/Harriet Burleson Flache; p/Noyce (dec) and Ara Mae Jennings, Lake Charles, TX; ed/BA, MA Tex Tech Univ; pa/Lang Arts Tchr & Drama Dir, Meadow HS; Former Pres Tex Speech Communs Assn; Chm K-12 Curric Guide Standing Com Tex Speech Communs Assn; Tex Ednl Theater Assn; Chm Univ Interscholastic Leag Adv Com; Speech Communs of Am; NCTE; Am Theater Assn; Former Pres Terry Co Tchrs Assn of Tex St Tchrs Assn; Former Mem SW Theater Conf; Am Forensic Leag; Guest Lectr Lubbock Christian Col & Guest Drama Coor Drama Dept HS Student Retreat Tex Tech Univ, Summer 1979; cp/Precinct Chm, St Dem Delegate 15 Yrs; r/Meth; hon/Speech Tchr Tex 1977; Drama Dept Recip of $1000 Ahmonson Foun Grant Record Holder for St One-Act Play Contest.

BURLESON, OMAR T oc/Congressman; b/Mar 19, 1906; h/4101 Cathedral Ave NW, Apt #917, Wash DC 20016; m/Ruth DeWeese; p/Joseph and Bettie Couch Burleson (dec); ed/LD Cumberland Univ; Abilene Christian Univ; Hon LLD Hardin-Simmons Univ; Univ Tex; mil/USN 3½ Yrs, Lt Cmdr; pa/Cong-man: Com on Ways & Means, Subcom on Hlth, Subcom on Misc Revenue Measures, Com on Budget Tax Expenditures, Govt Organ & Regulation, Nat Security Subcom; cp/Former Dist Gov Lions Intl; Var Civic, Ser & Vets Orgs; r/Ch of Christ; hon/Num Hons & Awds.

BURMAHLN, ELMER FRED oc/Director Business Education (Retired 1967); b/Oct 6, 1897; h/3716 Manton Dr, Lynchburg, VA 24503; m/Elizabeth L Butler; p/John and Emma Klopfer Burmahln (dec); ed/BS (Acctg & Bus Ed) Boston Univ 1930; MA (Bus Ed & Sch Adm) NYU 1934; Tchrs Col, Columbia Univ; Univ Cal-B; Harvard; Univ Wash; Univ Chgo; Univ Va; Spec Schs: Gregg Col, Fred Gurtler Sch of Ct Reporting, La Salle Ext Univ (Bus Adm), Stenotype Sch, Tulloss Sch (Prof Tw), Zanerian Col of Penmanship, Sheldon Sch of Salesmanship, Knox Sch of Salesmanship; pa/E C Glass HS, L'burg: Dir Bus Ed & Controller HS Fins 1923-67; Treas L'burg Tchrs Clb 1935-52; Hd Comml Dept: Lead HS, Lead, SC 1918-22, Escanaba HS, Escanaba, Mich 1917-18; Conslt, Contbg Editor, *The Catering World of Mgmt Mag Inc Chgo* 7 Yrs; Moderator Indust Coun Panel Conf 1952-56, RPI, Troy, NY; Conslt, Advr Today's Bus Law Goodman & Moore, Pitman Publ Corp NY, NY 1956-75; Va St Comml Contest Mgr (Covering Typewriting, Bkkpg & Shorthand) 1926-29; Bud Ed Assns: Nat, En, So, Va (Pres, Chm Bd Dirs 1931-34); Chm Va St Prodn

Bus Ed; Va Ed Assn; NRTA; Nat Assn Penmanship Tchrs & Supvrs; Nat Handwriting Coun US; Am Voc Assn; Intl Soc for Bus Ed; Va St Col Profl Cert; Am Acctg Assn; Spkr City, St, So, Nat Bus Ed Convs; Lectr Columbia, So & Nat Scholastic Press Assns; Nat Assn Accts: VP L'burg Chapt #151 1960-61, Mbrship Dir L'burg Chapt 1969-73; Charter Mem Richmond, Roanoke & L'burg, Va; NAA Intl Execs Ser Corps; Conductor Fgn Tours & World Traveler; Exec Secy to Clarence Hatzfeld Arch, Tribune Bldg Chgo 1914; cp/Life Mem Kazim Temple, Roanoke, Va; Life Mem Naja Temple, Deadwood, SD; 32 Deg Mason, Black Hills Consistory (Life Mem), Deadwood; K Templar Dakota Commandery #1 (50 Yrs Mem), Lead, SD; Master Mason Golden Star Lodge #9 AF&AM (50 Yrs Mem), Lead, SD; Dakota Chapt #3 Ram (50 Yrs Mem), Lead, SD; Black Hills Coun #3 R&SM (50 Yrs Mem), Lead, SD; Mem 100 Million Dollar Clb, Shriners Hosps for Crippled Chd, Kazim Temple & Naja Temple; Mem & Auditor L'burg Shrine Clb; Nat Travel Clb; Cunard White Star Travel Clb Inc; Track Meet Ofcl Local & St; Chm L'burg Gasoline Rationing WW II, Lttr of Apprec 1944, US Pres F D Roosevelt; Houston U Clb & C of C; U Clb Seattle; Schoolmasters Clb, L'burg; Boston Univ Alumni Assn (Life Mem); NYU Alumni Fdn; hon/Sigma Chi; Pub'd Author; Honorary Legion of Hon, Intl Supr Coun Order of DeMolay; DIB 1974-76; Personalities of S 1976-77; Men Achmt 1975-77; W/W S&SW 1977; Ldrs in Ed 1976; Outstg Edrs of Am 1977; Notable Ams of Bicent Era 1976; Commun Ldrs & Noteworthy Ams; Cert of Apprec: Va Bus Ed Assn 1963, L'burg Sch Bd 1967; Climbed Pikes Peak (14,108 Feet), Colo Sprgs, Colo 1918; Crossed Equator near Panama Canal 1915.

BURNS, BARBARA REID oc/Manager; b/Mar 25, 1946; h/Winston-Salem, NC; ba/RJ Reynolds Ind, WHQ-4A Systems Planning, Winston-Salem, NC 27102; c/Elizabeth S; p/William Lowry and Mary Nell Manley Reid (dec), Oak Ridge, TN; ed/BS 1968, MS 1971 Univ Tenn Knoxville; pa/RJ Reynolds Industs: Sys Analyst, Sr Sys Analyst, Proj Mgr, Mgr Corp Data Base Plan'g, Mgr Corp Info Sys Plan'g 1975-81; Union Planters Nat Bank 1971-75; Univ Tenn Computing Ctr 1967-71; DPMA; NAA; r/Presb; hon/Alpha Lambda Delta 1965; Phi Kappa Phi 1968; Beta Gamma Sigma 1967; Freshman Thesis Pub'd in *Harbrace Handbook* 6th Edition.

BURNS, FRANCES WILLETTA HILL oc/Community Relations Manager; b/Sept 13, 1931; c/Robert III, David Kanoa, Kevin Stuart; p/David B (dec) and Marzelle Cooper Hill, Dallas, TX; ed/Att'd Tenn St Univ 1948-52; BA magna cum laude Bishop Col 1970; pa/Dallas Housing Auth 1953-55; Tacoma, Wn Housing Auth 1955-57; San Antonio Housing Auth 1957; Martin Luther King Ctr 1969-: Social Wkr, Intake Supvr, Commun Relats Mgr; Assn Black Social Wkrs, Charter Mem; Tex Area 5 Hlth Sys Agcy Bd; Black Adoption Bd; Nat Caucus on Black Aged; Delta Sigma Theta, Pan Rep; cp/Wom's Ctr of Dallas; Adv Bd Ret'd Sr Vol Prog; Soroptomist Intl of Dallas; Anderson PTA; EOC-DISD Interagcy Adv Bd; Concerned Citizens for Public Hlth; Jr Black Acad Arts & Lttrs Adv Bd; hon/W/W Am Wom 1981-82; Black Wom Against Odds Awd, E Oak Cliff Subdist, Dallas Indep Sch Dist 1980; Plaque, Martin Luther King's Birthday Celeb, Anheuser Busch Co 1980.

BURNS, GROVER PRESTON oc/Mathematician, Physicist; b/Apr 25, 1918; h/600 Virginia Ave, Fredericksburg, VA 22401; ba/Dahlgren, VA; m/Julia Foster; c/Julia Corinne Jefferson (Mrs John N), Grover Jr; p/Mr and Mrs J A Burns (dec); ed/AB Marshall Univ 1937; MS WVa Univ 1941; Addit Study: Duke Univ, Univ Md; mil/Info & Ed Br 1945-46; pa/Mary Wash Col: Asst Prof & Chm Physics Dept 1948-68, Assoc Prof & Chm 1968-69; Supvr Quality Control FMC 1950-67; Res Physicist Naval Res Lab 1947-48; Pres Burns Enterprises Inc 1958-; Mathematician Naval Weapons Lab 1967-; Reviewer Am Jour Physics; cp/Dahlgren Golf Clb; Capitol Hill Clb, Wash DC; WVa Soc of Wash DC; r/Bapt; hon/Life Fellow Intercont Biog Assn; Life Mem Am Def Preparedness Assn; Am Men Sci; DIB; W/W: S&SW, Am Ed; DSc Colo St Christian Col 1973.

BURRELL, LAFAYETTE oc/Retired Debit Manager; b/Mar 16, 1909; h/705 E 11 Ave, Corsicana, TX 75110; m/Willie B; c/Pauline Annette Banks Alderson, Edewina Y Henderson; ed/Prairie View Col 1926-27; pa/Ret'd Debit Mgr, Universal Life Ins Co; cp/Telephone Chm & Past VP City Coun; Past Pres Unlimited Neighborhood Org; Basic Ed Adv Com; Dist Parent Adv Coun; r/Meth; hon/City Coun PTA Life Mbrship Awd 1973; Cert Merit 1964-66 from Nat Ins Assn.

BURRIS, FRANCES oc/Homemaker; b/Jan 26, 1914; h/Jonesboro, AR; c/Willa D Wiggins; p/John Francis (dec) and Sarah Keedy Rorex (dec); ed/Ark St Univ; pa/Elem Sch Tchr; cp/Pres LWV; Regent of DAR 1971-73; Jonesboro Chapt PTA Sr High Pres 1949-51; r/Bapt.

BURRIS, JOHN LOUIS oc/Poet, Writer; b/Mar 14, 1924; h/Rt 1, Box 1638, Belleview, FL 32620; m/Janice M; c/Linda Carol Garrett, Karen Irene Buchanan, Gregory Alan; ed/2 Yrs Col; mil/USN 15 Yrs; Survivor Pearl Harbor Attack, Dec 7, 1941; pa/Poet, Freelance Writer; Law Enforcement, Grad of Police Acad, Wichita, KS; Am Assn Ret'd People; cp/Hon Mem Belleview-S Marion C of C; hon/Cert Apprec,

Belleview-S Marion C of C 1980; Author: *Quiet Thoughts; The Honey Creek Anthology of Contemporary Poetry; Poetic Treasures, Past and Present.*

BURRIS, MAUREEN SMITH oc/Assistant Professor; b/May 14, 1943; h/109C Bush Circle, Americus, GA 31709; ba/Americus; c/Clifton Louis; p/Lonnie L and Frances McNeill Smith, McComb, MS; ed/BS; MEd; EdD; pa/Asst Prof Phy Ed, Ga SWn Col; AAHPER; r/Bapt; hon/Kappa Delta Pi.

BURRIS, WILFORD C oc/College President; b/July 1, 1929; h/Altus, OK; ba/2801 N Main St, Altus, OK; m/Joan; c/Jon Michael; p/Delbert and Iva Mae Burris, Mangum, OK; ed/BS SWn Okla St Univ 1951; MS 1957, EdD 1968 Okla St Univ; mil/AUS WWII; pa/Tchr 1951-57; Cnslr 1957-61; Dean of Students, SWn Okla St Univ 1961-71; Pres Wn Okla St Col 1971-; NEA; OEA; Am & Okla Pers & Guid Assns; Okla Univ & Col Deans Assn; Okla Col Pres's Coun; Okla Jr Col Ath Conf Chm 1978-80; cp/Civil Defense Prog; YMCA; Okla Mtl Hlth Assn; C of C Bd Dirs; Kiwanis Clb; City of Altus Airport Adv Bd 1973-79; Bd Dirs Okla Ed TV Auth; hon/W/W Am Ed.

BURROW, T BRUCE oc/Executive; b/Jan 11, 1943; h/1001 Merrywood, PO Box 974, Jonesboro, AR 72401; m/Sharon Young; c/Terri, Shelley, Ross, Debbie; ed/Att'd Harbor Jr Col; Savings & Loan Inst; pa/Wilmington Mutual Savings & Loan 1961-66; Real Est Mgr, New Site Acquisition, Taco Bell 1966-68; Pres Rlty Assocs Inc (Formerly Burrow & Co Rltrs) 1968-; Fdg Mem Nat Assn Corp Real Est Execs; Nat Assn Rltrs; St Assn Rltrs; Intl Coun Shopping Ctrs; Urban Land Inst; cp/J'boro C of C; J'boro Country Clb; hon/Real Est Million Dollar Clb; Top Vol Sales Prodr, J'boro Bd Rltrs.

BURROWAY, JANET oc/Professor; b/1936; h/240 De Soto St, Tallahassee, FL 32303; ba/Tallahassee; c/Timothy Alan Eysselinck, Tobyn Alexander Eysselinck; ed/Univ Ariz 1954-55; AB cum laude Barnard Col 1958; BA 1st Class hons 1960, MA 1965 Cambridge Univ; Yale Sch Drama 1960-61; pa/Fla St Univ: Prof 1977-, Assoc Prof Eng Lit & Writing 1972-77; Asst to Writing Lab, Spec Ed Opports Prog, Univ Ill 1972; Lectr in Sch of Eng & Am Studies, Univ Sussex, England 1965-70; Fiction Reviewer, *New Statesman* Mag, London 1970-71, 1975; Costume Designer, Belgian Nat Theatre at Ghent 1965-70 & Gardner Centre for the Arts, Univ Sussex 1965-71; Reg Dir NY St Expansion Prog for Yg Audiences Inc 1962-63; Author Books incl'g: *Raw Silk*, 1977, *The Giant Jam Sandwich*, 1972, *The Truck on the Track*, 1970, Others; Also Poetry, Short Stories, Articles, & Reviews; hon/Nat Endowmt for Arts Creative Writing F'ship; AMOCO Awd for Excell in Tchg, Fla St Univ; NBC Spec Fellow in Playwrighting, Yale Sch of Drama; Prize for S'ship, Newnham Col; Phi Beta Kappa; Others.

BURT, MARVIN V oc/Production Supervisor; b/Aug 11, 1926; h/239 Van, Dermit, TX; ba/Eunice, NM; m/Jessamine Virginia; c/Camma Elizabeth Kasner; p/Shelly G (dec) and Sarah Elizabeth Burt (dec); pa/Prod Supvr; cp/Pres Saddle Clb; Pres Square Dance Clb; Boy Scout Ldr; r/Meth.

BURTON, CLELAND PATRICIA oc/Historical Abstractor, Writer; b/July 15, 1918; ba/Box 1774, Bolar, VA 24414; c/Melissa Bragg Brown; p/Fred (dec) and Frances Louis McCloy Burton (dec); ed/Att'd Fairfax Hall 1937-39; Univ Mich 1939-40; pa/Exec VP Fred Burton Abstract Co 1947-59; Owner Burton Farms, Reg'd Shetlands, Mich, Calif, Va 1960-64; Title Examr, Palm Bch Co, Fla 1967-69; Histl Conslt, Writer 1965-; Hist Conslt Mason Co Bicent Comm, Pt Pleasant, WV 1974-77 & City of Pt Pleasant 1977-79; Review Bd, Pt Pleasant 1975-79, Bolar, Va 1979-; Histl Abstractor for Am's Frontier Ltd, Bolar, Va 1965-; Foremost Auth on Battle of Pt Pleasant, Oct 10, 1774; cp/Nat Trust for Hist Preserv; WV Hist Soc; WV Press Wom; Detroit Hist Soc; Hon Order of Ky Cols; r/Presb; hon/Awd, Freedoms Foun at Val Forge for Radio Series "200 Yrs Ago Today on Va's Frontier" 1975; Oct 10, 1975 "Patricia Burton Day" at Pt Pleasant, WV; Cert of Recog, Nat Soc DAR 1976; Martha Washington Medal, Geo Wash Cleek Chapt Va Soc SAR 1977; Ky Col 1979; Cert of Apprec, City of Pt Pleasant 1981; Author *The Augusta County Regiment 1774* 1975, *Andrew Lewis 1720-1781* 1978, *Virginia Begins to Remember* 1980; Many Articles Pub'd in Hist Jours; Presented Exhibs of Hist in Num Sts; Compiled & Filed 82 Hist Affidavits Dealing w Battle of Pt Pleasant.

BURTON, LUCILLE PEARSON oc/Coordinator, Director; b/July 10, 1915; h/45 Grail St, Asheville, NC 28801; ba/A'ville; m/Willie B; p/John Franklin (dec) and Emma Alice Clayton Pearson (dec); ed/AB; MA; pa/Coor, Dir Asheville-Buncombe Optional Sch; NCAE; NEA; Prin's Assn; NCTA; cp/YWCA Vol; Bd Mem St James AME Ch; Girl Scout Vol; Commun-Area Devel Org; City-wide Beautification Org; Vol City Pks & Rec Dept; hon/1st Hon Student HS; 2nd Hon Student Col; Highest Average, Sci Inst, Duke Univ.

BURTS, FRIEDA CULBERSON oc/Homemaker; b/Sept 20, 1920; h/1102 S Russell St, Jefferson City, TN 37760; m/Robert Milton; c/Robert Jr, Amanda; p/H B (dec) and Anne Gibson Culberson (dec); ed/AB; cp/Mem City Coun; Past Pres LWV; AAUW; Mem City Plan'g Comm; r/Bapt; hon/Jefferson City Citizen of Yr 1971.

BUSBEE, ELIZABETH DIVERS oc/Director Department of Social Service, Retired; b/May 15, 1912; h/Taliaferro Ave SW, Rocky Mt, VA 24151; ba/Same; m/Charles M (dec); p/Alfred and Bessie Ramsey Divers (dec); ed/Martha Wash Col; Milligan Col; BS Radford Col 1934; Past Grad Wk; pa/Dir Dept Social Sers Ret'd 1942-74; Franklin Co Va, Social Wkr, F C Dept of Social Sers 1938-72; Instr & BB Coach: Gretna HS 1937-38, W Jefferson HS, NC 1936-38, Franklin Co 1934-36; St-wide Hlth Coor'g Coun; Bd of Va, Area III, Hlth Ser Agy; Designated by SHCC as Rep to Mtl Hlth Adv Coun; cp/Pres: Va Leag Local Wel Execs, UDC, Woms Clb Rocky Mt (Orgr); Bd Dirs SW Soc for Crippled Chd; W Piedmont Planning Comm of Aging; Tech Hlth Plan'g Com of W Piedmont Comprehensive Hlth Plan'g Coun; Treas Franklin Co Chapt Nat Foun for Infantile Paralysis; Orgr Jr Woms Clb; Others.

BUSEK, BERNICE AMANDA WYSONG oc/Nurse; b/July 13, 1902; h/2230 Nursery Rd Apt J-111, Clearwater, FL 33516; ba/Dunedin, FL; m/Joseph R (dec); c/Joseph Ralph, Richard Collum; p/Will (dec) and Daisy Maude Houser Wysong (dec); ed/Cinci Univ, Ohio; pa/RN Spanish Gardens Nsg Home; r/Meth; hon/W/W Am Wom 1979.

BUSH, DANNY ELWARD oc/Minister; b/Oct 24, 1939; h/Oak Ridge, TN; ba/Oak Ridge; m/Nadine W Bush; c/Mark Allen, Charlotte Elizabeth; p/T and Blennie Keller Bush, Charlotte, NC; ed/UNCC 1957-60; BA Belmont Col 1963; MRE SWn Bapt Theol Sem 1968; Cert Billy Graham Sch of Evangelism 1974; pa/Assoc Min in Charge of Ed, First Bapt Ch, Oak Ridge, TN; Former Min Ed & Mus: Glenwood Bapt Ch, Nashville, Tenn; Loves Creek Bapt Ch, Siler City, NC; Univ Bapt Ch, Hyattsville, Md; First Bapt Ch, Everman, Tex; Justin Bapt, Justin, Tex; North Riverside Bapt, Newport News, Va; First Bapt Ch, Newport News; First Bapt, Fayetteville, NC; New Bridge Bapt, Richmond, Va; Pres Oak Ridge Min Assn; Moderator, Clinton Bapt Assn 1979-80; So Bapt REA; REA of US & Canada; Var Tnr Positions in NC, DC, Va & Tenn; cp/PTA Pres 1971-72; Fed Parole Advr 1971-75; Contact Support Wkr 1980-; Substitute Public Sch Tchr; Oak Ridge Lions Clb; r/So Bapt; hon/Alpha Psi Omega Nat Dramatic Frat 1962; Col Deans List 1962; Outstg Yng Men of Am 1970; Pub'd in *The Religious Herald; The Ministers Manual;* Others.

BUSH, ESTHER LOREAN oc/Assistant Director; b/Oct 26, 1951; h/Balto, MD; ba/500 E 62nd St, NY, NY 10021; p/Willie C and Ola Mae Bush, Pgh, PA; ed/BS Morgan St Univ 1973; Cert Boston Univ 1976; MS Johns Hopkins Univ 1977; pa/Asst Dir Wom's Affairs, LEAP, Nat Urban Leag 1980-; Asst Dir/Career Cnslr, Career Plan'g & Placement Ctr, Coppin St Col 1977-80; Tchr Balto City Public Schs 1973-77; Nat Vol Guid Assn Nat Employment Cnslrs Assn; APGA; Pi Lambda Theta, Dem Recording Secy 1978; cp/Dem Party; NAACP; Nat Urban Leag Wom's Crusade Against Crime, Balto Chapt Co-Chm; r/Bapt; hon/William Wallace Lanaham S'ship 1975; Gen Elect Guid F'ship 1976; W/W Am Wom 1981-82; Author "Summary of a Proposal for a Career Planning Course" *A Model Career Counseling and Placement Program* 1980; "The Converted Resume" *Journal of College Placement* Summer 1980; Author of Course Proposal for Career & Life Plan'g, Coppin St Col.

BUSH, MILLER WAYNE oc/Farmer; b/Aug 12, 1935; h/Rt 1 Box E74, Schlater, MS 38952; ba/Same; m/Celeste Ferguson; c/John, David, Chris; p/John Miller and Bennie Aford Bush; ed/BS Miss St Univ; mil/USAR; pa/Miss Farm Bur Dir; ASCS Co Com; Farmer's Home Adm Com; cp/C of C Dir; r/Bapt: Deacon; hon/Outstg Conservation Farmer of Yr 1978-79.

BUSLIG, BELA STEPHEN oc/Research Scientist; b/Aug 27, 1938; h/Auburndale, FL; ba/Fla Dept Citrus, c/o USDA, PO Box 1909, Winter Haven, FL 33880; m/Bertha Joanne Horsfall; c/Aileen, Bela Stephen; p/Gyula (dec) and Ilona Balazsy Buslig, Budapest, Hungary; ed/BA Queen's Univ 1962; MS Fl St Univ 1967; PhD Univ Fl 1970; pa/Res Sci (Biochem), Fla Dept Citrus 1967-; Can Soc Plant Physiol; Am Chem Soc; Am Soc Plant Physiol; Genetics Soc Am; AAAS; NY Acad Sci; Am Soc Horticultural Sci; Fla St Horticultural Soc; Sigma Xi; Refrigeration Ser Engrs Soc, Mem Bd Citrus Ctr Chapt; r/Roman Cath.

BUSSARD, DENNIS R oc/Assistant Athletic Director; b/Feb 16, 1947; ba/Asst Dir Athletics, Univ Tenn-Martin, Martin, TN 38238; m/Cynthia Day; c/Jennifer Nicole, Todd Stuart; p/Reba D Bussard, Springfield, Ohio; ed/BS Ed Ashland Col 1969; MEd Xavier Univ 1971; pa/Asst Dir Intercol Aths, Univ Tenn-Martin; Tennis Coach Univ Tenn-Martin; AAUP; NCAA Div III Tennis Selection Com; Nat Assn Basketball Coaches; AAHPER; c/Kiwanis; r/Meth; hon/Old Dominion Ath Conf

PERSONALITIES OF THE SOUTH

Tennis Coach of Yr 1976, 1977; Wash & Lee Univ Tennis Teams NCAA Div III Team Runners-Up 1976, 77; Author "Game Tempo and the Inside-Outside Offense" 1974; "Statistics: Little Things That Make a Difference" 1975; "Get More Out of Your Basketball Statistics" 1975.

BUSWELL, ARTHUR WILCOX oc/Army Medical Officer; b/Jan 6, 1926; h/68 St Lo Road, Fort Lee, VA 23801; m/Jane Fuksa; c/Arthur L, Robert J, Barbara J, Brian A, Gayla S, Richard A; p/Albert C Buswell (dec); Enid M Buswell, Kingfisher, OK; ed/BS Univ Okla 1950; MD Univ Okla Sch Med 1952; mil/AUS: 1944-46 China Burma India Theater Ser, Active Reserve 1946-61; Recalled Active Duty 1961; Cmdr 372nd Med Detachmt 1961-62 Ft Sill, Okla; Chief Outpatient Ser USAH Ft Sill 1962-63; Chief Profl Ser Bassett USA Hosp Ft Wainwright, Alaska 1963-65; Div Surg 1st Armored Div Ft Hood, Tex 1966-67; Div Surg 1st Inf Div Repub Vietnam 1967-68; Chief Experimtn Div & Human Factors USA Combat Devel Command Experimtn Command Ft Ord 1968-72; Chief Profl Ser Reynolds USA Hosp, Ft Sill 1972-73; Cmdr USA Med Dept; Activs Ft Stewart/Hunter Army Airfield & Cmdr USA Hosp Ft Stewart 1973-77; Chief Profl Sers Kenner Army Hosp, Ft Lee, Va 1977-; Adj Asst Profl Med Sci, Baylor Univ 1973; pa/Surg Resident Wesley Hosp, Okla City; Pvt Pract Med & Surg Hennessey, Okla 1955-63; Supt Hlth, Kingfisher Co 1960-61; Chief Staff Kingfisher Commun Hosp 1957; Fellow Royal Soc Hlth; Other Profl Assns; cp/Pres Sch Bd Ft Stewart, Ga 1977; hon/Legion of Merit w 1 OLC; Soldiers Medal, Bronze Star w 1 OLC; Air Medal w 3 OLCs; Vietnamese Gallantry Cross w Palm; Vietnamese Armed Forces Honor Medal 1st Class; Others.

BUTCHER, LOIS M oc/Secretary; b/Mar 21, 1938; h/1606 S Magnolia Ave, Sanford, FL 32771; ba/Sanford; m/J Gordon; p/James H and Nina V Messer, Sanford, FL; pa/Legal Secy; Past Ofcr Seminole Co Legal Secys Assn; r/Prot; hon/Valedictorian, Covington Sr High 1956; Secy of Yr, Seminole Co, Fl 1980-81.

BUTCHER, VERA ROBINSON oc/Instructor; b/Oct 18, 1922; h/200 Holmes St, McComb, MS 39648; m/K C; s/Willye Powell, Immel August; p/Immel Sr and Julia R Robinson, McComb, MS; ed/BS Alcorn St Univ 1944; MEd Prairie View Univ 1957; AAA Spec, Tex Wom's Univ 1970; MEd SEn Univ 1978; pa/Sec Voc Home Ec Instr, McComb HS; NEA; AHEA; AVA; SER-ACT; Chp MACT Resolution Com; Miss Assn Ed Bd Dirs; Chp Elem, Second & Adult MAE, Dist V Secy; Pres Elect McComb Assn Edrs; Ed Home Ec Section NEA; Govs Qual Ed Com; cp/NAACP; VP Pike Co Tchrs Fed Credit Union; Ga Westbrook Fed'd Clb VP; Pike Lib Bd; Secy Commun VB Sch; Secy Pike Co; Unity Chapt Alcorn Alumni Clb; Local Mgr & Poll Asst; FHA Ldr; r/Bapt; hon/NEA Wom's Hall of Fame 1976; Mother of Yr 1976; Gov's Cert Apprec 1976; MAE 1979; Ldr of Yr, McComb Public Schs 1979-80; MAE Dist V 1979-80; Alcorn Alumni Chapt 1980; McComb PTA Coun 1980; MS FHA Coun 1977; Articles Yrly to MS Misses for McComb High FHA.

BUTLER, BROADUS NATHANIEL oc/Academic Institute President; b/May 28, 1920; h/10014 Branch View Ct, Silver Spring, MD 20903; ba/Wash DC; m/Lillian Rutherford; c/Bruce Nathaniel, Janet B Reid (Mrs Leon Asbury III); p/John Nathaniel Butler (dec); Mary Lillian Broadus (dec); ed/Grad Talladega Col; BA 1941, MA 1947, PhD 1952 Univ Mich-Ann Arbor; mil/USAF WWII, 332nd Fighter Group (now hon'd as famed Tuskegee Airmen); pa/Pres Robert Russa Moton Meml Inst; Positions held at following: St Augustine's Col, Raleigh, NC, Wayne St Univ, Detroit, Mich, Tex So Univ, Houston, Tex, Dillard Univ, New Orleans, La; Asst to US Commr of Ed & Spec Asst to Assoc Commr for Higher Ed 1964-67; Former Staff Exec Am Coun on Ed; cp/Mem: St Ednl TV Auth, St Mus Comm, St Soc for Perf'g Arts of La; Mem & Chm Bd Dirs New Orleans Br, Fed Resv Bk of Atlanta; Mem Selection Bd I, US St Dept; Adv Com, Ofc of Hlth Manpower Opport, Nat Insts Hlth; Adv Com on Minority Instns Sci Devel, NSF; Bd Mem CEMREL Nat Ednl Lab; Nat Bd Dirs NAACP; Bd Advrs Nat Ctr for Career Life Planning; Bd Trustees, Ctr for Study of Presidency, Gulf S Res Inst; Former Chm Ad Hoc Com to Study & Assess the Tuskegee Syphilis Study, US Dept HEW; Former Chm Task Force Com on Africa to Study & Recommend Future Policy on Africa, Nat Bd of NAACP; Others; hon/Pub'd Author; Grand Cmdr Order of Star of Africa, Liberia; Cert Of Merit & Hon Citizen, NO; Hon Citizen, Mobile, Ala; Cert Dist'd Ser: Fed Resv Bk Atlanta, Nat Merit S'ship Corp, NW C of C; Fellow, ABI; Other Dist'd Ser Awds; Biogl Listings.

BUTLER, CHARLES E oc/Custodian, Student; b/Jan 8, 1950; ed/Dip AUS Aviation Ctr, UH-1 1979; AA Jefferson Commun Col 1981; mil/AUS 1971-76; pa/Custodian Vet Adm; Col Student; r/Meth; hon/Good Conduct Medal 1976; High Motivation Awd, Jefferson Commun Col, Title IV Prog 1978; Hon Men, Ky St Poetry Soc for "The Unknown" 1979; 1st Pl Jefferson Commun Col Art Exhib 1980; 1st Pl Poetry Contest, Jefferson Commun Col 1981; Ed Creative Achmt Awd 1981; Writing & Lit Creative Achmt Awd 1981; Poems "Prisms", "A Thousand Images in Words", "Inky Trails", Poetry & Photo has Rec'd Ext Coverage in Local Newspapers; Poetry & Photo Displayed in Sev Art Exhibs.

BUTLER, CHARLES LEO oc/School Principal; b/Apr 18, 1914; h/1240 Kent St, Augusta, GA 30901; ba/Augusta; m/Julia Collier; c/Charles Jr, Lillie Frances B Jurgurtha, Georgene Nettie; p/William Henry Butler; Beulah Butler (dec); ed/BA Paine Col 1938; MA Atlanta Univ 1943; DHL Allen Univ 1966; Further Study; pa/Ga Tchrs & Ed Assn: Pres 5th Reg 1953, Bd Dirs, Bd Trustees; Am Tchrs Assn; Nom'd to Bd Dirs NEA 1959 (Served 9 Yrs); NEA Del to World Conf of Orgs Of Tchr's Profession 1959; Mem Gov'd Conf on Ed 1964, 65, 66, 67; Chm Bd Trustees GTEA; Bd Trustees Ga Assn Edrs; Others; cp/Former Editor Black Notes, Augusta Chronicle Daily Newspaper; Former Mem Bd Dirs Weekly Review, Inc; Fdr Dukes Social & Civic Clb; Former Mem Exec Com Negro Col Fund Dr, SEn Ga Area; Former Campaign Dir Negro Col Fund; Bd Dirs SERA Div Easter Seal Soc Ga; Heart Fund Commun Drs; YMCA; Others; r/Mt Calvary Bapt Ch: Bd Deacons, Supt SS 8 Yrs; hon/Cert of Merit, Cong of Colored Parents & Tchrs; Plaque for Dist'd Ser to Cause of Ed, Ga Tchrs & Ed Assn; NEA Human Relats Awd; W/W S&SW; Others.

BUTLER, KELLEY W oc/Craftsman; b/Sept 7, 1953; h/PO Box 128, DeKalb, TX 25559; ba/Same; m/Kimberly; c/Amanda Lynn; p/Kelley and Lois E Butler, Avery, TX; pa/Leather Craftsman; Rodeo; r/Bapt.

BUTLER, MANLEY CALDWELL oc/Lawyer, US Representative; b/June 2, 1925; h/Roanoke, VA; ba/PO Box 869, Roanoke, VA 24005; m/June Nolde; c/Manley, Henry, Jimmy, Marshall; p/Dr (dec) and Mrs M W S Butler, Roanoke, VA; ed/AB Univ Richmond 1948; LLB Univ Va Sch Law 1950; Hon LLD Wash & Lee 1978; mil/USN Ofcr WWII; pa/Pract'd Law, Roanoke 1950-Election, Ptnr Law Firm Eggleston, Holton, Butler & Glenn; cp/Va Ho of Dels 1962-72; Chm Jt Repub Caucus 1964-66; Minority Ldr 1966-72; r/Epis.

BUTLER, MICHAEL BERNARD oc/General Surgeon; b/Feb 10, 1939; h/Longwood, FL; ba/695 Douglas Ave, Altamonte Springs, FL 32701; m/M Jean; c/Michele, Brian; ed/BA Talladega Col 1959; MD Howard Univ Col of Med 1963; mil/USN 1964-66, Lt Comdr; pa/Surg, Pvt Pract; Univ S Fla, Asst Prof; Am Cancer Soc, Fla Div; SEn Surg Conf; Intl Col Surgs; Exec Com Orange Co Med Soc; Bd Dir PRSO of Ctrl Fla; Am Col Surgs; Fla Div Intl Col Surgs, Secy-Treas; Former Chief of Surg, Fla Hosp & Mercy Hosp, Orlando; cp/Am Cancer Soc, Pres Orange Co Unit 1976-77; Rotary Seminole Co, S, Bd Dirs 1977-79; Christian Ser Ctr, Bd Dirs 1976-79; Seminole YMCA, Bd Dirs 1971-, Chm Bd 1979; Metro YMCA, Bd Dirs 1977-80; Bd Elders, Rolling Hills Moravian Ch; VP Fla Dist Bd of Moravian Ch; Bd Dirs ComBank, Seminole Co; r/Moravian Ch.

BUTLER, RAYMOND PRESTON oc/Therapist; b/Sept 10, 1947; h/Rt 5, Box 184, Alexander City, AL 35010; ba/Alexander City; m/Connie Campbell; c/Christopher Todd; p/James Roy and Ruby Skinner Butler, Graceville, FL; ed/AA Chipola Jr Col 1967; BS Univ W Fla 1969; MS Troy St Univ 1974; MEd Auburn Univ 1979; mil/USAF 1971-75; pa/Therapist/Elderly Sers Field Supvr, E Ala Mtl Hlth Ctr; AAHPER; Alliance of Info & Referral Sers; Ala Pers & Guid Assn; Lake Martin Runners; Tallapoosa Co Coun on Aging; Ala Mtl Hlth Cnslrs Assn; r/Prot.

BUTLER, SHIRLEY GEE oc/Secretary; b/Sept 22, 1943; h/Rt 4 Box 99A, Columbus, MS 39701; ba/Columbus; m/Jimmy L; c/Rhonda, Arnie, Pamela; p/Scott S and Vergie Junkin Gee, Columbus, MS; pa/Secy to Judge Ellis S Dale; cp/New Hope Sch PTA; Lowndes Rec Coach; Ran for Just Ct Judge, Dist 3, Lowndes Co, MS; r/Bapt; hon/Awds in Sports & Area Personality.

BUTLER, WILLIAM CURTISS oc/Attorney at Law; b/Aug 4, 1944; h/PO Box 91, Sandersville, MS 39477; ba/Laurel, MS; m/Alma Lee; c/William Brett, Brandon Rhett; p/James Curtiss and Myrtle Henry Butler, Shubuta, MS; ed/AA Jones Co Jr Col; BS Univ So Miss; JD Jackson Sch Law at Miss Col; mil/USN; pa/Atty at Law; Construc Bus-man; Assn Trial Lawyers of Am; ABA; Miss Trial Lawyers; cp/JCs; Dem Nominee for Rep Dist 82 Jones Co, Miss; r/Prot.

BUTLER, WILLIAM GILBERT JR oc/Physician; b/Oct 1, 1928; h/1708 Monticello Rd, Florence, AL 35630; ba/Florence; m/Winifred T; c/William G III, Ann, Robert W; p/Mr and Mrs W G Butler, Laurinburg, NC; ed/AB Univ NC 1949; MD Duke Univ 1953; mil/USAF Med Corp 1955-57; pa/Phys, Obst & Gyn; Alpha Epsilon Delta; Phi Delta Theta; Phi Chi; Am Bd Obst & Gyn; Fellow Am Col Obst & Gyn; Fellow Am Col Surgs; SEn Assn Obst & Gyn: Exec Com, Bd Dirs; Bayard Carter Soc Obst & Gyn Pres Elect; Exec Com Ala Assn Obst & Gyn; Rep Interspec Coun Med Assn Ala; Past Pres Lauderdale Co Med Soc; VP Med Staff ECM Hosp; Bd Censors Lauderdale Co Med Soc; Past Chm Lauderdale Co Hlth Dept; Fellow Am Soc Study Fertility; AMA; Med Assn St Ala; Lauderdale Co Med Soc; Admissions Com Dist VII; Am Col Obst & Gyn; England Hypnosis Soc; Phys Univ N Ala; cp/Metro YMCA of N Ala; Past Pres

Florence Rotary Clb; Bd Dirs Univ N Ala Sportsmans Clb; Bd Mem NW Ala Chapt Am Cancer Soc; Bd Dirs Lauderdale Co Chapt Am Red Cross; Exec Bd Lauderdale Co United Way; BSA; Explorer Scouts; Muscle Shoals Mtl Hlth Assn; Hope Haven Sch; Fdr, Chief Obst & Gyn, VP, Bd Trustees Colonial Manor Hosp; r/Presb; hon/Citizen of Yr, Shoal Area, Ala.

BUTTS, KENNETH OLIN oc/Biologist; b/Jan 22, 1948; h/PO Box 100, Austwell, TX 77950; ba/Austwell; m/Sharla R; c/Monte O, Brent D; p/Ted K and Vivian M Butts, Higgins, TX; ed/BS magna cum laude Bethany Nazarene Col; MS Okla St Univ; pa/Wildlife Biol; Wildlife Refuge Mgr; Tex Wildlife Soc; Phi Kappa Phi; cp/1st VP Austwell-Tivoli Lions Clb; Treas PTO; r/Ch of the Nazarene; hon/Outstg Yng Layman Awd JC Clb, 1974; Author 3 Tech Wildlife Pubs.

BUTTS, MICHELE TUCKER oc/Assistant Professor; b/Dec 23, 1952; h/118 Westminister St, Prestonsburg, KY 41653; ba/P'burg; p/Ray Runyon and Ruth Bumpus Butts, Clarksville, TN; ed/BA Austin Peay St Univ 1973; MA 1974, Postgrad Studies 1975 Univ Ky; Univ NM 1976-80; pa/Asst Prof Hist & Jour, P'burg Commun Col 1979-; Asst Editor, Bus & Ad Mgr, ASU Student Newspaper 1971-72; Tchr Houston Co Schs, Tenn 1974-75; Conslt Indian Lore & Wn Hist; Am Hist Assn; Orgr Am Hists; Ky Assn Tchrs Hist; Ky Assn Commun Col Profs; Order of Indian Wars; Phi Alpha Theta; Alpha Mu Gamma; cp/Big Sandy Area Devel Dist Envir Qual Com; Sierra Clb; Wilderness Soc; Ky Conserv Com; r/So Bapt; hon/Halbert Harvill Citizenship Awd, APSU 1973; Ser Awd Lonesome Pine Coun Order of Arrow, BSA 1977; Ser Awd GSA 1980; W/W S&SW 1981.

BYASSEE, EYRL LEON oc/Merchant; b/Nov 22, 1908; h/3250 Madison St, Maury City, TN; m/Jessie Edith Lax; c/Eyrl L Jr, Esther Fay Brown; p/John Edgar (dec) and Mattie Mayoma Agee Byassee (dec); mil/AUS 1945-46; pa/Merchant; cp/Ruritan Clb; Chm Crockett Co TB Assn; Sch Bd; r/Meth; hon/Duke of Paducah 1975.

BYE, RAYMOND SIGURD oc/Management; b/May 30, 1919; h/7596 Silver Fork Dr, Salt Lake City, UT 84121; m/Mary; c/Monte, Marianne, Joseph, Christine, Virginia; p/Raymond A and Mary E Bye, Salt Lake City, UT; ed/Att'd Hamline Univ, Univ Minn; pa/Dist Mgr, Am Fam Life Assn; Inventor w 3M Co; Former Packing List Inserter, Shipping Indust, Scotchlite Reflective Fabric.

BYERS, DAVID WILBURN oc/General Manager; b/Nov 3, 1931; h/Monticello, KY; m/Sally Ann; c/David Martin, Mark Campbell, Amy Ruth; p/David Colston and Flonnie Campbell Byers, Monticello, KY; ed/Georgetown Col 1950-51; En Ky Univ 1952 & 54; mil/AUS 2 Yrs; pa/Hwy Gen Mgr, Dept Trans, Ky Dist 8; Cardiac Pacemakers; r/Bapt; hon/W/W Ky 1974; Outstg Am of South 1975.

BYERS, KATHLEEN L oc/Physician; b/Oct 28, 1916; h/396 Wimbledon Rd, NE, Atlanta, GA 30324; ba/Atlanta; m/Atlanta; William John Lindsey; c/Patricia Ann Lindsey Weiss, John Byers Lindsey; p/Nell Elizabeth Byers, Naples, NC; ed/BS Univ Ga 1938; MD Ed Col Ga 1943; Intern Flower 5th Ave Hosp 1943-44; Residency Bellvue Hosp 1944-46; Dip

Am Bd Anesthesiology 1952; pa/Anesthesiology 1944-72; Adm Vet Adm; Staff Piedmont Hosp 1947-; Med Assn Atlanta; Am Soc Anesthesiol; Ga Soc Anesthesiol; Fulton Co Assn Anesthesiol; AMA; AMWA; cp/Atlanta Symph Orch Leag; High Mus Art; DAR, Atlanta Chapt; Atlanta Hist Soc; LWV; r/Disciples of Christ.

BYNUM, JACK L oc/Dean of Students; b/Mar 5, 1942; h/Pineville, LA; ba/Box 557, La Col, Pineville, LA 71360; m/Judy Smith; c/John, Jeffrey; p/Reba Bynum, Lovelady, TX; ed/BA Houston Bapt Univ 1970; MRE 1975, EdD 1980 SWn Bapt Theol Sem; mil/USAFR; pa/Tchr Tarrant Co Jr Col; Tchr SWn Bapt Theol Sem; Dean of Students, La Col; Am Assn Marriage & Fam Therapists; Am Ednl Res Assn; APGA; r/Bapt.

BYNUM, JODIE oc/Farmer, Janitor; b/Apr 10, 1907; h/815 Bethel NE, Hartselle, AL 35640; ba/Hartselle; m/Berzina; c/Jodie Jr, Minnie L Griffin, Emma Jean, Benjamin F, Cleveland B, Curtis L, Willie E, Eddie L, John S; p/Jim (dec) and Addie Bynum (dec); pa/Farmer; Shoeshine Stand; Janitor, Crestline Sch; r/Mission Bapt.

BYNUM, L S oc/Board of Supervisors; b/May 21, 1917; h/Rt 2, PO Box 244, Ellisville, MS 39437; ba/Same; m/Mary Esther; c/Eleanor McMillan, Sherwood; p/Leon S (dec) and Martha Bynum (dec); pa/Mem Jones Co Bd Supvrs; cp/Former Constable & Just Ct Judge; r/Bapt.

BYRD, IDA FAY oc/Educator; b/May 28, 1938; h/PO Box 126, Roaring River, NC 28696; ba/Wilkesboro; m/Kenneth Edwin; c/Teressa Rene, Edwin Scott; p/Nelson Hall (dec) and Tracy Jane Croce Caudle, Roaring River, NC; pa/Educator, Wilkes Commun Col; Pres NCAECT; NCCAEA; LRA; NC Media Coun; cp/Wilkes Co Bd Ed; r/Bapt.

BYRD, JOE W oc/Pastor; b/Aug 3, 1923; h/549 Packing Rd, Kingsport, TN 37660; ba/Kingsport; m/Eileen Barker; c/Ronald Lynn, Joseph Stephen, Carolyn Yvonne, Phyllis Teresa; p/Allie Roscoe Sr (dec) and Gussie Katherine Frazier Byrd (dec); mil/AUS 1942-46 Reconnaissance Sgt; pa/Pastor Bloomingdale Bapt Ch 1951-; K'port Bapt Pastor's Conf; Clk, Sullivan Bapt Assn; Tenn Bapt & So Bapt Convs; cp/Chaplain, Am Legion Hammond Post #3; Chaplain on Call, Holiday Inns of K'port; Co-Chaplain, Bloomingdale Ruritan; Probation Ofcr, Gen Sessions Ct, Div II; DAV; Masonic Lodge 688; Lynn Bachman Chapt, K'port Commandry; K'port Coun; hon/Life Mem PTA 1966; Ser to Mankind Awd, K'port Sertoma Clb 1970; Ser Awd, Ketron HS 1970; Probation Ofcr of Yr Awd 1975-76; Ser Awd, Am Legion 1981; Write Mthly Article for *Kingsport Legionnaire*, Hammond Post #3.

BYRD, MARQUITA LAVON oc/Assistant Professor; b/Mar 24, 1950; h/Hattiesburg, MS; m/Henry Wilbanks Jr; c/Henry Wilbanks III; p/Robert Byrd; Alma Byrd, San Jose, CA; ed/BS Ctrl Mo St 1972; MA So Ill Univ-Edwardsville 1975; PhD Univ Mo-Columbia 1979; pa/Asst Prof Speech Communs, Univ So Miss 1979-; Grad Tchg Asst, Univ Mo 1975-78; Grad Tchg Asst, So Ill Univ 1975; Grad Tchg Asst, Ctrl Mo St Univ 1973-74; cp/VP So Region Grad Advrs Coun Alpha Kappa Alpha; hon/Outstg Yng Am Wom 1980; W/W Intell 1980; Author "The Effects of Vocal Activity and Race of Applicant on Job Selection Interview Decisions" 1980.

C

CABAGE, GRAYCE MARIE HANNAH oc/Food Service; b/Dec 17, 1919; h/2306 Old Knoxville Pike, Maryville, TN 37801; ba/Maryville; m/Harold N; c/George Clayton, William Harold; p/Dr & Mrs George Franklin Hannah (dec) ed/Draughron's Bus Col 1940; Univ Tenn 1969; pa/Blount Co Sch Food Serv; Pres, Treas, Tenn Sch Food Ser Assn; Pres, Treas, E Tenn Sch Food Ser Assn; Pres Blount Co Sch Food Ser Assn; TEA; NEA; ETEA; cp/Recording Secy Tenn Fed Repub Wom; Pres, Secy, Treas Blount Co FRW; Recording Secy Mary Blount Chapt DAR; 4-H Ldr; PTA; Blount Co Repub Exec Com; hon/Blount Co Vol.

CAGLE, CHARLES WAYNE oc/Field Representative; b/Oct 5, 1956; h/921 E Tenth St, Cookeville, TN 38501; ba/C'ville; p/James M (dec) and Barbara S Cagle, Sweetwater, TN; ed/BS 1978, MA 1980 Tenn Tech Univ; pa/Asst Dir Fin Aid, Tenn Tech Univ 1979-80; Field Rep for Gov Lamar Alexander (R-TN); Dir Gov's C'ville Regional Ofc; Tenn Assn Student Fin Aid Amdrs; So Assn Student Fin Aid Admrs; r/Bapt; hon/Outstg Yng Men Am 1979; Kappa Delta Pi 1979, 1980; Author *The Techniques of Financial Aid - A Student's Guide to Financial Aid* 1980.

CAHOON, JOHN TILLMAN oc/Sanitation Superintendent; b/Mar 18, 1933; h/Augusta, GA; ba/PO Box 2207, Augusta, GA 30903; m/Lorna J; c/Debborah, Ralph, Wendy, Angel, Randy, Jaclyn; p/John G and Alda L Cahoon, Mt Carmel, PA; ed/CID Sch, AUS 1951; FBI Sch for Criminal Sex & Fingerprinting 1954-55; AIB Sch 1970; mil/AUS 1950-54 M/Sgt; pa/Sanitation Supt, Beatrice Foods 1973-; Sanitation Supt, Interstate Brands 1963-73; Mgr Triangle Shoe Store 1959-62; Asst Mgr Woolworth's Stores 1957-59; Chief Police, Mohnton, Pa 1956; Mt Carmel, Pa Police Force 1953-56; Envir Mgrs Assn, Secy-Treas So Region; EMA, Pres NE Chapt St Ga; Ga Envir Hlth Assn; r/Meth; hon/Envir Mgrs Assn Pres Citation 1979.

CAIN, MURRAY LELAND oc/Salesman; b/Aug 15, 1946; h/109 Oakhill Dr, Natchez, MS 39120; m/Debra; c/John Mark; p/M L (dec) and Sibyl Cain, Durant, MS; ed/Holmes Jr Col 1965; AA Whitworth Col 1965-68; mil/Civil Air Patrol 2nd Lt; pa/Salesman, Salesmanship Motivator, Cain & Assocs; Toastmasters; cp/Adams Co Exec; Dem Party; Past Pres JCs; Civil Defense Adv Coun; Moose; Lions Clb; Former Scoutmaster; EMT; Vol Rescue & Fireman; r/Bapt; hon/Outstg Yng Man 1973; Official St Santa Claus; St Jude Hosp Apprec Awd.

CALATAYUD, JUAN BAUTISTA oc/Associate Director Medical Education Doctors Hospital; b/May 17, 1928; h/Falls Ch, Va; ba/1712 Eye St, NW, Suite 1004, Wash DC 20006; m/Helen Lupton; c/Mary Carmen, Juan Cesar; p/Augustin and Carmen Calatayud, Valencia, Spain; ed/MD Univ Valencia Med Sch 1952; Dipl The ECFMG 1961; Var Postgrad Courses; mil/Spanish Mil Ser 6 Mos, 2nd Lt, Castellon, Spain 1952-53; pa/Intern Cardiac & Med Clins Valencia Med Sch 1953-55; Intern Alexian Brothers Hosp, Elizabeth, NJ 1956; Resident in Med St Paul Hosp, Dallas, Tex 1956-57; Fellow in Med Cardiovas Disease, DC Gen Hosp & Geo Wash Univ Hosp, Wash DC 1957-60; Res Asst Inst de Med et Chirurgie Experimentales Universite de Montreal, Canada 1960-61; Asst Resident Dept Med Montreal Gen Hosp, Univ Clin of McGill Univ 1961; Geo Wash Univ Hosp (Conslt Cardiac Clin) 1962-70, DC Gen Hosp Att'g in Med 1964-70; Res Com Wash Heart Assn 1966-68; Assoc Clin Prof of Med, Geo Wash Univ Sch of Med 1977-; Pan Am Med Soc DC Chapt; Att'g Ward Rounds in Med DC Gen Hosp GW Med Div 1967; Prog Dir Heart in Reg Med Prog Wash Metro Area, GWU Med Ctr 1967-70, GWU Sch Med; Fellow Am Col Angiology; AMA; Dir Heart Sta & Exercise EKG Lab, Drs Hosp 1974-; Advr to AAMA 1972-; Secy, Profl Staff of Drs Hosp 1973-; Bd Dirs Drs Hosp; Hon Mem Edit Adv Bd, Am Biog Inst 1975; Arbitration Assn 1974; Num Other Profl Orgs; hon/Hom Mem Peruvian Angiology Soc & Cardiac Soc; W/W: Sci, S&SW; Pub'd Author; Commun Ldrs Am; DIB; Intl W/W Commun Ser; 2000 Men Achmt.

CALDWELL, WILLIAM (BILLY) THOMAS oc/Businessman; b/Nov 15, 1938; h/N Franklin St, Christiansburg, VA 24073; m/Jacqueline Williams; c/Kenneth Edward, Tamela Leann; p/Dode G and Gertrude C Caldwell, Newport, VA; mil/USAF 9 Mos; pa/Owner & Opr Willard Monument Co; r/Christian.

CALDWELL-BURKE, MAXINE oc/Director Career Planning and Placement; b/July 6, 1936; ba/Career Placement/Plan'g, So Univ Shreveport, 3050 Cooper Rd, Shreveport, LA; c/Michelyn; p/Mittie Fields; ed/BA So Univ 1957; MFA Howard Univ 1972; MEd Prairie View A&M Univ 1981; pa/Dir Career Plan'g & Placement; Alpha Kappa Alpha; cp/YWCA; Urban Leag; NAACP; r/Cath; hon/Art Tchr of Yr 1979-80; Cert of Achmt, SUSBO's Art Clb 1980-81.

CALENDER, A D oc/Retired Service Assistant in Psychiatric Nursing; b/Oct 19, 1914; h/507 N Pk Ave, Terrell, TX 75760; m/Odaysel Fay White; c/Jack, Robert, Kenneth, Jeffery; Stepchd: Dan, Dewey, Jim, Dwaine, Elaine, Royce and Joyce; p/Lee Andrew Calender (dec); Maggie Elizabeth Tankersley (dec); mil/AUS 1943-45; pa/Ret'd Ser Asst in Psychi Nsg, Terrell St Hosp; cp/Am Legion; VFW; r/Ch of Chrsit; hon/Purple Heart 1945; Good Conduct 1945; Dip Psychi Aide 1971; Bronz Star 1956; Psychi Aide of Yr 1974.

CALHOUN, JAMES WALTER oc/Minister; b/Apr 23, 1950; h/302 Bethesda Dr, Huntsville, AL 35803; ba/H'ville; m/Shirley McCallister; c/Jennifer Leigh, John Marcus; p/Charles Walter Calhoun, Wetumpka, AL; Mary Agnes Smith, Opelika, AL; ed/BS Troy St Univ 1976; MA Ch of God Sch of Theol 1978; mil/USAF 1970-74; pa/Min Whitesburg Ch of God; Chilton Co Min Assn; Gtr H'ville Full-Gospel Min Assn; r/Ch of God; hon/Outstg Yng Man of Am 1979; Alpha Sigma Lambda Hon Soc; Nat Beta Clb.

CALL, CHARLES ALTMAN oc/Dentist; b/Apr 16, 1914; h/2509 Lake Oaks Rd, Waco, TX 76710; ba/Waco; m/Elizabeth; c/Charles Altman Jr, Carol Eve; p/Samuel Frost (dec) and Elizabeth Call (dec); ed/DDS; pa/Life Mem ADA; Tex Dental Assn, Life Mem; cp/Past Potentate & Life Mem Karem Shrine Temple; Past Dir Royal Order of Jesters, Waco Ct 113; Master Mason; 32° Scottish Rite; Knight Templar Mason; r/Meth.

CALLAWAY, CATHERINE (CATHY) LEWIS oc/Project Consultant; b/Dec 17, 1934; h/1135 Stillwood Dr NE, Atlanta, GA 30306; ba/Atlanta; m/Mayson A Jr; c/Mayson A III, Eugene Lewis, Louise Ann; p/Horace and Mildred Lewis, Avondale Ests, GA; ed/BA Agnes Scott Col 1955; MPA Ga St Univ 1981; pa/Social Wkr, Fulton Co 1956-58; Pers Acctg, Sears, Roebuck & Co 1970-75; Team Ldr & Revenue Agt, Dept Revenue, St of Ga 1975-77; Accts Payable & Accts Receivable Supvr, Dept Adm Sers, St of Ga 1977-79; Proj Conslt, Dept Adm Sers, St Ga 1979-81; Secy/Treas Namano Inc, Tucker, Ga; VP SEn Co, Tucker, Ga; Bd Dirs Calack Inc, Tucker, Ga; Fiscal Ofcrs of St of Ga; cp/High Museum of Art; r/Meth; hon/W/W Am Wom.

CALLEN, JEFFREY P oc/Physician; b/May 30, 1947; h/Louisville, KY; ba/554 Med Towers S, Louisville, KY 40202; m/Susan M; c/Amy M, David S; p/Irwin R and Rose P Callen, N Miami Beach, FL; ed/BS Univ Wis 1969; MD Univ Mich 1972; pa/Dermatologist, Internist, Univ L'ville Sch Med; Fellow Am Col Phys; Fellow Am Acad Derm; cp/L'ville C of C; Bd Dir L'ville Alumni Clb for Univ Mich; hon/Pub'd Author *Manual of Dermatology*, 1980; *Cutaneous Aspects of Internal Diseases* 1980; Over 75 Articles in Reference Jours; Editorial Bds: Cutis, Intl Jours of Dermatol.

CALLOWAY, WILLIAM oc/Assistant Master Brewer; b/Feb 10, 1939; h/Memphis, TN; ba/5151 E Raines Rd, PO Box 18309, Memphis, TN 38118; m/Lois; c/Michael, E Sharron; p/Mrs Walter Calloway, Longview, TX; ed/BS; pa/Asst Master Brewer, Jos. Schlitz Brewing Co, Memphis; Master Brewers Assn of Ams; r/Bapt; hon/W/W Black Ams 1977; Black Achievers Awd 1974.

CALLOWAY, WILLIAM BENNETT oc/Teacher; b/Oct 30, 1945; h/630 Stuart St, Christiansburg, VA 24073; m/Mary C Campbell; c/Kendra Malaka; p/Gentle Lynn (dec) and Malaka Calloway (dec); ed/Dip C'burg Inst 1965; BS Bluefield St Col 1969; pa/Tchr Montgomery Co Sch Bd 1969-; Montgomery Co Ed Assn 1969-; Va Ed Assn 1969; NEA 1969-; Corres Secy Alpha Phi Alpha 1979; cp/Prince Hall Grand Lodge of Va F & AM; St John #35 1977; C'burg Commun Ctr Bd Mem 1972-75; NAACP; r/Meth; hon/Outstg Yng Men of Am 1980.

CALVERT, RICHARD L oc/Security Systems Company Executive; b/Jan 15, 1932; h/2300 Redbud Dr, Jonesboro, AR 72401; ba/J'boro; m/Carolyn Lavin; c/E Scott, Chris; p/Thomas and Jean M Griffiths Calvert; ed/BS Fairleigh Dickinson Univ 1958; MBA Ark St Univ 1971; pa/Huffman-Koos, Hackensack 1957; Sales Mgr Leonard Motors, New Milford, NJ 1957-59; Prodn Engr, Buyer ADT Security Sys, Clifton, NJ 1959-65, Plant Mgr, Jonesboro, Ark 1965-; Guest Spkr Memphis St Univ 1972-73, Ark St Univ 1974-75, 80-; Am Soc Pers Admrs, Pres NE Ark Pers Mgmt Assn; cp/Gtr Jonesboro C of C; Ark C of C; New Indust Comm C of C; Ark Indust Devel Comm; Repub; Jonesboro Country Clb; Paragould Country Clb; Stonebridge Country Clb; Elks; United Way J'boro; r/Epis.

CALVERY, THOMAS CLEATON SR oc/Businessman; b/Mar 22, 1940; h/Corinth, MS; ba/404 Franklin St, Corinth, MS 38834; m/Faye Potts; c/Thomas Cleaton Jr, Elizabeth Ashley; p/Myrtle Calvery, Corinth, MS; ed/Att'd Miss Jr Col; mil/Miss Army NG 1957-67; pa/Owner-Operator Frames by Ashley; Agt Berryhill Bail Bond Ser; Cost Clerk Wurlitzer Co; Prod Control Ofc Supvr; Profl Picture Framers Assn; cp/Corinth Lions Clb; Miss Lions Sight Foun; Pres Alcorn Co Elec Comm; r/Bapt; hon/Lion of Yr 1971.

CAMERON, DON DAVIS JR oc/Laboratory Manager; b/Mar 17, 1931; h/3408 S Mntn Rd, Knoxville, Md 21758; ba/Frederick, Md; p/Don Davis Sr and Helen Josephine Timmons Cameron; ed/BS Maryknoll Col; mil/USN; pa/Mgr Ctrl Histotechnol Lab, Frederick Cancer Res Ctr; Pres

48

Frederick Co Soc Med Tech; Pres Va Soc of Histology Techns; Budget & Fin Com, Nat Soc Histolotechnol; ASCP Reg'd Histotechnol; r/Cath; hon/W/W Indust & Fin 1979.

CAMP, TONYIA MARIE oc/Model; b/Aug 14, 1960; h/819 Surrey Dr, Shelby, NC 28150; p/Lamar and Linda Camp, Shelby, NC; ed/Bauder Fash Col 1978; Libby Stone Finishing & Modeling Sch; pa/Modeling; Hlth Occupations; cp/Fash Shows; Plays; r/Bapt; hon/Intl Thespian Soc; WNCS Debutante 1978; Cert Merit from Wilhelmina Models Inc.

CAMPBELL, AGNES KNIGHT oc/Retired Social Agency Executive; b/Jan 10, 1911; h/6515 Sherwood Dr, Knoxville, TN; 37919; m/John Franklin (dec); p/George Allen (dec) and Nora Clark Knight (dec); ed/BS Tenn Tech Univ; MSSW Univ Tenn; pa/Profl Exec Coun Knoxville; Nat Assn Social Wkrs; Acad Cert'd Social Wkrs; Tenn St Conf on Social Wel; cp/Tenn Tech Univ Circle Omicron Delta Kappa; John Sevier Meml Assn; Gov John Sevier Org for Descendants; r/Prot; hon/Social Wkr of Yr 1976 Knox Area Chapt Nat Assn Social Wkrs; Dist'd Alumni Awd from Tenn Tech Univ 1977.

CAMPBELL, CAREY WALTON oc/Neurological Surgeon; b/Nov 24, 1937; ba/Suite 5A, 132 Lone Oak Rd, Paducah, KY 42001; c/Phyllis Catherine; p/Brutus Randolph Campbell, Hattiesburg, MS; Maggie Smith Campbell (dec); ed/BS Miss So Univ 1960; MD Univ Miss 1964; mil/AUS 1967-69; Maj; pa/Neuro Surg Pract, Paducah 1975-; Others; Cert'd by Am Bd Neuro Surgs; Res: Univ Miss Med Ctr 1965-66, Walter Reed Army Hosp 1968-69, George Washington Univ Med Ctr 1969-71; Am Assn Neuro Surgs (Harvey Cushing Soc); Diplomate Am Bd Neuro Surgs; Cong Neuro Surgs; Intl Soc for Study of the Lumbar Spine; cp/Pi Kappa Alpha; Masons; Dem; Bd Mem Paducah Art Guild; r/Bapt; hon/Contbr articles to Profl Jours; W/W in S&SW.

CAMPBELL, CAROLYN HOLCOMBE oc/District Sales Representative; b/Mar 2, 1942; h/3614 Dale Hollow Rd, Anniston, AL 36201; ba/Atlanta, AL; c/Randy; p/Charlie and Ola Holcombe, Oxford, AL; ed/Alverson Draughn Col; pa/Dist Sales Rep Ralston Purina Co; r/Bapt; hon/W/W Am Wom; Top Perfr Ralston Purina Co 3 Times.

CAMPBELL, DAVID GWYNNE oc/Company President; b/May 2, 1930; h/6109 Woodbridge Rd, Okla City, OK 73132; ba/Okla City; m/Janet Gay Newland; c/Carl David; p/Lois Raymond Henager; LaVada Ray Henager Campbell; ed/BS Tulsa Univ 1953; MS Univ Okla 1957; mil/USNR 1949-53; AUS 1953-55; pa/Pres, Earth Hawk Exploration, Petro Exec, Geol 1980-; Exploration Mgr Leede Exploration 1977-80; Dist Geol & Geol Conslt, Mid-Cont Div Tenneco Oil Co 1965-77; Geol Lone Star Prod Co 1957-65; Am Assn Petro Geols; Am Petro Inst; Okla Indep Petro Assn; Okla City Geol Soc; Okla City Geol Discussion Grp; Tulsa Geol Soc; cp/Last Frontier Coun BSA 1960-65; Okla City Rep to Cherokee Nation 1976-78; Pi Kappa Alpha; Okla City Petro Clb; hon/Sigma Xi 1957; W/W S&SW 1980-81.

CAMPBELL, J ROBERT oc/Administrator in Higher Education; b/Aug 6, 1927; h/2401 Dartmouth, Wichita Falls, TX; ba/Wichita Falls; m/Eloise Treaster; c/Barry, Lynn, Brian, Danny; p/Daniel Cavitt & Alice Pinnock Campbell (dec); ed/BA Sterling Col 1949; PhD Univ Ks 1953; pa/VP for Acad Affairs, MWn Univ 1968-; Chm, Div Natural Scis & Prof of Chem, Tarkio Col 1964-68; Sr Res Chemist, Monsanto Co 1952-64; Night Col Instr, Wash Univ 1954-64; So Assn Acad Deans; Assn Tex Cols & Univs; Am Chem Soc; cp/U Way Exec Com; Wichita Falls Symph Bd; Advr Jr Leag; r/U Presb Ch: Ruling Elder, Bd Dirs Presby Lay Com Inc, Mem Area Synod Coun; hon/15 US Patents; Sev Fgn Patents; 6 Scientific Papers Pub'd.

CAMPBELL, L ADONIS oc/Senior Industrial Engineer; b/Sept 21, 1948; h/115 NE 28th Ave, Ocala, FL 32670; ba/Gainesville, FL; m/Gail; c/Shayne, Shanda; p/H B and Jean Campbell, Cleveland, TN; ed/BS Univ Tenn 1974; Indust Mgmt Chattanooga St 1976; mil/AUS; pa/Indust Engrg; Pres Oster Mgmt Clb; cp/Sertoma Clb; hon/Bronze Star; Army Commend Medal w OLC.

CAMPBELL, MARSHAL oc/Company President; b/Aug 5, 1930; ba/1786 S Beltline Hwy, Mobile, AL 36609; m/Betty; c/Sue, Sharon, June; p/Murdock Scott and Ella Campbell, Satsuma, AL; ed/Mobile Col; pa/Pres Ala Furniture & Appliance Co; Pres Scotts Furniture Whsl & Showroom; Pres Inst Whsl Dist; Pres SEn Furniture Assn; Pres Mobile Furniture Assn; Dir Nat Home Furniture Assn; cp/32° Mason; Shriner; r/Bapt; hon/Mr Furniture Retailer, St of Ala 1978.

CAMPBELL, ROBERT CRAIG III oc/Attorney; b/Dec 11, 1942; h/1067 Greenway Dr, Mobile, AL 36608; ba/Mobile; m/Carol Elaine; c/Brett William, David Philip Lee; p/Joseph R and Gertrude Campbell, Drexel Hill, PA; ed/BA Georgetown Col 1964; JD Cumberland Sch Law Samford Univ 1967; Cert of Attendance NWn Univ Sch Law 1971; Cert Attendance Ams for Effect Law Enforcement Inc 1976; pa/Attorney for Bd of Sch Commissioners of Mobile Co; Instr Univ S Ala 1974-; Mobile Co Yth Ctr Asst Juvenile Judge 1975-78; Asst City Atty, Mobile 1973-; Sr Ptr Sintz, Pike, Campbell & Duke 1973-; St of Ala, Mobile Co, DA Chief Asst

1971-73; Mobile Bar Assn; Licensed to Prac before Supreme Ct of Ala 1967-; Am Bar Assn 1967-; Ala Trail Lawyers Assn; Mobile Bar Assn Grievance Com 1974-; Moblie Claims Assn; Ala Defense Lawyers Assn 1975; Ala Criminal Defense Lawyers Assn 1976-; Licensed to Prac US Ct of Appeals 1974-; Phi Alpha Delta; Pi Kappa Alpha; Licensed to Prac Supreme Ct of US 1972-; Appt'd to Adv Com US Comm on Civil Rights; cp/Mirror Lake Racquet Clb; r/Cath; hon/AUS Commend Medal 1969; USS Ala Battleship Comm Commend for Exceptionally Merit Ser 1973; Gov St of Ala Hon Lt Col Aide de Camp 1975; St of Ala Spec Asst Atty Gen 1977, 78, 79; Outstg Yng Men Am 1977, 78; Personalities of South 1976-77, 1979-80; Notable Americans 1977, 78, 79; Book of Honor, Tenth Anniv Ed 1978; Men of Achmt 1979; Intl W/W Intells 1979.

CAMPBELL, VIRGINIA PATRICE oc/Director Social Services; b/Aug 14, 1946; h/PO Box 42, New Hope, VA 24469; ba/Verona, VA; p/John Webster and Virginia Thomas Campbell; ed/BA Mary Baldwin Col 1968; MEd Univ Va 1972; MSW Va Commonwlth Univ 1979; pa/Dir Social Ser, People Places Inc (Pvt, Non Profit Spec Foster Care Agcy); Fdg Mem Bd Dirs People Places Inc; Assn for Advmt of Behavior Therapy; Am Pers & Guid Assn; Am Rehab Cnslrs Assn; Nat Assn Social Wkrs; Coun for Except Chd; r/Meth.

CAMPBELL-GOYMER, NANCY RUTH oc/Assistant Professor and Co-Director; b/July 1, 1949; ba/Box A-37, Psychology, Birmingham Southern Col, B'ham, AL 35254; m/George; p/T C and Nora Campbel, Westville, FL; ed/BA Fla St Univ 1971; MA Univ Ala 1972; Doct Study, Univ Ala 1974-; Clin Psych Internship UNC-Chapel Hill Med Sch, Psychi Dept 1976-77; pa/B'ham So Col: Asst Prof Psych 1977-, Co-Dir Cnslg Sers 1978-; Psych Asst II, Dept Insts, Social & Rehab Sers, Okla City, Okla 1973-74; Master's Level Psych, Univ Ala Psych Clin 1974-75; Psychometrist, Vocational Rehab Sers & W Ala Rehab Ctr 1975-76; Ala Psych Assn; Assoc Mem Am Psych Assn; r/Meth; hon/Alpha Lambda Delta; Psi Chi; Phi Kappa Phi; Phi Beta Kappa; Nat Merit Schlr 1967-71; NDEA F'ship 1971-72; Nat Sci Foun Summer Res Prog 1970; Undergrad Prog for Col & Univ Tchrs 1969-71; Recip Martin S Wallach Awd for Outstg Clin Psych Intern 1977; Ala's Outstg Yng Wom 1979; Danforth Foun Assoc 1980-; Outstg Yng Wom Am 1979; W/W Am Wom 1980; Co-Author: "Item-specific retroactive inhibition in mixed-list comparisons of A-B, B-C and A-B, D-C paradigms" *Journal of Verbal Learning and Verbal Behavior* 1971, "Strategy of multiple-baseline evaluation: Illustrations from a summer camp" *Perceptual and Motor Skills* 1974, "Mutual group hypnosis and creative problem solving with a weight-loss group," Presented at the Annual Sci Prog of Am Soc of Clin Hypnosis, Atlanta 1977.

CANALES, MODESTO oc/Government Administrator; b/Mar 31, 1929; h/1715 Saddle Creek Dr, Houston, TX 77090; ba/Houston; m/Mary I; c/Michele, Mark, Steve, Kevin, Marcia; p/Modesto (dec) and Aurora Canales (dec); ed/BBA St Mary's Univ 1962; mil/USAF 1951-55; pa/Govt Admr, US Customs Ser; Bd Dirs Govt Accts Assn; cp/Fed Bus Assn; Aircraft Owners & Pilots Assn; Bd Dirs Hispanic Univ; hon/W/W Govt.

CANGEMI, JOSEPH PETER oc/Administrator; Educator; b/Jun 26, 1936; h/1305 Woodhurst Dr, Bowling Green, KY 42101; ba/Bowling Green; m/Amelia Elena Santalo; c/Michelle, Lisa Anne; ed/BS St Univ NY, Oswego; Master's Syracuse Univ; Doct Ind Univ, Bloomington; Adv'd Study Wn Ky Univ; pa/Assoc Prof, Dept of Psychol, Wn Ky Univ 1968-; Proj Dir, Organizational Analysis: Lib Sys, Computer Sers Sys, Student Sers, Universidad de Los Andes, Merida, Venezuela, 1975-77; Proj Dir, Organizational Analysis: US Info Ser, Columbian Bi-Nat Ctrs, US Embassy, Bogota, Columbia 1978; Tchg Assoc, Dept Ed Psychol, Ind Univ, Bloomington 1972-73; Ed Columnist, *Daily Jour*, Caracas, Venezuela 1968; Asst Dir to Acting Dir Tng & Devel, US Steel Corp Orinco Mining Div, Puerto Ordaz & Ciudad Piar, Venezuela 1966-68; Ed Supr, US Steel Corp, Orinoco Mining Div, Ciudad Piar, Venezuela 1965-66; Vis Lectr, Dept of Psyhcol, St Univ NY Commun Col Syracuse 1966; Chm & Lectr, Dept of Psychol, Evening Ext Div, St Univ NY Syracuse Commun Col 1962-65; Other Past Positions incl: Asst Basketball Coach, Voc Rehab Coor, Res Assoc, Asst Sch Dir, Elem Instr, Eng & Reading Instr; Conslt to Corps, Assns, Govts, Schs & Univs; Mem Var Edit Bds; Profl Orgs; cp/Bowling Green CC; Syracuse Alumni Assn; Life Mem, Ind Univ Alumni Assn; SUNY Oswego Alumni Assn; Past Pres, NAm Assn of Venezuela; Others; hon/Cert, City of Bucaramanga, Colombia 1976, 77; Decreto, St of Santador, Colombia 1977; Awd, Colombian Nat Assn Indust Engrs 1977; Cert, ICETEX, Colombia 1977; Finalist, Creativity & Res Awd, Wn Ky Univ 1974, 77; Escudo, Nat Autonomous Univ of Nicaragua 1976; Medal, Brazilian Acad of Humanities 1976; Pi Kappa Delta; Psi Chi; Sigma Delta Psi; Sigma Tau Delta; Phi Delta Kappa; Num Biogl Listings; Pub'd: *Higher Education and the Development of Self-Actualizing Personalities*, 1977, *Readings for Managers* 1978, *La Psicologia De La Gerencia* 1978, *Psicologia Y La Educacion Universitaria* 1978, *La Educacion Universitaria* 1978, *La Educacion Y La Salud Mental* 1977, Num Articles.

CANN, MARJORIE MITCHELL oc/Professor; b/Aug 25, 1924; h/4740 Peacock Dr, Pensacola, FL 32504; ba/Pensacola; p/Douglas Robert Mitchell (dec); ed/Profl Cert VI, Nova Scotia Tchrs Col; BS Acadia Univ, Nova Scotia 1940; MA Mich St Univ 1953; PhD Univ Mich 1957; pa/Prof Ed in Dept Behavioral Sci, Pensacola Jr Col 1974-; Assoc Prof Ed & Hd Dept Behavorial Sci, Pensacola Jr Col 1967-74; Lectr Univ W Fla 1967-68; Grad Prof Ed 1964-67; Adm Hd Gtr Cleveland Math Prog 1963-64; Author & TV Tchr 1961-62; Dir Math Delta Col 1961-62; Instr Col Math, Acadia Univ 1957-60; Com Chm of Ser & Prog Devel United Cerebral Palsy of Fla 1973-; Human Rights Advocacy Com Mem, Dist 1 of HSR 1976-; Conslt/Spec, Mgmt & Ldrship Sems in Pensacola Area Hosps & Industs 1975-; Math Assn Am; Nat Coun Tchrs Maths; NEA; Am Assn Supervision & Curric; Canadian Ed Assn; Bd Dirs Victorian Order Nurses; r/Christian; hon/W/W: Am Ed, Am Wom; Intl Bios; Contemporary Authors; Cert of Apprec United Cerebral Palsy of NW Fla 1974; Dist'd Ser Awd Univ Cerebral Palsy Fla 1975; Intl Author *A Synthesis of Teaching Methods* 1964; Editor & Author *An Introduction to Education: Selected Readings* 1972; Res Asst & Co-Author *A Survey of Grand Ledge Community Schools* 1954; Other Profl Pubs.

CANNON, ISABELLA McLEAN BETT WALTON oc/Retired Mayor; b/May 12, 1904; h/212 Brooks Ave, Raleigh, NC 27607; m/Claude Marcus (dec); ed/AB Elon Col 1924; Grad Work Am Univ 1947-49, NC St Univ 1970-73; LLD Hon Elon Col 1978; mil/US Fgn Ser, Dip Corp; pa/Hd Dept Stats, French Purchasing Comm, Wash DC; Lib NCSU Adm Ofc; Ret'd Mayor, Raleigh, NC; cp/Charter Mem Wake Co Dem Wom: 1st VP Precinct 1; Hon Chm, Friends of Wake Co Lib; Wake Aid to Abused Wom, Bd Dirs; YWCA Bd of Advocates; r/U Ch of Christ; Quaker; hon/First Wom Mayor, Raleigh, NC; Salutatorian, Elon Col 1924; Wom of Yr, Sept Days Clb 1980-81; Editor *Library Focus*; Author Num Newspaper Articles.

CANNON, MARK WILCOX oc/Administrative Assistant; b/Aug 29, 1928; h/8404 Martingale, McLean, VA 22101; ba/Wash DC; m/Ruth Marian Dixon; c/Lucile, Mark, Kristen; p/Joseph Jenne Cannon (dec); Ramona Wilcox Cannon, Salt Lake City, UT; ed/BA Univ Utah; MPA, MA, PhD Harvard Univ; pa/Adm Asst to Chief Justice of US 1972-; Inst of Public Adm: Dir 1968-72, Dir Intl Progs 1965-68, Dir Venezuelan Urban Devel Proj 1964-65; Chm Polit Sci Dept, Brigham Young Univ 1961-64; Leg Asst to Sen Wallace F Bennett 1961-63; Adm Asst to Cong-man Henry Aldous Dixon 1956-60; Chperson Leonard D White Awd Com, Am Polit Sci Assn 1977; Supr Ct Histl Soc Yrbook Adv Bd 1976-; Adj Fac Mem, Antioch School of Law 1975-; Edit Adv Bd, *Judicature* 1974-76; Nat Acad Public Adm; Bd Trustees, Inst Public Adm; 1st Non-Lwyr Admitted to Am Bar Assn in Judicial Assocs Prog; Participant in Lects & Sems; r/Ch of Jesus Christ of LDS; hon/Pub'd Author.

CANTRELL, TRUETT VAUGHN oc/Retired US Air Force; b/July 27, 1919; h/Rt 4 Box 277, Palestine, TX 75801; m/Doris Beasley; c/Diane Saucier, Kathy Bacon; p/J J (dec) and Ivy Bailey Cantrell, Palestine, TX; ed/E Bapt Col; Col of Marshall; mil/USAF: 39th Air Div Chief of Intell; 4th Air Div; NE Air Command; Far E Air Command; Dir Adm Barksdale AFB, La w Contengency of 12,500 People; Ret'd Dec 1960 Lt Col; pa/Aerial Photog; Intell Gathering & Reporting; Second Combat Ops & Targeting; Adm & Staff Judge Advocate; cp/Past Master Aomori Lodge 139, Grand Lodge of the Philippines, F & AM; Past Master Neches Lodge 535, Tex AF & AM; Regional Dir No Region De Molays, Japan; Aomori Coun De Molays; Pres Anderson Co Farm Bur of Tex; Pres Neches Commun Improvement Assn; St Pres Tex Alpha Delta Kappa Assn; r/Bapt; hon/DD Form 214, ALFSA w 4 BOLC; GC MDL; NDSM; AF Res Med OM; ADSM; WWII V MDL; ACM.

CANTU, ANNA MARIA ABREGO PEÑA oc/Interior Designer; b/Dec 6, 1942; h/1900 E Elizabeth 5009, Brownsville, TX 78520; ba/B'ville; m/Rodolfo; c/Lawrence Anthony; p/Raul Hernandez (dec) and Concepcion Abrego Pena (dec); pa/Interior Decorator, A&R Enterprises; cp/B'ville Wom's Polit Caucus; Polit Action Chair; Mem Tex Wom's Polit Caucus & Nat Wom's Polit Caucus; r/Cath.

CANTU, RODOLFO oc/Consultant and Designer; b/Aug 26, 1946; h/1900 E Elizabeth #5009, Brownsville, TX 78520; ba/B'ville; m/Anna Maria; c/Lawrence Rocha, Melinda, Cindy & Chris; p/Melchor and Angelita Cantu, Corpus Christi, TX; ed/Assoc Arch Tech; mil/USMC; pa/Gen Mgt, Ctrl Kitchen Equip Inc; Food Facities Conslt & Designer; Tex Rest Assn; cp/Harlingen C of C; Cameron Co Bus'man Adv Coun; Mr Amigo Assn; r/Cath.

CAPEN, EDGAR A oc/Retired Electrical Contractor; b/Jan 26, 1895; h/1300 S Burden Ave, Waslaco, TX 78596; c/Mrs J W Jones, Edgar C; mil/Active & Reserve Serv, 31 Yrs Capt; pa/Local Mgr CP&L Co 1931-47; Telephone, Electric Co Wn Union Elec Contractor; Pres Last Mans Clb; c/Post Cmdr Am Legion, La Feria, TX; Pres La Feria Rotary Clb & Donna

Rotary Clb; City Coun & Mayor Donna, Tex; City Judge; Dir Civil Defense; Mgr Donna C of C; SAR; Mason; hon/Hon Citizen Winnipeg, Canada.

CAPLETON, EDDIE LEE oc/Principal; b/Jul 30, 1949; h/C-27 Village Green Apts, Montgomery, AL 36117; ba/Roba, AL; c/Brian Keith, Demond (dec); p/Evans Capleton (dec); Mary Capleton, Montgomery, AL; ed/BS; MEd; EdS; pa/Prin S Macon HS; Ed Assn Macon Co; NEA; Ala Ed Assn; Ed Assn Montgomery Co; cp/Kappa Alpha Psi; r/Zion Hill Bapt Ch; hon/Highest Hons Throughout Grad Sch.

CAPPS, BRUCE J oc/Clinical Administrator; b/Feb 18, 1949; h/Sipsey, AL; m/Cheryl Jolly; c/Bradley Judson; p/Gordon and Jetter Lou Cole Capps, Empire, AL; ed/MA Univ Ala 1971; pa/Clin Adm, Rural Hlth, Dept Hlth, Ed, Wel; The Chd's Hosp, Birmingham; pa/Nat Inst Acctg; cp/Bd Dirs Chd's Hosp; r/Ch of God.

CARAS, ROBERT LAWRENCE oc/Health Planner; b/Apr 12, 1950; h/2052 S Clack #570, Abilene, TX 79606; ba/Abilene; p/George and Hilde Brabee Caras, San Antonio, TX; ed/BA Bowling Green St Univ 1972; MPH Univ Tex Sch Public Hlth 1976; pa/Prog Mgr Plan Devel, Tri-Region Hlth Sys Agcy; Am Public Hlth Assn; Tex Perinatal Assn; r/Epis; hon/Sigma Tau Delta; Phi Alpha Theta; Confed Air Force.

CARATTINI, CESAR oc/Materials Manager; b/Oct 24, 1949; ba/Carolina, Puerto Rico; m/Neyzza Oparrill; c/Victor C, Luis M; p/Victor and Providencia Melendez Carattini, Cayey, PR; ed/BA Psych; mil/AUS; pa/Mats Mgr, Baxer Labs, Carolina; Baxter Labs, Campo Rico: Mats Supt, Mats Analyst; Inventory Control, Univ PR; r/Cath; hon/Good Conduct Medal; Parachutist Badge.

CARBON, FRANK HENRY JR oc/Certified Public Accountant; b/Aug 17, 1948; h/Metaire, LA; m/Janice Brown; c/Stephanie, Courtney; p/Frank H Sr and Beatrice Carbon, New Orleans, LA; ed/BBA Loyola Univ of the South 1970; mil/USMC 1970-76; pa/CPA; Am Inst CPAs; La Soc CPAs; EDP Auditors Foun; cp/Fin Plan'g Com of La St Supreme Ct; Chm Fin Com Big Brothers of Gtr New Orleans; Bd Dirs Yng Men's Bus Clb of Gtr New Orleans; Metro Ldrship Forum; Pres Cres City Toastmasters Clb; r/Cath.

CARDIN, BENJAMIN L oc/Attorney; State Legislator; h/2509 Shelleydale Dr, Baltimore, MD 21209; ba/Balto; m/Myrna Edelman; c/Michael, Debbie; ed/BA Univ Pgh 1964; LLB, JD 1967 Univ Md (Grad 1st in Class); pa/Pract Atty, Balto 1967-; Am Bar Assn; Md Bar Assn; Balto City Bar Assn; cp/Md Ho Dels: Elected 1966, Re-elected 1970, 74, Chm Ways & Means Com, Jt Budget & Audit Com, Leg Policy Com, Gov's Comm on Revision of Domestic Relats Law, Gov's Comm for Funding Spec Ed, VChm Gov's Comm to Study Ednl Funding Gov's Comm to Study Financing of Farmland Preserv in Md, Other Previous Com Assignments; Bd Mem: Cheswolde Improvemt Assn, Safety 1st Clb of Md; St John's Lodge # 34 AF&AM; Yedz Grotto; Past Pres, Golden Eagle Square & Compass Clb; Past Chm, New Ldrship Div-Israel Bonds; Assoc VChm, Israel Bonds Com from Md; r/Beth Tfiloh Synagogue; Greenspring Valley Synagogue; Dir Assoc'd Jewish Charities & Welfare Fund; Bd Mem, Balto Jewish Coun; hon/Profl Pubs; Num Acad Awds incl'g William Stroble Thomas Awd for highest acad achmt at Univ Md Law Sch; Order of Coif; Omicron Delta Epsilon Ec Hon; Safety Crusader Awd; Save-a-Heart Humanitarian Awd 1975.

CARDOSO, ANTHONY A oc/Instructor, Department Head; b/Sept 13, 1930; h/3208 Nassau St, Tampa, FL 33607; ba/Tampa; m/Martha; c/Michele Denise, Toni Lynn; p/Frank and Nancy Cardoso; ed/BS; BFA; MFA; pa/Art Instr; Dept Hd; Art Coun; FEA; FAEA; cp/Chm WEDU Ed Station Art Auction; r/Cath; hon/XXII Biennieh; Smithsonian Awd; Minn Mus Purchase Awd; Prix De Paris Art Awd; Salon of 50.

CAREY, HARVEY LOCKE oc/Attorney, Judge; b/Jan 19, 1915; h/Star Rt, Jamestown, LA 71045; ba/Jamestown; m/Nellie D (dec); c/Thomas D, Richard D, Katie Carey Sims; p/Gregory and Willie Belle Carey (dec); mil/USNR, Lt Cmdr; pa/US Atty; Wn Dist of La Asst Atty Gen; Judge City Ct of Shreveport; cp/Dem Ctl Com; Clk, La Ho of Reps; r/Meth; hon/Nat VCmdr, Mil Order of Purple Heart.

CARGILE, MARY CHASTEEN oc/General Manager; b/Apr 24, 1939; h/1902 Maywood Pl, NW, Atlanta, GA 30318; ba/Atlanta; c/William H Nichols III; p/William H Chasteen, Pt Arthur, TX; Mrs Ralph D Chadwick, Beaufort, NC; ed/Att'd Duke Univ 1959; AA Ga St Univ 1962; Bus Mgmt Courses, Ga St Univ 1980; pa/Secy & Real Est Agt, Ec Homes, Morehead City, NC 1961; Exec Secy & Asst Ofc Mgr, Lloyd A Fry Roofing Co 1961-64; Data Processor, So Railway Sys, Atlanta 1966-74; Equip Locator, So Railway Sys 1974-80; Sales Analyst Hal Eason Assoc 1974-80; Gen Mgr, Christmas Southeast Inc 1980-; Conslt to Small Bus Firms & Minority Grps 1968-; Inter-Racial Fam Cnslr 1970-; Nat Assn Female

Execs; cp/Dem Party; Vol Atlanta Labor Coun 1973-74; hon/Recip Danforth Foun Awd 1957; Contbr Articles on Inter-racial Fams to Local Pubs; W/W Am Wom 1981; Miss Down East 1957; Miss Dairy Princess 1958.

CARGILL, PAULA MARIE oc/Geriatric Social Worker, Director Social Services; b/Sept 18, 1943; h/1 Kenilworth Dr, Greenville, SC 29615; ba/Simpsonville, SC; p/John Edwin (dec) and Mabel Bridges Cargill, Greenville, SC; ed/BA Winthop Col 1965; MRE So Bapt Theol Sem 1973; MSSW Univ Louisville 1975; pa/Geriatric Social Wkr, Dir Social Sers, J Hlth Care Ctr Inc; Second Tchr 5 Yrs; Adult Ed Instr, Indust Prog, Greenville Co Schs 1979-; Field Instr & Adj Asst Prof, Col Social Work, Univ SC; Acad Cert'd Social Wkrs; SC Bd Social Wkr Reg; SC Nat Assn Social Wkrs; SC Social Welfare Forum; SC Gerontological Soc; Social Wkrs of SC Hlth Care Assn; So Bapt Social Ser Assn; The Gerontological Soc; Nat Assn Social Wkrs Inc; cp/Flutist, Greenville Civic Band; Gtr Greenville Commun Concert Assn; Lucille Wall Mus Clb; BPW; Chm Mission Action; Coun of Intl Progs; hon/Hon Socs: Alpha Kappa Delta, Pi Delta Phi, Kappa Delta Pi; Exch Social Wkr w France Summer 1980.

CARITHERS, HELEN oc/Instructional Coordinator; b/June 20, 1944; h/College Pk, MD; ba/Atlanta, GA; p/Ellis and Janice M Carithers, Commerce, GA; ed/BA Spelman Col 1966; Univ Vienna 1967; MAT Vanderbilt Univ 1971; pa/Instr Coor, Benjamin E Mays Acad Sci & Maths; Atlanta Public Schs, Sci Tchr, Sci Dept Chp, Data Collector & Indep Study Coor; Nat Sci Tchrs Assn; Ga Sci Tchrs Assn; cp/YWCA; Kappa Omega Chapt, Alpha Kappa Alpha; Spelman Alumni Assn; Nat Beta Clb Advrs; r/Meth; hon/W/W Am Cols & Univs 1965; $3000 Merrill Fgn Study S'ship 1966; Tchr of Yr, SW HS 1976; Curric Writer for NCCCD at SUNY, Stony Brook.

CARLO, MICHAEL J b/Dec 27, 1937; h/Box 10986 ASU Station, San Angelo, TX 76901; ba/San Angelo; oc/Professor of Chemistry; c/Michael; p/Joseph F and Anne Carlo, San Antonio, TX; ed/BS 1961, BA 1961, MS 1962, PhD 1970 Tex A&M Univ; pa/Angelo St Univ, San Angelo: Prof of Chem 1970-, Grad Fac 1971-, Asst Prof 1967-68; Thermodynamic Res Ctr, Tex A&M Univ, Col Sta, Tex: Res Assoc 1968-70, Conslt'g Expert 1970-; Conslt'g Toxicol: Tom Green Co Probation Dept, San Angelo 1976-, P&P Lab, San Angelo 1975-, Wohler Livestock Prods Co, San Angelo 1975-, St Prog on Drug Abuse, Austin, Tex 1974-, Mtl Hlth/Mtl Retard, San Angelo 1973-, Three Rivers Agy for Drug Ed, San Angelo 1972-; Editor *Tex Jour of Sci,* Angelo St Univ, San Angelo 1974-; Other Past Positions; Tex Assn of Col Tchrs: Past VP Angelo St Univ Chapt, Past Pres ASU Chapt; Bd Dirs, ASU Chapt, AAUP; Other Profl Assns; cp/San Angelo Downtown Lions Clb: Dist 2A-1 Cabinet Chm, Pres, Former 1/VP (Twice), Lion of Yr Awd 1974-75, Former Tail Twister, Past Dir; Past Pres, Holy Angels Cath Sch Bd of Ed; Lambda Chi Alpha Alumni: Past Pres Beta Alpha House Corp, VP Beta Alpha House Corp, Beta Alpha Alumni Chapt Advr High Pi, Beta Alpha Alumni Nat Rep; Stephenville JCs: Past Dir Yth & Sports, Outstg New JC, Outstg Yg Men of Stephenville; Bd Dirs: Halfway Ho (Pres 1977-), San Angelo Alcohol Detox (Pres 1978-), San Angelo Coun on Alcoholism, San Angelo Civic Theatre, Coun for Human Growth & Devel (Chm 1977-); Chm: Mtl Hlth/Mtl Retard Drug Treatment & Prevention Adv Bd, Concho Val Coun of Govts Reg Alcohol/Drug Adv Bd; Others; r/Rom Cath; hon/Felow: Tex Acad of Sci, World-Wide Acad of Scholars; Outstg Yg Men Am; Personalities of S; DIB; Notable Ams; Outstg Edrs Am; Intl W/W in Commun Ser; W/W in S&SW; Tarleton St Col Fac Res Grant; NSF Col Tchr Participation Grant; San Angelo Drug Ctl Res Grant; Angelo St Univ Org'd Res Grant; Sigma Xi; Phi Delta Kappa; Gamma Sigma Upsilon; Author: *General Chemistry: First Semester Laboratory* (w D G Tarter), *Technicians Manual: Laboratory Procedures for Street Drug Analysis,* 35+ Sci Wks, Num Papers.

CARLTON, FRAN oc/State House of Representatives; Jan 19, 1936; h/1250 Henry Balch Dr, Orlando, FL 32810; ba/Orlando; m/Ernie; c/Lynne, Julie; ed/AA Univ Fla 1956; BS Stetson Univ 1958; pa/Host Syndicated Exercise Prog on TV "The Fran Carlton Show"; Adv Coun on Preventive Hlth Strategy, Pres's Coun on Phys Fitness & Sports; So Dist Nat Rec & Pk Assn; Bd Dirs Commun Mtl Hlth Bd of Ctrl Fla; cp/Mem Fla Ho of Reps 1976-; Nat Con of St Legislatures Leg Info Needs Com; Exec Com of Bd Dirs Univ Fla Nat Alumni Assn; r/Bapt; hon/Dist'd Ser Awd, Fla Assn Htlh, Phys Ed & Rec 1977; Hon Awd, Pres Coun on Phys Fitness 1979; Friend of Ed Awd, Orange Co Clrm Tchrs Assn 1977; Author *A Time for Fitness* 1976; W/W: Wom in Polits, Am Polits, Wom in Public Ofc.

CARMICHAEL, DOROTHY S oc/Homemaker; b/Oct 10, 1925; h/PO Box 161, Tuscumbia, AL 35674; ba/Tuscumbia; m/Charles E Jr; c/Constance, Charles III, Dot, William; p/Maxwell Burns (dec) and Lydia Elizabeth Springer, Tuscumbia, AL; ed/Univ N Ala; pa/Tax Assessor, Colbert Co 1979; cp/Bd Trustee Univ Montevallo 1981; Del to Nat Dem Conv 1980; Ala Dem Exec Com; Ala Affirmative Action Comm; Dem Nat

Com-wom; Del to Dem Nat Conv 1960 (Served on Platform Com); Bd Dirs: U Fund, Colbert Co Dept of Pensions & Securities; Past Pres, Salvation Army Aux; r/1st U Meth Ch: Bd Trustees, Adm Bd, Chm Bd Dirs of Mission Home; hon/Hon Dr Humane Letters, Athens St Col 1978; Wom of Yr, Colbert BPW Clb 1980; Served on Host Com from Ala on Inaugural Com for Jimmy Carter's Inauguration.

CARMODY, SEAMUS oc/General Surgeon, Chief of Surgery; b/July 2, 1931; m/Barbara Lee; c/Maura, Brennan, Colleen, Kathleen, Kevin; p/Mrs John Carmooy, Buffalo, NY; ed/BS St Bonaventure Univ 1959; MD St Univ NY 1964; mil/AUS 1954-56; pa/Self Employed Gen Surg; Chief of Surg, Midland Meml Hosp, Midland, TX; FACS; Diplomate of Am Bd Surg; AMA; TMA; Midland Co Med Soc; cp/Midland C of C; r/Roman Cath.

CARMON, BARBARA A oc/Senior Consultant; b/June 30, 1942; h/607 E Losoya, PO Box 1411, Del Rio, TX 78840; ba/Del Rio; m/James Ray; c/Curtis Ray, Cathryn Rene; p/Mrs Leo Lacey, Camp Wood, TX; pa/Sr Conslt, Mktg Dept, Gen Telephone Co of the SW; BPW Clb; c/C of C; r/Ch of Christ; hon/BPW Clbs Wom of Yr 1979.

CARNEVALE, DARIO oc/General Manager; b/Jan 11, 1935; h/1325 NE 138th St, N Miami, FL 33161; ba/Des Plaines, IL; m/Franca; c/Daniela, Flavia, Fulvia, Dario Jr; p/Emilio (dec) and Olinda Carnevale, Rome, Italy; ed/DEng; pa/Gen Mgr Colombian Br, Mktg & Mgmt Oil & Petro Chem Plants; r/Cath; hon/W/W E; Personalities of Am; Personalites of South; Book of Honor; Men & Wom of Dist; IPA; ABI.

CAROON, EDNA EARL WHITLEY oc/Nurse, Executive Director; b/July 19, 1926; h/4028 Tanglewood Trail, Chesapeake, VA 23325; ba/Norfolk, VA; m/Earle Norman (dec); c/Deborah Lynn, Nell Gwendolyn, George Norman, James Earl; p/Ayer Manny Duncan Whitley (dec); Esther C Mangum, Charlotte, NC; ed/RN Mercy Hosp Sch Nsg 1951; pa/RN; Exec Dir Ear, Nose & Throat Hosp, Norfolk, Va; Adv Panel *Am Jour Nsg;* cp/Vol Hlth Relat'd Commun Drives; r/Bapt; hon/W/W Am Wom.

CARPENTER, MARJ COLLIER oc/News Director; b/Aug 23, 1926; h/5555 Roswell Rd NE, Atlanta, GA 30308; ba/Atlanta; m/C T (dec); m/Catherine, Carolyn, Jim Bob; p/W D Collier (dec); Beatrice Collier, Mercedes, TX; ed/BM Tex A&I; pa/News Dir, Presb Ch US; Music Tchr, Kingsvil!e, Tex; News Editor, *Pecos Independent, Andrews News; Big Spring Herald:* Area News Editor, Daily Columnist; cp/Bd Dirs: Heritage Mus, Permian Basin GSA Coun; Num Civic Bds; r/1st Presb Ch, Big Spring: Clk of Session; hon/1st in News Writing, Nat Press Wom; 1st in Columns, W Tex Press; 21 Top Jour Awds incl'g 5 Assoc'd Press Awds; Big Spring C of C Wom of Yr 1978.

CARPENTER, NORMA ROWE oc/Retired Journalist; b/Dec 27, 1910; h/3704 Tanglewood Ln, Davidson, MD 21035; m/Jarrott Elmo Brogdon (dec); 2nd Maurice Cecil; c/Jennie Lou Brogdon, Jarrott Alfred Brogdon, Linda Jane Brogdon; Stepchd: Paul David, Joanne Judkins; p/Leslie L (dec) and Melissa Jane Rowe, Davidsonville, MD; ed/AB; pa/Corresp: *Evening Capitol,* Annapolis, Md, *Hyattsville Independent,* Hyattsville, Md; cp/Ext Homemakers; Fed'd Woms Clb; Woms Dem Clb; r/U Meth; hon/Co Heart Assn Plaque for Merit Ser 1963; 3 Life Mbrships U Meth Wom.

CARPENTER, SUSAN oc/Founder-Director; b/Dept 27; h/3415 W End Ave, Nashville, TN 37203; m/Bill; c/Susan; p/William Dallas (dec) and Ellie Ruth Mann Chester (dec); ed/John Robert Powers Sch of Modeling; pa/Tchr John Robert Powers Sch; Fdr, Dir Jo-Susan Modeling & Finishing Sch for Girls; Modeling Assn Am; cp/Assn for Preserv of Tenn Antiquity; Nashville Symph Guild; Vanderbilt Chd's Hosp; Hillwood Country Clb; r/Prot; hon/W/W Am Wom; 1 of N'ville's 10 Best Dressed Ladies 1980; Recip Awds, WSM-TV 1965-67, For Fashion Show & TV Chm for Cerebral Palsy Telethon.

CARR, DAVID SHEPHERD oc/Aviator; b/Aug 31, 1945; h/1710 Plainview Dr, Murray, KY 42071; m/Donna Morgan; c/Allison Faye, Michael David; p/James R and Alice A Carr, Irvington, TX; ed/BS, MA Murray St Univ; mil/AUS Transp Corp, Aviator, Ranger; pa/Phi Delta Kappa; Scabbard & Blade; Ranger Advr; Big M Clb; cp/Alpha Tau Omega; Alumni Advr Sigma Delta; Rec Clb; Ath Fund Dr Vol; Lions Clb Dr; Chm Sid Syndrone; r/Meth; hon/Army Commend Medal; Air Medal; Bronze Star; Dist'd Mil Grad; Aviator Wings; Ranger Tab; Viet Nam Ser Medal; Nat Defense Ser Medal; Repub of Viet Nam Campaign Medal; Ky Col Awd.

CARRABBA, MICHAEL PAUL oc/General Manager; b/Jan 31, 1945; h/10175 SW 53rd St, Cooper City, FL 33328; ba/Hialeah, FL; m/Carol Frances; p/Paul and Margie Carrabba; Miami, FL; mil/USMC; pa/Owner & Gen Mgr D+ C− Airports Corp; NBAA; HAA; PAMA; AMFI; Profecional Pilots Assn; r/Cath.

PERSONALITIES OF THE SOUTH

CARRELL, CHARLOTTE RAY PETERSON oc/Realtor; b/May 20, 1938; h/1615 Inglewood Dr, Charlottesville, VA 22901; ba/C'ville; m/Finis Dixon; c/Catherine Ray, Elizabeth Anne, Jean Hylton, p/Robert Elmer and Dorothy Burnett Peterson, Memphis, TN; ed/Att'd Univ Colo 1957; Memphis St Univ 1959; Piedmont Va Commun Col 1979-80; pa/Rltr, Honn Real Est Co; Hostess Welcome Wagon Intl 1972-; Nat Bd Rltrs; C'ville-Albermarle Bd of Rltrs; cp/Pres C'ville Welcome Wagon Clb 1972; Repub Party; r/Presb: Ordained Elder, Mem Choir; hon/Pres 1st Jr Achmt Co to be formed in Tenn (and Gave It Its Name) 1955; Chosen Miss City Beautiful 1956; Alpha Omega Pi 1956.

CARRELL, FINIS DIXON oc/Regional Personnel Manager; b/June 25, 1938; h/1615 Inglewood Dr, Charlottesville, VA 22901; ba/C'ville; m/Charlotte Peterson; c/Catherine Ray, Elizabeth Anne, Jean Hylton; p/Homer Evott and Erna McKnelly Carrell, Memphis, TN; ed/BA SWn Univ 1960; mil/USNAF 1960-65 Helicopter Pilot; pa/St Farm Ins Co: Claims Adjustor 1965-70, Asst Pers Mgr 1970-; Past Pres C'ville Pers Assn; cp/Repub Party; r/Presb: Ordained Elder.

CARRINGTON, SHARON REID oc/Supervisor; b/Oct 3, 1942; h/812 Rogers Ct, Ashland, KY 41101; ba/Ashland; c/Becky, Brianne; p/Leo Carrington, Russellville, IN; ed/BA Berea Col 1964; MS Univ Bridgeport 1979; pa/Supvr Career Plan'g, Ashland Oil Inc; Counterparts; Org Devel Network; Human Rights Comm.

CARSON, SONJA YVONNE oc/Drug Coordinator; b/July 31, 1949; p/Nelson and Iva Carson, Ashdown, AR; ed/BS E Tex St Univ 1971; MEd Wn Wash St; Cand PhD E Tex St Univ; pa/Drug Coor, SW Ark Cnslg & Mtl Hlth Ctr, Texarkana; Guid Cnslr, Tacoma Sch Dist, Tacoma, Wash; cp/Comm on Ed for Fgn Field Missions; Vol Purdy Sers, Purdy Treatmnt Ctr for Wom; Good News Intl Missions Assn; Delta Sigma Theta; r/Ch of God in Christ.

CARSON, SYLVIA oc/Nursing Service Administrator; b/Nov 8, 1936; h/110 Barcelona Ct, Paducah, KY 42001; ed/BSN Univ RI 1959; MA Antioch Univ 1979; pa/Dir Nsg Ser, Wn Bapt Hosp, Paducah; VP Nsg Sers, Providence Hosp, Wash DC 1976-78; Preceptor for Kuait 1977; Wom's & Infant's Hosp of RI: Assoc Admr Nsg Sers & Ed 1973-76, Dir Nsg Sers & Ed 1970-73, Coor'g Instr 1965-67, Instr Student Nurse Affiliation Prog 1960-65; Staff Nurse Labor & Delivery 1959-60; AAAS; Am Col Hosp Admrs; AHA; ANA; APHA; ASNSA; Childbirth Ed Assn; Plan'g Sub-Com, Com on Help to Profls & Parents of Chd w Birth Defects; Hosp Coun of Nat Capital Area; Interfaith Hlth Car Min; Nsg Adv Bd; Guest Lectr, Dept Nsg Murray St Univ; NLN; Nurses Assn Am Col of Obst & Gyn; cp/Operation Foster Child, Taipei, Taiwan; St Labre Indian Sch; Mem Corp Wom's & Infants Hosp of RI; hon/W/W Wom 1980; Pub'd Author: "Reassessment of Newborn Transitional Care Unit"; "What Every Head Nurse Should Know About Management"; "Preparation of the Professional Nurse for a First Line Management Position."

CARSON, WILLIAM EDWARDS oc/Nuclear and Electrical Engineer; b/July 31, 1930; h/2625 Morningside Dr, Clearwater, FL 33519; ba/Dunedin, FL; c/Kathryn E Reed, William E Jr, John E; p/Joseph E and Elinor E Carson, Danville, VA; ed/BSEE 1952, MS 1959 Va Polytech Inst; pa/Test Engr, ERCO Div, ACF Industs Inc, Riverdale, Md 1952-53; Field Engr, ERCO Div SCF Industs, Tex, Fla, NC 1953-56; Nuclear, Elect Instrumentation, Propositions Engr, Babcock & Wilcox Co, Lynchburg, Va 1957-71; Sr Elect Engr, Burns & Roe Inc, Oradell, NJ 1971; Staff Engr, So Nuclear Engrg Inc, Dunedin, Fla 1971-73; Prin Engr & Proj Mgr, NUS Corp, Clearwater, Fla 1973-81; Nuclear & Elect Engr, So Sci Applications Inc 1981-; Am Nuclear Soc; Sr Mem IEEE; Sigma Xi; Am Mgmt Assn; Intl Platform Assn; cp/Chm Yng Repubs Fdn of Va 1965-67; Chm 6th Congl Dist Va 1964-65; Lynchburg City Repub Com 1962-68: V-Chm 1967-68, Publicity Chm 1962-67; Va Repub St Ctrl Com 1965-67; 6th Congl Dist Co 1965-67; Sertoma; Former Mem JCs; r/U Meth; hon/LFABI; ABIRA; W/W S&SW; 2000 Notable Ams; Personalities of Am; Men of Achmt; Book of Hon; Commun Ldrs & Noteworthy Ams; Men & Wom Dist; Intl W/W Intells; Contbr Tech Articles to Sev Pubs.

CARTER, CHARLES F JR oc/Executive Housekeeper; b/Sept 14, 1938; h/84 Terrapin Dr, Brandon, MS 39042; ba/Jackson, MS; m/Johnnie Katherine Chapman; c/Robert Carlton, Katherine Ruth, Charles Kevin; p/Charles F (dec) and Ruth Boone Carter (dec); ed/E Ctrl Jr Col 1959-60; mil/USN 1956-59; pa/Exec Housekeeper, Miss Bapt Med Ctr; Dir Bldg Ser Dept, Miss Bapt Med Ctr 1964-; SEn Assn Hosp Exec Housekeepers: VP 1969-70, Pres 1971-72; Miss Assn Hosp Exec Housekeepers: VP 1967, Pres 1968-69; Natchez Trace Chapt Exec Housekeepers, Charter Pres 1968; cp/Hosp Disaster Coor, Hinds, Rankin & Warren Cos; r/Bapt; hon/W/W S&SW 1980-81; Contbr to Hospital Journal, Spectum Magazine.

CARTER, CHARLES FINLEY oc/Planning Director; b/Oct 17, 1949; h/Rt 1 Box 28, Boston, VA 22713; ba/Culpeper, VA; m/Robin Lee Ahrens; p/Everett Finley and Ann Terriberry Carter, Hudson, WI; ed/BA Lehigh Univ 1972; pa/9 Yrs Profl Plan'g Exper w Va Co Multi-Discipline Cnsltg Firm, Large City Agcy & Public Utility Plan'g/Engrg Grp; AICP; APA; Rural Plan'g Caucus Va; cp/Culpeper Mtl Hlth Adv Bd; Rappahannock-Rapidan Commun Sers Gov'g Bd; hon/Nat Yth Conf on the Atom 1967; Pub'd Author: "Hagerstown Comprehensive Development Plan"; "Waynesboro Comprehensive Plan Proposals"; "Virginia Avenue Revitalization Plan"; "Comprehensive Plan for Community Development/Borough of Emmaus."

CARTER, FREDDYE JO oc/Supervisor of Women's Activites; b/May 23, 1935; m/Jesse L; c/Emma, Mable, Jesse II (Bill), Lorye; p/Freddie Kinney, Corpus Christi, TX; Jo Thelma Oliver, Houston, TX; ed/BA magna cum laude Paul Quinn Col 1956; MA Univ Tex-Austin 1962; pa/Supvr Wom's Activities, Carter's Temple Ch of God of Christ; Claims Clerk, Fed Govt 1965-74; Hd Mus Dept Paul Quinn Col 1958-65; Mus Tchr Butler HS, Butler, Tex 1957-58; cp/Mbrship Chm, Yng Wom's Christian Coun; St Pres Min's Wives, Tex NE Jur; r/Pentecostal; hon/Hons for Mass Choir 1976; Hons for Ser as Mus & Supvr of Wom 1975; Hons for Outstg Ser as Supvr of Wom 1981; Author "A Study of Approaches to Teaching Rhythm in the General Music Class of the Junior High School."

CARTER, HARRIET VANESSA oc/Teacher; b/Dec 19; p/Gerard F and Eugenia Carter, Miami, FL; ed/BA Newcomb Col 1969; MEd Univ Ill 1974; Att'd Summers: Inst Technol, Monterrey, Mexico 1969, Univ Aix-en-Provence, France 1972, Univ Nice 1974, Univ Montreal 1979, Univ Vienna 1980; pa/Fellow & Tchg Asst, Univ Ill 1969-71; Tchr King Philip HS, W Hartford, Conn 1971-76; Instr Univ Conn Med Sch Summer 1974; HS Tchr: Irvington, NY 1976-77; Bergen Co (Closter) 1977-78; Sch for Gifted Chd, Fla 1978-; MLA; Am Assn Tchrs of Span & Portuguese; NEA; German Assn Fgn Lang Tchrs; Fla Assn Fgn Lang Tchrs; Intl Biog Assn; So Fla Assn Phi Beta Kappa; Dir Sigma Delta Pi; cp/Alumni Admission Com, Tulane Univ & Newcomb Col; hon/Phi Beta Kappa; Schlrs Prog Tulane Univ; Nom Woodrow Wilson, Fulbright Fellow; S'ship Univ Vienna 1980; Author "Air Pollution and Hazardous Noise" 1965; Editor Focus on Multi-Cultural Happenings.

CARTER, JOHN ALBERT PRENTISS JR oc/Board of Supervisors; b/Mar 27, 1920; h/Rt 6 Box 115J, Hattiesburg, MS 39401; m/Vivian Byxbee; c/John A P III, Earl Lindsey, Gary Ross; p/John Albert Prentiss Sr (dec) and Kitty McCardle Carter (dec); ed/Univ So Miss; mil/USAF ATC Glider Pilot; pa/Supvr Beat Four 30 Yrs; cp/Supvrs Assn; Dem; Alumni Assn USM; Am Legion; VFW; Mason; Shriner; r/Meth; hon/Citizen Awd Salvation Army; FCAHS Alumni Assn; Miss Ext Forum; Miss Wildlife Assn.

CARTER, JUANITA oc/Salvation Army Officer; b/Mar 15, 1919; h/11543 92nd St, N, Largo, FL 33540; m/Leslie B; c/David, Kathleen, John, Timothy; p/James T (dec) and Florence Mason (dec); ed/Grad Salvation Army Sch Ofcrs Trg, Atlanta, Ga; pa/Salvation Army: Ofcr, Min, Social Work; cp/Altursa Clb; Orange Commun Coun; U Ch Wom; Home Hlth; Home Care; r/Prot; hon/Nom'd 1 of 5 Outstg Wom of Orange by BPW Clb 1974; Outstg Citizens Awd w Husband by Eagles Lodge 1969.

CARTER, LILLIE MAE oc/Author, Instructor; b/Dec 16, 1919; h/Toledo, OH; ba/Martin L King Sch, 1415 Lawrence Ave, Toledo, OH 43607; m/Leon John Jr; c/Leonyl Janice House, Leon J III, Michael Curtis; p/John S and Maude Bland (dec); ed/BS Tenn St Univ 1941; Grad Studies Univ Toledo; MA Tenn St Univ 1961; pa/Instr Remedial Rdg, Martin L King Sch; Delta Kappa Gamma; Phi Delta Kappa; Alpha Kappa Alpha; cp/Afro-Am Heritage Clb; NAACP r/Cath; hon/Black Am Writers 1975; Ky in Am Letters 1976; W/W Black Am; Golden Asterisk; Valedictorian St Street HS; Author: Black Thoughts 1971; Doing It...Our Way 1975; The Grass That Grew in the Trees; Others.

CARTER, MACK KING oc/Pastor, Visiting Professor; b/Feb 4, 1947; h/503 Quail's Run Apt A-3, Louisville, KY 40207; m/Patricia Thomas; p/Mrs Modlea Carter, Ocala, FL; ed/AA Ctrl Fla Commun Col 1967; BA Univ Fla 1970; MDiv 1976, DMin 1978 So Bapt Theol Sem; pa/Pastor Green Castle Bapt Ch, Prospect, Ky; Vis Prof So Bapt Theol Sem; hon/Guest Lectr Morehouse Sch Rel 1979-81; Guest Min Progressive Nat Bapt Conv 1980; Lectr Throughout US; Book to be Pub'd 1981.

CARTER, MARY MAGDALENE HEADS oc/Retired Principal; b/Dec 10, 1905; h/5640 Spring Valley Rd, Dallas, TX 75240; m/Ray; p/Jesse Harrison (dec) and Georgia Jackson Heads (dec); ed/AB Wiley Col 1939; MEd Prairieview Col 1951; Post Grad Study, N Tex St Univ & Tex Wom's Univ, SMU, Tex So Unit, Bishop Col; pa/Tchr Over 40 Yrs; Prin 16 Yrs, Dallas Public Indep Schs, Booker T Wash HS; NEA; Am Tchrs Assn; Tex St Tchrs Assn; Zeta Phi Beta; NTTA; PTA; cp/Secy Faith Outreach Mission; Life Mem YWCA; Vol Work w Sr Citizens; r/Meth: Trustee, VP Wom's Missionary Soc; hon/Wom of Dist of Am; W/W Am Wom; Cert of Hon 1978, 81; Contbn to Rel Edn & Chs.

PERSONALITIES OF THE SOUTH

CARTER, NANCY LUCRETIA oc/Homemaker; b/May 30, 1918; h/808 E Highland Ave, Atlanta, TX 75551; m/Albert W; c/Willis Thomas; p/Otis Dawson (dec) and Nellie Gertrude Rhodes Willis, Gibsland, LA; ed/Beauty Sch 1936-37; pa/Ret'd Regional Mgr Sev Cosmetic Firms; Owned Spec Catering Shop; Apple Head Doll Maker 29 Yrs; cp/Former Mem Am Legion Aux; DAV; r/Bapt; hon/Presented an Am Flag Flown Over US Capitol 1978.

CARTER, THOMAS AUBREY oc/Radial Drill Operator; b/July 6, 1914; h/30251 13 Mile Rd, Apt 29D, Farmington Hills, MI 48024; ba/Detroit, MI; m/Geneva Evelyn Gouge; c/Audrey Mae Clark; p/Thomas Abram Carter (dec); Allie Mae Martin (dec); ed/Tool & Die Journeyman 1958; pa/Radial Drill Opr, Johnson Die & Engrg; DTA; Intl Union; United Auto; UAW; r/Bapt.

CARTER, VIRGINIA NELL oc/Life Underwriter, Insurance Agent; b/Aug 26, 1930; h/1119 S Crockett St, Sherman, TX 75090; ba/Sherman; m/Paul David; c/David Clyde, Elaine, p/Gussie G (dec) and Effie Gaddie, Whitesboro, TX; ed/Fire & Casualty Agcy Sch, Life Underwriters Sch; 2 Yrs Grayson Co Col; Pvt Voice; pa/Co-Owner Paul D Carter Ins Agcy; Fire & Casualty Gen Agt; Life Underwriter; Bnk/Loan Dept; cp/Bd Dirs Sherman C of C; Dist Dir of Dist 12, BPW Clbs; Pres City Coun PTA; Heart Fund; U Way; Muscular Distrophy, Cancer Crusade; r/Ch of Christ; hon/Wom of Yr Twice.

CARVALHO, JULIE ANN oc/Psychologist; b/Apr 11, 1940; h/11668 Mediterranean Ct, Reston, VA 22090; ba/Wash DC; m/Joao M P De Carvalho; c/Alan R, Dennis M, Melanie D, Celeste A, Joshua E; ed/BA; MA; PhD Work; pa/Child Care Spec; Federally Employed Wom; cp/Pres Fairfax Co Assn for the Gifted 1979-80; hon/Commends from Fed Ofcls.

CARVER, J A oc/Company Owner/Operator; b/Sept 6, 1920; h/206 Delono Ave, Dunn, NC 28334; ba/Dunn; m/Mabel Starling; c/Anthony Steven; p/Herbert Charles and Geneva Patterson Carver (dec); ed/Acctg & Bus Adm; mil/USCG 1942-45; pa/Salesman; Owner/Operator Carver Equip Co Inc; cp/Am Legion; St Com, Fgn Relats Comm; Dem Ho & Sen Adv Coun; r/Presb.

CASE, EUGENE CLIFF oc/Pastor; b/Dec 26, 1947; h/Box 851, Woodville, MS 39669; p/Coburn C and Stella Ham Case, Ripley, OH; ed/BA Morehead St Univ 1970; MDiv Reformed Theol Sem 1974; pa/Min Woodville Presb Ch & Bethany Presb Ch; Pt-time Ofcr Woodville Police Dept; Wilkinson Co Sheriff's Dpty; Former Modr Grace Presb; Miss Law Enforcement Ofcrs Assn; cp/Former Mem Wilkinson Co Dem Exec Com; r/Presb.

CASE, JACK W oc/Personnel Officer; b/Apr 5, 1931; h/8201 Alvin Ln, Little Rock, AR 72207; ba/Little Rock; m/Janece Morgan; c/Michael L, Susan E Armstrong; p/John W (dec) and Belle Case, Tulsa, OK; ed/AA Ctrl Christian Col 1952; BSBA Harding Univ 1969; Study Univ Tulsa 1955-58; mil/AUS 1953-55; pa/Pers Ofcr, VA Regional Ofc 1977-; Pers Mgmt Spec IRS 1967-77; Ofcr IRS 1960-67; cp/Chm Govt Recruiting Coun Ark 1980; Adv Coun Ctrl Ark Consortium 1978-79; Ctrl Ark Pvt Indust Coun 1979-; St Ark Pvt Indust Coun 1980-; Admissions Com Enterprises for the Blind 1968-78; r/Ch of Christ; hon/Spec Achmt Awd IRS 1970; Outstg Perf Awd VA Regional Ofc 1979 & 80; W/W S&SW 1980-81.

CASEY, OFFA LUNSFORD oc/Attorney; b/Apr 22, 1912; h/1006 Broadway, Laurel, MS; m/Naomi K; c/Thomas L, Michael R; p/Benjamin Dudley (dec) and Ethel Lou Shivers Casey (dec); ed/BS, LLB 1936, JD 1968 Univ Miss; mil/2nd Lt - Lt Col 1942-46, Fgn Ser India & China; pa/Miss Leg 1980-83; Gen Law Prac 1970-80; Circuit Judge Jones Co, Miss 1955-70; Co & Yth Ct Judge, Laurel, Miss 1951-55; Judge City Ct, Laurel, Miss 1947-48; Asst to Gen Counsel, Adm of Export Control, Wash DC 1940-42; Atty Lands Div Dept Just, Wash DC 1938-40; Miss Bar Assn; Jones Co Bapt Assn; Pres Miss Assn Crime & Delinquency 1953-55; cp/Rotarian; Mason; KP; Pi Kappa Phi; Phi Alpha Delta; Jones Co Dem Com; Pres Laurel Rotary Clb 1967-68; hon/Pub'd in *Miss Law Journal* Aug 1959; Author *Circuit Court Practice: The Form & Content of Pleadings.*

CASH, FRANCIS W oc/Marriott Corporation Vice President and Corporate Controller; b/Mar 16, 1942; h/1050 Cedrus Ln, McLean, VA 22101; ba/Wash DC; m/Judith R; c/Jeri Lynn, Lori Ann, Robin Elaine; p/Winsford M Cash (dec); Elsie A Yates, Charlottesville, VA; ed/BS Brigham Yg Univ; pa/Fin Execs Inst; Am Inst of CPAs; cp/Pres PTA; r/Ch of Christ of LDS; Exec Secy; hon/Outstg Yg Men of Am; Fellow Am Biogl Inst.

CASSON, LUELLA HOWARD oc/Assistant Placement Director; b/Nov 27, 1935; h/11893 Rivercrest, Little Rock, AR 77207; ba/Little Rock; c/Sandranetta Cecilia; p/(dec); ed/BS 1956, MEd 1957 Ala St Univ; Addit Study: Wn Resv Univ, Univ NC, Ohio St Univ, Univ Mo, Memphis St Univ; pa/Dir Affirmative Action, Ind St Univ 1977-; Career Planning &

Placement, Univ Ark, Little Rock: Dir 1976-77, Asst Dir 1975-76; Philander Smith Col: Dir Career Cnslg, Coop Ed & Placement 1973-75, Dir Career Cnslg & Placement & Asst Prof Ed 1970-73, Dir Career Cnslg & Placement & Student Recruitment 1969-70, Dir Placement & Fin Aid 1967-69, Dir Placement 1966-67, Dir Guidance Sers & Instr of Ed 1965-66; Chm Social Studies Dept & Hist Instr, Harris Jr Col 1957-65; Am Pers & Guidance Assn; Am Col Pers Assn; Assn for Sch Col & Univ Staffing; Ark Col Pers Assn; Col Placement Coun; Coop Ed Assn; Nat Voc Guidance Assn; SW Placement Assn (Life Mem); AAUP; AAUW; Ark Assn of Placement Pers: Pres 1973-74, Secy-Treas 1970-71; Am Assn for Affirmative Action; cp/Dir SW Placement Assn 1977; Adv Bd, Govt Recruiting Coun of Ark; Gov's Comm on Status of Wom 1971-74; Citizen's Adv Com to Mayor of Little Rock 1968-69; VChperson, Title III Prog Bd Col Placement Sers 1972-75; Urban Leag Bd; r/St Bartholomew Ch: Parish Coun; hon/Kappa Delta Pi; Alpha Kappa Mu; Sigma Rho Sigma; R J Reynolds F'ship; NDEA F'ship; NSF F'ship; Ford Foun F'ship; DIB; World W/W Wom; Yg Edr Am; W/W Am Ed; Ldrs Black Am; Others.

CATECHIS, SPYROS oc/Psychologist; b/Nov 29, 1945; h/6218 Rutherglenn, Houston, TX 77096; ba/Houston; m/Marian G; c/Nicholas, Christopher; p/Anastasios S and Grace M Catechis, Houston, TX; ed/BS Stephen F Austin Univ 1968; MS E Tex St Univ 1969; EdD Univ Houston 1978; pa/Pvt Prac Psychol; Tex Res Inst of Mtl Scis 1974-77; Am Grp Psychtherapy Assn; Houston Grp Psychotherapy Soc; Houston Psych Assn; Coun for Except Chd; Am Soc Clin Hypnosis; Am Psych Assn; cp/Bd Mem Harris Co Mtl Hlth Assn 1976-78; Chm Chds Com MHA 1977-78; Com Mem Protection of Human Subjs, Univ Tex Hlth Sci Ctr at Houston 1979-80; Bd Mem Chd's Resource & Info Ser; r/Greek Orthodox; hon/W/W S&SW 1980; Chapt Contbn *Autism: Diagnosis, Instruction, Management and Research* 1979.

CATES, STELLA OATES oc/Teacher; b/Aug 31, 1937; h/26 Estate Ln, Forney, TX; m/Don Tate; c/Bill, Margaret, John, Harry; p/Joe Will (dec) and Grace Oates (dec); ed/Baylor Univ 1956-57; pa/Pvt Piano Tchr; Mesquite Area Mus Tchrs Assn; TMTA; NMTA; Nat Guild Piano Tchrs; Jr Cnslr Tex Fed Mus Clbs; Cnslr Forney Jr Mus Clb; Schubert Study Clb; Mus & Drama Clb; cp/Accompanist HS Yth Choir; Accompanist Ch Choir; r/Bapt.

CATO, THOMAS (TOMMY) L oc/Artist, Art Insturctor; b/Jun 30, 1951; h/1718 Northside Dr, Apt L-2, Valdosta, GA 31601; c/Thomas Christopher, Jonathan Stuart; p/James H and Mildred D Cato, Valdosta, GA; ed/BFA 1973, MEd 1978 Valdosta St Col; pa/Artist-in-Residence, Lowndes Co Arts Comm 1976-78; Chd's Art Instr, VSC Public Sers 1975-; Art Instr, Valwood Sch 1973-; Art Instr, Summer Playground Prog, Valdosta Parks & Recreation Dept 1973-74; Other Positions; Shows incl: Space Coast Art Fest 1977, House of 10,000 Picture Frames & the Walnut Gallery (2 1-man shows 1977), Santa Fe Commun Col 8th Annual Sprg Art Show 1977, Fernadina Sprg Art Show, Americus Sidewalk Art Show 1976, Douglas Art Show 1976, Thomasville Col Art Show 1973, 75, Others; hon/Awds incl: 2nd Pl Painting, VSC Sprg Art Show 1973, 3rd Pl Drawing Thomasville Col Art Show 1973, 1st Pl Drawing Nashville Art Show 1973, Langdale Purchase Awd, VSC Sprg Art Show 1973, 2nd Pl Painting, VSC Sprg Art Show 1974, 1st Pl Watercolor Douglas Art Show 1976, 2nd Pl Mixed Media/Oil, Douglas Art Show 1976, Coffee Co Bk Purchase Awd in Watercolor, Douglas Art Show 1976, Merit Awds, Americus Sidewalk Art Show 1976.

CATRON, JENNIE RACHEL oc/Retired; b/Feb 22, 1916; h/200 Jasper St, Somerset, KY 42501; m/Harold Lewis (dec); c/Harold Jr, Samuel Wilson, Nancy Elizabeth; p/Wilson Boyd Morrow (dec); Florence E Strecker (dec); ed/Univ Miami 1934-35; Bowling Green Bus Univ 1935-36; Somerset Area Voc Sch 1972-73; pa/Ret'd Legal Secy; Adm Asst Am Red Cross; Ins Agt; cp/Repub Wom's Clb 2nd VP; Histn, 1st VP DAR; Girl Scout Ldr; Pres BPW Clb; r/Presb; hon/Thanks Badge Girl Scouts 1973; Ky Col 1968.

CATRON, WILLIAM RICHARD oc/Dentist; b/Apr 22, 1953; h/110 Kittison Dr, Winchester, KY 40391; ba/Winchester; m/Debbie; p/William Raymond (dec) and Faye M Catron, Winchester, KY; pa/Clark Co Dental Soc; Bluegrass Dental Soc; Ky Dental Assn; Am Dental Assn; cp/Am Cancer Soc; r/Meth.

CATURANO, CARLO oc/Interior Designer; b/June 26, 1939; h/1547 SE 27 St, Ocala, FL 32671; ba/Same; c/Ann Marie; p/Vincent Sr (dec) and Mary Caturano, Silver Springs, FL; ed/Cert Parson Sch Design 1963; mil/AUS 1964-66; pa/Carlo Caturano Interiors 1978-; Pres Interior Design Archl Interiors Unltd 1971-78; Interior Designer CID Ltd 1968-71; Homefurnishing Coor Woodward & Lothrop 1966-68; Inst Bus Designers 1973-80; cp/Intl Rotary 1971; Dir Am Red Cross Dr 1971; Loyal Order of Moose; C of C Ocala-Marion Co; Small Bus Com; Plan'g & Growth Com; r/Roman Cath; hon/Designed Commemoration Medalion for Town of Kennebunk, Maine for 150 Anniv.

CAVANAGH, HARRISON DWIGHT oc/Professor; b/July 22, 1940; h/1365 Clifton Rd NE, Atlanta, GA; m/Lynn Ayres Gantt; c/Catherine DuVal; p/William Edwards Cavanagh; Marie Logue; ed/AB 1962, MD 1965 Johns Hopkins Univ; PhD Harvard Univ 1972; mil/USAR Major; pa/Prof & Chm Dept Ophthalmology, Emory Univ Sch Med; Ophthalmic Surg, Subspec Corneal Transplants; Am Acad Ophthalmology; Am Col Surgs; Assn for Res in Vision & Ophthalmology; New Eng Ophthalmological Soc; Contact Lens Assn of Ophthalmologists; Assoc Secy Am Acad Ophthalmology 1979-; Visual Scis Study Section A Nat Eye Inst; r/Prot; hon/Phi Beta Kappa 1962; Joseph Collins Schlr Med 1964; Held Foun Fellow 1973-74; W/W Am 1982; Author Over 50 Pubs.

CAVIL, WILLIE MAE oc/Maid; b/July 17, 1933; c/Cassandra Renee, Denise Olanda, Lei Lani, Marta J Jr, Darwin Dwayne; p/Anderson (dec) and Alberta Lee (dec); pa/Maid; r/Ch of God in Christ; hon/Kicker Awd 1980-81; PTA Mbrship Awd 1978-79, 1979-80; Pres PTA 1981-82; Life Mem PTA.

CAVIN, BRUCE WAYNE oc/Financial Officer; b/Aug 4, 1949; h/127 Rawley Ct, Longview, TX 75601; ba/Longview; m/Barbara L; c/Jeffrey W; p/David and Lucille Cavin; ed/BBA 1975, MBA 1979 Stephen F Austin Univ; mil/AUS 1972-74; pa/Controller, Hydrolex Corp 1980-; Suprv Job Cost Analysis, Marathon-Letrouneau Co 1979-80; Cost Acct Antenna Ops, Harris Corp 1978-79; Regional Planner E Tex Coun Govts 1975-78; Suprv Com Marathon Fed Credit Union; Am Mgmt Assn; cp/Brotherhood of St Andrews; r/Epis; hon/Omicron Delta Epsilon; W/W S&SW; Author: *Feasibility Study: Regional Administration of Section 8 Existing Housing 1978; Regional Housing Plan 1976 1977; Housing Demonstration Project 1976*.

CAZALAS, MARY WILLIAMS oc/Attorney; ba/1116 City Park Ave, New Orleans, LA 70119; ed/RN St Joseph's Infirm Sch of Nsg 1948; BS Oglethorpe Univ 1954; MS Emory Univ 1960; JD Loyola Univ 1967; pa/Gen Duty Nsg 1948-68; Instr Maternity Nsg, St Joseph's Infirm Sch of Nsg 1954-59; Med Res, Urology, Tulane Univ Sch of Med 1961-65; Legal Res, Law Clk to Judge Godfrey Z Regan, 4th Circuit Ct of Appeals 1965-67; Gen Pract Law 1967-71; Asst US Atty, New Orleans 1971-79; Trial Atty, US Equal Employment Opport Comm 1979-; Am Bar Assn 1968-79; Am Judicature Soc; La St Bar Assn; New Orleans Bar Assn 1968-79; Fed Bar Assn; Phi Delta Delta; Phi Alpha Delta; Nat Assn Wom Lwyrs; Nat Hlth Lwyrs Assn; cp/DAR: BPW Clb; New Orleans Art Assn; New Orleans Mus of Art; Alumni Assn: Emory Univ, Oglethorpe Univ, Loyola Univ; Fed Employed Wom Inc 1976-79; Jefferson Parish Hist Soc; Wom's Polit Caucus; PEO; hon/Best Comment in Loyola Law Review 1966-67; Three Am Jurisprudence Awds; 1st Pl for Oil Painting, Fed Bus Assn Art Exhib 1973; Hon St Sen 1974; Superior Perf Awd, US Dept Just 1974; Cert of Apprec, Fed Exec Bd 1975, 76, 77, 78; Rev E A Doyle Awd, Outstg Cardinal Key 1976; Commend from Guam Leg for Tchg in Forensic Psychi Conf 1977; Ser as Pres New Orleans Bar Assn 1975; Pres New Orleans Fed Bus Assn 1978; Alpha Epsilon Delta; Leconte Hon Sci Soc; Cardinal Key Nat Hon Soc; Phi Sigma; Law Review, Loyola Univ; W/W: Am Law, Am Wom, S&SW; DIB; Martindale-Hubbel Inc (Listed as High Legal Ability & Very High Gen Recommends); Intl W/W Intells; Personalites of Am; Pubs Incl "Nursing and the Law" 1978 & "Private Practice and the Law" Chapt 12 of *Private Practice in Nursing* 1979.

CESAR, THOMAS EUGENE oc/Executive Director Outpatient Clinic; b/Aug 25, 1944; h/Raleigh, NC; ba/Rehabilitation and Cerebral Palsy Ctr of Wake Co, 3004 New Bern Ave, Raleigh, NC 27610; m/Amber Henson; c/Todd Alan, Eric Thomas; p/Annette Rieger, Culver City, CA; ed/AA Santa Monica City Col 1965; BA Cal St LA Univ 1969; MA Boston St Col 1976; mil/USAF 1965-68; pa/Exec Dir Rehab & Cerebral Palsy Ctr 1978-; Unit Mgr Mt Auburn Hosp 1976-78; Staff Asst Mass Bd Regional Commun Cols 1974-75; Tchr Pilgrim Sch LA 1971-73; Assn Med Rehab Dirs & Coors; Nat Rehab Assn; Assn Retard Citizens; Am Hosp Assn; cp/Raleigh Arts Comm, Arts & Spec Pop Subcom; BSA, Scoutmaster Troop 389; Wake-Up Chd, Wake Child Advocacy; r/Christian.

CESSNA, PHYLLIS K oc/Guidance Counselor, Educator; b/Oct 9, 1938; h/3017 Tanbridge, Martinsburg, WV 25401; ba/M'burg; m/Gary; c/Maria Kessel, Michael Kessel, Todd Kessel; p/Leo and Lettie Sites, Petersburg, WV; ed/BS 1966, MA 1971 WV Univ; pa/Cnslr, Tchr, Curric Spec Tuscarora Sch; NEA; Am Pers & Guid Assn; Assn Supervision & Curric Devel; cp/Am Bapt Wom; WVU Alumni; OES; r/Bapt, hon/Regional Tchr of Yr 1965; Benedum S'ship 1966; W/W S&SW 1980; Author: *Student Career Guide; English/Communications Cross Reference Catalog; Career Education Cross Reference Catalog; Other Reference Works*.

CHACKO, JOHN KABZEEL YESUDAS oc/Vascular Surgeon; b/Sept 26, 1941; h/5610 NW 28 Terrace, Gainesville, GA 32601; ba/Lake City, FL; m/Jeanne Marie; p/John C and Mariam P Chacko; ed/MD Univ Kerala, India 1964; Master Surg 1969; Internship NY Infirmary & NY Univ Hosp 1970-71; Residency Mt Sinai Hosp 1971-72, Westchester Co Med Ctr

& Columbia Univ 1972-75; F'ship Vascular Surg Mt Sinai Hosp 1975-76; pa/Act'g Chief of Surg Sers, VA Med Ctr, Lake City; Clin Asst Prof Surg, Univ Fla; Fellow: Am Col Surg, Intl Col Surg, Intl Acad Proctology; Mem Assn Mil Surgs, Peripheral Vascular Surg Clb; cp/Exec Dir Evangelical Social Sers; r/Christian; hon/Am Col Surgs Awd.

CHAHINE, ROBERT A oc/Physician; Educator; b/Feb 8, 6111 Chimney Rock #116, Houston, TX 77081; ba/Houston; p/Antoine H and Jamie R Chahine, Tripoli, Lebanon; ed/BS 1962, MD 1966 Am Univ of Beirut; pa/Former Postdoct Fellow: Univ Miami, Harvard Univ, UCLA; Asst Prof UCLA 1972; Baylor Col of Med: Asst Prof of Med 1972-76, Assoc Prof of Medd 1976-; Chief, Sect of Cardiology, VA Hosp; Lebanese Order of Physicians; Am Heart Assn; Houston Cardiol Soc; AAUP; Am Fdn for Clinical Res; cp/Chm Com for Salvation of Lebanon; Bd Dirs Houston Chapt Am Heart Assn; r/Cath Ch: Mem; hon/Fellow: Am Col of Cardiol, Am Col of Phys, AHA Coun on Circulation, AHA Coun on Clin Cardiol, Am Biogl Inst; Num Pubs in Sci Jours w Ldg Res & Contbns in: Coronary Artery Spasm, Unstable Angina, Hypertrophic Cardiomyopathy & Exercise Testing.

CHALKER, JESS FRANK oc/National Sales Manager; b/Sept 29, 1947; h/Charlotte, NC; ba/1 Julian Price Place, Charlotte, NC; m/Marissa Kay; c/Ericka Marie and Alexis Jean; p/Herbert Frank and Demetra Jean Chalker, Southfield, MI; ed/BA Wn Mich Univ 1970; pa/TV Dir WKZP-VT, Kalamazoo; HS & Col Instr; St Mgr WMPX, Midland, Mich; Regional Mgr-Media Dir, Patten Corp; Nat TV Rep, Petry TV Inc, Troy, Mich; Grp Sales Mgr Petry TV Inc, Chgo, Ill; Nat Sales Mgr, WBTV, Jefferson-Pilot Broadcasting, Charlotte; Past Mem Advtg Clb of Detroit; cp/Adult & Contg' Ed; Past Mem: Big Bros/Little Sis of Midland, Mich; Jr Achmt, C of C Midland; r/Greek Orthodox.

CHAMBERLIN, LINDA GREGG oc/Chief Dietitian; b/May 19, 1949; h/4409 Prairie Dog Rd, Muskogee, OK 74401; ba/Muskogee; m/Gregory L; c/Byron Kevin, LaVanda LaVette; p/Frank and Doris Gregg; ed/BS; MS; pa/Chief Dietitian VA Med Ctr; Foun for Advmt Minorities in Dietetics; ADA; Am Hosp Assn for Food Ser Dirs; cp/Girl Scout Coun; Ever Ready Civics & Art Clb; NAACP; r/Ch of Christ; hon/Boss of Qtr; 1st Runner Up Miss KVAEA Contest.

CHAMBERS, CARL DEAN oc/Corporation Executive; Educator; Administrator; b/Oct 30, 1934; h/17345 SW 112 Ave, Miami, FL 33157; m/Kathryn M Keplar; c/Christine Elise; ed/BA; MS; PhD; mil/USAF 1953-57; pa/Pres, Personal Devel Inst, Miami; Prof & Dir, Inst for Public Hlth Res, Antioch Col, Columbia, Md; Editor: *Addictive Diseases: An Internal Journal, Spectrum Books in Sociomedical Sciences;* Adv Bd: *Sage Annual Reviews of Alcohol and Drug Abuse,* Medicine in the Public Interest Inc; Am Soc Criminology Com on Problems of Drug Dependence; US Food & Drug Adm Controlled Substances Adv Com; hon/Pub'd 150+ Jour Articles, Book Chapters & Monographs in Socio-Med Scis; Author: *Epidemiology of Drug Abuse, Employee Drug Abuse, Methadone Maintenance, Drugs & Crime, Chemical Coping, Heroin Epidemics.*

CHAMBERS, LOUISE PIERCE oc/Media Specialist; b/Apr 17, 1942; h/4120 Sarnia Ln SW, Atlanta, GA 30331; ba/Atlanta; m/Samuel Jr; c/Keelan Devoy; Che Louise; p/Jeff and Mattie Pierce, Atlanta, GA; ed/Morris Brown Col 1959-63; MS Atlanta Univ Sch of Lib Sci 1972; Adv'd Studies Atlanta Univ 1973-; pa/Media Spec w Atlanta Bd Ed 1969-; Tchr 1963-68; NEA; GEA; Atlanta Assn Ed; Ga Lib Assn; cp/Secy L P Miles Sch PTA; Zeta Phi Beta; r/Bapt; hon/R E Cureton Nat Hon Soc 1957; Num S'ships to Var Cols 1959; Hon Student Morris Brown Col 1959-63; W/W Students in Am Cols & Univs 1961; First Lady to Hold Ofc of Fin Secy at Iconium Bapt Ch.

CHAMBERS, MARGARET M HORSWELL oc/Engineer, Technician, Lapidary, Calligrapher, Currently Retired; b/Jan 19, 1916; h/402 Bluebonnet, LaMarque, TX 77586; ba/LaMarque; m/William Franklin (dec); c/William F Jr; p/Alred H Sr (dec) and Margaret Maloney Horswell (dec); pa/Musician; Sculptor; Artist; Writer; Illustrator; Bluebonnet Lapidary-Art Studio; Orig Design Lost Wax Cast Jewelry & Gem Stone Scuptures; cp/Sponsor Pediatric Patients & Orphans 'Treats for Tots'; Mainland Choral & St Michaels Choirs; Alliance of Galveston Co Sr Adults; Galveston Gem & Mineral Soc; CP on Com for Aiding Handicapped; r/Epis; Mem Daughs of Kings; Min, Order of St Luke; hon/Wom of Yr, Sweetheart, Phi Sigma Alpha; Poetry Pub'd in *Courier*.

CHAMBERS, MICHAEL LEE oc/Assistant Professor; b/Dec 9, 1949; h/Orlando, FL; ba/2503 E Kaley Ave, Orlando, FL 32806; m/Pamela J Goodman; c/Christopher Michael, Cara Beth; p/Mr and Mrs B N Chambers, Lincoln, IL; ed/AB Lincoln Christian Col 1972; MA 1979, MDiv 1979 Lincoln Christian Sem; Add'l Study Concordia Sem; pa/Asst Prof Phil, Dean Students, Ctrl Fla Bible Col; First Christian Ch, Collinsville, Il: Assoc Min 1970-72, Sr Min 1972-77; Assoc Min Lakeside Christian Ch 1977-79; Instr St Louis Christian Col 1976-77; Inst for Theol

Encounter w Sci & Technol; Evangelical Philosophical Soc; Am Sci Affiliation; r/Ch of Christ; hon/Pub'd Author *The Message of God in the Language of Man* 1973; *What They Did Right* 1974; "A Christian Response to the Energy Crisis" 1977.

CHAMBLESS, RALPH PROCTOR JR oc/Minister; b/Sept 16, 1949; h/Huntsville, AL; ba/307 Gates Ave SE, Huntsville, AL; m/Virginia Smith; c/Jason Orne, Kate Elizabeth; p/Ralph Proctor Sr and Betty Holmes Chambless, Atlanta, GA; ed/BA Univ Ga 1971; DMin Union Theol Sem 1977; pa/Pastor First Presb Ch, H'ville; Pres Mecklenburg F'ship of Christian Edrs; H'ville Area Clergy Assn; cp/N Ala Fball Ofcls Assn; Kiwanis Clb of S H'ville; Pres Hosp Hospitality House of H'ville Inc; Madison Co Council CASA; Fin Com Interfaith Mission; Yth Homes Inc; r/Presb.

CHAMBLISS, MARVIN HENRY oc/Retired; b/May 31, 1915; h/214 Charlotte, Roanoke Rapids, NC 27870; m/Mae S; c/Sylvia C Finch, William R, p/William Joseph (dec) and Minnie B Chambliss, Roanoke Rapids, NC; mil/USN; pa/Ret'd After 21 Yrs w A&P Tea Co; cp/Roanoke Val Rescue Squad; r/Meth; hon/Cert Apprec from Roanoke Val Rescue Squad 1979; Cert Hon A&P Tea Co; Cert from Red Cross & EMT Course.

CHANCE, ELIZABETH (BETH) MOORER oc/Teacher; b/Jan 23, 1954; h/105 Mellard Dr, Goose Creek, SC 29445; ba/Hanahan, SC; m/Sam L; p/John M and Betty W Moorer, N Charleston, SC; ed/BS; MEd; pa/Tchr; Intl Rdg Assn; NEA; SCEA; Berkeley Co Ed Assn; PTA; PTA Exec Bd; Citizens Adv Coun; Beta Sigma Phi; cp/St James Civic Clb; Y Clb Sponsor; Christian Fam Y; Student Coun Sponsor; r/Bapt; hon/Advr of Yr 1978-79, Christian Family Y; Yng Career Wom of Yr 1979, N Charleston BPW Clb.

CHANDLER, BARBARA ETTA oc/Baker; b/Apr 21, 1940; h/N Charleston, SC; m/Brice Sr; c/Bricena Elginetta, Bernette Elaine, Brice Elgin Jr; p/Marion and Carrie Gantt (dec), N Charleston, SC; pa/Mem Lunchroom Staff, Ben Tillman Sch, N Charleston; r/Bapt; hon/Most Contributing Band Parent, Bonds Wilson HS Band 1976.

CHANDLER, BOB J oc/Minister; b/June 20, 1946; h/Marshall, TX; m/Cheryl; c/Robert, Jeffrey, Christina; p/E J and Wanda Chandler, Shawnee, OK; ed/BA Tex Wesleyan Col 1968; MDiv SWn Bapt Theol Sem 1972; pa/Min First Christian Ch, Marshall 1978–; Assoc Min First Christian Ch Midland 1975-78; Assoc Min Woodlawn Christian Ch San Antonio 1974-75; Pres Marshall Min Assn 1980-81; VChm U Chs Care 1980; Camp & Conf Coor NE Tex Area Christian Ch 1978-80; r/Disciples of Christ.

CHANDLER, VENITA S LOVELACE oc/Chairperson; b/July 29, 1949; h/Mabelvale, AR; ba/Univ Central Ark, 1211 Wolfe St, Room 235, Little Rock, AR 72201; m/Ben Lovelace-Chandler; c/Marty, Alex, Sheriann; p/Jesse S and Reba Bonner Lovelace, Dallas, TX; ed/BS Univ Tex 1971; MACT UNC-Chapel Hill 1976; Cand PhD Tex A&M Univ 1981; pa/Chp, Dept Phys Therapy, Univ Ctrl Ark 1980–; Supvr Boston Chd's Hosp Wrentham Proj 1976-77; Asst Dir Clin Sers, Univ Ala at Birmingham, The Chd's Hosp 1973-74; Therapist, Dallas Soc for Crippled Chd 1971-73; APTA; Neuro Devel Alumni Assn; Phi Delta Kappa; r/Unitarian; hon/Pub'd Author "Employment of Physical Therapist Assistants in a Residential State School" 1979; "Supporting Clinical Research with Foundation Funds."

CHAPMAN, CARLTON JOHNSON oc/Banker; b/Sept 13, 1921; h/410 Jacksboro St, Snyder, TX 79549; ba/Snyder, TX; m/Lurlyne Pettit; c/Carla Cox, Myrna, Steven E; p/Nell D Hoover, Nocona, TX; ed/Hardin-Stevens Univ; BS 1951, MS 1952 Tex A&M Univ; Doct Study: Univ Wis, Tex A&M Univ; mil/USAAC 3½ yrs, WW II; pa/1st Nat Bk, Weatherford: Exec VP 1978–, VP 1975-75; Real Est & Investments 1973, 74; Pres: Peoples Nat Bk, Nocona 1967-73, Bowie Nat Bk, Bowie 1967, Wolfforth St Bk, Wolfforth 1965-67; VP, St Nat Bk, Big Sprg 1959-65; Farm Loan Supvr, Farmers Home Adm, USDA 7 yrs; Loan Analyst, Commodity Credit Corp, USDA 1945-49; Past Pres, Big Sprg Chapt, Am Inst Bkg; Past Chm, St Bkrs Adv Bd; Past Mem, Tex Bkrs Assn Agri Com; cp/Mayor, City of Wolfforth, Tex 1966-67; Bd Dirs, Girlstown USA; Past Pres & Bd Dirs, Nocona C of C; Past Mem Bd Dirs, W Tex C of C; Pres Nocona U Fund 1972-73; Chm Montague Co Chapt Tex Heart Assn 1967-68; Pres Tex-Okla Area Devel Foun, 2 terms; Weatherford Indust Com 1975-77; Gov's Com on Agri 1977–; Chm Parker Co Agri Com 1978–; 32 deg Scottish Rite Mason; Shrine; r/Bapt; hon/Outstg Citizen Awd, Big Sprg 1963; Alpha Zeta; Phi Kappa Phi; Outstg Personalities of S; Creative & Successful Personalities of World; W/W SW; Hon Lone Star Farmer, St of Tex 1972.

CHAPMAN, ELMA SINES oc/Teacher; b/Oct 25, 1930; h/6668 Big Seven Mile, Lesage, WV 25537; ba/Huntington, WV; m/Walter G Jr; c/Angela, Karen; p/Raymond and Katie Smith Sines, Lesage, WV; ed/AB 1951, MA 1956 Marshall Univ; pa/Nat, So, W Va Bus Ed Assn; Pi Omega Pi; cp/Adv Com Cox Landing Commun Sch; PTA; OES; r/Meth; hon/W/W Am Wom 1979-80.

CHAPMAN, ROBERT E oc/Brigadier General; b/Jan 8, 1932; h/432 East Dr, Maxwell AFB, AL 36113; ba/Maxwell AFB; m/Helen; c/Robert E II; p/James Winston and Floy B Chapman, Russellville, AR; ed/BS US Mil Acad 1954; MSEE Univ Mich; PFE Carnegie Mellon Univ; mil/USAF, Brigadier Gen; pa/Cmdr, Ldrship & Mgmt Devel Ctr, Maxwell AFB; Past Mem Air Univ, Maxwell AFB; Past Assignments: Fighter Pilot & Flight Cmdr w Air Def Command, Aircraft Maintenance Ofcr & Mem 316th Air Div Tactical Eval Team (Morocco), Cmdr (Col) 42nd Bomb Wing (Loring AFB, Maine) 1974, Plans Ofcr Air Proving Ground Ctr (Elgin AFB), Mem USAF Inspector Gen Group (Norton AFB, Cal),Plans Ofcr Mil Assistance Command (Saigon, Vietman), Chief Fighter Opers Br (Hickman AFB), VCmdr 380th Bomb Wing & Dep Cmdr for Opers (Plattsburgh AFB, NY); NAm Conf Mgmt Conslts; cp/Air Force Assn; Socio Technological Working Group; r/Meth; hon/Alternate White House Fellow 1965; Bronze Star; Legion of Merit; Meritorious Ser Medal; Commend Medal.

CHAPPELL, CLAUDIA B oc/Realtor, Company President; b/Oct 12, 1929; h/4616 NW 61st St, Okla City, OK 73132; ba/Okla City; m/J W (Bill); c/Glenna C Downing, Nancy, Stanfa Neil, Chris; p/Claud and Lena Botts, Amarillo, TX; ed/Profl Designations GRI, CRS; pa/Rltr, Broker, Pres Chaparral Properties Inc; Ofcr & Dir Okla City Bd Rltrs; Okla Assn Rltrs; cp/C of C; BBB; RPAC Chm; r/Meth; hon/1978 Rltr of Yr, Okla City.

CHAPPELL, EUGENE WATSON JR oc/Management Consultant; b/Jan 1, 1945; h/6101 W Edsall Rd #1213, Alexandria, VA 22304; ba/Alexandria; p/Eugene W and Virginia Lee Chappell; ed/BSEE Univ Va 1967; mil/Navy 1967-72 Submarine Ofcr; pa/Chm Bd Fiscal Assoc Inc; Dir Omnetics; DPMA; r/Bapt; hon/Navy/Esquire Nat Essay Grand Prize; W/W Fin & Indust.

CHARITY, RUTH HARVEY oc/Attorney; b/Apr 18; h/514 S Main St, Danville, VA 24541; ba/Danville; m/Ronald K; c/Khris Wayne; p/C C and Annie L Harvey (dec); ed/BA Howard Univ; JD Howard Univ Law Sch; pa/Atty, Gen Pract of Law, Civil & Crim 1953–; Spec Counsel: Spec Rep for 1st St Bank, D'ville, NAACP Legal Def & Ednl Fund, So Christian Ldrship Conf, Harvey's Funeral Home Inc; Pres Com on Civil Rts Under the Law; Past Pres Old Dominion Bar Assn; Nat Bar Assn: Orgr Woms Sect, Bd Dirs; Intl Fdn Wom Lwyrs; Nat Assn Wom Lwyrs; St Conf NAACP Brs, Legal Staff; D'ville City Coun-wom 1970-74; Va St Adv Com to US Civil Rts Comm; Former Mem Va Comm on Status of Wom; AAUW; cp/Alpha Phi Omega Chapt, Alpha Kappa Alpha Sorority; U Order of Tent; Grand Temple Daughs, IBPOEW, Grand Asst Legal Advr; Past Nat Ofcr, Nat Coun Negro Wom; Chums Inc: Past Nat Parliamentn, Treas; Trustee Va Sem & Col, Lynchburg, Va; Former Trustee: Palmer Meml Inst, Sedalia, NC, Howard Univ; LWV; YWCA: 1st Wom Chm, Va St Adv Com, US Civil Rts Comm; Bd Dirs, Nat C of C for Wom Ldrs; NOW; Exec Com, Dem Nat Com (1st Black Wom from S to be Elected to Major Polit Party in this Capacity); Va Dem Party Steering Com & Ctl Com; OES; r/High St Bapt Ch, D'ville: Mem, Sr Choir; hon/Num Awds: AKA, NCNW, Wom for Polit Action, Other Polit Action Groups; W/W: Am Law, Polits.

CHARLESTON, OLLIE BEATRICE PETERS oc/Teacher; b/Mar 2, 1919; h/476 Ashby St, NW, Atlanta, GA 30314; m/Rufus; p/Tobe (dec) and Violet Peters (dec); ed/Dip Tchrs Normal Col 1935; Corresp Course w Credit in Elem Ed; BS 1954; Spec Ed Courses 1972; pa/Tchr; Lead Tchr, Eng Adoption & Curric Guide Com; Pres & Secy Local Tchrs Assn; cp/Vol Wkr & Mem YWCA; Vol Ser & Funds for Ga Regional Hosp; Vol Wkr to Help Fight Emphysema; Vol Wkr to Help Fight Cancer; Child Welfare Ser, Coun of Parents & Tchrs; PTA Chaplain; Phi Delta Kappa; Chp Black Hist Progs; Contbr & Mem Nat Coun Negro Wom; Atlanta Chapt Min's Wives; r/Flipper Temple AME Ch: Secy Steward Bd #2, Co-Chp for Cheer & Condolence Com, VP Art Guild, Matron SS Class, Chp Wom's Day Activs; Dean's List 1934-35; Tchr of Yr 1964, 74; Cand Tchrs Hall of Fame 1974; Cand Edrs Hall of Fame 1974; Cert of Achmt, Merit Ser in Phi Delta Kappa 1980; Cert of Merit, Child's Wel Ser in PTA Coun 1966; Tchr Recog Social Sci Regional Awds 1969-71; Cert of Sers for Col Guid Grp 1977; Journalist for *Krinon Magazine* of Phi Delta Kappa 1975-76.

CHATMAN, JERRY MATTHEW oc/Executive; b/Mar 18, 1933; h/106 N Main St, Granite Falls, NC 28630; ba/Granite Falls; m/Virginia McGillen; c/Matthew Jr, Ronald, Brian, Mickey, Susan; p/Earl M and Beatrice Chatman, Johnson City, TN; pa/Retailer; Grocer; Restaurant Exec; cp/Past Pres Granite Falls Rescue Squad; Rotary; Town Commr 4 Yrs; r/Ch of God; hon/EMT.

CHAUDHURI, TAPAN K oc/Medical Researcher, Administrator, Teacher, Clinician; b/Nov 25, 1944; h/304 Rudisill Rd, Hampton, VA

23669; ba/Hampton; m/Chhanda; c/Lakshmi; p/Taposh K and Bulu Rami Chowdhurg; ed/ISc 1961; MBBS 1966; ECFMG 1967; DABNM 1972; FACP, FACG 1975; pa/Prof Radiology (Nuclear Med), En Va Med Sch 1979-; Chief, Nuclear Med, V A Med Ctr 1974-; Assoc Prof, Nuclear Med En Va Med Sch 1974-79; Asst Prof, Nuclear Med, Univ Iowa 1971-74; Soc of Nuclear Med; Biophys Soc; Am Physiol Soc; AMA; Am Fed Clin Res; Am Col Phys; Am Col Nuclear Phys; Am Col Gastroenterologists; Bengal & Brit Med Couns; AAAS; Am Heart Assn; Former Mem: Johnson Co Med Soc, Ia St Med Soc, Radiol Soc NAm, Am Geriatrics Soc, Am Assn Mil Surgs, Am Col Nuclear Phys, Computerized Tomography Soc; hon/Author 100 Pubs in Nat & Intl Sci & Med Jours; Calcutta Univ: 1st Cert Hons, Calcutta Univ Hons, Gold Medal (Physiol), Silver Medals (Forensic & Clin Med), Hons in Intl Med, Obstetrics & Gyn, Bengal Govt S'ship, Tuition S'ship, Best Perf in Autopsy Prize; Fellow Am Biogl Assn; Intl W/W Commun Ser; Book of Hon; Others.

CHAUDLER, GUY EDWARD oc/Lumberman; b/Dec 27, 1925; h/904 Anderson, Hearme, TX 79859; ba/Hearme; m/Dorothy Darlington; c/Wendy Lynn March James, James Edward; p/James Guy and Katherine Chaudler, Cameron, TX; ed/BS Tex A&M; mil/USAF 1943-45; pa/Lumberman; cp/Mayor of Hearme 5 Yrs; r/Bapt.

CHEATHAM, JOEL W oc/Executive Vice President; b/Aug 17, 1948; h/2002 Cherry, Pine Bluff, AR 71601; ba/Pine Bluff; m/Gary Lynn; c/Emily Anne; p/W O and Dorothy L Cheatham, El Dorado, AR; ed/BSBA; mil/USN; pa/Exec VP S Ark Savings & Loan Assn; Pine Bluff Bd of Rltrs; Dir Pine Bluff Home Bldrs Assn; cp/Pine Bluff Downtown Lions Clb; Dir U Way of Jefferson Co; Past Dir Easter Seal Bd; r/Meth.

CHENG, BIN-LUH oc/Associate Professor; b/June 6, 1941; h/2332 Hampshire Way, Tallahassee, FL 32308; ba/Tallahassee; m/Vera P; c/Jimming V, Winston; p/Hai-Chu and Shu Tsan Lo Cheng (dec), London, Ont, Can; ed/BSEE Nat Taiwan Univ 1964; MSCPS Nat Chiao Tung Univ 1967; MSEE Colo St Univ 1968; PhD Mich St Univ 1972; pa/Assoc Prof & Chm Dept EET, Fla A&M Univ; Reg'd Profl Engr Fla; Former: Instr Detroit Inst Technol, Devel Engr Honeywell Inc, Sr Engr Wn Elec Ill; IEEE, Secy Tallahassee Subsect 1979-80; ASEE; FEA; hon/Recip CTU Alumni F'ship 1966 & 67.

CHERRY, WILLIAM A oc/Secretary of Louisana Department of Health & Human Resources; b/Oct 25, 1924; h/4828 St Charles Ave, New Orleans, LA 70115; ba/Baton Rouge; m/Flora F; c/William Neal, Darrell Keith, Philip Allan, Susan Elizabeth; p/Bessie R Cherry, Halls, TN; ed/BS 1946, MD 1949 Tulane Univ; mil/USN 1943-46, 50-53; USNR 1953-63, Cmdr; USPHS 1963-; Asst Surg Gen; pa/Secy, La Dept Hlth & Human Resources 1977-; Chief Med Ofcr, USCG, Wash DC, 1974-77; Reg Hlth Dir, DHEW, HSMA, PHS, Reg VI, Dallas, Tex 1971-74; USPHS Hosp, New Orleans: Dir 1966-71, Surg Staff 1963-66; Pvt Pract Gen & Thoracic Surg, New Iberia, La 1957-63; Hosp Appts: Tulane Univ Sch Med: Clin Prof Surg 1970-, Clin Assoc Prof 1967-70; Tulane Univ Sch Public Hlth & Tropical Med: Adj Prof Hlth Sers Adm 1970-73, Adj Assoc Prof 1969-70; La St Univ Sch Med: Clin Asst Prof Surg 1966-67, Clin Instr 1963-66, Clin Assoc Instr 1953-57; Asst Chief Fracture Ser, La St Univ Div, Charity Hosp 1963-65; La TB & Respiratory Disease Assn (Bd Mem, Past Pres); La Thoracic Soc (Past Pres); USPHS Clin Soc; Nat TB Assn; James D Rives Surg Soc; Comm'd Ofcrs Assn (Past Pres); Mil Order of World Wars; La Public Hlth Assn; Assn Mil Surgs US; Diplomate, Am Bd Surgs; Fellow, Am Col Surgs; Profl Pubs & Presentations; r/U Meth Ch; hon/Phi Beta Kappa; Alpha Omega Alpha; Querens-Rives-Shore Awd, Tulane Univ; Delta Omega; USCG Meritorious Ser Awd; USPHS Meritorious Ser Awd; USPHS Commend Medal; Hon Mem, Nat Environmental Hlth Assn; W/W: Govt, La, NAm, US, S&SW; DIB; Commun Ldrs & Noteworthy Ams; Men Achmt; Outstg Ams S; Others.

CHEZEM, CURTIS GORDON oc/Corporate Executive; b/Jan 28, 1924; h/13121 NE 21st St, Amarillo, TX 79111; ba/Amarillo; c/Joanne, David; p/Clinton Daniel and Vera Veneta Forrester Chezem; ed/BA 1951, MA 1952 Univ Oreg; PhD Oreg St Univ 1960; mil/Oreg NG 1939-40; USNR 1945-46; pa/Staff Physicist Los Alamos Sci Lab 1952-67; Br Chief AEC 1967-69; Hd Nuclear Engrg Dept, Ks St Univ, Manhattan 1969-72, Black & Veatch Prof Nuclear Engrg 1971-72; Partner Casa Tlaloc, Los Alamos 1960-68, Manhattan 1969-72; Dir Nuclear Activs Middle South Sers Inc, NO 1972-77; Gen Mgr, Waterman Inc 1978-; Supvr Reactor Prog US Atoms for Peace Prog, Bogota, Columbia 1963; Vis Prof Tex A&M Univ 1966-67; Adj Prof Univ NM 1962-65; Ks St Univ Rep Atomic Indust Forum 1969-72, Middle S Utilities Inc Rep 1973-77; Inst Nuclear Materials Mgmt: Chm Profl Tng Com 1968-70, Profl Standards & Certification 1970-71, Exec Com 1973-74, Editor Jour 1972-74; Instr Airplane & Instrument Flight 1966-; Chm Adv Coun on Ed, Atomic Indust Forum 1972-77; Reg'd Profl Engr; Profl Orgs; Contbr Articles to Profl Jours; cp/Am Radio Relay Leag; Sierra Clb; Nat Audubon Soc; Tau Kappa Epsilon; hon/Sigma Xi; Pi Mu Epsilon; Sigma Pi Sigma.

CHICCA, VIVIAN THERESA oc/Director Nursing Services; b/Mar 26, 1934; h/1717 Briar Ln, Wharton, TX 77488; ba/Wharton; c/Daniel P, Karl T, Marcella C, Daniel G; p/Napoleon and Theresa Francoeur, Fall River, MA; ed/AD; pa/Dir Nsg Sers, Caney Valley Meml Hosp; ANA; Nat Assn Am Col of Obst & Gyn; hon/W/W Am Wom.

CHILDERS, BILL SANFORD oc/Sales and Marketing; b/Jan 5, 1940; h/Matthews, NC; ba/2707 Hinsdale, Charlotte, NC 28210; m/Hona; c/Billy, Beth; p/Andrew and Lena Cook, Connelly Springs, NC; ed/Univ Neb 1959-62; mil/AUS 1963-65; pa/Sales & Mktg, Childers Co; cp/Citizens Choice; Kiwanis Clb; JCs; Masons; r/Assembly of God; hon/Num Awds Given for Lectg to Over 50,000 People a Yr in Var Locations Around World; Book on Success Principles to be Pub'd Fall 1981.

CHILDERS, TERRY OLIVER oc/Professor, Coach; b/June 4, 1947; h/417 Aumon Rd, Augusta, GA 30909; ba/Augusta; m/Lynne Barfield; c/Terry Jr, Scott, Jason, Matthew; p/H D (dec) and Violet W Childers, Augusta, GA; ed/AS S Ga Col 1967; BS 1970, MS 1976 Ga So Col; mil/Ga ARNG 1970-; pa/Asst Prof & Hd Baseball Coach Augusta Col 1979-; Asst Prof Hlth, PE & Rec, So Ga Col 1975-79; Profl Baseball Player, Chgo Cubs, Milwaukee Brewers, Montreal Expos 1968-75; Assn Profl Baseball Players Am; AACBC; Nat Jr Col Ath Assn; Ga Jr Col Ath Assn; Ga Rec & Pk Soc; Ga So Col Alumni Assn, Pres Pk & Rec Chapt; cp/Pres 2 Yrs Westside Elem Sch PTO; hon/Coach of Yr Region XVII NJCAA 1978; Outstg Yng Men of Am 1977 & 78; OCS Hon Grad 1972; NAIA All-Tourn Team, Recip Silver Glove Awd 1968; MVP So Ga Col 1967; MVP Richmond Acad 1965; Drafted 10th Round by NY Yankees 1965.

CHILDRESS, GRAHAM HUGH oc/Rancher; b/Feb 17, 1936; h/PO Box 53, Dryden, TX 78851; ba/Same; m/Marion Lois Ward; c/Connie, Hugh Ward; p/Hugh Jr and Rachel Graham Childress, Ozona, TX; ed/BA Rice Univ 1958; mil/USN Lt Cmdr; pa/Rancher; Tex Sheep & Goat Raisers Assn; cp/Co Commr, Terrell Co Pct 4; Masonic Order; r/Meth; hon/Trustee, Scottish Rite Hosp for Crippled Chd.

CHILDRESS, THOMAS BURNS oc/Law Student; b/Dec 16, 1945; h/Box 391, Pocahontas, VA 24635; p/Sidney Burns Chldress, Clintwood, VA; Frances B Childress, Pocahontas, VA; ed/BS 1968, MA 1972 E Tenn St Univ; Att'g Antioch Sch Law; mil/AUS 1969-71; pa/Juvenile & Domestic Relats Probation Cnslr 1974-80; Va Juv Ofcrs' Assn; cp/Taze Co, Va Trans Safety Comm 1975-; Tazewell Co, Va Devel Corp 1975-76; Del Va St Dem Conv 1976, 78, 80; Precnt Com-man 1976; Yng Dems; r/1st U Meth Ch; hon/Pi Gamma Mu.

CHILDS, JAMES RIVES oc/American Ambassador (Retired); Writer; Scholar in Residence; b/Feb 6, 1893; h/Hotel Jefferson, Richmond, VA 23220; ba/Ashland, VA; p/John William and Lucy Brown Childs (dec); ed/BA Randolph-Macon Col; MA Harvard Univ; mil/AUS, 2/Lt 1917; pa/Scholar-in-Residence, Randolph-Macon Col; In Charge of Cipher Bur, GHQAEF & Liaison Ofcr, French & British War Ofcs 1918; Am Comm to Negotiate Peace, Paris 1918-19; Am Relief Adm, Kazan, USSR 1921-23; cp/London, Va Writers Clb; Pres Pvt Lib Assns; r/Meth; hon/Medal of Freedom; Recommended for Medal of Merit as Charge d'Affaires in Tangier, 1941-50.

CHILES, DAVID LEE oc/Executive; b/May 10, 1937; h/Alice, TX; ba/PO Box 669, Alice, TX 78332; m/Cora Lee Duke; c/Wade Lee, Jace Ray, Viki Lyn; p/Roger Lewis and Gertrude Imogene David Chiles; mil/AUS 1957-60; cp/Owner Oilfield Ser Co; Owner Simmental & Simbrah Cattle; Nat Fed Indep Bus; Am Simmental Assn; cp/Nat Rifle Assn; Alice Fair Assn; r/Prot; hon/Tex Hist Inst.

CHIODO, VINCENT MICHAEL PAUL oc/Student; b/July 18, 1959; h/125 Brooke View Dr, Follensbee, WV 26037; p/Vincent J and Josephine D Chiodo, Follansbee, WV; ed/Att'g WVU, Med Tech Prog; cp/K of C; Mus St Theresa's Roman Cath Ch; r/Rom Cath; hon/Dean's List Each Sem 1977-80; Col 4-H Clb; W/W Am HS Students; Grad Pt Aver 3.91 on 4.0 Scale.

CHISAMORE, RUTH MARION TREVORROW oc/Artist; b/Mar 7, 1927; h/PO Box 213, Bellows Falls, VT 05101; PO Box 8, Bethel Springs, TN 38315; m/Glenn I; c/Theodore J, Ruth C Towsley; p/William Bryant Sr and Ruth Fanny Trevorrow, Bellows Falls, VT; ed/Westminster, Vt Commun Col 1975; Jackson St Commun Col 1980; Ext Courses Jackson St 1981; pa/Free-Lance Artist; Exhib Chester Art Guild; Adamsville Art Assn; Chester Art Guild; Tenn Art Leag; Miniature Art Soc of Fla; cp/Past Brownie Troop Ldr; Past Mem Falls Neighborhood Action Coun Inc; r/Meth; hon/1st Prize Ribbon Acrylic Painting, 2nd Prize Ribbon Oil Painting, 1980 McNairy Co Fair; Featured Artist, Chester Art Guild.

CHISHOM, ANDREW JAMES oc/Criminology; b/Oct 17, 1942; h/124 Forest Fern Rd, Columbia, SC 29210; ba/Columbia; m/Lottie

Screen; c/Mark, Andre, Wendi; p/Junious and Janie Chishom, Augusta, GA; ed/BA Univ Md 1969; MA 1972, Doctorate 1975 Univ Ga; Studies Harvard Grad Sch of Ed 1980; mil/USAF 1962-66; pa/Spec Asst to Pres, Prof Univ SC, Dept Crim Just 1979-; US Marshall 1977-79; Dept Just Transition Team Mem 1977; Dir Minority Affairs, Carter-Mondale Pres Campaign, 1976; Asst Prof USC 1975-77; Instr Univ Ga 1973-75; Coor Ofc of Gov SC 1972-73; Coor Vol Ser, Dept Probation, Ga 1971-72; Field Dir Urban Leag 1970-71; Chm Bd Co & City of Greenville Commun Org for Drug Control 1970-71; Juvenile Plcmt Ofcr 1960-70; Prog Planner Metro Police Dept, Wash DC 1968-69; Adm Aide Ho of Rep Ga 1967; Police Foun 1978-; Police Exec Res Forum 1977-; So Assn Crim Just Edrs 1975-; Nat Assn Blacks in Crim Just 1974-; Am Soc Criminology 1973-; Nat Coun Crime & Delinquency 1973-; Am Correctional Assn 1972-; cp/U Way of the Midlands; Chm Seven-Thirty Breakfast Clb; Pop Warner Fball Meadowlake Falcons Coach 1975-78; r/Bapt; hon/Men of Achmt 1979 & 1981; DIB 1981; Intl W/W Commun Ser 1980; Commun Ldrs Am 1980; Intl Dic World Figures 1979; Personalities of South 1979; Plaque for Outstg Commitment & Contbn, Nat Assn Blacks in Criminal Just at Sixth Annual Conf 1979; Book of Honor 1979; Dept Just Spec Achmt Awd 1978; Nom'd Ten Top Yng Men in Am 1978; Commun Ldrs & Noteworthy Ams Awd 1978; W/W: Black Am, Fed Govt 1977; Outstg Personality of South Awd 1977; Presented Key to City of Columbia 1977; Outstg Humanitarian Awd, Polit Action Com, St of SC 1977; Dist'd Achmt Awd in Criminal Just by Palmetto St Law Enforcement Ofcrs Assn 1977; Cert Apprec for Profl & Dedicated Ser to Law Enforcemnt by Palmetto St Law Enforcement Ofcrs Assn Ladies Aux 1977; Presented Key to City of Phila; 1976; Presented Key to City of Dallas 1976; Presented Plaque for Outstg Work & Co-Fdg Nat Assn Blacks in Crim Just 1976; Outstg Legal Ed, Ga Bar Assn 1975; Andy Chishom Day, Greenville 1971; Outstg Citizen, Greenville 1971; Outstg Commun Awd Black Coun for Progress Greenville 1971; Outstg Citizen, Miss Black SC Beauty Pageant Inc 1971.

CHITTY, JAMES R JR oc/Retired Postmaster; b/Feb 23 1921; h/PO Box 823, Olar, SC 29843; m/Nadine B; c/Phillis, Rusty; p/James R Sr and Fannie Allen Chitty, Olar, SC; ed/Wofford Col 1939-42; mil/WWII Sgt; pa/Appt'd Postmaster, Olar, SC Dec 1 1952 by Pres Harry S Truman; Comm'd Postmaster 1955 by Pres Dwight D Eisenhower; Ret'd 1980; Nat Assn Postmasters; Natl Leag Postmasters; Ret'd Leagr, Nat Leag Postmasters; cp/Charter Mem Olar Lions Clb; r/Bapt; hon/Ser Awd 1980; Philippine Liberation Medal; APT Ser Medal; Am Theater Ribbon; WWII Victory Medal.

CHITWOOD, LORENE McDANIEL oc/Retired Principal; b/Dec 1, 1914; h/110 Val Dr, Dalton, GA 30720; m/Claude D; c/James L; p/D M and Nettie L McDaniel, Ringgold, Ga; ed/AB magna cum laude Carson Newman Col; MA UTC; pa/Ret'd Elem Sch Prin; DAE; GAE; NEA; GAESP; NAESP; cp/Lesche Wom's Clb; Hist Soc; ADK Hon Soc; r/Bapt; hon/Sec Hon Grad for HS.

CHLAPEK, CALVIN JOE oc/Controller-Vice President, Secretary; b/Oct 19, 1941; h/309 W Walker, Temple, TX 76501; ba/Temple; m/Joyce J Fuchs; c/Christopher Charles, Matthew Brian; p/Joe V and Mary R Chlapek, Temple, TX; ed/BBA Tex A&M Univ; pa/Am Desk Mfg Co, Wood-Arts Plas Clad, Inc, Temple Prods Inc; Arthur Andersen & Co, Superior Oil Co; cp/Cultural Activities Ctr; r/Evangelical Brethren Ch, Bd of Elders.

CHRIETZBERG, BERTHA CLARK oc/Assistant Professor; b/Oct 2, 1919; h/1715 Elrod St, Murfreesboro, TN 37130; ba/M'boro; m/James; c/Susan C, James III, Dinsie C; p/Dwight G (dec) and Bertha C Clark, Greenville, AL; ed/BS Univ Ala 1941; MEd MTSU 1968; Post Grad Studies; pa/Asst Prof Rec, Aquatics & First Aid, MTSU 1969-; AAHPER; Tenn Rec & Pks Assn; Tenn Secy, Bd Dirs Am Camping Assn; Bd Dirs Tenn Trails Assn; Bd Dirs Tenn Scenic Rivers Assn; Bd Dirs Am Red Cross; cp/Chm M'boro Bikeways Com; MTSU Energy Coun; r/Meth; hon/Girl Scout Thanks Badge 1972; Article "Wild Flowers, Trees and Nature's Bounty."

CHRISTIAN, LINDA KAY oc/Human Resources Management; b/May 7, 1952; h/4155 Essen Ln #202, Baton Rouge, LA 70809; ba/Baton Rouge; p/John Edward and Catherine Spooner Christian, W Lafayette, IN; ed/BS Purdue Univ 1974; MS 1975 & 76; pa/Human Resources Mgmt, Exxon Chem Co USA; AAAS; ACS; NEHA; Intl Communs Assn; Ind Acad Sci Purdue Alumni Assn; Pres Coun Purdue Univ; cp/Pres Purdue Alumni Assn of Baton Rouge; Adv Jr Achmt Baton Rouge; r/Presb; hon/Sigma Xi; Iota Sigma Pi; Rho Chi; Eta Sigma Gamma; Grad F'ship Purdue Univ; Nat Sci Foun Res Grant; Inst for Envir Hlth Res Grant; Dist'd Student Awd; 1974 Purdue Wom of Yr.

CHRISTIAN, MARY T oc/Educational Administrator; h/1104 West Ave, Hampton, VA 23669; ba/Hampton; ed/BS Hampton Inst 1955; MA Columbia Univ 1960; PhD Mich St Univ 1967; Hampton Inst: Dir Div of Ed & Exec Dir Non-graded Follow Through Model 1975-, Chperson Dept Elem Ed 1970, Instr Dept Elem Ed 1960-65; Instr, Dept Elem & Spec Ed, Mich St Univ 1966 (Sum); Elem Tchr, Aberdeen Sch, Hampton 1955-60; Vis Lectr; Conslt; Spkr; Workshop Dir; Profl Presentations & Pubs; Intl Reading Assn; Nat Coun Tchrs Eng; AAUW; Caucus for Black Sch Bd Mems; Va Ed Assn; AAUP; cp/Bd Dirs: Peninsula Assn Retarded Chd, CENTEX Telecommunications; Hampton Sch Bd; St Adv Bd on Tchr Cert; Bd Trustees: Cornell Univ, Peninsula Nature Sci Ctr; Life Mem NAACP; Delta Sigma Theta; Others; r/1st Bapt Ch: F'ship Choir; hon/Kappa Delta Phi; Alpha Kappa Mu; Pi Beta Theta; Ebony Awd; Cert of Merit, Wom's Senate, Hampton Inst; Phi Kappa Phi; Nat Coun Negro Wom Awd; Christian R and Mary F Lindback Awd; Merit Awd for Commun Ser, NAACP; Outstg Alumni Awd, Hampton Inst; Hampton Ed Assn Cit; Delta Sigma Theta Merit Awd; NAACP Ser to Yth Awd; Others.

CHRISTIAN, SAMUEL TERRY oc/Research Scientist, Professor, Author; b/Dec 4, 1937; h/1004 Riverchase Pkwy, W Birmingham, AL 35244; ba/B'ham; m/Nancy Lee Naylor; c/Teri Lei, Samuel Lawrence, John Eric; p/Homer B Christian, Kenova, WV; Marie Christian (dec); ed/BS; PhD Biochem; pa/Univ Ala Med Ctr: Prof Neurobiol, Assoc Prof Biochem, Assoc Prof Physiol & Biophysics, Chief Neurochem Sect (Neurosics Prog); hon/NDEA Fellow; Fellow Am Inst Chems; Hon Order Ky Cols.

CHRISTIANSEN, KENT M oc/College Professor; b/Dec 31, 1928; h/18 W Palmcroft, Tempe, AZ 85282; ba/Tempe; m/Margaret B; c/Maureen, Mary Ann, Susan, Stephen, Karen, Jane, John, Carolyn; p/James Loran and Thelma Park Christiansen, Moreland, ID; ed/BS 1954, MS 1958 Brigham Yg Univ; PhD Mich St Univ 1965; pa/Col Prof, Ariz St Univ, Tempe; Dir of Student Sers, Col of Ed 1966-; Vis Lectr, Gonzaga Univ 1970; Asst Prof, Counselor Ed, Univ Wyo 1965-66; Instr, Counselor-Lansing Commun Col 1965; Social Sci Instr, Asst Coach-Snake River HS 1954-55; Adj & Pers Ofcr USAF 1955-57; Chm Rocky Mtn Reg of Acad Affairs Admrs 1977-78; Prog Chm 5th Annual Conf of Rocky Mtn Reg of Acad Affairs Admrs 1977; Participant in World Assembly of Intl Coun on Ed for Tchg, Wash DC, 1976; Prin Investigator of Selected Studies in Ed Prog; Kappa Delta Pi: Nat VP for Chapt Devel 1972-74, CoChm on Multi-Cult & Intl Ed Conf Ariz St Univ 1970; Prog CoDir on Ed & the Intl Ed Conf Ariz St Univ 1970; Nat Coun on Accreditation for Tchr Ed, Sub-Chm 1970-71; Career Devel Conslt for Hd Start Supplementary Tng Prog 1967-69; Fac Grant-in-Aid 1967-68; Others; Assn of Mormon Counselors & Psychologists; Am Pers & Guid Assn; Am Col Pers Assn; Intl Coun on Ed for Tchg; Assn of Acad Affairs Admrs; Kappa Delta Pi, Life Mem; cp/Notary Public; LDS Bishop; Unsuccessful Cand for Local Sch Bd; Past ASU Rep to Ariz Col Assn; Registrars Adv Com; Univ Adms Bd; Col of Ed; Blue Ribbon Task Force on Certification, St of Ariz; Standards Com Chm, Adm-Rentention Standards Com Chm; r/Ch of Jesus Christ LDS; Bishop, Tempe 3rd Ward; hon/USAF ROTC Dist'd Grad; Kappa Delta Pi; Grad Asst; Fac Grant-in-aid; Pub'd Articles in Profl Jours.

CHRISTOPHER, CHARLES AUGUSTUS oc/Physician; b/Aug 13, 1943; h/Corpus Christi, TX; ba/2601 Hosp Blvd #218, Corpus Christi, TX; 78405; m/Marjon Alicia King; c/Melissa Charlene, Charles Augustus II; p/Roscoe (dec) and Emily Christopher, Pecos, TX; ed/BS Huston-Tillotson Col 1966; MD Meharry Med Col 1974; mil/AUS 1968-70; Tex NG 1978- Capt; pa/Phys Fam Med 1977-; Meml Med Ctr 1974-77; IBM Br Ofc Adm 1969; US Job Corps Prog 1965-69; AMA; TMA; TMF; Nueces Co Med Soc; AAFP; APPA; Am Soc Clin Hypnosis; Gulf Coast Chapt AAFP; Spohn Hosp: Emer Ser Com, Fam Prac-Med Care Eval Com, Patient Care Com; Meml Med Ctr: Fam Prac-Med Care Eval Com, Utilization Review Com; cp/Omega Psi Phi; M W Prince Hall Grand Lodge F&AM: Lyons Jr Lodge #290; Webb Smith Consistory 32° Mason Consistory #247; Ancient Egyptian Arabic Order Nobles of Mystic Shrine Cheops #200; Cand 33° Prince Hall F&AM in Orlando, Fla 1980; NAACP; Gulf Coast Golfers Assn; r/Meth; hon/W/W Students in Am Cols & Univs 1965; Student of Yr Meharry Med Col 1974; DeWitt Wallace S'ship 1970; Kendall Foun S'ship 1973-74; Bd Trustees Meharry Med Col 1974-75; Outstg Yng Men Am 1974 & 76; W/W Black Ams 1977-78; Humanitarian Awd Yng Mens Progressive Clb 1979.

CHURCH, AVERY GRENFELL oc/University Teacher; Author; b/Feb 21, 1937; h/351 Azalea Rd, Apt B-28, Mobile, AL 36609; ba/Mobile; p/Avery M & Eulah Lowe Church, Winston-Salem, NC; ed/BA cum laude Baylor Univ 1962; MA 1965, Addit Grad Work Univ Colo; mil/USN 1955-57, Hon Disch; pa/Lectr of Anthropology, Univ S Ala, Mobile; Res Staff & Bd Dirs Sociological & Anthropol Sers Inst Inc, Mobile; Asst Prof Anthropol, Memphis St Univ 1965-66 & 69-72; Indian Ed Proj, Univ Colo 1966-69; Tchg Asst, Univ Colo 1965; Navaho Urban Relocation Proj, Univ Colo 1964-; Sev Profl Orgs; Ala Acad Sci: VChm Anthropol 1975-76, VPres 1976-77, & Exec Com 1975-77; cp/Panelist Symposium on Drug Use for PTA Ldrs, Memphis St Univ 1970; Conf on Suicide, Univ Tenn Med Units, Memphis 1971; & Race & Mem Am Mus of Natural Hist, Nat Hist Soc, & Smithsonian Inst; Monetary Contbns to UF & Others; Vol Work for Cands; r/Guest Lectr Sev Rel Orgs; hon/Alpha Kappa Delta; Sev F'ships; Sev Profl Papers & Pubs; Num Pubs in Poetry; Other Biogl Listings; Fellow Am Biogl Inst.

CHURCH, LLOYD EUGENE oc/Dentist; Oral Surgeon; Teacher; b/Sept 25, 1919; h/7005 Glenbrook Rd, Bethesda, MD; ba/Bethesda; m/Hildegard Cascio; c/Pamela Gail; p/Howard Church (dec); Mary Naomi Henderson (dec); ed/Univ Wis-Madison; BA WVa Univ 1942; DDS Univ Md Dental Sch 1944; MS 1951, PhD 1959 Geo Wash Univ; mil/AUS Dental Corps 1946-48, Capt; 2 Medals; pa/Pract of Oral Surg 1948-; Vis Scientist Armed Forces Inst of Path, Wash DC 1962-63; Vis Prof Anatomy & Oral Surg, Bangalore Univ Dental Col, India 1966; Assoc Professorial Lectr in Surg (Oral), Geo Wash Univ Med Ctr 1973-74; Num Other Tchg Positions; Hosp Affils: Suburban Hosp Bethesda, Holy Cross Hosp Silver Sprg, Md, Wash Hosp Ctr, Wash DC & Num Others; Pres's Com on Employmt of Physically Handicapped 1961-75; Govs Com on Employmt of Physically Handicapped 1966-75; Chm Sub Com on Med Rehab 1965-67; Adv Com Dental Lab Technol Tng Prog of Montgomery Jr Col 1968-75; Profl Orgs; Profl Spkr; Conslt; cp/Sev Alumni Affils; Num Masonic Activs; Bethesda Kiwanis Clb; Bethesda-Chevy Chase C of C; Others; r/Bethesda Meth Ch: Past Pres Mens Clb, Past Usher, Past Mem Ofcl Bd & Steward, Past Mem Adm Bd, Other Activs; hon/Pub'd Author; Cited in *Congl Record*; Biogl Listings; Mil Order of WW's Cit; Cert of Dist'd Citizenship, St of Md; B'nai B'rith Awd of Merit: Gaithersburg, Md, Wash DC; Hon Mem Order of the Alhambra; Other Awds; Num F'ships; Num Hon Frats.

CHURCHWELL, JOHN RICHARD oc/Minister; b/Mar 8, 1919; h/Hazel, KY; m/Lois V; c/Lois Loretta Franks, Angela Louise Duffy, Florence Loraine Dunnavant; p/John Lewis and Florence Larue Churchwell; ed/Bailey Meter Schs 1958-60; Mid-South Bible Inst 1961-61; Emory Univ 1968-72; pa/Meth Min; Computer Spec; ARL; Intl Mission Radio Assn; r/Prot; hon/Hon Awd Lambuth Col 1975.

CINTRON, EMMA V oc/Counselor, Columnist; b/Aug 8, 1926; h/Box 3263, Inter-Am Univ, San German, PR 00753; m/Jorge N; c/Emma L, Ileana T; p/Jose Wargas Bocheciamppi (dec); Maria Teresa Rivera (dec); ed/BA 1973; MA 1975; Doct Cand; pa/Newspaper Columnist *El Mundo*; Student Clin Psych; AGPA; PRGPA; Humanist Assn; Phi Delta Kappa; Psych Assn; cp/Ladies Lions Clb; Grandmothers Clb; Partido Popular Democratico; r/Meth; hon/Kappan of Yr 1979; W/W S&SW; Articles in *Impacto, Colinas, PR Evangelico, El Mundo*.

CISSELL, WILLIAM BERNARD oc/Assistant Professor; b/Apr 21, 1941; h/1418 Meadowbrook Dr, Johnson City, TN 37601; ba/Johnson City; m/Mary Ellen Siebe; c/Lisa Kyung Mi; p/James Sylvester and Lucille Marie Bagsby Cissell; ed/BS So Ill Univ-Carbondale 1967; MSPH Univ Calif-LA 1970; mil/USAF 1961-64; pa/Asst Prof E Tenn St Univ Dept Hlth Ed 1979-; Univ Tex Dept Phy & Hlth Ed 1977-79; Dept Defense Schs 1972-77; APHA; AAHE; SPHE; cp/Adv Explorer Post #81 1975-77; Explorer Coor Far East Coun 1974-75; Mem Sev Alcohol & Drug Abuse Control Coms 1972-75; Bd Mem Am Cancer Soc 1979; hon/Phi Kappa Phi 1971; Articles: "Health Education in America"; "I Looked at Hooked"; Contbr to *Death and Dying* 1979.

CIVEY, GEORGE ARNOTT III oc/Art Historian, Critic; b/Jan 20, 1944; h/Richmond, KY; m/Mary Janet Eberwein; c/Jorgianne Irene; p/George Arnott Civey II, McComb, MS; Annette Newcomer Foley Civey (dec); ed/BA Transylvania Univ; MA Univ Ia; Cand PhD UNC-Chapel Hill; mil/USAF 1966-68; pa/Art Hist; Asst Prof Art, En Ky Univ 1975-; Tchg Asst Univ NCCH 1974-75; Instr Art Hist & Crit Memphis St Univ 1971-74; AAUP En Ky Univ; Col Art Assn; SE Col Art Conf; cp/Lions Intl; Nat Adv Bd Am Security Coun; hon/Acad S'ship Transylvania Univ 1962-66; Nat Defense F'ship; Univ Ia 1969-70; Excell in Tchg Awd, Fac Arts & Scis, En Ky Univ 1977-78; Reg Contbr *Goldsmith's Journal Metalsmith*.

CLAPP, JOHN VAN oc/Data Design Organization; b/June 24, 1946; h/1510 Woods Rd, Winston-Salem, NC 27106; ba/Winston-Salem; m/Susan B; p/Hugh Van (dec) and Irene Tilley Clapp, Greensboro, NC; ed/Miami-Dade Jr Col 1966; Brevard Engrg Col 1968; mil/AUS Signal Corp 1968-69; pa/Supvr Western Elec Co 1970-; Boeing Co, Kennedy Space Ctr Fla 1966-70; Ryan Elec Div of Gables Engrg 1964-66; STC; Toastmasters Intl Area Gov 1980-81; cp/4-H; Boy Scouts; Explorers; JCs; FBLA; DECA; Coach Yth Fball, Baseball, Ice Hockey; VP Winston Salem Amateur Ice Hockey Assn; Chm Engrs Week Symposium for Wn Elec Co; Pres Top Toastmasters Clb in St NC 1979; Won Num Speech Contests.

CLAPP, LAWRENCE EVERETT oc/Pastor; b/July 26, 1955; h/18 Oteen Ch Rd, Asheville, NC 28805; ba/Asheville; p/E W and Virgie Culler Clapp, Marshville, NC; ed/BA Gardner Webb Col 1977; MDiv SEn Bapt Theol Sem; pa/Pastor Oteen Bapt Ch; NC Assoc Pastor & Yth Dir First Bapt Ch Gibsonville 1976-80; First Chaplain in Guilford Co Sheriff's Dept

& Jail 1980; cp/Pres Assnl Evangelism 1971-73; Hon Lifetime Dpty, Guilford Co Sheriff's Dept; r/Bapt; hon/Mus Awd 1968-69; 2nd Prize Constitution Essay, DAR 1972; FOCUS S'ship 1974-75; Cert of Ordination 1979; Basketball Champs 1980.

CLAR, BARRY DAVID oc/Attorney; b/May 6, 1948; h/208 Burnet, Pt Lavaca, TX 77979; ba/Pt Lavaca; m/Lois Jane; p/Simon and Adele Clar, Rockville, MD; ed/BA Univ Md 1970; JD Univ Houston 1977; mil/AUS Security Agcy 1970-73; pa/Atty at Law, Asst Criminal DA, Calhoun Co, Tex; Am Bar Assn; cp/Pres Pt Lavaca JCs 1979-80.

CLARK, ALPHONSO H oc/Pastor; b/Dec 27, 1903; h/Charleston, SC; m/Anna L; p/Thomas (dec) and Flora E Clark; ed/BDiv Benedict Col 1950; BA Morris Col 1972; pa/Pastor Meml Bapt Ch, Charleston; cp/Exec Com Chaston NAACP; Bd Dirs Robert Gould Shaw Boys Clb; Exec Bd Ednl & Missionary Conv of SC; VModr Chaston Co Bapt Ass n; Trustee of Morris Col; Religious Tchr Bapt Ednl Foun Ctr; Mason; Phi Beta Sigma.

CLARK, ANNIE FRANCES oc/Auditor; b/Feb 26, 1922; h/107 Pine Needle Trail, Anderson, SC 29621; ba/Anderson; m/Gushion B Jr; c/William Martin; p/Hoyt Z Sr (dec) and Savannah C Martin (dec); pa/Anderson Co Auditor's Ofc 1948-; Assn Assessing Ofcls; 2nd VP SC Auditors & Treas Assn 1980-81; SC Assn; City of Anderson Mayors Com; cp/BPW Clb; r/Bapt.

CLARK, CHARLES DOUGLAS oc/Physician; b/Feb 6, 1924; h/801 516th, Murray, KY 42071; ba/Murray; m/Mary Ann; c/Pamela, Charles D Jr, Hollis J; p/Urban P and Virgie M Clark, Kirksey, KY; ed/MD Univ Tenn-Memphis; mil/AUS 1943-45; pa/Pres Ky Acad Fam Phys; Dir AHES 1977-78; Preceptor UK & UL Med Schs 1975; r/Meth; hon/Chief of Staff Murray Hosp 1953, 1960, 1971; Fellow AAFP 1972.

CLARK, CYDNE ERICCA oc/Student; b/Feb 23, 1963; h/1 Peach Orchard Hill, Rt 1, Box 71A, Watauga, TN 37694; p/Leif Ericsson and Annas Thompson Clark, Watauga, TN; pa/Student, Elizabethton HS; cp/Mem 1980 Olympic Clb; Newspaper Staff 2 Yrs; JTeens; Ski Clb; Lang Clb; Girls Basketball; Track Team; r/Christian; hon/Elizabeth Assembly #71 Intl Order of Rainbow for Girls, Received Grand Cross of Color Deg 1978, Appt'd Grand Rep to Alaska from Tenn 1979; Jr Miss Rhododendron 1979; First Class Awd Girl Scout 1978.

CLARK, DORIS JEAN WRIGHT oc/Part-time Nurse; b/Dec 17, 1930; h/1220 S Crockett St, Sherman, TX 75090; m/Donald J; c/Bruce Edward, Keith Edwin, Leigh Ellen; p/Gertrude L, Sherman, TX; ed/Decatur Bapt Col 1950; AN Grayson Co Col 1975; pa/Pt-time OB Nurse; Pres Grayson Co Guid Clin; Pres Sherman Ser Leag; cp/Pres Sherman Mus Arts; Pres Needlework Guild of Am; Pres Sherman City Coun PTA, Hon Life Mem; Bd Tex Wom's Assn for Symph Orch; Bd Sherman Hist Mus; Bd Sherman Girls Clb; r/Bapt; hon/Hon Life Mem PTA; Beta Sigma Phi Girl of Yr.

CLARK, ELIZABETH ADAMS oc/Property Mistress; Instructor; b/Jan 16, 1944; h/703 Orchard St, Hendersonville, NC 28739; ba/Flat Rock, NC; m/Eugene; c/Mary Corry, Walter Emmett; p/Calvin Emmett Adams, Arcadia, FL; Ruth Gertrude Paxton, Arcadia, FL; ed/BS Ga Col; pa/Prop Miss Flat Rock Playhouse, St Theater of NC; Instr Geneal, Blue Ridge Tech; AAUW; cp/Corres Secy Henderson Co Dem Wom; Bd Hendersonville Little Theater; Org'g Pres French Broad River Soc Chd Am Revolution; Pres Mt Bloomers Garden Clb; r/Epis; hon/Outstg Wom in Commun, Ardairsville, Ga 1974.

CLARK, MARIE TRAMONTANA oc/Businesswoman; b/Apr 21, 1940; h/16350 Hanna Rd, Lutz, FL 33549; ba/Same; m/Robert Julian Jr; c/Julie Ann, Robert Julian III; p/Joseph S and Nadean Weeks Tramontana, Tampa, FL; ed/BA Univ So Fla; mil/USO Entertainment; pa/Dir T Clark Modeling & Talent Agcy; cp/Krene of Venus; Latin Am Fiesta Assn; Goodwill Tour Spain-Portugal; Tampa Christian Wom's Clb, Proj Advr 1978-80; hon/Nat Model of Yr 1972; W/W Am Wom 1979-80; Univ Fla Singing Sweethearts 1958-59.

CLARK, NILES CRAIG JR oc/US Army Officer; b/May 29, 1933; h/PO Box 21, Waterloo, SC 29384; ba/Corpus Christi, TX; m/Ruth Amis; c/N Craig III; Thomas A, Steven M; p/Niles C (dec) and Agnes Anderson Clark, Waterloo, SC; ed/BS Clemson Univ 1955; MBA Univ Tenn 1971; AUS Command & Gen Staff Col 1972; Nat Defense Univ 1980; mil/Col AUS Transp Corps; Mil Occupl Specs of Aviation Mat Mgmt & Transp Mgmt; pa/Dir Maintenance, Corpus Christi Army Depot; Designated to be Army Depot Cmdr June 1981; Army Aviation Assn Am; Assn AUS; r/Meth; hon/Bronze Star Medal for Valor & 3 Oak Leaf Clusters; Merit Ser Medal 1977; Air Medal w 24 Oak Leaf Clusters; Jt Ser Commend Medal 1973; Army Commend Medal 1973; Purple Heart 1968; Master Army Aviator Badge 1978.

CLARK, WILLARD oc/Retired Merchant; b/Jan 16, 1915; h/Lacey

PERSONALITIES OF THE SOUTH

Springs, AL; p/Henry F and Nancy Mae Clark, Lacey Springs, AL; mil/AUS 1942-46; pa/Ret'd Merchant; cp/Am Legion Cmdr; r/Bapt.

CLARKSON, CHARLES ANDREW oc/Real Estate Investment Management; b/Sept 9, 1945; h/5201 Atlantic Blvd, Jacksonville, Fl 32207; ba/J'ville; m/Patricia H; c/Thomas Byerly, Blair Elizabeth; p/Harold William Clarkson; Jean Henrietta Jaxtheimer; ed/AB Princeton Univ 1963-67; JD Geo Wash Univ 1968-72; pa/Real Est Invest Mgmt; cp/C of C Com of 100; Ponte Vedra, Sawgrass, River Clb.

CLARKSON, LAWRENCE WILLIAM oc/Business Executive; b/Apr 29, 1938; h/272 Via Marila, Palm Beach, FL 33480; ba/W Palm Beach; m/Barbara Stevenson; c/Michael Warren, Elizabeth Louise, Jennifer Lynn; p/Harold William and Jean Jaxtheimer Clarkson, Palm Beach Shores, FL; ed/BA DePauw Univ 1960; JD Univ Fla 1962; mil/USAF 1962-66 Capt; pa/Mktg VP; Am Bar Assn; Am Judicature Soc; Fla Bar; cp/Palm Beach Co Coun of Arts; r/Epis.

CLARY, JOHN PAUL oc/Plant Manager; b/Mar 20, 1937; h/212 N 2nd St, Smithfield, NC 27577; ba/Clayton, NC; m/June Livingston; c/Mary Kathrine, Damon Garner, Dirk Elliot, Candace Elise; p/John S Clary, W Palm Beach, FL; Mary G Wettig, Homestead, FL; mil/AUS Signal Corps 1957-60; pa/Plant Mgr PCB Mfg, NC Div Data Gen Corp; IEEE; AIIE; cp/Johnston Co Commun Devel Com; Rep Data Gen at Clayton C of C; r/Presb; hon/Awd of Excell for Essay on the Role of Bus in Fight Against Communism 1967; Author *The Art of Hiring Supermen*; Wrote Articles & Made Presentation at IEEE Conv 1970.

CLAYTON, BILLY WAYNE oc/Speaker of Texas House of Representatives; b/Sept 11, 1928; h/PO Box 38, Springlake, TX 79082; ba/Austin; m/Delma Jean; c/Thomas Wayne, Brenda Jean Smith; p/William Thomas (dec) and Myrtle Clayton, Springlake, TX; ed/BS Tex A&M Univ 1950; pa/Farmer, Rancher 1950-; Exec Dir Water Inc, Lubbock, Tex 1968-72; Pres Springlake Enterprises Inc, Texhold Inc; cp/St Rep Dist 74 1962- & Spkr Tex House 1975-; Chm Aero Com, Cos Com, Livestock Com, Interim Water Com, V-Chm Banks & Bnkg Com; W Tex Adv Com Water Devel Bd; Chm Interst Conf Water Probs 1973; Coun St Govts 1977-78; Exec Bd W Tex Water Inst; Exec Com So Envir Resources Conf 1973-74; Chm Intergovtl Relats Com, Nat Leg Conf 1973; Mem for Tex Nat Water Cong; Chm So States Spkrs Conf 1975-75; Exec Com So Leg Conf 1973-74, Chm 1975-76; Adv Bd Yng Ams for Freedom; W Tex C of C; W Tex Water Inst; Lions Clb, Past Pres; Trustee High Plains Res Foun, Halfway, Tex; r/Bapt; Deacon; hon/Outstg Farmer in Lamb Co 1967; Hon Water Well Digger 1968; Recip Dist'd Ser to People of Tex Awd 1967; Dist'd Ser Awd, Dem Party Tex 1968; Commend Tex Water Rights Comm 1970; Outstg Ser Awd in Water Conserv 1972; 1st Awd W Tex Water Inst 1971; Chm Coun of St Govts; Past Chm So Legs Conf.

CLAYTON, BOYD LEE oc/Military Officer; b/Mar 29, 1945; h/5273-C Broadway, Eielson AFB, AK 99702; ba/Eielson AFB; m/Jerrolyn; c/Eric Lee, John Buchanan; p/F D and Emily Clayton, Earth, TX; ed/BS Abilene Christian Univ; MA Webster Col; mil/USAF; pa/Maj, USAF; Air Force Assn; r/Ch of Christ; hon/Air Force Commend Medal; Merit Ser Medal; Merit Ser Medal 1st OLC; Merit Ser Medal 2nd OLC.

CLAYTON, DEWAYNE LAMONT oc/Director of Community Development; h/613 N Upper St, Lex, KY 40508; ba/Winchester, KY; m/Marsha; c/Kim, Sheri, Stratford, Gilbert, Jaquita; p/Richard Clayton, NY, NY; Maugaret Clayton, Lex, KY; ed/Univ Ky; mil/AUS Pers Spec; pa/Dir Commun Devel, Winchester, Ky; Nat Urban Leag; Vol in Corrections; r/Bapt; hon/Ky Col; Hon Co Judge.

CLAYTON, JERRY MACK oc/Attorney; b/July 28, 1944; h/Gordon Rd, Alexander City, AL 35010; ba/Alex City; m/Fran; c/Colleen; p/Wilson and Inez Clayton, Alex City, AL; ed/BS Auburn Univ; Jones Law Sch; mil/AUS 1969-71 2nd Lt; pa/Ala Safety Coun; Ala St Bar; cp/Lions Clb; Former JC; r/Bapt.

CLAYTON, ROBERT L oc/Director for Minority Programs; b/Feb 25, 1934; h/Atlanta, GA; m/Minnie Harris; c/Robert Joel III, Myrna Audenise; ed/AB Talladega Col 1955; MDiv Hood Sem 1959; STM Interdenom Theol Ctr 1965; pa/Dir Minority Progs, Am Col Testing Prog; ACPA; AMEG Editorial Bd; ANWC; ASCA; ACES; NAACP; APGA; NVGA; SACES; NACADA; cp/Concerned Citizens of SW Atlanta; Nat Black Edrs Think Tank; Black Fundraisers Assn; r/AME Zion; hon/Danforth Foun Assoc; Contbr to Num Jours.

CLEMENT, JANYE MATTISSON oc/Executive Director Development Center; b/Jan 25, 1916; h/1802 Maxwell Pl, Orangeburg, SC 29115; ba/O'burg; m/Walter Albert; c/Charles Ernest McClinton; p/Ernest Truman Sr (dec) and Nannie Armstrong Mattison, Belton, SC; ed/BA; MS; pa/SC Funeral Dirs Assn; Ch Wom U Org; Secy-Treas Newton Funeral Home; Mem O'burg Area Neighborhood Devel Comm; Treas Mt

Pisgah Bapt Ch Deaconess Bd; O'burg Co Coun on Aging; O'burg Nominating Com for Coun on Aging; Intl Platform Assn; U Way of O'burg Panel 11; cp/Com Chm BSA; Indian Waters Coun; Christian Burial Aid Soc; Wom Missionary Soc; r/Bapt; hon/Intl Reg of Profiler 1979; Intl W/W Intells 1978; Commun Ldrs Am Bicent Meml; DIB; Vital Reg Human Accomplishment; Awd Ldrship Devel Prog 1975-76; Plaque Commun Ldrs Am in Recog of Past Achmt & Outstg Ser to Commun & St 1976-78; Plaque Woman of Yr, O'burg Alumni Chapt Kappa Alpha Psi 1978; St Rec Awd 1978.

CLEMENTS, MASON CARTER SR oc/Wholesale Grocer; b/Oct 5, 1925; h/526 Scotts Way, Augusta, GA 30909; ba/Augusta; m/Fay; c/M Carter Jr, James Bert, Beverly; p/James William Cowan; c/Julia, Clements, Ray City, GA; ed/BS Ga So Col; mil/USMC; pa/Past Pres Ga Wholesale Grocers Assn; Bd Dirs First Nat Bank of Atlanta; cp/Past Pres Exch Clb of Augusta; r/Bapt; hon/Hall of Fame, Ga So Col; W/W 1950.

CLEMONS, CLAIRE NELL oc/Writer; b/June 4, 1937; h/9011 Hempstead Ave, Bethesda, MD 20034; m/James William Cowan; c/Julia, Janet; p/Freela Clemons, Okla City, OK; ed/BA Okla Col Wom 1958; MA Penn St Univ 1961; ed/Educator: Penn St Univ, Am Commun Sch, Am Univ Beirut, Beirut Col Wom, Univ Wis; hon/Author: *Job's Wednesday 1974*; *Monday Morning Magazine*; *Aramco World*.

CLEVELAND, ADOLPHUS oc/Minister; Social Worker; b/Oct 26, 1942; h/PO Box 1791, Lubbock, TX 79408; ba/Lubbock; p/W D Cleveland Sr (dec); Etna J Cleveland, Plainview, TX; ed/BA Wayland Bapt Col 1961; Tex Tech Univ; pa/Pastor, New Jerusalem Bapt Ch 1978-; Tchr, Utah Elem Sch, LA, Cal 1978; Commun Sers Coor, Housing Authority, City of Lubbock; 1976-78; Job Placemt Spec, Goodwill Industs, Lubbock 1976; Attendant, Lubbock St Sch 1974-75; Outreach Worker, Commun Action Bd of Lubbock Co 1973-74; Juvenile Probation Ofcr, Lubbock Co 1968-70; Pastor, Triangle Bapt Ch, Colvis, NM 1966-67; Prog Chm, Lubbock Ministers Assn; Exec Secy, New Zeal Bapt Dist Assn; Lubbock Interdenominational Ministerial Alliance: Past Pres, Past Secy; Former Asst Secy, Bapt Min's Union of Lubbock & Vicinity; cp/Parks & Rec Bd; Neighborhood House Bd Dirs; Good Neighbor Comm; Bd Mem, Interagy Action Coun; Sr Citizens Proj Coun Adv Com; Others; r/Bapt; hon/Outstg Yg Men Am; W/W Am Polits.

CLEVELAND, LYNDA GAIL oc/Company President; b/Oct 26, 1946; h/7006 Kingsbury Dr, Dallas, TX 75238; ba/Dallas; p/Mr and Mrs Ray O Cleveland, Dallas, TX; ed/BA Baylor Univ 1968; MA Tex Tech Univ 1973; ABD; pa/Pres AV Prod Co; Pi Kappa Delta; Sigma Tau Delta; AAUW; Tex St Tchrs Assn; Speech Communs Assn; Tex Speech Assn; AAUP; Tex Assn Col Tchrs; P Merville Larson Debate & Interpretation Soc; Phi Kappa Phi; r/Bapt; hon/Outstg Yng Wom of Am 1979; 6 Nat Freedom Foun Awds 197477; W/W Am Cols & Univs; St & Nat Tchr Awds; Chm Assoc Adv Com DSA 1979-80.

CLICK, PAULA TAMMIE oc/College Student; b/Oct 27, 1957; h/Rt 6, Box 365, Ashland, KY 41101; p/Paul E and Elaine Click, Ashland, KY; ed/AA; BA Marshall Univ; Master's Cand; Univ Ky; mil/Ky Army NG; r/Liberty Missionary Bapt Ch; hon/Outstg Enlisted Guardsman of Yr 1977; Phi Alpha Theta.

CLIFT, ANNIE SUE oc/Nurse Educator; b/Nov 29, 1931; h/Rt 2, Newbern, TN 38059; ba/Martin, TN; p/James Lee (dec) and Mollie Sue Gelzer Clift, Newbern, TN; ed/BSN Univ Tenn Sch Nsg 1954; RN by Exam 1954; Cert Japanese Lang, Tokyo 1944; MRE SWn Bapt Theol Sem 1967; MN Nell Hodgson Woodruff Sch Nsg, Emory Univ 1969; pa/Asst Prof Nsg, Univ Tenn Martin 1973-; RN: Fgn Mission Bd of So Bapt Conv, WI Cook Meml Hosp Ctr for Chd 1960; Harris Hosp 1959-60; Parkview Hosp 1956-59, 1961-62; John Gaston Hosp 1954-55; Newbern St Bank 1949; Am Congress of Rehab Med; Assn Rehab Nurses; Local Hlth Conslt, Head Start, Westinghouse Hlth Sys; AAUP; Co Chm Dept Nsg Eval Com UTM Dept Nsg Lib Com UTM; Dept Nsg Admission, Retention & Policy Com UTM; UTM Res Com; UTM Bldg Com; Dept Nsg Fac Assn UTM; ANA; TNA; Past Pres, Treas, Secy Bd Mem of Dist 12 TNA; Dist 12 TNA Continuing Ed Com; r/So Bapt; hon/W/W S&SW 1980; Articles Pub'd.

CLIFT, MICHAEL E oc/Attorney at Law; b/Apr 6, 1947; h/1106 N Maple Ave, Cookeville, TN 38501; ba/Shelbyville; m/Martha; c/Allison; p/Floyd E and Helen P Clift, Shelbyville, TN; ed/BS 1970, JD 1974 Univ Tenn-Knoxville; pa/Partner Law Firm Moore, Jones & Radr PC; Former Clk, Tenn Ct of Crim Appeals; Former Dir Alumni Affairs, Univ Tenn; Admitted to: US Supr Ct, Tenn Supr Ct, US Dist Ct Appeals 6th Dist, US Dist Ct En Sect, US Dist Ct Middle Sect; Tenn Bar Assns (Pres Yng Lwyr's Sect, Mem Bd Govs); Am Bar Assn; Am Trial Lwyrs Assn; Tenn Trial Lwyrs Assn; Pres Shelbyville & Bedford Co Bar Assn; cp/Rotarian; Shriner; 32° Scottish Rite Mason; Bd Dirs Child Devel Ctr; Bd Trust Bedford Players; Spec Div Chm Heart Fund; BSA; UCF Drives; Scoutmaster Troop 390; VChm BSA Dist; VP, Exec Com, Bd Govs Univ

PERSONALITIES OF THE SOUTH

Tenn Nat Alumni Assn; Dist Chm Two Rivers Dist; Past Pres, Bedford Co Univ Tenn Alumni Assn; Co Chm for Jimmy Carter; Co Chm for Bobo Clement for Gov; Past Treas Bedford Co Dem Clb; r/1st Christian Ch; hon/JC Outstg Yng Man for Bedford Co; Recip Long Rifle Awd, BSA; Phi Sigma Kappa Outstg Alumnus 1973.

CLIMER, TERRY oc/Editor; b/Jan 29, 1951; h/Nashville, TN; ba/1813 Eighth Ave S, Nashville, TN 37203; p/Howard and Willette Bass Climer, Lebanon, TN; ed/Tenn Tech Univ 1969-71; BA Wn Ky Univ 1972-74; pa/Vitdeotape Computer Editor: WLAC-TV/WTVF Nashville, Opryland Prods; Chief Editor Complete Post Prod Ctr, H'wood, Calif; Sr Editor Pacific Video, H'wood; Soc Motion Picture & TV Engrs; r/Bapt; hon/4 Time Emmy Nom; Emmy Finalist 1980; Editor Num Network Specs & Series.

CLINE, ERNESTINE WOLFE oc/Artist, Businesswoman; b/Dec 27, 1936; h/413 Gregory St, Winston-Salem, NC 27101; ba/W-S; c/Lee Malynne, Derek Steven; p/Grover S Cline, Winston-Salem, NC; Ernestine Cline, Winston-Salem, NC; ed/Burton Institute; 5 Pvt Instrs; pa/Owner-Operator Ernestine Originals; cp/Bd Mem Assoc'd Artists of W-S; Vol Art & Pub for Dem Party; r/Bapt; hon/Many Prizes for Paintings & Designs in Art; Paintings in 80 Pvt Collects Across US.

CLINE, JEANIE M oc/Legal Secretary; b/Dec 28, 1940; h/960 S Blvd, Lenoir, NC; m/Vernon S Sr, c/Joey, Vernon H Jr; p/George A Martin, Lenoir, NC; ed/Cert Office Mgmt Inst Govt; Cert Communs Skills Cont'g Ed Ctr Boone; Cert Psych, Hickory, NC; pa/Mem Caldwell Co Bd Ed; Campaigning for Caldwell Co Bd Commrs; Presented "Women in Politics" Prog to ABWA; Former Leg Secy, 25th Jud Dist Secy of Juvenile Cnslg Sers; Dem Wom's Org; Past Mem Sub-Jr Wom's Clb; Past Mem NC St Employees Assn; Assn NC Dist Secys; Fdr Caldwell Chapt Am Bus Wom's Assn; cp/Chm Steering Com to Form Caldwell Co Diabetes Chapt; Area Capt Mothers March on Birth Defects; r/Bapt; hon/Best Secy for Nat Secy Wk 1977; Recog'd for Hard-Wkg Efforts as Area Capt Cystic Fibrosis 1974; Atuhor Short Stores & Poems.

CLINTON, BILL oc/Governor; b/Aug 19, 1946; ba/State Capitol, Little Rock 72201; ed/BS Georgetown Univ 1968; Rhodes S'ship, Univ Col, Oxford, England 1968-70; Yale Law Sch 1973; pa/Gubernatorial Campaign of Just Frank Holt 1966; Asst Clk, US Sen Com on Fgn Relats 1966-68; Re-Elect Campaign, Sen J William Fulbright 1968; Tex St Coor Dem Pres Campaign 1972; Instr Constl Law, Crim Just Adm, Univ New Haven 1972-73; Prof Law, Univ Ark Sch of Law at Fayetteville 1973-79; Ark Bar Assn; Am Bar Assn; cp/Gov Ark, 1979-; Dem Cand for Cong, 3rd Cong Dist 1974; Chm Ark Dem Part Affirm Act Com; Chm Bd, Ark Housing Devel Corp; Atty Gen, 1976; Coor Carter for Pres Campaign in Ark 1978.

CLONTZ, JEAN TONEY oc/Homemaker; b/Aug 16, 1939; h/8 Stone Gate N, Longwood, FL 32750; m/Franklin D; c/Lisa, Todd; p/James B (dec) and Alice E Toney, Sanford, FL; ed/Cornet Acad Modeling; cp/Pres Med Aux Seminole Co Med Soc; Bd Dir Am Cancer Soc; Bd Dirs Ballet Guild Sanford Seminole; Secy En Air Lines Silver Lines, Stewardess Alumni; Chm Breast Cancer Prog for 9th Grade Girls, Seminole Co; CPR Instr; Gator Booster Univ Fla; Bayhead Tennis Team; Seminole Yth Plan'g Coun; Ronald McDonald House; Chm Ladies Golf Tourn for Cancer Soc; Chm Fashion Show Am Heart Assn; Charter Mem Jr Wom's Clb; Cancer Soc Bike-a-Thon; Chm Leg Med Wives; Com on Friends to Elect Sheriff; Past Chm Mother's March of Dimes; Garden Clb; Profl Wives Plan'g Coun; Sch Adv Bd; Fla Med Assn Ednl Res Foun; Chm Hlth Careers; Homeowners Assn; r/Presb; hon/Am Heart Assn Fashion Show for Am Cancer Soc for Outstg Ser & Apprec 1973.

CLOSSER, PATRICK D oc/Printer, Radio-TV; b/Apr 27, 1945; h/3875 Dunhaven, Dallas, TX 75220; ed/Dip Am Sch of Cinema; pa/Printer, Radio, TV, Film: Dr Pepper Commercials; Chiropractic Assn Commercials; Network TV Commercials; Network TV Shows; KVTT 917 FM, KDTX 102.9 FM, KXVI 1200 Am, KBFI Channnel 33; Feature Movies, Films, Theatre Plays; SMPTE; NABET Local 4441; IBEW Local 1257; Nat Rel Broadcasters; Fellow Intl Biogl Ctr; cp/Dallas JCs; r/Epis; hon/Awd from Repub Party 1962; Commemorative Awds; Awds Intl Biogl Ctr; Author Radio Scripts; Artwork for KBFI Chanell 33.

CLOTHIER, JULIETTE CROXTON oc/Court Clerk; b/Oct 10, 1919; h/204 Kingswood Dr, Williamsburg, VA 23183; ba/W'burg; m/John D Jr; c/Juliette Dale Carroll; p/William Edwards Croxton (dec); Sophie Chapman Robinson (dec); ed/AB Col of William & Mary 1936; pa/Clk, Circuit Ct; Mortar Bd; Phi Mu; Va Ct Clk's Assn, Exec Com; cp/W'burg Gdn Clb; Soroptimist Clb; r/Bruton Parish Ch; hon/Gdn Clb of Va.

CLOWER, WILLIAM DEWEY oc/Executive; b/Oct 9, 1935; h/1098 Fairbank St, Great Falls, VA 22066; ba/Wash DC; m/Shirley T; c/Candice D, Michael D, Catherine D; p/Alton O and Addie Y Clower, Salem, VA;

ed/BSEE; MS; mil/USAF 2nd Lt; pa/Pres Food Processing Machinery & Supplies Assn; ASAE; AOPA; Trust FPI; WSAE; Fdr Commonwlth Band & Trust Co; cp/White House Staff 1970-75; RNC Adv Com; r/Presb; hon/Regional Schlr Univ VA 1954-58.

CLUNN, PATRICIA ANN oc/Nurse Educator; b/Apr 17, 1930; h/3500 NW 29th Terr, Gainesville, FL 32605; ba/G'ville; c/Jeffrey, Steven; p/Leslie and Pauline Clunn; ed/RN; MA; MEd; EdD; pa/Nurse Edr, Child Advocate, Univ Fla-G'ville; ANA Test Specification Com; Gen & Clin Spec; Cert Clin Spec, Child & Fam Psych/MH Nsg; r/Prot; hon/W/W Am Wom 1979; Awd from ANA Div Adv'd Nsg for Contbn to Adv'd Prac.

COATS, WAYNE ALFRED oc/Leasing and Management; b/Mar 3, 1954; h/102 Briarcliff Dr, Dunn, NC 28334; m/Rita; c/Steven; p/Thadius A and Darlene Coats, Erwin, NC; ed/Mitchell Jr Col 1973; pa/Pres J&W Leasing & Mgmt; cp/NC JCs; r/Bapt.

COBB, JACK LeROY oc/Superintendent of Grounds; b/Feb 24, 1934; h/3758 Winfield, Ft Worth, TX 75109; ba/Ft Worth; m/Patricia Kay; c/Deborah, Eddie, Larry, James; p/Clyde C Cobb; Nell V Onley; mil/USNR; pa/Supt Grounds, Tex Christian Univ; Tex Turf Assn; cp/Mason; r/Bapt; hon/Nat Red Cross Life Saving Awd.

COBB, JAMES THOMAS oc/Teacher, Coach; b/Aug 7, 1949; h/822 John Mark Dr, Dyersburg, TN 38024; ba/D'burg; c/James Thomas III; p/Harry J Sr and Muriel Cobb, Newbern, TN; ed/BS, MS Univ Tenn-Martin; mil/Tenn ARNG; pa/Tchr & Coach D'burg Middle Sch; DEA; TEA; NEA; D-PACE; T-PACE; N-PACE; cp/1st Chm D'burg PACE; Pres W Tenn Mid Sch Ath Assn; Bd Dir D'burg JCs; Del to Tenn Ed Assn Assem; r/Presb; hon/Keyman of Qtr 1978, Proj of Qtr 1978, Org of D'burg JCs.

COBURN, DAVID THAYER oc/Consultant; b/Aug 2, 1938; h/108 S Columbus St, Arlington, VA 22204; ba/McLean, VA; p/William (dec) and Gladys Louise Thayer Coburn (dec); ed/BS Tulane Univ 1961; MBA Columbia Univ 9163; mil/USAF 1955-57; pa/Cnslt to Retail Auto Dlrs, Nat Auto Dlrs Assn 1976-; Dept Conslg So Buying Assocs 1972-76; Am Mgmt Assn; cp/Oyster Harbor Assn; Antique Auto Clb Am; Randolph Country Clb; r/Prot.

COCHRAN, IVA DELL oc/Artist, Writer; b/Dec 1, 1904; h/1508 Stafford Dr, Ft Worth, TX 76134; ba/Ft Worth; m/George J; c/Billie Louise Janecki; Delaine Carl Duckworth; p/Bryce Monroe (dec) and Pearl Simmons Cochran (dec); ed/Brownwood Christian Col; pa/Mem 4 Clbs; 30 Yrs in CAA; cp/Pres Wom's Good Gov Leag; Highland Commun Clb; Former Mem Wom's Clb; Many Others; r/Bapt; hon/1st Place in Many Art Works, Poems & Stories.

COCHRAN, MARY JO oc/Teacher, Department Head; b/June 12, 1928; h/Chattanooga, TN; m/Walter L Jr, c/Walter L III, Joseph Lynn, Charles Lee; p/Haden P (dec) and Jimmie Alice B Copeland (dec); ed/BS 1948, MS 1970 Auburn Univ; pa/Head & Asst Prof HOEC, Univ Tenn Chat 1971-; Adj Fac, Univ Chat 1964-70; Casewkr Public Asst & Child Ser, Tenn Dept Public Wel 1952-54; Asst cC Agt, Auburn Univ Ext Ser 1950-51; Home Ec, Ala Gas Co 1949-50; Grad Asst, Auburn Univ Sch Home Ec 1949-50; Omicron Nu; Kappa Omicron Pi; Am Home Ec Assn; Tenn Home Ec Assn; Chat Area Nutrition Coun; SEn Regional Assn Home Mgmt; Tenn Col Home Ec Adm; Nat Coun Adm in Home Ec; cp/Consumer Alert; Landmark Inc; Chat Regional Mus; Houston Antique Mus; Chat Hist Soc; Nat Trust for Hist Preserv; r/Meth; hon/W/W S&SW 1980-81; Wrote & Dir'd Res Proj: *Survey of the Uses and Limitations of Computerized Dietary Analysis as a Diagnostic Tool in Medical Practice as Perceived by Selected Chattanooga Physicians;* Monographs: *Public Relations and Communications in Family and Consumer Services; Management for Effective Living.*

COCHRAN, THAD oc/Congressman; Attorney; b/Dec 7, 1937; ba/Wash DC; m/Rose Clayton; c/2; ed/Univ Miss; Univ Miss Law Sch; Univ Dublin, Ireland; mil/USN 2 yrs; pa/Entered Law Pract, Jackson 1965; Pres Yg Lwyrs Sect, Miss St Bar; Chm Miss Law Inst; cp/US Ho of Reps: Elected 1972, Re-elected 1974, 76, Mem Var Coms incl'g Public Works, Trans, Ethics & Select Com on Aging, So Rep on Ho Repub Pol Com; r/Bapt; hon/Watchdog of Treasury Awd; Cits for Exemplary Congl Ser from Citizens Orgs; Rotary Foun F'ship; Jackson's Outstg Yg Man 1971; 1 of 3 Outstg Yg Men in Miss 1971; Omicron Delta Kappa.

COCILOVA, NORMA JANE oc/Nurse; b/June 30, 1939; h/107 Shady Ln, Vicksburg, MS; ba/V'burg; m/Nick; c/Ronald Glen; p/Charles and Annie Freeman, Natchez, MS; ed/Dip Mercy Hosp Sch Nsg 1960; a/Staff Nurse, Hd Nurse, Inservice Instr, Mercy Regional Med Ctr, 1960-; Former Mem ANA; Assn Practitioners in Infection Control; r/Bapt.

COCKRELL, CLAUDE O JR oc/President of Six Companies; b/May

60

PERSONALITIES OF THE SOUTH

19, 1937; h/PO Box 90387, Nashville, TN 37209; ba/Same; c/Cana Lyn, Claude O III; p/Claude O Sr (dec) and Aubrey R Cockrell (dec); mil/USAF; ANG; pa/George Wallace for Pres Campaign Chm; r/Presb; hon/Dist'd Flying Cross, USAF.

COCKRELL, PATRICIA KERON oc/Claims Auditor; b/July 14, 1946; h/6312 NW 24th, Okla City, OK 73127; ba/Okla City; m/Gary; c/Scott Douglas Duren, Tara Nicole; p/RD McLain; Billie McLain, Bethany, OK; pa/Claims Auditor, Security Gen Life Ins; SW Ins Assn, OKC Chapt: Pres 1979-80, VP Progs 1978-79, Secy-Treas 1977-78; cp/Del City JC Jaynes; r/Ch of Christ.

COCKRELL, PEARL HAND oc/Freelance Writer; b/Jan 2, 1921; h/4408 Murray Hills Dr, Chattanooga, TN 37416; m/Harold R; c/Pamela C White, Jan C Mitchell, Doris C Schweizer; p/Arthur H and May J Hand (dec); ed/Massey Bus Col; Cleveland St Commun Col; pa/Freelance Writer; Poems Pub'd in Var Brochures & Mags incl'g: *The So Dem, The Vol Gardener, Home Life, Modern Maturity, Progressive Farmer, Music Min, The American, The Braille Forum*, Others; Poetry Readings: Deep-South Reg Conv of Garden Clbs, St Conv Tenn Fdn Garden Clbs, So Railways Ladies Clb, Others; Poems Pub'd in Anthologies & Jours: *Tenn Voices, Old Hickory Review, Alalitcom, Pegasus, The Sampler*, Others; r/Bapt; hon/Pub'd *Of Men and Seasons* (Poetry) 1978, *Sing On, America* (Poetry) 1976; 1st Pl Writing Awds: Utah St Poetry Soc Nat Contest 1977, Mid-South Poetry Fest 1977, St Lttrs, Nat Leag Am Pen Wom 1975, 77, Ala Writers Conclave 1977, Ky St Poetry Soc Nat Contest 1976, Mid-South Poetry Fest 1976 (Poet Laureate's Awd), Nat Fdn St Poetry Socs 1974, Cleveland Creative Arts Guild 1973, 74, Authors & Artists Clb of Chattanooga 1973; Num Other Lit Prizes & Hon Mentions; Am Legion Cit of Merit 1974; Poet Laureate Awd, Tenn Fdn Garden Clbs; Freedom Foun Awd 1977; Finalist Clover Intl Poetry Competition 1975 (5th Pl); Poem of the Month, The Pacesetter 1974; Notable Ams of Bicent Era; World W/W Wom; W/W Am Wom.

COFFEE, MACK oc/Salesman; b/May 10, 1945; h/Fitzgerald, GA; c/Venetta L; p/Wardell and Vicey Coffee, Fitzgerald, GA; mil/AUS; ed/HS Grad; Studying to Preach Gospel; pa/Salesman; cp/VA; r/Bapt; hon/Automobile Sales Awd 1973.

COFFEY, THOMAS HENDERSON oc/Insurance Agent; b/Oct 12, 1943; h/2302 Brookway, Geneva, IL 60134; ba/Chgo; m/Donna Davis; c/Diana Lin, Martha Elizabeth; p/William Shelby and Lancy Elizabeth Coffey, Somerset, KY; ed/BA En Ky Univ; Grad Yale Univ; mil/AUS Intel Capt; pa/Gen Agt Fin Analysis & Ins Corp; Gen Agts & Mgrs Assn; Chgo Assn Life Underwriters; r/Meth; hon/Recruiting Region of Yr Awd 1974-75; Bronze Star; Army Commend; Vietnamese Cross of Gallantry.

COFFMAN, JERRY RAYMOND oc/Pastor; b/Nov 23, 1939; h/1403 Nabors Ln, Odessa, TX 79761; ba/Odessa; m/Sarah Nell; c/Stephen Odell, Karen Lee, James Randell; p/Lee Maurice and Marcella Marie Coffman, Denison, TX; ed/SEn St Univ; DDiv Tex Bapt Inst; Further Study Odessa Col; p/Min Westwood Bapt Ch; r/Bapt; hon/Author *Discovery Hour Manual* 1975; *Bible Studies* 1977; "Tongues" A Study Course 1974.

COGGINS, PATRICK CHURCHILL oc/Associate Professor; b/Jan 25, 1943; h/Atlanta, GA; p/Edward (dec) and Hermin Coggins; ed/AS Brit Inst Engrg Tech 1962; BS Springfield Col 1964; LLB Blackstone Sch LAw 1966; MS So Conn Col 1971; JD Univ Conn Sch Law 1975; p/Asst Prof & Dir Alcoholism Trg Prog, Atlanta Univ 1979-; Chp Policy, Plan'g & Adm, Grad Sch Social Work, Atlanta Univ 1980-; Dir Yale Drug Dependency Inst 1976-70; Dir NE Regional Support Ctr 1979; Coun Social Work Ed; NASW; Am Bar Assn; Assn Govt Accts; Am Inst CPAs; AAUP; APHA; Notary Public Comms in Conn, NY, & Ga; cp/Pres New Haven Legal Asst Assn; Mem Alpha Phi Alpha Frat; Trg & Credentialing Task Force, Alcohol & Drug Abuse Div, St Ga; Adv Bd Nat Drug Abuse Ctr; r/Cath; hon/Fulbright Schlr 1963-65; Yng Men Intl Hon S'ship Awd 1964; YMCA Nat S'ship Awd 1965; W/W Cols & Univs 1970; Outstg Ung Man Yr JC Nat Awd 1971; Spec Awd Conv & Visitors Bur, Hartford, Conn 1978; Author *Confidentiality of Alcohol and Drug Abuse Patient Records*; Other Profl Pubs.

COHEN, SHERYL E oc/Public Relations Practitioner; b/Sept 10, 1954; h/Miami Bch, FL; ba/100 N Biscayne Blvd, Miami, FL 33132; p/Arnold (dec) and Shirley Cohen, Miami Bch, FL; ed/BA Univ S Fla 1977; Dip Intl St Univ 1975; AA Miami Dade Commun Col 1975; pa/Public Relats Coor, The Keyes Co, Rltrs; Free Lance Public Relats for Theatre, Mus, Dance & Var Prods; Pt-time Instr Miami-Dade Commun Col New World Ctr Campus in Public Relats; Wom in Communs Inc; Public Relats Student Soc of Am; Phi Rho Pi; Alpha Omega; Phi Lambda; cp/U Way Dade Co, Broward Co & Palm Bch Co Campaign Coor for The Keyes Co Rltrs; r/Jewish; hon/U Way of Dade Co Awd for Campaign Ldrship; Pub'd Article "Real Estate - A Concrete Security Blanket" 1980.

COKER, LILLIAN JOHNSON oc/Retired Educator; b/June 29, 1906; h/Greenville, AL; m/Albert Steinhart; c/Margie C Lee; Albert S Jr, Marsha; p/John Bomar (dec) and Emma Avant Johnson (dec); ed/AB Judson Col 1927; Post Grad Study Troy Univ 1953; Auburn Univ 1959-60; pa/Jr HS Eng Tchr 1942-44, 1960-69; Tchr W O Parmer Sch 1929-35, 1953-60; Prin Liberty Sch 1928-29; Eng Tchr McKenzie HS 1927-28; HS Mat Tchr 1950-51; Secy Butler Co Tchrs Assn; AEA; NEA; NETA; Butler Co Eng Tchrs Assn; Mem Curric Visitation Team 1966-68; cp/Pres Pilot Clb Greenville 1966-67; Pres Greenville Fed Garden Clbs 1977-79; Chm Butler Co Flower Show 1978-80; Pres Camellia City Garden Clb 1976-78; Chm Artistic Arrangements Camellia Show 1978-80; Secy Hist Soc 1965-68; r/Bapt.

COKER, ROY AKINYELE oc/Entomologist; b/Apr 14, 1940; h/4405 Old Colony Rd, Raleigh, NC 27612; ba/Raleigh; m/Sheila Clark; c/Che Nathaniel, Joy Roseanne Lolade; p/Comfort Lolade, Agege, Nigeria; ed/BS 1968, MS 1970 Calif St Univ-Long Bch; PhD Univ Calif-Riverside 1973; mil/RAF 1962-64; pa/Stauffer Chem Co 1977-; Intl Inst Trop Agric 1974-77; CIBA Geigy, Lagos, Nigeria 1973-74; Entomol Soc Am; Am Registry Profl Entomologists; Am Weed Sci Soc; r/Christian; hon/Sigma Xi 1971; Ford Foun Fellow 1971-73.

COKER, THEODORE JAMES oc/Consultant; b/May 20, 1938; h/2467 Birken Head Dr, Charleston, SC 29407; ba/Chas'ton; m/Amelia Thompson; p/A C (dec) and Hazel Coker (dec); ed/BS Allen Univ 1960; MEd SC St Col 1969; EdD Univ SC 1979; mil/AUS 1961-63 Cpl; pa/Career Ed Conslt Chas'ton Co Sch Dist; Supvr Hd St, NYU, Bronx Campus 1969; Crippens Lab, Balto, Md; Bonds-Wilson HS 1963-71; ASCD; DDK; NEA; cp/Chm Bd Gtr Chas'ton YMCA; Treas Speech & Hearing Clin; Omega Psi Phi; Mt Sinai AME Ch; r/Meth; hon/W/W Am Cols & Univs 1960; Achmt in Ed 1977; Omega Man of Yr 1980.

COLBE, BONNIE LEE oc/Marketing Supervisor; b/Apr 15, 1948; h/9105B Town & Country Blvd, Ellicott City, MD 21043; ba/Silver Spring, MD; p/Marvin R and C Irene Smith, Glen Burnie, MD; ed/BS Univ Balto; AA Strayers; MBA Univ Balto; pa/Mktg Supv, Residence Hdqtrs, Chesapeake & Potomac Telephone Co; r/Presb; hon/W/W: Am Col & Univs 1971-72, Am Wom 1979-80; Beta Alpha Hon Frat; Cert Merit from Univ Balto 1970-71; Golden Key Awd, Univ Balto 1971.

COLBURN, BETTYE LYNN VAUGHN oc/Author; b/June 28, 1934; h/229 E 3rd, Lusk, WY 82225; ba/Lusk; m/Walter Edward Jr; c/Melanie Diane McCarthy, David Edward; p/Clarence Lyn Vaughn, Frederick, OK; La Vesta Brand, Midland, TX; pa/Author *A Tapestry of Childhood*; cp/Lusk Wom's Clb; r/Prot; hon/Valedictorian 1952; Outstg Wom in Wy 1978.

COLBURN, KATHLEEN GRAHAM oc/Administrative Manager; b/Aug 10, 1945; h/1008 Forrest Dr, Arlington, TX 76012; ba/Grand Prairie, TX; c/Jimaleen, Richard; p/R W and Ayleen Barrett Graham, Decatur, TX; ed/BS; MBA; pa/Adm Mgr Intl Wildlife Pk; Ft Worth Regional Coun of Alcoholism; Ambassador Arlington C of C; Am Bus Wom's Assn; Tex & Am Med Records Assn; cp/Tex Assn Commun Ser & Cont'g Ed; Alpha Kappa Xi; Pres Beta Sigma Phi; Suburbia City Coun; r/Meth; hon/Danforth Awd; W/W Am Wom 1979-80; Alpha Kappa Xi Wom of Yr 1979; Valentine Queen Beta Sigma Phi 1979.

COLDIRON, FANNIE LEE OWENS oc/Retired Teacher; b/Sept 6, 1919; h/RR 3, Crab Orchard, KY 40419; pa/Crab Orch; m/John Casper; c/Phyllis Ann C Durham, Virginia Lee C Thomas; p/Harry and Mary Childress Owens; e/Bach Deg; pa/Ret'd Elem Tchr; PTA; KEA; NEA; Lincoln Co Clsrm Tchrs Assn; r/Ch of Christ; hon/Outstg Elem Tchr of Am 1972.

COLDIRON, PEARL McHARGUE oc/Teacher; b/Aug 29, 1903; h/PO Box 24, Corbin, KY 40701; m/Howard T (dec); c/Robert David; p/John R (dec) and Sarah Elizabeth Elliott McHargue (dec); ed/AB; pa/Org'd, Owned & Op'd Small Pvt Bus Col Over 40 Yrs; hon/Ky W/W Edrs 1956; Ky Col; Commun Ldrs & Noteworthy Ams 1977; Past Pres BPW Clb.

COLE, JUDY B SHELL oc/Registered Nurse Practitioner; b/Feb 16, 1940; h/1310 Peachtree St, Sweetwater, TN 37874; m/Leslie W; c/Ceri S, Shonna Lee, Jason L; p/Carl E Shell (dec); Carrie Lee Nichols, Johnson City, TN; ed/Undergrad Studies: Kan St Univ & Univ Md 1960-64; Nsg Grad E Tenn St Univ 1973; Grad Studies Univ Kan Med Ctr 1975-76; pa/Pvt Pract Ob-Gyn, Independence, Mo 3 Yrs; Planned Parenthood Assn of So Mtns, Oak Ridge, TN; NLN; ANA; r/Bapt; hon/Author Num Articles on Ob-Gyn, Self-Care & Patient Tchg.

COLE, MARY ELIZABETH F oc/Teacher; b/July 1, 1923; h/1500 Peartree Rd, Elizabeth City, NC 27909; m/Henderson Franklin Jr; c/Henderick Toloso; p/Joseph and Rosa S Felton, Eliz City, NC; ed/BS;

MS; p/Elem Tchr; NEA; NCAE; Secy Eliz City Edrs Assn; Am Clsrm Tchrs Assn; Nat Assn Univ Wom; ECSU & NCCU Alumni Assns; cp/Nsg Home Adv Com; Delta Sigma Theta; Hood Chapt #33 OES; Arabia Ct #23 Daughs of Isis; Order of Golden Circle; New Ednl Growth & Devel Org; r/Bapt; hon/Tchr of Yr Sheep-Harney Sch 1972-73, 1979-80; Queen of Wom's Fed'd Clbs of NC Dist 7 1978; Rec'd Num Awds as Yth Dir of Ch & Sers to Ch.

COLE, RANDY D oc/Psychologist; b/Apr 18, 1949; h/9106 Tooley, Houston, TX 77031; ba/Houston; c/Erika Michelle; p/Claude Abraham Jr and Cleo Del Wood, Amarillo, TX; ed/BA Tex Tech Univ 1970; MA Stephen F Austin St Univ 1972; PhD Tex A&M Univ 1976; pa/Psych, Marriage & Fam Cnslr Pvt Prac 1977-; Dir Pers Cnslg Ctr W Tex St Univ 1976-79; Psych Conslt Kilgore Chds Psychi Hosp 1977-78; Psych Conslt Conroe Indep Sch Dist 1979-; Psychol Conslt Aldine Indep Sch Dist 1980; Tchg Asst Ednl Psych Dept Tex A&M Univ 1974-76; Staff Psychol, Outreach Dept, Travis St Sch Mtlly Retard 1972-74; Tchg Asst Stephen F Austin St Univ 1970-72; Therapist Tech Lufkin St Sch Mtlly Retard'd 1971; Psychol Intern Tex A&M Univ 1975-76; Psych Intern Rusk St Mtl Hosp 1971; SWn Psych Assn; Am Marriage & Fam Assn; Kappa Delta Pi; Phi Kappa Pi; Psi Chi; Tex Assn Col Student Pers Admrs 1976-79; Nat Assn Cnslg Ctr Dirs 1976-79; Tex Assn Cnslg Ctr Dirs 1976-79; Nat Exch Clb 1979-; hon/Outstg Yng Men of Am Awd 1980; Pub'd "The Use of Hypnosis in a Course to Increase Academic and Test-taking Skills"; "Adolescent Psychology and Psychotherapy"; Other Profl Pubs.

COLE, ROBERT A JR oc/Telecommunications Systems Manager; b/Feb 21, 1947; h/7949 E 60th St, 65-103, Tulsa, OK 74145; c/LaWanda Marie; c/Robert A Sr and Cleatrice D Cole, St Louis, MO; ed/BS Univ Mo 1971; pa/Telecommuns Sys Mgr SWn Bell; IBM Corp Mktg Rep; McDonnell Douglass Physicist; Am Inst Physics; cp/Kappa Alpha Psi; r/Cath.

COLEMAN, CAROBEL BLAIR oc/Writer, Homemaker; b/June 28, 1896; h/2004 Avondale St, Wichita Falls, TX 76308; ba/Wichita Falls; m/Joseph Pickens; c/Blair Pickens, Carolyn Merrill C Sanders; p/William Wiely and Carrie May Merrill Blair (dec); ed/BA St Mary's Dominican Col; pa/Writer; cp/Study Clbs, Mus, Hosp & Symph Auxs; r/Epis; Presb; hon/Valedictorian; W/W; Author *Lines From A Life*; Recip Violet O'Reilly Awd for Dist'd Ser 1979; Recip Silver Bowl from St Mary's Dominican Col as Outstg Alumni.

COLEMAN, CLAUDETTE TONIA oc/Nurse Educator; ; b/Jan 17, 1949; h/2539 Montreat Dr, Montgomery, AL 36116; ba/Montgomery; p/Claude A (dec) and Mildred Coleman, Mont, AL; ed/BSN, MSN Univ Ala Sch Nsg; pa/Asst Prof & Dept Chp Auburn Univ Sch Nsg; Assoc Prof Nsg Univ S Ala; Nurse Edr, Auburn Univ-Mont; Former Nsg Instr, Brookley Campus, Univ S Ala; ANA; Nat Leag for Nsg; Sigma Theta Tau; Sponsor AUM Student Nurses Assn; cp/Edited Cookbook for Local Nsg Soc; Fac Sponsor USA Student Nurses Assn; Advr Med Explorers Post BSA; r/Bapt; hon/Outstg Yng Wom of Am; W/W

COLEMAN, JANETTE SHAW McGEACHY oc/Administrator; b/Aug 18, 1951; ba/Radford, VA; p/Dr and Mrs C L Coleman, Richmond, VA; ed/Att'd VPI & SU 1974: BA Va Commonwlth Univ 1976: MEd James Madison Univ 1977; pa/Dir, Career Plan'g & Placement, Radford Univ 1978-; Higher Ed Rep, Grant Funding, Va Voc Guid Prog 1979-; Guest Lectr, Grad Ed, VPI & SU 1979-; Reviewer, Current Lit, Network Career Plan'g & Adult Devel, *Journal of Col Placement* 1979-; Va Commonwlth Univ; Placement Asst 1978, Cnslr Cont'g Ed Vol 1978; Commonwlth of Va, Dept Corrections 1978; Cnslr James Madison Univ 1977; Instr, Law, Washington & Lee Univ 197; Substitute Tchr, Henrico Public Schs 1976; Mgr Carriage House Books 1975; Buyer, Schwarzchild Jewelers Inc 1973-74; Am Assn Affirm Action; AAUW; Am Soc Profl & Exec Wom; Col Placement Coun; Mid-Atlantic Assn Sch, Col & Univ Staff'g; Mid-Atlantic Placement Assn; So Col Placement Assn; Va Col Placement Assn; VPGA; Wom's Equity Action Leag; cp/Bklyn Botanical Gdns; Alumni Assn, Mary Baldwin Col; Smithsonian Inst; Tuckahoe Wom's Clb; Va Mus; Whitney Mus; r/Presb; hon/Invit to Wom's Equity Action Leag's Ec Equity Awds Dinner 1980; Nom'd to Read for Wom's Ednl Equity Prog, Ofc of Ed 1980; Appt'd to Selection Com, Voc & Guid Proposal Funding for Commonwlth of Va 1979-80; St Plan'g Com; Nom W/W S&SW; Nom Young Careerist, Nat Fed BPW Clbs Inc 1980-82; Judge for Future Bus Ldrs Am; Chp, Univ Sers Com, Radford Univ 1980; F'ship Awd 1977; Author Num Reports & Profl Pubs.

COLIGADO, EDUARDO Y oc/Physician; b/Apr 18, 1936; h/Borger, TX; m/Eladia Clemente; c/Eric Joseph, Edwin Joseph, Edward David, Emy Lee; p/Jose B and Pacita Ylanan Coligado, Cebu, Philippines; ed/MD Univ of the Philippines 1962; Residencies: St Vincent Charity Hosp, Cleveland 1963-64; Luthern Hosp 1964-65; Cleveland Gen Hosp 1965-67; Univ Utah 1967-68; pa/Pvt Prac North Plains Hosp 1976-80; Demonstrator in Med, Geneva Meml Hosp, Geneva, Ohio 1970-76;

Highland View Hosp, Cleveland 1968-70; ASTABULA Med Soc 1970-76; AMA 1970-76; cp/Geneva Kiwanis Clb; 1970-76; r/Cath; hon/W/W S&SW; Author: "Reversible Vascular Occlusion of the Colon"; "Neutral Amino Acid Absorption in Humans"; "The Effect of Side Chainlengths."

COLL, ALBERTO RAOUL oc/Writer, Public Speaker; b/June 13, 1955; h/Box 451, Stuarts Draft, VA 24477; ba/Charlottesville, Va; m/Nancy Robertson Jones; p/Silvio and Celia Coll, Miami, FL; ed/BA Princeton 1977; MA 1980, JD 1980 Univ Va; pa/Spec in Intl Polits; Yng ·Schlr, White Burkett Miller Ctr for Public Affairs; cp/Coun on Relig & Intl Affairs; Intercol Studies Inst; World Vision Intl; r/Christian; hon/Nat Champ'ship in Public Spkg 1974, 76; MacLean Prize, McConnell Fellow 1976; Lynoe Prize 1977; Richard M Weaver Fellow, Eisenhower Fellow, Thomas Jefferson Fellow 1980-81; Preparing *Normative Approaches to International Politics*.

COLLE, BARBARA W oc/President China Doll Rice and Bean Company; b/Sept 15, 1915; h/PO Box 1487, Mobile, AL 36611; ba/Mobile; p/Henry C and Mena Ery Colle (dec); ed/Acctg La Salle Univ; pa/Mem: Trade Mart, Ala Grocers Assn, Gen Mgr China Doll Rice & Bean Co; cp/Bd Dirs; Better Bus Bur, C of C; Mobile CC; hon/Outstg Wom Am; W/W Ala; Commun Ldrs & Noteworthy Ams; Book of Hon; Intl Reg Profiles; Fellow Am Biogl Inst.

COLLIER, GARY SAMUEL oc/Minister; b/Nov 21, 1950; h/Rt 2, Paris, Tn 38242; m/Linda Lyn Thompson; c/Candi Lyn, James Stephen; p/Sam and Madeline Collier, Paris, TN; ed/Cont'g Min Ed Through Ch Sponsored Prog in Independence, Mo; pa/Exec Min, Reorg'd Ch of Jesus Christ of Latter Day Sts; Gen Dir & Asst Mgr Local Funeral Home 7 Yrs; Henry Co Hwy Dept Gen Foreman & Maintenance Supvr 3 Yrs; Pres Tenn & Ky Dist RLDS 2 Yrs; r/RLDS; hon/Ordained 1973.

COLLIER, JUDSON WAVERLY JR oc/Attorney; b/Dec 4, 1947; h/4621 Archduke Rd, Glen Allen, VA 23060; ba/Richmond, VA; m/Debra Skaggs; p/Judson W Collier Sr, Richmond, VA; ed/BA VMI; JD T C Williams Sch Law, Univ Rich; mil/USMC 1970-73 Capt; pa/Commonwlth Atty for Co of Henrico, Va; Am, Va & Henrico Bar Assns; Va Trial Lwyrs Assn; Va Bch Police Dept 1974; Delta Theta Phi; Va Assn Commonwlth's Attys; cp/JCs; r/Bapt; hon/Outstg Yng Men Am 1977 & 78; W/W Am Cols & Univs; 10 Outstg Yng Men Am 1979; Kappa Alpha Hon Soc 1970; Yth Achmt Awd for Richmond/Metro Area 1966; Best Spkr Awd VMI 1970; Intl Men Achmt 1979; Recip Richard A Simpkins Meml Awd; Intl W/W Intells 1979-80; Intl Man of Achmt 1979; Outstg Personality of South 1980.

COLLIN, MARY A oc/Author, Poet; b/Mar 20, 1909; h/123 Lockwood Ct, Columbus, GA 31906; c/Barbara Jean Rigsbee, Robert Arthur, Margaret Collin Klitch; p/Webster Wright (dec) and Mary Hammons Briggs (dec); ed/Martha Wash Sem 1930; pa/Author Non-Fiction, Fiction, Textbooks; Exec Secy The Upjohn Co, Kalamazoo, MI 15 Yrs; Owner & Opr Scotch Ridge Herb Farm, Kalamazoo 10 Yrs; Nat Leag Am Penwom, Columbus Chapt; DAR; cp/Carter Campaign Wkr; Chm Bd Ed, Grand Prairie Sch, Kalamazoo; r/Roman Cath; Author: *Everyday Cooking with Herbs* 1974; *Medical Terminology and the Body Systems* 1974.

COLLINS, ADA LATRELLE oc/Businesswoman; b/Jan 15, 1928; h/Star Rt Box 181, Ochopee, FL 33943; ba/Copeland, FL; m/James; c/James, Wayne, Richard, Vicki, Dale, Della, Cindy; p/Alfred L and Mary H Haynes; r/Bapt.

COLLINS, BERTHA KNOX oc/Mayor's Assistant for Youth Affairs; b/Jul 13, 1914; h/1920 Sedgewood Ter, Ft Worth, TX 76105; p/Warren B and Ollie Appling Knox (dec); ed/BS cum laude Paul Quinn Col; Univ Okla, Norman; SWn St Col; pa/Coor, Mayor's Coun on Yth Opportunity 1969-; Ft Worth City Parks & Rec Dept: Dist Supvr 1963-64, Ctr Supvr 1963-64; USAF Testing Spec & Tchr, Clinton-Sherman AFB 1958-62; Tex Rec & Parks Soc; Tex U Commun Sers; Altrusa Clb of Ft Worth; Bd Mem: McDonald Br YMCA (Hon), Ft Worth Girls Clb, Ft Worth Orch Bd, Sickle Cell Anemia Assn of Tex; Altrusa Clb of Ft Worth; Nat Coun Negro Wom Inc: Fdr & Pres Ft Worth Sect, Area Coor; Longhorn Coun, BSA Dist 28 Bd; Ft Worth Ballet; Alpha Pi Sigma Chapt, Sigma Gamma Rho; Num Other Civic Activs; r/St James AME Ch; hon/Hon Doct, St Stephens Col; Ft Worth C of C "Tip of the Hat Awd"; YMCA Apprec Awd; Ft Worth Municiple Cts Apprec Awds; Univ Miami Apprec Awd; 1977-78 Easter Seal Soc Ser Awd; U Way Commun Ser Awd; U Negro Col Fund F D Patterson Awd; Nat Coun Negro Wom Bicent Awd; Ft Worth USA Bicent Awd; Nat Arts Fest Awd; Nat Sigm Gamma Rho Inc Hall of Fame Awd; City of Ft Worth "Bertha Collins Day", Feb 13, 1974; Black Bus Men Assn of Tex, Outstg Contbn to Yth in Tex Awd; Nom'd Newsmaker of Yr 1972, 73, Ft Worth Press Clb; KJIM Civil Servant of Wk; Num Others.

COLLINS, C D JR oc/Retired Engineer; b/Nov 27, 1919; h/105 Peg-

PERSONALITIES OF THE SOUTH

Wen Blvd, Statesboro, GA 30458; m/Ida; c/Sunni, Sharon, Doug, David; p/C D Sr (dec) and Josie Cooper Collins, Atlanta, GA; ed/The Citadel 1937-39; LLB Atlanta Law Sch 1942; Univ Ga Ext 1952-53; Univ So Calif 1973; mil/USAAC 1942-45 Fighter Pilot; USAF 1950-52 Jet Fighter Pilot; ARNG 1964-80 Helicopter Pilot; pa/Ret'd Engr Dept Trans; Ga Engrs Assn: Pres, Bd Dirs; cp/Kiwanis Clb; r/Bapt; hon/Recip Trophy Outstg Public Relats Employee; Gov's Staff: Gov Carl Sanders 1963, Gov Lester Maddox 1967, Gov George Busbee 1975.

COLLINS, CLARENCE CECIL oc/Executive Director; b/May 11, 1908; h/307 Hardin Circle, Gadsden, AL 35903; ba/Gadsden; m/Helen Trout; c/Barbara Helen Whatley; p/David H (dec) and Ola Mae Wood Collins (dec); ed/AB Earlham Col; DD McKendree Col; mil/USAAF 1943-46 Chaplain; pa/Exec Dir U Givers Fund, U Way; United Meth Min 1932-74; Ind Min Assn Dist Supt 1 Term; cp/32° Mason; Rotary Intl; r/Meth; hon/Hon DD from McKendree Col.

COLLINS, CLINTON oc/Police Dispatcher; b/Apr 23, 1950; h/1509 W Jackson St, Covington, VA 24426; p/Dorothy Collins, Covington, VA; ed/Dabney Lancaster Commun Col 1969-71; BA Elon Col 1975; pa/Police Dispatcher Covington Police Dept; cp/Covington Qtrback Clb; Bd Dirs Red Cross; Bd Dirs Alleghany Heart Assn; Adv Bd on Spec Ed; r/Meth; hon/Mr Heart 1979.

COLLINS, JACQUELYN E oc/Businesswoman; b/Nov 9, 1936; h/4551 SE 3rd Ave, Ocala, FL 32670; ba/Ocala; m/A M; c/Mark, Craig; p/B J and Dorothy Hammonds, Oklawaha, FL; ed/BAGeo Wash Univ 1955-59; pa/Owner Jacquelyn's Shop for Women; Public Relats, St Regis Paper Co Sales Dept; PBW; Retail Com; Com of 100; Bd Dirs C of C Ocala; Prime Indust Coun; cp/Pres Jr Woms Clb; VP Yng Repub; r/Epis.

COLLINS, LINDA G oc/General Manager; b/Aug 5, 1944; ba/1001 Oak Towers, N Wilkesboro, NC 28659; m/Paul D; p/Charlie Thomas and Novella Kendrick Greene; ed/Ferrum Jr Col; Holiday Inn Univ; pa/Currently Gen Mgr Holiday Inn, N Wilkesboro; Bkkpr, Front Ofc Mgr, Asst Innkeeper, Innkeeper, Allen-White Inc 1972-Present; Danville Foods 1964-72; Intl Org Hotel & Motel Mgrs; St Pres NC Motel Assn; r/Meth; hon/Recip Cert'd Hotel Admr Cert 1980.

COLLINS, LOU ANN oc/Instructor; m/Jerry; c/Charles, Michael, Matthew; p/Mrs Strother Hoge, Bluefield, WV; ed/BS WVU 1969; Perinatal Nsg Cert 1976; pa/Instr Nsg, Bluefield St Col; ANA; cp/Prenatal Instr; r/Bapt.

COLLINS, RAYMOND L JR oc/Business Manager; b/Dec 22, 1938; h/Albany, GA; m/Ann; c/Tami, Gary, Sharon; p/Irma C Morris, Ayden, NC; ed/BS UNC 1960; MBA Syracuse Univ 1973; pa/Bus Mgr Lindsey & Ritter Inc, Consltg Engrs; Ret'd from USMC Nov 1980 After 20 Yrs Ser; cp/BSA; Albany Coun Navy Leag; Albany Am Legion Post 30; USMC Assn; Ret'd Ofcrs Assn; Nat Rifle Assn; US Tennis Assn; Profl Sers Mgmt Assn; r/First Christian Ch of Albany; hon/Bronze Star; Merit Ser Medal; Combat Action Ribbon; Navy Unit Cit; Merit Unit Cit; Nat Defense Medal; Armed Forces Expeditionary Medal; Vietnam Ser Medal w 5 Stars; Vietnam Armed Forces Merit Unit Cit; Vietnam Civil Action Merit Unit Cit; Vietnam Campaign Medal; Tennis Champ USMC Logistics Base 1980; 1st Place in Jr Vet Div Singles & Doubles Tennis Competition in USMC E Coast Regional Tourn 1980; 3rd Place in Jr Vet Div Doubles Competition in All Marine Tennis Tourn 1980.

COLLINS, RUTH HARVEY oc/State Training Officer; b/June 4, 1917; h/1433 Willivee Dr, Dacatur, GA 30033; ba/Atlanta; c/Theresa Ruth McNamara, Theron Tilford III, Jane Elizabeth Strzyzewski; p/Clair Lloyd (dec) and Iva Bell Whiton Harvey (dec); ed/BA Lawrence Univ 1945; MA 1966, MSW 1967 Mich St Univ; pa/St Trg Ofcr, Ga Dept Human Resources; Regional Secy Wom's Div Bd of Missions U Meth Ch; Grp Wkr Meth Commun House, Grand Rapids, Mich; Social Worker Hd Start, Lansing, Mich; Expmtl Ednl Prog Camps of Spanish-Spkg Migratory Agric Wkrs Traverse City, Mich; Ga Assn Yng Chd; SACUS; NAEYC; NASW; cp/AAUW, Chm Wom's Issues; YMCA; US-China People's Friendship Assn; Altrusa Intl; r/Presb; hon/W/W Am Wom 1981-82; AAUW Res Grant 1972; NIMH S'ship 1965-67; Author: "Introduction to Child Care"; "Why Do Women Work?"; Others.

COLLINS, SADIE BELL oc/Retired Teacher; b/Dec 27, 1908; h/PO Box 315, Unadilla, Ga 31091; ba/Unadilla; m/Robert A Sr (dec); c/Geraldine C McNeill, Miriam, Robert A Jr, Patricia C Everett, Martha C Cheek; p/Ira and Martha Noach Hankamer (dec); ed/BA Sam Houston St Univ; na/NEA; GEA; Dooly Ed Assn; Chm of Eng Dept; Life Mem PTA; cp/Past Pres BPW Assn; r/Meth: Mem Bd of Stewards; hon/STAR Tchr 3 Times; W/W Am HS Tchrs.

COLMER, NEIL ALAN oc/Bicycle Mechanic; b/Aug 14, 1949; h/Rt 3, Berea, KY 40403; m/Mary; c/Yosa, Orien; p/Orien and Mary Colmer,

Pomeroy, OH; ed/BA Berea Col 1972; pa/Weaver; Tradl Craftsman; VP Harvest Moon Crafts Guild; Asst Suprvr Shaklee Corp; r/Quaker; hon/Red Foley Awd 1971; Ky Col 1977; Sarah Fuller Prize Loom 1971.

COLSON, SHARON KAY THOMPSON oc/Educator, Producer; b/July 13, 1937; h/1116 Neal Pickett St, College Station, TX 77840; ba/Col Sta; m/C Lynn; c/Cynthia Xane Colson Holland, Lesa Lynn, Steven Craig; p/William McKinley (dec) and Homa McGee Thompson, Gainesville, TX; ed/BS, MEd E Tex St Univ; PhD Tex A&M Univ; pa/Edr Col of Ed, Tex A&M Univ; TV Prodr; Resr; Writer; Spkr; TV Personality; cp/Bd Dirs Brazos Co U Way; r/So Bapt.

COLVIN, GEORGE RAY JR oc/Fiscal Officer; b/July 31, 1936; h/Big Spring, TX; ba/PO Box 231, Big Spring, TX 79720; m/Veta L; c/Tom Barr, Susie, Linda, James, Shawna, Tatia; p/George R (dec) and Ella P Colvin; ed/AA 1967; mil/AUS; pa/Fiscal Ofcr, St Psychi Facility; Big Spring St Hosp: Asst Acct, Chief Acct, Staff Sers Ofcr, Bus Mgr; Assn Mtl Hlth Admrs; Tex Public Employees Assn Pres; cp/Staker Plains Lodge No 598 AF & M; Big Spring Civitan Clb; Tex Dist Foun Civitan Intl; r/Meth; hon/Civitan of Yr 1975; Big Spring St Hosp Commend 1980.

COMBS, SONYA REA HOROWITZ oc/Employment Agency Owner; b/Oct 5, 1948; h/3101 Lorna Rd, Suite #1224, Vestavia Hills, AL 35216; ba/Bluff Pk, AL; m/Douglas L; p/Murray W Horowitz, Lakeland, FL and Sallye Finman Horowitz (dec); ed/BS Univ Fla 1971; MPC Troy St Univ 1975; pa/Owner, Dir AAA Employment 1972 & 1977-; Mgmt Conslt Alexander Proudfoot Co 1976; Public Relats Asst, Troy St Univ 1974-75; Conv Sales Gov's House 1974; Pers Dir Combs & Assocs 1971; Corres Secy ABWA 1979-80; Soc Profl Jours; Alpha Delta Sigma; AAUW; cp/Temple Agudath Israel Sisterhood; Birmingham C of C; HADASSAH Life Mem; Beta Sigma Phi; r/Jewish; hon/Awd of Excell AAA Employment 1978.

COMER, HAROLD DEE oc/Department Superintendent; b/July 1, 1951; h/Rt 2 Box 168, Adamsville,TN 38310; ba/A'ville; m/Brenda Ann Finley; c/Roger Hylton, Lori Ann; p/Alexander (dec) and Hazel Comer, Selmer, TN; pa/Water & Street Dept Supt; cp/BSA; Pee Wee & Little Leag Ball Teams; Asst Chief Vol Fire Dept; r/Bapt; hon/Murphy Snoderly Awd.

CONAGHAN, DOROTHY DELL oc/State Representative; b/June 24, 1930; h/PO Box 402, Tonkawa, OK 74653; m/Brain Francis (dec); c/Joseph Lee, Charles Alan, Roger Lloyd; p/Joe J (dec) and Wilhelmina Miller, Auburndale, FL; ed/Att'd Univ Okla; pa/St Rep, Okla Ho of Reps; Delphi Study Clb; Cher-Ok-Kan Gateway Assn; PEO; cp/Tonkawa C of C; Am Legion Aux; OES, Worthy Matron 1959; Bd Mem Alpha II Alcohol Treatment Ctr; Org Wom Legs; Kay Co Yth Ser Liaison Coun; St Bd Mem Yn Ams for Freedom 1981; Adv Mem No Okla Col Nsg Sch 1980; St Dir Am Leg Exch Coun 1980-81; Secy Okla St Yng Repubs 1957; Rep Chm, Dist 1, Tonkawa; Kay Co Repub Exec Com Mem; Chm Tonkawa Repub Party 1962: VChm Kay Co Repubs 1961-65; Mem Okla Repub St Exec Com 1967-71; Del Repub Nat Conv 1968; Mem Ho of Reps, 34th Leg, 2nd Session, Re-elect'd to 35th -38th Leg; Repub St Com 1961-65, 1971-; r/First Christian Ch; hon/W/W: Am Polits, Am Wom, S&SW; Intl Hon Mem Beta Sigma Phi; Hon Mem Soroptimist Intl; Wom Helping Wom Awd, Soroptimist Clb 1975; World W/W Wom 1981.

CONARD, RICHARD T oc/Physician; b/Mar 15, 1937; h/1707 71st St, NE, Brandenton, FL 33529; ba/B'ton; m/Betty; c/Scott, Kimberly, Christy; p/Marie Conard, B'ton, FL; ed/MD Univ of Fla Sch of Med 1966; Intership 1966-1967, Post Grad Studies 1967, Lloyd Noland Foun; pa/Prac'g Phys 1968-; Gen Prtnr: Avondale Estates, Manacare Ltd, Trinity Lakes Ltd, Trinity Shores Ltd; Past Pres Manacare Corp; Past Pres Alpha Med Land Corp; Pres BAC Corp; Pres Manatee Fam Phys; Mng Ptnr CBSD Ptnrship; Pres Sun Hill Med Ctr; Chm Bd Retirement Corp of Am; Secy-Treas Westbay Med Ctr; Mng Ptnr Alpha Land Ptnrship; Manatee Co Med Soc; Staff Mem L W Blake Meml Hosp; Assoc Mem Am Col Surgeons Com on Trauma; FMA; AMA; Charter Mem Am Col of Emer Phys; Fla Acad Fam Phys; cp/Manatee Co C of C; Ec Coun Manatee C of C; Nat Fed Indep Bus; B'ton Country Clb; B'ton Yacht Clb; Tower Clb of Tampa; Manatee Co Dem Exec Com; Dem Men's Clb of Manatee Co; Yng Pres's Org; Masonic Org Warren Lodge #53 AF & AM of Indianola, Ia; Chm Paramed Ed Com for Voc Sch of Manatee Co; VChm Manatee Co Emer Med Sers Com of Co Comm 1970-76; Chm Manatee Co Med Ed Foun Inc; Fla Regional Med Prog Areawide Dir 1972-75; Chm Emer Med Sers Adv Com to the Div of Hlth 1973; Conslt Dept Hlth, Ed, Wel of Region IV 1976; Med Dir Manatee Co Sheriff's Dept; Med Adv Bd Dept of Hwy Safety & Motor Vehicles; Bd of Med Examrs of St of Fla; r/Meth.

CONKLIN, DEBORAH JEANNE oc/Mental Retardation Specialist; b/Sept 26, 1950; h/Rawlwood Arms 1-F, 1302 E 14th St, Greenville, NC 27834; ba/G'ville; p/Edward Gordon and Jeanne Clayton Conklin, G'ville, NC; ed/BA 1972, MS 1973, E Carolina Univ; pa/Pitt Co Mtl Hlth

63

PERSONALITIES OF THE SOUTH

Ctr, Area Mtl Retard Spec 1975-; Dir Winterville-Ayden-Grifton Child Devel Ctr 1973-75; Psych Asst Caswell Ctr, Kinston 1970-71; Nat Assn Retard Citizens; NC Assn Retard'd Citizens; Pitt Co Assn for Retard'd Citizens; AAMD; r/Bapt; hon/Outstg Yng Wom Am 1979; W/W S&SW 1980-81.

CONLEY, LOIS JEAN oc/Homemaker; b/May 13, 1935; h/2400 Barbecue Rd, Catlettsburg, KY 41129; m/Allen Jean; c/Bobette C Wilson, Allen Jr (dec), Gretchen McDowell, Steven; p/Lowell Cordial Durbin, Catlettsburg, KY; Olive Newkirk Cordial (dec); cp/Ashland Parliamentary Procedure Clb; Yost PTA; C'burg Wom's Clb; Campfire Girls; CSA; Explorer Scouts; Vol for MS, Cystic Fibrosis, Arthritis, Cancer & Heart Fund Drs; Dem; r/Oakland Ave Bapt Ch.

CONLON, KATHLEEN PARKER oc/Assistant Professor; b/Mar 28, 1934; h/7120 Dogwood Dr, Knoxville, TN 37919; ba/K'ville; c/Christopher Phillip, Timothy Paul; p/Wilbur (dec) and Ethel A Parker, Versailles, NY; ed/BS; MS; RN; mil/USN; pa/Asst Prof Col of Nsg, Univ of Tenn; Tenn Leag of Nsg; NLN; Fac Devel Proj for SREB; Conslt; ARA; r/Roman Cath; hon/Sigma Theta Tau; Kappa Delta Pi.

CONNELL, SUZANNE McLAURIN oc/Librarian; b/Sept 12, 1917; h/502 Brunswick St, Southport, NC 28461; c/John Alexander (dec); p/John Bethea and Aleine McLeod McLaurin (dec); ed/AB NC Wom's Col 1938; AB Univ NC-CH 1940; pa/Libn (Ret'd); ALA; NC Lib Assn; SEn Lib Assn; cp/Dem; Hosp & Nsg Home Vol; Past Pres, Hosp Libs Div, ALA; Pub'd Profl Articles in British & Am Jours; r/Meth; hon/Phi Beta Kappa; Biogl Listings.

CONNELLY, SUSAN JONES oc/Choreographer; b/Apr 9, 1922; h/701 Marion Sims Dr, Lancaster, SC 29720; ba/Lancaster; m/Charles K Jr; c/Luther C Williams III; p/Ira B Jr (dec) and Minnie Craig Taylor, Lancaster, SC; ed/Winthrop Col 2 Yrs; pa/Owner Dance Schs; Choreographer St Jr Miss Pageant; Franchise Holder Miss Lancaster, Little Miss, Wee Miss & Jr Miss of Lancaster, SC; Choreographer Lancaster HS Band; cp/Lancaster Co Devel Comm; Trent Town Achmt Prog; r/Presb; hon/Wom of Yr 1974.

CONNER, JERRY H oc/Executive Vice President; b/Aug 23, 1950; m/Grace; p/Walter I and Louise Conner, Dallas, TX; ed/Christian Col of SW 1969-71; BS Abilene Christian Univ 1972-75; Inst for Org Mgmt, So Meth Univ 1978; Mng Mgmt Time Wkshop 1978; Tex A&M Univ 1979; Dale Carnegie Course in Human Relats 1980; pa/Exec VP Waxahachie C of C; Acct Exec KTAB-TV 1980-; Adm Asst W Ctrl Tex Oil & Gas Assn 1979-80; Mgr Abilene Conv & Vis Bur 1977-79; Am C of C Execs Assn; Tex C of C Execs Assn; C of C Execs Assn of W Tex; Intl Assn Conv & Vis Burs; Tex Assn Conv & Vis Bur; Discover Am Assn; Tex Tourist Coun; Tex Tour Devel Assn; Am Soc Assn Execs; Tex Soc Assn Execs; Nat Assn Exposition Mgrs; Religious Conv Mgrs Assn; Meeting Planners Inc; cp/Key City Kiwanis; Am Red Cross Lifesaving Cert; Red Cross First Aid Cert; Lions Clb; U Way; r/Ch of Christ.

CONNER, LEWIS H JR oc/Judge; b/Mar 21, 1938; ba/Supreme Court Bldg, Nashville, TN 37219; m/Ashley Whitsitt; c/Holland Ashley, Lewis Forrest; p/Lewis H Sr and Cleo Johnson Conner; ed/BA 1960, JD 1963 Vanderbilt Univ; mil/USAR 1963-66 Capt; pa/Judge Tenn Ct of Appeals Mid Sect; Fdg Ptnr Dearborn & Ewing 1972-80; Atty at Law Ptnr Bailey, Ewing, Dale & Conner 1966-72; Am, Tenn, N'ville Bar Assns; Am, Tenn & N'ville Trial Lwyr Assns; Bd Govs Tenn Trail Lwyrs Assn 1976-80, Treas 1978-79; cp/N'ville Exch Clb; Richland Country Clb; Bd Dirs 1976-79, Pres 1979; N'ville Cumberland Clb; r/Presb: Deacon 1976-78, Elder 1978-; Author Var Articles in Legal Periods; hon/Order of the Coif 1962-63; Mng Editor Vanderbilt Law Review 1962-63; Pres Alpha Tau Omega 1960; Amateur Golfer of Yr, St of Tenn 1973; Winner of Over 20 St, Regional & Local Amateur & Open Golf Tourns.

CONNOR, BETTE ROSALIE oc/Business Executive; b/July 28, 1922; m/Jerry; pa/Secy Purchasing Agt, Rock Island Arenal 1942-45; VP Nat Bridal Ser, Rock Island, Ill & Atlanta, Ga 1952-72; Comptroller, Connor's Jewelers; Advr to Bridal Conslts on Wedding Etiquette; Past Mem Tchg Fac Nat Bridal Ser; Editor Dynamic Personal Achmt Soc's Home Study Course; hon/W/W Am Wom; World W/W Fin & Indust; Appt'd Adv Mem Marquis Lib Soc; DIB; Royal Blue Book; World W/W Wom; Contbr to Var Profl Pubs.

CONNOR, JERRY oc/Executive; m/Bette Rosalie; pa/Fdr & Pres Dynamic Personal Achmt Soc & Author of Its Home Study Course 1973-; Entered Retail Jewelry Indust 1921, Jeweler Num Yrs; Fdr Nat Bridal Ser 1951, Pres & Chm 21 Yrs; Fdr & Pres Retail Pers Devel Inst, Div of Nat Bridal Ser 1961; Spkr Before Sales, Trade & Mgmt Grps in US; Sales & Mkgt Execs, Atlanta & Intl; Intl Platform Assn; Am Inst Mgmt; hon/W/W S&SW; World W/W Fin & Indust; Blue Book; DIB; Ky Col 1974; Contbr to Trade Pubs & Jours.

CONSTANT, CLINTON oc/Chemical Engineer; b/Mar 20, 1912 (US Citizen); h/PO Box 1221, Atlanta, GA 30301; ba/Atlanta; ed/BS cum laude Univ Alberta 1935; PhD Wn Reserve Univ 1939; pa/Reg'd Profl Engr; Designed Automatic Napalm Plant; Superphosphoric Acid Plant; Phosphoric & Fertilizer Plants; R&D & Engrg Facils; Mgmt Positions; Assoc Fellow & 50 Yr Pioneer Mem Am Inst Aeronatics & Astronautics; Am Chem Soc; Am Astronomical Soc; Astronomical Soc Pacific; Royal Astron Soc Canada; Fellow: Am Inst Chem Engrs, Am Inst Chem, AAAS; Am Water Works Assn; Ga Water & Pollution Control Assn; NY Acad Scis; Soc Mfg Engrs (Cert'd Mfg Engr); hon/Patents & Papers; Author.

CONWAY, COLLEEN oc/Professor; b/Apr 26, 1944; h/1313 Williams St, Denver, CO 80218; ba/Denver; p/John and Lorraine Conway, Boynton Bch, FL; ed/BSN Georgetown Univ 1965; MSN Catholic Univ 1969; PhD NYU 1973; pa/Prof Nsg Univ Colo Sch Nsg 1980-; Assoc Prof Calif St Univ Long Bch 1978-80; Assoc Prof Geo Mason Univ 1976-78; Asst Prof Georgetown Univ 1974-76; Asst Prof SUNY Downst Med Ctr 1970-74; ANA; Am Public Hlth Assn; Am Col Nurse Midwives Bd Dirs; cp/Jr Leag; r/Roman Cath; hon/Invited Student Guest ANA 8th Annual Res Conf 1972; NYU Fdr's Day Awd for Excell in S'ship 1973; Va Nurses Assn/Am Nsg Annual Awd for Excell 1977; Pubs incl: "Fears of Abortion Patients"; "Progmatics of Research"; "Human Sexuality and the Child Bearing Process"; Others.

CONWAY, MARTHA (MARTY) ANN oc/Secretary-Treasurer; b/May 24, 1940; h/2413 Fairway, Orange, TX 77630; ba/Orange; m/R J; c/Elizebeth Ann, William Alan, Jinger Joanne; p/Jack Purifoy Weldon (dec); Willie Valerie Cothran, Orange, TX; ed/Grad Rltrs Inst, CRS Designation Nat Assn Rltrs; pa/Secy-Treas Conway & Co Inc; Tex Assn Rltrs; Orange Co Bd Rltrs; cp/Bd Dirs Orange C of C; Bd Dirs Lamar Univ Friends of the Arts; r/Presb; hon/Outstg Com Chm 1977 Orange C of C.

COOK, DEBORAH SUE oc/Treasurer; b/Oct 2, 1951; h/8922 Stroud, Houston, TX 77036; ba/Houston; m/Richard G; p/Larry Robert and Madalyn Mahan Mangold, Midland, TX; ed/BA Univ Houston 1974; pa/Treas Ins Corp Am; CPCU Student; cp/Kidney Foun of Houston & Gtr Gulf Coast.

COOK, DORIS MARIE oc/Educator; b/June 11, 1924; h/1115 Leverett St, Fayetteville, AR 72701; ba/F'ville; p/Ira and Mettie Jewell Dorman Cook; ed/BA 1946, MS 1949; PhD Univ Tex 1968; pa/Staff Acct, Haskins & Sells, Tulsa 1946-47; Univ Ark, F'ville: Instr Acctg 1947-52, Asst Prof 1952-62, Assoc Prof 1962-69, Prof 1969-; CPA: Okla, Ark; Arb Foun BPW Clbs, Treas 1979-80; F'ville BPW Clb (Pres 1973-74, 75-76); Ark Fdn BPW Clbs (Chm Foun Com 1975-77, Treas 1979-80); Ark Soc CPA's (VP 1975-76); Am Acctg Assn; Am Inst CPA's; Am Wom's Inst CPA's; NW Ark Chapt of CPA's (Pres 1980-81); hon/Mortar Bd; Beta Gamma Sigma; Beta Alpha Psi (Pres Nat Coun 1977-78, Newslttr Editor 1973-77, Dir Regional Meeting 1978-79); Phi Gamma Nu; Alpha Lambda Delta; Delta Kappa Gamma (Secy 1976-78, Pres 1980-81); Phi Kappa Phi; Contbr to Profl Jours; Wom of Yr F'ville BPW Clb 1977; Beta Alpha Psi: Outstg Fac Mem Awd 1976, 1978-79, 1979-80 & Outstg Ser Awd 1978.

COOK, JAMES COLUMBUS oc/Disabled Veteran; b/Sept 2, 1934; h/Rt 3, Box 189, Lawndale, NC 28090; m/Margie; c/Deborah, Tracy, Annette and Anita; p/McOvie Larn and Darlas Cook, Hickory, NC; mil/USN 4 Yrs Active Ser, 4 Yrs Inactive Ser; r/Bapt; hon/Permanent Display Mint Mus Charlotte, NC; Permanent Display NC Mus Raleigh, NC; Has Work in Basset Hall, Home of John D Rockefeller; Has Work in Metro Mus in NY.

COOK, SHIRLEY oc/Hospital Administrator; b/June 16, 1940; ba/Ashdown, AR; c/Teresa, David, Janet; p/John W and Dovie Terrell, Cookville, TX; ed/Univ Ind 1965; Further Study E Tex St Univ; r/a/Hosp Acctg & Adm, Little River Meml Hosp; Am Assn Hosp Accts; Am Acad Hosp Admrs; Am Hosp Assn Hosps; Ark Hosp Assn; Tex Soc Hosp Admrs; cp/Former 4-H Ldr; Bd Govs Tri-St Shared Sers; r/Bapt; hon/Employer of Yr, VOE Class Mt Pleasant Sch Dist 1973; Golden Cleaf Clover Awd, 4-H Ldrship 1978.

COOKE, DON EMMETT oc/General Fixed Operations Manager; b/Oct 10, 1940; h/Levelland, TX; ba/202 Ave H, Levelland, TX; c/Charles Emmett, Thomas Emett, Melissa Kathryne; p/Juanita Evelyn Cooke, Roswell, NM; ed/W Tex St Univ 1959-60; Inter Law Enforcement Cert, Tex Dept Public Safety 1963-64; pa/Gen Fixed Ops Mgr, Keeling Buick Olds Pont Inc 1979-; Tex Dept Public Safety Hwy Patrol 1963-70; Auto Dlrship Parts & Ser Mgmt 1970-; Past Pres El Paso Parts & Sev Clb; Bd Dirs El Paso Commun Col Ser Trade Sch; El Paso Coor Nat Auto Dlrs Assn Trg Prog; r/Meth; hon/Composer 20 Songs to be Pub'd 1981.

COOLEY, CAROLYN ANN oc/Secretary; b/June 28, 1956; h/1106 S Pk, Little Rock, AR 72202; ba/Same; m/J F; c/Stephen Lamar; p/Eddie and Ruby Chatman Butler, Marion, LA; ed/Att'd La Tech Univ & Ark

64

Bapt Col; pa/Clerk-Typist, La Tech Univ, La Tech Concert Assn 1975-76; Typist Ark Bapt Col, Bus Ofc 1976-; Secy Parolee Referral & Sers 1976-; Co-Owner *Arkansas Wkly Sentinel* Newspaper; cp/OES; Urban Leag of Gtr Little Rock; ACORN; Ark Law Enforcement Ofcr's Assn; Former Mem & Pres Delta Sigma Theta Interest Grp; 4-H Clb 1973-74; Staff Mem Commun Relats Com, Atty Gen's Ofc 1977; Hon Dept Circuit Clb 1977, Pulaski Co Circuit Clb; Montgomery Ward Auto Clb; Fin Aid Ofcr Ark Bapt Col; Nat Sheriff's Assn 1978-79; Vol Wkr Cystic Fibrosis Foun 1976 & 78; Hon Spec Investigative Aid for Circuit Clk's Ofc Pulaski Co; Hon Probation Ofcr & Investigator N Little Rock Municipal Ct; hon/Community Ldrs & Noteworthy Ams 1977; DIB 1977; Ark Traveler Cert 1977; Cert of Recog, Gov David Pryor 1977; Cert of Mbrship Co Contact Com; Outstg Yng Wom Am 1978; Dpty Sheriff Pulaski Co 1978; Men & Wom of Dist 1979; Personalities of Am 1978-79; Cert of Recog Constable's Ofc Dist 3-A & Cert of Merit; Assoc Mem Ark Constable's Assn; Nom'd Intl W/W Intells; Others.

COOLEY, J F oc/Minister, Educator, Civil Rights Activist; b/Jan 11, 1926; h/4117 Barrow Rd, Little Rock, AR 72204; ba/Same; m/Carolyn A Butler; c/Virginia M Lewis, James F, Gladys M Taylor, Franklin D, Stephen Lamar; p/James Franklin (dec) and Martha Buie Cooley (dec); ed/AB 1953, BD, MDiv 1973, Johnson C Smith Univ; MA E Neb Christian Col; mil/AUS 1944-46 Chaplain, 1st Lt; pa/Chaplain Tucker Intermediate Reformatory 1971-; Ark Tchrs Assn; Intl Platform Assn; SANE; Am Security Coun; Nat Com of Black Chmen; Omega Psi Phi; cp/NAACP; AF & AM; Ark Coun on Human Relats; Com for Peaceful Co-Existance; Wel Rights Org; ACORN; Nat Hist Soc; St Dem Party; Nat Sheriff's Assn; Vets Org; Urban Leag; Ark Law Enforcement Assn; Press Agt; Early Am Soc; Min Alliance of Gtr Little Rock; Inspirational Trio; Juvenile Correctional Assn; Nat Conf Christians & Jews Inc; r/Meth; hon/Hon Dpty Circuit Clerk of Pulaski Co 1977; Dpty Sheriff Pulaski Co 1978; Leg Aide to Rep Grover Richardson in Prison Reform 1977; Book of Honor 1977-78; Ark Traveler's Cert; Personalities of South 1976-77; Cert of Awd, Walter E Simpson, Little Rock Police Dept; Hon Lt Col 1978; Commun Ser Awd 1978; W/W Black Ams 1977-78; Cert of Recog from Gov David Pryor 1978; Intl W/W Intells 1978-79; Intl Reg of Profiles 1978-79; Men and Wom of Dist 1978-79; Elect'd Pres Ark Constables Assn 1978; Month of Sept 19, 1978-Oct 10, 1978 Proclaimed as Dr J F Cooley Month in N Little Rock by Mayor Eddie Powell; Featured in RIP Mag 1979; Men of Achmt 1979; DIB 1979; W/W: Am, S&SW; Letter of Recog Prison Reform & Rehab, St Rep Robert Johnston; Apprec Night for Dr J F Cooley Dec 1, 1978, Num Awds of Recog, Plaques, Letters from War Law Enforcement Agcys; Cert of Good Citizenship, Mayor Don Mechlburger, City of Little Rock 1978; Cert of Recog, Gov Bill Clinton 1979; Fdr, Owner, Editor *Arkansas Weekly Sentinel* 1978; Ark Comm on Law Enforcement Standards Cert Law Enforcement Ofcr 1980; Fdr & Exec Dir Ex-Inmate Mission & Talent Ctr 1980; Commun Ser Prog US Dept Commerce Cert Apprec 1980.

COOLEY, JAMES FRANCIS oc/Social Worker; b/Dec 18, 1948; h/PO Box 4520, Little Rock, AR 72114; c/Latricia D; p/James Franklin Cooley, Little Rock, AR; Louvania Graham, Wilmington, NC; ed/BA Univ Ark Pine Bluff 1971; MSW Univ Md Sch of Social Work 1977; r/Prot; hon/US JCs Outstg Ung Men of Am 1978; Intl Biogl Ctr Vol 16, 1979-80.

COOLEY, JANE F oc/Executive Secretary; b/Nov 12, 1945; h/3505 Princeton, Midland, TX 79703; ba/Midland, TX; m/Philip; c/Philip; p/Harold T Jr and Barbara Cook Frost, Midland, TX; ed/Commercial Col of Midland 1964; pa/Exec Secy, Ortloff Corp; NSA; r/Meth.

COOPER, AGNES PEARSON oc/Dean of Student Services; b/Oct 18, 1910; h/Rt 2 Box 105, Kodak, TN 37764; ba/Knoxville, TN; m/David A Sr; c/David Jr; p/James P (dec) and May B Pearson (dec); ed/BS; MS; Adv'd Grad Work, Harvard Univ; pa/Dean of Student Sers, Cooper Inst Inc; cp/Past Intl Pres Quote Intl Inc; r/Bapt; hon/W/W: S&SW, Am Wom.

COOPER, BENNIE L JR oc/Emergency Medical Instructor; b/Oct 26, 1940; h/PO Box 962, Murray, KY 42071; ba/Murray; m/Mary Jo; p/Bennie L Cooper Sr, Lake Alfred, FL; Beatrice Cooper (dec); ed/BS; MS; mil/AUS 20 Yrs Med Corps; pa/Emer Med Instr, Murray St Univ; Many Emer Med Assns; cp/Red Cross Instr; Dem St Emer Adv; r/Meth; hon/Ky Col; Num War Decorations.

COOPER, BOBBY G oc/Instructor, Division Chairman; b/Nov 3, 1938; m/Della Larkin; c/Christopher, DeMetria, LaCarole; p/Larry (dec) and Mary Gray, Bolton, MS; ed/BS Tougaloo Col 1961; MS Univ Ill 1970; ECS 1972, EdD 1977 Univ Colo; c/Chp Humanities Div, Music Instr Utica Jr Col; Cnslr Spec Ednl Opportunities Prog, Univ Ill; Cnslr Camp Treetops, Lake Placid, NY; Music Tchr E T Hawkins HS, Forest, MS; Phi Delta Kappa; Music Edrs Nat Conf; Am Choral Dirs Assn; Nat F'ship Meth Musicians; cp/Indep Benevolent Protective Order of Elks of the World; r/Meth; hon/Ford Foun Grant 1968; Ofc of Ed Grant 1971; Univ Ill Sch of Mus S'ship 1969; Univ Colo S'ship.

COOPER, CAROLYN oc/Company Owner/Operator; b/Aug 17, 1939; h/Savannah, GA; m/Alfred C; c/Phyllis, Vivian; p/Collie M and Olga Vivian Brannen Usher; ed/Los Medanos Col; pa/Pres & Mgr Mktg Res Interviewing Ser; BBB; Nat Mktg Res Assn; Atlanta/SE Chapt MRA; Exec Female; cp/Nat Trust for Hist Preserv; Bd Dirs Poetry Soc Ga; Telfair Acad of Arts & Scis; Vol "Night in Old Savannah" fund raising activity for Girl Scouts; Mem Savannah Symph Chorale; r/Epis: Choir Mem; hon/Contra Costa Co Poetry Competition 1977: 2 1st Pl Awds, 3 2nd Pl Awds, 2 3rd Pl Awds.

COOPER, CELESTINE JULIET oc/Case Manager II; b/Dec 20, 1950; h/PO Box 31, Manning, SC 29102; ba/Manning; p/Jessie L and Maxie W Cooper, Gable, SC; ed/BA Bennett Col 1972; pa/Case Mgr II, Child Abuse & Neglect Sers (Invest & Treatment), SC Dept Social Sers; Clarendon Co Foster Parent Assn; SC St Employees Assn; cp/Clarnedon Co Alcohol & Drug Abuse Adv Coun; OES Red Hill Lodge #157; r/Bapt; hon/Outstg Child Protective Sers Wkr 1980-81.

COOPER, CHARLOTTE MALISSA HERVEY oc/Civic Worker; b/July 3, 1943; h/3016 Glasgow Dr, Arlington, TX 76015; ba/Same; m/James N; p/H A and Marie Cochran Hervey, Dallas, TX; ed/BA Speech & Eng; cp/Nat Bd Girls Clbs Am; Nat VP Zeta Tau Alpha; Jr Wom's Clb Pres; U Way Allocations Com Tarrant Co; Bd Dirs Arlington Gymnastics Inc; Pres/Fund Raising Chm Arlington Girls Clb; Bd Dirs Univ Tex Curtain Call Assn; Pres Arlington Newcomers Clb; Pres Scotswood Garden Clb; r/Meth; hon/W/W Am Wom; Newsmaker of Yr; Zeta Tau Alpha Cert of Merit & Hon Ring.

COOPER, DONALD PAUL oc/Minister; b/Aug 4, 1924; h/1127 Jimree Ave, Fayetteville, NC 28301; ba/F'ville; m/Annie Lois; c/Donnie Pual Jr, Edward L, Sunny Gale Flower, Brenda K Morgan, Robert H, David F; p/Paul Fonso (dec) and Lela B Cooper, Franklinton, NC; ed/AA Campbell Col; mil/USN; pa/Bapt Min; hon/Merit of Hon.

COOPER, ELLIS EWEN oc/Pastor, Beekeeper; b/Dec 4, 1916; h/125 E 17th St, Cookeville, TN 38501; ba/C'ville; m/Ann Treadwell; c/Shelby Jean Harper, Carolyn Ann Daniel; p/Cullie Robert (dec) and Bessie Dabbs Cooper (dec); pa/Pastor First United Pentecostal Ch of Jesus Christ; Past 2-Term Sect Presbyter; Past Sect Dir Home Missions; Past Sect Dir Tenn U Pentecostal Ch; hon/Weekly Writer of Rel Article "Truth for the Truthseeker"; Fdr & Bldr Mt Zion U Pentecostal Ch, Honewald, Tenn & Cookeville.

COOPER, JAMES IVIN oc/Assistant Hotel Manager; b/Nov 19, 1926; h/Rt 1 Box 134, Park City, KY 42160; m/Mary Evelyn; c/Judith Faye Scott, James Douglas; p/Charles Kelton (dec) and Mary Frances Cooper, Cane City, KY; mil/AUS 1946-47 Paratrooper; pa/Asst Mgr Mammoth Cave Hotel; cp/Pres Lions Clb 1965-66, 1977-79; 43 E Lions Clb of Ky Zone Ch 1974-75; PTA Pres Pk City Sch 1958-59; r/Meth: Chp Local Ch Bd, Chp Bd Trustees, Chp Coun on Ministries; hon/Good Conduct Medal; Paratrooper Wings; Occupational Ribbon.

COOPER, KENNETH DEAN oc/Corporate Manager; b/Dec 20, 1943; h/1302 River Oaks Dr, Flower Mound, TX 75028; ba/Dallas, TX; m/Ellen Elyse Shuler; c/Bucknell Dean; p/Robert Lee (dec) and Lois Mae Cooper, Glenshaw, PA; ed/Univ Richmond 1972-74; Orange Jr Col 1968; J Seargent Reynolds 1975; Inst Computer Mgmt 1963; Univ Colo 1962; Pitt Univ 1963-64; Dale Carnegie Inst 1979; mil/USAF 1963; Penn ANG 1963-68; pa/Staff Mgr, Trg & Ed, Staff Ops, Tech Evaluation, Logistics, Adm, Orient, Cutler-Williams 1976-; Mgr Systems Support, Garfinckles 1972-76; Pres D&E Conslts 1970-72; Mgr Programming Automatel Bus Sers 1969-71; Analyst Martin-Mariette 1968-69; Programmer Mobay Chem Co 1965-69; Supvr Mellow Nat Bank Computer Ctr 1964-65; Toastmasters Lewisville Clb 4137; Past Ednl VP, Current Pres; Dallas Darts Assn; Intl Platform Assn; NAm Darts Assn; cp/VFW; Am Legion; r/So Bapt; hon/CTM 1980; Outstg Clb Ednl VP Dist 25 Toastmasters 1980; W/W 1980; Author: *The Employee and Employer versus Mobility and Motivation* 1968; *The Evaluation Method* 1969; *Evaluating the Performance of Computer Professionals* 1971; *R&R of the Computer Technician* 1980.

COOPER, MARY BERRY oc/Legal Assistant; b/July 27, 1923; h/3909 Albert Dr, Nashville, TN 37204; ba/N'ville; m/Raiford Wilson Sr; c/Raiford Wilson Jr, Jack Glenn; p/Wilson Ray (dec) and Mrs W R Berry, Stockbridge, GA; pa/Legal Asst, Farris, Warfield & Kanaday; Pres Tenn Assn Legal Secys; Charter Mem Nat Assn Legal Assts; Past Pres Nashville LSA; cp/Secy Human Relats Comm of Metro Govt; Bd Mem Nashville, Davidson Co ARC & Fam & Ednl Adv Bd; Former Com-wom Davidson Co Dem Party; Magistrate, Davidson Co; Secy Tenn Citizens for Ct Modernization; r/Glendale U Meth Ch; hon/Legal Secy of Yr 1977.

COOPER, MICHELE ABINGTON oc/Home Economist; b/Mar 7, 1947; h/2603 Loop Rd, Winnsboro, LA 71295; ba/Winnsboro; m/Dennis

PERSONALITIES OF THE SOUTH

A; c/Michael Raymond; p/William H and Corinne C Abington, Keatchie, LA; ed/BS NE La St Col 1970; MEd NE La Univ 1971; pa/LSU Coop Ext Ser: Asst Home Ec 1971-74, Assoc Home Ec 1974-79, Home Ec 1979-; Nat Assn Ext Home Ecs; La Assn Ext Home Ecs, St Regional Cnslr 1978-80, St 1st VP 1981-83; Nat Hosp Comm 1980-81; Am Home Ec Assn; La Home Ec Assn, Nat Job Inf Exch 1978, Dist VP 1981-82, St Awds Chm 1980-81; cp/Nat Assn Ext 4-H Agts; La Assn Ext 4-H Agts, Charter Mem; Epsilon Sigma Phi; Kappa Omicron Phi; ABWA, Prog Com, Hospitality Com; r/Bapt; hon/Outstg Yng Home Ec, LAEHE 1978; Outstg Yng Wom, W'boro Jaynes 1980, Top 10 in St.

COOPER, WARREN oc/Retired Minister; b/Oct 8, 1910; h/Rt 4, Box 198 AA, Selma, AL 36701; ba/Same; m/Christine Williams; c/Warren William, Carol, Robert, Joy; p/Fletcher Leach (dec) and Eliza Easley Cooper (dec); ed/BS Tex Wesleyan Col; Dip Theol, SWn Bapt Sem; DMin Luther Rice Sem; pa/Sr Pastor Ctrl Bapt Ch, Selma, AL 1960-76; Past Mem Exec Bd Ala Bapt Conv; r/Bapt; hon/Man of Yr, Tenn St Exch Clbs; Pres Gavel Clb.

COOTS, HERMAN WOODROW oc/Retired Comunity Development Specialist; b/Feb 12, 1914; h/330 N 38th St, Paducah, KY 42001; m/(dec); c/Mary Carol Katzel, Lou Anna, p/Herman (dec) and Florence Montgomery Coots (dec); ed/BS 1936, MS 1969 Univ Ky; mil/ROTC Univ Ky 1 Yr; pa/Co Agric Agt & Commun Devel Spec as Staff Mem Univ Ky 37 Yrs; Pt-time Instr Univ Ky Commun Col; Pres Ky Assn Co Agric Agts & Pennyrile-Purchase Dist Agcy Devel Com; Gamma Sigma Delta; Epsilon Sigma Phi; cp/Pres Rotary Clb of Franklin, Ky; Rotary Clb Dir 8 Yrs; Pres Simpson Co Univ Ky Alumni Assn; Dir Franklin-Simpson C of C; Ky Cold; Duke of Paducah; r/Paducah First Bapt Ch: Deacon; hon/Nat Dist'd Ser Awd, Nat Assn Co Agri Agts 1947; Designated Rotary Paul Harris Fellow 1980; 25 Yrs Perfect Attendance Rotary Awd 19781; St 4-H Clb Alumni Awd 1978; 4-H Ldrship Awd 1980.

COPELAND, MARY L JONES oc/Registered Nurse; b/Feb 4, 1930; h/2760 Luther Dr, E Pt, GA 30344; m/Harold William; c/Mary Ellen, Sally Ann; p/John R (dec) and Mattie Low Beckam Jones (dec); ed/Lutheran Hosp Sch of Nsg 1951; BSA St Joseph Col 1978; Cert'd Hlth Admr by ANA 1979; pa/Hd Nurse Newnan Hosp, Newnan, Ga 1951-52; Supvr Grady Meml Hosp, Atlanta 1953-57; S Fulton Hosp, E Pt, Ga: Nsg Staff Mem 1963-79; Asst Dir Nsg, Dir Nsg Sers 1971-79; ANA; Ga St Nurses Assn; Ga St Leag for Nurses; Ga Soc Nsg Ser Admrs; Ga Hosp Assn; cp/Fulton Co Cancer Soc Bd of Dirs; Metro Atlanta Coun on Drug & Alcohol; Bd Dirs Ga AGAP & Adoption Agcy; r/Ch of Christ; hon/W/W S&SW 1980-81; Author: "Straight Talk to Christian Women" 1977; "God Himself Shall Be With Them and Be Their God" 1972.

CORBETT, WILLIAM PAUL oc/Instructor; b/Nov 19, 1948; h/Tonkawa, OK; ba/Division of Social Sciences, No Oklahoma Col, Tonkawa, OK 74653; p/S Paul and Marybelle D Corbett, Clarion, PA; ed/BS Ed Clarion St Col 1970; MA Univ SD 1976; PhD Cand Okla St Univ 1976-; mil/USN 1970-74; pa/Instr Forest Area Schs, Tionesta, Pa 1974-75; Tutor, Dept Hist, Univ SD 1976; Grad Tchg Fellow, Dept Hist, Okla St Univ 1976-80; Adj Instr, Seminole Jr Col; Instr No Okla Col 1980-; Pi Gamma Mu; Phi Alpha Theta, Pres Nu Chapt 1979-80; Wn Hist Assn; Okla Hist Soc; SD Hist Soc; Tonkawa Hist Soc; cp/Kiwanis Clb; Tonkawa Diamond Jubilee Com; r/Presb; hon/Homer L Knight Grad S'ship, Dept Hist, Okla St Univ 1979; Jefferson Davis Awd, Okla Div UDC 1979; Muriel Wright Awd, Okla Hist Soc 1981; Author: "Confederate Strongholds in Indian Territory: Fort Davis and Fort McCulloch" 1978; "Men, Mud, and Mules: The Good Roads Movement in Oklahoma" 1980.

CORBITT, SARAH CARUTHERS oc/Professor; b/Jan 7, 1936; h/4230 Santee Rd, Jacksonville, FL 32209; ba/J'ville; c/Maurice, Mark, Monique, Michael and Michelle; p/Sarah Caruthers Corbitt; ed/BS; MS; EdS; pa/Nat Sci Tchrs Assn; r/Bapt; hon/St Dist'd Tchr Awd; World W/W Wom in Ed; Miss Eve Finalist.

CORNWELL, RUBY PENDERGRASS oc/Retired Teacher, Retired Director of Child Development Center; b/Mar 31, 1904; h/95 Congress St, Cahrleston, SC 29403; m/A T (dec); p/Durant P (dec) and Maud Chavis Pendergrass (dec); ed/BA Talladega Col 1925; Grad Study Columbia Univ 1928, 1929; Cert in Early Ed, Peabody Tchrs Col 1967; pa/Tchr HS Eng & Hist, Avery Normal Inst 1925-29, Laing HS 1936-40; Dir St Mathew Child Devel Ctr 1966-77; cp/Chm Arts Com, Charleston Links Inc; Bd Mem NAACP; Bd Dirs Carolina Art Assn; Co-Chm of Vols; Citizens Adv Bd Piccolo Spoleto Arts Fest; Steering Com for Annual Black Arts Fest; Former St Pres Wom's Aux to Med Assn; Exec Bd Avery Inst Ctr for Afro-Am Culture; r/U Ch of Christ; hon/Writer Editorial Columns for *Evening Post*; Rec'd Awd & Plaque Upon Retirement from Charleston Hd Start Prog.

CORPREW, ANNETTE M oc/General Office Clerk; b/Jan 22, 1960; h/Chesapeake, VA; p/Ossia S and Annie D Corprew, Chesapeake, VA;

ed/Student Va St Univ 1978-; pa/Ofc Clerk, Va St Univ; Future Ldrs of Am 1976-78; Freshman Class Secy, Va St Univ 1978-79; Phi Beta Lambda 1978-; Bus Ed & Ofc Adm Clb 1979; r/Bapt; hon/Red Awd 4-H Poster Contest 1974; Cert of Awd, Yng Miss Am Pageant 1974; Cert of Completion, Secys Telephone Sem, Tidewater Commun Col 1977; Cert of Attendance, Tidewater Chapt The Nat Secys Assn 1977; Superior Rating on Essay 1978; 3rd Place Team Rating, Parliamentary Procedure Regional Event, Norfolk St Regional Chapt FBLA 1978; Dean's List Student 1978-; Cert of Acad Achmt, Freshman Coun of Va St Univ 1979; Sterling Silver Charm for Acad Achmt, Bus Ed & Ofc Adm Dept, Va St Univ.

CORPRON, CARLOTTA M oc/Teacher, Photographer; b/Dec 9, 1901; h/Denton, TX; ed/BS En Mich Univ; MA Tchrs Col, Columbia Univ; pa/Assoc Prof, Tex Wom's Univ; Kappa Delta Pi; Nat Ret'd Tchrs Assn; hon/Author: *Recollections-10 Women of Photography* 1979; *Light Abstractions* 1980.

CORRELL, CHARLES E oc/Developer; b/June 23, 1936; h/Somerset, KY; m/Doris N; c/Charles E Jr, Joseph A, Paula; ed/Deg En Univ 1955; ThM Bapt Theol Sem 1959; pa/Developer Shopping Ctrs, Subdivisions, Residential; Pres Correll Funeral Home; Pres Charles E Correll Evangelist Assn; Hon Ky Col; cp/Pres Class at En Univ; Dem Chm of Precinct; r/Bapt; hon/Most Outstg Thesis, Bapt Sem 1959; Articles: "My First Trip to the Holy Land" 1959; "What the Bible Teaches Concerning Baptism" 1962; "What the Bible Teaches Concerning The Tithe" 1959.

CORSELLO, LILY JOANN oc/Guidance Counselor; b/Mar 30, 1953; h/4521 NE 18 Ave, Ft Lauderdale, FL; ba/Lauderdale Lakes; p/Joseph DiFalco and Antonietta Gandolfo Corsello, Ft Lauderdale, FL; ed/BA Fla St Univ 1974; MEd Fla Atlantic Univ 1977; pa/Guid Cnslr Boyd Anderson HS; Nationwide Lectr-Spkr for Singles' Confs, The So Bapt Conv; Free-Lance Author Christian Single Magazine; APGA; NEA; Nat Edrs F'ship; NCTE; Fla Tchg Profession; Classroom Tchrs Assn; Lambda Iota Tau; cp/Pilot Intl; Repub Exec Com, Ft Lauderdale; r/So Bapt; hon/W/W S&SW 1980-81.

CORUM, B H oc/Hospital and Health Care Administrator, Professor; b/Nov 13, 1933; h/San Antonio, TX; ba/USAF Med Ctr, Lackland AFB, TX 78236; m/Carol Hill; c/Renee; p/Bulford H (dec) and Novia T Corum (dec); ed/BS Auburn Univ 1951-55; MHA Baylor Univ 1960-62; PhD Univ Fla 169-72; mil/USAF Col; pa/Admr Wilford Hall USAF Med Ctr; Am Col of Hosp Admrs 1976-; Am Acad Med Admrs 1976-; Acad Mgmt 1971-; Am Mgmt Assn 1975-; Assn Mil Surgs of US 1976-; Alamo Hosp Div, Tex Hosp Assn 1979; Tex Hosp Assn 1979; Ala St Bd Pharm, Lic'd Pharm 1956-; Am Hosp; Assn 1961-68; Am Pharm Assn 1955-57; cp/Trinity Bapt Ch: Chm Com on Coms 1976-77, Bd Deacons 1973-, Ed Com 1975-77; Mem Local PTA; r/Bapt; hon/Cert of Merit, Nat Hlth Agcys 1968; Cert Merit Intl Serv Agcys 1968; AF Commend Medal; Sem Coor Ctl Regional Conf Am Col of Hosp Admrs 1975; Pers Coun of Am Acad Med Admrs 1976; Merit Ser Medal; Nom'd Ray Brown Awd as Fed Hlth Care Exec of Yr 1978; Nom'd Legion of Merit (Highest Peacetime Mil Awd) for Outstg Ser as Dir Pers for Aerospace Med Div; Num Profl Pubs.

COSTA, MANUEL A oc/State Representative Department Industry and Trade; b/Oct 26, 1933; h/94 Hornet Dr, Brunswick, GA 31520; ba/Augusta; m/Barbara Susan; c/David M, Julia Lynn, Jeffery D; p/Manuel (dec) and Nellie Costa; ed/Jour; mil/USMC; pa/Classic So Rep Ga Dept Indust & Trade (Promo & Public Relats); TV News Dir; Dir Miami Marine Stad; Dir Advt & Prom VPA; Dir Helen, Ga C of C; cp/Augusta C of C; r/Cath; hon/2 World Speed Boat Endurance Records; Recip Silver Anvil Awd; Commends Orange Bowl Comm; 6 Yrs Commend Helen, Ga C of C.

COSTELLO, PAUL A oc/Commercial Investment Broker; b/Aug 8, 1924; h/Longboat Key, FL; m/Hanna M; ed/MBA Col of Holy Cross 1950; mil/USAR Major; pa/Former Chm & Chief Exec Ofcr, US Data Corp; 35 Yrs Tax Conslt & Former Spec Agt, US Treas Intell; Rltr Cnslr CCIM; Prof Univ Sarasota; Nat Assn Accts; Nat Assn Rlts; Fla Real Est Exch VP; Rltrs Nat Mktg Inst; Farm & Land Inst; Manatee Co, Fla Bd Rltrs; Nat Real Est Exch; Intl Real Est Exch; Data Processing Mgmt Assn Past Pres; Acad Real Est; cp/USCG Aux; US Power Squadrons; Manatee Co C of C; Mil Order of World Wars; Benevolent & Protective Order of Elks; Am Legion; Order of Ky Cols; r/Cath.

COSTON, ROBERT DONALD oc/Department Head; b/Apr 26, 1942; h/3 Wimbledon Ct, Statesboro, GA 30458; ba/Statesboro; m/Jacquelin Schmidt; c/Elizabeth Celine; p/Ralph and Frances Coston, Monroe, LA; ed/BSBA 1965, MBA 1967 NE La Univ; PhD Univ Ark; pa/Hd Dept Ec, Ga So Col; So Ec Assn; Atlantic Ec Assn; cp/Lt Gov Ga Dist Optimist Intl; r/Epis; hon/Pub'd Author.

COTHRAN, GLENDA MARIE oc/Writer, Photographer, Investor; b/Nov 21, 1955; h/701 Provine, Memphis, TN 38126; c/Eureka

McDowell; p/Qutesta Cothran, Memphis, TN; r/Bountiful Blessings Ch; hon/W/W Am Wom.

COTTEN, FRANCES LOUISE oc/Minister; b/Oct 3, 1929; h/904 Ave B, McComb, MS 39648; p/Sylvester and Florida W Cotten, McComb, MS; ed/AA Jr Col 1949; Corresp Course by Bd Ordained Min; pa/Assoc Min Centreville Charge; Bkkpr 17 Yrs SW Jr Col; Miss Conf Mins U Meth Ch; Brookhaven Dist Mins; cp/McComb BPW Clb; Nat & Miss Ednl Secys Clb; r/Meth; hon/Wom of Yr 1975, Miss Enthusiasm 1973, BPW Clb of McComb.

COTTON, ELEANOR LOVE GREET oc/Associate Professor; b/Jan 30, 1923; ba/El Paso, TX; m/Donald Reed (dec); c/Cabell Gillette C Capshaw; p/William Dement (dec) and Eleanor Love Martin Greet (dec); ed/BA 1950, MA 1962, PhD 1973 Univ Tex-El Paso; pa/Univ Tex-El Paso: Prof Eng Dept 1960-71, Prof Ling Dept 1971-, Prog Dir Freshman Eng for Fgn Students 1973-80; MLA; Tex Jt Eng Com; SW Coun for Fgn Lang Tchrs; Mex-Am Ednl Assn, Secy 1969; Tex Tchg Eng to Spkrs of Other Langs: VP 1974, Pres 1975; Ling Assn SW; cp/Jr Leag of Mpls; Chi Omega; Dem Party; Bd Mem El Paso Assn of Day Care Ctrs 1975-; r/Epis; hon/Outstg Fac Wom of Yr 1970-71; W/W Am Wom; DIB; Author 2 Chapts in *The Mexican-American Curriculum* 1970; "Noun-Pronoun Pleonasms: The Roles of Age & Situation" *Journal of Child Language* 1978; "Linguistic Design in a Poem by Cummings" *Style* (in press) & "Hypersemanticization in Neologistic - ear/iar Verbs in Mexican-American Spanish" w John Sharp.

COUSINS, SHARON DAVES oc/Nurse, Supervisor; b/Sept 12, 1953; h/321 Woodfield Circle, La Grange, GA 30240; ba/La Grange; m/A Lucian; c/Holly, Luke; p/Otis Wells (dec) and Jewel Dotson Daves (dec); ed/Assoc Deg Nsg So Ga Col 1974; BS St Joseph's Col 1979; pa/RN, Med Nsg Supvr, W Ga Med Ctr; Ga Heart Assn; cp/Dem Party r/Bapt; hon/W/W Am Wom 1979-80.

COVIN, THERON MICHAEL oc/Psychologist; b/Feb 27, 1947; h/Rt 3 Box 117-A-5, Abbeville, AL 35310; p/Fisher Bert Covin (dec); Doris S Knight, Evergreen, AL; ed/AA Jefferson Davis Col 1968; BS 1969, MS 1971 Troy St Univ; EdS Univ Ala 1973; EdD Univ Sarasota 1975; pa/Staff Psych, SE Ala Yth Sers 1979; Asst Prof Sch Ed, Adj Fac, Auburn Univ 1978-80; Dir Child & Fam Mtl Hlth Proj, HEW, Troy, Ala 1977-; Marriage & Fam Cnslr, Pvt Pract, Troy, Ala 1971-; Spec Ed Conslt & Psychometrist, Ala Public Schs 1971-; Num Previous Positions; Kappa Delta Pi; Phi Delta Kappa; AAUP; APGA; Am Mtl Hlth Cnslrs Assn; Ala Mtl Hlth Cnslrs Assn; Assoc Mem Am Assn Marriage & Fam Therapy; Gulf Coast Assn Marriage & Fam Therapy; APGA; Ala Coun on Fam Relats; Am Humanist Assn; hon/Beta Clb 1963; Pres's & Dean's Hon Lists 1966-69; Psi Lambda Psychol Clb 1968-75; Kappa Delta Pi 1970; Zeta Gamma Chapt VP 1970-71; Gamma Beta Phi 1971; Phi Delta Kappa 1973; Outstg Yng Men of Am 1974 & 1980; Contemporary Authors 1974; Compatriot in Ed 1976; W/W S&SW 1980; Num Profl Pubs Incl'g *Basic Statistics for Teachers*; *Basic Statistics for Educators*; *The Psychological Case Study*; "How to Improve Your Child's Performance."

COVINGTON, GEORGIA VERTELL PENDLEY oc/Homemaker; b/Feb 4, 1924; m/Charles Franklin; c/Charlotte Ann, Cynthia Geraine, Cary Gene, Cheryl Royetta; p/Dewey Christopher (dec) and Hannah Dovie Lee Pendley, Madisonville, KY; pa/Past Owner-Oper Drug Store; Typist for Bowling Alley Mfg; cp/Reporter PTA; Com Chp for Consolidation of Schs; 4-H Ldr 9 Yrs; r/So Bapt; hon/Mother of Yr, Hopkins Co 1965; Lttr of Commend for Trippling Donations for Am Red Cross 1971; Friend of 4-H 1975, 1979.

COWEN, DORA REVELLE oc/Homemaker; b/Nov 4, 1922; h/1715 N Union, Shawnee, OK 74801; m/Earnest A; c/E Allen, Mrs Norman Hanks; p/Clifford (dec) and Lillian Revelle (dec); ed/2 Yr Tex Col for Wom; cp/Jr Leag; Vol Shawnee Med Ctr; r/Presb; hon/Deacon 5 Yrs; Secy for Spiritual Life & Stewardship.

COX, ALMA EUGENE VAN HOOK oc/Director of Department of Planning; b/Feb 18, 1946; h/Jackson, MS; m/Frederick Gardiner Jr (dec); c/John Joseph Connors III, Jan Connors Coulson; p/Benjamin Ormond and Helen Van Hook; ed/BS 1955, MA 1958 Memphis St Univ; MEd Miss St Univ 1974; pa/Dir Dept of Plan'g, Miss St Dept Public Wel; Miss Medicaid Comm; Miss Employment Security Comm; Jackson Public Schs; Lausanne Girls Sch; Am Public Wel Assn; ABWA; Am Statistical Assn; cp/Le Bonheur Clb; Le Dejeuner Clb; Miss Repub Party; r/Presb; hon/1st in Class Scholastically.

COX, ARTHUR BOYCE oc/Salesman; b/Sept 15, 1944; m/Shirley; c/Paul, James; p/Arthur and Leora Cox, Old Glory, TX; ed/Lubbock Barber Col 1964; Att'd Tex Tech; Grad Acctg, Draughon's Col 1972; pa/Sales & Sales Mgmt; Motivational Spkr; cp/Mason; r/Bapt; hon/#1 Salesman for LTU-ESI 1970-71; Outstg Sales Mgr Awd 1972; Staff Writer

Texas Barber Journal 1964-66; Free-Lance Writer for LTU-ESI Mthly Pub.

COX, BETTIE LORINE KINARD oc/Administrative Clerk and Legal Clerk; b/Aug 10, 1933; h/2802 Hartnett Blvd, Isle of Palms, SC 29451; c/Cheryl Rose Cox Kornegay; p/Harry T and Lois Allen Kinard; ed/Draughon's Bus Col 1952; Assoc Deg Trident Tech Col; pa/Adm Clerk & Legal Clerk, US Attys Ofc, Charleston, SC 1956-; Adm Clerk En & Wn Dists of SC 1965; Adv Com Wom's Prog, Trident Tech Col; Bd Mem Ednl Foun SC Fed BPW Clbs; Coor Naturalization Ct & Reception for Newly Naturalized Citizens; Dist 6 Chm, SC Fed BPW Clbs 1975-76 & 1976-77; Past Pres Charleston BPW Clbs 1973-74; Press Clb; cp/Am Red Cross; Easter Seal Telethon; Heart Assn; Hotline; r/Bapt; hon/Nat Beta Clb; Merit Ser Awd, US Dept Justice 1972.

COX, BRENDA D oc/Teacher; b/Sept 5, 1952; h/PO Box 538, Richlands, NC 28574; m/Donald C; c/Billy Paul; p/Herbert P and Ella Frances Davis, Bladenboro, NC; ed/AA Mt Olive Col; BA UNC-Wilmington; r/Bapt; hon/Tchr of Yr, Richlands Elem Sch 1979.

COX, COY GENE oc/Minister; b/Feb 21, 1940; h/5712 Madison Pike, Independence, KY 41051; pa/Clarence E and Emma Cox, Middlesboro, KY; pa/Min First Bapt Ch Independence.

COX, DAVIS GRIFFITH oc/Architectural Restorationist, Painter, Sculptor, Designer; b/July 24, 1941; h/803 First St, Terrell, TX 75160; ba/Terrell; m/Kimberly Lairson; p/Jefferson Davis Cox (dec) and Netta Griffith Cox, Terrell, TX; ed/Att'd Stephen F Austin Univ 1959-60, Univ Americas 1960-62; Univ Tex 1962-64; BFA Univ Tex 1966; MFA Boston Univ 1970; pa/Assistant Professor, Head of the Div of Interior Design, E Tex St Univ 1981-; Owner Landmark Restorations 1971-; Wkly Feature Column "Designer's Sketchbook" *Denton Record Chronicle* 1971-; Painting Instr, Dallas Adult Ed Ctr 1964; Art Instr Ctrl Intermediate Sch, Brownsville, Tex 1967-68; Gtr Boston YMCA Art Dir & Crafts Instr 1968-69; Sculpture & Pottery Instr, Boston YMCA 1969-70; Interim Hd, Div of Interior Design, Asst Prof Art, Tex Wom's Univ 1970-71; Exec Dir Grove House Art Sch, Drawing, Anatomy, Painting Instr, Miami, Fla 1973-74; Asst Gallery Dir, Fox-Huddleston Gal, Dallas 1964-65; Free Lance Interior Designer: Dallas, Kan City, Providence (RI), London, Boston, Terrell, Denton (TX) 1964-73; Asst Gal Dir, Boston Univ Art Gals 1969-70; Exhibs: Stephen F Austin Univ Grp Show, E Tex Annual Art Fair, Univ Ams Grp Show, Instituto Americano Norte Americano Grp Exhib, Carriage Ho Gal, Univ Tex Mus Grp Exhib, St Fair of Tex Annual Exhib, Fox-Huddleston Gal, Eugene Frazier Gal, Boston Univ Art Gal; Collections: Univ of Ams, Univ Tex, Boston Univ Sch of Fine & Applied Arts; r/Epis; hon/Stacey Hunt S'ship Awd of Excell 1960; Tex Good Neighbor Comm S'ship 1960, 61; Univ Tex Tuition S'ship 1963-64; Boston Univ Asst'ship 1969-70; E Tex Art Competition 2nd Prize in Painting 1959; 1st Pl Painting, St Fair Tex 1962; 1st Prize Painting, 2nd Prize Sculpture, St Fair Tex 1966.

COX, GAIL WILLBERN oc/Administrator; b/Nov 20, 1924; h/1635 Bissonnet, Houston, TX 77005; ba/Same; m/F Joyce; c/David M, Philip R, Mary J Tevis, Jim L H, Kathryn G; ed/BS Art Ed; pa/Admr Pers Est; Tchr; Lobbyist; Bldr; Cnslr; Mgr; Artist; cp/Sierra Clb; NOW; Cherokee Civic Clb; r/Ch of Christ; hon/W/W Am Wom 1979.

COX, GLENDA oc/Legal Administrator; b/Apr 5, 1937; h/Houston, TX; ba/16th Floor, 2200 Milam Bldg, Houston, TX 77002; m/Don D; c/Janice, Larry; p/John and Eula Barkley, Brownsboro, TX; ed/Fed Inst (now Tyler Commercial Col) 1956; pa/Legal Adm Reynolds, Allen & Cook Inc 1966-; NatAssn Legal Admrs; Houston Chapt Assn Legal Admrs: Secy 1977-78; VP 1978-79, Pres 1979-80; cp/Adv Bd Bus Dept, N Harris Co Col 1978-80; r/Bapt; hon/Valedictorian Whitehouse HS 1955; Articles; Secy Course.

COX, HOLLIS UTAH oc/Veterinarian, Educator; b/Mar 4, 1944; h/1323 Kenilworth Pkwy, Baton Rouge, LA 70808; ba/Baton Rouge; m/Debra Campbell; c/Lindy Belle, Hollis Utah Jr, Matthew Christopher; p/Hollis Roy and Molinda Powell Cox, Midwest City, OK; ed/BS 1965, DVM 1967 Okla St Univ; PhD La St Univ 1973; mil/USAF 1967-69 Capt; pa/Assoc Prof Vet Bacteriology, Dept Vet Microbiol 1975-; Chief, Clin Diagnostic Sers, Vet Microbiol, Vet Tchg Hosp & Clin, Sch of Vet Med 1980-; Auburn Univ Dept Microbiol, Sch of Vet Med, Asst Prof 1973-75; Diplomate, Am Col Vet Microbiols; Spec Microbiol Am Acad Microbiol; Spec in Microbiol Am Soc Clin Pathols; AVMA; La Vet Med Assn; Baton Rouge Area Vet Med Assn (Pres 1980, Pres Elect 1979, Secy-Treas 1977 & 78); Am Soc Micrbiol; Phi Zeta; Sigma Xi; Alpha Psi; Phi Eta Sigma; Assn Wom Vets; Assn Am Vet Med Cols (Elec'd Del to Coun of Edrs for LSU 1977-83); cp/Masonic Lodge; Knights Templar; Scottish Rite; Shriners Rosicrucian; Kenilworth Civic Assn; U Way 1978 Campaign, Sect Chm for Vets; r/So Bapt; hon/Pitman-Moore Res Awd 1966; NDA Postdoct F'ship 1972-73; Sigma Xi Res Awd 1974; Contbr of Articles to *Am Jour of Vet Res*; *Jour of Am Vet Med Assn*; *Vet Med/Small Animal Clin*; *La Agric*.

PERSONALITIES OF THE SOUTH

COX, JOHN WESLEY oc/Assistant Sports Information Director; b/Oct 10, 1955; h/705 Grace Ave, Hattiesburg, MS 39401; ba/H'burg; m/Bettie Hatcher; c/Matthew; p/John W and Margaret S Cox, Middletown, OH; ed/BS Radio & TV; cp/Dir Rosedale Summer Basketball Leag 1973-77; r/Presb; hon/Outstg Broadcaster, Univ So Miss 1977; Outstg Sr Broadcastg, Univ So Miss 1978.

COX, MARK STEPHEN oc/Carpenter; b/Dec 23, 1938; h/Rt 1 Box 61A, Hiwassee, VA 24347; ba/Same; m/Barbara Sue; c/Mark Stephen Jr, Marica Stephanie; p/Hiram Wirt and Violet Tarpin Cox; Hiwassee, VA; mil/AUS; pa/Local 319 Carpenters; r/Prot; hon/Soldier of Month, Ft Stewart, Ga 1958.

COX, MORGAN SAMUEL oc/Farmer, Rancher; b/July 18, 1957; h/Box 1108, Stanton, TX 79782; ba/Same; p/Darrell Robert and Jo Jon Hall Cox, Stanton, TX; ed/Howard Col; cp/VP Stanton JCs; Pres Martin Co Old Settlers Reunion; Chm Martin Co Fair Assn; Martin Co Farm Bur; Martin Co Yng Farmers; Past Pres Tex Jr Hereford Assn; Campaign Wkr St Sen E L Short; r/Meth; hon/4-H Clb: I Dare You Awd, Gold Star Boy Awd; JCs: Rdrunner Travel Awd, Rookie of Yr Awd, Outstg Dir; W/W Am HS; 1st Place St Proj Awd JCs; 2nd Place St Proj Awd JCs.

COX, WILLIAM ANDREW oc/Surgeon; b/Aug 3, 1925; h/5214 Wooldridge Rd, Corpus Christi, TX 78414; ba/Corpus Christi; m/Nina Recelle Hobby; c/Constance Lynn Rogers, Patricia Ann Brown, William Robert, Janet Elaine; p/Virgil Augustus Jr and Dale C Jackson Cox; ed/BS 1950, MD 1954 Emory Univ; Intership Brooke Gen Hosp 1954; Residency: Brooke Gen Hosp 1955-60, Walter Reed Gen Hosp 1960-62; Postgrad Baylor Univ 1961; mil/AUS Col; pa/Thoracic and Cardiovascular Surgery; Attending Staff Driscoll Foun Chd's Hosp, Corpus Christi 1973-; Attending Staff Meml Med Ctr, Corpus Christi 1973-; Chief of Thoracic & Cardiovascular Surg Sect, Meml Med Ctr 1976-; Attending Staff, Drs Hosp, Corpus Christi 1973-; Attending Staff Phys & Surgs Hosp, Corpus Christi 1973-; Courtesy Staff Robstown Riverside Hosp 1973-; Chief of Staff Elect Meml Med Ctr 1979; Chief of Staff Meml Med Ctr 1980; Conslt in Cardio-Thoracic Surg, San Antonio St Chest Hosp 1978-; Clin Prof Thoracic & Cardiovascular Surg, The Univ of Tex Med Sch at San Antonio 1973-; Conslt Thoracic & Cardiovascualr Surg, Brooke Army Med Ctr, San Antonio 1973-; Conslt Thoracic & Cardiovascular Surg, Corpus Christi Naval Hosp 1974-; Diplomate Am Bd Surgery & Am Bd Thoracic Surgs; Soc Thoracic Surgs; AMA; San Antonio Surg Soc; Bexar Co Med Soc; Tex Med Assn; So Thoracic Surg Assn; Dirs of Thoracic Surg Residency Progs; Nueces Co Med Soc; Denton A Cooley Surg Soc; Am Col of Chest Phys; Corpus Christi Surg Soc; cp/Past Commodore Presidio Yacht Clb, San Fran; r/Presb; hon/W/W S&SW 1980-81; Legion of Merit Awd, AUS 1973; Prefix Awd, Thoracic Surg AUS Chest Hosp 1967.

COYNE, MARGARET PURCELL oc/Public Relations Consultant; b/May 9, 1905; h/Apt 1418, 524 N Charles St, Balto, MD 21201; p/Thomas James Coyne (dec); Mary Agnes Purcell (dec); ed/LLB John Randolph Neal Col of Law 1937; Dip Palmer Sch of Authorship 1956; Attended Schs of Jour: Tulane Univ, Georgetown Univ; pa/Corresp Tenn Dailies; Mem In Attendance Eleanor Roosevelt's White House Press Conferences; Free Lance Writer of Feature Articles; Self-Employed Public Relats Conslt 1966-; Wash & Am Newspapers Wom's Clbs; Nat Press Clb; Engr Soc of Balto; Balto Br Nat Leag Am Pen Wom: Pres 1970-72, 1980-82; Treas 1976-80; cp/Md Geneal Soc Archivist 1974-80; Wom's Clb Leag of Balto; r/Roman Cath; hon/Awd of Merit Cit, Md Geneal Soc 1979; Nat Fed of Press Wom Contest Awd for Best Pub'd Interview.

COZAD, JOHN ERVING oc/Rancher, Cattlefeeder; b/Aug 3, 1933; h/PO Box 2948, McAllen, TX 78501; m/Celine; c/Carla, John, Monica, Mary; ed/DVM Tex A&M 1957; mil/ROTC 2 Yrs Tex A&M; pa/Rancher 1973-; Small Animal Pract, Houston 1957-76; Tex Vet Med Assn; AVMA; Soc for Range Mgmt; TIPRD; cp/Past Pres Co Vet Med Assn; r/Cath; hon/W/W Am Cols & Univs 1956-57.

CRAFTON, PAULA MARITA oc/Deputy Commissioner of Agriculture; b/Jan 19, 1954; h/Rt 1, Robards, KY 42452; ba/Frankfort, KY; p/George R and Mary R Crafton, Robards, KY; ed/BS Georgetown Univ Inst; pa/Dpty Commr Agric, St of Ky; Transp Com, So Assn, St Dept of Agric; r/Meth; hon/Yng & 1st Female Dpty Commr in Ky Agric Dept.

CRAFTON-MASTERSON, ADRIENNE oc/Real Estate Executive; b/Mar 6, 1936; h/8200 Rolling Rd, Springfield, VA; 22153; ba/Alexandria, VA; m/Francis T; c/Mary Victoria Powers, Kathleen Joan, John Andrew, Barbara Lynn; p/John Harold (dec) and Adrienne Crafton; w/Student No Va Commun Col 1971-74; pa/Mem Staff T F Green of RI 1944-47, 1954-60; Mem Staff US Sen Com on Campaign Expenditures 1944-45; Clerk House Govt Cps Com 1948-49; Ho Campaign Expenditures Coun 1950; Asst Appt Secy Ofc of Pres 1951-53; w Hubbard Realty, Alexandria 1962-67; Owner Mgr Adrienne Investment Real Est

1968-; No Va Bd Rltrs; Nat Assn Rltrs; Mcht Broker Exch; cp/Exec Secy Leg Chm Richmond Diocesan Coun Cath Wom; Alexandria C of C; Friend of Kennedy Ctr; Nat Hist Soc; Nat Trust Hist Preserv.

CRAIGHEAD, CECELIA JO ROSE oc/Instructor; b/Nov 26, 1942; h/NW of City, Seiling, OK 73663; m/Gordon; c/Tahni, Kimberly; p/Ralph G Jr and Dorothirose Rose, Woodward, OH; ed/BA 1964; Cert'd Aerobics Instr 1977; Cert'd Stained Glass Artisen 1978; pa/Jr HS Eng Instr; OEA; NEA; SEA; cp/Seiling Gold & Country Clb; Okla Flying Farmers; Intl Flying Farmers; r/Meth; hon/W/W Am Cols & Univs 1964; Okla Flying Farmers Queen 1980; Intl Flying Farmers Queen 1980.

CRAIN, LACY E oc/Chemical Company Executive; ba/PO Drawer 20973, Dallas, TX 75220; m/Margie Lynn Cowan; pa/Crain Chem Co: Fdr 1945, Chm of Bd; Pres, Quimicos Crain de Mexico, SA; Chm of Bd & Pres: Crain Indust Products Corp, Petro Mfg Corp; Pres, Crain Chem Intl; Bd Mem, Multinational Mfg Corp; Bd Mem: Conaid Inc, Chem Specs Corp; Am Inst Chem Engrs; Past Pres, Intl Sanitary Supply Assn; Chem Spec Mfrs Assn; Intl Trade Assn; cp/32 deg Mason & Shriner; Past Bd Mem, YMCA; Indust & Ec Devel Com, C of C; Trustee, Tex Meth Home; Dallas Exchange Clb; Lancers Clb of Dallas; Intl Good Neighbor Coun; Bd Dirs, Preston St Bk; Others; r/Highland Park U Meth Ch, Dallas: Ofcl Bd Mem; hon/DHL, London Inst Applied Res 1972.

CRANE, KENT BRUCE oc/Investment Company Executive; b/Jul 25, 1935; h/5597 Seminary Rd, Falls Ch, VA 22041; ba/Wash DC; m/Catherine D; c/Jeffrey, Andrew; p/Willard L and Beth Ewart Crane; ed/BA cum laude Dartmouth Col 1957; Am Univ; mil/AUS 1957-59, 2/Lt to 1/Lt; pa/Pres, Crane Group Ltd; Chm of Bd, Crane Pub'g Co, Ridgewood, NJ; Proj Dir, US Comm on Org of Govt for Conduct of Fgn Pol 1974-; Adm Asst to Rep Peter H B Frelinghuysen (R-NJ) 1974-75; Asst Dir for E Asia & Pacific, US Info Agy 1972-74; Nat Security Affairs Advr to VP US 1969-72; Spec Asst to Sen George Murphy 1968-69; Sr Res Assoc for Fgn Affairs & Secy to Task Force on Conduct of Fgn Relats, Repub Nat Com 1967-68; 2/Secy (Polit Sect), US Embassy, Accra, Ghana 1965-67; Vice Consul, US Consulate, Zanzibar 1964-65; US Dept of St 1963-64; 3/Secy (Polit Sect), US Embassy, Jakarta, Indonesia 1960-62; Others; cp/Explorers Clb; Mt Kenya Safari Clb; Game Conserv Intl; Smithsonian Inst; Metro Clb, NYC; Intl Clb, Wash DC; Inst Strategic Studies; Others; hon/DIB; W/W: Am Polits, S&SW.

CRANSTON, JOHN W oc/Associate Professor; b/Dec 21, 1931; h/Holly Springs, MS; p/Mildred Cranston, Claremont, CA; ed/BA Pomona Col 1953; MA Columbia Univ 1964; PhD Univ Wis-Madison 1970; mil/US Armed Forces in Germany 1953-55 Public Info Spec; pa/Assoc Prof Hist, Rust Col 1974-; Asst Prof Hist, W Tex St U 1970-74; Am Hist Assn; Phi Alpha Theta; Social Sci Hist Assn; r/Epic; hon/Reviews in *Am Hist Review*; Paper Presented; Res in Germany 1977.

CRAPO, DOROTHY S oc/Merchant; b/Dec 3, 1930; h/1700 Father Ryan, Biloxi, MS 39530; ba/Biloxi; m/(dec); c/Deborah C Batia, Pamela C Bozema; Gregory K; p/L B and Dessie A Stewart, Ocean Springs, MS; pa/Pres & Gen Mgr Merchiston Hall Gals, Retail Furniture; cp/Am Heart Assn, Chm Spec Grp; Bd of Dirs C of C; U Way, Bd Dirs & Chm Spec Grp; Bd Dirs Red Cross; Miss Coast Crime Com Secy-Treas; Chm MCTA, Past VChm & Secy; r/Cath.

CRAWFORD, JOHN ARTHUR oc/Formerly in Aeronautics; b/Sept 12, 1911 (dec Dec 31, 1978); h/Formerly 10084 Sunny Ln, PO Box 194, Collegedale, TN 37315; m/Margaret Watkins; c/Margaret Catherine; p/Walter Scott and Mattie Craig Crawford (dec); ed/Wake Forest Col; AB Univ NC 1935; mil/Cmdg Ofcr, Naval Aviation VS-44 Squadron, WWII; Ret'd Lt Cmdr; pa/Flight Instr, Serv-Air Inc, Raleigh Municiple Airport 1946-48; Mgr & Flight Instr, Greenville Aviation Inc 1948-52; Motel Oper, Myrtle Bch, SC 1952-58; Mgr Raleigh Municiple Airport 1958-59; Supvr for AF & Army ROTC Flight Tng Prog; Flight Instr, Justice Aero Co; Owned & Oper'd Small Bus (Motel), Kinston; r/Seventh Day Adventist.

CRAWFORD, LARRY GENE oc/Artist; b/Apr 3, 1949; h/PO Box 193, Chappell Hill, TX 77426; p/Edward and Lois O Kleman, Deville, LA; ed/Computer Programming of Houston 1968-69; La Col 1969-70; pa/Interest Theaters Advt for 13 Theaters; La Pecan Fest Booklet; Alexandria Art Leag 1969-70; r/Meth; hon/Editor of Sch Paper 1967-68; Artist for Sch Yr Book 1967-68; Blue Ribbon for Painting, Alexandria Art Leag 1969; 2nd Place in Beaumont Art Show 1967; Blue Ribbon Washington Co St Fair 1980; 2nd Place Art Show Pensacola, Fla 1973; 1st Chair Flutist, HS Band 1966-68; Artist & Hist Lib Clb 1968; Show Each Yr Westheimer Art Fest; Show Each Yr Blue Bonnet & Scaracron Fests; Painting Comm'd by Burmah Oil & Gas Co 1975; In Process of Compiling Book on Hist Homes of Chappell Hill, Tex.

CRAWFORD, MARGARET WATKINS oc/Secretary, Homemaker; h/10084 Sunny Ln, PO Box 194, Collegedale, TN 37315; m/John Arthur

68

(dec); c/Margaret Catherine; p/Riley Linwood and Eula O Lassiter Watkins (dec); ed/Hoyle Bus Col; pa/Former Typing & Shorthand Instr, Hoyle Bus Col, Raleigh, NC; Former Secy to Mgr, VA Hosp, Durham, NC; r/Seventh Day Adventist.

CREECH, L T oc/Craftsman; b/Dec 22, 1929; h/Rt 1 Box 77, Selma, NC 27576; m/Erdine B; c/Judy, Jerry, Barby, Dwight; p/Luther Thomas Sr (dec) and Elizabeth Creech, Selma, NC; r/Bapt; hon/Ribbons for Crafts.

CREECH, ROGER ARON oc/Supervisor; b/Aug 20, 1935; h/1020 Brookrun Rd, Henderson, NC 27536; ba/Henderson; m/Doris Bryan; c/Bryan, Leigh; p/William T and Sally Creech, Raleigh, NC; ed/Real Est Broker's Lic 1974; Cert Am Mgmt Assn 1976; mil/NC NG 10 Yrs; pa/Supvr Right-of-Way Acquisition, Henderson Dist Carolina Power & Light Co; Am Right-of-Way Assn; cp/Scoutmaster Cape Fear Coun 1961-65; Vance Co U Way Campaign, Commercial Div Chm 1965, Drive Chm 1977, VP 1978, Pres 1979-80; Adv Com CP&L's Polit Action Com 1980; Pres Henderson Kiwanis Clb; r/Meth: Assoc Lay Ldr Rep'g Vance/Granville Cos in Durham Dist.

CREEK, JOHN DENNIS oc/Vice President Sales and Operation; b/May 4, 1951; h/4811 Tamanaco Ct, Arlington, TX 76017; b/Arlington; m/Billie Lou; c/Courtney Aulyne; p/Webster Bennett and Edna Ore Lott Creek, Hagerman, NM; ed/BA Tex Tech Univ 1974; Grad Studies 1975-76 Tex Tech Univ; pa/Field Tech Tait-Andritz 1976, Sales Staff 1977, Dir Mktg 1978; Instr Univ Wis 1979; VP Arus-Andritz 1980-; TAPPI; Am Inst Mining Engrs; cp/Rotary Clb; Repub Party; r/Bapt; hon/W/W S&SW; Awd for Contbn to Univ Wis 1979; Papers Pub'd TAPPI & AIME.

CREEK, JOSEPH WILLIAM oc/Assistant Professor, Assistant Director; b/Apr 18, 1921; h/Troy, AL; ba/Troy St Univ, Troy, AL 36081; m/Gloria Kilpatrick; c/William Judson, Jon Michael; p/Olivia Burkhardt Creek, Morristown, MI; ed/BS 1962, MBA 1964 Auburn Univ; mil/USN 1941-64; pa/Fac Auburn Univ, Tenn Tech Univ & Troy St Univ; Asst Dir, Ctr for Bus & Ec Sers, Troy St Univ; Conslt for St, Sev Local Govts, Bus & Non-Profit Orgs; Am Ec Assn; Delta Sigma Pi; Midsouth Acad Ecs; Assn Univ Bus & Ec Res; Secy Auber Editors; Omicron Delta Epsilon; cp/Lions; hon/Creator and Editor TSU Business and Economic Review 1976-.

CREGGETT, CARUTHA EARNESTYNE oc/Teacher; b/Jan 20, 1927; h/Rt 3, 2800 Ohio St, Pine Bluff, AR 71601; ba/Pine Bluff; m/Joe; c/Barbara Lorraine Johnson, Sherrie Lynn; p/Lee L (dec) and Lanie Thorns, Pine Bluff, AR; ed/BS UAPB; MS Univ Ark; pa/AEA; NEA; cp/Social & Art Clbs; Former Secy Commun Devel Com; r/African Meth-Epis; hon/Outstg Elem Tchrs of Am 1973.

CREW, PAMELA JO SCALES oc/Travel Counselor; b/July 19, 1951; h/Orange, TX; ba/PO Box 126, Orange, TX 77630; m/Walter Earl Crew; p/Grover Allen and Virgie Mansfield Scales, Orangefield, TX; ed/Att'd Lamar Univ 1970; pa/Travel Cnslr, St of Tex; Permit Clerk; cp/Orange Co Sheriff Posse; Uniform Com for St Dept Hwys & Public Transp, Travel & Info Div; r/Bapt; hon/Orange Co Sheriff Posse Rodeo Queen 1970; Tex St Roadrunner Awd 1980.

CREWS, HAROLD RICHARDSON oc/Research Clinical Chemist; b/Aug 31, 1934; h/Hialeah, FL; m/Barbara; c/Mark Richardson, Karen Hope; p/George Mills Crews (dec); Eva Marie Scott, Sylvania, GA; ed/S Ga Col 1958-60; Ga SWn Col 1960-62; Med Col of SC 1963-66; Univ Miami 1966-67; Univ Penn, Wharton Bus Sch 1980-; mil/USN; pa/Res & Devel, All Biol Applictions Relat'd to Applied Biol Scis in Med Indust; NY Acad Sci; AAAS; Am Chem Soc; Am Assn Clin Chem; Can Soc Clin Biochem; r/Prot; hon/Patentee in Relat'd Fields of Interest; W/W 1980.

CRISP, HAROLD oc/Welder; b/Jan 30, 1927; h/1105 Peerless Dr, Cleveland, TN; m/Sue; c/Melissa, Kim, Jeffrey, Jonathan, Joshua; p/J B (dec) and Amanda Crisp, Robbinsville, NC; ed/Att'd Greer Col; mil/USN 1943-46; pa/Knifemaker; cp/Secy Bradley Co Elect Com 1967-77; Chm Bradley Co Dem Party, 1968-70, 1974-76; r/U Meth; hon/Hon Tenn Col 1969; 1st Pl Custom-made Knives 1977, Cleveland Hunting, Rifle & Pistol Clb.

CRISWELL, LEONARD L (DICK) oc/Retired; b/Jan 29, 1908; h/Forney, TX; m/Kathryn W; c/Jim Dick, John Samuel; p/(dec); ed/Att'd Tex A&M; mil/AUS 1942-45; pa/Maintenance Foreman, N Tex Municipal Water Dist 17 Yrs; Farmer; cp/Am Legion Post 591; r/Bapt.

CRITCHER, B LEONARD oc/General Agent; b/Dec 14, 1944; h/Shreveport, LA; ba/S'port; m/Mary Tullie Wyrick; c/Merritt Martin, Leonard Wyrick; p/Calvin Lenard and Alice Critcher, Houston, TX; ed/BA Centenary Col 1967; Mary Ann Ohio Univ 1968; pa/Gen Agt for Pilot Life; Former Mgr Pan Am Life Ins Co; La Yng Mens Com, N La Rep; St Conv Spkr; Outstg Yng Men La Assn; La St Public Ser Com Chm; Past Speech Pathol-Audiol; VP S'port Speech & Hearing Assn; Other Profl Assns; cp/S S'port Kiwanis Clb: Num Ofcs, Outstg Clb Bldg Awd (Kiwanis Intl), Indiv Mbship Awd, Intl Conv Del, Others; S'port JCs: Moderator TV Forum, Spoke Awd of Qtr, Del Nat Conf, Speak-up of Yr, St La; Mar Dimes: Exec Bd Dirs, Walkathon Ldr, V-Chm Bd; Others; Exec Bd Polit Action Coun Caddo Parish; Bd Caddo Parish Repub Party; VP Ohio Repub Clb; Others; r/Broadmoor U Meth Ch: Tchr SS, Bd Coun on Evang, Pres Cornerstone Class, Vis Tchr, Adult Ch Sch Class, Lay Spkr, Adm Bd, Coun on Mins, Num Others; hon/Runner-up Outstg Yng Man S'port; Outstg Yng Men Am; Mayors Commun Ser Awd; Centenary Col: Outstg Grad, Centenary Gentleman, Outstg in Debate Awd, Varsity Tennis Lttrman, Intl Man of Yr, Outstg Jr, Grand Master, Grand Master of Ceremonies, Deans List, Sports Editor, Pres Soph & Jr Classes, Others; Num Biog Listings; Num Hon Socs; Others.

CRITCHER, MARY TULLIE oc/Homemaker; b/Feb 19, 1946; h/Shreveport, LA; m/Leonard; c/Merritt Martin, Leonard Wyrick; p/Tullie and Mary K Wyrick, Magnolia; ed/BFA Ohio Univ 1968; Centenary Col 1964-67; pa/Tchr Speech, Debate & Eng, Nelsonville, Ohio & S'port, La; Debate Coach; Ohio Yng Career Wom; Host Own Radio Prog 1963-64; TV Commercials; cp/Secy AAUW; Ofcr JC Jaynes; Com Chm Centenary Homecoming; Am Mothers Assn; Vol Alexander Speech Ctr; Area Chm Mar Dimes; Chm Cancer Dr; Bd Dirs Easter Seal Dr; Repub Action Coun; r/Broadmoor U Meth Ch: Yth Dir, SS Supt & Ofcr Ofcl Bd, Bd Evang, Pres Cornerstone Class; hon/Zeta Tau Alpha Alumnae Pres; Miss Centenary; Homecoming Maid.

CROCKETT, DELORES LORAINE oc/Regional Administrator; b/June 18, 1947; h/East Pont, GA; ba/Women's Bureau, US Dept Labor, 1371 Peachtree St, NE, Room 323, Atlanta, GA 39367; c/Ayanna Tiombe; p/Mrs A L Latson, Daytona Bch, FL; ed/BA Spelman Col 1969; MA Atlanta Univ 1972; pa/Regional Admr, Wom's Bur, USDOL SEn Region 1979-; Communs Supvr Avon Prods 1977-79; Minority Wom's Employment Prog 1974-77; cp/Gov's Appointee to Ga Adv Coun on Voc Ed 1980-83; Bd Trustees Ldrship Atlanta 1980-83; Bd Dirs Pvt Indust Coun 1979-83; 1 of 17 Sponsors, Atlanta Wom's Network 1979-80; Selected by Gov Busbee as 1 of 23 Georgians to Revise Ga Constitution, Exec Articles & Bd & Comms 1979-80; Ga Comm on Status of Wom 1976-79; Gov's Appointee to Ga Employment & Trg Coun 1978-82; Ad Bds Fulton Co CETA, Coun on Battered Wom, YWCA Proj FOCUS; Ga Del to IWY Conf 1977; BPW Clb Inc, Pres Local Chapt 1975-77, Dist Nom'g Chm 1977-78, St Leg Com 1978-79; r/Epis; hon/Wom in Round for Outstg Ser in Bus & Indust, Hillside Chapel & Truth Ctr 1980; 1 of 10 Outstg Yng People of Atlanta 1979; Wom of Achmt, BPW Clbs 1977 & 1979; Ldrship Ga 1978; Outstg Yng Wom of Am 1977; Ldrship Atlanta 1976-77.

CROFT, AMELIA KENNARD oc/Executive Director; b/July 28,1 916; c/Randell III, Mary C Alley, Thomas D, Philemon K; p/Philemon K (dec) and Mary Hardcastle Wright (dec); ed/AB Bryn Mawr Col 1937, MSW Smith Col 1939; pa/Exec Dir Fam Cnslg Ser 1959-; NASW, ST Bd Mem, VP & Pres; SC Wel Forum, BD Mem, Secy, Prog Chm, St Pres; cp/St James Epis Ch: Pres Wom of Ch, Mem of Vestry of Ch; r/Epis.

CROFT, H COLBERT oc/Evangelist; b/May 4, 1941; h/PO Box 125, Jasper, FL 32052; m/Joyce Smith; p/Arley William (dec) and Josephine G Croft (dec); ed/AA Norman Col 1969; BD Luther Rice Sem 1971; pa/Pastor 11 Yrs, Evangelist 5 Yrs; r/So Bapt; hon/W/W Rel 1977; Nom'd for Gospel Songwriter of Yr 1973; Pub'd Croft Songs for Church Vol I 1976, Vol II 1979.

CROFT, JOYCE oc/Music Evangelist; b/June 16, 1944; h/PO Bxo 125, Jasper, FL 32052; m/H Colbert; p/Daniel (dec) and Jewell C Smith; ed/BCM 1971; pa/Mus Evangelist, So Bapt Conv; r/Bapt; hon/Miss Jasper HS 1962; Author Croft Songs for Church Vol I & II.

CROMER, CHARLES MARION oc/Poet, Musician; b/Sept 15, 1943; h/117 Bostick Dr, Longview, TX 75602; p/Hiram Elisha (dec) and Mary Cromer, Longview, TX; pa/Poetry; Music; cp/Yth Ldr 1967; Bible Sch Wkr 1968; r/Bapt; hon/4 Yr S'ship Letourneau Col 1962.

CROMWELL, CHERYL DORSEY oc/Director Community Services; b/Aug 27, 1946; h/1128 Ocala Rd, Tallahassee, FL 32304; ba/Tallahassee; p/William and Anne C Dorsey, Catonsville, MD; ed/BA Morgan St Col; MSS Bryn Mawr Col; pa/Nat Coun Social Wel; Nat Assn Black Social Wkrs; Coun Social Work Ed; cp/Bd Mem: U Way, Green Thumb, Fla Legal Sers; hon/W/W Am Wom 1979-80; Outstg Yng Wom Am 1974.

CRONAN, HARVEY BERT oc/General Foreman; b/Aug 1, 1947; h/Rt 5 Box 160, Cleveland, TN 37311; m/Virginia Alene Davis; c/Sherry Denise, LeAnn Michele, Jessica Nichole; p/William and Viola Cronan, Benton, TN; ed/Att'd Cleveland St Commun Col 1975 & 77; mil/AUS; pa/Gen Foreman of Steel Fabrication, Magic Chef Inc; r/Ch of Christ.

CRONKHITE, PAT A oc/Rancher, Minister; b/Dec 6, 1942; h/RR 1 Watonga, OK 73772; ba/Same; m/Kelly (dec); c/Kaci Anne, Kelly, Kimbri Kay, Kipton; p/LeRoy and Alma York, Nash, OK: ed/Enid Bus Col; pa/Recording Artist; Pres Cronkhite Christian Ctr.

CROSS, EDNA MORRIS oc/Homemaker; b/Jan 24, 1932; h/601 Northside Dr, Enterprise, AL 36330; m/Allen; c/Debra Ann Middleton; p/Walter E Morris (dec); Mary E Wills Morris Cook, Red Land, AL; pa/Ala Textile Corp, So Bell Telephone; cp/Pres Azalea Garden Clb; Am Red Cross; Leukemia Soc Am; Hosp Vol; Chm, Bd Dirs Pilot Clb; r/Meth.

CROSS, VIRGINIA ROSE oc/Senior Research Chemist; b/Mary 15, 1950; h/Houston, TX; ba/High Performance Polymers, Exxon Chemical Co, PO Box 4309, Houston, TX 77210; m/John P; p/Remi J and Rose M Coussens, Hillsboro, OR; ed/BS Oregon St Univ 1972; PhD MIT 1976; pa/Sr Res Chem, Exxon Chem Co, High Perf Polymers Div 1980-; Sr Res Chem Am Hoechst Corp, Films Div 1979-80; Res Chem Celanese Plastics Co, Films Div 1976-79; Am Chem Soc; Sigma Xi; hon/Author Sev Pubs; 2 Patent Applications.

CROSSLEY, GEORGE LESLIE JR oc/Evangelist, Missionary; b/Apr 3, 1941; h/Deltona, FL; m/Agnes J; p/George L and Katherine Crossley, Sanford, FL; ed/BD 1978; MMin 1979; DMin Luther Rice Sem 1980; mil/AUS 1959-62; pa/Preacher; Missionary Sev Countries; Dir or Publicity Coor, Christian Fests, Orlando-Miami Area; cp/Pres Sanford-Seminole JCs; r/So Bapt; hon/Medal Mayor of Daejon, Korea for Crusade; Plaques from Coms in Daejon, Okgoen, Buyo Crusades.

CROWE, RICHARD A oc/Police Officer; b/July 26, 1936; h/Mound Bayou, MS 38762; p/Henry A and Altie M Thompson Crowe; mil/USAF 1952 MP Trg; pa/Police Ofcr Chgo Police Dept 1961; Wire Ser & Security for VP Hubert Humphrey 1966-69; Pt-time Investigator for Security Ofcr for Standard Oil 1966-69; Org'd Police Dept Mound Bayou & Served as First Chief of Police 1970-79; Ran for Ofc Sheriff Bolivar 1979; Comm Dpty Sheriff Bolivar Co 1970-80; Fdr & Served As Exec Dir Intl March Against Drug Abuse Inc; Nat Police Assn; Intl Police Assn; Chgo Police Assn; Ill Police Assn; St Jude Police Assn; Frat Order of Police; hon/25 Hon or Creditable Mention Awds; 5 Lttrs of Commend.

CROWNOVER, KENNETH ANDREW oc/Combustion Engineer and Energy Coordinator; b/July 6, 1930; m/Mildred Louise Harris; c/Danny Kenneth; p/Charles Perry (dec) and Lela Wilder Crownover, Hillsboro, TN; ed/EE Univ TEnn 1955; BAHY 1975, MAHY 1979 Univ Ala; mil/USN 1951-54; pa/Repub Steel Corp: Meter Inspector Helper 1956, Asst Test Engr 1958, Test Engr 1963, Combustion Engr 1967, Energy Coor & Chm of Energy Conserv Com for So Dist 1979; Ala Indust Assn; cp/Ala Hist Assn; Gadsden Concert Assn; Repub Steel's Spkrs Bur 1978-; Ch Deacon & Ednl Dir 1964-69; Noccalula Civitan Intl, Secy 1969-70 & VP 1970-71; PTA Record Book Chm 1964; BSA Com Chm 1965; r/Ch of Christ; hon/W/W S&SW 1980-81.

CROWTHER, JOHN BELCHER oc/Attorney at Law; b/Mar 20, 1945; h/635 Montclair Ave, Orange City, FL 32763; ba/Orange City; m/Margaret Smith; c/Jennifer Lynn, John Edward, Thomas Millard; p/James O and Betty T Crowther, Hamden, CT; ed/BA 1964, MA 1969, JD 1974 Stetson Univ; mil/AUS Mil Police Corps 1967-79 Capt; pa/Atty at Law; Am Bar Assn; Fla Bar Assn; Volusia Co Bar Assn; cp/Chm Coun, Coun-man Orange City 1977-; Mayor Orange City 1978-79; r/Meth; hon/Outstg Yng Men Am 1979; SW Volusia JCs Outstg Yng Man Awd 1978-79; Fla JCs St Good Gout Awd 1978-79.

CROXTON, THOMAS CLYBURN JR oc/Electronics and Photography Executive; b/May 3, 1942; h/9619 Alexis Dr, Charlotte, NC 28212; ba/Matthews, NC; m/Sylvia Joan Newell; c/Renee, Dawn, Tracie, Matt; p/Thomas Clyburn Sr and Willie Inez Young Croxton, Kershaw, SC; ed/Clemson Col 1960-62; Deg in Elecs Tech, Massey Tech Inst 1965; pa/ElecMaintenance Tech, Kinderfoto Intl, Charlotte 1965-69, Asst Plant Mgr 1969-72; Mgr Production Equip, PCA Intl, Matthews 1972-75, Dir Equip Mfg 1975-; Soc Mfg Engrs; Am Mgmt Assn; cp/Nat Rifle Assn; Woodmen of World; r/Presb; hon/Recip Employer of Yr Awd, NC Assn Retard'd Citizens 1977; W/W S&SW 1980.

CRUMP, FREIDA oc/Manager; b/July 13, 1950; h/1938 Tahiti Ln, Alabaster, AL 35007; ba/Pelham; m/Walter D; c/Michael Anthony; p/Fred W and Melba Jackson Boyd, Alexander City, AL; ed/BS Jacksonville St Univ 1972; MS Univ Ala-B'ham 1980; pa/Owner-Mgr Crump's Sporting Goods; Cleburne Co Bd of Ed; Shelby Co Bd of Ed; Anniston YMCA; Ala St AHPE; Nat Sporting Goods Assn; Ala Dlrs Assn; AAHPER; Hoover Ath Assn; cp/Hoover Ath Assn; Assn Girls Aux, Dir; Local Girl's Aux Dir; WMU Dir; Bapt Yng Wom; r/Bapt; hon/Ala St Softball Tourn 1972-80; All Star Coach 1981; Author: "Cashing in on Physical Education" 1981; "Crump's Sporting Goods Physical Education Catalogue" 1981.

CRUMP, MARY QUINN oc/Company President; b/July 31,1939; h/PO Box 944, Waycross, GA 31501; ba/Same; c/Carla Genetta; p/Hubert G and Etta Belle White, Northport, AL; ed/Patricia Stevens Career & Flnishing Sch; Savannah Sch Interior Decorating; pa/Pres Mary Quinn's Interiors; Pres Mary Quinn's Finishing & Modeling Sch; Profl Model; Mem ITMSA; IM; r/Epis; hon/Bd Dirs ITMAS.

CRUMPTON, MARILYN ELIZABETH oc/Health Officer; b/Sept 29, 1948; ba/Dothan, AL; m/Stanley Rodes Forston, Jr; c/Erin Leah Forston; p/Weymon Richard and Faye Cotton Crumpton, Birmingham, AL: ed/BS Birmingham So Col 1970; MD Univ Ala-Birmingham 1974; Residency Chd's Hosp, Birmingham 1974-77; pa/Pediatrician, Jefferson Hlth Foun 1977-78; Pediatrician, Ped Clin, Lyster Army Hosp 1978-80; Houston Co Hlth Ofcr 1980-; Fellow Am Acad Peds; Ala Chapt Am Acad Peds; Ala Public Hlth Assn; AMA; Del 1981 Ala Med Assn; r/Meth; hon/Chief Resident in Pediatrics at Chd's Hosp in Birmingham 1976-77

CRUSE, IRMA RUSSELL oc/Free Lance Writer, Former Rate Supervisor; b/May 3, 1911; h/136 Memory Ct, Birmingham, AL 35213; ba/B'ham; m/J Clyde (Dec); c/Allan Baird, Howard Russell; p/Charles Henry and Nellie Ledbetter Russell (dec); ed/B'ham-So Col; BA Univ Ala-Tuscaloosa 1975; pa/Current Free Lance Writer, Num Pub'd Writings; S Ctl Bel Co: Ret'd 1976, Rate Supvr in Rates & Tariffs, Former Public Relats Supvr, Editor Employee Mag, Coor Co Advtg Prog in Ala, Total 36 Yrs Ser; Ala Area Rate & Tariff Org; Coor Ala Share Owner-Mgmt Visit Prog; Traffic & Commercial Depts: Sales Clk, TWX Instr, Ser Rep, Tng Coach in Bus Ofc Methods; Secy: Naval Air St, B'ham (for Public Works Ofcr), Chief of Plan'g, Anniston Ordnance Depot; Prog Chm & Editor Newslttr, Ala St Newslttr, Ala St Poetry Soc; St Public Relats Chm, Ala Fdn BPW Clbs; Ala Writers Conclave: Am Prog Chm, Corresp Secy, Rec'g Secy, Prs; Ala Bapt Hist Assn; B'ham Bus Communicators: Past Pres, Corresp Secy, Nat Rep to Intl Coun of Indust Editors, So Coun of Indust Editors; Annual Inst SCIE Del, Outstg Chapt Pres 1978; Past Pres Wom in Communs; cp/Myasthenia Gravis Foun of B'ham: B Mem, Secy; Pres B'ham Quota Clb; Govs Com on Employmt of Handicapped; Actor & Dir Plays & Pageants; W Woodlawn Dramatic Playmakers; Drama Chm Woms Clb B'ham; Wom's C of C; Past CoChm Parent Ed for B'ham City PTA Coun; Proj Vol Power; Jefferson Co Radio & TV Coun; B'ham Coun of Clbs: 1/VP, Bd Dirs Rec'g Secy; Others; r/Mtn Brook Bapt Ch: Tchr Sev SS Classes; hon/9 Awds in Spring 1966 Ad Comp, B'ham Ad Clb; Edit Awds, B'ham Assn of Indust Editors; Soc Coun of Indust Editors; 1st Awd Best Photog, Writing Achmt Awd; Hon Mention, Intl Assn Indust Editors; 1st Place, Assn of Writers for Tech Pubs; 1st Place Best Feature in Jr Comp Sponsored by BAIE & Jefferson Co U Appeal; Freedoms Foun Awd for Public Affairs Emphasis; Nat Hon Soc; B'ham Metro BPW CLb: Wom of Achmt, BPW Mem of Week, Beautiful Activist for 1972; Foremost Wom in Communs; W/W: Am Wom, Ala Notable Wom; Personalities of S; 2000 Wom Achmt; Worlds W/W Wom; Nom'd: Wom of Yr 1975, B'ham Bar Assns Liberty Bell Awd; ARC David Daniel Eleemosynary Awd; Pub'd Num Articles.

CRUTCHFIELD, CAROLYN ANN oc/Physical Therapy Educator; b/Apr 2,1942; h/901 Briarwood St, Morgantown, WV 26505; ba/M'town; p/Leland Arnold Crutchfield; Josephine Katherine Leppink; ed/BA Wn St Col of Colo 1964; MS 1970, EdD 1976 W Va Univ; pa/Phy Therapy Edr, WVU Med Ctr; Staff Phy Therapist, Woorow Wilson Rehab Ctr 1966; Dir Rockingham Crippled Chds Ctr 1967-68; Prof & Acting Dir, Div Phy Therapy WVU 1970-; Univ Coun on Plan'g, Chm Com on Capital Improvements 1977-80; Interim Chm Med Ctr Plan'g Coun 1978; WVU Res Grantee 1968-76; Am Phy Therapy Assn (VP & Pres, Del & Cief Del for WV Chapt; Lectr at Nat Meetings; Chm-Elect of Comm for Cert of Adv'd Clin Competence); Soc of Behavioral Kinesiology; Am Assn Electromyographers & Electrodiagnosticians; So Soc Anatomists; Clin Study Tour of Soviet Union 1978; Author Num Pubs; cp/Mountaineer Camera Clb, Public Relats Chm; r/Roman Cath; hon/Kappa Delta Pi; Phi Delta Kappa; W/W Am Wom 1979-80.

CRUZ, GILBERT RALPH oc/Professor; b/Dec 6, 1929; h/407 Senova Dr, San Antonio, TX 78216; ba/Edinburg, TX; m/Martha O; c/Andres Antonio, Miguel Luis; p/Gilbert and Lottie Cruz, San Antonio, TX; ed/BA, MA St Mary's Univ; PhD St Louis Univ; pa/Prof Am Hist, Pan Am Univ; r/Roman Cath; hon/Sr Fulbright Schlr; Tex Hist Comm Cit; Presidio Hist Awd.

CULBERTSON, HARVEY REX oc/Corporation President, Company Vice President; b/Aug 29, 1919; h/3624 Wosley Dr, Ft Worth, TX 76133; ba/Ft Worth; c/Richard Donnell; p/Harvey D Culbertson (dec); Sarah Ann Primrose (dec); ed/BS Tex Christian Univ 1949; mil/Staff Sgt WWII; pa/Pres Corvette Oil Corp; VP Tex Natural Gas Co; Petro Clb; r/Roman Cath.

CULBERTSON, KATHERYN CAMPBELL oc/State Librarian and Archivist, Attorney; b/Aug 14, 1920; h/800 Glen Leven Dr, Nashville, TN

37204; ba/N'ville; p/Robert Fugate and Mary Campbell Culbertson; ed/BS E Tenn St Univ 1940; BS George Peabody Col Lib Sch 1942; LLB 1968, JD 1971, YMCA Night Law Sch; pa/St Libn & Archivist, Tenn St Lib & Archives 1972-; Atty in Pvt Pract; Dir Ext Ser, Pub Lib of N'ville & Davidson Co 1961-72; Regional Libn, Tenn St Lib & Archives, Johnson City 1953-61; Kingsport Public Sch 1949-51; Ref Libn & Cataloger, Tech Lib, US Bur of Ships, Wash DC 1945-49; Pres Tenn Fed BPW Clb 1974-75; Am & Tenn Bar Assns; Am, SEn & Tenn Lib Assns; cp/DAR; Zonta Intl, N'ville Chapt; YMCA Alumni Assn; Lib Com, Pres's Com Employment of Handicapped 1966-; Bicent of N'ville Century III Com Mem 1979-80; Coor Tenn Conf on Lib & Info Sers 1978; Lib Related Alternate to WHCLIS 1979; AAUW; hon/W/W: Am Wom, S&SW, Am; Eminent Tennesseans of 80's; Tenn BPW Clb Wom of Achmt 1970; N'ville Banner & Davidson Co BPW's 1 of 5 Wom of Yr 1979; Contbr to *Encyclopedia of Education*, vol 7, pages 596-599, 1971.

CULBERTSON, RICHARD DONNELL oc/Attorney; b/July 26, 1945; h/6423 Arthur Dr, Ft Worth, TX 76134; ba/Ft Worth; p/Harvey Rex and Loyce Linnell Ellen duMenil Culbertson, Ft Worth, TX; ed/BA Tex Christian Univ 1967; Univ Tex Law Sch, Univ Tex-Arlington 1967-69; pa/Atty, St Govt Ofcl in Charge of Child Support Collect for 10 Co Area for Tex Dept Human Resources; Am Bar Assn; Tex Bar Assn; Ft Worth-Tarrant Co Bar Assn; Assn Trial Lwyrs Am; Ft Worth-Tarrant Co Yng Lwyrs; Tex Archaeol Soc; cp/Tex Hist Assn Tri-C Clb Pres; Ft Worth JCs; Tarrant Co Hist Soc; Cand Tarrant Co Water Bd 1971, 1972, 1974; hon/Contbr to *Foard Co; Texas History*; & Var Geneal Pubs.

CULLUM, ROBERT FRANCIS oc/Chaplain Coordinator; b/Aug 9, 1932; h/446 Saipan, San Antonio, TX 78221; ba/San Antonio; m/Shirley Rose Harvengt; c/Pamela Kay, Barbara Lynn, Christi Coleen; p/Ralph Francis Cullum, Villa Grove, IL; Mildred McMeekin; ed/BA So Ill Univ 1960; BD 1965, MRE Cand SWn Bapt Theol Sem; ThD Luther Rice Sem 1973; Other Studies Hon DD; mil/USAF 1951-55, S/Sgt; pa/Chaplain Bapt Meml Hosp 1965-66; Chaplain/Cnslr, Masonic Home & Sch, Ft Worth, Tex 1962-65; Pulpit Supply & Revivals, 1959-81; Chaplain/Coor, Tex Dept Mtl Hlth & Mtl Retard 1981-; Exec Dir Intl Marriage & Pastoral Cnslrs Assn; Tchr Num Rel & Related Areas Study Courses & Wkshops; Lectr; Assoc Mem Am Assn Pastoral Cnslrs; Pres, Tex Mtl Hlth & Mtl Retard Chaplains; Projs Com, Coun of Pres; Fellow, Col Chaplains; Am Prot Hosp Assn Certn 1969; Profl Mem So Assn Marriage Cnslrs; Life Fellow, St Andrews Ext Res; Other Profl Assns & Former Activs; cp/Past Pres Half-way House San Antonio, Acad Rel & Mlt Hlth, SASHTPEA Chapt #15; Current Pres Mtl Hlth Assn Bexar Co; r/Ordained Min, So Bapt Conv 1963; hon/W/W Rel; Featured in Articles.

CUMBEE, JOHNNIE GLENN JR oc/Football Coach; b/Sept 2, 1948; h/2902 Newbern Dr, Johnson City, TN 37601; ba/Johnson City; m/Susan Rickenbaker; c/Meredith Kay; p/Johnnie and Mildred Cumbee, Ridge Spring, SC; ed/BS; MEd; pa/Fball Coach, E Tenn St Univ; Am Fball Coaches Assn; F'ship of Christian Aths; cp/US JCs; UPI Bd of Coaches; r/Bapt: Chm of Yth Com, Mem Ch Coun, Bapt Brotherhood Assn; hon/Outstg Yng Men of Am 1976 & 1978.

CUMBIE, MICHAEL HOWARD oc/Systems Director; b/Oct 9, 1947; h/Fayetteville, AR; ba/440 N College Ave, F'ville, AR 72701; m/Aven; c/Matthew; p/Howard F and Bobbie Cumbie, Searcy, AR; ed/Att'd Univ Ark 1966-68 & 75; AA Sacramento St Univ 1972; pa/Chief Exec Ofcr, Computer Div Mother Lode Bank; Mktg Dir Actuarial Assocs of Am Inc; Life Underwriters Tng Coun; NW Ark Underwriters Assn; cp/JCs; r/Luth; hon/Outstg Yng Men Am 1980; Author "The Future of the American Farmer" 1965-66.

CUNNINGHAM, BETHEL PAYTON oc/Assistant Professor; b/Oct 22, 1924; h/1439 Viewpoint Dr, Fayetteville, AR 72701; ba/F'ville; m/Leslie Paul; c/Paul Ray, Leslie Clark; p/James Elmer (dec) and Mamie Lee Payton, Ruidoso Downs, NM; ed/BSHE; MS; RD; pa/Asst Prof Foods & Nutrition, Univ AR; Am Dietetic Assn; Am Home Ec Assn; cp/LWV of Ark; Bd Mem Infant Devel Ctr; hon/Phi Upsilon Omicron; Gamma Sigma Delta; Kappa Kappa Iota; Alpha Delta Kappa.

CUNNINGHAM, KARON LYNETTE oc/Assistant Professor; b/Mar 24, 1950; h/1029 Sante Fe Trail, Canyon, TX 79015; ba/Canyon; p/Orville Weldon and Ruth Aileen Cunningham, Reed, OK; ed/BS H-SU 1972; MEd SWOSU 1977; EdD Okla St Univ 1979; pa/Asst Prof Bus Ed-Ofc Adm, W Tex St Univ; NBEA; MPBEA; Delta Pi Epsilon; Phi Delta Kappa; Kappa Delta Pi; Beta Gamma Sigma; cp/Coor Graded Mus, Adult Choir, First Bpat Ch; r/Bapt; hon/Outstg Yng Wom Am 1978.

CUNNINGHAM, PATRICIA JENKINS oc/Executive Director;

b/May 28, 1936; h/Smithfield, NC; ba/213 N Seventh St, Smithfield, NC 27577; c/Bill Jr, Kathy, Curt, Mike, Mary; p/Knox Vaughan and Eloise Darden Jenkins (dec), Smithfield, NC; ed/UNC-G 1954-55; Peace Col; pa/Exec Dir Johnston Co Coun on Aging; Asst Dir Reimbursement/Patient Relats Rep, O'Berry Ctr/St Mtl Retard Ctr 1974-80; cp/Pres Jr Wom's Clb 1971-73; Pres PTA 1969-79 & 1972-73; Appt'd to Bd, Dept Child & Fam Sers, Child Abuse Div; r/Meth.

CUNNINGHAM, SANDRA oc/Occupational Therapist and Educator; b/Nov 25, 1939; h/#2 Thrasher St, New Orleans, LA 70124; ba/New Orleans; p/Glenn Verniss Cunningham, Conway, AR; Margaret Spein Cunningham, Seattle, WA; ed/BA Univ Iowa; MA USC; pa/Assoc Prof & Head Dept Occupational Therapy, LSU Med Ctr 1977-; Asst Prof & Hd Dept Occupl Therapy, Sch of Allied Hlth Professions, LSU Med Ctr 1973-77; Dir Occupl Therapy Dept, NW Hosp, Seattle, Wash 1970-73; Instr & Coor Clin Internships, Div of Occupl Therapy, Dept of Phys Med & Rehab, Univ Wash 1968-70; Sr Therapist & Supvr, Functional Treatment Prog, Occupl Therapy Dept, Highland View Hosp, Cleveland, Ohio 1965-66; Staff Therapist, Dept Occupl Theray, GM&S, Hines V A Hosp, Hines, Ill 1962-64; AOTA 1959-; WFOT 1965-; LOTA 1974-; ACRM 1978-; New Orleans Area/Bayou-River Hlth Sys Agcy Inc 1978-; WOTA 1969-73; NW Clin Coun 1959-73; hon/Author *Development of a Conceptual Model for the Analysis of Behavioral Adaptations by Occupational Therapists* 1972; *Occupational Therapy Department Capital Improvement Plan (5-10 Year Period)* 1965; *The Instinct Concept: Theoretical Formulations for Evaluating the Adaptiveness of Human Behavior in Activites of Daily Living* 1967; Co-Author *An Educational Model for Occupational Therapy* 1970; Num Presentations Given & Wkshops Attended.

CURTISS, GUINEVERE CLARKSON oc/High School Librarian (Retired); b/Dec 9, 1908; h/208 W Philadelphia Ave, Salisbury, MD 21801; m/Richard Parmele (dec); c/Hilary Richard, Alan Clarkson, Linda C Prause (Mrs Robert H), Gail C Boardman (Mrs Edward); p/Douglas Reid and Annie Mitchell Clarkson (dec); ed/AB Univ Rochester; Rutgers Univ; St Univ Grad Sch Lib Sci; Grad Study: Univ Md, Univ Del; pa/Worked in Rush Rhees Lib, Univ Rochester; Staff Writer, Fortnightly Bultn of Bklyn Inst of Arts & Sci, Bklyn, NY; Chd's Libn, Laurel Public Lib, Laurel, Del; Libn, James M Bennett Sr HS, Salisbury, Md 1962-; Ednl Media Assn of Md; Md St Tchrs Assn; Wicomico Co Free Lib: Bd Dirs 1967-74, Chm Book Com 1971-74; 1961 Initiated Formation of Friends of Lib Wicomico Co Free Lib; cp/AAUW Salisbury Br: Nat Conv Del Chm 1977, Fund-raising Chm 1973, 74, 75, Status of Wom Chm 1953-54, Fine Arts Chm 1955-58, Histn 1956-59, Pres 1962-64. Budget Chm 1965-66, 1954 Org'd Great Books Discussion Groups Sponsored by AAUW & Open to Public, Chm 1954-58, Mem Bd Dirs 1953-59, 1962-66; AAUS Mid St Div; Publicity Chm 1960-61; 1956 Org'd Citizens Com to Promote Fluoridation for Salisbury; U Fund of Wicomico Co: Chm Ho-to-Ho Canvass 1948, Publicity Chm 1956, Mem Bd Dirs 1948-60; Wicomoco Co GSA Coun: Secy 1948, Prog Chm 1950, Mem Bd Dirs 1948-56, Public Relats Chm 1952-56; Wicomico Co Coun for Prevention & Treatmt of Juvenile Delinquency: Secy 1959, Publicity Chm 1959, Mem Bd Dirs 1959; Area Residential Chm, Salisbury Cancer Dr 1975; Bd Dirs, Wicomico Co Dept Social Sers 1974-76, 77-; r/Pres Salisbury Unitarian F'ship 2 yrs; Trustee 1958-; Chm Coms at Var Times: Publicity, Prog, Rel Ed.

CUSHING, HARRELL RICH oc/Pastor; b/Mar 22, 1931; h/702 Brookmont Dr, Gadsden, AL 35901; ba/Gadsden; m/Ann Weed; c/Charlotte Ann, Jama Joy, Constance Jeanne; p/Malcolm A Cushing (dec); Etha I Rich (dec); ed/BS Fla St Univ 1952; MDiv 1956, ThM 1961 SWn Bapt Theol Sem; DMin 1978 New Orleans Bapt Theol Sem; pa/Pastor: First Bapt Ch Gadsden; First Bapt Ch Andalusia, Ala; Woodstock Pk Bapt Ch, Jacksonville, Fla; First Bapt Ch, Florala, Ala; Trinity Bapt Ch, Pauls Val, Okla; Mem Mission Bd, Fla Bapt Conv; Exec Bd & Adm Comm, Ala Bapt Conv; Fgn Mission Bd So Bapt Conv; cp/Former Mem Rotary Clbs in Florala, Ala & Andalusia, Ala; r/So Bapt; hon/Awd Hon DD 1976 Mobile Col; Writer of Mats for "The Baptist Program" and "Stewardship Sermons."

CUSHMAN, LAURA oc/Educator; b/Nov 1, 1887; h/589 NE 57 St, Miami, FL 33137; ba/Miami; p/Albert and Elisabeth Cushman; ed/AB Morningside Col; pa/Owner Pvt Sch; Fla Coun Indep Schs; NEA; cp/Zonta Clb; r/Meth; hon/Hon LLD, Morningside Col; Theta Sigma Phi.

CYPHERS, CARROL KERLICK oc/Homemaker; b/Mar 8, 1938; h/Rt 3, Box 25, Palestine, TX 75801; ba/Palestine; m/Phillip; c/Deborah, Dusty, Chris, Stephen; p/Ed and Selma Kerlick, College Station, TX; ed/RN; cp/C of C; Dogwood Trails Bd; r/Luth.

PERSONALITIES OF THE SOUTH

D

DABNEY, HUBERT O'DONALD oc/Teacher, Athletic Director; b/Jan 26, 1915; h/411 E Main St, PO Box 866, Leesburg, FL 32748; m/Rebecca B; c/Debra O'Donna Dabney Austin; p/John Morgan (dec) and Bama Morse Dabney (dec); ed/BA Xavier Univ; pa/Coach of Aths & Rec; Babe Ruth Umpire; Red Cross Instr; cp/Redevel Agcy Mem; r/St Pual AME Ch: Supt & Trustee; hon/FACA Awd; Omega Psi Phi; Water Safety Instr; CPR Awd.

DABNEY, JOSEPH EARL SR oc/Public Relations Coordinator, Writer; b/Jan 29, 1929; h/3966 St Clair Ct, Atlanta, GA 30319; ba/Marietta; m/Susanne Knight; c/Geneva D Llewelyn, Joseph Earl Jr, Mark, Scott, Chris, p/Wade Vertell (dec) and Edmona F Dabney (dec); ed/BS Berry Col 1949; pa/mil/AUS Psych War Br 1951-52 Propaganda Writer; pa/Public Relats Coor, Lockheed-Ga Co; Sigma Delta Chi; Altanta Press Clb; cp/Dekalb Co Dem Com; r/Bapt; hon/Knight of Mark Twian; So Nieman Travel Study Grant to Poland/USSR 1958.

DABNEY, WILLIAM ROBERT oc/Police Detective Sergeant; b/Nov 7, 1946; h/420 E Fayle, Baytown, TX 77520; ba/Baytown; c/William David; m/Rebecca F Dabney, Houston, TX; ed/Lee Col; mil/USAF 1965-71 Staff Sgt; TANG; pa/Tex Narcotic Ofcrs Assn; Am Law Enforcement Ofcrs Asn; cp/Tex Fathers for Equal Rights; Police Insignia Collectors Assn; r/Meth; hon/Outstg Jr Ofcr 1968; Outstg Law Ofcr 1972.

DACBERT, DAVID MAURICE oc/President of San Antonio Piano Technicians Guild; President and Member of the International Piano Technicians Guild; Corporate Secretary; Band Instructor & Conductor; b/Jul 2, 1938; h/San Antonio, TX; ba/Dacbert Music Plaza, 1400 Nogalitos St, San Antonio, TX 78204; m/Roberta; 2nd, Carol; c/Maurice David, Dorris (Mother, Roberta); p/Leon (Born in France): Charter Pres of SW Lions Clb of San Antonio) and Dorris Fuller Dacbert, San Antonio; ed/Drum Major in HS, 2 Yrs; Full S'ship to St Marys Univ; Music Maj Deg; S'ship Grant to Play in St Marys ROTC Symphonic Band During Col Career; Asst Drum Maj; pa/HS Drum Major, 2 Yrs; Led All City Bands at Band Festival on High Platform at Alamo Stadium During Battle of the Flowers Fiesta (17 Yrs Old); Band Instr; Piano Tuner; Secy, 2 Dacbert Music Plaza Stores; Mem, Intl Piano Technicians Guild; Keeper of Bees; Famous Throughout San Antonio & SW for Getting Swarms, Appearing on TV (Shown Removing Swarms on Telephone Pole on Houston St, San Antonio, Where Crowds & Police Gathered & Traffic Was Blocked); cp/32° Shriner; Mem, 2 Shrine Bands; Mem, Beethoven Band; Mem, Sons of Am Revolution; Ancestor Col John Bradford & Col Wm Bradford (NC); Descendent of the 1st Families of Va 1607-24, Ancestor Capt Samuel MacOck; r/Presb; hon/5 Gold Contest Medals: Baton Twirling (1), Drum Major (2), Trumpet Playing (2).

DACBERT, DORRIS FULLER (MRS LEON) oc/First Vice President, Dacbert Music Plaza; Civic Leader; b/h/400 Broadview Dr W, San Antonio, TX 78228; ba/San Antonio; m/Leon (born in France; Charter Pres of SW Lions Clb of San Antonio); c/David Maurice; p/Zack A and Lillian Belle A Fuller; ed/Music Studies: Harp, Piano, Organ, Accordian, Voice, Others; Tchrs Deg, Lake Col; Music Tchrs Deg, St Louis; pa/1st VP, 2 Dacbert Music Plaza Stores; Bus Career & Music Trnr, 6½ Yrs; Pres Sev Clbs; Re-orgr & Past Pres, San Antonio Musical Clb, Hon Mem & Husband Hon Mem; Life Mem, Tuesday Musical Clb; cp/Assoc Mem, Daughs of Republic of Tex; DAR: Bd Mem, San Antonio De Bexar Chapt, Chm Motion Picture & TV 12 Yrs, Ancester Col John Bradford & Col Wm Bradford (NC), Descendent of the 1st Families of Va 1607-24, Ancestor Capt Samuel MacOck; Mem, Civic Opera Bd; Past Pres, Fdr, Woms Breakfast Clb; Life Mem, San Antonio Garden Ctr 1974-; Co Chm Mar of Dimes of Whole City San Antonio; Only One To Give Silver Tea for Whole City in Home; An Orgr, Red Carpet Com; San Antonio Conservation Soc; VP & Life Mem, Woms Clb of San Antonio; Chm Spirit of 76 Com of St Fdn of Woms Clbs; Chm Outstg Clb Wom of Tex; Pres Num Clbs; PTA & Coun; Raised Rare Exotic Tropical Fish; Raised & Sold Snow White Canaries; Promoted Litterbug Campaign & Beautify San Antonio Proj; San Antonio Civic Opera; San Antonio Chamber Music Soc; Pres Am Home Round Table of the Woms Clb; 27 Variety Style Shows; Est'd 4 Meml S'ship Funds: San Antonio Woms Clb, San Antonio Musical Clb, Downtown Opti-Mrs Clb, San Antonio Woms Breakfast Clb; Num Others; hon/2 Cit Awds, Daughs of Republic of Tex of Alamo Mission 1976; Emmy Awd from St Pres of Austin; 8 Oscars for Ldrship (Cit), Gen Fdn of Woms Clbs, Wash DC; Num Alamo Dist & Tex St Awds for Ldrship & Programming Outstg Projs; Life Mem Alamo Dist, Oscar 1976; San Antonio Woms Fdn Inc: Life Mem, Oscar 1978; Dorris Dacbert Gen Tex Fdn Woms Clbs Meml Fund Est'd in Her Hon; San Antonio Woms Fdn Dorris Dacbert LVN (Nurses) S'ship Fund Est'd in Her Hon; Num 1st Place Awds; Won 3 Times Tri-Color Highest Awd for Flower

Arrangements in Fiesta Flower Show over entire city & 60 Blue 1st Place Ribbons in Num Shows of Fiesta San Jacinto; Achmt Awd, Gen Fdn Woms Clbs When Nat Convention Held in San Antonio; Hon'd by Being Queen 3 Consecutive Yrs for Lions-Optimists Charity Baseball Games for Selling Largest Amt of Tickets for Boysville; Friendship Awd & CARE Awd, Tex Fdn of Woms Clb; Lib Sers Cit Awd, Gen Fdn; Friend of the Yr, French Legation in Austin, Cit 1976; Featured in Mass Media; Donated Personal Effects & Rifle of Davie Crockett to DRT to be Placed in the Alamo; 1 of 10 Outstg Wom of San Antonio in Clb Category, *Express-News* 1975, Oscar Awd; Hon Mem & Cit, SW Geneal Soc; Hon Citizen of Boysville, Gold Medal 1975; Notable Ams; Personalities of Am; Dorris Dacbert Gen Fund Est'd By Tex Fdn of Woms Clbs of St of Tex; Wom of Wk 1960; Hon'd with a few others on Bronze Plaque at the Entrance of Sunken Garden Theatre in Brackenridge Park of City for Preserving & Preventing City From Putting City Ball Park There; At Beginning of Fiesta of Kings Night River Parade, Hon'd by Rep'g Woms Clb of San Antonio on Float; Much Recog for Clb Work from City, St, Nation.

DALE, RUSSEL oc/Pipe Fitter, Foreman; b/Oct 10, 1944; h/2816 Moore Ave, Bay City, TX 77414; c/Angela, Kervin, Lajuan, Sherryl; p/Lewis and Emma Dale, Bay City, TX; ed/Tex So Univ; Jump Master Sch; mil/AUS Paratrooper; pa/Pipe Fitter, Foreman, S Tex Proj Brown and Root; r/Bapt; hon/2 Silver Stars; 2 Bronze Stars; Army Commend Medal; Good Conduct Medal; Ser Medal w Oak Leaf Cluster; Nat Defense Ser Medal, Vietnam Campaign; Vietnam Cit; Combat Infantry Badge; Sr Paratrooper Jump Wings; Expert Infantryman Badge.

DALLAIRE, ANDREW R oc/Quality Control Supervisor; Bird Tamer; b/July 7, 1939; h/Spainhour Rd, Morganton, NC 28655; m/Eunice R; c/Donna Jeanne Reddy and Diane Marie Bodine; mil/USAF 4 Yrs; pa/QC Supvr, Marantz Co; Display Bus, Providence, RI 14 Yrs; Tame Exotic & Tropical Birds; cp/Seekonk, MA Taxpayers Assn; r/Roman Cath.

D'AMICO, SALVATORE J oc/Chief Counsel, Subcommittee on Surface Transportation; b/Feb 11, 1924; h/8331 Wagon Wheel Rd, Alexandria, VA; ba/Washington, DC; m/Mary Rafferty Rowe; p/Santo D'Amico (dec); Frances Saggio D'Amico, Garfield, NJ; ed/AB; LLD; pa/Mem: NY, Va, Wash, DC Bars; cp/Chief Counsel, Sub-Com on Surface Transport, US Ho of Reps; Nat Com on Uniform Traffic Laws & Ordinances; Alt Mem Exec Com; hon/Lectr, NYC Police Acad.

DANIEL, EUNICE BACON oc/Retired; b/Jan 31, 1922; h/23 Culverton Ct, Savannah, GA 31406; m/Curtis Warren (dec); p/John Henry and Marietta Bacon (dec); ed/Culver-Bacon; Bus Adm Temple Univ 1955-56; Cert Programmer Computer Ednl Inst 1968; Cert Adm Supv for Wom, Drake Univ 1972; Cert Mgmt Concepts Ia St Univ 1972; Cert Ofc Mgmt Kirkwood Commun Col 1974; pa/Ret'd 1977 After 32 Yrs, 7 Mos w US Govt Ser (VARO-GS-11, Chief, Interviewing Unit); Coun Mem Am Soc Public Adm 1972-73; Conf Minority Public Admrs; Bus Indust Mgmt Clb; Intl Mgmt Coun 1972-73; Equal Employ Opport Com of VA 1972-73; Fed & Am Bus Wom Assns; Asst VP Cir Mission Ch Home & Tng Sch NCY & Phila 1951-56; Rosebud Choir 1946-56; Co-Owner Divine Hotel Riviera, Newark, NJ; cp/Ga St Notary Public; Mem & Secy Bd of Dirs Wesley Commun Ctrs 1978-79; NARFE; AARP; Musolits & Pinochle; r/Asbury U Meth Ch: Trustee 1978-79, Choir, UMW, Adm Bd, Coor Fam Mins; hon/Ser Pin & Cert Apprec (Career Ser Awd) for Completion 25 Yrs Ser w US Govt V Actr 1969; 4 Outstg Rating Awds, 4 Superior Perf Awds, Quality Increase Awd, Lttr of Mo Awd; 30 Yrs Ser Awd & Pin 1974; Personalities of W&MW 1973; Community Ldrs & Noteworthy Ams 1974-76; Notable Ams of Bicent Era 1976; Notable Ams 1977; World W/W Wom 1979.

DANIELL, VANCE LYNDALL oc/Minister; b/Jan 12, 1953; ba/PO Box 116, Newport, VA 24128; p/Jack Matthews and Colleen Woodruff Daniell, Asheville, NC; ed/BA UNC-A 1976; MDiv Lexington Theol Sem 1979; pa/Min First Christian Ch, Newport; cp/Ruritan Clb; r/Christian.

DANIELS, CAROL DEAN oc/Coal Miner; b/Nov 29, 1953; h/Rt 1 Box 149-D, Pineville, KY 40977; /Sonya Jean, Kris Edward; p/Elwood and Helen Davis Robbins, Pineville, KY; ed/S Ctrl Bell Telephone Co Poleclimbing Tng; Cert'd Impoundment Inspector; Att'g Lincoln Meml Univ; pa/Lineman S Ctrl Bell Telephone Co, 1977-78; Coal Miner Bell Co Coal Corp 1978-; cp/PTO; r/Pentecostal; hon/Grad Salutatorian, Bell Co HS; S'ship to Lincoln Meml Univ 1980.

DANIELS, DOUGLAS BRYAN I oc/Guidance Counselor; b/Feb 22, 1933; h/1318 S Shivers St, Poplarville, MS 39470; ba/Poplarville; m/Phyllis Gwendolyn; c/Darla Yvonne, Dana Roxanne, Douglas Bryan II; p/Robert Clifton Daniels (dec); Oneita Irene Moody (dec); ed/BS; AAA Cert Guid & Sch Adm; mil/AUS; pa/Guid Cnslr Poplarville HS; NEA; MAE; PEA; MPGA; PBGA; PTA; cp/C of C; 32° Mason; r/First Bapt Ch: Trustee, Former SS Tchr; on/Citizen of Yr Poplarville; 1 of USM Top 4 St-

72

wide Guid Cnslrs Awds; Coach of Yr; All-St Jr Col Qtrback; Most Outstg Ath Awd in HS & Jr Col; European Mil All Star Qtrback.

DANIELS, TONJA ANNE oc/Social Worker; b/Feb 23, 1957; p/David and Claraetta Daniels, Mobile, AL; ed/BA Dillard Univ 1979; pa/Social Worker, Mobile Co Dept Pensions & Security, Food Stamp Ofc; NASW; cp/Mobile Co Urban Leag; Mobile Sicle Cell Foun; r/Roman Cath.

DANNER, CAROLYN DAVIDSON oc/Florist; b/Dec 6, 1910; h/814 Hidalgo, New Orleans, LA 70124; ba/Same; m/Daniel Lawrence; c/Carolyn E Lastrapes, Julie A Clevenger, Jane E Anderson; p/Clarence Edward Davidson; Evelyn Lewis Machen; pa/Florist; Creator Ribbon Rose Design; r/Christian.

DARLAK, JOSEPH JOHN oc/Diagnostic Radiologist; b/March 18, 1931; h/422 Lowerline, New Orleans, LA 70118; ba/New Orleans; m/Gloria Jean Ross; c/Laurie Ann, Jeannie Marie, Joseph John III, Jeffrey Eugene; p/John and Stella Darlak (dec); ed/Pre-Med, Univ Buffalo 1952; MD Univ Buffalo Med Sch 1956; Intern Boston City Hosp 1957; Tng in Radiology, Madigan Gen Hosp; mil/AUS Med Corps 1957-79; pa/AUS Radiology Pract 22 Yrs, Ret'd Oct 1979 as Chm Radiol, Walter Reed Army Med Ctr; Assoc Prof Radiol, LSU Med Ctr, Hd Spec Procedures & Head Chest Radiol Sect; AMA; ACR; RSNA; Bavarian Am Radiol Soc, Pres; r/Rom Cath; hon/Army Commend Medal; Nat Defense Medal; Armed Forces Exped Medal; Merit Ser Medal; Author "Calcifications of the Liver".

DARMAN, RICHARD GORDON oc/Lecturer, Harvard University; b/May 10, 1943; h/1137 Crest Ln, McLean, VA 22101; ba/Cambridge, MA; m/Kathleen Emmet; c/William Temple Emmet; p/M H and E F Darman, Lincoln, MA; ed/BA cum laude 1964, MBA 1967 Harvard Univ; pa/Asst to Secy of Def 1973; US Asst Secy of Commerce 1976-77; US Rep for Law of Sea Negotiations 1977; Lectr, Public Policy & Mgmt, Harvard Univ; Mem: Coun on Fgn Relats, Intl Law Assn; Editor *Harvard Education Review* 1970; hon/Fellow Woodrow Wilson Ctr for Scholars, The Smithsonian 1974; Outstg Yg Men of Am.

DARNELL, DAVID R oc/Minister; b/July 3, 1931; h/Perryton, TX; ba/PO Drawer D, Perryton, TX 79070; m/Sarah Kelly; c/Timothy, Anthony, David, Krista; p/Dewey R (dec) and Margaret Darnell, Las Cruces, NM; ed/BS 1953; MDiv 1962; PhD 1973; pa/Min Christian Ch; Bible Lectr; cp/Bd Dirs, The Christian Ch (Disciples of Christ) in US & Can; Bd Dirs The Christian Ch in SW; Bd Dirs Hi-Plains Area Christian Ch; Bd Dirs Beehive Day Care Ctr; U Way; hon/Author *Rebellion, Rest and the Word of God* 1973.

DASCHKE, CARL EDWARD oc/Intelligence Analyst; b/Feb 18, 1946; h/Honolulu, HI; ba/Directorate for Combat Developments, US Army Aviation Ctr, Ft Rucker, AL 36362; m/Kathy Cooper; c/Kimberly Ann, Carl Victor; p/Leonard Victor and Frances Leach Daschke, Shawnee, KS; ed/BSEd Cameron Univ 1973; MBA Embry-Riddle Univ 1981; mil/AUS Capt; pa/Authority on Soviet Attack Aircraft & Their Employment; Assn AUS, Armor Assn; r/Roman Cath; hon/Outstg Armor Lt 1974; 3 Time Monthly Writers Awd, Aviation Digest; Pub'd "Air-to-Air Fact or Fiction" 1979; "The Artillery Threat" 1979; Sev Other Mil Articles.

DASHER, CHARLOTTE ANN oc/Senior Vocational Rehabilitation Counselor; b/Sept 11, 1948; h/1478 Twila Dr, Tifton, GA 31794; ba/Tifton; p/Johnny Vestus and Alma Lee Griner Dasher, Nashville, GA; ed/AA DeKalb Jr Col 1972; BS Ga St Univ 1974; MEd Univ Ga 1979; pa/Sr Voc Rehab Cnslr 1980-; Ga Regional Cnslg Assn; Nat Rehab Assn; Past Pres SW Dist Chapt Ga Rehab Cnslg Assn; Spec Ed Adv Com; Ga Assn Retard'd Citizens; Coun Exceptl Chd; Adv Com Handicaped Ben Hill-Irwin Tech Sch; cp/Tiftarea Civitan Clb; r/Bapt.

DAUBENSPECK, WAYNE MARTEL oc/Clergyman, Chaplain; b/Nov 25, 1904; h/208 W 22nd, Kannapolis, NC 28081; m/Ethel Mason (dec); 2nd Ollie Blackwelder Allman (dec); 3rd Christine Helen Dunn; c/Richard Edward, Ruth Elizabeth Kistler, Henry Mason; p/Lloyd Mashine Daubenspeck (dec); Della A Burns (dec); ed/AB Susquehanna Univ 1927; Dipl Susquehanna Univ Theol Sch 1930; Clin Tng Greystone Mtl Hosp 1936; Chaplain Sch Courses; mil/USAR Col Ret'd 1964; pa/Ordained 1938-; Pastor Oshkosh-Lewellyn, Neb 1930-35; Comm'd 1/Lt Chaplain Corps USAR 1935; Chaplain Neb Dist CCC 1935-38; Chaplain US Fed Prison Sys Lewisburg-Ft Leavenworth, KS 1938-40; Chaplain AUS 1940-54; 34th Inf Regt 1941; Ft McCoy, Wis & ETO 1943-45; Ft Sam Houston, Tex 1945-47; Wnd Armored Div Cp Hood, Tex 1947-49; HQs TRUST, Trieste, Italy 1949-52; Camp Pickett, Va 1952-54; Pastor Luth Ser Comm, Japan 1954-59 & Seoul, Korea 1960-63; Pastor Parish of St David, Kannapolis, NC 1964-69; Ret'd 1969; Supply Pastor Var Congress 1970]-75; cp/Resv Ofcrs Assn; Am Legion; VFW, Past St Chaplain; Mason 32°; r/Ministerial Assn; hon/Bronze Star & 7 Ser Medals; 4 Nat Awds, VFW; 4 Commun Ser Awds; 1 Local Ser Awd; Cit, Luth Ser Comm; Cit Nat Luth Coun; Pastor Emeritus, St David, Kannapolis; W/W S&SW; Men Achmt; Life Sketches of Luth Mins in NC; Fellow Mem ABI.

DAUGHERTY, FRED oc/Judge; b/Aug 18, 1914; h/1800 Coventry Ln, Okla City, OK; m/Marjorie E Green (dec); 2nd Betsy F Amis; ed/LLB Cumberland Univ 1934; Att'd Okla City Univ 1934-35, Okla Univ 1936-37; mil/AUS WWII; Major Gen 45th Inf Div 1960; pa/Admitted to Okla St Bar 1937; Gen Pract, Okla City 1937-40; Mem Firm Ames, Ames & Daugherty 1946-50; Mem Firm Ames, Daugherty, Bynum & Black 1952-56; Appt'd Judge Dist Ct, 7th Judicial Dist, St of Okla 1955-61; Appt'd US Dist Judge, Wn, En & No Dists of Okla 1961-, Chief Judge 1972; Mem Judicial Conf of US 1973-76; Okla Co Bar Assn; Okla Bar Assn; Am Bar Assn; Am Bar Foun; Fed Bar Assn; cp/Kiwanis Clb of Okla city: Pres 1957, Lt Gov Div 19 Tex-Okla Div 1959; Am Nat Red Cross: Nat Fund V-Chm for Okla 1956-57 & 57-58, Regional Fund V-Chm for Okla 1958-59 & 59-60, Chm Okla Co Chapt 1958-60, Mem Mid-Wn Area Adv Coun 1959-62, Chm Resolutions Com Nat Conv 1962, Mem Nat Bd Govs 1963-66 & 66-69, 3rd V-Chm 1968-69; Okla City C of C: V-Chm Mil Affairs Com 1958-60, Bd Dirs 1960-61, 66-67, 71-72 & 77-78, Corp Bd of Dirs 1969-70; U Fund of Gtr Okla City: Chm Public Employees Div 1957 & 58, Bd Dirs 1958-62, V-Chm 1959, VP 1960, Exec Com 1960-61, Pres 1961, Bd Trustees 1963-; Okla Co Assn Mtl Hlth, Profl Adv Com 1963-70; Okla Sci & Arts Foun, Adv Bd 1964-; Commun Coun of Okla City & Co: Bd Dirs 1962-66, VP 1965-66, Prse 1967-69; Okla City Coun on Alcoholism, Exec Com 1964-; Okla Med Res Foun, Exec Com 1966-69; Men's Dinner Clb of Okla City: Exec Com 1963-70, Pres 1966-69; Okla Heritage Assn, Bd Dirs 1970-73; 33° Mason, Guthrie Scottish Rite; Shriner, India Temple, Jester, Ct 78, Okla City: Dir 1967; Guthrie Scottish Rite, AASRFM: Pres Guthrie Scottish Rite Charitable & Ednl Foun 1971-, Bd Dirs Guthrie Scottish Rite Bldg Co 1971-, Inspector Gen's Adv Con 1975-, Scottish Rite Coun of Okla 1975-; Sigma Alpha Epsilon; Phi Delta Phi; Chm 45th Inf Div Mus Bd Dirs 1974-; NG Assn of US: Chm Army Affairs Com 1962 & 63, Chm Roles & Missions Com 1964; 45th Infantry Div Assn; AMVETS; Am Legion Post 35; Assn of AUS: Okla St Pres 1962-65, Nat Adv Bd of Dirs 1964-70; Okla NG Assn, Pres 1947; VFW Post 1857; Mil Order of World Wars, Comdr Okla City Chapt 1968-69; Nat Sojourners; hon/Combat Infantryman's Badge; Legion of Merit Medal w 2 OLCs; Bronze Star Medal w OLC; Philippine Pres Unit Cit; Invasion Arrowhead; Philippine Liberation Medal; UN Ser Medal; Okla Dist'd Ser Medal; NG Assn Dist'd Ser Medal.

DAUGHTRIDGE, PARTHA COUNCIL oc/Marketing Administration and Finance Manager; b/June 6, 1952; h/927 Tarboro St, Rocky Mt, NC; ba/Rocky Mt, NC; m/William Gray Jr; p/Addison W Council; Newport News, VA; Sarah Baker, So Pines, NC; ed/BS ECU 1974; pa/Mgr Mktg Adm & Fin Hardee's Food Sys Inc; cp/JCettes, Rocky Mt Chapt; r/First Presb Ch Rocky Mt: SS Tchr, Yth Grp Dir.

DAUPHIN, DONALD MAX oc/Insurance Agent; b/July 11, 1932; h/3617 Cheyenne Dr, Woodward, OK 73901; ba/Woodward; m/Ramona Stout; c/Martin M, Debra D, Lisa L, Karen K; p/Ted F and Alma Wylie Dauphin, Mooreland, OK; ed/NWn Okla St Univ 1957; Casualty & Life Ins Lic 1959; mil/AUS Infantry Div 1953-55; pa/Don Daupin Ins Agcy; Farmers Ins Grp Preferred Underwriting Agt 1970-; Life Masters & Commercial Masters Clbs; cp/Exalted Ruler Woodward Elks Lodge 1969; Charter Mem Woodward Rotary Clb, Pres 1970; r/Meth; hon/Watch Band w Farmers Ins Grp Emblem for 20 Yrs Ser 1979; Watch for 1979 Mem Commercial Round Table; Ruby Ring for Prod, Life Masters & Commercial Masters 1977; Dist Agt of Yr 1973, 74, 75, 76, 77, 78, 79.

DAVENPORT, EVELYN CORA oc/Policewoman; b/Apr 21, 1946; h/431 Davenport Rd, SW, Resaca, GA 30735; ba/Dalton, GA; m/Tommy; c/Billy; p/Millard and Gladys Tuggle, Dalton, GA; ed/Lic'd Beautician; mil/Wom's Army Corp; r/Bapt; hon/WAC of Qtr; Co-Capt Dril Team; Homecoming Queen Cand.

DAVENPORT, JOHN PAUL oc/State Chaplain; b/Apr, 1920; h/500 Orange Ave, Circle Belle Glade, FL 33430; ba/Same; m/Tessie C; c/Patricia Lucile Fuller, Daniel Lonny, Debra Lee Kerston; p/John Agusta Davenport (dec); Beatrice Hartman Davenport, Miami, FL; ed/BA; MTh Dallas Theol Sem; pa/Chaplain for St of Fla; Mem: ACCA, APCA, Fl Chaplains Assn; cp/Dem Party; r/U Meth; Mem Fla Annual Conf; hon/Endorsed by Chaplains Comm of U Meth Ch.

DAVES, DORYES oc/Receptionist; b/Jan 21, 1931; h/Hot Springs, AR; m/Arvel R; c/Drenda Clemons, Dalton, Derrol, Dwight; p/Robert B and Mary Belle Raper, Hot Springs, AR; ed/Att'd Garland Co Commun Col 1979; Cert of Tng, Degray Lake St Pk Poetry Wkshop 1979; pa/Recept for Public Acct; Nat Fed St Poetry Socs Inc; Poets Roundtable of Ark; Ark Authors, Composers & Artists Soc; cp/Past Mem Firemens Aux of Hot Springs; Past Mem Ark PTA; r/Pentecostal; hon/Ark Poetry Day 1977:

1st Prize, 3rd Prize, Hon Mention; Ark Poetry Day 1978: 2nd Pl, 2nd Pl Illus Poetry, Hon Mention; Ozark Writers & Artists Guild 1978 Hon Mention; Ark Poetry Day 1979: 1st Pl, 2nd Pl, 3rd Pl Illus Poetry, 3rd Luncheon Awd; Nat Fed Contest 6th Hon Mention; Annual Ark Anthol Contest 5th Pl 1979; Author *Spendrift Words* 1979; *Bible Based Poetry* 1979; Pub'd in Jours, Anthols, Newspapers.

DAVIDSON, JOY A oc/Nurse; b/Nov 21, 1937; h/1424 S Peninsula, Daytona Bch, FL 32018; m/Edward Bourke; c/Kathy, Karen; p/John and Helen Rogers, Cinci, OH; ed/DIP, RN; pa/Oncology Nsg; Jai Alai Nsg; Daytona Intl Speedway Nsg; Room Tchr & Tchr Aide; r/Roman Cath.

DAVIDSON, MABEL ELIZABETH oc/Writer, Speaker, Homemaker; b/May 20, 1901; h/233 Bay Shore Dr, Cape Coral, FL 33904; RR #1, Colfax, IN 46035; m/Dwight L; c/Evelyn Mae Potvoricky; p/Richard Matthew and Lida Jane Steele Farlow (dec); ed/Ind Univ; Purdue Univ; Hon Lttr & Cert, Famous Writers Sch 1966; pa/Writer, Spkr, Pubr; Intl Travel Study Clb; IPA; cp/Homemakers Clb; Intl Toastmistress Clbs; r/Meth U Woms Org; SS Tchr 25 Yrs; Other Ch Ofcs; hon/Pub'd Author: *Legend and Lore From America's Crossroads* (1 of Ind Univ's Most Dist'd Bks of Yr Awd, Ind Days at Lafayette Bk of Yr 1972), *Recollections of A Country Gal* (1st Awd Winning Bk at Age 70), *Out Of The Past --Into The Future*; Bk Awds; Public Sch Spkr Awds, Intl Toastmistress Clbs in Ind, Fla; Accomplishmts & Bks Featured in Brochure of Eicent Yr for Famous Writers Sch; Chosen 1 of 8 Outstg Students of Famous Writers Sch; Fellow Mem ABI.

DAVIS, ANDREW GANES oc/Chaplain; b/Jan 10, 1948; h/706 Winston St, Opelika, AL 36810; ba/Opelika; m/Margaret Ann; c/Andrew Greer; p/Van Buren (dec) and Lola Hawkins Davis, Laurel, MS; ed/BA Univ So Miss; MDiv Emory Univ; ThM Columbia Theol Sem; pa/Chaplain Lee Co Hosp; Ala Coun on Fam Relats; Assn for Clin Pastoral Ed; Ala Div Nat Coun on Alcoholism; r/U Meth.

DAVIS, ANNE MALLARD oc/Writer; h/Rt #2, Box 236, Whittier, NC; ba/Same; m/Harry E (dec); p/George Howard Osterhout (dec); Carriemae Morrall Osterhout, Beaufort, SC; ed/AB English, MA Dramatic Art UNC-Chapel Hill; pa/1950-65: Producer's Asst, Production Asst, Author, Profl Actress; 1965-70: Editorial Res Asst, Carolina Playmakers, UNC, Author Histl Articles, Publicity Releases; Asst to Dir Paul Nickell on 4 TV Shows Produced by Univ: "The Medium", "Days Between", "Box and Cox", "Lion in Winter"; Production Coor for "Unto These Hills", Cherokee, NC; Author 1st Novel: *None to Comfort Me*, 1978; r/Bapt; hon/Rockefeller F'ship.

DAVIS, BEATRICE GRACE oc/Lecturer, Lawyer, Retired Immigration Judge; b/Dec 7, 1913; h/1900 S Eads St, Arlington, VA 22202; p/Maurice W and Anne G Davis (dec); ed/BA cum laude Hunter Col 1935; MPA 1947, JD 1968 NY Univ; pa/Spkr & Lectr, Immigration & Naturalization 1976–; Immigration Judge (1st Wom) 1971-75; Gen Atty, US Dept Justice, Immigration & Naturalizaion Ser 1963-71; Pvt Law Pract, Immigration & Naturalization Specialist, Intl Conslt 1956-63; US Dept Justice, Immigration & Naturalization Ser 1941-55; Supvy Clk, Law Clk, Law Libn, Naturalization Exmr & Exec Asst to Dist Counsel; Secy 1937-41; Tchr Sch Bus Pract & Spch, RKO Bldg, NYC, NY 1936-37; Am Inst Acad: Fellow, Hon Life Mbrship; Nat Assn Wom Lwyrs, Intl Law Com; Fed Bar Assn, Immigration Com; Am Soc Public Adm 1948-63; Nat Bus & Profl Coun, Pres 1962-63 (1st Wom); Bronx Woms Bar: Past Dir, Spkrs Panel; Ill Woms Bar: Intl Law & Public Relats Coms 1965-66; BPW Clb, World Affairs Com 1967-68; r/Luth; hon/Phi Beta Kappa; DHL Philathea Col, London, Ontario, Canada 1963; W/W: Am Wom, E, Commerce & Indust; DIB; Cert Merit; 2000 Wom Achmt; Fellow Mem ABI.

DAVIS, BETTIE BEDFORD SLAGLE oc/Teacher; b/June 3, 1933; h/Canyon, TX; ba/Sunrise Sch, 5123 E 14th, Amarillo, TX 79104; c/Dwight Franklyn, Lesley, Douglas Edward; p/Anne Slagle Keehner, Tucson, AZ; ed/BS 1968, MEd 1975 W Tex St Univ; pa/Spec Ed Tchr, Amarillo Indep Sch Dist; NEA; TSTA; TCTA; ACTA; Amarillo Assn for Retard'd Citizens, Secy 1978-81; Nat Assn Retard'd Citizens; N Plains Assn for Chd w Lrng Disabilities; cp/Tex Dept Human Resources, Past Mem Bd Dirs; Chm Bi-City/Bi-Co Hlth Dept 1978–; r/Bapt; hon/Outstg Elem Tchr Am 1973; W/W Biogl Record, Child Devel Profls 1976.

DAVIS, EDWARD WALLER oc/General Manager, Instructor; b/Jan 30, 1940; h/205 Adams St, Berea, KY 40403; ba/Berea; p/George E and Lois W David, Gladys, VA; ed/BS Berea Col 1962; Sheraton Mgmt Prog 1964; Ramada Mgmt Prog 1975; pa/12 Yrs w Sheraton Corp Am; Kayu Aya Resort, Bali, Indonesia; Boone Tavern, Berea Col; Instr Hotel Mgmt, Berea Col; Hawaii Hotel Assn, Bd Dirs; Kaanapali Bch Ops Assn, Pres; Ky Hotel Assn; cp/Garland Hill Neighborhood Assn; Rotarian; Bd Dirs Hawaii Heart Assn; Past Pres Kauai Heart Assn; r/Bapt; hon/Ky Col 1968; Outstg Yng Men of Am 1968; W/W Am Hotels, Motels, & Inns 1975; FFA St Farmers Deg 1958; Phi Kappa Phi; Pi Gamma Mu.

DAVIS, FRED P oc/Retail Jeweler, Owner Radio Station; b/Aug 23, 1918; h/Elizabethton, TN; ba/405 Elk Ave, Elizabethton, TN 37643; m/Marguerite C; c/Marguerite Elaine Costner, Elizabeth Clark; p/Blanche Boyd David, Elizabethton, TN; ed/Milligan Col; E Tenn St Univ; mil/Ret'd AUS Col; pa/Retail Jewelry & Gifts 1946–; Ptnr Radio Sta WIDD; Owner Millrace Vil Rental Complex (Apts); Bd Dirs Tenn Retail Merchants Coun; Regional Dir Tenn Retail Jewelers Assn; cp/VFW; Am Legion; Elks; Masonic Lodge; Scottish & York Rite Bodies; Shriners; Past Pres E'ton Golf Clb; Kiwanis Clb; E'ton JCs & Watauga Chapt Reserv Ofcrs Assn; Chm E'ton Indust Comm; r/Meth; hon/E'ton JC Yng Man of Yr 1947.

DAVIS, GORDON WILLIAM oc/Associate Professor Physics, Biology & Chemistry; b/Oct 7, 1910; h/10545 NW 28th Ave, Miami, FL 33147; ed/AB Knox Col 1934; MS Wash Univ St Louis, Mo 1938; Addit Study: Knox Col 1935, Wash Univ 1939; mil/Civil Affairs Ofcr 1944-45, Mil Gov 1945-47, Br Advr Chem Corps & Res for NY & NY St 1951-53, Chem Corps Br Advr SC Dist & Chem Res Units Charleston, SC 1953-57; pa/Fdr, 1st Pres Miami-Dade Jr Col N Chapt AAUP 1966–; Del Fla Conf AAUP 1966–; Mem U Prof for Acad Order; Fla Assn Jr Cols; r/Cong Ch Mem; hon/Sigma Xi, Life Mem; DIB; Royal Blue Bk; Nat Social Dir; W/W: E, MW, Am, S&SW, Intl Commun Ser; IPA Dir; 2000 Men Achmt; Chem Clb; Pres Cit, Pres Truman 1948; Nat Reg Prom Ams; UNA-USA; Blue Bk; Gtr Miami Area Social Reg; Nat Ed Specs Reg; Life Fellow Intercont Biog Assn; Pres Miami-Dade Jr Col N Chapt AAUP 1972–; Fellow Mem ABI.

DAVIS, HENRY JR oc/Associate Professor; b/Nov 29, 1922; h/Rt 1 Box 14, Theodore, AL 36582; ba/Mobile; p/Henry (dec) and Edna Foval Davis (dec); ed/BM Boston Univ; MA La St Univ; mil/WWII Vet; pa/Assoc Prof Eng, Spring Hill Col; Free-Lance Writer on Lit; cp/Organist St James Epis Ch; r/Epis; on/Phi Mu Alpha; Crois du Guerre, Charles De Gaulle.

DAVIS, JOHN ALTON JR oc/Accountant; b/Oct 31, 1955; h/Rt 1, Coffee Springs, AL 36318; ba/Enterprise, AL; m/Wendy N; p/John A and Ruth David, Coffee Springs, AL; ed/BS magna cum laude; pa/Ala Assn Public Accts; Nat Assn Public Accts; Pres Wiregrass Chapt Ala Assn Public Accts; r/Bapt; on/Lion of Yr for Dist 34 G; Outstd First Yr Lion for Enterprise Lions Clb.

DAVIS, JOHN CLARENCE JR oc/Chief Executive Officer; Professional Clergyperson Affiliate College of Chaplains USA; b/June 14, 1921; ba/Dr Davis Media Ministries Study and Studios, 1728 Fair Dr, NE, Knoxville, TN 37918; m/Alma Coleen Beets; c/John Clarence III; p/J Clarence Sr and Cora Jane Martin Davis; ed/Att'd Univ Tenn-Knoxville, NWn Univ; BS Metro Univ Calif 1958; MA magna cum laude Kingdom Bible Inst; Hon DLitt Metro Univ of Glendale 1959; PhD Metro Univ Calif 1960; mil/AUS 1951-53 Chaplain, Ofc of Public Info Radio & TV; pa/Fdr *The Chaplain Hour* Radio & TV Armed Forces Network Prog; Ordained to Min 1959; Int Pastor Stamps Meml Bapt Ch Atlnta 1959, Glenbrook Bapt Ch Atlanta 1959-61, Other Chs in Atlanta So Bapt Mins Conf; Served in Var Capacities of Ldrship: Forest Pk Bapt Ch & Druid Hills Bapt Ch; Interim Supply Pastor, Knox Co (Tenn) So Bapt Mins 1970–; Serv Appts, US Civil Ser; Midland So Bapt Conf; Life Mem Atlanta So Bapt Mins Conf; Spkr "A Look At Your Bible" Radio Prog, Commun Awd Series, 1966–; Writer Column, Nat Bi-Cent Rel Awd Series, "Reach Out, America" for *Knoxville News-Sentinel* & Syndication, 1973–; cp/Act Chaplain, Civil Air Patrol 1970-71; Ofcr Chaplain, Am Legion Post 1973-76, USCG Aux 1972-73; Chm Div of Rel Affairs 1973–; K'ville Min Assn Bd of Chaplaincy & Coms; Nat Alumni Assn Univ Tenn; NWn Univ Alumni Assn; Metro Univ Alumni Soc; Assn for Advmt Higher Lrng in Theol Ed through Princeton Univ; Nat Rel Broadcasters Affils; r/Bapt; hon/Recip Nat Bicent Writers Awd, Bicent Comm of Ky 1975; W/W Rel; Nat Rel Broadcasters Blue Book of Ofcl Info; Commun Ldrs & Noteworthy Ams; Book of Honor; Nat Thespian Dramatic Hon Soc Awd; Heart Fund Cert of Merit; Tenn Bar Assn Cert of Apprec; Deafness Res Fun Dist'd Public Ser Awd; Pilot Clb Cert of Apprec; Am Red Cross Dist'd Public Ser Awd; JC Cert of Apprec; Civitan Intl Public Benefactor Awd; Ky Col; Hon Citizen Boys Town; Other Awds & Hons; Author of Nat Bicent Awd Series *Reach Out America*; Actively Enrolled in Kesler Grad Theol Grad Lib Studies Prog, Vanderbilt Univ.

DAVIS, JOHN CLEMENT SR oc/Education Administrator; b/Feb 13, 1936; h/1923 E Monroe St, Lake City, FL 32055; ba/Lake City; m/Maryann Eddy; c/John C Jr; p/Joe B (dec) and Lora E Davis, Chiefland, FL; ed/BS Fla St Univ; EdD Auburn Univ; mil/AUS 1955-58; pa/Ed Admr, Lake City Commun Col; Iota Lambda Sigma; Phi Delta Kappa; Fla Assn Trade & Indust Ed; Am & Fla Voc Assns; cp/Lake City Lodge 27 F&AM; Minnie Lee 113; OES; r/Bapt; hon/Outstg Edrs Am 1970, 1973.

DAVIS, JOY DURHAM oc/Lecturer, Book Reviewer, Dramatist; b/Sept 19, 1930; h/2108 Kesslen Ct, Dallas, TX 75208; m/Jewell A Jr;

c/William Jewell, Drew Ann; p/Kate Durham Morgan, Jackson, MS; ed/BA Miss Col 1952; pa/Public Spkr 15 Yrs; r/Bapt; Pub'd *Sentence Sermons* 1980.

DAVIS, LOURIE BELL oc/Computer Systems Manager; b/Apr 8, 1930; h/2403 W Okla St, Tulsa, OK 74127; ba/Tulsa; m/Robert Eugene; c/Judith Anne, Robert Patrick; p/Currie Oscar and Irene Rodgers Bell; ed/BS W Tex Univ 1959; pa/Tchr Elem Sch 12 Yrs; Computer Sys & Prog'g 12 Yrs; Blue Cross & Blue Shield of Okla 1971-75, 1977-; Assn of Sys Mgmt, Chm Seminars 1978, Chm Directory 1974, Newsltr Editor 1979; Tulsa Area Sys Ed Assn, Recorder 1978-80; ASTD-Tulsa Chapt; Am Mgmt Assn; Facs of Okla Col & Univ; NEA; OEA; cp/US Sen Bus Adv Bd 1980-81; Adv Bd Computer Sci Tulsa Jr Col 1971-81; r/Presb; hon/MENSA; INTERT&L; Cert of Data Processing; ASM Tulsa Awd of Merit 1978, Intl Awd of Merit 1980; W/W S&SW; Alpha Chi Hon Soc.

DAVIS, MARGARET FRANCES oc/Supervisor; b/Jan 1, 1937; h/50 Roberts Lane, Jackson, TN 38301; ba/Jackson; m/Harrial; c/Darrell Elder, Debbie Lynn Barnett; p/Clifton (dec) and Rusha Holt, Jackson, TN; pa/Supvr Bendix Aftermkt; Am Prod & Inventory Control; Bendix Auto Aftermkt Mgmt Clb; r/Bapt.

DAVIS, OUIDA SUE RISTOM oc/Retired Assistant Professor; b/Sept 17, 1926; h/PO Box 126, Hwy 109, Starks, LA 70661; ba/Same; p/George A (dec) and Susie L Ristom, Starks, LA; ed/BS USL; BS NWn; ME LSU; EdD Univ So Miss; pa/Nat Ret'd Tchrs Assn; La Ret'd Tchrs Assn; Nat Sci Tchrs Assn; Early Childhood Ed Assn; Alumni Assn USL, LSU, USM; r/Meth; hon/W/W Students in Am Cols & Univs 1946; W/W Am Wom; Alpha Sigma Alpha.

DAVIS, PAMELA JO oc/Director Detention Center; b/Oct 9, 1943; h/12230 SW 68 Ave, Miami, FL 33156; ba/Miami; m/J Brower III; c/Darrell Jo, J Brower IV; p/Henry and Ruth Esther Weaver, Coral Gables, FL; ed/BBA 1965; MEd 1972; PhD 1979; pa/Dir Dade Co Wom's Detention Ctr; Am Correct Assn; Am Soc Public Adm; Phi Delta Kappa; AAUW; cp/Wom's Comm of 10; Ctr for Wom Policy Studies; r/Meth; hon/Outstg Yng Wom; Commun Ldr Awd.

DAVIS, PAUL LAVERE oc/Retired; b/May 15, 1909; h/407 S Collins, Tulia, TX 79088; p/(dec); mil/USAF 1942-43; pa/Photographer; Reporter; Salesman; cp/Lions Clb; Helping Vets; r/Bapt; hon/Hon Mention Welfare Commun Wkr.

DAVIS, ROGER WARREN JR oc/Minister; b/Jan 28, 1947; h/2001 Fairview Rd, Gadsden, AL 35901; ba/Same; m/Sarah Frances Davis; c/Jerrery Scott, Steven Keith; p/Roger Warren Sr and Vassie Mae Davis, Douglasville, GA; ed/BS Ala Christian Sch of Rel 1978; MA Ala Christian Grad Sch of Rel 1980; pa/Min Ch of Christ; Preachers Clb Freed Hardenman Col 1965; Col Chorus 1965 & 66; cp/Chaplain Kiwanis Clb 1976; hon/W/W Students Cols & Univs 1978.

DAVIS, ROSIE LEE BURNES oc/Bookkeeper; b/Apr 4, 1934; h/209 W Arlo Rd, Killeen, TX 76541; m/Gordon A; c/Audie L Willingham, Carla Day Willingham, Anthony J DiMaggioo; p/Joseph J (dec) and Abbie Burnes; ed/Monterey Pen Col; mil/Ret'd AUS; pa/Bkkpr Dairymen Assn in Calif; Secy, Bkkpr GA Davis Patio, Sidewalk Construction; cp/Citizen Com for City of Harker Heights, Tex 2 Yrs; VFWA; Pres 1974-75, Dist Ofcr 1976, Dist Pres 1979-80; r/Bapt; hon/Silver Bowl VFWA 1975; Silver Bowl 1979 Outstg Work in Aux 1978; Nat Cert Dept of Tex Americanism & Loyalty.

DAVIS, ROY LAVELLE SR oc/Retired Merchant; b/June 10, 1917; h/504 SW Van Buren, Idabel, OK 74745; m/Ruby Lucille Campbell; c/Roy Lavelle Jr, Theresa Lucile, Vivian Rae; p/John Carrol (dec) and Nancy Maude Davis; mil/AUS 1942-46; pa/Ret'd from Grocery & Furniture Bus 1977; cp/City Coun-man, City of Idabel 1955-56; Qtrmaster VFW Post 4777 4 Yrs; r/Bapt; hon/Nat Aid-de-Camp Recruiting Class Awd for Outstg Recruits 1978-79, 1979-80; Num Outher Awds & Recogs Inclg Nat Aid-de-Camp Recruiting Cup, Sev Tie Tacks & Tie Bars; VFW Leather Bill Fold & Wall Plaque; 2 Cash Awds.

DAVIS, RUTH ESTHER oc/Assistant Professor; b/June 2, 1948; h/303A Eastbrook Dr, Greenville, NC; ba/G'ville; p/Wilbur Chamberlain and Ruth Drake Davis, Hyattsville, MD; ed/BS 1973, MS 1977 Univ Md Sch Nsg; Post Grad Studies, Georgetwon Univ 1979; pa/Asst Prof Psychi Nsg, ECU; NC Assn for Emotionally Troubled 1979-; ANA; Assn Retard Citizens; Mtl Hlth Assn; Phi Kappa Phi; Sigma Theta Tau; r/Presb; hon/W/W Students in Cols & Univs 1976; Outstg Student Contbn to Sch of Nsg, Univ Md 1973; Md St S'ship Grant 1971; DAR S'ship Awd for Outstg Girl's Stater 1962.

DAVIS, RUTH ROGERS oc/Assistant Professor, Nurse; b/Feb 20, 1950; h/Rt 2 Box 238, Berea, KY 40403; ba/Richmond, KY; m/Ben W;

c/Ben Jeromy; p/Charles Franklin (dec) and Rachel Wilson Rogers, Berea, KY; ed/BS Berea Col 1972; MS Indiana Univ 1978; pa/Staff Nurse, Mtn Maternal Hlth Leag 1972-73; Trg & Outreach Coor, Bluegrass Birth Plan'g Coun 1973-74; Clin Coor & Fam Plan'g Nurse Practitioner, Mtn Maternal Hlth Leag 1974-75; Instr En Ky Univ 1975-76, Asst Prof 1979-; Sigma Theta Tau; Nat Leag Nsg; Ky Leag Nsg, Co-Ed Newslttr; Ky Nurses Assn, 2nd VP; cp/Bd Mem Parents Anon of Ky; Sponsor Madison Co Parents Anon; Bd Mem Bluegrass Regional Mtl Retard Inc; hon/DHEW Profl Nurse Traineeship 1977-78; World W/W Wom 1981.

DAVIS, SAMUEL ADAMS oc/Retired Forester; b/June 7, 1917; h/2138 W Minnehaha Ave, Tampa, FL 33604; m/Mary Lona Forgy; c/Lona Francis Spencer, Mary Dee (dec); p/Samuel Pasco (dec) and Eleanor Russel Davis (dec); ed/BS Univ Fla 1950; Naval Aviation Sch, Corpus Christi 1943; Fed Aviation Authority Sch for Air Controllers 1950; mil/USN Aviator WWII & Korea, Ret'd Lt Comdr USNR; pa/Ret'd Forester Fla St Dept Agric, Div of Forestry, Co Forester Hillsborough Co; Am Lumber & Treating Co; Koppers Co; Fed Aviation Auth; Fla Dept Agric; Soc Am Foresters, Chm Caribbean Chapt Fla Section; Fla Forestry Assn; Am Forestry Assn; Intl Soc Ardoriculture, Past Pres So Chapt; cp/Rotary Intl; Fla Farm Bur; Fla Cattlemens Assn; Fla Nurseryman's & Growers Assn; Naval Reserve Assn USN Inst, Reserve Ofcrs Assn; Ret'd Ofcrs Assn; Mil Order of WWII, Staff of Fla Dept; Reg'd Scouter; Tampa Mens Garden Clb; r/So Bapt; hon/Spec Commend for Co Forester, Bd Co Commrs; 1979; USN Cross for 2nd Successful Landing & 1st Successful Take Off From Open Sea at Night in Seaplane; Air Medal & Pacific Area Ribbon w 2 Battle Stars; BSA Silver Beaver Awd; Writer of Newslttr for Tampa Mens Garden Clb.

DAVIS, SARA JEWELL oc/Designer, Author; b/Nov 5, 1906; h/Quincy, FL; m/Henry Jefferson III (dec); c/Henry Jefferson IV, Sara Margaret Marywoods; p/George Walton (dec) and Emma Cornelia Massey Davis (dec); ed/AB Huntingdon Col; pa/Eng Tchr, Public Schs; Visiting Tchr; cp/Nat Leag Am Pen Wom; Nat Accredited Master Flower Show Judge; Nat Fed St Poetry Socs; Nat Soc Colonial Dames XVII Cent; St Ofcr Fla Fed Wom's Clbs; St Ofcr Fla Fed Gdn Clbs; Lectr on Poetry & Floral Designs; r/So Bapt; hon/FFWC St-Wide Fest of Arts; Nat Flower Arrang Calendar; Writings or Designs Incl'd in: *Florida Poets*; *Poets of the Southern States*; Editor *Children's Corner*; Contbr to *Tropical Living*; Others.

DAVIS, SIDNEY D JR oc/Bank Executive Vice President; b/Mar 17, 1945; h/417 Simpson Circle, Mendenhall, MS 39114; ba/Mendenhall; m/JoJo; c/Dee, Brad; p/Sidney and Neddie Davis, Mendenhall, MS; ed/BBA Ole Miss; MA Ala Univ; pa/Asst NBE, Adm Assn Nat Bank Examr Ofc US Treas 1967-74; Exec VP Simpson Bank 1974-; CPA; MSCPAs; AICPAs; Grad Sch of Banking of S; cp/VChm Co Repub Exec Com; Miss Ec Coun Com; Little Leag Coach; Mendenhall Booster Clb & Civitan Clb; Past Exec Com Mem of Miss Yng Bnkrs; r/Meth; hon/Beta Gamma Sigma.

DAVIS, SKEETER oc/Entertainer; b/Dec 30, 1931; ba/PO Box 120276, Nashville, TN 37212; p/William Lee and Sarah Penick, Thompson Station, TN; pa/Entertainer, Singer, Recording Artist; Traveled & Performed w Hank Snow, Eddy Arnold, Elvis Presley; Recorded, Released 60+ Single Records, 30+ Albums for RCA Records 1953-73; TV Appearances on: "The Steve Allen Show", "American Bandstand", "The Mike Douglas Show", "The Midnight Special", Others; Mem Country Music Assn; r/Christian; hon/Grammy Noms: 1959, 64, 65, 67; Cash Box Awds; BMI Awds; ASCAP Awds; Gold Record for "The End of the World" 1963.

DAVIS, VIOLET AMY oc/Poet, Writer, Public Relations, Publicity, Secretary; b/Jan 18; h/6404 S Lindsay, Okla City, OK 73149; m/H H (dec); c/Mrs Sondra L Martin, Steven Conway; p/Edward Augusta Prosser (dec); Lily V Gatewood Prosser Allen (dec); ed/Att'd Okla Bapt Univ; pa/Mem: Nat Fed of St Poetry Socs Inc, Acad of Am Poets, Poetry Soc of Okla, Poetry Soc of Neb, AR's Poetica, Southwesterners Poetry Wkshop, Discovery Poetry Wkshop, Edmond Poetry Forum, Okla Writers Fed, Intl Toastmistress Clb; cp/Former Ldr Okla City & Madison 4-H Yth Clbs; Wrote Plays; Publicity Chm; Del for Okla Co to Attend Nat 4-H Adult Ldrs' Forum, Wash DC; Poetry Soc of Okla: Commun Chm Prog 1970, Publicity Chm 1970-75, Spec Events Chm 1971-74, 75; r/Christian; hon/Num Civic Hons & Awds Inclg: Okla Co 4-H Ldrships Devel Awd 1969, Nat 4-H Recog Awd, Okla City Kiwanis Awd 1971; Num Cultural Hons & Awds Inclg: Poet Laureate Awd 1969, Kolbe Awd 1969, The Mize Awd 1971, Poetry Soc of Okla Awd 1974, Intl W/W in Poetry Awd of Cert of Merit 1977, Poetry Soc of Okla Bicent Awd 1977; Num 1st Prize Awds for Pub'd Poems; Other Awds Incl NFSPS Random Rhyme Awd 1978; 7th Hon Men Manningham Awd 1978; Won NFSPS Poet Laureate of Tex Awd 7th Hon Men 1980; NFSPS SD Poetry Awd 7th Hon Men 1980; "The Freight Train" Pub'd in NFSPS *Prize Winning Poems* 1978; Rec'd Intl W/W Awd 1977; Won LSPS Mary B Wall Awd 1980; Won PSO

Inspirational Awd 1980; Won PSO Anon Humorous Awd 1981; Held Public Poetry Rdgs 1971-75; Quoted in The Acad of Am Poets Envoy 1979; 3 Articles Pub'd *National 4-H News* 1969 & 1970.

DAVIS, W HUBERT oc/Police Department Communications Officer; b/Jan 3, 1926; h/308 12th Ave N, Alexander City, AL 35010; m/Clara; c/Gina Anne; p/John L and Mary E Davis, Alexander City, AL; pa/Alexander City PD 28 Yrs; Ala Police Ofcrs Assn; r/Bapt; hon/Awd for Outstg & Loyal Ser to PD for 28 Yrs 1980.

DAVIS, WILLIAM RALPH oc/Missionary; b/Sept 4, 1921; h/314 S 23rd Ave, Hattiesburg, MS 39401; ba/Ghana, W Africa; m/Cora Joyce Merritt; c/Nan Lucia Davis Davis, David Carson; p/Thomas Watts (dec) and Nannie Alden Wright Davis (dec); ed/BA William Corey Col; MA Univ So Miss; mil/AUS 1940-45; pa/Missionary 1950-; r/Bapt; hon/Outstg Alumni Wm Corey Col 1976.

DAWSON, F D JR oc/Minister; b/Mar 13, 1913; h/2012 Wood St, Texarkana, TX 75501; m/(dec); c/F D Jr, Earl H, John Von, Adelia Goetter; ed/AB Lon Morris Col 1933; BA SWn Univ 1935; MBA Perkins Sch Theol 1939; pa/Meth Min 42 Yrs; hon/Wiley Col DD 1979; S'ship Wiley Col by Tex Meth Col Assn 1980.

DAY, JAMES TERRY JR oc/Insurance Agent; b/Nov 17, 1951; h/PO Box 944, Harriman, TN 37748; ba/Same; m/Edde Gilliland; p/James T Sr and Eva J Day, Harriman, TN; ed/BS Univ Tenn; mil/AUS 3 Yrs; pa/J T Day Ins Agcy; Insurors of Tenn; cp/Pres Harriman JCs; r/Meth; hon/Grad UT Knoxville w Hons.

DAY, MAGGIE LEE oc/Teachers Assistant; b/Feb 4, 1909; h/Rt 1, Denmark, TN 38391; ba/Jackson, TN; m/James Otha; p/Perry and Callaie Fuller, Denmark, TN; pa/Tchrs Assn; Avon Rep; r/Bapt; hon/Maggie's Day Awd Happy Hollow Sch.

DAY, RICHARD R oc/Director of Research and Staff Development; b/Jan 2, 1944; h/50 Kingspark Rd, Little Rock, AR 72207; m/Priscilla Ann Grist; c/Lisa, Leslie, Lori; p/Robert William and Bernice Ethyl Hocutt Day, B'ham, AL; ed/BS 1965, MS 1972 Auburn Univ; PhD Univ Va 1974; mil/USAR; pa/Dir of Res & Staff Devel, Ark Enterprises for Blind Rehab Ctr 1978-80; Asst Prof George Peabody Col 1976-78; Admr Commun Col Work; APGA; Am Psych Assn; Phi Delta Kappa; Am Assn Wkrs for the Blind; cp/Lions Clb; r/Bapt; hon/W/W SSW 1980; Pub'd in *Journal of Visual Impairment & Blindness* Apr 1980.

DAYHUFF, CHARLES HAL III oc/Broker; b/Oct 8, 1937; h/Box 7, Concord, GA 30206; ba/Same; m/Barbara Slade; c/Martha Claire, Richard Edward, Charles Hal IV; p/Charles Hal Jr and Marion Perry Dayhuff, Paoli, PA; ed/BA VMI; mil/Lt Col Reserve; pa/Broker, U Farm Agcy; Real Est; cp/Rotary; Coun Man City of Concord, Ga; Exec Bd FLint River Coun BSA; CoChm Co Adv Com; r/Epis; hon/Silver Beaver BSA; La Ordean de Espiritu de Las Buenas Obras, Canal Zone Coun.

DEAL, LILLIE MAE T oc/Homemaker, Clubwoman, Cultural Leader; b/Aug 21, 1911; h/Rt 2 Box 788, Lenoir, NC 28645; m/Marcus; c/William Marcus; p/Gaither Leroy (dec) and Judy Sigman Teague; ed/Att'd Caldwell Commun Col 1966-69; Home Ext from NCSU; cp/Cedar Val U Meth Ch: Mem Ofcl Bd, Pastoral Relats Com, Choir, Communion Steward 30 Yrs, Former SS Tchr, Pres & Charter Mem UMW; Past Pres Ext Homemakers Clb Caldwel Co, 2nd VP SWn Dist Coun 1955, Del 16th Annual Nat Coun Meeting 1952; Del Nat Conf on Citizenship 1963; Del Safety Citizenship Seminar 1977; Charter Mem Altrusa Clb Caldwell Co; NC Commun Devel Assn Beautification Chm; Prod'd 1st Caldwell Co Beauty Pageant 1973; Helped Org 4-H Clb; Blue Ridge EMC Doers Coun 1972-74; NC EMC Wom's Com 1973; r/Meth; hon/Blue Ridge EMC Commun Ser Awd 1973; Blue Ridge EMC Doers Coun Best in NC & 1 of Best in Nat 1972-74; Cert of Apprec; Coveted NC Ext Homemakers Ldrship Awd 1980; Caldwell Co Homemaker of Yr Awd 1968; UMW Spec Life Mbrship 1962; UMW Pin for Dist Work 1966.

DEAN, ANNE GWYNNE FREY oc/Nurse, Operating Room Supervisor; b/Sept 9, 1942; h/2102 Orange Blossom, San Antonio, TX 78247; ba/San Antonio; c/Heather Elizabeth, Michael Bruce, Stephanie Lara Anne; p/Robert F Frey, Waverly, OH; Anne Wynn Crace, Waverly, OH; ed/Assoc Deg Nsg, San Antonio Col; BSN Univ Tex Hlth Sci Ctr 1979; pa/RN; Assn Operating Nurses; Guest Lectr Metro Gen Hosp; Continuing Ed UTHSC; Critical Care Course Bexar C Hosp; UTHSC at Galveston; Chm Inserv Comm Bexar Co Hosp; r/Epis; hon/W/W Am Wom 1979.

DEAN, LYDIA MARGARET CARTER oc/Food and Nutrition Consultant, Author; b/Jul 11, 1919; h/7816 Birnam Wood Dr, McLean, VA 22101; m/Halsey Albert; c/Halsey Albert Jr, John Carter, Lydia Margarea; p/Christopher C and Hette Gross Carter; ed/Averett Col; BS

Madison Col 1941; MS Va Poly Inst & St Univ 1951; Postgrad Study, Univ Va, Mich St Univ; pa/Dietetic Intern, Therapeutic Dietitian, St Vincent De Paul Hosp, Norfolk, Va 1942; Physicist US Naval Operating Base, Norfolk, Va 1943-45; Clin Dietitian Roanoke Meml Hosps 1946-51; Assoc Prof Va Poly Inst & St Univ 1946-53; Commun Nutritionist, Roanoke, Va 1953-60; Dir Dept Nutritions & Dietitics SWn Va Med Ctr, Roanoke 1960-67; Food & Nutrition Conslt, Nat HQs ARC, Wash 1967-73; Staff Vol 1973-; Nutrition Scist, Conslt Dept Army, Washington 1973-, USDA 1973-; Pres DEAN & Assoc; Conslt, Assoc Dir Am Dietitic Assn 1975; Coor New Degree Prog, Univ Hi 1974-75; Task Force White House Conf Food & Nutrition 1969-; Chm Fed Com Interagy Com on Nutrition Ed 1970-71; Tech Rep to AID; Chm Crusade for Nutrition ed, Washington 1970-; Participant, Conslt Nat Nutrition Policy Conf 1974; Fellow Am Public Hlth Assn; Intl Inst Commun Ser; Am Dietetic Assn; Conslt BPW Clbs 1970-; Am Home Ec Assn: Rep, Treas Jt Congl Com; AAUW; Food Ser Execs Assn; Contbr Articles to Profl Jours; cp/Zonta Clb; hon/IPA; W/W: Am, Wom of World; Intl W/W in Commun Sers; Nat Social Dir; Pub'd Author.

DEAN, PETER W oc/Attorney, Broadcast Executive; b/Feb 8, 1947; h/Brownsville, TX; ba/2035 Price Rd, Brownsville, TX 78521; m/Paulette S Dean; c/Leslie R; p/Stuart E Dean, Brandenton, FL; Dorothy Dean, Austin, TX; ed/BA Univ Tex Austin 1969; JD St Mary's Univ San Antonio 1975; LLM Taxation NYU 1976; mil/USNR Lt J G; pa/Pres, Dean, Ludica, Harrison & Johnson PC w Ofcs in Brownsville, Corpus Christi, Houston & Denton, Tex; Chm Bd & Chief Exec Ofcr Tierra Del Sol Broadcasting Corp, Owners & Oprs of Channel 23, Brownsville; Am Bar Assn; St Bar of Tex; Nat Assn Broadcasters; Broadcast Fin Mgmt Assn; r/Epis.

DEAN, VALLIE LOLETA oc/Educator, Consultant; b/Mar 5, 1944; h/12133 Hunterton St, Upper Marlboro, MD 20870; ba/Wash DC; m/Richard D; c/Richard D II, Clifton S, Mensah M; p/Ralph and Lucille Johnson (dec); ed/BA; MA; pa/DC Bus Ed Assn; BPW Leag; Forrestal Toastmistress Clb; cp/DC Dem Wom; LWV; Kettering Civic Fed; r/Prot; hon/Nat Public Ser Awd; 1st Place Grad in Modeling Sch; 3rd Place Winner of Speech Contest.

DEARMAN, DEBORAH KAY oc/Consumer Loan Officer, Assistant Vice President; b/May 12, 1949; h/Midland, TX; ba/1100 Andrews Hwy, Midland, TX 79701; m/Kenneth; c/Kim, Chris; p/James H and Madalyn Curry, Levelland, TX; ed/Sev Courses Tex Tech Savings & Loan Sch; pa/Avco Fin Sers 5 Yrs; Gen Elec Credit Corp 2 Yrs; Credit Mgrs Assn; Nat Assn Credit Mgmt W Tex; r/Bapt.

DEAS, CATHERINE L oc/Executive Director; b/Jan 11, 1937; h/136 Hillcrest, Florence, SC 29501; ba/Sumter, SC; m/Aubrey; c/Jaimie, April, Joseph; p/Thomas Demetrious Liakos (dec); Louise Goff Teasley, Florence, SC; ed/RN; AA Sci; BA Hlth Care Adm; pa/Exec Dir, En Carolina Hlth Ed Sys; Bd Dir, Pres for SC to Carolinas Soc Hlth Ed & Tng; Bd Dir SC Leag of Nurses; Sem Ldr, N & S Carolina; Com for Commun Action, SC Leag Nsg; Nat Conslt for Shared Sers in Hlth Ed; Pub'd Article in Profl Jour; Com to Est Criteria for Nat Recog of Hlth Edrs; r/Bapt; hon/Rec'd Awd, CSHET, in Recog for Achmt in Hlth Ed 1981.

DEASON, DANIEL ARTHUR oc/Musician, Pianist; b/Aug 3, 1948; h/608 Richardson Dr, Henderson, TX 75652; ba/Dallas; p/Graham and Gwen Allen Deason, Henderson, Tex; ed/BMus Baylor Univ; pa/Asst Chorus Master, Dallas Civic Opera 4 Seasons; Ft Worth Opera Assn; Summer Staff Art Song Fest, Westminster Choir Col, Princeton, NJ; Staff Chatauqua Inst; Num Mus Comedy Dinner Theaters, Dallas Area Concerts & Pers; Lamar Univ Symph Orch Soloist, Beaumont, Tex; Soloist (Organ), Baylor Univ Oratorio Chorus; r/Luth: Ch Organist & Choir Master; hon/Gamma Fisher Foun S'ship for Adv'd Study at Am Inst for Mus Stuides, Gratz, Austria; Nat Opera Inst Grants 1977-78.

DEASY, STEVE HOWARD oc/Teacher; b/Jan 15, 1949; h/1010 North Ave, Portland, TN 37148; ba/Portland; p/Howard Deasy, Portland, TN; Lee Deasy (dec); ed/BS David Lipscomb Col 1971; MEd Tenn St Univ 1977; pa/Past Band Dir, Macon Co HS & David Lipscomb Col; Elem Tchr, Riggs Elem Sch; TEA; NEA; cp/Bd Dirs Portland Ath Boosters; hon/W/W Am Cols & Univs 1971; Tchr of Mo, SCEA 1981.

DEATHERAGE, OCTAVIA HUDSON oc/Professional Artist; b/Nov 5, 1911; h/Imboden, AR; m/Noble; c/Deanna Sexton, Carolyn, Steven; p/William (dec) and Edna Hedrick Hudson (dec); ed/Studied Art No Ill Univ; cp/Co-Fdr & Corresp Secy Spring River Art Leag; Arts Dept Chm & 2nd VP Altrurian Clb Ark; Gen Fed of Wom's Clbs; VP Ext Homemkrs Clb; Ark Hist Soc; r/So Bapt; hon/Blue Ribbon Profl Art Dept: Oil, Dekalb Fair; College Dekalb Co Fair; Portrait in Pastels, Dekalb Co Fair; Num Other Awds.

DeBAKEY, LOIS oc/Professor; ba/Baylor Col of Med, 1200 Moursund Ave, Houston, TX 77030; p/S M & Raheeja Z DeBakey (dec);

ed/BA Newcomb Col, Tulane Univ; MA, PhD Tulane Univ; pa/Prof Sci Commun, Baylor Col of Med, Houston; Lectr in Sci Commun, Tulane Univ Sch of Med, New Orleans; Usage Panel *Am Heritage Dictionary*; Edit Bd "Forum on Med," "Grants Magazine," Hlth Commun and Informatics," & "Cardiovascular Res Ctr Bultn"; Biomed Lib Review Com, Nat Lib Med; Bd Dirs Plain Talk Inc; Exec Coun, Comm on Cols, So Assn Cols & Schs; Spec Comm on Writing, Coun for Basic Ed; Former Mem Panel Judges, Writing Awds; Am Acad Fam Phys; Past Mem Bd Dirs Coun of Biol Editors; Com on Tech & Sci Writing, NCTE; Num Profl Orgs Incl'g: AAAS, Am Soc Info Sci, Intl Soc Gen Semantics, Inst Soc, Ethics & Life Scis, Com of 1000 for Better Hlth Regulations, Nat Inst Hlth Alumni Assn, Nat Assn Sci Writers, Soc for Tech Commun; Edited Num Med & Sci Articles, Chapts & Books; Sr Author *The Scientific Jour: Editorial Policies & Practices*; Conductor Progs in Sci Commun at Annual Profl Meetings, Var Med Schs & Hosps throughout US, Canada & Abroad; r/Epis; hon/Phi Beta Kappa; Dist'd Ser Awd, Am Med Writers Assn 1970; Biogl Listings.

DeBAKEY, MICHAEL E oc/Surgeon; b/Sept 7, 1908; h/5323 Cherokee St, Houston, TX 77004; ba/Houston; m/Katrin Fehlhaber; c/Michael M, Ernest O, Barry E, Denis A; p/dec; ed/BS 1930, MD 1932, MS 1935 Tulane Univ; p/Certs: Am Bd Surg, Am Bd Thoracic Surg, Nat Bd Med Examrs; Acad Affils: Instr, Assoc & Asst Prof Surg Tulane Univ; Pres, Dist'd Ser Prog, Prof & Chm Cora & Webb Mading Dept Surg Baylor Col Med; Clin Profl Surg Univ Tex Dental Br 1971-72; Hosp Affils: Dir Nat Heart & Blood Vessel Res & Demo Ctr, Houston; Sr Att'g Surg Meth Hosp Houston, Surg in Chief Ben Taub Gen Hosp; Editorial Bd, Nat & Intl Med Jours Incl'g: Iranian Cardiovascular Jour (Hon Chm), New Technique for AV Ed for Surgs' Bd Govs Am Acad of Achmt; Pres 1959 Am Assn Thoracic Surg; Fdg Mem Am Heart Assn; Dir 1966 Assn for Advmt of Med Instrumentation; Bd Dirs 1968 Bio-Med Engrg Soc, Adv Coun 1968-69 Houston Heart Assn, Pres 1964 Nat Assn on Standard Med Vocab, Bd Govs 1965 Soc for Cryobiology, Pres 1954 Soc for Vascular Surg, Pres 1952 SWn Surg Cong; Com for Preven of Heart Disease, Cancer, Stroke, Am Heart Foun; Hon Sponsor Draper World Population Fund; Bd Advrs Intl Med Complex of Iran; Adv Bd Nat Coun Drug Abuse; Ofc Technol Assessmt Hlth Adv Com; Hon Chm Art Rooney Benefit Dinner; Asociacion Mexicana de Cirugia Cardiovascualr A C (Hon Mem); Albert Lasker Clin Med Res Jury Awds Chm 1973; Citizens for Treatmt of High Blood Pressure Chm 1974; Intl Heart & Lung Inst Sci Adv Com; Nat Insts Hlth Nat Heart & Lung Adv Coun 1974; Hon Fellow Royal Col Surgs England; Hon Mem Acad of Med Scis USSR; cp/Press Clb Houston; Rotary Clb; hon/Hon DSc Hahnemann Med Col & Hosp Phila 1973; Hon DSc Albany Med Col; Am Col Surgs SW Pa Chapt Annual Awd 1973; Acmt Awd Am Soc Contemp Med & Spec Awd; Intl Prize "La Madonnina"; NYU Med Col of Dent, Alumni Awd; USSR Acad Sci 50th Anniv Jubilee Medal; Lib Human Resources; Alpha Omega Alpha; Alpha Pi Kappa; Sigma Xi; Hon LLD; AMA Dist'd Ser & Hektoen Gold Awds, Eleanor Roosevelt Humanities Awd, St Jude Man of Yr & Medal of Freedom Press Awds; Tex Med Ctr Medallion 1972; Rotary Clb Dist'd Citizen Awd 1972; Am Col Chest Phys Pres Cit; Michael E DeBakey Day, Baylor Col of Med; St Francis Hosp F'ship Awd, Roslyn, NY; Dir Ednl Specs; Intl Scholars Dir; Intl W/W Commun Ser; Intl W/W; Ldrs Ed; Nat Reg Prom Ams & Intl Notables; Outstg Edrs Am; W/W: Am, Am Col & Univ Adm, Sci, World.

DeBRIYN, NORMAN F oc/Head Baseball Coach and Assistant Professor; b/Nov 1, 1941; h/1680 Hammond St, Fayetteville, AR 72701; ba/F'ville; m/Caroline M; c/Todd Travis, Martin Mock, Carrie Jo; p/Henry and Esther DeBriyn, Ashland, WI; ed/BS; MA; pa/Hd Baseball Coach & Asst Prof Hlth, Phys Ed & Rec, Univ Ark; Am Assn Col Baseball Coaches, Clin Com; Clin Spkr; Fball & Basketball Officiating; r/Cath; hon/SW Conf Baseball Coach of Yr 1978; Dist VI Baseball Coach of Yr 1979.

DeCATSYE, ROBERT JR oc/Director Criminal Justice Program; b/Aug 24; h/109 Amesbury Ln, Cary, NC 27511; ba/Rocky Mount, NC; m/Patricia F; c/James E, John F, Jeffrey A; p/John Dawson (dec); Betty Dawson, Port Orange, FL; ed/AS Gen Ed; BA Criminal Justice; MA Criminal Justice Adm; mil/USAF 21 Yrs, SM Sgt Ret'd; pa/Spec Agent, Air Force Ofcl of Spec Investigations 1964-73; Dept Hd, Police Sci Tech, Wake Tech Inst, Raleigh 1973-78; Dir Crim Justice Prog, Wesleyan Col, Rocky Mt 1978-; Mem: Intl Narcotics Ofcrs Assn, Intl Assn Chiefs of Police, NC Law Enforcemt Ofcrs Assn, NC Crim Just Edrs Assn, So Assn of Crim Just Edrs, Adv Coun to Crim Just Prog, Shaw Univ, Bd Dirs NC Crim Just Edrs Assn; VP Wake Co Crim Just Coun; cp/Dem Cand for Sheriff of Wake Co 1978; r/Meth; hon/Merit Ser Medal, Pres of US, upon retiremt from mil; Merit Ser Medal, Pres of US for superior investigative accomplishmts.

DECHERT, DANIEL STRATTON oc/Computer Services Company Executive; b/Mar 31, 1934; h/1601 Barnard's Cove Rd, Va Bch, VA 23455; ba/Norfolk, VA; m/Mary Ellen MacDonald; c/Elizabeth, Stratton;

p/Robert Beck and Mary Katherine Dechert, Sarasota, FL; ed/AB Col of Wm & Mary 1956; mil/AUS 1957-59 Signal Corps; pa/Proj Dir Newport News Shipbldg & Dry Dock Co 1959-66; Mgr in Charge, Mgmt Consltg Sers, Ernst & Ernst 1966-72; Pres Hosp Data Ctr of Va Inc 1972-; Data Processing Mgmt Assn, Pres 1977; Nat Hosp Collectors Assn, Pres 1980; Nat Shared Hosp Sys Assn, Pres 1979; Va Hosp Assn; Nat Miocrofilm Assn; Am Hosp Assn; Assembly of Shared Sers, Bd Govs 1980; Soc Cert'd Data Processors; Acad Adm Mgrs; Soc Computer Med; r/Epis; hon/Inst for Cert of Computer Profls, Cert in Data Processing 1970; Adm Mgmt Assn Cert in Adm Mgmt 1971; Data Processing Mgmt Assn Gold Awd for Indiv Perf 1979; Co-Author *Managerial Accounting* 1971.

DECKER, JOSEPHINE oc/Clinic Administrator; b/May 24, 1933; h/308 SE Sam Houston, Muldrow, OK 74948; ba/Ft Smith, AR; m/William A; c/Peter A; p/Ralph and Ada Snider, Muldrow, OK; pa/SWn Bell Telephone Co 1951-52; Clin Admr, Holt Krock Clin 1952-; Credit Wom, Intl, Past Pres; Soc Cert'd Consumer Credit Execs; cp/Bd Dirs Ft Smith Credit Bur; Bd Dirs Sparks Credit Union; Adv Coun Ft Smith Public Schs; r/Prot.

DEDMON, BOBBY GENE oc/Personnel Manager; b/Oct 7, 1946; h/Westchester Apt A-2, Scottsboro, AL 35768; ba/Scottsboro; c/Richard Ronald; ed/AS NESJC; Att'd Ala A&M Univ; mil/USA Sgt; pa/Pers Mgr Gay-Tred Mills Inc; Bd Dirs Carpet & Rug Inst-Indust Relats Clb; Adv Coun TARCOG; cp/Pres Nelson Elem PTO; Adv Coun Title I Rdg Prog; Commun Adv Coun; Chm Indust Div So Grp Jackson Co UGF; Coach for T-Ball, Volleyball, Softball, Basketball; Gov Col Civitans 1974; Pres Col Civitan 1973; VP Toastmasters; Secy, Bd Dirs, Chaplain JCs 1970-73; r/So Bapt; hon/Outstg Yng Man 1971; Civitan of Yr 173; Phi Theta Kappa Nat Hon Frat for Jr Col 1976.

DEERE, EDWARD oc/County Agricultural Extension Leader; b/Dec 26, 1919; h/1001 Ray Ave, Maryville, TN 38701; ba/Maryville; m/Mabel E; c/Michael, Randall; p/E D (dec) and Laura Deer, Lexington, TN; ed/BS 1949, MS 1957 Univ Tenn; mil/AUS 1944-46; pa/Voc Agric Tchr 1950-59; Blount Co, Tenn Agric Ext Ldr 1959-; Tenn Co Agts Assn; Nat Co Agts Assn; cp/Alcoa Kiwanis Clb; r/So Bapt; hon/Dist'd Ser Awd, Nat Co Agts Assn.

DEESE, RUTHA MERLE oc/Nurse; b/Sept 22, 1942; h/Rt 1 Box 40, Silver Creek, MS 39663; ba/Prentiss, MS; m/Douglas (dec); c/Douglas Dewayne; p/Laney and Burnice W King, Silver Creek, MS; ed/BS; RN; pa/ANA; DNA; MNA; Soc on Nsg Adm; cp/Dem Party; r/Ch of God; hon/W/W Am Wom; St S'ship.

DeHAVEN, SANDRA MAE oc/Secretary-Treasurer; b/July 14, 1947; h/17 Oakwood Estates, Parkersburg, WV 26101; ba/P'burg; m/Clifford L Roberts; p/William J and Evelyn Jackson DeHaven, P'burg, WV; ed/AA Mtn St Col 1969; pa/Secy-Treas Franklin & DeHaven Jewelers; Mng Dir, Downtown Retail Merchants Assn; cp/Downtown Retail Merchants Assn; P'burg Revitalization Comm; P'burg C of C; Nat Fed Indep Bus; Nat Retail Merchants Assn; WV Retail Jewelers; r/Meth; hon/W/W Am Wom 1980-81.

DeHOFF, GEORGE W oc/Publisher, Minister; b/Sept 20, 1913; h/1106 Houston Dr, Murfreesboro, TN 37130; ba/M'boro; m/Marie Turner; c/George W Jr, Bonnie Fakes, Paul T, Theresa Anne; p/Orville O (dec) and Adah Gaskins DeHoff (dec); ed/Freed-Hardeman Col; BA, LLD Harding Univ; MA Peabody Col; ScD Am Christian Univ; mil/102nd Evacuation Hosp Unit, Staff Ofcr 1939-41; pa/Pres Magie Val Col 1957-64; Pres DeHoff Pubs 1939-; cp/Rotary Clb, Pres Tenn Clb 1969-70, Dist Gov Dist 676 1971-72; Tenn Constitutional Convs 1971, 1977; Del Dem Nat Conv 1976; r/Ch of Christ; hon/Hon Degs Harding Col, Magic Val Col, Knox Col; Author *DeHoff's Commentary on Bible* 6 Vols.

DEISON, HARRIETT SCHOELLKOPF oc/Homemaker; b/Feb 6, 1947; h/3910 1027 Carter Dr, Chatt, TN 37414; m/Peter Van; c/Mary Virginia, Helen Anne; p/Hugo W Schoellkopf Jr, Dallas, TX; Mrs Wm C Johnston, Dallas, TX; ed/Univ Tex 3 Yrs; cp/Jr Leag; r/Presb.

DEITZ, EDDIE JAMES oc/Evangelist; b/Sept 11, 1947; h/Sylva, NC; ba/PO Box 698, Sylva, NC 28779; m/Sandra Kaye; c/April Lynn, Brandon James; p/Coy and Dorothy Deitz, Sylva, NC; ed/Wn Carolina Univ 1965-68; pa/Profl Gospel Singer w Inspirations Quartet 1969-; hon/Appeared on Gospel Singing Jubilee Syndicated TV 1970-79; Appeared on Roger Mudd Newscast 1970; Accepted w Inspirations, Awd for Am Fav Gospel Singing Grp 6 Times; Voted #1 Baritone in Am Gospel Mus 3 Times; Hon DDiv, Calvry Bible Col 1974; Outstg Yng Men Am JCs 1977.

DEITZ, ROBERT LEE JR oc/Director of Purchasing; b/Mar 15, 1945; h/Charleston, WV; ba/Charleston; p/Robert Lee Deitz Sr; Eva Mae Boggess McCown; ed/BSBA WV St Col; pa/Dir Procurement Ser CAMC

(WV Univ Med Sch); Am Soc Hosp Purchasing & Mat Mgmt; Nat Assn Hosp Purchasing Mgmt; Tri-St Hosp Purchasing Agts Assn, Pres 1978-79; WV Purchasing/Mat Mgmt Assn; SEn Hosp Assn, Purchasing Grp, Mem of Bd 1981; r/Bapt.

de la CRUZ, HUGO LUIS oc/Radio Announcer; b/Feb 13, 1945; ba/KGBT Radio 1530, 1519 Harrison, Harlingen, TX 78550; m/Rebecca; c/Victor Hugo, Rebecca, Cynthia, Christian, Roxanne; p/Apolonio and Concepcion Gomez De La Cruz; ed/Deg Fed Communs of Mexico City 1964; mil/Ser in Mexico 1964-65; pa/KGBT Radio Announcer 13 Yrs; r/Cath; hon/Dist'd Guest of Commr Gen; Delta Area Civic Org 1974; Man of Yr; Awd'd Best Fball Score Board Prog of St of Tex 1979-80.

de la GARZA, S M JR oc/Bank Assistant Vice President; b/Feb 15, 1948; h/Edinburg, TX; m/Edna; c/Sam; p/S M (dec) and Maria I de la Garza; Edinburg, TX; ed/BBA Tex A&I Univ; pa/Asst VP First Fed St Bank & Trust Co; cp/Past Dir Brownsville JCs 1973; Past Pres Edinburg Bobcat Booster Clb 1976-79; Past VP Edinburg C of C 1979-80; Pres Elect Edinburg C of C 1980-81.

DeLaPENA, CORDELL AMADO oc/Physician; b/Apr 30, 1934; h/209 Candlelight Dr, Clarksburg, WV 26301; ba/Clarksburg; m/Erlinda Lapuz; c/Leslie, Nina, Cordell Jr;p/Eusebio de Guzan DeLaPena (dec); Virginia DeCosta, LA, CA; ed/AA 1952; DMed 1958; mil/Public Hlth 1959-63; pa/Phys; Pathol; Dir Labs; Pres Med STAH UHC Pres 1974-75 ; WV Soc Pathol Pres 1980-81, VP 1978; ; Pres Harrison CTY Med Soc, Pres 1980-81, Secy 1978; Pres WV Soc of Hematology 1981-82; Pres Philippine Pathol Am 1981-82; Asst Clin Prof of Pathol, WV Univ 1980-; Diplomate Am Bd Path; Fellow: CAP, ASCP, ASH, ICP, AMA, WV Med Assn; Adj Lectr Fairmont Col 1977-78; Dir MLT UHC 1978; Pres Cancer Soc 1974, 75, 76; hon/AMA Phys Recog Awds 1974-78; Diplomate Am Bd of Path AP 1967, CP 1978, HEM 1980.

DeLATTIBEAUDIERE, ALFRED GEORGE oc/Building Inspector; b/Nov 1, 1919; m/Juanita L; p/dec; pa/Owner Square Deal Construction Co, Sanford, Fla; cp/Seminole Co Voters Leag; Chm Mbrship Com, Seminole Chapt NAACP; Conslt Seminole Jt Tenant Coun; Chm Adv Com, Rural Yth Housing Ptnrship Prog; Bd Mem & Past Prog Com Mem SEEDCO; Past Chm Bd of Seminole Commun Action; Past Pres Georgetown Commun Improvement; Past Bd Mem Nat Tenant Org; Orgr of Seminole Jt Tenant Coun; Treas Seminole Neighborhood U Coun; Past Treas Fla Tenant Org; U Minority Contractors Assn of Fla; Past High Priest Holy Royal Arch Mason, Amos Chapt 4; Sanford Command #5, Knights Templar; Treas Ctrl Fla Masonic Coun; Min of St, City Beautiful Consistory #297, 32° Mason; Malta Temple #143, Nobles of Mystic Shrine; Past Worthy Patron of Rebecca Chapt #83, OES; K of P; r/Bapt; hon/Cert of Hons; Perfect Attendance SEEDCO Bd Meetings 3 Yrs; Outstg Ser Rendered to Commun; Apprec of Ser Org Tenants; Apprec of Ser SEEDCO Mbrship Dr; Apprec for Vol Ser ESAP; Cert for Wkg w Tenant Coun; Cert of Apprec from Westside Improvemnt Assn; Cert for Relig Commun Ser; Cert for Outstg Ser NAACP; Cert of Achmt, Team Assn Inc; Cert of Achmt Bd Trg, Fla Atlantic Univ; Cert of Achmt CSA.

DE LA VINA, ROBERT oc/Public School Teacher and Administrator; b/Apr 9, 1914; h/211 E Kuhn St, Edinburg, TX 78539; m/Grace; c/Robert Jr; p/Plutarco De La Vina; Irene Garza; ed/Edinburg Jr Col; BA Tex A&I; Addl Studies PanAm Univ; mil/USAF 1942-46; pa/Tchr; Prin Edinburg Jr HS 1955-68; Asst Dir Fed Progs 1968-69; Dir Spec Sers 1969-80; Ret'd 1980; PTA; Tex Clrsm Tchr Assn; Tex St Tchr Assn; Assn Compensatory Edrs of Tex; Rio Grande Val Assn Sch Admrs; r/Spanish Meth Ch: Pres Ch Bd Dirs, SS Tchr, Layman Spkr, Local & Dist Pres Meth Men Frat; hon/Carbine Marksman Medal; Good Conduct Medal; Am Theatre Campaign Medal; Asiatic-Pacific Campaign Medal; Victory Ribbon; Ser Stripe; Overseas Ser Bar; Resolution by Edinburg Sch Bd of Trustees; Plaque as Outstg Admr; Diamond Pin for 35 Yrs Dedication in Field of Ed by Edinburg Tex Clsrm Tchrs Assn & Tex St Tchrs Assn; De La Vina Fam Selected as 1 of "All Am Fams" During US Bicent Celeb.

DELCO, WILHELMINA RUTH oc/State Representative; b/July 16, 1929; h/1805 Astor Pl, Austin, TX 78721; ba/Austin; m/Exalton A Jr; c/Deborah Diane, Exalton III, Loretta Elmirle, Cheryl Pauline; ed/BA Fisk Univ; pa/Bd Trustees, Austin Indep Sch Dist 1968-74 (Secy 1972-74); cp/St Rep, Dist 37-D 1975-; Leg Session 66: Chm House Higher Ed Com, Mem Liquor Regulation Com; Interim Session 65: Chm Subcom on Curric Reform; Leg Session 65: V-Chm Public Ed Com, Mem Hlth & Wel Com, Mem Rules Com; Bd Trustees Austin Commun Col, Secy 1973-74; Bd Dirs Univ Tex YWCA; Pres Sims Elem Sch PTA; Pres Allan Jr HS PTA; Pres Travis Co PTA Coun; Secy & V-Chm Citizens Adv Com to Juvenile Ct; City of Austin Human Relats Comm; Girl Scout Jr Troop Ldr & Mem Coun Public Relats Com; Key Vol Trainer, Vol Bur; Vol Social Wkr, Travis Co Wel Dept; Eye Screening Ser, Travis Co Wel Dept; Mo Voter Bltn Mailer, LWV; Bd Vol Bur; Well-Child Conf Bd; St Adv Comm, Tex Study Public Sch Instrl Resources; Adv Com Tex Employment Commn; Bd

Dirs Lone Star Girl Scout Coun; Bd Mem Caritas; Bd Mem Child Care '76; Adv Bd Mem KTBC & KVUE; Bd Mem TRI-MAC Proj; Others; r/Cath; hon/Outstg Wom, Austin *Am Statesman* Newspaper 1969; Life Mem Tex Cong Parents & Tchrs 1969; Liberty Bell Awd, Austin Jr Bar Assn 1972; Public Sch Ser Awd, Zeta Phi Beta 1970; Public Ser Merit Awd, Omega Psi Phi 1971; Apprec Awd, NAACP 1971; Hon Mem Delta Kappa Gamma 1972; Coronat Medal, St Edward's Univ 1972; Arthur DeWitty Awd, NAACP; Apprec Awd, Blanton Sch 1973; Ser Awd, Sakarrah Temple #1 AAONOMS 1973; Ser Cit, Optimist Clb of E Austin 1973; Zeta Phi Beta, Austin's First Black Female Legislator 1975; Notable Ldrship & Dist'd Public Ser Alpha Kappa Alpha; Inspirational Support for Yth of Upward Bound, Huston-Tillotson Col; W/W Am Polits 1979-80; Wendell Phillips HS Hall of Fame 1979; Co-Author "Opportunities and Responsibilites for Developing Human Resources" *Liberal Education* 1969.

DELGADO, GEORGE HENRY oc/Vocational Agricultural Instructor; b/Oct 29, 1956; h/Deweyville, TX; m/Sherry Sue; p/Joe and Opal L Delgado; ed/AA Henderson Co Jr Col 1977; Grad N Tex Horseshoing Sch 1975; BS Tex A&M Univ 1979; pa/Asst Vet, Syler Vet Clin; Voc Agric Instr, Deweyville HS; Adv of FFA; Nat Voc Agric Tchrs Assn; Ctrl Rodeo Assn.

DELL, ANNIE WHITE oc/Elementary Teacher; b/June 27, 1920; h/Idabel, OK; p/James Madison (dec) and Nettie B White (dec); ed/BS Langston Univ 1942; Further Study Okla St Univ; pa/5th Grade Tchr; NEA; OEA; IEA; Ec Coun, VChm for Dist; r/Bapt; hon/First Runner-Up Liberty Nat Bank 1975-76; First Runner-Up Wilson Foods 1976-77; Third Place in St 1977-78; First Place in St, Third Place in Nat 1979-80.

DELLA VALLE, DOROTHY MUIR oc/Entrepeneur; b/Dec 2, 1930; h/6107 Dartmoor Ct, Bay Hill, Orlando, FL 32811; ba/Longwood, FL; m/Robert Stephen; c/James Robert, Perry, Nathan (dec); p/James E and Mary O Muir, Frostburg, MD; ed/AA; BA; pa/Owner-Opr Jim's Mobile TV Sales & Ser; Commercial Real Est Assn; Assoc/Conslt Fla Fin Agcy; cp/Nat & Local C of C; Nat & Local Profl Elects Assn; r/Jewish; hon/Outstg Ser Awd, Hadassah; Bus Person of Month, Longwood, Winter Springs C of C.

DEL-ROSARIO, ERNESTO oc/Insurance Executive, CPA; b/Nov 17, 1911; h/M-207 Villa Caparra, Guaynabo, PR 00657; ba/Hato Rey, PR; m/Josefina Masini; c/Elliette R De Pico; p/Ulises and Josefa Olivieri Del-Rosario (dec); ed/CPA PR; pa/Resident VP, Nationwide Ins Cos of Ohio in PR (Ret'd 1977), Conslt to 1978; Currently Exec Dir PR Ins Guaranty Assns; cp/Elk; Bankers Clb & Casino de PR; r/Roman Cath; hon/Exec Dir PR Ins Guaranty Assn.

DELVES, JOHN ALISTAIR oc/Corporate Director of Training and Development; b/Feb 2, 1944; h/3540 Mill Creek Ln, Marietta, GA 30060; ba/Atlanta; m/Sandy Dianne Englett; c/Jennifer Dianne, John Jason; p/Frederick W (dec) and Barbara Clay Delves, Smyrna, GA; ed/ABA Kennesaw Col; BBA, MEd Ga St Univ; mil/AUS Spec 4; pa/Am Soc Trng & Devel, St Pres; Intl Cong of Assessment Ctr Admr, Dir; cp/Ga JCs: Local Pres 1976, Dist Pres 1977, St Public Relats Chm 1978; Cobb Co Dem Exec Com, Ed Chm; PTA VP; r/Rom Cath; hon/Outstg JC USA 1977; Outstg JC GA 1977; Outstg Yng Men Cobb Co 1978; Outstg Spkr Ga 1977.

DeMAIO, ANTHONY FRANCIS oc/Retired Stevedore; b/Feb 4, 1922; h/6805 20th Ave W, Brandenton, FL 33505; m/Irene; c/Bruce, Yvonne; p/Patsy (dec) and Anna DeMaio; mil/NJNG 1938-41; USMM 1942-45 pa/Stevedore, NY-NJ Waterfront 31 Yrs; Ret'd 1971; cp/Past Grand Knight, K of C; Past Grand Knight, Pope John XXIII Council #5837 1977-78; Mem Desoto Coun #5604 Brandenton; 4° Monseigneur Eslander Assem; Color Corps Sarasota; r/Cath; hon/Ser Ribbons for Atlantic, Pacific, Mediterranean, Mid-East Theaters of Ser; Combat Ribbon w Silver Star for Ship Sunk by Torpedoes; Dist'd Ser Awd, W NY Guttenberg PBA 1967; Awd'd Knight of Yr, Desoto Coun 5604 1979-80; Knight of Yr Awd, Pope John XXIII Coun 5837 1974-75; Awd'd Bronze Pelican 1976, St George Awd 1978, Cath Com on Scouting; Scouters Awd 1962; Scouters Key 1964; Arrowhead Awd 1965.

DeMENT, IRA oc/Lawyer; b/Dec 21, 1931; m/Ruth Lester Posey; c/Charles Posey; p/Ira Jr and Helen Sparks DeMent (dec); ed/AB 1953 Univ of Ala; JD 1969 Univ of Ala Sch of Law; mil/USAR Comm'd 2nd Lt; AUS Extended Active Duty 1953; Army of Occupation, Germany 1st Lt 1953-55; Currently, Col USAFR-JAGD, Ofc of Staff Judge Advocate, HQs, Air Univ, Maxwell AFB, Ala; pa/Admitted to Pract: Supreme Ct of Ala 1958, US Dist Ct for No 1977, Middle 1958 & So 1967 Dists of Ala, DC 1972, US Ct of Appeals for 5th Circuit 1958, Supreme Ct of US 1966; Pvt Pract Montgomery, Ala 1961-69; Asst City Atty & Legal Adv to Montgomery Police & Fire Depts, City of Montgomery 1965-69; Spec Asst Atty Gen, St of Ala 1966-69; Instr Montgomery Police Acad 1971, 75; Adj Prof, Dept of Psychol Univ of Ala 1975-; Pvt Pract, Montgomery 1977-; Mem: Adv Bd Law Enforcemt Acad Univ of Ala 1972-, Auburn Univ-

PERSONALITIES OF THE SOUTH

Montgomery 1975-, Nat Panel of Arbitrators, Am Arbitration Assn, Nat Dist Attys Assn, Montgomery Co, DC, Fed, Am Bar Assns; cp/Repub Party; 32° Scottish Rite Mason & Shriner; Sigma Chi; r/Meth; hon/Num Mil Awds inclg: Meritorious Ser Medal 1976, Army of Occupation Medal 1954, Nat Ser Def Medal 1954, Armed Forces Ser Medal 1973, Air Force Longevity Ser Awd Ribbon w Oak Leaf Cluster; W/W: S&SW, Govt, US, Commun Ser, Am Law; DIB; Men of Achmt; Commun Ldrs & Noteworthy Ams; Others.

DeMERE, McCARTHY oc/Surgeon; b/Jan 20, 1918; h/Memphis, TN; p/Clifton and Leona McCarthy DeMere (dec); ed/BS SWn Memphis; MS Wash Univ; MD UTCMS; LLB MSU Law Sch; FACS; ACLM; ASPRS; mil/AUS Med Corps Capt; pa/Plastic & Reconstructive Surg; Pres Memphis & Shelby Co Med Soc; Bd Dirs Memphis & Shelby Co Bar Assn; Pres SE Soc Plastic Surgs; Pres Hosp Plastic Surg; Am Bar Assn; Diplomate Am Bd Plastic Surg; Diplomate Am Bd Gen Surg; Dir Inst Legal Med, Memphis St Univ Law Sch; Assoc Prof Surg Univ Tenn Med Units; Bd Govs Am Col Legal Med; Bd Editors Am Jour Legal Med; cp/Past Gov Tenn Sertoma Intl; Grad Jim Russell Sch of Race Driving; Grad So Inst Aviation; Breeder of Black Angus Cattle; r/Cath; hon/W/W Am; Pres Awd for Outstg Ser 1973; 27 Pub'd Sci & Legal Treatises.

DEMPSEY, NEAL III oc/Sales Vice President; b/Mar 20, 1941; h/2507 Springpark Way, Richardson, TX 75081; ba/Dallas, TX; m/Janet R; c/Sean, Heather; p/Neal Jr and Katherine S Dempsey, Tacoma, WA; ed/BA Univ Wash; MBA Univ Santa Clara; mil/Calif ARNG 1st Lt; pa/Sales VP Harris Corp, Data Communs Div; Sales Execs Clb; Am Mktg Assn; cp/Richardson & Tex YMCA Fund Raising Com; Richardson & Tex YMCA Indian Guides Prog Com; r/Roman Cath.

DENGLER, JOHN CHARLES oc/Boat Sales and Service; b/Jan 1, 1912; h/119 Pauline Ave, Del Rio, TX 78840; ba/Del Rio; m/Helen C; c/Nancy, David, Ian, Mark, Lorinda, Lissa; p/John C and Emma M Hirsch Dengler; ed/AB; MA; Cand EdD; pa/Fdr Pres SITA; World Travel Inc 1933-; Owner-Opr White Sun Guest Ranch; Dir Priorities Northrop Aircraft; Dir Manpwr Utilization Survey for Aircraft War Prodn Coun 1942-45; Mem Coun on Student Travel; Pacific Area Travel Assn; Am Soc Travel Agts; Phi Delta Kappa; Alpha Phi Alpha.

DENIS, SANDRA SMITH oc/Decorator; b/July 13, 1948; h/Decatur, AL; m/Mike A; c/Mike Jr, Mark and Tim; p/James L Smith, Bay City, MI; Ella Mae Weeks Smith, Big Rapids, MI; ed/Att'd Delta Col 1966-67; pa/Decorating Conslt; Owner Images Decorating & Display; cp/Decatur Jr Ser Leag; Student Theatre; Owner Images Decorating & Display; cp/Decatur Com; Chwom Dixie Yth Mother's Aux; Publicity Chm Oak Park Mid Sch PTA; Gordon Bibb PTA; Past 1st VP & Prog Chm Decatur Newcomer's Clb; Fomer Mem Bd Dirs Spirit of Am Fest; Ala Repubs; Mich Poetry Soc; Former Mem Mich Mother of Twins Clb; Den Ldr, Den 3 Pack 239 Arrowhead Dist; Chm Chds Parade on 4th of July; r/Bapt.

DENN, DONALD EUGENE oc/Teacher, Rancher; b/Jan 29, 1916; h/Rt 2 Box 95A, Montgomery, TX 77356; p/dec; ed/BS 1950, MEd 1954 Sam Houston St Univ; mil/USCG 1942-45; pa/Voc Agric Tchr 1950-74; Asst Coach Montgomery HS 1950-65; Montgomery Co Dem Com 1955-70; cp/Pres Montgomery Lions Clb 1962; r/Bapt.

DENNARD, CLEVELAND L oc/University President; b/Feb 17, 1929; h/691 Beckwith St SW, Atlanta, GA 30314; ed/BS 1948 Fla A&M Univ; MS 1958 Colo St Univ; EdD 1964 Univ of Tenn; pa/Pres Wash Tech Inst, Washington, DC 1967-77; Pres Atlanta Univ 1977-; Lectr in 16 countries sponsored by US Info Agcy; Spkr; Conslt; Editorial Conslt: *Career Opportunities Encyclopedia*; Contbr Chapt: *Courage to Change* 1971; Spec Editor: *The Bureaucrat* 1974; cp/Former Dir Metro Wash Bd of Trade; Trustee Robert F Kennedy Meml Foun; Dir & Chm Dist Communs Inc; Chm of Bd So Ed Foun, Atlanta; Trustee Aerospace Ed Foun; Trustee Martin Luther King Jr Ctr for Social Change; Former Dir Washington Performing Arts Soc; Others; hon/Mem on-site team to assess impact of US aid to Nigeria, as conslt to St Dept 1970; Appt'd by Pres Lyndon B Johnson & Richard Nixon to consecutive terms as a mem of Nat Adv Com on Adult & Cont'g Ed, HEW; Others.

DENNIS, C WENDYL oc/Steel Company Executive; b/Sept 30, 1939; h/9516 Regal Ln, Okla City, OK 73132; ba/Norman, OK; m/Rozanne Swick; c/Marc Anthony, Khristin Wyn; p/Carlice Garland (dec) and Mary Lois Dennis, McAlester, OK; ed/BBA Ctrl St Univ 1970; mil/AUS 1957-60; pa/W&W Steel Co 1961-71, Gen Mgr Norman, Okla Plant 1971-73, VP & Gen Mgr 1973-80, Sr VP 1980-; Norman Mfg Assn; cp/Norman C of C; Repub Party; r/Meth; hon/W/W S&SW.

DENNIS, CHERRE NIXON oc/Artist, Painter, Printmaker; b/Sept 2; h/Lakeview Rt 1 Box 304-B, Wagoner, OK 74467; 3000 Monterey SE, Albuquerque, NM 876106; m/Thomas D (dec); p/Howard Thomas Nixon

(dec); Ida May Pursol (dec); ed/Att'd Univ Tulsa, Okla St Univ, Univ NM; pa/Exhibs: St, Regional, Nat Juried Shows Incl'g Philbrook Art Ctr, Tilcrease Inst, Oakland Art Mus & Mus of NM Santa Fe; Alpha Rho Tau: Histn 1956-64, Treas 1965-66, Pres 1967-69; Pres & Chm Bd Adah M Robinson Meml Fund Inc 1967-70; NM Art Leag; Lake Region Art Colony; Public Info Ofc, Civil Air Patrol, Okla Wing 1951-56; r/Christian; hon/Watercolor & Graphic Awds; Cert of Apprec, Art Dept Univ Tulsa; Others.

DENNIS, LINDA H oc/Publisher, Executive; b/May 30, 1947; h/P Box 2712, Spartanburg, SC 29304; c/Caroline C; p/Clarence A Hiers, Springfield, SC; Willie J Hiers, Columbia, SC; ed/Att'd USC 1966, Middlesex Commun Col 1970-72; pa/Pres Linda Dennis Finish Line Inc; Pubr-Designer Needlework Booklets; Nat Needlework Assn; Soc of Craft Designers; Spartanburg Co Legal Aux; r/Meth; hon/Author *Finishing Techniques for Counted Cross Stitch, Needleworks for Children, Now That I Can Count...How Do I Finish?* & Others.

DENNIS, PAUL T oc/Lieutenant Investigator; b/Mar 23, 1938; h/PO Box 493, Smiths, AL 36877; ba/Opelika, AL; m/Anne C; c/Paule J, Barbara A, Terrie J, Donna Chapman, Elaina M; p/Ivey W and Edna B Dennis, Newman, GA; ed/EMT Sch 1973; Crimes Scene Invest 1974; Homicide Invest 1975, Enterprise Police Acad 1973; FBI Acad 1973; Police Photo 1977; Supervision of Police Pers 1979; mil/USN; pa/Lee Co Sheriff Dept, Lt Invest Felony; FOP, Pres 1975, VP 1974; r/Meth; hon/Promotion to Invest 1973; Promotion to Sgt Invest 1976; Promotion to Lt Invest 1980.

DENNIS, ROBERT HOWARD oc/Corporation Vice President; b/Aug 22, 1955; h/Rt 2, Jacksonville, TX 75766; ba/Tyler, TX; p/Donald J Dennis, Tyler, TX; Reba J Dennis, Jacksonville, TX; ed/AA Lon Morris Jr Col 1976; BA Baylor Univ 1978; pa/VP Am Plasti-Plate Corp; cp/Repub Party; r/So Bapt.

DENNISON, JERRY LEE oc/Retail Office Supply Executive; b/May 22, 1947; h/Rt 1, Box 104-A, Russell Springs, KY 42642; ba/Russell Springs; m/Patricia Jeanette Davis; c/Sonya; Staci, Jarred; p/Ronald M (dec) and Alice Marie Dennison, Clarkson, KY; ed/Automation Acctg Dip Spencerian Bus Col 1969; T&I Ed Wn Ky Univ 1975; pa/Mgr EDP Ky So Col 1965-67; Supr EDP Wn Ky Univ 1967-68; Asst Mgr Bank Data Ctr 1968-79; EDP Instr Spencerian Bus Col 1971-72; EDP Instr Somerset Voc-Tech Sch 1972-76; Mgr EDP Crane Co 1977-70; Owner-Mgr Dennison Ofc Supply 1979-; DPMA; NOMDA; cp/Russell Co C of C; Russell Springs Elem PTA, Pres 1973-74; VP 1974-75; r/Ch of Christ; hon/W/W S&SW 1980-81.

DENNISON, KATHLEEN MULVEY oc/Account Executive Trainee; b/Nov 14, 1949; h/PO Box 459, Lake Charles, LA 70602; c/Bradley Bartol; p/(dec); ed/BS 1972, MA 1976 Univ Ctrl Fla; pa/Acct Exec Trainee, Merrill Lynch, Pierce, Fenner & Smith Inc; Formerly w Suburban Real Est Inc, Better Homes & Gdns; Real Est Broker & Tchr; Nat Assn Rltrs; Rltrs Nat Mktg Inst; So Speech Commun Assn; La Rltrs Assn; Gtr Calcasieu Bd of Rltrs, Secy Bd Dirs; cp/LWV of La, Lake Charles Chapt Bd Dirs; Quota Clb; Newcomers of Lake Charles; r/Cath; hon/Million Dollar Clb of Gtr Calcasieu Bd of Rltrs 1978, 1979.

DENNY, WILLIAM ALOYSIUS JR oc/Management Consultant; b/Apr 27, 1936; ba/Professional Development Inc, 452 Derby Ln, Montgomery, AL 36109; m/Ilga; c/Frank Robert, Iveta Elizabeth, Kimberly Ann; ed/BS St Univ NY 1963; MS Pepperdine Univ 1975; Air Command Staff Col 1976; Dept Defesnse Computer Inst 1976; mil/USN; USAF; pa/Mgmt Conslt, Profl Devel Inc; Am Mgmt Assn; Kappa Delta Phi; cp/Mgmt Conslt to St of Ala JCs; r/Epis; hon/Bronze Star Medal; Merit Ser Medal w 1 Oak Leaf Cluster; Commendation Medal; Navy Good Conduct Medal; Outstg Unit Awd w V, Outstg Univ Awd w 2 Oak Leaf Clusters; Nat Defense Ser Medal, Vietnam Ser; Longevity Awd w 4 Clusters; Small Arms Expert Marksmanship Ribbon; PACAF Outstg Jr Pers Mgmt of Yr 1971; HQ Comd, USAF, Outstg Sr Pers Mgr of Yr 1975; Author: "Improve Productivity with Effective Goals and Controls" 1980; "Remedies for Excelsior Syndrome" 1980; Other Articles; *The American Promotion System* 1978; *Systems Analysis and Decision Making Handbook* 1978.

DENT, WOODY G oc/General Manager; b/Sept 7, 1952; h/PO Box 71, St Matthews, SC 29135; ba/Columbia; m/Jeanette C; c/Michelle Elizabeth, Edie Carroll; p/William P and Mary Guidry Dent; ed/Grad USC 1974; Att'd Univ Ga & Orangebery Calhoun Tech; mil/AUS 1971; NG 1972-77; pa/Past St Dist Mgr Progressive Farmer Ins; Former Owner & Mgr: The Back Door Night Clb, Woody's Outlet Clothing Store; Former Mgr QA Dept, TeePak Inc; Gen Mgr Dent Ins Agcy 1981-; Am Mgmt Assn; Am Soc Qual Control; cp/JC; Repub Party; r/Rom Cath; hon/W/W S&SW 1980-81; Eagle Scout; DAR Excell in History; Dean's List USC 1972; Order of Arrow.

DENTICI, PATRICIA DIANE oc/Family Nurse Practitioner; b/Dec

11, 1950; h/Comanche, OK; ba/PO Box 977, Velma, OK; p/Anthony Vincent and Maudine Long Dentici, Winnfield, LA; ed/AS 1974; Nurse Clinician Prog Cert 1981; pa/Self-Employed Indep Fam Nurse Practitioner; ANA; ONA; Dist II Nurses Assn; cp/Oak Ridge Volunteer Fire Dept; Lic'd FCC as Radio Sta Opr; r/Cath.

DENTON, BETTY ANN GRANT oc/Medical Technician; b/Feb 19, 1929; h/1403 Yows, Borger, TX 79007; ba/Borger; m/Beale B; c/Deborah Ann Huffman, Daniel Beale, David Patrick, Karen Ethel Writhe, Mary Elizabeth, Dollie Waucel; p/William Russell Grant, Macon, GA; Ethel Gladys Mullis Grant (dec); ed/Att'd LaGrange Col; pa/Lab & X'Ray in 3 Hosps & 7 Clins; Hamra & Powells Clin 17 Yrs; Secy Tex AMT; Asst Cook Harmony Hill; cp/Past Secy-Treas, Current Pres Hutchinson Co & Amarillo Geneal Soc; Girl Scout Ldr; Cub Scout Den Mother 4 yrs; Tchr Red Cross Swimming; r/Primitive Bapt; hon/3rd Place Stamp Show 1978; 3rd & 2nd Place Stamp Show 1979; Best in Show 1980; GSA Thanks Plaque; Author "The Baptist Trumpet."

DENTON, SARAH LEE CREECH oc/Business Education Research; b/Oct 30, 1926; h/963 Pine Crest Heights, Madisonville, TN 37354; m/Rex Carl (dec); c/Rex Carl Jr, Melanie Maria; p/Ollie William and Lydia Lee Odom Creech (dec); ed/AA 1953 Hiwassee Col; BA 1957 Scarritt Col for Christian Wkrs; MS 1971 Univ of Tenn-Knoxville; pa/Prof of Secretarial Sci, Dept of Bus Ed Hiwassee Col 1972-; Tchr of Bus Ed, Madisonville HS 1962-69; VP, Charter Mem Fort Loudoun Charter Chapt of Am Bus Wom's Assn; Mem: NEA, Tenn Ed Assn, Nat Bus Ed Assn, Tenn Bus Ed Assn, So Regional Bus Ed Assn, AAUP, Smithsonian Assocs; cp/Past Mem Houston Pk Comm; Former Cub Scout Den Mother; Treas Madisonville Housing Assn; Am Cancer Soc; Am Heart Fund; Sequoyah Trail Garden Clb: Mem, Former Pres, VP, Corresp Secy, Histn, Flower Show Chm; r/First U Meth Ch, Madisonville: Mem, Secy to Adm Bd, Yth Cnslr, Sub-Dist Yth Cnslr, Choir Mem; Mem U Meth Wom; hon/Fellow Mem ABI; Notable Ams of Bicent Era; World W/W Among Wom in Ed.

DENTON, THOMAS STEWART oc/Corporate Executive; b/Oct 12, 1945; h/812 N 20th St, Murray, KY 42071; ba/Murray; m/Janet Lee Scott; p/Stewart Benjamin Denton, Louisville, KY; Jane Alma Wiggins Denton, L'ville, KY; ed/Univ Miss 1964-68; BS Murray St Univ 1969; mil/USAF 1969-73 SSgt; USAFR 1973-74 SSgt; pa/Exec VP, Secy-Treas Scoden Inc 1979-; Am Numismatic Assn #2412; cp/Am Against the Union Control of Govt Liberty Lobby; Com to Establish the Gold Standard; Masons; Murray St Big M Clb; Murray St Alumni Assn; Century Clb Mem; Friends of KET; Citizens Com for the Right to Keep and Bear Arms; NCPAC; Am Securites Coun; Cong Clb; r/Prot; hon/W/W S&SW 1980-81.

DERRICK, HOMER oc/Retired Banker and Insurance Executive; b/Dec 10, 1906; h/315 Overhill Dr, Lexington, VA; m/Mabel Ellison Beckham; c/Homer Jr, Jeanne Morris, Betsy Calvo; ed/Univ SC; Grad Am Inst Banking; pa/VP SC Nat Bank, Columbia & Greenville 1926-50; Pres Carolina Nat Bank, Easley & Pendleton, 1951-54; Fdr & First Pres Great En Life Ins Co; Atlantic & Gulf States Ins Co; En Fire & Casualty Ins Co; Former Dir Freedom Life Ins Co; Chm Bd & Pres First Nat Bank, Lexington 1956-73 (Current Hon Chm Bd); Chm Bd First En Securities Corp; First En Fin Corp; Former Pres & Dir Fin Intl Corp; Dir Lexington Cadillac-Pontic Inc; Appalachian Fruit Growers Co; cp/Repub Party; Lexington Golf; English-Speaking Union; r/Epis.

DERRICK, MARY VIRGINIA DuBOSE oc/Teacher, Guidance Counselor; b/June 30, 1946; h/Pawleys Island, SC; m/Jean DuBose; c/Ashely DeTreville; p/Robert Newsome and Marie King DuBose, Pawleys Island, SC; ed/BA Columbia Col 1968; MEd USC 1980; pa/Tchr: Eng, Rdg, Lang Arts; Guid Cnslr; SCTE; NCTE; Presented St-wide Wkshop on Creative Writing at SCISA Meeting 1980; cp/Jr Wom's Clb of Columbia; Civitan Intl; Am Cancer Soc; Columbia City Ballet; r/All Sts Epis Ch; hon/Winner of Send a Mouse to Col Dr, Am Cancer Soc 1972; Outstg Sponsor Jr Clbs 1979; Editor "Stars to Steer By" 1980; Freelance Writer for *Pawleys Island Perspective*.

DERUCHER, KENNETH NOEL oc/Professor of Civil Engineering; b/Jan 24, 1949; h/Apt 1211, 13006 Old Stagecoach Rd, Laurel, MD 20811; ba/College Park, MD; m/Barbara Eileen; p/K J Derucher (dec); Vienna May Derucher, Utica, NY; ed/BSCE; MSCE; PhD; pa/Prof of Civil Engrg Univ of Md-College Park; Mem: ASCE, TRB, ASTM, AAAS, ASEE; r/Rom Cath; hon/Sigma Xi; Res Initiation Grant NSF; Fellow Mem ABI; Book of Hon; Notable Ams; Personalities of Am.

DeRUSSO, MITCHELL LANCE oc/Project Design and Cost Analysis; b/Mar 16, 1955; h/Steele, AL; m/Rebecca Lynn; p/Alfred Louis and Gwendolyn DeRusso, Steele, AL; ed/Gadsden St Jr Col 1973-75; Univ Ala-Birmingham 1975-76; BS Auburn Univ 1978; Enrolled Jacksonville St Univ Grad Sch; pa/Anniston Army Depot Methods Improvement Dept; 1 Yr w City of Gadsden Plan'g & Engrg Dept; 6 Mo Ser w Jones, Blair, Waldrup & Tucker Inc; 6 Mo w W S Dickey Co; 2 Yrs w So Co Sers Inc, Hydro Projs

Dept; Am Soc Civil Engrs; Am Soc Profl Engrs; Nat Soc Profl Engrs; cp/City Coun-man; Stelle Nat JCs; r/Meth; hon/St Mem Piano Guild; Var Sports Awds; Articles Pub'd in Newspapers.

DeSEAR, VERNON L JR oc/Retail Dealership; b/Apr 17, 1948; h/2601 Nightingale Ln, Brandenton, FL 33529; ba/Brandenton; m/Peggy; p/Vernon Sr and Cloyce De Sear, Brandenton, FL; ed/BA Stetson Univ; MRE So Bapt Sem; Masters Deg from Univ Louisville; pa/Guidance Cnslr Sch Bd Manatee Co; Retail GE Appliance Dlrship; Retail & Contractor Sales; cp/Bd Dirs: Bradenton JCs (Past VP), Brandenton Kiwanis, U Cerebral Palsy, Fla W Coast Symph, Miss Fla Pageant, Hernando DeSoto Hist Soc, Manatee Co Nursery Sch; Mem: Dem Exec Com, Manatee Symph Guild; r/Bapt; hon/JC Awds: JC of Qtr 5 Times; Key Man 1978, US Outstg Proj Chm 1979; Fla JCs Outstg Proj Com 1979; Hist Soc Awds: Outstg New Conquistador 1978, Outstg Creation & Initiative 1979; Ky Col 1979; W/W Students in Am Cols & Univs 1970.

DeSHIELDS, LINDA J oc/Chief Deputy Clerk of Court; b/Jan 1, 1942; h/Rt 2, Honea Path, SC 29654; ba/Anderson; m/Joe C; p/L C and Ruby Johnston, Honea Path, SC; ed/Secy Sci, Anderson Jr Col; pa/Chief Dpty Clk of Ct; r/Bapt.

deSTEIGUER, JOHN RODOLPH oc/Businessman; b/Feb 6, 1934; h/507 Normal St, Tahlequah, OK 74464; ba/Tahlequah, OK; m/Mary Jo Deem; c/John R Jr, Mary Elizabeth, Stephanie Anne; p/Joseph E and Ione Hudson deSteiguer, Port Arthur, TX; ed/MAPA Univ Okla; BS SW Tex St Univ; mil/USN Cmdr; pa/Naval Aviator; Civil Air Patrol; Am Soc Public Admrs; cp/Bd Regents Okla Cols; VChm City Plan'g & Zoning Comm; Am Legion; VFW; Kiwanis; r/Ch of Christ: Deacon & Treas.

deTREVILLE, RUTH SAFFOLD oc/Retired; b/Nov 26, 1892; h/701 Greene St, Box 27, Beaufort, SC 29902; m/Benjamin Ellis (dec); c/B Ellis Jr, R J, Ruth Richeter Spieler; p/Thomas P and Matilda Claghorn Saffold (dec); pa/Organiast; Tchr: Voice, Violin, Piano; Now Ret'd; r/Epis; hon/Achmt Intl, US Govt.

DETTWILLER, GEORGE FREDERICK oc/Beer Wholesaler; b/Oct 8, 1932; h/151 Valley Forge Dr, Nashville, TN 37205; ba/Nashville; m/Martha; c/Kimberly, Sally, George, Helene, Ann Kathryn; p/E E (dec) and Elsie Dettwiller, Nashville, TN; ed/AB Vanderbilt Univ 1954; pa/Det Dist'g Co; Bd Dirs Tenn Malt Beverage Assn; Life Assoc Vanderbilt Univ; cp/Bd Dirs UN Assn; Exec Com Muscular Dystrophy Assn Middle Tenn; Past Mem Qtrly Ct, Clarksville; Past Mem Airport & Library Comms; Bd Dirs Red Cross & Kiwanis Clb; hon/Miller Masters Awd 1977, 78, 79; Chm of UN Day for Nashville/Davidson Co 1979.

DEUTSCH, EBERHARD PAUL oc/Lawyer; b/Oct 31, 1897; h/Pontchartrain Hotel, 2031 St Charles Ave, New Orleans, LA 70140; ba/New Orleans; m/Rhea Loeb (dec); c/Brunswick G; p/Gotthard Deutsch (dec); Hermine Bacher (dec); ed/Tulane Univ 1924-25; Hon LLD Loyola Univ 1972; Hon LLD Univ Messina, Sicily; mil/AUS Col; pa/Spec Asst to Atty Gen of US 1950-53; Dir Am Judicature Soc 1938-56; St Rep for La, The Selden Soc 1993-; Am Bar Assn: Chm Com on Admiralty & Maritime Law 1961-62, Chm Com on Peace & Law through UN 1962-63, 1965-68, Chm Com on Law Treaties 1968-; Editor *The International Lawyer* 1968-74, Mem Coun of Sect of Intl Law 1967-, Foun Fellow 1972, Del of Sec of Intl Law to House of Dels 1972-74; La St Bar Assn: Chm Com on Law Reform 1956-76, Chm Common Revision of La Corp Laws 1961-68; Civilian Aide to Secy of Army for La 1962-76; Civilian Aide at Large to Secy of Army 1976-; Hon Consul Gen of Repub of Austria for La & Miss 1959-77; Chm Bd Visitors of Judge Advocate Gen's Sch of AUS 1967-76; Spec Conslt To White House on Pwrs of Pres as Cmdr-in-Chief 1970-76; Am Judicature Soc 1971-; Am Doc Intl Law; Assn Average Adjusters; Assn Bar of NYC; Assn Interstate Commerce Practitioners; AAUS; Braniff Intl Coun; Bur Govtl Res; Fed Bar Assn; Fgn Policy Assn; Fgn Relats Assn of New Orleans; France Amerique de la Louisiana; Grand Consistory of La; Indian Soc of Intl Law; Insurance Clb of New Orleans; Inter-Am Bar Assn; Intl Bar Assn; Intl House (Dir 1967-, Exec Comm 1967-); Intl Law Assn; Intl Legal Aid Assn; Intl Platform Assn; Intl Soc Mems of Consular Corps; Ionosphere Clb; Many Other Profl Orgs; cp/Admirals Clb; Alumni Assn Tulane Univ; Ambassador's Clb; Audubon Soc; Blue Key Nat Hon Frat; B'nai B'rith; C of C of New Orleans Area; City Clb of Baton Rouge; Confrerie des Chevaliers du Tastevin; Nat Trust for Hist Preserv; Cosmos Clb, Wash DC; Costeau Soc; CODIFIL; Downtown Athletic Clb; Intl Order of Blue Goose; Jerusalem Temple; Lamplighter Clb; Le Petit Theatre de Vieux Carre; Lotos Clb; La Hist Soc; New Orleans Lodge #30 BPOE; New Orleans Opera House Assn; New Orleans Philharmonic Symph Soc; Notaries Assn of New Orleans; Round Table Clb; Scottish Rite Temple; Shakespeare Soc of New Orleans; Other Civic Orgs; hon/US: Silver Star, Legion of Merit, Bronze Star for Valor, Army Commend, Purple Heart, Pres Unit Citation, WWI Victory w 4 Battle Stars, WWI German Occupation, Am Sector, European Sector w Bch-Hd Arrow & 8 Battle Stars, WWII Victory, WWII German

PERSONALITIES OF THE SOUTH

Occupation, 2 Certs of Apprec for Patriotic Civilian Ser; French: Crois de Guerre w Palm and Fourragere, Verdun St Mihiel, Order of Lafayette; Austrian Gold Cross of Merit; Consul of Yr, Intl Consular Corps Acad 1975; Assn of AUS for Ser as Mem of Adv Bd of Dirs 1975; La St Bar Assn on Occasion Marking 50th Yr Pract'g Law 1975; Num Biogl List'gs; Pub'd Author.

d'EVEGNEE, CHARLES PAUL oc/State Director for Benefits Development; b/Aug 4, 1939; h/10307 Pebblebrook Pk, Richmond, VA 23233; ba/Richmond; m/Marie-Therese Barnich; c/Chantal E, Charlie D; p/Charles Clement Devignez and Fernande Francoise Godet d'Evegnee, Herstal, Belgium; ed/BA Brigham Young Univ 1966; MA Univ Ct 1969; JD Univ Conn Law Sch 1974; mil/AUS 1960-63; pa/Grp Pension Underwriter, Conn Gen Life Ins Co 1969-72; Legal Conslt, Frank B Hall & Co 1974-76 Regional Counsel, Meidinger & Assocs 1976-78; St Dir Benefits Devel, Commonwlth of Va 1978-; Intl Foun of Employee Benefits Plans; Am Mgmt Assn; cp/Metro Richmond C of C; Kiwanis; hon/Legal Res & Writing Awd 1971; Co-Author: *European Antitrust Law* 1976; "The Continental Can Case" 1974; "The French Legal and Tax Aspects of the Formation of Subsidiaries in a European Context" 1975.

de VILLAR, DELIA DIAZ oc/Adjunct Instructor; b/Apr 2, 1910; h/510 SW 8th Ct, Miami, FL 33130; m/Gabriel S; c/Gabriel J Jr; ed/PhD Havana Univ; PhD Univ Havana; Certs of Methods of Tchg Spanish to English Spkg Students, Barry Col; Cert in SS, Diocesis of Miami; pa/Adj Instr Spanish Grammar & Hispanoam Lit, Biscayne Col; cp/Cuban Woms Clb; Miami Cuban Lions Clb Ladies Aux; r/Cath; hon/Lincln-Marti Dip of Hon, US Dept of HEW 1973; Plaque of Hon, Woms of Life, Latin BPW 1977.

DEWBERRY, INEZ STEPHENS oc/Teacher; b/Aug 28, 1915; h/Rt 1 Box 100, Lineville, AL 36266; ba/Wedowee; m/James Lawrence; p/Oscar Lee Stephens (dec); Bessie Gibson Stephens, Lineville, AL; pa/Spec Ed Tchr, Wedowee Elem; NEA; AEA; REA; CTA; r/Bapt; hon/Hall of Fame; Hon Roll; World W/W Wom; W/W Am Wom; Notable Ams.

DEWBERRY, MARVIN LARRY JR oc/County Extension Agent; b/Aug 31, 1950; h/PO Box 1058, Carrollton, GA 30117; ba/Carrollton; m/Debra Williams; c/Jennifer Nicola; p/Marvin L Sr and Florence Isom Dewberry, Moultrie, GA; ed/Assoc Deg Vet Med; BSA Animal Nutrition; pa/Co Ext Agt Univ Ga; Ga 4-H Assn; Co Agricl Agts; cp/Optimist Clb; Active St Andrew Meth Ch; Independent Party; ASSI; r/Meth; hon/Recog 4-H Assn: Devel'd Carroll Co into One of Strongest in 4-H Activs in Ga; Coach'd Sev of St 4-H Judging Teams.

DeYOUNG, MURIEL H oc/Professional Artist; Teacher; b/May 12, 1916; h/2605 Frederick Blvd, Delray Beach, FL 33444; m/John Charles; p/Louis Charles Maurer (dec); Anna B Maurer, Pompano Beach, FL; ed/2 Yrs Col; Ringling Sch of Art; Betty B Bentz of NC; Juan Cedeno & Alberto Dutary of Panama; Wallace Bassford, Palm Bch, Fla; pa/Profl Artist; Tchr; Mem: Intl Soc of Artists, NY, Delray Art Leag (Past Pres); Exhibiting Artist, Ctr for the Arts, Boca Raton, Fla; "DeYoung Studio of Fine Arts" cp/Mem, Past Pres, St Pres Nat Leag Am Pen Wom Inc; r/Presb; hon/Intl Register of Profiles; 2000 Wom Achmt; Commun Ldrs & Noteworthy Ams; World W/W of Wom; Fellow Mem ABI.

DHILLON, HARPAL SINGH oc/Engineer, Consultant, Company President; b/Dec 7, 1939; h/132 N Ithaca Ct, Sterling Pk, VA 22170; ba/Vienna, VA; m/Sarjit Kaur; c/Gurpreet, Manpreet; p/Harnand Singh (dec) and Mohinder K Dhilloh, Sterling Pk, VA; ed/BS 1958, BS 1962 Punjab Univ; MS Okla St Univ 1969; PhD Univ Mass 1973; pa/Lectr Thapar Col of Engrg, Punjab, India 1962-64; Grp Engr Brooke Bond Tea Co 1964-68; Grp Ldr Mitre Corp 1973-79; Pres Engrg & Ecs Res Inc 1979-; Operations Res Soc of Am; The Inst of Mgmt Scis; cp/Trustee of Guru Nanak Foun of Am; r/Sikh; hon/Merit S'ship of Punjab Univ 1960; Grad F'ship of Univ Mass 1971-73; Hon Mem Phi Kappa Phi Hon Soc 1969-; Pub'd Articles in *Journal for Policy Sciences*, Geothermal Jours & Tech Reports.

DIAL, JOHN HALVIN oc/Plant Manager; b/Sept 24, 1937; h/2505 Lakeview Dr SW, Decatur, AL 35601; ba/Decatur; m/Marsha P; c/Dietlinda Anne, Dirk Steven, Elizabeth Grace; p/Mary Moss Dial, Rome, GA; ed/BCE Inst of Tech, Atlanta 1963; MBA Berry Col 1976; mil/AUS 1963-65 1/Lt; pa/Plant Mgr, Aeroquip/Tomkins-Johnson 1979-; Plant Mgr Johnson Steel & Wire Co 1978-79; Prod Supvr, Maintenance Supvr, Proj Eng, Bekaert Steel Wire 1971-78; Strength Analyst/Engr McDonnell Douglas 1968-71; Reg'd Profl Engr in Ga, Ohio, Tenn, Mass, Miss; Mem Nat Soc Profl Engrs; c/Mayor Of Akron Ohio's Labor/Mgmt Relats Com; r/Cath; hon/Prof of Mil Sci Awd for Ldrship, Ga Tech 1962.

DIAL, MAUREEN oc/Extension Agent; b/Feb 11, 1944; h/Pembroke, NC; p/Danford and Reece G Dial, Pembroke, NC; ed/BS 1965; MS 1975; pa/Tchr; Home Ec Ext Agt; NCHEA: Pres, Treas, Secy; NCEHEA: Dist

Pres, Treas; r/So Bapt; hon/Outstg Yng Wom Am 1978; Native Am & Alaska Wom 1978; W/W Am Wom 1981.

DIAMOND, FAYE oc/Businesswoman; b/Aug 17, 1918; h/609 Country Club, Cleburne, TX 76031; ba/Cleburne; m/Donald; c/Sylvia, Patricia, Jannette, Janice, Donald II, Dianna; p/John D (dec) and Mabel A Plumlee (dec); pa/Co-Owner Metroplex Sign Mfg Co; Real Estate Invests; cp/Vol in Fund Drs for MD, Heart Fund, Am Cancer Soc; Past VP City Coun, Cleburne HS; Org'd 1st Girl's Little Leag Softball Team; Ofc Holder & Vol PTA 1945-60; Budget & Fin Ch Cooke Sch 1953; Asst Ldr Blue Birds & Camp Fire Girls 1956-62; Den Mother For Cub Scouts 1951-55; Pythian Sister w K of P Lodge 39 Yrs; r/Bapt; hon/25 Yr Pn & Awd for Faithful Ser to Home for Orphan Chd from Pythian Sisters.

DICK, W ARSENE SR oc/Director and Coordinator Emergency Services; b/June 23, 1915; h/Rt 4, Summit, MS 39666; ba/McComb, MS; m/Madelyn; c/Wilfred A Jr, Donald A; p/M W (dec) and Jessie E Dick (dec); mil/USN Sea-Bees; pa/Emer Preparedness & Plan'g; cp/St Pres Miss Civil Defense Assn; Pres Summit Rotary Clb; VP SW Shrine Clb; r/Bapt; hon/Dist'd Ser Cit, Dept Defense 1975; Public Ser Awd, US Dept Commerce 1975; Outstg Sr Awd, Miss Civil Defense Assn 1975; Ser Above Self Awd, Rotary Intl 1979; St of Miss Ho of Rep & Sen Jt Resolution #557 Outstg Ser 1975; Outstg Ser Awd, Sunnyhill Fire Dept 1976; Outstg Ser Awd Osyka Fire Dept 1977; Outstg Ser Resolution Bd Alderman, Summit, Miss 1978; US Civil Defense Assn Resolution 1977; Merit & Dist'd Ser Awd 1980; Dedicated Efforts Awd, Miss Civil Defense Assn 1977.

DICKERSON, ADOLPHUS SUMNER oc/Minister; b/May 25, 1914; h/Atlanta, GA; m/Juanita W; p/Dixie (dec) and Mary B Dickerson (dec); ed/AB Clark Col 1942; BD Gammon Theol Sem 1945; MA Atlanta Univ 1959; STM Boston Sch Theol 1960; DD Clark Col 1974; pa/Meth Pastor; Meth Dist Supt; Pt-time Chaplain Atlanta Fed Prison; Pt-time Chaplain Atlanta Vets Hosp; Editor Atlantic Coast of the Meth Ch; Pt-time Prof Interdenominational Sem; Pres Metro-Atlanta Christian Coun; Del Meth Gen Conf; Pres Hinton Rural Life Ctr; cp/Pres Atlanta Bi-Partisan Leag; Life Mem NAACP; Alpha Phi Alpha Frat; hon/Min of Yr Omega Frat 1959; Aldolphus Dickerson Day Jan 10, 1980 by Mayor Atlanta; Trustee Rhunhard Col.

DICKERSON, DOROTHY M oc/Bookkeeper, Receptionist; b/Apr 19, 1931; h/Rt 1, Earlsboro, OK 74840; ba/Seminole, OK; m/Leon; c/Barbara McGehee, Kenneth; p/Harvey C Moneypenny, Holdenville, OK; Beulah P Moneypenny (dec); ed/GED Cert; pa/Bkkpr, Receptionist, Austin Drilling Co; cp/Elect'd Ofc St Treas, Okla Fed BPW Clbs; r/Bapt; hon/Seminoles Bus Wom of Yr 1973.

DICKEY, LYNN CARTER oc/Interpreter for Deaf, Homemaker; b/Dec 1, 1948; h/3109 Greg, Tyler, TX 75701; ba/Same; m/Mill O; c/Laura Lynn, David Carter; p/Fred Band and Erna M Carter, Frankston, TX; ed/Certs: Manual Communication I & II, RID Provisional & TSID Coor Classes Sign Lang Tyle Jr Col; pa/Secy Christian Sers of SW; Interpreter: Doctors, Tyler Jr Col, Police, Job Interviews, etc; cp/Civic Clb Spkr; Child Nurture Clb; E Tex Dea & Hearing Assn; Gen Elect Wives Clb; Sec Friends of Chd, Child Care Aux; r/Glenwood Ch of Christ: Interpreter, Singer for Weddings, Spec Occasions; hon/Outstg Wom in Am; 2 Yr S'ship Tex Wom's Univ.

DICKEY, RONALD NEAL oc/Teacher; b/June 3, 1951; h/Rt 2, Selmer, TN 38375; ba/Selmer; m/Judy Lynn Davis; c/Ryan Neal; p/Wilburn and Mary Ruth Dickey, Selmer, TN; ed/BSEd Sec'dy Ed; pa/7th & 8th Grade Tchr, Selmer Middle Sch, McNairy Co Sch Sys; r/Bapt; hon/Tchr of Mo.

DIENES, SARI oc/Artist; Poet; b/1899; h/Stony Point, NY; ba/Same; m/Paul; ed/Studied Dance & Philosophy in Vienna & Paris; pa/Worked w Fernand Leger & Andre Lhote, Paris; Henry Moore, London; Asst Dir Amedee Ozenfant'd Acad; 1st Com-wom Show: New York Sch of Social Res 1942; Summer Residency, Cummington Sch of Art 1954; Comm'd by Univ of Wash to prepare 400 rubbings of prehistoric Indian carvings on stones bordering the Columbia River; Worked in Japan 1957-58, exhibs in Tokyo & Kyoto; Works shown in MOMA's "Art of Assemblage" 1962; Comm'd by St of NY to do 2 screens for hearing rooms in Legislative Bldgs; Poetical Work Appeared in *Tracks*, a Mag for Artist's Writings; Spkr, Nat Inst of Design, India 1975; Artist-in-Residence, Va Ctr for Creative Arts (VCCA), Sweet Briar, Va 1979; Lectrs; Set Designs; hon/Num Group Shows; Num Collects incl'g: Brooklyn Mus, MOMA, Univ of Vermont, Pvt collects; Num Solo Shows incl'g: Tokoyo Gallery, San Diego Gallery, Malik Col, Univ of Mont; Pub'd Num Articles & Reviews in Profl Jours incl'g: *Art Digest* 1950, 54, *Art International* 1973, *New York Herald Tribune* 1942, 54, 59, *San Francisco Chronicle* 1957, *Life* 1954, *The Rockland Review* 1977, *Ear Magazine* 1976, 77, *Emergence* 1977; Grants; F'ships; Residencies; Intl Wom's Yr Awd 1976.

81

DIETSCHE, H BRENT JURGEN oc/Clinical Psychologist; b/Aug 2, 1919; h/PO Box 69, Vinita, OK 74301; ba/Vinita; m/Jewell Anna; c/Michael, Marcelle, Elizabeth; p/Erwin and Erna Dietsche, Klamath Falls, OR; ed/BA; MA; PhD; Hon PhD; mil/AUS ASTP, US & Overseas; pa/En St Hosp, Vinita, Asst Chief Psychol, Dir Psychol Dept, Conslt Voc Rehab Mtl Retarded Home, Head Start; cp/Am Legion; C of C; Bd Mem, Camp Fire Girls; r/Bapt; hon/Notable Ams of the Bicent Era; Plaque: Intl Register of Profiles, Ser to the Commun from Intl W/W Commun Ser; Fellow Mem ABI.

DIETZ, GUENTHER oc/Head Soccer Coach, Assistant Professor; b/Nov 4, 1941; h/PO Box 1146, Buies Creek, NC 27506; ba/Buies Creek; m/Ivy Munsey; p/Fritz and Anna Klingler Dietz, Heidelberg, W Germany; ed/BA, MS Tenn Tech Univ; pa/Hd Soccer Coach & Asst Prof, Campbell Univ; VP Aths Advrs Inc; AAUP; AAHPER; r/Prot; hon/VISA Coach of Yr 1975; Outstg Col Aths 1970; Kappa Delta Pi 1970.

DIGGS, CHRISTINE HEATH oc/Director of Consultation and Education; b/June 5, 1950; h/3210 Longview Dr, Killeen, TX; m/Robert Allen; c/Robert Allen Jr; p/Robert Lee Sr and Wadella C Heath, Killeen, TX; ed/AA Ctrl Tex Col 1969; BA N Tex St Univ 1971; MS Univ Tex-Arlington 1974; pa/Dir Conslt & Ed, Ctrl Cos Ctr for MH/MR Sers; Proj Dir FACE Proj, McLennan Commun Col; Sr Social Wkr, Fam Plan'g, John Peter Smith Hosp; Nat Assn Black Social Wkrs; cp/Active in Ch Activs; r/Bapt; hon/W/W Am; Outstg Yng Wom Am 1977.

DIGGS, STEVEN FRANKLIN oc/Executive; b/July 3, 1952; h/22 Music Square W, Nashville, TN 37203; m/Bonita Louise; c/Megan Ruth; p/Herbert B and Verna Calvert Diggs, Oak Ridge, TN; ed/BS David Lipscomb Col 1974; pa/Sales Mgr Dave Floyd & Assocs Rltrs; Pres & CEO Franklin Grp (Parent Firm of Nashville-based Advtg Agcy & Radio/TV Commercial Prod Firm); ASCAP Pub'g Firm 1974-; TV Weatherman 1970; Recording Artist Until 1974; cp/Bus Advr Bd David Lipscomb Col; Exec Bd Dirs Christian Voice; Repub Party; Omega Chi; r/Ch of Christ; hon/Hon Tenn Col 1975; W/W S&SW 1980-81; Club 100 Awd 1970; Top 30 Crew Awd 1070; Salesmanship Awd 1976; Forensic Awd 1973; 2 Musical Compositions Pub'd: "Flight 408" & "Raggady Ann.".

DI GRAPPA, GERALD PETER oc/Clinical Social Worker; b/June 29, 1921; h/1601 Kiowa Dr, Big Spring, TX 79720; ba/Big Spring; m/Mary Maxine Clark; ed/BA, MS; mil/USMCR; USPHSR; pa/ACSW; NASW; cp/Bd Dirs Cath Charities.

DILL, ANNE HOLDEN oc/Professor; b/Mar 7, 1920; h/850 Walnut St, Gadsden, AL 35901; ba/Gadsden; m/Elmer; c/Winston Elmer, Jane Anne D Rozier, Caroll Elizabeth; p/James Houston and Florence Elizabeth Henley Holden (dec); ed/BS, MA, EdS Equiv, Univ Ala; pa/Prof English, Gadsden St Jr Col; Instr Ext Div, Univ Ga, Dublin; AAAU, Liaison Rep, Gadsden St Jr Col; NEA; AEA; S Ctrl Mod Lang Assn; cp/Gadsden Concert Assn; The Pres's Clb (Dem); r/1st Bapt Ch, Gadsden: Mem, Co-Dir Ednl Tng Prog; hon/World's W/W Wom; Fellow, IPA; Fellow Mem ABI; Hon Lt Aide-de-Camp, Ala St Militia, Terms of Gov G Wallace.

DILLON, TERRY LYNN oc/Bank Loan Officer, Assistant Cashier, Collection Officer; b/Jan 31, 1951; h/2912 Mimosa Dr, Newport, AR 72112; ba/Newport; m/Deborah Allbright; c/Christopher Allbright; p/Norman and Ruby Dillon, Newport, AR; ed/BA SWn Univ; cp/Bd Dirs Ozark Gateway Tourist Coun; Bd Dirs C of C; Pres Newport Kiwanis Clb; r/Epis; hon/Outstg Yng Men Am 1979; Grp Study Exch Prog through Rotary Intl which Traveled to Japan for 6 Wks.

DILWORTH, DERBERT L oc/Principal; b/Nov 16, 1940; h/Biloxi, MS; ba/Biloxi; c/Duane, Derbert Jr, Darrell; p/Dermit and Mattie Dilworth (dec); ed/Ariz St Univ 1960-61; BS Miss St Univ; MEd Univ So Miss; pa/Coached Fball, Basketball, Track 1964-68; Asst Fball & Baseball Coach 1968-69, 1969-71; NYC Dir 1971-72; Asst Prin Fernwood 1972-74; Asst Prin Nichols 1974-75; Prin Michel 1975-; Bd Dirs Miss Assn Edrs; NEA; Bilox Ed Assn; Biloxi Fed Credit Union; Miss HS Art Assn; cp/NAACP; Kiwanis; JCs; Zeta Mu Lambda Chapt of Alpha Phi Alpha; r/Bapt.

Di MASSIMO, E FAYE oc/Assistant Professor; b/July 20, 1914; h/116 Cambridge Pl, Little Rock, AR 72207; ba/Little Rock; m/Nicholas F; c/Richard, Lisa Griffith; p/Samuel Oather (dec) and Cora Duncan Jones (dec); ed/BSE Ark St Univ Tchrs Col 1937; MA Emerson Col 1945; Post Grad Study Univ Tex, Univ Ark, UALR; pa/Asst Prof UALR Dept Speech Communs 1968-; Asst Prof Boston Univ 1944-45; Asst Prof Univ Bridgeport 1945-47; Eng Tchr Little Rock Public Schs & Other Ark Public Schs; HCI; Ark Speech Communs Assn; So Speech Communs Assn; cp/Nat Soc Arts & Lttrs, Nat Fin Chm; Delta Kappa Gamma; Cub Scouts; PTA: PTO; Girl Scouts; Garden Clb; Wom's Caucus; Ark Wom's Network; Westport Co Playhouse; r/Prot; hon/Delta Kappa Gamma Res Grant; Ark Ed Assn Grant; Conslt to Mary Ann Campbell's Money Mngmt.

Art Ed TV Network which Rec'd Bronze Awd at 1980 Intl Film & TV Fest of NY.

DINCULEANU, NICOLAE oc/Professor; b/Feb 24, 1925; h/610 NW 22nd St, Gainesville, FL 32603; ba/G'ville; m/Elena Nineta; p/Frusina Dinculeanu, Padea, Romania; ed/PhD Univ Bucarest 1956; pa/Prof Maths, Univ Fla; r/Christian; hon/Prize of Romanian Acad 1964; Author 2 Monographs "Vector Measures"; Textbooks on Math Analysis; Papers for Math Jours.

DINGFELDER, JAMES RAY oc/Obstetrician/Gynecologist; b/Feb 15, 1938; h/Chapel Hill, NC; ba/109 Conner Dr, Chapel Hill, NC; m/Karen; c/Thomas, Andrew, Michael; p/Ray John and Norrine M Dingfelder, Erie, PA; ed/AB Thiel Col 1961; MD Jefferson Med Col 1965; mil/USAF 1966-68 Capt; pa/Chapel Hill Fertiltiy Sers; AMA; Am Col Ob & Gyn; r/Luth; hon/50 Articles & Books.

DINNING, ADA ROZELL oc/Cosmetologist; b/Jan 10, 1916; h/PO Box 212, Adairsville, GA 30103; ba/Calhoun, GA; m/Herbert F; c/James C Quinn; p/dec; pa/Cosmetologist; r/Bapt.

DITTMANN, WAYNE ROY oc/Mathematics Department Chairman; b/Jul 3, 1926; h/White Oaks Farm, Rt 2, Box 897, Stafford, VA 22554; ba/Woodbridge, VA; m/Evelyn Lois; c/Wayne Jr, Robert L, Daniel D, Dale D, Darryl B; p/Roy Dittmann, Stafford, VA; ed/BS Mil Sci Univ of Md; MAEd George Mason; Post Grad Univ of Va; mil/USMC 24 yrs, Major Intell Ofcr; pa/Chm Maths Dept, Rippon Sch; Proj Dir & Instr New Dimensions in Math; Mem Pres White House Conf on Yth; cp/Charter Mem & 1st Chm Stafford Indust Devel Auth; Dist Chaplain Am Legion; r/Presb; Superintendent Hartwood Ch Sch; hon/Tchr of Yr, Prince William Co; Mr Legionnaire Post 290; Most Outstg Dist Cmdr Va, Am Legion of Va.

DIX, BARBARA LOUISE oc/Homemaker; b/Sept 27, 1956; h/Rt 6 Box 194, Cadiz, KY 42211; m/Ronnie Leroy; c/Mandy; (Stepchd:) Kimberly, Anthony; p/Winchester W Pike; Dorothy L Fontes; ed/Cert for Voc Child Care Sers Level III 1974; AA 1979; hon/Phi Theta Kappa; Creative Writing Awd; Trophy Blue Grass Fest; Cert of Merit, Coop Ed Clbs Fla.

DIXON, PEGGY LEE oc/Restaurant Owner; b/Aug 6, 1939; h/210 Gandy Ave, Hattiesburg, MS 39401; c/Kimberly, Helen; p/Howard Lee, Hattiesburg, MS; Helen Lee (dec); pa/Owner PJs Fam Restaurant; cp/Cand for Just Ct Judge; hon/HS Ath Awd.

DOBBINS, LOY HENDERSON oc/Professor of Counselor Education; b/Nov 4, 1920; h/3045 Potomac Dr, Baton Rouge, LA 70808; ba/Baton Rouge; m/Joyce Baker; c/Ruth Anne Bennett, Denise Joyce; p/W M and Vera C Dobbins (dec); ed/BS 1947, MS 1949, PhD 1968 La St Univ; mil/Pacific Theater of Operations 1942-45; pa/Former Positions: Res Assoc, Instr La St Univ; Currently Prof of Cnslr Ed So Univ, Baton Rouge; Mem: Am Voc Assn, APGA, Assn for Measuremt & Evaluation in Guid, Nat Voc Agri Tchrs Assn, Nat Voc Guid Assn; cp/Shriner; Lions Clb; r/Meth Ch; hon/Alpha Gamma Rho; Phi Delta Kappa; Kappa Delta Pi; Alpha Zeta; Alpha Tau Alpha; Num Awds for Outstg Performance as a Tchr, La; Fellow Mem ABI.

DOBBS, VIRGINIA ELIZABETH oc/Bookkeeper, Secretary, Office Assistant; b/Mar 3, 1911; h/312 Hickory Hill Rd, Nicholasville, KY 40356; ba/N'ville; p/Charles Alvin (dec) and Rosa Bishop Dobbs (dec); ed/Alayco Col 1933; Cert Crump Commerce Col; BS Bus Col; pa/Secy 37 Yrs; Charter Mem: Lena Madesin Phillips BPW Clb; Charter Mem Jessamine Hist Soc, CWF 1950; r/Prot; hon/Ky Col 1963; Att'd 51 Quadrennial Assem 1957.

DOBSON, THOMAS RAY oc/Locomotive Engineer; b/Aug 24, 1948; h/PO Box 127, Jellico, TN 37762; m/Debra Lynn; c/Stacey, Lana; p/Joe C Sr (dec) and Bessie Dobson, Jellico, TN; ed/Att'd Cumberland Col 1 Yr; mil/AUS 1968-70; pa/Owner Making Tracks Shoe Store; Elect'd Jellico City Coun-man 1980; Appt'd Chm Fin Comm; Ser'g on Civic Devel Com; cp/Kiwanis Clb; r/Bapt; hon/Best HS Ath 1966.

DOCKERY, ORVILLE DON oc/Professional Housekeeper; b/Aug 25, 1933; h/1307 N Ninth St, Conroe, TX 77301; ba/Conroe, TX; m/Patricia; c/Laura, Donna, John; p/dec; ed/GED 1954; Reg'd Barber's Lic; mil/USN 4 Yrs; pa/Dir Housekeeping Dr's Hosp; Owner of Dockery Ser Co; Conslt for Hosp Affils Intl; Nat Exec Housekeepers Assn: Pres 1980, VP 1979, Bd Mem 1978; Ednl Chm Tex Hosp Assn Soc of Exec Housekeepers; r/So Bapt; hon/Mgmt Awds from Rollins Sers 1971, 72, 73, 74.

DOD, STEVE BARE oc/Beer Distributor; b/Mar 5, 1932; h/1012 Ridgemont Dr, Staunton, VA 24401; ba/Verona, VA; m/Jean W; c/Deborah Jean, Nancy Lee, John B II; p/John B and Annie B Dod,

82

Lexington, VA; ed/Att'd VMI & Univ Tenn; mil/USN 1953-55; pa/Bd Dirs First & Merchants Bank; cp/Elks Clb; Eagles Clb; Moose Clb; Masons; Shriners; r/Presb; hon/4 Times Winner Jos Schlitz Brewing Co Awds.

DODD, TEDDY oc/Minister; b/Feb 25, 1941; m/Mary; c/Teddy, Joyce, Jeremy; p/Rex and Opal Dodd, Bartlesville, OK; ed/Att'd Pilgrim Holiness Col 1 Yr, Vennard Bible Col 4 Yrs; pa/Min Ch of God 20 Yrs; Dir Sr Citizens, Superior, Neb 1971-72; Secy Bd of Properties, Ch of God, St of Ala; VP Ch of God N Ctrl Dist; Pres Blackwell Min Alliance.

DODDS, NAOMI JEAN C oc/Nurse; b/Sept 25, 1929; h/4310 Anderson Pike, Signal Mtn, TN 37377; ba/Chattanooga, TN; c/Andrew James III, Charles Owings; p/Porter (dec) and Frona Clark (dec); ed/RN; pa/AHA; Assn Critical Care Nurses; cp/Walden's Ridge Hist Soc; Alumni BEH; Guild Gardeners; Chattanooga Kennel Clb; Signal Mtn Wel Coun; r/Epis; hon/Past Pres Num Orgs.

DODSON, MARGARET oc/Bookkeeper, Tax Consultant, Poet; b/June 7, 1924; h/152 Carroll, Shreveport, LA 71105; ba/Same; m/Lewis E; c/Jeaneva Spriggs, David Rose, Myron Gibson; p/Charles Boothe; Elizabeth C Wolfe, Shreveport, LA; ed/AB; Masters Cand; mil/USO Entertainment Sers; pa/Tchg; Bkkpg; Conslt; cp/Campaign for Comservatives; r/Bapt; hn/Num Pub's.

DOMENICI, PETE V oc/United States Senator; b/May 7, 1932; h/11110 Stephalee Lane, Rockville, MD 20852; ba/Washington, DC; m/Nancy Burk; c/Lisa Ann, Peter, Nella, Clare, David, Nannette, Paula and Helen; p/Cherubino Domenici (dec); Alda Vichi Domenici, Albuquerque, NM; ed/BA Univ of NM; JD Univ of Denver Law Sch; mil/AF ROTC Univ of NM 1952-54; pa/US Senator: Asst Minority Whip; Mem: Com on Energy & Natural Resources, Environmt & Public Wks, Budget Com, Sen Select Com on Aging: Ranking Minority Mem; cp/Mayor, City of Albuquerque 1967; As Sen, Deleg for US to 1st World Food Conf, Rome 1974; Mem 1st Inter-Parliamentary Delegation from US Sen to Soviet Union 1975; r/Cath; hon/Hon'd by: Leag of U Latin Am Citizens Nat Ed Ser Ctrs, Nat Fedn of Indep Bus-men, Nat Assn Bus, Others.

DONAHUE, KATHERINE CAROLINE CLARK oc/Coordinator; b/Sept 10, 1949; h/Rome, GA; ba/Coosa High School, Rt 5, ALA Hwy, Rome, GA 30161; m/Arthur Lee III; c/Arthur Lee IV; p/James Walter and MaeDell Browning Clark, Thomaston, GA; ed/BS Berry Col 1971; MBED W Ga Col 1977; pa/CVAE Coor & VOCA Sponsor, Coosa HS 1972-; Pvt Secy to Ga Coor Early Childhood Tri-St Proj 1971; cp/Rome BPW Clb; r/Bapt; hon/Chm VOCA St Exec Coun 1976-77.

DONLON, MICHELE LYNN oc/Curriculum Coordinator; b/Aug 24, 1951; h/41 Brinkwood Dr, Brookeville, MD 20729; ba/Rockville; p/William James and Jo Donlon, Brookeville, MD; ed/BA Eureka Col 1973; MEd Univ Ill 1975; Att'd Nat Col 1974; So Ill Univ 1981; IBM Computer Programmer 1981; pa/Curric Coor, BRAC Manpwr Tng, Dept Labor 1981; Relief Field Ednl Rep 1980; Field Ednl Rep 1977-80; CNW RR 1975-77; Nat Bus Ed Assn; cp/Railway Clks Polit Leag; r/Cath; hon/Cortez Peters Typing Awd 1980; Author BRAC File Kit 1981, Indiv'd Eng 1981.

DONNELLY, BRADFORD HILTON oc/Policeman; b/Oct 21,1953; h/Auburn, AL; ba/141 N Ross St, Auburn, AL; p/Edward Daniel and Beatrice Hilton Donnelly; ed/Jr Standing Auburn Univ; Cert EMT; Ala Adv'd Crim Just Acad 1976; Burglary Invest Sch 1978; Adv'd Traffic Invest Class, NWn Univ; pa/Corp Over Trg of Shift, Auburn Police Dept; Frat Order of Police.

DONNELLY, DANIEL HERRING oc/Police Officer; b/Oct 21, 1953; h/Auburn, AL; ba/Auburn Police Dept, 141 N Ross St, Auburn, AL 36830; p/Edward Daniel and Beatrice Hilton Donnelly, Auburn, AL; p/Criminal Justice, Law Enforcement: Lt Auburn Police Dept; Frat Order of Police; r/Epis.

DONNELLY, EDWARD DANIEL oc/Plant Breeder; b/Dec 5, 1919; h/Auburn, AL; ba/Agronomy & Soils Dept, Auburn Univ, Auburn, AL 36849; c/Bradford Hilton, Daniel Herring, Janet Lynne; ed/BS 1946, MS 1948 Auburn Univ; PhD Cornell Univ 1951; mil/AUS 1942-45; pa/Plant Breeder, Dept of Agron & Soils, Auburn Univ 1951-; Am Soc Agron; Crop Sci Soc of Am; r/Epis; hon/Fellow Am Soc Agron 1966; Approx 75 Articles in Sci Jours.

DONNELLY, PHYLLIS BESWICK oc/Reading Consultant, Curriculum Writer; b/Nov 19, 1939; h/10494 Lake Shore Blvd, Cleveland, OH 44108; ba/Cleveland Hghts; m/John V; c/Deirdre, Sean, Patrick; p/Colin A J and Ruby Ellen Beswick, Enderby, British Columbia, Canada; ed/Att'd Univ Alberta 1957-58, NWn Univ 1961-62, Ind Univ 1962-63; BS Bethel Col 1964; MS Ind Univ 1967; pa/Rdg Conslt & Curric Writer,

Cleveland Hgts-Univ Hgts Bd of Ed 1967-; Tchr Culver, Ind Commun Schs 1964-66; Tchr Harris Sch, Chgo 1961-62, Tchr Strathearn Elem Sch, Edmonton, Alberta 1958-61; Prog Dir Right to Read 1974-; Intl Rdg Assn; Mary C Austin Rdg Coun; Am Fed Tchrs; Ohio Fed Tchrs; Cleveland Hgts-Univ Hgts Fed Tchrs; cp/Pres Judson Pk Evening Aux Vols; AAUW; r/Prot; hon/Ohio Roster of Wom 1977; Author *Reading Evaluation* 1964, *Primary Reading, Writing and Listening Skills* 1977; Co-Author *Developmental Reading Guides* Vol 1 & 2 1974, Vol 3 1976.

DONOHUE, JOHN W JR oc/Insurance Sales and Consultation; b/Feb 3, 1935; h/228 Stratus Rd, El Paso, TX 79912; ba/El Paso; m/Elaine A; c/Lori Elaine; p/Jack W (dec) and Marie R Donohue, El Paso, TX; ed/BS Univ Tex-El Paso; mil/AUS Lt; pa/Past Pres Tex Assn Life Underwriters; Assn Adv'd Life Underwriters; Million Dollar Round Table; cp/Chm Adv Coun Ldrship El Paso; Bd Dirs El Paso C of C; r/Cath; hon/El Paso Assn Life Underwriters Man of Yr.

DOPICO, ELVIRA MARTA oc/Public Schools Area Director; b/Oct 20, 1923; h/1400 SW 90 Ave, Miami, FL 33174; ba/Miami; p/J Claudio Dopico (dec); Marcelina Urquia, Miami, FL; ed/MS Barry Col; PhD Univ de la Habana, Cuba; pa/Area Dir S Ctl Area, Dada Co Public Schs; Mem: Epsilon Chapt Delta Kappa Gamma, Kappa Delta Pi; Nat Adv Bd "Sourisas" Bilingual TV Prog KLRN, Austin; cp/Treas U Fam & Chd's Sers; Exec Bd: DC BSA; Bd Dirs: Cuban Mus of Art & Culture; Past Pres, Charter Mem Cuban Wom's Clb & Latin BPW Clb; r/Rom Cath; Mem St Agatha's Parish; hon/Dipl of Hon "Lincoln-Marti", US DHEW; Dipl of Hon "Juan L Remos", Cruzada Educativa Cubana; Gran Orden Martiana del Merito Ciudadano, Liceo Cubana; Others.

DORMAN, JACK EUBANK JR oc/Town Manager; b/Apr 2, 1946; h/Culpeper, VA 22701; ba/118 W Davis St, Culpeper, VA 22701; m/Mary Jo; c/Jacquelyn Elise, Christopher Jackson Eubank; p/Jack E Dorman Sr, Raymond, MS; Martha L Barnes, Mobile, AL; ed/BS Univ So Miss 1976; pa/Town Mgr Culpeper; City Mgr Manassas Pk, Va; Pvt Conslt, JE Dorman & Assocs 1980; SEn Commun Devel Assn Bd Dirs; Am Plan'g Assn; Intl City Mgmt Assn; r/Epis; hon/Willa Bolton Awd for Excell in Geog, USM 1976; Pi Gamma Mu; Nat Scholastic Hon Soc; Pres USM Chapt Student Plan'g Network of NAm 1975-76; Chosen by Adm of Univ S Miss to Sit on Campus Plan'g Com as Student Mem & Student's Rep; Miss Chapt of Am Inst of Planners, Student Rep of Exec Com 1975-76; Dean's List Student.

DORMAN, PAMELA ANN oc/Associate Professor, Counselor; b/Sept 19, 1950; h/PO Box 7022, Hampton, VA 23666; ba/Hampton; p/Edward and Inez Dorman, Hampton, VA; ed/AA Thomas Nelson Commun Col; BA Christopher Newport Col; MA Hampton Inst; ADC William & Mary; pa/Nat Orientation Assn Bd Dirs; cp/Newport News Citizens Adv Com; hon/Phi Theta Kappa; Outstg Alumnus TNCC.

DORMAN, ROY LOIL oc/School Administrator, Teacher; b/Nov 8, 1915; h/2400 54th Ave, Meridian, MS 39301; ba/Meridian; m/Verna Mae; c/Wanda Medina, Sheila Martin, Belinda Gordon, Deborah, Roy Jr; p/Ulyss G Sr (dec) and Pomelia F Dorman, Meridian, MS; ed/BS; MA; MST; Post Grad Studies; mil/Capt WWII; pa/Pres Meridian AFT Local 3317; Phi Delta Kappa; Ed Coms; Life Mem Alumni Univ Ariz; co/Red Cross CPR Instr; Cand Co Supt Ed; Former Scoutmaster BSA; Indep Order Foresters; Mason; r/So Bapt; on/Dean's Schlr; Bronze Star; Combat Ribbon, Nat Sci Foun Awd.

DORN, WILLIAM DENTON oc/Administrator; b/Feb 25, 1943; h/PO Box 318, Irvine, KY 40336; p/Lynn V and Dorthy A Gordon, Newark, CA; ed/BS, BA Wash St Univ; MPH Univ SC; mil/USNR 1961-63 Medic; pa/Admr Cestill Co Hlth Dept; APHA; SOPHE; hon/Pub's in *Journal of American Medical Assn.*

DORSEY, JASPER NEWTON oc/Communications; b/Jan 19, 1913; h/366 Blackland Rd NW, Atlanta, GA 30342; ba/Atlanta; m/Callender Weltner; c/Sally D Danner (Mrs William), John Tucker (dec); p/John Tucker and Annie Coryell Dorsey (dec); ed/AB 1936 Univ of Ga; Postgrad Law 1935-36; mil/AUS WWII, Lt Col Infantry; pa/VP, Chief Exec Ofcr Southern Bell's Ga Operations 1968-; Dir Fulton Nat Bank, Fulton Nat Corp; Secy, Mem Exec Com Ga World Cong Ctr Authority; Univ of Ga: Former Pres, Chm Bd Alumni Soc, 1st Pres Adv Bd Henry W Grady Sch of Journalism, Visiting Dist'd Lectr Col of Bus Adm; Charter Mem Pres Adv Bd of Med Col of Ga; Trustee Ga Foun for Indep Cols; Hon Dir of Ga Engrg Foun; cp/Chm Bd Govs of Atlanta Commun Ser Awds; Hon Gen Chm 1977 Atlanta JCs Empty Stocking Fund Drive; Hon Chm Fund Drive for Ga Trust for Hist Preservation; Dir of Metropolitan Atlanta Boys Clbs; Adv Bds: Salvation Army, Kidney Foun of Ga; r/Presb Ch: Elder; Former Tchr, Deacon, Trustee, SS Supt; hon/Atlanta Salesman of Yr Awd 1977, Atlanta Sales & Mktg Execs; Ga Foun for Indep Cols Free Enterprise Booster of Yr Awd; William Booth Awd, Salvation Army; Atlanta JCs Hon Lifetime Mem Awd; Commun Ser Awd, Wom's C of C; Beta Gamma Sigma, Univ of Ga Chapt; Num Others.

DORSEY, LEONIA COLLINS oc/School Librarian; b/June 21, 1941; h/232 Wiley St, Greenville, MS 38701; ba/G'ville; m/Isaac Jr; c/Bonita Annette, Brandon Isaac; p/John (dec) and Willie Mae Collins, G'ville, MS; ed/BS Sociol; MS Lib Sci; pa/NEA; MEA; G'ville Assn Edrs; cp/Alpha Kappa Alpha; Nat Coun Negro Wom; NAACP; Ch Wom U; Nat Fed Colored Wom Clbs; r/Bapt; hon/Wom of Yr; Nom Outstg Black Ams; Personalities of S 1976; Nom Ebony Awd, Civic & Clb Work.

DOUGHERTY, FRANCIS KELLY oc/Manager; b/May 15, 1953; h/10500 Val Forge #179, Houston, TX 77042; ba/Houston; m/Bonnie Burch; c/Anne Katherine; p/Francis Kelly and Mary Ann Odell Dougherty, Okla City, OK; ed/BS Univ Dallas 1975; Rice Univ 1975-76; pa/Mgr Time Sharing Sers, Phila Life 197-; Ranger Nat Life, Houston 1976-77; Data Processing Mgmt Assn; FLMI Soc; Soc CLU; c/Repub Party; r/Roman Cath; hon/Fellow Life Mgmt Inst 1979; Chartered Life Underwriter 1980; Cert'd Data Processor 1980.

DOUGLAS, JANICE HENDON oc/Accountant; b/Sept 18, 1944; h/606 Russell St SE, Decatur, AL 35601; ba/Decatur; m/James Troyce; c/Stephanie Lynn, Stepch: Denise Renee, Troyce Anthony; p/Euthrea C and Mavis R Hendon, Decatur, AL; ed/Dunn & Bradstreet Credit & Fin Analysis 1979; Cont'g Ed at John C Calhoun Col; pa/Acct Wolverine Div, UOP Inc; cp/Acctg Adv of Wolvco, A Jr Achmt Co Sponsored by Wolverine Div; r/Bapt; hon/W/W Students Am Jr Cols 1977.

DOUGLAS, ROBERT WALTER SR oc/Cosmetologist; b/Oct 9, 1933; h/PO Box 243, Orange City, FL 32763; ba/Daytona Bch, FL; m/Dorothy Marie; c/Debra Gail, Robert Walter Jr, Kimberly Katrina; p/Isiah Caldwell (dec); Janice Douglas, Bronx, NY; ed/Grad DBCC 1977; mil/USAF 1954-57; pa/Pres Cosmetologist Unit 53; Daytona Bch OBCA; cp/Hd Start Policy Coun Chm 3 Yrs; Bd Dirs OCCIA; r/Union Bethel AME Ch: Trustee, Choir Dir; hon/Hd Start Pres's Awd 1977.

DOUGLAS, ROSSLEE GREEN oc/Nurse; b/Aug 12, 1928; h/Mt Pleasant, SC; m/W Earl (dec); c/Lynne Victoria Simmons, Sherman Elliot; p/Anglin and Rozenia Parker Green, Charleston, SC; ed/Lincoln Sch for Nurses 1952; Med Univ SC, Col of Nsg 1972; pa/Visiting Nruse ser of NY 1953-56; Staff Nurse 1963-67; Franklin C Fetter Fam Hlth Ctr Charleston 1969-789; SC Indust Comm 1978-80; ANA; SC Public Hlth Assn; Sigma Theta Tau, Gamma Omicron Chapt; SC Nurses Assn; Trident Nurses Assn; Chi Eta Phi; cp/VP Palmetto Low Country Hlth Sys; Wando HS Band Boosters; Wando PTA; Charleston Co Mtl Retard Bd; Hlth Com Trident 200; Adv Coun SC St Dept Mtl Hlth; St Hlth Car Adv Bd to DHEC; Conf on Hlth Care Delivery in SC; r/Prot; hon/Organizational Devel Awd Fetter 1975.

DOUGLASS, JOHN W oc/State Legislator; Businessman; b/Mar 19, 1942; h/1535 E N Ave, Baltimore, MD 21213; m/Married; ed/AB cum laude Lincoln Univ 1964; MA Johns Hopkins Univ 1966; pa/Mem M House Dels 1971-; Chm Jt Budget & Audit Com, Md Leg 1975-; House Approp Com; Instr Morgan St Col 1966-68; Salesman: R L Johnson Realty Co 1967-, Fin Indust Fund (Lic'd), Mutual Funds 1967-68; Clk Balto City Coun 1967-68; Partner-Mgr D & N Liquiors 1968-69; CoChm Dunber HS Charette 1969; Pres, Beta Kappa Chi, Lincoln Univ Chapt 1964; Beta Kappa Chi; Former Mem Assoc'd Bldrs & Contractors; Bus Opports Adm 1968; Pres: Bus-mens Leag Balto 1968, Lincoln Univ Chapt Am Chm Soc 1964, Others; cp/Adjacent Neighborhood Improvemt Assn; Former Indust Analyst, Conslt to Balto City Planning Dept; Former 1/VP, Yg Dems Md; Past Pres, Nu Chapt, Alpha Phi Alpha; Former Mem Exec Com & Policy Steering Bd, Model Cities Prog; New Dem Clb; Former Treas, Eastside Dem Org; Former Secy, Bd Dirs, Glenwood CC; Former Mem: Mt Royal Dem Clb, New Dem Coalition; r/So Bapt Ch: Mem; hon/En Ll Awd; NE Gaskins Prize; Morgan St Col: CoDir 9th Annual Small Bus Wkshop, Fac Res Grant, Cert Achmt; Am Legion Awd; ACS Awd; F'ships, S'ship; W/W Am Cols & Univs; Johns Hopkins Univ: Gilman F'ship, Asstship.

DOUTHAT, THOMAS ALEXANDER JR oc/Architect; b/May 13, 1950; h/Rt 2 Box 94, Pulaski, VA 24301; ba/Pulaski; p/Thomas Alexander Sr and Lena Faye Douthat, Pulaski, VA; ed/VPI & St Univ 1973; pa/Arch: Smithey & Boynton Architects & Engrs, Byron R Dickson, Echols-Sparger & Assocs; Presently Self-Employed; Am Inst Archs; cp/Pulaski Co Tech Review Bd; Pulaski Co C of C; r/Prot; hon/Outstg Sr 1968; Dean's List VPI 1972.

DOW, CHARLES DAVID oc/International Development Vice President; b/Nov 2, 1939; h/400 High Brook Dr, Richardson, TX 75080; ba/Bedford, TX; m/Dian Darby; c/Scott David, Ted Andrew, Kurt Daniel; p/Charles Harris and Marian Elizabeth Fernsler Dow, Dallas, TX; ed/BSEE Ind Inst Tech 1965; Postgrad Res Fla Inst Tech 1965-66; Hon Deg Tsinghua Univ, Peking 1980; mil/USAF 1958; pa/Engr Spec Circuits Gen Telephone 1961-65; Mgr Data Retransmission Br ITT Fed 1965-66; Sr Engr Prog Mgr, Westinghouse Co 1967-69; Tech Dir Sys Tech Div, Varo Inc 1970-72; Dir Mktg & Bus Devel Reliance Elect Telecommuns Corp 1973-;

Am Mktg Assn; Inst Mgmt Scis; Ops Res Soc Am; Ind Telephone Pioneer Assn; AAUP; cp/Lectr in Field; Pres Plano Sports Auth 1973-74, VP 1974-75; Active Tex Amateur Baseball Cong 1976-80; Adv Bus Plan'g First Bapt Acad 1978-79; r/Bapt; hon/Recip Awd for Excell EDN Mag 1969.

DOW, NORMAN G oc/Executive; b/Sept 29, 1936; h/Stafford, TX; m/Norma Dee; c/Teresa, Jim, Melinda, Billy; p/William P and Adyce Dow, Odessa, TX; ed/BBA Calif St Univ 174; MBA Pepperdine Univ 1980; mil/USAF 1956-60; pa/Exec Oilfield Equipment Mfg; Am Petro Inst; Instrument Soc of Am; Assn Mech Engrs; Am Nuclear Soc; r/Bapt.

DOYLE, ELIZABETH LEWIS oc/Advertising Executive, Writer, Medical Journalist; h/3284 Paris Pike, Lexington, KY; ba/Lexington; m/Walter Arnett; p/Alvin Edward Lewis, Davis, CA; Doris Joyce Lewis (dec); ed/Att'd Univ Calif Berkeley; BA, MS Mich St Univ; pa/Pres Doyle Advtg; Book Editor *Apothecary Magazine*; Columnist *American Druggist*; Editor *Beacon Magazine*; Kappa Delta Pi; Theta Sigma Phi; Lexington Advtg Clb; Am Advtg Fed; cp/C of C; hon/3 Regional Awds in Am Advtg Fed Contest 1978; 20 Local Awds in AAF Sponsored Contest 1979; 2 Regional Awds in AAF Competition 1979; 20 Local Awds in AFF 1980; 5 Regional Awds in AAF 1980; 1 Nat Awd AAF 1980; 2 Printing Industs of Am Graphic Arts Awds 1980; Author: *Momma Miser Finds Electronic Solutions to the Problems of Everyday Life* 1979.

DOZIER, CARROLL T oc/Bishop; b/Aug 18, 1911; h/Memphis, TN; ba/1325 Jefferson, Memphis, TN 38104; p/Curtis M Dozier (dec); Rosa Ann Conaty (dec); ed/PhB & Sacred Theol, Gregorian Univ, Rome, Italy; BA College of Holy Cross; pa/Appt'd Bishop, Diocese of Memphis 1971 Ordained 1937, Rome, Italy; Author Best Known For: *Peace: Gift & Task* 1971, *Justice: God's Vision Man's Discipleship* 1972, *Woman: Intrepid and Loving* 1975; cp/World Conf of Rel for Peace, Pres 1972; NCCB "Nat Hon Com for Black Cath Concerned" 1972; r/Cath; hon/Citizen of Yr 1980; Teresa of Avila Awd, Col of St Teresa 1976; Hon Deg DLitt, Col of Holy Cross 1973; Cath Human Relats Awd 1973; Bill of Rights Awd, Am Civil Liberties Union of W Tenn Chapt 1972; Brotherhood NCCJ 1967; Author Num Books & Articles.

DRACH, MARIAN CAPOZZI oc/Supervisor of Library Services; h/205 E Joppa Rd, Towson, MD 21204; ba/Towson; m/Joseph John; p/Daniel Michael (dec) and Frances Jane Capozzi, Baltimore, MD; ed/BS Univ Md; MSLS Cath Univ of Am; pa/Supvr Lib Sers, Balto Co Public Libs; ALA; Am Assn Sch Libs; Assn Lib Sers to Chd; Md Ednl Media Org; r/Cath; hon/Beta Phi Mu.

DRAGOO, BARBARA ELLEN oc/Clinical Nurse Coordinator; b/June 18, 1942; h/241 Applewood Dr, Ft Mitchell, KY 41017; ba/Cinci, OH; m/David Maurice; c/Christy Lee Ann; p/William R (dec) and Lelia Drake Hewitt, Erlanger, KY; ed/RN St Elizabeth Hosp 1963; BES Thomas Moore Col 1978; pa/Emer Dept Nurses Assn; cp/Thomas Moore Alumni; St Elizabeth Alumni; r/Prot; hon/Ky Col; W/W Am Wom 1979.

DRAGOO, CHARYL WAYNE oc/Artist; Art Instructor; b/Nov 5, 1948; h/Rt 1, Box 523A, Belton, TX 765131 ba/Same; m/Era Franklin; p/Troy D and Evelyn Kennedy, Beeville, TX; ed/BFA Mary Hardin-Baylor 1973; Addit Courses & Tng; pa/Devised Individualized Art Prog, devel'd Record Keeping Devices & Resource Materials; Conducted Prog Res & Eval; Adm'd & Taught This Prog Grades 1-8, 4 Yrs, Grade 9, 3 Yrs; Participated 3 Yrs Title III, 1 Yr Leag of Schs, Talents Unlimited Prog, Use of CITE, DSII Sch; Worked w Student Cnslg, Scheduling, Spec Courses; Dir Student Art Shows; Conslt for ESC Reg XII Proj ARTS; Author Pub'd Profl Articles; A-V Dir & Tchg Materials Resource Ctr Cokoor; Tchr Addit Pvt Art Lessons; Dir Sum Camp Art/Craft Activs; Free-lance Design, Layout, Lettering, Illustration; Participant in St Wide Shows, Exhibs, Sales; Dir & Prodr Murals; Promotional Designs & Layout; Set Design & Prodn; Title III Team Mem & Secy, Cultural Activs Ctr 1975-; Profl Assns; Area Yth Art Month Chm; NAEA Conv Evaluator 1978; TAEA; Others; cp/GSA; Rainbow Girls; r/Meth; hon/Evelyn McFatridge Brashears Art Awd; Kappa Phi; Nat Hon Soc; 1-Wom Art Shows: Morgans Pt Resort 1972, Holiday Inn 1972, 73, Bell Fine Art Assn 1973; Num Art Awds inclg: Best of Show, HM Landscape, Beeville Art Guild 1972, Num 1st Still Life paintings, Num Exhibs for Sale, Sev Galleries; Pub'd Works; Fellow Mem ABI; Others.

DRAKE, ANNE BILLINGSLEA oc/Instructor; b/Nov 29, 1931; h/557 E Creswell Ave, Greenwood, SC 29646; ba/G'wood; m/Charles E; c/Mary Ann, Nancy B, Jane E, Yung Le, Charles E Jr; p/Arthur Clement and Eula Mae Billingslea; ed/BS Fla St Univ; Cert'd Sem Tutor, Laubauch Literacy Intl 1980; ESL Tchg Cert, AUA, Bangkok, Thailand 1971; pa/Instr Lang Inst, AUA, Bangkok 1971-73; Instr Rdg Dept, Piedmont Tech Col 1975-78; Instr Adult Perf Level & Eng as 2nd Lang, Piedmont Tch Col 1978-80; VP St of SC Literacy Bd; Bd Mem Wil Lou Gray Adult Rdg Coun; cp/Chm G'wood Co Literacy Coun; VP Ward I Precnt G'wood Repub Party; Fin Com Main St U Meth Ch; r/Meth: Adm Bd; Secy U

Christian Mission Outreach Bd; hon/Dist'd Tchr of Yr 1980, Wil Lous Gray Adult Rdg Coun.

DRAKE, PAUL DAVID oc/Pastor; b/Mar 7, 1955; ba/First Baptist Ch, PO Box 697, Bushnell, FL 33513; m/Jody Riley; c/Jolene Elizabeth; p/Roger Q Drake, New Port Richey, FL; Elizabeth Becraft L'rake (dec); ed/AA St Petersburg Jr Col 1975; BD 1977; MDiv 1979 Luther Rice Sem; pa/Pastor, First Bapt Ch Bushnell; Var Coms Alackua Bapt Assn, Fla Bapt Conv; cp/Pres S Sumter Min Assn; r/So Bapt.

DRAKE, ROBERT ELDON oc/Ophthalmologist, Author, Genealogist; b/Jan 291, 1924; h/842 N Laurel Ave, Orlando, FL 32803; ba/Orlando; m/Jo Ann Williams; c/Robert Eldon Jr, Suzanne Elene, Kenneth Boss, Jesse Joseph; p/Edward Plummer (dec) and Carolyn Lucille Redding Drake; ed/La St Univ 1942-43; Tulane Univ 1943-44; MD La St Univ Med Sch 1948; Intern Touro Infirmary 1948-49; Eye F'ship Smith Eye Clin N O La; 1965-67; Mobile Gen Hosp 1967-68; Scheie Eye Clin 1974; mil/USNR 1942-45; USAF 1951-53 Capt; pa/Self-Employed Pvt Pract, Winter Pk 1953-64, Orlando 1968-; Orange Co Med Soc; Fla Med Assn; AMA; Am Acad Ophthalmology; So Med Assn; Am Soc Contemporary Ophthalmologist; Am Intra-Ocular Implant Soc; cp/Dem Party; Owner Orlando Broncos Fball Team 1972-74; Pres Winter Pk Little Leag 1958-64; r/Meth; hon/W/W S&SW 1980-81; AMA Phys Recog Awd; Num Lions Clb Awds for Work w Sight Prog; Author: *Descendants of Exum Drake* Vol III 1977, Vol IV 1978, Vol V 1980.

DRAKE, SUZANNE LEE oc/Owner and Manager Realty Company; b/Apr 26, 1942; h/Elizabeth City, NC; ba/305 S Hughes Blvd, Elizabeth City, NC 27909; m/David; c/Kimberly, Steven, Douglas; p/Albert & Leah Billings, Rye, NH; ed/Att'd Boston Univ 1960-61; pa/Owner-Mgr Sue Drake Rltrs; Elizabeth City Bd Rltrs Mbrship Chm; cp/Yng Careerist Chm BPW Clb; USCG Ofcrs Wives Clb; r/Prot; hon/Finished 11th In Real Est Grad Sch Chapel Hill.

DRAPER, LINE BLOOM oc/Artist, Educator, Printmaker, Enamelist, Engrosser; h/3134 Lakeview Dr, Delray Beach, FL 33444; m/Glen C; c/Andre L, Darlene J Lohmeyer, Gary G, Cheron; p/Leopold Voisin (dec); Mathilde Tache (dec); ed/Ecole des Arts Decoratifs, Belgium; Academie Royale des Beaux Arts, Belgium, Bowling Green St Univ; Emerson Burkhart; Skowhegan Sch of Art; Henry Vernum Poor, Willard Cummings, Kenneth Callahan, Harry Ballinger; pa/Num One-man Shows inclg: Elliott Mus, Stuart Fla 1977, Defiance Col 1975, Park Lane Hotel 1964, 65, 66, 67, Studio 100, Boca Raton, Fla 1978; Touring Exhibs; Pvt Collects; Mem: Am Watercolor Soc, Art Interests Inc, Athena Art Soc (Life, Pres 1967-69, VP 1972-73, Pres 1973-74), Intl Soc of Artists (Charter Mem), Phi Delta Phi (Hon Mem), Sigma Beta Phi (Hon Mem), Others; Work Pub'd in Num Jours Inclg: *American Artist, D'Art, The News Messenger, Sylvania Sentinel*; cp/Toledo Orch Assn; Toledo Wom's Art Leag; Zonta of Delray Beach; hon/Num Hons & Awds inclg: Nat Cassein Show, NY 1970, Ohio Gold Medal Exhib, Hon Mention 1966, Nat Bank Show, Sev Awds: 1960, 64, 66, 67, 73, Popular Awd 1967, Miniature Painters, Sculptors 39th Annual Exhib Washington, DC 1972; Nat Register of Prominent Ams & Intl Notables; Intl W/W in Commun Ser; 2000 Wom of Achmt; W/W: Am Art, Am Wom, MW; World W/W of Wom; Others.

DRAPER, MARY WANDA oc/Associate Professor, Author, Consultant; b/Feb 19, 1935; h/838 NE 21st, Okla City, OK 73105; p/Emil T Kachtik, Fredericksburg, TX; ed/BS 1962, MS 1967, PhD 1969 Tex Wom's Univ; Post Doct Study Harvard Univ Summer 1976; Post Doct Study Int Ctr for Genetic Epistemology, Geneva, Switz; pa/Full Time Fac Child Devel Spec; Dir Diagnostic & Therapeutic Ctr for Yng Chd, Univ Okla Col of Med; Author Sec'dy Sch Textbooks; Conslt in Child Devel, Parenting, Handicapped Chd; Adv Bd Ed Futures Intl; Okla Assn Chd Under Six; Pres, Bd Dirs Parents Assistance Ctr; cp/Fdr & Dir Okla Child & Fam Inst; Appt'd By Gov to Gob's Com on Chd & Yth 1974-80; Nat Assn Ed of Yng Chd; r/Meth; hon/OACUS Outstg Cltizen in Okla; Life Mem Meth WSCS; Author *Caring for Children* 1975; *Studying Children* 1977; Others Pubs on Chd & Fams.

DRAUGHON, JOHNNIE EARL oc/Librarian, Coach; b/Dec 20, 1951; h/PO Box 163, Jefferson, NNC 28640; ba/Jefferson; c/Erica Lynn; p/Esther J Draughon, Clinton, NC; ed/BS Wn Carolina Univ 1979; MA Appalachian St Univ; mil/USN 1973-77; pa/Libn, Fball, Softball & Weight Trg Coach, Ashe Ctrl HS; 10 Yrs in Radio & TV Communs; ALA; NEA; NCAE; Assn Clrm Tchrs, Fac Rep 1980, 1981; NC Assn Sch Libns; cp/Ashe Co Little Theatre, Actor, Dir, Tech; Jefferson U Meth Ch Choir; r/Eckankar; hon/Gov's Sch of NC 1969; Hon Grad Defense Info Sch, Adv'd Info Spec Course 175.

DRIFTWOOD, JIMMY oc/Folklorist; b/June 20, 1907; h/Timbo, AR 72680; m/Cleda Johnson; p/Neal (dec) and Allie Morris (dec); ed/BS Univ Ctrl Ark; Hon Dr Am Folklore, Peabody Col; pa/Records & Ranches; Folklorist; hon/Rec'd 3 Grammy Awds: Song of Yr 1959 "Battle of New Orleans"; Album "Wilderness Road"; Billy Yank & Johnny Reb.

DRINNON, DORIS JEAN oc/Leader Nurtition Program; b/Apr 29, 1930; h/902 17th Ave E, Cordele, GA 31015; ba/Cordele; m/Ralph E; c/Cheryl Jean Butler, Jackie Leah Wert; Garfield Robert II; p/S J (dec) and Magaret Sevier Grace, Cumberland, KY; ed/Lake Sumpter Jr Col; Lincoln Meml Univ; pa/Wkg in Homes on 1 to 1 Basis to Improve Dietary Level of Fams & Yth through Ed; Ldr Nutrition Prog; Asst EFNEP; cp/Chm St Jude's Chd Res Hosp; Bike-a-Thon; Pilot Clb Dir & Coor of Projs Div; r/Meth; hon/SW Prog Asst of Yr 1977; St Winner Prog Asst of Yr 1979.

DRISCOLL, JOHN ALBERT oc/Psychologist; h/Alexandria, VA; m/Eileen; p/Phyllis Driscoll, Warren, MI; ed/BA Univ Notre Dame 1947; MA Holy Cross Col 1967; MEd Loyola Univ 1971; MA, PhD Cath Univ Am; pa/Pvt Prac Child, Adolescent, Fam Cnslg; Indiv & Grp Cnslg for Adult as Mtl Hlth Practitioner; DCPA; VPA; APA; APGA; AAMFT; AMHA; r/Roman Cath; hon/3 Dissertations.

DRUCKER, MEYER oc/Professor; b/Aug 10, 1937; h/231 Heathwood Dr, Spartanburg, SC 29302; ba/Spartanburg; m/Barbara Loewe; c/Kenneth, Deborah; p/Morris and Ida Bella Drucker, Denmark, SC; ed/BS USC 1959; MA Am Univ 1962; JD USC 1966; mil/AUS 1956-58; pa/Prof Acctg Bus Law USC 1975; Assoc Prof Acctg, UNCC 1970-75; Hd Acctg Prog, Midlands Tech 1968-70; Controller, Maxon Shirt Co 1967-68; Sr Auditor, Burlington Ind 1966-67; Supvry Acct, US GAO 1959-63; Am Inst CPAs; Am Bar Assn; Am Acctg Assn; Inst Internal Auditors; SC Bar Assn; Adm Mgmt Soc; Nat Assn Accts; cp/B'nai B'rith; r/Jewish; hon/W/W: S&SW, Intl Ed; Contbr Var Articles & Book Reviews to Profl Jours.

DRUM, EMILY A oc/Psychotherapist, Administrator of Mental Retardation Services; b/Jan 6, 1936; h/5213 Shady Dell Trail, Knoxville, TN 37914; ba/K'ville; c/Lorin Maurice; Hilary Annette; p/James E Swanton Sr (dec); Helen E Harker (dec); ed/BA Maryville Col; MSSN UT Knoxville; pa/Dir Commun Client Sers; Nat Assn Social Wkrs; Am Soc Trg & Devel; Intl Transactional Analysis Assn; cp/Adv Coun Alcoholism; Exec Com Knoxville Dem Party; r/Unitarian-Universalist; hon/W/W Am Wom 1978; Article Pub'd in Profl Jour.

DRUMMOND, GARRY NEIL oc/Coal Executive; b/June 8, 1938; h/Rt 4 Box 141, Birmingham, AL 35210; ba/Jasper, AL; c/Garry Jr, Michael Allen, Douglas Bryan, Cynthia Ann; p/Heman E (dec) and Elza Stewart Drummond, Sipsey, AL; ed/BS Univ Ala 1961; pa/Chief Exec Ofcr, Drummond Coal Co; Chm Bd Ala Py Prods Corp; Chm Mining & Reclamation Coun of Am; Bd Dirs Nat Coal Assn; Past Pres & Currently on Exec Com Ala Surface Mining & Reclamaton Coun; Past Mem Bd Dirs Am Inst Mining, Metal & Petrol Engrs; Past Mem Bd Dirs Ala Mining Inst; Past Mem Bd Dirs Ala World Trade Assn; Bd Dirs Ala Great So RR; cp/Bd Trustees Ala Assn Indep Cols & Univs; Exec Com Univ Ala Diabetes Hosp; Bd Trustees Walker Co Med Ctr; Pres Cabinet Univ Ala; Exec Bd BSA; Black Warrior Coun; Bd Dirs Commun Chest-United Way; Patron B'ham Mus of Art; Hon Mem Ala Sheriffs Boys & Girls Ranches; Ala Wildlife Fed; r/Bapt.

DRUMMOND, KATHLEEN oc/Professor; b/Sept 22, 1918; b/1427 Everett Ave, Louisville, KY 40204; ba/L'ville; p/Thomas H (dec) and Golda Wells Drummond (dec); ed/BS Ind St Univ; MS Univ Ill; PhD NWn Univ; mil/USMC Wom's Reserve 1943-46 Capt; pa/Prof Adm Sers; Adm Mgmt Soc; Assn Records Mgrs & Adm; Intl Word Processing Assn; Nat Secys Assn Int; Nat Bus Ed Assn Conslt in Ofc Mgmt; Lectr for Profl Sems for Secys, Ofc Mgrs, & Bus Tchrs; Lectr Caulfield Inst of Technol 1974; cp/Zonta Intl; r/Meth; hon/Delta Pi Epsilon; Kappa Delta Pi; Pi Omea Pi; Phi Kappa Phi.

DRURY, JOHN TERRY oc/General Manager; b/Mar 11, 1947; h/4800 River Farm Rd, Marietta, GA 30067; ba/Atlanta; p/Carroll R and Runell S Drury, Athens, GA; ed/BBA Univ Ga 1969; pa/Gen Mgr Celebrity Pool & Spa 1980-; Owner Great Am Pool & Spas Inc 1980-; Mktg Dir Aquabrom-Tesco Div Great Lakes Chem Corp 1977-80; VP Mktg Tesco Chems 1974-77; Reg Sales Mgr Premier Fastener 1973; Nat Swimming Pool Inst; Intl Spa & Tub Inst; cp/Bd Dirs Coun on Aging 1970; Bd Dirs Fam Cnslg Ser 1970; Fund Raising Chm Camp Hallinan 1970; r/Ch of God; hon/W/W S&SW 1980-81.

DUBEY, SATYA DEVA oc/Supervisory Mathematical Statistician; b/Feb 10, 1930; h/7712 Groton Rd, Bethesda, MD 20034; ba/Rockville, MD; m/Joyce; c/Jay Dev, Dean Dev, Neal Narayan; p/Jagdish N Dubey, Bihar, India; Sahodara Devi, Bihar, India; ed/BS w hons Patna Univ 1951; PhD Mich St Univ 1960; Human Relats Cert Lincoln Ext Inst; Dale Carnegie Dipl; Num Spec Courses; pa/Acting Dir, Div Biometrics 1975-76, Br Chief, Stat Eval Br, Bur Drugs, Food & Drug Adm, Public Hlth Ser, Dept HEW 1973-75 Assoc Prof Dept Indust Engrg & Opers Res NYU 1968-73; Prin Statistician & Hd Stats & Opers Res Group Ford Motor Co 1966-68; Procter & Gamble Co: Hd Stats Sect 1965-66, Sr Math Stat 1960-65; Instr, Tchg & Res Asst Mich St Univ 1957-60; Res Asst Carnegie

Inst Tech 1956-57; Tchr, Res Asst Indian Inst Tech 1953-56; Conslt Pvt & Public Insts; Prin Investigator & Res Proj Dir USAF Res Contract; Fdg Mem Indian Soc Theoretical & Applied Mech; Charter Mem Intl Assn Survey Stats; Exec Com Mem W Chester-Rockland Sect Am JSoc Quality Control; Dep VChm NYU Chapt AAUP; Bd Editors Jour of Clin Data & Analysis; Edit Bd Mem Jour Indust Math Soc; Edit Collaborator Jour Am Stat Assn & Technometrics; Referee, Abstracter & Bk Reviewer Res Manuscripts & Other Pubs for 13 Sci Jours; Am Stat Assn: Fellow, Pres Cinc Chapt; Chm Indian Dels MSU UN; Ed Chm MSU Howland Coop House; Del Intl Stat Inst Confs; Adv Bd Mem Biometric Soc, ENAR 1974-76; Fellow: Wash Acad of Scis, AAAS, Royal Stat Soc, NY Acad Sci; Engrg Soc Detroit; Intl Assn Stats in Phy Scis; Sr Mem Am Inst Indust Engrs Inc, Am Soc Quality Control; Am Acad Conslt; cp/U Appeal; Spkr Kiwanis Clb; Judge Intl Toastmistress Clb; r/Spkr Var Chs; hon/Hon Mem Inst Math Stats; NSF Grant Doct Res; Sigma Xi; Author 50+ Res Pubs; Apprec Cert: ASQC, IEEE; Creativity Recog Awd Intl Pers Res; Am Men & Wom Sci; World Dir Maths; Spkrs List IEEE; Fellow Mem ABI; W/W: Computer Ed & Res, in E, in Govt; Creat & Success Personalities of World; Intl Dir of Res & Devel Sci; Men Achmt; DIB; IPA.

DUCWORTH, GEORGE MARION oc/Solicitor; b/Mar 31, 1949; h/2312 E North Ave, Anderson, SC 29621; ba/Anderson; m/Dale Haynie Ducworth; c/William Austin; p/Edward Thomas and Harriet Martin Ducworth, Anderson, SC; ed/AB Clemson Univ 1971; JD Univ SC Law Sch 1975; mil/USAR Capt; pa/Solicitor 10th Judicial Circuit 1981-; Asst Solicitor 10th Judicial Circuit 1977-79; Pvt Law Pract 1979-81; Leg Asst to Sen Strom Thurmond 1975-77; Am Bar Assn; SC Bar Assn; SC Trial Lawyers Assn; Solicitors Assn; cp/Anderson Co IPTAY Clb Pres; Am Legion; Anderson Co Dem Party; Anderson Co Yng Dem; Anderson Co Tax Accessor's Ofc Bd; Exec Sales Clb of Anderson C of C; r/Bapt; hon/Outstg Col Aths of Am; Outstg Yng Men Am 1977.

DUFFEE, BETTY BROWN oc/Teacher; b/Dec 25, 1928; h/PO Box 627, Old US Rd, Marianna, FL 32446; ba/Marianna; m/Ernest McGill; c/Ernest M Jr, Diane, Alan; p/Ausburn Allen and Rose Lee Brown, Banks, AL; ed/BS Auburn Univ; MS Univ Miss; pa/NEA; Fla Tchg Profession; Past Pres Jackson Co Ed Assn; Delta Kappa Gamma; r/Meth; hon/Jackson Co Tchr of Yr 1974.

DUFFER, MICHAEL IRAD oc/Minister of Youth and Music; b/Jan 10, 1955; h/210 E Oio Ave, Apt A, DeLand, FL 32720; ba/DeLand; p/Joseph M and Helen B Duffer, Wylliesburg, VA; ed/BS Roanoke Bible Col 1978; pa/Min Yth & Mus, Plymouth Ave Christian Ch; r/Christian.

DUGAN, MILDRED CLAIRE oc/Physician; b/Sept 21, 1929; h/7158 Tamarack Rd, Ft Worth, TX 76116; p/Hugh Dugan Jr (dec); Florine Schnieder Dugan Stubbs, Ft Worth, TX; ed/BA Tex Christian Univ 1951; MD SWn Med Sch, Univ Tex 1955; Postgrad Deg Adolescent Med, Harvard Med Sch 1962; Intern, Harris Hosp, Ft Worth 1955-56; Residency St Louis Chd's Hosp, Wash Univ Sch of Med 1959-61; Fellowship Harvard Med Sch, Chd's Med Ctr & Hosp Adolescent Med 1961-62; pa/Clin Instr Peds, Wash Univ Sch Med 1959-61; Ped Conslt, City Public Hlth & Co Public Wel Baby Clins, St of Tex 1970-74; Coor CHAP Child Study Grp 1967-69; CHAP Ofcr & Med Advr 1967-69; Conslt Ped, Ft Worth Public Sch Bd of Spec Ed 1968-70; Med Advr N Tex Chapt Nat Cystic Fibrosis Res Foun 1972-75; Com for Coor of Chd's Activs Tarrant Co Med Soc 1972-73; Bd Mem, N Tex Chapt Nat Cystic Fibrosis Res Foun 1973-75; USAF Civil Ser, Carswell Hosp 1956-59, 1962-73; Diplomat Am Bd Peds; Fellow Am Acad Peds; Fellow Tex Acad Peds; Charter Mem Soc of Adolescent Phys; Tex Assn Chd w Lrng Disabilities; Am Med Wom's Assn; Med Wom's Intl Assn; Am Sch Hlth Assn; Am Public Hlth Assn; Tarrant Co Med Soc; Tex Med Assn; AMA; Fellow Royal Soc of Hlth (England); Tex Public Hlth Assn; Assn Am Phys & Surgs; Fellow Ped Sect, Pan Am Med Assn; Tex Chapt Am Assn Phys & Surgs; Ft Worth Acad Med; Tex Med Foun; So Med Assn; Am Profession Pract Assn; Dallas So Clin Soc, Assoc Mem 1976-78; cp/Alpha Chi; Alpha Epsilon Iota; Tex Christian Univ Wom's Execs; L.I.F.E. Mem Tex Christian Univ 1967-69; SWn Med Sch Alumni Assn; St Louis Chd's Hosp Alumni Assn; Chd's Hosp Alumni Assn (Boston); Wash Univ Ctr Med Assn; Intl Platform Assn; Fed Bus Assn 1969-75; Ft Worth Zoo Soc 1970-72; Am Mus of Natural Hist; Am Heritage Soc; Mercedes Benz Clb of Am; Nat Geo Soc; Physicians Epicurean Soc; r/Bapt; hon/Cert of Proficiency in Basic Sci 1955; W/W Dir of Med Specs 1962; Am Pediatric Dir 1963; Hon Hillbilly Cert, Teen Trumpeters Dept, High St Bapt Ch 1964; SAC Lttr of Apprec 1967; Spec Ser Awd, SAC, Carswell CHAP Work 1968; Personalities of S 1969-77; Commun Ldrs & Noteworthy Ams 1972-78; 2000 Wom of Achmt 1972; World W/W Wom 1973-77; Nat Register of Prominent Ams & Intl Notables 1974-77; Fellow Intercontl Biogl Assn 1974-76; Hon Editorial Conslt, Personalities of the S 1975; W/W: S&SW 1977, World of Intells 1978; Men & Wom of Dist 1978; Personalities of Am 1977; Biog Dir Am Public Hlth Assn 1978; Author "Occipital Neuralgia in Adolescents and Young Adults" *New England Journal of Medicine* 1962; "Patterning the Unpatterned Youth" *Journal of Texas Public School Teachers Association* 1969; Others.

DUKE, ALVAN EUGENE oc/Project Engineer; b/May 12, 1946; h/406 Dixie St, Carrollton, GA 30117; ba/Carrollton; p/Emory M (dec) and Sara E Duke, Flovilla, GA; ed/Mech Technol; mil/Ga ARNG 6 Yrs; cp/Masonic Lodge #69; r/Meth; hon/Awd'd US Patent & 1 Pending; Outstg Yng Man of Am.

DUKE, DONALD EDWARD oc/Professor; b/May 5, 1930; h/9005 Forest Lawn Dr, Brentwood, TN; m/Katherine Billingsley; c/Donald E Jr; p/John W (dec) and Leona D Duke, Summitville, TN; ed/BS Univ Tenn-Knoxville 1955; MS Columbia Univ 1958; PhD Univ Ga 1974; mil/AUS 1951-53 1/Lt; pa/Prof Acctg, Tenn St Univ; Pres Don Duke Investments Inc; Cert'd Public Acct; Am Acctg Assn; Am Inst CPAs; cp/Repub Party; r/Bapt; hon/Author Var Acctg & Tax Articles.

DUKE, JOSEPH BENJAMIN oc/Judge; b/Aug 18, 1926; h/1726 Columbine Rd, Milledgeville, GA 31061; ba/Milledgeville; m/Angelyn Brown Amis; c/Joseph Benjamin III, Lucy Ciaire, Nancy Angelyn; p/Joseph Benjamin and Martha English Turner Duke (dec); ed/AB, LLB (JD) Emory Univ; mil/US Infantry WWII Staff Sgt 1944-46; pa/Judge, Superior Cts, Ocmulgee Judicial Circuit; Mem: Baldwin Co Bar Assn, Ocmulgee Circuit Bar Assn, St Bar Assn, Am Bar Assn, Am Judicature Soc; cp/Mason; Am Legion; OES; r/1st Meth Ch.

DUKE, JULIE ANNE oc/Project Director; b/Sept 27, 1953; h/PO Box 742, Albany, GA 31702; ba/Albany; p/Aaron L (dec) and Phyllis B Duke, Albany, GA; ed/BS Ga So Col 1975; pa/Proj Dir River House, Child Wel Sers; Ga Co Wel Assn; cp/Dougherty Co Juvenile Ct Adv Coun; Dougherty Co Social Sers Coor'g Coun; St Teresa's Cath Wom's Coun; r/Cath.

DUKE, R L (BILL) oc/Director of Development; b/Nov 9, 1920; h/PO Box 654, Washington, GA 30673; ba/Altanta, GA; m/Judy Martin; c/Richard L Jr, Carol Inez Cloer (Mrs); p/John R and Adie Inez Duke (dec); pa/Pastor; Dir of Missions; Promo Sect; cp/Kiwanis; Mason; r/So Bapt.

DULMADGE, ELIZABETH ANN oc/Research Biologist; b/Oct 13, 1922; h/1612 S 29th Terrace, Birmingham, AL 35209; ba/Birmingham; p/William Blake Dulmadge (dec); Katherine Morell Dulmadge, Birmingham, AL; ed/BS Biol 1944, MS Biol 1962 Birmingham-So Col; MT 1945, MMicrobiol 1971 Univ of Ala Sch of Med Tech; pa/Clin Bacteriology Supvr Univ of Ala Hosp Clin Labs, Birmingham 1945-56; Res Biol So Res Inst, Birmingham 1956-; Mem: AAAS, Am Soc for Microbiol, Am Soc of Med Techs, Sigma Xi, Tissue Culture Assn, NY Acad of Scis; Affiliate Mem Am Soc Clin Pathols; Author 20 Pubs on experimental cancer chemotherapy & applied microbiology, 16 abstracts; r/Presb; hon/W/W of Am Wom.

DUMMER, DYEANN REDDIG oc/Publisher; b/May 11, 1939; h/410 Santa Maria Way, Longwood, FL 32750; m/Richard; c/Ken Croll, Sharon Croll, Cathy Croll, Geoffrey; p/Henry S (dec) and Thelma Reddig, Boca Raton, FL; ed/NWn Univ 1957-59; Ohio St Univ 1960; pa/Pres Gidder House Pub'g Inc; Pubr *Mobile Home & RV News, Fla Mobile/Mfd Home Guide, Orlando Mobile Home Finder*; Fla Press Assn; Fla Mag Assn; Intl Toastmistress Clb; Fla Mfd Housing Assn; cp/Gtr Seminole C of C; Citrus Coun of GSA; Bd Dirs Yng Repubs; Chm Seminole Co Repub Exec Com; hon/W/W S&SW 1980-81; Author *Big Book of Florida's Best Housing Buy* 1978.

DUNAGAN, OTIS THEODORE oc/Retired Chief Justice; b/Nov 9, 1908; h/8319 Oxford Dr, Tyler, TX 75703; m/Louise Thomas; c/Otis Theodore Jr; p/James Lee and Ella Lee Hawkins Dunagan (dec); pa/Atty for 7 Yrs; Trial & Appellant Judge 36 Yrs; Chief Justice 12 Ct of Civil Appeals of Tex, Ret'd 1978; r/So Bapt; hon/Assn of Broadcasting of Tex; Profl Jour of Tex; Judicial Sect of St Bar of Tex.

DUNCAN, DONN ROBERT oc/Counseling Psychologist; b/Nov 18, 1922; h/Lakeland, FL; m/Donna Hiers; c/Donn Robert II, Phillip James, James Robert; p/R W A Duncan (dec); Vera M Duncan, Frostproof, FL; ed/Univ Fla: BSBA 1946, MA 1950, MRC 1960, EdD 1962; mil/Real Est Ofcr ADMAC, New Delhi, India 1943-46; Hosp Treas Army Hosp, Tokyo, Japan 1950-52; pa/Am & Fla Psych Assns; Life Mem Diplomatic Courier Assn; Previous Pos: Diplomatic Courier US St Dept, Bus Mgr Alcoholic Rehab Prog for St Fla; Current Cnslg Psych, Lakeland; Pres Duncan Groves Inc; cp/CoChm Mtl Hlth Planning Com 1965-66.

DUNCAN, JOHN EBLEN oc/Director of Associational Missions, Shelby Baptist Association, SBC; b/Aug 1, 1925; h/101 Myrtle St, Columbiana, AL 35051; ba/Columbiana; m/Kathleen Gardenhire; c/John Charles; p/Ronald C and May Gray Duncan (dec); ed/AB Howard Col; MS Samford Univ; mil/US Air Corps 1943-50, Air Force Resv 1951-57, Army Nat Guard 1957-60; pa/ Ala Conf of Dirs of Associational Missions,

Pres 1976-77; APGA; Assn for Specialists in Group Work; Ala Pers & Guid Assn; Nat Conf for Dirs of Mission; cp/Mem Bd of Advisors Shelby Yth Aid Bur; Past Pres Local Chapt Civitan Intl; Involved in Mtl Hlth Projs, Am Heart Assn; hon/Sev Articles Pub'd on Bapt Associationalism & Chs in Transition; W/W Rel; DIB; Notable Ams; W/W in S&SW.

DUNCAN, SYLVIA ANNA oc/President Advertising/Public Relations Firm; b/Feb 28, 1944; h/10220 Memorial, Houston, TX 77024; ba/Houston; a/Monique; p/Clifford and Octavin Paisley, Galveston, TX; ed/Jour; pa/Advtg Fed; cp/Special Gifts, Mus Fine Arts; Civic Soc; r/Epis; hon/Overall Outstg Achmt in Communs 1978.

DUNLAP, ESTELLE CECILIA DIGGS oc/Educator, Retired; h/719 Shepherd St, NW, Washington, DC 20011; m/Lee Alfred; c/Gladys C D Kimbrough, Dolly A D Sparkman; p/John F and F C Diggs (dec); pa/Edr, Math Instr, Ret'd; Lectr; AAAS; NEA; Other Profl Assns; Intl Platform Assn; AAUW; Num Civic & Cult Orgs; r/Cath; hon/Nat Sci Foun F'ship; Math F'ship Howard Univ; Num Certs of Awd & Apprec; Biogl Listings; Fellow Mem ABI.

DUNN, EDRA NORRIS oc/Director of Nursing; b/Aug 9, 1945; h/217 W Troy St, Brundidge, AL 36010; ba/Troy, AL; m/Johnny; c/Sonya, Teresa; p/Ralph and Mary Norris, Troy, AL; ed/Dip in Nsg; pa/ANA; Ala St Nurses Assn; cp/SS Tchr Yng People; r/Bapt.

DUNN, ELSIE HYDER oc/Teacher, Department Chairman; b/May 18, 1912; h/670 W Pearl St, Bartow, FL 33830; ba/Bartow; m/W Sam; c/Joyce D Stewart (Mrs), W Sam Jr; p/Dan L and Sarah A Hyder, Elizabethton, TN; pa/Tchr, Social Studies Dept, Bartow, JR HS; Ofcr Polk Co Social Studies Coun; Delta Kappa Gamma; PTA; NEA; FUSA; cp/Regent of Bartow Chapt DAR; Polk Histl Soc; r/Mem 1st Bapt Ch, Bartow; hon/Outstg Sec'dy Tchr for 1974.

DUNN, ERNESTINE LONG oc/Retired Principal; b/Feb 11, 1898; m/C K (dec); c/William Elliott, Forrest Stapleton; p/William Elliott (dec); Ida Stapleton (dec); ed/BS 1942, MS 1946 Auburn Univ; pa/Tchr; Prin Elem Sch; Pres Lee Co Tchrs Assn 1953; AAUW; Delta Kappa Gamma; Pres E Ala Geneal Soc; Mem Bd Pensions & Security; r/Meth; hon/All Awds to 4-H Clb Local Ldrs; Life Mem APTA.

DUNN, FLOYD oc/Retired Certified Public Accountant; b/Mar 14, 1906; h/306 LaVerne Dr, Chattanooga, TN 37421; m/Chlora Curtis; c/Charlie Ann D Mendez, Barbara D Rigsby; p/Jim E (dec) and Laura Buchanan Dunn (dec); ed/Att'd Pan Am Col 1928; Univ Ala 1933-35; Dip LaSalle Extension Univ 1940-44; pa/CPA; Tenn Soc CPAs; Chattanooga Chapt Tenn Soc CPAs Prog Chm; cp/Rotarian; r/Meth; hon/Cert of Hon For Outstg & Dedicated Ser to the Arley, Ala Commun 1979; Author: *Swimmin' Holes 'n' Fishing' Poles: Tales from Brushy Creek* 1979; Contbns to Var Newspapers.

DUNN, MICHAEL RATLIFF oc/Director of Music; b/Apr 13, 1954; h/426 N Green St, Glasgow, KY 42141; ba/Glasgow; m/Sandra; /Frank R and Barbara M Dunn, Bowling Green, KY; ed/BA W Ky Univ 1977; MCM New Orleans Bapt Theol Sem 1979; pa/Dir Mus First U Meth Ch; Am Choral Dirs Assn; Am Musicological Soc; Am Guild Organists; Choristers Guild; F'ship of U Meth Musicians; hon/Ky's Bass Rep to ACDA Bicent Celeb, Interlochen Nat Mus Camp 1976; Perf Awd New Orleans Bapt Theol Sem 1977-78.

DUNN, MILDRED ELAINE oc/Consultant for Home & Family Living Education; b/Sept 27, 1930; h/64 Cedar Lawn Cir, Galveston, TX 77550; ba/Galveston; m/David E (dec); p/Fletcher L and Mildred Meredith Pool, Millican, TX; ed/BS Sam Houston St Univ; pa/Conslt for Home & Fam Living Ed, Galveston Indep Sch Dist; Galveston Ed Assn; Living in Ed, Galveston Indep Sch Dist; Galveston Ed Assn; Tex St Tchrs Assn; NEA; Am Home Ec Assn; Houston Area Home Ec Assn; Voc Homemaking Tchrs Assn of Tex; Am & Tex Voc Assns; Nutrition Today Soc; Assn for Supervn & Curric Devel; Tex Assn for Dir & Supvn of Occupational Ed & Technol; Assn of Childhood Ed Intl; cp/Secy, Cedar Lawn Assn; Galveston Hist Foun; Chd's Coun of Galveston Co; Others; r/Moody Meml 1st U Meth Ch: Chancel Choir; hon/Dist IV TSTA Homemaking Sect Chm; Outstg Ser Awd, Area III Homemaking Tchrs; Encouragemt, Coop & Personal Meritorious Ser Awd, St Voc Ofc Ed; 25 Yr Ser Awd, VHTAT; World W/W of Wom; W/W Biogl Record of Sch Dist Ofcls; Notable Ams; Commun Ldrs & Noteworthy Ams; Fellow Mem ABI.

DUNN, NORMA oc/Site Manager, Senior Citizens Services; b/Sept 22, 1935; h/PO Box 295, DeKalb, TX 75559; m/Morris Jr; c/Wilbur, Kathy; p/Major and Mae Graham, Farmington, NM; pa/Site Mgr Sr Citizens Ctr; cp/JCettes Past VP; ABWA; Del Dem Co Conv; r/Meth.

DUNN, RICHARD VAN oc/Director Economic Development; b/Jan 31, 1946; h/1030 Woodbrook Dr, Largo, FL 33540; ba/St Petersburg, FL;

p/Raymond C and Marion J Dunn; ed/BS Univ Ala 1969; MA Univ So Calif 1970; pa/Dir Ec Devel City of St Petersburg; Nat Assn Devel Orgs Bd; Am Ec Assn; Coun for Urban Ec Devel; cp/World Future Soc; US JCs; r/Bapt; hon/Pres's Awd Panama City, Fla Jr C of C.

DUPREE, MAXINE NELSON oc/Retired; b/Sept 9, 1927; h/1228 S Brand St, Sherman, TX 75090; c/Barbara Ford, Freddie J Savage Jr, Jerry De Mars Savage, Charlie Du Wayne, Marla; ed/Att'd Tex Col 1964; pa/Profl Cook 9 Yrs in Sch Lunch Prog; Cafeteria Mgr; Salad Mgr Wyatts Cafe & Ramada Inn; r/Meth; Queen of Yrly Tea 4 Yrs, Chm 1 Yr; hon/Crowned Queen of Ch w Diamond Crowns; Others.

DURBIN, ALAN CURTIS oc/Attorney; b/Jul 29, 1942; h/1231 Barkley Ave, Norman, OK 73071; ba/Oklahoma City, OK; m/Linda Culp; c/Lisa Rae, Laura Ann; p/Lowell C and Beatrice F Durbin, Shawnee, OK; ed/BA 1965, MA 1966, JD 1972 Univ Okla; pa/Atty, Ptnr: Andrews Mosburg Davis Elam Legg & Bixler Inc, Okla City; Spec Instr Home Mortgage Lending, Am Inst of Bkg, S Okla City Commun Col, Okla City 1976-; Instr in Polit Sci, Macomb Co Commun Col, Warren, Mich 1966-69; Am Judic Soc; Okla Co Bar Assn; Okla Bar Assn; ABA, Sect on Local Govt Law; cp/Commr Norman, Okla Cable Communications Comm 1978-; Mem Ec & Trade Devel Com, Norman C of C; Mem Residential Real Est Transactions Panel; Past Mem Adv Com, Norman Point of Entry Prog (Sub-Com on Ex-Offenders, Norman Human Rights Comm); Adv Bd, Norman Dept of Parks & Rec Softball Prog; Univ Okla Alumni Assn; Univ Okla Col of Law Assn; Univ Clb; r/Prot; hon/Pi Sigma Alpha; Phi Delta Phi; Co-Author *Contemporary International Politics* 1972.

DURFEE, HAROLD ALLEN oc/Professor; b/May 21, 1920; h/12405 St James Rd, Rockville, MD 20850; ba/Washington, DC; m/Doris G; c/Peter Allen, Gary Robert; p/Lynn S and Ethel F Durfee, Cambridge, NY; ed/PhB 1941 Univ of Vermont; BD 1944 Yale Univ; PhD Columbia Univ 1951; pa/The American Univ, Washington: William Frazer McDowell Prof of Philosophy 1957-, Chm Dept of Phil & Rel 1957-73, Chm Div of Humanities 1957-68, Assoc Prof of Phil 1955-57; Exch Prof, The Cath Univ of Am 1972; Author Articles, Papers, Books; Dir Sems; Mem: Am Acad of Rel, AAUP, Am Phil Assn, Intl Soc for Metaphysics, Kappa Sigma, Metaphysical Soc of Am, Phi Kappa Phi; Others; Bd Dirs Forum on Psychiatry & The Humanities of Wash Sch of Psychiatry 1973-; Co-Editor Am Univ Pubs in Phil 1972-; Bd Trustees Wash Consortium of Univs 1970-; Dissertation Com, Georgetown Univ; Conslt, Nat Endowmt for the Humanities 1967; Fdr, Dir Sem in Contemporary European Phil, The Univ of Oxford, Univ of Paris, Univ of Tubingen 1963; Lectr: Christian Col, Georgetown Univ, Johns Hopkins Univ, Univ of Md, William & Mary Col, Others; hon/Dir of Am Scholars; Intl Scholars Dir; Men of Achmt; W/W: Am, Md.

DURR, SHEILA AVERY oc/Teacher; b/Apr 13, 1952; h/Rt 1 Box 118L, Guys, TX 38339; m/Paul E; c/Nikki Neshauna, Paul Aviance; p/Albert C and Ora L McKinnon Avery; ed/AS Jackson St Commun Col 1971; BS Univ Tenn 1974; pa/5th Grade Tchr, Selmer Middle Sch; PTO Chm Ways & Means Com; r/Bapt; hon/Tchr of Month, Sept 1980, Selmer Middle Sch.

DWYER, LEONA DEMERE oc/President Aesthetic Medical Art; b/May 1, 1928; h/Memphis, TN; m/John Thomas Sr; c/John T Jr, DeMere, Patrice, Brian, Anne-Clifton, McCarthy-DeMere; p/Clifton (dec) and Leona McCarthy DeMere (dec); ed/BA SWn Univ 1949; Assoc Med Illus 1974; Att'd Memphis Acad Art; pa/Medical Artist; Apprentice Emblamer; Apprentice Funeral Dir; Speech Therapist 30 Yrs; Guest Lectr: Memphis St Univ Law Sch, Univ Tenn, Am Assn Med Assts, Dalinde Med Sem Mexico City, USAF Base Tokyo, Japan; Columns for *Sports Car Magazine*; Assn Med Illustrators; Am Assn Med Assts; Emer Depts Nurses Assn; Am Phys Nurses Assn; Guest Mem Am Soc of Plastic & Reconstructive Surgs; Sound-Slide Com of Ednl Foun of Am Soc Plastic & Reconstrctive Surgs; Exhibr AMA Convs; Chm of Assocs Wom in Law; Bd Mem Exec Wom of Am; Adv Nat Kappa Delta Soc; Orgr Danny Thomas Ladies of St Jude; Brandeis Univ Wom; Brooks Art Gal Leag; cp/Past Pres N Memphis Civic Clb; Chm Chd's Cotton Carnival Ct; hon/Wom of Yr Awd Cand; Holder of Nat Competition Lic in SCCA to Race Formula Cars; Holder of Federation Internationale de l'Automobile, FIA to Race Intlly 1972; Descendant of Raymond & Paul De Mere, Fdrs of First English Colony in Tenn.

DYE, BRAD oc/Lieutenant Governor; b/Dec 20, 1933; h/5015 Meadow Oaks Pk Dr, Jackson, MS 39211; ba/Jackson; m/Donna Bess Bailey; c/Hamp, Ford, Rick; p/Bradford Johnson Sr (dec) and Maylise Dogan Dye, Grenada, MS; ed/BBA 1957, Law Sch 1959 Univ Miss; pa/Lt Gov, St of Miss 1980-; Pres Jackson Savings & Loan Assn 1976-79; St Treas 1972-76; Dir Miss Agric & Indust Bd 1968-71; Workmen's Comp Comm 1965-67; Appt'd Atty, US Sen Judiciary Com 1961-64; St Sen 1963; Miss Ho of Reps 1959; Pract'd Law w Father 1959-61; Page under Jamie

PERSONALITIES OF THE SOUTH

Whitten, US Ho of Reps 1950; Pi Kappa Alpha; Phi Alpha Delta; cp/Chm Grenada Co Cancer Dr 1959; Charter VP Granada JCs 1959-60; St Heart Assn Chm 2 Yrs; Ctrl Miss Am Red Cross Chm 1 Yr; U Way Bd Dirs 3 Yrs; St Ofcr U Way Fund Chm 1968; Former Mem Rotary Clb, YMCA; Coached Minor Leag Baseball, Basketball, Fball, Northside YMCA, Currently Coach'g Basketball; Bd Andrew Jackson Coun, BSA 10 Yrs; Charter Pres Univ Miss Bus Alumni Assn; r/Meth: Adm Bd.

DYER, CAROLYN ELIZABETH oc/Nurse, Operating Room Supervisor; b/July 11, 1945; h/PO Box 269, Demopolis, AL 36732; ba/Demopolis; p/Horace Edward Dyer II, Rutland, VT; Dorothy Lavelle Gibson Dyer, Demopolis, AL; ed/Assoc Deg in Nsg; pa/RN; Operating Room Sprvr; ANA; Marengo Co Nurses Chapt, ANA; cp/Am Horse Protection Assn Inc; Univ Ala Alumni Assn; r/Bapt; hon/W/W Am Wom.

DYER, ROBERT FRANCIS JR oc/Specialist in Internal Medicine; Medical School Professor; Clinic Director; b/Nov 18, 1926; h/Stonehaven, 5608 Albia Rd, Bethesda, MD 20016; ba/Washington, DC; m/Doris Anne S; c/Robert F III, William Edward, Anne Marie Helen; p/Robert F Sr and Sallie A Worley Dyer (dec); ed/AB Mich 1951; MD George Washington Univ Med Sch 1955; ScD Univ Madrid 1967; mil/AUS Med Corps, Col; Ser: WW II, Korean Occup; pa/Conslt in Internal Med; Clin Prof of Med, George Washington Univ; Dir Protective Sers Clinic, Washington, DC; Med Soc Ofcr; Contbg Mem DOC-PAC of DC Med Soc 1977; Secy Wash Med & Surg Soc; Pres-elect Occupl Med Sect, DC Med Soc; Past Pres Hippocrates-Galen Med Soc; r/Presb: Ruling Elder; hon/Osler Awd 1954; E H Hill Awd 1951; S'ship Awd 1950; Commun Sers Awds 1968, 70; Mayors Awd for Outstg Ser 1971; War Cross, Soc of Colonial Wars 1963; SAR Past Pres Awd 1977; Pub'd Author, Med Pubs 1956-77; Fellow Mem ABI.

DYKES, MARGARET HIMMEL oc/Social Worker; b/Apr 7, 1918; h/923 Park Forest Ln, Jacksonville, FL 32211; ba/J'ville; c/Denise A, Barbara J; p/John Peter (dec) and Hazel Carmer Himmel (dec); ed/BS Iowa St Univ; MA Univ Chgo; pa/Social Wkr, Buckner Foun; NASW; Acad of Cert'd Social Wkrs; NASW Reg of Clin Social Wkrs; r/Meth; hon/W/W Am Wom.

PERSONALITIES OF THE SOUTH

E

EADDY, BETSY JO oc/Medical Social Worker; h/PO Box 3051, Florence, SC 29502; ba/Florence; p/Mr and Mrs Jack J Eaddy, Johnsonville, SC; ed/BA Winthrop Col; MSW Fla St Univ; pa/Med Social Wkr, Crippled Chd's Clinic; McLeod Meml Hosp; Hospice of Pee Dee Bd Dirs; NASW; Sc Public Hlth Assn; cp/Florence Jr Wel Leag; r/Presb; hon/SC Social Wkr of Yr Awd 1979.

EADES, BASCOMB GALLOWAY oc/Priest; b/Apr 10, 1924; h/1503 Cedar Hill Ave, Dallas, TX 75208; ba/Athens, TX; p/Bascomb G Sr (dec) and Lavinia Dashiell Eades, Dallas; ed/Att'd Holy Trinity Sem & Unv Dallas; pa/Artist; Author; Tchr; Priest St Edwards Cath Ch; cp/Lectr in Art & Rel; r/Roman Cath; hon/Hon Life Mem Intl Mark Twain Soc.

EADER, MICHAEL EDWARD oc/Regional Program Director; b/Aug 17, 1943; h/712 Forest Hill Ln, Port Charlotte, FL 33952; ba/Orlando, FL; m/Jeanne; c/Scott, Shannon; p/Mr and Mrs Cecil Estill, Lincoln Park, MI; ed/BS Univ Mo; MA Univ Miss; pa/Reg Migrant Coor Fla Dept Ed 1977-; Charlotte Co Sch Bd: Asst to Supt/Coor of Exceptl Student Ed 1975-77, Coor Exceptl Student Ed/Spec Projs 1973-75, Coor Exceptl Student Ed 1971-73; Tchr/Coor Except Student Ed, Charlotte HS 1970-71; Tchr/Supvr Exceptl Student Ed, E Alton-Wood River Sch Dist, Wood River, Ill 1969-70; Tchr Belleville (Ill) Twp Sr High 1966-69; Reg Dir Fla Ednl Negotiators; Pres Fla Coun for Admrs of Spec Ed; Treas Fla Fdn Coun for Exceptl Chd; hon/Pubs incl: "Teacher Union Master Analysis Mgmt Counterproposals" & "Picture Voc Interest Inventory"; David A Blanton S'ship Awd; W/W Am Sch Dist Ofcls.

EADS, SHERRY LYNN oc/Administrator, Medical Clinic Consultant; b/July 4, 1946; h/4117 Antelope Trail, Temple, TX 76501; ba/Temple; m/James R; p/Erlene Pope Smith, Georgetown, TX; ed/San Antonio Col 1963; Tex A&M Univ 1963-65; pa/Admr Hassmann Clin; VP Med Mgmt Assocs; Med Grp Mgmt Assn; Am Mgmt Assn; cp/Ctrl Tex C of C; r/Meth; hon/Top Prodr ERA Rltr Contrac, Tex 1979.

EAKER, SYLVIA BRITTON oc/Instructor, Businesswoman, Coordinator; b/Feb 9, 1939; ba/Florence, Al; m/Paul D; p/Nannie B Britton, Ramer, TN; ed/GED 1967; Spec Student Univ N Ala 1975; Bus Sch Tuscumbia, Ala 1957-58; cp/Past Radio Announcer; Owner, Instr Inner Devel (Modeling); Coor Beauty Pageants, Fashion Shows; MC; Modeling Assn Am & NY; Intl Model's & Talent Agcy; cp/Tenn Val Art Ctr; r/Prot; hon/Articles Pub'd In Newspapers 1973-74.

EARLES, PAT S oc/Teacher; b/Nov 5, 1938; h/525 Joe Clifton Dr, Paducah, KY 42001; m/Melvin; c/Cheryl; p/Knox (dec) and Ruby Brinn, Paducah, KY; pa/PE Tchr; Pres Ky PTA; PEA; KEA: NEA; r/Ch of Christ; hon/Life Mbrship KCPTA; NCPTA; Thanks Badge; Ky Col.

EARLEY, DEBRA GEORGETTE oc/Student; b/May 10, 1959; h/Jacksonville, NC; p/George W and Elizabeth B Earley, J'ville, NC; ed/Att'g UNC-W; pa/Student Wkg for Vocal Perf Deg in Mus; r/Meth; hon/3rd Runner Up Regional Contest for Bob Hope's Search for Tops in Col Talent; 2nd Runner Up 1981 Miss Wilmington Pageant; Winner Hannah Block Awd; Miss Greenville/So Flue Cured Tobacco Queen 1981.

EARLY, JACK JONES oc/College President; b/Apr 12, 1925; h/Limestone Col, Gaffney, SC 29340; ba/Same; m/Nancye Whaley; c/Lela Katherine, Judith Ann, Laura Hattie; p/Joseph M Early, Corbin, KY; Lela Early (dec); ed/BA Union Col 1948; MA Univ Ky 1953; BD Lexington Theol Sem 1956; EdD Univ Ky 1956; pa/Pres Limestone Col, Gaffney 1973-; Exec Dir-Ed The Am Bkrs Assn, Wash DC 1971-73; Pres: Pfeiffer Col, Misenheimer, NC 1969-71, Dakota Wesleyan Univ, Mitchell, SD 1958-69; Ia Wesleyan Col, Mt Pleasant, Ia: VP & Dean Col 1956-58, Prof Ed & Psychol 1956-58; Instr Grad Sch Univ Ky, Lexington Sum 1956; Asst to Pres & Dean Fac Athens Col, Athens, Ala 1954-55; Other Previous Positions; Rel News Commentator WLAP, Lexington; Past Pres Upper Ky River Ed Assn; Past VP Classroom Tchrs, Ky Ed Assn; Former Rep Ky Ed Assn Planning Bd; Nat Assn for Indust-Ed Cooperation; Former Mem SD Ed Assn Leg Comm; Pres SD Assn Cols & Univs; Former Secy-Treas So Assn Ch-Related Cols; IPA; cp/Former Chaplain Ky Mtn Clb; Sigma Phi Epsilon; Univ Ky Alumni Assn; Union Col Alumni Assn; Mitchell C of C; Mason; Shriner; VP Rotary Clb; Bd Dirs YMCA; Rep Upper MW Res & Devel Coun; Eng-Spkg Union; Univ Clb, Wash DC; Bd Dirs Gaffney Boys' Clb; Adv Coun ARC for Carolinas; Adv Bd 1st Fed Savs & Ln Assn, Gaffney; Bd Trustees Rel Heritage of Am, Wash DC; Crustbreakers; Gaffney CC; Arts Coun Limestone Col, Cherokee Co; Mem SC St Tuition Grants Com; Others; r/U Meth Ch: Wn NC Conf; hon/Mitchell JCs: Spoke Awd for Outstg Commun Ser, Dist'd Ser Awd as "Yg Man of Yr"; Outstg Yg Man, SD JCs; Elected to Dist'd Hall of Fame, Univ Ky; O'Tucks

Awd for Outstg Former Kentuckian; Hon Citizen Awds; Bus & Profl Ldr Awd in Field of Ed, Rel Heritage Am; Mem Hon Frats; Hon Degs; Num Biogl Listings; Others.

EARNEST, JAMES EZRA oc/Retired Coal Miner; b/July 12, 1915; h/Rt 1 Box 9, Parrish, AL 35580; m/Eunice; c/Charles Ray, Grace Nell, William Edward, Paul Howard; p/John and Lula Earnest (dec); pa/Coal Miner 40 Yrs; Coun-man City of Parrish 1972-76, 1976-79; cp/City of Parrish Lib Assn; UMWA Local 8982; r/Zion Ch of Christ; hon/Hon Lt Col Ala St Militia 1971; Awd'd Gold Pin & Hard Hat for 27 Yrs Accident Free Safety 1975; Author *Our History, Parrish, Alabama 1878-1976.*

EARWOOD, MARGARET OGDEN oc/Artist; b/Aug 26, 1908; h/PO Box 901, Belle Glade, FL 33430; m/Henry O (dec); c/Carolyn Ogden Dugan; p/Hayden Thomas (dec) and Margaret Rouster Ogden (dec); ed/AB Stetson Univ 1932; Studied Art Univ Ind 1929-30, Fla St Univ 1958; Grad Studies Univ Fla & Univ Tenn Grad Sch; pa/Art Instr Belle Glade HS 1950-68; Art Instr Glade Day Sch 1968-75; FAEA; NAEA; Lake Worth Art Leag; Norton Gal WPBH; Artists Guild, Norton Gal; cp/Delta Kappa Gamma; NRTA; FRTA; r/Bapt; hon/1st Awd, Fla Amateur Artists 1947; 1st Awd Univ Fla Summer Session 1954; Awds w Lake Worth Art Leag: 1st in Batik 1973 & 81, 2nd Silk Screen 1977, 1st Stitchery 1973 & 79, 2nd Water Color 1954 & 47, 1st Awd Copper Enameling 1978 & 80; 3 One-Man Shows.

EASLEY, LOUIS T (TEX) oc/Press Assistant; b/Jul 29, 1907; h/1404 Crestwood Dr, Alexandria, VA 22302; ba/Wash DC; m/Bonita Carlson; c/Rex C, Rita E Percival (Mrs William F); p/L T and Della Mae Kerr Easley (dec); ed/BJ Univ Mo 1930; pa/Press Asst to House Agri Com, US Ho of Reps; Assoc'd Press Wash Bur 1937-67; Reporter Dallas Times Herald 1936-37; Reporter Denver Post 1930-36; cp/Staff of House Agri Com 1967-; r/Meth.

EASON, FRANCES ROGERS oc/Associate Professor, Nurse; b/July 25, 1944; m/Walter G; c/Walter Brian; p/Ella P Rogers, Youngsville, NC; ed/Dip Nsg Park View Hosp Sch of Nsg 1965; BSN E Carolina Univ 1970; MEd NCSU 1976; EdD NCSU 1980; MN ECU 1980; pa/Assoc Prof Nsg Ed: ECU 1976-78 & 1979-, NC Wesleyan Col 1978-79, Atlantic Christian Col 1973-76; NCNA; NC Adult Ed Assn; Salvation Army Nurse F'ship; cp/St Commr of Hlth; St Commr Radiation Safety Protection; r/Meth; hon/Outstg Yng Wom Am 1979.

EASON, SHARON EILEEN HANNA oc/Teacher's Aide, Bus Driver, Secretary; h/Goodwater, AL; m/Herold C; c/Sharonda Rebecca, Herold Wade; p/Woodrow W Hanna, Goodwater, AL; Arliene B Hanna (dec); pa/Remedial Math Tchr's Aide; Sch Bus Driver; Ch Secy; ESPO; AEA; NEA; cp/Ath Booster Clb; PTA: Past Pres & Secy; r/Bapt; hon/3 Vol Ser Awds for Cystic Fibrosis 1979 & 80.

EAST, LOYD EDDIE oc/Medical Technologist; b/Dec 12, 1931; h/Rt 2 Box 41A, Gainesville, TX 76240; ba/G'ville; m/Marilyn Joyce Boynton; c/Loyd Jr, Cecilia Randall, Cynthia, Scot, Tamera, Melainie, Tina (dec), Helen, Patricia Russell; p/Jessie (dec) and Mamie East (dec); ed/BS; mil/AUS 6 Yrs; pa/Am Soc Clin Pathol; cp/Foster Parent; r/So Bapt.

EASTER, MARTHA CORBIN oc/Registered Nurse Supervisor; b/Nov 18, 1946; h/PO Box 792, Galax, VA 24333; ba/Galax; m/Royce R; p/GailB (dec) and Besie Corbin, Greenville, VA; ed/Dip Nsg; BS Cand Univ Va & Wytheville Commun Col; pa/AACN; Am Heart & Va Heart Assns; cp/Galax Fireman's Aux, VP; Red Cross; Twin Co Commun Hosp: Ch-wom Nsg Care Plan'g Com, Mem Nsg Audit Com; r/Bapt; hon/W/W Am Wom 1979-80.

EASTMAN, WALTER DALE oc/Businessman; b/Oct 9, 1957; h/5329 Annette, El Paso, TX 79924; ba/El Paso; p/Walter and Sallie Eastman, El Paso, TX; ed/BS; pa/Pt-time El Paso Natural Gas Co; UTEP Band; Med Professions Org; Sec'dy Edrs Assn; Tex St Tchrs Assn; Nat Assn Jazz Edrs; Bapt Student Union; cp/Coach for Little Leag Baseball Team 3 Yrs; Cand UTEP Student Activities Corr; r/Bapt; Ldr of Ch Singing Grp "Inspiration"; hon/Student Del Chm of Public Affairs Com at UTEP; SPURS (Soph Class Hon Soc).

EATON, FRANK HOLLIS oc/Manager; b/Aug 6, 1952; h/2311A Judy, Odessa,TX 79762; ba/Odessa; p/Teresa S Eaton, El Paso, TX; ed/3 Yrs Toward BSCE; pa/Mgr Plant Constr, Holloman Constr; cp/Nat Rifle Assn; Repub Party; r/Cath; hon/Valedictorian El Paso HS; Stevens Schlr to UTEP.

EATON, JAMES WOODFORD oc/Pension and Profit Sharing Specialist; b/Nov 8, 1944; h/1420 Walnut St, Pine Bluff, AR 71601; ba/Pine Bluff; m/Pamela; c/Cristina, Courtney, James; p/Ortis A Eaton, Tampa, FL; Mildred G Veach Eaton (dec); ed/BS SE Mo St Col; mil/USAR 1969; pa/Assoc Am Soc Pension Actuaries; cp/Lions Intl; Toastmasters Intl; r/Presb; Deacon.

EAVES, A REGINALD oc/County Commissioner; b/Mar 29, 1934; h/1158 Cardinal Way, SW, Atlanta, GA 30311; ba/Atlanta; p/Rabbi Cecil R and Gladys Eaves, Jacksonville, FL; ed/BA Morehouse Col 1956; Att'd Atlanta Univ & Boston Univ; LLB New England Law Sch 1966; pa/Exec Dir Boston's S End Neighborhood Action Prog 1966-69; Commr Penal Insts for Boston & Suffolk Co 1972-74; Exec Asst to Mayor Atlanta 1974; Commr Public Safety, Atlanta 1974; Fulton Co Commr 1978; VChm Fulton Co Bd Commrs; VChm Nat Steering Com for Envir & Energy 1979; hon/Cert of Merit for Sers Rendered on Bd Dirs, Action for Boston Commun Devel; 1 of 10 Outstg Yng Men Boston 1970; Outstg Yng Man Am 1970; Awd for Courage Exemplified in Fight Against Crime in City of Atlanta 1975; Bankhead Peace Prize 1975; Outstg Job in Crime Reduction; Spirit of Atlanta Awd 1975; Outstg Ser Awd, Atlanta Assn Fed Execs 1975; Apprec for Concern for Yth & Crime Prevention 1975; Citizenship Day Awd 1975; Awd for Bringing Pride & Profism to Bur of Police Sers 1975; Cert of Apprec, Nat Defense Transp Assn 1975; Cert of Apprec for Generous & Outstg Ser, Mar of Dimes 1976; Achmt Awd, Nat Black Police Assn 1976; Apprec Awd, Forum of Dist'd Ams 1976; Apprec Awd Douglas Commun & City Civic Clb 1976; Cit for Outstg Ldrship in Field of Law Enforcement 1976; Dist'd Ser Awd, Black Alliance of Ga St Univ 1976; Yng Man of Yr Awd, Omega Y's Men 1974; Achmt Awd, Beta Gamma Sigma 1976; Apprec Awd for Outstg Commitment & Humanitarian Effort, Atlanta St Acad 1979; Commun Ser Awd 1979; Cert of Apprec Atlanta Yth Devel Ctr 1979; Outstg Black Am 1980; Num Other Awds for Ser to Commun.

EBERT, REVA JANETTE oc/Retired Teacher; b/June 11, 1914; p/Daniel William (dec) and Jennie Eva Pates Ebert (dec); ed/BEd Ill St 1935; MS Univ Wis 1943; pa/Ret'd Phys Ed Tchr; Supvr Phys Ed N Tex St Univ; AAHPER; TAHPER; Assn for Student Tchg; Tex St Tchrs Assn; Delta Psi Kappa: Secy, Pres, Editor, Province Dir; cp/Zeta Tau Alpha Alumnae; r/Presb: Elder; hon/Nat Hon Pres, Delta Psi Kappa.

ECHOLS, MICHAEL WAYNE oc/Chief of Police; b/Feb 18, 1945; h/Trinidad, TX; ba/PO Box 403, Trinidad, TX 75163; m/Victoria L; c/Leah Ann, Theresa Lynn, David Wayne, p/Robert Wayne and Betty Echols, Gainesville, TX; ed/Att'd: Cooke Co Jr Col, SMU; Dip Tex Security Ofcrs Acad 1974 & 76; Masters Dip in Conservation 1970; Dip E Tex Police Acad; Red & White Proficiency Cert, St of Tex; Dip: Civil Liabilities for Police Ofcrs 1980, Burglary Investigation 1980, Narcotics Investigation 1980, Rural Fire Defense 1979, Fire Control Sch 1980; pa/Chief of Police for One Man Force; cp/Treas: Trinidad Vol Fire Dept; r/Ch of Christ; hon/Awd'd Highest Scholastic Average of Grad'g Class Tex Security Acad 1974 & 1976.

ECK, KENNETH FRANK oc/Pharmacist; b/Feb 4, 1917; h/E Tex Rd, Healdton, OK 73438; ba/Healdton; m/Ouida Landon; c/Alan G, Mark W, Dana L; p/CJ and Rosa B Eck (dec); ed/BS SWn St Univ; mil/USN 3½ Yrs WWII, Chief Pharmacists Mate; pa/Pres Eck Drug Co Inc; Past Pres Okla St Bd Pharm; Dist Pres OPhA; Off-Campus Fac Mem SW St Univ Sch Pharm; cp/Lions Clb: Zone Chm, Dpty Dist Gov Elect; Cmdr VFW; Cand Lt Gov 1978; Past Pres Chickasaw Multi-Co Lib Sys; Pres Healdton Med Soc; Post Cmdr Am Legion; Treas C of C; r/Ch of Christ: Deacon; hon/Syntex Preceptor Awd; SW St Spec Recog Awd; SW Alumni Ser Awd; Healdton Man of Yr Awd.

ECKELS, ROBERT YOUNG JR oc/County Commissioner; b/Jul 24, 1929; h/4035 Trey Dr, Houston, TX 77084; ba/Houston; c/Robert Allen, Carol Ann; p/Robert Y Eckels Sr (dec); Mildred Daniel Eckels, Houston, TX; ed/BA; MA; mil/AUS; pa/Tchr; Sch Admr; Ins Agt; Safety Advr; cp/Elected Co Commr, Harris Co Precnt 3; Past Pres HISD Bd Ed; PTA; Mason; Bd Dirs Nat Assn Counties; r/Presb; hon/Dist'd Alumni, Sam Houston Alumni Assn.

ECKERT, ELAINE BERG oc/Retired Therapist, Homemaker, Civic Worker; b/July 17, 1946; h/605 Washington, Camden, AR 71701; c/Leah, Emily; p/H M Sr (dec) and Mrs Mike Berg, Camden, AR; ed/BA William Woods 1968; pa/Ret'd Therapist; Tenn Psychi Hosp; Jr Aux Fin Chm Ouachita Sheltered Workshop Dir; cp/Chm Heart Fund 1978; Vol for U Fund, Cancer Fund, Arthritis Fund; r/Jewish.

ECKHARDT, ROBERT CHRISTIAN oc/US Congressman; b/Jul 16, 1913; ba/1741 Longworth House Ofc Bldg, Wash DC 20515; m/Celia Bucan Morris; c/Sarah, Orissa E Arend, Rosalind; p/Joseph Carl Augustus and Norma Wurzback Eckhardt, Houston, TX; ed/BS 1935, LLB 1939 Univ Tex; mil/USAAC 1942-44; pa/Atty; St Rep; US Rep 1967-; cp/Chm S/Com on Consumer Protection & Fin; r/Presb.

ECKHARDT, RUTH HUYCKE FERGUSON oc/Retired Public School Teacher; b/July 3, 1913; h/Morrill Rd, PO Box 486, Mississippi St, MS 39762; m/Robert C (dec); c/William George, Karl Robert, Elizabeth Ann Geer (Mrs J Michael), Myrna Lorraine Lott (Mrs N Bryan); ed/BS Univ Manitoba (Canada) 1935; MS Ia St Col 1937; Miss St Univ Grad Sch;

pa/Ret'd as Sci Tchr S'ville (Miss) Mid Sch 1978; Tchr S'ville Public Schs 1959-78; Asst Prof Univ Manitoba 1935-36, 1937-39; Active in Local, St & Nat Ed Assns; Past Pres S'ville Ed Assn; Com Mem Miss Ed Assn Dept Clrm Tchrs 1969-70; Dir Dist I DCT 1970-73; Past Pres AAUW; Others; cp/Cub Scouts; 4-H Clb; Civic Wom Clb; Past Pres: Miss St Univ Wom's Clb, Nocturn Mus Clb, S'ville PTA; Pilot Clb S'ville; Delta Delta Delta; r/1st Presb Ch, S'ville: Former SS Tchr, Soloist in Ch Choir; Miss St Univ Commun Choir; hon/Miss Mother of Yr, St of Miss Archives; 1968 St Miss Merit Mother; 1969 St Miss Mother of Yr; Delta Kappa Gamma; Hon Life Mem Miss Cong of PTA; Tchg F'ship, Ia St Col; Gold Medalist Univ Manitoba; The Acad of Am Edrs 1973-74; Outstg Edrs Am 1978-79; Biogl Listings.

EDGEMON, CONSTANCE KAY oc/Staff Psychologist; b/Nov 27, 1947; h/112 Lincoln, Big Spring, TX 79720; ba/Big Sprg; p/R P and Verna Graham Edgemon, Mercedes, TX; ed/BA Pan Am Col 1969; MA Chapman Col 1975; pa/Staff Psychologist, Big Sprg St Hosp Adolescent Prog; Assoc Mem: SWn Psychol Assn, Tex Psychol Assn; Psychol Assn for Gtr W Tex: Charter Mem, Secy; Author 'The Relationship Between Physical Attractiveness, Physical Effectiveness, & Self-Concept in Hospitalized Adolescents", *Psychosocial Rehab Jour*, 1979; Presentation at SWPA Conv 1978; Spkr to Sch & Civic Orgs; cp/Beta Sigma Phi, Mu Zeta Chapt; Girl Scout Ldr; Kappa Delta Sorority, Delta Epsilon Chapt; Life Mem Order of Rainbow for Girls; r/Bapt.

EDGENS, DANA BYINGTON oc/Homemaker; b/Aug 2, 1940; h/Rt 10, Horseshoe Bend, Rome, GA 30161; m/Jack R; c/Jefferson Gordon, Samuel Byington, Branan Reece; p/E C (dec) and Mrs E C Byington, Irwinton, GA; ed/AB Ga St Col for Wom 1961; pa/Math Tchr 1961-66; cp/Treas Floyd Co Med Aux; Pres Four Seasons Garden Clb; Ed Chm The Nature Conservancy-Marshall Forest; Secy Floyd Co Audubon Soc; r/St Peters Epis Ch: SS Tchr 4 Yrs.

EDGERTON, WILBERT DELANO oc/Professor; b/Jan 2, 1934; h/Virginia Bch, VA; ba/Norfolk St Univ, 2401 Corprew Ave, Norfolk, VA 23504; p/Wiliam Henderson (dec) and Victoria Wilder Edgerton (dec); ed/Dip Norfolk St Univ 1954; AB Va St Univ 1956; MS & EdS Ind Univ 1961; EdD Columbia Univ 1972; mil/AUS 1956-61 Capt; pa/Instr Va St Univ 1961-63; Dir Ednl Media Prince Edward Free Schs Assn 1963-64; Instr Va St Univ 1964-65; Asst Prof-Prof, Dept Hd Norfolk St Univ 1965-; Nat Assn Ednl Broadcasters; BEA; SCA; AECT; Phi Delta Kappa; Kappa Delta Pi; Kappa Phi Kappa; Alpha Epsilon Rho; Am Film Inst; Nat Film Soc; Life Mem Ind Univ & Norfolk St Univ Alumni Assns; Life Mem Kappa Alpha Psi; hon/Ford Founs F'ships 1959-70, 1970-71; Contbr Over 20 Articles to Jours & Books.

EDMONDS, DONALD RAY oc/Systems Engineer; b/Mar 16, 1937; h/5004 Regina Dr, Annandale, VA 22003; ba/McLean, VA; m/Clydene Jones; c/Catherine Joy, Douglas Jones; p/Clarence Raymond and Marilyn Edmonds, Roselle, NJ; ed/BS, BA Rutgers Univ 1960; MS 1966, PhD 1973 Ohio St Univ; mil/USAF 1960-63; pa/Res Assoc/Asst, Ohio St Univ 1963-66; Sr Oprs Res Analyst, N Am Rockwell Corp 1966-68; Res Assoc Ohio St Univ 1968-69; Lectr Univ So Calif 1969-70; Asst Prof Univ Utah 1971-74; Sr Res Analyst, Presearch Inc 1974-76; Sr Staff Scist, Geo Wash Univ 1977-78; Conslt, Summit Res Corp 1977-79; Dept Staff MITRE Corp 1979-; Assoc Professorial Lectr, Geo Wash Univ, Dept of Oprs Res & Sch of Gen Studies 1977-; Oprs Res Soc of Am; Mil Oprs Res Soc; IEEE; AIIE; AAAS; Wash Oprs Res/Mgmt Sci Coun; cp/Repub Party; Beta Theta Pi; r/Unitarian; hon/Pi Tau Sigma; Pi Mu Epsilon; Alpha Pi Mu; Sigma Xi; W/W: MW 1969-70, S&SW 1980-81.

EDMONSON, HAROLD W oc/Associate Rector; b/Aug 16, 1925; h/4218 N Stanton, El Paso, TX 79902; ba/El Paso; m/Ava V; c/H Alan, Jeffrey S, Sarah J; p/Willard F and Ruth B Edmonson, Plainfield, IN; ed/BS Canterbury Col; MS Ind Univ; MD Sem of SW; mil/USN 1943-46; pa/Fdg Mem, ESP Res Assocs; Order of Unknown Saints; Assoc Rector, St Clement Epis Ch, El Paso; cp/Crisis Counseling; r/Epis; hon/Fellow, ABI; W/W Rel; Men of Achmt.

EDMONDSON, JEANNETTE B oc/Chairman of the Board; b/June 6, 1925; h/Rt 6 Box 10, Edmond, OK 73034; ba/Okla City; m/J Howard (dec); c/James H Jr (dec), Jeanne E Watkins, Patricia E Zimmer; p/A Chapman (dec) and Georgia S Bartleson (dec); ed/BA Univ Okla; pa/Chm Bd, Am Heart Assn, Okla Affil; cp/Kappa Alpha Theta; Chapt D PEO; r/Meth.

EDMONSON, MARY LOUISE (dec) oc/Poet; Civic Worker; b/Oct 30, 1904; h/4003 Dobbs Dr, Huntsville, AL 35802; m/Nat Jr; c/Nathan; p/(dec); ed/BS Tex Tech Univ 1931; pa/Poet; Tex Agric Ext Ser, 1927-30; cp/Madison Co Stop ERA, Chm; Past Pres AAUW, H'ville Br; Eagle Forum of Ala, Co-Chm 5th Dist of Ala; Photo Soc of Am; r/Presb; hon/Slides to Illustrate "Evangeline", "The Blessed Damozel" & 'The Lady of Shalott"; Hon'd by H'ville AAUW; Pub'd in *The National Review* & *National Observer* as well as Local Newspapers.

EDMUNDS, EDWARD WAYNE oc/Market Research and Development Manager; b/June 29, 1945; ba/Anchor Darling Indust Inc, PO Box 300, Kulpsville, PA 19443; m/Diane Kasten, c/Shawn Michael, Jarret Christian; p/Edward Edmund and Shirley Barbara Edmunds, Monmouth Bch, NJ; ed/AB Colgate Univ 1967; mil/USNR 1964-69; pa/Am Soc Metals 1967-; Past Ofcr & Chm Elect Old S Chap ASM; NACE & Its Tech Coms T-5 & T-1F; AWS; MTS; ASTM & Chm Sub-Com G1.13 "High Temperature Oxidation & Corrosion by Gases" & B10.05 "Corrosion of Titanium and Other Refractory Metals"; TMS & the SPE of Am Inst Mining, Metal & Petro Engrs; TAC of MPC & Active on Coms 7, 8, 9; TAPPI; cp/Delta Upsilon; Colgate Alumni Assn; r/Epis; hon/W/W: Fin & Indust 1979, S&SW 1980.

EDRINGTON, GEORGE ELDEN oc/Divisional Sales Manager; b/Aug 17, 1954; h/Cleveland, TN; ba/Hardwick Stove Co, Cleveland, TN 37311; p/Mr and Mrs Raymond J Frohling, Sterling, IL; ed/Att'd Acad of Hlth Scis, Sauk Valley Jr Col; mil/AUS 1972-77 Food Inspection Spec; pa/Div Sales Mgr, Hardwick Stove Co; Former Owner-Oper Johnson's Appliance; NARDA; cp/Lions Intl; r/Nazarene; hon/Nat Defense Awd; Good Conduct Ser Awd.

EDWARDS, DAN W oc/Educator; Marriage, Family & Sex Therapist; b/Jul 19, 1941; h/561 E State St, Baton Rouge, LA 70802; m/Janet Stephens; p/Mr and Mrs Dan W Edwards, Tallahassee, FL; ed/MSW Fla St Univ; PhD Fla St Univ 1972; Addit Studies; pa/Chm Fields of Social Work Pract Curric Area, Sch of Social Wel, La St Univ; Assoc Editor, *Jour of Intl & Comparative Social Welfare*; Pub'd Author; Contbr Num Articles to Profl Jours; Presenter/Contbr at Nat Convs & Confs inclg: Nat Adult Ed Res Conf, Nat Coun of Commun Mtl Hlth, 3rd Nat Annual Inst on Social Work Pract in Rural Areas, Am Correctional Assn, Soc of Police & Correctional Psychologists Nat Meeting, 39th Annual Conf of Am Assn of Mtl Hlth Profls in Corrections, Others; Treas, Fla NASW 1966-67; Pres, La Assn of Criminal Justice Social Workers Inc 1981-82 (Affiliate, Am Correctional Assn); Coun on Social Work Ed; Nat Assn Social Workers; Cert'd Clin Mem, Nat Alliance for Fam Life; Cert'd Clin & Supervisory Mem, Am Assn Marriage & Fam Therapists; Cert'd Clin Mem, Am Assn of Sex Edrs & Cnslrs; Bd Dirs, Fla Coun Alcoholism Prog Directors Inc 1975-77; Fla Coun for Commun Mtl Hlth Inc; Bd Dirs, Mtl Hlth Assn of Escambia Co Inc 1975-77; Pres, La Assn of Criminal Justice Social Workers Inc 1981-82; Others; r/Prot; hon/Phi Delta Kappa; Alpha Kappa Delta; W/W Human Sers, The Am Acad of Human Sers; Rec'd Grants for Res; Others.

EDWARDS, DEL M oc/Wholesale and Manufacturing; b/Apr 12, 1953; h/4821 Trenton St, Tyler, TX 75703; ba/Tyler; p/Welba C and Davida M Edwards, Tyler, TX; ed/AA cum laude Tyler Jr Col 1974; BBA Baylor Univ 1976; pa/Exec VP W C Supply Co; Pres Walker Auto Spring Mfg; VP WC Square Shopping Ctr; VP W C Edwards & Assoc; Coun of Fleet Specs; Auto Ser Indust Assn; cp/Sustaining Mem Smith Co Hist Soc; Treas Jas P Douglas Camp #124 SCV; r/Bapt; hon/Hon Awd Tex Div SCV 1977; Contbr *Chronicles of Smith County* Winter 1974.

EDWARDS, EDWIN WASHINGTON oc/Governor; b/Aug 7, 1927; h/1001 Capitol Access Rd, Baton Rouge, LA 70801; ba/Baton Rouge; m/Elaine Schwartzenberg; c/Anna, Victoria, Stephen, David; p/Clarence and Agnes Brouillette Edwards; ed/Grad La St Univ Law Sch; mil/USN Air Corps WWII; pa/Pract Law, Crowley, La 1949-64; cp/Gov St of La 1972-; Former Chm Interst Oil Compact Comm; St CoChm Ozarks Reg Comm; Host Gov 1975 Nat Govs' Conf (Held in New Orleans); Mem Energy Com, So Govs' Conf; Nat Govs' Conf: Mem Sev Coms, Mem Task Force on Fgn Trade & Tourism; Previous Elected Positions: Mem US Ho of Reps, La St Senate, Crowley City Coun; Lions Clb; Intl Rice Fest; Gtr Crowley C of C; Am Legion; r/Cath.

EDWARDS, ELLA CHANDLER oc/Librarian; b/July 17, 1934; h/928 Monrovia, Shreveport, LA 71106; ba/Shreveport; c/Clarence Jeptha Jr, Marguerite Herries, Mathilde Hollingsworth; p/Robert Gray (dec) and Nell Orman Chandler, Shreveport, LA; ed/BA NWn St Col 1968; MS La St Univ 1973; pa/Magale Lib, Centenary Col of La: Cataloging Asst 1969-72; Acquisitions Libn 1972-74, Cataloger & Hd Tech Processer 1974-75; Asst Dir 1975-; Acting Dir 1975-76; Ptnr EMS Lib Conslts 1980-; Exec Libn for So Cols & Univs Union to Jt Univs Lib at Nashville 1972; AAUP; La Lib Assn; Kappa Delta Pi; cp/Nat Soc Colonial Dames; La Trails Coun; Shreveport Jr Leag; DAR; Ozark Soc; Shreveport Preserv Soc; Repub Party; r/Epis; hon/Author: "Henry Marshall, Confederate Congressman from Louisiana" *North Louisiana Historical Association Newsletter* 1968.

EDWARDS, ELWYN GERALD oc/Minister, Retired US Army Chaplain; Teacher; b/June 10, 1928; h/PO Box 104, Homosassa Springs, FL 32647; ba/Crystal River, FL; m/Joyce Lavonne Trawick; c/Lawyn Clayton, Dawana Jo; p/Seeber I and Beula Franklin Edwards, Tampa, FL; ed/AB Stetson Univ 1952; BD 1958, MDiv 1973 SWn Bapt Sem; mil/AUS Chaplain (Col); pa/Tchr Crystal River Mid Sch; Bapt Min; Mil Chap Assn; Fla Chap Assn; Am Corectional Chap Assn; cp/Pres Sierra Vista Min Assn 1976-77; r/So Bapt; hon/14 Mil Awds & Decorations Incl'g Legion of Merit; W/W Rel 2nd Ed.

EDWARDS, JAMES BURROWS oc/Governor; Oral Surgeon; b/Jun 24, 1927; h/101 Venning St, Mount Pleasant, SC 29464; m/Ann Norris Darlington; c/James Burrows Jr, Catherine; p/O M Edwards; Bertie Ray Hieronymus; ed/BS Univ Louisville 1950; DMD Sch Dentistry, L'ville 1955; Postgrad Studies: Grad Med Sch Univ Pa 1957-58, Henry Ford Hosp, Detroit (Mich) 1958-60; mil/US Maritime Ser 1944-47, Lic'd Merchant Marine Ofcr at Age 19; USN 1955-57; USNR Until 1967, Lt Comdr; pa/Oral Surg; Am Dental Assn; SC Dental Assn; Charleston Dental Soc; Past Pres Coastal Dist Dental Soc; SEn Soc Oral Surgs; Am Soc Oral Surgs; Brit Assn Oral Surgs; Fdn Dentaire Internationale; Intl Soc Oral Surgs; Oral Sur Polit Action Com; Fellow: Am Col Dentists 1966, Intl Col Dentists 1968; L D Pankey Dental Foun, Inc; Appt'd Mem Fed Hosp Coun 1969 (4 Yr Term); cp/Gov St of SC; SC Dental Assn Rep on Gov's Stwide Com for Comprehensive Hlth Care Planning 1968-72; Past Dir Coastal Carolina Boy Scouts; Past Mem Bd Trustees: C'ton Co Hosp, Gtr C'ton YMCA; Bd Trustees Col Preparatory Sch, C'ton; Mem C'ton Coun Navy Leag US; Chm So Govs' Conf 1978; Other Elected Positions; r/Hibben Meth Ch, Mt Pleasant: Mem, Adm Bd; hon/Var Hon Degs; Alumni of Yr, Col of C'ton; Grad w hons, Univ L'ville Sch Dentistry; Outstg Grad, Univ L'ville; Delta Sigma Delta; Omicron Delta Kappa; Phi Delta; Others.

EDWARDS, JAMES DON oc/J M Tull Professor of Accounting; b/Nov 12, 1926; h/325 St George Dr, Athens, GA 30601; ba/Athens; m/Clara; c/Jim; p/T T Edwards, Albany, LA; Reitha Mae Cranford, Albany; ed/BS La St Univ 1949; MBA Univ Denver 1950; PhD Univ Tex 1953; mil/USN WWII 2 Yrs, Disch'd 3rd Class Petty Ofcr; pa/Res Prof, Dept of Acctg & Bus Law, Col of Bus Adm, Univ Ga, Athens; Other Tchg & Adm Positions: Univ Denver, Univ Tex, Mich St Univ, Univ Minn; CPA, Tex; Vis Scholar Stanford Univ 1967-68; Clem-King, Univ Manitoba, Lectr 1971; Dist'd Lectr Tour Soc of Indust Accts 1973; Past Pres, Chmships & Coms Am Acctg Assn; Public Review Bd Arthur Andersen & Co 1974-78; Grad Sch Coun, Univ Ga 1974-77; Acctg Forum Com, Ga Soc CPAs 1974-75; Hon Mem Edit Adv Bd Am Biogl Inst; NAA Res Foun; Beta Alpha Psi Nat Adv Coun 1975; Res Com Nat Assn Accts 1972-75; Bd of Examrs for CPA Exam, Am Inst CPAs 1972-77; Trustee Fin Acctg Foun; Bd Regents Bank Adm Inst 1975-78; Conslt USAF Controller Gen; Contbg Editor to "What to Read" (*Jour of Accountancy*); Bd Stds, Schs of Profl Acctg; Other Profl Activs; hon/1st Outstg Acct Awd, Nat Coun Beta Alpha Psi; Outstg Acctg Edr Awd, Am Acctg Assn; Pub'd Author; Biogl Listings.

EDWARDS, JAMES HARRELL oc/Senator; b/Nov 25, 1926; h/PO Box 524, Rt 3, Granite Falls, NC 38630; ba/Raleigh, NC; p/James J and Ella R Edwards, Ayden, NC; ed/Att'd: Atl Christian Col, E Carolina Univ, Univ Miami; mil/USNR; pa/Former Staff Adjuster, NC Farm Bus Mutual Ins Co; SEn Adjustmt Co, Hickory: Assoc'd w 1959-, Owner/Mgr SEn Hickory Ofc, Pres; Pres Edwards & Assocs, Hickory (Pvt Detective Firm); cp/Elected to Serve in 24th Senatorial Dist, NC; Elected to Serve in Ho of Reps, 34th Dist 1975-76, 1977-78; Mem Num House Coms; Appt'd Mem Public Sch Employees' Salaries Study Comm; Life Mem VFW; Am Legion; Moose Lodge; 32° Mason; York Rite Mason; Shriner; r/Bethlehem Luth Ch.

EDWARDS, JOE E oc/Director of Evangelism and Home Missions of Alabama; b/Sept 25, 1939; h/Birmingham, AL; ba/Ch of God St Hdqtrs, Drawer A, B'ham, AL 35228; m/Pansy Harrison; c/Pamelia Jo, Shelia Ann, Donna Sue; p/Emmette O and Estelle Edwards, Florala, AL; ed/S En, Lee Col; pa/Min, Dir Evangelism & Home Mission of Ala; r/Chs of God; hon/Awd of Excell Ldrship; Contbr *Sylacauga News, Sylacauga Nurse's School, On Guard Magazine.*

EDWARDS, JULIAN WARD oc/State Representative; b/Feb 28, 1930; h/Garward Cir, Butler, GA 31006; m/Billie Salmon; c/Hallie Ward; p/Julian Willis and Lillian Edwards; ed/Ga Mil Col; Univ Ga; John Gupton Sch of Mortuary; mil/Entered as Pvt, Released as Sgt, Ser in NEn Air Command 1952-54; pa/Mortician Edwards Funeral Home, Butler; cp/Aide to Lt Gov of Ga 1958-62; Liaison Ofcr, St Hwy Dept 1963-64; Ga St Rep 1967-; Dem Majority Whip, Ga Ho of Reps 1970-71, Secy 1973-; Del Ga St Dem Exec Com 1970-; Mem St Dem Exec Comt, Ga 1974-; Chm 3rd Dist Legis Caucus; Former Secy Dem Caucus; Del Nat Conv in Miami, 1972; VFW; Elks; Kiwanis; r/Meth.

EDWARDS, LYMAN M oc/Engineer; Technical Consultant; b/Jan 13, 1908; h/3638 Aberdeen, Houston, TX 77025; ba/Houston; m/Thelma W; c/James Paul, Robert Bruce, Kent Martin; p/L P and Lela L Edwards (dec); ed/BA, BS Univ Okla; mil/USN Capt, Ret'd; pa/Tech Conslt to Pres Petrol & Minerals Group, Dresser Industs, Inc; Mgr Engrg Dresser Atlas Corp, Dresser Ctr; Mgr Res & Engrg Pan Geo Atlas Corp; Sr Field

Engr Schlumberger Well Surveying Corp; Design Engr (Geophy Instrumentation) Champlin Refining Co; Soc Profl Well Log Analysts; Houston Geological Soc; AIME; Chm 1st NASA Technol Transfer Conf 1974; Mem Steering Com: Dept Energy Geothermal Instrumentation, Dept Energy Geothermal Drilling, NASA, Dept Energy Magma Drilling Prog, Others; Tech Adv Com Los Alamos Sci Labs, Geothermal Hot Dry Rock Prog; Tech Adv Com Univ Houston, Clear Lake City Technol Prog; Adv Com for Doct Sci Degs, Univ Tex-El Paso; cp/Chm Houston C of C Sci & Technol Com; r/Meth; hon/Mexican Govt Aztec Awd; Holder Num US & Fgn Patents in Elect Technol; Bronze Star Medal.

EDWARDS, MARTHA JO GEREN oc/Associate Professor and Director of Radiologic Sciences; b/May 1, 1947; h/Maitland, FL; m/Gordon L; p/G L and Minnie Sue Geren, Cleveland, TN; ed/BS Univ Ala 1972; MEd Memphis St Univ 1975; Doct Cand Univ Fla; pa/Asst Prof Univ Tenn Ctr for Hlth Sci; Asst Prof Brevard Commun Col; Dir & Assoc Prof Rad Scis, Univ Ctrl Fla; Fla Soc Radiologic Technol, VP 1980; Ctrl Fla Soc of Radiologic Technol, Pres 1980; Am Soc Radiologic Technol, Cand Secy-Treas 1980; r/Prot; hon/Excell in Tchg Awd 1979, 1980; Author: "Evaluating Students' Clinical Performance in the Health Sciences" 1977; "Curriculum Guide in Cardiovascular Imaging Technology" 1978.

EDWARDS, RICHMOND SUMMERS oc/Instructor; b/July 11, 1945; h/614 Fruitwood, Hot Springs, AR 71901; ba/Same; m/Zelda; c/Shannon, Bryan; p/Daniel R (dec) and Mary E Edwards, Royal, AR; ed/BS Ark Tech Univ; MSE Univ Ark; pa/Instr Garland Co Commun Col & Hot Springs HS; NEA; AEA; FEA; HSEA; HSCTA; Ark Sci Tchrs Assn; r/So Bapt; hon/Ark St Del to Nat Sci & Humanities Symposium at West Point; Jr Acad of Sci Awds; Nat Sci Yth Congress; Westinghouse Awd; Tomorrow's Scists & Engrs.

EDWARDS, THELMA CLIETT oc/Teacher; b/Aug 26, 1908; h/1940; W Greenbriar Ave, Orange, TX 77630; ba/Orange; m/Earl C; c/Jack C; p/W T (dec) and Lucy Murray Cliett (dec); ed/BSE; MSE; Psychological Examr Lic; pa/Tchr in Blind Coop, Little Cypress Sch; CTA; TSTA; NEA; Delta Kappa Gamma;cp/Lit Clb; Jury Ser; Wk for Local Cands; r/Bapt.

EDWARDS, WILLIE GEORGE oc/Administrative Assistant and Classroom Teacher; b/May 11, 1945; h/Albany, GA; m/Portia T McLaurin; c/Joseph, Michael; p/Douglas Atkins (dec); Willie Mae Edwards (dec); ed/BS Albany St Col 1966; MEd Univ Ga 1973; Cand Masters Deg Valdosta St Col; pa/Adm Asst M C King Jr HS; Pres Elect Ga Coun of Social Scis; Past Pres Dorgherty Co Assn Classroom Tchrs, Dist II Chm Social Scis; cp/Omega Psi Phi; r/River Rd Ch of Christ: Music Dir; hon/Tchr of Yr 1969; Omega Man of Yr 1978; JCs Outstg Yng Man Am 1979.

EGAN, BRIAN J oc/Pastor; ba/St Bernard, AL; p/James Egan (dec); Bridget Egan, Holmes, PA; ed/BA (Phil), BA (Sociol) Benedictine Col; MA Notre Dame Univ; ThM Princeton Theol Sem; Grad Work Univ Ala; pa/Pres So Benedictine Col, St Bernard; Former Pastor 2 Mission Chs in Appalachia, Ky & Tenn; Pres St Bernard Col, Cullman, Ala; Chaplain Penn St Univ, St Col, Pa; Dir Pax Romana, Intl Cath Student Movemt, NY; Chaplain to Students of Georgian Ct Col & Ocean Co Col, Lakewood, NJ; Mem Bd Trustees: Friendly Sons of St Patrick of Jersey Shore, Nat Conf of Christians & Jews, NY; Bd Trustees Nat Newman Foun; Mem Exec Bd Nat Cath Ednl Assn; Pres Ch Related Cols of S; Pres Ala Assn Col Admrs; Exec Bd NJ Cath Campus Min 1972-73; 3 Yr Term Served on Priests' Coun of Trenton Diocese; Exec Bd Coun of Priests 1972-75; VP Coun Priests 1974-75; cp/Bd Dirs YMCA, Lakewood; r/Cath; hon/Nom for 1 of Nation's 10 Outstg Yg Men in US 1959; Ldr in Ecumenical Activs in S; Featured in *Time*, 1958; Outstg Yg Man Ala, JCs.

EHRLE, SALLY RENE ALLEN oc/Educator; Government Official; h/8327 Donoghue Dr, New Carrollton, MD 20784; m/Raymond A; p/Lawrence C Allen, Lakewood, OH; Irene Siegal Allen (dec); ed/BA w hons; MA; Doct Cand Univ So Cal; pa/Educr; Govt Ofcl Brookings Inst; Exec Coun Nat Area Chapt Am Soc for Public Adm; cp/LWV, Prince George's Co (Md); hon/Am Polit Sci Assn Congl Fellow; Under-Secy of HEW Awd.

EHRLICH, BERNARD HERBERT oc/Lawyer, Trade Association Executive; b/Apr 3, 1927; h/507 Bonifant St, Siver Spring, MD 20910; ba/Wash DC; m/Edna Kraft; c/Vivian Rose, Beverly Denise, Brenda Susan, Lisa Jean; p/Zachary and Elsie Klein Ehrlich, Silver Spring, MD; ed/LLB 1949; JD, MA 1950; mil/USNR 1943-45; pa/Am Bar Assn; Bar Assn DC; Am Soc Int Law; Am Hist Assn; cp/Pres Com on Employment of Handicapped; Phi Beta Kappa; Nu Beta Epsilon; Phi Delta Pi; r/Jewish; hon/Num Awds Incl'g Signif Ser Am Inst Laundering; NATTS; NACS; NHSC.

EICHENLAUB, RICHARD JEFFREY oc/Minister; b/June 18, 1952; h/PO Box 186, Hookerton, NC 28538; m/Nancy Evelyn Edinger;

p/Valentine Dennis and Shirley Ann Gardner Eichenlaub, Cherry Hill, NJ; ed/BA Atlantic Christian Col 1974; MDiv SEn Bapt Theol Sem 1980; Cert'd by St NC EMT 1980; pa/Pastor: Aldine Univ Meth Ch 1974-75, Spotswood U Meth Ch 1975-77, Mattamuskeet U Meth Ch 1977-78, Ctrl Christian Ch 1978-79, Hookerton Christian Ch 1979-; Houseparent Haven House Inc 1978; Disciples Grp; Lectionary Grp; Asst Dir Camp Agape 1980; cp/Chaplain of Hookerton Vol Fire Dept & Resque Squad & Greene Co Rescue Squad; NC St Firemen's Assn; NC St Assn Rescue Squads; r/Christian Ch; Ordained Min 1980; hon/Sigma Pi Alpha; Hookerton Rescue Squad Man of Yr 1980.

EIDSON, JOHN OLIN oc/Educator; b/Dec 10, 1908; h/362 Valley Green Dr, NE, Atlanta, GA 30342; ba/Atlanta; m/Perrin Cudd; p/Oin Marvin and Margaret Rushton Eidson (dec); ed/AB Wofford Col 1929; MA Vanderbilt Univ 1930; PhD Duke Univ 1941; mil/AUS Inf 1942-46 Maj; USAR Lt Col; pa/VChancellor Univ Sys of Ga, Atlanta 1971-76; Pres Ga Soc Col 1968-71; Dean Arts & Sci, Univ Ga 1957-68; Dir Univ Ctr in Ga 1953-57; Fac (Eng Instr to Prof Am Lit) Univ Ga 1936-68; Editor "Ga Review" 1950-57; Bd Dirs Intl Inst Ed; cp/Pres 50 Yr Clb of Wofford Col 1980-; Pres Univ Ga Botanical Garden 1981-; BSA: Former VP Coastal Empire Coun, Exec Bd Atlanta BSa; Dem; r/Meth; hon/M B Michael Awd for Res; Fulbright Prof of Am Lit, Univ Freiburg, Germany; Fulbright Prof Am Studies, Univ Bonn, Germany 1977-78; Phi Beta Kappa, Ofcr.

EILERMAN, CHARLES BERNARD oc/Economic Consultant; b/Mar 5, 1947; h/22 Swain Ct, Covington, KY 41011; ba/Louisville; p/Arthur (dec) and Carmen Eilerman, Covington, KY; ed/AB Thomas More Col 1968; MBA Harvard Univ 1970; pa/Ec Conslt; Am Plan'g Assn; Ky Plan'g Assn; Ky Ec Assn; cp/V-Chm 3rd Cent; Dir Mar of Dimes, Ohio Val; Trustee Commonwlth Preserv Coun; r/Rom Cath; hon/Outstg Yng Men Am 1975; Trustee Spirit of L'ville Foun.

EL-BAYADI, NAGUI RIZK oc/General Surgeon; b/Nov 16, 1934; h/Montieth Br Rd, Sylva, NC 28779; ba/Sylva, NC; m/Marion Openshaw; c/Karen Mona, Sandra Lynn; p/Rizk El-Bayadi, Sylva, NC; Mounira El-Bayadi (dec); ed/MB; ChB Cairo 1957; FRCS Edinburgh 1963; FACS 1972; pa/Att'g Sur CJ Harris Hosp: Past Chief of Staff & Chief of Surg; Am Bd of Surg 1970; cp/Rotarian, Past Dir; r/Epis.

ELBJORN, CHARLES DAVID oc/Assistant Trust Officer and Assistant Cashier; b/Dec 19, 1955; h/4800 N Stanton #15, El Paso, TX 79902; ba/El Paso; p/V E Nielsen, Fabens, TX; ed/Cand Deg Univ Tex El Paso; pa/Asst Trust Ofcr & Asst Cashier, St Nat Bank of El Paso; El Pso Estate Plan'g Coun; cp/Bd Dirs St Marguaret's Ctr for Chd; r/Meth; hon/W/W Am HS Students 1973.

ELDER, MARK LEE oc/University Research Administrator; Novelist; b/May 3, 1935; h/1157 Robin Hood, Norman, OK 73069; ba/Norman; m/Wanda; c/Staci; p/Mark Gray Elder (dec); Ethel Kiker; ed/BA 1965, MA 1973 OU; mil/AUS 1954-56; pa/Univ Res Admr Univ Okla; Tech Editor; Sem Spkr; Author Novels: *Jedcrow, Wolf Hunt, The Varga Cross*; hon/Univ Okla Profl Writing Awd.

ELEBASH, HUNLEY AGEE oc/Episcopal Bishop; b/Jul 27, 1923; h/1905 Live Oak Pkwy, Wilmington, NC 28403; ba/Wilmington; m/Maurine Ashton; c/David Hunley, Brett Randolph; p/Eugene Perrin and Ann Hunley Elebash (dec); ed/BS Univ S 1944; BD 1950; DD 1969; mil/USMC 1/Lt; pa/Epis Bishop of Diocese of E Carolina; Rector, Exec Secy, Bishop Coadjutor; r/Epis Ch: Ordained Priest 1951; Consecrated Bishop 1968.

ELIAS, HAROLD J oc/Department Head, Advertising and Marketing Services Manager, Director Corporate Communications; ed/BFA, MFA Sch of Art Inst of Chgo; Further Study Mich St Univ, DePaul Univ, Univ Mich; PhD Hamilton St Univ; mil/USAF 1941-45; pa/Asst/Acting Dir, Hackley Art Gal, Muskegon, Mich 1952-57; Lectr/Demonstrator Grumbacher and Winsor & Newton Cos 1976-80; Art Instr, Muskegon Commun Col 1952-57; Cont'g Ed, St Joseph, Mich 1959-60; Art Instr: Lake Mich Col 1964-67, Kilgore Col 1969-72, LeTourneau Col 1974-75; Asst Prof Art, Ambassador Col, Big Sandy, Tex 1973-77; Instr Stephen F Austin St Univ 1977-78, Kilgore Col 1978-80, Tarrant Co Jr Col 1980-; Mgr Advtg & Mktg Ser, R G LeTourneau Inc; Hd Indust Art Dept, Clark Equip Co, Constrn Machinery Div 1957-67; Mktg Ser Supvr, Stemco Mfg Co 1971-72; Dir Corp Communs, Wellman Industs Inc 1972-74; Mktg Sers Dept, Lebus Intl Inc 1974-77; Pres Indust Illust'd 1977-80; Asst Dir Art/Creative, Radio Shack/Tandy Corp 1980; Am Artists Profl Leag; Am Fed Arts; Am Assn Museums; Artists Equity; Chgo Soc Artists; Intl Coun Museums; Intl Inst Arts & Lttrs; Col Art Assn Am; Mich Acad Sci, Arts & Lttrs; Mich Watercolor Soc; Ala Watercolor Soc; Bd Dirs Nat Mgmt Assn: Mgmt Devel Com 1966, Public Relats Com 1967 (Resigned When He Moved from St); cp/Muskegon Commun Theatre 1952-54; VP Fine Arts Assn, Muskegon 1952-53; Chm Fine Arts Fest, SWn Mich 1961; Mich Dir Am Art Wk 1962-65; Regional Dir Am Art Wk 1964-65; Appt'd by Gov of

PERSONALITIES OF THE SOUTH

Mich to Mich Coun for the Arts 1964; Appt'd by Gov of Tex to Tex Comm on the Arts & Humanities 1970-77; Pres E Tex Fine Arts Assn 1971; Advr Bd of Dirs Longview Symph Assn 1971; Bd Dirs Longview U Fund 1971; Chm Public Relats Com, BSA, E Tex Chapt 1971; Longview C of C: Chm Info & Public Relats Com, Civic Affairs Com; Art Coun of Ft Worth & Tarrant Co: Govt Com, Mktg Com; hon/Exhib'g Artist in Over 90 Juried Regional & Nat Exhibs Incl'g Am Art Today, Metro Museum of Art, Penn Acad of Fine Arts, Detroit Inst of Art, Chgo Art Inst, Creative Gal NY, Denver Art Museum & Others; Represented in Intl Sculpture Competition, Brussels, Belgium; Over 200 One-Man Shows throughout US; Winner Many Awds; W/W: Am Art, Fin & Indust, Mid-W, S&SW; Personalities of W&MW; Men of Achmt; Intl W/W: Commun Ser, Art & Antiques; DIB; Contemporary Personages; Am Artists of Renown.

ELIAS, KAREN LYNN oc/Advisor; b/July 2, 1949; h/2404 W 8th #10, Stillwater, OK 74074; ba/Stillwater; p/Julius Berman, Ponca City, OK; Dorothy Berman, Ponca City, OK; ed/BS Ed; MS Distb Ed; pa/St DECA Advr for Voc Ed; Dir Yth Sers, Ldrship Devel Inst; Delta Pi Epsilon; Yth Rallies; Summer Camps for Yths; Conslt Work for Ldrship Activs; cp/Alpha Gamma Delta; Okla City Ldrship Bd; r/Presb; hon/LDI Fdr's Awd.

ELIZONDO, ALFREDO GERUSA oc/Funeral Director; b/Sept 17, 1951; m/Margaret Majia; c/Alfredo Rolando, Orlando Alberto, Margaret Lleanna, Gleida Denise; p/Mr and Mrs Alfredo A Elizondo, San Benito, TX; ed/Att'd Pan Am Univ; MS Commonwlth Col of Scis 1973; pa/Garza Funeral Home 7 Yrs; Mgr Thomae-Garza Funeral Dirs; cp/Lions Clb Intl; Denldr BSA Den 2 Pack 21; Rio Grande Val Coun; Coach Little Leag Baseball; Bowie Elem PTA.

ELKINS, JAMES ANDREW JR oc/Attorney at Law; b/Jan 24, 1940; h/6130 Canterbury Dr, Columbus, Ga 31904; ba/Columbus; m/Martha Lee; c/James A III, Allen Lee, Martha Lee; p/James A (dec) and Dorris Elkins, Columbus, GA; ed/AB Univ of S 1962; JD Univ Ga 1965; pa/Am Trial Lwyrs Assn; Ga Trial Lwyrs Assn; Ga Assn Criminal Defense Lwyrs; Columbus Lwyrs Clb; St Bar Ga; cp/Commun Org on Drug Abuse 1971-76; Bd Dirs Pioneer Little Leag of Columbus 1977-79, Secy 1978-79; r/Epis.

ELKINS, RUSSELL KEITH oc/Special Assignment News Reporter; b/Aug 8, 1955; h/Huntsville, AL; ba/WHNT-TV News, PO Box 19, H'ville, AL 35804; p/C Houston and Frances Elkins, Tanner, AL; ed/BA Univ Ala 1977; pa/TV News; H'ville Press Clb Bd Dirs; Bd Dirs Univ Ala Sch Communs Alumni Assn; cp/Madison Co Yng Dems VP; r/Prot; hon/Ala Broadcasters Assn S'ship Recip 1976; Univ Ala S'ship Recip 1977; Cahaba Temple Awd of Merit 1979; H'ville JCs Commun News Ser Awd 1979; Outstg Yng Men of Am Nom 1980.

ELLINGER, RICHARD ALVIN oc/Sales Representative; b/Apr 22, 1942; h/1305 Barterbrock Rd, Staunton, VA 24401; ba/Staunton; p/Otho Elwood and Katherine Neese Ellinger, Staunton, VA; p/Farming & Truck Leasing, Obaugh Ford; r/Seventh Day Adventist; hon/Mem Profl Sale Coun; Mem Gold Clb 1978.

ELLIOT, SIMON oc/Attorney at Law, Industrialist; b/Feb 4, 1912; h/Siera Gorda 39 Mexico 10 D F; c/Helen; ed/LLB, JD NYU Law Sch; pa/Fdr & Pres Industrias Sorel SA VP Fibras Mexianas SA, Encajes Mexcanos SA; Fdr & Pres Park Realty Co & S7 E Realty Co, NY; Contbr to Textile Pubs; Wkly Review in *La Voz de Mexico*; cp/Active in charitable, Hlth & Sport Orgs; hon/Men of Achmt; W/W S&SW; DIB.

ELLIOTT, DOROTHY VIRGINIA oc/Professor; b/Feb 12, 1911; p/dec; ed/Grace Hosp Sch of Nsg 1932; BS Ohio St Univ 1937; MS 1943; MA Columbia Univ; EdD 1955; mil/AUS Nurse Corps Lt Col, Ret'd; pa/Prof Hlth Care Mgmt & Res Techniques; Nsg Ser Adm; Dir Nsg Ed; Ednl Conslt Army Nurse Corps; Kappa Delta Pi; Pi Lambda Theta; Delta Kappa Gamma; The Ret'd Ofcrs Assn; Ret'd Army Nurse Corps Assn; cp/DAR; Am Legion; hon/Mil Campaign Medals; Army Commend Medal; Author Med & Tech Manuals for AUS.

ELLIOTT, FRANK DWIGHT oc/Author, Playwright; b/July 15, 1928; h/905 E King St, Boone, NC 28607; ba/Boone; m/Betty Barnes; c/Deborah E Carrol, Mark, Lydia; p/Adlai Elzy and Lula Gantt Elliott, Fallston, NC; ed/Acctg Evans Col of Commerce; mil/USAF 1950-54, Airman of Month, Chateauroux AFB Apr 1954; pa/Partner Black Bear Motel; cp/Ofcr, Dir Gastonia Jr C of C, Spoke Awd, Cert of Merit; Ofcr, Dir Forest City Lions Clb & C of C; Pres, Ofcr & Dir Grandfather Mtn Motel Assn; Area & Alt Gov NC Motel Assn; Boone Area C of C; Boone Lions Clb; Watuaga Swim Assn; Scoutmaster Troop 14, Gastonia BSA; r/Boone Meth Ch: Mem; Deacon & SS Supt Linden ARP Ch, Gastonia; hon/Best Supporting Actor 1949, Shelby Little Theater; Merit Awd "Novels," Reg Writers Conf Appalachian St Univ; Pub'd Author: *God Made Little Green Apples, Goodnight Angel in Heaven, Mancha;*

Personalities of S 1976-77, 1977-78; Chm Spring Fest in Mtns 1979; Lion of Yr Awd, Boone Lions Clb 1978-79; Editor *The Mountain Lion* 1978-79; Top Broom Salesman Boone Lions Clb 1978-79; Partner & Gen Mgr Scottish Inns of Boone 1979.

ELLIOTT, J ROBERT oc/Bank Vice President; b/Mar 31, 1951; h/Dallas, TX; ba/Dallas; m/Stephanie; p/Andrew C (dec) and Virginia M Elliott (dec); ed/BBA Tex A&M Univ 1974; pa/VP, Commercial Loan Ofcr, Energy Dept, Mercantile Nat Bank 1974-; Am Assn Petro Landmen; Dallas Assn Petro Landmen; Intl Assn Drilling Contractors; cp/Dallas Aux Edna Gladney Home of Ft Worth; r/Meth.

ELLIOTT, SHIRLEY RAE oc/Supervisory Medical Technologist; b/Oct 21, 1922; h/1007 Bentley Circle, Gallatin, TN 37066; ba/Nashville, TN; m/Floyd S; c/Linda Rae, Teresa M, Rita Kay, Susan I, John Roger, Katherine C, Floyd S Jr; p/John R (dec) and Carrie K Reynolds (dec); ed/Duke Univ 1942-43; Univ Tex 1942-43; pa/VA Med Ctr: Med Tech 1973-80, Adm Fee Basis Tests 1973-80; ASMT; ASCLT, Nom Com 1977, 2nd VP 1980; TSCM; Royal Soc Hlth; Affil Mem ASCP; cp/Sumner Co Hist Soc; r/Meth; hon/Gallatin C of C Mother of Yr 1976; Middle Tenn Nom Profl & Tech VA Employee of Yr 1976.

ELLIOTT, STEPHEN MARION oc/Real Estate Development and Investment; b/Oct 15, 1945; h/9204 Flickering Shadow, Dallas, TX 75243; ba/Dallas; m/Carol Anne; p/John Franklin and Winifred Key Elliott, Fort Worth, TX; ed/BBA Univ Tex-Arlington 1968; Cert in Real Est So Meth Univ 1974; Furthur Study; pa/Self-employed Real Est 1976-; VP Baldwin-Harris Inc, Dallas 1971-76; Asst Property Mgr Mayflower Investmt Co, Dallas 1969-71; Proj Mgr San-Suz Apts, Arlington 1968-69; Life Mem Delta Sigma Pi; Assoc Mem Dallas Bd Realtors; Bd Dirs NW Dallas Co C of C; Inst Real Est Mgmt; Bd Dirs Dallas Chapt BOMA; Others; r/Presb; hon/NWDCCC: Most Mbrships Sold, Largest Amount in Chamber Mbrships, Pavement Pounder Awd, Teamwork Awd; Life Mem Hustler's Clb, NWDCCC; Outstg Yg Men Am; W/W: S&SW, Am.

ELLIOTT, WILLIAM WAYNE oc/Company President, Manufacturing Representative; b/Dec 16, 1943; h/444 Birch Ln, Richardson, TX 75081; m/Wilma; c/Michelle Paige; p/Helen Rose Wagner, Great Bend, KS; ed/BA St Thomas Univ 1964; mil/USAF 1964-66 Flight Engr; pa/Pres Bumper Inc; Furniture Mfg Rep, Wholesale Furn Sales, Deville Furn; Schwadic Corp 1970-74; Stock Broker Stiefel Nicholaus Corp 1968-70; ADU Sales, Wichita Eagle 1966-68; SW Roadrunners Assn; Furn Mfg Assn; Nat Home Furn Assn VGov; cp/Dallas Golf Assn; Bd Govs Canyon Creer Country Clb; K of C; Cath Mens Clb; r/Roman Cath; hon/Indust Salesman of Yr Awd 1972, 73, 75; Outstg Perf Awd 1979.

ELLIS, BONNIE LEE oc/Dental Assistant, Homemaker; b/Sept 5, 1929; h/6018 Reefridge, San Antonio, TX 78242; ba/San Antonia; m/Bobbie A; c/Michael, Cynthia, Barry; pa/Dental Asst.

ELLIS, ROY FRAZIER oc/School Superintendent; b/Jan 22, 1944; ba/Rt 9 Box 8, Elizabethton, TN; m/Barbara; c/Corey Frazeir, Kala Brooke; p/Clarence Ellis (dec); Hazel Ellis Woods, Knox, TN; ed/BS; MS; EdD; pa/Supt Elizabethton City Schs; Am Assn Sch Admrs; Tenn Org Sch Supt; Phi Delta Kappa; Phi Kappa Phi; Kappa Delta Phi; r/Bapt; hon/Outstg Sec'dy Edr in Am 1973; Kappa Delta Phi.

ELLIS, VERNE R oc/Chief of Police; b/May 30, 1929; h/1101 Lou Ann, Corsicana, TX 75110; ba/Corsicana; m/Beulah Leona; c/V Richard Jr, David E, Timothy P; p/C W and Ruth Ellis, Bellaire, TX; ed/BA Psych; pa/Intl Chief's of Police; cp/Rotary Clb; Lions Intl; r/Bapt; hon/Nat FBI Acad 116th Session; Adv'd Cert in Law Enforcement.

ELLIS, WILLIAM L oc/World Witness Director; b/Dec 7, 1940; h/PO Box 1081, Dunn, NC 28334; m/Barbara; p/Mr and Mrs L W Ellis, Whiteville, NC; ed/ThB, Att'd NC Wesleyan, Moody Bible Inst; BD, MDiv, DMin Luther Rice Sem; pa/World Witness Dir, Pentecostal Free Will Bapt Ch Inc; Instr Heritage Bible Col.

ELLISON, DARRELL F oc/Executive; b/Jan 19, 1941; h/1900 Piedmont Rd, Marietta, GA 30062; m/Linda; c/Ty D, Tracie L, Tonya J, Tara J, Craig S; p/Ode O and Ruth Faye Ellison, Monticello, IA; ed/BS Univ Neb; mil/USAF; pa/Pres Help Unltd Inc; Pres Transworld Sers Inc; r/Luth.

ELLISON, DOROTHY S oc/Teacher; b/Oct 5, 1916; h/Sumiton, AL; c/Curtis W, Anne E Hobbs, James M, Jeanne E Meyer; p/William S (dec) and Carrie Dunsieth Standfield (dec); ed/AB Judson Col 1941; MA Univ Ala 1961; pa/Sci Tchr: Dora HS 1952-77, Sumiton Jr HS 1944-49, Damascus HS 1941-42; Chem Control Lab, Ammonia Plant, TVA 1943; Walker Co Ed Assn, Sci Sect Chm 2 Terms; Ala Ed Assn, Sci Sect Chm; NEA; Nat Assn Ret'd Tchrs; Ala Acd Sci, Ed Sect V-Chm; Suiton PTA,

Pres; Dora HS PTA; Delta Kappa Gamma, Walker Co Chapt 1st VP; Nat Assn Bio Tchrs; cp/Dora HS Sci Clb, Orgr & Sponsor; Sumiton Lib Bd Chm; Carl Elliot Reg Lib Bd, Chm, V-Chm; r/U Meth: Adm Bd; hon/Dora HS Yrbook Dedication 1956, 68; Top 10 in *McCalls* Magazine's Nat Outstg Tchrs 1958; Nat Assn of Biol Tchrs Outstg Bio Tchr Awd, St of Ala 1976; Author Decorating Craft *Ideas Magazine* June 1980.

ELLISON, ROBERT ALEXANDER oc/Assistant Attorney General; b/Jan 21, 1915; ba/Virgin Islands Dept of Law, PO Box 1074, Christiansted, St Croix, Virgin Islands 00820; m/Vivian; c/Robert, Charles; p/Robert (dec) and Marie Carter Ellison (dec); ed/AB NYC Col 1941; JD Brooklyn Law Sch 1952; pa/Chief, Crim/Fam Law Div, VI Dept Law; Instr Police Sci & Bus Law, Col of VI; Asst Atty Gen, VI Dept Law; Acad Crim Just Scis; Nat Dist Atty's Assn; Am Arbitration Assn; VI Bd of Parole, Past Chm; VI Bar Assn, Past Pres; cp/Rotary Intl; Counsel to VI Parole Bd; Gov's Con on Hwy Saftey; r/AME; hon/Phi Eta Sigma, Ohio Univ.

ELLSWORTH, LINDA DIANE VOLLMAR oc/Historian & Bureau Chief; b/Nov 22, 1945; h/9330 Scenic Hwy, Pensacola, FL 32504; ba/Pensacola; m/Lucius Fuller; p/R E and Julia A Vollmar, Montgomery, MN; ed/BA Macalester Col; MA Univ Del; pa/Histn & Chief Bur Res & Pub, Hist Pensacola Preserv Bd; AASLH; Fla Hist Soc; Record'g Secy Gulf Coast Hist & Humanities Conf; AAUW, Pensacola Br: 1/VP 1974-76, Pres 1976-78; hon/Phi Alpha Theta; NEH Awd for Mus Profls; Hagley F'ship, Univ Del.

ELLZEY, FRANCIS LINDSEY (SAM) oc/Professional Bail Bondsman; b/Dec 10, 1951; h/Rt 1 Box 278, Soso, MS 39480; ba/Same; m/Shelia R Harris; c/Fred Lindsey; p/Fred (dec) and Willie Mae Knight Ellzey (dec); ed/AA Jones Count Jr Col; mil/AUS; pa/Owner Ellzey Bonding Co; Former Hd of Fugitive Investigations & St Supvn fo Sentinel Bonding Co; cp/Am Legion; Master Mason, Hebron Lodge 515; Notary Public; Soso JCs; W Jones JCs; r/Bapt; hon/Expert M14, M16 AUS; Outstg Promotion of Intl Newspaper Carrier Day 1975.

ELMORE, PONCE LEROY oc/Retired; b/Sept 4, 1914; h/205 Vinewood Dr, Sanford, FL 32771; m/Mary E; c/Lawrence L, Sandra L Atchley, Marylee Haddon; p/Wheller (dec) and Virginia Elmore (dec); mil/USN 20 Yrs, Ret'd Chief Aviation Mech; pa/Former: Real Est Salesman, Cashier Dog Track, Heating & Air Conditioning Repairman; Editor USS Wasp Stinger Clb; cp/Life Mem Elks; Fleet Reserve Assn; r/Bapt; hon/Stinger of Yr 1981; Life Mem #8, USS WASP Stinger Clb; Real Est Salesman of Yr, Sanford; Rocky Mtn Golden Gloves Champ, Middle Weight 1937.

EMANUEL, ALICE HARRIET oc/Social Worker; b/Jan 12, 1947; p/Stuart J (dec) and Esther W Emanuel, Ocean Springs, MD; ed/BS Alcorn St Univ 1967; MSW LSU Sch of Social Work 1976; Further Study Univ So Miss, Gulf Coast Campus & William Carey Col on the Coast; pa/Harrison Co Dept Public Wel: Social Wkr in Tng 1967-71, Social Wkr III 1971-75, Supvr II 1976-81; Co Dir, Jackson Co Dept Public Wel 1981-; Assn of Black Social Wkrs, Secy St Chapt; Acad of Cert'd Social Wkrs; NASW, Secy St Chapt Bd Dirs; cp/Harrison Co Head Start, Policy Coun 1977-81, V-Chp 1979-80, Chp 1980-81; Alpha Kappa Alpha, Theta Zeta Omega Chapt, Chp 1983 Regional Conf; Bd Dirs Saraland Devel Corp; Am Cancer Soc, Minority Involvement Coun; U Meth Ch, Miss Conf, Coun on Yng Adult Mins; St Pauls U Meth Ch: Chm Coun on Mins, Com on Evangelism, Fin Com; r/Meth; hon/Outstg Yng Wom Am 1980; Cert of Apprec, St Hd Start Dirs 1981; Cert of Apprec, Harrison Co Hd Start Prog 1981.

EMBREE, THOMAS E oc/Loan Officer; b/Oct 14, 1936; h/512 Jupiter Way, Casselberry, FL 32707; ba/Orlando, FL; m/Beulah Ann LaForce; c/Paula Kay, Brian Keith, Darel Eugene; p/Willie M Embree, Madison, MO; Georgia C Freels Embree (dec); ed/HS Grad; mil/USN Ret'd Sr Chief Pers; pa/Coun-man, City of Casselberry 1972-75; Loan Ofcr, Navy Orlando Fed Credit Union; Ctrl Fla Chapt Fla Credit Union Leag, Secy 1979; cp/JCs: Local Dir, St VP/Intl Relats Dir; r/Meth; hon/Dist'd Ser Awd 1967; Elkton, Md JCs 1 of Md's 5 Outstg Yng Men 1967-68; Md JCs Outstg Yng Men Am 1968; JCI Senator #6658, Bel Air, Md, US JCs 1967.

EMBRY, CARLOS B JR oc/Administrator; b/Jul 29, 1941; h/Old Hartford Rd, Box 202, Beaver Dam, KY 42320; ba/Hartford, KY; m/Wanda Lou; c/Laura Ann, Barbara Ann, C B III; p/Carlos B Embry Sr (dec); Zora Romans Embry, Beaver Dam; ed/BS Wn Ky Univ; BD Adler Univ; MA Edison Col; pa/Dir Commun Devel for Ohio Co; cp/Treas Repub Party of Ky; Mayor City of Beaver Dam 1970-73; Former Ohio Co Judge; r/Beaver Dam Bapt Ch: Mem; hon/Outstg Yg Repub in Nation 1973-75.

EMDEN, KAREN ANNE oc/Assistant Professor, Lawyer; b/Mar 8, 1947; h/45 Mile Course, Williamsburg, VA 23185; ba/W'burg; m/Willard

F Jr; c/Patricia; p/John A and Helen R Gallucci, Piermont, NY: ed/AB, JD, Cert of Adv'd Study in Ed, Col of William & Mary; pa/Asst Prof Bus Adm, Col of William & Mary; Va St Bar; Va Wom's Bar Assn; Am Bar Assn; Va Trial Lwyr's Assn; Trial Lwyrs Assn of Am; Am Bus Law Assn; Real Property Com; 2nd VP & Former Secy-Treas Mid-Atlantic Bus Law Assn; Atty at Law, W'burg, Va 1976-; cp/Bd Dirs Va Peninsula Swim Union; Referee, Va Peninsula Swim Union Summer Swim Progs; r/Rom Cath; hon/Author "Interstate Succession, Wills and Estate Administration" in *Layman's Guide to Virginia Law*; Phi Beta Kappa; Kappa Delta Pi; W/W Am Wom.

EMMICK, ROGER SR oc/Registered Professional Nurse, USAF Officer; b/Jan 24, 1948; h/Orlean, NY; m/Paula Anne Batesky; c/Roger Jr, Heather, Steven; p/Walter J Jr and Eva Kathleen Passmore Emmick, Ellington, NY; ed/AAS Jamestown Commun Col 1971; BSN W Tex St Univ; mil/USN 1967-68 Hospitalman; USAF 1977- Capt; pa/Worked in Intensive Care Units; Primary Care Nurse Practitioner; ANA; TNA, Bd Mem & Govtl Affairs Rep 1979-80; AMA Nsg Br; cp/K of C, 3rd & 4th Deg Formations; Big Bros 1979; r/Cath; hon/Outstg Unit Awd 1978; Grad w Hons W Tex St Univ 1979; Jr Ofcr of Qtr, Reese AFB 1980.

EMMONS, JUDITH FLORENCE DILLEY oc/Nurse; b/Dec 18, 1942; h/308 Norton Dr, Longview, TX 75602; ba/Longview; m/James Franklin; c/Mark, Kristi, Jamie; p/Orville Lee Dilley (dec); Ophelia Key Dilley Brooks, Longview, TX; ed/AA 1975, LVN 1964 Kilgore Col Sch of Nsg; pa/RN Good Shepherd Hosp; TNA; ANA; cp/Beta Sigma Phi; PTA; r/Prot; hon/W/W Am Wom 1979-80; 15% Nat Ranked St Bds Exam Nsg 1975.

EMMONS, TETTA WANDA oc/Retired Laboratory Technician, Amateur Photographer; b/Aug 11, 1914; h/3629 Drexel Ave, Pt Arthur, TX 77640; m/Leroy G (dec); p/William Taylor (dec) and Sarah Addie West (dec); cp/Photo Soc of Am, Area Rep 1975; Pt Arthur Camera Clb: Color Slide Div Chm 2 Yrs, Pres 1961 & 73, VP 1978; Chm Color Slide Div CavOILcade Intl Photo Salon 1960 & 65, Dir 1970, Co-Dir 1972; Fin Chm Gulf Coast Camera Clb Coun 1965; GSCCC Color Slide Cnsltg Ser 1965; Dir GSCC 1966; Past Mem PTA; r/Ch of Christ; hon/Hon Mentions in Photo Intl Salons; Winner, Photo Contest, C of C; Judge Intl Salons in Houston, San Antonio & Pt Arthur, Tex & Shreveport, La; Silver Medal NY Salon; PSA Distbr of Instrn Slide Sets 1976.

EMORY, EMERSON oc/Physician, Psychiatrist, Editor-Publisher; b/Jan 29, 1925; ba/2814 S Beckley, Dallas, TX 75224; m/Peggy; c/Sharon, Karon, Emerson Jr; p/Mrs C B Emory, Dallas, TX; ed/Att'd Prairie View A&M 1940-43; BA cum laude Lincoln Univ 1948; MD Meharry Med Col 1952; mil/AUS 1943-46 Cpl; USNR 1949-80 Ret'd Capt; pa/Pvt Pract Psychi & Med; Chief Psychi Sers, Fed Correctional Inst, Seagoville, Tex 1972-73; Staff Psychi, Terrell St Hosp 1969-72; Acad Psychi & Law; World Med Assn; Nat Med Assn; Fellow Acad Psychosomatic Med; cp/Fdr & Past Pres Nat Naval Ofcrs Assn; Nat Pres Wash-Lincoln Alumni Assn of Dallss Inc; Former Cand for Mayor, City of Dallas; Cand for St Leg; Elks; K of C; Alpha Phi Alpha; r/Cath; hon/St Dept & AMA Cit for Vol Ser in Vietnam 1966; Editor-Publisher *Freedom's Journal* 1978-.

EMRICK, RAYMOND TERRY oc/Professor; b/Aug 9, 1915; h/108 Dogwood Dr, Olney, IL 62450; ba/Olney; p/Terry C Emrick (dec); M Pearl Emrick, Paris, IL; ed/BS, MS Ind St Univ; PhD Walden Univ; mil/USAF 1942-45, 1951-52, Ret'd Ofcr; pa/Prof Psychol & Human Relats; IPA; Phi Delta Kappa; ISU Alumni Assn; AAUP; WUMAA; cp/ROA; SCO; MOWW; VFW; r/Christian; hon/Mem Intl Biogl Assn; Intl Register Profiles; DIB; Men Achmt; Book of Honor; W/W in Am; Commun Ldrs & Noteworthy Ams; Col Acad Hons, ISU; Fellow ISU.

ENGELS, JANICE JEANNE oc/Religious Educator; b/Nov 16, 1931; h/2417 Caron Ln, Falls Ch, VA 22043; ba/Falls Ch; m/William A; c/Rebecca Lynn, William Arthur Jr; p/Thomas Raymond and Lucille Yann Jones, Jeffersontown, KY; ed/Att'd Columbia Bible Col 1949-52; pa/Dir Childhood Ed, Columbia Bapt Ch 1973-; No Va Pvt Sch Assn; Supt: Wom's Mission Union of Rappahanock Assn & Wom's Mission Union of Mid-Tidewater Assn; r/Bapt.

ENGERRAND, DORIS A DIESKOW oc/College Professor; b/Aug 7, 1925; h/1674 Pine Valley Rd, Milledgeville, GA 31061; ba/M'ville; m/Gabriel H; c/Steven, Kenneth, Jeannine; p/William J Sr and Alma Cords Dieskow (dec); ed/BS N Ga Col 1958, 59; MBE 1966, PhD Ga St Univ; pa/Prof Ga Col, M'ville; Bd Dirs ABCA; STC; ICA; NBEA; GAE, Secy Ga Col Chapt; AVA; GVA; VP GBEA; NSA; Acad Mtmt; So Mgmt; Sev Pubs; VP M'ville Br AAUW; r/Meth; hon/Beta Gamma Sigma Hon Frat; Delta Pi Epsilon Hon Soc; Pi Omega Pi Hon Soc; Star Tchr Lumpkin Co 1963, 66; Pilot of Yr, N Ga Chapt 99s Intl 1973; Outstg Fac Mem Bus Dept, Ga Col 1976.

ENGLAND, ARTHUR J oc/Justice; b/Dec 23, 1932; h/1002

Kenilworth Rd, Tallahassee, FL 32303; ba/Tallahasee; m/Morley Tenenbom; c/Andrea, Pamela, Ellen, Karen; p/Arthur J England (dec); Elsbeth Garber, Tallahassee; ed/BS; LLB; LLM; mil/Counter Intell Corp 1955-57; pa/Admitted to Bars of NY & Fla 1961; Pract Tax & Corporate Law: NY 1961-64, Fla 1964-70, 1973-74; Spec Tax Counsel to Fla Ho of Reps 1971, 72; Consumer Advr & Spec Counsel to Gov of Fla 1972, 73; Elected to Supreme Ct 1978; Adj Prof Law Fla St Univ Col Law 1971, 1978; Fla & NY Bars; ABA; Am Law Inst; Am Judic Soc; Inst Judicial Adm; Dade Co Bar Assn; Fla Rep to Nat Ctr for St Cts; Former Chm Fla Supreme Ct Judicial Ed Com & Adv Com on Appellate Rules; Other Profl Activs; cp/Bd Dirs Am Heart Assn, Fla Affil; Bd Trustees Temple Israel, Tallahassee; SEn Reg Bd Mem Anti-Defamation Leag B'nai B'rith; r/Hebrew; hon/Beta Sigma; Grad Magna Cum Laude; Order of Coif; Pub'd Author.

ENGLAND, DICKIE WEST oc/Editor; b/Aug 22, 1953; h/Springfield, VA; ba/Informatics Inc, 6811 Kenilworth Ave, Riverdale, MD; m/Thomas F; c/Daniel Grey; p/R H and Nola B West, Limestone, TN; ed/BA magna cum laude 1974; MA summa cum laude Univ Pgh 1976; Post Grad Studies Univ Pgh; pa/Application Mgr, Pubs Sers, Informatics Inc 1980-; Asst to Pres, Am Technol Univ, Killeen, Tex 1977-79; Speechwriter, Rockwell Intl 1976; Phi Kappa Phi; Delta Sigma Rho-Tau Kappa Alpha; So Speech Assn; Speech Commun Assn; Penn Speech Assn; cp/Mar of Dimes; r/Epis; hon/Valedictorian Schlr, Univ Tenn 1971-72; Mellon Fellow Univ Pgh 1974-76; Mortar Bd Dist'd Grad; Tchg Fellow Univ Pgh 1975-77; Author "The Republicans in 1976: Rhetorical Nemeses" SCAP Conv 1976.

ENGLAND, JAMES CALVIN oc/Emergency Medical Technician; b/Dec 13, 1952; h/151 Pk Manor, Middlesboro, KY 40965; ba/M'boro; m/Brenda Jean Dalton; p/Earl and Bernadine Mays England, M'boro, KY; pa/CPR Instr; hon/Dr Jack Carey Awd for Outstg EMT, St of Ky 1979.

ENGLAND, LYNNE L oc/Audiologist and Speech Pathologist; b/Apr 11, 1949; h/New Orleans, LA; m/Richard E; p/Sally Goldman, Owings Mills, MD; ed/BA cum laude Univ Mich 1970; MA Temple Univ 1972; Student Tulane Sch of Law; Cert of Clin Comp, Am Speech & Hearing Assn; pa/Speech Therapist, Est'd Audiol Dept, Rockland Chd's Hosp; Est'd Audiology Div of Speech Pathol Dept, Rehab Inst of Chgo; Pvt Pract 1973-; Am Bar Assn, Student Div; Am Speech, Hearing & Lang Assn; Am Cong of Phys Med & Rehab; r/Jewish; hon/Clin Asst'ship, Temple Univ 1970-72; Author "Significance of Patient Preference in the Hearing Aid Evaluation" 1973 & "Effect of Diabetes on Hearing in Stroke Patients" 1976.

ENGLAND, PERRY LEWIS oc/Manager, Paramedic; b/Sept 23, 1954; h/Rt 8 Derby, Apt D2, Somerset, KY 42501; ba/Somerset; m/Sandy K; p/Ira Jr and Marge England, Campbellsville, KY; ed/HS Grad; pa/Mgr Pulaski Co Div, Lake Cumberland Emer Med Ser; cp/Mason; Past Secy & Treas 4th Dist Wildlife Fed; r/Bapt.

ENGLE, EDGAR V oc/Retired; b/May 29, 1915; h/Rt 1, Parksville, KY 40464; m/Mary Lettie; c/Bill, Jim and Dick; p/William (dec) and Ollie Engle (dec); mil/USN WWII; cp/Master Mason; Dem Party; r/So Bapt; hon/Ky Col; Sportsman's Awd 1968-69; Am Greeting Bowling Leag 1970-71.

ENGLISH, ALFRED L oc/City Judge; b/Aug 29, 1918; ba/PO Box 5, Shelbyville, TN 37160; m/Alene Delk; c/Alfred Burton, Dwight Forrest; p/Guy S English (dec); Florence Grady English; ed/LLB Vanderbilt Univ 1948; mil/USAF WWII; pa/City Judge 1966-; Atty; Pres S'ville Bar Assn; Gen Sessions Judge 1949-66; Tenn Bar Assn; Am Judic Soc; Gen Sessions Judge Assn; Mun Judges Assn; cp/Nat Cmdr Disabled Am Vets; Col Staff of Govs in Tenn, Ky & Ga; Freedom Trip to Germany; Am Freedom Foun Trip to Korea; Trip to Israel Rep'g DAV; Pres S'ville Lions Clb; 32nd Deg Mason; Shriner; Mem Pres' Com on Employmt of Handicapped; Mem Gov's Com on Employmt of Phy Handicapped; Bedford Co Bk S'ville 1965-78; Fdr, Gen Counsel, Dir; r/Ch of Christ: Mem, SS Ldr; hon/Hon'd in Resolution by St Tenn Ho of Reps; Men Achmt; Tenn Blue Book; Tenn Govtl Guide; Am Bk Attys; Phi Delta Phi; Hon Sgt-at-Arms, Tenn Ho of Reps; W/W Am Law.

ENGLISH, ROBERT JAMES oc/Executive, Writer; b/Apr 28, 1948; h/1419 Mimosa, Abilene, TX 79603; ba/Abilene; m/Patricia Ann Wade; c/BaKari Robert; p/Robert M and Ressie English, Ft Worth, TX; ed/BA Abilene Christian Univ 1971; pa/Exec VP Abilene Black C of C; Free-Lance Writer; Radio Reporter & Producer TV Documentories; cp/Abilene C of C; Tex Dem Party; Cultural Arts; r/Eucumenical; hon/Outstg Yng Men Am; Intl Biog; Personalities of Am; W/W Intells; Men of Achmt.

ENRIQUEZ, GUADALUPE oc/Store Manager; b/Sept 25, 1945; ba/212 N Hwy 35, Pt Lauaca, TX 77979; m/Maggie; c/Sonia, Mirasol; p/Manuel and Anita Enriquez, Edinburg, TX; ed/Student; mil/USAF;

pa/Retail St Mgr; cp/Advr VOE & OE; Advr Tex Employment Comm; r/Cath.

EPLER, CHARLES A oc/Personnel Research Psychologist; b/Jun 8, 1936; h/2583 Calle Delfino, Santa Fe, NM 87501; ba/Santa Fe; m/Janis E DeBardeleben; c/Kristen Michele; p/Mrs E R Vanaman, Santa Fe; ed/BS Ball St Univ 1958; MEd 1968, EdD 1973 Memphis St Univ; mil/USAF1961-67; pa/Pers Res Psychologist, Res & Test Devel Div, NM St Pers Ofc, Santa Fe; Eval Coor for St Dept Ed, Santa Fe 1975-77; En Ky Univ: Adj Prof Ed, Vis Prof Ed Sum 1974, Asst Prof Ed, Res Dir for Handicapped Pre-Sch Hdstart Prog, Dept Spec Ed 1973, Adj Prof Ed 1973, Others; Res Asst Bur Ednl Res & Sers Memphis St Univ 1971-72; Other Previous Positions; Charter Mem: Am Ednl Studies Assn, M-S Ednl Res Assn; Am Ednl Res Assn; Assn for Supvn & Curri Devel; Intl Pers Mgmt Assn; Kappa Delta Pi; NM Assn for Bilingual Ed; NM Assn Sch Admrs; Phi Delta Kappa; Tau Kappa Alpha; Others; cp/Civitan Intl; CoChm Jerry Lewis Telethon for Santa Fe, 1978; r/1st Christian Ch, Santa Fe: Bd Mem, Chm Stewardship Com; hon/Pub'd Author; Post-Doct F'ship, NW Univ.

EPPS, ANNA CHERRIE oc/Academician and Administrator; b/July 8, 1930; h/3333 Annette St, New Orleans, LA 70122; ba/New Orleans; m/Joseph M; p/Ernest Sr and Anna J Cherrie, New Orleans, LA; ed/BS Howard Univ 1951; MS Loyola Univ 1959; PhD Howard Univ 1966; Internship Our Lady of Mercy Hosp, Sch of Med Technol 1952-53; Further Study, Dillard Univ 1951; Grad Work La St Univ 1952; Adv'd Work Univ Cinci 1952-53; Wkshops Gen Hosp, Univ Cinci; Studies at Univ Calif-Berkeley Summer 1960; pa/Technol, Clin Lab Dept, Our Lady of Mercy Hosp, Cinci, Ohio 1953-54; Technol, Pt-Time, Clin Lab Dept, Flint-Goodridge Hosp, New Orleans 1954-55; Xavier Univ: Asst Prof 1954-60, Instr & Acting Hd of Dept of Med Tech 1954-58, 59-60; Chief Technol, Clin Lab Dept, Mercy Hosp, Hamilton, Ohio 1954; Technol, Dept Med, La St Univ, Sch of Med 1959-60; Blood Bank Technol Spec, Clin Labs Blood Bank Dept, Freedman Hosp, Wash DC, Summers 1957, 58; Blood Bank Spec, Clin Lab Dept, NIH Clin Ctr, Wash DC Summer 1959; Howard Univ Sch of Med: Asst Prof of Microbiol, Col of Med 1961-69, Prog Dir for Acad Reinforcement Prog 1961-62; Fellow, Dept of Med, Johns Hopkins Univ Sch of Med 1969; Tulane Univ Sch of Med: Asst Prof & USPHS Fac Fellow, Dept of Med 1969-71, Assoc Prof 1971, Prof Dept of Med 1975, Dir Med Ed Reinforcement & Enrichment Prog 1969-; Am Soc Clin Pathols; Am Soc Med Technol; Am Assn Blood Banks; AAUP; Albertus Magnus Guild; Washington Helminthological Soc; Am Soc Bacteriols; Sigma Xi; Am Soc Tropical Med & Hygiene; Musser-Burch Soc; Ad Hoc Adv Com on Recruitment of Minority Scis, NIAID; Nat Adv Res Resources Coun; Chp, Standing Com on Student Support Sers, Tulane Med Ctr 1977-; Mem Nat Res Coun, Nat Acad of Scis, Post-Doct F'ship Evaluation Panel for Nat Sci Foun; Adv Bd Dept of Hlth & Human Resources; Chd's Hosp, New Orleans, Bd of Trustees 1977-; Past Mem Num Other Profl Orgs; r/Cath; hon/Ldrs in Am Sci 1960; Interstate Postgrad Med Assn of N Am's Awd for Merit Res 1966; Num Exhibs Incl'g: AMA Annual Meeting, San Fran, Calif 1968 & Nat Med Assn Annual Conv 1968; Nat Cancer Insts-Spec Fac F'ships: Johns Hopkins Univ Col of Med 1969, Tulane Univ Col of Med 1969-71; Author/Co-Author Num Pubs Incl'g: *The Sickling Phenomenon in a College Population & Experimental Schistotomiasis 1 Electrophoretic Studies.*

EPPS, MIEKE N oc/Counselor; b/Apr 16, 1940; h/1534 E 17 Pl, Tulsa, OK 74120; m/Latimer A Jr; c/Zachary, Kyle, Adriaan; p/Willem and Coosnje Neunenhuysen; ed/BA 1977; MSW 1980; pa/Social Work Cnslr; NASW; OHWA; cp/Rel in Action Bd, All Souls Unitarian Ch; Prog Com, Yth Sers of Tulsa; Ad Hoc Com, Indian Nations Coun of Govt; r/Unitarian; hon/Phi Theta Kappa; Pi Gamma Mu; Psi Chi; Alpha Kappa Delta.

EPPS, WILLIAM DAVID oc/Minister; b/Jan 15, 1951; h/308 Holland Dr, Kingsport, TN 37663; ba/Johnson City; m/Cynthia Douglas; c/Jason Douglas, John Peyton; p/William Jr and Kathleen L Epps, Kingsport, TN; ed/Min Studies Deg, Berean Sch of the Bible; BSW E Tenn St Univ; DMin Cand Berean Christian Col; mil/USMC 1970-73; Tenn NG 1977-78; pa/Tenn Conf of Social Wel; Fac Mem Moody Ctr of Biblical Lrng; ETSU Chi Alpha Campus Min; Fam Cnslr in Child Abuse; cp/Vol Probation Ofcr; Boy's Clb Vol Coach; r/Assem of God; hon/Phi Alpha; Hon Mem Christian Ed F'ship.

EPPS, WILLIAM SAXE oc/Minister; h/2719 Reynolds Pk Rd, Winston-Salem, NC 27107; ba/W-S; m/Agretta Denise Holloway; c/Jacqueline Jeannelle; p/Charles T Sr and Pauline Jacqueline Jones Epps, Jersey City, NJ; ed/BS Bishop Col; MDiv Union Theol Sem; MEd Tchrs Col, Columbia Univ; Matriculating Student: Andover Newton Theol Sem, Boston Univ & Columbia Univ; pa/Min: Calvary Bapt Ch (Haverhill, Mass), Abyssinian Bapt Ch; Tchr: Boston & Jersey City; Adm Asst to Supt Dist 9, NY Public Schs; Old Testament Tchr, No Bapt Sch of Rel; Bapt Min Conf & Assocs; Forsyth Clergy Assn; Am Bapt Chs; Nat Bapt Chs; cp/Precinct Chm SE Ward; Fam Sers Bd; Bd Mem YMCA; 3rd Cent

Priorities Com of W-S; r/Prot; hon/W/W Rel 1978; W/W of Intl Biogl Ctr; Men & Wom of Dist.

ERICSON, RUTH ANN oc/Physician, Psychiatrist; b/May 15; h/Dallas, TX; ba/2339 Inwood Rd #22, Dallas, TX 75235; p/William Albert (dec) and Anna M Ericson, Dallas, TX; ed/BS Bethany Col; MD Univ Tex Med Br 1951; Internship Calif Lutheran Hosp 1951-52; Residency, Psychi, Univ Tex 1952-55; pa/Pvt Pract Psychi, Dallas 1955-; Clin Instr, SWn Med Sch 1955-; Conslt for Dallas Indep Sch Dist, AUS & Var Rel & Other Grps; Bd Mem Chd's Devel Ctr 1958-61; Dallas Intertribal Ctr Clin 1974-81; Adv Bd Dallas Intertribal Ctr 1976-81; Conslt Tribal Concern: Alcoholism 1977-; Am Med Soc 1955-79; Tex & Dallas Co Med Socs; Am, Tex & Regional Psychi Assns; Fellow Am Geriatric Soc; So Med Assn; Alumni Assn Univ Tex Med Br; Dallas Area Wom Psychi; Am Med Woms Assn, Corresp Secy 1980; cp/Tex Archeol Soc: Audit Com 1976, 77, Med Dir, Field Schlr 1980-; Dallas Archeol Soc: VP 1971-72, Pres 1972-73, Pres Elect 1981; Life Mem Navy Leag of US; AF Assn; r/Luth; hon/W/W: Am Wom, S&SW; DIB; Delta Psi Omega; Alpha Psi Omega; Pi Gamma Mu; Lambda Sigma; Alpha Epsilon Iota; Alpha Omega Alpha; Other Hon Socs; Author: "107° on the Tigua: Survival in the Desert" *The Record* Dallas Archeol Soc, Apr 1979.

ERNOUF, ANITA BONILLA oc/Teacher; b/Feb 22, 1920; h/312 Randolph St, Farmville, VA; ba/F'ville; m/Edward; c/Edward III, Roderic; ed/BA Hunter Col 1944; MA 1946, PhD 1970 Columbia Univ; Addit Study Mex, Spain, France; pa/Longwood Col: Prof, Chm Dept Fgn Langs; French, Spanish & Portuguese Examr, USA Postal Sers; Res Asst, Hispanic Inst, Columbia Univ 1945-47; Assoc Prof, Hollins Col 1947-60; Universidad Iberoamericana; Tchr Grad Sems (Sums) & Dir of Thesis Intl Dept; Past Pres F'ville Dist Chapt AAUW; Alpha Delta Kappa: VP Alpha Delta Chapt 1972-74, Pres 1974-76; Mod Fgn Lang Assn of Va: Pres-elect 1972, Pres 1973; Pres-elect Mod Fgn Lang Assn Va 1977; Pres Va St Coun on Study Abroad 1977; Sgt-at-Arms, St Alpha Delta Kappa 1977; ACTFL; VEA; NEA; LEA; V-PAK; AAUW; AATSP; cp/F'ville Woms Clb; Sponsor YWCA 10 Yrs; hon/Fellow, ABI.

ESCOBAR, LUIS oc/Deputy Executive Secretary; b/Feb 10, 1927; h/4620 N Park Ave, Apt PHO4E, Chevy Chase, MD 20015; ba/Wash DC; m/Helga; c/Luis Eduardo, Maria Cristina, Elsa Patricia, Gisela; p/Luis and Elsa Cerda Escobar, Santiago, Chile; ed/Economist Univ of Chile 1949; MPA Harvard 1957; pa/Intl Monetary Fund & World Bk: Exec Dir 1963-70, Dep Exec Secy, Devel Com 1975-; Profl Lectr Var US Univs 1974-; cp/Min of Economy, Devel & Reconstrn, Chile 1961-63; hon/"Mejor Ingeniero Comercial", Chilean Economists Assn; Univ of Chile: "Miembro Academico" & "Profesor Extraordinario".

ESKEW, ROBERT LEWIS oc/Athletic Director; b/Dec 30, 1945; h/3343 Ravenwood Dr, Augusta, GA 30907; ba/Augusta; m/Eleanor; c/Candace; p/Mable Ivey, Chgo, IL; ed/BS Hlth & Phys Ed; MS Guid & Cnslg; mil/AUS NG Pvt 2nd Class; pa/Ath Dir, Hd Coach Men's Basketball; NEA; Nat Basketball Coaches Assn of Am; Nat Assn of Intercol Aths; cp/NAACP; Oper PUSH; Urban Leag; r/U Meth; hon/MacDonald Prep All Star Coach of Ind 1979.

ESKRIDGE, OLLIE oc/Teacher; b/Dec 27, 1948; h/Tunica, MS; p/Louis and Mandy Eskridge, Tunica, MS; ed/BS Jackson St Univ 1971; Further Study Delta St Univ & Univ Miss; pa/Math Tchr, Rosa Ft HS; Miss Assn Edrs; NEA; Bldg Rep MAE-NEA; VP S Yalobusha Co Tchrs Assn 1979-80; r/Bapt; hon/Yalobusha Co Tchr Assn Cert of Apprec 1976; N Miss, Miss Tchrs Assn, NEA Outstg Ldrship Awd 1976; Outstg Yng Wom Am 1978.

ESKUT, BILLIE LEE oc/Teacher; b/Dec 3, 1931; h/5709 Fair Oaks Ave, Baltimore, MD 21214; ba/Balto; m/Frances Hall; c/Ginger Kay, Vicky Lee, Frances Janice, Ruth Ann, Sandra Lynn, Billy Lee; p/Frank Steve Eskut Jr (dec); Kathleen Eskut, Balto; ed/BA N Tex St Univ 1957; MA Univ Tex 1969; LSU; Tex A&M; Stephen F Austin St Col; mil/USAF; pa/Current Assoc Prof Math, Univ Balto; Balto Polytech Inst: Dept Hd Math 1973-74, Tchr Adv'd Math 1963-, Curric Com Hd of Adv'd Calc & Probability; Former Engr, Westinghouse Aerospace & Bendix Div, Balto; Former VP Inst of Envir Scis, Chesapeake Chapt; Profl Assns; Judge, Nat-Intl Sci Fair, Balto; Features Spkr, Nat Conv IES 1970; Former Nt Bd Mem IES; cp/Civil Def Tchr; Others; r/Ch of Christ: Preacher 10 Yrs, Bible Tchr 15 Yrs, Admr of Tchg Prog; hon/Articles Pub'd in Scholarly Jours; Fellow, ABI.

ESPARZA, THOMAS oc/Director of Intramural Sports; h/811 S 16th Ave, Edinburg, TX 78539; m/Esther LaMadrid; c/Tommy Jr, Steven, Teylene; ed/Allen Mil Acad; BS, MS Tex A&I Col; PhD Clayton Univ; mil/USN WWII; pa/Hlth, Phys Ed & Rec Conslt, Edinburg Schs; Instrnl Media & Ath Events Dir Edinburg; Asst Supt Edinburg; Past Pres Edinburg Tchrs Fed Credit Union; Past Pres Pan Am Univ Fed Credit Union; Coor Tex HPE & Sports Wk, Pan Am Univ; Dir Intramural Sports, Pan Am

Univ, Appt'd Full-Time Dir 1968; Life Mem NEA; Life Mem Tex St Tchrs Assn; Nat Intramural Assn; Auditing Com Tex Assn Hlth, Phys Ed & Rec; Conslt to Ednl Ser Ctr Region I Spec Olympics; Rep Assem H&PER Assn of Tex; cp/VP 1st Am Cancer Soc Unit, Edinburg; Hidalgo Co Hist Soc Bd Dirs; Hidalgo Co Housing Auth Bd of Dirs: Co-Dir Spec Olympics Dist I; Life Mem Disabled Am Vets; Am Legion 15th Dist Baseball Chm; Am Leigon Baseball Div Chm; Resolution Assigmtns Com, Tex Am Legion; Americanism Com, Am Legion of Tex; Org'd First Panocha Bread Cook-Off, June 1979; Past Comdr Am Legion Post 408; Former Secy City of Edinburg Pk Bd; Former Ed Chm Hidalgo Co Cancer Soc; Steering Com, Fdr Metro National Bank, McAllen, Tex; hon/Tex Legion Hall of Fame; Author Many Mag Articles on Sports & Phys Ed; Compiled Booklet "Physical Education Activities for the Elementary Grades"; Hon'd by Gov's Com on Phys Fitness; DIB; Men of Achmt; W/W: Commun Ser, SW; Ldg Ams & Their Fams; Intl W/W Intells; Intl Register of Profiles; World Wide Acad of Schlrs; Commun Ldrs & Noteworthy Ams; Notable Ams; Personalities of Am; Men & Wom of Dist.

ESPINOLA, AURELIO AURELIO oc/Forensic Pathologist; b/June 25, 1940; h/9503 Hexham Ct, Spring, TX 77373; ba/Houston; m/Rosa V Molle; c/Rommel, Leilani; p/Victorino L and Esperanza A Espinola, Houston, TX; ed/MD Manila Ctrl Univ 1963; Pathol Intern, Detroit-Macomb Hosp Assn 1971-72; Pathol Resident, Wayne St Univ 1972-76; Fellow in Forensic Pathol, Wayne Co Med Examrs Ofc 1976-77; pa/Asst Med Examr, Harris Co; Am Soc Clin Pathol; Harris Co Med Soc; Houston Soc of Clin Pathols; Tex Assn Philippine Phys; Tex Med Assn; Nat Assn Med Examrs; Col of Am Pathol; r/Cath.

ESPOSITO, ALBERT CHARLES oc/Ophthalmologist, Eye Surgeon; b/Nov 9, 1912; h/171 Woodland Dr, Huntington, WV 25705; ba/H'ton; m/V Elizabeth Dodson; c/Bettina E Kelly (Mrs Peter F), Gregory CJ, Mary Alice Tartler; p/Charles CJM S and Elizabeth Ellen Esposito; ed/BS Univ Pgh; MD cum laude Loyola Univ; pa/Chief Ophthal Hosp #97; Past Pres: Cabell Co Med Soc, So Med Assn, WVa Acad Ophthal, Am Assn Ophthal; Regent for WVa; Fellow Intl Col Surgs; Clin Prof Ophthal & Active Chm Dept Ophthal Marshall Univ Med Sch; Pres WVa St Med Assn; cp/Bd Dirs Gtr H'ton C of C; Former Mem WVa St Leg, Elected Minority Whip 1976; Lions Clb; Guyan Golf & CC; r/Rom Cath; hon/Stritch Medal Awd, Chgo; Alpha Omega Alpha; Outstg Ophthalmologist in S Awd 1972; Hon DSc Deg, Marshall Univ Sch of Med; Apprec Awd, City of H'ton; Man of Yr Public Ser Awd 1974, JCs.

ESSENWANGER, OSKAR MAXIMILIAN KARL oc/Research Physicist, Adjunct Professor; b/Aug 25, 1920; h/610 Mtn Gap Dr, Huntsville, AL; 35803; m/Katharina D; p/Oskar (dec) and Anna Essenwanger (dec); ed/MS (Dip); PhD (Dr.rer.nat.); mil/German AF 1939-45; pa/Chief Aerophysics Br, Army Missile Command; Adj Prof, Envir Sci, Univ Ala-H'ville; Sigma Xi Clb, Univ Ala-H'ville, Pres 1977-; Ala Acad Sci, VP 1973; Other Profl Orgs; r/Rom Cath; hon/Missile Command Sci & Engrg Achmt Awd 1965; Cert'd Consltg Meteorologist 1967; Cert'd Qual Engr 1966; Sigma Xi Awd for Outstg Res 1977; Listed in Var Nat & Intl W/W; Life Fellow ABI Res Assoc 1979; Fellow Intercontl Biog Assn; Author *Applied Statistics in Atmospheric Science*; Over 100 Articles & Reports in Am & European Jours.

ETTIEN, JAMES THOMAS oc/General and Vascular Surgeon; b/Mar 23, 1941; h/2345 Kings Pointe Dr, Largo, FL 33540; ba/Largo; m/Janey Cureton; c/James Keith; p/Todd and Rosa Jane Verhey Ettien, Chattanooga, TN; ed/BA Univ of the S 1963; Att'd Ga St Univ 1966-67; MD Med Col of Ga 1971; Internship Vanderbilt Hosp 1971-72; Med Col Ga: Ophthalmic Residency 1972, Orthopedic Residency 1973-74, Surgical Residency 1973, 1974-76; mil/Active Duty 1963-66, Reserves 1963-73 1st Lt; pa/Gastonia Surg Assocs 1976-78; Diagnostic Clin 1979-; Asst Prof, Dept of Surg, Med Col Ga; Att'g Surg, VA Hosp, Forest Hills Div, Augusta, Ga; Med Records Com; Med Res Foun of Ga: Opers Review & Plan'g Com; Surg Conslt, Eisenhower Med Ctr; Surgeon, Med Ctr Hosp; Editorial Advr, Resident & Staff Phys: Pinellas Co Med Soc; Med Assn Fla; AMA; SEn Surg Cong; William H Moretz Surg Soc; Assn for Acad Surg; Pancreas Clb; So Med Assn; Am Col Surgs; Fellow Intl Col of Surgs; r/Epis; hon/W/W S&SW; Mosby S'ship Awd; Alpha Omega Alpha; Author Num Profl Pubs Incl'g: "Psychomotor Seizure Activity Precipitated by Exposure to Erotic Stimuli" 1978 & "The Hypothenar Hammer Syndrome: Case Report" In Press.

EUDALY, HAZEL MARIE oc/Foreign Missionary, Editor, Author; b/Dec 22, 1911; h/PO Box 4255, El Paso, TX 79914; ba/El Paso; m/Nathan Hoyt Sr; c/Dick, Katharine E Hart, Nathan Hoyt Jr; p/Russell Godby Sadler (dec); Bertha Mae Sadler, Appleton City; ed/BS Ctl Mo St Tchrs Col 1936; MRel Ed 1939, Postgrad Study 1956, 63 SWn Bapt Theol Sem; pa/Tchr Public Schs, Amsterdam, Mo 1931-37; Editor, Writer, Bapt Spanish Pub'g House, Fgn Mission Bd, El Paso 1948-; Curric Conslt Bapt World Alliance 1966; cp/Past Pres Local PTA; Chm Parent & Fam Life Ed Com, Dist XV PTA, Tex; Austin HS Chapt Am Field Ser; Pres,

PERSONALITIES OF THE SOUTH

PTA; hon/Author 19 Books in Spanish & English, incl'g: *My Friends, My Family, Stories of the New Testament;* Life Ser Awd to Dist'd Alumnus, SW Bapt Col, Bolivar, Mo; W/W: Am Wom, S&SW; World W/W Wom; Nat Reg Prom Ams & Intl Notables; Am Bicent Res Inst, Human Resource of USA; DIB; Intl W/W in Commun Ser.

EULER, ARTHUR R oc/Pediatric Gastroenterology; b/Oct 20, 1942; h/3208 Breckenridge Dr, Little Rock, AR 72201; ba/Little Rock; c/Elizabeth Suzanne, Katherine Anne; p/John Stanley and June Alice Biestek, Hammond, IN; ed/BS Purdue Univ 1965; MD Ind Univ 1969; Pediatric Internship, Riley Hosp, Ind Univ 1969-70; Pediatric Residency, Riley Hosp 1970-71; Pediatric Residency Harbor Gen Hosp, Torrance, Calif 1973-74; Pediatric Gastroenterology F'ship, UCLA 1974-76; mil/USN 1971-73; pa/Asst Prof, Univ Ark for Med Scis; Hd Div of Pediatric Gastroenterology, Ark Chd's Hosp, Little Rock; N Am Soc Pediatric Gastroenterology; So Calif Soc Gastrointestinal Endoscopy; Wn Gastroenterology Assn; So Calif Soc Gastroenterol; Am Soc Parenteral & Enteral Nutrition; Ctrl Ark Pediatric Soc; Mid-W GUT Clb; So Soc Pediatric Res; Am Acad Pediatrics; Am Fed Clin Res; Am Gastroenterol Assn; AAAS; NY Acad Scis; cp/YMCA; Ark Symph Guild; Friends of the Ark Zoo; Ark Advocates for Fams & Chd; r/Luth; hon/Cit of Merit Ser, from Comdg Gen USMC 1973; Recip So Calif Soc for Gastrointestinal Endoscopy Olympus Prize Assay Awd 1976; Outstg Yng Men Am 1978; W/W S&SW 1980; Author 21 Articles in Med Lit.

EVANS, BERNIECE BARWICK oc/Church Secretary; b/Sept 4, 1918; h/Paducah, KY; m/Cecil R; c/Beverley Humer, Mrs Ron Love, Richard L; ed/Assoc Deg; Secy Dip, Draughon's Bus Col; pa/Secy Bapt Tabernacle 27 Yrs, Trinity Bapt Ch 4½ Yrs; Past Pres, Past Secy-Treas ABWA; cp/Jackson Purchase Hist Soc; r/Bapt; hon/Ky Col; Hon Chm Belle of Louisville; Personalities of S 1972.

EVANS, BRUCE A oc/Library Administrator; b/Aug 6, 1947; h/Townhouse #11, Corinth, MS 38834; ba/Corinth; m/Carol; p/Albert and Claire Evans, Okla City, OK; ed/BA SUNY-Stony Brook; MSLS Fla St Univ; mil/USAF 1969-73; pa/Asst Dir Reference-Ext Sers, NE Reg Lib Sys; Miss Lib Assn: Intell Freedom Com, VChm Public Lib Sect 1977-78, Chm 1978-; Miss Museums Assn; 1/Pres-elect Alcorn Co Libn's Cooperative 1976-77; Chm NE Reg for 1st Very Spec Arts Fair in Miss 1977-78 (Handicapped Art); Del to 1979 Miss Gov's Conf on Libs; cp/Reviewer for *Library Journal;* Former Mem Civitans; Rel Ed Instr; Del Miss St Cath Conv; Actor & Stagehand Corinth Commun Theatre; Vol: Mar Dimes, Cancer Dr, Dr for St Jude's Hosp; Polit Campaign Activs; r/Cath; hon/Spec Cert of Achmt, Confrat Home Study Ser (Vincentian Fathers).

EVANS, CHARLES WESLEY oc/Attorney; State Representative; b/Feb 19, 1939; h/809 Bedford Ct W, Hurst, TX 76053; ba/Hurst; m/Patricia Anne; c/Lisa Anne, James Wesley; p/Robert and Leona Evans, Fort Worth, TX; ed/BA; JD; mil/USN; pa/Ft Worth-Tarrant Co, NE Tarrent Co, Tex Bar Assns; Phi Alpha Delta; ABA; cp/Dir Hurst-Euless-Bedford C of C; Haltom-Richland C of C; Lions Clb; Univ Tex-Arlington Alumni Assn; St Wide Com for Town Meeting, Tex; Chm House Com on Judicial Affairs; r/Bapt; hon/Phi Kappa Theta; Good Conduct Medal, USN; Man of Month, Hurst JCs; Spec Recog, Haltom-Richland C of C; Outstg Ser to St of Tex, Tex Chiro Assn; Spec Recog, St Bar Tex; Dist'd Ser to People of Tex, St Bar Tex; W/W: Tex, Am, Am Polits, Govt; Outstg Ams in S.

EVANS, DE ETTE BRITT oc/Educational Diagnostician, Writer; b/May 30, 1938; h/300 Meadowlake Dr, Longview, TX 75604; ba/Carthage, TX; c/Aurelia Joyce, Cara Lynn; p/Denman R and Lomer W Britt, Carthage, TX; ed/BS N Tex St Univ; MEd Stephen F Austin St Univ; pa/Ednl Diagnostician: Panola Co Co-op, Cathage 1974-, Marshall Indep Sch Dist, Marshall, Tex 1973-74; Tchr Educable Retard, Shelby Co Co-op, Ctr, Tex 1971-73, Eskimo Chd, Bur Indian Affairs, Emmonak, Alaska 1965-68; Chperson: Lang and/or LD Sect Tex St Tchrs Conv 1976, Assessmt Techniques, APGA Conv 1977; Num Papers Presented; APGA; Tex Pers & Guid; Assn for Measuremt & Eval in Guid; E Tex Assn for Ednl Diagnosticians; Tex St Tchrs Assn; E Tex Sch Wom's Coun; r/Meth; hon/Grad w Hons; Phi Delta Kappa; Kappa Delta Phi; Alpha Delta Kappa; Pub'd Author; W/W S&SW.

EVANS, EVA VIRGINIA oc/Public Information Specialist; b/Mar 20, 1931; h/209 Jefferies St, Hot Springs, AR 71901; ba/Hot Sprgs; p/Coley Marvin Evans, Hot Sprgs; Clara Scott Evans (dec); pa/Public Info Specialist Forest Ser, USDA; Coor Wom's Conservation Activs, Ouachita Nat Forest 1969-: Fed Wom's Prog, Hispanic Employmt Prog Coor; Clerk-Stenographer/Secy Fed Ser 29 Yrs: VA, Dept of Army, Dept Agri; Nat Fdn BPW Clbs Inc: Yg Careerist Com 1978-79, Bd Dirs 1976-77; Ark Fdn BPW Clb: Past Pres, Pres Elect, 1st & 2nd VP, Dist Dir, Bd Dirs Chm Bylaws; Hot Sprgs BPW Clb; Ark Adv Coun on Envir Ed 1970-75: Past Pres, VP, Mem Steering Com; cp/Ark Arbor Day Com; Fed Wom's Prog Coun of

Ark; Ark Fdn Garden Clbs Inc; Nat Coun St Garden Clbs Inc; Ark Fdn Wom's Clbs; Gen Fdn Wom's Clbs; Hot Sprgs Wom's C of C; Ark Wom's Com on Public Affairs; Bd Dirs Hot Sprgs Coun of Garden Clbs; First Nighters Garden Clb; Demoiselle Clb; Bd Advrs Salvation Army; r/Bapt; hon/Superior Ser Hon Awd, US Dept Agri; Individual Ser Awd for Outstg Achmt, Ark Fdn Garden Clbs; Wom of Yr, Hot Sprgs BPW Clb; Sustained Superior Perf Awds, Ouachita Nat Forest.

EVANS, JO FRED oc/Businesswoman; b/Dec 18, 1928; h/PO Box 283, Junction, TX 76849; ba/Junction; m/Charles Wayne II (dec); c/Charles Wayne III, John Burt, Elizabeth Wishart Burt; p/John Fred (dec) and Sadie Oliver Burt, Junction, TX; ed/Att'd Sul Ross St Col 1962 & Univ Houston Sch Law 1963; BA Mary Hardin-Baylor Col 1948; MA Trinity Univ 1967; Dip Intl Graphanalisis 1968; pa/Bus Mgr Fam Owned Ranches & Rent Property 1948-; Part Owner & Mgr TV Translator Corp 1967-; Owner-Mgr Radio Sta KMBL 1958-59; Real Est Broker 1964-75; Advr to Nelson Wilff on Ec & Water Probs During Polit Canpaign for US Ho of Reps; Nat Translator Assn; BPW: Secy 1979-81, Pres 1981-82; cp/Hist Survey Comm: Histn 1980-; AAUW: Book Fair Chm 1967-70; Daughs of Repub of Tex; Intl Platform Assn; Study Grp Chm - We The People 1971; Treas & Asst Coor, Citizens for Tex 1972; Treas & Coor, Citizens for a New Constitution for Tex 1974; Tex Film Conserv, Edwards Aquifer 1975; Money's Worth 1972; r/Ch of Devine Sci; hon/Fellow Named in Her Hon 1972; Tex St Sen Resolution #721 Commend'g Her as an Outstg Texan 1973; W/W Am Wom 1981-82.

EVANS, MARILYN BAILEY oc/Florida House of Representatives; h/Melbourne, FL; c/Hugh Jr, Dan, Cecile, Mary Louise; ed/BA Duke Univ; pa/Rltr Assoc, Evans-Butler Rlty; cp/Fla Ho of Reps, Repub Dist 46 1976-; Ed, Hlth & Rehab Sers & Natural Resources Coms; Curric, Living Resource Mgmt & Social & Rehab Sers Subcoms; Repub Caucus Chm; Sponsor Safe-Drinking Water Act 1976; Secy of Leg Affairs, Fla Conf of U Meth Wom; St-Wide Exc Bd, U Meth Wom; LWV; Melbourne Br AAUW; Melbourne Area C of C; S Brevard Co Panhellenic PEO; Concern Inc; Fla Forestry Assn; Repub St-Com-Wom, Brevard Co; Sr Am Pilot Proj Chm, Nat Fed Repub Wom, Bd Dirs; Am Leg Exch Coun; Nat Leg Task Force on Wom; Adv Coun BCC WENDI & WOW; Adv Coun Ret'd Sr Vol Prog; Hon Chm Mothers Mar of Dimes 1979; Hon Brevard Co Campaign Chp, Arthritis Foun 1977-78; Mem En Test Range Action Com 1977; Bd Dirs Brevard Co Mtl Hlth Ctr 1977-74; Life Mem Friends of Eau Gallie Lib; r/Meth; hon/Outstg Polit Contbns Awd 1978, Fla Coun for Commun Mtl Hlth; VIP Awd 1978, Human Rights Advocacy Com for Mtlly Retard'd, HRS Dist VII; W/W Am 1978-79; Good Govt Awd 1977-78, Melbourne JCs; Personalities of the S 1976; Juvenile Guid Awd, Brevard Co PTA Coun; W/W Am Polits 1978-79; Personalities of Am 1978-79; Susan B Anthony Awd 1979, NOW, S Brevard Chapt; Selected 1 of 2 Wom in Fla to Part in Wkshop for St Legislators by Wash Inst for Wom in Polits.

EVANS, MICHAEL LEE oc/Advertising Manager; b/Nov 11, 1950; h/Rt 8 Box 5520, Lufkin, TX 75901; ba/Lufkin; m/Patricia Kaye; p/George William and Clara Cecilia Evans, Lufkin, TX; ed/AA Angelina Jr Col 1971; BBA Stephen F Austin Univ 1974; pa/*Lufkin News:* Ad Salesman 1974, Asst Advtg Mgr 1977, Advtg Mgr 1978-; INAE; TNAMA; Tex Daily Newspaper Assn; cp/Hudson Vol Fire Dept, Histn; Advtg Advr Angelina Co Bike-a-Thon Cancer Com 1979; Div Chm U Way of Angelina Co 1980; r/Cath; hon/W/W S&SW 1980.

EVANS, PHILLIP RANDOLPH oc/Manager; b/Feb 2, 1939; h/4605 Royale Ct, Ashland, KY 41101; ba/Ashland; m/Doris Ingram; c/Kimberly Jan, Kay Lynn; p/Reginald Desmond and Mabel Claire Brown Evans, Houston, TX; ed/BS 1961, MBA 1962 Tex A&M Univ; Fundamentals of Fin, Wharton Sch, Univ Penn 1980; pa/Engr, Data Mktg Mgr, SWn Bell Telephone 1962-68; Mktg Rep, Control Data Corp 1968-69; Corp Communs Mgr, Occidental Petro Corp 1969-74; Mgr Telecommuns & Radio/Elects, Ashland Oil 1974-; Bd Dirs Petro Indust Elect Assn; Bd Dirs Intl Communs Assn; Ctrl Com on Telecommuns, Am Petro Inst; Telecommuns Adv Com, Tex A&M Univ & Ohio Univ; cp/Pres Candlelight Plaza Civic Clb; Fdg Pres, Ashland Tri-St Rec Assn; Pres-Elect Ashland Rotary Clb; Area Chm Citizens Advocacy Com; Div Chm, U Way Ashland; Chm BSA Fam Fund Dr; Advr Jr Achmt, Houston; Bd Dirs JCs, Houston, C of C Ashland; Repub Party; r/So Bapt: Deacon, SS Tchr, Fin Chm; hon/Mosher Steel Schlr 1959-61; Ashland Bicent Awd 1976; W/W S&SW 1980; Ky Col 1978; Contbr to Intl Communs Assn's Internal News Jour 1969-; Author "Management by Objectives" *Texas Engineer* 1965.

EVANS, ROBERT THOMAS oc/Minister, Music Evangelist, Seminar Instructor, TV Show Host; b/July 26, 1935; h/Rt 1 PO Box 433, Lebanon, TN 37087; m/Peggy Bellar; c/Laurie Lynn, Lisa Ann, Susan Elizabeth; p/Allie Mai Evans, Lebanon, TN; ed/Att'd TPI Inst, Cumberland Col; Grad High Pt Furniture Inst, Dip in Interior Design 1970; Certs of Completed Min, S Bapt SS Bd Tng Ctr 1976-80; pa/Rel Evangelism; Pres Towne & Country Home Furnishings; Pres Bryant Prods of Lebanon; Pres

97

Love One Another Mins; Pres Wilson Co Pastor Conf; cp/Lebanon C of C, VP; Pres Retail Div LHS Band Boosters; Secy JCs & Rotary Clb.

EVANS, THOMAS IRVIN oc/Director of Pharmacy; b/Sept 24, 1947; h/Hamilton, AL; ba/1315 Military St, Hamilton, AL 35570; p/Pet (dec) and Jewel Irvin Evans, Hamilton, AL; ed/BS Univ Miss 1970; EMT II, Univ Ala-Huntsville 1977; Shelton's Adv Sch of Floral Design 1980; pa/TKE Drug Co 1970-72; Relief Pharm, NE Miss 1972-74; Conslt Pharm, Primary Hlth Care, Tupelo, Miss 1973; Dir Pharm, Lister Hill Hosp, NW Ala Med Ctr 1974-; Conslt Pharm, Marion Co Nsg Home 1974-; N Miss Pharm Assn: VP 1973, Pres 1974; cp/Ala St Singing Conv: VP 1976, Pres 1981; Nat Singing Conv: VP 1975, Adv Com 1980; r/Meth; hon/I Dare You Awd 1965; Composer of Rel Mus 1977-79.

EVERETT, KARL MENOHER JR oc/Gerontologist, Consultant, Educator; b/Aug 13, 1935; h/1305 Spruce Dr, Norman, OK 73069; ba/Norman; m/June Kay Lenz; c/Dianna Lynn, Christopher Douglas; p/Karl Menoher Everett (dec); Nell Irene McCullogh (dec); ed/Grad w Hons NY Univ Col of Med, Div of Nsg 1958; Grad Defense Lang Inst W 1964; Grad US Fgn Ser Inst 1971; BA cum laude Univ Md-College Park 1974; Postgrad Study Univ Okla-Norman 1978-; pa/Gerontology Conslt, Ctrl St Griffin Meml Hosp & SW Ctr for Human Relats Studies, Univ Okla; Conslt Am Univ, Wash DC; Clin Instr NYU-Bellevue Med Ctr; Instr LA City Col (Overseas), Seoul, Korea; Vis Fac, John F Kennedy Ctr, Ft Bragg, NC; Pres & Chm of Bd, Okla World Conslt Inc; Sr Assoc, Karl M Everett & Assocs; Gerontological Soc of Am; Am Geriatric Soc; Am Acad of Polit & Scial Sci; cp/Cleveland Co Christmas Store; Co Chm, Mbrship Co, C'land Co Dem Party Ldrship Clb; Bd Dirs Mtl Hlth Assn in C'land Co; Chm Public Affairs Com, Mtl Hlth Assn in C'land Co; Adv Bd Mem, Mtl Hlth Assn of Okla; Mem Ad Hoc Com, Nat Security Coun, 1968-69; Pvt Negotiator UN Command, Korea, w People's Repub of China & Dem People's Repub of Korea 1971-75; r/Prot; hon/Bronze Star Medal 1967; Joint Sers Commend Medal 1979; Var Other Mil Awds; Min Level Awds, Govt Repub of Korea 1971-75; Ogden D Mills S'ship Awd for Achmt 1958; W/W S&SW.

EVERETT, LOU WHICHARD oc/Nursing Instructor; b/Feb 21, 1944; h/Greenville, NC; ba/Sch of Nsg, ECU, Greenville, NC 27834; m/Lester L Jr; c/Lester L III, Andrew Fate; p/James Andrew and Essie O Whichard, Bethel, NC; ed/Dip Park View Hosp Sch of Nsg 1965; BSN 1976, MSN 1979 ECU; pa/Psychi-Mtl Hlth Nsg Instr, ECU Sch Nsg; Marriage & Fam Therapist; Sigma Theta Tau, Beta Nu Chapt: Pres & Prog Chm 1980-81; Assoc Reg Mem Intl Transactional Analysis Assn, Pres-Elect 1981; NLN; ANA; NCNA; Assoc Mem Am Assn Marriage & Fam Therapy; cp/Pitt Co Mtl Hlth Assn; Profl Conslt, Pitt Co Mtl Hlth Ctr; Westhaven Home & Gdn Clb; r/Meml Bapt Ch: Chp Nursery Com; hon/Outstg New Mem's Awd, Rocky Mt Jr Wom's Clb 1971; Pres Grad Student Org, ECU Sch Nsg 1978; Sigma Theta Tau 1978; Nom'd to Rep Sigma Theta Tau, Beta Nu Chapt in Contest for W/W Am Cols & Univs; Writing "Childbearing Practices of Nurses as They Approximate Selected Social Class Values."

EVERHART, FRANKIE DARLENE GEORGE oc/Buyer; b/Oct 5, 1937; h/1914 N Fenton, PO Box 292, Tyler, TX 75710; ba/Addison, TX; c/Pamela Da'Juan, Terence Lea Maurier, Felencia LaGayle E Thompson; p/William (dec) and Mabel Franklin George (dec); ed/AA Bus Adm; BS Home Ec; pa/Buyer Xerox Corp; Former Mem: NEA, E Tex & Tex St Tchrs Assn; cp/PTA; Former: Alternate Election Judge, Precnt Chm, Del to Repub St Conv, Sponsor Campfire Girls, Jack & Jill of Am; Mem Acad Motion Pictures & TV Viewers; r/St Mary's Bapt Ch: Secy; hon/W/W Am Wom; Alpha Kappa Mu; Grad summa cum laude.

EVERY, RAYMOND CALVIN oc/Acting Chief; b/July 5, 1927; h/Metairie, LA; ba/BA Med Ctr, 1601 Perdido St, New Orleans, LA; c/Brant, Monique, Paul; p/Karl O'Bryant (dec) and Victoria Taylor Every (dec); ed/BA magna cum laude Furman Univ 1951; Post Grad Univ Utah 1954; MSW Univ Washington 1957; Doct Courses: UCLA, Ariz St Univ; mil/AUS 1946-47; pa/Social Wkr w VA Med Ctrs 1957-; Asst Chief Social Work Ser-VAMC, Lyons, NJ & New Orleans, La 1967-; Ctrl Ariz Chapt NASW, Pres; Editor in Chief NASW St of La Newslttr; Acad of Cert'd Social Wkrs; Cert'd Sex Therapist, Am Assn Cert'd Sex Edrs, Cnslrs & Therapists; Bd Cert'd Social Wkr, St of La; cp/Krewe of Hercules, Mardi Gras Assn; hon/W/W: W 1962, S&SW 1980-81.

F

FABRE, LOUIS FERNAND oc/Psychiatrist; b/Sept 13, 1941; h/5503 Crawford St, Houston, TX 77004; ba/Same; m/Betty Murray; c/Amy, Holly; ed/BS Akron Univ 1962; PhD Case-Wn Reserve Univ 1966; MD Baylor Col Med 1969; Internship, Residency; pa/Clin Assoc Prof Psychi, Univ Tex Med Sch, Houston 1974-76; Assoc Lectr, Alcoholism Cnslrs Prog, Univ Houston 1973-; Owner-Dir: Crawford St Clin, Houston 1973-, Champions Clin, Houston 1973-74, Portland Clin, Houston 1974-75, Fabre Clin, Houston 1975-; Pres Fabre Leasing Inc, Houston 1973-; Med Dir, Res Testing Inc, Houston 1973-; Active Staff Mem, Psychi Dept, St Josephs Hosp, Houston 1973-; Num Other Former Profl Positions; Fellow Am Col Clin Pharmacol; Profl Assns; World Cong Mbrships; hon/Assoc S'ship Awd, Univ Akron; Phi Sigma Alpha; NIH Travel Fellow to 3rd Intl Cong Endocrinol, Med; AMA Physicians Recog Awd; W/W: Tex, S&SW; Nat Reg Prominent Ams & Intl Notables; Men Achmt; Am Men & Wom Sci; IPA; Fellow Intercont Biog Assn (England); Pub'd Author.

FAGGETT, HARRY LEE oc/Professor; b/Jan 10, 1921; ba/PO Box 2042, SC St Col, Orangeburg, SC 29117; c/Frances, Walter, Jacquelyn, Heather, Barry; p/Walter (dec) and Lucy Faggett (dec); ed/BS Hampton Inst 1941; AM 1945, PhD 1947 Boston Univ; pa/Prof Eng, SC St Col; NCTE; MLA; r/Epis; on/Abstract Selected for Pub For Schlrs in 55 Fgn Countries by Univ Mich *Language and Language Behavior Abstracts*; Author *Blacks and Other Minorities in Shakespeare's England* 1970, *Lines to a Little Lady* 1976.

FAGLIE, KAY MARIE RUNDQUIST oc/Registered Nurse; b/Feb 4, 1948; h/Rt 5 Box 278A, Moncks Corner, SC 29461; ba/Moncks Corner; m/Jerry C; c/Shawn Christopher; p/Gust William and Betty Mae Parsons Rundquist, Seminole, FL; ed/Att'd Ga St Col 1966-67; Grad'd St Joseph's Infirm Sch of Nsg 1969; pa/Staff Nurse Med Intensive Care Unit, Pediatrics, Renal Dialysis St John's McNamara Hosp 1969; Staff Nurse Surgical & OB Recovery Sers 1972-73; Staff Nurse Emer Dept, Asst to Dir Nsg Ser, Nurse Coor Utilization Review, Supvr Emer Dept Candler Gen Hosp 1973-78; Commun Hlth Nurse Women, Infants & Chd Prog; Well Child Assessment & Devel Screening Clin, Berkeley Co Hlth Dept 1979; Ofc Nurse, Berkeley Fam Pract 1979-; Emer Dept Nurses Assn; Am Heart Assn; Ga Affil Am Heart Assn; Cert'd Instr Basic Life Support; RN SD, Ga & SC; r/Luth; hon/Awd for Naming Ofcl Newslttr of Am Heart Assn, Ga Affil 1980; W/W S&SW.

FAIN, ANNIE LOVE oc/Nurse, Registered Midwife; b/June 16, 1920; h/916 Campbell St, Palestine, TX 75801; ba/Palestine; m/Cleo Sr; c/Cleo Jr; p/Enoch W Sr (dec) and Ophelia Henry, Palestine, TX; ed/AA Mary Allen Jr Col; Voc Sch Nsg; Jones Bus Sch; Post Grad Sch of Nsg Chgo; Att'd Tyler Jr Col; Glover & Davenport X-Ray Trg Classes; pa/Lic'd Voc Nurse; Reg'd Midwife St of Tex; Asst Admr Patton's Clin & Voorhies Hosp; Charge Nurse So Heritage Nsg Home; cp/Assoc Charaties, Civic, Sch & Rel Orgs; r/Christian Ch; hon/Miss Lincoln High Class of 1938-39; Ser Awd Twilight Yrs Com of Palestine; Alpha Kappa; Most Versatile Yng Lady fr Commun; Tex Christian Missionary F'ship; Tchr of Yr Awd, Ch Sch Dept Fulton St Christian Ch; E W Henry Fam Plaque; Sojourner Truth Awd, Nat Assn Negro BPW Clb.

FAIR, MATTHEW DEWEY oc/Assistant Principal; b/June 13, 1927; h/808 S Thompson Ave, Deland, FL 32720; ba/Deland; m/Flora V; c/Kathy Ann, Matthew Dewey Jr; p/dec; ed/BS; MEd; mil/AUS Medic 2 Yrs; pa/Asst Prin Deland HS; NEA; FTP; cp/Kiwanis; Pres Sch Bd St Peters Cath Ch; Past Cmdr Am Legion; Past Pres Vet Clb; r/Cath; hon/Human Relats Man of Yr 1970.

FAIRBANKS, DOUGLAS JR oc/Actor; Writer; b/Dec 9, 1909; h/The Vicarage, 448 North Lake Way, Palm Beach, FL 33480; ba/New York, NY; m/Mary Lee Epling; c/Daphne, Victoria, Melissa; p/Douglas Fairbanks Sr (dec); Anna Beth Fairbanks Whiting (dec); ed/Polytech Sch, Pasadena, Cal; Harvard Mil Sch, Los Angeles, Cal; Privately Tutored in London, Paris; mil/USNR Lt (jg) to Cmdr, Sea Duty 1941-44; Released to Inactive Duty 1946, Promoted to Capt 1952; Retired Resv 1974; Spec Advr to Cmdr in Chief US Naval Forces Europe; Staff C-in-C US Naval Forces, NATO; US Naval Deleg to SEATO Conf London 1971; pa/Actor in Num Films incl'g: "The Prisoner of Zenda", "Having Wonderful Time", "The Exile"; Plays: "My Fair Lady", "The Pleasure of His Company", "The Secretary Bird"; Num Radio & TV Broadcasts; Writing & Spkg Engagemts; Est'd Criterion Film 1935, Douglas Fairbanks Ltd 1952; Currently: Pres Fairtel Inc, Pres Boltons Trading Co, Pres Westridge Inc, Assoc Mus Mgmt Conslt; London: Chm Douglas Fairbanks Ltd, Dir Norlantic Recordings Inc, Dir Norlantic Devel Co Ltd, Dir Cavalcade Films Ltd; cp/Appt'd by Pres Roosevelt as Presl Envoy for Spec Mission to Brazil, Argentina, Uruguay, Chile, Peru, Panama 1940-41; Var Temporary Diplomatic &/or Mil Duties in Europe, Asia, NAm for: Ofc of Pres, St Dept, ECA, USN,

USIA, Var US Embassies; Other Appts; Mem: Coun on Fgn Relats Inc, Am Acad of Polit & Social Scis, Acad of Motion Picture Arts & Scis 1935-64, Denver Ctr for Performing Arts (Adv Coun 1972-); England: Pilgrims Soc, Royal Shakespeare Theatre, Spec Com Order of St John of Jerusalem, Others; hon/Num Hons & Awds for Diplomatic, Public or Philanthropic Sers; Citations for Mil Sers; Medals for Mil Campaigns; Civilian Medals or Citations; Hon Degrees; F'ships.

FAIRBANKS, HAROLD VINCENT oc/Professor Metallurgic Engineering; b/Dec 7, 1915; h/909 Riverview Dr, Morgantown, WV 26505; ba/Morgantown; m/Marilyn M; c/Elizabeth M, William M; p/Oscar W Fairbanks (dec); Muriel A Fairbanks, Holland, MI; ed/BS 1937, MS 1939 Mich St Univ; Metallurgy S'ship MIT 1939-40; pa/WVa Univ, M'town: Prof Metallurgic Engrg, Chm Engrg Dept & Metallurgical Engr, Engrng Experimt Sta 1955-, Assoc Chm Dept Chem Engrg 1973-, Res Fellow, Coal Res Bur 1972-, Former Positions; Advr for Mining & Metallurgical Engrg Dept, Taiwan Provincial Cheng Kung Univ, Tainan, Taiwan (Formosa), Free China, Purdue-Taiwan Engrg Proj 1957-59; Conslt: Coal Res Bur of WVa Univ 1966-, M'town Machine & Hydraulic Inc 1965-, Preiser & Wilson, Charleston, WVa 1974, Ethyl Corp, Ferndale, Mich 1967, U Fidelity & Guarantee Co, Clarksburg, WVa 1965-66, US Bur of Mines 1964-67, Num Others; Res, Grants & Contracts: NSF 1975-, Nat Steel F'ship 1951-66, Senate Res Grants 1960, 64, NASA Space Oriented Res 1964-66, Nat Steel Corp 1960-62, Others; Duties as Overseas Advr: Est'd Separate Mining Engrg & Metallurgical Ed Curric Approved by Min of Ed for Cheng Kung Univ, Est'd Sys of Accreditation for Engrg Dept in Taiwan Adv'd by Chinese Inst Engrs, Assisted Mining & Metallurgic Engrg Dept of Cheng Kung Univ in Introducing New Metallurgy Courses, Conslt for Sci Ed Prog in Taiwan Under Min of Ed for Repub of China, Pt-time Advr for Chem Engrg Dept at Cheng Kung Univ; Fellow AAAS; Num Profl Assns; Pres M'town Chapt Profl Engrs 1962-64; St Chm Profl Engrs in Ed 1966-69; Am Chem Soc; Chm Wabash Valley Sect (Terre Haute, Ind) 1945-46, Chm WVa Sect (M'town) 1954-55, Nat Com Mem 1955-57; Chm Engrg Sci Sect, WVa Acad Sci 1969; Ext Res; Reg'd Profl Engr: Ind, WVa; Cert'd Corrosion Specialist, Nat Assn of Corrosion Specialist, Nat Assn of Corrosion Engrs; Other Former Positions & Activs; r/U Presb; hon/Num Profl Pubs; Sigma Xi, Past Pres WVa Chapt; Tau Beta Pi, MSU S'ship; Phi Kappa Phi; Phi Mu Alpha; Grad w High Hons, MSU; Cheng Kung Univ Labs Named in Hon: Fairbanks Applied Metallurgic Engrg Lab, Fairbanks Quality Control Lab; Num Biogl Listings.

FAIRCHILD, JAMES D oc/Executive; b/Mar 26, 1942; h/1316 Westover Ave, Norfolk, VA 23507; ba/Norfolk; m/Pamella Tutton; c/Patricia, Tamara, Thomas James; p/George C Fairchild, Buffalo, NY; Harriett Kepley (dec); pa/Exec VP Norfolk C of C; cp/Bd Am Red Cross, Tidewater Chapt; Chm Norfolk Yng Life; Bd of Regents, Inst for Org Mgmt; Bd V Assn Chamber Execs; Mgr Sev Polit Campaigns in SC (St & Local); Greenville Tax Appeals Bd 1972-74; r/Presb; hon/Toastmaster of Yr, Greenville, SC 1972.

FALLS, LEE WAYNE oc/Statistician; b/Mar 17, 1929; h/6200 Stratford Ct, Huntsville, AL 35806; ba/Space Flight Center, AL; m/Patricia Y; c/Tad Lee, David Wayne, Randall Allan; p/George B Falls (dec); Winifred A McVeigh, Madison, AL; ed/BS Geol; BS Maths; MS Math Statistics; pa/Statistician George C Marshall Space Flight Ctr; Mem Am Statistical Assn; r/Prot; hon/NASA Outstg Perf Awd; NASA Tech Utilization Awds, 1970, 71, 73, 77; NASA Skylab Achmt Awd; Apollo Achmt Awd.

FANNINGS, SHIRLEY McGEE oc/Teacher; b/Jan 18, 1937; h/725 Laverne Dr, NW; Atlanta, GA 30318; ba/Atlanta; m/Charles Carl Sr; c/Vivian Cecelia, Charles Carle Jr; p/Bud and Josephine H McGee, Pine Mtn, GA; ed/BA Spelman Col 1958; MA 1970, DAS-5 Cert 1974 Atlanta Univ; pa/Rdg Tchr; Atlanta Bd Ed; Bd Dirs Atlanta Assn Edrs; Public Relats Com Chp Ga Assn Edrs; NEA; Intl Rdg Assn; Assn Classroom Tchrs; Assn Supervision & Curric Devel; Assn Childhood Ed Intl; cp/Delta Sigma Theta; Am Bus Wom's Assn; Nat Coun Negro Wom; NAACP; YWCA; r/Meth; hon/Outstg Elem Tchr of Am 1974; Plaque for Dedication to Tchg Profession 1974; Plaque for Outstg Ser to PTA 1979; Tchr of Yr 1980-81; Plaque for Perfect Attendance 1974-80.

FANT, CHARLES W III oc/Minister of Youth Education; b/Nov 29, 1952; h/2791 Meadowlake Dr E, Apt 2A, Memphis, TN 38118; ba/Memphis; p/Charles and Betty Byrd Fant, Anderson, SC; ed/Att'd Clemson Univ; MDiv, MRE SWn Bapt Theol Sem; pa/Min Yth Ed, First Bapt Ch of Memphis; r/Bapt; hon/Pres Student Body SWn Bapt Theol Sem; Outstg Yng Man Am 1978-79; W/W Am Cols.

FANT, ELENA B oc/Executive; b/Aug 15, 1908; h/508 W Baylor St, Weatherford, TX 76086; ba/Weatherford; m/George; p/John Wesley (dec) and Beatrice Acord Newsom (dec); pa/Savings & Loan Exec; cp/Hon Mem 4-H Clbs Parker Co; E D Farmer Relief Fund Bd Trustees; Nat Trust Hist Preserv in US; Past Mem Bd Dirs Weatherford C of C, A I M; Mem Jim

Wright Cong Clb; r/Bapt; hon/W/W: Fin & Indust, Am Wom; DIB; World W/W Wom.

FARBER, ERICH ALEXANDER oc/Distinguished Serivce Professor and Director; b/Sept 7, 1921; h/1218 NE 5th St, Gainesville, FL; 32601; ba/G'ville; m/Ellen W; c/Hans F, Webb W; p/I (dec) and Hilde Farber, Phoenix, AZ; ed/BS 1943, MS 1945 Univ Mo; PhD Univ Iowa 1949; mil/AUS; pa/Dist'd Ser Prof; Dir Solar Energy & Energy Conversion Lab; Pioneer in Fields of Heat Transfer, Fluid Flow & Engergy Conversion; Built Solar Energy Lab, Univ Fla to Level of Intl Reputation; Devel'd Boiling Curve; NSF/NASA Solar Energy Panel; Mem Solar Energy Working Grp; cp/Fla Energy Comm; Boy Scoutmaster; r/Presb; hon/Battle Field Comm; Purple Hearts; Silver Star; Other Mil Decorations; Cit from AF for Work in Solar Energy Conversion; Worcester Reed Warner Gold Medal for Outstg Contbns to Permanent Lit of Engrg; Fla Blue Key Dist'd Fac Awd 1973; Col of Engrg Outstg Ser Awd 1974; Hon of Resolution of Ala Conservancy 1977; Crosby Field Awd, Am Soc of Heating, Refrigeration & Air-Conditioning Engrs for Best Tech Paper & Best Paper of 1976; Invited by Austrian Govt to Give Sci Lect in Vienna 1977; Cit & Cert of Recog, NASA, for Invention & Devel of Fluidic Gas Analyzers; Dist'd Lectr 1977, Univ Fla; Cit NASA for Contbns to Space Prog; Charter Mem Solar Hall of Fame; Frontiers of the Mind Lectr; Nom'd Dist'd Ser Prof 1979; Engrs Jt Coun Engrs of Dist; Outstg Floridians; W/W: Am, World; World W/W Sci; Ldrs in Am Sci; Am Men of Sci; Others; Author Over 400 Pubs; Co-Author 6 Books.

FARLEY, GRACE LOUISE oc/Homemaker; b/Jan 3, 1942; h/Pgh, TX 75686; m/Joe Jr; c/Aaron, Stephanie, Angelia, Byron, Frederick; p/Lucius and Eunice Johnson, Natchitoches, LA; cp/Cookie Chm, Day Camp Dir, Gilr Scout Cadette Ldr (Germany), Jr Ldr (Ariz), Asst Ldr & Cadett Ldr (Pgh); Boy Scouts Den Ldr & Asst Den Mother; r/Bapt; hon/Letter of Apprec for Jr Scouts for Vol Sers; Plaques for Contbns to Girl Scouts; Poem to be Pub'd in 1980 Anthology of Dreams.

FARMER, CHARLES RICHARD oc/Minister; b/Oct 7, 1933; h/Rt 3, Box 105, Walnut, MS 38683; ba/Same; m/Faye Wilbanks; p/Robert E Farmer, Columbia, MO; Martha L Farmer (dec); ed/BA Okla Bapt Univ; MDiv New Orleans Bapt Theol Sem; mil/AUS Signal Corps 1954-56; pa/Min Sems; Miss Bapt Sem Instr; Evangelist; Tchr; Chm Num Bapt Assn Coms; cp/Rotary Intl; NE Miss CB Clb; r/So Bapt; hon/Pres Elect Rotary Clb.

FARMER, GEORGE oc/Instructor; b/Dec 15, 1937; h/Longwood, FL; ba/Seminole Commun Col, Sanford, FL; c/Tammy, Beverly, Michael; p/Tom (dec) and Virgie Farmer, New Smyrna Bch, FL; ed/Cand BA Univ Ctrl Fla 1981; pa/Instr Voc-Tech Air Conditioning, Refrig, Heating; Lead Mechanic Armstrong Heating & Air Conditioning; Mechanic Pan Am World Airways; Seminole Voc Assn; Fla Voc Assn; Am Voc Assn; Fla Assn Trade & Indust Ed; Fla Assn Commun Cols; Refrigeration Ser Engrs Soc; hon/New Smyrna Bch JCs Outstg Com Chm 1969; Outstg JC 1969; Outstg Yng Men Am Awd 1970; Nom'd Outstg Voc Edr From Seminole Commun Col 1976 & 77.

FARMER, JAY PRATT oc/Regional Marketing Director; b/Aug 21, 1954; h/289 Landcaster Circle, Marietta, GA 30066; ba/Atlanta; p/James L and Elveta Y Farmer, Hazlehurst, GA; ed/BS Public Relats; pa/Regional Mktg Dir, Carter & Assocs Inc; Intl Coun Shopping Ctrs; Public Relats Ser of Am; cp/Yng Repubs Ga; r/Ch of Christ; hon/Outstg Commun Ser 1978; Eagle Scout; Citizen of Wk 1977.

FARMER, MILDRED LaVERNE oc/Associate Professor; b/July 12, 1931; b/3113 Ginn Rd, Knoxville, TN 37920; ba/K'ville; p/Clark (dec) and Lou Ella Abbott Farmer, Townsend, TN; ed/BS 1953, MS 1959; pa/Assoc Prof Fam Ecs, Agric Ext Ser, Univ Tenn; Am Home Ec Assn; Tenn Home Ec Assn; Nat Assn Ext 4-H Agts; Tenn Assn Ext 4-H Agts; Am Coun Consumer Interests; Elect Wom's Roundtable; cp/Chm Bd of Trustees Bethel Bapt Ch & Cemetery; Ch Organist & SS Tchr; Bd Dirs Smoky Mtn Passion Play Assn; r/Bapt; hon/Omicron Nu Nat Home Ec Hon Soc; Epsilon Sigma Phi Nat Hon Ext Frat; W/W Am Wom.

FARMER, WADE ODICE oc/General Manager; b/Aug 26, 1928; h/3432 Sheffield Dr, Mtn Brook, AL 35223; ba/B'ham, AL; m/Freda M; c/Anne F Lipscomb, Lynne, Kimberley; p/Wade Thomas (dec) and Maggie Farmer (dec); ed/BS VPI; mil/AUS Capt; pa/Gen Mgr Union Ctrl Life Ins Co; GMAC; Sales Mkt Exec; Nat Assn Life Underwriters; Inverness Clb; cp/Kiwanis; Elks; Sertoma; B'ham C of C; r/Epis; hon/W/W W 1974-75.

FARMER, WILLIAM ALTON oc/Minister; b/Sept 15, 1905; h/Gen Del, Como, TN 38223; m/Edna Powers; c/Donald, Ramona; p/Oscar L Farmer, Martin, TN; Beulah Richee Farmer, Gleason, TN; ed/AB Union Univ; pa/Pastor 40 Yrs; Modr of 5 Different Bapt Bodies; Exec Bd Tenn Bapt Conv; Trustee Mid-Cont Bible Col; r/Bapt.

FARQUHAR, BETTY MURPHY oc/Artist, Poet; b/June 17, 1924; h/PO Box 127, Marion, TX 78124; ba/Same; m/Winfred G; c/Frank Mruphy, Hans Michael, Cynthia Jean; p/Hans Karl (dec) and Emma Edelmann Ritter, Kirchenlamitz, Germany; pa/Poetry Pub'd in Anthols & Mags; cp/Vol Work in Chs, Hosps, Libs, PTA, Yth Grps; r/Luth; on/New Worlds Poetry Awd 1978; Patriotic Achmt Cert 1978; Other Poetry Awds.

FARR, DAVID T oc/General Sales Manager; b/May 28, 1943; h/106 Larkwood Dr, Sanford, FL 32771; ba/Sanford; m/Joyce E; c/June, Jackie, Debbie, David; p/T H Jr and Dallas P Farr, Orlando, FL; ed/BA Polit Sci; Master City Plan'g Ga Tech; pa/Gen Sales Mgr, Sales Assoc, Stentstrom Realty; Chm C of C Roads & bridges Comm; c/Former Secy Kiwanis Clb; Sanford City Comm; Bd Dirs Kiwanis; r/Bapt; hon/Million Dollar Salesman 1978; JC Dist'd Ser Awd; Outstg Yng Rel Ldr.

FARR, ROY H oc/Bus Driver; b/May 25, 1916; h/Sylacauga, AL; m/Agnes; c/Rebecca Hagan, Connie; p/Lester (dec) and Jessie Farr (dec); mil/USAF WWII; pa/Trailways Bus Driver; r/Meth; hon/Safety Pin Each Yr w/out Accident; One Millon Mile Safety Plaque; Two Million Mile Safety Plaque.

FARRAR, BEVERLY JAYNE oc/Associate School Psychologist; b/Nov 6, 1928; h/10220 Mapleridge Dr, Dallas, TX 75238; ba/Dallas; m/R L; c/Dorothy Jane; p/Jack Murphy (dec) and Jane Thomas Clark, Dallas, TX; ed/BA 1949, MA 1967 So Meth Univ; MEd E Tex St Univ 1972; Post Grad Studies TCU, TWU, SHSU & ETSU; pa/Assoc Sch Psychol, Richardson Indep Sch Dist; Edr 16 Yrs; Speech Pathol 6 Yrs; Assn Richardson Ed; TSTA; NEA; Dallas Psych Assn; Tex Psych Assn; Am Speech & Hearing Assn; cp/AAUW; Alpha Delta Pi Alumnae; r/Meth; hon/Zeta Phi Eta; Achmt Awd Delta Kappa Gamma; W/W S&SW; Devel'd Resource Book on Classroom Mgmt 1980; Hon Mem Alpha Psi Omega.

FARRAR, C EDWIN oc/Assistant Regional Administrator, Student Financial Assistance; b/Jan 4, 1941; h/1219 E Marvin Ave, Waxahachie, TX 75165; ba/Dallas; m/Carol Reglin; c/Louis Christopher, Eric Winston, David Ryan; p/C Randall and Mary Eleanor Green Farrar, Palmer, TX; ed/BS Tex Christian Univ 1963; Num Other Courses & Progs; mil/AUS Med Ser Corps 1st Lt; pa/Asst Regional Admr, Claims & Collections, Student Financial Asst, Dept of Ed 1971-; Univ Tex 1968-71; Naval Audit Ser 1967; Army Dispensary, Pentagon 1965-67; Jack T Holmes & Assocs Advtg 1964-65; Nat Contracts Mgmt Assn; Delta Sigma Pi; cp/Waxahachie Symph Assn: Chm Bd Dirs 1978, Treas 1979, Publicity Chm 1980, Chm Bd Dirs 1981; Hist Waxahachie Inc: Bd Dirs & Prog Com 1980, Bd Dirs & Treas 1981; Ellis Co Museum; Gingerbread Trail: Home on Trail 1976, 79, Equipment Chm, Trail Com 1980; Waxahachie Chorale; Waxahachie Commun Theatre; Smith Cemetery Assn, Trustee; Waxahachie City Coun 1981-; Waxahachie HS Ex-Students Assn, VP Pubs 1981; TCU Alumni Assn; r/First U Meth Ch-Waxahachie: V-Chm Adm Bd 1977 & 78, Chm Adm Bd 1979 & 80, Mem Adm Bd 1981, Chm Evangelism 1981, Fin Com 1979 & 80, Pastor/Parish Com 1979, 80, 81, Chancel Choir, Pres Bldrs Sunday Class 1978, 79, 80, Chm Piano Com 1981; hon/Cash Awd 1974; Quality Step Increase 1978; Cert of Apprec, Regional Admr 1979; 1 of 3 Nat Finalists for John E Fogarty Public Pers Awd 1980; Tex Employer of Yr Awd, Tex Chapt Am Assn of Wkrs for Blind 1980; Quality Step Increase 1980.

FARRIS, JEFFERSON D JR oc/University President; b/Sept 30, 1927; h/140 Donahecy, Conway, AR 72032; ba/Conway; m/Patricia Camp; c/Rebecca F Jessup, Elizabeth Camp, Jeff D III; p/Jeff Farris (dec); Loretta Gragson Farris, Conway, AR; ed/BSE; MA; MPH; EdD; mil/USN 1946-48; pa/Pres, Univ of Ctl Ark; Nat Endowmt for the Humanities Liaison; Chm Bd Dirs Ark Hlth Manpower; Chm Ark Coun for Hlth Careers Bd Dirs; Conslt to: AMA Conf on Physicians & Schs, So Reg Ed Bd Mtl Retardation Wkshop, Univ of Tex Sch of Public Hlth, Others; cp/Bd Dirs Conway Meml Hosp; Pres Rotary Clb; Conway C of C; r/Meth; hon/Layman of Yr, Ark Soc of Dentistry for Chd; Outstg Edrs of Am; Men of Achmt; W/W: Hlth Ed, S&SW.

FARRIS, TERRELL ELEANOR oc/Student; b/Jan 1, 1965; h/Van Vleck, TX; p/Jack Truett and Sara A Terrell Farris, Van Vleck, TX; ed/HS Student; r/Nazarene; hon/DAR Essay Awd 1976; Hon Student, Treas Student Coun 1981; UIL 1st Div Piano 1981; Wharton Co Piano Fest 1978, 79, 80, 81; Outstg Soph Band Student 1981.

FASCELL, DANTE B oc/Member of Congress; b/Mar 9, 1917; h/6300 SE 99 Terrace, Miami, FL 33156; ba/Washington, DC; m/Jeanne-Marie; c/Sandra Jeanne F Diamon (Mrs Frank), Toni Francesca, Danta Jon; p/Charles Fascell (dec); Mary Fascell, Coral Gables, FL; ed/JE 1938 Univ of Miami-Coral Gables; mil/Fla Nat Guard 1941; Comm'd 2nd Lt 1942; Ser'd in African, Sicilian & Italian Campaigns; Disch as Capt 1946; pa/Atty; Mem: Fed, Am, Fla, Coral Gables, Dade Co Bar Assns, Omicron Delta Kappa, Kappa Sigma; cp/Elected to 84th Cong of US 1954 & to each

PERSONALITIES OF THE SOUTH

congress thereafter; Appt'd by Pres to Rep US at 24th Gen Assmebly of UN 1969; Com on Intl Relats 1957-; Chm Comm on Security & Cooperation in Europe 1976-; CoChm US-Canadian Inter-Parliamentary Group; C of C; Project Hope; Am Legion; Loyal Order of Moose; Others; r/Prot; hon/Num Hons & Awds incl'g: Doctor of Humanities Awd, Pan Am Med Assn 1976, Freedom Awd, Nat Conf on Soviet Jewry 1977, Dist'd Ser Awd, Partners of the Americas 1974, Italian-Am of Yr, The Italians Inc 1977, Dist'd Ser Awd, Coun of Jewish Fedns 1978, Num Others.

FAULK, LILLIAN T oc/Retired Teacher; b/Aug 3, 1912; h/508 Gibson, W Memphis, AR 72301; m/Raymond D (dec); p/Charles D (dec) and Aurelia J Tibbels (dec); ed/BSE; MA; EdS; pa/Mem Local, St & Nat Ed Assns; Intl Rdg Assn; Assn Supervision & Curric Devel; Nat Assn Elem Sch Principals; cp/W Memphis Quota Clb; OES; Civic Auditorium Comm; r/Bapt; hon/Fav Tchr Ark 1959; W Memphis Wom of Yr 1965; Rec'd Sustaining Mbrship in W Memphis Jr Aux 1973; W Memphis Sch Bd Named New Elem Sch "The Lillian T Faulk Elem Sch" 1978.

FAULK, WAYNE STEPHEN oc/Minister; b/Dec 12, 1948; h/Rt 3 Box 822, Marianna, FL 32446; ba/Marianna; m/LuAnne Pierce; c/Jennifer Paige, Jeffrey Wayne, Jacqueline Ann; p/A J Faulk (dec) and Frances Faulk Fisher, Selma, AL; ed/Lab & X-Ray Tech; Dip in Theol; BA Rel & Psychol; pa/So Bapt Min; Asst Chr Trg Dir, Butler Co, Ala; Evangelism Dir, Vernon Parish, LA; Cp/Hm Steering Com; Concerned Citizens of Ward 8, Vernon Parish, LA; r/So Bapt; hon/Alpha Mu Gamma.

FAWLEY, OKEY BROWN JR oc/Executive Director; b/June 8, 1938; h/Morgantown, WV; m/Pamela Shelton; c/Joshua, Zachary; p/O B Fawley Sr (dec); Ruth Louise Fawley Hadsell, Masontown, WV; ed/BS 1960, MSW 1965 WV Univ; mil/AUS; pa/Bell Telephone of Pennsylvania 1960-64; Psychi Social Wkr Veteran Hosp, Salem, Va 1965-68; Exec Dir Valley Commun Mtl Hlth Ctr 1968-; Assoc Prof WV Univ Dept of Psychi 1969-; Assoc Prof WV Univ Sch of Nsg 1969-; NASW; Orgr & First Pres WV St Assn of Mtl Hlth/Mtl Retard Progs; cp/Rotary Intl; Morgantown Little Leag Assn; All-Star Coach; Org'd & Chaired NEED (24 Hr Telephone Answering & Referral Ser); r/Meth; hon/W/W S&SW 1980; Selected Tech Asst Conslt, Nat Inst Mtl Hlth.

FEAGANS, ROBERT RYAN oc/Farming; b/Jan 11, 1918; h/Rt 5, Box 324, Madison Heights, VA; ba/Roanoke, VA; m/Helen C; c/Helen F Smith; p/Charles B and Minnie C Feagans, Lynchburg, VA; ed/BS w Hons; mil/Capt Inf PTO; pa/Bus Farming; hon/W/W Fin & Indust.

FEATHERS, CHERYL ANN WRIGHT oc/Teacher; b/Apr 23, 1952; h/9912 Old Third St Rd, Louisville, KY 40272; ba/L'ville; m/Charles Leo Jr; p/Arthur William and Verna Mae Bandy Wright, L'ville, KY; ed/BA w High Hons 1974, MEd w Highest Hons 1977 Univ L'ville; pa/Tchr Eng & Humanities, Jefferson Co Bd of Ed; Jefferson Co Tchrs Assn; KEA; NEA; Assoc Mem Nat Ret'd Tchrs Assn; r/Bapt; hon/Outstg Teenager Am 1969-70; Phi Kappa Phi; Woodcock Soc; W/W S&SW; DIB; Altrusa Clb & Thomas S'ship 1972-74, Univ L'ville; Elected to Cwens.

FECHTEL, VINCENT JOHN JR oc/State Legislator; b/Aug 10, 1936; h/PO Box 1675, Leesburg, FL 32748; ba/Same; c/Vincent John III, Kara; p/Vincent Sr and Joanne Fechtel, Leesburg, FL; ed/BA Bus Adm Univ of Fla; pa/Real Est; Retail Merchandising; cp/St Legislator; Kiwanis Clb; Elks Clb; Conservation Coun; Jacksonville Bch Histl Soc; C of C: Leesburg, Mt Dora, Eustis, Lake Co, Others; r/Cath.

FEDOR, SHARON JEANNE oc/Teacher; b/Jan 22, 1950; h/1555 NE 148 St, N Miami, FL 33101; p/Leo (dec) and Jeanne Fedor, N Miami, FL; ed/BA Psych; MEd; pa/Tchr Spec Ed-Autistic; r/Cath; hon/Phi Kappa Phi, Univ Fla Chapt 1975.

FEENEY, KEVIN oc/Library Director; b/May 30, 1954; ba/302 WS Henderson, Cleburne, TX 76031; m/Vicki; c/Catherine F Feeney, Plano, TX; ed/BA So Meth Univ 1976; MLS Tex Wom's Univ 1979; Doct Cand TWU; pa/Data Line Info Mgr 1980; Lib Dir Cleburne Public Lib 1981; ALA; PLA; TLA; Tarrant Regional Lib Assn; Tex Municipal Lib Dirs Assn; hon/Beta Phi Mu 1980.

FELDER, VADA PHILLIPS oc/Director of Training Union Publications; b/Jan 27; h/1331 Stewart St, Ft Worth, TX 76104; m/O P (dec); p/Cornelius Phillips (dec); Parthenia Bennett (dec); ed/AB summa cum laude Wiley Col; MRE Tex Christian Univ; pa/Dir Tng Union Pubs, Nat Bapt Conv, USA Inc; Dean U Christian Ldrship Sch; Instr Bishop Col, Dept Christian Ed, Dallas, Tex 1965-71; Chm Christian Ed Wkshop, Bishop Col; Group Convenor, Ft Worth Area Coun of Chs, Christian Ed Com; Coun Chm, Christian Edrs Assn; Former Basileus of 2 Chapts, Zeta Phi Beta Sorority Inc; Other Former Assns & Activs; cp/NAACP: Former Sponsor Yth Coun, Bd Mem; Urban Leag: Bd Mem, Chm Prog Com; YWCA: Bd Chm, Secy, Bd Mem, Life Mem; Tarrant Co Grand Jury (1st Negro Wom); No Dist US Jury (1st Negro Wom); Mayors Com of Status of Wom; Ldr in Wkshops & Confs; Num Others; r/Instr, Classification Com, Nat SS & BTU; Instr; Registrar, Galilee Griggs Dist SS & BTU Cong; St James Bapt Ch: VP WMU, Sponsor Deaf Mute Prog; OES; Others; hon/Pub'd Author; Wom of Yr, F B Brooks Lit & Art Clb 1955; Num Dist'd Ser Awds; Rel Achmt Trophy, Delta Sigma Theta; Outstg Citizen Awd, KNOK Radio Stn; Achmt Trophy, N Tex Conf MAE Mins Wives Guild; BSA Awd; GSA Plaque; W/W Black Men & Wom in Tex; VP Felder Day Proclamation, Ft Worth; 100 Most Outstg Wom in Rel, Nat Bapt Conv; Num Others.

FELTS, JAMES DONIVAN oc/Band Instrument Repair Technician; b/Jan 24, 1944; h/620 4th Ave, SW, Decatur, AL 35601; ba/Decatur, AL; m/Margaret Freeman; p/Louis J (dec) and Ethel A Felts, Waverly, TN; ed/BS Austin Peay St Univ 1968; Band Instr Repair Deg, Wn Iowa Tech 1974; pa/Decatur Band Instr Co; Repair Sems, Univ Ala; Charter Mem Nat Assn Profl Band Instr Repair Techs; Assoc Mem Middle Tenn St Band & Orchestra Assn; Phi Mu Alpha Symphonia; r/Presb.

FELTY, RONALD GENE oc/Attorney; b/May 5, 1953; h/2807A Edgemere Dr, Plainview, TX 79072; ba/Plainview; m/Susan; p/J W and Jean Felty, Lubbock, TX; ed/BA Tex Tech Univ 1975; JD Tex Tech Univ Sch of Law 1978; pa/Asst Dist Atty, Hale & Swisher Cos of Tex 1978-80; Co Atty, Hale Co 1980-; St Tex Bar Assn; Hale Co Bar Assn; Am Bar Assn; Am Trial Lwyrs Assn; Tex Trial Lwyrs Assn; cp/Dem Nom for Co Atty, Nov 1980 Gen Elect; r/Meth; hon/Outstg Yng Men Am 1980.

FENDLEY, CHARLES ROBERT oc/Company Vice President; b/Mar 9, 1946; h/Rt 1 Box W35A, Jasper, GA 30143; ba/Jasper; m/Linda Sue Mull; c/Michael Shane; p/Robert W and Ruby Lee Fendley, Jasper GA; mil/AUS 1966-68; pa/Salesman Moore Furn Co 1967-72; Supvr H D Lee Co 1965-67; Gen Mgr Glen Head Inc 1972-79; VP Jasper Yarn Processing 1979-; Owns 50%: Jasper Yarn Processing In, Jasper Leasing Inc, Custom Yarn Co; 33% NEn General Ins of Jasper Inc; Amicalola Elect Mbrship Corp, VP 1976-; Am Assn Chemist & Colorist; Aircraft Owners & Pilots Assn; cp/Qtrback Clb; Pickens Co JCs; Booster Clb; r/Bapt; hon/W/W S&SW; Bronze Star; Purple Heart.

FERGUSON, GEORGE ROBERT oc/Lawyer; Legislator; b/Aug 13, 1933; h/PO Drawer 89, Raymond, MS 39154; ba/Same; m/Martha Gillespie; c/Martha Elizabeth, George R III, Cade Drew; p/George R Ferguson Sr (dec); Eugenia Williams Ferguson; ed/BS Miss St Univ; LLB Jackson Sch of Law; mil/AUS 2 Yrs; pa/Mem: Hinds Co, Miss, Am Bar Assns; cp/Mem Miss Ho of Reps; Lions Clb; Dem Party; r/Presb, Elder.

FERGUSON, PETER ROWLAND oc/International Recycling Consultant; b/Oct 29, 1945; h/PO Box 11794, Atlanta, GA 30355; ba/Eugene, OR; m/Andrea Carole Hamilton; c/Charles Hamilton; p/William C and Sarah Jane Rowland Ferguson, Roswell, GA; ed/BS, MA: Ed; mil/USMC, Hon Disch 1967; pa/Intl Recycling Conslt; Trader; Mem: ISIS, NACR; Owner/Dir Camp Pinnacle; cp/Repub Liberal; Master Instr w Am Nat Red Cross; r/Ch of Christ; hon/Commandant Meritorious Mast, Oct 9, 1967; Past Pres Recycling Sers Ltd 1976; Intl Lectr on Recycling Waste Probs.

FERNANDEZ, ERIC oc/Physician; b/Sept 19, 1944; h/Miami Lakes, FL; ba/1550 W 84th St, Suite 27, Hialeah, FL 33014; m/Cheryl Ann Burr; c/Katrina Lorenne, Candice Ann, Lorene Carin; p/Ceferino and Dolores Fernandez-Brito, Miami Lakes, FL; ed/BS Univ Md 1965; MD Med Sch, Univ Salamanca, Spain 1972; Internship & Residency Univ Miami Sch Med Affil'd Hosps 1972-75; mil/ROTC Univ Md 1962-63; pa/Internist-Cardiologist, Pvt Pract 1972-; Clin Asst Prof Med, Univ Miami Sch Med 1978-; VP Med Staff Palm Springs Gen Hosp; Am Col Phys; Am Soc Internal Med; Dade Co Med Assn; Fla Med Assn; Palmetto Gen Hosp, Mem ICU-CCU Com, Pharm & Therapeutics Com, By-Laws Com; cp/Nat Repub Cong Com; Am Red Cross; Am Security Coun Ed Foun; Nat Jogging Assn; NAm Vegetarian Soc; Editorial Res Bd, Postgrad Med Jour; Police Surg, Mem Am Law Enforcement Ofcrs Assn; Nat Police Reserve Ofcrs Assn; r/Christian; hon/Winner Nat Asthma Ctr Bike-a-Thon 1980; Author "Acetaminophen Liver Toxicity" *New England Journal of Medicine* 1977.

FERNSTROM, MEREDITH M oc/Director of Consumer Affairs; b/July 26, 1946; h/1124 Westmoreland Rd, Alexandria, VA 22308; ba/Wash DC; m/John R; p/Mr and Mrs Lee W Mithcum, Rutherfordton, NC; ed/BS 1968 Univ NC-Greensboro; MS 1972 w Hons Univ Md, Col Pk; pa/Dir Consumer Affairs 1974-76; Spkr; Sems; Ednl Activs for Consumers & Bus; Mem: Bd Dirs Soc of Consumer Affairs Profls, Am Coun on Consumer Interests, Am Soc of Testing & Mats, Am Home Ecs Assn, Am Nat Standards Inst; Advr; Author Articles in Profl Jours; hon/Phi Kappa Phi; Omicron Nu; Commend for Superior Perf, Mayor Wash 1975; Dist'd Yng Alumni, Univ Md; Outstg Yng Wom Am; W/W Fin & Indust.

101

PERSONALITIES OF THE SOUTH

FERRELL, NORMA A oc/Nurse; b/Jan 17, 1938; h/PO Box 1132; Florence, SC 29503; b/Florence; m/John Henry; c/John Henry Jr, William Eugene, Barbara Ronalyn, Brenda Lee; p/Fred Ira Ely, Coshocton, OH; Thelma Susan Turner (dec); ed/AA; RN; LPN; pa/RN; Charge Nurse, Bruce Hosp; AACN: Pee Dee Chapt SC & Nat; cp/Dem Party; r/Bapt; hon/Nolan Awd, SC Area Voc Sch 1967; W/W: SC Student Nurses 1977, Am Jr Cols 1977, Am Wom; Pres SC Student Nurses Assn 1977-78; Nat Del Student Nurse Conv 1977; Nom'd Del SC Nurses Assn Nat Conv 1977; Mem Am Assn Critical Care Nurses; Highest Scholastic Average Assoc Deg Nsg Prog, Florence Darlington Tech Col 1977.

FERRIS, DIXIE RHINEHART CALDER oc/Instrumentation Detailer; b/June 29, 1951; h/PO Box 18952, Raleigh, NC 27619; ba/Research Triangle Park; m/Richard B; c/(Stepchd:) Leigh Ann, Deborah Denise; p/Leroy A and Jessie R Calder, Lumberton, NC; ed/BA UNC-Chapel Hill 1973; Post Grad NC St Univ 1977, 80; Dip Fonville-Morisey Ctr for Real Est Studies 1979; pa/Misc Steel Detailer 1973-76; Legal Assoc 1976-79; Fabricator-Metal 1979; Instrumentation Detailer 1979-; Am Soc Metals; Am Soc Notaries; Am Soc Tng & Devel; Instrument Soc Am; Nat Soc Female Execs, Former Network Dir; cp/Precnt Secy, Wake & Mecklenburg Cos, NC; Notary Public; Gtr Raleigh C of C; r/Bapt; hon/Former Bus Mgr *The Bulletin.*

FESS, RICHARD ALLEN oc/General Manager; b/Aug 15, 1945; h/142 W Wagon Wheel Way, Lake Mary, FL 32746; ba/Altamonte Springs, FL; m/Linda S; c/Lisa A, Bradley Allen; p/John H Fess, Pamona, CA; Opal G Boyl, New Albany, IN; ed/BS Ind Univ 1969; mil/AUS 1963-64; USAR 1964-69; pa/Retail Mgmt, Gen Mgr Robinsons of Fla 1975-; L S Ayres, Ayr-Way Stores 1969-75; Am Soc Trg Dirs; Nat Retail Merchants Assn; Altamonte Mall Bd Dirs VP; cp/City Coun-man Lake Mary, Fla; 1st VP & Campaign Chm U Way of Seminole Co 1981; Pres Lake Mary Community Improvement Assn 1981; Lake Mary C of C; Orlando C of C; Life Mem Ind Univ Alumni Assn; r/Meth.

FETTER, ELIZABETH ANNE oc/Coordinator, Services for Handicapped Students; b/Feb 6, 1948; h/11419 Flamingo Ln, Dallas, TX 75218; ba/Mesquite, TX; p/Theodore and Sarah Fetter, Philadelphia, PA; ed/BA; MA; MEd; pa/Coor, Sers for Handicapped Students, Eastfield Col; Mem: Jr Col Student Pers Assn of Tex; cp/Mem: Am Coalition of Citizens w Disabilities (ACCD); r/Presb; hon/Outstg Yg Wom of Yr, Tex 1977; 1 of 10 Outstg Yg Wom in US 1977.

FEZ-BARRINGTEN, BARIE oc/Professor; b/Dec 28, 1937; ba/College Station, TX; m/Christina; p/Henry Joseph and Anne Fez-Barringten; ed/BFA Pratt Univ 1962; MArch Yale Univ 1968; mil/ROTC; pa/Prof Tex A&M Univ Col of Arch, Dept of Bldg & Construction; Pres & Fdr Labs for Metaphoric Environs; Proj Mgmt Inst, Houston Chapt, Ednl Dir; Nat Assn Corp Real Est Execs; Intl Real Est Fed; Nat Coun Arch Reg Bds; Former Treas & Urban Design Subcom Mem; Am Inst Archs; Tex Real Est Tchrs Assn; Am Real Est & Urban Ecs Assn; Yale Univ Asst for S'ship & F'ships; cp/Fdr & Pres Pratt Inst Broadcasting Clb; Tenn St Com of Arts; Editor Yale's Archl Jour; Editor Chermsyeff's Report on Urban Plan'g to Bur of Standards; Nat Trust for Hist Preserv; C of C: Houston, College Sta, Bryan; r/Luth; hon/Pub'd Author.

FIELD, ELIZABETH ASHLOCK oc/Community Volunteer in Historic Preservation; b/Nov 27, 1915; h/2451 Brickell Ave, Apt 8G, Miami, FL 33129; m/H Lamar (dec); c/Elizabeth Field Wassell; p/Jesse Vernon (dec) and Felecia Bruner Ashlock (dec); ed/Grad'd Litle Rock Jr Col 1934; Att'd Wash Univ 1934-35; pa/Dir "Villa Marre," Angelo Marre House; Dir: Ark Commem Comm, Ark First St Capitol, Ark Confederate Capitol; Former Govt Ofcl; cp/The Vizcayans; Fla Trust for Hist Preserv Inc; Miami Design Preserv Leag; Trustee Dade Heritage Trust, VP 1975-76; Nat Trust for Hist Preserv; Metro Mus & Art Ctr; r/Epis; hon/Quapaw Qtr Assn Dedicated Ser Awd 1974.

FIELDS, B H oc/Associate Professor; b/Oct 20, 1922; h/Marshall, TX; p/Floyd (dec) and Willette H Fields (dec); ed/BA Wiley Col 1944; MS Tex So Univ; Further Studies Tex Christian Univ, Lamar St Univ, Atlanta Univ, Rice Univ, Okla City Univ, N Tex St Univ; pa/Assoc Prof Natural Scis, Wiley Col; Envir Protection Agcy; Nat Sci Tchrs Assn; AAUP; cp/Kappa Alpha Psi; Citizens' Adv Com; r/Evergreen Bapt Ch: Deacon, Sr Choir Soloist; hon/Awd for Dist'd Ser, U Negro Col Fund 1980; Outstg Instr Awd; Pioneer in Field Ed Awd; Article "Creative Teaching" to *Science Journal.*

FIELDS, BETTY JO oc/Thoroughbred Trainer; b/Mar 18, 1934; h/Box 819, Miami, OK 74354; ba/Miami, OK; m/Bobby Joe; c/Tommy, Debra; p/Frank Shamblin (dec); Opal Beck, Los Alamitos, CA; pa/Lady Horse Tnr; Pres Ladies Aux, HBPA So Ill Div; cp/Dem Party; r/Christian; hon/Contbr to *Horseman's Journal.*

FIELDS, DEARIE WHITE oc/Instructor; b/May 15; c/Melonie Rene Lee, Felicia Rochelle White, Deirdre White; p/Tyree Bishop Fields, Dallas, TX; Junaita Miller, Mt Pleasant, TX; ed/BS Paul Quinn 1962; MEd Prairie View AM Univ 1978; PhD Cand N Tex St Univ 1980; pa/Tchr Voc Ed Subjs, Bus & Mgmt Magnet Sch 3 Yrs; Alex W Spence Acad Occupl Invest Tchr 2 Yrs; Extra 3 Movies; 2 Commercials; Tex St Tchrs Assn; Beverly Hills Bapt, Clrm Tchrs of Dallas; Tchrs Nat Assn; Tex Occupl Clb of Am; Dallas Urban Leag; cp/Former Editor, Jack & Jill of Am; r/Bapt; hon/Curric Writer of Ofc Duplication Procedures at BMC 1978; Creator Grooming & Hygience Dept 1978.

FIELDS, GLADYS DOLORES oc/Nurse; b/Mar 10, 1927; h/Bartlesville, OK; c/Nancy Ann Wake, Linda Lee Ferguson, John Robert, Janis Sue Dragon; p/Gladys A Dodson, Niotaze, KS; ed/RN Wesley Sch of Nsg 1945; cp/Hosp RN, House Supvr OB 20 Yrs; Surveillance Nurse 1977-; ANA; ONA; APIC; cp/Repub Party; r/Meth; hon/Cert in Epidemiology, So Calif Sch of Med.

FIELDS, JUNE NASH oc/Partner Insurance Agency; b/Aug 30, 1940; h/Rt 1 Box 272, Baxter, TN 38544; ba/Cookeville, TN; c/Terry Lynn, Jennifer Maria; p/Ben Hooper Nash (dec); Herdley Nash McCowan, Cookeville,TN; ed/Dip Nashville Bus Col 1959; Att'd Tenn Tech 1 Qtr; pa/Ptnr Maynard-Fields Ins Agcy; Ofc Mgr & Commercial Ins Rating & Placement Poteet Ins & Assoc; cp/Coach Jr Pro Basketball Leag; r/Bapt; hon/S'ship to Play Basketball w Semi-Profl Team 1958.

FIELDS, KENNETH WAYNE oc/Pastor; b/Jan 7, 1947; h/PO Box 236, Killen, AL; ba/Killen; m/Terry Ann Tucker; c/Paula Kay, Angela Gay, Rebecca Joice; ed/BA Hist 1973 Athens Col; MA Christian Ed 1975 Scarritt Col; Certs: Parliamentarian Procedure 1974, Biblical Hebrew 1975 John C Calhoun Commun Col; DMin 1978 Luther Rice Theol Sem; pa/Pastor Killen Meml Bapt Ch 1976-; Morgan Assn: Assnl SS Dir 1973-74, Assnl Missions Com 1974-75, Assnl Yth Com 1973-74; Colbert-Lauderdale Assn: Assnl Nom'g Com 1976-77, Assnl Evangelism Com 1977-78; Has preached in: Jamaica, Trinidad, Venezuela, Barbados, other sections of West Indies; Pub'd Article in *Outreach Magazine* 1972; cp/Ch Growth Conslt; r/So Bapt; hon/Phi Tau Chi; Sigma Tau Delta.

FIELDS, ROBERT I oc/Insurance Agent; b/Jan 26, 1934; h/Dale City, VA; m/Carole Hundley; c/Robert W, Monique L, Nicole L; p/Taft I Fields, Mt Vernon, NY; Valaria Brown Fields (dec); ed/BA Va Union Univ 1961; Grad Study: Univ Del & Universite de Besancon, France; pa/Ins Agt w NY Life 1967-; Tchr 4 Yrs; No Va Assn Life Underwriters, Pres 1979-80; Va Union Univ, Immediate Past Pres, Nat Alumni Assn; cp/Prince William Co Park Authority, Charter Mem; r/Bapt; hon/W/W: S&SW 1980, Black Ams 1980.

FIFER, CLIFTON JR oc/Teacher, Coach; b/Feb 10, 1952; h/Kerrville, TX; c/Clifton Curtis Scott; p/Mr and Mrs Clifton Fifer Sr; e/BS Hist, Hlth & PE 1976; pa/VP Local Chapt F'ship of Christian Aths; TSTA; cp/VP Local Beauty Pageant; Dir Local Black Awareness Prog; r/Meth; hon/Recog'd for Ldrship in Commun 1980; All W Tex Track Man 1971.

FIGHTMASTER, DONALD C oc/Administrator; b/June 13, 1932; ba/Commonwlth of Ky, Dept of Pks, Frankfort, KY 40601; m/Pauline; c/Donna Holland, Walter, Debra Curby; p/Judd and Amanda Fightmaster, Louisville, KY; ed/BS Univ L'ville 1958; MS Ind Univ 1960; mil/USAF 4 Yrs; pa/Dpty Commr, Ky St Pk's Sys; Dir Golf Assn; cp/Past VP Sportsman Supper Clb; Past Pres Univ L'ville Lttrman's Clb; Past VP L'ville Qtrback Clb; r/Christian; hon/Nat One-Arm Golf Champ: 1970, 72, 73, 75, 76, 77, 78; Intl One-Arm Golf Champ 1975 & 77; First Golf Inductee into L'ville Sportsman Hall of Fame 1975; Ath of Yr, L'ville Qtrback Clb 1977.

FIGUEREDO, NANCY oc/Physician; b/July 3, 1937; h/5521 SW 64 Pl, Miami, FL 33155; ba/Miami; c/Carrie, Rafael Miguel, Alexia; p/Jose (dec) and Georgina Hernandez (dec); ed/Dr Med & Surg; pa/Phys; r/Cath.

FILLYAW, HAROLD oc/Professor and Administrator; b/June 25, 1942; h/Houston, TX; ba/PO Box 2684, Prairie View, TX 77445; p/William and Mable J Everett, Wilmington, NC; ed/BA Fayetteville St Univ 1965; AM 1971, PhD 1975 Univ Mich; pa/Dir Freshman Studies Eng Dept, Prairie View A&M Univ 1976-; Dir Rdg & Learning Skills Ctr, Prairie View A&M Univ 1975-76; Prin Bader Sch, Ann Arbor, Mich 1974-75; Dir Rdg Staff Devel, Ann Arbor Public Schs 1972-74; Interim Prin Mack Elem Sch, Ann Arbor 1971; Tchr, Ann Arbor Public Schs 1970; Visiting Lectr, En Mich Univ 1970; Tchg Fellow, Dept Behavioral Scis, Univ Mich 1969-70; Res Asst, Sch Ed, Univ Mich 1968-70; Resr, Urban Sociol Prog, Univ Mich 1968; Indiv Res Proj, Univ London 1969; Elem Public Sch Tchr, Pontiac, Mich 1965-67; Life Mem Univ Mich Alumni Assn; NAACP; Am Psychol Assn; Mich Rdg Assn; Intl Rdg Assn; Intl Cross-Cultural Psychol Assn; Alpha Phi Alpha Frat, Epsilon Tau Lambda Chapt; Tex Psychol Assn; Am Psychotherapy Assn; NCTE;

cp/Hearthstone Civic Assn; Hearthstone Country Clb; r/Bapt; hon/Phi Kappa Phi; Phi Delta Kappa; NDEA Tchg F'ship 1967-65; Special Rackham F'ship 1968-69.

FINCH, CHARLES CLIFTON oc/Governor of State of Mississippi; b/Apr 4, 1927; h/Governor's Mansion, PO Box 139, Jackson, MS 39205; ba/Same; m/Zelma Lois Smith; c/Janet Herrington, Virginia Anne, Charles Clifton II "Chuck", Stephen Nicholas "Nicky"; p/Carl Bedford and Ruth Christine McMinn Finch (dec); ed/BA Polit Sci, Public Adm; JD Univ of Miss; mil/AUS 1945, Gunner in field artillery division; pa/Mem, Ofcr Miss Bar Assn; Mem Am Bar Assn; cp/St Rep 1960-64; DA 17th Circuit Ct Dist 1964-72; Gov 1976-80; Mason; Lions Intl; Civitans; Moose; OddFellows; Am Legion; VFW; r/Mem 1st Bapt Ch; hon/Num Awds & Hons.

FINCH, RAYMOND LAWRENCE oc/Judge; b/Oct 4, 1940; h/81 TanTan Terrace, Christiansted, St Croix, USVI 00820; ba/Christiansted; m/Lenore L; c/Allison, Mark, Jennifer; p/Wilfred C and Beryl E Finch, Christiansted, St Croix; ed/AB; JD; mil/1966-69 Armor, Capt; pa/Judge, Territorial Ct of VI; Mem: Am Judges Assn, Am Bar Assn, Nat Bar Assn; cp/Dem Party; Dir BSA; r/Luth; hon/Cert of Apprec; Army Commend; Bronze Star; Admitted: VI Bar, 3rd Circuit Ct of Appeals.

FINCH, THOMAS WESLEY oc/Manager; h/200 Bridgeway Dr #202, Lafayette, LA 70506; fam/Married; 1 son; cp/Area Mgr for CORRINTEC/USA, Cathodic Protection Sers Inc 1980-; Engr, Cathodic Protection Sers Inc (Denver, Colo) 1973-80; Other Former Positions; Reserv Ofcrs Assn; Nat Assn Corrosion Engrs; Soc Am Mil Engrs 1966-75; Am Security Coun, Nat Adv Bd 1978-; hon/W/W: W, Technol; Men of Achmt; Other Biogl Listings.

FINCHER, FREEMAN O oc/Pharmacist; b/Jan 12, 1892; h/306 Semmes St, PO Box 92, Alexander City, AL 35010; ba/Alexander City; m/Aulsie Mae Edwards (dec); c/Mrs Sam Damson, Mrs R Taylor Abbot; p/William G (dec) and Louise Chester Fincher (dec); ed/Pharmacy; pa/Ala St Bd Pharmacy; cp/Num Civic Orgs; r/Meth; hon/Awd & Plaque for 50 (67) Yrs Ser as Pharmacist.

FINK, KENNETH ERNEST oc/Program Director; b/Apr 18, 1944; h/Rt 1 Box 454, Claremore, OK 74017; ba/Claremore; m/Jessie Pauline; c/Herschel, Sarah, Sam, Tracy; p/Harry (dec) and Lillian Fink, Southfield, MI; ed/BA; PhD; mil/USPC Uganda; pa/Dir Nat Am Studies Prog, Claremore Col; Co-Editor *Race to Power*; Author *A Cherokee Notion of Development*; cp/Adv Mem Rogers Co Cherokee Assn; r/Jewish; hon/Photo Exhibs; Exchequer of Yr Awd; Sigma Alpha Mu.

FINNELL, CHARLES ADKINS oc/Businessman; Attorney; State Legislator; b/Sept 16, 1943; h/PO Box 468, Holliday, TX 76366; ba/Austin, TX; p/Leslie B Sr and Mary Frances Finnell (dec); ed/Univ of Tex; St Marys Univ Law Sch; pa/Mem Tex Ho of Reps Dist 53, 1967-; cp/Dir W Tex C of C; r/U Meth Ch, Holliday, Tex.

FINNELL, SCOTT oc/Minister of Youth; b/June 22, 1956; h/2209 Gorman #3, Waco, TX 76707; ba/Waco; m/Pamela Kay; p/Billy Bob and Lawana Finnell, Grand Prairie, TX; ed/BA & MA Rel, Baylor Univ; pa/Grad Student; Min Yth; Tex Bapt Hist Soc; r/Bapt.

FINNEY, ERNEST A oc/Third Circuit Court; b/Mar 23, 1931; h/24 Runnymede Blvd, Sumter, SC 29150; ba/Sumter; m/Frances Davenport; c/Ernest A III, Lynn Carol, Jerry Leo; p/Ernest A Sr and Collen Godwin Finney; ed/BA cum laude 1952; JD 1954; pa/3rd Circuit Ct Judge; Am Bar Assn; SC Bar Assn; Sumter Co Bar Assn; Black Lwyr Caucas; Nat Bar Assn; cp/SC Elect Comm; NAACP; Claflin Col Bd of Trustees; r/Meth; hon/Native Son Awd; Bedford-Styvesant JC Awd.

FINNEY, MARY BAILEY CREWS oc/Social Work in Gerontology; b/Oct 18, 1922; h/15 Blue Ridge Dr, Liberty, SC 29657; ba/Liberty; m/William Bert Finney; c/Sondra F Bowie (Mrs), Jan F Garner (Mrs), William Bert II, Robert Bailey; p/Joseph and Flossie Bailey Crews (dec); ed/Fla St Univ; pa/US Dept of Commerce; Welcome Wagon Intl; SC Employmt Security Comm; E T Kelley Jewelry & Gift Shop; cp/Mayor City of Liberty; Secy-Treas SC Small Municipal Assn; VP Pickens Co Municipal Assn; Holds Positions in Num Civic Orgs; r/Bapt; Var Coms, Tchr, Choir; hon/Pres Greenville Metro Ladies Golf Assn; Winner Greenville Metro Golf Assn Championship 2 Yrs; Pres Pickens Co CC Wom's Golf Assn 14 Yrs; Recip JCs Presl Awd for vigorous & effective support while serving as Mayor; Commun Ldrs & Noteworthy Ams; DIB; World W/W of Wom.

FIORENTINO, CARMINE oc/Attorney; b/Sept 11, 1932; h/2164 Medfield Trail, NE, Atlanta, GA 30345; p/Pasquale and Lucy Coppola Fiorentino; ed/Att'd Hunter Col 1951; Att'd Columbia Broadcasting Sch 1952; LLB Blackstone Sch Of Law 1954; LLB John Marshall Law Sch 1957;

pa/NY 1st Wkmens Com Bd, NY St Dept Labor 1950-53; Ct Reporter, Hearing Stenographer for Gov Thomas E Dewey's Com of St Counsel & Attys 1953; Public Relats Secy, Indust Home for Blind 1953-55; Legal Stenographer, Resr, Law Clrk 1955, 1957-59; Secy For Import-Export Firm 1956; Pvt Law Pract 1959-63; Atty-Advr, Trial Atty US Dept Housing & Urban Devel & Ofc of HUD Gen Counsel 1963-74; Acting Dir Disaster Field Ofc, US Dept Housing & Urban Devel 1973; Bars: St of Ga, Dist of Columbia; US Supreme Ct; US Dist Ct; US 2nd Circuit Ct of Appeals; US Dist Ct, No Dist Ga; US 5th Dist Ct of Appeals; Pract'd US Ct of Claims; Am Bar Assn; Fed Bar Assn; Atlanta Bar Assn; Decatur-DeKalb Bar Assn; Am Judicature Soc; Old War Horse Lwyrs Clb; Assn Trial Lwyrs; cp/Jr C of C; Toastmasters Intl; Intl Platform Assn; Smithsonian Inst; Century Clb; Repub Nat Comm; Columbian Repub Leag; Nat Hist Soc; Atlanta Hist Assn; Atlanta Botanical Gardens; Gaslight Clb; hon/Most Progressive Commercial Student Awd, NYC Public Sch Sys 1950; Pitman Shorthand Achmt Awds 1948, 49, 50; Commend US Crusade for Freedom 1951; Commend US House Un-Am Activs Com 1951; Commend from Dir US Dept Housing & Urban Devel for Excel in Disaster Relief Work 1972; Num Biogl List'gs.

FISCHER, DOMINIC PETER oc/Artist-in-Residence; b/May 20, 1949; h/Harbour W Apts E-1, Rocky Mt, NC 27801; ba/Rocky Mt; p/O'Niel and Natalie Fischer, Pgh, PA; ed/BA Colgate Univ; pa/Artist-in-Residence, Nash Tech Inst; Mime; r/Christian; hon/All-East & Hon Mention All-Am Fball Teams 1969-71; NCAA Record for Most Rushes in Fball Games.

FISH, WILLIAM STERLING oc/Educational Administrator, Part-time Farmer; b/Aug 18, 1933; h/PO Box 7, Anthony, FL 32617; ba/Same; m/Betty T; c/Connie, Tim; p/Foy (dec) and Sara C Fish (dec); ed/Bach Deg w Hons Univ Fla 1956; Masters Deg Univ Fla 1965; pa/Marion Co Sch Bd; Marion Co Prin's Assn, Pres 1970; Fla Assn Sch Admrs; cp/Kiwanis, Pres; Shrine, Secy; C of C; Com of 100, Dir; Farm Bur; Cattleman's Assn; Chm, Dem Party, Marion Co; Supt Schs, Marion Co, Fl; r/Meth: Chm of Bd; hon/Selected as Top Admr Marion Co by PTA 1968; Selected as 1 of 100 Top Sch Execs by Exec Edr 1980; Golden Sch Awd, Fla 1978; Pub'd Author.

FISHER, CHARLES HOWARD oc/Research Professor; Consultant; b/Nov 20, 1906; h/1941 Braeburn Dr, Salem, VA 24153; ba/Salem; m/Lois Carlin; p/(dec); ed/BS 1928 Roanoke Col; MS 1929, PhD 1932 Univ Ill; pa/Dir So Utilization & Devel Div, USDA, NO, La 1950-72; Conslt & Res Prof, Roanoke Col, Salem 1972-; Pres Sci Fair of Gtr NO Area 1967-69; cp/Pres Roanoke Col Alumni Assn 1978-79; hon/So Chemists Awd 1956; Herty Medal; Chem Pioneer Awd, Am Inst of Chemists; Hon DSc Tulane Univ 1953; Hon DSc Roanoke Col 1963; Am Men of Sci; W/W World; Cosmos Clb, Wash, DC; Intercont Biog Assn.

FISHER, ELIZABETH CAVITT BOUSHALL oc/Executive Director; b/Mar 11, 1941; h/312 Marguerite Rd, Metairie, LA 70003; ba/Metairie, LA; m/Michael Stewart Kilpatrick; c/Ann Cavitt, Carolyn Stewart; p/Francis McGee and Ruth Cavitt Taliaferro Boushall; ed/BA La St Univ 1963; pa/Exec Dir, Fdr Intl Desgin Counsel Inc; cp/Fin Adv Bd LWV; Repub Wom; Wom in Communs; New Orleans Mus Art; AAUW; 1st Wom Editor Tex Aggie Mag; r/Presb; hon/Del Govs 1st Conf Womn 1976; W/W Am Wom; World W/W Wom.

FISHER, JIMMIE LOU oc/Auditor of State; b/Dec 31, 1941; h/606 N Ridgeway, Little Rock, AR 72205; ba/Little Rock; p/Tollie H and Joyce E Cooper, Paragould, AR; pa/Green Co Treas 8 Yrs; Currently Auditor of St; cp/Dem Nat Com; Ark St Dem Com; Ark Dem Wom's Clb; r/Bapt.

FITZGERALD, ALBERT JOSEPH oc/Management Executive, Vice President; b/Aug 24, 1949; h/1206 Kingsway Dr, Huntsville, AL 35802; c/Patrick Joseph; p/Thomas Wilbert and Sophia Beatrice Fitzgerald, H'ville, AL; ed/BA Univ Ala-H'ville 1971; MA Psychol 1974; MS Computer Sci 1977; DSc Cand Technol Mgmt; pa/Computer Software Devel Mgmt Exec, VP Colsa Inc; IEEE; ACM; ASM; DPMA; cp/Mgmt Dir H'ville JCs 1973-74; Dir, Fin Chm, First VP, Pres U of Ala Huntsville Alumni 1976-80; Fdr, Dir, SEn Inst Alumni 1979-80; r/Bapt; hon/JC of Yr 1974, H'ville & Ala JCs; Life Mbrship Univ Ala Alumni Assn.

FITZGERALD, DIXIE oc/Businesswoman; b/Jan 2, 1932; h/6 Dogwood Rd, Lake Brenda, Mineola, TX 75773; ba/Mineola; m/J D; c/Dwight, Diane, Donna; p/Ellen Brashier, Garland, TX; ed/HS Grad; pa/Co-Owner: Mineola Motor Lodge, Carl's Pest Control; cp/Pilot Intl; 3rd Lt Gov 1979-80, 2nd Lt Gov 1980-81; r/Bapt.

FITZGERALD, MARY ELLEN oc/Student, Program Director; b/Apr 1, 1937; h/PO Box 512, Boiling Springs, NC 28017; m/Charles; c/Denece Fite, Charles B Jr, Clifton Frank, Mark Steven, John Michael; p/Robert W Davis (dec); ed/Student Gardner-Webb Col; pa/Prog Dir WGWG FM; Piano & Organ Tchr 12 Yrs; Radio & Communs; cp/Little Leag Bd Dirs;

Pres Band Clb; Homemakers Clb; Rdg Sci for Blind; r/So Bapt: Organist, Yth Dir, Ch Mus Dir; hon/Fam of Yr 1958; Sigma Tau Delta.

FITZSIMONS, AGNES MARIE oc/Hospital President; b/Dec 29, 1904; h/PO Box 3927, Lafayette, LA 70501; p/James and Mary Elizabeth McCauley Fitzsimons; ed/RN Our Lady of the Lake Sch of Nsg 1928; BS St Louis Univ 1942; MS Cath Univ Am 1950; pa/US Citizen 1933; Professed in Franciscan Missionaries 1925; Mgr Bus Ofc, Our Lady of Lake Hosp 1938-39, Med Supvr Instr 1936-41, Dir Sch of Nsg 1943-46, Asst Adm 1960-65; Lab Tech Inst Sci, St Francis Hosp, Monroe, La 1929-36, Purchaing Agt 1946-49; Pres Our Lady of Lourde Hosp, Lafayette 1966-; Diocese Coor of Hlth Affairs; Mem La St Bd Nurse Examrs; NCEA; NLN; Am Adult Ed Assn; Nat Fed VPW Clbs; Nat Polit & Social Sci Assn; cp/US Nat Travel Clb; Nat Hist Soc; Cath Lib Assn; L'Heure de Music Clb.

FLACK, WILMA LEE oc/Saleslady; b/Aug 17, 1924; h/857 Scenic Dr, Cullman, AL 35055; ba/Same; m/Benford Loyd; p/Robert and Myrtle Burks, Cullman, AL; pa/Salelady; r/Bapt; hon/Gold Cups; Co Pres Awd.

FLAHERTY, DAVID THOMAS JR oc/Attorney; b/June 17, 1953; h/Mtn Circle, Cedar Rock Ests, Lenoir, NC 28645; ba/Lenoir; p/D T and Nancy H Flaherty, Lenoir, NC; ed/BS Math; JD Law; pa/ABA; NCBA; NC St Bar; NC Acad Trial Lwyrs; cp/Work w JCs; Repub Party of NC; r/Meth; hon/Blue Key.

FLAKE, JANICE LOUISE oc/Professor; b/Nov 24, 1940; h/1065 Merritt Dr, Tallahassee, FL 32301; ba/Tallahassee; p/Berlen and Eloise Flake, Decatur, IL; ed/BS Fla St Univ; MA, PhD Univ Ill; pa/Prof Fla St Univ; Author; r/Meth; hon/EH Taylow Awd, Outstg Math Major; NSF Part for Num Insts; W/W Am Wom.

FLANNERY, GERALD V oc/Professor, Executive; b/Dec 27, 1930; h/Lafayette, LA; ba/USL Box 43809, Lafayette, LA 70504; m/Laura; ed/BA Univ Miami 1948; MA Univ Fla 1963; PhD Ohio Univ 1966; mil/US Army Signal Corps 1952-54; pa/Owner Media Cnslts Co; Prof Dept of Commun 1978-; Prof Mass Commun, Mid Tenn St Univ 1973-77; Prof Commun, Univ So Miss 1971-73; Assoc Prof, Dept Commun Arts, William Paterson Col 1969-71; Asst Prof, Chm, TV-Radio-Film, Dept of Speech, Auburn Univ 1966-68; Tchg Fellow, Ohio Univ, Col of Communs 1963-66; News Writer, Reporter, Editor, Producer, WTVJ-TV, CBS News Affil, Miami 1958-61; Sigma Delta Chi; NAEB; SCA; AEJ; SSCA; LSA; LAB; NEA; LEA; BEA; r/Cath; hon/Author Num Poems & Articles.

FLANSBURG, MARGARET A oc/Instructor and Adjunct Professor; b/Jan 8, 1936; h/NW 28th, Okla City, OK 73107; ba/Okla City; m/Leonard D; c/Sundra, Mark, Miles; p/Durward B (dec) and Neesa G McMahon, Marie, MI; ed/BFA Painting 1958 Univ Okla; MA Hist of Art 1971 Univ Iowa; PhD Cand Renaissance Studies Univ Okla; pa/Instr, Humanities Dept, Ctrl St Univ, Edmond, Okla; Adj Prof, Art Hist, Okla City Univ; Docent Tnr, Okla Mus of Art; Dir of Ed Okla Mus of Art 1978-80; Art Gal Staff: Cedar Rapids, Iowa & Bristol, England; Journalistic Writing; Practicing Artist; cp/LWV; Common Cause; Commun Music; r/Unitarian; hon/Rosenblum Watercolor Awd, Carnegie Mus; Leitzeiser Awd 1958, Univ Okla; Delta Phi Delta; World W/W Wom 1980, 81.

FLANZER, JERRY PHILIP oc/Social Worker, Professor, Consultant; b/June 25, 1943; h/Little Rock, AR; ba/Grad Sch of Social Work, Univ Ark Little Rock, 33rd and Univ, Little Rock, AR 72204; m/Sally Manesberg; c/Matthew, Douglas; p/Marcella S Flanzer, Chgo, IL; ed/BS Roosevelt Univ 1965; MSSA Wn Reserve Univ 1967; DSW Univ So Calif 1973; pa/Assoc Prof Clin Social Work Pract; Dir Mid-Am Inst on Violence in Fams & Fam Ctr, Grad Sch of Social Work, Univ Ark Little Rock; Cnslt; Pvt Pract; Fellow Am Orthopsychiatric Assn; AASW; NASW; Fellow Res Soc Alcoholism; cp/Bd Mem LR Jewish Fed; Bd Mem Ark Gov's Conf on Fams; r/Jewish; hon/W/W SW 1980; NIMH F'ship 1970-72; Num Papers Pub'd.

FLEETWOOD, CAROLINE LANE oc/Teacher; b/June 8, 1900; h/Box 6, Conway, NC 27820; m/Joseph A (dec); c/Joseph A Jr; p/R Y (dec) and Annie G Lane (dec); ed/Grad Mary Baldwin Col; Spec Student Staunton Univ; pa/Tchr Mus Chowan Col 3 Yrs; Violinist in Orch; cp/Pres Conway Wom's Clb; Kirly Mus Clb; Garden Clb; PTA; Bapt Missionary Soc; OES; Delta Kappa Gamma; r/Bapt; hon/Num Mus Awds; Fam of Yr Awd, Conway, NC.

FLEGLE, LARRY VERNON oc/Investment Advisor; b/Aug 9, 1948; h/Sheffield, AL; ba/931 Avalon Ave, Muscle Shoals, Al 35660; m/Janice Marie; c/Krista; p/Vernon Frederick and Hazel Maxine Flegle, Lithia, FL; ed/BA Univ S Fla; MA Pepperdine Univ; Enrolled DPA Prog, Nova Univ; mil/USN 1968-72; pa/Reg'd Rep U Capital Securities; VP Slatton & Assocs Broadcasters (WBTG-FM); Intl Assn Fin Planners; cp/Secy Sheffield Kiwanis Clb; Bd Mem Colbert Co C of C; r/So Bapt.

FLEISCHER, ARTHUR CARROLL oc/Radiologist; b/May 15, 1952; ba/Nashville, TN; m/Leona Lynn; c/Branden Matthew; p/Eugene and Lucille Fleischer, Augusta, GA; ed/BS cum laude Emory Univ 1973; MD Med Col of Ga 1976; pa/Dept Radiology, Vanderbilt Univ Med Ctr; Region Grps VChm Am Inst Ultrasound in Med; Sigma Chi; Am Col Radiology; AMA; Radiological Soc of N Am; cp/Bd Mem Couples Clb, Temple; r/Jewish; hon/Pres's Awd Am Roentgen Ray Soc 1977; Miami Herold's Silver Knight Awd for Sci 1970; Author Over 30 Sci Pubs.

FLEMING, JAMES FURMAN oc/Vice President for Governmental Relations; b/Mar 31, 1937; h/4184 Idlevald Dr, Tucker, GA 30084; ba/Decatur, GA; m/Martha Capps; c/James F Jr, William Keith; p/Mrs I M Fleming, Conway, SC; ed/Grad N Greenville Jr Col 1960; St Bernard Col; Off-Campus Deg Prog, Upper Iowa Univ 1975; pa/VP for Govnmtl relats, U Egg Prodrs, Atlanta 1970-; Ala Poultry Indust Assn, Cullman, Ala: Exec Secy 1966-67, Exec VP 1967-70, Secy-Treas Ala Poultry & Eg Coun 1966-70; Other Former Positions: Profl Assns; cp/Tucker (Ga) Yth Coun; Assoc, Smithsonian Inst; Atlanta Coun of Intl Visitors Bur; Intl Cult Exc; PTAs; Other Orgs; r/Bapt; Clarkston Bapt Ch, Clarkston, Ga: Mem, Bd Deacons, Others; hon/Outstg Ldrship Awd in Poultry Indust, Poultry & Egg Nat Bd, Chgo, Ill 1963; Outstg Red Meat Promotion Awd, Nat Livestock & Meat Bd, Chgo 1964, 65, 66; Outstg Dairy Promotion Awd, Am Dairy Assn, Chgo 1965-66; Overall Commodity Awd, Am Farm Bur Fdn, Chgo 1964-65; Mgmt Achmt Awd, Am Soc Assn Execs, Wash, DC 1970; Num Biogl Listings; Others.

FLEMING, LACIE THERESA WADSWORTH oc/Homemaker; b/July 2, 1913; h/Sanford, FL; m/Sully Ward; c/Faye Elizabeth; p/Smauel Warren (dec) and Fannie Bennett Wadsworth (dec); ed/Att'd Chowan Col 1932-33; Att'd Motts Bus Sch 1943; Att'd Michael Stoffa's Oil Painting Sch 2 Yrs; Att'd Gladys Phillips China Painting Sch 6 Yrs; cp/Secy Kingston, NY Hosp Aux 1957-61; r/Meth; hon/St Fla Fed'd Wom's Clb First Prize Art Fest.

FLEMING, RICHARD M oc/Baseball Coach, Assistant Football Coach; b/Mar 31, 1948; h/514 S Maple, Nowata, OK 74048; ba/Nowata, OK; m/Vicki Lynn; c/Christopher Lance; p/Robert E and Alama Fleming, Tulsa, OK; ed/AA; BS; MS; pa/Hd Baseball Coach, Asst Fball Coach; Am Hist Tchr, Nowata HS; OEA; NEA; Okla Coaches Assn; Okla Baseball Coaches Assn; cp/Nat Hist Soc; r/So Bapt.

FLETCHER, DIXIE CHAFIN oc/Nurse; b/May 11, 1950; h/2525 Brookwater Circle, Birmingham, AL 35243; ba/B'ham; m/Oliver Mayo; p/Richard and Ann Lakewood, LuGoff, SC; ed/BS Nsg NWn St Univ 1972; pa/RN; ANA; Ala Nurse Assn; cp/Vol Wkr Mar of Dimes, Cancer, Arthritis; r/Meth; hon/W/W Am Wom 1979.

FLETCHER, JOHN CALDWELL oc/Bioethicist; Theology Educator; b/Nov 1, 1931; h/202 Vassar Place, Alexandria, VA 22314; ba/Bethesda, MD; m/Adele Woodall; c/John C Jr, Page Moss, Adele Davis; p/Robert C and Estelle C Fletcher, Birmingham, AL; ed/BA 1953 Univ S; MDiv 1957 Va Theol Sem; PhD 1969 Union Theol Sem, NY; pa/Bioethicist NIH, Bethesda; Theol Edr; Fdg Fellow Inst for Soc, Ethics, Life Scis; Fellow Kennedy Ctr for Bioethics, Georgetown Univ; cp/Dem City Com, Alexandria; r/Epis; hon/Fulbright Scholar; W/W: Am, Am Rel.

FLINT, CHARLES oc/Instructor, Department Chairman; b/June 8, 1931; h/809 Luella, Deer Park, TX 77536; ba/Pasadena, TX; m/Peggy Shepherd; c/Nancy, Julia, Amy; p/Robert L (dec) and Jane Flint (dec); ed/AA Kilgore Jr Col 1951; BBA E Tex St Univ 1955; mil/AUS 1953-55; pa/Instr-Coor Mgmt Devel Dept, San Jacinto Col; Tex Jr Col Tchrs Assn; Tex Jr Col Mgmt Edrs Assn; Jr Col DECA; E Tex St Univ T Assn; r/Bapt; hon/W/W S&SW 1980-81.

FLOOD, JOAN MOORE oc/Legal Staff Research Specialist; b/Oct 10, 1941; h/Irving, TX; ba/Associates Ins Grp, 800 W Airport Freeway, Irving, TX 75062; c/Angie; p/Harold W and Estanlena Fancher Moore, Grand Prairie, TX; ed/BMus N Tex St Univ 1963; MLA Prog SMU 1968-69; Mus Prog TWN 1978-79; pa/Ins Res & Legal Reference; Am Assn Law Libns; Spec Libs Assn; r/Epis; hon/W/W: SW, Lib Sci; NAII Res Dir; Author: "Current Trends in US Insurance"; "US Regulations of Insurance."

FLOURNOY, RICHARD LYNN oc/Minister of Music and Youth; b/Sept 26, 1957; h/1612 W 13, Plainview, TX 79072; ba/P'view; m/Debbie; p/Harold and Marva Fournoy, Lubbock, TX; ed/Att'g Wayland Bapt Col; pa/Dir 3 Choirs & Supvr 4th; r/Bapt; hon/Sports Editor HS Paper; Yrbook Photog; 2 Yrs All-Region Band.

FLOWERS, JOHN T oc/Postal Clerk; b/May 15, 1922; h/PO Box 492, Camden, TN 38320; ba/Camden; m/Doris Farrar; c/Donna Jean, Linda Kaye, Judy Anne, John Steven, James Nelson, Cynthia Louise, Christinia Jo; p/Thomas (dec) and Eva Flowers (dec); mil/WWII 1943-45 Ordnance Grp HQs; cp/VFW, Mason; r/Bapt; hon/Wk'd w Scouts as Scoutmaster 10 Yrs.

FLOYD, HENRY BASCOM III oc/Consulting Engineer; b/Sept 6, 1927; h/4017 Dobbs Dr, Huntsville, AL 35802; m/Rubie Fore; c/Rebecca, H B IV (Chip), Jennette, Tina; p/H B Jr and Isabelle Sanders Floyd (dec); ed/BSCE, MSIM; pa/Conslt'g Engr, Semi-Ret'd, H'ville; Reg'd Profl Engr: Ala, SC; cp/Scout Cnslr; Civitan Intl; Fdg Bd, Boys Home of NC; r/Meth; hon/NASA Exceptl Ser Medal; 12 Commends for Outstg Contbns to Space Scis; Fellow Mem ABI.

FLOYD, LEWIS EARL oc/Retired Navy, Antique Dealer, Amateur Actor; b/Mar 24, 1923; h/Oak Forest Est, PO Box 1431, Corinth, MS 38834; ba/Same; m/Florence; c/Sheila, Carl, Cynthia; p/Claud C (dec) and Lillian Floyd, Corinth, MS; mil/USN 30 Yrs Master Chief Petty Ofcr; pa/Past Asst Admr, Naval Hosp; cp/Elks Clb; VFW; Am Legion; Fleet Reserve Assn; Adj VFW; r/Epis; hon/Mil: 14 Medals & Awds Incl'g Purple Heart; 6 Pers Commends for Ldrship & Job Accompls; Merit Promo to Chief Petty Ofcr During Combat Action in Korea; Civ: Magnolia Awd for Supporting Actor of Yr for Role of W O Gant in "Look Homeward Angel," Crossroads Theater, Corinth Theater Arts; Nom'd Actor of Yr for Role of Capt Keller in "Miracle Worker."

FLUDD, WILLIE EDWARD oc/Territory Manager, Male Model Instructor; b/July 3, 1953; h/3510 Kaiser Ave, Columbia, SA 29204; c/Kristal Alana, Wesley Jarrod; p/John M and Julian S Fludd, Summerton, Sc; ed/Benedict Col 1974; Millie Lewis Finishing Sch 1975; pa/Territory Mgr, NCR Corp; Male Model Instr, Millie Lewis Modeling Agcy; r/AME Ch; hon/Modeling Assn of Am Intl 1st Place Runway; Male Model of Yr, Columbia, SC 1977; Selected to Travel w Belk Store, Sers Fashion Travel Show 1980.

FLURY, SCOTT L oc/Radio News Director; b/Oct 14, 1949; h/4512 Wilshire, Midland, TX 79703; ba/Midland; m/Linda; c/Kevin, Amanda; p/William Flury, Albuquerque, NM; Thelma Flury (dec); ed/Att'd NM St Univ 1967-69; FCC 1st Cl Lic, Radio Elects Inst 1969; pa/Radio News Dir, Broadcaster; cp/Bd Dirs Optimist Clb of Midland; Bd Dirs JCs, Belen, NM; r/Cath; hon/Over 12 Plaques in Hon of Civic Work in NM 1973-79; Citizen of Yr, Belen, NM 1979; Fdr Girls Softball Prog, Belen 1973; Coached St Champs Yng Am Leag Fball Team, NM 1969; Yngest U Way Dr Chm, Ulysses, Kan 1972.

FOGELMAN, JOHN ALBERT oc/Associate Justice, Supreme Court of Arkansas; h/67 Cherry, PO Box 50, Marion, AR 72364; ba/Little Rock, AR; m/Annis Adell Appleby; c/John Albert Jr, Annis Adell F Rector (Mrs Henry M), Mary Barton F Williams (Mrs Charles L Jr); p/John Franklin and Julia McAdams Fogleman, Marion, AR; ed/Att'd Univ of Ark-Fayetteville; LLB 1934 Univ of Memphis (Now Memphis St Univ); mil/Pvt to 1st Lt 1944-45; pa/Past Pres: Crittenden Co Bar Assn, NE Ark Bar Assn, Ark Bar Assn; Mem: Am Bar Assn, Delta Theta Phi, Nat Com for Preparation of Model Set of Rules for Admission to Bar, Ark Com for Criminal Code Revision; cp/Past Pres Rotary; Mason; Am Legion; VFW; Former Chm Dem Ctl Com; Secy to Bd of Election Commrs, Crittenden Co; r/Marion Meth Ch: Mem Ofcl Bd 30 yrs, Chm 3 Yrs, Tch of Men's Class; hon/W Memphis Man of Yr 1961; Fellow Am Col Trial Lwyrs; W/W Am.

FOGLEMAN, BILLYE SHERMAN oc/Anthropologist, Professor; b/Dec 6, 1927; h/Quail Call, Rt 3 Box 44, Moscow, TN 38057; ba/Memphis; m/Robert Emerald Taylor Jr; c/Douglas Sherman, Stanley Elton, Gregory William; p/Walton Everett and Oressa Hembree Sherman, Dallas, TX; ed/BA; MA; PhD; pa/Chm Behavioral Sci; Adv Com to Students, Undergrad Ed Com; Editor, Cultural Sect, *Tenn Anthropologist*; Editor Dept of Psychi Newslttr; Team Tchr, Social & Commun Psychi; Lectr; Small Grp Ldr; Fellow: Am Anthropol Assn, Soc for Applied Anthrol, AAAS; cp/Thesis Com, Masters Deg Students, Memphis St Univ; r/Prot; hon/BA w Hons; Tau Gamma Epsilon; Sigma Delta Pi; Sears-Roebuck Foun S'ship; Hockaday S'ship; Nat Defense Ed Act F'ship; W/W Am Wom; World W/W Wom; Fellow Inst for Study of Earth & Man; Assoc Current Anthrop.

FOLEY, CHARLES BRADFORD oc/Instructor, Performer; b/Jan 30, 1953; h/104 Westwood Dr, Greenville, NC 27834; ba/G'ville; m/Diane Berger; p/Charles L and Barbara Foley, Indpls, IN; ed/BA Ball St Univ 1975; MMus 1977, DMA Cand Univ Mich; pa/Instr Saxophone, E Carolina Univ 1979-; Instr Woodwinds, Stephen F Austin St Univ 1977-79; Pt-Time Instr Woodwinds, Jordan Col of Mus, Butler Univ 1977; Grad Tchg Asst, Saxophone, Univ Mich 1975-77; N Am Saxophone Alliance; Phi Mu Alpha Sinfonia; Pi Kappa Lambda, Chapt VP; NC Mus Edrs Assn; MENC; r/U Meth; hon/En NC Bandmasters All-St Clins 1981; Perf NC Mus Edrs Conv 1980.

FONTANA, PAUL ANDRE oc/Chief of Occupational Therapy; b/May 23, 1954; h/4847 Monroe St, Gary, IN 46408; ba/Gary; p/Tony and Evelyn Fontana, Abbeville, La; ed/BS LSU; pa/Chief Occupl Therapy, St Mary's Med Ctrs, Gary & Hobart, Ind for Phys's Phy Therapy Sers; Past Staff Occupl Therapy for VA Med Ctr & Med Col of Ga in Augusta; Past VChm Am Occupl Therapy Assn Student Com; Past Sch Rep AOTA for LSU Med Ctr; Active Mem AOTA; Ga OTA; Ind OTA; cp/Co Rec Progs: Coach 11-12 Yr Old Boys Fball, Basketball, Baseball; Yth Mus Prog; Vol Handicapped Girl Scouts; r/Cath; hon/W/W Am HS Students; Am Legion Awd; Supvr Perf Awd VA Med Ctr; Am Heart Fund Perf Awd.

FORD, ALLENE MAY oc/Director of Christian Education; b/Mar 29, 1920; h/5353 Inst Ln #11, Houston, TX 77005; ba/Houston; p/Milo Westel (dec) and Ella Fay King Ford, Dayton, TX; ed/AA Lon Morris Col; BS So Meth Univ; MA Columbia Univ Tchrs Col; pa/Deaconess, Dir Christian Ed, St Paul's U Meth Ch; Chm Cntrl Com, N Am Diakonia; VP Diakonia World Fed Deaconess Assn; Animator Koinonia/Diakonia Encounter, Lyon, France 1976; Served 17 Yrs w Bd Global Mins of U Meth Ch, NY; r/Meth; hon/Dist'd Alumnae Awd, Lon Morris Col; Cert of Apprec w Gift of $1660 to Diakaid.

FORD, BARBARA GAY oc/Professor; b/Aug 1, 1947; h/St Charles, IL; ba/236 Graham Hall, No Ill Univ, DeKalb, IL 60115; m/Ronald David; c/Vanessa Meghan, Hadley Morgan; p/Bert W and Loye Baumgartner, Garfield, AR; ed/BS 1969, MS 1971 Univ Mo; PhD Univ Conn 1975; pa/Dir Region II Area Ser Ctr for the Gifted, No Ill Univ 1976-79; Prof, No Ill Univ 1975-; Phi Delta Kappa; Coun for Excptl Chd; VP Ill Coun for the Gifted 1976-78; Adv Bd Prog for Promising Chd; Assn for the Gifted; Nat Assn for Gifted Chd; r/Epis; hon/Author: *New Directions in Creativity, Mark A* 1976, *New Directions in Creativity, Mark B* 1976, *Developing the Creativity of Exceptional Children* In Press.

FORD, FREDERICK WAYNE oc/Attorney; b/Sept 17, 1909; h/519 S Lee St, Alexandria, VA 22314; ba/Washington, DC; m/Mary Margaret; c/Mary Carter F Beary (Mrs Rodney), Frederick W Jr; p/George M and Annie Laurey Linn Ford (dec); ed/AB, JD WVa Univ; mil/USAF 1942-46 Major; pa/Ptnr Law Firm Pittman, Lovett, Ford & Hennessey 1970-; Pres NCTA 1965-70; FCC: Chm 1960-61, Pres Appt 1957-64; US Dept Justice 1953-57: 1st Asst in Ofc Legal Counsel, Act'g Asst Atty Gen in Charge of Ofc, Asst Dept Atty Gen; Former 1st Chief of Hearing Div, FCC; Former Law Pract, Clarksburg, WVa; r/Epis.

FORD, GORDON BUELL JR oc/Educator, Author, Financial Management Specialist; b/Sept 22, 1937; h/PO Box 7847, St Matthews Station, Louisville, KY 40207; p/Gordon Buell Sr and Rubye Ann Allen Ford; ed/AB Princeton Univ 1959; AM 1962, PhD 1965 Harvard Univ; Add'l Studies Univ Oslo, Univ Uppsala, Univ Stockholm, Univ Sofia, Bulgaria, & Univ Madrid; pa/Prof Eng & Ling, Univ No Ia, 1972-76; Prof Gen Lings, Hist & Comparative Lings & Slavic & Baltic Lings, SEn Res & Devel Corp, L'ville, Chgo, & Delray Bch, Fla 1972-; Fin Mgmt Spec, Humana Inc, The Hosp Co, L'ville 1978-; Lings Soc of Am; Intl Lings Assn; Societas Linguistica Europaea; Am Philological Assn; Mediaeval Acad of Am; MLA; Am Assn Tchrs of Slavic & E European Langs; Assn for Advmt of Baltic Studies; Inst Lithuanian Studies; cp/Princeton Clb of NY; Princeton Alumni Assn of L'ville; Harvard Clb of Chgo; Harvard-Radcliffe Clb of Ky; SAR; Hon Order of Ky Cols; L'ville Country Clb; hon/Phi Beta Kappa 1959; NWn Univ Fac Res Grant 1966; Univ No Ia Fac Res Grant 1972-73; Author *Readings in Comparative Linguistic Methodology* 1980; Num Other Books & Articles.

FORD, HAROLD EUGENE oc/United States Congressman; b/May 20, 1945; h/3631 Shady Hollow Ln, Memphis, TN 38116; ba/Memphis; m/Dorothy Bowles; c/Harold Eugene Jr, Newton Jake, Sir Isaac; p/Newton Jackson and Vera Davis Ford, Memphis, TN; ed/BS Bus Adm; r/Bapt.

FORD, WENDELL HAMPTON oc/United States Senator, Commonwealth of Kentucky; b/Sept 8, 1924; h/4974 Sentinel Dr #202, Sumner Village, Sumner, MD 20016; ba/Washington, DC; m/Jean Neel; c/Shirley F Dexter (Mrs William), Steven Milton; p/E M Ford (dec); ed/Student Univ of Ky; Grad Md Sch of Ins; mil/AUS WWII, Disch'd as Sargeant 1946; pa/Mem: Energy, Nat Resources Com; Commerce, Sci & Transport Com; Chm Consumer Subcom US Senate; Chm Dem Senatorial Campaign Com; r/Bapt; hon/Past Intl VP JCs; Past Nat Pres JCs; Past Chm Nat Dem Govs; W/W.

FORD, WILLIAM EDWIN JR oc/Teacher, Department Head; b/Mar 30, 1932; h/Rt 1 Box 159, Owensboro, KY 42301; ba/O'boro; m/Anne Dawson; c/William Edwin III, Sarah Douglas; p/Edwin and Ethel Ford, O'boro, KY; ed/BS 1955, MA 1972 Wn Ky Univ; mil/USAF 1956-59; USAFR 1959- Lt Col & USAF Acad Liaison Ofcr; pa/HS Indust Arts Tchr & Dept Hd; KEA; NEA; USAF Assn; Reserve Ofcrs Assn; cp/Optimist Clb Bd Dirs; r/Bapt; hon/Wn Ky Outstg Liaison Ofcr 1979; Outstg Edrs, Wn Ky Univ Col of Ed.

FORDYCE, MICHAEL W oc/Psychologist; b/Dec 14, 1944;

ba/Cypress Lake Profl Ctr, Suite 4, Cypress Lake Dr, Ft Myers, FL 33907; p/Joseph W Fordyce, Ft Lauderdale, FL; Grace Fordyce (dec); ed/AB Emory Univ 1967; MA 1968, PhD 1971 US Intl Univ; pa/Prof Psychol Edison Commun Col; Pvt Pract Psychol; Public Lectr; Wkshop Ldr; APGA; Am Mtl Hlth Coun Assn; hon/Sev Articles Pub'd in Jours & Mags.

FOREMAN, CAROL TUCKER oc/Government Official; b/May 3, 1938; h/5408 Trent St, Chevy Chase, MD 20015; ba/Washington, DC; m/Jay H; c/Tucker, Rachel; p/James Guy and Willie Maude White Tucker; ed/AA 1958 William Woods Col; AB 1960 Washington Univ-St Louis; Am Univ; pa/Asst Secy for Food & Consumer Sers, US Dept of Agri; Mem; Wom's Equity Action Leag, Nat Wom's Polit Caucus; cp/Wom's Nat Dem Clb; hon/Hon LLD, William Woods Col 1976; W/W: Am Wom, Am.

FORGY, BYRON KEITH oc/Surgeon; b/Nov 14, 1946; h/108 Woodstream Dr, Valdese, NC 28690; ba/Morganton, NC; m/Dianne S; c/Kelli Michelle, Jennifer Kristi; p/Byron L and Jean H Forgy, Ft Lauderdale, FL; ed/AB Duke Univ 1968; MD Univ Miami Sch Med; Internship 1973, Residency 1973-77 Emory Affil'd Hosps; pa/Gen & Vascular Surg, Grace Hosp, Morganton; AMA; Burke Co Med Soc; Am Soc Abdominal Surgeons; Soc Contemporary Med & Surg; cp/Burke Co C of C; r/Bapt; hon/Cert'd by Am Bd Surg 1978; Alpha Omega Alpha Hon Med Soc 1972.

FORKNER, CLAUDE ELLIS SR oc/Physician; Educator; Foundation Executive; b/Aug 14, 1900; h/PO Box 820, DeLand, FL 32720; m/Marion Sturges DuBois; c/Claude E Jr, Helen F Farley, Lucy F Greene (Mrs Thomas A); ed/BA; MA; MD; pa/Clin Prof Med (Emeritus), Cornell Univ Med Col, Ithaca, NY; Conslt in Med, The NY Hosp; Lic'd to Pract Med: NY, Mass, Fla, Repub of China, Dominican Repub; Cert'd Nat Bd Med Examiners & Am Bd Internal Med; Num Profl Assn Mbrships & Ofcs; Century Assn, NYC; Harvard Clbs of NYC & Ctl Fla; Other Civic Assns; r/Ctl Presb Ch, NYC: Mem; hon/Medal of Hon'd Merit, Repub of China; Companionship in Royal Order of Homayun (Ks), Shahinshah of Iran; Gold Medal, Harvard Med Alumni Assn; Sigma Xi; Fellow, NY Acad Scis; Hon Mem Rotary Intl, DeLand.

FORRESTER, JOYCE DUNCAN oc/Sales Representative; b/May 27, 1939; h/404 Galphin Dr, Greenville, SC 29609; m/Harvey C Sr; c/Harvey Jr (Butch), Steven Lee; p/John L and Lillian Wilson Duncan, Greenville, SC; pa/Sales Rep; Nat Secy Assn; cp/Pres & Secy Basketball Leag; Commun Concert; PTA Treas; Booster Clb Ofcr; r/First Assem of God; hon/W/W Am Wom 1979-80.

FORSGARD, EDDIE CAMILLE oc/Retired Elementary Principal; b/Nov 10, 1908; h/1122 N 4th St, Waco, TX 76707; p/Edward F (dec) and Annie M Forsgard (dec); ed/BA, MA Baylor Univ; Att'd Univ Tex, Univ Houston; pa/Tchr: Ctr Hill 1930-34, Chalk Bluff 1934-36, McLennan Co, Tex; Sul Ross Elem, Waco Indep Sch Dist 1936-71; Bi-Co Sch for Deaf, Waco 1971-72; Hillcrest Elem, Waco Indep Sch Dist 1972-79; Prin: Sul Ross Elem 1947-71; Bi-Co Sch for Deaf 1971-72; Hillcrest Elem 1972-79; Life Mem Delta Kappa Gamma; Life Mem Tex St Tchrs Assn, NEA, Tex Cong Parents & Tchrs; Waco Adm Clb; Tex Elem Prins & Supvrs Assn; Former Mem Nat Elem Prins; Past Pres Waco Assn Childhood Ed Intl; cp/Bd Dirs EOAC 1966; Asst'd Oral Polio Immunization Campaign McLennan Co 1963; Wkd w Literacy Prog Baylor Univ; Dir'd Prog for Non-English Spkg Chd, Waco 1960; Editor Sul Ross News 1947-71; r/Epis; hon/Windowbox Dedicated in Hist Hall of Yth Cultural Ctr, Hillcrest PTA 1976; Cert of Cit for Dedicated Ser to Waco Indep Sch Dist from Tex Ho of Reps 1979; 4 Paintings To Tribute Miss Eddie C Forsgard, Prin Hillcrest Elem Sch 1979.

FORSYTH, PRESCOTT oc/Insurance Salesman; b/Sept 24, 1937; h/Bainbridge, GA; ba/Jeffords Realty, Bainbridge, GA; m/Jane; c/Cole, Scott; p/Mrs Charles Forsyth, Rome, GA; ed/Deg 1960; pa/Tchr; Fball Coach; Ins Salesman, Jeffords Realty; Nat Life Underwriters; c/Rotary; r/Presb; hon/Scotch Foursome Golf 1967.

FORTSON, BENJAMIN WYNN JR oc/Georgia Secretary of State; b/Dec 19, 1904; h/PO Box 428, Washington, GA 30673; ba/Atlanta; m/Mary Cade (dec); c/Ann F Mandus; p/Benjamin Wynn and Lillie Wellborn Fortson (dec); ed/Hon LLD John Marshall Law Sch; Assoc Humanities Reinhardt Col; pa/Nat Assn Secys of St; Surveying & Mapping Soc; Nat Assn Securities Admrs; r/Meth.

FORTUNE, HILDA ORR oc/Consultant, Researcher, Writer; b/Aug 31, 1913; h/Lauderhill, FL; m/Roland K (dec); c/Lois Joyne Fortune Maginley; p/Henry (dec) and Mettie Orr (dec); ed/AB Morgan St Col 1938; EdD summa cum laude NYU 1963; pa/Sr Res Planner, Voc Acad, Behavioral Scis Ctr, Nova Univ 1980; Sociol Prof, York Col, CUNY 1968-79; Psychol Sers, Ofc of Dean of Students; Instr Sociol & Cnslg & Guid 1963-68; Dir Commun Sers, Urban Leag of Gtr NYC 1955-63; Dir

Commun Sers, Westchester Urban Leag 1952-55; Dir Employment Dept, YWCA, Harlem Br 1947-52; Mem Emerita APGA; Pi Lambda Theta; Kappa Delta Pi; Intl Platform Assn; Delta Sigma Theta; Hon Trustee Broward Commun Col; NASW; cp/Chm Ad Hoc Com Brotherhood Man Series, Broward Commun Col 1980; Broward Urban Leag, Annual Dinner Com 1980; U Negro Col Fund 1980; Inst Review Bd, Nova Univ, Behavioral Scis Ctr 1980; Inner City S'ship Selection Com 1979; Chp Cnslg & Guidance Subcom Instructl & Support Servs SCOPEK 1980; r/Bapt; hon/Wom of Yr, York Col 1975; Fdrs Day Cert of Achmt for Outstg S'ship, NYU 1963; Outstg Profl Cit, Voc Guid Wkshop Ctr 1970; Conslts Cit, Harlem Teams for Self-Help 1976; S'ships: Delta Sigma Theta, Prince Vance Hall Masons, Jesse Smith Hoyes Fdn, Warburg S'ship; Many Cits for Commun Sers; Author "Pros and Cons of Sensitivity Training" 1970; *Shared Leadership and New Concepts 1965.*

FOSDICK, FRANKLIN LAWRENCE o/Aircraft Executive; b/Sept 12, 1919; h/1639 Whitedove Dr, Dallas, TX 75224; ba/Dallas; m/Bette H Burns; c/Franklin L Jr; p/Horace G and Maude P Fosdick (dec); ed/BBA w Hons So Meth Univ 1962; MBA Pepperdine Univ 1978; mil/AUS 1944-46 WWII 1st Lt Inf Ser'd as Traffic Mgr, AES, Yokohama, Japan; pa/LTV Aerospace Corp 30 Yrs: Mgr Mat Control, Past Mgr Traffic & Transp 1970-73; Mgr Opers Control Mich Div 1963-70; Detroit Purchasing Mgmt Assn: Bd Dirs 1969, Mem 1963-70; Am Airlines Freight Adv Bd; Pres, Prin Owner Bali-Hi Apts, Dallas; Dallas Apt Assn; cp/Shrine; 32° Scottish Rite Mason; r/Southwood U Meth Ch: Chm Adm Bd 1974-75; Holds Delta Sigma Pi Key for Highest Scholastic Record in Grad'g Class; Pres Alpha Sigma Lambda; Secy Sigma Iota Epsilon; Beta Gamma Sigma Jr Yr.

FOSTER, ALBERT LAWING oc/Plant Engineer; b/Oct 30, 1950; h/Rt 1 Box 215-F, China Grove, NC 28023; ba/Charlotte, NC; m/Deborah Bass; p/Lester Jr and Myra Lawing Foster, Charlotte, NC; ed/AAS-MEt Ctrl Peidmont Commun Col 1977; BET w Hons UNCC 1981; mil/USN 1969-71 Boiler Tech 3rd Cl; pa/Steam Plant Supvr UNCC 1972-80; Catawba Chapt Am Inst Plant Engrs, Pres 1980-81; Opers Farm Prod'g Cattle, Hay & Cert'd Seed Wheat 1976-; Univ Senate, UNCC, Pres 1978-79; Univ Plan'g Com, UNCC, Chm 1977-78; cp/Oakhurst Vol Fire Dept 1968-74; r/Luth; hon/AIPE Chapt Activ Awd 1980; Cert'd Plant Engr #1437; Mecklenburg Co Life Saving Awd 1972; Merit Unit Commend USN 1971; Engrg Efficiency Awd USN 1970; Navy Expert Pistol Medal 1969; Author Chapt "Information Gathering for Energy Management" for *Countering the Conflicts: Arming the Plant Engineer for Inflationary Times.*

FOSTER, ANNE S oc/Realtor Associate; b/Jan 28, 1934; h/838 SE 8th St, Ocola, Fl 32670; m/E Hunter; c/William Timothy, Edward Jr, Julia Anne Floor, June Lurose; p/Harry P and Rose P Sloane, Lexington, KY; pa/Wom's Coun of Rltrs; cp/C of C; Wom's CLb; OES; r/Bapt.

FOSTER, BETTY V oc/Retired Vocal Teacher; b/Jan 29, 1912; h/803 Western Ave, Waterloo, IA 50702; 9 Ithaca, Lakeland, FL 33801; m/Jess M; c/Sharon kay Brown, Herbert Neubauer Jr; p/Russell and Nettie Hatch (dec); ed/BA; MA; pa/Vocal Mus Tchr 20 yrs; Dance Classes, Dirs Rhythmairs; Mem: NRTA, Phi Omega Pi Alumnae; Ch Choir Dir; cp/Wom's Clb; RSVP; r/Presb.

FOSTER, CAROLINE ROBINSON oc/Regional Blood Services Recruiter; b/Oct 2, 1937; h/5778 Honor St, Mobile, AL 36608; ba/Mobile; c/Robin Caroline, Edward Eugene Jr; p/Lucius Waite (dec) and Vassar Bowling Robinson, Chickasaw, AL; ed/Att'd Troy St Univ 1956-57, Univ S Ala 1972-; pa/Exec Asst, Mobile Co Commmr Jeff Mims 1979-; Pers Dir-Asst to Pres, Goodwill Industs of Mobile Area 1968-79; Sect to Dir & Asst Dir of Social Sers, Mobile Gen Hosp 1966-68; Pacific Fin Corp, Yuma, Ariz 1957-58; Am Soc Pers Admrs: Dist Dir Region VI 1979, Com Mem Ldrship & Devel Com 1979; Past Pres Mobile Pers Assn, Mem Student Com; Pers & Indust Relats Sem; Indust Mgmt Coun; cp/Regional Recruiter, Blood Sers, Am Red Cross; r/Bapt; hon/Part in Student Tour of Europe 1974; Finalist, Annual Career Wom's Awd Prog, C J Gayfers Inc 1976; W/W: S&SW 1978, Am Wom 1979.

FOSTER, CARY DON oc/Executive; b/Aug 14, 1951; h/Clinton, OK; ba/Rt 1 Box 133, Clinton, OK 73601; p/John D and Alma R Graybill Foster, Thomas, OK; ed/BS Okla St Univ 1973; pa/Pres Foster Contruc Co Inc; cp/Chm Custer Co Dem Party 1976-; Chm Custer Co Ec Devel Coun 1978-79; High Plains Water Adv Task Force 1978-; Wn Okla Home Bldrs Assn; Clinton Rotary Clb; hon/Alumni Fund Devel S'ship, Okla St Univ 1973; W/W S&SW 1980.

FOSTER, EVA CLYDE GARGUS oc/Retired Teacher; b/Feb 16, 1897; h/Decatur, AL; m/Earl L; p/Pink Gargus (dec); Mary Abigail Britnell (dec); ed/BS Univ Ala 1935; pa/Ret'd Elem Sch Tchr; AEA; NEA; Org'd Morgan Co Ret'd Tchrs 1961; cp/Org'd First Girl Scout Troop in Decatur, Ala & Ldr 25 Yrs; DAC; r/Meth.

FOSTER, LUTHER H oc/College President; b/Mar 21, 1913; h/520 Montgomery Rd, Tuskegee Inst, AL 36088; ba/Tuskegee; m/Vera Chandler; c/Adrienne F Williams, Hilton Foster; p/Luther H Foster (dec); Daisy Poole Foster, Ettrick, VA; ed/BS Hampton Inst; MBA Harvard Univ; PhD Univ of Chgo; pa/Pres Tuskegee Inst; Mem Bd Dirs Nat Foun March of Dimes; Sears, Roebuck & Co; Norton Simon Inc; College Retiremt Equities Fund; r/Epis; hon/Hon LLD's: Univ of Liberia, Va St Col, Univ of Mich, Colby Col, Univ of Ala; Hon DHL's: Colby Col, Loyola Univ of Chgo, NEn Univ.

FOSTER, MAURAE H oc/Service Representative; b/Aug 12, 1923; h/603 Columbia Ave, Glasgow, KY 42141; ba/Glasgow; m/Wilton; c/Stephen Edwards, David Hunley; p/Aubrey (dec) and Elsie Hunley (dec); pa/Serv Rep, Public Relats, So Ctrl Rural Telephone Co 25 Yrs; cp/Glasgow BPW Clb; Dem Wom's Clb; C of C Bd Dirs; r/Bapt; hon/Wom of Achmt, Kiwanis Clb; Wom of Yr BPW Clb; Ky Col.

FOSTER, ROBERT J oc/Retired; b/Dec 26, 1925; h/1750 Holly Hill, Camden, AR 71701; m/Betty A; c/Janis L, Cynthia D, Rebecca J, Robin E; p/dec; mil/USMC; cp/VFW; Masons; Shriners; r/Bapt; hon/Outstg Dist Comdr VFW.

FOSTER, SPURGEON HOLMES JR oc/Grain Farmer; b/July 11, 1947; h/Rt 3 Box 404, Mocksville, NC 27028; m/Sherry M; c/Bryan C, Wesley A; p/Spurgeon H and Lucille M Foster, Mocksville, NC; pa/Grain Farming 1200 Acres; Bd Dirs NC Soybean Assn; Bd Dirs Davie Co Farm Bur; cp/Mason; r/Prot; hon/Outstg Yng Farmer Awd, Davie JCs 1969; Outstg Yng Farmer & Rancher Awd, Davie Co Farm Bur 1976; So Piedmont Runner Up, NC Corn Contest 1977; Runner Up Davie Co Corn Growing Contest 1978; Winner NC St Corn Contest, Setting New St Record 1980.

FOSTER, THOMAS LANE oc/Real Estate Broker, Auctioneer; b/Feb 21, 1949; h/301 DeKalb St, McMinnville, TN; ba/McMinnville; m/Donna Kay; c/Craig, Chad, Robin; p/Thomas D and Christine Foster, McMinnville, TN; ed/Att'd Univ Tenn; Cert'd Real Est, Appraisal & Fin; pa/Methods Engr, DeZurik Corp; cp/Secy JCs; r/Ch of Christ.

FOSTER, WILLI KRAPELS oc/Marriage and Family Therapist; b/Feb 6, 1946; h/202 Grand Ave, Raleigh, NC 27606; ba/Raleigh; m/William Thomas III; p/John (dec) and Jetty Hobijn Krapels, High Point, NC; ed/BA Wake Forest Univ 1968; MEd NCSU 1972; pa/Dir New Careers Prog, NC Dept Correct 1973-74; Dir Diagnostic Ctr, NC Correctl Ctr for Wom 1974-76; Clin/Dpty Dir Drug Action of Wake Co 1976-; Chm/VChm NC Foun Alcohol & Drug Studies 1979-80; cp/Assn Drug Abuse Preven; Wake Co Mtl Hlth Assn; NC Grp Behavior Soc; hon/Drug Cnslr Cert 1980; W/W S&SW 190; Cert'd Tnr Nat Inst Drug Abuse 1976-80.

FOUNTAIN, L H oc/Representative; h/Leggett, NC; m/Christine Dail; c/Nancy Dail; p/Lawrence H (dec) and Sallie Barnes Fountain; ed/AB 1934, JD 1936 Univ NC; mil/AUS 1942-46 Maj; Ret'd Lt Col USAR; pa/Law Pract, Tarboro, NC 1934-42; En Orgr Yng Dem Clbs of NC, Chm 2nd Congl Dist Exec Com, Rdg Clk NC Senate 1936-41; Elected to St Senate 1947; Elected to 83rd Cong as Rep from 2nd Congl Dist of NC 1952-; Serves on Ho Coms on Govt Opers (Chm Intergovtl Relats & Human Resources Subcom) & Fgn Affairs; cp/Exec Com E Carolina Coun BSA; Local & Other Bar Assns; Elks; Kiwanis Clb; Lt Gov 6th NC Div Kiwanis Intl; Former JC; Appt'd to & Served as US Del to 22nd Session of UN Gen Assem; r/Presb: Elder; hon/Dist'd Ser Awd, Man of Yr, Tarboro JCs 1948; NC Citizens Assn Dist'd Public Ser Awd 1971; Univ NC Sch of Med Dist'd Ser Awd 1973; Assn of Am Univ Presses Dist'd Ser to Higher Ed & Scholarly Commun Awd 1975; Spec Cit for Dist'd Cong Ser, Nat Leag of Cities 1976; Ldrship & Dist'd Ser Awd, Assn Fed Investigators 1978.

FOURCARD, INEZ GAREY oc/Executive Director of Southwestern Sickle Cell Anemia Foundation Inc; b/Sept 26, 1930; h/1414 St John St, Lake Charles, LA 70601; ba/Lake Charles; m/Waldren Arthur Sr; c/Chrystal Frances, Sharon Lynne, Waldren Arthur Jr, Andrea Renee, David Marguard, Anita Lynn; p/Georg W and Lucille Garey, Philadelphia, PA; ed/BFA; pa/Exec Dir SWn Sickle Cell Anemia Foun Inc 1974-; Spec Adv Com of Spec Ed, Calcasieu Sch Bd 1977-; VP La Assn for Sickle Cell Anemia 1974-; Adv Coun of Child Centered Parents; La Task Force on Commun Ed 1974-75; Profl Artist, Paintings in Pvt Collects in US, France & Spain; Num Wkshops; cp/Calcasieu Parish Bicent Com; hon/Hon Citizen of Ft Worth 1977; Certs of Merit; Awd for Sers Rendered to Sickle Cell Disease, Sigma Gamma Rho Soc; Outstg Ser to Commun, Phi Beta Sigma; Var Plaques; Num Biogl Listings incl'g: Intl Artist Directory, Book of Hon, DIB, Commun Ldrs & Noteworthy Ams, Intl W/W in Art & Antiques, World W/W of Wom, Intl Register of Profiles, Notable Ams, W/W: Am Wom, S&SW.

FOUCHARD, JOSEPH JAMES oc/Director of Public Affairs; b/Jun 6, 1928; h/4840 Flower Valley Dr, Rockville, MD 20853; ba/Washington, DC; m/Martha J Swiney; c/James, Melissa, Lisa; p/Joseph N and Nell G Fouchard; ed/BS Jour Univ of Ill; mil/Ser'd w Ofc Chief of Info, Dept of Army 1951-52; pa/Dir of Public Affairs, US Nuclear Regulatory Comm; r/Presb.

FOUSHEE, OLA MAIE (MRS J McIVER) oc/Painter, Writer, Lecturer; h/Box 877, Chapel Hill, NC 27514; ba/Same; m/John McIver Jr; c/June Keaton; ed/UNC 1953-57; pa/Tchr Arts & Crafts Army Convalescent Hosp 1954; UNC 1946; Tchr Art Allied Arts Durham 1955-56; Current VP, Adv Mgr Foushee Realty & Ins Co Chapel Hill; 1-Man Shows in NC, SC; Exhibited in Group Show in NC, SC, Pa & Va; Lectr Art to Woms Org, PTA, Art Orgs, Sch & Profl Groups; Fdr Chapel Hill Art Guild; Co-Fdr Assn Artists NC; Art Columnist Greensboro *Daily News*, Durham *Morning Herald*, Rocky Mt *Evening Telegram*, High Point *Enterprises*, Charlotte *Observer*, Wilmington *Star* & Others 1958-63, Chapel Hill *Weekly* 1963-; Wrote Column in "Art in NC" 1958-65; "Hist of Art in NC" 1972; Other Profl Assns; r/Chapel Hill Presb Ch; hon/Cit from St Art Soc for Promoting Art in NC; 5 Biogl Listings; Phi Mu; Pub'd Author; incl'g: *The Suttenfield Family - A Sentimental Journey* 1976; Prod'd TV Series 'NC Artists"; Prod'g TV Special on outdoor murals & sculpture and corporate support of the arts, UNC TV.

FOWLER, BRUCE WAYNE oc/Physicist, Concepts Analyst; h/202-3 Utica Place, Huntsville, AL 35806; ba/Redstone Arsenal, AL; p/James Kenneth and Helen Christine Towers Fowler, Guntersville, AL; ed/BS Ch 1970 Univ Ala; MS 1972 Univ Ill; PhD 1978 Univ Ala; pa/Mem Am Physical Soc, Am Chem Soc; Author Num Pubs; Mem Var Coms; r/Prot; hon/Gorgas Fellow; Var Gov't Awds.

FOWLER, E BERT oc/Retired Life Insurance Agent; b/Apr 3, 1910; h/Jasper, AL; c/Bert Jr, Patricia, Jeff; p/James (dec) and Nancy Josephine Fowler (dec); ed/Att'd John H Snead Sem, Emory Univ, Henry Brady Sch Bus Law, Clara Bell Smith Bus Col; Grad Watkins Inst-Nashville; pa/Life Ins 50 Yrs; cp/Pres Walker Co Div Am Heart Assn; St Bd Dirs Mtl Hlth Assn; Pres Walker Co Mtl Health Assn; Pres Kiwanis Clb of Jasper; Secy-Treas Jasper Assn Life Underwrtiers; Chm St & Fed Leg Com of Life Underwriters 1980-81; Former Yth Dir, Tenn Conf U Meth Ch; r/Meth; hon/Pres Plaque, Jasper Underwriters Assn.

FOWLER, MEL oc/Sculptor; b/Nov 25, 1921; h/PO Box 255, Liberty Hill, TX 78642; ba/Same; c/James E, Robert M, William W; p/Walter Fowler, Marble Falls, TX; Thelma Gregory, Austin, TX; ed/Att'd: Univ of Tex, Univ of Md; SWn Univ Norfolk Sch of Art; mil/USAF Lt Col, Fighter Pilot: WWII, Vietnam; pa/Num One-Man Exhibs incl'g: Galerie Monika Beck, Homburg, Germany 1977, 78, Giornata Michealangelo Intl Sculpture Exhib, Azzano, Italy 1978, La Bilancia Intl Exhib, Pietrasanta, Italy 1978, Abilene Fine Arts Mus 1977, Galerie im Savoy, Kaiserslauten, Germany 1977, Italian Intl Sculpture Exhib, Pietrasanta 1977, US Cong, Washington, DC 1976, Others; Sculptures in Num Pvt & Public Collects; Dir 1st Intl Sculpture Symposium in S - Conducted as Bicent Proj 1976; Mem: So Assn of Sculptors, Tex Soc of Sculptors, Artists Equity; hon/Num Awds in Europe & US; Notable Ams; W/W: German Art, Tex.

FOWLER, WATSON RODNEY oc/Counselor Educator; Criminal Justice Educator; b/Jan 30, 1938; h/3510 Oak Knoll Dr, Chattanooga, TN 37415; ba/Chattanooga; m/Ann Carter Bass; c/Travis Lindley-Park, Margaret Alyse, Shannon Marie; p/Watson Francis and Margaret Elizabeth Douglass Fowler; ed/BS 1965 Lock Haven St Univ; MA 1968 Cal St Univ-San Diego; EdD 1974 Ball St Univ; mil/AUS 1957-59; pa/Exec Dir Correctional Psychol Assn Inc, Muncie, Ind 1973-76; Police Psychol Del Co Police, Muncie 1973-76; Asst Prof Psychol Ball St Univ, Germany, England, Greece, Spain 1974-76; Asst Prof Cnslr Edn Univ of Tenn, Chattanooga 1976-; Conslt Ind St Police, Muncie Police, Cambridge Home, Ind Woms Prison, Weathers Med Corp, Parkridge Hosp, Hamilton Co Police, Chattanooga; Exec Dir Green River Crime Coun, Ky 1969-71; Mem: Am Acad Crisis Interveners, Am Assn Sex Edrs, Cnslrs, Therapists, APGA, Assn Cnslr Edrs & Supvrs, Am Assn Correctional Psychols, Assn for Specs in Group Work, Ind Assn Profl Police Ofcrs, Tenn Psychol Assn, Tenn Assn Pers & Guid Workers, Lookout Mt Pers & Guid Assn; cp/Black Dragon Fighting Soc, Imua Kwan Tae Kai Karate Soc Sho-dan (1st Black Belt) Kodakan Judo 1966; Kwan-Tao Kai Karate 1968, Hapkido 1968; hon/Pub'd Articles in Field.

FOX, CHARLES LEIGH oc/Town Administrator; b/Aug 29, 1946; h/PO Box 306, Hudson, NC 28638; ba/Hudson; m/Janet T; c/Jonathan, Christina; p/Levi C and Blanche C Fox, Hudson, NC; ed/BS UNC-CH 1972; mil/USN 1966-70; pa/Acctg Supvr, Bottling Co; Asst Acctg Mgr, Metal Container Co; Gen Acctg Mgr Winston Mills; Town Admr, Hudson, NC; Nat Assn Accts; Intl City Mgmt Assn; cp/Mem Hudson Postal Adv Coun; r/Bapt; Dir Yng Adults Dept; hon/USN Honorman 1966.

FOX, CURTIS HOWARD SR oc/Minister of Music and Youth; b/Feb 17, 1949; h/Sedalia, KY; ba/PO Box 306, 220 W Farthing St, Mayfield, KY 42066; m/Janet Carnes; c/Curtis Jr, Karen Marie, Kenneth Michael, Sara Elizabeth; p/Howard Lenord Fox (dec); Alice Nielsen, Mayfield, KY; ed/BRE, Cert Mus, Mid-Cont Bapt Bible Col 1981; Num Certs & Dips through Ch Study Course Prog, So Bapt Conv; mil/USN; pa/Retail Sales-Mgmt, Grand Union Co 10 Yrs; Cnslg, Snelling & Snelling Employment Ser 1 Yr; High Pt Bapt Ch 1½ Yrs; Pt-Time Tchr Mid-Cont Bapt Bible Col; Assoc Dir of Mus, Graves Co Assn of Bapt in Ky; So Bapt Ch Mus Conf; Ky HS Ath Assn, Basketball Ofcl; r/Bapt.

FOX, EDGAR LEROY oc/Pastor; b/Oct 8, 1934; h/Box 356, Quanah, TX 79252; p/John and Mary Fox, Pettus, TX; ed/BA 1957, BD 1960, DDiv 1975; pa/Ser'd Film Libn Tex Christian Univ 1959-60; Exec Dir w Yakima Indian Nation 1965-70; Pastor, Disciples of Christ Christian Ch, Quanah, Tex 1976-; Quanah Min Assn, VP 1978-; cp/Lions Clb; BSA; Ctrl Area Christian Ch Bd; VP Min Assn; Past Pres Post Min Assn; F&AM 32°; r/Disciples of Christ; hon/Dist'd Ser Awd 1970; Dist'd Ser to Commun 1980; Dist'd Ser to Wapto C of C 1966; Secy Sundown M Ranch, Helped Est Alcoholic Rehab Ctr; W/W Rel ;Author *It Must Be Done* 1968, *It Can Be Done* 1970.

FOX, IRENE LEINART oc/Music Specialist; b/Dec 17, 1933; h/607 S Main St, Clinton, TN 37716; ba/Oak Ridge, TN; m/Walter Alvin; c/Karen F Barreira, Thomas Dale; p/Millard and Bonnie Greene Leinart, Lake City, TN; ed/BS 1971, MS 1975 Univ Tenn; pa/Piano Tchr, Clrm Mus Spec, Woodland Elem Sch; U Tchg Profession; Mus Edrs Nat Conf; Tenn Vocal Assn E Tenn Vocal Assn; Chm E Tn Elem Mus Tchrs 1968-69; cp/Orgr & Dir Clinton Commun Chorus; Timely Topics Clb; hon/Phi Kappa Phi 1971; Pi Kappa Lambda 1971; AAUW Outstg Sr Wom, Col of Ed 1971; Nom Outstg Wom of Yr, Clinton 1979; Gov's Outstg Tennessean Awd 1980; Tenn Tchr of Yr 1980.

FOX, LUCY REED oc/Extension Assistant; b/Apr 17, 1922; h/1004 E Main St, Richmond, KY; m/Harold; c/Harold Jr, Edwin Reed; p/dec; pa/Ext Asst w Expanded Food & Nutrition Prog 10 Yrs; r/Bapt; hon/Cert for Work w Local Nutrition Progs for Inter-City Yth.

FOX, MARY ELIZABETH oc/Journalist, Lecturer; h/Plantation Square #C-3, 2411 S 61st St, Temple, TX 76501; p/J S and Frances West Fox (dec); ed/BA; BS; MA; Grad Study toward PhD; pa/Journalist; Lectr; Free-Lance Writer; cp/Del to Co, St & Nat Convs of Dem Party; r/Meth; hon/Working On 3 Books to be Pub'd Simultaneously.

FOX, PATRICIA GRIFFITH oc/Homemaker; b/Feb 5, 1930; h/275 W Lakeview Ave, Lake Mary, Fl 32746; m/Raymond George Jr; c/Raymond G III, Caroline Ann, Earl Philip; p/Earl (dec) and Vea Wimes Griffith, Pensacola, FL; ed/Fla St Univ 1948-50; cp/Epsilon Sigma Alpha 1961-75; Naval Ofcrs Wives Clb 1975-; Naval Trg Equip Ctr Wives Clb 1975-; Lake Mary C of C 1976; PEO, Chapt AX (Cottey Col Chm 1980-81, Corresp Secy 1980-81); DAR; Lake Mary Wom's Clb (Treas 1978-80; Chaplain 1980-82); r/Lake Mary U Presb Ch: Ruling Elder 1980-82; hon/Recipes Pub'd *Cecil Field Officers' Wives Cookbook; Recipes on Parade; Vegetables; Florida Daughters of the American Revolution Cookbook.*

FOX, PAUL JOHN oc/Chiropractor; b/Aug 22, 1945; h/241 North, Gainesville, FL 32601; ba/G'ville; m/Patricia Tudor; c/Paul Jason, Debra Ann, John Matthew, Trisha Ann; p/Paul John Fox Sr (dec); Bertie Seigler Cheshire, Florahome, FL; ed/BS; DC; pa/Dr of Chiropractic; Backachers Farm, Reg'd Jerseys; Nat Assn Intensive Day Care Ctrs; Nat Fed Indep Chiropractic Phys; cp/Charter Mem Kiwanis Clb of Kendale; r/Prot; hon/W/W S&SW; Ambassador Awd, Palmer Col 1977.

FOX, PORTLAND PORTER oc/Consulting Engineering Geologist; b/Aug 10, 1908; h/500 Hiwassee St NE, Cleveland, TN 37311; m/Sarah Pearl Monk; p/William Ross Fox (dec); Dora Mayes (dec); ed/BS UNC 1937; pa/Geol: USGS, US Soil Erosion Ser, TVA, US Bur of Reclamation, Brazilian Traction Light & Power, Ebasco Sers; Bd of Conslt: Dez Dam in Iran, Swift, Blenheim-Gilboa, Northfield Mt Cornwall, Bear Swamp & Rock Island Dams; r/First Christian Ch; hon/Wisdom Hall of Fame.

FOX, RAYMOND GEORGE JR oc/Business Executive; b/Sept 5, 1926; h/Lake Mary, FL; ba/PO 2810, Lake Mary, FL 32746; m/Patricia Griffith; c/Raymond G III, Caroline Ann, Earl Philip; p/Raymond George Fox (dec); Ida Lou Conoley Fox Marz (dec); ed/BS Auburn Univ 1949; Cert Grad Aviation Safety Course, Univ So Calif 1955; Cert Gen Line Sch, US Naval Post Grad Sch 1959; Cert Explosive Safety Course, Univ Ind 1971; mil/USN Aviator, Cmdr, Ret'd After 35 Yrs; pa/Owner Fox Distributors; US Naval Inst; Sanford Area Ret'd Naval Ofcrs Assn; Naval Trg Equip Ctr Retirees' Assn; cp/Sigma Alpha Epsilon 1945-; Orlando Area Auburn Univ Clb, Pres 1978-80; Kiwanis 1967-68; Lake Mary Rotary Clb, Bd Dirs 1978-79; Lake Mary C of C, VP & Bd Dirs 1978-79; Lake

Mary Plan'g & Zoning Bd 1976-78; Lake Mary City Coun-man 1980-82; r/Lake Mary U Presb Ch; hon/Eagle Scout 1939; DeMolay 1940-44; Key Clb 1941-44; 21 Mil Awds Incl'g Campaign, Area & Pers Cits from USA & Fgn Govts 1943-78.

FOX, ROXANNE ELAINE oc/Senior Technical Operations Manager; b/June 22, 1946; h/110 E H St, Brunswick, MD 21716; ba/Frederick, MD; m/Raymond Dale; c/Rodney Redford, Roxanne Renee; p/William Ralph and Ruth Pauline Elliott, Alexandria, VA; ed/Assoc of Liberal Arts 1966; BS 1971; Postgrad Work in Mgmt; pa/Sr Tech Opr Mgr, Animal Resource Prog, Frederick Cancer Res Ctr, Litton Bionetics, Frederick, MD; Am Assn for Lab Animal Scis; Frederick Co Soc for Advmt of Med Technol; r/Epis; hon/Outstg Ser 1964; W/W Am Wom.

FOX, SANDRA ELAINE oc/Nursing Inservice Education Coordinator; b/Apr 23, 1947; h/Box 296, Senoia, GA 30276; ba/Newnan, Ga; p/Thomas A and Emily R Fox, Senioa, GA; ed/AA 1970; BSN 1974, MSN 1976 Ga St Univ; pa/AACN; Chp PCEC, Mem Procedure Com & Disaster Com; r/Bapt; hon/Top Student Awd LPN Prog 1968; Outstg Instr Awd 1978; SS Perfect Attendance 15 Yrs.

FOX, VIVIAN E SCRUTCHIN oc/Director Special Education; b/Jan 3, 1914; h/Rt 3 Box 472, Corpus Christi TX 78415; ba/Corpus Christi; m/V B (dec); p/William A Scrutchin (dec); Attala W Scrutchin, Corpus Christi, TX; ed/BA; MA; pa/Dir Spec Ed, Calallen ISD; TSTA-NEA; TACLD; TCASE; CEC; ASCD; AAUW; cp/OES; r/Meth.

FOY, RONALD THOMAS oc/Quality Control Manager; b/May 3, 1942; h/Humble, TX; ba/Bama Food Prods, Div of Bordens; PO Box 15068, Houston, TX 77020; m/Ruth Ann; p/Milo and Opal Foy, Red Oak, IA; ed/Assoc Deg Clarinda Commun Col 1962; BS NW Mo Univ 1964; pa/Armour & Co 1966-69; Borden Food Div 1970-; Inst Food Technols; cp/Houston Zoo Soc; r/Presb.

FRAGALE, ANTHONY FRANCIS oc/Retired Civil Service; b/June 13, 1931; m/Florence Douglas; c/Lewis Anthony, David Francis, Danial Allan; p/(dec); ed/HS Grad; mil/USAF WWII; pa/Ret'd USN Civil Ser; Gen Foreman Naval Aircraft Overhaul; r/Seventh Day Adventist; hon/Trophy Each Yr, Gtr Jax Fair for Outstg Leather Craftsman; Author "Make it with Leather" & Other Articles.

FRANCIS, NAN oc/Concert Artist and Voice Teacher; b/June 19; h/305 Mustang Dr, Spartanburg, SC 29302; m/Robert S Gregg (dec); c/David London Gregg, Grace Lee Gregg; p/Max C Francis, Shelby, NC; Minnie Lee Crowder Francis (dec); ed/BMus Westminster Choir Col; Master's Equiv, Hofstra Univ & LI Univ, C W Post Campus; pa/Voice Tchr: Gardner Webb Col, Limestone Col, Converse Col; Perf'd w Num Symphs in E, Wash Opera Wkshop & Charlotte Opera Assn; Has Appeared in Commun Concerts & Extensively at Cols & Univs.

FRANCIS, PAULETTE KROPP oc/Teacher, Coordinator; b/Jan 14, 1944; h/195 Reynolds Ln, Vidor, TX 77552; ba/Beaumont, TX; m/Tommy E; c/Brady Bennett; p/Paul (dec) and Beth Kropp, Lockney, TX; ed/BS Tex Tech Univ; Cert Courses from Wayland Bapt Col & Prairie View A&M Univ; pa/Secy-Treas Tex Indust Voc Assn; Tex Voc Tech Assn; Am Voc Assn; Beaumont Clrm Tchrs; Tex St Tchrs Assn; NEA.

FRANCOVILLA, MARY ANN oc/Assistant Vice President and Regional Sales Manager; b/Aug 31, 1954; h/8110 Skillman #2034, Dallas, TX 75231; ba/Dallas; p/Anthony Peter (dec) and Josephine Genevieve Francovilla, Bronx, NY; ed/St Univ NY-Oswego 1972-74; Fordham Univ 1975-77; pa/Asst VP & Regional Sales Mgr, Barclays Bank Intl, Visa Travelers Cheques; Asst Dir CBS Radio Network; Acct Exec Merrill Lynch & Co; Nat Assn Female Execs; Dirs Guild of Am; r/Cath; hon/W/W: Am Wom, E; Recip NY Regents Col S'ship 1972.

FRANK, KATE oc/Retired Public School Teacher; b/Feb 5, 1890; h/Kate Frank Manor, Muskogee, OK 74401; p/C G (dec) and Julia Frank (dec); ed/MA Univ Mo; MS SW Mo Tchrs Col; p/Hon Mem Delta Kappa Gamma; Tchrs & Ret'd Tchrs Assns; Life Mem NEA; OEA; NRT; cp/Chm, Bd Trustees YWCA; Gov's Mini Cabinet to Rep the Aging; Pres Okla Resident Com; Pres Muskogee Transp Sys for Elderly; Part Bd City Devel; r/Meth; hon/Nat Ret'd Tchr of Yr 1972; Outstg Older Oklahoman 1980.

FRANK, LUANNE THORNTON oc/Associate Professor; b/Dec 27, 1932; h/4708 Kelly Perkins Rd, Arlington, TX 76016; ba/A'ton; m/Ted Earl; p/King N and Mabel M Thornton, W Palm Beach, FL; ed/MA Lib Sci 1960, MA Comp Lit 1963, Emory Univ; PhD Univ Mich 1970; pa/Assoc Prof Comp Lit, Dept Eng, Univ Tex-Arlington; MLA; Am Comp Lit Assn; Am Soc 18th Cent Studies; Intl Soc Germanists; Am Assn Tchrs of German; Col Coun of Tchrs of Eng; hon/Nat Endowment for Humanities F'ship for Yngr Humanists 1972; Univ Mich Grad Fellow 1966.

FRANK, RUBY MERINDA oc/Executive President, Bank Director; b/June 28, 1920; h/534 Longmeadow Circle, St Charles, IL 60174; ba/St Charles; m/Robert G (dec); c/Gary Robert, Craig Allen; p/John J and Olise Hanson, McClusky, ND; ed/Bus Major Mankato Col; pa/Exec Pres Frank's Employment Inc; Dir St Charles Savings & Loan; Exec's Clb of Chgo; Ofcr Kane-Dupage Pers Assn; Ill Pers Conslts; cp/St Charles Country Clb; St Charles C of C; Wom's Repub; 20 Yrs Trustee Delnor Hosp; r/Luth; hon/W/W Am Wom.

FRANKLIN, CALVIN G oc/Chief of Mob Improvement Management Office; Director MOBEX Task Force; b/Mar 31, 1929; h/3-E Wheeler Dr, Ft McPherson, GA 30330; ba/Ft McPherson; m/Betty Marie; c/Gail, Steve, Kevin; p/Scott and L B Gail Franklin (dec); ed/AA; BA; MBA; PhD Cand; pa/Dir MOBEX Task Force & Chief Mobilization Improvemt Mgmt Ofc, Mobilization Planning Div, DCSOPS, US Army Forces Command; Previous Assignmts in 4 Commands; Var Staff Positions; Mgmt Conslt, Gen Dynamics, San Diego, Cal 1976-78; Fdr, Pres Biomedical Technologies Inc; Nat Mgmt Assn, Past Secy; Inst of Environmtl Scis, Bd Dirs, Past Ednl Chm, San Diego Chapt; Am Soc for Quality Control; Author Pubs; cp/Intl Rotary Clb, Treas & Past Mbrship Chm; r/Prot; hon/Nat Mgmt Assn: Extraordinary Ldrship Awd 1970, Excell Awd 1972, Pres Awd 1974; Gen Dynamics: Corporation Awd for Outstg Ldrship 1972, Pres Awd 1963, Certs of Commend 1974, 76.

FRANKLIN, DOUGLASS EVERETTE oc/Plant Operations; b/June 17, 1943; h/1752 Sawaga NE, Orangeburg, SC 29115; ba/Denmark, SC; m/Alfreda Delores; c/James Vincent; p/Earvin J Sr and Addie M Franklin, Bamberg, SC; ed/BD; BPhB; DD; STD; pa/Pastor Shiloh & Calvery Bapt Chs; Plant Opers, Div of Support Sers, Voorhees Col; cp/Bull Swamp Masonic Lodge #312 FAAYM; r/St Paul Missionary Baptist Union, Modr.

FRANKLIN, HERBERT oc/Director Greater Franklin County Teacher Center; b/May 1, 1935; h/179 Blueridge Dr, Frankfort, KY 40601; ba/Frankfort; m/Dorothy Ann; c/Marcus Byron, Lori Teaneale; p/Arthur (dec) and Margaret Taber Franklin (dec); ed/BS Ky St Univ 1967; MA Univ Louisville 1967; EdD Ind Univ 1974; mil/AUS 1960-62; 1st Lt USAR; pa/Dir Gtr Franklin Co Tchr Ctr 1979-; Asst Prof Univ Fla 1974-79; Prin Dyer Middle Sch, Bloomington, Ind 1973-74; Cnslr, Ednl Placement, Ind Univ 1972-73; Louisville Public Schs: Asst Prin Wash-Meyzeek Schs 1968-72, Team Ldr Tchr Corps 1967-68, Cnslr 1965-67, Tchr 1962-65; Nat Assn Sec'dy Sch Prins; Life Mem NEA; Phi Delta Kappa; cp/Bd Mem Frankfort Chd's Theater; Reserve Ofcrs Assn; NAACP; r/Bapt; hon/Outstg Tchr, Bych Elem; Kantana (Men's Acad of Hon); Father of Yr; W/W: Am Cols & Univs; S&SE; Pub'd Author.

FRANKLIN, SYLVESTER JR oc/Associate Plant Technician; b/Jan 12, 1942; h/1007 Mulberry Ave, Sanford, FL 32771; m/Willie Mae; c/Bruce, Dexter; p/Sylvester Sr and Thelma Franklin, Sanford, FL; ed/NC A&T 1962-63; mil/AUS 1964-66 Spec 4th Class, 82nd Airborne Div; pa/Assoc Plant Tech; cp/Sanford Yth Baseball Assn VP; Coach Sanford Baseball, Fball, Basketball Assn; r/Bapt; Deacon New Mt Calvary Missionary Bapt Ch; hon/Man of Yr Awd, New Missionary Mt Calvary Ch 1977.

FRANKLIN, WILLIAM DONALD oc/Government Economist; b/Nov 26, 1933; h/509 Lewis St, Vienna, VA 22180; ba/Washington, DC; m/Elizabeth Ann Giles; c/Braden, Kimette, Laura, Thomas, Amy; p/Thomas Kimsey and Lora Claudia Martin Franklin; ed/BS Austin Peay St Univ 1961; MS Tex A&M Univ 1961; Grad Advanced Mgmt Prog Harvard Univ 1973; mil/AUS to Maj 1953-58; pa/Data Processing Mgr, Bollin-Harrison Inc, Clarksville, Tenn 1959-61; Economist, Tex A&M Univ, Col Stn 1961-63; Asst Prof Upper Iowa Univ, Fayette 1963-64; Transport Economist Tex Trans Inst, Tex A&M Univ 1964-69; Hd Dept Ecs, Dir Comml Sers & Mgmt Devel, Tenn Wesleyan Col 1969-75; Pres Econoter Res Co, Athens, Tenn 1969-75; Dpty Div Chief, Trade & Indust Analysis Bur, Intl Affairs Dept Labor, Washington 1975-77; Indust Economist, Planning & Analysis Fed RR Adm Dept Transport, Washington 1977; Energy Sys Res Div, Ofc of Vehicle Sys Res Nat Hwy Traffic Safety Adm 1977-; Conslt, Ctr for Govt Trng, Univ of Tenn 1969-75; Fed Coor Emergency Transport, St of Tenn 1973-76; Mem: Presl Exec Res, Exec Ofc of US Pres 1967-73, Tenn St-wide Coun on Commun Ldrship 1973-75, St-wide Consumer Ed Planning Coun 1970-75, Am Econ Assn, Am Statistics Assn, Am Acad Polit & Social Sci, IPA, Phi Sigma Kappa, Phi Alpha Theta; cp/Harvard Bus Sch Alumni Assn; Lions; Rotary; Capital Yacht Clb; r/Meth; hon/Hons List, Woodrow Wilson Fdn 1961; Author: Highway Cost and Special Benefits 1967, (W Maj Gen John Doyle) Federal Emergency Transportation Preparedness 1968, Supervisory Management 1972, Community Leadership Development 1975; Contbr Articles to Profl Jours.

FRANTZ, ANN BROWNING oc/Training Instructor; b/Oct 23, 1950; h/Box 41, Frontier Ct, Summersville, WV 26651; ba/Craigsville, WV; p/Richard Alden and Louraine Martin Frantz, Montgomery, WV; ed/AB Glenville St Col; MS WV Univ; pa/Trg Instr, Island Creek Coal; r/Presb; hon/W/W Am Wom 1979-80.

FRAZE, DENNY T oc/Professor; b/May 28; h/2219 S Hayden, Amarillo, TX 79109; ba/Amarillo; m/Gwen Woodson; c/David A, Michael W, Jennifer B, Byron W, Wendy W; p/Oran Lester (dec) and Ima Laveine Fraze, Weatherford, TX; ed/Weatherford Col 1958-59; BFA Univ Tex-Austin 1962; Att'd Tex Christian Univ Summer 1963; MFA Univ Colo-Boulder 1964; Att'd N Tex St Univ Summer 1965; pa/Amarillo Col: Instr Art 1965, Acting Chm Dept Art 1967-68, Assoc Prof Art 1968-70, Prof Art 1970, Chm Dept Art 1968-; Tex Jr Col Tchrs Assn; Col Art Assn Am; Hon Mem Amarillo Fine Arts Assn; Hon Mem Tex Fine Arts Assn; Tex Coun on Arts in Ed, Bd Mem 1970-72; St Chm St of Tex Nat Art Ed Assn 1971-72; Tex Assn Schs of Art, Chm Acad Standards Com 1968-70, Pres 1970-72, Bd Mem 1970-74, Acad Standards Com 1976-; VChm, Coor'g Bd Tex Col & Univ Sys; Intl Biogl Assn; Num Exhibs; cp/Amarillo Art Ctr Assn, Bd Devel; Amarillo C of C Fine Arts Coun; Bd Trustees Amarillo Montessori Acad 1975-77; Amarillo C of C Decade 1980 Com; r/Epis; hon/Amariloo Globe-Times Accolade 1970; W/W Am Art; Men of Achmt; DIB; Blue Book of Tex Panhandle; W/W S&SW.

FRAZIER, THOMAS W III oc/Insurance Agent; b/Sept 3, 1952; h/155 Dorsey Pl, Henderson, NC; ba/Henderson; m/Patricia Rainey; c/Elizabeth Ann; p/Thomas Worth Jr and Rebecca Clayton Frazier, Henderson, NC; ed/BS UNC-Chapel Hill 1974; Grad Rltrs Inst, UNC-CH 1975; Chartered Property & Casualty Underwriter Deg 1980; pa/Secy-Treas Wester Rltr & Ins Agcy Inc; Kerr Lake Bd of Rltrs; Past Secy-Treas Soc CPCU; NC Assn Rltrs; cp/Henderson JCs; U Way Campaign Chm; Bd Dirs Vance Co Cancer Soc; VP UNC Alumni Assn, Vance Co Chapt; Coun on Mins Chm; Ecumenical Affairs Com; r/U Meth Ch; Adm Bd.

FREEMAN, ARTHUR MERRIMON III oc/Physician; Psychiatrist; Educator; b/Oct 10, 1942; h/3233 E Briarcliff Rd, Birmingham, AL 35223; ba/Birmingham; m/Linda Poynter; c/Arthur Merrimon IV, Katherin Leigh, Edward Todd; p/Arthur Merrimon Jr and Katherine Lide Freeman, Birmingham, AL; ed/AB 1963 Harvard Univ; MD 1967 Vanderbilt; mil/USN Lt Cmdr, Med Corps 1972-74; pa/Prof, Dept of Psychiatry Univ of Ala Sch of Med; Editor; Admr; Chief Psychiatric Ser, VA Hosp, Birmingham; Author: Psychiatry for the Primary Care Physician; cp/Adm Bds: Canterbury Meth Ch, E Side Mtl Hlth Clin, Creative Montessori Schs; r/Meth; hon/Fellow Am Psychi Assn; Nat Merit Scholar, Harvard 1959-63; F'ships: Karolinska Inst 1965, Univ of London 1970, 76; Examiner Am Bd of Psychi & Neurology.

FREEMAN, BETTY DELAINE oc/Caretaker for Horses, Homemaker; b/Feb 10, 1939; h/Crowell Ln, Rt 10 Box 226, Lebanon, TX 37087; ba/Same; m/John Bryan; c/Elizabeth Delaine, John Bradford; p/T Lester and Loucile Bradford, Lewisburg, TN; ed/Am Med Technol; Att'd MTSU; pa/Tenn Walking Horse Breeders & Exhibrs Assn; Chm Charity Classic Horse Show; Activs Chm Middle Tenn Trails Coun; cp/Yr Round Garden Clb; Bldg Com Mem Humane Soc; r/Ch of Christ; hon/Past Pres Lebanon JCettes.

FREEMAN, FRANK RAY oc/Professional Counselor; b/Sept 16, 1936; h/6905 Edgebrook Dr, Springfield, VA 22150; ba/Annandale, VA; p/William Stanford (dec) and Amanda V Fentress Freeman (dec); ed/Ball St Univ 1954-55; AB Bellarmine Col 1968; Georgetown Univ 1958-60; MEd Spalding Col 1967; Post Grad Work Cath Univ Am, Current; pa/Hd of SS, Providence HS 1960-64; Tchr De Sales HS, Louisville, KY 1964-66; Prin Carr Twp Schs 1966-67; Instr Univ Va 1967-70; Cnslr-Assoc Prof No Va Commun Col 1970-; Pvt Cnslg Pract; APGA; No Va PGA; VEA; NEA; AAUP; ACLU; Assn Measurement & Evaluation in Guid; cp/Dem Party; hon/Ten Yr Ser Awd from St of Va; W/W S&SW 1980-81.

FREEMAN, JAMES DREW SR oc/Controller; b/July 13, 1924; h/225 Randles St, Sparta, TN; m/Zella Wise; c/Josie D, James D Jr, Nell Woolf; p/Jesse Bryan Sr (dec) and Nell Cornelia Freeman (dec); ed/Intl Accts Soc 1952; mil/USN 1942-45; pa/Works Acct HK Porter Co Inc, Asbestos Works 1951-72; Controller Thomas Industs 1971-; Nat Assn Accts; cp/Repub Party; r/First Christian Ch; hon/Achmt Awd HK Porter 1956; 25 Yr Awd from Masons.

FREEMAN, JEROME W oc/Executive Director; b/Jul 3, 1928; h/PO Box 148, Danville, KY 40422; ba/Oklahoma City, OK; m/Helen Beatrice Jackson; c/Jerome Warren Jr, Michael Louis Freeman; p/George L and Ida Helen Freeman (dec); ed/BA; MEd; MA; EdD; pa/Exec Dir Okla Comm on Deaf & Hearing Impaired; Tchr, Supv'g Tchr, Prin, Asst Superintendent: NC, Miss, Tex, La, Tenn, Ky Schs for the Deaf; Asst Prof & Dir Univ of Sci & Arts of Okla; Phi Delta Kappa; Conf of Am Instrs of the Deaf; Conf of Execs of Am Schs for Deaf; cp/Nat Fraternal Soc of the Deaf; Gallaudet Col Alumni Assn Chapt; Secy, Mem Bd Dirs: La Assn of the Deaf; r/Bapt; hon/Kiwanis S'ship, Ind Sch for the Deaf; Olaf Hanson Ldrship Awd, Gallaudet Col; W/W Cols & Univs; Commun Ldrs & Noteworthy Ams; Pers of Am.

FREEMAN, JOE PHILLIP oc/Mechanical Technician, Real Estate

Associate; b/June 16, 1940; h/4700 Paris, Orange, TX 77630; ba/Orange; m/Janice; c/Angela, Joe Jr, Brian; p/D L and Ruth Freeman, Lufkin, TX; cp/Lions Clb Pres; Charter JC; hon/Coach of Yr, Orange Jr Fball.

FREEMAN, JUDY DELK oc/Kindergarten Teacher; b/Dec 2, 1941; h/Rt 1 Box 35 B, Swansea, SC 29160; m/Kenneth D Sr; c/Ken, Katie; p/Wilbur R (dec) and Bertie Lee Delk, Hilda, SC; ed/BS Winthrop Col 1973; MEd SC St Col 1979; Prin's Cert 1979; pa/Tchr 8 Yrs; SCEA; NEA; Palmetto St Tchrs Assn; cp/Swansea Hay Day Fest Fin Com; Mothers Clb Chp; r/Bapt; hon/Swansea Elem Tchr of Yr 1979-80; Lexington Dist #4 Tchr of Yr 1980-81.

FREEMAN, KATHERINE oc/Director Day Care, Co-Owner Business; b/June 18, 1931; h/33 Andrews Dr, Daleville, AL 36322; ba/Daleville, AL; m/Tom G; c/David, Michael, Stephen; p/dec; pa/Co-Owner Freeman Ser Co; Dir Christian Day Care, Daleville Bapt Ch; Regional Day Care Assn; Nat Assn Housing & Redevel Ofcls; cp/Pres Lovely Touch Garden Clb; Daleville Ath Boosters; PTA; Sr Citizens & Nsg Home Sponsor; r/So Bapt: Ch Hostess, SS Tchr, Ldr Adult Trg.

FREEMAN, MARY BERTHA oc/Retired Teacher; b/Jan 20, 1903; p/Rolland Harvey and Bertha Lee Howard Freeman; ed//Grad Andrew Col 1921; BS Ga So Col 1937; MA Univ NY 1940; Att'd George Peabody Col for Tchrs; pa/Tchr Public Schs Ga 1921-36; Supvr, Bryan, Evans & Liberty Cos, Ga 1936-40; Tchr Ga So Col 1940-62; Ret'd 1962; Past Mem: NEA, GEA; Mem: Nat Ret'd Tchrs Assn, Ga Ret'd Tchrs Assn; Bulloch Co Tchrs Assn; Assn Supvn & Curric Devel 1936-40; Assn Chd Ed Intl, Ga St Pres; Kappa Delta Pi; cp/DAR: Nat, St, Local Levels, Regent of Archibald, Bullock Chapt; Eta Chapt, Phi St Delta Kappa Gamma; r/Meth; hon/Ga So Col Yrbook Dedication; Author 94 Histories of DAR Ancestors.

FREEMAN, RICHARD MERRELL oc/Director, Tennessee Valley Authority; b/Jul 2, 1921; h/1539G Coleman Rd, Knoxville, TN 37919; ba/Knoxville; m/Joanne S; c/Randy, Mark, Candy, Marcia; p/F Rider Freeman (dec); Ruth Freeman, Crawfordsville, IN; ed/AB Wabash Col; LLB Columbia Univ; mil/USNR 1943-46; pa/Dir TVA; Mem Am Bar Assn; cp/Dem Party; r/Prot; hon/Phi Beta Kappa.

FREEMAN, RONALD BRUCE oc/Group Home Manager; b/July 19, 1939; h/PO Box 51, Weldon, NC 27890; ba/Roanoke Rapids, NC; m/Mary Ann Glenn; c/Leslie Elaine, Ronald Harry; p/Harry D and Callie M Freeman, Randleman, NC; ed/BS Biol & Psychol; MA Cnslg; mil/USAF 1961-65; pa/Grp Home Mgr, Devel Disabled Chd; Phi Delta Kappa; cp/Assn Retard'd Citizens; r/Epis; hon/Psi Chi.

FRENCH, JOHN H oc/Attorney; b/Mar 16, 1946; h/3509 Turkey Run Ln, Tallahassee, FL 32312; ba/Tallahassee; m/Jeana T; p/John H (dec) and Sara T French, Tallahassee, FL; ed/BA 1967, JD 1971 Fla St Univ; pa/Fla Bar Assn; Am Soc Law & Med; Fla Ecs Clb; Capital Tiger Bay Clb; cp/Exec Dir Fla Dem Party 1973-75; Gen Counsel Sunshine Amendment 1976; Gen Counsel No Casino Inc 1978; r/Meth; hon/Gold Key; Omicron Delta Kappa, Homecoming Chm 1970.

FREUND, EMMA FRANCES oc/Lab Supervisor; b/Oct 8, h/Richmond, VA; ba/Surgical Pathology Dept, Med Col of Va Hosp; 12th and Broad Sts, Richmond, VA 23298; m/Frederic Reinert (dec); c/Frances, Daphne, Fern, Frederic; p/Walter Russel Ervin, Kensington, MD; Mabel W Loveland Ervin (dec); ed/BS Wilson Tchrs Col 1944; MS Cath Univ 1953; Cert Mgmt Devel, Va Commonwlth Univ 1975; Cert Electron Microscopy, St Univ NY 1977; Att'd J Sargent Reynolds Commun Col 1978; Reg'd Harvey and Bertha St Peter 1979; pa/Tech, Parasitology Lab, Zoo Div, US Dept Agric 1945-48; Histologic Tech, Pathol Dept, Georgetown Univ Med Sch 1948-49; Clin Lab Tech, Kent & Queen Anne's Co Hosp 1949-51; Histologic Tech, Surg Pathol Dept, Med Col Va Hosp 1951-; Supvr Histology Lab, Surg Pathol Dept, Med Col Va Hosp 1970-; Am Soc Med Technol: Rep to Sci Assem Histology Sect 1977-78, Histology & Cytology Sects 1980-81; Va Soc Med Technol; Richmond Soc Med Technol, Corresp Secy 1977; Nat Soc Histotechnol, Charter Mem Ho of Dels 1979-80; Va Soc Histology Techs: Bd Dirs 1979-, By-Laws Com 1975 & 1979-80; Nat Geographic Soc; Smithsonian Inst; AAAS; Assn Wom Sci; Va Govtl Employees Assn; Am Soc Clin Pathols; cp/YWCA; Asst Cub Scout Den Ldr; Robert E Lee Coun BSA 1967-68, Den Ldr 1968-70; r/Presb; hon/Phi Beta Rho 1940; Kappa Delta Pi 1944; Phi Lambda Theta 1946; Sigma Xi 1953; NY Acad Scis 1979; W/W S&SW 1980-81; Author "A Method of Staining Trichomonas Foetus in Smears of Bovine Vaginal Secretions" *Proceedings of the Helminthological Society of Washington DC* 1949.

FREVELE, JANICE MARIE CLEMENT oc/Teacher; b/Sept 28, 1938; h/801 W Mulberry, Enid, OK 73701; m/Charles L Jr; p/Virgil A (dec) and Stella Clement, Memphis, TN; ed/BS Univ Tenn; MA George Peabody Col; Add'l Study Memphis St Univ; pa/Tchr Vocal Mus; Former Soloist

Memhis & Knoxville, Tenn; MENC; NEA; cp/Alamance Choral, Burlington, NC; Commun Chorus; r/First Bapt Ch; hon/Outstg Yng Wom of Am 1971.

FREYLER, WILLIAM JOHN oc/Cashier, WV Alcohol Beverage Control Commission; b/Nov 23, 1940; h/61 Burkham Ct, Wheeling, WV 26003; p/Gus W and Edna B Freyler, Wheeling, WV; ed/AB W Liberty St Col; pa/Cashier Store #106, WVa ABC Comm; cp/Asst 4-H Ldr, Omaha 4-H Clb; VP Ohio Co 4-H Ldrs Assn; Ohio Co 4-H Publicity Chm; WV 4-H All Stars; Wheeling JCs, Past Chaplain, Reception Chm & Dir; Emorclew Clb, Past Treas, Secy & Pres; YMCA; Ohio Co 4-H All Stars, Past Secy-Treas; r/Stone U Presb Ch: Past Deacon, Mem Sanctuary Choir, Ruling Elder, Chm Worship Com; hon/4-H Awds: Charting Pin 1961, Alumni Pin 1965, WV 4-H All-Star 1966; Outstg 4-H Ldr 1973; Friend of 4-H 1977; Wheeling JCs: Keyman of Yr 1975, 77, Spark Plug Winner 1977, JC of Month 1975, 75, 77, Pres Awd 1979, Citizen of Month Oct 1979; WV JC St Awds: Wheelchair Awareness Day 1st Place 1976; Bicycle Rodeo 1st Place 1979, WV JCs Statesman 1979, MD Toll Road 2nd Place 1980; Pub'd Articles.

FRIEDMAN, RICHARD NATHAN oc/Lawyer; b/June 13, 1941; h/Miami, FL; ba/Miami, FL; m/Catherine H; c/Melissa Danielle; p/Martin Harry Friedman (dec); Caroline Shaines, No Bay Village, FL; ed/BA Univ Miami 1962; JD Univ Miami Sch of Law 1965; LLM Georgetown Law Ctr 1967; pa/Staff Atty, SEC 1965-66; Feldman & Warner Attys At Law 1966-67; Sole Pract of Law 1968-; Adj Prof Law, Univ Miami Sch Law 1972-76; Arbitrator, NY Stock Exch 1973-; Fla Bar 1965; Unified Bar of Dist of Columbia 1966-; cp/Am Stockholders Assn, Fdr-Pres 1971-74; Stop Transit Over People 1975-; Univ Miami: Soc Univ Fdrs 1980-, Pres's Clb 1976-, Endowment Com 1970-; hon/Cert of Merit, Dade Co Bar Assn 1972 & 73; Certs Apprec: Opa Locka-Carol City JCs 1977, Ponce de Leon Devel Assn 1976, Kiwanis Breakfast Clb of Miami 1977, Kiwanis Clb S Miami 1977, Kiwanis Clb N Miami 1977, Kiwanis Clb Miami-Midtown 1977, Allapattah Lions Clb 1977, Bayshore Ser Clb 1970, Nor-Isle Optimist Clb of Miami Bch 1973, 100 Clb Dade Co 1978, Optimist Clb of N Shore 1977, N Dade C of C 1977, Exch Clb of Miami 1978, Exch Clb Miami Lakes 1978, SW Miami JCs 1978; W/W: S&SW, Am Law; DIB; Frichard N Friedman Wk Apr 1978; Hon Citizen St of Tenn 1970; Citizen of Day 1980; Featured in Num TV & Theatrical Films; Columnist: *Miami Review* 1971-73, *Business Leader* 1974-76.

FRIEDMAN, BARBARA JO BAXTER oc/Student, Houseparent; b/July 18, 1948; h/302 Hargrove Rd, Tuscaloosa, AL 35401; m/William Robert; c/Michael Payne, Jonathan Courtney, Jeremy William, (Foster:) Elizabeth Louise Skelton, Thomas Franklin George Jr, Michael Alexander George, Frederick Dale George, Charles Ray Baber; p/Oscar Albert and Elizabeth Ivey Baxter, Tavares, FL; ed/Fla Tech Col; IBM Prog Grad 1967; Att'g Univ Ala; p/Houseparent Ctrl Ch of Christ Chd's Home; Ala Soc Profl Engrs; Nat Soc Profl Engrs; Soc Wom Engrs; r/Ch of Christ; on/Recip Hardaway Foun S'ship Engrng.

FRIEND, EDITH OVERTON oc/Extension Home Economist; b/June 5, 1928; h/Lovingston, VA; ba/L'ton; m/Kathryn Louise; c/Mary Elizabeth (dec), Samuel Warren (dec); p/George Hiram (dec) and Carrie Elizabeth Overton, Lovingston, VA; ed/BA Asbury Col 1950; MA WV Univ 1961; pa/Ext Home Ec, VPI & SU 1968-; Instr Home Ec, Concord Col 1966-68; Home Ec Tchr, Mercer Co Bd of Ed 1966; Elem Tchr Preston Co 1965; Substitute Tchr 1961-65; Home Demo Agt, Ext Ser, WVU 1954-61; Home Economist, Appalachian Power Co 1954-54; Nat Home Demo Agts Assn, Nat Chm of St Pres's Grp 1958; WV Wom Ext Wkrs Assn, St VP 1957-58, St Pres 1958-60; WV Home Ec Assn: Chm Ext Sect 1956-58, St Mbrship Chm 1958-60; Nat Assn Ext Home Ecs; Va Assn Ext Home Ecs; Am Sch Food Ser Assn 1967-68; Am & Va Home Ec Assn; E Ctrl Dist Ext Home Ecs, Secy 1970-71; Epsilon Sigma Phi, Alpha Gamma Chapt, E Ctrl Dist Dir 1976-77 & 77-78; Va Del to NAEHE Meeting 1971, Nat Arrangements Com 1971; Pres VESA 1979-80; cp/OES #95, Worthy Matron 1973-74, 78-79; Asbury Col Alumni Assn 1967-72; Nelson Co Gdn Clb, Scrapbook Chm 1977-79; Beta Sigma Phi; Nelson Co BPW Clb; r/Meth; hon/W/W Am Wom 1959; DIB 1963, 73; Nat Register of Prominent Ams 1967; Royal Blue Book 1969; 2000 Wom of Achmt 1970, 71; Personalities of the S 1971-72; World W/W Wom 1973; Intl W/W Commun Ser 1973; Personalities of the S Bicent Meml Ed; Notable Ams of Bicent Era 1976; Commun Ldrs of Va 1976-77; W/W Commonwlth's Commun Ldrs; Personalities of Am 1978.

FRIEND, HARLAN DILLMAN oc/County Judge; b/Jan 20, 1924; h/1505 Bowie St, Liberty, TX 77575; ba/Liberty; m/Karen Lee Shannon; c/Shelley Anne, Harlan Jefferson, Shannon Lee, Sean Arthur, Patrick Dillman; p/Harlan Downs and Erba Dillman Friend; ed/BBA 1949, LLB 1956, JD 1969 Baylor Univ; mil/USN 1942-46, So Pacific Theatre; pa/Co Judge, Liberty Co, Tex 1975-; Partner Cain & Friend 1957-61, Zbranek & Friend 1961-75; Mem: Chambers-Liberty Co Bar Assn (Secy 1958, VP 1959, Pres 1960-61), St Bar of Tex, Tex Trial Lwyrs Assn, Am Bar Assn,

PERSONALITIES OF THE SOUTH

Am Judicature Soc; cp/Deleg Tex Dem St Conv 1956-; Solely Org'd 4th Senatorial Dist of Tex for Jimmy Carter's Candidacy for Pres; Chm Jimmy Carter Nat Deleg Selection Com 4th Senatorial Dist of Tex; Mem, Elected Secy of Electoral Col 1977; Ofcr Masonic AF&AM 48, Houston; Scottish Rite Temple; Arabia Shrine Temple, Houston; Elks; VFW (Hon Life Mem); Cmdr Am Legion; Doberman Pinscher Clb of Am; Newport Yacht & CC; Valley Players, Liberty; Pres Hull Rotary Clb; r/Trinity Epis Ch, Anahuac, Chambers Co: Mem, Lay Reader; hon/Sigma Delta Ci; Delta Sigma Phi; Phi Delta Phi; Mil: Asiatic Theater Ribbon, Good Conduct Medal, Hon Disch.

FRINK, BETTYE oc/State Auditor; b/Feb 19, 1933; h/1943 Talbot Terrace, Montgomery, AL; m/William D Sr; c/Victor, William D Jr, Bettye Lynn, Leigh Allen; p/Lester Love and Edna Leora McMillian Haynes; ed/Bus Col; pa/Secy of St, Ala 1959-63; St Auditor 1963-67, 75-79; Dem Nominee for St Auditor 1979-83; r/Born Again Christian; hon/W/W: Am Wom, Am Polits, Wom Govt.

FROEHLICH, SUE ANN oc/Advertising Executive; b/Dec 28, 1946; h/3004 Cherry Ln, Austin, TX 78703; ba/Austin; m/Travis Dean; c/Stephen Brent; p/Jack and Bee Wertherimer, Dallas, TX; ed/BJour Univ Tex-Austin; pa/Pres Fralix Inc; Austin Advtg Clb; Austin Exec Assn; Guest Lectr Univ Tex; on/Local, Regional, Nat Addy Awds 1975, 76, 77, 79.

FROHLICH, EDWARD DAVID oc/Vice President of Education & Research; b/Sept 10, 1931; h/5353 Marcia Ave, New Orleans, LA 70124; ba/New Orleans; m/Sherry; c/Margie, Bruce, Lara; p/William and May Zneimer Frohlich, Silver Spring, MD; ed/BA cum laude 1952 Washington & Jefferson Col; MD 1956 Univ of Md Sch of Med; MS Physiol 1963 NWn Univ; mil/AUS Capt 1960-62, Chief Circulation Sect, Environmtl Med Div, AUS Med Res Lab, Fort Knox, Ky; pa/Ochsner Medical Foun, New Orleans: VP for Ed & Res, Staff Mem & Hd Div of Hypertensive Diseases; Tulane Univ & La St Univ: Clin Prof Dept of Med, Adjunct Prof, Dept of Physiol; Mem: AAAS (Fellow), Am Bd of Internal Med, Am Col of Cardiol, Am Col of Physicians, Am Fedn for Clin Res, Am Heart Assn, Am Physiological Soc, Am Soc of Nephrology; Others; Conslt; Adv Bds; Editorial Bds; r/Hebrew; hon/F'ships; Dist'd Fac Awd, Student Coun Univ of Okla Hlth Scis Ctr 1970; So Med Assn Annual Awd, Univ of Louisville 1971; George Lynn Cross Res Prof'ship, Univ of Okla 1975; Chi Epsilon Mu; Phi Sigma; Alpha Kappa Alpha; Others.

FROST, ELTON JR oc/Chief Log Analyst; b/Oct 6, 1951; h/Houston, TX; ba/10205 Westheimer, Houston, TX 77042; m/Katherine Lois; c/Jennifer Ann, Jonathon Teague; p/Elton and Dorothy Mae Frost, Lampasas, TX; ed/BS 1973, MA 1975 SW Tex St Univ; pa/Chief Log Analyst, Dresser Atlas, Div Dresser Indusrs; SPWLA; SPE-AIME, CWLS; r/Bapt; hon/Nat Hon Soc; Author/Co-Author Num Papers Incl'g "Some Aspects of the Calculation of Gypsum Free Porosity" & "Some Basic Mathematical Considerations in Complex Reservoir Analysis."

FRUEAUFF, SUE ADCOCK oc/Teacher; b/Mar 7, 1940; h/801 W 17th Terr, Russellville, AR 72801; c/David Arthus, Anna Katherine; p/A E and Fannie Sue Adcock, Little Rock, AR; ed/BS; MEd; pa/Clrm Tchrs Assn; AEA; NEA; cp/Policy Coun Ark Wom's Polit Caucus; Gov Com on Status of Wom; Former Mem Bd Dirs Yth Home Inc; Past Pres Little Rock & R'ville Brs AAUW & Ark Div AAUW; r/So Bapt; hon/Outstg Yng Wom Am 1971.

FRY, BARBARA ANN WILFORD oc/Regional Fiscal Management Officer; b/Nov 10, 1937; h/1511 Montevallo Cir, Decatur, GA 30033; ba/Atlanta; m/Ron; c/Kim Buskirk, Gena Buskirk; p/Robert N and Marianne E Wilford, Lakeland, FL; ed/BS Univ III 1959; MBA Roosevelt Univ 1976; mil/USAF 1959-61 Lt; pa/Navy Elects Supply Ofc: Budget Analyst 1962-65, Hd Budget Sect 1965-73; Chief Budget Sect, Midwest Region IRS 1973-75; Chief Budget Sect, SE Region IRS 1975-76; Regional Fiscal Mgmt Ofcr, IRS, SE Region 1976-; Atlanta Chapt Fed Employed Wom Inc: Pres 1980-81, Co-Chm Inter-agcy Coun 1979-80; Atlanta Assn Fed Execs: Treas 1981-82; AAUW, Past Treas; cp/Atlanta Wom's Network; PTF; Pal in Pioneer Girls; r/Fund-Evang; hon/W/W Am Wom 1981-82.

FRYAR, MARIDELL FISHER oc/Coordinator Fine Arts and Speech; b/Aug 18, 1935; h/3401 Humble, Midland, TX 79703; ba/Midland; m/Jack Delane; c/Eric, Delanna; p/Fred L and Leah Fisher, Orange, CA; ed/BA Hardin Simmons Univ; MA Tex Tech Univ; pa/Coor Fine Arts & Speech, Midland Schs; Nat Coun AFA; Pres TFA; Nat Student Cong Parliamentarian NFL; cp/Ky, Md & Midland Geneal Assns; r/Bapt; hon/Outstg Tex Speech Tchr; Dist'd Ser Awd Trinity Univ; Double Diamond Coach NFL; Outstg Coach Awd Notre Dame HS.

FRYE, MARY LOIS oc/Educator, Administrator; b/June 22, 1925; h/702 Lakeshore Dr, Stillwater, OK 74074; ba/Stillwater; m/E Moses;

c/Lynette Chapman, Camille Henson, Renee; p/Lyle H Rulifson, Anaheim, CA; Elsie Whitson Rulifson (dec); ed/BS cum laude Hamline Univ 1947; BS Okla St Univ 1966; Grad Studies Oregon St, Univ Oregon, Univ Nev, Portland St, Okla St Univ; Doct 1979; pa/Okla St Univ: Asst Dir Sch Hlth, PE & Leisure Sers 1975-79, Asst Prof Hlth, PE & Rec, Asst Dir Rec Sers 1968-75; GSA ACA Camping & Aquatic Instrn 1963-68; Instr Okla City Parks & Rec Dept 1958-61; Aquatics, Fitness & Gymnastics Instr YWCA 1955-57; Univ Nev: Instr HPER 1951-54, Dorm Hd Res 1951-52; Instr Psychol & Phy Ed Gallup Sr HS 1950-51; Instr HPER Gallup Jr HS 1949-50; Instr Hlth & Phy Ed Roseberg, Oregon Jr HS 1947-49; Am Camping Assn; Nat Intramural-Rec Assn; Nat Rec & Park Assn; Okla Hlth, Phys Ed & Rec Assn, VP for Rec 1971-72 & 1977-78; AAHPER; Okla Parks & Rec Soc: Secy-Treas 1969-70, Hon & Awds Chm 1978-80; cp/Bd Dirs Arts & Humanities Coun; Girl Scout Cnslt; Lahoma Clb; Stillwater Tennis Assn; Stillwater Sailing Clb; U Fund Bd; YWCA Aquatic Bd; Stroke & Turn Judge, Big 8 Men & Wom AAU Swimming; Sierra Clb; AAUW; BPW; Nat Wildlife Fed; r/Presb; hon/Fac Dist'd Ser Awd, Arts & Sci Col 1979; W/W Am Wom; Personalities of S; World W/W Wom; 30 Yrs Ser w Am Red Cross; Sigms Sigma Psi; Torch & Cycle Hon; Phi Epsilon Kappa; Author *Compilation of the Leisure Services Opportunities in the City of Stillwater*; Num Other Profl Articles.

FRYMIRE, LESLIE HAYNES oc/Gulf Distributor and Jobber; b/Aug 18, 1926; h/101 Spring St, Irvington, KY 40146; ba/Irvington; m/Blanche Stith; c/Elizabeth Ann, Junius Leslie; p/Junius M and Anna A Frymire, Webster, KY; ed/Wn Ky St Tchrs Col, Bowling Green; mil/USN WWII So Pacific; pa/Gulf Distributor & Jobber; Constitutional St Offcr; Ky RR Commr; cp/Dem Party; Former Commr of Dixie Leag & Baseball; r/Meth; hon/30 Yrs Ser to Yth & Recreation; World's Only Treeologist.

FRYXELL, GRETA ALBRECHT oc/Oceanographer; b/Nov 21, 1926; h/210 Redmond Dr, College Station, TX 77840; ba/College Station; m/Paul Arnold; c/Karl Joseph, Joan Esther, Glen Edward; p/Arthur Joseph Albrecht (dec); Esther Miriam Andreen Albrecht, Moline, IL; ed/BA Augustana Col; MEd, PhD Tex A&M Univ; pa/Editorial Bd, Jour of Phycology; Intl Diatom Coms; Mem Algal Com, Smithsonian Oceanographic Sorting Ctr 1978-83; cp/Adult Ed; AAUW; ACLU; r/Unitarian; hon/Outstg PhD Cand; Sigma Xi; Phi Sigma; Grants: NSF, DEB 77 - 15908, Marine Diatom Genus Thalassiosira, Smithsonian Oceanographic Sorting Ctr, Antarctic Diatoms.

FUCCI, LINDA DEAN oc/Assistant Vice President; b/July 2, 1947; h/Auburn, AL; ba/PO Box 711, Auburn, AL 36830; m/Bob; p/Alton H (dec) and Irma T Dean, Opelika, AL; ed/AS So Union St Jr Col 1974; Grad Am Inst Real Est 1978; Flight Trg Auburn Univ/Air Univ 1980; Basic/Standard Cert Am Inst Bkg 1979; pa/Asst VP Auburn Nat Bank; Flight Instr, Auburn Univ; Nat Assn Bank Wom, Ed Com 1979; Am Inst Bkg, E Ala Chapt, 1st VP 1980-81, Pres 1981-82; cp/Auburn Heritage Soc 1978; Treas Lee Co Chapt Am Heart Assn 1978-79; Crusade Chp Lee Co Chapt Am Cancer Soc 1979-80; Pres Lee Co Chapt Am Cancer Soc 1980-81; r/Cath; hon/Nat Jr Hon Soc; W/W Am Wom 1980.

FULFORD, SARAH SEARS oc/Music Teacher; Professional Harpist; b/Mar 29, 1947; h/Rt 2, Box 421-A, Waycross, GA 31501; ba/Waycross; m/Paul Durwood; p/Marvin Hugh and Helen Chiles Sears, Cocoa Beach, FL; ed/BA Music Ed 1969 Fla St Univ; MMus 1974 Ga St Univ; pa/Elem Music Tchr, McDonald St Sch; Mem: Delta Kappa Gamma, Am Harp Soc, Ga Music Edrs Assn, Music Edrs Nat Conf; cp/Waycross Commun Concert Assn; Former Harpist: 2nd, Atlanta Symph Orch; Principal Harpist Atlanta Commun Orch; Kingsport, Tenn Symph Orch; Emory Univ Orch; Savannah, Symph Orch; r/Meth; hon/Recip Valley Forge Freedom's Foun Tchr Awd, Ga 1971; Intl W/W in Music & Musicians.

FULLER, CLAUDE CONYER oc/Professor; b/Mar 19, 1927; h/Monroe, LA; c/Claude C Jr, Randall D, Galey S Harrison; p/dec; ed/BS 1953, MA 1954 W Tex St Univ; PhD La St univ 1972; mil/AUS 1944-46; USAF 1950-51; pa/Prof: NE La Univ 22 Yrs, Frank Phillips Col 4 Yrs; Speech Comm Assn; La Speech Assn; Acadic Foun of NLU; Alpha Psi Omega; cp/La Assn Hi 12 Clbs, Past Pres; Masonic Lodge & Shrine; Monroe Scottish Rite Bodies; r/Meth.

FULLER, GARY LEE oc/Policeman; b/Apr 23, 1936; h/1115 Fulton St, Albertville, AL 35950; ba/Albertville; m/Linda S; c/Richey Holsonback, Robbey Holsonback; p/Charlie (dec) and Lois Y Fuller, Albertville, AL; mil/USAF; pa/Asst Police Chief; cp/Albertville Chapt #278 OES; Masonic Lodge #430; r/Bapt.

FULLER, JAMES WALKER oc/Surgeon; b/Jan 5, 1945; h/Inverness, FL; ba/411 W Highland, Inverness, FL 32650; m/Suzanne; c/Dana, Kevin; p/Mary Francis Fuller, Dyersburg, TN; ed/BS 1966, MD 1970 Univ Tenn; mil/USAF 1976-78 Chief of Surgical Sers; pa/Surg & Med; AMA; Diplomate Am Bd Surg; Fellow Intl Col Surgs; Assoc Fellow Am Col Colon-Rectal Surgs; SEn Surg Assn; hon/W/W S&SW.

111

FULTON, FRED FRANKLIN oc/Retired Management Analyst; b/Sept 27, 1920; h/5121 Harlan Dr, El Paso, TX 79924; ba/Ft Bliss, TX; m/Mary Elizabeth Ryan; c/Sharon Rosenthal, Sue Paulson, Kathleen Sutton, Timothy; p/Fred Fulton, Grass Valley, CA; Ora L Fulton (dec); ed/BIE 1970, BCE 1971 Univ E Fla; mil/USAF 1950-51 T/Sgt; USN 1942-45; pa/Artist; Poet; Engr; Ret'd Mgmt Analyst, US Govt; Pres Far W Mining & Exploration Corp; Former Indust Engr US Govt: Anchorage, Alaska, Sacramento, Cal, Lathrop, Cal; Aero-Jet Gen Corp: Mgmt/Sys Analyst, Human Factors Engr, 2 Pubs; Profl Assns; cp/Tchr Art Classes to Underprivileged Mex Yth, World Changers Inc; Bd Dirs NE El Paso Civic Assn; Others; r/LDS 70s Quorum; hon/Purple Heart; Num ZD Awds; Nom Civil Ser Employee of Yr 1973, Ft Bliss; 1-Man Art Exhibit, Instituto Mexicano Norteamericano Culturales de Relaciones de Chihuahua 1972, USIS Cult Exc Prog.

FULTON, MICHAEL NELSON oc/Surgeon; b/June 8, 1947; h/Deland, FL; ba/500 Lakeview Dr, Lake Helen, FL; m/Nancy J; c/Brent N, Christopher M; p/William N and Patsy S Fulton, Columbus Jnct, IA; ed/BA Coe Col 1969; MD Univ Ia 1973; Internship Gundersen Clin, La Crosse, Wis 1974; Residency, Dept Orthopedics, Univ Ia 1978; pa/Orthopedic Surg; Sports Med; Nat Orthopedic Conslt, Nautilus Sports/Med Industs; r/Meth; hon/Article Pub'd "Ringman's Shoulder Lesion" *The American Journal of Sports Medicine* 1979.

FULTON, ROY JR oc/Businessman; b/May 27, 1923; h/527 Thorne Ridge Cove, Memphis, TN 38117; m/Gloria A; p/Florence C Fulton; mil/AUS WWII Amphibious Tractor Batt; pa/Contractor, Fulton Plumbing & Heating Co Inc; cp/Am Qtr Horse Assn; Am Paint Horse Assn; Mid-S Qtr Horse Pres; Cub Scout Master; So Amateur Saddle Clb Assn; Girl Scout Rep; r/Bapt; hon/Recommend'd for Pres Unit Cit; Red'd Silver Buckle for Outstg Job as Pres Mid-S Qtr Horse; Sev Articles Pub'd in Am Qtr Horse Mags.

FULTON, VIRGINIA oc/Music and Education Secretary; b/Sept 16, 1937; h/376 Walthall St, Grenada, MS 38901; ba/Grenada; m/John D; c/John David, Karen Diane; p/Mary E Spain; pa/Mus & Ed Secy, First Bapt Ch; cp/2nd Lt Gov La-MS Dist Pilot Intl; r/Bapt: Ch Clerk, Dir Chd's Mus; hon/Past Pres Exchangettes; Past Pres PTA; Dir Grenada Co Lung Assn.

FUQUA, JOHN BROOKS oc/Business Executive; b/Jun 26, 1918; h/3574 Tuxedo Rd NW, Atlanta, GA 30305; ba/Atlanta; m/Dorothy Chapman; pa/Chm of Bd, Chief Exec Ofcr, Fuqua Industs Inc; Chm of Bd, Fuqua TV Inc; Dir Ctl of Ga RR; Mem: Chief Execs Forum, World Bus Coun, The Conf Bd; cp/Ga Legislature 1957-64; Chm House Banking Com 4 Yrs; Chm Senate Banking & Fin Com 2 Yrs; Bd Trustees: Ga St Univ Foun, Hampden-Sidney Col, Duke Univ; Former Bd Dirs Atlanta C of C; Former Pres Augusta C of C; Former Mem: Ga Sci & Technology Comm, Hd Visitors Emory Univ; hon/Hon LLDs: Hampden-Sidney Col, Duke Univ; Golden Plate Awd, Am Acad of Achmt; Ga Broadcaster Citizen of Yr 1963; Augusta Jr C of C Boss of Yr 1960; Ga Pioneer in Broadcasting Awd 1979.

FUQUA, WILLIAM ANDREW oc/Retail Merchandiser; b/Sept 16, 1946; h/2516 W Brooks #8, Norman, OK 73069; ba/Norman; p/W D and Patricia Fuqua, Dallas, TX; ed/RN; mil/AUS 3 Yrs Staff Sgt; pa/Sooner Theatre Guild, Am Guild Var Artists; r/Epis; hon/Nat Vol of Yr 1965.

FURR, FRANK oc/Minister; b/May 31, 1924; h/406 Gibson St, Enterprise, AL 36330; ba/Enterprise; m/Juanita I; c/Steven Paul, Kenneth Eugene; p/James Franklin (dec) and Lula Mae Furr (dec); ed/BS Troy St Univ; mil/AUS WWII; pa/Min St Luke U Meth Ch; Phi Alpha Theta; Past Pres Min F'ship, Emory Univ; Registrar Bd of Ordained Min; Conf Comm on Equitable Salaries; Ala-W Fla Conf U Meth Ch; r/Meth; hon/Ala Rural Min of Yr 1966; Awd from Daughs Fdrs & Patriots of Am; Plaque for Outstg Ser to Bd of Ordained Min.

FURR, MARY ELIZABETH SUGG oc/Homemaker; b/Sept 14, 1906; h/1927 Old Aberdeen Rd, Columbus, MS 39701; m/Ray Albert (dec); c/William Hal (dec), Ray Albert Jr; p/Amos Watson (dec) and Virginia Cooper Sugg (dec); ed/BA Blue Mtn Col; pa/Hon Mem Miss Wom's Press Assn; cp/Trustee Lowndes Co Dept Archives & Hist; r/So Bapt; hon/DAR; DAC.

FURR, QUINT E oc/Company Vice President; b/Sept 21, 1921; h/9232 3 Oaks Dr, Silver Spring, MD 20901; m/Helen W; c/Tiffany Grantham, Quentin, R Luke, Pamela Lacy, Erik Erickson; p/Walter Luther and Mary Ceclia Barnhardt Furr (dec); ed/BA Polit Sci Univ of NC; 1 Yr Law Sch Univ of NC; mil/USNR Lt (jg) WWII, Korea; pa/VP Corporate Mktg Textilease Corp; Reg Mgr Top Value Enterprises; Reg Mgr J F Pritchard Co; SMEI; IIL Chm Mktg Com 1974-76; Pi Kappa Alpha; cp/Moose; Elks; Am Legion; VFW; r/Cath; hon/Mktg Awds 1970, 71, 72, 73, 1st Pl 1974; Fellow Mem ABI; DIB; Notable Ams; Commun Ldrs & Noteworthy Ams; W/W in Advertising.

FURR, RAY A (dec) oc/Formerly Executive; m/Elizabeth Sugg; c/William Hal (dec); Ray Albert Jr; ed/BJ Univ Mo 1930; MA George Peabody Col 1935; Adv'd Grad Study Geo Peabody & NYU; pa/Asst Supt Oxford, Miss City Schs 1929-35; Assoc Prof Eng, Winthrop Col 1936-38; Hd Dept Jour & Dir Winthrop News Ser, Winthrop Col 1938-43; Prog Dir WIS Radio 1943-47; Mgr WIST Radio 1947-52; Mgr Opers WSGN 1952-53; Asst to Pres WAPI 1953-54; VP for Prog'g WAPI 1954-60; cp/Dist Gov Carolinas Kiwanis; Editor Carolina Kiwanian 1940-52; Pres Charlotte, NC Sales Exec Clb 1950; Bd Dirs Ala Broadcasters Assn 1956-60; VP Ala Broadcasters Assn 1959-60; 1st VP Birmingham BBB; Hd Jour Dept Dir Public Info & News Bur, Miss St Col for Wom 1960-70.

G

GABBARD, RALPH W oc/General Manager and Vice President; b/Dec 14, 1945; h/1809 Joan Dr, Lexington, KY 40505; ba/Lexington; m/Jackie; c/Joey, Jason, Matt, Jesse; p/Ralph and Maggie Gabbard, Versailles, KY; ed/Harvard TV Sales Mgmt; pa/VP & Gen Mgr WKYT-TV; Mem Ky Broadcasters; TVB; NAB; cp/Bd BSA; Ky Transp; r/Bapt; hon/Outstg Yng Man 1979; Yngest VP & Gen Mgr of Maj TV Sta (27 Yrs Old 1974).

GABLE, ELLEN MORPHONIOS oc/Judge; b/Sept 30, 1929; h/8640 SW 84th Ave, Miami, FL 33143; ba/Miami; m/Vincent L; c/Dale, Dean; p/Wesley Leroy and Lydia James, Miami; ed/JD Univ Miami; pa/Judge Circuit Ct of Fla, 11th Judicial Ct; Trial Atty, Chief Prosecutor Crim Ct 1961-70; Asst St's Atty, St of Fla 1961; Pract, Miami 1958-61; Fla Bar Assn; ABA; Am Judic Soc; Admitted to Pract: US Supreme Ct, US Circuit Ct of Appeals, US Dist Ct, Supreme Ct of Fla, Others; cp/Guest Commentator Stas WKAT, Miami & KMOX, St Louis; Spkr to Var Civic, Polit & Frat Orgs; r/Prot; hon/Citizen of Yr 1978, Dade Co Police Benevolent Assn; Gen Douglas McArthur Meml Awd, Leag Am Ideals; Good Citizenship Awd, Dept Fla Ladies Aux, Jewish War Vets; Lady of Yr 1972, Miami Beach Dem Clb; W/W Am Wom.

GADE, CLIFFORD WALLACE oc/Minister; b/Nov 10, 1934; m/Heidi Sievers; c/Dorothy, Werner, Stephen, Rebecca; p/Louis Hebert and Dorothy Hellis Gade; ed/BTh Concordia Col & Theol Sem 1962; Clin Oncology Residency 1977; mil/USMC 1952-56; Chaplain, Maj, Civil Air Patrol 1977-; pa/Missionary Red Lake Dist, Christ Ch, Ont, Can 1962-65; Pastor: St Peter's Ch, Antigo, Wis 1965-69; Trinity Ch, Danbury, Our Redeemer Ch, Webster, Immanuel Ch, Frederic, Wis 1969-73; Our Redeemer Ch, Webster, Trinity Ch, Danbury, Wis 1969-75; St Matthew. Ch, Eau Claire, Wis 1975-80; Immanuel Ch & Sch, Alexandria, Va 1980-; Chm N Wis Dist LCMS Bd of Missions 1976-80; Dist Campus Coor N Wis Dist LCMS 1977-80; Co-Ed *Kyrios* 1974-76; Ed-in-Chief *Kyrios* 1972-74; Bd Mem N Wis Dist Doct Concerns Prog; Zone Pastoral Advr Intl Luth Laymen's Leag; Zone Pastoral Advr Luth Wom' Missionary Leag; cp/Langlade Co Resource & Devel Com 1968-69; Chm Citizen Adv Comm 1972-72; Bd Dirs Burnett Co Chapt ARC 1974-75; Chm Regulatory Comm Wis Tri-Co Network 1976-80; Ec Communs Clb CD 1976-80; BSA; Antigo Area C of C; Am Legion; r/Luth; hon/CAP Chaplain of Yr 1979; W/W Rel; Intl W/W Commun Sers; Personalities W&MW; Men of Achmt; Personalities of Am; Notable Ams; Personalties of S.

GAINER, RUBY JACKSON oc/Counselor, Dean; b/Mar 9, 1915; h/1516 W Gadsden St, Pensacola, FL 32501; ba/Pensacola; m/Herbert P; c/James Herbert, Ruby Paulette, Cecil P; p/Will Bart and Lovie Jones Jackson (dec); ed/BS Ala St Univ; MA Atlanta Univ; Postgrad Fla Univ; 6 Hon Docts; pa/Tchr, Adm Dean, Cnslr, Dean; cp/NAACP; Dem; Unsuccessful Cand for City Coun, Ward 5, Group I; r/Mt Zion Bapt Ch; hon/Wom of Yr, Fed'd Wom of Yr, AKA Wom of Century; Fellow ABI.

GAINES, RUTH MAY CARPENTER oc/Teacher; b/May 1, 1937; h/708 S Oak Ave, Sanford, FL 32771; ba/Longwood, FL; m/Frederic Frelinghuysen; c/Elizabeth, Frederic III; p/Lewis O (dec) and Bessie N Carpenter, Fernandina Bch, FL; ed/BS Univ Tenn; MS Syracuse Univ; pa/Home Ec Tchr, Lyman HS; Am & Fla Home Ec Assns; Am & Fla Seminole Voc Assns; PTA; cp/Sanford Wom's Clb; Seminole Mutual Concert Bd Dirs; Bd Dirs Ballet Guild of Sanford/Seminole; Winter Springs C of C; Beta Sigma Phi; r/Meth; hon/Dist'd Ser Awd, Fla Assn FHA 1976; Outstg Mem Awd, Jr Wom's Clb 1977; Ctrl Fl Home Ec Tchr of Yr 1979.

GAINEY, EDITH ESTELLE MARLER oc/Teacher, Principal; b/Jan 18, 1915; h/Dunn, NC; m/Onslow Kesler; c/Onslow Kesler Jr; p/Martin Luther (dec) and Swannie Geneva Tart Marler (dec); ed/AB Atlantic Christian Col 1935; MA E Carolina Univ 1968; pa/Tchr & Prin Sampson Co Sch Sys; Tchr Harnett Co Sch Sys; NEA; NCAE; CAT, Chm Sev Coms; cp/BPW Clb, Chm Fin Com; Wom's Clb, Secy; Just-A-Mere Garden Clb, Pres; Newton Grove Chapt #267 OES; 4-H Ldr Sev Yrs; r/Presb; hon/4-H Ldr Awds.

GAINOUS, RABIE J JR oc/College Executive Vice President; b/Sept 10, 1919; h/804 Second Ave, Daytona Bch, FL 32014; ba/Same; m/Theresa C; p/Rabie J Gainous Sr (dec); Alonia Hassell, Daytona Bch, FL; ed/BS, MEd, DMS; mil/AUS; pa/Exec VP Bethune-Cookman Col; NEA; Alpha Phi Alpha; Nat Morticians Assn; cp/JCs; Daytona Bch Kiwanis Clb; NAACP; Lions Clb for Blind; r/Bapt; hon/Alpha Kappa Mu; Beta Kappa Chi; Beta Beta Beta.

GAITHER, DOROTHY WRIGHT oc/Executive Director; b/Apr 30, 1906; h/1766 Johnson Rd NE, Atlanta, GA 30306; ba/Atlanta; m/Fannye

H; c/Ellen H, Renee Werbin (Mrs Samuel N); p/Ellis Hyman and Dena Dora Galanty (dec); pa/Org, Ed, Atlanta Jewish News; Org, Ahavath Achim Bible Sch; Ed, Scroll, Ahavath Achim Bull; Supt HS Dept, Ahavath Achim Sch; Exec Dir, Ahavath Achim Congreg; Cons Bienniel Convs U Synagogue of Am; Nat Assn Synagogue Admrs; cp/32 Mason, Shriner; r/Jewish; hon/Scroll of Hon, Bonds of Israel; Plaque of Apprec, Jewish War Vets; Plaque of Dedicated Ser, Coun Jewish Fdns Welfare Funds; Cit Nat Jewish Welfare Bd; Awd Ahavath Achim Synagogue; Fellow ABI.

GALLAGHER, WILLIAM JOHN JR oc/Environmental Scientist; b/Dec 13, 1953; h/Clarkston, GA; ba/Permits Sect, Enforcement Div, US EPA, 345 Courtland St, Atlanta, GA 30308; m/Sue Thomas; p/William John Sr and Alice A Gallagher, Hopkinsville, KY; ed/Att'd Austin Peay St Univ 1971-73; BS E Tenn St Univ 1975; Att'd Chattanooga St Tech Commun Col 1977, Univ Tenn-Chat 1978-79; MPH Univ Mich 1980; pa/Reg'd Profl Envir w St Tenn; Cert'd Pesticide Applicator, Tenn Dept Agric, EPA; Public Hlth Environmentalist, Tenn Dept Public Hlth 1975-79; Envir Sci, US Envir Protect Agcy, Region IV Atlanta Ofc 1980-; Nat Envir Hlth Assn 1975-79; Tenn Envir Hlth Assn 1976-79; Secy-Treas Lower E Affil, Tenn Envir Hlth Assn 1979; Tenn Public Hlth Assn 1976-79; Student Nat Envir Hlth Assn 1973-75; Treas E Tenn S Univ Chapt, Student Nat Envir Hlth Assn 1975; cp/Jasper JCs 1976-79: Secy 1977, External VP 1978; r/Presb; hon/Nom'd for Annual Lynn B Hearn Meml Awd for Outstg Environmentalist in St Lower E Affil, Tenn Envir Hlth Assn 1979; Cert of Merit, Tenn Envir Hlth Assn; Pres Aid Awd, Pres Jasper JCs 1976.

GALLE, WILLIAM PRESTON JR oc/Professor, Director Graduate Studies; b/Nov 19, 1942; h/Rt 5, Box 162, Johnson City, TN 37601; ba/Johnson City; m/Julia W; c/Julie Michelle, William Preston III; p/Willaim P and Lillian W Galle, New Orleans, LA; ed/BS 1967, MBA 1969 LSU; PhD Univ Ark 1972; pa/LSU-New Orleans; Univ Ark-Fayetteville; Univ Ark European Grad Studies Prog; Presently Prof & Dir Grad Studies, Dept Mgmt, E Tenn St Univ; Acad Mgmt; Am Bus Communs Assn; Adm Mgmt Soc, VP; Am Inst Decision Scis; cp/Pers Com, St Bd Regents; r/Meth; hon/Nat JCs Outstg Yng Man 1977; Delta Sigma Pi Fac Awd 1978, 79; Author "Telecommunications: Tying the World Together" *Management World* 1977; *Business Communications: Theory and Practice* 1980.

GALLIMORE, TELLUS (MACKIE) oc/Teacher; b/Jan 28, 1943; h/310 Jackson St, Puryear, TN 38251; ba/Puryear; m/Janet; c/Jeff, Mitch; p/Donnie Gallimore, Puryear, Tn; ed/BS 1966, MA 1969 Murray St Univ; pa/Classroom Tchr, Puryear Elem Sch; NEA; TEA; HCEA; cp/Lions Clb; Dem, Alderman City of Puryear; r/Ch of Christ; hon/Puryear Lions Clb Lion of Yr 1977; Region I Dist 12-2 Lion of Yr 1977.

GALLOWAY, DAVID OLIVER oc/Lieutenant Commander; Facility Director; b/Feb 26, 1932; h/1810 Cardinal Ln, McAlester, OK 74501; ba/McAlester; m/Nancy Jean; c/Justin Rea, Shauna Kay, Tamara Lynn; p/Charles R Galloway (dec); Dorothy Fern Galloway, Venice, FL; ed/BS; MPH; mil/Lt Cmdr USPHS Comm'd Corp; pa/Dir IHS Indian Hlth Ctr; Adj Instr Parasitology & Lab Pract 1972; Mem Adv Bd for Pittsburg Co Home Hlth Care Prog; Pittsburg Co Coor, Lung Assn; cp/Pres McAlester Kiwanis Clb; Chm McAlester Alcoholism Coun; Reg Guid Ctr Adv Coun; Chm Adv Com Kiamichi Area Alcoholism; Mem Okla Assn on Alcohol Abuse & Alcoholism; r/U Meth Ch: Mem; hon/Wonder Worker Awd, SE Reg Okla Lung Assn; Author "Quality Control: A New Dimension", *Med Lab Observer*, 1973.

GANAWAY, BETTYE JEAN oc/Special Education Teacher; b/June 30, 1937; h/PO Box 221, Dyersburg, TN 38024; ba/D'burg; m/Marvin Sr; c/Marvin Jr, Morey Allen; p/Odell (dec) and Betty Hudson (dec); ed/BS; mil/20 Yr Dependent USAF; pa/D'burg Ed Assn; TEA; Nat Tchrs Assn; Coun for Exceptl Chd; cp/W Side Home Demo Clb; Missionary Soc; Sunshine Clb; r/Meth; hon/Outstg Yng Wom Am 1970; Cert of Apprec USAF.

GANDIN, WILLIAM BAILOUS SR oc/Staff Auditor; b/July 17, 1921; h/1927 Viking Dr, Houston, TX 77018; ba/Houston; m/Mildred Snowden; c/William Bailous Jr, Paul Snowden, David Lee; p/Jacob William (dec) and Leona Stone Gandin (dec); ed/BBA 1957, Post Grad 1957-59 Univ Houston; Rice Univ 1946-49; Indust Col of Armed Forces Hon Grad 1970; mil/USAF 1942-45, 50-52 Col, in Brig Gen Position as Mobilization Asst to Logistic Ctr Comdr 1971-75; pa/Pipeliner, Guager, Hd Stock Guager 1946; Draftsman 1947; Acct 1948-66; Hd Spec Studies, Esso-Libya 1966-67; Auditor 12 St Wn Region 1967-76; Hdq Controllers Staff Auditor, Exxon Co 1976-; AF Assn; Reserve Ofcr Assn; cp/Mil Affairs Com, Houston C of C; Sam Houton Area Coun BSA 1959-81: Fin Chm, Asst Dist Com Chm, Dist Commr; Cubmaster, Scoutmaster 1959-66; Little Leag Mgr 1961-64; Scouting Coor, Libya 1966-67; Loan Exec U Way 1977; Master Mason; Scottish Rite; Shriner; r/Meth; hon/Silver Beaver, BSA 1974; Dist'd Awd of Merit, BSA 1974; Outstg Shriner Hosp Awd 1950-70; Tex Life Mem PTA 1962; Flying Col Delta Air

Line; Flying St-man, Continental Airline; USAF Merit Ser Medal 1975; Cert'd Artic Circle Crossing 1975.

GANDY, EDYTHE EVELYN oc/Attorney; Lieutenant Governor State of Mississippi; b/Sept 4, 1922; h/727 Arlington St, Jackson, MS 39202; ba/Jackson, MS; p/Kearney C Gandy (dec); Abbie Whigham Gandy, Jackson, MS; ed/LLB; pa/Began Pvt Law Pract, Hattiesburg, Miss 1947; Elected to Miss St Leg from Forrest Co 1947; Former Asst Atty Gen of Miss; Atty, St Dept of Public Wel; St Treas 1960-64, 68-72; Commr of Public Wel 1964-67; Former Commr of Insurance; Elected Lt Gov of Miss 1975; Currently Serving: Bldg Comm, Comm of Budget & Acctg, Agri & Indust Bd, Miss Bicent Comm; H'burg BPW Clb; Former Pres Miss Fdn BPW Clbs; Bar Assns: Forrest Co, Hinds Co, Miss St, Am; Am Judic Soc; Univ Miss & Univ So Miss Alumni Assns; r/Bapt; hon/Biogl Listings; Life Mem Miss Cong PTA; Named 1 of Top 10 Wom of Mid-S for Decade of 60s.

GANNON, LEROY COLUMBUS JR oc/Retired; b/Mar 4, 1914; h/208 W King St, Jefferson City, TN 37760; m/Imogene E; p/Leroy C Sr and Annie H Gannon, Murfreesboro, TN; ed/BS Andrew Jackson Bus Univ; cp/Lions Clb; Civitan Clb; r/Bapt.

GANTT, CHARLES DAVID oc/Law Student; b/Oct 2, 1956; h/Rt 1 Box 340, Coats, NC 27521; m/Charise Lowery; p/Charles Herman (dec); and Augusta Gantt, Sanford, NC; ed/BA Univ NC-Chapel Hill 1978; JD Campbell Univ Sch Law 1981; cp/Pres Verbal Abuse Chapt of Toastmasters, Buies Creek, NC; hon/Student Citizen of Yr, Sanford, NC 1974.

GARBIRAS, SUSAN E oc/Medical Secretary; b/Dec 21, 1950; h/804 Claiborne St, Johnson, TN 37601; m/Raymond; c/Bonnie, Raymond, Damian; p/James and Bonnie Shuffler, Astoria, NY; ed/AS; pa/Med Secy; cp/Wom of Moose Lodge #1831; r/Cath; hon/4.0 Average, Dean's List Each Qtr; Recip Victor Frenkil Foun S'ship 1979.

GARCIA, LINO JR oc/Professor; b/Jan 7, 1934; h/Edinburg, TX; ba/Pan Am Univ, Edinburg, TX 78539; m/Amalia; c/Cynthia Y, Linus; p/Lino Sr and Felipa Lopez Garcia, Brownsville, TX; ed/BA St Mary's Univ 1959; MA N Tex St Univ 1966; ABD Tulane Univ 1972-; mil/USN 1952-56; pa/Prof Span Our Lady of the Lake Univ 1966-67; Prof Span Pan Am Univ 1967-; Pres Alamo Val Chapt Am Assn Tchrs of Span & Portuguese; Tex Col of Tchrs; Span Heritage Soc; Inter-Am Soc; cp/City Commr 1977-; Past Chm Commun Devel Coun; Past Chm Edinburg Bicent Comm; Past Pres St Joseph Sch Bd; Chm Public Responsibility Com MH-MR; r/Roman Cath; hon/Citizen of Wk KGBT 1979.

GARCIA-PALMIERI, MARIO R oc/Physician; b/Aug 2, 1927; ed/BS magna cum laude Univ Puerto Rico 1947; MD Univ Md 1951; Intern Fajardo Inst Hosp 1951-52; Resident: Bayamon Dist Hosp 1952-53, San Patricio VA Hosp & Asst in Med, Sch of Med 1953-54; Fellow in Cardiology, Nat Heart Inst, Sch of Med, Univ PR 1954-55; FACP 1961; FACC 1962; Fellow Coun of Clin Cardiology of Am Heart Assn 1963; Fellow Coun on Epidemiology of Am Heart Assn; FRSH 1972; pa/Lic to Prac Med: St of Md 1951, PR 1953; Diplomate Am Bd of Internal Med 1958; Diplomate Am Bd Cardiovascular Disorders 1962; Hd Dept Med, Fajardo Dist Hosp 1955-56; Hd Dept Med & Sect of Cardiology, Univ Hosp 1961-; Conslt to Presb, San Jorge, San Juan City, Auxilio Mutuo, Dr, Tchrs & San Patricio VA Hosps, San Juan, PR; Instr Med, Sch of Med 1955-56; Assoc in Med, Sch of Med, Univ PR 1956-58; Asst Prof of Med, Sch of Med Univ PR 1958-60; Dir of Comprehensive Med Prog, Sch of Med -1959; Dir Outpatient Dept of Univ Hosp 1959-61; Assoc Prof, Sch of Med 1960; Prof & Hd, Dept Med & Chief Sect of Cardiology, Sch of Med 1961-66; Prof of Med & Chief Sect of Cardiology, Dept of Med, Sch of Med 1967-68; Prof & Hd, Dept of Med & Chief Sect of Cardiology, Sch of Med 1968-; Lectr in Cardiovascular Epidemiology, Dept of Preventive Med & Public Hlth, Sch of Med, Univ PR; Prof Sch of Dentistry, Univ PR 1975; AAAS; So Soc Clin Investigation; Assn Profs of Med; Am Fed for Clin Res; Am Soc of Tropical Med & Hygiene; Assn Am Med Cols; Local Chapt, Am Soc of Internal Med; PR Med Assn; PR Soc Cardiology: Pres 1968 & 69, 1976-77, 77-78; PR Soc of Gastroenterology; Sect of Cardiology, PR Med Assn: Pres 1968-69, 76-77, 77-78; Am Public Hlth Assn; PR Public Hlth Assn; Soc for Epidemiologic Res; Assn of Univ Cardiologists; Assn of Am Phys; Royal Soc of Hlth; Intl Epidemiological Assn; Assoc Mem by Invit, Sociedad Mexicana de Cardiologia; Secy of Hlth of PR & Pres Bd Dirs of PR Med Ctr 1966-67; Latin Am VP, Sect of Cardiovascular Diseases PAMA 1967-; Editor Bltn of PR Med Assn 1960-66, Mem Bd 1966-; Gov 38th Anniv Cong of Pan Am Med Assn 1963; Editorial Bd, Am Heart Jour 1965-; PR Acad of Arts & Scis; Bd Dirs Interam Soc of Cardiology 1964-68, 72-76; Gov of PR Chapt Am Col of Cardiology 1966-69; Fdr & Mem Sci Coun on Epidemiology & Prevention of Intl Soc of Cardiology 1968-; Past Mem Num Other Profl Orgs & Coms; hon/Alpha Omega Alpha; Cert of Merit, Fajardo Dist Hosp 1965; Cert of Merit, PR Med Assn; Hon Mem Alumni Assn of Sch of Med, Univ PR

1973; Cert of Dist, Asociacion de Hospitales de Puerto Rico 1970; 2000 Men of Achmt 1969; Recog Awd, PR Med Assn 1972; 200 Yrs of Med in Balto 1976; Part in Num Nat & Intl Sci Meetings or Spec Lects; Pub'd 98 Sci Papers on Electrocardiography & Vectorcardiography in Congenital Heart Disease; Book *The Electrocardiogram and Vectorcardiogram in Congential Heart Disease* 1965.

GARDNER, DONALD ANGUS oc/Architect; b/June 2, 1944; h/104 Westover Pl, Greenville, SC 29615; ba/Greenville; m/Gloria Orr; c/Angela Renee, Donald Jr, Sonia Dale; p/Angus John and Mary Shaw Gardner, Thomasville, AL; ed/BArch Clemson Univ 1968; mil/AUS 1968-70 1st Lt; pa/Draftsman, JB Lindsay Arch 1970-74; Proj Arch, Vickery Allen Baker, 1974-75; Ptnr Gardner, Edelblut & Assocs 1975-76; Proj Arch Daniel Intl, Daniel Engrs 1976-79; Pres Donald A Gardner Arch Inc 1978-; AIA; NCARB; NAHB; Reg'd Arch SC & Ga; cp/Rotary Clb 1975-76; Repub Party; r/Meth; hon/Home Designs Pub'd in *Country Living Magazine, Hudson Home Magazine, Gold Medal Home Plans, Premium Home Plans; Architect's Choice Home Plans.*

GARDNER, HERBERT F oc/Photographer; b/Jan 14, 1917; h/408 4th Ave, Decatur, AL 35601; ba/Same; m/Nellie R; c/Herb Jr, Mary K Boyle, Mike D, John Mark; p/C Field (dec) and Minnie Brooks Gardner (dec); pa/Photog, Platemaker, Press Opr, CS; Rep'd Major Graphic Arts Mfr; Photo Staff *Nashville Banner, Nashville Tennessean, Birmingham News, Birmingham Post Herald;* Ala Post Card Co & Scenic S; hon/Ala Press Assn 1st Place Awd 1959-60.

GARDNER, LELA M oc/Speech Pathologist; b/Feb 6, 1908; m/John Hall (dec); c/Marvel Jean; p/Virgil Ralph (dec) and Jeanie Mae Warriner Marshall (dec); ed/BS Univ Neb 1930; MS Wash Univ 1932; Post Grad Study: Columbia Univ 1958-59 & 1961-62, Bowling Green St Univ 1950-60; NJ Cert Speech & Hearing 1960, Life Cert 1965; Provl Cert Speech & Hearing, Md 1966; Adv'd Profl Cert 1969; pa/Speech Pathol: Toledo Hearing Leag 1959-60, Newark Bd of Ed 1960-63, Edward R Johnstone Tng Sch 1963-66, Frederic Co Bd of Ed 1966-76; Conslt in Speech, St Home for Boys, Jamesburg, NJ 1964-67; Speech Pathol, Wn Md Ctr 1976-77; Am Speech & Hearing Assn 1960-; Pi Lambda Theta, Secy 1961-64; cp/AAUW: Bd Dirs, Arts Chm 1953-55; Wom's Univ Clb, Phila, Publicity Chm 1954-55; Northampton Co Soc for Crippled Chd & Adults, Bd Dirs 1951-55, Public Relats 1953-55; Nat Adv Bd, Am Security Coun 1973-; Charter Mem, Coalition for Peace through Strength 1978; Fdr Ctr for Intl Securities Studies 1977; Am Coun for World Freedom 1972; Bd of Policy, Liberty Lobby 1973-; WV Panhandle Chapt, Eagle Forum, Pres 1978-; Am Conserv Union, Life Mem 1973; Com to Restore the Constitution 1974-; Foun for Law & Soc 1978; Repub Clb of Jefferson Co, Prog Chm 1980; John Birch Soc, Life Mem 1972; hon/Contbns to Jours: Wkly Lttr on Nat & Intl Affairs; Palladian Lit Soc Short Story Contest 1st Prize 1929; Hooper Orital Contest 3rd Pl 1980; Provident Assn Schlr 1930-31.

GARLAND, JACK RICHARD oc/Director Special Services Program; b/Dec 22, 1943; h/Box 53, Emory, VA 24327; ba/Johnson City, TN; m/Carole Evonne Crabtree; c/Brett Ryan, Vaughn Whitney, Holly Beth; p/Frank N and Tilda Courtney Garland, Erwin, TN; ed/BA Emory & Henry Col 1969; MA 1974, EdD 1979 E Tenn St Univ; mil/AUS 1963-65; pa/Fed Progs Admr, Dir Spec Sers Prog, E Tenn St Univ; Phi Gamma Mu; Phi Delta Kappa; Tenn Assn Spec Progs: APGA; SEn Assn Spec Progs Pers; Am Col Pers Assn; cp/Kiwanis; Dem Party of Va; r/Bapt; hon/Author "An Analysis of the Educational Experiences and Views of Jesse Stuart."

GARLAND, RUTH TAYLOR oc/Homemaker; b/Sept 28, 1936; h/Brandenton, FL; m/James Alfred; c/Scott Ashley, Susan Bartow; p/John Harris (dec) and Dellion Davis Turner, Brandenton, FL; ed/Att'd Fla So Col 1954-56; cp/Manatee Players: Bd Dirs, Treas; Sigma Sigma Sigma; Brandenton Country Clb; Brandenton Yacht Clb; Commun Thrift Shop: Pres, Secy, Bd Dirs; Entre Nous Reporter; Wom's Com S Fla Mus; Pres Univ Fla Law Dames; Jr Wom's Clb; r/Christ Epis Ch, Brandenton: Epis Chwom: Pres, VP.

GARLAND, VIRINDA LEE oc/Paralegal; b/Oct 20, 1947; h/Newport, KY; c/Donna LaRene, LeNora, Daryl D'Wayne, Juan, Daylin, Dickie; p/Johnny S Garland; Johnnie Nelson Dean, Newport, KY; ed/AA No Ky Univ; BS Cand 1981; pa/Human Rights Comm; Cnslr NKU 1976-78; r/Christina; hon/Recited Poems at NKY SW Class for 3 Yrs; NKU Commencement Com 1977.

GARNER, C WAYNE oc/Photographer; b/July 31, 1946; ba/Garner's Studio, 610 W Kings Hwy, Paragould, AR 72450; m/Anna Darlene; c/Dee Ann, Bryce Lee; ed/A C (dec) and Edna Garner, Paragould, AR; ed/Mil Trg, Nuclear Power Trg; mil/USN 6 Yrs; pa/Self Employed Photog; Profl Photogs of Ozarks; Ark Profl Photogs Assn; r/Ch of Christ; hon/Profl Photog of Ozarks, Fall Conv 1980; Gen Exhib 1st Place Commercial.

PERSONALITIES OF THE SOUTH

GARNER, GERALDINE MARIE O'DONNELL oc/Educational Researcher and Administrator; b/June 10, 1946; h/802 Toms Creek Rd, Blacksburg, VA 24060; ba/Falls Ch, VA; m/Jerry L; c/Lauren Christine, Adrian Derek; p/John James O'Donnell; Geraldine Marie Sowers; ed/BA 1976, MEd 1978 Col of William & Mary; EdD VPI & St Univ; pa/Proj Dir, Nat Voc Guid Assn 1980-; Doct Intern & Postdoct Res Fellow, Career Guid Div of Appalachia Ednl Lab 1979-80; Coor for Coop Ed, Va Tech 1976-78; Prog Planner & Voc Cnslr, Williamsburg James City Co Commun Action Agcy 1975-76; Staff Editor, Bur of Nat Affairs 1973-74; Fdr & Dir Clearinghouse for Wom's Career Info 1972-74; Res Spec in Career Info, APGA 1972; Res & Prog Analyst, FORERA Corp 1969; Tchr, Fairfax Public Schs 1968; AMEG; AERA; VPGA; VVGA; AAUW; APGA: NVGA, Newslttr Ed, Comm on Career Devel of Yng Adults, Comm on Occupl Status Wom, Pubs Com; Equalization of Opport in Employment Com; cp/Rep Lt Gov of Va to Conf on Voc Guid; Bd Dirs NRV Commun Action Agcy; hon/Outstg Grad Student S'ship, Va Tech; William & Mary F'ship; Phi Kappa Phi; Phi Delta Kappa; Kappa Delta Pi; Recip Cert of Ser; Author *The Career Development of College Women Through Cooperative Education;* Articles in *National Business Woman, Engineering Education;* Chapt in *Financial Counseling.*

GARNER, JAMES oc/Associate Dean; b/May 4, 1942; h/4013 Summerhill Pl, NW, Huntsville, AL 35810; ba/Normal; m/Anita B; c/Anita D; p/Daniel Garner, Batesville, MS; Cora Garner, Memphis, TN; ed/BS; pa/Assoc Dean Student Life, Ala A&M Univ; NAPW; SCPA; APGA; Kappa Alpha Psi; cp/Dem Party; r/Cumberland Presb.

GARRETSON, CASEY CHARLENE oc/Fire Fighter; b/June 30, 1959; h/508 S 2nd, Marlow, OK 73055; ba/Marlow; m/Robert Paul; p/Virgil and Mary Janis Brooks, Ninnekah, OK; ed/Col of Engrg, Basic Firefighting Acad; pa/Remodeling Old Houses; Bldg Furn; Firefighter, Marlow Fire Dept; hon/Dip Basic Firefighting Acad.

GARRETT, JAMES HERSCHEL oc/Hospital Associate Director and President Specialized Medical Management; b/Nov 26, 1943; h/Ft Worth, TX; ba/1300 W Cannon St, Ft Worth, TX 76104; m/W Lee; c/Kyle Connell, Kristin Brooke; p/Raymond Cleaver (dec) and Helen Dean Connell Garrett; ed/BA 1966, MA 1969 Tex Christian Univ; MHA Wash Univ Sch Med 1971; mil/USAR Capt; pa/Assoc Admr Sparks Regional Med Ctr 1973-76; Fac Wash Univ Sch of Med 1971-73; Assoc Dir Harris Hosp Meth 1976-80; Pres Harris Meth Corp 1980-; Tex Soc Hosp Ed, Pres 1979-80; Am Soc Hosp Edrs; cp/Rotary; Optimist; Lions; JCs; Kiwanis; Ft Worth C of C; r/Meth; hon/Dist'd Ser Awd; 10 Outstg Yng Men Ark.

GARRETT, JUDSON PAUL JR oc/Assistant Attorney General; b/Oct 26, 1937; h/663 Rhone Ct, Glen Burnie, MD 21061; ba/Annapolis, MD; m/Judith Schall; c/Kathleen Patrice, Karen Denise, Kimberly Anne, Kristine Therese, Judson Schall; p/Judson P and Irma Grubbs Garrett, Charleston, SC; ed/AB St Mary's Sem & Univ; LLB Univ Md; mil/USAR 1959-65; pa/Asst Atty Gen; Counsel to Md Gen Assembly; Mem Comm to Revise Annotated Code of Md; Md Bar Assn; cp/Pres Andover Rec, Inc, Linthicum, Md; r/Rom Cath.

GARRETT, MARY LAURA oc/Student, Biological Aid; b/Nov 27, 1951; h/606 5th St, Leland, MS 38756; ba/Stoneville, MS; p/Louis T Garrett (dec); Mary Garrett Porter, Greenville, MS; ed/BS Cand, Delta St Univ; pa/Biol Aid, US Forest Ser; r/Epis; hon/Dean's List, Delta St Univ; Gooch S'ship.

GARRETT, MELVIN R oc/Building Contractor; b/Mar 21, 1929; h/1652 Ash, Russell, KS 67665; ba/Same; m/Eunice; c/Bonita, Ronald; p/Chloie, Russell, KS; mil/Korean War; pa/Self-Employed Bldg Contr; Ctrl Ks Bldrs Assn, 1st VP; cp/Past Dist Comdr Am Legion 1966; Past Post Comdr Dorrana Am Legion 1959; Past Russell Co Coun Cmdr Am Legion 1960-62; r/Luth; hon/Best Percentage Co Coun Goal 1960; Plaque at Dorrana Bldrd Dinner 1976; Bldrs Assn Outstg Bldr Awd.

GARRISON, JUANITA oc/Nurse; b/Dec 1, 1939; h/1773 Blue Licks Rd, Lexington, Ky 40504; ba/Lexington; p/William J (dec) and Artie May Garrison, Lexington, KY; ed/Dip St Joseph Hosp Sch of Nsg; pa/RN; SEn Cancer Grp; Oncology Nsg Soc; Soc Hemopheresis Specs; cp/Fayette Co Wom's Dem Clb of Ky; r/Meth; hon/W/W Am Wom.

GARRISON, LAWRENCE oc/Attorney, Contracting Officer; b/Oct 14, 1917; h/2509 Lagrand St SW, Huntsville, AL 35801; ba/H'ville; m/Willodean W; c/Rory G Stratton, Thalia, Laurel Davis; p/Vivian and Florence Brindell Garrison (dec); ed/AB; LLB; JD; mil/USAF, Counter Intell, WWII; pa/Atty, Contracting Ofcr, George C Marshall Space Flight Ctr; Fed Bar Assn; Nat Lwyrs Clb; cp/Big Sprg Civitan; Dem; r/Prot; hon/W/W Govt.

GARRITY, JOHN JOSEPH oc/State Senator; Attorney at Law; b/Dec 3, 1933; h/3801 Calverton Dr, University Park, MD 20782; ba/Hyattsville, MD; m/Bertha Ann; c/Kevin Michael, John Joseph Jr; p/John J and Agnes McDermott Garrity (dec); ed/BA; JD; mil/USN; pa/Mem US Supreme Ct Bar; Md & DC Bars; cp/Former Asst Sts Atty; Former Asst Atty Gen Md; Former Co Commr, Prince George's Co (Md); Past Chm Co Coun; Mem Md Ho of Dels 1974-77; r/Cath; hon/Outstg Leg 1973, 77, 78.

GART, JOHN JACOB oc/Mathematical Statistician, Section Head; b/Apr 15, 1931; h/3406 Kenilworth Dr, Chevy Chase, MD 20015; ba/Bethesda, MD; m/Sheila N Sinclair; c/Matthew, Thomas, Jacqueline, Rebecca; p/Jacob P and Bertha M Gart, Chgo, IL; ed/BS DePaul Univ 1953; MS Marquette Univ 1955; PhD VPI 1958; pa/Math Statistician, Sect Hd, Nat Cancer Inst, Bethesda; Assoc Editor *Biometrics,* 1975 & *Epid,* 1977-; cp/Conslt Food & Drug Adm, World Hlth Org; r/Rom Cath; hon/Hon Fellow: Am Stat Assn, Inst Mat Stat, AAAS; Sigma Xi; Vis Res Scholar, VPI 1971.

GARTH, GWENDOLYN ADDIFRA oc/Counselor; b/June 4, 1916; h/PO Box 868, Enterprise, AL 36331; ba/Enterprise; m/Benjamin F; c/Benita Jean G Sills; p/James Curtis and Blanche Harris Sharpley (dec); ed/BS Ala St Univ 1950; MA Hampton Inst 1968; pa/Tchr: Opelika 1 Yr, Elba 5 Yrs, Enterprise 32 Yrs; Enterprise City Ed Assn; Ala St Ed Assn; NEA; APGA; Dist IX Guid Assn; Past Secy-Treas, Parliamentn Dist IX Guid Assn; cp/VP Salem Enterprise Wom's Conv; OES, Hosannah Chapt #80; Heroines of Jericho; Sons & Daughs Levi; Ladies Aid, Mattie Donald Soc #7; Semper Fidelis Clb; Hist Geneol Soc; r/Pleasant Grove Bapt Ch: Pres Deaconesses, VP Matrons, Chm Ch Prog Com; Matron's Choir; hon/Black Wom of Yr 1980.

GARTON, CHARLES E oc/Real Estate Broker, Developer, Contractor; b/Dec 25, 1921; h/421 Main Ave, Weston, WV 26452; ba/Weston; m/Opal Dunham; c/Stephen S, Deborah K, Melissa J, Charles G; p/George (dec) and Christina Mason Garton (dec); ed/Grad Univ Okla 1945; mil/USNAR 1944-46; pa/Real Est Broker; Pres & Gen Mgr Garton Real Est Inc; Pres Garton Real Est & Construc Inc; Pres GCH Devel Inc; WV Assn Rltrs; cp/Lewis Co C of C; Repub; Deerfield Country Clb; Am Legion; Moose; K of C; r/Roman Cath.

GARVIN, BARNEY WILLARD oc/Oil Executive; b/Aug 15, 1904; h/Wagener, SC; m/(dec); p/Luther Ernest (dec) and Annabel Courtney Garvin (dec); ed/Att'd Clemson 1924-25; BS NCSU 1927; mil/USAR Infantry 1st Lt; pa/Dist Mgr, SC Elect & Gas 1935-42; Hd Engr, SC Public Ser Auth 1943; Cotton Broker 1944-45; Farmer 1932-; Owner & Opr Garvin Oil Co 1958-; SC Oil Jobbers Assn; Nat Cotton Assn; cp/Bd Dirs C of C, Florence 1941-42; Bd Dirs Shriners Chds Hosp 1945; Sigma Chi; OES 1930-; Past Potentate Omar Temple Shrine 1945; Shrine Clubs of Columbia, Pres 1937-39, Aiken, 1st Pres 1946; Jesters; Rotary Clb, Pres 1939-40; Chm Utilities Com Rotary Intl, 1939; r/Bapt.

GARY, LAWRENCE E oc/Professor, Social Scientist; b/May 26, 1939; h/1213 Kathryn Rd, Silver Spring, MD 20904; ba/Wash DC; m/Robenia Baker; c/Lisa Che, Lawrence Charles Andre, Jason Edward; p/Ed Gary (dec); Henrietta M Gary, Birmingham, AL; ed/BS, MPA, MSW, PhD; pa/Am Public Hlth Assn; Nat Assn Social Wkrs; Nat Mtl Hlth Assn; DC Inst Mtl Hygiene; DC Mtl Hlth Assn; Black Social Wkrs; r/AME; hon/Alpha Kappa Mu Hon Soc; W/W S&SW; Res Grants: NIMH, NIH.

GARZA, DAVID CHAMPION oc/Attorney; b/Aug 15, 1948 h/Brownsville, TX; ba/PO Box 2025, Brownsville, TX 78520; m/Diane M; p/Reynaldo and Bertha Champion Garza, Brownsville, TX; ed/BA St Edwards Univ 1969; JD Univ Tex Sch Law 1973; pa/Ptnr Garza & Garza; Former Staff Tex Constitutional Revision Comm & Tex Constitutional Conv; Cameron Co Bar Assn; Am Bar Assn; Tex Trial Lwyrs Assn; Diocesan Attys Assn of US; Tex Assn Bnk Counsel; cp/U Fund of Brownsville, Chm of Bd 1979; Kiwanis Day Breakers, Past Pres; Sierra Clb, Past Pres; K of C, Past Advocate; Order of the Alhambra, Dpty Regional Dir for St of Tex; Rio Grande Val Boy Scout Coun, Bd Dirs; Boys Clb of Brownsville, Past Dir; Tex Lyceum Assn, Dir; Dir Val Commun Hosp; Dir Tex Bank & Trust; r/Cath; hon/W/W: Students in Univs & Cols 1969-70, Am Law; Outstg Yng Men Am; Order of Coif 1973.

GARZA, JUAN oc/District Sales Manager; b/May 15, 1939; h/Harlingen, TX; m/Genoveva R; c/Troy, Sylvia Lynn, Velma Lisa, Juan Jr; p/Candelario (dec) and Juana Garza, Santa Rosa, TX; ed/LUTC 1971; mil/USAF 3 Yrs; pa/Life Ins Dist Mgr In Charge 16 Agcys; Dir Life Underwriter Assn; X-Oficio Mem C of C; cp/Pres Mexican Am C of C, Harlingen; r/Cath; hon/Ldr in Sales of Co 1972.

GARZA, NOE ELIBERTO oc/Postal Clerk; b/Mar 24, 1935; h/116 W Martha Louise, Edinburg, TX 78539; ba/McAllen, TX; m/Lydia F; c/Marissa; p/Humberto R (dec) and Antonia B Garza, Edinburg, TX; ed/Att'g Pan Am Univ; mil/USAF 1954-74 TSgt; pa/Distribution Clerk

115

PERSONALITIES OF THE SOUTH

(Manual) 1979-; Paralegal Immigration Secy 1977; Mgr Fashion Retail Store 1976; cp/Masonic Lodge #1036 AF&AM; Worshipful Master Masonic Lodge #1036; 32° Scottish Rite, Val of Houston; Am Legion Post#37; St Joseph's Mens Clb, Pres 1980-81; Little Leag Coach; APWU; VP Masters, Wardens & Secys Assn, Masonic Dist 40A & 40B of Grand Lodge of Tex; r/Cath; hon/Merit Ser Medal; Jt Ser Commend Medal; Air Force Commend Medal; Expeditionary Forces Medal; Vietnamese Ser Medal; Vietnamese Campaign Medal; Small Arms Expert Medal; Air Force Longevity Awd; Air Force Good Conduct Medal; Army Good Conduct Medal; Sev Commend Lttrs & Lttrs of Recog for Civic & Commun Involvement.

GASPERONI, EMIL oc/Realtor; b/Nov 13, 1926; h/2510 E Commercial Blvd, Ft Lauderdale, FL 33308; m/Ellen Jean; c/Sam, Emil Jr, Jean; p/Rose Gasperoni, Ft Lauderdale, FL; mil/1945-46; pa/Nat Fee Appraiser, Intl Real Est Fed.

GASQUE, DAVID H JR oc/Resident Hall Director; Retired US Air Force; b/Sept 24, 1932; m/Joyce; c/Mark, Louise, Lisa; p/David H Sr and Ruby Gasque, Whiteville, NC; ed/BS Lee Col 1981; mil/USAF 22 Yrs Ret'd; pa/Tchr; Pres Vets Clb 1978-79; VP SNEA 1980-81; 1 of 8 Student Voting Del, Ofcl Leg Body, SNEA; cp/Optimist Clb, Chm Yth Activs 1979-80, 80-81; r/Prot; hon/Pres's People to People Awd 1959; AF Commend Awds 1971 & 72; Dean's List, Spring 1981.

GASTON, CHARLES L JR oc/Counselor; b/Jan 3, 1934; ba/4070 Lancewood Dr, S, Mobile, AL 36609; m/Linda F; c/Linda, Tami, Angela, Lori; p/Doris E Gaston, Prichard, AL; ed/BA William Carey Col 1960; BD New Orleans Bapt Theol Sem 1963; DD Bapt Bible Inst 1975; ThD So Bible Sem 1977; mil/USAF 1951-55; pa/Clin Psychol; Fam Cnslr; Pastor; Min; So Bapt Conv; Mobile Bapt Assn, Exec Bd Ala Bapt St Conv; Am Pastoral Cnslrs; cp/Civitan Intl, Chaplain; Vol Chaplain Univ Hosp, Mobile Psychi Unit; r/Bapt; hon/W/W Am Rel 1976-77 & 78-79; Bronze Star, Good Conduct Medal; Author "The Interaction of Guilt, Grief and Hostility" 1970.

GASTON, THOMAS DALE oc/District President Labor Union; b/Oct 9, 1940; h/Hwy 70 W, Central City, KY 42330; ba/Madisonville, KY; m/Judith Elaine; c/Kirk, Wendy, Amy; p/Howard Thomas and Carolyn Laine Gaston, Cleaton, KY; pa/Dist Pres U Mine Wkrs Am, Dist 23; UMWA Bargaining Coun; 4 Union Negotiating Teams; cp/Bd Mem M'ville Area Voc Col; r/Ch of Christ; hon/Ky Col; W/W Am Labor.

GATES, BETTY RUSSELL oc/Professional Artist; b/Aug 10, 1927; h/4900 Wondol Ct, Hurst, TX 76053; m/David W; c/Jerry R (dec), David E, Patricia Ann, Julie Russell, Lisa, Alexander; p/Robert Russell, Hunt, TX; Lela Creekmore, Tulsa, OK; ed/Att'd Ark A&M; Grad Art Instrn Inc; pa/Comml Artist Until 1960; Painter & Sculptor; Num Solo Exhibs; Artist Mem & Juried Exhibr: Nat Leag Am Pen Wom, N Shore Arts Assn (Gloucester, Mass), Artist & Craftsmen (Dallas, Tex), Catherine Lorillard Wolfe Art Clb (NY, NY), Tex Fine Arts (Austin), Others; Slides Included in Nat Leag Am Pen Wom Travelling Exhbn Out of Wash DC; Work Has Been Accepted by MONAC Live Art Auction & Show, Held Annually in Spokane, Wash, 4 Yrs; r/Unity Ch; hon/Slides of Work Sent to Gloucester, England by N Shore Arts Assn in Exc Exhbn; 1st Pl, Nat Leag Am Pen Wom 1978 St Conv in Dallas; W/W Am Wom 1981-82; Contemporary Personalities; Academia Italiabelle Artie bel Lavoro; Best of Show, Spec Awd & 2nd Pl in Nat Leag Am Pen Wom 1981 Dallas Show.

GATLIN, WALTON EUGENE oc/Chiropractor; b/May 15, 1924; h/129 N Cherry St, McComb, MS 39648; ba/McComb; m/Naomi Tomlinson; c/William T, Danny E, Paul L, Betty Sue, John W; p/Bennie W (dec) and Anna Bell Hawkins Gatlin (dec); ed/Palmer Chiropractic Col; mil/USAF; pa/Chiropractor in Pvt Pract 23 Yrs; Past Grand Cnslr Miss-La U Commercial Travelers; Pres Pike Co Retard'd Chd Assn; 4 Yrs Pres Miss Chiropractic Assn; Pres Miss Assoc Chiropractors; Bd Dirs Chiropractic Assn; cp/Charter Pres McComb Evening Lions Clb; Secy McComb Coun U Commercial Travelers #576; Pike Co Park & Rec Commr; r/Bapt; hon/Chiropractor of Yr, Miss 1979.

GAUNCE, JAMES RICHARD oc/Principal; b/June 19, 1932; h/PO Box 195, Pauline, SC 29374; m/Avanelle G; c/Deborah Kay, Carol Sue, Belinda Frances, Teresa Elaine; p/Herman Francis and Helen Marie Young Gaunce, Edinburgh, IN; ed/BA Asbhury Col 1957; MA WCU 1973; EdS USC 1976; Grad Studies: Univ S Ala, Clemson Univ, Converse Col; mil/AUS 1952-54 SCARWAF; pa/Pastor EMC 1958-65; Tchr Whitfield Co Schs 1958-65; Pastor Evangelical Meth Ch 1965-68; Tchr-Guid, Alba HS 1965-68; Pastor Evangelical Meth Ch, Spartanburg 1968-72; Tchr Spartanburg Co Sch Dist #6 1968-74; Prin Spartanburg Co Sch Dist #6 1974-; NEA; GEA; WEA; AEA; MEA; SCEA; SPEA; SCDA; APGA; Elem Prin Assn SC; cp/Westview Ath Org; Lions Clb; S Mobile Co Min Assn, VP 1966; Westview Ruritan, Chaired Sev Comms; r/Bapt; hon/W/W S&SW; Outstg Elem Admr; Ordained Bapt Min 1973.

GAUTHIER, THOMAS RUGG oc/Consulting Metallurgical Engineer; b/Apr 15, 1918; h/228 Gingham Ln, PO Box 953, Pinehurst, NC 29374; m/Phyllis Irene Peterson; c/Sherry Irene Slawski, Gwendolyn Lucille Weller; p/Thomas Louise and Alice Edna Rugg Gauthier, Waterloo, IA; ed/BS Ia St Univ 1940; MS Case Inst Technol 1941; Att'd Princeton Univ 1972-74; Postgrad Studies Allegheny Col 1973-78; Att'd Sandhills Commun Col 1978-80; pa/Staff Metal Alumninum Co of Am 1940-45; Chief Control Metal 1945-51; Chief Metal of Forgings 1951-57; Chief Metal of Cleveland Opers 1957-62; Chief Metal of Tenn Opers 1962-65; Chief Staff Metal Pgh 1965-69; Chief Metal & Exec Secy Res & Devel 1965-78; Cnsltg Non Ferrous Metal 1975-; Lectr Univ Tenn 1962-65; Advr Dept of Metal, Vanderbilt Univ 1962-65; Bd Visitors Univ Penn 1965-78; Bd Visitors Metal Dept, Univ Pgh 1965-78; Bd Trustees Univ Pgh 1968-71; Advr Ser Corps of Ret'd Execs; Exec Bd Metals Properties Coun 1965-78; Adv Jr Achmt, Pgh 1967-75; Bd Dirs Renaissance for Gifted (Retard'd) Chd 1975-80; Am Soc Metals 1941-78; Am Inst Mining & Metal Engrs; Brit Inst Metals; Navy Leag; Nat Geog Soc; Wilderness Soc; Nat Wildlife Soc; Audobon Soc; Pi Delta Theta; Exec Sponsor World Golf Hall of Fame; Patron US Gold Assn; cp/Duquesne Clb 1965-75; Repub; Pres Men's Clb of Commun Presby Ch; Cleveland Ath Clb; Boston Heights Country Clb; Green Meadow Country Clb; St Clair Country Clb; Pinehurst Country Clb; Exec Bd Am Cancer Soc of Moore Co; Chm Am Cancer Soc Pinehurst; Chm BSA; r/Presb; hon/Sigma Xi Mem at Large; Pioneer in Forging of Berillium & Titanium for Space Capsules 1940-; Inventor Sev Aluminum & Magnesium Casting & Forging Methods; Lectr Intl Titanium Conf, London, England; Num Articles on Metal to Sci Pubs.

GAVORA, BETTY J oc/Communications Manager; b/July 6, 1935; h/4006 Ramsgate, San Antonio, TX 78230; ba/San Antonio; c/Mark Jerome; p/Frank (dec) and Dorothy Steitle, San Antonio, TX; ed/Bob Jones Univ 1953-54; San Antonio Col 1955-56, 68-72; Trinity Univ 1972-79; pa/Communs Mgr/Asst to Pres; Wom in Communs; Sigma Delta Chi; Intl Assn Bus Communrs; Exec Wom Intl; cp/C of C, Leg Affairs Coun Chm, Free Enterprise Coun; Editorial Adv Task Force; Bd Advrs St Philip's Col Sch of Bus; hon/Chromalloy's Top Mgmt Awd, Communs 1973, Public Affairs 1977; Editor of Yr, IABC/San Antonio; Hdliner, Wom in Communs.

GAWLIK, PAULINE GREEN oc/Teacher; h/Rt 4 Box 950, Edinburg, TX 78539; ba/McAllen, TX; m/Sam J; c/Samuel Lee; p/Charles G (dec) and Ruth Paull Green, Edinburg, TX; ed/BA Pan Am Univ; pa/Art Tchr, McAllen HS; Tex St Tchrs Assn; NEA; Rio Grande Val Art Ed Assn, Past Prs; Tex Art Ed Assn, Treas; Nat Art Ed Assn; cp/Past Mem Edinburg Jr Ser Leag; Past Pres St Joseph Altar Soc; r/Cath; hon/Presenter Nat Art Ed Conv 1979; Master Tchr of Art by Columbia Col, Columbia, Mo; Delta Kappa Gamma.

GAY, MARJORIE LOUISE ANDERSON oc/Realtor; b/Oct 18, 1909; h/Tampa, FL; ba/100 Madison St, Tampa, FL 33602; m/Forrest Theodore Jr; c/Forrest Theodore III, Marjorie Anderson; p/Louis Markham Anderson; Bertha Marjorie Graham; ed/Att'd Scott Col 1926-27; BS Fla St Col for Wom 1930; Post Grad Studies: Univ Tampa 1942, Drake Univ 1961, Univ Fla 1962; pa/Tchr Woodrow Wilson Jr HS 1930-32; Tchr St Petersburg HS 1938-45; Saleswom W H Toole & Sons Rltrs 1962-63; Real Est Broker, Tampa 1964-; Dir L M Anderson Dental Supply Co 1961-70; Dir & VP Decoa 1970-75; Dir Codesco 1975-77; Pres Marjorie Gay Realty Inc 1977-; Fla Assn Rltrs; Tampa Bd Rltrs; Nat Assn Rltrs; Rltrs Nat Mktg Inst; Wom's Coun Rltrs; cp/Panhellenic; Alpha Delta Pi; Coral Gables Jr Wom's Clb; St Petersburg Jr Wom's; Edgebrook Wom's Clb; Des Moines Wom's Clb; Vil Garden Clb; Tower Clb of Tampa; Tampa Yacht & Country Clb; Carrollwood Vil Golf & Country Clb; Gtr Tampa C of C; Com of 100 of Tampa C of C 1977-; Pilot Clb of Tampa; Dir Fla Gulf Coast Symph; Dir St Joseph's Hosp Devel Coun; Downtown Coun of Tampa; r/Presb; Deacon; hon/GRI.

GAYNOR, LEAH oc/Occupational Specialist; b/Dec 22, 1931; h/1255 NE 171 Terr, N Miami Bch, FL 33162; ba/Miami; m/Robert M; c/Michael David, Lisa Hedi, Tracy Lynn; p/Jack Kamish, Long Branch, NJ; Sophia Kamish, N Miami Bch, FL; ed/AA Miami Dade Commun Col; BA Fla Intl Univ; pa/Occupl Spec, Lindsey Hopkins Tech Ed Ctr, Dade Co Public Schs; Wom in Communs; Am Wom in Radio & TV; cp/Common Cause; Dem Party; hon/W/W Am Wom.

GEER, GEORGE H oc/Assistant Chief Deputy; b/Mar 19, 1925; h/Rt 10, Whorton Bends, Gadsden, AL 35904; m/Emma J; c/G David; p/J P Sr (dec) and Mrs J P Geer, Gadsden, AL; ed/Att'g Etowah Co Sch Sys; pa/Dpty Etowah Co Sheriffs Dept; cp/Dwight Masonic Lodge 550; Intl Brotherhood of Elec Wkrs #136; Ala Girls & Boys Ranch; Hds Reserve Dpty Assn of Etowah Co; r/Bapt.

GEHO, CLAUDIA G WALDREP oc/Store Manager; b/Sept 16, 1951; h/Algood, TN; ba/105 Main St, Algood, TN 38501; p/Lester and Dorothy Waldrep, Birmingham, AL; ed/BA St Leo Col 1974; pa/Upper

116

Cumberland Human Resource Agcy, Manpwr Ser Rep; Adams, Rains & Assocs Inc Acct Exec; Charles Sales Corp Ofc Mgr & Sales Rep; Adm Asst Price Waterhouse & Co; Mgr Custom Order Furniture Store; St Leo Col Alumni Bd Dirs; VP MENC; r/Cath; hon/Alpha Gamma; Nat Thespian Soc; Pres & VP Assn Wom Students 1974; W/W Am Cols & Univs; Delta Phi Delta; Outstg Female Senator for Student Govt Assn; Asst'd in Formulating New Trg Sales Manual for Acct Exec Trainees.

GELDART, DONALD BLAIR oc/Family Physician; b/Oct 5, 1940; h/1545 Oleander Dr, Avon Park, FL 33825; ba/Avon Pk, FL; m/Ruth Alice Brace; c/Michael David Donald, Crystal Lillian Ruth, Kimberly Rose Florynce; p/William Guy Geldart (dec); Margaret Cormier Moncton, New Brunswick, Can; ed/BA Kingsway Col 1960; MD Dalhousie Med Sch 1968; Cert Fam Pract 1979; Diplomate of Am Bd Fam Pract 1979; Fellow Am Acad of Fam Pract 1979; pa/Pract Fam Med Avon Pk; Clin Prof, Dept Fam Med, Univ S Fla; Walker Meml Hosp Med Staff; Med Dir Respiratory Sers; Chm Emergency Room & Critical Care Unit; Highlands Co Med Soc; FMA; AMA; Fla Acad Fam Pract; CME Rep for Highlands Co; Am Acad Fam Prac; Nat Assn Med Dirs of Respiratory Sers; Bd Trustees PHH PSRO; Chm Concurrent Review Com PSRO; Bd Dirs & Med Advr West Coast Chapt Am Mar of Dimes; Am Geriatrics Soc; cp/Avon Park C of C; Bd Tri-Co Alcoholic Sers; Bd Dirs Envir Protective Assn; r/Seventh Day Adventist.

GELTZ, CHARLES GOTTLIEB oc/Forester, Educator; b/Feb 21, 1896; h/1521 NW 7th Ave, Gainesville, FL 32603; m/Mildred Harry Julin; c/Charles Gottlieb, Betty Anne Swanson; (Stepchd:) Helen Julin Reiley, Jane Julin Keenen; p/William and Mary Ditter Geltz (dec); ed/BS Pa St Forest Sch 1924; MSF Univ Calif 1927; mil/13th US Cav, Mex Border Campaign, WWI; US Cav Res 1920-41; WWII 1942-46; Adj Gen's Corps Resv, Apr 1946-56; Maj AUS (Ret'd 1956); pa/Forester, Ala Comm of Forestry 1924-25; Instr Forestry, Registrar, NY St Forest Ranger Sch, Col of Forestry, St Univ of NY, Wanakena 1925-26; Res Asst, Div of Forestry, Univ Calif 1926-27; Jr Forester, US Forest Ser 1927-29; Instr Forestry, St Forest Sch, Pa Univ 1929-30; Asst Prof, Purdue Univ 1930-34, Assoc Prof 1934-46; Dir Purdue Forestry Summer Camp 1930-42; Prof Silviculture Sch Forestry, Univ Fla 1946-66; Dist'd Prof, Silviculture Emeritus 1966-; So Regional Counsel for Nat Sch Forestry & Conserv; Wolf Springs Forest, Minong, Wis; Oper, Owner, & Chief Forester, Charles G Geltz Assocs: Forestry, Conserv, and Conslt; Conslt Forest Rec & Fam Camping, Fla Fam Camping Assn; Outdoor Rec Conslt to Dir Resource Progs Dept Interior 1963; Lectr on Envir, Conserv; Reg'd Forester Ga & Fla; Fellow Am Geog Soc; Soc Am Foresters; Am Soc Ecological Edn; Am, Fla Forestry Assns; Forest Farmers Assn; Fla Forestry Coun, Secy; Fla Conserv Foun; Fla Forestry Coun; Fla Fam Campus Assn, Hon Life Mem; Ret'd Ofcrs Assn, Life Mem; Xi Sigma Pi; Phi Sigma; Phi Delta Kappa; Kappa Delta Pi; Scabbard & Blade; Alpha Phi Omega; cp/C of C; 32° Mason; Shriner; Mem Fla Gov's Resource Use Ed Com; Neighboorhood Commr BSA; r/Epis; hon/Unit Cit Awd & Plaques; Commend Ribbon; Silver Beaver Awd, BSA 1951; Wisdom Hon Awd, Wisdom Soc 1970; Outstg Forester Awd, Fla Sect Soc Am Foresters 1966.

GENTRY, CHARLES MELVIN JR oc/Executive Director; b/Feb 11, 1952; h/614 Crockett, Greenwood, MS 38930; ba/Greenwood; m/Anne Roddy; p/Charles and Mary Catherine Gentry, Clinton, MS; ed/BS Univ So Miss; pa/Exec Dir C of C & Indust Bd Greenwood-LeFlore Co; Miss Indust Devel Coun; r/Bapt; hon/Barett, Harris, Kelso Indust Devel Lit Awd.

GENTRY, MARLENE ANN MENDOZA oc/Steno-Clerk; b/Oct 22, 1935; h/216 Fifth St, Nederland, TX 77627; ba/Port Arthur, TX; m/Marshall J; c/Jackie Ann Stanley, Deborah Ann; p/Emile Joseph Mendoza, LaMarque, TX; Melba Hebert Mendoza (dec); ed/Att'd Port Arthur Col & Lamar Univ of Beaumont; Rec'd Secy Sci Dip 1954; pa/Steno for Prod Contrl Div & Clerk for Engrg Div TEXACO Inc; Bd Dirs Texaco PAW Employees Fed Credit Union; Pres, 1st VP, Treas Sabine Chapt Credit Unions; cp/1st VP Pilot Clb Intl; Pres, VP, Secy Preceptor Beta Mu Chapt Beta Sigma Phi Intl; Pres & 1st VP Port Arthur Area Coun Beta Sigma Phi; Bd Mem Steering Com of Nederland Heritage Fest; r/Roman Cath; hon/Hon Grad LaMarque HS 1953.

GENTRY, T RUDENE oc/School Superintendent; b/Aug 8, 1932; h/Hwy 32, Irwinville, Ga 31760; m/Ida Carr; c/Garry L, Tommy L, Cheerie D; p/Lee (dec) and Effie L Gentry; ed/BA 1957, MEd 1958 Univ SC; EdS Valdosta St Col 1973; mil/AUS 1953-55; pa/Tchr; Coach; Prin; Supt; GAE; NEA; GASSP; GAEL; AASA; cp/Lions Clb; r/Bapt; hon/Coach of Yr, Region 1 Ga 1967; Ga Sch Supt of Yr 1980.

GENTRY, WILLIAM NORTON c/Safety Consultant; b/May 29, 1908; m/Margaret Whaley (dec); c/Susan Margaret, William David; p/William N Gentry, Little Rock, AR; Margaret Whaley Gentry (dec); ed/BA Univ Ark-Fayetteville 1929; Att'g Univ Ark-Little Rock; mil/AUS Signal Corps 1942-46 Capt; Ret'd USAR 1968 Lt Col; pa/SWn Bell

Telephone 1929-42 & 1946-73; Charter Mem Ark Chapt Am Soc of Safety Engrs 1956-; Chm Annual Safety Inst 1972-76; So Safety Conf, Pres 1968-69; cp/Little Rock Safety Comm 1966-, Chm 1970-71; Little Rock Ctrl YMCA Bd 1972-74; Org'g Pres U Cerebral Palsy of Little Rock 1959-60; Org'g Bd Contact 1968-76; r/Meth; hon/W H Sadler Trophy Commun Chest of Little Rock 1950-51; Ser Awd U Cerebral Palsy of Ctrl Ark 1969; Safety Awd of Commend, Ark Dept Labor 1973; Booklet "How to Prevent Electric Shock" 1954.

GEORG, TERRY ALICE oc/Assistant Manager; b/Sept 26, 1960; h/207 Hatcher, San Antonio, TX 78223; ba/San Antonio; p/Arlon Raymond and Norma Jo Georg, San Antonio, TX; ed/Att'g Col to Obtain Law Deg; pa/Asst Mgr Town & Country Carpets Inc; hon/W/W Am HS Students 1977-79.

GEORGE, LOUIE B JR oc/Minister, Principal; b/Dec 4, 1938; h/3106 Carver Circle, Texarkana, TX 75501; ba/Texarkana; m/Aberstine J; c/Louie B III, Leornard B, Carl L, Lamar B, Larry B; p/Louie B George Sr, Ft Worth, TX; Elizabeth C Rutherford, Mt Pleasant, TX; ed/BS 1960, MEd 1968; pa/Prin 15th St Sch, Texarkana; Min Oak St Bapt Ch; Tex St Tchrs Assn; Tex Elem Prin Assn; Tex Cong of Parents & Tchrs; Alpha Phi Alpha; Christian F'ship Union; Past Pres Texarkana Rural Unit of Tex St Tchrs Assn; Past Pres Dist VIII Tex Elem Prins Assn; St of Tex Spec Ed Adv Com; cp/Master Mason; Am Woodman; r/Bapt; hon/Hon Life Mem Tex Congress PTA.

GEORGE, RAYMOND CHARLES oc/State Coordinator; b/May 21, 1941; h/16 Lee Dr, Wheeling, WV 26003; ba/Wheeling; m/Elizabeth Ann Blanar; c/Christopher Raymond, Raymond Michael, Jason Andrew; p/Nicholas George, Bethlehem, WV; Irene McGinnis George, Cleveland, OH; ed/BA W Liberty St Col 1975; pa/WV Progs Ofcr, US Envir Protection Agy; Am Inst Chem Engrs; Pgh Soc: Analytical Chemists, Spectroscopists; cp/Cand Wheeling City Coun 1975 & 1979; Chm Ch Parish Coun; Co-Chm Energy Expo 82; r/Cath; hon/W/W: Govt, S&SW.

GERATO, ERASMO GABRIELLE oc/Associate Professor; b/Mar 24, 1943; h/20-16 Ted Hines Dr, Tallahassee, FL 32308; ba/Tallahassee; m/Lorilyne Earnest; p/Mario and Natalina Cristina Capogrosso Gerato, Formia, Latina, Italy; ed/BS; MA; PhD; pa/Assoc Prof French-Italian-Humanities, Fla St Univ; Am Assn Tchrs Italian; S Atl MLA; SCMLA; RMMLA; Am Assn Tchrs of French; Pi Delta Phi; Sigma Alpha Iota; r/Rom Cath; hon/Ward Medal, BS Hons; Fulbright S'ship; W/W S; Author *A Critical Study of the Life and Works of Alessandro Poerio Parma* 1975; Num Articles in Am & European Jours.

GERMAN, FINLEY LaFAYETTE oc/Mobile Homes Dealer; b/May 30, 1910; h/104 Auld Farm, Lenoir, NC 28645; m/Gladys Bell; c/John W, Anita Denuis; p/John Finley and Malona Eller German; ed/Spec Courses UNC & Chrysler Sales Inst; pa/Fdr, Mgr, Pres F L German Motor Co Inc 1940-; Org'd N C Mfc'd Housing Assn; cp/Dem Party; Kiwanis Clb; K of P; Former Dpty Rev Commr NC Field Forces; r/Tabernacle Advent Christian Ch: SS Tchr, Chm Bd Trustees.

GERSHOWITZ, SONYA oc/Administrative Director; b/July 31, 1940; h/2307 Hidden Glen Dr, Owings Mills, MD 21117; ba/Balto, MD; c/Benjamin, Sharon; p/David (dec) and Rose Ziporkin (dec); ed/AA; BSN; RN; pa/Owner & Adm Dir: Gtr Penn Ave Nsg Ctr, Lafayette Square Nsg Ctr, Federal Hill Nsg Ctr; Dir Nurses Multi-Med Convelescent & Nsg Ctr of Towson 1974-75; Camp Nurse, Med Dir & Coor Timber Ridge Camp Reservation 1969-73; Conslt Harbor View Nsg Ctr 1973; Dir Nurses at Mt Sinai Nsg Home 1968-71, 1973-74; Dir Nurses Ashburton Home 1963-64; Evening Supvr Happy Hill Convelescent Home 1963-64; Staff Nurse Sinai Hosp 1960-63; ANA; Md St Nurses Assn; Sinai Hosp Nurses Alumni; Fellow Am Col Nsg Home Admrs; Labor Mkt Adv Com; Mayors Ofc Manpwr Resources; Adv Com Nsg Home Aides/Orderlies Trg ACNHA; cp/Leag of Md Horses; Md Law Enforcement Ofcrs Inc; Am Fed Police; S Balto Bus-mens Assn; Mt Royal Improvement Assn; r/Jewish; hon/W/W: Am Wom, Hlth Care, Fin & Indust.

GERSTUNG, KATHERINE oc/Director of Public Relations and Volunteer Services; b/Jan 15, 1925; ba/2829 10th Ave N, Lake Worth, FL 33460; c/Ann Miller, Paul Gray; Allison LaMonde; p/Laura T Grosskopf, Louisville, KY; ed/Mgmt Trg Prog, Fla St Univ 1977; pa/Dir Public Relats & Vol Sers, Drs Hosp of Lake Worth; Am Soc Dirs of Vol Sers of Am Hosp Assn; Fla Assn Dirs of Hosp Vol Sers; Am Soc Hosp Public Relats Dirs; Fla Hosp Assn of the PR Coun; Fla Public Relats Assn; Am Hosp Assn; So Public Relats Fed; cp/Zonta Intl, Lake Worth II Chapt; Rep for Drs Hosp, Lake Worth C of C; r/Meth; hon/Life Mem Drs Hosp Aux; Hon Life Mem Chds Hosp Aux; Cert of Apprec from Spec Olympics Prog 1978.

GEVEDON, MILLARD LEE oc/Real Estate Vice President; b/June 29, 1933; h/1101 W Main St, Richmond, KY 40475; ba/Richmond, KY; m/Carolyn; c/Larry; p/Tenny (dec) and Nettie Gevedon, W Liberty, KY;

mil/AUS 1953-56; pa/VP Real Est & Internal Audits; cp/Ky Com for Employer Support of Guard & Reserve; r/Epis; hon/Ky Col.

GHOLSTON, BETTY JEAN oc/Educational Specialist and Project Director; b/Feb 1, 1942; h/Rt 1 Box 283, Wagram, NC 28396; ba/Hoffman, NC; m/Willie G; c/Lisa Regina, Betty Corneilia, Saranarda, Willie Jr; p/Lacy and Sarah Blue, Wagram, NC; ed/BS NC Ctrl Univ 1963; MS NC A & T St Univ 1979; Att'd UNC-CH 1978; pa/Ednl Spec & Proj Dir, Cameron Morrison Yth Ctr 1977-; Libn Scotland Co Schs, Richmond Co Schs & Cameron Morrison Sch 1966-77; Pres ACT 1976; Treas & Secy NCAE; NEA; cp/Secy Wagram Precinct; Secy Scotland Co NAACP; Fdr & Orgr Newtown Commun Org, Mayor Pro-Tem 1976, 77, 80-81; Wagram City Coun 1974-; r/Bapt; hon/Tchr of Yr, NC Dept of Yth Sers 1977; W/W Am Wom.

GIAM, C S oc/Professor and Department Head; b/Apr 2, 1931; h/Rt 3 Box 651, Bryan, TX 77801; ba/Col Sta, TX; m/M Y; c/Benny Y-B, Patrick Y-Y, Michael Y-Y; p/C H and E K Giam, Singapore; ed/BSc; BSc w hons; MS; PhD; pa/Prof & Hd Chem Dept, Tex A&M Univ; Am Chem Soc; Can Inst Chem; Chem Soc; Royal Inst Chem, London, England; hon/Nat Reg Coun of Can: Undergrad & Postgrad F'ships; US Nat Inst Hlth Spec F'ship; Dist'd Fac Awd, Tex A&M Univ.

GIBBS, GEORGE FORT JR oc/Retired; b/June 9, 1902; h/Venice, FL; m/Mary Frances Loud; c/George Fort III; p/George Fort and Maud Harrison Gibbs; ed/BA Princeton Univ 1923; pa/Advtg; Playwright; Hollywood Scenario Writer; Real Est; Land & Resort Develr; Owner-Opr Seaside Resort; Fdr & 1st Cmdr Venice Yacht Clb; Co-Fdr Fla W Coast Symph; cp/Zero Population Growth; Coalition for Survival; Prevention of Juvenile Drug & Other Yth Problems; Dir Sr Friendship Ctrs; Planned Parenthood; S Co & Venice Bd of Sarasota Hist Comm; Adv Bd S Co Fam YMCA; r/Epis; hon/Ch Choir 30 Yrs; hon/Winner Sunshine Press Awd.

GIBERSON, MICKIE LYNN oc/Homemaker, Publisher; b/Oct 28, 1959; h/414 W Park, Enid, OK 73701; m/Paul; c/Stephanie Lynn, Jennifer Leah; p/Boyd L and Nona Toy Hoskins, Lawton, OK; ed/BS Okla Col of Liberal Arts; pa/Tchr Enid Sch Sys 2 Yrs; Pubr; cp/BPW Clb 3 Yrs; Pres & 9th Dist Leg Ch; Beta Sigma Phi; r/Ctrl Christian Ch.

GIBSON, BEATRICE oc/Student; b/Sept 5, 1959; h/Rt 3, Calhoun, KY 42327; p/Mr and Mrs Juett Gibson Sr, Calhoun, KY; ed/Att'g Ky Wesleyan Col; pa/Seeking Perf Deg in Piano; MTNA; r/Bapt; hon/Dean's List 1979-80; Nat Dean's List 1980; Winner Mitchell Keyboard Awd 1980; Nom'd for Oak & Ivy Awd 1980.

GIBSON, EDWARD L oc/Retired Surgeon; b/Jan 3, 1889; m/Theda Metcalf; c/Edward L Jr, Charles Lewis; p/Franklin and Minnie Lee Gibson (dec); ed/Univ Ala Med Col 1913; mil/1918; pa/Phys, Surg; Ala St Med Assn Life Cnslr; cp/Coun City Enterprise 1928-32; Charter Mem Rotary Clb 1926; Bd Ed 1932-40; Pres C of C 1923; r/Meth; hon/Outstg Ser to Humanity Beyond Profl Duty.

GIBSON, JON LEE oc/Professor, Head of Department; b/Mar 22, 1943; h/120 Beta Dr, Lafayette, LA 70506; ba/Lafayette; m/Mary Beth Sellers; c/Erin Lea; p/Claude Lee and Kathren M Maxwell Gibson; ed/BA NWn St Univ 1965; MA La St Univ 1968; MA 1970, PhD 1973 So Meth Univ; pa/Archaeol Res Ctr, So Meth Univ 1967-69; Univ SWn La: Asst Prof 1969-73, Assoc Prof 1973-76, Prof Anthrop 1976-, Hd Dept SS 1975-; Pres Archaeology Inc 1978-; Pres La Achaeol Soc: Pres 1976, Editor 1974-; Tex Archaeol Soc, Regional VP 1974-75; La Archaeol Survey & Antiquities Comm 1975-79; Num Nat & Regional Archaeol Soc Mbrships; r/Bapt; hon/Dist'd Prof, Univ SWn La 1975; Dist'd Alumni NWn St Univ; Sigma Xi Resr of Yr, Univ SWn La 1977; Editor Emeritus La Archaeol Soc 1979; Author: *The Culture of Acadiana; Caddoan and Poverty Point Archaeology*; Over 70 Jour Articles & Monographs.

GIBSON, RANDY A oc/Health Care Technician, Minister, Genealogist; b/June 25, 1952; h/120 Union Grove Rd, Lenoir, NC; m/Wanda Runyon; c/Alisha Jeanine, Jamison Curtis; p/Earl Edward and Floye Smith Gibson, Lenoir, NC; ed/Att'd Fruitland Bible Inst; Tenn Temple Col; Intl Bible Inst & Sem; ThB 1980; pa/Ordained Bapt Min; Med Hlth Tech, Broughton Hosp, Morganton; NC Christian Edrs Assn; NC St Employers Assn; cp/Dir Caldwell Co Hist Soc; Burke Co Hist Soc; SW Va Hist Soc; Former Mem Yng People Repub Soc of Caldwell Co; Bd Dirs Caldwell Christian Sch; Bd Reps Bapt Haiti Mission; r/Bapt; hon/Caldwell Co Bicent Com 1976; Pub'd Author.

GIBSON, RAY ALLEN oc/Physician; b/Jan 15, 1941; h/Glasgow,

KY; m/Nancy Bailey; c/Rachel; p/Mildred Caton, Poole, KY; ed/BS Berea Col 1962; MD Univ Louisville 1968; mil/AUS 1972-74 Major; pa/Gyn, Howard Clin; Barren Co Med Soc; Ky Med Assn; Am Fertiltiy Soc; Am Col Ob-Gyn; Diplomate Am Bd Ob-Gyn; Ky Ob-Gyn Soc, Exec Com; cp/C of C; 32° Mason; r/Bapt: Deacon Glasgow Bapt Ch; hon/Chief of Staff TJ Samson Commun Hosp 1976; Chief of Ob-Gyn TJ Samson Commun Hosp; Co-Author.

GIBSON, ROXIE E oc/Author, Secretary; b/Jan 24, 1934; h/898 Van Leer Dr, Nashville, TN 37220; ba/Same; m/James G; c/James C Jr; p/Ethel Cawood, Spring City, TN; pa/Secy Oak Hill Sch; Am Soc Composers, Authors & Pubrs; Nashville Press & Author Clb; Nat Leag Am Pen Wom; r/Presb.

GIDDENS, BEULAH oc/Newspaper Editor; b/Dec 26, 1921; h/PO Box 333, Burgaw, NC 29425; ba/Burgaw; m/John O; c/Judy Schutt; p/Garris Lee (dec) and Beulah Jones Pridgen, Wilmington, NC; pa/Editor *Pender Chronicle* 26 Yrs; cp/Ladies Aux of Gideon Intl; r/Calvary Bapt Ch: SS Tchr, Dir Yng Married Couples; Mem Choir; Publicist & Past Hist for Wilmington Bapt Assn; Del Annually to So Bapt Conv; Del to World Bapt Cong; hon/W/W: NC, S&SW, Profl Wom Am; Intl Reg of Profiles 1980; Hons from: 4-H, JCs, Lions, UNS, AUS, USAF.

GIDEON, JODIE SUGGS oc/Senior Clerk; b/Oct 6, 1918; h/Midland, Tx; m/Edward Nunnelee Sr; c/Edward Nunnelee Jr, Michael Logan, Rebecca D'Arvin Gideon Johnson; p/Joseph Jefferson Suggs (dec); Mrs J J Suggs, Midland, TX; e/Grad Bus Col 1936; pa/Sr Clerk, Accts Receivable & Sales; cp/Charter Mem Ft Bend Chapt & Col Theun Dey Chapt DAR; Regent of Lt William Brewer Chapt DAR; Charter Mem Norm Pride Chapt DAC; Santa Rita Clb & Pioneers of the Permian Basin; r/Org'g Mem Meml Christian Ch.

GIECK, JOE HOWARD oc/Athletic Trainer, Physical Therapist; b/Dec 15, 1938; h/Wentworth Farm, Rt 6, Box 147, Charlottesville, VA 22901; m/Sally Grymes; c/Elizabeth DeJarnette, Katherine Wentworth; p/Ralph Herman and Clarice Coots Gieck, Altus, OK; ed/BS Univ Okla 1961; MEd 1965, EdD 1975 Univ Va; pa/Univ Va: Hd Trainer 1962-, Ser Phy Ed 1962-, Dir Adapted Ser Ed Prog 1962-, Dir Ath Tng Masters Prog 1975-, Grad Ed Sch Instr 1965-; All Star Lacrosse Tnr 1963, 1976; Host Tnr NCAA 1977 Finals; Tnr US Olympic Basketball Devel Camp 1971; Tnr US Pan Am Games 1971; Va All Star Baseball 1976; Pvt Pract Phy Therapy 1961-; Phy Therapy, Univ Va Student Hlth 1962-; Phy Fitness Conslt, Fed Exec Inst; Item Writer-Certn Exam-Nat Ath Tnrs Assn; Item Writer-Sports Med Sect-Am PT Assn; Coor Va Ath Tng Lic'g Bill; Num Ofcs Hld Nat Ath Tnrs Assn; Am Col Sports Med; Am PT Assn; Va & Okla PT Assns; Phi Delta Kappa; AAUP; Am Orthopedic Soc for Sports Med; APGA; Num Sci Presentations; Pub'd Author; r/Epis; hon/Dist'd Ser Awd, Va HS Coaches Assn; W/W in S&SW.

GILBERT, ADAM HILL oc/Television and Film Producer, Writer; b/Aug 28, 1935; h/306 Park Ave, Culpeper, VA 22701; ba/Hollywood, CA; p/Henry Dudley and Dorothy Fant Gilbert, Culpeper, VA; ed/Att'd Duke Univ; mil/USNR; pa/TV & Film Prodr Such Shows as "Circus of the Stars," "Steve Allen Show," etc; Screen Actors Guild; Writers Guild of America; cp/Repub Party; r/Bapt; hon/Clio Awd 1979; Recruit Cmdr of Troops, USN Recruit Trg; Author "I'm the Guy Who Gets...." 1966; Num TV Scripts.

GILBERT, BILLIE (VIRGINIA) oc/Homemaker; b/Oct 12, 1912; h/Midland, TX; c/Pat Humes; p/William and Anna Willis; cp/Dir Midland Wom's Clb; Pres Yucca Gdn Clb 1954-55; r/Bapt: SS Tchr; hon/Awd of Apprec for Display of Dried Flowers, Ector Co Fair; Hon Citizen Boys Town; Num Blue Ribbons in Flower Shows 1955-; Num Other Hons & Awds.

GILBERT, LEONARD H oc/Attorney; b/Apr 3, 1936; h/Tampa, FL; ba/PO Box 3239, Tampa, FL 33601; m/Jean; c/Jonathan S, Suzanne E; p/Sidney Gilbert, Lakeland, FL; ed/BA Emory Univ 1958; LLB Harvard Law Sch 1961; pa/Admitted to Fla Bar 1961 (Pres 1980-81); Atty w Carlton, Fields, Ward, Emmanuel, Smith & Cutler; Am Bar Assn; Am Judicature Soc; Am & Fla Socs of Hosp Attys; Lectr: Am Bar Nat Inst, NY Law Jour Progs; Fla Bar CLE Progs & Pract'g Law Inst; Commercial Law Leag; Am Trial Lwrs Assn; Fla Acad Trial Lwyrs; cp/Pres Harvard Clb W Coast of Fla; City of Tampa Charter Revision Com; Pres Midtown Kiwanis Clb; Chm Arts Coun Tampa & Hillsborough Co; Chm Cultural Affairs Com, Tampa C of C; Dir Gasparilla Sidewalk Art Fest;

Hillsborough Co Bicent Comm; US Coast Guard Reserve; Chm U Way, Attys Div; Pres Emory Univ Alumni Clb; Bd Trustees Patrons St John's Parish Day Sch; Congreg Schaari Zedek; VP Friends of Gal, Univ Tampa; Secy Harvard Law Sch Assn of Fla; hon/Author Var Legal Articles.

GILDRED, VICTORIA oc/Foundation President; b/Feb 8, 1934; h/LL Island Ave, Belle Island, Miami Bch, Fl 33139; ba/Miami; m/Albert; c/John, Bill, Victoria Alejandra Albornoz; p/William A (dec) and Susana R de Petersson (dec); pa/Pres Victoria Gildred Foun (For Latin Am Hlth & Ed); Intl Coor Sci Exchs, Univ Miami, Sch Med; Chp Med Com of Fla-Columbia Partners of Ams; r/Cath; hon/Order of Los Lanceros Gobernment of Colombia, SA; Num Awds.

GILES, ALTHEA oc/Director of Public Information; b/July 14, 1935; h/703 Oakwood Trail, Ft Worth, TX 76112; ba/Grand Prairie, TX; m/David N; c/Roxanne, Jennifer, Randy, Melynda; p/Louis A (dec) and Ardythe Oden, Ft Worth, TX; ed/Att'd Tex Wom's Univ; pa/Dir Public Info, Meth Affil'd Hosps; Edna Gladney Home, Dir of Aux & Public Info; Casa Manana Theater, Dir of Audience Devel; U Way of Metro Tarrant Co, Asst to Dir, Communs Dept, Div of Spec Projs; Wom in Communs Inc: Bd Dirs, Recording Secy; Am Wom in Radio & TV: Bd Dirs, Mbrship Chm; Tex Soc Hosp Public Relats; Nat Assn Hosp Sers; cp/Bd Dirs C of C; Soroptomist Intl; Am Heart Assn, NE Tarrant Co Chapt Publicity Chm; r/Meth; hon/Am Bicent Vol; Hon Citizen of Baton Rouge, La.

GILES, CECILE JEWEL MARKS oc/Teacher; b/Nov 18, 1943; h/1210 Chatham Rd, Waynesboro, VA 22980; m/Schuyler M; c/Stephen M, Stephanie M; p/Mr (dec) and Mrs Cecil Winfield Marks, Willard, NC; ed/BA Campbell Col 1966; Further Study ECU & Univ Va; pa/Social Sci Tchr, Kate Collins Jr HS; Student Coop Assn Advr; Past Chm Communs & Commun Transitional Com; Former Positions: Atkinson HS, Atkinson, NC & Sunset Pk Jr HS, Wilmington, NC; Mem: NEA, VEA; Past Mem: W'boro Ed Assn & NCEA: Dist Chm, VP; cp/AAUW, Hospitality Chm; Hoe & Hope Gdn Clb, Corresp Secy; r/Presb: SS Tchr; hon/DAR Awd 1962.

GILES, STEPHEN RICHMOND oc/Attorney; b/Feb 26, 1947; h/319 E Maple, Fayetteville, AR 72701; ba/Fayetteville; m/Nancy Jo Meyer; c/Aaran Meyer; p/Fred R and Catherine J Giles, Little Rock, AR; ed/BA 1969, JD 1973 Univ Ark; pa/Am Bar Assn; Ark Bar Assn; Real Est Law & Bnkg Law Coms; cp/F'ville C of C; Rotary Clb; r/Christian.

GILHOOLEY, GEORGE oc/Civil Engineer; b/Mar 25, 1955; h/Rt 3 Box 318G, Deland, FL 32720; p/Thomas and Gladys Gilhooley, Deland, TX; ed/BCE Univ Dayton 1977; pa/Civil Engr, Fla Dept Transp; Am Soc Civil Engrs; cp/VP Delta Upsilon; VP, Treas Deland JCs; r/Cath; hon/Bill Wren Awd Outstg JC of Yr 1980; Spoke Awd Outstg First Yr JC 1979.

GILLASPIE, MARGARET ELIZABETH oc/Religious Administrator; b/Apr 1, 1934; h/6640 W 11th St, Indianapolis, IN 46224; ba/Indpls; p/Joanna E Gillaspie, Arkadelphia, AR; ed/BA 1960, MA 1963 Ouachita Bapt Univ; MRE So Sem 1966; Am's Missionary Dir, St Conv of Bapts, Ind 1968–; Social Wkr Wesley Commun House, Louisville, Ky 1964–68; Tchr Delight Public Sch Sys 1962–64; Tchg Fellow Ouachita Univ 1960–61; Operator & Ser Asst SWn Bell Telephone Co, Arkadelphia 1955–62; Other Previous Positions; Assnl Wom's Missionary Union Dir 1976–77; Bapt Public Relats Assn 1974–78; Writer for: Ind Bapt & Accent Mag; NEA; Ark Ed Assn; cp/Alpha Chi; Former Mem L'ville PTA; Dem; Former Mem: L'ville Coun of Chs, E L'ville Area Coun, Jackson Area Coun, Dept Agri, Consumer & Mktg Ser; ARC; Pres' 1970 White House Conf for Yth; Farley Neighborhood Assn; r/Chapelwood Bapt Ch, Indpls; Bible Tchr, Day Care Com Mem, Acteen Ldr, GA Ldr, Missions Com Ctl Bapt Assn; hon/Gov's & Mayor's Commend for Literacy Work Among Intls in Ind; Outstg Yg Wom Am.

GILLIAM, SHARON LYNN oc/Teacher; b/July 2, 1948; h/Borger, TX; ba/Borger HS, Borger, TX 79007; m/Patrick; c/Stefanie; p/Keith and Doris Thomas, Elmwood, OK; ed/BA 1970; pa/HS Eng Lit Tchr, Borger HS; NCTE; TCTE; Delta Kappa Gamma, Chm Pers Growth & Sers Com; cp/Borger Study Clb; Fed'd Wom's Clb, 2nd VP; Borger Commun Concert Assn; r/First Christian Ch: Dean, SS Tchr, Chm Ed & Outreach Dept.

GILLILAND, CLAUDIA JO oc/Teacher, Coordinator; b/Oct 13, 1925; h/1901 S Voss #58, Houston, TX 77057; ba/Houston, TX; c/Michael, Mark Jay Hernandez; p/dec; ed/Att'd San Antonio Jr Col 1961–63; BA Univ Houston 1969; Att'g Univ Houston; Voc Cert Tex A&M & Prairie View A&M 1976; pa/Tchr-Cnslr-Coor Out-of-Sch Yth Prog, Houston Indep Sch Dist; Am Voc Assn; Tex Indust Voc Assn; cp/Nat Writers Clb; r/Unitarian.

GILLILLAND, CORA LEE CRITCHFIELD oc/Art Historian; Numismatist; b/Apr 12, 1932; h/3713 N Glebe Rd, Arlington, VA 22207; ba/Wash DC; m/Thomas; c/Shaun, Ruth, Virginia; p/Edward J Critchfield (dec); Hazel Ratekin (dec); ed/AB Lindenwood Col for Wom 1954; AM Univ Chgo 1960; Postgrad St Univ Ia; pa/Ednl Specialist Dept of Ed, Trust Ty of Pacific Isls 1957-58, 1962-65; Prin Truk HS, Caroline Isls 1962-63; Smithsonian Instn, Wash DC: Mus Specialist Div of Numismatics 1965-71, Collaborator 1971–; Lectr Art Hist Montgomery Col, Takoma Pk, Md 1975-, & No Va Commun Col, Annandale 1976–; Mem Profl Socs; cp/Repub; Citizen ARt Adv Group; r/Prot; hon/Heath Awd for Literary Merit, Am Numismatic Assn; Pub'd Author.

GILLION, MARGUERITE COPELAND oc/Retired; b/Dec 11, 1922; m/Joseph H; c/Michael, Sharon; p/Walter S (dec) and Ethel Copeland (dec); ed/Att'd Troy St Univ; pa/Ret'd from Indep Life Ins Co; Owner St Crafts Store & Tiffany Bakery; Owned & Oper'd Marguerites Drugs-Sundries 1946-52; Million Dollar Round Table; cp/OES; r/Bapt.

GILLISPIE, VIC oc/Professional Artist; b/Mar 6, 1943; h/Manteo, NC; ba/Same; m/Barbara; c/Barry; p/Gratton V and Jessie Marie Gillispie, Manteo, NC; ed/AAS Tech Col Alamance; mil/AUS; pa/Profl Artist; NC Watercolor Soc; So Watercolor Soc; r/Bapt; hon/Awd of Excell 1975-77; 1st Pl in Watercolor, Alamance Art Assn 1977; Num Other Art Awds; W/W Am Cols & Jr Cols; Best in Show Azalea Fest 1978-79; 1st Place Watercolor, Occasion for the Arts, Williamsburg, Va 1977.

GILMAN, ALBERT FRANKLIN III oc/Professor; b/June 25, 1931; h/PO Box 22, Cullowhee, NC 28723; ba/Cullowhee; m/Mia Lindsay Peterson; c/Albert III, Eugenia, Clifford, Patience, Anastasia, Nicholas, Alexandra, Georgia; p/Albert F Gilman Jr (dec); Mrs A F Gilman Jr, Lombard, IL; ed/BS NWn Univ 1952; MA Univ Mont 1958; MA 1962, PhD 1963 Ind Univ; mil/AUS 1954-56; pa/Instr & Asst Prof, Bowdoin Col 1963-66; Assoc Prof, Prof Col of the Virgin Islands 1966-69 & Chm Div of Sci & Maths; Prof Math, Wn Carolina Univ 1969- & Asst VP Acad Affairs 1969-72, Acting VP 1972; Exec Dir Repub Steering Com, US Ho of Reps 1973-74; Vis'g Prof of Maths, Bulgarian Acad of Scis, Sofia, Bulgaria, 1978; cp/Repub Cand Cong, NC 11th Dist 1974; Rotary Clb of Sylva, NC, Pres 1981-82; r/Holy Trinity Greek Orthodox Ch: Mem Bd & Pres.

GILMORE, JOAN ELIZABETH oc/Editor; b/May 14, 1927; h/3321 NW 52, Okla City, OK 73112; ba/Okla City; m/Alfred W McLaughlin Jr; p/Joseph Gilmore (dec); Helen Parks Gilmore, Waukegan, IL; ed/BA Drury Col; Spec Work Columbia Univ, Okla City Univ; pa/Owner Public Relats Firm: Joan Gilmore Inc; Past Pres Okla City Profl Chapt Wm in Communs Inc; Past Bd Mem Sigma Delta Chi; cp/Past Pres Okla City Reg Fashion Grp; Bd Mem Ballet Okla; Bd Mem Wom's Comm of Okla Symph Orch; Okla City's Charter 100 Steering Com; r/Epis; hon/Outstg Wom in Communs, WICI.

GIMENEZ, JOHN oc/Pastor; b/Nov 28, 1931; h/Virginia Bch, VA; ba/PO Box 62524, 640 Kempsville Rd, Va Bch, VA 23462; m/Anne N; c/Robin Anne; p/Stella G Cassiano, Va Bch, VA; ed/Att'd Elim Bible Inst; Hon Deg ARE Rock Bible Inst 1977; pa/Min Rock Ch; Chm Nat Steering Com for "Washington for Jesus"; hon/Author "Up Tight" and "Upon This Rock" 1979.

GINZEL, FRANKLIN L oc/Attorney, Rancher; b/May 21, 1922; h/Colorado City, TX; ba/117 W 2nd St, PO Box 1090, Colorado City, TX 79512; m/Doris Ann; c/Carol Johnson, Marsha Elaine, Franklin Carl; p/dec; ed/LLV Univ Tex Sch Law 1950; mil/143rd Inf 1940-45, Prisoner of War 1943-45; pa/Co Atty, Mitchell Co 1954-70; Dist Atty 32nd Judicial Dist 1970-80; Counsel & Ranch Agt for Coleman Ranch; Pres Mitchell Co Bar Assn 1966; Pres 32nd Dist Bar 1966; VP 32nd Dist Bar Assn 1962; Tex Bar Assn; Am Bar Assn; cp/Pres Colo City Kiwanis Intl 1964; Dem Party; Mitchell Co Atty 1954-70; Nom for 32nd Judicial Dist Atty 1970, Elect'd 1972, 1976; r/Presb: Elder; hon/Plaque Awd for 26 Yrs Law Enforcement Ser to 32nd Judicial Dist 1980; Plaque Awd for 26 Yrs Law Enforcement Ser Mitchell Co Law Enforcement Ofcrs Assn 1980.

GIOLITO, CAROLYN HUGHES oc/Congressional Staff Assistant; h/13912 Northgate Dr, Silver Sprg, MD 20906; ba/Wash DC; m/Caesar A; c/Glenn, Antoinette; p/Eunice B Hughes, AL; ed/BS Ala Col; Geo Wash Sch 1956-58; pa/Staff Asst (Projs), Senator Robert C Byrd 1977–; Spec Asst to Sen Kenneth Keating of NY 1960-65; Spec Asst to Rep Richard L Ottinger of NY 1965-66; Asst to Rep Russell Tuten of Ga 1966-67; Aide to Rep John Dellenback of Oreg 1967-68; Leg Aide Rep Richard White of Tex 1968-71; Asst to Rep G Elliott Hagan of Ga 1971-73; Adm Asst Rep John B Breckinridge of Ky 1973-77; IPA; Adm Assts Assn; r/Presb.

GIPSON, THOMAS ALLEN oc/Personnel Specialist II; b/July 28, 1948; ba/Brown & Root, Adams Rd, Bay City, TX 77414; c/Rene, Thomas Jr, Kim; p/James Lee Gipson; Cora Lee Lewis; ed/Sec'dy Ed; pa/Oakland Raiders 1971-75; World Fball Leag 1975-76; Personnel Spec II, Brown & Root; cp/Brown & Root Softball; Brown & Root Basketball; Chess Player; r/Bapt; hon/All Am 1962 & 67; All Am Wharton Jr Col Track 1968 & 69; Other Sports Awds.

PERSONALITIES OF THE SOUTH

GIRARD, CHARLES M oc/Training, Research and Evaluation Executive; b/Mar 2, 1943; h/Fairfax, VA; ba/1301 Penn Ave NW, Wash DC 20004; m/Roberta C Jeorse; c/Charles John; p/Charles George and Meta Ann Geschwend Girard; ed/BA Park Col 1965; MGA Univ Penn, Wharton Sch; PhD Wayne St Univ 1971; oc/Dir Human Sers, Public Technol Inc 1980-; Chm of Bd & Pres Intl Trg, Res & Eval Coun 1971-; Asst Dir SW Mich Coun of Govt 1969-71; Instr-Trg Coor Wayne St Univ, Dept Polit Sci 1967-69; Asst to City Mgr, Port Huron, Mich 1966-67; Analyst, Pers & Labor Relats, Ford Motor Co 1965-66; First Nat Adv Bd, Nat Crime Preven Inst, Univ Louisville; Security Mgmt Trg Bd, Motorola Teleprogs Inc; Adj Prof Am Univ; Reviewer, Nat Criminal Just Ref Ser, Law Enforcement Assistance Adm; Am Polit Sci Assn; Am Soc Public Adm; Nat Assn Dirs of Law Enforcement Trg; Am Soc Trg & Devel; Intl Soc Law Enforcement & Criminal Just Instrs; Intl Assn Chiefs of Police; Am Mgmt Assn; Nat Assn Clock & Watch Collectors; Smithsonian Assoc; Wilsonian Assoc; Nat Geog Soc; cp/Villa-Lee Commun Assn; Chm Budget & Fin Coms 1973-, Chm Arch Com 1974-; hon/Rec'd Fels S'ship & F'ship to Univ Penn 1965-67; Rec'd Spark Plug Awd, US Jr C of C 1967; Phi Sigma Alpha; Hon Tex Citizen by Gov Dolph Briscoe 1974; Cert of Apprec, El Paso Police Dept 1976; Hon Col, Salt Lake City Police Dept 1978; Dist'd Ser Awd, Mass Crime Prevent Ofcrs Assn 1978; W/W S&SW 1980-81; Author & Co-Author Num Pubs Incl'g *Pro-Cop: Professional Growth Exercises* & *Small Police Agency Consolidation: Suggested Approaches.*

GIRGUS, SAMUEL D oc/Engineer and Investment Executive; b/Mar 21, 1932; h/600 Paseo Canada, San Antonio, TX 78232; ba/San Antonio; m/Lequetta Sue Tacker; c/Mark Daniel, Glen Samuel, Todd John; p/Nicholas (dec) and Mary Girgus (dec); ed/AA Union Col 1955; BS Rutgers Univ 1957; mil/USAF 1948-52; pa/Chm of Bd Shield Invest Corp 1979-; Pres K-A South, Elects 1974-79; VP Intell Kuras-Alterman Corp 1970-74; Dir ITT Avionics 1957-70; MIL-COM Elec Bd Dirs; Competitive Bus Forms Bd Dirs; Am Inst Mgmt, Pres Coun; Am Inst Indust Engrs; Elec Defense Assn; cp/Am San Antonio C of C; Commun Nursery Dir; N San Antonio C of C; Nat Assn C of C; r/Presb; Elder; hon/Tex First Govs Awd 1975; Develr Energy Plaza 1980; Num Articles on Elec Intell to Classified Pubs.

GITTNER, CORY HUGH oc/Student; b/Oct 23, 1958; h/Gainesville, FL; p/Charles H Gittner, Ormond-by-the-Sea, FL; Lois Clark, Allandale, FL; ed/AA Daytona Bch Commun Col 1978; BS Univ Fla 1980; pa/Intern Fla Sea Grant Marine Adv Prog Editorial Ofc; Intern Col of Engr Info Sers; Public Relats Student Soc of Am; Nat Liaison Ofcr Alpha Chapt; cp/Fla Blue Key Spkrs Bur Dir of Res; hon/Author Sev Articles Incl'g "Acoustic Navigation for Divers" 1980.

GLASSMAN, EDWARD BURTON oc/Professor; b/Mar 18, 1929; h/112 Kenan St, Chapel Hill, NC 27514; ba/Chapel Hill; c/Lyn, Susan, Ellen, Marjorie; ed/BA 1949, MS 1951 NY Univ; PhD Johns Hopkins Univ 1955; pa/UNC Med Sch: Prof Biochem & Genetics 1967-, Assoc Prof 1963-67, Asst Prof 1960-63; Ednl & Org Devel Conslt; Staff Mem Dept Genetics, City of Hope Med Ctr, Duarte, Cal 1959-60; Res Assoc Dept Genetics Univ Edinburg, Scotland 1958-59; Res Assoc Dept Biochem, City of Hope Med Ctr 1957-58; Res Assoc Dept Biol Cal Inst Tech 1955-57; hon/Adam T Bruce F'ship; Sigma Xi; Am Cancer Soc Postdoct F'ship; NIH Postdoct Fellow; NIH Career Devel Awd; Fellow John Simon Guggenheim Meml Foun.

GLAZE, DIANA LISOWSKI oc/Principal; b/June 29, 1939; h/1409 Stafford Rd, Sherwood, AR 72116; ba/Little Rock, AR; m/Johnny; p/Roman and Appolonia Lisowski, Milwaukee, WI; ed/BS; MS; EdS; pa/Inter Sch Prin on Sabbatical for Doctorate; AEA Human Relats Comm; AEA; AAUW; Kappa Kappa Iota; Alpha Delta Kappa; AAESP; Prin's Round Table; Alumni Assns of Univ Wis & St Mary's Acad; Life Mem PTA; Textbook Selection Com; Curric Guide Com; cp/Am Wom's Polit Caucus; ERA Coalition; Panel of Am Wom; NLR Dem Wom's Clb; Urban Leag; Altar Soc; r/Cath; hon/Kappa Kappa Iota Nat S'ship 1979; Outstg Yng Wom of Am 1973; Bowling & Golf Awds.

GLENN, CAROLYN LOVE oc/Teacher of Choral Music; b/June 30, 1933; h/2310 Don Andres Ave, Tallahassee, FL 32306; ba/Tallahassee; c/Lawson Hilman and Geneva Foster Glenn, Raleigh, NC; ed/BME Fla St Univ; pa/Tchr Elem & Jr HS; Recital Carnegie Recital Hall 1965; Concerts NC, NJ, Ga, Fla; Tchr Pvt Voice HS & Col Levels; r/St Pauls Meth Ch; Soloist; hon/Delta Kappa Gamma; Rockefeller Foun Grant to Oberlin Univ.

GLICK, PERRY AARON oc/Retired Entomologist-Ecologist; b/Dec 21, 1895; Los Cedros Apts 901 A, 1025 Wild Rose Ln, Brownsville, TX 78520; p/M M (dec) and Eva Alice Moran Glick (dec); ed/AB, MS Univ Ill; mil/Tex St Guard 1944-45; pa/Ret'd From US Dept Agric after 42 Yrs Ser w Govt; Int Coop w Gladys Porter Zoo; Pioneer in Field of Insect Dissemination & Migration, Authored Maj Pub on His Res which was Pub'd By Govt; Author on Ecology of Aerial Insect Dissemination & Ref to

Wk & Pubs Appeared in Num Ldg Profl Jours, Newspapers, Mags & Sci Books in US, England, France, Italy, USSR & Brazil; Owns World-wide Collection of Exotic & Rare Butterflies & Moths; Photog of Merit in Pictorial Compositon; Travelled Extensively in US & Europe; Made Investigaton of Inca Ruins in Peru & Ecol Study on Amazon River; Observations & Study of the Wild Animal Life in Kenya & Tanzania 1975; A Spec Guest on "Adventure in Butterflies" Safari in S Africa 1978 Sponsored by KLM, Royal Dutch Airlines & Allyn Mus of Entomology, Sarasota, Fla; Conslt on Insect Density & Population: NSF, Chance Vought Aircraft, Mil Aircraft Sys, Div of Boeing Airplane Co; Mem Num Profl, Sci & Civil Orgs in US, Mex, England, France & New Zealand; cp/Lions Intl, Waco, Tx; Nat Assn Ret'd Fed Employees; Am Adv Coun; Intl Good Neighbor Coun; r/Presb; hon/USDA Awd; Dist'd Alumni Awd, Park Col, Ks City, Mo; Pub'd Author; Others.

GLOD, STANLEY JOSEPH oc/Attorney; b/Jun 28, 1936; h/2331 Creek Dr, Alexandria, VA 22308; ba/Wash DC; St Gallen, Switzerland; ed/AB w high hons John Carroll Univ 1958; JD Georgetown Univ 1961; Cert Hague Acad Intl Law, Holland 1964; SJD Univ Munich, Germany 1967; mil/AUS 1962-69, Maj Judge Advocate Gen's Corps USAR Col; pa/Admitted to Pract: DC Bar 1962, Va Bar 1970, US Supr Ct Bar 1969; Adj Instr Bus, Intl & Mil Law, Univ Md European Div, Verdun, France 1963-65, Munich 1965-67; Assoc Prof Intl & Comparative Law JAG Sch Univ Va 1968-69; Partner: Sutton & O'Rourke, Wash 1969-71, Boner & Glod, Wash 1971-72, Glod & Oesch, St Gallen; Indiv Pract, Wash 1972-; Chm 1st & 2nd Polonia Press Confs, Wash 1974, 75; Pres Adv Com for Trade Negotiations 1975; Pres Trade Del to Polish Min Fgn Trade 1976; Mem Bar Assns; Am Soc Intl Law; Intl Law Assn; World Peace Through Law Ctr, Geneva; Intl Soc Mil Law & Law of War; Wash Fgn Law Soc; Am Fgn Law Assn; Contbr to Num Profl Jours; cp/Assn Alumni Hague Acad Intl Law; Polish Inst Arts & Scis Am; Grotius Foun; Polish-Am Arts Assn Wash; Polish Am Cong, Bd Dirs Wash Chapt 1975-77; Fac Smithsonian Instn Assocs; Adv Coun for Ec Affairs, Repub Nat Com; Nat Treas Repub Heritage Groups Coun; hon/Alpha Sigma Nu; Phi Alpha Delta; Eisenhower Awd Repub Nat Com 1978; W/W: Am Cols & Univs, Am Law, E; Others.

GLOVER, KENNETH S (SAM) oc/Pharmacist; b/Dec 3, 1940; ba/Glover Pharmacy, Sumiton, AL 35148; m/Sarah C; c/Ken, Beth, Martin; p/Martin (dec) and Rose Glover, Sumiton, AL; ed/BS Samford Univ; pa/Owner Glover Pharm 11 Yrs; Kappa Psi; Walker Co Pharm Assn; cp/E Walker Co C of C; r/Ch of God.

GLOVER, MARION SUE oc/Director Acute Care Department; b/June 17, 1941; h/2417 Gunpowder Rd, Little Rock, AR 72207; ba/Little Rock; m/Earl S; c/Lisa Renee, Lana Sue; p/David Loy and Myrtle Ara Tullos Cheek; ed/Dip 1962; pa/Dir Acute Care Dept, Bapt Med Ctr; Pres Dip Nurses Ark 1978-79; Tech Nsg Procedures Conslt, Area Hosps 1977; Secy-Treas Earl S Glover Constr Co; Dir Trg Prog CPR for Residents of Little Rock 1976-77; ANA; Ark St Nurses Assn; Dist 10 Nurses Assn; Am Assn Critical Care Nurses; Ctrl Ark Hlth Sys Agcy; Nat Leag Nurses; Ark Leag Nurses; Dip Nurses Ark; cp/Ark JCette 1968-72; Gtr Little Rock JCettes 1968-72: Bd Mem 1969-72, 1st VP 1972; McDermott Elem Sch PTA 1973-78; Henderson Middle Sch Band Parents Clb, 1st VP 1978-79; hon/W/W Am Wom 1979-80; Cert'd Coronary Care Nurse; Ark JC Aux Spoke Awd 1968; Ark JC Aux JCette of Month 1968.

GLOVER, RALPH oc/Director of Emergency School Aid Act; b/June 4,1938; h/1221 Alpha St, Henderson, NC 27536; ba/Henderson; m/Francine J Carr; c/Lynette J, Ralph C Jr; p/Daisy Glover; ed/BS Elizabeth City St Univ 1961; MS NC St A&T Univ 1977; pa/Past Pres Vance Co Unit NCAE; NCAE-NEA; Ofcl Black Caucus NEA; Past Mem NCAE Leg Com; Booster Clb Elizabeth City St Univ; Elizabth City St Univ Alumni Chapt; cp/VP & Past Pres COOBS Clb; Past Pres Hammock Bch Clb; Henderson-Vance Biracial Coun; Bicent Forum Com; Voters Leag; NAACP; Fin Secy Pride of Vance Elks Lodge #1263; Baxter P E R Coun #127 IBPOE of W; Chm Ed Dept Fifth Dist IBPOE of W; Recorder & Asst Fin Secy NC St Assn IBPOE of W; Beacon Light Masonic Lodge #249: Chm Auditing Com, Chm Social Com, Worshipful Master; Chm Bd Dirs Goodwill Baxter-Beacon Light Housing Projs; r/Big Ruin Creek Bapt Ch: Asst Ch Clerk, Trustee, Treas Bldg Fund, Usher, Chm Study Plan Com for Bldg Ch; Vance Co SS Conv; Exec Mem Vance Co Bapt Conv; hon/Hon Awd NCAE 1972-73; Outstg Ser, Pres Vance Co Assn Edrs 1972-74; Faithful & Loyal Ser Awd, Beacon Light Masonic Lodge; Outstg Ser as Fin Secy Pride of Vance Elks Lodge; Cub Master of Yr 1973; Dist'd Ldrship Ser 1974 & 75; Silver Beaver Awd 1978.

GOBER, PEGGY GRACE NELSON oc/Secretary-Treasurer, Office Manager; b/Aug 12, 1934; m/David; c/Jana W G Zimmerman, Dana F G Sandison, Rhonda Gale; p/Matthew E (dec) and Vere Belle Green Nelson (dec); ed/Att'd Odessa Col 1953; Burroughs BMS Course 1975; Night Sch, Odessa Col, cum laude Real Est 1978-79; pa/Ofc Mgr, W Tex White Trucks Inc 1970-74; Secy-Treas, Ofc Mgr, Bob's Casing Crews & Emco Machine Works Co 1974-80; Real Est Sales Person, Zant & Assocs 1978-;

120

Secy-Treas Royal Mud Inc 1980-; Dir Bob's Casing Crews Wives Clb 1974-80; Jour Clb, Odessa Col 1953; Staff Odessa Col Newspaper 1953; cp/Cystic Fibrosis Campaign; Precnt Rep Ector Co Dem Conv 1976; r/Meth; hon/W/W Am Wom 1981-82.

GODDARD, JOHN HUNTER JR oc/Attorney; Judge; b/Jun 8, 1912; h/530 E College St, Griffin, GA 30223; ba/Griffin; m/Loula Byne Walker; c/John Hunter III, Edmund Walker; p/John Hunter and Harriot Cope Mills Goddard (dec); ed/PhB 1934, LLB 1936, LLD 1970 Emory Univ; mil/USN 1942-46, Lt Cmdr, European, African & Atl Oceans; pa/Judge St Ct of Spalding Co 1949-; Appt'd Judge Mun Ct, City of Griffin 1949; Asst Atty Gen 1947-48; Spec Dep Asst Atty Gen 9 Yrs; Law Pract w Firm Beck, Goddard, Owen & Murray, Griffin; Griffin Fed Savs & Ln: Fdr, VP; Ga & Griffin Bar Assns; Writer Uniform Traffic Code for Gen Assembly of Ga; Past Pres Phi Delta Phi; Author: *The Mills, Cope and Related Families of Ga*, 1962, *History of First Baptist Church of Griffin*, 1978; cp/Past Chm Bd Dirs: Salvation Army, ARC; Former Chm UF; Past Pres: Griffin JCs, Griffin Hist & Presv Soc, Phi Delta Theta; Former Mem Bd Dirs Griffin-Spalding Co C of C; Former Mem Ga Hist Comm; Ga St Leg; Dem; Masons; Elks; Shrine; Moose; VFW; Am Legion; Griffin CC; Exc Clb; r/1st Bapt Ch: SS Tchr, Exec Com, Bd Deacons 8 Yrs, Ofcl Histn, Past Chm Memls Com.

GODFREY, HORACE CHILTON oc/Retired; b/June 9, 1893; h/Waxahachie, TX; m/Katie Elizabeth Wheatley (dec); p/Samuel McClung (dec) and Eloise Henderson Godfrey (dec); mil/USN 1917-1919; pa/Tex Elect Railway; Tex Power & Light 1925-1958 (Ret'd); cp/Waxahachie Masonic Lodge #90; K of P, Howard & Waxahachie Lodges; Vets of WWII; Am Legion Post #137; Trustee Am Assn Ret'd Persons; Charter Mem Ellis Co Mus, Ellis Co Hist Comm, Ellis Co Geneol Assn; Trustee Waxahachie Sr Citizens Ctr; r/Bapt.

GODLEY, WILLIAM LARRY JR oc/Retired, Volunteer Prison Chaplain; b/Feb 27, 1927; h/4938 Shelley Dr, Wilmington, NC 28405; m/Dorothy F; c/William Larry III, Joycelyn; p/William Larry Sr, Wilmington, NC; Lee Clory Godley (dec); mil/USNR RMNSA 1948-53; pa/Vol Prison Chaplain, St of NC 8 Yrs; Ret'd City Of Wilmington Police Ofcr; cp/Work w Boys Home, Nsg Homes, Foster Homes, Juvenile Detention Ctrs, Schs, Alcoholic Ctrs, Orphanages, Num Chs; r/Bapt; hon/City Coun Cit, Wilmington 1952; Respect for Law Commend 1974; Lttrs of Commend from: Gov George Wallace 1973 & 74, Gov James Holshouser Jr 1975, Sen Birch Bayh 1973, Sen Carl T Curtis 1973, Billy Graham Evangelistic Assn, Oral Roberts Evangelistic Assn, Rex Humbard Outreach Evangelistic Assn, Thomas W Bradsaw (Secy Dept Transp, NC), Sen Jesse Helms; Intl W/W Comun Ser.

GODSMAN, MITCHELL SIDNEY oc/District Manager; b/Mar 25, 1923; h/Richmond, VA; ba/Richmond; m/Katherine G; c/Francis Charlotte, Paul Bromley II, Cornelia Mitchell Stearns, Elizabeth Allen, William Pickett, Thomas Gregory; p/Sidney Paul and June Mitchell Godsman, Denver, CO; ed/BSCE Univ Denver 1949; mil/USAF WWII, Mich Nat Guard 1956-61; pa/Dist Mgr, Mid-Atlantic St, Bennett Pump Co 1972-; Ser Mgr Bennett Pump Co 1961-72; Spec Agt Prudential Inst Co 1958-61; Standard Oil Co: Dist Sales Rep 1956-57, Engr 1949-55; Nat Conf Weights & Measures, Chm Assoc Mbrship Com 1971; Wn Weights & Measures Assn, Chm Indust Com 1966-72; Mich Weights & Measures Assn, Chm Indust Com 1964-72; Va Weights & Measures Assn, Chm Indust Relats Com 1979-80; Va Oil Men's Assn; NC Oil Jobbers Assn; Md Petroleum Coun; Bd Dirs SW Mich Life Underwriters 1959-61; Chm Weights & Measures Com Gasoline Pump Mfrs Assn 1964, 1967, 1971; cp/Pres Kiwanis 1961 & 67; Masons; VFW; Am Legion; Pres Ctrl-Elliott Sch PTA 1964; Asst Ottawa Dist Chm BSA 1964-67; Repub Precinct Chm 1957-61, 1964-72, 1973-76; Repub Co Com 1963-72 Ottawa Co Mich, 1973- Henrico Co, Va; Del Repub Co & St Convs 1965-; Parade Marshal, Meml Day Assn, Grand Haven Mich 1965-72; r/Epis; hon/Hon Awd Nat Conf Weights & Measures; Spec Recog Awd Wn Conf Weights & Measures 1971 & 78; Resolution by Va W & M Assn 1980; Contbn to Jours; Spkr Nat Conf on W & M.

GODWIN, FRANCES MAE oc/Homemaker, Volunteer Worker; b/July 27, 1941; h/1000 Morningside Dr, Rockingham, NC; m/A C Jr; c/Tony, April, Rodney; p/J Leon and Mae J Godwin, Dunn, NC; ed/Att'd E Carolina Col 1960 & Sandhills Commun Col 1965; cp/Rockingham Jr Wom's Clb: Charter Mem 1971, Charter Hist 1971, Pres 1978-79; NCFWC; Leak St Sch PTA: Pres 1977-78, 1st VP 1976-77, 1975-76; Secy L J Bell Sch 1974-75; Richmond Co Parents Adv Coun 1978-80, 1974-75; Richmnd Co Commun Concert Assn, Bd Dirs 1976-78; Richmond Co Band Boosters; Craft Chm Richmond Co; r/First Bapt Ch; hon/Clb Wom of Yr, Rockingham Jr Wom's Clb 1976 & 79.

GOFF, DOYLE ROGER oc/Clergyman; b/June 19, 1950; h/PO Box 54, Everglades City, FL 33929; ba/Chokoloskee, FL; m/Terrie Lane Roberts; c/David Roger, Duane Richard; p/Vernon Harry Sr and

Elizabeth Amanda Bostick Goff, Everglades City, FL; ed/Att'd Lee Col 1968-71; BA 1974, MS 1979 Fla Intl Univ; PhD Prog Fla St Univ 1981-; pa/Ordained in Min 1974; New Field Evangelist 1974-75; Pastor Carrabelle, Fla 1975-76; Min Ch of God, Chokoloskee, Fla 1977-80; Dist Dir Yth & Christian Ed in Ch of God 1977-80; APGA; Am Sch Cnslr Assn; Am Mtl Hlth Cnslrs Assn; cp/Scoutmaster BSA 1973-75; Campaign Chm Cystic Fibrosis Foun 1978 & 80; Lee Col Alumni Assn, Secy-Treas Fla Chapt 1976-; Repub; r/Prot; hon/W/W S&SW 1980-81.

GOFF, ERIS HUGHS oc/Free-Lance Writer, Homemaker; b/Aug 10; h/708 Ridgewood Ave, Monticello, KY 42633; ba/Same; m/Thomas A; p/Milton A (dec) and Vida Hughs (dec); ed/Dip Inst Mtlphysics; Dis Merit Leonardo Da Vinci Acad Sci, Rome, italy 1972; pa/Nat Leag Am Pen Wom; Asst & Secy-Treas T A Goff Nat Gas Co 1933-68; Nat Adv Coun NY World's Fair 1939; r/Intl Ch Mystical Christianity; hon/Cert Merit; W/W Poetry 1971-73; Poet's Parchment NY World's Fair; Hon Mem Intl Mark Twain Soc 1945; 2000 Wom of Achmt 1972.

GOFF, JACQUELINE ANN oc/Expeditor; b/May 25, 1943; h/2155 Winrock, Apt 2, Houston, TX 77057; ba/Houston; p/Jacob B M and Leila A Camp Goff, Baton Rogue, LA; ed/BMus; pa/Assn Profl Expeditors; cp/Repub; r/Presb; hon/W/W Am Wom.

GOFF, KENNETH DALE oc/Deputy Sheriff; b/July 1, 1927; h/PO Box 1054-2005 6th Ave, Tuscaloosa, AL 35401; ba/Same; m/Roberta Morrison; c/Maddona Dale Anderson, Tommie Diane Newby; p/Lloyd Dale Goff (dec); Estelle Lawson; ed/Adv'd Fire Arms Instr; mil/AUS WWII; pa/DAV; VFW; FOP; cp/St, Co, City Handicapped Advr; r/Prot; hon/Handicapped Shooter Yr.

GOINS, LOUISE COPENING oc/Teacher; b/Nov 18, 1913; h/Lenoir, NC; m/Walter L; c/Bessie Louise; p/Vance (dec) and Bessie Jones Copening (dec); ed/BA Bennett Col 1935; MEd Boston Univ 1952; Further Study Lenoir-Rhyne Col & Appalachian St Univ; pa/Tchr Lenoir City Schs 1934-47, Morganton City Schs & Burke Co Public Schs 1949-80; ACT; NEA; NCAE; Delta Sigma Theta; NWn Profl Wom's Clb Treas; cp/Past Pres Wom's Civic Clb of Lenoir; Civitan Intl; r/Meth; hon/Tchr of Yr 1980, Hillcrest Sch.

GOLD, ARCHIE oc/Government Executive; b/Jun 15, 1926; h/7713 Persimmon Tree Ln, Bethesda, MD 20034; ba/Alexandria, VA; m/Joy Pearl; c/Fran Maureen, Laurie Ann; p/Morris Gold (dec); Esther B Gold, Atlantic City, NJ; ed/BSME 1949, MSAE 1954 Drexel Inst Technol; mil/USN 1944-46, Pacific Theatre; pa/Asst for Integration, Ballistic Missile Def R&D; Sr Mem AIAA; IEEE; AAAS; Chm AIAA Jt Strategic Scis Mfg; Nat Res Coun; NBS Review; Others; r/Jewish, Wash Hebrew Congreg; non/Sev Patents; AUS Outstg Commend; Exemplary Perf, St Dept; Others.

GOLDEN, WOODROW WILSON JR oc/Attorney; b/Feb 15, 1948; h/6163 Lake Trace Circle, Jackson, MS 39211; ba/Jackson; m/Mary Lewis Herndon; c/Wilson Harris, Lewis Hamilton; p/Woodrow Wilson Golden (dec); Constance H Golden, Holly Sprgs, MS; ed/BPA 1970, JD 1977; mil/USAR, JAG Corps CPT; pa/Atty, Watkins, Ludlam & Stennis; ABA; Miss Bar; Jackson Yng Lwyrs Assn; cp/Mem Exec Comm, Dem Part St of Miss; r/Presb; hon/Outstg Yng Men Am.

GOLDFARB, RONALD L oc/Attorney; Author; h/7312 Rippon Rd, Alexandria, VA 22307; ba/Wash DC; m/Joanne Jacob; c/Jody, Maximilian, Nicholas; ed/AB Syracuse Univ 1954; LLM Yale Law Sch; mil/USAF, JAG 1957-60, Ret'd Capt; pa/Partner Goldfarb, Singer & Austern & Predecessor Firms 1966-; Spec Prosecutor Dept of Justice, Org'd Crime & Racketeering Sect 1961-64; Chm Spec Review Com, Est'd by US Dist Ct for DC 1975-76; Conslt Num Orgs incl'g: Pres' Task Force for Devel of Poverty Prog, Pres' Adv Comm on Civil Disorders, Nat Comm on Reform of Fed Crim Laws, Brookings Instn, Nat Coul of St Judiciary, Cal Leg, Assembly Judiciary Com, Ford Foun, Twentieth Century Fund, Fac Am Trial Lwyr's Assn, Others; DC, NY & Cal Bars; Bar of US Supreme Ct; Chm Bd Dirs, The Law-Sci Coun, Off-Season; Nat Gov'g Bd: Am Jewish Com, Nat Alliance for Safer Cities; Am-Jewish Cong; Past Pres DC Citizens' Coun for Crim Justice Inc; VP Wash Ser Bur; Others; hon/W/W: Am, S&SW, Am Law; Dir British & Am Writers; Blue Book; Other Biogl Listings; Author Books; Contbr Num Profl Pubs to Law Jours & Articles to Newspapers & Mags.

GOLDSBY, WILMER DEAN oc/Executive Director; b/June 9, 1935; h/2024 Summit St, Little Rock, AR 72206; ba/Little Rock; m/LaVerne; ed/AA Campbell Jr Col 1955-57; BA Allen Univ 1959; MEd Univ Ark 1965; Labor Relats Cert, Ark-Okla Labor Sch 1968; Human Sers Deg, Univ Houston 1969; Mgmt Study, Harvard Univ 1973; pa/Exec Dir Economic Opport Agcy of Pulaski Co Inc 1971-; Dir Prog Opers, Ec Opport Agcy Pulaski Inc 1970; New Careers Spec, EOA New Careers Prog 1969; Cnslr EOA Neighborhood Yth Corps Pulaski Co 1967; Tech Asst Spec, Volt

Tech Corp 1970; Dean Shorter Col 1969; Dir Fed Col Work-Study Prog & Work Aid 1966-67; Dean Students, Shorter Col 1964-67; Varsity Ath Coach, Shorter Col 1960-67; Instr 1960-17; Dir Aths 1961; Dean Men, Shorter Col 1960-64; cp/Pres Elect Ldrship Roundtable; Chm Oper'g Engrs Appren Trg Prog; Chm Pulaₓki Co A Philip Randolph Inst; Pres N Little Rock Coun Human Relats; VP Progress Assn Ec Devel, Little Rock Affil; Chm Pers Com Progress Assn Ec Devel; Little Rock JCs; Pulawski Co Hlth & Wel Coun; Exec Bd AFSCME Coun 38 of St of Ark; Basileus of Omega Psi Phi; Chm Interim Com Control of Shorter Col; Pres Am Fed St, Co, & Municipal Employees Union of EOA Local 1934; Exec Bd Pulaski Co Fair Housing Coun; Chm Policy Adv Bd Shorter Col Day Care Ctr; Chm Com on Housing of N Little Rock Coun Human Relats; Secy-Treas Nat Assn Commun Devel 1973-; Bd Trustee Shorter Col; Bd Trustee Nat Commun Action Trust Fund; Nat Leg Forum; Nat Commun Action Agcy Exec Dirs Assn & Fin Com; Commr Gov's Ec Devel Study Comm; Ark Commun Action Agcy Assn; VChm EOA Ec Devel Com; N Little Rock Civic Leag; Optimist Clb Gtr Little Rock; Num Other Civic & Polit Orgs; r/Meth.

GOLDSTEIN, J JEFFREY oc/General Manager; b/July 10, 1943; h/4602 Kemper St, Rockville, MD 20783; ba/Silver Spring, MD 20906; m/Rebecca E; c/Scott Edgar; p/Louis Goldstein, Venice, FL; ed/Dale Carnegie Sales Course Grad; Grad Nat Inst Drycleaning; pa/Gen Mgr Overall Opers Taro Cleaners 1979-; Tech Sales Rep Drycleaning & Laundry Chems 1978-79; Owner J&K Valet 1971-78; Asst Sales Mgr Country Clb Cleaners 1969-71; Life Ins Slaes, Fidelity Bankers Life 1965-69; Electro-Mech Draftsman, Ord-Marine Engrg 1962-65; Past Pres Suburban Md Cleaners & Launderers Assn; Past Chm Md St Drycleaners Muscular Dystrophy Campaign; Co-Fdr & Past Pres Wash-Balto Mustang Sports Car Clb; Orgr & Past Pres 199 Dalmatians; r/Bapt; hon/Am Drycleaner Mag Plant Design Contest Merit Awd Winner; W/W Bus & Indust 1979.

GOLDWATER, MARILYN oc/Nurse; State Legislator; b/Jan 29, 1927; h/5508 Durbin Rd, Bethesda, MD 20014; m/William H; c/Charles A, Diane L; p/Frederick and Rebecca Rubin; ed/RN Mt Sinai Hosp Sch of Nsg 1948; pa/Camp Nurse, Camp Ramblewood, Darlington, Md 1960, 62; Emer Room Nurse San Mateo Commun Hosp, San Mateo, Cal 1956-58; Gen & Pvt Duty Nsg New Orleans, La 1949-50; Gen Duty Nurse Mt Sinai Hosp, NY, NY 1948; Am Nurses Assn; Nurses Coalition for Action in Polits; Mt Sinai Hosp Sch of Nsg Alumnae; Red Cross; Mem Metro Wash Coun of Govt's Hlth & Envir Protection Policy Com 1976-; Mem So Reg Ed Bd's Comm on Mtl Hlth & Human Sers 1976-; Lectr; cp/Elected Md Ho of Dels 1974; Num Polit Activs; Bd Mem Jewish Social Ser Agy; Concerned Citizens for Juv Justice; Sisterhood Bd, Temple Sinai, Wash DC; Former Red Cross Instr; Order Wom Legs; Others; r/Jewish; hon/Yr of Nurse; Cits from: VFW, Heart Assn, Mar of Dimes; W/W Am Polits.

GOLIGHTLY, ANNIE LUCILLE oc/Professor; b/Dec 26, 1920; h/4749 Audubon View Cir 2, Memphis, TN 38117; ba/Memphis; p/Renfro Selman (dec) and Zenobia Morris Golightly (dec); ed/Att'd Am Col for Wom 1939-42; BS Auburn Univ 1946; MS Univ Tenn 1955; Att'd Iowa St Univ 1964, Colo St Univ 1970; PhD Utah St Univ 1974; pa/Prof Home Ec (Textiles & Clothing), Memphis St Univ; Assn Col Professors of Textiles & Clothing; AAUW; Am Home Ec Assn; Tenn Home Ec Assn; W Tenn Home Ec Assn; Alpha Delta Kappa; Kappa Omicron Phi; r/Bapt.

GOMEZ, JORGE oc/Physician; b/May 22, 1938; h/Longwood, FL; ba/819 1st St, Sanford, FL 32771; m/Lu-Stella; c/Angela Maria, Jorge Octavio, Isabel Cristina; p/Jorge Sr (dec) and Eulogia E De Gomez, Tunja, Columbis, SA; ed/Colegio de Boyaca, Columbia 1956; MD Nat Univ Med Sch 1964; Intern Cleveland 1969; Spec Cardiovascular Diseases, Miami 1971; pa/Pvt Pract, Sanford, Fl 1971-; Chief of Med, Seminole Meml Hosp 1972-80; Pres Sem Co Med Soc 1977; Bd Dirs Am Heart Assn, Ctrl Fla Chapt 1978-79; Fla Med Assn; AMA; Am Soc Internal Med; Past Mem Bd Trustees Seminole Meml Hosp; r/Cath.

GÓMEZ BERRIOS, NÉLIDA oc/Instructor and Consultant; b/Nov 6, 1935; h/312 32nd St, Villa Nevarez, Rio Piedras, PR 00927; c/Edmund, Conrado, Norman Luis, Yamira Santiago; p/Salomon Gomez (dec); Josefa Berrios (dec); ed/BBA; MBA; pa/Univ Univ; Conslt Ins Co; cp/Coop Movement of PR; r/Cath; hon/W/W S&SW; Grad magna cum laude MBA.

GONCE, MARION WILSON oc/Teacher; b/Aug 8, 1944; h/Rt 6 Box 354, Alexander City, AL 35010; ba/Alexander City; m/Nicki Carol; c/Jason; p/Ollie A Gonce, Stevenson, Al; Gretchen Gonce (dec); ed/BS 1967, MS 1974 Auburn Univ; pa/Agric-Bus Tchr, Benjamin Russell HS; AEA; NEA; Nat Voc-Agric Tchrs Assn; r/Ch of Christ.

GONZALES, ALBERT PEDRO oc/Adult Probation Officer; b/Feb 3, 1929; h/1505 McCreary St, Killeen,TX 76541; ba/Killeen; m/Rosa Kim; c/Alexander Jerome, Anna Kim, Albert Pedro II, Ambrose Francis, Angela Kim, Anthony Paul; p/Pedro Marez (dec) and Casimira Baca Gonzales (dec); ed/Dip Mil Intell Sch 1951; Dip Army Lang Sch 1951; Dip AUS Mil Police Sch, Crim Invest 1963; BS 1979, MS 1980 Am Technol Univ; mil/AUS 1951-77; pa/Interrogator of Prisoners of War, Korea & Vietnam; Criminal Investigator, Adult Probation Ofcr, 27th Judicial Dist, TX; Mbrship Chm, Nat Criminal Just; Alpha Phi Sigma, Omega Lambda Chapt; Tex Police Ofcrs Assn; Ctrl Tex Peace Ofcrs Assn; cp/K of C, Grandknight 1975-76, Coun 4724, Killeen; Bd Dirs Cath Men's Corp Killeen; Bd Dirs Alumni Assn of Am Technol Univ; Am Legion; 4° Knight, St Joseph's Assem Coun 4724; r/Rom Cath; hon/AUS Merit Medal; Good Conduct Medals (8); Army Commend Medals (2); Combat Infantryman's Badge; Knight of Yr, K of C.

GONZALEZ, ANTONIO oc/Lawyer, Educator; b/Mar 14, 1943; h/1207 Blalock Rd, Houston, TX 77055; ba/Houston; m/Elma De Luna; c/Julissa Priscilla; p/Manvel and Natalia Torres Gonzalez, Edinburg, TX; ed/BA Univ Md 1971; MA Univ Tenn 1973; JD Miles Col 1979; mil/USAF 1966-70; pa/Lwyr Crain, Caton, James & Oberwetter, Houston 1979-80; Spitler & Lyon, Ala 1978; Instr Tex A&I Univ 1975; Dept Asst Univ Tenn 1973; Am Bar Assn; Am Hist Assn; AAUP; Delta Theta Phi; Cand Ind Bar Assn; cp/Leag U Latin Am Citizens; Dem; r/Cath; hon/W/W S&SW 1980-81; Am Jurisprudence Awd 1978; Corpus Juris Secundum Awd 1979; USAF Commend Medal 1969; Law Day Awd 1978; Cross of Gallantry, Vietnam Repub Awd 1969.

GOOCH, HUBERT LEE JR oc/School Administrator; b/May 28, 1935; h/Rt 2 Box 201, Oxford, NC 27565; ba/Oxford, NC; m/Geraldne; c/Katrina, Aubrey, Annette, Sheila; p/Hubert L Sr and Willie A Gooch, Oxford, NC; ed/BS NC A&T Univ 1957; MA NC Ctrl Univ 1976; mil/Capt; pa/Prin Mary Potter Sch; NC Assn Sch Admrs; Nat Assn Elem Sch Prins; cp/Phi Beta Sigma; Former Co Commr Granville Co; r/Ordained Bapt Deacon.

GOOCH, PATRICIA CAROLYN oc/Cytogeneticist; b/Mar 28, 1935; h/226 Tusculum Dr, Oak Ridge, TN 37830; ba/Oak Ridge; p/James Lide Gooch, Michie, TN; Mary Frances Hyneman Gooch (dec); ed/BS Univ Tenn 1957; pa/Biol Div ORNL 1958-70; Univ Tex Grad Sch Biomed Scis 1970; Northrup NASA Manned Spacecraft Ctr, Houston 1970-73; Biol Div Oak Ridge Nat Lab 1973-; AAAS; Am Genetic Assn; Envir Mutagen Soc; Genetics Soc Am; Org'g Com 1st Mammalian Cytology & Somatic Cell Genetics Conf, San Juan, PR; Local Org'g Com, Symposium of Human Cytogenetics, Univ Tenn, Knoxville 1962; cp/Knoxville Area Delta Gamma Alumnae Assn; Univ Tenn Delta Gamma Col Advr, 1957-63, 1975-80; Big Orange Clb of Oak Ridge; Anderson Co Chapt Univ Tenn Alumni Assn, Treas 1980-81; r/Ch of Christ; hon/Outstg Yng Wom Am 1968; Univ Tenn Pan-Hellenic Outstg Tenn Wom 1974; Sigma Xi 1975; W/W S&SW 1980-81; Author Books & Profl Jour Articles.

GOOD, ELIZABETH LEATHERWOOD oc/Director Nursing Services; b/Jan 9, 1921; h/10575 Cromwell Dr, Dallas, TX 75229; ba/Dallas; m/Robert O (dec); c/Carolyn Johnson, Robert O II; p/Robert Lee and Martha Francis Stovall Leatherwood, Bryson City, NC; ed/BSN Duke Univ; MN Emory Univ; Mil/1st Lt 65th Gen Hosp ANC; pa/Dir Nsg Ser, Parkland Meml Hosp; ANA; TNA; NLN; THA; TSH; NSA; cp/BSA; GSA; PTA; Spkrs Bur; r/Presb; hon/W/W Am Wom; Sigma Theta Tau; Others.

GOODE, WADE CALVIN oc/Teacher; b/Nov 30, 1925; h/PO Box 3322, Cleveland, TN; ba/Cleve; m/Bettie Christina; c/Vicki, Sharon, Floyd; p/William Calvin and Lela Mae Goode, Cleve; ed/MS; mil/USMC 3 Yrs; AUS 1 Yr; USAF 17 Yrs, Ret'd; pa/5th Grade Tchr E L Ross Elem Sch; Past Pres Cleve Ed Assn; NEA: TEA; CEA; cp/Cmdr Dept Tenn DAV; Am Legion; VFW; r/Union Grove Ch of Christ; hon/Sev Mil Hons; DAV Hons.

GOODING, ERLE STANLEY oc/Historian; b/Sept 8, 1948; h/Red Clay Hist Area, Rt 6 Box 733, Cleveland, TN 37311; m/Ingrid Butler; p/Edward Jr and Christine Tolbert Gooding, Pensacola, Fl; ed/BA Univ Tex-El Paso 1978; mil/AUS 1967-71; pa/Res Asst U Negro Col Fund 1978; Fed Residential Cnslr, Opport House 1979-80; Hist Area Supvr, Red Clay St Hist Area 1980-; E Tenn Hist Soc; Bradley Co Hist Soc; Tenn Hist Soc; cp/Kappa Alpha Psi; Polemarch Theta Xi Chapt Kappa Alpha Psi 1975-76; r/Bapt; hon/Men of Mines, Univ Tex El Paso 1977; Mobil Oil S'ship, Univ Tex El Paso 1978; Achmt Awd, El Paso-Las Cruces Chapt Kappa Alpha Psi 1977; Outstg Achmt Awd AUS 1968.

GOODLETT, ANNIE BETH oc/Nurse; b/Oct 21, 9120; h/204 Fairpark, Henderson, TX 75652; m/B H Rowe; c/Lynda Beth Trent, Jon David Rowe; p/Andrew Gibson and Zelma Needham Goodlett, Henderson, TX; ed/Grad Henderson Meml Hosp Sch Nsg 1951; pa/Spec Duty Nurse Henderson Meml Hosp 8 Yrs; Drs Nurse in Ofc 9 Yrs; cp/Thomas J Rusk Chapt, Nat Soc DAR; r/Meth; hon/Coming Home Queen, Kilgore Col 1980; Hon'd by St Tex Heritage Prog for Continuous Prod by Same Fam for Over 100 Yrs on MD & Annie Needham Ranch.

GOODMAN, JEAN CLARENCE (JC) oc/Retired; b/June 8, 1910; m/Inez; c/Barbara Pyles, John Steven; p/John L (dec) and Barbara Elizabeth Goodman, Claremore, OK; pa/Artist; r/Prot; hon/Painting Hangs at US Naval Acad; Painting Owner By Egyptian Pres Anwar Sadat.

GOODSON, ANNIE HARRIS oc/Teacher; b/Sept 19, 1944; h/Box 711, Bluefield, Va 24605; ba/Berwind, WV; c/Philip, NIcholas, Katrina; p/Howard Hobert (dec) and Annie Harris, Bluefield, VA; ed/BS Hlth & PE; pa/NEA; WVEA; McDowell CEA; cp/Logan St Sch PTA; Berwind Sch PTA; r/Bapt; hon/W/W Am Wom; Va St Col S'ship; Perfect Attendance Awd HS; Valedictorian HS.

GOODSON, SHANNON L oc/Human Resources Consultant; b/May 26, 1952; h/7707 Meadow Pk #204, Dallas, TX 55230; ba/Dallas; p/James E and Lorayn Goodson, Dallas, TX; ed/BS, MS Lamar Univ; pa/APGA; Assn Measurement & Evaluation in Guid; Inst for Adv'd Study in Rational Psychotherapy; SEn Psych Assn; hon/Invit'd to Present Res Involving Achmt Behavior in Wom, SEn Psych Assn Conv 1978 & 79.

GOODWIN, BRADY ROY oc/Sales Manager; b/July 1, 1946; h/Arlington, TX; ba/Cleburne; m/Patricia L; p/(dec); ed/BA N Tex St Univ; pa/Retail Mgmt 11 Yrs; Sales Mgr Tex Lime Co 3 Yrs; Am Mgmt Assn; cp/C of C, Mbrship Com, Lib Bd Dirs; hon/Pub'd Author.

GOODWIN, FRANCES ELIZABETH oc/Registered Nurse; b/Aug 16, 1924; h/Rt 2 Box 98, Carrollton, MS 38917; ba/Greenwood, MS; m/Marvin Doyle Sr; c/Marvin Doyle Jr, Myron Anderson; p/James Franklin Anderson (dec); Lenora Elizabeth Cooper Walters, Pope, MS; ed/AD Nsg Sci; 3 Yr Study Sec'dy Ed; pa/RN; MNA; ANA; AHA; HH Nurse Coor, Leflore Co; CERP; cp/OES Chapt 70; r/So Bapt; hon/Recog from MNA on CEU's.

GORDON, CARSON A oc/Credit Union Manager; b/Mar 4, 1940; h/1914 Hilton St, Camden, SC 29020; ba/Lugoff, SC; m/Kathleen; c/Robin, Stephen; p/C J and Annie Lee Gordon, Rembert, SC; ed/BS Newberry Col; mil/AUS; pa/Mgr Dupont May Plant Credit Union; Bd Dirs CUAC Inc; cp/Little Leag Coach & Fball Ofcl; r/Bapt.

GORDON, JERRY L oc/Music Teacher; b/Sept 15, 1938; h/2601 Rockview, Waco, TX 76710; ba/Waco; m/Nena; c/Zachary; p/Morris L and Bernice J Gordon, Greenville, OH; ed/BS, MMus; DMA; mil/USAF 4 Yrs; pa/Soloist w Cinci & Honolulu Symphs; Recorded on Decca Records; Mus Tchr Baylor Univ; cp/Yth Activs; Coach Ch Leag Basketball & Softball Teams; r/Prot; hon/Gorno & Baur S'ship in Voice; Intl W/W Mus.

GORDY, JOE C oc/Educator, Football Coach; b/June 29, 1947; h/Box 836A Lake Serene, Hattiesburg, MS 39401; ba/H'burg; m/Janice S; c/Shana; p/Mrs E A Ross, Sumrall, MS; ed/BS 1970, MS 1976, Post Grad Work 1979 Univ So Miss; pa/Edr, Fball Coach Oak Grove HS 4 Yrs; Miss Assn Coaches: Bd Dirs & Exec Com Mem; Am Fball Coaches Assn; Nat HS Coaches Assn; MEA; cp/Oak Grove Lions Clb; Lake Serene Property Owners Assn; W Lamar Water Assn Bd Dirs; Dem Party Lamar Co; r/Temple Bapt Ch; hon/Staff Mem Ole Miss All Sports Camp 1977; Clin Lectr S Miss Fball Coaches Clin 1977.

GORE, BILLY MAC oc/Investigator; b/Oct 7, 1946; h/PO Box 29, Vardaman, MS 38878; ba/Starkville, MS; m/Mary Jane Ellard; c/Dusten Douglas, Mary Dare; p/Samuel LeRoy and Mattie Virginia McQuary Gore, Houston, MS; ed/Miss Law Enforcement Trg Acad 1975; Adv'd Invest Sch 1980; mil/Miss Nat Guard 1963-67; AUS 1967-69; pa/Patrolman & Investigator, Miss Hwy Patrol Bur of Criminal Invest; Miss Hwy Patrol Assn; r/Bapt; hon/Purple Heart & Vietnam Cits 1967; Interdeptl Pistol Champion 1977; Nom'd Patrolman of Yr 1974; Bruce JCs Outstg Law Ofcr 1973.

GORE, DEAN FRANKLIN III oc/Policeman; b/Apr 2, 1942; h/Albany, GA; m/Linda A; c/Tina Michelle, Dean F, Sherri Belinda; p/Dean Franklin Sr (dec) and Edna Gore, Albanay, GA; mil/NG 1960; USAFR 1967; pa/Albany Police Dept, Traffic Div Supvr 1963-; FOP; Flint River Long Rifle Assn, Pres 2 Yrs; r/Meth.

GORE, JOHN HOWARD oc/Director Health Education Program; b/June 30, 1944; ba/145 McDowell St, Welch, WV 24801; m/Carolyn Sue; c/Kristy Sue; p/Howard (dec) and Bessie I Gore (dec); ed/BA 1972, MA 1974 Marshall Univ; mil/USAF 1963-67 Sgt; pa/Dir McDowell Co Hlth Ed Prog 1979-; Dir Elkhorn Mtl Hlth Clin 1977-79; Dir Adams Co Mtl Hlth Clin 1976-77; Alcoholism Treatment Spec, Lansdowne Mtl Hlth Ctr 1973-76; APGA; Am Col Pers Assn; Am Rehab Cnslrs Assn; WV Primary Care Study Grp; Rural Am; McDowell Co Hlth Action Coun Inc; hon/W/W S&SW 1980-81; Lttr of Commend, Asst Surg Gen 1979.

GOSS, EUNICE RUTH ASHWORTH oc/Librarian; b/Sept 18, 1919;

h/PO Box 36, White, GA 30184; ba/Cartersville, GA; m/C L; c/Malcolm Charles, Kenneth Harold, Ronald Michael; p/Hugh Malcolm and Mary Magdline Jarrett Ashworth, Ranger, GA; ed/BS Ed; pa/Libn Cass Comprehensive HS; cp/Past Grand Martha OES; Past Pres Wom's CLb; St Treas Roadrunners Clb; Other Commun Clbs; r/Bapt.

GOSSAGE, EDNA JENKINS oc/Senior Social Counselor; h/12 Grassy Cove Rd, Rt 3, Box 202, Crossville, TN 38555; ba/C'ville; m/Roy (dec); c/Dorothy Lucille, Daniel Arthur, Margaret Solomon (Stepdaugh), Roy Lee Jr (Stepson), Helen Kendall (Foster Daugh); p/Arthur A Jenkins (dec); Lennie Belle Bailey (dec); ed/Tenn Tech Univ; Univ Tenn; Mars Hill Col; pa/Writer "Cumb Hds" 1934-55; Poet; Public Relats Chm; Painter; Woodcarving; Weaving; Actress Cumb Co Playhouse; CC Commun Theatre Assn; Tenn Conf Social Wk; BPW, Pres 4 Terms, Dist Dir Tenn Fdn; IPA; Dist Dir Save Chd Fdn; NYA Supvr; Dist Mgr 3 Cosmetic Firms; Tenn Theatre Assn; Wrote Hist Hds Meth Ch; ARC; Cousteau Soc; Mtl Hlth; Chm Planning Com to Devel Ctr Handicapped; Fdr Daniel Arthur Rehab Ctr, Oak Ridge & Clinton; Bd Dirs Hill Toppers Inc; cp/Orig Homesteader Ldr Commun Projs; Esp Mtl Hlth Prog; Dem Woms Clb; r/Hds Meth Ch, SS Tchr, Adm Bd, Comm, Treas & Fin Mgr 13 Yrs, Pres Hds U Meth Wom; Prog Chm Dist UMW; hon/Anderson Co Mother of Yr 1951; Cumb Co Wom of Achmt; 2nd Place Oratorical Contest; 25 Yr Pin: Laurel Chapt OES, Tenn Dept Public Wel; Cumb Co Bicent Wom of Hist 1976; Fellow, ABI; Notable Ams Bicent Era; Intl Dic Biog; Intl W/W: Wom, Intells; Intl Reg Profiles; Intercont Biogl Assoc Mem.

GOSSETT, JOHN SARTAIN oc/Professor; b/Dec 18, 1951; h/117 E Third, Tyler, TX 75701; ba/Cedar Falls, IA; p/Phil and Dorothy Gossett, Tyler, TX; ed/BS Univ Houston 1974; PhD Univ So Calif 1979; pa/Prof Speech, Dir Debate Univ No Ia; cp/Dem Party; r/Bapt; hon/Coach 2nd Pl Team, Nat Debate Tourn 1977 & 78.

GOTTSCHALK, CONSTANCE oc/Musician, Teacher; b/Dec 30, 1940; ba/Cocoa, FL; m/Charles; c/Lisa; p/Ben and Madelyn Maestranzi, Niles, IL; ed/BMus 1964; MMus 1970; pa/Tchr Brevard Commun Col; Pianist; hon/Solo Concert, Italy 1979; S'ship Nice, France for 2 Mos Study 1960; Solo Concert w Fla Symph Orch 1979.

GOUGH, E C HELEN oc/Homemaker; b/Aug 20, 1927; h/3504 31st St, Meridian, MS 39301; m/Edward Connell Sr; c/Edward Connell Jr, Jerrerson Lee; p/John J and Marie Mienhardt Gartman; ed/AA; cp/Pres Meridian Flower Show Judges Coun; 2nd VP Miss Flower Show Judges Coun; Pres Meridian Coun of Garden Clbs; Dist Dir Garden Clbs of Miss; r/Bapt; hon/Den Mother Awd; BSA Silver Bowl; Flower Show; Many Top Awds in Artistic & Horticulture Divs of Local & Nat Flower Shows.

GOULD, LYNDA GAY oc/Teacher; b/June 9. 1940; h/2946 Elliott, Wichita Falls, TX 76308; ba/Wichita Falls; c/Guardian of Bobby Gould Jr; p/J B (dec) and Gladys Gould, Wichita Falls, TX; ed/AA BA Midwestern Univ; pa/4th Grade Tchr; cp/Beta Sigma Phi; Water Safety Instr; ARC; Toastmistress Clb; Art Assn; r/Rom Cath; hon/Pres Asedo Sorority; VP Wesley Foun; W/W Am Wom; Pres Clb of Avon Inc.

GOULD, PAUL FREDERICK oc/Physicist; b/Jan 12, 1938; h/123 Woodlawn Dr, Panama City, FL 32407; ba/Panama City; m/Janet Ann; c/Laura Ann, Scott Frederick, Cynthia Ann, Robb Kayser; p/Wilber J and Cleo Kayser Williamson, Des Moines, IA; ed/BA Duke Univ; MS Univ So Cal; mil/Ia NG 1956-62; pa/Physicist, Mgr Range Data & Control Ctr, Nav Coastal Sys Ctr; Am Def Preparedness Assn; cp/Pres Bch Optimist Clb; Treas Employees Wel Assn, NCSC; r/Luth; hon/3 Patents; 11 Tech Reports; Jr Col Hon Soc; W/W S&SW.

GOULD, ROBERT A oc/Insurance Executive; h/206 Guadalupe Cir, Athens, TX 75751; m/Peggy L Lubben; ed/Att'd Henderson Co Jr Col, Tarleton St Col, Hartford, Conn Ins Col, Sev Schs while in Navy; mil/USN 4 Yrs; pa/Owner Gould Ins Agcy & Robert A Gould Investments; cp/JC Intl, Senator from Athens; Loop Adv Bd, City of Athens, Secy; Indust Foun, Hwy Com; Henderson Co Jr Col, Ex-Students S'ship Fund Dir; Dir 1st Nat Bank Athens; Part in Var Law Enforcement Projs; VFW Life Mem; Fdr & Charter Pres Athens Ambassadors Clb; Co-Fdr, Charter Secy, Life Mem Tex HS Basketball Hall of Fame; r/Epis; hon/Henderson Co Jr Col, Outstg Ex-Student; Athens JCs, JC of Yr Twice; Rec'd 45 Local & St Awds.

GOWER, DOUGLAS oc/Veteran's Benefits Counselor; b/Jan 10, 1944; h/222 Picardilly Dr, Winston-Salem, NC 27104; ba/Winston-Salem; m/Virginia M; c/Kimberly Louise; p/Conley H and Vivian Gower, Vandalia, MO; ed/AA Gaston Col 1977; mil/AUS 1967-70 Sgt; pa/Cnslr Vet's Adm; cp/Life Mem Disabled Am Vets Post 9; Nat Amputee Post 76; Am Legion Post 119; r/Meth; hon/Outstg Handicapped Fed Employee of VA 1980; Outstg Disabled Am Vet of NC 1978-79; NC Handicapped Citizen of Yr 1978; Handicapped Employee of Yr, City of Winston-Salem 1978.

GRADDY, WILLIAM HENRY IV oc/Attorney; b/Sept 29, 1947; h/Versailles, KY; ba/Versailles, KY; m/Lisa Todd; c/Tevis Garrett, Lucy Hart; p/Wiliam Henry III and Katherine Churchill Graddy, Versailles, KY; ed/BA Wash & Lee Univ 1969; JD Univ Ky 1975; mil/USNR 1969-75; pa/Atty McCauley & Elam Law Firm; Asst Commonwlth's Atty, 14th Judicial Dist 1978-; ABA; KBA; Am Trial Lwyrs Assn; Ky Assn Trial Attys; Am Soc Intl Law; cp/Chm Cumberland Chapt Sierra Clb 1980-; Pres Ky Conservation Com 1976-; Bd Dirs Ky Conservation Foun 1980-; Bd Dirs Land & Nature Trust of Bluegrass 1975-; Bd Dirs Ctrl Ky Legal Sers 1975-79; Bd Dirs Appalachian Res & Defense Fund 1979-; Treas Woodford Co Rupub Party 1975-80; r/Presb.

GRAHAM, BOB oc/Governor of Florida; b/Nov 9, 1936; m/Adele Khoury; c/Gwen, Cissy, Suzanne, Kendall; p/Ernest R and Hilda Simmons Graham; ed/BA Univ Fla 1959; Law Deg Harvard Law Sch 1962; pa/Gov St of Fla 1979-; Elect'd to Fla Ho of Reps 1966 & Fla Senate 1970; Chm: Ed Com of the Sts, So Regional Ed Bd & Intergovtl Adv Coun to Dept of Ed; Addressed Nat Conv of NEA 1980; Delivered Nom'g Speech for Pres Jimmy Carter, Dem Nat Conv 1980; Hd Caribbean/Ctrl Am Action Grp 1980-; Former Dairy & Cattle Mgr; Develr Commun of Miami Lakes; Owns & Manages Ranch in So Ga; cp/4-H Yth Foun; Nat Comm on Reform of Sec'dy Ed; Nat Foun for Improvement of Ed; So Regional Ed Bd; Nat Com for Citizens in Ed; Sr Ctrs of Dade Co; hon/Allen Morris Awd 1967 for 2nd Most Outstg First Session Mem of the House; Fla JCs 1 of 5 Most Outstg Yng Men of Fla 1970-71; Allen Morris Awd 1971-72 for Outstg First Term Mem of Senate; St Petersburg Times Awd for Most Valuable Mem of Senate 1972; Conserv 70s, Fla Wildlife Fed & Sierra Clb Leg Awds 1972; Allen Morris Awd 1973 for Most Valuable Mem of Senate; Fla Assn of Commun Coils & Fla Sch Bds Assn Leg Awds 1974; Allen Morris Awd 1976 for 2nd Most Effective Senator.

GRAHAM, CECIL DEWAYNE oc/Reporter, Producer & Host; b/Sept 16, 1949; h/610 10th St, McComb, MS 39648; ba/McComb; m/Carolyn Holland; c/David Wayne, Sheila Renee; p/Cecil V and Ozella Graham, Birmingham, AL; ed/HS Grad; pa/WAPF-WCCA FM: Chief Announcer, Program Dir, Mus Dir 1974-80; News & Public Affairs Director 1975-80, Mem Sales Staff 1976-80; News Reporter, "Contact 9"; Producer & Host of "The Morning Show", WAFB-TV; cp/Kindergartern Parent's Adv Com, Chm; McComb Sch Dist Adv Com, Chm; McComb Sch Dist Energy Mgmt Com; McComb C of C Leg Com, Chm; Pike Co Arts Coun: Mem, Coffeehouse Com; Bright Hope Foun Exec Bd; Work w: Lion's Clb, Exch Clb, Rotary Clb, JCs, JCettes, McComb Gdn Clb, Jr Aux, Co-Op Ext Ser Clb & Other Civic Orgs; Staff/Publicity/Tech Dir, Miss Mississippi-USA Pageant 1979; r/Jehovah's Witnesses; hon/Sch Bell Awd, Miss Assn Edrs 1979-80; Ser to St Jude's Awd 1978; Ser to March of Dimes 1979; Ser to Pike Co Arts Coun 1979; Holder 3rd Class Lic w Broadcast Endorsement.

GRAHAM, GORDON MARION oc/Aerospace Executive; b/Feb 16, 1918; h/4018 N 27th St, Arlington, VA 22207; ba/Wash DC; m/Vivian F; c/Eloise L Brooks, Gordon A E, Helen H Stubbs; p/(dec); ed/BS Univ Cal; MS Univ Pgh; AF Inst Tech; mil/USAF 1940-73, Ret'd Lt Gen; Last Tour Cdr US Forces Japan; pa/McDonnell Douglas Corp: Corporate VP Far E 1973-77, Corporate VP Wash 1978-; Tau Beta Pi; Am Inst Mining; Metallurgical & Petrol Engrs; Am Fighter Aces Assn; Red River Val Fighter Pilots Assn; AF Assn; Am Logistics Assn; Nat Def Trans Assn; Confederate AF Col; Life Mem Nat Rifle Assn; Order of Daedalians; r/Presb; hon/Num Mil Hons incl'g: Dist'd Ser Medal, Silver Star, Legion of Merit, Dist'd Flying Cross w Oak Leaf Cluster, Air Medal w 27 Oak Leaf Clusters, Jt Ser Commend Medal, AF Commend Medal.

GRAHAM, REBEKAH NEWMAN oc/Legal Secretary; b/Jan 12, 1952; h/2102 Westbriar, Duncan, OK 73533; ba/Duncan; m/Glenn D; c/Joshua Newman; p/Denver L and Viola M Newman, Duncan, OK; ed/Cand Paralegal Deg; pa/St Treas Okla Assn Legal Secys 1979-80; Tch Trg Course for Legal Secys Red River Area Voc-Tech Sch; Past Pres, Secy-Treas, Gov & NALS Rep of Stephens Co Legal Secy; hon/BPW 1976-77 Yng Careerist; Legal Secy of Yr, Stephens Co 1977.

GRAHAM, SUSANN BURFORD oc/Producing Director; b/Apr 6, 1950; h/206 Alberta Dr, Atlanta, GA; ba/Marietta, GA; p/William Bascum (dec) and Lorene C Graham, Ft Worth, TX; ed/BFA Lamar Univ 1972; pa/Prod & Dir Plays, Barn Dinner Theatre (Oldest Dinner Theatre Metro Atlanta Area); cp/DAR; Marietta C of C; Atlanta Conv & Visitors Bur; hon/Recog of Outstg Achmt, Ga Land Devel Assn 1975, 76; Outstg Layout & Desgin-Commercial Art Category, Waterford Inc 1978; Outstg Advtg Achmt, Regional Enterprises 1978; Advtg Awd-Copywriting Category & Advtg Awd-Layout & Design Category, Highgate Devel Corp 1978; Outstg Achmt, Four Color Advtg, Bio-Sci Res Inc 1978.

GRAHAM, WILLIAM THOMAS oc/Superior Court Judge; b/Oct 24, 1933; h/1000 Arbor Rd, Winston-Salem, NC 27104; ba/W-S; m/Nancy Kent Hill; c/William Thomas Jr, Ashton Cannon; p/James Monroe and Margaret Virginia Goodwin Graham, Waynesboro, VA; ed/Fishburne Mill Sch 1952; AB Duke Univ 1956; JD Univ Va 1962; Wake Forest Univ Law Sch; mil/AUS 1957-58; pa/Assoc Law Firm Craige, Brawley; Partner Law Firm: Craige, Brawley, Horton & Graham 1965-69, Billings & Graham 1971-75; Superior Ct Judge 1975-: NC, DC, Va, US Dist Ct, Mid Dist NC, Tax Ct US & US Supr Ct; cp/Bd Dirs Am Cancer Soc; Forsyth Co Bd Elections; Others; Del Num Repub Convs, Co, Dist, St, Nat; Var Yg Repub Convs; NC Steering Com 1972, Metro Coor, Holshouser for Gov; Com to Re-elect Pres: Co-Mgr Forsyth Co, NC Com; Repub Precnt Chm; Chm Forsyth Co Repub Party 1966-69, 1973-75; Repub Cand for Mayor W-S 1970; Others; hon/NC Yg Repub Sr Party Awd; W/W Am Polits; Hon Mention Westinghouse Nat Sci Talent Search.

GRAMM, PHIL oc/US House of Representatives; b/July 8, 1942; ba/Wash DC; m/Wendy Lee; c/Marshall Kenneth, Jefferson Philip; ed/BBA 1964, PhD 1967 Univ Ga; pa/Prof Ecs, Tex A&M Univ 1967-78; Ptnr Gramm & Assocs 1971-78; Former Conslt, US Bur of Mines, Nat Sci Foun, Arms Control & Disarmament Agcy & US Public Hlth Ser; cp/Cong-man, US Ho of Reps 1978-; Coms: Interst & Fgn Commerce, Subcoms: Energy & Pwr, Hlth & Envir; Vet Affairs, Subcoms: Med Facilites & Benefits, Compensation, Pension, Ins & Meml Affairs, Ed, Tng & Employment; r/Epis; hon/Outstg Yng Man of Yr 1976, Brazos Co JCs; 1 of 5 Outstg Yng Texans 1977, Tex JCs; Author Sev Books & Monographs; Articles Pub'd in Am Ec Review, Jour of Money, Credit & Banking, & Jour of Ec Hist; Guest Editorials in Wall St Jour & National Observer.

GRAMS, IRVING JOHN II oc/Government Employee; b/Nov 4, 1948; h/Box 800, Hooks, TX 75561; ba/Texarkana, TX; m/Carolyn M; c/Dawn Marie, April Joanna; p/Irving John and Rose Marie Grams, Denison, TX; ed/AS 1970; BS 1979; MBA 1976; Dept Army Maintenance Mgmt 1974; mil/USAF; pa/Govt Mgmt in Govt Indust Opers; Entrepreneur, Owner Grams Enterprises & McMichael Trailer Park; cp/Alderman, City of Hooks 1977-79; Hooks C of C; Pres E Hooks PTA 1979-; r/Presb; hon/Suggestion Awd 1979; W/W 1980; Pres Lttr 1979.

GRANDISON, QUEENETTE FAYE oc/Records Clerk; b/Aug 21, 1950; h/Rt 1, Box 66-B, Surry, VA 23883; p/Walter Ray and Gracie Ester Grandison, Surry; ed/BA, AA; pa/Records Clk, Sta Records, VEPCO Surry Nuclear Power Sta, Surry; Phi Delta Kappa; Surry Power Sta First Aid Team; UEA Union at Work; Chrysler Mus at Norfolk; Former Mem NCTE; Cert'd Tchr English Grammar & Composition, Lit, Public Spkg; cp/Surry Co Bicent Com; NAACP; Voter Ed Proj; Notary Public, St-at-Large; Former Mem YWCA; Contbr to Va Bapt Chds Home; Vol Cystic Fibrosis Campaign; Public Spkr; Orgr Surry Co GSA; r/Mt Nebo Bapt Ch, Surry: Mem, Yth Com, Usher Bd, Ex-Dir Bd Public Relats; hon/Fellow, ABI; Notable Ams..

GRANT, HARRISON oc/Minister; b/Apr 28, 1917; h/Pinewood, SC; m/Louise Singleton; c/Fannie, Elaine, Martha, David, Dennie, Derrie; p/Julius (dec) and Pauline Grant (dec); ed/Att'd Morris Col Sch of Rel; mil/WWII 4 Yrs Sgt; pa/Pastor, Calvary Bapt Ch; Chm Exec Bd Black River Assn; cp/NAACP; r/Bapt.

GRANT, IKE oc/Instructor, Coach; b/May 22, 1953; h/812 N Long St, Opelika, AL; ba/Lafayette; p/William and Lillie Grant, Alexander City, AL; ed/BS; MA Ed; MA Saftey; pa/Dr Ed Instr & Hd Fball Coach, Lafayette HS; Coaching Assn; r/Meth; hon/Drafted by NY Jets 1976; Num Ath Awds.

GRANT, MONROE CLEVELAND oc/Pastor; b/Sept 20, 1930; h/1109 Maple Dr, Griffin, GA 30223; ba/Griffin, GA; m/Shirley Clarke; c/Robert Cecil; p/Monroe Grant; Evelyn Jordan; ed/BA; MDiv; pa/Pastor First Christian Ch (Disciples of Christ); cp/Rotary Clb.

GRANT, WILLIAM ALEXANDER JR oc/Mining Executive; b/Nov 7, 1918; h/Jasper, AL; m/Marion Bankhead; c/William A III, Blossom, Walter; p/William A (dec) and Louise Hooper Grant (dec); ed/BA Univ Richmond 1941; mil/USN WWII Aviator; pa/Fdr Bankhead Mining Co, Cobb Coal Co, Jefferson Coal Co, Bankhead Devel Co; Secy Crumpton Lands Inc; Pres Chattanooga Found Inc; Pres GMC Broadcasting Co Inc; Pres Taterland Broadcasting Inc; Secy Viking Oil Co; Dir Energy Inc; Secy Tri W Broadcasting Inc; cp/Past Dir Jasper C of C; Past Secy & Pres Jasper Rotary Clb; Nat Assn Accts; Past Pres Jasper JCs; Musgrove Country Clb; B'ham Downtown Clb; No River Yacht Clb; Bd Assocs Univ Richmond; r/Meth.

GRANTHAM, KELLY ROSE oc/College Student; b/Jan 8, 1961; h/3608 Patetown Rd, Goldsboro, NC 27530; p/James E and Mary Lou Grantham, Goldsboro, NC; ed/BS Cand; r/Free Will Bapt; hon/All-Conf Basketball 1975 & 76; Queen of Wayne Co Fair 1977; Sportsmanship Awd Tennis 1978; All-Conf Tennis 1979; Sr Rep on Homecoming Ct 1979; 1st Runner-Up Miss Aycock Pageant 1979; Acad S'ship Mt Olive Col 1980; Freshman Rep on Pickle Classic Ct, Mt Olive Col 1980; 1st Runner-Up

PERSONALITIES OF THE SOUTH

Miss Greenville/So Flue-Cured Tobacco Fest & Miss Congeniality 1980.

GRANTHAM, ROY EMERY oc/Oklahoma State Senator; b/Jan 26, 1907; h/325 S 12th St, Ponca City, OK 74601; m/Martha Elizabeth Young; c/Marcia Lea Courtney (Mrs Kenneth V), Linda Roy McNew (Mrs Thomas A); p/Amos Dean and Flora Lillian McCarty Grantham; ed/AB 1934, LLB 1934, EdM 1938 Univ Okla; mil/AUS 1/Lt to Lt Col 1942-47, ETO; pa/Co Atty, Kay Co, Okla 1941-42; Gen Pract of Law 1947-; Num Profl Assns; cp/Okla St Senator, Dist 20 1950-, Secy, St Sen Dem Caucus 1954, Presiding Ofcr, Okla St Senate, Sitting as Ct of Impeachmt 1965, Chm Com on Coms & Rules 1965 & Judiciary Com 1969-; Del All Dem Conv 1972; Alt Del, Dem Nat Conv 1968; Am Legion; ROA; C of C; Mason; r/Christian Ch NAm; hon/Commend Ribbon for Outstg Ser in Judge Adv Sect HQs, Berlin Command; Order of the Coif; Pub'd Author.

GRAVES, GARY WAYNE oc/Concert Pianist and Teacher; b/July 25, 1957; h/Centreville, MS; ba/1419 Esic #7, Edwardsville, IL 62025; p/Jame A and Mary K Graves, Centreville, MS; ed/BMus Univ So Miss 1979; MMus So Ill Univ 1981; Studied w Mr George Imbragulio & Miss Ruth Slenczynska; pa/Concert Appearances in S & Mid-W; Tch Piano Pvtly & at So Ill Univ; Organist First U Meth Ch Collinsville, Ill; cp/Alumni Mu Phi Epsilon; hon/Selected to Perf at Annual Awds Concert 1979, Univ So Miss; Guest Perf w Jackson, Miss Symph 1981; Outstg Mu Phi Epsilon Sr of Yr 1979.

GRAVES, JUNE oc/Fashion Coordinator, Personal Grooming Consultant; b/June 4, 1931; h/Hurst, TX; m/Lawrence B; c/Kirk, Lesa; p/Jennie Scott, Salina, KS; ed/Grad Patricia Stevens Modeling Sch 1950; Grad Sci of Pers Achmt; pa/Grooming Instr Flight Attendants, Am Airlines Learning Ctr, Ft Worth, Tex; Pres June's Fashions: Fashion Coor & Grooming Cnslt; Public Relats House of Esther; Grooming Instr & Chaperone for Miss Tex St & Local Pageants; Pageant Judge; cp/Hurst-Euless-Bedford C of C; r/Bapt.

GRAVES, THOMAS JAMES oc/Government Official; b/Apr 25, 1914; h/6015 Avon Dr, Bethesda, MD 20014; ba/Wash DC; m/Nan D; c/Thomas John, Barbara, Jill; p/Thomas James Graves (dec); Agnes Rodgers (dec); ed/BA; MA; PhD; pa/USNR WWII, Lt; pa/Govt Ofcl, Nat Endowmt for the Arts; Am Soc Public Adm; Govt Res Assn; cp/Former Staff Dir, US Sen Cte on Appropriations; White House Ofc Mgt & Budget; r/Christian.

GRAY, FREDERICK THOMAS oc/Attorney; State Senator; b/Oct 10, 1918; h/4701 Bermuda Hundred Rd, Chester, VA 23831; ba/Chesterfield, VA; m/Evelyn Helms Johnson; c/Frederick T Jr, Evelyn Cary G Skaltsounis; p/Franklin Pierce and Mary Gervase Pouder Gray (dec); ed/BA, LLB Univ Richmond; mil/USAAF WWII, 1/Lt, Navigator; pa/Atty Williams, Mullen, Christian, Pollard & Gray; Va St Bar Assn; Am Col Trial Lwyrs; Atty Gen Va 1961-62; cp/Mem Senate 1972-; Mem Ho of Dels 1966-71; Bd Dirs Va Meth Foun Inc; Past Pres: C'field Co Lions Clb, Meadowbrook CC, Jordan Point CC; Bd Trustees Randolph-Macon Col; Va Constitutional Conv 1956; Va Comm Constitutional Govt; Va Code Comm; So Bd Reg Ed; r/Meth; hon/JCs Man of Yr; Phi Beta Kappa.

GRAY, GWENDOLYN ELOIS WHITE oc/Assistant Professor; b/Oct 25, 1945; h/3241 Shoal Lake Dr, Lexington, KY 40503; ba/Keith, KY; m/William A; p/Oscar White, Richmond, KY; Lucy White (dec); ed/BS, MA En Ky Univ; pa/Asst Prof Rdg & Study Skills, Dept Lrng Skills, En Ky Univ; Jesse Stuart Chapt IRA; Phi Delta Kappa; r/Bapt; hon/Excell in Tchg Awd 1979-80; Assoc Editor *Resource-ery* An Annotated Bibliography for Interdisciplinary Academic Support Ctrs.

GRAY, HENRY BRAMLETTE III oc/Adjutant General, State of Alabama; b/Jan 29, 1929; h/Woodland Dr, Eufaula, AL 36027; ba/Montgomery, AL; m/Mary Adams; c/Henry IV, Dorothy, John; p/Henry Bramlette Jr and Dorothy Davis Gray (dec); ed/BS Yale Univ; BS Auburn Univ; Army War Col; mil/Ala NG, Maj Gen; pa/Past Pres Ala Cattlemen's Assn; cp/Past Gov Ala Dist Kiwanis Intl; r/Meth; hon/1969 Eufaula Citizen of Yr; Ala Cattleman of Yr 1971.

GRAY, JOHN CHARLES oc/Attorney at Law, Rancher; b/Apr 26, 1932; h/Gemini Springs Farm, Star Rt 1, DeBary, FL 32713; ba/Orlando, FL; m/Saundra Hagood; c/Terese, John, Lee; p/G Wayne (dec) and Mary A Gray, Winter Pk, FL; ed/BA 1955, LLB, JD 1958 Univ Fla; pa/Pres Gray, Adams, Harris & Robinson, PA, Attys at Law; Owner Gemini Springs Farm, Purebred Santa Gertrudis Cattle Ranch; Co Atty, Orange Co, Fla 1978-; City Solicitor, City of Orlando 1960-61; Chm Fla St Tpk Auth 1965-67; Fdg Dir Atty's Title Sers Inc (now Lwyrs Title Sers Inc); Fdg Dir & Gen Counsel, SE Nat Bank Orlando; Phi Alpha Delta; Am Bar Assn; Fla Bar; Pres Santa Gertrudis Breeders Intl, Former VP & Treas; Orange Co Bar Assn; St Assn Co Attys; Dir Nat Assn Co Civil Attys; Arbitrator, Am Arbitration Assn; cp/Chm Univ Ctrl Fla Pres's Coun of Advrs; Past Pres Univ Fla Alumni Assn of Ctrl Fla; Past Dir Orlando C of C; Comm on Future of Fla's Public Univs; Dir Intl Cultural Ctr; Past Pres Pi Kappa Alpha Alumni Assn; Past Dir Orlando C of C; Past Mem Fla Coun 100; Fdg Dir Fla Epilepsy Foun; Dir Univ Clb Orlando; r/Epis; hon/Univ Fla Hall of Fame; Fla Blue Key; Outstg Yng Men Am 1966-67; W/W: Am Law 1978-79, S&SW 1967; Prominent People in Fla Govt 1979.

GRAY, JONNIE E oc/Retired; b/July 10, 1901; h/146 N Hyland St, Scottsburg, IN 47170; m/Ben R (dec); c/Margaret Joyce, Mary Catherine; p/Peden B Haynes (dec); Margaret C McRae (dec); pa/Ret'd City Clerk, Longwood, Fla; cp/Pres Civic Leag; Chp U Fund; Pres PTA; Pres Home Demo Clb; Mem First Fla St Chorus; r/Bapt; hon/Dedicated Commun Ser Awd 1980; Jonnie Gray Day, First Bapt Ch, Longwood 1980.

GRAY, MINNIE DELL CROMWELL oc/Retired Teacher; b/June 13, 1912; h/1613 W 14th, Stillwater, OK 74074; m/Allen Delane; c/Allen Jr, James Cromwell, John Paul; p/Sheldon Winfield and Martha Jane Cromwell, Sulphur, OK; ed/BA; MA; pa/DAR; PEO; Delta Kappa Gamma; Eng Tchr of Fgn People; cp/VP Gamma Phi Beta Alumni; r/Meth; SS Tchr; hon/Tchr of Yr; Ed Awd from PTA; Pres Stillwater Ed Soc; Notable Am of Bicent Era; Commun Ldrs & Noteworthy Ams.

GRAY, ROBERT WARD oc/Director; b/Jun 26, 1916; h/17 Botany Ct, Asheville, NC 28805; ba/A'ville; m/Verdelle Connell; p/(dec); ed/Att'd Univ Fla, Tri-St Col; mil/USM WWII; pa/Dir So Highland Handicraft Guild; Dir Worchester Craft Guild Ctr 1951-61; Pottery Shop, Old Sturbridge Village 1949-51; Proj Engr Fla St Rd Dept 1946-47; Chm Com Coor'g New England Craft Sem Progs 1953-55; Past Secy New England Craft Coun; Mem NE Reg Jury, Syracuse, "Nat Ceramic Exhbn" 1956; Juror for St Craft Exhbns: Conn, NH, Pa, Mass, SC, Local Exhibits; Bd Dirs Handweavers Guild Am 1970; Others; Craft Cnslt: Small Bus Adm, US Dept Ed, US Dept Agri, Appalachian Reg Comm; Exhbn Aid Panel, Nat Endowmt for Arts 1976; cp/Former Mem Bd Dirs: A'ville Tourist Assn, A'ville C of C; Chm Craft Adv Bd, Mtn Empire Commun Col; Adv Bd Appalachian Consortium, Inc; Others; r/Meth; hon/W/W: Am Art, SE.

GRAYSON, JACOB HENRY oc/Businessman; b/May 16, 1916; h/Rt 5 Box 483, Hattiesburg, MS 39401; ba/H'burg; m/Mildred H; c/Donna G Ward, William E, Robert L, James R; p/William C (dec) and Lou Blakney Grayson (dec); pa/Self-Employed; cp/32° Mason; Odd Fellows; r/Bapt.

GREATHOUSE, GLADYS MILLARD oc/Professor Emeritus; b/May 22; h/114 E Main St, Wilnore, KY; p/Robert E; c/Richard F, June Dickinson; p/Richard Montgomery (dec) and June Millard (dec); ed/AB magna cum laude Asbury Col 1932; MEd Univ Ky 1943; Doct Study Univ Wis;p/Prof Speech & Drama; VP Ky Speech Assn; cp/Ladies Aux to Ky RCA; VP & Pres; Ladies Aux to Nat Rural Carries Assn; Pres Home & Garden Clb; DAR; OES; r/Meth; hon/Kappa Delta Pi; Pi Alpha Theta; W/W: Am Wom, Ed; Commun Ldrs Am.

GREEN, G CARL oc/Minister, Educator; b/July 1, 1918; h/1740 S St, Winston-Salem, NC 27107; ba/W-S; m/Martha Grace Sarber; c/Stephen Clark, Stanley Norris; (dec); p/Roy A and Bethona Clark Green (dec); ed/AB Samford Univ 1943; MA Bob Jones Univ 1944; pa/Prof Wake Forest Col Ext 1946-48; Prof & Chm Bible Dept, Tenn Temple Col 1950-63; Prof Piedmont Bible Col & Dean Piedmont Evening Sch, Winston-Salem 1970-; Pastor: Bapt Chs in Ala 1939-50, Ga 1950-63, SC 1963-64, Ga 1964-70; r/Bapt; hon/LLD, Tenn Temple 1958; DD Bob Jones Univ 1958.

GREEN, HUGH EDWARD JR oc/Attorney; b/Sept 28, 1950; h/Lebanon, TN; ba/Lowery Bldg, Public Square, Lebanon, TN 37087; m/Jan Butler; p/Hugh Edward Sr and Mildred Porter Green, Carthage, TN; ed/BS Univ Tenn 1973; MS Memphis St Univ 1975; JD Univ Tenn Col Law 1978; pa/Atty w Lowery & Green; Tenn Trial Lwyrs Assn; Tenn Bar Assn; Tenn Assn Criminal Defense Lwyrs; cp/Tenn Repub Party; Wilson Co Repub Party; r/Bapt.

GREEN, JAMES H oc/Farmer; b/Jan 4, 1898; h/Spring Hope, NC; m/Annie Bryant; c/Idalene Benson, Warren H, John Willis, Blua Jean Upchurch; p/James Rufus (dec) and Alvareta Edwards Green (dec); pa/Tobacco Farmer; Livestock Farmer; r/So Mission Bapt.

GREEN, JOE RALPH oc/Supervisor of Employment; b/Sept 18, 1932; h/Benton, KY; ba/Pennwalt Corp, Personnel Dept, PO Box 187, Calvert City, KY 42029; m/Pat D; c/Kelli Green Cornwell, Carla Green Ivey, Lea Allison; p/John A (dec) and Ada Green (dec); ed/BS Murray St Univ 1961; mil/USN; pa/Supvr Employment, Pennwalt Corp; Nat Mgmt Assn; r/Ch Grove U Meth Ch.

GREEN, JUDY F oc/Student Loan Director; b/Apr 29, 1941;h/2708 St, Little Rock, AR 72206; ba/Little Rock; m/Earnest; c/Richardo DuValle Washington, Billye Valese Washington, Tanya LaVette Washington; p/Thurman Lee Freeman (dec); Ann Lee Freeman Williams (dec); ed/BA;

PERSONALITIES OF THE SOUTH

mil/Ark ANG 1975-78 SP4; pa/Dir Nat Defense Student Loan, Philander Smith Col; r/St Andrew AME Ch.

GREEN, MARTHA GRACE oc/Professor, Department Chairman; b/July 25, 1919; h/1740 S St, Winston-Salem, NC 27107; ba/Winston-Salem; m/G Carl; c/Stephen Clark, Stanley Norris; ed/AB Samford Univ; MEd cum laude Univ Tenn-Chattanooga; pa/Prof Eng & Chm Speech Dept, Piedmont Bible Col 1970-; McEvoy Jr HS Eng Dept Chm 1965-70; Tchr Weir Elem Sch 1964-65; Greenville Jr HS 1963-64; Tenn Temple Schs, Speech Dept Chm 1950-63; Tenn Temple Elem Sch Prin 1951-57; Elmore Co Schs Mus 1948-50; Bob Jones Acad Hist Tchr 1943-44; Tchr Gibson Elem Sch 1942-43; Tallassee HS 1941-42; NEA; NCTE; Bibb Co Ed Assn; Ga Speech & Drama Assn; SCEA; Greenville Co Ed Assn; AEA; Jefferson Co Ed Assn; Edmore Co Ed Assn; Tallassee Ed Assn; Nat Debating Soc; Overseas Tour Grps Coor; cp/Drama Clb; Creative Writing; Intl Relats; Booklovers; Nat Debate; r/Bapt; hon/Winner Dramatic Rdrs Medal 1940; Original Oration Medal 1939; Govt Grant, NDEA Eng Inst, Univ Ga 1968; Contbr to Profl Pubs.

GREEN, ROBERT LEO oc/Shift Commander; b/June 26, 1941; h/PO Box 1194, Marshall, TX 75670; ba/Marshall; m/Sandra Kay; c/Elaine, Joe, Brenda, Michael; p/Mrs J C Green, Breckenridge, TX; ed/Att'd Tex A&M 1960-61, Kilgore Jr Col 1972, E Tex Bapt Col 1974; Panola Col 1976-79; Grad of Floydade Police Acad 1967; Basic, Intermediate & Adv'd Certs from Tex Comm on Law Enforcement Ofcr Standards of Ed; pa/Lt Shift Cmdr in Patrol Div, Marshall Police Dept 11 Yrs; Tex Parks & Wildlife Game Warden 1½ Yrs; Police Dept, Plainview, Tex 5½ Yrs; Marshall Police Ofcr Assn: Past Pres & VP, 8 Terms as Chm; Tex Police Ofcr Assn; Nat Police Marksman Assn; NRA; cp/Police Exploring Advr; Cub Scout Master; Master Mason; r/Ch of Christ; hon/Dist Awd Merit 1975; G O Cooper Awd 1975; Police Ofcr of Yr, Govt Affairs Com 1975; Police Ofcr Merit Awd for Public Ser, C of C 1979; Num Marksmanship Awds & Scouting Awds.

GREEN, RUTH GOSWICK oc/Retired Librarian and Teacher; b/Aug 30, 1916; h/3543 Ala Hwy SW, Rome, GA 30161; m/James E; c/Maryann Green Hupf; p/Marion A (dec) and Roxie Pearl Loughridge Goswick (dec); ed/BS West Ga Col 1959; Att'd Jacksonville St Col, Berry Col, Shorter Col, Univ Ga; pa/Tchr & Libn Coosa Sch 39+ Yrs; St Ga Ret'd Tchrs Assn; Alpha Delta Kappa, Alpha Xi Chapt; Charter Mem Kappa Kappa Iota Conclave; Past Mem: Mtl Htlh Assn, Floyd Co Tchr Assn, Ga Tchrs Assn, NEA; cp/Past Mem Rome LWV; Rome BPW, Parlimentn; r/Bapt; hon/Golden Eagle Awd 1971; Wom of Achmt 1979-80.

GREENE, MARIANNE oc/Coordinator; b/Oct 12, 1935; h/San Antonio, TX; c/Barbara, Andrea, Janette; p/Mathias (dec) and Johanna Finkler, Wertheim, Germany; ed/BA 1977, MS 1981 Univ Tex-San Antonio; pa/Coor Supportive Sers for Elderly, Dept Human Resources & Sers, City of San Antonio; Alamo Area on Aging Adv Bd; Recording Secy Incarnate Word Col, Sch of Nsg Adv Bd; Recording Secy, Hlth Inc Day Care Ctr for Elderly Adv Bd; cp/Bltn Editor AAUW; r/Epis Ch of the Holy Spirit; hon/Outstg Wom of Yr Awd, AAUW 1980; $500 S'ship Awd, AAUW 1979.

GREENE, RANDALL ALLAN oc/Unit Executive and Field Representative; b/Oct 16, 1953; h/1326 W Poplar St, Griffin, GA 30223; ba/Griffin; m/Ketina Dell Griswell; p/Bernard Joseph and Margaret Jane Greene, Hampton, GA; ed/BA Ga St Univ; r/Meth; hon/Alpha Kappa Delta.

GREENE, RAY JOSEPH oc/Advertising Executive; b/Feb 4, 1933; h/4701 Monroe, Hollywood, FL 33021; ba/Hialeah, FL; m/Carol Marie Meier; c/Tom, Tim, Terry, Cheryl, Kevin, Kerry, Kris, Jenny, James, John, Jeff, Darrin, Heather; p/Charles Estus and Anna Marie Pfieufauf Greene; ed/Sacred Heart Acad 1948-51; pa/Copy Boy, Retail Sales, Mgr Classified Advtg, Oreg Statesman 1951-53; Statesman and Jour 1953-66; Mgr Classified & Real Est Advtg Balto News-Am 1966-73; VP Newpaper Advtg Bur, NYC 1973-76; Pres Chief Exec Ofcr Classified Intl Advtg Sers Inc, 1976-; Pres Greene House of Printing 1977-; Assn Newspaper Classified Advtg Mgrs; Pacific NW Classified Advtg Mgrs, Pres 1954; Intl Newspaper Advtg Execs; Wn Classified Advtg Mgrs Assn, Dir 1968; cp/BSA 1956-66; Bd Dirs Exec Search Prog; K of C, Grand Knight 1961-63; r/Rom Cath; hon/Dist'd Ser Awd 1963; Author Double the Payoff of Your Real Estate Advertising 1974; Contbg Author to Real Est Manuals.

GREENE, RICHARD LARRY oc/State Senator; Attorney; h/1910 Birchwood Way, Macon, GA 31206; ba/Macon; m/Sheila Waters; c/Richard Russell; p/Bruce B and Vernita D Greene, Savannah, GA; ed/BS; JD; mil/AUS, 1/Lt Mil Intell; pa/Partner Law Firm of Berlin, Hodges & Greene; cp/St Senate, Dist 26; r/Bapt; hon/Am Legion Awd of Merit.

GREENTREE, ELEANOR M oc/Associate Professor; b/Aug 8, 1928; h/9208 Swiven Pl, Balto, MD 21237; ba/Balto; m/James L; p/Hazel Harrison, Balto; ed/BSN, MS, RN Univ Md; pa/Assoc Prof Nsg, Essex Commun Col; ANA; KNA; MNA; MLN; Univ Md Alumni; Nurses Alumni; cp/Am Cancer Soc; Md Heart Assn; hon/Phi Kappa Phi; Sigma Theta Tau; Phi Delta Gamma.

GREENWELL, LULA MAY SMITH oc/Retired Nurse; b/Aug 24, 1915; h/Box 333, Terrell, TX 75160; m/Lawrence A (dec); c/Diane Todd, Donna Mullins, Deborah Kirsner, Mindy Lovell, Nicki Otto, (Stepchd:) Sid, Helen Turledge, Anne Hargrove; p/Walter Julian (dec) and Ellen Bates Wilson Smith; ed/RN Scott & White Sch of Nsg; Att'd Univ Tex-Austin & UCLA; pa/RN; Hosp Nsg; Ofc & Indust Nsg; Dir & Instr Sch Voc Nsg 20 Yrs; ANA; Tex Leag Nsg; NLN; cp/Am Cancer Soc; Kaufman Co Heart Assn VP; r/Epis; hon/Lula May Greenweel Day; Collabr on Workbooks for Voc Nsg, Univ Tex; Contbns to Am Jour Nsg.

GREENWOOD, PAT MINTER oc/Executive; b/Oct 4, 1906; h/#3 Briarwood, Houston, TX 77019; ba/Houston; m/Isabelle; c/Jimmy M, Betty G Reese, Kay G Brown, Ann G Kolb, Bill; p/Elmore Patrick and Edna Minter Greenwood (dec); pa/Chm Exec Com Great So Corp; Past Chm Bd & Pres: Great So Corp, Great So Life Ins; Dir 1st City Nat Bk, Houston; Past Chm St Savs & Loan Assn, Salt Lake City, Utah; cp/Past Pres Salesmanship Clb Dallas; Past VP River Oaks CC; Past Dir Houston Horse Show Assn; r/Meth; hon/Best Sport Story of Yr, St of Mo.

GREER, PATRICIA FAY RYALS oc/Homemaker; b/Jan 24, 1947; h/Rt 2 Box 231B, McComb, MS 39648; m/Carroll S; c/Carroll Anthony, Travis Wendell; p/Ella Mae Ryals, Kosciusko, MS; r/Bapt.

GREER, WESLEY DWAINE oc/Administrator, Researcher, Artist; b/Nov 25, 1937; h/10068 Ellis Ave, Fountain Val, CA 92708; ba/Los Alamitos, CA; m/Beverley Jean; c/Todd Alexander, Kevin Anthony; p/Donald R and Gloria C Staples, Vancouver, BC, Can; ed/BEd, MEd Univ British Columbia; PhD Stanford; pa/Arts Ed Admr, Res, Artist, SWRL; Past Pres Calif Art Ed Assn; Bd Dirs LA Artists Equity; cp/Cultural Arts Com, City of Fountain Val; r/Presb; hon/Pub in Schlrly Jours & Books; Conslt to St & Nat Arts Ed Projs; One-Man Exhib 1978.

GREGG, ALICE JOAN oc/Teacher; b/Nov 15, 1937; h/Wagoner, OK; ba/Box 188, Okay, OK 74446; m/Donald L (dec); c/Paul Byrum, Carissa Dawn; p/Edwin (dec) and Rose Olson (dec); ed/BA Oberlin Col 1960; MS NEOSU; pa/Rec Ldr, Am Red Cross 1960; Wel Wkr, Ga St Dept Wel 1962-63; German-Eng Tchr 1975-; NEA; OEA; Wagoner Co OEA Pres; Okay OEA Chm of Profl Devel Com & Mem Negotiation Com; Pres Dist Eng Dept, Past Secy & VP; cp/Esther OES: Past Matron, Past Adah, Past Chaplain; Study Clb Unltd: Secy, Past Treas; Wednesday Night Bridge Clb; PTA; r/Meth: Trustee, SS Tchr; hon/Hon Bulldog of Wagoner Fball Team 1979; Tchr of Yr 1980.

GREGG, WILLIE RUTH oc/Executive Secretary and Credit Manager; b/Jan 18, 1946; h/4765 Meadow Ave NW, Cleveland, TN 37311; ba/C'land; m/Daryll Lee; c/Jamie Myles; p/John H (dec) and Jessie V Crumley, C'land, TN; ed/Cert'd Credit Exec 1978; pa/Cert'd Consumer Credit Exec, Bledsoe's Retail Clothing Store; Pres C'land Credit Wom Intl; 1st VP Tenn Credit Wom Intl; cp/Ladies Aux VFW; r/Bapt; hon/C'land Credit Wom of Yr 1977 & 79; Tenn Credit Wom of Yr 1979.

GREGORY, YVONNE BELMONT oc/Teacher, Concert Artist, Actress, Painter; b/Aug 7, 1919; h/300 Gateway Ln, Hopkinsville, KY 42240; ba/H'ville; m/Joseph E (dec); c/Joseph E II, Suzanne Gregory Keith, William Belmont; p/B L (dec) and Loraine Cobb Belmont (dec); ed/AA Univ Ky; BS, MS Austin Peay St Univ; Cand PhD Murray St Univ; pa/Art Tchr H'ville Mid Sch; Singer; St Hist of Ky Art Ed Assn; KAEA; cp/Pennyrile Players; H'ville Art Guild; Commun Chest; r/Cath; hon/Winner Gateway to Hollywood 1939; Alumni of Mo, Univ Ky; Hon Ky Col; Golden Key Awd, No Fulton HS.

GREGSON, THOMAS LARRY oc/Training Officer; b/Oct 1, 1942; h/411B S Porter, Stuttgart, AR 72150; ba/Stuttgart; p/Frank and Alice M Gregson, Little Rock, AR; mil/AUS 1961-70; pa/Trg Ofcr, Stuttgart Police Dept; cp/VFW; Am Legion; JCs; Cert'd EMT; r/Bapt.

GRESHAM, ROY MILTON JR oc/Minister of Youth and Music; b/Sept 17, 1945; h/902 Main St, Murray, KY 42071; ba/Murray, KY; m/Jacqueline Wolford; c/Jonathan Christian, Benjamin Royce, Steven Noel; p/Roy M and Dorothy Hendrick Gresham, Seymorn, IN; ed/BME Georgetown Col; MMus So Bapt Sem; pa/Ky Opera Soc; Choristers Guild Am; Ky Bapt Choral; Am Guild Organists; Am Soc Tchrs Mus; r/So Bapt.

GRIDER, SYLVIA ANN oc/Assistant Dean and Associate Professor; b/Oct 21, 1940; h/Bryan, TX; ba/Dept English, Tex A&M Univ, Col Sta, TX 77843; p/Mr and Mrs R C Grider, Pampa, TX; ed/BA 1963, MA 1967

126

PERSONALITIES OF THE SOUTH

Univ Tex-Austin; PhD Ind Univ 1976; pa/Asst Dean Grad Col, Assoc Prof Eng, Tex A&M Univ; Tex Folklore Soc: VP, Pres-Elect; Am Folklore Soc; Intl Soc Folk Narrative Res; Phi Kappa Phi; Delta Kappa Gamma; r/Prot; hon/Author Articles & Reviews on Folklore & Hist in Var Profl Jours, Anthologies & Textbooks.

GRIFFIN, BETTY DON oc/Teacher, Coach; b/Aug 28, 1947; h/Snyder, TX; ba/Snyder, TX; m/Merle; c/John, Jim Pat, Jay Don; p/Don and Betty Bruner, Sweetwater, TX; ed/BS Ed Tex Tech Univ 1969; pa/Sec'dy Eng & Hist Tchr, Girl's Volleyball, Basketball & Track Coach, Snyder Jr HS; TSTA; NEA; AAHPER; Tex Coaches Assn; r/Meth: UMW; hon/Coach of Yr 1970.

GRIFFIN, DANIEL WATSON oc/Museum Director; b/July 5, 1954; h/PO Box 5773, Meridian, MS 39301; ba/Same; p/Daniel Carner and Marguaritte Germany Griffin, Phila, MS; ed/BS Miss St Univ; pa/Dir Meridian Mus Art; Miss Mus Assn; Miss Art Assn; Tchr Art Classes Meridian Mus Art; cp/Meridian JCs; Meridian Little Theatre; r/Christian: Choir & Yth Work; hon/Outstg Sr; Beta Tau Chapt Kappa Alpha Order; Winner Var Art Awds Miss; Purchase Awd 1976; Awd of Merit, Red Hills Art Show 1978.

GRIFFIN, DOROTHY ROPER oc/Dean of Student Affairs; b/May 11, 1946; h/Augusta, GA; ba/1235 15th St, Augusta, GA 30910; c/Robert; p/Nathan and Sarah Roper, Grove Hill, AL; ed/BS 1968, MEd 1973 Tuskegee Inst; PhD Penn St Univ 1977; pa/Dean Student & Dir Cnslg Ctr, Paine Col; Title III Coor, Shaw Col; Cnslr Penn St Univ; Asst Dir Student Activs, Lincoln Univ; Am Assn Higher Ed; APGA; Am Col Pers Assn; Assn Non-White Concerns in Cnslg; AAUW; So Col Pers Assn; Nat Assn Student Pers Admrs; Inst Rational Emotive Therapy; r/Bapt; hon/Tuskegee Inst Gen S'ship 1964; Awd for Acad Achmt 1966-68; Dean's List 1965-68; Outstg Yng Wom Am 1980.

GRIFFIN, JAMES (JIM) ELBERT oc/Administrator; b/Nov 3, 1945; h/1204 Ninth Ave, Albany, GA 31707; c/James Wesley, Rhonda Carol; ed/BA La Bapt Col 1968; MPEAdm Univ Ctl Ark 1972; pa/Currently on Med Leave; Admr Dougherty Co Mtl Retard Tng Ctr, Albany Feb-Dec 1978; Job Voc Coor Bryant Public Sch Sys, Bryant, Ark 1977-78; Dir Civitan Ctr, Benton, Ark 1974-77; Resource Coor Ark Assn for Retard Citizens, Little Rock, Ark 1973-74; Ed & Tng Dept Supvr, Ark Chd's Colony, Conway, Ark 1968-73; Other Past Positions; Former Mem: Saline Co Assn for Retard Citizens, Am Assn on Mtl Deficiency, Day Care & Child Devel Coun of Am, Albany Assn for Retard Citizens; Former Assoc Mem Bd Dirs, Albany Assn for Retard Citizens; Coor 1st Invitational Bass Tournamt, Greers Ferry Lake (All proceeds assisted in devel'g facility for Mtly Retard of Cleburne Co) 1974; Coor 18 Co Reg Meeting on Sers for Mtly Retard, Walnut Ridge 1974; Conslt; Other Profl Activs; cp/Mem Dougherty Civitan Clb; Former Mem: Inter-Agy Coun Saline Co, Bd Dirs Benton Civitan Clb, Saline Co Hlth Coun; hon/Recipient S'ships; Civitan Clb Intl Media Awd for MR Preven 1977; Ark ARC Dir of Day Ser Ctr Awd; Hon Mention, Fitzhuggs Boggs Rec Awd, NARC; Nom for Outstg Yg Men Am.

GRIFFIN, JAMES OLIVER oc/Director of Volunteer Services; b/Aug 18, 1930; h/2721 Maceo Circle, Dallas, TX 75216; ba/Richardson, TX; m/Giley Nixon; c/Pamela Renee Mitchell, James Dale; p/John and Thelma Griffin, Greenville, TX; ed/BS 1952, MEd; mil/AUS 1952-54; pa/Dir Vol Sers, Richard Indep Sch Dist; Richardson Ed Assn; Tex Elem Prins & Supvrs Assn; Nat Assn Elem Prins & Supvrs; Dallas Co Admrs Assn; Nat Sch Vol Prog; Tex Sch Vol Assn Pres; cp/Phi Beta Sigma; Jarvis Alumni Assn (Past Nat Pres; Pres Nat Treas); r/Christian Ch; hon/Coach of Yr 1961; Life Mem Tex Cong PTA; Won St Fball Championship 1961; Dist'd Alumni Awd, Jarvis Christian Col 1978; Outstg Ldrship Awd, Nat Assn Equal Opport in Higher Ed 1979.

GRIFFIN, LARRY DON oc/Assistant Sales Manager; b/July 17, 1937; h/2481 W Bridge Pl, Marietta, GA 30062; ba/Atlanta, GA; m/Nancy May; c/John, Christine, Michael, David; p/Don and Martha Griffin, Marietta, GA; mil/ANG; pa/Engrg & Sales; So & SWn Railway Clb; Assoc AREA; Grad Am Mgmt Assn Profl Salesmanship; cp/Past Pres Fairoaks Ath Assn; Past Treas Osborne Ath Assn; r/Prot.

GRIFFIN, RODNEY LEVERETT oc/Manager; b/Nov 4, 1946; h/735 Stephanie Dr, Missouri City, TX 77489; ba/Houston; m/Jan Faye West; c/Elizabeth Ann, William Leverett, Omari Akil; p/William Lewis and Margaret Louise Griffin, Houston, TX; ed/BA Univ Tex 1970; Nat Cable TV Inst 1980; pa/Engr Cable & Telephone Consults; Nat Org Telecommuns Engrs & Scists; cp/Presiding Judge, Precinct 13, Fort Bend Co, Tex; Nat Clients Coun, Wash DC; Nat Consumer Law Ctr, Boston, Mass; r/Bapt; hon/Jesse H Jones S'ship 1965-69; Human Opports Corp Commun Ser Awd 1972.

GRIFFITH, THOMAS E oc/Chief of Police; b/Aug 17, 1953; h/500 S

Denny, Howe, TX 75059; ba/Howe; m/Marilyn E; c/Mike, Kristina, Jamisson, Jennifer, Juleen; p/Eddie and Betty Griffith, Hot Springs, AR; ed/Adv'd Trg w Certs in Field Law Enforcement; mil/Sgt Mil Police & Crim Invest; pa/Chief Police, Howe PD; Ctrl Tex Peace Ofcrs Assn; r/Jehovah's Witness; hon/Pres L B Johnson Funeral 1973; Num Mil Hons.

GRIFFITHS, MURIEL ANNE oc/Teacher; b/Apr 9, 1932; h/176 Ocean Terrace, Ormond Bch, FL 32074; ba/Holly Hill, FL; p/John L Jr and Mary Boyd Griffiths, Ormond Bch, FL; ed/BS Ed Ohio Univ; pa/Fla St Rdg Coun; Alpha Delta Kappa; NEA; FTP; VEA; r/Presb; hon/VP Fla St Rdg Coun; Right to Read Adv Coun, St Fla.

GRIGORY, MILDRED A oc/Executive; b/Jan 31, 1948; h/318 Swan Ridge Pl, Duncanville, TX; ba/Dallas; m/Larry David; p/Ruby C McGhee, Richmond, VA; ed/BA magna cum laude Col William & Mary; DHS Harvard Univ; pa/Pres, Cert'd Resources Corp 1979-; Dir Data Processing: Judd, Thomas, Beasley & Smith CPAs, Parish Murrel & Co CPAs, Best Prods Co; Pres's Adv Coun for Small Bus Reform 1979, 79, 81; Data Processing Mgmt Assn; Assn for Sys Mgmt; Data Processing Mgmt Assn; Intl Entrepreneurs Assn; EDP Auditors Assn; Am Film Inst; PBW; cp/Nat Hist Soc; Nat Trust for Hist Preserv; Smithsonian Assocs; Intl Platform Assn, Profl Public Spkr; C of C of USA; F'ship of Christian Aths, Nat Lectr; hon/W/W Am Wom; Oustg Wom of Yr in Am 1980; Wom of Yr 1973, 76, 78, Data Processing Mgmt Assn; Dist'd Am, ABI 1981; W/W World 1981; Great Personalities of S 1981; Dir Dist'd Ams; Author *Eagles Aren't Found in Flocks* 1979.

GRIGSBY, ROBERT LEE JR oc/College President; b/Jan 25, 1924; h/Rt 2 Box 344, Leesville, SC 29070; ba/Columbia, SC; m/Martha L; c/Robert L III; p/Robert Lee and Juell Gregory Grigsby; ed/Att'd Clemson Col 1941-43, Purdue Univ 1944; BS Clemson Univ 1947; MS NC St Col 1952; Att'd Union Col 1956; Gen Elect Co Mfg Trg Prog 1957-59; pa/Pres Midlands Tech Col 1974-; Exec Dir Midlands Tech Ed Ctr 1969-74; Dir Richland Tech Ed Ctr 1962-69; Mfg Supvr, Gen Elect Co, Irmo, SC 1956-62; Asst Prin, Irmo HS 1952-56; Asst Prin Gilbert HS, Gilbert, SC 1947-51; Am Coun on Ed; Am Soc Engrg Ed; Am Voc Assn; Lexington Co Bd Ed; SC St Employees Assn; SC Tech Col Pres Assn; SC Tech Ed Assn; So Assn Cols & Schs; Wardlaw Clb; cp/Org'd & Cmdr Am Legion Post 142; Org'd & Bd Dirs Ruritan Clb Gilbert; Past Pres Ruritan Clb Irmo; Past Pres Rotary Clb SC; Rotary Intl; SC Crippled Chd's Assn r/Meth; hon/40 & 8; Phi Kappa Phi; W/W: Meth Ch, S&SW, Am Cols & Univ Adm; Intl Notables; Personalities of S; Commun Ldrs of S; Dist'd Edrs Am.

GRIMES, ROBERT GERALD oc/Insurance Commissioner; b/Jan 29, 1941; h/1120 Larchmont Ln, Oklahoma City, OK 73116; ba/Okla City; m/Linda Jo; c/Amy Gretchen; p/Weldon and Lucille Grimes, Okla City; ed/BS Ctl St Univ; pa/Okla Ins Commr; Gov's Com on Employmt of Handicapped; Nat Assn Ins Commrs; Col of Ins, NY, NY; r/Prot.

GRIMM, BETTY J oc/Professor; b/Feb 8, 1920; h/2310 Don Andres, Tallahassee, FL 32306; ba/Tallahassee; p/W C and Leah Harris Grim, Huntington, WV; ed/BA, Prof Dip Opera Sch NYC; pa/Prof Mus Fla St Univ; Performer: Records, Films; cp/Dir FSU Wom's Glee Clb; Dir Ch Choirs; r/Meth; hon/Pi Kappa Lambda; SAI; Pub'd Voice Book.

GRISSOM, MAURICE WARREN oc/Clergyman; b/Aug 31, 1926; h/717 Fernwood Dr, PO Box 35, Clayton, NC 27520; ba/Clayton; m/Doris B; c/Charles Michael, Robert Fuller; p/Robert M (dec) and Nettie S Grissom (dec); ed/BA; BD; MDiv; DM; pa/Min First Bapt Ch Clayton; Writer; Col & Hosp Trustee; cp/Rotary; Mtl Hlth Bd; Mayor's Adv Coun; r/Bapt.

GRONOUSKI, JOHN AUSTIN oc/Professor; b/Oct 26, 1919; h/216 Bonnieview, Austin, TX 78704; ba/Austin; m/Mary Metz; c/Stacy G Jennings, Julie; p/John Austin Gronouski; Mary Riley Gronouski (dec); ed/PhD Univ Wis 1955; Hon Degs; mil/USAAC 1942-45, 1/Lt Navigator, 24 Combat Missions, ETO; pa/Lyndon B Johnson Sch of Public Affairs: Dean 1969-74, Prof Public Affairs & Ecs 1974-; Prof Ecs: Univ Main 1948-50, Wayne St Univ 1957-59; Wis Commr Taxation 1960-63; Exec Dir Wis Tax Study 1959-60; Postmaster Gen of US, Cabinet of Pres' Kennedy & Johnson 1963-65; Spec Master US Dist Ct En Dist Wis, Desegregation of Milwaukee Public Sch Sys 1976-; Ambassador to Poland & US Rep in Talks Between US & Communist China 1965-68; Chm Bd for Intl Broadcasting; Nat Acad Public Adm; Polist Inst Arts & Scis in Am Inc; Am Ec Assn; Nat Tax Assn, Tax Inst of Am; Other Profl Activs; cp/Former Mem Bd Trustees, Nat Urban Leag; r/Cath.

GRONWALD, VIOLA HILL oc/Cosmetologist, Artist; b/Dec 4, 1918; h/Rt 1, Redfield, AR 72132; m/Joseph Peter; c/Joseph Francis, Linda Kay; p/George W (dec) and Ethel B B Hill (dec); ed/Att'd Univ Ark; pa/Intlly Known Artist; cp/Commun Affairs; r/Bapt; hon/180 Awds from Art Shows; 100+ Flower Show Ribbons.

127

GRUBER, ELLEN JOAN oc/Professor, Marriage and Family Therapist; b/June 21; h/Atlanta, GA; ba/W Ga Col, Carrollton, GA 30118; m/Morton M; c/Lee, Lloyd, Lane; p/Henry and Mary Carlish, Santa Monica, CA; ed/BS 1958; MEd 1972; PhD 1974; JD 1979; pa/Prof, Sch Ed, Dept Early Childhood, W Ga Col; Marriage & Fam Therapist; APA; AAMT; ASCD; Bd Mem AHE; ACEI; hon/Author: *Creative Fun for Everyone; Learning Can Be Fun; Could I Speak to You About This Man, Piaget, A Minute?; Tell It Again: An Integrated Approach to Children's Literature.*

GUAJARDO, DERLY oc/High School Equivalency Program Director; b/May 30, 1945; h/Edinburg, TX; ba/1201 W Univ Dr, HS Equiv Prog, Emilia Hall Rm 207, Edinburg, TX 78539; m/Ofelia E; c/Debra; p/Jose Maria and Altagracia Guajardo, Laredo, TX; ed/BS 1972, MEd 1979 Pan Am Univ; mil/AUS 1965-68 Paratrooper; pa/Social Worker Tex Dept Human Resouces 1973; Coor Vets Cost of Instr Prog, Pan Am Univ 1975; Student Employment Coor Pan Am Univ 1979-80; Dir HS Equivalency Prog, Pan Am Univ 1980-; Pan Am Univ Alumni Assn; Nom Com for Bd Dirs San Antonio/Houston Vietnam Vets Civic Adv Coun, Pres 1979-80; cp/Hidalgo-Willacy Cos Plan'g Adc Coun 1975-79; Tex Assn Retard'd Citizens, Pres 1980; Am GI Forum, Chm 1979-80; Am GI Forum of Tex, Bd Dirs 1979-80; r/Cath; hon/Outstg Yng Man Am 1978; Co Hidalgo Cert of Apprec 1979.

GUDE, WILLIAM D oc/Supervisor Histopathology Laboratory; b/Feb 27, 1914; h/128 Pembroke Rd, Oak Ridge, TN 37830; ba/Oak Ridge; m/May Stebbins; c/Patricia L Creekmore, Katie L Dripps; p/William D (dec) and Mary C (dec); ed/AB Tulane Univ 1940; MS Univ Tenn 1952 & 1959; mil/WWII 1942-46; pa/Clin Lab Tech Hotel Dieu Hosp 1940-42; Hist Tech Tulane Univ Sch Med, Dept Anatomy 1946-48; Supvr Histopathol Lab, Biol Div, Oak Ridge Nat Lab 1948-; Assn SEn Biologists; Gerontological Soc; AAAS; NY Acad Scis; Tenn Acad Scis; Oak Ridge Unit Recording for Blind; r/Luth; hon/Author *Autoradiographic Techniques 1968; Histological Atlas of the Laboratory Mouse* In Press.

GUDNASON, HALLDOR VIKTOR oc/Physician; b/Jul 16, 1932; h/PO Box 450, Culpeper, VA 22701; m/Drofn Markusdottir; c/Haukur Markus, Ingi Valdimar, Gudbjorg Helga, Kristin Halldora; p/Gudni Krisjansson and Ingibjartardottir Gudnason, Reykjavik, Iceland; ed/MD; pa/Med Socs: Iceland, Am, Va, Md-DC; Anesthesiology Assns: Am, Va, Md-DC; Am Profl Pract Assn; r/Luth; hon/AMA Phys Recog Awd; Fellow, ABI; Biogl Listings.

GUELKER, NORA LEE oc/Farming; b/Oct 3, 1923; h/Rt 1 Box 525, Edinburg, TX 78539; m/Willie Fritz (dec); c/Gene, Lois Weaver, Ronnie, Willie Fritz Jr, Edward; p/Eddie (dec) and Selma Rust Hopmann (dec); r/Luth; hon/1st Pl Plaque Awd for Essay Written on Dist Ldrship Sch 1978-79.

GUENTHNER, LOUIS ROBERT JR oc/Attorney; Member House of Representatives; b/Aug 9, 1944; h/6103 Rodes Dr, Louisville, KY 40222; ba/L'ville; m/Betty Carol; c/Melissa, Louis Robert III; p/Louis R Sr and Gladys Guenthner, L'ville; ed/JD Univ L'ville; mil/AUS 1962-68, Lt Col; pa/Am, Ky, L'ville-Jefferson Co Bar Assns; Am Judic Soc; Former Mem Bd Dirs Am Trial Lwyrs Assn; Ky Trial Assn; Am Acad Polit Sci; cp/Kiwanis Intl; Bellarmine Alumni Assn; Univ L'ville Alumni Assn; Ky Hist Soc; Smithsonian Inst; Ky JCs; St Rep, 48th Dist: 1973, 74, 75, 76, 77, 78; Mem Num Coms; So & Nat Couns of St Legs; CoFdr Tri-Col Yg Repub; Del to Nat Repub Ldrship Conf, Wash DC; r/Cath; hon/Winner Senator Thurston Morton, Outstg Repub Awd; W/W: Am, S, St Govt.

GUERRANT, DORIS JEANNE oc/Psychologist; b/Sept 23, 1931; h/2415 S Jefferson St, Roanoke, VA 24014; ba/Roanoke; c/Priscilla Jeanne, Diane Nadine, Douglas Gordon, Margaret Anne; p/William Speer (dec); Matilda Eichhorn, Keyport, NJ; ed/BA Roanoke Col 1968; MS Radford Col 1972; pa/Psych; Am Psych Assn; Va Psych Assn, Chm Public Relats Com; r/Presb; hon/Grad cum laude Roanoke Col.

GUEST, RAYMOND RICHARD JR oc/Farmer; State Legislator; b/Sept 29, 1939; h/Rock Hill Farm, Front Royal, VA 22630; ba/Front Royal; c/Mary Elizabeth, Raymond Richard III; p/Raymond Guest Sr, King George, VA; Elizabeth Polk Guest, Wash DC; ed/BA Yale Univ; mil/USMCR; pa/Va Farm Bur; cp/Mem Va Ho of Dels; Va St Crime Comm; Front Royal Rotary; Am Legion; Izaak Walton Leag of Am; Ruritan; r/Epis.

GUETTNER, PATRICK DAVID oc/Engineer, Attorney; b/Mar 10, 1946; h/1710 Oak Hills Dr, Kingston, TN 37763; ba/Oak Ridge, TN; m/Devera; p/Frank and Mary Jane Guettner, Kingston, TN; ed/BS; JD; pa/Engr Union Carbide Corp; Atty; Phi Delta Phi; cp/Kingston JCs; Civil Air Patrol; hon/Most Outstg Bd Mem, Kingston JCs 1978-79

GUILLEN, WANDA VAUGHN oc/Records Administrator; b/Nov 3,

1935; h/3600 Keith St, Cleveland, TN 37311; ba/Chattanooga, TN; c/David, Kara, Kim; p/Bertha Hudson, Eton, Ga; ed/AS Dalton Jr Col 1973; Passed Am Med Record Nat Accred Exam 1973; BMS Emory Univ 1975; Passed Am Med Record Nat Exam for Med Record Amdrs 1975; pa/Intern Tri-Co Hosp, Ft Oglethorpe, Ga 1971 & Meml Hosp, Chattanooga, Tenn 1973; Hlth Record Analyst, Meml Hosp Chat 1973-75; Review Coor, Tenn Foun Med Care Inc 1975-77; Dir Med Records, Baroness Erlanger Hosp, T C Thompson Chd's Hosp, Willie E Miller Eye Ctr, Chat 1977-; Cnslt Tri-Co Hosp, Ft Oglethorpe 1975-; Cnslt Med Records, Dodson Ave Hlth Ctr, Chat 1977-; Cnslt Patient Info, Alton Park Hlth Ctr Chat 1977-; Clin Instr Emory Univ Sch Med, Div Allied Hlth Professions, Emory Univ Hosp 1977-; Clin Instr, Univ Ala-B'ham Med Ctr/Sch Allied Hlth; Clin Dir Chat St Technol Commun Col, Div Allied Hlth Professions, Chat; Am Med Record Assn; Tenn Med Record Assn; Chat Area Med Record Assn; Tenn Assn Review Coors; BPW; cp/Am Cancer Soc; Am Heart Assn; hon/Merit Awds Am Cancer Soc; Nat Recog for Outstg Work Am Heart Assn; Phi Theta Kappa; Adv Coun Dalton Jr Col; Cert for Serving As Clin Instr, Chat St Tech Commun Col 1979; Cert for Part in Multidisciplinary Audit Sem; Cert for Part in Prog on Hosp Accred Standards; Cert Pract Pharm, Chat St Tech Commun Col 1977; Cert for Completion of Principles in Supervision 1979.

GUMER, INDERPAL SINGH oc/Civil Cost-Estimating Engineer; b/Oct 17, 1942; h/5507 Edgebrook Forest, Houston, TX; ba/Houston; m/Manjit Kaur; c/Anjleen, Saminderpaul; p/Presm Singh and Harbans Kaur Gumer, Ludhiana, India; ed/Dip Civil Engr 1964; BS 1971; MS 1973; pa/Sr Cost Engr, Bechtel Power Corp; Reg'd Profl Engr, St Tex; cp/Secy Bechtel Toastmasters Clb 1980; hon/Student Gov Tenn Tech Univ 1970-71.

GUNKEL, FRANCES MARIE oc/Nurse, Public Relations Director, Inservice Director; b/Jan 11, 1952; h/1709 Beverly, Odessa, TX 79761; ba/Odessa; p/Jack Elvin and Ada Marin Gunkel, Odessa,TX; ed/Grad Odessa Col 1972; BS Univ Tex-Permian Basin 1973; BS W Tex St Univ 1975; pa/Odessa Wom & Chds Hosp: RN, Inservice Dir for Physicians & Employees, Infection Control Nurse, Public Relats Dir 1975-; Midland Meml Hosp 1972-73; Odessa Wom's & Chd's Charter Clb 1975- Odessa Wom's & Chd's Charter Candystripers Sponsor 1975-; Assn Infection Control Practrs 1975-; Tex Hosp Assn 1976-; Tex Soc Hosp Edrs 1976-; Tex Nurses Assn 1976-77; ANA 1976-77; Tex Perinatal Assn 1977-; Tex Soc Infection Control Practrs 1978-; Org'd: Mended Hearts Clb, Parents of High Risk Infant Clb, Candystripers, 4th Annual W Tex Perinatal Assn Wkshop; cp/Am Soc Trg & Devel 1975-77; Commun Ser Org 1977-; Am Diabetes Assn, Bd Dirs; Bd Dirs & Prog Task Chp Am Heart Assn; W Tex St Univ Alumni Assn 175-77; Am Red Cross Disaster Nurse 1975-; W Tex Blood Sers Com 1975-77; Candystriper Hosp Sponsor 976-; Shakespeare Fest Com Mem 1978-; Globe of Great SW Juliet Soc, Parliamentn 1981-82; Bd Govs Globe of Great SW 1980-81; Altrusa Clb Bd Dirs; HS Adv Com 1980-81; Am Bus Wom's Assn, Bulletin Com; Civic Concert Assn; Midland/Odessa Symph Guild; r/Luth; hon/Phi Theta Kappa, Eta Tau Chapt; Spec Recog for Being Yngest RN at Midland Meml Hosp 1972; Perfect Attendance Awd, Altrusa 1976-77, 1979-80; Cert of Apprec for Ser to Child Devel Prog Odessa Col 1977; Odessa Wom's & Chd's Hosp Booster of Yr 1977; Cit of Apprec Am Bus Wom's Assn 1978; Am Heart Assn Cert 1978; Odessa Wom's & Chd's Hosp Employee of Month Mar 1979; W/W S&SW; Nom'd Wom of Yr 1980; Nom'd Outstg Yng Wom Am 1980.

GUNN, DANNY E oc/Machinist; b/Feb 20, 1955; h/Sycamore St, Mortons Gap, KY; m/Cathy J; c/Bradley; p/Clyde and Hazel Gunn, Mortons Gap, KY; pa/Machinist, Ky Birmingham Bolts; cp/VP Mortons Gap JCs; r/Bapt; hon/JCs Awds: Unselfish Ser to Commun 1979, Recruitment Awd 1979, Outstg JC of Qtr 1979.

GUNN, GEORGE ROBERT oc/Director Crime Prevention Unit; b/Feb 3, 1949; h/Waverly, AL; ba/Auburn Police Dept, 141 N Ross St, Auburn, AL 36830; m/Beverly Dean; p/Emory Cable and Beatrice Gunn, Daleville, AL; ed/AS Entreprise St Jr Col 1973; BS magna cum laude Troy St Univ Montgomery 1978; mil/AUS 1967-71; ARNG; pa/Dir Crime Prev Unit, Detective Div, Dir Plan'g & Res, Dir Public Relats, Grantsmanship Admr, Auburn PD; FOP; Ala Peace Ofcrs Assn; Am Soc Indust Security; cp/VFW; r/Meth; hon/W/W Students Am Univ & Cols 1977-78; Gamma Beta Phi; Alpha Sigma Lambda; Ala Peace Ofcrs Assn Cert First Alternate for Ala Criminal Just Col 1978; Contbns to *Ala Peace Ofcrs Magazine, Ala Law Enforcement Ofcr Magazine, Opelika-Auburn News, Auburn Bulletin.*

GUNNELS, AUBREY ALONZO oc/Member US House of Representatives; b/Apr 20, 1918; h/7000 Aronow Dr, Falls Ch, VA 22042; ba/Wash DC; c/John Robert, Mary Louise G Baxter, James Andrews; p/S A Gunnels, Dallas, TX; Ada M Gunnels (dec); ed/AA Am Univ; mil/USMCR Col, Ret'd; pa/Staff Advr House Appropriations Com, US Ho of Reps; r/Prot; hon/Dunham-Devor Fellow, Am Univ.

GUNTER, AUBREY MURRAY oc/Restaurant Manager; b/Dec 31, 1938; h/1607 Merle Circle, Opelika, AL 36801; c/Cindy Annne, Sheri Denise, Charles Edward, Aubrey Murray Jr; p/Aubrey Milford and Mildred Jackson Gunter, Chattanooga, TN; ed/Att'd Univ Chat; mil/AUS; pa/Owner-Mgr Sonic Restaurant; cp/Welcome Wagon; C of C; K of C; Lions Clb; JCs; r/Cath; hon/Million Dollar Salesman 1978.

GUNTER, WILLIAM DAWSON JR oc/State Treasurer, Insurance Commissioner; b/Jul 16, 1934; h/3802 Leane Dr, Tallahassee, FL 32308; ba/Tallahassee; m/Teresa Arbaugh; c/Joel, Bart, Rachel; p/William Dawson Sr and Tillie Gunter, Orlando, FL; ed/BSA Univ Fla 1956; mil/AUS, Outstg Hon Grad of Basic Army Adm Course; pa/Sr VP Southland Equity Corp, Orlando, Fla; Pres Southland Capital Investors Inc, Orlando; cp/St Treas & Ins Commr, St of Fla 1976-; Mem US Cong 1972-74; St Senator 1966-72; Mem & Ofcr JCs; Ctl Fla Fair Assn; Orlando Area C of C; Orange Co Farm Bur; Sportsman's Assn; Kiwanis Clb; Masons; U Appeal; Others; r/Bapt Ch: SS Tchr, Deacon; hon/Elected as 1 of Fla's "Five Outstg Yg Men", St JCs; Univ Fla Hall of Fame; Fla Blue Key; 1972 St JC Good Govt Awd for Outstg Public Ser.

GUSTE, WILLIAM JOSEPH oc/Attorney General; b/May 26, 1922; h/4 Richmond Pl, New Orleans, LA 70115; ba/NO; m/Dorothy Schutten; c/William III, Bernard, Marie Louise, Melanie, Valerie, Althea, Elizabeth, James, Anne, John Jude (dec); p/William J Guste Sr (dec); Marie Louise Guste, NO; ed/AB; LLB; mil/AUS, Tech Sgt; pa/Atty Gen for St of La 1972-; Housing Auth of NO: Atty & Chief Counsel 1957-69, Assoc Coun 1947-57; cp/Position of Pres Held: Yg Men's Bus Clb, Metro Crime Comm, Cancer Assn Gtr New Orleans Inc, U Cancer Coun (Nat Pres), La Housing Coun, Assoc'd Cath Charities; Xavier Univ: Chm Bd Lay Regents, Bd Trustees; Bd Adrs Charity Hosp; Chm Bd Nat Housing Conf; Chm of Coun of Civic Clb Presidents; Brotherhood Week Spkr; Chm 1st Human Relats Com in La; Former Parennial Chm Annual Orphans' Christmas Tree Party, NO; Assoc'd Cath Charities: Bd Dirs, Pres; Former St Senator; Former Chm & Mem Juv Ct Adv Com; Orgr Monsignor Wynhoven Apts Inc; Orgr NO Metro Crime Comm; Mem Adv Com Gov's Comm on Law Enforcemt & the Adm of Justice; Nat Assn Attys Gen: Consumer Protection Com, Anti-Trust Com, Chm Offshore Resources & Revenue Sharing Com; Num Other Activs to Better Commun & St; r/Cath: Num Layman Activs; hon/Gautrelet Awd, Springhill Col; Named Housing Man of Yr 1976, Nat Assn Housing & Redevel Ofcls; Hon LLD, Loyola Univ; John F Kennedy Ldrship Awd, Yg Dems of La St Univ-NO;

Outstg Yg Man in NO, Nat JCs; Others.

GUTHRIE, SYLVIA EUGENE oc/Principal; b/Aug 19, 1945; h/The Villas, 12-F, Greenwood, SC; ba/Greenwood; p/Floyd Guthrie, Charlotte, NC; Bertha Guthrie, Burlington, NC; ed/BA Furman Univ 1967; MEd 1971, EdD 1979 Univ SC; pa/Prin Merrywood Elem, Greenwood 1980-; Prin McDonald Elem, Georgetown, SC 1978-80; Asst Prin, Leaphart Elem, Columbia, SC 1976-78; Tchr Leaphart Elem 1973-76; Tchr Seven Oaks Elem, Columbia 1967-73; Nat Assn Elem Sch Prins; Assn Elem & Mid Sch Prins VP; SC Assn Supervision & Curric Devel; Nat Assn Supervision & Curric Devel; Palmetto St Tchrs Assn; Phi Delta Kappa; r/Bapt; hon/Lexington Co Sch Dist Five's Tchr of Yr 1976; Co-Author *Planned Activities for Learning* 1975.

GUTOWSKI, EDWARD PAUL oc/Physician; b/Aug 3, 1943; h/Port Charlotte, FL; ba/350 Mary St, Punta Gorda, FL 33950; m/Lourdes; c/Edward Jr, Alexander; p/Franz Gutowski, Turomoari, NM; Anna Gutowski (dec); ed/BS Univ ND 1965; MD Harvard 1969; mil/USPHS 1970-72; pa/Bd Cert'd Fam Pract; Fellow Am Acad Fam Phys; Charlotte Co Med Soc, Pres 1980; Med Ctr Hosp Chief of Staff 1979-80; Air Med Examr FAA; cp/Repub Party; r/Cath; hon/Phys Recog Awd AMA.

GUTTMAN, HELENE N oc/Health Science Administrator; b/Jul 21, 1930; h/5306 Bradley Blvd, Bethesda, MD 20014; ba/Bethesda; p/Arthur and Mollie Nathan, Brooklyn, NY; ed/BA; AM; MA; PhD; pa/Hlth Sci Admr, Nat Heart, Lung & Blood Inst; Civil Ser Com, Am Acad Microbiol; Mem Edit Bds, J Am Med Woms Assn; Creative Wom Qtrly; Am Soc Cell Biol; Am Soc Biol Chem; Assn for Wom in Sci; Am Soc Microbiol; Fed Org Profl Wom; Fed Profl Soc; Reticuloendothelial Soc; hon/Silver Key Awd, Bklyn Col Student Govt; Sr Prize, Soc Biol & Med, Bklyn Col; Fellow Grad, Wom in Sci; Fellow, AAAS; Andelot Fellow in Med Scis, Harvard Med Sch; Fellow, Dazan Fdn Med Sci; Scholar Rutgers Univ; Thos Jefferson Murray Awd, Theobald Smith Soc; Pres' Fellow, Soc Am Bacteriologists; Spec Awd; Others.

GWALTNEY, MILDRED B oc/Assistant Professor; b/June 1, 1946; h/621 Cabell Dr, Apt 4, Bowling Green, KY 42101; ba/Bowling Green; ed/BA Longwood Col; MLS George Peabody Col; EdD Cand Univ Ky; pa/Asst Prof, Dept Lib Sci & Instrl Media, Wn Ky Univ; SE Lib Assn; Ky Lib Assn; r/Presb.

PERSONALITIES OF THE SOUTH

H

HAAS, MERRILL WILBUR oc/Geologist; b/Jul 9, 1910; h/10910 Wickwild, Houston, TX 77024; m/Marie Lara; c/Mariella, Merrill Wilbur Jr, Maria Cecilia, Frederick Harold; p/Frederick William and Ella Keller Haas (dec); ed/Att'd Univ Ks 1928-31; BA 1932 Univ of Mich; Postgrad Studies Harvard Univ; pa/Num Former Positions as Paleontologist & Geologist incl'g: Chief Geol, Exploration Mgr, VP, Dir: The Carter Oil Co, Tulsa, Okla 1950-60; VP for Exploration, Exxon USA 1960-75; Current: Petroleum Conslt; Chm Resvs & Prodn Capacity Com, Am Petroleum Inst 1971-73; Chm Manpower Com, Am Geol Inst 1967-69; Fellow Geol Soc of Am; Mem: Houston Geol Soc, Tulsa Geol Soc, Assn of Profl Geological Scists; Author Num Profl Articles; Spkr; Resch; Recruitmt & Ed of Geols; cp/Explorers Clb; Sigma Gamma Epsilon; Acacia; Mason; r/Meth Ch; hon/Erasmus Haworth Dist'd Alumni Awd 1961, Citation for Dist'd Ser 1966: Univ of Ks; Merrill W Haas Dist'd Visit'g Prof'ship Est'd in Hon, Univ of Ks; Fellow Mem ABI; Am Men of Sci; W/W: S&SW, Fin & Indust, World Oil & Gas, Am.

HABAL, MUTAZ B oc/Plastic Surgeon; b/Apr 27, 1938; h/Tampa, FL; m/Randa; c/Rula, M Bassam; p/M M and Rasia R Habal, Tampa, FL; ed/MD Am Univ Beirut 1964; Att'd St Univ NY 1968; PBBH Harvard Med Sch 1972; pa/Ret'd Prof & Chief Plastic Surg USF; Am Col Surgs; Royal Col Surg; Intl Col Surgs; c/Moslem; hon/Awds in Plastic Surg & Craniofacial Surg; Over 200 Articles Pub'd in Profl Jours.

HABERECHT, ROLF R oc/Company Vice President; b/June 4, 1929; h/10984 Crooked Creek Dr, Dallas, TX 75229; m/Ute; c/Michael Frank, Caroline Ann; p/Olga Heberecht, Germany; ed/PhD; MBA; MS; pa/VP Tex Instruments Inc; Electrochem Soc; r/Luth; hon/Bd Trustees St Marks Sch Tex; Beta Gamma Sigma.

HACKERMAN, NORMAN oc/College President; b/Mar 2, 1912; h/President's House, Rice Univ, Houston, TX 77001; ba/Houston; m/Gene Colbourn; c/Patricia, Stephen, Sally, Katherine; ed/AB 1932, PhD 1935 Johns Hopkins Univ; pa/Pres Rice Univ; Electrochemical Soc: Past Chm Corrosion Div, Past VP, Past Pres, Past Interim Editor *Electrochemical Technology*, Past Field Editor *Journal of Electrochemical Society*; Num Mbrships on Bds, Coms & Couns; Adv Edit Bd *Corrosion Science* 1965-; Chm Nat Sci Bd 1974-; Elected Mem: Nat Acad of Scis 1971, Am Philosophical Soc 1972; hon/Whitney Awd of Nat Assn of Corrosion Engrs; Joseph L Mattiello Awd; Palladium Medalist of Electrochem Soc; SW Reg Awd of Am Chem Soc; Recip Am Inst of Chems Gold Medal 1978; Num Hon Socs; Author & Co-author 170+ Pubs.

HACKNEY, (FRANCIS) SHELDON oc/University President; b/Dec 5, 1933; h/2 Audubon Pl, New Orleans, LA 70118; ba/New Orleans; m/Lucy Judkins Durr; c/Virginia Foster, Sheldon Fain, Elizabeth Morris; p/Cecil Fain and Elizabeth Morris Hackney, Birmingham, AL 35213; ed/BA 1955 Vanderbilt Univ; MA 1963 Yale Univ; PhD 1966; mil/USN to Lt 1956-61; pa/Princeton Univ: Instr in Hist 1965-66, Asst Prof 1966-69, Assoc Prof 1969-72, Prof of Am Hist 1972-75, Provost 1972-75; Tulane Univ: Prof of Hist 1975-, Pres 1975-; cp/Bd Dirs Am Coun on Ed; Mem: Carnegie Foun for the Advancemt of Teaching, Intl House, YMCA, Ednl Testing Ser; hon/Albert J Beveridge Prize, Am Histl Assn; Charles S Sydnor Prize, So Histl Assn: 1970, for *Populism to Progressivism in Alabama* 1969.

HACKNEY, HOWARD SMITH oc/Farmer, County Executive Director; b/May 20, 1910; h/2003 Inwood Rd, Wilmington, OH 45177; ba/Wilmington; m/Lucille Morrow; c/Albert M, Roderick Allen, Katherine Ann Becker; p/Volcah Mann and Gusta Anna Smith Hackney (dec); ed/BS cum laude Wilmington Col; pa/Co Exec Dir ASCS; Mem: NASCOE, St Nat Duroc Swine & Southdown Sheep Assn; Ohio NASCOE Leg Conslt; r/Quaker; hon/Chi Beta Phi Sci Awd; Ohio St & Midwest Area NASCOE Awds for Ser to Agric; Num Awds for Duroc Swine & Southdown Sheep; Wilmington Col Agric Adv Coun; Commun Action Coun; Regional Plan'g Comm.

HADDON, JOHN HERBERT oc/Veterinarian; b/Feb 6, 1942; h/245 Florence St, Aiken, SC 29801; ba/Aiken; p/Herbert Deacon and Phylis Mary Haddon, Devon, England; ed/BVM; pa/Vet; Secy S African Equine Practrs 1970-71; r/Meth.

HADLEY, JIMMY R oc/Mud Engineer; b/Aug 1, 1950; h/PO Box 1262, Seminole, OK 74868; p/Emerson (dec) and Letha Hadley, Holdenville, OK; ed/Att'd Altus Jr Col & Seminole Jr Col; mil/USAF 1971-73; pa/Tchr Mud Engrg Seminole Jr Col; Owner Seminole Mud Engrg Supplies; cp/Mem at Large Seminole Elks Clb; r/Bapt; hon/Author Drilling Fluids Manual.

HADSEL, FRED LATIMER oc/Research Foundation Director; b/Mar 11, 1916; h/306 Letcher Ave, Lexington, VA 24450; ba/Lexington; m/Winifred Nelson; c/Christine, Winifred R, Jane L; p/Fred L Sr and Mary Perine Hadsel (dec); ed/AB Miami Univ; MA Clarke Univ; PhD Chgo Univ; mil/AUS 1942-46, Ret'd as Maj; pa/Dir, George C Marshall Res Foun 1974-; Former Ambassador 1969-74; Fgn Ser Ofcr, US Govt 1946-74; r/Christian; hon/Hon DDS Miami Univ 1977; Superior Ser, St Dept.

HAGEDORN, JUDY W oc/Psychologist; Author; Lecturer; ba/2626 East 21st St, Suite 6, Tulsa, OK 74114; ed/Doctorate, Univ of Okla; pa/Co-host "Psychologists Corner" TV Show; Other TV Appearances; Lectr, Tchr: Cols & Univs in US; Mem: Am Psychol Assn, Tusla Psychol Assn (Past Pres), Am Assn for Sex Edrs, Cnslrs & Therapists; Co-author: *GEMINI: The Psychology and Phenomena of Twins* 1974; *The Use of Post-Hypnotic Suggestions for Recall & Amnesia to Facilitate Retention & to Produce Forgetting for Previously Learned Materials in a Classroom Situation*; Others Forthcoming; cp/Bd Dirs March of Dimes; Mem: Am Wom in Radio & TV, NOW, OK-ERA; hon/w Sister: Outstg Yg Wom of Okla, Outstg Yg Wom of Am, Dist'd Alumnae Awd, Univ of Tulsa, Fellow Intl Soc for Twin Studies; Past Pres Intl Twins Assn; DIB; Commun Ldrs & Noteworthy Ams; Outstg Yg Wom of Am; Intl W/W in Commun Ser; W/W: Am, Am Wom, S&SW, Am Cols & Univs.

HAHN, ALAN THEODORE oc/Senior Programmer Analyst; b/Nov 18, 1950; h/3119 Hiss Ave, Balto, MD 21234; ba/Balto; m/Maureen; p/Donald Hahn, S Amboy, NJ; Helen Hahn (dec); ed/BS magna cum laude St Mary's 1972; MBA Loyola Col 1979; pa/Assn Exec MBAs; Ec Advr to Chris Smith, Cand to House of Rep from NJ; US Olympic Soc; cp/K of C; Nat Capital Hist Soc; CYO Basketball Dir; r/Cath; hon/W/W: Am Univs & Cols, Indust & Fin; Phi Alpha Theta; Alpha Sigma Nu.

HAHN, LORENA GRACE oc/Nurse; b/Apr 16, 1914; h/2431 Sichel St #207, Los Angeles, CA 90031; p/Albert Hicks Barnes (dec); Myrtle Mae Bingham (dec); ed/RN; CCRN; pa/Supvg Nurse, LA Co, Univ So Calif Med Ctr; Critical Care Nurse White Meml Med Ctr; cp/PTA; Sr Citizens; Commun Affairs; Wesleyan Oriental Missionary Soc; r/Salvation Army; hon/Nat Hon Soc; 35 Yr Ser Awd LAC USC Med Ctr; Dedicated Ser Awd White Memel Med Ctr; Outstg Employee Awd 1965; Cert Hon LAC USC Med Ctr 1979.

HAHON, NICHOLAS oc/Research Virologist; b/Mar 24, 1924; h/1375 Headlee Ave, Morgantown, WV 26505; ba/Morgantown; m/Katheryn E; c/Nicolette Kay; p/Samuel A and Catherine Hahon (dec); ed/BS cum laude David & Elkins Col 1948; ScM Johns Hopkins Sch Public Hlth & Hygiene 1950; mil/AUS 1943-46, Bronze Star Medal; USNR, MSC, Lt 1952-58; pa/Lab Instr Med Bact, Johns Hopkins Med Sch 1950; Microbiologist, Dept Army, Ft Detrick, Md 1951-68; Chief Aerobiology Br, Dept Army, Ft Detrick 1968-71; Lab Dir USPHS, ALFORD, Morgantown 1971-; Instr Microbiol & Asst Prof Pediatrics, WVa Univ Sch Med 1971-; Conslt: WHO, US Civil Ser Exam Bd for Microbiol; Profl Orgs; cp/North Hills Civic Assn; hon/Scientific Res Soc of Am Awd; AUS Cert of Achmt; Kellogg Scholar, Johns Hopkins Univ; Tech Writing Awd 1977; Biogl Listings.

HAIRE, CAROL DIANE oc/Professor, Consultant, Pathologist; b/June 24, 1949; h/4810 Stonehedge Rd, Abilene, TX 79606; ba/Abilene; p/Lloyd Frederick and Martha Vera Haire, Muleshoe, TX; ed/BA Tex Tech Univ 1970; MA N Tex St Univ 1971; EdD Tex Tech Univ 1976; pa/Speech Pathol, Cooke Co, Tex Public Schs 1972; Speech Pathol, Muleshoe Tex Public Schs 1973-74; Pt-time Instr Col of Ed, Tex Tech Univ 1974-76; Asst Prof & Clin Supvr, Communicative Disorders Ctr, Howard Payne Univ 1976-77; Dir Speech Pathol & Audiology, Hardin-Simmons Univ 1977-; Conslt Speech-Language Pathol & Ednl Diagnostician, W Tex Rehab Ctr 1977-; Speech-Lang Pathol Diagnostician, W Ctrl Tex Homes Hlth Agcy 1980-; Big Country Speech & Hearing Assn, Pres 1979-80; Tex Speech-Lang-Hearing Assn; Am Speech-Lang-Hearing Assn; Am Soc Allied Hlth Professions; Phi Delta Kappa; Coun Exceptl Chd; Div For Chd w Commun Disorders of Coun for Exceptl Chd; Hardin-Simmons Univ Gen Fac & Fac Assem Ofcr, Secy 1980-81; r/Bapt; hon/Phi Kappa Phi; W/W S&SW; Author: "Speech, Language and Hearing Therapy Materials" 1975 & "Effects of an Inservice Education Model for Supportive Personnel on Factors Regarding Exceptional Children" 1976.

HAIRRELL, WILLIAM BLAGOVEST oc/Manager; b/Mar 6, 1939; h/1821 Crestwood Rd, Athens, TN 37303; ba/Athens; m/Bonnie Hatfield; c/English Hatfield, Elizabeth Nicole; p/William Dewey (dec) and Gertrude Karaivanoff Hairrell (dec); ed/BS Ga Tech 1964; pa/Mgr Taylor Implement Div, Pgh Forgings Co; c/Co Coun McMinn Co Tenn; Bd Mem Athens Area C of C; Kiwanis Clb; Pres Adv Coun, Tenn Wesleyan Col; Past Pres & Fund Dr Chm U Fund of McMinn Co; r/Meth.

PERSONALITIES OF THE SOUTH

HAIRSTON, IRENE JEANETTE oc/Teacher; b/July 28, 1950; h/Gen Del, Squire, WV 24884; ba/Berwind, WV; p/Timothy Logan (dec); Viola Hairston, Berwind, WV; ed/BS Ed, Eng, Home Ec; mil/Pershingette Mil Drill Team; pa/Home Ec Tchr; PTA; WVEA; CEA; cp/Alpha Kappa Alpha; Sister's Clb; Berwind Angels Softball Team; r/Rose of Sharon Bapt Ch.

HALBERT, JEAN F oc/Instructor; b/Aug 3, 1924; h/1614 Bell Ave, Columbus, MS 39701; ba/Columbus; m/Thomas Ira; pa/Voc Rehab Instr.

HALE, JAMES RAY oc/Office Manager; b/Oct 31, 1939; h/Elk City, OK; ba/Box 927, Elk City, OK; m/Billie Jean; c/Jeffrey, Jeana, Joy; p/Ernest C and Beatrice Hale, Guymon, OK; ed/BS Panhandle St Col 1964; pa/Job Ser, St of Okla 13 Yrs; NE PTO Pres; cp/Kiwanis Clb: Secy, Pres; r/Ch of Christ: Dir Mus.

HALE, NORMAN FISHER oc/Teacher; b/Dec 25, 1939; h/2125 Moss, Searcy, AR 72143; ba/Searcy; m/Mary Lou; c/Gerri, Norman, Judy; p/M T and Ruth Hale, Newport, AR; ed/Att'd Harding Col 1958-60; BS 1966, MS 1969 Ark St Univ; Further Study Ark St Univ; pa/Grocery Clerk 1961-62; Milk Route Salesman 1962; Natural Gas Compressor Sta Maintenance 1962-64; Monument Sales & Engraving 1964-66; Voc Agric Tchr, McCrory HS 1966-70; Prin, McCrory Elem Sch 1970-73; Asst Prin,Thomas Jefferson Elem Sch 1973-75; Prin R E Baker Inter Sch 1975-77; Sci & Bible Tchr, Harding Acad 1979-80; FFA Advr; VATA; AVATA; AEA; NEA: AAES; NEASP; Pres McCrory Ed Assn; Rep AEA Gen Assem; NW Ark Zone Dir AAESP; Grp Dis Ldr NAESP Nat Conv; Chm NCA Steering Com, Thomas Jefferson Elem; NCA Reviewing Com, Chgo; NCA Study Team, McCrory; Parlimentn PTA; cp/Kiwanis: 1st & 2nd VP; Bicent Com Mem; Charter Mem Bentonville Mus Assn; Mayor's Comm on Deciency; 4-H Ldr, Benton Co; r/Ch of Christ.

HALEY, GLADYS MURPHY oc/Retired High School Teacher; b/Aug 12, 1910; h/607 East College, Homer, LA; m/Forney Chleo; c/Benjamin Paschal, Robert Edward, Elizabeth Gertrude; p/Paschal E and Gertrude Saxon Murphy (dec); ed/BA 1930 Hendrix Col; Grad Studies: Univ of Ark, La St Univ, La Tech Univ, La Tech Rome (Italy), Am Univ; pa/HS English & History Tchr: Junction City, Mount Holly, El Dorado (Ark), Summerfield, Homer (La); Pres Claiborne Parish Tchrs Assn; Mem: AAUW, Exec Coun 4th Dist Classroom Tchrs Assn, Delta Kappa Gamma; cp/DAR: Chapt Regent, V Regent, Chaplain, Nat Def Chm, Indian Schs Chm; Am Legion Aux: Pres at Unit, Dist, St Levels; Nat Exec Com-wom; Org'd Homer's 1st Sidewalk Art Show; N La Hist Assn; Others; r/Homer U Meth Ch: Mem, SS Tchr, Lay Spkr, Lay Reader; Charter Mem Wom's Soc of Christian Ser; Charter Mem U Meth Wom; Participant: World Conf, Buck Hills, Pa, Christian Crusade Conf, Salisbury, Rhodesia; hon/Freedoms Foundation Tchr Awd; Red Cross Citation; Nat Leg Medal; Nat Americanism Plaque of Am Legion for Ed; Articles Pub'd in *Claiborne Sketches*; Fellow Mem ABI; DIB; Commun Ldrs & Noteworthy Ams; World W/W of Wom.

HALEY, JESS LEE oc/TV News Director; b/Nov 3, 1938; h/4800 Parktowne Way, Montgomery, AL 36116; ba/Montgomery; m/Heather Burns; c/Pegeen Mike; p/Jess L Jr and Preston Kimbrough Haley, Clarksdale, MS; ed/BA Univ Ala 1963; mil/USAF 1956-60; pa/TV New Dir, WSFA-TV; Former Mem, Bd Dirs Ga Assn Newscasters; Commercial Pielot; RTNDA; r/Bapt; on/SDX Excell in Jour; Emmy-News Prodr; Emmy-Edl Writing; UPI Outstg News Opr; UPI Outstg Edl.

HALL, ANTHONY WILLIAM JR oc/Texas State Representative; b/Sept 16, 1944; h/3709 Rio Vista, Houston, TX 77021; ba/Houston; m/Carolyn Middleton; c/Ursula Antoinette, Anthony William III; p/Anthony William Hall Sr (dec); Quintanna Wilson Allniece, Houston, TX; ed/BA Howard Univ 1967; mil/AUS 1967-71, Capt; pa/Current Dir Hlth Testing Prog, So Tex Laborers Dist Coun; Asst to Harris Co Commr 1971-72; cp/Tex St Rep 1973-; Mem St Dem Exec Com 1972-; Bd Mgrs S Ctl Br YMCA; Past VP Harris Co Coun of Orgs; Houston BPM: Past VP, Bd Dirs, Pres; Adv Com to Bd Dirs Eliza Johnson Ctr for Aging; Del: 1971 St & Nat Dem Convs; r/Gtr Zion Bapt Ch: Mem; New Mt Carmel Bapt Ch: Mem; hon/Black Achiever Awd, S Ctl Br YMCA; Cotton Hook of Yr, ILA Local 872; Purple Heart; 3 Bronze Stars; Air Medal Meritorious Ser Medal; Other Mil Decorations; Kappa Alpha Psi; Biogl Listings incl'g: DIB; Men of Achmt; Notable Ams; W/W: Tex, Am Polits, Govt.

HALL, BEN HUMBLE oc/United States Government, Retired; Writer; h/402 Knox St, Huntington, TN 38344; ba/Huntington; c/Vivian Therese Inman (Mrs), Ben Humble II; pa/Former Ofcl & Admr in Intelligence Work w Ofc of Strategic Ser, Mil Intelligence Ser, CIA, Exec Ofcr & Security Ofcr for US Info Agcy, Attache for Adm & Security at Embassies for St Dept; Currently: Reporter-Writer; Asst Advertising Mgr, Grocery Chain; Public Relats & Pers Dir, Md Co Govt; cp/Mem Town Coun; Past Pres, Past Public Relats Ofcr, Carroll Co Chapt Cancer Soc; Pres Co Chapt Am Assn Retired Persons 1978; Past Legislative Rep, 3 Co Chapt

Nat Assn of Retired Fed Employees; Co-Chm McKenzie-Huntington Airport Com; Mem Co Comm on Aging; Past US Govt Advr; Ex-officio Mem Am Sch Bds: Monrovia, Liberia, Accra, Ghana, W Africa; r/Mem Ch of Christ; hon/Commends US Civil Ser Comm 1944; Meritorious Hon Awd, US Dept of St 1966; Lttrs of Commend: late VP Hubert Humphrey, Am Assn Sch Admrs; Dir's Ser Awd, Huntington C of C 1976; Others.

HALL, CELIE oc/Assistant Professor; b/May 4, 1940; h/313 Hillcrest Ave, Baton Rouge, LA 70807; ba/Baton Rouge; c/Ronald Dexter, Byron Dwayne; p/Octavia Williams, Greensburg, LA; ed/BA 1958, MEd 1961 So Univ; Further Study: La St Univ, Univ Mich; EdD Univ Houston 1977; Further Study So Univ & SEn Univ; pa/Asst Prof, Col of Ed, So Univ Lab Sch 1977-80; Asst Prof Univ Houston 1974-77; Asst Prof So Univ Lab Sch 1966-67; Elem Tchr 1962-68; Jr HS Tchr 1958-61; LEA; So Univ Alumni; Univ Houston Alumni; Phi Delta Kappa; NEA; IRA; hon/Leg S'ship; Most Outstg FHA; Multicultural F'ship.

HALL, CHARLES WORTH LEO oc/Educator; b/Dec 18, 1946; h/Box 4036 So Sta USM, Hattiesburg, MS 39401; m/Diane Lee Olson; c/Charlotte Ann; p/Worth Leroy Hall; Gertrude Omega Greenwell; ed/AA Hartnell Col 1975; BS Univ So Miss 1976; Postgrad Study SD St Univ 1977; MEd Univ Louisville 1979; Postgrad Study Univ Louisville 1980; mil/AUS; p/Cnslr; Instr Human Relats, Data Processing, Career Assessment, Employment Orientation; Admissions Ofcr, Fin Aid Cnslr, Asst Dir Student Sers, Ivy Tech Col, SCtrl, Sellersburg, IN 1979-; Chm, Pres Pers Sers Co Inc, Jackson, MS 1976-; Fdr, Pres, Dir New Horizons Devel Co, Louisville 1978-; Am Soc Pers Admrs; Am Col Pers Assn; APGA; Nat Assn Student Pers Admr; Ind Assn Col Registrars & Admissions Ofcrs; Ind Assn Col Admissions Cnslrs; Ind PGA: Public Relats Ofcr SE Chapt 1980-81, Pres Elect SE Chapt 1981-82; So Assn Student Pers Admr; Ky PGA; Col Pers Assn Ky; Ind Tchrs Lic; Data Processing Mgmt Assn; Am Mktg Assn; cp/Voters Registration Com 1974-75; Del Forrest Co Dem Conv 1975; Chm Pinecrest Conservative Precinct Caucus 1975; Pres Yng Dems Univ So Miss 1975-76; Dist Commr Monterey Bay Coun BSA 1971-72; Asst Dir Commr Pine Burr Coun 1972-75; Beauvoir Devel Foun; Am Mensa Soc; Kadets of Am/Intl; CAP; Sons Conf Vets; Mil Order Stars & Bars; Confed Meml Lit Soc; Res Ofcrs Conf Alliance; Confed Alliance: Col Adj Ofcrs Corps 1980-, Col Dpty Dir Spec Opers 1980-, Conductor, Order Battleflag ROCA 1980-; Friends of Confed Soc; Nat Eagle Scout Assn; Am Legion; VFW; Alpha Phi Omega; Notary Public Hinds Co, Miss 1976-80; Notary Public At Large, Ky 1980-84; Nat Rifle Assn; r/Roman Cath; hon/Decorated Vietnam Cross of Gallantry 1971; Army Commend Medal w Oakleaf Cluster 1973; Army Res Achmt Medal 1976; Mil Ser Medal 1974; Mil Ser Cross 1978; Recip Eagle Scout Awd 1963; Commr's Tng Key 1969; Dist'd Ser Key 1976; Dist'd Recruiting Cup 1977; Hon Ky Col 1979; Phi Delta Kappa 1979; Phi Kappa Phi 1976; Omicron Delta Kappa 1976; Pi Gamma Mu 1975; Delta Tau Kappa 1980; Epsilon Delta Chi 1975; Order Battleflag ROCA: Comdr Class 1980, Knight Class 1980; Dixie Clb Gold Medal 1975.

HALL, KENNETH KELLER oc/United States Circuit Judge; b/Feb 24, 1918; h/2025 Quarrier St E, Charleston, WV 25311; ba/Charleston; m/Gerry Tabor; c/Kenneth K Jr; p/Jack Hall (dec); Ruby G Hopkins, Charleston, WV; ed/JD WVa Univ, Morgantown; mil/USNR 1942-45; pa/US Circuit Judge, US Ct of Appeals, 4th Circuit; cp/Past Dist Gov; Rotary Intl; r/Bapt; hon/Silver Beaver Awd, BSA 1962.

HALL, MICHAEL T oc/Chaplain, US Navy; b/Sept 9, 1951; h/Ofc of Chaplain, USCG Support Ctr, Elizabeth City, NC 27909; m/Regina Kaye; p/James Lester and Nelma Taylor Hall, Benoit, MS; ed/AA Wood Jr Col 1971; BS Delta St Col 1973; MDiv SWn Bapt Theol Sem 1976; Further Study US Naval War Col 1976; mil/Chaplain Corps, Lt; pa/Pastor Kent Bapt Ch & Shoals Bapt Ch 1978-80; US Naval Inst; cp/Elizabeth City Min Assn; r/So Bapt; hon/Eagle Scout; Contbr to *All Hands* 1977; Chaplaincy 1979.

HALL, ROBERT EVANS oc/US Army Drill Sergeant; b/May 31, 1947; h/2 Pratt St, Fort Monroe, VA 23651; ba/Fort Monroe; m/Carolyn c/Apra, Rea Anne; p/Pittman Hall, Gaffney, SC; mil/AUS 1968- Drill Sgt; r/So Bapt; hon/Sgt Morales Clb; Drill Sgt of Yr 1979-80.

HALL, SAMUEL JONATHAN IV oc/News Director, Anchorman; b/Feb 18, 1947; h/140 Camelot, 2222 W Main St, Dothan, AL 36301; ba/Dothan; p/Samuel J Hall III, Ashford, AL; Mary Egbert Hall (dec); ed/BS Troy St Univ; mil/Ala NG; pa/News Dir-Anchorman WDHN-TV; Soc of Profl Jours; Sigma Delta Chi; cp/Elks Clb; Sigma Chi; r/Presb; hon/Sigma Delta Chi Recog for Invest Reporting.

HALL, SUE HAMMACK oc/Bank Assistant Vice President; b/June 25, 1937; h/124 Holly Dr, Statesboro, GA 30458; ba/Statesboro; m/J Leonard; c/Kim Sylvester, James L Jr; p/Mrs H E Hammack, Cochran, GA; ed/ABA Middle Ga Col 1956; pa/Ofc Mgr, Ga Elect Mbrship Corp; Asst Ed "Rural Ga" (St REA Mag); Asst VP Island Bank 1968-; Charter

131

Pres Lotts Creek Charter Chapt ABWA; Nat Assn Bank Wom; Am Inst Bkg; Ga Bankers Assn; Woms Conf Com of Ga Bankers Assn; r/Meth; hon/Inner Circle.

HALL, THOMAS FRANCIS JR oc/Plant Studies; b/Jan 21, 1913; h/PO Box 68, Sheffield, AL 35660; m/Louise Tabor; c/Frances Ann Hurt; Robert Lee (dec); p/Thomas Francis (dec) and Lea Mandot Hall (dec); ed/BS 1935, MS 1938 Tulane Univ; PhD Cornell Univ 1948; pa/Ret'd Botanist TVA; NY Acad Sci; Weed Sci Soc Am; St Pres Ala Wildflower Soc; cp/Sheffield Kiwanis Clb VP; r/Epis; hon/Plaque for Spearhdg Fund Raising of $50,000 for Nature Ctr for Chd of NW Ala 1979; Co Ldrship Awd 1978; Kiwanis Plaque 1979-80; Author *Aquatic Plant Control in Pest Control Research* 1961; Var Articles on Swamp Forests 1939-46.

HALL, VIC oc/Associate Justice; b/Feb 4, 1926; h/300 Rainbow, Waco, TX 76710; ba/Waco; m/Bettye Joyce Sheridan; c/Lisa Jo, Brian Sheridan, Keith Arnett, Nancy Edith; p/Arnett D Hall Sr (dec); Mrs Arnett D Hall Sr, San Angelo, TX; ed/JD 1953 Baylor Univ; mil/USNR 1944-46 Pacific Theatre; pa/Assoc Justice 10th Dist Ct of Civil Appeals of Tex; Mem: St Bar of Tex, Waco-McLennan Co Bar Assn, Am Judicature Soc; cp/Salvation Army Adv Bd; r/Prot (Bapt); hon/Silver Beaver Awd, BSA.

HALL, WILLIAM CLIFTON oc/Instructor; b/Nov 6, 1954; h/2410 Botanical Dr, Killeen, TX 16541; m/Patricia; c/Cody; p/Mr and Mrs A J Hall, Belton, TX; ed/BS Tex A&M Univ 1977; pa/Voc Agric Instr; Tex Voc Agric Tchr Assn; Tex Voc Tech Assn; Killeen Jr Livestock Show Assn; cp/Killeen C of C; r/Bapt; hon/W/W Am HS Students 1972, 73; Lone Star Farmer Deg FFA 1973; Am Farmer Deg FFA 1975; Star Am Farmer FFA Area 8, 2nd in St Tex 1975; Var Champships in Showing Breeding Cattle, Market Steers, Burrows & Lambs; Beef Showmanship Awds 1970-74; Mem Jr & Sr Meats Judging Team & Livestock Judging Team Tex A&M; Outstg Public Relats Awd, Killeen C of C 1973; Ctlr Tex Col Agric S'ship 1073; Moormans Agric S'ship 1973; Tex Angus S'ship 1973; Dist'd Student Tex A&M 1977; Champion Ham Trimmer & Champ Beef Showman 1976.

HALL, WILLIAM STONE oc/Administrative Psychiatry; b/May 1, 1915; h/1427 Summerville Ave, Columbia, SC 29201; ba/Columbia; m/Oxena Elizabeth Gunter; c/William Stone Jr, Carol Lynn, Richard Furman; p/Henry F Sr and Mary Gantt Hall (dec); ed/MD Med Univ SC 1937, Dist'd Alumnae Awd 1974; Addit Studies; mil/AUS 1942-46 Maj, Chief Neuropsych Sects, Army Hosps; pa/St Commr SC Dept Mtl Hlth 1963-; Assoc Examr Cert Mtl Hosp Admrs 1962-; Clin Prof Psychi, Med Univ SC 1957-; Prof Psychi Univ SC Sch Med 1976-; Former Supt Num Hosps; Other Past Positions: Pres Assn Med Supts Mtl Hosps; Nat Inst Mtl Hlth, Conslt Nat Adv Mtl Hlth Coun 1972-; Remotivation Tech Org, Adv Bd 1972-; Am Bd Neurol & Psych, Diplomate Psych 1974-; Jt Comm Accred of Hosps 1973-; Tchg Conslt, Wm S Hall Psych Inst 1964-; Gov's SC Couns: Hlth & Social Devel Policy & Plan'g 1974-; St-wide Hlth Coor'g 1976-; Chm: Coor Coun SC Comm on Aging, F'ship Nom Com SC Dist Br Am Psychi Assn; Past Pres SE Soc Neurol & Psych; Nat Asn St Mtl Hlth Prog Dirs: Past Pres & VP; Num Other Profl Assns; cp/Pres SC St Employees Assn; UF Bd Dirs; Bd Trustees U Communn Fund; Others; SC Gov Legis Com St Employees & Their Employmt 1973-; hon/Fellow Am Col Psychs; Dist'd Ser Awd SC Hosp Assn; Awd for Meritorious Ser, Nat Assn Med; Dist'd Public Ser Awd, Am Legion; Wm S Hall Psych Inst, Columbia, Named in his Hon; SC Hall of Fame 1975; Num Biogl Listings.

HALLADAY, DANIEL WHITNEY oc/University System Chancellor; b/Oct 13, 1920; h/14224 Playa del Rey 9-D, Corpus Christi, TX 78418; ba/Corpus Christi; m/Cherie Longeway; c/Steven Owings, Whitney Sue H Whitelaw (Mrs Ernest); p/Harlow Monroe and Marion Winans Halladay (dec); ed/BA Pomona Col 1942; MA Claremont Grad Sch 1947; EdD Columbia Uiv 1955; mil/AUS Inf 1942-46 Capt, Maj 1951-53; pa/Pres: Tex A&I Univ, Corpus Christi 1972-, E Tex St Univ 1966-72; Other Past Positions; Bd Dirs Am Assn of St Cols & Univs; Past Pres: Coun of Pres of St Sr Cols, SW Assn of Student Pers Admrs; Other Profl Assns; cp/Bd Dirs: Corpus Christi Area Conv & Tourist Bur, E Tex C of C; Chm Sulphur River Mun Water Dist Bd; Others; r/Meth Ch: Mem; hon/Silver Star; Bronze Star w 2 OLCs; Commend Medal; Purple Heart w OLC; Combat Inf-man's Badge; Num Biogl Listings.

HALLINAN, LINDA D oc/Psychiatric Nurse; b/Aug 13, 1951; h/Sumter, SC; ba/Tuomey Hosp, 16-18 W Calhoun St, Sumter, SC 29150; m/John Dennis; c/Shawn Evan; p/Evelyn H Sniecinski, Sumter, SC; ed/BSN Med Univ SC, Col of Nsg 1972; MSN Cand Univ SC; pa/Staff Nurse Charleston VA Hosp 1972-73; Staff Nurse Tampa VA Hosp 1973-76; Nurse III Home Hlth Sers, Santee-Wateree Mtl Hlth Ctr 1976-77; Hd Nurse Psychi Unit, Tuomey Hosp 1977-; Adv Bd Visiting Nurse Assn, Ctrl SC; Bd Sumter Co Mtl Hlth Assn; Problems/Activs Com, Quality Assurance Prog, Tuomey Hosp; r/Bapt; hon/Personalities of S; Newspaper Article.

HALLION, RICHARD PAUL JR oc/Museum Curator; Adjunct

Professor; b/May 17, 1948; h/1003 Montrose Ave, Laurel, MD 20810; ba/Washington, DC; p/Richard P Sr and Marie E FLynn Hallion, Laurel, MD; ed/BA 1970 Univ of Md; PhD 1975 Univ of Md; pa/Curator Nat Air & Space Mus, Smithsonian Institution; Adjunct Prof Univ of Md; Mem: Am Inst of Aeronautics & Astronautics, Soc for Hist of Technology, Am Astronautical Soc, US Naval Inst; cp/Fac Rep Univ of Md; r/Rom Cath; hon/Phi Alpha Theta; Phi Kappa Phi; Pi Sigma Alpha; AIAA Hist Manuscript Awd; Daniel & Florence Guggenheim Fellow.

HALLMAN, GRADY LAMAR oc/Physician, Cardiovascular Surgeon; b/Oct 25, 1930; h/3443 Inwood, Houston, TX 77091; ba/Houston; m/Martha Suit; c/Daniel Suit, David Lamar, Charles Harlow; p/Grady Lamar Hallman (dec); Mildred Kennedy Hallman, Tyler, TX; ed/BA w Hons 1950; MD w Hons 1954; mil/USAMC, Capt; pa/Chm Cardiovas Disease Records Screening Com, St Lukes Epis & Tex Chds Hosps; VChm Cardiovas Surg Com of Am Col Chest Physicians; Mem: Coun on Cardiovas Surg, Am Heart Assn; Pres Am Heart Assn, Houston Chapt; Mem: Adv Com Congenital Heart Prog, Crippled Chds Sers; Num Profl Assns; cp/Patron Houston Friends of Music; Bd Dirs Houston Symph Orch; Supporter of all Houston Arts; Repub Party; r/Epis; hon/Phi Beta Kappa; Alpha Omega Alpha.

HALPERIN, SANFORD B oc/Professor; b/July 14, 1923; h/26 Lakeview Dr, Monroe, LA 71203; ba/Monroe; m/Joan L; c/Jack L, Jill H Roberts (Mrs Timothy C); p/Clement J Halperin (dec); Bertie V Hollander; ed/BS NYU 1947; MA Univ Penn 1948; PhD Mich St Univ 1972; mil/AUS 1943-46; USAR 1942-43, 1946-78 Ret'd Col; pa/Tchg Fellow & Instr, St Univ of NY at Buffalo 1948-50; Ins Agt, Asst Mgr Brokerage Supvr, Ed & Tng Conslt 1950-66; Asst Prof & Assoc Prof Ins & Bus Adm, Ferris St Col 1966-74; Prof Ins, NE La Univ 1974-; Exec Dir NE La Ed Foun; Am Soc CLU; Soc CPCU; cp/Nat Defense Exec Reservist, Fed Emer Mgmt Assn; Bd Trustees Little Theatre of Monroe 1975-78, Chm 1977-78; Scabbard & Blade: Dist Advr 1975-, Dpty Nat Coor 1981-; r/Hebrew-Unitarian-Eclectic; hon/W/W S&SW 1980-81; Outstg Edr Am 1974; Bronze Star; Merit Ser Medal; Purple Heart; Combat Infantry Badge; Co-Author: *Study of Industrial Linkages in Monroe, La* 1976; Author of Articles in Profl Jours Incl'g *Journal of Risk & Insurance, CLU Journal, Physician's Management.*

HALPIN, GLENNELLE oc/University Professor; b/Nov 12, 1939; h/112 Norwood Ave, Auburn, AL 36830; ba/Auburn; m/Gerald; c/Mike, Mark; p/Henry and Ruby McCollum, Lineville, AL; ed/BS; MA; PhD; pa/Am Psychological Assn; Am Ednl Res Assn; Nat Coun on Measuremt in Ed; Nat Soc for the Study of Ed; cp/Phi Beta Kappa; Phi Kappa Phi; r/Meth: Coun on Worship, Grace Ch; hon/W/W in Am Cols & Univs; Outstg Yg Wom of Am; Fellow Mem ABI.

HALVERSTADT, DONALD BRUCE oc/Surgeon; b/Jul 6, 1934; h/2932 Lamp Post Lane, Oklahoma City, OK 73120; ba/Oklahoma City; m/Margaret; c/Donna, Jeffrey, Amy; p/Lauren Oscar Halverstadt (dec); Lillian Frances Halverstadt, San Diego, CA; ed/BA magna cum laude Princeton Univ; MD cum laude Harvard Med Sch; mil/Chief of Surgery, USPHS Indian Hosp, Shiprock, NM, Hon Disch; pa/Clin Prof Urology Okla Univ Col of Med; Okla Chds Meml Hosp, Okla City: Chief Pediatric Urology Ser, Chief of Staff; Pvt Pract Urology, Okla City; cp/Okla City C of C; Com of 100, Okla City; r/Presb; hon/"The Best Med Sers & Specialists in the US" *Town & Country* Mag, Feb 1978; Am Bd of Urology 1970; Physicians Recog Awd, AMA 1969, 72, 77; "Who Are The Best Doctors in Am".

HAM, ROBERT ELLIS oc/Division Manager; b/Mar 7, 1940; h/2596 Rocky Springs Dr, Marietta, GA 30066; ba/Norcross, GA; m/Goldie Smith; c/Jeffrey Mark, John Michael; p/Cleon Audley (dec) and Lucille Eva Smith Ham (dec); ed/Mech Engrg Deg Intl Corresp Schs 1971; mil/Va NG 1962; pa/Div Mgr, Proj Mgmt/Proj Devel, EDS Nuclear Inc; ASME; r/Meth; hon/Outstg Freshman, Va Tech 1959.

HAMBLETON, BERNIECE CAMPBELL oc/Nurse, Operating Room Supervisor; b/Feb 9, 1926; h/360 N Second, E Soda Springs, Idaho 83276; ba/W Soda Springs; m/Clarence Earl Jr; c/Juliana Marie, Clarence Earl III; p/Clarence Henry Campbell (dec); Nellie Marie Stubblefield, Texarkana, AR; ed/Dip Warner Brown Sch Nsg; pa/RN; OR Supvr Caribou Meml Hosp; Assn OR Nurses; ANA; INA; cp/Repub Party; r/Bapt; hon/W/W Am Wom.

HAMER, BRENDA JOYCE oc/Administrator; Facilities Management; b/Sept 23, 1945; h/2170 Kessler Ct, Dallas, TX 75208; ba/Dallas; p/Alexander Sr and Bernice Davis Hamer, Washington, DC; ed/BA Hist w Hons; JD; pa/Dallas Indep Sch Dist: Admr of Facilities Mgmt, Asst Sch Atty, Staff Counsel to Real Est Adv Com, Purchasing Com, East Oak Cliff Adv Com; Former Positions incl: Spec Asst to Asst Secy, US Dept of Housing & Urban Devel, Washington, DC, White House Assoc Gen Coun, Presl Clemency Bd, Washington; Past Chapt Pres Delta Sigma Theta;

Mem: Phi Alpha theta, Dallas Sch Admrs Assn; cp/Former Mem Bd Dirs Dallas Fam Guid Ctr; BPW, Dallas; Mem Senator John Tower's Fin Com, Dallas; 1st VP Oak Cliff Repub Wom's Clb; Mem, ex-officio, St Repub Exec Com; r/Meth; hon/1st Place Winner, Am Bar Assn 6th Circuit Moot Ct Competition; Outstg Oral Advocate, Appellate Ct Competition, 6th Circuit Ct; Recip Kennedy Book Awd for Outstg Legal Writing.

HAMILTON, ROBERT oc/Pastor, Truck Driver; b/July 10, 1936; h/1467 Merlin Ave, Memphis, TN; m/Betty; c/Cathy Coleman, Robin Johnson, Regina, Pamela, Robert Jr, Norman; p/Mr and Mrs Jacob Hamilton Sr, Byhalia, MS; pa/Truck Driver, Red Ball Truck Line; Pastor & Evangelist, Ch of God in Christ; cp/NAACP; r/Pentecostal.

HAMMER, MICHAEL WALLACE oc/Store Manager; b/Sept 29, 1953; h/Oakmont Manor Apt 1-A, Vicksburg, MS 39180; ba/V'burg; m/Dora Faye; c/Joshua Michael; p/Henry Howard Jr and Nita Gay Hammer; ed/HS Grad w Hons; pa/Bus Mgmt & Acct; cp/US JCs: Chm Sev Coms; r/U Meth; hon/Miss Jr & Sr Bowling Leag: 1st Pl St Champ'ship Singles 1971, 6th Pl 1972, 1st Pl Doubles Category 1969; Many Other Bowling Awds; Scholastic Awd, Pearl HS 1971: "I Dare You" Awd, Pearl HS 1971.

HAMMERSCHMIDT, JOHN PAUL oc/Representative to Congress; b/May 4, 1922; h/Harrison, AR 72601; ba/Washington, DC; m/Virginia Sharp; c/John Arthur; p/Arthur P Hammerschmidt (dec); Junie Taylor Hammerschmidt, Harrison, AR; ed/Att'd: The Citadel, Okla St Univ, Univ of Ark; mil/USAAC Pilot w 3rd Combat Cargo Group, China-India-Burma Theatre 1942; pa/Chm of Bd, Hammerschmidt Lumber Co, Harrison; Mem: Ark Lumber Dealers (Past Pres), SWn Lumberman's Assn, Ks City (Past Pres), Nat Lumber & Bldg Material Dealers (Past Nat Dir); cp/Elected US Rep, 3rd Dist Ark; Coms: Public Works & Transport, Ec Devel Sub-Com, Aviation Sub-Com, Water Resources Sub-Com, Vet's Affairs, Aging, Housing & Consumer Affairs Sub-Com; Harrison City Planning Comm (Former Chm); Harrison City Coun; Elks; Am Legion; VFW; Mason; Scimitar Shrine; Future Farmers of Am Alumni Assn (Hon Mem); r/Presb: Ordained Elder, Deacon; hon/Mil: Air Medal w 4 Oak Leaf Clusters; Dist'd Flying Cross w 3 Oak Leaf Clusters; 3 Battle Stars.

HAMMOND, JACK ARNOLD oc/Mill Manager; b/Jan 29, 1938; h/Valley Ridge, Covington, VA 24426; ba/Covington; m/Mitzi; c/Tamyra Jo, Jack Arnold II, Ross Alan; p/Wendell B and Maude Hammond, Monroe, OH; ed/BChem Engrg Ohio St Univ; mil/AUS Air Def, Ft Bliss, Tex; pa/Mill Mgr, Westvaco Corp; Mem: Am Mgmt Assn, Nat TAPPI, Va-Carolina TAPPI, Va Mfrs Assn; cp/Former Mem Bd Dirs Gtr Alleghany C of C; Past Pres Alleghany CC; Mem Hot Springs-Covington Rotary Clb; r/Prot; hon/Co-Holder Westvaco Semichemical Pulping Process Patent; Boss of Yr, Covington Chapt NSA 1976.

HAMMOND, WILLIAM JACKIE oc/Physician; b/Nov 24, 1947; h/Rt 2, Box 181, Fitzgerald, GA 31750; ba/Fitzgerald; m/Jan R; c/Heather Rae; p/Jack and Carolyn Shackelford Hammond, Abbeville, GA; ed/BA; MS; BS; MD; pa/Am Acad Fam Phys; r/Bapt; hon/Nat Sci Foun S'ship.

HAMPTON, BESSIE YVONNE HENSLEY oc/Educational Diagnostician, Special Education Supervisor; b/Oct 12, 1945; h/Mt Pleasant, TX; m/Gerald E; c/Scott Anthony, Sheri Renee, Robert Charles, Jeremy Roy; p/Roy Vaughan and Eva Mae Hensley, Mt Pleasant, TX; ed/Att'd Scottish Rite Lang Sch, Summer 1967; BS 1966, MA 1969 E Tex St Univ; pa/Elem Tchr; Jr HS Choir Tchr; Ednl Diagnostician & Spec Ed Suprvr; Tex St Tchrs Assn/NEA Del to Nat Conv 1980; NE Tex Assn of Ednl Diagnosticians, Org'g Pres; Assn for Chd w Lrng Disabilities; Assn for Retard'd Chd; Tex Assn Ednl Diagnosticians; Tex Assn Supvrs & Curric Dirs; Choristers Guild; cp/Jr Regent Martha Laird Chapt DAR; Titus Co Gospel Mus Assn; Euterpean Clb, Yrbook Com 1981; Commun Concert Assn; St Andrew UMC: Choir Dir, Organist, Chd's Choir Dir; OES #305; r/U Meth; hon/Valedictorian w S'ship 1963; Nom'd for Awd to Wom for Dist'd Ser; Nom'd Outstg Jr Mem Martha Laird Chapt 1980 & Outstg Jr Regent 1981.

HAMPTON, CAROL CUSSEN McDONALD oc/Historian; b/Sept 18, 1935; m/James Wilburn; c/Jaime Jennifer, Clayton Christopher, Diana Elizabeth, Neal McDonald; p/Denzil Vincent McDonald; Mildred Juanita Cussen; ed/BA 1957, MA 1973 Univ Okla; Doc Cand Univ Okla; pa/Tribal Hist, Caddo Tribe Okla; Grad Tchg Asst Univ Okla; Lectr on Am Hist & Rel; Wn Hist Assn; Olde Hist Soc; Am Hist Assn; Org Am Hist; cp/Jr Leag Okla City; Caddo Tribal Coun; Okla City Area Indian Hlth Bd; Nat Cong Am Indians; r/Epis; hon/W/W S&SW; Ency Am Indian 1978; W/W Am Indian Wom 1980; Author "Indian Colonization in the Cherokee Outlet of Western Indian Territory."

HAMPTON, CAROLYN HUTCHINS oc/Professor; b/Dec 11, 1936; h/103 Lamont Rd, Greenville, NC 27834; ba/G'ville; m/Carol D; c/Frederick Bennett; p/Hugh Caldwell (dec) and Mary Elarnor Patton

Hutchins, G'ville, NC; ed/BS Appalachian St Univ 1959; MS 1961, PhD 1963 Univ Tenn; pa/Grad Tchg Asst, Univ Tenn-Knoxville 1959-60; Res F'ship, Atomic Energy Comm, Univ Tenn-K'ville 1960-63; Asst Prof Biol, UNC-Charlotte 1963-65; Asst Prof Natural Sci, Longwood Col 1965-66; E Carolina Univ: Asst Prof Sci Ed 1966-70, Assoc Prof Sci Ed 1970-76, Prof Sci Ed 1976-; Sigma Xi; Delta Kappa Gamma; Nat Sci Tchrs Assn; Am Inst Biol Sci; NC Acad Sci; NC Sci Tchrs Assn; AAUP; r/Luth Ch in Am: Ch Coun 1977-; hon/W/W Students of Am Univs & Cols 1959; Outstg Yng Wom Am 1973; W/W: Am Wom, S&SW; World W/W Wom; Am Men & Wom of Sci; DIB; Ldrs in Ed; Personalities of Am; Nat Sci Foun F'ship, Univ PR, 1967; Dir NSF Inst in BSCS Biol for HS Biol Tchr 1969-70; NSF Ldrship Conf in SCIS, Univ Calif 1972; NSF F'ship to Attend Ldrship Conf in SCIS 1972; Cert for Placing in Top 10% on Tchr Evaluation by Pupils 1972; NSF Ldrship Conf in OBIS Univ Calif 1975; Dir OBIS Resource Ctr 1975-; Gustaf-Ohaus Awd 1975; Dir Num Projs; Author Num Profl Articles Incl'g "Duckweed" & "Crayfish" Science and Children 1979 & "Ecology and the Biology Teacher" North Carolina Education 1971.

HAMPTON, GENE EDWARD oc/Sheriff; b/Aug 26, 1942; h/Durant, OK; ba/Courthouse, Durant, OK; m/Brenda Sue; c/Ronald Gene, Scott Dewayne; p/Lewis Virgle and Mary May Hampton, Bennington, OK; mil/AUS 1961-64; pa/Sheriff Bryan Co; cp/Odd Fellows Lodge; r/Holiness; hon/AUS Good Conduct Medal.

HAMPTON, OPHINA (PEGGY) R oc/Nurse; b/Nov 19, 1924; h/500 Oak Ave, S Pgh,TN 37380; ba/S Pgh; m/N Scott Sr; c/Scott Jr, George L, J Thomas; p/Oscar B Lawson (dec); Mary L Vann (dec); ed/Dip Baroness Erlangen Sch Nsg; Post Grad St Mary's Hosp; pa/RN; Quality Assurance Coor; Suprvr CCU; AACCN; ANA: BEH Alumni; cp/Ch Wom for Brock; Cub Scouts Troop 3008; r/Presb; SS Tchr; hon/JCs Oper Pincushion; W/W Am Wom 1979-80.

HAMRA, ARMEL JEAN 4oc/Senior Buyer; b/May 10, 1932; h/Kerbey Jennings Trail, Hamlin, KY 42046; ba/Murray, KY; c/Philip; p/Elvin Ferris and Metta Allene Claxton; ed/Attg Murray St Univ; pa/Sr Buyer, Purchasing & Gen Sers, Murray St Univ; Ky Chapt Nat Ednl Buyers; Ky Wom Admrs & Deans; r/Meth; hon/Chm Ky Chapt Ednl Buyers 1979.

HAMROCK, MARILYN ANGELA oc/Speech-Language Pathologist; b/Dec 21, 1946; h/10931 SW 177 St, Miami, FL 33157; ba/S Miami, FL; p/Aloysius Thomas and Angela Salreno Hamrock, Campbell, OH; ed/BS Kent St Univ 1968; MA NWn Univ 1969; pa/Pres Hamrock & Gram PA: Speech Pathol Assocs; Am Speech-Lang-Hearing Assn; Fla Speech-Lang-Hearing Assn; Intl Assn Phoniatrics & Logopedics; Miami Assn Commun Scis; cp/S Miami C of C; r/Roman Cath; hon/Kappa Delta Pi; W/W S&SW 1980-81; Author Speech Pathology Outcome Criteria in Quality Assurance Book.

HANCE, KENT ROLAND oc/United States Congressman; b/Nov 14, 1942; ba/Federal Building, Lubbock, TX 79401; m/Carol; c/Ron, Susan; p/Raymond Hance, Vernon, TX; Beral Hance, Dimmitt, TX; ed/BBA Tex Tech Univ; JD Univ of Tex; pa/St Bar of Tex; cp/Rotary; Lions Clb; r/Bapt.

HANCOCK, CYNTHIA CHAPMAN oc/Public Relations Director; b/Dec 15, 1936; h/516 Bontona Ave, Ft Lauderdale, FL 33301; ba/Same; m/Dane Reed; c/Cheryl Ann, Scott Reed; p/Edward Markus Chapman (dec); Hazel Chapman Pisini, Hampton, CT; ed/AA Daytona Commun Col 1960; AB Stetson Univ 1963; pa/Public Relats Dir, Am Lrng Sys; Public Relats Conslt, Dane Reed Hancock PE; Wom in Communs Inc: Regional VP S 1980-82, Atlantic-Fla Chapt Pres 1977-79; cp/Wk of the Ocean: Co-Chm 1981, Publicity Chm 1980; Chamber Marine Task Force 1979-81; r/Unitarian; hon/Wom of Yr in Communs, Broward Co 1980.

HANCOCK, JOYCE ANN oc/Scholar, Critic, Administrator, Photographer; b/Jan 30, 1945; h/Box 111, Sulphur, KY 40070; ba/Berea, KY; p/Forest Dunlap (dec) and Minnie Ruth Hancock, Sulphur, KY; ed/BA Univ Ky 1967; MA Univ Fla 1968; PhD Univ Ky 1978; pa/Instr Lit & Writing Univ Ky, Ky St Univ, Univ Louisville; Dir Res & Photog/Writer for Folklore Proj, Berea; Exec Secy The Settlement Insts of Appalachia; Regional Coor Ky Oral Hist Comm; Bd Dirs Henry Co Hist Soc; cp/Gov's Task Force on Ed; LWV Ed Com; r/Bapt; hon/Phi Beta Kappa; Woodrow Wilson F'ship; Author "Dynamic Tension in Kurt Vonnegut's Cat's Cradle"; "Squaring the Circle: The System of Conflicts in Little Big Man"; Num Other Pubs & Presentations.

HANCOCK, SAMUEL LEE oc/Educator and Consultant; b/Dec 2; h/Rt 1 Box 291, Blacksburg, VA 24060; ba/Blacksburg; p/Samuel Eldridge and Gladys Maupin Hancock Jr; ed/BS Cedarville Col 1969; MEd Univ Cinci 1971; ED D VPI & St Univ 1980; pa/Conslt Min of Ed, Jamaica & US Agcy for Intl Devel; Admr Coop Ext Prog; Conduct Mnly TV Show & Contbr to Local Newspapers; Past Prof Australia, Papua New Guinea,

Japan; US Dept St Part in Rural Devel Botswana, Swaziland, Kenya; Charter Mem Va Commun Ed Assn; Co-Chm Leg Com Va Commun Ed Assn; Va Ext Agts Assn; Va 4-H Ext Agts Assn; Past St VP Va 4-H All Stars; Adm Asst/Leg Aide, Va Gen Assem; cp/Secy Blacksburg JCs; Com Chm Freedom Guard/Polit Awareness, Blacksburg JCs; St Com Chm Freedom Guard/Polit Awareness, Va JCs; Bd Dirs Kisumu, Kenya-Roanoke, Va Sister Cities Intl Com; Planning Com Roanoke Val Intl Fest; Spkr Bus, Civic & Profl Orgs on Topics of Intl Affairs, Ecs & Ed; r/Meth; hon/Springboard Awd, Blacksburg JCs; Search for Excell, Va Coop Ext Ser 1977; Profl Ldrship Devel Grant, US Dept of Ed 1978 & 79.

HAND, G OTHELL oc/Director-Senior Vice President Motivation; b/Oct 10, 1920; h/1660 Flournoy Dr, Columbus, GA 31906; ba/Columbus; m/Martha Pillow; c/Kerry Wayne, Steven Mark; p/George Loftin (dec) and Velma Clay Hand, Collinsville, MS; ed/BS Miss St; PhD So Bapt Theol Sem; pa/Bd Dirs Am Family Life, Trust Co of Columbus, Florence Marina Inc; Sr VP Motivation Am Fam Life; cp/Rotary Clb of Columbus; Execs Clb; Columbus Country Clb; Trustee Shorter Col; Pres's Coun Mercer Univ; Candun Lit Clb; r/Bapt; hon/Geo Wash Medal of Hon, Freedoms Foun at Val Forge; Lib Named in His Hon.

HANFORD, PATRICK JOSEPH oc/Medical Student; b/Nov 26, 1952; h/8801 N Normandale, Ft Worth, TX 76116; m/Sharon Roach; c/Ryan Joseph; p/Ralph J and Marguerette Hanford, Abilene, TX; ed/BS Angelo St Univ 1976; Deg Cand Tex Col Osteopathic Med; p/Student Osteopathic Med Assn; Beta Beta Beta; Student Govt Rep TCOM; Atlas Clb; r/Meth; hon/Med Student S'ship From Cogdell Meml Hosp.

HANKS, JOANNA EMILY DAVIS oc/Associate Professor; b/Mar 25, 1948; h/Mechanicsville, VA; ba/PO Box 12084, Richmond, VA 23241; m/W Roger; c/Leann Davis, Lawrence Ryland; p/Lawrence Hall and Leona P Davis, Warsaw, VA; ed/BS Longwood Col 1969; MS Va Commonwlth Univ 1974; pa/COE Coor Henrico Co Public Schs 1969-74; Prog Hd, Secy Sci Dept, J Sargeant Reynolds Commun Col 1974-79; Assoc Prof J Sargeant Reynolds Commun Col 1979-; Delta Pi Epsilon; Va Bus Ed Assn; Conslt & Ed SWn Pub Co; cp/Past Mem Brook Run Jr Wom's Clb; Am Legion Aux; Sev Ofcrs Cool Spring Bapt Ch; r/Bapt; hon/W/W S&SW 1980-81; Author "An Individualized Approach to Teaching Typewriting in an Urban Environment."

HANLON, FREDA ANDREA WHITSON oc/Special Education Resource Specialist; b/Oct 12, 1950; h/207 Norcross Dr, Apt 43D, Knoxville, TN 37923; ba/Strawberry Plains, TN; m/Cary B; p/Fred B and Verdie C Whitson, Charleston, SC; ed/BA David Lipscomb Col 1971; MA The Citadel 1975; pa/NEA; TEA; KCEA; Childhood Ed; r/Ch of Christ; hon/W/W: Am, S&SW, Early Childhood.

HANNA, DONNA F oc/Student; b/Jan 3, 1947; h/409 Mars, Altus, OK 73521; m/Charles RE; c/Steven Charles, Michael Carl; p/Mike (dec) and Christina Semkoff, Clinton, OK; ed/AS; BS Cand; cp/NCO Wives Clb; r/First Christian (Disciples of Christ); hon/Phi Kappa Phi; Pi Mu Epsilon; Winner NCO Wives S'ship for 3 Yrs.

HANNER, RICHARD RAYFIELD oc/Clerk and Foreman; b/Dec 8, 1906; h/815 Emma Rd, Asheville, NC 28806; m/Leila Mitchell; c/Richard R Jr (dec), Terrence Edward, Henry David, Thomas Issac, Linda Leila; p/Henry Littleton (dec) and Lillie Reynolds Hanner (dec); mil/USN; pa/Post Ofc Clerk & Foreman 41 Yrs; cp/Dem Party; r/Meth; hon/Treas Nat Assn Ret'd Fed Employees 1969-81; Life Mbrship U Meth Men 1971; Cit For Merit Ser, Nat Assn Ret'd Fed Employees 1975.

HANNIGAN, JAMES EDWARD oc/Aerospace Engineer, NASA; b/Apr 30, 1930; h/102 Shady Oak Dr, Dickinson, TX 77539; ba/Houston, TX; m/Harriett E; c/Linda Lucile, Richard Edward, Thomas James, Mary Kathleen; p/Edward S Hannigan (dec); Marian H Hannigan, Jacksonville, FL; ed/Bach Aero Engrg 1952 Ga Tech; mil/USAF Capt Ret'd; pa/Asst Div Chief, Flight Control Div, Johnson Space Ctr; cp/Explorer; BSA; Rotary Intl; r/U Meth; hon/NASA Exceptional Ser Medal; Apollo 11 Cert of Commend; Apollo 13 Cert of Commend.

HANNS, CHRISTIAN ALEXANDER oc/Vocational/Educational Consultant; b/Sept 12, 1948; h/312 Jefferson Ave, Linden, NJ 07036; ba/Newark, NJ; p/Christian J Hanns, Parlin, NJ; Elizabeth Branch Hanns (dec); ed/BA 1972, MA 1973 Kean Col of NJ; Doct Cand Rutgers Univ; mil/AUS 1966-69; pa/Voc/Ednl Conslt, NJ Dept Hlth, Div Narcotic & Drug Abuse Control; Coor CLEP Prep Progs, Lakewood Commun Schs; Dir Cnslg Ednl Resource Inst; Dir Cnslg Union Col; Co-Chm Cnslr Sect Assn Adult Ed of NJ; NJ Assn Commun Ed; Am Voc Ed; NJ Voc Assn; Nat Psychi Assn; cp/Chm Fund Raising Spec Projs Am Red Cross; Allocations Team, U Way of En Union Co; Pastoral Com, Linden U Meth Ch; Adv Coun Vietnam Era Vets; r/Meth; hon/Vol of Yr, Am Red Cross 1980; W/W E 1979-80; Commun Ldrs of Am; DIB; Author: Job Prep Manual for NJ Dept Hlth 1980, "Language Curiosities", "Too Many Irons in the Fire."

HANSFORD, WILLARD oc/County Clerk; b/Mar 10, 1940; h/Somerset, KY; m/Lois Faye; c/Todd Shane; p/Arthur and Helen Irene Hansford, Somerset, KY: mil/USAR 8 Yrs; pa/Pres Ky Co Clerk Assn.

HARALSON, LINDA oc/Community Service Specialist; b/Mar 10, 1951; h/721 Windward Rd, Jackson, MS 39201; ba/Jackson; p/Roosevelt (dec) and Alice Haralson (dec); ed/BA Jackson St Univ; Att'd NC Ctrl Univ Sch Law; pa/Commun Ser Spec, US Bur Census; Am Soc Public Adm; Conf of Minoirity Public Adm; cp/Nat Coun Negro Wom; Nat Landowner Assn; Proj Media; JSU Pre-law Adv Com; r/Bapt; hon/Achmt of Excell Awd in Prog Plan'g & Res.

HARB, MITCHELL ABRAHAM oc/Professional Inventor, Master Craftsman, Master Mechanic; b/Oct 15, 1919; h/1 Harb Dr, Lexington, NC 27292; ba/Lexington; m/Marilee Cruse; c/Mithcell Joseph, Marilee Priscilla; p/Fareed J and Catherine Mae Harb; ed/Att'd Univ Wis 1972-74; USAFI; mil/AUS 1942-44; USAF 1944-45; pa/Owner Harb Tire Ser; Owner & Mgr Harb Foundry 1949-; Patent Cons 1957-; Instr Nat Rifle Assn 1957-; Designer Patterns & Molds for Plaques & Medals 1949-; Created Silver Jubilee Medallion for Queen of England 1977; Miniature Models of Am Ships Monitor and Merricmac & Cannons Rep'd in Permanent Display at Mariners Mus, Beaufort, NC, Var Davidson Co Libs & St Mus; Special Request from Miss NC USA to Make Favors for Every Contestant in Miss USA Pageant Held at Biloxi, MS 1980, Spec Request from Contestant's Parents to Make Favors for Miss La Petite Contest in Wingate, NC 1980; Inventor: Daul Tire Cutting Machine; cp/Nat Rifle Assn; High Rock Lake Assn; Dem Party; Eagle Coin; r/Bapt; hon/Recip Pres Sports Awd 1977; Nom to Nat Inventors Hall of Fame 1979; W/W Tech 1980; 3 US Patents.

HARBERT, BARBARA KOCH oc/Violinist, Organist; b/Mar 15, 1904; h/501 Ocean Ave, Melbourne Bch, FL 32951; m/Jason T Jr, Barbara H Finger, William Bruce; p/William D (dec) and Frances Runkle Koch (dec); ed/Violin Grad Cert, Cinci Col of Mus 1924; pa/Ch Organist; Life Mem Delta Omicron; Am Guild Organists, Ctrl Fla Chapt; cp/Mil Wives Org; r/Presb; hon/Certs from 9 European Summer Ecumenical Courses; 50 Yr Mem PEO.

HARBERT, JASON TALMAGE oc/Clergyman; b/Aug 11, 1899; h/Melbourne Bch, FL; m/Barbara Kock; c/Jason T Jr, Barbara H Finger, William Bruce; p/Lincoln Lafayette (dec) and Ollie Teuton Harbert (dec); ed/BA Univ Tenn 1920; BD Lane McCormick Sem 1925; MA Vanderbilt Univ 1954; mil/AUS Ret'd Army Chaplain; pa/Pres Clergyman; St Chaplain Am Legion 1929-30; Mem Scottish Rite; Life Mem ROA; Nat Chaplains Assn; Savannah Am Legion; VFW; Sojourners; Lions Clb; hon/Certs for 9 Summer Sems in Europe.

HARBISON, MARGARET ANN WARLICK WATERS oc/Professor; b/Dec 19, 1935; h/2824 McCarley Dr, Commerce, TX 75428; ba/Commerce; m/Paul D; c/Jack Hilton Waters; p/Walter Theodore (dec) and Lessie Lawrence Downs Warlick (dec); ed/BS 1957, MA 1963 Appalachian St Univ; EdD Univ Miss 1974; pa/Tchr: D Matt Thompson Jr HS (NC) 1957-61, Meadowlawn Jr HS (Fla) 1961-62; Grad Asst Appalachian St Univ 1962-63; Asst Prof Univ Miss 1963-67; Asst Prof Kennesaw Col 1967-70; Assoc Prof Delta St Univ 1970-74; Prof E Tex St Univ 1974-; Exec Com, Nat Assn Intercol Aths; TAHPER; SAPECW; AAHPERD; NAPEHE; Delta Kappa Gamma; Kappa Delta Pi; cp/U Way, Bd Dirs, Treas 1977-80; C of C Bd Dirs; Chp Beautification Com 1977-80; Pres Psych Clb, Fed Wom's Clb; r/Bapt; hon/Dist'd Commun Ser Awd 1981; W/W Am Wom 1981.

HARD, GORDON WAYNE oc/Manager; b/Sept 17, 1955; h/Rt 2 Box 16 B, Seminole, OK 74868; m/Dawn Amber; c/Joseph Allen; p/George Washington and Betty Lou Hard, Remus, MI; mil/AUS 3 Yrs; cp/Lions Clb; r/Evangelistical.

HARDEE, HOYT JAMES oc/Secretary and Business Manager; b/Oct 17, 1927; h/Rt 4 Box 316, Loris, SC 29569; ba/Loris; m/Martha Florence Prince; c/Janice H Lyerly, Edwina; p/Thelton C (dec) and Martha Lezettie Cox Hardee, Loris, SSC; ed/Dip Columbia Commercial Col 1947; Att'd Clemson Univ 1976, Horry-Georgetown Tech Col 1967; Dale Carnegie Course 1969; pa/Asst Mgr Farmers Coop Exch 1956-60; Mgr Allied Security Ins Branch Ofc 1960-63; Secy & Bus Mgr Hardee Mfg Co Inc 1963-; Past Pres Horry Indust Coun; cp/Past Chm Loris HS Adv Bd; Loris Lions Clb, Pres 1970-71; Past Chm & Secy, Deacon Loris First Bapt Ch; r/Bapt; hon/Pvt Pilot's Lic 1968; Lions Intl "Lions Dist'd Ser Awd" 1980.

HARDEE, WILLIE JR oc/Registered Medical Assistant; b/July 13, 1931; h/PO Box 361, Homerville, GA 31634; m/Carrie; p/Willie Sr and Alma Hardee, Homerville, GA; ed/EMT; 3 Yrs Col; mil/AUS; pa/Reg'd Med Asst, Clin; cp/City Coun-man; Mayor Pro-Tem; Police Commr; r/Meth.

HARDEMAN, CAROLE HALL oc/Curriculum Developer, Researcher, Project Director; b/Mar 24, 1945; h/1709 NE 58th St, Oklahoma City, OK 73111; ba/Norman, OK; c/Paula Suzette; p/Ita D Sr and Rubye Hibler Hall, Okla City, OK; ed/BA Fisk Univ; MA, PhD Univ Okla; pa/Curric Develr, Resr, Proj Dir, Univ Okla; AERA; Phi Delta Kappa; ASCD; Wom in Maths; NABSE; NAFEO; cp/Links Inc; Jack & Jill of Am; AKA; Urban Leag; YWCA; YMCA; NAACP; Afro-Am Arts Coun; r/Bapt; hon/Doct F'ship Okla St Regents for Higher Ed; Resolution for Outstg Mus Perf, Okla St Leg.

HARDESTY, GEORGE K C oc/Consulting Engineer; b/Nov 15, 1909; h/Box 130, Mayo, MD 21106; m/Elizabeth M; c/Kathleen H; p/George Knox and Sarah Sedoms Hardesty (dec); pa/Conslt'g Engr, Electro - Optical - Illumination Fields; Contbr to Sci Lit; Mem Sev Nat Engrg Soc Coms; Fellow Illumination Soc of NAm; Sr Mem ISA; Mem: OSA, SID, ISCC; Holder 40 Patents in field of naval ship instrumentation, man-machine interface displays & controls; cp/Kiwanis Intl: Past Dir, VP; BPOE; Past Pres Cloverlea Boat Clb; Cloverlea Citizen's Assn; Life Mem Fish & Game Assn; hon/Aero-Space Awd 1969, Soc of Automotive Engrs; Commends & Awds, Secy of Navy; Num Awds for inventions of value to Navy.

HARDIN, ELEANOR oc/Retired; b/Apr 9, 1911; h/Rt 2 Box 85, Corinth, MS 38834; p/John Marion Hardin (dec); Martha Louvernia Gipson (dec); pa/Ret'd Dept Army Communs Spec; cp/OES; Pilot Clb; Homemakers Ext Clb; Leave of Absence from Beta Sigma Phi Exemplar; r/Bapt; hon/Outstg Perf Awds by Dept Army.

HARDIN, MARGARET G oc/Teacher; b/Feb 28, 1916; h/Rt 9 Box 402, Elizabethton, TN 37643; ba/E'ton; m/Paul A; c/Joyce Hardin Mann; p/Charles (dec) and Ina Woulf Carr (dec); ed/BS Milligan Col; pa/Tchr Hunter Sch; TEA; NEA; Life Mbrship PTA; r/Christian.

HARDING, FANN oc/Scientist; Administrator; b/Jan 29, 1930; h/5306 Bradley Blvd, Bethesda, MD 20014; ba/Bethesda; p/James Hilary Harding (dec); Caldwell Harding, Henderson, KY; ed/BA; MS; PhD; pa/Scist, Admr: Nat Insts of Hlth; Spec Asst to Dir, Div of Blood Diseases & Resources, Nat Heart, Lung & Blood Inst; Mem: Intl Soc on Thrombosis & Hemostasis, Reticuloendothelial Soc, Assn for Wom in Sci; Fdg Pres Fedn of Orgs for Profl Wom; cp/Nat Wom's Polit Caucus; r/Epis; hon/Magna Cum Laude Grad, Coker Col; Ruth Patrick Awd; Elected to Sophiades.

HARDMAN, PATRICIA KIRVEN oc/Researcher, Author, Educator; b/May 6, 1944; h/4745 Centerville Rd, Tallahassee, FL 32308; m/Robert S; p/Wilds Wallace and Stella Davis Kirven, Summerton, SC; ed/Att'd Campbell Col 1962-64; BS Univ SC 1967; MAT Citadel 1976; PhD Walden Univ 1980; pa/Dir Dyslexia Res Inst Inc & Woodland Hall Acad; Orton Soc; Assn for Chd w Lng Disabilities; Fla Assn Indep Spec Ed Facilities; r/Presb; hon/Pub'd 42 Textbooks; *Sugarless Cookbook, or How to Keep Cool, Calm, & Collected* 1979; Other Profl Pubs.

HARDY, JOYCE POUNDS oc/Teacher, Volunteer; b/Nov 23, 1925; h/4067 Merrick, Houston, TX 77025; m/Tom C; c/Tom Jr, Lynn Brotherton, Horace, Mike, Larry; p/Horace Earle (dec) and Christine Lewis Pounds (dec); ed/BA Rice Univ 1967; pa/Ret'd Eng Tchr; r/Presb; Ordained Elder; hon/First Wom Pres Assn of Rice Alumni 1977-78; Pres Soc Rice Univ Wom 1972-73; Exec Bd ARA 1973-76; Recip Hugh Scott Cameron Rice Univ Ser Awd, Given By Sr Class at Commencement 1978; First Wom to Ser on: Bd Dirs Owl Clb, Rice Univ 1979 & Rice Univ Standing Com on Aths 1979; Assoc Jones Col; Hon of Highest Wom's Varsity Ath Awd Given in Her Name Annually; Mem Leg Com Harris Co Med Aux.

HARDY, LANE HENRY (JIMMY) oc/District Superintendent; b/Feb 24, 1918; h/3009 Denison, Snyder, TX 79549; m/Irene; c/Jimmy, Don, Sandra; p/L C (dec) and Prebble Hardy (dec); mil/Sea Bees WWII; pa/Dist Supt Tex Elec Ser Co; r/Bapt; hon/Tex Elec Ser Awds.

HARDY, PAUL JUNE oc/Secretary of State; b/Oct 18, 1942; h/1721 Sherwood Forest Blvd, Baton Rouge, LA 70804; ba/Baton Rouge; m/Sandra Gatlin; c/Yvette, Gregory; p/Florent Hardy; Agnes Angelle; ed/BA; JD; pa/Secy of St, St of La; Mem: Am, La, St Martin Parish Bar Assns; cp/St Senator 1971-75; St Chm: Heart Assn, Cerebral Palsy Assn; r/Cath; hon/Outstg Newcomer in Senate; Legislative Conservationist of Yr.

HAREN, JAMES HARRISON oc/Executive; b/Mar 25, 1935; h/3701 S George Mason Dr, #2015 N, Falls Church, VA 22304; c/James Harrison, David Michael, Susan Joan, Jeffrey William, Gregory Patrick, Jamie Lynn; p/Mrs W F Haren, Dalton, GA; ed/BS Va Tech 1955; MS NM St Univ 1958; mil/AUS 1956-58; pa/Pres Safe Baby Prods 1960-70; Pres Intl Inventors Inc 1971-; Chm of Bd Intl Bartending Inst 1977-; Va Pvt Trade Schs Assn; r/Prot; hon/W/W: Adult Cont Ed, S&SW; Author "Blocking, The First Fundamental of Football" & "Who Motivates the Motivator."

HARGROVE, LINDA oc/Songwriter; Entertainer; b/Feb 3, 1949; ba/809 18th Ave S, Nashville, TN 37203; p/James Thomas Hargrove, Longview, FL; Ann T Peragino, Nashville, TN; ed/HS Grad; pa/Songwriter; Recording Artist; Entertainer; Mem: Country Music Assn, Am Fedn of Musicians, Am Fedn of TV & Radio Artists, Acad of Country Music, Nashville Songwriter Assn Intl: Bd Dirs, Exec Bd; Affiliate Broadcast Music Inc; Recorded for: Elektra, Capitol, RC; Exclusive Writer for Window Music Inc 1971-; r/Non-Denominational Christian; hon/3 Broadcast Music Inc 1976, Country Music; 1 Broadcast Music Inc, Pop Music.

HARITUN, ROSALIE ANN oc/Professor; b/May 30, 1938; h/206 N Oak St, Apt 8, Greenville, NC 27834; ba/Greenville; p/George and Helen Ternosky Haritun, Great Bend, PA; ed/BME Baldwin-Wallace Conservatory of Mus 1960; MS Univ Ill 1961; Profl Dip Tchrs Col, Columbia Univ 1965; EdD Columbia Univ 1968; Postdoct Study 1971; pa/Asst Prof Mus Ed, Soc Mus, ECU 1972-; Instrumental Mus Instr NYC Bd Ed 1971-72; Instr Mus Ed, Temple Univ 1968-71; Doct Tchg Fellow, Columbia 1966-68; Jr HS Instrumental Mus Dir, LI, NY 1963-65; Elem Instrumental Mus Tchr, LI, NY 1961-63; Clarinetist/Saxophonist, Greenville Summer Wind Ensemble 1975-79; Num Other Performances; cp/Dir Ch Yth Orch, Patchogue Bapt Ch 1962-65; Dir Patchogue Adult Mus Recorder Soc 1964-65; Choir Dir, Landmark Bapt Ch, Greenville 1975-79; Vol Mem Pitt Co Res Com Concerning Liquor-by-the-Drink 1979; Stering Com Greenville City Commr Cand 1978; Yng Dems, Columbia Univ 1966-68; r/Bapt; hon/Personalities of Am 1979; Men & Wom of Dist 1979; Intl Reg Profiles 1978; W/W: Intells, S&SW; Annual Mbrship Intl Biogl Soc; World W/W: Wom in Ed, Wom; Personalities of S; Intl W/W Mus; DIB; Outstg Yng Wom Am 1972; Author: "A Sequential Approach to Behavioral Objectives in Music Education," "Television for Developing Teaching Skills," "Basic Skills for Teaching Music."

HARLEY, JOSEPHINE ANNE od/Restaurant Owner; b/Oct 15, 1939; h/5103 Springwod Dr, New Bern, NC 28560; c/Meredith, Clay, Heather; p/F D Bundy, Longwood, FL; Josephine Pearson Bundy (dec); ed/Att'd USc 1957-59; pa/Restaurant Owner; c/Trent Woods Garden Clb; r/Meth: Adm Bd, Exec Bd UMW; hon/Most Improved Wom Golfer 1974.

HARLOW, FREEDA oc/Author, Lecturer, Foster Mother; b/Aug 5, 1937; h/Nocona, TX; m/Ray; c/Cathy, Tammy, John; Foster Mother of 15 Chd; p/Ethel Ford, Nocona, TX; ed/Beauty Col 1956; Accredited Hours in Foster Parenting 1977-81; pa/Secy-Treas Harlow Chd's Ranch Inc; r/Full Gospel; hon/Book in Process of Being Pub'd.

HARLOW, JOYCE MORGAN SOUTHARD BRECHT oc/Executive Director; b/Sept 1, 1932; h/Houston, TX; ba/PO Box 218103, Houston, TX 77218; m/Eugene Harrison; c/Amy Brecht, Stephen Brecht, David Brecht, Peter Brecht; p/Frederick Reynolds (dec) and Eleanor Plumb Southard (dec); ed/AB DePauw Univ 1954; EdM Boston Univ 1962; pa/Tchr: Fairburn, Ohio 1955-57; Weston, Mass 1957-61; Rockville, Md 1973-77; Pres Joyce Brecht Enterprises 1975-77; Exec Dir Park Ten Commun Assn 1980-; Ptnr J&N Pubs 1976-; Bd Dirs S Lawn Child Care; Pi Lambda Theta; cp/Harvard Bus Sch Wives Assn; Pi Beta Phi; r/Epis; hon/Author "Sing Noel" 1975; Edwin W Broome Awd for "Sing Noel" 1975..

HARMAN, CODY JR oc/General Manager and Vice President; b/July 24, 1949; h/Box 225, Cedar Bluff, VA 24609; ba/Cedar Bluff; m/Connie De Reene; c/Julia De Reene, Jennifer Renee, Richard Wade; p/Cody Sr and Reva Harman, Jewell Ridg, VA; pa/Owner Mine Controls Inc, Julie Coal Co; Co-Owner Messick Branch Coal Co; VP & Gen Mgr Triangle Mining Equip Co Inc; r/Free Penetecostal Holiness: Preacher; hon/W/W Fin & Indust 1979-80.

HARPER, BERNICE CATHERINE oc/Social Worker, Medical Care Administrator; h/11801 Rockville Pike, Rockville, MD 20852; ba/Wash DC; m/Alpha Lorenzo; c/Reginald; p/Raymond (dec) and Mary Saunders Wright (dec); pa/NASW; NCSW; ICSW; AHA; cp/Alpha Kappa Alpha; Mayor's Com on Long Term Care; r/Bapt; hon/ACHA's Better Life Awd; PHS Superior Ser Awd; Ida M Cannon Awd; Public Hlth Traineeship Awd; Univ So Calif Alumni Awd.

HARPER, JAMES WELDON III oc/Financial Consultant; b/Mar 31, 1937; h/233 9th St NE, Wash DC 20002; ba/Wash DC; p/James Weldon Harper Jr (dec); Mildred Conaway Harper Switzer, Frederick, MD; ed/AB; pa/Apt & Ofc Bldrs Assn; Bd Dirs Caliban Prods Ltd; Pres US Energy Conservations Sers Inc; Pres Weldon Enterprises; cp/Repub; Var Coms; r/Meth; hon/Num Acad S'ships; Quill & Scroll; Hon Soc.

HARRELL, BARBARA ELLEN oc/Registered Brangus Cattle Breeder, Office Manager; b/Apr 2, 1944; h/Sabinal Canyon Ranch, Utopia, TX 78884; ba/Same; m/John Kenneth Sr; p/Cecil Martin and Ethel Samantha Sinyard Tucker; ed/Att'd Univ Tex; pa/Ofc Mgr Sabinal Canyon Ranch; Nat VP Tex Soc So Dames of Am; Org'g Regent Capt Francis Eppes Chapt DAC; Charter Mem Intl Brangus Aux; cp/Bandera C of C; Regent Bandara Chapt DAR; St Chm Jr Mbrship & House & Platform TSDAR; r/Epis; hon/Outstg Jr Mem TSDAR 1979; Outstg Jr Mem Tex Soc Colonial Dames XVII Century 1978; Nat Outstg Jr CDXVIIC 1978.

HARRELL, JAMES ALFRED oc/Consultant; b/Apr 10, 1941; h/904 Twin Oaks Dr, Broken Arrow, OK 74012; m/Helen Jennifer Timbers; c/James Bradley, Jennifer Adrienne; p/Alfred Emanuel (dec) and Dorothy Mae Smith Harrell, Broken Arrow, OK; ed/Chem Engr: Univ Okla 1959-61, Okla St Univ 1962-64; mil/USAF 1965, Ofcr Cand 1967; pa/Bus Sys Mgmt Conslt, Invest Conslt, Chem Sales & Purchasing Conslt; Nat Paint Varnish & Laquer Assn; Propeller Clb; cp/Sts & Hwys Com; r/Meth; hon/W/W S&SW 1980-81.

HARRELL, HARDY MATTHEW oc/Executive; b/Oct 15, 1905; h/2228 Lake Shore Blvd, Jacksonville, FL 32210; ba/Same; m/Edna Mae Richardson; c/Hardy Matthew Jr, Edward Monroe, George Mark; p/George Monroe and Willie Harrell (dec); ed/Bus Col: Corr Courses, Lasalle Bus Life Ofc Mgmt Assn Inst, Assoc Degree Nat Ofc Mgmt; pa/Elected Exec Secy-Treas Affiliated Bapt Hosps Inc, New Orleans; Corp Secy & Asst VP, Gulf Life Ins Co, J'ville 38 Yrs, Ret'd 1965; Bd Dirs: Bapt Hosp of J'ville, Bapt Meml Hosp, J'ville (Past Pres), Affiliated Bapt Hosps Inc (& Predecessors) Past Pres & Past Chm Exec Com; cp/Masonic Lodge, 32° Scottish Rite Mason: Riverside Lodge #266 F&AM, J'ville, Past Master of Riverside Lodge #266, Num Coms, Grand Lodge F&AM of Fla (Num Coms); J'ville C of C; Others; r/So Bapt Ch: Mem since 1921, Deacon, Tchr Sr Men's Bible Class 35+ Yrs, SS Supt, Dir Bapt Yg People's Tng Union, Num Coms; Other Ch Related Activs; hon/Dist'd Awd for Civic Wk: Stetson Univ, Bethune Cookman Col, So Bapt Conv; Cits: Am Cancer Soc, Patron J'ville Univ; Fellow Mem ABI.

HARRELL, ROSALIND KNOTT oc/Missionary; b/May 23, 1929; h/Box 32, Limuru, Kenya; ba/Raleigh, NC; m/Ralph W; c/R Stephen, Beverly Jean, Samuel P; p/Samuel Lee (dec) and Lois Daniel Knott (dec); ed/BA Meredith Col; Att'd So Bapt Theol Sem 1951-52; pa/Asst Dir of Coor'd Lit Prog for En & So Africa & Intl Editor for Jr Sunday Sch Lit (Missionary) So Bapt Conv, Kenya; Tchr 1952-53; Portland Ave Commun Ctr, Louisville 1951-52; Dir Lang & Orientation, Limuru, Kenya 1976-77; Editorial Dept Bapt Pubs, Nairobi 1969-75; Cateress Bapt Conf Ctr, Limuru 1964-69; Evangelistic Work Nairobi Chs 1962-64; Adult Tchr Bapt Commun Ctr, Dar es Salaam, Tanzania 1959-61; cp/Kenya Horticultural Soc; r/Bapt; hon/Contbr to *The Commission*.

HARRELL, ROXANN oc/Businesswoman; b/July 16; h/PO Box 112, Pike St, Osyka, MS; ba/Osyka; m/Favirot Holyne; c/Tabetha Ann, Cara Terann; p/Bill and Bernice Carcara, Osyka, MS; ed/Att'd Gulf Coast Bus Sch; pa/Co-Owner Harrell's Furniture & Appliances; La Dept Hwys 1963-65; cp/Osyka Civic Clb, Treas 1979-80; Chm Osyka Mtl Htlh Assn Campaign 1980; Osyka Lib Bd 1978-80; Pres PTO 1980-81; r/Bapt.

HARRILL, FLORENCE HENDERSON oc/Retired High School Teacher; Retired Federal Government Worker GAO; b/Jan 2, 1908; h/Rt 1, Bostic, NC 28018; m/Jacques William; p/Ernest Wilmot and Edith Campbell Henderson (dec); ed/BS Univ ND; MS Duke Univ; pa/HS Tchr 15 Yrs; Fed Govt Wkr GAO 15 Yrs; Retired Tchrs of NC; cp/NC Repub Wom; DAR; Colonial Dames of 17th Century; Colonial Daughs 17th Century; Daughs of 1812; Mayflower Descendants; Nat Huguenot Soc; N S Ams of Royal Descent; Plantagenet Soc; Daughs of the British Empire; Dames of the Loyal Legion; Magna Charta Dames; Daughs of Am Colonists; Num Others; r/Epis; hon/Mary Mildred Sullivan Awd & Cit, Lincoln Meml Univ, Harrogate, Tenn; 2000 Wom of Achmt; W/W Am Wom; DIB; 500 1st Fams of Am; W/W S&SW; Fellow Mem ABI.

HARRIS, DAVID oc/Minister; b/Apr 12, 1932; h/Dallas, TX; p/David Sr and Annie Mae Harris, Dallas, TX; ed/BS Wiley Col 1957; BD, MRE SWn Sem; Att'd Princeton Univ & Howard Univ; mil/AUS 1952-54; pa/Pioneer Fdr & Min 2nd Corinthian Ch; cp/Masons AF&AM; Commun Chest of Dallas; NAACP; Big Brothers of Dallas; Dallas Voters Leag; Dallas Black C of C; Dallas Interdenom Ins Alliance; World Neighborhood Ctr for World Peace; Epsilon Delta Chi, Sigma Chapt; hon/W/W: S&SW, Black Ams; Outstg Min Awd, 1980; Hon'd by Dallas Times Herald 1976; Mem Gtr Dallas Commun of Chs; Mem Conf of Christians & Jews; Resolution of Commrs Ct of Dallas for Outstg Ser to Urban Black Commun 1977.

HARRIS, EVA HALL oc/Retired Teacher, Principal, County Supervisor; b/June 17, 1902; h/105 Harris St 212, Brookhaven, MS 39601; m/Versie H; p/Beauregard (dec) and Dora Williams Hall (dec); ed/BS;

MA; HHD; pa/Local, St, Nat & Ret'd Tchrs Assns; cp/Mem 2 Commun Clbs; r/Bapt; hon/Num Local, St, Nat Awds & Cits.

HARRIS, FLORENCE CATHERINE oc/Social Worker; b/Dec 28, 1941; h/6102-2 Turnabout Ln, Columbia, MD 21044; ba/Balto; p/Wilber Fiske and Melda Beitzel Harris, Edgewater, MD; ed/BS Highpoint Col 1963; MSW Univ Md 1972; pa/NASW; Adv Coun NW Mtl Hlth, Balto Co; Fam Life Ctr; cp/Bd Dirs Christian Cnslg Assocs; Contact Balto; r/Presb; hon/LCSN; ACSW.

HARRIS, GLADYS B oc/Retired Teacher; b/Oct 8, 1908; h/Rt 1 Box 84, Rickman, TN 38580; m/Millard L; c/Linda Taylor; p/William Perry (dec) and Lee Ola Ramsey Bowmer (dec); ed/BS 1961; pa/Elem Tchr & Prin; HS Eng Tchr; Nat, St & Co Ret'd Tchrs Assns; cp/Co & St Ladies Aux of Tenn Soil Conservation Assn: Pres 4 Yrs; r/Meth; hon/Tenn Conservaton Edr of Yr 1979.

HARRIS, HENRY LEE oc/Patrolman; b/June 18, 1950; m/Olivia Mayberry; c/Marquis Jackson, Jessie Ilin; p/John and Mabel Bacon, Natchez, MS; ed/Assoc Deg, Copiah Lincoln 1974; pa/Patrolman, Natchez Police Dept; cp/Natchez Bowling Leag; World Tennis Assn; Basketball & Fball Referee Assn; Natchez Police Aux Assn; hon/First 1st Mixed Doubles Winners of Am Cancer Tourn 1979 & 80; 1st Pl Mixed Doubles Winner Lipton Tea Tennis Tourn 1980; 1st Pl Semi-Pro Basketball Team Named Hawks 1979; Natchez Police Dept Softball Team Mbrship 1978-79; Asst Coach N Natchez B Adams Tennis Team.

HARRIS, IMOGENE HARRELL oc/Assistant City Attorney; b/Jan 9, 1930; h/5847 S Richmond, Tulsa, OK 74135; ba/Tulsa; m/Allen Klein; c/John Jason Harrell Harris Jr; p/J C Hairrell, Clayton, OK; Janie Watkins, Blackfork, AR; ed/BS; LLB: JD; pa/Legal Com Am Public Transp Assn; Am, Okla & Tulsa Co Bar Assns; cp/Ldrship Tulsa; Metro Tulsa Transit Auth; r/Unitarian; hon/Judge Alternate, City of Broken Arrow, Okla.

HARRIS, JAMES ROBERT oc/Field Sales Representative; b/Dec 9, 1935; h/2705 Pisces Dr, Orlando, FL 32809; ba/Huntsville, AL; m/Barbara O; c/Rob, Jennifer; p/Clarence E (dec) and Gladys B Harris (dec); ed/BS Tenn Tech Univ 1959; mil/USNR; pa/Field Sales Rep, Prudential Ins Co; Pres Huntsville Life Underwriters; Past VP Huntsville Chapt Am Inst Indust Engrs; cp/Past VP JCs; Bd Dirs: YMCA, Red Cross, Multiple Sclerosis, Mlt Hlth; r/Presb; Elder; hon/Huntsville Outstg Yng Man of Yr Nom 1969, 70; Eagle Scout; Nat Multiple Sclerosis Hope Chest Awd.

HARRIS, JANE MADDOX oc/Plant Manager; b/Sept 27, 1936; h/PO Box 157, Kellyton, AL; ba/Alexander City, AL; m/Charles L; c/Ronald, Randall, Elaine, Diane, Joseph; p/Joseph Leslie (dec) and Marjorie Morrow Maddox; pa/Plant Mgr, Double Knit, Russell Corp; cp/Dpty Sheriff Coosa Co; r/Meth.

HARRIS, JOHN FRANKLIN oc/Dean of Students; b/Feb 22, 1946; h/527 Columbus Dr, Selma, AL 36701; ba/Selma m/Mildred Smith; c/1, 72, 73, 1st Pl 1974; Fellow Mem ABI; DIB; Notable Ams; Commun Ldrs & Noteworthy Ams; W/W in Advertising.

HARRIS, KEITH CORLEY oc/Assistant Finance Officer/Purchasing Agent; b/July 29, 1957; h/Rt 4 Box 361, Granite Falls, NC 28630; ba/Lenoir, NC; p/Paul H and Virginia C Harris, Granite Falls, NC; ed/BS Social Science; pa/Asst Fin Ofcr/Purchasing Agt Caldwell Co; Nat Inst Govtl Purchasers; NC Fin Ofcrs Assn; cp/U Fund, Heart Fund.

HARRIS, MARTIN HARVEY oc/Aerospace Company Executive; b/Mar 14, 1932; h/2845 Summerfield Rd, Winter Park, FL 32792; ba/Orla J F Pritchard Co; SMEI; IIL Chm Mktg Com 1974-76; Pi Kappa Alpha; cp/Moose; Elks; Am Legion; VFW; r/Cath; hon/Mktg Awds 1970, 71, 72, 73, 1st Pl 1974; Fellow Mem ABI; DIB; Notable Ams; Commun Ldrs & Noteworthy Ams; W/W in Advertising.

HARRIS, MAUDE EDWARDS oc/Retired; b/May 6, 1920; h/911 14th St, Bradenton, FL 33508; m/Adrian; c/Adrian; p/General (dec); and Ethel Edwards, Donalsonville, GA; ed/BS Savannah St Col; pa/NEA; Early Childhood Assn; AAUW; Manatee Ed Assn; Fla Ed Assn; Manatee Co Kindergarten Assn; Orange Ridge PTA; cp/GSA; Girls Clbs; Zeta Phi Beta; Links Inc; OES Chapt 121 of Bradenton; Lilly White Lodge 151; r/St Paul Missionary Bapt Ch: Co-Chm Decoration Com; hon/Citizen of Yr; Delta Queen; Tchr of Yr of Orange Ridge Elem Sch 1979; 1 of Manatee Co 5 Finalist for Tchr of Yr Manatee Co.

HARRIS, MILDRED MARSHALL oc/Teacher; b/Feb 20, 1923; h/405 S Hine St, Athens, AL 35611; m/Oliver P; c/Myrdis Pauletta Lindsey, Oliver Marshall, Harriet Yvonne; p/John Sterling and Hattie Saunders Marshall, Birmingham, AL; ed/BS Ala St Univ; MS Ala A&M Univ;

pa/Limestone Co Ed Assn; AEA; NEA; Biol Sci Curric Studies; Sec'dy Sci In-Ser Chp for Limestone Co Sch Sys; Hd Sci Dept East Limestone, Athens; cp/RSVP Adv Bd, Athens St Col; Epsilon Gamma Omega Chapt Alpha Kappa Alpha; Nat Coun of Negro Wom; OES; NAACP; Profl Wom's Clb; Chartered Pres of Am Legion Aux of Willie D Griffis Post of VFW; r/Village View U Meth Ch: Ed Com of N Ala Conf of U Meth Chs; 1980 Nom Bd of Pensions of N Ala Conf of U Meth Ch; hon/W/W Am 1973; Outstg Sec'dy Edr of Am & of Limestone Co Sch Sys; Sec'dy Nom to Jacksonville Tchr Hall of Fame; US SEn Alpha Kappa Alpha Neophyte of Yr Awd 1973.

HARRIS, PAMELLA DECOYISE oc/Social Worker; b/Aug 28, 1957; h/3764; Rockport Place, SW, Atlanta, GA 30331; ba/Cedartown, GA; p/Mr and Mrs Perry Harris, Atlanta, GA; ed/BA Wesleyan Col 1979; MA Cand W Ga Col 1982; pa/Social Wkr Ethel Harpst Home for Chd & Yth Inc; Coun of Chd; N Ga Child Care Assn; cp/NAACP; r/Antioch Bapt Ch; hon/Gov's Internship to Ga Mtl Htlh Inst 1978; W/W Black Ams 1981.

HARRIS, PAT oc/Director of Volunteers, Hospital Administrator; b/June 12, 1923; h/8200 Walnut Hill Lane, Dallas, TX 75231; c/Paul Wakefield, Patricia Dianne Stephenson; p/dec; ed/Basic Course in Hosp Mgmt 1969; Inst on Mgmt Principles 1971; Adult Ed Course, Dallas Jr Col 1974; pa/RN, Dir Vols, Hosp Admr Presb Hosp of Dallas; Fac Univ Tex Sem on Proflism 1972; Fac THA Sem Roles & Responsibilities of Dir of Vols 1975; Am Hosp Assn; Coun on Adm Pract, Dir of Vols 1979; THA Creative Mgmt of Vol Sers 1980; Mbrship Chm THA, Dirs of Vols; Charter Mbr Am Soc Dir of Vol Sers; Am Hosp Assn; Tex Nurses Assn; Charter Mbr Tex Assn Staff Dirs Hosp Vol Sers; cp/Notary Public, St of Tex; Assn Staff Dirs of Hosp Vol Sers St of Tex; Am Hosp Assn; r/Epis; hon/Article in *Texas Hospitals.*

HARRIS, PATRICK BRADLEY oc/Realtor; b/Apr 19, 1911; h/706 E Mauldin St, Anderson, SC 29621; ba/Anderson; m/Elizabeth Orr; c/Patrick Bradley Jr; p/Calhoun and Frances Morrah Harris; ed/Att'd Presb Col 3 Yrs; pa/VP Exec Sers & Planning Inc; Anderson Bd of Realtors; cp/Anderson Cancer Soc; Rotary Clb; Mem SC Ho of Reps 1969-; r/Young Meml ARP Ch: Mem, Ruling Elder; hon/Cits: Nat Coun on Aging, Am Nsg Home Assn; 1 of 10 Outstg Legislators in Nation; Outstg Freshman Legislator during first term in Gen Assembly 1969, Gen Assembly of SC.

HARRIS, RUTH N GILLMAN oc/Educator, Counselor; b/Aug 5, 1932; p/Fred (dec) and Annie Belle Ward Harris, Henderson, NC; ed/BS Va Union Univ; MA Howard Univ 1970; pa/Tchr-Lectr St Francis Col Bklyn Sch Dept; Acad Advr SUNY, Farmingdale Student Affairs Dept; APGA; Am Public Hlth Assn; Am Col Pers Assn; AAUW; cp/Delta Sigma Theta: NY Alumnae Chapt Pres, Nat Nom'g Com En Region; NYC Sch Bd Dist #5 Secy; Nat Coun of Negro Wom; Harlem Terms for Self-Help Adv Coun; Manhattanville Housing Coun; Addicts Rehab Ctr Exec Bd V Chp & Corresp Secy; r/Bapt; hon/Kappa Delta Pi; Eta Sigma Gamma; NY St Social Action Comm Outstg Achmt 1979.

HARRIS, SAMUEL MARCUS oc/Loan Officer, Bank Vice President; b/Sept 16, 1951; h/Roanoke, AL; ba/Bank of Wadley, Wadley, AL 36276; m/Jill Jordan (dec); c/Courtney Brook; p/George R (dec) and Cenus Burton Harris, Roanoke, AL; ed/BS Auburn Univ; Grad Ala Bnkg Sch 1979; pa/Citibanc of Ala 5 Yrs; VP & Loan Ofcr Bank of Wadley 1980-; Yng Ala Bnkrs; cp/JCs, Roanoke Immediate Past Pres; Roanoke Qtrback Clb; Auburn Alumni Assn; Adm Bd Roanoke First Meth Ch; Roanoke Country Clb; Roanoke Moose Lodge; r/Meth.

HARRIS, SHARAH RENEA oc/Student, Apartment Manager; b/Jan 9, 1959; h/1017 Engolio St, Plaquemine, LA 70764; p/Gehrig Leonard Sr and Louise Lewis Harris, Plaquemine, LA; ed/AS 1979, BS 1980 Grambling St Univ; Att'g So Univ Sch Law; pa/Student; Apt Mgr w Father; Lambda Alpha Epsilon; Pi Sigma Alpha; cp/Frontlash; r/Bapt; hon/W/W Students Am Univs & Cols 1979-80; Nat Dean's List; Outstg Acad Achmt in Polit Sci 1980; Versatility Awd 1980; Outstg Acad Achmt in Crim Just 1979; Most Outstg Polit Sci Clb Mem 1979-80.

HARRIS, THOMAS LEE oc/Industrial Engineer; b/Nov 13, 1941; h/6515 Marsh Ave, Huntsville, AL 35806; ba/Redstone Arsenal, AL; m/Lynn Marie Sharpless; c/Thomas Lee II, Johanna Lynn, Elizabeth Juanita, Margaret Pauletta; p/John Pearson and Bertha Viola Townsend Harris, Huntsville, AL; ed/BS Indust & Sys Engrg 1973 Univ of Ala-Huntsville; mil/USNR 1959-64; pa/Indust Engr Huntsville Hosp 1973; US Army Missile Res & Devel Command, Redstone Arsenal 1974-; Acting Chief Spec Projs & Planning Div Progs Mgmt Ofc, US Army Missile Command 1975-77; cp/Co-Chm Barry Goldwater for Pres Campaign 1964; Mem: Franklin Mint Collectors Soc, Huntsville Sci Fiction Assn, Am Legion; Dem Party; r/Ch of Christ; hon/Recip Lttrs of Commend: Gov George C Wallace 1970, Sen Edward M Kennedy 1975, Cmdr US Army Missile Res & Devel Command 1977.

HARRIS, VANDER E oc/Director of Physical Plant; b/Dec 27, 1932; h/1417 Pine St, Columbia, Sc 29204; ba/Columbia, SC; m/Janie Greenwood; c/Vander E Jr, Jason G; ed/BS Fisk Univ 1957; IBM Data Processing Sch Dip 1960; Further Study Fisk Univ & Tenn St Univ; mil/AUS Med Corps; pa/Benedict Col; Univ Tenn at Nash; Fisk Univ; Ala A&M Univ; Macon Area Voc & Tech Sch; Fort Val St Col; Douglas Air Craft Missile & Space Sys; A D Harris Construction Co; J E Crain Contractors; Soc Profl Engrs; Am Inst Plant Engrs; Assn Phy Plant Adm of Univ & Cols; cp/VFW; r/Meth; hon/Trinity Bapt Awd 1964; Pub'd Energy Paper & Rec'd $10,000 AED Awd for Benedict Col.

HARRIS, VERSIE H oc/Retired Minister; b/Dec 12, 1890; h/105 Harris St, PO Box 212, Brookhaven, MS 39601; m/Eva H; p/Wallace (dec) and Lucy Williams Harris (dec); ed/ThB; pa/Evangelistic Min; cp/Advr to Mayor; Mem Civic Bds; 33° Mason; r/Bapt; hon/Inspector Gen of St Masonic Lodge; Num Hons.

HARRIS, VIRGINIA D oc/Reference Librarian; b/July 4, 1925; h/Pine Bluff, AR; ba/Univ Ark Pine Bluff, Watson Meml Lib, Pine Bluff, AR 71601; m/Robert; c/Cheryl H Williams; p/Mattie B Carter, Elyria, OH; ed/BA Univ Ark Pine Bluff; MLS N Tex St Univ; pa/Branch Lib, Pine Bluff; Ref Lib, Univ Ark Pine Bluff; Ark Lib Assn; SWn Lib Assn; cp/OES; r/Prot; hon/Lectr for Acad Lectr Series 1981, "Study Abroad, Col of Libnship - Aberystwyth, Wales."

HARRISON, ALBERT CURTIS oc/Music and Choir Director; b/June 21, 1940; h/Ridgeland Rd, Box 140, Greenwood, MS 38930; ba/Greenwood; m/Beverly Gains; c/Keith Bernard, Neidra La Bertha; p/Earmon Harrison, Heidelberg, MS; Bertha Harrison (dec); ed/BS Mus Ed; MMus; pa/Public Sch Mus & Choir Dir, Amonda Elzy Sch; Leflore Co Tchrs Assn; NEA; r/Meth; hon/Star Tchr Amonda Elzy 1977-79, 1978-79.

HARRISON, ALBERTIS SYDNEY JR oc/Justice of Supreme Court of Virginia; b/Jan 11, 1907; h/Saddletree Farm, Lawrenceville, VA 23868; ba/Lawrenceville; m/Lacey Virginia B; c/Albertis S III, Antoinete H; p/Albertis S and Lizzie Goodwin Harrison; ed/LLB; mil/USN Lt (jg); pa/Var Bar Assns; cp/Gov of Va; Atty Gen of Va; St Senator; r/Epis; hon/LLD William & Mary Col.

HARRISON, DAVID FRANCIS oc/Computer Systems Engineering Consultant; b/Aug 1, 1936; h/13922 Mango Dr, Del Mar, CA 92014; ba/San Diego, CA; m/Susan J Luttringhaus; c/Bryon Scott, Grant David; p/Horace Earl Harrison (dec); Lottie M Overby, Hollister, MO; ed/B Mus Ed St Louis Inst Mus 1961; MMus Univ Neb 1965; Post Grad Work Univ Ia 1965-71; pa/Edr; Musician; Broadcaster; Elecs Tech; Computer Sys Analyst/Conslt, Control Data Corp; Nat Assn Ednl Broadcasters; Mus Pers Profl Interest Grp; hon/W/W S&SW; Logo Awd Control Data Corp Profl Sers Div 1978; Pi Kappa Lambda; 1st Prize Priscilla Parsons Composition Contest 1966; Pi Kappa Lambda Composition Awd 1965; Article: "MUSPROG: An Automated Music Programmer."

HARRISON, HENRY FORD oc/Retired; b/Dec 18, 1913; h/108 Rowell Dr, Selma, AL 36701; m/Mary Grice; c/Mary Hudson, Ann Maas, Jean Wehr, Patti Ivey; p/Joseph Charles (dec) and Amelia Hughes Harrison (dec); mil/USN WWII; pa/Designed & Copywrited Selma to Montgomery Freedom March Medal; Writer of Chd's Stories; Antique Collector & Appraiser; cp/Past Cmdr VFW; 32° Mason; Alcazar Shrine Temple; r/Presb; hon/Aide-de-Camp to Nat Cmdr of VFW.

HARRISON, HENRY MILTON JR oc/Announcer and Co-Host; b/Jan 21, 1928; h/2401 Roundabout Ln, Charlotte, NC 28210; ba/Charlotte; m/Susan Lancaster Wadsworth; c/Henton Rymil, David Robert; p/Henry Milton Sr and Sally Ina Hill Harsion, Snow Hill, NC; ed/Grad Coyne Radio & Elec Sch 1948; Hon DD Gulf Coast Sem 1978; Ordained Bapt Min 1976; pa/Announcer & Co-Host Daily Syndicated PTL Clb TV Prog; NCAB; NAB; NRB; cp/Optimist Clb; Full Gospel Businessman's F'ship Intl; r/Bapt; hon/Hon DD 1978; Author *Second Fiddle* 1977.

HARRISON, IRCEL COLUMBUS JR oc/Campus Minister; b/Aug 16, 1943; h/Rt 1 Box 115E, Lakewood Dr, Jefferson City, TN 37760; ba/Jefferson City; m/Rita Fairchilds; c/Sharon Elizabeth, John Richard, Stephanie Kay; ed/Ircel C Sr and Mildred B Harrison, Mobile, AL; ed/BS Univ So Miss 1965; MDiv SWN Bapt Theol Sim; DM Cand So Bapt Sem; mil/AUS 1965-67; pa/Dir Bapt Student Min, Middle Tenn St Univ 1970-76; Dir Bapt Student Union, Miss St Univ 1976-80; Dir Campus Mins, Carson-Newman Col 1980-; Assn So Bapt Campus Mins; Nat Inst Campus Mins; Nat Assn Fgn Student Advrs; cp/Pres Elect & Prog Chm Optimist Clb of Starkville 1977-79; r/So Bapt; hon/Outstg Yng Man Am 1979; Num Profl Inclg.

HARRISON, YEWELL oc/Retired; b/Feb 21, 1907; h/522 N Broad St, Lexington, TN 38351; m/Crystal Lee; c/Magaret Lee; p/Otis (dec) and Dovie Harrison (dec); ed/Murray St Col; pa/Org'd & Instr'd First Band:

Lone Oak HS, Reidland HS, Heath HS; Fulton HS, Lexington HS, Caywood City Sch, Montgomery HS; Prin Carr Inst; Played Sax w Irvin S Cobb Hotel Orch, Ritz Hotel Orch & Jack Stalcup Orch; Tchr Instrumentl Mus Farley & Hendron Grade Schs, McCracken Co, KY; cp/Plays for Ret'd Tchrs & Sr Citizens Meetings; hon/Selected to Play for Tenn St Conv of Ret'd Tchrs; First Bnad Dir Grad'd Through Mus Prog Murray St Univ.

HARSHBARGER, ROLLIN MAURICE oc/Building Contractor, Land Developer; b/Dec 27, 1919; h/Rt 1 Box 95, Mt Solon, VA 22843; m/Betty W; c/Pamela S; p/Jess L and Margaret W Harshbarger; mil/AUS 1st Sgt; pa/Pres R M Harshbarger Inc; Wayne Apt Inc, Pres; Va Nat Bank Dir; cp/Chm Augusta Co Supvrs; Giddian; N River Ruritan Clb; Augusta Co Repub Party; r/U Meth.

HARSTON, HAZEL TOLER oc/Retired Teacher; b/May 2, 1912; h/301 W Park, Farmerville, LA 71214; m/John B (dec); p/William R (dec) and Emma Dawkins Toler (dec); ed/BA N La Univ; pa/Ret'd Elem Sch Tchr; cp/Nat Leag Am Pen Wom, N La Branch, Secy & Hist; Alpha Delta Kappa, Hist & Chap; r/Bapt; hon/Pub'd Num Chd's Stories, Units, Plays, Articles & How-Tos.

HART, ELOISE oc/Real Estate; b/Feb 12, 1930; h/219 Circle Dr, Statesboro, GA 30458; ba/Statesboro; m/dec; c/Vicki Hart Santarone, William Gregory; p/Pearl Steptoe, Soperton, GA; ed/Real Est Lic 19978; pa/Real Est Sales, Lanier-DeLoach Realty; Statesboro Bd Rltrs; Ga Bd Rltrs; Nat Bd Rltrs; cp/Pres Cherokee Rose Garden Clb; Past Secy Bullock Coun Garden Clbs; r/Bapt; hon/Top Listing Real Est Assc Savannah Dist 1978.

HART, JOSEPH TATE oc/College President; b/May 5, 1930; h/Ferrum College, Ferrum, VA 24088; m/Carolyn Evans; c/James David, Mary Catherine, Sally T, Nancy L, Brian Joseph, Evan A; p/Ilva Tate Hart, Lake Junalaska, NC; ed/BA Emory & Henry Col 1951; MA Duke Univ 1953; PhD Am Univ 1967; mil/Intell Ofcr 1953-56; pa/US Govt, Johns Hopkins, Res Analyst Corp; Intl Planning Assocs; World Future Soc; Am Polit Sci Assn; Nat Planning Assn; Bd Dirs Nat Coun Indep Jr Cols; r/Rotary; Commun Ctrs; Bd Dirs Yth Rehab Inc; r/Meth Ch: Lay Ldr; hon/Mil & Govt Commends.

HARTE, EVA MARY oc/Retired; b/Mar 3, 1915; h/381 Cedar Pl, Land O' Lakes, FL 33539; m/Neville A; c/Jo Ann Morton, Flora Copley (dec); c/Ludwik (dec) and Josephine Agnes Maczak Mikolajczyk (dec); pa/Archaeol Field Trips; Petroglyphs; Gemology; cp/Commun Charities; r/Cath; hon/Many Ribbons in Gem & Min Shows.

HARTKE, VANCE oc/United States Senator; b/May 31, 1919; m/Martha Tiernan; ed/AB Evansville Col; JD Ind Univ; pa/Mayor of Evansville 1955-58; US Senate 1958-, Coms: Fin, Commerce, Sub-Coms: Surface Transport, Communs, African Trade; Deleg to: Atlantic Conf, NATO, Parliamtns Conf, Canadian-Am Parliamtry Exc, UN Food & Agrl Org; Atty; cp/Dem Party; Chm Vanderburgh Co Ctl Com 1952-58, VChm Dem Senatorial Campaign Com 1959-60, Chm Dem Senatorial Campaign Com 1961-63, Deleg Dem Nat Conv 1960; r/Mem: St Paul's Luth Ch, Evansville, St Paul's Luth Ch, Falls Ch, Va.

HARTLEY, HERBERT CLIFTON oc/Businessman; b/Feb 21, 1938; h/1202 Nassau, Plainview, TX 79072; ba/P'view; m/Judy; c/Leah, Susan Seago, Gloria Hoggett, Donnie Meikle; p/C Herbert Hartley, P'view, TX; Margaret Cole, P'view, TX; ed/BS Sec'dy Ed; mil/Tex NG; pa/Owner Burger Train Drive-In; Owner Blue Lakes Miniature Golf; cp/P'view C of C; Campaigned for Morris Sheats for Cong; r/Calvary Temple Interdemon; hon/Basketball S'ship NTSU; Letters in Track & Boxing; Plainviews Man of Day 1979.

HARTLINE, JEFF oc/Marketing Representative; b/Oct 14, 1955; h/299 Heck Rd, Kennesaw, GA 30144; ba/Atlanta, GA; m/Melodie; p/John William and JoAnne Hartline, Juliet, TN: ed/BA Freed-Hardeman Col 1976; pa/Mktg Rep Jackson & Coker; Ldr Phys Recruiting in SE; r/Ch of Christ.

HARTSELL, DONALD WAYNE SR oc/Preacher; b/Nov 17, 1939; h/700 Hwy 8 N, New Boston, TX 75570; ba/New Boston; m/Sandra Lee Hearn; c/Donald Wayne Jr, Jonathan Dwayne, Timothy Ray, Joshua Lee; p/James Grover and Hazelene Elizabeth Hartsell, China Grove, NC; ed/Cert Theol, Ala Christian Sch of Rel; mil/USAF 5 Yrs Airman 1st Cl; pa/Christian Camp Cnslr; Lectr & Preacher Ala, Ark, NC, Calif, Utah, Tex; cp/Chm New Boston Rehab Com, VP NB Little Leag; r/Ch of Christ; hon/Num Achmt Awds Sears & Roebuck; VP Student Body Fruitland Bapt Bible Inst; 2nd Pl Orators Contest, Ala Christian Col.

HARTSFIELD, BETTY T oc/Instructor; b/May 31, 1943; h/190 Alabama Dr, Jacksonville, AR 72076; m/Wayland M; c/Brent, Bart; p/Russell and Jamie Thomas, Leoma, TN; ed/BS Athens St Col 1972; MA Univ Ala 1978; AA Cert in Tchg Jacksonville St Univ 1980; pa/USAF Employee; Tch Nights, Eng Dept Ark St Univ; cp/Ofcrs Wives Clb; PTO; Prot Wom of Chapel; r/So Bapt; hon/Staff Writer for "La Petite Roche."

HARTSFIELD, WAYLAND MARSHALL oc/Chaplain; b/June 27, 1942; h/Jacksonville, AR; ba/LRAFB, AR; m/Betty T; c/Brent, Bart; p/Austin and Addie B Hartsfield, Loretto, TN; ed/BA Belmont Col 1966; MDiv 1975; DMin 1978; mil/USAF Chaplain; Guid Cnslr Sec'dy Ed 7 Yrs; Chaplain USAF; Giles Co Bapt Assn Modr; Etowah Bapt Assn V-Modr; Lawrence Co Bapt Assn Ch Trg Dir; Pres Pastor's Assn; cp/Chaplain: Civitan Intl, Gile Co Tenn & Masonic Order in Glencoe, Ala; r/So Bapt; hon/Author "Where Are the Men?" 1978.

HARVARD, BEVERLY JOYCE oc/Affirmative Action Specialist; b/Dec 22, 1950; h/3541 Cumberland Rd, E Pt, GA 30344; ba/Atlanta, GA; m/Jimmy; p/Arcelious Sr (dec) and Irene Perkins Bailey, Macon, GA; ed/BA Morris Brown Col 1972; MS Ga St Univ 1980; pa/Affirmative Action Spec, City of Atlanta; Public Affairs Dir, Atlanta Dept Public Safety; ABWA; Am Mgmt Assn; Bur Nat Affairs Pers Policy Forum; W Atlanta Elem Sch Adv Bd; cp/Delta Sigma Theta; U Yth Adult Conf; r/Meth.

HARVEL, ROSS oc/Superintendent of Schools; b/Mar 5, 1917; h/201 Bourland, Keller, TX 76248; ba/Keller; m/Lillie Mae; c/Paul, Norma Helm; p/dec; ed/BS; MS: EdD; mil/AUS, USAF WWII; pa/Bd Dirs Occupl Plan'g for TEA 3 Yrs; St Bd Dirs Voc Admrs Assn 3 Yrs; Past St Pres Voc Admrs Assn; St Bd Dirs Tex Profl Edrs Assn; Adj Prof E Tex St Univ; Tex Assn Sch Admrs; Am Assn Sch Admrs; Tex Profl Edrs; cp/Keller City Coun 2 Yrs; Past Mayor Keller; Lay Preacher 1st Bapt Ch Keller; Lions Clb; 3 Local PTAs; r/Bapt; hon/Hon Life Mem Tex PTA; Hon Admiral Tex Navy; Spec Awd for Outstg Ser to Keller Commun; Spec Awd Outstg Ser to PTA; Hon Mem FHA; Spec Awd Outstg Ser to FFA.

HARVEY, GERALD oc/Educational Therapist; b/Feb 21, 1950; h/20 80 Mason St, Macon, GA 31204; p/Johnny L and Maggie E Mills, Macon, GA; ed/BS Tuskegee Inst; MEd Ga Col; pa/Ednl Therapist.

HARVEY, WILLIAM ROBERT oc/President of Hampton Institute; b/Jan 29, 1941; h/612 Shore Rd, Hampton, VA 23669; ba/Hampton; m/Norma; c/Kelly Renee, William Christopher; p/William B and Claudis P Harvey, Brewton, AL; ed/BA 1961 Talladega Col; MA 1966 Va St; DEd 1971 Harvard Univ; mil/Army Histn 1962-65; pa/Pres Hampton Inst; Profl Mbrship: Am Assn Higher Ed; r/Bapt; hon/Woodrow Wilson F'ship; Harvard Univ Higher Ed Fellow.

HARVILLE, JEAN ELLEN oc/Teacher; b/Mar 13, 1940; h/702 Wildwood Rd, Daingerfield, TX 74538; m/Morris Vernon; c/Brian Clark, Stanley Keith; p/Mae Oakmail Baine, Fordyce, AR; ed/Att'd Miss Univ for Wom; Att'd Univ So Miss; Grad Univ Ark-Monticello; pa/Elem Sch Tchr: Harmny Grove, Ark; Dierks, Ark; Daingerfield, Tex 15 Yrs; Tex St Tchrs Assn; NEA; Tex Classroom Tchrs Assn; Morris Co Tchrs Assn; cp/BSA; Ladies Aux Daingerfield Vol Fire Dept; r/Bapt; hon/Commun Commr BSA 1978-80; Den Ldr Coach 1980-81; Den Ldr Awd 1980; Water Safety Instr; Article "Famous People Auction."

HARVILLE, LEONARD BARRINGTON SR oc/General Manager; b/July 13, 1936; h/Box 11, Rt 1, Ringgold, VA 24541; ba/Danville, VA; m/Betty Sue; c/Leonard Jr, Mark Steven, Deborah Sue, Algie Dwight; p/Elijah (dec) and Louella Harville, Danville, VA; mil/USMC; pa/Gen Mgr Yellow Cab of Danville & Allied Devel Corp; Va St Taxicab Assn; cp/Am Legion; r/Bapt.

HARVILLE, MORRIS VERNON oc/Teacher, Coach; b/Sept 11, 1941; h/PO Box 602, Daingerfield, TX 75638; m/Jean; c/Brian Clark, Stanley Keith; p/Vernon and Wootie Harville, Bogata, TX; ed/Att'd Paris Jr Col; BSE Univ Ark-Monticello 1964; MEd Stephen F Austin Univ 1980; pa/Asst Coach & Tchr Bearder, Ark & Fordyce, Ark; Hd Coach, Dierks, Ark 1965-70; Asst Coach & Tchr, Daingerfield, Tex; Pres Local Clrm Tchrs Assn; cp/Asst Chief of Daingerfield Vol Fire Dept; Dir Ambulance Ser; Capt DVFD; Alderman City of Daingerfield; r/Bapt; hon/Outstg Coach Dist 7-B 1965, 68, 70; Outstg Fireman 1976.

HASSELL, DOROTHY HOWARD oc/District Manager; b/Apr 13, 1928; h/PO Box 10, Holly Pond, AL 35083; ba/Same; m/David C Jr; c/Carmalita H Krupp, David C III, Anita Brumleve; p/Tomie (dec) and Bertie H Howard, Cullman, AL; pa/Dist Mgr Avon Prods Inc; cp/C of C; Love Polits; r/So Bapt; hon/Circle of Excell, 3 Yrs Avon Mgr, Most in Div 1977-78.

HASSELL, HERMAN oc/Retired; b/Mar 23, 1915; h/220 59th St W, Bradenton, FL 33505; m/Florence; c/Barbara, Terrence, Florence, Gerald, Daniel; p/Herman (dec) and Cecelia Hassell (dec); ed/BA CCNY 1942; AS Manatee Jr Col 1977; mil/USNR 1942-51; pa/Ret'd Foreman PO Dept Mil Mail & Fgn Sects; cp/Past Cmdr Am Legion; Past Grand Knight K of C; Faithful Navigator 4° Saratoga; r/Cath; hon/Fam of Yr, K of C 1979; Life Mem Am Legion 1959; Superior Accomp Awd PO Dept 1964; Cert Awd PO Dept 1969.

HASTINGS, PETER COLEMAN oc/Chemical-Mining Management; b/Dec 12, 1940; h/Mulberry, FL; m/Linda Watts; c/Monica Lynn, Peter Coleman Jr; p/Coleman Livingston and Locri Pecholis Hastings, Columbia, SC; ed/BS 1964, MS 1972 Univ SC; MBA Va Commonwlth Univ 1979; pa/Chem Mgmt, Engrg Mgmt, Mobil Chem Co; pa/Am Inst Chem Engrg; r/Epis; hon/Sigma Xi; W/W S&SW; Paper Pub'd.

HASTY, RICHARD SPENCER oc/Minister; b/Sept 12, 1928; h/178 Pleasant Ave, Portland, ME 04103; ba/Portland; m/Margaret Lawrence Howlett; c/Margaret Lawrence, Christopher Spencer, Victoria Merritt; p/Harold Clyde (dec) and Jennie Sanborn Hasty, Dover, NH; ed/AB Univ NH; STB Harvard Div Sch; mil/Mil Intell; 1st Lt 1952-57; 2nd Lt 1950-52; pa/Minister; r/Unitarian Universalist; hon/DIB 1978-79; Notable Ams 1978-79.

HATANAKA, MASAKAZU oc/Head, Cell Physiology Section; b/Mar 23, 1933; h/14003 Shippers Lane, Rockville, MD 20853; ba/Bethesda, MD; m/Kazuko; c/Iwao, Takeshi; p/Kazuo Hatanaka, Mieken, Japan; Yasue Hatanaka (dec); ed/MD; PhD; pa/Hd Cell Physiology Sect Nat Cancer Inst, Nat Inst of Hlth, Bethesda, MD; r/Buddhism; hon/Visiting Scholar Awd, US-France Cancer Prog 1977.

HATCHER, CHARLES ROSS JR oc/Professor of Surgery; Clinic Director; b/Jun 28, 1930; h/1105 Lullwater Rd NE, Atlanta, GA 30307; ba/Atlanta, GA; c/Marian Barnett, Charles Ross III; p/Charles R Sr and Vivan Miller Hatcher, Attapulgus, GA; ed/BS magna cum laude Univ of Ga; MD cum laude Med Col of Ga; mil/USMC Capt, Walter Reed Army Med Ctr, Washington, DC; pa/Emory Univ Sch of Med: Prof of Surg, Chief Thoracic & Cardiovascular Surg; Dir Emory Univ Clinic; Bd Trustees: Woodruff Med Ctr; Mem: Am Col of Surgeons, Am Col of Cardiology, Am Col Chest Physicians, Am Surgical Assn, So Surgical Assn, Am Assn for Thoracic Surgery, Soc of Thoracic Surgeons, Am Heart Assn, AMA, Others; cp/Atlanta Rotary Clb; Ga Heart Assn; r/Meth; hon/Phi Beta Kappa; Sigma Xi; Alpha Omega Alpha; W/W in Am.

HATCHER, WILLIAM BIGGS oc/Assistant Superintendent; b/June 23, 1914; h/Radford, VA; m/Nell; p/Clark C and Emma Day Hatcher, Montvale, VA; ed/Att'd Lees McRae Col, High Pt Col; BS, MS VPI & SU; Grad Work Univ Va; pa/Tchr; Asst Prin; Assoc Prof; Tchr Ext Classes, Univ Va; Asst Supt Schs; Am Assn Sch Admrs; NEA; VEA; Radford Ed Assn; Phi Delta Kappa; cp/Radford Rotary Clb, Pres Bd Dirs; Commun Chest Chm; Employ the Handicapped Com, Radford Co C of C; r/Presb: Elder, SS Tchr, Sponsor Westphel Col Girls; hon/Life Scout; Old Dominion W/W-Virginia Lives 1964; Radford Rotary Clb Hon Plaque 1980; Tng Room, Radford HS, Dedicated to & Named for 1980.

HATFIELD, BENJAMIN FRANK oc/Professional Engineer; Public Utility Consultant; b/Jul 31, 1906; h/3916 Land O' Lakes Dr NE, Atlanta, GA 30342; ba/Same; m/Ada Ella Hatcher; c/Ada Joyce H Coleman, Benjamin Frank Jr (dec); p/Henry and Katie Corinne Scholl Hatfield (dec); ed/BS Elect Engrg, BS Mech Engrg, summa cum laude Grad, #1 Engrg Grad, Univ Tenn 1930; So Bell T&T Transmission Sch 1931; Addit Studies; mil/2nd Lt Corps of Engrs Resv to Col of Resv 1930-66; Ret'd Col 1966-; pa/So Bell T&T Co: Equipmt Engr Atlanta, Ga 1930-32, 36-41; Switchman Louisville, Ky 1932-36; Maintenance & Practices Engr, Co HQs 1946-49, La Chief Engr New Orleans, La 1949-53, Asst VP Co HQs 1953-71, Ret'd 1971; Tech Mem Steinhauer, Hatfield & Good, Assocs, Public Utility Conslts 1971-; VP A L Groce, Assoc, Public Utility Conslts 1972-; Mem Fac Bell Sys Ctr for Tech Ed, Lisle, Ill 1971-72; Reg'd Profl Engr, Ga & Formerly La; Active in Devel of Telephone Circuits & Profl Groups on Telephone Bus 1949-71; Instr So Bell Engrn Ec Courses 1962-68; Conducted Num Sems 1960-68; Bell Sys Regulatory Adv Panel for Regulatory Res 1969-71; Other Past Positions; Dir Am Inst of Elect Engrs 1952-53; GA Arch & Engrg Soc; Sr Mem, IEEE; Life Mem, Telephone Pioneers of Am; NC Indep Telephone Assn; cp/Yaarab Temple Shrine Band: Trumpet Player, Secy; Land O' Lakes Civic Clb: Past Treas, VP, Past Pres, Past Dir; Past VP, 8th Ward Civic Assn; Am Heritage Soc; Nat Geographic Soc; Others; r/Grace U Meth Ch, Atlanta: Mem, Tchr Adult Classes, Altar Guild Steward, Mem Com on Hist & Records, Lay Spkr, Ch Trustee, Mem Coun on Mins, Other Past Positions; hon/Fellow, Intl Inst of Commun Serv; Jr Engrg Prize, Univ Tenn; Krusi Prize in Elect Engrg, Univ Tenn; #1 Grad, AUS Engr Sch 1935; Am Defense Medal; Am Theatre Campaign Ribbon; Past VP Univ Tenn Chapt: Phi Kappa Phi, Tau Beta Pi;

Pacific-Asiatic Theatre Campaign Ribbon w Bronze Star for N Burma Campaign; Cmdr, Meritorious Ser Unit 1945; WW II Victory Medal; Bronze Star Medal; Fellow Mem ABI; Num Biogl Listings.

HAUSE, ROBERT LUKE III oc/Professor, Conductor; b/Dec 12, 1935; h/2208 Charles St, Greenville, NC 27834; ba/Greenville; m/Karen McCann; c/Eric M, Jonathan M, Evan R; p/Robert L Jr (dec) and Mary Lucile Morehead Hause (dec); ed/B Mus Ed cum laude 1958, MMus 1960 Univ Mich; pa/Jacksonville Public Schs 1960-62; Asst Conductor, Jacksonville Symph Orch 1960-62; Stetson Univ 1962-67; E Carolina Univ Prof Mus & Conductor Symph Orch 1967-; Nat Sch Orch Assn, So Div Chm 1965-67; Phi Mu Alpha Sinfonia, Gov Province 20 1976-; cp/Greenville Boys Choral Assn, Chm 1975-77; Candlewick Swim & Tennis Clb, Pres 1971-73; En Mus Fest Bd Dirs 1962-76; hon/James L Babcock S'ship 1958; Oreon E Scott Awd 1958; Elsa Gardner Stanley Awd 1960; Phi Beta Kappa; Phi Kappa Phi; Pi Kappa Lambda; 2 Pub'd Mus Works: *Toccata in G Major by J S Bach*, Transcribed for Orch by R Hause; *Sonatina for Violin and Piano* 1979.

HAUSE, WILLIAM HARRY oc/Electronic Technician; h/116 Locust St, Clinton, MI 49236; cp/Elect Technician, Nn Telecom Sys Corp; Poet; Lenawee Area Writers Assn; Stella Woodall Poetry Soc; Trustee Steering Com, Yana Ctr of Saline (Mich); Author, "Red River", "Trail of the Bigots", "The Mountain Duke", "Tools of God", Others; hon/AUS Commends & Good Conduct Medals.

HAVAR, VASCHAHAR oc/Programmer, Analyst; b/July 20, 1950; h/7951 Woodpecker Way, Alexandria, VA 22306; ba/Alexandria; p/Robert H and Muriel D Hughes, Whitesboro, NY; ed/Att'd Hartwick Col 1967-68, St Univ NY-Oneonta 1968-69; Hon Grad Computer Lng Ctr 1974; pa/Data Processing Sr Progr/Analyst, Software Consltg/Ser Bur; Assn Computer Progrs & Analysts; cp/ABWA, Treas 19978; OES.

HAVELOS, SAM GEORGE oc/Restauranteur, Numismatist; b/Dec 4, 1915; h/305 Cork Dr, PO Drawer E, Blacksburg, VA 24060; ba/Blacksburg; m/Diana; p/George D (dec) and Spyridoula Havelos, Athens, Greece; ed/Bus Col; The Zasserian Col of Penmanship; pa/Restauranteur; Numismatic; c/C of C; Frat Orgs; r/Greek Orthodox; hon/Cert of Merit Ser, Nat Soc SAR; W/W S&SW 1978-79.

HAVENS, DOLORES D oc/Research Speech Pathologist; b/Jan 19, 1938; h/207 W Strickland St, Del Rio, TX78840; m/Rudolph E; c/Ralph C, Frances Y; p/Ernest J and Rosalia Rosas Draeger, Del Rio, TX; ed/BS 1959, MEd 1972 SW Tex St Univ; PhD Univ Wis-Madison 1975; pa/Res Speech Pathol; Prin Investigator; Ongoing Res in Lings; Am Speech-Lang-Hearing Assn; Tex St Tchrs Assn; Am Acad Pvt Pract Speech Pathol & Audiol; r/Prot; hon/Del Rio HS Valedictorian 1956; W/W S&SW 1980-81; Pub'd Author.

HAVILAND, LEONA oc/Librarian; b/Nov 10, 1916; h/809 Penn Ave, St Cloud, FL 32769; m/Warren John Burke; p/Howard Brush Haviland, Lincoln, DE; Ada Grace Jewell; ed/BS Ed; MS LS; pa/ALA; NY Geneal/Biogl Soc; cp/LI Hist Soc; Nat Assn Ret'd Fed Employees; hon/W/W: Am Wom, E.

HAWKINS, HERMAN HERBERT oc/Product Design Engineer; b/May 7, 1954; h/6075 Alpine Circle Apt #8, Beaumont, TX 77708; ba/Beaumont; p/Calvin Sidney (dec) and Alice Blanch Hill Hawkins, Borger, TX; ed/AA Frank Philips Col 1973; BSME Tex Tech Univ 1975; Postgrad Work W Tex St Univ 1978-80; pa/Sr Engr Mason & Hanger, Silas Mason Co Inc 1975-80; Engr NL Rig Equip 1980-; Am Soc Mech Engrs; VChm Panhandle Plains Subsect 1979-80; Tau Beta Pi; Pi Tau Sigma; r/Pentecostal Holiness; SS Supt 1972-80; hon/W/W S&SW 1980-81; Profl Engr St of Tex 1980.

HAWKINS, JIMMY W SR oc/Professional Truck Driver; b/May 15, 1943; h/Rt 2 Box 272, Reedy Creek Rd, Bristol, TN 37620; ba/Bristol; m/Gloria; c/Tarina Kay, Jimmy W Jr; p/Jimmy W Hawkins, Bristol, VA; Ruby E White Hawkins (dec); mil/USAF 1st Lt; pa/Profl Truck Driver, Onite Transp Co; Past Ruritan Mem Va; cp/Ctrl Heights Citizen Com for Better Ed PTA Pres; r/Missionary Bapt; hon/Hon Mem Tenn Public Safety; 10 Safe Driver; 10 Yr Safe Wkr; 1st Pl 6 Times Truck Rodeo Awd; 1st Pl St Rodeo 2 Times; 2nd Pl St Rodeo 2 Times; 3rd Pl 1 Time; Pres Ctrl Heights PTA.

HAWKINS, ROBERT A oc/Director of Guidance; b/Aug 21, 1924; h/3305 Providence Dr, Midland, TX 79703; ba/Midland; m/Nina Jo; c/Paul Clark, Sheila Ann H Jordan (Mrs); p/Lawrence R Hawkins (dec); Grace O Lauer, Canada; ed/BA 1948, MA 1967 Abilene Christian Univ; EdD 1974 Tex Tech Univ; pa/Dir of Guid, Midland Col; Instr in Phil; Contbr Articles to Profl Jours; Translator of *Bible Student's New Testament*; cp/Active in Civic Affairs; Spkr Num Orgs; r/Active in Local & Area Rel Emphasis; hon/Phi Kappa Phi; DIB; Notable Ams; W/W in S&SW; Book of Hon; Fellow Mem ABI.

HAWKINS, SARAH MARGARETT oc/Retired Hospital Advisor; b/Mar 9, 1915; h/6801 Alter St, Balto, MD 21207; p/James Henry (dec) and Barbara Barclay Hawkins (dec); ed/BS; RN; pa/Adm Phys Meml Hosp, La Plate, Md; Fac Sch of Nsg Md Gen Hsop; Dir Nurses, Md Gen Hosp; Hosp Adv Md St Dept Hlth & Mtl Hygiene; Past Treas Md St Nurses Assn; Sigma Theta Tau; Bd Dirs Md Gen Nurses Alumnae; Taught Red Cross Nurses Aides; Charge Nurse, Casualty Sta WWII; cp/Regent John Eager Howard Chapt NSDAR; Past Pres Wom's Aux Old St Paul's Ch; Public Ser Progs St SCAO; Past Pres Bd Linwood Chd's Ctr; Am Wom in Radio & RV; English Spkg Union; Md Hist Soc; Past Pres Pilot Clb Balto; r/Epis; hon/Freedom's Foun Val Forge for Radio Prog "Hist of Flag"; Citizen's Ser Awd, Heart Assn of Ctrl Md; Bronze Good Citizenship Medal, Md SAR; Nurse of Yr 1979.

HAWS, RONALD WILLIAM oc/Insurance Co Executive; b/Mar 25, 1941; h/Jacksonville, FL; m/Rebecca Lynn Wright; c/Matthew Lloyd, Heather Leigh; p/Ernest Robert and Clara Louise Haws; ed/BS Univ Tampa 1965; MA Univ S Fla 1970; CLU Am Col 1978; RHU NAHY 1979; FLMI Loma 1980; pa/Mgr-Owner Gen Agcy Operation 1975-76; Dir Mktg & Tng, Fdrs Life 1976-79; Dir Sales Devel & Tng Profl Ins Corp 1979-; Nat Assn Life Underwriters; Am Soc CLU; Nat Assn Hlth Underwriters; Sales & Mktg Execs Intl; cp/Dir Woodmere Homeowner's Assn 1980-81; r/Meth; hon/W/W S&SW 1980; Contbr to Profl Jours.

HAY, BETTY JO oc/Volunteer, Homemaker; b/June 6, 1931; h/7236 Lupton Circle, Dallas, TX 75225; m/Jess T; c/Patricia, Deborah Werner; p/Duncan and Kathryn Peacock, McAlester, OK; ed/BA So Meth Univ 1952; cp/Coor'g Bd Tex Col & Univ Sys 1972-; Chm Fin Plan'g Com, Prog Devel Com; Mtl Hlth Assn 1978-: Fin Com, Childhood & Adolescent Com; Mtl Hlth Assn Tex 1974-; Mtl Hlth Assn, Dallas Co 1972-: VP Public Info, Chm Child Abuse Conf 1978, Chd's Com, Mbrship Com; Dallas Lwyrs Wives Clb; Dallas Coun World Affairs, Wom's Div; Mortar Bd Alumni Assn; Dallas Symph Orch Leag; Hist Preserv Leag; Dallas Wom's Clb; Bard & Ballad Review Clb; Com to Plan Dallas Co Strategy for Intl Yr of Child; r/Meth; hon/Intl W/W Commun Ser; World W/W Wom.

HAY, GEORGE AUSTIN oc/Actor, Director, Producer; b/Dec 25; h/2022 Columbia Rd NW, Washington DC 20009; p/George and Mary Austin Hay; ed/BS; MA; MLitt; mil/AUS WWII; pa/Tchr; Writer; Actor, Broadway: "Inherit the Wind", "What Every Woman Knows"; TV Shows, Commercials, Feature Movies: "Child's Play" w James Mason, "Being There" w Peter Sellers; Artist, Exhibs: Duncan Gals, NY, Lincoln Ctr, Carnegie Inst, Am Painters in Paris; Prodr-Dir: Def Dept Documentaries, Army Tng Films, US Dept of Transp; Mem: Wash Film Coun, Fed Design Coun, Am Artists Profl Leag, Nat Acad TV Arts & Scis, Mus Lib Assn, Inst for Bach Studies, Shakespeare-Oxford Soc, SAR, Nat Press Clb, Screen Actors Guild, Others; cp/Nat Trust for Hist Preserv; Cambrian Co Histl Soc; Donated Turn-of-Century Period Room to Museum; Bd Govs & Trustee Wash Arts Clb; hon/Fellow Mem ABI; Artists USA; Notable Ams of Bicent Era; DIB; Men of Achmt; W/W.

HAYES, BETTY JO BATES oc/Real Estate Broker and Instructor; b/Jan 26, 1932; h/916 E Georgia Ave, DeLand, FL 32720; ba/Deland; m/Clifford; p/Elbert and Nellie Bates, Ooltewah, TN; ed/Daytona Bch Commun Col 1970; BS Rollins Col 1972; pa/Real Est Broker & Instr; Dist 2 VP Fla Assn Rltrs 1980; Pres DeLand & W Volusia Bd Rltrs 1979; Pres Volusia Wom's Coun Rltrs 1978; Dist 2 VP Wom's Coun Rltrs 1978; cp/Pres Friends of DeLand Pub Lib 1979; Campaign Mgr Volusia Co Cthouse Beautification Com; Pilot Clb DeLand; BPW; DeLand Wom's Clb; r/Bapt; hon/Rltr Assoc of Yr, DeLand Bd Rltrs; 1976; Rltr of Yr DeLand Bd Rltrs 1977.

HAYES, DEANNE oc/Head Librarian; b/Aug 31, 1937; h/PO Box 384, Hollis, OK 73550; ba/Hollis; p/L G Bell, Ind, MO; Pauline Smollock, Nampa, Idaho; ed/AA Wn Okla St Col; BS Oscar Rose Col; pa/ALA; OLA; Harmon Co Hist Assn; cp/Okla Arts & Humanities Coun; Okla Image Prog; r/Bapt; hon/World W/W Wom; W/W Am Cols & Univs; Outstg Wom of Am; DIB; Commun Ldrs Am; Book of Honor.

HAYES, MARLENA NELSON oc/Welcome Wagon Hostess; b/Aug 29, 1941; h/Bay City, TX; m/Daniel E; c/Lisa Kay, (Stepch:) Keith, Royce; p/Neal McMaster Nelson; Dorothy Brugman Nelson; ed/Grad w Hons Alvin Jr Col 1961; BS Ed Univ Tex 1963; pa/Tchr 15 Yrs; Welcome Wagon Hostess, Bay City Tex; Tex St Tchrs Assn 1963-78; Secy Westgate PTA 1964-65; Charter Reporter Delta Upsilon Chapt Alpha Delta Kappa 1978-79; cp/Cystic Fibrosis Dr 1976; Cancer Dr 1978; Bay City Day Care Bd; r/Meth; hon/Outstg Student Alvin Jr Col 1961; Good Neighbor Comm Tex Awd 1961; Sears Foun F'ship Ec Ed 1974; Grand Prize Rice Dish Round-Up Contest 1975; Poems Pub'd.

HAYES, MAXINE DELORES oc/Physician; b/Nov 29, 1946; h/2507 Meadow St, Jackson, MS 39213; ba/Brandon, MS; p/Isaac (dec) and Myrtle Hayes, Jackson, MS; ed/AB; MD; MPH; pa/Dir Hinds-Rankin Urban Hlth Innovations Proj; cp/Instr Pediatrics Univ Miss Med Sch; Co-Dir Nurse-Practitioner Prog UMC; r/Prot; hon/Miss's Outstg Yng Wom of Yr 1978; Upjohn Awd for Excell in Med 1973.

HAYES, OSCAR LAWRENCE oc/Operations Manager; b/Jan 1, 1935; h/2308 Stuart Ave, Albany, GA 31707; ba/Albany; m/Margie Nell; c/Donna Elaine, Debra Lynn, Christopher Joe; p/Lawrence Carroll Hayes, La Grange, GA; Ruby Mae Hayes (dec); ed/La Grange Bus Sch; mil/USN; pa/GAC Fin Corp 1959-66: Br Rep, Asst Mgr, Br Mgr, Co Intl Auditor; Franklin Fin 1966-69; Finance America Corp 1969- (Formerly GAC); Past VP & Trustee Albany Lenders Exch; cp/Past Pres Hasan Cartoon Capers; Elect'd to Exec Bd, SW Ga MD Assn; r/Bapt; hon/Hon Mem Fin Am Pres Clb 1979; Elect'd for Good Citizen Awd, Fin Am 1980.

HAYES, PHYLLIS oc/Chemistry Instructor and Department Chairperson; b/Nov 29, 1943; h/Rt 2, Magnolia, MS 39652; p/Willam Neil Sr and Dorothy Laura McGehee Hayes; ed/AA SW Jr Col; BS Millsaps Col; MS Univ So Miss; EdS Univ Miss; PhD USM-Hattiesburg; pa/Chem Instr, Copiah-Lincoln Jr Col 16 Yrs; Miss Sci Tchr Assn; Miss Jr Col Fac Assn; Copiah-Lincoln Jr Col Fac Assn; Alpha Epsilon Delta Pre-Med Hon; Am Chem Soc; r/Bapt; hon/Nat Sci Foun Part; Memphis St Part in Instrumtl Analysis; Outstg Yng Wom Am; Delta Kappa Gamma Ednl Hon; 1 of 10 Jr Col Chem Instrs chosen by "Ole MIss" Pharmacy Sch to Tour Pharm Houses: Eli Lilly & Abbot, Chgo & Indpls; CMA Awd, 1 of 5 Outstg Chem Tchr in US & Can; Chem Mfr Assn Awd 1980; Outstg Instr of Yr, Copiah-Lincoln Jr Col 1980.

HAYES, RAYBURN PAUL oc/Investment Banker; b/Aug 10, 1947; h/10230 Deermont Trail, Dallas, TX 75243; ba/Dallas; m/Linda Ruth; c/Todd, Jennifer; p/Rayburn D and Kathryn Hayes, Lufkin, TX; ed/BA Unv Houston 1971; pa/Reg'd Rep for Rauscher, Pierce, Refsnes Ins of Dallas; Tex Municipal Adv Coun; Dallas Bond Clb; Full Gospel Businessmens F'ship Intl; cp/Yng Repub Party; r/Full Gospel.

HAYES, TEDDIE NARVER oc/Commercial Pilot, Instructor, Electronic Technician; b/Jan 24, 1942; h/Rt 5 Box 218, Durham, NC 27704; m/Addie Adams; p/Jake Hayes, Laurel Hill, NC; ed/Att'd NC Col 1961-64; US Signal Sch, AUS 1964-65; Assoc Deg Spartan Sch Aeronautics 1981; Commercial Pilot Rating, Airplane Single Engine Land; Rotorcraft Helicopter, Harvey Young Airport 1980; mil/AUS 1964-78; pa/Avionics Instr; Pilot & A&P Mechanic; Civil Air Patrol 2nd Lt; Command Pilot & Tng Ofcr; Negro Airmen Intl; Aircraft Owners & Pilots Assn; NAACP; r/Morning Star Bapt Ch; hon/USO Ser-man of Yr 1972; Comdrs Awd, Civil Air Patrol 1972; Hon Grad Spartan Sch of Aeronautics 1979.

HAYLES, JASPER A oc/Associate Professor; b/Nov 19, 1922; h/Jonesboro, AR; ba/PO Box 1080, State Univ, AR 72467; m/Winona; c/Richard, p/J A Sr and Mildred Hayles, Frisco City, AL; ed/BS, MS Auburn Univ; PhD La St Univ; mil/USN; AUS; NG; pa/Prof Agric Ed, Ark St Univ Col of Agric; Ark Voc Agric Tchrs Assn; Ark Voc Spec Needs Assn; Ark St FFA Foun; Ark St Adv Bd Spec Needs Progs; So Region Agric Edrs; Am Assn Voc Instrl Mats Bd Dirs; Nat Voc Agric Tchrs Assn; Nat Voc Special Needs Assn; Nat FFA Alumni Assn; Delta Tau Alpha; Alpha Tau Alpha; r/Presb; hon/Pub'd Author.

HAYNES, MARY MARGARET oc/Teacher, Recorder-Treasurer; b/Mar 2, 1923; h/PO Box 42, Washington, AR 71862; p/Thomas Giles (dec) and Callie Bailey Haynes (dec); ed/BA Ouachita Bapt Univ 1951; pa/Elem 34 Yrs; Recorder-Treas for City of Wash, Ark; Delta Kappa Gamma; cp/Bd Dirs & Recording Secy Pioneer Wash Restor Foun; r/Bapt; hon/Awd of Merit, Grade Tchr Mag 1969; Tchr of Yr, Hope-Hempstead Co Ark C of C 1978.

HAYRE, RICHARD WILLIAM oc/Farmer, Power Linesman, Scuba Diver and Instructor, Law Enforcement; b/Mar 30, 1929; h/Adamsville, TN 38310; m/Nancy Alice Foot; p/Lester B and Johnny L Hayre; ed/Tampa Police Acad; US Intl Underwater Instrs Assn; US Power Squadrons Piloting of Seaman; mil/AUS 1951-52; NG 1955-56; pa/Past Law Enforcement Ofcr, Tampa Police Dept; Former Co-Owner Tampa Skin Divers & Inc; Farmer; cp/32° Mason, Val of Tampa, 3rd Adamsville Blue Lodge 338; r/Bapt; hon/UN Ser Medal; Nat Defense Ser Medal; 3 Bronze Stars; Dist'd Unit Emblem; Good Conduct Medal; 3 Lttrs Commend while on Tampa Police Dept; 1 Lttr Commend for Tchg Underwater Safety for Red Cross.

HAYS, EDWIN KEITH oc/Personnel Manager; b/July 16, 1945; h/Rt 2 Box 166A, Murray, KY 42071; ba/Murray; m/Marybeth; c/Vonnie Sue, Christopher Keith; p/Curtis (dec) and Ann Hays, Murray, KY; ed/BS Murray St Univ; pa/Pers Mgr Fisher Price Toys; cp/Secy Murray Lions Clb; Chm Mtl Hlth Bd; Pres PTO Murray Middle Sch; r/Ch of Christ.

HAYS, JAMES EDWIN oc/Pastor; b/Nov 28, 1951; h/Little Rock, AR; m/Beverly Diane Phillips; c/Philip Edward, Rachel Elizabeth;

PERSONALITIES OF THE SOUTH

p/Julian James and Hazel Griffis Hays, Judsonia, AR; ed/BS w Hons Ark St Univ 1972; ThM Mid-Am Bapt Theol Sem 1977; pa/Pastor Cedar Hgts Bapt Ch; Calvary Bapt Assn, Modr; N Pulaski Bapt Assn, Modr; Pres Mid-Am Alumni Assn, Ark Chapt; VP Mid-Am Bapt Theol Sem Alumni Assn, Nat Chapt; r/So Bapt; hon/HS Valedictorian 1969; Outstg Freshman Awd, Ark St Univ 1970; Outstg Sr in Col of Bus, Ark St Univ 1972; Grad of Dist, Ark St Univ 1972; Pres Mid-Am Bapt Theol Sem Student Body 1977.

HAYS, TINA SWANK oc/Free Lance Artist; b/Apr 10, 1922; h/1329 E Cherry, Enid, OK 73701; ba/Enid; m/D Swank (dec), 2nd Joel LeRoy Jr (dec); c/Earnest D Swank, John C Swank, (Stepchd:) Gary Hays, Connie Williamson; p/John and Sylvia Pulos (dec); ed/Commercial & Advtg Art; mil/Ladies USMC; pa/Free Lance Advtg, Sign Painting; Charter Mem ABWA Red Carpet Chapt; cp/VFW; Am Legion; Moose Aux; Life Mem Alpha Tri Child Study Clb; Cub Scouts: Past Den Mother, Coor; Wom of the Moose, Chapt 1587; r/Greek Orthodox; hon/Wom of Yr 1981-82, ABWA Red Carpet Chapt; Dist 11 Pres of Yr, VFW Aux for St, 1977; Pres Sev Orgs.

HAYTER, DARLENE CAROL HOLLAND oc/Regional Coordinator; b/Oct 29,1951; h/PO Box 146, Crystal River, FL 32619; m/Henry Bruce; c/Shannon Noelle, Henry Culver; p/Oliver C (dec) and Alice V Holland, Brandon, FL; ed/Nsg Student; pa/Regional Coor Nat Reyes Syndrome Foun; Drug Abuse Cnslr, Birth Control Cnslr, Med Asst, St Petersburg Free Clin & Clearwater Free Clin 1970-71; cp/Chp Vol Sers for Crystal River Prim Sch; Orgr The Door (Drug Abuse Hotline) 1970; Orgr Spring Inc (Spouse Abuse Ser) 1976-77; Vol Juvenile Cnslr 1978; Friends of the Elderly 1977-80; r/Agnostic; hon/Cert of Apprec, Bd Public Instr, St of Fla, Co of Citrus 1980.

HAZARD, FLORENCE McLEOD oc/Homemaker; b/Sept 17, 1919; h/916 College, Columbus, MS 39701; m/George Stephenson; c/George Stephenson Jr, Florence H Winton, Eulalie McLeod; p/Harry Augustus (dec) and Florence Richardson McLeod, Columbus, MS; ed/BA Miss St Col for Wom; pa/Dir Columbus & Lowndes Co Hist Soc Mus; r/Epis.

HAZEL, DELORES SIMMONS oc/Financial Examiner; b/May 13, 1943; h/2419 Bettys Dr, Albany, GA 31705; ba/Same; m/James A; p/Booker T and Carrie E Simmons, Newton, GA; ed/BBA Albany St Col; MBA Valdosta St Col; pa/Soc of Fin Examrs; AAUW; NAFE; Iota Phi Lambda; Alpha Kappa Mu; cp/NAACP; Dem Party; r/Meth: Stewardess Bd, Choir, SS Tchr, So Ga Conf Secy; hon/W/W Am Wom; Wall St Jour Achmt Awd; Kellogg Awd.

HAZEL, JAMES ANDREW oc/Minister, Teacher; b/May 14, 1937; h/2419 Bettys Dr, Albany, GA 31705; m/Delores S; p/D C Sr and Lucy J Hazel, Albany, GA; ed/BA Albany St Col; MEd Ga St Univ; pa/Pastor, Williams Tabernacle Christian Meth Epis Ch; GAE; NAE; Nat Elem Sch Prins Assn; PACE; cp/NAACP; Urban Leag; Albany St Alumni Assn; Dem Party; r/Williams Tabernacle CME Ch: Mem Bd of Social Concerns, Bd Christian Ed; Treas S Ga Conf.

HAZLEWOOD, HOPE oc/Secretary-Treasurer, Homemaker; b/July 16, 1906; h/503 Mason, Stanton, TX 79782; m/L C; c/Cliff Jr, Elaine Eiland; pa/Secy-Treas W Tex Telephone Corp Inc.

HEAD, MARILYN ELEANOR oc/Registered Real Estate Broker; b/Nov 21, 1945; h/Ocala, FL; ba/1021; SW 17 St, Ocala, FL 32670; m/Jimmie O Jr; c/Steven M, Thomas M; p/Lois F Hilton, Miami, FL; ed/Gold Coast Sch Real Est: Salesman 1978, Broker 1979; Fla Real Est Comm Broker 1979; pa/Hotel/Motel Sales; r/Johovah's Witness; hon/VP John J Piccione Real Est Inc.

HEALD, TEE D oc/Retired; b/Aug 28, 1904; h/1902; W Lafayette, Marianna, FL 32446; m/Thomas; c/Lee B Talley; p/Sanders L Davis (dec); Viola Harriet Wachob; pa/Ret'd Restaurant Owner-Opr; cp/Wom's Clb; BPW Clb; OES; Mystic Ladies Clb; Past Matrons & Patrons Clb; Lib Friend; r/Meth; hon/Daugh of Nile.

HEARN, JOYCE C oc/Legislator; h/1316 Berkeley Rd, Columbia, SC 29205; ba/Columbia; m/Thomas Harry; c/Terri H Potts, Kimberly Ann, Carolyn Lee; p/J C and Carolyn Carter Camp; ed/Att'd Ohio St Univ; Adv'd Study Fin Univ of SC; pa/Rep for Richland Co House Dist 76, SC House; Ofcr SC Judicial Nom'g Com; VP Ct Update; cp/Dist VChm Cou Repub Party; Chm Co Repub Party; 2nd Congl Dist Mgr US Census; U Fund Capt; r/Bapt; hon/Awds for Judicial Reform & Sexual Assault Legislation: Claims Mgmt Assn of SC, Columbia Rape Coalition.

HEATH, BOBBY JERRELL oc/Cardiac Surgeon; b/Feb 19, 1943; h/5150 Shirlwood Dr, Jackson, MS 39211; m/Linda C; c/Ashley; p/Earnest Heath, Duck Hill, MS; Louise Corder Heath (dec); ed/Att'd Holmes Jr Col 1961-63; Univ Miss 1963-64; MD Univ Miss Med Ctr 1968;

Residency 1972-78; mil/USAF 1970-72; pa/Chief of Cardiac Surg, Univ Hosp, Jackson, Miss; AMA; Miss St Med Assn; Ctrl Med Soc; Jackson Surg Soc; Am Heart Assn; Am Col Cardiology; Am Col Chest Phys; So Med Assn; SEn Pediatric Cardiology Soc; r/Presb; hon/Alpha Omega Alpha; Commend Med USAF 1972; Phi Kappa Phi; Author Chapt in Critical Surgical Illness & Rhoads Textbook of Surgery.

HEATH, GLADYS LEVONIA MOYERS oc/Owner, Teacher & Barber at Beauty College; b/Mar 7, 1908; h/2812 North Haltom Rd, Ft Worth, TX 76117; m/Alfonso B (dec); c/Kathey Levonia; p/Samuel Edgar and Mintie Elizabeth Moyers (dec); ed/Att'd Jacksonville Bapt Col; pa/Owner/Tchr Barber & Beauty Col, Ft Worth; Mem: U Barbers Assn, Nat Fedn of Indep Bus; cp/Wom's Clb; Ladies Oriental Shrine; Police Resv; Past Matron Southside Chapt OES; r/Meth; hon/Worthy Matron Jewel, OES; Fellow Mem ABI; DIB; World W/W of Wom.

HEATH, WILLIAM HENRY oc/Farmer; b/Jan 24, 1943; h/Rt 1, Box 316, Hookerton, NC 28538; m/Evelyn Albritton; c/Karen, Stephanie, Jennifer, Beverly; p/Thomas Jarvis (dec) and Maude Lineberry Heath, Hookerton, NC; ed/Assoc Agric, Agric Inst 1963; pa/Tobacco, Grain, Hog Farmer; cp/Pres Lenoir Co Farm Bur; Bd Dirs: First Citizen Bank of Hookerton, N Lenoir Water Assn, Lenoir Livestock Assn, Lenoir Co Pest Mgmt Assn; cp/Past Dist Dpty Grand Master 11th Masonic Dist 1977-79; r/Disciples of Christ; hon/Outstg Yng Farmer 1969 & 78.

HEATHERINGTON, J SCOTT oc/Medical Director; b/Apr 22, 1919; h/7224 S Birmingham Place, Tulsa, OK 74136; ba/Tusla; m/Geraldine V; c/Jeffrey Scott, Douglas Linder, Marc Gilbert; p/Clarence Linder Heatherington (dec); Nora B Scott, Newton, KS; ed/BS Westmar Col; DO COMS Iowa; pa/Okla Osteopathic Hosp: Med Dir, Dir of Med Evaluation; Editor: Osteopathic Medicine; Mem: Am, Okla Osteopathic Assns; Pres-Elect Am Acad Osteopathy; cp/Advr to Okla Physician Manpower Tng Comm; r/Boston Ave U Meth Ch, Tulsa: Mem; hon/Hon Life Mem: Am Osteopathic Assn, Okla Osteopathic Assn; Hon Degrees: LLD Westmar Col, LLD Philadelphia Col Osteopathic Med, Dr Lttrs Col of Osteopathic Med & Surg.

HEATHERLEY, ELINOR ELIZABETH oc/Clinical Nurse Leader; b/Aug 10, 1949; h/1003 Waverly Dr, Arlington, TX 76015; ba/Ft Worth; c/Charlotte Kelly; p/Eli John and Thelma Parent, Trenton, NJ; ed/ADN Tarrant Co Jr Col; mil/1967-68 MSN; pa/RN; Vol Am Red Cross; cp/GSA; Dem Party; r/Presb; hon/Nat Jr Hon Soc 1964; W/W Am Wom 1979-80.

HEATHERLY, JERRY RONALD oc/Chief of Juvenile Probation Services; b/Mar 16, 1945; h/PO Box 192, Cullman, AL 35055; ba/Cullman; m/Charlotte Jasper; c/Amy Karen; p/Mack R (dec) and Dora J Heatherly, Cullman, AL; ed/BS Miss St Univ; pa/Ala Coun Crime & Delinquency; Ala Juvenile Just Assn; cp/Yng Dems, Cullman; Pres's Clb Ala; r/Bapt.

HEAVNER, JOHN MILTON JR oc/Principal; b/Sept 27, 1948; h/1030 Montego Bay Dr S, Jacksonville, FL 32218; ba/Atlantic Bch, FL; m/Esther Kay Daniel; c/Johnna Daniel; p/John M Sr and Ilease Fisher Heavner, Cherryville, NC; ed/BS 1970, MA 1973 Appalachian St Univ; pa/Nat Assn Elem Prins; Fla Assn Sch Admrs; Duval Elem Sch Prins; cp/Jacksonville Northside Bus-man's Clb; r/Meth.

HEBERT, CAROLYN MAE ST AMANT oc/Physician, Cardiologist; b/Dec 21, 1939; ba/Thibodaux, LA; m/Leo P Jr; c/Anne Marie, Catherine, Elizabeth, Leo, Maria, Julie; p/Julius Clement and Marie Pauline Martin St Amant, New Orleans, LA; ed/BS St Mary's Dominican Col 1961; MD LUS Sch of Med 1965; pa/Pvt Phys; Dir Heart St & ICU, Thibodaux Gen Hosp; Diplomat Am Col Phys; Am Soc Internal Med; hon/Alpha Omega Alpha; Phi Kappa Phi; Delta Epsilon Sigma; Cardinal Key 1959; W/W Am Cols.

HEDGEPETH, LUTHER LAWRENCE oc/Farmer; b/Aug 10, 1923; h/c/o Postmaster, Falkland, NC 27827; m/Aldine C; c/Lawrence Dean, Kenneth Randal; p/Collin Elias and Dollie B Hedgepeth, Fountain, NC; ed/Elec Welding Cert; EMT; mil/AUS; pa/Farmer; cp/Am Legion; VFW; Belvoir-Falkland Ruritan; Bd Dirs Falkland Fire Dept; r/Bapt; hon/Outstg Ruritan 1979; Falkland Rescue Squad 1980; Good Conduct Medal.

HEDRICK, LARRY DOUGLAS oc/Thiokol, Fibers Division; b/Mar 29, 1944; h/Rt 1 Box 122, Lyndhurst, VA 22952; ba/Waynesboro, VA; m/Freda Virginia; c/Larry Douglas Jr, Christine Dian; p/Homer H and May Hedrick, Fayetteville, WV; pa/Wayne Tex Inc; cp/Rural Div Chm U Way of W'boro; St Chm Big Brothers, Va JCs; Pres Big Brothers, Big Sisters W'boro; Gem & Mineral Soc; JCs; BSA; Augusta Co Liaison to Intl Yr of Disabled Person; Area 5 Coor Va Spec Olympics; Va Fine Arts, W'boro Chapt; r/Mt Vernon Ch of Brethren; hon/JC of Mo; 10 Most Active JCs; Outstg Yng Man W'boro.

HEFLEY, PAULINE M oc/Sales, Insurance; b/Feb 6, 1936; ba/Amarillo, TX; m/C W Jr; c/Josephine D McKnight, Alexis D; p/Lea A Elliott, Quanah, TX; Margaret Jackson Elliott (dec); ed/Var Ins Schs; Wkg on CLU Designation; pa/Ins Sales: Life, Hlth, Pension, Profit Sharing, Property-Casualty; First Wom Pres Amarillo Assn Life Underwriters Assn; cp/First Wom Pres Toastmasters Intl Clb; 1875 Natural Gassers; First Wom Pres Coun One of Am Heart Assn, Tex Affil Inc; r/Ch of Christ; hon/Won Trips; Wrote Column for Canyon Newspaper 2 Yrs.

HEHL, LAMBERT LAWRENCE JR oc/Attorney; County Judge; b/Jul 22, 1924; h/46 Madonna, Fort Thomas, KY 41075; ba/Newport, KY; m/Helyn; c/Susan Snyder, Barbara; p/Lambert Lawrence Sr and Martha Hehl (dec); ed/JD 1952 Chase Col of Law, No Ky Univ; mil/USMC 1943-46, Pacific; pa/Atty; Co Judge/Exec: Campbell Co; Mem: Campbell Co Bar Assn (Past Pres), Ky Bar Assn, Am Judicature Soc; Bischoff-Hehl-Howe Law Firm; cp/Mem Ky Senate 1960-63; Past Pres Ky Magistrates & Commrs Assn; 1st VP No Ky Area Devel Dist; Past Pres Ky Co Judge/Exec Assn; Others; r/Cath; hon/Lifesavine Awd, VFW 1976.

HEIDEN, EDWARD J oc/Government Executive; b/Sept 12, 1938; h/318 South Lee St, Alexandria, VA 22314; ba/Washington, DC; m/Mary Doherty; c/Stephen, Tory, David, Carrie; p/(dec); ed/Govt Exec, US Consumer Product Safety Comm; Mem: Am Ec Assn, Am Mktg Assn, Econometric Soc; r/Rom Cath; hon/Summa Cum Laude 1960; Dist'd Ser Awd 1975.

HEIDRICH, HERMAN JOSEPH oc/Civic Worker; b/Dec 5, 1895; m/Sarah Frances Devlin; c/Herman Joseph Jr, Francis Xavier, Helen Jeannette (dec), Paul Daniel; p/George Herman and Wilhelmina Josephine Meier Heidrich; c/Wholesale Produce Mkt 1916; Org'd Herman J Heidrich & Sons, Orlando, Fla 1930; Org'd Oakfield & Elba Growers Inc 1936; cp/Knight, Equestrain Order of Holy Sepulchre of Jerusalem; Knight Sovereign Mil Order of Malta; Knight of Grand Cross, Equestrian Order of Holy Sepulchre of Jerusalem; Donated Shrine of Our Lady of Lordes to St James Cath Ch 1954; Donated Alter of Sacred Heart in Immaculate Conception Chapel, N Am Col, Vatican City 1954; Bd Govs St Bernard Col; Charter Mem Com of 100 of Orange Co 1956; Donated Interior Furnishings of St Juliana Ch, Ft Val, Ga 1956; Built & Donated St Joan of Arc Cath Ch, Louisville, Ga 1962; Built & Donated Heidrich Cultural Ctr, Bishop Moore HS, Orlando 1965; Donated Acreage to Diocese of Orlando 1970; Bd Govs Rom Cath HS, Phila, Pa 1974; Bd of Trustees, Rom Cath HS 1974; Built Chapel Adjoining St James Cath 1979; hon/Man of Yr, Rom Cath HS, Phila 1956; Man of Yr, Woodsmen of World 1957; DLitt, St Bernard Col 1960; Commun Ldrship of Orange Co Awd 1973; Herman J Heidrich Lib, St Bernard Col 1973.

HEINS, MARY FRANCES (LILLIAN) oc/Co-Principal, Teacher; b/Nov 12, 1927; h/811 Donovan, Houston, TX 77091; ba/Same; p/George Sr (dec) and Rosella Heins, Tex City, TX; ed/BA Dominican Col 1954; MEd Lamar Univ 1973; pa/Tchr Parochial Schs in Tex 1948-58; Tchr St Francis de Sales Sch, Riverside, Calif 1958-61; St Pius X HS, Houston, Tex 1961-66; St Agnes Acad, Houston 1966-68; Kelly HS, Beaumont, Tex 1968-80; Tchr & Admr, Sponsor Student Coun, Pius X HS 1980-; Sabine Area Sci Tchrs Assn 1968-80; STAT; NSTA; Nat Assn Student Activ Advrs; Tex Assn Student Couns; Gtr Metro Houston Assn of Chem Tchrs; Assn for Supvn & Curric Devel; Delta Kappa Gamma, Pres Eta Chapt 1978-80, Mem Eta Chapt 1972-80, Mem Iota Gamma Chapt, Var Coms, Chm Prog Com; Lamar Univ Ex-Students Assn; Nat Assn Physics Tchrs; Tex Assn Physics Tchrs; Ex-Officio Mem Kelly HS Bd 8 Yrs; Diocesam Com, Diocesan Sch Bd, Beaumont, Tex; Ex Officio Mem St Pius X HS Bd; Former Mem Ed Bd for Dominican Sisters, Houston; Task Force for Study of Commun-Owned Schs, Dominican Sisters; cp/Ed Task Force for Goals for Beaumont, Beaumont C of C; LVW; Arch Soc; Mar of Dimes Prog, Sabine Area; r/Cath: Mem Dominican Order; hon/Outstg Classroom Tchr, Kelly HS 1971; Outstg HS Clrm Tchr, City of Beaumont 1971; Outstg Sci Tchr, St of Tex for Grades 9-12 1980; Nat Sci Foun Grants: Notre Dame Univ 1960, Sam Houston St Univ 1966 & 67, Trinity Univ 1968; Tchr of Mo, Kelly HS 1979; 3rd Pl 1976, 1st Pl 1979, Alpha Omega SS Class Comp; Num Certs of Part & Apprec Certs from Wkshops & Drs.

HELD, JOE ROGER oc/Director Division of Research Services; b/Jun 23, 1931; h/16305 Grande Vista Dr, Rockville, MD 20855; ba/Bethesda, MD; m/Carolyn Ann; c/Lisa Lynn, Robert Joseph, Leslie Ann, Teresa Jeanne; p/Edward Samuel and Carmen Antoinette Held; ed/AA; BS; DVM; MPH; mil/Comm'd Ofcr, US Public Hlth Ser; pa/Dir Div of Res Sers, Nat Inst of Hlth; Devel & maintenance of resources for the support of biomedical research; hon/Outstg Alumnus 1977, Tulane Univ Sch of Hlth; PHS Meritorious Ser Awd 1972.

HELLER, JOHN RODERICK JR oc/Physician; b/Feb 27, 1905; h/5604 McLean Dr, Bethesda, MD 20014; ba/Bethesda; m/Susie May; c/John Roderick III, Winder McGabock; p/John R and Elizabeth Smith Heller; ed/BS Clemson Univ; MD Hon Emory Univ; mil/USN Rear Admiral; pa/Former Dir Nat Cancer Inst; Physician; Former Pres Meml Sloan Kellering Cancer Ctr; r/Presb; hon/Num Hons & Awds incl'g: SC Hall of Fame 1979.

HELLER, MAX M oc/Mayor; b/May 28, 1919; h/36 Pinehurst Dr, Greenville, SC; m/Trude Schonthal; pa/Left Austria 1938; Worked as Stock Boy, Piedmont Shirt Co, Greenville; Fdr Own Co: Maxon Shirt Co 1948; Ret'd 1968; cp/Elected to Greenville City Coun 1969; Elected Mayor 1971, Re-elected 1975; Appt'd Chm St Devel Bd 1978; Mem Adv Coun to Bd of Trustees Furman Univ; Past Pres Bd, Greenville Housing Foun; Mem Bd, Fam & Chd's Ser; Adv Coun on Drug Abuse; Chm: St Francis Commun Hosp Bd of Trustees, U Fund Bd, C of C, Nat Conf of Christians & Jews, Phillis Wheatley Ctr, Others; Hejaz Shrine Temple; Kiwanis; hon/Man of Yr Awd, Nat Coun Jewish Wom 1970; Man of Yr Awd, N & S Car Bnai Brith Lodges 1972; DAR Freedom Awd 1973; Hon LLD, Furman Univ 1975; Dist'd Ser Awd, Gtr Greenville Ministerial Alliance 1976; Others.

HELLER, RONALD HOWARD oc/International Economist; b/Mar 18, 1948; h/Rt 3, Box 284, Harpers Ferry, WV 25425; ba/Washington, DC; m/Marsha D; p/Morris I and Faye B Heller, Cleveland, OH; ed/BMus w Distn 1969 Ind Univ; MA 1972 Ohio St Univ; pa/Intl Economist; Musician: Columbus Ohio Symph Orch, Springfield Ohio Symph Orch, Henry Mancini Orch, Johnny Mathis Orch, Les Grands Ballets Canadiens Orch; Col Tchr: Ohio St Univ, Ind Univ, Otterbein Col, Wittenburg Univ; hon/Performer's Cert Awd, Ind Univ 1969; Phi Eta Sigma; Pi Kappa Lambda.

HELM, BOYD EDWARD oc/Cardiologist; b/Jan 28, 1942; ba/4045 N Blvd, Baton Rouge, LA 70806; m/Barbara; c/Shannon, Boyd, Eric; p/James Boyd Helm, Gulfport, MS; Helen Friloux Helm, New Orleans, LA; ed/BS Loyola Univ of S 1964; MD LSU Med Sch 1967; Intern LSU Div of Charity Hosp 1968, Residency 1971; F'ship Cert Univ Tenn 1975; mil/USN 1971-73 Lt Cmdr; pa/Consltative Cardiology & Cardiac Catheterization; Fellow: Am Heart Assn, Am Col Chest Phys, Am Col Cardiology; Bd Dirs Am Heart Assn of La; r/Rom Cath; hon/Bd Cert'd Spec Internal Med 1972; Bd Cert'd Spec Cardiology 1975.

HELMS, JOHN BENJAMIN oc/Company President; b/June 18, 1946; h/PO Box 305, Wingate, NC 28174; ba/Wingate; m/Anne Rushing; c/Paul Christopher; p/Lester L and Mary Smith Helms, Wingate, NC; ed/BS UNC-CH 1968; Yng Exec Inst UNC 1972; mil/USAR 1968-74; pa/Pres MaLeck Industs Inc; Dir NCNB, Monroe; NC Del to White House Conf on Small Bus; cp/Rotary; UCS Soc Plan'g Coun; BSA; r/Bapt; hon/Silver Beaver Awd, BSA; W/W Am.

HELTSLEY, THOMAS ALLAN oc/Comptroller; b/Apr 15, 1946; h/1950 Sand Lake Rd, Orlando, FL 32809; m/Carolyn; p/Charles M (dec) and Jeannette S Heltsley; ed/BSBA Univ Ctrl Fla 1974; mil/USN 1965-69; pa/Comptroller, Southland Midwest Distribution Ctr; Nat Soc Public Accts; r/Prot; hon/Phi Theta Kappa.

HEMBREE, BEVERLY KATE oc/Homemaker; b/Jan 4, 1933; h/7630 S Richmond, Tulsa, OK 74136; m/Raymond C; c/Teresa Lynne, Julia Marie, Raymond Craig; p/E Grant (dec) and Lylas V Covell, Harlingen, TX; pa/Past VP, Pres-Elect St Francis Hosp Aux; VP Asst Leag of Tulsa; Pres & Past VP Tulsa Opera Guild; cp/Tulsa Ballet Guild; Wom's Assn; Tulsa Philharmonic; VP St Mary's Wom's Clb; Rotary Anns; Chm Hosp Aux Conv; Immed Past Pres Cascia Hall Mother's Clb; Regional Rep, Leg Com, Okla Hosp Assn; hon/Pi Omega Pi; Alpha Mu Gamma.

HEMPHILL, ROBERT WITHERSPOON oc/United States District Judge; b/May 10, 1915; h/167 York Street, Chester, SC 29706; ba/Columbia, SC; m/Isabelle Anderson; c/Forrest H Stewart, Harriett H Crowder, Robert W Jr; p/John McLure Hemphill (dec); Helen Witherspoon Hemphill, Chester, SC; ed/AB 1936 Univ of SC; LLB 1938 Univ of SC; mil/USAAF 1941-45, Hon Disch; pa/US Dist Judge; cp/Mem SC Legislature 1947-48; Solicitor 6th SC Jud Circuit 1951-56; Mem US Ho of Reps, 5th Congl Dist 1957-64; r/Purity Presb Ch, Chester: Mem; hon/Algernon Sidney Sullivan Awd; Judicial Awd of Merit, Am Trial Lwyrs Assn; Dist'd Public Ser Awd, Am Legion.

HEMPSTONE, SMITH JR oc/Journalist, Columnist; b/Feb 1, 1929; h/7611 Fairfax Rd, Bethesda, MD 20014; ba/Same; m/Kathaleen Fishback; c/Katherine Hope; p/Smith Hempstone (dec); Elizabeth Noyes Hempstone, Bethesda, MD; ed/BA, Hon PhD Univ of the S; mil/USMC, Former Capt; pa/Author 4 Bks: *Africa, Angry Young Giant*; *Rebels, Mercenaries & Dividends*; *A Tract of Time*; *In The Midst of Lions*; Num articles in mags; syndicated column; r/Epis; hon/Sigma Delta Chi; Overseas Press Clb; Citations for Fgn Corresp.

HENDERSON, CAROL MORNER oc/Assistant Dean; b/Oct 12, 1941; h/2904 Starlit Dr W, Mobile, AL 36609; ba/Mobile; m/Joe B Jr;

c/Alicia, Angela, Shannon; p/Lester Arthur Morner (dec); Mildred Kindshci, Madison, Wis; ed/BSN; MA; RN; pa/Asst Dean, Sch Nsg, Univ S Ala; ALN; NLN; ANA; U Cerebral Palsy Bd; Adv USA Nurse Hon; cp/Bd Profl Home Hlth Care Ser; PTA; r/Cath; hon/W/W Am Wom; Nurse of Yr, Mobile Co 1977-78; Sigma Theta Tau.

HENDERSON, DENNIS S oc/Minister, Youth Pastor; b/Apr 19, 1947; h/2846 Bay Meadow Cir, Dallas, TX 75234; ba/Dallas; m/Billie S; c/Stephanie Donnell, Sharon Deann, Shannon Denise, Dennis Scott; p/James E and Helen L Henderson, Albuerquerque, NM; ed/BS; pa/Guest Spkr Success Motivation Inst; Reg Spkr Num Yth Confs & Sems; cp/Little Leag; Var Yth Orgs; r/Bapt; hon/Hon Grad from Col.

HENDERSON, MARYLEA oc/Program Director; b/May 4, 1929; h/Waco, TX; c/M'Lane; p/Clyde (dec) and Audrey Henderson, Coleman, TX; ed/BA Howard Payne Univ 1950; MRE SWn Sem 1952; EdD Tex Tech Univ 1969; MS Univ Ore 1978; pa/Professor; Cnslr; Displaced Homemakers; Delta Kappa Gamma; Am Assn Marriage & Fam Therapists; APGA; r/Disciples of Christ; hon/Personalities of the S 1972; Author *Persons Not Things* 1971.

HENDERSON, RICHARD DELANO oc/Trainman; b/Sept 18, 1933; h/PO Box 463, Ellerbe, NC 28338; m/Ruby Foyles; c/Regina Elaine; p/Thomas A and Katie McRae Henderson (dec); ed/HS Grad; mil/AUS 2 Yrs; pa/Trainman for Seaboard Coastline RR; r/1st Presb Ch Ellerbe; Deacon; hon/Plaque, $50 bond for heroic efforts in saving a man from being run over by a train.

HENDERSON, WANDA MARIE oc/Head Teller; b/June 4, 1931; h/Junction Star Rt, Box 61, Ingram, TX 78025; ba/Ingram; m/Temple; c/Bert Thomas, Emily Jan, James Warren, William Russell; p/William Warren and Junaita Towers Fannin, Marlin, TX; ed/N Tex St Univ 1947-48; Num Spec Schs, Wkshops, Sems, Tex Sch Assessors Assn & Tex Bnkrs Assn; Cont'g Ed Tivey HS; pa/Hd Teller, Ingram St Bank 1978-80; Savings & Loan Dept Charles Schreiner Bank 1977-78; Tax Assessor-Collector, Ingram Indep Sch Dist 1971-76; Radio Sta KERV Traffic Mgr, Local News Editor, Copy Writer, Bkkpr 1963-70; Am Inst Bnkg; Tex Assn Assessing Ofcrs; Tex Sch Assessors Assn; cp/Circle of Gold Chapt of Am Bus Wom's Assn, Pres 1979-80, VP 1978-79, PR Chm 1977-78; PTA, Pres; 4-H Adult Ldr 20 Yrs; Home Demo Clb, Pres; r/Bapt; hon/Wom of Yr 1980, ABWA; Dist'd Vol Adult Ldr, Tex 4-H Yth Devel Foun 1970; Gov's Conf on Yth & Chd 1970.

HENDLEY, GRAHAM FISHER oc/Retired; b/Jun 19, 1927; h/2400 Howell Br Rd, 78 Sorrento Cir, Winter Park, FL 32792; p/W Fisher Hendley (dec); Margaret C Hendley, Alexandria; ed/BS Univ SC 1948; BS 1954, MHA 1969 Med Col of Va; mil/AUS 1954-56; USAR 1949-53; pa/Hosp Adm Ofcr; Reg'd Pharmacist; Jazz Musician; Band Ldr; Am Col of Hosp Admrs; Am Hosp Assn; Am Pharm Assn; cp/Past Mem Rotary, Lions; Life Mem DAV; r/Meth; hon/Phi Delta Chi Awd for Scholastic Achmt; Scholastic S'ship; Rho Chi; Sigma Zeta; Kappa Sigma Kappa; Alpha Epsilon Delta; Fellow Mem ABI; Biogl Listings.

HENDON, DONALD WAYNE oc/Professor and Department Chairman; b/Jun 1, 1940; h/1212 W Henrietta St, Kingsville, TX 78363; m/Brenda Bradford; p/Jesse M and Jennie M Hendon, San Antonio, TX; ed/BBA 1962, PhD 1971 Univ Tex-A; MBA Univ Cal-B 1964; mil/1962-63; pa/Prof & Chm Dept of Mgmt & Mktg, Col of Bus Adm, Tex A&I Univ 1977-; Resident Admr, MBA Prog, Col of Commerce & Indust, Univ Wyo, Casper 1976-77; Assoc Prof of Mktg, Div of Bus & Ec, Columbus Col, Ga 1972-76; Former Tchr: Univ Tex-A, Univ Nev-LV, Columbus Col; Vis Prof; Conslt Sev Firms incl'g: Am Mgmt Assn, Australian Assn of Nat Advertisers, Australian Inst of Mgmt, Colgate-Palmolive, Kodak, Others; Testified on Mkgt Practs before Employees of Fed Trade Practs Comm & Bur of Stats in Australia & before Num Govtl Ofcls; Mem Num Profl Assns incl'g: Acad of Intl Bus, Am Acad of Advtg, Am Coun on Consumer Interests, Am Mktg Assn, Assn for Consumer Res, Am Psychol Assn, Others; Res in Consumer Behavior, Advtg, Consumerism & Intl Mkgt; Num Res Papers Presented at Nat & Intl Confs of Profl Assns & Pub'd in Profl Jours; cp/Arbitrator for Better Bus Bur & Am Arbitration Assn; Mem Jr Achmt, Minority Bus Conslts Task Force & Public Policy Resources Panel of Am Mktg Assn; JCs; Columbia Ad Clb; Others; Conslt to Var Govtl Groups; hon/Alpha Delta Sigma; Delta Sigma Pi; Sigma Iota Epsilon; Div of Bus & Ec Awd for Outstg Perf & Competence in Res & Pub, Columbus Col 1973; Author: 33 Pub'd Articles, 23 Unpub'd Articles, 4 Pub'd Case Studies, 2 Monographs *The Economic Effects of Advertising*, *Today's Ways to Increase Your Market Share*; Men Achmt; Outstg Edrs Am; Commun Ldrs & Noteworthy Ams; Notable Ams; DIB.

HENDRICK, LEONARD EARL oc/Chief of Police; b/Jan 15, 1946; h/Humble, TX; ba/110 W Main, Humble, TX 77338; m/Paula Jean Janssen; c/Stephanie Lynn; p/L Paul and Inez J Hendrick, Midfield, TX; mil/USCG 4 Yrs; pa/Chief of Police, Humble; r/Bapt; hon/Hon Grad Ctrl

Tex Regional Police Acad 1970; Outstg Yng Law Enforcement Ofcr of Yr, Matagorda Co, TX 1974; Recog Awd, Bay City Kiwanis Clb 1977; Lttr From Bay City for 9 Yrs Faithfull Ser 1979.

HENRION, ROSEMARY PROVENZA oc/Registered Nurse; b/Oct 2, 1929; h/19 Wenmar Ave, Pass Christian, MS 39571; ba/Biloxi VA Ctr, MS; m/Albert Joseph Sr (dec); c/Albert Joseph Jr; p/Vincent Provenza (dec); Camille Portera Provenza, Greenville, MS; ed/BSN Univ Tex Med Br 1963; MSN Vanderbilt Univ 1972; MEd Univ So Miss-H 1974; pa/Current Psychi Clin Nurse Specialist, VA Ctr, Gulfport Div, Biloxi, Miss; Asst Clin Prof, Psychi-Mtl Hlth Nsg, La St Univ Grad Sch Nsg, New Orleans, La 1975; Co-Therapist, Couple Therapy, Alcohol Treatmt Unit 1975-; Cnslr & Therapist, Marriage Cnslr 1973-; Co-Therapist, Transactional Analysis 1972-74; Therapist & Co-Therapist, Logoanalysis 1973-; In-House Conslt for Biloxi VA Ctr; Psychi Clin Nurse Specialist, 3 Yrs; Gen Hosp: Dist Nsg Ser 1 Yr, Asst Dir Nsg Ser 1 Yr, Dir Inservice Ed 1 yr; Pvt Duty Nsg; Nsg Instr; Other Profl Positions; Dist Nurses Assn: Chm Mbrship Com 1966-67, Mem 1964-66; Miss Nurses Assn: VChm Psychi-Mtl Hlth Spec Interest Group 1972-75, Prog Chm Psychi-Mtl Hlth Spec Interest Group 1972-75; Panelist, Inst on Ldrship Devel, Keesler AFB, Miss; Participant, Planning Com, Dissemination Conf For Dirs of Nsg Ser, SREB Nsg Curric Res Proj 1975; Pres Miss Bd Nsg (Appt'd by Gov) 1976-; ANA Coun of Adv'd Practitioners for Psychi-Mtl Hlth Nsg; Intl Transactional Assn; Am Nurses Assn; cp/Sev Alumni Assns; ARC; Former Mem Planning Com, Woms Worry Clin, Gulf Coast Mtl Hlth Assn; Gulf Coast Mtl Hlth Assn; Ofcrs Wives Clb; Pass Christian Carnival Assn; r/St Thomas Ch, Long Bch, Miss: Formmer Mem Planning Com for Fam Cnslg, Min of Canonical Affairs; hon/Worlds W/W Wom; Sigma Theta Tau; NIMH F'ship, VU; Exceptional Ser Awd, Biloxi VA Ctr; Fed Traineeship, UT Med Br; Hon Student of St Marys Sch Nsg; Pub'd Author.

HENRY, DOLLIE MAE oc/Security Officer; b/Feb 22, 1929; h/1225 Pennsylvania Ave, Dallas, TX 75215; ba/Dallas; p/Johnnie and Mattie L Ross; pa/Security Ofcr; r/Bapt; hon/Perfect Attendance 1969, 1976, 1978.

HENRY, JOHNNIE oc/Transportation Supervisor; b/Dec 5,1929; h/Denton, TX; m/Sara P; c/Jimmy C, Johanna K Reed; p/Charlie Rubin (dec) and Margie May Henry (dec); mil/22 Yrs AUS & USAF; pa/Transp Supvr Moving & Hauling, NTSU; Past Pres Tex Employment Assn; cp/USAF Sgts Assn; UCT; VFW; r/Bapt; hon/Purple Heart; Bronze Star; Combat Infantry Badge; Silver Star; 4 Oakleaf Clusters; Good Conduct Medal; Cit for Little Leag to All Alaskian Prog 1956; Man of Yr Local Ch 1979; Man of Yr St Ch 1980.

HENSCHEL, BEVERLY JEAN oc/Program Analyst; b/Nov 1, 1927; h/12701 Epping Terrace, Wheaton, MD 20906; ba/Wash, DC; c/Laura Jane, Linda Jean, Karl Bruce, Lisa Margaret; p/Theodore Smith (dec); Laura F Smith (dec); ed/BA Univ Wyo; MFA; EdD Univ Utah; Cert of Achmt, Univ Heidelberg (Germany); pa/Prog Analyst, US Dept Energy & Atomic Energy Comm; Hon Mem Wyo Assn Petro Landmen; Brit & Am Nat Adv Bd Mem, Oddo Pub'g Inc; Spkr, Jt Engrg Coun Tech Assessmt Panel (Nat Level); Exhib'd New Styles Painting at Lib for the Arts, Martin Luther King Meml Lib 1980; hon/W/W Am Wom; Dist'd Citizens of Am; DIB.

HENSLEY, JEANNETTE CATHERINE oc/Company Manager and President; b/Dec 24, 1935; h/283 E Main St, Sylva, NC 28779; ba/Sylva; m/Paul C; c/Kathy Lynn; p/Georgia Allison, Whittier, NC; ed/Dip Interior Design; pa/Pres & Mgr Massie Furniture Co; Secy Sylva Merchants Assn; C of C Bd Dirs; r/Meth.

HENSLEY, R E JR oc/Farmer; b/Jan 26, 1933; h/Rt 5 Box 96; Levelland, TX 79336; ba/Levelland; m/Ellea; c/Dusty, R E III, Murray, Scott; p/R E Hensley, Burnett, Tx; pa/Farmer; Oilfield Lease Opr; cp/Sundown Lions Clb; Past Pres Hockley Co Farm Bur; Sundown Sch Bd; r/Bapt; hon/Recog'd by Tex St Tchrs Assn.

HENSON, BERNICE A oc/Lunchroom Manager; b/June 22, 1938; h/1810 Church St, Orange, TX 77630; ba/Orange; c/Linda Lowe, Billy W, Elizabeth A, Doris A; p/Lucian and Elizabeth A James, St Martinville, LA; pa/Lunchroom Mgr; Work w Rel Class; r/Cath.

HERBST, ROBERT LeROY oc/Assistant Secretary for Fish, Wildlife & Parks; b/Oct 5, 1935; h/4109 Wynnwood Dr, Annandale, VA 22003; ba/Washington, DC; m/Evelyn Clarice Elford; c/Eric Elford, Peter Robert, Amy Jo; p/Walter Peter and Bernice Mickey Mikkelson Herbst, Long Lake, MN; pa/Asst Secy for Fish, Wildlife & Parks, Dept of the Interior; VChm Great Lakes Fishery Comm; Mem US Nat Comm for UNESCO; Mem Pres Carter's Interagency Coun; hon/Dist'd Ser Awd, Nat Trout Unlimited Org; Archaeologist's Awd, St of Col; Num Plaques & Certs.

143

PERSONALITIES OF THE SOUTH

HERMANN, BRENDA LOUISE ANN oc/Executive Director; b/Apr 4, 1939; p/Charles and Agnes Hermann, Balto, MD; ed/BA Holy Fam Col 1968; MSW Fordham Univ 1970; pa/Exec Dir Cath Social Sers, Montgomery-Dothan Deaneries of Archdiocese of Mobile, Ala 1978-; Fam Life Dir, Diocese of Greensburg, PA 1975-78; Social Work Supvr 1974-76; Am Ortho-Psychi Assn; Nat Conf of Cath Charities; Am Grp Psychotherapy Assn; r/Rom Cath; hon/To be Pub'd: *Parish As Community of Service.*

HERNÁNDEZ, MARÍA C oc/Public Relations Director; b/Nov 23, 1931; h/4761 SW 4 St, Miami, FL 33134; ba/Miami; p/Arturo (dec) and Angelica Carbrera-Hernandez (dec); ed/BS & BLit, Instituto de Marianao 1940; DPharm Univ Havana 1953; Cert Post Grad Prog in Med Sci, Sch of Med, Univ Miami 1966; Cert Fgn Pharm Prog, Sch of Pharm Univ Fla 1976; Grad Dip, Am Savings & Loan Inst 1969; Cert Home Bldg & Commercial Constrn Prog, Nat Assn Wom in Constrn 1974; pa/Chase Fed Savings & Loan Assn: Public Relats Dir 1979-, Public Relats Ofcr 1975-79, Mortgage Loan Ofcr 1975, Mortgage Tng Ofcr 1973-75, Mortgage Loan Ofcr 1971-73, Loan Processor 1971, Disburser-Mortgage Clk 1963-71; Pharm in Cuba; Am Savings & Loan Inst, SE Chapt 29 1964-; Fla Fed BPW Clbs: St Talent Bank Chp 1975-76; Dist 11: Treas 1976-78, Asst Dist Dir 1978-79, Dist Dir 1979-80 & Latin Clb: Fin Chp 1971-72, Editor of *Latin Chatter* 1971-72, 1st VP 1972-73, Pres 1973-74, Leg Chp 1976-77; Dade Co Pharm Assn; Colegio Farmaceutico de Cuba en El Exilio; AAUW 1974-; Asociacion Interamericana de Hombres de Empresa 1977-; Am Assn Wom in Commun & Jr Cols 1977-; cp/Trustee Miami-Dade Co Commun Col 1975-79; Pres Cuban Wom's Clb 1978; Bd Dirs Girl Scouts Coun of Tropical Fla 1977-; Bd Dirs Miami Mtl Hlth Ctr 1977-; Bd Dirs Nat Assn Cuban-Am Wom 1977-; Bd Dirs Yng Woms Christian Assn of Gtr Miami & Dade Co 1976-; Hlth Sys Agcy of S Fla 1974-; Fla Intl Univ, Adv Bd, Inst for Wom 1975-; Adv Com, Rape Ctr 1976; Exec Com, Child Care Prog, City of Miami 1976-78; Cuban Wom's Mus of Arts & Culture 1977-; Herstory of Fla Inc 1974-, Budget & Fin Chp 1975-77; Adv Bd Encuentro, Univ Miami 1977-78; City of Miami Comm on Status of Wom 1975-78; Del to Intl Wom's Yr Conf 1977; Fla Del to Intl Wom's Decade Nat Conf 1977; Bd Dirs Fla Endowment for the Humanities 1978-; Screening Com to Select the Architect to Build Dade Co Govt Ctr 1978; Judge Hist Essay, Jr & Sr HS Students of S Fla Hist Assn 1978; Conslt, Social Security Adm, Task Force on Hispanic Affairs 1978-; r/Cath; hon/Cit City of Miami Bch's Safety Coun 1969; Marti Citizenship Awd, Cuban Lyceum 1973; Excptl Ldrship Awd, Dist 11, Fla Fed BPW Clb 1975; Commun Ser Awd, Cuba Lions Clb 1975; Hdliner Awd, Wom in Commun 1976; Trail Blazer Awd, Wom's Com of 100 1977; Commun Ser Awd, AAUW 1977; Gran Orden del Bicentenario, Cuban Lyceum 1976; Outstg Mem Commun, Cuban Wom's Clb 1977; City of Miami Plaque for Vol Sers, Child Care Exec Com 1977; "Wom Who Are Making It," *Miami Magazine* 1976; 'The Hot 100" (Top 100 Cuban-Am Ldrs) *Miami Magazine* 1977; Maria C Hernandez Ctr, Miami-Dade Commun Col, S Campus, Fine Arts & Student Ctr 1978; Metro Dade Co Plaque for Dedication & Devoted Efforts 1978; City of Miami Plaque for Commun Dedication 1978; Maria C Hernandez Day, City of Hialeah, Nov 18, 1978; Outstg Citizen of Day, Citizens Fed Savings & Loan & WINZ News Radio Nov 29, 1978; 1 Day Hon Mention, WQBA Radio Nov 26, 1978 & Jan 4, 1979; Bus Wom of Mo, Asociacion Interamericana de Hombres de Empresa, Jan 1979.

HERNÁNDEZ, MIGDALIA A oc/Director Inservice Division; b/July 6, 1936; h/Carolina, PR; ba/San Juan, PR; m/Rafael Hernandez Cardona; c/Francisco Antonio Almodovar; Alejandrina Tirado; ed/Grad Bayamon Dist Hosp Sch of Nsg; Profl Studies, Univ PR; pa/Neurosurg Nurse, Bayamon Dist Hosp; ICU Supvr, Univ Hosp; OR Nurse Presb Hosp; Nurse Instr Presb Sch Nsg; Inservice Instr Presb Hosp; Acting Dir Nsg Dept, Dir Inservice Div, Ashford Commun Hosp; Col Profl Nurses; VP Credit Coop Col of Profl Wom; Ec Asst Comm of Col of Profl Nurses; Secy Inservice Assn; cp/Pres Am Legion Aux Unit 60 1980-81; Secy Am Legion Aux Dept of PR 1979-80; Secy Am Legion Aux Unit 66 1979-80; Treas DAMAS Columbinas 1975-76; r/Cath; hon/W/W S&SW 1980; Merit Awd for Ser in Presb Hosp 1974-75.

HERNÁNDEZ, RAMON FRANCISCO oc/Linguist, Educator; b/Oct 10, 1935; h/655 Villa Verde Dr, Brownsville, TX 78521; ba/Brownsville; m/Esther R; c/Ramon F Jr, Esther, Josefina, Prisciliano, Teresa; p/Prisciliano Hernandez Martinez (dec); Josefina Garza de Hernandez, Brownsville, TX; e/Grad Instr's Sch, Amarillo Tech Trg Ctr 1959; Tchr Recog Nat Autonomous Univ of Mex 1962; mil/USAF 1953-61; pa/Dir Intl Sch of Languages; Lang Tchr, Interpreter, Translator; Am Soc Intl Law; Soc Fed Linguists; cp/Am GI Forum; Am Red Cross; Past Mem City Charter Revision Com; Past Mem Bicent Comm; hon/Citizen of Week, KGBT Radio 1976; Charter Mem La Esperanza Home for Boys 1972; Hon'd 3 Times as Judge in Philip C Jessup Intl Law Moot Ct Competition; Author Unpub'd Textbook.

HERNANDEZ, TANILA TANIS oc/Manager and Attendant; b/July 12, 1927; h/PO Box 1333, Plainview, TX 79072; ba/Plainview; m/Robert Sr; c/James, Robert Jr, Linda, Gloria, Lisa, Carolyn; p/Alfredo Rodrigus (dec); Angela Arionia, Lockney, TX; r/Cath.

HERNDON, BETTY LOU BOCK oc/Teacher; b/Nov 28, 1930; h/Bradenton, GL; m/John B; c/Sandra Louise, Debra Louise, John Charles; p/Charles H Bock, Bradenton, FL; Beatrice F Bock (dec); ed/BS Fla St Univ 1953; MS Univ S Fla 1975; pa/Tchr Grades K, 1 & 2, Tallahassee, Leesberg & Bradenton; Owner & Dir Pvt Nursery & Kindergarten; Manatee Ed Assn, Treas, VP, Pres; First Full Time Release Pres, Chm Negotiating Team Fla Ed Assn; U Dist VP Am Fed Tchrs; cp/Manatee Co Dem Exec Com; Dem Wom's Clb; r/Luth; hon/Phi Kappa Phi.

HERNDON, CHARLES PRESLEY oc/Minister, Christian Educator; b/Jan 24, 1922; h/2300 Greenwood Cir, Carrollton, TX 75006; ba/Dallas, TX; m/N Elizabeth; c/Charles Presley Jr; Ronald S; Deborah N Pearce, Rebecca L Pegram, Mary B Thompson, Joseph Mark; p/Presley Herndon, Auburn, KY; Mary Hannah Herndon (dec); ed/BA Wn Ky Univ; MA Univ Ky; Hon DLS Lexington Christian Bible Col; mil/AUS 14th Armored Div WWII; pa/Min Clearview Christian Ch; Prof Bible, Mins & Humanities Dallas Christian Col; Pres New Sch of Min, Texarkana, TX 1981-; Past Mem So Christian Conv & N Am Christian Conv; cp/Ky Col; r/Christian; hon/Num Articles in Brotherhood Jours; Contbg Author Parts of 2 Books.

HERNDON, JUDITH A oc/Lawyer; State Senator; b/Jun 5, 1941; h/27 Elmwood Place, Wheeling, WV 26003; ba/Wheeling; p/Richard G and Virginia H Herndon, Wheeling, WV; ed/Mary Washington Col, Univ of Va; AB Ecs 1963 Duke Univ; NWn Col of Law; JD 1967 WVa Univ Col of Law; pa/Ptnr w Herndon, Morton & Herndon Law Firm; Mem: WVa St, Ohio Co, WVa, Am Bar Assns; Bd Dirs: The Good Zoo, Russell Nesbitt Home, Wheeling Dollar Savs & Trust Co, Wesbanco, Wheeling Col, Others; cp/St Senator, 1st Senatorial Dist of WVa; Coms: Banking & Ins, Confirmations, Ed, Elections, Judiciary, Local Govt, Others; Chm Reagon for Pres 1976; r/Rom Cath; hon/W/W: Wom, Politics.

HEROLD, CRYSTAL LEE WOODS oc/Pre-School Teacher; b/Oct 5, 1946; h/3317 2nd Ave W, Bradenton, FL; m/William Matthew Jr; c/Matthew, Jason, Kenneth; p/Wandal Lee and Helen Hamann Woods, Roanoke, VA; ed/BA Radford Col; Att'd Univ Md; Attg Univ S Fla; pa/Tech Asst Disabilty Claims for Social Security Adm 1968-74; Pre-School Tchr Palma Sola; Parent-Instr for Parent Resource Prog; Rep World Book Ency; Alpha Psi Omega; cp/Beta Sigma Phi: Past Pres, VP, Recording Secy, Corresp Secy; Treas; BSP; Bradenton City Coun Treas; Christian Wom's Clb; r/Luth; hon/Dean's List Radford Col 1967-68; DHEW Commr's Cit 1973; Girl of Yr, Zeta Chi Chapt Beta Sigma Phi 1980; First Pl Slide Contest BSP; Best Supporting Actress, Radford Col 1967; Ritual of Jewels Runner-Up, St Girl of Yr, Beta Sigma Phi, Fla St Conv 1980.

HERR, ARBA OWEN oc/Editor, Curriculum Consultant; b/Nov 17, 1912; h/6832 Highland Park Dr, Nashville, TN 37205; ba/Liberia, W Africa; m/Paul S (dec); c/Paula Jo Arwood, Paul Arden; Nora Beth Allen; p/Harry Garman (dec) and Rebecca Stine Owen (dec); ed/BS Ed; MS Ed Temple Univ; pa/Conslt Curric Design to Min Ed, Monrovia, Liberia; cp/Intl Altrusa Clb; Common Cause; r/Meth: Spec Assgmt Bd of Global Mins; hon/Grad'd Cum Laude, Elizabethtown Col.

HERRING, CLYDE LEE oc/Senior Minister; b/July 30, 1935; h/5739 S Victor, Tulsa, OK 74105; ba/Tulsa; m/Betty Jo; c/Jeffrey Lance, Boyd Lee; p/Ruby Lee Herring, Plainview, TX; ed/BA, MA Baylor Univ; BD SWn Bapt Theol Sem; DMin Cand Phillips Univ; pa/Sr Min So Hills Bapt Ch; Clin Mem Am Assn Marriage & Fam Therapists; r/Bapt; hon/Author: *If God Talked Outloud; Home Sweet (?) Home; Determining Your Values;* Many Articles & Denom Lit.

HERRING, ROBERT RAY oc/Corporation Chairman; b/Feb 11, 1921; h/3195 Inwood Dr, Houston, TX 77019; ba/Houston; m/Joanne; c/Robert R Jr, Randolph W, Sylvia Diane, (Stepchd:) Beaufort King, Robin King; p/L R (dec) and Clara Herring, Stephenville, TX.

HERRINK, RUTH JONES oc/Director, Department of Commerce; b/Sept 8, 1926; h/4028 Mount Vernon St, Richmond, VA 23227; ba/Richmond; c/Sarah, l everly, Jessica; p/Basil B and Ruth S Jones, Richmond, VA; ed/BS Social Sci Simmons Col; pa/Dir, Dept of Commerce Commonwealth of Va; Former Positions: Chm Comm for Profl & Occupational Regulation, C'wealth of Va, Acting Dir, Dept of Hlth Regulatory Bds, C'wealth of Va, Va Comm on the Status of Wom, Va Equal Employmt Opportunity Com; cp/Chm U Way Dr for St Govtl Agcies 1977; Past Pres Nat Coun on Occupational Licensing; Mem Post Sec'dy Ed Adv Com, St Coun of Higher Ed, C'wealth of Va; Mem Richmond Public Forum 1963-72; hon/Stylemaker of Yr, Richmond Affiliate, Va St Hairdressers & Cosmetologists Assn Inc 1978; Stylemaker of Yr, Va St Hairdressers & Cosmetologists Assn Inc 1978.

144

HERRON, EDWIN HUNTER JR oc/Energy Consultant; b/June 7, 1938; h/McLean, VA; ba/2001 Jefferson Davis Hwy, Suite 701, Arlington, VA 22202; m/Frances Hunter; c/Edwin, David, Ashley; p/Edwin H (dec) and Helen R Herron, Shreveport, LA; ed/BS 1959, MS 1963, PhD 1964 Tulane Univ; pa/Res Engr Exxon Res & Engr Co 1959-61; Sr Res Engr Exxon Prod Res Co 1964-66; Corp Plan'g Advr, Esso Europe, London, England 1966-74; Proj Analyst Exxon Corp 1974-78; VP Gruy Fed Inc 1978-; Soc Petro Engrs of AIME; Am Inst Chem Engrs; Sci Res Soc; Tau Beta Pi; Am Mgmt Assns; Soc Tulane Engrs r/Epis; hon/Levey Awd, Tulane Univ 1970; W/W S&SW 1980; Author Tech Articles.

HERSHEY, ROBERT EARL oc/State Geologist; b/Sept 27, 1921; h/862 Bresslyn Rd, Nashville, TN 37205; ba/Nashville; m/Suzanna Wiesehan; c/Dianne Grace, Catherine Claudinia; p/John Christian; Grace Ethyl Hershey (dec); ed/BA Vanderbilt Univ; mil/USAAF WWII 2nd Lt; p/St Geologist; Mem Sev Profl Socs; cp/Intl Lions Clb; r/Belle Meade U MethCh: Mem; hon/W/W: Govt.

HESTER, ELLEN NORA oc/Homemaker, Part-time Enumerator; b/Sept 25, 1916; h/PO Box 55, Hargill, TX; m/Burton C; c/Frances Ruth H Atkins, Lynnette H Rigney, Glenn Burton; p/Julius Henry (dec) and Donia Ruth Berthold (dec); pa/Enumerator Tex Crop & Livestock Reporting Ser, Tex Dept Agric & US Dept Agric; cp/PTA; r/Cath; hon/Life Mbrship Awd: Tex Cong Parents & Tchrs Branch Nat Cong of Parents & Tchrs.

HESTER, JAMES TIMOTHY oc/Airline Pilot; b/Jan 17, 1955; h/2619 NW 123 Ave, Coral Springs, FL 33065; ba/Miami, FL; m/Virginia Guy; c/Douglas Landon, David Barry; p/James Edward and Jamie Louise Hester, Benoit, MS; ed/BA Miss St Univ; pa/Second Flight Engr on Boeing 727; Assoc Mem Airline Pilot's Assn; cp/Former Scoutmaster Troop 79, Cleveland, MS; r/Bapt; hon/Grad'd w Highest Distinction from Miss St Univ 1977.

HESTER, RUTHIA McCLOUD RIGGINS oc/Field Specialist; b/Mar 15, 1932; h/Sanford, FL; ba/1017 W 13th St, Sanford, FL 32771; m/Jerry; c/Charles, Joseph, Sharron, Cleoria, Joyce, Durrell, Kelvin, Felita; p/R B and Annie McCloud, Sanford, FL; ed/Sunlight Beauty Col 1951; pa/Ruthia House of Beauty, LA, Calif 1963-66; Field Spec, Seminole Commun Action Inc 1969-; Seminole Employment Ec Devel Corp Inc: VChm, Bd Dirs; The Grove Inc, Treas Bd Dirs; cp/Region IV Citizen Part Coun; Fla Tenant Org, Past Pres; Nat Coun Commun Reps, Chm; r/Mt Sinia MBC; hon/Commend Cert City of LA 1968; Seed Co Ser Awds 1973, 75, 76, 78, 79; Westside Bd Dirs 1973.

HEWETT, ROBERT JOSEPH SR oc/Business Consultant; b/July 17, 1933; h/12406 Caisoon Rd, Fairfax, VA 22030; ba/Fairfax; m/Martha R; c/Douglas, Michael, Karen, Sally, Jeffrey, Robert Jr; p/Wilber Dougals Hewett (dec); Ola M Sawyer (dec); ed/BBA Washburn Univ; mil/AUS 1953-58; pa/Delta Sigma Pi; Nat Soc Accts for Coops; cp/Fairfax C of C; r/Bapt; hon/Cert of Merit, US Dept Agric; Cert of Achmt, AUS.

HEWITT, HELEN SMITH oc/Chief Ground Instructor; b/Feb 12, 1921; h/840 Poleman Rd, Shreveport, LA 71107; ba/Shreveport; m/Forrest A; c/Jeffrey Alan, Forrest Clark, Mark Christopher, David Smith; p/Ralph Royal (dec) and Ruth Wiard Smith (dec); ed/BA Allegheny Col; MEd La St Univ; pa/Chief Ground Instr, Shreveport Aviation Co; Ninety-Nines Inc; Pres Northwood Golf Assn; cp/Repub; St Mark's Episc Women's Hope Guild; r/Epis; hon/Airman of Yr 1973; Flight Instr of Yr 1974; Zonta Awd 1975.

HIBBS, BETTY LOUISE ELLIS oc/Correctional Facility Director of Males; b/Nov 5, 1938; h/5072 Pine Ridge Dr, Macon, GA 31210; ba/Macon, GA; c/Ray III, Dana Elizabeth; p/Ernest Crawford Ellis (dec); Willie Mae Smith Ellis Best, Macon, GA; ed/AA TCJC 1972; BA Wesleyan Col 1975; MEd Ga St Univ 1977; Wkg on CPM; pa/Dir Macon Diversion Ctr, Ga Dept Offender Rehab 1978-; Mgr Peach & Crawford Co Probation Ofc, Dept Offender Rehab 1977-78; Probation & Parole Ofcr, Ft Val Probation Ofc, Dept Offender Rehab 1975-77; Macon Restitution Shelter 1974-75; Mgr Moody AFB Aero Clb 1967-68; Lic'd Pvt Pilot 1967-; Ga Probation Parole Assn; Public Offenders Cnslg Assn; APGA; Am Correctional Assn; Pi Gamma Mu; cp/Middle Ga Coun Commun Agcys; r/Unitarian; hon/Probation Ofcr of Yr, St of Ga 1978; Nat Social Sci Hon Sci 1975; Gov's Intern Prog 1974-75; Att'd First Gov's Conf on Criminal Just 1979; Only Female Dir of Male Diversion Correctional Fac, St of Ga; W/W S&SW 1980-81; Presented *Evolution and Development of the Diversion Restitution Program in Georgia* at Nat Symposium on Restitution and Commun Ser Sentencing 1980.

HICKEY, ELIZABETH JOAN GRANDOFF oc/Executive, Artist; b/May 6, 1932; h/2506 Parkland Blvd, Tmapa, FL 33609; ba/Tampa, FL; c/Joan, Linda, John, Suzanne, Diane, Michael, Patrick; p/Anthony Bernard and Frances Evelyn Grandoff, Trenton, FL; ed/AA Georgetown Visitation Jr Col; pa/Pres & Owner Rent All of Tampa; VP & Dir Grandoff Invests; Nat Leag Am Pen Wom; Intl Platform Assn; r/Rom Cath; hon/12 One-Wom Shows throughout S; Paintings in Ringling Art Mus & Archives of St of Fla; Hon'd at Bellair Art Ctr, The Art Clb of Fla & Annual St Petersburg Invitational; World W/W Wom.

HICKS, GLORIA JEAN oc/Credit Analyst; b/Jan 21, 1937; h/1605 W Commerce St, Aberdeen, MS 39730; ba/Aberdeen; m/Bobby; c/Tom, Lynn, Angela; p/Clarence and Louise Odom Hickman, Aberdeen, MS; pa/Credit Analyst, Fin Am; Retail Merchants Assn; cp/Pilot Clb; Christian Wom; VP Todays' Wom; Miss St Bd Am Cancer Soc; Bd Mem Aberdeen-Monroe Co C of C; r/Pentecostal; hon/Outstg Citizen, Fin Am Corp; Awd of Excell, Aberdeen C of C.

HICKS, ROBERT STEPHEN (STEVE) oc/Draftsman; b/June 8, 1952; h/208 E Denman #8, Lufkin, TX 75901; ba/Lufkin; p/Robert and Katherine Hicks, Lufkin, TX; ed/BFA; pa/Draftsman Tex Forest Ser, Fire Control Dept; cp/Lufkin JCs, Pres 1979-80; r/Bapt; hon/Outstg Local Pres for 1st Qtr of 1979-80 JC Yr; JC of Yr Awd 1978-79; JC of Mo Oct 1977 & July 1974; Brownfield Meml Awd, First Yr JC 1975; Armbruster Keyman Awd, Over 1 Yr JC 1976, 77, 78.

HICKS, SELMA LOUISE oc/Teacher; b/Apr 29, 1929; h/2613 Lynn, Big Spring, TX 79720; ba/Big Spring; m/Anderson Clayton; c/John C, Joe D; p/Ewell Ethridge Sr (dec) and Eula G Crawford, Ft Worth, TX; ed/BS Tex Christian Univ 1949; Att'd: Univ NM, Univ Albuquerque, Sul Ross St Univ, Univ Utah; pa/Tchr 29 Yrs Tex & NM; Secy & Histn Marcy PTA; TSTA; NEA; Delta Kappa Gamma; cp/Meml Bd Staffettes; Beauceants; r/Bapt; hon/Hon Life Mbrship Tex PTA 1980; W/W Tex Ed; VA Vol 1000 Hr Cert 1980; Big Spring TSTA Tchr of Mo; 5 Articles Pub'd.

HICKSON, FRANCES ASPINWALL oc/Musician; b/June 1, 1897; h/218 W 12th St, Sanford, FL 32771; p/dec; ed/Piano Emma Willard Sch; pa/Organist & Tchr of Pianoforte; r/Disciples of Christ; hon/"This is Your Life" Sunday, 1968; Rec'd Engraved Silver Tray 1977.

HIEBERT, CHERYLE JEANNE oc/School Nurse; b/May 30, 1938; h/Rt 1, Deer Creek, OK 74636; m/Daniel D; c/Tracie Michele; ed/Blackwell Sch of Nsg; Okla St Univ; pa/Bd Dirs Okla Heart Assn; Nat Rural Water Comm; cp/Grant Co Fair Bd; r/Cath & Mennonite; hon/Grant Co Wom of Yr 1978.

HIGGINBOTHAM, KATIE SOWELL oc/Kultural Krafts; b/Dec 5, 1929; h/Rt 2 Box 50, Laurel, MS 39440; ba/Laurel; c/Janet Marie, Jeana Murl, Joby Michael; p/Lavell (dec) and Mamie Hester Stewart; pa/Nat Assn Ret'd Fed Employees; Ret'd Med-Surg Asst; cp/Past Mem OES; Am LWV; Past Cmdr Disabled Am Vets Aux; r/Bapt; Pianist & Organist.

HIGGINBOTHAM, SARA oc/Director Human Resources Development; b/June 21, 1926; h/Rt 2 Box 155, Gadsden, AL 35903; ba/Gadsden; m/Manning E; c/Nancy June, Miles Dudley; p/Donald Pepe, Hackensack, NJ; Theresa (dec); ed/BS Alfred Univ 1948; MS Jacksonville St Univ; pa/Dir Human Resources Devel Bapt Meml Hosp; Chm Inservice Ed Com, Ala Leag Nsg 1977-78; Am Hosp Assn; Am Heart Assn; Am Cancer Soc; Nat Leag Nsg; hon/W/W Am Wom.

HIGGINS, JAMES WATSON oc/Retail Store Manager; b/Nov 30, 1951; h/2035 Robert Grey, Vidalia, LA 71373; ba/Vidalia; m/Pamela; c/James W II; p/Watson Walter Higgins Sr, Lucey Dale, MS; Mrs Leslie E Holmes, Nathcez, MS; mil/AUS Vietnam 1970-71; pa/Mgr Big Star Supermkt; r/Bapt; hon/Boss of Yr 1980.

HIGGS, WILLIAM ROBERT oc/Surgeon; b/Apr 10, 1943; h/3909 McGregor Ct, Mobile, AL 36608; ba/Mobile; m/Marilyn E; c/Lauren Meredith, Meagan Caroline; p/William Reginald and Catherine Covington Higgs, Ruston, LA; ed/BS summa cum laude La Tech Univ 1968; MD Baylor Col Med 1969; Intern City of Memphis Hosps, Univ Tenn 1969-70; Res Gen Surg Baylor Col Med Affil'd Hosps 1970-73, Chief Res Gen Surg 1973-74; Res Thoracic & Cardiovascular Surg Emory Univ Sch Med 1974-75, Chief Res Thoracic & Cardiovascular Surg 1975-76; mil/AUS Med Corps Maj; pa/Cardio-Thoracic & Vascular Surg; Clin Asst Prof Surg, Univ S Ala Med Sch 1976-; Active Staff: Mobile Infirmary, Providence Hosp, Doctors Hosp, Univ S Ala Med Ctr, Springhill Meml Hosp; AMA; Am Heart Assn; Michael E DeBakey Intl Cardiovascular Soc; Am Trauma Soc; Am Thoracic Soc; FACS; Mobile Co Med Soc; Med Assn St Ala; Am Med Joggers Assn; FACC; Soc Thoracic Surgs; So Med Assn; FACCP; So Thoracic Surg Assn; cp/Kiwanis Intl; C of C Mobile; Dixie Leag Baseball Team; Adv Bd US Sports Acad; Adv Bd Ohio St Profl Adv Com of Circulation Technol Div of Sch of Allied Med Professions; r/Epis; hon/Phi Kappa Phi; Omicron Delta Kappa; Sigma Tau Delta; Beta Beta Beta; W/W Am Cols & Univs; Arnold Air Soc; Co-Author "Malignant Mixed Tumor of the Gallbladder."

PERSONALITIES OF THE SOUTH

HIGH, ROBERT EDWARD oc/Teacher; b/Apr 13, 1947; h/Paris, TX; ba/Paris, TX; m/Carol J; c/Robert, Donald, Donna; p/Edward and Darnetta High, Marshall, TX; ed/BS E Tex St Univ; pa/Clrm Sci Tchr, Crockett Ind Sch 1971-; Paris Clrm Tchrs Assn, Pres 1978-79; Tex Clrm Tchrs Assn, VP 1978; Tex St Tchrs Assn, Treas 1977; cp/Bd Dirs Lamar Co Human Resource Coun, Paris Pks & Rec Dept, Tex Clrm Tchrs Assn; r/Meth; hon/Dean's List in Col; Outstg Edr of Yr 1977; Dist'd Edr Awd 1979.

HILDABRAND, HERBERT LOGAN oc/Businessman; b/Jan 28, 1932; h/512 S Madison, Enid, OK 73701; ba/Enid; m/Debra Ann; c/Sabrina N, Sonrisa C, Sharlton S, Starlene T, Shaunette G, Sharilyn J; p/Harry C (dec) and Narcissus P Hildabrand, Enid, OK; ed/Bach Liberal Studies; mil/USAF Tech Sgt, Ret'd; pa/Cabinet & Appliance Sales, Ser & Installation; Pres NW Okla & SW Kan Mil Retirees Assn; cp/US Senatorial Clb; Adv Bd Mem Am Security Coun; Sustaining Mem Repub Nat Com; AF Sgts Assn; r/Bapt; hon/AFCM; AFOUA; GCM w 4 Loops; NDSM; KSM; AFGCM w 1 Br OLC; AFLSA w 4 Br OLC; ROKPUCE; UNSM; SAEMR; Master Missleman Badge.

HILDEBRAND, GEORGE JR oc/Police Chief; b/July 8, 1930; h/1504 S Porter, Stuttgart, AR 72160; ba/Stuttgart; m/Pauline; c/Cheryl, Terry; p/George and Mollie Hildebrand, Stuttgart, AR; mil/AUS 1948-57; pa/Ark Municipal Police Assn; cp/C of C; Alcohol Awareness Com; VFW; r/Luth; hon/Nat Defense Ser Medal; UN Ser Medal; Korean Ser Medal; Good Conduct Medal w 2 Loops; Marksman Medal; 3 Bronze Stars; 1 Silver Star.

HILDEBRAND, JOYCE BRUFF oc/Teacher, Artist, Civic Worker; b/Feb 4, 1930; h/2701 Trail of the Madrones, Austin, TX 78746; m/Frank; p/Albert Griffith (dec) and Hazel Smith Bruff, San Antonio, TX; ed/BA Sophie Newcomb Col, Tulane Univ 1951; pa/Libn, Hist Ctr 1980; Libn Comm for the Blind 1978-80; Rehab Tchr, Austin St Hosp 1962-68; Sec'dy Sch Tchr, Austin & Baytown Tex 1957-68; Society Editor Jennings Daily News 1953-55; Dir Jennings La Little Theatre 1952; Ref Libn, San Antonio 1951; cp/Austin St Ofcl Ladies Clb, Secy 1973, VP 1978-79, Pres 1979-80; St David's Hosp Aux, Bd Mem 1968-74, Secy 1973, Coor of Vols 1973-74; San Antonio Speech Arts Assn 1962-81, Secy 1973, Poet Laureate 1972; Pan Hellenic Coun 1950-51; Pres Beta Sigma Omicron 1950-51; r/Epis; hon/Phi Beta Kappa, Alpha of La Chapt 1951; Sweetheart of Sigma Chi 1950; Sweetheart of Ct of Engrs 1949; Nat Forensic Leag Judge 1980.

HILL, ARNOLD P JR oc/Industrial Maintenance Specialist; b/Nov 25, 1939; h/Murfreesboro, TN; p/dec; ed/Att'd Madison Col 1959-61; Elec Sch Missile Sys 1962-65; mil/AUS; pa/Indust Maintenance Spec; r/Primitive Bapt; hon/Archaeol Site Reports for SEn Antiquity Soc.

HILL, JOE DENNIS oc/Sales Manager; b/July 29, 1939; h/Rt 1 Box 201, Decatur, TX 76234; ba/Decatur; m/Janis Elizabeth Branscum; c/Jennifer Dee, Joe Dennis, Johnathan Duane; p/Denman C and Mary Jo Crane Hill, Dallas, TX; ed/BBA So Meth Univ 1961; mil/USNR Cmdr; pa/Direct World Wide Distbr Network in Sale of High Technol Graphite Prods; Frequent Tech Lectr; Soc Mfg Engrs; Naval Reserve Assn; USN Leag; cp/Fdr-Chm Bd Wise Co, Tex U Fund; Chm Decatur Ser Unit The Salvation Army; Bd Dirs Decatur C of C; Immediate Past Pres Decatur Rotary Clb; Mem Brazos Basin Hlth Plan'g Coun; SMU Lttrmens Assn; r/Bapt; hon/Decatur Rotarian of Yr 1979; Author "Fundamentals of Electrical Discharge Machining."

HILL, LAURA FREEMAN oc/Teacher; b/July 4, 1926; h/2800 Dowell Ct, SW, Birmingham, AL 35211; ba/Goodwater, AL; m/Rosell; p/L William (dec) and Bessie M Freeman, B'ham, AL; ed/BS; MEd; pa/Coosa Ed Assn; AEA; NEA; cp/B'ham-Jefferson Co Civil Defense; r/Bapt; hon/Coosa Co Tchr of Yr 1963; Nom to Tchrs Hall of Fame 1978.

HILL, LUCILLE MILLER oc/Resource Teacher; b/Dec 8, 1916; h/4033 Cain Ave, Chattanooga, TN 37410; ba/Chat; m/Oscar M (dec); p/S H (dec) and Eliza Miller (dec); ed/BS Childhood Devel; Cert'd Spec Ed; pa/Resource Tchr, Chat Public Schs; cp/Profl Wom's Clb; Dem Clb; Tchr Orgs; r/Christian; hon/W/W Profls 1977; W/W Am Wom 1978.

HILL, PAUL ANTHONY oc/Campus Minister; b/Oct 29, 1952; h/Denton, TX; ba/Univ Min Ctr, PO Box 13765, N T Station, Denton, TX 76203; p/Thomas C Hill Jr (dec); Martha R Pickens, Dallas, TX; ed/BA N Tex St Univ 1977; MDiv Boston Univ 1980; mil/AUS 1972-74; pa/Campus Min, U Meth Ch, N Tex Conf; Nat Assn Campus Mins; Min to Blacks in Higher Ed; NAACP; Black Meth for Ch Renewal; r/U Meth; hon/Crusade S'ship 1978-80; Bass S'ship 1977; Charles D Tadlock S'ship 1978-79.

HILL, RICHARD LEE oc/Assistant Professor; b/Feb 25, 1935; ba/Abingdon, VA; m/Evelyn; c/Richard Lee II, Anne Elizabeth; p/Thelma E Hill, N Port, FL; ed/BS Univ Tenn-Knoxville 1959; MEngrg Univ S Fla-Tampa 1967; mil/AUS 1954-56; pa/Asst Prof & Ext Spec-Tech

Resources, VPI & SU 1975-; Arcata Corp 1970-75; Magnavox 1968-70; TRW Inc 1966-68; Intl Minerals & Chem Corp 1964-66; Sperry Rand Corp 1959-64; Regional VP, Chapt Pres, AIIE; Nat Assn Co Agric Agts; Treas Am Soc QC; cp/Dir Optimists Intl; Chaplian US JCs; r/Presb; hon/W/W S&SW 1980; Unit Superior Ser Awd, US Dept Agric 1978; W/W Engrg 1977; Outstg Indust Engr 1973; Author *Annual Conference Proceedings*, AIIE 1971, 1973.

HILL, ROSEMARY AUGUSTA oc/Speech-Language Pathologist; b/Dec 19, 1952; h/7709 Byrum Dr, Charlotte, NC 28210; ba/Charlotte; p/Robert Perry and Avalo Donovan Hill, New Smyrna Bch, FL; ed/BS Ed Univ Ga 1974; MA Ed Wn Carolina Univ 1975; pa/Speech-Lang Pathol (Deaf, Hearing Impaired & Orthopedically Handicapped), Charlotte-Mecklenburg Schs; Am Speech, Hearing & Lang Assn; hon/Rec'd Grad Asst'ship to Attend Grad Sch; W/W S&SW.

HILL, THOMAS NORMAN oc/Petroleum Landman; b/Sept 29, 1952; h/Box 8351, Midland, TX 79730; ba/Midland; m/Lori Kathleen; p/Gordon Hill, Canadia, TX; ed/BA Trinity Univ 1975; pa/George W Arrington Oil Co Inc 1976-78; Sr Landman, Tex Oil & Gas Corp 1978-; Okla Landman's Assn; Amarillo Landman's Assn; Permian Landman's Assn; r/Midland Bible Ch; hon/Pres Student Body Canadian HS 1971; 4-Yr Fball S'ship Trinity Univ 1971-75.

HILLER, E A STURGIS JR oc/Business Consultant; b/Jan 20, 1928; h/205 S Courtenay Pkwy, #206, Merritt Island, FL 32952; ba/Same; c/Wyatt T M, Christine M LaGarde, Susan R Buchanon, James R; p/Edward Abbor Sturgis (dec) and Ruth Helen Bursley Hiller, Foxboro, MA; ed/USCG Radio Sch 1945-46; Cert USAF Col Level 1952; Cert Fed Aviation Agcy; Dip Dale Carnegie Ldrship Trg 1959; USDA Grad Sch; Am Mgmt Assn; Cert Ofc of Civil Defense 1962; mil/USCG 1945-58; pa/Fdr & Pres People & Orgs Inc (Nat Human Resources Devel & Consltg Firm); Food & Drug Adm 1965-78; Fed Aviation Adm 1965; Martinsburg Bus Sers 1965-66; Martinsburg Veneer Corp 1964; Fed Aviation Agcy 1958-64; Am Mgmt Assn; Am Soc Public Adm; Am Soc Trg & Devel; Adm Mgmt Soc; Soc Advmt Mgmt; Intl Word Processing Soc; Nat Small Bus Assn; Intl Entrepreneurs Assn; cp/Lions Intl; FOP; Civil Defense Communs Unit; Opequon Amateur Radio Soc; r/Prot; hon/Recip Outstg Perf Awds: FAA 1950, FDA 1966; Author: *Leadership Skills for Office Supervisors* 1977; *Managing the Administrative Services Function* 1978; *Managing Human Resources* 1978; Num Others.

HILLIARD, EARL F oc/Attorney; State Legislator; b/Apr 9, 1942; h/1625 Castleberry Way, Birmingham, AL 35214; ba/Birmingham; m/Mary Franklin; c/Alesia, Earl F Jr; p/William Hilliard (dec); Iola Hilliard, Birmingham, AL; ed/BA Morehouse Col; JD Howard Univ; MBA Atlanta Univ; pa/Atty; Mem: Ala Bar Assn, Nat Bar Assn, Ala Black Lwyr Assn; cp/St Rep, Dist 45; Chm Ala Black Legislature Caucus; Life Mem NAACP; r/Bapt; hon/Bus-man of Yr; Omega Phi Psi.

HILLIER, GEORGE THOMAS oc/Broadcaster; b/June 19, 1930; h/1064 Ocean View Ave W, Norfolk, VA 23503; ba/Norfolk; m/Etta Louise Stender; c/Bruce Thomas, Paul Thomas; p/George Robert (dec) and Thelma Laura Lowery Hillier (dec); ed/Att'd William and Mary 1949-51; mil/USAF 1951-54; pa/Broadcasting WVEC TV Inc 1964-; Soc Motion Picture & TV Engrs; Soc Broadcast Engrs; cp/Expmtl Aircraft Assn; Aircraft Owners & Pilots Assn; Fac Adv Norfolk Voc/Tech Sch; r/Bapt; hon/Rec'd Cert of Merit Expmtl Aircraft Assn 1973; Purple Heart.

HILLIS, SHELBY ROSS oc/Professor; b/Jan 27, 1940; h/Snyder, TX; m/Lisa; c/Michelle Rhea, Morgan Leigh; p/M O and Mary Louise Hillis, AR; ed/BS 1965, MS 1970 Stephen F Austin St Col; PhD Univ Tex Austin 1975; mil/USMC 1958-62; pa/Ecton Co ISD 1965-72; Univ Tex Austin 1973-75; Univ So Miss 1975-77; Prof Sci, Chm Div Sci & Math, Coach Judo Team, Wn Tex Col; Nat Sci Tchrs Assn; Nat Assn Res in Sci; US Judo Fed; US Judo Inc; Tex Judo Black Belt Assn, Col Chm & Registration Chm; Tex Judo Inc, Registration Chm; r/Bapt; hon/NSF Acad Yr Inst Univ Tex Austin 1972-73; 3rd Deg Black Belt in Judo; 3rd Deg Black Belt in Aikido; Author Num Profl Articles.

HILLMAN, JON G oc/Saddlemaker, Businessman; b/July 2, 1951; h/2203 Morrison, Big Spring, TX 79720; m/Kim A; p/Jay G Hillman, British Columbia, Can; Marg Beaver, Alberta, Can; ed/Att'd Sul Ross St Univ 1970-71; pa/Saddlemaker; Owner-Opr Saddle Shop & Western Wear Store; cp/C of C, Big Spring Area; Pres Univ 312 Woodmen of World; r/Bapt; hon/Patent Holder.

HILLS, CARLA ANDERSON oc/Lawyer; b/Jan 3, 1934; h/3125 Chain Bridge Road NW, Washington, DC 20016; ba/Washington; m/Roderick M; c/Laura Hume, Roderick Maltman Jr, Megan Elizabeth, Alison Macbeth; p/Carl Anderson (dec); Edith Hume Anderson Wagner, Lake San Marcos, CA; ed/AB cum laude 1955; LLB 1958; pa/Asst Atty Gen, Civil Div Dept of Justice, Wash, DC 1974-75; Secy, Dept of Housing

146

& Urban Devel, Wash, DC 1975-77; Partner in law firm of Latham, Watkins & Hills, Wash, DC 1978-; Mem: Bar of Supreme Ct of US, Cal St & DC Bars, Am Bar Assn: Mem/Coun Sect of Antitrust Law, Fed Bar Assn, Wom Lwyrs Assn, LA Co Bar Assn: Var Coms; Co-Author: *Federal Civil Practice, Antitrust Adviser*; Bd Dirs: Intl Bus Machines, The Signal Cos Inc, Standard Oil Co of Cal, Am Airlines Inc; cp/Mem: Trilateral Comm 1977-, Am Com on E-W Accord 1977-, Intl Foun for Cultural Coop/Devel, Bd Dirs Intl Exec Ser Corps 1977-, Bd Trustees Brookings Institution, Carnegie Comm on Future of Public Broadcasting, Sloan Comm on Govt & Higher Ed, Num Others; r/Epis; hon/Hon Degrees: Pepperdine Univ 1975, Washington Univ 1977, Mills Col 1977.

HILT, NANCY ELAINE oc/Nursing Supervisor and Clinical Specialist; b/Sept 9, 1943; h/210 Harvest Dr, Charlottesville, VA 22901; ba/C'ville; p/Paul A Hilt (dec); Harriet Hilt Grove, Rochester, NY; pa/Nsg Supvr & Clin Spec.

HINDMAN, JANET LANELL TIPTON oc/Art Educator; b/Jan 26, 1953; h/Borger, TX; ba/Borger High School, Borger, TX 79007; m/Scott Dwayne; p/J C and Evelyn LaJune Tipton, Stavanger, Norway; e/BS W Tex St IUniv 1974; MA Cand WTSU 1981; pa/Eng Tchr Hereford HS Abilene HS, Amarillo HS; Art Tchr Borger HS; Girls Volleyball Coach, Cross Country Track Coach, Plainview HS & Abilene HS; TSTA; NEA; Nat Art Assn; Nat Eng Assn; BCTA; ACTA; cp/Potpourri Jr Wom's Fed'd Leag; r/Christian; hon/Nat Eng Hon Frat 1972-74.

HINDMARSH, JAMES WESLEY oc/Administrative Coordinator; b/Sept 30, 1946; h/3106 Kendall Ave, Ft Smith, AR 72903; ba/Ft Smith; m/Roberta Darlene; c/Darrell Ray; p/Darrell Wesley and Ruth Ellen Hindmarsh, Ft Smith, AR; ed/Att'd West Ark Commun Col 1966-68; Dip Bell & Howel Sch of Accty 1971; pa/Adm Coor Arkhola Sand & Gravel Co 1964-; Nat Assn Accts; cp/UCT #86; Ft Smith Exch Clb; W Ark Postal Customers Coun Chm; r/Bapt; hon/W/W S&SW 1980; Panelist Nat Postal Forum S 1979; Editor *Mailroom Messenger*.

HINDSMAN, BILLIE FAYE PARKER oc/Director of Nurses; h/111 Posey, Vivian, LA 71082; ba/Vivian; c/Debra, Rebecca, Sheni; p/Jack K (dec) and Dessie Crumpler Parker (dec); ed/Dip Schumpert Sch of Nsg 1955; pa/Schumpert Med Ctr 1957-65; VA Hosp, Shreveport, LA 1955-57; Dir Nsg N Coddo Meml Hosp 1965-; ANA; Shreveport Dist Nurse Assn; OR Nurse Assn; Am Heart Assn; Dir Nsg Ser Soc; cp/L Allergo Clb; Am Legion Aux; r/Bapt; hon/Nurse of Yr 1971; W/W 1980-81.

HINDSON, EDWARD E oc/Professor, Director of Counseling, Associate Pastor; b/Dec 21, 1944; h/Lynchburg, VA; m/Donna Jean; c/Linda, Christy, Jonathan; p/Edward J and Helen J Snyder Hindson, Allen Park, MI; ed/BA Univ Detroit; MA Trinity Div Sch; ThM Grace Theol Sem; ThD Trinity Grad Sch of Theol; DMin Westminster Theol Sem; pa/Assoc Pastor Skokie Val Bapt Ch, Wilmette, Ill 1966-67; Pastor Fulton Bapt Ch, Fulton, Ind 1967-69; Assoc Dir Life Action Mins, St Petersburg, Fla 1970-74; Prof Rel, Liberty Bapt Col 1974-; Assoc Pastor Thomas Rd Bapt Ch; Nat Assn Nouthetic Cnslrs; Evangelical Theol Assn; Assn Christian Ed Tchrs; cp/St Repub Del; r/Bapt; hon/Outstg Yng Men Am 1979; W/W S&SW 1980; Author Num Rel Pubs.

HINER, LOUIS CHASE oc/Washington Correspondent and Columnist; b/Apr 19, 1919; h/3426 Farm Hill Dr, Falls Church, VA 22044; ba/Wash DC; m/Phyllis Clark; c/Mary Carolyn H Wright, Gregory C, Bradley C; p/Louis C (dec) and Rubye Marie Hiner (dec); mil/USAAF Pilot WWII; pa/Wash Corresp & Newspaper Columnist; Sigma Delta Chi; Nat Press Clb; Wash White House Corresp Assn; Smithsonian Assoc; r/Prot; hon/Nom'd Pulitzer Prize 3 Times; Cited For Efforts to Aid Paragon, IN, in Getting A Sewage Disposal Plant 1957.

HINOJOSA, LOUIS JR oc/Manager; b/Aug 28, 1949; m/Patricia N; c/Patricia Marie; p/Louis Lopez Sr and Gloria Lopez Hinojosa, B'ville, Tx; ed/AA 1970; BBA Cand 1981; mil/USMC 1971-74 E-6; pa/Owner-Mgr, Pers Dir & Admr, EEO Ofcr, Recruitment Spec; ASPA; Am Entrepreneurs Assn; IPMA; cp/Cameron Co Good Govt Leag, VP & Exec Dir; Kiwanis Intl; r/Cath; hon/Keynote Spkr, Social Security Symposium 1979; Author "Withdrawal in Cameron County."

HINSON, JOY LOU EDWARDS oc/Cosmetologist; b/Nov 6, 1937; h/803 S Washington Ave, Dunn, NC 29334; ba/Dunn; m/James Marshall Sr; c/James Marshall Jr, Joy Dianne; p/Thurman Kevitt Edwards, Jacksonville, FL; Martha Linda Baggett Edwards (dec); ed/Dunn Col of Beauty Culture 1967; Adv'd Cosmetologist Course Sampson Tech Inst 1976; Adv'd Cosmetol Course Johnston Tech Inst 1978; Acctg Johnston Tech Inst 1979; pa/Cosmetologist & Shop Owner, Dunn Plaza Shopping Ctr; Former Dental Asst; Johnston-Harnett Co Dental Asst Assn Secy; Harnett Cosmetol Affil #2; cp/Dunn BPW Clb; r/Bapt; hon/Miss Plain View 1954-55; 3rd Pl for Skit At Parade of Affiliates, Annual Conv at Winston-Salem 1980.

HINTON, BETTY B oc/Assistant Cashier, Loan Officer; b/Oct 8, 1936; h/715 S Sixth St, McComb, MS 39648; ba/McComb; c/Bill, Rick, Keith, Janel, Kyle; p/J L and Cora Butler, Jackson, MS; ed/Grad SW Jr Col 1956; Data Processing & Computer Programming 1976; Basic Bnkg Courses; pa/First Nat Bank, McComb: Asst Cashier, Branch Mgr, Loan Ofcr; r/Bapt.

HIRT, ROBERT EDWARD JR oc/Mechanic; b/Mar 5, 1960; ed/HS Grad; pa/Mech, Clark & Hirt Constrn; r/Bapt: Song Ldr; hon/Am Farmer Deg 1980; St Farmer Deg 1978; St Winner Agric Mechanics 1977.

HITCHCOCK, WALTER LeVANOIS JR oc/Pastor; b/May 4, 1928; h/264 28th Ave Pl NE, Hickory, NC 28601; ba/Hickory; m/Naomi Jane Orr; c/Pamela Jane, Mary Ann, David Walter, Stephen Andrew; p/Walter L Sr (dec) and Louisa Smith Hitchcock (dec); ed/BA Muhlenberg Col; ThM Lutheran Theol Sem; Dip Spanish Lang Inst; mil/AUS 1950-52 Supply Sgt; pa/Asst Pastor St Paul's, Lansdowne, Pa; Mission Develr, 1st Pastor of Trinity, Fairless Hills; Evangelist Missionary, Santiago, Chile; Missionary-in-Residence, Atlanta; Pastor Mt Olive, Hickory, NC; pa/World Missions Com Chm; Area Dir Strength for Missions; Synodical Evangelism Comm; Am Missions Com; cp/Hickory Coop Min Dir; The Bridge Dir; Hickroy Rotary Clb; Am Cancer Soc, Catawba Co Unit 1st VP, Co Crusade Chm, St Dir, St Crusade Chm; Little Leag Coach; r/Luth; hon/Num Awds from Am Cancer Soc; Cert of Merit, Home Bldrs Assn.

HIXON, CHRISTINE P oc/Guidance Counselor; b/May 13, 1918; h/1827 Paulette Dr, Birmingham, AL 35226; ba/Homewood, AL; m/Daniel Alexander Sr; c/Daniel Alexander Jr, Charlotte Lisa H Taylor; p/Hoy Ellsworth (dec) and Rosa M Bridges Pritchard (dec); ed/BS; MS; AA; pa/Guid Cnslr, Homewood HS; Kappa Delta Pi; Kappa Delta Epsilon; r/Bapt: Long Rang Plan'g Com; hon/Ala Poetry Soc; Ala Writers Conclave.

HIXON, ROBERT CHARLES oc/United States Army Officer; b/Feb 12, 1932; h/51 Fenwick Road, Fort Monroe, VA 23651; ba/Fort Monroe; m/Frances Peele Acree; c/Robert Charles Jr, Thomas Edward, James Andrew, William Oliver; p/Charles Edward and Edna Grace Wickham Hixon, Washington, DC; ed/BS Univ of Md; MA George Washington Univ; mil/AUS Maj Gen; pa/Mem Bd of Mgrs, Army Emergency Relief Soc; Mem Dept of Army Histl Adv Com; cp/Mem Steering Com, Assembly on Dimensions of Hunger & Malnutrition; r/Epis; hon/Dist'd Ser Medal; Silver Star; Legion of Merit w 2 OLCs; Dist'd Flying Cross; Bronze Star Medal w OLC; Air Medal V Device 17 Awds; Joint Ser Commend Medal; Army Commend Medal.

HO, MINH VUONG oc/Physician; b/May 7, 1940; h/Houston, TX; ba/Med Arts Bldg, 1215 Walker, Suite 1024; Houston, TX 77002; m/Hanh; c/Nghiem, Nghi, Thanh, Trang; p/Chanh Van Ho and An Thi Vuong, Saigon, S Vietnam; ed/MD Univ Saigon Med Sch 1959-65; pa/Fam Pract; AAFP; ACEP; r/Bapt; hon/Phys's Recog Awd; Diplomate of Am Bd Fam Pract; Fellow Am Acad Fam Phys.

HOBBS, BEN T oc/Partner in Building Firm; b/Feb 7, 1930; h/3313 Garden Val Rd, Tyler, TX 25702; ba/Henderson, TX; m/Mary Sue; c/Linda Carol Farrell, Marilyn Diane Farrell; p/R L Hobbs (dec); Blrdie Hobbs Tyler; pa/Ptnr Superior Bldrs; r/Bapt; hon/Cert of Merit for Outstg Lyric Writing.

HOBBS, CAROLE CORNELL oc/Homemaker; b/Aug 14, 1921; h/1503 N B St, Midland, TX 79701; m/Robert A; c/Carole Leslie; p/Russel E (dec) and Carol Witter Cornell, Midland, TX; ed/Att'd Olivet Col; cp/Ofcr Sev Civic & Social Grps; 12,000 Hrs Ser to Hosp Aux; Symph Guild; Garden Clb; Book Review Clb; Parliamentary Law Study; Arthritis Foun; Hist Soc; r/Presb; Deacon, Presbytery & Synod Coms, Ch Wom U; hon/Hon Life Mem Hosp Aux & Wom of Presbytery; Nom Wom of Yr.

HOBBS, HORTON HOLCOMBE JR oc/Curator; b/Mar 29, 1914; h/3438 Mansfield Rd, Falls Church, VA 2041; ba/Washington, DC; m/Georgia Blount; c/Horton H III, Nina H Singleton; p/Horton H and Johnnie Strickland Hobbs (dec); ed/BS 1935, MS 1936, PhD 1940 Univ of Fla; Univ of Va Mountain Lake Biological Stn Summers 1935; pa/Smithsonian Institution: Hd Curator, Dept of Zoology 1962-64, Sr Zoologist, Dept of Invertebrate Zoology 1964-; Num Former Positions as Prof: Univ of Fla, Univ of Va, Universidad Nacional Autonoma de Mexico; Mem: Sigma Xi, Phi Kappa Phi, Phi Beta Kappa, Alpha Epsilon Delta, Phi Sigma, Am Soc Nat, Am Soc Zool, Soc Systematic Zool, AAAS, AIBS, Others; Lectrs; Sems; Pubs: 150+ articles & books; Res on the freshwater decapod crustaceans of the Americas; r/Presb; hon/Fla Acad of Scis Res Awd 1958; Seven Soc Awd, Univ of Va 1961; J Sheldon Horsley Awd, Va Acad of Sci 1968; Ivey F Lewis Dist'd Ser Awd, Va Acad of Sci 1971; Meritorious Tchrs Awd, Assn of SEn Biologists 1973.

HOBBS, JUDY LEE oc/Sales Auditor and Cashier; b/July 7, 1951;

h/Rt 3 Box 438, Lebanon, TN 37087; ba/Lebanon, TN; m/Ronnie Lee; c/Madana Lee, Jason Ron; p/Houston and Allie Lee Cummings, Lebanon, TN; pa/Sales Auditor & Cashier Johnson's Dairy Inc; VP BPW Lebanon; r/Bapt; hon/Mem Immanuel Bapt Ensemble Appearing on Local TV Station Wkly.

HOBBS, SONIA AKOL BLANCO oc/Nurse; b/Feb 3, 1945; h/Nashville, TN; ba/230 25th Ave N, Nashville, TN 37203; m/George Ira (dec); c/Christopher Alan; p/Antonio R (dec) and Francisca de Tomas Akol Blanco (dec); ed/Dip Nsg, Univ of the Philippines; BS Ctrl Philippine Univ; pa/RN; Am, Middle Tenn Heart Assns; Am Assn Critical Care Nurses; r/Rom Cath; hon/Timawer Schlr.

HOBBY, NELLIE LEILLA oc/Manager; b/Nov 12, 1925; h/10025 SW 80th Ter, Miami, FL 33173; ba/Miami; c/George, Padget H Williams, Betty H Kallestad, Patricia; p/Albert Quillian Harper (dec); Nelie Lea Anglin (dec); ed/Att'd So Col, Atlanta 1944-45; pa/Processor Disability & Benefits, VA, St Petersburg, Fla 1945-48; Exec Secy Fla St Sch Architects 1951-52; Mem Staff Capital Outlay & Debt Sers, Dept Ed, St of Fla 1952-53; Exec Secy to Mgr, Ryder Systems Inc 1961-; cp/Beta Sigma Phi; Dem Party.

HOBBY, ROBERT DONALD JR oc/Student, Minister of Music; b/Feb 2, 1959; h/233 Carolina Dr, Tifton, GA 31794; p/Mr and Mrs R Donald Hobby, Tifton, GA; ed/Att'd Presb Col; pa/Pt-time Min of Mus in Bapt Chs; cp/Pres Circle K Clb; r/Bapt; hon/Hon Grad HS; Dean's List 4 Sems; Cert of Merit; Sigma Kappa Alpha; Exch Clb Yth of Yr 1977; Presb Col Jr Fellow; Ga All-St Chorus 1974-77.

HOBBY, WILLIAM PETTUS oc/Newspaper President; b/Jan 19, 1932; h/1506 South Boulevard, Houston, TX 77006; ba/Houston; m/Diana Poteat Stallings; c/Laura, Paul, Andrew, Katherine; p/William Pettus Hobby Sr (dec); Oveta Culp Hobby; ed/BA 1953 Rice Univ; mil/USN Intell, Lt Jr Grade, Disch'd 1957; pa/Houston Post: Var Positions 1955-, Currently Pres; cp/Lt Gov of Tex 1973-; r/Epis; hon/1 of 5 Outstg Yg Texans, Tex Jr C of C 1965.

HOBSON, FRED COLBY JR oc/Associate Professor of English; h/12113 Northwood Lake, Northport, AL 35476; ba/University, AL; m/Linda Whitney; c/Jane; p/Fred C and Miriam Tuttle Hobson; ed/AB 1965, PhD 1971 Univ of NC-Chapel Hill; MA Duke Univ 1967; pa/Current Assoc Prof Eng, Univ Ala; Past Edit Writer for Winston-Salem Journal & Sentinel; Mod Lang Assn; English Inst; cp/Dem Party; r/Univ Pres Ch, Tuscaloosa, Ala: Mem; hon/Pub'd Serpent in Eden: H L Mencken & The South; F'ship, Nat Endowmt for the Humanities 1976-77; Co-Recip Pulitzer Prize in Jour 1970.

HOBSON, KATE EVANGELINE (EVE) oc/Educational and Career Consultant; b/Feb 21, 1910; h/Lone Fountain, Star Route, Box 24, Churchville, VA 24421; ba/Waynesboro, VA; m/George Hull; c/Stepson: George; p/Ernest (dec) and Kate Elizabeth Jones (dec); ed/Bd Ed Tchg Cert, B'ham Univ, England 1930; BS 1963, MEd 1963 James Madison Univ; EdD Univ Va 1973; pa/Ednl & Career Conslt; Delta Kappa Gamma; Fine Arts Ctr, Staunton; cp/Soroptimist Intl of Staunton, Past Pres; Lit Vols of Augusta Area; Bd Mem Home Care Sers; r/Epis; hon/Apprec to Eve Hobson for Outstg Contbn to Ctrl Shenandoah Hlth Adv Coun 1977-80; Author Handbook & Guide to a Perceptual Motor Program; Author Sev Articles for Profl Pubs.

HOBSON, JOANNA KIRK oc/Artist, Teacher; b/Sept 9, 1942; h/1300 S Main, Del Rio, TX 78840; c/Roger Dwight, Jessica; p/Dwight Louis and Wylene Cassity Kirk, Lubbock, TX; ed/BFA Art Ed; p/Art Tchr; cp/Bd Mem Del Rio Coun for the Arts; r/Epis.

HODGE, LOUISE oc/Realtor; b/May 30, 1934; h/Greenville, NC; ba/Box 123, 226 Commerce St, Greenville, NC 27834; m/James D; c/Sharon Rachel, Marcia Ann, James A; p/Rufus A and Dora Frady, Toccoa, GA; e/BS Bob Jones Univ 1955; pa/Rltr 1973-; Greenville-Pitt Co Bd Rltrs; Nat Assn Rltrs; NC Assn Rltrs; Wom's Coun Rltrs, VP 1979-80, Pres 1980-81; NC Assn Rltrs, St Dir 1978, Profl Standards Com 1979-80, Make Am Better Com 1980-81; cp/Pitt-Greenville Co of C; Local Concerns Com 1980-81; r/Bapt; hon/Greenville-Pitt Co Bd Rltrs Rltr of Yr 1980.

HODGES, HAROLD D oc/Medical Research Associate; b/Jun 29, 1936; h/432 Maple Ave, Oliver Springs, TN 37840; ba/Oak Ridge, TN; m/Charlene; c/Julia, Kirk; p/Mrs Harold C Hodges, Crossville, TN; ed/BS; pa/Med Res Assoc; Mem: Soc of Nuclear Med Technologists Sect, SEn Chapt Soc of Nuclear Med Technologists, Tenn Soc of Nuclear Med Technologists, E Tenn Org of Nuclear Med Technologists; Assoc Mem Soc of Nuclear Med; Author num papers; Participant in Num Meetings; Lectr; Conds Labs; hon/Winner of Mbrship Drive Awd, Technologist Section of SE Chapt Soc of Nuclear Med; Named Assoc Editor of Journal of Nuclear Medicine Technology; Cand for Treas of Soc of Nuclear Med Technologist Sect; Recip letter of recog, Cong-wom Marilyn Lloyd.

HODGES, JOSEPH EDWARD oc/Artist-in-Residence; b/Dec 31, 1929; h/Byrd's Creek, Rt 3, Box 398, Crossville, TN 38555; ba/C'ville; m/Maureen Cullen; c/Kathleen Mary; p/Harold Christopher (dec) and Ruth Taylor Hodges, Crossville, TN; ed/BA Univ Tenn; MA Duke Univ; mil/AUS Signal Corps; pa/Tchr Art & Humanities, Artist-in-Residence, Cumberland Co Schs; cp/Mem Hist Preserv & Commun Arts Coun; r/Christian; hon/Am Inst Arch Spec Awd for Preserv; Tenn Arts Comm Spec Awd for Outstg Art Tchg.

HODGES, SHARON MANON KAUFFMAN oc/Substitute Teacher, Student; b/Jan 19, 1951; h/Box 54, Pettit, TX 79354; m/Bill R; c/Bryan Randall; p/Jeff and Betty Kauffman, Levelland, TX; ed/AA S Plains Jr Col 1971; Att'd W Tex St Univ 1971-72, Tex Tech 1978; pa/W Tex Watercolor Soc; Levelland Area Art Assn: Secy 2 Yrs, Exhib Chm 1 Yr; r/Presb.

HOFFMAN, ELISE oc/Administrator Technical Programs II; b/Mar 10, 1922; h/609 Front St, Richmond, TX 77469; ba/Richmond; m/Billy C; c/Rosilyn Overton, Billy May Peschel; p/James E (dec) and Laura Jack Gay (dec); ed/BA Univ Houston; MEd Prairie View A&M Univ; EdD Nova Univ; Post Grad Studies Univ Tex; pa/AAUP; Tex Jr Col Tchrs Assn; ANA; TLN; cp/Life Mem PTA; Parliamentn Dem Clb; Pres Band Boosters; Pres PTA; Adv Coun Am Red Cross; r/Meth; hon/W/W Am Wom; Intl W/W Ed.

HOFFMAN, LEAH JANE oc/Director of Exceptional Children Programs; b/June 10, 1953; h/1305 Wychwood Rd, Charleston, WV 25314; ba/Madison, WV; m/Randall J; p/Matt (dec) and Betty J Fisher, Charleston, WV; ed/BS cum laude 1974, MS 1975 WV Univ; Post Grad Studies Col of Grad Studies 1976-80; pa/Dir Exceptl Chd Progs, Boone Co, WV 1979-; Adj Instr WV Col Grad Studies, Spec Ed 1979-; Coor Speech-Lang Dept, Kanawha Co, WV 1977-79; Public Sch Speech-Lang Pathol 1976-77; Hd Start Conslt 1976; WV Ed Assn; WV Speech & Hearing Assn; Am Speech & Hearing Assn; Coun for Exceptl Chd; cp/Windsor Forest Garden Clb; r/Prot; hon/Cert Clin Competence Am Speech & Hearing Assn 1976-77; W/W S&SW 1980.

HOFMASTER, RICHARD NAMON oc/Entomologist, Scientist; b/Apr 12, 1915; h/Box 26, Belle Haven, VA 23306; ba/Painter, VA; m/Doris M; c/Donna Margaret; p/Harry A (dec) and Clara R Hofmaster (dec); ed/BS 1937, MS 1941, PhD 1948 Ohio St Univ; pa/Entomologist, Va Truck Experimt Sta 1947-80; Instr Entomology Dept OSU 1946-47; Res Asst OSU 1938; Tech USDA Sugarbeet Insects Lab 1938-41; Am Assn Ec Entomologists; Reg Profl Entomologists; Va Acad Sci; cp/Belle Haven Zoning Comm; Northampton Co Fair Bur; Am Legion; VFW; Masons: Blue Lodge & 32°; Moose; cp/Presb: Elder, SS Supt; hon/1st L O Howard Awd in Entomology 1974; 1st DAGA Awd for Excell 1979; Awd for Outstg Contbn to Mid Atlantic Food Processors 1979; Sigma Xi; Gamma Sigma Delta.

HOGAN, CLEO GREER oc/Meteorologist; b/Mar 31, 1946; h/PO Box 2132, 89 Cumberland Ave, Asheville, NC 28802; ba/Asheville; m/Donna Louise Bankey; p/Byron Gordon and Lathas Belle Haynes Hogan, Clarksville, TN; ed/BS Austin Peay St Univ 1968; Att'd Univ Mich 1969; mil/USAF 1970-77 Capt; pa/Meteorologist, Nat Climatic Ctr (NOAA) 1978-; Am Meteorol Soc 1969-; SEn Mich Chapt 1969-70; Ctrl NC Chapt 1970-71; Derby City Chapt, Louisville, KY 1973-75; Asheville Chapt 1978-; cp/Am Mensa; Tenn Geneal Soc 1966-; Tenn Hist Soc; NC Geneal Soc; Wn NC Hist Assn; Va Geneal Soc; Ky Hist Soc; Hogan Fam Assn; Haynes Surname Assn 1966-77; Pennington Res Assn; Mensa Geneal Spec Interest Grp; Old Buncombe Co NC Geneal Soc; Unitarian-Universalist Geneal Soc; SAR; SCV; r/Unitarian-Universalist; hon/Armed Sers Expeditionary Ser Medal 1971; Repub of Korea Pres Unit Cit 1971; AUS Commend Medal 1972; Century Farm Cert, Tenn Dept Agric 1976; Cert Apprec, Neb St Geneal Soc 1978; War Ser Medal, SCV 1980; Dist'd Ser Awd, Old Buncombe Co Geneal Soc 1980; War Ser Medal SAR 1981; Author Cemetery Records of Montgomery County, Tennessee.

HOGAN, SUSAN LYNN WILSON oc/Marketing and Public Relations Specialist; b/Dec 31, 1952; h/5717 Del Roy Dr, Dallas, TX 75230; ba/Dallas; m/Philip Courtney; p/Howard E and Alyce Velma White Wilson; ed/BFA So Meth Univ 1974; MA Cand So Meth Univ; pa/Mktg Coor & Editor Beck Bulletin Henry C Beck Co; 1977-; Intl Assn Bus Communrs; Am Mgmt Assn; cp/The 500 Inc; Innovators of Dallas Symph Orch Leag; Chd's Arts & Ideas Foun, Adv Bd; r/Meth; hon/W/W S&SW 1980; Vol Ser Awd Dallas Indep Sch Dist 1978, 79, 80; Contbr Articles to Texas Contractor Magazine.

HOGG, JACK oc/Senior Recreation Supervisor; b/Nov 15, 1937; h/Eau Gallie, FL; c/Suzanne p/John and Helene Hogg, Melbourne, FL; ed/BS cum laude Fairleigh Dickinson Univ 1963; pa/Sr Rec Supvr, Brevard (Responsible for Brevard Handicapped Prog) 1977-; Fla Rec & Pks Assn; Assn Retard'd Citizens; US Parachute Assn; hon/Nom'd Handicapped Div Recreator of Yr 1980, Nom'd for Heart of Gold Awd 1980.

PERSONALITIES OF THE SOUTH

HOLBROOK, EDWARD LIONEL oc/Retired Pneumatic Control Consultant; b/Oct 27, 1911; h/Rt 4, Brushy Creek Rd, Taylors, SC 29687; m/Annie Lou (dec); c/Edward L Jr, Cynthia Counts, Elizabeth Shelton; p/Frederick L and Eliza Lott Holbrook (dec); pa/Ret'd Pneumatic Control Conslt; Reg'd Profl Engr & Cert'd Sr Engrg Fluid Power Tech; Pneucon, Inc: Part Owner, VP, Mem Bd, Formed in 1967-; Devel'd Pneumatic Valve Logic & Valve Series; Lectr; Devel'd Hinge-block Control Valve Symbol & Cybergram Method of Control Design; Artists, Paints in Water Colors & Oils; Composer of 400+ Compositions; Plays Piano & Organ, Cartoons, Composes Poetry; Contbr 150+ Articles & Several Handbooks to Tech Writing Field; Num Profl Assns; r/Epis; hon/Patentee in Field; Elected to Profl & Exec Hall of Fame; Fluid Power Design Awd; Fluid Power Achmt Awd; Num Biogl Listings incl'g: Men of Achmt, DIB, Notable Ams, Intl Register of Profiles, People Who Matter, W/W of Intells; Fellow Mem ABI.

HOLCOMB, MILDRED oc/Teacher; b/Dec 27, 1907; h/Jacksonville, FL; m/Hoyt F; c/Hoyt F Jr; p/Roscoe and Ethel Scarborough; ed/Dips in Ceramics, Handmolding, Doll Making, Doll Repair, China Painting; pa/Traveling Tchr Ga, Ala, Fla; Lectr at Jacksonville Fla Lib; Fdr Ceramic Art Guild of Jacksonville; Am Pen Wom; cp/Nat Leag Am Pen Wom; r/7th Day Adventist; hon/Plaques for Art Work, Sers of Donated Times in Art Fields; Ribbons & Plaques in Art 1951-79.

HOLCOMB, PATRICIA ANN HORNE oc/Homemaker; b/June 23, 1946; h/3308 Highland Dr, Vicksburg, MS 39180; m/Barry W Sr; c/Barry, Julie; p/William C Jr and Eleanor S Horne, Jackson, MS; ed/BAE Univ Miss 1968; pa/Latin Tchr, Libn & Hist Tchr, Rankin Co Schs & Brandon Acad 1968-69, 1973-74; cp/V'burg Jr Aux; West Miss Med Aux: Secy, 2nd VP, Pres; r/Presb: SS Tchr Jr Dept; hon/W/W Among Am Univs 1968; Mins Ec Coun, STAR Tchr 1968; St C of C Awd.

HOLDER, ADOLPHUS DOYLE oc/Vocational Teacher Training; b/Sept 9, 1934; h/1226 Clover Ln, Denton, TX 76201; ba/Denton; m/Marion R; c/Madeleine Renee; p/Adolphus (dec) and Cora Ella Reeves Holder (dec); ed/BS Sec'dy Ed 1963, BS Hist 1964 Lamar St Col of Technol; MEd Colo St Univ 1970; PhD 1992; ed/USMC 1952-55; pa/Tchr Coor, Midland, TX ISD; Dir Mid-Mgmt Program Howard Col, Big Spring, Tex; Asst St Dir Distb Ed, State Dept Ed, Ala; Post-Sec'dy Tchr Edr, N Tex St Univ 1973-78; Div Chm, Voc Ed, NTSU 1978-80; Am Voc Assn; Nat Coun Distb Tchr Ed; Phi Delta Kappa; Alpha Delta Epsilon; Iota Lambda Sigma; Nat Assn St Supvr of DE; Tex Assn Tchr Edrs; Tex Assn Admr & Supvrs of Voc Ed; r/Bapt; hon/Hall of Fame Distb Ed 1966; Ednl Profl Devel Act Fellow 1970-73; Author "National Trends in Distributive Education" & "Mid-Management, The Texas Story."

HOLDER, CLINTON L oc/Manager of Shipping; b/Aug 11, 1926; h/1303 Tony Dr, Jonesboro, AR 72401; m/Mary E; p/Clinton W (dec) and Telitha Holder, Jonesboro, AR; mil/AUS 1952-54; pa/Mgr Shipping, Storall Mfg Co; cp/Jonesboro Optimist Clb, Past Pres; r/Free Will Bapt, Ordained Min 1963-.

HOLDERMAN, JAMES BOWKER oc/University President; b/Jan 29, 1936; h/President's House, University of South Carolina, Columbia, SC 29208; ba/Columbia, SC; m/Carolyn Meadors; c/Elizabeth Ann, Nancy Rae, Jamie Lynn; p/Samuel James Holderman, Morris, IL; Helen Boynton Bowker (dec); ed/BA w hons Denison Univ, Granville, Ohio; PhD NWn Univ, Evanston, Ill; pa/Pres, Univ of SC 1977-; Sr VP & Dir, Public Policy Progs Acad for Ednl Devel Inc 1976-77; VP for Ed, Lilly Endowmt Inc 1973-76; Num Former Positions at Var Univs; cp/Mem Task Force on the Financing of Higher Ed, Nat Coun of Indep Cols 1972-; Elmhurst Sch Bd: Mem 1967-73, Pres of Bd 1971-73; Mem Gov's Task Force on Hlth Planning, Ill 1970-73; r/Presb; hon/Hon Degrees incl: DePaul Univ 1971; Dr of Philanthropy, St Joseph's Col 1975; LLD McKendree KCol 1976; Recip Ford Fdn grant for 5 months to complete study on experiences in Ill 1973; Others.

HOLLAND, GENE GRIGSBY (SCOTTY) oc/Artist; b/June 30, 1928; h/1080 Errol Pkwy, Apopka, FL 32703; ba/Seffner, FL; m/George William; c/Shereta Lee, Harvelyn Georgene, Alicia Hope; p/Edward and Virginia Watson Grigsby (dec); ed/BA Univ S Fla 1968; NEn St Tchrs Col; Tulsa Univ; pa/Elem Sch Tchr, Hillsboro Co, Fla 1968-72; Clk, Fogarty Bros Moving & Transfer, Tampa & Miami, Fla 1954-57; News Reporter & Photographer, Bryan Daily News, Bryan, Tex 1952; Pvt Secy, Burroughs Adding Machine Co, Tampa & San Antonio, Tex 1951-52; Discount Clk & Cashier, GMAC, Tampa 1950-51; Acctg, Wilcox Oil Co, Tulsa, Okla 1948-50; cp/Past Pres Hillsborough Co Fdn Woms Clb; Past 1 VP, Bd Incorporators Musicale & Fed'd Clbs Inc, Tampa; Past Chm Dist #696 Intl Inner Wheel (Rotary Wives); Past Pres Inner Wheel Clb of Tampa; Past Rec'g Secy & Mbrship Chm Tampa Civic Assn; Nat Trust for Hist Preserv; SC Hist Soc; Charleston Mus; S'ville Hist Preserv Soc; Alumni Assn Univ S Fla & NEn Okla St Univ; Fdr Mem & VP Summerville Inner Wheel; Charter Mem & Wkshop Chm, Summerville Artist Guild; Pres Apopka

Wom's Clb, FFWC; r/Bethany U Meth Ch, Summerville: Mem, Rec'g Secy, U Meth Wom; hon/Hon Ky Col; Winner 1st, 2nd & Purchase Awds in Art; Am Artists of Renown.

HOLLAND, HAL DERRINGTON oc/Corporation Controller and Executive Director; b/Mar 22, 1925; h/28 Chelsea Dr, Ft Walton Bch, FL 32548; ba/Ft Walton Bch; m/Theresa Margaret; c/Mark Christian, John Derrington; p/Charles Philip (dec) and Gertrude Marie Witte Holland, Ft Walton Bch, FL; ed/BS Univ W Fla 1971; Dip Acctg Long Bch Bus Col 1947; mil/Ret'd Ofcr 1969; pa/Corp Controller & Exec Dir Cnsltg Firm; Nat Assn Accts, Dixie Coun; cp/Bd Dirs Kiwanis Clb; FWB/Bd Dirs U Way, Okaloosa Co, Inc; r/Rom Cath; hon/Bronze Star, Air Medal, Commend Medal, Num Others.

HOLLAND, KEN oc/United States Congressman; b/Nov 24, 1934; h/Rock Hill, SC 29730; ba/Washington, DC; m/Diane; c/Lamar, Beth, Amy; p/James A and Ruby B Holland, Gaffney, SC; ed/BA Jour 1960 Univ of SC; LLB 1963 Univ of SC Law Sch; mil/USAR 1952-59, Hon Disch, Sgt E-5; pa/2nd Term Congress; Pvt Law Pract; Mem SC Hwy Comm; cp/Former St VP, JCs; Former Mem Kiwanis; r/St John's Meth Ch, Rock Hill: Mem; hon/Euphradian & James Patterson Hons in Oratory.

HOLLEY, ANNA MARIE GAY oc/Enterostomal Therapist; b/Dec 19, 1929; h/4008 Lee Pl, Martinez, GA 30907; ba/Augusta, GA; m/Earnest Ray; c/Charlene P Hess; Stepch: Peggy Salter, Douglas, Jerry, Tommy; p/John Albert (dec) and Hannah Bell Gay (dec); pa/Enterostomal Therapist, Univ Hosp Spec Sers; 10th Dist GNA; ANA; Augusta Chapt UOA; IAET; cp/Publicity Chm Augusta Chapt UOA; r/Bapt; hon/Achmt Awd Univ Hosp; Employee of Yr Awd 1979; Wom's Missionary Soc Pres Awd 1964.

HOLLIN, SHELBY W oc/Attorney and Counselor at Law; b/July 29, 1925; h/7710 Stagecoach, San Antonio, TX 78227; ba/Same; m/Martha Jane Fisch; c/Sheila K, Henry J, Richard G, Charlotte A, Jacob C; p/Herbert (dec) and Maggie Hollin (dec); ed/BBA St Mary's Univ; JD St Mary's Univ Law Sch; mil/USAFR Major; pa/ABA; Tex & San Antonio Bar Assns; cp/ROA; DAV; VFW; Delta Theta Phi; r/Bapt; hon/W/W: Am Law, Tex; Men of Achmt; DIB; Men & Wom of Dist; USAF Commend Medal; Air Medal; Outstg Am in S.

HOLLINGS, ERNEST FREDERICK oc/US Senator; b/Jan 1, 1922; ba/Wash DC; m/Rita Liddy; c/Michael, Helen, Salley, Fritz; p/Adolph G and Wilhelmine Meyer Hollings; ed/BA The Citadel 1942; LLD Univ SC 1947; mil/WWII Capt; pa/Pract'g Atty 1947-58, 1963-66; SC Ho of Reps 1949-55; Spkr Pro-Tem 1951-55; Lt Gov SC 1955-59; Gov SC 1959-63; US Senator 1966-; Charleston Co, SC & Am Bar Assns; Admitted to Pract Before SC Supreme Ct, US Dist Ct, US Circuit Ct of Appeals, US Tax Ct, US Customs Ct & US Supreme Ct; Fdr Albert Einstein Sch of Med, Yeshiva Univ; cp/Hibernian Soc; Elks Clb; Shrine, Omar Temple; Am Legion; Arion Soc; C'ton C of C; VFW; German Friendly Soc; r/Luth; hon/Woodruff Awd, Assn AUS 1980; Am Speech & Lang Hearing Assn Awd 1980; Hon DDL Univ SC 1980; So Assn Textile Awd 1980; Dist'd Ser to Ed 1979; Awd for Dist in 95th Cong 1979; Textile Man of Yr, NY Bd of Trade 1979; Silver Medal Awd, No Textile Assn; Am Legion Public Servant Awd 1979; Charleston Naval Shipyard Awd 1979; SC Trail Lwyrs Assn Awd 1979; Neptune Awd, Am Oceanic Org 1978; Nat Fisheries Awd 1977; Awd for Ser to Disadvantaged Yth 1976; Guardian of Small Bus Awd 1973, 76; Legislator of Yr 1975; SC Wildlife Fed Awd 1975; Nat Soc Autistic Chd Awd 1975; Hon LLD Bapt Col 1975; 1st Recip Friend of Ed Awd, SC Ed Assn 1974; 1st Recip SC Envir Law Soc Awd 1974; Cotton Warehouse Assn Awd 1974; Num Other Awds 1947-; Author *A Case Against Hunger: A Demand for a National Policy* 1970.

HOLLINGSWORTH, DENVER oc/Meat Director; b/Jan 16, 1919; h/301 College Blvd, Statesboro, GA 30458; m/Janie Martin; c/James Philip; p/Andrew (dec) and Effie Hodges Hollingsworth (dec); ed/Dip Nat Sch Meat Cutting Inc 1949; mil/AUS 1942-45 Master Sgt; pa/Market Mgr, Colonial Stores 20 Yrs; Meat Dir T J Morris Co 18 Yrs; cp/VChm Altamaha Area Commun Action Auth Inc; Com for the Humanities in Ga; Chm Altamaha So APDC Hlth Resources Adv Com; Statesboro HS Band Booster, Pres 1971-72; Pres Bulloch Co Hist Soc 1974-76; Bd Mem & Chm Arts & Craft Fest; r/Pastor Emmaus Ch; hon/Bronze Star; Recog of Dist'd Achmt, Named Hist Buff of Yr 1974; Cert of Apprec, Statesboro Optimist Clb 1975; Optimist of Yr 1976-77; Intl Pres Presented Golden Circle Cert of Mbrship Optimist Clb 1977-78; Mem Nat Geog Soc 1973-.

HOLLMANN, ROBERT EMMETT oc/Division Chairman; b/Sept 9, 1944; h/2608 Northrup, Midland, TX 79701; ba/Midland; m/Sally; c/Kelly, Carrie, Rob; p/Adolph Hollmann Jr, Lamesa, TX; ed/BA 1968, MA 1972, EdD 1976 Tex Tech Univ; mil/USMC 1968-70; pa/Div Chm Midland Col; Am Polit Sci Assn; Acad Polit Sci; SWn Polit Sci Assn; Tex Jr Col Tchrs Assn; Permian Hist Soc; Wn Polit Sci Assn; Soc Petro Engrs;

149

Pi Sigma Alpha; Phi Delta Kappa; cp/Delta Tau Delta; Westside Optimist Clb; Midland Col JCs; Reserve Ofcrs Assn; Marine Corps Leag; r/Epis; hon/Purple Heart; Combat Action Ribbon; Merit Unit Commend; Nat Defense Medal; Vietnam Ser Medal; Vietnam Cross of Gallantry; Vietnam Campaign Medal; Vietnam Civic Action Medal; Lttr of Commend from Cmmdr-in-Chief Atlantic Forces.

HOLLOWAY, CARL DEWITT oc/Educator; b/Oct 18, 1935; h/515 Moak St, Brook Haven, MS 39601; ba/Brook Haven; m/Johnette Tillman; c/Carl Dexter, Charles; p/Eddie Hue Holloway, Las Vegas, Nev; Emmaline Holloway, Brook Haven, MS; ed/BS, Masters, AAA Adm & Supervision; mil/AUS 1954-57; pa/Brook Haven Ed Assn; Miss Ed Assn; NEA; cp/Bd Dirs Brook Haven Rec Dept; SW Plan'g & Devel Dist; r/Meth; hon/Grad cum laude Alcorn St 1960; Past Pres Lincoln Co Tchrs Assn.

HOLLRAH, GRACE FRENCH oc/Coordinator; b/Feb 25, 1920; h/Rt 5, Box 82, Enid, OK 73701; ba/Enid; m/Roy E; c/Richard Eugene, Kenneth Roy, Robert Warren, Terry Lewis; p/Clifford C Horner (dec); Mrs Earl Harting, Glencoe, OK; pa/Coor Garfield Co Sr Citizens; cp/Ext Homemakers, Co Pres 1976-78; Helped Estb 2 Parks in City of Enid; r/Luth; hon/Outstg Homemaker of Yr; Homemaker of Yr 1979 (Garfield Co, 16 Co Dist, St of Okla).

HOLLUMS, JOHN R oc/Manager, Executive Director; b/Aug 23, 1956; h/Midland, TX; ba/3200 Andrews Hwy, Midland, TX; m/Lezlye Ann; p/Donald and Jo Ann Hollums, Midland, TX; ed/Att'd Abilene Christian Univ; mil/AUS Capt; pa/Mgr, Exec Dir Golden Life Fitness Ctrs; Profl Karate Fighter; W Tex Martial Arts Assn; Pres & Fdr; Amateur Ath Union, Tae Kwon Do, S Tex Chapt; Intl Phys Fitness Assn; World Karate Assn; r/Cath; hon/Ranked 9th in World, Full Contact Karate, World Karate Assn; Hon Thespian in Col; #1 Light-Heavyweight Fighter in US (Karate); Working on Volume in Devel of Karate in US.

HOLLY, LEWIS REYNOLDS oc/Manager, Employee and Community Relations; b/June 7, 1939; h/2106 Burningtree Dr, Decatur, AL 35603; ba/Decatur; m/Barbara Hobson; c/Jonathan, Christopher; p/dec; ed/Att'd Marietta Col & NYU; AUS Staff Sgt; pa/Mgr, Emloyee & Commun Relats, Gen Elec Co; Mem Var St & Regional Pers & Indust Assns; cp/U Way; C of C; Tech Sch Adv Panels; r/Bapt; hon/Army Commend Medal; Va AP News Awd; GE Mgmt Awd.

HOLMES, ELIZABETH ANN oc/Educator, Assistant to President; b/June 6, 1927; h/704 NE 20th, Okla City, OK 73105; ba/Edmond, OK; m/Abe B; c/Beverly Ann Holmes-Smith; p/Timothy McCurdy, Okla City, OK; Maggie McCurdy (dec); ed/BA; MEd; EdD; pa/Edr, Asst to Pres, Ctrl St Univ; Am Assn Univ Admrs; Intl Rdg Assn; Coor Wom's Caucus Am Assn Higher Ed; ABWA; NEA; OEA; Nat Assn Wom Deans & Admrs; Delta Kappa Gamma; Phi Delta Kappa; cp/YWCA; Alpha Kappa Alpha; Urban Leag Guild; r/Meth; hon/Ldrs in Am Ed 1971; W/W Okla 1974; Intl Biog 1976; W/W Wom of World 1976; Co-Author *Smuggling Language Into Reading* 1972 & *Really Reading* 1976.

HOLMES, JEFFREY L oc/District Commercial and Marketing Manager; b/Apr 6, 1945; h/6807 Uppingham Rd, Fayetteville, NC 28306; ba/F'ville; m/Judy T; c/Jeffrey O'Neal; p/H J and G H Holmes, Dunn, NC; mil/AUS; pa/Dist Commercial & Mktg Mgr, Carolina Telephone & Telegraph Co; cp/Kiwanis Clb; Rotary Clb; Mason; Shriner; U Way;r/Meth; hon/Man of Yr, Ahoskie, NC 1975.

HOLMES, ROBERT A oc/University Professor; b/Jul 13, 1943; h/Atlanta, GA; ba/Atlanta; m/Jean Ann Patterson; c/Donna Lee, Darlene Marie, Robert Jr; p/Clarence Holmes, Shepherdstown, WVa; Priscilla Holmes, NYC, NY; ed/BS Shepherd Col 1964; MA 1966, PhD 1969; pa/Prof: Currently at Atlanta Univ, Columbia Univ, So Univ, Hunter Col; Coor Harvard-Yale Intensive Sum Studies Prog; Other Past Positions; Pres Nat Conf of Black Polit Sci Group; Other Profl Assns; cp/Pres: Adams Pk Residents Assn, Cascade Sch PTA, SW Commun Groups; Big Brothers Assn; Others; r/Friendship Bapt Ch: SS Tchr, Trustee Bd; Chm Task Force on Yth; pa/St Rep 39th Dist to Gen Assembly; Adv Coun on Govtl Sers, Atlanta, Reg Comm; hon/Num F'ships; SW Atlanta Good Neighbor Awd; Cert Apprec, Atlanta Public Schs; Columbia Univ Intl Fellows Prog Awd; Pub'd Author; 10 Outstg Persons of Atlanta 1977; Layman of Yr, Metro Atlanta YMCA 1977; Am Assn of Adult Edrs Outstg Legislators Awd 1977; St Com on Life & Hist of Black Georgians Ser Awd 1977; Atlanta New Impact Coalition Awd for Outstg Commun Ser 1976; Ldrship Atlanta 1976-77.

HOLMES, ROY ANDERSON oc/Minister, Teacher; b/Apr 13, 1951; h/Elizabeth City, NC; ba/320 Culpepper St, Elizabeth City, NC; m/Lovetta Jean Goodson; c/Krista Marie; Kimberly Michelle; p/Tommy (dec) and Rubye Holmes, Greenwood, MS; ed/AB Morris Brown Col 1974; MDiv Hood Theol Sem; pa/Min Mt Lebanon AME Zion Ch; Tchr Biblical Studies Col of the Albemarle; pa/Secy Nat Alumni Assn Hood Sem; Former VP Elizabeth City Area Min Assn; Fdr-Orgr & VP Black Mins Coalition; Alpha Phi Alpha; NC Coun Chs, Bd Migrant Mins & Bus & Fins Com; cp/Bd Dirs Elizabeth City Heart Fund; Housing Com Elizabeth City; Past Pres Pasquotank Co Branch NAACP; Chm Adv Bd Pasquotank Co Credit Union; Adm Asst to Pres NAACP; r/AME Zion; hon/Del to 14th World Meth Conf 1981; Outstg Ser to Ch & Commun; Del Gen Conf AME Zion Ch 1980; Epis & Sub-Com of AME Zion Ch; Morris Brown Col Hon Roll; Hood Theol Sem: Student Govt Pres Awd, E L Burton Awd for Humanitarian Ser, I D Blumenthal Awd, Rev J M Hoggard Meml Awd; Fac Commend Ldrship.

HOLMES, WILLIAM WALKER JR oc/Professor, Writer; b/May 20, 1921; h/1119 Kathleen, Kingsville, TX 78363; ba/K'ville; m/Jean Houston; c/William Thomas, Jeananne, Robert Keith; p/Mr and Mrs William W Holmes (dec); ed/BA Tex A&I; MA Univ Colo; mil/USAAF WWII Ret'd Lt Col; pa/Prof Jour; Tex Sports Writer Assn, Past Pres; Hall of Fame Selection Com; cp/Am Cancer Soc; Kiwanis; Scout Troop Com; Bicent Comm; r/Meth; hon/Col Sports Info Dirs Hall of Fame; Order of Golden Quill (Univ Interscholastic Leag).

HOLSTI, OLE RUDOLPH oc/Research and Teaching; b/Aug 7, 1933; h/2439 Tilghman Circle, Chapel Hill, NC 27514; ba/Durham, NC; m/Ann; c/Maija, Eric Lynn (dec); p/Rudolph W and Liisa Franssila Holsti (dec); ed/BA Stanford Univ 1954; MAT Wesleyan Univ 1956; PhD Stanford Univ 1962; mil/AUS 1956-58; USAR 1954-56, 58-62; pa/George V Allen Prof, Dept Polit Sci, Duke Univ 1974-; Dept Polit Sci, Univ British Columbia: Assoc Prof 1967-71, Prof 1971-74; Dept Polit Sci, Stanford Univ: Instr 1962-65, Asst Prof 1965-67; Assoc Editor *Western Political Quarterly* 1970-; Bd Editors: *Computer Studies in the Humanities & Verbal Behavior 1968-, American Journal of Political Science* 1975-; Profl Assns; r/Prot; hon/Pub'd Author: Books, Chapts, Articles; F'ships & Grants; Fellow Ctr for Adv'd Study in the Behavioral Scis 1972-73.

HOLSTON, JAMES JR oc/Postmaster; b/Mar 12, 1935; ba/Eldridge, AL 35554; m/dec; c/Pamela; p/James Sr and Susie Holston, Jasper, AL; ed/Grad Walker Jr Col; Att'd Univ Ala-B'ham; mil/USAF 1956-60; pa/Postmaster, Eldridge, AL; Holston's Real Est; cp/SS Supt 8 Yrs; r/Bapt; Deacon.

HOLT, DOUGLAS EUGENE oc/Office Manager and Secretary to Board of Directors; b/Jan 5, 1925; h/Rt 5, Johnson City, TN 37601; ba/Elizabethton, TN; m/Elizabeth Ann; c/Douglas E Jr, Lisa Gail, John Timothy, Jeffery Daniel; p/John H and Alcyone C Tate Holt, Johnson City, TN; ed/Att'd E Tenn St Univ 1942 & 45; Att'd Ariz St Univ 1944; BS Univ Tenn 1948; mil/USAAC 1943-45; pa/Ofc Mgr & Secy Bd Dirs Elizabethton Elec Sys 1956-80; Johnson City Water & Sewer Dept 1955-56; Jellico Elec & Water Dept 1948-55; En Div Public Power Acctg Assn VP; Tenn Val Public Power Assn; Am Public Power Assn; cp/Past Pres Carter Co C of C; Carter Co Indust Com; Past Pres Elizabethton Rotary Clb; Bd Dirs E Tenn Christian Home; Pt-time Instr Elizabethton Voc Sch; PTA; 4-H Clb Ldr; Adv Com Elizabethton Voc Sch, Elizabethton HS & Carter Co Voc Schs; r/Ch of Christ; hon/W/W S&SW 1980-81; Outstg Citizenship Awd U Fund 1962; Outstg Citizenship Awd C of C 1964.

HOLT, FLORENCE S oc/First Vice President and Corporation Secretary; b/Oct 2, 1921; h/3001 S Memorial Dr, Greenville, NC; ba/Greenville; m/Ernest H; c/Emily Freida Lucas, Buddy; pa/Semi-Ret'd 1st VP & Corp Secy, Holt Olds/Datsun; Hon Life Mem: LCW & NC Fed Wom's Clbs; cp/Past Treas BPW Clb; Past Pres Lady Lions; Past Pres Greenville Wom's Clb; Dist Pres & 2nd VP NCFWC; Precinct Registrar for Pitt Co Bd Elects; Gov Task Force IYC; r/Presb; Pres WOC; hon/NCFWC Bicent Poetry 1976, Sonnet 1979, Best Short Story 1979; Eva Berry Harris Awd, Lyric Poem 1977 & 78.

HOLT, FRANCES GOODWIN oc/Materials Engineer; b/Dec 26, 1939; h/129 Dennis Dr, Williamsburg, VA 23185; ba/Yorktown, VA; m/H Milton; p/Edgar Lee (dec) and Octavia Logan Goodwin, Apex, NC; ed/BS; MS; CAGS; pa/Mats Engr, Naval Mine Engrg Fac; Am Chem Soc; Am Defense Preparedness Assn; r/Meth; hon/Navy Outstg Perf & Sustained Superior Perf Awds.

HOLT, HUGH MILTON oc/Electrical Engineer; b/Oct 27, 1938; h/129 Dennis Dr, Williamsburg, VA 23185; ba/Hampton, VA; m/Frances G; p/Hugh McAdams and Helen Frances Holt, Burlington, NC; ed/BS; MS; pa/Elec Engr, NASA, Langley Res Ctr; IEEE; r/Meth; hon/NASA Exceptl Ser Medal; Outstg Pers Awds; Goddard Meml Trophy.

HOLTMAN, DARLINGTON FRANK oc/Professor; b/Oct 12, 1903; ba/Dept of Microbiol, Univ Tenn, Knoxville, TN 37916; ed/AB Univ Kan 1927; MA Univ Tenn 1930; PhD Ohio St Univ 1937; pa/Asst Bacteriol, Tenn 1927-29, Instr 1929-32; Asst Ohio St Univ 1932-36, Instr 1936-42; Asst Prof Bacteriol & Hygiene, Wn Reserve Univ 1942-43; Prof Bacteriol & Hd Dept, Univ Tenn Knoxville 1943-68; Prof Microbiol, Univ Tenn-K'ville 1968-; Conslt TVA 1944-48, Oak Ridge Nat Lab 1954-58; Chief Med Ecol Br, Chem Corps Biol Labs, Ft Detrick, Md 1949-50; Diplomate Am Bd Microbiol; AAAS; Soc Exp Biol & Med; Am Soc Microbiol; Radiation Res Soc; Am Acad Microbiol; hon/Am Men & Wom of Sci; W/W Am; World. W/W Sci.

HOLYOAK, HUGH KENNETH oc/Aquatic Developer; b/Nov 23, 1936; h/Rt 1, Alapaha, GA 31622; ba/Alapaha; m/Judye Wilson; c/Hugh Kenneth II, Jason Ken; p/Josiah Hugh Holyoak, Enigma, GA; Elsie Jewell Dorminey Holyoak (dec); ed/BS Univ Ga 1959; Att'd Auburn Univ 1975; Att'd Univ So La 1980; mil/USAF 1959-65; pa/Owner & Opr Ken's Fish Hatchery & Fish Farms, H K Holyoak Farms & Pres Ken's Farms, Inc (Devels New Breeds Fish Through Genetic Work & Hybridization; Devels Aquaculture Techs & Equip); Am Fisheries Soc; AAAS; Res Com Catfish Farmers of Am; cp/Repub Nat Party; Nat Security Coun; r/Ch of Jesus Christ of Latter Day Saints: High Coun-man; hon/US Steel Corp, Albany, Ga Div, Awd for 100% Sales Performance 1966; Author: "FISH KILL: A Step by Step Guide for Avoiding Disaster" & "Ken's Fish Hatchery - Guide for Culturing Fish."

HONEYCUTT, JERRY RANDELL oc/Supervisor; b/Nov 6, 1949; h/9099 Homewood Dr, Riverdale, GA 30274; ba/Atlanta; m/Deborah C; c/Jason, Karen and Kevin; p/Jobie J and Irene S Honeycutt, Mars Hill, NC; ed/BS Berea Col 1972; pa/Hd of Interior/Exterior Landscape & Bldg & Grounds Maintenance Supvr, Lenox Sq (Shopping Mall); r/Bapt.

HONOR, DAISY BISHOP oc/Teacher; b/May 1, 1927; h/829 32nd Ave, Columbus, GA 31906; ba/Same; m/Edward; c/Alexia; p/Wyatt and Lula Bishop (dec); ed/BA Philander Smith Col; MA Tuskegee Inst Reading; Specialist & EDS, Ga St Univ; pa/Intl Reading Assn; GAE; MAE; FAB; Century Clb; cp/Jack & Jill of Am Inc; LWV; YMCA; Nat Coun of Negro Wom; r/1st African Bapt Ch, Columbus: Mem; hon/FAB Wom of Yr 1974; Century Clb Achmt Awd; Fellow Mem ABI.

HOOBLER, JAMES FERGUSON oc/Director, Program Review & Budget Staff; b/Aug 2, 1938; h/7425 Democracy Blvd, Bethesda, MD 20034; pa/Washington, DC; p/Frank M and Jane Ferguson Hoobler, Naples, FL; ed/BS 1963 Kent St Univ; MA 1967 Univ of Md; mil/AUS 1958-61; pa/Dir Prog Review & Budget Staff, Ofc of Mgmt & Fin, US Dept of Justice; Mem: Am Soc Public Adms, Am Acad Polit & Social Sci, Acad Polit Sci, Nat Register Sci & Tech Personnel; r/Presb; hon/Fellow, Univ of Md 1968-69; Fellow, Nat Inst Public Affairs 1968-69.

HOOD, BURREL SAMUEL oc/University Professor; b/Dec 14, 1943; h/411 Myrtle St, Starkville, MS 39759; ba/Mississippi State, MS; m/Billie Lane Williams; c/Kelli Elizabeth; p/Chief B S and Rosemary Juel Boyd Hood, Starkville, MS; ed/BS; MME; EdD; mil/AUS; Miss Army Nat Guard; pa/Prof of Music Ed, Miss St Univ; Mem: Music Edrs Nat Conf, Menc Res Soc, Alliance for Arts Ed, Phi Delta Kappa, Phi Mu Alpha Sinfonia, Nat Assn of Col Wind & Percussion Instructors, Phi Kappa Phi, Miss Music Edrs Assn; Music Conslt; cp/Master of Masonic Lodge; Knight Templar; Shrine; Starkville Shrine Clb; Shrine Band; r/1st Bapt Ch: Mem, Deacon, Music Ministry; hon/Intl W/W in Music; Men of Achmt; DIB; Book of Hon; Commun Ldrs & Noteworthy Ams; Fellow Mem ABI.

HOOD, EDWIN CORNELL oc/Corporation President; b/Apr 19, 1939; ba/4137 S Sherwood Forrest Blvd, Baton Rouge, LA 70816; m/Phyllis J; c/Michael, Erie, Ervin, Amy; p/Helen E Martin, Indep, MO; ed/BA Univ Md; Ext Courses LSU; mil/AUS Spec 4; pa/Pres Profl Ins Planners Inc & Petro Invest Plan'g Inc; Nat Life Underwriters; Indep Assn Fin Planners; cp/Masons; Shriners; Bapt Men's Clb; Kiwanis; Shenandoah Home Owners Assn; r/Bapt; hon/Soldier of Qtr 1962; Lttr Commend; Top Salesman of Yr 1974-76; Million Dollar Sales Clb 1979; Apptmnt to La Ins Comm Bd of Life-Hlth Ins Advrs 1980.

HOOD, SUSAN DIANE oc/Student; b/May 28, 1959; h/106 Parkview Dr, Hot Springs, AR 71901; p/John and Billie Hood, Hot Springs, AR; pa/Studnet, Sports Commentating of Razorback Games; cp/Vol Mar of Dimes, MD Telethon; r/Bapt; hon/Pres Sigma Nu Little Sisters; Finalist in St Patricia Pageant; Razorback Beauty; Delta Delta Delta Song Ldr & Entertainment Chm; Sigma Delta Chi; TV Commercial; Outstg Yng Am; Nat Black Girl 1977; Miss U Way; Miss Ark Teen-Ager; Miss Diamondhead; Seen on Cover of Sev Nat Magazines.

HOOF, DAVID LORNE oc/Physical Scientist; b/Dec 2, 1945; m/Bethea Leigh Gledhill; c/Laura Louise; p/Wayne and Mary Eleanor English Hoof, Rockville, MD; ed/AB Cornell Univ 1969; PhD Purdue

Univ 1974; pa/NSF Postdoct Fellow, Georgetown Univ 1974-75; Fac Montgomery Col 1974-76; US Energy Res & Devel Adm 1977-78; Phy Scist US Dept Energy 1978-; Toastmasters; Am Nuclear Soc; NY Acad Scis; AAAS; Sigma Xi; r/Epis; hon/All Am Interscholastic Swimming Team 1962-64; Contbr to Sci Jours.

HOOKER, BILLIE J oc/Director of Development; b/Nov 29, 1938; h/1618 West 15th St, Pine Bluff, AR 71603; ba/Pine Bluff; c/Brian Casey; p/William Shaifer, Port Gibson, MS; Hazel Shaifer (dec); ed/BA Eng; MSLS; pa/Dir of Devel, Univ Ark-Pine Bluff; Mem: Coun for Advmt & Support of Ed, AAUW, Intl Assn Bus Communs; cp/Pine Bluff C of C; Delta Sigma Theta; r/Bapt; hon/Alpha Kappa Mu; Beta Phi Mu; Rockefeller F'ship 1966-67.

HOOKER, HOLLY DUANE oc/Deputy Director; b/Dec 17, 1946; h/911 Elden St, Herndon, VA 22070; ba/Wash DC; p/William Lester and Vera Gertrude England Hooker, Manchester, CT; ed/BS Cornell Univ; pa/Dpty Dir Ofc Public Affairs, US Small Bus Adm; Free-Lance Writer & Editor; Wash Press Clb; Nat Wom's Bus Ownership; cp/Adult Advr AFS Intl Exch Student Assn; r/Meth; hon/Cornell Nat Schlr.

HOOPER, MARJORIE SEATON oc/Editor Emeritus, Researcher; b/Feb 29, 1908; h/2731 Blairstone Rd, #125, Tallahassee, FL 32301; p/Junius Thomas Sr and Maude Darling Seaton Hooper (dec); ed/BA Mt Holyoke Col 1929; pa/Am Printing House for the Blind, Louisville, KY: Editor 1943-73, Var Positions 1933-43; US Del to UNESCO Confs on Braille, Paris, France 1949, 50; Res Assoc, Fla St Univ, Work on Standardization of Braille Codes (Grant from BEH Ofc of Ed, Wash); Secy-Treas Braille Auth for US 1950-76; Del to Num World Profl Confs; Conslt; Past Pres (1st Wom) Am Assn of Wkrs for Blind; Bd Dirs: Nat Braille Assn, Am Foun for Blind; Other Activs; hon/Migel Medal for Ser to Blind, Am Foun for Blind; Master of Art of Living, Class of 1929, Mt Holyoke Col; Medal for Achmt, Round Table on Lib Ser to Blind, Am Lib Assn; Outstg Ser Awd, Nat Accred Coun of Agys Serving the Blind; Ky Lives; Vol of Yr Awd, Tampa Lighthouse for the Blind 1976.

HOOPER, ROY B JR oc/Realtor; State Representative; b/Mar 19, 1947; h/1515 N 31st, Lawton, OK 73505; ba/Lawton; m/Sue; c/Blake, Mark; p/Roy B Hooper (dec); Frances C Hooper, Lawton, OK; ed/BS Bus; mil/USAF, SFC 1968-74; pa/Realtor; Ins Sales; Mem: Lawton Bd of Realtors, Indep Ins Agents Assn; cp/Dem Party; St Rep Dist 64 1975-78; r/Bapt; hon/Outstg Yg Men of Am; W/W in Am Polits.

HOOVER, EVA V oc/Retired Public Nurse; b/Oct 10, 1903; m/Ellis A; c/Doris Ann Herrera, David Westerman, Sharolyn Stinger, Elaine Gammon, Carol Moon; p/Warren (dec) and Anna Myrtle Hardy (dec); ed/Ngs Dip Colo Trg Sch 1929; pa/Surgical & OB Nsg 1931-48; Pvt Duty Nsg 1948-50; Public Hlth Nsg 1950-74; 8th Dist Nsg Assn; Okla Nurses Assn; cp/C of C; Blackwell BPW, Pres 1964-65; Public Relats Chm 1970; Yth Power Chm 16 Yrs; Red Cross Vol; r/Meth; hon/Wom of Yr 1981; Hon Kiwanian; Pres AARP 1980-82; Author Sev Newspaper Articles.

HOOVER, MARY ALICE SMITH oc/Director of Special Education; b/July 19, 1946; h/2711 Bayshore Dr, Bacliff, TX 77518; ba/Alta Loma; m/John Samuel; c/Amanda Gaye; p/W E and Ethel Lizetta Kingrea Smith, Mabank, TX; ed/BA, MAT; Ednl Psych F'ship; pa/Dir Spec Ed, Santa Fe ISD; Pres-Elect Gulf Coast Admrs of Spec Ed 1979-80; r/Ch of Christ; hon/Presented Papers to 1975 Intl Coun of Excptl Chd.

HOOVER, MIRIAM JACKSON oc/Technical Writer, Chemist, Teacher; b/Mar 13, 1931; h/7706 Teal Dr, Huntsville, AL 35802; m/Richard B; c/Brenda; p/Joseph Able Jackson, Clanton, AL; Estelle Onderdonk Jackson, Williamsville, NY; ed/BS magna cum laude Samford Univ 1952; MS Syracuse Univ 1957; pa/Aerospace Engr, NASA & Lockheed; Chemist; Tchr Sci & Math; Tech Writer & Free-Lance Writer; r/Presb; hon/Author Num Profl Articles Incl'g "Solar Home Heating and Cooling - New Method for Using Clean Energy" & "Optical Phenomena in Diatoms."

HOPE, DAVID LEE oc/Instructor; b/Oct 1, 1952; h/2406 Dublin St, Florence, AL; ba/Florence; m/Cathie Ann; p/Jesse and Evelyn Hope, Huntsville, AL; ed/BS Univ N Ala 1976; pa/Speech & Drama Instr, Coffee HS; Dir "Miracle Worker" Perf'd at Ivy Green (Birthplace of Helen Keller); Dir "Play it Again Sam"; Writer & Performer of Radio Commercials; Ala Speech Commun & Theatre Assn; Alpha Sigma Rho; Tau Kappa Alpha; Alpha Psi Omega; cp/NW Adv Panel, Ala Film Comm; r/Bapt; hon/Ala Speech Tchr of Yr 1980; Nom'd SEn Speech Tchr of Yr.

HOPEWELL, PAUL DENNIS oc/Divisional Marketing Manager; b/Jan 27, 1949; h/3110 Hunt Master Dr, Bowling Green, KY 42101; ba/Bowling Green; m/Billie Hammons; c/Paul Thomas, David Myron; p/Jerome Cull (dec) and Bernice Hopewell (dec); pa/Div Mktg Mgr, Schwan Sales Enterprise; cp/C of C Bowling Green; r/Christian; hon/Exec & VP Com Awds.

HOPKINS, GEORGE BERNARD oc/Management Information Systems Director; b/Sept 21, 1949; h/9600 Golf Lakes Trail #2020, Dallas, TX 75231; ba/Dallas; p/George and Lola B Hopkins, Ocala, FL; ed/BS Morris Brown Col 1971; Att'd Whittier Col, Copenhagen, Denmark 1970; Further Study Ohio St Univ 1971-72; pa/Programmer-Analyst, Gen Motors Truck & Coach Div 1972-74; Proj Mgr Hooker Chem & Plastics Corp 1974-79; Dir Mgmt Info Sys Zoecon Industs, Div Hooker Chems 1979-; Assn Sys Mgmt; cp/Alpha Phi Alpha; r/Bapt; hon/Valedictorian Howard HS 1967; Grad cum laude Morris Brown Col 1971.

HOPKINS, GEORGE MATHEWS MARKS oc/Patent Lawyer; b/June 9, 1923; h/765 Old Post Rd NW, Atlanta, GA 39328; ba/Atlanta; m/Betty M; c/Laura M, Edith C; p/C Allen (dec) and Agnes Marks Hopkins, Montgomery, AL; ed/Att'd Ga Inst Technol 1943-44; BSChE Auburn Univ 1944; JD Univ Ala; Grad Studies George Wash Univ; mi/WWII Submarine Ser; pa/Patent Lwyr; Ptnr Newton, Hopkins & Ormsby; Formerly: Asst Dir Res, Auburn Res Foun & Instr Maths Univ Ala; Am Bar; Ga Bar; Am Patent Law Assn; cp/Cherokee Town & Country Clb; Nat Lwyrs Clb; Phoenix Soc; Univ Yacht Clb; SAE; Phi Delta Phi; Submarine Vets of WWII, Pres Ga Chapt; r/Epis; hon/Reg'd Profl Engr; Reg'd Patent.

HOPKINS, LARRY J oc/Congressman; b/Oct 25, 1933; ba/514 Cannon House Ofc Bldg, Wash DC; m/Carloyn Pennebaker; c/Tara, Shae, Josh; ed/Att'd Murray St Univ; Hon LLD Morehead St Univ 1975; mil/USMC; pa/Mem JJB Hilliard & W L Lyons Inc, Brokerage Firm; Fayette Co Clk, 1969; St Rep, Ky's 78th Leg Dist; St Sen 12th Senatorial Dist; Elect'd to US Ho of Reps 1978: Ho Agric Com: Subcom on Tobacco, Subcom on Dairy & Poultry, Subcom on Conserv & Credit; House Armed Sers Com: Subcoms on Investigations & Mil Pers; cp/Kiwanis Intl; Masonic Lodge #1; Olieka Shrine; Am Legion; r/U Meth; hon/Leg of Yr 1974, 76, 78.

HOPPER, EUGENE oc/Civil Engineer; b/July 3, 1918; h/26 Oakhurst Dr, Natchez, MS 39120; b/Same; m/Katherine K; c/Thomas Eugene, John Leslie, Benjamin Harris, Stephen Alexander, Edwin Key; p/Thomas J (dec) and Sara Edna S Hopper (dec); ed/Att'd Millsaps Col & Miss St Univ; mil/AUS 3 Yrs WWII; pa/Ret'd Civil Engr; Reg'd PE in Miss; ASCE; NSPE; PEG; NSPE in Miss; NSPE in La; SAME; ASCE, Miss Chapt; ASCE, La Chapt; cp/Spkr Rotary, Kiwanis, Lions Clbs Miss & La; r/Meth; hon/Sustained Superior Perf 1959; Ofcl Commend 1963; Commend for Exemplary Perf During 1973 Flood 1973; Cert Achmt During 1973 Flood 1974; Miss River Comm Cert Apprec During 1974 & 74 Floods 1974; Ofcl Commend for High Quality Perf 1977; Decoration for Merit Civilian Ser 1979.

HOPPER, FRANK JAY oc/Internationally Known Painter and Illustrator; b/Oct 15, 1924; h/1050 Ranchero Dr, Sarasota, FL 33582; ba/Same; m/Marjorie B; c/Pat, James, Carol; p/George and Elizabeth Anne Hopper; ed/BArts Art Inst of Chgo; MFA Am Acad; mil/USN WWII, Combat Artist, Pilot; pa/St Mary Star of the Sea: 26' x 21' Mural, 14 Stations of the Cross; Unicef Painting for Annual Telethon; Prints, Portraits of Pres Nixon, Senators; Pvt Comms; r/Prot; hon/Best of Jewish Intl Show Mus Fine Arts of the S, Mobile, Ala; Famous Am Series, Histl Mus, Washington, DC; Mural Chateau Pyrenees, Denver, Colo.

HORGAN, MICHAEL CORNELIUS oc/Executive Director; b/Aug 13, 1919; h/301 Yacht Clb Dr, Ft Walton Bch, FL 32548; ba/Ft Walton Bch; m/Joan L; c/Candace, Michael, Timothy, Patrick, Stephen, Daniel, Dennis, Maureen Ann; p/James (dec) and Catherine K Horgan (dec); ed/BSBA; mil/USAF 31+ Yrs 353 Fighter Sorties (Flew in 3 Wars); pa/Exec Dir Ft Walton Bch Housing Authority; cp/Red Cross; Kiwanis; Ret'd Ofcrs Assn; Daedalians; U Way; r/Cath; hon/Leg of Merit w 2 Cluster; DFC w 3 Clusters; AM w 35 Clusters; Others.

HORN, CARL JR oc/Chairman of the Board, Duke Power Company; b/Oct 21, 1921; h/2111 Wendover Rd, Charlotte, NC 28211; ba/Charlotte; m/Virginia J; c/Carl Horn III, Claire E, Kathrine W, Thomas E; p/Carl Horn (dec); Freda W Horn, Salisbury, NC; ed/BA, LLB Duke Univ; mil/AUS 4 Yrs, Capt; pa/Duke Power Co: Asst Gen Counsel 1954-71, Pres 1971-76, Chm of Bd 1976-; Former Law Pract, Charlotte; Public Utility Law Sect of ABA; Kappa Alpha; Phi Delta Phi; Order of the Coif; cp/Past Pres Mecklenburg Kiwanis Clb; Dir Anderson Foun, Charlotte-Mecklenburg Hosp Auth, U Commun Sers, Gtr Charlotte Foun, UNC-C Foun, Edison Elect Inst, Res Triangle Foun, SC Foun Indep Cols & Indep Col Fund of NC; Trustee Arts & Sci Coun Inc of Charlotte-Mecklenburg; Others; r/1st Presb Ch, Charlotte: Mem, Elder; hon/Outstg Chief Exec of Yr in Public Utilities Indust.

HORN, HAZEL oc/Businesswoman; b/Mar 27, 1926; h/Sherman, TX; ba/117 E Lamar St, Sherman, TX 75090; m/Earl D (dec); c/Hazel Ilaine Horn Elkins; p/Frank R Sr (dec) and Mae Cottongin, Nederland, TX; ed/Att'd Bus Col, Mobile, Ala & Beaumont, Tex; Fin Sch, Mobile, Ala; Bus Mgmt, Beaumont, Tex; Credit Mgmt Univ Tex 1972; pa/Owner

& Opr Fin Co; Owner Sales & Rental Bus (Appliance, TV, Stereos, etc); Secy-Treas Mobile Fin Assn; Only Female on Bd Dirs Tex Fin Assn; Exec VP Tex Fin Assn; cp/C of C; Pythian Sisters; Texoma Racquet Clb; Sev Ofcs w Am Legion Aux of Downtown Sherman; Secy Sherman Rebekah Lodge #297; r/Pentecostal; hon/Hon Cert Cosmopolitan Inv Corp 1972; Won TV from TEA 1974, Sewing Machine 1972; Hons for Having Lowest Delinquency in Co for Num Yrs.

HORN, MARION JR oc/Financial Consultant; b/Aug 9, 1942; h/2964B Candlelight Way, Lexington, KY 40502; ba/Inez, KY; m/Elaine Bright; c/Stuart M, Sonya E; p/Marion and Gladys Bowen Horn, Inez, KY; ed/BS English; Deg NY Inst Fin; mil/USNR; pa/Fin Conslt & Coal Exec; Am Coal Assn; cp/Secy Martin Co Farm Bur; Mason; Scottish Rites; Repub; r/Bapt; hon/W/W Fin & Indust 1979-80; Ky Lake Cumberland Hlth Com 1973; Adv Coun St Dept Voc Ed 1974.

HORNE, ANNIE PEARL COOKE oc/Civic Worker; b/Nov 2, 1918; h/1107 Anderson St, Wilson, NC 27893; m/Elmer Lee; c/Patricia Smith, Elmer Lee, Doris Pruitt, Hacie Cooke; p/Erastus and Pearl Coley Cooke; ed/Grad Wilson Tech Inst 1972; pa/JC Penny Co Inc 1939-41; Secy Horne Scale & Equip Co 1942-77, VP 1942-; cp/Vol Wilson Co Rescue Squad Aux 1968-75; Vol Wilson Crisis Ctr 1968-75; Vol Worker Wilson Meml Hosp 1965-; Cnslr Jr Garden Clb 1966-72; Dist Chm Jr Garde Clb of NC 1970-75; Org'd Jr Garden Clb for En NC Sch for Deaf 1971; Mem Lois Rainwater Ext Homemaker Clb 1968-, Pres 1969-73; Vol Cherry Hosp 1968-70; Secy-Treas Dem Precinct #2 1970-75; Cub Scout Den Mother 1952-77; Altrusa; Wilson Wom's Clb; BPW; r/First Christian Ch; Deaconess 1965-69, Ofcr SS Class 1938-75; hon/Recip Ser to Mankind Awd, Sertoma Clb 1971; Green Band Awd, Wilson Dist Scouting Com 1968; Silver Tray Awd, The Garden Dept of Wilson Wom's Clb 1972; Merit Awd Altrusa 1971.

HORNE, PAMELA SWAN oc/Administrator and Coordinator; b/Mar 7, 1949; h/Bryan, TX; ba/Bizzell Hall, Tex A&M Univ, College Station, TX 77843; m/Doyle Jackson; p/Forrest and Mary Louise Swan, Granite City, IL; ed/BA Univ Ill 1971; MA Univ Calif 1973; PhD Tex A&M Univ 1980; pa/Title XII Strengthening Grant Admr & Wom in Devel Coor; Dir New Dimensions-Displaced Homemakers Prog, Tex Engrg Ext Ser, Tex A&M Univ Sys 1978-79; Assessor, Adult Perf Level Comp Based HS Dip Prog, Houston Indep Sch Dist 1976-77; Lectr Eng, Tex A&M Univ 1974-76; Adm Asst to Dir Cont'g Ed in Hlth Scis, Alaska Meth Univ 1974; Instr Speech, Univ Alaska 1973-74; Conf of Col Tchrs of Eng; LACUS; LSA: Phi Delta Gamma; hon/Cert of Apprec for Outstg Ldrship of New Dimension-Displaced Homemakers Prog, St of Tex, Ho of Reps 1979; Grad F'ship to Study Wn Indo-European Langs 1975; Grad w High Hons in Liberal Arts & Scis w Dist in Eng 1971; Recip Child of Vet S'ship & Work-Study S'ship 1068-71; Co-Author "An Analysis of College Classroom Discourse" 1976.

HORNER, MARY LOU oc/Newspaper President; b/Nov 21, 1924; h/3717 Thrall Dr, Knoxville, TN 37918; ba/Knoxville; c/Robert H; p/Lonas H Vittetoe (dec); Mae L Major (dec); ed/Att'd Univ of Tenn; pa/Pres, Holston Review Newspaper; Sales Rep, Pt-Owner Commun News Group; Am Bus Wom's Assn; C of C; cp/Knox Co Ct, 7th Dist Mem; Chm Fountain City Town Hall; Pres Ctl HS PTSA; Bd Mem: Knox Co Unit Am Cancer Soc, E Tenn Chapt Easter Seals Soc, Family Crisis Ctr, Sex Abuse Help Line, Task Force for Handicapped & Elderly; Others; Treas, Bd Mem Knoxville Commun Theatre; Urban Leag; LWV; Beck Cultural Ctr; Knoxville Symph Soc Guild; Others; r/Bapt; hon/Fountain City Wom of Yr 1975.

HORNER, PATRICIA IRENE oc/Administrative Director; b/June 26, 1934; h/6006 Westchester Pk Dr, #301, College Park, MD 20740; ba/Bethesda, MD; m/Kenneth R; p/Charles L and Dorothy I Fox, Carnegie, PA; ed/Conv Mgmt Cert; Att'd Univ Pgh & Prince Geo's Commun Col; pa/Assn Exec-Adm Dir Alliance for Engrg in Med & Biol; Intl Fed Med & Biol Engrg, US Del to Gen Assem 1976-; Am Soc Assn Exec; Prof Conv Mgmt Assn; Am Mgmt Assn; Wash Soc Assn Exec; Editor Intl Dir Biomed Engrs 1978; cp/Sustain'g Mem Repub Nat Com; r/Meth; hon/World W/W Wom; DIB.

HORNSBY, J RUSSELL oc/Lawyer; b/July 3, 1924; h/480 S Lake Sybelia Dr, Maitland, FL 32751; ba/Orlando, FL; c/Lawrence H, James Russell, Kevin L, Tonya Lisa, David Brandon, Richard Earl; p/Benjamin Franklin (dec) and Lillie Weiss Hornsby (dec); ed/LLB 1950; mil/USMC; pa/Am Bar; Fla Bar; Orange Co Bar; Acad Fla Trial Lwyrs; Intl Acad Law & Scis; cp/Order of Moose; Legion of Moose; Am Legion; C of C; Rolling Hills Country Clb; r/Epis; hon/Awd for Outstg Commun Sers 1978.

HOROWITZ, EMANUEL oc/Deputy Director for Resources and Operations; b/Mar 29, 1923; h/14100 North Gate Dr, Silver Spring, MD 20906; ed/BS 1948 The City Col of NY; MS 1956, PhD 1963 George Washington Univ; pa/Nat Bur of Standards: Supvry Chemist 1951-61, Res Chem 1961-65, Chief Polymer Characterization Sect 1965-67, Dpty Chief

Polymers Div 1967-69, Dpty Dir Inst for Material Res 1969-77, Dpty Dir for Resources & Opers, Nat Measuremt Lab 1978-; Mem: Am Standards for Testing & Materials, Intl Standards Org, Am Chem Soc, AAAS; Pub'd 30+ papers on chemical analysis & characterization of polymers & test methods & standardization of textiles, rubber, plastics & surgical implants; hon/Phi Lambda Upsilon; Sigma Xi; Alpha Chi Sigma; Gold Medal, Inst for Materials Res; Rosa Awd, Nat Bur of Standards 1972; Repub of China Standards Awd 1974; ASTM Cert of Apprec 1972; NBS Spec Achmt Awd 1974; Num Others.

HORTON, AMOS L SR oc/Minister; b/May 12, 1960; h/913 Clark St, Lufkin, TX 77351; ba/Same; m/Tina R; c/Bruce Jerome, Shywanda Denise, Amos L Jr; p/Jessie and Lorriane Paxton, Livingston, TX; ed/Wkg on Deg in Theol; pa/Bapt Min; Ins Salesman; Basketball Umpire; Clothes Salesman; cp/Min Alliance; r/Bapt; hon/Cert of Study for Complete Study of Bible; Proj Love; Little Dribbler Asst.

HORTON, ROBERT G oc/Engineering Assistant; b/Sept 18, 1950; h/Abilene, TX; m/Dorothy Ann; p/J T Jr and Billie Louise Horton; ed/Att'd Commercial Col 1971; pa/Engrg Asst, W Tex Utilities Co; r/Bapt.

HORTON, SARAH CAROLINE HAMILTON oc/Nurse; b/Dec 18, 1945; h/1224 Josephine Ave, Prattville, AL 36067; m/Stephen A; c/Sarah Scott, Edward Alton; p/Ed (dec) and Sara Jo Harvill Hamilton, Jasper, AL; ed/Carraway Meth Hosp Sch Nsg 1967; pa/RN, Nat Med Conslts; Am Red Cross Nurse; Formerly: Hd Nurse, Psychi Unit, Carraway Meth Hosp; Mtl Hlth Nurse, Muscle Shoals Mtl Hlth Ctr; Dir Nsg, Burns Nsg Home; cp/Org'r & Past Pres Decatur Jr Wom's Clb; Charter Mem & Past Treas, Secy & Pres of Potpourri Jr Wom's Clb, Rusellville, Ala; r/Meth; UMW Coor of Christian Personhood; hon/C N Carraway Surg Awd 1967; Apprec for Ser UMW 1980.

HORTON, WILLIE MAE oc/Teacher; b/Dec 17, 1946; m/Linton; c/Linton Cornell; p/Mary Benton, Spokane, WA; ed/BS Morris Brown Col 1969; MA Cand Ga St Univ; pa/Tchr Atlanta Bd Ed, Peyton Forest Elem Sch; AAE; GEA; NEA; cp/Chaplain, Altanta Chapt Tots & Teens; VP Parents Clb of Happy Time Child Devel Ctr; r/Pentecostal; hon/Featured in Concert, Atlanta 1980, Spokane 1979; Traveled w MBC Concert Choir 1965-69; Num Other Concerts.

HOSEA, ADDISON oc/Episcopal Bishop; b/Sept 11, 1914; h/PO Box 610, Lexington, KY 40586; ba/Same; m/Jane Marston; c/Nancy Jane, Addison III, Anne-Cameron; p/Addison and Alma Eugenia Bowden Hosea (dec); ed/AB 1938 Atlantic Christian Col; MDiv 1949 Univ of the S; Postgrad Studies: Union Theol Sem 1948, Duke Univ 1950-53; mil/AUS; pa/Ordained to Min Epis Ch as Deacon 1948, Priest 1949; Early Positions as Priest, Rector; Rector St John's, Versailles, Ky 1954-70; Prof New Testament Lang & Lit, The Epis Theol Sem, Ky 1954-59, 65-70; Mem Standing Com 1957-58, 60-64; Examining Chaplain 1964-70l Hon Canon Cathedral of St George the Martyr, Crystal, Ky 1964-70; Dpty to Gen Conv 1955, 58, 64, 67, 69; Bishop Coadjutor, Diocese of Lexington 1970-71; 4th Bishop of Lexington 1971-; r/Epis; hon/Hon DD, Epis Theol Sem, Ky 1968; Hon DD, The Univ of the S 1970.

HOSTETTER, CARLISLE oc/Athletic Director; b/June 6, 1936; h/Banner Elk, NC; ba/Lees McRae Col, Banner Elk, NC 28604; m/Geneva; c/Stanley, Sheila; p/Herbert and Helen Hostetter, Buena Vista, VA; ed/Att'd Gardner Webb Jr Col 1953-55; BS Lynchburg Col 1965; MS Radford Univ 1970; pa/Hd Basketball & Baseball Coach, Parry McCluer HS, Buena Vista, Va 1965-69; Ath Dir, Asst Prin, Hd Basketball Coach Radford HS 1969-75; Ath Dir, Hd Basketball Coach Lees McRae Col 1975-; Chm Basketball Com in Wn Carolina Conf; VP Wn Carolina Conf; Secy & Treas Region X; r/Bapt; hon/Coach of Yr 1970-71-72; Hd Coach of West Team, First Va East-West All-Star Game 1972; Dir'd 1972 Radford Team To An Unbeaten Season (Only One in Hist of the Sch); Author Articles in Ath Jours.

HOUCK, EDWARD B II oc/Marriage and Family Counselor, Psychotherapist; b/May 13, 1948; ba/809 Robinson Rd, Suite 1A, Deerfield Bch, FL 33441; p/Edward B and Evelyn Houck, Highland Bch, FL; pa/Pvt Pract Marriage & Fam Cnslg; Am Assn Marriage & Fam Therapy; APGA; Am Mtl Hlth Cnslrs Assn; Fla Assn Prac'g Psychos; cp/Gov's Com on Employment of Handicapped; Adv Bd Fla St Dept Labor, Bus of Workman's Comp; hon/Blue Key 1976.

HOUCK, LEWIS DANIEL JR oc/Management Consultant, Author, US Government Official; b/July 9, 1932; h/Kensington, MD; ba/451 Seventh St SW, Wash DC 20410; c/Marianne Jennifer, Leland Daniel; p/Lewis and Mary Houck, Princeton, NJ; ed/AB Princeton Univ 1955; MBA w Dist 1964, PhD 1971 NYU Grad Sch Bus Adm; mil/USAR 1955-56 1st Lt; pa/Mgr Spec Res in Mdsg, Young & Rubilam 1957-59; Mktg Mgr, Selling Res Inc 1959-62; Mgmt Conslt to Pvt Indust 1962-64; Instr NYU

Grad Sch Bus Adm 1966-69; Ednl Projs Mgr, Nat Assn Accts 1969-71; Spec Conslt, US Dept Agric 1971-73; Proj Ldr, Ec Res Ser, US Dept Agric 1973-78; Pres Houck Mktg & Mgmt Conslts Inc 1979-; Spec Asst to Dir, Ofc of Prog Mgmt & Control, US Dept Housing & Urban Devel 1980-81; Intl Platform Assn; Am Acctg Assn; Am Inst Mgmt; Am Ec Assn; Acad Polit Sci; Am Acad Polit & Social Sci; Am Mktg Assn; r/Epis; hon/Fellow Ford Foun 1964-66; Fdrs Day Awd, NYU 1971; Fellow ABI 1977-; Fellow Intl Biogl Assn 1978-; Hon Fellow Anglo-Am Acad 1980-; Chm Mktg & Communs Discussion Sems, Fourth IBC Cong, London, England 1977; Author *A Practical Guide to Budgetary and Management Control Systems* 1979.

HOUGE, TRINA MOSSETT oc/Student; b/May 27, 1961; h/Rt 3 Box 399, Cherryville, NC 28021; p/Joe B Houge, Cherryville, NC; Lois E Houge, Cherryville, NC; cp/Girl Scouts; r/Bapt; hon/Awd Recog W/W.

HOUGH, MARGARET LEE oc/Packaging Engineer; b/Mar 11, 1949; h/6904 NW 5th St, Plantation, FL 33317; ba/Ft Lauderdale; m/Ernest H Haller; p/John W and Lillian Rymsza Hough, Indiana, PA; ed/BS, MS Mich St Univ; pa/Soc Pckg & Handling Engrs; MSU Alumni; cp/Toastmasters Intl; Repub Party; hon/W/W Am Wom 1979-80.

HOUSE, ERANA NASH oc/Secretary; b/Nov 19, 1942; h/13008 Halwin Cir,Dallas, TX 75243; ba/Dallas; m/Everett W; c/Marvena B Maynard; p/Elijah Sr (dec) and Odessa Nash (dec); ed/IBM Keypunch Cert, OSU Tech 1964; Secy Trg, Okla Sch Bus 1969; Att'g Sch Communs, Howard Univ; pa/Secy Adv'd Sys Div, Equip Grp, Asst Engrg Supvr w Col Recruiting, Tex Instruments Inc; r/Ch of Christ.

HOUSE, JERRY BRENT oc/Cotton Farmer; b/Mar 4, 1944; h/Clairemont Rd, Snyder, TX 79549; m/Rita; c/Brent, Shea, Perry, Justin, Raymond, Jeremy; p/Raymond and Pauline House, Snyder, TX; ed/Att'd Howard Jr Col; pa/Cotton Farmer; Feedlot Owner; cp/JCs: Dir 2 Yrs, Elec Judge 4 Yrs; Commun Com Mem ASCS; Db Dirs Scurry Co Prodrs Assn, Past Pres; r/Bapt; hon/Outstg Yng Farmer Scurry Co 1978, 2nd Runner-up in St Contest.

HOUSER, LOUISE KELLEY oc/Health Care Administrator; b/Feb 22, 1919; h/121 Jackson St, Rome, GA 30161; ba/Rome, GA; m/John W Jr; c/George, John W III; p/George (dec) and Byrdie Stephens Kelley (dec); ed/BS 1941, MS 1959 SC A&M Col; Further Study Berry Col, Univ Ga, Atlanta Univ & La Salle Ext; pa/CD Instr, Red Cross & Civil Defense 1941-43; Sci & Home Ec Tchr, Marion Co Trg Sch 1941-44; Sci Tchr, Ga Sch for Deaf 1959-61; Elem Tchr, Rome City Schs 1961-68; Hlth Care, Dir Pers, Brentwood Med Care Home 1967-71; Admr, Nsg Home 1972-77; Admr, Brentwood Park, Three Rivers Hlth Care Co 1977-; N Ga Coun Hlth Care Assn; Ga Hlth Care Assn, Vols & Activs Com; Am Hlth Care Assn; Ga Soc Activ Dirs, Past VP NW Coun; Aux N Ga Dental Soc; Aux Ga Dental Soc, Pres 1970-72; Ladies Aux to Nat Dental Assn, Pres 1974, Zone VP 1959-70, Fin Secy 1972-74, Exec Bd Mem 1976-; Am Cancer Soc, Pres, Floyd Co Colored Div 1952-60; Rome Coun Human Relats; Delta Sigma Theta; Bd Dirs Sara Murphy Home 1972-; Bd Dirs Brentwood Corp 1964-77; Past Mem Ednl & Sci Assns; r/Meth; Past Chm Ed Comm, Ch Sch Supt, Yth Dir, Chmm Fin, Lay Spkr, Chm Hlth & Wel Min, Coor Christian Global Concerns; hon/Ideal Delta of Alpha Xi 1941; H E Trophy for Hon & Achmt 1941; Rome Tchr of Yr 1967; Dist Tchr of Yr 1967; Dynamic Delta 1968; W/W: Ga, Hlth Care, Am Wom; Delta of Yr 1977; Nat Social Dir 1938; Notable Ams 1977.

HOUSEWRIGHT, RILEY DEE oc/Microbiologist; b/Oct 17, 1913; h/147 Fairview Ave, Frederick, MD 21701; ba/Wash DC; m/Artemis; c/Kim Bryant, Stepch: Rudi Jegart, Nike Jegart; p/Vick and Lillie Housewright, Wylie, TX; ed/BS N Tex St Univ; MA Univ Tex; PhD Univ Chgo; mil/USNR Ret'd Capt; pa/Past Pres Am Soc Microbio; Antibiotic Res; cp/Bd Frederick Meml Hosp; Am Type Culture Collection; r/Meth; hon/Diplomat Am Bd Microbiol; Patent Awds; Exceptl Civilian Ser Awd AUS.

HOUSTON, LAWRENCE J oc/Accountant; b/Dec 25, 1938; h/2208 Boyd, Midland, TX 79701; ba/Midland; m/Phyllis Smith; c/Joyce Elaine Peterson, Marvin Dean, Luetta Milbrandt, Jean; p/Walter Charles (dec) and Mayre Helm Houston, Albuquerque, NM; ed/AA Ctrl Col 1948; Cert in Mod Bus Alexander Hamilton Inst 1964; pa/Acct I, Revenue Acctg Sect, ARCO Oil & Gas Co; r/Free Meth.

HOUSTON, OLIVIA NASH oc/Education Specialist; b/Jan 18, 1930; h/2809 NE 25th St, Oklahoma City, OK 73111; p/Luther; c/Arlene; p/dec; ed/BS Ed 1956; MEd 1973; AS 1976; pa/Ed Spec US Dept Transp, Fed Aviation Adm Acad, Air Traffic Control Branch; Kappa Delta Pi; cp/YWCA; r/Ch of Christ; hn/Outstg Tech Writing Student 1975-76; Three Zero Defect Awds (Bronze, Silver, Gold); Ofcl Lttrs of Commend for Devel'g & Writing Air Traffic Trg Courses 1977, 78, 79.

HOVIS, CHARLES PATRICK oc/Deputy Assistant General; b/Jul 26, 1928; h/11800 Magruder Ln, Rockville, MD 20852; ba/Washington, DC; m/Janet Fowler; c/Carol, Katherine, Brenda; p/Robert H Hovis (dec); Alma Jobe Hovis, Guntersville, AL; ed/AB; LLB; pa/Dpty Asst Gen Coun, US Gen Acct'g Ofc; Mem Fed Bar Assn; cp/Past Pres 500 Fam Civic Assn; Lions Clb; r/Presb; hon/W/W in Govt.

HOWARD, BARBARA BURROW oc/Cultural Affairs Consultant, Free-Lance Editor; b/May 17, 1929; h/2305 Sherbrooke Way, Rockville, MD 20850; ba/Rockville; m/William J Jr; p/E Dick (dec) and Alyce Faught Burrow, S Pgh, TN; ed/AA w Hons Gulf Park Col 1948; BA w Hons Univ Ala 1950; pa/Feature Writer *Daily Mountain Eagle* 1945-48; Wom's Editor *Tuscaloosa News* 1950-51; Leg Asst to Cong-man Carl Elliott 1951-53; Press Secy to Cong-man Arminstead I Selden 1953-62; Mgr Gerald G Wagner Assocs Public Relats Firm 1962-73; Cultural Affairs Advr 1973-; Free-Lance Editor 1973-; Assoc Prodr, Annual UN Concert & Dinner 1964-71; Editor Commemorative Pubs 1962-72; Writer-Editor Cultural Pubs 1963-; cp/VP Univ Ala Nat Alumni Assn 1965-66, Pres Nat Capital Chapt 1965-67; Chi Omega; Vol Hosp Aide; Com Chm Rockville Art Leag & Montgomery Co Arts Coun; Smithsonian Nat Assocs; r/Bapt; hon/Dist'd Alumnae Awd, Univ Ala 1970; Cert Merit BPW's Clbs 1950; Recip Theta Sigma Phi Awd for Outstg Wom Grad Sch of Jour 1950.

HOWARD, CURTIS DAMONE oc/MBA Candidate; b/June 27, 1954; h/7313-B Gardner Hills, Ft Campbell, KY 42223; m/Arnia A; p/Margaret S Howard, Kinston, NC; ed/BA UNC-CH 1975; Dale Carnegie Human Relats 1979; MBA Cand Austin Peay St 1982; pa/Prodr-Dir WCTI TV 1975-77; Promo Mgr WTVD TV 1977-78; TV Prod Coor WPTF TV 1978-79; Alpha Kappa Psi; U Order Master Mixologists; cp/F&AM; Omega Psi Phi; US JCs; r/Prot; hon/Outstg Yng Man Am 1978, 79, 80; Alpha Kappa Psi Bad Guy Awd 1981; Author "Dante's Inferno - A Concise and Personal Statement on the Art of Mixology."

HOWARD, GENE C oc/State Senator; b/Sept 26, 1926; h/748 S 94 Ave, Tulsa, OK 74112; ba/Tulsa; c/Joe, Ted, Jean Peterson; p/Joe W Howard (dec); Nell L Howard, Tulsa, OK; ed/JD Univ of Okla; mil/USAF Lt Col Resv; Active Duty 1961-62, 1944-46; pa/Atty; cp/Ho of Reps 1958-62; Okla Senate 1965-; Pres Pro Tem Okla Senate 1975-; r/Disciples of Christ; hon/Outstg Yg Atty of Tulsa Co 1953.

HOWARD, HARRY L oc/Executive Vice President; b/Feb 23, 1909; h/1015 Carolina Ave, N Augusta, SC 29841; ba/Augusta; m/Isabel Lefler; c/Cyrus Lee, Harriet Howard Day, Donald; p/Cleveland F and Anthia Sigman Howard; pa/Exec VP Belk Grp Stores; r/Meth; hon/Ser to Mankind Awd, Sertoma Clb 1974; Citizen of Yr, N Augusta C of C 1969.

HOWARD, KARAN ANICA oc/Bank Officer; b/Dec 23, 1939; h/6432 Brownlee Dr, Nashville, TN 37205; ba/N'ville; m/Samuel; c/Anica Lynn, Samuel H II; p/Charles C Wilson, Ottawa, KS; Wilmenta M Wilson (dec); ed/BS Ed; pa/Ofcr, Retail Sers Dept, 3rd Nat Bank; Exec Wom of Am; CABLE, Bd Dirs; cp/Cumberland Val Girl Scouts Bd of Dirs; Florence Crittenton Home Bd of Dirs; Jack & Jill of Am; Exec Com N'ville C of C; hon/World W/W Wom.

HOWARD, LEONARD (LENNIE) AMBERS oc/Chaplain; b/Aug 9, 1952; h/5733 Hyde Pk Dr, Montgomery, AL 36117; m/Elizabeth Meyer; p/William Leonard Howard (dec); Nelwyn Johnson, Americus, GA; ed/AS; BS; MS; MDiv; mil/USAF 1971-75; pa/Chaplain, Green River Boys Camp; r/So Bapt.

HOWARD, MARJORIE ELAINE oc/Administrator; b/May 15, 1923; h/Rt 2 Box 265E, Salem, AL 36874; m/Robert N; c/Sheryl M Siniard, William Eugene Mims; p/Charles Eugene (dec) and Cora Marquis Holstein, Salem, AL; ed/Att'd Auburn Univ; pa/Adm-Registrar's Ofc, Chattahoochee Val Commun Col (on leave of absence); cp/Bd Dirs Ala Div, Am Cancer Soc, Exec Secy; Past Vol: Red Cross, Mar of Dimes, PTA; Indian Val Chapt Am Bus Wom's Assn; Wom's Civic Clb of Phenix City; r/Meth; hon/Life Mem Wom's Civic Clb; Mardi Gras Queen 1979.

HOWE, COURTNEY EVERETT SR oc/Chief Executive Officer; b/Aug 30, 1932; m/Marie F; c/Linnea C, Karen A, Lisa C, Courtney E Jr; p/Madiline T Howe, Cuba, NY; ed/BS Penn St Univ 1954; MS St Bonaventure Univ 1963; pa/ACME Elec Corp, Pers Dir 1959-63; Labor Relats Supvr, Celanese Fibers Co 1963-65; Internal Conslt, N Am Rockwell Corp 1965-67; Jordan Howe Assoc Inc 1967-, Pres & Chm; Pres & Chm Bd Cape Coral Med Clin Inc; Am Col Med Grp Mgrs; Pres Fla St Med Grp Mgrs Assn 1978; cp/Secy Rotary; Pres Indust Mgmt Clb; YMCA Bd Dirs; r/Prot; hon/W/W: Hlth Care, S&SW; Contbr to *Computer Based Collections* 1980.

HOWELL, WINSTON C oc/Sheetmetal Mechanic; b/Jan 22, 1942; p/T B and Jennie Mae Howell Hartford, AL; pa/Mech Hayes Intl Corp; r/Ch of God; hon/Winner Over 200 Trophies, Ribbons, Certs & Plaques

For Running 1974-; Has Run 20,000 Miles 1974-; Competed in Boston Marathon 2 Times; Competed in 52 Major Road Races in 1980.

HOWERTON, JAMES WILLIAM oc/Judge; b/Oct 22, 1931; h/3954 Primrose Pl, Paducah, KY 42001; ba/Paducah; m/Eva; c/John, Jane, Clay; p/Walter C and Nell Bass Howerton, Paducah, KY; ed/BS Bus Adm; JD; mil/USAF Active Duty 1953-55; Resv to date, Lt Col; pa/Judge, Ct of Appeals of Ky 1976-; City Mgr & Assoc Coun, City of Paducah 1972-76; Corp Coun, City of Paducah, 1967-72; Other Former Positions; Mem: Am Bar Assn, Ky Bar Assn, McCracken Co Bar Assn; cp/Rotary Clb, Pres 1969-70; Gtr Paducah Industl Devel Assn, Pres 1972-73; Paducah Commun Col, Lifetime Trustee; C of C, VP 1974, Dir 1969-72; Ky Comm for Improving Mgmt in Local Govt, Chm 1975-76; Others; r/Epis.

HOWINGTON, LEW HAYWOD oc/Sales Manager; b/June 14, 1932; h/Houston, TX; ba/2400 W Loop S, PO Box 22605; Houston, TX 77027; m/Ava Merle; c/Loretta Jane, Michael Lew; p/Benjamin Franklin Howington, Petal, MS; ed/Att'd La Salle Ext Univ 1953-54, Univ So Miss 1954-56; mil/USN 1950-54; pa/Sales Mgr, Div Halliburton Co; API; AIME (SPE); Nomads; r/Meth.

HOYLE, EMMA JEAN oc/Food Service Staff; b/Jan 1, 1936; h/1307-A J St, Alexander City, AL 35010; ba/Alexander City; m/Earnest; c/Bettie Jean Thomas, Otis, Earl, Patricia, Roger; p/Johnny (dec) and Mattie Marshall, Wetumpka, AL; ed/Cert in Bible Studies; pa/Pastor Alexander City No 2 AOH Ch of God; Food Ser Staff, Jim Pearson Sch; cp/Ala Sheriff's Boys & Girls Ranches; Mar of Dimes; Heart Fund; Am Cancer Soc; r/Holiness; hon/5 Yr Pin, Alexander City Sch Sys.

HRDLICKA, ROBERT JAMES oc/Insurance Agent; b/May 16, 1932; h/4614 Atlas #216, El Paso, TX 79904; ba/El Paso, TX; m/Mary Lou; c/Stephen John; p/Henry (dec) and Nancy Hrdlicka, Clark, NJ; ed/BSA Univ Tex-El Paso; Assoc Technol NW Mo St Univ; mil/AUS Ret'd Chief Warrant Ofcr; pa/Bd Dirs Tex Assn Life Underwriters; cp/Repub Nat Com; VFW; r/Christian; hon/Past Pres El Paso Assn Life Underwriters; 3 Time Recip Army Commend Medal from Secy Army for Merit Ser.

HUANTES, MARGARITA RIVAS oc/Social Worker; b/Mar 21, 1914; h/251 Quill Dr E, San Antonio, TX 78228; ba/San Antonio; m/Santos; p/Octaviano Rivas (dec); Maria de los Reyes Hernandez (dec); ed/BA summa cum laude Univ Tex-Austin 1937; MSW w Hons Wn Reserve Univ; Doct Cand Nova Univ; pa/Prog Dir, Inman Christian Ctr 1948-65; Exec Dir San Antonio Lit Coun; Chp S Tex Chapt NASW; Nat Bd NASW 1977-80; cp/Chp YWCA; Chp SA Coalition for Human Sers; Chp SA Immigration Task Force; r/Prot; hon/W/W Am Wom; Nat Assn Social Wkrs Dir; 200 Wom of Acht; AAWU Ednl Foun F'ship Prog; Recog of Significant Ser 1973; Top's In Texas, For Commun Ser; Fed Tex Repub Wom 1968; Commun Ser Awd as Outsg Edr 1971; Cert Awd for Dist'd Achmt in Commun Progress 1971; Ambassador WOAI TV 1974; Awd for Outstg Civic Work 1973; Recip Golden Yr Apprec Awd; Mexican Am of Month May 1976; Recip Hidalgo Awd for Commun Ser 1976; Recip Awd in Apprec for Contbns in Field of Social Work & Lit 1977; Recip Monfrey Commun Awd 1980; Today's Wom 1980.

HUBBARD, BILLIE YVONNE oc/Resource Consultant; b/Dec 10, 1951; p/Billie Charles and Mildred Loree Hubbard, Jackson, MS; ed/BS Lee Col 1973; MSSW Univ Tenn-Knoxville; pa/Psychi Social Worker; Resource Conslt, Cleveland HS; cp/Hiwassee Student Sers Assn; r/Ch of God.

HUBBARD, CARROLL oc/Member of Congress; b/Jul 7, 1937; h/1025 Delf Drive, McLean, VA 22101; ba/Washington, DC; m/Joync Lynn Hall; c/Kelly, Krista; p/Carroll Sr and Addie Beth Hubbard, Louisville, KY; ed/BA Georgetown Col, Georgetown, Ky; JD Univ of Louisville Sch of Law; mil/Air Nat Guard, Capt; Ky Army Nat Guard; Active Duty: Lackland AFB, Brooks AFB; cp/Elected to Ky St Senate, US Ho of Reps 1974; Former Rotary Clb Pres; r/Bapt; hon/1 of 3 Outstg Yg Men of Ky 1968; Outstg Yg Dem Legislator 1972; Outstg Yg Men in Am.

HUBBARD, EDWARD SIMS oc/Journeyman Carpenter; b/Sept 17, 1923; h/2106 Dadeville Rd, Alexander City, AL 35010; m/Hilda Jeannette Tapley; p/Henry Austin and Jennie Brince Glenn Hubbard; ed/Journeyman Cert Lindsey Hopkins Voc Sch 1950; mil/USN 1943-46; pa/Gaines Constr Co; Miami Prefab Inc; Indep Constr Co; Blount Intl Ltd; Am Fed Labor; U Brotherhood of Carpenters & Joiners of Am; r/Bapt; hon/Am Victory WWII; Outstg Craftsman Awd 1981.

HUBBARD, EMILY R oc/Homemaker; b/Feb 19, 1935; h/163 Huntington Rd NE, Atlanta, GA 30309; m/Larry M; c/Cathy H Raborn, Larry M Jr, Christian Scott; p/Virgil A and Lucille W Rose, Memphis, TN; pa/La St Univ Former Positions: Exec Secy to Provost & V/Chancellor, Pres & Bd Mem Campus Fed Credit Union, Chm Staff Rep Com, Staff Senate Pers Policies Com, Bd Dirs Fac Clb, Others; Past VP Hubbard Inc;

cp/Past Exec Dir Polit Party HQs; St Dir ERA U La; Pres Wom in Politics; Mem Coms La Woms Polit Caucus; Del Intl Woms Yr Conf; Mem Gov's Task Force on Wom & Credit; r/St Ann's Epis Ch: Mem; hon/Invited Spkr & Participant Num Confs; Notable Ams; Book of Honor; Fellow Mem ABI.

HUBBARD, FRANK MULDROW oc/Chairman of Board; b/Feb 15, 1920; h/729 Alba Dr, Orlando, FL 32804; ba/Orlando; m/Ruth Scorgie; c/Leonard Evans, Ruth Converse Hanberry; p/Francis Evans (dec) and Mildred M Hubbard, Summerville, SC; mil/Capt 342nd Engr Reg 3½ Yrs; pa/Chm Bd Hubbard Constr Co; r/Presb.

HUBBARD, MARQUETTA LYNN oc/Bookkeeper; b/Jan 12, 1955; h/914 E Beech St, La Follettel, TN 37766; ba/La Follette; m/Michael S; p/Robert E and Frances Brantley, Jacksboro, TN; ed/Affil Brokers Lic; cp/Chp Mtl Hlth Assn Tenn; r/Bapt.

HUBENAK, JOE A oc/State Representative; b/Jul 2, 1937; h/2635 Sequoia, Rosenberg, TX 77471; ba/Rosenberg; m/Sandra Lynn; c/Elizabeth Lynn, Joe Anthony, Michael Andrew; p/John Joe Sr and Rose Marie Hubenak, Rosharon, TX; ed/AA Alvin Jr Col; BBA Univ Houston; mil/Tex Army NG 8 Yrs; pa/St Rep, Dist 21 10 Yrs; Chm Tex Ho of Reps Com on Agri & Livestock 6 Yrs; Cand, Tex Commr of Agri; Agri & Food Supply Task Force, Intergovtl Relats Com, Nat Conf of St Legs; Chm Subcom on Mktg; So Leg Conf Com on Agri & Rural Devel; Tex Coastal & Marine Coun; cp/Lifetime Mem: Houston Fat Stock Show & Rodeo, Ft Bend Co Fat Stock Show & Rodeo; Dir Ft Bend Co Mar Dimes; Zone Chm, Tex Lions Clb, Fgn Exc Student Prog; Others; hon/Dist'd Leg Awd, Voc Agri Tchrs Assn; Citizen Who Contributed Most to Ed from His Area, Tex St Tchrs Assn; The Tex Lawman, 62nd Leg's Outstg Rep; Outstg Yg Men of S; W/W Govt.

HUCKABAY, GEORGIA ANNE oc/Assistant Professor; b/Oct 11, 1941; h/1405 St John Ave, Ruston, LA 71270; ba/Ruston; m/Houston Keller; c/Georgia Anne; p/George Thomas and Levetia Rosa Danne Filligham; ed/BMEd, MM Univ So Miss; pa/Asst Prof Mus, La Tech Univ; Dir Summer Mus Camp; Tau Beta Sigma; Mu Phi Epsilon; Nat Assn Col Wind & Percussion Instrs; cp/Godchaux Mus Clb; r/Epis; hon/W/W Am Wom.

HUCKABY, JERRY oc/Congressman; b/Jul 19, 1941; ba/228 Cannon House Office Bldg, Washington, DC 20515; m/Suzanne Woodard; c/Michelle, Clay; ed/BSEE 1963 La St Univ; MBA 1968 Ga St Univ; Doctoral Studies in Ecs La Tech Univ; pa/Western Elect Co 1963-73; Farmer; Mem: La Farm Bur, N La Milk Prodr Assn, La Cattleman's Assn; cp/US Rep, 5th Congl Dist 1977; Mem Coms: House Agri, House Interior & Insular Affairs, Exec Com 95th Cong New Mems Caucus, Rural Caucus, Dem Study Group; Dem Resch Org; Nat Bd Dirs, Citizen's Com for the Right to Keep & Bear Arms; Bd Dirs Distributive Ed Clbs of Am; Lions Clb; BSA Scout Master; r/Meth Ch.

HUCKS, LARRY A oc/Automobile Dealer; /Dec 12, 1947; h/PO Box 444, Aynor, SC 29511; ba/Aynor; p/W A Jr and Mary T Hucks, Aynor, SC; ed/AAS; BS; mil/AUS 3 Yrs; cp/Nat Assn Accred'd Talent & Beauty Pageant Judges; Aynor JCs; r/Bapt.

HUDDLESTON, FRANK HENRY oc/Electrician; b/Nov 9, 1933; h/Rt 1, Central City, KY 42330; ba/Same; m/Gynon B; c/Terry Dewayne, John Kohl, Judy Ann; p/John Henry (dec) and Mary Annie Huddleston (dec); mil/AUS 2 Yrs; pa/Pres Townhouse Inc; Owner Huddleston Elec & Huddleston Insulation; cp/Lions Clb; C of C; Repub Party; r/Missionary Bapt; hon/W/W Fin & Indust 1979-80.

HUDGENS, BETTIE WARREN oc/Department Chairman; b/Sept 27, 1935; h/Mobile, AL; ba/Communication Arts Dept, Spring Hill Col, Mobile, AL 36608; m/A Neil; c/Lew, Margaret; p/Lewis and Margaret Warren, Portsmouth, VA; ed/BA Westhampton Col, Univ Richmond 1957; MA Univ Ala 1958; pa/Assoc Prof, Dir Commun Arts Dept, Spring Hill Col; Advtg Fed of Gtr Mobile; Public Relats Coun of Mobile; Speech Commun Assn; So Speech Assn; Am Forensics Assn; Nat Assn Ednl Broadcasters; cp/Gulf Coast Public Broadcasting, VP; Public Relats Chm, Sr Bd Florence Crittenton Home; Mobile Co Sch Bd Plan'g Com; Proj Dir CPB Grant, HEW Grant & NEH Plan'g Grant; Channel 42 Ednl TV Adv Bd; hon/1 of 10 Outstg Career Wom of Mobile 1979; Outstg Edr of Am 1975; Elected to Nat Coun of Delta Sigma Rho-Tau Kappa Alpha; M O Beale Scroll of Merit 1962.

HUDSON, MARIAN SUE PARSONS oc/Director of Pharmacy; b/Sept 24, 1951; h/307 Selkrik Trail, So Pines, NC 28387; ba/McCain, NC; c/Stephen Ray; p/Solomon Lankester and Doris Bost Parsons, Biscoe, NC; ed/AA Sandhills Commun Col 1971; BS Univ NC-CH 1974; pa/Dir Pharm, McCain Hosp, St NC Div Human Resources; Am Soc Hosp Pharms; NC Soc Hosp Pharms; NC Pharm Assn; NC St Employees Assn,

VChm Area 16, 1980-81; NC Drug Adv Com for Purchase & Contract; Kappa Epsilon Alumnae; cp/Aberdeen JCettes; Sandhill BPW Clb; Wallace O'Neal Day Sch Mother's Assn; Highland Trails Homeowners Assn; NC Pharm PAC, Bd Dirs 1979-81; Dem Party; r/Presb; hon/W/W S&SW.

HUDSON, MARY GAIL CARNEAL oc/Speech, Hearing, Language Pathologist; b/Jan 4, 1953; h/3828 Silverstone, Plano, TX 75023; ba/Dallas; m/Paul William; p/Virgil Eugene Jr (dec) and Mary Sigrid Lanum Carneal, Dallas, TX; ed/BS w Hons 1974, MS 1975 So Meth Univ; Cert Tchr St Tex 1974; Cert Clin Competence, Am Speech & Hearing Assn 1977; pa/Speech, Hearing, Lang Pathol, Richardson Indep Sch Dist, Spring Creek Elem Sch; Intl Assn Logopedics & Phoniatrics; Am Speech & Hearing Assn; Tex Speech & Hearing Assn; Dallas Assn Speech Pathols & Audiologists; Assn Tex Profl Edrs; Richardson Assn Tex Profl Edrs (Treas); Richardson Ed Assn; Zeta Phi Eta; cp/Smithsonian Assn; Nat Geog Soc; Dallas Mus Fine Arts; Repub Party; r/Meth; hon/W/W S&SW 1980-81.

HUEBNER, RICHARD ALLEN oc/Executive Director; b/July 31, 1950; h/2700 Leeds Ln, Charlottesville, VA 22901; ba/C'ville; m/Marsha Lawrence; c/Angela Carol, Holly Anne; p/Otto LeRoy Huebner (dec); Audrey Elizabeth James, Racine, Wis; ed/BBA Univ Wis-Madison; pa/Exec Dir Kappa Sigma Frat; Am Soc of Assn Execs; Frat Execs Assn; Intl Platform Assn; Assn of Frat Advrs; Assn of Col Frats; Wis Alumni Assn; Edgewater Conf; Kappa Sigma; cp/US JCs, C'ville-Albemarle Chapt, St Dir; r/Luth: Lay Catechist & Yth Advr; hon/JC Key Man Awd 1979; W/W S&SW; Personalities of Am; Outstg Yng Men Am; Notable Ams; Men & Wom of Dist; Book of Hon; Men of Achmt; DIB; W/W Assn Mgmt.

HUEY, ADRIENNE COCHRAN oc/Artist, Lecturer, Teacher; b/Sept 2, 1921; h/5920 N Meridian Pl, Okla City, OK 71322; ba/Same; m/George Owen (dec); c/Nancy Runner, Barbara Brennan, Shirley Hastings, Peggy Ann; p/Paul R and Fan Alexander Cochran, Okla City, OK; ed/Studied Batik, New Delhi, India 1965-67; Att'd Treveni Khala Sangham; pa/Pres Okla City Branch Nat Leag Am Pen Wom 1978-80; Ofcl Bd Am Wom's Clb, Buenos Aires, Argentina 1975; Ofcl Bd Inter-Am Wom's Clb 1970-73; Treas US Info Ser Bi-Nat Ctr, Panama 1971; r/Prot; hon/1st & 3rd Ribbons NLAPW Juried Art Show 1979; Num Other Ribbons for Batik Paintings & Wall Hangings as Well as Oil Paintings; 2000 Wom Achmt 1972; Intl Dic Biogs.

HUEY, MARY EVELYN BLAGG oc/University President; b/Jan 19, 1922; h/2801 Longfellow Lane, Denton, TX 76201; ba/Denton; m/Griffin B; c/Henry Griffin; p/Henry H and Melissa Evelyn Manning Blagg (dec); ed/BA 1942, MA 1943 Tex Woms Univ; MA Univ Ky 1947; PhD Duke Univ 1954; Addit Studies; pa/Pres, Tex Woms Univ, Denton; Other Former Ednl Positions: N Tex St Univ, Univ Miss, Tex Woms Univ; Am Coun on Ed, Comm on Wom in Higher Ed; AAUW; Ariel Clb; Spkr, Panelist; Other Profl Activs; cp/DAR; Daughs of Repub of Tex; Nat Geneal Soc; N Ctl Tex Coun of Govts; Am, SWn, So Polit Sci Assns; SWn Social Sci Assn; City Denton, Bd Adjustmt (Planning & Zoning); 2/VP U Way; Others; r/1st Presb Ch, Denton; hon/Dist'd Alumni Awd, Tex Woms Univ 1974; Public Admr of Yr, N Tex Chapt AAPA; W/W: Am Wom, S&SW, Am Ed, Am Men of Sci; DIB; Intl Gold Book; 500 1st Fams of Am; Pub'd Author; Others.

HUFFER, DAVID STONE oc/Teacher; b/June 27, 1957; h/350 Mary Grey Lane, Staunton, VA 24401; ba/Waynesboro, VA; m/Roy S and Betty S Huffer, Staunton, VA; ed/BS Phy Ed; pa/Tchr Kate Collins Jr HS; VEA; r/Bapt; hon/HS All-Dist Qtrback.

HUFFMAN, DIXIE MATHERLY oc/Retired Teacher, Hostess; b/Jan 5, 1928; h/Mackville Rd, Rt 6, Harrodsburg, KY 40330; ba/H'burg; m/Hugh (dec); c/Wanda Jo Hurlbert, Leonna Milburn, Cheryl Lester; p/Dewey L (dec) and Ruby Graves Matherly, H'burg, KY; ed/AA Midway Jr Col; BS En St Univ; pa/Ret'd Elem Tchr; Hostess Shakertown; MCEA; KEA: NEA; KRTA; r/Bruner's Chapel Bapt Ch.

HUFFMAN, DONALD R oc/Lawyer, Retired Officer USMC; b/Aug 11, 1936; h/Rt 1 Box 403, Fayetteville, AR 72701; m/Marilyn J; c/Leslie Anne, Wade; p/Elmer Huffman (dec); Claudia Beatrice Pierce Huffman Sarten, Rogue, AR; ed/BS Math & Natural Sci; BS Communs; MBA; JD; mil/USMC 1956-76; pa/Student Bar Assn; Delta Theta Phi; r/Ch of Christ; hon/Top Student in All Mil Classes; Silver Star Medal; Legion of Merit w Combat V.

HUFFMAN, GEORGE E oc/Administrator; b/June 27, 1944; h/4001 Terrace, Amarillo, TX 79109; ba/Amarillo; m/Jane Cooper; c/Steven Eugene, Aaron Bradley; p/Lawrence W and Nyra Everett Huffman, Lewis, KS; ed/BS Ed; MS Ed; pa/Admr Amarillo Col; ALA; AECT; TAET; CCAIT; cp/Vol Ldr Boy Scouts; r/Paramount Bapt Ch; hon/Nom'd Outstg Edr, Olathe, Kan; Outstg Yng Man Am 1978.

HUG, RICHARD E oc/Corporation President; b/Jan 11, 1935; h/247 Oak Ct, Severna Park, MD 21146; ba/Balto; m/Lois; c/Donald, Cynthia; p/Gustave Hug, Pocono Summit, PA; ed/BS 1956, MF 1957 Duke Univ; pa/Pres Envirl Elements Corp; AWPA; IGCI; FPRS; cp/Bd Dirs: U Way, Boy Scouts, Loyola Col, Cols of Md, Balto Aquarium; r/Presb; hon/Chm Wash-Balto Yng Pres Org; Gen Campaign Chm U Way of Ctrl Md.

HUGHES, BRENDA LYNN oc/Land Manager; b/Mar 24, 1948; h/801 Shell, Midland, TX 79701; ba/Midland; m/Ronald Blanks; p/Thomas Lewis Gale, Cottonwood, AZ; Dorothy Myers Nettles, Midland, TX; ed/HS Grad; pa/Land Mgr, NRM Petro Corp; Am Assn Petro Landmen; Permian Basin Landman's Assn, Bd Dirs; cp/Vol Wkr Midland Commun Theatre; Perf'd Midland Summer Mummers 1971-; Secy-Treas HamHocks (Vol Org of MCT); r/Epis.

HUGHES, EDITH M oc/Chief Program Assistant; b/Jan 26, 1937; h/Rt 1, Rienzi, MS 38865; ba/Corinth, MS; m/Billy T; c/Keith Wade, Josie Ann; p/John E and Minnie Burcham Moore, Rienzi, MS; pa/USDA-ASCS Chief Prog Asst; cp/Bus & Profl Clb of Corinth; 4-H Adv Coun Alcorn Co; r/Prim Bapt; hon/Admr's Ser to Agric Awd.

HUGHES, EDWIN McCULLOC oc/Educator, Minister, Psychologist; b/Feb 22, 1911; bh/205 N Grand, Searcy, AR 72143; ba/Same; m/Ruby Jo McGehoe; c/Eddy Jo, Philip Edwin; p/S H Hughes (dec); Epsie A McEachern (dec); ed/BA; MS; EdD; pa/Ret'd Civil Ser; Public & Pvt Elem & Sec'dy Schs 1938-52; Asst Prof Ed, Harding Col 1953-55; Assoc Prof Psycho, Harding Col 1956-58; Spec Lectr Psycho Little Rock Univ 1960-65; Tchg Asst, Psycho-Ed, Denver Univ 1955-56; Instr-Cnslg Univ Ark 1961; Clin Psychol, VA Hosp, N Little Rock 1960-77; Gov's Adv Coun Mtl Retard 1970; Ark Bd Examrs in Psychol 1970-75; Exec Secy, Ark Bd Examrs in Psychol 1976-; Pvt Prac Psychol 1961-; Am Psychol Assn; Ark Psychol Assn; Ark Soc Clin Hypnosis; Assn Mil Surgs of US; Am Assn Suicidology; Intl Platform Assn; Phi Delta Kappa; cp/Searcy C of C; r/Ch of Christ; hon/Personalities of the S, 1973, 74, 74, 76, 77, 78, 79; Notable Ams of Bicent Era; Notable Ams; Commun Ldrs & Noteworthy Ams; Fellow Mbrship ABI; DIB; Ark St Cert of Merit 1976; Intl Biogl Assn 1975; Intl Reg of Profiles 1976; Intl W/W: Commun Ser, Intells; Men of Achmt; Nat Reg Hlth Ser Providers in Psychol; W/W S&SW.

HUGHES, MIKE oc/Rancher; b/Sept 2, 1939; h/Sanger, TX; m/Linda; c/Cynthia, Jana; p/Bill (dec) and Mildred Hughes, Gainesville, TX; mil/USMC; pa/Rancher Spec'g in Qtr Horses; Pres Mike Hughes Inc; VP Wn Images Inc; Pres Rose Classic Inc; VP & Dir Trinity Qtr Horse Assn; Bd Dirs Lone Star Qtr Horse Assn & Tex Qtr Horse Assn; Instr Horse Mgmt, Eastfield Col; cp/Pres Civitan Clb; Bd Dirs & Ofcr JCs; Bd Dirs Sanger C of C; Dir Spec Events Am Cancer Soc; hon/TQHA Awd 1980; Key to City of San Antonio & Mayor for a Day; Yearling Awd; Silver Belt Buckles from Am Cancer Soc; Winner & Grand Champ w Qtr Horse Stallion 1979, All Am Qtr Horse Cong; Articles in Tex & So Qtr Horse Jour 1980.

HUGHES, ROBERT B oc/Nursing Home Administrator; b/Apr 22, 1946; h/Rt 1, Cleveland, MS 38732; ba/C'land; m/Brenda H; c/Jennifer Lee, Robert Jason; p/W F and Nonnie B Hughes, Canton, MS; ed/Att'd Copiah Lincoln Jr Col & Univ So Miss; pa/Miss Nsg Home Assn; Nat Assn Mtl Retard'd Citizens; r/Bapt.

HULL, DONNA JEAN oc/Service Forester; b/Apr 26, 1956; h/Woodward, OK; ba/USDA Field Station, 2000 18th St, Woodward, OK 73801; p/Donald A and Betty C Hull, Torrance, CA; ed/Att'd El Camino Commun Col 1976; BS Utah St Univ 1979; pa/Forester, Coop Forest Mgmt & Urban Forestry, Okla Dept Agric; Soc Am Foresters; Xi Sigma Pi; BPW; cp/Majority Mem & PHQ, Intl Order of Job's Daughs; OES; r/Christian; hon/Gov's Schlr; Calif Scholastic Fed Hon Soc Life Mem; Dean's Hon Roll.

HULVEY, LARRY WILLIAM oc/Psychologist; b/May 16, 1943; h/525 S Sixth St, Jesup, GA 31545; ba/Jesup; m/Judy Kay Hensley; c/Michael Christopher, Jonathan Patrick; p/John William (dec) and Lelia Radford Hulvey, Abingdon, VA; ed/Att'd Univ Va 1961-62; BA Berea Col 1965; MEd Univ Tenn 1972; EdS Univ Ga 1973; pa/Dade Co Bd Ed: Tchr, Coach, HS Cnslr, Coor Progs Ed & Career Exploration 1966-72; First Dist Coop Ednl Sers Agcy, Statesboro, Ga 1973-78; Sch Psychol Wayne Co Bd Ed, Jesup, Ga 1978-; NEA; GAE; Dade Assn Edrs, Pres 1970-72; Ga Assn Sch Psychos; Chm Leg Com 1976-77; r/Ch of Th Brethren; hon/Star Tchr Awd, Dade Co Bd Ed 1971.

HUMPHREY, DOROTHY ANN PRATT oc/Customer Service Manager; b/Nov 29, 1929; h/2748 Amherst, PO Box 8541, Shreveport, LA 71108; ba/S'port; m/Henry; c/Stephen Craig, Robin Dale, Barry Glenn; p/James J Pratt (dec); Mary Thomas Leonard, S'port; ed/Credit & Collection Sems; PBX Telecommunications; pa/Credit-Collection Mgr; Traffic Mgr; Public Relats; Advt'g; Charter Mem (since 1952), Intl Telecommunications: Local Pres 6 times, Secy 8 times, St Treas, St VP, St Pres, St Secy; r/Bapt; hon/La St PBX Operator of Yr 1975.

HUMPHRIES, JOAN oc/Psychologist; b/Oct 17, 1928; h/1311 Alhambra Cir, Coral Gables, FL 33134; ba/Miami; c/Peggy Ann, Charlene Adele; p/Lawrence (dec) and Adele Ropes (dec); ed/BA Univ Miami 1960; MS Fla St Univ 1955; PhD La St Univ 1963; pa/Assoc Prof Psychol, Miami-Dade Commun Col 15 Yrs; Intl Platform Assn; Bd Govs; Am Psychol Assn; Dade Co Psychol Assn; Secy AAUP; r/Prot; hon/Phi Lambda Plaque for Outstg Devotion 1976; Am Assn Univ Wom Cert of Apprec for Dedicated Ser to Wom in Commun 1977; Author Sev Articles.

HUNKAPILLER, BARBARA T oc/Management Analyst; Programs Analyst; b/Aug 22, 1939; h/409 Westchester Ave SW, Huntsville, AL 35801; ba/Flight Center, AL; m/Kyle; p/M G and Grace M Tompkins, AL; ed/Certs, Profl Studies; Grad Massey Col; 2 Yrs Bus Adm & Computer Sci; pa/Mgmt Analyst, Computer Progs Analyst, Marshall Space Flight Ctr, NASA, Ala; BPW; Am Bus Wom; Federally Employed Wom; AMC, Computer Mgmt Assn; Soc for Advancemt of Mgmt; cp/Nat Histl Assn; Intl Wom's Yr Com; Arts Coun; Parton Huntsville Mus of Art; hon/Commend Awds: MSFC, NASA; Profl, Civic Org Awds; ASTP Awd; Astronaut's Personal Silver Awd; Apollo Soyuz Prog Awd; Skylab Achmt Awd, NASA; Skylab Medallion Aerospace Awd, NASA; Others.

HUNSAKER, EDWIN LUAINE oc/Art Director; b/Oct 27, 1940; h/1582 Caribbean Dr, Melbourne, FL 32935; ba/Kennedy Space Ctr; m/Betty Lou Hixson; c/Tamra Sue, Mysti Yvette, Tayne Edwin, Sholette Nicole, Benjamin West; ed/Att'd Weber St Col; pa/Owner Hunsaker & Assoc Advtg; cp/Boy Scout Coun; PTA Pres; Singing Grp Perf'g for Var Grps; r/Ch of Jesus Christ of Latter Day Saints; hon/Perf'd for Kennedy Space Ctr, Different Chs & Civic Grps.

HUNT, ELIZABETH S oc/Office Manager; b/May 17, 1947; h/103 Tiffany Dr, Waynesboro, VA 22980; ba/Charlottesville, VA; m/Joseph Thomas; c/Victoria, Robin; p/J R Sutherland, Shepherdsville, KY; ed/Att'd Univ Ky 3½ Yrs; pa/Ofcr Mgr, Recruitment & Placement Cnslr, Hayes Temporary; cp/Ladd PTA, Pres 1979, VP 1978; Pres Newcomers 1978; Chm Cancer Crusade 1979; Jr Wom's Clb; JCettes; Waynesboro Hosp Aux Bd Mem; r/Bapt.

HUNT, KOLETA GLOVER oc/Real Estate Broker; b/Nov 5, 1933; h/2137 Pembrooke, Denton, TX 76201; ba/Denton; m/Vaughn B; p/C Tillman Glover, Odessa, TX; Hazel Alexander Glover (dec); ed/Att'd Odessa Col, Univ Tex, NY Inst Fin; pa/Real Est Broker; Sales Mgr, Barnes Realty Co; Nat Assn Rltrs; Tex Assn Rltrs; Denton Bd Rltrs; Wom's Coun Rltrs; cp/Mean Green Ath Assn of N Tex St Univ; r/Ch of Christ.

HUNT, SUSANNE CAROL oc/Nurse; b/Dec 25, 1943; h/9006 Traveller St, Manassas, VA 22110; ba/Falls Church, VA; c/Kenneth George Jr, Kristen Susanne; p/Rudolph A and Helen A Kraft; ed/Dip E Orange Gen Hosp Sch of Nsg; pa/RN; ANA; VNA; No Va Dirs of Nsg Assn; r/Meth; UMW.

HUNTER, CANNIE MAE oc/Educator; b/July 16, 1916; h/4626 30th St, Lubbock, TX 79410; c/Darline H Gamble, Bob Ray; p/Jesse Daniel Cox, Nolanville, TX; Mary Alice Hamilton Cox (dec); ed/BS Mary Hardin Baylor 1940; MS San Marcus St Univ 1942; Grad Studies Univ Tex, Baylor Univ, Tex Tech Univ, St Mary's Univ; pa/ACEI; NEA; AAUW; Nat PTA; Tex Clrm Tchr Assn; ABWA; cp/Am Red Cross; YWCA; Contract Intl; Lubbock C of C; Cert'd Profl Edr 1972; r/Bapt; hon/Outstg Ser Awd ARC 1966; Bronze Hon Roll Contact Telemin 1977.

HUNTER, EDWARD oc/Editor; Author; Psychological Warfare Specialist; b/Jul 2, 1902; h/4114 N 4th St, Arlington, VA 22203; c/Robert, Tate Ann; p/William and Rose Weiss Hunter; ed/Self-educated; pa/Reporter & News Editor Var Newspapers incl'g: Newark Ledger, New Orleans Item, NY Post, NY American; Reporter Paris Edit Chicago Tribune 1924-25; News Editor Japan Advertiser, Tokyo 1927, Editor Hankow (China) Herald 1928-29, Peking Leader 1929-30; Covered Japanese Conquest of Manchuria, Spanish Civil War, Italian Conquest of Ethiopia, Intl News Ser 1931-36; Pioneered in Revealing Brainwashing, Introducing It to Written Word; Chm Anti-Communist Liaison Inc 1962-; Conslt, Psychol Warfare USAF 1953-54; Propaganda Warfare Specialist AUS w Morale Operations Sect, OSS, Asia, WWII, Similarly CIA; Pubr-Editor Monthly Tactics, also Bound in Annual Vols, Indexed 1964-; Contbr Articles on Psychol Warfare, Polit Extremism to Num Periodicals; Mem Overseas Press & Silurians Clbs; hon/W/W: World, Am; Freedom Awd, Order of Lafayette 1976; Bella V Dodd Meml Awd, NY Co Com, Conservative Party 1976; Pub'd Author: Guide to Peking 1930, Brain-Washing in Red China 1951, Revised ed 1971, Brainwashing: The Story of Men Who Defied It 1956, Revised as Brainwashing: From Pavlov to Powers 1971, The Story of Mary Liu 1957, The Black Book on Red China 1958, The Past Present: A Year in Afghanistan 1959, In Many Voices: Our Fabulous Foreign-Language Press 1960, Attack By Mail 1963.

PERSONALITIES OF THE SOUTH

HUNTER, EVELYN JOYCE oc/Instructor, Coach; h/226 Hempstead Pl, Charlotte, NC 28207; ed/BS Phieffer Col 1963; pa/Phys Ed Instr, Volleyball & Girl's Basketball Coach, Garinger HS; US Tennis Assn; Clrm Tchr Assn, Charlotte-Mecklenburg Sch Sys; cp/UDC; hon/Basketball Coach of Yr 1979-80.

HUNTER, JEAN C oc/Homemaker; b/May 1, 1944; m/Walter; c/Walter Jr; ed/GED; r/Jehovah Witness.

HUNTER, JOHN ROBERT JR oc/Deputy Federal Insurance Administrator; b/Nov 20, 1936; h/602 S Lee St, Alexandria, VA 22314; ba/Washington, DC; m/Carole; c/Laura Jeanne, James Douglas, John Robert III; p/John Robert Sr, Alexandria, VA; Alberta Cox (dec); ed/BS Physics Clarkson Col of Technol; pa/Dpty Fed Ins Admr, Dept of Housing & Urban Devel; Fellow, Casualty Actuarial Soc; Mem Am Acad of Actuaries; cp/Pres, Rockville Musical Theatre; Pres, Freeport Commun Chorale; r/Presb.

HUNTER, PATRICIA FINN oc/Teacher, Librarian; b/Jan 1, 1927; h/6732 Bonneville Dr, Knoxville, TN 37921; ba/K'ville; m/Reuben Andrew; c/Donna Jane, Mary Andrea; p/David Ewing Finn (dec); Dona Esther Whitlock (dec); ed/BS Univ Tenn 1955; MA Unv No Colo 1979; Att'd: Berea Col 1944-46, Dip Berea Foun Sch 1942-44; pa/Camp Cnslr, Camp Algonquin 1947-49; Libn Powell HS, Knox Co, Tenn 4 Yrs; Book Cataloguer & AV Coor, Knoxville City Schs 2 Yrs; Libn Park Jr HS, Knoxville City Schs 9 Yrs; Libn NW Jr HS, K'ville 6 Yrs; Libn Tyson Jr HS, K'ville 7 Yrs; Knoxville Ed Assn; TEA; NEA; E Tenn Ed Assn, Chm AV Sect 1958-59; Am Assn Sch Libns; Tenn Assn Sch Libns; Intl Rdg Assn; cp/DAR; Alpha Delta Kappa; Pi Lambda Theta, Alpha Xi Chapt; AAUW; r/Meth; hon/Presently Writing Finn Fam Hist.

HUNTER, REUBEN ANDREW oc/Teacher, Guidance Counselor, Principal; b/Nov 29, 1924; h/6732 Bonneville Dr, Knoxville, TN 37921; m/Patricia Finn; c/Donna Jane, Mary Andrea; p/Jerdon Elisha Hunter (dec); Nora Louise Bowman (dec); ed/BS Berea Col 1947; MS Univ Tenn 1953; pa/Civics Tchr, S Jr HS 1947-50; Civics & Am Hist Tchr, Guid Cnslr Rule HS 1950-63; Tchr Pers Cnslr, Ctrl Ofc 1963-64; Asst Prin, Holston HS 1964-66; Prin W View Elem Sch 1966-69; Prin Lonsdale Elem Sch 1969-71; Prin Ridgedale Elem Sch 1971-; PTA; TEA; KEA; NEA; Nat Assn Elem Sch Prins; Phi Delta Kappa; K'ville Elem Prins Assn; Former Mem E Tenn Pers & Guid Assn; Mem Tenn Adv Coun on Tchr Cert & Ed 1975-77; Nat Commun Ed Assn 1978-81; Pres K'ville Meth Layman's Assn 1975-76; Pre Holston-Chilhowee Swim Clb 1968-70; Pres Kiwanis Clb of E K'ville, Prog Chm 14 yrs; Pres K'ville Chapt Berea Col Alumni Assn; r/Meth; hon/Life Mem Tenn Cong of Parents & Tchrs 1969; Commend, K'ville City Schs 1954; Hon Life Mem K'ville-Knox Co Ret'd Tchrs Assn 1968; Citizenship Awd, K'ville Coun of PTA 1980; Life Mem Nat Cong of Parents & Tchrs 1980.

HURT, ALLIE TEAGUE oc/Real Estate Executive; b/Aug 28, 1923; h/Dallas, TX; m/Charles E (dec); c/James Taylor, Daniel McLane Jr, Gwendolyn McLane, Winfred McLane, Eric C, Gregory B; p/Lucious T (dec) and Mary Whitley Teague (dec); ed/El Centro Commun Col 1968; BS Bishop Col 1973; Post Grad Work N Tex St Univ 1974; pa/Owner & Broker Allie T Hurt Real Est Co 1975-; Real Est Sales Agt 1967-75; Sub Sch Tchr, IDSD 1973-75; Soc Editor, Dallas Express 1960-65; Ins Agt, Universal Life Ins 1957-58; Pianist Chs 1959-69; Secy Excelsior Life Ins; Chatelaine, Eta Phi Beta, Epsilon Chapt 1978-79; cp/NAACP; PUSH; Rosicrucian Order; Bishop Col Alumni Assn; N Tex St Alumni Clb; r/Bapt; hon/W/W S&SW 1980-81; Cert Iota Phi Lambda 1979; Cert Recog Eta Phi Beta.

HURT, NELLIE GRAY oc/Professional Nurse; b/June 15, 1919; hy/2925 Rivermont Ave, Lynchburg, VA 24503; b/Lynchburg; p/Robert Henry (dec) and Lottie C Hurt, Lynchburg, VA; pa/Reg'd Profl Nurse, Lynchburg Gen Hosp; ANA; VNA; Alumnae Assn; cp/Rebekah Lodge; r/Meth; hon/Rec'd 35 Yrs Ser Pin 1979; W/W Am Wom 1979-80.

HUTCHENS, EUGENE GARLINGTON oc/College Administrator; b/Nov 26, 1929; m/Betty Goode; c/Dale, Wayne, Wade; p/Mr and Mrs Luther Hutchens, B'ham, AL; ed/BA Samford Univ 1952; ThM New Orleans Bapt Theol Sem 1970; MS Univ Mo 1972; pa/No Brenton Bapt Ch 1952-56; First Bapt Ashland 1956-63; Highlands Bapt Ch 1963-67; Huntsville City Sch Sys 1967-71; NW Ala St Jr Col, Dir Branch Campus 1972-; Bapt St Ex Bd; VP Ala Bapt Pastors Conf; AEA; NEA; ACSAS; cp/Tuscumbia Kiwanis Clb; Dem Party; r/Bapt.

HUTCHINS, MYLDRED FLANIGAN oc/Retired Social Worker, Teacher, Counselor, Writer; b/Jan 19, 1908; h/413 Princeton Way, NE, Atlanta, GA 30307; m/Arthur L; c/Anne H Harper; p/Thomas C (dec) and Elveda Elder Flanigan (dec); ed/BPh Emory Univ; MS Tulane Univ; EdS; Univ Ga; pa/Acad Cert'd Social Workers; NEA; GAE; Epsilon Kappa Delta; cp/AAUW; DAR; Druid Hills Civic Assn; Rose Soc Garden Clb; r/Meth; hon/W/W Am Wom; Articles Pub'd in Profl Cnslrs Mags.

HUTCHINSON, JANET LOIS oc/Director; b/May 2, 1917; ba/888 NE MacArthur Blvd, Stuart, FL 33494; c/Jefferson Troy Siebert; p/Lewis Orin and Gertrude Elizabeth Hutchinson (dec); ed/LLL Drew Sem; Opo Sem; Blackstone Col for Wom; pa/Dir Martin Co Hist Soc, Elliott Mus & House of Refuge Mus; Nat Trust Hist Preservation; Nat Hist Soc; cp/Bd Trustees, St Michaels Sch; DAR; Completed 1875 Restoration House of Refuge; r/Unitarian; hon/Wom of Yr 1974; Fellow Mem ABI.

HUTH, DOUGLAS WERNER oc/Law Enforcement Professional; b/July 27, 1940; h/PO Box 3501, 130 E Alma Ave, Lake Mary, FL 32746; ba/Sanford, FL; m/Valerie Ann; c/Douglas Shane; p/Werner E and Darlene W Huth, Lake Mary, FL; ed/AS Seminole Commun Col 1976; BS Rollins Col 1980; Cert Achmt Univ Va, Div Cont'g Ed 1979; FBI Nat Acad 119th Session; pa/Dir of Trg, Plan'g & Res, Police Liaison Ofcr, Ofc of Sheriff, Seminole Co 1971-; Adv Bd Seminole Co Law Awareness Prog; Arbitrator Seminole Co Juvenile Commun Arbitration Prog; Vol Cnslr Yth Progs; Police Liaison Ofcr, Ofc of St Atty, 18th Jud Circuit, Sanford 1978-79; cp/Seminole Co Animal Wel Adv Bd 1976-; r/Cath; hon/Author "Florida Criminal Law Handbook for Peace Officers."

HUTTENSTINE, MARIAN LOUISE oc/Assistant Professor of Journalism; b/Jan 26, 1940; h/4527 18th Ave E, 1224, Tuscaloosa, AL 35405; ba/University, AL; p/Ralph Benjamin and Marian Louise Engler Huttenstine, Wapwallopen, PA; ed/BS 1961; MEd 1966; PhD Cand 1981; pa/Lake Lehman HS 1961-66; Lock Haven SC 1966-73; UNC; Assn Ed in Jour; AAUW; Am Adv Fed; Kappa Tau Alpha; Nat Fed Press Wom Inc; Sigma Delta Chi; Am Acad Advtg; Radio TV News Dirs Assn; cp/NAACP; r/Lutheran; hon/W/W S&SW; World W/W Wom; Author.

HUTTO, BETTE BRASWELL oc/Executive Director; b/Feb 14, 1942; h/52 Odd Rd, Poquoson, VA 23662; ba/Norfolk, VA; m/Fred Kent; c/Fred, Michael, Ramona, Rebecca; p/Grover O and Agnes Y Braswell, Columbia, SC; ed/BS Univ So Miss 1963; pa/Tchr Prof Bus & Med Inst 1978-, Bd Dirs 1977, Dir 1974-77, Assoc Dir 1973-74; Tchr Baylake Pines Pvt Sch 1972-73; Tchr Aurora Gardens Acad 1969-72; Tchr Gretna Jr HS 1968-69; La Power & Light 1963-66; Va Assn Proprietary Schs; Tidewater Va Assn Tech & Trade Schs; VEA; Tidewater Assn Proprietary Schs; cp/Panhellenic Del, Tidewater, Va; Theta Phi Bd Dirs; Charter Mem Theta Kappa House Corp; Theta Kappa House Bd Dirs; Charter Mem Epsilon Mu House Corp; Hist New Orleans Speech & Hist Guild; Block Ldr, Penbroke Manor Civic Assn; Dir HS Yth Activs, Aragona Bapt Ch; Dir VBS Aragona Bapt Ch; Dir Girls in Action; r/Bapt; hon/Best Radio Prod, Univ So Miss 1963; Awd'd Keys to City by Mayor of Lafayette, La 1972; Outstg Yng Wom Am 1973; W/W Am Wom 1977; World W/W Wom 1979; DIB 1979; Book of Hon 1979.

HUTTON, SCOTT oc/Police Officer; b/Apr 1, 1957; ba/Killeen Police Dept, Killeen, TX 76541; m/Roberta L; c/Larry, Kristin; p/Frederick L and Davie Ann Hutton, Ottumwa, IA; ed/AAS Indian Hills Commun Col 1977; BS Am Technol Univ 1971; Grad Ctrl Regional Police Acad 1980; MS Cand Am Technol Univ 1980; mil/AUS 1977-80 Sgt; pa/Law Enforcement; r/Meth; hon/Soldier of Qtr 1979; Awd'd Army Commend Medal for Exceptlly Merit Ser; Good Conduct Medal; W/W Students Am Univs & Cols 1979-80; Alpha Phi Sigma; Outstg Yng Man Am 1979; Am's Outstg Names & Faces 1979.

HYDEN, JERRY W oc/Contractor; b/Aug 24, 1948; h/Rt 6 Box 159, Somerset, KY 42501; m/Mary Ann Gallagher; c/Kenneth Dale, Anthony Craig; p/Leonard (dec) and Clara Sears Hyden, Mt Victory, KY; mil/1969; pa/Self-Employed Contr'g Timber Work; Small Bus Mgmt; cp/Repub Precinct Chm; Yng Repub Clb Pulaski Co; Sch Bd Pulaski Co 2nd Dist; Hd Com to Form Water Assn; r/Bapt: SS Tchr, Bd Trustees; Dist Messenger So Bapt Conv.

HYDER, BRIAN DOUGLAS oc/Wildlife Biologist; b/Mar 17, 1950; h/PO Box 908, Franklin, NC 28734; m/Anne Semaschko; c/Stephanie Nicole; p/Gus H and Elaine Y Hyder, Flat Rock, NC; ed/BS Univ SC 1972; pa/Wildlife Biol & Wild Turkey Proj Ldr, NC Wildlife Res Comm 1973-; Rep for NC on Tech Com of Nat Wild Turkey Fed; Past Pres & Mem Exec Com WNC Chapt Wild Turkey Fed; Wildlife Soc; Nat Wildlife Fed; r/First U Meth Ch Franklin; Adm Bd; hon/Area Awd Wildlife Conserv 1975; Capt NC St Champ HS Track & Field Team 1968.

HYLAND, WILLIAM GEORGE oc/Senior Fellow, Center for Strategic and International Studies; b/Jan 18, 1929; h/501 Wolftrap, Vienna, VA 22180; ba/Washington, DC; m/Evelyn Virginia; c/William G Jr, James Edward; p/Dora A Hyland, Kansas City, MO; ed/BA Washington Univ, St Louis; MA Univ of Mo; mil/AUS 1951-52; pa/Sr Fellow, Ctr for Strategic & Intl Studies, Georgetown Univ; Mem Coun on Fgn Relats; Author: The Fall of Kruschev; cp/Dpty Asst to Pres for Nat Security 1975-76; Dir, Bur of Intell, Dept of St; hon/Nat Intell Dist'd Ser Medal.

157

HYNDS, TOHNIE E   oc/Attorney at Law; b/Aug 20, 1951; h/2700 S Travis #237, Sherman, TX 75090; ba/Sherman; m/Dennis M Robertson; p/Robert H and Uldine H Hynds, Van Alstyne, TX; ed/BA Austin Col 1973; JD So Meth Univ 1976; pa/Assoc Atty w David H Brown 1976-78; Assoc Atty w Munson, Munson, Hynds, Watkins, Gordon & Wilkes 1978-; Am Bar Assn; St Bar of Tex; Grayson Co Bar Assn, Treas 1979-80; Tex Assn Bank Counsel; Phi Delta Phi; cp/Sherman BPW Clb, 1st VP 1978-79, Pres-Elect 1979-80; Altrusa Clb of Sherman; Bd Dirs First Nat Bank of Van Alstyne, Bd Dirs Easter Seal Soc for Crippled Chd & Adults of Grayson Co; Grayson Co Child Wel Bd; Former Mem Bd Dirs Mtl Hlth Mtl Retard Sers of Texoma; r/Disciples of Christ; hon/Outstg Yng Wom Am 1977; Dist 12 BPW Yng Careerist 1977; Dist 12 BPW Wom of Yr.

HYNUM, BEN F   oc/City Manager; b/June 16, 1926 ba/Coalgate, OK; m/Janice C; c/Sandra Sebring, Theresa Montgomery, Biff; p/Benjamin F Sr and Billie E Hynum; ed/Att'd NE Okla A&M, Miami, Okla, & Ozark Bible Col; mil/Ret'd Major; pa/Mayor & V-Mayor Grove Okla 1973-75, 1979-81; Okla Assn City Mgrs; Internat Assn City Mgrs; cp/Lions Clb; Moose Lodge; C of C; r/Bapt; hon/11 Mil Medals Incl'g Bronze Star for Ser in Vietnam; 2 Army Commend Medals & Pres Unit Cit.

HYRE, CHARLES STEVEN   oc/Research and Development; b/Apr 19, 1947; h/1120 Wilkie Dr, Charleston, WV 25314; ba/C'ton; p/Charles Gordon and Mary Grace Hyre, Circleville, WV; ed/BA Sec'dy Ed; MEd Spec Ed; pa/Res & Devel in Trg & Ed; Phi Delta Kappa; Am Ednl Res Assn.

PERSONALITIES OF THE SOUTH

I

IGBOKWE, EMMANUEL CHUKWUEMEKA oc/Professor; b/Jan 18, 1941; h/5900 Enterprise, El Paso, TX 79912; m/Gwendolyn Mattie Capers; p/Aaron and Edna Igbokwe; ed/BS; MS; PhD; pa/Prof Biol; Res & Tchg; r/Epis; hon/W/W Dist Citizens of N Am 1976-77.

IGBOKWE, GWENDOLYN MATTIE CAPERS oc/Counselor, Administrator; m/Emmanuel Chukwuemeka; p/Eddie Williams, Detroit, Mich; Juliet Capers; ed/BS Tuskegee Inst; MEd; pa/APGA; Phi Delta Kappa; SAEOPP; cp/YWCA; r/Bapt; hon/W/W Am Wom 1979-80.

IKERD, FRANK HELLER JR oc/Coal Miner; b/Apr 14, 1927; h/Somerset, KY; m/Willene Wager; c/Frank H III, Jasie Nell, Richard Andrew; p/Nell Barringer Ikerd; mil/USN; pa/Pres Ikerd-Bandy; r/Meth.

IMPARATO, EDWARD THOMAS oc/Financial Consultant; b/Jan 5, 1917; h/155 Bayview Dr, Belleaire, FL 33516; m/Jean Catherine deGarmo; p/Charles and Romilda Delilbove Imparato (dec); ed/BS Univ Tampa 1963; Univ Pa Inst Investmt Bkg; mil/USAFF 1939-42, 2nd Lt to Col; pa/Merrill Lynch, Pierce, Fenner & Smith, Clearwater 1971-, VP 1973-; Goodbody & Co: Acct Exec 1963-69, Mgr 1969-71; Instr, St Petersburg Jr Col 1964; Bd Mem & Fdg Dir: Med Sci Intl Corp 1968-71, Vikintactin Instrument Co 1968-71, Snibbe Pubins Inc 1969-71; Fin Com for Town of Belleair; Am Soc Profl Conslts; cp/Order of Daedalions; Pinellas Co, Fla Com of 100; Past Pres, Clearwater Chapt ARC; Past Trustee, St Petersburg Mus Fine Arts; Past Pres Fla Gulf Coast Art Ctr; Bd Dirs Clearwater Concert Assn; Ret'd Ofcrs Assn; Delta Sigma Phi; Sword & Shield; Am Security Coun; IPA; Mil Order World Wars; Pres & Chm of Bd Morton F Plant Hosp Foun Inc; r/Epis; hon/Outstg Ser Awd Seacoast YMCA; Ser to Mankind Awd, Sortoma Clearwater; Father of Foun; One of A Kind Awd, Morton F Plant Hosp Foun; Legion of Merit; Air Medal w 2 OLC; Belin Airlift Medal; Author *How to Manage Your Money* 1967; W/W Fin & Indust.

INMAN, IMOGENE J oc/Teacher, Church Music Director; b/Feb 9, 1946; h/Tuscaloosa, AL; ba/Jasper, AL; m/Arthur; c/John W, Richard R; p/Henry S (dec) and Vera E Reed, Jasper, AL; ed/BMusEd So Col 1962; MA 1965, PhD 1980 Univ Ala; pa/Pvt & Public Tchr 25 Yrs; Ch Mus Dir 20 Yrs; MENC; cp/OES: r/Meth; hon/Kappa Delta Pi; Article in *The School Musician* May 1979.

INMAN, LARRY JOE SR oc/Head Women's Basketball Coach; b/Jan 3, 1948; ba/Murfreesboro, TN; m/Clydell Parker; c/Larry Joe Jr, Latrice Clydell; p/Joseph S and Norma Jean Inman, Gallatin, TN; ed/BS Austin Peay St Univ; MA Tenn St Univ; pa/Tchr & Coach Middle Tenn St Univ; TAHPER; NEA; TEA; cp/Kiwanis Intl; Exch Clb; Optimist Intl; r/Bapt; hon/Kelloggs Most Outstg Wom's Basketball Coach in St of Tenn 1977; 16th Dist Coach of Yr 1975; Dist Coach of Yr 1974; Ohio Val Conf Coach of Yr 1979-80; Optimist Intl Sportsman of Yr 1979-80.

INMAN, LUCY DANIELS oc/Clinical Psychologist, Fiction Writer; b/Mar 24, 1934; h/5113 Shamrock Dr, Raleigh, NC 27612; ba/Raleigh; c/Patrick, Lucy, Jonathan, Benjamin; p/Jonathan W Daniels, Hilton Hd, SC; Lucy Cathcart Daniels (dec); ed/BA 1972, PhD 1977 UNC-CH; pa/Clin Psych Pvt Pract; Am Psych Assn; NC Psych Assn; r/Agnostic; hon/Guggenheim Fellow in Lit 1957; Phi Beta Kappa 1972; Author *Celeb, My Son* 1956 & *High on a Hill* 1961.

IRBY, PAUL DANIEL oc/Psychotherapist; b/Apr 21, 1934; h/210 Crescent Dr, Dothan, AL 36302; ba/Dothan; m/Wanda Olivia Strickler; c/Rebecca Lynn, Deborah Elaine; p/Wiley Edward (dec) and Hattie Mae Collins Irby (dec); ed/BS William Carey Col 1956; MDiv 1959, MRE 1961 New Orleans Bapt Theol Sem; EdD Univ So Miss 1971; pa/Pvt Pract Cnslg & Psychotherapy 1975-; Prof Cnslg & Dir Cnlsg Ctr, Troy St Univ 1970-75; Am Psychol Assn; APGA; Pres 1980-81; Ala Mtl Hlth Cnslrs Assn; Intl Assn Cnslg Sers; cp/Dothan Kiwanis Clb, Chaired Yth Activs Com 1974-80; Bd Mem: SE Ala Hlth Sys Agcy, Human Resources & Devel Corp; Ala Elect Law Comm; Demo Pres Clb in Ala; Masonic & Scottish Rite Lodges; Constable Houston Co 1981-85; r/So Bapt; hon/Lt Col Aide-de-Camp Ala St Militia.

IRELAND, KATE oc/Volunteer; b/Aug 25, 1930; h/Willow Bend, Wendover, KY 41775; ba/Same; p/R L Ireland, Cleveland, OH; ed/Att'd Vassar 1949; pa/Ky Primary Care Assn; Nat Primary Care Assn; Ky Home Hlth Acgy; Nat Assn Home Hlth Agcys; Nat Leag Nsg; Nat Coun Homemaker Home Hlth Aide Sers; cp/Ky River Area Devel Dist; Leslie Co Coop Ext Ser; Human Resources Coun; Ky Coun Area Devel Dists; r/Epis; hon/Dr Humane Letters, Allegheny Col; Dist'd Ser Awd, Midway Col.

IRLAND, MARQUITA L oc/Department Chairperson; b/Dec 10,

1921; h/475 N Highland 8G, Memphis, TN 38122; ba/Memphis; p/Ray (dec) and LaDore Irland, Memphis, TN; ed/BS, MS Mich St Univ; EdD Wayne St Univ; pa/Chp Dept Home Ec, Memphis St Univ; Am Home Ec Assn; Tenn Home Ec Assn; Am Voc Assn; Nat Coun Home Ec Admrs; Tenn Coun Home Ec Admrs; Assn Tchrs Edrs; Bd Dirs Memphis BBB; Regional Chm Penneys Ednl Bd; r/Meth.

IRONS, WILLIAM LEE oc/Lawyer; b/Jun 9, 1941; h/316 Gran Ave, Birmingham, AL 35209; ba/Birmingham; m/Karen; p/George Vernon Irons Sr, Birmingham, AL; Velma Wright Irons (dec); ed/BA Univ Va 1963; JD Samford Univ 1966; mil/USAF 1966-70, Capt; pa/Law Firm Partner: William L Irons 1972-, Speir & Irons 1971-72, Speir, Robertson, Jackson & Irons 1970-71; Legal Coun: USAF Hosp Recovery Claims 1968, Maj Gen Walter B Putnam 1968, Negotiation & Settlemt of Sonic Boom Claims 1966-67; Dir Mil Justice, Maxwell AFB 1968-69; Acting Trial & Def Coun for USAF 1967-68: Perrin AFB, Offutt AFB, Tyndall AFB, Whiteman AFB, Maxwell AFB, Robbins AFB, Hunter Air Field, Ft Monroe; Asst Staff Judge Advocate, Gunter AFB 1967-68; Law Clerk: James L Shores 1965-66, Speir, Robertson & Jackson 1964-65; B'ham Bar Assn; Ala Bar Assn; Am Trial Lwyr's Assn; Am Bar Assn; Sigma Delta Kappa; Nat Assn Cert'd Judge Advocates; Fed Bar Assn; Bar Ct Mil Appeals; Nat Assn Judge Advocates; Am Judic Soc; Nat Lwyr's Clb; cp/Cand Ala Ho of Reps 1966; Nat Resv Ofcrs Assn; Planned Parenthood Assn, B'ham: Bd Dirs, Legal Cnslr; B'ham Exec Clb; Nat Trust for Hist Preserv; SAR; Sons Confed Vets; Order Stars & Bars; Soc Sons of Revolution; Jamestowne Soc; B'ham Geneal Soc; Descendents of Wash's Army at Val Forge, Pa; r/Mountain Brook Bapt Ch: Mem, Former Assoc Deacon, SS Tchr, SS Supt, Girl's Basketball Coach; hon/ Dupont Reg Scholar; USAF Commend Medal & Cit; Dist'd Personalities of S; S'ship; Outstg Jr Ofcr of Command, Air Univ, Maxwell AFB 1969; Nat Social Dir; W/W: Ala, Am Law, S&SW, Hon Soc Am.

IRVIN, CHRISTINE FRELIX oc/Teacher; b/Nov 29, 1930; h/PO Box 572, Picayune, MS 39466; ba/Picayune; p/Johnnie Frelix, Columbia, MS; Johnnie Mae Frelix Jefferson, Columbia, MS; ed/BS Alcorn St Univ; MS Univ Wis; pa/Home Ec Tchr, Picayune Jr HS; PAE, Pres 1977-78; PAE-MAE-NEA Del 1978; FHA St Adv Bd; III-C Dist Advr MHEA Task Force; cp/MAE - M-Pact Steering Coun; Ladies Amicable Clb; r/Bapt; hon/FHA Dist'd Ser; MAE Outstg Ldrship & Dedication Pilgrim Bound Apprec for Sers.

IRWIN, JOHNIE DEE oc/Industrial Designer; b/June 19, 1951; h/3702 Brushwood, Corpus Christi, TX 78415; m/Margo K; c/D Dee and Inez Irwin, Ingleside, TX; ed/Assoc Deg Del Mar Col; Del Mar Real Est Deg; pa/Indust Conslt on Process Designs; r/Bapt.

IRWIN, PAT oc/Supreme Court Justice; b/Jun 12, 1921; h/1325 Andover Ct, Oklahoma City, OK 73120; ba/Oklahoma City; m/Margaret Boggs; c/William J, Margaret; p/Marvin J Irwin (dec); Ollie D Irwin, Leedey, OK; ed/LLB, JD Univ Okla, Norman; mil/USMCR 1942-46, Capt; cp/Okla St Supr Ct: Elected 1969-, Chief Justice 1969-70; Presiding Judge, St Ct on Judiciary 1971-74; Secy, Okla Land Commr 1954-58; Okla St Sen 1950-54; Dewey Co Atty 1949-50; r/Prot.

ISENBERG, CHARLES CLAYTON oc/Minister; b/Nov 18, 1942; h/Glasgow Rd, Edmonton, KY 42129; ba/Edmonton; m/Elsie; c/Todd, Tracy; p/Edmond and Delsie Isenberg, Cave City, KY; ed/Grad Sunset Sch Preaching; pa/Min; cp/Past Pres PTA Mocksville Elem Sch; r/Ch of Christ; hon/Hon Sen of Ky 1971.

ISENHOUR, GRADY EUGENE JR oc/Air Traffic Control Chief; b/Nov 26, 1951; h/PO Box 404, Granite Falls, NC 28630; ba/APO, NY; m/Lenora Jean; c/Brian Eugene; p/Grady E Sr and Joann Isenhour, Granite Falls, NC; ed/Bach Profl Aeronautics; mil/AUS 1970- Air Traffic Control Chief; pa/Mil Career; r/So Bapt; hon/Silver Star; Bronze Star w OLC & V Device; Air Medal w 7 OLC & V Device for Valor; Army Commend Medal w OLC; Purple Heart; Good Conduct Medal; Vietnam Campaign Medal; Vietnam Ser Medal; Nat Defense Medal; Mem AUS Europe Sgt Morales Clb; Hon Grad: Air Traffic Control Sch, Non-Com Ofcrs Acad, Adv'd Non-Com Ofcrs Sch.

ISGETT, RAYMOND "RAY" OSWALD oc/Crime Prevention Specialist; b/Jul 9, 1939; h/216 Lee St, Sumter, SC 29105; ba/Columbia, SC; m/Carol Jean Pilson; c/Vicki Lynn, Ed Rey Eugene, Daniel Glenn; p/Eugene Raymond and Fema Mary Dirby Isgett, Florence, SC; ed/AA Palmer Col; Bach Gen Studies, Univ SC; Addit Study, Univ Louisville; mil/USAF; SC NG; pa/Crime Prevention Spec, Gov's Ofc Crim Justice Progs, St of SC 1978-; City of Sumter Police Dept: Lt Reg Crime Prevention Unit (VCmdr) 1976-78, 75 Patrol Div (Patrol Sgt) 1974-75, 73 Detective Div (Narcs) 1972-73, 71 Patrol Div (Patrolman) 1967-71; Asst Mgr, Edwards Inc 1962-67; Fdg Mem, Nat Assn Crime Prevention Practioners; St Assn Crime Prevention Ofcrs: Charter Mem, Bd Dirs, Pres 1978-79; SC Law Enforcemt Ofcrs Assn: Mem, Chm Commun

159

Relats/Crime Prevention Com; cp/BSA; Optimist Clb; W Ashley Jaycees; SC Lung Assn (Wateree Br Bd Dirs); Pres, Intl Martial Arts Fdn; r/Eastside Bapt Ch: Mem; hon/Bravery Awd, SC Am Leg; Dale Carnegie Highest Awd for Achmt; Police Ofcr of Yr, City of Sumter; Gold Medallion Awd, Optimist Intl; Police Ofcr of Yr, Am Legion Post #15; Citizenship Awd, City of Charleston; God & Country Awd, BSA.

IVES, TOM oc/District Manager; b/Jan 13, 1946; h/804 Shady Creek Dr, Cleburne, TX 76031; ba/Cleburne; m/Martha Jane; c/Jeffrey, Lesli; p/Ernest R and Fronie Ives, Palestine, TX; ed/BBA Sam Houston St Univ 1967; AMA Exec Dev 1977, AMA 1981 Tex A&M; pa/Mgmt, Tex Power & Light Co; cp/Dir & Past Pres C of C; Past Pres & Bd Mem YMCA; Chm Boy Scouts; Dir Am Heart Assn; Past Pres Johnson Co Livestock & Agric Assn; SWn Adventist Col: Commun Coun; Cleburne Indust Foun; Rotary; Cleburne Forum, Christian Bus-man's Clb; Citizens Adv Com on Commun Devel of Cleburne; Past Dir & Chm BSA; Past Pres & Dir JCs; Past VP & Dir Optimist; r/Meth: Ofcl Bd; hon/Outstg Chm 1976; Chm of Yr 1977.

IVY, MARGARET ONEIDA MAY oc/Business Executive; b/May 31, 1947; h/3302 Pritchett, Irving, TX 75061; ba/Carrollton; m/Jess Lawrence; c/James Daniel; p/Fred and Mary Lou McGowan May, Irving, TX; ed/Grad Byrnes Commercial Col 1968; pa/Secy, Ofc Mgr, Security Rlty 1965-68; Bldg Mgr, Carpenter Freeway Med Ctr 1968-69; Ofc Mgr, Runaway Bay 1970-71; VP, Corp Secy Metro Warehouse Co 1971-; Am Warehousemen's Assn; Nat Assn Exec Secys; r/Ch of Christ; hon/W/W Am Wom; World W/W Wom; Dir of Dist'd Ams.

PERSONALITIES OF THE SOUTH

J

Cnlsg; cp/Pres Red River Reg Coun on Alcoholism; Mem Var Bds; Dem Party; r/Epis; hon/Spec Recog FCI JCs; Awd from Toastmasters Clb.

JACK, BETTY LEE oc/Secretary-Treasurer; b/Aug 23, 1932; h/2105 Glenway Dr, Sanford, FL 32771; m/William T; c/Dianna Lynn Foster, Paula Sue Simpson; p/Roy and Freda Webster, Sebestain, FL; ed/Bus Dip 1963; pa/Secy-Treas Sanford Heating & Air Conditioning; cp/Beta Sigma Phi; Sanford Wom's Clb; Sanford Gdn Clb; Bd Mem Sanford-Seminole Ballet Guild, Treas; hon/Girl of Yr, Beta Sigma Phi, Xi Beta Chapt 1979-80; Girl of Yr, Beta Sigma Phi, Xi Beta Eta Chapt 1975-76.

JACKSON, ANTHONY D oc/Student; b/Mar 13, 1959; h/5048 11 St NE, Wash DC 20017; p/(dec); ed/NC A&T St Univ 1977-; pa/Tech Aide, John Hopkins Univ Applied Physics Lab, Summers; Nat Soc Profl Engrs; DC Soc Profl Engrs; IEEE; Kappa Alpha Psi; cp/Student Govt Assn; Student Jud Coun; r/Meth; hon/Tau Alpha Tau; Minority in Engrg S'ship Awd; Xerox S'ship; Part in Nat Consortium for Grad Degs for Minorities in Engrg Inc Prog; Dean's List.

JACKSON, BERENICE LLOYD oc/Homemaker; h/Rt 2 Box 62, Gage, OK 73843; m/Brice P; c/John Lloyd; p/Landom (dec) and Clara Childress Lloyd (dec); pa/Rancher's Wife; Chp Cultural Arts Com; Past Pres Beaver Co Hist Soc; r/Bapt; hon/Outstg Citizen Awd, Beaver JCs 1972; Awd Recog, Okla Living Legends Prog 1973; Awd Spec Merit 1974; Stanley Draper Dist'd Ser Awd, Okla Heritage Assn 1981; Co-Author *Man and the Oklahoma Panhandle.*

JACKSON, BETTY RUTH oc/Nurse Educator; b/Oct 12, 1930; h/1907 Ward St, Midland, TX 79701; ba/Odessa, TX; m/James Robert; c/Jamie Beth, Julie Anne, George Robert; p/William Roy and Mary Anne Underwood Hutchins; ed/BSN W Tex St Univ; MSN Univ Tenn Austin; pa/ANA; NLN; AAUP; Tex Nurses Coalition Action Politically; r/Luth; hon/Sigma Theta Tau; Phi Kappa Phi; W/W Am Wom.

JACKSON, CAROLYN JANE oc/Educational Librarian; b/May 2, 1937; h/1502 N Grove, Marshall, TX 75670; p/Frank W Jackson (dec); Sallie Belle Towers Jackson; ed/BA, MLS Tex Wom's Univ; Postgrad Study: MWn Univ, Tex Wom's Univ; pa/Asst Libn, E Tex Bapt Col 1969-; Acquisitions Libn, MWn Univ 1960-68; Periodicals Libn, Sul Ross St Univ 1968-69; Campus Rep, AAUP 1973-77; Treas Fac Dames, MWn Univ 1971-72; Tex Lib Assn; SWn Lib Assn Am Lib Assn; AAUW; cp/Col Wom's Clb, E Tex Bapt Co; Conslt, Am Security Coun 1971-72; Am Hist Assn; Nat Trust for Hist Preserv; Smithsonian Instn, U Fund OES; r/Ctl Bapt Ch, Marshall; hon/Fellow Am Biogl Inst; DIB; W/W: Am Wom, S&SW, US; Book of Hon; Notable Ams Bicent Era.

JACKSON, COLON STONEWALL JR oc/USN Chaplain; b/May 24, 1928; h/218 E Palmer Dr Rt 4, New Bern, NC 28560; ba/Cherry Pt, NC; m/Doris; c/Gayle, Mark; p/Colon S Jackson Sr, Hertford, NC; ed/BA Waker Forest Univ 1954; MA Webster Col 1979; MDiv SEn Bapt Theol Sem 1958; mil/USN Chaplain; pa/Chaplain USN; Am Assn Pastoral Cnslrs; Col of Chaplains; Am Assn Marriage & Fam Therapy; cp/Rotary Clb; r/Bapt; hon/Navy Commend Medal 1970; Navy Achmt 1975; Humanitarian 1979.

JACKSON, DANIEL H oc/Master Sergeant USAF; b/Jun 26, 1946; h/520 Gold St, Shelby, NC 28150; ba/APO San Francisco, CA 96519; m/Reiko; c/Lisa Ann, Michael Scott; p/William K and Hazel D Jackson; mil/USAF; Implemented Transportation Priority-4 cargo movement prog at NCOIC Freight Terminal Facilities, Mem Misawa AB Air Force Sr Enlisted Assn & VFW Post 9681, Consolidated Freight Section w Packing & Crating Sect, Others; r/Bapt; hon/Rec'd 2 AF Commendation Medals; Nom'd for Outstg Noncommissioned Ofcr of the Yr at Misawa AB, Air Force Transportation Awds Prog 1979.

JACKSON, EARL JUNIOR oc/Pastor; b/Mar 11, 1943; h/804 Gilbert St, Bowling Green, KY 42101; ba/Bowling Green; m/Barbara Faye Anderson; c/Earl Darelwin, Roderick Lamar; p/James C (dec) and Keathryn C Jackson (dec); ed/ThB; ThG; BA; MRE; MDiv; DD; pa/Pastor & Radio Min; cp/King of Kings Masonic Lodge #126 A&ASR of F&AM, Nashville, Tenn; Kiwanis Clb of Bowling Green; Bowling Green Alumni of Kappa Alpha Psi; NAACP; Ky Wel Assn; IAPES; r/Misson Bapt.

JACKSON, HENRY HOLMAN oc/Private Counseling, Investor; b/Sept 1, 1927; h/3004 College Dr, Texarkana, TX 75501; ba/Texarkana; m/Shirley Ann Haselbarth; c/Henry Holman III, Hugh Harold, Melissa Etta, Martha Opal; p/Ephraim (dec) and Etta Jackson (dec); ed/AA Texarkana Col; BA Univ Tex; MA Stephen F Austin Univ; PhD Univ Mexico; mil/USN; USMC; pa/Cnslg Ofc in Fed Prison until Ret'd; Pvt

JACKSON, MAJORETTE oc/Supervisor; b/Nov 7, 1956; h/Magnolia, MS; c/Kevin Early; p/Beulah J Jackson, Magnolia, MS; ed/Secy Sci Deg, SW Miss Jr Col 1975; pa/Fabric Warehouse Supvr; r/Holiness; hon/3 Yr Ser Awd Kellwood Co 1979; Bus Awd 1974, S Pike HS.

JACKSON, MARTHA S oc/Teacher; b/Sept 24, 1945; m/James E; c/James Kendric; p/G W and Birdia Smith, Koscius Ko, MS; ed/BS 1968; MS 1976; AAA 1979; pa/Tchr GT, S Pike Schs; Cheerldr Sponsor 1970-72; cp/Pike Co Yth Advr; Advr S Pike Old Fashion Spelling Bee; r/Announcing Secy & Asst Secy of Ch; Pres of Choir; hon/Am Outstg Edr in Elem Ed 1970.

JACKSON, MAYNARD HOLBROOK JR oc/Mayor; b/Mar 23, 1938; h/Atlanta; m/Valerie Richardson; c/Elizabeth, Brooke, Maynard III, Valerie Amanda; ed/BA Morehouse Col 1956; JD w Hons NC Ctrl Univ Sch of Law 1964; pa/Mayor, Atlanta, Ga 1974-; V-Mayor, Atlanta 1968-74; Co-Fdr Jackson, Patterson, Parks & Franklin (Ga's First and Largest Afro-Am Law Firm); Pres Nat Conf Dem Mayors 1979-80; Chm US Conf of Mayors Transp Com; Dem Nat Com; Bd Mem: Nat Leag of Cities, US Conf of Mayors; Am Soc Public Adm, Nat Inst for Public Mgmt; Chm Local Govt Energy Policy Adv Com; Am Bar Assn; Ga Bar Assn; Atlanta Bar Assn; Gate City Bar Assn; Exec Com Dem Party of Ga; Ams for Dem Action, Nat VChm; Ga Assn Black Elected Ofcls, Chp Municipal Sect; NBC/LEO; So Conf of Black Mayors, Exec Com; cp/33° Prince Hall Mason; Nat Gun Control Ctr, Nat Chm; NAACP; Am Cancer Soc, Hon Bd Mem; Martin Luther King, Jr Ctr for Social Change, Bd Mem; Am Jewish Com; NOW; Atlanta Legal Aid Soc; Nat Conf on Christians and Jews, Hon Bd Mem; Ctrl Atlanta Prog; Atlanta C of C; Resurgens Atlanta; Nat Wel Rts Org; Ga Conservancy; Atlanta Urban Leag; Nat Adv Coun from So Regional Task Force; So Task Force, Ex-Officio Mem; Alpha Phi Alpha; Morehouse Col Bd Trustees; John F Kennedy Sch of Govt; Co-Chm Pres Carter's Com on Windfall Profits Tax; r/Friendship Bapt Ch: Trustee; hon/Hon LLD, Morehouse Col, Del St Col & Howard Univ; Recog'd for Outstg Achmts in Field of Public Mgmt, Babson Col; 1 of Yngest Mayors of Major US City; Only Mayor Appt'd by Pres Jimmy Carter to Nat Comm on Neighborhoods.

JACKSON, ROY L oc/Executive Director; b/Oct 21, 1939; h/PO Box 431, Grambling, LA 71245; ba/Grambling; m/Shirley Johnson; c/Darryl Roi, Dolphus Carl; p/J C and Estella Walter Jackson, Shreveport, LA; ed/BS Grambling St Univ 1961; MA Ball St Univ 1970; Post Grad: Kan St, Okla Univ, Univ Hawaii, La St Univ; pa/Exec Dir Devel/Alumni Affairs, Grambling St Univ (La St Dept Ed & Caddo Parish Sch Bd); La Assn for Adult & Commun Ed; Nat Assn Equal Opport; Coun for Advmt & Support of Ed in Higher Ed; cp/Regional Occuptl Work Assn; Nat Alliance of Bus; RSVP; Voter Registration Coor; Omega Psi Phi; Vol Cnslr for Juvenile Delinquent Boys; r/Bapt; hon/Leg Schlr 1957; Edr of Yr, Caddo Parish 1972; Outstg Cnslr for Juveniles 1973; Outstg Sec'dy Edrs in Am 1973; Outstg Yng Men Am; Contbr "Grambling-Cradle of the Pros" 1980.

JACKSON, RUBY FERN oc/Personnel Assistant and Secretary; b/Sept 5, 1923; h/1517 30th St, Lubbock, TX 79405; ba/Lubbock, TX; m/William L Jr (dec); c/William N; p/Guy Worth (dec) and Cora E Cathey McNeely, Lubbock, TX; ed/AAS S Plains Col; BS Wayland Bapt Col; Cert'd Profl Secy, Nat Inst Cert Secys; pa/Pers Asst & Secy to Dist Engr, Dist 5 St Dept Hwys & Public Transp; Nat Secys Assn, Intl Toastmasters, Intl; Tex Public Employees Assn; cp/Chm Bus Adv Com; S Plains Col; r/Asbury U Meth Ch: Ofcl Bd, Choir, Wkshop Work, Area & Coun of Mins; hon/Cert'd Profl Secy; Secy Of Yr, Caprock Chapt NSA, Intl 1966, 1977-78; Secy of Yr Finalist in Tex-La Div NSA Intl 1978.

JACKSON, SAMUEL WATSON (WATT) JR oc/General Superintendent; b/Mar 28, 1938; h/1212 Spring Dr, Shelby, NC 28150; ba/Lawndale, NC; m/Margaret H; c/Lauren Marie, S W; p/Samuel W and Lucy M Jackson, Rock Hill, SC; ed/BS Clemson Univ 1961; Ga St Mgmt Skills for Plant Mgmt Prog 1977; AMA Top Mgmt Briefing 1980; pa/Asst Overseer Milliken Inc; Cleveland Mills: Quality Control Supt, Supt Knitting Div, Gen Supt; So Textile Mfc Assn; Tech Adv Com for Inst Textile Technol; cp/Mason; Elk; Lions Clb; U Fund Bd Dirs; Clemson Univ Dit Dir; Cleveland-Rutherfordton Clemson Alumni Clb Treas

161

PERSONALITIES OF THE SOUTH

1978-79, Pres Elect 1980, Pres; r/Shelby Presb Ch: Elder & Deacon; hon/Alumni Nat Coun Awd 1979.

JACKSON, SHIRLEY JOHNSON oc/Grant Director; b/July 6, 1941; h/Grambling, LA; ba/PO Drawer 8, Grambling, TX 71245; m/Roy L; c/Darryl Roi, Dolphus Carl; p/Samuel L (dec) and Elzadie Coleman Johnson, Shreveport, LA; ed/BS Grambling St Univ 1963; MS La St Univ 1974; Cert Mtl Retard LSU 1975; Further Study: Geo Peabody, Ball St Univ, So Univ & Univ SEn La; pa/Dir Proj Upward Bound, Grambling St Univ; Phi Delta Kappa; Coun Exceptl Chd; La Assn Edrs; La Rehab Assn; SW Assn Student Asst Progs; La Assn Student Asst Progs, VP; cp/YWCA; Delta Sigma Theta, Mbrship Chm; La Assn Mth Hlth; Nat Coun Negro Wom, Precinct Wkr; r/Bapt; hon/Outstg Yng Edr 1976; Outstg Yng Wom in Am 1976; Finalist OYE in La 1976; Hon Citizen, City of Lake Charles, La 1976; Colonel on the Staff of Gov Edwin E Edwards 1978; Co-Author Tchg Unit for "Specialized Job Directory" 1977.

JACKSON, VADER L oc/Tariff Specialist; b/Jan 8, 1942; h/PO Box 1452, Bay City, TX 77414; ba/Houston; p/Roxie M O'Neal, Bay City, TX; ed/BS Tenn St Univ 1964; MEd De Paul Univ 1977; pa/Sec'dy Ed Tchr-Supvr; Tariff Spec, Continental Airlines; AFT; NEA; NOLPE; cp/Yng Dems 1965-69; Operation Breadbasket 1967-69; NAACP; r/Meth; hon/Cert Ill Sch Law 1975; Cert Airline Trg, Eastern Airlines 1973.

JACKSON, VELMA MAE ALSTON oc/Supervisor; h/225 25th St NW, Winston-Salem, NC 27105; ba/Winston-Salem; m/Elijah L Sr; c/Elijah L Jr; p/George and Bessie Alston, Kinston, NC: ed/BS, MA, Profl Dip Columbia Univ; pa/Supvr Adult Students, Forsyth Tech Inst; Kappa Delta Pi; Delta Sigma Theta; cp/Precinct Chm Exec Com Mem; r/Missionary Bapt; hon/Gov's Com.

JACKSON, VIDA KAY oc/Pediatrics Nurse; b/Sept 2, 1957; h/1910 C Franciscan Terrace, Winston-Salem, NC 27107; ba/Winston-Salem; p/Robert M and Sylva Dale Jackson, Dunn, NC; ed/BSN ECU; pa/RN Ped, NC Bapt Hosp; NC Nurses Assn; Past Mem Student Nurses Assn; Pres ECU SNA; cp/Former 4-H Mem; r/Bapt; hn/Sigma Theta Tau; Nat Dean's List 1979.

JACOBS, KEITH WILLIAM oc/Associate Professor; b/Feb 24, 1944; h/PO Box 102, Pearlington, MS 39572; ba/New Orleans, LA; p/Cyril William and Sylvia Woodrum Jacobs, Cedar Falls, IA; ed/BA Univ No Ia; MA E Ill Univ; PhD Univ So Miss 1975; mil/AUS 1968-71; pa/Assoc Prof Dept Psychol, Loyola Univ 1975-; Adj Instr, Sch Nsg, William Carey Col 1979-80; Lectr Psychol, Our Lady of Holy Cross Col 1976-79; Am Psychol Assn; Am Ednl Res Assn; Am Assn Sex Edrs, Cnslrs & Therapists; La Acad Scis; SEn Psychol Assn; cp/Intl Childbirth Ed Assn; Childbirth Ed Assn of New Orleans, Nat Abortion Rights Action Leag; Am Civil Liberties Union; hon/Nat Tchr Awd, Div 2 of Am Psychol Assn 1980; Author Approx 50 Papers Pub'd in Profl Jours; Photos Exhib'd in Intl Salons.

JAFFE, HERMAN oc/Certified Public Accountant and International Tax Consultant; b/Jan 24, 1903; h/7920 Royal Ln, Dallas, TX 75230; ba/Dallas; m/Hannah Louise Blum; c/Richard R, David B, Kenneth P; p/Morris S and Rose Weiss Herman; ed/BS NYU 1924; pa/Admitted to Pract before US Tax Ct 1928; Instr NYU & Yale Univ; Intl Fiscal Assn; Mem Com to Investigate Bondholders Re-org for Ho of Reps; Mem Com of Truman Investigating Com for US Sen; Am Inst CPAs; NY St Soc CPAs; Conn Soc CPAs; Tex Soc CPAs; cp/Yale Clb; hn/Author Texts on: Heavy Constn Indust, Short Term Trust & Charitable Contbns, Merger & Acquisitions, Corp Orgs & Re-orgs, Others; Author Maritime Comm Act, Vinson Act, Sect 351 to 368 of Revenue Code of 1954, Others.

JAGGERS, ZACK oc/Retired Teacher and School Administrator, Federal Employee; b/Sept 26, 1909; h/Bonham, TX; m/E Kate Armstrong; c/Wanda Kirleen Hiett; p/Marvin Eugene (dec) and Viola Chloe Seay Jaggers (dec); ed/BS Tex Tech Univ 1941; MEd W Tex St Univ 1954; pa/Public Sch Ser 17 Yrs; US Fed Ser 20 Yrs; Co Agric Agt, Tex 9 Yrs; NEA; TSTA: Tex Co Agts Assn; cp/Pres Lions Clb, Secy-Treas 1974-; Secy-Treas Masonic Lodge; r/Ch of Christ.

JAKSHA, JOHN TIMOTHY oc/Radio Announcer, Music Director, Production Manager; b/Feb 17, 1949; h/3531 Willie Way, Spring, TX 77380; ba/Spring; m/Cheryl; c/Jason; p/Joseph (dec) and Louise Jaksha, Pasadena, TX; ed/BA Radio-TV Communs; pa/Featured on Local NBC News Prog "Live at 5:00"; Staff Announcer & Salesman for Pasadena Cablevision 1975-76; cp/Ch Work; r/Full Gospel; hon/Dean's List, Sam Houston St Univ.

JAMES, ADVERGUS DELL JR oc/College Administrator; b/Sept 24, 1944; m/Anna; p/Advergus D Sr and Helen G James, Muskogee, OK; ed/BS Langston Univ 1966; MS Okla St Univ 1969; pa/Asst Registrar, Langston Univ 1966-69; Dir Admissions & Records, Langston Univ 1969-70; Dir Student Fin Aid, Prairie View A&M Univ 1970-; Nat Assn

Student Fin Aid Ofcrs; SWn Assn Student Fin Aid Ofcrs; Tex Assn Student Fin Aid Ofcrs; Nat Assn Fin Asst for Minority Students; cp/Prairie View Optimist Clb; Phi Delta Kappa; Order of Rising Star; 32° Mason Lodge; r/Bapt.

JAMES, DAVID oc/Associate Dean; b/Sept 2, 1940; h/8937 Tamar Dr #202, Columbia, MD 21045; m/Janie; c/Lauren, Joi; p/John Oscar (dec) and Lula F James, Greenville, NC; ed/BS Elizabeth City St Univ 1962; MA Georgetown Univ 1971; EdD Nova Univ 1978; pa/Assoc Dean Ext Ctrs & Spec Progs, Prince George's Commun Col 1971-; Wash Public Sch Sys 1967-71; Clarke Co, Va Public Sch Sys 1963-67; Pitt Co Public Sch Sys 1962-63; Nat Coun Commun Sers & Cont'g Ed; Adult Ed Assn USA; Nat Civil Ser Leag; AAUA; Md Assn Adult Ed; Nat Coun for Staff, Prog & Orgl Devel; cp/VP Jeffers Hill Elem Sch; r/Presb; hon/W/W Black Ams; Requested by Cong-wom Shirley Chisholm of Congl Black Caucus to be a Mem "Brain Trust Com" to Study Ednl Issues Involving Minorities & Poor 1977-; Phi Alpha Theta; Outstg Tchr, Wash DC Public Sch Sys, DC Bd Ed 1971; Nom'd Coach of Yr 1966; Hon Grad Elizabeth City St Univ 1962.

JAMES, EARL EDWARD oc/General Manager; b/May 9, 1949; h/404 Kiowa Dr E, Lake Kiowa, TX 76240; ba/Gainsville, TX; m/Melodie Elaine; c/Penelope Elaine, Crystal Juanita, Earl Edward Jr; p/Artie and Addie James, Colo Springs, CO; ed/BS Bethany Nazarene Col; pa/Gen Mgr K-Mart Retail Dept Store; cp/G'ville C of C; r/Prot.

JAMES, FLORINE DELORIS oc/Teacher, Missionary Worker; b/Nov 25, 1924; h/910 Russell, Orangeburg, SC 29115; ba/Same; m/J E; p/Clarence (dec) and Sebelle Walters (dec); ed/AB SS; MA Ed; Cert'd in Cnslg; pa/Public Sch Tchr; Missionary Wkr AME Ch; Pres Clarendon Ed Assn; SCEA; NEA: SCPGA; SCAPCAE; cp/NCHW; NAACP; CC for Chd & Yth; PTA; Voter's Leag; 4-H Clb; Summerton Civic Com; Fdr & Orgr Girl Scouts Summerton; r/AME Ch; Pres Wom's Missionary Soc; Secy IMWA & CWU; hon/SC Assn Clrm Tchr Awd 1972; AUS Recruiting Awd 1974; SC Human Relats Awd 1976; SC WMS AME Ch Pres 1974-78; S'ship Urban Causeway CWU.

JAMES, NONA FAYE oc/Office Manager, Insurance Agent; b/Aug 13, 1939; h/PO Box 41, Seminole, OK 74868; ba/Seminole; m/Vernon; p/Fred Snell, Seminole, OK; Dora Snell (dec); ed/Att'd E Ctrl, OBU, Shawnee & Seminole Jr Col; pa/Lic'd Ins Agt; Pt Owner Dacus Ins Agcy; cp/2 Terms Pres Seminole BPW Clb, Dist Dir over 8 Clbs; r/First Assem of God Ch; hon/1st Prize Best Speech in Dale Carnegie Course.

JAMESON, WILL ALLEN oc/Artist, Writer; b/Dec 5, 1927; h/2107 W 11th St, PO Box 996, Plainview, TX 79072; ba/Same; m/Robert Ray; c/Robert Alan, David Ray; p/Thomas Dromgoole Stodghill, Quinlan, TX; Garnet LaEunice Palmer Stodghill, Amarillo, TX; ed/Grad Amarillo Col; Att'd W Tex St Univ & Wayland Bapt Col; pa/Real Est Salesman, Tullis Real Est; Past Mem Okla Press Assn; Fdr & 1st Pres McAlester Writers Guild; Org'd Toastmistress Clb, McAlester; Wroter "Art Chatter" (Wkly Column) 2 Yrs; Wrote "Shopping in the City" for McAlester News Capital; Acct Exec 2 Yrs; Spec Dir Plainview Daily News; cp/Past Pres Plains Art Assn; Past Pres Coronado Study Clb; r/Bapt; hon/Awds for Bronze Sculpture & Blue Ribbons for Paintings.

JAMIESON, FRANK MARTIN oc/Mortgage Loan Analyst; b/Sept 26, 1948; h/703 12th St, Galveston, TX 77550; ba/Galveston; p/Frank and Mary Catherine Martin Jamieson, Onalaska, TX; ed/BBA 1970 & 77, MBA 1978 Tex A&M Univ; Am Inst Real Est Appraisers Courses; mil/AUS 1970-73 1st Lt Signal Corp; pa/Mortgage Loan Analyst, Am Nat Ins Co; Instr, Dept Fin, Col Bus Adm, Tex A&M Univ; Dist Mgr, Wickes Corp; Asst Fin VP & Controller, Univ Mobile Sers Corp; Acct, Corp Hdqtrs, Universal Sers Corp; cp/Bd Dirs, Treas Am Cancer Soc; Bd Dirs Galveston Co YWCA; Proj Chm Galveston Hist Foun; Instr Col of the Mainland; Kiwanis Clb; r/Cath; hon/W/W Am 1979-80; Guest Lectr, Grad Real Est Courses, Tex A&M Univ 1980.

JAMISON, CHRISTINE MORRIS oc/Nurse; b/May 24, 1931; h/255 W Hunt Rd, Alcoa, TN 37701; ba/Same; m/Haley M; c/Jamie M; p/John W Morris, Rocky Mount, VA; Ossie D Morris (dec); ed/Grad Roanoke Meml Hosp Sch Nsg; pa/RN; ANA; cp/Bd Ed Alcoa City 14 yrs; Bd Govs Voc Ed; Leg Com Tenn Sch Bd Assn Tenn Fed Repub Wom; Dist Dir Tenn Fed Garden Clbs, Pres Chilhowee Clb; Tenn Fed Wom's Clb; Pres Alcoa Garden Clbs; Pres Blount Co Coun Garden Clbs; Bd Dirs Child & Fam Sers; Bd Dirs Heart Fund Assn; r/First U Meth Ch Alcoa: Coor Chd Min & Elem SS Tchr; hon/Cert Achmt, So Region Sch Bd Res & Trg Ctr; Nat Coun BSA Den Mother's Awd; Richard Allen Ser Awd for Outstg Ser to Yth of Alcoa; Life Mem Tenn Fed Garden Clbs Inc.

JANOSKY, THOMAS ALAN oc/Behavioral Optometrist; b/May 28, 1952; h/Floyd, VA; ba/PO Box 223, Floyd, VA 24091; p/Francis R and Alberta S Janosky, Pittsford, NY; ed/BA Hamilton Col 1974; BS 1977, OD 1979 Penn Col Optometry; pa/Optometrist Spec'g in Develmntl Vision &

Vision Trg; Beta Sigma Kappa; Optometric Ext Prog, Clin Assoc; Col of Optometrists in Vision Devel, Assoc Mem; SWn Va Optometric Assn, Treas; Va Optometric Assn; Am Optometric Assn; cp/Floyd Lions Clb; New River Val Assn Retard'd Ciitizes, Bd Dirs; Roanoke Val Assn Chd w LD; r/Rom Cath; hon/Clin Excell Hon Mention 1979, Acad Excell Hon Mention 1979, Penn Col Optometry.

JARKOWSKI, BOLESLAW ZENON oc/Retired Engineering Educator; b/July 6, 1913; h/4424 San Clerc Rd, Jacksonville, FL 32217; m/Stefania; p/dec; ed/BAS; MS; Dr Eng; mil/RAF WWII Wing Cmdr; pa/Engrg Ed; Res; Conslt; ASME; ASEE; AAUP; cp/Am Security Coun; Am Legion; r/Rom Cath; hon/Pi Tau Sigma; Num Mil Decorations; Polish, British, Dutch, French; Outstg Edr Am.

JARRELL, NANA BELLE (MRS R C) oc/Insurance Office Work; Substitute Teacher; b/Mar 23, 1895; h/68 Riverside Dr, S Charleston, WV; m/R C; c/Lucy Whisman, Betty Carter (both adopted); p/Mrs A B Clay (dec); ed/AB Marshall Univ 1939; MA WVa Univ 1950; pa/Prin US Nav Ordnance Sch S C'ton 14 yrs; Tchr Kanawha Co Jr & Sr HSs; Audio Visual Dir S C'ton Jr HS, Supvr Student Tchr Tng WVa St Col; Sub Tchr S C'ton; Mem all Tchr Orgs, Ret'd Tchrs, NRTA Leg Com 1962-, Tchr 43 Yrs; cp/Past Matron Tickelwah Chapt #45 OES C'ton, Past High Priestess C'ton Shrine #7, Mother Advr Rainbow Girls 4 Yrs, Chm Bd Dirs 4 Yrs, Past High Priestess & Help Org 1st Ct C'ton, Life Mem; AAUW, Arts Chm S C'ton; Chm Num Fund Drs; Centennial: Cent Artists Assn, Invitation Gov Barren All Functions, Tea Hostess DAR Chapt House Wash, DC 72nd Cong; NSDAR: Past Regent Kanawha Val Chapt, Former Chaplain, Past Corr Secy, Past Regent C'ton Chapt, Num Chm'ships; Wom's Clb: Charter & Life Mem Clb S C'ton, Pres 2 Terms, S C'ton 1st Lady, Parliamentn; Mtl Hlth: Kanawha Chapt WVa Assn, Oper Santa Claus; UN: Treas Kanawha Co Chapt, Panel Moderator, Bd Dir Co; Recording Secy, Past Regents Clb of DAR C'ton; Wife 1st Mayor S C'ton, Com Polit Party Ward 3 4 Consecutive Terms, Com-Wom Ward 4; hon/Alpha Delta Kappa: Charter Mem, 2/Pres C'ton, WVa Expansion Chm, Chm Nom'g Com WVa, Intl Favors Com Denver Conv, WVa Conv Chm Ks City, Orgr Chapts, Commend Nat, VP WVa, Life Mem, Guest Spkr, Lttr Commend: S C'ton C of C Display Arts & Crafts, Ruth Jones Chm Wom's Participation WVa Centennial; Book of Hon; Fellow Am Biogl Inst.

JARY, ROLAND SAUNDERS oc/Civil Engineer; b/Jan 26, 1936; h/1600 Trail Glen Ct, Arlington, TX 76013; ba/Ft Worth; m/Linda Gordanier; c/Janiece Lorraine, Matthew Saunders; p/Roland Edmund Jary (dec); Jane Elizabeth Saunders, Ft Worth, TX; ed/BA Tex Christian Univ 1959; Post Grad Study, Univ Hawaii 1961-62; BS Tex A&M Univ 1965; Further Study George Washington Univ 1967-68; Grad Defense Lang Inst, Wash DC 1970; MS Tex Christian Univ 1977; Command & Gen Staff Col 1974; mil/US Corps of Engrs 1959-74 Maj; pa/Constrn Engr & Topographic Engr: Ft Belvoir, Va; Honolulu, Ha; Saigon, Vietnam, Korea, Thailand; Col Fac, Sch of Ams, Ft Bulick, Canal Zone; Proj Dir, Inter-Am Geodetic Survey, Santiago, Chile & Quito, Ecuador; SWn Labs, Constrn Mats Engr; Conslt Gen Contractor, Ft Worth; Reg'd Profl Engr, Tex; Nat & St Soc Profl Engrs, Secy, Treas, VP Ft Worth Chapt; Am Soc Civil Engrs; Am Water Works Assn; Soc Am Mil Engrs, VP Ft Worth Post; Dir Tex Coun Engrg Labs 1981-; cp/Kappa Sigma; Steeplechase Clb, Ft Worth; City Coun-man, Town of Pantego 1979-80; Ambassador's Country Team, Ecuador & Chile 1970-73; Mayfest Vol, Ft Worth 1976; Advr to Tarrant Co Jr Col 1979-81; r/Presb: Deacon; hon/Bronze Star, Merit Ser Medal; Army Commend Medal; Vietnam Campaign Medal; Cross of Gallantry, Vietnam; Nat Defense Medal; Contb'd Articles to *Civil Engineer Journal & Military Engineering Magazine.*

JASPER, DANNY oc/Quality Control Director; b/Oct 29, 1948; h/Rt 1 Box 448, Science Hill, KY 42553; ba/Somerset, KY; m/Norma Jean; c/Scott Daniel; p/Hoit E Jasper, Science Hill, KY; Jewell Jasper (dec); ed/BS Col Agric, Univ Ky 1970; pa/QC Dir, So Belle Dairy; VP Ky Dairy Prod Assn; Dir Ky Assn Milk Food Envirl Sanitarians; r/Bapt.

JASPER, JUDITH CAMILLE oc/Student; b/Aug 30, 1959; h/606 Lynn, Lufkin, TX 75901; ba/Lufkin; p/John C and Sue Jasper, Lufkin, TX; pa/Pt-Time Ofc Wkr; cp/Bapt Yng Wom; r/So Bapt; hon/Townsend S'ship; Select Student S'ship, Stephen F Austin St Univ.

JAVELLAS, INA J oc/Administrator; Consultant; Social Worker; b/Jun 15, 1934; h/3447 SE 44th St, #231, Del City, OK 73105; ba/Oklahoma City, OK; ed/BA 1956, MSW 1958 Univ Okla-N; pa/Conslt: Nat Inst Mtl Hlth, Rockville, Md 1972-, Dept HEW, Public Hlth Ser, Dept Hlth Sers, Alcohol, Drug Abuse, & Mtl Hlth Adm, Adm Sers Sect Reg VI, Dallas, Tex 1976-; Chief, Commun Mtl Hlth Planning & Devel, Dept Mtl Hlth, Okla City; Coor Commun Mtl Hlth Div, Dept Mtl Hlth Div, Dept Mtl Hlth, Okla City; Okla 1965-; Psychi Social Wkr, Commun Sers Proj, Commun Mtl Hlth Div, Dept of Mtl Hlth, Tulsa, OK 1963-65; Other Former Social Work Positions; NIMH Conslt Core Advr Group 1978-79; Edit Com, *Health & Social Work,* 1977-79; Nat Assn

Social Wkrs: Exec Com Wn Okla Chapt 1972-, Steering Com of Social Leg Proj Ctr 1976, Num Coms, Sev Chmships; Com on Compendium of Goals & Objectives, Okla Hlth Planning Comm 1975-76; Dept HEW, Public Hlth Ser, Dept Hlth Sers, Alcohol, Drug Abuse, & Mtl Hlth Adm, Adm Sers Sect, Reg VI, Dallas: Commun Mtl Hlth Ctrs Tech Assistance Planning & Adv Com 1976-, Commun Mtl Hlth Ctr Newlttr Adv Bd 1976-; NCSW Mem, Task Force for Long-Term Care in the US, Co-Sponsored by Div of Long-Term Care, Ofc of Admr, Hlth Resources Adm 1976; Acad Cert'd Social Wkrs; Conf of Social Wkrs in St & Territorial Mtl Hlth Progs: Editor Newslttr 1966-76, Chm Interorgnl & Cont'g Ed Coms 1976-77, Other Ofcs; Okla Bd Registration of Social Wkrs; Interagy Hlth Manpower Data Task Force; Govs Adv Com on Employment of Handicapped 1969-70; Num Other Assns & Former Ofcs; Num Speeches/Lectures & Papers; cp/Phi Mu Sorority: Life Mem, Col Fin Advr for Univ Okla Bldg Corp, Former Alumnae Dir of Dist IX, Other Former Ofcs; Com Assignments, AAUW; Former Class Rep, Okla Univ Alumnae Assn; Okla Hlth & Wel Assn: Coor Resource Ctr for St Conf, Conslt Prog Com, Former Chm Prog Com for St Conf, Bd Dirs, Others; hon/Profl Pubs; Social Wkr of Yr NASW, Wn Okla Chapt 1970; Num Biogl Listings; Phi Mu Frat Scholar; Outstg Yg Wom in Am 1965; Awd of Recog for Dist'd Ser, Okla Hlth & Wel Assn 1977; Num Others.

JAYSON, JOSEPH MORTON oc/Parole Case Analyst; b/Jan 17, 1955; h/118 Castle Cir, Smithfield, NC 27577; ba/Raleigh, NC; p/Ben D and Evelyn M Jayson, Clinton, NC; ed/Cand MPA NC St Univ; BA Univ NC-Wilmington; pa/NC Dept Correction, Pre-Release & Aftercare Sers: Field Ser Cnslr 1977-80, Parole Case Analyst 1980-; Am Correctional Assn; NC Probation-Parole Assn, Exec Com 1977-78, Treas 1978-79; cp/NC JCs, Institutional Rep; Smithfield JCs, VP; NC Assn EMTs; Johnston Co Yng Dems, VP 1980-81; hon/Pres Awd of Hon, NC JCs 1979; Goerge W Randall Awd, Most Outstg Correctional Ofcr in NC 1979, 1980; Dist'd Ser Awd, Johnston Co JCs 1980; Order of Tar Heel Corps NC JCs 1979.

JECKO, PERRY TIMOTHY oc/Actor; Educator; Author; b/Jan 24, 1938; h/207 Inwood Ave, Upper Montclair, NJ 07043; m/Mary Louise Painter; c/Christopher Brendan, Nicholas Benjamin; p/Perry Joseph and Cora Timothy Jecko, Bethesda, MD; ed/BA, MFA Yale Univ; mil/USNR, Lt; pa/Worked as Prin Performer in TV Drama *All My Children* & Appeared in 2 Off-Off-Broadway Prodns *(Faces of O'Neill & The Friday Bench)* & Var TV Commercials While On Extended Leave from Tchg in Arlington, Va; Am Fdn TV & Radio Artists; Screen Actors Guild; r/Epis.

JEFFREY, MARY MADELINE oc/Assistant Director Nursing Service; b/July 9, 1928; h/978 Lakeside Ct, Venice, FL 33595; ba/Venice, FL; m/Lawrence E; c/Kathryn Jane Braswell, Lawrence E II, Cheryl Ann Schramm, Barry D; p/Louis J (dec) and Mary J Andreolli; ed/Shadyside Hosp Sch Nsg 1949; BS Hlth Sers Adm Fla Intl Univ 1980; Lic'd RN: Fla 1964-, Penn 1949-; pa/Staff Nurse & Pvt Duty, Ind Hosp 1946-63; Venice Hosp: Staff Nurse 1963-65, Hd Nurse Med Surg Unit & OB 1965-68, Adm Supvr 1968; Asst Dir Inser Ed & Adm Supvr 1969-72; Acting Dir Nsg Ser 1968-69, 1974-74, 1978, 1979-80; Asst Dir Nsg Ser 1972-; ANA; FNA; Dist 44 Nurses Assn; Fla Soc Nsg Ser Admrs 1980; cp/Wom's Clb; Beta Sigma Phi, Upsilon Pi Chapt; Co-Chm U Way, Venice Hosp; Past Pres Wom's Soc of Christian Sers; Reg'd Dem; r/Meth.

JEFFRIES, WILLIAM WORTHINGTON oc/Museum Director and Archivist; b/July 23, 1914; h/716 Melrose Ave, Annapolis, MD 21401; ba/Annapolis; m/Mary Ruth Franklin; c/John Worthington, Susan J Clinton, Gertrude Parker, Margaret McKee, Virginia Oxford; p/Frank Mauzy (dec) and Gertrude Worthington Jeffries (dec); ed/AB B'ham So Col 1935; MA 1936, PhD 1941 Vanderbilt Univ; mil/USNR 1942-46, Cmdr Ret'd; pa/Tchg Fellow, Vanderbilt Univ 1936-38, 1940-41; Instr, B'ham So Col 1938-40; Asst Prof Univ Miss 1941-42; USN Acad: Ofcr Instr 1942-46, Asst Prof 1946-48, Assoc Prof 1948-55, Prof 1955, Sr Prof Eng, Hist & Govt 1955-70; Naval Acad Archivist 1970-; Dir USN Acad Mus; So Hist Assn 1973-; Middle Atlantic Archives Conf; r/Meth; hon/Co-Author: *American Sea Power Since 1775; International Relations; Geography and National Power.*

JENKINS, ANDREA SHARON oc/Teacher; b/May 9, 1947; h/7 Wytchwood Ct, Apt 2, Balto, MD 21209; ba/Balto; c/Dawn Marie; p/Henry A McKee Sr, Hackensack, NJ; ed/BS Elec Ed; Grad Prog Spec Ed; pa/Elem Ed Tchr; Tchr's Adv Coun; r/Meth; hon/Tchr's Adv Coun Rep to Regional Adv Coun Region 5.

JENKINS, CLARA BARNES oc/Professor; h/920 Bridges St, Henderson, NC 27536; b/Lawrenceville, VA; p/Stella G Barnes, Henderson, NC; ed/BS Winston-Salem St Univ; MA NC Ctrl Univ; EdD Univ Pgh; pa/Prof St Paul's Col; AAUP; Nat Soc for Study of Ed; AAUW; NEA; Assn Tchr Edrs; VEA; Hist of Ed Soc; Doct Assn of Edrs; Am Acad Polit & Social Sci; Am Hist Assn; AAAS; Am Assn Higher Ed; Acad Polit Sci; Am Psych Assn; Marquis Biog Lib Soc; Intl Platform Assn; Phi Eta

PERSONALITIES OF THE SOUTH

Kappa; Bd Dirs Winston-Salem St Univ; Soc for Res in Child Devel; Jean Piaget Soc; r/Epis; hon/Fac Fellow, U Negro Col Fund; Grantee, Am Bapt Conv, Val Forge, Pa; Plaque Awardee, NC Agric & Tech St Univ; W/W: S&SW, Am Ed, Am Wom, Black World, US; Nat Gold Book of Dist'd Wom; Nat Social Dir of USA; Nat Register of Prominent Ams; Intl Platform Assn Dir; Creative & Successful Personalities of World; DIB; Intl Blue Book; 2000 Wom Achmt; Dir Ednl Specs; Ldrs in Ed; Intl Schlrs Dir; Blue Book (Ldrs of Eng Spkg World); Biog Dir of Am Psych Assn; Ldrs of Black Am; Personalities of Am; W/W Biog Record: Child Devel Profls.

JENKINS, EDWARD E oc/Minister; b/Dec 5, 1924; h/Rt 1, Taylors, SC 29687; ba/Greenville, SC; m/Margaret M; c/Patricia A, E E Jr, Alonzo C; p/J E C (dec) and Maggie Jenkins (dec); ed/AB; MDiv; DD; mil/USN 3 Yrs 1st Class Petty Ofcr; pa/Trustee Wofford Col; cp/NAACP; r/Meth; hon/Awds for Outstg Ser to Florence & Columbia Dists of Meth Ch.

JENKINS, GELAH EVELYN LONG oc/Dairy Farmer; b/Dec 7, 1916; m/Andrew; c/Reva Harper, Beverly Bobo; p/James Monroe (dec) and Ollie Parker Long (dec); ed/HS Grad; pa/Dairy Farmer; cp/Active in Commun & Sch Activs; r/Christian; hon/St 4-H Alumni Awd 1965.

JENKINS, JAY oc/Attorney-at-Law; b/Aug 6, 1937; h/604 Club Ln, Marietta, GA 30067; ba/Atlanta, GA; m/Elizabeth Byrd Sheetz; c/Jay McClellan, Lewis Turner, John Paul; p/Jewell Jenkins (dec); Fannie McClellan Jenkins, Munford, AL; ed/LLB, JD Woodrow Wilson Col of Law; mil/USMC 1955-59; pa/Chm of Bd, The Gentry Co 1972-; Pvt Law Pract 1968-; Public Affairs Dir, Petroleum Coun of Ga 1966-68; Press Secy to Lt Gov of Ga 1964-66; Editor & Publr, The Gentry Report; Free Lance Writer w Pub'd Articles in Newsweek, Real Estate Atlanta, Contemporary Living, Municipal South and Num Newspapers; Atlanta Bar Assn; St Bar of Ga; Cobb Co Bar Assn; Intl Assn Fin Planners Inc; Nat Small Bus Assn; cp/Atlanta C of C; Am Horse Coun; r/Presb; hon/Hon Mem, Gridiron Secret Soc, Univ Ga; Hon Lt Col Aide-de-Camp, Staff Ala Gov George C Wallace; Commun Ser Awd, Nat Edit Assn 1963.

JENKINS, WARREN MARION oc/Minister; b/Mar 8, 1915; h/190 Muller St, Orangeburg, SC 29115; m/Alma W; c/Patricia Elaine; p/J E C and Maggie E Walker Jenkins; ed/AB Claflin Col 1937; BD Gammon Theol Sem 1944; MA Drew Univ 1947; Att'd Yale Sch Alcohol Studies & Tex Christian Univ; pa/United Meth Communs 1972-; Asst Secy for Field Cultivation & Bus Mgr Div Interpretation, Prog Coun, U Meth Ch 1969-72; Dist Supt 1968-69; Full-time Exec Secy SC Conf Bd Ed 1962-68; Chaplain SC St Col 1949-53; Chaplain & Tchr Claflin Col 1945-49; Public Sch Tchr 4 Yrs; Min SC Conf 1939-; SC Conf; Gen Bd Ed of Meth Ch 1956-68; Assn Meth Hist Socs 1964-; SEn Region Exec Secys Assn, Pres 1966-68; VChm Exec Secys & Bd Pres Sect Meth Conf on Christian Ed 1965-67, Chm 1967-68; cp/Mason; Phi Beta Sigma; Commission on Rel & Race 1969-72; r/Christian.

JENKINS, WILL M JR oc/Captain US Air Force; b/Sept 27, 1951; h/Jacksonville, AR; m/Theone Lynn; p/William D and Madreen T Abbott, Bullard, TX; ed/Att'd Del Mar Col & Sch of the Ozarks 1971-73; BA summa cum laude Tex A&I Univ 1974; MA Univ No Colo 1980; Grad Work Univ Ga Inst Correctional Rehab 1978; Air Force Inst Technol, Tech Contract Trg 1979; FFC Broadcast Oprs Lic Univ Corpus Christi 1973; Air Force Squadron Ofcrs Sch 1980; Air Force Ofcrs Trg Sch 1976; Marine Corp Command & Staff Col 1980; mil/USAF 1975- Capt; pa/Roustabout Continental Oil Co 1970-71; Newspaper Editor Sch of the Ozarks 1971-73; Spec Agt Prudential Ins Co of Am 1975; Info Spec Corpus Christi Area Tchrs Credit Union 1974-75; Newspaper Editor, F E Warren AFB 1975-76; Security Police Flight Cmdr Carswell AFB 1976-79; Chief Security Police, Ghedi AB, Italy 1979; Govt Contract Admt, Prod Ofcr 1979; Govt Contract Negotiator, Kelly AFB 1979-80; Titan II Launch Crew Ofcr, Little Rock AFB 1980-81; Nat Contract Mgmt Assn 1979-80; Purchasing Mgmt Assn 1979-80; Air Force Assn 1976-; Air Force Sgts Assn 1976-80; Speech Communs Assn Am 1979-80; cp/Tarrant Co Big Brothers Assn 1976-78; Am Qtr Horse Assn; Appaloosa Horse Clb of Am 1976-81; Tex Appaloosa Horse Clb 1976-80; Sierra Clb of Am 1979-80; Credit Com Carswell Fed Credit Union 1978; PR Conslt Security Police Explorer Scout Post 1977-78; Dean's Adv Coun Tex A&I Univ 1973-74; Jr Plan'g Coun, City of Corpus Christi, Tex 1979; Order of DeMolay, Past Master Cnslr, Knight; r/First Bapt Ch: Trg to Become Full-Time Min; Outreach Ptnr Jimmy Swaggert Evangelist Assn; hon/Jr Ofcr of Qtr, Kelly AFB 1980; Outstg Security Police Ofcr of Yr: Strategic Air Comand 1977, 8th Air Force 1977, 19th Air Div 1977, 7th Bombardment Wing 1977; Jr Ofcr of Qtr, Carswell AFB 1978; Airman of Qtr, FE Warren AFB 1976; Dist'd Hon Grad, Defense Info Sch 1975; Hon Grad Basic Mil Trg, Lackland AFB 1975; All Deans List Del Mar Col, Univ Corpus Christi 1971-73; W/W Am Student Ldrs 1973; Outstg Yng Men Am 1977, 78, 79, 80, 81; 3rd Outstg DeMolay in Tex 1970; AF Commend Medal 1979; AF Trg Ribbon 1980; Outstg Unit Ribbon 1978; Good Conduct Medal 1976; Longevity Ser Ribbon 1979; Small Arms Expert Marksman 1976.

JENKS, SALLIE ANNE oc/Medical Technologist; b/Nov 13, 1935; h/6140 SW 65th Ave, S Miami, FL 33143; ba/Miami; p/Dan Hugh Jenks Jr, Dunedin, FL; Zoe Ellen Lashbrook Jenks (dec); ed/Univ Miami 2 Yrs; Fla Col Med Technol 1 Yr; Lic'd Lab Technol, Fl St Bd Hlth; pa/Am Soc Med Technol; Am Soc Microbiols, Local & Nat Chapts; AAAS; Fla Soc Med Technols; cp/Secy Kappa Delta Chapt Beta Sigma Phi; Yng Repubs Org; Mus Comedy Act in Wesley Minstrels 1970-76, Proceeds for Philippine Missionaries; r/Presb; hon/W/W Am Wom; Pub'd Author: Num Profl Articles.

JENNINGS, BRENDA M oc/Instructor, Nurse; b/Feb 16, 1947; h/Wedowee, AL; ba/So Union St Jr College, Wadley, Al 36276; p/Jack and Arzelia Brown Messer, Roanoke, AL; ed/Grad Univ Ala Hosp Sch Nsg; Post Grad Studies UAB 1972-73; EMT Basic 1978; EMT Intermediate 1979; pa/Emer Room Charge Nurse, Carraway Meth Med Ctr; ER Staff Nurse, Univ Hosp B'ham; EMT Instr 2 Yrs; Tchg Adv'd Cardiac Life Support, St Ala; BCLS Affil Fac 3 Yrs; Bd Dirs Randolph Co Ambulance Assn; Bd Dirs E Ala EMS Region; Am Heart Assn; BCLS & ACLS Instr; cp/Trg & Ed Com, E Ala EMS; r/Meth; hon/Wom of Yr, Randolph Co 1980.

JENNINGS, THOMAS HAROLD oc/Vice President Manufacturing; b/Dec 26, 1932; h/811 Double Churches Rd, Columbus, GA 31904; ba/Columbus; m/Bettie Ellen; c/Deborah Sue, Jeanne Sue; p/James (dec) and Ruby Williams Silvey (dec); ed/BS Univ Tenn-Chat 1965; Postgrad Ga St Univ 1971; mil/USAF 1953-57; pa/VP Mfg Lummus Industs Inc; Soc Mfg Engrs; Am Inst Indust Engrs; Am Prod & Inv Cnl Soc; cp/Columbus C of C; Pres Joel Chandler Harris Homes Assn 1957; r/Nazarene; hon/William Danforth Awd; W/W Fin & Indust 1979.

JENRETTE, JOHN WILSON JR oc/United States Congressman; Attorney; b/May 19, 1936; h/N Myrtle Beach, SC; ba/Cannon Ho Ofc Bldg, Wash DC 20515; m/Rita Carpenter; b/Mary Elizabeth, Harold Hampton; p/John Wilson Sr and Mary Herring Jenrette; ed/BS Wofford Col 1958; LLD Univ SC 1962; mil/USAFR, Maj; SC NG; pa/Atty & City Judge for Ocean Dr Beach; Am Bar Assn; SC Bar Assn; Horry Co Bar Assn; Am Trial Lwyrs Assn; Atty, N Myrtle Beach; cp/US Ho Reps 1975-81; SC Ho Reps 1965-72; C of C; Jaycees; Lions Clb; SC Huguenot Soc; Kappa Sigma Frat; SE Forestry Adv Bd; Others; r/Trinity Meth Ch: Mem, Ofcl Bd, Former Chm Fin Com; hon/Nom'd for Ten Outstg Yg Men of Am; Dist'd Ser Awd, SC Municipal Assn 1966.

JENSEN, JACKSIE ANN oc/Nurse; b/Mar 4, 1932; h/Rt 2, Cedar Hill, TN 37032; ba/Springfield, TN; m/Roy Stanley; c/Chris Stanley, Timothy Floyd, Rebecca Louanne; p/Floyd Oscar (dec) and Annie Elizabeth Whitehurst, Portsmouth, VA; ed/BNA FWBB Col 1957; Nsg Dip, Tenn Regional Cardiovascular Nsg Ctr 1971; Critical Care Nsg Cert 1979; pa/Profl Nurse Metro Nashville Gen Hosp; AACCN; Tenn Hosp Assn; Mid Tenn Hlth Assn; Am Hlth Assn; cp/Robertson Co Repub Wom's Clb; r/Bapt; hon/Best All Around Girl Awd FWBBC 1956; Scholastic Awd, 1960; W/W Am Wom 1979-80.

JESSIE, PAULA BLANTON oc/Teacher; b/Jan 27, 1947; h/120 Sunset, Campbellsville, KY 42718; ba/C'ville; m/Keith H; c/Katherine Shea; p/Paul F and Lyda F Blanton, Orleans, IN; ed/BS; MA; pa/NEA; KEA; MCEA; cp/Dem Party; C'ville Country Clb; Ladies Golf Assn; r/Bapt; hon/W/W Am Wom 1979-80.

JETER, LARRY JOE oc/General Manager, Associate Publisher; b/Aug 27, 1943; h/Odessa, TX; ba/Wall at Lorraine, Midland, TX 79702; m/Janice Kay; c/Steven Patrick, Brandy Suzanne; p/Jasper Lee and Treva Nell Jeter, Abilene, TX; ed/BBA McMurry Col 1978; mil/AUS 1964-73 Capt; pa/Advtg Acct Exec, Abilene Reporter News 1974-78; Gen Mgr, Basinweek 1978; Gen Mgr & Assoc Pubr, Hart Pubs 1978-; r/Meth; hon/Bronze Star; Air Medal for Valor; 19 Other Air Medals; Army Commend Medal.

JEWETT, HUGH JUDGE oc/Surgeon; b/Sept 26, 1903; h/100 E Melrose Ave, Baltimore, MD 21212; ba/Baltimore; m/Margaret V Moseley; c/Rosalind Nelson; p/Hugh Judge Jr and Anne Ingraham Van Lent; ed/AB 1926, MD 1930 Johns Hopkins Univ; pa/Johns Hopkins Univ Sch of Med: Prof Emeritus 1969-, Instr in Urol to Prof Urol 1936-69, Resident Urologist 1935-36, Asst Resident 1933-34, Asst in Gen Pathol 1932-33; Resident Urologist, Ancker Hosp, St Paul, MN; Vis Urologist: Johns Hopkins Hosp, Ch Home & Hosp, Baltimore City Hosp; Conslt Staff, Walter Reed Army Hosp, Wash DC 1948-59; Chm Registry Genito-Urinary Pathol, Armed Forces Inst Pathol 1958-64; Trustee, Am Urological Res Foun 1952; Past Pres, Md Med Ser Inc (Blue Shield); Former Councilor, Med & Surg Fac, St of Md; Past Pres: Mid-Atlantic Section AUA, Clin Soc Genito-Urinary Surgs; Am Urol Assn; Am Assn Genito-Urinary Surgs; Am Col of Surgs: Fellow, Past Gov; Am Bd Urol Inc: Diplomate, Past Gov; Soc Univ Urols; Intl Soc Urol; Sociedad Venezolana de Urologia; Editor-in-Chief: Urological Survey 1951-, Journal of Urology

1966-77; cp/Elkridge Clb; Hamilton St Clb, Johns Hopkins Fac Clb; Chevy Chase Clb;r/Epis; hon/Ramon Guiteras Awd, AUA 1963; Phi Beta Kappa; Alpha Delta Phi; Author 90 Sci Papers & Num Book Chapts.

JINKS, KENNETH ALLEN SR oc/Executive Vice President; b/Mar 18, 1938; h/104 Rowell Dr, Selma, AL 36701; ba/Selma; m/Peggye Wallace; c/Kenneth A Jr, Jon Mark; p/A H Jinks, Fayetteville, AR; Edith Christine Jones, Hillsboro, AL; ed/Att'd Tenn Val Jr Col & Univ Ala; pa/Exec VP Disco Intl Inc; cp/Dir Geo C Wallace Jr Col; r/Meth.

JOE, YOUNG-CHOON CHARLES oc/Professor; b/Jan 23, 1936; h/1113 Chickering Park Dr, Nashville, TN 37215; ba/Joelton, TN; m/Hee-Mee Yoo; c/Jeannie, John and Jeffrey; p/Kyoung Hwan and Geel-Hwa Kim Joe, Seoul, Korea; ed/Pre Med Col of Yonsei Univ 1955-57; MD Med Sch Yonsei Univ 1961; MS Univ Wash Grad Sch 1973; pa/Med Dir Wash St Dept Social & Hlth Sers, Wash St Pen Hosp 1973-75; Assoc Prof Fam Pract, E Tenn St Univ Col Med 1976-77; Assoc Prof Fam Med, Meharry Med Col 1975-; Pvt Pract Fam Med & Ear-Nose-Throat 1977-; Diplomate Am Bd Fam Pract 1974-; Fellow Am Acad Fam Phys; Fellow Am Soc Abdominal Surgs; Am Col Emer Phys; Soc Tchrs of Fam Med; Assn Am Med Cols; Pan Am Med Assn in Sects of ENT & Med Ed; cp/Chm Bd Dirs Mid Tenn Korean Assn; r/Nashville Korean Meth Ch; Lay Ldr; hon/1st Prize Michael A Gorman Awd 1967; AMA Phys Recog Awds 1969, 72, 75, 78; Num Med Papers & Articles in Var Med Jours.

JOGLAND, HERTA HELENA b/Nov 22, 1922; h/2579 Benson Dr, Charleston, WV 25302; ba/Institute, WV; oc/Professor; p/Joseph and Margaret Vogl Stoessel; ed/PhD; pa/Prof of Sociol, WVa St Col; Res; r/Cath; hon/Res Grants Fulbright & German Res Coun; Danforth Coun; Danforth Assn; Intl W/W Intells; Intl Reg Profiles; DIB; World W/W Wom; Am Men & Wom of Sci; Ldrs of Black Am; Personalities S; Book of Hon; Fellow Am Biogl Inst.

JOHNS, CLARENCE BENJAMIN JR oc/Pastor, Teacher; b/Jan 11, 1925; h/25 Van Buren St, Farmingdale, NY 11735; m/Jeanette Turner; c/Cynthia J Marve, Fabienne Ruth, Clarence B III, Felicia Ellen, Reddick Earl; ed/BS Hampton Inst; MA NYU 1973; mil/AUS 2 Yrs; pa/Tchr Emotionally Disturbed Chd, PS 9; Pastor St Paul AME Ch; cp/Past Pres LI Chapt Nat Hampton Alumni Assn; Chap 2 Yrs Nat Exec Bd, Nat Hampton Alumni Assn; Chap N Atlanic Region NHAA.

JOHNS, GLENN M oc/Minister; b/Apr 9, 1924; h/400 Charles St, Spencer, NC 28159; m/M Ruth Cundy; c/David Hoyt, Dan Jeffery; p/St Patrick (dec) and Rosa Frazier Johns (dec); ed/Dip Univ Mortuary Sci; AB Kan St Col at Pgh; mil/USN WWII; pa/Min 195]-; YMCA Exec 1956-61; Edr 1975-; cp/Mason; Loyal Order Moose; BPO Elks; Bd Mem Rowan Salisbury Arts Coun; Pres Spencer Optimist Clb 1980-81; r/Presb; hon/Psi Chi Nat Hon Soc 1955.

JOHNS, RANDALL L oc/Director of Data Processing; b/Jan 10, 1937; h/727 So Hill Ave, Deland, FL 32720; ba/Sanford, FL; m/Elaine A; c/Mark L, Lorraine A, Heather L; p/Ottie J (dec) and Gertrude Johns, Orange City, FL; ed/Att'd Stetson Univ; mil/AUS 2 Yrs; pa/Dir Data Processing, Seminole Co Schs; Past Bd Mem, Past Pres Fla Assn Ednl Data Sys; cp/Pres Edith I Starve Elem Parent Tchr Grp r/Bapt; SS Tchr.

JOHNSON, ADA BERNICE STRONG oc/Retired Teacher; b/Aug 24, 1907; h/314 W Franklin St, Warrenton, NC 27589; m/Matthew Alva (dec); c/Melba B J King, Jennie A J Franklin; p/Peter (dec) and Channie Little Strong (dec); ed/BS Fayetteville St Tchrs Col 1947; Further Studies: NC Ctrl Univ; Howard Univ, Univ NC-Chapel Hill; pa/Elem Tchr, Warren Co, NC Public Schs 38 Yrs; Pres Hawkins HS PTA; Secy Warren Co PTA; Pres & Histn, NC Cong Colored Parents & Tchrs, Dist 3; Pres Warren Co Negro Tchrs Assn; NC Tchrs Assn; NCAE, Life Mem; NEA; Nat Ret'd Tchrs Assn; cp/Chm Warren Co Students Legal Defense Fund; NC Crim Just Ed Tng Sys Coun; Warren Co Coor'g Coun for Sr Citizens; 2nd V-Chm NC Wom & Polit Caucus; Ldr & Conslt, Warren Co Girl Scouts; Nom'g Com, Pines of Carolina Girl Scout Coun; Warren Co Bd of Elects; NC & Warren Co Repub Party; Am Civil Liberties Union; Interfaith Comm, Soul City, NC; Ladies Aux, Warren Gen Hosp; Sound & Print U (WVSP-FM Radio); r/AME Ch: Pres Mission Soc, Asst Dir of Public Relats; hon/Layman of Yr, 2nd Epis Dist of AME Ch 1971; S'ship Com, John R Hawkins Alumni & Friends 1979; Spec Recog, Nat Com of Repub Party 1976-81.

JOHNSON, AGATA PALMISANO oc/Businesswoman; b/Nov 2, 1920; h/528 Brook Circle, Griffin, GA 30223; ba/Griffin; m/William W Sr; c/Noneal Archer, Kay Ramsey, W Whitfield Jr, Taina Taylor; p/Leon A (dec) and Hattie K Palmisano (dec); pa/Restaurant Owner; cp/C of C; Garden Clb; Griffin Devel Auth; r/Bapt.

JOHNSON, ANNE CURTIS oc/Realtor Associate; b/Oct 9, 1931; h/2425 Craig Cove, Knoxville, TN 37919; ba/K'ville; m/James White;

c/Lucy Holloway, Margaret Tyler, James Jr, Andrew Price; p/Gerald R (dec) and Louise R Curtis (dec); ed/BFA Univ Tenn; pa/Rltr Assoc, R M Moore & Assocs; Knoxville Real Est Bd, Prog Com; cp/U Way Bd; Chm Commercial Div UW Campaign; r/Epis; hon/Million Dollar Awd; K'ville's First Lady 1968; Bd Gov's Univ Tenn Nat Alumni Assn; Pres Tanasi Girl Scout Coun; Past Pres YWCA; Girls Clb; K'ville Sym Wom's Guild.

JOHNSON, BESSIE MAE (BETH) COOK oc/Teacher; b/Dec 26, 1912; h/Arlington, TX; m/Loren W (dec); c/Forrest D, Karen Kennedy, Marjorie Warner; p/William T and Bessie Mae Caldwell Cook; ed/Tchr's Cert Sam Houston St Tchrs Col; pa/Primary Tchr; Tex St Tchrs Assn; NEA; Hill Country BPW Clb, 1st VP; Past Mem DAR & Beta Sigma Phi; r/Meth; hon/Hunt Elem Sch Mother of Yr and Granny of Yr 1976-77, Tchr of Yr 1973.

JOHNSON, BEVERLY KIM oc/Teacher, Coach; b/Nov 12, 1955; h/Magnolia, AR; ba/Texarkana, AR; p/Beverly and Nelle Johnson, Magnolia, AR; ed/BSEd So Ark Univ 1978; pa/Phy Ed & Sci Tchr & Coach Girls Volleyball & Basketball, North Heights Jr HS; AAHPER; Phy Ed Majors & Minors Clb, Pres; r/Bapt; hon/W/W Am Cols & Univs 1978; Outstg Yng Wom Am 1979; Yth in Achmt 1979; Nat Hon Soc Alpha Chi 1978.

JOHNSON, CARLENE FRANKLIN oc/Tax Commissioner; b/Dec 26, 1947; ba/Statesboro, GA; m/John Roy; c/Jason Christopher, John Mitchell; p/Oscar Carl Franklin (dec); Pat Conner, Statesboro, GA; pa/Dpty Tax Commr 9 Yrs; Elec'd Tax Commr, Bullock Co 1979-; ABW; VPW; Leg Chm Co Ofcrs Assn; Ga Tax Ofcls Assn; cp/Leg Com Ga ASssn Ofcls; Fed Dem Wom; Bd Dirs U Way; Pres Am Heart Assn; r/Prim Bapt; hon/DAR Good Citizenship; Fac Awd for Excell; Sch Ser Awd; ABW Wom of Mo June 1980.

JOHNSON, CHARLES ELBERT oc/Superintendent of Education; b/July 1, 1946; h/PO Box 763, Woodville, MS 39669; ba/Woodville; m/Bessie H; c/Vanessa La Shea; Adrianne Monique & Andrea Melita; p/Fenimore J (dec) and Olivia B Johnson, Woodville, MS; ed/BS Alcorn St Univ 1968; MEd So Univ 1971; pa/Tchr 6½ Yrs; Coor Neighborhood Yth Corp for Wilkinson & Amite Co 4 Summers; Supt Ed, Wilkinson Co Sch Dist; Miss Assn Edrs; NEA; Miss Assn Sch Supt; Am Assn Sch Adm; Miss Ec Coun; cp/Adv Coms, St Miss: ESEA-Title I, Tchr Cert, Brookhaven Lng Resources Ctr; r/Bapt.

JOHNSON, CHARLIE JAMES oc/Minister; b/Sept 24, 1923; h/Rt 3 Pond Creek Rd, Sweetwater, TN 37874; ba/Sweetwater; m/Mary Ellen Upton; c/Marcus Anthony, Michael A (dec); p/Emory Moses (dec) and Ruth B Johnson; ed/BA Morehouse Col 1956; BD ITC 1960; MDiv 1973; ThD Trinity Col of Bible & Theol Sem 1980; mil/AUS 1942-45; pa/Pastor, U Presb Ch USA; Columnist (Wkly) *Daily Post-Athenian*, 1967-; cp/Mayor's Com on Human Relats, Athens, Tex 1969-70; r/Christian (Reform Tradition); hon/W/W Rel.

JOHNSON, DONALD MARK oc/Para-Medic, Respiratory Therapist, Skills Instructor; b/May 31, 1957; h/1620 Gribble, Gainesville, TX 76240; ba/G'ville; m/La Wanda Diane; p/Donald E and Venita R Johnson, Denison, TX; ed/Assoc Deg EMT; pa/Mbrship Chm Cooke Co Chapt Tex Assn of EMT; hon/Cert of Merit for Life Saving, Garland Police Ofcrs Assn 1976.

JOHNSON, DOROTHY LOUISE oc/Homemaker, Civic Worker; b/Jan 11, 1935; h/203 N Slaughter, Sundown, TX 79372; m/Don R; c/Dennis Ray, David Lind; p/Louise Hackler, Sundown, TX; ed/Att'd S Plains Col; Dale Carnegie; Profl Flower Design Schs; Profl Cake Instn; pa/Profl Cake Decorator 8 Yrs; Reg'd Brangus Cows; Thoroughbred Race Horses; Oil Interests; cp/Pres Sundown Gdn Clb; Pres Boomtown Days Mus; Dir, VP VBS; Dem Alternate Judge Sundown C of C; r/Bapt; hon/Runner-Up Mother of Yr, Hockley Co; Pub'd in *Las Cruses Journal, Hospitality House News, Levelland Sun-News.*

JOHNSON, DOROTHY PURNELL oc/Teacher; b/Aug 23, 1930; h/829 Ormond St, Macon, GA 31204; m/Frank J; c/Cheryl Teresa; p/James Thomas Purnell, Macon, GA; Willie Mae Purnell, Macon, GA; ed/BS Savannah St Col; MA NYU; pa/Bibb Assn Edrs; GAE; NEA; cp/Zeta Phi Beta; Unionville Improvement Assn; r/Meth; hon/Outstg Elem Tchr Am 1972; W/W Am South Wom 1977-78; Matilda Hartley Tchr of Yr 1976.

JOHNSON, E C oc/Director of Parks and Recreation; b/Nov 25, 1926; h/Toney, AL; m/Julia B; c/David Brian, Jeffrey Keith, Ronald Stephen, Anna Jeronda; p/Bernice V Johnson; ed/Att'd Anderson Col 1952 & N Ala Col of Commerce 1953; mil/AUS 1944-46; pa/Exec Secy Madison Co Rec Dept 1964-; Phys Ed Instr 1950-63; Ala Park & Rec Soc; Ala Phy Ed Soc; Am City & Cos; cp/Huntsville Qtrback Clb; Huntsville

Bowling Assn, Life Mem; Ala Bowling Assn Bd Dirs, Life Mem; Kiwanis Clb; r/Bapt; hon/Yngest Person Ever Inducted into Ala Bowling Hall of Fame; Ala Ho of Reps Resolution for Extraordinary Achmt 1980; Nom'd By Madison Co Comm for Part & Rec of Yr.

JOHNSON, ESTA DODSON oc/Consultant; b/Aug 25, 1907; h/715 N 11th St, Columbus, MS 39701; ba/Columbus; m/E B (dec); p/Richard and Rosa Dodson (dec); ed/BS So Miss Univ; PA, MA NWn Univ; pa/Prof, ECU; Eng Tchr, Columbus; Prin & Tchr, Oak Pk, Ill; cp/Pres Mus Study Clb; Bd Mem Columbus Concert Assn 1979-81; Model for Pryors 1978-81; r/Bapt; hon/Kappa Delta Pi; Pi Lambda Theta.

JOHNSON, FRANK J oc/Facilities Planning Specialist; b/June 11, 1927; h/829 Ormond St, Macon, GA 31204; ba/Warner Robins, GA; m/Dorothy Prunell; c/Cheryl Teresa; p/Thomas (dec) and Cherry Johnson (dec); ed/BS Savannah St Col; mil/USMC WWII; pa/Facilities Plan'g Spec, Warner Robins AFB; Homosophian Clb; cp/Pres Unionville Improvement Assn; NAACP; SCLC; Bibb Voter's Leag; Bd Mem Boy Scout Troop 217; Ga Coun Human Relats; Warner Robins ALC Minority Com; Macon-Bill Co Ath Adv Com; Substandard Housing Adv Com; Bd Dirs Thomas Meml Funeral Home; r/Bethel CME Ch: Steward Bd, Chm Evangelism; hon/Hon'd for Having Served on Macon Mayor's Rec Adv Com; Cert of Apprec, Ga HS Ath Assn; Macon-Bibb Co Rec Dept Ser to Commun Awd.

JOHNSON, FRANK MINIS JR oc/US District Judge; b/Oct 30, 1918; h/3106 Old Farm Rd, Montgomery, AL 36111; ba/Montgomery; m/Ruth Jenkins; c/James Curtis (dec); p/Frank M Sr (dec); ed/LLB Univ Ala 1943; mil/AUS WW II; pa/Temp Emergency Ct Appeals of US 1972-; Judicial Ethics Com 1978-; Judicial Conf Jt Com on Code of Judicial Conduct for Federal Judges 1972-; r/Prot; hon/Hon Doct Law: Univ Notre Dame 1973, Princeton Univ 1974, Univ Ala 1977; Hon JD, St Michael's Col 1975; Am Acad Achmt 1978; Bronze Star.

JOHNSON, GERALDINE MEADOR oc/Guidance Counselor; b/Mar 10, 1921; h/Texarkana, AR; m/John Charles; c/John Charles Jr; p/Jacob Erwin and Bertha Gilley Meador; ed/BS 1948, MS 1951; Univ Ark; PhD E Tex St Univ 1971; pa/Texarkana, Ark Schs; APGA; Am Sch Cnslr Assn; Ark PGA; Ark Sch Cnslr Assn; SW Ark Sch Cnslr Assn; NEA; AEA; Texarkana Clrm Tchr Assn; Alpha Delta Kappa; Phi Delta Kappa; Kappa Delta Pi; Phi Sigma; SW Ark Tchr Ctr; cp/Altrusa Clb; AAUW; OES; Social Order Beauceant; Texarkana USA Geneal Soc; UDC; Haven Home Bd; Ark Ednl TV; r/Bapt; hon/PTA Life Mem 1975; ADK St S'ship 1966; Articles Pub'd in Profl Jours.

JOHNSON, GLADYS R oc/Donation Coordinator; b/Mar 24, 1911; c/Travis L; pa/Donation Coor WPS Yth; Social Work; r/Bapt.

JOHNSON, GLEN ERIC oc/Assistant Professor; b/May 29, 1951; h/1429 Forest Ridge Rd, Charlottesville, VA 22903; ba/C'ville; m/Kathryne Anne; c/Edward Lindgren, Eric Anders; p/Ray Clifford and Helen Lindgren Johnson, Webster, NY; ed/BSME Worcester Polytechnic Inst 1973; MSME Ga Inst Technol 1974; PhD Vanderbilt Univ 1978; pa/Mech Engr, Tenn Eastman Co 1974-76; Asst Prof Mech Engrg, Vanderbilt Univ 1978-79; Asst Prof Mech Engrg, Univ Va 1979-; Reg'd Profl Engr; Am Soc Mech Engrs; Acoustical Soc Am; Math Programming Soc; hon/Pres's Fellow GIT 1973-74; HSV Grad Schlr VU 1976-78; Dupont Summer Fellow VU 1978; Pi Tau Sigma 1971; Tau Beta Pi 1973; Sigma Xi 1978; 14 Articles Pub'd in Profl Jours or Books.

JOHNSON, GUERRY WAYNE oc/Corporation President and Treasurer; b/Nov 8, 1947; h/Charleston, SC; ba/C'ton; m/Diane P; c/Angela E; p/Thaxton C Johnson, Lawrenceburg, TN; Mable R Johnson, C'ton, SC; ed/AS Trident Tech Col 1977; mil/AUS 1966-68 Sgt; pa/Proj Mgr & Cost Estimator Gen Contr'g Co; Pres & Treas Johnson Bldg Corp; Assn Gen Contrs Am; cp/Trident C of C, Amvets, Dem Party; r/Prot; hon/Soldier of Mo 1968; Hon Grad Army Engrg Sch 1967-68; Num Certs of Achmt, AUS.

JOHNSON, HUGH CHRISTOPHER oc/Director of Indian Programs; b/June 28, 1933; h/Norman, OK; ba/Okla City, OK; m/Sonya Eileen Hively; c/Tracy Lynn, Michael Christopher, Scott Andres, Todd Patrick; p/Harber Johnson (dec); Bettie McHenry (dec); ed/BS Okla St Univ 1958; mil/USMC 1951-54 Sgt; m/25 Yrs w HUD: Presently Dir of Indian Progs; Bd Dirs Native Am Ctr, Okla City; cp/Masonic Lodge #28; 32° Mason, Val of Springfield; Shriner, Ansar Temple; V Chief Creek Nation 1971-75; r/First Christian Ch; hon/Little Leag Fball, Basketball & Baseball Coach; Rec'd Cert of Apprec from US JCs as Guest Spkr 1977.

JOHNSON, JAMES ARTHUR oc/Priest; b/Nov 22, 1947; h/3908 Palisades Dr, Weirton, WV 26062; ba/Weirton, WV; m/Betty Jean; c/Laura Elizabeth, Jacob Nathaniel; p/Herbert Charles and Lily Ruth

Johnson, Midland City, AL; ed/BA Shorter Col; MDiv Va Theol Sem; DMin Cand Pgh Theol Sem; mil/USAF 4 Yrs; pa/Rector St Thomas Epis Ch, Weirton; Vicar St Matthew's Epis Ch, Chester, WV; Order of St Luke; Order of Holy Cross; Assn Creative Change; cp/Lions Clb; Rotary; Dem Party; Nat Eagle Scout Assn; r/Epis; hon/Air Force Commend Medal; Author WV Sch Lay Min Core Course in Theol.

JOHNSON, JAMES FRANKLIN JR oc/Nursing Home Administrator; b/Jan 19, 1944; h/Harriman, TN; ba/Rt 7 Box 290, Harriman, TN 37748; m/Beverly G; c/Kelly, Derek, Perri; p/James F Sr and Thelma G Johnson, Lenoir City, TN; ed/BA Carson Newman Col 1966; Att'd SEn Theol Sem 1966-68; pa/Admr Johnson's Hlth Care Ctr Inc; Tenn Hlth Care Assn: Dist Pres, 1st VP, Pres, Chm Leg & Govt Relats Com, Chm Tenn Ed & Polit Action Com, Chm Nom'g Com, VChm & Org Charter Endorser Tenn Hlth Care Ednl Foun; Tenn Dept Public Hlth: Chm Tenn Bd Examrs for Nsg Home Admrs, Medicaid Med Adv Com, Gov's Task Force for Reduction of Paperwork in Nsg Homes; Am Col Nsg Hme Admrs; Roane Co St Area Voc Sch LPN Adv Com; cp/Harriman Rotary Clb VP; Walden Ridge Antique Car Clb Pres; Early Ford V-8 Clb; r/Bapt: Deacon, Fin Com, Ch Coun, Dept Dir, SS Tchr; hon/Tenn Hlth Care Assn Spec Apprec Awd 1977; Pres's Awd 1980; Col Aide de Camp, Gov's Staff 1979.

JOHNSON, JOSEPH E III oc/Physician, Medical Education & Research; b/Sept 17, 1930; h/3500 Quarterstaff Pl, Winston-Salem, NC 27104; ba/Winston-Salem; m/Judith Haynes Kemp; c/Joseph E IV, Judith Ann, Julie Marie; p/Joseph E Johnson Jr (dec); Marie Dowson, Coral Gables, FL; ed/BA cum laude Vanderbilt Univ 1951; MD Vanderbilt Univ Sch Med 1954; mil/USN 1955-57; Cmdr USNR 1965-; pa/Prof & Chm, Dept of Med, Bowman Gray Sch of Med, Wake Forest Univ 1972-; Chief of Med, NC Bapt Hosp 1972-; Univ Fla Col of Med: Assoc Dean 1970-72, Prof of Med & Chief Div of Infectious Diseases 1968-72, Assoc Prof & Hd Infectious Diseases Div 1966-68; Johns Hopkins Univ Sch of Med: Asst Dean for Student Affairs 1963-66, Asst Prof of Med 1963-66, Instr in Med 1961-62; Physician, Johns Hopkins Hosp 1961-66; Sigma Alpha Epsilon (Pres Vanderbilt Chapt 1950); Omicron Delta Kappa; Phi Chi (Pres Vanderbilt Chapt 1953-54); Alpha Omega Alpha; Fellow Am Col Physicians; Fellow Royal Soc Med; BG Govs, Am Bd Internal Med 1977-; Num Profl Assns; r/Prot; hon/Royal Soc Med Foun Traveling F'ship 1970; Phi Beta Kappa; Am Col Physicians Postgrad Scholar 1960-61; John & Mary R Markle Scholar in Med Sci 1962-67; Pub'd Author.

JOHNSON, JOYCE DUNDALOW oc/Nurse; b/June 21, 1933; h/3008 Catalina Ave, Suffolk, VA 23434; ba/Suffolk; m/James Marshall; c/John Nelson; p/Anne E Dundalow, Suffolk, VA; pa/BPW Clb; Vol Am Red Cross; Owner Home for Adults; Va Assn Home for Adults Inc; r/Meth; hon/Outstg Pilot 1974-75; Pilot Clb of Suffolk, Va; Recog for Vol Ser, Dept of Mtl Hlth & Mtl Retard.

JOHNSON, JOYCE K oc/Psychophysical Therapist; h/5837 Mariner Dr, Tampa, FL 33609; ba/Same; c/Mark, Ken, Greg, Hilary; p/Edward I Kalt, CA; Rose Orkin Oser, Miami Bch, FL; ed/AA; MA; PhD; RMT; pa/Healing Arts Coun; Mtl Hlth Assn; St Dance Assn of Fla; Nat Rehab Coun Assn; r/Unitarian; hon/Hon Student; HCC Human Sers Awd.

JOHNSON, LINDA RUSSELL oc/Psychotherapist; b/Sept 14, 1950; h/51 Springbrook, Tuscaloosa, AL 35405; ba/University, AL; m/David P; p/William B and Hazel Capwell Russell, Bruce, MS; ed/BA Miss St Univ 1974; MSW Univ Ala 1976; pa/Psychotherapist, Univ Ala Cnslg Ctr 1976-; NASW; NACSW; AAMFC; NAWDAC; AAUW; Clin Social Worker, Pinebelt Mtl Hlth Ctr 1976; r/Ch of Christ; hon/Outstg Yng Wom Am 1978; Phi Alpha; Todd Meml S'ship 1975.

JOHNSON, MARK O oc/Minister; b/Jan 29, 1953; h/125 S La Salle Rd, Oak Ridge, TN 37830; ba/Oak Ridge; m/Carol; c/Cristi, Traci; p/Mr and Mrs Andy L Johnson, Oak Ridge, TN; ed/BA Cumberland Col 1975; Att'd So Bapt Theol Sem; pa/Ord'd 1972; Pastor Royce Bapt Ch; Spiritual Life Dir Yth Encounter Mins; r/So Bapt; hon/W/W Am Cols & Univs 1975.

JOHNSON, MARY ANN LEE oc/Assistant Community Development Director; b/July 5, 1940; h/Burnside, KY 42519; m/Ben W Jr; c/Carryn Kay, Joel Douglas; p/Matter Lee, Burnside, KY; ed/Beauty Col; pa/Hairdresser; Case Wkr Big Brother & Big Sister; Asst CD Dir, Pulaski Co Commun Devel; Pres Pulaski Co Dem Wom; Pres Ky St Treas Dem Wom; 5th Dist Dir Dem Wom; cp/Past Pres Fireside Homemakers; Pres Burnside Civic Clb; r/Meth; hon/Dem Wom of Yr, Pulaski Co 1980.

JOHNSON, MARY LOUISE oc/Homemaker; b/May 23, 1922; h/216 W Boyle, Earlington, KY 42410; m/Alonzo Edward (dec); c/Jennifer June McKissic, Margaret Luzennia; p/Lucian (dec) and Lassie Bowles, Madisonville, KY; cp/PTA; Homemakers Clb; Centennial Com 1976; r/Bapt; hon/PTA Life Mem; Wom of Yr; Foods, Nutrition, Hlth Chm for Hopkins Co Homemakers Coun.

PERSONALITIES OF THE SOUTH

JOHNSON, MICHAEL ROY oc/Instructor; b/July 2, 1952; h/SS Box 8166, Hattiesburg, MS 39401; m/Rebecca; p/Roy R and Marilyn Johnson, Meridian, MS; ed/BMus, Univ Ala; pa/Fac Univ Ala; Instr Mus Univ So Miss; Recitals & Tours Throughout US & Spain; Calgary Philharmonic Orch; hon/Fred Waring Awd for Composition 1970; Pi Kappa Lambda.

JOHNSON, NANCY CAROL oc/Teacher; b/June 5, 1946; h/Copperas Cove, TX; ba/Copperas Cove, TX; p/Mr and Mrs Hal R Hunnell, Brownfield, TX; ed/BS Sul Ross St Univ 1976; pa/Title I Math, Elem Level, Copperas Cove ISD; Tex St Tchrs Assn, Local Unit Pres Elect 1980-81, Pres 1981-82; Former Exec Bd Mem & VP TSTA Alternate to St Meeting in Dallas 1978; r/Ch of Christ; hon/Tex St Tchrs Assn Merit Awd 1980.

JOHNSON, NELLIE oc/Retired Teacher; b/May 26, 1915; m/dec; c/Bobby A, Bernice Hart, Doris Williams, Jerry F, William, Beverly Hall, Melvin D Rogers, Barbara Tardy, Vera Little, Larry R, Leemorris C, Pamela J Jackson, Delilah O, Kenneth L; p/dec; ed/BS Miss Indust Col 1960; Grad Studies Univ Wis-Milwaukee; pa/Clrm Tchr 39 yrs; Tunica Co Tchrs Assn; NEA; Miss Assn Eng Tchrs; NCTE; cp/U Voters of Tunica; NAACP; Homemakers Clb; r/Meth; hon/Plaque for Dedicated Ser DHEA Bd 1978; Star Tchr 3 Times 1965, 72, 74; Wom of Yr, Tunica Co 1979.

JOHNSON, NORMA W oc/Executive Director; b/Sept 4, 1935; h/249 Juniper Dr, Frankfort, KY 40601; b/Frankfort; c/Teresa Ann Brown, Charles Martin; p/Henry Jack and Mabel Jones Wilson, Mayfield, KY; pa/Exec Dir, Gov's Ofc of Vol Ser; cp/Exec Bd Ky Fed Wom's Clbs; VP Heritage Wom's Clb; Bd Dirs Assn Adm of Vol Sers; Chm St Govt U Way Campaign; Kellogg Foun Vol Ldrship Regional Coun; Task Force Intl Yr of the Child; r/Bapt; hon/W/W: Am Wom, Lib; Outstg Yng Wom Am 1966; Reg of Prom Ams 1972; World W/W Wom 1979; Cit Bur of Vol Sers 1978; Cit Ky Fed Wom's Clbs 1975; Cit Mar of Dimes 1968; Cit Am Cancer Soc 1967; Cit ABWA 1975; Cit U Fund Bd 1967; Pres Cit Ky Lib Assn 1972; Pres Cit SEn Lib Assn 1970.

JOHNSON, ODIE QUITMAN oc/General Superintendent; b/Aug 24, 1924; h/1102 6th Ave SE, Cullman, AL 35055; ba/Cullman; m/Faith Hendrix; c/John David, Fran Johnson Hammond; p/George Coggins (dec) and Etta Busby Johnson (dec); ed/Cont'g Col Credit Courses & Profl Sems; mil/USN WWII; pa/Gen Supt Cullman Elec Coop; Ala Rural Elec Fed Credit Union; Cullman Co Merit Bd, Chm; Assoc Basketball Ofcls; cp/Past Pres Cullman Lions Clb; Co Fair Bd of Dirs & Chm Public Relats; r/Meth; hon/Won Nat Thrift Hon Awd for AREFCU Success; 100% Pres Hon Awd, Lions Clb.

JOHNSON, OLIVETTE K oc/Extension Home Economist; b/Feb 14, 1926; m/Robert A; c/Pamela Michelle; p/James (dec) and Ethel Kuykendall (dec); ed/BS Jackson St Univ 1950; MS Univ So Miss 1978; pa/Ext Home Ec, Marion Co, Columbia, Miss; Miss Ext Home Ec Assn, Conv Chm; Nat Ext Home Ec Assn; Miss Home Ec Assn; Am Home Ec Assn; r/Bapt; hon/Miss Dist'd Ser Awd 1976; Miss Outstg Expanded Food & Nutrition Ed Awd 1976; Nat Assn Exec Home Ec Awd 1979; W/W Am Wom 1981-82.

JOHNSON, PATRICIA ANN oc/Editor, Public Relations; b/Dec 2, 1952; h/25 Adler Circle, Galveston, TX 77550; ba/Galveston; p/E E and Jean Cain Johnson, Galveston, TX; ed/BS Univ Mo 1975; pa/Ed "Star Bulletin" & "The Tower" for Am Nat Ins Co, Public Relats Dept 1975-; cp/Jr Leag of Galveston Co; Upper Deck Theatre, Chm Gov'g Bd 1976-77 & 79-80, Secy Gov'g Bd 1977-78 & 78-79, Public Relats Com Chm 1975; Galveston Co Unit, Am Cancer Soc 1977-79, Secy 1978-79; r/Presb; hon/Life Ins Advtrs Assn Awd for Excell of Publicity 1976; Blood Donor Progs Inc Pioneer Awd 1978, 79, 80; W/W S&SW 1980.

JOHNSON, PETER MICHAEL oc/Director of Operations Planning; b/Oct 21, 1945; h/332 Meadowbrook Dr NE, Atlanta, GA 30342; ba/College Park, GA; m/Vivian Langsdorf; p/Raymond Lawrence and Evelyn McGowan Johnson, Minneapolis, MS; ed/BS Univ Minn 1967; mil/AUS 1967-70; pa/Dir Opers Mgmt, Trg & Prod Intro Restaurant Grp, Del Taco Corp; Inst Food Technols; Am Assn Cereal Chemists; Nat Railway Hist Soc; cp/Dir Long-Range Plan'g Comm City of Crystal, Minn; Dir Envirl Comm; r/Luth; hon/W/W S&SW 1980; Articles for Profl Jours.

JOHNSON, REBECCA CORLEY oc/Corporate Secretary-Treasurer; b/Mar 8, 1929; h/3512 Lawson Rd, Aiken, SC 29801; ba/Aiken; m/Dan L Sr; c/Nancy J Ross, Dan L Jr; p/Oscar P Corley (dec); Irene C Gringrey, Trenton, SC; ed/BS Winthrop Col; pa/Corporate Secy-Treas; cp/Bd Dirs Aiken Co Mtl Retard Assn; Aiken Co Hosp Aux; r/St Paul's Luth Ch.

JOHNSON, RICHARD ALVIN oc/Engineering Management; b/July 8, 1934; h/Gulfport, MS; ba/ARAMCO, Box 5734, Dhahran, Saudi Arabia; m/Linda O; c/Richard, William, Terry; p/Elma B Ryan, Largo,

FL; ed/BS Mich St Univ 1963; pa/Supt, Prog Control Div, Arabian Am Oil Co 1977-; Johnson & Assocs 1976-77; VP & Prin, Amco Constr Co 1974-76; Dir Miss St Univ Res Ctr 1971-74; Res Coor, Prog Analysis Engr Gen Elec Co 1966-71, Mgr Engrg Sys Text ITT Fed Labs 1965-66; Sr Field Engr Gen Dynamics-Elecs 1959-65; hon/Author & Co-Author.

JOHNSON, ROBERT CLIFFORD oc/Retail Gasoline; b/July 18, 1908; h/906 W Ninth, Weslaco, TX 78596; ba/Weslaco; m/Madeline Martin; cp/Nathan Harris (dec) and Margret Ethel Caffey Johnson (dec); ed/Miss St Univ; pa/Mgr, Dist Engr, Dist Mgr Miss Power & Light Co 1929-45; Retail Hardware Firm 1945-48; Part Owner Wholesale Hardware Firm 1945-54; Var Positions Gas Firms: Billups Petro Co 1954-64, Ec Oil Co 1968-, Pres & Owner Cliff Johnson Petro Co 19544-; cp/Weslaco Rotary Clb, Pres 1961-62; Weslaco C of C, Pres 1963; Weslaco Lib Bd, Chm 1970; Hidalgo Co Lib Bd 1978-; Tex Oil Jobbers 1978-; r/Bapt; hon/W/W S&SW 1980-81; Weslaco Outstg Citizen Awd 1977.

JOHNSON, ROSA T oc/Insurance Agent; b/June 28, 1928; ba/Durham, NC; m/Charles B (dec); c/Lydia; p/Forest and Laura Townsend, Atlanta, GA; ed/Att'd Spelman Coll 1945-48; LUTU Tng 1975-76; Ga St Univ 1977-; pa/Ordinary Ins Agt, Pers & Grp, NC Mutual; ABWA: Past Publicity Chp, Prog Chp, Chp Enrollment Event 1979; pa/Bd Dirs Ralph C Robinson Boys Clb; r/Bapt; hon/Wom of Yr, Greensboro Chapt ABWA 1980-18; All Around Agt of Yr 1976, Runner-Up Agt 1977, Ordinary Agt 1979, Runner-Up Agt 1980; 1st of 3 Wom to Produce Over $2 Million for NC Mutual.

JOHNSON, RUBY E oc/Postmaster; b/Aug 15, 1929; h/Granite Quarry, NC; c/Constance, Joyce, Leander Jr, E Katrina; p/dec; ed/Bus Dip 1958; Assoc Deg Postal Mgmt CPCC 1978; pa/US Postal Ser; Nat Assn Postmasters; Nat Leag Postmasters; cp/Fed Wom's Clb; hon/Spec Achmt US Postal Ser, White Rock AM Zion Ch, Mt Lion Bapt Ch, JC Smith Univ.

JOHNSON, RUFUS WINFIELD oc/Attorney at Law; b/May 1, 1911; h/Rt 2 Box 220A Hogeye, Prairie Grove, AR 72753; ba/Same; m/Vaunda L; p/Charles L (dec) and Margaret Smith Johnson (dec); ed/AB 1934, Grad Study 1939 Howard Univ; mil/ROTC 2nd Lt; WWII, Korea, Ret'd Lt Col; pa/Pvt Pract of Law: Wash DC 1945-48, Calif 1952-77, Ark 1979-, Sem-Ret'd; Am Judicature Soc; Am Acad Polit & Social Sci; Judge Advocate Assn; cp/NAACP; ACLU; Masonic Lodge; r/Bapt; hon/Purple Heart; Bronze Star; CIB; Spec Regimental Cit for Bravery; Completing Personal Memoirs of Mil Expers & Cases Involving Law Pract.

JOHNSON, SAM D oc/Supreme Court Justice; b/Nov 17, 1920; h/1811 Exposition Blvd, Austin, TX 78703; ba/Austin; m/June Page; c/Page J Harris (Mrs Barney), Janet J Clements (Mrs Scott), Sam J; p/Sam D Sr and Flora Brown Johnson (dec); ed/BBA Baylor Univ 1946; LLB Univ Tex 1949; mil/AUS WW II; pa/Justice, Tex Supr Ct 1973-; Justice, 14th Ct Civil Appeals 1967-72; 1st Dir, Houston Legal Foun 1965-67; Dist Judge, 66th Judicial Dist 1959-65; Co Atty & Dist Atty, Hill Co, Tex 1953-59; Pvt Law Pract, Hillsboro, Tex 1949-53; Am Bar Assn: Coun Mem & Exec Com Judicial Adm Sect, Chm Appellate Judges Conf 1976-77, Others; St Bar Tex: Past Secy-Treas, Past Exec Com Mem & Past Chm Com on Legal Sers Judicial Sect; Travis Co Bar Assn; Houston Bar Assn; Hill Co Bar Assn (Past Pres); Ctl Tex Bar Assn (Past Pres); Nat Legal Aid & Defender Assn; Edit Bd, *The Judges' Jour* 1976-77; Am Judic Soc; Inst Judicial Adm; Nat Conf St Trial Judges; Lectr; cp/Phi Delta Chi; Bd Dirs, Presb Chd's Home & Ser Agy; Baylor Ex-Students Assn: Past Pres, Past Dist Dir; Initial Life Mem, Baylor Alumni Assn; Bd Dirs, U Urban Coun of Austin; r/Covenant Presb Ch: Elder; hon/Bronze Star; Purple Heart; 3 Battle Stars; Combat Infantryman's Badge; 1 of 3 Dist'd Alumni, Baylor Univ 1978; Hon Order of Coif, Univ Tex Law Sch 1977; Arthur von Briesen Awd, NLADA 1978; Fellow, Am Bar Foun; Others.

JOHNSON, SCOTT EDWIN oc/Retired School Principal; Educator; b/Oct 14, 1894; h/716 10th, PO Box 1400, Huntsville, TX 77340; ba/Huntsville; m/Ethel Mae Downs; c/Ethel Ruth Daniels, Saundra Daniels, Selma LaVerne (Granddaugh); p/Scott and Caroline Houston Johnston (dec); ed/BA, MA Hampton Inst; mil/Pfc, WW I; pa/Ret'd Sch Prin, Tchr; NEA; TSTA; Local Tchrs Assn; cp/32 Deg Mason; Day Care Ctr; Chld Wel; Credit Union; City Coun; Others; r/Bapt; hon/Plaques: City, St, Credit Union; Mayor for a Day, Co; Commun Ldrs & Noteworthy Ams; Book of Hon; Fellow Am Biogl Inst; Others.

JOHNSON, THOMAS KENNEDY SR oc/Free Will Baptist Minister; b/Feb 15, 1932; h/Rt 3 Box 520, DeQueen, AR 71832; ba/DeQueen; m/Ada Majorie Harris; c/Thomas Kennedy Jr, Timothy Clyde, Archie Eugene; p/Atlas Thomas and Iris Elizabeth Kennedy Johnson, Smithfield, NC; ed/BA Bob Jones Univ; Postgrad Study: Univ NC, Univ Ark; mil/NC NG 1949-50 Pvt-Sgt, 1953-54 M/Sgt; AUS 1950-52, 1954-56; pa/Migrant Ed Coor, DeQueen Public Schs 1979-; Missionary Pastor: Grace Free Will Bapt Ch 1975-, Friendship Free Will Bapt Ch, Wilmington, NC 1966-75,

Brookwood Free Will Bapt Ch, Fayetteville, NC 1960-62; Tchr-Coor, Coop Distbv Ed, John T Hoggard HS, Wilmington 1969-73; Pastor, Ahoskie Free Will Bapt Ch, Ahoskie, NC 1963-65; Revenue Collector, NC Dept Revenue 1963; Others; Past Mem, Chm & V-Chm Credentials Com, Little Mo River Assn FWB Ark; Little Mo Assn FWB Ark: Asst Moderator 1976-78, Moderator 1978-79; Past Asst Moderator, Coastal Assn FWB NC; Past Moderator, NEn Assn FWB NC; Past Pres, Cape Fear Min's Conf FWB; Nat Assn FWB; Ark Assn FWB; Little River Assn FWB; r/Free Will Bapt; hon/Korean Ser Medal w 3 Bronze Stars; UN Ser Medal; Good Conduct Medal.

JOHNSON, W R SR oc/Minister; b/Mar 4, 1908; h/426 N College St, Covington, TN 38019; ba/Covington; m/Mabel Elain; c/William R Jr, Raymond (dec), Robert M, Herman A, Harold C, Allen C, Bernard Coutroulis; p/Jonas and Perla Mae Johnson (dec); ed/BS Fla A&M Univ 1942; pa/Pastor, Collins Chapel Christian Meth Epis Ch; Former Pastorates (Fla): Quincy, Mt Pleasant, Marianna, Tallahassee, Campbellton, Clearwater, Bradenton, Florence Villa, St Petersburg, Ocala; Pastor & Tchr 11 yrs; Past Pres, Covington Min Alliance; Past Ruling Elder, Jacksonville Dist, Ocala; cp/Co-Orgr, CIO Fruit Pickers Union, Florence Villa, Fla; Florence Villa Civic Coun; Past Commr, BSA; Pinellas Co Dem Com; Citizens Adv Coun, Co Bd Public Instrn; r/Meth; hon/Commun Ldrs & Noteworthy Ams; Book of Hon; Fellow Am Biogl Inst.

JOHNSON, WALTER THANIEL JR oc/Attorney; b/May 18, 1940; h/Greensboro, NC; ba/831 W Morgan St, Raleigh, NC 27603; m/Yvonne Jeffries; c/Walter Thaniel III, Vernon Kennedy, Lisa Yvonne, Shannon Tamara; p/Walter Thaniel Sr and Gertrude Alexander Johnson, Greensboro, NC; ed/BS A&T St Univ 1961; JD Duke Univ Law Sch 1964; pa/Chm NC Parole Comm; Formerly Sr Ptnr Frye, Johnson & Barbee; NC Bar Assn; Former Mem NC Bd Govs, Greensboro Bar Assn; cp/Chm G'boro Bd of Ed; Bd Dirs G'boro C of C; VP for Plan'g, G'boro U Way; r/Providence Bapt Ch: Bd Trustees; hon/1 of 5 Outstg Yng Men NC 1971.

JOHNSTON, ADA CLARA oc/Teacher, Coordinator; b/Mar 16, 1944; h/1005 Sixth Ave, Marianna, FL 32446; ba/Marianna; m/Heyward Lynn; c/Ted, Cynthia, Fred; p/Joe Dee and Lyndal Hicks, Ponce de Leon, FL; ed/BS Bus Ed; MEd Voc Adm; pa/Tchr Chipola Jr Col; Fla Assn Mktg & Distb Ed Tchrs, Pres 1979-80, VP 1977-78; Bd Advrs Jr Col Div DECA, Chm 1979-80; Exec Bd Fla Voc Assn; Fla Coun Mktg & Distb Ed; St Adv Com Mktg & Distb Ed; Task Force for Jr Col DECA; Chipola Jr Col DECA Advr; In-Ser Ed Com, Secy 1979-80; Coun Chipola Edrs 1979-81; Disciplinary Bd, Secy 1978-80; Bd Student Pubs; Chipola Fac Assn 1978-; Fla Assn Commun Cols; Jackson Co Tchrs Credit Union; cp/PTO Marianna Middle Sch; Lady of Elks; r/First Bapt Ch SS Tchr; hon/Vernon HS Tchr of Yr 1974; Nom to Outstg Yng Wom of Am 1977, 78, 79.

JOHNSTON, BETTY JO oc/Bookkeeper, Secretary; b/Feb 9, 1930; h/Rt 3, Box 41, Robstwon, TX 78380; ba/Same; m/Alton P; c/Linda Lee Jonas, Jerry B, John W, Kay Lynn, Lou Ann, Jeffrey P; p/W Bailey and Era S Cooper, Macon, MS; ba/NFSA; Dir Assoc'd Tel Directory Pubrs Inc; cp/Chm Local Chapt 99s; r/Bapt.

JOHNSTON, JAMES E oc/Construction Supervisor; b/Jan 21, 1947; h/310 Loruna St, Gulf Breeze, FL 32561; ba/Pensacola; m/Sandra E; c/Heather, Rudy, Ashley, Amber; ed/Grad Macon Acad; mil/USAF; pa/Supvr Constr, So Bell Telephone Co; cp/Past Pres Gulf Breeze Sports Assn; Pres Gulf Breeze JCs 1980-81; Coach Little Leag Baseball/Softball; Gulf Breeze Vol Fire Dept.

JOHNSTON, JAMES FRANKLIN oc/Teacher; b/Nov 12, 1937; h/617 Forrest Ave, Griffin, GA 30223; ba/Griffin; m/Sally Ruark; c/Mary Carol, Elizabeth Alice; p/Arthur and Fannie Alice Johnston, Albany, GA; ed/MEd; mil/Ga ANG 1960-66; pa/Tchr French & Humanities, Yrbook Advr, Griffin HS; Past Pres Griffin Spalding Assn Edrs; GAE; NEA; cp/Mus Dir Firt Bapt Ch, Hampton; r/Bapt; hon/John Hay Fellow 1965.

JOHNSTON, RICKY E oc/Pastor; b/Jan 25, 1952; h/PO Box 514, Aberdeen, MS 39730; m/Jo Nell Grubbs; c/Jennifer Elise, Carrie Danielle; p/George W and Mavis Elaine Wallace Johnston, McComb, MS; ed/AA SW Miss Jr Col 1973; BS Univ So Miss 1975; MDiv New Orleans Bapt Theol Sem 1977; pa/Pastor Southside Bapt Ch; VP Franklin Co Bapt Pastors Conf; Mem Num Coms Pike Bapt Assn, Franklin Bapt Assn, Lincoln Bapt Assn, Monroe Bapt Assn; r/So Bapt; hon/Outstg Yng Men Am 1979.

JONES, ANNIE GAY oc/Teacher; b/Mar 11, 1919; h/PO Box 264, Rochelle, GA 31079; m/dec; c/Charles K Taylor; p/George Gray Sr, Rochelle, GA; Della M Gay (dec); ed/BS Fort Valle St Col; MEd Tuckegee Inst; pa/SS Tchr; GAE; NEA; AAUW; cp/GAE PACE; NEA PAC; Nat Assn Smithsonian Inst; Assn Matron Fairfield OES: Hon Mem Boys Town; Ga Sheriff Assn; r/Bapt: Adult SS Tchr; hon/Tchr of Yr 1970; Val Forge

Tchrs Medal Awd 1976; Compiled Activ Book Won for Rochell Elem Sch Val Forge Hon Cert 1976.

JONES, ANNIE RUTH oc/Professor; b/Sept 23, 1943; h/1803 Vine Ave, Demopolis, AL 36732; ba/Marion, AL; m/Jerry Allen; c/Jessica Leah; p/Thomas C and Addie Rivers Morgan, Sweet Water, AL; ed/BS; MEd; PhD; pa/Prof, Chp Div Ed, Judson Col; Am Assn Col for Tchr Ed; Ala Assn Col for Tchr Ed; So Assn Col & Schs; Ala Comm on Elem Ed; cp/AAUW; Pilot Clb; BPW; Tyrolean Clb; r/Bapt; hon/Kappa Delta Pi; Honors Day Fac Recog at Univ of Ala 1976.

JONES, BEATRICE GIROUX oc/Real Estate Broker; Civic Worker; Artist; b/Oct 27, 1912; h/Rt 1, Box 81, Penrose, NC 28766; 2780 Punta Gorda, FL 33950; m/G Russell; c/Gary W Jenkins, Tamara Jenkins Edge; p/Benjamin William Giroux (dec); Gertrude Montreuil, Pembroke Pines, FL; ed/Manatee Jr Col; Edison Commun Col; pa/Reg'd Real Est Broker, Own Bus; Charter Mem Englewood Bd Realtors; Sarasota Co, Fla Lot Clearing Bd; Secy-Treas Gtr Charlotte Co, Fla Indust & Aviation Comm; Ret'd 1970; cp/Num Art Assns; Charlotte Co Meml Auditorium Inc: Org'g Mem, 1/Pres; Area Chm: Heart Fund 2 Yrs, Cancer Crusade 1 Yr; Fla BPW Leg Chm 2 Terms; Englewood C of C: Mem, Chm Indust Comm; Englewood BPW Clb: Pres, Charter Mem, Treas; Sarasota Co, Fla Farm Bur Woms Comm: Orgr, Chm; Secy & Dir Sch Dist #6 Arcadia Twp, Attica, Mich, Lapeer, Mich; Lapeer Co, Mich Fed'd Woms Clbs: Secy, VP; Chm Lapeer Co, Mich Farm Bur Woms Comm; Home Ext Ldr; 4H Clb Ldr; Precnt #9 Repub Com-wom; Pres Englewood Repub Clb; Orgr, Pres Englewood Repub Woms Clb; Corresp Secy, Sarasota Co, Fla Repub Exec Bd; hon/Num Art Awds in Juried Shows; Paintings Rep'd in Pvt Collections; Wom of Yr, Englewood, Fla 1968; IPA; Commun Ldrs & Noteworthy Ams; Am Biogl Inst Res Assn.

JONES, BETTY VIRGINIA BOOKER oc/Nurse; b/Nov 23, 1941; h/979 Pelham St NW, Atlanta, GA 30318; m/Charles L Jr; c/Nefertiti II; p/George II (dec) and Virginia Booker, Atlanta, GA; ed/LPN Atlanta Area Tech Sch 1968; Att'g DeKalb Commun Col; pa/LPN Grady Meml Hosp; Student Nsg Assn; cp/PTA Pres; NAACP; PTSA; LPN Assn; r/Bapt.

JONES, BETTYE G oc/Receptionist; b/Mar 17, 1937; h/101 W Russell Dr, Enterprise, AL 36330; m/Wallace O; c/Roxanne, Jeffery, Rusty; p/Daniel S Green, Chancellor, AL; ed/Cosmetology 1964; pa/Cosmetologist; Receptionist; r/So Bapt.

JONES, CHRISTINE ANN HATCH oc/Nurse, Assistant Professor; b/Feb 13, 1944; h/7227 N Mesa #304, El Paso, TX 79912; ba/El Paso; p/Lewis Fredric Hatch, Saudi Arabia; Mildred Norseth Hatch, Austin, TX; ed/BSN Univ Tex-Austin 1965; MSN Univ Tex Sys Sch of Nsg 1976; pa/Asst Prof Col of Nsg, Univ Tex El Paso; Instr Cont'g Ed, Univ Tex-El Paso Col of Nsg 1976-77; Asst Dir Nsg Ser, Dir Ed & Staff Devel, Matagorda Gen Hsop 1973-75; Spec Lectr Tex Wom's Univ 1974-75; Clin Instr Alvin Jr Col 1973; St Joseph Hosp; Instr 3-Week Intensive & Coronary Care Course for RN's 1971-73; ANA; Cont'g Ed Coun ANA; Am Assn Critical Care Nurses; Tex Hsop Assn; Am Heart Assn; cp/Univ Tex Alumnae Assn; Chi Omega Alumnae Assn; Wn Hills U Meth Ch Chancel Choir; r/Meth; hon/Sigma Theta Tau; Cert'd Critical-Care RN II; Cert of Achmt, Am Heart Assn 1972 & 73; W/W Am Wom 1979-80; Author "A Kidney Donor: Providing Life After Death" & 'The Concept of Critical Care Nursing."

JONES, CLARENCE EUGENE II oc/Assistant Superintendent; b/Aug 18, 1945; h/2852 Neeses Rd NW, Orangeburg, SC 29115; ba/Holly Hill, Sc; m/Joyce A Tyler; c/Kelvin Clarence III; p/Clarence E Sr and Georgia Anna Jones, Bowman, SC; ed/MA; MEd; mil/Staff Sgt; pa/Asst Supt Orangeburg Sch Dist #3; Phi Delta Kappa; NEA; SCEA; APGA; NASA; O/C/BAA; cp/Yng Repub; r/Meth; hon/cum laude Undergrad; ACM 1st Oak Leaf Cluster; Decorated for Valor 2 Purple Hearts; ACM w/v Device; Bronze Star; Good Conduct; Expert Rifleman's Badge; Vietnam Ser Medal; Airborne Badge.

JONES, DONALD REGINALD oc/Attorney at Law; b/Nov 7, 1952; h/Box 436, Liberty, MS 38645; ba/Liberty; m/Gay Lee; c/Reg; p/R C and Della Jones, Liberty, MS; ed/AA SW Jr Col; BA Millsaps; JD Univ Miss Law Sch; pa/Atty Town of Liberty; Amite Chm for Law Day 1979; cp/Bd Trustees SW Jr Col; Bd Dirs Liberty JCs; BD Dirs C of C; r/Meth.

JONES, DOROTHY DIX oc/Bank Teller; b/Dec 3, 1939; h/Rt 6 Box 266, Meridian, MS 39301; ba/Meridian; m/J L; c/Doris Elaine, Emily Joyce, Gregory, Irish Denise; p/Julius and Ora L Fox, Meridian, MS; ed/Certs in Fin; pa/OES Victory Chapt #652; Secy; Fin Secy; cp/Lauderdale Co Dem Com; r/Bapt; hon/Credit Mgr of Yr 1974; Credit Mgr Merit Awd 1973, 74, 75, 76, 77; Banker of Month, June 1979.

JONES, ED oc/Congressman; b/Apr 20, 1912; h/PO Box 128,

Yorkville, TN 38389; ba/Wash DC; m/Llewellyn Wyatt; c/Mary Llew Jones McGuire (dec), Jennifer Jones Kinnard; ed/BS Univ Tenn 1934; Att'd Univ Wis 1944, Univ Mo 1945; pa/Tenn Dept Agric 1934-41; Inspector Tenn Dairy Prods Assn 1941-43; Agric Agt, Ill Ctrl RR 1943-49, 1952-69; Tenn Commr Agric 1949-52; Chm Tenn Agric Stabilization Conserv Com 1952-69; Dir Nat Telephone Coop Assn 1965; cp/Congressman 1969-; Chm Agric Subcom on Conserv & Credit; Mem Subcom on Livestock & Grains; Ranking Dem, Subcom on Cotton; Chm Subcom on House Sers; Com on House Adm; Pres Memphis Agric Clb; VP Am Dairy Assn of Tenn; Co-Fdr, Pres W Tenn Artificial Breeding Assn; Mem Bd & VP Dyersburg Prod Credit Assn; Bd Dirs, Mid-S Fair; Pres Y'ville Telephone Coop; Assoc Farm Dir, Radio Sta WMC, Memphis; Pres Am Railway Devel Assn; Gibson Co Bd of Ed; Nat Cotton Adv Com; Bd Mem Nat Telephone Coop Assn; Chm Bd of Trustees Bethel Col; r/Presb; Elder; hon/Progressive Farmer's Man of Yr 1951; Memphis Agric Clb's Man of Yr 1957; Hon DLitt, Bethel Col 1963; Univ Tenn Dairy Clb's Dist'd Dairy Ser Awd 1966; Am RR Devel Assn Dist'd Public Ser Awd 1970; FFA Dist'd Nat Ldrship Awd 1970; Univ Tenn Block & Bridle Clb Awd 1972; 4-H Alumni Awd 1973; Md Egg Coun's Friend of Yr 1974; Presented U Egg Prodrs Awd for Sponsoring Leg Vital to Egg Indust 1975; Nat Telephone Coop Assn Ldrship Ser Awd 1978.

JONES, ELSIE WILLIAMS oc/Teacher, Supervisor; b/Oct 4, 1896; ba/College Station, Box 849, Berea, KY 40403; m/H Clyde; c/Russel Clyde, Robert Lee; p/Nathan Bradley (dec) and Dovie Baker Williams (dec); ed/Audited Col Art Classes 1962-66; pa/Tchr Rural Sch 3 Yrs; Supvr Berea Col Candy Kitchen 31 yrs; cp/DAR, Past Regent; Ky Col; Wom's Clb; White Shrine; OES, Worthy Matron; Berea Gdn Clb; Berea Col Pres's Clb; Pres Kiwanis Clb; r/Berea Union Ch; hon/Spec Merit Awd, Berea Col, for 31 Yrs Ser; Author Hist of Berea Col Candy Kitchen.

JONES, ERNEST LEE oc/Minister, Artist, Educator; b/May 10, 1931; h/1015 Elkin St, Norfolk, VA 23523; m/Paulette L; c/Dawn, Mary, Mia; p/Lee (dec) and Mary A Jones (dec); ed/BA Johnson C Smith Univ; Cert Va Union Univ 1979; Nationwide Tech Inst 1973; Famous Artist Sch 1967; Oakatree Art Sch 1961; pa/Shaklee; cp/VISTA Commun Orgr; Inter City Social Prob; U Christian Front for Brotherhood; r/Bapt; hon/Mid City Art Show Hon Mention 1977; Father of Yr.

JONES, EVELYN LEE oc/Registrar; b/July 29, 1926; h/Rt 3 Box 45, Dawson, GA 31742; ba/Americus, GA; m/Robert P; c/Elaine J Fowler, Paula J Blankenship, Donna J Morgan; p/Howard L and Elline Bruner Lee, Dawson, GA; ed/BS Ed 1974; MEd 1976; pa/Registrar Ga SWn Col; Ga Assn Adm Ofcrs & Registrars; Phi Delta Kappa; So Ann Adm Ofcrs & Registrars; cp/Dawson BPW Clb; Dem Party; r/Meth; hon/W/W Am Wom 1978-79, 1979-80.

JONES, H CLYDE oc/Bakery Executive; b/Oct 13, 1894; ba/Berea, KY; m/Elsie E Williams; c/Russel Clyde, Robert Lee; p/Charles Emerson (dec) and Lela Bell Bowman Jones (dec); ed/Att'd Berea Col Acad 1913-16; Grad Am Inst Baking 1926; mil/USN 1917-19 Baker; pa/B F Goodrich Tire & Rubber Co 1920; Supt Berea Col Bakery 1921-Retirement: Devel'd Berea Col Bakery & Candy Kitchen (Mgr 42 Yrs); Am Soc Bakery Engrs; cp/C of C; Am Legion; Mason; Shriner; OES, Past Worthy Patron; Kiwanis, Past Lt Gov; So Madison 4-H Coun 17 Yrs; Trustee & Bus Mgr, Ch of Christ Union, Treas 7 Yrs; r/Meth; hon/Spec Merit Awd, Berea Col Alumni; Ky Col; 39 Yr Perfect Attendance, Kiwanis; World W/W Commerce & Indust; W/W S&SW.

JONES, HARRY EDWARD oc/Minister, Professor; b/Sept 18, 1926; h/3744 Sunset Ave, Rocky Mount, NC 27801; m/Mable M; c/Gwendolyn, Harriett; p/Harry George and Elizabeth Jones; ed/BRE; ThM; mil/USN 6 Yrs; pa/Pastor Great Branch Evangelical Bapt Ch; Prof William Carter Col; cp/NC St Ofcr Woodmen of World; r/Bapt; Dir Christian Ed; hon/Carter Col Trustee of Yr 1978.

JONES, HERB oc/Artist; b/Mar 25, 1923; h/238 Beck St, Norfolk, VA 23603; ba/Same; m/Barbara D; c/Robert Clair, Louis Herbert; p/Leon Herbert Jones, Norfolk, VA; Edna May Jones (dec); ed/Att'd William & Mary Col 1942-44; pa/Free-Lance Artist; Paint Maker; IBA; Nat Soc Arts & Lit; cp/Bd Intl Kidney Foun; r/Meth; hon/Over 200 Awds & Hons 1962-; Subject of Articles in Num Jours.

JONES, HUTTON REESE oc/Retired Technician; b/July 3, 1914; h/1497 W Crestwood Dr, Memphis, TN 38117; m/Margaret C; p/Jon (dec) and Lou Jones (dec); mil/AUS WWII; pa/Ret'd Tech; r/Bapt.

JONES, JANET HAIR oc/Evening Supervisor; b/Mar 2, 1957; h/Jackson, TN; ba/Jackson-Madison Co Gen Hosp, Med Records Dept, 708 W Forest, Jackson, TN 38301; m/Alan L; c/Christopher Alan; p/Sam H and Margaret S Hair, Adamsville, TN; ed/BS Lambuth Col 1979; BS UTCHS 1980; pa/RRA Supvr, Quality Assurance Coor, Jackson-Madison Co Gen Hosp; W Tenn Med Records Assn; Memphis Med Record Assn;

Tenn Med Record Assn; Am Med Record Assn; r/Meth; hon/Dean's List 1980; Sigma Phi Omega Little Sister 1979.

JONES, JESSIE MAE oc/Teacher; b/Aug 3, 1929; h/1604 Chase St, Rocky Mount, NC 27801; p/Lela B Goffney, Rocky Mount, NC; ed/BS Shaw Univ 1951; MS Penn St Univ 1959; Att'd: Union Col, Brooklyn Col, Holy Cross Col, Ctrl Wash St Univ, Ohio Wesleyan Univ, Unit Dayton, UCLA; Univ Calif-Berkeley, Fla Technol Univ, E Carolina Univ, Univ Wyo, NC St Univ; pa/Tchr Chem & Phys, Beddingfield HS 1978-; Sci & Math Tchr Elm City Grade Schs 1962-78; Sci & Math Tchr McIver HS 1951-62; NC Sci Tchrs Assn; NC Acad Sci; Nat Sci Tchrs Assn; NCAE; NEA; En NC Sci Tchrs Resource Coop; AAAS; NC Tchr Ctr for Sci & Maths; cp/Rocky Mount Energy Adv Bd; Tri-Co Industs for the Handicapped; Dem Wom Edgecombe Co; NC Dem Wom; Nat Dem Com; Human Relats Comm; Precinct Com Mem Edgecombe Co; Delta Sigma Theta; Wilson-Rocky Mount-Tarboro Chapt Links Inc; AAUW; NC Wom's Equity Action Leag; Rocky Mount Br NAACP; NC Black Wom's Polit Caucus; r/Bapt; hon/Austin D Bond Awd for Dist'd Ser to Sci Ed, ECU 1978; Past WEST Assocs Energy Tour 1978; Gen Elec Sci Fellow 1953; Pi Lambda Theta 1959; NC Sci Tchr Awd for Dist'd Sert to Sci Ed 1980; Contbns to NC Sci Tchrs Assn Jour.

JONES, JOHN D oc/Data Control I/O Clerk; b/Aug 16, 1961; h/Rt 5 Box 111, Midland, TX; p/R D Jr and Darlene Livingston Jones, Midland, TX; ed/Att'd W Tex St Univ 1979-81; pa/Data Control I/O Clerk, Eagle Computing Corp; cp/4-H Coun Mem 1970-79; FFA 1976-80: Local Reporter & Pres, Dist VP; hon/St Farmer Deg 1979; Am Farmer Deg 1980.

JONES, JOHNNYE MAE oc/Assistant Professor; b/Apr 3, 1943; h/803 Honeysuckle St, Henderson, TX 75652; ba/Hampton, TX; p/Roy (dec) and Lovie B Jones, Henderson, TX; ed/BS; MA: PhD; pa/Asst Prof Biol, Hampton Inst; Beta Kappa Chi; Nat Inst Sci; Mycological Soc Am; Botanical Soc Am; cp/Alpha Kappa Alpha; r/Bapt; hon/MARC Fac Fellow 1974-79; Res Assoc Brookhaven Nat Lab 1979; NSF Grantee 1969-70.

JONES, LORA LEE oc/Nurse; b/Aug 24, 1942; h/410 S 11th Ave, Madill, OK 73446; ba/Kingston, OK; m/David Duke; c/Gregory David, Kimberly Ann, Amy Lee; p/Marion Dodd (dec) and Lora B Clark Sims, Jasper, AL; ed/Assoc Deg Nsg; pa/Sch Nurse; Am Sch Hlth Assn; Okla Public Hlth Assn; CPR Instr; Am Heart Assn; PTA; cp/All Sports Booster Clb, Secy-Treas 1977-79; Wildcat Teen Town, Pres 1977-79; OES; r/Meth; hon/W/W Am Wom.

JONES, MAGGIE O'NEAL oc/Teacher; b/Apr 11, 1901; h/14 Boatner Ave, Cartersville, GA 30120; m/Saxon (dec); c/John Paul; p/William Newton (dec) and Mary Anna Caldwell O'Neal; ed/BS Univ Ga; pa/Ga Ret'd Tchrs Assn; Cartersville-Bartow Ret'd Tchrs Assn; cp/AARP; r/Bapt; hon/Phi Kappa Phi.

JONES, MARGARET O oc/Travel Consultant; b/July 28, 1942; h/2503½ Thomas Ave, Dallas, TX 75201; ba/Dallas; p/Robert Lee (dec) and Bessie Lee Oliver, Longview, TX; ed/Grad Viking Intl Sch Travel; mil/USNR; pa/Pacific Area Travel Assn; Nat Assn Female Execs; Navy Leag Dallas; Urban Leag; Discover Tex Assn; cp/Vol Dallas Taping for the Blind; r/Bapt; hon/W/W Am Wom.

JONES, MARY WHITLEY oc/Retired Teacher; b/Dec 22, 1904; h/Granite Falls, NC; m/Melvin Hayes; c/Herbert Whitley; p/Herbert Lafayette (dec) and Jessie Patton Whitley (dec); ed/BS Appalachian Univ; pa/Ret'd Primary Tchr; cp/Life Mem Granite Falls Garden Clb; r/Meth; hon/Granite Falls Wom of Yr 1964; Ruth Landolin Prog Awd 1975; Fireman's Sweetheart Awd 1974-80.

JONES, MICHAEL D oc/Evangelist; b/Jan 14, 1947; h/7128 Sweetbriar Ct, Ft Worth, TX 76180; m/Mary E; c/Jennifer, Michael II, Russell Keith; p/Lonnie R and Iris Ione Jones, Dallas, TX; ed/BA E Tex Bapt Col 1965; Grad Work SWn Bapt Theol Sem; pa/Gospel Singer & Preacher, So Bapt Conv; Mus & Yth Dir, Chs in Tex & Tenn 1965-72; Pastor 1973-77; Led Soda Lake Assn in Baptisms 1976; r/First Bapt Ch of Eules, Tex; hon/Record'n Rainbow Recording Studio.

JONES, MILDRED ERWIN McDOWELL oc/Civic Worker; b/Oct 12, 1905; h/Rt 10 Box 592, Lenoir, NC 28645; m/David J Jarrett Jr (dec); 2nd Eugene Patterson (dec); p/Frank Craige (dec) and Ella Lee Jones McDowell (dec); cp/Helped Launch Campaign to Restore Hist Ft Defiance; Ft Defiance Inc: 1st Chm Bd dirs, Fdr, Orgr, Promoter, Charter Mem, Life Mem Bd Trustees; Guest Panelist "Generations: 6 Decades of Transition in Caldwell Co" at Caldwell Commun Col; 1st Pres Blackstone Homemkrs Clb, Riverside, Yadkin Val 1945; Chapt Chaplain & Dist II Histn, Ninian Beall Chapt DAR; NC Preserv of Antiques; Nt Trust for Hist Preserv; Caldwell Co Hist Soc, Past Pres; Contbr Column "Happy Valley Views" to

Granite Falls Press; Part in Bicent Pageant; Contbr Hist Info to Lenoir HS Mag *Sweet Bess*; r/Epis: Publicity Chm Epis Ch-wom; hon/Lttr of Commend for Fund Raising Efforts, Bob Wright, NBC News Corresp 1965; Awd from Gov Hunt for Restoration Efforts 1979; Ruth Cannon Cup; Colonial-Era Pistol for Great-Great Grandfather Maj Joseph McDowell for Patriotic Sers During Rev War at King's Mtn; Hon Mem NC Sheriffs Assn; Hon Col, Over Mtn Vic Trail Assn; Key to City of Lenoir; Key to Ft Defiance; Grand Marshall of Patterson Sch Homecoming Parade 1980; Awd of Merit, Am Assn St & Local Hist; Hon'd w Dinner & Dance, Ofcrs & Trustees of Ft Defiance Inc.

JONES, MILDRED JOSEPHINE oc/Real Estate Broker; b/Jan 29, 1927; h/3024 Biltmore Ave, Montgomery, AL 36109; ba/Montgomery; p/Howard M (dec) and Gladys Eulala Carr Jones, Montgomery, AL; pa/Nat Assn Rltrs; Farm & Land Inst; Montgomery Bd Rltrs; cp/Point Aquarius Country Clb; Nat Adv Bd Am Christian Col; r/Trinity Presb Ch; hon/Recip Num Sales Awds for Top Salesperson, Which Resulted in Being Appt'd to Pres Adv Com Field Enterprises Ednl Corp.

JONES, MILDRED LUCILLE SINGLETON oc/Administrative Assistant; b/Jan 8, 1927; h/9909 El Mada Ln, Dallas, TX 75220; ba/Dallas; m/Bobby H; c/Randall Harrison, Gerald Wayne; p/Arthur Frank (dec) and Media Jordan Singleton (dec); pa/Adm Asst Mtl Hlth Clin; Mtl Hlth Assn; U Way Spkrs Bur; Conslt on Psych, Clin Adm Procedures; cp/Cub Scout Ldr; PTA Ofcr; Jr H SS Tchr; r/Bapt; hon/W/W Am Wom.

JONES, MIRIAM ESTHER CRISLER oc/Director of Central Service Department, Nurse, Enterostomal Therapist; b/Nov 10, 1923; h/136 Miller Dr,SE, Winter Haven, FL 33880; ba/Winter Haven, FL; p/Thomas Russell and Mary Olga Crisler, Rushsylvania, OH; ed/Cert'd OR Tech 1971; AD Nsg Polk Commun Col 1974; Emory Univ 1976; pa/Dir Ctrl Ser Dept, Enterostomal Therapist Winter Haven Hosp; Intl Assn Hosp Ctrl Ser Mgmt, Recording Secy 1975; Intl Assn Enterostomal Therapists; Advr to Winter Haven Ostomy Clb; cp/Dem Party; r/Indep Christian Ch; hon/Hon Grad Polk Commun Col 1974.

JONES, NANCY ANN oc/Extension Agent; b/Jan 3, 1944; h/606 Ch, Providence, KY 42450; ba/Dixon; m/Virgil W; c/Brian Keith, Anita Marie; p/Frank Urey (dec) and Marie Elizabeth Blackburn Young, Princeton, KY; ed/BS 1966, MS 1970 Murray St Univ; pa/Voc Home Ec Tchr, Carlisle Co HS 1966-67; Home Living Tchr, Outwood Hosp & Sch 1968-73; Webster Co Ext Agt for Home Ec 1974-; Am Assn Mtl Deficiency; Am Home Ec Assn; Nat Assn Ext Home Ecs; cp/Dixon BPW Clb, Pres 1978-80; r/Bapt; hon/Epsilon Sigma Phi.

JONES, NANCY OWINGS oc/Manager; b/July 4, 1934; h/Greenville, NC; ba/510-A Greene St, PO Box 1190, Greenville, NC 27834; m/Robert W; c/Susan S Fletcher, Charissa S Peterson; p/Addison D Sr and Elizabeth S Owings, Terry, MS; ed/BS Miss Wom's Univ 1955; Further Study So St Col 1972; pa/Ansherphone: Mgr Greenville Ofc 1979-, Secy-Customer Relats Rep 1978-79; Exec Secy Telephone Communs Inc 1977-78; Nat Mktg Inc: Mktg Spec 1976, Ofc Mgr 1974-76; Ofc Mgr El Dorado Answerfone 1973-74; Union Meml Hosp: Pers Dir 1968-73, Adm Secy 1963-68; Stenographer & Secy, Lion Oil Co 1955-63; r/Repub Party; r/Luth; hon/HS Salutatorian 1952.

JONES, NEAL THOMAS (BUDDY) oc/District Attorney; b/Oct 20, 1950; h/Rt 3 Box 3, Hillsboro, TX 76645; ba/Hillsboro; m/Theresa Oden; p/Neal T and Betty Adams Jones, Falls Ch, VA; ed/BA Baylor Univ 1974; JD Baylor Law Sch 1975; pa/Dist Atty 66th Jud Dist; Pres Hill Co Bar Assn; St Bar of Tex; cp/Secy Hill Co Dems; Bd Dirs Hillsboro C of C; r/Bapt; hon/W/W; Editor Baylor Law Review.

JONES, NICHOLAS oc/Retired Teacher; b/Nov 14, 1915; h/326 Catalpa Ave, Hampton, VA 23661; m/Etta Mae; p/Lee and Pattie Jones, Spring Hope, NC; ed/BS Fayetteville St Tchrs Col; Att'd Va St Col, Col William & Mary, Old Dominion Univ; mil/AUS; pa/Ret'd Tchr, Coach, Ath Dir; Newport News Ed Assn; NEA; VEA; r/Bapt.

JONES, PAUL O oc/Sales Manager; b/Nov 4, 1935; h/Rt 4 Box 14, Alexander City, AL 35010; ba/Opelika, AL; m/Romonia K; c/Sharon, Dale, Roderick; p/Homer (dec) and Mary Sue Jones, Alexander City, AL: ed/Mgr Course, Auburn Univ; mil/USNNG; pa/Wn Dist Sales Mgr, Meadow Gold; cp/Alexander City C of C; Tallapoosa Co Bd Ed; r/Bapt; hon/Big Cheese Awd 1973; Outstg Achmt Awd 1979; Pres Hon Clb 1977.

JONES, REBA A oc/Retired Bookkeeper; b/Apr 14, 1912; h/Rt 1 Box 210B, Dunn, NC 28334; m/Furney (dec); p/Eddie (dec) and Vida Naylor Aman (dec); cp/Mingo Home Demo Clb & Grange; r/So Bapt; hon/1st Pl Winner Nat Grange Sewing Contest Cat A.

JONES, ROBERT FRANKLIN oc/Manager, Engineering; b/Feb 21, 1940; h/Rt 2 Box 485, Seneca, SC 29678; ba/Clemson; m/Nancy Norbeck;

c/Catherine, Douglas; p/John Wilson Jones; Lula Whitehurst; ed/BSME NC St Univ 1962; Att'd Kent St Univ 1966-67; mil/AUS Lt; pa/Mgr Engrg TRW; Mfg Engr Westinghouse Elect; Mgr Plant Engr, Browning Mfg Div, Emerson Elect; Proj Engr, Fiber Industs Inc; ASM, Exec Bd Old S Chapt; SME; cp/Toastmasters, Foothills Chapt; Bayshore Assn, Treas; r/Presb.

JONES, RUBY WILLIAMSON oc/Salary Administrator; b/May 1, 1932; h/1912 Carlton Ave, Greensboro, NC 27406; ba/Greensboro; m/W I; c/Walton Jr, Michael L, John Eric; p/James E (dec) and Bertha Williamson (dec); ed/BS 1954, MS 1980 NC A&T Univ; pa/NC A&T Univ: Dir Contracts & Grants, Asst Dir Learning Asst Ctr, Salary Admr; Nat Coun Univ Res Admrs, Mbrship Com; Nat Fed BPW Clbs, NC St Pres; cp/Guilford Co Info & Referral Coun Mem; 1st VP Dem Wom of NC; Vol Action Coun; r/Bapt; hon/HS Valedictorian 1950; Grad summa cum laude NC A&T Univ; Cert of Merit Coop Ed Prog.

JONES, SARAH LILLIAN oc/Homemaker; b/Sept 5, 1917; h/1080 Fairway Dr, Waynesboro, VA; m/Malcolm G; c/Elizabeth Matthews Morgan, Mary Matthews Reed; p/James Thomas (dec) and Daisy Tribbett Maupin (dec); ed/Assoc Deg Mary Baldwin Col 1937; pa/Alumnae Secy, Mary Baldwin Col 1961-62; PEO; cp/Trustee Waynesboro Commun Hosp, Trustee Devel Com Chm; Hon Bd Mem W'boro YMCA, Corp & Endowment Chm; r/Presb: Elder; hon/Thanks Badge, GSA 1951.

JONES, THOMAS M JR oc/Assistant Professor; b/Oct 7, 1938; h/Elizabeth City, NC; ba/Elizabeth City St Univ, Park View Dr, Elizabeth City, NC 27909; m/Maxine; c/Gregory; p/Thomas M Jones Sr, Detroit, MI; ed/BS Ft Valley St Col 1959; MS 1976, PhD 1980 NC St Univ; MEd Ind Univ 1968; pa/Instr Ed & Psychol, Fayetteville Univ; Instr Ed Dept Morris Col; Instr Psychol Kennesaw Col; Asst Prof Psychol Unit, Coor, ECSU; AAUP; ABP; NCAE; NEA; cp/Former Pastor Siloam Bapt Ch, Kingstree, SC; Bd Dirs Cobb-Marietta Vol Assn; r/Bapt; hon/Author "A Model for Adult Education Programs Based Upon Maslow's Near Heirarchy."

JONES, VIRGIL CARRINGTON oc/Retired Journalist, Professional Writer; b/June 7, 1906; h/15000 Lee Hwy, Centreville, VA 22020; m/Geneva Carolyn Peyton; c/Virgil Carrington Jr, Judith Watkins Jones Robinson; p/Alonzo Lewis Jones (dec); Virginia Terrell Graves (dec); ed/BA magna cum laude; pa/City Editor *The Huntsville Times* 1931-37; Reporter *The Times-Dispatch* 1937-41; Reporter *The Evening Star* 1941-43; Reporter *The Wall Street Journal* 1943-45; Mgr Wash Public Relats Ofc of The Curtis Pub'g Co 1945-61; Free-Lance Writer 1961-63; Adm Asst to Cong-man William M Tuck of Va 1963-69; Profl Writer Nat Aeronautics & Space Adm 1969-76; Ret'd 1976; r/Disciples of Christ; hon/Phi Beta Kappa; Author First Ofcl Govt Account of Moon Landing *Log of Apollo 11*; Author Num Hist Narratives.

JONES, WALTER BEAMAN oc/Congressman; b/Aug 19, 1913; m/Doris Long; c/Dotdee Moye, Walter B II; p/dec; ed/BA NC St Univ 1934; pa/Dem Rep 1st Dist NC, US Ho of Reps 1966-; Mem House Com on Agric & Ho Com on Merchant Marine & Fisheries; Chm Agric Subcom on Tobacco; Mem Subcoms: Oilseeds & Rice, Dairy & Poultry; Mem Merchant Marine & Fisheries Subcoms on Coast Guard & Navigation & Panama Canal; NC Ho of Reps 1955, 57, 59; cp/Past Trustee Campbell Col & UNC; Former Mayor Farmville; Moose; Shrine; Elk; Rotary Clb; r/Bapt; hon/Awd for Each Yr in Cong, Ams for Constitutional Action.

JONES, WALTER SAMUEL JR oc/Minister, State Employee; ba/Dept Transportation, Raleigh, NC; b/Apr 23, 1931; m/Elsie Peterson; c/Angela Gail, Martin Samuel; p/Walter Samuel Sr (dec) and Lillian Dennign Jones, Smithfield, NC; ed/Grad Wayne Commun Col 1968; Dip Johnston Tech Inst 1970; Ord'd 1972; mil/USMC 1951-53; pa/St Employee, NC Dept Transp; Min Faith Bapt Ch; r/So Missionary Bapt; hN/Awd in Apprec of Recog for Exceeding the Goal in St Employees Combined Campaign 1978; Hon'd By Ch Each Yr Since 1972.

JONNALAGADDA, MURALI MOHAN RAO oc/Assistant Clinical Director, Psychiatrist; b/June 29, 1941; h/531 Parkwood Ln, Goldsboro, NC 27530; ba/Goldsboro; m/Venkata Thirumala-Devi Vutla; c/Devi Penusila, Venkata Ramanamba; p/Ramaniah and Venkata Subbamma Vinjamuri Jonnalagadda, Nellore, India; ed/MBBS (MD) Guntur Med Col 1964; DPM All India Inst Mtl Hlth 1968; pa/Lectr, Hd Dept Psychi, Rangaraya Med Col, Kakinada, India 1968-71; Sr Registrar Mtl Handicap & Child Psychi, Bristol, England Clin Area 1971-74; Consltg Psychi, St Davnet's Hosp, Monaghan, Ireland 1974-75; Staff Psychi, Cherry Hosp 1975-; Asst Clin Dir 1978-; Asst Clin Prof, Dept Psychi, ECU 1978-; Mem Royal Col Psychi; Royal Soc Med; Brit Med Assn; Irish Med Assn; Soc Clin Psychi; Am Assn Mtl Deficiency; Am Psychi Assn; AAAS; AMA; Fed Am Scist; r/Hindu; hon/Author, Co-Author Num Profl Articles.

JORDAN, JOHN R JR oc/Attorney at Law; b/Jan 16, 1921; h/809 Westwood Dr, Raleigh, NC 27607; m/Patricia Exum Weaver; c/Ellen

Meares, John Richard III; p/John R Sr and Ina Love Mitchell Jordan; ed/Chowan Col 1938; BA UNC 1942; LLD UNC Law Sch 1948; pa/Mem NC Senate, Gen Assem of NC 3 Reg Sessions & 1 Spec Session; Bar Assns: Intl, Am, NC, Wake Co; Am Judicture Soc; NC Acad Trial Lwyrs; Mem Staff of Atty Gen of NC 1948-51; NC Comm on Higher Ed Facilities 1964-; Bd Govs UNC 1973-; Trustee Ravenscroft Foun 1971-; NC Rep on Nat Com for Support of Nat Pub Schs 1962-; VChm NC Common Intl Coop 1970-; cp/Past Pres: NC Div Am Cancer Soc, NC Arthritis Foun, Wake Co Hist Soc, Wake Co Chapt Arthritis Foun, Friends of Lib of NCSU; Active Mem Dem Party; Past St Pres Yng Dem Clbs of NC; Cand for Ofc of Lt Gov of NC 1964; Editor "Why the Dem Party" 1955; Author of Newspaper & Mag Articles & Book Reviews on Polits & Govt; hon/Raleigh Yng Man of Yr 1955; Tar Heel of Wk 1955; Am Cancer Soc Gold Medal Awd; Others.

JORDAN, PEGGY oc/Associate Broker, Director of Sales; b/May 18, 1928; h/Ruidoso, NM; c/Kelly Louis; p/Roma Ayres, Midland, TX; ed/Att'd Univ Okla 1945-47, Albuquerque Univ 1973-74; pa/Assoc Broker & Dir Sales, Innsbrook Vil Real Est; Past Altruistic Chm Alpha Gamma Delta Alumni, San Antonio; Proj Chm Wom's Home Bldrs Assn; r/First Christian Ch; Secy 1976-78; hon/Million Dollar Clb; Top Wom Prodr & Runner-Up to Top Real Est Salesman 1980.

JORDAN, SAMUEL III oc/Associate Professor; b/July 4, 1939; h/PO Box 268, Pace, MS 38764; ba/Itta Bena, MS; m/Eunice; c/Samuel IV, Felicia; p/Samuel and Lovely Jordan, Clarksdale, MS; ed/BS; MEd; EdD; mil/AUS; pa/Assoc Prof Ed, Miss Val St Univ; Phi Delta Kappa; Coun Exceptl Chd; cp/Commun Clb; Voters Leag; r/Cath; hon/Alumni & Civic Awds.

JOTHI, S P oc/Internist; b/July 26, 1939; h/2801 Partridge, Parsons, KS 67357; ba/Parsons; m/Bala; c/Suresh, Krishnan, Raja; p/G Subramoniam and V Mangalam Jothi, Houston, TX; ed/Att'd Mar Ivanios Col, Trivandrum, India 1959; Pre-Med Intermediate Col, Trivandrum 1960; MD Med Col, Trivandrum 1965; Internship, Gen Hosp, Trivandrum 1966-67 & Mercy Hosp, Denver, Colo 1970-71; Residency, Menorah Med Ctr, Kansas City, Mo 1971-74; pa/Tutor in Radiology, Med Col Hosp, Trivandrum 1966-67; Med Ofcr, Sacred Heart Hosp, Tuticorin, India 1967-70; Pvt Prac, Parsons, Kan 1974-; Staff Labette Co Med Ctr, Parsons; Past Pres Labette Co Med Soc; VP Labette Co Med Ctr Staffs; Chm Kan Heart Assn, Labette Co Br; AMA; Am Thoracic Soc; Dir Respiratory Dept at Labette Co Med Ctr; cp/Past VP Indian Assn Kan City; Chm Heart Assn Fund Raising in Oswego 1975; Chm Heart Assn Fund Raising Labette Co 1980; r/Hindu; hon/Bd Cert Internal Med 1978; Sev Prizes Won in Tennis Tournaments, SE Kan.

JOYE, LEBON oc/Student; b/Sept 30, 1959; h/Barnwell, SC; p/L M and Edna M Joye, Barnwell, SC; ed/BS Cand Austin Peay St Univ; r/Bapt; hon/Nat Hon Soc; Best Defensive Player, APSU Baseball 1980; All OVC 1980; Co-Capt 1980, Capt 1981 APSU.

JOYNER, DELORES oc/Teacher; b/Sept 16, 1936; h/Rt 2, Box 62A, Fort Val, GA 31030; m/James P; c/Robin J Callahan, Connie J Hall; p/John P and Mildred Wilson Williams; ed/BA Mercer Univ 1973; MS Ft Val St 1976; Further Study Univ Ga; pa/Elem Tchr 6 Yrs; cp/Dem Party.

JUDD, JEAN T oc/Secretary, Bookkeeper; b/Sept 3, 1928; h/Rt 10 Box 208A, Cookeville, TN 38501; ba/Cookeville; m/Robert P; c/Tana J Davis, Parker Taylor; p/Cecil G and Janye H Taylor, Shelbyville, TN; pa/Secy-Bkkpr: Bussell Construc & Realty Co, Home Component Mfg Co; Pilot Clb of Cookeville: Pres 2 Terms, VP 3 Terms, Div Coor & Area Ldr; Div Coor St of Tenn Pilot Clb; Past Pres Jere Whitson Sch PTA; cp/Past Girl Scout Ldr; Past Girl Scout Dist Camp Dir; Girl Scout Camp Ldr 1 Yr for St; Past Cub Scout Ldr; Past Cub Scout Ldr in Trg Other Ldrs; Hosp Vol Aux; r/Bapt; SS Secy; hon/Long Rifle Awd, Given by Boy Scouts for Outstg Work 1960; Pilot of Yr 1976.

JUMPER, W A (WOODY) oc/Chief of Police, Instructor; b/July 6, 1943; h/115 E Muskogee, Sulphur, OK 73086; ba/Sulphur; m/Pamela Ann Scott; c/Sheila June, Chad Alan, Christa Lynn, Hilary G; p/John F Jumper (dec); Adell Jumper Shoptaugh, Ada, OK; ed/EMT Dip 1976; Grad St Gregory's Col 1971; Grad E Ctrl Okla St Univ 1975; Grad Okla Hwy Patrol Acad 1976; mil/USAF; pa/Chief of Police, Sulphur Police Dept; Instr Murray St Col; FOP; Okla Sheriff & Peace Ofcr's Assn; cp/Am Legion, Chaplain; Lions Clb; r/Free Will Bapt; hon/Winner Shooting Contest, Ada & Sulphur, Okla; Letter of Apprec from Late Sen Dewey Bartlett.

JUSTICE, CHARLES CHAPPELL oc/Architect; b/July 11, 1909; h/204 Sunset Dr, Richmond, VA 23229; ba/Richmond; m/Mary B; c/Roberta Shelton, Bruce Morgan, Irene Bailey Myers; p/Edward (dec) and Blanche M Justice (dec); ed/BArch Ohio St Univ 1935; mil/ROTC Ohio St Univ, Arch Naval Oper Base WWII; pa/Ptnr Ballou & Justice, Arch & Engrs; Va St Registration Bd for Archs, Engrg & Land Surveyors 1958-68, Pres 1963, VP, Chm Arch Sect; Am Inst Arch: Va Chapt, Past Pres, VP, Secy, Treas; Nat Coun Arch Reg Bd; St Exam'g Bd for Arch, Engrg & Landscape Arch; cp/Past Mem Richmond Red Cross; Westham Civic Assn; r/Unitarian; hon/Pres Va Chapt AIA; Misc Amateur Radio Awds; Chm Atlantic Div NCARB; Pres St Exam'g Bd Arch, Engrg & Landscape Arch.

K

KAERWER, BOBBY NEWTON oc/Golf Professional; b/Aug 9, 1941; h/1278 Stubing Ct, El Paso, TX 79925; ba/Ft Bliss, TX; m/Joy Marie; c/Melissa Rene; p/Bob and Ruth Ellen Kaerwer, El Paso, TX; ed/BS, MEd Tex Tech Univ; mil/AUS 1st Lt; pa/PGA Golf Pro; Profl Golfers Assn Am; cp/Cielo Vista Mall Optimist Clb; r/Meth hon/Sun Country PGA 1977 Horton Smith Awd Winner; Profl of Yr, Sun Country PGA 1978.

KAHLER, TAIBI oc/Clinical Psychologist; Counselor, Consultant, Author; b/June 30, 1943; ba/PO Box 5129, Little Rock, AR 72205; m/Sandra Payne; c/Stepch: Laura; p/George and Madelyn Kalena, Highland, TX; ed/BA 1968, MS 1971, PhD 1972 Purdue Univ; pa/Co-Dir Human Devel Assocs 1977-; Dir Transactional Analysis Inst for So Calif 1975-76; Dir Clin Trg for San Diego Inst Transactional Analysis 1974-75; Assoc Dir Halcyon Inst 1972-74; Res & Tchg Asst Child Devel & Fam Life Dept 1969-72; Dir VISTA Prog Summer 1968; Intl Grp Psych Assn; Am Grp Psych Assn; Ark Grp Psych Assn; Calif Assn Marriage, Fam & Child Cnslrs; Am Assn Marriage, Fam & Child Therapists Clin Mem; Bd Trustees Intl Transactional Analysis Assn, Clin Tchg Mem, VP 1980-82; Guest Editor *Transcational Analysis Journal*; Ark Psych Assn; Am Soc Trg & Devel; Ark Soc Trg & Devel; Adj Tutor Intl Col, LA, Calif; Psych Conslt NASA Astronaut Prog; Conslt: ALAT, Interactional Sers, San Diego Inst Transactional Analysis, Fam Ser Agcy Little Rock, Suspected Child Abuse and Neglect Little Rock, Bapt Med Ctr Sys Little Rock; Fac Mem San Fernando Val TA Trg Inst; Res Conslt Child Psych Inst of San Diego; Active Conslt Staff Cedarstone Psychi Inst, N Little Rock; cp/Mensa; Intertel; Soc Philosophical Inquiry; Triple Nine; hon/Originator of "Miniscript" Concept, Which Rec'd Eric Berne Meml Sci Awd 1977; Guest Spkr World Cong ITAA, Villars, Switz 1974; Guest Spkr World Cong ALAT, Rio DeJaneiro, Brazil 1976; Guest Spkr World Cong ITAA, Brighton, England 1980; Guest Spkr Nat Cong Marriage & Fam Cnslrs, Newport, Calif 1974; Guest Spkr ITAA Mid-Wn Conf, Detroit, Mich 1979; Guest Spkr at 10 Convs for Therapists & Bus People 1972-; W/W S&SW; Hon Fellow Association Lationoamericana de Nuevas Ciencias de la Conducta; Psych Chosen by NASA to Consult in Selection of Astronauts; Author & Co-Author Num Profl Articles.

KALBHIN, NORA EVELYN oc/Educator, School Administrator; b/Jun 2, 1928; h/2714 Delor Ave, Louisville, KY 40217; ba/L'ville; m/Donald L Sr; c/Donna K Asbury, Donald Lee Jr; p/George Robert and Ruth Evelyn Steiden Scott (dec); ed/BS Ed; MA Adm; Rdg Specialist; pa/IRA Exec Bd; r/Christian Cath; hon/Notable Ams of Bicent Era; W/W Ky; Outstg Ams of S; Fellow Mem, ABI.

KALE, W WILFORD JR oc/Newspaper Bureau Chief; b/Sept 2, 1944; h/107 Oxford Cir, Williamsburg, VA 23185; ba/W'burg; m/Louise Lambert; c/Anne-Evan Lambert; p/Wilford and Martha Irwin Kale, Matthews, NC; ed/Att'd Col of William and Mary 1962-67; BA summa cum laude Park Col 1971; Grad Studies Geo Wash Univ 1974-75; mil/AUS 1968-70 1st Lt; pa/Pt-time Sports Writer, *Charlotte Observer* 1960-64, Full-time 1965; Info Assoc Col William and Mary 1965-66; Staff Writer *Richmond Times-Dispatch* 1966-68; Asst to Dir Minn Pvt Col Fund 1971; *Williamsburg Bur Chief Richmond Times-Dispatch* 1971-; Sigma Delta Chi; Richmond Chapt Awds William & Mary Pubs Coun Chm 1974-77; Williamsburg-James City Co Bicent Com 1972-77; Exec Com Medallion Com 1975-77; Songs of the Am Revolution, Williamsburg Chapt 1976, Hist 1978-; r/Presb, Ruling Elder 1974; hon/US Army Commend Medal 1969; Bronze Star; William & Mary Soc of the Alumni 175th Anniv Medal, 1 of 94, 1968; Pi Delta Epsilon Medal of Merit 1975; Soc for Col Journalists Medal of Merit 1980; Author "Robert Andrews: A Forgotten Professor"; "The Brafferson"; "Private Homes in Williamsburg Today."

KANDIL, OSAMA A oc/Associate Professor; b/Oct 25, 1944; h/7212 Midfield St, Norfolk, VA 23505; ba/Norfolk; m/Rawia A; c/Dalya O, Tare K O; p/Abd El-Mohsin Kandil and Attiat El-Shazli, Giza, Egypt; ed/BS Cairo Univ 1966; MS Villanova Univ 1972; PhD VPI 1974; pa/Assoc Prof Mech Engrg & Mechs, Old Dominion Univ 1978-; Asst Prof Engrg Sci & Mechs VI 1975-78; Res Asst VPI 1972-74; Tchg Asst, Villanova Univ 1971-72; Instr Cairo Univ 1966-70; AIAA; SES; AAUP; Phi Kapa Phi; Sigma Xi; ASEE; Va Acad Sci; r/Moslem; hon/Invited to US Del to 11th & 12th Cong Intl Coun Aeronautical Scis 1978, 80; Invited as US Del to Agardinato 1977, 78; W/W S&SW 1980; NASA, ASEE F'ships 1978, 79; Phi Kappa Phi; NASA Grants 1975-81; Army Ofc Res Grant 1975-78; Navy Contract for Res 1980-81; Hon Deg Cairo Univ 1966; S'ships Villanova Univ 1971-72; Res Asstships VPI 1972-74.

KAPPA, MARGARET McCAFFREY oc/Director of Housekeeping; b/May 14, 1921; h/The Greenbrier, White Sulphur Springs, WV 24986; ba/Same; c/Nicholas Joseph, Christopher Francis; p/Verna Anderson McCaffrey, Wabasha, MN; ed/BS Cornell Univ 1944; Dale Carnegie Course 1978; Ext Courses: Univ Minn 1945 & NYU 1947; pa/Dir Housekeeping, The Greenbrier; Conslt Hotels; Tchr Hotel Housekeeping: Soviet Union, Singapore, W Germany, Bahamas, Aruba, USA; Cornell Soc of Hotelmen: Pres 1980-81, 1st VP 1979-80, 2nd VP 1978-79; Nat Exec Housekeepers Assn, Pres NY Chapt 1950; cp/St Charles Parish Assn: VP 1981, Pres 1960; White Sulphur Springs Wom's Clb; r/Rom Cath; hon/Recip Dip of Hon Societe Culinaire Philanthropique 1961; NYU Hotel & Rest Soc Hon Life Mem; Vis'g Lectr Cert, Cornell Univ; Author Num Profl Articles for *Nat Exec Housekeepers Mthly*.

KARELS, JAMES D oc/Senior Buyer; b/Mar 14, 1928; h/405 Prairie Ave, Cleburne, TX 76031; ba/Ft Worth; m/Judy B; c/Karolyn Kay, William Brice, Liesa Jo Ann, Kelly Sue, Jerry Duane, Jerry Stephen, Michael Lee, Tracy Gail, James Darren; p/Fred W Karels, Waco, TX; Lucille Fellers, Hico, TX; mil/AUS; pa/Purchasing Agts Assn; cp/Elks Lodge; r/Bapt; hon/Golo Titan Awd.

KASPERBAUER, JAMES CLEMENS oc/Commander AFROTC, Professor; b/Sept 12, 1937; h/2576 Tigrett Cove, Memphis, TN 38138; ba/Memphis; m/Margaret Craig; c/Susan, Jean, Jamie; p/Clare Kasperbauer, Manning, IA; ed/BA Univ Neb-Omaha 1965; MA 1973 & 75 Ctrl Mich Univ; mil/USAF; pa/Prof & Dept Hd, Memphis St Univ 1979-80; Div Chief Space Missile Elec Contractors 1971-79; Br Chief, R&D Contracts, Wright-Patterson AFB 1972-75; Flight Cmdr, Instr, Navigator 1963-72; Soc Pen & Sword; AF Assn; Nat Contract Mgmt Assn; cp/Mem C of C; r/Cath; hon/Commun Ldr Am 1980; W/W E 1979; Set AF Record For Most Hours Flown in 1 Yr 1968; Dist'd Flying Cross & 57 Other Mil Awds & Decorations.

KATAHN, ENID oc/Artist, Teacher; b/Apr 10, 1932; h/4607 Belmont Pk Terr, Nashville, TN 37215; ba/N'ville; m/Martin; c/David, Terri; p/David E Miller (dec); Rae L Miller, Miami, FL; ed/BM Hartt Col; MM Geo Peabody Col; Studied at Juilliard Sch; pa/Artist-Tchr Blair Sch Music; Concert Pianist; Town Hall Debut 1961; European Tour 1962; Over 50 Concerts Annually Throughout Country & Abroad; hon/Highly Praised by Music Critics Throughout World; 3 Albums Recorded on *Peacetree* Label.

KAUFFMAN, GLENN EDWARD oc/Executive; b/Dec 14, 1944; h/3127 Sumac Dr, Doraville, GA 30360; ba/Norcross, GA; m/Ann Robinson; c/Brian Charles, Sherry Lynn; p/Walter L and Lillian Geisler Kauffman, Lancaster, PA; ed/AB Lycoming Col 1966, BSEE Bucknell Univ 1967; MSEE Rochester Inst Technol 1972; pa/Engr, Buyer Eastman Kodak 1967-72; Tech Sales Data Gen Corp 1973-75; Sales Gentry Assocs 1974-76; Pres Atlanta Minicomputer Assocs Inc 1976-; Data Processing Mgmt Assn; Atlanta Area Microcomputer Hobbiest Clb; cp/BSA, Adult Advtr Sponsoring Com Button Gwinnett UCC; Ctrl Congregl Ch: Social Action Com, VChm, Pledge Campaign Chm; War Control Planners; r/U Ch of Christ; hn/W/W S&SW 1980-81; Author "Digital Executive Control of a Hybrid Computing System" 1972.

KAUFMAN, IRENE MATHIAS oc/Principal; b/Jan 28, 1942; h/936 Fairway Dr, Waynesboro, VA 22980; p/Ted and Mary Mathias, Waynesboro, VA; ed/BA Mary Baldwin Col; MEd Univ Va; pa/Elem Sch Prin; Life Mem NEA; VEA; WEA, Bd Dirs 1970-74; Dist G Elem Prins: Secy-Treas 1974-76, Pres 1976-77; Nat Assn Elem Sch Prins; Va Assn Elem Sch Prins; Bd Dirs WPSE Credit Union 1976-; Leg Rep WPSE Credit Union 1976-; Ctrl Va Chapt Credit Unions: Secy 1972-74, Pres 1974-75; Leg & Liaison Com, Va Credit Union Leag 1974-; cp/Adv Bd Waynesboro Salvation Army 1978-; Pres Staunton-Augusta Repub Wom's Clb 1970-77; Secy Augusta Co Repub Com 1969-70, 75-76, 78-; 6th Dist Repub Wom's Rep 1974-78; Augusta Co Repub Com 1969-; 6th Dist Repub Com 1974-78; Chm Wayne Dist Repub Com 1977-; Treas Augusta Co Repub Wom's Clb 1977-; r/Presb; hon/Personalities of the S 1974; W/W: Polits in S&SW 1973, Am Polits 1973-74; Commun Ldrs & Noteworthy Ams 1977; World W/W Wom; Intl W/W Intells; Del Repub Nat Conv 1972.

KAUNDART, WES oc/Teacher, Coach; b/June 25, 1954; h/PO Box 98, Fordyce, AR 71742; ba/Fordyce; m/Sandra Curtis; p/Gayle and Ruth Kaundart, Ft Smith, AR; ed/AA Westark Commun Col; BSE Univ Ctrl Ark; pa/Hd Basketball Coach & Tchr, Fordyce HS; Ark Activs Assn; AEA; NEA; r/Presb; hon/W/W Am Jr Cols 1974-75 & 75-76.

KAUTZ, JAMES RUSSELL oc/Student; b/Apr 5, 1960; h/106 Sherwood Forest, Morehead, KY 40351; p/Aubrey Salyer Jr and Donna Jean Kautz, Morehead, KY; ed/BBA Cand Morehead St Univ 1981; r/First Ch of God; hon/Phi Kappa Phi; Intl Yth in Achmt 1982; Nat Dean's List 1980; Pres's List, Fall 1980; MSU Acad S'ship 1979-80.

KAY, KASMIR STANLEY oc/Executive Administrator; Educator; Consultant; b/Sept 15, 1918; h/4820 Kingston Dr, Annandale, VA 22003; m/Beverley B; c/Sherryl B; p/William B Kay (dec); Margaret R Kay, Terryville, CT; ed/BCS; MBA; DPA; mil/USAR Lt Col, Fin Corps, Ret'd;

pa/Adjunct Prof Public Adm, SEn Univ, Wash DC 1977-78; Fin Exec & Admr, US Dept Interior 1956-77; Chief Acctg Sys Staff, Dept Treas, Internal Revenue Ser, Wash DC 1954-56; Liaison Ofcr, US Atomic Energy Comm, Wash 1952-54; Fin Ofcr, VA 1946-52; AAUP; Am Soc for Public Adm; Resv Ofcrs Assn; Am Soc Mil Comptrollers; Army Fin Assn; Budget Execs Inst; Fed Execs Leag; Fed Govt Accts Assn; Other Profl Activs; hon/Num Biogl Listings.

KEARNEY, HELEN REVENDA oc/Psychologist; Professor; b/Dec 4, 1941; h/1305 St Mary, Apt 5, New Orleans, LA 70130; p/Edward Thomas Kearney (dec); Revenda Elizabeth Rynard Kearney, Harrisburg, PA; ed/BS, MS, PhD; pa/Prof Dept Psychol Newcomb Col, Tulane Univ, NO; The Alan Guttmacher Inst; AAUP; Am Psychol Assn; Am Public Hlth Assn; The Groves Conf on Marriage & the Fam; hon/Predoct Fellow Interdisciplinary Grad Prog in the Humanities, Col of Lib Arts, Pa St Univ 1974-75; Fellow, ABI; W/W Among Students Am Univs & Cols.

KEATING, WILLIAM F oc/Business Executive; b/Aug 6, 1932; h/3218 39th St NW, Wash DC 20005; ba/Wash DC; m/Ann; c/William F Jr, Jon, Kenneth, Edwin Loyd, Marina Jane; p/William F and Florence D Keating, Holyoke, MA; ed/BA/BS; MS; TD; mil/AUS; pa/Bus Exec; cp/Kiwanis; r/Rom Cath; hon/Indust Mktg Gold Medal.

KEATON, EDWIN ALEXANDER oc/Attorney at Law; b/June 13, 1952; h/PO Box 524, Bearden, AR 71720; ba/Camden; m/Opal Y; c/Kimberly Dione, Carmen Renea; p/William T and Theresa S Keaton, Arkadelphia, AR; ed/BA Univ Ark; JD Univ Ark Law Sch; pa/Am, Ark, Ouachita Co & Ark Black Lwyrs Assns; cp/Camden JCs; Camden NAACP; r/Bapt.

KEDIA, PRAHLAD RAY oc/Associate Professor, Department Chairman; b/July 4, 1937; h/Choudrant, LA; ba/Criminal Justice Dept, Box 383, Grambling St Univ, Grambling, LA 71245; m/Sushila Podar; c/Kavita, Sarita, Anita; p/Shri Kaluramji (dec) and Kanchan Devi Kedia (dec); ed/BS Univ Rajasthan 1957; LLB 1961, LLM 1965 Univ Bombay; pa/Asst Mgr Jaipur Hotel, Jaipur, India 1954-57; Asst Acct-Acct Indore Malwa U Mills Ltd, Bombay 1958-65; Called to Bar 1965; Pract'g Atty, High Ct, Bombay 1965-71; Grambling St Univ, Asst Prof, Law 1971-78, Dir Crim Just & Law Adm Ctr 1975-; Acad Crim Just Scis; Am Crim Just Assn; Bombay Bar Assn; La Crim Just Edrs Assn; r/Hindu; hon/Assoc Editor *International Journal of Comparative Criminal Justice Sciences.*

KEE, JOYCE MARIE oc/Postmaster; b/Mar 6, 1929; h/PO Box 125, Melissa, TX 75071; ba/Melissa; m/John Monroe; c/Jaqueta Marie Hardin, Joseph Simon, Julie Melissa, Jonna Merri Eve; p/Leslie Simon (dec) and Clefa Belle Settle, Anna, TX; pa/Stengrapher Tex Power & Light Co 1946-51; Secy Dist Atty of Collin Co 1952-54; Postmaster, Melissa, Tex 1954-; Tex Br Nat Leag Postmasters VP 4 Yrs, Pres 1979-80; cp/Melissa Garden Clb, Reporter; Melissa PTA, Parliamntn, Hist, Treas, Reporter; Ch Treas; News Corresp *McKinney Courier Gazette;* Chm Num Fund Dirs in Commun & Co; r/First Bapt Ch; Tchr SS Classes, Trg Union & Girls Aux Ldr; hon/Valedictorian Grad Class 1946, Westminster HS; Awds for Num Fund Raising Projs; Good Housekeeping Awd at PO 1971; Awd'd Gold Watch for Recog of Ser as Pres Tex Br Nat Leag Postmasters of US.

KEEL, ALTON GOLD JR oc/US Senate Armed Forces Committee; b/Sept 8, 1943; h/PO Box 4178, Silver Spring, MD 20904; ba/Wash DC; c/Kristen Ann, Patricia Dean; p/Alton Gold (dec) and Ella Clair Kennedy Keel (dec); ed/BS 1966, PhD 1970 Univ Va; Post Doct Univ Calif 1970-71; pa/Profl Staff Mem, US Sen Armed Sers Com; Am Inst Aerospace & Astronautics; Sigma Xi; Phi Eta Sigma; Tau Beta Pi; cp/Prog Com, Unitarian Universalist Ch; Bd Dirs Commun Co-Owners Assn 1975; r/Unitarian Universalist; hon/Recip Air Force Ofc of Sci Res, Nat Res Coun Post Doct Res Awd 1970; Sustained Superior Perf Awd, Navy Dept 1973; AIAA Congl Sci Fellow 1977; Yng Engr/Sci Awd, AIAA Nat Capitol Sect 1978.

KEEL, H WAYNE oc/Drilling Technician; b/Dec 3, 1952; m/Kellie; p/James H and Marjorie Keel, Seagraves, TX; ed/Att'd Midland Col; Exxon Drilling Sch; mil/USAF 1971-75 Fuels Spec Sgt pa/Equip Opr Wn Co of N Am 3 Yrs; Gas Plant Opr Montex Drilling Co 1 Yr; Roustabout, Lease Opr, Drilling Tech Exxon Co USA 1½ Yrs; r/So Bapt hon/Airman of Qtr 1973; Outstg Unit Awd, Ellsworth AFB 1972; Winner 2 Motocross Races, Lubbock, Tex 1978.

KEELEY, ROBERT VOSSLER oc/Diplomat; b/Sept 4, 1929; h/850 Old England Ave, Winter Park, FL 32789; ba/Port Louis, Mauritius; m/Louise Benedict Schoonmaker; c/Michal Mathilde, Christopher John; p/James Hugh and Mathilde Julia Vossler Keeley, Winter Park; ed/AB Princeton Univ 1951; mil/USCG 1953-55, Lt (jg); pa/Career Fgn Ser Ofcr, US Dept of St; Am Ambassador to Mauritius 1976-78; hon/Superior Hon Awd, Dept of St.

KEENE, SUSIE oc/Librarian; b/Nov 8, 1929; m/Bruce E; c/Rebecca L; p/Joe and Jessie Ison Horne, Robinson Creek, KY; ed/BS Pikeville Col 1961; MA En Ky Univ 1969; pa/Libn George F Johnson Elem Sch 1967-; Art Tchr Robinson Creek Elem 1961-67; NEA; KEA; KLA; Ky Sch Media Assn; En Ky Lib Assn; Pike Co Ed Assn, Treas 197-78; 1st Pres Pike Co Art Ed Assn 1958-61; 1st Pres Pike Co Sch Media Assn 1977-79; AAUW, Treas & Publicity Chm Pikeville Chapt; Nu Chapt Delta Kappa Gamma, Public Relats Chp 1972-78, 1st VP 1978-; Com Publicity & Pubs Alpha Gamma St; St Media Cadre; Bd Dirs Ky Lib Assn 1978-80; cp/Co-Editor 'The Third Century Woman" 1975-78; Pikeville Chapt DAR; Pikeville Chapt BPW; r/Virgie Bapt Ch: Public Relats Dir, Tchr Adult Wom; Mission Study Chm for Bapt Wom; hon/Outstg Elem Tchr of Am 1973; Kentuckiana Cook from *Courier-Journal* 1974; Tchr of Mo, Nu Chapt Delta Kappa Gamma 1978.

KEEPLER, MANUEL oc/Professor; b/Nov 4, 1944; h/Box 1656 SCSC, Orangeburg, SC 29117; ba/O'burg; m/Dannie Lee Hornsby; c/Adrianne Kapayl; p/Gus H Keppler, Atlanta, GA; Charssie N Keppler (dec); ed/BS; MA; PhD; pa/Prof Math & Computer Sci, SC St Col; Math Pubs Incl'g Series of Articles on Random Evolutions; Statistical Conslg; cp/Advr for Local Chess Clb; r/Bahai; hon/Num S'ships & F'ships Incl'g: Woodrow Wilson 1966-67 & NASA/Hamtpon Inst Fellow, Langley Res Ctr Summer 1981; Num Biogl Listings Incl'g: W/W S&SW; Men Achmt; Commun Ldrs & Noteworthy Ams; Recip Sev Plaques for Excell in Tchg.

KEES, TERRY ELIZABETH SIMMON oc/Computer Systems Analyst; b/Jan 9, 1946; h/5001 Liberty Bell Ct, Burice, VA 22015; Sundance #29, New Market, VA; ba/Wash DC; p/Peter and Billie D Simmon, Waco, TX; ed/BA Tex Christian Univ 1968; pa/Data Processing Career, Ctrl Intell Agcy 1968-; r/Epis; hon/Cert of Dist.

KELLEY, CALLIE IMOJEAN oc/Counselor; b/Aug 7, 1932; h/Rt 2 Box 43, Greenwood, SC 29646; ba/G'wood; c/Paula Elizabeth; p/A B Kelley, G'wood; Callie Jane Klaus, G'wood; ed/AB Lander Col; MEd Clemson Univ; pa/Southside Jr High: Cnslr, Beautification Chm, Former Mem Adm Coun, Former Chm Sci Dept, Advr to Jr Yth Bd of SC Lung Assn, Fin Chm, Former Beta Clb Advr, Former Student Coun Advr; Dist 50 Tchr Coun: Pres, Southside Jr High Rep; NEA; SC Ed Assn; G'wood Co Ed Assn: Past Secy, Former Mbrship Chm; Resource Person for Commun Adv Couns of Dist 50; Mem Steering Com for Study of Traditional Schs; Co-Chm Spec Com for Bond Issue Dist 50; Former Mbrship Chm Delta Kappa Gamma; AAUW: Past Secy/Treas; SC Area Six Lung Assn: Pres, Mem Exec Com, Meml Gifts Chm, Adv Bd Dirs; VP SC Lung Assn; Chm Resolutions Com for G'wood Co Ed Assn; Spec Rep, Clemson Univ Innovations Day; Test Coor Southside Jr High; Rep Piedmont Tech Col Guidance Com; Lander Col Alumni Clb; r/Presb: Secy Rock Presb Ch Wom in Ch Coun, Secy Pulpit Com; hon/Tchr of Yr, G'wood Dist 50, 1974-75; Outstg Sec'dy Edr of Am; Advr to Sci World Mag of Scholastic Mags; Tchr of Yr in Conserv Ed 1976; Notable Ams 1978-79; Personalities of S 1978-79; Commun Ldrs & Noteworthy Ams 1978; Personalities of Am 1978-79; DIB 1980; Dir of Dist'd Ams 1981; Am Registry Series, First Edition.

KELLEY, CARLTON WILLIAM oc/Retired; b/Mar 19, 1906; h/1022 Sherman St SE, Decatur, AL 35602; m/Louella Masterson; c/Carlton William Jr, Ellen Frances; p/Monroe Marvin (dec) and Nancy L Kelley (dec); ed/BA B'ham So Col; MA Univ Ala; LHD Athens Col; pa/Ret'd Pres Emeritus Calhoun Commun Col; Writing Hist Calhoun Commun Col; cp/Lions Clb; r/Meth.

KELLEY, DUANE NEIL oc/Comptroller, Vice President Finance; b/Aug 13, 1953; h/3700 Hickory Hill Dr, Somerset, KY 42501; ba/Somerset; m/Debra Lynne Keeton; c/Jalayna Lynne; p/Billy Gene and Jane Hill Kelley; ed/Grad Morehead St Univ 1977; pa/Dir & Ofcr: Correll Enterprises Inc: Comptroller & VP Fin, Correll Holding Co Inc, Correll Properties Inc, Correll & New Invests Inc, G&C Devel Co Inc, C&N Real Est Co Inc, A-1 Bldrs Inc; Am Mgmt Assn; Nat Fed Indep Bus; cp/Sumerset-Pulaski Co C of C; Ky C of C; US C of C; r/Bapt; hon/W/W: S&SW, Fin & Indust.

KELLEY, JOHN H oc/Assistant Principal; b/July 4, 1946 h/PO Box 81, 29 Lovingood Ave, Walhalla, SC 29691; ba/Walhalla; p/John and Earlene Kelley, Walhalla, SC; ed/BA Ctrl Wesleyan Col; MEd Clemson Univ; pa/Asst Prin Walhalla Middle Sch; Oconee Co Ed Assn; SCEA; NEA; cp/Walhalla JCs; Walhalla Adv Coun; r/Col St Bapt Ch; hon/Outstg Yng Edr; Key Man; Dist'd Ser Awd; B Anderson Meml Awd.

KELLEY, JUDY RAE oc/Speech-Language Pathologist, Lecturer; b/Jan 10, 1945; h/1411 Fairfield St Apt 6, Star City, WV 26505; ba/Morgantown, WV; p/Orville Jr and Ruby Charleen Williams Kelley, Salem, WV; ed/BA Salem Col 1967; MS WVU 1969; Post Grad Work 1969-76; pa/Hd Speech-Lang Pathol, Monongalia Co Bd Ed 1976-; Lectr WVU 1979-; Speech Pathol Monongalia Co Bd Ed 1969-76; Instr WVU

1969-79; Clin Supvr Student Clinicians from WVU Dept Speech Pathol; Coor Summer Speech, Lang, Vision, Hearing, Dental Screening & Immunization Prog 1972-; Am Speech-Lang-Hearing Assn; WV Speech & Hearing Assn, St Treas 1974-76; Assn Supervisoio & Curric Devel, Pres & VP Both Regional & Local Chapts, Gen Chm WVASCD Conv 1977; Phi Delta Kappa; Coun Exceptl Chd; cp/Zonta Intl, Morgantown VP 1980-, Treas 1979-80, Bd Dirs 1978-79; Bd Dirs Riding for Handicapped; Spec Ed Adv Coun VP 1978-79, 1980-; Repub Party; r/Meth; hon/W/W S&SW 1980-81; Outstg Yng Wom Am 1976; W/W Students Am Univs & Cols 1966-67.

KELLEY, LOUISE SALTER oc/Educational Administrator; b/Aug 19, 1907; h/1724 Wrightsboro Rd, Augusta, GA 30904; m/George W Sr; c/George W Jr, Helen K Cleaveland; p/James Blaine Salter (dec); Flewda Parker Salter, Augusta, GA; ed/AB Ga St Col for Wom; MEd, Specialist Deg Univ Ga; Certn in Supvn; pa/Dir of Right to Read & Coor Devel 1st Grade; Former Classroom Tchr & Coor Devel Rdg; Richmond Co Schs: Lang Arts Coor 1976, Rdg Coor 1966-76; Instrnl Supvr Devel Rdg, CEP, Title I, ESAA; Coor Career Prog for Elem Schs 1974-76; Info Ctr & Clearinghouse; GDIS; Assn for Supvn & Curri Devel; IRA; Orgr & 1st Pres CSRA Rdg Coun & Richmond Co Eng Coun; Past VP AAUW; Org'd Tutorial Prog, Richmond Co Bd of Ed; r/Hill Bapt Ch; hon/Alpha Delta Kappa; Kappa Delta Pi; Recipient 2nd Annual Awd for Outstg Ldrship & Ser, Ga Coun of IRA; Fellow, ABI; Book of Honor.

KELLEY, MICHAEL FRANCIS oc/Assistant Professor; b/Apr 30, 1951; h/259 Oak St, Auburn, AL 36830; ba/Auburn; m/Elaine; p/Frank J Kelley, Scottsdale, AZ; Betty J Kelley, Phoenix, AZ; pa/Asst Prof Fam & Child Devel, Auburn Univ; Phi Delta Kappa; Jean Piaget Soc; Am Ednl Res Assn; r/Prot; hon/Univ Ga Phi Delta Kappa Original Res Awd 1979.

KELLY, BARBARA ANN oc/Associate Director Athletic Programs; b/Mar 28, 1937; h/Rt 1 Box 297-C, Keswick, VA 22947; ba/Charlottesville; m/Carson H (dec) and Esther May Hales Kelly, Beaufort, NC; ed/AA Campbell Col 1958; BS ECU 1961; MEd Col William & Mary 1970; pa/Univ Va: Assoc Dir Ath Prog 1979-; Gen Fac 1971-, Dir Wom's Sports Prog 1973-79, Wom's Varsity Basketball Coach 1973-75, Dir Wom's Intramurals 1971-73; Tchr Hlth & Phy Ed, Booker T Washington HS 1970-71; Dir Norfolk Rec Dept Day Camp 1965-70; Dir Girl's Intramural Dept, Granby HS 1964-70; Chp Girl's Phy Ed Dept Granby HS 1964-70; Cnslr Camp Yng-Disadvantaged Yths (Wkends), Norfolk City Sch Sys 1965-70; Clin Coor Norfolk Rec Dept 1963-71; Game Ofcl, Norfolk Rec Dept 1963-71; Assn Intercol Aths for Wom, Ofcl Rep Univ Va 1971-; Va Assn Intercol Aths for Wom, Ethics & Eligibility Com 1979-, Restructuring Com 1979-; Assn Intercol Aths for Wom, Chp Ath Dirs 1978-; Assn Intercol Aths for Wom Region II TV Com 1978-; Atlantic Coast Conf Wom's Basketball Champ'ship, Tourn Dir 1978; Ednl & Employment Opports, Obligations & Rights Com, Univ Va 1978; Invitational Basketball Tourn, Tourn Dir, Univ Va 1976, 77; Fdr & Dir Univ Va Summer Swim Clin 1975-; Nat Assn Col Dirs of Aths 1976-; AAHPER 1961-; VAHPER 1961-; Phi Delta Kappa 1974-; Va Sports Halls of Fam, Bd Dirs 1978, Chp Mbrship Com 1978; AAUW 1979-; Wom's Equity Action Leag 1979-; hon/Editor *Official Wom's Lacrosse Scorebook* 1976.

KELLY, ERIC LEROI oc/Marketing and Business Management Consultant; b/July 10, 1946; h/5009 Bass Pl SE, Wash DC 20019; ba/Same; m/Elizabeth A G; c/Derek Christopher Hobier; p/Alex Sr and Ruth B Kelly, Tallahassee, FL ed/BA; MA; pa/Toastmasters Intl; cp/JCs; Dem Party; r/Meth CME; hon/Public Ser Awds; Personal Achmt Awd.

KELLY, ERNEST E JR oc/Realtor, Tax Practitioner; b/Oct 16, 1924; h/Ponca City, OK; ba/221 S 2nd, Ponca City, OK; m/Mable Marie; c/Sharon Kay, Karen Kim, Erin Kit; pa/Ernest E (dec) and Francis B Kelly, Murfreesboro, AR; ed/BA Draughons Bus Univ 1946; MA Okla St Univ 1952; mil/USN WWII; AUS Korea; pa/Rltr CRS CRI; NAIPT; ASTC; Tax Conslt; NASD & OSC Reg Rep; Ponca City Bd Rltrs; Wom Coun Rltrs, VP Ponca City Chapt; cp/Ponca City C of C, Ed Com; Repub Party; r/Disciple of Christ.

KELLY, JOHNNY MOODY oc/Sanitation Engineer; b/Apr 28, 1928; h/412 Sycamore St, Weldon, NC; ba/Halifax; m/Doris W; c/Michael T, Jeb S, John L, Jeffry A; p/(dec); ed/Att'd Univ Tex & Univ Md; mil/AUS 23 Yrs Ret'd Sgt Maj; pa/Dir Halifax Co Solid Waste Dept; cp/Mason; Shriner; Am Legion; PM AF&AM; r/Bapt; hon/Merit Ser Medal 1968, 1970; Bronze Star 1963; Army Commend Awd 1958, 64; 9 Ser Awds; Author Sev Articles.

KELLY, STANLEY DURHAM oc/Consultant; b/May 12, 1916; h/Box 25, Rt 7, Harriman, Tn 37748; ba/Same; m/Clella Ramsey; c/William Nelson, Richard Perry; p/James Nelson (dec) and Dixie Durham Kelly (dec); ed/Dip in Engrg; mil/Grad AF Cadets, Command & Staff Col & Indust Col of Armed Forces, Pilot; cp/VFW; Reserve Ofcr Assn; r/Meth; hon/Purple Heart.

KENAN, SEBASTIAN REGINALD oc/Attorney; b/Oct 3, 1955; h/PO Box 68, Rose Hill, NC 28458; ba/Goldsboro, NC; p/Walter and Margaret Kenan, Rose Hill, NC; ed/AB 1977; JD 1980; pa/Atty; Am Bar Assn; NC St Bar; NC Bar Assn; r/Bapt; hon/W/W: HS Students 1973, Col Students 1977, Law Students 1980; All-Am Fball Player 1977; Dean's List 1974-77; Nereus English Awd 1977; MVP on Fball Team 1977.

KENDRICK, BOYCE ABNER oc/Artist, Teacher; b/Dec 12, 1927; h/4708 Oglukian Rd, Charlotte, NC 28211; p/Bonnie Boyce Kendrick; Effie Jane Lowery; ed/Studied Ringling Art Sch 1948-50, Ammagansette Art Sch 1951-54; mil/11th Airborne Div 1946-47; pa/Profl Artist 10 Yrs; Instr Water Color, Oil Painting, Drawing, Design, Ctrl Piedmont Commun Col; Past Adv Mem NC Water Color Soc; r/Bapt; hon/Circus Show Purchase Awd 1949; 2 Times 1st Prize Winner, Firt Nat Bank Catabaw Co; 3 Times 1st Prize Winner Lincolnton Art Show.

KENMAR, DANIEL J oc/Auctioneer; b/Apr 28, 1959; ba/Lucedale, MS; m/Cheryl Elain; c/James Edward; p/Gerald Dee and Geneva Sue Kenmar, Mobile, AL; pa/Auctioneer, Buying & Selling Mdse; r/Bapt.

KENNEDY, PAUL JENNINGS SR oc/Photographer; b/Aug 20, 1907; h/626 Margaret Rd, Statesville, NC 28677; m/Isabel McGill; c/Paul Jr, John Lowry, Margaret Jane; p/Ladd Brooks (dec) and Maggie Green Kennedy (dec); pa/Maxwell Brothers Chain Furniture Stores 1931-51; Mgr & Part Store Owner Maxwell-Morris & Kennedy 1939-51; Blackwelder Furniture Chain 1951-70; Ret'd 1970; Photog; Past Pres Merchant Assn; Ldr Org'g Jr C of C; cp/Masonic Lodges, Gastonia 369, Shelby 202, Charlotte 31, Statesville 27; Past Pres Statesville Rotary Clb 1976; r/Meth; Mem Ofcl Bd; hon/Silver Beaver Awd Scouting 1944; Man of Yr Lions Clb 1947; Pres Hoey Bible Class; Golden Deeds Awd, Exc Clb 1980; Perfect Attendance Rotary Clb, Shelby 15 Yrs, Statesville 14 Yrs.

KENNEDY, SHERRON MAE oc/Secretary, Public Affairs Director; b/June 16, 1944; h/McComb, MS; ba/PO Box 573, McComb, MS 39648; m/Jerry; c/Gregg, Raine; p/Dewey L and Mae J Matthews, McComb, MS; ed/CPS 1979; pa/Secy, Radio Persnality WAKK Radio; Oil & Gas Land Work; Nat, Intl, Miss Secys Assn, Div VP 1977, Pres-Elect 1978, Pres 1979, Dixie Chapt Pres 2 Yrs; cp/Secy to Mayor John S Thompson 1969-76; Secy to McComb Plan'g Comm; Secy Bldrs Trades Com; Secy Gov'g Bd; r/Bapt; hon/Nom'd Outstg Yng Wom Pike Co 1975; Secy of Yr 1980.

KENNEDY, SUSAN ESTABROOK oc/Historian; b/June 8, 1942; h/8200 Notre Dame Dr, Richmond, VA 23228; ba/Richmond; m/E Craig Jr; p/Austin Lovell (dec) and Dorothy Ogden Estabrook, Richmond, VA; ed/BA summa cum laude; MA; PhD; pa/Fac Mem Va Commonwlth Univ; Author; Researcher; cp/Co-Fdr & Former Secy & Pres Richmond Oral Hist Assn; hon/John Simon Guggenheim Meml Assn Fellow 1978-79.

KENNEY, GILBERT oc/Insurance Sales; b/Sept 22, 1933; ba/#2 Metz Ct, Midland, TX 79701; m/Ruth H; c/Scott, Katherine, Christopher; p/Gilbert L (dec) and Josephine P Kenney, Pine Bluff, AR; ed/BSBA Univ Ark 1957; mil/USN 1956-68; pa/Liberty Mutual Ins Co: Claims Adjuster 1959-63, Resident Adjuster 1963-65, Claims Supvr 1965-68, Bus Salesman 1968-71, Sales Mgr 1971-; pc/N Ctrl Little Leag, VP, Pres; Midland Jr Baseball Assn, Sponsor Chm; Midland-Lee Yth Ctr Bd Dirs; Gtr Midland Fball Leag, Commr; Midland C of C; Midland YMCA, Chm Boys Sports Com; r/Meth; hon/Liberty Mutual's Top Prodrs Clb 1968-80; Liberty Ldrs Clb 1969, 70, 72-75, 77-79; Liberty's Millionaires Awd 1974, 76-80; Liberty's Sales Hall of Fame 1979; Midland Optimist Clb Friend of Yth Awd 1980.

KERN, BLAINE S oc/Business Executive; b/May 17, 1927; h/#23 Carriage Ln, New Orleans, LA 70114; ba/New Orleans; c/Thais, Blaine Jr, Barry, Brian, Blainey Katherine; p/Roy A (dec) and Josephine M Kern, New Orleans, LA; ed/New Orleans Acad Art; mil/AUS Sgt; pa/Pres & Owner: Blaine Kern Artists Inc, Blaine Kern Advtg Specialities, Blaine Kern Productions Inc; Produces Mardi Gras Parades & Extravaganzas; cp/Tourist Comm Bd; Algiers Homestead Dir; La Film Comm; Dir Info Coun of the Ams; VP Police & Fireman Tragedy Fund; Am Legion; YMBC; VFW; C of C; r/Cath; hon/Cits Rotarians, Kiwanians; Selected Top 10 Best Dressed Men in New Orleans; Cath Charities Horizons Awd, Prizes & Awds from Major Parades in Am.

KERNS, EDITH BAILEY oc/Foster Mother; b/Oct 27, 1920; h/6427 Old Carolina Rd, Haymarket, VA 22069; c/David Thomas (dec), George Franklin; p/Joseph (dec) and Annie Elizabeth Bailey, Haymarket, VA; pa/Foster Mother; Pres Gainesville Dist Fire Dept Aux 1965-71; r/Bapt.

KERR, ANDRÉ FIELDING oc/Amateur Musician; b/Nov 22, 1951; h/PO Box 297, Buffalo, SC 29321; ba/Same; m/Patti G; c/Leslie Mishea; p/Truesdale and Thelma Kerr, Jonesville, SC; pa/Mus; r/Bapt; hon/HS Friendliest & Most Dependable; Col Friendliest.

PERSONALITIES OF THE SOUTH

KERR, CATHERINE EARL oc/Artist, Teacher; b/July 4, 1928; h/1412 W Hindricks, Roswell, NM 88201; m/J K; c/David, Terry; p/A K and Lynn Bailey (dec); ed/AB Mason Col Music and Fine Art; Post Grad Art Student Leag 1962; pa/Exhib'd: Ligoa Duncan Gal, NYC 1962, 63, 77; Raymond Duncan Gals, Paris 1973; David's Gal, Roswell, NM 1975-77; Security Nat Bank, Roswell 1978; Num Other Exhibs in US & Europe; Rep'd in Permanent Collects US & Europe; Allied Artists WV; r/Presb; hon/Recip Awd Association Beigo-Hispanica 1973, 74; Las Palmas de Ora al Mierte Belgo Hispanico, Raymond Duncan Gal 1975, 76; Prix du Centenaire Diploma plus Medaille Ciencias Humanisticas Relaciones Diploma, Santo Domingo, Dominican Repub 1977.

KERR, DOUGLAS MOSELEY oc/Life Insurance Agent; b/Sept 25, 1947; h/Valley View Farm, Rt 2, Lascassas, TN 37085; ba/Murfreesboro, TN; m/Patricia Skinner; c/Andrew Thomas, Kathryn Eleanor; p/Willard Augusta and Eleanor Wade Moseley Kerr, Murfreesboro, TN; ed/BA 1969, MA 1971, Post Grad Studies Tulane Univ; mil/USAF; pa/Est Plan'g Spec; Nat Assn Life Underwriters; Mid Tenn Assn Life Underwriters; Tenn Folklore Soc; cp/Tenn Repub Party; Rutherford Co Repub Primary Bd, Past Pres, Current Secy; Past Treas, Current Nat Foun Chp, BPOE #2585; r/Disciples of Christ; hon/Cit for Fulfilling Life Underwriters Trg Coun's Course on Bus Ins; Num NY Life Ins Co Awds & Nat Assn Life Underwriters Awds; Author Num Articles.

KETCHUM, CHARLES RAYMOND oc/School Food Services Director; b/Dec 21, 1941; h/7201 Spencer Hwy, #438, Pasadena, TX 77505; ba/Pasadena, TX; m/Anna Darlene Holloway; c/Darla LeeAnn; p/John W Sr (dec) and Lydia E Ketchum (dec); ed/BS Ed; MS Food & Nutrition; mil/USN 1960-64; pa/Dir Sch Food Sers, Pasadena ISD; Am Sch Food Ser Assn; Tex Sch Food Sers; Tex St Tchrs Assn; NEA; Clrm Tchrs Assn Tex Restaurant Assn; cp/Kiwanis Clb; r/Disciples of Christ; hon/Pres Tex Sch Food Ser Assn; Mbrship Chm Am Sch Food Sers; Boss of Yr, ABWA, Snyder Chpt.

KEYS, RAYMOND R oc/US Air Force Officer; b/Jun 10, 1929; h/421 Eagle Dr, Satellite Beach, FL 32937; ba/Patrick AFB, FL; m/Gloria P; c/Kimberly A Wells, Sharon K Wilkins, Karen L, Raymond R Jr; p/Audra R Keys, St Petersburg, FL; ed/BSC Ohio Univ 1951; BSEE Okla St Univ 1962; MBA George Wash Univ 1965; UCLA; Grad: Air Univ Sqdrn Ofcrs Sch 1958, Air Univ Command & Staff Col 1965, Indust Col Armed Forces 1974; mil/USAF, Lt Col; pa/Instr & Dir, USAF Elects Sch: Keesler AFB, Lowry AFB; Spec Wk in Elects, Mechanics, Physics & Geol for USAF in Spain; US Electronics Staff & Liaison Ofcr w Canadian Govt for Churchill Res Range (Rockets), Ft Churchill, Canada; Prog Mgr for USAF Res Satellites, USAF Ofc of Aerospace Res; Sci Prog Mgr for USAF Tech Applications Ctr, Wash DC & Patrick AFB, Fla; Chief Contract Mgmt, En Test Range Oper (Satellite Launching), Patrick AFB; Cert'd Bldg Contractor, Fla; Brevard Co Elect Contractor; IEE; Intl Electronics Adv Panel 1974, 75; cp/Chm Adv Bd, Delaura Jr HS 1977-78; BSA Merit Badge Cnslr; r/Lay Ldr; Lay Spkr; hon/Delta Sigma Pi; Outstg Mem Engrg Toastmasters, Okla St Univ 1962; USAF Commend 1962, 69; USAF Meritorious Ser Awd 1978; DIB; Commun Ldrs & Noteworthy Ams; Res Opportunities for AF Ofcrs; Pub'd Author; Others.

KHUEN-KRYK, BARBARA COTTOM oc/Advertising Executive; b/May 7, 1925; h/1533 Pleasant Rd Apt H-4, Bradenton, FL 33507; ba/B'ton; m/dec; c/Stewart W Damon, Michael Allen Damon; p/L M Cottom, Bradenton, FL; ed/Att'd Penn St 1944; ICS 1948; mil/USWAC 1944-46; pa/Owner Steno-Pad Inc (Secy Ser); Owner Consortium Inc (Advtg Agcy); r/Meth.

KIDD, CATHERINE JUNE oc/Social Worker; b/May 25, 1940; h/New Orleans, LA; ba/1532 Tulane Ave, New Orleans, LA 70140; p/Cecil C and Jane Gregory Kidd, Baton Rouge, LA; ed/Att'd So Meth Univ 1961; BA La St Univ 1965; pa/Social Ser Dept, Chanity Hosp of La at New Orleans; NASW; Assoc Mem to St Bd NASW Hlth Unit; Assn Care of Chd in Hosps; cp/Jr Com of New Orleans Philharmonic Symph; Jr Com New Orleans Opera Assn; Friends of the Cabildo; hon/W/W Am Wom.

KIDD, VIRGINIA STEADMAN oc/Vice President Finance, Secretary, Treasurer; b/June 21, 1931; h/Athens, GA; ba/855 Sunset Dr, Athens, GA 30606; m/W Howard; c/Joy K Patterson, Martha Gay; p/Alec Hamilton (dec) and Ruth Amason Steadman (dec); ed/Att'd Elberton Commercial Col 1948-49; pa/University Chevrolet Co 1950-56; Ga Outdoor Advtg Inc 1961-; VP Adm Mgmt Assn, Athens Chapt; cp/Athens LWV; r/Bapt; Dir Chd's Dept; hon/W/W S&SW 1980-81; 1st Hon Grad HS Class.

KIESEWETTER, FRANK HOWARD oc/Retired Senior Design Engineer; Registered Engineer, Ohio; b/Oct 27, 1909; h/3520 Milam Ln, Apt 409, Lexington, KY 40502; m/Evelyn V Cundiff (dec); c/Frank Reid; p/Frank John and Lynda Pursifull Kiesewetter (dec); ed/Univ Cinc; BSME Univ Ky 1935; mil/USAF 1942-46, Maj; USAFR Ret'd 1956; pa/Air Conditioning Engr Thomas Emery Sons Inc, Cinc, Ohio 1935-38; Mech

Consltg Engr, Warren & Ronald Consltg Engrg, Louisville, Ky 1938-42; Mech Engrg Conslt for Design & Constrn of Camp Breckenridge, Allied Arch Engrs, Morganfield, Ky 1942-; Ret'd Ser Design Engr, Emery Industs Inc 1948-71; Profl Assns; cp/Life Mem Univ Ky Alumni Assn; Henry Clay Meml Foun; Blue Grass Trust for Hist Preserv; Nat Trust for Hist Preserv; Former Pres, Green Township Ohio Sch Bd; Former VP Oak Hills Sch Bd, Ohio; Ky Civil War Roundtable; Mason; Realm of King Neptune; Res Ofcrs Assn US; Others; r/Presb: Deacon, Trustee; hon/DeMolay Legion Hon; Scouters Awd; Ky Admiral 1970-; Nat Social Dir; W/W S&SW; DIB; Book of Hon; Intl W/W Intells; 2000 Men Achmt; Men Achmt; Lib Human Resources; Notable Ams of Bicent Era; W/W Am; Life in Blue Grass; Fellow Am Biogl Inst.

KILGORE, DONNA SUE oc/Patient Accounts Manager; b/Mar 13, 1948; h/1525 SW 79th Terr, Okla City, OK 73159; ba/Okla City; p/George Riley and Maybelle Timmons Kilgore, Okla City, OK; pa/Patient Accts Mgr, Okla Med Res Foun; SW Ins Assn; Instr Okla Cancer Ctr, Adv'd Oncology Wkshop; cp/Am Red Cross; r/U Pentecostal Ch Intl; hon/W/W Am Wom 1979-80.

KILLIAN, MICHAEL GENE oc/Educator; b/Jan 8, 1948; h/712 Kennedy, Alice, TX 78332; ba/Alice; m/Jennifer Kay; c/Michael James, Christi Denise; p/Travis Killian, Ft Worth, TX; Faye Killian, Ft Worth, TX; ed/BA 1970; MEd; PhD; pa/Public Sch Prin; Author Num Profl Articles; NASSP; TASSP; PDK; cp/Coor Prog of Parental Involvement in Ed; Cancer Soc; r/Ch of Christ; Deacon, SS Tchr; hon/PTA S'ship; C S Mott Foun F'ship; Grapevine Tchr of Yr.

KIM, SUKKI oc/Anesthesiologist; b/Dec 25, 1942; h/301 Leitchfield Rd, PO Box 1026, Owensboro, KY 42301; c/Susan, Joseph, Jane; p/Shihee and Sunshim Kim; ed/MD Med Sch of Korea Univ 1967; mil/ROK Army 1967-70 Capt; pa/Asst Prof Univ Louisville 1978; Pvt Pract'g Anesthesiologist; AMA; KMA; ASA; KSA; Am Heart Assn; Ky Alcoholism Coun; r/Seventh Day Adventist.

KIMBER, ALICE MAE oc/Retired Teacher and Social Worker; b/Mar 24, 1921; h/1421 Valencia St, Sanford, FL 32771; m/Victor Daniel; p/James Dee and Buena Nee Perkins, Altamonte Springs, FL; ed/BA So Missionary Col; Att'd La St Univ & Tulane Univ; pa/Social Wkr Miss & Fla; Home Ec Missionary Tchr to Rhodesia at Inyazura & Lower Gwelo 1951-55; Bethel Col of SDA 1979-80; Dietician Fla Hosp SDA 4 Yrs; r/Seventh Day Adventist.

KIMBER, VICTOR DANIEL oc/Retired Technician; Author; b/May 23, 1914; h/14212 Valencia St, Sanford, FL 32771; m/Alice Mae Perkins; c/Betty June K Whitten; p/George Jack Kimber (dec); Annette Doyle Kimber Steyn (dec); ed/Att'd Natal Tech Col, Natal, Africa; Att'd RR Col, S Africa; mil/WWII S African Engrs; pa/Tech, Fla Hosp of 7th Day Adventists; Author *Stagecoach to Lusisisiki*; cp/Vol to Indians in Arizona; r/7th Day Adventist; hon/Defense Medal; War Medal 1939-45; Africa Ser Medal; Great Grandson of Lord Peer-McKay, Scotland.

KIMMITT, JOSEPH STANLEY oc/Secretary of the US Senate; b/Apr 5, 1918; h/6004 Copely Ln, McLean, VA 22101; ba/Wash DC; m/Eunice Wegener; c/Robert M, Kathleen A, Joseph H, Thomas P, Mary P, Mark T, Judy J; p/(dec); ed/BS Utah St Univ; mil/AUS 1941-66, Pvt to Col; pa/Secy for Majority, US Sen 1966-77; Adm Asst to Majority Ldr, US Sen 1966; r/Cath; hon/Silver Star; Legion of Merit; Bronze Star V w 3 OLC; Order of Mennelik II, Ethiopia.

KINCAID, BETSY STRAUSE oc/Secretary; b/Jan 12, 1949; h/1212 River Rd, Suffolk, VA 23434; ba/Suffolk; m/James W Jr; c/Steven B, James W; p/Bernard H and Elizabeth C Strause, Richmond, VA; ed/Att'd Univ Col 1970-71, Westhampton Col 1971; pa/Secy Kincaid Distributing Co Inc (Beer Distbrs); Secy Harrell's Hams Inc; Nat Assn Female Execs; Intl Platform Assn; cp/Nat Neurofilanmatosis Foun; Yng Dems Suffolk; Virginians for Horseracing; r/Meth; hon/W/W Am Wom 1981.

KINCHEN, THOMAS ALEXANDER oc/Minister; b/Dec 28, 1946; h/3939 Gentilly Blvd, Box 483, New Orleans, LA 70126; b/New Orleans; m/Ruth H; c/Alex, Lisa; p/George H and Annie L Kinchen, Thomasville, GA; ed/BA Ga So Col; MEd Uni Ga; MDiv New Orleans Bapt Theol Sem; mil/USANG; pa/Ga Juvenile Sers Assn; Sev Bapt Orgs; cp/Past VP & Pres Elec Kiwanis; r/So Bapt; hon/Grad summa cum laude; Phi Kappa Phi; W/W Am Col & Univs; Alpha Pi Omega; Outstg Student New Orleans Sem; Outstg Yng Men Am; S'ship Awd; Ldrship Awd.

KINDALL, LUTHER MARTIN oc/Professor; b/Nov 1, 1942; h/257 Newport Rd, Concord, TN 37720; ba/Knoxville; m/Alpha J; c/Kimberley, Katrina; p/Bruce and Lucy Kindall, Nashville, TN; ed/BS; MS; PhD; pa/Prof Cnslg & Ednl Psych, Univ Tenn-K'ville; APA; APGA; AERA; cp/PUSH; NAACP; Pres Tenn Alliance Black Voters; r/Bapt; hon/Nat Tchg Fellow, Nat Sci Foun; Fdr Assn Black Psychs.

175

KINDER, EUGENE HARRILL oc/Counselor; b/Apr 5, 1943; h/2002 York Rd, Martinsburg, WV 25401; ba/Hedgesville, WV; m/Patricia Ann; c/Eric Eugene, Raymond Harrill; p/William Harrill and Gustava Marjorie Kincaid, S Charleston, WV; ed/BS 1967, MA 1971 WVU; Post Grad Work 1977-; pa/Yth Employment & Trg Prog Cnslr, Hedgesville HS 1978-; Sch Cnslr, Jefferson HS 1972-78; Sch Cnslr Harpers Ferry HS 1970-72; Tchr Chem & Physics, Mingo Junction HS 1967-69; APGA; Am Sch Cnslrs Assn; NEA; WVEA; Berkeley Co Ed Assn; WVPGA; W Va Sch Cnslr Assn; Jefferson Co Ed Assn; WV St Guid Adv Com; cp/En Panhandle Chapt Mar of Dimes Birth Defects Foun, Treas 1978-; Civitan Intl; Chm Martinsburg Civitan Clb Yth Activs 1977-; r/Christian; hon/Recip Num Cits & Awds for Profl & Civic Involvement; Author & Co-Author Profl Articles.

KINDER, FREDERICK EARL JR oc/Retail Management; b/Nov 17, 1948; h/1101 11th Ave N, Columbus, MS 39701; p/Fred E Sr and Mary Jane Kinder, Kenansville, FL; ed/BS Fla St Univ; cp/Pres Columbus Commun Theatre 1976-79; Secy Columbus Civic Arts Coun 1979-80; Pres Miss Theatre Assn 1980-81; Miss Theatre Assn Conv Chm 1980; r/Meth; hon/Delta Chi; Outstg Acting Awd 1977.

KING, BONNIE EZZELL oc/Executive Director; b/July 17, 1952 h/Merritt Island, FL; ba/95 Merritt Square, Merritt Island, FL 32952; m/Charles J; c/Chad; p/Richard and Connie Ezzell, Cocoa Bch, FL; ed/AA 1972; Cont'g Ed Bus Mgmt; pa/Public Relats, Announcer & Copywriter WEZY Radio 1972-77; Mktg Dir Merritt Square 1977-; Intl Coun Shopping Ctrs; Fla Coun Shopping Ctrs; Exec Bd C of C; cp/Cape Canaveral Public Relats Assn Exec Bd; Coop Distbr & Mktg Adv Com Brevard Commun Col & Merritt Island HS.

KING, CALVIN RICHARD oc/Marketing Director; b/Nov 8, 1952; h/Rt 1 Box 211, Marianna, AR 72360; ba/Forrest City, AR; m/Sara; c/Kimberly; p/Sterling and Jessie King, Marianna, AR; ed/BA; pa/Conslt Work w Different Agcys; cp/Alpha Phi Alpha; r/Bapt; hon/Farm Improvement Awd, Mr Lee Sr HS.

KING, DANIEL GRAY oc/Company President; b/Aug 28, 1948; h/3409 Red Rock Rd, Okla City, OK 73120; ba/Edmond, OK; m/Linda Kay; c/Amy Kay; p/Robert and Dorothy King, Midland, TX; ed/BBA; pa/Pres Rolynn's Enterprises Inc; cp/St & City C of C; r/Luth; hon/Del to Wash on Pres's Com Small Bus.

KING, ISAAC MONROE JR oc/Retired; b/Feb 25, 1912; m/Jesse Faye Latham; c/Martha Kay, Isaac Monroe III; p/Isaac Monroe Sr (dec) and Birdie Hasley King (dec); ed/Att'd Okla A&M; pa/Ret'd from Exxon; Ret'd from Farming & Ranching; Pres FFA 1931; Intl Arabian Horse Assn; Gulf Coast Arabian Horse Clb; Arabian Horse Clb of Tex; r/So Bapt; hon/Top Ten Nat Arabian Stallion, Am Horse Show Assn; Num Arabian Horse Champ'ships.

KING, LYNN HAWKINS oc/Social Worker; b/Mar 24, 1945; h/205 Mountain Dr, Gadsden, AL 35901; ba/Gadsden, AL; m/George Dodgen Jr; c/George Dodgen III; p/Chad B and Frank Elrod Hawkins, Gadsden, AL; ed/BA Univ Montevallo; pa/Child Wel Social Wkr; VP Gadsden AAUW; cp/Pres Wom Comm Concert Assn; VP Arts Coun; Mayors Adv Coun; VP Friends Gadsden Lib; DAR; Gadsden Ser Guild; Chm Commun Ambassador Prog; r/Meth; hon/Dean's List; Hon Day; Zeta Phi Eta.

KING, RALPH DONALD oc/Veterinarian; b/Oct 3, 1932; ba/Rockmart, GA; m/Shirley Gober; c/Glenn Ralph, Janet Marie; p/Hancel Clifton and Maggie Rae King, Rockmart, GA; ed/BS Univ Ga 1958; DVM Univ Ga Sch Vet Med 1961; mil/AUS 1952-54; pa/Vet; GVMA; AVMA; cp/Rockmart Kiwanis Clb, Past Pres & Dir; Rockmart C of C, Past Pres & Dir; Rockmart Indust Devel Corp, Dir; Rockmart-Aragon Hosp Auth, Chm; r/Bapt; hon/Man of Yr, Rockmart C of C 1980.

KING, ROBERT BURDICK oc/Operational Controller; b/Dec 21, 1949; h/503 Sweet Hollow Rd, Melville, NY 11747; ba/Jamaica, NY; m/Ursula Czulak; c/Eric Michael, Lisa Marie, Loraine Ann; p/William Burdick King (dec); Justine Brewi King, Melville, NY; ed/BA Salem Col; pa/Operational Controller Crew, Trans World Airline; cp/Fdr, Huntington Citizen's Com for the Preserv of Ferguson's Castle; r/Rom Cath; hon/Author *Ferguson's Castle: A Dream Remembered* w Forward by Vincent Price & Intro by Jeanne Dixon; hon/W/W Among Students in Am Cols & Univs.

KINGDON, DOUGLAS ERNEST oc/Director-Professor; b/Oct 9, 1929; h/Chattanooga, TN; ba/Chat; m/Mary Nichols; c/Dwight Douglas, Kim Allison; p/Ivor C and Bertha L Kingdon, Ontario, Can; ed/BA Houghton Col 1957; MS St Col for Tchrs 1959; EdD St Uni NY Buffalo 1971; pa/Tchr Iroquois Ctrl Sch, Elma, NY 1957-60; Dir-Instr Elem Ed Dept Houghton Cl 1960-63; Tchr Amherst Ctrl Schs 1963-68; Co-Dir/Supvr Ghetto Prog Elem Ed, SUNY Buffalo 1968-69; Tchr Rdg E

Aurora Mid Sch 1969-71; Instr US Ofc Ed, EPDA Rdg Inst, Savannah St Col 1971-72; Prof, Coor Rdg Univ Tenn Chat 1972-; Nat Rdg Conf; NCTE; Col Rdg Assn; Org Tchr Edrs in Rdg; Phi Delta Kappa; Intl Rdg Assn; cp/Chat Boy's Clb; PTA; Chat Coun Commun Action Agcy; Hd Start Policy Coun, Chm Vol Sers; Commun Sers Clb; r/Presb; hon/Cert of Merit, St of Tenn Right to Read; W/W S&SW; Author Num Articles in Profl Jours; *Handbook for Student Teachers; Every Student Can Write Creatively*.

KINNEY, MARY ALICE oc/Homemaker; b/May 2, 1919; h/804 Atkinson Dr, Dalton, GA 30720; m/Hinton Eugene; c/Jannie Gail, Donald Eugene; p/John Samuel Sr (dec) and Alice Elizabeth Moreland Jones (dec); ed/BS Ga Col at Milledgeville; r/Meth.

KIRBY, HENRY VANCE oc/Physician; b/Apr 3, 1908; h/1001 W Nicholson Ave, Harrison, AR 72601; ba/Harrison; m/Elva Hudson; c/Henry Hudson, Carol Anne K Fordyce, Helen Vance K Daniel; p/Leander Bender and Virgie May Vance Kirby (dec); ed/BS Univ Ark 1931; MD Wash Univ; Sch Med St Louis, Mo 1933; mil/Capt MC AUS 1942-45; Med Ofcr Gen Duty w 85th Inf Div No Africa & Italy; Bronze Star Medal; EAME Theatre Ribbon w 3 Bronze Ser Stars; pa/Phys, Gen Pract, Harrison 1934-; Ark St Med Soc 8 yrs; Ark Foun; Dir of Ark Acad Gen Pract; Charter Fellow Am Acad Family Pract; cp/Harrison Rotary Clb Since 1934, Sr Mem, Past Pres; Harrison Sch Bd 11 Yrs, Past Pres; Co Bicent Comm Mem; Co Coroner 12 Yrs; r/Presb Ch: Mem, Served on Session 2 Terms; hon/Cert of Apprec w 3 Stripes From Pres F D Roosevelt for 3 Yrs Ser Without Pay as Exmr for Boone Co Draft Bd; Combat Medic Badge; Book of Hon; Fellow Am Biogl Inst.

KIRBY, MAYME C oc/Retired Writer; b/Nov 15, 1900; h/Birmingham, AL; m/(dec); c/Herbert Andrew Jr (dec), Mildred N Kirby-Phillips; p/William Jackson and Willie A Conville Clark (dec); ed/BA Howard Col; Samford Univ; Am Bible Sch; pa/Ret'd Tchr & Social Ser Admr; Govt Employee 23 Yrs; Writes Articles on Civic & Ed Issues; Writes Own Paper "World Hope" 4 Times Yr; Nat Assn Ret'd Fed Employees; cp/Vol w Eldergarten (Sr Citizens Grp); Contbr to Humanitarian Orgs; r/Assem; hon/Nat Liberty Awd, Cong of Freedom, 3 Yrs; World W/W Wom; Commun Ldrs & Noteworthy Ams; DIB; Personalities of Am; Pub'd Poems, Articles & *Tapping Secrets in Silence*.

KIRKLAND, WILLIAM MINOR oc/Golf Professional; b/Dec 26, 1950; h/Owensboro, KY; ba/Pro Shop, Windridge Country Club, Rt 2, Millers Mill Rd, Owensboro, KY 42301; m/Ginger; p/Alfred and Marjoe Kirkland; ed/Grad Univ Ky 1979; USN 1970-74; pa/Hd Golf Profl, Windridge Country Clb; Dir Ky Sect Tri-St Pro Am Golf Assn; r/Meth; hon/Ky St Intercol Golf Champ 1976.

KIRKSEY, FLOYD THOMAS oc/Pastor; b/Apr 6, 1928; h/Rt 6, Box 525, Loncolnton, NC 28092; ba/Same; m/Dorothy Agnes Lynch; c/Carol Ann; p/Victor and Viola Holt Kirksey, Catawba, NC; ed/Deg Theol Fruitland Bapt Inst 1964; pa/Pastor Massapoag Bapt Ch; Missionary S Fla 1960-61; Ordination Comm; White House Comm for Elderly; Panel to Study Brand New Mdse; Plan'g Comm S Fork Pastors Conf; Interdenom Pastors Conf; Former Mem Missions Comm & Bapts Chds Home & Hosp Comm; Bapt St Conv; r/So Bapt; hon/Hon'd by AA Concert for Work w Yng People 1971; W/W Rel; Men Achmt.

KIRKWOOD, EL WANDA J SHIELDS oc/Insurance Agent; b/July 7, 1943; m/Daniel Edward; c/Kimberly Jo Nance; Dana Lenora, Daniel Edwin; p/Louise E Sr and Lenora M Richters Shields, Madisonville, KY; ed/Univ Ky; pa/St Farm Sect Ofc Mgr 1965-68; All St Ins 1976-80; Past Secy, Treas, VP, Pres Elec Nat Assn Life Underwriters; Working Wom Am; Nat Assn Female Execs; Nat Assn Wom's Clbs; cp/Dem; r/Pentecostal; hon/Life Millionaire 1980; Conf of Champs 1977-80; Hon Ring 1977-80; W/W Am Wom 1981-82; W/W Life Ins in Ky 1981.

KIRVEN, LEO E JR oc/Commissioner Mental Health and Mental Retardation; b/July 18, 1923; h/PO Box 1797, Richmond, VA 23214; ed/BS Clemson Univ 1949; MD Med Col SC 1954; mil/USAF 1942-45 Pilot; pa/Commr Va Dept Mtl Hlth & Retard 1976-; Task Force Commun Mtl Hlth Progs, Nat Assn St Mtl Hlth Prog Dirs; Task Force Hlth Plan'g, Nat Assn St Mtl Hlth Prog Dirs; Chm Com Mtl Hlth & Human Sers 1979, So Regional Ed Bd; Steering Com Va Coun Hlth & Med Care; Ex-Officio Mem Gov's Adv Coun Medicaid-Medicare; Adv Com Va Ctr on Aging; Ex-Officio Mem, Va Comm to Study Containment of Hlth Care Costs; Va Coun for Deaf; Va Devel Disabilities Plan'g Coun; CETA Balance St Plan'g Coun; Clin Assoc Prof Psychi, Dept Psychi, Univ Va Med Ctr; Psychi Conslt Va St Penitentiary; Psychi Conslt Petersburg Psychi Inst; Neuropsychi Soc Va; Am Psychi Assn 4th Dist Med Soc; Med Soc Va; AMA; SMA; Nat Assn Mtl Hlth Supts; Nat Assn St Mtl Hlth Prog Dirs; Assn Mtl Hlth Admrs; hon/Author Num Profl Articles.

KISER, S CRAIG oc/General Counsel; b/Dec 20, 1946; h/Tallahassee,

PERSONALITIES OF THE SOUTH

FL; ba/Office of the Comptroller, The Capitol, Tallahassee, FL 32301; m/Gail S; c/Patricia S, Pamela R; ed/BA Fla St Univ 1972; JD Fla St Col Law 1974; pa/Pvt Law Pract 1975; Asst City Atty, Davenport, Ia 1976; Asst Gen Counsel, Tallahassee, Fl 1977; Dpty Gen Counsel Ofc of Comptroller, Tallahassee 1979; Gen Counsel Ofc Comptroller Tallahassee 1980; pa/Fla Bar; Iowa Bar; Am Bar Judicature Soc; cp/Nat Fed Blind, Pres Tallahasse Chapt 1973-74; Nat Repub Party; Hearing Ofcr, Davenport Civil Rights Comm 1975; r/Presb.

KISH, LAWANA FREY oc/Realtor; b/July 13, 1930; h/104 Highland Ct, Sanford, FL 32771; ba/Sanford; c/Teddie K Stuart, Paul M; p/Beulah E Frey, Charlotte,TN; ed/Cert'd Grapho Analyst 1957; pa/Rltr 1973-; Seminole Co Bd Rltrs, Secy, 2nd VP, 1st VP, Pres; Fla Assn Rltrs; cp/Sanford Wom's Clb; Sanford Garden Clb; LWV; Dem Exec Com; r/Ch of Christ; hon/Cert of Hon & Apprec from Emperor of Japan 1963 (Highest Awd Ever Given to Fgn Female); Rltr of Yr 1971, Seminole Bd Rltrs.

KITTLEMAN, MARTHA ADRIENNE HAYWOOD oc/Interior Decorator, Florist; b/Dec 31, 1936; h/B'ville, OK; ba/B'ville; m/Edmund Taylor Sr; c/Adrienne Eloise, Martha Elizabeth, Edmund Taylor Jr, William Marley and Whitaker Haywood; p/Benjamin Whitaker Haywood (dec); Maria Dolores Welder (dec); ed/Att'd Ole Miss, UNC, Longwood, La Salle, Univ Tulsa, Intl Summer Sch Oxford (England); mil/ROTC Btln Major; pa/Owner Decorating Bus & Pineapple Tea Room; cp/DCXVIIC; UDC; ESU; Nat Trust; cp/Hist Socs; r/Cath; hon/Book of Poetry, Var US & British Pubs.

KIZER, CHARLES RAYMOND oc/Paramedic; b/Oct 5, 1944; h/Rt 1 Box 164, St George, SC 29477; ba/Charleston; p/Raymond and Annie Ruth Kizer, St George, SC 29477; mil/USANG 6 Yrs; pa/EMT Instr; Fdr Dorchester Co Emer Med Assn; cp/Fdr Upper Dorchester Co Rescue Squad; Tchr First Aid & CPR; r/Meth.

KLEIN, BERNARD oc/Publisher, Author; b/Sept 20, 1921; h/7309 Corkwood Terr, Tamarac, FL 33321; ba/Coral Springs, FL; m/Betty Stecher; c/Cheryl Rona, Barry Todd, Cindy Ann; p/Joseph J and Anna Wolfe Klein; ed/BA Col City NY 1942; mil/AUS 1942-45; pa/Fdr & Pres US List Co 1946-; Fdr, Pres & Chief Editor B Klein Pubs 1958-; Conslt on Direct Mail Advtg & Reference Book Pub 1950-; Direct Mail Advtg Assn; cp/Mason; hon/Author's Guide to Am Directories; Guide to Am Ednl Directories; Mail Order Bus Directory; Directory of Col Media; Others.

KLEIN, MELVYN NORMAN oc/Attorney, Business Executive; b/Dec 27, 1941; h/4270 Ocean Dr, Corpus Christi, TX 78411; m/Annette Grossman; c/Jacqueline Anne; p/Harry and Bertha Gleicher Klein, Griffith, IN; ed/AB Colgate Univ; JD Columbia Univ; pa/Pres & Chief Exec Ofcr, Altamil Corp; Am Bar Assn; Corpus Christi Indust Comm; Yng Pres Org; cp/Bd Gov's Art Mus of S Tex; Dir So Tex Ednl Broadcasting Sys; hon/Edward Johns Noble Ldrship Awd 1963-67; NY St Col Debating Champ 1961-62; 1st Pl Colgate V Julius Turner Meml Awd.

KLEINHANS, JOHN JAMES oc/Law Enforcement; b/Nov 5, 1954; h/Midland, TX; m/Karen Beth; c/Katherine, Jacob; p/E R Jr and Ann Marie Kleinhans, Brownwood, TX; ed/Att'd Sam Houston St Univ & Tarrant Co Jr Col; pa/Law Enforcement Ofcr; r/Cath; hon/Most Valuable Law Enforcement Ofcr of Midland Co Sheriff's Dept 1979-80.

KLEPPER, PAMELA J SMITH oc/Free Lance Designer, Advertising Consultant; b/July 12, 1950; h/Ada, OK; ba/The Studio, 116 E Main, Ada, OK 74820; m/Jim C; c/James Bradley; p/(dec); ed/BS SWn Okla St Univ 1973; Masters E Ctrl Univ 1976; Post Grad Study Okla Univ & Okla St Univ 1980-; pa/Designer & Owner The Studio; TV, Radio & Newspaper Advtg Conslt; Teacher; Am Home Ec Assn; NEA; Okla Ed Assn; Ada Ed Assn, Local Rep 2 Yrs; OEA Del; Am Clrm Tchrs Assn 1980 Del; cp/Tanti Study Clb: Yrbook Chm, Nom'g Chm, Prog Chm; Kiwannians VP; Okla Polit Action; Dem Del; Arts & Humanities Coun; Scout Merit Badge Cnslr; Commun Chest; Retail Merchants Assn; Oak Hill Golf & Country Clb; Ladies Aux; r/Meth; hon/Outstg Regional Tchr, SE Okla Region 1978-79; Contbg Editor Co-Ed Magazine 1979-80, 80-81; W/W 1973; Duke Awd, Outstg Sr 1972; Outstg Home Ec Major 1973.

KLIEWER, WILLIAM PHILIP oc/Insurance and Real Estate Executive; b/Feb 13, 1950; h/708 Illinois, Killeen, TX 76541; ba/Killeen; m/Mary Helen Bigham; c/John William; p/William Gerald and Ollie DeCou Kliewer, Kenner, LA; ed/BA Nicholls St Univ 1972; MS Am Technol Univ 1979; mil/AUS 1972-77; pa/Ptnr Bigham Ins & Real Est 1978-; Indep Ins Agts ofAm; Indep Ins Agt of Tex; Ind Ins Agents fo Ctrl Tex, Pres 1980; Nat Assn Rltrs; Tex Assn Rltrs; Ft Hood Area Bd Rltrs; Nat Assn Life Underwriters; cp/Gtr Killen Col of C, Com Chm 1978-80; Assn AUS, Chapt VP 1979-80; Killeen-Harker Heights U Way, Dir 1980; Killeen Downtown Inc, Pres 1979; Cen-Tex Kiwanis Clb, Dir 1978-80; hon/Author "Planning for Growth" & "Independent Agent" 1979.

KLINGBIEL, PAUL HERMAN oc/Systems Analyst; b/Nov 3, 1919; h/7480 Jayhawk St, Annadale, VA 22003; ba/BWI, MD; m/Mildred Lawson; c/Alice Jane Blessley, Jo Ann Grayson; p/Herman Carl and Elsa Zilisch Klingbiel (dec); ed/PhB, BS Univ Chgo; MA Am Univ; mil/AUS 1943-46; pa/Sys Analyst, Plan'g Res Corp; Sr Conslt, Aspen Sys Corp; Res Linguist, US Govt Civil Ser; Am Soc Info Sci; Assn Computational Linguistics; Linguistic Soc Am; r/Luth; hon/Merit Civilian Ser Awd; W/W Govt.

KLOPFENSTEIN, CONNIE LEE BECKER oc/Assistant Professor; b/Aug 30, 1945; h/4406 Dolphin Dr, Tampa, FL 33617; ba/Tampa; c/Kimberly Anne, Kelly Lynne; p/Nathan and Juanita Becker, Woodburn, IN; ed/BSN Goshen Col 1968; MN Univ Fla 1974; pa/Asst Prof, Univ S Fl Col of Nsg; Pvt Cnslg Prac; r/Presb; hon/Sigma Theta Tau; W/W Am Wom 1979-80.

KNAUB, DONALD E oc/Museum Director; b/Dec 18, 1936; h/902 Kennamer Dr, Huntsville, AL 35801; ba/H'ville; m/Karen Palmer; c/Zackary Daniel, Andrea Rachael; p/Mary Keeney Knaub, Dallastown, PA; ed/AB Elizabethtown Col; MFA Boston Univ, Mass Sch Fine and Applied Arts; pa/Mus Dir, Huntsville Mus Art 1979-; Exec Dir Muckenthaler Cultural Ctr 1978-790; Civic Arts Dir, City of Davis, Calif 1973-78; Info Asst I, NY Public Lib 1962-68; Assoc'd Coun for Arts; Nat Assem Commun Agcys; Wn Assn Art Mus; Am Assn Mus; SEn Mus Conf; cp/Com for Arts & Lectrs, Univ Calif; Cultural & Rec Com, Davis Area C of C; Leisure Sers Policy Com, Leag of Calif Cities; Exec Com & Bd Mem Alliance of Calif Arts Coun; Chm Fine Arts Com, Orange Co Spec Mus Task Force; hon/Harvard Univ, Inst Arts Adm Cert in Arts Adm; Recip Nat Endowment for Arts F'ship; Cert Prins of Mgmt for Cultural Inst, Columbia Univ Grad Sch; Presented Paper 1978 UCLA Conf of Profl Arts Mgrs.

KNIGHT, EUGENE oc/Salesman; b/Nov 3, 1921; h/1814 30thSt, haleyville, AL 35565; m/Margaret; c/Greg, Steve, Debbie, Len, Phillip; p/Mrs J W Knight, Haleyville, AL; mil/USN WWII; pa/Devvy Inst, Chgo, Ill; Bell & Howell Sch, Chgo; cp/Qtrmaster VFW; Com-man Dem Party; r/Bapt; hon/Ford Soc Profl Sales Cnlsrs 1978 & 79; Pres Clb, Bell & Howell.

KNIGHT, KAREN LINDA oc/Executive; b/Mar 19, 1940; h/1011 4th St, Gretna, LA 70053; ba/Same; p/Nat B Jr and Ada Brunies Knight; ed/JD; pa/Pres Jefferson Savings & Loan Assn; Am & Jefferson Bar Assns; Phi Delta Delta; cp/Adv Bd Eye Foun Am; r/Rom Cath.

KNIGHT, MARY L oc/Assistant; b/May 12, 1938; h/Drawer 10, Hwy 511 E, Quitman, MS 39355; m/Harmon; c/Cathy Sollie, Sherri Bates, Fran; p/Otis and Mary E Kile, Mt View, AR; pa/Miss Nsg Home Admrs; r/Bapt; hon/W/W Am Wom.

KNIGHT, RICHARD GENE oc/Blacksmith; b/Mar 21, 1933; h/Rt 3, Box 427, Murray, KY 42071; ba/Same; m/Barbara; c/Cynthia Ann; p/Thurman Knight (dec); Mildred Cook, Murray, KY; mil/2 Yrs; pa/4th Generation Blacksmith; r/Bapt; hon/Recog by TV & Radio Stations and All Major Newspapers.

KNOPP, WILLIAM EARL oc/Businessman; b/Aug 5, 1932; h/501 Holloway, Hartselle, AL 35640; ba/Cullman; m/Maxine Y; c/Garry, Darrel, Carolyn; p/Harvey W and Alma Knopp, Cullman, AL; mil/USN 1950-54; pa/Co-Owner & Mgr Sonic Drive-In Rest; cp/VFW Post 4190; r/Bapt; hon/Showmanship Awd, Martin Theatres.

KNORI, BETTY JOYCE oc/Manufacturer's Representative; b/Oct 30, 1944; h/2305 Airline Dr, Friendswood, TX 77546; ba/Friendswood; m/Gerald W; p/Otto and Lettie Lou Castleberry Penner, Oologah, OK; ed/AS San Jacinto Col 1970; pa/Self-Employed Mfrs Rep; Nat Rec & Park Assn; Tex Rec & Park Soc; Phi Theta Kappa.

KNOWLES, MARJORIE FINE oc/Assistant General Counsel; b/Jul 4, 1939; h/815 C St SE, Wash DC 20003; ba/Wash DC; p/Jesse J and Roslyn L Fine, NY, NY; ed/AB magna cum laude Smith Col 1960; PhD Cand Radcliffe Grad Sch 1960-62; LLB cum laude Harvard Law Sch 1965; pa/Asst Gen Counsel, Inspector Gen Div, Dept HEW 1978-; Univ Ala Sch of Law: Prof 1975- (on leave), Assoc Prof 1972-75; Exec Dir, Jt Foun Support, NY, NY 1970-72; Asst Dist Atty, NY, NY 1967-70; Asst US Atty, So Dist of NY 1966-67; Law Clk to US Dist Judge Edward C McLean, So Dist of NY 1965-66; Others; Am Bar Assn; Alas Bar Assn; AAUW; cp/ACLU; NOW; LWV; Ala Wom's Polit Caucus; Wom's Equity Action Leag; Bd Dirs Ms Foun for Wom; Adv Bd, Nat Wom's Polit Caucus; Past Chperson, Adv Com, Wom's Rights Proj, ACLU; Edit Bd SIGNS: Women in Culture & Society; Past Mem Exec Com, So Reg Coun; Conslt, ERA Proj, Cal Comm on Status of Wom 1974; Bd Dirs, Wom's Action Alliance; hon/Pub'd Profl Articles; Phi Beta Kappa; Dawes Prize in Govt, Smith Col; F'ship, Radcliffe Grad Sch; Joseph H. Beale Prize, Harvard Law Sch;

177

Rockefeller Foun/Aspen Inst Fellow 1976; 1 of 10 Outstg Yg Wom Am, Bd Advrs for Outstg Yg Wom Am 1975; Wom of Achmt Awd, Tuscaloosa BPW Clb 1974.

KNOWLES, MARK ANDREW oc/Physician's Assistant; b/Aug 8, 1952; h/Spring Lake, NC; ba/Anderson Creek Med Ctr, Rt 1 Box 547, Spring Lake, NC 28390; m/Madonna Cathrine Manning; c/Shane Andrew; p/Phyllis Knowles, Chevy Chase, MD; ed/Att'd Fla Inst Technol; Phys Asst Cert Geo Wash Univ 1978; mil/ROTC; pa/Phys's Asst w HEW; NC Phys's Asst's Assn: Am Acad Phys's Assts; cp/Ruritan Clb; Anderson Creek Vol Rescue & Fire Dept; r/Rom Cath.

KNOWLES, OLA FAYE BOTTOMS oc/Professional Writer, Dog Breeder; b/June 7, 1940; h/Rt 1, Lake Georgia, Chula, GA 31733; m/James P III; c/Jae, Kandy, Kristopher, Scotty; p/Roy Hunt Bottoms, Williamson, GA; Emma Elizabeth Buchanan Bottoms, Griffin, GA; ed/BA Univ Ga 1962; pa/Wom's Pages, City News, Feature Writer *Moultrie Observer* 1965-70; Brigadoon Collie Kennels; Collie Clb of Am; cp/UDC, 3rd VP Tifton Chapt, 9th Dist Dir; Past Secy Ga Div 1976-78; Ga Editor UDC Mag 1966-71; r/Bapt; hon/Faye B Knowles Tray, Awd Given Yrly to Ga UDC Chapt w Most Mat in UDC Mag.

KNOX, JANE WEATHERLY M oc/Oil Company Executive; b/Mar 8, 1911; h/PO Box 397, Wise, VA 24293; m/Sam A (dec); c/Joseph R Morton, Jimmy W Morton (dec), Sam A III; p/Joseph P (dec) and Ida F Weatherly (dec); ed/RPI & Clinch Val Col; pa/One of Fdrs Clinch Val Col; Mgr Sears, Roebuck Co 1940-50; Pres & Chm Bd Knox & Sons Oil Co 1960-80; Adv Bd Nat Petro News; Com UN 35th Anniv; cp/BPW Clb; Pres, Dist Dir St Bd Va Petro Jobbers Assn; St Chm Va DAR; r/Presb; hon/Cert Achmt, US Oil Week 1976.

KNUDSON, HELON oc/Nurse; b/Aug 28, 1936; h/Cranfills Gap, TX; ba/Goodall-Witcher Hosp Found, 101 S Ave T, Box 549, Clifton, TX 76634; m/Trent H; c/Ruth Jana K Taylor; p/Ernst W and Caroline Kachuig Viertel, Cranfills Gap, TX; ed/Dip Providence Sch Nsg 1957; pa/Dir Nurses, Helt Hosp, Meridian Tex 1957-60; Clin Nurse S L Witcher MD, Surgery Nurse Goodall-Witcher Clin 1960-72; Surg & Ctrl Supply Supvr, Goodall-Witcher Hosp Foun, Bd Cert'd Chief of Surg D L McCord MD 1972-; Secy Cranfills Gap Lions Booster Clb 1960; Secy W Olaf Luth Ch 1970-73; Ctrl Tex Assn OR Nurses 1973; Secy CTAORN 1980-81; r/Luth; hon/W/W S&SW.

KOBERT, NORMAN oc/Engineering Consultant; b/Apr 15, 1929; h/161 S Ocean Dr, Ft Lauderdale, FL 33316; ba/Ft Lauderdale; m/Natalie Toby; c/Robyn Beth, Roy Scott, Jay Stuart, Lisa Ellen; p/Murray and Rose Kobert, Tamarac, FL; ed/BSIE NY Univ Col Engrg; MBA Marquette Univ; pa/Prin, N Kobert & Assocs, Ft Lauderdale; Former VP, Stevenson Jordan & Harrison Mgmt Conslts Inc; Conslt to Clients in Metalwork, Ceramics, Electronics, Textiles, Pressure Vessiles, Refineries, Instrumentation, Plastics & Others; Chief Indust Engr, Picantany Arsenal (during Korean Conflict); Former Spec Asst to US Comptroller of Ordnance Corps; Former Chief of Mgmt Engrg Sers, Ordnance Corps in Pentagon; Panel of Experts, *Boardroom Report*; r/Jewish; hon/Hon DCS; Euril Vanes Chair, Cambridge; Man of Yr Awd, Rutgers Univ 1959; W/W S&SW; Alpha Pi Mu; Beta Gamma Sigma; Hon Mem, Ft Logistics Mgmt Ctr; W/W Am Ed; Poor's Reg Corporate Dirs & Ofcrs; Contbr to Profl Jours.

KOENINGER, JIMMY GLEN oc/Associate Professor, Executive Director; b/Dec 10, 1942; h/1424 Liberty Ave, Stillwater, OK 74074; ba/Stillwater; m/Barbara; c/Jeffrey Glen, Jason Charles; p/Glen and Dorothy Koeninger, Duncan, OK; ed/BA; MS; PhD; pa/Assoc Prof Bus Ed, Okla St Univ; Exec Dir Ldrship Devel Inst; r/Ch of Christ; hon/Pub'd Num Articles, Instrl Packages & Mats.

KOFFMAN, EARLDENE oc/Corporate Secretary and Administrative Assistant; b/Sept 3, 1927; m/James C; c/Sheila Jean Braune Pappas, Paula Jane Braune Schubert; p/Ira V (dec) and Jessie L Johns, Onawa, IA; ed/Grad Var Courses & Sems; pa/Exec Secy & Ofc Mgr, Ardaman & Assoc 1961-67; Adm Asst to Pres, So Gold Citrus Prods 1967-73; Corp Secy & Adm Asst to Pres, Albertson Intl 1973-; Secy-Treas D A Intl Inc 1975-; Delta Nu Alpha; Nat Assn Female Execs; Am Bus Assn; 1980-81 Pres City Beautiful Chapt ABWA; cp/Nela Isle Commun Clb: VP 1979-80, Secy-Treas 1980-81; Tohopekaliga Yacht Clb: Ways & Means Chm, Editor News Sheet; r/Prot; hon/W/W Am Wom; Personalities of Am; Wom of Yr, City Beautiful Chapt ABWA.

KOGELSCHATZ, JOAN LEE oc/Psychotherapist; b/Nov 26, 1940; ba/1015 Honeysuckle Rd, Dothan, Al 36301; p/Edgar Rolfe and Helen J Kogelschatz; ed/BA Univ Fla 1963; Att'd Wayne St Univ 1964-65; MSW 1967, PhD 1975, Fla St Univ; Internship V A Hosp, Bay Pines Fla & Dev Child & Adolescent Psychi, Univ Fla Med Ctr 1966; pa/Instr in Psychi, Dept Psychi, Div Child & Adolescent Psychi, Univ Fla Med Ctr, Shands

Tchg Hosp & Clins 1967-72; Field Supvr/Instr for Grad & Undergrad Students, Fla St Univ Sch Psychi Social Work 1973; Field Supvr/Instr, Fla St Univ Sch Social Work 1973-74; Conducted Num Wkshops for Fla St Univ 1973-74; Pvt Pract w E P Pruitt MD, Dothan, Ala 1975; Pvt Pract 1975-; Conslt to Lyster Army Hosp, Dept of Pediatrics Ft Rucker, Child & Fam Probs Clin 1975-78; Conslt & Bd Mem Stop Child Abuse Today 1978-; Appt'd by Gov Fob James to LEPA 1980-; Bd Mem Ala Soc Crippled Chd & Adults 1981-; Am Psychol Assn; Div 29, Psychotherapy, Am Psychol Assn; Acad Psychosomatic Med; Am Orthopsychi Assn; Am Assn Psychi Sers for Chd; Am Soc Clin Hypnosis; Am Assn Marriage & Fam Therapists, Clin Mem; NASW; Acad of Cert'd Social Wkrs 1969-; Nat Coun on Fam Relats; SEn Coun of Fam Relats; Am Assn Sex Edrs, Cnslrs & Therapists; Gulf Coast Assn for Marriage & Fam Therapy; Lic'd: Clin Psychi Social Wkr, Profl Cnslr, Psychol; Cert'd Sex Therapist; Nat Cert'd Psychi Social Wkr; r/Epis; hon/Alpha Kappa Delta; W/W Am Wom; Dist'd Ldrs in Hlth Care; Personalities Am; Commun Ldrs Am; Co-Author *Fatherlessness in Perspective* (in process); Pub'd Sev Profl Articles & Book Reviews.

KOHLER, HELEN ROSALIE oc/Professor, Epidemiologist, Nurse, International Health Consultant; b/Apr 16, 1932; h/Satyr Hill Farm, 2175 Cromwell Br Rd, Balto, MD 21234; ba/Balto; p/Edwin P (dec) and Rosalie Redman Kohler, Allentown, PA; ed/RN; BS; MS; PhD; pa/Prof Univ Md; Active in Epidemiology, Public Hlth, Ed & Nsg Orgs; cp/Yth Cnslg; Common Cause & Ch Affils; r/Luth; hon/Sigma Theta Tau; Delta Omega; W/W: Hlth Care 1977, Am Wom 1978.

KOHLER, KARL EUGENE oc/Architect, Developer; b/Oct 26, 1932; ba/301 Maple Ave W, Vienna, VA 22180; m/Betty Sampson; c/Mark Allen, Eric Leslie, Janis Lynn, James Robert; p/Frederick Leslie Kohler; Nora Gibson; ed/BS 1954; MS 1957 VPI; mil/AUS Corps of Engrs 1954-56 Lt; pa/Pres 301 Plaza Inc 1980-; Prin Karl E Kohler Assocs 1980-; Exec VP-Secy Windmill Point Marine Resorts Inc 1980-; Pres-Treas Kohler-Daniels-Harrelle Assocs 1977-79; Num Archl Positions 1955-; No Va Bldrs Assn; Am Inst Archs; cp/Mill Creek Park Civic Assn, Treas 1962, Pres 1963-64; Past Mem Annandale Jr C of C; Vienna Sertoma Clb, Bd Dirs 1965-67; Vienna C of C, Bd Dirs 1970-72; Fairfax Co C of C; Northumberland Co Va Hist Soc; Fairfax Co Jr Achmt, Bd Dirs 1975-77; r/Bapt; hon/Tchg F'ship VPI 1956-57; Tau Sigma Delta; Cert'd Arch Va, Md, DC, NY; Cert'd Mem Nat Coun Archl Reg Bds; Fairfax Co Fist Annual Bldg Beautificaion Awd 1969; No Va Bldrs Assn Annual Bdlg Awds 1969-75; Fairfax City Annual Bldg Beautification Awds 1976; Am Soc Landscape Architects Hon Awd 1979; Designed JKJ Chevrolet, Vienna, Va (Largest Dlrship in Wash Area) 1976; Designed Hilton Hotel, Williamsburg (Largest Indep Opr'd Motel in W'burg).

KOKENZIE, HENRY FAYETTE oc/Veterans' Affairs Officer; b/July 13, 1918; ba/Key West, FL; m/Irene Mildred Owens; c/Antoinette Irene, Henry F Jr, John Robert, Nicholas Alexander; p/John Kokenzie; Antonia Philimonova; ed/BA Univ Denver 1948; mil/AUS 1939-46 Capt; pa/Dir Vets Affairs, Monroe Co, Fla 1972-; Exec Secy Vets Coun Monroe Co, Fla 1972-; Mgr, Truck Sales, Key West Ford Inc 1961-72; Dpty Clerk, Municpal Ct, Savannah, Ga 1952-58; Bus Mgr Aths, Univ Denver 1948-49; Co Vets Ser Ofcrs Assn of Fla, Pres 1977-79; Fla Public Relats Assn, Pres Fla Keys/Conch Chapt 1977-78; cp/Kiwanis Clb of Key West; Life Mem: DAV, Navy Leag of US, Ret'd Ofcrs Assn, Non-comm'd Ofcrs Assn, AMVETS; Am Legion; Mil Order of World Wars; Civilian Conserv Corps Alumni; Kay West C of C; r/Cath; hon/Phi Beta Kappa; Omicron Delta Kappa; Pi Gamma Mu; Recip Thomas H Gigniallet Awd (Outstg Citizens Cultural Awd) 1958.

KOLENDRIANOS, CAROL ANN oc/Homemaker, Teacher; b/Nov 27, 1948; h/115 Ginger Dr, Danville, VA 24541; m/Harry Thomas; c/Elizabeth Ann, Anastasia Maxine; p/Peter C and Bettie H Athans, Danville, VA; ed/BS Univ So Calif; AA Am River Col; pa/AAUW; Hellenic Profl Assn Am; Va Assn Sci Tchrs; cp/Campaign Rep for Local Coun Elecs; Greek Ladies Philoptochos Soc; r/Greek Orthodox; hon/Grad USC cum laude; Alpha Gamma Sigma.

KONERT, ANN MARIE oc/Director of Nursing Services; b/Dec 20, 1921; h/1440 N 35, Ft Smith, Ar 72904; ba/Van Buren, AR; m/Adolph M; c/James Michael, Peggy, Jo Ellen, Thomas Paul; p/Frank (dec) and Dora Furstenberg (dec); ed/Dip Grad; mil/AUS Nurse Corp 1943-46; pa/ANA; ASNA; Ark Soc Dirs Nsg; Adv Bd Nsg Dept, W Ark Commun Col; Adv Bd Nsg Dept Ark Val Voc Tech Sch; Ark Hosp Assn; cp/NARC; Sele Co Red Cross Bd Mem; r/Cath; hon/W/W Am Wom 1979-80.

KONES, RICHARD JOSEPH oc/Physician; b/Apr 8, 1941; h/356 Horseshoe Hill Rd, Pound Ridge, NY 10576; ba/Bridgeport, CT; New Orleans, LA; m/Sandra Lee Morrissey; c/Kimberly Susan, Robin Melissa (dec), Melanie Ann, Sabrina Lee; p/Joseph I and Ruth Murphy Winkler Kones; ed/BS NYU Hgts 1960; MD NYU 1964; mil/USAF; pa/Assoc Vis Physician, Clinica Cardiol, Tulane Univ Sch of Med, Sect Cardiol 1975-;

Pvt Pract 1971-; Asst Prof Clin Cardiol, NY Med Col 1971-; USPHS Nat Heart Inst Res Fellow in Cardiol, Tulane 1970-71; Instr in Med, Tulane 1969-71; Fellow in Cardiol, VA Hosp, New Orleans 1969-70; Tchg Fellow in Cardiol, Arthur C Logan Meml Hosp, NY; Med Resident, Lenox Hill Hosp, NY 1966-68; Surg Resident, Bronx Mun Hosp, NY; Med Intern, Kings Co Hosp, Brooklyn, NY 1964-65; Staff Mem: Park E Hosp, Park W Hosp, NYU Med Ctr Midtown Hosp, Logan Meml Hosp, Madison Ave Hosp, Parkchester Gen Hosp, Westchester Square Hosp, Kings Highway Hosp, Commun Gen Hosp, Cabrini Hlth Care Ctr, Flatbush Gen Hosp, Mt Sinai Sch Med, Lefferts Gen Hosp, Mt Eden Gen Hosp (all NYC), Park City Hosp, Bridgeport, Conn; Conslt Cardiologist to Hosps & Conn Burs of Disability Determinations Social Security Adm; Mem Num Profl Assns incl'g Am Col Angiology (Fellow), Am Col Cardiol (Fellow), AAAS, Am Col Phys, Am Col Clin Pharmacol, Am Soc Internal Med, Others; cp/Am Mus Natural Hist; Nat Geographic Soc; US Lawn Tennis Assn; Am Med Tennis Assn; E African Wildlife Soc, Kenya; Nat Wildlife Fedn; hon/Lectr in Field; NY St Regents Scholar; Eshborn Scholar; Arthritis Rheumatism Foun Scholar; Freshman Chem Achmt Awd, NYU; Cont'g Ed Awds, AMA 1969, 71, 76, 78; Consltg Editor Profl Pubs; Pub'd Articles; Biogl Listings.

KONIS, BEN oc/Artist, Art Instructor; b/Apr 28, 1924; m/Junni; c/Kelly, Jade; ed/Caton-Ruse Inst Fine Art 1950; Art Students Leag 1953; New Sch 1967; mil/AUS 1944; pa/Artist Oil & Pastel Media Impressionistic Paintings of SWn Subjects & Landscapes; Salamagundi Clb; cp/Bd Dirs Amarillo Panhandle Humane Soc; Art Adv Bd Amarillo Col; r/Cath; hon/Num SWn Exhibs, Mus, One-Man Shows; Pub'd in *Southwest Art* 1978 & *American Artist* 1979.

KOOCK, MARY FAULK oc/Author; b/July 11, 1910; h/1202 Wild Basin Ledge, Austin, TX; m/Chester; b/Kenneth, Karen, Gretchen, Bill, Tim, Judy, Martha; p/Henry Faulk (dec); Martha Miner (dec); ed/Asst'd Univ Tex & So Meth Univ; pa/Fd'd & Devel'd Elite Restaurant in Family's Hist Home Austin 1943-68; Nat Restaurant Assn; Wom in Commun; Nat Assn Bank Wom; cp/Charter Mem & Pres Austin Symph Leag; LWV; Austin Wom's Forum, Exec Bd Wild Basin Wilderness Park; Bd U Fund; Austin Wom's Forum; Pan American Round Table; Bd Mem Ctr Stage Inc; r/Roman Cath; hon/Outstg Wom in Austin 1972; 1 of 3 Tex Wom Innovators 1978; Outstg Wom in Bus & Fin, AAUW 1979; W/W/: Am Wom, Am; Wom of Achmt; Author 3 Best Selling Cookbooks.

KOPLON, MANUEL oc/Businessman; b/Sept 22, 1911; h/Opelika, AL; ba/Koplon's Shoe Store, Opelika, AL; m/Sadye; c/Beverly; p/(dec); ed/Grad Auburn Univ; pa/Owner Koplon Shoe Store; Real Est & Developer; Auburn Univ Alumni, Life Mem; Opelika Plan'g Bd 25 Yrs; Treas Downtown Bus Assn, Opelika; Life Mem Alpha Epsilon Pi (Org'd Auburn Univ Chapt); r/Jewish.

KORDUBA-UNDERWOOD, OLGA MARIA CEHELSKY oc/Music Therapist, Consultant; b/Apr 6, 1946; h/2156 Cedar Forks Dr, Marietta, GA 30062; ba/Atlanta; m/Benjamin Hayes; p/George Michael and Veronica Bronislava Drozdovska Cehelshy, Miami Bch, FL; ed/B Mus Ed Temple Univ 1968; MMus Univ Miami 1979; pa/Reg'd Mus Therapist; Conslt DeKalb Co Hlth Dept; Nat Assn Mus Therapy; Therapeutic Activs Assn of Ga; Day Treatment Assn of Ga; Atlanta Mtl Hlth Assn; Nat Mtl Hlth Assn; Mtl Hlth Assn of Ga; Nat Assn Flight Instrs; cp/Ukrainian-Am Assn of Ga; Ukrainian Wom's Leag of Am; Aircraft Owners & Pilots Assn; r/Ukrainian Cath; hon/Alumni Awd, Temple Univ 1968; Pres's Awd Temple Univ 1967; Grad Res Awd SEC-NAMT, Univ Miami 1975.

KORNICKER, LOUIS SAMPSON oc/Curator; b/May 23, 1919; h/10400 Lake Ridge Dr, Oakton, VA 22124; ba/Washington, DC; m/Beatrice; c/Lance, Steven, William; p/Howard and Lena Kornicker (dec); ed/BS; BSChE; MA; PhD; pa/Curator, Dept of Invertebrate Zoology, Nat Mus of Natural Hist, Smithsonian Inst; Assoc Editor Antartic Res Series; r/Messianic Jew.

KOZLOWSKI, THEODORE JAMES oc/Head Hispanic Apostolate; b/Mar 16, 1933; ba/733 Bridge St NW, Grand Rapids, MI 49504; p/Theodore and Estelle Hankiewicz Kowalski, Grand Rapids, MI; ed/BS Univ Montreal 1954; Study Univ Mex City, Assumption Sem; pa/Pastor St Joseph Ch, Grand Rapids 1965-69; Assoc Pastor St Andrews Cath 1958-65, Pastor 1968-72; Pastor St Francis de Sales, Holland, MI 1972-76; Rector, St Joseph Sem, Grand Rapids, MI 1976-79; Dir Migrant Apostolate, Diocese of Grand Rapids, MI; Chm Pastoral Formation Comm, St Joseph Sem; Adv Bd Commun Action House, Hope Col, Holland, MI; Pres Human Relats Comm, Diocese of Grand Rapids; Human Relats Comm Grand Rapids; Gov's Bd Commun Action, Kent Co, MI; r/Rom Cath; hon/Dist'd Ser, Leag of Cath Home & Sch Assn; Brotherhood Awd, Lambda Kappa Mu.

KRAETSCH, GAYLA ANNE oc/Program Officer; b/Sept 16, 1949; h/4740 Connecticut Ave NW, Wash DC 20008; ba/Wash DC; p/Vernon W and Mildred E Kraetsch, Pgh, PA; ed/BS NWn Univ; MEd Tufts Univ;

PhD Univ Va; mil/VISTA Vol; pa/Prog Ofcr, Acad Ednl Devel; Fairfax Co Public Schs 1972-76; Perkins Sch for Blind 1971-72; Ctr for Yth & Fam Sers 1976-78; Coun for Exceptl Chd; NWn Univ Alumni Admissions Coun & Alumni Clb Bd Govs, Wash DC Chapt; hon/Woodrow Wilson Nat F'ship 1978-80; Phi Beta Kappa; Outstg Tchrs Exceptl Ed 1974; Outstg Yng Wom Am 1979; Mortar Bd; Shi-ai; Alpha Lambda Delta; Dean's List.

KRANERT, VEDA PROCTOR oc/Piano Teacher; h/1119 Locust Ave, SW, Huntsville, AL 35801; m/LeRoy William; p/Mr and Mrs Reuben Finis Proctor; ed/Att'd Judson Col; BMus Chgo Mus Col; pa/Sigma Alpha Iota; First Mem Nat Guild Piano Tchrs Madison & Jackson Cos; Org'd & Lead Jr Mus Clbs Num Yrs; Pres Huntsville Mus Study Clb; Dir Dist 1 Mus Clb; Pres Ala Fed Music Clb 2 Yrs; Life Mem Nat Fed Mus Clbs; Bd Mem from Ala to Bd Dirs Nat Fed Mus Clbs; Nat Chm Biennial Conv Nat Fed Music Clb; Nat Chm Ed Dept NFMC; cp/Huntsville Symph Orch Guild; Former Bd Mem Huntsville Yth Orch.

KRANOWSKI, NATHAN oc/Assistant Professor; b/Sept 26, 1937; h/1212 Keffield St, Roanoke, VA 24019; ba/Radford, VA; m/Muriel; c/Steven, Daniel; p/dec; ed/BA CCNY 1959; MA Middlebury Col 1960; PhD Columbia Univ 1977; Master Acctg Va Tech; pa/Tchr French: CCNY 1960-62, Rutgers Univ 1962-70 Hillins Col 1970-74; Tchr Acctg Radford Univ 1977-; Am Acctg Assn; Nat Assn Accts; Acad Acctg Hists; Am Assn Govt Accts; Exec Com & Editor Newslttr SW Va Chapt AAGA; r/Jewish; hon/Phi Bata Kappa 1959; Grad CCNY magna cum laude 1959; Beta Alpha Psi; Beta Gamma Sigma; Author Book *Paris Dans Les Romans D'Emile Zola*; Article "The Historical Development of Standard Costing Systems Until 1920."

KRASHEY, PAT JETT oc/Homemaker; b/Dec 17, 1918; h/84 Crestview, Calhoun, TN 37309; ba/Calhoun; m/Ralph; p/Joseph Herman (dec) and Bertha Owen Jett (dec); pa/Restaurant Owner-Mgr; cp/Am Red Cross; Bloodmobile Registration Chm; Charleston Wom's Clb, VP; Bradley Co Humane Soc; r/Epis; hon/Plaque for 12 yrs Wkg Every Bloodmobile in Bradley & McMinn Cos 1980.

KREBS, NANCY ANDREA oc/Actress/Singer; b/Feb 19, 1950; h/11249B Snowflake Ct, Columbia, MD 21044; ba/Same; p/Alcuin H and Mary Josephine Krebs, Baltimore, MD; ed/BA Theatre Univ of Md-Balto Co; pa/Mem: AEA, AFTRA, SAG; Performed at: Ctr Stage, Garland & Oregon Ridge Dinner Theatres; Host of "The Bloomin' Place"; r/Rom Cath; Columbia Bapt F'ship; hon/Outstg Yg Wom of Am; W/W; Emmy Awd for "Once Upon A Town"; Best Actress, Univ Md-Balto Co 1969, 70, 71, 72; Phi Kappa Phi; Alpha Psi Omega.

KREDER, CATHERINE JEAN oc/Legal Secretary, Administrative Assistant; b/June 24, 1946; h/514 Wildflower Dr, Grand Prairie, TX 75051; ba/Arlington, TX; c/Alexander Kurt; p/Robert W and Annabella M Burden, Dallas, TX; ed/BA Univ Tex; pa/Adm Asst Dallas SPCA; Legal Secy; Am Humane Assn; Humane Soc of US; Tex Fed Animals; Tex Animal Control Assn; Humane Assn; Soroptimist; Legal Secy Assn Pers Assn Dallas; LWV; Tex Notary Public Assn; r/Epis; hon/Soroptimist Wom of Yr 1976; W/W Am Wom 1979; Lic'd Tex Dept Child Wel & Adult Ed 19745-79; Hon MA Univ Tex, Given for Humane Resources Devel.

KREPS, JUANITA MORRIS oc/US Secretary of Commerce; University Vice-President; Professor; b/Jan 11, 1921; h/1407 W Pettigrew St, Durham, NC 27705; ba/Washington, DC; m/Clifton Holland Jr; c/Sarah Blair, Laura Anne, Clifton H III; p/Elmer M and Cenia Blair Morris (dec); ed/AB; MA; PhD; pa/Secy, US Dept of Commerce; Duke Univ: Sr VP, J B Duke Prof of Ecs; Pres, Am Assn for Higher Ed 1975-76; Pres, So Economic Assn 1975-76; r/Epis; hon/Phi Beta Kappa; S'ships and F'ships, Duke Univ 1942-45; Ford Faculty Fellow 1964-65; NC Public Sers Awd 1976.

KRIDER, JOHN SAMUEL oc/Retired; b/June 27, 1907; h/Sanford, FL; m/Sarah Keith; c/John S Jr, James N; p/Samuel F (dec) and Ella M Williams Krider (dec); pa/Profl Baseball Player; Exec Mgr Gtr Sanford C of C; cp/City Commr, Sanford; Co Comm Chm, Seminole Co; r/Prot; hon/Topper Awd for Commun Devel 1972; 25 Yrs Selective Ser Bd; Adv Bd Salvation Army; Pres Fla St Baseball Leag 1947-54; Chm Waterways Assn of Fla; Kiwanis Citizen of Yr 1978.

KROEGER, CARROLL VINCENT oc/Management Consultant and Educator; b/Jan 3, 1926 h/1617 17th Ave St, Nashville, TN 37212; m/Grace Lee Bolton; c/Carrol Vincent, Sheryl Lynn; p/August Carl Kroeger (dec); Sarabel Newman (dec); ed/NROTC Prog Rice Univ; BA 1949, MBA 1973 Vanderbilt Univ; Doct Qualification Vanderbilt Univ 1975; Dip Natural Gas Engrg, Penn St Univ 1950; mil/USNR 1950-52 Lt; pa/Engr: Blackstone Val Gas & Elec 1949-50, Ctrl Indiana Gas Co 1952-56, Wash Natural Gas Co 1956-59; Conslt: Stone & Webster Mgmt Conslts 1959-64; Sr Advr Standard Oil of NJ, The Hague, The Netherlands 1964-66, Esso Europe Inc, London 1966-69; Fdr & Pres Kroeger & Smith

PERSONALITIES OF THE SOUTH

SA, Zug, Switz 1969-71; Res Assoc Grad Sch Mgmt, Vanderbilt Univ 1972; Proj Conslt, Vanderbilt Univ 1973; Dir Tenn Energy Ofc 1974-75; Mgmt Conslt Pvt Pract 1976-; Assoc Prof Mgmt, Belmont Col, Sch of Bus 1978-; Fellow Inst Gas Engrs, Inst Energy; Chartered Engr, Mem ASME, Am Gas Assn, Acad Mgmt; cp/Gov's Staff, Energy Advr to Gov & Dir Tenn Energy Ofc 1974-75; Com of Nat Acad Sci 1974-77; r/Epis; hon/Stokley Foun S'ship for Dissertation Res 1978-81; Cert of Merit for Part in Proj Indep, Fed Energy Adm; Cert Apprec Outstg Contbns to Gov's Task Force on Energy; Author Over 60 Articles in Profl Jours 1954-.

KRONK, ANNIE KING oc/College Administrator; b/May 9, 1944; h/Rt 1 Box 113, Smithsburg, MD 21783; ba/Frederick; m/Aubrey Eugene; p/Kenneth and U Imogene King, Smithsburg, MD; ed/BA; MLS; Post Grad Study; pa/Col Admr, Hood Col; Lectr; Conslt in Field; NAWDAC; NEA; MSTA; RAWDAC; NOW; WEAL; Other Mbrships & Ofcs; cp/Dem Party; Commun Ser Vol; r/Meth; hon/Beta Phi Mu; Hons in All Acad Work; W/W Wom in Am; Outstg Yng Wom Am 1976, 78.

KRUSE, RICHARD HARRY oc/Microbiologist; b/June 3, 1927; h/Bourbon Arabians, N Middletown, KY 40357; ba/N Middletown; m/Eloise Christenberry; c/Cynthia Jo; p/Harry J (dec) and Carla M Kruse, N Middletown; ed/Att'd Duke Univ 1944-45; BS Univ Richmnd 1952; mil/AUS 1946-49; pa/Indust Hlth & Safety Div, Ft Detrick 1953-63; Chief Res Sect Indust Hlth & Safety Div, Ft Detrick 1963-72; Dir Mycology Lab, St Mycology Ctr, Paris, Ky 1973-77; Pres MEDI Inc 1977-; Am Soc Microbiol; Intl Soc Human & Animal Mycology; S Ctrl Assn Clin Microbiol; SEn Assn Clin Microbiol; Med Mycological Soc Am; Sigma Xi; Chm 23rd Biol Safety Conf 1980; hon/Am Assn Lab Animal Sci Res Awd for Outstg Paper Pub'd in *Lab Animal Care* 1970; W/W S&SW; Author Num Profl Pubs.

KUCSERA, ABBIE KENT oc/Author; b/Mar 14, 1916;h/45 Seminole Trail, Whispering Pines, FL 32939; ba/Georgetown, FL; m/Carl Coleman; c/Lorraine Joan, Carl Walter; p/Walter Green and Marion Ella Szekrak-Miller Kent; ed/Detroit Inst Technol 1954; pa/Editor Pontiac Press 1947-57; Mng Editor *Inter-Lake News*, Walled Lake Bur 1959-61; Promo Publicity Writer City of Sunrise 1961-62; Writer-Editor *On-the-Go* Mag 1963; Copywriter Fla Advtg Inc 1963; Author *Prize Winning Watercolors, North America* 1964; *Best of Show, Flower Arrangements, America* 1964; Editor *Hell Turned Wrong Side Out* 1965-66; r/Bapt; hon/Recip Apprec Cert Palm Bch Co Bar Assn 1975; Poet Laureate SE Fla Dairy Inst 1965.

KUHN, ANNE WICKER oc/Professor; h/Wilmore, KY; ba/Wilmore; m/Harold B; p/Annie Hicks, Richmond, VA; ed/AB John Fletcher Col 1939; AM Boston Univ 1942; Addit Study: Boston Univ, Harvard Univ, Trinity Col, Univ Ky, Liverpool Univ, England, Univ Munich, Germany; pa/Prof Asbury Col, Wilmore 1962-; Var Other Tchg Vis Prof, Union Biblical Sem, Yeotmal, India 1957-58; Tchg, US Armed Forces, Germany 1951-52; Other Tchg Positions; Libn Harvard Univ, Cambridge 1939-44; Lectr Armenian Biblical Inst Beirut, Lebanon 1958; Profl Orgs; Del Var Convs; AATG Cong of Germanists, Bonn 1974; Intl Cong on World Evang, Lausanne, Switzerland 1974; Tour Dir E & W Germany 1976, 77, 78; Travel-Ministry in Germany, W Berlin, France, Belgium 1948-75 (Sums), Hungary & Czechoslovakia 1972, Poland 1973, E Germany 1975; cp/Former Refugee, Relief & Rehab Work Europe; Rel Ed Clb; Harvard Dames; Asbury Sem Dames; Wilmore Woms Clb; Other Activs; Contbr Var Pubs; r/Prot Wom of Chapel; hon/Biogl Listings; Delta Phi Alpha; Grad F'ship Ed Harvard Univ; Grad Asstship Boston Univ; Delta Phi Alpha Awd; German Consular Awd; Thomas Mann Awd Boston Univ; Goethe Inst for Germanistern Munich, Germany; Retreat Ldr PYCC Cons; USA & AF Europe; Harvard Alumni Dir 1970, Fac Clb; Vis Prof, Seoul, Korea Theol Sem Fall 1978; Further Spkg Engagemts, Far E, Taiwan, Hongkong.

KUHN, HAROLD BARNES oc/Professor; Clergyman; b/Aug 21, 1911; h/Wilmore, KY; ba/Wilmore; m/Anne Wicker; p/John William and Ida Alice Kuhn (dec); ed/AB John Fletcher Col 1939; STB 1942; STM 1943; PhD 1944; Hopkins Fellow; Postdoct Scholar Harvard; DD Houghton Col 1970; Postgrad Study Univ Munich, Germany; mil/AUS, USAF Europe 1953-65; pa/Travel-Ministry W Germany, Berlin, Czechoslovakia & Hungary Sum 1972, Poland Sum 1973; Recorded Min Soc Friends 1935; Res Fellow Phil Univ Ky 1944-45; Asbury Theol Sem, Wilmore: Prof Phil 1944-; Chm Div Theol, Phil Rel 1959-; Former Pastor Va & Mass; Res

Scholar Univ Mainz, Erlangen, London, Free Univ Berlin 1960; Observer World Coun Chs, Amsterdam, Netherlands 1948; Fellow Goethe Inst Munich, Germany Sum 1967; Retreat-master USA Europe Sums 1957, 60, 65, 68-77; Del World Conf Methodism Oslo, Norway 1961; Evangelischer Kirchentag, Munich, Germany 1961; Dortmund, Germany 1963; Chaplains Supply; Dir, Lectr Flying Sem to Bible Lands 1954; Inst Social Change, Norman, Okla 1965, 190th Anniv US Chaplains Corps Berlin 1965; Position Paper, Intl Cong on Evang 1966; Prot Del Notre Dame Conf on Vatican II 1966; Position Paper & Respondent Intl Cong World Evang, Lausanne, Switzerland 1974; Tour Dir E & W Germany 1976, 77, 78; Staly Lectr, Wheaton Ill Col 1976; Lectr Univs & Cols; Profl Orgs; cp/1st Aid Instr ARC, Active Refugee Relief & Rehab Germany; Trustee Malone Col; Bd Dirs Christian Freedom Foun; Soc Bible Lit; hon/Delta Phi Alpha; Harvard Fac Clb; Theta Phi; Pub'd Author; Sev Edit Positions; Alumnus of Yr: Malone Col 1968, Vennard Col (Ed) 1975; Editor-at-Large *Christianity Today* 1963-; Vis Prof, Seoul, Korea Theol Sem Fall 1978; Further Spkg Engagemts, in Far E, Taiwan, Hongkong.

KUNATH, ANNE ROBINSON oc/Consultant, Minister; b/Jan 21, 1932; h/3631 Highcliff, San Antonio, TX 78218; ba/San Antonio; m/Donald W; c/Robin Brown, Bonnie, Cindy, John and Stan; p/F Tyer Ronbinson, Columbia, SC; ed/Grad Divine Sci Ednl Ctr; pa/Fdg Min, Divine Sci Ch of Today; Ordained Min Divine Sci Fed Intl; Tchr; Cnslr; Motivation Expert, Gives Classes & Sems to Bus's; Writer Brochures, Pamphlets & Articles; SW Soc for Clin Hypnosis; cp/Am Mensa Ltd; San Antonio Symph; SW Soc for Res & Devel; Treas Perrin Beitel Little Leag; San Antonio Opera Guild; r/Divine Sci; hon/Nat Hon Soc; Author Var Articles & Short Stories in Postitive Thinking and Rel Magazines.

KUNKEL, MARY ELIZABETH oc/Nutrition Scientist; b/Sept 8, 1953; h/Rt 3 Box 770, Newport, AR; ba/B'ham; p/Karl E and Mary F Kunkel, Newport, AR; ed/BSE Univ Ctrl Ark; MS, PhD Univ Tenn; pa/Nutrition Sci, Inst Dental Res; Gerontological Soc; Inst Food Technols; hon/Alpha Chi; Gamma Beta Phi; Omicron Nu; Sigma Xi; Univ Tenn Chancellors Cit For Extraordinary Profl Promise.

KUPPER, MARJORIE LAKIN oc/Education Specialist; b/Nov 28, 1943; h/3508 Needles Pl, Alexandria, VA 22309; ba/Wash DC; c/Mark L; p/Charles T Lakin, Fredericksburg, VA; Gloria P Lakin, Ocala, FL; ed/BA w Hons; MEd; pa/Ed Spec, Instrl Designer, Internal Revenue Ser; Assn Ed Commun Technol; Secy-Treas Fed Ed Technol Assn; Nat Soc Perf & Instr; cp/NOW; hon/Salutatorian HS; W/W Am Wom; Achmt Awd AUS Engr Sch; Pub'd Articles in Profl Jours.

KUPTZIN, HAROLD oc/Labor Economist; b/Mar 28, 1921; h/1316 Xaveria Ct, Silver Spring, MD 20903; ba/Washington, DC; m/Lenore; c/Michelle, Janis; p/Bernard and Sadie Kuptzin (dec); ed/Bach Social Scis; MA; mil/AUS WW II 3 Yrs, Tech Sgt; pa/Dir, Ofc of Tech Support, US Dept of Labor; cp/Bd Mem, DC Chapt, Intl Assn Personnel in Employmt Security; r/Jewish; hon/Num Hon Awds, US Dept of Labor.

KUTZMAN, SONDRA L KLEMENTIS oc/Assistant Professor; b/Oct 11, 1944; h/424 Fox Ct, Mobile, AL 36608; ba/Bay Minette, AL; m/Gerald; p/Alexander Klementis (dec); Thelma Nottingham, College, AK; ed/BS; MS; Phd; pa/Asst Prof, Troy St Univ; Instl Rdg Assn; Phi Delta Kappa; Col Rdg Assn; cp/Garden Clb Huntleigh Woods; r/Prot; hon/Outstg Yng Wom Am 1970.

KUYKENDALL, MACK LAWRENCE oc/Loan Agent; b/Feb 4, 1943; h/3508 Evans Dr, Okla City, OK 73121; m/Saundra Maureen; c/Michael, Michelle; p/Lawrence Kuykendall, Lawton, OK; Navana Kuykendall, Anadarko, OK; ed/Masters Deg Pepperdine Univ 1972; pa/Profl Baseball Player 1960-68, Chgo Cubs & Calif Angels; Bank Ofcr 1972-77, Liberty Nat Bank; Loan Agt Wells Fargo Credit Corp 1979-; Okla Bankers Assn; Gov's Indust Devel Coun; cp/Okla City Jr C of C, St Rep 1978 & 80; Last Frontier Coun Adv Coun; r/Ch of Christ; hon/Outstg Yng Man Yr, Okla City JCs 1976; Mayor's Ser Awd, LA, Calif 1971; Ch of Christ Ser Awd 1978; Okla All-St Player in 3 Sports 1960.

KUZBYT, RAYMOND oc/International Marketing; b/Sept 30, 1933; h/PO Box 25496, Tamarac, FL 33320; ba/Ft Lauderdale; c/Raymond Jr, Gustave, Rudolph; p/Demetrio Kuzbyt (dec); Tanish O'Gorman, Buenos Aires, Argentina; ed/BS Indust Engrg; pa/Intl Trade in Elecs Field; hon/W/W Am.

PERSONALITIES OF THE SOUTH

L

LaBARBERA, FRANK THOMAS oc/Sales Representative; b/Mar 13, 1944; h/PO Box 1395, Plant City, FL 33566; ba/Lakeland, FL; m/Joyce M; c/Frank T III, Paul, Michelle; p/Florence LaBarbera, Plant City, FL; ed/AA; BA; pa/Sales Rep, Lakeland Ford Leasing; cp/Plant City JCs, Past Pres; Fla JCs, Past St VP; Sertoma Clb; r/Cath; hon/W/W Am; Outstg Yng Men Am.

LA BARRE, WESTON oc/Educator; b/Dec 13, 1911; h/Sycamore Slough, Mt Sinai Rd, Rt 1, Durham, NC 27705; ba/Durham; m/Maurine Boie; c/John Boie Keasbey, David Quinton Lefebvre, Louise Anne Stephens; p/l Weston (dec); Artemisia van Meter Hannah (dec); ed/AB summa cum laude Princeton Univ 1933; PhD w hons 1937, Sterling Fellow, Yale Univ; Res Intern Menninger Clin; mil/Parachuter, Off Nav Intell, Calcutta, Kunming; Nav Liaison Off, Adv Ech HQ, Chungking; OSS China-Burma-India, Delhi; OSS SE Asian Comman, Kandy; Att Staff, Cmdr Destroyers, Atl Fleet, Casco Bay; Att Staff, Cmdr-in-Chief Atl Fleet, Bermuda; pa/Jas B Duke Prof of Anthrop, Writer; Res Fellow: Santa Fe Lab Anthropol, Am Mus Nat Hist & Yale Inst Human Relats, Soc Sci Res Coun, Viking Fund & NSF, NSF (Sr); Fellow, Am Anthropol Assn, Current Anthropol; Editor-in-Chief *Landmarks in Anthropology*; r/Sponsor Durham Friends Sch; hon/Geza Roheim Meml Awd; Guggenheim Fellow.

LACEY, V DUANE oc/Hospital & Health Care Consultant; b/Nov 11, 1932; h/7913 Patriot Dr, Annandale, VA 22003; m/Joan; c/Lauren Joan; p/John Vearl and Rose Leah Lacey; ed/BA Univ Wash 1960; MA St Univ Ia 1962; pa/Hosp & Hlth Care Conslt; Intl Mktg of Med Prods & Sys; Dir Projs Mgmt, Am Health Sers Inc; Managed Planning, Devel, Design, Org & Constrn Coor of Med Sers, PT Intl Nickel Indonesian Proj for Nickel Min Locations of Hosps, Outpatient Clins, First Aid Posts, Others; VP & Mng Dir, MW Hosp Planning & Hlth Conslt Firm; Had Developed New & Expanded Hosp Facilities for US Dept of St & Pvt Hosps; Num Profl Orgs; Conslt, Res Assoc w Staff, Div of Human Ecology, Dept Pediatrics, Sch of Med & Grad Sch Public Affairs, Univ Wash; Other Profl Activs; hon/Fellow Mem, ABI; Author Num Profl, Trade & Tech Articles & Papers; W/W in E; Notable Ams Bicent Era; Intl W/W Intells; Book of Honor.

LACY, ELSIE HALSEY oc/Writer, Poet; b/July 31, 1897; h/Rt 1 Box 241, Grassy Creek, KY 41435; m/William Paris; p/Joseph M and Martha A Gevedon Halsey (dec); ed/Tchr Ed, Hazel Green Acad; pa/Tchr Halsey Fork Sch, Centerville, Bethel Chapel, Sycamore Grove; Author 16 Books Incl'g *Verseland of Kentucky* 1956; *Characteristic Traits of Kentuckians* 1961; *A Lacy Sampler!* 1963; *From Kentucky Hills* 1970; *Thoughts Voiced in Poems, Voice of Appalachia, Poem Echoes* and *From Cumberland Hills* all in 1974; Mem Am Soc of Composers, Authors & Publishers; cp/SS Tchr; hon/Life Danae Mem, Clover Poetry Assn; NIA Cert 1967; Received Num Merits & Hons; W/W Poetry.

LADSON, BARBARA MARIA REYNOLDS oc/Tax Consultant, Commissioner; b/Sept 25, 1933; h/Charleston, SC; m/Charles E; c/Eugene Reynolds Jr, Cheryl D Reynolds, Daron F Drahiem and Darryl P Reynolds, Keith Charles Reynolds (dec); p/Lawson and Lorraine T Johnson (dec); ed/Cortez Peters Bus Sch 1955-56; Agric Grad Sch 1968-70; Univ Md 1972-74; pa/Commr, James Island PSD; Tax Conslt & Notary Public; Distbr for Amway; Real Est Salewom, Security Rlty; Asst Entr AT&T; Adm Asst US Cts; Med Secy VA; Housing Ofcr USN; Union Steward Communs Wkrs of Am AT&T; Mbrship Mgr Nat Fed Govt Enployees; cp/Past Mem: Yng Wom's Leag Inc, Secy Longview Bch Assn, Lucky 13 Social Clb; Secy James Island #1 Precinct; Cert'd Poll Mgr; James Island Improvement Assn; Dem Wom; r/Cath; hon/Outstg Communs Work AT&T 1967; 2 Merit Awds US Cts; Merit Awd USN.

LADSON, LUCIA ZACHERT oc/Organizational Psychology; b/July 19, 1926; h/Box 20, Good Hope, GA 30641; ba/Monroe, GA; m/Lonnie L; c/Robert, Mary Virginia, George Massee; p/Reinhold Edward Zachert (dec); Cora Massee, Good Hope, GA; ed/BA; MA; EdD; pa/Orgl Psych, Walton Co Bd Ed; Early Childhood Ed; cp/Civitannette; GAEYC; SACUS; r/So Bapt; hon/Grad cum laude CNC 1946; Devel'd "Ladson Orientation Test" 1978.

LAERM, JOSHUA oc/Museum Director; b/Sept 27, 1942; h/Nowhere Rd, RR1, Athens, GA 30601; ba/Athens; p/Rolf Laerm, Las Vegas, NV; Della B Laerm, Blue Ridge Summit, PA; ed/BA Penn St Univ 1965; MS 1972, PhD 1976 Univ Ill; pa/Asst Prof Zool & Dir Museum Natural History Univ GA 1976-; AAAS; Am Soc Mammalogists; Am Soc Zoologists; Soc for Study of Evolution; Soc Vertebrate Paleontology; hon/Num Grants; Author Approx 20 Sci Articles.

LAGUERUELA, EARLINE VEVE oc/Executive; b/Aug 4, 1952; h/San Antonio, TX; ba/9933 Broadway, San Antonio, TX 78217; m/Andy; p/Rafael F and Lisette Ortiz Veve, Fajardo, PR; ed/Att'd Univ Geneva, Switz 1971; BA Manhattanville Col 1973; pa/Pres Sounds & Creations Inc, Advtg Agcy; cp/Nat Hispanic Repub Assem, San Antonio Chapt, Del Bd Dirs; hon/Nat Hon Soc; W/W Am Wom 1981-82.

LAHR, NIELS LONGFIELD oc/Electrical Engineer; b/Apr 18, 1933; h/27 Valencia Rd, Rocklege, FL 32955; ba/Kennedy Space Ctr, FL; m/Mary Ann Newman; c/Sharon Denise, Susan Longfield, Kelly Anna, Shanna Lynn; p/Ralph Oliver Lahr (dec); Muriel L Longfield-Smith Lahr, Babson Park, FL; ed/BSEE Univ Fla 1957; pa/Engr, The Boeing Co, Kennedy Space Ctr, Fla 1957-74; Prin Engr, Planning Res Corp, Kennedy Space Ctr 1974-; IEEE; cp/Bd Dirs Rockledge HS Band Parents Assn; r/Meth: Adm Bd; hon/Apollo/Saturn V Roll of Hon 1972.

LAING, BETTY JEAN oc/Director of Inservice Education; b/Jan 29, 1925; h/2807 52nd St, Lubbock, TX 79413; ba/Lubbock; m/Robert William (dec); c/John Leslie, Mary Lou Munnecke, Jo Ann; p/Elic Garland (dec) and Lettie Emilie Cook Sanders, Amarillo, TX; ed/BA Redland Univ; RN Northwest Tex Hosp Sch Nsg; mil/Nurse Cadet WWII; pa/Dir Inservice Ed, St Mary of the Plains Hosp; Fac Mem Am Heart Assn; Hosp Coun Edrs of Lubbock; Tex Hosp Assn Edrs; Am Hosp Assn; Reg'd RN in St Tex & Calif; r/Presb; hon/W/W Am Wom 1978-79; W/W Am HS Students; Best All Around Student 1942.

LAIRD, ROBERT DONALD oc/Manager; b/May 1, 1942; b/Clarksville, AR; p/Russell and Jean Laird, Coshocton, OH; ed/Assoc Deg Cleveland Engrg Inst 1961; Mech Technol LeTourneau Col 1963; mil/USMC; p/Mgr Mfg & Facilities Engrg, Singer Co Motor Prods Div; Soc Mfg Engrs; Robotics Intl SME; Am Soc Metals; Am Mgmt Assn; cp/Am Legion; VFW; Order of Eagles; Loyal Order Moose; r/Bapt; hon/Navy Commend 1970.

LAKE, WENDELL WILKIE oc/Company Vice President; b/Nov 27, 1941; h/97 Hughes Ave, Berea, KY 40403; ba/Richmond, KY; m/Jacqueline Combs; c/Kirk, Lisa, Jeff; p/Algan Lake (dec); Zayda Williams, Sand Gap, KY; pa/VP Begley Drug Co; r/Christian.

LAM, CHARLOTTE NELL oc/College Professor; b/Jun 17, 1924; h/826 Bryan, Weatherford, OK 73096; ba/W'ford; c/Vicki Nell Parks, Mary Lynn Lenz, Bradford Earl; p/Arden E and Maude Dawson, W'ford; ed/BE; MT; PhD; pa/SWn Okla St Univ: Prof, Pres Fac Senate 1978-79, Lectr; cp/ACBL; r/Meth; hon/St HEACO, Let's Hear It Awd, 1978.

LAMB, FRED F JR oc/Music Supervisor; b/Nov 17, 1945; h/2409 Temple Ave, Albany, GA 31707; m/Bobette B; c/Lacey, Jeremy; p/Fred F Sr and Freddie Mae Armstrong Lamb, Pensacola, FL; ed/AA Pensacola Jr Col 1966; B Mus Ed Fl St Univ 1968; MEd Auburn Univ 1976; mil/AUS; pa/Mus Supvr Dougherty Co Sch Sys; Ga Mus Edrs Assn, Past Dist VChm & Secy-Treas; Mus Ed Nat Conf; Ga Assn Curric & Instr Supvrs; cp/Prot.

LAMB, MARY KAY oc/Program Coordinator; b/Apr 22, 1953; h/124 E Monore St, Sturgis, KY 42459; ba/Morganfield, KY; m/Donald W; c/Chad Pryor; p/Charles Jr and Martha Lewis Pryor, Sturgis, KY; ed/BS Murray St Univ 1975; Grad Studies Guid & Cnslg Murray St Univ 1976-; pa/Prog Coor, Higgins Lrng Ctr 1978-; Cnslr Breckinridge Job Corp Ctr 1975-78; Am Assn Mtl Deficiences; Nat Rehab Assn; Ky Rehab Assn Nat Assn Rehab; Profls in Pvt Sect; r/Bapt; hon/W/W S&SW 1980.

LAMBERT, AURORA BLANCHE h/Frankston, TX; ba/Tex College, 2404 N Grand Ave, Tyler, TX 75701; p/Abe (dec) and Ora Smith (dec); pa/E Tex Rdg Coun, Past Pres; Intl Rdg Assn; cp/Secy to Precinct Elec Judge; Palestine Civic Leag; r/Bapt; hon/Author "Evaluative Criteria for a Secondary School Library" 1967.

LAMBERT, DORIS LYNN oc/Performer, Teacher; b/Dec 27, 1953; h/422 NW 68th St, Lawton, OK 73505; m/James William; p/Billy and Verda J Reed, Long Bch, MS; ed/BME magna cum laude SWn Okla St Univ; MMus Mid-Wn St Univ; pa/Performer & Tchr Vocal Mus; Soc Mus Theory; Lawton Phil Orch; Mu Phi Epsilon; Nat Mus Tchrs Assn; r/Bapt; hon/Pi Kappa Lambda; Soloist w Wichita Falls Civic Chorus.

LAMBERT, MARTIN LEE JR oc/Executive; b/July 3, 1937; h/1401 Grainger Ave, Knoxville, TN 37917; ba/Knoxville; m/Kathryn Burns; ed/BSPH Auburn Univ 1958; MPH 1976, PhD 1978 Univ Tenn; RPh; CF; COAC; FACA; ABDP; mil/USAR 1960-66; pa/Pharm Ritch's Pharm 1958-60; Pharm NeSmith Pharm 1960-61; Med Ser Rep ER Squibb & Sons 1961-62; Pharm: Good Samaritan Hosp, C-B Lab, Pearl Drug Co, Lewis Drug Co 1962-64; Med Ser Rep ER Squibb & Sons 1964-66; Pres Lambert's Pharm I Inc, Pres Lambert's Pharm II; Pres Medicare Equip Sers of E Tenn Inc, Proprietor Hlth Care Mgmt Sers; Proprietor Fling River Farm; Adj Asst Prof Samford Univ Sch Pharm 1966-; Knoxville Area Assn Retail

Druggists 1971-72; K'ville Pharm Assn Inc, Author Constitution & By-Laws 1973; Am Col Apothecaries, Chm Bd Dirs 1979-81; Am Col Apothecaries Res & Ed Foun, Mem Bd 1979-81; Univ Tenn Col Pharm, Asst Prof Pharm Pract 1978-80; Nat Assn Retail Druggists; Am Pharm Assn; Acad Pharm Pract; Am Col Apothecries; Am Bd Diplomates in Pharm, Cert'd in Fam Pract; Am Assn Cols of Phars, Coun Faculties; Am Inst Hist of Pharm; Am Public Hlth Assn; Soc Public Hlth Ed; United Ostomy Assn; Assn Indep Med Equip Suppliers; Tenn Pharm Assn; Tenn Pharm Polit Action Com; Tenn Med Equip Providers Assn; K'ville Pharm Assn; K'ville Ostomy Assn; Kidney Foun E Tenn; Samford Univ Mortar & Pestle Soc; Phi Kappa Phi; Phi Delta Chi; Delta Sigma Phi; BBB; Gideons Intl; Num Other Profl Assns, Activs & Coms; cp/YMCA Bd Mgmt, Eastside Br 1975-80; YMCA Heritage Clb; St Mary's Med Ctr Devel Coun, Annual Support Com 1979-80; Brownlow Commun Org; E Tenn Substance Abuse Coun, Bd Dirs 1979-80; Univ Tenn Pres's Clb; Samford Univ Prof's Clb; Gtr Knoxville C of C; BSA Asst Scoutmaster Troop 25; r/Epis; hon/Regional Dir Am Col Apothecaries 1976; Ky Col 1977; Ark Traveler 1978; W/W S&SW 1980; Intl Biog 1980; Author Num Profl Pubs Incl'g *How I Started My Pharmacy with a Bankroll that Totaled a Mere $200!* & *Drug and Diet Interactions.*

LAMBERT, RUSSELL R oc/General Contractor; b/June 23, 1928; h/Trenton, TX; m/Jackie; c/Russ Richard Jr, Cathy Jean; p/Emma Marie Gordon, Le Mars, IA; mil/USAF 18 Mos; pa/Gen Contractor Bldg & Invests; r/Prot.

LAMBETH, JAMES ERWIN oc/Executive; b/Feb 2; h/PO Box 308, Thomasville, NC 27360; m/Katharine Evermond Covington; c/James Erwin III, Richard Covington, Mary Katherine Cullens, William Roderick; p/James Erwin Lambeth Sr (dec); Helen McAulay Lambeth Yankey (dec); ed/AB Duke Univ 1937; Att'd Harvard Bus Sch 1978; pa/Secy-Treas Erwin-Lambeth Inc; cp/Rep NC St Ho of Reps 1977-80; NC Wildlife Comm; r/Meth.

LAMMERDING, JOHN JUDE oc/Executive; b/July 3, 1929; h/Jacksonville, Fl; ba/1045 Riverside Ave, Suite 235, Jacksonville, FL 32204; m/Jane Annette Haglund; c/Mark John, Amy Annette, Eric Richard; p/John Charles Vincent Lammerding (dec); Mary Margaret Elmiger (dec); ed/BS Univ Ala; MBA NY Inst Fin 1970, Inst Fin Plan'g 1972, Univ N Fla 1978; mil/USAF 1956-67; pa/Broker-Rep Walston & Co 1969-73; Conslt Intl Mgmt Firm 1973-74; Sr Fin Analyst Single Source Bnkg, Capital Efficiences 1974-; Pres Lammerding & Assocs; AMBA; Intl Platform Assn; Aircraft Owners & Pilots Assn; Nat Automated Clearing House Assn Panelist; c/J'ville C of C; Westside Bus-man's Clb; Captain's Clb; Ala Alumni Assn; Gator Bowl Sunbelt Conf Basketball Tourn Com; r/Rom Cath; hon/W/W S&SW 1980-81; Shareholder's Mgmt Co One of the Outstg Broker-Reps in Country; Panelist & Part 4th Annual NACHA Nat Conv 1979.

LANCASTER, JAMES FRANKLIN oc/Businessman; b/Feb 9, 1923; h/Rt 5 Box 170, Live Oak, FL 32060; ba/Same; m/Elaine V; c/Richard, Larry, Rodney, Sharon Williams, Sandy West; p/Ben and Mae Lancaster, Live Oak, FL; mil/AUS; pa/Restaurant & Grocery; r/Prot.

LANCE, LaBELLE D oc/Author; Homemaker; b/May 8, 1931; h/10 Habersham Way NW, Atlanta, GA 30305; ba/Calhoun; m/Thomas Bertram Sr; c/Thomas Jr, David J, Stuart A, Claude Beverly; p/Claude Barker David Sr (dec); Ruth McDavid Chance, Calhoun; ed/Att'd Univ Ga; pa/Public Spkr; cp/Wom's Clb; Grey Lady; Scout Ldr; Red Cross Swimming Instr; Bd Mem: The Washington Home, Smithsonian Woms Assocs, Nat Symph, Am Univ Trustee (all in Wash DC); Bd Govs Atl Commun Ser Awds Inc; Bd Ga Mtl Hlth Assn; r/Meth Ch: Local Pres, Dist & St Ofcs Held; hon/Wom's Clb Citizenship Awd for St; Dist Homemakers Awd; Author *This Too Shall Pass,* 1978; Valedictorian, Calhoun HS.

LAND, JOSEPH HAROLD SR oc/Attorney-at-Law; b/Apr 1, 1913; h/8204 N May Ave, Oklahoma City, OK 73120; ba/Okla City; m/Lucille Lackey; c/Virginia Lee Mills, Pammela Sue Ash, Joe H Jr; p/Joseph Henry and Hattie Bell Land (dec); ed/BA OS Univ 1935; LLB SE Univ Wash DC 1941; mil/45th Div NG 4½ Yrs; pa/Lwyr 32 Yrs; Mun Judge 3½ Yrs; Asst Co Atty, Okla Co; cp/C of C; Shriner; 32nd Deg Mason; Var Ofcs, Dem Party; r/Bapt; hon/Am Bar Assn Del; Pres US Cit; Nat Col Judiciary Certs; Univ Nev, Phi Beta Gamma.

LAND, MARY ELIZABETH oc/Professor of Music; b/Dec 17, 1925; h/5511 Bradshaw St, Jacksonville, FL 32211; ba/J'ville; m/William Anderson; c/Mary, Martha, William A II; p/William B Burrus (dec); Mary W Burrus, New Bern, NC; ed/BA Univ NC-Chapel Hill 1947; MA E Carolina Univ 1960; Addit Study: Juilliard Sch Music Sum 1948, New Sch for Music Study Sum 1969, Others; pa/Fla Jr Col-J'ville: Chm for Presenting Sev Master Piano Classes, CoDir Fine Arts Enrichmt Centre 1975, Full-time Mem Music Fac 1974; Presenting Piano Wkshops 1975-76;

Dir Music Arlington Presb Ch, J'ville 1960-73; Developed Music Prog, St Andrews Epis Day Sch, J'ville 1963-; Music Resource Tchr (Grades 1-6), Duval Co Schs, J'ville 1960-62; Org'd Mary Elizabeth Land Studio of Music 1948-60; Other Previous Positions; Appt'd Adjudicator Nat Guild Piano Tchrs 1973; 1st Dir J'ville Music Tchrs Piano Ensemble 1975-76; Org'd 1st Jr Choir Fest, J'ville 1970; J'ville, Fla St Music Tchrs Assns; Music Tchrs Nat Assn; Sigma Alpha Iota; Beta Rho Chapt Delta Kappa Gamma; Var Perfs; r/Presb; hon/St & Nat Certn in Piano; Hon'd by Jr Choir Fest Org at Last Concert.

LANDERS, JAMES WALTER JR oc/Real Estate Broker; b/Jan 4, 1926; h/Borger, TX; m/Willa Mae; p/James Walter Landers, Quanah, TX; Verdie M Landers (dec); ed/AA Frank Phillips Col 1955; BBA Univ Okla 1957; mil/USN 1944-46; pa/Owner Landers Real Estate; VP & Secy Borger Bd Rltrs; cp/Precinct Chm, Precinct II Hutchinson Co, Tex; Comdr Smokey City Post #671 Am Legion; hon/Sophomore Class Pres, Frank Phillips Col 1954; Pres Vet's Clb, Frank Phillips Col 1953-55; W/W Frank Phillips Col 1955.

LANDISS, FRED LEVI oc/Assistant Director of Alumni & Placement Services; b/Jul 18, 1947; h/468 Rivermont Dr, Clarksville, TN 37040; ba/C'ville; m/Judy Ann Powell; c/James Phillip; p/G L Jr and Katherine Gillahan Landiss, Cumberland City, TN; ed/BS, MA Austin Peay St Univ; pa/Asst Dir Alumni & Placemt Sers, Austin Peay St Univ, C'ville; Tenn Assn of Supvn & Curri Devel; Nat Assn of Supvn & Curri Devel; IRA; Tenn Assn of Middle Schs; Kappa Delta Pi; Bd Trustees, C'ville Acad; cp/Cubmaster, C'ville Acad Cub Scout Pack 521; Former Mem Civitan Intl; r/U Meth Ch; hon/Pres-elect Austin Peay St Univ Alumni Assn; Outstg Yg Men in Am 1977.

LANDMAN, GEORGINA BARBARA oc/Attorney at Law, Professor of Law; b/Feb 16, 1938; h/3241 S Troost, Tulsa, OK 74105; ba/Tulsa; c/Nathaniel Martin; ed/BA Trinity Univ; MA St Louis Univ; JD Univ Denver; LLM Univ Mo-Kansas City; pa/Atty at Law, Williams, Landman & Savage, Tulsa; Atty at Law, Rogers & Bell, 1976-78; Univ Tulsa Col Law: Asst Dean & Assoc Prof Law 1974-76, Asst Prof Law 1973-74; Spec Asst to Reg Admr, US Dept of Justice, Law Enforcemt Assistance Adm, Ks City, Ks 1972-73; Legal Asst & Urban Intern US Dept Housing & Urban Devel, St Louis, Mo 1971-72; Com Mem, Tulsa Co Bar Assn & Okla Bar Assn; ABA; Fed Energy Bar Assn; Editor & Chm Tulsa Co Bar Assn Pubs Com; cp/Mem Metro Tulsa Citizens' Crime Comm; hon/Intl Law Awd 1970; Boettcher Foun Judicial Clerkship; John B Gage Hons Fellow, Urban Law; Pub'd Author; Biogl Listings.

LANDRAM, CHRISTINA LOUELLA oc/Librarian; b/Dec 10, 1922; h/1478 Leafmore Ridge, Decatur, GA 30033; ba/Atlanta, GA; m/Robert E; c/Mark O; p/Ralph Oliver (dec); Bertie Oliver, Decatur; ed/BA; MSLS; pa/Am Lib Assn: Life Mem, VChm, Chm Elect Cataloging Norms Discussion Group, Cataloging & Classification Sect, Resources & Tech Sers Div; SEn Lib Assn; Mem Budget Com Ga Lib Assn; r/Presb.

LANDRENEAU, RODNEY EDMOND JR oc/General Surgeon; b/Jan 17, 1929; h/1311 Williams, Eunice, LA 70535; ba/Eunice; m/Colleen Fraser; c/Rodney J, Michael D, Denise Margaret, Melany Patricia Savoy, Fraser E, Edythe B; p/R E Sr and Blanche Savoy Landreneau, Eunice; ed/MD LSU Med Sch 1951; Charity Hosp New Orleans, La: Internship 1951-52, Gen Surg Residency 1952-54, 1956-58; mil/AUS Med Corps 10th Spec Forces Group ABN Group Surg 1954-56; Colonel Confederate AF 1977; pa/Chief Med Staff, Moosa Meml Hosp 1977-79; Gen Surg Eunice, La 1958-; Clin Instr Nsg Dept LSU-E (EMT Tng); Conslt Staff: Lafayette Charity Hosp, Savoy Meml Hosp, Opelousas Gen Hosp; cp/Rotary Clb; BSA; Centurion LSU Alumni Fund; Bd Mem Acadiana Bk & Trust Co; Am Legion; SAR; VP Fraquetique Chapt Imperial St Landry Hist Soc; Others; r/Rom Cath: K of C; hon/AOA Med Soc; LSU Med & Surg Soc.

LANDRÓN VILLAMIL, JOSÉ M oc/Personnel Director and Management Consultant; b/Feb 4, 1936; h/274 Larrinaga St, Urb Baldrich, Hato Rey, PR 00918; m/Judith Baralt; c/Lindy A, Bianca A; p/Jose M Landron; Blanca R Villamil; ed/BS Clemson Univ 1963; Att'd Univ PR 1960; mil/Adv'd Course ROTC; pa/Indust Relats Dir; Mgmt Conslt; Past VP E Region ASPA; Dir Public Relats ASPA 1975; PR Mfrs Assn Soc Accident Prevention; Instr PR Industs Sems; VChm Nat Alliance Bus; VChm Pvt Indust Coun PR; r/Chat; hon/Cit Jr Achmt Cnlsr 1971 & 72; U Funds Outstg Citizenship Awd 1972; Red Cross Recog for Fund Raising 1977; Author "Duties and Responsibilities of Good Supervision" 1972.

LANDRY, WALTER JOSEPH oc/Attorney at Law; Professor of Political Science; b/Jan 23, 1931; h/501 Tulane Ave, Lafayette, LA 70503; ba/Lafayette; m/Carolyn K; c/Celeste, John, Joseph, Catherine, Walter Jr, James; p/John T Landry (dec); Lelia Peltier Landry, Lafayette; ed/BSME Notre Dame 1952; JD Tulane 1958; MA 1969, PhD 1975 Am Univ; mil/USMC 1952-54, Maj; pa/Gen Elect Co 1954-55; Patent Examr US Commerce Dept, Wash 1955-56; Leg Asst to Senator Russell Long of La,

Wash 1956-57; Indiv Pract Law, New Orleans 1958-61; Fgn Ser Ofcr US Dept St, Wash 1961-70; 3rd Secy Embassy, Paraguay 1962-64; Vice Consul Spain 1964-66; Assoc Ops Ofcr, Editor Exec Secretariat Dept 1967-68; Advr to US Mission to OAS 1968-70; Sr Reschr La Constl Conv 1973-74; Asst Prof Polit Sci Univ SWn La 1970-74, 1976-; w Law Firm Landry, Poteet & Landry, Lafayette 1974-79; Partner, Firm of Poteet & Landry 1979-; La St Bar Assn; cp/Mem Dem St Ctl Com; Chm Lafayette Parish Dem Exec Com; Chm Carter-Mondale Campaign Lafayette Parish, 1976; Cub Scouts, Lafayette; Past Pres: La Assn Dem Exec Coms, Intl Relats Assn of Acadiana; Pres Acadiana Chapt Intl Good Neighbor Coun; VChm Clb of Elected Dems of La; Del Dem Nat Conv 1974, 78; hon/Contbr Articles to Profl Pubs; W/W in Am Law.

LANDTROOP, MICHAEL EUGENE oc/Plant Manager; b/June 5, 1948; h/Camdem, AR; ba/North American Car Corp, Box 3199, E Camden, AR 71701; m/Tammie; c/Rene Michele, Michael Eugene II; p/Loyd and Helen Landtroop, Ranger, TX; ed/Att'd Ranger Jr Col; mil/AUS; pa/Regional & Plant Mgmt & Adm Freight Rail Car Repair Indust; Profl Conslt Rail Car Repair; Cert'd by Tex Ed Assn for Welding Metallurgy; cp/Past Pres Ranger JCs; r/Bapt; hon/Outstg JC Awd 1975; Co-Author of Assn Am Rail Road Interch Rules Course Used at Tex Railway Car Corp.

LANEY, RUTH HUNLEY oc/Filmmaker; Writer; b/Sept 24, 1944; h/2126 B Jackson St, Alexandria, LA 71301; ba/Alexandria; p/Rex and Ruth Laney, Baton Rouge, LA; ed/BA, MA LSU; pa/Free-lance Writer; Pub'd in Mags & Newspapers.

LANG, FRANZ oc/Director of Library Services; b/Sept 7, 1921; ba/11300 NE 2nd Ave, Miami, FL 33161; p/Andrew (dec) and Elizabeth Winczner Lang; ed/BA Siena Heights Col 1959; AMLS Univ Mich 1964; Postgrad: Univ Ill, Univ Chgo, Siena Heights Col, St Dominic Col, Barry Col, Marywood Col; mil/USAF 1942-45; USAFR 1946-50; pa/Dir Lib Sers, Barry Col 1970-; Dir St Dominic Col Lib 1963-70; Asst Libn Siena Heights Col 1962-63; Tchr Bishop Qtr Mil Acad 1956-62; Tchr St Joseph Sch 1952-56; Cath Lib Assn 1962-; ALA; AAUA; Assn Col & Res Libs; Dade Co Lib Assn; Fla Assn Univ Admrs; Fla Chapt Cath Lib Assn; Fla Lib Assn Coun Fla Libs; SEn Lib Assn; cp/Human Relats Coun, St Charles, Ill 1967-70; Common Cause 1977-; Network 1977-; r/Adrian Dominican Congreg of Most Holy Rosary; hon/Contbr to *Catholic Library World & Florida Libraries*; Cert of Merit for Outstg Ser to Commun, St Charles, Ill 1970; Barry Col Profl Achmt Awd 1979; Del to Fla Gov's Conf on Lib & Info Sers 1978; Del to White House Conf on Lib & Info Sers 1979.

LANGDON, JAMES LLOYD oc/Executive; b/Oct 6, 1918; h/3614 Bristol Hwy, Johnson City, TN 37601; ba/Johnson City; m/Madelyn Pope; c/Madelyn L Baker, Sheila L Pierce; p/James Uriah Langdon (dec); Ruth Langdon, Raleigh, NC; ed/BS NC St Univ; mil/USAFR Lt Col; pa/Group Pres Pet Inc; Past Pres Intl Assn Ice Cream Mfrs; So Assn Dairy Food Mfrs; Bd Mem Milk Indust Foun; cp/VP: Meml Hosp, JCs; Bd Mem: Hamilton Bk, US Indust Coun; r/Downtown Christian Ch: Mem; hon/Phi Kappa Phi; W/W in Am.

LANGFORD, MABEL HAYES oc/Activities Director; b/Aug 23, 1907; h/2 Baptist Vil of Dothan, Dothan, AL 36303; ba/Dothan; m/Joseph Edgar (dec); p/Jesse Franklin (dec) and Odie Thompson Hayes (dec); ed/Att'd Livingston Tchrs Col; AB Ala Col 1941; pa/Ret'dButler Co Bd Ed Prin & Tchr; Butler Co Dept Public Wel, Caseworker, Child Wel Worker, Dir; Mission Ser Corps Vol Activs Dir, Bapt Vil of Dothan Retirement Ctr; Alpha Epsilon Chapt Delta Kappa Gamma, Pres; Butler Co Ret'd Tchrs Assn; AEA; ARTA; NRTA; AARP, Greenville Chapt; Cp/Butler Co Hist Soc; Ala Hist Assn; r/So Bapt: Past WMU Dir & Asst Libn; Mission Ser Corps Vol.

LANGHAM, CECIL DURWOOD oc/Insurance Company District Manager; b/Apr 27, 1916; h/1756 Romain Dr, Columbia, SC 29210; ba/Columbia; m/Virginia N; c/Cecile L Cothran; p/Ernest Langham (dec); Carrie E Langham Cottrell, Mobile, AL; ed/Bus Col; mil/US Inf, Ret'd Capt; pa/Indep Life & Accident Ins Co: Dist Mgr 1957-, Agt, Supt 1951; Past Pres Columbia Gen Agts & Mgrs' Assn; SC Assn Life Underwriters: Past Pres, Past Mbrship Chm, Mem Pioneer Clb; cp/Chm Police Com; Developed Rec Pk, 1st Dir; Mem Selective Ser Bd; Org'd 1st "Fund Raising Carnival", Hammond Hills Sch, N Augusta, SC; "Can Do" Mbrship Clb, Gtr Columbia C of C; Manpower Resources Com, Columbia Urban Leag; Indust Div UF; Past Pres PTA, N Augusta; Past Treas Columbia High Booster Clb; Past Mem Richland Co Bd; Dir ARC; Am Legion; Charter Mem St Andrews Lions Clb; Former Coun-man N Augusta; Others; r/Park St Bapt Ch, Columbia: Mem; SS Tchr; Supt SS; hon/Pres' Clb Awd, Indep Life & Accident Ins Co; Recipient Nat & St Certs for Outstg Ser in Adv'g Heart Prog & Stimulating Public Suport; Commend for Outstg Ser, Mar Dimes; Combat Inf Badge; Purple Heart; Bronze Star; Awd'd Key to City of Columbia for Americanism, Mayor John T Campbell.

LANGLEY, JANIE S oc/Management Consultant, Controller, Accountant; b/Aug 21, 1940; ba/100 W Bank Expressway, Gretna, LA 70053; m/Charles E Sr; c/Teri, Eric, Tina, Charles E Jr; p/Ben R and Leonor DeLeon Salazar, Temple, TX; ed/AB Univ PR 1962; Att'd Ctrl Tex Col 1967, Cameron Commercial Col 1964; p/Mgmt Conslt, Controller, Acct Sheraton Gretna; ABWA, Quelles Nouvelles Chapt, Pres 1979-80; Globe Chapt ABWA, Pres 1970-71, VP 1969-70, Treas 1968-69; ABWA Nat Conv in New Orleans 1982, Secy; San Antonio Hospitality Accts, Pres 1974-75, Chm of Bd 1975-76; Tex Hotel & Motel Assn, Secy 1968, 69, 70 & 75, 2nd VP 1970-71, 1st VP 1971; cp/Chm Bus Dist Heart Fund Assn, Killeen, Tex 1970; Intl Maritime Propellor Clb Ladies Aux; Stella Maris Ctr Fund Raiser 1978-79; r/Cath; hon/San Antonio Hospitality Accts Proclaimed Feb 15, 1979 Janie Langley Evening; ABWA Quelles Nouvelles Chapt Wom of Yr 1979-80; ABWA Inner Circle 1970; ABWA Gold Star Awd 1974; ABWA Emerald Star Awd 1978.

LANGLEY, LUCILLE TOLBERT oc/Teacher, Travel Assistant; Beautician; b/Aug 30; h/Denmark, SC; m/Sterling Russell Sr; c/Beverly L Gilrerth, Sterling Russell Jr, Michael; p/Ernest and Ida Tolbert (dec); ed/Dip Apex Beauty Col 1943; BS Fla A&M Univ 1948; Cert Wilfred Acad 1968; Cert Clairol Inst 1970; Awd SC St Col EPDA Sem; Certs Univ SC Ldrship Inst & Cont'g Ed; MEd SC St Col 1976; pa/Tchr; Former Dept Hd, Cosmetology, Denmark Tech Col; Past Owner Beauty Salon; SCTEA; Am Voc Assn; SC Voc Assn; Phi Beta Lambda; Delta Sigma Theta; SC St Employees Credit Union; Whoozits Travel Clb; Quettes; AAUW; Cosmetology Tchrs Guild, Secy 1957-64; Mem Accred Team So Assn Col & Sch 1977; cp/Den Mother BSA 1965; White House Conf Fams; Adv Coun Cosmetology, Denmark Tech Col; r/Mt Carmel ME Ch; Mem Choir; hon/Sweetheart Runner-up Omega Psi Frat 1964; Judge SC St Trade Contests; Judge Trade Shows & Beauty Contests; Cert of Ser Awd, St of SC, 30 Yrs Ser as St Employee 1978; Pin 30 Yr Ser, St SC 1978; Cert Recog, White House Conf on Fams; VIP Awd, Richard Carroll Mid Sch 1980.

LANGLEY, NINA STILL oc/Homemaker; b/July 30, 1922; h/Rt 1 Box 354, Lafayette, AL 36862; m/William Thomas; c/Sharon Elizabeth L Tankersley, Victoria L Ford, Janet L Eason; p/Frank Sanford (dec) and Mary Elizabeth Jones Still (dec); ed/HS Grad; pa/Ala Ext Homemakers Coun: Pres 1981-, VP, Treas, Dist Dir; r/So Bapt; hon/Ldrship Awd, Auburn Univ 1976; Recog Awd, Ala Coop Ext Ser 1978; Cert of Apprec Awd, Ala Coop Ext Ser 1979, 80.

LANGLEY, WELBORN JAMES oc/Physician; b/Sept 12, 1926; h/8260 San Leandro, Dallas, TX 75218; ba/Dallas; m/Dorothy Jean; c/Beverly Jo, Debra Jean, Roger James, Brenda Diane, Rebecca Jane; p/Floyd Alton Langley (dec); Willie Frances Langley, Cleburne, TX; ed/BS, BA, MD; mil/AUS 5 Yrs; pa/Dallas Co Med Soc; Tex Med Assn; AMA; cp/Fdr of Foun "The Origin & Destiny of Man"; r/Ch of Christ; hon/AUS Commen, Gen Walker.

LANGLEY, WILBUR H SR oc/Well Drilling; b/Dec 17, 1934; h/PO Box 305, Lecanto, FL 32661; ba/Inverness, FL; m/Helen; c/Wilbur H Jr; Kelvin; p/Will T (dec) and Annie H Langley, Lecanto, FL; pa/Water Well Drilling; 1st VP Fla Water Well Assn; Chm Withlacoochee Regional Water Supply Auth; VChm Withlacoochee Regional Plan'g Coun; cp/Dir, Bd Dirs St Assn Co Commrs; Mem Each of 3 Dem Clbs of Citrus Co; Bd Co Commrs Citrus Co; Dir Citrus Co Fair Assn; Past Pres Citrus Co Fair Assn; r/First Bapt Ch Lecanto: SS Supt, Chm Bd Deacons.

LANGNER, MILDRED CROWE oc/Medical Librarian; b/Jul 30, 1911; h/1408 SE Bayshore Dr, #505, Miami, FL 33131; ba/Miami; m/Julian (dec); ed/BA Univ Chatta 1933; BS Peabody Col for Tchrs 1945; pa/Univ Miami Med Lib: Dir & Prof 1968-, Hd Libn & Assoc Prof 1955-61, 1963-68; Chief Ref Sers Div Nat Lib of Med 1961-63; Libn & Asst Prof Univ Ala Med Lib 1945-55; Intern & Asst Vanderbilt Univ Med Lib 1944-45; Med Libn Med Soc Lib Chatta Public Lib 1940-44; Div Hd City & Co Brs 1935-39; Lib Asst Chatta Public Lib 1933-35; Med Lib Assn: Chm Num Coms, Secy, Editor, Pres; Spec Lib Assn: Pres-elect & Com Mem Ala Chapt, Dir Fla Chapt; Am, Fla & Dade Co Lib Assns; Am Assn Hist of Med; hon/Alpha Soc, Univ Chatta; Med Lib Assn's Editor's Awd; Med Lib Assn's Noyes Awd for Outstg Libnship 1976.

LANGSTON, AARON J oc/Director; b/Mar 29, 1937; h/PO Box 448, Columbus, MS 39701; ba/Columbus; p/Arnold E and Ethel E Wooten Langston (dec); ed/BS, MEd Miss St Univ; pa/Dir Golden Triangle Voc-Tech Ctr; Miss Voc Assn; Post Sec'dy Dirs Assn; cp/Kiwanis; BSA; Past Pres Exc Clb; r/So Bapt; hon/Silver Beaver, BSA; Outstg Voc Edr 1976-77; Wildlife Conservation Awd.

LANIER, CAMPBELL BROWN JR oc/Telephone Company Executive; b/Dec 30, 1925; h/PO Box 510, West Point, GA 31833; ba/W Point; m/Sydney Louise Gaines; c/Campbell Brown III, David Gaines, John Thompson; p/Campbell Brown Sr and Bertie Acree Thompson

Lanier, W Point; ed/Engrg; mil/USN 1946, Ensign; US Merchant Marine Acad; pa/Pres: Interst Telephone Co, Val Telephone Co; cp/Dir USITA Tel Assn; Dir Val Estates; Rotary Clb; r/Christian Ch: Mem, Deacon.

LANIER, GENE DANIEL oc/Educator; b/Mar 13, 1934; h/526 Westchester Dr, Greenville, NC 27834; ba/G'ville; m/Susan Roberts; c/Leigh Katherine, Nicole McLean; p/Jeanne D Lanier (dec); Gertrude M Lanier, Conway, NC; ed/BS; MSLS; PhD; mil/US Counterintelligence Corps, Wn Europe; pa/Chm & Prof Dept Lib Sci, E Carolina Univ; Past Pres NCLA; Editor Bd NC Libs; ALA; SELA; AALS; NCASL; LRA; Alpha Beta Alpha; r/1st Christian Ch: Deacon.

LANKFORD, JOE ANN oc/Executive Secretary, Real Estate Salesperson; b/July 20, 1937; h/1213 N 65th, Waco, TX 76710; ba/Waco; m/Marion D; c/Richard, Julie; p/Joe F and Ann Loy, Waco, TX; ed/Secretarial, 4 C Col; Cont'g Ed McLennan Commun Col; pa/Exec Secy Farmers Supply Corp; Real Est Salesp Chester Thompson Real Est; cp/Huaco Chapt ABWA: Mbrship Chp, Ways & Means Chp, Recording Secy, VP, Presently Pres; Regional Meetings & Nat Convs Tex, Miss, Ga ABWA; Campaign John Connally for Pres; r/Bapt; hon/Sweetheart Nom Beta Sigma Phi 1961; Wom of Yr Huaco Chapt ABWA 1979; Top 10 Wom ABWA 1979.

LAPOSKY, BEN FRANCIS oc/Commercial Artist and Designer; b/Sept 30, 1914; h/301 S Sixth St, Cherokee, IA 51012; ba/Same; p/Peter Paul (dec) and Ledna A Laposky (dec); mil/Sgt 43rd Div HQ WWII; pa/Oscillons; Elec Abstractions; 225+ Exhibs; Over 180 Pubs, US & Abroad; r/Rom Cath; hon/NY Art Dirs Clb Gold Medal Awd.

LaPRINCE, KENNETH R oc/Educator; b/Oct 6, 1944; h/21½ Nunan, Charleston, SC 29403; ba/C'ton; p/Thomas and Elizabeth LaPrince, C'ton, SC; ed/BA, MEd The Citadel; pa/AFT; cp/C'ton Neighborhood Housing Ser; Bd of Fire Masters; r/Epis; hon/Outstg Yng Man Am 1977-78; Personality of S 1977-78.

LARDE, ENRIQUE ROBERTO oc/Insurance Executive; b/Feb 7, 1934; h/80 King's Ct, Apt 601, Condado, PR 00911; ba/San Juan, PR; m/Ida Maria Hess (dec); p/Enrique Rafael Larde-Arthez and Marina Bellegarrigue de Larde, Woodside, NY; ed/BA Columbia Univ 1956; MGA Intl Graphoanalysis Soc 1965; mil/AUS 1957-59; pa/Dir S Cont Ins Agcy 1972-; Dir & Exec VP Corporacion Insular de Suguros 1973-; Dir Centro de Informacion de Seguros 1976-; Dir PR Joint Underwriting Assn for Med-Hosp Profl Liability Ins 1976-78; Dir & Pres Asociacionde Companias de Seguros Incorporadas en PR Inc 1978-79; Adv Com Ins Sers Ofc PR; Ins Inst PR 1975-; Life Mem Instl Graphoanalysis Soc; cp/Bnkrs Clb PR; C of C of PR; USN Leag 1979-; hon/DIB; Notable Ams; Intl W/W: Intells, Commun Ser; Book of Hon; Men of Achmt; Intl Regis of Profiles; Men and Wom of Dist; Quien es Quien en El Serguro Latinoamericano; Author Sev Newspaper Articles; Chapt to "Simposio Sobre la Industria de Seguros de Puerto Rico"; Sev TV Appearances.

LAREY, BERT B oc/Attorney at Law; b/Feb 23, 1896; h/Texarkana, AR; ba/612 St Line Plaza, Box 8001, Texarkana, AR; m/Mayno I Britt; c/Bert W, Bethel B, Carolyn, Lance L; p/Roland L (dec) and Mary Cathron Larey (dec); ed/Att'd St Tchrs Col 1915-18; LLB Vanderbilt Univ (Converted to LD 1969); mil/AUS WWI; Govt Appeal Agt Miller Co WWII; pa/Gen Prac Law; Tchr, Prin, Taylor HS, Taylor, AR 1920-21; Supt N Benton HS 1921-23; Miller Co Bar Assn, Secy-Treas 1945-47, VP 1947-48, Pres 1948-50; Ark Municipal Judge's Assn, Secy-Treas 1967-69, VP 1969-70, Pres 1970-71; cp/Dem Pres Elector 1944; Ark Bar Assn; Miller Co Bar Assn; Am Bar Assn; Chm Com on Public Relats, Ark Bar 1947-48; r/Meth; hon/Trustee Ark St Tchrs Col 1939-41; Cert Ark Bar 1973 for 50 Yrs Pract.

LARGEN, MARY ANN oc/Director; b/June 30, 1943; h/955 S Columbus St, #402, Arlington, VA 22204; ba/Bethesda, MD; c/Stacia Alana; p/Justic E and Ruth A Hawks, Alexandria, VA; ed/BA Univ Md; pa/Dir New Responses Inc 1977-; Nat Ctr for Preven & Control of Rape, Nat Inst Mtl Htlh, US Dept HEW 1975-77; Coor Nat Rape Task Force NOW 1973-74; Campaign Schedule for Flora Crater for Va Lt Gov 1972; Leg Com, Nat Coalition Against Sexual Assault 1978-; Public Safety Com, Wom's Agenda, Comm on Intl Wom's Yr 1975-77; Conf Coor NOW 1972; Am Acad Polit & Social Sci; NOW; Rural Am Wom; cp/Subcom on Law, Arlington Co Common the Status of Wom; Bd Dirs No Va Chapt NOW; Coor No Va NOW Rape Task Force; Cnslr Wash DC Rape Crisis Ctr; Com on Crim Just; LWV; Co Chm Fairfax Co Com on Sexual Assault; Arlington Co Crim Just Adv Com; White House Conf on Fams 1979-80; r/Prot; hon/Commend for Commun Sers, Prince Georges Co Coun, Md 1974; Women Today: Nat Dir Wom Ldrs 1974-76; Nom'd W/W Am Wom 1975; Author Num Pubs Incl'g "Every Woman A Potential Victim of Rape" & "Child Sexual Abuse: A Bibliography" 1978.

LARIMER, GREGG oc/Coach; b/Dec 16, 1955; h/3964 Candlenut Ln,

Dallas, TX 75234; ba/Richardson, TX; p/Harold and Jestina Larimer, Dallas, TX; ed/BS N Tex St Univ 1978; pa/Gymnastics Coach & Tchr, JJ Pearce HS; Gymnastics Coach, Farmers Br Boys Gymnastics Team; AAHPER; GAT; NHSGCA; NTWGJA; THSGCA; USGFWC; cp/FCA; FCAGDCC; r/Bapt; hon/TAAF Boys St Gymnastic Champs 1977, 78, 79, 80; USGF Tex Class III St Champs 1979, 80; F'ship of Christian Aths Dallas Coach of Yr 1980; Dist II-AAAA JV Track Champs, H Grady Spruce HS 1980.

LARIMORE, LEON oc/Minister; b/Jul 22, 1911; h/1041 En Parkway, Louisville, KY 40217; ba/L'ville; m/Blanche Lile; c/Marjorie Bell Broady (Mrs Levy); p/William C and Myrtie D Isenberg Larimore (dec); ed/Grad 1946, DD 1962 Campbellsville Col; Georgetown Col 1946; AB Wn Ky Univ 1949; BD So Bapt Theol Sem 1952; pa/Pastor: Third Ave Bapt Ch 1957-, Bapt Chs Hart, Edmonson, Green, Metcalfe & Monroe Cos, Ky 1937-57; Field Supvr Boyce Bible Sch, So Bapt Theol Sem; Chm Campus Min Com, Ky St Bd; St Mission Bd 1952-55, 58-61, 72-; Ky Bapt Conv: VP 1965, VChm Adm Com 1972-73; Moderator Long Run Assn Bapt 1971-72, Pres Exec Bd 1971-72; Chm Assembly & Camps St Mission Bd 1973; Trustee Wigginton Bapt Home for Men 1967-; Dir Bapt Homes for Elderly 1962-; VP Ky Bapt Pastors Conf; Other Former Positions; cp/Dir S Ctl Rural Telephone Coop; Chm Hart Co Unit Am Cancer Soc; Pres Rotary Clb; Past Grand Chaplain, Grand Lodge Ky Masons F&AM; Others; hon/Ky Col; Ky Admiral; Dist'd Awd, ACS; W/W: S&SW, Ky; Commun Ldrs & Noteworthy Ams; Lib Human Resources; DIB; Num Others.

LARKIN, BARBARA SHORES oc/Social Worker; b/Nov 23, 1945; h/1516 5th Ave, W Birmingham, AL 35208; ba/B'ham; m/Tom Larry; c/Danielle Renee and Damien Laurent; p/Arthur D and Theodora W Shores, B'ham, AL; ed/BA Talladega Col; MSW Univ Ill; pa/Bd Mem Chd's Aid Soc; Soc Serv Com of Am Red Cross; NASW; Ala Chapt NASW for Minority Affairs; Am Public Hlth Assn; Phi Delta Kappa; cp/Links Inc; NAACP; Urban Leag; AAUW; Alpha Kappa Alpha; Support Com of Ballet Barre for the Ala Sch Fine Arts; r/U Ch of Christ; hon/Presented Paper to Am Assn Sch Psych 1976; Co-Author Article "Educating the Disadvantaged Child."

LARKIN, GERTIE MAE oc/Charge Nurse; b/Oct 1, 1930; h/3716 Robinhood Dr, Temple, TX 76501; ba/Cameron, TX; m/William Clayton Jr (dec); c/Sue Ann; p/Urbane Aaron Sr (dec); Willie Mae Aaron, Temple; ed/Tchr Cert, Mary Hardin Baylor Col 1975; BS Tex Wom's Univ 1978; Addit Studies; pa/Charge Nurse, Cameron Commun Hosp 1980-; Staff Nurse, Santa Fe Meml Hosp 1976-80; Pvt Secy, First Nat Bank (Temple) 1956-57; 1st Grade Tchr, Sinclair Elem Sch (Hampton, Va) 1953-55; EKG Technician, Scott & White Meml Hosp 1951-52; Am Nurses Assn; Tex Nurses Assn; Regional Nsg Assn; Reg'd Nurse; r/First Bapt Ch: Former Nursery Age Tchr; hon/W/W Am Wom; Personalities of Am; DDA; World W/W Wom.

LAROUERE, JOSEPH G oc/Hospital Administrator; h/Rt 2, Box 1F, Hayes, VA; m/Beverly; c/Tina, Kristy; p/Regis P and Alice M Larouere, Gulfport, FL; ed/2 Yr Assoc Deg Food Mgmt; Va Polytech Inst; pa/Hampton Gen Hosp, Hampton, Va: Dir Envir Sers 1975-, Dir Food Ser Dept 1974-75; Food Ser Dir Specialized Mgmt Inc, Northampton Accomack Meml Hosp 7 Yrs; Asst Food Ser Dir Specialized Mgmt Inc, Macke Co; Greyhound Food Mgmt Inc 5 Yrs; Past St Pres, Tri-St Food Handlers Soc; cp/Northampton JCs: Past Pres, Life Mem; Past St VP Va St JCs; Fund Raising Chm Northampton Red Cross; Moose Lodge; Past Pres: Exmore Fire & Rescue Co, NAM Credit Union, Hampton Gen Credit Union; hon/Food Ser Dir of Yr 1976, Tri-St Food Handlers Soc; "Top Tenn" Awd for Hosp Food Ser Dir, Intl Food Handlers Assn; Culinary Art Exhbn, St-wide Hosp Div Awd, Va Restaurant Assn; VA Jcs: Outstg Local Pres, Outstg St Chm, Key Man Awd; JC of Yr, Northampton JCs, 1970, 71, 72.

LA ROWE, GEORGIA ANN oc/Teacher; b/Oct 22, 1923; h/Apt C-4, 2755 NE 28 Ave, Lighthouse Point, FL 33064; m/Donald P; p/Hershel H (dec) and Mary E Jennings; ed/EdB magna cum laude Univ Miami; MS Fla St Univ; pa/Classroom Tchrs Assn; NEA; r/Presb; hon/Kappa Delta Pi.

LARRIMORE, THOMAS ALSTON oc/Music Evangelist; Minister; b/Sept 9, 1929; h/1156 Winnrose St, Jackson, MS 39211; ba/Same; m/Florence Ann Kull; c/T Van, Margaret Ann, Janet Renee; p/David DeLoach Larrimore (dec); Margaret Aletha Jackson Larrimore, Lucedale, MS; ed/BA Miss Col; MRE, BSM New Orleans Bapt Theol Sem; mil/AUS, Resv Ofcr, 10 Yrs; pa/Recording Artist, 8 LPs; Song Writer; 4 Songs Pub'd; r/Min of Music 24 Yrs; Evangelism 8 Yrs; Preacher; hon/W/W in Rel.

LARSON, JOHN CHRISTOPHER oc/Historic Preservationist; b/Jan 28, 1949; h/454 S Church St, Winston-Salem, NC 27101; ba/Winston-Salem; m/Sharon; p/James E and Eleanor Larson, Columbia, SC; ed/BA, MA Univ SC; mil/AUS 1/Lt; pa/Hist Res & Arch Preservation of Old Salem Inc; r/Presb; hon/Newcomb Awd, Dept Hist USC.

LARSON, MURIEL KOLLER oc/Writer; Author; Composer; h/10 Vanderbilt Cir, Greenville, SC 29609; ba/Same; c/Gay L Verhey, Lori Joy; p/Eugene L Koller Sr (dec); Helen M Koller, G'ville; pa/Author 11 Books Pub'd by Moody Press, Bible Voice, Warner Press, Pillar Books, Pyramid, & Baker Book House; Author 2000 Articles; r/Bapt.

LARSSON, DONALD ERIC oc/Director of Sales; b/July 27, 1941; h/3046 NW 119 Ln, Coral Springs, FL 33065; ba/Miami; m/Irene B; c/Douglas, Linda; p/Erik J (dec) and Della P Larsson, Jacksonville, FL; ed/BA Univ Fla 1963; mil/USN; pa/Sales & Mkgt Mgmt, Bldg Mats, Gory Assoc'd Industs Inc of Miami; Conslt Coun of Nat Insts of Bldg Scis; Nat Assn Homebldrs; Fla Homebldrs Assn; Construction Specifications Inst; Am Mktg Assn; Am Mgmt Assn; So Bldg Codes Cong Intl; cp/Yng Repubs; Gator Bowl Assn; Univ Fla Alumni Assn; Gen Chm J'ville Public TV Auction; r/Epis.

LARY, GENE oc/Lawyer; b/Nov 28, 1906; h/100 Lorenz, #605, San Antonio, TX 78209; ba/Same; ed/Att'd Univ Tex 1925, 1976-77; Ft Worth Sch Law 1926; So Meth Univ 1943; Trinity Univ 1977; Univ Tex San Antonio 1977; LLD Universidad Autonoma de Puebla, Mexico 1964; El Illustre Colegio de Puebla 1964; Academico, Academia Mexican de Derecho Internacional 1964; pa/Admitted to Tex Bar 1927, Repub of Mex Bar 1944; US Supreme Ct Bar 1944; Assoc & Ptnr Firm Phillips, Trammell, Chizum, Price, & Ester 1927-36; Atty-Cnslr Mexican Consulate 1944-68; Judge Municipal Ct, City of University Park 1950-60; Intl, Inter-Am Bar Assn; San Antonio Bar Assn; Colegio de Abogados de Puebla, AC, Puebla, Mex; Tex Police Assn; Coun Intl Relats; Bd Dirs 1973-76; Kappa Alpha; Alpha Lambda Delta; Phi Eta Sigma; hon/St Bar of Tex 50-Yr Awd 1977; Decorated by Order Aztec Eagle, La Cruz Laureda, la Orden Mexicana del Derecho y La Cultura; Recip Homenaje de Samptia Wwd La Asociacion Nacional de Abogados 1944; Nat Awd Am Bar Assn 1957; Contbr of Articles to Profl Jours; W/W: Tex, Am Law; Nat Alumni Dir 1980; Commun Ldrs & Noteworthy Ams; Notable Personalities of Am; Dir of Dist'd Ams; Pers of Am; Men of Achmt; Men & Wom Dist.

LASATER, JOHN PORTER oc/District Sales Manager; b/July 21, 1943; h/585 Wakefield Ct, Naperville, IL 60540; ba/Oak Brook, IL; m/Diana Sellers; c/John Jr, Mary C; p/Mr and Mrs Robert L Lasater, Bunnlevel, NC; ed/Att'd Campbell Col 1961-62, Meth Col 1973-74, ABA Lafayette Col 1974; Ga St Univ 1977-79; mil/AUS 1964-67; pa/Piedmont Aviation Inc 1963-64, 1967-; Denver Airline Mgrs Assn, Past Pres; Atlanta Airline Sales Mgrs Assn; Chog Airline Mgrs Assn; SKAL Clb of NAm; Piedmont Airlines Ski Clb, Pres-Treas; r/Presb.

LASHARE, CAROLINE ANN oc/Psychology, Music; b/Dec 3, 1951; h/8608 Willowick, Austin, TX 79759; ba/Same; m/Darrell; c/Michael James; p/John Hudson and Emma Elizabeth Schlueter, Austin, TX; ed/BA 1979; pa/Internships & Practicum in St Psych Agcys; cp/Wednesday Morning Music Clb; Nat Guild Piano Tchrs; r/Bapt; hon/1st Pl Gold Medal Winner Nat Recording Contest.

LASSETER, DAVID F oc/Retired Funeral Director and Embalmer; b/Oct 5, 1928; h/709 Willow Ct, Dothan, AL 36301; m/Jean Saunders; p/Cecil Herman (dec) and Linnie Forrester Lasseter (dec); paj/Lic'd Funeral Dir & Embalmer, St of Ala; cp/Jr C of C; r/Missionary Bapt; hon/NRA Coor Tri-St Gun Clb 1979-; Mbrship Chm Benefactor Life Mem Nat Rifle Assn Mem of Yr 1979-80; Master Mason 1952; York Rite Mason 1952; Shriner 1952; Scottish Rite Mason 32° 1964; OES 1964.

LASSON, KENNETH LEE oc/Writer; Law Professor; b/Mar 24, 1943; h/3808 Menlo Dr, Baltimore, MD 21215; ba/Balto; m/Barbara; c/Tammy; p/Nelson B and Nanette M Lasson; ed/AB; MA; JD; pa/Asst Prof Polit Sci & Commun Arts, Loyola Col 1972-; Guest Scholar The Brookings Instn 1975-77; Goucher Col: Lectr in Eng 1970-72, Asst to Pres 1970-71; Edit & Adm Conslt, Ralph Nader's Ctr for Study of Responsive Law 1969-; Asst to Dean Univ Md Sch of Law 1967-69; Tchg Fellow & Lectr, The Johns Hopkins Univ 1966-68; Other Former Positions; Md Bar; Supreme Ct Bar; Am Civil Liberties Union; Md Chapt Legal Panel; Others; Contb'g Editor *The Washingtonian*; hon/Author: *The Workers/Portraits of Nine Am Jobholders*, 1971, 72, *Proudly We Hail/Profiles of Public Citizens in Action*, 1975, *Private Lives of Public Servants*, 1978; Contbr Articles to Profl Pubs.

LATHAM, FRANK W JR oc/Executive; b/Jan 3, 1945; h/10011 Burgandy, Waco, TX 76710; ba/Waco; m/Jeannie Brown; c/Frank III, Robert, John; ed/Baylor Univ; mil/USAF 1963-67; pa/VP R E Cox Co; cp/Pres Heart of Tex Goodwill Industs 1980; Adv Bd Tex Ranger Commemorative Foun; Bd Dirs Hist Waco Foun; Adv Bd Scottish Rite Foun; Nat Bd Am Soc Prevention of Cruelty to Chd; VP Waco Chapt SAR; Ofcr SCV; Chm Retail Adv Com McLennan Commun Col; Hon Life Mem Tex Ranger Hall of Fame; Permanent Contbg Mem Shriner's Hosp for Crippled Chd; Mason; Shriner; Active Mem DeMolay Legion of Hon; hon/Recip Good Citizenship Medal, SAR; CCP Am Soc Indust Security;

W/W S&SW 1980-81; Hon Mem Hood's Tex Brigade Assn; Instr Cont'g Ed Div McLennan Commun Col; Royal Order of Jesters; Order of Red Cross of Constantine; Waco Scottish Rite Bodies; Waco York Rite Bodies; Austin Ex Bd BSA, Heart of Tex Coun.

LATHEM, BETTY BROOKS oc/Administrative Assistant; b/Aug 16, 1931; h/599 Holly Dr, NW, Gainesville, GA 30501; m/Charles Malcolm; c/Charles Thomas, Richard Lee, Betty Kathryn Parrish; p/Raymond England (dec) and Ezelle Chappell Brooks, Griffin, GA; pa/Intl Mgmt, Spec in Org, Res & Prep of Books & Articles for Pub; Nat Assn Female Execs; cp/CONTACT, Hall Co 1981-82; r/Bapt; hon/W/W Am Wom 1981-82; Wkg on Fam Hist.

LAUGHLIN, BEVERLY ANN oc/Marketing Executive; b/Aug 24, 1937; h/9226 Highridge, Dallas, TX 75238; ba/Dallas; m/Lea Anne, Lori Lynn, Lisa Kay; p/Sarah Turpin (dec); Gordon A and Ruth L McCallum (Foster Parents) (dec); pa/Dir Mktg for Wom, SWn Life Ins Co; Former Lic'd Career Agt; Tex & Nat Assn Life Underwriters; Exec Wom Dallas, Dallas Assn Life Underwriters; Tex Ldr's Roundtable; Wom Ldr's Roundtable; cp/Bd Mem: Heart of Tex Chapt Mar Dimes (Immed Past Chm of Bd), Metro Dallas Chapt Nat Foun Mar Dimes, McLennan Co Heart Assn; Waco (Tex) C of C, Wrangler's Clb; Am Bus Woms Assn, Pres Cen-tex Chapt; Past VP PTA, Lake Air Jr HS, J H Hines & Viking Hills Elem; r/1st U Meth Ch: Mem 23 Yrs, Pres U Meth Wom 3 Yrs, Bd Mem & Past Chm Laura Edwards Christian Commun Ctr; hon/Outstg Yg Wom Am; Wom of Yr, Cen-tex Chapt ABWA 1972; SWn Life Co Grand Newcomer 1971; Waco Assn Life Underwriters Assn Rookie of Yr 1972; Nat Quality Awd; Nat Sales Achmt Awd; SWn Life Top Clb 1972, 73, 75; SWn Life Pres's Hon Clb 1974; Nat Top Ten Wom of Yr 1976, Am Bus Woms Assn.

LAUGHLIN, RAY E oc/Computer Operator; b/Oct 5, 1931; h/Rt 1 Box 309, Dale, OK 74801; ba/Okla City; m/I JoAnn; c/Mike, Karen; p/Raymond E and Laura B Laughlin, Meeker, OK; ed/HS Grad; mil/USN 1951-54; pa/Computer Oper, Civil Ser, Tinker AFB; cp/Dale Sch Bd of Ed 5 Yrs; Orgl Ldr Dale 4-H Clbs; St 4-H Energy Devel Com; St Fair 4-H Improvement Com; Coach Dale Summer Baseball & Softball; St 4-H Ldrs Bd of Dirs, VP; r/Bapt; hon/St Hon 4-H Awd; Co Hon 4-H Awd; Dale FFA Chapt Hon Awd.

LAUGHLIN, REVA BENTON oc/Executive Vice President; b/Sept 9, 1921; h/1810 W 3rd Ave, Stillwater, OK 74074; ba/S'water; m/Glenn E; c/Glenda Joyce L Tucker (Mrs James H), Sidney Calvin, Sheri Gay; p/C D Benton, Sand Springs, OK; Birdie Stephenson Benton (dec); ed/BS 1949, MS 1950 Okla St Univ; pa/Thomas N Berry & Co: Exec VP, Dir; VP & Dir Marietta Royalty Co; Dir Okla Petrol Coun; Nat Supply & Demand Com, Indep Petrol Assn Am; cp/Past Pres Am Legion Aux; Gamma Phi Beta; S'water Golf & CC; Life Mem Freedoms Foun; r/Bapt; hon/Hon Cert, Freedoms Foun at Val Forge; Ser Awd, Altrusa Clb; Author, "St Hist of Am Legion Aux".

LAUKHUFF, PERRY oc/Editor; b/Aug 14, 1906; h/PO Box 689, Amherst, VA 24521; ba/Same; m/Jessie Coburn; c/Louise Argyle; p/Frank Edward and Laura Perry Laukhuff (dec); ed/AB Otterbein Col; AM Harvard; Cert Acad Intl Law, The Hague; mil/Hon Mem, Ofcr's Mess, Essex & Kent Scottish Regiment, Windsor, Ontario, Canada; pa/Editor *The Certain Trumpet*; Pres-Emeritus F'ship Concerned Churchmen; Coun on Fgn Relats; Am Fgn Ser Assn; r/Anglican; hon/Keble Awd, Am Ch Union; Ofcr Companion, Mil & Hospitaller Order of St Lazarus of Jerusalem.

LAVELY, PHILIP ELSON oc/Associate Professor; b/Nov 29, 1943; h/200 Todd St, Martin, TN 38237; ba/Martin; m/Marcia Marvin; c/William Calvin, Laura; p/Calvin E and Hazel P Lavely; ed/BS 1967, MS 1969 Univ Ga; PhD Tex A&M Univ 1974; mil/USAR; pa/Assoc Prof, Sch Agric, Univ Tenn; Nat Rec & Park Assn; Tenn Rec & Park Soc; Interpretive Naturalists; Tenn Assn Nat Trails Coun Bd Dirs; cp/Lions Clb; r/Bapt; hon/Alpha Zeta; Xi Sigma Pi; Phi Kappa Phi; Gamma Sigma; Editor *Trails Bibliography*; Author Num Profl Articles.

LAVENDER, EULA MAE TAYLOR oc/Artist; b/Apr 14,1923; h/Star Route Box 47, Black Mountain, NC 28711; m/Howard H; c/William R Morris, Gerald L Morris, H Taylor Mirris (dec), David Andrew Morris; p/John Randolph Taylor, Black Mtn, NC; Ida Oma Marlowe Taylor (dec); pa/Handcrafts, Oil Paintings, Rock Crafts, Blue Prints; r/Pentecostal Holiness; hon/Ribbons & Awds on Afghans.

LAW, WALTER CHARLES oc/Institutional Researcher; Management Information Specialist; b/Mar 26, 1951; h/1820 Binz #8, Houston, TX 77004; ba/Houston; p/Wilkie Gilhart Law Sr (dec); Eloise M Law, Houston; ed/BA; MA; pa/Tex So Univ: Instnl Reschr, Mgmt Info Specialist; Res, Eval, Transactional Sys Design, Tchg; cp/UF Dr; U Negro Col Fund Dr; BSA; r/Ch of God in Christ; hon/Career Achmt Awd, Houston Com; Career Achmt in Ed Awd, Atlanta Com; W/W S&SW.

PERSONALITIES OF THE SOUTH

LAWANDALES, ROCHELLE W oc/Grants Administrator; b/Dec 6, 1955; h/Melbourne, FL; ba/900 E Strawbridge Ave, City Hall, Melbourne, FL 32901; m/Frank; p/Philip Wittenberg, Sumter, SC; ed/Att'd Oglethorpe Univ 1973-74 & Alliance Francais, Paris 1976-77; BA 1977; MCRP 1979; pa/Grants Admr, City of Melbourne, 1980-; Plan'g Dir, City W Melbourne 1979-80; Asst Planner, Anderson Co Plan'g & Devel Bd, Anderson, SC 1978-79; Asst Planner, Clemson Arch Foun Plan'g Res Div 1979; Prog Coor & Dir, Coastal Zone Mgmt Wkshop, Clemson Univ, Feb 1979; Acad Tutor, Clemson Univ Ath Dept, Fall 1977, 1978-79; Intern, Anderson Crisis Ctr, Spring 1977; Assoc Mem Am Plan'g Assn; Fla Plan'g & Zoning Assn; APA, SC Student Rep; Nat Assn Plan'g Students, Clemson Univ, Chapt Chm; Sociol Clb Pres, Clemson Univ; cp/S Brevard Museum Complex, Bd Mem; r/Jewish; hon/Dept of Housing & Urban Devel F'ship; Grad Asst'ship; Dean's List.

LAWRENCE, HARDING LUTHER oc/Executive; b/Jul 15, 1920; ba/Exchange Park, Dallas, TX 75235; m/Mary G Wells; c/James B, Deborah M, State R, Pamela, Katy; p/Muncey Luther and Helen Beatrice Lawrence (dec); ed/BBA Univ Tex 1942; LLB S Tex Col of Law 1949; Hon LLD Univ Portland 1968; JD S Tex Col of Law 1972; mil/USAF; pa/Chm of Bd & Chief Exec Ofcr, Braniff Intl; Dir of Air Transport Assn; Dir First Intl Bancshares Inc; hon/Order of Balboa, Republic of Panama 1965; Order of the Sun, Republic of Peru 1966; Cmdr in Order of O'Higgins, Chile 1968.

LAWRENCE, ROBERT LANDY IV oc/Head Start Director; b/Dec 25, 1949; h/112 E 22nd St, Owensboro, KY 42301; ba/Owensboro; m/Jeannette; p/Robert L Lawrence III, Owensboro, KY; Mary Brown Henderson Lawrence (dec); ed/AB Centre Col 1971; MS Univ Ky 1975; Doct Studies Univ Ky 1979-80; pa/Dir Audobon Area Hd Start Prog; Sr Staff Mem Audobon Area Commun Sers Inc; Soc for Res in Child Devel; Cousteau Soc; Friends of the Earth; Nat Assn Ed of Yng Chd; Nat Geog Soc; Nat Hd Start Assn; Smithsonian Soc; cp/Exec Com Mem TRUST Inc; r/Agnostic.

LAWSON, ARCHIE DAVID oc/Physician's Assistant; b/Aug 29, 1947; h/206 Harding St, Florence, AL; ba/Florence; m/Judith Ann; c/Melissa Ann, Christopher David; p/Archie Delmer Lawson, Florence, AL; Helen Mae Lawson (dec); ed/Att'd Florence St Univ 1965-67; Clin Spec Course, Womack Army Hosp 1968; Phys's Asst Prog, Bowman Gray Sch of Med; Att'd Wake Forest Univ 1970-72; pa/Phys's Asst, Fam Pract 1972-; Am Acad Phys's Assts; 1st Elec'd VP, Charter Mem Ala Soc Phys's Assts; r/Ch of Christ; hon/Bd Cert'd Nat Comm on Cert of Phys's Assts 1973.

LAWSON, BARBARA A oc/Homemaker; b/July 21, 1952; h/Philadelphia, PA; m/John E; c/Aishia, Alishia, Lydia; p/Mary Etta Bradley, Phila, PA; ed/Att'd Univ Penn, Wharton Sch; pa/Secy; Evangelist; Songstress; r/Penecostal.

LAWSON, CARRIE O oc/Retired; b/Dec 14, 1906; h/Camden, AR; m/Samuel David; c/Ersaline I, Emogene L, Docia Joyce, Samuel David Jr; pa/Retired, Orlando Hotel & Camden Hotel; cp/Camden Commun Action Coun; Pres Gen Mission Soc; OES, Order of Golden Circle; hon/Samuel D and Carrie O Lawson Ednl S'ship Fund.

LAWSON, DOROTHY MAE oc/Banking; b/Dec 21, 1941; h/Louisville, KY; ba/Liberty Nat Bank, 2300 W Market St, Louisville, KY 40211; c/Tammy D, Delon David; p/Robert M and Janie L Garr, Louisville, KY; ed/Att'd Nazareth Cl; pa/Asst Cashier & Br Mgr Liberty Nat Bank & Trust Co; Nat Assn Negro BPW; Portland Bus Assn; cp/NAACP; W L'ville Med Ctr, Bd Mem; r/Bapt; hon/Black Achiever 1979-80.

LAWSON, GALE LELAND oc/Retired; b/Jan 29, 1906; h/930 Oak St NW, Cleveland, Tn 37311; m/Elsie Mae Grittenden; c/Peggy Ann Eagan, James Gale, Clyde Leland; p/James Franklin and Mary Emma Lawson; pa/Ret'd After 38 Yrs w US Postal Ser; Real Est Broker 1961-73; cp/Pres Tenn Skeet Shooting Assn; r/Disciples of Christ; hon/Var St Skeet Titles 1938-77; Bradley Co Old Timers Hall of Fame 1980.

LAWSON, INEZ G oc/Teacher; b/Sept 8, 1931; h/2342 Smiley Ave, Prichard, AL 36610; ba/Prichard; c/Gerald F, Lynnette A; p/Charles Sr (dec) and Rebecca Goldsby (dec); ed/BS; MA; pa/Tchr 25 Yrs; AFT; MCEA; NEA; AVA; cp/Voter Registration; Public Ser; Polit Campaign Orgr; NAACP; r/Bapt; hon/Mother of Outstg Ath 1975; 25 Yrs Public Ser Delta Sigma Theta.

LAWSON, JENEANNE JOHNSTON oc/University Administrator; b/Aug 8; h/620 Wellesley, Houston, TX 77024; ba/Houston; m/Robert L; p/James Wesley and Dorothy Nichols Johnston, Lawton, OK; ed/BA, MA Univ Okla; Adv'd Work: Univ Tex, Univ So Cal; pa/Dir Col Relats/Pubs, Dir Info Sers, Univ Houston Downtown Col; Col Public Relats & Tchg;

Mgr of Art Gallery 1975-76; Dir Student Activs 1975-76; Instr of Communs 1976-77, 73-74; Other Past Positions; Continuity Dir, KCCO-FM, Lawton, Okla; Continuity-Promotion Dir, KSWO-TV (ABC), Lawton; Woms Page Editor, "Morning Press", Lawton; Opers Mgr, Houston Press Clb Gridiron Show; Consumer Conslt, Am Heritage Dic, Houghton Mifflin Pub'g Co; Publicity Conslt, Proj EVE (Equal Voc Ed) funded by Tex Ed Agy; Art Show Publicity, Advtg Conslt, Art Barn Gallery, N Post Oak; Num Profl Assns; Wkshop Spkr; cp/Chm 1977 Annual Meet'g, Harris Co Mtl Hlth Assn; Chm Houston/Harris Co Mtl Hlth Assn; Com Mem Main St 1977; Cult Affairs Com, C of C; Exec Com Alley Theatre Gala; Others; r/Bapt; hon/F'ships; Biogl Listings; Achmt Awd, NCCJ Assn 1976; Outstg Yrbook Advr by Nat Col Pub Advrs 1966; Others.

LAWSON, JOHN E oc/Musician; b/July 31, 1950; h/Phila, PA; m/Barbara A; c/Aishia, Alishia, Lydia; p/John Lawson, Phila, PA; Adeline A Sanford, Williamston, NJ; ed/US Sch Mus 1977; Att'd Bapt Col 1979; mil/USN 1975-80; pa/Entertainer while in Mil; Recording Gospel Artist; Traveling Evangelist; r/Pentecostal; hon/Lttr Apprec Mil 1977; Lttr Commend Mil 1976; "Mr and Mrs Gospel" (w Wife).

LAWSON, KENNETH RAY oc/Educator; b/July 7, 1945; h/773 NE 9th St Apt G, Crystal River, FL 32629; ba/Crystal River; p/Virgil and Freela W King Lawson, Brooksville, FL; ed/AB En Ky Univ 1968; MA Univ Dayton 1971; EdD VPI & St Univ 1976; pa/Tchr NEn HS 1968-74, Crystal River HS 1979- Lectr Ctrl Fla Commun Col 1979-; Editor *A New Concept* 1976-79; Adj Prof VPI 1976; Am Psych Assn; Am Hist Assn; Am Ednl Res Assn; Assn Supervision & Curric Devel; Nat Coun SS; Fla Coun SS; Fla Assn Supervision & Curric Devel; US Tennis Assn; Fla Tennis Assn; Am Acad Polit & Social Sci; Phi Delta Kappa; Kappa Delta Pi; Phi Alpha Theta; Phi Kappa Phi; cp/Dem Party; Plantation Tennis Clb; Fla Ath Coaches Assn; r/Rom Cath; hon/W/W S&SW 1980; Tchr Spotlight *Senior Scholastic Magazine* 1973; Va Fellow & Grad Tchg Asst; 26 Tennis Trophies; Co-Author *Mastering the Art of Winning Tennis: A Psychology of Strategy*.

LAWSON, MARSHALL LEE oc/Counselling Psychologist; b/July 8, 1934; h/16 Colonial Dr, Newnan, GA 30263; ba/Newnan; m/Joyce; c/Debra Lynn, Marshall Jr, Bev James, Angela Denise, Crystal Camille; p/Melvin and Edna M Lawson, Omaha, TX; ed/BA; MS; PhD; mil/Basic & Adv'd Airborne; pa/Mgmt & Job Conslt; Career Cnslr; Sex Therapist; Marriage & Fam Cnslr; cp/Ret'd Ofcrs Assn; NAACP; hon/Merit Ser Medal; Bronze Star; Air Medal; Vietnamese Cross of Gallantry w Palm; Master Parachutist; Ranger; Combat Infantryman's Badge.

LAWSON, SAMUEL DAVID oc/Retired; b/Oct 7, 1904; h/Camden, AR; m/Carrie O; c/Ersaline I, Emogene L, Docia Joyce, Samuel David Jr; pa/Ret'd Edr; Camden Commun Coun; Fdr New Haven Bapt Ch; cp/32° Mason; hon/Establishment of Samuel D and Carrie Lawson Education S'ship Foun.

LAWSON, SOPHIA GREGSON oc/Real Estate; b/Jan 13, 1924; h/1417 S Anderson Blvd, Topsail Bch, NC 29445; ba/Topsail Bch; c/Jerry B Reeves Jr, William D Reeves; p/William D and Willkings Smith Gregson (dec); pa/Real Est; cp/Ext Homemkrs; Penslow Hlth Clinic; Pender Co Dem Com; r/Epis; hon/Outstg Civic & Commun Ldrs.

LAWTER, J MIKE oc/State Representative; b/Dec 9, 1947; h/8104 NW 7, Okla City, OK 73127; ba/Okla City; m/Martha A; c/Michael Jay; p/Z H and Loucile Lawter, Okla City, OK; ed/BS Ed Ctrl St Univ; JD Okla City Univ; ml/Okla NG 1st Lt; pa/Okla Bar Assn; Am Bar Assn; OTLA; Okla Co Bar Assn; cp/Mason; S Okla City C of C; St Rep; r/Meth; hon/Pres Sr Law Clas; Alumni Awd; Pres Hon Rol.

LAYMAN, JOYCE ANNE BARTLEY oc/Teacher, Department Chairman; b/Oct 8, 1943; h/Rt 1 Box 33-H, Swoope, VA 24479; ba/Staunton, Va; m/L Allen; c/Kendra Anne, Wendy Alana; p/Henry Grafton (dec) and Virgina Barnhardt Bartley, Stuarts Draft, VA; ed/BA Hist; pa/Tchr, Chm SS Dept, Shelburne Jr HS; SEA; VEA; NEA; cp/Repub Party; r/Luth.

LAYTON, T ETHEL oc/Coordinator; b/Oct 18, 1934; h/100 St Johns Dr, Dothan, AL 36301; ba/Dothan; p/John Lewis and Ethel Mae Tolar Layton, Ashford, AL; ed/BS 1963, MA 1969 Univ Ala; pa/Dothan HS: Bus & Ofc Ed Coor 1978-, Bus & Ofc Ed Instr 1965-78, Bus Ed Tchr 1963-65; Fla Bus Ed Tchr, Escambia HS 1963; Ch Secy 1958-59; Clerk 1952-58; NEA; AEA; DEA; Nat Bus Ed Assn; So Bus Ed Assn; Alpha Delta Kappa; Delta Pi Epsilon; Am Voc Assn; Ala Voc Assn; SE Ala Bus Ed Assn; r/Bapt; hon/Plaque of Apprec, BOE Coop Students 1981; BOE St Acctg Curric Com 1980; Tchrs Ctr Com; Profl Devel Com; Supvr Student Tchrs, Troy St Univ; Sponsor Future Bus Ldrs Am Clb.

LAZENBY, WILLIAM DOUGLAS oc/Surgeon; b/Mar 2, 1931;

h/Opelika, AL; m/Peggy Shugart; c/Audrey Jane, William Douglas Jr, Allen Warren; p/Adolphus Leroy and Mamie Thompson Lazenby, Auburn, AL; ed/BS Auburn Univ 1953; MD Emory Univ 1957; Surg Spec Grady Meml Hosp 1958-64; mil/Asst Chief Surg, AUS Hosp Wuertzburg, Germany 1960-62; pa/Gen Surg; Pres Med Arts Assn E Ala; Angus Breeder; Dist 14 PSRO St Com of Public Hlth Cont'g Med Ed; Com Diplomate Am Bd Surg; Fellow Am Col Surgs; Fellow SE Surg Cong; cp/Opelika C of C, Past Pres; Farmers Nat Bank, Dir; Traffic Study Com, Chm; Lib Bd; Achmt Ctr Bd; Lee Co Hosp Bd; r/Bapt; Deacon; hon/Citizen of Mo, Opelika Civitan Clb; Outstg Profl Citizen of Yr, Lions Clb; Author Num Profl Articles.

LEAHY, MIRIAM KRAMER oc/Homemaker; Volunteer; b/Nov 6, 1891; h/3325 Garfield, Washington DC 20008; m/William Edward (dec); p/Thomas Best and Luanna Crook Kramer; ed/Att'd Geo Wash Univ 1912-13; Hon LLD Georgetown Univ 1975; cp/Vol Tchr ARC, Wash DC 1917-20, 1939-41; Chm Motor Corps 1942-45; Gray Lady Walter Reed Hosp 1945-56; Chm Blood Donor Ser 1956-59; Former Chm Nsg Sers; Past Pres Ladies Bd, Georgetown Univ Hosp; Nat Capital Law Leag; Inner Wheel; Twentieth Century Clb; Columbia CC; The Washington Clb; Cosmos Clb; Am Newspaper Wom's Clb; r/St Albaus Ch: Rectors' Aide; hon/Fellow, ABI; ABIRA Mem; Notable Ams; W/W Am Wom.

LEARY, WILBUR TALMADGE oc/Pharmacist; b/July 23, 1912; h/41 Burtis St, Portsmouth, VA 23702; c/Richard Lee, Thomas Rhoads, Katherine Lee, William; p/William Henry (dec) and Grace Halstead Leary (dec); ed/Med Col Va 1933; pa/Owner Cradock Pharm & Leary's Pharm; Asst Mgr Peoples Drug Store; Va Pharm Assn; cp/Va House Dels 1950-60; Portsmouth City Coun 1960-68; IOOF; r/Bapt; hon/Va Ho Dels Com Fin, Roads & Internal Navigation; Chm Retrenchment & Ec, Chesapeake & Its Tributaries.

LEAVELL, JAY C oc/Advertising Executive; b/May 8, 1921; h/1640 S Perry St, Montgomery, AL 36104; ba/Montgomery; m/Josephine Krebs; c/Winston, Candice, Tracy, Wiley; p/J C Sr and Vera Mae Leavell (dec); ed/Undergrad Study Univ Ala; mil/USAAC 1941-45, Overseas, ETO; pa/Chm Leavell, Wise & Ticheli; Mem Ala St Coun on the Arts & Humanities; Mgmt Art Guild; cp/Montgomery Rotary Clb; r/1st U Meth Ch, Montgomery: Mem; hon/Hon Mem: Pi Tau Chi, Am Inst Architects; Silver Medal, Man of Yr Awd, Mgmt Advtg Clb 1967.

L'ECUYER, ELEANOR CREED oc/Retired Military Officer; b/Jun 13, 1922; h/PO Box 553, Sun City Center, FL 33570; p/Eugene W L'Ecuyer (dec); Eleanor Creed L'Ecuyer, Sun City Ctr; ed/BA; JD; Hon Doct Juridical Sci; mil/Seaman Recruit 1944 (Ret'd Sr Wom Ofcr Active Duty); Presently Capt USCGR (Ret'd); pa/Mil Judge; cp/Dem; Cmdr Post 246 Am Legion; Resv Ofcrs Assn of US; Fleet Resv Assn; NCOA; TROA; Mass Assn of Wom Lwyrs; Intl Fdn Wom Lwyrs; Bd Trustees Trinity Lakes Retiremt Ctr; r/Rom Cath; hon/Only Wom Awd'd Coast Guard Meritorious Ser Medal.

LEDBETTER, ANNIE JEANNETTE GIVEN oc/Purchasing Agent, Transportation Agent; b/Dec 9, 1938; h/621 Holly Ridge Dr, Vicksburg, MS 39180; ba/Vicksburg; m/Walter W; c/Robert C Aldredge Jr, Mary Annette Aldredge Sims; p/John L annd Mary Clyde Logue Given, Vicksburg MS; ed/St Francis Xavier Acad 1956; MTMC Gen Traffic Mgmt 1978; GSA Small Purchases 1979; HDP; AUS Logistics Mgmt Ctr; mil/AUS; pa/AUS Engr Dist, Purchasing Agt, Transp Agt; ADP Coun SEn Sts; r/Rom Cath; hon/Spec Ser Awd 1973; Suggestion Awd 1976; Emerg Opers Awd 1979; Suggestion Awd 1980; Sustained Superior Perf Awd 190; Hon Grad Mgmt Defense Acquisition Contracts, Commandants List 1980; Lttrs of Commend 1979 & 80.

LEDWELL, JO STARNES oc/Clinical Psychologist; h/Rt 1 Box 274, Independence, WV 26374; ba/Morgantown, Wv; m/John D; ed/BA; MS; PhD; pa/Am Psych Assn; WV Psych Assn; Conslt Monongalia Yth Care Assn 1972-73; Secy, Bd Dirs Monongalia Co Yth Care Assn 1973-74; hon/W/W Am Wom; Lambda Soc; Phi Kappa Phi; Psi Chi.

LEE, BILLIE RAY SPIVEY oc/Library Technician; b/July 5, 1925; h/Kilgore, TX; m/Foy L; c/Mac L, Gene R; p/William Asberry (dec) and Joe Alice Johnson Spivey (dec); ed/Kilgore Jr Col 1962-64; pa/Lib Tech Kilgore Jr Col; Cattle Ranch; Tchrs Assns; Fac Clb; cp/Dem Party; r/First Christian Ch: SS Tchr; hon/Donated to Cookbook; Nom for Beauty in HS.

LEE, DAVID LENNOX oc/Manager; b/Feb 8, 1949; h/1511 Marion St Sw, Decatur, AL 35601; ba/Decatur; m/Angela West; p/Elizabeth M Lee, Tuscaloosa, AL; BS 1972; mil/Ala NG 1st Lt; pa/Mgr Dist Ofc Dept Indust Relats, St Ala; Pres Middle Tenn Val Chapt Ala St Employees Assn; Intl Assn Pers in Employment Security; Nat Guard Assns of Ala & US; cp/Past Secy Tenn Val Exposition; Pres Commun Sers Plan'g Coun of Morgan Co; VP Decatur JCs; Com Mem Tenn Val Rehab Ctr; r/Meth; hn/Outstg Dir of Yr, Decatur JCs; Outstg Yng Man of Yr, Decatur 1979.

LEE, JOSEPH R oc/Group Vice President; b/Dec 18, 1940; h/PO Box 38, Gotha, FL 32734; ba/Orlando; m/Carolyn Dale Bowen; c/Michael F, Kenna Rene; p/J Pope and Audice Lee Davis Lee, Blackshear, GA; pa/Grp VP-Restaurants, Gen Mills Inc; Dir Nat Restaurant Assn; Dir Sun First Nat Bank of Ctrl Park; cp/Marine Adv Com, US Dept Commerce; r/Bapt.

LEE, LA JUANA WILLIAMS oc/Professor and Department Chairman; b/May 16, 1930; h/2238 17th St, Lake Charles, LA 70601; ba/Lake Charles; m/Dr Richard H Jr; c/Richard H III; p/John B (dec) and Bessie Whitlock Williams, Mansfieold, LA; ed/BS, MEd Pan Am Univ; PhD Univ No Colo; pa/McNeese Univ, Lake Charles: Prof & Hd Dept Ofc Adm, Sch of Bus 1964-, Supvr Student Tchrs at LaGrange Sr HS 1962-63; Doct Grad Asst Univ No Colo 1968-69; Bus Ed Tchr LaGrange Sr HS, Lake Charles 1958-64; Bus Tng Instr Sowela Tech Inst, Lake Charles 1961-63; Other Previous Positions; McNeese Fac Coun; Delta Kappa Gamma; Nat Secys Assn, Intl (Assoc Mem); La Assn Cert'd Profl Secys; Calcasieu Exec Secys Assn (Hon Mem); Nat Bus Ed Assn; La Bus Ed Assn; La VocAssn; La Tchrs Assn; La Assn Higher Ed; La Assn Tchr Edrs; McNeese Coun on Tchr Ed; AAUW; BPW Clb; Am Bus Commun Assn; Other Profl Assns; cp/Lake Charles Commun Concert; Buccaneers, Civic Promoters for City of Lake Charles; Lake Charles Vis Artists Grp; Arbitrator Better Bus Bur; Indust Mgmt Org; Phi Sigma Alpha; r/Prot; hn/Grad summa cum laude; Phi Kappa Phi; Delta Pi Epsilon; Pi Omega Pi; Kappa Kappa Iota; Phi Lambda Pi.

LEE, PAMELA DIANE oc/Physical Therapist, Executive; b/Dec 14, 1946; ba/Gainesville, FL; c/Tanya Brookshire, Shelby Brookshire; p/Noble F and Virginia Lee, Woodruff, MS; ed/Att'd Univ So Fla 1964-65; AA Lake Sumpter Commun Col 1969; BS Univ Fla 1973; Further Study Univ Fla 1975-76; Num Other Courses & Wkshops; pa/Instr Sunrise Wkshop Inc 1966-67; Phys Therapy Aide, Howard Yng Med Ctr Summer 1972; Phys Therapy Intern: Happiness House Rehab Ctr Apr 1973, U Cerebral Palsy May 1973, Shands Tchg Hosp Aug 1973; Staff Phys Therapist, Sunland Tng Ctr 1973-75; Owner-Admr, Chief Phys Therapist: Phys Therapy Inc 1974-, PERT Inc 1980-, Physiotherapy Assn 1981-; Am Phys Therapy Assn, Nat & Fla Chapts, Sect of Pediatrics, Sect of Pvt Pract; Alachua Co Assn for Retard'd Citizens; Beta Sigma Phi, Corresp Secy; U Cerebral Palsy of N Ctrl Fla: Past Pres, Treas; Phys Therapy & Rehab Sers of Gainesville Inc: Pres, Chm Bd Dirs.

LEE, SAMUEL C oc/Professor; b/May 4, 1937; h/Norman, OK; ba/Sch Elec Engrg & Computer Scis, Univ Okla, 202 W Boyd, Norman, OK 73019; m/Elisa T; c/Jennifer, Vivian; p/Chou-Ying and Fu-Teh Chang Lee; ed/BS Nat Taiwan Univ 1960; MS Univ Calif-Berkeley; PhD Univ Ill; pa/Tech Staff Bell Labs 1965-67; Assoc Prof, NYU 1967-70; Assoc Prof Univ Houston 1970-75; Prof Univ Okla 1975-; Sr Mem IEEE; Mbrship Chm Biomed Pattern Recog Com of Computer Soc; Gen Chm Micro 77; Gen Chm 1979 Intl Micro & Mini Computer Conf; Gen Chm 11th Intl Symposium on Multiple Valued Logic; Profl Engr Okla & Tex; cp/AAWB; r/Cath; hon/IEEE Okla City Sect Outstg Achmt Awd 1980; Okla Soc Profl Engrs Outstg Engrg Achmt Awd 1980; 1 of 10 Outstg Achmt Awds, Nat Soc Profl Engrs 1980; Author 4 Books.

LEE, STEVEN MICHAEL oc/Computer Programmer; b/Oct 10, 1956; h/PO Box 184, Georgetown, KY 40324; ba/Lexington, KY; p/Estill H and Juanita Lee, Georgetown, KY; ed/BS Morehead St Univ 1978; pa/Programmer Trainee Chem Abstracts 1978; Computer Programmer Ky Ctrl Life Ins 1979-; Phi Beta Lambda; Phi Kappa Phi; cp/Morehead St Univ Alumni Assn; r/Corinth Christian Ch; hon/Nom'd Outstg Yng Man Am 1981; Wall St Jour Outstg Achmt Awd 1978; Ky Phi Beta Lambda Data Processing II Competition 1st 1978, 2nd 1977.

LEEPER, LINDA GAYLE oc/Teacher; b/Sept 27, 1943; h/100 S Iowa, Weslaco, TX 78596; ba/Weslaco; p/WW Leeper, Houston, TX; Trudy Karrer Marble Falls, TX; ed/BA Houston Bapt Col; MEd Pan Am Univ; pa/Elem Tchr; Kappa Delta Pi; Tex St Tchrs Assn; r/Presb; hon/W/W Am Wom.

LEETZOW, LEONARD ERMOND JR oc/Senior Vice President Investments; b/Mar 29,1 938; h/7007 Clark Rd, Sarasota, FL 33583; ba/Sarasota; m/Cherie Lee Cuthbert; c/Joni Lynn, Michael Leonard, Mark Winston; p/Leonard Herman and Alvina Elizabeth Meinke Leetzow, Bradenton, FL; ed/BS US Naval Acad 1962; mil/USN 1956-59; pa/Chm Pres's Coun 1976; Mgmt Adv Coun 1969-79; cp/Bd Dirs Girls Clb of Sarasota Co 1975-, Treas 1977-79; Bd Dirs Sarasota Co 4-H Foun 1975-80; Bd Dirs Sarasota Co C of C 1975-81; Com of 100 1978-80; Univ Clb; Gator Greek Golf Clb; Field Clb; Masons; Shriners; r/Presb Ch of the Palms; hon/Outstg Pres Emerald Div Fla Kiwanis Intl 1972-73; W/W Fin & Indust 1978-79 & 1979-80.

LEFEVRE, MARGARET CLARK oc/Professor Emeritus; b/Nov 11, 1911; h/7210 Grevilla Ave, 1A, S Pasadena, FL 33707; c/Anne Kent, May King; p/dec; ed/AB Wn Mich Univ 1932; MA Univ Minn 1946; PhD Wn

Reserve Univ 1957; pa/Kabat-Kaiser Insts; Wn Reserve Univ & Cleveland Hearing & Speech Ctr; Univ Akron; Univ Vt & Vt Rehab Ctr; Bloomsburg Penn St Col; AAUP; Am & Penn Speech & Hearing Assns; IBA; cp/Am Civil Liberties Union; Common Cause; NOW; Pinellas NOW Del to Fla NOW & Nat; hon/Fellow Am Speech & Hearing Assn 1971; Life Mem Am & Penn Speech & Hearing Assns 1976; Num Articles & Conv Papers.

LeMASTER, DAVID R oc/Educator; b/Dec 4, 1935; h/3312 W Mich, Midland, TX 79703; ba/Midland; m/Mosolete Fowlkes; c/David James, Marvin A B II, Chyree Mosolete; p/Arthur Brookshire (dec) and Ruth Denham LeMaster; ed/AA Odessa Col; BS W Tex St Univ; MEd Sul Ross St Univ; EdD Cand 1981; mil/USAFR Maj; pa/Edr, Midland Indep Sch Dist; NEA; Tex St Tchrs Assn; Clrm Tchrs Assn; Reserve Ofcrs Assn; PTA; cp/Pres James Mims SS Couples Class; r/Bapt; hon/W/W Tex Ed; Outstg Sec'dy Edrs of Am; Awd Life Mem PTA; Commend by Korean AF Chief of Staff; Commend by Korean AF Acad Supt; Commend USAF; Appt'd by Tex Gov Bill Clements to Tex Profl Practs Comm.

LEMLEY, BARBARA F oc/Administrator; b/Nov 3, 1949; h/Carmichael Rd, Montgomery, AL 36196; ba/Rockford, AL; p/Howard and Selma Lemley, Grant, AL; ed/BS Sociol; MSW; pa/Admr Dept Pensions & Security; APWA; Co Dir's Assn; cp/Montgomery Commun Coun; U Way; hon/BS w Hon, Univ N Ala.

LEONARD, CLARENCE LEO oc/Missions Representative; b/Feb 7, 1932; h/430 S 25th NW, Cleveland, TN 37311; ba/Cleveland; m/Joyce Johnson; p/dec; ed/Grad Demo HS at Univ So Miss; Bible Inst NC; Dist Overseer Chs of God, Asheville, NC; St Bd Chs of God NC; cp/HUD, Mt Holly, NC; Pres Min Assn, Mt Holly; r/Ch of God.

LEONARD, NELS JR oc/Music Educator; b/Feb 16, 1931; h/15 Crestview Dr, Wheeling, WV 26003; ba/W Liberty, WV; m/Barbara Jean; c/Thomas Nelson, Susan Anita; p/Nels (dec) and Rachel Marie Leonard (dec); ed/AB; MM; PhD; mil/AUS; pa/Prof Mus, Hall of Fine Arts, W Liberty St Col; Past Pres WVMEA; Former Editor Notes a Tempo; cp/Dir Mus 1st Presb Ch, Martins Ferry, OH; r/Presb; hon/Recip S'ship from Spanish Govt to Perf.

LEONHARD, JOHN R SR oc/Shoe Repairer; b/May 20, 1929; h/1312 Jackson Landing Rd, Picayune, MS 39466; ba/Picayune; m/April Elaine; c/Michelle, Tina, Paula, John, Steven; p/John Paul and Ella Anna Leonhard, Lake Genevs, WI; mil/AUS 22½Yrs; pa/Shoe Repair & Sales; r/Cath; hon/Purple Heart; Silver Star; Commend w Cluster.

LEONHART, WILLIAM HAROLD oc/Reinsurance Broker; b/May 2, 1906; h/550 4th Ave S, Naples,FL 33940; ba/Towson, MD; m/Martha Curtis; c/Valerie L Smalkin, Mery Curtis, Jean L Anfossi, John Lawrence, James Chancellor, William H Jr; p/William Henry and Dorah Chancellor Leonhart (dec); ed/Marshall Col Model Sch, Huntington, WV 1917-18; Balto City Col Night Sch 1921-26; mil/Md St Guard 1931-35; pa/Pres Leonhart & Co Inc (Reinsurance), Balto 1943-; Instr Ins Soc of Balto; Instyr Ins Inst of Am; Indust Com to Define Reinsurance; cp/Past Pres Civitan Clb; Chm Boystown Homes of Md 1969-72; SAR, Md Chapt; ARC, Past Mem Exec Com Balto Chapt; Past Rep En Vols (Nat), Chm Blood Prog (Korean War) Balto Chapt; Dem; Treas Dems of Eisenhower (Both Campaigns); Others Activs; r/Rom Cath; hon/Life Mem Civitan Clb of Balto; Past Intl Com for Mtly Retard'd Chd, Civitan Intl.

LERMA, EVERARDO C oc/Administrator and Instructor; b/June 2, 1915; m/Lydia C; c/Patricia C Unsinn; p/dec; ed/BA Tex A&I Univ 1938; MA 1950 Tex A&I Univ; pa/Coach 28 Yrs; Elem Prin, HS Prin, Supt Schs; Prin Lincoln Elen Sch, Edinburg CISD 1978-80; Instr Evening Classes, Pan Am Univ 1977-80; AASA; Life Mem PTA; Dallas Sch Admrs Assn; Tex Suprvrs & Curric Assn; Tex Assn Sec'dy Sch Prins; Tex Assn Elem Sch Prins; NEA; cp/Sports Trail Century Clb 1957; r/Cath; hon/Hall of Hon, Tex HS Coaches Assn 1968; Intl Platform Assn 1972-76; Laredo Intl Hall of Fame; Com to Select Worthy Cands for Tex HS Coaches Assn Hall of Fame; Ath Hall of Fame, Tex A&I Univ 1977.

LEROY, WALTER WILLIAM JR oc/Executive; b/Apr 25, 1937; h/70 Springlake Pl, Atlanta, GA 30318; ba/Atlanta; m/Ina Sue Marlin; p/Walter William and Louise Honiker Leroy, Baltimore, MD; ed/BA Ga Inst Technol; mil/AUS 1964; pa/Pres Info Resources Inc; TIMS; ACM; LOMA; IASA; cp/Optimist; r/Epis; hon/Cert'd Data Processor; LOMA Cert.

LESLIE, JOE NEWLAND oc/Safety Administrator; b/Feb 27, 1919; h/273 ALabama Ave, Kingsport, TN 37660; m/Margaret W; c/Betty J Pendleton; p/Walter F and Vessie Newland Leslie (dec); ba/Dir Safety Sullivan Co Hwy Dept; Tenn Law Enforcemnt Ofcrs Assn; U Comml Travelers of Am; FOP; cp/U Citizens for Better Govt; Burgess-Mills Lodge #11; Moose Lodge 972; Sullivan Co Assn Taxpayers; r/Bloomingdale Bapt Ch; hon/Bloomingdale Ruritan.

LESSENBERRY, ROBERT ADAMS oc/Retail Executive; b/May 7, 1926; h/913 S Green St, Glasgow, KY 42141; ba/Glasgow; m/Mary Lloyd Howard; c/Robert Howard, Hugh Barret Adams, Leigh Langford; p/Robert Long and Hugh Barret Adams Lessenberry (dec); ed/AB Centre Col of Ky 1950; mil/AUS Inf 2/Lt 1944-46, Field Arty Capt 1950-52; Decorations; pa/Pres: Lessenberry Bldg Ctr Inc, Lessenberry Elect & Plumbing Ctr Inc (1973); Glasgow Railway Co: Dir-Treas 1946, Pres 1965; Partner Parkview Devel Co 1959; Pres Lessenberry Devel Co Inc 1969; VP Mod Manor 1971-76; Lessenberry Real Estate (Broker) 1972; Hardware Wholesalers Inc 1973-: Dir, Treas, Secy, VP, Pres; Ind-Ky Hardware Assn 1975-: Dir, Secy; Dir-Pres Ky Retail Lumber Dealers; cp/Former Mayor City of Glasgow; Pres: PTA, Glasgow Concert Assn, Rotary Clb Glasgow; Dir: Barren River Area Devel Coun, C of C; Barren Co Red Cross; Pres Bd Trustees, Westminster Terr Presb Home for Sr Citizens & Hlth Care Ctr, Louisville; Mason; York & Scottish Rite; Shriner; r/1st Presb Ch: Elder, Choir Dir, Ch Sch Tchr; VChm L'ville Presby; hon/Ky Col Comm; Orgl Chm, Prs Glasgow Commun Concert Assn 1953-58; Balfour Awd, Ky-Tenn Province; Omicron Delta Kappa Awd; Hon Citizen, Metro Nashville; Num Biogl Listings; ODK Ldrship Frat 1950.

LESTER, DEBORAH MOORE oc/Teaching Assistant; b/June 26, 1953; m/Edgel Celsus; c/Whitney Dawn; p/Richard Earl and Lorene Pollard Moore; ed/BS 1973, MA 1978 Univ Ala; PhD Cand Univ Ky; pa/Tchr Hamilton HS & Lupton Elem Sch; Tchg Asst Univ Ky, Sch of Mus; Mu Phi Epsilon; Mus Edrs Nat Conf; Ky Mus Edrs Nat Conf; r/Disciples of Christ Christian Ch; hon/Outstg Yng Wom Am 1978.

LESTER, EDGEL C oc/Psychologist, Mental Health Administrator; b/Aug 2, 1950; m/Deborah M; c/Whitney; p/Edgel and Norma E Lester, Owensboro, KY; ed/BA Vanderbilt Univ 1972; MA Mid Tenn St Univ 1975; JD Cand Univ Ky Sch of Law; pa/Dir of Adm & Devel, NW Ala Mtl Hlth Ctr; cp/BSA, Asst Dist Commr; r/Disciples of Christ.

LESTER, JAMES LUTHER oc/Attorney at Law; b/Jan 12, 1932; h/770 Camellia Rd, Augusta, GA 30904; ba/Augusta; m/Gwendolyn Gleason; c/James Jr, Frank G; p/William M Lester, Augusta; Elizabeth Miles Lester (dec); ed/AB The Citadel; JD Univ Ga Sch of Law; mil/AUS Arty 1952-54; 2/Lt, Discharged Capt; pa/Ga & Am Bar Assns; cp/Former Chm Richmond Co Dem Exec Meeting; Senator Ga Gen Assembly 1971-; Dir YMCA; Mem St Adv Coun for Mtl Hlth & Mtl Retard; r/Meth; hon/1973 Outstg Ser to Mtly Retard Awd, Augusta Assn for Retard Chd; 1976 Public Affairs Awd, Mtl Hlth Assn of Metro Atlanta; Outstg Ser to Ed Awd, Richmond Co Edrs Assn; Dist'd Ser Awd, Ga Assn for Mtl Hlth.

LESTER, SHIRLEY RIFE oc/Senior Buyer; b/Aug 17, 1952; h/Richlands, Va; ba/S&S Corp, Rt 3 Box 70, Cedar Bluff, VA 24609; c/Tracey Denise; p/Mack and Clara Sword Rife, Richlands, VA; ed/Attd'd Sw Va Commun Col 1971-73; pa/Sr Buyer Corp Purchasing, S&S Corp; Past Pres S&S Machinery Credit Union Inc; Past Pres Nat Secys Assn, Va Div Lonesome Pines Chapt; Nat Assn Purchasing Mgmt, Network Dir Nat Assn Female Execs; Am Soc Profl & Exec Wom; r/Christian; hon/Comm of Col, Hon Order of Ky Cols; W/W Am Wom.

LESTER, VIRGINIA LAUDANO oc/College President; b/Jan 5, 1931; h/240 Kable St, Staunton, VA 24401; ba/Staunton; c/Valerie, Pamela; p/Edmund F and Emily Downs Laudano, Philadelphia, PA; ed/BA; MEd; PhD; pa/Mary Baldwin Col: Pres, Prof Interdisciplinary Studies 1976-; Empire St Col, St Univ NY, Saratoga Sprgs: Act'g Dean St-wide Progs 1976, Sr Assoc Dean & Assoc Prof St-wide Progs 1975-76, Assoc Dean & Asst Prof 1973-75; Vis Fac Fellow, Harvard Univ Grad Sch of Ed, Cambridge, Mass Spring 1976; Conslt'g Core Fac Union Grad Sch, Union for Experimenting Cols & Univs, Yellow Sprgs, Ohio 1975-; Other Previous Positions; Conslt; Am Assn Higher Ed; AAUP; Am Acad Polit & Social Scis; Mem Num Profl Bds; Others; cp/Former Mem: Saratoga Sprgs Housing Bd of Appeals, Promotion Com Saratoga Sprgs C of C, Citizen's Adv Com Saratoga Sprgs Bd of Ed; Var Ofcs Held Hosp Aux; Former Dir Saratoga Sprgs Yth Employmt Ser; Former Chm Saratoga Sprgs HS Site Selection Com; r/Quaker; hon/Pub'd Author; Freshman Sch of Ed Awd; Chimes, Jr Wom's Hon Soc; Pi Lambda Theta; Pi Gamma Mu; Pioneer of Yr, Dist'd HS Alumni Awd 1977, Frankford HS Alumni Assn; W/W in Am.

LEVINE, JACK H oc/General Contractor; b/Nov 25, 1952; h/7845 Camino Real, #0-305, Miami, FL 33143; ba/Coral Gables, FL; p/Murray I Levine (dec); Eileen Seitlin, Miami, FL; ed/BS cum laude Univ Miami 1973; pa/Owner Levine Properties (Gen Contractor, Mortgage Broker, Real Est Broker); Am Soc Civil Engrs; Tau Beta Pi; cp/Bd Dirs Gtr Miami Jewish Fed; Camp Judaea Com; Chm Yng Adult Div Gtr Miami Jewish Fed; Public Relats VP B'nai B'rith Ko-ach Lodge; r/Jewish.

LEVINE, LEON oc/Chairman of Board, Chief Executive Officer; b/June 8, 1937; h/1818 Cloister Dr, Charlotte, NC 28211; ba/Charlotte; m/Sandra P; c/Howard Russell, Lori Ann, Mindy Ellen; p/Harry (dec) and Minnie Ginsberg Levine (dec); ed/Att'd Wingate Col & Univ Miami; pa/Chm Bd, Chief Exec Ofcr Family Dollar Stores; Trustee U Jewish Appeal; cp/Bd Dirs Adv Coun U Synagogues of Am; Trustee Temple Israel; Adv Bd Duke Univ Hosp; r/Jewish; hon/Holy City Peace Awd 1974.

LEVY, DEBORAH oc/Educational Consultant; b/Aug 5, 1949; h/2740 Hollywood Blvd, Hollywood, FL 33020; m/Elliot; c/Jonathan, Emily; p/Irvin and Esther Benovitz, W Palm Bch, FL; ed/BA w Hons Univ Ill 1971; MA w Hons Wash Univ 1973; EdD w Hons Nova Univ 1979; pa/Ednl Conslt, Devel Resource Ctr; CEC; ACLD; cp/Orton Soc; r/Jewish; hon/James Schlr 1971; Most Outstg Tchr 1972; Article Pub'd in Profl Jour.

LEWINS, THOMAS M IV oc/Superintendent; b/June 8, 1947; h/PO Box 857, Warren, AR 71671; ba/Warren; m/Cheryl; p/Thomas M III and Elizabeth J Lewins, Little Rock, AR; ed/BS St Col Ark 1969; MS Univ Ctrl Ark 1975; pa/Cottage Life Dir, Alexander Unit, Ark Chd's Colony; Supt Jonesboro Unit Ark Chds Colony; Supt SE Ark Human Devel Ctr; Am Psych Assn; Ark Psych Assn; Am Sch Psych Assn; SE Ark Psych Assn; Ark Assn Mtl Deficiency; Am Assn Mtl Deficiency; Lic'd Psych Examr; Lic'd Nsg Home Admr; cp/Intl Lions Clb; Benevolent & Protective Order of Elks; r/7th Day Adventist; hon/Cert of Acknowlegement Miss Co Commun Col 1980.

LEWIS, ANNA ELIZABETH oc/Production and Circulation Assistant; b/Oct 24, 1946; h/21 Pine Dr, Myrtle Bch, SC 29577; ba/Conway, SC; m/Gary Elizabeth, Laura Ellen; p/Samuel C Sr (dec) and Ruth G Weaver Laster, Myrtle Bch, SC; ed/AA Stratford Col; Att'd Wake Forest Univ; pa/Prod & Cir Asst Weekly Advtg Pub; Grand Strand Press Clb; cp/Grand Strand Humane Soc; Var Polit Compaigns; Beta Sigma Phi; r/Epis; hon/W/W Am Wom 1979-80.

LEWIS, BESSIE RUTH oc/Postmaster; b/Mar 18, 1927; h/Rt 1 Box 18, Buckner, AR 71827; ba/Buckner; m/Charles W Jr; c/Nancy Ruth Grimmett, Charles Winston; p/Calhoon Milner (dec) and Ruth Lee Owen Jackson (dec); pa/Postmaster Buckner PO; NAPUS of Ark Exec Com 1976-80; Past VP 3rd Class 1976-77; r/Bapt; SS Tchr; Past Pres Bpat WMA; hon/Top Avon Saleswom 1971 & 72; Florist Designer 1963-72; Cert of Trg.

LEWIS, CALLIE ANN oc/Nursing Supervisor; b/Oct 7, 1936; h/5719 Wqaterford, Houston, TX 77033; ba/Houston; m/Joseph Nathaniel; c/Debra Denise Kizzare, Roy Anthony Hunt, Paula Yvette Williams; p/Irvin Daniels (dec); Florence Jenkins, Houston, Tx; ed/RN; pa/RN Supvr, Tex Med Ctr; Eta Phi Beta; Past Pres LVNA; cp/Past Pres LVN's St Luke, Tex Chd Hosp; r/Bapt; hon/LVN of Yr, St Luke's Hosp; Eta Phi Beta S'ship Queen.

LEWIS, CHARLES B oc/Teacher, Missionary; b/Sept 20, 1913; h/908 N Union, Natchez, MS 39120; ba/Natchez; p/Mr and Mrs Irvin Lewis; ed/AB; BD; ThM; pa/Asam Bapt Profs of Rel; Nat Assn Adukt Ed; cp/Civic & Bus Ctrs; r/Bapt; hon/W/W: Ed, Rel, Black Ams.

LEWIS, DALE PAUL oc/Executive; b/Aug 20, 1932; h/6124 Ramshorn Dr, McLean, VA 22101; ba/Wash DC; m/Ann M; c/Leonard J, Kimberly A, Amanda E, Christian F; p/Floyd B (dec) and Elizabeth A Lewis, Los Angeles, CA; ed/AA USCG Acad; mil/USCG Lt; pa/Pres & Chm Bd ICX Aviation Inc, Lewis Aircraft Corp; cp/McLean Citizens Assn, Bd Mem Chm Budget Com; r/Cath; hon/Public Ser US Dept Commerce Burs E-W Trade.

LEWIS, ELIZABETH (LIBBY) JOHNSON oc/Sales Representative; b/Mar 27, 1943; h/Rt 2, Kinards, SC 29355; ba/Newberry, SC; c/Chuck, Nicole; p/Morris Pinckney (dec) and Mary Frances Miller Johnson (dec); ed/Att'd Winthrop Col; Completed Var Sems on Fin Plan'g, Est Analysis & Bus Ins; pa/Life Ins Sales Rep; Nat Assn Life Underwriters; Bd Mem Clinton-Laurens-Newberry Assn Life Underwriters; Wom Life Underwriters Conf; cp/Former Mem Newberry BPW; Steering Com Newberry HS Band Parents Assn; r/Bapt: Choir Mem; hon/Challenger Awd 1977; Wom's Ldrs Roundtable, Nat Assn Life Underwriters 1978; Nat Sales Achmt Awd 1978.

LEWIS, EMMA GOLDMAN oc/Instructor; b/Sept 1, 1929; h/1566 Schoolview, Jackson, MS 39213; ba/Jackson; m/Jesse C; p/Peggy Ann Rebertson, Valerie; p/James and Augustine Goldman London, New Orleans, LA; ed/Artist Dip; BMus; pa/Mus Instr, Jackson St Univ; NATS; NMTA; LWV; r/Cath; hon/Diuguid F'ship.

LEWIS, ERV oc/Singer, Songwriter, Recording Artist; b/Aug 19, 1936; h/Box 218, Wellman Heights, Johnsonville, SC 29555; m/Frances; c/Hal, Pam, Steve, Cindy; p/Henry Jackson and Lila Ruth Rogers Lewis, Hemingway, SC; ed/Att'd The Citadel; Intl Corresp Sch; Cert Purchasing Mgr, Nat Assn Purchasing Mgmt; pa/Pres & Dir Herald Assn (Corp Home for Herald Records, Klesis Records & Mark Five Records); Records for Herald Records; Gospel Mus Assn F'ship Christians in Arts, Media & Entertainment; F'ship Christian Aths; F'ship Contemporary Christian Mins; Teen Crusade Inc, Dir; Jerry Arhelger Evangelistic Assn Dir; Albert Long Happenings Inc; Erv Lewis Christian Outreach, Pres; Purchasing Mgmt Assn of Carolinas & Va; r/Presb; hon/Nat Communs Awd, Nat TV Prod 1972; Hon Citizen Awd, City of Myrtle Bch 1973; Key to City, Florence, SC 1979; Author Songbooks.

LEWIS, JOHN OLIVER oc/Plant Manager; b/Aug 8, 1923; h/200 Broadmoor St, Borger, TX 79007; m/Virginia D; c/Susan E Byrd, Cynthia Ann Hopkins, Nancy J; p/Hazel F Lewis, Danville, Ill; ed/BS Univ Ill 1948; mil/AUS 1943-46; pa/Phillips Petro Co: Mgr Toledo, Ohio Philblack Plant 1969-73; Plant Engrg Mgr, Teesside Opers 1973-78, Mgr Woods Cross Refinery 1978-; Profl Engr St Tex; r/Presb.

LEWIS, GEORGE MARVIN JR oc/Soft Drink Bottler; b/Feb 16, 1916; h/1108 Honeysuckle Rd, Dothan, AL 36301; m/Jean Coleman Brock; c/George Marvin III, William Brock; ed/Att'd Starke Univ Mil Sch 1929-31; mil/USAAF 1943-46; pa/Coca-Cola Bottling Co, Ptnr & Stockholder; Pres Jenmar Corp; Orig Stockholder So Discount Corp; Stockholder WDHN-TV; Pres Dothan Soft Drink Advtg Com; cp/Past Chm Houston Mar of Dimes; V-Chm & Past Chm Rec Bd of Dothan; Chm Dothan Rec Proj Com; Dothan Country Clb; Elks Lodge; Masonic Lodge; Alcazar Temple, Montgomery; Hon Mem Dept Public Safety, Daleville; Past Chm Bogardus S Cairns Adv Coun, Assn of AUS; Exec Com Bogardus S Cairns Chapt Assn AUS, Pres 1972-73; Bd Dirs & Exec Com AUS Aviation Mus, Ft Rucker; V-Chm Dothan Housing Auth; Pres Ala Leasee Housing Assn; Bd Dirs Dothan-Houston Co C of C: V-Chm of Bd, Past Treas, Past Chm Air Transp Com; Dothan-Houston Co Homebldrs Assn; Bd Dirs Ctrl Bank of Dothan; Adv Bd Trustees, Troy St Univ; Dept of Defense Jt Civilian Orientation Conf; r/U Meth: Adm Bd; hon/U Fund Merit Awd 1970; Dist'd Ser Awd, Ala Soft Drink Bottlers Assn 1981.

LEWIS, GLADYS SHERMAN oc/Free-Lance Writer, Registered Nurse; b/Mar 20, 1933; h/3620 Ridgehaven Dr, Midwest City, OK 73110; ba/Midwest City; m/Wilbur Curtis; c/Karen, David, Leanne, Cristen; p/Andrew Sherman, Wynnewood, OK; Minnie Sherman, Okla City, OK; ed/RN; BA; pa/ANA; Okla Co Med Aux; Okla Med Aux; Columnist, Editor "Sooner Physician's Heartbeat"; cp/Dem; PTA; Girl Scouts; AAUW; OK ERA: Nat Rel Com ERA Evangelical Wom's Caucus; r/Bapt; hon/W/W Am Wom; Midwest City Pilot Clb's Wom-of Yr 1979.

LEWIS, OLEE oc/Director; b/July 30, 1927; h/Rt 1 Box 46, Puryear, TN 38251; b/Paris, TN; p/Elvuren and Cursell Gray, Puryear, TN; ed/Att'd Nat Bapt Missionary Tng Sch 1954-55; Grad Nurse Aide, Murray-Calloway Co Hosp 1955; Cert Gerontology Wkshop, Univ Tenn 1976; Cert Tenn St Univ 1977; pa/Henry Co Dir NWTEDC 1967-; Dir Henry Co NW Tenn Devel Dist Elderly Nutrition Prog 1975-; cp/Easter Seal Soc, Adv Bd Weakley Co; Title I Fed Ed Prog, Co Wide Parent Adv Bd Henry Co; State Human Sers Dept; Area on Aging; W Tenn Hlth Improvement Assn, Bd Dirs & Mem Plan Devel Com; Henry Co Life-Line Vol Blood Prog; r/Missionary Bapt; hon/Ky Col 1971; Cert Apprec, NW Tenn Ec Devel Coun 1978; Dist'd Ser Awd, Outstg Contbns in Fields of Communs, Human Relats & Civic Endeavors, Civic Leag Paris-Henry Co 1979; Cert Achmt Child Check Campaign 1980; Ten Yr Ser Cert, Tenn Commun Sers Adm 1980; Cert Contbg to Success of Older Am Hlth Fair 1979.

LEWIS, ORVAL L oc/Engineering Director; b/July 27, 1916; h/569 N Post Oak Ln, Houston, TX 77024; ba/Houston; m/Debbie; c/James, Robert; p/Roy and Anna Lewis (dec); ed/BSME Tex Tech Univ; MBA Univ So Calif; pa/Engrg Dir, Davy Inc; Pres Am Soc Mech Engrs; cp/Repub Party; r/Meth; hon/Fellow ASME; Engr of Dist; Engr of Mo, LA; W/W: Tex, S&SW, Kan Bnkrs Assn.

LEWIS, PAULINE EVANS oc/Teacher; b/Aug 13, 1938; h/1055 Glenwood Dr, Orangeburg, SC 29115; ba/Orangeburg, SC; m/Otis W; c/Gary Jason; p/John Gary Evans, Orangeburg, SC; Florence Evans (dec); ed/BS Elem Ed; MS Ed; pa/Rdg Tchr Felton Lab Sch; Edisto Rdg Coun; Intl Rdg Coun; Ednl Assns Local, St, Nat; cp/Zeta Phi Beta; Dem Party; r/Bapt; hon/Outstg Elem Tchr 1974; Dist'd Tchr 1976; Inspiration Cert Yng Wom's Missionary Circle 1977; Served on Lang Arts Adv Bd.

LEWIS, ROMEO oc/Physician; b/May 16, 1909; h/Clinton, NC; ba/Clinton; m/Rena; c/Romeo H II, Yvonne L Edey; p/James A (dec) and Yvonne Lewis (dec); ed/AB New Mex Univ 1931; MD Howard Univ Med Sch 1940; MPH Harvard Univ Sch Public Hlth; mil/Maj 93rd Div; pa/Gen Pract, Migrant Clin; Old N St NMA; AMA; Fam Pract Assn Public Hlth Soc; Geriatric Soc; cp/Omega Psi Phi; Blind Comm Clinton City Sch Bd; r/Meth; hon/Awd from Omega Psi; Awd Tri-Co Clin.

LEWIS, ROSA MAE oc/Homemaker; b/Apr 10, 1915; h/312 Main St,

Griffin, GA 30223; c/Charles Merlin, Thomas Eugene, Nancy Louise Smith; p/George S (dec) and Clara Mae Rawls (dec); r/Bapt.

LI, CHOH-LUH oc/Neurosurgeon; b/Sept 19, 1919; h/7001 Buxton Terr, Bethesda, MD 20034; ba/Bethesda; m/Julia Y R; c/Claire, David, Anne; p/Chein-Chi and Mei-Ching Li (dec); ed/MS; MS; PhD; pa/Neurosurg, NIH; Res, Study Function of Nervous Sys; hon/Awd for Dist'd Sci Achmt, Am-Chinese Med & Hlth Assn.

LIBLICK, MARVIN MAX oc/Technician, Musician; b/Mar 16, 1939; h/705 Westmount Dr, LA, CA 70069; p/Nathan (dec) and Sophie Liblick (dec); mil/AUS Med Corps 2½ Yrs; pa/Motion Picture & TV Sound Tech; Film & Mus Lyricist; cp/ASCAP; r/Hebrew; hon/Mus TV 1957, 59.

LICHOLAT, RUTH TAYLOR oc/Communications Consultant; b/July 17, 1949; h/1722 Granada Dr, Arlington, TX 76014; ba/Dallas; m/John Edward; c/Edward Anthony; p/Calvin E Taylor, Dallas, TX; Jessie Richards, Gladwin, MI; ed/Ferris St Col 1967-70; pa/Lab Asst, Res Asst, Profl Asst Ferris St Col 1967-70; Receptionist, Secy Wash Steel Corp, Warren, Mich 1970-71; Sales Rep Avon Prods, Royal Oak, Mich 1970-74, Stand-By Mgr Kansas City, Mo 1972-74, Dist Sales Mgr, Dist 707, Fort Worth-Arlington 1974-78; Ser Cons Outside Sales, Mktg Dept SWn Bell 1978–; Bus-Consumer Ethics Task Force; cp/Arlington, Tex C of C 1974–, VChm 1977-78; hon/Recip Dist'd Sales Mgmt Awd, Avon Prods 1977, Recruiting Awd 1977.

LICK, DALE W oc/College President; b/Jan 7, 1938; h/Rt 5, Statesboro, GA 30458; ba/S'boro; m/Marilyn K; c/Lynette M, Kitty I, Diana K, Ronald W; p/John R and Florence M Lick (dec); ed/BS; MS; PhD; pa/Pres Ga So Col 1978–; Old Dominion Univ, Norfolk, Va 1974-78: Dean Sch of Scis & Hlth Professions, Prof Math & Computing Scis; Drexel Univ, Philadelphia, Pa 1969-72: Hd & Assoc Prof Dept Math; Adj Assoc Prof Dept Pharm, Temple Med Sch, Temple Univ 1969-72; Other Former Acad Positions; Conslt; Chm Bd Dirs, Shared Staff Devel Prog, EVIMEC Hosps & En Va Med Auth 1975–; Sci Mus Assn of En Va 1976–: Chm Bd Trustees, Pres; Num Other Profl Activs; AAAS; Am Assn for Higher Ed; AAUP; Am Assn Univ Admrs; Am Math Soc; Am Soc Allied Hlth Professions; Assn for Computing Machinery; Math Assn Am; Pi Mu Epsilon; Sigma Xi; Soc for Indust & Applied Math; Va Acad Sci; Va Assn Allied Hlth Professions; Others; hon/Mich St Univ: Entrance S'shp, J C Plant Awd, Grad w Honor, Grad Coun F'ship; NSF Sum Res F'ship, Univ Cal-Riverside; Postdoct Res F'ship, Brookhaven Nat Lab; Biogl Listings; Pub'd Author.

LIESEN, DOROTHY ANN THIEL oc/Nurse Epidemiologist, Associate Clinical Professor; b/Dec 13, 1944; h/14101 Cherry Orchard Run, Tampa, FL 33618; ba/Tampa; m/Richard Philip; p/Roman Aloise and Mary Ann Viola Thiel, Milwaukee, WI; ed/RN St Joseph's Hosp Sch of Nsg 1966; BS Carroll Col 1975; MS Univ S Fla 1979; Infection Control Trg 1973; mil/AUSR 1978- Capt; pa/Surg Staff Nurse, Charge Duty Evening & Night Duty St Michael's Hosp 1966-67; Clin Instr Sacred Heart Sch Pract Nsg 1967-73; Infection Surveillance Ofcr, Waukesha Meml Hosp 1973-76; Nurse Epidemiologist, James A Haley Vet Hosp 1976–; Assoc Clin Prof Univ S Fla Sch Nsg; Lectr & Conslt US & Carribean in Infection Control; Fac Mem Hillsborough Commun Col, Cmmun Sers Sect; Assn Practitioners of Infection Control Nat Assn; Wis Lung Assn; Fla Practitioners of Infection Control; Bay Area Practitioners of Infection Control; Am Public Hlth Assn; cp/Nat Trust Hist Preserv; hon/Phi Kappa Phi 1978; Sigma Theta Tau, Delta Beta Chapt 1981; Author Num Profl Pubs.

LIFQUIST, ROSALIND CARIBELLE oc/Retired Food Economist; b/Jun 5, 1903; h/1727 Massachusetts Ave NW, Wash DC 20036; m/Milton Wilcox Lifquist (dec); p/John D and Frances Myrtle Wilcox Lifquist (dec); ed/Dipl Univ Wis 1921; BW w High Distn 1935, MS 1937 Univ Minn; mil/USN Waves 1942-46; pa/Tchr Home Ec Public Schs Algoma, Gillette & Shawano, Wis 1921-26; Dietetics Intern: Univ Minn Hosp 1926, Univ Wash 1941; Dietitian City Hosp Lock Haven, Pa 1926-33; Instr Foods Univ Minn, St Paul 1935-37; Asst Prof Foods and Nutrition Ia St Col, Ames 1937-41; Food Economist Bur Human Nutrition & Home Ec USDA, Wash 1946-55; Consumer Ec Spec Agri Mktg Ser, Ec Res Ser 1955-73; Am Home Ec Assn, Nat Chm Public Relats Com 1958-61; Capital Press Wom; hon/Caleb Dorr Awd Univ Minn; Cert Merit USDA; Dist'd Sr Awd, Univ Wis; Fellow Mem, ABI; Intl Reg Profiles; DIB; 2000 Wom Achmt; W/W S&SW; Omicron Nu; Pi Lambda Theta; Phi Upsilon Omicron; Pub'd Author.

LIGHTFOOT, HARRIETT ANNA GRIMM oc/Executive; b/Dec 7, 1897; h/1155 Lake Miriam Dr, Lakeland, FL 33803; ba/Same; m/Edwin H Sr (dec); Edwin N Jr, Esther Audred L Ehlert; p/Erenest A and Emile D Grimm (dec); ed/Concert Soprano, Univ Ill, Am Conservatory of Music; pa/Pres Niblock Inc, Teen Inc, Alee Inc; Mgr Lightfoot Groves; cp/Pres Music, Garden, Wom Writers; Others; r/Presb; hon/Wom of Yr; Mother of Yr; Plaque for Outstg Ser; Key to City; Others.

LILES, DONALD MELVIN oc/Personnel Officer; b/Apr 30, 1941; h/Rt 1 Box 73--C, Spring City, TN 37381; ba/Spring City; p/Alice Liles Roach, Scottsboro, AL; ed/AS NEn St Jr Col 1972; BS Univ N Ala 1975; mil/USAF 1962-66; pa/TVA Pers Ofcr 1976–; Pers Mgr John Blue Co 1973-76; Pers Mgr SCI Elecs Inc 1969-71; Pers Mgr Hayes Intl Corp 1966-69; pa/Am Soc Pers Adm; Nat Mgmt Assn; r/Meth.

LILJENQUIST, L BLAINE oc/Mortgage Banking, International Transactions; b/Apr 5, 1912; h/1234 Meyer Ct, McLean, VA 22101; ba/Same; m/Patricia L Charters; c/John Eric, Blaine Lee, David Floyd, Thomas Richard, Kathryn, Mark Douglas; p/Ezra Lorenzo Liljenquist (dec); Mary Malinda Wilcox (dec); ed/BS Univ Idaho 1938; JD Geo Wash Univ 1959; CAE; Further Study; mil/USN 1944-46, Lt; Hdqtrs Staff, 7th Fleet, SW Pacific & Philippine Sea Frontier; pa/Agri Ext Agt Pueblo Indian Agy, Albuquerque, NM 1938-41; US Dept Agri: Amarillo, Cincinnati, Indianapolis, Wash DC 1941-44; Wn Sts Meat Packers Assn Inc: Wash DC Rep 1946-58, VP 1958-61, Pres & Gen Mgr 1961-70; Chm Wash Intl Fin Corp; Pres Wash Intl Devel Co Inc; Past Pres: Nat Assn Execs Clb, Wash Soc Assn Execs; Past Dir Am Soc Assn Execs; Past Chm The Food Group; Alpha Zeta Agri Frat; r/Ch of Jesus Christ LDS: Ordained Bishop & High Priest 1951, Bishop Wash Ward (Wash DC) 1951-56, Mem Wash & Potomac Stake High Couns 1957-64; hon/World W/W Fin & Indust; W/W S&SW; Wash Blue Book.

LILLARD, RONALD KIM oc/Minister; b/Aug 2, 1945 h/PO Box 187, Andice, TX 78626; ba/Same; c/Allyson Marie; p/R D (dec) and Cleo Lillard, Waco, TX; ed/BA Baylor Univ; MA, ThD Univ Heidelberg, Germany; pa/Vis Prof Ch Hist, Intl Bapt Sem, Rushlikon, Switz; Min Andice Bapt Ch; cp/Adv Bd Parents w/out Partners; r/So Bapt; hon/W/W: Red, Intells; DIB; Men Achmt.

LILLY, THOMAS GERALD oc/Lawyer; b/Sept 17, 1933; h/4408 Deer Creek Dr, Jackson, MS 39211; ba/Jackson; m/Constance Ray Holland; c/Thomas G Jr, William Holland, Carolyn Ray; p/Sale Trice and Margaret Evelyn Butt Lilly, Belzoni, MS; ed/BBA Tulane Univ 1955; LLB 1960, JD 1968 Univ Miss; mil/USNR 1955-58 Capt; pa/Mem Law Firm Wise, Carter, Child, Steen & Caraway; Pres Fed Bar Assn 1979-80; cp/Asst US Atty, No Dist Miss 1962-66; r/Meth; hon/Navy Commend Medal 1977.

LIMPUS, PAT LONGINO oc/Author; b/Oct 13, 1946; h/511 Bitterfield Dr, St Louis, MO 63011; m/Lawrence L; c/Alicia, Christopher, Michelle; p/James F and Nan Longino, New Boston, TX; ed/BA Sam Houston St Col 1969; pa/AAUW; cp/DAR; Wom's Assn St Louis Symph Soc; Metro St Louis Lwyrs Wives Assn; New Neighbors Leag; r/Bapt; hon/Author *The Nest* 1979.

LIN, CHIANG oc/Political Scientist and Educator; b/Mar 28, 1936; h/Ruston, LA; ba/PO Box 960, Grambling, LA 71245; m/Chi H; c/Susan; p/Kai Y Lin, Chishan, Taiwan; Mei L Lin (dec); ed/BA 1960, MA 1964 Taiwan Univ; PhD Univ Paris 1969; mil/Chinese AF 2nd Lt 1960-61; pa/Grambling St Univ: Asst Prof 1970-74, Assoc Prof 1974-80, Prof 1980–; Am Polit Sci Assn; Pi Sigma Alpha; r/Luth; hon/Intl W/W & W&SW 1980-81; Cert Merit, Intl Biogl Ctr 1979; Cert Achmt Gamma Sigma Upsilon & Omega Phi Chapts Lambda Alpha Epsilon 1979; Author Num Profl Articles.

LINDAHL, IVAN LEROY oc/Research Chemist; b/May 8, 1919; h/12508 Sir Walter Dr, Glenn Dale, MD 20769; ba/Beltsville, MD; m/Angie Rhodes; c/Janice L; p/Carl Joseph and Dolly Speer Lindahl (dec); ed/BS Neb Ctl Col 1941; Geo Wash Univ: Univ Md; pa/USDA, B'ville: Chemist 1943-48, Biochemist 1948-51, 1954-57, 1957-59, Animal Nutritionist 1951-54, Res Chemist 1959–; cp/Lions: Dir, 1st, 2nd & 3rd VP, Pres; Prince George Audubon Soc: Charter Mem, Dir; Mtl Hlth Assn, Prince Geo Co; r/Meth: Adm Bd; Gideons Intl; hon/Fellow Mem, ABI; Hon Fellow, ASAS; Dist'd Ser Awd, NE Sect ASAS; Fellow, Am Inst Chemists; DIB; W/W in E; 2000 Men Achmt; Am Men of Sci.

LINDER, DONALD E oc/Research Scientist; b/Oct 4, 1938; h/2409 Cardinal, Ponca City, OK 74601; ba/Ponca City; m/Cecilia; c/Julianne, Joel Dean, Jeffrey Don; p/Oscar W Linder (dec); Lillian Linder, Yoakum, TX; ed/BS; MS; PhD; pa/Res Scist Continental Oil Co; cp/Chm Kay Co Repub Party; St Pres Okla Bass Fdn; r/Meth; hon/Am Men & Wom of Sci; W/W: Am Cols & Univs, Am Polits.

LINDH, PATRICIA SULLIVAN oc/Government Official; b/Oct 2, 1928; h/1124 Kensington Rd, McLean, VA 22101; m/H Robert Jr; c/Sheila L Valle, Deborah, Robert L; p/Lawrence W Sullivan (dec); Lillian Devlin, Scottsdale, AZ; ed/BA Trinity Col; pa/Dep Asst Secy of St; Spec Asst to Pres, The White House; cp/Adv Coun, Repub Nat Com; Bd Trustees, La Arts & Sci Ctr; Others; r/Rom Cath; hon/Hon Degs (LLD): Trinity Col, Jacksonville Univ, Walsh Col.

LINDLEY, J G oc/Banker, Tax Lawyer; b/May 2, 1917; h/7111 Stonetrail Dr, Dallas, TX 75230; m/Ruth A; c/Judy Ruth Lindley-Hodge; p/Tom E (dec) and Jewell B Lindley (dec); ed/Att'd Tex Tech Univ 1934-37; BBA 1938, JD 1940 Univ Tex-Austin; mil/AUS 1941-45; pa/VP, Trust Ofcr, Mgr Tax Div, Trust Dept, Mercantile Nat Bank, Dallas; St Bar Tex; Tex Reg'd Public Acct; Dallas St Plan'g Coun; r/Disciples of Christ: Chm Bd Elders; hon/W/W Tex 1973-74.

LINDLEY, RUTH ALEXANDER oc/Attorney at Law; b/Feb 26, 1915; h/7111 Stonetrail Dr, Dallas, TX 75230; ba/Dallas; m/Jay G; c/Judy Lindley Hodge; p/Hartwell (dec) and Alwilba Bouldin Alexander (dec); ed/BA Sophie Newcomb Col 1937; LLB 1940, JD 1969 Univ Tex Austin; pa/Prudential Ins Co of Am, Legal Dept 1941-49; Murray Investment Co 1968-75; Indiv Prac Law 1975-; Tex Bar Assn; cp/Bd Dirs Dallas Camp Fire Girls; r/Northway Christian Ch.

LINDSEY, CHARLES ALBERT oc/Chiropractor; b/Dec 9, 1942; h/605 Ivy St, Ellisville, MS 39437; ba/Ellisville; m/Clare Claudia; c/Susan Angela, Lacinda Charleen; p/Charles Ray and Mary Eunice Lindsey, Ellisville, MS; ed/DC; PhD; pa/Miss Chiropractics Assn, Past Pres, VP & Parliamentn; cp/Past Mem Lions Clb; Commun Devel; r/Lic'd Min Assem of God; hon/Hon by Peace Ofcrs Assn for Homeless Boys.

LINDSEY, EVELYN G oc/Staff Records Officer, Micrographics Specialist; b/Oct 2, 1934; h/PO Box 215, Daisy Dallas Rd, Hixson, TN 37343; ba/Chattanooga, TN; m/William A; c/Lee Henderson (dec); Yvonne E Henderson; pa/Charles L and Beulah S Gentry, Hixson, TN; ed/BS Tenn Technol Univ 1968; Univ Tenn 1970-72; MS Middle Tenn St Univ 1974; pa/Instr Walker Co Tech Sch, St Area Voc-Tech Sch, Edmondson Col; Legal Secy to US Atty, US Dept Justice 1963-66; Staff Records Ofcr, Coor'g Micrographics TVA 8 Yrs; Co-Owner N Co Carpet Cleaning Inc; Co-Owner Lindsey Distributors Inc; Am Voc Assn; Ga Voc Assn; Tenn Voc Assn; Charter Mem Chat Paralegal Assn; Past Pres & Prog Chm Rock Cit Chapt Assn Records Mgrs & Admrs; Tenn Val Chapt Nat Micrographics Assn Bd Dirs; Chat Engrs Clb, Publicity Dir for Engrg & Sci Fair; Nat Coor Del to Nat Micrographics & Assn Records Mgrs & Admrs; Wkshop Instr Chat Area Literacy Movement Tchrs; cp/Past Pres Daisy Jr Wom's Clb; Past Pres ABW Assn; Atlanta Skylarks Flying Clb; Hixson Chapt Toastmasters Intl; r/Bapt; hon/Broke Typing Record Tenn Tech 1967; Author Outstg Tech Ednl Handbook 1969-70; W/W S&SW; Awd of Merit Rock City Chapt Assn Records Mgrs & Admrs 1980; Chapt Mem of Yr Rock City Chapt ARMA 1980; Author "You, Too, Can Type" 1971 & "Teaching All to Type" 1971.

LINDSEY, HIRAM EDWARD JR oc/Executive; b/Dec 17, 1926; h/1611 Gulf Ave, Midland, TX 79701; ba/Midland; m/Vangie; c/Krisitn, Stephen C; p/H E (dec) and Carolyn Lindsey, Atlanta, GA; ed/BS Ga Tech; mil/USNR 1943-46; pa/Pres MWL Tool Co; SPE of AIME; PEA; API; cp/Midland Rotary Clb; Mason; Shriner; r/Bapt; hon/Pub'd Author: Num Profl Articles; W/W S&SW; Dist'd Lectr SPE of AIME 1981-82.

LINDSEY, JUDGE B oc/Retired Pastor and Evangelist; b/Sept 17, 1912; h/Russellville, AR; m/Lila Fay; c/Judge C; p/Elbert Shelby (dec) and Maggie Lenora Holder Lindsey (dec); pa/Pastor Largest Assem of God Ch in Ark 8 Yrs & in So Calif 18 Yrs; Chm Min Alliance LA, Calif & R'ville, Ark; r/Assem of God: Sect Presberty Exec, Gen Coun 1946-53; hon/Merit Ser Awd, So Calif Col 1964 (Mem Bd Dirs).

LINEBAUGH, NATHANIEL LEE JR oc/Judge; b/Mar 17, 1911; h/11007 Aladdin Dr, Dallas, TX 75229; ba/Dallas; m/Kathlyn Elizabeth Woolverton; c/Daniel Hollis; p/Nathaniel Lee Sr and Lucy McKinney Sims Linebaugh (dec); ed/BA So Meth Univ; LLB Univ Am Sch Law Judge, HHS; Tex Bar; US Supreme Ct Bar; ABA; SW Legal Foun; Fed Trial Examrs Conf; Assn Adm Law Judges Conf; cp/Mason; r/Meth; hn/Author: Volenti Non Fit Infuria, The Texas Application, Others.

LINER, OLGA L oc/Nutritionist; b/May 13, 1932; h/438 Sheffield Cir, Augusta, GA 30909; ba/Gracewood, GA; m/Cornelius Ewell; c/Stephen Ewell, Constance Ann; p/Humberto Leignadier Clare (dec); Olga Arica de Leignadier, Panama, Repub of Panama; ed/BS St Mary-of-the-Woods Col 1955; pa/Dietitian w US Govt Overseas 1956-58; Chief Dietitian: Dale Co Hosp 1958-59, Geneva Co Hosp 1960; Rec Spec, US Govt Overseas 1965; Kan St Univ Sch Home Ec, Inst Mgmt Dept Instr 1971; Asst Mgr & Acting Mgr, Kan St Res Hall Food Ser; Lang & GED Prog Instr, AUS 1972; Therapeutic Dietitian, Univ Hosp 1973-76; Chief Dietitian, Patient Ser, Aiken Commun Hosp 1976-77; Dir Dept Dietetics, Gracewood St Sch & Hosp 1977-; Am Dietetic Assn; Instr-Preseptor Food Ser Supvr Coorsp Course Univ Fla; Pre Elec Augusta Dist Dietetic Assn 1979-80; Asst Chm Food Com AAUW Mbrship Tea; Block Chm Neighorhood MS Collect; Mem CAMP Menu Bd; Hist Augusta Patron; Gov's Ad Hoc Com, White House Conf on Am Fams 1980; Ga Heart Assn; Gracewood Employees Assn; Ga St Employees Assn; AAUW; Am Soc

Hosp Food Ser Admrs; Augusta Dist Dietetic Assn; cp/Westlake Country Clb; Cranford Flower Clb; Augusta Symph Patron; Hist Augusta; r/Cath; hon/Apprec Neighborhood Yth Corp; Apprec VOT; W/W Am Wom in S 1980.

LINTZEN, WILBERT (BUDDY) oc/Area Manager; b/Oct 28, 1933; h/2307 Culpepper, Midland, TX 79701; ba/Hobbs, NM; m/Anita M; c/Jennifer Lynn, Mitchell Frank, Stephen Mark; p/dec; ed/BS Univ Sw La 1971; mil/USAF 4 Yrs; pa/Area Mgr, Stimulation & Cementing Ser, Petro Indust, Western Co N Am 19 Yrs; Soc Petro Engrs of AIME.

LIPSCOMB, BUFORD MILTON oc/Pastor; b/Oct 9, 1951; h/9 Pine Vista Cir, Cartersville, Ga 30120; ba/C'ville; m/Ann; c/Christopher, Tara, Joshua; p/Jack and Francis Lipscomb, Atlanta, GA; ed/Att'd Kennesau Jr Col & Beulah Bible Col; pa/Jr Achmt; Pastor Victory Temple Ch; cp/Cand City Coun of White, Ga 1975; r/Interdenom; hn/Recog Awd from Gov for 2 Yrs Wk w Jr Achmt.

LIPSTATE, EUGENE J oc/Petroleum Geologist; b/Dec 6, 1927; h/Lafayette, LA; m/Jo Ann Davis; c/Jame M, Betsy Ann; p/Philip H (dec) and Gertrude Faber Lipstate (dec); ed/BS Univ Tex 1949; mil/USAF 1st Lt; pa/VP Exploration NW Oil Co; Pres Eugene J Lipstate Inc; Am Assn Petro Geols; Lafayette Geol Soc, Bd Dirs; Gulf Coast Assn Geol Socs; cp/Longhorn Clb; Repub Party; r/Jewish.

LIPTON, KENNETH ALBERT oc/Auctioneer; b/Jan 29, 1944; h/1014 E 4th St, Alice, TX 78332; ba/Alice; m/Mary Frances Foster; c/Mark Allen, Lori Lynn; ed/AS Del Mar Col 1968; Cert Nat Auction Inst 1969; Dale Carnegie Sales Course 1973; Dale Carnegie Effective Speaking & Human Relats Course 1979; mil/AUS 1961-62; pa/Auctioneer & Owner LAW Auctioneers 1976-; Pres Lipton Enterprises Inc; Auctioneer, Auctioneers Assocs 1975-76; Austin Sales Br Mgr, AIM Inc 1973-75; Mat Controller, Hudson Engrg 1970-73; Engr, Brown & Root 1968-70; Nat Auctioneers Assn; Tex Auctioneers Assn; Am Entrepreneurs Assn; Rotary Intl; JC Intl; US C of C; Nat Fed Indep Bus-man; cp/Alice C of C, Dir 1979 & 80; Jim Wells 4-H Clb, Pres 1980-81, Cnslr 1980; Pres St Elizabeth's Parents Clb 1979-80; Boy Scout Show Chm, Mesquite Dist 1979 & 80; U Way of Alice, Adv Coun 1980, Secy 1980, Dir Chm 1979; Dir Jim Wells Co Fair Assn 1980; Dir Alice Rotary Clb 1979-; Alice JCs, Internal VP 1977-80, Dir 1976-77; r/Jewish; hon/Key Man Awd, Bellaire, Tex JCs; JC of Yr, Bellaire JCs; Spark Plug of Yr, Bellaire JC; JC of Mo, Bellaire JCs; JC of Mo Austin, Tex JCs; JC of Mo, Alice JCs; Outstg Yng Men Am 1975; "Velocity & the Chronograph", 1st Pl Student Paper Awd 1968; Cert of Apprec, Dale Carnegie Courses 1973; Brown Bldrs WW, Brown & Root Inc 1969; Spec Recog, BSA 1970, 79 & 80; Cert of Apprec, Jim Wells Co Fair Assn 1979 & 80; Outstg Mem Alice Rotary Clb 1978; Nom'd W/W Fin & Indust 1980.

LISKA, DARIN VLADIMIR oc/Civil Structural Engineer; b/Nov 12, 1915; h/14015 Briarworth, Houston, TX 77077; m/Millie Anna; c/Peter John; p/Vladimir and Emille Liska; ed/Civil Structural Engrg; pa/Conslt; Writer Theoretical Articles; r/Rom Cath; hon/Patentee in Structural Engrg; St Awd Design.

LISTER, DORIS WATFORD oc/Administrator; b/Oct 11, 1925; h/1402 Hagood Ave, Columbia, SC 29205; ba/Columbia; p/Lucas Furman (dec) and Vera Inez King Watford (dec); ed/BS; MS; pa/Nurse Admr; ANA; NLN; Am Pulbic Hlth Assn; r/Meth; hon/Aurelia Potts S'sip; Sigma Theta Tau.

LITTLE, FLORENCE ELIZABETH HERBERT oc/Retired Teacher; b/July 7, 1911; h/1093A Belle Terre Dr, La Place, LA 70068; m/Alfred Lamond (dec); c/Alan Rush, Barbara Jean Little Votaw; p/Charles Arthur (dec) and Bertha Schlachter Herbert (dec); ed/BA; MSE; pa/Kappa Kappa Iota; Mu Phi Epsilon; ABWA; NEA ISEA; DMEA; cp/Friends of the Cabildo; Jefferson Orchid Soc; River Parishes CB Clb; Commun Home Owners Assn; St John Civil Defense Unit; AARP; r/Presb; hon/NSF Grant 1963-64.

LITTLEFIELD, CAMILLIA HUGHES oc/Office Manager; b/Aug 17, 1936; h/109 N Elm St, Adamsville, TN 39310; ba/Selmer, TN; m/James Otis; p/David M (dec) and Allie Hughes, Adamsville, TN; ed/Att'd Jackson St Commun Col; pa/Ofc Mgr, McNairy Co Gen Hosp; Nat Hosp Fin Mgmt Assn; W Tenn HFMA; cp/OES; r/Bapt; hon/Appt'd Grand Ofcr OES 1971; Personal Page to Most Worthy Grand Matron OES, Grand Chapt Tenn 1979.

LITTLEFIELD, RICHARD WELLS JR oc/Attorney, Senator; b/Sept 17, 1948; h/1308 Oak St, St Simons Island, GA; ba/Brunswick, GA; m/Elizabeth; c/Stephanie Ann, Richard Wells III; p/Richard W Litlefield, Jesup, GA; Hazel Harper Littlefield (dec); ed/BA Emory Univ 1970; JD Univ Ga Law Sch 1973; pa/Att'd DA Brunswick Judicial Curcuit 1975-76; Ptnr Littlefield, Ossick & Rivers; Ga Bar Assn; Am Bar Assn; Ga Trial

Lwyrs Assn; cp/Brunswick JCs; Northside Kiwanis; Dem Party, St Senator 6th Dist; r/Presb; hon/Most Outstg Legislator Awd 1980; W/W S.

LITTRELL, TERRIL D oc/College President; b/Mar 9, 1941; h/1840 Falcon Dr, Cleveland, TN 37311; ba/Cleveland; m/Chloe Ann Johnson; c/Donald, Terrie; p/James Edward (dec) and Leola William Littrell (dec); ed/BR Williams Col 1969; BS Evangel Col 1970; MA SW Mo St Univ 1975; DD Col of Biblical Studies 1976; PhD Pacific NWn Univ 1979; pa/Pastor, Joplin, Mo 1966-70; Public Sch Tchr 1970-75; Dean Sch of Min, Cleveland, Tenn 1975-78; Pres Kent Col 1978-; Exec Dir Bible Sabbath Assn Intl 1971-79; Am Intell Assn; Christian Cnslrs Assn; Soc Pentecostal Studies; Am Intell Assn; Pres's Clb, Wash DC; Nat Chaplains Assn; Alpha Psi Omega; Chm Ch Work NAACP; r/Ch of God; hon/Hon Lt Col Ala St Militia; Hon Col Ten & Ky Militia; W/W Commun Ser; Men of Achmt; W/W Intells; Notable Am Awd; Man of Dist; Commun Ldr Awd.

LIU, Y A oc/Professor; b/June 6, 1946; h/Auburn, AL; ba/Chem Engrg Dept, Auburn Univ, Auburn, AL 36830; m/Hing-Har; p/Cheng-Hsian and Ya-Shan Han Liu; ed/BS Nat Taiwan Univ; MS Tufts Univ; MA 1971, PhD 1974 Princeton Univ; pa/Chem Engrg Dept, Auburn Univ; Asst Prof 1974-77, Assoc Prof 1977-80, Alumni Assoc Prof 1980-; Am Chem Soc; Am Inst Chem Engrs; IEEE; Guest Editor, IEEE Transactions on Magnetics 1976; Chm Technicam Com on Magneticc Separation, IEEE Magnetics Soc 1977-; r/Christian; hon/Alumni Prof'ship Awd, Auburn Univ 1980; Outstg Chem Engr Tchr Awd 1975 & 1980; Cert of Apprec, Engrg Foun, U Engrg Trustees Inc 1978; Author: *Preceedings of Magnetic Desulfurization of Coal Symposium 1976*, *Industrial Applications of Magnetic Separation 1979*; *New Physical Methods for Cleaning Coal 1980*; Over 30 Pubs in Profl Jours.

LLOYD, EVA JO oc/Banker; b/Mar 24, 1919; h/1706 Hoyt Dr, Longview, TX 75601; ba/Longview; m/Lawrence W Jr; c/Kathryn A Snow; p/Joe (dec) and Cora McCormack (dec); ed/AB Am Inst Bnkg; Univ Colo Mktg; pa/VP Longview Bank & Trust; Nat Assn Bank Wom; E Tex Chapt NABW; cp/Zonta Intl; ABWA; C of C; Bd Mem Am Heart Assn; YMCA; Adv Bd Voc Ofc Ed; r/Bapt; hon/Hdliners Awd, Profl Jours Inc; Sales & Mktg Exec Awd; C of C Ambassador of Yr 2 Times & Life Mem; 1 of Top 10 Wom Execs, Tex Bus Mag.

LOCHRIDGE, WILLARD FISKE IV oc/Executive; b/Dec 14, 1942; h/2613 Steeplechase Dr, Reston, VA 22091; ba/McLean, VA; m/Vija; c/Whitney K, Brenton S; p/Willard F (dec) and Patricia M Daugherty Lochridge, St Augustine, FL; ed/BS Wn Carolina Univ; mil/USMC Capt; pa/Sales Rep Control Data Corp 1968-69; Dir Mktg US Time Sharing Inc 1969-70; Sr Staff Engr TRW Sys 1970-71; Mktg Mgr Plan & Res Corp 1971-74; Sr Mktg Rep Grumman Data Sys 1974-75; VP, Fed Mktg Opers, Informatics Inc 1975-; ADAPSO; Time Sharing Users Assn; Intl Game Fish Assn; Wn Carolina Univ Alumni Assn; Informatics Sr Staff Assn; r/Presb; hon/Silver Star 1966; 2 Bronze Stars; Purple Heart; 3 Pres Unit Cits; 23 Navy Unit Cits; Vietnamese Cross of Gallantry w Silver Star; Vietnamese Medal of Hon; Vietnamese Public Ser Awd; 100% Clb, 1977, 78, 79, Informatics; Employee of Yr 1979 Informatics.

LOCKARD, BETTY PINE oc/Professor, Attorney at Law; b/May 12, 1933; h/Rt 7, Warrensburg, MO 64093; ba/W'burg; m/Lawrence A; p/Gayles R Pine, W'burg, MO; Meda M Pine (dec); ed/BS Ed, MS Ed CMSU; JD UMKC; pa/Assoc Prof Crim Just Adm, Ctrl Mo St Univ 1971-; Conslt & Instr Nat Traffic Mgmt Inst CMSU 1971; Pract'g Atty & Ptnr Pine & Lockard 1966-71; Probate Judge & Ex-Ofcl Magistrate Judge, Johnson Co, Mo 1962-66; Pract'g Atty & Ptnr Pine, Welling, Jones & Lockard 1961-62; Tchr Warrensburg, Mo Public Sch Sys 1956-58; Tchr, Topeka, Kan Public Sch Sys 1955-56; Mem: Mo Bar Assn; Johnson Co Bar Assn, Past Secy-Treas; Am Judicature Soc; Mo Police Chief's Assn; Mo Tchrs Assn; Commun Tchrs Assn; Nat Safety Coun; cp/Heart Fund, Cancer Fund; U Fund; Spkr Var Local Grps; Campaign Mgr Repub Cand, Circuit Clerk, Johnson Co, Mo 1978; Advr to Campaigns of Co Clerk, Probate Judge & Co Collector, Johnson Co 1978; Johnson Co Repub Clb; r/Meth; hon/Phi Kappa Phi; Alpha Phi Sigma, Gamma Chapt; Recip Emily Gates Alumni Achmt Awd, Sigma Sigma Sigma 1977; W/W: Students in Am Univs & Cols, Am Wom, US, Am Law; World W/W: Wom, Wom in Ed; Nat Register of Prom Ams & Intl Notables; Commun Ldrs & Noteworthy Ams; DIB; Personalities of W&MW; Best Lwyrs of Am; Intl W/W Ed.

LOCKE, DON C oc/Associate Professor; b/Apr 30, 1943; h/1509 Shelley Rd, Raleigh, NC 27612; ba/Raleigh, NC; m/Marjorie P Myles; c/Tonya Elizabeth, Regina Camille; p/Willie Raymond and Carlene Elizabeth Lovely Locke, Sunflower, MS; ed/BS 1963; MEd 1964 Tenn St Univ; EdD Ball St Univ 1974; Post Doct Studies Stanford Univ 1979; pa/SS Tchr, Ft Wayne Commun Schs 1964-70; Sch Cnslr, Ft Wayne Commun Schs 1971-73; Cnslr Edr, Ball St Univ European Prog 1974-75; Cnslr Edr, NC St Univ 1975-; APGA; ASGW; NVGA; ACES; Phi Delta Kappa;

NCPGA, Pres 1980-81; r/Luth; hn/Author & Co-Author 15 Articles in Profl Jours & Co-Author Chapt in Book.

LOCKE, JOHN P oc/Executive; b/Oct 7, 1950; h/2200 N Rose Isl Rd, Prospect, KY 40059; ba/Louisville; m/Cynthia Teekell; c/Regan Lindsay, Ryan Kelly; p/Patrick Roger (dec) and E Maurine Holtsclaw Locke, Shreveport, LA; pa/Pres Topco Mktg & Devel Inc; Pres Topco Prods Inc; Sales & Mkgt Execs of L'ville; Phi Sigma Epsilon; Notary Public; BBB; cp/C of C; Bd Dirs Jr Achmt of Kentuckiana; r/Epis; hon/W/W Fin & Indust 1979-80.

LOCKLAR, WAYNE EVERETT oc/Teacher and Coach; b/Aug 6, 1948; h/109 Dale Dr, Troy, AL 36081; ba/Troy; m/Alyene Williams; c/Julianne Kristin; p/Care Franklin and Mary Frances Locklar, Troy, AL; ed/BS 1970, MS 1976 Troy St Univ; Add'l Studies 1980; mil/USN 1970-74; pa/US & World Hist Tchr, Coach Fball & Baseball, Henderson HS; NEA; AEA; TEA; cp/Coach Dixie Majors Baseball Prog; Dist V Basketball Elimination Chm for Ala Royal Ambassador Prog; r/Bush Meml Bapt Ch: Cnslr Royal Ambassadors.

LOCKWOOD, BOBBY oc/Minister; b/Feb 26, 1953; h/20 Shallowford Rd, Chattanooga, TN 37404; ba/Chat; m/Linda Morrison; c/Robert Jason, Elizabeth Ann; p/James A and Francis Joy Lockwood, W Columbia, SC; ed/Theol Deg Tenn Temple Bible Sch; BA Tenn Temple Univ; pa/Min Highland Park Bapt Ch; r/Bapt; hon/1 of 50 Outstg Alumni Tenn Temple Univ; Pres Tenn Temple Univ Alumni Assn 1980.

LOCKWOOD, DAVID M c/Head of Department; ba/Cumberland Col, Williamsburg, KY 40769; ed/BA, MA, EdD Univ Tulsa; Further Study: Univ Buffalo, Syracuse Univ, Ohio St Univ, Univ Tulsa; pa/Hd Art Dept, Campbell Col 1957-59; Hd Art Dept Cumberland Col 1959-; hon/Num Exhibs Incl'g: Wn NY St Annual, Carnegie Inst Tulsa Annual, Okla Annual, NC Annual, The Ogunquit Art Ctr 59th Annual Nat Exhib of Paintings (Maine) 1979; 7th Annual SWn Invit Show (Ariz) 1979; Num One Man Shows Incl'g: Campbell Col, Cumberland Col, Sue Bennett Col, Univ Tulsa, Defiance Col, La Patre Gal (Manford, Okla), SWn Bell Telephone, Berea Col.

LOCY, WADE DALLIS JR oc/Minister of Music, Instructor, Supervisor; b/July 6, 1937; h/Rt 1 Box 595, Forest, VA 24551; m/Sandra C; c/Sharon Renee, Jonathan Edward; p/Wade D Sr and Alice E Locy, Bedford, Va; ed/BA Bob Jones Univ; MEd Lynchburg Col; pa/Elem & HS Tchr 18 Yrs; Instr & Student Tchr Supvr Liberty Bapt Col 1 Yr; Min Mus Timberlake Bapt Ch 17 Yrs; Assn Tchr Ed; r/Bapt; hon/Mus Edrs Nat Conf Chm 1956; Annual Mus Awd 1974; S'ship Shenandoah Mus Conservatory 1957.

LODOWSKI, RUTH ELLEN oc/Personnel Administrator; b/Feb 15, 1951; h/715 Green Hill Rd, Dallas, TX 75232; ba/Dallas; p/Charles H and Genevieve G Lodowski, Dallas, TX; ed/BA Univ Tex-Austin 1972; MBA N Tex St Univ 1976; pa/Res Asst, Castilian Dorm, Austin 1971-72; Hd Resident 1972-74; Bank Teller, Greenville Ave Bank, Dallas 1974-75; Employment Interviewer, Tex Employment Comm, Grand Prairie 1975-76; Pers Intern, US Dept Just, Seagoville 1976-77; Pers Asst, Army & AF Exch Ser, San Antonio 1977-78; Staffing Admr & Pers Admr, Tex Instruments, Dallas 1978-; Am Soc Pers Adm; Dallas Pers Assn; cp/Am Red Cross Vol; Presb Hosp Vol; Bd Dirs Chd Inc; r/Rom Cath; hon/Top 10 Medal of Hon, Kiwanis Intl 1969; Phi Theta Kappa.

LOEWENSTEIN, GEORGE W oc/Medical Consultant, Director, Instructor; b/Apr 18, 1890; h/880 Mandalay Ave #522, Clearwater, FL 33515; ba/same; m/Johanna S Sabath; c/Peter Lansing (dec), Ruth Gallagher; ed/MD; Spec Courses: Hygiene, Tropical Med, Preventive Med; mil/WW I 40 Mos; pa/Med Dir; Prof Berlin Acad Postgrad Med Tng; Dir Public Hlth & Yth Wel; Hlth Ofcr; Med Conslt; MD 57 Yrs; Fellow: Royal Soc Hlth, AAAS; Charter Mem, Fellow Emeritus Am Col Sportsmedicine; Corr Mem Berlink Med Soc; Life Mem Fla Public Hlth Assn; Am Acad Fam Physicians; Life Charter Mem, Fellow; cp/Pres UNA Clearwater, Peace Medal; Dir & Hon Pres, IFA Paris, France; Rotarian; Shrine; Musicologist, Richey Symph Soc; Num Books & Papers; Fellow Am Public Hlth; Fellow Emeritus AAAI; ARC Vol 52 Yrs; hon/Cert of Commend of USA Pres; Am Medal DAR; Sertoma Ser to Mankind Awd; Hon Awd Clearwater Jr Woms Assn; Commun Ser Awd, Fla Acad Fam Physicians; Gold MD Dipl, Univ Berlin 1973; Pres Sports Awd.

LOGAN, FRENISE AVEDIS oc/Professor; b/Sept 30, 1920; h/Greensboro, NC; m/Mary Whitfield; c/Jewel Denise, Frenise Avedis II; p/dec; ed/BA Fisk Univ 1943; MA 1947, PhD 1953 Case-Western Reserve Univ; Post Doct Studies, Univ Bombay 1953-54; pa/Prof Hist, Bennett Col, A&T Univ 1948-60, 1980-; Fgn Ser Ofcr, US Dept St & US Info Agcy, 1961-80; Assn Study of Afro-Am Life & Hist; Indian Hist Cong; E African Acad; Smithsonian Inst; cp/Rotary Clb, Kaduna, Nigeria; r/Epis; hon/RWD Conner Awd for Best Article in *North Carolina Historical*

PERSONALITIES OF THE SOUTH

Review 1959; Ford Foun F'ship, India 1953; Fulbright Prof, India Univs of Calcutta & Madras 1969-61; Am Philosophical Assn Awd for Res in England 1972; St & Local Hist Assn Grant for Res on Blacks in NC 1959; Conslt for Am Hist Wkshops, India 1960, 61, 62; Commend for Outstg Achmts in Intl Ed & Cultural Exch, US Dept St, Bur Ednl & Cultural Affairs 1977; W/W E Africa 1965; NC Lives; Dir Am Schlrs; Dir Fgn Area Schlrs; Author *Negro in North Carolina 1876-1894* 1964; Pub'd Over 50 Profl Articles in India & US.

LOGUE, BRUCE WAYNE oc/Minister; b/Mar 3, 1947; h/1625 Lock Lomond, Murray, KY 42071; ba/Murray; m/Beverly Holeman; c/Angela Kaye, Jonathan Wade; p/William V and Helen P Logue, Shreveport, LA; ed/BA; MS; pa/Min Univ Ch of Christ; APGA; cp/Kiwanis; Repub Party; r/Ch of Christ.

LOKEY, ESTHER GENEVA oc/Retired; b/Sept 1, 1912; h/Rt 3 Box 157, Shawnee, OK 74801; m/Olane Willie; c/Donald Eugene Allen, Terry Don Allen; p/Arthur B (dec) and Elizabeth Popline Akins, Shawnee, OK; cp/Vol Work; r/Bapt; hon/Okla Outstg Vol Awd, Dist V.

LOKEY, GEORGE HARRISON oc/Oil Company President; h/2801 S Hughes, Amarillo, TX 79109; ba/Amarillo; m/Sheri Mimms; c/Alexander; p/Ted H and Stella Yeatts Lokey, Amarillo; ed/BBA; mil/USMC, Disch'd as 1/Lt, 1st Marine Air Wing in Japan; pa/Pres Ted Lokey Oil Co, Oil Jobber for Diamond Shamrock Corp; Pres Tex Oil Marketers Assn; Nat Oil Jobbers; cp/Dir Discover Tex Assn; Pres Panhandle Heritage Foun, Prodrs Musical Drama "TEXAS"; Chm Bicent Comm; Dir: Chm of Commerce, Gtr SW Music Fest, Les Amis du Vin (Friends of Wine); Pres Amarillo Zoological Soc; Mem Amarillo Art Ctr; Panhandle Cult Arts Ctr; Bailli, Confrerie de la Chaine des Rotisseurs (Gourmet Org); hon/Outstg Yg Texans; W/W S&SW.

LOMAN, JAMES HAROLD oc/Evangelist; b/Sept 27, 1917; ba/PO Box 1, Salisbury, NC 28144; m/Elizabeth; c/Larry, Richard, Janice, Lane, Leslie; p/dec; ed/Grad John Wesley Col 1939; ThB Clarksville Theol Sem 1954; Hon Doct Clarksville Theol Sem 1954; mil/Civil Air Patrol Chap; pa/Owned & Oper'd Funeral Home, Gibsonville, NC & Greensboro, NC 1947-52; Lic'd Funeral Dir, St of NC 1947-; Gen Conf Evangelist, Wesleyan Ch; Bd Lakeland, Fla Camp Meeting; Bd Wesleyan Bible Conf Assn; cp/Past Mem Lions Intl & Civitan Clb; hon/Author "If Christ Had Not Come" & "What God Can Do."

LONG, BERNICE H oc/Administrative Assistant; b/June 19, 1910; h/121 Princeton Ave, Oak Ridge, TN 37830; ba/Oak Ridge; c/Howard Allan; p/Charles A (dec) and Althea French Hilderley (dec); ed/Att'd: Univ Rome, Univ Heidelberg, Univ Tenn; pa/Adm Asst, Rural Legal Sers of Tenn; cp/City Bds: Human Resources, Elder Citizens; Adv Bd Spec Nsg Home Com; Anderson Co Coun on Aging; C of C Com on Elder Citizens; Pres Oak Ridge Am Assn Ret'd Person 1977 & 78; Past Regent DAR; r/Meth.

LONG, CHARLES ALEXANDER oc/Minister, Educator, Social Worker; b/Aug 22, 1881; m/dec; p/Martin D (dec) and Caledonia S Hamilton Long (dec); ed/BS Okla Univ 1905; BD 1911, MDiv 1973 Vanderbilt Univ; pa/Pastor US & Brazil; Missionary to Brazil 1911-52; r/Meth; hon/Alumni Assocs Okla Univ 1981; Title "Bldr of Chs & Develr of Fields" Given by Jour "Expositor Cristao", Brazil; Hons for Rehab & Expansion Gtr Granbery Col, Brazil; W/W: Meth Ch, Am; Personalities of S; DIB; 2000 Men Achmt; Notable Ams of Bicent Era; Manchester Ctl Lib Ctr, Manchester, England; Hon Mem Cherokee & Choctaw Indian Tribes of Okla.

LONG, ELSIE S oc/Real Estate Saleswoman; b/Apr 27, 1937; h/Berea, KY; c/Lance; p/Henry W (dec) and Earley B Steele (dec); pa/Saleswom, Don Foster & Assocs; cp/Pres Beta Sigma Phi 1956; Pres Berea Yngr Woms Clb 1969-71; Berea Hosp Aux; Chm Candy Striper Prog 1968; Yngr Woms Clb; Dir Berea C of C 1980-81; Dir & Secy Madison Co Bd Rltrs 1980; Berea Country Clb, Social Chm 1977; Arlington Assn; r/Christian; hon/Nat Hon Soc; Personalities of S.

LONG, INEZ HENDERSON oc/Retired Teacher; b/Jan 4, 1912; h/4237 Sheridan Dr, Charlotte, NC 29205; m/Thurman Baxter; p/Henry Silas (dec) and Vida Hartley Henderson (dec); ed/BS Appalachian St Univ; MA Univ NC-CH; pa/Tchr: Severn HS, Severn, NC 1938-43; Pikeville HS, Pikeville, NC 1943-46 Battle Sch, Rocky Mt, NC 1946-49; Harding HS, Charlotte, NC 1949-60; Eastway Jr HS, Charlotte, NC 1969-70; NC Assn Edrs; NEA; Clrm Tchr Assn; Nat Coun Tchrs of Maths; NC Lit & Hist Assn; NC St Mus Soc; AAUW; Charter Mem NC Alpha Chapt Alpha Delta Kappa; Intl Sorority for Wom Edrs: Past Pres, VP, Corresp Secy & St Treas; Bd Govs Intl Platform Assn; Life Mem Charlotte-Mecklenburg Assn Edrs; cp/Chm Alpha Delta Kappa S'ship Com; Am Red Cross Instr; hon/NC Lives; W/W: Am Wom, S&SW; Commun Ldrs Am; World W/W Wom; Cert Apprec, Charlotte Clrm Tchrs Assn.

LONG, KATHLEEN E oc/Music Therapist; b/May 23, 1950; h/1802 Pawnee, Enid, OK; m/Daniel A; c/Ryan M; p/Albert J and Maurine Rummel, Enid, OK; ed/BS Elem Ed; pa/Mus Therapist for Mtly Retard'd 3 Yrs; Pres, VP, Secy Okla Gas & Elec Co's Wom's Com; r/Meth; hon/Enid Delta Zeta Alumnae Wom of Yr 1977; Nom'd Okla's Outstg Alumni in Delta Zeta.

LONG, RICHARD L JR oc/Professor, Consulting Engineer; b/June 5, 1947; ba/Dept CHE, PO Box 10053, Lamar Univ, Beaumont, TX 77710; m/Sharon Ann; c/Christine; p/Richard L Long, Pahala, HI; Alta Marie Long (dec); ed/BA 1969, PhD 1973 Rice Univ; mil/USAR 1977-79 1st Lt; pa/Res Engr, El DuPont 1974-78; Prof Chem Engrg Lamar Univ 1978-; AICHE; ACS; NSPE; TSPE; ISES; cp/US Senatorial Bus Adv Bd; r/Meth; hon/Sigma Xi Res Awd 1973; Author "On Phenomenological Muscle Models, I, II"; "Evaporator Tube Collapse by Combustion Detonation."

LONG, RUSSELL B oc/Senator; b/Nov 3, 1918; m/Carolyn Bason; c/Rita Katherine Mosely, Pamela Rust McCardell; p/Huey P and Rose McConnell Long; ed/BA 1941, LLB 1942 La St Univ; mil/USNR Lt; pa/Admitted to La Bar 1942; Elected to US Senate 1948-; Asst Senate Majority Ldr 89th & 90th Congresses; Chm Merchant Marine Subcom of Commerce Com 1969-76; Chm Sen Com on Fin 1966; Chm Surface Transp Subcom, Commerce Com 1977; Mem Dem Steering Com which Makes Sen Com Assignments 1973; cp/Delta Kappa Epsilon; Omicron Delta Kappa; Order of the Coif; Tau Kappa Alpha; Phi Delta Phi; Lions Clb; Elk; Am Legion; hon/Selected as Most Effective Senate Com Chm & Most Persuasive Sen in Debate by Congressman & Senators; Featured in Num Periodicals.

LONG, SAM HOLDEN oc/Attorney at Law; b/Jan 30, 1894; h/1013 Jackson St, Tupelo, MS; m/Genevieve Mathis; c/Genevieve M Jr; Sam H Jr; p/Charles Phillip (dec) and Augusta Holden Long (dec); ed/LLB Univ Miss 1914; mil/WWI & WWII; pa/Lwyr Adams, Long & Adams; r/Bapt; hon/Croix de Guerre w Palm; Legion of Hon.

LONG, SARAH oc/Counselor; b/Sept 17, 1932; h/36 Avon Rd, Asheville, NC 29905; ba/Asheville; m/dec; c/Carl Edward Harris II, Richard DeLos Harris; p/Richard Ottis and Thelma Sowers Long; ed/BA Bennett Col 1955; MS NC A&T St Univ 1978; pa/Cnslr S French Bd Jr HS; NEA; NCAE; NCPGA; NC Sch Cnslrs Assn; APGA; Am Sch Cnslrs; NC Assn Non-White Concerns; r/Rom Cath; hon/W/W S&SW.

LONG, SHIRLEY DOBBINS oc/Contractor, Land Developer; b/Feb 5, 1943; h/PO Box 19123, Guildford College Station, Greensboro, NC 27410; ba/Same; m/dec; p/Matt J (dec) and Louiva Davis Dobbins; ed/BS Math; Post Grad Studies Sch of Design; pa/Gen Contractor, Land Develr, Shirley D Long Bldrs Inc; Tennis, Golf Designs by Shirley Dee; r/Meth; hon/W/W S&SW; Men & Wom Dist; Intl Biogl Ctr; Intl Platform Assn.

LONG, THURMAN BAXTER oc/Retired; h/4137 Sheridan Dr, Charlotte, NC 28205; m/Inez H; p/Wiliam Locksley and Pinckney Reinhardt Long (dec); ed/Davidson Col; Univ Colo; Columbia Univ; mil/NCCG Aux; pa/Org'd Citizens Trust Co, Past Pres; Past Mgr Sunlife Assurance Co; Real Est Broker; Santa Fe & El Paso & SWn RRs; Ret'd Stock Broker After 31 Yrs, Bache & Co; Profl Golfer; Fdr Intl Security Studies of Am Securtiy Coun Ed Foun; cp/Charlotte Mfrs Clb; Qtr Century Clb; Charlotte Sr Forum; hon/First Fams Am; Eminent Dist of Nat Register Prominent Ams.

LONGMIRE, SIOTHIA R oc/Region Supervisor; b/Jan 5, 1935; h/Creekwood Apts #122, Rt 3, Leesburg, GA 31763; ba/Albany; ed/BS Carson-Newman Col 1956; Postgrad Studies PE & Rec Univ Tenn; pa/Region Supvr, Ga Dept Natural Parks, Rec & Hist Sites; PE & Hlth Tchr, Coach: Tullahoma HS, Enka HS; PE Instr, Staff Mem: Berea Col, Tenn Sch for Deaf, Bethel Col; YWCA Camp Dir, Adm Asst: Atlanta, Ga, Memphis, Tenn; Camp Staff: Ridgecrest Bapt Assem, Crestridge for Girls, Rockmont for Boys; Rec Admr, Will-a-Way Rec Area for Handicapped; Nat Pks & Rec Assn; Coms, Ga Rec & Pks Soc; Chm Promotional Com, Am Camping Assn; Ga Assn for Hlth, PE & Rec; cp/Ga & Nat Assns for Retard Citizens; Rec Com, Winder-Barrow C of C; Pilot Clb Intl; hon/Outstg Ser Awd, Ga Dept Natural Resources; Featured in "Ch Adm" Mag; Pub'd Author, Num Profl Articles.

LONTOS, PAM oc/Corporate Director of Sales, Author, Management Consultant; b/Feb 28, 1945; h/7055 Merriman Pkwy, Dallas, TX 75231; ba/Dallas; m/Ernest; c/Anna-Marie, Ryan; p/Steve and Mary Congas, Dallas, TX; ed/BS 1967, MLA 1971 SMU; pa/Corp Dir of Sales, Shamrock Broadcasting; Motivational Spkr; Mgmt Conslt; Sales Tnr; Am Wom in Radio & TV; Nat Assn Broadcasters; Nat Spkers Assn; hon/Spec Recog for Contbn to Radio Advtg Bur Mng Sales Conf 1981; Spec Recog, Nat Assn Broadcasters Conv, Apr 1981; Author *Fundamentals of Broadcast Selling* & Video Course.

PERSONALITIES OF THE SOUTH

LOPER, MARILYN SUE oc/Contractor, Real Estate Salesperson, Counselor; b/June 7, 1944; h/Pt Richey, FL; ba/PO Box 64, Pt Richey, FL 33568; m/Gregory C Miller; p/Elmer Charles and Thelma Pearl Haferkamp Loper, New Pt Richey, FL; ed/BS 1967, MA 1971 En Mich Univ; pa/Hlth & Rehab Sers, Ofc of Voc Rehab: Supvg Cnslr 1978-, Cnslr 1973-78; Marriage & Fam Cnslr 1975-; Salesp Henry Dingus Jr Rlty 1978-; Residential Contractor 1977-; Bd Public Instr, Land O Laks, Fla 1970-73; Elem Tchr, Fitzgerald Public Schs, Warren, Mich 1969-70; Elem Tchr, Nankin Mills Public Schs, Westland, Mich 1968-69; Anne Arundel Co Schs, Annapolis, Md 1967-68; NASW; Fla Assn Hlth & Social Sers; Nat Rehab Assn; Fla Rehab Assn; Nat Rehab Cnslr Assn; Fla Rehab Cnslr Assn; Nat Rehab Admr Assn; Fla Rehab Admr Assn; Pasco Bldrs Assn; Nat Assn Home Bldrs; cp/W Pasco C of C; Nat Repub Com; hon/W/W Am Wom.

LOPEZ, ADAN C oc/Deputy Sheriff; b/June 3, 1944; h/Levelland, TX; m/Julia R; c/Israel, Raymundo, Ruben; p/Faustino and Rosilita Lopez, Levelland, TX; ed/Att'd S Plains Col; mil/AUS; pa/Investigator, Hockley Co Sheriff's Dept; cp/Past Pres St Michael's Sch Bd; Past Jr V-Comdr Levelland VFW Post 4506; r/Cath.

LOPEZ, NICOLASA oc/Peace Officer; b/Feb 13, 1957; h/Edcouch, TX; ba/Edinburg Police Dept, c/o City of Edinburg, 117 N 10th, Edinburg, TX 78539; p/Pedro and Emilia Y Lopez, Edcouch, TX; ed/Att'd Pan Am Univ; Basic Law Enforcement Ofcr Cert, Rio Grande Valley Police Acad; pa/Police Ofcr, Edinburg PD; r/Cath.

LOREY, WILLIS EDWARD II oc/Management Consultant; b/Apr 14, 1926; h/740 Bandit Trail, Smithfield, TX 76180; ba/Smithfield; m/Nell Marie; c/Sandra Christine, Sara Robertta, Marcia April and Melissa Barbara; p/Willis Edward (dec) and Myrle Agnes Lorey (dec); ed/BS 1950; USAF Air Intell Sch 1951; Air Command & Staff 1954; Adv'd Intell Sch 1966; Dept of Defense Intell Sch 1968; MA Ed 1979; PhD Indust Psych 1979; mil/USMC 1943-46; USAF 1950-70 Ret'd Col; pa/Course Chm & Prog Ldr, Am Mgmt Assn; Adj Prof Richland Col & N Lake Col, Dallas, Tex; Pvt Mgmt Cnsltg for Non-Profit Orgs, Commun Grps & Fortune 500 Cos; Pres, Dallas Chapt, Am Soc Trg & Devel; Past Pres Soc Humanistic Mgmt; Bd Dirs Dallas Chapt ASTD; Past Nat SIG Chm Am Soc Trg & Devel; cp/Scoutmaster BSA; Chm U Way; r/Meth; hon/Jt Ser Commend Medal 1964; USAF Commend Medal w 2 Clusters 1950-69; Bronze Star 1968 & 69; Vietnamese Hon Medal 1969; Pub'd in Profl Jours.

LOTT, NANCY BRASHER oc/Homemaker; b/May 23, 1942; h/Rt 6, 169 Mifflin Rd, Jackson, TN 38301; m/Claude Edward Jr; c/Emily, Carol, Richard, Mark and Scott; p/Charles Joseph and Martha Arnold Brasher, Jackson, TN; cp/Former Mem Yng Farmers & Homemakers St Com; Farm Bur Ladies Chm, Madison Co; Jackson Commun Chorus; 4-H Adult Ldr, Madison Co; r/So Bapt; hon/Runner-up to St YF&H Queen 1970; On Dist & St Progs for Farm Bur 1979.

LOUIS, HELEN LOUISE oc/Businesswoman; b/Oct 24, 1927; h/1724 Airport Dr, Laurel, MS 39440; m/Sidney Ellis Sr; c/Linda Annette, Sidney Ellis Jr; p/Leon Miller (dec); Bessie Mae Carroll, De Ridder, LA; pa/Co-Owner Stub's Trading Post; cp/VFW Aux; Laurel Shrine Aux, Past Pres; PTA; OES: Laurel Chapt #24 Past Worthy Matron, Dist Dpty Grand Matron of Dist 22, Current Pres Past Matron's Clb, Star Point Ofcr, Prog Chm & Social Events Chm; Justice Heights Garden Clb, Pres; BPW Clb; r/Bapt; hon/Trophy for Having Most Certs OES.

LOVE, GERALD DEAN oc/Government Executive; b/Aug 4, 1927; h/1413 Celesta Ct, Vienna, VA 22180; ba/Wash DC; m/Mildred Lois Casey; c/Laura, Cynthia, Gregory, Linda, Geoffrey; p/Guy Dewey and Grace Elva Gray Love (dec); ed/BS Ia St 1949; MS 1956; Cert in Traffic Eng, Bur Hwy Traffic, Yale 1959; DEng Rensselaer Polytech 1975; mil/USN 1950-54, Capt, USNR; pa/Exec US Dept Trans; Assoc Profl Lectr Civil Engrg, Geo Wash Univ; r/Meth; hon/Sustained Superior Perf Awd, DOT; Secy's Awd for Meritorious Achmt.

LOVE, HOWARD L oc/Agency Executive; b/Dec 8, 1942; h/6509 Sherry Dr, Little Rock, AR 72204; ba/Little Rock; m/Carol A; c/Howard L Jr, Netra Lashawn; p/John M Love (dec); Willie Mae Love Pointer, Tulsa, OK; ed/BA; Master's, Commun Ser Cnslg; pa/Exec Com Nat Urban Leag Coun of Exec Dirs; Pres So Reg Exec Dirs Coun; cp/Ldrship Roundtable; Ark Black Caucus; NAACP; r/U Meth; hon/Distn in Field; 1977 Bapt Pastors Conf Layman of Yr; Dist'd Ser & Awds of Recog: City of Little Rock, Hope Inc, GYST House.

LOVE, LOUISE GARDNER oc/Nurse; b/Oct 20, 1916; h/3057 Spottswood Ave, Memphis, TN 38111; ba/Memphis; m/Robert Lyles (dec); c/James Gordon II, Robert Lyles Jr, Thomas Mitchell; p/Robert Bruce (dec) and Minnie Floy James Gardner (dec); ed/Dip RN; ba/RN Bapt Meml Hosp; ANA; Am Red Cross; Bapt Meml Hosp Alumnae; cp/Spottswood Gdn Clb; Tenn BPW Clb; r/Bapt.

LoVECCHIO, JOSEPH VICTOR oc/Regional Coordinator; b/Aug 8, 1947; h/504 W 1st St, Weatherford, OK 73096; ba/Weatherford; m/Patricia Sue; c/Kimberly Jo, Kristy Lynn; p/Salvador V and Frances L LoVecchio, Norman, OK; ed/BS Psych; pa/Regional Coor Drug Abuse Prog, Wn Okla St Univ; Recording Star; r/Christian; hon/Nat Drug Ed Ctr Grad.

LOVELACE, KATIE W oc/Area Controller, Office Manager; b/Nov 6, 1933; h/1807 Morningside Dr, Hartselle, AL 35640; ba/Decatur, AL; m/Harold; p/Jesse E Woods, Nashville, TN; Allie H Lee, Gray, KY; ed/La Salle Inst Acctg 1964; Att'd John C Calhoun Col 1970-71; Dip Dale Carnegie; pa/ConAgra Inc 27 Yrs; Am Feed Mfc'd Assn; Nat Assn Accts; Adm Mgmt Assn; cp/ABWA, Past Pres; Bd Mem U Way 6 Yrs; VP Am Cancer Soc; Morgan Co Mtl Hlth Assn; r/Bapt; hon/Wom of Yr ABWA; Boss of Yr, ABWA 1980.

LOVELL, CLAYTON C oc/Executive; b/Oct 21, 1942; ba/PO Box 31608, Charlotte, NC 28231; p/Charles Frederick Lovell Sr, Winston-Salem, NC; Rachel Arnold Lovell, Pilot Mtn, NC; ed/NYC Commun Col; Am Inst Bnkg, NY Chapt; pa/VP & Regional Pers Ofcr, Wachovia Bank & Trust Co; cp/NC JCs: St VChm Proj Mainstream 1974-75, St Chm Proj Mainstream 1975-76, Miss NC Pageant Treas 1975-76; Winston-Salem JCs: Dir 1972-73, VP 1973-74, 1st VP 1974-75, Dir at Large 1975-76, Pres 1976-77, Chm of Bd 1977-78; Chd's Ctr Dir 1977-80; Coun on Drug Abuse, Dir 1977-80; Urban Leag: Dir 1976, Treas 1977-80, VP 1978-80; Experiment in Self Reliance: Dir 1975, 1980, 1st VP 1976, Pres 1977-80; Salvation Army Boys Clb, Dir 1975-80; hon/JC: Freedom Guard of Yr, NC Freedom Guard, Pers Awd, Bob Bain Meml Awd, JC of Mo August, Dist'd Ser Awd, 5 Outstg Yng Men; Nat Coun of Negro Wom Dist'd Ser Awd; Hon Life Mem 70001 Career Assn; Delta Sigma Pi; C of C Ldrship Tng Conf.

LOVING, GARVIS INEZ oc/Cosmetologist and Instructor; b/Feb 19, 1932; h/Okla City, OK; m/George; c/Gloria, Deborah Akindele; p/Arthur (dec) and Nettie Rogers, Okla City, OK; ed/Bach Cosmetology 1965; Masters Cosmetology 1967; Doct Cosmetology 1968; pa/Owner, Instr Loving's Beauty Col; VP Aquarius Hair Designers; Accred'g Comm Team Wash DC; Ednl Chp St Beauty Culture Leag; Nat Beauty Culture Leag; Past Soloist Anti-Basilus of Theta Nu Sigma; cp/YWCA; Yng Dem Clb; Small Bus Adm Assn; Chm Christian Ed; r/Ch of Christ; hon/Hair Styling Trophy, Wichita, Kan 1970; Judge Cert, Miss Wiley Pageant, Marshall, Tex 1973; Outstg Artist, Dallas, Tex 1975; Lady of Yr, Theta Nu Sigma 1975; Millinary Trophy 1978; NBCL Conv Talent Show 1979.

LOWDER, EDWARD LEWIS oc/Retired Insurance Executive; b/Sept 12, 1913; h/Montgomery, AL; m/Catherine Kennedy; c/Robert E, James K, Thomas H; p/H S (dec) and Ollie C Lowder (dec); ed/BS Auburn Univ; mil/AUS WWII Capt; pa/Helped Form Ala Farm Bur Ins Cos 1946, Exec VP; Bd Govs Nat Assn Indep Insurers, Exec Com, Pres 1964-65; Bd Dirs: Ctrl Bank of Montgomery, Exch Bank of Attalla, Exch Nat Bank B'ham, First Nat Bank of Commerce of New Orleans, First Nat Bank Cobb Co, Carolina Energies, Kinder-Care Lrng Ctrs, Eye Foun of B'hm; Bd Visitors for Univ Ala Col of Commerce & Bus Adm; Adv Bd Auburn Univ; Auburn Univ Foun Bd; 4-H Clb Foun Bd; Ala Indep Cols Bd; cp/Past Pres U Way of Montgomery; Men of Montgomery; r/Presb.

LOWERY, DWIGHT NELSON oc/Training Officer and Fire Inspector; b/Mar 15, 1943; h/1021 Crestline Dr, Hartselle, AL 35640; ba/Hartselle; m/Linda White; c/Jonathan Paul, Lara Susan; p/Jetta Elkins Lowery, Sheffield, AL; ed/Florence St Col 1961-64; John C Calhoun Col 1967-68, 1978-79; mil/Ala NG 1960-66, 73-; pa/Firefighter City of Hartselle 1971-; EMT II; cp/Ala JCs, Treas 1964; r/Bapt; hon/Hartselle C of C Humanitarian Awd 1978; Am Legion Firefighter of Yr for Ala 1979.

LOWERY, HATTIE PERRY oc/Home Economist; b/July 12, 1920; h/1006 E Cheves St, Florence, SC 29501; ba/Florence; m/Moses; c/Ulysses; p/Adam and Sallie Perry, Florence, SC; ed/BS Home Ec; MSHE Ed; pa/SC Employees Assn; Nat & St Home Ec Assn; Epsilon Sigma Phi; cp/Elks; OES; Dem Party; U Order of Lents; Metro Coun of Wom; r/Bapt: Choir, Missionary; hon/Outstg Home Ecs of St, Nat Home Ec Assn 1965; 20 Yr Ser Awd, US Dept Agric.

LOWERY, MICHAEL DOUGLAS oc/Paralegal; b/Feb 21, 1950; h/Madisonville, KY; ba/M'ville; p/Arthur J Lowery, New Bedford, MA; Lila Mae Hendrix, Earlington, KY; ed/BS 1974, MA 1976 Murray St Univ; Dip Hopkinsville Col of the Bible; pa/Paralegal, Commun Ed Person 1979-; Elliott Mortuary Gen Asst 1960-; Outreach Wkr, Hopkins Co Lib 1978-79; Rdg Instr, Breckinridge Job Corps Ctr 1976-78; Rec Wkr, City of Madisonville 1975; Rec Dir First Christian Ch 1974; Orderly Hopkins Co Hosp 1973; Maintenance Wkr, St Hwy Dept 1973; Instr Madisonville Day Care Ctr 1971; cp/NAACP, Local Pres; Urban Leag; White House Conf on Chd & Yth; Masonic Lodge; Omega Psi Pi; Yng Dems; Nat Bapt Conv of Am; Progressive Nat Bapt Conv of Am; Bd Mem Bapt Unified Christian

194

Ldrship Conf; Asst Dean First Dist SS & Bapt Trg Union Cong; Min & Deacons Meeting of Hopkins Co; SCLC; Operation Push; r/Bapt; hon/Org'd Black Student Union, Murray St Univ; Org'd Cultural Com Murray St Univ; Org'd Alpha Beta Chapt Omega Psi Phi; Del Ky Yng Dems Conv; Org'd Christian Chs Coffee House Madisonville; Outstg Yth for Yth Day, E View Bapt Ch; Nat Student Register 1971-74; Spec Recog African Meth Epis Zion Ch for Sers to Commun; NAACP Awd for Commun Ser 1980.

LOWRANCE, MURIEL EDWARDS oc/Data Analyst; b/Dec 28, 1922; h/2038 Mackland Ave, NE Albuquerque, NM 87106; ba/Albuquerque; c/Kathy Gutierrez; p/Warren E (dec) and Mayme Barrick Edwards, NE Albuquerque, NM; ed/BS E Ctlr Univ; pa/Data Analyst, Dept Orthopaedics, Univ NM Sch Med; Nat Contract Mgmt Assn; AAUW; cp/Pres Pilot Clb Albuquerque Inc; Past Pres ABWA; Bd Dirs Amigos de las Americas; r/Meth; hon/Designated Certified Profl Contracts Mgr, NCMA 1976; Wom of Yr, ABWA 1974; W/W Alumni Assn, E Ctrl Univ 1978.

LOWRIE, BONITA ANN oc/Educator; b/July 24, 1936; h/6427 Honey Hill, San Antonio, TX 78229; ba/San Antonio; m/Glen W (dec); c/Michael Landis, Norman Ray, Bonita Glenette; p/Bertram Ashby Patterson, Garrison, TX; Jodie C Patterson (dec); ed/EdD 1972; MEd 1965; BMEd 1958; pa/Dean Univ Instrn; AAUW; Okla Mus Edrs Assn; Okla Col & Univ Adm; Okla Bd Control; Am, Tex, S Tex PGAs; Tex St Tchrs Assn; Tex Mus Edrs Assn; Mus Edrs Nat Conf; cp/GSA; BSA; Explorer Scouts of Am; Sierra Clb; Coun of Intl Relats; r/Epis; hon/Kappa Delta Phi; Danforth Assn Cand; W/W Am Wom; World W/W Wom; Intl W/W Intells.

LOWRY, K PATRICIA HARDY-BEARDSLEY oc/Professor; b/Apr 29, 1927; h/Rt 3 Box 143-2, Lowry Ln, Huntsville, TX 77340; ba/H'ville; m/S Douglas; c/Fred, Patty; p/Robert Paul Beardsley, Fredrick R E S Hardy; Kathleen C Heilman Beardsley; ed/BS, MA EdD Ball St Univ; pa/Nat Poetry Judge; Tchr Wkshops; Rdg Methods for HS & Elem; Wom's Studies; Prof Dept Ed Sam Houston St Univ; Delta Sigma Theta Sponsor; Intl Rdg Coun Pres; cp/Prog Chp St NOW; Kappa Delta Pi; Phi Delta Kappa; Audubon Soc; 4-H Ldr; Girl Scout Ldr; Blue Bird Ldr; r/Christian Sci; hon/Outstg Alumnus Ball St Univ; World W/W Wom; Ldr in Ed; Intl Biog Bicent Awd; Notable Ams; Num Pubs.

LOWRY, LESTER LEE oc/Minister, Teacher; b/Aug 9, 1939; h/Spiro, OK; m/Mary A; c/Davene, Lesley, David, Lorraine; p/Oren Emory and Sybil Lorraine Lowry, Bartlesville, OK; ed/AA Tulsa Jr Col; BA Ed NEn Okla St Univ; mil/USAF 5 Yrs; pa/Min Assem of God 21 Yrs; HS Tchr 5 Yrs; Gen Coun Assems of God; NEA; OEA.

LOWRY, VINIE LANGLEY oc/Instructor; b/May 13, 1909; h/1304 Hwy 29, S Lawrenceville, GA 30245; ba/L'ville; m/George R; c/James F, Gloria L Clayton; p/J F and Zella Langley; r/Meth; hn/Ga Chd Friendship Awd; Gwinnett Co Wom of Yr in Home Demo; Homemaker of Yr.

LOYOLA, ANDREA A oc/Community Relations Director; b/July 28, 1952; h/Metairie, LA; ba/Community Relations Ofc, De Paul Hospital, 1040 Calhoun St, New Orleans, LA 70118; p/Angel M and Carmelite Richter Loyola, New Orleans, LA; pa/Dir Commun Relats, DePaul Hosp 1980-; Asst Chachere Advtg Assocs 1979-80; Dir Public Relats & Devel, Mercy Hosp of New Orleans 1974-79; Newscaster WGNO TV 1974-76; Hotel Public Relats Asst 1973-74; Stringer WGSO Radio 1972-73; Intl Assn Bus Communrs, Public Relats Chp; Am Assn Hosp Public Relats; WICI; Nat Assn Hosp Devel; So Assn Bus Communs; cp/C of C; NAPPH; Press Clb; r/Cath; hon/2nd Pl Awd Bus Pubs NO Press Clb 1977; Outstg Yng Wom Am 1975; W/W Public Relats 1975.

LUCAS, AUBREY KEITH oc/Educator; b/Dec 7, 1934; ba/So Station, Box 5001, Hattiesburg, MS 39401; m/Ella Ginn; c/Frances, Carol, Alan, Mark; p/Keith C (dec) and Audell Robertson Lucas; ed/BS w Hons 1955, MA 1956 Univ So Miss; PhD Fla St Univ 1966; pa/Asst Dir Rdg Clin, Univ So Miss 1955-56; Instr Hinds Jr Col 1956-57; Dir Admissions & Assoc Prof Ed, Univ So Miss 1957-61; Res Asst, Computer Ctr & Ofc of Instl Res & Ser, Fla St Univ 1961-63; Registrar & Assoc Prof Ednl Adm, Univ So Miss 1963-70; Dean Grad Sch, Coor Res & Prof Higher Ed, Univ So Miss 1970-71; Pres Delta St Univ 1971-75; Pres Univ So Miss 1975-; St Comm Postsec'dy Ed; Miss Rep to So Regional Ed Bd; Com on Fed Relats & Com on Policies & Purposes, Am Assn St Cols & Univs; Past Pres Miss Assn Cols; Team Conslt, So Assn Cols & Schs; Omicron Delta Kappa; Phi Kappa Phi; Pi Kappa Pi; Pi Gamma Mu; Pi Tau Chi; Kappa Delta Pi; Phi Delta Kappa; Red Red Rose; Newcomen Soc of N Am; Kappa Pi; Pi Kappa Delta Miss Arts Com; Miss Com for Humanities; Phi Theta Kappa, Nat Bd 1980-; cp/Hub City Kiwanis Clb; Miss Forestry Assn; Miss Ec Coun; H'burg Ch of C Bd Dirs; Forrest-Lamar U Way Bd Dirs; Pine Burr Area Boy Scouts Bd Dirs; Miss Crusade Chm Am Cancer Soc 1979; Chm Forrest-Lamar U Way 1980; r/Parkway Heights U Meth Ch: Coun Mins, Dist Lay

Ldr, Wesley Foun, Bd Dirs Chm; hon/W/W: Am, S&SW, Am Cols & Univs; DIB; Ldrs in Ed; Author *The Mississippi Legislature and Mississippi Public Higher Education 1890-1960* & *Higher Education Opportunities and Needs in the Meridian Area;* Contbg Author to *History of Mississippi;* Author of Conslt Studies & Reports.

LUCAS, JULIA McDONALD oc/Assistant Professor; b/Sept 9, 1946; h/Rt 2, Box 332, Cochran, GA 31014; ba/Cochran; m/Wallace; c/Robert Patrick; p/Daniel Patrick McDonald (dec); Helen Booth McDonald, Jesup, GA; ed/BSEd Ga So Col 1969; MEd Univ of Ga 1971; Specialist in Ed, Univ of Ga; pa/Asst Prof Home Ec, Middle Ga Col 1977-; Dir of Bleckley Co Trng Center for Mtly Retarded (Cochran) 1974-77; Instr Home Ec, Mid Ga Col 1970-73; HS Tchr (Atlanta) 1968-69; Past Secy, Mid Ga Col Chapt of Ga Assn Edrs; St Exec Bd & Chm for Cont'g Ed, Ga Home Ec Assn; Voting Del from Ga to AHEA Conv in Atlantic City (NJ) 1981; Delta Kappa Gamma; Chm Bd of Regents, Acad Com on Home Ec 1981-82; VP Ga Student Home Ec Assn 1967-68; Others; cp/Charpter Pres & 2nd VP, Pilot Clb of Cochran; Charter Mem C of C; Pres & Bleckley Co Hike-Bike Chm, Bleckley Co Assn for Retarded Citizens; Trades Chm, Am Heart Assn; Past Secy-Treas, Ga 4-H Clbs; Others; r/Trinity Epis Ch; hon/W/W Am Wom; Plaque for Outstg Ldrship, Pilot Clb of Cochran; Wom of Yr, Cochran Jr Wom's Clb; HS Valedictorian.

LUCAS, TOM M oc/County Treasurer, Rancher-Farmer; b/July 17, 1946; h/RR 2, Box 168, Woodward, OK 73801; ba/Woodward; m/Margaret; c/Amy; p/E T and Claris Lucas, Selman, OK; ed/BS, MS Okla St Univ; mil/USAR Capt; pa/Woodward Co Treas; Pres St Co Treas Assn; Immed Past Pres NW Dist Co Treas Assn; cp/Past Pres Woodward Chapt Kiwanis Intl; Okla Adv Task Force for High Plains Coun; Adv Bd Okla Polit Action Com; Bd Dirs OSU Alumni Assn; Bd Dirs Okla Water Inc; Doane Country Wide Farm Panel; Okla Ec Devel Adv Coun; hon/Past Pres OSU Student Body 1967; Past St Secy Okla FFA Assn; Hon Lt Gov Okla; 9 Pubs on Agric & Ed; Woodward Co Soil Conservation Awd Winner 1978.

LUCCASEN, RAPHEAL ANDREW JR oc/Health Care Administration; b/Feb 22, 1948; h/531 Cliff Pl, Homewood, AL 35209; ba/B'ham; m/Linda Mary Charlet; c/Rapheal Andrew III, Racheal Anne, Russell Abraham; p/Rapheal A Sr and Sarah Piper Luccasen, Baton Rouge, LA; ed/BS 1970, MSW 1972 La St Univ; MPH Univ Ala-B'ham 1981; Post-Masters Cont'g Ed: Menninger Foun, Columbia Univ, Va Commonwlth Univ, Univ Tenn, La St Univ; pa/Vol Staff Mem, Res Assoc, Baton Rouge Mtl Hlth Ctr 1971; Dir Social Sers, Prog Hd Start, LeMoine Commun Action 1971; Guest Lectr, LSU 1972; Staff Mem LSU Hosp, Cnslg & Mtl Hlth Unit 1972; Prog Conslt, Dept Hlth, Ed & Wel 1972; Team Psychi Social Wkr, Hill Crest Hosp 1972-73; Dir Hosp Therapeutic Prog, Hill Crest Hosp 1973; Psychi Social Wkr Pvt Grp Pract 1973-77; VP Pvt Grp Pract, B'ham Psychi Med Sers 1977-79; Conslt, Hill Crest Hosp 1974-79; Adj Med Staff Mem, Hill Crest Hosp 1974-79; Dir Human Sers, St Vincent's Hosp 1979-; Am Public Hlth Assn; Am Acad Psychotherapists; Am Grp Psychotherapy Assn; Intl Assn Grp Psychotherapy; S En Grp Psychotherapy Soc, Ala St Chm 1975-79; Am Orthopsychi Assn; Acad Cert'd Social Wkrs; Ala Soc Clin Social Wkrs, Bd Dirs 1975-77, Licensing Com; NASW, Prog Plan'g Com, Ala Chapt; Soc Hosp Social Work Dirs Lic'd Cert'd Social Worker; Ala Public Hlth Assn; hon/Nat Registry of Hlth Care Providers in Clin Social Work; Nat Register Clin Social Wkrs; W/W S&SW; Author *The Use of Group Therapy in Pathlogical Grief Patients* 1975; *Preparing Families for the Psychiatric Admission of the Wife-Mother* 1977; *An Overview of the Development of Alternate Care Programs for the Terminally Ill* 1980.

LUCE, DWAIN GREGORY oc/Banker; b/Apr 25, 1916; h/2012 N Levert Dr, Mobile, AL 36607; ba/Mobile; m/Margaret Wilson; c/Dwain Gregory Jr, Margaret L Brown; p/Jex Howard (dec) and Emily Terrill Luce (dec); ed/BS Auburn Univ; mil/WWII Ret'd Major Airborne Artillery; pa/Dir First Miss Corp; Dir First Chem Corp; Miss Export RR Co; Columbia Ventures Inc; Bank of Lucedale, Miss; cp/Past Dir C of C; Past Chm & Dir U Fund; BSA; Jr Achmts; Art Gal; St Safety Coun; r/Epis; hon/6 Battle Stars; Bronze Star; Oak Leaf Cluster; 2 Arrow Hds.

LUCIUS, DENNIS JOE oc/Vocational Director; b/Mar 11, 1945; h/Rt 2 Box 182, Senatobia, MS 38668; ba/Senatobia; m/Loretta; c/Laurie, Suzanne; p/Dennis Eugene and Matter Mae Lucius, Eupora, MS; ed/Masters Guidance & Cnslg, Voc Evaluation; mil/USN Medic; pa/Nat Rehab Assn; St Secy AVEWAA; cp/VP Civitan; r/Bapt; hon/Profl St Awd, Ala 1978; Outstg Yng Man Am 1979; Cert of Merit 1979, Alumni Assn.

LUCKEY, DIANE VIRGINIA McKENNEY oc/Office and Financial Accounting Manager; b/July 16, 1946; m/Richard Anthony; c/Stepch: Tina, Tonya, Theresa; p/Warren Harold and Adriance Imogene Coosey McKenney; ed/Ricker Col; Hillsborough Commun Col; pa/US Govt 42nd Transp Sqdn 1964-65; US Govt Social Security Adm 1965-67; Guaranty

PERSONALITIES OF THE SOUTH

Loan & Real Est Co, W Memphis, Fla 1967-71; Computer Spec & Supvr Kandell Construction Co 1971-75; Full Charge Bkkpr & Ofc Mgr Universal Coach, Hollywood, Calif 1975-76; Ofc & Fin Acctg Mgr, Hillsboro News Co, Tampa, FL 1977-; Am Mgmt Assn; Wom in Contruction Org; Wom in Mgmt Assn; Am Soc Profl & Exec Wom; Advr Jr Achmt; cp/Notary Public, St of Fla 1974-; Secy N Me Br NDTA; Am Qtr Horse Assn; Am Horse Show Assn; Fla Comancheros; Fla Qtr Horse Assn; Palomino Horse Breeders Assn; Rainbow Girls; OES; r/Bapt; hon/Cert for Outstg Ldrship w 4-H Horse Grp; Treas & Show Com Chm Fla Comancheros Inc.

LUDWIG, RAY WOODROW oc/Teacher; b/June 10, 1941; h/PO Box 550, Moorefield, WV 26836; ba/M'field; p/Branson G Ludwig (dec); Nerva L Ludwig, Rio, WV; ed/AB Sec'dy Ed, Shepherd Col 1964; AM Sec'dy Adm 1966, MA Cnslg & Guid 1972, WV Univ; pa/Hardy Co Schs: Eng Tchr M'field HS 1976-, Dir Sec'dy Ed & Coor Spec Projs 1969-76; Reg II WVa Curric Improvement Ctr, Math Spec 1968-69; Math Tchr, Asst Prin Morgan Co Schs 1967-68; Math Tchr Ohio Co Schs 1964-67; Pres HCEA; VP Clrm Tchrs Assn; Del: WVEA, NEA; Assn for Supvn & Curric Devel; Editor, Asst Editor Cohongoroota 1962-64; cp/Org Pres & VP: Sperry's Run Yth F'ship, Cir K Clb, Student Christian Assn; Treas Kappa Delta Pi; Nat Geog Soc; Am Mus Natural Hist; 4-H Clb; r/U Meth; hon/W/W: Sch Dist Ofcls, Am Cols & Univs; Kiwanis Cir K Man of Yr 1964; FFA Hon Farmer's Deg 1970; Am Legion Citizenship Awd; Outstg Yng Man of Am; Notable Ams; Commun Ldrs & Noteworthy Ams; DIB.

LUMMUS, EILEEN DAVIS oc/Retired; b/Oct 28, 1921; h/1576 Alamo Dr, Orange, TX 77630; m/Willard R; c/Sanford W; p/Wiliam E Davis (dec); Belle D Luce, Orange, TX; pa/Coor Vols at Jones Rest Home; Local Chm Buckners Benevolences; Ret'd Pt-time Tchr; 20 Yrs Wom's Credit Clb; cp/Red Cross; PTA; Dem Clb; r/Bapt: SS Tchr, Supt, Secy Trg Union, Wom's Missionary Soc; hon/Red Cross Ser; Miss Liberty; Most Valuable Person in Credit to Salesmen.

LUND, BONNIE RAE oc/Credit Counselor; b/Jan 12, 1940; h/1211 DeLeon Ct, Clarkson, GA 30021; ba/Atlanta; m/William G; c/Marsha K Cox; p/Raymond George and Melba Lobb Brocksieck, Rushville, IL; ed/Cert'd Consumer Credit Exec 1979; pa/Credit Cnslr, Wom's Loan Prog, Assocs Fin Ser Co Inc; Credit Wom Intl: Atlanta Chapt Pres 1980, 1st VP 1979 & Orlando Chapt Pres 1974-76, Secy 1973; Atlanta Consumer Credit Assn, Bd Dirs 1980-81, 81-82; cp/Dekalb C of C VIBES Prog; Wom's C of C; r/U Meth; hon/Credit Wom of Yr, Orlando 1974, St of Fla 1975, Atlanta 1980, St of Ga 1980, Dist 1981; "Woman and the Credit They Deserve" in Coca-Cola's Employee Newslttr.

LUSTER, RONNIE LEE oc/Comptroller; b/Nov 19, 1947; h/Fairway Apts #13, Johnson City, TN; p/Lee G and Hazel B Luster, Church Hill, TN; ed/BS 1973, MBA 1982 ETSU; mil/USMC 1966-70; pa/Comptroller Lancaster Assocs Inc 1977-; Adm Mgmt Soc, Bd Dirs; Am Fin Assn; Japan Karate Org; cp/BPOE Elks; r/Meth; hon/W/W: S&SW 1980, Fin & Indust 1981.

LUTES, CANDIDA J oc/Associate Professor, Assistant Dean; b/June 18, 1948; h/College Station, TX; ba/Dept Psychology, Tex A&M Univ, College Station, TX 77843; m/Russell A Dunckley; p/Willard J (dec) and Jean M Lutes, Waterbury, CT; ed/BA Boston Univ 1970; BA 1973, PhD 1976 So Ill Univ; pa/Assoc Dept Psychol Univ Calif-Santa Barbara 1974-75; Tex A&M Univ: Asst Prof Dept Psychol 1975-81, Assoc Prof Dept Psychol 1981-, Asst Dean Col of Liberal Arts 1980-; Gerontological Soc of Am; Soc Res in Child Devel; SWn Soc Res in Human Devel; MWn Psychol Assn; Brazos Val Psych Assn; Nat Assn Acad Affairs Admrs; Am Assn Higher Ed; hon/W/W: S&SW, Am Wom; Author "Early Marriage & Identity Foreclosure"; Co-Author "Nontraditional Approaches to Therapy with the Rural Aged."

LYLES, YVONNE BRIGMAN oc/Educator; b/Sept 9, 1931; h/Rt 8 Box 264, Texarkana, AR 75502; c/Deneise Birmingham; T B (Dec) and Eva A Brigman, Atlanta, TX; ed/BA, MA Prairie View A&M Univ; Post Grad Studies: N Tex St Univ, Ind Univ, Mich St Univ, Concordia Col, Kesgraves Adult Ctr; Tchr 29 Yrs; Profl Sponsor: Class Sponsor, Nat Jr Hon Soc, Jour, Student Coun, Debate, UIL Activs, Drama, Basketball, Track; TSTA; NEA; AAUP; cp/PTA; TSTA; Band Booster Clbs; Las Amigas Social & Civic Clb; r/Bapt; hon/Superior Rating, Most Outstg Tchr 1973; Mem of Instrl Adv Com for Dist VIII; Dir Sev In-Ser Trg Prog in Eng.

LYMAN, RUTH ANN oc/Mental Health Administrator; b/Feb 2, 1948; h/3228 Highland Dr, Birmingham, AL 35205; ba/B'ham; m/Robert D; p/Oren E and Frances E Frerking, Florence, AL; ed/BS, MA, PhD Univ Ala; pa/Dir Bur of Mtl Hlth & Dir Wn Mtl Hlth Ctr, Jefferson Co Dept Hlth 1975-; Adj Asst Prof, Dept Psych, Univ Col, Univ Ala-B'ham 1977-; Chief, Mtl Helth Sect & Clin Psych, Univ Hlth Ser, Col of Commun Hlth Scis, Univ Ala 1973-75; Conslt, NW Ala Commun Mtl Hlth Ctr 1974-75; Profl Dir, Tuscaloosa Pregnancy Cnslg & Rape Relief Ser 1973-75; Assoc,

Resource Design & Devel Corp, 1973-78; Psychometrist, Psych Clin, Dept Psych, Univ Ala 1972; Trg Grp Ldr, Tuscaloosa Commun Crisis Ctr 1972; Conslt Lowndes Co Sch Sys 1971; Clin Psych Montgomery Area Mtl Hlth Auth 1971; Cnslr & Res Assoc, Camp Ponderosa 1969-70; Instr Div Spec Studies Univ Ala-B'ham 1977-78; Instr Jefferson St Jr Col 1975-77; Adj Asst Prof, Dept Psych Univ Ala-Tuscaloosa 1973-75; Am Psych Assn; Ala Coun Mtl Hlth/Mtl Retard Dirs; Ala Acad Neurology & Psychi; Assn Lic'd Psychs Ala, B'ham Area Coor 1978-; SEn Psych Assn; Ala Psych Assn, Chm Profl Sers Review Com 1978-79; Am Public Hlth Assn; Ala Public Hlth Assn; cp/Pers Adv Coun, Jefferson Co Pers Bd, Leg Review Com 1978-; Profl Adv Com, Mtl Hlth Assn Jefferson Co 1978-; Hd Start Policy Coun, Jefferson Co Com for Ec Opport, Commun Rep to Coun 1976-, Chm Bylaws Com 1977-; Bd Dirs Alcoholism Recovery Sers Inc, B'ham, Appointee of Jefferson Co Bd Hlth 1977-; Profl Adv Bd Sch Social Work, Univ Ala-B'ham 1977-; Grp Home Adv Com, Jefferson-Blount-St Clair Mtl Hlth/Mtl Retard Auth 1976-; r/Meth; hon/W/W: Am Wom, Hlth Care; Nat Register of Hlth Ser Providers in Psych 1975-78; Lic'd by Ala Bd Examrs in Psych 1975; Outstg Yng Career Wom Awd 1974; Martin S Wallach Awd 1973; Fellow Ala Dept Mtl Hlth 1969-71.

LYNCH, MARY LYNN PORTER oc/Nurse; b/Nov 14, 1944 ;h/PO Box 311, Kosciusky, MS 39090; ba/Kosciusky; m/David J Sr; c/David Joel Jr, Carol Lynn; p/Houston Phiffer (dec) and Myrtis Lee Brewer Porter (dec); ed/AA Nsg Hinds Jr Col 1968; pa/Cert'd CPR Instr, Am Heart Assn; Assoc Adv Med Explorer Post BSA; Am & Miss Nurses Assn; Wn St Assn Intravenous Therapy; Miss Hosp Assn; Soc of Nsg Ser Admrs, Charter Mem & Dir; Am Fed BPW; Am Heart Assn; Miss Heart Assn; Lectr CPR, First Aide; Chm BPW Clb CPR Com; r/Bapt; hon/W/W Am Wom 1979-80.

LYNCH, WALTER KENNETH oc/Professor and Department Head; b/Apr 17, 1929; m/Martha Jeffreys; c/Carol Anne, Frances Kaye; p/Eva K Privette; ed/BS 1959, MS 1966 NC St Univ; PhD Univ Leeds, England 1971; pa/Superior Yarn Mills Inc 1950-56; Union Carbide Chem Co 1959-62; NC St Sch Textiles 1962-75; Textile Engrg, Auburn Univ 1975; Textile Quality Control Assn; Assn Textile Technols; Am Assn Textile Chems & Colorists; Acad Mgmt; Rayon Acetate Coun, Chm of Bd; cp/Delta Kappa Phi; Sigma Tau Sigma; Phi Kappa Phi; Nat Coun Textile Ed, VP; r/Meth; hon/Acad Outstg Tchrs 1971; Ldrs in Textile Indust 1979; Phi Psi Lambda Chapt Hon Mem; US Del to Intl Standards Org 1980; Chm SC-5 Yarn Testing Intl Standards Org 1980; Author *The Influence of Wire Profile on the Quality of Wool Type Carded Webbs: Conventional Flexible Wire, Non-Conventional Flexible Wire, The Assessment of Card Wire Sharpness.*

LYNCH, WILLIAM WRIGHT JR oc/Real Estate Developer; b/Aug 26, 1930; h/5463 Haynie, Dallas, TX 75205; ba/Dallas; m/Sandra McVay; c/Mary Margaret, Katherine; p/William W and Martha Hirsch Lynch, Dallas, TX; ed/BS Ariz Univ 1959; MBA Stanford Univ 1962; mil/AUS 1959-60; pa/Pres Ins Bldg Corp 1965-; Secy, Dir Lynch Properties Corp 1972-; Dir Llano Inc, Broadmoor Properties Inc, N Mex Elec Ser Co, Hobbs Gas Co, Ins Bldg Corp, Bd Dir Dallas Civic Mus 1970-77; Ednl Opports Inc 1973-; Dallas Symph Orch 1966-74; r/Epis.

LYNN, BYRON STEPHEN oc/Veterinarian; b/July 22, 1952; h/108 Wilburn Rd, Statesboro, LA 30458; m/Miriam Lunsford; p/Byron and Carolyn W Lynn, Reidsville, LA; ed/AS Abraham Baldwin Agric Col 1972; BS cum laude 1974, DVM 1977 Univ Ga; pa/Dockery Vet Hosp 1977-80; Statesboro Animal Hosp 1980-; Am Vet Med Assn; Ga Vet Med Assn; Am Assn Swine Practrs; Am Soc Theriogenology; cp/Ga JCs; r/Meth.

LYNN, JAMES WILLIAM (BILL) JR oc/Executive; b/Aug 25, 1939; h/1817 Helen Dr, Alice, TX 78332; ba/Alice; m/Suzanne; c/Jamie Suzanne, Brenton; p/Jacqueline Lynn, Alice, TX; ed/BBA Tex A&I Univ 1962; mil/USAFR 1963-68; pa/Pres Lynn Ranches Inc; Sr VP & Trust Ofcr Alice Nat Bank; Indep Cattlemens Assn, Treas; Tex & SW Cattle Raisers Assn; Santa Gertrudis Breeders Intl; S Tex Santa Gertrudis Breeders Assn; cp/City-Co Airport Bd Chm; C of C, Dir 1976-78; Alice Ambassadors 1978-79; City Bd Adjustments 1978-79; Mary Dinn Reynolds Meth Foun, Trustee & Treas; Alice Cemetery Assn, Treas; Alice Pee Wee Baseball Treas; Rotary Clb of Alice, Dir 1975-76; r/Meth.

LYON, REBECCA MAY SAXON oc/Marriage and Family Therapist; b/Oct 14, 1933; h/1100 Amherst Dr, Dothan, AL 36301; ba/Dothan; m/Gerald Dean; c/Janice Ruth, Patricia Kay, Deborah Sue; p/John Davis (dec) and Sara Conner Saxon, Saltillo, MS; ed/BS; MS; PhD; pa/Marriage & Fam Cnslg; Tchr; Admr in Higher Ed; cp/AAUW; Zonta Clb; r/Ch of the Nazarene; hon/Borden S'ship Awd; S'ship Troy St Univ; F'ship Fla St Univ; Phi Kappa Phi; Omicorn Nu; Alpha Kappa Delta.

LYONS, KIRK DAVID oc/Student, Director and Curator Historical Museum; b/June 17, 1956; h/Austin, TX; ba/Box 1047, Galveston, TX

196

PERSONALITIES OF THE SOUTH

77553; p/Clarence Jay Jr and Mildred Modena Morris Lyons; ed/BA Univ Tex-Austin; 2nd Yr Law Student, Univ Houston; pa/Dir-Curator Galveston Co Hist Mus; Dir Battle of Galveston Reenactment 1980; Tex St Hist Assn; Walter Prescott Webb Hist Soc; Am Living Hist Assn; Nat Reenactment Soc; Magruders Brigade; cp/Comdr & Fdr Major G W Littlefield Camp SCV; Albert Sidney Johnston Camp SCV; SCV; Fdr NBFFC; Yng Ams for Freedom; Christian Legal Soc; r/Epis; hon/Jefferson Davis Awd 1977; Author Profl Pubs Incl'g "Bondage in Retrospect: The Biblical & Legal Justification of Slavery by Antebellum Southerners."

M

MABERRY, LOUISE JONES oc/Executive Director; b/Jan 24, 1929; h/Rt 4 Box 904, Orange, TX 77630; ed/Bus Col; Att'd Lamar Univ, Univ Tex, Univ Okla; Preceptors Lic; Nsg Home Admrs Lic; pa/Exec Dir & Part Owner Jones Hlth Ctr Inc 1958-; Est'd Home Hlth Acgy 1969-; Tex-Jones Hlth Ctr of Vidor 1976-; cp/Orange Co C of C: Com on Aging 1977, Bd Dirs 1974-76, VP 1977; Nom for Col of Nsg Home Admrs; Tex Nsg Home Assn: Chm Ed Com 1974, 75, 76; Gtr Sabine Area Chapt 16, Tex Nsg Home Assn: Past Pres; Gtr E Tex Hlth Sys Agcy: Hlth Plan'g Com, Gov'g Body Com; SE Tex Regional Plan'g Comm: Com on Aging; Task Force on Hlth Sers for Orange Co: Chm 1976-77.

MACHEN, ROY WALTER oc/Minister; b/Jul 5, 1906; h/Rt 2, Box 233, Olive Hill, KY 41164; ba/Same; m/Estha Omega Slone; c/Patricia J M Jordan, Russell W, Mary C M Springer, Roy W II, Elizabeth A M Greenhill; p/Harvey Lee and Mary Jane Marshall Machen (dec); ed/BA magna cum laude Okla City Univ 1927; MA Morehead St Univ 1965; ThD Clarksville Sch Theol 1956; DD 1958, DRE 1959, DMin 1978; Postgrad Studies, Marquette Univ 1966; pa/Reg'd Profl Engr, Tex 1938-; Chemist, Natural Gasoline & Refinery Plant 1927-35; Constrn Engr & Opers Supt, Natural Gasoline & Petrol Refining Plants 1935-48; Supvr Sulphur Co Warehouse & Motor Trans 1950-59; Owner & Pres Sulphuric Engr'd 1948-; Former Mem: NEA, OEA, WOEA, Xenia EA; Vis Prof Bible Studies, Doctrine & New Testament, C'ville Sch Theol 1957-; HS Math Tchr (Covington, Okla) 1927; HS Intrumental & Vocal Music Tchr (Olive Hill) 1960-61; Sr HS English & Journalism Tchr/Dept Chm (Hamersville, Ohio) 1962-67; Sr HS English Tchr & Dept Chm (Xenia, Ohio) 1967-76; Ordained to Min, Bapt Gen Conv of Tex 1950; Pastor: 1st Bapt Ch (Pledger, Tex) 1950-53, 1st Bapt Ch (Magnet, Tex) 1953-59, 1st Bapt Ch (Olive Hill) 1959-62, 1st Bapt Ch (Mount Orab, Ohio) 1962-77; Revival Evang: Tex, Okla, La, WVa, Tenn, Ohio, Wis, Wyo, Ky, NC; Interim Pastor, 1st Bapt Ch (Olive Hill) 1981; VP Repent or Perish Gospel Mins 1973-; Author: *Research Paper Manual* (1981), *Notes on the Book of Colossians* (1973), *Synthetic Bible Studies* (1980); Contbr Articles to Sci Jours; cp/Former Mem: Lions Clb, Rotary; Former ARC 1st Aid & Life Saving Instr; BSA: Scoutmaster, Dist Commr, Merit Badge Instr 16 Yrs, Mem Sam Houston Area Coun; Former Dep Sheriff in Okla & Tex; r/Bapt; ho/Ky Col; Xenia Disaster Commemorative Awd; W/W Rel; Eagle Scout; Order of Arrow; Silver Beaver Awd; Men of Achmt; Notable Ams; Other Biogl Listings.

MACIK, HELEN MARIE oc/Educational Diagnostician; b/Sept 6, 1950; h/2576 Interstate Blvd, Mesquite, TX 75150; p/Stanley and Evelyn Macik, Hutchins, TX; ed/BS 1973, MEd 1977 E Tex St Univ; Cert'd Lang Therapist, Dean Meml Lrgn Ctr; Profl Tchr Cert, St Tex: Elem Ed, Mtl Retard; Lang Lrng Disabilities, Ednl Diagnostician, Supvr Spec Ed; pa/Ednl Diagnostician w Mesquite Indep Sch Dist; Orton Soc Inc, Dallas Br, Treas 1980-81, 3rd VP 1979-80; Mesquite Ed Assn, Fac Rep 1977-78; cp/Czech Clb of Dallas, Secy 1977; Hist Soc of Czech Clb; Cath Daughs of Am; r/Cath; hon/Co-Editor "Generation to Generation: Czech Food, Customs & Traditions Texas Style" 1980.

MACK, JANIS C oc/Real Estate Broker; b/Mar 25, 1940; h/Rt 3, Breenbriar, AR 72058; ba/Greenbrier; m/Ralph L Jr; c/David Wayne, Roy Glenn; p/Exel and Esther Howard, Greenbrier, Ar; pa/Broker, Mack Rlty; Conway Bd Rltrs; cp/Greenbrier PTA & Band Boosters; r/Missionary Bapt; Organist.

MACKEY, DAN B II oc/Executive Director; b/Oct 30, 1939; h/204 Yosemite Dr, Greenwood, SC 29646; m/Pearce Webb; c/Dan III, Ben; p/Dan B and Olive Nettles Mackey, Camden, SC; ed/AB Univ SC 1963, Univ Okla 1967, Univ Ga 1966; mil/USMC 1957-59; pa/Exec Dir Savannah Coun of Govts; Pres SC Indust Develrs Assn; Chm SC COG Exec Dirs Com; Adv Bd Mem Nat Assn Regional Couns; cp/Pres Greenwood Co Gamecock Clb; Bd Mem Greenwood Rotary Clb; r/Epis; hon/Outstg Yng Man Am 1976; Nat Walter A Scheiber Regional Ldrship Awd, Nat Assn Regional Couns 1980.

MacKINNON, F T oc/Retired; b/Aug 25, 1898; h/609 W Lafayette St, Marianna, FL 32446; m/Inez S; ed/Deg Agronomy, Univ Fla; mil/WWI Sgt; pa/Food Stores, Cattle Auction Mkt; Meat Pckg Plant; Hardware Store; cp/City Comr; Secy C of C; Rotary; r/Epis; hon/Fed Savings & Loan Plaque for 44 Yrs Ser; WTOT Radio Plaque for 10 Yrs Ser.

MacMILLAN, JUDITH RUTH oc/Assistant Professor, Department Head; b/Feb 21, 1943; h/1422 Shiloh Trail E, NW, Kennesaw, GA 30144; ba/Waleska, GA; p/Walton L and Gertrude Winston Payne MacMillan, Kennesaw, GA; ed/BS Carson-Newman Col 1965; MMU Ga St Univ 1971; pa/Choral Dir, Gen Mus Tchr, Powder Springs Elem Sch 1965-66; E Cobb Jr HS 1966-67; Choral Dir, Gen Music Tchr, Hd Mus Dept, Cobb Co Bd Ed; Mae Smythe Elem Sch, Parks Elem Sch 1968-70; Beverly Hills

Intermediate Sch 1970-72; Accompanist for Orchestra, Guest Dir for Dist 6th Grade Choral Fest, Pasadena Indep Sch Dist, Houston, Tex; Ga St Univ, Grad Asst'ship 1973-74; Asst Prof Mus, Hd Mus Dept, Reinhardt Col 1971-; Mus Dir Camp Crestridge for Girls; Entertainment Dir Hugh O'Brian Intl Yth Ldrship Seminar; Interim Mus Dir, Holly Springs Bapt Ch; Am Choral Dirs Assn; Mus Edrs Nat Conf; AAUP; cp/Commun Concert Assn, Canton, Ga 1974-81; r/Bapt; hon/Grad Asst'ship Ga St Univ; Awd for 10 yrs Dedicated Ser to Camp Crestridge for Girls; W/W S&SW; World W/W Wom; Articles Pub'd in Profl Jours.

MADDOX, JOE WAYNE oc/Teacher; b/Mar 13, 1939; h/1741 Lake Hill St NW, Cullman, AL 35055; ba/Hanceville, AL; m/Kathryn Walker; c/Melanie Kaye, Kathy Michelle; p/Jay Maddox, Cullman, AL; Hettie Jennings Maddox, Cullman, AL; ed/BA St Bernard Col; MA, EdD Univ Ala; Post Doct Study Penn St Univ, Univ Ala-B'ham; pa/Math Tchr, Tchr Ed Advr, Wallace St Commun Col; ATE; AACTE; NEA; PDK; TASCD; NSSE; cp/Dem Party; r/Bapt-Meth Rural Country Ch Org; hon/Sr Class VP; Nat Task Force ATE; Dedicated Tchr Awd.

MADDOX, NOVA C oc/Librarian; b/Sept 26; h/6710 Lake Cliff Dr, San Antonio, TX 78244; ba/Brooks AFB, TX; m/Clemon; p/Earnest Sr (dec) and Daisy S Carter, San Antonio, TX; ed/BS; MEd; MSLS; pa/Lib, Base Lib; ALA TLA; BLA; AAUP; NAACP; Aerospace Toastmistress; cp/Zeta Phi Beta; HTC Alumni; r/Meth; hon/Sustained Superior; Outstg Zeta of Yr.

MADRIGAL, ROBERTO oc/Director; b/Feb 8, 1946; h/11919 Westmere, Houston, TX 77077; ba/Houston; m/Patricia; c/Ivan, Christina; p/Alfonso Madrigal; Judith Quevedo; ed/Deg Indust Engrg; 2 Yrs Doct Work Paris XII; pa/Dir Fgn Crude Trading; r/Nondenom.

MAGEE, SADIE E oc/Coach and Instructor; b/Oct 27, 1932; h/Jackson, MS; ba/HPER Dept, Jackson St Univ, Jackson, MS 39217; p/Julius C and Alice D Magee, Mt Olive, MS; ed/BS Alcorn St Univ 1954; MS Ed Jackson St Univ 1975; pa/Wom's Basketball Coach & Instr Hlth, Phy Ed, Jackson St Univ; NAWS, Pres Elect; MAIAW, Pres for Devel; AAHPERD; MAHPERD; MAE-NEA; JSU Higher Ed Assn; JSU Alumni Assn; NRP-Ethnic Minority Soc; MAADS; cp/NAACP; YWCA; Miss Dem Party; r/Bapt; hon/Cert of Merit for Outstg Ser, New Orleans 1978; Alumnus of Month, Jackson Hinds Alumni Chapt of Jackson Nat Alumni Assn 1978; Cert of Apprec for Exceptl Ser & Loyalty to City of Jackson 1978; Coach of Yr Nat Sports Foun 1978; Beverly Savlcy Awd, NSF 1978; Coach of Yr, Nat Assn Wom Sports 1978 & 80; Nat Assn Wom Sports Nat Tourn Coaching 1979-80; Outstg Achmts Awd, Dept HPER Jackson St Univ 1978-79; Ldrship Awd Jackson St Univ 1979; Nat Alumni Awd in Sports, Jackson St Univ 1978; Jackson Daily News Coach of Yr 1980.

MAGUIRE, ROBERT O JR oc/Educator, Performer, Arranger; b/Jan 31, 1948; h/Sanford, FL; m/Maureen Jennifer; p/Robert O Sr and Shirley S Maguire, Orlando, FL; ed/AA Seminole Commun Col 1971; BME Fla St Univ 1975; MA Rollins Col 1978; Internship Rickards HS, Tallahassee; mil/USAF 1966-70; pa/Profl Entertainer: Hilton Inn S, Club Lui, Ramada Inn 1971-75; Fla St Univ Jazz/Rock Ensemble 1974-75; Choir Dir, First Presb Ch of Bainbridge, Ga 1974; Min Mus, First Bapt Ch of Perry, Fla 1975; Seminole HS: Band Dir 1975-76, Choral Dir 1975-81; Seminole Commun Col, Adj Fac: Pvt Voice Instr 1976-81, Col Vocal Jazz Ensemble 1979-81; Profl Arranger & Band Conductor, Vision Enterprises 1980-81; Fla Tchg Profession-NEA; Nat Assn Jazz Edrs; Fla Vocal Assn: Dist Chm, Adjudicator; Mus Edrs Nat Conf; Fla Mus Edrs Assn; Am Choral Dirs Assn; r/Prot; hon/Grad cum laude Seminole Jr Col; W/W Am Jr Cols; Phi Mu Alpha; Grad cum laude Fla St Univ; Kappa Delta Pi; Outstg Yng Edr; Sanford JCs 1981; Seminole Co Tchr of Yr 1976.

MAHAFFEY, CHARLES EDWARD oc/Dentist; b/Jan 19, 1941; h/Elizabeth City, NC; ba/322 Kramer Bldg, Main St, Elizabeth City, NC 27909; m/Brenda Heath; c/Charles Edward II, Molly Heath; p/John William and Lena Garrett Mahaffey, Elizabeth City, NC; ed/AB ECU 1963; DDS UNC 1968; mil/US Public Hlth Ser 1968-71; pa/Dentist; Am Dent Assn; NC Dent Soc; Bicent Dent Study Clb; Acad Gen Dent; En Carolina Hlth Systems Agcy; cp/Bd Dirs First Citizens Bank; Chm Exec Com BSA; Mastor Mason, Past Master 1979; York Rite Mason; Scottish Rite Mason; Shriner; Pres Albemarle Ed Foun; Chm Bd Albemarle Acad; r/Bapt; Deacon, Chm Diaconate, SS Tchr.

MAHAFFEY, MARGARET MICHELE oc/Chief of Food Service Management; b/Nov 5, 1945; h/Big Spring, TX; p/Bennett Rogan Sr and Frances Margaret Bearden Mahaffey, Canton, TX; ed/BS w Hons Tex Wom's Univ 1971; pa/Chief Food Ser Mgmt, Big Spring St Hosp; Gaston Epis Hosp; ARA Food Sers; Tex Agric Ext Ser; City of San Antonio Nutrition for the Elderly; Tex Home Ec Assn; Tex Public Employee Assn; Tex Hosp Assn; Tex Soc Hosp Food Ser Dirs; World Hlth Org; cp/Humane Soc; 4-H Adult Ldr; r/Bapt; hon/Intl Farm Yth Exch Prog to India 1968-69.

MAJOR, FLORENCE RUBY BENNETT oc/Homemaker; b/Jan 5, 1923; h/119 Hillcrest, Madisonville, KY 42431; m/William Morris; c/Ruby Ann M Hartwig, William Morris III, Robert Bennett; p/Eli L (dec) and Lissis Ann Carder Bennett, Madisonville, KY; cp/Wom's Clb of Madisonville; r/First Chrsitian Ch; hon/Ky St Winner "Bright of Am" Art Contest; Paintings Exhib'd in & Winner of Many Awds in Local, St & Nat Competition.

MALONE, NANCY BOYD oc/Nurse; b/Mar 6, 1948; h/PO Box 60, Rt 1, Cadiz, KY 42211; m/Anthony Glenn; c/Michelle Dawn, Glenda Annette, Anthony Durwood; p/Walter F Cameron, Cadiz, KY; Inez B Cameron (dec); ed/Assoc Deg Nsg, Midway Jr Col 1969; pa/RN, Hd Nurse 3-11 Shift Trigg Co Hosp; Chm Nsg Audit for Trigg Co Hosp & Marshall Co Hosp; cp/PTA; Relief SS Tchr; r/Meth; hon/Cert for 4 Wk Adv'd Critical Care Course 1979; Cert for 16 Hour Course Responsibilities of Hd Nurse 1975; 7 Yr Perfect Attendance Pin at Ch.

MANDRELL, REGINA ANGELA MORENO oc/Retired Teacher; b/Mar 10, 1906; h/Fairhope, AL; m/George F Kirchoff (dec); 2nd William F Mandress (dec); c/George F Kirchoff Jr, Margaret K Handler; p/Cameron Anderson Sr (dec) and Seana Barkley Crary Moreno (dec); ed/AB B'ham So Col 1926; Post Grad Studies: Univ Ky 1964, Smith Col 1965; pa/Fields of Hlth Ed, Genealogy, Hist; Ala Hist Soc; Baldwin Co Hist Soc; Pensacola, Fla Hist Soc; Baldwin Co Writers Clb; Alpha Chi Omega; Pi Gamma Mu; Chi Delta Phi; Kappa Delta Epsilon; cp/Nat Soc DAR; Nat Soc Colonial Dames XVII Century; r/Meth; hon/Recip Geo Wash Medal, Freedom Foun 1961; 1st Pl Lit Awd, B'ham Fest Arts; Author Hist & Ednl Pubs.

MANERY, CAROL SUE oc/Musician; b/July 25, 1944; h/1022 W Chase St, Denison, TX 75020; p/J U and Hazel B Manery, Denison, TX; pa/Levi Strauss & Co; Gospel Mus, Manery Ribble Trio; hon/Awd for Instrumentalist of Yr; Awd for Gospel Band of Yr 1981.

MANESS, BETTY oc/Secretary; b/June 23, 1924; h/123 Tall Oaks Ct, Kingsport, TN 37663; ba/Kingsport; m/Eugene C; c/Gary Eugene; p/Everett H and Ann Munsey, Kingsport,TN; ed/Dip Whitney Sch of Bus 1944; pa/Secy Holston Defense Corp; BWA, Com Chmships; cp/Am Legion, Bd Dirs; Wom of the Moose, Coms; Kingsport Commun Aid; Ladies Aux to VFW, St Pres & 4 Nat Dir'ships; MD Assn of Sullvan Co, Secy & Bd Mem; r/Prot; hon/Jt House Resolution #491 1980, Tenn Gen Assem for Outstg Ser to Commun & Ser in Ladies Aux to VFW.

MANFULL, DANIEL MALCOLM oc/Banker; b/Feb 25, 1917; h/Killeen, TX; ba/Church & Gray Sts, PO Box 609, Killeen, TX 76541; m/Ruth J; c/Marilyn Ruth Griffin, James Daniel, Wanda Kaye; p/Daniel V (dec) and Mary S Manfull (dec); ed/BS Kent St Univ; Grad Work Akron Univ; OCS 1942-43; Reserve Ofcrs Sch 1942-43; Amphibious Warfare, Staff & Command Sch 1948; mil/USMC Ret'd Lt Col; pa/VP Mktg Am St Bank 1979-; Exec VP Gtr Killeen C of C 1959-79; Pres CCMSAET 1965; Exec VP Gtr Killeen C of C 1959-70; Mgr C of C 1956-59; Marine Ofcr Instr, NROTC Unit, Univ Okla 1954-56; Adm & Exec Ofcr, Ext Sch, MC Schs 1951-54; Trg & Exec Ofcr, 1st Provisional Casual Co 1950-51; Other Mil Positions; Adv Dir Bd Dirs Am St Bank; Chm Bus Relats Coun, Gtr Killeen C of C; Am Ednl Complex Adv Coun; VChm Pvt Indust Coun, Ctrl Tex Manpwr Consortium; Ctrl Tex Col Bus Adv Com; Past Pres C of C Mgrs & Secys Assn of E Tex; cp/VFW; Am Legion; Disabled Am Vets; Bells Co Sheriff's Posse; Killeen Riding & Roping Clb; Campaign Dr Chm U Way 1980; r/Presb; hon/Bronze Star; Lttr of Commend w Ribbon; Am Campaign WWII; Nat Defense Medal; Asiatic Pacific Campaign; Korean Ser Medal; Commend Ribbon; Cert'd Reg'd C of C Exec; Hon St Farmer 1974; Hon Chapt Farmer 1975 & 80; Boss of Yr, ABWA, Globe Chapt 1973; W/W S&SW 1968; 1 of 75 Businessmen in US to Attend the 39th Jt Civilian Orientation Conf & to Tour Mil Installations in US as Guest of Defense Dept.

MANGIERI, TERESA ANN oc/Band and Chorus Director; b/June 20, 1958; h/PO Box 281, Tabor City, NC 28463; ba/Tabor City; p/Margaret Mangieri, Rockville, MD; ed/BME E Carolina Univ 1980; pa/Band & Chorus Dir, Tabor City Primary HS; NCAE; MENC; NCMEA; Phi Kappa Phi; Pi Kappa Lambda; r/Luth; hon/Outstg Col Grad Register; Grad magna cum laude ECU.

MANGOLD-CLARK, LANA CAROLE oc/Professor; b/July 30, 1943; h/Dallas, TX; ba/Sch Home Economics, N Tex St Univ, Denton, TX 76203; m/James L Clark; c/Juston L Clark; p/Curtis E and Bennie J Paramore, Kilgore, TX; ed/BS Tex Wom's Univ 1965; MA 1972, PhD 1973 Univ Tex Austin; pa/Div Dir Profl Ed in Home Ec, Col Ed, N Tex St Univ 1974-; Field Coor Title III Accountability Proj, Comal & Eanes Indep Sch Dist, Austin, Tex 1973; Res Assoc Curric & Instr Dept Univ Tex Austin 1972-73; Tchg Assoc Dept Curric & Instr, Univ Tex Austin 1971-72; Ednl Adm Intern, Brazosport Indep Sch Dist 1971; Tchg Asst Home Ec Dept Univ Tex Austin 1970; Curric Spec Inst for Study of Hlth & Soc, Wash DC

1970; Voc Home Ec Tchr, John H Reagan HS, Austin Indep Sch Dist 1967-69; Sub Tchr Austin Indep Sch Dist 1966; Dallas Indep Sch Dist Clrm Tchr of Home Ec, Marsh Jr HS 1965-66; Asst for TASCO 1970; Conslt-Grp Ldr for Ctr for Public Sch Ethnic Studies Grp Technique-Culture Awareness Sems & Wkshops 1972-; Nat Coun on Fam Relats 1971-73; Am Home Ec Assn; Tex Home Ec Assn; Tex St Tchrs Assn 1965-71; Austin Assn Tchrs 1967-70; NEA; Voc Homemaking Tchrs Assn of Tex; Assn for Supervision & Curric Devel; Tex Assn Col Tchrs; Home Ec Ed Assn; Am Voc Assn; hon/Hon Grad Tex Wom's Univ 1965; Rec'd Home Ec Dept S'ship 1969; Rec'd Ima Hogg S'ship UT at Austin Home Ec Dept 1969; Spec Scholastic Recog, Univ Tex Austin 1972-73; Outstg Yng Wom Am 1977; Phi Theta Kappa; Omicron Nu; Phi Lambda Theta; Kappa Delta Pi; Phi Dalta Kappa; Delta Kappa Gamma, VP 1978-80; Author *Great Ideas: Teaching Home Economics Through Bulletin Boards* 1979; Co-Author Num Profl Articles.

MANN, CHARLES KENNETH oc/Executive Director; b/Aug 16, 1914; h/601 Eden Dr, Longview, TX 75601; ba/Longview; m/Vivien A; c/David K; p/Charles J (dec) and Thresa B Mann (dec); ed/Grad Nyack Bible Col 1933; BA Gordon Col 1942; MDiv Gordon-Conwell Theol Sem 1945; mil/Tex St Guard Chaplain Lt Col; pa/Chap LeTourneau Col 1946-55; Min of Pastoral Care, First Bapt Ch, Longview 1955-78; Exec Dir Longview Fam Cnslg Ctr 1978-; Clin Mem Assn Marriage & Fam Cnslrs; Christian Assn Marriage & Fam Cnslrs; Prot Hosp Assn, Col of Chaps; cp/Rotary Intl; Am Cancer Soc, Gregg North Unit; Bd Dirs Salvation Army; Longview Mtl Hlth Assn; r/Bapt; hon/Mayors Awd, Cert of Achmt for Exceptl Ser 1980; Phi Alpha Theta 1972; Tex St Guard Assn Cert of Achmt 1978.

MANNING, ALTHA oc/Educator; b/Aug 23, 1939; h/1405 Suwanee Rd, Daytona Bch, FL 32014; m/George Russell; c/George Russell II; p/William Doby and Aldonia H Flowers, Tallahassee, FL; ed/BS Fla A&M Univ 1961; MS III Inst Technol 1971; Further Study Univ NC Greensboro, Duke Univ; pa/HS SS Tchr 1961-68, 1971-72; Prog Assoc Lrng Inst of NC 1968-70; Coor Early Childhood, Region 5 NC Dept Public Instr 1972-75; Commun Col Instr, Child Devel 1976-78; Coor Spec Sers 1978, Coor Lrng Support Ctr, Daytona Bch Commun Col; Pres Fla Assn Ed Oppor Prog Pers 1981-83; Exec Br & Conf Chm So Assn Ed Oppor Prog Pers; Fla Assn Commun Cols; APGA; NARDSPE; Fla Devel Ed For Commun Cols; cp/Pres U Child Care; Pres So Ridgewood Elem PTA; VP St Timothy's Lrng Ctr Bd; Chm AAUW Study Grp; Dem Wom's Clb; Daytona Fine Arts Coun; Past Pres Volusia Assn for Chd Under Six; Past Conf Chm Fla Assn Chd Under Six; Coalition for Commun Action; NAACP; Epis Chwom; r/Epis; hon/Exemplary Progr Awd, Fla CC Assn Div of Student Devel 1979; W/W S&SW 1980; Vols of Public Schs 1980; Adm for Child Yth & Fams Awd for Outstg Ser; Contbr to Ednl Jours.

MANNING, BETH SHELTON oc/Artist, Educator; b/June 29, 1935; h/601 N Ave D, Kermit, TX 79745; m/John Ridder; c/John Rory, Jeffrey Britton; p/Henry Shelton, Kermit, TX; Stella Vida Shelton (dec); ed/BA W Tex St Univ 1965; MA Tex Tech Univ 1970; Post Grad Study Univ Tex Permian Basin; pa/Owner Little Porch Frame & Gal; Former Owner M&M Fin; Profl Cnslr; Edr GT Chd; Profl Artist; Tex PGA; SW Watercolor Soc; Sands Art Assn; Odessa Art Assn; Tex St Tchrs Assn; cp/Fdg Mem October Affairs Art Show; Exec Mem October Affair Bd; r/Bapt; hon/Winner Num Awds & Ribbons in Art; Paintings in Pvt Collects in Tex, Okla, NM, Ga.

MANNING, DAVID A oc/Minister of Music, Teacher, Piano Tuner; b/Dec 5, 1943; h/122 E Holly Ave, Dunn, NC 28334; ba/Dunn; m/Glenda G; c/Dana, Gina, Carla; p/Samuel David Manning, New Bern, NC; Mary Irene Mitchell Manning (dec); ed/Cert US Army Sch Mus; Att'd ECU; mil/AUS 440th Army Band 82nd Div Band, Green Beret Drum & Bugle Corps; pa/Composer; Tchr; Piano Tuner-Tech; Min Mus; cp/Full Gospel Bus Mens F'ship Intl; r/Pentecostal Holiness; hon/Citizenship Awd; Superior Ratings 4 Yrs Intl Piano Guild Auditions.

MANNING, LEAH V oc/Retired Dress Maker; b/June 23, 1920; m/James Baliver Jr; c/Joseph Clifton; p/Benjamin Smith (dec) and Sarah Williams Vick, Nashville, NC; pa/Retired Dressmaker; Ordained Min Ch of Gospel Min; hon/Hon DD, Ch of Gospel Min Inc.

MANSFIELD, ASA oc/Oilfield Driller, Shipyard Operator; County Commissioner; b/July 7, 1907; h/Rt 1 Box 256, Orange, TX 77630; m/Mabel; p/Bouregard (dec) and Melina Mansfield (dec); pa/Orange Co Commr; cp/Mason; Odd Fellow; Lions Clb; Rotary; hn/Rec'd Plaque from S Regional Plan'g 1980; Rec'd Plaque K of C 1981; Plaque of Ser Commr 1951-80.

MANSON, FREDERICK LEE oc/Guidance Counselor; b/Mar 2, 1917; h/Baton Rouge, LA; ba/Plaquemine, LA; m/Evelyn B; c/Cheryl LaVerne Thompson, Frederick L II; p/S L and Laura A Manson, Keystone, WV; ed/BS So Univ 1947; Masters Deg Tex So Univ, Houston 1969; Guid Cert,

St of La; mil/AUS 1942-45; pa/Guid Cnslr, Plaquemine Sr HS; Iberville Parish Sch Bd; APGA; NVGA; JK Haynes Foun; Legal Defense Fund; NCTE; cp/Dem Party; NAACP; r/Bapt.

MANUEL, PAUL NEAL oc/Retired Postal Clerk; b/Mar 25, 1918; h/PO Box 121, Pulaski, VA 24301; m/Aileen Reed; c/Paul Neal Jr; p/Guy N (dec) and Ada Manuel, Max Meadows, VA; mil/AUS WWII; r/Ch of the Brethren; hon/Purple Heart; 26 Yrs Ser Awd US Postal Ser.

MARANTZ, BART oc/Musician, Instructor; b/Apr 6, 1950; h/819 Duane St, Hattiesburg, MS 39401; ba/Ellisville, MS; m/Sara Mann; p/Herbert and Florence D Marantz, Miami, FL; ed/Att'd Ind Univ; BMus Univ Miami 1973; att'd New England Conservatory 1975-77; pa/Jazz and Big Band Mus; Instr Mus Jones Co Jr Col; r/Hebrew.

MARBURY, LARRY A oc/Pharmacist; b/Nov 13, 1948; h/228-3A Robert Jemison Rd, Homewood, AL 35209; b/B'ham; c/Jumaane; p/James Jr (dec) and Lula Mae Marbury, Alexander City, AL; ed/AS Alexander City St Jr Col 1969; BS Auburn Univ 1973; pa/Reg'd Pharm; Owner-Mgr: Marbury's Discount Pharm, Marbury's Variety & Gift Shoppe, Marbury's Laundramat; B'ham Metro Pharm Soc, VP; Ala Pharm Assn; Jefferson Co Pharm Assn; Nat Assn Retail Druggists; Nat Pharm Assn; cp/32° Mason; r/AME; hon/Booker T Washington Bus Col, Bus Mgmt Merit Awd; W/W SE; Intl Achievers.

MARCHMAN, JAMES FRANKLIN JR oc/Merchant; b/Apr 27, 1913; h/303 Morgan St, Forest City, NC 29043; ba/Forest City; m/Alva C; c/James F III, Philip R, Marilyn Sue Veal; p/Rev & Mrs J F Marchman (dec); ed/BA Georgetown Col 1933; AF Pilots Trg, Ottawa Col 1942; Harrisburg Air Intell Sch 1943; mil/USAF 1942-46 Capt; pa/Western Auto Supply Co: 1935-52, 1946-53 (Store to Dist to Div to Home Ofc Sales Promo Mgr); NC Airports Assn Chm of Bd; Rutherford Co Aviation Auth Chm; Intl Execs Ser Corp; Pilot for 51 Yrs; cp/Kiwanis Clb, Sr Mem, Past Pres, Past Lt Gov; Aircraft Owner & Pilots Assn; OX5 Aviation Pioneers; r/Bapt; Coor Bapt Mens Overseas Missions Proj for NC; Deacon; hon/NC Bapt Mens Outstg Layman of Yr 1979; Kiwanis Man of Yr 1969; Pres Forest City C of C 1969.

MARCUM, GORDON G II oc/Attorney, Executive; b/July 4, 1942; h/2607 Lockheed St, Midland, TX 79701; ba/Midland; m/Margaret Burleson; c/Michal Elizabeth, Gordon Matthew, Jeffrey Wallace; p/Gordon G Sr and Marjorie Shelton Marcum, Midland, TX; ed/BBA w Hons 1964, JD 1967 Univ Okla; mil/AUS Capt; pa/Dir Oil & Gas, St of NM 1969-71; VP, Atty Marcum Drilling Co 1971-78; VP, Exploration Mgr, Olix Industs Inc & Olix Energy Co 1978–; Tex Bar Assn; Am Assn Petro Landmen; Intl Assn Drilling Contractors, VP 1978; Cert'd Profl Landman; cp/City Coun-man Place #2 (Mayor Pro-Tem); C of C; Midland Country Clb, VP 1981; Permian Civic Ballet, Pres 1979; Mid-Tran Comm; Am Cancer Soc; r/Presb: Deacon, Treas; hon/Outstg Resident, Cross Ctr, Univ Okla 1961; True Gentleman Awd, Sigma Alpha Epsilon 1962; J C Mayfield Awd, Outstg Ldrship, Univ Okla 1963; Dist'd Mil Student 1963-64; Am Assn Petro Landmen S'ship 1963-64; Dist'd Mil Grad 1964; Dean's Hon Roll 1963-64; Julian Rothbaum Awd, Outstg Grad Awd 1964; Ldrship Awd, Ofcr Basic Course 1968; Upper 2% of All Capts in Adj General Corps, AUS; AUS Commend Medal 1969.

MARCUM, HILDA BERNIECE oc/Teacher; b/Apr 5, 1954; h/Louisa, KY; p/James and Imogene Courtney Marcum, Louisa, KY; ed/AB Berea Col 1977; Elem Cert by Commonwlth of Ky & Dept of Ed 1977-87; pa/Elem Tchr, Lawrence Co Bd Ed, Louisa, KY; NEA; KEA; PTA, Treas 1980-81; cp/Louisa Commun Choir; Berea Col Alumni Assn; r/Bapt; hon/Berea Col Chapel Choir 1972-76; Jr Wom's Clb S'ship 1972; Hall of Fame 1975, Berea Col Dramatics Dept.

MARIAH, BRYMER BRADFORD oc/County Agent; b/May 11, 1926; h/PO Box 275, Rockford, AL 35136; ba/Rockford; p/George W (dec) and Easter D Bradford (dec); ed/BS; MEd; pa/Co Agt Home Ec; AAEHE; AEHE; ACESEO; NEA; AEA; AHEA; IHEA; cp/ARC; Chm ARCV; SEASHA; NAACP; CCCC; RMB; Dem Party; r/Bapt; hon/Alpha Kappa Mu; W/W: Am Wom, World Wom.

MARKER, DAN E oc/School Director; b/Nov 29, 1937; h/Rt 6 Box 610, Shawnee, OK 74801; ba/Shawnee; m/Midge; c/David, Chele; p/Perry and Madge Marker; ed/BA Eng; MEd Cnslg; PhD Cnslg-Psych; pa/Dir Liberty Acad (Pvt Christian Sch); cp/Active in Cvic & Commun Affairs; r/Prot; Ordained to the Gospel Min.

MARKHAM, WILLIAM HUBERT oc/Pastor; b/Mar 8, 1937; h/306 Hundred Oaks, Ruston, LA 71270; ba/Ruston; m/Pauline McKinney; c/William Blain, Patricia Rene, Lori Ann, Carla Yvette; p/C H and Hazel Markham, Texarkana, TX; ed/BA E Tex Bapt Col; pa/Bapt Pastor; hon/W/W: S, Rel; Commun Ldrs & Noteworthy Ams; DIB.

MARKS, ALPHONSE MICHAEL oc/Instructor; b/May 29, 1957; h/Christina Apts #263, Hattiesburg, MS 39401; ba/Lumberton, MS; p/Alphonse and Mary B Marks, Magnolia, MS; ed/BS 1977, MS 1981 Univ So Miss; pa/Instr of Debate, Drama & Mus Theatre, Lumberton HS; Dir Travelling Song & Dance Show Grp "Company"; Outreach Chm, Lumberton Chapt Miss Assn Edrs; Miss Speech Assn; Nat Forensic Leag Affiliate; cp/Pres Lamar Co 4-H Adv Coun; Exec Dir Miss Lamar Co S'ship Pageant; Dir Lumberton Little Theatre; Dir Lumberton Forensic Leag; Alumni Rep Omega Psi Phi; Hist Gamma Chi Chapt Kappa Kappa Psi; r/Bapt; Dir Mus; hon/Interfrat Coun Awd Acad Excell 1977; Outstg Bandsman of Kappa Kappa Psi 1975; Outstg Dir Miss St Talent Hunt 1979; Guest Spkr Nat 4-H Conf 1975; Guest Perfr Miss SLAM Conv 1980; Lions Clb Plaque for Outstg Involvement in Commun Affairs 1981.

MARKS, JOHN COURTNEY oc/Systems Engineer; b/Mar 1, 1924; ba/Med Ctr at Bowling Green, 250 Pk St, Bowling Green, KY 42101; m/Henrietta Horton; c/Barbara, Lynn, Michael, Paul, Debra; p/dec; ed/BS Univ Scranton 1953; mil/AUS 1942-44; pa/Mgmt Engr, Med Ctr at Bowling Green 1979–; Mgr Support Sys, Ky Hlth Sys Agcy 1977-79; Admr Shalomwald Hosp 1976-77; Sys Engrg Conslt, Sts Mary & Elizabeth Hosp 1974-76; Sys Engr, Humana Inc 1969-73; Res Engr Kentec Labs 1967-69; Res Engr-Prod Engr Am Air Filter Co 1963-67; Chief Engr Louisville Med Ctr 1956-63; Asst Chief Engr, Air Pollution Control Dist 1953-56; Conslt to Battelle Meml Inst 1953-54; Instr, Univ Louisville 1954; Conslt to US Public Hlth Ser 1955; Conslt to Inst of Indust Res Univ L'ville 1962; L'ville Sci Couns, Com on Sci Sem in Sec'dy Schs 1957-61; Pres Chapt 1 Nat Assn Power Engrs 1960; Chm L'ville Engrg & Sci Socs Coun 1961; Nat Chm Com on Air Pollution, Nat Assn Pwr Engrs 1961; Instr Sys Design Course, Bellarmine Col 1975; Past Pres L'ville Engrg & Sci Coun; Past Pres Nat Assn Pwr Engrs Ky #1; Am Assn Comprehensive Hlth Plan'g; Hosp Mgmt Sys Soc; Am Soc Engrg Ed; Am Meteorological Soc; cp/Bd Appeals, Jefferson Co Bldg Dept, L'ville 1957-63; Metro Plan'g Coun, L'ville 1958; Acute Care Tech Adv Grp, Ky Hlth Sys Agcy West; Barren River Sub-Area Hlth Coun; hon/Commend, US Public Hlth Ser 1956; Awd'd Mem-at-Large, L'ville Engrg & Sci Socs Coun for Ser to Coun 1960; Ser Awd, Air Pollution Control Assn 1960; Commend Berg Sci Foun 1961; Commend Engrs Coun for Profl Devel 1961; Num Profl Publs Incl'g "Air Pollution Enabling Acts" 1953 & "Cost of Health Planning & the Certificate of Need Process" 1978.

MARKS, MARY ELIZABETH oc/Newspaper Feature Writer/Reporter, Free-Lance Writer, Poet; b/Sept 3, 1909; h/10 Alina Ln, Hot Springs Village, AR 71909; ba/Same; m/R G; c/Carol Ann Evans, Jeanne Beth Jones, Gale Bender; p/Wayne and Mary Jane Pierson Mettler (dec); ed/Eng Maj; pa/Newsroom *LaVilla*; Life Mem Ill Wom's Press Assn; r/U Meth Ch; hon/Wom of Yr, IWPA 1972; Prizes for Prose & Poetry.

MARKUSSEN, JERRY V oc/Research Hydraulic Engineer; b/Mar 22, 1955; h/220 Rhodes Dr, Vicksburg, MS 39180; ba/V'burg; p/Kenwood and Lillian Markussen, Vienna, VA; ed/BS VPI & SU 1977; Att'g Miss St Univ; pa/Res Hydraulic Engr, Waterways Expt Sta, Vicksburg; cp/Pres V'burg Men's Soccer Leag 1980-81; Cadet Commdr, Old Dominion Cadet Squadron 1971-73; Fairfax, Va Civil Air Patrol; r/Bapt; hon/Lttr of Commend James Madison HS 1973; Spec Ser Awd, Waterways Expt Sta 1980.

MARLIN, JEFF THOMAS oc/Evangelist, Author, Businessman; b/Sept 23, 1914; h/PO Box 667, Duncan, OK 73533; ba/Same; m/Ora McBroom; c/Sue Garner, Jerry; p/R D (dec) and Bertha Davis Marlin (dec); ed/LLD Magic Val Christian Col; pa/Delivered Over 3000 Illustr'd Lects on the Bible Lands; Author *Bible Land Illustrated*; Invited by Turkish Tourism to Write First Biblical Guide to the Seven Churches of Asia; Marlin Tours; Hall Mark Gift Stores; cp/Kiwanis; Spec Lects on Capitol Punishment & Other Issues; r/Ch of Christ; hon/Tenn Vol; Ky Col; Hon Lt Col Aide-de-Camp.

MARMO, FRANKLIN CHRISTOPHER oc/Editor; b/Jan 9, 1930; h/Box 1735 North Bch St, Daytona Bch, FL 32015; ba/Ormond Bch, FL; m/Stella; c/Marie Mullaney, Christopher; Carloyn Sofie; p/Louis and Marie Errico Marmo, Newark, NJ; ed/BS; MA; PhD; pa/Editor *North Florida Times-Journal*; Sports Editor *Halifax Reporter*; Fla Press Assn; Secy-Treas U Fed Col Tchrs; AFL-CIO Local 1841; Pres Essex Co Bd Ed; Commr Essex Co Bd Sch Estimate; cp/FOP; Fla Lodge #22; Florida on Patrol Pub; Hon Mem Fla Sheriff's Assn 1979; r/U Ch of Christ; hon/Good Citizenship Medal; SAR; W/W: Am, En US & Can; Men of Intl Achmt.

MARQUISS, JANE CHATTEN oc/Building Contractor, Interior Designer; b/Sept 30, 1927; h/Rt 4 Box 200A, Clinton, TN 37716; ba/Same; m/John H; c/Christine M Ganzer; p/Carney E (dec) and Elsie Mae Chatten (dec); ed/Cert Arts Monticello Col 1947; Dip Chgo Sch Interior Design 1960; pa/Assoc, E V Murphy Construction Co 1961-64; Interior Decorator, Interiors by Marie Wilde 1965-67; Pres Marquiss &

Bice Construction Inc 1967-74; Owner-Mgr Jane Marquiss Construction Co 1976-; Nat Small Bus Assn; cp/Repub Party; r/Epis; hon/W/W Am Wom 1979.

MARRERO, FRANK oc/Manager; b/Oct 28, 1916; h/Rt 1 FM 2965, Wills Point, TX 75169; ba/Wills Pt; m/Ruby M; c/Frankie, Mike, John, Frankie A; p/Isidro (dec) and Mercedes Marrero (dec); ed/Cand BBA 1981; mil/AUS Ret'd Chief Warrant Ofcr; pa/Mgr C of C Wills Pt; Num Mil Positions; cp/YMCA; Rotary Intl Bd Dirs Meth Ch Wills Pt; Cubmaster Pack 379; Wills Pt Ath Clb; Band Booster Clb; r/Meth; hon/2 Nat Defense Medals; UN Ser Medal 1955; Dept Army Suggestion Awd Cert 1961; Cert of Achmt 1964; 4 Army Commend Medals; 2 Merit Ser Medals; 2 Bronze Stars; 2 Vietnam Ser Medals; USAR Ser Medal, 30 Yrs Ser 1975; Ethiopian Star Order Medal 1955; Korean Ser Medal 1955; Vietnam Ordnance Badge 1970; Vietnam Commend Medal 1970; Vietnam Cross of Gallantry w Palm 190; Vietnam Armed Forces Hon Medal 1971; Over 50 Lttrs of Commend &/or Apprec; Author Sev Mil Handbooks.

MARRERO, RUBY M oc/Continuing Education Coordinator; b/July 10, 1940; h/Rt 1 FM 2965, Wills Point, TX 75169; m/Frank; c/Frankie, Mike, John, Frankie A; p/Michael Moss and Reppie B Rushing Rasbury, Terrell, TX; ed/Dip Profl Nsg, So Meth Univ, Meth Hosp of Dallas Sch of Nsg 1962; Futher Study in Coronary Care & Respiratory Therapy; BS E Tex St Univ 1979; MBA Cand ETSU; pa/Cont'g Ed Coor, Staff Devel Dept, Tex Dept MH Hlth & Mtl Retard 1978-; Coor Mtl Hlth & Mtl Retard Sers Series Tng, Terrell St Hosp, Tex Dept MH/MR 1976-78; RN Supvr 1975-76; Travel in Europe 1972-75; RN Supvr, Martha T Berry Med Care Facility, Mt Clemens, Mich 1967-72; Profl Nsg Staff Mem, VA Hosp, Dallas 1965-67; Dispensary Nsg Ser Coor, Nelingen AUS Dispensary 1963-67; Dir Nsg Sers, Colonial Hosp, Terrell, Tex 1962-63; ANA; Cont'g Ed & Approval Prog, Tex Nurses Assn; TNA; Am Heart Assn; Intergovtl Tng Coun; Am Red Cross; cp/Dallas Metro Intergovtl Coun; r/Meth; hon/Nom'd Trainer of Yr Awd, Dallas Metro Intergovtl Coun; Awd of Merit, Am Red Cross 1962; CPR Task Force Chm.

MARRS, WILLLIAM L oc/Public Relations; b/Dec 3, 1910; h/PO Box 781, Johnson City, TN 37601; ba/Same; m/Pauline Scott; c/Patricia M Wilson, Sandra M Dimick; p/Batter and Minnie Pogue Marrs, Fayetteville, TN; pa/Newspaper Column; Radio & TV; cp/Scottish Rite; Sportsman's Clb of Am; Outdoor Writers of Am; Better Sport's Inst; r/U Meth; hon/Mr Heart 1977; Fishing Hall of Fame; Hon Mem Ruritan.

MARSDEN, RUTH ELIZABETH oc/Retired Teacher; b/Jan 31, 1909; h/1 Azalea Rd, PO Box 125, Toccoa Falls, GA 30577; p/Thomas LeRoy and Julia Koehn Marsden, Springfield, IL; ed/BA; BMus; MMus; EdD; pa/Spec in Keyboard & Ch Mus; Composer-in-Residence, Toccoa Falls Col; r/Prot; hon/World W/W Ed; Personalities of Am.

MARSH, JOSEPH VIRGIL oc/Research Specialist; b/Apr 28, 1952; h/PO Box 12, Rt 1, Ararat, NC 27007; p/Gilliam Hughes and Dovie Elizabeth Watson Marsh; ed/Surrey Commun Col 1970-72; Coop Engrg Prog, US Govt Schs, Md, SC, Wash 1972-74; pa/Jt Armed Sers Tech Liaison, Wash 1974-75; Conslt US Govt 1975-76; Conslt Indivs & Bus on Tech Matters, Ararat, NC 1977-; Intl Entrepreneurs Assn; Ind Conslts Assn; Inst Assn Sci Devel; Coun on Civilian Tech Advrs; cp/VFW; Armerd Forces Assn; Repub Party.

MARSH, RANDALL CONWAY oc/Teacher; b/Dec 5, 1948; h/1526 17th St S, Birmingham, AL 35205; ba/B'ham; m/Haden Gaines; c/Kimberly Ann; p/Jack Huey and Katherine Jennings Marsh, B'ham, AL; ed/BA Samford Univ; MA Univ Ala 1974; pa/Eng Lit Tchr, Ala Sch Fine Arts; Dir B'ham Fest Theatre; r/Bapt; hon/Marian Galloway-Ralph Belamy Awd for Acting 1974; B'ham Fest Arts Silver Bowl for Drama 1977; Obelisk Awd for Directing 1978.

MARSHALL, ARTHUR GLENN oc/Retired Accountant; Director United Way; b/Jan 9, 1906; h/304 Wilson Ave, Maryville, TN 37801; ba/M'ville; m/Dorothy Alexander Huff; c/Virginia Carol Ramsey; p/Gates McMahan (dec) and Mary Houston Marshall (dec); ed/Att'd Univ Tenn 1925, 26, 27, 28; Dip Ldrship Trg Meth Epis Ch 1935; pa/Tchr Blount Co, Tenn 1924-29; Alumninum Co of Am, Alcoa, Tenn 1929-71; Dir U Way, Blount Co 1980-; 25 Yr Ser Clb Alcoa: Pres, VP, Dir, Secy; Alcoten Clb, Secy; Blount Co Tchrs Assn, Past VP; Nat, St & Blount Co Tchrs Assns; cp/Blount Co Rec Coun; M'ville Bd Charities, Past Pres; Vol Blount Co U Way; M'ville City Sch Bd 26 Yrs, Chm 20 Yrs, VChm 4 Yrs; Tenn Sch Bd Assn, Dir E Dist; r/U Meth; hon/Hon'd First U Meth Ch, M'ville 1977; Scroll of Apprec First U Meth Ch 1959; Cert of Apprec in Recog of Sers, U Meth Men of M'ville First U Meth Ch 1974; Tenn Sch Bds Assn Dist'd Ser Awd 1975; Tenn Sch Bds Assn, Qtr Century Clb Cert from Outstg Ser Rendered to M'ville City Bd Ed 1975; Plaque for Outstg & Dedicated Ser 1975; Dist'd Mem Awd, M'ville First U Meth Ch 1976; Rec'd U Way of Blount Co, Tenn Champaign Awd 1977; U Way Gold Awd for Outstg Ser to People of Blount Co 1978; Heisman Trophy Awd for

Successfully Reaching the Industry Section Goal in 1979 Blount Co U Way Campaign 1979.

MARSHALL, DAVID oc/Executive; b/Sept 25, 1937; ba/PO Box 241, Memphis, TN 39126; m/Catherine W; c/Valerie, Amelia, David Jr; p/Freeman (dec) and Carrie L Marshall, Columbus, GA; ed/Att'd Geo Wash Univ 1955-56; Univ Houston 1973-79; mil/USAR; pa/Afro Am Life Ins Co 1958-76; Asst VP-Regional Agcy Dir Universal Life Ins Co 1976-; cp/Frontiers Intl, Past Pres; r/Wall Chapel Amez Ch; Chm Trustee Bd; hon/Mgr of Yr 1964, 65, 67, 71, 73, 74.

MARSHALL, H RICHARD JR oc/Dentist; b/Nov 16, 1941; h/Lewisburg, WV; ba/120 Maplewood Ave, Ronceverte, WV 24970; m/Gail M; c/Mary Page, Lucy MacLee; p/Clair A and Mary Board Carter; ed/BS WVa St Col 1966; DDS WV Univ Sch Dentistry 1970; pa/Pvt Prac Dentist 1971-; Dir ESEA Title I Dental Prog 1970-71; Am Dental Assn; WV Dental Assn, Secy 1976-, Exec Coun Rep 1971-75; Greenbrier Val Dental Soc, Pres 1977-78, VP 1976, Secy-Treas 1973-75, Chm Chd's Dental Hlth Month 1980-; Am Acad Operative Dentistry; George M Hollenbeck Operative Dentistry Sem; Greenbrier Val Hosp Staff 1979-; Bd Dirs WVa Div Am Cancer Soc; Dental Conslt: Greenbrier Manor Nsg Home, Potomac House Nsg Home, Greenbrier Ctr for Retard'd Chd; cp/Phi Kappa Psi; Psi Omega, Editor Alumni Chapt 1978-80; Lewisburg Elks Lodge; Lewisburg Lodge #42 AF & AM; Ronceverte Chapt #2 RAM; Greenbrier Commandry #15 KT; Beni Kedem Shrine Temple; Ath Coun WVa Univ; Chm Mountaineer S'ship Fund, Greenbrier Val Chapt; r/Old Stone Presb Ch: Bd Deacons, Chm 1979; Fin & Budget Com; Pers Com; Christian Ed Com; hn/WVa Univ Sch Dentistry Periodontics Awd 1970.

MARSHALL, KATHRYN AMY oc/School President; b/Nov 11, 1951; h/PO Box 1570, Altamonte Springs, FL 32701; p/Raymond Marshall, Odenwald, W Germany; Loretta Marshall, Arlington, VA; ed/BA Wheaton Col; Att'd Dartmouth Col; Grad Studies: Aiglon Col, Villars, Switz 1970; SMC Dorset, England 1968; pa/Pres & Secy Small Corp; Pres Nat Trade Sch; Intl Bartending Inst Inc; Va Assn Trade & Tech Schs; cp/BBB of Metro Wash DC; C of C; r/Cath; hon/Author of Intl Bartending Inst Inc's Copyrighted Textbook.

MARSHALL, ROBERT ARCILLIOUS oc/Assistant Pastor, Machine Operator; b/Feb 5, 1945; h/Tulsa, OK; ba/419 N Elgin Ave, Tulsa, OK; m/Marie; c/Dee Dee, Charles R; p/Preston Marshall, Las Vagas, NV; Margaret Marshall, Houston, TX; ed/Att'd Moody Bible Inst 1979-80; Tulsa Jr Col 1981; mil/AUS 1963-69 Paratrooper; pa/Am Airlines: Ramp Supvr, Temp Instr, Blast Machine Oper; Fdr Berean Evangelistic Outreach Mission; cp/Chaplain A Phillip Randolf, Tulsa Br; r/Bapt; hon/Purple Heart; Vietnam Medal of Hon; Author "Jesus, Yesterday, Today and Forever" & "The Christian and Halloween."

MARSICOVETE, JOSEPH CHARLES oc/Communications Consultant; b/Mar 6, 1955; h/1123 Westview Terr, Laurel, MD 20810; ba/Wash DC; p/Joseph R and Jean Marsicovete, Mine Hill, NJ; ed/BA Rider Col 1977; MA Univ Md 1978; pa/Mgr Consumer Res Wn Union Telegraph Co, Communs Const, Trg & Res; Am Soc Trg & Devel; SCA; ECA; SOCAP; r/Cath; hon/W/W Students in Am Cols & Univs 1975; Grad summa cum laude Rider Col 1977.

MARTIN, CAROLYN SUE oc/Lumbermill; b/Nov 25, 1962; h/Box 393, Rt 3, Baxter, TN 38544; p/Allon Terry and Mary Dimple Martin, Baxter, TN 38544; ed/HS Grad; cp/VP Dist FFA 1980; Treas Chapt FFA; Treas HS Sr Class; r/Ch of Christ; hon/Best Defensive Player, Basketball; Best Sportsman Awd; Star Greenhand Awd; Indust Arts Awd.

MARTIN, CLIFFORD WELLS oc/Farmer, Teacher; b/Aug 16, 1903; h/Box 368, Wrens, GA 30833; m/Jean H; c/Clifford W Jr (dec), Walter B, Joseph Burch (dec); p/Millard P Martin Sr (dec); ed/Univ Ga Agric; mil/USN Signalman WWII; pa/Feed & Farm Supplies; Cotton Ginner; Tchr; Farmer; cp/Wrens Kiwanis Clb, Prog Chm 12 Yrs, Past Pres, VP; r/Meth; hon/Aghon Gridiron; Pres Soph Class; Pres Ag Hill Coun; Blue Key; X Clb; Saddle & Sirloin Clb; W/W Am Col & Univs.

MARTIN, DEBORAH LOUISE MORGAN oc/Realtor Associate; b/Oct 21, 1917; h/Newport News, VA; m/John Dick Jr; c/John Dick III; p/Jimmie Jubal (dec) and Callie Maude Wright Morgan (dec); ed/Att'd Roanoke Nat Bus Col 1937; Univ Va; Class A Rltrs Inst, St Leo Col; Peggy Newton Cosmetics Sales Trg Course 1956; Newport News Adult Ed, Real Est Dip 1971; Tailoring & Adv'd Tailoring 1971; Other Trg Courses; pa/Secy Westinghouse Elec Supply Co 1937; Receptionist-Secy Grace Hosp 1937-39; Secy Vicco Fuel Corp, Sales Div of Va Iron Coal & Coke Co 1939-41; Secy Blue Diamond Coal Corp 1941; Housing Mgr Fed Public Housing Auth 1942-45; Asst Housing Mgr, Fed Public Housing Auth 1945-46; Asst to Proj Mgr, Erection of Low Rent Housing for City of Roanoke 1946-47; Br Mgr Peggy Newton Cosmetics 1948-58; Br Mgr

House of Hollywood Cosmetics 1956-58; Housing Construction Mgr John D Martin Co 1947-49; Rltr Assoc: Ward Rlty & Ins Co 1972, Landon Rlty 1972, Chuck Klein Rlty 1973, Eagle Properties Ltd 1977-79, Atkins & Co Inc 1979, Powell & Morewitz Rlty Inc 1980; Mktg Conslt Universal Equipment & Supply Co 1980; Newport News Bd Rltrs; MLS Va Assn Rltrs; Richmond Nat Assn Rltrs; Chgo Wom's Coun Rltrs; Va Wom's Coun Rltrs; Va Peninsula Wom's Coun of Rltrs; cp/Lady of Khedive Shrine Temple; Lady of Kazim Shrine Temple; Santa's Elf for Clbs & Orgs; Howard Baker Pes Campaign Task Force Mem 1980; Gov John N Dalton Campaigner for Elect 1978; US Hist Soc; Richmond Area Friendship Force Assn; Spkrs Bur, Richmond Area Friendship Force Assn 1980; Friendship Force Clb of En Va 1980; Elec Night Watch, Wash DC; r/Meth; hon/W/W Am Wom 1981; Intl Platform Assn 1981; Rec'd Sev Ribbons for Short Stories in Wom's Clb Contests; Won Trip to NY by Peggy Newton Cosmetics; Author "A Compact Cottage."

MARTIN, DOLORES LEONARD oc/Teacher; b/Dec 30, 1937; h/104 Mina St, Enterprise, AL 36330; ba/Ft Rucker, AL; m/Joseph I Jr; c/Catherine Ann, Joseph I, Sandra Elizabeth; p/Willie Hoyd (dec) and Margaret Viola Yarbarough Leonard, Lexington, NC; ed/BS UNC-Greensboro; MA Troy St Univ; mil/1st Lt USA Phys Therapist 1960-62; pa/Phy Ed Tchr, Ft Rucker Prim Sch; AEA; NEA; AAHPER; Alpha Delta Kappa; SACUS; NAYEC; PDK; AAUW; Coffee Co Arts Allicance; Reg'd Voter; YMCA Bd; Ofcrs Wives Clb Ft Rucker; r/Cath; hon/Wom of Yr 1979, Enterprise.

MARTIN, DORIS-MARIE CONSTABLE oc/Artist; b/May 7, 1941; h/65 Woodland Rd, Asheville, NC 28804; m/Russell Maylon Jr; c/Robert Matthew, Lisa-Marie; p/Clifford Matthew (dec) and Doris-Marie Gray Constable (dec); ed/AA Miami-Dade Commun Col 1971; BA UNC-Asheville 1976; MA Goddard Col 1980; pa/Self-Employed Artist; Art Tchr Asheville Country Day Sch; Num Art Exhibs; Fdr, Incorporator; First Pres Bd Mem WNC Fibers-Handweavers Assn; Asheville Art Mus; Am Crafts Coun; Handweavers Guild of Am; Fla Craftsmen; NC Art Soc Style & Technique; r/Prot; hon/W/W Am Art 1978; World W/W Wom 1979; IDB 1980; Best Sculpture, Craft Work 1976, Am Crafts Coun; Best Sculpture & One-Man Show, Durham Arts Guild Inc, Allied Arts Ctr, NC 1976; Awd for Sculpture, Springs Mills Traveling Show 1975 & 77.

MARTIN, FRANK MICHAEL (MIKE) oc/Free Lance and Commercial Artist; b/Dec 7, 1950; h/214 Chapman Dr, Lebanon, TN 37087; ba/Same; p/Frank and Willye Harris Martin; ed/Grad Cumberland Col; Att'd MTSU; pa/Free Lance & Commercial Artist; Act'd in Num Prods Incl'g "The Crucible" & "Life with Father"; cp/Bd Trust Sound & Light Co; Lebanon's Commun Theatre; r/Meth; hon/Richard D Lawlor Meml Awd 1980; Completing Illust'd Versions of *Dracula* & *A Christmas Carol*.

MARTIN, LINDA REID oc/Government Manager; b/July 1, 1940; h/408 Watts Br Pkwy, Rockville, MD 20854; ba/Wash DC; m/Howard Truman; c/Kelley Rene Shields; p/Frederick Sherman Reid (dec); Kathryn Elizabeth Jaynes Lindberg, Pacific Palisades, CA; ed/BA Univ Calif Berkeley; pa/Fed Wom's Prog Coun, San Fran, Calif 1973-75; r/Epis; hon/IRS 2 Spec Act Awds; 2 Outstg Achmt Awds.

MARTIN, MELVIN D oc/Dairy Equipment Dealer, Farmer; b/Feb 1, 1930; h/Rt 5, Campbellsville, KY 42718; ba/Same; m/Reba Lee; c/Peggy Ann M Cauld, Stephen D, Janet Lee; p/Cloyd and Amelia Martin, Greensburg, KY; mil/USAF 1951, Korean War; pa/Secy Soil Conserv Dist; Agric Coun; Farming Profl; Dairy Equip Dlr; Agric Rep; cp/Dem Clb; 4-H Clb Ldr 22 Yrs; Pres Fair Bd; Chm Local Commun Ctr; Mason; Kiwanis Clb: r/Bapt; hon/JC Awd; Am Legion Awd; Agric Awd; Dairy Shrine; JC Outstg Yng Farmer; Intl W/W; Notable Ams; Men of Achmt; Book of Hon.

MARTIN, PATTY LOUISE ADAMS oc/Realtor; b/Nov 14, 1928; h/Opelika, AL; m/B J; c/Stan, Joel; p/Andy Claycomb (dec) and Orah McGullian Adams (dec); ed/Ext Courses Auburn Univ 1949; Att'd So Union Jr Col 1974-75; pa/Piano Tchr 1960-74; Real Est Salesp 1974-80; Lee Co Bd Rltrs; Ala Assn Rltrs; Nat Assn Rltrs; cp/Pilot Clb of Lee Co; Opelika Arts Assn, Past Treas 1974; Past Pres Garden Lovers Garden Clb; Past Pres Opelika Fed Garden Clbs; Fdr Opelika Newcomers Clb & Opelika Bridge Clb; r/Meth, Pres SS Class; hon/Sales Assoc of Yr 1979, E B Odom Real Est; Valedictorian HS Grad Glass, Knobel HS 1947; Best All Round Girl, by Fac Knobel HS 1947.

MARTIN, ROBERT L oc/Assistant Professor; b/Jul 6, 1929; h/PO Box 579, Alva, OK 73717; ba/Alva; m/Mary Jo; c/Robert L Jr, Dana C; p/Leo H Martin (dec); Mabelle A Martin, Pueblo, CO; ed/BS 1951, MS 1956 KSTC-Emporia; Addit Study Okla St Univ; pa/Asst Prof Spch & Drama, Debate Coach NWn Okla St Univ; cp/Dir-Actor & Past Pres, Alva Commun Theatre; Dir-Narrator, Outdoor Christmas Pageant, Little Sahara St Park 15 Yrs; PDGER; BPOE; PSVP; Okla Elks Assn; PER, Elks Lodge #1184; Past Pres Rotary; Bd Dirs UF; Co Chm Heart Fund 6 Yrs;

r/Presb; hon/Nescatunga Arts & Humanities Coun Awd for Theatre 1974; Okla Heart Assn Outstg Achmt; BSA Com Th 1975; Cameo Awd, Commun Theatre; Book of Honor; DIB; Intl W/W Commun Ser; Personalities of Am; Intl Register Profiles; Intl W/W Intells; 2000 Notable Ams.

MARTIN, ROBERT R oc/Salesman; b/June 8, 1930; ba/Levelland, TX; m/Ruby; c/Kaua Lattimore, Tony; p/Audrey Chapman, Lamesa, TX; ed/Sev Profl Sales Schs 1969-74; Acctg Schs; mil/USN 4 Yrs Submarine Ser in Pacific & Instr at Submarine Sch 18 Mos; pa/Auto Sales, Ford-Mercury; Grand Master Sales Coun; cp/Square Dance Clb; Lions Clb; Levelland City Coun-man; BSA Dist Chm; hon/Top Salesman in St w Ford Motor Co 1977 & 78.

MARTIN, SHERRILL VIRGINIA oc/Department Chairman; b/Apr 20, 1940; h/2064F Vestavia Pk Ct, Birmingham, AL 35216; ba/B'ham; p/Ollin V and Jewell L Martin, Daleville, AL; ed/BMus Samford Univ; MMus Univ Ala; PhD Univ NC; pa/Chm Mus Dept, Univ Ala-B'ham; Nat Musicology Chm, Mus Tchrs Nat Assn 1976-79; Nat Am Mus Chm 1976 MTNA; Nat Pre-Col Chm for Piano 1973-77, Nat Com Student Activs 1969-77 MTNA; Nat Known Pedagogue, Lectr, Musicologist, Pianist, Harpsichordist; Pi Kappa Lambda; Alpha Lambda Delta; Delta Omicron; MENC; MTNA; Exec Bd Dirs Ala Sch Fine Arts; Yng Artist Auditions Chm, Nat Fed Mus Clbs; cp/Exec Clb of B'ham; B'ham Symph Wom; B'ham Chamber Mus Soc; B'ham Opera Bd; r/Bapt; hon/1 of 7 Musicians in US to Receive Awd of Merit for Outstg S'ship & Perf in Field of Early Am Mus, Nat Fed Mus Clbs 1979; 1 of 11 Adjudicators for Am Mus S'hip Assn Intl Competition 1980.

MARTIN, TERRY JOE (SPARKY) oc/Service Clerk; b/Jan 22, 1956; h/13 Horse Shoe Dr, Paris, KY 40361; m/Karen Johns; p/George and Exona Martin, Corbin, KY; ed/BS En Ky Univ; Att'd Cumberland Col; pa/Ser Clerk, Whayne Supply Co; cp/Corbin Optimist Clb; Corbin Bd Ed; Boys Work Chm; hon/Optimist of Mo, Sept 1980; Best Redhound Support 1970-74.

MARTIN, THOMAS HOWARD oc/Pastor; b/Aug 22, 1952; h/Dallas, TX; ba/6810 Samuell Blvd, Dallas, TX 75228; m/Vicki L; c/Tara Catherine, Aubrey Lynn; p/Howard V Martin, Clovis, NM; Gertrude E Martin (dec); ed/Att'd Baylor Univ; BBA En NM Univ 1974; MDIv SWn Bapt Theol Sem 1978; pa/Owner Michael's Gift & Bridal Shop 1974-75; Pastor: Hilltop Bapt Ch 1976-77, Pioneer Dr Bapt Ch 1977-80, Buckner Terrace Bapt Ch 1980-; Missions Com Tarrant Bapt Assn; Evangelism Com Dallas Bapt Assn; Preparation Com Chm Tex Bapt Evangelism Conf; Chm Bd Call for Action; cp/Lions Clb, Treas; Exec Com U Fund; DeMolay; Clovis Retail Merchants Assn; r/So Bapt; hon/Order of Knights Templar DeMolay 1969; Rep DeMolay 1969; Outstg Yng Men Am 1981; Lic'd to Preach 1974; Ordained to the Gospel Min 1977.

MARTIN, WILLIAM E oc/Professional Engineer; b/July 9, 1925; h/3001 N Midland D1 C-8, Midland, TX 79703; ba/Midland; m/Naomi V W; c/Richard E, William C, Lynn M Hullinger; p/Everett W Martin, St Cloud, FL; Pearl Atchley Martin (dec); ed/BS Civil Engrg 1951; BS Mech Engrg 1953; mil/AUS WWII; pa/Proj Mgr Ortloff Corp Oil and Gas Engrg & Construction; cp/Masonic Temple; Alpha Phi Omega; Sertoma Intl; r/Meth; hon/Author "Understanding Project Management" & "Understanding Construction Management."

MARTIN, WILMA JEAN QUEEN oc/Hospital Administrator; b/July 30, 1937; h/171 Nighbert Ave, Logan, WV 25601; m/James P; c/John F Cook II, James Michael Cook; p/Donald Queen (dec); Elberta Lucas Queen Ellis, Logan, WV; ed/Att'd So Commun Col; pa/Hosp Admr, Guyan Val Hosp Inc; VP & Co-Owner Logan Park Care Ctr; VP & Co-Owner Mingo Co Care Ctr Nsg Home; Pres & Owner Guyan Distbg Co; Ofcr Hosp Corp, Secy; Ofcr Hosp Bd Dirs; cp/Hon Order Ky Cols; Smithsonian Inst; Jr Wom's Clb; Ladies VFW Org; Bowling Leag; Co-Chm Cancer Soc; Crippled Chd Assn; U Fund; Heart Assn; Red Cross; r/Presb.

MARTINEZ, BETTY ELNORA oc/Sales Representative; b/Jan 7, 1937; h/4033 NW 33rd St, Okla City, OK 73112; ba/Okla City; p/Jim Smith (dec) and Jewell Smith, Okla City, OK; ed/BS 1974, MBA 1975 OCU; pa/Solvent Sales Rep, Kerr McGee Ctr; cp/MBA Clb of OCU, Pres 1975-; Del to Okla Dem Conv 1972; hon/W/W Am Wom 1979-80

MARTINEZ, INEZ N oc/Nurse, Associate Professor; b/Mar 19, 1926; h/1707 Rosewood Dr, Greenville, NC 27834; ba/Greenville; m/Raymond H; c/Linus Ray, Suzanne Alice; p/Thomas W and Susie Norris, Ft Deposit, AL; ed/Dip Providence Hosp Sch Nsg 1947; BS 1959, MA Ed 1966 E Carolina Univ; ba/ECU: Assoc Prof Sch Nsg 1975-, Asst Prof Sch Nsg 1966-75, Instr Sch Nsg 1962-66, 1960-61; OR Staff Nurse, Pitt Co Meml Hosp 1955; Indust Nurse, Haspel Brothers Inc 1952-54; Pvt Duty Nurse, Touro Infirm 1952; Staff Nurse Ochsner Foun Hosp, New Orleans 1947-52; Staff Nurse, Providence Hosp 1947; ANA; NC Nurses Assn, Dist

30: VP 1963-64, 68-69, 75-76, Bd Dirs 1962-63, 68-69, 73-74, Var Coms; NLN; NCLN; Sigma Theta Tau, Beta Nu Chapt, Nom'g Com 1972-73, Eligibility Com 1973-74; cp/Am Cancer Soc, NC Div, Pitt Co Unit: Bd Dirs 1969-, 2nd VP 1975-76, 1st VP 1976-77, 77-78, Pres 1978-79, 79-80, Var Coms; En Lung Assn; Pitt Co Mtl Hlth Assn; Am Heart Assn; PTA Rose HS; LWV; r/Cath; hon/Sigma Theta Tau.

MARTINEZ, JOEL oc/Orthodontist; b/May 27, 1952; ba/1007 Sycamore, McAllen, TX 79501; m/Norma Vasquez; p/Aurelia R Martinez, McAllen, TX; ed/DDS 1977; Post Grad Cert 1979; pa/Self-Employed Orthodontist; Am Dental Assn; Am Assn Orthodontics; SWn Soc Orthodontics.

MARTINEZ, MILTON E oc/General Surgeon; b/Oct 13, 1930; h/Miami, FL; ba/2541 SW 27 Ave, Suite 301, Miami, FL 33133; m/Caridad N; c/Milton E, Eduardo M, Rebecca M; p/Andres and Aida Martinez, Miami, FL; ed/MD Univ Havana Sch of Med 1954; pa/Self Pract, Gen Surg; AMA; FMA; Dade Co Med Assn; SE Med Assn; Fla Assn of Surgs; Bd Cert in Gen Surg; cp/Repub Party; r/Cath.

MARTINEZ, RICARDO ARGUIJO oc/Health Care Administrator, Consultant, Educator; b/Jan 25, 1951; h/1804 Brunswick Blvd, San Antonio, TX 78211; ba/San Antonio; p/Robert R and Lupe A Martinez, San Antonio, TX; ed/AA San Antonio Jr Col 1971; BS Univ Tex Sys Sch Nsg 1973; MS SW Tex St Univ 1975; MPH Univ Tex Sch Public Hlth 1981; pa/RN, Hlth Care Cnsltg & Adm, Commun Med Ed Sers; So Assn Commun Hlth Ctrs; Am Red Cross Nurse; r/Cath; hon/Outstg Student, Univ Tex Sch Nsg 1973; All St S'ship 1972; Nsg Alumni Schlr 1972; US Public Hlth Traineeship 1980; Author *Hispanic Culture and Health Care* 1978 & *Thanksgiving* (Novel) 1981.

MARTINEZ, ROBERT oc/Supervisor; b/Apr 6, 1934; h/3312 Cornwall, El Paso, TX 79925; ba/El Paso; m/Lupe; c/Robert Anthony, Sylvia Yvonne, Cynthia Annette, MeLissa Myra; p/Joe (dec) and Dolores Vega Martinez, El Paso, TX; ed/BA Tex Wn Col; MA Univ Tex-El Paso; MS Ed UTEP; mil/USMCR Lt; pa/Supvr Driver & Safety Ed Ctr, Region XIX ESC; Phi Delta Kappa; TSTA; TCTA; ASCD; ATSEA; TSTEA; cp/WTCOG Adv Com; Crime Preven; Peer Cnslg; Optimist; r/Cath; hon/Pres, VP, Treas TSTA; Ariz St Univ Stipent, SW Tex St Univ Recip.

MARTINEZ, ROBERTO GUTIERREZ oc/Coordinator; b/Feb 1, 1952; h/1513 Richard, Killeen, TX 76541; m/Debbie L; c/Robert Neil; p/Pete H and Delia G Martinez, Harker Heights, TX; ed/Att'd Johnson & Wales Col; pa/Fashion Mdsg F W Woolworth Co; cp/K1000 Civic Art Guild; Alumni of Distb Ed Chapt; Phi Delta Alumni; r/Cath; hon/First in Body Jewelry, Killeen Art & Craft Show 1980; Best of Show in Craft Copperas Cove 1978 & 80.

MARTINEZ, SERGIO ERNESTO oc/Executive; b/Aug 4, 1919; h/8520 SW 80th Pl, Miami, FL 33143; m/Adeline; c/Sergio Alberto, Maria Linda; p/Sergio Martinez (dec); Clara de la Vega (dec); ed/BS in EE 1940, BS in ME 1947 MIT; MS NYU 1972; Profl Indust Engr Columbia Univ 1972; pa/Chief Engr, Textilera Ariguanabo, Bauta, Cuba 1942-49; Field Supt, Frederick Snare Corp, Venezuela, Cuba & Colombia 1949-55; Mill Mgr, Papelera Pulpa Cuba, Trinidad, Cuba 1955-69; Chief Proj Engr, Dir Budgeting & Plan'g, Parsons & Whittemore, NY 1960-77; VP & Gen Mgr Miami Subsidiary Resources Recovery Inc 1977-; Reg'd PE Saskatchewan, Can; TAPPI; SAME; ASTM; cp/VP Local Am Assn Coast Engrs; r/Cath; hon/W/W S&SW 1980; Pt-Time Instr NYU Grad Sch Engrg 1969-73; Author "Cost Control of Solid Waste Plants" 1981.

MARTZ, IRENE oc/Administrative Assistant; b/Aug 5; h/Jonesboro, AR; ba/Office of Academic Affairs, State Univ, AR 72467; m/J Eugene; p/R F Meredith (dec) and Elizabeth Brewer Garland (dec); ed/Dip Jonesboro Bus Col 1960; AB Ark St Univ 1974; CPS Cert Inst Certifying Secys 1977; pa/Adm Asst Acad Affairs, Ark St Univ; Nat Assn Exec Females; Profl Secys Intl, A-O Div Pres-Elect 1980-81, VP 1979-80; NE Ark Chapt NSA Chart Pres 1975-77; Jonesboro BPW, Pres 1979-80; cp/Altrusa Clb of Jonesboro, Yrbook Chm; ERArkansas; r/Meth; hon/Beta Gamma Sigma; Miss Secy of SW Region of US 1960; Wom of Yr, Jonesboro BPW Clb 1980; Secy of Yr NEA Chapt NSA 1977.

MARXER, ELLEN oc/Assistant Professor, Retired/Disabled; b/Dec 29, 1931; h/4002 Devon St SE, Huntsville, AL 35802; ba/Carbondale, IL; m/David; c/Carl L, Catherine E Keeton, Margaret E, p/Armstrong H and Catherine M Kolb, Brevard, NC; ed/BS; MS Ed, SIU-C; pa/SIU, C'dale: Asst Prof Elect Data Processing, Sch of Tech Careers, Reschr in Follow-Up of Grads & Non-Grads; 3 Textbooks Currently in Pub; cp/Former PTA Activs, Tuscaloosa & H'ville, Ala; Profl Musician in SE; Local Coor Tax-Aide for Elderly, NRTA/AARP; Writer for UAB Newslttr, Dept of Rheumatology & Arthritis Foun, Ala Chapt; r/Presb; hon/Music S'ship; Wayne St Univ; Deans List, Univ Ala-Tuscaloosa; Fellow ABI; Phi Kappa Phi, Psi Chapt; Iota Lambda Sigma; Life Mem AVA; Mem Ala Voc Assn.

MASKA, EDWIN CHESTER oc/Railroad Executive; b/Nov 5, 1929; h/8419 Doyle Dr, Alexandria, VA 22308; ba/Wash DC; m/Geneil Clay; p/Frank and Anna Maska, Dalton, MA; ed/BS Univ Pa, Wharton Sch Fin & Commerce; LLB Geo Wash Univ Nat Law Ctr; mil/USMC Capt; pa/RR Exec So Railway Co; Dist Columbia Bar; Am Bar Assn; Tax Exec Inst; cp/Treas Citizens for Better Govt, Fairfax Co 1967-68; Investigator US Senate Com Labor; Pres Comm on Govt Security 1956-57; r/Presb.

MASON, MARJORIE SMITH oc/Home Economist; b/Mar 1, 1937; h/1281 Brockett Rd, Clarkston, GA 30021; ba/Decatur, GA; m/dec; p/Tracy J and Eleanor Goddard Smith, Stone Mtn, Ga; ed/BS Home Ec; pa/Home Economist, Ga Ext Ser; Am & Ga Home Ec Assns; NAEHE; GAEHE; BPW; Ga Nutrition Coun; Atlanta Farmer's Clb; cp/Atlanta Theatre Guild; Ga Heart Assn; Am Cancer Soc; r/Prot; hon/Nat Dist'd Ser Awd, NAEHE; W/W Am Wom.

MASON, ROSCOE C oc/Minister, Teacher; b/Jan 5, 1920; p/dec; ed/AB Tex Col; Rel Work SMU; mil/AUS 5 Yrs; pa/Tchr Christian Co HS; Phi Beta Sigma; Ky Col; NEA; KEA; cp/Min Assn; St Hlth Coun; PAD; r/Meth Epis; hon/Ky Col; Grad Cum Laude.

MASSELL, SAM oc/Business Executive; b/Aug 26, 1927; h/2750; Wyngate NW, Atlanta, Fulton, GA 30305; ba/Atlanta; m/Doris M Middleborrks; c/Cynthia Diane, Steven Alan, Melanie Denise; p/Sam and Florence Rubin Massell; ed/Emory Univ 1944-45; Univ Ga 1947-48; LLB Atlanta Law Sch 1949; BSc 1951, Postgrad Cert in Selling 1952, Postgrad Dip in Real Est 1953 Ga St Univ; mil/USAAF 1946-47, Adm Sch Instr; pa/Chief of Pubs, Nat Assn of Woms & Chds Apparel Salesmen Inc 1949-51; VP Allan-Grayson Rltr Co 1955-69; Instr in Real Est, Smith-Hughes Atlanta Voc Sch 1956; VP Mallin Develrs Inc 1956-65; Dir: Security Fed Savs & Ln Assn of Atlanta 1961-67, U Trust Life Ins Co 1964-68; Pres Allan-Grayson Devel Assocs 1974-75; Dir CONCAPCO of Ga Inc 1975-; Proprietor, Your Travel Agt Sam Massell 1975-; cp/Commerce Clb; Standard Clb; Dem Party; Coun-man, City of Mtn Pk, Ga 1950-52; Secy Atlanta City Exec Com 1953-61; Pres Bd of Aldermen & V-Mayor, Atlanta 1962-69; Mayor, Atlanta 1970-74; r/Hebrew Benevolent Congreg; hon/W/W Am.

MASSETT, WILLIAM AUGUST oc/Teacher; b/Sept 2, 1941; h/8248 Gladewood Dr, Baton Rouge, LA 70806; ba/MS; p/William August (dec) and Dolores S Massett, Baton Rouge, LA; ed/BA, MEd, EdS La St Univ; mil/USN 1959-65 Petty Ofcr; pa/Spec Ed Tchr; Presently Doct Cand Miss St Univ; cp/Dem Party; Polit Action Com Tchrs in La; r/Cath; hon/Phi Delta Kappa; W/W Fin & Indust.

MASTERSON, ADRIENNE CRAFTON oc/Realtor; h/8200 Rolling Rd, Springfield, VA 22153; fam/4 chd; cp/Realtor Spec'g in Investment Properties; Nn Va Bd Realtors; Va Assn Realtors; Nat Assn of Realtors; Alexandria C of C; Fairfax Co, Va Envir Quality Adv Coun; Lee Dist, Land Use Adv Com; Others; hon/No Va Million Dollar Sales Clb 1963-65; W/W Am Wom; World W/W Wom.

MATHENY, TOM HARRELL oc/Lawyer; h/PO Box 221, Hammond, LA 70401; ba/Hammond; p/Whitman (dec) and Lorene Matheny; ed/BA SEn Univ; JD Tulane Univ; Dr Law Centenary Col & DePaul Univ; pa/Ptnr Law Firm Pittman & Matheny; Am Bar Assn; La St Bar Assn; Secy-Treas-VP 21st Judicial Dist Bar Assn; Gen Chm La St Bar Assn Com on Legal Aid; World Peace Through Law Ctr's Com on Conciliation & Mediation of Disputes; Trust Counsel, First Quaranty Bank, Hammond, La; La Trial Lwyrs Assn; Nat Lwyrs Clb; Assn Nat Colls & Univs Attys; Am Col Mortgage Attys; VP So Brick Supply; Fac Holy Cross Col 3 Yrs; Fac SEn La Univ 5 Yrs; Intl Soc Barristers; cp/Dist Gov Supreme Coun Order of DeMolay 1964-; Pres Masonic Yth Foun of St La 1970-71; Baton Rouge Consistory; Jerusalem Temple of New Orleans; Tangipahoa Parish Shrine Clb; Livingston Lodge #160 Free & Accepted Masons; Pres SEn Alumni Assn; Bd Dirs Tangipahoa Parish Chapt SEn Alumni Assn; Exec Bd Istrouma Coun BSA; Chm Advmt Com Boy Scouts Dist; Adv Com Dist Area Coun Boy Scouts; Nat Libera Clb of England; Pres Tangipahoa Parish Mtl Hlth Assn; Bd Dirs La Mtl Hlth Assn, Pres; Am Acad Rel & Mtl Hlth; La Hist Assn; Friends of Cabildo; Hon Fellow Harry S Truman Lib Inst; U Nat Assn; Intl Platform Assn; Nat Hist Soc La Annual Conf; Chm Crime Control Com Goals for La; Com on Commun Action & Crime Preven of La Comm on Law Enforcement & Adm of Crim Just; Bd Dirs La Moral & Civic Foun; Public Affairs Res Coun; La Assn Bus & Indust; Coun for Better La; Num Other Orgs & Coms; hon/Layman of Yr, La Annual Conf U Meth Ch 1966 & 73; 1 of 3 Outstg Men La 1964; Recip Dist'd Ser Awd 1960 & 64, Hammond Jr C of C; Layman of Yr La, Miss, W Tenn Kiwanis Intl 1972; Citizen of Yr, Hammond Kiwanis Clb 1978; W/W: Ed, Am Law Enforcement, Bus, S&SW, Methodism, World; DIB; Outstg Yng Men Am; Outstg Civic Ldrs Am; Royal Blue Book; Commun Ldrs of Am.

MATHEWS, ALLEN McLEOD oc/County Agricultural Agent; b/Nov

14, 1923; h/411 Junaluska Ave, Dothan, AL 36303; ba/Dothan; m/Jeanette Carleton; c/Larry Allen, Ronald Carleton; p/Albert Sidney Sr (dec) and Juddie Williams Mathews (dec); ed/BS, MS Auburn Univ; mil/Field Artillery 102nd Inf Div ETO; pa/Ala Co Agts Assn; Gamma Sigma Delta; Alpha Delta; Nat Co Agts Assn; cp/Lions Clb; Kiwanis Clb; Bd Dirs Nat Peanut Fest; r/Bapt; hon/St 4-H Awd; Dist'd Ser Awd, Nat Co Agts Assn; Agribus Awd, Dothan C of C; "Allen Mathews Awd" Given Annually.

MATHEWS, RICHARD LEE oc/Assistant Manager; b/Mar 4, 1923; h/331 Rowland St, Henderson, NC 27536; ba/Henderson; m/Alma Holtzman; p/George Washington (dec) and Martha Catherine Riggan Mathews (dec); pa/Asst Mgr Aycock's Shoe Store; cp/VP Henderson Clb 1968 & 73; Pres Henderson Exch Clb 1969; Maria Parham Hosp Host Clb 1966-; Vance Co Rescue Squad; NC Assn Rescue Squads; Vance Co React Team; r/Tabernacle Meth Ch: Ch Choir, SS Tchr, Cert'd Lay Spkr; hon/Man of Yr, Henderson Exch Clb 1968; Cert of Apprec, Warren Co 4-H Clbs 1965-.

MATHEWS, WALTER MASON oc/Clinical Psychologist and Psychotherapist; b/Aug 2, 1903; m/Berth Beyer; c/Frederic Mason, Schael Ann Engle; p/Thomas Edgar (dec) and Anna Leota Mathews (dec); ed/BA 1930, MA 1934, PhD 1937 Univ Ia; mil/USNR Cmdr; pa/Clin Psychol & Psychotherapist; Am Psych Assn; An Ortho Psychi Assn; Diplomate Am Bd Profl Psych; Assn Marriage Cnslrs; cp/Highland Pk, Mich Sch Bd; Soc Mtl Hlth; r/Prot.

MATHEWS, WANDA PHILLIPS oc/Teacher; b/Mar 20, 1935; h/936 Riviera St, Venice, FL 33595; ba/Venice; m/James L; c/Jeanie Lynn, Sharon Kay; p/Jackson D and Verna Lee Phillips, Atlanta, GA; ed/BA W Va St Col; pa/Christian Sch Tchr; cp/SS Tchr; Choir Dir; hon/Written & Pub'd Inspirational & Metaphysical Articles.

MATHEWS, WILFORD DALE JR oc/US Air Force; b/July 4, 1935; h/700 Canterbury Blvd, Altus, OK 73521; ba/Altus AFB; m/Bonnie Louise; c/Joey Lee, Raymond Phillip Maull, Timothy William Maull, Wilford Dale III; p/Wilford D Sr and Hazel L Mathews, Leon, IA; ed/Bach Bus; Master Mgmt; mil/Squadron Ofcrs Sch; Air Command & Staff, Indust Col of the Armed Forces; Air War Col; pa/USAF; cp/Masonic Lodge; OES; r/Bapt; hon/Bronze Star Medal; Merit Ser Medal w OLC; Air Medal; AF Commend Medal w 2 OLC; Combat Readiness Medal w OLC; Good Conduct Medal; Nat Defense Medal; AF Expeditionary Medal; Vietnam Ser Medal w 7 Stars; Vietnamese Hon Medal First Class; RVN Gallantry Cross w Palm; Repub of Vietnam Campaign Medal.

MATHIS, GWENDOLYN ANN oc/Sales Manager; b/Feb 24, 1936; h/124 D St, Lindale, GA 30147; ba/Atlanta; m/Jack M; c/Thomas David; p/James Darrell Simpson, Rockmart, GA; Kathleen Davis Thacker (dec); pa/Sales Mgr Alchem Plastics; So Sect: Past Secy, Spec Events Chp, Nom'g Com Chp, Gen Staff Oper'g Com; Pres 1978; Bd Dirs; Nat Coun-wom & Mng Editor; Intl Level: Region 7 VChm Mbrship Com, Chm Radiack Dot Mbrship Campaign, VChm Sects Com, Ad Hoc Com to Improve Coun Effectiveness; cp/Floyd Co Dem Assn, Secy 4 Yrs; Pres Yng Dems Ga; 4th Dist Pres Am Legion Aux; C of C; r/Lindale Meth Ch; hon/Jules Lindau Awd 1980, Soc Plastic Engrs.

MATTHEWS, D ERNEST oc/Insurance and Securities Sales; b/Apr 21, 1916; h/112 E Isabella St, Salisbury, MD 21801; ba/Same; m/Dorothy H; c/Ernest C, Daniel H, Theodore P, Robert L, Mary Ellen Donaway, Patricia A Schrawder, Dorothy K; p/Ernest (dec) and Mary A Matthews (dec); ed/Cert'd Fin Planner 1975; pa/IAFP; ICFP; NAEP; NASD; cp/Fin Adv Delmarva Poultry Indust; hon/W/W Fin & Indust; Salisbury JC Yng Man of Yr 1951; Univ Md Agric Awd 1952; Dist'd Citizen Awd, Delmarva Poultry Indust 1961.

MATTHEWS, ELSIE C SPEARS oc/Assistant Editor, Book Reviewer, Writer; b/Aug 8, 1901; h/926 Sandstone, Bartlesville, OK 74003; m/Thomas M (dec); c/Thomas A II, Byron S; ed/AB Wheaton Col 1923; NW Univ Law Sch; pa/Writer, Author; Compiler; Asst Ed Current Mun Probs w Son Byron, Supplements & Mun Ordinance & Revision Vol 2 of Same; Press & Publicity Chm, Conserv of Rec Lands; Rocky Mtn Fdn Mineralogical Socs; Publicity & Public Relats Chm, Osage Hills Gem & Mineral Soc Inc; cp/Wash Co Chm Keep Am Beautiful; Green Country; Beautification Chm, City Bartlesville, C of C; Johnny Horizon Rep; Author Anti-Litter Skit; Wilderness Soc; Smithsonian Assoc; Nat Park Assn; Am Forests Assn: Costeau Soc; Pres Indep Repub Woms Clb, River Forest, Ill; r/1st Presb Ch: Mem; hon/Green Country Cert Merit; W/W: Wom, Am Wom, Commun Ldrs, S&SW, Commun Ser; 2000 Wom Achmt; Fellow, Intl Biogl Soc; Intl Reegister Profiles; Stella Woodbell Intl Poetry Soc.

MATTHEWS, JAMES A oc/Manager of Manufacturing; b/Apr 5, 1950; h/Anderson, SC; ba/Singer Co, PO Box 1110, Anderson, SC;

m/Penny; c/Kelly, Meghan; p/Elizabeth Matthews, Rocky Mount, NC: ed/BSIE NC St Univ 1972; pa/Indust Engr Square D Co; Singer Co: IE Supvr, IE Dept Mgr, Div IE Mgr, Mgr Mfg & Facilities Engrg; Am Inst Indust Engrs, Chapt Treas, VP Chapt Devel, Pres; Indust Adv Bd, Engrg Tech Dept Clemson Univ; r/Presb; hon/Awd of Excell AIIE 1977-78, 1978-79.

MATTHEWS, PAUL THOMAS oc/Bookkeeper; b/Aug 24, 1929; h/Riceville, TN; m/Mary Ruth; c/William Thomas, Susan Elizabeth; p/William Thomas (dec) and Bonnie Wade Matthews, Riceville, TN; pa/Ret'd After 30 Yrs Ser w McMinn Co Bd Ed; Self-Employed Farmer & Saw Mill Oper; VChm ASCS Co Com; cp/Past Pres Riceville Ruritan Clb; Past Treas Cherokee Dist Ruritan; Dem Precinct Chm; r/Ch of Christ; Elder.

MATTOX, JOHNNY LYNN oc/Instructor; b/Apr 13, 1951; h/Rt 5 Box 208, Corinth, MS 38834; ba/Fulton, MS; m/Jean Eaton; c/Jason Lynn; p/O L Jr and Joyce Mills Mattox, Corinth, MS; ed/AA NE Miss Jr Col; BAE, MCS, PhD Univ Miss; pa/Biol Instr, Itawamba Jr Col; Kappa Delta Pi; Phi Kappa Phi; Phi Delta Kappa; Miss Sci Tchrs Assn; Nat Sci Tchrs Assn; Miss Acad Scis; Nat Assn Biol Tchrs; Soc Col Sci Tchrs; r/Bapt; hon/Phi Delta Kappa Awd, Univ Miss 1973; W/W Students in Am Jr Cols 1971; Star Tchr, Kossuth HS 1975-76; Grad Spec Dist Univ Miss 1973; Chosen to Part in Miss-Ala Sea Grant Consortium 1979.

MATYI, MARIE FRIEDLEY oc/Model, Homemaker; b/May 16, 1931; h/Deland, FL; m/Floyd Sr; c/Floyd Jr, JoAnn, George, Fred, Irving, Linda, Ted; p/Alexander Matyi (dec); Mary Matyi Starego, Edison, NJ; ed/GED Md 1965; Att'd Glassboro St Col; pa/Rockette Radio City Mus Hall 1948-; Staff John Robert Powers 1980; Tchr: Blackwood, NJ 1969, Folsum, NJ 1968; hon/Skating Roller 1979; Date & Skate 1979.

MAULDIN, JEAN oc/Business Executive; b/Aug 16, 1923; h/1013 W Elliott Pl, Santa Ana, CA 92704; 102 E Forty Fifth Ave, Savannah, GA 31405; ba/Seal Bch, CA; m/William Henry (Bill); c/Bruce Patrick, William Timothy III; p/James Wiley Humphries Northridge, CA; Lena Leota Crain Humphries (dec); ed/BS Hardin Simmons Univ 1943; MS Univ So Calif 1961; Westfield Col, Univ London 1977; Marlborough Col, Oxford, England 1977; pa/Pres Stardust Aviation; Former Pres Mauldin & Staff, Public Relats; Pubs: *Cliff Winters, The Pilot, The Man* 1961, *The Consummate Barnstormer* 1962, *The Daredevil Clown* 1963, *Schumacher Presss*; Am Mgmt Assn; Experimental Aircraft & Pilots Assn; cp/Past Mem Tulare Co Dem Cent Com, Calif; Former Del Calif Dem Caucus 5 Yrs; Former VP Dem Wom Tulare Co, Dem Wom Orange Co; Del: Nat Conv 1976, Nat Wom's Polit Caucus, Wash DC 1973-75, Nat Issues Conv 1976; Past Treas Dem Coalition; Orange Co Dem Cent Com; LA Dem Wom's Forum; Friends of Santa Ana McFadden Public Libs, Pres & Chm; Fed Dem Ctrl Com; Exec Bd Calif Dem Ctrl Com, Nat Fed Dem Wom; Intl Platform Assn; r/Epis; Chm Wom's Missionary Soc; hon/Wom of Yr 1960; W/W: Am Polits, Am Wom; FIBA; ABIRA; Intl W/W.

MAUND, LINDA KAY oc/Professional Nursing Instructor; b/July 27, 1943; h/10950 Jefferson Hwy, River Ridge, LA 70123; ba/New Orleans, LA; p/Robert Dixon and Sibyl Smith Maund, Boyce, LA; ed/Dip RN; BSN; MSN; pa/AORN; r/Meth; hon/Grad cum laude BSN & summa cum laude MSN; Sigma Theta Tau; LSU Med Ctr Hon Soc; W/W Am Wom 1979-80.

MAXEY, JOE O oc/Director of Bands; b/Feb 4, 1948; h/Albany, GA; ba/Albany Jr Col, 2400 Guillonville Rd, Albany, GA 30707; m/Marilyn W; p/Mrs Lewis Maxey, Lithonia, GA; ed/Att'd DeKalb Jr Col; BMus Ed, MMus Ga St Univ; mil/Ga ANG Cmdg Ofcr; pa/Principle Trumpet, Albany Symph Orch; Dir Bands Albany Jr Col; GMEA; MENC; Reserve Ofcrs Assn; Intl Trumpet Guild; r/Bapt.

MAXWELL, FRANCES MARION oc/Homemaker; b/Dec 8, 1942; h/3340 Audubon Dr, Laurel, MS 39440; m/Earle Wilson Jr; c/Tripp; p/Franklin M Mitchell (dec); Mary Mitchell Stewart, Westminster, SC; ed/Att'd Clemson Univ; cp/Laurel Jr Aux; Laurel Little Theatre; Commun Concert; Charter Mem Laurel Needlework Guild; Lauren Rogers Mus; Docent Ofcr Town & Country Garden Clb; r/Meth: SS Tchr, Altar Guild, Past Circle Chm, Mbrship Chm WSCS.

MAXWELL, LEONA V McWILLIAMS oc/Businesswoman; b/Feb 16, 1914; h/Box 1225, Seminole, OK 74969; ba/Same; m/James Sinclair; c/Patricia Violet Ogden, Leona Colleen Ogden; p/Fred Haden McWilliams, Cinci, OH; Ada Mae Stamper, La Grange, KY; pa/Bldg Contractor & Real Est Broker; Oilfield Equip; Maxwell Engine & Supply; cp/Am Heart Assn, Okla Affil, Secy; r/Meth; Ordained Deacon; hon/BPW Wom of Yr; Am Heart Assn, Okla Affil, Wom of Yr; Okla St Yth Ldr Awd.

MAXWELL, LOUIS oc/Dean of Student Affairs; b/Jan 23, 1948;

h/PO Box 102, Tuskegee, ALA 36088; ba/Tuskegee; m/Janice Middleton; c/Brenda, Kiwanda Latrice, Deanah Darnell; p/James and Mary B Maxwell, Benoit, MS; ed/Assoc Deg Coahoma Jr Col 1968; BS 1972, MEd 1974 Tuskegee Inst; pa/Dean Student Affairs, So Voc Col; Ala Vets Affairs Assn, VP 1976; Nat Assn Concern Vets; cp/Macon Co Polit Org; r/Bapt.

MAXWELL, RUTH LEDBETTER oc/Police Officer; b/June 12, 1952; h/130 N Erwin St, Apt D-2, Cartersville, GA 30120; ba/C'ville; c/Sidney E Jr; p/Matthew and Hattie Jackson Ledbetter, C'ville, GA; pa/FOP; Afro-Am Patrolman's Leag; cp/Afro-Am Social Civic Assn; r/Bapt.

MAY, JUANITA W oc/Insurance Agent; b/Oct 28, 1942; h/Rt 1 Box 33 G, Swoope, VA 24479; ba/Staunton, Va; m/Jerry L; c/Jeffrey; p/Wilmer R (dec) and Ruby M Wheelbarger, Bridgewater, VA; pa/Ins Agt, Staunton Ins Agcy; cp/Assoc Mem Florence Nightingale Hosp Aux; Secy-Treas Abbington Hills Homeowners Assn; Secy Hebron Boy Scout Ladies Aux; r/U Meth.

MAY, SUE LOUISE oc/Nurse; b/Aug 5, 1947; h/PO Box 33, Soper, OK 74759; ba/Hugo, OK; m/Carl Dean; c/James Lyles Wariner, Lisa Leann Wariner; p/Hubert and Dale Parker, Ringling, OK; ed/RN NW Tex Hosp Sch Nsg; pa/Am Assn Oper'g Nurses; cp/CPR Instr Am Heart Assn; r/Bapt.

MAYFIELD, MARY SUE oc/Director of Nurses; b/Aug 3, 1932; h/1207 Navaho Trail, Richardson, TX; ba/Denton, TX; m/Ben Earl; c/Lorrie Lei Garre, Ben Joseph; p/Edwin J (dec) and Elsie Stitt Brown, St Johns, MI; ed/BS Incarnate Word Col; MS Abilene Christian Univ of Dallas; pa/RN, Dir Nurses Westgate Hosp & Med Ctr; Tex Hosp Assn of Nsg Ser Admrs; cp/Dallas Co N Repub Clb; r/Presb; hon/Scholastic S'ship St Paul Sch Nsg; W/W Am Wom 1978; Spec Ser Awd, Abilene Christian Univ 1978.

MAYNARD, KENNETH DELANO oc/Superintendent; b/Aug 30, 1914; h/Rt 4 Box 32 A, Sylvester, GA 31791; ba/Sylvester; m/Kathleen Henning; c/Gregory Owen, Mignon; p/Lorenza and Nancy Dow (dec); ed/Freed-Hardeman Col; pa/Min; Supt Sowega Yth Home, Ch of Christ Chd's Home; cp/Civitan Clb; Am Cancer Soc; Parent Adv Coun; r/Ch of Christ; hon/WOW; Commend Ser Awd; Pres's Awd; Intl Civitan.

MAYNOR, HAL WHARTON III oc/Student; b/Mar 20, 1956; h/PO Box 605, Auburn, AL 36830; ba/Auburn; m/Donnie Love; c/Hal Wharton IV; p/Hal Wharton Jr and Marjorie Baker Maynor, Auburn, AL; ed/Student Auburn Univ; r/Pentecostal; hon/W/W Am HS; Nat Hon Soc; God & Country Awd; John Phillip Sousa Awd; Most Musical in Sr Class; Band Pres.

MAYS, BENITA BANISTER oc/Education Coordinator; b/Mar 16, 1937; h/5227 Duncanville Rd, Dallas, TX 75211; ba/Dallas; m/James E; p/Charley T (dec) and Maude Blake Banister, Mt Vernon, TX; ed/BS Univ Tex-Arlington; MA Univ Tex SW Med Sch; PhD Tex A&M; pa/Ed Coor, El Centro Col.

MAYS, RITA DIANE oc/Coach, Athletic Trainer; b/Sept 16, 1953; h/Rt 6, Pleasants Apts #6, Elizabethton, TN 37643; ba/Milligan Col, TN; p/Lawrence and Florence Mays, Greeneville, TN; ed/BS; MA; Cert Sports Med; pa/Coach, Ath Tnr Miligan Col; NATA; AAHPER; r/Bapt; hon/First Aid Instr; CPR Instr.

MAZE, MARTHA MALONE oc/Professional Career Counselor; b/May 4, 1942; h/Rt 3, Limestone, TN 37681; ba/Johnson City, TN; m/Roger W; c/Anthony; p/Thomas Luke and Jessie Dora Clark Malone, Greeneville, TN; ed/BS Univ Tenn 1963; Post Grad Work ETSU & Univ Tenn 1967, 74-76; pa/Sec'dy Sch Tchr, Sci Hill HS, Greeneville City Schs, Knoxville City Schs 15 Yrs; Mdsg Mgr The Paty Lumber Co 1½ Yrs; Employment Cnslr 1980-, Snelling & Snelling Employment Agcy; TEA; NEA; Elec Wom's Roundtable; Home Ecs in Bus; Tenn & Am Home Ec Assns; cp/C of C, Wom's Div Johnson City, Washington Co, Tenn, Pres Elect 1981-82; Lobbyist for Ed, St of Tenn 1972-79; US Congl Contract Team for Ed 1976-79; Exec Bd Tenn-Appalachia Mar of Dimes 1974-78; Alpha Delta Kappa; hon/Cert Merit, Tenn Dept Clrm Tchrs, Dist'd Tchr 1976; Tenn Polit Action Comm for Ed PACE Setter 1976-79; Author Occupational Home Economics for the Mentally Handicapped 1972.

McALISTER, THOMAS EDWARD oc/Businessman; b/Aug 27, 1950; h/818 Scott Ave, PO Box 96, Russellville, AL 35653; ba/R'ville; m/Rhonda; p/Thomas B and Dorothy J McAlister, Russellville, AL; ed/Att'd Univ N Ala; Am Real Est Sch 1974-78; US Govt Bur 1970; cp/Sustaining Mem Nat Repub Party; Franklin Co Repub Exec Com 1970-; Past Chm Yng Repub of Franklin Co; Cand Circuit Ct Clk, Franklin Co 1976; Chm Yng Repubs to Elect Nixon 1972; Chm Red Bount for Senate 1972; Campaign Mgr, McDuff for Sheriff, Franklin Co 1974; Chm Jim Martin for Sen 1978; Past Pres Dist 11 Ala JCs; Past Pres R'ville JCs; Franklin Co Fair, Dir & Treas; Chm of Bd, R'ville Public Lib 1976, V-Chm & Dir 1974-76; Ala Small Bus Adm Adv Bd 1975-77; R'ville Booster Clb; Am Judiciatory Soc; Phi Gamma Delta; Intl Entrepreneurs Assn; Am Security Coun Nat Adv Bd; R'ville Bicent Com 1975-76; Dir Civitan 1979-80; R'ville C of C; r/Bapt; hon/Nom R'ville Citizen of Yr 1976; JCs Speak-Up Awd, Spark Plug Awd, 6 Yr Awd, Past Pres Awd, Ala Awd of Hon, US Spec Pres Cit, US Pres Awd 6, 15, 25 Men Awd, US Pres Awd of Hon, Achmt, Ldrship; Citizen's Bank & Savings Awd of Hon; Blue Chip Awd of Hon 1976; Outstg Yng Men Am 1976, 77; Personalities of the S 1976-78; Intl W/W Intells 1978; #1 JC Chapt in St of Ala in 3-A Div, Pres 1975-76.

McATEE, ROBERT W oc/Realtor and Land Designer; b/Sept 2, 1919; h/112 Stephen Ct W, Athens, TX 75751; ba/Athens; m/Louise M; c/Robert W Jr, Linda K, Stephen Edward; p/Frank (dec) and Alma McAtee (dec); ed/BBA SMU; Tex Rltrs Inst; mil/USAF 13 Yrs; pa/Real Est Broker, Cnslr, Investments Analyst; Nat Assn Rltrs; Farm & Land Inst; Henderson Co Bd Rltrs, Pres; Life Mem Tyler Bd Rltrs; hon/DFC; Air Medal; Pres Cit; GRI; AFLM; Sev Articles Pub'd in Farm and Land Realtor.

McAULEY, FLOREE COX oc/Homemaker; b/Oct 8, 1903; h/108 Shubuta Dr, Greenville, NC 29611; m/Stephen Floyd; c/Louis Floyd, Van Alfon, Hariett M Bryson; p/William Shermon and Sallie Murphy Cox (dec); ed/Att'd New Orleans Sem 1935, Furman Univ; pa/Elem Sch Tchr 1920-24, 27-30; r/So Bapt; hon/WMU; Prayer Chapel Named for Her and Her Husband.

McAULEY, STEPHEN FLOYD oc/Minister; b/Oct 22, 1896; h/108 Shubuta Dr, Greenville, SC 29611; m/Floree Cox; c/Louis Floyd, Van Alfon, Hariett M Bryson; p/John Davison and Harriett Sammons McAuley (dec); ed/Att'd N Greenville Col, Furman Univ, New Orleans Sem, Appalachian St Tchr Col; Pastoral Orientation Course, Gen Hosp G'ville; mil/AUS; pa/Pastor 36 Yrs; r/So Bapt; hon/Pastor Emeritus; St Chaplain for WWI Vets; Chaplain G'ville Barracks #2529.

McBIRNEY, EDWIN TILLOTSON oc/Executive; b/Aug 10, 1928; h/Rt 2 Box 329, Edgewood Manor, Bunker Hill, WV; ba/Winchester, VA; m/Barbara Jean Milam (dec); 2nd Jeanne Clements Gaston; c/Edwin T III, Teri Linn, (Stepchd:) Robert C Gaston III, Elisa Paige Gaston; p/Edwin T and Helma Margaret Spreng McBirney; ed/BS Univ Cinci; pa/Nat Fruit Prod Co, Inc: VP Sales & Mktg, Corp Bd Dirs, Corp Exec Com; Processed Apple Int; Dir Vinegar Inst; Past Mem Mdsg & Mktg Com, Nat Food Brokers Assn; Nat Food Procesors, Statistical & Public Relats Coms; Am Mgmt Assn; Grocery Mfrs Assn; Sales Exec Clb, San Fran & NYC; Intl Apple Inst; cp/Dir, Mem Exec Com, Montgomery Co, Penn Repub Com 1969-71; Corp Chm U Fund, Oakland; Rotary Clb, Winchester; Lions Clb, Phila; hon/W/W Fin & Indust 1979-80.

McBRIDE, MICHAEL HONSON oc/Associate Professor and Department Chairman; b/Nov 23, 1944; h/PO Box 561, Snyder, TX; ba/Snyder; c/Michelle Elaine; p/Mary Margaret McBride, Rocksprings, TX; ed/AA San Angelo Col 1965; BA Angelo St Col 1967; MA 1973, EdD 1979 Tex Tech Univ; pa/San Angelo Indep Sch Dist 1967-73; Assoc Prof & Chm Dept of Jour, Wn Tex Col 1973-; Tex Intercol Press Advrs Assn, Past Pres; Nat Coun Col Pubs Advrs, Past St Pres; Tex Jr Col Jour Assn, Past Reporter; Commun Col Jour Assn; Rocky Mtn Col Press Advrs Assn; Tex Jr Col Tchrs Assn; Assn for Ed in Jour; cp/Repub Party; Former Mem: Kiwanis Clb, Lions Clb, Scurry Co Poetry Soc; r/Meth; hon/Phi Delta Kappa; Phi Kappa Phi; Outstg Yng Men Am 1975-76; Personalities of S 1972; Intl W/W Poetry 1971; W/W S&SW 1980; Author Silhouettes of Sincerity 1969; Editor Catalog Course Description Guide to Texas Jr Colleges Offering Journalism and Photography 1975; Author "We Know Who We Are in Texas" Community College Journalist Summer 1977.

McBURNEY, MILLARD LYLE oc/Associate Professor; b/Mar 10, 1939; h/Alexander, AR; ba/Henderson St Univ, Arkadelphia, AR 71923; m/Ruth Evelyn Percefull; p/Millard Jennings and Rinner Mae Adams McBurney, Athens,TX; ed/BS 1961, MS 1963 E Tex St Univ; pa/Assoc Prof Biol, Henderson St Univ 1966-; Beta Beta Beta, VP 1962-63; r/Meth; hon/Charter Mem Alpha Epsilon Chapt, Beta Beta Beta; Co-Author Laboratory Exercises in Biology 1978.

McCAIG, TRAVIS HOWARD oc/Businessman; b/July 9, 1919; h/Rt 2, Lincoln, AL 35096; ba/Same; m/Doskey C; c/Roy Mitchel; p/John M and Inez Smelser McCaig (dec); pa/Owner & Oper Motel; r/Ch of Christ.

McCALL, CAROLYN SUE WILSON oc/Nurse, Club Woman; b/Jan 14, 1937; h/6516 Aberdeen, Dallas, TX 75230; m/Thomas Screven; c/Thomas Kevin, Carol Kathleen; p/Otis Wilford and Mary Elizabeth Barnes Wilson, Bullard, TX; ed/Grad Brackenridge Hosp Sch of Nsg, Austin, Tex 1958; AA Blinn Col 1958; Att'd Biola Col 1959, E Tex St Univ

1979; pa/Charge Nurse Shriner's Hosp for Crippled Chd, Los Angeles 1959; Nurse, Nursery Dept: Presb Hosp, Whittier, Calif 1959-60, Midway Hosp, LA 1961-62, Baylor Hosp, Dallas 1962-63; Nurse Presb Hosp, Dallas 1968-74; cp/James Campbell Chapt DAR: Nat Defense Chm 1976-78, Corresp Secy 1980-, Recording Secy 1978-80; 3rd VP Dallas Chapt 6 UDC 1970-80, Pres 1980-82, 3rd VP Tex Div 1976-78; Soc Mayflower Descs; Nat Soc Magna Charta Dames; Daugs Am Colonists; Dallas So Meml Assn; Friday Forum; Dallas Symph Orch Leag; Repub Party; Brookhaven Country Clb; OES; Marianne Scruggs Jr Gdn Clb; Freedoms Foun at Val Forge, Dallas Area Chapt; r/Bapt; hon/Jefferson Davis Medal, UDC 1978.

McCALL, TRISTRAM BETHEA oc/Citrus Grower and Real Estate Investor; b/July 13, 1903; h/1313 Eastlake St, Longwood, FL 32750; m/June Morrison; c/Tristram Bethea III; p/Marvin and Mary Higgins McCall (dec); ed/Att'd Auburn Univ, G C Mil Acad; pa/Ret'd Citrus Grower & Real Est Investor; r/Meth.

McCANDLESS, MICHAEL DANE oc/Insurance Agent; b/Sept 24, 1948; h/315 Seay St, Glasgow, KY 42141; ba/Glasgow; m/Alma; c/John, Michelle; p/Bill Tom McCandless (dec); Mrs Donald Lycan, Louisville, KY; ed/HS Grad; pa/Agcy Mgr & Exec VP Pedigo-Lessenberry Ins Agcy Inc; Indep Ins Agts of Ky, Dir; cp/Glasgow Rotary Clb; Glasgow-Barren Co JCs, Dir; Barren Co Dem Party Com-man; r/Bapt.

McCANDLESS, PAUL LESLIE oc/Business and Financial Consultant; b/Sept 27, 1947; h/Houston, TX; ba/1177 W Loop St, Suite 1177, Houston, TX 77027; m/Margie Jean Bier; c/Erin Elizabeth, Brian Christoper; p/Ernest Ervin (dec) and Eleanor V McCauley McCandless, Omaha, NB; ed/BBA Univ Notre Dame 1969; MBA Creighton Univ 1977; pa/Arthur Anderson & Co 1969-72; Controller Swanson Enterprises 1972-78; Pres Erin Mgmt Acctg Inc 1978-; Am Inst CPSs; Tex & Neb Soc CPAs; Nat Assn Accts; Inst Mgmt Accts; cp/Exch Clb of Magic Cir-Houston, Secy; r/Rom Cath; hon/CPA Cert 1972; Cert in Mgmt Acctg 1978.

McCARTHY, ROSEMARY oc/Registered Nurse; b/June 25, 1948; h/Houston, TX; ba/3200 Shenandoah, Houston, TX 77021; p/Peter J and Alice V Conlon, Staten Island, NY; ed/BSN Niagara Univ 1970; MS Tex Wom's Univ 1979; pa/Fac ADN Prog, Acting Dir, Houston Commun Col; ANA; TNA; Am Lung Assn; r/Rom Cath; hon/W/W S&SW; Author 'The Predictive Value of Three Pre-Entry Criteria for Success on the Practical/Vocational Nursing Licensing Examination'' 1979.

McCARTY, ORICE DELBERT oc/Retired Mail Carrier; b/Mar 5, 1912; h/Rt 1 Box 651, LaFollette, TN 37766; m/Molly B; c/Russell Odel, Olen Osro, Herschel D, Cobia Inez Stagnolia, Orice David; p/Dapney C (dec) and Nancy Catherine Petree McCarty (dec); pa/US Mail Carrier; Farmer; Carpenter; Pres 3 Terms & VP 7 Terms Farm Bur; ASCS Com-man 4 Yrs; cp/SS Supt 21 Yrs; Ch Deacon 22 Yrs; r/Primitive Bapt; hon/Rural Mail Carrier Awd 1979; Farm Bur Bldrs Awd 1967-77.

McCARTY, RAYMOND M oc/Tax Attorney, Author; b/July 27, 1908; h/1247 Colonial Rd, Memphis, TN38117; ba/Same; m/Margaret Burton; ed/LLB So Law Univ 1948; Validated by Memphis St Univ 1967; Taxation Law Memphis St Univ Fall 1972; mil/AUS 1942-43, Corporal; pa/Chief Planning & Control Bch Real Est Div, Memphis Dist Corps Engrgs 1951-72; Secy Memphis Chapt Fed Bar Assn 1971-72; 1st Pres Poetry Soc Tenn 1953-54, Obtained Charter of Incorp; Author: Bk Poetry *Harp in a Strange Land* 1973 & *Trumpet in the Twilight of Time* 1981; Other Pub'd Works; cp/Appt'd Parliamentn Poetry Soc Tenn; r/Colonial Bapt Ch, Deacon, Tchr Mens Bible Class; hon/Commend from Chief Engrgs; Spec Cit World Poetry Soc.

McCLAIN, RODGER EUGENE oc/Administrative Officer; b/Dec 3, 1918; h/Tifton, GA; ba/Tifton; m/Ruth Brantley; c/Ruth Elizabeth, Carolyn Judy; p/James Lowell McClain, Tifton, GA; Mable Elizabeth McClain (dec); ed/AA Jacksonville Jr Col 1954; BSBA Univ Fla 1957; mil/AUS 1942-46 S/Sgt; pa/Adm Ofcr, US Dept Agric; cp/Past Pres Northside PTA; Annie Belle Clark PTA 1964; Life Mem PTA; Am Legion: Past Fin Ofcr, Past Adj & Past Comdr Post #21, Past Dist Comdr 12 Dist 1976 & Comdr Elect 1980-81; Past Pres Meth Men; Past Chef-De-Gare Post 909 Soc 40/8 1975, Grand Chef 1976; r/U Meth.

McCLAIN, RUTH BRANTLEY oc/Teacher; b/Oct 13, 1919; h/521 E 18th St, Tifton, GA 31794; m/Rodger Eugene; c/Ruth Elizabeth, Carolyn Judy; p/Count J M (dec) and Mollie Williams Brantley (dec); ed/AA Ga So Col 1940; Att'd Univ Fla 1954-55, Valdosta St Col 1967-69; pa/Tchr: Tifton, Ga 1978-80; Tiftarea Acad 1970-78; Len Lastinger Elem Sch 1968-70; Manor Sch 1940-43; Waycross, Ga US Civil Ser Com 1943-45; Jacksonville, Fla US Civil Ser Cost Acct 1945-53; cp/Tifton Mtl Hlth Assn, Bd Dirs 1975-81; Am Legion Aux Unit 21, Tifton Chm Ed & S'ship 1979-81; Albany, Ga 909 40/8 La Societe De Femme; Former Brownie & Girl Scout Ldr; SS Tchr; Chd of Confeds; PTA; r/U Meth; hon/Beta Sigma Phi Girl of Yr 1962-63; Beta Sigma Phi Hon Order of the Rose 1966.

McCLANAN, REBA JOYCE SALYERS oc/Civic Leader; b/Oct 25, 1937; h/3224 Burnt Mill Rd, Virginia Bch, VA 23452; m/Glenn B; c/Martin Whitehurst, Anne Laura, Glenn Jr; p/Mrs Hudson Salyers, Eastern, KY; ed/Att'd Merill Palmer Inst of Human Devel & Fam Life 1958-59; BS Berea Col 1959; MS VPI & SU 1979; Further Study Old Dominion Univ, Univ Va, George Wash Univ; pa/Home Demo Ext Agt, Univ Ky 1960-63; Elem Tchr, Waynesboro, VA 1963-64; Tchr Home Ec, Va Bch HS 1964-66; Home Ec Tchr Kellam HS 1967-68; Va Home Ec Assn; Am Home Ec Assn; Chm Va Bch Home Ec Tchrs; cp/Mem Va Bch City Coun; Former Pres Va Bch Coun Civic Orgs; Former Pres Va Bch Coun of Gdn Clbs; Former Pres Va Bch Friends of Lib; Former Pres Plaza Elem PTA & Plaza Gdn Clb; Va Bch Cancer Crusade Chm 1981; Part Va Bch Ct Docent Prog 1978-81; Va Bch Clean Commun Comm; Princess Anne Hist Soc; Adv Bd Va Bch Beautificaion Comm; Former Mem Exec Bd, Norfolk & Va Bch LWV; 1980-81 Mbrship Chm Coun of Civic Orgs; r/Meth; hon/W/W Am Wom 1981-82; Hon Life Mem Va Assn Parents & Tchrs; Hon Life Mem Citizens U for Boys.

McCLELLAN, HAROLD GREGORY oc/Bank Auditor; b/Nov 4, 1951; h/PO Box 492, Alexander City, AL 35010; m/Patricia Shores; p/Harold and Clara Mae McClellan, Alexander City, AL; ed/AS Alex City St Jr Col 1972; BS Auburn Univ; pa/Chief Auditor, Citibank Grp Inc; cp/Alex City JCs: Treas 1979-80, Pres 1980-81; r/Bapt; hon/Phi Theta Kappa; Alex City JCs Key Man of Yr Awd 1979-80.

McCLENDON, BILLY W oc/Preacher; b/Oct 8, 1951; h/Terrell, TX; ba/500 S Frances, Terrell, TX 75160; m/Bernetta; c/Billy Jr, Athena LaShun, Demetrius, Kristina; p/Leroy (dec) and Leora McClendon, Enterprise, TX; ed/BA LeTourneau Col 1974; Cert Polit Sci, Univ Tex 1978; Further Study: Tex Bapt Sem, So Bible Inst, Bishop Col, Richland Jr Col, Perkins Sch of Theol at So Meth Univ; pa/Min Bethlehem Bapt Ch; Tchr 5 Yrs Longview HS; TSTA; NEA; r/Bapt.

McCLURE, FREDERICK DONALD oc/Law Student; b/Feb 2, 1954; h/1314 James, Waco, TX 76706; m/Harriet; p/M N and F D McClure, San Augustine, TX; ed/BS Tex A&M Univ; pa/Former Agric Asst to US Sen John G Tower; White House Intern 1975; St Real Est Res Adv Com 1979-; St Adv Coun for Tech-Voc Ed 1975-77; r/Bapt; hon/Former St Pres & Nat Secy FFA 1972-74; Student Body Pres Tex A&M Univ 1976-77; Outstg Grad Tex A&M 1977; Yng Am Awd, BSA 1976; Golden Eagle Awd Am Acad Achmt 1976.

McCLURE, GEORGE GILLEN oc/Citrus Grower-Processor, Indoor Foliage Plant Grower; b/Aug 1, 1925; h/Apopka, FL; ba/PO Drawer 1010, Apopka, FL 32703; m/Nancy Brower; c/Michael, Patricia, Marilyn, John Peter, Nancy Carol; p/Gillen (dec) and Betty Moses McClure (dec); ed/BS Univ Fla 1949, Grad Asst 1950; mil/USMC 1943-46; pa/Asst Prod Mgr, Minute Maid Groves Corp 1950-53; Grove Owner 1948-; Nurseryman 1954-; Owner-Mgr Ctrl Fla Grove Ser Inc 1966-; Past Conslt: Conn Gen Ins Co, Minute Maid, Libby McNeil & Libby, Olin-Mathesin, Prudential Ins Co, Am Agrinomics; Dir Silver Springs Citrus Coop 1967-79; Past Dir Apopka Growers Supply; Fla St Horitculture Soc; Fla Citrus Prod Mgrs Assn; Fla Citrus Comm 1972-79; cp/Past Pres Apopka Jr C of C; Former City Commr, Apopka; r/Meth.

McCLUSKEY, PATRICIA ANN oc/Secretary, Teacher; b/Mar 6, 1957; h/Rt 3 Box 156, Starkville, MS 39759; p/James Robert and Frances Watkins McCluskey, S'ville; ed/MEd Miss St Univ 1981; pa/Pi Omega Pi; Phi Beta Lambda; Miss Bus Ed Assn; r/1st Bapt Ch, S'ville; hon/Nat 4-H Poultry Achmt Winner; St Del XV World's Poultry Cong, New Orleans, La; Cook of Wk, *S'ville Daily News*, 1975; Miss 4-H All Stars; S'hip, Nat Secys Assn, S'ville Chapt; W/W Am HS Students, Miss Phi Beta Lambda.

McCOLLUM, ERDINE IMBLER (DEE) oc/State Employee; b/Feb 22, 1926; h/Rt 5 Box 125A, Frankfort, KY 40601; pa/Frankfort; m/Bruce B Jr; c/Bruce B III, Jack B, Richard L; p/Jessie Alvin Imbler (dec); Margaret Miller Lewis (dec); mil/USAF 1944-45; pa/St of Ky Bus Ofc; Intl Wom's Pilot; Towing Gliders; cp/Maj Civil Air Patrol; Bd Ky Aviation Pilot; r/Prot; hon/Safety Awd, Hughes Air W Classic Race 1979.

McCONNELL, J KNOX oc/Banker; b/Dec 13, 1926; h/Drawer AA, Keystone, WV 24852; p/J Knox Sr (dec) and Marie Rice McConnell (dec); ed/BS Waynesburg Col; PhD Elysion Col; mil/AUS 1950-51; pa/Pres & Dir First Nat Bank Keystone; Dir Nat Assn Review Appraisers; Dir Consumer Fin Assn of WV; Dir St Adv Bd of Small Bus Adm; cp/Rotary Clb of Keystone; hon/Author "How to Get a Loan" 1975 & Others.

McCOOL, CHARLES W oc/City Manager; b/Jan 8, 1955; h/Holly Hill, FL; ba/1065 Ridgewood Ave, Holly Hill, FL 32017; m/Laura J; c/Christoper E Powers; p/Charles E and Mary L McCool, Jacksonville, Fl; ed/BA Stetson Univ 1979; pa/Adm Asst, City of Orange City 1979; Field Opers Asst, US Census Bur 1980; City Mgr, City of Holly Hill 1980-; Am

Soc Public Adm; ICMA, Coop'g Mem; Fla City & Co Mgrs Assn; cp/Volusia Co Dem Exec Comm 1977-; Orange City Am Red Cross, Bd Dirs 1979-80; Orange City Kiwanis 1978-79, Secy 1979; r/Bapt; hon/6th Pl Extemporaneous Spkrs Nat Tourn, Plattsburg, NY 1974; Outstg Yng Men Am 1980.

McCORD, AMELIA ADAMS oc/Homemaker; b/Mar 17, 1912; h/Trinity Pl, 300 Airline Rd, Apt D-13, Columbus, MS 39701; m/Malcolm Marvin; p/James Louis Sr (dec) and Rachel White Adams (dec); ed/Att'd Cumberland Univ & Union Univ; cp/Past Pres Stephen Foster Mus Clb; Past Mem DAR: Nat Cong Page 1933, Pers Page to Nat Curator Gen 1934; Past Mem UDC; r/Presb; hon/Valedictorian Class of 1929.

McCORMICK, RALPH EUGENE oc/Executive; b/May 11, 1948; h/Charlotte, NC; ba/PO Box 3446, Charlotte, NC 28203; m/Eugenia K; c/Darby E; ed/AS King's Col; mil/AUS; pa/VP Fin & Adm, W A Buening & Co Inc, Mercy Hosp; Nat Assn Accts; Am Mgmt Assn; Am Soc Pers Mgrs; r/Epis.

McCOY, LEE BERARD oc/Buyer and Sales Promotion Manager; b/July 27, 1925; h/Box 717, Theodore, AL 36590; c/Bernadette, Raymond, Richard, Joan; p/Damase Joseph (dec) and Robena Bruce Berard (dec); ed/Att'd Univ Ala 1958-60; pa/Mgr Custom Color Div, Promoter, Mobile Paint Co; Spectromatic Assocs; Nat Paint Distbrs; cp/Quota Clb: Corresp Secy 1977-78, Pres 1978-80, Bd Dirs 1977-81, Editor *Quota Care-Gram* 1980-, Chm Pres's Coun 1979, Chm 44th Dist Conf 1980, Chm Commun Ser Com Quota Intl 1980-82, Intl Ser Com S Area 1978-80; Del Civic Roundtable 1977-78; First VP Civic Roundtable 1980-81; Bd Dirs Friends of Museum, City of Mobile 1978-81; Bd Dirs Miss Wheelchair Ala 1980-84; Curator Shepard Meml Lib 1972-; Bd Dirs Old Dauphin Way Assn 1977-79; Hist Preserv Soc; Eng Spkg Union; Mobile Area Retard'd Citizens; Heart Fund; r/Meth; hon/Merit of Hon, Civic Roundtable 1979, 80; Quota Ser: Ser Awd Wom's Com of Spain Rehab Ctr 1980, Ser Awd Dist 8 1979, Intl Awd for Serving Quota Objs 1980; Wom of Day; W/W S&SW; Nom Gayfer's Career Wom; Patriot's Awd; Num Pubs.

McCRACKEN, LLOYD H oc/Executive; b/Sept 25, 1932; h/605 Elm, Jonesboro, AR 72401; ba/J'boro; m/LaVida J Shelton; c/Lloyd H Jr; p/E H (dec) and Vitrie McCracken, J'boro, AR; ed/Att'd Ark St Uiv, J'boro & Ark Col; AA Univ of St of NY 1974; pa/Real Est Appraiser; VP & Chief Appraiser, U Fed Savings & Loan, J'boro; IFAS Designated Mem; SRA Designated Mem; CRA Designated Mem; Nat Assn Indep Fee Appraisers: Pres NE Ark Chapt 1978-80, So Regional Gov 1979, Ark St Dir 1980, Nat Pubs Com 1978-, Chm Nat Pubs Com 1981, Nat Dir 1980-83; Secy-Treas NE Ark Chapt Nat Assn Home Bldrs 1979; Bd Assessors J'boro Downtown Improvement Dist; cp/Craighead Co Hist Soc: Pres 1978, Bd Dirs 1980-82; Editor Craighead Co Hist Qtrly 1973-75; r/U Meth; hon/V G Warner Trophy as Man of Yr, Nat Assn Indep Fee Appraisers 1980; Wrote Hist Huntington Ave U Meth Ch 1970.

McCRARY, BURMAH M oc/Retired Contract Negotiator; b/Feb 3, 1908; h/Rt 3 Box 719, Ft Payne, AL 35967; m/Arthur J (dec); p/Joseph Oliver (dec) and Elizabeth Durham McCracken (dec); ed/Grad Jacksonville St Univ 1927; LLB George Washington Univ 1939; pa/Mem Bar DC; Fed Bar Assn; Ret'd Contract Negotiator & Liaison in Missile Prog; Gen Counsel's Ofc, Atty; Ofc of Comptroller Gen, Wash; DC; cp/Pres Gdn Clb of Ala Inc; DeKalb Co Dem Assn; r/Bapt; hon/Local Awds in Area of Civic Concern; Appt'd by Gov & Serving on Jury Comm.

McCRARY, GUY RICHARD oc/Assistant Vice President; b/June 28, 1953; h/1712 Douglas, Midland, TX 79701; ba/Midland; m/Marion; p/Edwin D and Bettye McCrary, Garland, TX; ed/MS Am Technol Univ; BS Tex A&M Univ; mil/AUS 1975-79; pa/Asst VP, First Nat Bank (Previously Ec Res Ofcr); Am Inst Bnkg; cp/C of C; Midland JCs; U Way; Am Cancer Soc; r/Prot; hon/Dist'd Student; Dist'd Mil Grad Tex A&M; Army Commend Medal.

McCREIGHT, CARLOS ROBERT JR oc/Firefighter; b/July 11, 1946; h/3402 Rollingwood Dr, Gastonia, NC 28052; ba/Gastonia; m/Mary Mercks; c/Carla Dawn; p/Carlos R McCreight Sr, Brunswick, OH; Ruby Clark McCreight, Gastonia, NC; ed/AS Fire Sci; AA Bus Adm; mil/AUS 1966-68; pa/Intl Assn Fire Fighters; NC EMT; r/Salvationists; hon/Gastonia Father of Yr 1979.

McCREIGHT, MICHAEL JOE oc/Superintendent; b/June 22, 1948; h/Alexander, AR; ba/PO Box 320, Alexander, AR 72002; m/Barbara; c/Melisa; p/Mr and Mrs Joe C McCreight, Silver Springs, MD; ed/BA 1970, MS 1971; pa/Adm Positions, St Residential Facilities for the Mtlly Retard'd; Supt Ark Chd's Colony; Psi Chi; Phi Kappa Phi; Fla Assn Retard'd Citizens; r/Meth; hon/Grad F'ship 1970-71.

McCRICKARD, RUBY ASHWELL oc/Director of Nursing Services,

Assistant Administrator; b/Apr 19, 1931; h/Rustburg, VA; ba/Lynchburg General-Marshall Lodge Hosp, Lynchburg, VA 24506; m/George; c/Tom; p/(dec); ed/Dip Riverside Hosp Sch of Nsg 1953; Cert Univ So Calif 1976; BA Goddard Col 1975; MSN Med Col Ga 1977; pa/Dir Nsg Sers/Lynchburg Gen-Marshall Lodge Hosps: Asst Admr 1978-, Dir Nsg Sers 1969-78, Asst Dir Nsg Sers 1966-69, Intensive Care & Ctrl Supply Supvr 1962-66; OR Staff Nurse, Asst OR Supvr, Acting OR Supvr, Kecoughtan Vet Hosp 1955-62; OR Staff Nurse, Hd Nurse Med Unit, Riverside Hosp 1953-55; ANA: Past Mem Mbrship Com & By-Laws Com; VNA: Chm Profl Nsg Pract Com, Past Bd Mem, Past Chm Nsg Ser Admrs Sect, Past Chm & Secy OR Conf Grp, Past Chm-Secy-Treas Gen Duty Sect, Past Com on Noms, Past By-Laws Com, Past Chm Ec & Gen Wel; NLN; VLN: Past Mem Nom'g Com; Nat Forum for Adm of Nsg Sers of NLN; Am Soc for Hosp Nsg Ser Adm of Am Hosp Assn: By-Laws Com 1978, Recog Prog for Excell in Field of Nsg Adm: Nom Level 1979, Cand Level 1980; Va Chapt Am Soc Nsg Ser Admrs: Pres 1981, Pres-Elect 1980, Treas 1979, Chm Nom'g Com 1978, Mbrship Com 1977; Piedmont Heart Assn: Past Chm Nsg Com, Past Bd Mem; Lynchburg Col Nsg Ed Adv Coun; Ctrl Va Commun Col Adv Com for Respiratory Therapy; Ctrl Va Hlth Plan'g Emer Med Adv Coun: Past Chm By-Laws, Past Mem Transp & Patient Transfer Adv Com; Ctrl Va Commun Col Child Care Prog; SW Va Hlth Sys Agcy Inc: Primary Care Com; Riverside Hosp Sch of Nsg Alumnae: Pres 1959-60, 1st VP 1958, Secy 1957; Num Other Coms & Part in Many Sems on Local & St Level in ANA & NLN; cp/OES, Rustburg Chapt #23; Scottish Rite Wom's Clb; Nat Soc Lit & Arts; Parent Tchr F'ship, Timberlake Christian Sch; Nobletts Clb of Lynchburg Shrine Clb; AAUW; r/Chestnut Hill Bapt Ch; hon/Ella T Whitten Awd 1966; Beta Omicron Chapt Sigma Theta Tau; Del for US Nsg Ser Adm Ldrs Goodwill Travel Prog Del Vis'g Wn Europe 1980; W/W S&SW 1980-81.

McCUEN, WILLIAM (BILL) JAMES oc/Commissioner of State Lands; b/Aug 19, 1943; h/PO Box 269-108 Horseshoe Dr, Hot Springs, AR 71901; ba/Little Rock; m/Nancy Sue; p/Garland Granville McCuen (dec); Sallie E McCuen, Ft Smith, AR; ed/BS Col of Ozarks; MS Henderson St Univ; pa/Commr of St Lands, St of Ark, 1980-82; Previously Judge Garland Co; Prin Goldstein Elem Sch 1971-76; Tchr Grades 2 & 4, Rix Elem Sch 1969-71; Tchr Grade 6, Pomona, Calif 1968-69; Former St Pres Ark Assn for Chd's Ed; Past Pres Garland Co Elem Prin's Assn; Former Mem: Ark Elem Prin's Assn, Ark Ednl Assn; Ark Assn Devel Orgs: Pres; Former Mem Ark Manpwr Coun; cp/Former Alderman, Ward 6, Hot Sprgngs; W Ctrl Dist Policy Bd; Ark Weatherization Policy Bd, Dept Local Sers: Former Ex-Oficio Mem Ouachita Hosp Bd; Hot Sprgs: JCs, Elks Lodge, Foun Perf'g Arts, Pks & Beautification Com, C of C; S Hot Sprgs Lions; Former Bd Mem Webb Commun Ctr; Wkshop for Informed Dems; Others; r/Presb.

McCULLOGH, PAULINE WINTERS oc/Homemaker; b/Dec 14, 1921; h/1706 Chilton Dr, Baytown, TX 77520; m/Emery Leroy Jr; c/Lois Marie M Fassino, Patricia Anne M Cargill; p/James Carvin (dec) and Laura Elizabeth Carter Winters (dec); cp/Life Mem Bay Area Heritage Soc & Museum; Winters Meml Assn; Charter Mem Goose Creek Chapt DAR: Regent 1979-81; Charter Mem Daughs of Repub of Tex: Treas 1979-81, Hist Pubs Com 1979-71; UDC, Lum Roark Chapt 1978-80, Histn, Yrbook & Prog Chm, Conv Del-St & Dist; Descs of San Jacinto Vets, Houston Chapt; OES Goose Creek Chapt 798; r/Bapt; hon/DAR: Cert & Blue Ribbon 1976, Bicent Cert Awd 1978, Nat Tri-Color Ribbon Awd for Yrbook, St Blue Ribbon Cert Awd.

McCULLOUGH, HELEN LOUISE oc/Executive; b/Mar 9, 1929; h/413 Oak Hill Dr, Conroe, TX 77304; ba/Conroe; c/Harold Wayne Stockdale, Charlotte Elizabeth Stockdale, Thomas Waters; p/Cora Lee Smith, Conroe, TX; ed/BS SWn Bus Col 1952; pa/Pres & Owner Conroe Marine Inc; School Bus Driver, Conroe Indep Sch Dist; Previously: Production/Proration Clk, Superior Oil Co & Clk/Steno Humble Oil & Refining Co; Agt Tex Pks & Wildlfe Dept; Notary Public Comm, Montgomery Co & Harris Co 30 Yrs; VP BPW Clb; Tex Tchrs Assn; r/Bapt; hon/Secy of Wk, Conroe Radio Sta KIKR 1979; W/W S&SW 1980-81.

McCUTCHEN-WENDLANDT, GAY oc/Clinical Laboratory Manager; b/Sept 20, 1938; h/2600 Belle Fontaine, D24, Houston, TX 77025; ba/Houston; p/Vonly Buel and Wilma Irene Crosby McCutchen; ed/BA 1960, Pre-Med 1961, La St Univ; Med Tech Internship, Charity Hosp 1962; Att'g Tex Wom's Univ 1979-; Other Courses & Sems; pa/Pt-Time McCutchen Constrn Co, Jennings, La 1950-62; Field Corresp, *Horse World Magazine* 1961-62; Bench Technol in Hematology Feb 1962, Supvr Hematology Sect Oct 1962, Mercy Hosp 1962-67; Chief Med Technol, Sect on Clin Pathol, Univ Tex Sys Cancer Ctr, M D Anderson Hosp & Tumor Inst 1967-70; Clin Lab Mgr, Dept Lab Med, M D Anderson Hosp & Tumor Inst 1970-; Acting Admr, Inst of Hemotherapy, Houston 1974-77; Conslt, Inst of Hemotherapy 1977-; Am Soc Med Technol: Elect Com Mem 1971, Adm Sect Awds Com 1971, Chm Elects Com 1972-74, Leg Conslt Region VII 1974-, Donor Recruitment Task Force of Am Blood Comm 1975-77,

207

V-Chm Noms Com 1976, Chm Elects Com 1976, Noms Task Force 1976, Del 1970-, Chm Noms Com 1976-79; Tex Soc for Med Technol: Noms & Elects Com 1970-71, Assoc Editor Newslttr 1970-73, Prog Com Chm TSMT Conv 1972, Bd of Dirs 1972-75, Leg Co 1973-, Att'd St Meeting as Del 1969-79, Chm Hotel Arrangements for 1978 Conv 1977-78; Houston Dist Soc for Med Technol: Chm Noms & Elects Com & Chm Standards & Studies Com 1968-69, Pres-Elect 1970-71, Pres 1971-72, Chm Leg Com 1971-74, Bd Dirs 1973-77; Am Assn Blood Banks: Blood Bank Public Policies Com 1975-, S Ctrl Dist Liaison Com & Com on Plan'g & Action 1976-; S Ctrl Assn Blood Banks: Adm Prog Com 1976-77; Tex Blood Bank Dirs: Hosted Jan 1976 Meeting; Houston Antibody Clb 1974-; Tex Hosp Assn 1975-; Omicron Sigma; Alpha Delta Pi; cp/Bd Mem & Pres Barclay Homeowner's Assn; Adv Coun Nat Hlth Labs for "Older Ams Hlth Fair Day"; Designed & Devel'd Model of Vol Blood Procurement Prog for Am Cancer Soc; Recip for Am/Meth; hon/Nat Hon Soc; Nat Thespian Awd; La St Univ S'ship; La St Univ Band; Guest Editor *Am Jour of Med Technol* June 1975; Appt'd to Donor Recruitment Task Force of Am Blood Comm as Rep of Am Soc Med Technol 1975-77; Vis'g Fac Mem, Mayo Clin, Dept Lab Med, Sept 1975; Assoc Editor of Mgmt/Instrumentation Sect *Am Jour Med Tech* 1976-; Omicron Sigma, Pres's Hon Roll, Am Soc Med Technol 1977, 78, 79; Pres Awd, Am Soc Med Technol 1978 & 79; W/W: Fin & Indust 1979 & S&SW 1980; Num Presentations at Meetings & Confs; Author/Co-Author Num Profl Articles.

McDANIEL, JAN LEE oc/Music Instructor; b/June 18, 1957; h/522 Montague St, Nocona, TX 76255; ba/Same; m/Len E; p/William A (dec) and Jenice McDaniel, Nocona, TX; ed/BMus Cand Mid-Wn St Univ; pa/Nat Guild Piano Tchrs; Pi Kappa Lambda; r/Grace Ch; hon/Presser Schlr 1979; Clark Schlr 1975-76.

McDAVID, MARY ELLEN FARRIS oc/Speech-Language Pathologist; b/Nov 4, 1954; h/5 Dairy Rd, Poca, WV 26169; ba/S Charleston; m/Daniel; p/Ramon A and Evelyn Starr Farris, Charleston, WV; ed/BS 1975, MS magna cum laude 1977, WVU; pa/Speech-Lang Pathol, Kanawha Co Bd Ed 1978-; Am Speech & Hearing Assn; WV Speech & Hearing Assn; cp/Beta Sigma Phi, Treas; Scarlet Oaks Country Clb; r/Rom Cath; hon/WV Rehab Ctr Grantee 1975; Cert of Clin Comp, Am Speech & Hearing Assn 1979; Thesis Presented at Am Speech & Hearing Assn Conv, San Fran, Calif 1978.

McDERMOTT, EMMAJEAN oc/Retired Teacher; b/Feb 19, 1898; h/807 S Ponca, Norman, OK 73071; m/Hugh V; c/Jack, Caroline M Kennedy; p/William V (dec) and Carrie Hopkins Provost (dec); ed/BS; BFA; BIA; MIE; pa/Ret'd Tchr; BPW Clb, St Pres; Indust Arts, Treas; cp/Hd Unit U Fund; Chm Mobile Meals; r/Presb; hon/Wom of Yr, BPW; S'ship Named in Her Hon; Outstg Greek Wom of Yr.

McDONALD, LESTER L oc/Retired Teacher; b/Sept 12, 1918; h/Rt 2 Box 34, Preston, MS 39354; m/Edna E; c/Jimmy Leo; p/Charlie (dec) and Agnes Jones McDonald (dec); ed/BS; mil/AUS 4½ Yrs; pa/Ret'd Basic Elem Instr; r/Assem of God.

McDONALD, MARY HELEN oc/Administrator; b/Oct 24, 1942; h/Rt 3 Box 180B, Magnolia, AR 71753; ba/Magnolia; m/Robert Foster; c/Maria Lynn, Genevieve Nanette, Paul Robert; p/William Welcome Dodson, McNeil, AR; Margaret McAlister, McNeil, AR; ed/Assoc Deg Nsg So Ark Univ 1976; LPN Oil Belt Voc Sch 1970; pa/Adm Leisure Lodge Nsg Home; Ark Reg'd Nurse Assn; cp/Quota Clb; BPW Clb; r/Bapt.

McDONALD, MORTON oc/Board Chairman; b/May 2, 1904; h/PO Box 105, DeLand, FL 32720; ba/DeLand; m/Thelma S; c/William R (dec), Francis Morton, Thomas Smedley, Rebekah M Bostic; p/William Jamison (dec) and Daisy Stummer McDonald (dec); pa/Bd Chm The Abstract Corp, Land Title Ser; Pres Fla Land Title Assn 1940-41; Am Land Title Assn 1966-56; cp/Pres DeLand Rotary Clb 1936, Dist Gov 1948-49; r/U Meth; hon/Algernon Sydney Sullivan Awd, Stetson Univ 1974; Paul Harris Fellow, Rotary; Hon Mem Am Land Title Assn.

McDONALD, STEPHEN LAMAR oc/Funeral Director; b/June 4, 1950; h/310 Essex, Picayune, MS 39466; ba/Picayune; p/Claiborne III (dec) and Edith R McDonald, Picayune, MS; mil/Miss NG; pa/VP McDonald Funeral Home; Miss Funeral Dirs Assn; NFDA; Order of Golden Rule; cp/Picayune C of C; Picayune Rotary Clb; 32° Mason; Knight Templar; Shriner; r/U Meth; Ofcl Bd; hon/Rotary Pres's Cup.

McDONALD, THERESA oc/Music Teacher; b/Sept 16, 1945; h/Winona, MS; ba/Winona Acad, Hwy 51 S, Winona, MS 38967; c/Jeffrey Wayne; p/Mrs E S Fletcher, Cleveland, MS; ed/BMus 1966; BME 1969; pa/Piano & Voice Tchr, Winona Acad; Miss Mus Ed Assn: Dist Chm, St V-Chm; Miss Pvt Sch Choral Assn, St Pres; cp/Miss Fed Wom's Clbs; Montgomery Co Repub Wom's Clb; r/Meth; hon/Choral Grp Listed in W/W Am HS Students 1980; Hon'd at St Conv of Delta Kappa Gamma as Outstg Mem of Fine Arts 1981; Superior Grps in Miss Mus Ed Assn

1966-72; St Choral Fest Accompanist of MMEA & MPSCA; Superior Grps in Miss Pvt Sch Choral Assn 1973-80; Outstg Yng Wom Am 1972; Cnslr Fred Waring Wkshop 1970; Delta St Univ Mus Hall of Fame 1980.

McDUFFIE, PAUL WAYNE oc/Electronic Technician; b/Mar 8, 1945; h/203 Brentwood, Petal, MS 39465; ba/Hattiesburg, MS; m/Evelyn Lee Styron; c/Joseph Scott, Sean Paul, James Wayne; p/Joseph Paul McDuffie, Kokomo, IN; Eunice Lee Newsome, Hattiesburg, MS; ed/Crim Just USM; mil/173 Abn Div 1965-66; pa/2nd Class FCC Commercial Amateur Radio Oper N5AAM; cp/Am Legion; McDuffee Clans Am; Miss Magnolia Repub Clb; r/Prot; hon/Grad Miss Law Acad.

McELMON, ALBERT NOBLE oc/US Postal Carrier; b/Oct 25, 1928; h/PO Box 1001, Morehead City, NC 28557; ba/Morehead City; m/Frances Rice; c/Sandra Marie Green, Janet Sue McKinney, Albert Noble Jr; p/Byron Noble (dec) and Laura LeFurgy McElmon, Eatontown, NJ; mil/USMC; pa/US Postal Carrier; Dir Mus; cp/Past Secy Lions Clb Morehead City; NALC; r/Free Will Bapt; hon/Salesman of Mo, REA Express Jan 1957; Hon for 30 Yrs Ser, First Free Will Bapt Ch; Key to Morehead City 1979.

McENTIRE, RICK E oc/Minister; b/July 30, 1954; h/PO Box 1862, Lawton, OK 73502; ba/Lawton; m/Marsha Lynn Johnson; c/Allison Lynn; p/Vic and Joyce McEntire, Comanche, OK; ed/Att'd Cameron Univ; Att'g Luther Rice Sem; pa/Min Evagelism, First Bapt Ch, Comanche, OK; Min Yth, Cameron Bapt Ch, Lawton; Pastor Letitia Bapt Ch, Lawton; Okla Assn Evangelists; Assn of Evangelists, So Bapt Conv; r/Bapt; hon/Lic'd into Gospel Min May 1974; Ordained into Min Apr 1977; Pres Cameron Univ BSU 1975, 76; Outstg Yng Men Am 1977; Orgr & Dir Drug Abuse Sems in Schs, Chs & City Meetings; Spkr at Num Retreats, Confs & Clbs.

McGAHEE, SELVIN oc/Rural Rental Specialist; b/Feb 2, 1954; h/Rt 6 Box 931, Pk St, Lake Placid, FL 33852; p/Leroy Jr and Margaret McGahee, Lake Placid, FL; ed/Att'd Bethel Col 1972-73; BBA En Ky Univ 1977; pa/Rural Rental Spec, Fla Non-Profit Housing Inc 1980-; Soc for Advmt of Mgmt; cp/NAACP; Highlands Co Home Hlth Agcy; S Fla Jr Col's Equal Access-Equal Opport Com; Hwy Park Housing Inc, Bd Dirs, Treas; r/Meth; hon/W/W S&SW 1980-81.

McGEE, H GLENN oc/Architect, Interior Designer; b/June 26, 1937; h/415 Harden St, Columbia, SC 29205; ba/Columbia; p/James Gladney Sr and Elizabeth W McGee, Hartsville, SC; ed/BArch Clemson Univ 1960; mil/USAR; pa/Pres Am Inst Archs; Am Soc Interior Designers; cp/Palmetto Hist Preserv Soc; Columbia Coun Archs; r/Epis; hon/Nat Awd NSID 1972; W/W SE 1980-81.

McGIMPSEY, EDWARD R oc/Funeral Executive; b/Jan 31, 1949; h/220 Avery Ave, Morganton, NC; m/Lydia Yvonne Logan; p/Edward R Sr and Hazel C McGimpsey, Lenoir, NC; ed/BA Gardner-Webb Col; Grad Gupton-Jones Col 1972; pa/Mgr & VP Ebony Funeral Ser; r/Presb.

McGINLEY, ANTHONY JOSEPH oc/Professor; b/Sept 2, 1920; h/4352A Lee Hwy, Apt 103, Arlington, VA 22207; ba/Arlington; p/Anthony Joseph Sr and Elizabeth Mary Schoeffler McGinley (dec); ed/BA St Charles Col 1941; Post Grad St Charles Sem 1942-45; MA 1971, PhD 1993, Cath Univ Am; pa/Campus Min Conslt, Susquehanna Univ, Selinsgrove, Pa 1954-60; Advr/Conslt Dickenson Col & Dickinson Law Students, Carlisle, Pa 1960-70; Grad Students Res Dir, Cath Univ Am, Wash 1971-73; Prof Psych Marymount Col Va 1979-; Prof Psych Georgetown Univ, Wash 1977-79; Prof Psych, Dir Dissertations & Master Theses Georgetown Grad Sch, Dept Orthodonics, Wash 1977-79; Doct Dissertation Conslt, Hot Line Conslt, Arlington 1978-79; AAUP; APGA; DCPA; Am Psych Assn; Delta Epsilon Sigma, Marymount Col of Va Chapt; cp/Active Var Civic Orgs; Chaplain VA Hosp, Lebanon, Pa 1953-54; Dem Party; Hon Life Mem K of C; Washington Golf & Country Clb; r/Cath; hon/Orgr & Mem Psi Chi Hon Soc, Marymount Col of Va Chapt; Delta Epsilon Sigma; W/W S; Man of Yr, Carlisle City Com, Pa 1966; Recip 5 Yr Awd, Marymount Col 1979; Contbr Articles to Profl Pubs.

McGINNIS, JOHN SHELDON oc/Sales and Marketing; b/Sept 2, 1934; h/Pounding Mill, VA; ba/S&S Corp, Rt 3 Box 70, Cedar Bluff, VA 24609; m/Joyce Bolyard; c/Jon Lincoln, Jo Ellen; p/Francis Guy and Nola Agnes McGinnis; ed/Num Ser Schs Incl'g Ofcr Cand 1957; Ingersoll-Rand Sr Mgmt Sch; mil/AUS 1950-70 Ret'd Maj; pa/Sales-Mktg, S&S Corp; Am Mining Cong; Coal Opers Assn 1980; cp/Adm Bd Meth Ch, Dir 1980; Dir Marion C of C 1976-77; Mason; r/Meth; hon/Legion of Merit; Bronze Star Medal; Air Medal w OLC; Vietnamese Cross of Gallantry w Silver Star; W/W S&SW.

McGLON, EVANGIE HYTCHE oc/Assistant Professor; b/Oct 10, 1932; h/6104 Branniff Dr, Okla City, OK 73105; ba/Stillwater; p/Hayes

PERSONALITIES OF THE SOUTH

and Bethel Hytche, Okla City, OK; ed/BS; MT; MS; PhD; pa/Asst Prof OSU; Coun Excptl Chd; Phi Delta Kappa; Okla Assn for Chd w Lrng Disabilities; Okla Psych Assn; Assoc Mem Grad Fac; cp/Delta Sigma Theta, Sponsor Chapt OSU; YWCA; Urban Leag; r/Presb; hon/Doct Fellow Okla St Regents for Higher Ed; Reviewed the Prospectus for Revision of Textbook *Assessment in Special and Remedial Education.*

McGRADY, ANN A oc/Child Development Specialist, Social Worker; b/May 16, 1947; h/Hillsville, VA; m/Joseph H; c/Jonathan Lee, Chadwick Paxton; p/John and Lena Abbate, Orange, CT; ed/AA Marymount Col 1967; BS 1972, MS 1976 Radford Col; Post Grad Work VPI & SU 1977-; pa/Buyer Firelite Bridal Shop, Orange, Conn Summers 1965-68; Salesclerk Malley's Dept St, New Haven, Conn Summers 1963-65; Ft Lauderdale Res Lab for Mtlly Retard'd Chd 1965-67; Little Flower Montessori Sch, Orange, Conn 1967-68; Master Tchr, Carroll Co Hdstart Ctr 1972-73; Summer Hdstart & Kindergarten Prog 1972; Kindergarten Tchr, Hillsville Elem Sch 1973-75; Summer Bible Sch, H'ville Christian Ch 1973, 76, 77; Task Force for Kindergarten for Carroll Co & Kindergarten Cnslt 1972-76; Tchr H'ville Elem Sch 1977; Dir Carroll-Grayson-Galax Early Childhood Devel Prog 1977-80; Child Devel Wel Spec, Carroll Co Dept Social Sers 1981-; Delta Kappa Gamma, Corresp Secy 1979-; Va Ed Assn, Early Childhood Div; NEA; Carroll Ed Assn; Am Assn Elem-Kindergarten-Nursery Sch Edrs; So Assn for Chd Under Six; Va Assn for Early Childhood Ed; Nat Assn Ed of Yng Chd; Am Montessori Soc; Va Govtl Employees Assn Inc 1981; Assn for Childhood Ed Intl; Twin Co-Galax Assn for Retard'd Citizens; Notary Public for Commonwlth at Large; cp/H'ville Wom's Clb: VP, Corresp Secy, Chm Ed Dept, Mem SWn Dist's Nom'g Com, Past Pres; Bd Mem Rep'g Carroll Co on Galax-Carroll-Grayson C of C & Chm Merchant Consumer Relats Div; VP C of C 1976-; Chm Carroll Co Human Sers Advocate Adv Com 1976-; Bd Mem Plan'g Dist 3 Subarea Hlth Coun, SW Va Hlth Sys Agcy 1976-; Past Pres Univ Tenn Law Wives 1970; Past Brownie Troop Ldr 1973; Plant & Pluck Gdn Clb 1972; Past Neighborhood Chm, Mother's March of Dimes, Knoxville, Tenn 1968-69; Chapt 10 Mount Rogers Mtl Hlth & Mtl Retard Sers, Bd Mem Rep'g Carroll Co 1978-; Chm Parent to Parent Org, Carroll Co 1977-; Spec Ed Adv Com, Carroll Co 1978-79; Va Div Chd & Yth Com Adv Panel to Review Revised St Plan to Meet Needs of Handicapped Chd in SWn Va 1978-; Carroll Co Rec Comm Bd Dirs 1979-; Bd Dirs Va Infants Prog 1978-; SW Va Agric Assn Inc, Chd & Fams Com 1980-; r/H'ville Christian Ch; hon/Outstg Elem Tchrs Am 1973-74, 74-75; W/W Am Wom 1981; Author Var Articles Concerning Child Growth & Devel, Infant Stimulation & Early Childhood Techniques & Parent Effectiveness 1977-.

McGREGOR, FRANK BOBBIT JR oc/Attorney and Counselor at Law; b/Dec 30, 1952; h/Hillsboro, TX; ba/H'boro; m/Brenda Ruth Battles; c/Jason Bobbitt, Aaron Lee; p/Frank Bobbit and Doris Mason McGregor, Hillsboro, TX; ed/BS Baylor Univ 1974; MEd Tarleton St Univ 1976; JD S Tex Col Law 1979; pa/Atty & Cnslr at Law; Cert'd Speech & Eng Tcr; Am Bar Assn; St Bar Tex; Hill Co Bar Assn; Am Judicature Soc; cp/H'boro Lodge #196 AF&AM; Lions Clb of H'boro; r/So Bapt; hon/Outstg Teenager Am 1971; Pres Hill Co Bar Assn 1980-81; Dean's Hon List, Baylor Univ; Bancroft-Whitney Am Jurisprudence Awd Winner.

McGRIGGS, LEE AUGUSTUS SR oc/Professor; b/Feb 25, 1945; h/Houston, TX; ba/Tex So Univ, 3201 Wheeler Ave, Houston, TX 77004; m/Virginia Peters; c/Lee Augustus Jr; p/Sampson Sr and Lenora McGriggs, Pt Gibson, MS; ed/AB Jackson St Univ 1967; MS Tenn St Univ 1969; PhD Univ Ill 1975; pa/Prof Public Adm, Tex So Univ; Nat Assn Schs of Public Affairs & Adm; Am Polit Sci Assn; Am Soc Public Admrs; cp/Gulf Coast Brotherhood Assn; r/Bapt; hon/Author *The Odyssey of Martin Luther King, Jr & Black Legislative Politics in Illinois.*

McHAM, ALLEN EARL oc/Minister; b/Aug 10, 1948; h/Rt 3 Box 418, Minden, LA 71055; m/Teresa S; c/Scott, Lorie; p/Dub Hulen and Marion Vivian McHam, Homer, LA; ed/BS Dallas Bapt Col 1975; Att'd SWn Sem; pa/Pastor Emmanuel Bapt Ch, Big Spring; Exec Bd Mem Big Spring Bapt Assn; Former Mem Exec Bd & Past Assoc Yth Coor, SEn Bapt Assn NM; r/Christian; hon/Psych Awds 1974 & 75.

McHENRY, WILLIAM EARL oc/Assistant Professor; b/July 22, 1950; h/PO Box 202, Starkville, MS 39762; ba/Miss St; m/Barbara Phillips; p/Louie and Evelyn McHenry, Camden, AR; ed/BS So Ark Univ 1972; PhD Miss St Univ 1977; pa/Am Chem Soc; AAAS; Miss Acad Sci; cp/Chm Coun on Minority Affairs; r/Bapt.

McHUGH, CAROLYN MARLOW oc/Coordinator of Graduate Placement; b/July 5, 1941; h/240 Pine Valley Dr, Athens, GA 30606; ba/Athens; c/Catherine, Carol, Starr; p/Chiel Watson (dec) and Sara Daniell Marlow, Bogart, GA; ed/BBA; MBA Cand; pa/Coor Grad Placement, Col of Bus Adm, Univ Ga-Athens; cp/Athens Jr Assem; Am Cancer Soc Aux; r/Bapt; hon/Phi Kappa Phi; Beta Gamma Sigma; Alpha Lambda Delta; W/W Am Wom.

McILLWAIN, GEORGE ANNE oc/Nurse; b/Dec 30, 1930; h/1717 Hobbit Glen, Germantown, TN 39703; m/Benard Wood; c/Lillian Antoinette Bargagliotti; Barbara E Hodge, Margaret Anne; p/Bedford Frank (dec) and Lillian Lowe (dec); ed/RN; pa/TNA, Chm, V-Chm Local Unit; r/Ch of Christ.

McINERNEY, JOHN WAYNE oc/Administrator, Executive; b/Apr 1, 1942; h/4347 W 108th Pl, Oaklawn, IL 60453; ba/Clinton; m/Donna S Stanish; c/John P, Jenipher D, Sean M, Timothy C; p/John A and Elaine Briney McInerney, Bull Shoals, AR; ed/BA Grace Col 1976; Att'd Reformed Theol Sem, Jackson, Miss; mil/USMC 1961-65; pa/Admr, Pres & Chm Bd, The Word & the World Inc; Polit News Commentator, "McInerney Report" on Var Miss Stas; Am Fed Police, Nat VP; cp/Cand for US Ho of Reps, 4th Dist of Miss; r/Presb.

McINNIS, ALMA RUTH B oc/Retired Sewing Machine Operator; b/Oct 8, 1916; h/904 W Simmons, Enterprise, AL 36330; m/James A; c/Jimmie L Watson, Clifford A Watson, Mrs Charles E Ellis Jr; p/James W (dec) and Lela C Bradley (dec); pa/Employed by Ofc of Res & Devel, WV Univ; cp/Served on Mayor's Adv Com on Streets 4 Yrs; Ch Work; Am Legion Aux; Org'd Labor; Local, St & Nat Polits; r/Presb; hon/Cert of Merit, So Labor Sch AFL-CIO; Ldrship Tng Cert, ACTWU.

McINTOSH, WILLIE BRIDE JR oc/Airborne Infantryman; b/Apr 12, 1951; h/Rt 1 Jones Rd, Box 522, Lawndale, NC 28090; ba/Ft Bragg, NC; m/Jeannette Haynes; c/Quandra Michelle, Avril Natasha; p/Aron and Virginia McIntosh Logan, Bostic, NC; ed/Instrnl Tng Course; Sniper Instrs Sch; Ldrship Tng Sch; mil/AUS Airborne Infantryman & Sniper Instr; cp/Pistol & Karate Comps; r/Bapt; hon/Pres Awd Hon, Camp Lincoln JCs 1974; Cert of Recog, Lincoln JCs 1974; AUS Trainee of Wk, Basic Combat Tng, Ft Jackson, SC 1976; Am Aprit Hon Medal, Ft Jackson 1976; Airborne Parachutist Badge 1977; Expert Rifleman & Grenadier Badge 1977; XVIII Airborne Corps & Ft Bragg Heavy Weight & Grand Champ, Taekwondo Karate Champ 1977; Soldier of Mo Awd, 1st Battallion 508th Airborne Infantry Div 1977.

McINTYRE, LUCILE DEW oc/Teacher; b/May 16, 1943; h/Rt 1, Ivanhoe, NC 28447; ba/Vanceboro, NC; m/Johnny Lee; c/Sunday, John Christopher; p/Jasper Hinson and Grace Barefoot Dew (dec); ed/BS ECU 1965; pa/Eng Tchr, W Craven HS; Pres Craven Co Assn Clrm Tchrs 1978-79; Pres Elect Craven Co NCAE 1978-79; cp/Charter Pres Ladies of Craven Civitan Clb (Best Clb of Yr Awd During Charter Yr); NC Dist E Jr Civitan Adv Com; Secy Crave Commun Arts Coun; Past Pres & Secy ECU Playhouse; r/Bapt; hon/Charter Mem Alpha Psi Omega; Recip Laurel Awd for Character Acting; Outstg Yng Edr, Orange Co 1974; 2nd Pl in NC Outstg Yng Edr Awds 1974; Craven Co Tchr of Yr Awd 1977; Civitan of Yr, Area 9 of NC Dist E (1st Wom of Area 9 to Win Awd) 1978; Civitan Hon Key, Ladies of Craven Civitan Clb 1978; Best Fac Advr Awd 1976-77 & 77-78, Jr Civitan Clb of NC Dist E.

McINTYRE, MICHAEL TODD oc/Student; b/Dec 7, 1964; h/Rt 7 Beyer St, Albertville, Al 35950; p/Malcolm Andrew and Mary Frances McIntyre, Albertville, Al; ed/Att'g Albertville HS; r/Meth; hon/Eagle Scout 1979; God & Country Awd 1979; Best Band in Dixie (AHS) 1980.

McKEAN, RICHARD LEE oc/Director of Choral Activities; b/Apr 18, 1941; h/Kilgore, TX; ba/Kilgore Col, 1100 Broadway, Div of Fine Arts, Kilgore, TX 75662; m/Mary Ann; c/Donald Christian; p/Lee F and Mary McKean, Hastings, NB; ed/AFA Del Mar Col 68; BME Tex Christian Univ 70; Att'd So Meth Univ Summer 1971; MMus N Tex St Univ 1976; Att'd SWn Univ Summer 1974, Aspen Sch Mus Summer 1978, Presb Col Summer 1979; mil/USN 1959-63; Org'd Ship's Choir 1962-63; pa/Dir Choral Acts & Comprehensive Musicianship Instr, Skyline Ctr for Career Devel, Dallas, Tex 1970-72; Dir Commun Chorus & Class Voice, Eastfield Commun Col, Mesquite, Tex 1971-72; Dir Choral Activs & Instr of Theory, Richardson HS 1972-77; Dir Choral Activs, Voice & Theory Instr, Kilgore Col 1977-; Dir Longview Civic Chorale 1978-; Mus Dir, Longview Commun Theatre 1979-; Min Mus, Elmira Cumberland Presb Ch 1979-; Am Choral Dirs Assn; Tex Choral Dirs Assn; Tex Mus Edrs Assn; Tex St Tchrs Assn, Voca Div Chm 1970; cp/Org'd & Dir'd Richardson Commun Choir 1973-77; hon/Vocal S'ship, Hastings Col 1959; Pres Cit 1962; Violin S'ship, Del Mar Jr Col 1965; Acad S'ship, Del Mar Jr Col 1966; Acad & Choir S'ship, Del Mar Jr Col 1967; Persichetti Composition Competition 1st Pl Awd, Juilliard Sch Mus 1967; Conducting & Acad S'ship, Tex Christian Univ 1968-70; Richardson HS Choirs Rec'd Superior Ratings at Univ Interscholastic Leag Comp 1972-75; Richardson HS Concert Choir Selected by Panel of Intl Judges as 1 of Top 10 HS Choirs in Nation & Invited to Perform at Intl Choral Fest, Graz, Austria; Superior Rating, Buccaneer Mus Fest, Corpus Christi, Tex 1975; Outstg AAAA Choir, Six Flags Over Mid-Am Choir Fest 1976; Pi Kappa Lambda; Richardson HS Madrigal Singers Selected as Outstg Ensemble, St Univ Interscholastic Leag Comp 1976; Hon Mention, Buccaneer Mus Fest 1977; Adv'd Conducting S'ship, Aspen Sch Mus 1978; Kilgore Col Madrigal

209

Singers Invited to Perform at Renaissance Arts Fest, New Orleans 1980; Guest Conductor, Shreveport Symph Oct 1980.

McKEE, ARTHUR JR oc/Treasure Hunter, Marine Archaeologist; b/Nov 2, 1910; h/Tavernir, FL; ba/PO Box 165, Tavernier, FL 33070; m/Janet Gay Bodden; c/Phyllis, Wayne Morris (dec), Patricia K, Richard A, Arthur III, Terry (dec), Karen T, Kevin D; p/Arthur and Mabel A Chain McKee; ed/HS Grad; mil/USN 1941-43 Diver; pa/Rec Dir Bridgeton, NJ 1935-36; City Rec Dir, Homestead, Fla 1940-50; Org'd & Pres McKee's Museaum of Sunken Treasure, Fla Keys; Marine Archaeologist, St of Fla 1952-62; Fdr of Divers Technol Sch of Underwater Archaeol 1960; Conducted 32 Treasure Diving Expeditions to Bahamas, Fla Keys, Caribbean & Ctrl & S Am; Excavated Sunken City of Pt Royal; Promo Campaigns for Nat Airlines; Commercials for Delco Battery & Hiram Walker; cp/Islamorada C of C, Pres 1967-68; Upper Keys C of C: Dir 1973-76, Pres 1977-78; Standing Mem Elks; r/Prot; hon/Mr Treasure Hunter of Yr 1966; Pioneer in Underwater Archaeol in Wn Hemisphere, Nat Geog Soc 1973-74; Subject of Num Documentary Films; Appeared on Num TV Shows Incl'g *To Tell the Truth, The Mike Douglas Show, & Danger is My Business*; Appeared in *Nat Geographic, Life, Skin Diver, Sport Diver* & Other Magazines; Mentioned in Num Books Incl'g *Sea Fever* by Robert F Marx & *The Lost Treasure of the Concepcion* by John Grissim; Patentee of Underwater Motion Picture Camera & System of Excavating Wreck Sites.

McKENSZIE, JACKIE KEVIN oc/Student; b/Oct 6, 1959; h/Pinehurst, NC; p/Jackie B and Marlene J McKenzie, Pinehurst, NC; ed/Att'g ECU; mil/AFROTC Field Tng, Plattsburg AFB, NY 1979; pa/Cnslr BSA; cp/Comdr of Arnold Air Soc; Rep Moore City, Am Legion Post 350; r/Luth; hon/Awd of Merit, Wake Forest Univ 1976; Phi Alpha Theta; Eagle Scout 1976; Boys St 1976; Am Scholastic Excell Awd AFJROTC 1976.

McKINLEY, FRANK ARNOLD oc/Professor; b/June 13, 1915; h/2316 Houston Pl, Denton, TX 75201; m/Marilyn Rights; c/Alec William, Bruce David, Lyn Ann; p/ Mr and Mrs D F McKinley (dec); ed/BS Muskingum Col 1937; Att'd Westminster Choir Col 1937-40; MMus Tchrs Col, Columbia Univ 1946; Att'd Syracuse Univ Summer 1947, Indiana Univ 1951-52; mil/AUS 1942-46 Warrant Ofcr; pa/N Tex St Tchrs Col 1940-42; Ky Wesleyan Univ 1946-47; N Tex St Col 1947-51, Prof Mus, Choral Dir, Coor Voice 1953-80; Exch Prof, Poland 1980-81; Mus Edrs Nat Conf; Am Choral Dirs Assn; cp/Denton Rotary Clb; r/Presb; hon/Alumni Cit of Merit for Dist'd Achmt as Choral Conductor & Tchr, Westminster Choir Col 1978; Pres's Awd, N Tex St Univ Hons Day 1979.

McKINNON, B E oc/Textile Management; b/Feb 17, 1940; h/Hickory, NC; ba/Valdese Weavers Inc, PO Drawer 70, Valdese, NC 28690; m/Della Vickers; c/Kelly, Rob; p/Carl E and Beulah S McKinnon, Burlington, NC; ed/BA Elon Col 1962; Grad Studies, Univ Ky St 1964-65; mil/AUS 1963-66, Grad OCS Prog, 1st Lt; pa/Pres, CEO, Treas Valdeses Weavers Inc; VP Lavonia Mfg Co, Lavonia, GA; Bd Dirs Shuford Industs, Hickory, NC; NC Textile Mfg Assn; Am Textile Mfrs Inst: V-Chm Uphol Fabric Com, Communs Com; Assoc Mem Nat Assn Decorative Fabric Distbrs; cp/Valdese Rotary Clb, Bd Dirs; r/Presb.

McKINNON, RUSSELL FRANCIS DANIEL oc/Association Executive; b/Feb 11, 1944; h/Alexandria, VA; ba/ADRA, 1000 Vermont Ave, NW, Wash DC 20005; p/John Joseph Phee and Margret Louise Bates MacKinnon, Falmouth, MA; ed/AB Col Holy Cross 1966; Cert Profl Devel Prog, Am Soc Assn Execs, Univ Md 1976; mil/USN 6 Yrs Lt; pa/Dir Communs Yth for Fed Union 1972-73; Asst Exec Dir Fed Bar Assn 1973-77; *Fed Bar News:* Mng Editor 1974-77, Bus Editor 1975-77; Pubr *Dismantlers Digest* 1977-; Exec VP Automotive Dismantlers & Recyclers Am, Wash 1977-; Am & Wash Socs Assn Execs; cp/Army-Navy Country Clb; US Yth Coun, Exec Com Mem 1973-75; Hunting Creek Clb Tennis Assn, Pres 1977 & 78; hon/Bronze Star w Combat V; Navy Commend Medal; Staff Medal of Hon, Repub of Vietnam; W/W Fin & Indust; DIB; Best Thesis, Profl Devel Prog, Am Soc Assn Execs, Univ Md.

McLAUGHLIN, WILLIE oc/Teacher; b/Aug 2, 1927; h/214 N Bethune St, Grenwood, SC 29646; m/Flora Louise Graves; c/Gearlean, Ronald, Bruce; p/Adornia (dec) and Bertha Davis McLaughlin (dec); ed/BS 1956, MS 1965, St Col; Adv'd Study, Clemson Univ; mil/AUS 1946-51; pa/Tchr Agric Mechs, Grenwood Voc Ctr; cp/Tarrant-McGriier Post 224, Am Legion SC: St V-Comdr, St Exec Com, St HS Oratorical Contest Com; Past Post Comdr, Post Adj, Bus Mgr, Past V-Comdr, Past Dist 15 Comdr; Past Mem St Credentials Com & Go Getters Clb; Past Chm of Bd, Greenwood Co Civic Leag; Past Secy & Mem Bd Dirs Greenwood Museum; Pres Greenwood Clb, SC St Col Alumni Assn; Past Nat VP SC St Col Alumni Assn; Past Chm on Advmt, Boy Scouts Greenwood & Newberry Cos, Local & Dist Neighborhood Commr & Mem Dist Com; Pres Greenwood Co Ed Assn; SC & Nat Ed Assns; St & Nat Agric Tchrs Assns; SC & Am Voc Assns; Past Pres Greenwood Co Tchrs

Assn; Past Parliamentn Palmetto Agric Tchrs Assn; Past Secy-Treas SC Voc Agric Tchrs Assn; Del Assem SC Ed Assn; r/Trinity U Meth Ch: SS Tchr, Ch Sch Supt, Adm Bd, Past Yth Advr, Former Mem Trustee Bd & Bd Stewards; hon/Am Legion Outstg Ser Awd 1962 & 1966; Dist'd Ser Awd & 20 Yr Ser to Agric Ed Awd 1976.

McLENDON, MARY VONDELL oc/Secretary; b/July 18, 1923; h/215 Fairview St, Marshall, TX 75670; ba/Marshall; m/Don; c/Jo Ann M North, Donald Wayne, Ronald Gene, Annette M Smith; p/E D (dec) and Myra Ramey, Dallas, TX; pa/Secy Co Ext Agts; Formerly Bkkpr F W Woolworth Co; cp/Harrison Co Ext Homemkrs Clb, Publicity Chm, Co Homemkr Coun Chm; r/Ch of Christ; hon/KKYR Radio's VIP 1976; Secy for Wk 1979; Outstg Ext Homemkr 1978; Sweepstake Winner in Gregg Co Fair 1976, 77, 79.

McMANUS, MICHAEL FRANKLIN (MICKEY) oc/Coordinator; b/Jan 30, 1942; h/434 Granville Dr, Winston-Salem, NC 27101; ba/Winston-Salem; m/Mona Faye Willis; c/Mark Franklin; p/Stanley Ray (dec) and Louise Claxon McManus, New Boston, OH; ed/Att'd Bob Jones Univ 1960-61; BRE Piedmont Bible Col 1968; Cert'd Instr Evangelical Tchr Tng Assn; pa/Ordained Bapt Min 1978; Min Yth & Ed, Fayetteville St Bapt Ch, Asheboro, NC 1967-72 & Temple Hgts Bapt Ch, Tampa, Fla 1973-74; Assoc Pastor of Yth & Ch Ed, W Hill Bapt Ch, Akron, Ohio 1974-78; Yth & Vis Pastor, Salem Bapt Ch, 1978-; Christian Camping Intl; Dir Salem Bapt Ch Charter of Positive Action for Christ; 1st VP Alumni Assn of Piedmont Bible Col 1979-81; cp/VP PTA, Balfour Elem Sch; Chaplain Advr, Temple Hgts Christian Sch, Tampa, Fl; r/Bapt; hon/Outstg & Dedicated Ser Awds in Christian Ldrship; Guest Lectr Piedmont Bible Col.

McMILLAN, MICHAEL REID oc/Orthopaedic Surgeon; b/Aug 28, 1941; h/1400 Ninth Ave, Conway, SC 29526; ba/Same; p/Hoyt and Sara Sherwood McMillan, Conway, SC; ed/BS The Citadel 1963; MD Duke Univ 1967; Intern in Med, Balto City Hosps 1967-68; Fellow in Med, Johns Hopkins Hosp 1967-68; Resident in Orthopaedic Surg, Greenville Hosp Sys, Greenville Hosp 1971-75; mil/USN 1968-71 Lt Comdr; pa/Orthopaedic Surg, Staff Conway Hosp 1975-; SC Med Assn; Horry Co Med Soc; AMA; SC Orthpaedic Assn; Am Fracture Assn; Stelling Soc; cp/Trustee Burroughs Foun 1980; Assn of Citadel Men; Horry Co Citadel Clb; r/Bapt.

McMULLAN, PAUL W oc/Chairman of the Board; b/Feb 6, 1929; h/2 Cherokee Cir, Hattiesburg, MS 39401; m/Mary George Watkins; c/Paul Wilson Jr; ed/BS Univ Miss 1954; Att'd Grad Sch of Bnkg of S, La St Univ 1958; Hon DBA William Carey Col 1974; mil/USAF 1951-52; pa/Chm Bd & Chief Exec Ofcr, First Miss Nat Bank, Hattiesburg; Chm of the Bd, Newton Co Bank, Newton, Miss; Chm of the Bd, Farmers & Merchants Bank, Forest, Miss; Dir & Mem Exec Com, Consolidated Am Life Ins Co, Jackson, Miss; Pres Trend Lands Inc, Biloxi, Miss; Ptnr McMullan Stys & Real Est, Newton, Miss; Ptnr Tanglewood Plantation, Newton Co, Miss; Treas Cayman Energy Ltd; Dir & V-Chm Bd, Bay Springs Bank, Bay Springs, Miss 1961-75; Past Mem Regional Adv Com on Bnkg Policies & Practs of 8th Nat Bank Region 1974-75; Past Ptnr Scott Co Ins Agcy, Forest, Miss 1974-75; Past VP Palmer Ins Agcy, Forest, Miss 1975-76; Past Ptnr Beaver Creek Ranch 1973-75; Am Bankers Assn: Commercial Lending Div Minority Lending Com 1978-79; Pres-Elect Miss Bnkrs Assn; Fund for Ed in Ecs, Bd Trustees, Am Bnkrs Assn; cp/Bd Trustees Miss Arts Assn; Adv Coun US Sister City Prog; Bd Dirs Miss Foun Indep Cols; Chm Bank Adv Coun Com of Miss Foun Indep Cols; Dir Miss Ole Miss Alumni Assn; H'burg Rotary Clb; Pres's UN Day Nat Com; Coun Rep of Pine Burr Area Coun BSA; Miss Safety Coun; Newcomen Soc N Am; V-Chm, Bd Trustees Forrest Co Gen Hosp; Bd Dirs AAA Ambulance Sers Inc; Chm, Adv Com, St Jude Chapt of H'burg; Ambassador, New Orleans Mid-Winter Sports Assn (Sugar Bowl); Adv Bd, H'burg Civic Light Opera; Lamar Soc; Miss Com for the Humanities, Treas; Bd Dirs, Miss-Ala Div Mid-Cont Oil & Gas Assn; Policy Bd Technol Commercialization Ctr, Jackson, Miss; Hon St Campaign Chm, Cystic Fibrosis Foun, Miss Chapt; Past Mem Num Other Civic Orgs & Coms; r/Presb; hon/Recip Nat Awd for Excell, US Commerce Dept; Miss JCs Awd for Outstg Yng Man Yr, St of Miss 1963; Silver Beaver Awd, BSA 1972; Class of Eagle Scouts Honoree, Pine Burr Area Coun BSA 1975; Sales & Mktg Execs of H'burg Man of Yr Awd 1975; Irwin Province Ct of Hon of Kappa Alpha Order; W/W: Banking, US; Omicron Delta Kappa 1974; Credit Wom Intl Boss of Yr 1968; Liberty Bell Awd, S Ctrl Miss Bar Assn 1976; 1 of Miss Most Influential Men 1978; WHSY Awd of Excell in Bnkg.

McMULLAN, WILLIAM PATRICK JR oc/Bank Executive; b/Nov 20, 1925; h/4140 Dogwood Dr, Jackson, MS 39221; ba/Jackson; m/Rosemary Lyons; c/W P III, Robert J, Michael L, Mary Charlotte, Julie M Kehoe; p/William Patrick Sr (dec) and Charlotte McMullan, Memphis, TN; ed/BS; Masters Bkg & Fin, Univ Pa; mil/USAF 1943-45; pa/Miss Bank: Chm Bd, Chief Exec Ofcr 1975-; Deposit Guaranty Corp: Pres & Chief Oper'g Ofcr 1973-75; Deposit Nat Bank: V-Chm 1973-75, Pres 1969-73,

Exec VP 1961-69, VP & Asst to Pres 1960-61; St Comptroller Dept Bank Supvn 1957-60; Other Past Positions; Bd Dirs: Newton Co Bk, Merchs & Planters Bk Tchula, Mobile Communs Corp Am, Cal-Maine Foods Inc, Magna Corp, First City Bank Gainesville (Fla), Others; Chm Alcorn Bank & Trust Co, Corinth, Miss; Chm Exec Com, Fin Security Life Ins Co; Exec Com Miss Bus & Indust Corp; cp/Bd Trustees Miss Bapt Hosp; Chm Jackson Mun Airport Auth; Exec Com Dem Nat Fin Coun; Fin Chm St of Miss 1976 Jimmy Carter for Pres Campaign; Miss Banker's Assn; Fed & St Leg Coms; Former Activs Inc: Pres Jackson Boys' Clb, Dir Jackson C of C, Dir Jackson Symph Leag, Nat Fund V-Chm Red Cross Fund Dr, Nat Dir & St Pres Nat Assn Mtl Hlth, Dir Jackson Mus Assn, Others; r/Bapt.

McMULLIN, BOYCE DALE oc/General Contractor; b/June 27, 1944; h/Rt 3 Box 301, Purvis, MS 39475; ba/Hattiesburg, MS; m/Lottie; c/Missy, Amanda; p/T G and Bloomie McMullin, Purvis, MS; ed/Arch Constrn Technol; mil/AUS; pa/Assoc'd Bldrs Contractors; cp/Elks Clb; Hattiesburg C of C; Miss Ec Coun; Col on Staff of Gov of Miss; r/Bapt; hon/Boss of Yr, Gtr Hattiesburg Chapt Nat Assn Wom in Constrn 1978.

McMURRAY, JAMES PETER oc/University Lecturer; b/June 14,1907; h/311-C 72nd Ave N, Myrtle Bch, SC 29577; m/Frances Roesch; ed/AB NJ St Tchrs Col-M 1930; AM Columbia Univ 1932; EdD Rutgers Univ 1939; pa/Tchr Sci Vernon L Davey Jr HS, E Orange, NJ 1930-36; Instr Newark Tech Sch, NJ 1930-38; Instr NJ St Tchr Col, Newark 1936-40; Prof Ed, Hd Dept Ed, Seton Hall Col 1940-43; Asst Engr Wn Elec Co, Kearny, NJ 1943-44; Acting Dir, PR, NJ Ed Assn, Trenton 1944-45; Chief Pers Potomac River Nav Command 1947-48; Sup Ed Spec USN Tng Pubs Ctr 1948-58; Sr Analyst Bur of Ships Navy Dept 1958-64; Nat Referral Ctr Lib Cong 1964-68; Dir Admissions, Prof Ed Coastal Carolina Reg Campus USC 1968-70, Dir Acad Affairs, Prof Ed 1970-72; Lectr Grad, Golden Gate Univ 1972-77; Contbr Ed Jours; cp/Rotary Clb; Past Pres Optimist Clb of the Oranges, NJ; hon/W/W: Am Ed, E; DIB; Ldrs in Ed.

McNABB, MARTHA SUE WILLIAMS oc/Writer; b/Mar 18, 1936; h/Road M Route 3, Green City, MO 63545; c/M Ronald Marshall (dec), Deborah Sue Marshall; p/Cecil M (dec) and Sue Forbes Williams (dec); ed/Att'd Kirksville St Tchrs Col 1953-54; NE Mo St Tchrs Col 1962-64; BSE Univ Calif-Berkeley 1965; Hon D Aetiology, Fillmore Inst 1966; pa/Tchr, Dudgeon Sch, Fayette, Mo 1965-75; Employment Spec, Dept Labor 1977; Older Ams Supvr, Mo Green Thumb 1978; Manpwr Dir, NE Mo Commun Action Agcy, CETA 1979-; Distbr Lord Jim's Parlour Rest 1978-; Adv Bd Regional Manpwr Adv Coun; Asst Tchr Dale Carnegie; Nat Assn Female Execs; Nat Ret'd Tchrs Assn; Intl Entrepreneurs Assn; Am Fed Tchrs; ASCAP; Mo Assn Commun Action; cp/NOW, Task Master Nat Action Ctr 1975-76; AAUW; Mo Div Ext Ser; Nat Fed BPW, Regional Dir 1971; r/7th Day Adventist; hon/Recip Cert of Apprec & Commend, Disadvantaged/Handicapped NE Mo 1978; World W/W Wom 1981; Author *The Basic Aspects and Concepts of Play Therapy* 1965; *DAP - A Catalogue for Interpretation* 1965; *Culture and Personality* 1966; *Praimeri Kaer* 1981; *Testament of Seasons* and *Climbing the Crystal Stairs* 1981-82.

McNAIR, THOMAS WILEY oc/Banker; b/Aug 23, 1947; h/Box 1767, Fayetteville, AR 72701; ba/F'ville; m/Donnealia; c/Becky, Carrie; p/David M and Feriba T McNair; ed/BA Univ Ark; pa/Heritage Fed Savings & Loan; r/Bapt.

McNALLY, JAMES RAND III oc/State Representative; b/Jan 30, 1944; h/11 Mona Ln, Oak Ridge, TN 37830; ba/Nashville; m/Janice Rebecca; c/Melissa Kathleen, Margaret Diane; p/James Rand Jr and Margaret McKenna McNally; ed/BS Memphis St Univ; Pharm Univ Tenn; pa/Tenn Pharm Soc; Am Soc Hosp Pharms; cp/Tenn St Rep; Pres Bd of Commun Sers for Excptl Citizens; Bd Mem Red Cross; Girls Clb; r/Cath; hon/JC Yng Man of Yr.

McNATT, LESTER ALLAN oc/Youth and Music Director; b/July 11, 1954; p/Thomas L McNatt, Douglasville, GA; Edith L McNatt, Memphis, TN; ed/BA Freed-Hardeman Col 1978; Further Study: Mercer Univ, Memphis St Univ, Union Univ; pa/Min Mus & Yth; Dir Cumberland Val Yth Chorus; Am Choral Dirs Assn; cp/Warren Co Adv Com; r/Ch of Christ; hon/Nom'd Outstg Yng Men Am 1980; Co-Sponsor Philomathean Social Clb 1979-80; Co-Chm Makin' Music 1979; Dir Freed-Hardeman Col Chorus Ensemble 1976-78; Dir Freed-Hardeman Col Chamber Singers 1978-79; Lambda Delta Phi.

McNEAL, RAYMOND THOMAS oc/County Judge; b/Apr 9, 1946; h/1115 NE 42nd Ave, Ocala, FL; ba/Ocala; c/Ray J, Christopher; p/Raymond L and Helen McNeal, Ocala, FL; ed/BA 1969, JD 1973 Univ Fla; pa/Welch & McNeal, Attys at Law 1973-75; Asst St Atty, 5th Judicial Circuit 1974-78; Marion Co Div Chief 1976-78; Co Judge, Marion Co 1979-; Am Judicature Soc; Marion Co Bar Assn; Am Bar Assn, Judicial Mbrship Com on Small Claims Cts; Fla Bar Assn; Am Trial Lwyrs Assn, Judicial Mem; Nat Dist Atty's Assn, Judicial Mem; Lwyr's Title Guaranty Fund, Inactive Mem; cp/Ocala Lions Clb: Corresp Secy 1975, Bd Dirs

1976, 2nd VP 1977, 1st VP 1978, Pres 1979-80; Benevolent Protective Order of Elks Lodge #286; BSA: Cubmaster Pack 355 1975-78, Marion Dist Cub Com Chm 1978, Troop 196 Com 1978-, Webelos Liaison 1978, Marion Dist Mbrship Chm 1980; Marion Citrus Mtl Hlth Assn 1975; Law Enforcement & Corrections Adv Com, Ctrl Fla Commun Col; NE Fla Safety Coun, Student Safety Coun, Marion Co 1979-; r/Bapt; hon/BSA: Century Awd 1979-80, Scouter's Key 1978; Citizens Commend, Ocala Police Dept 1978; W/W Am Law 1978; Prominent People in Fla Govt 1979; Ocala JCs Dist'd Ser Awd 1980.

McNEELY, CYRUS CARMI JR oc/Textile Executive; b/Sept 17, 1922; h/1231 May Ct, Burlington, NC 27215; ba/B'ton; m/Barbara May; c/Cyrus Carmi III, Benjamin Kilpatrick, Barbara Louise, Nancy Annette; p/C C (dec) and Alice Cloaninger McNeely, Mooresville, NC; ed/BS Davidson Col; mil/Capt 78th Infantry Div WWII; pa/Exec Burlington House; cp/Dir: B'ton Day Sch, Meml Hosp of Alamance Co, May Meml Lib, NC Div Am Cancer Soc; Past Pres: Osteogenesis Imperfecta Foun, Lions Clb; r/Presb: Elder; hon/Bronze Star; Army Commend Ribbons.

McNORRILL, NORMAN LONNIE oc/Life Underwriter; b/Jan 10, 1949; h/Statesboro, GA; ba/NWn Mutual Life, PO Box 204, 220 N Ofcs, Statesboro, GA 30458; m/Jo Ann Delk; p/Elaine Dickey, Waynesboro, GA; ed/AB Ga So Col 1971; Num Ins Courses; Grad LUTC 1978; pa/Self-Employed w Own Agcy, NWn Mutual Life, Statesboro; Former Sales Mgr, Life Ins Co of Ga; Nat Assn Life Underwriters; Ga St Assn Life Underwriters; S'boro Assn Life Underwriters, Pres; Assn of Agts, NWn Mutual Life; cp/Kiwanis Clb of S'boro, Bd Dirs; Sigma Phi Epsilon Bd of Ga So Col, VP; r/So Bapt.

McQUARY, JEANNE oc/Postmaster; b/Apr 29, 1944; h/Trinidad, TX; m/Steve; c/Kimberly, Ronald, Karla, Craig; p/Loyd E Goode, Casper WY; Fern Irene Goode (dec); ed/Att'd Casper Jr Col 1963-64; pa/Postmaster: Evansville (WY), Trinidad (TX); ABWA, Secy, Ways & Means; PTA, Natrona Co Secy; cp/Trinidad C of C; r/Bapt.

McWHORTER, ANDREA ALFREDO oc/Therapeutic Counselor; b/Oct 14, 1954; h/1962 Duncan St, Mobile, AL 36606; ba/Same; m/Le'Verne Joyce Davis; p/Priscilla P McWhorter, Century, FL; ed/BS Alcorn St Univ 1975; MA Ohio St Univ 1976; Post Grad George Wash Univ; pa/Therapeutic Cnslr, Piney Woods Sch; APGA; hon/W/W S&SW 1980.

MEAD, ANN oc/Executive; b/Jan 10, 1943; h/6003 Liberty Bell Court, Burke, VA 22015; ba/Alexandria; p/Lester Segerman, Encino, CA; ed/BBA Univ Cinci 1966; pa/Adm Asst, Appalachian Regional Comm, Wash DC 1966-69; Pers Cnslr, Metro Wash Area 1969-74; Pres A Job Bank Ltd 1974-; Pres J B Temps Inc 1978-; Va Assn Pers Sers; Wash Metro Temp Sers; Nat Assn Indep Bus; Alexandria Hosp Corp Bd; ABWA; cp/Alexandria C of C; Hyatt Regency Clb; r/Jewish; hon/W/W Am Wom 1980-81.

MEALING, ESTHER MORRISON (MOLLIE) oc/Free-Lance Artist, Publisher; b/Aug 8, 1916; h/809 Cooper Ave, Columbus, GA 31906; m/John P; c/Robert Adams, Esther Lee M Lehew, Marguerite Anna M Ozley; ed/Att'd Draughon's Bus Col, Columbus Col; pa/Free-Lance Artist; Poet; cp/Secy-Treas Moscogee Co Citizens Assn 1955-59; Asst Den Mother, BSA 1953-54; Asst Ldr & Ldr, GSA 1952-57, 62-67; Bd Dirs Muscogee Co Wel Dept 1957-72, Chm Adv Bd 1971-72; Rep Dist 3 1971-72, Mem Adv Bd, St of Ga 1957-72; Secy-Treas Wom Christian Temperance Union 15 Yrs; Supvr Art Dept, Chattahooche Val Fair 1973-76; Artist Guild Huntsville; Benning Hills Wom's Clb, Past Pres; Hist Columbus Foun; Hist Trust for Preserv; Columbus Art Guild; Past Pres Columbus Br Nat Leag Am Pen Wom, Ga St Pres 1976-78; Neighborhood Chm Am Cancer Soc; Assoc Mem Ga Water Color Soc; Columbus Mus Arts & Crafts; r/First Christian Ch Columbus; hon/Book of Haiku Verse *Memories of Studio 10;* 1st Prize in Oils, 2nd Prize Water Color, Chattahoochee Val Fair; Hon Mention, Cross Counry Art Show; Num Other Awds and Prizes; 2 Vol Work *Sketch Book - Century Old Houses of Columbus and Vicinity.*

MEDLIN, CATHLEEN LEWIS oc/Cafeteria Supervisor; b/Aug 28, 1929; h/Kenly, NC; ba/Smithfield-Selma Sr HS, PO Box 1497, Smithfield, NC 27577; m/William Harvie; c/William Roger, Janie Medlin Rogerson, Ricky Douglas; p/dec; ed/8 Certs in Sch Food Ser; pa/Cert'd Food Ser Mgr; Cater Dinners, Banquets, Wedding Receptions, etc; Pres Johnston Co Chapt Sch Food Ser 3 Yrs; Dist Dir Dist XII NC Sch Food Ser Assn; r/Free Will Bapt.

MEEKS, PHILIP T SR oc/Retired Railroad Conductor; b/Aug 6, 1918; h/2416 Myrtle Ave, Sanford, FL 32771; ba/Sanford; m/Jewell S; c/Philip T Jr; p/Waldo (dec) and Clara M Meeks (dec); ed/Att'd Ga Bus Col; mil/MM; pa/RR Conductor, Seaboard Coastline; Furniture; cp/Dem Party; r/Presb.

PERSONALITIES OF THE SOUTH

MEETZE, JANETTE JACKSON oc/Artist, Teacher; b/Jan 19, 1955; h/Rt 13, Box 806M, Ft Myers, FL 33908; ba/Cape Coral, FL; m/Francis R Jr; c/Francis R III; p/Frank W and M Janice Vaughn, Merritt Isl, FL; ed/BA Art; pa/Tchr Quilting, Crocheting, Gen Art & Crafts Progs; Tutor for Art Hist; cp/Judge for Local Craft Events; r/Luth; hon/Grad w Hons Univ Fla 1976; One Mo Show of Quilts, Cape Coral Art Studio 1978.

MEIBUHR, ARTHUR C oc/Retired Banker; b/Nov 21, 1905; h/2505 E Hartford #17, Ponca City, OK 74601; m/Mabel C; c/Caralee; p/dec; ed/Grad Bus Col 1918; Att'd Cleveland Col; pa/VP & Trust Ofcr, Security Band and Trust; Treas, VP, Pres Cleveland, OH Chapt Nat Assn Bank Auditors & Comptrollers; Treas & Bd Mem C'land, OH Chapt Am Inst Bnkg; cp/Past Pres Lions Clb; Men's Rose Clb; Local C of C; 32° Mason; Deacon, Elder, Trustee First Presb Ch, Ponca City; Past Pres Pioneer Hist Soc; Repub Party; r/Presb; hon/Okla Bnkrs Assn 50 Yr Clb 1975; Past Pres, Charter Mem The Pioneer Hist Soc.

MEIGS, WALTER R oc/Corporate Attorney, Assistant Secretary; b/Sept 7, 1948; h/3505 Springwood Dr E, Mobile, AL 36608; ba/Mobile; m/Sharmon E; c/Nancy; p/Mrs Ralph Meigs, Centreville, AL; ed/BA B'ham So Col 1970; JD Univ Ala 1973; Grad Study Auburn Univ 1974; pa/Judicial Dept St Ala 1973-74; Assoc Law Firm Hubbard, Waldrop & Jenkins 1974-75; Ala Dry Dock & Shipbldg Co, Atty & Asst Secy 1975-; Ala St Bar Assn; Am Bar Assn; Mobile Bar Assn; Maritime Law Assn of US; Am Forestry Assn; Ala Forestry Assn; Phi Delta Phi; cp/Ala Hist Assn; So Hist Assn; Propeller Clb of US, Mobile Chapt; Kiwanis Clb; r/Meth.

MEISTER, PETER WILLIAM oc/Teacher; b/Aug 31, 1948; h/Box 71, Woodberry Forest, VA 22989; ba/Woodberry Forest; p/John William (dec) and Miriam George Meister, Titusville, NJ; ed/BA Univ Penn 1976; MA Univ Va 1979; pa/German Tchr, Lang Ofc, Woodberry Forest Sch; Fellow Intl Biog Assn; r/Quaker; hon/Undergrad Poetry Prize, Univ Penn 1975; Author *This My Dream* 1965; Entries in Anthologies.

MELCHOR, OLLIE MAE oc/Principal, Treasurer; b/Nov 12, h/104 5thSt, Clarksdale, MS 38614; ba/C'dale; m/John C; c/Ginise Johnson Climent; p/Leon Johnson; Emma Johnson Roberson, Clarksdale, MS; ed/AB; MS; Grad/Elem Sch Prin; Corp Treas; St Tchrs Assn; Local & Nat Tchrs Assns; cp/Pres Am Legion Aux; Pres VFW Aux; r/Meth; hon/Math Awd; Dr Deg.

MELGAR, JULIO oc/Mechanical Engineer; b/July 4, 1922; h/6108 Menger Ave, Dallas, TX 75227; ba/Ft Worth, TX; p/Lorenzo (dec) and Maria Melgar, Dallas, TX; ed/BME Univ Detroit 1952; mil/USMAC 1943-45; pa/Fed Aviation Adm, Tinker AFB; Wyatt Metal & Boiler Works; AJ Boynton Co; Joe Hoppe Air Cond'g Contr; Zumwalt & Vinther Cnsltg Engrs; Wyatt C Hedrich Arch; Chance Vought Aircraft; Am Soc Heating Refrigerating & Air Cond'g Engrs; Ed Chm; Nat Soc Profl Engrs; Am Soc Mech Engrs; Fed Bus Assn; Metroplex Rec Coun; Fed Aviation Clb; cp/Ft Worth Opera Assn; Bd Dirs Ft Worth Opera Guild; Dallas Opera Guild; r/Cath; hon/NY St Bd Regents Gold Medal High Score Span Regent Test 1937; Ft Worth Handball Outstg Contbn to Handball 1965.

MELLERT, LUCIE ANNE oc/Writer; b/June 6, 1932; h/1017 W Va Ave, Dunbar, WV 25064; m/William J; c/James F III; p/Wilbur C Frame, Charleston, WV; Grace Martin Taylor, Charleston, WV; ed/Att'd WVU & Mason Col Music & Fine Arts; pa/Freelance Writer, Public Relats & Ofc Mgmt Cnslt, Dunbar, WV 1979-; Public Relats Exec, Ofc Mgr, Kanawha Stone Co, Nitro, WV 1975-78; Public Relats Exec, Ofc Mgr, Hallcraft Inc, Dunbar 1972-74; Public Relats Exec, Asst Treas, Ofc Mgr, J H Milam Inc, Dunbar 1959-71; Nat Fed Press Wom; WV Press Wom, Past Treas; cp/Beautification Commr, City of Dunbar 1969-72; Activ Coor, Prog Dir, Dunbar Bicent Comm 1971; Coor Dunbar City Wide Beautification & Improvement Comm 1969-72; Pioneer Wom's Clb, Past Pres; Wom of the Moose; hon/Cert of Apprec, Kanawha Co Beautification Campaign 1973.

MELTON, WILLIAM EMORY oc/Mortician; b/Apr 18, 1934; h/Statesboro, Ga; m/Vilette; c/Emerson F, Derrel E; p/Carie M Melton (dec); Mable M Tippins, Savannah, GA; ed/Grad 1958; mil/Korea Medic; pa/Mortician; Lic'd Emblamer; Lic'd Funeral Dir; cp/Lions Clb, Eye Conserv; 1st Embalming Cert in Eye Removal in Statesboro & Bulloch, Ga; JCs, Secy & Treas; Am Red Cross CPR Instr; CPR Instr Tnr; Multi-Media First Aid Instr; Am Cancer Soc, Memls Chm; Ch Camp Dir; BSA; r/Prim Bapt; hon/BSA: Scouters Key, Silver Beaver Awd, Trg Awd.

MENDELL, JAY STANLEY oc/Professor; b/Mar 13, 1936; h/11295 NW 38th St, Coral Springs, FL 33065; ba/Boca Raton, FL; m/Joan Brightman; c/Risa Sue, Eden Sharon; p/Emanual (dec) and Lillian Danenbaum Mendell, NY, NY; ed/MA Vanderbilt Univ 1958; PhD Rensselaer Polytech Inst 1964; pa/Vis Prof, Col of Bus & Public Adm, Fla Atlantic Univ 1975-; Assoc Prof, Technol Fla Intl Univ 1973-75; Prat & Whitney Aircraft Co 1963-73; World Future Soc; Acad Mgmt; Am Assn

Social Psychi; N Am Soc Corp Plan'g; r/Reform Jewish; hon/Co-Editor *Business Tomorrow* Magazine; Innovation Editor *The Futurist*; Contbg Editor *Planning Review* & *Creativity Focus*.

MERCER, SHARON ELI oc/Registered Nurse; b/Mar 29, 1951; h/4627 Beaver Rd, Louisville, KY 40207; ba/L'ville; m/Edward Lovell; c/Owen Edward; p/Mancil and Katherine Parker Eli, Crofton, KY; ed/Grad Norton Meml Infirm Nsg Sch; pa/AORN; NLN; SESNA.

MEREDITH, DOUGLAS RAYMOND JR oc/Draftsman; b/Jan 18, 1955; h/PO Box 2972, Radford, VA 24141; ba/Radford; p/Douglas Raymond and Merlyn Hartsock Meredith, Radford, VA; ed/AAS New River Commun Col; pa/Draftsman City of Radford; Transit Supvr; Engrg Aide; cp/U Fund; Coach Little Leag Sports; r/Meth.

MERIAN, AUDREY EILEEN oc/Agency Manager; b/July 19, 1926; h/Midland, TX; ba/605 W Ohio, Suite 1, Midland, TX 79701; c/Michelle L VanVoris, Jeffrey H, Susan R; ed/BA 1950; pa/Multi-Line Ins Agcy Mgr; BPW; r/Epis.

MERRILL, FRAN J oc/Free-Lance Writer; b/May 16, 1921; h/525 N Market, Shawnee, OK; c/Tom Palmer, Sheila Burns, Jackie; p/Joseph Higdon (dec); Mrs Bernie Lewis, Van Nuys, CA; ed/GED Okla Bapt Univ 1979; Courses Hadley's Sch for the Blind; pa/Free-Lance Writer; r/Tchr 2 Bible Classes, Victory Tabernacle; hon/Recog'd *Seminole Collegian*, *Seminole Producer, Shawnee News Star*.

MERRILL, MAURICE HITCHCOCK oc/Lawyer; b/Oct 3, 1897; h/800 Elm Ave, Norman, OK 73069; ba/Norman; m/dec; c/Jean Merrill Barnes; p/George Waite (dec) and Mary Lavinia Hithcock Merrill (dec); ed/BA 1919, LLB 1922 Univ Okla; SJD Harvard Univ 1925; mil/AUS 1918; pa/Instr Univ Okla 1919-22; Pract Law, Tulsa, Okla 1922-26; Tchr 1926-68, Full-time 1968-; cp/Okla Bar Assn; Norman Hosp Bd; r/Meth hn/Dist'd Ser Awd, Univ Okla 1968; Pres's Awd Okla Bar Assn 1972; Phi Delta Phi.

MERRIWEATHER, BETTY ROSE ATMORE oc/Teacher; b/July 3, 1945; h/1035 Tuscaloosa Ave, Gadsden, Al 35901; ba/Gadsden; m/J E; c/Johnny Jr, Tonya Elaine, Timothy Earl, Dionne Elise; p/B C and Lucy Atmore, Bessemer, AL; ed/BS 1976; BS 1978; Hon Doc Humanitarian; pa/Sub Tchr Drake Day Care; Credit Dept Sears Inc; Cnslr Gadsden Commun Ctr; Pers Secy Rev JE Merriweather; Pres Min Wives of the NE St Conv of Ala Aux to Nat Bapt Conv USA; cp/NAACP; SCLC; Voters Leag of Etouah Co; Girl Scout Ldr, GSA 652; r/Bapt; hon/Outstg Ser Awd for Neighborhood Ser to Poor & Underprivileged Chd 1970-74; Author *The Things That Women Live By*.

MERTZ, EDWARD PHILLIP oc/Retired Marine Officer; b/Aug 4, 1924; h/410 Chadwick Ave, Havelock, NC 28532; m/Ruth Evelyn Parks; c/7; p/Frank Edward and Mary Eleanor Mertz, Greensburg, PA; ed/Univ of Hi; St Olaf Col; E Carolina Univ; USMC Basic Sch; MCATS Flight Sch; mil/US Marine Corps: Rec'd Wings 1947, Ser'd 1943-66, Ret'd 1966; pa/Cert'd Tchr of Indust Tech Tng; Employed w AMF Hatteras Yachts; Past Treas, Armed Forces Retirees; Life Mem, Ret'd Ofcrs Assn; Marine Corps Leag; Naval Aviation Asssn; Naval Mutual Aid Assn; Past Spkr for Vietnam Returnees; cp/GSA Assoc 1956-; BSA: Scout Liaison Ofcr at MCAS (Kaneohe Bay, Hi), Troop Treas, Advmt Chm, Cubmaster, Scoutmaster, Instnl Rep, Dist VChm, Dist Chm, E Carolina Coun Exec Bd Mem 1963-; Past Pres, H'lock HS PTA; Past VP, HHS; Life Mem, NC Cong Ps & Ts; Past Treas, Repubs; Life Mem, Tailhook Assn; Silver Eagles; MAREPA; Craven Co Mtl Hlth Assn; Craven Co Commun Art Assn; Suicide Vol; Cystic Fibrosis; Cancer Soc; HALT; Horticultural Soc; Pres, Craven Commun Concert Assn; Past Nat Rifle Assn Yth Instr; ARC Blood Donor; Coastal Chapt TROA; Easter Seal Soc; Life Mem: NC Wildlife Fdn, Nat Right to Work Com, Am Security Coun; Others; r/Luth Ch of Am: Past Ch Coun Pres & Mem, Parrish Ed Chm, SS Tchr, SS Supt, Luth Ch Men, Conv Del; hon/BSA: Scouters Key, Green Band Awd; GSA Cert of Apprec; AMF Hatteras Yachts Outstg Ser Awd; Num Mil Awds.

MERTZ, RUTH EVELYN PARKS oc/Free-lance Writer; b/Oct 13, 1925; h/410 Chadwick Ave, Havelock, NC 28532; m/Edward Phillip; c/E Philip, Thomas Howard, Deborah Ruth, Cheryl Colleen, David Stephen, Jonathan Parks, Timothy Edward Parks; p/Howard A and Anna Palmquist Lintner Parks (dec); ed/E Carolina Univ; pa/Former Tchr Creative Writing & Tutorial Rdg, Craven Commun Col; Cert'd Instr in Tng Remedial Rdg Tutors; Former Newspaper Columnist, Current Stringer for Sev Others; Nat Ret'd Tchrs Assn; cp/GSA: Nat Del, Neighborhood Chm Camp Dir, Brownie Ldr, GS & Sr Ldr, Vol Tnr, Secy GS Coun of Coastal Carolina, Num Others; ARC: Gray Lady, PR Chm, 1000 Vol Hrs & Awd, Certs Apprec; H'lock Booster Clb; Band Parent; Pres H'lock HS PTA (5 times); Pres H'lock Jr HS PTA; State PTA: PR Chm (2 terms), Life Mem, Dist 15 Chm (2 terms), RISE Com, Ed Com, St Bltn Editor, S'ship Comm, Bd Mgrs, Cert Apprec; Sustaining Mem: Nat PTA,

Nat Repub Party; Past Treas, Local Repub Party; Intl CB Radio Operators Assn: Mem, Watch Ofcr; H'lock Art Guild: Fdr, Publicity Chm, Newslttr Writer, Former Rec'g Secy; Cherry Pt Ofcrs Wives Garden Clb: Original Mem, Bd Mem, Parliamentn, Publicity; Dist XI Garden Clb: Envir Improvement Chm, Beautification Chm, Civic Devel Chm, Publicity Chm; Cystic Fibrosis: Chm, Ed Chm; Cancer Soc: Bd Dirs, Former Crusade Chm, Ed Chm; Craven Co Mtl Hlth Assn: Bd Mem, Publicity Chm, Vols Com; NC Spina Bifida Assn; Craven Co Commun Concert Assn: Bd Dirs, Sponsor; Craven Arts Coun: VP, Fdg Mem; Publicity Com, NC Coun Wom's Orgs; NC PPHC; Nat Multiple Sclerosis Soc; Nat Archives Trust Fund; Nat Soc Lit & the Arts; Inter-Americas Soc; Order of the Golden Dragon; Craven Co Music & Cultural Arts; Chapt Chm, NC Arts Soc; Craven Co CoChm, NC Art Mus; Nat Trust for Hist Preserv; Am Land Trust; Sev City Coms; Ed Chm, H'lock Homemakers; Sustaining Mem, Roanoke Island Hist Assn; Nat Hist Assn; Smithsonian Assoc; Cherry Pt Ofcrs Wives Clb: Bd Mem 6 Yrs, Thrift Shop Vol; World Assoc Mem, Nat Wildlife Fdn; Am Heart Assn: Voting Mem, Fdrs Day Awd Cert & Pin; Num Other Activs; r/Luth (LCW); hon/GSA: Thanks Badge, Certs Apprec; BSA: Silver Fawn, Den Ldr Tng Awd, Certs Apprec, BS Statuette, Green Band Awd, Others; NC Cong Ps & Ts: Oak Leaf Awd, Life Mem; Outstg Wom Awd; Blue Ribbons, Flower Shows; Biogl Listings.

MERYMAN, CHARLES DALE oc/Fish Pathologist; b/Sept 14, 1951; h/Riverview, FL; ba/PO Box 765, Brandon, FL 33511; p/Charles Robert and Helen Lois Britt Meryman, Centralia, IL; ed/AS Kaskaskia Col 1971; BS 1973, MS 1974, Spec Fish Parasitology Psych En Ill Univ; Pharm St of Ill 1976; Cert'd Fisheries Sci 1977 Am Fisheries Soc; Restricted Aquatic Pesticide Applicator 1977 St of Fla; Doct Psych Animal Behavior 1978 Univ Metaphysics; pa/Ill Dept Conserv 1971-73; Instr En Ill Univ 1973-74; Fish Doctor Clin Ctr 1980-; Charles R Meryman Mus Natural Hist 1980-; Am Fisheries Soc; AFS Fish Admrs Sect; AFS Fish Culture Sect; AFS Fish Hlth Sect; AFS Water Qualtiy Sect; Fla Marine Life Assn; Fla Tropical Fish Farmers Assn; Goldfish Soc Am; Hillsborough Co Envirl Coalition Water Quality; Intl Oceanographic Foun; Intl Wildlife Fed; N Am Native Fish Assn; US Envirl Protection Agcy Nationwide Urban Runoff Prog; Tampa Bay Regional Plan'g Coun; cp/BSA; Gtr Brandon C of C Envirl Res Com, Hlth & Med Com; Gtr Brandon Citizens Envirl Alliance; Japan-Am Soc; Rotary Intl; Gtr Brandon Pres's Roundtable; r/Bapt.

METCALF, RALPH EDWARD oc/Area Sales Representative; b/Dec 21, 1953; h/2515 Brownsboro Rd, Apt 7, Louisville, KY 40206; ba/L'ville; p/Robert R (dec) and L Pearl Metcalf; ed/BS Univ L'ville 1979; Att'd Murray St Univ; pa/Area Sales Rep, R J Reynolds Tobacco Co; cp/Kappa Alpha Psi; JCs; r/Meth.

METZGAR, ROBERT DOUGLAS oc/Pastor; b/May 25, 1950; h/1301 Jefferson Pl, Plainview, TX 79072; ba/P'view; m/Sharon Marie; c/Cayce Michelle; p/W D Metzgar, San Angelo, TX; Janie Metzgar (dec); ed/AA Ctrl Bible Col; BA SWn; MA Maranatha Sem; pa/Sr Pastor First Assem of God Ch; cp/Rotarian; Pres Our Father's House Pub'g; r/Assems of God; hon/WC Field's S'ship; W/W: Am Cols & Univs, Rel.

MEYER, GRACE BERNSTEIN oc/Counselor; b/Sept 19, 1926; h/1180 NE 176 St, N Miami Bch, FL 33162; ba/Same; m/Joseph; c/Richard Paul; Hollis Jill M Barnett; p/Louis (dec) and Elizabeth Heilbrun Bernstein (dec); ed/BA 1970; MSW 1972 Barry Col; pa/Marriage & Fam Cnslr; NASW; Acad Cert'd Social Wkrs; Clin Mem Am Assn Marrriage & Fam Therapy; r/Jewish; hon/BA summa cum laude; Kappa Gamma Pi; W/W Am Wom.

MEYER, LOUIS B oc/Associate Justice; b/July 15, 1933; h/Wilson, NC; m/Evelyn S; c/Louis B III, Patricia Shannon, Adam B; p/Louis B Sr (dec) and Beulah Smith Meyer (dec); ed/BA 1955, JD 1960 Wake Forest Univ; mil/AUS 1955-57 1st Lt; pa/Assoc Just, NC Supreme Ct; Pract'd Law 18 Yrs w Lucas, Rand, Rose, Meyer, Jones & Orcutt; Spec Agt FBI; Law Clk to Late Chief Just R Hunt Parker; Adj Prof Atlantic Christian Col; Wilson Co Bar Assn; 7th Jud Dist Bar Assn; NC Bar Assn; Am Bar Assn; cp/Past Co Chm, Dem Party of Wilson Co; St Dem Exec Com; Former City Chm Wilson Co Chapts Am Heart Assn & Am Red Cross; Former Dir Wilson JCs, Wilson Sertoma Clb & Local Salvation Army; Elks Clb; Mason; r/Bapt.

MEYSTEDT, LUCILLE E oc/Nurse; AKC Dog Show Judge; b/Nov 21, 1923; h/RR #1, Box 259, Rusk, TX 75785; p/Harry E and Mary Ethel Collins Scheper (dec); ed/RN St Marys Sch Nsg 1946; pa/Pvt Duty Nsg 1952-55; Staff Nurse SE Mo Hosp 1962-66; Night Supvr Poplar Bluff Hosp 1966-68; Dir Nsg, Farmington Mineral Area Osteopathic Hosp 1968-70; Night Super: Rusk Meml Hosp 1970-74, Neuburn Meml Hosp, Jacksonville, Tex 1974-76, Rust St Hosp 1976-; Nsg Advr Fairview Rest Home 1958-64; Dist 8 Nsg Assn; Nat Nsg Assn; Past Mem SE Mo Kennel Clb; Past Chm Nat Dog Wk, Cherokee Co; Former Bi-Wkly TV Progs on Animal Care, Cape Girardeau, Mo; Guest Appearances on Lufkin, Tyler & Rusk TV (Animal Care); Fdg Mem Affenpinscher Clb of Am; Longview Kennel Clb; Assoc Mem Italian Greyhound Clb of Gtr Houston; Am

Kennel Clb Dog Show Judge; Mexican Kennel Clb Judge, Mexico; Author Num Articles on Dogs & Their Care; Affenpinscher Columnist for Popular Dog Mag; Chm Charity Dog Matches, Rusk St Hosp; Chm Pet Responsibility Wk for Rusk Area; Other; r/Bapt; hon/W/W Am Wom.

MEZIAN, WILLIAM SARKIS oc/Executive Chef; b/Nov 21, 1953; h/Lakeland, FL; m/Mary; c/Jonathan, Kenneth; p/John and Marian Mezian, Elmwood Pk, NJ; eed/Att'd Fla Inst Technol; pa/Marriott Corp; Red Coach Grill Corp; Sheraton Corp; Imperial Lakes Country Clb; Profl Culinary Assn Am; Profl Inst of Chefs of Am.

MICHAEL, MARBETH GAIL oc/Assistant Professor; b/Sept 12, 1933; h/El Paso, Tx; ba/1101 N Campbell St, El Paso, TX; p/Mrs R A Michael, Newport, OR; ed/BS Ind Univ 1960; MN Univ Wash 1966; mil/Army Nurse Corp 1958 2nd Lt; Asst Prof Wrain, Univ Md; Chief Nurse Gen Hosp Germany, Chief Nurse Inst Surg Res, Instr Acad Hlth Sci, Staff Ofcr Hlth Sers Command, Ret'd; pa/Asst Prof Col of Nsg, Univ Tex El Paso; ANA; NLN; Sigma Theta Tau; AAUP; Tex Nurses Assn; Ret'd Army Nurses Assn; Assoc AUS; r/Prot; hon/Merit Ser Medal w OLC 1972 & 74; Humanitarian Ser Medal 1976; Am Expeditionary Medal 1968; Legion of Merit 1978; Article Pub'd in Association of Operating Room Nurses Journal 1967; Annals of American Burn Assn 1972.

MICHAELIS, CAROL TINGEY oc/Assistant Professor; b/Sept 24, 1933; h/100 N Melrose #1412, Natchitoches, LA 71457; ba/Natchitoches; c/Richard, Blaine, Jim, Neil, Trish; p/Willia A and Lola Madsen Tingey, Logan, UT; ed/BS magna cum laude 1970, MEd 1971, PhD 1976 Univ Utah; mil/ROTC Sponsor in HS & Col; pa/Asst Prof Spec Ed NWn St Univ; CEC; AAMD; AAESPH; NARC; Phi Kappa Phi; cp/Mem At Large Adv Bd Co Rec Dept; r/Latter Day Sts; hon/HS S'ship, Girls St; Col 10 Dean's List; Masters F'ship; W/W Am Wom; Phi Kappa Phi; Author 8 Articles, Book Home/School Relations with Exceptional Children.

MIDDLEBROOK, DORTHEY RUTH LOWERY oc/Social Worker; b/Dec 4, 1935; h/524 Isaac Hayes Dr, Dyersburg, TN 38024; ba/D'burg; m/Perry L Sr; c/Perry L Jr, Danie Ruth Hickman, Charles Bernard, Victor Lowery; p/Dan Lowery, Mounds, IL; Mary L Guyton, Halls, TN; ed/Att'd Newbern Area Voc Tech Sch 1969; pa/Social Wkr, D'burg Housing Auth; Gospel Concert Performer & Recording Artist; Coor & Contact Clk, Saint Day Care Ctr 1978-; Contact Clk, Social Security Adm 1966; Sub Tchr Lauderdale Co Bd Ed 1959; Phys's Secy 1953; cp/New Homemkrs of Am 1949-51, Pres Local Chapt Ripley, Tenn Dist Histn; SS & Yth Dept Tchr 1947-; VP PTA, Bruce HS 1961-62; Bd Dirs NW Tenn Ec Devel Coun, D'burg 1966-68; W Tenn St Choir, Ch of God in Christ 1952-69; r/New Jerusalem Ch of God in Christ: Usher Bd, Pres Choir, Pres Nurse's Aid, Secy-Treas; hon/Cit, Lane Col, Stage Appearances 1940 Awd's Rec'd from Var Chs & Schs 1938-52; Stage Appearances Singing & Spkg; Awd for Public Spkg, St Conv, New Homemkrs Am, A&I St Col, Nashville 1950; Salutatorian of Class 1952; Vocalist on TV 1974; Nat TV 700 Clb 1974; Song Pub'd "The Real Meaning of Christmas Day" 1960.

MIDDLETON, MARIA DICKERSON oc/Polygraph Examiner; b/Sept 15, 1948; h/Rt 2 Box 195-1A, Magnolia, MS 39652; ba/McComb; m/James Lynn; c/Stuart; p/Theodore T Dickersn (dec); Etta D McCullough, Jayess, MS; ed/Dip Zonn Inst Polygraph 1980; Att'g SW Miss Jr Col; pa/Polygraph Sers Ltd; Miss Bd Polygraph Examrs, Adm Asst 1977-80; Sartin Polygraph Conslts Inc, Ofc Mgr 1977-80; Reeves & Reeves Attys 1972-77; Ofc of Co Prosecuting Atty, Legal Secy 1966-70; Am Polygraph Assn; Miss Legal Secys Assn; Miss Assn Polygraph Examrs (First & Only Female Mem); cp/Beta Sigma Phi, VP, Secy; Am Red Cross; Pike Co Arts Coun; r/Bapt; hon/Beta Sigma Phi: Ritual of Jewels Deg 1972, McComb Azalea Ct 1976, Prog of Yr Awd 1974, Valentine Queen 1977, Prog of Yr Awd 1976, Perfect Attendance Awd 1976, Examplar Deg 1977; Pike Co Arts Coun: Spec Recog for Part in Spring Fest 1979, Spec Recog & Awd for Perf in Coun's Prod "The Sound of Music" 1979, Spec Recog for Part in Spring Fest 1980; Outstg Yng Wom Am, S Pike C of C; Highest Grade Ever Made on Miss Polygraph Exam; Grad Zonn Inst of Polygraph w Highest Hons 1980.

MIEIR, CHARLES EDWARD oc/Minister; b/Jan 5, 1929; h/404 Broad St, Oxford, NC 27565; ba/Oxford; m/Helen Brown; c/Robert, Steven, Pamela, Sharon; p/William Herbert (dec) and Constance Louise Briggs Mieir (dec); ed/Att'd Univ Md 1955-57; BS magna cum laude Univ W Fla 1970; SEn Bapt Theol Sem 1974-76; mil/USAF 1948-69 Ret'd Master Sgt, Elec Instr 1964-68; pa/Pastor: Delrayno Bapt Ch, Oxford, NC 1978-; Shockoe Bapt Ch, Chatham, Va 1974-78; Dorcas Bapt Ch, Crestview, Fla 1968-74; Modr Okaloosa Bapt Assn 1973 & 74; Modr Flat River Bapt Assn 1979-; cp/Adv Com Granville Co Univ NC Dept Correction; Vol Chap Granville Care Nsg Home; r/Bapt; hon/Ordained Deacon 1964, Ordained Min of Gospel 1968; hon/Author of Wkly Newspaper Column "The Sunday School Lesson" Chatham, Va Star-Tribune 1974-78 & Oxford, NC Public Ledger 1979-.

PERSONALITIES OF THE SOUTH

MIESSE, MARY ELIZABETH oc/Educator, Writer, Composer; b/June 2; h/PO Box 31, Channing, TX 79018; p/Robert Leon (dec) and LaVeta Francis Humphrey Miesse (dec); ed/BA; BS; MBA; MA; MEd; MPS; Degs from Univ Colo & W Tex St Univ; Cert'd: Profl Cnslr, Spec Ed Cnslr, Profl Tchr, Tchr Mtlly Retard'd, Tchr Lang-Lrng Disabled, Diagnostician, Admr, Spec Ed Supvr; pa/Prof Amarillo Col 1948-64; Tchr-Cnslr Public & Pvt Schs 1964-80; Semi-Ret'd 1980-; Editor Mag of Tex Jr Col Assn 7 Yrs; Mem Nat, St & Co Gen & Spec Ed Assns; Col Assns; AAUP; cp/Num Profl, Social & Ser Orgs; hon/1 of Nat's Top 10 Wom of Yr, ABWA 1962; Awds in Ednl TV, Art-Typing, Speech; Hon Grad Col & HS; S'ship Univ Colo; W/W: Am Wom, S&SW, Child Devel Profls, Poetry in Am, World Wom; Author Sev Ednl Articles, Poetry & Short Stories; Many Musical Comps; Sev Radio-TV Series.

MIKRONIS, CHRISTOS EDGAR oc/Manufacturing Executive; b/Apr 16, 1921; h/2572 Tulip St, Sarasota, FL 33579; ba/Osprey, FL; m/Winnie Whitehead; c/Edgar Andrew, Robert Tucker, Gary Eugene; p/Christos B (dec) and Elizabeth B Mikronis (dec); ed/Att'd Sch Engrg, La St Univ; mil/USN 1941-45 Naval Aviator; pa/Hydraulic Valve Mfg Exec, Rexnord Inc; Bd Dirs Pan Am Bank of Sarasota; Past Pres & Bd Dirs Sarasota Area Mfcs Assn; cp/Past Ser BSA; Past Pres Sarasota Bay Rotary Clb; Bd Govs Sarasota Univ Clb; Bd Nat Conf of Christians & Jews; Bd Dirs WECU Channel 3 TV; Pres Elect Am Cancer Soc Crusade Chm; Pres Sarasota C of C; Bd Dirs Bay Village Retirement Ctr; r/Pine Shore Presb Ch: Past Deacon, Past Elder, Past Pres Bd Dirs, Bd Mem Endowment Com, Mem Bd Trustees; hon/Man of Yr Sarasota Area Mfcs Assn.

MILBURN, THERESA HOLTZCLAW oc/Retired Teacher; b/July 24, 1914; h/Rt 2, Harmon Hgts, Danville, KY 40422; m/William Isaac; c/Theresa Sue Sallee; p/Walter S (dec) and Ophelia Walker Holtzclaw (dec); ed/AB Georgetown Col; Masters Deg Univ Ky; pa/Local Ret'd Tchrs Assn; KEA: NEA: NRTA; AARP; cp/Former AAUW; BPW; r/Bapt; hon/World Traveler.

MILBURN, WILLIAM ISAAC oc/Retired; b/Mar 15, 1914; h/Rt 2 Harmon Hgts, Danville, KY 40422; m/Theresa Holtzclaw; c/Theresa Sue Milburn Sallee; p/John (dec) and Pearl Sparrow Milburn (dec); ed/Bus Deg Campbellsville Col; mil/AUS 1943-45; pa/Old Bank 1933-76: Exec VP 1966-76, Dir 1960-76; cp/Am Legion; VFW; Ch Commun Dr; Secy Boyle Sch Bd 1973-76; r/Bapt; hon/Ky Col.

MILBY, RUTH KITTRELL oc/Homemaker; b/Aug 8, 1922; h/Rt 12, Box 355, London, KY 40741; m/Robert L; c/Theodore Henry, Marcia M Ridings, Michelle M Gardner; p/Henry Harrison Kittrell, San Diego, CA; Amanda Lawrence Kittrell (dec); cp/GSA 1957-; Pres Bluegrass Repub Wom's Clb 1958; Wom's Clb of London, Pres 1962-64, 78-80; r/Bapt; hon/Thanks Badge, GSA.

MILES, CHARLES R oc/Investment Counselor; b/Mar 29, 1929; h/Venice, FL; ba/PO Box 1525, Venice, FL 33595; m/Mary Jane; c/Charles R Jr, William G, Frances F, Mark; ed/BS Ind Univ 1951; Cert'd Fin Planner, Col for Fin Plan'g 1978; Reg'd Prin, NASD; Reg'd Option Prin, CBOE & AMEX; Reg'd Investment Advr, SEC; mil/AUS 1951-61 Capt; pa/Pres The Men's Shop 1961-68; Reg'd Rep & Asst Mgr, Venice Br A G Edwards & Sons Inc 1968-73; Mgr OSJ Venice Br for Raymond James & Assocs Inc 1973-78; Investment Cnslr, Self-Employed 1978-; Ofcr & Dir Downtown Venice Merchants Assn 1962-68; Venice Hosp: Bd Trustees 1966-, Chm & Pres 1969-; Org'g Dir, First Venice Savings & Loan Assn 1978-; cp/Venice-Nokomis Rotary Clb, Ofcr & Dir 1963-68, Pres 1967; C of C: Ofcr & Dir, Pres 1966; Venice Yacht Clb: Ofcr & Dir, V-Commodore 1969; Fdg VP Com of 100, Venice Area; Campaign Chm, U Way 1968; Venice Lodge #301 F&AM 1951-; Egypt Temple, Tampa 1972-; Venice Shrine Clb: Ofcr & Dir 1973-78, Pres 1975; Venice Civic Ctr Plan'g Com 1971-77; Coached Little Leag Rotary Team; Served on Boy Scout Com; Org'd & Devel'd Parking Facility in Downtown Venice; r/St Mark's Epis Ch: Vestry 1964-67, 78-, Sr Warden 1979, Lay Reader 1965-.

MILHOLLAND, THOMAS ALVA oc/Assistant Director; b/Aug 19, 1944; h/Abilene, TX; ba/Abilene Christian Univ, Box 8185, Abilene, TX 79699; m/Sandra; c/Kay, Matt; p/Mrs F Milholland, Dallas, TX; ed/BS Okla Christian Col 1966; MS E Tex St Univ 1972; PhD Tex Tech Univ 1979; pa/Prof Marriage & Fam Therapy, Abilene Christian Univ; Pvt Pract Marriage & Fam Therapy; Am Assn Marriage & Fam Therapy; Nat Coun Fam Relats; Tex Assn Marriage & Fam Therapy; Tex Coun Fam Relats; r/Ch of Christ, Ordained Min; hon/Outstg Yng Men Am 1979; Pat E Harrell, Guest Lectr 1980; Author Num Profl Articles.

MILLER, BRUCE RICHARD oc/Personnel Executive; b/Mar 16, 1944; h/400 Madison St, #2103, Alexandria, VA 22314; ba/Alexandria; p/Robert Joseph and Marguerite Marie Fritz Miller; ed/BA Penn St Univ 1971; mil/AUS 1966-70; pa/Supvr Salary Adm, Govt Employees Ins Co, Chevy Chase, Md 1971-73; Asst to Pers Dir, MCI Telecommuns Corp, Wash DC 1973-74; Corp Pers Dir, Kay Jewelers, Inc, Alexandria, Va

1974-; Am Soc Pers Adm; cp/Metro Wash Bd of Trade; Alexandria C of C; Penn Retail Jewelers Assn; r/Luth; hon/Contbr to *Jeweler's Circular Keystone* & *National Jeweler.*

MILLER, GEORGE CRAWFORD oc/Marketing Manager; b/May 15, 1946; h/209 Grisdale Hill, Annapolis, MD 21401; ba/Hunt Valley, MD; m/Dianna R; c/Matthew, Mark; p/L Reed and Emilie Crawford Miller, Chevy Chase, MD; ed/BS Univ Tenn 1969; MBA Loyola Col 1979; pa/Mktg Mgr, Am Bank Stationery Co 1975-; Wallace Bus Forms 1970-75; IBM Wash DC 1968-70; BFMA; DPMA; DMCW; cp/US JCs, Chat, Tenn 1970-72; r/Presb; hon/Tenn JCs Pres Awd 1971; IBM 100% Clb 1969; Wallace Bus Forms Top 20 1979, 72, 74; Articles Pub'd in *Computerworld; Informs; Business Forms Mgmt Assn Jour.*

MILLER, GILBERT CARL JR oc/Executive Director; b/Oct 9, 1945; m/Karen Costello; c/Christopher Patrick, Kara Melissa, Adam Ryan; p/G Carl Sr (dec) and Leona C Miller, Wilmington, NC; ed/BS ECU 1967; Masters Psychi & Med Social Work, Med Col Va Commonwlth Univ 1969; Adv Studies UNC-CH 1979, Fla St Univ 1980; pa/Asst Dir Ofc Ec Oppors, Wilmington, NC 1967; Social Wkr Supvr, SEn Mtl Hlth Ctr 1969-70; Chief Supvr Area Prog Tideland Mtl Hlth Ctr 1971; Exec Dir, NC Dept Human Resources, Div Yth Sers; Am Assn Psychi Sers for Chd 1974-79; NASW 1967; Acad of Cert'd Social Wkrs 1971; Am Assn Marriage & Fam Cnslrs 1973; Past Chm U Way for St Employees 1979; NC Juvenile Sers Assn, Bd Mem 1980-81; Am Correctional Assn, Profl Mem 1980; cp/NC JCs, Past Pres, Past VP, Chm Bd 1969-80; Master Mason, Orr Masonic Lodge 10792; Sir Knight of York Rite; 32° Scottish Rite Mason 1972; Shriner Sudan Temple 1973; Past Chm Sr Vol Prog & Child Advocacy Coun 1975-78; r/Meth; hon/W/W: Human Sers, NC; NC St JCs Pres's Awd of Hon 1974-75; Hons from Easter Seal Soc 1974, Cerebral Palsy 1975, Ret'd Sr Vol 1975-76, U Way 1977; NC JC Past Pres Awd 1975; Carbarrus Citizen of Yr, Concord, NC 1979; Recip Dist'd Ser Awd, Concord JCs 1980; Presented Key to City of Concord 1980.

MILLER, GREGG EDWARD oc/Instructor; b/Mar 25, 1951; h/Camden, AR; ba/So Ark Univ, Tech Branch, PO Box 3048, Camden, AR 71701; m/Janey H; c/Glenn Eugene, Michael Christopher; p/Kenneth C and Genevieve E Miller, Webster, NY; ed/AAS AV Technol 1972; BS AV Communs 1975; MS Cand Instr Technol; pa/Photo Instr 1978-; Advr for Photo Option of Commercial-Advtg Art Dept, So Ark Univ; SAU-Tech Edrs Assn VP 1979-80, Pres 1980-81; Active Edr Mem Profl Photogs Am; cp/Palmyra-Macedon JCs 1976-78; r/Roman Cath; hon/Awd'd Best of Show, 1st Pl Portrait Category, 3rd Pl Sports in Action Category, Mall Invitational Sponsored by S Ark Arts Ctr, El Dorado, Ark 1980.

MILLER, JAMES VERNON (JAKE) oc/Postal Service; b/May 26, 1942; h/Rt 6 Box 365, N Wilksboro, NC 28655; m/Hazel A; c/Lena Kay, James V Jr; p/Claude N and Loan H Miller, N Wilkesboro, NC; ed/Att'd Wilkes Commun Col 1979; mil/USMC; pa/Post Master Mt Ulla, NC; cp/N Wilkesboro Fire Dept; Mulberry Fairplain Ruritan; r/Bapt; hon/Perfect Attendance Awd in Sch 1960; Fireman of Yr 1979; Citizen of Wk 1978.

MILLER, JANEL HOWELL oc/Psychologist; b/May 18, 1947; h/806 Walbrook, Houston, TX 77062; ba/League City, TX; m/Charles Rick; c/Kimberly, Brian, Audrey; p/John E and Grace H Howell, Louisville, KY; ed/BA 1969; MA 1972; PhD 1979; pa/HPA; TPA; APA; AAMFT; TSPA; HBTA; r/Prot; hon/De Pauw Alumni Schlr; NIMH Fellow; Cert'd Assoc Psych; Lic'd Social Psychotherapist; Psi Chi.

MILLER, JEWELL H oc/Retired Secretary and Accounting Clerk; b/Dec 15, 1910; h/Caryville, TN; m/dec; p/D M (dec) and Hattie P Hogan (dec); ed/Dip Alverson Bus Univ 1930; pa/Ret'd Secy, Acctg & Pers Clerk; cp/Past Mem Campbell Co Dem Exec Com; Dem Wom's Clb; r/U Meth.

MILLER, JOHN J oc/Computer Science and Engineering Writer; b/Oct 5, 1932; h/Rt 1 Box 331-C, Damascus, VA 24236; m/Evelyn L; p/Herman C and Nell M Miller, Elizabethton, TN; ed/Study in Elec Engrg, Physics, Chem, Indust Mgmt; mil/AUS 3 Yrs; pa/Instr Large Scale Computers; Supvr Prod of Nylon & Polyester; Engrg Writer Missile Sys; Prod & Control Mgr; Mgr Presentations & Pubs, Textile Machinery; Computer Technol; Sr Mem IEEE; Soc Tech Writers; Soc Logistic Engrs; cp/Pres Rotary Clb; Toastmaster Clb of Am; Vinifera Wine Growers Assn; 1st VP C fo C; Repub Party; r/Bapt; hon/VIP Awd 1963 & 69; C of C Spec Annual Achmt Awd 1968; Rotary Clb Annual Achmt Awd 1967.

MILLER, JUDITH A SHRUM oc/Associate Director; b/Sept 8, 1941; h/8623 Langport Dr, Springfield, VA 22152; ba/Wash DC; m/William L Jr; c/Steven William Shrum, Vickie Lynn White, Lisa Ann Shrum, Mark Allen Shrum, Brian David Shrum; p/Frank G and Kathryn M Bell, Indianapolis, IN; ed/Att'd Ind Ctrl Col, DePauw Univ; pa/Assoc Dir Interfaith Forum on Rel, Art & Arch; AAWA; Great Lakes Assn Sch, Col & Univ Staffing; cp/Co Coun Rep, Fairfax Co Schs 1978-; Comm on

214

Aging, Steering Com 1979-; Region of Capital Area, Outreach & Stewardship Comm 1978-; Nat City Christian Ch, Outreach Com 1979-; Nat City Christian Ch Fin Com 1978-; St Louis Chd's Home, Exec Com 1976-78; Citizens Adv Coun, Parkway Sch Dist, St Louis, Mo 1976-77; r/Disciples of Christ; hon/W/W Am Wom.

MILLER, LLOYD JACKSON oc/Educator; b/Sept 2, 1940; h/108 Yorkshire Pl, Gadsden, AL 35901; ba/Gadsden; m/Brenda Joyce Hughes; c/Todd Lloyd; p/dec; ed/AS Gadsden St Jr Col 1967; BA 1969, MS 1979 Jacksonville St Univ; pa/Prin Gadsden HS; Phi Delta Kappa; cp/Rotary Clb; r/Ch of Christ; hon/Outstg Yng Men Am 1974; Ala Most Outstg Prin 1980.

MILLER, LOREN G oc/Store Manager; b/Apr 21; ba/404 Merchant Dr, Knoxville, TN 37912; m/Anna L; c/Loanne, Tina; p/Mr and Mrs Joseph G Miller, Elizabethton, TN; ed/AA Mars Hill Col; BA Carson-Newman Col; BD, MRE SWn Bapt Theol Sem; Computer Programming Dip; pa/Mgr Bapt Book Store; r/Bapt; hon/Living Bible Awd; Keith C Von Hagen Awd.

MILLER, MARILYN EVE oc/Physical Therapy Instructor; b/Aug 4, 1948; h/#4 Club Rd, Jacksonville, AR 72076; ba/Little Rock, AR; m/William H; c/Eric William, Jeffrey Martin; p/Charles M and Eve K Miller, Hammond, IN; ed/BS Univ Wis 1970; AUS Med Field Ser Sch, Phy Therapy Cert; MA Univ Ark 1981; mil/AUS 1970-72; USAR 1972-; pa/Phy Therapy Instr Univ Ctrl Ark; Multidisciplinary Screening Team Auburn Univ-Montgomery; Phy Therapy Dir Ctrl Ala Home Hlth, Fairview Med Ctr, Rehab Ctr Albuquerque, NM; Staff Therapist VA Hosp Montgomery; Ark Chapt Am Phy Therapy Assn; APTA Geriatric Sect; Ark Gerontological Soc, Bd Dirs; AAUP; r/Unitarian; hon/Nat Hon Soc 1966; Outstg Yng Wom Am 1975; 5th US Army Mus Theatre, Best Choreography 1972; Author Monthly Article to *La Petite Roche*.

MILLER, MAXINE oc/Executive; b/Dec 15, 1940; h/2406 N Vine, Magnolia, AR 71753; m/J D; c/Linda, Derrell; p/Mr and Mrs John Loe; pa/Owner-Mgr Millers Cafeteria; Bd Ark Restaurant Assn; Nat Restaurant Assn; cp/C of C; Pres Pilot Clb Magnolia; Pres Boys Clb Wom's Aux; Bd Indep Living; r/College View Bapt Ch: SS Tchr; hon/Pilot of Yr 1976.

MILLER, PATSY oc/Antique Collector; b/Dec 8, 1928; h/Star Rt Box 27-B, Andrews, TX 79714; m/George; c/Janella Walls, Judy Franklin; p/Dave (dec) and Ruby Sisson, Andrews, TX; r/Bapt.

MILLER, PRESTON JOSEPH oc/Plantation Executive; b/Dec 12, 1921; h/Sweet Bay, Abbeville, LA 70510; ba/Abbeville; m/Dolores Ann; c/Preston J III, Fel N, John William, Mary Dolly; p/P J and Laura Miller, Abbeville, LA; ed/BS LSU 1940; pa/Farmer: Livestock; Timber; Oil & Gas; Real Estate; cp/C of C; Dem Party; r/Cath.

MILLER, REBECCA ELLISA oc/Clerical Worker; b/Nov 20, 1947; h/103 Dogwood, New Boston, TX 75570; ba/Texarkana, TX; m/James Howard; p/William T and Nellie Louise Hervey, Texarkana, TX; ed/Att'g Texarkana Commun Col; pa/Clerical Wkr Missile Maint Br Red River Army Depot; r/Meth; hon/2 Blue Ribbons for Cooking, Four States Fair.

MILLER, RICHARD L SR oc/Music Evangelist, Youth Counselor and Advisor; b/Mar 3, 1937; h/PO Box 1255, Glenmora, LA 71433; ba/Same; m/E Jeane; c/Richard L Jr; p/R L and Nell Miller, Glenmore, LA; ed/Att'd La Bapt Col & McNeese St Col; pa/Mus Evangelist Prisons, Schs, JC Meetings, Fball Stadiums, etc; r/So Bapt; hon/Ordained Mus Min.

MILLER, ROBERT GREGORY oc/Broadcast Executive; b/July 11, 1948; ba/KTSU-FM, 3100 Wheeler St, Houston, TX 77004; m/Prudence S; c/Marissa Marie; p/Robert F Miller, Chgo, IL; Marie L Miller (dec); ed/BSJ 1970, MSJ 1971 NWn Univ; PhD Cand Univ Tex; pa/Chief Exec Ofcr KTSU-FM Radio; Network TV/Radio News Corresp ABC News; Asst to Pres KERA TV, Dallas; Am Fed TV & Radio Artists; Writers Guild of Am E; cp/NAACP; Black Repub Party Chapt, Dallas; r/Bapt; hon/1st Pl Feature News Reporting, New Orleans Press Clb 1976; Feature Story in *Panarama Magazine*.

MILLER, THELMA CLAY oc/Nurse; b/Apr 30, 1914; h/923 Brazos, Graham, TX 76046; ba/Graham; m/Guy; c/Annie Belle Burdick, Juanita Gilliam, Olita (dec), Helen Waldrop, Howard, Joyce Hinson, Shirley Philips; p/Rufus (dec) and Anie Neill (dec); pa/LVN Graham Gen Hosp.

MILLER, THOMAS ALLEN oc/Surgeon, Associate Professor; b/July 7, 1944; h/Houston, TX; ba/Dept Surg, Univ Tex Med Sch, 6431 Fannin, Houston, TX 77030; m/Janet Ruth Walters; c/David Allen, William James, Laurie Ann; p/Joseph Edgar and Marion Ruth Corpman Miller, Harrisburg, PA; ed/BS Wheaton Col 1966; MD Temple Univ Med Sch 1970; Intern Univ Chgo Hosps 1970-71; Jr Resident Surg 1971-74, Sr

Resident Surg 1974-75 Univ Mich Hosps; Fellow Surg Res, VA Hosp, Ann Arbor, Mich 1972-73; Postdoct Res Fellow, Dept Surg, Univ Tex Med Br 1975-76; Postdoct Res Fellow, Dept Physiology, Univ Tex Med Sch 1976-77; pa/Univ Tex Med Sch: Asst Prof Surg 1977-79, Assoc Prof Surg 1979-; AAAS; FACS; Am Digestive Disease Soc; Am Fed Clin Res; Am Gastroenterological Assn; MA; Am Physiol Soc; Am Soc for Parental & Enteral Nutrition; Assn Acad Surg: Com on Leg Issues 1978-79, Chm 1978-79, Com on Issues 1979-; Harris Co Med Soc; Houston Gastroenterological Assn; Houston Surg Soc; NY Acad Scis; Pancreatic Clb Inc; Soc for Surg of Alimentary Tract; Soc of Univ Surgs; Splanchnic Circulation Grp; Tex Med Assn; r/Presb; hon/Grad cum laude Wheaton Col 1966; Conrad Jobst Awd 1973; Frederick A Coller Awd 1974; Frederick A Coller Traveling Schlr 1974-75; W/W: S&SW 1980-81, Houston 1980-81; Recip Nat Inst of Hlth Res Grant 1979-82; Editorial Conslt, *Am Jour of Physiology* 1979-, *Digestive Diseases & Scis* 1980-; Cert'd by Am Bd of Surg 1976; Author Multiple Articles on Surg Disease & Gastrointestinal Physiology.

MILLIGAN, THOMAS BRADEN JR oc/Musicologist; b/May 31, 1947; h/Rt 2, Timberlake, Talbott, TN 37877; p/Mrs Thomas B Milligan, Talbott, TN; ed/BA, BMus Carson-Newman Col 1969; MA 1974, PhD 1978 Eastman Sch Mus, Univ Rochester; mil/AUS 1969-71; pa/Musicologist, Pianist, Tchr: Univ Rochester 1975-76; Carson-Newman Col 1978-; Am Musicological Soc; Col Mus Soc; Pi Kappa Lambda; Phi Beta Kappa; Phi Mu Alpha Sinfonia; Alpha Chi; r/Bapt; hon/Fulbright Grant to Austria 1971-72; Intl W/W Mus 1980.

MILLS, DOLORIES MILES oc/Cosmetologist; b/Apr 28, 1943; ba/109 N Main St, Enterprise, AL 36330; c/Gary Lawrence, Dorothy Lynn, Larry Earl; p/Dennis C and Uvav Miles, Elba, AL; ed/Cosmetology; Nurse's Aide; pa/Nat Hairdressers Assn; r/Bapt.

MILLS, WANDA LEE oc/Tenant Service Director; b/Dec 30, 1936; h/628 8th St Ct, Henderson, KY 42420; ba/Henderson; m/Gilbert Earl; c/Mary Katherine Pierson, James Alexander Boatmon Jr, (Stepch:) Tina, Dwayne, Gill Lee; p/Edward and Mary E Schuck, Corydon, KY; ed/Assoc Deg; pa/Tenant Ser Dir, Housing Auth; cp/Moose; Eagles; Sportsman Clb; r/Bapt; hon/Vol Awds: 1000 Hosp Hours, Cystic Fibrosis, Rest Homes.

MILLWOOD, CLAYTON LAMAR JR oc/Florist, Teacher, Photographer; b/Sept 4, 1943; h/766 Mimosa Dr, Marietta, GA 30060; ba/Marietta; p/Clayton L Sr and Jeans S Millwod, Marietta, GA; ed/Att'd Carson-Newman Col, Univ Ga, Univ Tenn, Am Floral Arts Sch, NY Inst Photo; pa/Florist 12 Yrs; Tchr Florists; Photog; cp/Work w Florist Grps & Charity Orgs; Garden Clb; Cancer Soc; r/Bapt.

MILNE, NANCY HOBACK oc/Homemaker, Civic Worker; h/429 Allison Ave SW, Roanoke, VA; m/James Whitton; c/James W Jr, John Howard; p/Fred S and Lettie Lee Howard Hoback; ed/AB Roanoke Col; Mus Hollins Col; Att'd UNC; pa/Former Tchr & Choir Dir; Bd Va Fed Music Clbs, Past St Pres; cp/Past Pres Thursday Morning Mus Clb, Bd Dirs; Bd Dirs Greenwood Road Garden Clb, Past Pres; Bd Mem Nat Fed Mus Clb; Roanoke Country Clb; DAR; Dem Party; r/Presb; hon/Roanoke Valley Mother of Yr, Arts & Scis; Va Composer.

MILSTEAD, ELDON ANDREW oc/Businessman; b/Feb 25, 1928; h/2613 College Ave, Plainview, TX 79072; ba/P'view; m/Dorothy Marie; c/Richard, Diane McAninch, Cathryn Chandler, Virginia Young, David; p/Andrew Merton (dec) and Clara Simpson Milstead (dec); pa/Owner Hardware Store; S-Ctrl Fed Mineral Soc; Hi-Plains Rock Clb; cp/C of C; r/Sethward Bapt Ch: Deacon.

MILTON, JERRY MARTIN oc/Executive; b/Apr 28, 1940; h/716 Ogletree Rd, Auburn, Al 36830; ba/Auburn; m/Eunice Conerly; c/Jerry M Jr, Nan Conerly; p/Lloyd E and Gertrude Milton, McComb, MS; ed/BS Miss St Univ 1962; pa/Fac Cont'g Ed Columbus Col; Ins Fac Ala Indep Ins Agts; Pres University Acgy Inc (Gen Ins); Ala Indep Ins Agts: Bd Dirs 1979-; Chm Ed Com 1977-; c/Auburn Rotary Clb, Pres 1979-80; Auburn C of C, Pres 1975; Auburn U Fund, Pres 1975; Auburn Parks & Rec Bd 1973-77; Jr Achmt, Dir 1979-80; BSA, Dist Com 1974-78; Auburn Dixie Yth Baseball, Dir 1975-79; r/Auburn U Meth Ch: Ofcl Bd, Lay Spkr, SS Tchr; hon/Ala Indep Inst Agts Insuror of Yr 1980, Outstg Com Chm 1979.

MINES, ERAS ANTHONY oc/Businessman; b/June 22, 1948; h/2504 Jeffrey Dr, Chattanooga, TN 37421; ba/Chat; c/Jason Anthony; p/Kenneth K and Lillie F Mines, Chat, TN; ed/Att'd E Tenn St Univ 1967; mil/AUSSgt; pa/Little Art Shop 1964-67; Mgr Opers Little Art Shops 1971-72; Spec Agt John Hancock Ins Co 1972; Cert'd Welder Lorain Div Koehring Co 1972-73; Owner & Dir Opers Art Creations 1973-; Yng Wom's Christian Org & Chat St Tech Commun Col 1977-; cp/Chat JCs 1971-; E Ridge Merchants Assn, Bd Dirs, VP 1977; Profl Picture Framers Assn, Chapt Pres Tenn Val Chapt 1976, Assoc Dir SE Region; E Ridge JCs,

PERSONALITIES OF THE SOUTH

Bd Dirs & VChm 1973-76; Hamilton Co Yng Repubs, Bd Dirs 1976; Prog Chm 1977, Chm 1978; E Ridge Coun of Gtr Chat C of C, Bd Dirs 1977-79; Hamilton Co Repub Party, Exec Com & Steering Com, Ticket Chm Sen Richard G Lugar Dinner; r/Presb; hon/Vietnamese Cross of Gallantry, 1st, 2nd, 3rd Awds; Vietnamese Civic Action, 1st, 2nd, 3rd Awds; Army Commend Medal, 2nd & 3rd OLCs; Vietnamese Campaign Medal; Vietnamese Ser Medal; Art Awd 1966 & 76; Crandel Art Awd 1967.

MINOR, DAVID MICHAEL oc/Attorney; b/Apr 21, 1946; h/1409 S Houston, Kaufman, TX 75142; ba/Kaufman; m/Susan; p/Lillian Minor, Henrietta, TX; ed/BA Tex Christian Univ; JD S Tex Col of Law; pa/Pvt Pract Law, Austin 1978; Asst Co Atty, Hale Co 1979; Asst Crim Dist Atty, Kaufman 1979-; Kaufman Co Bar Assn; Tex St Bar; Am Bar Assn; Tex Co & Dist Atty Assn; cp/Kaufman Co Lib Bd; hon/Dir Yth Affairs, St Dem Exec Com, Austin 1970.

MINOR, JIM D oc/Coach and Teacher; b/Nov 1, 1919; h/303 W Grand, Tonkawa, OK 74653; ba/Tonkawa; m/Emma Jean Gray; c/James Gray, Mary Jean Ladd, Martha Anne; p/J L Minor, Russellville, AR; Stella Webb Minor (dec); ed/Ark Polytech Col; BSE Univ Ark; mil/AUS 1942-45; pa/HS Fball Coach: Asst Coach 13 Yrs, Hd Coach 21 yrs; Hd Coach Tonkawa HS; OEA; NEA; Nat HS Ath Coaches Assn; Okla Fball Coaches Assn; Okla Coaches Assn; cp/Lions Intl; Civil Defense, Communs Chm; Am Legion; hon/HS All-St Guard; Col All-Star & All-Conf; Dist A-9 Coach of Yr 1973, 77, 80; Region 2 Coach of Yr 1980; Cand Okla Coach of Yr 1981; Elect'd Okla Coaches to Coaching Staff for N All-Stars 1963; Elect'd Okla Coaches to Coach Okla All-Stars vs Tex All-Stars 1976; Omicron Delta Kappa.

MINSHEW, C GENECE oc/Manager; b/Mar 18, 1951; h/7400 Powers Ave, Apt 289, Jacksonville, FL 32217; ba/Jax, FL; p/John Wiley (dec) and Janece Bowles Minshew (dec); pa/Mgr So Bell Bus Sers Dept; cp/NOW: Pres 1979-; Treas 1976-79; Pres Jacksonville Chapt 1977-78; Secy Indian River Fla Chapt 1976; Att'd Nat Conf 1977 & 78; Att'd Regional Conf 1976, 77, 79; Att'd St Conf 1976, 77, 79; Devel'd & Wkrd on N Fla ERA Caravan; Att'd Fla IWY Conf; Com-wom Duval Co Dem Exec Com 1978-; Dir Wom's Ctr for Reproductive Hlth 1978-; VP BD Dirs Hubbard House 1978; r/Bapt.

MINTON, HUBERT LEE oc/Retired; b/Oct 15, 1890; h/526 Donaghey, Conway, AR 72032; m/Lucy Permelia Williams; c/Imogene A Holt, Sarah Lee Hindsman, Patricia A Newton, Hubert Lee Jr; p/Jesse Morris (dec) and Harriet Minton (dec); ed/BA Ed; PhD Univ Chgo 1937; mil/WWI 2nd Lt; pa/Ret'd Tchr; Past Pres & Life Mem Ark Sch Bd Assn; Past Pres AEA; Past Mem Phi Alpha Leag; cp/Kiwanis Clb; r/So Bapt; hon/Red Cross Ser Awd; 2 Dist'd Ser Awds Kiwanis Clb; 46 Yr Awd Univ Ctrl Ark; Prof Emeritus UCA; Author Hist UCA.

MINTON, MARVEL SUE oc/Math Supervisor; b/Nov 4, 1933; h/Box 615, Brookhaven, MS 39601; ba/Brookhaven; p/Albert Sidney (dec) and Ella Parker Minton (dec); ed/BS, MEd Univ So Miss; pa/Math Supvr Brookhaven Public Schs; Past Pres Brookhaven Ed Assn; Past Pres Brookhaven Dept Clrm Tchrs; Past Dir Dist 7 Dept Clrm Tchrs; Past Secy Dist 5 Miss Assn Edrs; Past Pres Rho Conclave, Kappa Kappa Iota; Pres Theta Chapt Delta Kappa Gamma 1978-80; Mumbling Mums; Nat Coun Tchrs Maths; Miss Coun Tchrs Maths; Miss Coun Supvrs Maths; NEA; Miss Assn Edrs; Brookhaven Assn Edrs; Miss Assn Public Cont'g Adult Ed; Brookhaven Adm & Tchrs Adv Coun; Leg & Noms & Elects Coms Miss Dept Clrm Tchrs; Profl Relats & Profl Consltg Sers Coms Miss Ed Assn; Miss Ed Conv Com on Credentials & Elects; Sect Chm Elem Div Miss Ed Conv 1968; cp/Brookhaven BPW Clb, 2nd VP; Heart Fund Vol Wkr 1979; Brookhaven Beautiful Vol Wkr 1980; Former Mem Bd Dirs Lincoln Co Cancer Dr; 1980 Lobbying Team, Miss Assn Edrs; Leg Com Brookhaven Assn Edrs; r/Bapt; hon/Nat Register Prom Ams; Outstg Yng Wom Am 1966; Rec'd Outstg Tchr Awd, Lincoln Co Urban S'ship Bd 1977-78; Wom of Achmt Awd, Brookhaven BPW Clb 1980; Order to the Rose Deg, Beta Sigma Phi 1978; Plaqe from Miss Assn Edrs, Dist 5, for Cont'd Dedicated Ser 1978; Cert Apprec, Am Heart Assn 1979; W/W Am Wom 1981-82.

MINTZ, RONALD LEE oc/Assistant to Chief Public Safety Emergency Communications; b/Aug 21, 1954; h/Shelby, NC; ba/PO Box 1406, Shelby, NC 28150; m/Donna Pierce; p/Rush Shull and Mary McDaniel Mintz, Shelby, NC; ed/Att'd WCU 1973, Gardner-Webb Col 1973-78; pa/Telecommunr II Cleveland Co Communs; NC Assn Public Safety Communs Ofcrs; cp/Shelby JC, Pres 1980-81, VP 1979-80; City of Shelby Human Relats Coun, Race Dir St Patricks Day Run 1979, 80; Shelby Christmas Parade Chm 1978; Firemans Meml Fund Chm 1979-80; Master Mason, Cleveland Lodge 202; r/Bapt; hon/Dist'd Ser Awd 1980 Vol Ser to Commun; Shelby JC Yr 1979-80; Richard Ferchaud Commun Ser Awd 1980; Spec Vol Awd, NC Govt's Ofc 1979.

MIRACLE, E VERN oc/Police Officer; b/May 15, 1943; h/A-9 Odessa

Apts, 235 Wayne Dr, Richmond, KY 40475; ba/Richmond; c/Cherae Michelle; p/Oscar Miracle, Chuckey, TN; Ida Mae Houser Miracle (dec); ed/Att'd En Ky Univ; mil/USMC 4 Yrs; pa/Ky St Police: Trooper 10 Yrs, Detective 4 Yrs; Charter Mem Ky St Police Profl Assn; cp/BSA: Advr for Law Enforcement, Explorers 3 Yrs; EKU High Adventure Clb 2 Yrs; r/Bapt; hon/Vietnam Ser Medal.

MIRACLE, JERENE oc/Real Estate Salesperson; b/Nov 26, 1940; h/Rt 1, Cleburne, TX; ba/Cleburne; m/Wilbur; c/Myrisha, Johnny; p/dec; ed/Ft Worth Adult Ed, Real Est 1968; pa/First Mark Rltrs; Ft Worth Bd Rltrs; Johnson Co Bd Rltrs; r/Bapt; hon/W/W Tex 1973-74; Outstg Am in S 1975.

MIRANDA, MERCEDES DIAZ-CUERVO oc/Manager; b/June 28, 1930; h/9800 Sunset Dr, Miami, FL 33173; ba/Miami; c/Mercedes Maria, Jose A, Maria Paloma, Maria Cristina, Javier A, Mary Ann, Maria Elena; p/Carlos Diaz-Valdes (dec); Esperanza Cuervo-Corrales, Havana, Cuba; ed/Social Sci, Bus Adm, Elect Data Processing, Mktg, Advtg; pa/Editor *Floridana*; Hispanic Commun Relats Mgr, The Miami Herald Pub'g Co; Public Relats; Promo & Human Relat'ship; Cultural, Charity & Civic Promotor; cp/Pres BPW Latin Clb; Bd Dirs Cuban Wom's Clb; Am Cancer Soc; Dade Lung Monroe Assn Big Bros & Sisters; Hemispheric Cong for Wom; Latin Orange Fest Coun; Interam Foun for the Fine Arts; Hispanic Heritage Wk; r/Roman Cath; hon/B'nai Brith Jewish Congreg Nom Wom of Yr 1978.

MIRANDA, OSMUNDO AFONSO oc/Professor; b/Dec 23, 1926; h/80 E Lake, Tuscaloosa, AL 35405; ba/Tuscaloosa; c/Nisa Miranda Bacon, Georgeolimpio Afonso, Cheyenne Afonso; p/Olympio Afonso de Miranda (dec); Laurinda Ferreira (dec); ed/Att'd Gammon Inst, Lavras, Minas, Brazil 1950; MDiv Presb Theol Sem, Campinas, SP, Brazil 1954; ThM 1957, PhD 1962 Princeton Theol Sem; pa/Stillman Col: Prof Rel & Phil 1972-, Assoc Prof 1968-72; Midwestern Col, Instr Mod Lang 1966-68; Pgh Theol Sem, Libn Asst Cataloguer 1965-66; Campinas Theol Sem, Prof Biblical Criticism & Interpretation 1962-65, Dean 1964-65; AAAH; AAUP; AAR; Soc Biblical Lit; So Conf Humanities; Chm So Conf AAUP Com on AAUP & Accred'g Assn Relats; Associacao de Seminarios Teologicos Evangelicos de Brazil; r/Presb; hon/Outstg Edr Am 1971; Dir Am Schlrs 1978; W/W S&SW 1980; Intl W/W: Intells 1980, Ed 1980; Author Num Profl Articles.

MISCHEN, BETTYE ANN SMITH oc/Coordinator; b/Feb 9, 1936; h/Plano, TX; m/John J; p/A A and Dora Mae Smith, Denton, TX; ed/BA 1956, MA 1962 Univ Tex-El Paso; Supvr's Cert, Tex Wom's Univ 1979; pa/English Coor-Conslt, Plano ISD 1977-; Eng Tchr-Dept Chm, Plano HS 1962-77; Eng Tchr, El Paso HS 1956-62; Delta Kappa Gamma: St 1st VP, St Com Chm of Prog & of Ldrship Devel, Chm St Conv & Instl Conv, Chapt Pres; Gtr Dallas Coun Tchrs Eng, Pres; Tex Jt Coun Tchrs Eng, Conv Steering Com, Dist Secy, Public Relats Chm; NCTE; TSTA Eng Sect Chm; N Ctrl Tex Assn Supervision & Curric Devel, Pres Elect; ASCD; TASCD; NEA; Tex St Tchrs Assn, Dist Del; Collin Co Tchrs Assn, Secy; Plano Ed Assn, Com Assignments; Kappa Delta Pi, Pres; Phi Delta Kappa; cp/Plano BPW Clb, Chm 3 Coms; Tex & Nat Feds BPW; Fdr Dallas-Ft Worth Chapt Univ Tex Ex-Students Assn; Sustaining Mem Plano YMCA; r/Meth; hon/Tex Tchr of Yr 1971; Plano Tchr of Yr 1970; Channel 8 Citizenship Awd for Contbn to Ed 1970; Part in Ldrship/Mgmt Sem Baylor Univ, Delta Kappa Gamma; Delta Kappa Gamma: St Achmt Awd, Chapt Achmt Awd.

MITCHELL, EDGAR ELLIOTT oc/City Attorney; b/Oct 26, 1952; h/1306 Wood St, Big Spring, TX 79720; ba/Big Spring; m/Linda Rae; p/Ted and Wilma Mitchell, Austin, TX; ed/BA Univ Tex-Austin 1975; JD St Mary's Sch of Law 1978; pa/St Bar of Tex; Tex Yng Lwyrs Assn; Am Bar Assn; Howard Co Bar Assn; cp/Big Spring Optimist Clb; Big Spring Area C of C; r/Epis.

MITCHELL, JANET WHITE oc/Teacher; b/Dec 24, 1950; h/PO Box 473, Collins, MS 39428; m/Rexford; p/Garland L and Thelma Wooten White, Brookhaven, MS; ed/BS 1974; MEd 1976; EdD 1980; pa/Col Tchg, Area Spec Ed; Coun Exceptl Chd; Kappa Delta Pi; Miss Arts Fair for Handicapped, Chm; Spec Olympics; Phi Delta Kappa; cp/Miss Lung Assn, Chm Covington Co Chapt; USM Alumni Assn, VP Covington Co Chapt; Collins Summer Rdg Prog Co-Dir; r/Bapt; hon/W/W Miss 1974; Outstg Yng Wom Am 1976; NAJA S'ship 1979; Miss Lung Assn Goal Breaker Awd 1975.

MITCHELL, JOSEPH CLOVIS oc/Educational Administrator; b/May 28, 1948; h/College Station, TX; ba/Tex A&M Univ, Ednl Adm, College Station, TX 77843; m/Janette Whitt; p/J Christopher and Julia Craig Mitchell, Mobile, AL; ed/BA Morehouse Col 1969; MA Univ S Ala 1973; CASE Univ Ala-B'ham 1979; pa/Ednl Adm; Phi Delta Kappa; Nat Commun Ed Assn; Ala Commun Ed Assn Intl Mus Union; Nat Therapeutic Rec Assn; cp/NAACP, Mobile Chapt; YWCA Assoc Mem;

216

Therapeutic Rec Assn; cp/NAACP, Mobile Chapt; YWCA Assoc Mem; Neighborhood Org'd Wkrs, Secy Info; r/AME; hon/Charles Stewart Mott Fellow 1978-79, 81-82.

MITCHELL, KELLY KARNALE oc/Evangelist, Counselor, Educator; b/May 18, 1928; h/3403 Santee Dr, Montgomery, AL 36108; ba/Montgomery; m/Audrea Marie; c/Kelyne Audrienne, Kelly Karnale; p/Jerry C (dec) and Marie Mitchell (dec); ed/BA Fisk Univ 1952, Adv Work in Rel 1953; DD Ala Christian Col 1968; MRE Ala Christian Sch Rel; pa/Min Southside Ch of Christ; Rel Supvr Radio Sta WRMA; Phi Beta Sigma, Chap; Pres Ecumenica Assn; cp/Chm Montgomery Commun Action Bd; hon/Danforth Foun Awd for Ldrsip; Cert Merit, Montgomery Heritage Movement; Cert Apprec Montgomery Commun Action; Author 15 Rel Tracts.

MITCHELL, MICHAEL WESLEY oc/Consultant; b/May 7, 1955; m/Mary Theresa; c/Karen, Moses Michael, Tina Marie; p/Wesley A Mitchell, Mansfield, OH; Ethyl M Kingan, Crestline, OH; ed/AS 1980; EMT 1979; LPN 1979; Conslt in Ctrl Ser 1980; mil/USN 2nd Cl Petty Ofcr; pa/Hosp Ctrl Ser Conslt; Emer Room Tech; Intl Assn Hosp Ctrl Ser; Australian Hosp Assn; Am Hosp Assn; Nat Assn for Pract Nurses; Nat Registry of EMT; Switz Hosp Assn; Hosp Fin Assn; r/Cath; hon/W/W S&SW 1980-81; Sailor of the Qtr, USN 1978; Author "Hazards of Ethylene Oxide" 1979.

MITCHELL, RUTH MAY oc/Retired; b/Oct 19, 1908; h/2601 Joliet #37, Plainview, TX 79072; m/Fred W (dec); c/Charles E Kennedy, Doris West, Sally Gwartney; p/Charles F (dec) and Sarah Murray Henry (dec); ed/Pgh St Tchrs Col; pa/Ret'd Dorm Cnslr, Wayland Bapt Col; cp/Plainview Theatre; Past Matron OES; Wom's Clb; Mus Arts Clb; r/Bapt; hon/Plaque for 10 Yrs Cnslr WBC; 25 Yr OES Pin.

MITCHELL, WILLIAM EASON oc/Attorney, Municipal Judge; b/Mar 13, 1950; h/Calera, AL; ba/PO Box 550, Calera, AL 35040; m/Janice Ruton; c/Susan Catherine; p/W S Mitchell, Calera, AL; Martha Love Johnston, Calera, AL; ed/Att'd Univ Montevallo 1968-69; BS B'ham-So Col 1972; JD Cumberland Sch Law, Samford Univ 1975; pa/Sr Ptnr Mitchell, Green, Pino & Greer; Municipal Judge, Wilton, Calera & Montevallo, Ala; Pres Shelby Co Bar Assn; Bd Govs Ala Trial Lwyrs Assn; Ala Bar Assn; Am Trial Lwyrs Assn; Am Bar Assn; Phi Alpha Delta; cp/FOP; Nat Riflemen's Assn; Ala Sheriff's Assn; Ala Cattlemen's Assn; Med-Legal Christian Soc; Calera Civitan Clb; Calera C of C; 32° Mason; r/Meth; hon/JC Outstg Yng Men Am 1979; Author "Tender Years - Who Suffers" 1977 *Alabama Trial Lawyers Journal*.

MITCHUSSON, STELLA HUDSON oc/Teacher, Social Worker; b/May 30, 1914; h/Paducah, KY; m/William Guthrie; c/Janette M Ferguson, Joan M Klinger; p/Joshua Boyd and Ferrel Choat Hudson, Eddyville, KY; ed/Att'd Murray St Tchrs Col 1935-37; pa/Tchr Rural Schs 1935-45; Social Wkr, Commonwlth Ky 1945-75; Ky Ret'd Tchrs Assn; Nat Ret'd Tchrs Assn; Ky Wel Assn; Tenure Clb, Ky Dept Human Resources; Am Assn Ret'd Persons; cp/Nat Fed BPW Clb, Pres Charter Clb, Kuttawa, Ky; BPW Clb Reidland: Pres, VP, Secy; Wn Bapt Hosp Aux; Joslin Diabetes Foun Soc; r/Bapt; SS Tchr, Dir Sr Citizens Grp; hon/Ky Col 1975; Duchess of Paducah 1975; Wom of Yr, Reidland BPW Clb 1980; Locality Reporter, *Lyon County Herald* 1930-34.

MIZE, MARK oc/Special Agent; b/Sept 16, 1952; h/McComb, MS; ba/PO Box 606, McComb, MS 39648; p/John D and Barbara Mize, Jackson, MS; ed/AA Clarke Col 1972; BS 1974, MEd 1976 Miss St Univ; pa/Spec Agt: Miss Farm Bur Ins Cos, So Farm Bur Life Ins Cos; cp/McComb JCs, Treas 1979, Recording Secy 1980; r/Bapt; hon/Miss Farm Bur Ins Cos: Rookie of Yr 1979, Million Dollar Round Table Winner 1979, All Star Winner 1979.

MOHR, GORDON (JACK) oc/Lecturer, Lay Evangelist; b/Jan 1, 1916; h/Bay St Louis, MS; m/Doris S; c/Gordon D Jr; ed/LLD 1976, ThM 1978 Freelandia Inst; mil/1941-68; pa/Lectr; Lay Evangelist; Am Pistol & Rifle Assn, VP Ctrl USA Area; cp/US Senatorial Clb; Nat Adv Bd Am Security Coun; Ret'd Ofcrs Assn; r/Bapt; hon/18 Mil Awds & Decorations Incl'g Silver Star, Bronze Star w 3 OLCs, Purple Heart w 4 OLCs; Author *Hyenas in My Bedroom*; *Formula for Survival*; *Destination Somewhere*; *The Point of No Return*.

MOIZE, JERRY DEE oc/Attorney; b/Dec 19, 1934; h/Houndhill, Rt 2 Box 185B, Canton, MS 39046; ba/Jackson, MS; m/Margaret Ann Wooten; c/Jerry Jr; p/Dwight Moody and Thelma Ozment Moize, Gibsonville, NC; ed/AB cum laude Elon Col 1957; JD Tulane Univ 1960; mil/AUS 1960-62 Capt; USAR 1964-; pa/Num Mil Positions; Law Clerk to Hon Eugene A Gordon, US Dist Judge, Middle Dist NC 1965-66; Dir Legal Aid Soc Forsyth Co, Winston-Salem, NC 1966-69; Exec Dr Forsyth Bail Proj, Winston-Salem 1966-69; Exec Dir Lwyr Referral Ser of Bar of 21st Judicial Dist, Winston-Salem 1968-69; Atty Ofc of Gen Counsel, Fed

Aviation Adm 1969-71; Chief Adm & Legal Sers Br, Ofc Gen Counsel Fed Aviation Adm 1971; Atty Ofc Gen Counsel, Dept Housing & Urban Devel 1971; Area Counsel, Jackson Area Ofc Dept Housing & Urban Devel, Jackson, Miss 1971-; Proj Adv Grp, Legal Sers Prog, Ofc Ec Opport 1968-69; Adv Com Housing & Urban Renewal Law, Miss Law Res Inst 1980-; cp/Pilot Mtn, NC Preserv & Pk Com 1968-70; Fdr Whitworth Hunt Clb, Pres 1973-76, Master Foxhound 1975-76; Jt-Master of Foxhounds, The Austin Hunt 1976-; Masters of Foxhounds Assn; r/Meth; hon/Awd'd: Army Commend Medal 1965, Army Reserv Components Achmt Medal 1977, Nat Defense Ser Medal 1965, Reserve Forces Ser Medal 1972, Army Certs of Achmt 1961 & 65; Pi Gamma Mu; Contbr to Legal Jours; Editor *North Carolina Legal Aid Reporter* 1968-69.

MOLINA, AGUSTINA R oc/Department Manager; b/May 28, 1931; h/100 NW 4th, Big Spring, TX 79720; ba/Big Spring; p/Jesus and Nicolasa R Molina, Big Spring, TX; pa/Catalog Sales Dept Mgr; cp/Vol Work at St Hosp; r/Cath; CCD Tchr 25 Yrs; hon/Montgomery Ward & Co, Diocese of San Angelo.

MOLLE, NORMA LEE oc/Truck Driver; b/July 2, 1947; h/Rt 1, Hanson, KY 42413; ba/Same; m/Edwin Henry; c/Devry, Dennis, Kevin; p/Earl and Norma Sigafus, Wisconsin Dells, WI; pa/Profl Truck Driver; r/Meth; hon/Safe Driving Awds.

MONTALVO, KAREN CLARK oc/Administrator; b/Nov 26, 1945; h/Brandon, MS; ba/2500 N State St, Jackson, MS 39216; m/J M; c/Jay Ratcliff; p/W W and Ann Wilson Clark, Clinton, MS; ed/BS Univ So Miss 1968; MS Miss Col 1973; pa/Edr 1968-73; Law Enforcement, Res & Plan'g 1973-76; Med Clin Admr 1976-; Med Grp Mgmt Assn, Nat & St; cp/DAR, Walter Leake Chapt; r/Bapt; hon/Nat Merit Schlr 1963; Dean's List & Pres's List 1964-68; W/W 1981.

MONTGOMERY, JOSEPH HORACE oc/Executive Director; b/Aug 24, 1913; h/Rt 1 Box 2, Vinemont, AL 35179; ba/Cullman, AL; m/Clara Cole; c/Darlene, Marlene, Joe, Gail, Charlie, Glenn, Bonnie, Gary, Anita, Cary, Mark; p/Charlie Crowe (dec) and Emma Stewart Montgomery (dec); pa/USDA-ASCS Co Exec Dir; ALASCOE; NASCOE; cp/Charter Mem Civitan Clb; Vol Scout Work; r/Meth; Ofcl Bd Mem 30 Yrs, Treas Over 20 Yrs; hon/ASCS Dist'd Ser Awd; ALASCOE Dist'd Ser Awd; Past ALASCOE Pres.

MONTGOMERY, LUCRETIA BROWN oc/Retired Teacher; b/Oct 23, 1921; h/PO Box 243, Daphne, AL 36526; m/John H; c/Corlis Gail, Eric Vincent; p/William E and Dorinda H Brown, Daphne, AL; ed/Masters Deg; pa/Ret'd Sch Tchr; Delta Sigma Theta; Life Mem NEA; cp/NAACP; r/Bapt; hon/Outstg Elem Sch Tchr Am; Dedicated Tchr Awd.

MONZA, LOUIS oc/Artist; b/Mar 21, 1897; h/604 N Guadalupe Ave, Redondo Bch, CA 90277; ba/Same; m/Heidi M; p/(dec); mil/WWI; pa/Artist: Painter, Sculptor, Graphics; Artists Equity Assn; hon/Subj of Book *Graphic Work of Louis Monza* 1973.

MOODY, SAMUEL BARNS oc/Retired; b/June 2, 1920; h/Longwood, FL; m/Madelene; c/Elizabeth, Steven; p/(dec); ed/Var Mil Schs & Ins Schs; mil/USAF Ret'd (Survivor of Bataan Death March, POW of Japanese in WWII 3½ Yrs); pa/Ins Underwriter, Mutual Life of NY; Life Underwriters Assn; cp/Kiwanis; Lt Gov NY 1965; AF Assn of Fla: Past Pres (Best Chapt in St 1980); Masons; Shriner: Sojourners; Past Nat Condr, Am Defenders Bataan & Corregidor; Past Comdr Am Fed Ex-POW's; Past Comdr DAV Chapt 124, Orlando; r/Meth; hon/AF Medal of Merit (Only Man in Fla to Receive One) 1980; AFA Pres's Awd for Best Pres 1979-80; Outstg Pres's Awd, AFA 1978; Awd of Excell, 27th Bombardment Grp 1977; Dist'd Achmt Awd, Am Defenders of Bataan & Cooregidor 1964; Dist'd Achmt Awd, City of Peekskill, NY 1955; 15 Mil Decorations Incl'g Purple Heart, AF Commend Medal & 3 Philippine Decorations; Num Other Awds from Var Clbs for Work in Common Affairs; 1 of 2 Witnesses to Testify at Intl War Crimes Trials, Tokyo, Japan 1947; Listed in *Guinesses Book of World Records* for Standing at Attention Longer Than Any Other Man in the World (While a POW); Author *Reprieve from Hell* 1961 & 67.

MOON, ELVIN O oc/Pharmaceutical Sales; b/Mar 27, 1935; h/Rt 10 Lakewood, Anderson, SC 29621; m/Juanita P; c/Deborah, Donna; p/Walter E Moon (dec); Grace M Howard, Landrum, SC; ed/AA N Greenville Jr Col 1955; BS Furman Univ 1957; mil/AUS 1958-60; pa/Pharm Sales, Parke Davis & Co 1963-; Past Pres Anderson Toastmasters; Past Dist Lt Gov St Toastmasters; Pres SC Traveling Mems Assn; Nat Spkrs Assn; cp/Image Task Force, Anderson Area C of C; r/Bapt; hon/The Dist'd Toastmaster; Regional Humorous Contest, 1st Pl 1974; Salesman of Yr.

MOORE, BETTYE JO REED oc/Teacher; b/Mar 9, 1933; h/384 E

Main St, Ashdown, AR 71822; p/Roosevelt Reed (dec); Georgia A Sandefur, Ashdown, AR; ed/BS AM&N Col 1953; MEd E Tex St Univ 1969; Further Study Univ Ark; pa/Math Tchr Ashdown HS; Chp Math Dept, Ashdown, AR; Math Dept Chp, Ashdown Sch Dist; Ashdown Clrm Tchrs, Past Pres; Ark Ed Assn; NEA; Nat Coun Tchrs Math; cp/Am Cancer Soc; Alpha Kappa Alpha; Phi Delta Kappa; OES, Grand Matron; Intl Masons; r/CME Clb; hon/Dedicated Tchr Awd 1967; Ldrship Awd 1980; Ser to OES 1980; Ser to Student Couns 1980.

MOORE, DAVID EUGENE oc/Vocational Instructor; b/Jan 11, 1945;· h/Rt 2 Box 396, Lily, KY 40740; ba/Corbin, KY; m/Brenda Joyce; c/David A, Melissa Renee, LaGonna Sharre; p/Bill Moore, Loyall, KY; Oreida Thomas, Austell, GA; ed/GED Harlan Area Voc Sch 1967; Dip Frigidaire Div, Gen Motors Corp 1968; Basic Elec Dip, Whirlpool 1974; AS En Ky Univ 1978; Other Voc Courses; pa/Corbin Area Voc Ed Ctr, Major Appliance Repair Instr 10 Yrs; KIEA; AVA; KVA, Dist Pres 13th Region; cp/Corbin Optimist Clb; Coached Little Leag 5 Yrs; Advr VICA; r/Nondenom; hon/Comm'd Ky Col 1977; KIEA Outstg Tchr for Trade & Indust Ed, St Ky 1980.

MOORE, ERCYLENE E oc/Assistant Vice President; b/Feb 2, 1932; ba/Marshall, TX; m/W Don; c/Alan, Rickey, Mitch; p/W Bennie and Ethel Lee Smith, Avinger, TX; ed/Grad Univ Of Installment Credit Sch, Univ Colo 1975; Dip Am Inst Bnkg; pa/Asst VP, Installment Loan Ofcr & Bank Card Mgr, First Nat Bank Marshall; Pisces Chapt ABWA; cp/Ed Com Marshall C of C; 1 Yr Dir Marshall Pilot Clb; 3 Yr Dir E Tex Chapt AIB; E Tex Grp-N, Nat Assn Bank Wom, Ed Com; r/Meth: Secy Fin Com & Parsonage Com; hon/Wom of Achmt, Marshall BPW Clb 1975; S'ship Recip NABW E Tex Grp 1975; ABWA Pisces Chapt Wom of Yr 1980.

MOORE, FRANCES SMITH oc/Legal Secretary; b/June 10, 1950; h/102 S Washington St, Remington, VA 22734; ba/Remington; c/Stacey Beth, Brandon Scott; p/Charles F and Maybelle Osborne Smith, Bealeton, VA; ed/Computer Prog'g Inst of Md & Del; No Va Commun Col; pa/Legal Secy Niles, Chapman & Dulaney; Asst Mgr So-Fro Fabrics; C & P Telephone Co; Legal Secys Assn, Corresp Secy, Editor Newspaper; cp/Fauquier Co Repub Com, Recording Secy; M M Pierce Elem Sch PTO, Past VP & Pres; Rappahannock Swim Clb, Bd Dirs, Past VP; r/Presb.

MOORE, FREDERICK ALVIN oc/Director of Nursing Service; b/July 3, 1952; h/New Orleans, LA; ba/2425 La Ave, New Orleans, LA 70115; guard/Mrs Beatrice Miller, Bartow, FL; ed/ASN Dekalb Col 1974; BSN William Carey Col 1977; MN La St Univ Med Ctr 1981; pa/Dir Nsg Ser, Flint-Goodridge Hosp of Dillard Univ; Am Assn Hemodialysis Nurses & Techs; New Orleans Chapt Am Critical Care Nurses Assn; La Hlth Care Assn, Dir Nurses In Action, Parliamentn St Org; Bd Advrs Sidney N Collier Meml Voc Tech Inst, Sch Lic'd Pract Nurses; La St Nurses Assn; New Orleans Dist Nurses Assn; La Nsg Ser Adm Soc, Mbrship & Promo Com; La St Univ Hon Soc, 1st VP; La St Univ Cont'g Ed for Emer Room Nurses; New Orleans Dirs of Nsg Ser Org; New Orleans Chapt Black Nurses Assn, Pres; Charity Hosp Sch of Surg Technol, Bd Advrs; La High Blood Pressure Control Prog, Bd Advrs; Ad Hoc Com LSNA Criteria for the New BSN Grad; Ad Hoc Com New Orleans Metro Hosp Assn; Nurses to Re-Elect Senator Fritz Eagan; New Orleans Area/Bayou-River Hlth Sys Agcys Nom'g Com; SE La Emer Med Ses Coun; r/Prot; hon/W/W Am Jr Cols 1974; SE La Emer Med Ser Awd 1980; Author "Nursing in Black Community Hospitals" 1981.

MOORE, GIBBS BERRY oc/District Superintendent; b/Mar 13, 1928; h/Grandview Rd, Rt 9, Box 300, Beaver, WV 25813; ba/Beckley, WV; m/Josephine Torch; c/David Gibbs, Susan M Wamsley; p/James Basil and Beatrice Berry Moore, Fairmont, WV; ed/Att'd Fairmont St Col & W Va Univ Sch Mines; mil/AUS 1950-52; pa/Dist Supt, Island Creek Coal Co; VP Keystone Div En Assoc'd Coal Corp; Am Inst Mining, Metall & Petro Engrs; VP Mid-St Mining Inst 1977-78, Coal Age Adv Panel; cp/Bd Dirs Fam Plan'g Bd 1971-72; r/Presb; Elder; hon/W/W Fin & Indust; Army Commend Medal.

MOORE, IONA JUNE oc/Breeder & Trainer of Horses; b/Nov 10, 1929; h/Rt 1 Box 130-M, Midland, TX 99701; m/dec; c/Shirley Bennington, Roger Lewis; p/West T (dec) and Zora C Pool, Midland, TX; pa/Breeder & Trainer of Horses; Owner Blue Acres Indoor Arena; r/Bapt.

MOORE, JAMES TURNER oc/Director of Nutrition and Food Service; b/Mar 20, 1927; h/4500 Greenbriar Ct, Austin, TX 79756; ba/Austin; m/Louise; c/Frances Louise, Deborah Sue, Leslie Ann, James T Jr; p/Frances Leilah Polk, Austin, TX; ed/BS Tex A&M Univ 1949; MS MIT 1955; mil/AUS Ret'd Col 1974; pa/Dir Nutrition & Food Ser, Tex Dept Mtl Hlth & Mtl Retard; Am Hosp Assn; Am Soc Hosp Food Ser Admrs; Tex Hosp Assn & Tex Soc Hosp Food Ser Admrs; Inst Food Technols: Nutrition Div, Food Ser Div, Sensory Evaluation Div; Am Dietetic Assn; Tex Dietetic Assn, Pres; Tex Restaurant Assn; Soc for Advmt Food Ser Res; cp/Masonic Order; PTA; BSA; Indian Guides;

r/Prot; hon/Legion of Merit w OLC 1974; Bronze Star Medal 1968; Merit Ser Medal 1974; Army Commend Medal w OLC 1967; Merit Unit Commend w OLC 1968; Vietnam Ser Medal w Silver Star 1969; Repub of Vietnam Hon Medal 1969; Korean Order of Mil Merit 1969; Intl Food Ser Mfrs Assn Silver Plate Awd; Food Mgmt Mag Gold Awd; Author Num Articles for Profl Jours.

MOORE, JON MILTON oc/Police Officer; b/Aug 14, 1954; h/1201 Berry Ln, Tifton, GA 31794; ba/Tifton; m/Ellen; c/Jon Douglas; p/Douglas G and Dorothy Jean Moore, Ont, Canada; pa/Patrol Ofcr; cp/FOP; POAG; Civitan; JC of Tifton; r/Epis; hon/Police Ofcr of Yr 1977; Rotary Clb Awd 1977; Law Day Awd 1979.

MOORE, JULIA SHIRLEY oc/Administrative Assistant; b/May 18, 1940; h/110 Maryland Ave NE, Box 35, Wash DC 20002; p/Julius A II and Mamie Harvey Moore, W Mifflin, PA; ed/BA Eng; MAT Eng & Ed; pa/Admin Asst to the Pres; AAUW; AAHE; cp/Former Peace Corps Vol (Liberia); NAFEO Supporter; r/Bapt; hon/W/W Students in Am Cols & Univs; Woodrow Wilson Fellow Hon Mention List 1961.

MOORE, MARY BULLUCK oc/Secretary, Nurse, Tax Preparer; b/July 30, 1968; h/613 Highland Ave, Rocky Mount, NC 27801; ba/Same; m/Charlie; c/Helena D Lee, Maggie B Barnes, Charles L, Raleigh M; p/Mance (dec) and Maggie Jenkins Bullock (dec); ed/Att'd Shaw Univ; pa/LPN; Notary Public; Secy; Tax Preparer; cp/Mary B Talbert Fed'd Clb BPW; r/Bapt; hon/Best Secy of Neuse River Bapt Assn 1978; Secy Edgecombe Co SS Conv; W/W Rel.

MOORE, MARY FRANCES oc/Student; b/Jan 8, 1960; h/Rt 1 Box 50, Booneville, KY 41314; ba/Morehead; p/Eugene D and Lexene Moore, Booneville, KY; ed/BBA Cand Morehead St Univ; cp/Phi Beta Lambda; Cardinal Key Nat Hon Soc; Gamma Beta Phi; F'ship of Christian Aths; r/Presb; hon/Basketball Awd 1975; Acctg Awd 1976; All-St Hon Mention, Basketball 1977-78; Typing Awd 1977; HS All Am 1977; W/W Aths 1978; Sr Class Queen 1978; Pres's Acad S'ship 1978; Sr 1st Pl Soil Conserv Essay Winner 1978; Morehead St Bus & Ed Dean's List 1979-80; Morehead St Wom's Basketball S'ship & Lttr 1979-82; Other Awds.

MOORE, PATRICIA ANN oc/Teacher; b/Oct 13, 1942; h/502 Albemarle, Marshall, TX 75670; ba/Marshall; m/James Allen; c/Kelly Gae, Kerri Glynn; p/James Herbert (dec) and Lucile Patterson Owens, Huntsville, TX; ed/BMus N Tex St Univ 1964; pa/Elem Mus Tchr, David Crockett Sch; Alpha Delta Kappa; Sigma Alpha Iota; Alpha Lambda Delta; TMEA; TCDA; TSTA; NEA; cp/Life Mem PTA; r/Bapt; hon/Mus S'ships 1960-64; 1st Pl NATS 1962; SAI Sword of Hon 1963.

MOORE, RONALD DEAN oc/Businessman; b/Mar 16, 1954; h/1755 Carolina Ave, Cleveland, TN 37311; ba/C'land; m/Debbie Stephenson; p/Jay Lake and Faye Moore, C'land, TN; ed/AS; pa/Moore Foam & Sales Inc; cp/Bradley Co Field Dpty; Tenn Assn Elec Commrs; C'land JCs; Chm Bradley Co Elec Com; hon/JC of Yr 1976; Pres C'land JCs 1977-78; Outstg Yng Bus-man of C'land 1975.

MOORE, VIVIAN MYERS oc/Homemaker; b/Jan 1; h/820 W Bch Dr, Panama City, FL 32401; m/Clifford C (dec); p/George Matthew (dec) and Mattie N Myers, Panama City, FL; cp/Chaplain Fla Fed Wom's Clbs; Tchr of Bible Class; Past Pres Gulf Coast Commun Col Foun; Bd Dirs C C Moore Meml Boys Clb; r/Bapt; hon/Milestone Awd, Boys Clbs; JCettes Humanitarian Awd; Hon PhD Gulf Coast Cummun Col; FFWC Pres Awd; Gtr Sanford C of C Awd.

MOOREHEAD, GEORGE A oc/Physician, Pharmacist; b/Apr 5, 1917; h/Estate Wintberg 373, PO Box 3668, Charlotee Amalie, St Thomas, VI 00801; ba/St Thomas; m/Ilse-Marie; p/George A Sr (dec) and Beatrice Eleanore La Frank Moorehead (dec); ed/MD; BS; pa/Dematologist; Pharmacist; Asst Phys Nat Inst Public Hlth, Oslo, Norway & Oslo Emer Med Ctr 1967; Res Dir & Conslt VI Law Enforcemt Comm, Task Force on Alcoholism & Narcotics, VI 1969-71; Exec Dir (Insular) VI Comm on Alcoholism & Narcotics, Dept Hlth, St Thomas, VI 1971-; Profl Assns; Contbr Papers on Drugs & Narcotic Problems (Local, Nt, Intl); r/Luth: Usher, VChm Luth Social Soc; hon/Biogl Listings.

MOOS, JOY oc/Art Dealer; b/Jan 17, 1932; h/1160 102nd St, Bay Harbor, FL 33154; ba/Miami; m/Walter A (dec); c/Howard, Suzanne; p/Harry (dec) and Irene Kaplan, Montreal, Quebec, Canada; ed/Att'd Fleishman Art Sch & Moore Inst Art; pa/Designer; Writer; Photog; Lectr; cp/Exec Mem Bd Miami Design Preserv Leag; Dir & Pres Art Deco Intl Soc; r/Hebrew.

MORA, ZEKE R oc/Retired; b/Dec 28, 1907; h/911 E Hill St, Alice, TX 78332; m/Marcela Kramer; c/Zeke Jr, Luis, Carmela Saenz, Arabela Hernandes, Frances Rogers; p/Silvestre (dec) and Santos Mora (dec); r/Cath; hon/Num Baseball, Basketball, & Fball Awds.

PERSONALITIES OF THE SOUTH

MORALES-NIEVA, IGNACIO oc/Associate Professor; b/Dec 18, 1928; h/Hato Rey, PR; ba/Instituto de Humanidades, Colegio Universitario de Turabo, Caguas, PR; m/Mercedes Vizoso Arandes; p/Dona Pilar Maria de los Dolores, Valdepenas, Spain; ed/Profl Dip Royal Conservatorio de Mus, Madrid, Spain 1949; Profl Dip Piano-Forte 1962; Manhattan Sch of Mus, NY 1967; pa/Assoc Prof Humanities, Prof Form & Analysis, Conservatory of Mus, PR; ASCAP; Soicedad de Musica Contemporanea de PR; cp/Intl Lions, Chapt of PR; r/Cath; hon/Cavaliere della Croce di Gerusalemme 1964; 1st Fest POP 1976; Commun Ldrs Am 1979-80; Primera Semana de las Humanidades CUT 1979; Num Pubs.

MORGAN, BRANCH JR oc/Dancer, Student; b/May 18, 1952; h/Atlanta, GA; p/Branch and Arneatha Morgan, Balto, MD; ed/BA Washington Univ 1974; MA Cand Emory Univ; Studied: L'Ecole Municipale de Danse Classique, Strasbourg, France 1973-74; Balto Sch of Ballet 1974-75; pa/Dancer Wash Univ 1971-73; Prin Male Dancer, Balto Dance Theatre 1975-80; Prin Male Dancer, Atlanta Dance Theatre 1980-; Perf'd in "My Fair Lady" 1978, The Nutcracker 1978, 79, "Don't Bother Me, I Can't Cope" 1979; cp/Dance Instr; Ebenezer Bapt Ch F'ship Choir; r/Bapt; hon/Russian Ballet Perf 1979; Instr Ballet & Mod Dance, Atlanta Dance Theatre 1980; Toured w Balto Dance Theatre Austria, Germany & Italy 1980; Judge Emory Univ's Dance Alive Dance Co 1980; Coor Dance & Theatre Perfs First Annual S Black Conf on Lit & Art, Emory Univ 1980; Dance Interview for Evening Mag 1981; Cand Ga's Gov's Arts Awd in Dance 1981; Ga Bronze Jubilee Awds Finalist in Dance 1981.

MORGAN, JULIAN EARL III oc/President and Chairman of the Board; b/Aug 14, 1950; h/Dyersburg, TN; ba/PO Box 708, 425 W Ct St, Dyersburg, TN 38024; m/Rickie Jeanette; c/Phillip Douglas, Laurie Anne, Mary Catherine; p/Julian E and Anne P Morgan, Memphis, TN; ed/BA cum laude Univ of S 1972; MA Baylor Univ 1973; pa/Ch of Bd & Pres Frontier Fed Savings and Loan Assn 1977-; First Citizens Nat Bank 1976-77; First Tenn Bank 1976; Union Planters Nat Bank 1973-76; US Leag of Savings Assn, Public Relats & Consumer Affairs Com; Tenn Savings & Loan Leag, Ins Com 1978-80, Prog & Ed Com 1978-81; Lic'd Ins Agt, St Tenn; Nat Assn Review Appraisers; cp/Min Mus & Mem Fin Com Cumberland Presb Ch; Tenn Bapt Conv, Com on Audits; Gideons Intl, Pres 1980; Breakaway; Gtr Dyersburg/Dyer Co C of C, Bd Dirs, VP, Pres Elect 1981-82; Dyersburg Rotary Clb, Bd Dirs 1978-79; Chm Mus Com 1978-79, Chm Prog Com 1979-80; NW Tenn Humanities Coun, Bd Dirs; Dyersburg Union Mission, Bd Dirs, Fin Com, Chm Yth Home; Bd Assocs & Exec Com Union Univ; Pt-time Instr for Am Inst Bnkg Dyersburg St Commun Col; r/Presb; hon/Dist'd Ser Awd, Dyersburg JCs 1979; Outstg Yng Man of Yr 1980 Dyersburg JCs; US JCs Outstg Yng Men Am 1979, 81; Intl Yth Achmt Awd 1979; Senate Resolution for Outstg Ser to Commun 1980; Baylor Univ Res F'ship & Tchg Asst'ship 1972-73; Acad S'ship The Univ of S 1968-72.

MORGAN, KARL ZIEGLER oc/Health Physicist; b/Sept 27, 1907; h/1984 Castleway Dr, Atlanta, GA 39345; ba/Atlanta; m/Helen Lee; c/Karl Ziegler Jr, Eric Lee, Joan Elen, Diana Matthews; p/Jacob Levi and Elizabeth Virginia Clay Shoup Morgan; ed/BA 1929, MA 1930 UNC; PhD Duke Univ 1934; pa/Hd Physics Div, Oak Ridge Nat Lab 1943-72; Prof Ga Inst Technol 1972-; Fellow Am Col Radiology, Am Nuclear Soc, Am Phys Soc; Am Indust Hygiene Assn; AAAA; Hlth Physics Soc; Radiation Res Soc; Intl Radiation Protection Soc; Nat Coun Radiation Protection; Intl Comm on Radiological Protection; cp/Dem Party; r/Luth; hon/Dist'd Ser Awd, Hlth Physics Soc; Editor Health Physics Journal; Pres Hlth Phys Soc; Recip 1st Gold Medal of Swedish Royal Acad 1962; Ofcl Advr US Del to Atoms for Peace Conf in Geneva, Switz 1955; Author Principals of Radiation Protection; Pub'd Over 350 Articles in Sci Jours.

MORGAN, MAXIE DELL oc/Principal; b/Feb 11, 1945; h/1709 N Ctrl, Cameron, TX 76520; ba/Cameron; m/Linda; c/Holly, Kent; p/Dee Sr and Florence Morgan, Rogers, TX; ed/BS; MS; Supvry Cert; Adm Cert; pa/Prin C H Yoe HS; VP Milam Co Tchrs Assn; Assn Sec'dy Sch Prins; NEA; TSTA; Adv Com Region VI Ed Ser Ctr; cp/Lions Clb; City Lib Bd; Civic Auditorium Comm; Chm Folk Fete Arts & Crafts Show; Unit Chm Salvation Army Boys Camp; r/Bapt; hon/1st Pl Sculpture, Lufkin Arts & Crafts Show 1975.

MORGAN, MICHAEL L oc/Dentist; b/May 7, 1941; h/30 Cherokee Blvd, Shawnee, OK 74801; ba/Okla City; p/Lafayette and Zula A Morgan; ed/BA; DDS; MPA; pa/Chief Dental Hlth Sers, Okla St Dept Hlth; ADA; ODA; Okla Public Hlth Assn; cp/Dem Party; r/First Ch of God; hon/OPHA Exceptl Merit Awd; W/W: Okla, Hlth Care.

MORI, MARIANNE McDONALD oc/Research; b/Jan 2, 1937; h/Box 929 Rancho, Santa Fe, CA 92067; ba/Irvine, CA; m/Torajiro; c/Conrad, Bryan, Bridget, Kristie; p/Eugene and Inez McDonald, LA, CA; pa/Instr Univ Calif-Irvine; Pub'd Books & Articles.

MORLEY, RONALD DAVID oc/Realtor; b/Sept 24, 1954; h/Rt 1 Box 377, N Garden, VA 22959; ba/Charlottesville, VA; m/Kathryn Wilson; p/Joseph Edward and Reba Alice Morley, Union Bridge, MD; ed/BA Univ Va; pa/Rltr 1977-79 Farms & Ests, Roy Wheeler Rlty; cp/Coach St Annes Belfield Sch 1977-79; Campaign Coor Allen Hahn for Ho of Dels 1979; hon/Sales Assoc of Month, Aug 1978, Mar 1979; Asst Coach of Yr, St Annes 1977, 78; Lttrman U Va Fball 1973-75; HS All Am Track; St Champ Shot Putt & Discus 1971-72.

MORMAN, SQUARE oc/Civil Rights Organizer; b/May 18, 1922; h/Star Rt Box 135, Rossville, TN 38066; m/Wilola; c/Little David, Seaarmy, S M, Bird Anner Jackson, Mae Anner Dadridge, Edna Cambell, Melva, Square Jr, Esau, Mildred Lee; pa/Assoc'd w: NAACP; So Christian Ldrship; Ctr for Hlth Ser; Primary Hlth Care; Civic & Wel Leag; Pres Poor Peoples Hlth Coun; Red Cross; Tenn Hunger Coalition; Wom Infant Chid; Pres Home Mission Burial; VP Stamping Plant; r/CME Ch; hon/Constitution Conv 1977; Tenn Public Ser 1975; Contbng Author Num Jours.

MORRIS, CECIL ARTHUR oc/Professor; b/May 20, 1943; h/Rt 3 Box 911, Williamsburg, KY 40769; ba/W'burg; m/Brenda Braswell; c/Cecil A II, Leah Elizabeth; p/A C Morris, NE Concord, NC; ed/AB Pfeiffer Col 1965; MA Appalachian St Univ 1967; PhD VPI & St Univ 1975; pa/Prof Math, Cumberland Col; Sys Analysis; Computer Programming; Math Assn Am; Nat Coun Tchrs Maths; Phi Kappa Phi; cp/Dem Party; r/Bapt; hon/NASA F'ship 1968; Pres's S'ship 1962, 63; Author "Consumer Problems."

MORRIS, CYNTHIA ELIZABETH oc/Hostess; b/Jan 30, 1960; h/32 Hillcrest Dr, Natchez, MS 39120; ba/Natchez; m/Fred Jr; p/Warren William Jr and Anabel Young Maxie, Natchez, MS; pa/Hostess Stanton Hall (Antebellum Mansion); cp/Pilgrimage Garden Clb; r/Bapt; hon/Bible Sch Tchr for Navajo Indian Chd, Mission in Gallup, NM 1980.

MORRIS, DELOUIS A oc/Merchandiser; b/Dec 23, 1955; h/Lawton, OK; p/Lorine Morris, Conway, AR; ed/BBA Univ Ark-Pine Bluff; pa/Mdse Mgr Chds Dept JC Penney; Pres Phi Beta Lambda 1977-78; r/Bapt; hon/Yth Fitness Achmt Awd 1971; Part in Ark Jr Miss Pageant (Among Top 10 for Outstg Talents) 1974; Ark Yth Coun 1974; Cert for Interactive & Creative Dancing 1974; Bus Awd 1978.

MORRIS, GLADYS H oc/Commissioner of Finance; b/Sept 20, 1904; h/1604 Anderson Pike, Signal Mtn, TN 37377; m/Mayfield Marvin (dec); p/Joseph William Hesse (dec) and Emma Rathoeber (dec); ed/Bus Col 1919; pa/Secy Trust Dept Am Nat Bank & Trust Co, Chat, TN; Commr of Fin, Town of Walden, Tenn; cp/Past Mem Bd Dirs Local Diabetes Chapt; Local Chapt Tenn Repub Wom; r/Epis.

MORRIS, HARRY LEE oc/Farmer; b/Apr 27, 1947; h/Shelbyville, KY; m/Twila Franklin; c/Rebecca Lee, Jacob Allen; p/C J Jr and Mabel Spaulding Morris, Shelbyville, KY; ed/BS En Ky Univ 1970; mil/AUS 1970-72; pa/Tobacco & Dairy Farmer; cp/Shelby Co Farm Bur Dir; Shelby Co Yng Dairyman, VP; Shelby Co Yng Farmers; Co Ext Forage, Dairy & Tobacco Couns; r/Bapt; hon/Ky Farm Bur Outstg Yng Farmer 1976; Burley Tobacco's Outstg Yng Tobacco Prodr 1979.

MORRIS, JULIA RUTH oc/Assistant Vice President; b/June 19, 1955; h/2013 NE 48th St, Ocala, FL 32670; ba/Ocala; p/Betty Jane Morris, Ocala, FL; pa/Asst VP, Data Communs Coor, Assn Hd Teller; cp/Ocala/Marion Co C of C; r/Bapt.

MORRIS, MARY LEE oc/Purchasing Assistant; b/Apr 8, 1941; h/2005 Denice Cir, Roanoke, VA 24012; ba/Roanoke; m/James Howard; c/Tonya; p/David C and Elsie Jackson, Marion, VA; ed/Att'd Marion Col; pa/Purchasing Asst, Adv Stores Co; Dist 4 VP ABWA; Trustee for Nat S'ship Fund ABWA; cp/Secy LaBellevue Garden Clb; Secy LaBellevue Civic Leag; Va St Coun Garden Clbs; Roanoke Repub Wom's Clb; Treas BWA Region Meeting; r/Meth; hon/ABWA Wom of Yr.

MORRIS, ROBERT WESLEY oc/Sales Manager; b/Dec 6, 1949; h/105 Fox Run Dr, Hopkins, SC 29061; ba/Columbia; m/Bonnie; c/Robert Wesley Jr; p/M L Sr (dec) and Elizabeth A Morris, Columbia, SC; ed/BS Univ SC 1972; mil/USCGR 1972-78; pa/Sales & Mktg, Lwyrs Title Ins Corp; SC Indust Devels Assn; cp/Cayce-W Columbia JCs; SC JCs; r/Prot; hon/Acad Achmt Awd, Univ SC 1970; Grad #1 in Class, USCG Pt Security Class 1973; Outstg Yng Men Am 1978; Outstg Local Pres, SC JCs 1978; Most Outstg Dist Dir, SC JCs 1979; Outstg Dist Dir, US JCs, Rec'd M Keith Upson Meml Awd 1979; Pres's Awd for Sales Achmt, Lwyrs Title Ins Corp 1980.

MORRIS, RUTH FALLS oc/Educator, Tutor, Lecturer; b/Jan 23, 1913; h/2419 Castletowers Ln, Tallahassee, FL 32301; ba/Same; m/Vestal Lee; p/Charles Newton Falls (dec); Bryte Elizabeth Stroupe (dec); ed/BS

UNC-Greenville; MA Tchrs Col, Columbia Univ; MS Laverne Col; pa/Tchr, Ednl Prescriptionist; Tutor; Supvr; cp/Pres Intl Rdg Assn 1975-76; Pres Soroptimist Intl, Colon, Panama 1960-61; Charter Pres Caribbean Col Clb 1953-54; Regional Gov Soroptimist Intl Panama & Costa Rica 1964-66; VP Atlantic Tchrs Guild of Canal Zone 1953-54; Atlantic Coor Fed Employed Wom 1975-77; Nat Leag Am Pen Wom; Intl Platform Assn; AAUW; Ph Delta Kappa; Cristobal Wom's Clb; Inter-Am Wom's Clb; Spec Ed Assn of Canal Zone; Caribbean Assn Ed of Yng Chd; Med Wives Soc of Canal Zone; Coun Exceptl Chd; Sierra Clb; Cousteau Soc; r/Presb; hon/Outstg Tchr Panama Canal Zone Schs 1967, 73, 75; W/W Am Wom; Nat Register Prom Ams; DIB; World W/W Wom; 2000 Wom Achmt; Royal Blue Book.

MORRISON, DOROTHY PERRY oc/Histologist, Diagnostic Laboratory Director; b/June 29, 1939; h/4748 Dawes Ct, Va Bch, VA 23455; ba/Norfolk; m/Frederick Stanley; c/Frederick Scot; p/Leslie E Huybert Jr, Va Bch, VA; Dorothy B Mayer, Norfolk, VA; ed/BS Elon Col 1965; So Theol Sem 1964; Norfolk Gen Shop Sch of Histology 1960; pa/Dir Diagnostic Lab, En Va Med Sch 1979-; Adm Asst Dept Comparative Med & Surg, En Va Med Sch 1978-79; Supvr Div of Exptl Surg, En Va Med Sch 1976-78; Asst Dir Cardiovascular Res, En Va Med Auth 1974-76; Instr Pacemaker Safeline Process 1975-78; Cardiovascular Res Asst, Res Inst En Va Med Sch 1971-74; Cardiovascular Res Technol, En Va Med Auth 1969-71; Histologist: Leigh Meml Hosp 1969, Norfolk Gen Hosp 1961-69; Histology Tech DePaul Hosp 1959-61; Am Soc Med Tech 1960-; Va Soc Med Tech; cp/Med Lab Tech Polit Action Comm Bd Trustees; r/So Bapt; hon/1st Pl Photo Awd; Med Tech of Yr; Alpha Mu Tau; ASMT Pres Commend; Hon Tex Citizen; Nom'd Outstg Yng Wom Am 1972; W/W Hlth Care 1977; Nom'd Am Soc Med Tech Mem of Yr 1976 & 78; Num Profl Pubs.

MORRISON, GRACE BLANCHE oc/External Relations Specialist; b/Dec 18, 1933; h/Rt 2 Box 178A, Commerce, TX 75428; ba/Dallas; m/Henry Joseph Jr; c/Gregory Alan Murphree, Gina Grace Murphree; p/Lyle M and Grace Luella Simpson, Mesquite, TX; ed/BS SMU 1956; MEd Univ Houston 1973; pa/External Relats Spec, Dept Energy; Reg'd Parliamentrn, Fed Employed Wom Inc; cp/Downtown Dallas Noon BPW Clb; r/Unitarian; hon/Wom of Yr BPW 1976; W/W Am Wom 1979.

MORRISSETTE, HATTIE MAE COLLINS oc/Housewife; b/July 18, 1910; h/Rt 1, Newbern, AL 36765; m/Swarner Warren; c/Walter E, John E, Willie J, Charlie W, Hattie Deloris Owens; r/Missionary Bapt.

MORSANI, AL oc/Freight Agent; b/Mar 13, 1924; h/PO Box 774, Rogers, AR 72756; ba/Same; m/Patricia; c/Rita Marie, James, Mary Ann, Virginia Rose; p/Elvidio Adolpho (dec) and Marie Morsani (dec); mil/MM 1942-47; p/Railway Freight Agt; Chief Cook & Bottle Washer St Vincents Mens Clb of Rogers; Past Telegrapher; r/Roman Cath; hon/Man of Yr St Vincents Mens Clb 1957.

MORSE, EUGENIA MAUDE oc/Architect, Educator; b/Feb 23, 1920; h/2621 33rd St, Lubbock, TX 79410; ba/Lubbock; p/Robert Emmett Morse (dec); Eugenia Maddox Fry, Houston, TX; ed/BA Arch, BS Arch Rice Univ; pa/Prof Div Arch Tex Tech Univ; Archl Pract Tex & La 1949-; cp/Nat Hist Soc; Storm Defense Clb; r/Bapt; hon/Treas: Altrusa Intl, Lubbock Art Assn 1960-62; Mem: Am Forestry Assn; Nat Geog Soc; Am Mus Natural Hist.

MORSE, SAMUEL A oc/Hospital Administrator; b/Feb 24, 1943; h/3620 Cross Bend Rd, Plano, TX 75023; ba/Farmers Branch, TX; m/Neville Janice Stromquist; c/Joshua Dean, Jeremy Scott, Mary Ann; p/Samuel A Sr and Dorothy Mae Morse, Woodlands, TX; ed/BS Christian Univ 1966; MS Trinity Univ 1971; MBA St Mary's Univ 1973; DBA Ind N Univ 1981; pa/DPH Cand Univ Tex Sch Public Hlth; PhD Cand Univ Tex; Cert Trg Bexas Co Hosp Dist 1971; pa/Exec VP Brookhaven Med Ctr 1979-; Dir Mgmt Sys Am Medicorp Inc 1978-79; Assoc Hosp Dir, Hermann Hosp 1977-78; Adm Asst, Am Medicorp 1977; Exec Dir Kaytona Commun Hosp 1974-77; Asst Admr Bexar Co Hosp 1972-74; Mgmt Conslt 1970-72; Yth Dir, Town N YMCA 1969-70; Yth Phys Dir, E End YMCA 1967-69; Chm Bd MPII Inc; Pres Hosp Resources Mgmt Inc 1978-79; Instr 1971-: Trinity Univ, San Antonio Col, Univ Tex, Stetson Univ, Univ Tex Sch Med, Tex Wom's Univ, Univ Dallas; Preceptor 1974-: Trinity Hosp, Washington Univ, Univ Fla, Univ Houston, Tex Wom's Univ, Univ Dallas; Lectr 1977-: Sch Hlth Scis, Sheppard AFB & Hlth Care Adm, Univ Dallas; Am Col Hosp Admrs; Am Hosp Assn; Am Acad Med Admrs; Am Public Hlth Assn; Hosp Fin Mgmt Assn; Am Soc Public Admrs; Am Inst Indust Engrs; Hosp Mgmt Sys Soc; Soc Public Hlth Edrs; Assn Mil Surgs; Assn MBA Execs; Hosp Soc Hlth; Inst of Hlth Ser Admrs; Fla Hosp Assn; Tex Hosp Assn; Fed Am Hosps; Res Ofrcs Assn; AF Assn; Eagle Scout Assn of Am; Tex Mfrs Assn; Assn Dirs of YMCA's of N Am; cp/Oak Cliff Lions; C of C Bd Mem; Bd Mem JCs; Westside Kiwanis Charter Mem; Rotary; Bd Mem: Daytona Bch Commun Col, Boy's Clb, YMCA, Mus Arts & Scis, Volusia Assn Retard'd Citizens, Daytona Bch Area C of C, Am Cancer

Soc, Daytona Bch Area Com of 100, Am Mended Hearts Assn, Am Heart Assn, Daytona Commun Hosp, U Way; SE Kiwanis; Num Other Civic Coms & Orgs; r/Ch of Christ; hon/Outstg JC of Mo Awd, July 1975; Pres's Citation Awd, Daytona Bch JCs 1975; Outstg Yng Med Am 1975-78; Personalities of S 1975-78; Personalities of Am 1978-79; Most Notable Ams, Bicent Era Awd 1976; DIB; Intl W/W Intells 1978; Cert Apprec Intl Yth Achmt 1978; Intl W/W Commun Ser 1978; W/W S&SW; Num Mil Awds & Decorations Incl'g: Air Force Accommodation Medal, Nat Defense Medal, AF Outstg Unit Awd w 2 OLCs; Num Other Awds & Hons.

MORTON, CHRISTINE RITA oc/Instructor; b/Aug 31, 1943; h/1879 Clearbrooke Dr, Clearwater, FL 33520; ba/Clearwater; m/Paul Douglas; c/William John Libengood, Michelle Lynn Libengood; p/Stanley Darwin, Castleton, NY; Rita MacDonald, St Petersburg, FL; ed/Grad Jackson Meml Hosp Sch of Nsg 1964; pa/Instr Hlth Related Technol, Pinellas Voc Tech Inst; NEA; AVA; FVA; Evaluation Team Mem So Assn Cols & Schs; cp/Am Heart Assn; CPR Instr; Vol Am Red Cross; Vol Ctr Prevent Child Abuse; r/Christian.

MOSBY, ROBERT SCOTT JR oc/Executive; b/Oct 14, 1941; h/2012 Millwood, Conway, AR 72032; ba/Conway; m/Elizabeth; c/Laurie, Rob; p/Scotty and Ruth Mosby, Little Rock, AR; ed/BAS; AS; mil/USAF Capt; pa/VP & Gen Mgr, Nabco Mech & Elect Contractors; ASHRAE; r/Bapt; hon/Tau Alpha Pi.

MOSELEY, MICHAEL oc/Director of Community Services; b/Jan 28, 1953; h/2412 Linden Ave, Kinston, NC; ba/Kinston; m/Cassandra Gail Lane; p/Emanuel and Mamie Moseley, Kinston, NC; ed/BA UNC-CH 1974; MA Ed ECU 1980; Profl Staff Cert, NC Rec & Parks Soc 1974; pa/Co-Dir Spec Populations Prog, Kinston Rec Comm 1975-76; Caswell Ctr: Vol Sers Rep 1976, Res Advocate 1976-78, Asst Dir & EEO Ofcr 1978-80, Dir Commun Sers & EEOO 1980-; Pt-Time Instr Mtl Hlth Curric, Lenoir Commun Col 1979-; NC Ass Vol Admrs 1976-77; Nat Rec & Parks Assn 1974-76; Nat Therapeutic Rec Soc 1975-76; NC Rec & Parks Soc 1974-76; Lenoir Co Interagency Coun for Mtlly Retard'd 1975-76; Carolina Wheelchair Assn 1975-76; Am Assn Mtl Deficiency; NC St Employees Assn; cp/Alpha Phi Alpha; Kinston JCs; NAACP; Masons; Lenoir Co Chapt Am Red Cross Bd Dirs; Our Homes Inc Bd Dirs; Mayor's Com for Employment of the Handicapped; Easter Seal Soc; Kinston Commun Relats Comm; Lenoir Co Assn Retard'd Citizens, VP & Bd Dirs 1975-77; Lenoir Co Special Olympics Orgr; Gov's Sch Alumni Assn; r/AME Zion; hon/Kappa Delta Pi; W/W S&SW 1980-81; Outstg Yng Men Am 1976, 78, 79; JC Rookie of Yr 1976; Merit Cert Masons 1977; Outstg Ser Cert, St Augustus Ch 1977.

MOSELEY, NANCY LEA oc/Teacher, Coach; b/July 28, 1947; h/541 N White St, 7 Village Square, Carrollton, GA 30117; ba/Carrollton; m/Wayne; p/Roy H and Kathleen Carter, Alma, GA; ed/BS Ga So Col 1969; MEd W Ga Col 1978; pa/Tchr & Coach, Dept Aths, W Ga Col; LaGrange Sr HS; Instr Phy Ed 1974-; Alpha Delta Pi; Wom's Intramural Assn; Ga Ath Coaches Assn; Nat HS Ath Coaches Assn; Phi Kappa Phi; AAHPER; GAHPER; r/Bapt; hon/LaGrange Daily News All-Area Coach of Yr 1978-79; W/W Am Cols & Univs 1969; Miss GSC 2nd Runner-Up 1967; Sweetheart of Phi Mu Alpha 1967-68.

MOSER, SHIRLEY O oc/Musician; h/210 S 3rd St, Richmond, KY 40475; c/Marcia, Robert Jr, Karen; p/Oscar E (dec) and Blanche Wessman Olson (dec); ed/AA Palomar Col; BMus NWn Univ; Grad Deg Cand E Ky Univ; pa/Am Guild Organists; Delta Omicorn; Beta Sigma Phi; AAUW; r/Prot; Ch Organist; hon/Tri-Delta S'ship NWn Univ; PEO Assistance NU 1945-47.

MOSES, FRED oc/Businessman; b/Mar 22, 1934; h/117 View St, Morganton, NC 28655; ba/Morganton; m/Mary Townsend; p/Beulah Del Moses, Morganton, NC; mil/USAF 1951-71; pa/Owner & Operator Starlight Fish House; r/Prot; hon/12 Mil Awds; Commend Awd 1980 Burke Co Profl Assn.

MOSIER, RONALD RAY oc/Internal Affairs Investigator; b/Jan 25, 1931; h/Rt 6 Manchester Rd, Murfreesboro, TN 37130; m/Gerry Smith; c/Michael Julian, Lisa Andrea, Leslie Ann; p/Andrew Thomas (dec) and Irene Frances Mosier (dec); ed/Grad Mid South Broadcasting Inst 1963; Dip Elkins Inst Elects; mil/USMC 1948-51; pa/Police Investigator, Dept Corrections, St Tenn; News Dir WGNS Radio; Public Relats Chm Middle Tenn Chapt MD Assn 1977-80; cp/Commr of Murfreesboro, Rutherford Co Coun for the Perf'g Arts 1978-79; Spec Events Coor Rutherford Co 1977-79; Kiwanis Clb; r/Christian; hon/2 Connie Awds: Best Coverage of Elect Returns 1964, Mus Prog'g Excell; Connie Awd w Boots Randolph for Best Live Jazz Show on Radio 1965; Diamond Awd, Nat Assn Advtrs 1965-66; UGF Awd for Campaign Kick-off Party Variety Show 1970; Jefferson Davis Awd for Outstg Res in So Hist 1978; Spec Awd Cancer Assn 1978; Am Red Cross Blood Prog Awd 1978; Jerry Awd 1979;

Commun Ser Awd, Seventh Day Adventist Ch 1980; Former Staff Writer *Nashville Magazine;* Former Field Corresp *Nashville Banner;* Battle of Stones River Tape.

MOSLEY, WILLIAM F III oc/Certified Public Accountant; b/Mar 2, 1948; h/11323 Chevy Chase, Houston, TX 77077; ba/Houston; m/Pamela; c/Ryan; p/William F Jr and Martha F Mosley, Richardson, TX; ed/BBA N Tex St Univ 1970; mil/USAF; pa/Ptnr Leavitt, Mosley, & Co CPA's; Am Inst CPA; Tex Soc CPA's; r/Epis; hon/W/W S&SW 1980-81.

MOSS, DIKE LEE oc/Rater and Underwriter; b/Apr 24, 1961; h/1619 E Park Shopping Ctr, Cullman, AL 35055; ba/Cullman; p/K G Moss, Hanceville, AL; V Nail, Cullman, AL; pa/DeMolay; cp/VICA; Interact Org; r/Luth; hon/Masonic Awds; 4-H Awds.

MOSS, FAYE K oc/Homemaker; b/Jan 31, 1940; h/Rt 1, Kittrell, NC 27544; m/Richard W; c/Richard Dale, Christopher Wayne, Elizabeth Faye, p/Leonard Ralph Kerly (dec); Ladie B Daniels, Henderson, NC; cp/Zeb Vance PTA; Zeb Vance Ext Homemaker Clb, Pres; Jr Yth F'ship Cnslr; Jr Girl Scout Troop 97; r/Meth; hon/Vance Co Den Mother of Yr 1968; Ext Homemaker Clb: Clb Secy Awd 1975, Indiv Vol Ldr Awd 1979, Clb Pres Awd 1980; Clb Wom of Yr Vance Co 1980.

MOSS, JERRY PAT oc/Executive Vice President; b/June 2, 1942; h/419 Town N Dr, Terrell, TX 75160; ba/Terrell; m/Judy; c/April, Amy, Pat, Allison; p/Pat and Mable Moss, Ft Worth, TX; ed/Assoc Mgmt Deg SEn Okla 1976; pa/Owner Retail Apparel Bus; Gen Mgr Dallum, Hartley Cos C of C; Exec VP Gtr Mgrs & Secys Assn E Tex; r/Bapt; hon/Recip Mgmt S'ships, Tex C of C Execs Assn 1978.

MOSS, MIKE oc/Insurance Executive; b/Feb 6, 1943; h/212 W Dilado Dr, Miami Bch, FL; ba/Coral Gables; m/Laurie; p/Rose Moss, Sebastian, FL; ed/Att'd Miami Dade Col 1961-63, Univ Miami 1963-64; pa/Mgr Home Life Ins Co; Gen Agts & Mgrs Assn, Past Pres; Est Plan'g Coun; Chartered Life Underwriter; cp/Yng Pres's Mt Sinai Hosp; hon/Nat Mgmt Awd 1976, 77, 78; St Fla Ram Awd 1978-79.

MOTT, BOBBY RICSHAN oc/Home Improvement; b/July 4, 1941; h/3927 Webb Ct, Columbia, SC 29204; ba/Columbia; m/Mary Kelly; c/Bobbie, Ricshan; p/Lester (dec) and Eulia Collins Mott, Crowley, LA; ed/Interior Design; mil/AUS 1962-64 101 Airborne Div; pa/Owner-Pres Bob Mott Inc; r/Bapt; hon/W/W S&SW 1980-81.

MOTT, JAMES RANDOLPH oc/Counselor; b/Sept 26, 1944; h/5818-B Highland Pass, Austin, TX 78731; ba/Austin; m/Janet Marie Luther Green; c/Paul Christopher, Samantha Beth; p/James Joshua and Anita Reppeard Motsenbocker Mott, Georgetown, SC; ed/BA 1967, MAPA 1973 Univ Okla; Post-Grad Chapman Col 1973-74; MA Univ Tex-Austin 1976; PhD Cand Univ Tex; mil/USAF 1967-74 Capt; pa/Psychometrist, Cnslg-Psych Sers Ctr, Univ Tex-Austin 1974-76; Psych Intern/Cnslr, Cnslg-Psych Sers Ctr 1976-78; Psych Trainee, V A Hosp, Temple, Tex 1976; Cnslr, Career Choice Info Ctr, Univ Tex 1978; Cnslr Student Sers Ofc, Rio Grande Campus, Austin Commun Col 1978-; Student Affil Am Psych Assn; Student Mem: APGA, Am Col Pers Assn, Ann for Cnslr Ed & Supvn, Nat Voc Guid Assn; Tex Jr Col Tchrs Assn; Jr Col Student Pers Assn of Tex; r/Epis; hon/O U Schlrs, Univ Okla 1963; Res Grantee, Univ Tex-Austin 1977; Phi Kappa Phi 1978; W/W S&SW 1980.

MOTT, JERRY oc/Maintenance Purchasing; b/Mar 29, 1946; h/PO Box 357, Shubuta, MS 39360; ba/Shubuta; m/Charlotte Ann; c/Kimberly Ann, Marie Anjanette, Jerry Jason; p/William J and Pearl P Mott, Tibbie, AL; pa/Maint Purchasing, Intl Paper Co; cp/VP Miss JCs; Cand for Ho of Rep, Miss Leg; r/Bapt; hon/Outstg Yng Men Clarke Co 1978; Outstg Yng Men Am 1979; Fireman of Yr 1979; Clint Dunagan Awd; Top 20 JCs in Nat 1979.

MOUNT, MARGARET ELIZABETH oc/Teacher and Minister; b/Sept 1, 1926; h/4601 18th Ave N, St Petersburg, FL 33713; ba/St Petersburg; m/Lewis Fillmore; c/Martin Fillmore, Arnold Adams, Cynthia Mary Boffoli; p/James Andrew (dec) and Cynthia Adams Doyle, St Petersburg, FL; ed/MA Rel Ed; MDiv; ThD; pa/Lic'd Psych; Tchr; r/Prot; hon/Rel of World; W/W Wom of World.

MOUNTAIN, CLIFTON FLETCHER oc/Physician, Professor of Surgery; b/Apr 15, 1924; h/1612 S Blvd, Houston, TX 77006; ba/Houston; m/Marilyn Isabelle Tapper; c/Karen Lockery, Clifton Jr, Jeffrey Richardson; ed/AB; MD Boston Univ Sch Med 1954; mil/USNR 1942-46, 1/Lt & Damage Control Ofcr; pa/Prof Surg & Hd, Dept Surg, Chm Thoracic Oncology, Univ Tex Sys Cancer Ctr, M D Anderson Hosp & Tumor Inst 1976-; Assoc Prof Surg, Univ Tex Sch Med, Houston 1970-76; Other Past Positions; Num Profl Assns incl'g: Am Bd Surg

(Fellow), Am Col Chest Phys (Fellow), Am Col Surgs (Fellow), AMA, Inst Envir Scis (Fellow), Sigma Xi, Am Assn for Thoracic Surg, Soc of Thoracic Surgs, Am Radium Soc, Soc of Surg Oncology; hon/Pub'd Author; Postdoct S'ship, Univ Chgo 1956; Kelsey-Leary Res Awd 1960; Mike Hogg Vis Lectr in S Am 1967; USA-USSR Sci Mission on Lung Cancer 1974-; USA-Japan Coop Cancer Res Prog & Hd USA Sci Del on Lung Cancer to Japan 1975; Pres Intl Assn for Study of Lung Cancer 1976-.

MOUTON, JANE SRYGLEY oc/Behavioral Scientist; b/Apr 15, 1930; ba/Scientific Methods Inc, PO Box 195, Austin, TX 78767; m/Jackson C Jr; c/Janie, Jacquelyn; p/Theodore Srygley; Grace Stympe (dec); ed/BA Univ Tex 1950; MS Fla St Univ 1951; PhD Univ Tex 1957; pa/Austin Public Schs 1953-55; Instr Univ Tex 1957-59; Asst Prof Univ Tex 1959-64; VP Sci Methods 1961-; Diplomate Am Bd Profl Psychs; Lic'd & Cert'd by Tex Bd Examrs of Psych; Am Psych Assn; Am Soc Grp Psychotherapy & Psychodrama; Interam Soc Psych; NY Acad Scis; hon/Am Col Hosp Admrs Book Awd for *The New Managerial Grid* 1980; Am Soc for Training & Devel Best Writing Awd 1961-62; Author Num Profl Works.

MOW, ANNA BEAHM oc/Retired Teacher, Lecturer, Writer; b/July 31, 1893; h/1318 Varnell Ave NE, Roanoke, VA 24012; m/Baxter M; c/Lars M Snavely, Joseph B, Merrill; p/I N H and Mary B Beahm (dec); ed/BA; MRE; BD; ThM; pa/Ret'd Tchr; Former Missionary to India; Author 10 Books; r/Prot; hon/DD (2); DLitt; Alumni Awd; Va St Mother of Yr.

MOWBRAY, JAMES ARTHUR oc/Dean of Student Services and Professor; b/Jan 7, 1941; h/1105 Cephia St, Lake Wales, FL 33853; ba/Babson Pk; m/Paulette Anne Rosbury; c/Renee Anne, Danielle Elizabeth; p/John Alexander and Wilma Louise Kronberg Mowbray, Maitland, FL; ed/PhB 1964; MA 1966; PhD 1975; ICAF 1974; Nat Staff Col, CAP-USAF 1979; Nat Search & Rescue Sch, USCG-USAF 1980; mil/USAF Aux, Civil Air Patrol 1957-; Lt Col, Dir of Tng, Fla Wing; pa/Dean of Student Sers, Prof Hist & Polit Sci, Webber Col 1980-; Dir Area Agcy on Aging, E Ctrl Fla Regional Plan'g Coun 1977-80; Asst Exec Dir, Mid-La HSA 1976-77; Dir Plan Devel, Acadiana Hlth Plan'g Coun 1974-76; Exec Coor, Ofc of Mayor, City of Lafayette, La 1973-74; Instr of Hist, Univ SW La 1971-73; Am Hist Assn; European Sect So Hist Assn; Mil Hist Soc; Dominion Students Hall Trust (London); US Armor Assn; cp/Bd Dirs Good Shepherd Hospice; Dem Party; Univ Clb of Winter Pk; Scottish-Am Soc Ctrl Fla; r/Luth; hon/Bronze Medal of Valor 1978; Merit Ser Awd 1973, 76, 80; W T Laprade Fellow, Duke Univ 1968-71; Author "Life in the Trenches in WWI" 1973; Contbr-Editor Manual for Org & Mgmt of HSAs 1975.

MOYER, ROBERT ALEXANDER oc/Special Projects Manager; b/Nov 12, 1944; h/7034 E 52nd Pl, Tulsa, OK 74145; ba/Tulsa; m/Kathleen Ann Moore; c/Richard, David, Michael and Steven; p/Benjamin Michael (dec) and Rita Marguerite Scheurich Moyer, Tulsa, OK; ed/BS Okla St Univ 1967; mil/USNR 1967-69; pa/Cities Ser Co: Employment Spec 1969-70, Ofcr Employment & Adm Supvr 1970-72, Compensation Analyst 1972-73, Indust Chems Complex, Labor Relats Spec 1973-76, Adm Supvr Employment Dept 1977-78, Col Recruitment Mgr 1978-79, Spec Projs Mgr in Pers Resources, Energy Resources Grp 1979-; Mid-Atlantic Placement Assn; En Col Pers Assn; Tulsa Pers Assn; Work Ed Coun of Tulsa; Houston Indust Immigration Assn; cp/Kiwanis Clb; Repub Clb; r/Roman Cath; hon/W/W 1980-81.

MTANGI, STANLAKE ANESU oc/Process Engineer; b/Mar 7, 1949; h/Shelby, NC; p/Chandiwira and Maideyi Mtangi, Ft Victoria, Zimbabwe; ed/BS St Univ NY Col-Buffalo; MS Atlanta Univ 1980; pa/Process Engr; Devel Chem Noury Chem Corp, Burt, NY 1976-77; Res Chem Polaroid Corp, Cambridge, Mass 1979; Am Chem Soc; r/Cath.

MUELLER, ROY C oc/Graphic Arts Company Executive; b/Aug 15, 1930; h/202 Forest Dr, Bristol, TN 37620; ba/Bristol; m/Patricia Robinson; c/Eric, Janet, Debra, Gregory; p/Adam and Bertha Mueller; ed/Att'd Rochester Inst Tech 1976; pa/Mgr Estimating-Billing Dept Editors Press 1962-66; VP-Gen Mgr Peninsula Press, Div A S Abell Corp 1968-70; Owner, Mgr Crown Decal & Display Co 1972-; Pres Bristol Screen Inc 1977-; Screen Printing Assn; Am Philatelic Soc; cp/Repub Party; r/Luth; hon/Ad Awd Tri City Advtg Fed 1975; Intl Exhibn Awd, Screen Printing Assn 1977.

MULLINS, HAROLD ALEXANDER oc/Dentist; b/Nov 6, 1928; h/Fayetteville, NC; m/Carol Waldron; c/Lori Carol, Amy Alexandria; p/Henry Porter (dec) and Brooxie Deshong Mullins (dec); ed/BS Univ Tenn 1950; DDS Univ Tenn Col Dentistry 1955; Post Grad Univ Penn Sch of Dental Med 1965-67; AUS Rotating Dental Internship, William Beaumont Army Hosp 1956-57; mil/AUS 1956-78 Ret'd Col; pa/Conslt in Oral Med to Surgeon, USAREUR 7th Army 1969 & 3rd Army 1972; Va Public Hlth Dentist 1958; NC Public Hlth Dentist 1980-81; Am Dental Assn; Sigma Alpha Epsilon; Delta Sigma Delta; r/Presb; hon/Certs of

PERSONALITIES OF THE SOUTH

Apprec, Calif Dental Assn, Am Dental Assn 1968; Prizes in Tennis Touns as Top Player En & Wn Divs AUS.

MULLINS, REBECCA JANE LOWE oc/Director of Alcoholism Services; b/Sept 29, 1951; h/PO Box 186, Moravian Falls, NC 28654; ba/Wilkesboro; m/William Sidney Jr; c/Emily Susan; p/Caney L and Jane Pennell Lowe; ed/BA Mars Hill Col 1973; pa/Ct Cnslr Wilkes Comm on Alcohol & Drugs; Social Wkr, Wilkes Infant Ctr; Day Care Tchr, Wilkes Dept Social Sers; Dir Alcoholism Sers, New River Mtl Hlth Ctr; cp/Former Mem: Wilkes Co Coun on Status of Wom (Secy 1977-78), Wilkes Co Yng Repubs (Secy 1978), Wilkes Co Repub Wom (Editor 1978), Legal Aid Soc for the Blue Ridge (Bd Dirs 1979-80), NC Gov's Wom in Ldrship Conf-Wilkes Co 1979-80 (Publicity Chm), & Shelter Available Fams in Emers, Trainer for Crisis Line Vol 1980; N Wilkesboro Jr Wom's Clb 1978-; Wilkes Co JCettes 1975-: Dir Civic Involvement 1975-76, Pres 1976-77, Parliamentn 1977-78, Histn 1978-79; NC JCettes 1976-, St Cancer Chm 1977-78; US JCettes 1976-; r/Epis; hon/NC JCettes Outstg Local Pres 1977; U Cerebral Palsy Cert of Apprec 1977; Wilkes Co JCettes: Pres Awd of Hon 1978, JCette of Mo 1979, Sparkette Awd 1979; NC JCettes: Pres Awd of Hon 1978, Sparkette Awd 1979; Am Cancer Soc Awd of Hon 1978; N Wilkesboro Jr Wom's Clb: Cert of Apprec 1978, Unsong Hero Awd 1979, Nancy Spencer Citizenship Awd 1979, Commun Ser Awd 1980, Jr Clbwom Awd 1980.

MULLINS, SHIRLEY RUTH oc/Assessor; b/Aug 11, 1942; h/Rt 1 Box 248, Selmer, TN 38375; ba/Selmer; m/Billy Gene; p/Robert Bruce Sr and Thelma Jewel Leonard, Selmer, TN; ed/Cert Univ Tenn Tng Ctr 1970 & 71 pa/Assessor of Property, McNairy Co, Tenn 1980-; Dpty Assessor 1969-80; Charter Mem McNairy Co Chapt ABWA: Ways & Means Chm, Past Corresp Secy, cp/McNairy Co Repub Wom's Clb; r/Meth.

MULLIS, MILDRED LOUISE oc/Retired Teacher and Librarian; b/Feb 22, 1908; h/Morganton, NC; p/John Hampton (dec) and Martha Alice Hendrix Mullis (dec); ed/Dip Davenport Jr Col 1927; AB Meredith Col 1929; Further Study in Lib Sci, Appalachian St Tchrs Col; pa/Tchr Public Sch Sys 1929-51; Morganton-Burke Lib Histl Room; Secy Morganton PTA; Past Pres Morganton Unit NCEA & Clrm Tchrs Assn; NWn Clrm Tchrs Assn; Past Dir NCAE; Past Chm Sch & Chds Sect NC Lib Assn & Mem Nom'g Com; NEA; NCAE; SELA; Past Pres Delta Kappa Gamma; Co/Repub Party; Past Pres Schubert Mus Clb; Past Chm Lib Com NC Fed Mus Clbs; Morganton Pilot Clb: Past Pres, VP & Dir; Past Dist Gov NC Pilot Clbs; Past VP Wom's Clb; Grace Hosp Guild, Pink Lady (Over 1000 Hrs Vol Work), Co-Cm Hostess Com, Past Co-Chm Lib Com; r/Bapt: Treas & Past Pres Choir, Hist & Archive Com, Pianist Adult S Dept, Dir Wom's Mission Union; hon/Contbr Devotional Selection in NC Fed Wom's Clb Devotional Booklet.

MUMBY, WILLIAM oc/Vice President for Planning and Development; b/Dec 13, 1926; ba/Bowie St Col, Bowie, MD 20715; m/Mattie L; c/William Wayne, Geralyn Rosina, Kim Evette; p/William (dec) and Anna Rosina Mumby (dec); ed/BS 1952 Morgan St Col; Grad Study Morgan St Col & Harvard Univ; mil/USN 1943-46 Petty Ofcr 2nd Class; pa/Asst to Pres, Charles Ctr-Inner Harbor Mgmt Inc; VP Institutional Plan'g & Devel, Coppin St Col; Asst to Pres Bowie St Col; Dir Admissions, Bowie St Col; MCEA; Omega Psi Phi; Theta Psi Chi; Soc for Univ Plan'g; cp/Charette Commun Plan'g Assn; AAMOA; Balto City/Morgan Tenth Cycle Tchr Corps Proj, Exec Coun; Metro Bus Resource Ctr; Forest Park Little Leag: Past VP, Pres & Treas; Past VP PSTA Lemmel Jr HS; Past Mem Exec Bd PSTA No Pkwy Jr HS; Past Treas Hilton Elem Sch; Past VP Ashburton Improvement Neighborhood Assn; Bd Mem Fam & Chds Soc; Past Mem Balto City People Mover Sys; Past Liaison Proposed Balto Aquarium Com; Bd Dirs Balto Aquarium; Past Bd Mem Proj Resource; Exec Search Com Fam & Chds Soc; Part Vol Coun of Balto; Bd Mem Nat Alumni, Bd Trustees Morgan St Univ; Bd Park W Hlth Ctr; Treas Park W Hlth Ctr; Secy Fam & Chds Soc; Ad Hoc Long Range Plan'g Com Gtr Balto YMCA; Bd Mem Gtr Balto YMCA; hon/Cert of Accommodation for Outstg Perf Aboard USS Chourre 1946; 1 of 16 Most Outstg Mems Class of 1952 Morgan St Col; Most Outstg Student Dept of Ecs, Morgan St Col 1952.

MUNITZ, BARRY A oc/University Administrator; b/July 26, 1941; h/924 Saddlewood, Houston, TX 77024; ba/Houston; m/Martha Sanford; c/Christine, Marci, Katherine; p/Ray and Vivian Munitz; ed/BA Bklyn Col 1963; MA 1965, PhD 1967 Princeton Univ; pa/Univ Houston-Ctrl Campus: Chancellor 1977-, VP & Dean Faculties, Interim Chancellor & Dean 1976-77; Univ Ill Sys: VP for Acad Devel & Coor 1972-76, Assoc Provost 1971-72, Mem Pres Staff 1970-71; Other Past Positions; Bd Mem Nat Corp for Yth Enterprises; V-Chm Bd SW Ctr for Urban Res; Vis Prof Autonomous Univ Guadalajara; Energy Foun of Tex Bd; AAUP; Am Assn Higher Ed; So Assn Cols & Schs; Am Assn Univ Admrs; Yng Pres's Org (in process); Com Urban Public Univs; Johnson Assocs Adv Coun; Other Profl Activs; cp/Govt Affairs Com Houston C of C; Anti-Defamation Leag Bd; Houston Area Wom's Coun Bd; Nat Ldrship Vitality Bd; VP

Houston Grand Opera; Bd Dirs Houston Symph; Intl Woodland Conf Bd; Trustee St Johns Acad, Houston; hon/Phi Beta Kappa; Woodrow Wilson Fellow; W/W Am; Change Mag 100 Ldrs in Ed; Pub'd Author.

MUNRO, NANCY JAMES oc/Communications Consultant; b/Jan 25, 1937; h/3700 Curry Ford Rd, Apt Y-20, Orlando, FL 32806; ba/Orlando; c/Michael Thomas, Elizabeth Edna; p/David Burt (dec) and Elizabeth Buchanan James, Forest Hill, MD; ed/BS; MBA Cand; pa/Communs Conslt, So Bell; cp/Dem Party; r/Unitarian; hon/Phi Beta Kappa.

MUNSON, WANDA M oc/Instructor; b/Jan 18, 1930; h/822; Bird St, Oroville, CA 95965; ba/Oroville; c/Deborah, Janet, Albert, Susan; p/Clarence M Penrod (dec); Pluma Brandenburg, N Manchester, IN; ed/BS Manchester Col; MA Ball St Tchrs Col; pa/Instr Butte Col; Acad Senate for Calif Commun Cols; FACCC; cp/Pres St Senate 1974-75; FACCC Leg Com 1978-80; r/Prot; hon/W/W Am Wom 1979.

MUNTER, PAUL H oc/Associate Professor; b/Apr 1, 1952; h/Lubbock, TX; m/A Lynn; p/Hal and Helen Munter, Lindsay, CA; ed/BS 1974, MS 1975 Calif St Univ-Fresno; DBA Univ Colo 1978; pa/Assoc Prof Acctg, Tex Tech Univ; Am Acctg Assn; Am Inst CPAs; Acad Acctg Hists; Tex Soc CPAs; r/Presb; hon/Dean's Medal Winner; W/W Am Cols & Univs; Outstg Grad; Author *Complete Handbook of Inflation Accounting*; Num Articles in Profl Jours.

MUNTZ, CHARLES EDWARD JR oc/Special Education Director; b/May 26, 1944; h/330 Senate Dr, Frankfort, KY 40601; ba/Frankfort; m/Charlene Spring; c/Christopher Aaron, Susan Lynn; p/Mr and Mrs Charles Edward Muntz Sr, Cynthiana, KY; ed/AB En Ky Univ; MA Univ Ky; pa/Spec Ed Dir, Franklin Co Schs; Pres Coun of Admrs of Spec Ed in Ky; cp/Bd Dirs Frankfort Habilitation Inc; r/Bapt; hon/Outstg Sr Social Sci Area Major 1967, En Ky Univ; Ky Col.

MURDOCH, HELEN HEMBREE oc/Division Vice President; b/Aug 22,1928; h/7159 Wade Rd, Austell, GA 30001; ba/Atlanta; m/John Andrew; p/James Homer (dec) and Elsie Ingram Hembree, Austell, GA; ed/Att'd Marietta-Cobb Voc Tech Sch & Ga St Univ; pa/VP Linen Supply Div, Am Associated Cos; Dir AMASO Inc; Linen Supply Assn Am; Am Hotel Motel Assn; Ga Restaurant Assn; Hopitality and Travel Assn; SEn Rental Textile Assn; cp/Past Secy C of C, Mableton Chapt; r/Prot; hon/W/W Am Wom 1979-80.

MURPHREE, WILLIAM R oc/Consultant, Executive; b/Dec 27, 1947; h/1104 Willow Run Dr, Opelika, AL 36801; ba/Auburn; m/Susan H; c/Alma Michelle; p/William H and Grace M Murphree, Gautier, MS; ed/AA Marion Mil Inst 1967; BS Auburn Univ 1970; Charter Life Underwriter 1979; Reg'd Hlth & Disability Underwriter 1979; mil/Cobra Helicopter Pilot 1970-73 1st Lt; pa/Conslt in Est, Bus & Employment Benefits, Pres, Smith-Murphree Inc; Nat Assn Life Underwriters; Nat Assn Hlth Underwriters; Am Soc Charter Life Underwriters; Ala Assn Life Underwriters; Charter Mem & Pres Est Plan'g Coun of Lee Co; cp/Kiwanis Clb of Auburn; Adm Bd 1st Meth Ch Opelika; VP Meth Men's Clb 1978-79; r/Meth; hon/Nat Quality Awd; Nat Sales Achmt Awd; Qualifying Mem Million Dollar Round Table; Gen Am Nat Conf of Champs, Maui, Hawaii 1979.

MURPHY, CHARLES FRANKLIN oc/Plant Breeder; b/Dec 13, 1933; h/820 Richmond St, Raleigh, NC 27609; ba/Dept Crop Sci, NC State Univ, Raleigh; m/Carol Parker; c/Charles Reid; p/Dr and Mrs H C Murphy (dec); ed/BS 1956, PhD 1961 Iowa St Univ; MS Purdue Univ 1953; pa/Plant Breeder, NC St Univ 1961-; Ext Res; cp/Dem Precnt Chm; Bd Dirs, Wake Co YDC; VChm Citizens for Ramsey Clark; Del 1970, 72 Co, Dist & St Dem Convs; Wake Co Dem Exec Com; r/Commun U Ch; hon/Man of Yr in Ser to NC Agri "Progressive Farmer" 1967; Yg Alumnus Awd, Iowa St Univ 1968; Outstg Yg Men Am.

MURPHY, JOHN FRANCIS oc/Coach, Counselor; b/Sept 5, 1947; h/Windsor Ave, Charlotte, NC 28209; ba/Belmont, NC; p/John F Sr and Mary L Murphy, Wantagh, NY; ed/BS Hist; MEd Guid & Cnslg; mil/USN 1969-73; pa/Soccer Coach, Ednl Psych/Cnslg, Belmont Abbey Col; cp/Spec Olympics; r/Roman Cath.

MURPHY, MARY KATHLEEN CONNORS oc/Educational Administrator, Writer; h/2892 Castlewood Dr NW, Atlanta, GA 30307; ba/Atlanta; m/Michael C; c/Holly Ann, Emily Louise, Patricia Marie; p/Joseph C and Eileen E Connors, Denver, CO; ed/AB Lure Ho Hghts Col 1960; MEd Emory Univ 1968; PhD Cand Ga St Univ; pa/Ednl Admr Gerontology Ctr, Ga St Univ; Ed Writers Assn; Gerontological Soc; Nat Assn Wom's Deans, Admrs, & Cnslrs; AAUW; Cont'g Ed Com & Exec Com Gerontology Ctr Ga St Univ; Contbg Editor *Education USA*; cp/Bd Rel Ed 1979-, Cathedral of Christ the King; r/Cath; hon/W/W Am Wom 1979-80; Pubs Com CASE 1976-77; Coun for Advmt & Support of Ed; Pubs Com Nat Assn Indep Schs 1974-77; Nat Defense Ed Act F'ship

222

1966-67; Adm on Aging Trg IV-A F'ship 1977-79; Nom'd Phi Delta Kappa; Applied for Dissertation Grant, Adm on Aging HEW, $5,500 Awd 1979; Gov's Intern, Summer 1977; Gerontology Cert, Ga St Univ Gerontology Ctr 1978.

MURPHY, MICHAEL CONLON oc/Lawyer; b/Nov 14, 1937; h/2892 Castlewood Dr NW, Atlanta, GA 30327; ba/Atlanta; m/Mary Kay; c/Holly Ann, Emily Louise, Patricia Marie; p/Patrick and Bessie Conlon Murphy, Brewster, NY; ed/BS USAF Acad 1959; MBA Ga St Univ 1964; JD Emory Univ 1966; mil/USAF 1959-64 Capt; Reserve Ofcr Capt 1964-69; pa/Ptnr Troutman, Sanders, Luckerman & Ashmire; Am Bar Assn; Ga Bar Assn; Atlanta Bar Assn; Lwyrs Clb Atlanta; cp/Bd Mem & Mbrship Chm Downtown YMCA 1978-; Adj Prof of Law, Emory Univ 1976-; r/Cath; hon/Outstg Atlantans 1978; Vietnam Campaign Ribbon.

MURRAY, AVERY oc/Purchasing Director; b/Aug 23, 1916; ba/613 W Mountain St, Kings Mountain, NC 28086; m/Inez Hawkins; c/Donald Avery, Donna Reginnia; p/H R Murray, Kings Mountain, NC; Bea Jones Murray (dec); ed/Att'd Nat Handwrite Inst 1050; BA Freedom Inst 1954; MA NC St Univ 1951; Att'd Dallas Sem 1957, Locksmithing Inst 1967, Liberty Sch Advtg 1959, Gaston Tech; mil/Army Air Evac Pilot; pa/Purchasing Dir, Salesman, Nu Prod Broker Sales & Murray's of Kings Mtn; NC St Notary Public 25 Yrs; Editorial Writer & Columnist; Grapholigist; Pres's Coun, Am Mgmt Assn; Men of Mfg; cp/C of C; Nat Geographic Soc; Smithsonian Inst, Contbg Mem; Va St Sheriff's & CS Assn, Life Mem; WOW Soc, Past Comdr, Life Mem; Fairview Lodge; Blue Mason Lodge of Perfection; 32° Mason; r/Ch of Gospel Ministry-Bapt, Ordained Min; hon/Mr Woodman 1957; Outstg Man of Yr 1960; Outstg Achmt in Psychographology 1963; Merit Awd for Outstg Commun Ser & Merit Achmt 1974; Gold Plaque for Outstg Editorial, *Exposure* Magazine 1979; 25 Yr St Notary 1979; Author *Minutes of Humor for the Speaker*; *Antiques to Live With*; *Writing Your Life*; *Murder Where You Find It*; *Murder on the Waterfront*; *Murder Rides Free*; Var Magazine Editorials.

MURRAY, CHARLES EDWARD oc/Educator; ba/C E Murray HS, Greeleyville, SC 29056; p/Willaim Murray (dec); EJ McCollum; ed/AB, MA S Carolina St Univ; PhD; mil/AUS 3 Yrs; pa/Prin & Dir Adult Ed CE Murray HS; Eng Tchr 23 Yrs; Prin 18 Yrs; cp/Claflin Col Assocs; r/U Meth: Conf Bd of Ed; Bd Laity; Com Fam Life; hon/Hon Doc Humanities, Claflin Col.

MURRAY, CROSBY L oc/Retired; b/Feb 17, 1902; h/5912 Holston View Ln, Knoxville, TN 37914; m/Lena Davis; p/Elmer (dec) and Lillie Wright Murray (dec); ed/BS Lincoln Meml Univ; pa/Chm Bd Trustees LMU; Life Mem 4-H Clbs; cp/Rotary; UT Ext Clb; Commun Improvement Clb; r/Bapt; hon/Algernon Sydney Sullivan Awd; Congressional Awd; Most Outstg Alumni LMU.

MURRAY, HAL J oc/Wildlife Artist; b/Oct 28, 1946; h/Rt 4 Box 322, Picayune, MS 39466; ba/Same; m/Annette J; c/Charles, Helen, Patricia, Luara, Michael, John; p/Harold J and Violia C Murray; mil/USN; pa/Artist; Fine Art for Investment; cp/Preserv of Worlds Wildlife Through Art; Loyal Order of the Moose; r/Roman Cath; hon/Best of Show; 1st & 2nd Pl Throughout Many Yrs In Art Shows.

MURRAY, JANET BAUM oc/Librarian; b/Jan 4, 1913; h/999 Cyress Way, Boca Raton, FL 33432; m/Warren Snyder; c/Jane M Kitchen; p/Charles A (dec) and Lillie M Baum (dec); ed/BS Marshall Col; pa/First Libn Boca Raton Public Lib; Adv Bd Boca Raton Public Lib; cp/Boca Raton Hist Soc; r/Meth.

MURRAY, PERCY EDWARD oc/Professor; b/Mar 12, 1948; ba/Durham, NC; m/Carol W; c/Amber Eulann; p/Sam Jr and Bertha Murray, Swan Qtr, NC; ed/BS 1970, MA 1972 NC Ctrl Univ; PhD Miami Univ (Ohio) 1977; pa/Instr Winston-Salem Univ 1971-72; Vis Instr Miami Univ (Ohio) 1972-73; Asst Prof Fayetteville St Univ 1976-79; Chm & Assoc Prof, Dept Hist, NC Ctrl Univ 1979-; Assn Study of Afro-Am Life & Hist, Chm Noms Com 1980, Prog Com 1981; NC Lit & Hist Soc; So Hist Soc; Org of Am Hist; Oh Acad Hist; cp/NC Hwy Hist Marker Adv Com; r/Bapt; hon/Outstg Yng Men Am Awd 1977; Phi Alpha Theta 1972; W/W Students in Am Cols & Univs 1969-70; Author "Crusading Editor, Harry C Smith"; Book Reviews for NIP Mags.

MYERS, CECIL EVERETT oc/Business Manager; b/July 1, 1921; h/725 E Union, Magnolia, AR 71753; ba/Magnolia; p/dec; ed/BSE Henderson St Univ; MA Geo Peabody Col; mil/USCG; pa/Bd Mem BSA; cp/Kiwanis Clb; Am Legion; Recorder-Treas 10 Yrs City of Strong; Past Lt Gov Kiwanis Intl; r/Meth; hon/First Pres Malvern, Ark Kiwanis Clb; Noted for Outstg Work For Polio Foun 1950s; Recog'd by Kiwanis for Ldrship in Commun.

MYERS, HELEN MACK oc/Nurse, Enterostomal Therapist; b/Aug 1, 1928; h/Louisville, KY; ba/L'ville; m/Wesley; c/Ralph E, Paula M Phillips; p/Abraham (dec) and Emma Mack; ed/Dip L'ville Gen Hosp Sch Nsg 1960; BSN Ind Univ Sch Nsg 1973; Cert'd Enterostomal Therapist Tucson Med Ctr 1975; pa/Hd Nurse, Med Surpvr, Dir Inservice Ed L'ville Gen Hosp; Staff Nurse, Hd Nurse, Instr Nsg Ed, Enterostomal Therapist L'ville VA Med Ctr; ANA; Instl Assn Enterostomal Therapy Inc; Sigma Theta Tau; cp/YWCA; NAACP; Iota Phi Lambda, VP; Intl Toastmistress, Past Secy & Pres; Fed Employed Wom; r/Bapt: Bd Trustees, SS Tchr; hon/Nat VA Awd, "VA May I Help You"; Nat VA Admrs 'Hands and Hearts Awd"; Nom'd Fed Employee of Yr Awd 1981; Author "Ostomy Patients Evaluation of Teaching Program."

MYERS, MARCEAU CHEVALIER oc/Music Educator and Administrator; b/Oct 9, 1929 h/1614 Highland Park Rd, Denton, TX 76201; ba/Denton; m/Judith May Kleine; c/Daraugh Anne; p/St Clair (dec) and Marcella C Myers (dec); ed/BS Mansfield St Col 1954; MME Penn St Univ 1957; Post Grad Ind Univ 1954-55; EdD Columbia Univ 1972; mil/USMC 1950-52; pa/Dean Sch Mus, N Tex St Univ; Dean Conservatory Mus, Capital Univ 1970-74; Asst Prof Mus, Dept Chm 1965-70, Wn Conn St Col 1960-70; Instruml Mus Instr, Bronxville Public Sch 1957-60; Nat Assn Schs of Mus, Mem Grad Com; Tex Assn Mus Schs, VP 1977-78; Mus Edrs Nat Conf; Mus Tchrs Nat Assn; Col Mus Soc; Phi Mu Alpha Sinfonia; cp/Chm City of Danbury Cultural Comm 1965-70; Adv Panel Mus Foun; Gtr Denton Arts Coun; Denton Bach Soc; Patron Columbus, Ohio Arts Coun; r/Prot; hon/Phi Mu Alpha Orpheus Awd 1974; 1:00 Lab Band Awd 1978; Num Profl Pubs.

MYERS, ROBERT LAWRENCE oc/Pharmacy Services Vice President; b/May 13, 1945; h/221 Ocala Rd, Belleair, FL 33516; ba/Clearwater; m/Kimberly Junius; c/Robert Bradley, Meghan Waldorf; p/Lawrence Myrl and Frances Thunander Myers, Elkhart, IN; ed/BS Pharm Butler Univ 1968; mil/USAR 1969-75; pa/VP Pharm Sers, Jack Eckers Drug Co; Am Pharm Assn; Roche Adv Bd; Sigma Chi; r/Meth.

MYERS, SAMUEL LLOYD oc/Executive Director; h/3608 Baskerville Dr, Bowie, MD 20716; ba/Wash DC; m/Marion Rieras; c/Yvette M May, Tama R Clark, Samuel L Jr; p/David Elkanah and Edith Reid Myers (dec); ed/AB w highest hons Morgan St Col 1940; MA Boston Univ 1942; MA 1948, PhD 1949 Harvard Univ; mil/AUS 1942-46, WWII, PRT Ribbon; pa/Exec Dir Nat Assn Equal Opportunity in Higher Ed; Past Pres Bowie St Col, Bowie, Md; Bd Dirs, Am Assn St Cols & Univs; cp/V-Chm Md Com for Humanities & Public Policy; r/Meth; hon/Alpha Kappa Mu.

MYERS, VIRGINIA HUNTER oc/Assistant Professor, Consultant; b/Mar 29, 1930; h/5214 87th St, Lubbock, TX 79424; ba/Canyon, TX; m/Donald R; c/Marcia Ann Swanson; p/Ray R and Ruth Hunter, Canyon, TX; ed/BS 1949, MEd 1965 W Tex St Univ; Grad Study Wis St Univ 1969, Univ Tex Austin 1971 & 74, Tex Tech Univ 1976, 78, 79; pa/Tchr Sec'dy Eng, Speech & Drama: Miami HS 1950-55, Denver City HS 1956-61; Panama HS 1963-67, Lubbock HS 1967-70, Monterey HS 1970-78, W Tex St Univ 1978-; Commun & Ed Conslt; St Dir Intl Thespian Soc 1970; Pres Tex Speech Commun Assn 1977; VP Tex Forensic Assn 1978; Am Forensic Assn Comm on Discussion & Debate for Nat Univ Cont'g Ed Assn & Nat Fed HS Activ Leags; Com on K-12 Guidelines & Curric, Tex Speech Commun Assn, Chp; Wording & Selection Com, Nat Univ Cont'g Ed Assn/Nat Fed HS Activ Leags Comm on Discussion & Debate; Mbrship Com Am Forensic Assn Chp; cp/Lubbock C of C, Wom's Div; People to People, Area Dir; r/Disciples of Christ; hon/Clark Foun S'ship for Tchg Excell 1959.

MYLES, PATRICIA GLASS oc/Director Day Care Center; b/Nov 18, 1954; h/3806 Marshall St, Gadsden, AL 35901; ba/Gadsden; m/Edward Marvin; c/Vanessa Jeanenne, Edward Marvin Jr; p/Samuel and Finous Glass, Leesburg, AL; ed/BS Early Chdhood Ed; pa/Dir Myles Day Care & Kiddie Sch; Orgr Assn Day Care Dirs; r/Bapt.

PERSONALITIES OF THE SOUTH

N

NACOL, MAE oc/Attorney; b/June 15, 1944; h/6012 Memorial Dr, Houston, TX 77007; ba/Houston; c/Shawn Alexander, Catherine Regina; p/William Samuel and Ethel Bowman Nacol, Houston, TX; ed/BS Rice Univ 1965; Admitted to Tex Bar 1969; pa/Diamond Buyer & Aprraiser, Nacol's Jewelry 1961-; Diamond Conslt Jewelry Stores & Ins Cos 1961; cp/Chm Cands Com 1970; Chm Mbrship Com 1971; Chm Lwyrs Referral Com 1972; Bar Assns; Tex Trial Lwyrs Assn; Nat Assn Wom Lwyrs; Am Jud Soc; Jewelers Bd Trade; hon/Mayor's Recog Awd, Houston 1972; Ford Fellow 1965.

NAKARAI, CHARLES F T oc/Music Educator; b/Apr 25 , 1936; h/3520 Mayfair St, Apt 205, Durham, NC 27707; p/Toyozo W and Frances A Nakarai, Elizabethton, TN; ed/BA 1958, MM 1967 Butler Univ; Grad Studies UNC-CH; mil/USAF 1958-64 Capt; pa/Asst Prof Mus, Milligan Col 1970-72; Pvt Tchr Mus 1972-; Am Musicological Soc; Col Mus Soc; Am Guild Organists; Mus Lib Assn; Mus Tchrs Nat Assn; NC Mus Tchrs Assn; Durham Mus Tchrs Assn, Publicity Chm; hon/Sev Mil Awds & Hons; Phi Kappa Phi; Contbr to *Performance Practice: A Bibliography*; Composer "Three Movements for Chorus" and "Bluesy."

NAKARAI, TOYOZO W oc/Educator; b/May 16, 1898; h/Rt 4 Box 240, Elizabethton, TN 37643; m/Frances A; c/Charles F T, Frederick L; p/Tosui and Wakae Nakarai (dec); ed/AB Kokugakuin Univ 1920; AB 1924, AM 1925 Butler Univ; PhD Univ Mich 1930; Postdoct Studies: Univ Mich, Univ Chgo, NY Univ; pa/Col Missions Instr 1923-25; Butler Univ & Christian Theol Sem: Instr 1927-28, Asst Prof 1928-29, Assoc Prof 1929-31, Prof & Hd Dept Old Testament 1931-65, Prof Emeritus 1965-; Emmanuel Sch: Rel Prof & Hd Dept Old Testament 1965-71, Dist'd Prof & Hd Dept Old Testament 1971-; Am Sch Oriental Res Jerusalem Vis Prof 1947-48; Hon Lectr 1962-63; Midwest Br Soc Biblical Lit, Pres 1951-52; Nat Assn Profs Hebrew, Pres 1956-58; Am Oriental Soc; AAUP; Soc Sci Study Rel; Am Acad Rel; Israel Explor Soc; Israel Soc Biblical Res; Nippon Kyuyaku Gakkai; r/Christian; hon/Phi Kappa Phi; Theta Phi; Eta Beta Rho; Baxter Foun Awd; Medal & Schroll Brit Abraham; J I Holcomb Prize; Cit & Scroll Histadrut Ivrit; Author *Japanese Conversation* 1922; *A Study of the Kokinshy* 1931; Others.

NAKASHIMA, TADAYOSHI oc/Research Associate Professor; b/Dec 1, 1922; h/7400 SW 159 Terr, Miami, FL 33157; ba/Coral Gables; m/Fukuko; c/Rieko; p/Chunosuke (dec) and Hina Nakashima (dec); ed/BP Nagoya Pharm Col 1943; BS Taihoku Imperial Univ 1946; PhD Kyushu Univ 1961; pa/Assoc Prof: Univ Hawaii 1962-64, Univ Miami 1964-; Inst for Molecular & Cellular Evolution; Am Chem Soc; Inst Soc Study of Origin of Life; Japanese Soc Food and Nutrition; Sigma Xi; r/Meth; hon/Japanese Nat Sci Foun Grantee 1957; Contbr Articles to Profl Jours.

NANCE, M MACEO JR oc/President, South Carolina State College; b/Mar 28, 1925; h/SC St Col, Orangeburg, SC 29117; ba/O'burg; m/Julie E; c/Robert Milton, I Maceo; p/Milligan Maceo and Louella Stewart Nance (dec); ed/AB 1949; MS 1953; LLD 1968; LHD 1975; mil/USN 1943-46; pa/Mem Bd Dirs & Treas Nat Assn Equal Opport in Higher Ed, Comm on Fed Relats of Am Coun on Ed, Financing Higher Ed Comm Nat Assn St Universities & Land-Grant Cols; VP Nat Bd Dirs, Col Placemt Services; Chm Coun of Presidents, SC St Supported Cols and Univs; cp/Mem: Bd Dirs Blue Cross & Blue Shield (SC), Bd Dirs Bkr's Trust (SC), Gov's Comm on Police & Commun Relats, Bd Dirs United Way(Orangeburg), St Coun Boy Scouts; r/Williams Chapel AME Ch; hon/1st Black to Deliver Comm'g Address of a Nuclear Attack Submarine (USS SEA DEVIL SSN664 Newport News, Va); Outstg Civilian Ser Medal by Dept of Army; Guest Lectr in Africa; Honored for Dist'd Ser in Ed & Commun by Kappa Alpha Psi; Mem: Delta Psi Omega Frat, Alpha Kappa Mu; Participated in 18th Annual Nat Strategy Sem (Army War Col); Guest Lectr Sem (Army War Col).

NAPIER, SHIRLEY RITA oc/College Official; b/Dec 6, 1932; h/4619 Sunflower Rd D59, Knoxville, TN 37919; ba/K'ville; c/James Roscoe Chambers Jr; p/Isaac Chauncey Sr and Johanna Edith Miller, Easton, MD; ed/AB Eng; MA Ed; EdD; pa/Col Ofcl, Knoxville Col; Phi Delta Kappa; Assn Wom in Psych; Nat Assn Wom Deans, Cnslrs & Admrs; Am Assn Sch Admrs; AAUW; Tenn Adult Ed Assn; cp/Col Bd Minority Affairs Adv Bd; r/Ch of Christ; hon/W/W Am Wom 1979-80; Senatorial S'ship; Acad Yr Inst Fellow.

NAPLES, ROBERT FRANCIS oc/Assistant Professor; b/Oct 20, 1948; h/Rt 4 Box 315B, Boone, NC 28607; ba/Boone; m/Mary Christine Quirion; c/Anna Christine; p/Francis P and Evelyn M Naples, Hamden, CT; ed/ABS Husson Col; BBA Col Ins; MBA Ga St Univ; CLU; FLMI; FALU; HIAA; ICA; pa/Asst Prof Ins, Dept Fin, Ins & Real Est,

Appalachian St Univ 1978-; Grad Res Asst, Dept Ins, Ga St Univ 1975-78; The Equitable Life Assurance Soc: Underwriter, Grp Ins Dept, 1974-75; Underwirter Mass Mkts Div, Underwriting & Issue Dept, 1973-74; Underwriter, Underwriting Div, Underwriting and Issue Dept, 1972-73; Var Pos, The Col of Ins & Equitable Life in Res & Devel, Agts Requirements, Ser & Inspec, Underwriting & Issue Dept 1969-72; Am Ec Assn; Am Fin Assn; Am Risk & Ins Assn; Pi Sigma Epsilon; Ins Soc NY; Am Mktg Assn; Alpha Kappa Psi, Chapt VP; Doct Fellows; Gamma Iota Sigma, Chapt Advr, Chapt Pres; Toastmasters Intl, Clb Ednl VP; So Risk & Ins Assn; Wn Risk & Ins Assn Boone Assn Life Underwriters; NC Ins Ed Foun, Bd Mem; Ins Co Ed Dirs Soc; Nat Assn Hlth Underwriters; hon/Beta Gamma Sigma; W/W: Am Student Ldrs, Students in Am Cols & Univs; Spec Commend HIAA; 100% Work-Study S'ship; Ga Assn Mutual Ins Agts S'ship; Ga Chapt CPCU S'ship; Alpha Kappa Psi Dist'd Ser Awd.

NATCHER, WILLIAM HUSTON oc/Member of United States Congress; b/Sept 11, 1909; h/638 E Main St, Bowling Green, KY 42101; ba/Wash DC; m/Virginia R; c/Celeste N Jirles, Louise N Murphy; p/J M and Blanche H Natcher (dec); ed/AB Wn Ky Univ; LLB; mil/USN; pa/Mem of Bar; cp/Kiwanis Clb; r/Bapt; hon/1971 Ky Am Legion Dist'd Ser Awd.

NAVA, ROBERT oc/Zoo Attendant; b/May 13, 1946; h/8928 Mt Delano, El Paso 79904; ba/El Paso; m/Martha; c/Sandra Marie; p/Robert and Rosa Nava, El Paso, TX; mil/USMC 6 Yrs; pa/Zoo Attendant; r/Cath; hon/Outstg Softball Player 1978.

NAVARRO, ALFRED oc/Assistant Foreman; b/Mar 27, 1947; h/102 Joe C Ln, Lufkin, TX 75901; ba/Lufkin; m/Ludin C; c/Alfred Jr, Juan Cleofas; p/Antonio and Gloria Rios Navarro, McAllen, TX; ed/HS Grad; mil/USMC 1966-69; pa/Asst Foreman, Lufkin Indust Inc; cp/Helping Latin Ams; r/Cath; hon/Tex Comm Base Cert; Grateful Apprec, DAV; Cert Good Conduct; 2 Purple Hearts; Combat Action Ribbon; Nat Defense Medal; Vietnam Ser Medal; Vietnam Campaign Medal; Rifle Marksmanship Badge; Num Other Awds.

NAVIAUX, LaREE DeVEE oc/Psychologist; b/Aug 18, 1937; h/1603 Longridge Rd, Charleston, WV 25314; ba/C'ton; m/Frank A D'Abreo; p/Prosper Leo (dec) and Dorothy DeVee Naviaux, Lewellen, NB; ed/BS; MS; PhD; pa/Dir Chd's Mlt Hlth, Shawnee Hills MH/MR Ctr; Asst Clin Prof WVU Col Med; Asst Dir Parents Annonymous of WV; WV Task Force for Foster Care; WV Action for Foster Chd; WV Child Welfare Resource Info Exch; Assn Humanistic Psych; Am Psych Assn; Nat Mtl Hlth Assn; r/Cath-Universalist; hon/Intl W/W Commun Ser; DIB.

NAYLES, LEE C oc/Pharmacist, Student; b/Nov 2, 1943; h/9417 Labette, Little Rock, AR 72204; m/Dorothy; c/David, Jon; p/Mattie Nayles, Camden, AR; ed/BS Pharm 1966; D Pharm 1967; MS Pharm 1970; MD Cand 1981; pa/Hlth Care Conslt HEW; Asst Admr MLK Hlth Ctr, Chgo; Chief Pharm MLK; Owner Lee's Apothecary, Little Rock; Nat Pharm Assn; Student Nat Med Assn; Student AMA; cp/Bd Dirs Carver YMCA; r/Congregationalist; hon/CIBA Awd 1979.

NEAL, FRANK ALBERT III oc/Manager; b/Apr 13, 1942; ba/Dallas; m/Darlene Johnson; c/Frank A IV, Benjamin Eric, David Patrick; p/Frank A Jr and Georgia Hudson Neal, Lebanon, TN; ed/Att'd David Lipscomb Col; BBA Cand Pacific Wn Univ; pa/Regional Parts Mktg Mgr, Intl Harvester Co; Sales & Mktg Execs of Dallas; r/Ch of Christ; hon/Nat Winner Sales Progs 1978 & 79 Intl Harvester; Designed & Printed 6 Trg Books for Intl Harvester.

NEAL, MONTFORD LEE oc/Pastor; b/Jan 25, 1942; h/3799 Amity Ln, Middletown, OH 45042; ba/M'town; m/Rita G; c/Robert Lee, Melissa Ann, Randy Alan; p/Howard C and Nannie Myrtle Neal, Clay City, KY; ed/BS Ind Univ; MA TTU; Dip Anderson Sch Theol, Anderson Sch of the Adv'd Pastoral Studies; MDiv Cand U Theol Sem; pa/Min; Author; Radio Spkr, WPFB-AM, Midd, Ohio; Men of Ch of God Inc Intl; Ohio Mins Pastoral/Ch Relats Com; Am Assn Christian Cnslrs; cp/Bd of Yng Life, Christian Ctr; Bd Evangelism; Bd Credentials; Warren Co Tutoral Grp; r/Prot; hon/W/W: Rel, Ind; Noteworthy Citizens; Author *Theories of Personality & History of Southwest Ohio Churches of God.*

NEAL, PATSY E oc/Writer; Lecturer; b/April 19, 1938; h/PO Box 732, Morristown, TN 37814; ba/same; ed/BS cum laude Wayland Col; MS Univ Utah; pa/Instr: Lincoln Jr HS 1960-62, Univ Utah 1963-66, Brevard Col 1966-77 (Asst & Assoc Prof); Graduate Asst Univ Utah; Instr 4th Nat Inst on Girls & Wom's Sports; Mem: AAU & DGWS Basketball Rules Com 1964-66 & 1973-75, Basketball Sub-com of US Col Sports Coun 1968-70; Lectr Medalist Sports Ed Camps in Sum; Has own Basketball Camp for Girls in Sum; Gives Num Clins, Wkshops, & Speeches at Univs & Cols (St); Only Wom Selected to Attend Multidisciplinary Symp on Sport & Means of Elevating Intl Understanding at St Dept Wash DC 1973; Pub'd Author: *Basketball Techniques For Women, Coaching Methods For*

Women, Sport And Identity, So Run Your Race, Coaching Girls And Women, Num Articles, Pub'd Poetry Nat Anthol of Col Poetry, Short Stories; hon/Many Biogl Listings; Wayland: Homecoming Queen, Beauty Pageant Participant, 1st Wom Student Body Pres, Citizenship Awd; Num Basketball Hons incl'g: Capt US Team in World B'ball Tournaments Peru, SAm 1964, AAU All-Am (1959, 60, 65), Played in 1959 Pan-Am Games; Has Ranked in Top Ten in Wom's Singles & Doubles Tennis in NC & Utah; Featured in Sev Pubs; Nat Spokeswom for Wigwam Socks.

NEAL, STEPHEN LYBROOK oc/United States Congressman; b/Nov 7, 1944; h/Winston-Salem, NC; ba/331 Cannon Hob, Wash DC 20515; m/Rachel Landis; c/Mary Piper, Stephen L Jr; p/Charles H Neal (dec); Mary Martha Spitemiller, Winston-Salem, NC; ed/BA Univ of Hi; pa/Newspaper Pubr; cp/Elected US Cong 1974, 76 (Dem); Chm Subcom on Intl Trade, Investmt and Monetary Policy; r/Epis.

NEAL, VINA ELDORA MILLER oc/Teacher; b/Nov 5, 1930; m/Earl Loyd; c/Mickie Carol Key, Diana Cheryl Pribble; p/Clifford Wesley Miller, Woodward, OK; Alta Mildred White Miller (dec); ed/BS Okla Bapt Univ 1953; Masters NWn Univ 1975; pa/Tchr: Wellston HS 1953-54, Bowlegs Jr HS 1954-55, Tangier HS 1956-61, Selman HS 1961-66, Mooreland Public Schs 1966-80; Okla Bapt Univ Home Ec Clb, Pres 1951-53; OEA; NEA; Little Sahara Rdg Coun; Mooreland Ed Assn; r/So Bapt; hon/1st Prize OGE Cake Baking Contest 1952; Valedictorian Sharon HS 1949; Pres's Honor Roll, NWn St Univ 1973-74.

NEE, LINDA ELIZABETH c/Social Worker; b/Dec 29, 1938; h/10201 Grosvenor Pl, Rockville, MD 20852; ba/Bethesda; p/Thomas Markham and Ellen Thomas Jamieson Nee; ed/BA Russell Sage Col 1961; MSSW Va Commonwlth Univ 1968; pa/Clin-Res Social Wkr, Nat Inst Mtl Hlth 1974-; Clin Social Wkr, Social Work Dept, Clin Ctr, Nat Inst Hlth 1968-74; Med Social Wkr, Tuberculosis Sanatorium of Med Ctr Va 1967; Social Wkr, Social Ser Dept NY Neurological Inst, Columbia-Presb Med Ctr 1961-66; NASW, Chp Ethics & Grievances 1978-; hon/W/W Am Wom 1979-80; Commencement Address Nat Cath Univ Grad Sch of Social Work 1977; Editor *Social Work, Metropolitan Washington* 1975-77; Author Nom Profl Articles Incl'g "Considerations Regarding Death and Termination: Casework with Nine Year Old Jerry, Referred After the Death of His Mother."

NEEDHAM, ALLYN BRYANT oc/Treasurer and Controller; b/Oct 10, 1955; h/6208 Longhorn Trail, Ft Worth, TX 76135; ba/Ft Worth; p/Jay H and Doris E Needham, Ft Worth, TX; ed/BA Austin Col; pa/Treas-Controller Jay Needham Inc; Tex Assn Bus; Spkr Sem on Small Bus 1979; cp/Alumni Bd Austin Col; Dem Party; r/Presb; Choir Mem; Aid to Yth Men; Mu Pi Gamma Mu; W/W Austin Cols; Hon Rol Univ of Tex at Arlington; Admiral in Tex Navy.

NEEDHAM, JAMES RAY JR oc/Sales Manager; b/July 25, 1947; h/167 Shiloh Pk, Conroe, TX 77302; ba/Houston; m/Karen K; c/Scott Christopher; p/James and Dorris Needham, Nacogdoches, TX; ed/BA Houston Bapt Col; mil/USMC; pa/Sales Mgr Motorola Communs & Elect Inc; cp/Coach on Yth Soccer Team; Referee Yth Soccer; Choral Dir Conroe Chorale; r/Presb; hon/W/W Am Cols & Univs; Regional Ranking Awd.

NEEF, HAZEL E MOUTON oc/Director of Dietary Department; b/July 4, 1926; h/Scott, LA; m/William G; c/Patricia Ann, Pamela Joan, Janette Lynn, Geralyn, William Stephen, Dorothy Marie, Thomas Michael; p/Rene F and Leah Martin Mouton, Scott, LA; ed/Att'd Univ SWn La 1946; Dietetic Internship, Touro Infirm 1947; Mgmt Credits Nichols St Univ 1965; Adv'd Nutrition La St Univ 1971; pa/Dir Dietary Dept, Our Lady of Lourdes Hosp; Formula Room & Pediatric Dietitian, Touro Infirm; Staff to Asst Chief Dietitian, VA Hosp, Alexandria; Hd Therapeutic Dietitian, Hermann Hosp; Hd Dietary Dept, St Joseph Hosp; Conslt Dietitian to Sev Insts; Lafayette Dist Dietetic Assn; Houston Dietetic Assn; Tex Dietetic Assn; La Dietetic Assn, Pres; ADA; cp/Acadiana Hlth Plan'g Coun, Bd Dirs; Mid-La Hlth Sys Agcy; Area Agcy on Aging; r/Cath; hon/W/W S&SW; Mu Sigma 1942 & 43; S'ship to USL; Lambda Omega; Home Ec Clb; Sigma Theta, Pres.

NEEPER, RALPH ARNOLD oc/Computer Specialist; b/Sept 29, 1940; h/13530 Delaney Rd, Woodbridge, VA 22193; ba/Ft Belvoir, VA; m/Nancy Diane; c/Rachel Claudine, Jennifer Alice; p/Guy Enoch and Alice Elizabeth Arnold Neeper, Toledo, OH; ed/BS 1963, MS 1971 Purdue Univ; mil/AUS; pa/Computer Spec, Defense Mapping Sch; ACM; ADPA; ANA; AAAS; Gideon's Mensa; Past Mem: MAA, AMA, ALA, AMS, ASP, ACSM, Toastmasters; cp/Lorton (Prison) Liturgical Com; r/Luth; hon/Dean's List 1964; Suggestion Awds 1974, 75, 77.

NEIGHBORS, JOE LARSON JR oc/Investigator; b/Sept 6, 1951; h/Rt 5 Box 263, Alex City, AL 35010; ba/Dadeville, AL; m/Susan Lee; c/Susan Renee, Freddie; p/Joe L and Jessie Ruth Neighbors, Montgomery, AL;

ed/Grad EMT; Grad NE Ala Police Acad, Jacksonville St Col; Burglary Invest Sch; Sgt Sch; Ala Crim Just Trg Ctr; pa/Tallapoosa Sheriff Dept; cp/Goodwater JCs; r/Bapt; hon/Awd'd at JC Conv.

NEIGHBORS, RICHARD HENRY oc/Pharmacist; b/July 5, 1926; h/PO Box 46, Goodwater, AL 35072; m/Deon D; p/Thomas Herbert (dec) and Nell Moon Neighbors (dec); ed/BS Auburn Univ 1960; pa/Neighbors Drug Co, Retail Pharmacy 1950-79; Carraway Meth Med Ctr, Ala IV Pharm 1941-; Am Pharm Assn; Ala Pharm Assn; NARD; cp/Rotary Clb; US C of C; NFIB; EMS Bd, City of Goodwater; Goodwater Airport Auth; G'water Lib Bd; G'water Housing Auth; G'water Plan'g Comm; Alderman Mayor Pro-Tem, City of G'water; r/Meth; hon/Num Civic Recogs Incl'g Lions & Rotary Clbs 1980.

NEILL, W MARTIN oc/Executive; b/Feb 7, 1921; h/2208 W Cuthbert, Midland, TX; ba/Midland; m/Genell Conner; c/Keneth Martin, Donald Morgan, Nancy Ann; ed/Intl Accty Soc 1942; mil/USAF 1942-46; pa/Pres Martin Neill Co; Assoc Mem Am Soc Heating, Refrig & Air Cond'g Engrs Inc; Nat Soc Public Accts; cp/Past Pres W Tex Chapt Arthritis Foun; Mem City Coun 7 Yrs, Mayor Pro-Tem 2 Yrs; Human Welfare Coor'g Bd, Bapt Gen Conv of Tex, Past VChm; Com of 200 Bapt Gen Conv Tex; Trustee Bapt Meml Geriatrics Hosp, San Angelo, Tex; Chm Region IV Tex Municipal Leag; Dir Downtown Lions Clb; VChm Christian Life Comm, Bapt Gen Conv of Tex; Former Chm City of Midland Plan'g & Zoning Comm; Objectives for Midland Prog; Bd Dirs Midland Co Hosp Dist; hon/W/W Tex 1973-74; Outstg Ams in S 1975.

NELSON, BRYANT McNEILL oc/College President; b/Feb 16, 1932; h/7222 Longleaf Dr NW, Roanoke, VA 24019; ba/Roanoke; m/Grace Moore; c/Faith Ann, Stephen Michael, Mark Andrew, Hope Elizabeth, Peter Eric; p/Laudies Ira (dec) and Nell A McNeill Nelson (dec); ed/BS Bob Jones Univ; Grad Studies Univ Del; mil/USAF 1949-52; pa/Pres Shenandoah Bible Col; Pastor; Missionary; Probation Ofcr; cp/Am Legion; Repub Party; r/Bapt; hon/Eagle Scout; Key to Panama City, Fla; Personal Invitation to White House by Pres Truman; Outstg Admr Awd 1979.

NELSON, EDWINA oc/Guidance Counselor; Consultant; b/Sept 14, 1937; h/3698 Oregon Trail, Decatur, GA 30032; m/William E; c/Melva Renee, Edwina Michelle; p/Daniel Williams Sr (dec); Ollie M Owen, Columbus, MS; ed/BA Bennett Col 1958; MA Boston Univ 1969; MA Wayne St Univ 1973; pa/Tchr of English & Stenography, Harwood Sch (Albuquerque, NM); Adm Asst, Asian Foun (SF, Cal); Tchr of Elem Sch, Chgo (Ill) Public Schs; Coor of Cultural Awareness Prog for Dependent Schs in Aviano & Rimini (Italy); Tchr of Students in US Dependent Schs in france, W Berlin & Italy; Staff Devel & Tng Specialist for Ga Dept of Human Resources, Fam & Chd Sers; Guid Cnslr, DeKalb Co Schs; APGA; Am Sch Cnslrs Assn; Ga Sch Cnslrs Assn; DeKalb Co Sch Cnslrs Assn; cp/Nat Urban League; SCLC Wom; Alpha Kappa Alpha; DeKalb Co BPW; Columbia Valley Commun Clb; hon/Awd for Superior Tchr, US Dependent Schs, Europe; Kiwanis Clb Grant; Albuquerque Spec Recog for Sers in Cultural Awareness; Certs for Vol Work w Var Orgs.

NELSON, ELIZABETH oc/Public Health Nurse; b/Jan 22, 1917; h/Roanoke, VA; m/Henry Clay Jr; c/Bonnie Eliabeth, Henry Clay III, Arthur Guthrie, Choon Wha Cho; p/Alonza Bernard (dec) and Bettie Nichols Guthrie (dec); ed/BS Tchrs Col, Columbia Univ 1946; Cert Public Hlth Nurse, Richmond Profl Inst 1942; RN Dip Emer Hosp Sch Nsg 1939; Att'd Wythville Commun Col 1975; pa/Adm Coor Child Devel Clin, Va St Hlth Dept; Va St Dept Hlth, Public Hlth Nurse Supvr Hlth Plan'g Dist; Instr OB, Roanoke Meml Hosp Sch Nsg; Supvr-Conslt, US Public Hlth Ser; Dir & Orgr Lunenburg Hlth Ser; Supvr Nurse, Instr Vis Nurse Assn; Staff Nurse Instr Vis Nurse Soc; ANA; VNA, Bd 1972-74, Pres Dist II 1972-74; NLN; VLN; Am Public Hlth Assn; So Br Va Public Hlth Assn; cp/Va Leag Planned Parenthood; Roanoke Val Leag Planned Parenthood; Roanoke Val Regional Hlth Sers Plan'g Coun; Leag Older Ams; Mtl Hlth Assn; AAUW; 4-H Clb Ldr; r/Presb; hon/Nance Vance Pin Awd, VNA 1980; Resolution & Lttr Commend'g Contbn Made in Devel'g SW Va Hlth Sys Agcy 1976; Outstg Nurse Awd, 5th Plan'g Dist 1974.

NELSON, GEORGE AGLE oc/Consulting Engineer; b/Mar 29, 1931; h/802 Springdale Rd, N Augusta, SC 29841; ba/Augusta, GA; m/Marcia Bailey; c/Jennifer, Eugene; p/Gordon V Sr and Myrtle A Nelson; ed/BSCE 1953, MS 1957 Kan St Univ; mil/USAF 1953-55 Capt; pa/ASCE, Pres SC Sect 1978; NSPE; ACEC; No Augusta Plan'g Comm, Chm 1972, 73; cp/Arts Adv Coun; No Augusta C of C; Repub Party; Mason; r/Luth; hon/Sigma Tau.

NELSON, LAWRENCE R oc/Division Chairman; b/Jan 13, 1931; h/Marianna, FL; m/Hazel Burns; c/Richard Alan, John Lawrence; p/Thomas J and Lucy Virginia Nelson, Mobile, AL; ed/AB Asbury Col 1957; MM Fla St Univ 1965; mil/AUS 1953-55; pa/Chm Div Fine Arts & Humanities, Chipola Jr Col 1960-81; Fla Mus Edrs Assn; Fla Assn

Commun Cols; cp/Secy Spanish Trail Fine Arts Coun Inc; r/Epis; hon/W/W SE; CART Residency Dir of Excell 1980; Adjudicator, Choral Contests in Fla, Ala, Ga; DIB.

NELSON, RALPH ERWIN oc/Land Planner, Executive; b/July 30, 1946; h/PO Box 8564, Bayshore Br, Bradenton, FL 33507; ba/Same; m/Elarie; c/Anne Marie; p/Vernon L and Astrid L Nelson; ed/BS McPherson Col; MA Cand Univ Sarasota; pa/Land Planner; Pres R E Nelson Inc, Plan'g & Arch Conslts; Am Inst Planners, Assoc Mem; Am Soc Plan'g Ofcls; cp/Repub Party; hon/W/W S&SW 1978-79, 80-81.

NELSON, RICHARD EARL oc/Retail Sales; b/May 21, 1928; h/808 W 10th St, Del Rio, TX 78840; ba/Del Rio; m/Dorothy Fuller; c/Deborah, Gayle, Ellen; p/George (dec) and Elsie Nelson, Steger, IL; pa/Owner, Mgr Kirby Co of Del Rio; Prin Pvt Sch; cp/Pres Antique Car Clb; AACA; Optimist; Repub Party; r/Meth; hon/Sev Awds for Antique Car Restoration.

NELSON, THOMAS DWIGHT oc/Director Information and Communications; b/Dec 24, 1945; h/1021 Louisville Rd, Frankfort, KY 40601; ba/Frankfort; c/Sean, Shane, Seth; p/Mary E Nelson, Springfield, MO; pa/Dir Info & Communs, Ky Dept Public Info; RTNDA; cp/Yng Dems; JCs; Big Brothers; Boy Scouts; r/Christian; hon/Am Legion Citizenship Awd; Broadcasting Man of Yr 1975.

NELSON, THOMAS HARRY oc/Life Insurance Salesman and Sales Manager; b/Jul 23, 1945; h/7407 Radcliffe Dr, Col Park, MD 20740; ba/Bladensburg, MD; m/Sandra Lorraine; c/Eric Anthony, Gwendolyn Renee, Thomas Harry, Valerie Nicole; p/Edward Joseph and Bernice Cecilia Nelson, Baltimore, MD; ed/Att'd: Univ Va, Inst of Mod Procedure Inc USMC 1968, Accounts Receivable Sch-IBM Corp 1970, Commun Col Baltimore 1971, Franklin Companies 1971-74; mil/USMC 1965-68; pa/Natl Assn Life Underwriters; Md Suburban Life Underwriters Assn; cp/Free & Accepted Masons of Md; r/Disciples of Christ; hon/Sev Biogl Listings; Many Mil Hons; Acad Hons; Outstg Ser Awd, Morning Star Lodge #14; Cert of Proficiency, Lodge of Instrn; Million Dollar Round Table, 2nd Full Yr in Bus; Natl Sales Achmt Awd; Natl Quality Awd; Num Co Hons Incl'g: Md St Volume Sales Ldr 1972, 73, 74, Life & Qualifying Mem Franklin Million Dollar Conf, Mem Franklin's Multi Million Dollar Faculty; Mid-Atl Reg: Outstg Salesman of Yr, Man of Yr 1974, Manager of Yr 1976; Mid-Potomac Agy: Star of Yr 1972, Man of Yr 1973, Manager of Yr 1974 & 76, Pyramid of Success Awd 1975 & 76; Contbr to *Life Insurance Selling* (July 1974); Fellow Mem ABI; Mem ABIRA.

NELSON, WESLEY JOSEPH oc/Librarian; b/Aug 13, 1935; h/Rt 3, Box 25D, Ferrum, VA 24088; ba/Ferrum; m/Annita Palmer; c/Deborah Ruth, Eugene Joseph, Michael Lee; ed/BA Beloit Col 1957; MTh SMU 1962; MLS Geo Peabody Col 1967; pa/Assoc Libn in Tech Sers, Ferrum Col, Ferrum 1970-; Catalog Libn, Div Lib, Jt Univ Libs, Nashville, Tenn 1966-70; Pastor: Monona Meth Ch, Monono, Wis 1963-66, Johnson Creek & Concord Meth Chs, Johnson Creek, Wis 1962-63; Lib Assns: Am, Va, Am Theol; AAUP; cp/Lions Clb; Credit Union; ARC; Mem, 1977 Secy/Treas Ferrum Vol Fire Dept; r/Meth Min.

NELSON, WILLIAM ROY oc/Audiologist; b/July 20, 1940; h/PSC Box 645, Ft Clayton, APO, Miami 34004; ba/APO Miami; m/Donna Toye MacPherson; c/Marnie, Roydon Bleak, William Aaron, Camron Blair; p/LeRoy Bleak Nelson (dec); Nola Lang Turner, Santa Ana, Calif; ed/BS 1966, MS 1972 Utah St Univ; Dip Electronystography Meth Hosp 1974; AMEDD Ofcrs Basic Course 1972, MFSS Ft Sam Houston; AMEDD Ofcrs Adv'd Course 1978; Hlth Care Adm Course, Acad Hlth Scis 1980; mil/USMCR 1963-69; AUS Med Ser Corps 1972-; pa/Audiologist, SEn Utah Commun Action Progs 1967-71; Chief Audiologist, Moncrief Army Hosp 1973-75; Conslt Pee Dee Speech Hearing Ctr 1973-74; Chief Audiometrics Br Bioacoustics Div AUS Aeromed Res Lab; Chief Audiologist USAMEDDAC, Panama, SA 1979-; Mil Audiology & Speech Path Soc; Soc Med Audiologist; Am Speech & Hearing Assn; Coun for Accreditation in Occupational Hearing Conservation, Cert'd Course Dir; cp/Wiregrass Coun; BSA; Panama Canal Zone Coun, Explorer Post Advr; r/Ch of Jesus Christ of Latter Day Saints; hon/Neurol & Sensoral Disease Ser Proj F'ship, HEW 1966-76; AUS TSGO Ad Hoc Com on Hearing Protectin; 2 Army Commend Medals for Merit Ser; Author 8 Books & Num Articles in Field of Profl Res.

NEMESH, ANNA oc/Personnel Officer; h/10304 Rockville Pike, #202, Rockville, MD 20852; ba/College Park, MD; p/Charles and Anna Nemesh, Vintondale, PA; ed/BS Penn St Univ; MEd, PhD Univ Md; pa/Dir TERP Ser & Pers Ofcr; Nat Bus Ed Assn; Intl Work Processing, Edrs Adv Coun; En Bus Ed Assn; Intl Soc Bus Ed; Pres Md Voc Assn; Past Pres Md Bus Ed Assn; Newslttr Editor Nat Assn Supvrs Bus Ed; Secy Phi Delta Kappa; Treas Col Park BPW Clb; Tchr Ed Task Force for Am Voc Assn; Exec Bd Md Voc Assn & Md Bus Ed Assn; Circuit Breaker Voc Ed in St of Md; Ex Bd Md Coun Ed; cp/Commun Enterprises Devel Assn; PG

Mtl Hlth Assn; Grosvenor Pk Clb; r/Russian Orthodox; hon/Annual Wilford White Small Bus Achmt 1976; Merit Ser & Ldrship Awd, Md Voc Assn 1979; MBEA Awd 1976; Co-Author 2 Yrbook Chapts for Nat Bus Ed Assn; Outstg Bus Edr 1978; Md Coun Ed Merit Ser Awd; Md St Future Bus Ldrs of Am Cert of Apprec 1977; Conslt: Nat Inst Hlth, SWn Pub'g Co, Stryer Col, Anne Arundel Co Bd Ed, Mid-Atlantic Placement Assn, Nat Housing Ctr; World W/W Wom; DIB.

NENTWICH, CARL ALBERT oc/Realtor; b/Jan 27, 1941; h/224 W Elmview, San Antonio, TX; ba/San Antonio; m/Carol Ann Cory; c/Cory Elizabeth, Cynthia Polk, Courtney Melissa; p/Arthur H (dec) and Thekla G Nentwich, San Antonio, TX; ed/BS, MBA Univ Tex-Austin; mil/USAR; pa/Pres Nentwich/Cory Rltrs Inc; Sr Residential Appraisal, Soc Real Est Appraisers: Past Treas, VP, Pres San Antonio Chapt 65; Residential Mem Am Inst Real Est Appraisers, Bd Dirs So Tex Chapt 29; Am Inst Real Est Appraisers: Nat Gov'g Coun 1974-75, Nat Public Relats Com 1975-76; San Antonio Bd Rltrs: Bd Dirs 1975-79, Treas 1976, 2nd VP 1977, 1st VP 1978, Pres 1979; Tex Assn Rltrs; Nat Assn Rltrs; Guest Lectr San Antonio Col & Univ Tex San Antonio; cp/Dir Gtr San Antonio C of C 1979; Dir Gtr San Antonio Bldrs Assn 1979; Dir San Antonio Ec Devel Foun Inc 1979; r/Epis; hon/Recip Profl Recog Awd, Am Inst Real Est Appraisers; Salesman of Yr, San Antonio Bd Rltrs 1969.

NESBITT, VANDA WHICKER oc/Teacher; b/May 29, 1917; h/Box 56, Mooresboro, NC 28114; ba/Same; m/Andrew W (dec); c/Philip Wincord, Wanda Kathryn, Patricia Anne; p/Pinckney E and Martha B Motsinger Whicker, Winston-Salem, NC; ed/BS; MA; pa/NEA; NCEA: Clrm Tchrs Assn; NCET; Kappa Kappa Iota; cp/Chm Plan'g & Zoning Com, Mooresboro; VChm Dem Precinct Cm; r/Bapt; hon/Star Tchr 1967; Outstg Ser 1959-79, Shelby HS.

NESS, JOHN HERBERT oc/Executive Secretary Commission on Archives and History, The United Methodist Church; b/Sept 29, 1919; h/29 Lakeshore Dr, Lake Junaluska, NC 28745; ba/Lake Junaluska; m/Naomi G; c/John Howard, Harry Albert, June Lucille; p/John Harrison Ness, Lebanon, OH; Myra Kiracofe Ness (dec); ed/AB; MDiv; MA; LHD; pa/Author ONE HUNDRED FIFTY YEARS (Hist of Pub'g in Evang U Brethren Ch); Exec Secy of World Meth Hist Soc; AASLH; cp/Waynesville (NC) Lodge #{59 AF&AM; En Star Chapt #☆65 (Waynesville); r/Ordained Clergy (Ctl Penna Conf, U Meth Ch); hon/Recip St George's Gold Medal Awd (St George's Ch Phila); Life Mem Balto Conf Hist Soc (UM Ch); U Meth Assn of Communicators.

NESTER, RUEL PAULLUS oc/Extension Agronomist; b/July 8, 1921; h/3808 Moreland, Little Rock, AR 72212; ba/Little Rock; m/Norma E; c/Paul Ruel; p/William Henry (dec) and Madge Isabel Nester (dec); ed/BS Univ 1953, MS 1954 Univ Ark; mil/1980-; pa/Ext Agronomist, Univ Ark Coop Ext Ser 1958-; Epsilon Sigma Phi; Am Soc Agric; AAPA; Alpha Zeta Farm House; Am Soybean Assn; Ark Agric Pesticide Assn, Pres 1937-74, Secy 6 Yrs; Secy Ark Seed Coun; Ark Soybean Assn; r/Cath; hon/Outstg Sers Recog, Ark Soybean Assn 1974; Cit, Ark Agric Pesticide Assn 1978; John White Awd 1978-79.

NETTLES, BARRY D oc/Assistant Superintendent; b/Jan 28, 1932; h/1706 Amy, Baytown, TX 77520; ba/Baytown; m/Lyla; c/Larry, Tanya, Barfield; ed/BS Univ Tex; MEd Univ Houston; pa/Asst Supt Schs; Pres Tex Assn Sch Pers Admrs; r/Presb.

NEUMANN, IDABELLE MARIE oc/Homemaker, Medical Technician; b/Apr 22, 1921; m/John E Sr; c/Theodore Henry, Kathryn N Spinniken, William T, John E Jr, Mary and Martha; p/Theodore H (dec) and Ida Hessell Nischwitz (dec); ed/Grad Gradwohl Sch of Lab & X-Ray Technique; pa/Med Tech Evansville, Ind & Granite City, Ill; cp/Province Dir Nat Coun Cath Wom's Exec Bd Dirs; Coor Sch Rel, Holy Cross Cath Ch; Lector Holy Cross Cath Ch; Paris Country Clb, Pres Bd Dirs 1978-; Poetry Chm Janusette Delphain Clb 1976-78; Pres Memphis Diocesan Coun Cath Wom 1974-76; r/Cath; hon/Mother of Yr, Paris-Henry Co, Tenn 1979; Finalist Tenn Mother of Yr 1979; Won Asa Giles Meml Sr Golf Tourn, Paris Country Clb 1978; First Pres Jackson Deanery Coun of Cath Wom 1974; Cath Wom of Tenn 1972; Wom's Golf Champ 1969.

NEW, DEANNA JANE MARBLE oc/Teacher, Artist; b/Aug 31, 1943; h/Star Rt Box 26, Ovalo, TX 79541; m/Donald Ray; c/Roland, Kalyn, Stacey, Jason; p/Daniel F and Pearleen M Antes, Las Cruces, NM; ed/BS NM St Univ 1965; MEd Hardin Simmons Univ 1978; pa/Tchr Art, Mus; Kappa Delta Pi; Tex Profl Edrs; cp/Adv Com BSA; r/So Bapt; hon/W/W Am Cols 1965; Pres Sr Wom's Hon Soc (Mortar Bd) 1965; Awd Grad Asst'ship 1977-78; Chi Omega; Outstg Artist Awd 1961.

NEW, MICHAEL W oc/Sales and Service Representative; b/Sept 21, 1951; h/31 Shady Ln, Conway, AR 72032; ba/Conway; m/Patricia Jane Stoltz; p/Otis W and Margie New, Conway, AR; ed/BSE Univ Ctrl Ark; mil/USAR 1st Lt; pa/Sales-Ser Rep, Polyvend Inc; r/Bapt.

PERSONALITIES OF THE SOUTH

NEWBERN, CAPTOLIA DENT oc/Professor of Social Work and Director of Undergraduate Social Work Education, Lincoln Memorial University (Harrogate, TN); b/Sept 22, 1902; h/5833 Cobbs Creek Pkwy, Philadelphia, PA 19143; ba/Harrogate, TN; m/Samuel H (dec); ed/BS cum laude Paine Col 1925; BMus 1937 Talladega Col; MSSW 1942, EdD 1954 Columbia Univ; Att'd: Univ Penn, U Theol Sem, Hampton Inst, NWn Univ, Case Wn Resv Univ; Faculty Intern at US Dept HEW in Atlanta; pa/Former Tchg Positions: Lane Col, Lambuth Col, Paine Col, Talladega Col, Howard Univ, Albany St Col; Pres of Harragate Br of Am Assn Univ Wom & Chaplaincy of Lincoln Meml Univ Lincoln Dames; Columbia Univ Acad Sci; Rel Ed Assn; Am Security Coun's Natl Adv Bd; Middlesboro (Ky) BPW Clb; Intl Platform Assn; Sev Social Welfare Orgs; cp/Life Mem NAACP; r/Mother CME Ch, Mem of Sev Orgs; White Meml AMEZ Ch: Lay Asst to Min, Dir Ch Music, Pianist, Trustee, Deaconness, Dir Christian Ed, Mem; hon/Num Awds incl'g Cit from US War Dept for Outstg Ser as 1st Negro Wom Appt'd Employee Coun at Pentagon, Columbia Univ Tchrs Col Highlight Hon; Num Biogl Listings; Fellow Mem ABI.

NEWMAN, BILL N oc/Oil Company President; b/May 28, 1918; h/7211 Aberdeen, Dallas, TX 75230; ba/Dallas; m/Marjorie Ann; c/Catherine Ann; p/George O and Carolyn Newman (dec); ed/BBA So Meth Univ; mil/AUS, Pvt to Maj; 4 European Campaigns WWII; pa/Pres: Newman Properties Corp, Leasebankers Inc; cp/C of C; 4-H Clb Co Chm; r/Congreg; hon/Pub'd Author; W/W Fin & Indust.

NEWMAN, BOBBIE SUE oc/Assistant Vice President; b/Sept 12, 1933; h/352 Third St, Henderson, TN 38340; ba/Henderson; p/Algie U Toss (dec) and Tracy Holloway Newman, Henderson, TN; pa/Asst VP, First St Bank; Nat Assn Bank Wom; Pres Tenn Fed BPW Clbs; cp/Chm Cerebral Palsy Drive for Chester Co; r/Ch of Christ; hon/Wom of Achmt 1973, Henderson BPW Clb.

NEWMAN, CLINTON HARLIN II oc/Assistant Secretary of State (Kentucky); b/Apr 5, 1942; h/Rt 4 Box 427, Versailles, KY 40383; ba/Frankfort, KY; m/Linda Emrick; c/Clinton Harlin III; p/C H and Gladys Ford Newman, Versailles, KY; ed/BS; MBA; JD; pa/Former Asst St Treas (Ky); r/Presb; hon/Outstg Yg Man; W/W St Govt; W/W Am Law.

NEWMAN, JAMES SAMUEL oc/Chemical Engineer; b/Sept 25, 1922; h/410 Glover St, Hendersonville, NC 28739; ba/H'ville; m/Sarah Kate; c/Jerry F, Jama Ruth Johnston; p/Sim O and Lola A Newman, Seymour, TN; ed/BS Univ Tenn 1951; mil/AUS 1942-46 & 1950-51; pa/Engr, Belding Heminway Co 1951–; AIChE; ACS; AATCC; cp/VFW; Past Cmdr Am Legion; Vol Fireman; Former Mem Henderson Co Rescue Squad; Henderson Co Coor of Civil Preparedness 8 Yrs; Past Mason; Ser'd on Ed Com, ACS Local Chapt; Ser'd on Pres' Adv Com of US Civil Defense Agy; Woodman of World Ins Frat; r/Bapt; hon/Man of Yr, Henderson Co Commun Devel 1975; CD Commend; Cert of Apprec, US Dept of Agri; W/W S&SW; DIB.

NEWMAN, WILLIE B oc/Student; b/Dec 10, 1954; h/1609 Peach Ave, Sanford, FL; ba/New Orleans, LA; p/Willie (dec) and Ethel Mae Newman, Sanford, FL; ed/BS Fla St Univ 1976; MD Tulane Med Sch 1980; pa/Medicine; AMA; SAMA; AMSA; Kappa Alpha Psi; cp/Big Brothers of Gtr New Orleans; r/Bapt; hon/Alpha Omega Alpha 1979; Outstg Yng Men Am 1979; Ciba Awd, Tulane Med Sch 1978; Martin Marietta S'ship 1972.

NEWTON, ELEANOR RUNELL oc/Dollmaker, Antique Dealer; b/Jan 28, 1935; h/Rt 2, Angier, NC 27501; ba/Lillington, NC; m/Grady S; c/Loretta N Pleasant, Trent; p/Walter and Christine H Norris, Angier, NC; pa/Doll Artisan Guild; r/Bapt; hon/Doll Doctor, Lifetime Career Sch.

NEWTON, LILLIAN HINSON oc/Technical Writer; b/Apr 17, 1921; h/Box 189, Dahlgren, VA 22448; ba/Dahlgren; m/John Norton (dec); c/Norton Byrd, Wanda N Atkins; p/George Washington and Mary Marks Hinson, Templemans, VA; ed/Att'd Am Univ; Charles Co Commun Col; Rappahannock Commun Col; pa/Naval Weapons Surface Ctr 1946-76: Math Tech, Computer Sys Analyst, Prog Analyst, Fed Wom's Prog Coor; Mgr, Profl Mgmt Sers, Fredericksburg; Engrg Writer, Sperry UNIVAC; cp/Past Pres King George & Potomac PTA; Past Pres Dahlgren Toastmasters Clb; Dahlgren Garden Clb; Dahlgren Home Demo Clb; Oakland & Potomac Bapt Ch Missionary Soc; Past VChm King George Plan'g Comm; Chm King George Bd Zoning Appeals; Chm King George Med Sers, King George C of C; r/Bapt.

NEWTON, WILLMA HUMPHREYS oc/Professional Genealogist and Semi-Retired Land Title Abstracter; b/Nov 2, 1908; h/PO Box 41, Hampton, AR 71744; ba/Same; c/William Fletcher Humphreys II; p/William Fletcher and Nellie Pledwell Himler Humphreys (dec); ed/AA

Stephens Col (Columbia, Mo); pa/Mem: Ark, Ky, & Randolph Co NC Geneal Socs; Author Geneal Articles; Columnist; DAR; cp/Co Com-wom, Calhoun Co, Ark; r/Christian Scist; hon/Plaque From Pres FDR For Giving Birthday Ball; Plaque Dist'd Ser Ark Gen Soc 1973; Var Other Awds.

NGUYEN, HUU DINH oc/Social Worker; b/Jul 1, 1930; h/1239 Shadowfox Dr, San Jose, CA 95121; m/Lien-Anh Tran; c/Huyen, Thuhuong, Hung, Lienhanh, Lienhao, Huan, Huy, Lienhoang; ed/Licencie es Lettres, Univ of Saigon; Master of Social Work, Univ of Ala; mil/Former Col, Mil Attache, Embassy of Republic of Vietnam in Thailand; pa/Social Worker III, Dept of Pensions & Security (B'ham); Nat Assn Social Workers; Ala Assn of Clin Social Workers; cp/Social Com, ARC of B'ham; hon/Vietnam Mil & Civilian Medals; French Croix de Guerre; Hon Lt/Col, Ala St Militia.

NICELY, GARY L oc/Assistant Cashier-Loan Officer; b/Nov 2, 1947; h/792 Jarvis Ave, Somerset, KY 42501; ba/Somerset; m/Helen; c/Angela Dawn; p/Walter Junior (dec); Anna Mae Nicely, Somerset, KY; ed/Am Inst Bnkg 1980; pa/Asst Cashier-Loan Ofcr, Mortgage Loan Processor, Student Loans, First & Farmers Nat Bank; pa/Am Inst Bnkg; Ky St Notary Public; cp/Woodstock Masonic Lodge #639 F & AM, Secy & Past Master; Oleika Shrine Temple; 32° Mason, Woodstock Chapt OES #521, Past Worthy Patron; Grand Chapt OES of Ky, Past Dist Dpty Grand Patron; r/First Bapt Ch: Chm Deacons, Ch Treas, SS Div Dir; hon/Cert of Apprec, C of C 1980; Ky St Farmers Deg 1965.

NICELEY, GILLON TRUETT oc/Farmer, Home Furnishings Dealer; b/June 5, 1923; m/Mary Ellen Oyer; c/Gillon T Jr, Richard Curtis Dyer, Nelle Kyer; p/Trailing Arbutus Niceley, Louisville, KY; ed/Att'd Union Univ 1939-40, Mercer Univ 1940-41, Union Col 1941-42; mil/USAF 1942-45; cp/Kosias Shrine Clb; Riasok Shrine Clb; r/Bapt; hon/Kiwanis Clb Intl Awd; Key to My Old Ky Home; Ky Col.

NICHOLS, AUBREY NORWOOD III oc/Ophthalmologist; b/June 17, 1950; ba/PO Box 220, 143 Howard St, Centreville, MS 39631; m/Gewndolyn G; c/Richmond Gordon, Todd Applewhite; p/Mr and Mrs A N Nichols Jr, Benton, MS; ed/BS Miss Col 1972; MD Univ Miss Sch Med 1976; Intern Bapt Meml Hosp, Memphis, Tenn 1976-77; Residency Univ Miss Sch Med 1977-80; pa/Pvt Pract Ophthalmologist; AMA; Am Assn Ophthalmology, Am Intra Ocular Lens Soc, Miss Eye, Ear, Nose & Throat Assn; Miss Med Frat & Ednl Soc; r/Bapt; hon/Balfour Awd 1968; Pres Alpha Epsilon Delta 1972; Bailey Biology Awd 1972; Hon Awd for Excell in Undergrad Study of Ophthalmology 1976.

NICHOLS, CHRISTINE LYNN McCURDY oc/Consultant; b/Sept 6, 1948; h/Christiansburg, VA; ba/Risk Services Inc, 519 Second St, Radford, VA 24141; m/Jeffrey Morris; c/Eric Douglas, Amy Christine; p/Malcolm L and Jean S McCurdy, Roswell, NM; pa/Risk Mgmt & Ins Conslt; Profl Ins Agts of Va/DC; hon/Cert'd Ins Cnslr 1980.

NICHOLS, GREGORY D oc/Composer, Pianist, Arranger; b/Sept 13, 1956; h/1603 Laurel St, Texarkana, AR 75501; p/Robert Nichols, Detroit, MI; Mattie Dawson, Texarkana, AR; ed/Schoolcraft Col 1977-78; Julliard Sch Mus 1978-79; Texarkana Col 1979–; pa/Musician, Have Worked w Barry Manilow, Aretha Franklin, Other Celebrities; Writing Mus for Movie "The Battle of Golialid"; Hired to Write Broadway Musical "Musical"; Pres Detroit Perf'g Arts Co 1976-77; VP Rejoursiance Ensemble 1978-79; r/African Meth; hon/Num S'ships; Samuel Barber Composition Awd "Music for Lisa Hackney" 1979.

NICHOLS, J HUGH oc/Assistant Secretary, Department of Budget & Fiscal Planning (State of Maryland); b/Nov 27, 1930; h/6117 Sebring Dr, Columbia, MD; ba/Annapolis, MD; m/Sue; c/Duane, Sharon, Hugh, Jonathan; p/J Gordon and Roberta Nichols, Tarrant, AL; ed/AB Univ Ala; MA The Am Univ; mil/AUS Signal Corps 1948-54; pa/AAAS; cp/Former Mem: Howard Co Coun, Md Ho Dels; r/Meth; hon/Phi Beta Kappa.

NICHOLS, JAMES DON (JIM) oc/Director; b/May 13, 1941; h/108 Choctaw Dr, Searcy, AR 72143; m/Edna; c/Chris, Holly, Jim Mark; p/Nishia Nichols, Hampton, AR; ed/BSE So Ark Univ 1966; MEd Auburn Univ 1970; Doctl Cand, Univ of Ark; mil/USN; pa/Dir of Pers Sers & Asst Prof of Ed, Harding Univ; Bd Mem SWn Region, Col & Univ Pers Assn; Bd Mem, N Ctl Ark Pers Assn; Bd Mem, Ark Elem Prin Assn; cp/Bd Mem, Ark Cancer Soc; r/Ch of Christ.

NICHOLS, MARGUERITE M oc/Teacher-Librarian; b/June 26, 1914; h/2005 E Ctrl St, Bentonville, AR 72712; ba/B'ville; c/Clyde Nichols Grace; p/Charles Nellens (dec); Florence Harris (dec); ed/MLS Univ Okla; pa/Am Lib Assn; Ark Lib Assn; AAUW, St Pres; cp/Lanbach Lit Affil, St Pres; r/Epis; hon/Gov Comm on Status of Wom, Del IWY, Mexico City.

NICHOLS, SARAH LETHA oc/Portrait Artist, Teacher; b/Mar 10, 1914; m/Earl O (dec); c/Gary Phillips; p/Elmer Lee (dec) and Florence N Holland Phillips, Broken Arrow, OK; ed/Att'd NEn St 1931-33; Okla St Univ 1940-42; Tulsa Univ; pa/Portrait Artist; Tchr; Spec Progs; TJC Guest Artist; Past Pres Alpha Rho Tau Art Clb; Past VP Tulsa Artists Guild; St Art Chm Nat Leag Am Pen Wom 1980-82; r/Prot; hon/Grand Prize for Pastel Portrait, Mutual of NY; Sev Awds in Juried Shows; NLAPW: St Show Awd 1977, Nat Show 1978, St Show Awd Pastel 1979; St Show Awd Sculpture 1979.

NICHOLSON, RICHARD SELINDH oc/Director, Chemistry Division, National Science Foundation; b/Apr 5, 1938; h/9031 Brook Ford Rd, Burke, VA 22015; ba/Wash DC; m/Lois Ann; c/Jeffrey, Gregory; p/Gene Nicholson (dec); Margaret Nicholson, Des Moines, IA; ed/BS, PhD Univ of Wis; mil/USN; p/AAAS; Am Chem Soc (Chm Local Sect); r/Prot; hon/Pub'd Author; Eastman Kodak Awd ($1,000); Govt Meritorious Serv Awd.

NICOLA, SANDRA ANN oc/State Art Education Consultant, Mississippi State Department of Education; b/Aug 10, 1943; h/4740 Chastain Dr, Jackson, MS 39206; ba/Jackson; p/Wadie and Latifie Nicola, Vicksburg, MS; ed/MEd 1975, BSE 1968 Delta St Univ; Addit Studies; pa/Art Ed Conslt, Miss St Dept Ed; Defined Perimeters of Positions as 1st Art Conslt; Conduct On-Going Tchr Cert Needs Assessmts in Arts Ed; Assist in Title IV-C Arts Projs; Conduct Wkshops on Arts & Serve on Adv Bd of St Special Arts Fair for Handicapped; Art Instr: Warren Central HS 1970-75, Madison Parish HS 1974, YMCA 1974, Adult Ed Classes 1972-74, Meridian HS 1970, Kate Griffin Jr HS 1968-70; Pt-time Fashion Coor 1970-75; Nat Art Ed Assn; Nat Assn St Dirs Art Ed; Nat Ed Assn; Miss Assn Sch Admr; Miss Art Ed Assn (Secy-Treas 1972-74); Miss Scholastic Art Awd Adv Bd; Miss Ed Assn; Miss Art Assn; Miss Alliances Art Ed (St Dept Ed Rep 1976-); Miss Theatre Assn (Secy 1974-75); SEn Theatre Assn; Vicksburg Theatre Guild (St Del 1973-75, VP 1974-75); Meridian Art Assn; Vicksburg Art Assn; Delta St Univ Alumni Assn; AAUW; Miss Museum Art Ed Coun 1978; Miss Lung Assn Christmas Seal Art Proj Chm 1978; SWn Reg Art & Crafts Dir; Judge Statewide Art Contest; Num Guests Lectures; r/En Orthodox Cath; hon/Alpha Sigma Phi; Beta Sigma Phi; Num Art Exhbns; Var 1st, 2nd, 3rd & Hon Mention Awds; Tupelo Ceramic Guild 2nd Place 1964; Outstg Yg Wom of Am 1975; Num Pubs & Media Resources.

NIEMEYER, JANICE MARIE oc/Social Worker; b/July 1, 1933; h/510 W 26th St, Austin, TX 78705; ba/Austin; p/Louis Frederick and Loretta Halloran Niemeyer (dec); ed/BA; MSW; pa/Lic'd Social Wkr: Calif, Ill, La; cp/Bds of Hosps, Cols, Neighborhood Orgs; r/Rom Cath; hon/W/W Am Wom; Num Local Hons.

NIEMIEC, JEROME PETER oc/Finance; b/July 4, 1941; h/2571 Elizabeth, Fayetteville, AR 72701; ba/Fayetteville; m/Janice; c/Jurie, Julie; p/James (dec) and Marie Niemiec (dec); ed/BS Ill Inst Technol; MBA Univ Chgo; mil/USAR 6 Yrs; r/Prot.

NIES, ROBERT JOHN JR oc/Financial Planner; b/Jan 25, 1943; h/1300 52nd Ave NE, St Petersburg, FL 33703; ba/St Petersburg; m/Cheryl C Carter; c/Brian Robert, Gregory Robert, Carter Robert, Jacqueline Mae; p/Robert J Nies Sr, St Petersburg, FL; Eula Mae Markert (dec); ed/Univ Pgh 1960-68; Cert Fin Planner Col for Financial Plan'g 1976-79; pa/Pres Nies Fin Sys Inc 1974-; First Investors Corp; Reg'd Rep 1968, Sys Mgr 1969, Br Mgr 1970-71, Regional Mgr 1971-72, Asst VP 1972-74; Adj Fac, Col for Fin Plan'g; Intl Assn Fin Planners, Sales & Mktg Exec of St Petersburg, Dir; St Petersburg Stock & Bond Clb, VP & Dir; Intl Platform Assn; Nat Assn Securities Dlrs; cp/C of C; Com of 100; St Petersburg Yacht Clb; r/Epis; hon/2nd Highest Grade Pt Average Class 1977, Col Fin Plan'g; Num Fin Plan'g Articles.

NILL, CARL JONATHAN oc/Publisher; b/Sept 7, 1938; h/7540; Hollyridge Rd, Jacksonville, FL 32216; ba/J'ville; m/Suzanne J; c/Kevin Jonathan; p/Carl M and Winifred L Nill, Mandarin, FL; ed/Att'd Wheaton Col 1957-78; Grad Am Inst Bnkg 1964; pa/Ptnr & Sr VP Homes & Land Pub Co 1974-; Commercial & Real Est Loan Ofcr 1972-73; cp/Sertoma Clb; Deerwood Clb; Univ Clb; Ponte Vedra Clb; Jax Chrisitan Men's Clb; r/Bapt; hon/W/W S&SW 1980; TV-Radio-Civic Clb Tenor Soloist & Recording Artist; Crusade Soloist in Seoul, Korea 1980.

NILSSON, BARBARA oc/Bank Executive; b/Apr 29, 1942; m/Weldon H; c/Gregory; pa/Asst VP, Commercial Lending Ofcr, Victoria Bank & Trust 1978-; FIRA & CRA Compliance Ofcr 1979-; Secy Trinity Epis Ch 1968-69; Secy, Psych Testing, Gulf Bend Ctr 1965-66; Secy to VP Tex Tan 1962-65; Nat Assn Bank Wom 1975-, Adv Bd, Chm Nom'g Com 1981; cp/C of C: Mbrship Com 1976-77, Ed Com 1978, City Co

Affairs Com 1979, VChm City Co Affairs 1980, Chm City Co Affairs 1981, Bd Dirs 1981, Chm Budget Com 1981, VIP Clb 1981; VP & Treas 1981; U Way: Bd Dirs 1976, VChm Bd 1977, Asst Campaign Chm 1978, Campaign Chm 1979, Pres Bd 1980, Chm Pers Com 1981, Chm Com to Find New Dir 1981, Co-Chm Area-Wide Com 1981; Tex U Way-St Bd; Victoria Boys' Clb, Bd Dirs 1979-; r/Luth; hon/Outstg Profl & Bus Wom Victoria 1981.

NIVER, PRUELLA CROMARTIE oc/Instructor; b/Dec 4, 1924; h/1271 Burtwood Dr, Ft Myers, FL 33901; ba/Ft Myers; c/Peddy Niver Mayhurst; p/Esten Graham (dec) and Mary Lee Jones Cromartie; ed/Grad Ga So Col 1944; Grad Work, Ga So 1947-48, Ala Polytech Inst 1948, Fla St Univ, Univ Miami, Univ Fla, Univ S Fla, Fla Atlantic Univ; mil/Civil Ser 1944-45; pa/Instr Mus Lee Co Schs; Tchr Bus Career Maths; Guest Dir Ft Myers Symph Chorus; Dir Commun Chorus; Mus Conslt Local Theatre Grps; Guest on TV & Radio; Soloist Singers Clb 1954-57; Mus Edrs Nat Conf; Fla Mus Edrs Assn; Am Choral Dirs Assn; Fla Vocal Assn, Past Coor St Bd; Charter Mem Lee Co Alliance of Arts; Nat Assn Tchrs of Singing in Am & Can; Gal Assocs, Edison Commun Col; Lee Co Dance Coun; Ft Myers Commun Concerts Assn; SW Fla Symph & Chorus Assn; Ft Myers Hist Mus; cp/Beta Sigma Phi; Bd Commun Concerts Assn; Lee Co Chapt Ringling Mus; r/Meth; hon/W/W Am Cols & Univs 1944; Appt'd by St Dept of Ed of Fla as Mem Sec'dy Mus Instrl Mats Coun 1978-80; Fla Vocal Assn Mus Spec for Vocal Solo Lit for St Fla 1978-79.

NIX, GORDON HILLIARY oc/Consultant; b/Nov 16, 1938; h/1094 Warrenhall Ln, Atlanta, GA 30319; ba/Atlanta; m/Marjorie Scruggs; c/Karen, Jennifer, David, Russell Scruggs, Randall Scruggs; p/Norman (dec) and Ruby Nix, Greenville, AL; ed/BSME; MSME; PhD Auburn Univ; pa/ASME; APCA; TAPPI; MFPG; INCE; cp/Dir OESC; r/Presb; hon/Fball S'ship 1957-62; NASA S'ship 1964-66.

NIX, JAMES CARROLL oc/Supervisor; b/July 2; h/707 S 7th Ave, Laurel, MS 39440; ba/Laurel, MS; c/Gregory, John, Vernon, Lee Carlton; p/Willie James Nix, Luarel, MS; Emma L Nix, Laurel, MS; mil/AUS 12 Yrs; pa/Supvr Tank Dept, Howard Industs, Supvr Bldrs of Distbr Transformers; cp/Dir Yth Choir; r/Bapt; hon/Good Conduct Medal; German Occupation Medal; Nat Defense Medal.

NOAH, SHIRLEY JEAN oc/Nursing Service Administrator; b/May 15, 1941; h/Rt 1 Windswept Subdivision, Lancaster, KY 40444; ba/Lancaster; m/Kenneth Eugene; c/Jeffrey; p/Powell James (dec) and Ida Marie Ellis, Mullens, WV; ed/BS Stephens Col 1975; RN St Mary's Sch Nsg 1962; pa/Nsg Ser Admr, Garrard Co Meml Hosp; NLN; KLN; Ky Soc Hosp Nsg Ser Admrs; cp/Cert'd Instr Am Heart Assn CPR; Ky Cancer Soc; hon/Ky Col 1975.

NOBLE, FRANCES ELIZABETH oc/Teacher; b/Sept 3, 1903; h/2915 NE Center Ave, Ft Lauderdale, FL 33308; ba/Same; p/George W (dec) and Clara Lane Noble (dec); ed/BA; MA; PhD; pa/French Tchr Kalamazoo & Ft Lauderdale; 43 Yrs Prof Wn Mich Univ; cp/Repub Party; r/Presb; hon/Grad cum laude; Palmes Academiques.

NOBLES, WILLIAM LEWIS oc/President of Mississippi College; b/Sept 11, 1925; h/PO Box 4186, Clinton, MS 39058; ba/Same; m/Joy Ford; c/Sandra Nash (Mrs Ben), Suzanne (dec); p/J S Nobles (dec); Ruby Rae Roper Nobles, Clinton, MS; ed/BS & MS Univ Miss; PhD Univ Ks 1952; Postdoct Study Univ Mich 1958-59; mil/Active Resv Duty in USN as Comm'd Ensign 1944-46; pa/Pres Miss Col 1968-; Sigma Xi; Rho Chi; Am Pharm Assn; Am Chem Soc; Chem Soc (Gt Brit); AAAS; NY Acad Sci; Kappa Psi; Com on Patent Policy of Acad of Pharm Scis of Am Pharm Assn; IPA; cp/Bd Trustees Clinton Sep Sch Dist; Lions Clb; Rotary Clb; BSA; r/1st Bapt Ch, Oxford, Miss & Clinton, Miss: Deacon; Bd Trustees New Orleans Bapt Theol Sem; hon/Biogl Listings; Pub'd Author; Am Pharm Assn Foun Awd 1966; Nat Rho Chi Awd, Montreal, Canada 1969; Am Foun for Pharm Ed Fellow 1949-52; Gustavas A Pfeiffer Meml Res Fellow 1955-58, 59-60; NSF Postdoct Fellow 1958-59.

NOBLIN, JAMES E oc/State Senator; b/Jan 24, 1937; h/2222 Wild Valley, Jackson, MS 39211; ba/Jackson; m/Camelia; c/David, Dawn, Jeff; p/Earl Noblin (dec); Ivadell Noblin, Forest, MS; ed/MS; MBA; pa/Chm, Ctl Data Processing Auth; Comm of Budget & Accounting; Natl Coun of St Legs Energy Task Force; Senate Approp Sub-Com on Conserv & Ed; Exec Contingency Expense, Ed, Highways Coms; r/Meth.

NOKES, GEORGIA WOODRUFF oc/Assistant Professor; b/Dec 31, 1949; h/Jonesboro, AR; ba/Col of Nursing, PO Drawer E, State Univ, AR 72467; m/Charles; c/Rusty, Morgan Marie, Adam; p/George and Dorothy Woodruff, Searcy, AR; ed/BSN Harding Col 1977; MNSc Univ Ark Med Sch 1981; PhD Univ Tex; pa/Asst Prof Nsg, Ark St Univ; Asst Dir Nsg Forest View Convalescent Manor; Critical Care Staff Nurse; ANA; ASNA; cp/AAUW; r/Ch of Christ; hon/Author "The Relationship Between Decision-Making Opportunities and Stress Levels in Hospitalized Patients."

NOLAN, OLLIE JEAN oc/Assistant Professor, Athletic Director; b/Sept 12, 1944; h/398 W Outer Dr, Oak Ridge, TN 37830; ba/Bluefield, VA; p/Zollie B and Viola M Nolan, Oak Ridge, TN; ed/BS 1972, MS 1973 Univ Tenn; pa/Demo Tchr Pediatric Lang Clin, Univ Tenn 1973-76; Sub Tchr Oak Ridge, Tenn Public Schs 1977-79; Asst Prof Hlth & Phy Ed, Wom's Ath Dir, Volleyball & Basketball Coach, Bluefield Col 1979-; TEA; NEA; Coun Exceptl Chd; AAHPER; So Assn HPER; VAIAW/AIAW; cp/Red Cross, Standard First Aid Instr & WSI; r/Presb; hon/Selected to Study Swedish Fitness & Hlth Care, Concordia Univ 1980; Outstg Yng Wom Am 1980; Author Sev Profl Articles.

NOLAND, PATRICIA HAMPTON oc/Writer; h/2400 Westheimer, Apt 215W, Houston, TX 77098; ba/Houston; p/L Maxwell and Clara Hampton Noland (dec); ed/Hon Doct for Ldrship in Poetry from Intl Acad of Ldrship (Quezon City, Philippines) 1969; Hon DHL L'Universite Libre d'Asie (Karachi, Pakistan) 1973; pa/The Intl Poetry Inst: Fdr, Pres; cp/Mem Ctl Arts Coun of Houston, Tex; r/1st Ch of Christ, Scientist (Boston, Mass & Houston, Tex): Mem; hon/Hon Intl Poet Laureate (U Poets Laureate Intl, Manilla, Philippines 1969); Var Lit Prizes.

NORMAN, RITA KAY oc/Nurse; b/Mar 13, 1946; h/PO Box 68, Bartlett, TX 76511; ba/Taylor, Tx; p/Erwin and Angeline Spinn, Holland, TX; ed/BS; MS; pa/Public Sch Nurse; Pres Taylor Unit Tex St Tchrs Assn; Leg Chm St Sch Hlth Assn for Nurses, Past St Pres; Exec Bd Dist 7 Tex Nurses Assn; Williamson Co Child Welfare Bd; Am Sch Hlth Assn; Exec Com Tex Sch Hlth Assn; ANA; TNA; NEA; Nat Assn Sch Nurses; cp/Dem Party; Chm & VChm Williamson Co Edrs Polit Action Com; Campaign Chm 1978-79 Williamson Co Edrs for Dem John Hill for Gov Tex; Bd Dirs & Ed Chm E Williamson Co Am Cancer Soc; PTA; r/Cath; hon/Awd from Dist VI Sch Nurse of St Sch Hlth Assn for Outstg Leg Efforts for Profl Nsg; Cert Tex Nurses Assn for Accumulating 100+ Cont'g Ed Pts 1976-78; Awd on Tex Nurses Day, Local Sch Dist, for Outstg Commun Hlth Ser.

NORMAN, RONALD LEE oc/Minister, College Administrator; b/Oct 28, 1957; h/Columbia, TN; m/Martha Goodall; p/Clarence and Virginia Norman, Columbia, TN; ed/BA Freed Hardeman Col 1979; pa/CASE; r/Ch of Christ; hon/Outstg Yng Men Am 1979, 80; W/W Am Univs 1979; Mr Freed Hardeman Col 1979.

NORMAN, ROSE LYNN oc/Technical Editor; b/Sept 30, 1949; m/Malcolm Richardson II; p/Ralph Reynard Jr and Iris Little Norman, Deposit, AL; ed/BA Judson Col 1970; MA Univ Ala 1972; PhD Univ Tenn 1979; pa/Editor, Dept Oceanography, Tex A&M Univ; Tchr, Dept Eng, Tex A&M Univ; Tech Editor, No Guild of Mex Topographic Features Study; Assn Tchrs of Tech Writing; Intl Assn Bus Communrs, Brazos Val Chapt Treas; MLA; SAMLA; SCMLA; cp/AAUW, Com Chm Chd's Movie Classics Series, VP in Charge Progs 1980-81; Arts Coun Brazos Co 1979-; Brazos Civil Liberties Union , Publicity Coor 1978-79, 81, VP 1979-81, Art & Craft Auction Coor 1980; King's English String Band, Pennywhistler 1979-; Stage Ctr, Bd Mem 1979-, Asst Dir *Richard III* 1980; Prod *Passion for Dracula* 1980; hon/Hodges Awd for Excell in Tchg, Univ Tenn 1976; Phi Kappa Phi 1977; Univ F'ship Univ Ala 1970-71; Hons Prog, Judson Col 1969-70; Jane Jewett Hon Soc 1969-70; Chi Delta Phi; Pi Delta Phi.

NORMAN, WALLACE oc/Executive; b/Feb 5, 1926; h/PO Box 208, Houston, MS 38851; m/Maurene C; c/Wallace Jr, Karen Jean, Emily June, Lauren Beth, John C; p/Leland F (dec) and Lucile B Norman, Houston, MS; ed/Att'd E Ctrl Jr Col 1942, Univ Miss 1946, Milsaps Col 1946; BS Okla City Univ 1948; mil/USNR WWII; pa/Owner Wallace Norman Ins Agcy 1949-; Pres Norman Oil Col 1956-; Pres Nat Leasing Co 1969-; Pres US Plastic Inc 1969-; Pres Calhoun Nat Co Inc 1974-; Pres Norman Trucking Co 1975-; Chm Running Bear Dist Boy Scouts 1971-73; Miss Assn of Ins Agts; Miss Mfrs Assn; Am Waterworks Assn; DAV; VFW; Am Legion; Exch Clb; r/Meth.

NORTH, MICHAEL R oc/Real Estate Sales; b/Mar 12, 1949; h/Terlingua Rt Box 220, Alpine, TX 79830; m/Delilah Womack; c/Mitzi Jean, Eric Ryan; p/Jack and Betty North; ed/Att'd Tex A&M Univ 1968-70; pa/Sales Mgr/Broker, Jack North & Assocs; Gen Ptnr/Mgr N&N Land & Cattle Co; Tex Assn Rltrs; Nat Assn Rltrs; cp/Big Bend Nat Park Lions Clb, Past Secy & Pres; Lions Dist 2-T-3, Zone Chm 1978-79; r/Prot; hon/W/W S&SW 1980-81.

NORTMANN, JOACHIM ROBERT oc/Business Executive; b/Sept 19, 1919; h/PO Box 3181, Wilson, NC 27893; ba/Wilson; pa/Prof Cooperating Univ of Am, Wilson; Pres & Owner Nortmann Est Trustee Adm Corp 1952-; Pres & Owner Inst of Economical & Financial Res Corp 1964-; Pres & Owner Muhling Banking Corp 1952-64; Assoc'd Press Staff Corresp (Ec) in Berlin, Bonn, London & Paris 1946-52; Fellow Mem ABI.

NORVELL, JOHN EDMONDSON III oc/Professor; b/Nov 18, 1929;

ba/Dept Anatomy, Oral Roberts Univ, 7777 S Lewis Ave, Tulsa, OK 74171; m/Rosemary Justice; c/John E IV, Scott Justice; p/Mathilde N Patteson, Charleston, WV; ed/BS Univ Charleston 1953; MS WV Univ 1953; PhD Ohio St Univ 1966; mil/USNR 1947-48; pa/Instr Johnstown Col, Univ Pgh 1956-60; Asst Prof Otterbein Col 1960-62; Asst Instr Ohio St Univ 1962-65; Asst Prof - Assoc Prof Med Col Va 1966-76, Prof & Chm, Oral Roberts Univ Sch Med 1976-; AAAS; Am Assn Anatomists; Am Assn Dental Schs; Assn Anatomy, Chm; Assn Am Med Cols; Cajal Clb; Okla Acad Sci; Okla St Anatomical Bd Chm 1978-; Sigma Xi; Soc Neurosci; So Soc Anatomists; Transplantation Soc; hon/Chi Beta Phi S'ship Key; Ldrs in Am Sci 1962-63; W/W Va 1974; Ohio St Univ Grad Sch F'ship 1964; Outstg Tchr of Yr, Chosen by Freshman Class, Sch Med, Med Col Va 1970, 71, 72, 75; Author Num Books, Abstracts & Articles Incl'g *Sectional Anatomy of the Head and Neck* & *Anatomia Humana.*

NOTORO, JOHN ANTHONY II oc/Club Manager; b/Jul 24, 1952; h/3208 S Main St, Anderson, SC 29624; p/John A Sr and Darline Notoro, Clarendon, PA; ed/BA Gannon Univ 1975; pa/Former Trouble Shooter w Howard Johnson Inc of Fla, Var Mgmt Positions; Pub'd in Col Pubs; r/Cath.

NOTTINGHAM, HARMON ALLEN oc/Cardio-Vascular Nurse Specialist; b/July 11, 1949; h/247 S 69th E Ave, Tulsa, OK 74112; ba/Tulsa; p/Harmon and Pauline Nottingham, Coweta, OK; pa/Cardio-Vascular Nurse Spec, Cardiac Catheterization Lab, Hillcrest Med Ctr 1978-; Staff Nurse ICCU, Hillcrest Med Ctr 1973-78; Beta Beta Beta; Psi Chi; Nat Critical Care Inst Ed; AACN; Am Heart Assn; r/Bapt; hon/AACN; Am Heart Assn.

NOVELL, EARL KENYON oc/Insurance Management; b/Sept 13, 1925; h/3937 River Run Trail, B'ham, AL 35243; ba/B'ham; m/Stephanie T; c/Michael K, Paula W Higgins, Stephen J; p/Michael and Allegra Novell; ed/Reg'd Profl Engr; Cert'd Hazard Control Mgr; mil/USAAF 1943-46; pa/ASSE; Nat Safety Coun; Ins Risk Mgmt; r/Roman Cath.

NOZAKI, MASAKO oc/Medical Scientist; b/Mar 24, 1941; h/Sapporo, Japan; ba/Dept Pharm, Sch Dentistry, Hokkaido Univ, Sapporo, Japan; p/Kennosuke and Sumi Nozaki; ed/BS Tohoku Pharm Sch 1964; PhD Dept Pharm, Sch Med, Hirosaki Univ 1976; pa/Res Assoc, Dept Pharm, Mich St Univ 1973-74; Vis Assoc, Nat Inst Drug Abuse, Addiction Res Ctr, Neuropharm Sect 1974-77; Res Assoc, Dept Pharm, Cornell Univ Med Col 1977-78; Vis Asst Prof, Dept Pharm, Univ Ky, Col Med 1978-79; Med Res Scist, Dept Pharm, Univ Ky, Col Med 1979-80; Adj Instr, Dept Pharm, Sch Dentistry, Hokkaido Univ 1980-; Author/Co-Author Num Profl Pubs.

NUNNELLEY, KENNETH SLOAN oc/Patrolman; b/Nov 9, 1957; h/Auburn, AL; ba/Auburn Police Dept, 141 N Ross St, Auburn, AL 36830; p/John R and Christine Sloan Nunnelley, Huntsville, AL; ed/BS Auburn Univ 1979; Grad Montgomery Police Acad 1980; Completed Basic EMT Trg 1980; pa/Police Ofcr, City of Auburn; Lambda Alpha Epsilon; r/Bapt; on/Grad First in Class, Montgomery Police Acad 1980; Police Expert w Revolver, Nat Rifle Assn; W/W Am HS Students 1975-76; Eagle Scout 1970.

NUNNERY, MELVIN ERNEST oc/Member, House of Representatives, District #44; b/May 11, 1951; h/PO Box 781, Chester, SC 29706; ba/Chester; m/Karen Kay Lowe; p/Jimmie E Nunnery, Fort Lawn, SC; Cora N Simpson, Rock Hill, SC; ed/BA Univ SC 1972; pa/Mem, SC Ho Reps; Dir of Vol Sers; Personal Aide to St Senator Nick Ziegler, Cand for US Senate 1972; Intern for US Senator Ernest F Hollings, Wash DC 1972; Mem: Chester Co Bd of Commerce & Devel & Appt'd to Govt & Leg Com (1975, 76, 77), Chester Co Mtl Hlth Assn (1975-76-77), Chester Co Yg Dems, Chester Co Assn for Retard Citizens & Appt'd as its Public Relats Person (1975, 76), SE Reg Cabinet of Assn for Retard Citizens, Speech & Hearing Bd for York, Chester, & Lancaster Cos; Chester Co Coun on Aging: Exec Com (1974, 75, 76, 77), Chm 1978; Pres: Yth SC Assn for Retard Citizens (1972-73, 1973-74), Mid-Carolina Yth Assn for Retard Chd 1971; Bd Dirs of Assn for Retard Citizens 1972-73, 1973-74; Org'd 1st Hike-Bike for Retard in SC; Elected Acting Presiding Ofcr for Yth-SEn Reg Conf; Elected as Delegation to Nat Dem Conv from SC 1972 (SC Ygest Del); Vice Chperson 1972, Exec Com-man 1974, 76 for Wylies Mill Precnt; Del to Co & St Dem Convs 1974; Appt'd to SC Dem Partys Govt & Leg Com; Asst Reg Nat VP of Yth-Nat Assn for Retard Citizen 1972; Appt'd by St Chperson of SC Dem Party to Com of Re-org of Dem Party 1973; cp/Chester Civitans 1975, 76, 77, 78; Chester Co Chm Univ SC Alumni Assn 1977, 78; Charter Mem & External VP (1976) of Lewisville JCs; Mem: Chester Moose Clb, Couples Clb, Fishing Creek Clb, Bd Dirs of Grover Pundts Developmental Ctr; Div Chm Chester Co U Fund 1977-78; Chm Chester Co Area U Fund 1978-79; Mar Dimes Marathon Chm & MC 1978, 79; r/1st Bapt Ch, Chester, SC: Mem, Mem Yg Couples Class; Former SS Tchr of 7th & 8th Grade Boys of Harmony Bapt Ch, Edgemoor, SC; hon/W/W: in Polits in S&SW US, in Polits in Am; Yth of Yr Awd 1974,

SC Assn for Retard Citizens; DAV Dist'd Ser Awd; Pres's Awd from Newberry Col Yg Dem.

NYABONGO, VIRGINIA SIMMONS oc/Professor of French; b/Mar 20, 1913; h/936 34th Ave N, Nashville, TN 37209; ba/Tenn St Univ, N'ville; c/Joel (Adoptive); p/Vester & Mary Warren Simmons (dec); ed/BA Bennett Col 1934; MA 1937, PhD 1944 Univ Wis; MA 1948, Profl Dipl Dean of Students Tchrs Col 1962 Columbia Univ; Cert d'Etudes Francaises, Cert de Phonetique, Diplome d'Etudes Avancees de Phonetique Univ Grenoble France, Franco-Am Fellow Inst Intl Ed 1939; Postdoct: Res Fulbright Grant 1952-53, Institut Pedagogique Paris, France, Study & Res 1954, 55, 62 Columbia Tchrs Col, Assoc Japan Studies Prog Syracuse Univ 1956; Certs: Newspaper Inst Am 1950, Indust Col Armed Forces 1963, Cashier Tng Inst 1965, Real Est Univ Tenn 1968; Num Others: pa/Presented Paper 10th Intl Cong Intl Fdn Fgn Langs & Lits Aug 1966 Univ Strasbourg, France; Presented Paper ICLA, Bordeaux, France 1970 & Ottawa, Canada 1973, Budapest 1976; Del NEA 1968, 69, 17th & 18th Assemblies of WCOTP; Del 50th Annual Meeting of Am Assn of Tchrs of French, Paris, France 1977; Alternate Del Intl Fed of Univ Wom, Univ Stirling, Stirling, Scotland 1977; Att'd Num Others; Asst Prof French Wilberforce Univ, Wilberforce, Ohio 1937-41; Bennett Col, Greensboro, NC: Instr, Acting Registrar 1934-36, Dean of Students 1941-42; Tenn St Univ, N'ville: Dir Student Personnel & Guid 1944-58, Res Univ 1958-63, Pt-time Fgn Student Advisemt 1968-69, Assoc Prof French 1944-45, Prof French 1944-; Life Mem: APGA, Nat Assn Wom Deans & Counselors, Col Lang Assn, NEA, Intl Inst Arts & Lttrs, MLA, Am Assn Tchrs French, YWCA, AAUW, Bennett Col & Univ Wis Alumni Assns; Past Pres Tenn Philological Assn 1967-68; Tenn Fgn Lang Tchg Assn: Bd Dirs 1969, 70, Co-Editor Newslttr 1971; Alliance Francaise, N'ville: Steering Com 1970-71, Bd Mem 1971; Am Assn Tchrs French, Tenn Chapt VP 1971-73, Pres 1972-73; cp/N'ville C of C: Mem 1965-, Ed Com 1970-71; Fac Clb TSU: Among Fdrs 1951, 1976, 25th Anniv Fac Clb, Meharry Med Col Fisk Univ, Community, N'ville Pres 1967-70, Exec Secy 1970-; UN Assn USA N'ville Chapt: Bd Dirs 1966-72, 74, 76-; 2/VP 1973-76; Pres 1977; N'ville Urban Observatory Housing 1970; U Negro Col Fund; VP N'ville Br AAUW; AAUW Sem on UN 1974-76, AAUW-IFUW Japan 1974; Davidson Co Dem Woms Clb: VP 1970, Bd Mem 1970-71, UN Rep 1974-; Bd Tenn Fdn Dem Wom, Spkrs Bur 1970-71, Corr Secy 1971-72; r/1st Bapt Ch; hon/Fellow: African Studies Assn, Soc for Values in Higher Ed, Intl Inst Arts & Lttrs; W/W: Am Ed, Colored Am, S&SW, Am Wom; Ldrs Am Sci; Dir Am Scholars; Commun Ldrs Am; Intl Sci Info Ser; DIB; Phi Delta Kappa; N'ville Outstg Wom Ed 1952; Omega Psi Phi; Alpha Kappa Alpha, N'ville Pearls 1958; Kappa Delta Pi; IPA; Nat Assn Pers Wkrs: Charter Mem, Cert Merit 16 Yrs Ser 1962; Bennett Col Cit; Tenn St Univ Golden Anniv 10 Yr Fac Ser Awd 1962; Ministere de l'Education Nationale, Republique Francaise, Chevalier, Ofcr dans l'Ordre des Palmes Academiques 1963; Hon Mem Edit Adv Bd Am Biog Inst 1971; Pub'd Author.

NYE, EDD oc/Insurance Agent; State Legislature; b/Sept 12, 1932; h/PO Box 8, Elizabethtown, NC 28337; ba/Elizabethtown; m/Peggy McKee; c/Shannon, Edward, Allison; p/Joseph Burke and Vera Johnson Nye, Council, NC; ed/AA NCSU; mil/USAF 1952-56; cp/Former Mem NC St Senate; Current Mem NC St House; r/Baptist.

O

OAKES, KENNETH WAYLAND oc/Businessman, Rancher; b/Mar 11, 1935; h/PO Box 147, Donie, TX 75838; ba/Donie; m/Helen Ruth; c/Pam, Debbie, Michele, Melinda; p/Tommie and Hazel Oakes, Donie, TX; ed/BA Sam Houston St Univ; Tchr Cert Baylor Univ; mil/USAFR; pa/Owner-Oper Feed, Fertilizer, Hardware Store; Rancher; Public Sch Tchr 10 Yrs; cp/Dir & Mem Indep Cattlemen's Assn; NFO; r/Bapt: Deacon.

OATES, GRADY REMBERT oc/Associate Minister; b/Sept 17, 1928; h/310 E Stuart, Bartow, FL 33830; ba/Bartow; m/Mable Young; c/Deborah, Dorcas, John, Elizabeth; p/John Hough and Isabel Jackson Oates, York, SC; ed/BA; BD; DD; mil/AUS Air Corps; pa/Pastor Bartow ARP Ch; cp/Rotarian; U Way; Hosp Dir; Housing Auth; r/Assoc Reformed Presb; hon/DD; Modr Gen Synod ARP Ch.

OATES, WILL ETTA (WILLIE) oc/Civic, Charity, Community Leader; h/485 Valley Clb, Little Rock, AR 72212; m/Gordon Page; c/Randolph Lee, Deborah O Erwin; p/Harry Lee Long (dec); Roberta Fern Long, Ark City, KS; ed/BA Univ Ark; Num Other Courses; mil/Defense Adv Com on Wom in the Sers: Exec Com 2 Yrs, Chm Planning Com for 20th Anniv; pa/Mem Ark Leg 1959-60 (1st Wom); Sponsor 1st Law Pertaining to Motorcycles & Motor Bikes; OWL; Model & Commentator Style Shows; Does Commercials & Spec Features; Former Interviewer of Own Wkly TV Show, KTHV, Channel 11, Little Rock; cp/Past Pres Kappa Kappa Gamma Alumnae Assn; Past Bd Mem: Univ Ark Alumnae Assn, Panhellenic Lib of Little Rock; Public Spkr: TV, Radio, Civic Clbs; Former Intl Hostess Chm, Gen Fdn Woms Clbs; Chm Little Rock Traffic Safety Comm; Past Dist Dir Quapaw Area DAR; Pres S Ctl Reg GFWC; VChm Ark Envir Com of Ed Dept; Public Relats Chm, Woms City Clb of Little Rock; Govs Comm on Status of Wom; Past Pres Bapt Med Ctr Aux; 1st Wom Pres, AF Assn, David D Terry Chapt; St Adv Bd for Bus & Ofc Ed for Dept Ed Ark; Chm Ark Wom Hwy Safety Ldrs Bd; Steering Com for Ark St Nurses Assn; Pres Carti Aux, Ctl Ark Radiation Therapy Inst; Chm Fund Dr, Coun on Aging Pres Deptl Clb; Chm Com on Nsg S'ships, Bapt Med Ctr Sys; Mem Com of 100 for Ozark Folk Ctr; Mem Ark Vol Coor Assn; Num Other Activs, Ofcs, Bds; r/1st Pres Ch: Circle Chm; Pres Ch Wom U 1978-79; hon/Little Rock Wom of Yr 1955; Wom of Yr 1961, Diamond Charter Chapt of Abwa; Ark Traveler Gov Awd; Lady of the Day in Ctl Ark 1964; Hon Life Mem Num Orgs & Comms; Hon Col & Goodwill Ambassador, USAR; Hon Recruiter, USA & USN; USAF Dr of Aerospacelogy; 1st Wom Appointee to Pulaski Co Grad Jury; Biogl Listings; Num Others.

OATMAN, TAMRA-SHAE oc/Executive Director; b/Feb 24, 1952; ba/910 B So Grant, Odessa, TX 79763; p/William Arthur and Audrea Lynne Cox Oatman, Maryneal, TX; ed/BBA Univ Tex Austin 1974; pa/Vista Vol; Cabin Creek Quilts; BPW of Odessa 1st VP; r/Epis.

OATS, REBECCA ANN oc/Math Coordinator for the State Department of Public Institute of North Carolina; b/Sept 27, 1978; h/1900 Charles Blvd, Apt 43-D, Greenville, NC 27834; m/William Russell Jr; c/William Russell III; p/Nathan Sr and Annie M Alford, Benson, NC; ed/BS (Math); Masters in Ednl Supvn & Adm; pa/NCTM'; r/Bapt.

OBERMAYER, HERMAN JOSEPH oc/Editor-Publisher; b/Sept 19, 1924; h/4114 N Ridgeview Rd, Arlington, VA 22207; ba/Arlington; m/Betty Nan Levy; c/Helen, Veronica, Adele, Elizabeth; p/Leon J and Julia Sinsheimer Obermayer, Phila, PA; ed/AB cum laude Dartmouth Col; mil/AUS 1943-46 Staff Sgt; pa/Newspaper Editor-Pubr; Am Soc Newspapers Editors Prog Com; So Newspaper Pubrs Assn, Editorial Com; cp/Nat Capital Coun of Boy Scouts, Pres 1971-77; Trustee No Va Chapt Am Heart Assn; Am Red Cross; r/Jewish; hon/Silver Beaver, BSA; Friends of Scouting Awd; Rhineland Campaign Star.

OBERT, PAUL M oc/Physician, Pathologist; b/Apr 25, 1924; h/303 Tampa Dr, Victoria, TX 77901; ba/Victoria; m/Gene M; c/Mary, Jeanne, Paul Jr, Elizabeth, Catherine; p/dec; ed/BS Stanford Univ 1944; MD Okla Univ Sch Med 1947; mil/AUS 1942-46, 52-56 Col; pa/Pathol-in-Chief, Citizens Meml Hosp, Champ Traylor Hosp; Pres Victoria-Goliad-Jackson Tri-Co Med Soc; Tex Med Assn; AMA; cp/Bd Dirs S Tex Hlth Sys Agcy; Bd Dirs & Med Dir S Tex Regional Blood Bank; r/Cath; hon/Tex Dept Hlth Cert of Apprec for Merit Ser to People of St 1980.

O'BRIEN, D SUSAN J oc/Architect, Planner; b/Aug 13, 1942; h/2705 Avonhill Dr, Arlington, TX 76015; ba/Ft Worth, TX; p/Jack Dallas and Jane Childs O'Brien, N Olmsted, OH; ed/BArch Tech Univ 1966; MArch Univ Tex-Austin 1975; pa/Am Inst of Archs; Tex Soc of Archs; Am Inst of Planners; Urban Land Inst; Nat Assn of Envir Profls; Reg Sci Assn; Metro Assn of Urban Designers & Envir Planners; cp/Dir & Chm of Bldg & Grounds Com, Save the Scott Home Preserv Soc, Aesthetics Com & Bicent Com, Streams & Valleys Inc, Ofc of the Mayor of Ft Worth; hon/Alpha Lambda Delta; Jesse H Jones S'ship; Nat Coun of Architectural Registration Bds Certn 1972; Fellow Mem ABI.

O'BRIEN, KEVIN MICHAEL oc/Physician, Nephrologist; b/July 13, 1942; h/Nashville, TN; ba/1900 Patterson St, Nashville, TN 37203; m/Suzanne; c/Danielle; p/William Michael and Helen Hughes O'Brien, Ft Lauderdale, FL; ed/BS Siena Col 1964; MS Adelphi Univ 1966; MD Univ Bologna 1971; pa/NIH Res Asst, Aldelphi Univ; Instr-Med, Vanderbilt Univ; Renal Conslt, Nashville VA Hosp; Med Dir, Dialysis Clin Inc, Madison, Tenn; Pvt Pract; Clin Asst Prof, Allied Sci, Trevecca Col; AMA; Davidson Co Med Soc; Tenn Med Soc; Intl Soc Nephrology; Am Soc Nephrology; Assoc Mem Sigma Xi; Arthritis Foun, Middle Tenn Bd Trustees; Kidney Foun, Middle Tenn; Renal Phys Assn; So Med Assn; Upper Cumberland Med Soc; r/Cath; hon/Author Num Profl Articles.

O'BRYANT, JAMES ARTHUR oc/Accountant; b/June 1, 1923; h/5215 Clubview Dr, Dallas, TX 75232; ba/Dallas; m/Billie Louise Birdwell; c/Betty Joyce, Jimmy Bruce; p/Arthur and Suejette Cherry O'Bryant; ed/Att'd Univ NM 1940-41; Durham Col 1946-47; mil/USAF Capt; Lt Col, Exec Ofcr MP Grp, Tex St Guard 1971-79; pa/Pers Ofcr-Insp Gen, Europe, Africe, Middle East 1942-45; Pers Br Chief, Korea 5th Army 1951-53; Var Assignments SAC; Gen Mgr Kleen-Air Tex, Inc 1962-64; Pres Chem Exhaust 1964-65; Sales Mgr Guardian Fire Protection 1965-69; Secy-Treas Whitel Mus Co 1969-75; Pres O'Bryant & Machtley Inc 1975-; Action Com Nat Fed Small Bus; Nat Soc Public Accts; Nat Soc Mgmt Consults; Tex Assn Public Accts; Tex Nat Guard Assn; Tex St Guard Assn; cp/Repub; r/Bapt; hon/Bronze Star.

OCHSNER, LENA FRANCES SCHMIDT oc/Homemaker; b/Apr 30, 1933; h/2215 Huntington, Midland, TX 79701; m/John Dorr; c/John Dorr II, Robert Frederick, Julie Kate; p/Frederick Harry (dec) and Willie Kate Meador Schmidt, Slaton, TX; ed/BS Tex Tech Univ; pa/Art Tchr, Public Schs, Seminole, TX; cp/Past Pres Midland Alumnae Clb of Pi Beta Phi; Past Pres Gwyn Garden Clb; Nat Yng Artists Comp, Midland Odessa Symp & Chorale, Com Chm; Midland Symph Guild; PEO Sisterhood; Petro Engrs Wives; Yng Life; Santa Rita Clb of Permian Basin Petro Mus & Lib Hall of Fame; Coach-Mgr & Chaperone Miss Softball Am; Vol: Visual Eye Screening, Lib, Meals on Wheels; Midland Country Clb; Univ City Clb; r/Presb; hon/Wom of Yr Tex Tech Univ 1954; W/W: Am Cols & Univs 1953, on Campus Tex Tech Univ 1954; Pres Assn Wom Students, Tex Tech; Pres Pi Beta Phi; Life Mbrship Awd, Tex Cong PTA 1980.

ODOM, ISAIAH oc/Minister; b/Apr 23, 1933; h/PO Box 548, Denmark, SC 29042; c/Loretta, Windell, Shanda, Deletha, Isaiah, Deona; p/Rosa Lee Brabham, Olar, SC; ed/Denmark Tech Col 1960; Att'd Morris Col Theologe Ext Class, Pinland, SC 1974-76; mil/AUS 1953-55; pa/Pastor of Second Bapt Ch (Barnwell, SC); Operator of Odom's Autor Parts; cp/Notary Public, St of SC; Am Legion Post #252; Elizabeth Wright Lodge #44, Past Sr Warden; Bamberg Co Coun 1978-, Chm 1981; r/Honey Ford Bapt Ch.

ODOM, LEON DAVID oc/Maintenance Engineer, Student; b/Jan 26, 1951; h/400 E Danforth, Apt 131, Edmond, OK 73034; m/Freda Faye; c/Kami Faye, Loralie; ed/Att'g Ctrl St Univ; mil/AUS 1968-70; USAR 1971-; Indust Arts Clb, Ctrl St Univ; r/Freewill Bapt; hon/Outstg Drill Sgt, 3rd Bn 1975-76.

ODOM, MARJORIE MORGAN oc/Librarian; b/July 22, 1924; h/PO Box 8374, San Antonio, TX 78203; ba/San Antonio; m/Steven Jr (dec); p/A J (dec) and Estella Phillips Morgan; ed/Lic'd Cosmetologist, Mme C J Walker Sch Cosmetology 1944; Adv'd Studies Cosmetology 1946-57; BA 1964, MEd 1979, Our Lady of the Lake Col; pa/Mgr Mme C J Walker Beauty Salon, San Antonio 19·4-52; Proprietor Ross Hotel Beauty Salon, San Antonio 1952-63; Asst Supvr, Chd's Dept, San Antonio Main Public Lib 1964-65; Sec'dy Sch Libn, San Antonio Indep Sch Dist 1965-; NEA, Life Mem; Tex Tchrs Assn; Tex Clrm Tchrs Assn; San Antonio Indep Sch Dist Libns Assn; Bexar Lib Assn; PTA; San Antonio Tchrs Coun; cp/Dem Party; St Senator Rothmann's Adv Coun on Leg Affairs; r/Mt Pleasant Bapt Ch: 1st Assoc Supt Ch Sch, SS Tchr, Chm Lib Comm, Dir Christian Ed; hon/Recip Our Lady of the Lake Div of Bus Studies Outstg Awd in Analysis & Design 1978; Num Rel Certs; Co-Author of Model for a Computerized Lib Prog 1978.

ODOM, RONNY DEAN oc/Teacher; b/Nov 30, 1943; h/1925 N Fairfax Dr, Corsicana, TX 75110; ba/Corsicana; m/Marsha J; c/Shannon, Alyssa; p/Rube L and Grace Lee Odom (dec); ed/BA 1972, MEd 1973 Sam Houston St Univ; Doct Work E Tex St Univ 1974-75; Att'd Univ Tex-Arlington, Stephen F Austin Univ; mil/AUS 1967-69 Sgt; pa/Spec Ed Resource Tchr, Lang Lrng Disabilites; Corsicana Edrs Assn: Pres 1978-79, VP 1976-77; Tex St Tchrs Assn; NEA; Tex Clrm Tchrs Assn; cp/Dem

Party, Precnt Chm; John Hill Ed Com 1979; Corsicana Edrs Polit Action Com; r/Bapt; hon/Profl Recog in Var St Ed & Polit Orgs; Author Var Newspapers Articles.

ODOM, STEPHEN JR oc/Area Extension Agent; b/Jan 9, 1945; h/255 Wisewood Cir, Greenwood, SC 29646; ba/Greenwood; m/Lou Amye C; c/Charlene Denise; p/Stephen Sr (dec) and Rometa Odom (dec); ed/BS SC St Col 1967; MS Clemson Univ 1978; mil/AUS 1968-71 Sgt; pa/Sci Tchr 1968; Asst Co Agt, Edgefield, SC 1971-74; Assoc Co Agt, Edgefield, SC 1974-80; Area Ext Agt, Spec Progs, Greenwood & McCormick Cos; SC Assn Co Agric Agts, Secy-Treas; Nat Assn Co Agric Agts; SC 4-H Agts Assn; SC St Employees Assn; cp/SC St Col Alumni Clb; r/Bapt; hon/AUS Commend Medal & Cert 1969; Good Conduct Medal 1971; SCACAA Cert of Merit 1978; SCACAA Public Info Awd, 3rd Pl Direct Mail Piece 1978, 2nd Pl 1979; Cert Apprec Thurmond HS FFA 1980; Co-Author "Growing Tomatoes at Home" 1975.

O'DONNELL, EDWARD BAXTER JR oc/Diplomat, Foreign Service Officer; b/May 19, 1946; h/434 S Reese St, Memphis, TN 38111; ba/Asuncion Paraguay; m/Beth; c/Christina, Susannah, Edward III; p/Edward Baxter and Velma Ruth Hensley O'Donnell, Memphis, TN; ed/BA So Meth Univ 1968; MA Am Univ; Postgrad Heidelberg Univ; mil/USAR, Capt 1968-72, Current Active Resv; pa/Diplomat/Fgn Ser Ofer, US Dept of St; Am Fgn Ser Assn; Am Mgmt Assn; cp/Kappa Sigma Alumni Assn; Memphis JCs; r/Meth; hon/Phi Kappa Phi; Army Commend Medal.

O'FARRELL, LUCY SHELTON oc/Real Estate Broker; Instructor; Investor; b/Dec 25, 1918; m/Oscar C; c/Carol Lynn; p/Bennett Gordon and Mary VanDella Dye Shelton; ed/Ga St Col for Wom 1936-37; Hurst Bus Col 1937-38; pa/Real Estate, Clover Realty Co 1971-; VP, Broker/Mgr Branch Ofc; Merritt & McKenzie Ins Agy (Atlanta, Ga): Ins Agent & Ofc Mgr 1941-71; Nat Assn Realtors; Ga Assn Realtors; Atlanta Bd Realtors; Woms Coun; Ga Chapt Cert'd Real Estate Brokers; Atlanta Assn Ins Wom; cp/Sandy Springs C of C (Atlanta); Toastmasters Intl; Nat Assn of Parliamentarians; Ga Assn Parliamentarians; r/Bapt; hon/W/W Am Wom; Real Estate Review's Dict of Real Est Profls; CRB Designation; GRI Designation.

OGDEN, FREDERICK DORRANCE oc/Executive; b/Oct 11, 1915; h/212 College View Dr, Richmond, KY 40475; ba/Richmond; m/Jessie Cupitt; c/Elisabeth Joan Churchill, Katharine Janet Cornell; p/Fred Dorrance Ogden (dec); Florance Caroline Young Ogden Clark (dec); ed/AB Tusculum Col 1938; PhD Johns Hopkins Univ 1951; mil/USAAF 1942-45; pa/Clk Edgewood Arsenal 1940-41; Asst Mgr Civilian Pers Field Ofc, Wright-Patterson Field 1941-42; Instr-Assoc Prof, Univ Ala 1946-61; En Ky Univ: Prof Polit Sci, Dept Chm 1961-65, Dean Col Arts & Scis 1965-79, Assoc VP Plan'g 1977-; Fulbright Lectr, Indian Sch of Intl Studies, New Delhi, India 1957-58; Dir Intl Relats, Appalachian St Univ Summers 1960 & 61; Mem Com to Select City Mgr, Richmond, Ky 1971; Ky Sci & Tech Adv Coun 1967-71; Citizens Adv Subcom Ky Leg Compensation 1974; Modr, Constit Conv, Ky Leg Res Com 1977; Commonwlth Fellow, Duke Univ Commun Studies Ctr 1959; Am Soc Polit Sci Assn; Ky Conf Polit Sci, Pres 1964-65; AAUP, Chapt Pres 1964-50; Nat, Ky Ed Assns; Am Conf Acad Deans: Dir 1974-77, Editor-Secy 1975-77; Coun Col Arts & Scis; Inst Intl Ed: Chm Select Com, Schlrs to S Asia 1975-76; UN Assn: VP Ky 1963-65; Coun Visitors, Tusculum Col 1978-; r/Epis; hon/Order of Ky Cols; Pi Sigma Alpha; Phi Kappa Phi; Author The Poll Tax in the South 1959; Contbg Author Analysis of Social Problems; Editor The Public Papers of Governor Keen Johnson 1939-43; Editorial Bd Univ Press of Ky 1969-.

OGG, E JERALD SR oc/Minister; b/June 30, 1933; h/18256 Pinebrook Dr, PO Box 3310, Kingsport, TN 37664; ba/Same; m/Janett N; c/E Jerald Jr, Judith Dawn, Jeffrey Alan, James Patrick; p/Cullom and Ethel Ogg, Hendersonville, TN; ed/BA Ctrl Bible Col; pa/Pastor, First Assembly, Kingsport, Tenn; Solotist; Asst Dist Supt for the Assems of God in Tenn; cp/Min Alliance, Pres Charleston, Mo & Dyersburg, Tenn; r/Assems of God.

OGLESBEE, HARRIET BARKLEY oc/Librarian; h/822 Osage Ave, NW Columbia, SC 29169; ba/Columbia; m/Tom; p/Harry E and Beatrice G Barkley, Statesville, NC; ed/AB Erskine Col; MS Fla St; pa/Libn, Univ SC, Columbia; ALA; SELA; SCLA; cp/AAUW, Jr Ser Leag; r/Presb; hon/Beta Phi Mu.

OGLESBY, HELEN AGNEW oc/Teacher; b/Apr 16, 1941; h/404 S Clay St, Salisbury, NC 28144; m/Phillip Daniel Sr; c/Phillip Daniel Jr; p/William C Sr and Virginia Agnew, Salisbury, NC; ed/AB Livingston Col 1962; Masters Cand UNC-Charlotte; pa/Elem Tchr; NEA; NCAE; cp/Zeta Phi Beta; NAACP; r/Bapt; hon/Tchr of Yr, Lundis, NC 1979-80.

OGLETREE, DAVID LAWRENCE oc/Minister; b/Mar 9, 1936;

h/1457 N Morningside Dr NE, Atlanta, GA 30306; ba/Atlanta; p/Mr & Mrs Robert Earl Ogletree, Perry, GA; ed/Att'd Emory-at-Oxford; BA LaGrange Col; Att'd Columbia Sem & Candler Sch Theol, Emory Univ; pa/Assoc Pastor Atlanta First Meth Ch; N Ga Conf U Meth Ch; cp/1st VP Ga St Poetry Soc; Hon Mem Hist Soc S Ga Conf U Meth Ch; Assoc Mem Chapt Am Guild Organists; Dixie Coun Authors & Jours; Poetry Soc Ga in Savannah; The Village Writers Grp Inc; Atlanta Assn Retard'd Citizens; Bd Cnslrs Oxford Col, Emory Univ; Lincoln Collector & Impersonator of Abraham Lincoln; Lincoln Grp of Boston; Abraham Lincoln Assn in Springfield; Friends of Hildene Inc; Com for Restoration of Dr Smauel A Mudd House Inc; r/Meth; hon/Yng Man of Yr, Cartersville JCs 1964; Poet of Yr Dixie Coun Authors & Jours 1977; Author Steeples, A Volume of Verse; Lanscapes; & Weavings; Co-Author Noel! Poems of Christmas.

OGUNSUSI, PATRICIA A oc/Teacher; b/Mar 5, 1951; h/2571 S Candler Rd, Q-9, Decatur, GA 39932; ba/Atlanta; m/Raphael T; p/George L (dec) and Bessie H Anderson, SE Atlanta, GA; ed/BS 1973, MEd 1977 Ga St Univ; pa/Elem Tchr, Atlanta Public Sch Sys, 8 Yrs; cp/Phyllis Wheatley YWCA; Eta Sigma Chapt, Sigma Gamma Rho; r/Bapt; hon/Tchr of Yr, Fred A Toomer Elem Sch 1980-81.

OLDHAM, DOROTHY A CLOUDMAN oc/Executive; b/Nov 25, 1925; h/261 Bal Cross Dr, Bal Harbour, FL 33154; ba/Bal Harbour; c/Carol Cloudman; p/Philip Horace Cloudman (dec); Mabel Ings Rigg (dec); ed/AB Univ Mich-Ann Arbor; pa/Pres Cloudman Oldham Advtg & Public Relats; Advtg Fed Miami; Nat Home Fashions Leag; Wom in Communs; Fashion Grp Miami; cp/Miami Design & Preserv Leag; r/Meth; hon/Advtg Excell 1st Prize, Profl Bldr Mag; Former Fashion Editor Detroit Free Press; Former Editor Detroit & Suburban Life Magazine.

OLDHAM, HENRY NEVEL oc/Aerospace Engineer; b/Apr 29, 1943; h/8801 Willow Hills Dr SE, Huntsville, AL 35802; ba/Redstone Arsenal, AL; c/John; p/Arthur S Oldham (dec); Florrie P Oldham, Athens, GA; ed/BS Univ Ga 1965; MAE Univ Va 1968; mil/AUS 1968-71; Maj Ordnance Corps USAR 1978; pa/Employed in Trajectory Analysis & Perf Analysis, Tech Mgmt Div, Gen Support Rocket Sys (GSRS) Prof Ofc (Provisional); Pub'd Reports on LANCE & SHILLELAGH Missile Sys Simulations; AIAA; IEEE; Phi Mu Alpha; Comml Pilot, Airplane Single & Multi-Engine Land; AOPA; N Ala Solar Energy Assn; cp/Pres Huntsville JCs 1975-76; H'ville C of C; H'ville/Madison Co Indust Devel Assn; Dir, N Ala Kidney Foun; AUSA; ROA; Friends of Public Radio; Prog Chm, Exploring, Tenn Valley Coun BSA; r/Valley U Meth Ch: SS Tchr, Chm Coun Social Concerns; hon/Phi Eta Sigma; NSF Traineeship 1965-66; Res Assstship Univ VA 1966-67; Ala JCs; Outstg JC Spkr 1972, 1 of 5 Outstg 1st Yr JCs 1973, 1 of 3 Outstg Sustaining JCs 1975; Outstg H'ville JC 1977; Outstg Perf Rating, US Army Missile Command, 1973, 74, 75; Outstg Yg Men of Am; Notable Ams of Bicentennial Era; Notable Ams of 1976-77; Commun Ldrs & Noteworthy Ams.

OLFERS, JUDITH ANN MOORE oc/Homemaker; b/Dec 24, 1950; h/10807 Bar X Trail, Helotes, TX 78023; m/Peter B; c/Amay Nicole, Stephanie Noelle; p/Theodore Richard Moore Sr, Houston, TX; Bertie Jo Moore, Houston, TX; ed/BS 1973, MS 1975 Tex Tech Univ; pa/HEIH; r/Meth; hon/Author "The Influence of Clothing on Advertising Effectiveness" 1975.

OLINGER, RALPH HARVARD oc/Instructor; b/May 14, 1949; h/Rome, Ga; ba/Floyd Jr College, Box 1864, Rome, GA 30161; m/Catherine Sheppard; c/Rebecca Elizabeth; ed/Cert'd MT 1972; BS Berry Col 1974; MACT Auburn Univ 1979; pa/MT Floyd Med Ctr; Cheif MT, Chattoga Co Hosp; Chem Supvr, W Ga Med Ctr; Instr Med Lab Technol, Floyd Jr Col; Am Soc Clin Pathols; Am Soc Med Technol; r/Meth; hon/Gamma Sigma Delta, Auburn Chapt 1976.

OLIPHANT, SONNY oc/Coach and Teacher; b/Feb 17, 1945; h/Box 71, Gamaliel, KY 42140; ba/Gamaliel; p/John and Virginia Oliphant, Scottsville, KY; ed/BS, MA Wn Ky Univ; mil/US Reserves & NG 7 Yrs E-7; pa/Asst Basketball Coach, Hd Baseball Coach, Gamaliel HS 11 Yrs; cp/Lions Clb; Sportsman Clb; r/Bapt.

OLIPHANT, THOMAS A oc/Photographer; b/July 22, 1954; h/Elk City, OK; ba/Blunck Studios Inc, 614 Frisco, Clinton, OK; m/Teresa L; p/Mr and Mrs Harry Oliphant, Benton, AR; pa/Holiday Inn 3 yrs; Olan Mills 4 Yrs; Photog, Blunck Studio; Profl Photogs of Am; SWn Region Profl Photogs; Profl Photogs of Okla; cp/US JCs, Elk City Chapt, Secy 1979-80; r/U Meth.

OLIVA, RALPH ANGELO oc/Manager; /July 1, 1946; h/Plano, TX; ba/Tex Instruments Lrng Ctr, PO Box 225012 M/S 84, Dallas, TX 75265; p/I Ralph and Raechel Oliva, Shoreham, NY; ed/BS Fordham Univ 1966; MS, PhD Rensselaer Polytech Inst 1966-73; pa/Staff Physicist, Army Elecs Command 1965-68; Grad Tchg-Res Asst 1966-73; Dir Tex Instrument Lrng

Ctr & Mgr Comsumer Mdsg Strategy 1973-; Nat Coun Tchr Maths; Nat Coun Supvrs of Maths; Am Assn Physics Tchrs; Am Phy Soc; r/Roman Cath; hon/Sun & Balance Awd for Excell in Reaching 1973; NSF Res/Study Grants 1959-64; Author Num Profl Articles.

OLIVER, ROBERT THOMAS oc/Teacher; b/Mar 24, 1946; h/305 Spring Creek Rd, Chattanooga, TN 37411; ba/Chat; m/Sandra McMillon; c/David Steven, Melanie Renee; p/R C and Virginia Jane Oliver, Henderson, TN; ed/AA Freed-Hardeman Col 1966; Cert in Bible Freed-Hardeman Col 1967; BS Murray St Univ 1972; MA Ball St Univ 1975; pa/Tchr Boyd Buchanan Sch; Kappa Delta Pi; Past Mem Pi Phi Delta; cp/Past Pres E Ridge Kiwanis Clb; Sponsor Jr Optimist & Octogon Clbs, Boyd Buchanan HS; r/Ch of Christ.

OLIVER, SHERYL LYNN oc/Sales Representative; b/Aug 1, 1944; h/333 Laurina St, Apt 137, Jacksonville, FL 32216; ba/J'ville; p/John M (dec) and Charleyn M Oliver, Richton Park, IL; ed/AA Stephens Col; BA So Meth Univ; pa/Sales Rep, Standard Register Co; Pres Assn Sys Mgmt 1979-80; Com Chm Data Processing Mgmt Assn; Intl Toastmistress Clb; GSA; r/Arlington Congreg Ch, Choir & Yth Advr.

OLSON, FLORA MAE oc/Homemaker, Artist; b/Aug 7, 1927; h/Rt 1, Avoca, TX 79503; m/Marvin C; c/Diane Grigsby, Denis; p/Alfred (dec) and Mary Rinn (dec); cp/Big Country Art Assn; Tex Fine Arts Assn; r/Prot; hon/Hon Men Big Country Cit Show; Artist of Mo of Aug, Stamford, TX 1980; Artist of Mo of Nov, Anson, TX 1980.

OLSON, JAMES ROBERT oc/Naval Officer; b/Nov 23, 1940; h/6416 Bluebill Ln, Alexandria, VA 22307; ba/Wash DC; c/Eric Robert; p/Robert August and Jean Elizabeth Olson, Lincoln, NB; ed/BA Univ Neb 1965; MA Ctrl Mich Univ; Att'd Alliance Francaise, Paris 1958; Midshipman US Naval Acad 1962; mil/USN 1965- Cmdr; pa/Fac Defense Intell Sch 1970-71; Nat Photo Interpretation Ctr 1971-73; Nav Air Facility 1973-77; Task Force 68, 1977-80; Naval Air Facility 1980-; US Naval Acad Alumni Assn; Phi Alpha Theta; Naval Reserve Assn; Ec Clb Detroit; cp/Nat Rifle Assn, Life Mem; Colo RR Hist Foun, Life Mem; Nat Rwy Hist Soc, Wash Chapt; Rwy & Locomotive Hist Soc, Baker Lib, Harvard; Pvt Car Assn; Nat Assn RR Psgrs; r/Meth; hon/Bronze Star w Combat V Air Medal; Combat Action Ribbon; Vietnam Cross of Gallantry; Recip Awds for Govt Norway, City Detroit, Civil Assns Detroit Area; Author Articles in Field.

ONDROVIK-BURRESS, JOANN CATHERINE oc/Clinical Psychologist; b/Feb 13, 1944; h/220 25th SE, Paris, TX 75460; c/Jodie, Tad; p/Frank and Jane Ondrovik, Gainesville, TX; ed/BS Tex Woms Univ 1965; MEd 1969, PhD Tex A&M Univ 1973; pa/Hd Speech Ser, Dept of Ed 1967; Pvt Pract, Speech Therapy (Bryan, Tex) 1966-73; CoFdr Bryan Coun of Stutterers 1971-73; Coor of Troubled Yth Prog (Bryan) 1973; Internship, Brazos Outreach & Austin St Hosp 1972-73; Social Worker-Psychol, Arlington Independent Sch Dist (Arlington, Tex) 1973-75; Psychol & Asst Dir of Psychol Sers, Dallas Independent Sch Dist 1973-75; Pvt Pract Psychol (Paris) 1975-; Adj Prof of Psychol, E Tex St Univ 1975-76; Cert'd by Nat Register of Hlth Ser Providers in Psychol; Am, Tex & E Tex Psychol Assns; Tex Speech & Hearing Assn; Am Assn Behavior Therapists; Dallas Psychol Assn; Assn of Psychotherapists; cp/Bd Mem, YWCA; LWV; Big Brothers/Big Sisters; City of Paris Airport Adv Bd; BPW; Lamar Co C of C; Round Table; r/Meth.

O'NEAL, ROBERT PALMER oc/Aircraft Aeronautical Engineer; b/Sept 20, 1912; h/Rt 1, Morehead City, NC 28557; m/Nancy Anne Monroe; c/Robert Monroe, Nancy Burke Arthur, Patricia McWilliam Colyer, Peggy Ford Perry; p/Robert McWilliam and Aimee Ford O'Neal; ed/AB 1935, MA 1936 Occidental Col; Att'd UNC Adv'd Ext Sci Courses 1949-51; pa/Monroe Chem: New England Rep 1937-39, En Sales Mgr 1939-41; Rep Bur Aeronautics, Pratt & Whitney Aircraft Corp 1941-44; Num Mil Positions; Pres Piksco Corp; Am Inst Aeronautics & Astronautics; Am Chem Soc; AAAS; Soc Am Mil Engrs; Am Ordnance Soc; Am Mgmt Assn; NC Acad Scis; Am Security Coun; Engrs Jt Coun Inc; Fleet Reserve Assn; cp/VFW; MC Aviation Assn; Delta Upsilon; Optimists Instl; Blue Key Assn; Occidental Col Alumni Assn; hon/Intl Reg Profiles; Intl W/W Intells; Book of Hon; Men of Achmt; Notable Ams; Life Patron ABA; Intl Platform Assn; 19 Mil Cits Incl'g Bronze Star w Combat V, Navy Lttr Commend w Combat V; Navy Uvit Cit.

ONG, ANTONIO LIM oc/Anesthesiologist, Family Practitioner; b/Oct 16, 1940; h/Hinesville, GA; m/Cecilia B; c/Bruce Anthony, Anna Rae, Antonio B Jr; p/Alfonso C and Ana Lim Ong, Manila, Philippines; ed/MD 1966; pa/Pvt Prac Fam Practitioner; Chief Anesthesia Dept, Liberty Meml Hosp; Am Med Fam Phys; Med Assn Ga; St John Med Soc; r/Cath.

ONI, CLAUDIUS ADESINA oc/Assistant Director and Counselor; b/Feb 8, 1953; h/PO Box 152, Huntington, WV 25706; ba/Bluefield;

p/Samuel Folarin (dec) and Tanimowo Omoseri Oni; ed/BS 1976; MA 1978; pa/Asst Dir/Cnslr, Spec Student Sers, Bluefield St Col; Commun Mtl Hlth Ctr; St Mary's Hosp; Marshall Univ; APGA; Am Col Pers Assn; Am Mtl Hlth Cnslrs Assn; WV Col Pers Assn; Pres Elect WV Assn Student Pers Admrs; WVPGA; hon/W/W: Students in Am Cols & Univs 1976, S&SW 1980.

ORLOFF, SUSAN NESSA SCHRIBER oc/Registered Occupational Therapist; b/Aug 25, 1946; h/4658 Pamlico Circle, Columbia, SC 29206; ba/Same; m/David Ira; c/Jenny Rebecca, Rachel May, Nathan David; p/Max and Lillian Schriber, Rockville, MD; ed/BS Ed; Grad Cert OTR; pa/SCOTA: Cont'g Ed Com, Lic Chm, VP, Acting Pres; Mem Am OT Assn; cp/Jewish Wel Fed, Bd Mem; r/Jewish; hon/W/W Am Wom; Danforth Assoc.

ORME, JEAN MARIE HARDY oc/Executive; Bookkeeper; b/Oct 8, 1935; h/284 NE 118 Terr, Miami, FL 33161; m/Harold D Jr; c/Linda Marie, Kenneth Michael; p/James Thomas Hardy (dec); Muriel Loesche Hardy Bryant, Gray Court, SC; pa/Pres & Bookkeeper, Orme Electric Inc (Electrical Contractors); With First Nat Bank of Miami 1953-60; cp/Vol w GSA 1969-75, Little Leag Baseball 1973-79, St Rose Lima Sch (Asst Libn Vol) 1973-79; N Miami Commun Concert Band: Libn/Sec/Public Relats 1976-81; hon/W/W Am Wom.

ORR, RACHEL LEONA oc/Assistant Superintendent; b/Aug 11, 1951; p/Eben and Mary Orr, Robbinsville, NC; ed/BS 1972, MA, EdS 1976, BS 1978 Wn Carolina Univ; Post Grad Study ECU 1980-81; pa/Asst Supt Instr, Roanoke Rapids Graded Schs 1980-81; Supvr Instr, Roanoke Rapids 1978-80; Instr Halifax Commun Col Evening Prog 1978-80; RN; Instr SWn Tech Inst Evening Prog 1977-78; Fac WCU, Instr Elem Ed & Univ Supvr Student Tchrs 1976-78; Duke Med Ctr PNA Traineeship Prog, Summer 1977; Grad Asst, Dept Adm & Sch Pers, WCU 1975-76; Grad Editorial Asst *WCU Journal of Ed and Psych;* Tchr Graham Co Sch Sys, NC 1972-75; Delta Kappa Gamma, Alpha Kappa Chapt; Phi Delta Kappa; Assn Supervision & Curric Devel; NC ASCD; NEA; NCAE; NC Assn Sch Admrs; r/Bapt; hon/W/W S&SE 1981; Spkr Nsg Ceremony for Capping & Pinning, Class of 1978 WCU; Sr Student Rep, Dean of Hlth Sci Adv Com, WCU 1977-78; Outstg Yng Wom Am 1974; Hon Student Throughout Col.

ORR, ROY oc/Dallas County Commissioner, District 4; b/Oct 2, 1933; h/320 Woodhaven, DeSoto, TX 75115; ba/Dallas, TX; m/Janice Gallagher; c/Valerie, Lei Ann, Tim, Roxie; ed/So Meth Univ; mil/USAF; pa/Nat Assn of Cos: Currently 3rd VP, Mem Taxation & Fin Steering Com, Mem Bd Dirs 1975-77; Dallas Co: Appt'd to Commissioners Court 1972 (Elected Twice), Mayor of DeSoto 1971, Pres DeSoto Sch Bd 6 Yrs, Chm DeSoto City Charter Comm; St & Reg: Chm TSDEC, Dir Tex Co Dist Retirement Sys Bd, Mem Exe Com St Dem Exe Com, Secy-Treas Exec Bd of N Ctl Tex Coun of Govts, 2/VP Tex Assn of Reg Couns; Del: Nat Dem Conv 1968-72, Mini Conv in Kansas City 1974; cp/Pres DeSoto C of C (Twice); Pres Lions Clb (Twice) & Deputy Gov of Lions 1956-57; r/Ch of Christ; hon/Oak Cliff Man of Yr 1976; Outstg Man Under 35, 1963; Outstg Man Over 35, 1975.

ORTABASI, UGUR oc/Head Solar Division; b/June 1, 1938; h/20-D Urb Villa Flores, Guaynabo, PR 00659; ba/San Juan, PR; m/Ilse; c/Melek, Oktay; ed/Diplom Physiker Deg, Univ Hamburg 1965; Study at Univs Gottingen & Hamburg, Germany; PhD Univ Fla 1969; pa/Ctr for Energy & Envir Res, Univ PR 1978-: Hd Solar Div, Chm Res Adv Com, Vis Res Sci, UN Assignment as Conslt to Turkey; Corning Glass Works: Sr Res Physicist, Tech Staff Div 1976-77, Sr Physicist 1973-76, Res Fellow in Physics, R & D Labs 1971-73; Asst Prof Univ Fla 1969-71; Grad Asst, Wn Reserve Univ & Univ Fla 1965-69; hon/DAAD F'ship 1961-65; Awd of Univ of Hamburg for Outstg Fgn Students, Hamburg 1965; Am Nuclear Soc Student Meeting Awd for Outstg Papers 1967; Recip 2 Yrs CGW F'ship Awd Physics; Sev US Patents; Num Profl Books & Papers.

ORTIZ, ARACELI oc/Professor; b/Jan 15, 1937; h/Hato Rey, PR; ba/Univ Puerto Rico, Sch Dentistry, GPO Box 5067, San Juan, PR 00930; m/Jesus Latimer; c/Paul; p/Jesus M Ortiz (dec) and Pura Martinez, Rio Piedras, PR; ed/BS Univ PR 1958; DMD Univ PR Sch Dentistry 1962; Residency Gen Pathol, Univ Dist Hosp 1962-65; MSD Ind Univ 1965-67; pa/Prof Univ PR Sch Dentistry; Am Dental Assn; Am Bd Oral Pathol, Diplomate; Am Bd Oral Med, Diplomate; Am Acad Oral Pathol; Am Acad Oral Med; cp/Zonta Intl; Clb Zonta San Juan, Pres 1978-79, Area V, Dist XI Dir 1980-82; r/Cath; hon/Outstg Alumnus, Colegio San Antonio 1964; Outstg Alumnus Sch Dentistry, Univ PR 1965; Student Clinicians of the Am Dental Assn Achmt Awd 1965; Outstg Wom in Field Med, PR C of C 1975; Dist'd Lady of PR, Fed Jours & Press Writers of PR 1977; SCADA Fac Advr Awd 1980.

ORWIG, ANNE LOUISE oc/Chaplain, Commuter Affairs Specialist; b/Nov 11, 1952; ba/Frederick, MD; p/James and Katharine Cook Orwig,

Berea, KY; ed/BA cum laude St Olaf Col 1973; MDiv Va Theol Sem 1978; pa/Chaplain, Hood Col; Epis Priest Feb 1980; cp/Zonta Intl; r/Epis; hon/Co-Authored Article on Commuters 1980.

OSBORN, MAURICE oc/General Manager; b/Dec 2, 1942; h/707 Georgetown Rd, Red Oak, TX 75154; ba/Dallas, TX; m/Glenda; c/Dennis, Dee Ann; p/Lester Osborn (dec); Gladys Osborn, Palestine, TX; ed/Att'd Pan Am Univ; AA HCJC; Addit Studies; pa/Gen Mgr, Convoy Servicing Co; Pers Mgr; Dir of Labor Relats; Asst Gen Mgr; Gen Mgr; Profl Instr; Profl Spkr; Am Mgmt Assn; Tex Motor Trans Assn; Reserve Law Ofcrs Assn; Sheriff's Assn of Tex; cp/Smithsonian Inst Assocs; Trustee, Red Oak Independent Sch Dist; Treas, RO C of C; CoChm, RO Area Industl Foun; hon/3rd Largest Thermo King Dealer in the World 1977; Thermo King Intl Million Dollar Sales Clb; Top Thermo King Dealer of Tex 1980.

OSBORN, THOMAS NOEL II oc/Economist, Professor, Researcher, Administrator; b/May 22, 1940; h/Ave Leon Felipe 42, Col San Angel, Mexico 20, DF Mexico; ba/Mexico; m/Diana Lynn Bergerhouse; c/Elise, Aaron-Emile; p/Thomas Noel (dec) and Georgia B Osborn, Denver, CO; ed/BA 1963, MA 1970, PhD 1973 Univ Colo-Boulder; mil/USNR 1963-LCDR; pa/Instr Univ Colo 1970, Adj Assoc Prof; Vis Prof Autonomous Univ Guadalajara 1970-73; Nat Univ Mexico: Prof 1980, Assoc Prof 1976-80, Vis Prof 1973-76; Prof & Acad Coor Inst Bnkg & Fin; Omicron Delta Epsilon, Pres Colo Chapt; r/Cath; hon/Fulbright Prof 1970-71, 73-76; Am C of C of Mexico Bicent Prof 1976-77; Author Num Profl Pubs; Articles in Many Jours & Reviews in US & Mex.

OSBORNE, BASIL ROYSTON oc/Executive; b/Sept 22, 1938; h/4635 WN 27 Ave, Miami, FL 33142; ba/Kingston, Jamaica; m/Lucille Joyce Ferron; c/Dawn, Sheldon, Rose Marie, Wayne; p/Conrad Constantine (dec) and Millicent Zara Campbell Osborne (dec); ed/Att'd Col Arts Sci Tech, Barry Col; pa/Owner Time Piece Bus Ser, Kingston, Jamaica 1962-68 & Welcome Aboard Tours, Miami, Fla 1970-; Pres Resort Fashions Inc 1977- & Travel & Resort Fashions Ltd 1977-; Airline Passengers Assn; Fla Regional Minority Purchasing Coun; Small Bus Assn; r/Bapt.

OSBORNE, JAMES SANFORD oc/Retired Mechanic; b/July 27, 1912; h/129 Magnolia Dr, Griffin, GA 30223; m/Emma; c/Linda, Jimmy; p/Robert H and Birdie Osborne (dec); ed/HS Grad; mil/USN; pa/Ret'd Mech, Delta Air Lines; r/Bapt; hon/Fisher Body Craftsman Guild, Sr First Trim Craft & Paint Craft 1932 & 33.

OSBORNE, KAREN oc/Instructor; b/June 19, 1954; ba/Box 1313, Stetson Univ, DeLand, FL 32720; p/Mrs G H Osborne, Sarasota, FL; ed/BS High Hons Univ Fla 1975; MA Univ Denver 1977; PhD Cand 1981; pa/Tchg Asst Univ Denver 1975-77; Tchg Fellow Univ Denver 1977-79; Instr Eng, Stetson Univ 1979-; Free-lance Editor & Tutor in Composition 1975-77; Kappa Tau Alpha; SAMLA; Presented Paper NEMLA Conv 1979; cp/Secy Arts & Scis Grad Student Assn, Univ Denver; Co-Fdr Moonsquilt Press 1979; hon/3rd Prize, Acad Am Poets Poetry Competition, Univ Denver 1979; Var Other Awds; Author Reviews and Short Stories.

OSBURN, CARROLL DUANE oc/Professor; b/Sept 2, 1941; ba/1000 Cherry Rd, Memphis, TN; m/Linda Carol Moore; c/Heather Denise, Valerie Michelle; p/J Gorman and Mattie Lee Osburn, Forrest City, AR; ed/BA Harding Univ 1963; ThM Harding Grad Sch Rel 1968; DDiv Vanderbilt Univ 1970; PhD Univ St Andrews, Scotland 1974; pa/Prof New Testament, Harding Grad Sch Rel 1973-; Vis Prof Univ St Andrews 1980; Assn Internationale d'Etudes Patristiques; Soc Bible Lit; Am Acad Rel; cp/Memphis Oratorio Soc; Camp Wyldewood Adv Coun; Wycliffe Assocs; r/Ch of Christ; hon/Intl W/W Ed 1980; Outstg Edrs Am 1974; W/W S&SW 1980; Author Sev Res Articles.

OSTERBERG, SUSAN SNIDER oc/Dramatist, Playwright, Teacher; b/Oct 12, 1945; h/518 Gingham, Houston, TX 77024; ba/Houston; m/Edward Charles Jr; p/Ray S and Helen Taubkins Snider, Pomona, NY; ed/BS NWn Univ 1966; MS So Ill Univ 1967; EdD Univ Houston 1979; pa/Alley Theatre 1970-; Alley Merry-Go-Round Theatre Sch; Tchr Virgil I Grissom Elem Sch, Houston Indep Sch Dist 1967-78; Actress Talent Assocs, Houston 1976-77; Writer, Dir Am Wom in Radio & TV, Houston 1976-77; Tchr Jewish Commun Ctr, Houston 1975-76; Tchr, Dir Contemporary Arts Mus, Houston 1975-76; Tchr Congreg Beth Yeshuran, Houston 1975; Tchr, Dir Conroe Little Theatre, Conroe, Tex 1971; Properties Theatre Under the Stars, Houston 1971; Lectr Public Spkg, Speech Dept Univ Houston 1967-73; Field Supvr Student Tchrs, Col Ed, Univ Houston 1975-76; Houston Grand Opera Assn: Properties Mistress 1970-71, Dir's Asst 1971-72, Editor Opera Cues 1972-74; Am Theatre Assn: Arts Adm Co-Chm, Profl Chd's Theatre Presenters & Prodrs Steering Com, Jobs for Theatre Grads Com, Convention Recorder; Assn Supervision & Curric Devel; Chd's Theatre Assn Am; Gtr Houston Area Rdg Coun; Intl Assn Theatre for Chd & Yth; Intl Rdg Assn, Tex St Coun;

Tex Assn Improvement of Rdg; Theatre Communs Grp; cp/Alley Theatre Guild; AAUW; Bayshore Area Preliminaries to Miss Am Pageant; Channel 8 Tele-Art Auction; Chi Omega Alumni; Commun Chd's Theatre; Contemporary Arts Mus; Cousteau Involvement Day; Harris Co Heritage Soc; Houston Area Feminist Credit Union; Houston Arts Coun; Houston Ballet Guild; Houston Grand Opera; Houston Indep Sch Dist, Perf'g Arts Bd; Houston Metro Racquet Clb; Kappa Delta Pi; Main Street 78; Mus Fine Arts; NOW; NWn Univ Alumni Assn; Panel Am Wom; Tex Arts Alliance; US-China People's Friendship Assn; Vinson and Elkins; Wom's Aux Houston Bar Assn; Yng Wom of the Arts; Wom's Polit Caucus; hon/World W/W Wom 1979; Univ So Ill Grad F'ship 1966-67; Zeta Phi Eta; Univ Houston Grad F'ship 1975-76; Kappa Delta Pi; Matching Grant S'ship to Alley Theatre Named in Hon of Susan Snider Osterberg; Mem Ednl Tour People's Repub China 1977; Outstg Yng Edr, Houston Jr C of C 1977; Outstg Wom of Yr, YWCA 1978; W/W: S&SW 1980-81, Am Wom 1979; Writer Num Merry-Go-Round Prods; Author "Behavioral Objective in Creative Drama" 1969 & "Bumper Snickers" 1978.

OSTROM, ALICE KOONTS oc/Retired; b/Oct 3, 1910; h/211 Glenview Dr, Marion, NC 28752; m/Ralph K; c/Ralph K Jr, Ralice O Gertz; p/Harvey Hill Sr (dec) and Elsie Tussey Koonts (dec); ed/LLB; mil/Civilian Instr USAFI; pa/Ret'd Textbook Supvr, McDowell Co Schs; Creative Writing Conslt; Former Pres McDowell Arts & Crafts Assn; Treas McDowell Arts & Crafts Assn, Chm Creative Arts Dept; Author & Publr Book of Verse; Judge for The Poetry Soc of SC Contests; NC Poetry Soc; Poetry Soc SC; cp/Chm Dept Corrections Adv Coun; Treas McDowell Dem Exec Com; Marion Gen Hosp Aux; Christian Wom's Clb; r/Epis; hon/Intl W/W Poetry; World W/W Wom; Poetry Pub'd in: Encore, SC Poetry Soc Handbook, New Voices in Am Poetry; Editor Odes to a West Wind.

OSWALD, WILLIAM JACK oc/Corporation President and Chairman of the Board; b/Feb 10, 1927; h/2200 S Ocean Ln, Ft Lauderdale, FL 33316; ba/Miami; m/Delores J; p/Yejo and Marie Oswald; ed/BS; Cert'd Employment Conslt; mil/USAAC; pa/Investor; Bus Mgmt; Writer; Composer; r/Prot; hon/Gtr Miami Social Register; W/W Fin & Bus.

OTTO, MARY VINCENT b/Aug 5, 1932; h/5918 Wigton St, Houston, TX 77096; ba/Ft Worth, TX; ed/BA 1965, MS 1979 Our Lady of the Lake Univ; pa/Congreg of Sisters of St Mary of Numur 1949-; Tchr-Admr Elem & Jr HS in Tex & Calif 1952-75; Resurrection Sch, Houston, Asst Prin 1954-58, Prin 1958-59; Field Dir Ofc of Camp Fire Girls, Wichita Falls, Tex 1968-69; Camp Dir of Resident Camp Fire Girl Camp, St Jo, Tex 1969; Prin Resurrection Sch 1969-73; Grad Student Our Lady of the Lake Univ 1976-79; Am Assn Marriage & Fam Therapy; APGA; TPGA; Mtl Hlth Assn; Houston Holistic Hlth Assn; Nat Assem of Wom Rel; cp/Vol Bexar Co Mtl Hlth/Mtl Retard Sys; SW Mtl Hlth Univ, Bexar Co MHMR Sys 1977; Bd Mem Mtl Hlth Assn in Bexar Co, Chp Aftercare/Rehab Com; Designer & First Coor Proj Friendship; Del Bexar Co Chapt Mlt Hlth Assn to Tex St Conv 1977, 78; Bd Dir Vol Sers Coun San Antonio St Hosp; San Antonio St Hosp Transitional Living Facility; Bd of Sponsors Houston Holistic Hlth Assn; Pvt Pract Marriage & Fam Cnslr & Rehab Cnslr 1979-; Conslt & Resource Person for St Thomas More Parish 1979-; hon/Kenneth Donaldson Awd, Mtl Hlth Assn Bexar Co for Outstg Contbns to Area Mtl Hlth 1977; 1st Annual Awd Reclamation Inc 1978; W/W S&SW 1980-81.

OUREDNIK, JOHN MATTHEW oc/Auditor; b/May 28, 1941; h/1621 Ruger Dr, Bel Air, MD 21014; ba/Aberdeen Proving Ground, MD; m/Patricia Ann Ruzicka; c/Patricia Ann, Lorraine Teresa; p/William Edward (dec) and Margaret E Ourednik, Balto, MD; ed/ABA En Col 1968; BS Univ Balto 1971; BD Balto Sch Bible 1977; MPA Anticoh Univ 1978; EdD Univ Sarasota 1978; pa/Govt Fin Sr Auditor; Am Soc Mil Comptrollers; Assn Govt Accts; Pres Mgmt Conslt Adv Sers; cp/Dir Source Light Mission, Assoc Sch Balto 1976; Dir Teen Challenge, Md Trg Sch for Boys 1974-76; r/Assems of God; hon/Sustained Superior Perf Awd, Dept Army 1976; Sustained Superion Perf Awd 1978; W/W Am Fin & Indust 1979-80.

OUTLAND, CHARLES MICHAEL oc/Insurance Agent; b/Feb 25, 1957; h/1700 Holiday Rd, Murray, KY 42071; ba/Murray; p/Charles D and Mary E Outland, Murray, KY; ed/BS Cand Murray St Univ; pa/Ins Agt, Personal Lines & Life Ins; Indep Ins Agts of Ky, Am; cp/Murray Lions Clb, Bd Mem, Ofcr; r/So Bapt; hon/W/W Am HS Students 1975; Sr Superlative.

OVASSAPIAN, ANDRANIK oc/Anesthesiologist, Associate Clinical Professor; b/Jan 27, 1936; h/Northbrook, IL; ba/333 E Huron St, Chgo, IL 60611; m/Ashghen; c/Nora L, Armen A, Vahe H; p/O and H Ovassapian; ed/MD Shiraz Med Sch, Shiraz, Iran 1962; Residency Hosp of the Univ of Penn 1963-66, Res Trainee 1966-67; pa/Assoc Clin Prof Anesthesia, NWn Univ Med Sch; Chief Anesthesia Ser, VA Lakeside Med Ctr; r/Christian; hon/16 Articles Pub'd in Med Jours.

OVERBY, GEORGE R oc/University President; b/Jul 21, 1923; h/5927 Windhover Dr, PO Drawer 16936, Orlando, FL 32811; p/T E Sr and Virginia H Overby (dec); ed/BA 1951, PhD 1966 Fla St Univ; MEd 1959, Specialist in Ed 1963 Univ Fla; mil/USN Aviator, WWII; pa/Pres Freedom Univ, Orlando 1974-; Life Ins Underwriter & Mgr; Tchr in Elem& Sec'dy Schs; Prin on Elem & Sec'dy Levels in Christian Ed; Assoc Prof, Prof, Dept Chm in Higher Ed; Conslt on All Ednl Levels; Univ Profs for Acad Order Inc: CoFdr Spec Ohio Com, Univ Campus Rep, Chm Nat Com on Textbooks & Lit, Nat Com on Accrediation; Fdr & Pres, Intl Assn for Christian Ed; Author; Editor; Spkr; Scholar; Charter & Life Mbrships, Num Profl Assns; cp/Bd Mem; BSA, Am Security Coun, Citizens for Decent Lit; Others; hon/Bd Mem: Christian & Missionary Alliance Ch, Faith Bible Ch, The Lord's Ch, Child Evangelism, Christian Boy's Clb, Christian Enterprises Inc; Others; hon/Num Biogl Listings; Life Fellow: Intercont Biogl Assn, Intl Inst of Commun Ser; Life Patron, Intl Biogl Assn: 3 Hon Degs; Num Ser & Ldrship Awds; Mem ABIRA; Others.

OVERBY, TALULAH EARLE oc/Librarian, Educator; b/May 30, 1913; h/2106 E Anderson Pl, Orlando, FL 32803; ba/Miami; p/Taylor Earl Sr (dec) and Rachel Virginia Overby (dec); ed/BA Univ Fla; MA Appalachian St Univ; pa/Miccosukee Commun Lib; Sch Social Wkr; Pres Fla Sec Vis Tchrs; FEA; Pres Pi Chapt Delta Kappa Gamma; cp/Fed Wom's Clb; Pilot Clb Intl; Friends of the Lib; Nat Cong Parents and Tchrs; r/Meth; SS Tchr, Supt Chd's Div; hon/Charter Mem Intl Christian Edrs Assn; Delta Kappa Gamma; Kappa Delta Pi.

OVEREND, PENELOPE JONES oc/Professor; b/Sept 16, 1916; m/George Duffield Jr; c/George D III, William Jones; p/William Pyott (dec) and Edna Durham Jones (dec); ed/BA 1938; MA 1972; pa/Prof Eng; Delta Kappa Gamma; NEA; TEA; ETEA; CEA; r/Meth.

OVERTON, BEN F oc/Chief Justice, Supreme Court of Florida; b/Dec 15, 1926; h/2929 Tyron Circle, Tallahassee, FL 32303; ba/Tallahassee; m/Marilyn S; c/William, Robert, Cathi; p/Benjamin H Overton, St. Petersburg, FL; Esther Wiese Overton (dec); ed/BS Bus Adm, JD Univ Fla; mil/AUS, Reserve Ofcr in Judge Advocate Gen Corps; pa/1st Supreme Ct Judge Selected Under New Merit Sel Process, Appt'd by Gov Askew & Elected to 6-Yr Term 1974; Chief Justice 1976-78; Exec Coun of Conf of Chief Justices, Chaired Coms on Judicial Ed & Cameras in Ctroom; ABA: Chm Com Which Drafted Standards for Enforcement of Judicial Discipline, Exec Com of Appellate Judges Conf (Mem of Standing Com on Standards for Crim Justice); Fellow Am Bar Foun; Mem Bd Dirs of Am Judicature Soc & Nat Judicial Col; Currently Chairs New Appellate Structure Comm in St of Fla; Formerly Served for Nearly 10 Yrs as Circuit Judge (Civil & Crim); Chief Judge of his Circuit 3½ Yrs, Chm of Fla Conf of Circuit Judges 1973; Fla Bar Continuing Legal Ed Com (1963-74), Chm (1971-74); Pt-time Faculty Mem Stetson Univ Col of Law; Faculty Mem of Nat Judicial Col Sponsored by ABA; 1st Chm of Fla Inst for Judiciary Created by Supreme Ct; Chm Fla Ct Ednl Coun; Admitted to Practice Law: All Cts in Fla 1952, All Fed Cts incl'g US Supreme Ct; cp/St Petersburg Boys Choir; Rotarian; r/Epis; Lay Reader; Vestryman; Sr Warden of Ch; hon/Phi Alpha Delta; Alpha Kappa Psi; Pi Kappa Phi; Fla Blue Key; Hon LLD Stetson & Nova Univs; St Thomas More Medal of Cath Lawyers Guild, Archdiocese of Miami.

OWEN, DOLORES BULLOCK oc/Documents Librarian; h/218 Antigua Dr, Lafayette, LA 70503; ba/Lafayette, LA; m/Travis E; c/Alexsandra, Gabrielle, Monique; p/Andrew Jackson Bullock (dec); Dolores N Bullock, Baton Rouge, LA; ed/BA, MS; pa/Documents Libn, Univ SWn Libs, Lafayette; Am Lib Assn; SW Lib Assn; La Lib Assn; Soc of SW Archivists; cp/Lafayette Little Theater; LWV; r/Unitarian.

OWEN, ROSS C oc/Retired Teacher and Coach; b/Feb 25, 1902; h/318 Bibb St, Tuskegee Inst, AL 36088; m/dec; c/Rosslyn O Taylor; p/dec; ed/BS SD St Univ 1925; MS Univ Mich 1940; Adv'd Study: Geo Williams Col 1931, NYU 1947-48, Sarah Lawrence Col 1948; pa/Kan Voc Sch, Dir Hlth 1925-26; Tuskegee Inst Asst & Coach Phy Ed 1926-33; Ft Scott Kan, Rec Supvr 1933-35; Philander Smith Col, Dir Hlth & Phy Ed

1935-37; Tenn St Univ, Instr Hlth & Phy Ed 1938-40; Tuskegee Inst Assoc Prof, Phy Ed & Aths 1941-72; So Intercol Conf Basketball Tourn, Chm 1956-75; Chm Local Chapt, Coun Rep Am Red Cross; WSI; Nat Tchrs Assn; Nat Coaches Assn; cp/NAACP; Optimist; r/Bapt; hon/Num Profl Pubs Incl'g Recently Completed Hist & Devels of Sports at Tuskegee Inst; Dist'd Ser Cert, Am Nat Red Cross 1979; US Olympic Assn Cert Apprec 1956; Apprec for Outstg Ser, Sch Ed, Tuskegee Inst; Spec Awd, Miami, Fl 1972; SD St Univ Ath Hall of Fame 1974; Ath Hall of Fame, Tuskegee Inst 1975; Apprec for Ser, Ala Div Am Red Cross; Spec Recog of Outstg Ser to Game of Basketball, Ross Owen Tourn 1980; Hon'd by Miller Brewing Co; Ross Owen Awd, for Dedicated Ser to SIAC.

OWENS, J LYNN oc/Manager, Secretary-Treasurer; b/Oct 14, 1936; h/1923 S Park, Pecos, TX 79772; ba/Pecos; m/Virginia L Campbell; c/Suzan Lynnette; p/B F Owens, Hobbs, NM; Nellie F Owens Van Noy, Artesia, NM; ed/Univ NM 1954-55; pa/Brown Pipe & Supply of Albuquerque 1954-55; Brown Pipe & Supply of Artesia 1956-62; Brown Pipe & Supply of Pecos 1962-; Chm Plumbing Adv Bd; Bldg Trades Adv Coun, Pecos Schs; cp/Secy-Treas Bd Em Pecos Vol Fire Dept; Asst Chief Pecos Vol Ambulance Ser; Charter Mem Tex Assn EMT; EMS Instr, Tex Dept Hlth; Basic Life Support Instr, Am Heart Assn; First Aid Instr, Am Red Cross; EMT Instr Odessa Col; r/Bapt.

OWENS, JOHN P JR oc/Manager, South Central Bell Telephone Company; m/Anne Soles; c/Kimberly, Christopher; ed/Undergraduate, Summa Cum Laude, William Carey College; Grad Sch, Univ of So Miss; mil/USAF Capt, Navigator; cp/Former Mem of Bd Dirs JCs & Kiwanis; Bd Mem & Pres-Elect Rotary Clb; Former Campaign Chm Mar Dimes; U Way (Lee Co): Campaign Chm 1975, V/Chm Bd Dirs 1976, Mem Bd Dirs 1972-76, Executive Bd Mem 1974-76; Chm Large Firms Div, Jackson Co U Way 1976; Mem MEC St & Local Govt Com; Mem Pascagoula-Moss Point C of C; Bd Dirs: Salvation Army, Boys Clb of Jackson Co, U Way of Jackson Co; Campaign Chm U Way Jackson Co 1977; Mem Jackson Co Devel Foun; Mem US Navy Leag; Mem Yg Exec Bd, 1st Nat Bk of Jackson Co; VP U Way; hon/Phi Delta Theta; Phi Alpha Theta; W/W in Am Cols & Univ.

OWENS, ORV oc/President, Orv Owens & Associates, Relationship Development Consultants; b/Dec 27, 1937; h/5810 Ashfield Rd, Alexandria, VA 22310; ba/Alexandria; m/Leona; c/Corey, Kirby, Kristopher, Codey, Candy; p/Orville K and Nel Owens, Everett, WA; ed/BA; MA; Dr Psychol; mil/USAF; pa/Conslt to Govt Agencies; Corps Personal Counseling; Am Soc of Prof Salesmen; Sales & Mkting Execs; cp/C of C; r/Prot; hon/Advisor to Senators, Congressmen & Govt Ldrs.

OWENS, WILLIAM GAYLON oc/Highway Safety Patrolman; b/Aug 31, 1953; h/Confederate Qtrs Apt 9-G, Vicksburg, MS; ba/Jackson, MS; h/Louise Ann Gorman; c/William Gaylon Jr, Edward Wilton; p/Wilton Author Owens (dec); Opal Harris Owens, Grenada, MS; ed/BSEd Delta St Univ 1979; pa/Miss Hwy Safety Patrol; r/Bapt; hon/5 Mile Clb; Expert Shooter, Pistol Range.

OWENSBY, EARL oc/Producer, Actor, Businessman; b/Sept 18, 1935; h/PO Box 184, Shelby, NC 29150; ba/Same; m/Elizabeth; c/Dennis, Elvis, Rhett; p/Thomas and Bertha Owensby, Cliffside, NC; ed/PhD; mil/USMC 5 Yrs; pa/Motion Picture Prodr; Actor; Bus-man; r/Bapt.

OZIAS, JANICE MARIE oc/Supervisor of School Nurses; b/Nov 19, 1947; h/10806 Yucca Dr, Austin, TX 78759; ba/Austin; m/Douglas K; c/OrinMichael; p/Ralph and Elsie Wilson, Vinton, IA; ed/BSN, MA Univ Tex Austin; pa/Tex Sch Hlth Assn, Bd Govs 1977-81; Tex Nurses Assn, Cont'g Ed Com 1978-80; Dist 5 Nurses Assn, Bd Dirs 1977-79, Pres 1976-77, 1st VP; St Tchrs Assn, Sch Nurse Sect, Exec Bd; Austin Assn Public Sch Admrs, Pers 1978-79; cp/Tex Soc Prevent Blindness, Prog Com 1979, Austin Chapt Bd Dirs 1977, Pres 1978; Austin Diabetes Assn Bd Dirs 1976-78; Capital Area Rehab Ctr, Bd Dirs 1977-80; City of Austin Med Asst Adv Bd 1979; hon/Sigma Theta Tau.

P

PABON, CARLOS BRUCE oc/Marketing Manager, South Central Bell Telephone Company; b/May 28, 1944; h/PO Box 414, Ocean Springs, MS 39564; ba/Gulfport, MS; m/Marilyn; c/Robin, Sabrina, Tracy, Heather, Carla; p/Carlos R and Amanda E Pabon, Ocean Sprgs, MS; ed/2 Yr Jr Col; cp/Chm Civil Suc Comm; r/Bapt; hon/Past Pres Ocean Sprgs Lions Clb-Eagle Scout-1st up Sales & Mktg Clb; 1st up of Sertoma Clb; Past Pres Meridians Lions Clb; Mem Moose Lodge; Past Dist Advmt; Chm BSA; Past Pres PTA OS Miss.

PACE, MARGARET ANN oc/High School Principal; b/Aug 7, 1943; h/106 Circle Dr, Princeton, WV 24740; ba/Bluefield, WV; p/Lawrence J and Nettie E Pace; ed/BA Marshall Univ 1965; MEd Univ Va 1968; MA Marshall Univ 1971; pa/Tchr Educable Mtly Retard; Whelling, WV 1965-67, Bluefield, WVa 1968-69; Prin Park Ungraded HS, Bluefield 1969-; Demo Tchr, Col of Grad Studies Sum 1974; Bd Dirs WVa Spec Olympics 1974-75; Mercer Co Spec Ed Adv Com 1970-; ESEA Title I Eval Com, Ohio Co, WVa 1966; Past Mem Dept of Mtl Hlth Day Care Review Bd; CEC: Past Secy WVa Fdn, Past St Mbrship Chm WVa Fdn, Past Rep Nat Bd Govs, Past Rep to WVEA Del Assembly, Past Pres Mountaineer Chapt; Ed Assns: Nat, WVa, Mercer Co; Nat & Mercer Co Sec'dy Prins Assn; WVa Sec'dy Prins Comm; Am Assn Mtl Deficiency; Nat Assn Coors of St Progs for Mtly Retard; Nat Assn Spec Edrs; cp/2/VP, Delta Kappa Gamma; Pres-elect Jr Woms Clb of Princeton; 2/VP, Bd Dirs Quota Clb of Princeton Inc; Bd Dirs Mercer Co Opport Wkshop for Handicapped; Past Secy Bd Dirs Disabled Citizens Home Inc; Assns for Retard Citizens Inc; Nat, WVa (Exec Bd, Secy Bd Dirs), Mercer Co (Mbrship Chm); Pres Jr Woms Clb of Princeton; Others; r/Sacred Heart Cath Ch Alter Soc; hon/Princeton JCs Awd of Apprec for Work w Spec Olympics; Outstg Yg Edr WVa (WVa JCs) 1971; Phi Delta Kappa; Fellow Member ABI.

PACE, WILLIAM EUGENE oc/Architect; b/Jan 3, 1954; h/1720 Shady Grove Rd, Jonesboro, AR 72401; ba/Jonesboro; m/Joanna; p/Harold B and Alice Sue Pace, Memphis, TN; ed/BArch; pa/Brackett-Krennerich & Assocs 1978; Draftsman, Johnson Controls Inc 1978; Scruggs Equip 1976-77; Designer Inn Keepers Supply Co 1972-75; Nat Trust Hist Soc; cp/Jonesboro JCs; r/Bapt; hon/Pub'd Author.

PACKARD, JEAN ROBERTS oc/Washington Representative, Federal Liaison for Urban Counties; b/Mar 6, 1923; h/4058 Elizabeth Lane, Fairfax, VA 22032; ba/Washington, DC; m/Fred E; p/Jean E; p/David W and Ernestine H Roberts, Cincinnati, OH; ed/BA Univ Mont; mil/USAF 1944-45; pa/Legis Rep & Fed Liaison for Urban Co; cp/Past Chm Fairfax Co Bd Supvrs; Am Motors Profl Conserv; Fairfax Co Conserv of Yr.

PADEN, CURTIS W oc/Retired; b/Oct 7, 1920; h/Rt 2 box 468, Corinth, MS 38834; m/James D; p/Wilson Guy and Lucy Curtis Wood, Booneville, MS; pa/Ret'd S Ctrl Bell; r/Bapt.

PADGETT, GERALDINE ANN oc/Chief Technologist; b/Aug 26, 1946; h/PO Box 174, Turon, KS 67583; m/Gary E; c/Michelle, Kim, Drew; p/G Truman and Kathleen A Tucker, Wichita, KS; ed/Att'd Sacred Heart Col; Med Tech Trg St Francis Hosp, BS 1968; pa/St Fracis Hosp: Med Tech Trg, Bench Tech in Chem; Pontiac Gen Hosp: Bench Tech Hematology; Our Lady of Lourdes Hosp: Bench Tech Chem; Norman Municipal Hosp: Gen Tech, Bench Tech Spec Chem; Aurora Presb Hosp: Bench Tech; Midland Meml Hosp: Bench Tech Chem, Chief Technol; ASCP; ASMT; r/Roman Cath.

PADILLA, HERNAN oc/Doctor; Mayor of San Juan, Puerto Rico; b/May 5, 1938; h/GPO 70170; ba/same; m/Miriam Vargas; c/Hernan Francisco, Ingrid Yamil, Gloria del Carmen, Maria Soledad, Fernando Luis; p/Hernan and Luisa Ramirez Padilla; ed/BS (cum laude) Univ PR; MD Univ Md; mil/NG - Maj and Chief Med Ofcr; pa/Mem Med Assn of Puerto Rico, Am Public Hlth and PR Public Hlth Assn; cp/Past Mem PR Ho of Reps, Mayor, PR 1976-; Mem Nat Leag Cities & US Conf of Mayors; Past Mem Num Coms; r/Rom Cath; hon/Chancellor Phi Sigma Alpha, chosen for cult exc prog at Univ Md, Spec Guest Gov of Md.

PADILLA, RAUL (PAT) oc/Chief Operator, Amoco Oil Company; b/Oct 8, 1921; h/2440 9th St N, Texas City, TX 77590; m/Mary L; c/Laura P Lopex, Rose Ann P Gallardo; p/Modesto and Mary De La Cerda Padilla (dec); mil/Staff Sgt USAF 1942-45; pa/Operator, Tin Process Corp 1946-57; Texas City Lab and Water Plant 1957-66; with Amoco Oil Co 1966-, operator, 1966-74, chief operator, 1975-; cp/Past Mem Commun Act Coun, Texas City; Mem Texas City Human Rel Coun, Galveston Co Manpower Coun, Galveston Co Ec Devel Coun, Mem Other Civic Orgs; Mem Dem Com; Mem Leag U Latin Am Citizens (Pres 1946-47, 56, 58, 71, Treas 1973-, Parliamentarian 1972, Secy 1968); r/Rom Cath; hon/Man of Yr Coun 1963, 71, dist 8, 1971; Recipient Plaque for Ser from Commun Action Coun.

PAFFORD, GLADYS LUCILE oc/District Supervisor; b/Aug 19, 1910; h/8 Preston Dr, Statesboro, GA 30458; m/Julian Aubrey; c/Julian Aubrey Jr; p/Mood (dec) and Augusta Pearl Dorsey Griffin (dec); ed/BS Univ Ga 1939; Grad Study Univ Ga & Ga So 1950; pa/Ga Public Schs 25 Yrs; Dist Supvr Fed Works Prog; Co, State, City, Nat Assns Edrs; Ga Ret'd Tchrs Assn; Ga & Nat Assn Mtl Retard; AAUW; Delta Kappa Gamma; cp/BPW Clb; Corresp Secy Ch Prog'd Yrbook Comm; By Laws & Constitutional Amends Comm, Bulloch Co Chapt DAR; Byrnes Downs Garden & Civic Clbs; Cherokee Garden Clb; Coun Garden Clbs; Mr & Mrs Garden & Civic Clb; Fac Dames Clb; r/Meth: Adm Bd, Coun Mins, Worship Com, Alter Guild, Chm Memls Com, Meml Garden Com, Bldg & Grounds Com, Chm Ch Supportive Com, Supt Nursery Dept.

PAGE, THORNTON LEIGH oc/Research Astronomer; b/Aug 13, 1913; h/18639 Point Lookout Dr, Houston, TX 77058; ba/Houston; m/Lou Williams; c/Tanya P Rice, Mary Ann, Leigh II; p/Leigh and Mary Thornton Page (dec); ed/BS Yale Univ; PhD Oxford, England 1938; mil/Cmdr USNR Ret'd, Legion of Merit 1945; pa/Author (with Mrs Page) of 9-volume *Library of Astronomy*, Macmillan, NY, 1968-76, *Apollo-Soyuz Experiments in Space*, NASA EP133-141, 1977; r/Congreg; hon/Rhodes Scholar, 1934-37; Hon DSC Deg, Cordoba, Argentina 1968.

PAINTER, CHARLOTTE L PORTER oc/Buyer; b/Dec 16, 1949; h/Martinsburg, WV; ba/Corning Glassworks, Rt 11 S, Martinsburg, VA 25401; m/Donald L; p/Ralph L and Janet W Porter, Greensboro, NC; ed/BS NC St Univ 1971; MS Frostburg St Col 1975; pa/Corning Glassworks: Buyer 1977-; Prod Supvr 1973-77; Guilford Tech Inst 1971-73; Am Inventory & Prod Control Soc; AAUW; hon/W/W Am Wom 1981-82.

PALLONE, SHARON RANEY oc/Executive Director; b/Aug 8, 1939; h/Rt 3 Box 336A, Little Rock, AR 72211; ba/Little Rock; c/Samuel Pete, Michael Bradford; p/D P (dec) and Helen Raney, Little Rock, AR; ed/Att'd Randolph Macon Wcm's Col; BA Univ Ark 1961; Grad Study Miss So Col 1961; Post Grad Trg in Treatment Child Abuse, Univ Colo Sch Med, 1972, 74, 76, 77; Hon Doct Humanities, Univ Ark 1976; pa/Fdr & Exec Dir SCAN Vol Ser Inc (Suspected Child Abuse and Neglect) 1972-; Child Psychi 1971; Fdr & Chm Little Rock Literacy Coun 1966-71; Fdr & Chm Ark Literacy Coun 1967; Child Protection Team, Univ Ark Med Ctr & Ark Chd's Hosp; Exec Mem Ark Coun Child Protect; Pulaski Co Task Force for Child Protect; Bd Dirs SCAN Vol Ser; Adv Bd Woodlawn Day Care Ctr for Abused Chd; BD Dirs Ark Assn Chd w Lrng Disabilities; Adm Bd Pulaski Hghts Meth Ch; Bd Dirs Ada Thompson Home; Dpty Investigator Pulaski Co Prosecuting Atty's Ofc; r/Meth; hon/Outstg Ser in Field of Human Relats Awd, Wesley Guild of Mile Chapel CME Ch 1974; Del to Gov's Conf on Early Childhood Devel 1972; W/W Am Cols & Univs 1961; Amy Burham Onkan Nat Awd 1961; Pi Beta Phi; 10 Outstg Wom Am 1975; Outstg Yng Wom Ark 1975; Wom of Yr 1975; W/W Am 1976, Am Wom 1976; Author "SCAN Volunteer Services: A Unique Program Helps Child Abusing Parents" *Dimensions*.

PAMOJA, IMANI oc/Teacher, Writer; b/Feb 3, 1947; h/PO Box 41453, Dallas, TX 75241; ba/Dallas; m/Duane Thomas; c/Hisani M, Idris, Aisha Z, Lamila H; p/Aron J P S (dec) and Carrie E Malone, Dallas, TX; ed/Bishop Col; pa/Tchr Bishop Col MAALC; Intl Platform Assn; Intercontl Biog Assn; Centro Studi E Scambi Intl; Mus African-Am Life & Culture; Akini Isl Pub'g Co; hon/Intl W/W Poetry; Writers Dir; Intl Authors & Writers; DIB; 1st Place Plaque Essay Contest; Commun Ldrs & Noteworthy Ams; Contemporary Poets in Am; IWW Silver Medal; Lit Medal, Jr Black Acad Arts & Lttrs.

PANNELL, RINALDO DIMITRI oc/Staffing Assistant; b/May 26, 1953; h/1128 Chgo St SE, Wash DC 20020; ba/Wash DC; p/Roland Hayes (dec) and Mary Alberta Pannell (dec); ed/BA Psych; pa/Tchr Wash Saturday Col 1976-77; r/Carron Bapt Ch, Pres Yth Dept.

PANTOJA, LUIS JR oc/Minister, Professor; b/Nov 21, 1946; h/11304 Estacado Dr, Dallas, TX a75228; ba/Dallas; m/Liwayway; c/Luis III, Calvin Wesley; p/Luis Pantoja Sr, Rupub of the Philippines; Eugenia Pantoja (dec); ed/ThB; MDiv; MST; ThD Cand; pa/Asst to the Pres & Prof Theol, Criswel Ctr for Biblical Studies; Assoc Pastor First Bapt Ch, Dallas; r/Bapt; hon/W/W Am Cols & Univs 1975; Outstg Yng Men Am 1977.

PANZER, DIANA GAIL oc/Sevice Correspondent; b/July 21, 1952; h/8101 Amelia #208, Houston, TX 77055; ba/Houston; p/Stanley and Estelle Rose Rubenstein, Houston, TX; ed/Ser Corresp Trg Grad 1979; pa/US Steel Corp: Steno Clerk 1972, Corresp 1972-76, Ser Corrrst 1979-; Pension Fund & Profit Sharing Dept, Mass Mutual Ins Co 1972; Ofc Mgr Repub Ins Agcy 1971-72; Secy Wendell Loomis & Assocs 1970; cp/Pres Tzadakah B'nai B'rith Wom 1974-75; Houston Coun B'nai B'rith Wom: Mbrhisp Chp 1975-76, Publicity Chp 1976-77, VP Communs 1978-79; Devel'd New B'nai B'rith Wom Chapt, Sabra 1977-78, Career & Cnslg Prog

Chm 1979; r/Jewish; hon/Plate Pwrhouse Awd, US Steel Corp 1978; Ser Corresp Trg Del, US Steel Corp 1979; W/W Am Wom 1979-80; Most Outstg Prog Awd, Career & Cnslg Proj, SW Region B'nai B'rith Wom 1979.

PAPASAN, MAVOUR RUTH oc/Teacher; b/Sept 15, 1914; h/Rt 1, Etta, MS 38627; ba/Myrtle; m/Robert Wayne (dec); c/Bobby Hugh, Larry Wayne, Ruth Ann Stroud; p/Huelet Sessom and Eula Myrtis Messer Gafford (dec); ed/BAE Ole Miss; MMA Am Col Mus; pa/Elem Tchr; Local, St & Nat Ed Orgs; Composer Hymns; Writer Wkly Column *New Albany Gazette*; cp/Repub Party; Del to Meth Annual Conf; r/Meth: Pianist, Adult Bible Tchr, Bd of Ed; hon/Outstg Tchr of W Union; Tchr of Am 1973; Intl W/W Mus.

PAPPAS, THOMAS M (TONY) oc/Congressional Liaison Officer at the Department of HEW Sec Office; b/Feb 3, 1941; h/Box 187 Pappenbauer Haus, Accokeek, MD 20607; ba/Washington DC; m/Maryanne Bauer; c/Parker Bauer; p/Harry George and Iva O'Dell Pappas, St P'burg, FL; ed/BA Pol Sci; pa/Dem Nat Comm Progs; cp/Mem Chas Co Dem Clb; r/Cath; hon/Outstg Yg Polit Ldr.

PARHAM, RUBY INEZ MYERS oc/Retired; b/Nov 4, 1914; h/215 S College, Tahlequah, OK 74464; m/Rufus K McCollum (dec); 2nd J A; c/Bill, Donald, Garry, Anne George; p/Ola T (dec) and Bursha Culver Myers (dec); ed/BS; Masters Deg; Grad Palmer Writers Sch; pa/Worthy Matron OES; WMU; Kappa Kappa Iota; r/Bapt; hon/Grand Cross of Colors, Rainbow Girls.

PARKER, AMOS PHILIP SR oc/Businessman; b/July 27, 1935; h/803 Lawrence St, Summit, MS 39666; ba/Summit; m/Colleen Fay McMahon; c/Amos Philip Jr, Michael James, Joseph Lee, Jonathan Andrew; p/James Burton Parker, Jackson, LA; Elvie Smith Wooten Parker (dec); ed/BS Univ SEn La 1960; mil/USMC; Miss NG; pa/Owner The Warehouse, Plumbing & Elec Supply; Miss Waterwell Drillers Assn; Bd Dirs Bank of McComb; cp/Summit Lions Clb, VP, Pres, Tailtwister; Dpty Dist Gov of Dist 30-B of Miss Lions; Pike Co Arts Coun; Summit C of C; Summit Dixie Yth Baseball; Scout Ldr Summit Troop 143; Del to Pike Co Dem Caucus; McComb HS Booster Clb; Sponsor Rotary Boys Basketball Leag; McComb PTA; r/So Bapt; hon/Dpty Dist Gov Lions Apprec Awd 1970-71; Awd of Merit BSA 1975; Good Shepherd Awd BSA 1980; Outstg Chancel Choir Mem, First Bapt Ch Summit 1978-79.

PARKER, BILL C JR oc/Insurance Agent; b/Oct 18, 1936; h/2205 Young Dr, Valdosta, GA 31601; ba/Valdosta; m/Nancy S; c/David, Timothy; p/B C and Gladys Tyler Parker, Hahira, GA; ed/Att'd Valdosta St Col 1954-55; Nat Retail Credit Assn, Public Relats Course 1958; Nat Life Underwriters Trg Course 1978; mil/USAR 1965; pa/St Farm Ins Co; Valdosta Life Underwriters Assn, Secy; cp/Valdosta Country Clb; Valdosta JCs; Charter Mem N Valdosta Rotary Clb, Sgt-at-Arms; Valdosta & Lowndes C of C; r/Bapt; Deacon, SS Tchr, Pers & Budget Coms, Yth Coun; hon/Liberty Nat Life Torch Clb Awd 1966; JC Outstg Clb Mem 1969; Legion of Hon 1975-79; Bronze Tablet Soc Awd 1980.

PARKER, BOOTS oc/Hostess, Model, Restauranture, Humanitarian, Philanthropist; b/Dec 25, 1929; h/724 Jamestown Dr, Winter Park, FL 32792; ba/Titusville, FL; m/Paul Hixson (dec); 2nd W Dale; p/Joseph P and Ida Mae Harmon Farthing (dec); ed/Modeling Instrn; Ohio St Univ; pa/Pres Multiple Sers, m/Mgmt Conslt, PR & Pub'g Firm; Former Chief Cashier of Firestones U Trading Co & Ofcl Hostess for Firestone Intl, Monrovia, Loberia, W Africa; Formerly Worked w: Holiday Inns of Am, F W Woolworths & Ronnies of Orlando, Fla, O'Neil Co in Akron, Ohio; Co-Owner (w husband) Worlds Largest Space Artifact Collection Containing 5 Moon Items; Owner Diversified Art Collection from Europe & Africa; cp/Mem Num CCs, Incl'g Royal Oak Golf & CC; BPOD; NY Vets Police Assn; Fla Frat Order of Police; Va Sheriffs Assn Former Mem Dem Exec Com; Supporter Var Charities; hon/Intl Humanitarian Awd, London, England 1972; Cert Merit for Dist'd Commun Serv, Cambridge, England; Fla Sheriffs Assns Dist'd Ser Awd; Hon Col, Ala St Militia; Num Biol Listings.

PARKER, E L oc/Law Enforcement; b/July 16, 1929; h/Orange, TX; ba/PO Box 1461, Orange, TX 77630; m/Carey Ruth; p/Otis Parker (dec); Emelia Coon, Saratoga, TX; ed/BS 1969; MS 1973; FBI Nat Acad 1977; Adv'd Cert Tex Law Enforcement Ofcr; Instr Cert Tex Law Enforcement Comm; mil/Tex St Guard 1st Lt; pa/Nat Sheriff's Assn; Tex Sheriff's Assn; Tex Police Assn; Law Enforcement Ofcrs Assn Tex; Assn Tex Law Enforcement Edrs; Tex Crime Preven Assn; Nat Acad Assocs of Tex; Nat Acad Assocs; Tex Div Intl Assn Identification; r/First Christian Ch; hon/Cert Apprec: City of Beaumont 1977, Ladies Aux of Vidor VFW 1978, Ladies Aux VFW 1979, Calvary Bapt Ch 1979, Orange Co Wel Bd 1970; Cert Dedicated Ser, Lamar Univ Regional Police Acad 1976; Parade Marshall: Bridge City C of C Parade 1978, Orange C of C Parade 1980.

PARKER, ELMER BLANEY III oc/District Supervisor; b/Feb 21, 1947; h/204 Fox Haven Dr, Greenville, NC 27834; ba/Greenville; m/Lynda Rogers; c/Kimberly, Marty, Stacey; p/Elmer B Jr (dec) and Evelyn Ward Parker, Stokes, NC; ed/BS Atlantic Christian Col 1969; Job In-Ser Trg Courses, NC St Univ 1970-71; mil/NC Army NG Platoon Sgt; pa/Dist Supvr NC Dept Agric (Pesticide & Plant Protect), Regulatory & Consumer Sers; NC St Employees Assn; NC NG Assn; Pitt Agric Bus Assn; Past Mem NC Bee Keepers Assn & NC Yam Prodr Assn; r/New Testament Christian; hon/NC Dept Agric Superior Ser Awd 1978; Ft Meade Outstg Ldr Awd 1980.

PARKER, EUDINE MARIE oc/Artist; b/Mar 26, 1927; h/310 N 17 St, Enid, OK 73701; m/Willmer B; c/Robert D, Karen Lea Nickel; p/Gordon Meech, Enid, OK; Clara Meech (dec); pa/Photo Retoucher 23 Yrs; Porcelain Artist; r/Fundamentalist.

PARKER, HERBERT GERALD oc/State Official; b/May 13, 1929; h/3510 Tullamore Ln, Tallahassee, FL 32308; ba/Tallahassee; m/Florida Lucylle Fisher; c/Christie Lynne; p/Otis James and Anna Berthina Parker, Fayetteville, AR; ed/BS Univ Neb 1962; MS A&T St Univ 1971; Doct Cand Fla St Univ 1977; mil/AUS 1947-77 Ret'd Col; pa/Dir Crimes Compensation Prog, St Fla 1979-; Bd Dirs Opports Indust Ctrs, Leon Co U Way 1977-; Nat Assn Social Scist; Reserve Ofcrs Assn AUS Civil Affairs Assn; Toastmasters Inst, Pres 1973; cp/Jack & Jill of Am; Am Bowling Cong, Pres Univ Men's Leag; Winewood Mens Gold Assn, Pres, VP; Bass Anglers Sportsmans Soc; Sigma Pi Phi; r/Meth; hon/W/W S&SW 1980-181; Phi Kappa Phi; AUS Civic Affairs Dist'd Ser Awd 1973; Recip BSA Dist'd Ser Awd 1969; Decorated: Silver Star, 2 Legion of Merit Medals, 3 Bronze Stars, Purple Heart, 3 Air Medals, Jt Ser Commend Medal; Ser Awds Received During AUS Career.

PARKER, JACQUELYN SUSAN oc/Aerospace Engineer; b/Jul 4, 1960; h/4605 NASA Rd 1 #4-308, Seabrook, TX 77586; ba/Seabrook; p/William Dale and Boots Lee (Farthing) Parker; ed/BS Gilford Col 1978; AA FTU 1977, PhD Cand; pa/Former Mem CAP (Pilot's Lic Jul 1977); Charter Mem Nat Space Inst; Former Mem Mensa Intl; cp/Featured PEOPLE magazine; her Alumni mag, also many newspapers; Num Radio & TV Shows; hon/Dean's List; Nat Hon Soc; Cert Merit Ed Cambridge, England 1976; "The Golden Eagle" Awd Am Acad Achmt 1979; Num Biogl Listings.

PARKER, JOANNA JAYNE oc/Pension Consultant; b/Aug 28, 1939; ba/7000 SW 62 Ave PH-C, S Miami, FL 33143; p/Jay Francisco and Neva Naomi Russell Gulbuena, W Palm Bch, FL; ed/AA Palm Bch Jr Col; pa/S Fla Employee Benefits Coun; Co-Author "Lucky Day!" Musical; r/Bapt.

PARKER, JOSEPH CHAPMAN oc/Minister; b/Feb 22, 1926; h/104 Sumner St, Selma, NC 27576; ba/Selma; m/Eunice Bray; c/Joseph Christopher, George Randolph; p/Wilbur Chapman and Linder Rhodes Parker, New Bern, NC; ed/AA 1962; BA 1976; mil/USN 1944-46; pa/Meth Min 22 Yrs; New Life Missioner; Havelock Min Assn, VP & Pres; Moore Co Min Asn; cp/Havelock Civitans, Past Chaplain; Ionic Lodge AF & Am, Past Master; Scottish Rite Mason 32°; r/Meth; hon/Carnegie Hero Medal 1966; Commendable Ser Awd 1973; Cert Apprec, Am Red Cross 1980; Woodmen of World; Author *History of Lanes Chapel Methodist Church* 1960 & *Descendants of William and Sally Parker* 1979.

PARKER, LOISLEE M oc/Teacher; b/May 14, 1930; h/1601 S Shade Ave, Sarasota, FL 33579; ba/Sarasota; m/L L; c/Renee, Wayne; p/(dec); ed/BS; MEd; PhD Cand; pa/SCTA/AFL; Grade Level Chm Hlth Adv Bd; Chm Hlth Instrl Improvement Coun; Sch Public Relats; SS Hlth Coor; Kappa Kappa, St Empathy Chm; Kappa Nat Resolutions Com; Kappa Epsilon, Charter Mem; cp/Repub Party; AAUW; OES; Nsg Home Vol; Mtl Hlth Assoc; Grad Student Assn: Pres, Past 1st VP; Bd Mem Coun on Aging; Pilot Clb; Co Chm Mtl Hlth Proj Cheer; Ch Sch Fac Coun; Precnt Com Wom; Hlth Adv Bd; Human Relats Bd; r/Prot; hon/Outstg Tchr Am 1973; Nat Alumni Recog Awd 1975; Nat Ed Awd 1969; Hlth Ser Awd 1978; Red Cross Recog Awd 1978; Co & Sch Public Relats Awd 1978-79; Mtl Hlth Ed TV Hon 1979.

PARKER, LUTRELLE FLEMING oc/Acting Commissioner of Patents and Trademarks, US Patent & Trademark Office; b/Mar 10, 1924; h/2016 S Fillmore St, Arlington, VA 22204; ba/Wash DC; m/Lillian M Cobb; c/Lutrelle F Jr, Wendell E, Raymond D; p/Edgar Parker; Cora Lee Deloatch Parker (dec); ed/BS, CE Howard Univ Engrg Sch 1944; JD Georgetown Univ Law Sch 1952; Fellow Dept Commerce Sci & Tech F'ship Prog 1964-65; mil/USN Ensign 1944-46; USNR-R Reserve, Captain 1946-; Cmdg Ofcr RRU 106 1975-; pa/Mem DC and Va Bars, Admitted to Practice before Highest Court in Both Jurisdictions and CCPA; Reg'd Civil Engr; Patent Ofc Soc; Past Chm and Mem Arlington Co Planning Comm; Acting Commr Patents and Trademarks 1977; Dep Commr Patents and Trademarks, Pres Appt; Chm Com Enrollmt of Patent; Attorneys and Agents, Hearing Ofcr, Dept Commerce; Other Profl Positions; cp/Mem

Bd Mgmt Vet Mem YMCA, Arlington, Va; Bd Dirs Metro YMCA; Past Pres Nauck Citizens' Assn; Shriner; 33 Deg Mason; Mem Bd Dirs Arlington Metro Chorus; VChm and Mem Bd Trustees Arlington Hosp; Howard Univ Engr & Arch Alumni Assn; Secy and Mem Bd Trustees A Pres Classroom for Yg Am; Others; r/Bapt; hon/Superior Accomplishment Awd; Meritorious Ser Awd (Silver Medal); Superior Perf Awd; Letter Commend for Law Examr; Pres Cert Commend (Pres Nixon); Howard Univ Sch Engr Outstg Alumni Awd 1961; Arlington Links Inc Outstg Citizens Awd 1968; W/W Govt; Alpha Phi Alpha Civic Awd; Nat Links Inc Outstg Citizens Awd 1976.

PARKER, MARY EVELYN oc/State Treasurer; b/Nov 8, 1920; h/9321 Hill Trace Ave, Baton Rouge, LA 70809; ba/Baton Rouge; m/W Bryant (dec); c/Mary Bryant Smith, Ann Graham; p/Racia E and Addie G Dickerson (dec); ed/BA NW St Col; Dipl Soc Wel-Grad Sch Soc Work, La St Univ; pa/Exec Dir La Dept Commerce and Indust 1948-52; Chm St Bd Pub Welfare 1950-51; Commr Pub Welfare, St of La 1956-63; Chm White Hous Conf Chd & Yth 1960; Commr Adm, St of La 1964-68; St Treas, St of La-Third Term 1968-; Pers Admr, War Dept 1943-47; Editor Wkly Newspaper 1947-48; Life Ins 1952-56 First Wom in US to Qualify for Mbrship in Million Dollar Round Table First Year in Business; cp/Nat Dem Com-wom; Secy Am Pub Welfare Assn; Bd Trustees Epis HS; Bd Dirs Wom's Hosp; Bd Trustees, Baton Rouge Gen Hosp Foun; Adv Coun, Col Bus Tulane Univ; r/Bapt; hon/W/W Am Wom, Wom in Govt, Wom in World; Wom of Yr 1976, Baton Rouge.

PARKER, MELISSA ANNE oc/Co-Manager; b/Apr 12, 1956; h/100 Clover St, Enterprise, AL 36330; ba/Enterprise; p/Yancey and Evelyn Mixson Parker, Enterprise, AL; ed/Finishing & Modeling Deg, Patricia Stevens Finishing & Modeling Sch 1973; BS Auburn Univ 1978; pa/Co-Mgr Yancey Parker's; Ala Retailers Assn, Assoc Bd Dirs; Nat Home Ec Assn; Omicron Nu; AAUW; Menswear Retailers Am; Haggar NAMBAC Trg Sem Tulane Univ; Fasion Inc; Am Assn Textile Chemists & Colorists; Kappa Kappa Gamma; cp/Assn AUS; Pres & Coor Devel Enterprise Co-Ed Hi-Y Clb; Del Nat Affairs Conf YMCA; Campaigned for Bill Dickinson for Ho of Reps; Ala Retailers Assn, Assoc Bd Dirs; r/Meth; hon/Only Wom Assoc Bd Dirs Ala Retailer's Assn; Omicron Nu; Treas Fashion Inc; Kappa Kappa Gamma; Chi Phi Little Sister; Del to Nat Affairs Conf YMCA.

PARKER, MILTON BICKLEY oc/Assistant Agricultural Extension Agent; b/Apr 16, 1948; h/204 Laurelwood Dr, Smithfield, NC 27577; ba/Smithfield; m/Tish; p/Milton B Parker Sr, Wallingford, PA; Mrs J D Rowley, Media, PA; ed/BS 1971; MA 1977; pa/NC Assn Co Agric Agts; cp/Kiwanis Clb; r/Assems of God.

PARKER, PATRICIA EVANS oc/Financial Executive; b/Jun 25, 1954; h/112 Overbrook Point Ct, Brentwood, TN 37027; m/James F Jr; c/Angela Beth; p/Robert and Elizabeth Evans, Madison, TN; pa/Exec VP & Secy-Treas, Business Machines Inc (Nashville); Exec Wom Intl; cp/Beta Sigma Phi (Local Chapt Pres); r/Bapt; hon/W/W Am Wom.

PARKER, WILLIAM DALE oc/Executive, Humanitarian; b/Apr 13, 1925; h/724 Jamestown Dr, Winter Park, FL 32972; ba/Titusville, FL; m/Frances Ross Jennings (dec); 2nd Boots Lee Farthing; c/Frances Lea, Elizabeth Dale, Kim Carolyn, Penny Jo Ann, Jacquelyn Susan; p/Otis Durie and Eva Estelle Dempsey Parker (dec); ed/Grad Col Wm & Mary 1949, Intl Correspondence Sch (IE) 1956, Univ Del 1959, Cal Wn Univ 1962, Univ Cal-SD 1964, Stetson Univ 1969; (Hon) DSc James Balmes Univ 1969; PhD Fla Inst 1970; (Hon) DD Univ Life 1971; mil/USCG, WW II; pa/Dir Intl Inst Human Relats, La Jolla, Cal 1964-; Aerospace Scist, Mgmt Specialist, Gemini & Expmts Prog Ofc, NASA, Houston 1964-67, Cape Kennedy 1967-69; Mftg Engr & Lectr, Gen Dynamics/Astronautics, San Diego 1961-64; Fam & Marriage Counselor, Titusville 1967-71; Mgmt Conslt & Pres Multiple Sers, T'ville & Portsmouth, Va 1969-; Dir & VP in Charge of Franchising, Am & Intl Model Festivals & Spangler TV Inc, NYC 1969-73; Chm Bd, Travel Intl Inc 1971-74; Mayor Monroe Park, Del 1951; Fdr Indust Mgmt Clb of Newark, Del 1952; Pres NFFE Local 1575, 1968; Former Columnist, Intl Mag Writer, & Asst Editor; Former Producer TV & Radio Shows; Art Collector; Edit Adv Bd, Am Biogl Inst; Other Former Profl Positions & Assn Mbrships; cp/Fdr Monroe Park Civil Def Org; Former Dir; New Castle Co Civil Def Coun, Del St Civil Def Warden Div, Del St Evacuation Comm, Boys & Girls Aid Soc & Marcy Manor Sch, San Diego; Former Chm & Pres, Del Am Legion Child Wel Com, Del, Md & Penn Tri-St Hosp Comm, Del St Safety Coun; Num Fraternal Orgs; Bd Advrs, Salvation Army; Alumni Assns; Former Mem Dem Exec Com; Life Mem: Am Legion, Nat Space Inst, Portsmouth BPOE Lodge #82; Num Others; hon/Designer Astronaut Celestial Navigation Tng Ctr Medallion & Owner Worlds Largest Collection of Space Artifacts on Display at the College of Wm & Mary in Williamsburg, Va; Designed Medallions for All Major Profl Sports Teams in USA 1975; Keys to Cities: Wilmington, Del, T'ville & Miami, Fla; Del Outstg Yg Man of Yr 1956; Del Vol Silver Awd 1957; GM Mgmt Awd; NASA Gemini Prog Group Achmt; Intl Dist'd Ser to Humanity 1969; Nat Spch Awd, Nat Dept Am Legion, St Louis, Mo

1959; Hon Sheriff, Portsmouth 1976; Ext Biogl Listings; Pub'd Author; Num Other Cits & Recog.

PARKINSON, BELVIDERA ASHLEIGH DRY oc/Retired Teacher; Civic Leader; b/Sept 4, 1887; h/PO Box 126, Albemarle, NC 28001; m/Burney Lynch (dec); p/G Martin Dry (dec); Laura Belvidera Dodge Myers (dec); ed/BA Humanities, Flora McDonald Col 1906; BS Home Ec, Geo Peabody Col 1919; BS Lib Sci Miss St Col for Wom; MA Psychol 1918; PhD Psychol w hons 1927 Univ SC; Grad Studies; Columbia Univ, Harvard Univ; pa/Edr; Lectr; Author; Scholar; Parliamentarian; Researcher; Formerly Involved in Activities Associated w Beign 1st Lady & Wife of Pres of Miss St Col for Wom, Columbus, Miss; Vis Prof Psychol, Wm Carey Col, Hattiesburg, Miss 1964; Dir Res Ala Ednl Assn 1930-32; Former Tchr 1914-27; (Hist) Chicora Col (now part of Queens Col), (Psychol) Furman Univ, Adult Night Schs in SC; Tchr NC & SC Public Schs 1906-14; Participant Num Confs, incl'g Centennial Cong, NYC 1940, Rural-Urban Conf, Wash DC, 1939, White House Conf 1944; Lectr Parliamentary Law Clb, Richmond, Va, 4 Yrs; Writer Articles & Res Papers for Variety of Pubs; AAUW; Nat 2/VP, Nat Bd, Rec'g Secy Nat Exec Com, Pres Miss Div 2 Yrs, Past Pres Sev So Brs; Nat Assn Parliamentns; 4/VP, Orgr Alpha Unit in Miss, Orgr & 1/Pres St Assn Miss, Orgr Va & NC Units, Nat Bd, VP 8 Yrs, Past NC Chm; cp/Num Philanthrophic Activs; Public Spkr; Conductor Forums; Ldr Adult Spec Study Courses; Addressed Sev St Convs, Univ Banquets, Assns; DAC; Colonial Dames of Am; Colonial Dames of 17th Century; Mortar Bd; Am Legion Aux; Alpha Delta Pi; Delta Kappa Gamma; Pi Kappa Delta; Regent, Shuhkota-Tomaha Chapt DAR, Columbus; Parliamentn & Chm Lowndes Co Plan, Miss DAR; Former Parliamentn Nat DAR Cong, Wash DC; Former VRegent, Chm Nat Def Wash-Lewis Chapt DAR; Albemarle Woms Clb; Past Pres, Past Chm Commun Ser Dept; Former Parliamentn Miss Fdn Woms Clb; Former Chm U China Relief for Loundes Co; Former NC St Chm Nat Def NSDAR; Chm Stanly Co Bicent Com on Ednl Contests, UDC, DAR, Woms Clb, Parliamentns; r/Presb, Active in Num Chs; SS Tchr: Albemarle, Columbia, SC, Montgomery, Ala, Fredericksburg, Va; Pres Sev Ch Woms Groups: Laurens, SC, Columbia, Montgomery, Columbus, F'burg; VP Ala Synodical; Pres: SC Presbyterial, E Ala Presbyterial; Tchr Mission Study Classes, Montreat, NC; Bd Trustees Stillman Inst; Spkr to Num Interdenom Groups; hon/Dera D Parkinson F'ship Est'd in Hon, Univ SC; 1st Wom Awd'd Doctorate, Univ SC; Cordon Awd, NC St DAR Conv; Phi Beta Kappa: Mem, Readers Coun of Am Scholar Mag, Banquet Address at Univ SC Dinner 1965; IPA; Cong of Freedom Liberty Awds (4); Albemarle Wom of Yr: 1963, 76; Featured in Media; Scholastic Hons; Num Biogl Listings; Author: "A Sch Prog for SC", "A Statistical Study of the Freshman Class in Univ of SC"; Dist'd Wom of Laurens Co, SC; Others; Fellow Mem ABI.

PARKMAN, JESSE L oc/Postmaster, Instructor; b/Oct 12, 1923; h/107 Bellview Dr, Palestine, TX 75801; ba/Memphis, TN; m/Ida Lee; c/Sheila Lynn Link, Jimmye Lee Brown; p/Jesse L Sr (dec) and Martha Clyde Parkman (dec); ed/Bus Col Deg; mil/USAF; pa/Mgmt Action Ser Instr; Nat Assn Postmasters US; cp/Rotary Clb; Sch Bd of Ed; Selective Ser; r/Ch of Christ; hon/Superior Accomplishment Awd.

PARKS, ANNA CONVERSE EVANS SINGLETON oc/Instructor; b/Dec 20, 1941; h/7225 Chef Menteur Hwy, New Orleans, LA 70126; ba/New Orleans; m/Larkin Vence; c/Larry B; p/James and Velma Joseph Converse, Napoleonville, LA; ed/BA So Univ of NO 1970; MA Howard Univ 1973; Cosmetic Therapy Cert for Tchrs 1979; Cert in Voc Ed 1979; Cosmetic Therapy Cert for Operators 1961; mil/AUS 1977; SSG, La Army Nat Guard 1976-; pa/Sr HS Cosmetology Instr; Cosmetician, Magee's Beauty Salon 1962-78; Secy, Cnslr, Howard Univ Dept of Sociology (Wash, DC) 1971-73; Sociologist, So Univ (Baton Rouge) 1974-77; Instr of Cosmetology, B T Washington Sr HS 1977-; Public Housing Instr & Conslt Planning & Operations Spec; AAUP; Alpha Kappa Delta; Author: *Behavioral Perspective of Housing Management* (1976), *Human Relats: A Study of the Social-Psychological Effects of Occupancy Patterns of Four New Orleans Projects* (1975); cp/Vol Ser Worker, Sr Citizens Group; r/Bapt; hon/Rec'd Lttrs of Commend, AT & AGI; La Commend Medal, La NG; Plaque, AGI; SUNO Honor Roll.

PARKS, SANDRA LOU oc/Social Worker; b/Jun 28, 1946; h/1225 Newbern Rd, Pulaski, VA 24301; p/Carl A and Frances J Parks, Pulaski, VA; ed/AA Hiwassee Jr Col 1966, BS VA Commonwealth Univ 1969; pa/Mem Va Coun on Soc Work; cp/Pres Alpha Tau Chapt of Beta Sigma Phi; r/Aldersgate U Meth Ch: SS Tchr, Adult Choir, Ofcl Bd Mem, Fin Com, Chm Com of Ed Bd; hon/Fellow Mem ABI; Personalities of S.

PARMER, CHARLIE D oc/Minister, Associate Director Development; b/Mar 27, 1938; ba/Belton, TX; m/Lyndal Joyce; c/Teri De Lyn, Deana Joy, Martin Ray; p/BA Tex A&M 1960; MDiv SWn Bapt Theol Sem 1968; pa/Tchr Belton Indep Sch Dist 1960-63; Min 17 Yrs; Assoc Dir Devel, Univ Mary Hardin-Baylor; TSTA; cp/Chaplain Lions Clb; Tex St Heritage Soc, Pres; Little Leag Orgs; Lib Bd; Co Chm Am

Cancer Soc; r/Bapt; hon/Stella P Ross Awd for Old Testament, SWn Sem 1967; Pastor Ch of Yr, Tex Bapt Gen Conv 1968, 71, 72, 73.

PARRISH, EMORY CONRAD oc/Deputy Commissioner, Georgia DOT (Engineer); b/Sept 26, 1929; h/3389 Dunn St, Smyrna, GA; ba/Atlanta, GA; m/Nelda F; c/Melanie P Johnson (Mrs William H Johnson), Danny; p/J J Parrish (dec); Ada Belle S Parrish, Adel, GA; ed/BS Ga Inst Tech; MS Ga Inst Tech; mil/Brigadier General; Mem Reserve Ofcr's Assn, Assn of US Army; pa/Am Assn of St Hwy and Trans Ofcls (AASHTO); SEn Assn of St Hwy and Trans Ofcls (SASHTO); Am Soc CE; Inst of Traffic Engrs; Nat and Ga Soc Profl Engrs; Am Public Works Assn; ARTBA; Mem and Past Chm Ga St Bd Registration for Prof Engrs and Land Surveyors; NCEE; Ga Planning Assn; Resident Engr, Fitzgerald and Sylvester, Ga; Served in US Corps Engrs; Chief Urban Planning Sect, Ga Hwy Dept; Asst Hwy Planning Engr; St Hwy Planning Engr; Exec Asst to Hwy Dir; Dep Commr, Ga DOT; cp/Past Mem Gov's Comm to Make Ga Beautiful; Am Legion; r/Meth; hon/Engr in Govt Awded by Ga Soc Prof Engrs; Nat Def Ser Medal; German Occupation Medal; Armed Forces Reserve Medal; Army Reserve Components Achmt Medal; Meritorious Ser Medal.

PARRISH, JUDITH BELCHE oc/Librarian; b/June 8, 1942; h/202 Oak Dr, Louisburg, NC 27549; ba/L'burg; m/Billy Glenn; c/Melissa Ruth, Felton Edward; p/Felton E and Ruth A Belche, Castalia, NC; ed/BS 1963, MA 1968 ECU; pa/Libn Cecil W Robbins Lib; NC Lib Assn; cp/VChm Franklin Co Lib Bd; Lit Book Clb; r/Bapt; hon/Outstg Yng Wom Am 1973.

PARRISH, MARGIE EMBS WOOD oc/Businesswoman; b/Aug 9, 1941; b/PO Box 1208, Belleview, FL 32620; m/Willie; c/Greg, Suzi; p/Chester and Edith Embs, Winchester, KY; pa/Owner-Operator Trucking Co; r/Ch of God.

PARRISH, WILMA KING oc/Businesswoman; b/Jan 6, 1910; h/1221 Audubon Dr, Helena, AR 72342; m/Chester (dec); p/Artie O (dec) and Willie Brantley King (dec); ed/Bus Sch; Dale Carnegie Grad; pa/Co-Owner Retail Furniture Store, Secy-Treas; cp/Altrusa Intl; Poets Roundtable, Ark; Ark Fed China Decorators; r/U Meth; hon/Pres & Wom of Yr, BPW Clb 1968; Pres Altrusa Intl; W/W Am Wom; Outstg Vol Awd, Nat Cystic Fibrosis Res Foun 1964.

PARROTT, GROVER W oc/Pharmacist; b/July 7, 1931; h/110 Champions Dr, Lufkin, TX 75901; ba/Lufkin; c/Janet Coffer, Denise Freeman, Cheryl, Robert; p/O L and Mabel Parrott; ed/BS Chem; BS Pharm; mil/AUS Paratroopers; pa/Pharm; Owner Profl Pharmacy; Rho Chi; Phi Delta Chi; Am Pharm Assn; Tex Pharm Assn; r/Bapt.

PARSLEY, ANDREW MENTLOW oc/Ordained Minister; b/Mar 1908; h/Rt 1, Box 185, Elkton, VA 22827; m/Idell Seay; 2nd Lucia Sanchez; c/Billie Joe, Bettie Jean; (adopted:) Mary, Teresa, Mentlow, Andrew Albert; p/William Drury and Vassie Varina Watson Parsley; ed/Attended Sem; Sul Ross Univ; Grad Wk Univ Tex-El Paso; Specialized in Spec Ed, Tex Tech-Lubbock; PhD 1996; pa/Ordained Bapt Min, So Bapt Ch; Served in Chs in Tenn, NM, Ariz & SW Tex; Missionary & Tchr of Math, Sci & Hist, Grades 1st through HS, 25 Yrs; Est'd Var Mission Chs & Med Clins; Tex St Tchrs Assn; Tex Prin & Classroom Tchrs Assn; NEA; cp/Rotarian; Ldr, BSA; Ldr, Royal Ambassadors; hon/Fellow Mem ABI.

PARSLEY, BRANTLEY HAMILTON oc/Library Director; b/Oct 15, 1927; h/114 Longview Dr, Campbellsville, KY 42718; ba/C'ville; m/Loyce Marie Franklin; c/Linda Marie, Brantley Hamilton Jr; p/Clarence Elroy and Florence Sally Barnes Parsley, Balto, MD; ed/AA; BA; BD; MRE; ML; pa/Lib Dir, C'ville Col; Former Chm: Ky Col & Res Lib, Coun Indep Col; cp/Former Chm: Ctrl Ky Arts Series; Dir Radio Broadcast; r/Bapt; Ordained Min; hon/Sunday Papers Boy of Mo; Am Legion Sch Awd.

PARSONS, PURNA LYNN oc/Internal Auditor; b/June 15, 1954; h/PO Box 4551, Tulsa, OK 74104; ba/Tulsa; p/Carl R and E Purna Parsons, Royal Oak, MI; ed/BSBA cum laude Ohio St Univ 1976; pa/Internal Auditor; Nat Fed BPW; Co-Chm Fin, By-Laws Chm; cp/Acctg Advr, Voting Mem, Fund Raiser, Theatre Tulsa; Programs Chm Ohio St Alumni Clb of Okla; hon/Beta Gamma Sigma; Beta Alpha Psi.

PARSONS, WILLIAM DOUGLAS oc/Attorney; b/Oct 7, 1950; h/Clinton, NC; ba/PO Box 1065, Clinton, NC 28328; p/Seth W and Erma Parsons, Clinton, NC; ed/AB Univ NC 1972; JD Wake Forest Univ Law Sch 1975; pa/Chief Asst Dist Atty, 4th Jud Dist 1975-78; Asst US Atty, En Dist NC 1978-79; Ptnr Warrick, Johnson & Parsons PA 1979-; NC Acad Trial Lwyrs; NC Bar Assn; NC St Bar; Am Bar Assn; Sampson Co Bar Assn; cp/Dem Mens Clb, Sampson Co; Y/ Clinton JCs; Adv Com Sampson Tech Col, Crim Just Dept & Bus Dept; r/Meth; hon/Commend Lttr from Dir FBI for Work as Asst US Atty 1979.

PARTAIN, MARTIN CLIFFORD oc/Master Mechanic; b/Mar 2, 1930; h/Rt 2 Box 414, Harlingen, TX; ba/Harlingen; m/Mary; c/Marty, Mike, Matthew, Marshall; p/Estelle Partain, San Juan, TX; mil/ROTC 2 Yrs; USAF Cook; pa/Sheet Metal Master Mech, Sechrist-Hall Co; r/Bapt; hon/Plaque Explorer Scouts Post 299, Asst Post Guide.

PARTIKA, JACOB F JR oc/Insurance Agent; b/May 25, 1942; h/Alexander City, AL; ba/PO Box 504, 208 Tallapoosa St, Alexander City, AL 35010; m/Louise C; c/Mandy Dore, Kimberly Louise; p/Jacob F Sr and Mamie L Partika, Goodwater, AL; ed/Att'd Alexander City St Commun Jr Col 1976-77, Jacksonville St Univ 1961-62, Oberlin Col 1975; Grad Sch for Mutual Ins Agts & Life Underwriting Trg Coun; pa/Property, Casualty & Life Gen Ins Agt; Nat Assn Life Underwriters, Pres 1974, 1st VP 1973, 2nd VP 1972; Cotton St Ins Cos, Pres Ctrl Ala Dist 1979; cp/Chm Local Medic-Alert Assn 1974; Alexander City C of C; r/Bapt; hon/Recip Nat Quality Awd 1972-73; Nat Hlth Ins Qual Awd 1972; Nat Sales Achmt Awd 1974.

PARTON, STELLA M oc/Singer and Song Writer; b/May 4, 1949; h/PO Box 2154, Nashville, TN 37214; ba/Nashville; m/James Edward Malloy; c/Timothy C Rauhuff; p/Robert Lee and Avie Lee Parton, Lebanon, TN; pa/Country Singer & Profl Song Writer, Nashville; Elektra/Asylum Label; Albums: Country Sweet, Stella Parton; I Want To Hold You In My Dreams Tonight; Hit Singles: Ode to Olivia, I Want To Hold You In My Dreams Tonight, I'm Not That Good At Goodbye, Standard Lie #1, You've Crossed My Mind, Danger Of A Stranger, Num Others; Cloud Dancer, Movie Appearance; TV Appearances: Merv Griffin, Dinah Shore Show, Mike Douglas, Flip Wilson Special, Good Ole Nashville TV, Marty Robbins, Dolly Parton Show, Acad of Country Awds Show, Dick Clark, Num Others; cp/Christ Chd Fund; Cancer Soc; r/Prot; hon/Most Promising Intl Act 1978, Intl Country Music Awds, Wimbly, England; Most Promising Female Vocalist Nominee, Acad of Country Music Awds 1978; 1 of 5 Top Finalist for New Female Vocalist; Music City New Awds 1978; ASCAP Awds; New Artist of Yr 1977, Record World; Num Others.

PASCOE, CHARLES THOMAS JR oc/Director of Data Processing; b/July 21, 1941; h/11580 Hicks Ct, Manassas, VA 22110; ba/Manassas; m/Carole Ruth Kouse; c/Charlotte Ruth, Cheryl Anne, Carrie Marie; p/Charles T Sr (dec) and Annie Pearl Grubb Pascoe; ed/BA Wittenberg Univ 1964; mil/USAF 1962-69; pa/Phi Mu Alpha Sinfonia; cp/Toastmasters; Repub Party; r/Luth; hon/W/W Fin & Indust.

PATANGIA, HIRAK C oc/Professor; b/Mar 11, 1943; h/Little Rock, AR; ba/School of Engrg Tech, UALR, Little Rock, AR 72204; m/Rita; c/Debi, David; p/Nabin C (dec) and Tarulata Patangia, Tezpur, India; ed/BTech Indian Inst Tech, Kharagpur, India 1965; MS Univ New Brunswick, Canada 1968; PhD McGill Univ 1977; pa/Assoc Prof, Sch Engrg Tech, Univ Ark at Little Rock; Sr Instr, Dept Elec Engrg, McGill Univ; Lectr Dept Elec Engrg, Gauhati Univ; Am Soc Engrg Ed; IEEE; r/Hindu; hon/Nat S'ship, India 1961-65; Proficiency Awds, India 1963-65; Nat Res Coun S'ship, Canada 1968-72; Author Res Articles for Profl Jours.

PATE, ALETHEA FENNELL oc/Homemaker; b/Oct 14, 1899; h/Rt 2, Greenville, SC; m/William Wilson; c/William Wilson Jr, Wallace Pennell; p/Willaim Wallace (dec) and Mary Lyle Fennell (dec); ed/Grad Converse Col; pa/Sch Tchr 3 yrs; r/Meth; hon/Col Awds.

PATE, JOHN RALSTON oc/Government Official; Organization Executive; b/Aug 27, 1906; h/1503 N Jefferson St, Arlington, VA 22205; ba/Wash DC; m/Alice Drew Chenoweth; c/John Ralston; p/Charles H and Nell Singletary Page; ed/AB; AM, USC 1927; BS, MD Duke 1933; JD U Louisville 1945; MPH Johns Hopkins 1948; Cert Hosp Administrn, U Rochester 1933; pa/Assoc Prof Commun Med & Intl Hlth, George Town U; Staff Ky Dept Hlth 1938-47; w DC Dept Pub Hlth 1948-; Dir Bur Disease Control 1953-64; Chief Bur Commun Disease Control 1964-; Admitted to Supreme Ct US Bar 1969; Mem Civitan Intl 1955-; Gov Chesapeake Dist 1961-62, VP Zone 3, 1962-64, Intl Pres-elect 1964-65, Pres 1965-66; Fellow Am Pub Hlth Assn; Am Col Legal Med, Royal Soc Hlth; Mem AMA; Assn Tchrs Preventive Med; Other Profl Assns; cp/Nat Coun BSA; Bd Vis Freedoms Fdn at Valley Forge; Pres Com for Handicapped; Mem Gov of Va Com for Handicapped Employmt; Dem; r/Epis; hon/Recipient 1st Albernon Sydney Sullivan Medallion USC; Cit for Ser Leag Wom Voters DC; Scroll of Hon Omega Psi Phi; Named Mr Civitan, Chesapeake Dist 1962.

PATRICK, GRACIE MAE BONNER oc/Head Nurse; b/Sept 15, 1933; h/224 Holy Hills, Biloxi, MS 39532; ba/Biloxi; m/Joe N Sr; c/Joe N Jr, Debra Elaine; p/R F Sr and Magaret C Upchurch Bonner, Sandersville, MS; ed/RN; pa/Hd Nurse VA Med Ctr; ANA; Intl Urological Scis; r/Presb; hn/W/W Am Wom.

PATRICK, JEAN FRASER oc/Clinical Social Worker; b/Sept 11,

1934; h/516 Lakeshore Dr, Lexington, KY 40502; ba/L'ton; m/Paul A; c/James, Paul Richard, Bob, Scott, Mary Ann; p/James A Fraser, Lexington, KY; Jean Lynn Fraser (dec); ed/BA; MSW; pa/NASW; Transactional Analysis Assn; ACSW; Soc Clin Social Wkrs; cp/Chd's Theatre Bd; Plan'g & Zoning Com; Hlth Sers Coun; r/Luth; hon/Most Creative Wom; Stylus Editor.

PATRICK, LYNNE PARKER oc/Training Manager Trainee; b/Mar 25, 1950; h/3904 Walker Ave, Greensboro, NC 27403; p/Elizabeth P Patrick, Spartanburg, SC; ed/AA Spartanburg Meth Col 1970; BS 1972, MA 1975 Appalachian St Univ; pa/Tchr Spec Ed 7 Yrs; Trg Mgr Trainee, Burlington Industries; r/Meth; hon/W/W Students in Am Jr Cols 1969-70; Am Legion Awd 1969-70.

PATRICK, VAN D oc/Bank Vice President; b/Apr 24, 1931; h/#8 Trailwood Ct, Lufkin, TX 74901; ba/Lufkin; m/Bobbie Nalaine; c/Michael Wayne, Sean Macon, James Thomas; p/Van D Sr and Cora Lou Redman Patrick, Shreveport, LA; pa/VP First Bank & Trust Lukfin; Bank Adm Inst; Am Inst Bnkg; cp/Rotary; r/Epis; hon/25 Yr Cert from the Grand Lodge of LA F&AM; Past Pres Tex-La Chapt Bank Adm Inst.

PATRICK, VICTOR EUGENE oc/Deputy Administrator; b/Mar 8, 1931; h/Baton Rouge, LA; m/Janet Ritter; c/Paul R, Margaret E, Jeffrey E; p/Harold V Patrick, Millen, GA; Mrs Edward M Murphy, Atlanta; GA; ed/BA Emory Univ 1951; MA George Washington Univ 1965; MPA Am Univ 1969; mil/USMC 1951-74, Ret'd Lt Col; pa/Ofcr USMC 1951-74; Gen Mgr Public Sys Inc 1974-76; Mdse Controller, Goudchaux's 1976-77; Dpty Admr, Ofc Mtl Htlh & Substance Abuse, Dept Hlth & Human Resources, St La 1978-; Ret'd Ofcrs Assn; Secy Gtr Baton Rouge Area Chapt TROA; Marine Corps Assn; ACM; Phi Kappa Phi; cp/Mason 32°; Heroes of 76; Toastmasters; Shriner; Sojourner; Bd Dirs Baton Rouge Alcohol & Drug Ctr; VP Gulf Coast Chapt 3rd Marine Div Assn; r/Epis.

PATTERSON, EARLINE C oc/Day Care Director; b/Feb 17, 1930; m/James W; c/Shirley A Garner, Marion, Sandra Jackson, Larry, Mark E, Alponso J, Pattye Johnson; p/Freddie Campbell, Huntsville, AL; Olla More Cmapbell (dec); ed/Att'd Univ Ala 1967-68; Samford Univ 1970, 72; pa/Dir Lawrence Co Day Care Inc; Admr Day Care Home Food Prog 4 Cos; Fed Child Care Ctrs Ala; Bd Dirs Salvation Army; N Ala Adv Bd Quality Child Care; cp/City of Decatur Energy Crisis Com; Girl Scouts N Ala Ser Unit Chm; r/AME Ch, Dir Yth Dept, Stewardess Bd Pres, Missionary Soc; hon/Recog Awd for Vol Sers 1967.

PATTERSON, JAMES K oc/Executive Vice President; b/Nov 14, 1949; h/Rt 3, 830 Meadow Dr, Lewisburg, TN 37091; ba/Franklin, TN; p/James R (dec) and Virginia H Patterson, Lewisburg, TN; ed/BS MTSU 1971; Tenn Ygn Bnkrs Sch 1976-77; Am Real Est Inst 1978; Am Inst Bnkg 1980; Sch Bnkg of the S, LSU; pa/Bank Exmr w Tenn Dept Bnkg 7 Yrs; VP First Nat Bank Rutherford Co, Smyrna & Murfreesboro, Tenn 1 Yr; Exec VP & Dir Bank of Franklin; cp/Kappa Alpha; MTSU Golden Century Clb; Elks Clb; Former Dir & Treas Elect Rutherford Co U Way; Tenn Squires; US Cong Page Alumni Assn; Pres Merchants Assn, Jackson Hgts Plaza 1980; r/Meth.

PATTERSON, JERRY LEE oc/Police Officer; b/Feb 5, 1948; h/Rt 2 Box 90, Shelby, NC 28150; ba/Boiling Springs, NC; m/Kay; c/William Scott, Micah Lee; p/William Howard (dec) and Ora Lou Patterson, Shelby, NC; ed/AA Police Sci; pa/Cleveland Co Law Enforcement Assn; Boiling Springs City Fire Dept; cp/Lions Clb; r/Bapt; hon/3 Cits from Region C Crim Just Plan'g Agcy; Gen Intermediate Law Enforcement Cert NC Dept Just, Crim Just Trg & Standards Coun; St NC Cert Apprec.

PATTERSON, LUCY PHELPS oc/Educator; b/June 21, 1931; h/2779 Almeda Dr, Dallas, TX 75216; m/Albert S; c/Albert Harllee; p/John C Jr and Florence Harllee Phelps, Dallas, TX; ed/AB cum laude Howard Univ 1950; MSW Univ Denver 1963; pa/Branham Prof & Dir Social Work Prog 1978-; Asst Prof & Field Coor, N Tex St Univ 1974-78; Plan'g Dir Commun Coun of Gtr Dallas 1973-74; Exec Dir Dallas Co Child Care Coun 1970-73; Dir Inter-Agcy Proj 1968-70; Casework Supvr, Dallas Co Dept Public Wel 1963-68; Casewkr, Dallas Co Dept Public Wel 1954-61; Tabulating Machine Supvr & Oper, Fed Govt 1950-54; Tex Chapt NASW: Secy 1976-80, Bd Mem & Exec Com 1976-80; Bd Mem Tex Coun NASW Chapts 1968-75; Bd Mem Dallas Chapt NASW 1968-75, Secy 1960-61; Coun on Social Work Ed; Tex Assn Col Tchrs; cp/City Coun-wom, City of Dallas 1975-76, VP 1973-75; Commr Dallas Housing Auth; Bd Mem Dallas/Ft Worth Airport Bd; r/Meth; hon/Num Awds & Hons; Author Num Profl Pubs.

PATTERSON, SUSAN FRANCES PIERCE oc/Clubwoman; b/Feb 4, 1927; h/Okla City, OK; m/Louis Winfield; c/Steven Thomas, David Edward, Reynolds West; p/Albert Edward Pierce (dec) and Sarah Frances Jarvis (dec); ed/BS Univ Tulsa; cp/Nat Soc Col Daughs of the 17th Century, Pres Gen; Nat Soc DAC, Hon Nat Pres; Nat Soc Daughs Colonial Wars, Okla St Pres; Nat Soc US Daughs of 1812, 2nd VP Nat; Nat Soc DAR, Hon St Regent; Colonial Dames of Am Chapt XII, Chapt Treas; Nat Soc Sons & Daughs Pilgrims, Nat Chm Bylaws & Const; Nat Soc New England Wom, Org'g Colony Pres; Freedoms Foun at Valley Forge, Okla City Chapt VP of Ed; PEO Sisterhood, Chapt Pres; Delta Delta Delta; Okla Heritage Assn, Com to Preserve Tchg of Okla Hist in Public Schs; Okla Hist Soc; Okla Geneal Soc; Order of Ams of Armorial Ancestry; Nat Soc Magna Charta Dames; r/U Meth Ch Nichols Hills: UMW, Pres 1979, Choir, Wom's Handbell Choir; hon/Okla City Ladies in the News 1975; Commun Ldrs & Noteworthy Ams 1978; Recog from Bacone Col 1979.

PATTERSON, SUZANNAH ANNETTE oc/Manager; b/Oct 4, 1945; h/102 Linton Ave, Natchez, MS 39120; ba/Natchez; p/Wallace Benjamin Sr (dec) and Grace Wallace Patterson, Columbia, MS; ed/BS Univ So Miss; MA Bowling Green St Univ; pa/Mgr Public Affairs, Natchez Mill, Intl Paper Co; Intl Assn Bus Communrs; Indust Mgmt Clb; Public Relats Assn Miss; cp/Natchez-Adams C of C; Am Nat Red Cross Bd Mem, Adams Co Chapt; r/Meth; hon/Outstg Yng Wom Am 1973; Grad Fellow BGSU.

PATTON, CELESTEL HIGHTOWER oc/Associate Professor; b/July 14, 1910; h/4934 Echo Ave, Dallas, TX 74215; ba/Baton Rouge, LA; m/Ural L; p/(dec); ed/DH Meharry Med Col 1947; BS Tenn St Univ 1952; MA Columbia Univ; MA Universidad Interamericana; Spanish Cert, Madrid, Spain; pa/Assoc Prof Hlth Ed, So Univ; Dir Hlth Ed, Wilberforce Univ; Dean of Wom & Hlth Tchr, Bishop Col; First Negro Dental Hygienist in Tex Public Sch Sys; AAUP; AAUW; APHA; HPEAR; ADHS; Tex DHS; Tex AAUW; PUBH; Tex PUHA; cp/YWCA; So Dallas BPW Clb, Past Secy; r/Warren Ave Christian Ch; hon/Outstg Ser Hlth & Dental Hlth; World Mem Intl House, NY; Intl Platform Assn; Pres's Awd; Dist'd Alumnus Awd, Meharry Med Col 1972; Author *Health Education in the Public* 1964.

PATWARDHAN, RAMESH VASANT oc/Surgeon; b/Jan 20, 1948; h/1003 Kathy Place, Elk City, OK 73644; ba/Elk City; m/Sheryl Ann; p/Mr and Mrs V C Patwardhan, Bombay, India; ed/PUC Loyola Col (Madras, India) 1964; MBBS Christian Med Col, Univ of Madras 1970; Intern, Christian Med Col Hosp 1970-71, House Ofcr 1971-72; Resident Dept of Surg, NJ Col of Med & Dentistry 1972-73; Resident Dept of Surg, Creighton Univ 1973-75, Chief Resident & Asst Clin Instr 1975-76; Clin Fellow in Oncologic Surg, Ellis Fischel St Cancer Hosp 1976-78, Adv'd Sr Fellow 1978-79, Att'g Staff Surg 1979-80; pa/Spec in Surg Oncology; Am Med Assn; Creighton Surg Soc; Contbr to Profl Jours; Presenter at Profl Confs; r/Hindu.

PAUL, M LEE oc/Director University Services, Instructor; b/July 13, 1951; h/2536 Dorrington Dr, Dallas, TX 75228; ba/Garland, TX; p/F M and Aileen Paul, Dallas, TX; ed/BS, MS Abilene Christian Univ; Post Grad Work ETSU, TSU; pa/Dir Univ Sers & Res, Psych Instr, Abilene Christian Univ; cp/Entertained w USO Show in Korea 1967; r/Ch of Christ; hon/Nat Hon Soc; Pres's S'ship ACU; Outstg Yng Man Am 1979; Evaluated as Superior as Psych Instr.

PAUL, PATSY LYN WITTENAUER oc/Free-Lance Commercial Artist; b/June 26, 1955; h/10 Timberlake Trail, Conway, AR 72032; ba/Conway; m/George S; p/William H and Frances J Wittenauer; ed/BA Univ Ctrl Ark; pa/Painted Mural of Hist Univ Ctrl Ark; Designed Progs for UCA Functions; cp/Painted Bicent Star in Middle of Conway Intersection; Red Cross Vol; r/Epis; hon/Dean's List; Alpha Chi; Former Pres Kappa Pi.

PAULEY, ALTA L oc/Project Director; b/Mar 3, 1924; h/Dothan, AL; ba/400 S Edgewood, Dothan, AL 36301; m/Warren P; c/Warren P Jr, Suzanne Pauley Mills, (Foster Chd:) Judi Fox Zuccaro; p/Oralee Sellers, Jasper, AL; pa/Dir Vol Sers, SE Ala Med Ctr 9 Yrs; Dir Ret'd Ser Vol Prog 1980-; Am Soc Dirs Vol Sers; GSA, Coun Field VP, Assn Chm; Dothan Wiregrass Art Leag, Pres; cp/Nat Peanut Fest, Bd Trustees; Assn Sers Agcys, VP; r/Prot; hon/Thanks Badge 1955; Awd in Apprec of Ser, Teenage Vols, SE Ala Med Ctr 1977; Cert Apprec, RSVP 1977.

PAYNE, G FREDERICK oc/Educator; b/Jan 29, 1941; h/Rt 1 Box 274, 32 Chinquapin Rd, Travelers Rest, SC 29690; ba/Tigerville, SC; m/Kay Martin; c/John Frederick, Mark Christopher, Janet Elizabeth; p/Fred N (dec) and Lota Griffith Payne, Donalds, SC; ed/BS 1963, MA 1966 Univ SC; MRE Luth Theol So Sem 1968; PhD Cand Univ Ga; mil/USN 1960-62; pa/Dir Devel, N Greenville Col 1980-; Dir Admissions, Brewton-Parker Col 1978-80; Asst Prof, Ga So Col 1966-78; Ga Assn Col Registrars & Admissions Ofcrs; Assn Am Geographers, SEn Div Steering Com 1973-75; Sigma Xi, GSC Clb Pres, VP, Secy; cp/Kiwanis Clb; C of C; Ldrship Greer; r/Bapt; hon/Dist'd Ser Awd, Brewton-Parker Col 1980; Predoct F'ship, Inst Higher Ed, Univ Ga 1969-71; Num Articles in Profl Jours.

PERSONALITIES OF THE SOUTH

PAYNE, GRACE LILLIAN oc/Retired; b/June 7, 1898; h/552 Wood Val Dr SW, Marietta, GA 30064; m/Talmadge; c/Priscilla Weese, Paul, Titus, Beulah Clement; p/James and Mary Ann Fraser; ed/RN; pa/Ret'd Nurse; r/Prot.

PAYNE, JAMES EDWARD oc/Industrial Engineer; b/Dec 23, 1944; h/4201 Corbett Dr, Del City, OK 73115; ba/ALC/MAWF, Tinker AFB, OK; m/Mary Gibson; c/James Michael, Mark Wayne; p/James Benton and Helen Henley Payne, Enid, OK; ed/BS Okla St Univ 1968; Further Study Towards MBA Okla City Univ; pa/Reg'd Profl Engr: Okla 1972, Ks 1975; Okla Soc Profl Engrs; Nat Soc Profl Engrs; Order of the Engr; Treas Am Inst Indust Engrs 1976-77; Am Soc ME; Tinker Soc Profl Engrs & Scists; Tinker Mgmt Clb; Am Inst Aeronautics & Astronautics, OSU Student Chapt Treas 1967; Dir & VP J B Payne & Assoc Inc, Enid; cp/Okla Co Foster Parent Assn; Tinker Mens Golf Clb; Little Leag Baseball Coach; Former Little Leag Basketball Coach; YMCA; PTA; Highland Park Baseball Assn; r/St Matthew U Meth Ch; Former Student Treas Wesley Foun Stillwater, Okla; hon/Nom to Participate in AF Logistics Command Incentive Orientation Prog; Rec'd Outstg Job Perf Rating; DIB; Men Achmt; Notable Am of Bicent Era; Commun Ldrs & Noteworthy Ams; Fellow Mem ABI.

PAYNE, JUANITA BRINKLEY oc/Executive Secretary, Psychic; b/Dec 1, 1939; h/413 Double Springs Rd, Murfreesboro, TN 37130; ba/Smyrna, TN; m/Barnett; c/Michael, Rachael, Elizabeth, Valerie; p/Floyd Cletis and Thelma Ruth Brinkley, Shady Val, TN; ed/BA 1960, MS 1964, MBA Cand, Univ Tenn-Knoxville; Cert'd Profl Secy 1978; pa/Exec Secy to VP Fin & Adm; Psychic & Astrologer; Tenn Life Cnslg Sers, Co-Dir 1980-81; AAUM; Assn for Res & Enlightenment; Nat Secy Assn Intl; Nat Assn Female Execs; cp/Nat Entrepreneurs Assn; Troop Ldr GSA; r/Congreg; hon/W/W Am Wom; Personalities of Am; Lectr in Field of Parapsychol.

PAYNE, KERRY MAXINE HANCOCK oc/Homemaker; b/Aug 12, 1944; h/2311 Woodley Rd, Montgomery, AL 36111; m/Gillis Lavelle Jr; c/Andrew Christian; p/Herman Huffman and Maxine Moore Hancock, McCalla, AL; ed/AB Ala Col, Univ Montevallo 1966; pa/Sch Tchr; cp/Montgomery-Autauga Med Aux, Pres; Montgomery Jr Leag; DAR; r/Prot.

PAYSINGER, VIRGINIA ALICE THOMPSON oc/Public School Teacher; b/Oct 19, 1918; h/2010 E Wells Park Dr, Newberry, SC 29108; ba/Newberry; m/Gerald Chapman; c/Nancy Virginia P Hove, Jane Thompson, Alice Louise; p/Percy Trimmier and Nancy Elizabeth Tanner Thompson (dec); ed/AB 1939; Spch & Drama Cert 1939 Columbia Col; Grad Wk Clemson Univ; pa/Tchr Speers St Sch, Newberry; Newberry Co Ed Assn; SC Ed Assn; NEA; cp/Columbia Col Alumnae Assn: Past Coun Mem, Past Mem Exec Bd; Past Pres, Newberry Col Wom's Leag (3 Terms); Literary Study Clb: Past Pres, Past VP, Past Publicity Dir; Past Secy, Am Legion Aux; Others; r/Luth Ch of Redeemer, Newberry: Ch Coun 4 Yrs, Past Secy & Mem Exec Bd, Adm Cabinet 3 Yrs, Social Min Com Chm 3 Yrs, SS Supt, SS Tchr, Weekday Ch Sch, Former Tchr; Luth Ch Wom: Pres Local Org 5 Yrs, Past VP, Past Treas, Past Chm Ed Com; SC Unit of Luth Ch Wom: Exec Bd 5 Yrs, Publicity Chm 2 Yrs, Ed Com Chm 2 Yrs, Past St Conv Chm, SC Unit Del to 1977 LCW Triennial Conv; hon/HS Top Hon Grad; Col Scholastic S'ship; Personalities of S; Notable Ams of Bicent Era; Fellow Mem ABI.

PEACOCK, CYNTHIA oc/Nurse; h/302 E Kennedy Cir, Benson, NC 27504; ba/Erwin, NC; m/Ernest; c/Casandra, Sterling; p/Thurman Bridgers, Durham, NC; Ledora Allen, Balto, MD; ed/Dip Durham Tech Col; pa/LPN Good Hope Hosp; cp/Mem US Dept of Compensatory Ed Adv Panel for Title I Dist Practices Study (Only Parent on Panel); Active in Johnston Co Schs Title I Parents Adv Coun 1978-; Chm Sch Title I Adv Coun for Benson Primary & Elem Schs; Chm Johnston Co Dist Sch Adv Coun for Title I; Del to Nat Coalition of Title I Parents 1979 & 80; Lectr for Parent Grps on Topic "Parents Rights and Responsibilities Toward Their Children's Education"; r/Benson Rivival Ch.

PEACOCK, SHERRILL EDWIN oc/Farmer; b/Mar 3, 1931; h/Rt 2 Box 14, Benson, NC 27504; ba/Same; m/Willadean J; c/Ronnie Edwin, Brenda P McLamb; p/Willie Eric (dec) and Bertha Webb Peacock, Benson, NC; mil/AUS Corp; pa/Farmer; Com-man Agricl Stabilization & Conserv Ser Joston Co; r/Advent Christian; hon/Conserv Farm Fam of Yr 1978.

PEARCE, CHARLES WELLINGTON oc/Surgeon; b/Nov 2, 1927; h/1662 State St, New Orleans, LA 70118; ba/New Orleans; m/Dorothy DeL; c/John Y, Charles W Jr, Andrew F, Margaret E; p/Frances Marion Pearce (dec); Fanny Chamberlain Brown (dec); ed/MD Cornell Univ 1953; mil/AUS 1946-48; pa/Cardiovascular & Thoracic Surg; Clin Assoc Prof Surg, Tulane Univ 1969-; Hd Sect Cardiovascular & Thoracic Surg 1967-69, Assoc Prof Surg 1966-69, Asst Prof Surg 1962-66, Instr Surg 1960-61; Instr Surg, Cornell Univ 1958-60; Vis Surg, Charity Hosp, New Orleans; Conslt in Surg, Huey P Long Charity Hosp, Lallie Kemp Charity Hosp, VA Hosp Alexandria; Staff Mem: Touro Infirm, So Bapt Hosp, Mercy Hosp, Hotel Dieu, E Jefferson Gen Hosp; Fellow, Am Col Surgs; Am Assn Thoracic Surg; Soc Thoracic Soc; Intl Soc Surg; Fellow, Am Col Cardiology; Fellow, Am Col Chest Phys; Am Heart Assn; La Heart Assn; So Med Assn La Thoracic Assn; New Orleans Postgrad Med Assem; Oscar Creech Sug Soc; Am Proctologic Soc; Orleans Parish Med Soc; La St Med Soc; Phi Chi, Pres, Cornell Chapt; cp/SAR; Soc Mayflower Descendents, Gov, La Soc; New Orleans Opera House Assn, Bd Govs; New Orleans Spring Fiesta Assn; Fgn Relats Assn; La Landmark Soc; New Orleans Mus Art, Sponsor; C of C of New Orleans Area; Intl Platform Assn; R Assn, Rice Univ; r/Presb; hon/Alpha Omega Alpha; Est'd Investigator, Am Heart Assn; Awd of Hon, Wisdom Soc; W/W S&SW; Am Men of Sci; Ldrs Am Sci; DIB; Men Achmt; Personalities So; Hereditary Register USA; Dir Med Specs; Commun Ldrs & Noteworthy Ams; Author of More than 75 Articles in Profl Jours.

PEARCE, DOROTHY DeLORENZO oc/Civic Worker; b/Mar 22, 1927; h/1662 State St, New Orleans, LA 70118; m/Charles W; c/John Y, Charles W Jr, Andrew Frances, Margaret Elizabeth; p/Andrew John (dec) and Margaret Robilotti De Lorenzo (dec); ed/BA Barnard Col Columbia Univ 1947; cp/Thrift Shop Rep, So NY Hosp's Wom's Aux 1959-60; Bd Govs New Orleans Opera House Assn Wom's Guild, 1965-73, Social Hostess 1966-71, Hist 1969-; Chm Uptown Subscription Com 1967-69; Mem Chd's Concerts Com 1964-66, Mem Tour Com New Orleans Spring Fiesta Assn 1966-67; Opera Orientation Com, New Orleans Opera House Assn 1964-72, Registrar, Hostess 1965; New Orleans Symph Preview 1968-; Fund Raising Com, De Paul Hosp Wom's Aux 1968-; Vol Crippled Chd's Hosp Guild 1965-66; La Coun Perf'g Arts 1967-; Gailler Hall Wom's Com 1967; Bd Commun Concerts Assn, New Orleans; Fund Raising Com Hotel Dieu Wom's Aux 1968-; Bd Dirs Mercy Hosp Wom's Aux 1965-72, Pres 1970; Bd Dirs Sara Mayo Hosp Guild 1964-; Chm Hosp Comm 1967-72; Bd Dirs Orleans Parish Med Aux 1969-71; Chm AMA Ed & Res Fund Com 1969-71; Bd Dirs Visiting Nurses Assn; New Orleans Garden Soc, Chm Christmas Decorations 1969-70; Fgn Relats Assn; AAUW; La Landmark Soc; Friends of the Cabildo 1978-; r/Roman Cath.

PEARMAN, REGINALD A SR oc/Professor; b/Aug 8, 1918; h/#1203 200 Ft Meade Rd, Laurel, MD 20810; ba/Bowie, MD; m/Barbara A; c/Jocelyn R, Reginald A Jr; p/Reginald J (dec) and Louise I Pearman (dec); ed/BS, EdM, CAGS Boston Univ; mil/AUS WWII; pa/Hlth Ed Specialist; Col Prof: Leland Col 1942-43, Morristown Col 1949-50, Bowie State Col 1951-; Tchr, Inkster (Mich) Public Sch Sys 1944-47; ASA; Col Hlth & PE Coms; Fellow: AAHPER, ASHA, APHA, Nat Parks & Rec Assn; Aristo Clb; cp/Boy's Clbs; Omega Psi Phi; Dem Party; r/Cath; hon/Certs of Merit St of Md; Cert Apprec, Bowie St Col; Biogl Listings.

PEAVY, JOHN WESLEY JR oc/Judge; b/Apr 28, 1942; h/5501 Blythewood, Houston, TX 77021; ba/Houston; m/Diane; c/Wendy, John III, Tiffany, Jason Christopher; p/J W Sr and Malinda T Peavy, Houston; ed/AB 1964, JD 1967 Howard Univ; pa/Judge-J of P Precnt 7 1973-; Assoc Counsel for Proj: Home 1970-71; Exec Asst to Co Judge Bill Elliot 1968-70; Assoc Field Coor Harris Co Commun Action Assn 1967-68; Nat Aeronauts & Space Coun, The White House, Wash DC; Adm Asst 1964-67, Acctg Clk 1962-64; Profl Orgs; cp/BSA: Area Chm W L David Div, San Houston, Eagle Scout, Order of Arrow; Alpha Phi Alpha; Urban Leag; Harris Co Coun Orgs; NAACP; Nom'g Com: Houston Bus & Profl Mens Clb, YMCA Century Clb; Adv Bd KYOK Radio Sta; Legal Advr Lions Clb; Bd Dirs: Mercy Hosp, C of C; Steering Com A Philliph Randolph Inst; Former Dem Precnt Chm, Precnt 292 Houston; r/Antioch Mission Bapt Ch: Parliamentn; hon/Chgo Tribune Awd, Outstg Mil Student; Acad S'ship; YMCA; Dist'd Achievers Awd, Outstg Ser to Commun; Biogl Listings; Hon Mem ILA; Others; Fellow Mem ABI.

PECK, BETTY LEE oc/Nurse; b/Feb 1, 1926; h/Rt 66, Box 296, Daniels, WV 25832; ba/Beckley, WV; m/Harry G Sr; c/Virginia P McCroskey, Harry G Jr; p/Russel Forrest (dec) and Irma L Newton, Daniels, WV; ed/Univ Va Sch Nsg; Cont'g Nsg Ed, WV Univ; pa/RN VA Med Ctr; cp/SS Tchr; Past Mem Beta Sigma Phi; Past Mem Shady Spring Wom's Clb; r/Meth.

PECK, DIANNE KAWECKI oc/Architect; Corporate Officer; b/Jun 13, 1945; h/11510 Wildflower Ct, Woodbridge, VA 22192; ba/Woodbridge; m/Gerald Paul; c/Samantha Gillian, Alexis Hilary; p/Thaddeus W and Harriet A Zlotkowski Kawecki, Ridgefield, NJ; ed/BA Carnegie-Mellon Univ 1968; pa/Peck Peck & Williams Inc: Partner 1974-80, Corp Ofcr 1980-; Partner, Peck & Peck Archs 1973-74; With Beery-Rio & Assoc (Annandale, Va) 1971-73; With Kohler-Daniels & Assocs (Vienna, Va) 1969-71; Other Former Positions; VP, Voc Ed Foun 1976; Chm, Arch & Engrg, United Way; Hlth Sys Agy 1977-; Wash Profl Wom's Corp; Chm, Indust Devel Auth of PW 1976-, VChm 1977, Mem 1975-78; PW Co Bd of Suprvs 1976; cp/Bd Dirs, PW C of C 1977-80; Repub Party; r/Rom Cath; hon/Pub'd Res on Inner City Rehab for FNMA; W/W: Am Wom, SE.

241

PERSONALITIES OF THE SOUTH

PEGUES, WENNETTE OSCEOLA WEST oc/Associate Academic Dean; b/Nov 25, 1936; h/1741 W Virgin St, Tulsa, OK 74127; ba/Tulsa; m/Julius; c/Mary Angela, Michael David, Angela Suzette; p/Wilbur Brown West (dec); Mary Josephine Cutts (dec); ed/BSN Carlow Col 1958; CCS Univ Tulsa 1974; mil/AUS Nurse Corps; pa/Assoc Acad Dean, Langston Univ Urban Ctr; Bd Dirs Tulsa Dist Nurses 1970-72; Bd Dirs Tulsa Leag Nsg 1969-71; APGA; OPGA; Nat Assn Acad Affairs Admrs, Mem Nat Bd Dirs, Minority Task, Judicial Affairs & Legal Issues; Nat Assn Wom Deans, Admrs & Cnlsrs; AAUW; Nat Conf Acad Advg, Chp Regional Publicity & Org, Mem Com on Orgl Plan'g & Structure, Exec Steering Com; Am Public Wel Assn; cp/Bd Dirs: Family & Chd Sers 1969-73, Margaret Hudson Prog for Teenage Parents 1970-73, Tulsa YWCA 1974-75, Magic Empire Coun of Girl Scouts 1975; Okla St Wel Com; Dep Sch Bd Dist 55, 1979-80; Intl Review Bd Hillcrest Med Ctr 1979; r/Cath; hon/Grad Asst'ship, Univ Tulsa 1974-75; Grad Res F'ship, Univ Tulsa 1975-76; Outstg Schlr in Okla 1976; Alpha Kappa Delta; Kappa Delta Pi; Phi Delta Kappa; W/W Am Wom 1978-79.

PEHL, LINDA KAY oc/Nurse Educator; b/Nov 8, 1942; h/Rt 5, Box 5803-W, Belton, TX 76513; ba/Belton; m/Charles A; c/Donna Denise, Daryl Dwayne; p/Lionel L (dec) and Earon Hood, Belton, TX; ed/BSN; MSN; PhD Cand; pa/ANA; TNA, Dist VII Bd Dirs; Chp: Nom'g Com, Public Relats Com, Mbrship Com; Vol Con'g Ed for RN's, Planner & Condr Progs; cp/Vol Am Heart Assn, Am Cancer Soc, Jerry Lewis MD Drive; Scott & White Hosp Sch Nsg Alumnae Assn; Tex-N-Cap; r/Bapt; SS Tchr; hon/Tchg Excell Awd; Outstg Yng Wom Am 1977.

PELTIER, FLOYD G oc/Locksmith, Minister; b/Jan 27, 1933; h/1406 Alta Mira, Killeen, TX 76541; ba/Killeen; m/Elsie B; c/Floyd G Jr, Patricia N, Jeffrey A, Christopher D; p/Michael and Nora Peltier, Detroit, MI; ed/Grad NJ Locksmith Inst 1968; Univl Bible Inst 1977; mil/1952-72; pa/Locksmith, Joyners Lock & Key Ser; Assoc Pastor, 2nd Bapt Chm, Lampassa, Tex; Tex Locksmith Assn; Assoc'd Locksmith of Am r/Bapt; Ordained Min 1979; hon/Kiwanis Clb Ser Awd 1977.

PELTON, WILLIAM ALLEN JR oc/Artist; b/Nov 22, 1944; h/1100 Parkwood Cir, Picayune, MS 39466; ba/Same; m/Rose D; c/William A III, Amanda Rose; p/William A and Grace J Pelton, San Antonio, TX; mil/USN 1962-65; pa/Custom Painting; Air Bursh T-Shirts; Oil & Acrilic Canvas; cp/Art Tchr; r/Prot.

PENAROQUE, ERNEST oc/Analyst; b/Aug 10, 1933; h/Rt 8 Box 9X, Orlando, FL 32817; m/Dorothy J Milcarek; c/Ernie Jr, Anita, Tony p/Braulia Penaroque, Humacao, PR; ed/AS Valencia Col 1976; BABA Univ Ctrl Fla-Orlando 1978; mil/USAF; pa/Prog Mgmt Analyst; Supply/Logistics Mgmt; Mktg Mem, Umpires Assn (ASA); cp/Paso Fino Horseman Assn; r/Cath; hon/Air Force Commend Medals (4) 1968, 69, 70, 72; Strategic Air Command Ednl Achmt Awd 1970; Cost Reduction Awd 1968; Outstg Yng Man Awd 1969; Dean's List UCF 1977; Dean's List Valencia Col 1976; Good Conduct Medals (5); Outstg Unit Cit Awd 1959; Vietnam Medal 1969.

PENDER, P EUGENE oc/Corporate Controller; b/Feb 5, 1931; h/7215 Lavendale Cir, Dallas, TX 75230; ba/Dallas; m/Lynelle; c/Gary Warren, Jeffrey Scott; c/R L Pender, Shreveport, LA; Annie C Penny (dec); ed/Att'd NWn St Col 1948-50, Centenary Col 1950-52; pa/Acct Pak-a-Sak Ser Stores 1950-52, Secy-Treas, Dir 1952-71; Southland Corp: Div Controller 1971-72, Asst Corp Controller 1972, Corp Controller 1973-; Pres Ark-La-Tex; Airmen's Assn 1967-69; Bd Dirs BBB 1971; Mtl Hlth Ctr 1964; U Fund; CPA La; CPA Tex; Am Inst CPAs; La & Tex Socs CPAs; QBs, Keyman 1971-72; cp/Dem Party; r/Epis.

PENDERGRASS, SUZANNE SHINGLER oc/Co-Director; b/Jan 31, 1957; h/2401 Nottingham Way 102, Albany, GA 31707; ba/Albany; p/S P (dec) and Mary S Pendergrass, Greenwood, SC; ed/Att'd Presb Col 1975-76; Deg Col of Charleston 1976-79; pa/Co-Dir Woodland Hall Acad; Greenwood Rdg Foun; SCALD; cp/Sat Sch Tutor, Greenwood Rdg Foun 1972-76; Summer Sch Tchr, Woodland Hall Acad 1977; Camp Cnslr Woodland Hall 1979; r/Meth; hon/DAR; Furman Schlr 1978; Presb Col Jr Fellow 1978; Sr Valedictorian 1975; Math Awd 1975; French Awd 1975; Dena's Highly Dist'd List 1978 & 79, Col Charleston.

PENDLETON, INEZ M oc/County Clerk; b/Aug 29, 1930; h/12 Lakeshore Dr S, Cherry Creek Hills, Valdosta, GA 31601; ba/Valdosta; m/Fred T Sr; c/Fred T Jr, Wiliam D; p/Royce D and Ava Clyde Moon, Valdosta, GA; ed/Cert'd Clerk-Admr, Univ Ga; pa/Co Clerk, Lowndes Co, Ga; Bd Commrs; Past Pres Assn Co Clerks of Ga; Ga Security & Investigation Bur Inc, Pres; Intl Acad Criminology; Intl Assn Clerks, Recorders, Elec Ofcls & Treas; Nat Assn Co Treas & Fin Ofcrs; Bd Mem & Past Pres Coastal Plain Area Ec Opport Auth; Orgr & Mgr LOCEA; cp/Past Mem & Ofcr, Valdosta Jr Wom's Clb; Charter Mem Azalea City Wom's Clb, Past Pres; Wymodausis of Valdosta, Dept Chm; OES, Chapt #244; Peace Ofcrs Assn of Ga Aux, Past Dist VP; BPW Clb of Valdosta; Bd

Mem Valdosta Girl's Clb; Charter Mem Pilot Clb Intl; C of C, Valdosta-Lowndes Co; Past Treas Viking Athletic Booster Clb; Coor Vietnam ERA Vets Recog for Pres Certs for Lowndes Co by Pres Jimmy Carter; r/First Christian Ch; hon/Ser Awd, Tchr-Instr Class of 1976; Cert Co Clerk Admr, Univ Ga; St Ga Clara Jordan Awd; Nom Wom of Yr for Valdosta 1972; W/W Govt; World W/W Wom 1974-75; U Way of Lowndes Co.

PENDLETON, JOYCE SHARP oc/Assistant Professor; b/July 24, 1951; h/213 Herbert St, Starkville, MS 39759; m/William; c/Tiffany Joyce; p/Clifton and Beatrice Sharp, Starkville, MS; ed/BSW 1973, MSW 1975; pa/Asst Prof Social Work, Miss St Univ; NASW; Coun Social Work Ed; AAUW; r/Pentacostal.

PENN, OJEDA LAMAR oc/Assistant Professor; b/Jul 29, 1943; h/555 San Remo Ct, College Park, GA 30349; m/Jacqueline S; c/Kwame Nyerere; p/Luther L Penn (dec); Sadie G Penn, Montgomery, AL; ed/BS 1966, MA Atlanta Univ; PhD Cand Emory Univ 1973; pa/Asst Prof of English, Atlanta Jr Col; Profl Musician & Artist; Recorded LP; NCTE; Musicians Union; African Heritage Assn; Writer of Monthly Column, "Jazz Forum"; cp/Bd Mem, Neighborhood Arts Ctr; VP, Ponderosa Neighbors; hon/MA with 4.0 GPA.

PENNER, LETTIE LOU CASTLEBERRY oc/Factory Worker; b/Feb 13, 1926; h/Oologah, OK; m/Otto; c/Betty Joyce, Otto Penner Jr, Tamma Lou; p/Flem Smith and Inez Lee Heady Castleberry; pa/Murphy Safety Switch 1976-80; Centrilift Hughs Tool 1980-; cp/OES, Past Worthy Matron, Oologah Chapt #473.

PEREZ, JOSEPHINE oc/Psychiatrist, Clinical Instructor, Assistant Director; b/Feb 10, 1941; ba/2525 SW 27 Ave, Suite 202, Miami, FL 33133; p/Jose Perez; Teresa Navarro; ed/BS Insituto C Avila 1961; Sr BS Univ Santiago, Spain 1971; MS Univ Santiago; Psychi Res Cert, Univ Miami/Jackson Meml Hosp 1978; pa/Clin Instr Psychi Univ Miami; Asst Dir Adolescent Unit Jackson Meml Hosp; Staff Psychi Jackson Meml Hosp; Pvt Prac Psychi; AMA; Am Psychi Assn; S Fla Psychi Assn; r/Cath; hon/Phys Recog Awd AMA 1979; Am Psychi Assn Cert 1981; Num Lectrs & Papers to Univ Miami.

PEREZ-SHIREY, ATILANO V oc/Consultant; b/Sept 4, 1937; h/1725 Lytle Shores, Abilene, TX 79602; ba/Abilene; m/Linda; c/Penny; p/Juan g and Maria V Perales, San Antonia, TX; ed/BA Univ Tex-Austin 1967; MBA Hardin-Simmons 1980; mil/USMC, USAF; pa/Real Est Invest Conslt; Nat Assn Rltrs; Tex Assn Rltrs; Abilene Bd Rltrs; cp/VP Fla Judo Black Belt Assn 1974-76; r/Unitarian; hon/Commun Ldrs & Noteworthy Ams 1978; St of Tex Master's Div Judo Champ 1978; Dist'd Flying Cross 1968; Air Medal 1968; AF Commend Medal 1974; AF Good Conduct Medal 1965; Vietnam Cross of Gallantry 1969.

PEREZ-SHIREY, LINDA oc/Division Chairperson; b/Aug 29, 1946; h/1725 Lytle Shores Dr, Abilene, TX 79602; ba/Abilene; m/Atilano V; p/W Wayne and Violet I Shirey, Rockport, TX; ed/BA Univ Tex-Austin 1967; MS Univ Miami 1975; MBA Hardin-Simmons Univ 1981; pa/Div Chp, Mktg & Distbg Div, Cisco Jr Col 1977-; Tech Editor, NASA 1969-73; Math Assn of Am; Tex Jr Col Tchrs Assn; Am Voc Assn; Tex Mgmt Edrs Assn; r/Unitarian; hon/World W/W Wom 1978; W/W Voc Ed 1980; Spec Recog Awd, Cisco Jr Col 1979.

PERKINS, ARLAND VINCENT oc/Personnel Director; b/May 24, 1936; h/103 Vail Mt Dr, Lawton, OK 73501; ba/Edmond, OK; m/Frances L; c/James D, Kathleen D, Karen D, Felicia D; p/Harry V Perkins, Long Bch, CA; Garland M Murray, Alden, KS; ed/BS; mil/AUS Ret'd; pa/Grad Ed/Labor Relats; cp/VFW; DAV; r/Prot; hon/Var Mil Medals Incl'g 4 Bronze Stars, Air Medal.

PERLMAN, EILEEN ELEANOR oc/Civic Worker; Investor; b/Oct 31, 1935; h/6401 Cellini St, Coral Gables, FL 33146; c/Jason Jefferson, Clayton Kyle, Ivy Lee; p/Bennett Viggo and Eleanor Lucille Christensen, Miami, FL; ed/NWn Univ 1954; Patricia Stevens Modeling Sch 1955; Liberty Bapt Col 1978-80; pa/Co-Fdr Lum's Inc (Miami Bch) 1958; Self-Employed Investor; cp/Repub Party; Protect Our Chd; Anita Bryant Mins; Anti-ERA Campaign; ARC; Bd Dirs, Exec Com, Corres Secy Wom for Responsible Leg & Polit Action, So Fla Chapt; Fdg Charter Mem, Nat Adv Comm to Bring Back Sch Prayer 1980; Floridians Against Casino Takeover; US Lawn Tennis Assn; US Figure Skating Assn, Dir Miami Chapt 1978; Am Bridge Clb; Am Security Coun, Nat Adv Bd Mem; Adv Coun Philip Crane for Pres; Sustaining Mem Repub Nat Com; Bd Dirs Christian Wom's Clb, So Fla Chapt; Interfaith Com Against Blasphemy; Christian Broadcasting Co, 700 Clb; Liberty Bapt Col Old Time Gospel Hour; Campus Crusade for Christ; Fdg Mem, Moral Majority 1978; Num Others; r/Presb; Chm Visitation 1973-75; Circle Chm 1978-80; hon/Spec Recog Awd 1979; Support of Masters Deg Prog in Nat Security Studies, Am Security Coun; Num Biogl Listings.

PERSONALITIES OF THE SOUTH

PERRITT, HENRY HARDY oc/Education and Communication Consultant; b/June 13, 1918; h/RR 2 Box 278, Whitehouse, TX 75791; ba/Same; m/Margaret Floyd; c/H H Jr, Margaret P Davis; p/F S (dec) and Blanche Bagley Perritt (dec); ed/BA 1938, MA 1942 La St Univ; PhD Univ Fla 1954; mil/USNR Comdr, Secy Navy Unit Commend WWII, Communs Ofcr WWII & Korean Emer; pa/Human Relats Advr Public Schs, Little Rock, Ark; Chm Div Humanities Miles Col, Birmingham, Ala 1962-71; Pres B'ham Univ Sch 1959-62; Assoc Prof Univ Ala 1956-59; Asst Prof Univ Fla 1954-56; Asst Prof Univ Va 1946-53; Instr La St Univ 1942; HS Tchr Miss & La 1938-41; Instr Adult Classes La, Va, DC, Ala & Ark 1939-71; Modr "Know Your News" Ala ETV Network 1960-62; Prof Linguistics Wichita, Kan St Univ Summer 1966; Ed Conslt 1968-; Ins Broker; Farmer; cp/U Fund; K of P; Kiwanis; Civitan; Active Indep Dem; r/Meth & Unitarian; hon/Tau Kappa Alpha; Kappa Phi Kappa; Phi Kappa Phi; Navy Unit Commend, WWII; Res Grants: Univ Va & Univ Ala; Fulbright Lectr Brazil 1964; W/W S&SW; DIB; W/W Am Ed; Dir Am Schlrs; Commun Ldrs Am; Conslt-Lectr Bi-nat Ctr Sems for Eng Tchrs Rio De Janeiro and Fortaleza, Brazil 1964; Pres So Speech Assn 1958-59; Grad Fellow Univ Fla 1952-54; Pub'd Author Books & Jour Articles.

PERRY, GLENN HUYLETT SR oc/Law Enforcement; b/Oct 5, 1924; h/115 E King St, Edenton, NC 27932; ba/Edenton; m/Agnes Jean Britton; c/Bonita Jean, Glenn Huylett Jr, Darren Randall; p/John Elmer (dec) and Mattie Knight Perry; ed/Law Enforcement Courses: NC Just Acad, Col of the Albemarle at Elizabeth City, Inst Govt at Chapel Hill; mil/UAS WWII; pa/Chief Dpty Sheriff, Chowan Co Sheriff's Dept; Nat Sheriff's Assn; NC Law Enforcement Ofcrs Assn; cp/VFW; Edward G Bond Post 40 of Am Legion; EMT; r/Bapt; hon/Awd of Merit, Outstg Law Enforcement Ofcr of Chowan Co 1980; Cert of Recog & Apprec, Am Legion Dept NC.

PERRY, MARCUS WOOTEN oc/Real Estate Broker; b/Apr 21, 1940; h/Halifax, NC; ba/207 Dobbs St, Halifax, NC 27839; m/Barbara B; c/Mark, Thad, Suzanne; p/Maye V Perry, Weldon, NC; ed/Att'd Guilford Col 1958-59, Univ NC 1959-60; AAS Halifax Commun Col 1976; mil/AUS 1961-64; pa/Acctg Clerk, NC Dept Corrections 1964-66; Real Est Salesman 1966-69; Farm Prods Mgr 1969-70; Farmer 1970-77; Pres Perry Realty Co 1977-; cp/Exec Secy NC Mtl Hlth Assn 1968; Pres Halifax Lions Clb 1980; Town Commr 1975-77; r/Bapt.

PERRY, MARGUERITE FREEMAN oc/Home Economist; b/Jan 20, 1923; h/PO Box 51, Stratford, OK 74872; ba/Duncan, OK; m/Boyd Glynn; c/Pamela P Thompson, Boyd Glynn Jr, Vicki P Tucker; p/Samuel Henderson and Jewell George Freeman, Stratford, OK; ed/BS 1970, MA E Ctrl Okla St Univ; pa/Home Economist, Okla St Univ Coop Ext Ser; Am Home Ec Assn; Okla Home Ec Assn; Okla Assn Ext Home Ec; OEA; cp/BPW; APA; r/Ch of Christ; hon/Farm Foun S'ship; Norma Brombaugh S'ship; Epsilon Sigma Phi.

PERUMALLU, TRIPURANENI ANJANADEVI oc/General Surgeon; b/June 14, 1937; h/330 E Goldsboro Rd, Goldsboro, NC 27530; ba/Same; m/Tripuraneni L; c/Tripuraneni Deepa; p/Ghatamaneni Raghavaiah and Ghatamaneni Varamalleswaramma; ed/MBBS; FRCS; Am Bd Cert'd in Gen Surg; pa/Surgeon; r/Hindu; hon/W/W Mid-W; Intl Biog, Cambridge.

PESTO, JOHN LAWRENCE oc/Director of Nursing Services; b/Apr 22, 1942; h/Rt 4 Box 839, Tifton, GA 31794; ba/Tifton; m/Susan Cecilia; c/Sarah Wison, Mary Laura; p/John H and Dorothy Pesto, Seminole, FL; ed/AA; BSN; MSN; mil/USN; pa/Dir Nsg Sers, Tift Gen Hosp; GNA; Com on Human Rights; ANA; cp/Clearwater, Fla JCs 1971; Sarasota, Fla C of C 1972; r/Cath; hon/Grad w Hons Fla Intl Univ 1977; Sigma Theta Tau, Beta Omicron Chapt.

PETERS, KATHLEEN JOY oc/Assistant Professor, Artist; b/Dec 19, 1946; h/Atlanta, GA; ba/Atlanta Jr Col, 1630 Stewart Ave SW, Atlanta, GA 30310; m/James D; p/William Kenneth and E Loretta Ballard, Wash DC; ed/BFA Howard Univ 1969; MFA Boston Univ; pa/Art Instr Atlanta Jr Col 1974-; Art Tchr Brookline Sch Sys 1969-72; Nat Conf Artists; Black Artists Atlanta, Treas 1979-83, Pres 1976-78; Coalition of Wom's Art Orgs, Nat Bd Dirs 1981-83; cp/Phoenix Cultural Arts, Adv Bd 1977-81; Neighborhood Arts Ctr, Bd Dirs 1980; Fulton Co Arts Coun; City of Atlanta Dept Cultural Affairs, Adv Funding Bd; r/Epis; hon/Juko Rissanen Pictorial Art Exhib 1st Prize 1980; WETV Bronze Jubilee Awd in Fine Arts 1980; Author Reviews & Articles for *Atlanta Art Papers*.

PETERSON, DONALD M oc/Financial Consultant; b/Aug 2, 1932; h/6620 Elgin Ln, Bethesda, MD 20034; ba/Same; m/Shirley; c/Katie, Sarah; p/Marvin (dec) and Helen Peterson, Delray, FL; ed/BME; MS; MBA; PhD; mil/USN; pa/NYSSA; r/Prot; hon/Author *Financial Ratios and Investment Results* 1975.

PETERSON, DOROTHY BURNETT oc/Retired Educator; b/Dec 17, 1908; h/3454 Scheibler Rd, Memphis, TN 38128; m/Robert Elmer; c/Dorothy Lee Banker, Charlotte Ray Carrell, Jean Lesesne; p/Henry Prince (dec) and Dora Branscome Burnett (dec); ed/Dip & Tchr's Cert Harrisonburg St Tchrs Col (now James Madison Univ) 1928; Mus Study, Memphis St Univ 1964-66; pa/Elem Tchr Public Schs Va & NC 1928-33; Kindergarten Tchr, Hughes Pvt Sch, Memphis, Tenn 1939-40; Pvt Piano Tchr Num Yrs; cp/Colonial Dames XVIIC; Magna Charta Dames; Ft Assumption Chapt DAR; Lunch Forum Clb; Repub Party; r/Presb.

PETERSON, JAMES H oc/State Director of Purchasing, State of Oklahoma; b/Jan 9, 1930; h/1421 Mill Creek Rd, Edmond, OK 73034; ba/Oklahoma City, OK; m/Helen B; c/Mark, Sarah, Paige; p/William and Grace Peterson (dec); ed/BA; Grad Studies; mil/USMC Reserve, Major; pa/Rotary; NIGP; NASPO; Elks; Colorado Col Alumni; C of C; cp/BSA Past Coun Pres, Asst Coun Treas; Trustee Ottumwa Heights Col; r/Presb; hon/Scouting Hon; Exec Com Nat Assn Purchasing Ofcrs.

PETERSON, PATRICIA GRIER oc/Economist; b/Feb 8, 1938; h/1932 McCalla Ave, Knoxville, TN 37915; ba/K'ville; c/Ellaina Carrine; p/Hoke Calvin (dec) and Ella Mildred Grier (dec); ed/BS; pa/Economist, TVA; Intl Coun Small Bus; Nat Ec Assn; Grp Rep TVAEA Engrg Assn; cp/Adv Bd Magnolia Fed Savings & Loan Assn; NAACP; Adv Bd Katie Miller Grp Home for Girls; YMCA; r/Bapt; hon/W/W Am Wom; World W/W Wom.

PETERSON, ROBERT ELMER oc/Retired Engineer and Plant Manager; b/Jan 1, 1910; h/3454 Scheibler Rd, Memphis, TN 38128; m/Dorothy Burnett; c/Dorothy Lee Banker, Charlotte Ray Carrell, Jean Lesesne; p/Axel Robert (dec) and Charlotte Olson Peterson (dec); ed/BS 1932, MS 1933 VPI; mil/USAR 1st Lt; pa/Plant Mgr & Engr, Va Bridge Co 1946-52; Plant Mgr & Engr Am Bridge Div US Steel 1952-56; Plant Mgr Pidgeon-Thomas Co 1965-73; Am Soc Profl Engrs; Tenn Soc Profl Engrs; cp/Violinist Memphis Phil Orch; Chickasaw Country Clb; C of C; Memphis Rotary Clb 1946-80; Repub Party; r/Presb.

PETERSON, ROBERT GLEN oc/Lawyer; b/Aug 30, 1954; h/Rt 1 Box 290, Leland, NC 28451; ba/Chapel Hill, NC; m/Dean Johnsey; p/H O Jr and Alma P Peterson, Leland, NC; ed/BA UNC-CH 1976; JD UNC-CH Law Sch 1981; pa/Law Clerk Ray H Walton Esp 1979-80; Juvenile Just Plan'g Com, Gov's Crime Comm 1980; Am Bar Assn, Law Student Div, Gen Pract Sect; cp/Yng Dems of NC, St Treas 7th Dist, Pres Brunswick Co; Col Fed YDNC St Treas; r/Bapt; hon/Johnston Schlr; Most Outstg Col Yng Dem; Outstg Yng Man Am 1980.

PETERSON, SHERRY C oc/Interior Designer, Real Estate Broker; b/Jan 2, 1936; h/110 Pine Cir, Smithfield, NC 27477; b/Smithfield; m/Sherrill R; c/Rhonda G; p/Will H (dec) and Mabel H Creech (dec); ed/Intl Corresp Schs; Chgo Sch Interior Design; Bacon Sch Real Est; p/Secy-Treas Interior Design Soc, NC & SC; r/Meth; hon/Gillett-Narron Awd of Excell, Smithfield Jr Wom's Clb; Outstg Yng Wom Am 1970.

PETTERSON, SYLVIA ROYSENE oc/Diagnostic Radiology; b/Aug 21, 1944; h/2430 Deer Creek Country Clb Blvd, Deerfield Bch, FL 33441; ba/Deerfield Bch; p/Roy G A and Miriam S Petterson, Fort Pierce, FL; ed/BS w Hons Fla So Col; MD Univ Miami; pa/AMA; RSNA; NERRS; SMA; AMWA; IRCMS; FMA; cp/Advr to Radiological Technol Prog, Indian River Commun Col; r/Meth; hon/W/W Am Wom 1979-80; Yng Alumnus of Yr, Fla So Col 1973; Phys Recog Awd, AMA 1973 & 76.

PEVETO, NATALIA LAVONNE BRACKIN oc/Reading Specialist, Title I Coordinator; b/Aug 30, 1943; h/Vidor, TX; c/Bradley Dale; p/John W and Ursula Dean Brackin, Vidor, TX; ed/BS Lamar Univ 1969; MEd McNeese St Univ 1971; EdS McNeese St Univ 1973; EdD La St Univ 1980; pa/Elem Tchr, Vidor Indep Sch Dist 1969-71; Rdg Spec Vidor Indep Sch Dist 1971-75; Rdg Spec Pt Arthur Indep Sch Dist 1975-78; Title I Coor, Orangefield Indep Sch Dist 1978-; Tex Clrm Tchrs Assn, Chm Tchr Pers Sers 1980, Pres 1974; AAUW; ABWA; Intl Rdg Assn; Tex Assn Improvement of Rdg; NEA Tex Assn Tchr Edrs; Tex St Tchrs Assn; Phi Delta Kappa; r/Bapt; hon/Guest Spkr: Tex A&M, Lamar Univ, Houston Bapt Univ, McNeese St Univ; Author "The Relationship of Biorhythms to Academic Performance in Reading; 1 of 4 Tchrs in Tex Appt'd to Study Textbook Laws & to Devel Recommends for Changes 1972.

PFLASTERER, LOUISE WOOD oc/Artist; b/May 10, 1907; h/230 W Vanderbilt Dr, Oak Ridge, TN 37830; m/Edward (dec); c/Peter Wood; p/dec; ed/Grad Nat Col Chiropractic 1928; pa/Prac Phys Therapy 18 Yrs; Artist Nature in Water Colors; cp/Charter Mem & 1st Treas Foothills Craft Guild; Oak Ridge Commun Art Ctr; Past Mem Oak Ridge Wom's Clb, Book Sect Chm; r/Luth; hon/Art Show at Oak Ridge Public Lib 1965; Num Art Shows Throughout Tenn.

PHELAN, P CAREN oc/Chief of Psychology; b/Nov 9, 1927; h/Rt 1 Box 168-WW, San Marcos, TX 78666; ba/Austin, TX; p/William T Tyler (dec); Grace T Silvers, Quinter, KS; ed/PhD Univ Md 1973; Cert'd & Lic'd by Tex Bd Psychs; Cert'd Hlth Ser Provider; Lic'd by Tex Bd Social-Psychotherapists; Cert'd by Nat Rehab Assn as Rehab Cnslr; pa/Chief, Psych Dept, Austin St Univ 1979-; Mtl Hlth Prog Dir, Div Mtl Hlth 1978-79; Asst & Acting Dpty Commr Mtl Hlth Sers, Tex Dept Mtl Hlth & Mtl Retard 1976-78; Unit Dir Alcohol/Narcotic Treatment Univ, San Antonio St Hosp 1974-76; Instr, Alcohol/Drug Ed, Behavior Sci Div, Acad Hlth Sci 1972-74; Supvr DC Voc Rehab Unit, St Elizabeths Hosp 1970-72; Tchg Aid, Ortero Co Sch Retard 1962-64; Psychodrama Conslt VA Hosp San Antonio 1975-; Am Psych Assn; Tex Psych Assn; Am Grp Psychotherapy Assn; San Antonio Transactional Analysis Assn; Nat Rehab Assn; AGPA; Tex Assn Mtl Deficiency; Am Assn Mtl Deficiency; Bexar Co Mtl Hlth Assn; Travis Co Mtl Hlth Assn; Assn Rural Mtl Hlth; Chp Regional Alcohol Adv Bd; Mem St Forum White House Com for Handicapped; Mem Citizens Adv Com on Alcohol Leg; Task Force on Autism, Tex Soc for Autistic Citizens; hon/World W/W Wom; W/W: S&SW, Am Wom.

PHELPS, SHARON SUE J oc/Distributor; b/Jan 6, 1946; h/9721 Kempwood, Apt 1324, Houston, TX 77080; m/George Irby Sr; c/George Jr, Lloyd Calvin; p/James Wesley and Veda Greer Johnston (dec); pa/Distributor for Poly-Carb in Houston Area; cp/Maracaibo Players; Faith Bapt Chorus (Maracaibo, Venezuela); r/So Bapt.

PHIFER, REBECCA ROLL oc/Attorney; b/Sept 30, 1950; h/601 W Union St, Morganton, NC 28655; ba/Morganton; m/Edward William III; c/Justin Matthew McLear; p/Robert D and Shirley J Roll, Greensboro, NC; ed/BS Ohio St Univ 1973; JD UNC Sch Law (Chapel Hill) 1979; pa/Staff Analyst, NC Govtl Evaluation Comm 1979-80; Law Firm Assoc, Patton, Starnes & Thompson PA 1980-; NC Bar; ABA; cp/Morganton BPW; r/Presb.

PHILLEY, IRMA CHRISTINE (McGUFFEE) oc/Home Economist; b/Jun 4, 1951; h/109 River Oaks Rd, West Monroe, LA 71291; ba/W Monroe; m/Freddie Maurice; c/Ronald Edward; p/Ronald R and Irma Dean Eubanks McGuffee, Enterprise, LA; ed/BS 1972, MEd NE La Univ 1973; Addit Studies; pa/Asst Home Economist (4-H), La St Univ 1973-76, Assoc Home Economist (4-H) 1976-79, Home Economist (Energy) 1979-; Charter Mem, La 4-H Agent's Assn: Author of Assn's First Newslttr, Reporter 1977-78, Awds Chm 1980-81; La Assn of Ext Home Economists: Secy 1980-; Past Dist Pres, La Home Ec Assn; Am Home Ec Assn; Epsilon Sigma Phi; Phi Kappa Phi; Writer "Focus on Energy", News Column; Energy Pamphlet, "Cut Kitchen Energy Costs"; Author, "Making Energy Interesting - Puppet Prodns"; cp/Charter Mem, Pilot Clb of Twin Cities (1st VP 1981-); r/Bapt; hon/Outstg Yg 4-H Clb Agent; Outstg Yg Home Economist; Florence Hall Awd St Nom; Nat Consumer Ed Awd; W/W Am Wom.

PHILLIPS, ALVON WAYNE oc/Businessman; b/Oct 3, 1960; h/1411 Brown, Little Rock, AR 72204; m/J F Cooley; p/Tommy Phillips, Little Rock, AR; Erma Phillips, Little Rock, AR; pa/CETA; Pizza Planet.

PHILLIPS, ANNE W oc/Ranching, Oil, Gas; b/Nov 10, 1938; h/Frisco, TX; ba/1212 First Nat Bank Bldg, Ft Worth, TX 76102; m/B F Jr; c/Windi; p/John Hall (dec); Anne Burnett Tandy (dec); ed/Grad Briarcliff Jr Col; Att'd Univ Tex & Univ Geneva, Switz; pa/Self-Employed Rancher; Bd Trustees Tex Christian Univ; Bd Overseers, Ranching Heritage Assn, Tex Tech Univ; Bd Regents Tex Tech Univ; Bd Trustees Hockaday Sch.

PHILLIPS, DONALD EUGENE oc/Assistant Professor; b/Dec 11, 1943; h/Erlanger, KY; ba/Highland Heights, KY; m/Glenda Claire; c/Rebecca Lyn; p/Dorothy Shaner, Kingfisher, OK; ed/BA Univ Ark 1967; MA Baylor Univ 1970; PhD Univ Okla 1977; pa/Asst Prof Commun, No Ky Univ 1978-; Chm Div Lang Arts, SWn Col, Okla City, Okla 1975-78; Life Mem Delta Tau Kappa; Speech Commun Assn; So Speech Commun Assn; Ky Assn Commun Arts; Intl Commun Assn, Philosophy of Commun Interest Grp; So Humanities Conf; r/Bapt; hon/Humphrey's Hall Honor Roll; Acad S'ship, Meml Bapt Ch, Tulsa, Okla; Baylor Univ Dean's Dist'd List; Author Student Protest, 1960-69: An Analysis of the Issues and Speeches 1980; Karl Barth's Philosophy of Communication 1981; Num Articles and Reviews.

PHILLIPS, ELEANOR Z oc/Teacher; b/Oct 29, 1932; h/6782 Georgia Ave, Bradenton, FL 33507; ba/Sarasota, FL; m/Charles Duval Jr; c/Edwin Sterling, Elizabeth Anne; p/Edwin Albert Zundel, Sarasota, FL; Eleanor Clay Lewis Zundel (dec); ed/Att'd Intl Col Sacred Heart, Tokyo, Japan; BA Mary Wash Col of Univ Va 1954; BS Fla So Col 1955; pa/Elem Tchr, Bay Haven Elem, Sarasota Co 1955-; Sarasota Co Tchrs Assn, Bldg Rep 5 Yrs; Fla Ed Assn; cp/Secy Bayshore Gdns Pk & Rec Dist Bd Trustees; AAUW; r/Epis.

PHILLIPS, FAYE oc/Museum Director; b/Mar 23, 1927; h/Meridian, MS; p/dec; ed/Dip Nsg Sch, Univ Ala & Miss 1949; pa/Jimmie Rodgers

Mus Dir; cp/Jimmie Rodgers Meml Fest; Country Mus Assn; Hon Mem All Fan Clbs in Country Mus; r/Bapt; hon/Chosen to Serve on Staff of Ridgecrest Bapt Assn, NC 1970; Chosen to Adv Bd of Tenn Tech Univ Staff.

PHILLIPS, FERNLEY oc/Woodworker; b/Mar 18, 1931; h/2833 Central Dr, Sanford, FL 32771; c/David, Daniel; p/(dec); pa/Woodworker, Teak Trimmer for Robalo Boats; AMF Robalo Boat Div; r/Meth.

PHILLIPS, GEORGE LANDON oc/Attorney; b/May 24, 1949; h/901 W Pine St, Hattiesburg, MS 39401; ba/H'burg; p/Gilbert L Phillips, H'burg, MS; Grace Staker; ed/BS Univ So Miss; JD Univ Miss; pa/Forrest Co Prosecuting Atty 1976-80-84; Pres Miss Prosecutors Assn 1978-79; VP S Ctrl Miss Bar Assn 1975-79; cp/Nat Dir Nat Dist Attys Assn 1979-80; S Ctrl Miss Red Cross Chapt 1978-80; r/Bapt.

PHILLIPS, JOHN WILLIAM JR oc/Insurance Agent; b/Oct 30, 1952; h/215 Robinson St, Decatur, AL 35601; ba/Laurel, MS; m/Donna N; c/Amber Rae; p/John William Sr and Betty Davis Phillips, Florence, AL; ed/BS Univ N Ala; Wn La Sch Life Ins Mktg; pa/Self-Employed Ins Agt; cp/JCs; Alpha Tau Omega; r/Presb; hon/Profl Ins Corp Pres Hon Clb 1978 & 79.

PHILLIPS, MARGARITA GOMEZ oc/Microbiologist, Medical Technologist; b/July 20, 1942; h/912 Linwood Tr, Lutz, FL 33549; ba/Pt Richey, FL; p/Jose Gomez Lozano, Jalisco, Mexico; Guadalupe Lams de la Torre (dec); ed/BA Univ S Fla; pa/Am Soc Microbiol; Am Soc Clin Pathols; Fla Assn Blood Banks; Soc Applied Anthrop; USF Alumni Assn; cp/Dem Party; r/Cath; hon/Notable Ams 1976-77; W/W: Am Wom 1977-78, 79-80, S&SW 1978; World W/W Wom 1978, 79.

PHILLIPS, REGINA KAY oc/Student; b/Sept 21, 1959; h/Rt 1 Box 1974, Demopolis, AL 36732; p/Neal and Carol C Phillips, Demopolis, Al; cp/Treas Biol Hon Soc; r/Nondenom; hon/W/W: Am Univ & Col Students, Am HS Students; Livingston's Loveliest; Eng Awd; Math & Sci Awd; Spirit Awd; HS Valedictorian.

PHILPOTT, HARRY MELVIN oc/President, Auburn University; b/May 6, 1917; h/430 S College, Auburn, AL 36830; ba/Auburn; m/Pauline; c/Melvin, Jean (Mrs Melvin Bankester); p/B Cabell and Daisy Hundley Philpott (dec); ed/AB (cum laude) Washington & Lee 1938; PhD Yale 1947; DD Stetson Univ 1960; LLD Wash & Lee Univ 1966, Univ Fla 1969, Univ Ala 1970; HHD Samford Univ 1978; mil/Lt Chaplains' Corps, USNR 1943-46; pa/Dir Rel Activities, Wash & Lee Univ 1938-40; Asst Prof-Assoc Prof Rel, Univ Fla 1947-52; Dean Rel Life and Head of Dept of Rel and Philosophy, Stephens Col 1952-57; VP, Univ Fla 1957-65; Pres, Auburn Univ 1965-; Chm, Ala Study Com on Ed 1967-69; Pres, So Assn, Land Grant Cols and St Univs 1968-69; Mem Adv Coun of Pres to the Assn of Gov Bds of Univs and Cols 1968-76; Pres SEn Conf 1972; Chm, SREB Com on Regional Cooperation 1972; VChm SREB 1973; Num Other Profl Positions; r/Bapt; hon/Kappa Alpha Order; Omicron Delta Kappa; Kappa Phi Kappa; Blue Key; Kappa Delta Pi; Phi Kappa Phi; Hon Alumnus, Univ Fla; Ala Educator of Yr 1970; Citizen of Yr 1970; Ala Acad of Hon; Ala Dist Exchange Court of Hon Awd.

PHINNEY, WILLIAM CLOVIS JR oc/Business Manager; b/Feb 21, 1931; h/Coahoma, TX; em/Joy Jane Echols; c/Ronald Scott, Lusara, Faron Lee; p/Mr and Mrs Clovis Phinney, Coahoma, TX; ed/Howard Col 1949; mil/USAF 1950-55 Staff Sgt; pa/Bus Mgr Oper'g Engrs Local 826 Intl Union 1980-; Oper, Cosden Oil & Chem Co 1949-80; Tex AFL-CIO; Disabled Am Vet Labor Orgr 1965-; cp/Coahoma Sch Bd VP, Pres Local 826 12 Yrs; Elks Lodge #1386 Trustee; Field Rep Tex Rehab Ctr; Area Dir Labor to Jerry Lewis MD Campaign; Pres Cosden 25 Yrs Clb; U Way Bd Mem; RA Dir; Precinct Chm Dem Party; r/Bapt; hon/Aide de Camp, NM 1970.

PICKEL, CONRAD L oc/Artist; b/Feb 10, 1906; m/Johanna Friedlmaier; c/Erma Obermayr, R Paul; p/Konrad (dec) and Katherin Pickel (dec); ed/Franz Mayer Studios, Munich, Germany; Acad Arts, Munich; Var Other Art Schs in US; pa/Self Employed Stained Glass Artist; Chief Designer Pickel Studios; Bldr Gal Fantasia; hon/Men of Achmt; W/W SE; Intl Biogl Assn; Intl Platform Assn; Awds from C of C for Bldg Deisgn; Cath W/W.

PICKENS, WILLODINE ROBBINS oc/Nurse; b/Dec 21, 1913; h/241 Springhill Rd, Alexander City, AL 35010; m/dec; c/Wilfrd McKay; p/Joseph Edward Robbins (dec); Leora McKay (dec); ed/DipHillman Hosp Sch Nsg 1939; pa/RN Russell Hosp 1950-; ANA; NLN; Ala St Nurses Assn; Am Red Cross Nsg Sers; Dir 16th Dist Nurses Assn, Chm Nom'g Com 16th Dist 1965, Secy & Treas; Bd Mar of Dimes; cp/Pres Klicker Clb 1953; r/Presb; hon/Sev Awds at Local Flower Shows; Nurse of Yr, 16th Dist Nurses Assn 1972.

PICKERING, MARTHA ELIZABETH oc/Retired; b/May 14, 1918; h/3619 Hycliffe Ave, Louisville, KY 40207; m/William Dale (dec); p/Shelby Burch (dec) and Ruby Gardner Parrott (dec); ed/AB Ky Wesleyan Col; MA Univ L'ville; pa/Wom's Polit Caucus; NOW; Ky Pro ERA Alliance Co-Chm; Wkr & Lobbyist for Wom's Rights; cp/Dem Party Wkr; LWV; r/So Bapt; hon/Citizens Awd, L'ville & Jefferson Co LWV 1979; Pioneer Feminist Awd, L'ville NOW 1975.

PICO, JOSE H oc/Administrative Law Judge With The SSA; b/Apr 8, 1939; h/60 Jaguas St, Milaville, Rio Piedras, PR 00926; m/Elliette; c/Jose E, Elliette J, Gerardo R; p/Jose Pico Pico (dec); Aurora Pico, Coamo, PR; ed/BBA; JD; LLM; pa/Pres PR Bar 1974-76; St Del to ABA; cp/Mem ATBWBO of PR; r/Cath; hon/Sev by PR Bar.

PIELAGO, BRUNILDA NUNEZ oc/Vice Consul; b/Aug 31, 1938; h/Coral Gables, FL; ba/PO Box 343337, Coral Gables, FL 33134; m/Ramon; c/Olga, Ana Victoria, Rafael, Carolina, Lourdes Garcia Navarro, Ramon Emilio; p/Plga Fabrega Nunez, Repub of Panama; ed/Merici Acad, Havana, Cuba; pa/Vice Consul, Repub of Panama in Miami; r/Cath.

PIERCE, ELNORA RETLEDGE COOPER oc/Educator; h/4822 Creekmoor Dr, San Antonio, TX 78220; ba/San Antonio; m/dec; c/Jerome Rutherford Cooper; p/J R (dec) and Sarah J Retledge (dec); ed/BA Bishop Col; MA Univ Tex SanAntonio 1976; pa/SATC; TSTA NEA; Mus Edrs Assn; cp/SAE-PAC; Tex Mins & Citizens Ldrship Coun; CAP; NAACP; r/Bapt; hon/Intl W/W Mus; DAR; Freedom Foun.

PIERCE, HAROLD FREDERICK oc/Retired Petroleum Engineer; b/Nov 8, 1912; h/8567 Sweetwater Dr, Dallas, TX 75228; m/Susie K; c/Randall Harold; p/Fred and Lola L Pierce (dec); ed/BS Mo Sch of Mines 1937; Att'd SMU; mil/US Coast Guard 1942: Comm'd Ensign 1943-46, Lt (Engrg Ofcr aboard Coast Guard Ships); pa/Geologist, Sun Oil Co 1937-39; Exploration Engr, Shell Oil Co 1939-62; Investigator, US Geol Survey 1962-65; Petro Engr, US Bur of Mines 1965-77; Petro Engr, US Dept of Energy 1977-78; Now Ret'd; Profl Engr, Tex; Am Assn Petro Engrg 1938-42; Pub'd Res for US Bur of Mines; cp/Civitan Clb: Secy, Pres, Lt/Gov; r/Bapt: Deacon; hon/W/W Tex; Cash Awd & Cit, US Bur of Mines.

PIERSON, JANE WILHELMINA oc/Retired Nurse; b/July 24, 1917; h/113 Bluebird, Berea, KY 40403; p/William (dec) and Barbara Elizabeth Pierson (dec); pa/Ret'd RN & Cert'd Nurse Midwife; r/Luth; hon/Nat Cit ACNM 1971; Nurse of Yr 1971.

PIGOTT, HELEN SUE oc/Teacher; b/May 24, 1947; h/Rt 4 Box 123, Tylertown, MS 39667; p/William Otis and Loice Brumfield Pigott, Tylertown, MS; ed/AA SW Miss Jr Col 1967; MS Delta St Univ 1970; MEd William Carey Col 1980; pa/SS Tchr: Am Acad Bogaulas, La 1970-75; S Pike Jr HS, Magnolia, Miss 1976-; NEA; MAE; S Pike Assn Edrs; Miss Jr Hist Soc; cp/Miss Easter Seal Soc; Miss Dist YWCA; M-Pact; OES; r/Bapt: Ch Hist, SS Tchr, Choir; hon/4-H Ldr Awd; Trophy La St Univ Coop Ext Ser 1975; Sponsor Y-Teen Clb, S Pike Jr Hist.

PILGRIM, RAYMOND W oc/Executive Vice President and Chief Operating Officer; b/June 14, 1936; h/Opelika, AL; ba/Diversified Products Corp, PO Box 100, Opelika, AL 36801; m/Katheryn H; c/Jeffrey K, Anthony W; p/Donnie Mae Pilgrim, Lafayette, GA; ed/BS 1959, MS 1962 Ga Inst Technol; mil/AUS Air Defense 1st Lt; pa/Exec VP & Chief Oper'g Ofcr, Diversified Prods Corp; Bayly Corp, Exec VP & Mem Bd Dirs, Denver, Colo; Oxford Industs, VP, Mktg & Adm, Atlanta, Ga; AAMA; Nat Sporting Goods Assn; cp/C of C Opelika, Bd Dirs; C of C Skeebeville, Tenn, Bd Dirs; r/Bapt.

PILLERT, PAT AKERS oc/Property Manager; b/Nov 21, 1934; h/6189 H St, Little Rock, AR 72207; ba/Little Rock; m/Frank D; c/Paul Fletcher; p/Andy (dec) and Vera Barham, Wilmott, AR; pa/Ark Chap Inst of Real Est Mgmt, Pres 1979; BOMA of Little Rock, Pres 1979; SW Conf BOMA Intl, Bd Dirs 1978-79; Past Pres Wom in Construction of Gtr Little Rock; r/Meth.

PINKERTON, GLEN IRVIN oc/Minister; b/July 25, 1947; h/1021 N Forrest, Altus, OR 73521; ed/Same; m/Marilyn F; p/John M Pinkerton, Wenatchee, WA; Josephine E Pinkerton, Olympia, WA; mil/USN; pa/Ordained Min, Ch of God; Dist Overseer Altus Dists; r/Pentacostal-Holiness.

PIRKLE, ESTUS WASHINGTON oc/Pastor and Evangelist, Christian Film Producer; b/Mar 12, 1930; h/PO Box 721, New Albany, MS 38652; ba/Myrtle, MS; m/Annie Catherine; c/Letha Dianne, Gregory Don; p/Grover W (dec) and Bessie Nora Jones Pirkle (dec); ed/BA Mercer Univ; BD, MRE, ThM SWn Bapt Sem; pa/Prodr 3 Christian Films: "Footmen"; "Burning Hell"; "Believers Heaven"; r/So Bapt; hon/Valedictorian Norman Jr Col; Grad cum laude Mercer Univ.

PIRNAT, JANET WENGER oc/Instructor; h/Rt 2 Box 7685, Deland, FL 32720; ba/Deland; m/Charles Raymond; c/Jeremy Joseph, Suzanne Rachelle; p/David S and Mary B Wenger, Brownstown, PA; ed/BS Lock Haven St Col 1961; MEd Temple Univ 1965; Adv'd Cert in Ed, Univ Ill 1970; pa/Instr Chd's House Montessori Sch; r/7th Day Adventist; hon/Intl W/W Ed 1980; W/W Am Wom 1979-80; Cert of Merit for Wkg w Handicapped Chd of Euclid.

PITCHER, LINDA RUTH TILLMAN oc/Executive Assistant; b/Jun 3, 1943; h/951 Brookwood Rd, Jacksonville, FL 32207; ba/J'ville; m/Griffith F; c/Lawrence Brooke, William T, Margaret W; p/Thomas J and Stella F B Tillman, Altamonte Springs, FL; pa/Exec Asst: Exec Wom Intl; cp/LWV; J'ville Bar Aux; Cummer Gallery; J'ville Mus of Arts & Scis; J'ville Art Mus: VP Wom of J'ville Art Mus 1979-80, Publicity Chm; r/Ch of Rel Sci; hon/W/W Am Wom; Nat Social Register; Orlando Social Register.

PITCHFORD, DAVID W oc/Law Clerk; b/July 30, 1954; ba/PO Box 193, Southaven, MS; p/Frank H Pitchford (dec); pa/Trial Lawyer.

PITMAN, RONNIE DALE oc/Director of Economic and Industrial Development, Cherokee Nation of Oklahoma; b/Jan 18, 1943; h/634 Kankakee, Muskogee, OK 74401; ba/Tahlequah, OK; c/Vance, Rhonda; p/Russell and Myrtle Pitman, Muskogee, OK; ed/BS, Indust Devel Inst; pa/Bd Dirs, Cherokee Nat Indust; cp/Rotarian, Lions Clb, ELK, Past Mem Retailers Assn; Fdr of Tennis Assn in Paris, Tex & McAlester, OK; hon/Grant in Aid S'ship, Tulsa Univ.

PITTMAN, JOYCE JANITA HOWARD oc/Consultant-Analyst; b/Aug 31, 1940; m/Clyde H Jr; c/Craig, Clarissa; p/O B and Thelma Louis Hiser Howard, Cairo, WV; ed/Masters Deg, Univ of Dallas 1980; PhD Cand; pa/Conslt to Bus, Govt & Polit Entities, TDB Ltd; cp/Toastmasters (Pres); Nat Leag of Cities; Conserv & Wom's Caucus (Chm Conserv Caucus); Irving Repub Wom's Clb: Pres, Treas, Secy; Pres, Heart Assn of Irving; Treas, Irving Repub Clb; Wom's C of C; Tex Repub Wom's Org; Jayceettes; DAL Proj Chm; Chd's Med Ctr Irving Fund Raising Chm; Dallas & Irving Symph Assns; r/Meth; hon/City Coun-Wom, City of Irving 1974-77; Outstg Wom of Tex; Outstg Coun Rep.

PITTMAN, RACHEL NEWBERN oc/Economist; b/Nov 26, 1924; h/Wynnewood, Rt 1 Box 255, Aulander NC 27805; ba/Colerain, NC; m/Otis Woodrow; c/Elizabeth Wynne Overton, Margaret Amy; p/George J Sr (dec) and Mary V Wynne Newbern, Ahoskie, NC; ed/AB UNC-G 1945; MA Columbia Univ 1946; pa/Tchg Appts: Meridian Jr Col, Wake Forest Univ; Prof Ec & Govt, Chowan Col 1966-78; cp/Pres Hertford Co Dem Wom; Chm Hertford Co Hist Properties Comm; Hertford Co Lib Bd; r/Meth; hon/Phi Beta Kappa; Weil F'ship, UNC-G; Pres S'ship, Columbia Univ.

PITTMAN, SANDRA LOWRY oc/Extension Home Economist; b/Oct 18, 1955; ba/PO Box 37, Halifax, NC 27839; m/James L; p/Robert Lee and Mary McKenzie Lowry, Cary, NC; ed/Att'd WCU 1973-75; BS Campbell Col 1977; pa/Ext Home Ec, NC Agricl Ext Ser; Nat Assn Ext Home Ecs; NC Home Ecs Assn; r/Presb.

PITTMAN, SIDNEY E oc/Director Environmental Services; b/Nov 14, 1941; h/Deland,FL; ba/W Volusia Meml Hosp, PO Box 509, Deland, FL 32720; m/Carolyn; c/Patrice; p/Adolph and Mary Pittman, Gulfport, MS; ed/AS Miss Gulf Coast Col; BS Univ So Miss; mil/USMC; pa/Dir Envirl Sers, W Volusia Meml Hosp; SEn Conf Hosp Housekeepers, Pres; Nat Exec Housekeepers Assn: Dist Gov 1980, Dist V-Gov 1980; Chapt Pres 1979; cp/BPOE; Am Cancer Soc, Gen Crusade Chm 1980; r/Cath; hon/W/W S&SW 1978-80; Pub'd in Num Profl Jours.

PITTS, BEN ELLIS oc/Associate Professor; b/Sept 29, 1931; h/Greenville, MS; ba/Box 3162, Delta St Univ, Cleveland, MS 38733; m/Gracie S; c/Ben E Jr; p/Mary Pitts, McLean, VA; ed/BS Lincoln Meml Univ 1954; MEd, EdS, EdD Univ Ga; MDiv Emory Univ; pa/Assoc Prof Media-Lib Scis, Delta St Univ 1979-; Asst Prof Lib Sci & Coor Lrng Resources Ctr, Tenn Technol Univ 1974-79; Media Spec, Gwinnett Co Bd Ed 1969-73; Clrm Tchr, Lee Co Sch Sys, Jonesville, Va 1951-55; Prin/Tchr Lee Co Sch Sys 1950-51; Min U Meth Ch Va 1955-69; Phi Delta Kappa; Phi Kappa Phi; Kappa Delta Pi; Miss Lib Assn; SEn Lib Assn; ALA; MEA; NEA; Soc Edrs & Schlrs; Produced Audio & Video Oral Hist Tapes: Alexandria, Tenn 1977, Celina, Tenn 1977, Gainesboro, Tenn 1976, Jamestown, Tenn 1977, Smithville, Tenn 1976; Prod'd Wkly News Prog for Cookeville, Tenn Cablevision 1975; Conslt to Upper Cumberland Regional Lib Sys 1977-79; r/Meth; hon/Bd Dirs Edrs & Schlrs; Author Num Profl Pubs.

PITTS, EMMA THOMAS oc/Assistant Professor; b/Sept 14, 1948; h/321 Roselawn St, Apt D, Houma, LA 70360; ba/Thibodaux, LA; m/David Monroe; p/Manvel and Dorothy Harrison Thomas, Baton Rouge, LA; ed/BS; MEd; PhD; pa/Asst Prof Ofc Adm, Nicholls St Univ;

Phi Delta Kappa; Nat Bus Ed Assn; La Bus Ed Assn; Am Voc Assn; La Voc Assn; Kan St Univ Alumni Assn; SW Adm Sers Assn; Nicholls St Univ Fac Assn; cp/S La Voc-Tech Crafts Adv Coun, Dept Ofc Occups, S La Voc-Tech Inst; r/Bapt; hon/Phi Delta Kappa; Pub'd Sev Articles; Outstg Personality of Wk, Houma, La; Secy of Yr; Awd for Yrbook; Featured as Fac Mem Personality in Nicholls St Yrbook; Yngest Recip PhD for 1976, Kan St Univ; Only Black PhD Nichlls St Univ; Only Black in Col of Bus Adm, Nicholls St Univ.

PITTS, KEEFFEE L oc/Bulk Mail Technician and Custom Service; b/Oct 3, 1926; h/1817 47 St Ct W, PO Box 494, Bradenton, FL 33506; ba/Bradenton; m/Edna; c/Lyn, Michael, Constance, Kenneth; p/James Hardy (dec) and Rosa Mae Pitts (dec); mil/USN 1945-48; pa/USPS 1944-; Spec Min to Elderly in Nsg & Retirement Homes 20 Yrs; r/Bapt.

PITTS, ROY L SR oc/Artist, Letterer, Minister; b/Dec 6, 1923; h/Rome, Ga; ba/PO Box 2662, Rome, GA 30161; m/Ruth M; c/Annette, Nancy, Terrie, Roy Jr; ed/Dip Gulf States Art Sch; Cert of Credit, Emory Univ; mil/AUS; pa/Cherokee Masonic Lodge; Metro Kiwanis; Pres Biblevision Inc; r/Meth.

PLATT, JAN KAMINIS oc/County Commissioner; h/4606 Bch Pk Dr, Tampa, FL 33609; ba/Tampa; m/William R; c/Kevin; p/Peter C and Adele Kaminis; ed/BA Polit Sci & Public Adm; pa/Hillsborough Co Commr; cp/Past Pres: Suncoast Girl Scout Coun (Hillsborough, Pinelas, Pasco & Hernando Cos), Bayview Gdn Clb, Citizens Alert; Past VP Hillsborough Co Bar Aux; LWV; Bd Dirs AAUW; Bd Dirs DAACO; Bd Dirs New Place; Hillsborough Co Coun Govts; Gov's Task Force on Coastal Zone Mgmt; Constituiton Revision Comm; VChm Tampa Bay Regional Plan'g Coun; Chm 7th Congl Dist Sunshine Amendment Dr; Past Chm Commun Devel Com, Tampa City Coun; Tampa Chamber Downtown Devel Auth Task Force; COG Water Coor'g Com; Chm COG Com to Coor Rec Sers; Temp Chm Charter Revision Com; Coun Screen Com; Past Chm Fin Com, Tampa City Coun; Pks-Rec Cultural Com, Tampa City Coun; Inebriate Task Force; Chm Tampa Housing Study Com; Chm Public Works Com, Tampa City Coun; Secy Hosp & Wel Bd; Chm: Envirl Protection Comm, Bd Tax Adjustment, Coun Govts; VChm Commun Act Agcy; Tampa Area Mtl Hlth Bd; Arts Coun; Expressway Auth; Chd's Sers Vol Leag; Metro Plan'g Org; r/Epis; hon/Athena Awd, Wom in Communs.

PLEDGER, EDWARD LEWIS SR oc/Landscape Designer, Vocational Coordinator; b/Sept 28, 1944; h/1901 N Minnesota, Shawnee, OK 74801; ba/Tecumseh, OK; m/Marsha Ann; c/Edward Lewis Jr, Kimberely Ann; p/Victor and Norma Pledger, Tecumseh, OK; ed/Bach in Horticulture & Landscape Design, Masters in Landscape Design Okla St Univ; Further Study Tex Tech Univ; mil/USAR Capt; pa/Am Voc Assn; Okla Voc Assn; NEA; cp/YMCA; Nat Taxpayers Assn; r/Bapt; hon/FFA; Pres's Hon Roll; Army Commend Medal; Vietnam Campaign Medal; Vietnam Ser Medal; Am Defense Medal; 2 Reserve Commend Medals.

PLITT, JEANNE GIVEN oc/Director of Libraries; b/Aug 27, 1927; h/6633 S Kings Hwy, Alexandria, VA 22306; ba/Alexandria; m/Ferdinand C Jr; c/Charles Randolph, Christine Marie; p/Charles R and Anna Given, Whitehall, NY; ed/AB Univ Md; MSLS Cath Univ; pa/Dir Libs, Alexandria Lib; Va Lib Assn; Intl Libs Tech Comm, Wash Metro Area Coun Govts, Chm 1970-71; Army Spec Sers Lib Div 1949-51; Lic'd Tchr Md & Va Sec'dy Area; cp/PTA; Little Theatre Grp; Co Civic Assn; Zonta Clb Intl, Past Secy Alexandria Chapt; Past Dir Alexandria Hist Soc; Manuscript Soc; Past Mem Urban Leag; r/Rom Cath.

PLIVKA, ANDREW DANIEL oc/Banker; b/June 1, 1947; h/840 SE 3rd Terr, Pompano Bch, FL 33060; ba/Pompano Bch; ed/BS NY Inst Tech; MS Hofstra Univ; Computer Fla Atlantic Univ; pa/Am Math Soc; hon/Var Hons & Awds.

PLUMMER, EDNA MAE oc/Secretary-Cashier; b/May 29, 1921; h/Louisville, KY; m/Kenneth W (dec); c/Jerald D; p/Elmer Leonard (dec) and Fern Haggin Schultz (dec); ed/Bus Deg Spencerian Col 1939; Att'd Univ Ky Ext; Sems Dun & Bradstreet; pa/Monarch Equipment Co 1939-42; Army Air Force 1942-46; Chevrolet Motor Div, Gen Motors Corp 1946-; Prod Distbn Mdsg, Secy-Cashier; ABWA: Corresp Secy, 1st VP, Secy, Pres; cp/Wom's Ky C of C: Leg Com 1979-80, Exec Bd 1980-81; Wom's Coun S L'ville Christian Ch, Past Pres; Woodson Bend Resort; r/Christian; hon/Wom of Yr 1979-80, ABWA; W/W Am Wom 1981-82.

PLUMMER, JACK MOORE oc/Psychologist; b/Apr 19, 1940; h/614 Ridge View Dr, Hot Springs, AR 71901; ba/Hot Springs; m/Rose Marie Taylor; c/Cynthia Marie, Edward Moore, Elizabeth Anne, Sarah Lorraine, Jack Moore; p/Jack Moore (dec); Sarah Carroll Cochran, Galveston, TX; ed/BA St Mary's Univ 1962; MS Trinity Univ 1968; PhD Tex Tech Univ 1969; AAS Garland Co Commun Col 1978; pa/Clin-Cnslg-Conslt Psych; Conslt & Adv Bd Mem Parents w/out Ptnrs; Fellow Ark

Psych Assn; Pres Hot Springs Psych Assn 1979-80; Chm Fellow Review Com of Ark Psych Assn; Assoc Mem FOP; Assoc Mem Intl Assn Chiefs of Police; cp/Chm Sight Conserv Com, S Hot Springs Lions Clb 1971-72; r/Rom Cath; hon/W/W S&SW 1976-77, 78-79, 80-81; Contbr to Var Profl Jours & Chapt on Projective Tech in *Handbook of Measurement and Evaluation in Rehabilitation* 1976.

PLYLER, BOB LEE oc/Executive; b/Dec 20, 1936; h/Box 26593, Houston, TX 77207; m/Paulette Durso; c/Vonda Lynn, Pamela Lee, Bobby Lee, Joseph Lane, Rick Todd; p/Lee Roy and Altha Cleo McSpadden Plyler; ed/AA Arlington St 1955; BA Tex A&M Univ 1957; Hon AFD London Inst 1972; mil/USAF 1955-56; pa/Fdr & Pres Acme Ladders Inc 1966-; Plant Mgr Lone Star Ladder Co 1957-66; cp/Past Pres Gulf Meadow Civic Assn; Former Spec Advr & MC of Consular Ball of Houston; MC Noches Americas Intl Ball; Former VP Gtr Houston Civic Foun; Former Protocol Rep to Ofc of Mayor; Houston JCs; Chm Galveston Co Drainage Dist; Bd Dirs Houston-Taipia Sister City Com; Master Mason; Shriner; r/Bapt; hon/Notable Ams of Bicent Era; W/W: Tex, Fin & Indust, S&SW; Book of Honor; Intl W/W Commun Ser.

POAGE, CYNTHA JEAN oc/Attorney; b/June 18, 1940; h/2602 Mountain Laurel Pl, Reston, VA 22091; ba/Herndon, VA; m/William H; c/Peter, Christopher, Matthew; p/Stephen M and Doris J Archer, Pt Charlotte, FL; ed/BA 1961; JD 1969; pa/Va, Md, US Supreme Ct Bars; cp/Dir: Herndon C of C, Dulles Com, Mid-Atlantic Band Fest; r/Meth.

POAGE, WILLIAM ROBERT oc/Congressman; b/Dec 28, 1899; h/600 Edgewood Ave, Waco, TX 76708; ba/Wash DC; m/Frances; p/W A and Helen C Poage (dec); ed/AB; LLB; LLD; LHD; mil/Navy; p/Was in Tex Legis Prior to Coming to US Congress 1937; r/Universalist.

POE, BOOKER oc/Physician; b/July 9, 1936; h/3518 Lynfield Dr SW, Atlanta, GA 30311; ed/BS Tenn St Univ 1957; MD McHarry Med Col 1963; mil/USAF 1964-66 Capt; pa/Internship Hurley Hosp 1963-64; Residency Trg Chd's Hosp of E Bay 1966-68; Chief of Pediatrics, Tachikawa AFB, Japan 1968-69; Pvt Pract Pediatrics, Atlanta 1969-; Atlanta Med Assn: Prog Chm 1970-76, Public Relats Chm 1976, Chm Awds Com 1977; Ga St Med Assn: Prog Chm 1970-76, Chm Med Leg Breakfast 1976; Mem Fulton Co Maternal & Infant Hlth Care Plan'g Task Force 1975-76; Treas Metro-Atlanta Hlth Plan 1977-80; Minority Dentist & Phys of Ga, Advr 1980; Atlanta Med Assn, Bd Dirs 1980; Assoc Clin Prof of Pediatrics, Ga St Univ 1970, 74; Hlth Prog Chm, W Manor Sch 1975-76; hon/Cit for Outstg Ser to Org, Ga St Med Assn 1973; Yng Phys of Yr, Atlanta Med Assn 1973; Commun Ser Awd, Ga St Med Assn 1974; Contbns Awd, Harper HS 1976; Hlth Care Contbn Awd, W Manor Sch 1977; W/W: Atlanta, Black Am; Atlanta Br NAACP Awd 1978; Cit for Efforts Ldg to 50 St Regulation, Atlanta Med Assn 1978; Dir of Dist'd Ams 1980; Author "EPSDT and the Black Medical Community of Georgia" 1979 & "Why Attend a Legislative Breakfast?" 1980.

POE, FRED W oc/Assistant City Manager; b/Sept 14, 1927; h/2611 W Shandon, Midland, TX 79701; ba/Midland; m/Truma L; c/Paula LaGrone, Keith W, Sherry Griffith; p/Fred C (dec) and Mrs Fred C Poe, Winters TX; ed/BS Tex A&M 1949; mil/WWII & Korea; pa/Asst City Mgr, Midland, Tex; Intl City Mgrs Assn; Tex City Mgrs Assn; Past Pres W Tex City Mgr Assn; Past Mem Tex City Mgrs Bd Dirs; cp/Lions Clb, Former Bd Dirs; Salvation Army, Bd Dirs, Chm Bd 1977; r/Bapt; hon/Boss of Yr, Permian Chapt Nat Secys Assn 1980.

POGUE, SUSAN SMALL oc/Director of Personnel and Payroll; b/July 11, 1947; h/Cookeville, TN; ba/Tenn Tech Univ, Box 5037, Cookeville, TN 38501; m/Ronald Van; c/Shawn, Dana, Mark, Barbara; p/Kenneth H and Margaret B Mansfield, Palm Bch Gdns, FL; ed/Colby Col 1965-67; BS Univ Maine 1976; pa/Sys Coor EEO/AA, Pers Spec Univ Maine 1974-77; Tenn Tech Univ, Univ Pers/Payroll Ofcr 1977-; Col & Univ Pers Assn, Nat Equal Employment Opport Com; Pres Upper Cumberland ASPA Chapt; Chm Upper Cumberland ASPA Profl Devel Com; St Tenn Job Ser Employer's Adv Com: St VChp, St Steering Com Mem, Chp Putnam, White, Cumberland, Smith Co Chapt; Tenn Pvt Indust Coun, Ex-Officio Mem; cp/Past Pres, Treas Beta Sigma Phi; Past Treas Parent's w/out Ptnrs; hon/W/W S&SW 1980-81; Recip Nat BPW Career Advmt S'ship 1975; Beta Gamma Sigma 1976.

POITEVINT, KATHERINE BROWN oc/Speech and Language Pathologist; b/Oct 5, 1949; h/3233 Wilmington Rd, Montgomery, AL 36105; ba/Montgomery; m/James William III; p/John C (dec) and Edna Louise Brown (dec); ed/Agnes Scott Col 1968-69; BA Univ S Ala 1972; MA Auburn Univ 1974; pa/Owner-Dir Speech Therapy Sers 1977-; Conslt to: Hosps, Nsg Homes, Montgomery Commun Action; Conslt Trg Outreach Prog for Sensory Impaired, Univ Ala 1978-80; Adj Prof Auburn Univ Montgomery 1978; Chief Speech Pathol Ala Mtl Hlth Clin, Auburn Univ 1974-76; ASHA, Cert of Clin Competence; Am Acad Pvt Practrs in Speech Pathol & Audiology; Montgomery Speech & Hearing Assn; Ala

Speech & Hearing Assn, Exec Coun 1979-; cp/Jasmine Hills Arts Coun 1979-80; Montgomery Mus Assn 1980-; Landmarks Foun 1979-80; Ashmolean Soc, Order of the Rogue; Montgomery Jr Wom's Clb; AAUW, Exec Coun 1980-81; r/Meth; hon/Psi Chi; Sigma Alpha Eta; Phi Kappa Phi.

POLATTY, ROSE CRYSTAL JACKSON oc/Freelance Journalist, Civic Volunteer; b/Sept 17, 1922; h/889 Mimosa Blvd, Roswell, GA 3005; m/George Junius; c/George Junius Jr, Robert Wilmot, Rose Crystal, Richard James; p/James Wilmot (dec) and Esther Sweeny Jackson (dec); ed/AB Univ Ga 1943; Post Grad Study Oglethorpe Univ 1962-63, Ga St Univ 1963; pa/Freelance Writer; cp/Wom in Communs; Delta Omicron; Phi Beta Kappa; Kappa Delta Pi; Roswell Hist Preserv Comm; Roswell Hist Soc; Roswell Wom's Clb; Roswell Gdn Clb; Univ Ga Alumni Soc; DAR; Colonial Dames XVII Cent; PEO Sisterhood; Kappa Delta; Nat Trust for Hist Preserv; Ga Trust for Hist Preserv; Ga Citizens for the Arts; r/Meth; Chm Altar Guild, Adm Bd; hon/Recog Awd, Nat 4-H Alumni 1959; Ser Awd, City of Roswell 1976; Commun Ser Awd, Roswell Optimist Clb 1977; Roswell JC Ldrship Awd 1977; Commun Ser Awd, Zion Bapt Ch 1977; Fabulous Fifty, Atlanta Symph Orch Assocs 1980.

POLLIO, MICHAEL A oc/Athletic Director, Instructor; b/June 12, 1943; h/4427 Taylor Dr, Owensboro, KY 42301; ba/O'boro; m/Ann; c/Lynn, Marty, Susan; p/dec; ed/BA Bellarmine Col 1965; MEd Univ L'ville 1971; pa/Va Commonwlth Univ, Asst Coach 1973-75; Asst Coach Old Dominion Univ 1975-80; Hd Basketball Coach, Ath Dir, Instr Spec Ed Ky Wesleyan Col; Bellarmine Col Bd Dirs 1966; Nat Assn Basketball Coaches; Nat Assn Ath Dirs; cp/K of C; r/Cath; hon/UPI Coach of Yr in Ky 1971; Dist Coach of Yr, L'ville Ky 1969, 71; Dist Coach of Yr, Orlando, Fla 1973.

POLOPOLUS, JEAN CALTON oc/Homemaker; b/June 4, 1945; h/4741 NW 8th Ave, Gainesville, FL 32605; m/Leonidias; p/Williams Jennings and Emma Adell Knight Stewart, Jacksonville, FL; ed/BA Bus Adm; pa/Former Shipping Exec; cp/Beta Sigma Phi; Agric Wom's Clb; r/Greek Orthodox; hon/W/W Am Wom 1979-80.

POLSTRA, LARRY JOHN oc/Attorney; b/June 28, 1945; h/Avondale Ests, GA; ba/250 Peidmont Ave NE, Suite 1402, Atlanta, GA 30308; m/Joan M; c/Shawn M Rozier; p/John E and Elizabeth Polstra, Lafayette, IN; ed/BS Bob Jones Univ 1968; JD 1976, LLM 1977 Atlanta Law Sch; mil/USMC 1968-71; USMCR 1971-80 Capt; pa/Atty, Ptnr Smith, Polstra & Kirsch; Atlanta Bar Assn; St Bar of Ga; Ga Assn Crim Defense Lwyrs; Assn Trial Lwyrs Am; Am Bar Assn; Intl Bar Assn; cp/Firm Com, Bethel Bapt Ch; r/Bapt; hon/S'ship Cert, Delta Theta Phi 1976; Various Ribbons & Medals for Ser in Vietnam.

POMER, OSCAR JAY oc/Administrative Law Judge, Bureau of Hearings and Appeals, HEW; b/Dec 14, 1908; h/54 Logan St, Charleston, SC 29401; ba/Charleston; c/Sarah Irene; p/Jerome and Sarah R Pomer (dec); ed/LLB; mil/AUS WW II, Cpl; pa/Fed Bar Assn; Fed Adm Law Judges Conf; r/Hebrew; hon/Purple Heart, Bronze Star.

PONDS, OTIS D JR oc/Psychotherapy; b/Sept 18, 1936; h/2115 Poinciana Dr, Clearwater, FL 33520; m/Barbara L; c/Gregory A, Debroa S; p/dec; ed/Att'd Stetson Univ 1959-60; BS Univ Neb 1971; MSW Fla St Univ 1974; Dr Public Adm Nova Univ; mil/AUS 1963-69; pa/Social Wkr Pasco Mtl Hlth 1971-72; Social Wkr VA, Bay Pines, Fla 1974; Assoc Dir Emer Mtl Hlth, Pinellas Co, Fla 1975-76; Pvt Prac Christian Psychtherapy, Clearwater, Fla 1976-; Conslt Home Hlth Sers; Assoc Dir Emer Mtl Hlth, Clearwater 1975-76; Nat Assn Christian Social Wkrs; r/Bapt; hon/Alpha Kappa Delta 1971.

POOL, NELDA LEE oc/Art Dealer and Appraiser; b/Jul 3, 1941; h/2610 E 21st, Odessa, TX 79761; ba/Odessa; m/Curtis A; c/Jeanna Lea; p/Olan C Lee (dec); Onis L Lee, Odessa; ed/AA Tarleton St Col 1961; BA N Tex St Univ 1963; Grad Studies: Tex Tech Univ, San Maguel de Allende Art Inst (Mex); Cert'd Fine Arts Appraiser, Am Soc Appraisers 1972; Cert, Nat Soc Lit & Arts; pa/Hd Art Dept, Ector HS, Odessa 1963-68; Former Ofcr Tex St Art Ed Assn; Art Gallery Businesswoman 1968-; Profl Artist Exhibiting Throughout US & Mex; Paintings Included in Tex Fine Arts Assn Touring Exhbn; Ector Co Com, Former of Tex Fine Arts Comm; Past Pres Odessa Art Assn; cp/Patron Mem Globe of SW, Odessa; Bd Dirs: YWCA, YMCA, Odessa; Odessa Knife & Fork Clb; Supporting Mem Mus of SW, Midland, Tex; Campaign Chm Ector Co Div, Am Heart Assn; Odessa-Midland Symph Guild; Com Chm, Ector Co UF; Altrusa Intl; Ector Co Pres Mus, Active Annual Mem; Active in Local, St, Nat Dem Party; Immed Past Pres, Ector Co Dem Woms Clb; CoChm Cong-man O C Fisher 1970 Campaign; CoChm Cong-man R C White 1975-76 Campaign Com; hon/Outstg Yg Wom Am; Intl W/W Arts & Antiques; IBD; Life Mem (Only Wom), Odessa C of C; Intl Dic Arts; Intl W/W Intellectuals; World W/W Wom; IPA; 1st Place Art Awds: Intl Designer/Craftsman Exhbn, El Paso, TX, "Artists of the SE", Tex Exhbn, NO, La; Pub'd Author; Fellow Mem ABI.

POOLE, WILLIAM OLIVER oc/Rancher, Investments, Drilling Contractor; b/Mar 20, 1917; h/1805 Encino, Alice, TX 78332; ba/Alice; m/Evalyn; c/Billy Roy (dec), George Ann Aycock, Cynthia Jane Fauth, Priscilla Lynn Urban, Patricia Louise Foster; p/Eugene Charlie and Mamie Jane Avery Poole; ed/Att'd Tex A&M 1935-36, Corps Christi Bus Col 1938; mil/USAAF 1942-46 Pilot; pa/Asst Airport Mgr, Cliff Maus Aiport, Corpus Christi, Tex 1938-42; Commercial Pilot for Pvt Cos 1946; Appell Drilling Co, Alice, Tex: Pilot, Ofc Mgr 1947-52, Gen Mgr, Drilling Supt 1952-64; Fdr Choya Drilling Co, Alice 1964, Pres 1964-75, Advr 1975-78; Owner-Oper Choya Ranches, Kerrville, Camp Wood, Tex; Owner Bill Poole Enterprises, Alice; Co-Fdr Magee-Poole Drilling Co 1979; Dir Ctrl Park Bank, San Antonio, Corpus Christi Bank & Trust; Intl Assn Drilling Contractors, Dir; Tex Indep Prodrs & Royalty Owners Assn; Tex Mid-Cont Oil & Gas Assn; Intl Brangus Breeders Assn, Dir; Hill Co Brangus Breeders; Tex Brangus Breeders; Indep Petro Assn; Am Clubs: Houston Petro; Corpus Christi Petro; cp/BSA 1964-78; Dir Gulf Coast Coun 1974-75; Pres Airport Bd Alice 1974-75; Jim Wells Co Master Plan'g & Devel Assn 1973-79; Capitol Improvements Com City of Alice 1974-76; Sch Trustee Alice 1971-78; Bd Dirs Bandina Christian Yth Camp 1975-; Trustee Corpus Christi Christian Sch 1975-78; Collector Fine Art (Esp 18 & 19th Cent Sporting Paintings); Corpus Christi Yacht Clb; r/Ch of Christ; hon/Intl W/W; Cattle Breeders Hall of Fame.

POPADIC, JOSEPH STEPHEN oc/Associate Professor, Director of Graduate Studies; b/Nov 6, 1945; h/Baton Rouge, LA; ba/Baton Rouge; m/Mary Katherine Rountree; p/Joseph Peter and Pauline Katherine Vrabel Popadic, Shelton, CT; ed/BLA 1967, MLA 1974 SUNY at Syracuse Univ; mil/USAR Capt; pa/Landscape Arch: New Haven Redevel Agcy 1967-68, Rermann & Buechner 1970-71, Moriece & Gary 1974, Haynes, Popadic, Abbey & Assocs 1978-; Assoc Prof Sch Landscape Arch, La St Univ 1972-; Am Soc Landscape Arch; La Soc Landscape Arch; r/Rom Cath; hon/W/W S&SW 1980; LSU Fac Senate 1977-80; Canoe Assn Cert'd Whitewater Canoe Instr, Am Red Cross; Chapt Entry *Wilderness Trails of Louisiana* 1981.

POPE, DALLAS HARRIS oc/City Manager; b/Dec 28, 1931; h/Box 973, Lillington, NC 27546; m/Dorothy E; c/Dallas H II, Jannette E Evans; p/Floyd E and Mazie M Pope, Lillington, NC; ed/BS NC St Univ 1955; AF Pilot Tng 1956; Air Univ 1959; AF Inst of Tech 1970; mil/Entered USAF 1955 as 2nd Lt, Ret'd as Col 1979; pa/Constrn Engr; USAF Pilot & Engr; Ret'd Ofcrs Assn; cp/Bd Govs, Rotary Clb; Harnett Co Arts Coun; r/Presb; hon/Legion of Merit Medal; 2 Merit Ser Medals; Bronze Star Medal; 3 AF Commend Medals; Nat Defence Ser Medal; Republic of Viet Nam Campaign Medal & Commend Medal; 3 USAF Outstg Awds; AF Longevity Ser Awd (5 OLC).

POPE, DOUGLAS LEE oc/Area Conservationist; b/Apr 10, 1924; h/Rt 3 Box 481, Albany, GA 31707; m/Delores Hendley; c/Rodney Lee, Michael Leon, Russell Sanders; p/James Sanders (dec) and Neva Williams Pope, Pinehurst, GA; ed/Abraham Baldwin Agric Col 1947; BS Univ Ga 1949; mil/USAAC 1942-45; pa/Area Conservationist, US Dept Agric (32 Yrs w Soil Conserv Ser); Dir Ga Natural Resources Conserv Wkshop 1977-81; Soil Conserv Soc Am; Land Improvement Contractors Am; r/So Bapt; hon/4 Sustained Above Average Awds 1958, 63, 68, 71; Conservationist of Yr; Voodman of World 1970; Outstg Perf Awd, Soil Conserv Ser 1976-77; Good Turn Awd, BSA 1978; Dist'd Conserv Awd, Ag Alumni, Univ Ga 1978; Commend Awd, Soil Conserv Soc 1978; Man of Yr, GACDS Awd for Superior Profl Support to Conserv Dists 1980.

POPE, GEORGE WASHINGTON III (BUDDY) oc/Superintendent; b/Aug 12, 1947; h/114 Franklyn Pl, Millen, GA 30442; ba/Millen; m/Linda Carmichael; c/Heather Renee; p/George W Jr (dec) and Marjorie G Pope, Millen, GA; ed/AB 1969, MEd 1974, EdS 1976 Ga So Col; pa/Supt Jenkins Co Sch Sys; Phi Delta Kappa; Phi Kappa Phi; GAE; GASS; NASS; GAE; NEA; NASSP; Ga So Col Bd Dirs Alumni Affairs; Nat Sch Bds Assn; cp/Millen Rotary Clb; Bd Dirs Am Cancer Soc; Past Pres Local GAE; r/Meth.

POPE, GROVER C ALLEN oc/Nurse; b/July 28, 1929; h/319 E Parkview St, Dyersburg, TN 38024; m/Ruth; c/Darwin Allen, Dana Ruth; p/G C (dec) and Glora Pope (dec); ed/AEd; BSN; pa/RN; Tenn Nsg Assn; Tenn Hosp Assn; r/Ch of Christ.

POPE, LELA WALKER oc/Retired Teacher; b/Oct 12, 1899; h/511 Vaughn St, Corbin, KY 40701; m/Willis Hamblin (dec); c/Jack H (dec); p/Frank Finley (dec) and Lucinda Bryant Walker (dec); ed/Tchr Tng Cumberland Col; Att'd George Peabody Col Summer 1924, Ashville Normal Summer 1927, Union Col Summer 1928; AB Univ Ky 1930; MA Duke Univ 1940; pa/Tchr: Whitley Co, Ky 1918-22, Cumberland Col, Williamsburg, Ky 1923-24, Corbin City Sch, Corbin, Ky 1925-66, Cumberland Col 1966-70; Ret'd 1970; KEA; Former Mem NEA; Ret'd Tchrs Assn of Ky; Nat Ret'd Tchrs Assn; Ky Assn

PERSONALITIES OF THE SOUTH

Commun Arts: Charter Mem & Mem Emeritus; cp/Pres Corbin Gdn Clb; OES; Past Pres & Parlimentn, Tri-Co BPW Clb; Rec'g Secy, Ky Fed BPWC; Dukes & Duchess Clbs of Corbin HS: Orgr & Sponsor 1935-65; r/Bapt: SS Tchr, Yth Grp Ldr; hon/Tri-Co Wom of Yr 1968; Tri-Co BPW Clb Wom of Achmt 1981; Other Hons.

POPE, MARY MAUDE oc/Pastor; b/Jan 27, 1916; h/1120 Cross Link Rd, Raleigh, NC; ba/Raleigh; m/(dec); p/Delia Smith (dec); ed/Am Sch of Chgo; Univ NC; NCSU-R; pa/Bishop, Fdr, Mt Sinai Saints of God Holy Chs & Mt Sinai Chs Worldwide; Over 100 Chs Alone in Africa; Built Orphanage Sch of Nigerians & 20 Room Home Called Popes Manse; Currently Wkg in Bishop Maude Pope's (Gospel Singing) & Healing Crusade; r/Holiness; hon/W/W NC (Only Black Wom Bishop & Fdr & Ldr in Book), Plaque; Cert Apprec, NTO AKPAN Village Coun; W/W Among Black Ams; Fellow Mem ABI.

PORTER, DARWIN F oc/Editor, Author; b/Sept 13, 1937; h/324 William St, Key West, FL 33040; ba/Staton Island, NY; p/Numie Rowan Porter (dec); Hazel Porter Triplett, Key West, FL; ed/BA Univ Miami 1959; pa/Bur Chief, *The Miami Herald* 1959-60; VP Haggart Assocs 1961-63; Ed, Author, Arthur Frommer Inc & Frommer/Pasmantier Pub'g Corp 1964-; cp/Intl Platform Assn; Key West Hist Soc; Am Soc Travel Writers; Sigma Delta Chi; Smithsonian Assn; F'ship Intl Biogl Assn; hon/Mae Bernice Jacobs Meml Awd 1967; Silver Awd, Film & TV Fest NY 1977; Author: (Novels) *Butterflies in Heat & Marika;* (Film) *The Last Resort* 1980; Dollarwise Guides to Italy, Spain, Morocco, Scandinavia, Germany, Portugal, England, Scotland, France, The Caribbean, Bermuda & the Bahamas; Guides to Lisbon, Madrid, Paris, Rome, Los Angeles & London.

PORTER, HENRY L oc/Pastor, Educator, Poet, Recording Artist; b/Jan 2, 1948; h/1986; 29th St, Sarasota, FL; ba/Sarasota; m/Cynthia E; c/Henry L II, Etienne Jaberly; p/Lee Ernest and Hazel Elkin Porter, Sarasota, FL: ed/BS Fla A&M Univ 1969; Grad Work Yale Univ 1969-71; pa/Edr, Dept Maths, Fla A&M Univ 1973-75; Fdr Westcoast Ctr of World Evangelism 1978-; Pres Henry L Porter Evangelistic Assn 1971-; r/Transdenom, Meth Background; hon/Ford Foun Doct F'ship 1969; Gtr Dist Grad, Fla A&M Univ 1969; Alpha Kappa Mu 1967.

PORTER, MICHAEL LEROY oc/Assistant Professor; b/Nov 23, 1947; h/3 Adrian Cir, Hampton, VA 23669; p/Leroy Porter, Hampton, VA; Doretha B Porter, Hampton, VA; ed/BA Va St Col 1969; MA Atlanta Univ 1972; PhD Emory Univ 1974; Fulbright-Hays Post-Doct Nom 1979; mil/AUS; pa/Asst Prof Black Studies, Wash St Univ 1974-75; Ednl Coor Target Projs Prog, Newport News, Va 1977; Asst Prof Hist, Hampton Inst, Dept Hist 1977-; So Hist Assn; Nat Hist Soc; Va St Col Alumni Assn; Atlanta Univ Alumni Assn; Emory Univ Alumni Assn; Yng Profls of Tidewater; Nat Assn Housing; Phi Alpha Theta; cp/Bach Benedict Social & Civics Clb; Peninsula Coun of Clbs, Recording Secy; Old Dominion Golf Clb, Hist; Bullseye Gun Clb; Ctr Ct Racquet Clb; Am Legion Post #31; Cand Hampton Sch Bd; Bd Dirs: Cath Home, Bapt Bur, Citizens Boys Clb, Sickle Cell Anemia, King St Commun Ctr, YWCA; hon/Alpha Kappa Delta; Cand for Alpha Kappa Mu; Author "Jim Crowism Atlanta Style" 1978 & "The Formation of a Black Community" 1978.

PORTER, STEPHEN MICHAEL oc/Programming Director; b/Jan 29, 1952; h/Lexington, KY; ba/1617 Fox Haven Rd, Richmond, KY 40475; p/Wayne Ray and Patricia Dixon Porter, Lexington, KY; ed/BA Univ Ky 1974; pa/Dir Prog'g & Commun Devel, OVC Telecommuns Inc; Intl Radio & TV Soc; Ky Assn Communs; r/Prot; hon/Prod'd Video Tape for Nat Wheelchair Basketball Assn 1978; Prod'd Series of 9 Video Tapes for Univ Ky Prog'd Envirs 1975.

POSTER, CAROL oc/Poet, Technical Writer; b/Aug 5, 1956; h/Alexandria, VA; ba/Control Data Corp, 1800 N Beauregard St, Alexandria, VA 22311; p/C H Poster, Carrollton, GA; ed/BA cum laude Hollins Col 1977; MA Ind Univ 1979; pa/Software Writer, Control Data Corp; Dir'd Plays Off-Broadway; VP Wom's Intl Theatre Alliance; hon/Author *Blackbird* 1979; Over 300 Poems, Translations & Short Stories in Periods & Anthols in US & Abroad.

POTTS, BERNARD oc/Attorney; b/Aug 22, 1915; h/3206 Midfield Rd, Pikesville, MD 21208; ba/Balto; m/Frieda; c/Phillip L, Neal A, Bryan H, Andrea M; p/dec; ed/ABA Col of Commerce, Balto; LLB En Univ; JD Univ Balta; Cert Mich St Univ Police Inst; mil/USCG; pa/Chm Police Commun Relats Coun; Alcoholic Adv Bd of Hlth Dept, Bd Mem; Correctional Prog, Md Coun Social Concern; Prison Alternative Coun of Md; cp/Safety First Clb Md, Pres 2 Yrs; Jewish War Vets of USA, Post Comdr, Star of David; Accident Preven Bur of Md, Chm 9 Yrs; Mary Dopkin Chd's Fund, Fdr & Pres; E Balto Chd's Fund, Fdr, VP; Boys Town Hmes of Md, Fdr & VP; hon/Alumnis of Yr: En Univ, Talmudical Acad of Balto; Dist'd Citizens Awd, Gov St of Md 1971; Fdr's Awd, Boys Town Homes Md; Md Achmt Awd, Metro Civic Assn Md; Outstg Pres Awd, B'nai B'rith, Dist 5; Num Other B'nai B'rith Awds.

POTTS, NANCY DEE oc/Marriage & Family Therapist; Writer, Program Consultant; b/Dec 21, 1947; h/3111 W Creek Clb Dr, Missouri City, TX 77459; m/Lloyd L; p/Sidney Boyd and Katie Sue Needham, Houston; ed/BA Baylor Univ 1970; EdM Sam Houston St Univ 1974; Clin Residency Marriage & Fam Consultation Ctr 1975; Doct Cand Univ Houston; pa/Partner, Bourne & Potts Marriage & Fam Conslts (Cnslr, Conslt, Wkshop Devel) 1977-; Cnslr, The Ctr for Counseling 1975-76 (Resigned to Complete Doct Studies); Cnslr & Prog Conslt, S Main Bapt Ch 1974-75; Other Past Positions; Num Profl Assns; Currently Preparing Arts for Var Jours & Other Pubs; Ldr Num Sems & Wkshop in Areas of Marriage & Fam Enrichmt, Premarital Wkshops, & Progs Designed for Singles, Widows & Formerly-Married; cp/LWV; Vol for Crisis Cnslng, Crisis Hotline; r/Bapt; hon/Pub'd Author; 1 of 30 Tchrs Selected to Participate in Wash DC Sum Sems at Am Univ; Fellow Mem ABI.

POWELL, ANDREW JEFFERSON JR oc/Corporate Director; b/Oct 12, 1936; h/518 Audubon Dr, Spartanburg, SC 29302; ba/Lyman, SC; m/Elizabeth Ann; c/Dawn Elizabeth, Andrew J III, Dianne; p/Andrew J and Mary Vann Powell, B'ham, AL; ed/BSIM Auburn Univ 1961; mil/USN 2 Yrs; pa/Dir Corp Indust Engrg, M Lowenstein Corp; AIIE; Auburn Univ Engrg Adv Coun; cp/SC Ed Res Foun Adv Coun; r/Bapt; hon/VP & Dir High Reach Equip Inc.

POWELL, IRIS LEE BURNETTE oc/Nurse; b/Jan 27, 1945; h/3509 16th Ave W, Brandenton, FL 33505; ba/B'ton; c/Sherrie Michele, Shellie Darlene, Marina Kay; p/Leroy and Sue Whisnant Burnette, Morganton, NC; ed/ASN Wn Piedmont Commun Col 1973; p/OR Nurse, Manatee Meml Hosp; AORN, Chm By-Laws Com 1976-77; Pres Elect Wn NC Chapt AORN 1976-77; Gulf Coast Chapt AORN: Editor Newslttr *The Opener* 1978-79, Pres Elect 1979-80, Chm By-Laws Com 1979-80, Pres 1980-81; Orgr Fla Coun AORN, Editor Fla St Coun Newslttr; r/Epis; hon/Del AORN Nat Cong 1977, 78, 80; 1st Pl Photo Awd, Gulf Coast Chapt AORN 1979; Accomplished Dancer.

POWELL, JODY oc/Press Secretary to US President; b/Sept 30, 1943; h/The White House, 1600 Pa Ave, NW, Wash DC 20500; m/Nan; c/Emily; ed/USAF Acad 3 Yrs; BA Polit Sci Ga St Univ 1966; Grad Work Polit Sci, Emory Univ; pa/Press Secy to Pres Jimmy Carter, Wash DC; Former Press Secy to Jimmy Carter as Gov of Ga, Elected 1970-74; Former Vol, then Aide to Cand Carter in Ga Gubernatorial Campaign 1970; Former Employee, Life Ins Co of Ga 1966.

POWERS, JOHNNY DON oc/Teacher, Coach; b/Aug 22, 1944; h/225 Lawrence St, Sumter, SC 29150; ba/Sumter; p/Donald Edward and Jean Weaver Powers, Lansing, NC; ed/BS Appalachian St Univ 1966; Grad Studies: Appalachian St Univ & Univ SC; pa/Tchr Chem & Biol, Hd Basketball Coach, Sumter Sch Dist #17; NEA; SCEA; SC Coaches Assn; SC Basketball Coaches Assn, Charter Mem; Sumter Clrm Tchr; Am Chem Soc; SC Acad Sci; r/Bapt; hon/Tchr of Yr 1968; STAR Tchr of Yr 1969; Area Coach of Yr 3 Times; Region Coach of Yr 5 Times; McDonald's All Am Coach; SC AAAA Coach of Yr 2 Times; Outstg AAAA Coach, Palmetto Scouting Ser; Achmt Awd, Nat Assn Basketball Coaches; Author Articles Pub'd in *Coach and Athlete*, *Athletic Journal*, *The Coaching Clinic*, and *The Basketball Clinic*.

PRESNAL, BILLY CHARLES oc/State Representative; b/Apr 26, 1932; h/1605 Brook Hollow, Bryan, TX 77801; ba/Bryan; m/Mickey; c/James Scott, Stephen Earl, DeAnna Kay; p/Will Presnal (dec); Majorie Presnal, Bryan, TX; ed/BS, MS Tex A&M Univ; mil/Ofcr USAF; pa/Mem Tex Ho of Reps; Chm of Appropriations Com; Mem: Legis Budget Bd, Legis Audit Com, Legis Reference Lib; Mem Task Force Com on St Fiscal Info and Mem of Sci and Tech Com of Nat Conf of St Legis; Mem Steering Com of Fiscal Affairs and Govt Operations Com of the 17 St So Legis Conf; cp/Masonic Lodge; r/Meth; hon/Tex Runner-up Outstg Yg Farmer; Gold Star 4-H Winner; Outstg Bryan Future Farmer; Hon Deg of Law, Univ of Tex-San Antonio; Hon Mem: Ctr Tex Assn Life Underwriters, Bremond C of C; Cert of Apprec for Tex Pub Commun-Jr Col Assn; Dist'd Ser Awd.

PRESNELL, JESSE GUY JR oc/Supervisor; b/Feb 23, 1929; h/1105 Porter St, Goldsboro, NC 27530; ba/G'boro; m/Ann Moses; c/George Michael; p/Jesse Guy (dec) and Marjorie P Presnell, Panama City, FL; mil/AUS 1950-52; pa/Line & Ser Supvr, Carolina Power & Light Co; cp/Boy Scouts; Wayne Co Boy's Clb; Wayne Masonic Lodge, Past Master; rp/Meth; hon/Grand Master's Masonic Awd 1971; Outstg Ser Awd, Wayne Co Boy's Clb 1979.

PRESSLER, HERMAN PAUL III oc/Judge, Fourteenth Court of Civil Appeals; b/Jun 4, 1940; h/282 Bryn Mawr Cir, Houston, TX 77024; ba/Houston; m/Nancy Avery; c/Jean Townes, Anne Lyle, Herman Paul IV; p/Herman Paul Jr and Elsie Townes Pressler, Houston; ed/BA (cum laude), Princeton Univ 1952; JD Univ Tex Law Sch 1957; mil/Lt, USN; pa/Vinson and Elkins Law Firm 1958-70; Judge, 133rd Judicial Dist of Tex, 1970-78; Judge, 14th Ct of Civil Appeals 1978-; cp/55th Tex Legis

Representing Harris Co; r/Bapt Deacon: Mem and SS Tchr, First Bapt Ch of Houston; Bd Dirs, Dallas Bible Col; hon/Houston Jr C of C Awd for Outstg Yg Man of Houston 1957; Faith in God Awd for a Non-JC; DAR Hon Medal.

PRESTRIDGE, CLARA ANN REACH oc/Homemaker; b/Mar 13, 1943; h/32 Royal Dr, Opelika, AL; m/Charles Walter; c/Mary Catherine, Charles David, Stephen Perry; p/Samuel Archie Reach (dec); Clara Fay Reach Owens, Helena, AL; ed/HS Grad; cp/Contbns to Sch Orgs Incl'g: Fair Booth Chm PTA, Ways & Means Chm Sch Band Booster Assn; Beta Sigma Phi, Chapt Pres 1980-81; r/Bapt; hon/St Hon Girl of Yr, Beta Sigma Phi 1980.

PREWITT, JUDITH MARTHA oc/Mathematician; b/Oct 16, 1935; h/8008 Aberdeen Rd, Bethesda, MD 20014; ba/Bethesda; c/David Joshua; p/Charles Shimansky (dec); Rebecca Shimansky, Brooklyn, NY; ed/BA w high hons Swarthmore Col 1957; MA Univ Penn 1959; PhD Univ Uppsala (Sweden) 1978; pa/Mathematician Nat Insts of Hlth, Bethesda; Editor, Jours, Num Pubs on Computers in Med; IEEE; BES; MAA; AMS; SIAM; IAC; Sigma Xi; hon/Phi Beta Kappa; Sigma Xi; USPHS, F'ships & S'ships; Vis Scist, Uppsala Univ.

PRICE, ALVA JACKSON JR oc/Pastor; b/Sept 3, 1953; h/PO Box 87, Hornsby, TN 38044; ba/Same; m/Linda Sheryl; c/Jeremy Jackson; p/Alva J Jr and Betty Jean Price, Williston, TN; ed/BS Univ Tenn Martin; MDiv So Bapt Theol Sem; pa/Pastor Hornsby Bapt Ch; cp/Ruritan Clb; r/Bapt.

PRICE, HENRY LEE oc/Chemical Operator; b/Mar 9, 1942; h/520 Chadwell Rd, Kingsport, TN; ba/Kingsport; m/Pearly; c/Judy Price Stacy, Barbara; p/Henry H Price, Kingsport, TN; Irene Hoytt, Long Bch, CA; mil/AUS 1960, 63; pa/Chem Oper, Eastman Kodak; cp/Tenn Constable's Assn Regional Comdr for Sullivan, Carter & Johnson Cos; hon/Most Outstg Constable in St Tenn 1979-80.

PRIMEAUX-SMITH, VALENTINE JOY oc/Student; b/Aug 12, 1929; h/PO Box 33, Tonkawa, OK 74653; ba/Same; m/Ross John; c/Jeffrey Clyde; p/Ira B Hagg (dec); Pauline Gordie Pyle, Tonkawa, OK; ed/Student No Okla Col; pa/Profl Appraiser & Conslt; Fdr & Pres LOVE Inc; cp/Ponca City Art Assn; hon/Men & Wom Dist 1979; Num Hons; Pub'd in *Harvest Magazine* 1978 & 79.

PRINCE, ELIZABETH COLLINS oc/Secretary, Bookkeeper; b/Apr 27, 1928; h/412 Griswold St, Selma, NC 27576; m/Willie Everette; c/Harold Steven Creech, Gregory Collins Creech; p/Andrew Barnes (dec) and Florence Perry O'Mary Collins (dec); ed/Raleigh Sch Commerce 1948; pa/Secy-Bkkpr; r/Meth.

PRINDLE, JIMMIE GLENN oc/Patrolman, Firechief; b/Dec 2, 1935; h/Keene, TX; ba/100 N Mockingbird, Keene, TX; m/Margie; c/Chris Allen, Freda Kay, Penny Elaine; p/Ralph Prindle, Charleston, SC; Margaret Prindle, Keene, TX; pa/Patrolman, Keene Police Dept; Firechief, Keene Vol Fire Dept; cp/N Tex Fireman's & Fire Marshal's Assn; r/7th Day Adventist.

PRINTUP, JOHN M oc/Retired Advertising & Marketing Consultant; b/Oct 14, 1919; h/210 Worth Dr NW, Atlanta, GA 30327; c/Bonnie, Michael, Richard, Susan; p/Edna Polka, Genoa, IL; ed/Att'd No Ill Univ 2 Yrs & No Ill Col of Optometry 3 Yrs; mil/USAF 1941-45; pa/Chm of Bd, John Printup & Assocs Inc (Pubrs Advtg Reps) 27 yrs; Bus & Profl Advtg Assn, Chm Ednl Com; Contbr to *Sales Mgmt Magazine*; r/Prot; hon/Eagle Scout w Bronze Palm, BSA; Shriner (Masonic); USAF Good Conduct Medal; Am Defense Medal (Pearl Harbor); WWII Medal; European Victory Medal; Merit Ser Awd.

PRITCHARD, LOUISE oc/Secretary; b/Sept 14, 1946; h/Box 2, Ayden, NC 29513; c/Andre, Tonya, Junior, Kiana; p/Paul C Hemby, Newark, NJ; Fannie H Gorham, Stamford, CT; ed/AAS Gen Ofc Technol 1980; AAS Med Secy 1981; pa/NC Comprehensive Commun Col, Student Govt Assn, Fin Com Secy 1979-80; Gamma Beta Phi; cp/Rose of Sharon; Ct of Calanthe; r/Bapt; hon/S'ship, Nat Secys Assn; Gamma Beta Phi Hons; Dean's List; Hon Roll; W/W Am Cols.

PRITCHETT, JEWELL G oc/Homemaker; Writer; b/Oct 25, 1907; h/3101 S 4th St, Abilene, TX 79605; m/Jester L; c/Charles Hart, Reva Marie Kennedy, Doris Ann Pittman; p/(dec); ed/Draughans Bus Col 1929; pa/Author: *From the Top of Old Hayrick* (1979), *Tagalong with Cody* (1980); cp/Charter Mem, Abilene Preserv Leag; Abilene Wom's Clb; r/United Meth.

PROCTOR, HOWARD BLAKE oc/Municipal Management; b/Oct 20, 1947; h/1827 Myrtle Jo Dr, Ormond Bch, FL 32074; ba/Orange City, FL; m/Laura Lynn Fenske; p/Howard L and Mary O Proctor, Rockledge,

FL; ed/BSBA Fla Technol Univ 1977; MPP Univ Ctrl Fla 1980; mil/USASA 1968-74; pa/Plan'g Asst, Ormond Bch, Fla; Adm Asst/City Planner, Lake Helen, Fla; Asst City Admr/Pers Ofcr, Orange City, Fla; Intl City Mgmt Assn; Am Soc Public Adm; r/Meth; hon/Cert Merit, Small Bus Inst 1977; Cert Apprec, Lake Helen City Comm 1970.

PROCTOR, RUTH ALICE oc/Extension Agent; b/Oct 14, 1930; h/11905 Grandview Ave, Silver Spring, MD 20902; ba/Gaithersburg, MD; m/Frank B; c/Gail, Jennifer, Suzanne; p/Leland H and Lula Mae Carson, Cicero, IN; ed/BS Purdue Univ 1953; MA Am Univ 1976; pa/Ind Coop Ext Ser 1953-55; US Dept Agric, Sch Lunch Ser 1957-58; Md Coop Ext Ser 1975-; Md Assn Ext 4-H Agts Assn, Secy 1978, Prog Chm 1976-77; Nat Assn Ext 4-H Agts Assn, Prog Regional Contact 1979, Host St Coor, 1982 Nat Meeting; cp/Montgomery Co Chapt Phi Mu, Pres 1979-80; r/Prot; hon/Nat 4-H Agt Assn Dist'd Ser Awd 1980; W/W Am Wom 1980; Md Epsilon Sigma Phi Ext Rookie of Yr 1977.

PROFFITT, THOMAS WILLIAM oc/Rural Letter Carrier; b/Oct 16, 1916; h/Paint Lick, KY 40461; m/Pauline Clark; c/Thomas W Jr, Mary Eve P Cleveland, John Daniel, Paul Clark, Martha Jean, Timothy Lee; p/William H (dec) and Martha Hardigree Proffitt (dec); mil/AUS 1940-45; pa/Rural Lttr Carrier; cp/Am Legion, Chaplain of Lancaster, Ky Post; Past PTA Pres, Paint Lick Sch; r/Prot; hon/Ky Col; 25 Yr Expert Rifle Awd, Safety Coun; Outstg Rural Lttr Carrier of Yr 1967; Purple Heart.

PROTOPAPAS, PANAYOTIS (TAKO) oc/Consulting Engineer; b/June 4, 1945; h/Reston, VA; ba/Fuel & Mineral Resource, 1760 Reston Ave, Suites 504 & 511, Reston, VA 22090; p/Elia Protopapas (dec); Vassiliki Protopapas Giagiannos, Athens, Greece; ed/Engrg Deg, Nat Tech Univ of Athens 1968; MS Carnegie-Mellon Univ 1970; MS 1972, PhD Applied Earth Scis 1975, MS Cand Chem Engrg 1975-, PhD Cand Mgmt & Adm 1972- Stanford Univ; pa/Pres Fuel & Mineral Resources Inc 1977-; Dir Wash Opers, Ford, Bacon & Davis Engrs & Constructors 1979; Dir Fossil Fuels & Geotech Scis, Sci Applications Inc 1977-79; Sr Phys Scist, TRW Energy Sys Grp, 1975-77; Dir Earth Scis & Technol, JJ Davis Assocs Inc 1974-75; Sr Res Assoc, Stanford Univ 1970-74; R&D Metall Engr, Mellon Res Inst 1969-70; Res Asst, Nat Tech Univ Athens 1963-69; Mng Ptnr, Proto Exports-Imports 1966-68; AIME; Sigma Xi; ASM; Brit Iron & Steel Inst; Brit Inst Metals; Can Metall Soc; Greek Chamber of Com; Nat Dem Clb; NY Acad Scis; Reviewing Com SME; Lectr Num Profl Socs; r/Greek Orthodox; hon/W/W S&SW; World Press Ser; Am Biog Inst; Men of Achmt; Intl W/W Intells; DIB; Author Num Profl Pubs & Documents Incl'g "Safety Economics of Underspoil Coal Haulage."

PROUD, JOHNNY D oc/Manager; b/Mar 4, 1953; h/921 Summer Dr, Dyersburg, TN 38024; ba/D'burg; m/Kay Curry; p/John and Geraldine Proud, Newbern, TN; ed/Grad Ky Sch Mortuary Sci; Nat Foun Funeral Ser; pa/Mgr J W Curry & Son Funeral Home; Nat Selected Morticians; Nat Funeral Dirs Assn; Tenn Funeral Dirs Assn; cp/D'burg JCs; D'burg Rotary; Treas Moose Lodge.

PRYOR, WALLACE CYRAL oc/Executive; b/Sept 16, 1922; h/PO Box 903, Griffin, GA 30224; ba/Griffin; m/Jeanette Altman; c/David Nelsen, Paul Richard, Mark Bernard, Peter Gwyn, Joel Phillip, Andrew George; p/Harry Gwyn (dec) and Maude Johnson Pryor (dec); mil/USN Aviation Radio Man 1st Class; pa/Pres Pryor Enterprises Inc; cp/Dem Party; r/Bapt.

PTASZKOWSKI, STANLEY EDWARD JR oc/Civil-Structure Engineer; b/June 11, 1943; h/12916 Greenway Chase Ct, Houston, TX 77072; ba/Houston; p/Stanley Edward Sr and Elsie Helena Ptaszkowski, Middle Village, NY; ed/AAS; BSCE; pa/Sr Structural Engr, Marathon-Letourneau; Am Soc Civil Engrs; AIAA; r/Luth; hon/Dean's List, Sch of Engrg 1974, Univ Mo-Columbia.

PUCKETT, IMOGENE GORDON oc/Teacher; b/Sept 4, 1911; h/1207 Runnels, Big Springs, TX 79720; m/Olen L; c/Philip Gordon, Sarah Ann, Lynne Louise; p/Edmond W (dec) and Irene Lusk Gordond, Lubbock, TX; ed/BA Tex Tech Univ; pa/Tex St Tchrs; NEA; NRTA; Rocky Mtn Poetry Soc; cp/Vol Coun TMHMR; Salvation Army Bd; r/Presb; Elder; Christian Ed Com; hon/Conserv Tchr of Yr; Poetry Awd.

PUGH, CHARLES WERNIS SR oc/Assistant Professor; b/Nov 25, 1931; h/Baton Rouge, LA; m/Amy Lea Brazier; c/Charles Jr, Charmaine, Eric Gerard, Regina; p/Ernest T (dec) and Madlyn A Pugh, Amite, LA; ed/BA 1955, MS 1957 Tenn St Univ; Further Study Univ Tenn 1959, Univ Denver 1960, 68, La St Univ 1979-80; mil/Sgt Korean War 1952-54; pa/Asst Prof Eng, So Univ, Baton Rouge, La; Am Fed Tchrs; Life Mem Callaloo Black Jour Arts & Lttrs; AAUP; cp/Jack & Jill of Am; Lt Reserve Dpty, E Baton Rouge Sheriff's Dept; Phi Beta Sigma; r/Bapt; hon/UN Ser Medal; Korean Ser Medal; Nat Defense Ser Medal; W/W S&SW 1980-81.

PULITANO, CONCETTA oc/Learning Center Coordinator; b/Jun

16, 1941; h/1813 Landrake Rd, Towson, MD 21204; m/Francis Joseph; c/Maria Anne, Margaret Theresa, Angela Marie; p/Umberto Norigenna (dec); Benedetta Triassi Norigenna, Joppa, MD; ed/Secretarial Deg; pa/Secy, Ka-Line Pool Prods (Hialeah, Fla) 1959-61; Bookkeeper for Gena's Dept Store (Opa-Locka, Fla) 1959-61; With Bendix Communs (Balto, Md) 1961-63; Cathedral Sch: Student Coun Moderator, Dir of Activs, Pt-time Secy, Lng Ctr Coor; r/Rom Cath; hon/W/W Am Wom.

PULLEY, WILLIAM PAUL JR oc/Attorney at Law, State Legislator; b/Aug 30, 1936; h/4720 Farrington Rd, Durham, NC 27707; ba/Durham; m/Elizabeth Dees Nelson; p/W Paul and Josie Bullard Pulley, Durham, NC; ed/BA 1958, LLB 1961 Univ NC-Chapel Hill; pa/Assoc w Manning, Fulton & Skinner 1961-62; Ptnr Weatherspoon & Pulley 1962-67; Pres Pulley, Wainio, Stephens & Lambe, PA 1968-; Mem Trial Lwyrs Acad; NC Bar Assn; NC Acad Trial Lwyrs; 14th Judicial Bar Assn; NC St Bar; cp/St Legislator, Ho of Reps; Pres Rogers Herr Jr HS PTA; Chm Ed Devel Coun; Ofcr 14th Judicial Bar; Chm Var Projs & Orgs; r/Bapt.

PULLUM, GEORGE WILLIAM JR oc/Painter; b/Mar 4, 1948; h/RR 1 Box 459-B, Henderson, KY 42420; ba/Henderson; m/Brenda Parker; c/Keith H; p/George William Sr and Opal R Pullman, Henderson, KY; pa/Custom Painter; Car, Bike, Van Bldr; r/Bapt; hon/Featured in Sev Mags; Num Paint Awds; Other Spec Awds.

PURDY, EDITH CALDWELL WILCOX oc/Travel Agent; b/Mar 5, 1928; ba/Travel Time, 1529 W Innes St, Salisbury, NC; m/Joseph Linn (dec); c/Roy Douglas Wilcox, Diance Lee Wilcox Strutz, Stephen Ray Wilcox, Gary Alan Wilcox; p/Glenn Morgan Wilcox Jr; Edith C Wilcox Purdy; ed/Att'd Mitchell Col 1947; McConnel Airline Trg 1948; Inst Cert'd Travel Agts 1977; pa/Owner & Mgr Travel Time of Salisbury; Ptnr Abstract Pubrs; Inst Cert'd Travel Agts; Past Mem Am Bus Wom, Secy, Treas, Var Coms; cp/Co-Chm Cool Springs Repubs; Clerk Elec Bd for Repub Party; hon/Contb'd 3 Fam Hists to Iredell Heritage Book, Iredell Co Geneal Soc; Pub'd Book on Abstract of Deeds for Iredell Co 1787-1798.

PURNELL, FRANK DELANO oc/Educator; b/Apr 5, 1933; h/732 Meredian, Normal, AL 35762; ba/Normal; m/Rosentene B; p/Walter and Ethel Purnell; ed/EdD; mil/AUS; m/Edr; r/Bapt; hon/All-Am Fball; Rockefeller Fellow.

PURTLE, VIRGINIA oc/Associate Dean; b/Aug 14, 1940; c/Buell and Mary Carol; p/Homer and Mary Barber Purtle, Prescott, AR; ed/BS 1961, MA 1963 Okla St Univ; PhD LSU; pa/Assoc Dean, Col of Arts & Scis, Prof Sociol, La St Univ; Rural Sociol Soc, Coun Mem; Am Sociol Assn; So Sociol Soc; hon/Author Num Pubs.

PURVIS, MARY BELLE b/Jun 12, 1932; h/426 W Main St, Greenville, TN 37743; ba/G'ville; ed/BA Tusculum Col 1953; MA E Tenn St Univ

1959; pa/Chem Lab Asst, Tusculum Col 1951-53; Self Employed: Bill Collector 1954-59, Bkkpr 1956-65, Chem Lit Reschr 1959-65; Pvt Res 1965-; Am Chem Soc 1953, 58, 59; AAUW: Life Mem, Charter Mem G'ville Br, Past Pres & Histn G'ville Br, Mem Tenn Div; cp/Sierra Clb; Nat Soc DAR Former: Dir, Corr Secy, Regent, 1/VRegent, Histn, Rec Secy; Nat Soc DAR: Personal Page to Tenn St Regent at Nat Cong Num Yrs, Page to Chaplain Gen NSDAR (2), Del to Cong Num Yrs; Past Regent Nolanchuckey Chapt DAR; Chd of Am Revolution: CoChm, Sr Pres Robert Sevier Soc, Tenn St, Nat & Life Promoter; Tenn Soc DAR: Former Chm Am Indians Com NSDAR, Past Mem: St Conf Ticket Com, Credentials Com, Flag Com Chm; Nat Soc So Dames of Am: Memphis Tenn Soc, Past Tenn Soc NSSDA Rec Secy; Life Charter Mem: Greene Co Hist Soc, Watauga Assn Genealogists, Bass Anglers Sportsman Soc, The Franklin Mint; Life Mem Geneal Clb of Am; Nat Hist Soc; UDC: Past Mem Stonewall Jackson Chapt, Knoxville, Tenn, Charter Mem; Gdn Fdn Woms Clbs; Tenn Fdn Woms Clbs, Andrew Johnson Clb, Past Mem Epsilon Sigma Oma-Cron w Torch; Assn for Preserv of Tenn Antiquities, Wash Co Chapt; Life Mem Soc of Descs of Colonial Clergy; IPA; Nat Fdn Press Wom; Tenn Woms Press & Authors Clbs; OES; G'ville Chapt #223, Martha 1953-55; Union Temple Home Demo Clb Past: Hlth & Safety Ldr, Reading Prog Ldr, Pres, Scrapbook Ldr, Rec Ldr; Home Demo Clb Greene Co Coun Past: Rec Secy, Reading Prog Chm, Mem Hospitality & F'ship Coms, Judge Co 4H Clb Public Spkg Contest; Applachian Zool Soc; Oceanic Soc, SF Bay Chapt; Nitecaps Intl Assn; GSA: Past Asst GSA Ldr, Earned Highest Rank in Scouting; ARC Past: Water Safety Instr, 1st Aid Instr, Home Nsg Instr; Mem Chd of Confederacy Rachel Carson Chapt, Knoxville; Rod & Gun Clb 1949, Marksman & Sharpshooter; Life Mem Am Fishing Assn; Fishing Clb of Am; Nat Travel Clb; Nat & Charter Mem Smithsonian Assocs; Assoc Mem Am Mus of Natural Hist; r/1st Presb Ch USA: Wom Assn Pres 1962-64, Ch Choir 21 Yrs, SS Tchr Adult Wom 1961-64, Nom'g Com; hon/Author *A Fungicidal Study*; Num Biogl Listings; Outstg Clb Wom of Yr, Union Temple Home Demo Clb 1964; Am Chem Soc Sr Student (Col) Awd; Fellow Mem ABI.

PYLE, RAYMOND JAMES JR oc/Regional Manager; b/Jan 15, 1932; h/1206 S Suffolk Dr, Tampa, FL 33609; ba/Clearwater, FL; m/Mabel Lee Freeman; c/Dale, David, Steven, Carol Lynn; p/Bessie Osborn Pyle, Winter Gdn, FL; ed/Att'd Univ Wis 1951-56; Univ Notre Dame 1968; Univ SC 1972; pa/Sales Rep Ldr Dept Store 1955-57; London Wholesale Hardware 1957-58; Martin Outdoor Adv: Sales Rep 1958-65, Gen Mgr 1965-66, VP 1966-69, Pres 1969-76; Reg Mgr & VP Foster & Kleiser 1976-; Inst Outdoor Adv SE, USA Treas, Outdoor Advt Assn Fla, Pres; Tampa Adv Fed, Past Pres; Sales & Mktg Execs, Tampa Past Pres; Univ Tampa Bd Fellows; Pi Sigma Epsilon; cp/Easter Seal Soc, Tampa Bd Dirs, Former Treas; ARC of Tampa, Bd Dirs; Fla Gulf Coast Symph, Bd Dirs; Past Dir Mchts Assn; Univ Clb; Rotary; Masons; r/Bapt; hon/Tampa Advt Fed: Advtg Man of Yr 1969, Silver Medal Awd 1979-80, Sales & Mktg Exec of Yr 1971.

Q

QUALLS, PATRICIA STEELE   oc/Mayor; b/May 13, 1940; h/201 Dogwood Ln, Lake City, AR 72437; ba/Lake City; m/Bill; c/Bret; p/J D and Mildred Steele, Monette, AR; ed/BSE, MSE Ark St Univ; pa/Mayor Lake City; Pres Alpha Delta Kappa; Mus Tchr; cp/Choir Dir Monette Bapt Ch; r/Bapt; hon/Hon Mem 4-H; Ark Choral Dirs Assn.

QUARLES, CHARLES ELLIS   oc/Career Guidance Consultant; b/June 10, 1929; h/RFD 4 Box 202, Louisa, VA 23093; ba/Wash DC; m/Leola D; c/Donna Knight, Linda R, C Ellis III; p/C Ellis Quarles, Phila, PA; Tessie Sutton, Louise, VA; pa/Bus, Career Guid & Employment Conslt; r/Bapt.

QUILLINAN, G CAROL   oc/Architectural Designer, Reporter, Editorial Consultant, Writer; b/June 2, 1927; h/Rt 1, Box 356A, Bokeelia, FL 33922; ba/Same; c/Kasia, William, Nicole, Kevin; p/William L (dec) and Belle Schwalbe (dec); pa/Writer-Pubr; Custom Homes Designer; Lectr; Conslt; cp/Cand City Coun, Sanibel, Fla 1976; Vol Hosp Work; r/Nonsectarian; hon/W/W Am Wom.

QUIÑONES, GILDA   oc/Rehabilitation Counselor; b/May 27, 1948; h/Homero #35, Alto Apolo, Rio Piedras, PR 00927; ba/Cagues, PR; p/Jose Auinones (dec); Hilda Pereyo, Rio Piedras, PR; ed/BA Col Sacred Heart 1969; MA Univ PR 1973; pa/Dept Social Sers, Voc Rehab Prog; Voc Rehab Cnslr, Trust Fund Sub-Prog; Rehab Cnslrs of PR Assn, Treas 1974-75; APGA; Am Rehab Assn; Nat Rehab Assn; Comm on Rehab; Cnslr Cert #9102; Lic'd Rehab Cnslr in PR; r/Cath; hon/Recip Awd Ospri Acad 1978; W/W S&SW 1980-81.

QUINTERO, ZANDRA   oc/Assistant Manager; b/Jan 10, 1954; h/106 Cameron, Alice, TX 78332; ba/Alice; p/Elias Valerio Quintero (dec); Josephine Ruiz; ed/Cert Notary Public; pa/Asst Mgr Hlth Clb; Pursuing Career in Real Est Sales; r/Cath.

R

RABIN, JACK oc/Professor; b/Jan 3, 1945; h/807 Wesley Dr, Montgomery, AL 36111; ba/Mont; m/Sandra Clar; p/Saul and Etta Rabin, Montgomery, AL; ed/BA 1965, MA 1967 Univ Miami; PhD Univ Ga 1972; pa/Prof, Auburn Univ at Mont; Conslt: Exec Ofc of Pres 1972-74; St & Local Govts 1971-; Am Soc Public Adm; Chair-Elect ASPA Sect on Pers Adm & Labor Relats; hon/W/W S&SW 1980-81; NSF & NDEA Fellow, Univ Ga; Editor 4 Acad Jours; Author Num Articles.

RADER, EUGENE BLACKWELL oc/Retired; b/Feb 17, 1912; h/412 E Concord St, Morganton, NC 28655; m/Lettie Walker; c/Eugene Michael, Robert Blackwell; p/Robert Blackwell (dec) and Della Mae Anderson Rader (dec); pa/Broadway Cafe 1926-47; Owner & Opr Boxwood Motel & Rest 1948-50; Owner & Mgr Gene's Drive-In Rest 1951-81; Ret'd 1981; cp/Catawba Val Masonic Lodge #217, York Rite & Accepted Masons; York Rite Shriner, Oasis Shrine Temple; Burke Co Shrine Clb; Charter Mem Morganton Elks Lodge, BPOE; Mimosa Chapt #269 OES; Active in Jim Hunt for Gov Campaign 1980, Precinct Capt; r/Bapt.

RADFORD, ANN GURLEY oc/Teacher; b/Sept 5, 1931; h/Rt 1 Box 80, Kenly, NC 27542; ba/Princeton, NC; m/Chester R (dec); c/Allen R, M Kay; p/Forest C (dec) and Mamie F Gurley (dec); ed/BS Atlantic Christian Col 1973; MA Ed ECU 1979; pa/Elem Math Tchr, Princeton HS 1973-; NEA; NCAE; Johnston Co ACT; NCCTM; NCTM; Johnston Co Br AAUW; Kappa Delta Pi; r/Free Will Bapt; hon/ACT Tchr of Yr, Princeton HS 1979-80.

RAHALL, NICK JOE II oc/Congressman; b/May 20, 1949; ba/Wash DC; m/Helen McDaniels; c/Rebecca Ashley, Nick Joe III; p/N Joe and Alice Rahall, Beckley, WV; ed/BA Duke Univ 1971; Grad Study George Washington Univ 1972; pa/Staff Asst to US Senator Robert Byrd of WV 1971-74; Pres Mountaineer Tour & Travel Agcy 1974; Pres WV Broadcasting; US Congressman, 4th Dist WV; cp/Elks, Rotary; Moose; YMCA; Shrine Clb; Beni Kedeem Temple; NAACP; r/Presb; hon/Yng Dem NC 1971; Yng Dem WV 1978; Ynd Dem of Yr, Dem Nat Com 1980; Coal Man of Yr 1980.

RALSTON, CLARICE McDUFFIE oc/Nursing Supervisor; b/Feb 11, 1932; h/815 Preston, Burkburnett, TX 76354; ba/Wichita Falls, TX; m/William Kent; c/Diana Lynn (dec), Stephen Kent; p/Welbourne C (dec) and Louise S McDuffie, Tampa, FL; pa/RN; Res; Writing; Tchg; ANA; TNA; cp/OES; Vol Red Cross; Dem Party; r/Meth; hon/W/W Am Wom 1979-80.

RAINEY, LOYD DANIEL oc/Professor; b/Aug 20, 1951; h/9407 Goshen Ln, Burke, VA 22015; ba/Fairfax, VA; m/Vivian Linda Hopper; p/J C and Lorene Rainey, Walnut, MS; ed/Att'd LSU-Baton Rouge 1969-71, So Univ 1970; BA 1973, MA 1975 Memphis St Univ; ABD Univ Pgh 1978; PhD Cand Univ Pgh; pa/Asst Prof Commun, Rhetoric & Mass Commun, George Mason Univ 1978-; Tchg Fellow, Univ Pgh 1975-78; Instr Wn St Correctional Inst 1975-78; Media Conslt, Amalgamated Clothing & Textile Wkrs Union 1977-78; Tchg Asst, Memphis St Univ 1973-75; SCA; Exec Bd, Div Chm, VSCA; Mem Editorial Bd *The Virginia Journal of Communication*; Fac Advr *Broadside*, George Mason Univ Student Newspaper 1979-80; Dir, Writing Conslt WRQX-FM, Wash DC; cp/Fairfax Co Dem Com; hon/Author & Co-Author Num Profl Papers Incl'g "Terrorism as Communication."

RAMEY, HAROLD THOMAS (PETE) oc/Highway Patrolman; b/Oct 23, 1954; h/3159 Berry Lane, Apt 28, Roanoke, VA 24018; ba/Salem, VA; p/Robert Howard and Frances C Ramey, Christiansburg, VA; ed/BS Radford Col 1978; Police Sci Deg, Va St Police Acad 1981; pa/Virginia St Patrolman; cp/NAACP; r/Bapt.

RAMSEUR, ALVIADEAN oc/Employee Development Specialist; b/Nov 1, 1943; h/4223 13th St NE, Wash DC 20017; ba/Wash DC; p/Hugh F and Eunice I Ramseur, Wash DC; ed/BS; mil/AUS; pa/Job Cnslr; Instr; Prog Develr; Trainee Coor; Am Soc Tnrs & Develrs; Am Tchrs Assn; Toastmasters Inc; NEA; Am Soc Spec Ed; cp/SE Commun Assn; Jr C of C; Wash Sat Col; DC Tutors Clb; r/Bapt; hon/Outstg Yng Men Am 1977; Tchr of Yr 1977-78.

RAMSEY, GARY ROBERT oc/Chief of Nursing; b/Oct 12, 1949; h/Rt 4 Box 107, Louisville, TN 37777; ba/Knoxville; m/Glenda Horvath; c/Christopher Matthew, Lori Ann; p/Glenn Everett and Bobbie Coker Ramsey, Maryville, TN; ed/Att'd Univ Tenn 1967-69; BSN E Tenn St Univ 1972; MSN Med Col Ga 1974; pa/Chief Nsg, Lakeshore Mtl Hlth Inst 1979-; Asst Prof, E Tenn St Univ 1974-79; Univ Hosp, Augusta, Ga 1973-74; Univ Tenn Hosp 1972-73; ANA; TNA, St Secy, Dist Pres; NLN; Tenn Hosp Assn; Tenn Soc Nsg Ser; Sigma Theta Tau, Beta Omicron

Chapt; cp/Mtl Hlth Assn, K'ville; Gtr K'ville Epilepsy Foun, Bd Dirs; r/Bapt; hon/W/W S&SW 1980; Outstg Yng Men Am 1980.

RAMSEY, THOMAS HARRISON oc/Department Manager; b/Oct 16, 1948; h/203 NE 4th St, Atkins, AR 72823; ba/Russellville, AR; m/Rachel Lucille; c/Michelle Danette, Susan Annette, William Daley III; p/William D and Irene Ramsey, Hector, AR; pa/Auto Dept Mgr; cp/Summer Yth Prog; r/Mission Bapt; hon/Var Hons for Sales & Ser; Plaque for Being #1 in Dist.

RANDALL, JAMES ALLEN oc/Contractor; b/Sept 19; h/12933 Northwood Lake, Northport, AL 35476; ba/Tuscaloosa; m/Kathleen Elizabeth; p/H Pettus (dec) and Ettie Beeland Randall, Tuscaloosa, AL; ed/BA Advtg & Public Relats; mil/USAR; pa/Homebldrs Assn; cp/JCs Bd Dirs; Yng Repubs, Pres; St Chm Tuscaloosa Co Exec Com & St Exec Com; r/Presb; hon/Outstg Yng Men Am 1979.

RANDOLPH, LESTER oc/Counselor; b/Jan 6, 1937; c/L K Jr, Roland, Kelvin, Valerie; p/Jesse and Katie Mae Randolph; ed/BS Edwards Waters Col; MS Fla A&M Univ; EdS Univ Fla; DHD Work Univ Fla; mil/USNR; pa/Tchr Phy Sci 1968-74; Asst Chief Therapist 1975-76; Cnslr Univ N Fla 1976-79; Cnslr Duval Co Public Sch 1979-80; APGA; ANWC; ASGW; AMEL; ASCA; cp/Dem Party; r/Prot; hon/Author Sev Articles.

RANDOLPH, MARGARET ANN SHERER oc/Teacher; b/Aug 11, 1947; h/Rt 4, Cleveland, TN 37311; ba/C'land; m/Sheridan Charles; p/Charles H Sr (dec) and Margaret Robertson Sherer, Jasper, AL; ed/BMus B'ham So Col 1969; Grad Studies Penn St Univ; MMus Univ Ill; pa/Mus Tchr; Dud-Piano & Chamber Mus Perf'g; Choral Dir; Vocal Accomp, Univ Ill; Past Fac, Univ Ill; Mu Phi Epsilon; MTNA; Past Bd Mem Tenn MTA; Co-Fdr & Past Pres Ocoee MTA; cp/MacDowell Clb; Cleveland Mus Clb; Pres Bradley Co Bar Aux; VP C'land AAUW; r/Christian; hon/Zonta Clb Carr Meml S'ship Winner; B'ham Mus Clb Yng Artists Audition Awd Winner; Others.

RANEY, L H oc/Minister; b/July 20, 1903; h/101 Harbin, Waxahachie, TX 75165; m/Myra; c/Howard G; p/Charley P (dec) and Mima Chaterine Raney (dec); ed/BA Baylor 1971; Post Grad Study SWn Theol Sem; Att'd E Tex St Tchrs Col, Burleson Bapt Col; pa/Pastor 1929-66; Dir Christian Ed, Bapt Missionary Assn of Tex 1966-69; Interim Pastor 4 Bapt Chs; Min of Outreach, So Pk Bapt Ch; Chaplain, WC Tennery Commun Hosp 1979-80; r/Bapt; hon/Outstg Ellis Co Citizen 1980; Author Sev Rel Tracts & Books on Christian Ed.

RANKIN, JULIUS EARLE oc/Publisher; b/Apr 11, 1922; h/Box 868, Driftwood Ests, Irvington, AL 36544; ba/Bayou La Batre, AL; c/Randy, Russell, Van; p/Ruby C Allen, Irvington, AL; mil/Maj; pa/Newspaper Publr; Sigma Delta Xi; cp/Hosp Bd; Proj Dir Med Clin; r/Presb; hon/3 Awds for Ser to Commun; "Rankin Day" Hon.

RAO, MAMIDANNA SESHAGIRI oc/Associate Professor; b/June 21, 1931; h/8830 Pineybranch Rd, Apt 602, Silver Spring, MD 20903; ba/Wash DC; m/G C Jayasheela; c/Surya Satya Sree, Gayatriveena; p/Mamidanna Suryanarayana and Satyavati Rao, Andhra Pradesh, India; ed/SCD; MS; MA; BS; pa/Assoc Prof, Dept Commun Hlth & Fam Pract, Howard Univ Col Med; Fellow Royal Soc Trop Med & Hygiene; APHA; ASA; Biometric Soc; Sigma Xi; cp/Gtr Wash Telugu Cultural Soc, Res Conslt; r/Hindu; hon/WHO F'ship; Am Men & Wom Sci.

RAPOPORT, MARTHA ANN oc/Speech Pathologist and Audiologist; b/Aug 27, 1951; h/2400 McCue #79, Houston, TX 77056; ba/Houston; p/Herman Leonard and Phyllis S Rapoport, Portsmouth, VA; ed/Att'd Beaver Col 1969-71, Univ London 1971; BS NWn Univ 1973; MEd Univ 1976; pa/Speech Pathol & Audiol, Cerebral Palsy Devel Disabilities Ctr; Speech & Hearing Conslt, Meml Lung & Diagnostic Ctr; ASHA; TSHA; Acoustical Soc Am; Houston Area Assn Commun Disorders; "Here-Say Inc"; Assn for Res & Enlightenment, Assoc; cp/Sponsor Christian Chd's Fund; r/Jewish; hon/Cert Clin Competence in Speech Pathol 1979; Cert Audiol, ASHA 1977; Grad F'ship Prog Univ Va; Author "Hearing Damage from Forest Fire Fighting Operations" *Fire Control News* 1976.

RAPPAPORT, HAROLD oc/Engineer, Writer; b/Feb 10, 1920; h/Miami, FL; ba/2650 SW 27th Ave, Miami, FL 33133; m/Bertha B; c/Paul M, Jill A; p/Louis J (dec) and Rebecca R Rappaport (dec); ed/BS cum laude NEn Univ 1950; Reg'd Profl Engr, Commonwlth Mass 1967; Cert'd Construction Specifier, Construction Specifications Inst 1978; mil/AUS 1942-44; pa/Mark Linenthal, Consltg Engr 1944-50; Goldberg, LeMessurier & Assoc Consltg Engrs 1950-67; Connell, Metcalf & Eddy, Archs & Engrs 1967-79; Civil-Structural Engr, Construction Specification Writer, Greenleaf Telesca, Planners, Archs & Engrs 1979-; Miami Chapt Construction Specifications Inst, Pres 1975-76; Fla Engrg Soc; Nat Soc Profl Engrs; Am Soc Testing & Mats; Am Arbitration Assn; c/Am Mensa

Ltd; r/Hebrew; hon/W/W S&SW; Nat Awd, James F Lincoln Arc Welding Foun Competition 1966; Editor Manuals of Engrg Ofc Pract.

RASBERRY, JUDITH ANN oc/Manager of Operations; b/Mar 2, 1943; h/31 Lincolnshire Circle, Bedford, TX 76021; ba/Ft Worth; m/Frank D; c/Chip; p/Reuben F and Maxine M Knight, Morgan Mill, TX; ed/Att'd Tarleton St Univ, TCJC-Ft Worth; pa/Fdr & Pt-Owner, Mgr Opers, Anago Inc; Prod Mgr & Dir Mktg, Precept Inc 10 Yrs; cp/Epsilon Sigma Alpha, Theta Chi Chapt; Mid-Cities Area Coun; r/Ch of Christ; hon/Outstg Epsilon Sigma Alpha'er; Epsilon Sigma Alpha Dist 7 of Tex Miss Congeniality; Mid-Cities Coun Girl of Yr; W/W Am Wom 1979.

RASH, LLOYD MONROE oc/Hospital Executive; b/Nov 3, 1911; h/1003 Olive Ave SE, Lenoir, NC 28645; ba/Lenoir; m/Margaret Rabb; c/James Dennis; p/James Warren (dec) and Bess Zoe Lingle Rash (dec); pa/Pres & Treas Blackwelder Hosp Inc; NC Hosp Assn; Nat Assn Accts; Catawba Val Exec Clb; cp/Rotary Clb, Past Pres 1951; Co Commr 1959-65; Dem Party; r/Meth: Steward, Lay Ldr, Trustee, Del of Conf; hon/Admiral USS NC Battleship; Hon Rotarian 40 Yrs Ser to Commun; Ky Col; DIB 1979-80.

RATCLIFFE, SHELIA PANNELL oc/Manager and Consultant; b/July 23, 1953; h/556 Lost Tree Ln, Knoxville, TN 37922; ba/K'ville; m/Carl R Jr; p/Craig Dennis and Mary Fisher Pannell, Sylva, NC; ed/Att'd Centro-Colombo Americano, Cali, Colombia 1973; BA WCU 1973; MA 1977; pa/Pers Conslt, Dunhill of K'ville 1980-; Per Mgmt Conslt, Ratcliffe & Co 1980-; Indust Relats Mgr, Am Thread Co 1978-80; Pers Admr/Employment Supvr, Litton Sys Inc 1974-78; Instr Evening Bus Adm Prog, Tri-Co Commun Col, Murphy, NC 1979-79; Adj Fac Mem, Mars Hill Col 1980; Am Soc Trg & Devel, VP & Prog Chm; Altrusa Clb of Asheville Inc, Ext Chm; WNC Safety Coun; Adult Basic Ed Adv Com, Tri-Co Commun Col, Chm; SEn Plan'g & Ec Devel Comm; Employers Adv Com for NC Employment Security Comm; cp/Cherokee Co U Way, VP; r/Bapt; hon/Estella M Bell S'ship 1970 & 71; Cherokee Co, NC Yng Career Wom 1978; W/W S&SW 1980-81.

RATHMELL, ARETTA JENNINGS oc/Psychiatrist; b/Mar 28, 1938; h/2200 Norben Dr, Lake Charles, LA 70601; ba/Lake Charles; c/Karen, Robert, Gregory; p/Noyce Ted (dec) and Ara Mae Pierce Jennings, Lake Charles, LA; ed/BA Chem; MD; pa/AMA; APA; La St Med Soc; Acad Psychosomatic Med; cp/Dpty Coroner; Med Advr Yth Conslg Grp; r/Meth; hon/Minnie Moffett F'ship; Fellow Psychosomatic Acad.

RATLIFF, DALE H oc/Professor; b/Mar 30, 1928; ba/Broward Commun Col-Central, Ft Lauderdale, FL; c/Todd H, Robin D, Scott H, Hale H; ed/MDiv, ThM, DMin, Louisville Presb Sem; PhD St Andrews, London, England; pa/Prof Psych & Sociol, Broward Commun Col & Nova Grad Sch; Am Assn Rel Therapists, Dir; Am Assn Marriage & Fam Therapists; Am Psych Assn; Acad of Psychotherapists; r/Prot; hon/Author *Minor Sexual Deviance* 1976 & *Bridal Beds Around the World* 1977.

RAUCH, MARSHALL ARTHUR oc/Executive; b/Feb 2, 1923; h/1121 Scotch Dr, Gastonia, NC; ba/Gastonia; m/Jeanne Girard; c/John, Ingrid, Marc, Peter, Stephanie; p/Nathan A and Tillie P Rauch; ed/Duke Univ; mil/Infantry, Overseas European Theater WWII, Combat Infantry Medal; pa/Rauch Industs Inc: Pres, Dir, Chm of Bd; Dir & Treas, E P Press Inc; Dir, Majestic Ins Financing Corp; Pres & Dir: P D R Trucking Inc & Magic Ltd; cp/NC State Senator, 25th Dist 1967-80: VChm Appropriations 1969-70, Chm Intergovt Relats 1971-72, Chm St Govt 1973-74, VChm Fin 1973-74, Chm Law Enforcement & Crime Control 1975-76, VChm Mfg, Labor & Commerce 1977-80, Num Coms; Past Mem, NC Adv Budget Comm; Past Chm: Legis Tax Study Comm, Wildlife Tax Study Comm, Bldg Comm of Legis Sers Comm, Gastonia Human Relats Comm, NC Com on Population & Fam, Employ the Handicapped Com; Past City Coun-man, City of Gastonia; Past Dir: Gastonia C of C, Salvation Army Boys Clb, United Fund, Gaston Mus of Natural Hist, Holy Angels Nursery, Planned Parenthood & World Population (NY), Others; Past Mem, NC Citizens Com for Dental Hlth; Past Mem Bd Advisors, Gardner Webb Col; Past Mem Bd Govs, NC Jewish Home for Aged; Past Pres: Temple Emanuel, Frank Goldberg Lodge (B'nai B'rith), Duke Univ Gaston Alumni Assn, Gastonia YMCA; Num Others; r/Jewish; hon/Man of the Yr: Gastonia Jr C of C 1957, Gastonia Jr Wom's Clb 1964, Gaston Co Omega Psi Phi 1966, NC Hlth Dept 1968, Gastonia Red Shields Boys Clb 1970; Nat Rec Cit, Nat Rec Assn; Nat Coun of Christians & Jews Brotherhood Awd; Human Sers Awd, NC Assn Jewish Men & St of NC.

RAVAL, PINAKIN MANUBHAI oc/Physician; b/Oct 1, 1943; ba/PO Box 1234, Palm Coast, FL 32037; m/Mayuri; p/Manubhai and Sharda Raval, Bombay, India; ed/MD; FACA; pa/Med Pract.

RAY, ALICE LOUISE HOLLY oc/Teacher; b/June 16, 1937; h/Idabel, OK; m/Eugene Blue; p/Luther Ray Sr and Mary Alice Stark Holly, Red

Oak, OK; ed/Assoc Deg En St Jr Col 1957; BS SEn Univ 1964; Grad Studies OSU & SEU; pa/Elem Tchr, Ctrl Elem Sch, Idabel Public Schs; NEA; IEA; OEA; cp/Nat, St BPW Clb, Local Recording Secy, Pres, Parliamentn, Chm Num Coms; Alpha Delta Kappa, Hist; Okla Coaches Assn; Okla Ofcls Assn; Coach Little Leag; r/Assem of God; hon/Awds from Jt Coun Ec Ed; Cert Apprec, Idabel U Way 1979-80; Class Selected to Part in Intl Twinning Prog, Lions Clb 1979-80; Recip Torch Awd, BPW 1975.

RAY, EUGENE COLLINS oc/Police Patrolman, Student; b/Feb 12, 1943; p/Arthur and Estella Mae Ray, Oxford, NC; ed/Att'g Piedmont Tech Col; AAS Vance Commun Col 1980; Cert Gen Surveying & Small Motor Repair 1972; mil/AUS 1969; pa/Policeman; Studying Mech Drafting; cp/Notary Public; Former 2nd Lt, Civil Air Patrol; Mason, New Johanthan Lodge 722; Law Enforcement Clb; Notary Assn; Mem of a Quartet (Plays Six String Lead Guitar); r/River Zion Holy Ch; hon/Outstg Ofcr of Yr 1980; Good Samaritan Awd; Selected to Police Hall of Fame; 2 Hero Awds; Story Pub'd in Profl Jour.

RAY, LEXIE B oc/Minister; b/Sept 19, 1932; h/Rt 5, Box 98, Kingston, TN 37763; ba/Kingston; m/Zann P; c/Karyn Joyce, Latetia Jill; p/Onyx B Ray, Murray, KY; Ola S Ray (dec); ed/AA Freed-Hardeman Col; BS Murray St Col; pa/Min Kingston Ch of Christ; cp/Former Mem Kiwanis Clb; Hon Life Mem Tenn PTA; r/Ch of Christ; hon/Outstg Yng Man Yr, Union City, Tenn Kiwanis Clb 3 Yrs.

RAY, MICHAEL THOMAS JR oc/Veterinarian; b/Mar 22, 1952; h/Rt 4 Box 30, Auburn, AL 36830; p/Michael Thomas and Annelu Moore Ray, Carthage, NC; ed/BSBA summa cum laude Pembroke St Univ 1974; BS NCSU 1977; DVM Auburn Univ Sch Vet Med 1980; pa/Vet, Maple Lawn Animal Clin, Vass, NC; Vet, Auburn Univ Large Animal Clin; AVMA; AAEP; AABP; Gamma Sigma Delta; r/Objectivist/Positivist; hon/Hon Grad NCSU; Cert Acad Excell NCSU; Contbr *Auburn Veterinarian* 1979.

RAY, NEWTON HARDMAN oc/Retired; b/Aug 18, 1931; h/120 Hawthorne Ct, Danville, VA 24541; m/Martha Fitchett; c/Newton Hardman Jr, Christopher Hyde; p/James Wilmer (dec) and Genevieve Hazlewood Ray (dec); ed/AB Wash & Lee Univ; mil/USAR 1954-56 1st Lt; pa/Cert'd Landscape Designer; Horticulturist; Lectr; cp/Pres Men's Gdn Clb 6 Yrs; Pres Mlt Hlth Assn; Pres City Beautiful Com 2 Yrs; r/Meth, Ch Bd 4 Yrs; hon/St Mlt Hlth Vol of Yr 1979.

RAYBURN, DENNIS HAROLD oc/Cab Driver; b/Oct 29, 1956; h/522 Harrison Meadows, Apt 2, Paris, TN 38242; m/Debra Lou Boothe; c/Alice Lynn; p/Thomas H and Martha Bowden Rayburn, Paris, TN; ed/Att'd Univ Tenn-Martin; pa/Driver, Paris Yellow Cab Inc; cp/Repub Party, Yng GOP Publicity Chm 1972-; Former Mem Paris-Lakeway Kiwanis Clb 1975; r/Full Gospel; hon/Hon Page to Tenn Ho Reps 1974; Author "Tribute to James Sego" *Paris Post-Intelligencer*.

RAYNOR, GEORGE MARION III (RICKEY) oc/Building Contractor; b/Nov 27, 1944; h/Rt 2 Box 6A, Louisburg, NC 27549; ba/Same; m/Betty Gilliam; c/Tammy Michelle, George Ryan; p/George Marion Raynor Jr, Louisburg, NC; Lillian Earl Gray Raynor (dec); ed/Att'd Campbell Col; mil/NCNG 1965-71 Spec 5; pa/Owner Raynor Bldrs; Pres Franklin Co Homebldrs 1980; Dir Kerr Lake Area Homebldrs 1980-82; cp/Bd Dirs Green Hill Country Clb 1982-84; Bd Dirs L'burg Area C of C 1981-82; Zoning Bd for Town L'burg 1979-82; Downtown Revitalization Com, Town of L'burg 1981, 81; r/Bapt; hon/Bdlr of Yr, Kerr Lake Area Homebldrs Assn 1980; Outstg Trainee, Co A 5th Bn 1st Bn USATC 1967.

READ, WILLIAM DAVID oc/Librarian; b/Oct 12, 1951; h/3354 Dalebranch #2, Memphis, TN 38116; p/George D Read Jr, Stonewall, MS; Carrie Lee Williams Read (dec); ed/AA; BS; pa/Miss Lib Assn; Fiji Lib Assn; r/Bapt; hon/Outstg Sch Libn/Media Spec, St of Miss.

RECIO, FRANCISCO HERNANDEZ oc/Management Consultant; b/June 18, 1944; h/2615 Alhambra Cir, Coral Gables, FL 33134; ba/Miami; m/Irene Canosa; c/Irene Maria, Francisco III, Ana Maria; p/Francisco Hernandez and Josefina Madrazo Recio, NY, NY; ed/BME 1964, MS 1966 Rensselaer Polytech Inst; pa/Methods Engr Huyck Corp 1966-68; Mgmt Conslt, Mgr Haskins & Sells 1968-76; Mgmt Consltg Prin, Prin in Charge of Latin Am Mgmt Conslt g, Peat, Harwick, Mitchell, & Co 1976-, Mem Exec Com in Latin Am; AIIE, VP S Fla; Nat Assn Accts; Cuban Public & Pvt Accts Assn; Fla Int CPAs Assoc; cp/Fla Phil Orch, Bd Dirs; r/Cath; hon/Best Paper in the Sys Area, XIII Interam Acctg Conf 1979; Author "Role of the CPA in the Implementation of Electronic Systems."

RECKER, CLIFTON SIMON JR oc/Executive; b/June 2, 1937; h/Rt 2 Box 860, Adkins, TX 78010; ba/San Antonio; m/Glenda J; c/June R Johnson, Brett Steven, Monelle Kathryn, Brent Clifton; p/Clifton S Sr (dec) and Agnes E Recker, San Antonio, TX; ed/Cert in Mechs of Air Cond'g 1972; Num Certs for Study in Auto Elec Sys, AC-Delco 1975; mil/AUS 1955-58; pa/Pres R&R Auto Parts 1971-; Dir SE Devel Foun 1973-77; cp/Pres La Vernia Lions Clb 1976-77, Dir 1977-79; r/Cath; hon/Awds for Tchg Elecs to on the Job Trainees; Awd for Most Improved Bowler 1970, Am Bowling Cong.

RECKER, GLENDA JUNE oc/Comptroller, Secretary-Treasurer; b/June 7, 1941; h/Rt 2 Box 860, Adkins, TX 78101; ba/San Antonio; m/Clifton Simon; c/June Michelle Johnson, Brett Steven, Monelle Kathryn, Brent Clifton; p/Luthor Clabourn and Viola Merle McBee Jones; Grad Durham's Sch Bus 1964; pa/Bkkpr, Girl Friday E&R Shannon, San Antonio 1964-65; Bkkpr K J Smith & Sons Inc, San Antonio 1965-69; Accts Receivable Clerk, Ace Brake Co 1969-70; R & R Auto Parts Co (Now R&R Auto Elec Rebldrs Inc), Corp Secy-Treas, Comptroller 1971-; Pres Wood Val Acres Home Owners Assn 1974-76; cp/ABWC; SE Devel Foun, Dir; La Vernia C of C; Nat Write Your Cong-man Clb; Wom's Intl Bowling Cong, Del to Nat Conv 1979 & 80; Tex Wom's Bowling Assn; San Antonio Wom's Bowling Assn, Dir; Nat Ind Bus-person's Assn; 600 Bowling Clb; Les Dames 700 Bowling Clb; PTA; Tex Farm Bur; Nat Motor Clb; Indep Party; Order Foresters; Sons of Hermann; Moose Aux; Turner's Bowling Clb; Highland Social Clb; Gtr San Antonio C of C; r/Assem of God; hon/Recip Num Bowling Awds & Champ'ships; Recip Apprec Trophy U Way 1975; Cert Apprec La Vernia Cystic Fibrosis Breath of Spring Bike-a-Thon 1979; Citizen of Month, Tex Bank 1976.

REDFEARN, BEVERLY YVONNE oc/Financial and Management Consultant; b/May 20, 1935; h/Dallas, TX; ba/8306 Londonderry Ln, Dallas, TX 75228; p/Raymond J (dec) and Ocie L Redfearn, Dallas, TX; ed/So Meth Univ; pa/Acct Annuity Bd, So Bapt Conv 1959-67; Bus Mgr Akin, Vial, Hamilton, Koch & Tubb Attys 1967-74; Bus Mgr Rain, Harrell, Emery, Young & Doke Attys 1974-77; Pres B Redfearn & Assocs Fin & Mgmt Conslts 1977-; Real Est Broker St Tex; Am Mgmt Soc; Nat Assn Legal Admrs; Dallas Chapt Assn Legal Admrs, Pres 1976-77; Adv Com Am Bar Assn Sect Ecs; Am Soc Bus & Mgmt Conslts; cp/Repub Party; Mid-Mgmt Adv Com, Dallas Co Commun Col Dist; Legal Asst Adv Com, Dallas Co Commun Col Dist; r/So Bapt; hon/Author *How to Develop Your Dynamic Dollar Sense* 1980; Fin Articles to Var Mthly Pubs; W/W S&SW.

REDMOND, STANLEY EDWARD oc/Assistant Coach and Instructor; b/Oct 6, 1954; h/Camden, AR; ba/So Ark Univ-Tech Br, Camden, AR 71701; m/Michelle Lynn; c/Christa Ann; p/Ralph and Elva Redmond, Independence, KY; ed/BA, MA Georgetown Col; pa/Asst Basketball Coach & PE Instr, So Ark Univ-Tech Br; AAHPER; AAA; cp/Optimist Clb; r/Christian; hon/Dean's List Grad; 4-Yr Basketball Lttrman.

REDWINE, ANGIE oc/Evangelist and Singer; b/Mar 18, 1959; h/PO Box 7223, Sparta, TN 38583; ba/Nashville, TN; p/Eugene and Naomi Redwine; pa/Gospel Singer; Recording Artist; r/Holiness; hon/Worked w J D Sumner & John Kell; Recorded "The Son is Rising in the Tomb" & "Bill Collector."

REDWINE, EUGENE oc/Evangelist & Singer; b/Feb 26, 1933; h/PO Box 7223, Sparta, TN 38583; ba/Nashville, TN; m/Naomi; c/Sherry Diane, Jerry Eugene, Angela Marketa, Amanda Dore; p/Jack and Cleo Redwine, Crab Orchard, TN; mil/AUS; pa/Welder; Evangelist; Gospel Recording Artist; Gospel Mus Assn; Skylite Sing Record Co; r/Holiness; hon/Worked w J D Sumner & John Kell; Recorded "The Son is Rising in the Tomb."

REDWINE, NAOMI oc/Evangelist and Singer; b/Oct 30, 1939; h/PO Box 7223, Sparta, TN 38583; ba/Nashville, TN; m/Eugene; c/Sherry Diane, Jerry Eugene, Angela Marketa, Amanda Dore; pa/Cert'd Seamstress; Gospel Recording Artist; Gospel Mus Assn; Skylite Sing Record Co; r/Holiness; hon/Worked w J D Sumner & John Kell; Recorded "The Son is Rising in the Tomb."

REECE, DONNIE RICHARD oc/Farmer; b/Oct 23, 1943; h/Knob Lick, KY 42154; ba/Knob Lick; m/Betty Jean Wilson; c/Kimberly Dawn, Scott Richard; p/Edgar Reece, Knob Lick, KY; Juanita Reece (dec); pa/Dairy Farmer; Bd Dirs, Mammoth Cave Prod Cred Assn; cp/Metcalfe ASCS Bd; r/Presb.

REED, CAROL ANN oc/Teacher; b/Mar 14, 1950; h/8120 Port Said St, Orlando, FL 32807; ba/Winter Pk, FL; p/William F and Betty L Reed, Orlando, FL; ed/AA; BA Ed; pa/Specific Lrng Disabilities Resource Tchr; Assn for Chd w Lrng Disabilities; Coun Exceptl Chd; r/Presb; hon/Outstg Yng Wom Am; W/W Am Wom 1979-80.

REED, JIMMY BURL SR oc/Executive; b/June 30, 1924; h/Radford, VA; ba/Giles Ave & Main St, Dublin, VA 24084; m/Lorene H; c/Jimmy Burl, William Michael, Helen Lynn; p/William Sidney and Mary Purdy Reed; ed/BS Univ Palm Bch 1949; mil/USN 1943-46; pa/Goodyear Tire & Rubber Co Inc: Retail Salesman 1949-51, Retail Store Mgr, Miami, Fla 1951-53, Retail Store Mgr, Tampa, Fla 1953-59, Dist Truck Tires Sales Mgr, Jacksonville, Fla 1959-62, Dist Petro Sales Mgr, St Ala 1962-65, Regional Petro Sales Mgr, So Region 1965-67; Owner & Pres Dublin Auto Supply Co 1967-; Pres & Owner Leisure Living Homes Inc 1973-; Nat Assn Indust Bus; cp/Pres Dublin U Way 1973-74; Chm Pulaski Co U Way 1975; New River Commun Col Adv Bd 1975-; Bd Dirs Pulaski Co Lifesaving 1974-75; Pulaski Co C of C, Dir 1976-77; PTO; Lions Clb, Dir 1974-76; r/Meth.

REED, MONIKA BEXTEN oc/Supervisor and Assistant Professor; b/Mar 7, 1950; h/128 Rocky Ford, Nolensville, TN 37135; ba/Nashville; m/Ronald E; p/Franz and Johanna Bexten, West Germany; ed/Lic'd Prof Bnkg & Fin; BA Sociology; MA Sociology Gerontology; pa/Supvr Res & Evaluation; Asst Prof Sociol; ACA; ASA; SSS; AACTP; ASC; SSCA; ACA Wom's Task Force, Smithsonian; cp/Alpha Mu Gamma; Phi Gamma Mu; Tau Omicron, BPW; r/Rom Cath; hon/W/W Am 1979-80; Yng Careerist of Nashville; Author 3 Res Pubs.

REED, ORALEE ELLA oc/Cashier; b/Feb 6, 1941; h/406 E First St, Mt Pleasant, TX 75455; ba/Mt Pleasant; m/J Harrell; c/Donna Pauline, James Andrew; p/Alton D Warren, Jacksonville, TX; Susie A Warren (dec); pa/Cashier, Am Nat Bank of Mt Pleasant; E Tex Chapt Am Bnkg Inst; cp/BPW Clb; r/Bapt.

REED, PROCTOR JR oc/Controller; b/Aug 2, 1927; h/203 N Colonial Dr, Hagerstown, MD 21740; ba/H'town; m/Dorothy Marie Jackson; c/George Michael, Susan Marie, Eric Gage, John Mark, Richard Scott; p/Proctor Reed Sr (dec); Florece P Groves (dec); ed/BA Univ Md 1969; Grad Study Frostburg Col; Grad AUS Command & Gen Staff Col; mil/USAR Lt Col Ret'd; pa/Controller, H'town Block Co; CPA Md; cp/32° AASR; Ali Ghan Temple; AAONMS; r/Luth; hon/W/W Fin & Indust 1979-80.

REES, JOHN oc/Associate Professor; b/Mar 25, 1948; h/Richardson, TX; ba/Sch of Social Sciences, University of Texas at Dallas, Richardson, TX 75080; m/Janet S; c/David Wynn, Mark Eirwyn, Catherine May; p/Thomas Eirwyn Rees, Barmouth, Wales, UK; Kitty A Rees (dec); ed/BA Univ Wales 1969; MA Univ Cinci 1971; PhD Univ London 1977; pa/Assoc Prof Geography & Polit Ec, Assoc Dir Ctr for Policy Studies, Univ Tex-Dallas; Regional Sci Assn; Am Ec Assn; Assn Am Geographies; cp/Metroplex Ec Adv Coun, N Tex Comm; r/Congreg; hon/Nat Sci Foun Res Grants 1976-77, 1978-80; Author Num Jour Articles & Book Chapts.

REESE, VIRGINIA DENYER oc/Professor; b/June 9, 1932; h/2302 Surrey Dr, Morgantown, WV 26505; ba/Shawnee, OK; m/Jack; c/Janelle, Steven; p/Thomas H (dec) and Nell Denyer (dec); ed/BMus Okla Col for Wom; MMus Univ Mich; PhD Univ Okla; Grad Study Syracuse Univ; pa/Prof of Mus, Okla Bapt Univ; Sigma Alpha Iota; Am Guild Organists; Pres Pi Zeta Kappa; AAUP; cp/Shawnee Fine Arts Clb; r/Bapt; hon/Outstg Edrs of Am 1972; Intl W/W Mus 1975; Sword Hon, Alpha Chi Chapt Sigma Alpha Iota.

REEVE, JOAN PRICE oc/Author; b/Sept 28, 1901; h/26 Lincoln Pk Dr, Burnsville, NC 29714; m/Warren Scott (dec); c/Eve Lynne Joan; p/Eustice Dickinson Price (dec); Mary Lillingston (dec); ed/BA Univ Lond; Dip Intl Lang Inst; MS Univ Oxford (England); pa/Fgn Missionary; Tchr Math & Mus; Chd's Authoress; Delta Kappa Gamma; Am Guild Organists; cp/Nat Fed Wom's Clbs, Pres B'ville Chapt; U Presb Wom, Pres, VP, Treas; Mus in the Mtns; Fdr & 1st Pres B'ville Gdn Clb; hon/NC Wom's Clbs 1st Prize Short Story Contest 1961,73; Author: *The Mystifying Twins* 1960; *The Secret of the Mystifying Twins* 1964; *Jerry and the Missing Cuckoo* 1971 & Others.

REEVES, ANNIE LAURA oc/Retired Teacher; b/Oct 15, 1902; h/Camden, AR; m/Carl Sr (dec); c/Mildred R White, Robert Z, Deloris A Clark, Evelyn A Broadwater; p/Robert E (dec) and Annie Pierce (dec); ed/Col Certs 1966, 75-59; pa/Ret'd Elem & Kindergarten Tchr; Mus Tchr; Missionary Pres, Secy of 3 Bds; cp/Mariah Craigen Chapt #172 OES, Secy; r/AME Ch; hon/Num Hons & Awds 1960-80.

REEVES, EARL LAMAR oc/Army Officer; b/June 17, 1950; ba/ROTC Dept, St Augustine Col, Raleigh, NC 27611; m/Annie Ruth; c/Walter, Angela; p/Calvin Coolidge Sr and Annie Mae Reeves, Seville, FL; ed/BS Stetson Univ 1972; mil/AUS Capt; pa/AUS Ofcr; r/Bapt; hon/Nat Defense Ribbon; Parachutist Badge; Army Accommend Medal; Merit Ser Medal.

REEVES, SAMUEL DWAIN oc/Minister; b/July 11, 1936; h/1004 76th St NW, Bradenton, FL 33529; ba/Bradenton; m/Geraldine Elizabeth Baker; c/Thomas Mark, Michael Dwain, ErikSamuel; p/Mr and Mrs Bryan E Reeves, Mt Pleasant, TX; ed/BA Mercer Univ 1961; BD 1964,

MDiv 1973 SWn Bapt Theol Sem; DM Columbia Theol Sem 1978; pa/Pastor First Bapt Ch; Missionary, Argentina & Costa Rica; cp/Douglas Co Sr Citizens Coun, Pres; Lithia Springs Elem Sch Enlargement Com, Chm; Lithia Springs Civic Clb, Pres; Bradenton Kiwanis Clb; r/Bapt; hn/Author Articles Pub'd in *The Commission*.

REGISTER, MILTON DEAN oc/Minister; h/Franklinton, LA; ba/Rt 7 Box 148, Franklinton, LA 70438; m/Sharon Giddens; c/Heather, Wesley; p/Carlton and Margaret Register, Adel, GA; ed/BA Valdosta St Col; MDiv New Orleans Bapt Theol Sem; pa/Pastor Enon Bapt Ch 1979-; Min of Outreach, First Bapt Ch, Brunswick, Ga 1976-79; Pastor: Talisheek Bapt Ch, Talisheek, La 1974-76, Crosland Bapt Ch, Norman, Ga 1972-73; New Orleans Bapt Sem Alumni, VP for St Ga 1979-80; Bapt Mins Assn of SE Ga 1976-79, Stewardship Chm 1979; Bapt Mins Assn Wash Parish, La, Stewardship Chm 1980, Credentials Chm 1981; cp/F'ship of Christian Aths, Bd Dirs SE Ga 1976-79; Rel Columnist, Franklinton ERA Ldr News 1980-81; r/So Bapt; hon/Outstg Yng Men Am 1979; Valdosta St Col, Dept Speech & Drama Awd 1970; Cook Co JCs Citizenship Awd 1969; Contbr to *Outreach Magazine* 1979 & *Sunday School Leadership* (Mnthly Feature Column) 1981-82.

REID, CLARENCE ALEXANDER oc/Music Director; b/Apr 15, 1911; h/Charleston, SC; m/Louise; c/Clarence A Jr, Donald; p/dec; ed/LHD 1975; DLMA 1979; pa/Dir C A Reid Sch Mus; Past Mem NTE; cp/SC St Col Alumni Assn, Former Prog Dir; SC Mus Tchrs Assn; r/Epis; hon/Composer "Song of Spring" 1950, "Where the Wild Flowers Grow" 1946, Sev Others.

REID, RICHARD STETSON JR oc/Air Force Logistician; b/Mar 4, 1945; h/Montgomery, AL; m/Karen Mills; p/Richard Stetson Reid Sr, Redlands, CA; Jean Burns Hartley, Biloxi, MS; ed/BS Auburn Univ 1968; MS USAF Inst Technol 1971; Profl Mil Ed Cert, AF Squadron Ofcrs Sch, Air Univ 1975; Profl Mil Ed Cert, AF Air Command & Staff Sch, Air Univ 1980; mil/USAFR 1963- Major; pa/USAF Logistician, Chief Data Sys Supply Mgmt Sect 1979-80; Many Other Positions USAF; Delta Sigma Pi; Soc Logistics Engrs, Mbrship Chm Local Chapt 1979; cp/Exec Com Gunter Air Force Station Jr Ofcrs Coun; YMCA Coach for Yth Soccer Leag 1978-80; YMCA Coach for Yth All-Star Team 1980; Gunter Air Force Station Teen Town Bd of Advrs 1978-80; Vol VA, Montgomery, Ala Med Ctr 1978-80; r/Epis; hon/Air Force Commend Medal; Merit Ser Medal; Bronze Star; Dist'd AFROTC Grad, Auburn Univ 1968; Sigma Iota Epsilon; Outstg Jr Ofcr, DaNang Air Base, Vietnam 1971; Top ⅓ of Class, Air Force Squadron Ofcrs Sch 1975; Dist'd Grad Air Force Staff Supply Ofcr 1976; Outstg Supply Ofcr, Air Force Data Sys Design Ctr 1979; Jr Ofcr of Yr, Air Force Data Sys Design Ctr 1980; W/W S&SW 1980-81; Assoc Author-Editor *USAF Supply Manual*.

REINL, HARRY CHARLES oc/Federal Employee; b/Nov 13, 1932; h/1111 Arlington Blvd, Arlington, VA 22209; ba/Same; c/Chawi Necha (daugh sponsored through Pearl S Buck Foun); p/Carl and Angela Plass Reinl (dec); ed/BS Fordham Univ 1953; AM Geo Wash Univ 1968; Grad Studies MIT 1972; mil/AUS 1953-55, Ser'd to 1/Lt; Comm'd Ofcr USAR 1955; Hon Discharge 1/Lt USAR, ORDC, AUS & Armed Forces of US 1962; pa/Transferred Labor Economist, CSC (now Ofc of Personnel Mgmt) 1968-; Applicant in Region III Appropriate Technology Prog, Dept of Energy (VA 195) 1979-; Am Security Coun; Fdr Ctr for Intl Security Studies of Am Security Coun Ed Foun 1977; Nat Archives (Assoc) 1976-; Am Police Hall of Fame; Smithsonian Inst (Nat Assoc); cp/Telethon Vol, Geo Wash Univ; Am Film Inst; Sustaining Mem, Repub Nat Com; Congl Com-mem, Nat Repub Congl Com; Life Mem, Repub Party; Summary in *Congressional Record* on Nat Defense; r/Rom Cath; hon/Nat Defense Ser Medal; Korean Ser Medal; UN Ser Medal; Cert of Ser, US Dept of Labor; Commemorative Medal, Repub Nat Right to Work Legal Defense Foun; Special Recog Awds, Ctr for Intl Security Studies; Cert of Commend, Exec Bd of Nat Congl Com; Fellow, ABI & IBC; Biogl Listings & Awds; Others.

RENDINE, PAUL oc/Executive; b/Feb 3, 1944; h/109 Williams St, Greenville, NC 27834; ba/G'ville; m/Nancy Jean LeCocq; c/Kristin Elizabeth; p/Lawrence A and Margaret I Rendine, Kitty Hawk, NC; ed/BS Salisbury St Col 1974; mil/USN; pa/VP & Br Ofc Mgr, Investment Bnkg Firm, Wheat First Securites Inc; Adj Prof Mgmt, Commodity Hedging Investments, Financial Planning, ECU; Adj Prof Ecs & Investments WOR-WIC Tech Commun Col; cp/VChm Wicomico Repub Ctrl Com, Rules Com Chm; Md Repub Party, Orgr & Bd Chm; Friends of Salisbury Zoo; Pres Wicomico Co Am Cancer Soc, Bus Chm; Wicomico Co U Way; Delta Upsilon; VP Cherry Oaks Civic Assoc 1981-; Bd Dirs Downtown Greenville Assoc 1981-; Fin Com Chm & Pres-Elect, Jr Achmt of Pitt Co 1981-; Mem Exec Com Pitt Co Ed Work Council 1981-; Chm Human Resources Task Force, Pitt-Greenville Co C of C Bus & Indust Devel Council 1981-; Greenville Noon Rotary Clb 1981-; Sr High Yth F'ship Advr, First Presb Ch 1981-; r/Presb; hon/Wall St Jour Awd 1974; Dist'd Ser Awd 1977; Outstg Yng Men Am, Salisbury JCs 1977; Achmt Awd, Am Cancer Soc 1978.

RENEAW, BEATRICE DENNIS oc/Instructor; b/Oct 24, 1914; h/704 Alice Ave, Lindsay, OK 73052; ba/Same; m/Wallace L; p/Thomas A (dec) and Ola G Dennis (dec); ed/BMus; Nat Cert Piano-Voice; pa/Lindsay Phil Soc, Past Pres; Nat & Okla Mus Tchrs Assn; Nat Guild Piano Tchrs; Pvt Instr Piano, Organ, Voice; r/First Christian Ch; Deaconess, Choir Dir; hon/W/W Wom; Sigma Alpha Iota; Intl W/W Intells.

RENTFRO, LARRY DEAN oc/Hospital Administrator; b/Mar 14, 1941; h/Texarkana, TX; ba/1000 E Pine, Texarkana, TX 75501; m/Clariece Van Valkenburgh; c/Donald Ray, Sheri Renee; p/Floyd and Helen Rentfro, Okmalgee, OK; ed/BS Okla St Univ 1964; MHA Wash Univ 1972; Adm Residency Wesley Med Ctr 1971-72; mil/AUS 1964-66; pa/Hd Basketball Coach, Edison HS, Tulsa, Okla 1966-70; Asst Admr St Johns Hosp Sch Nsg, Tulsa 1972-76; Asst VP St Johns Med Ctr, Joplin, Mo 1976-78; VP Wadley Hosp, Texarkana 1978-; Exec Com Tri-Sts Shared Sers Bd; Am Col Hosp Admrs; Exec Com ATCOG Emer Med Sers Bd; Am Hosp Assn; Tex Hosp Assn; cp/Onklawn Rotary Clb; Texarkana U Way Bd; Texarkana Little Leag Baseball; r/Meth; hon/Foster McGan S'ship Grant 1970; W/W S&SW 1980; Author "Management and Supervisory Development in the St Louis Area Hospitals" 1972.

RESLEY, GEORGE BOULTER oc/Regional Sales Manager; b/Nov 23, 1945; h/Broken Arrow, OK; ba/4343 S 118th E Ave, Tulsa, OK 74145; m/Virginia Beth Hopper; p/Horace Ernest and Annie Jane Resley, Ft Stockton, TX; ed/BBA Tex A&M Univ 1969; Grad Dale Carnegie Sales Course 1976; mil/ROTC Tex A&M; pa/Regional Sales Mgr, C-E Vetco Sers Inc; Soc Petro Engrs; Nat Assn Corrosion Engrs; Intl Assn Drilling Contractors; cp/Repub Nat Com; Life Mem Nat Rifle Assn; Tex Muzzle Loading Rifle Assn; Nat Muzzle Loading Assn; Osage Muzzle Loading Rifle Assn; Tex A&M Century Clb; Westerners; N Am Rod & Gun Clb; Green Country Model RR Clb; Nat Model RR Assn; r/Christian Scist; hon/10 Yr Awd, C-E Vetco Sers Inc 1979.

REUBEN, LUCY JEANETTE oc/Professor; b/Dec 15, 1949; h/Chapel Hill, NC; ba/Fuqua Sch of Bus, Duke Univ, Durham, NC 27706; c/Kwame Oliver; p/O R (dec) and Anna D Reuben, Sumter, SC; ed/AB Oberlin Col 1971; MBA 1974, PhD 1981 Univ Mich; pa/Prof Fuqua Sch Bus, Duke Univ 1979-; Grad Sch Bus Adm, Univ Mich; Tchg Asst 1978-79 & 1975-77, Tchg Fellow 1977-78; Fin Staff, World Hdqtrs, Ford Motor Co 1974-75; Nat Black MBA Assn; Nat Ec Assn; Am Fin Assn; Wn Fin Assn; AAUP; Nat Assn Female Execs; Conf Discussant: Assn Univ Bus & Ec Res 1979, Allied Social Scis Assn 1980; hon/W/W: Am Cols & Univs 1974, 78, Am Wom; Beta Gamma Sigma; Outstg Yng Wom Am 1979; Nat F'ships Fund Awd; Earhart Foun F'ship; Danforth F'ship, Finalist & Hon Mention; Author *Black Economic Development: Analysis and Implications* 1975.

REVISKY, CHARLES WAYNE oc/Pastor; b/Aug 8, 1946; h/PO Box 79, Fingerville, SC 29338; m/Gail Lawter; c/Joshua Charles; p/Margaret R Lawter, Inman, SC; ed/AB Gardner Webb Col 1978; mil/USN; pa/Pastor First Bapt Ch, Fingerville; Pastor's Adv Bd, Bapt Col Charleston; Missions Com, Spartanburg Bapt Assn; Presenter Spartanburg Bapt Assn Message, N Spartan Assn 1981; r/Bapt.

REYNOLDS, EUGENE JACKSON oc/Pastor; b/Oct 18, 1930; h/3521 Western Ave, Gadsden, AL 35904; ba/Gadsden; m/Violet; c/Randall, Richard, Rhonda, Renda; p/Mr and Mrs B J Reynolds, Gainsville, GA; ed/Att'd Lee Col 1956; Master Ser Dip, Ch of God Bible Inst 1975; pa/Pastor: Sheperd's Fold Ch of God 1960-70, Ala City Ch of God, Gadsden 1970-; Evangelist 1950-60; Pres Num Min Assns; Pres NAm Min Assn; Pres E Ctrl Min Assn; hon/Num Awds on Nat & St Level for Min Activs; Author "Echoes of Evangelism" 1957 & Others.

REYNOLDS, EVELYN C oc/Veterans Service Officer; b/Oct 19, 1931; h/1027 N 13th Ave, Laurel, MS 39440; ba/Laurel; m/Harry Leighton; c/Gordon Leigh; p/Lee J Clark (dec); Ruby K Beech, Ellisville, MS; ed/Att'd Jones Co Jr Col; pa/Jones Co Vet Ser Ofcr; Miss Assn Vets Ser Ofcrs; YWCA; Local Rep St Vets Affairs Comm; cp/Pres Am Legion Aux Univ 11; Past Matron OES Star Chapt 256; Past Pres PTA; Former Cub Scout Den Mother; Part'd in Heart Fund, Cancer Dr & Mlt Hlth Progs; Past Matron's Clb; r/Bapt; hon/Commun Ldrs & Noteworthy Ams; Nat Cit for Merit Ser, Nat Vets Affairs & Rehab Comm; Orchid for a Lovely Lady Awd for Commun Sers.

REYNOLDS, MILDRED DAWN oc/Entrepreneur; b/July 28, 1947; h/Huntsville, AL; ba/Techni-Core, 3315 Memorial Pkwy, Suite 5, H'ville, AL 35802; m/John; c/Laura, Christina; p/William F Shaffer, Germantown, TN; Majorie P Shaffer, Lowell, MA; ed/BSBA Univ Ala 1975; pa/Fdr & Owner Techni-Core Engrg Firm; Phi Kappa Phi; Pres Soc for Advmt of Mgmt; cp/Notary Public; Hon Dpty Sheriff; r/Bapt; hon/W/W Students in Am Univs & Cols; Phi Kappa Phi.

REYNOLDS, THOMAS WILLIAM oc/Printing Executive; b/May 31, 1949; h/Waynesboro, VA; m/Martha Trice; c/Thomas, Daniel; p/V

Francis and Susan Spilman Reynolds, Waynesboro, VA; ed/BA Emory & Henry Col 1971; Grad Study LSU 1971-72; pa/VP Impressive Advtg & Lithography Inc 1972-; Elem Sch Mus Tchr, City of Waynesboro 1972; Emory & Henry Col Alumni Assn 1971-, Class Agt, Shenandoah Val Chapt Pres; cp/Waynesboro Choral Soc 1972-77; W'boro Players; Oak Grove Theater; Theater Wagon; W'boro Marathon Assn; Friends of the Lib; W'boro Big Bros/Sisters; W'boro JCs 1977-; Va JCs, Regional Dir; Blue Key Nat Hon Frat; US JCs; JCs Intl; Theta Chi Epsilon; W'boro Chapt Am Cancer Soc; r/Meth; hon/W'boro JCs: JC of Mo, 10 Most Active JCs, Outstg Ofcr; Dist 29 JCs: Novice Speak Up Winner, Awd of Hon, Outstg Pres of Yr, Outstg Chapt of Yr, Outstg Newslttr of Yr; Skyline Region JCs: Novice Speak Up Runner-Up, Outstg Ser Awd, Outstg Chapt Yr, Outstg Pres of Yr, Outstg Newslttr of Yr; VA JCs: Novice Speak Up Winner, Overall Speak Up Winner, Parade of Chapts 1st Pl, Level of Excell Awd, Blue Chip Awd, Sidney D Peck Winner (Outstg Local Pres of Yr); Va JCs Metro Conf: Chapt of Mo, Awd of Hon; US JCs: Ldrboard Awds, Century Clb, Big City BUBBA, Pres Cit, 10 Mem Recruitment Patch, Cand's Patch, Outstg Regional Newslttr, En Inst Trg Session Dip, Pres Clb; Va JCs Ext Awd, Recruiter Awd, Outstg Regional Newslttr, Geissenbier Awd; Life Mem Freedom JCs; Other JC Awds.

REYNOLDS, WANETTA oc/Freelance Writer; b/Feb 19, 1915; h/Shawnee, OK; m/Glen; p/dec; ed/Att'd Seminole Jr Col 1963-65; BA 1968, Grad Work 1970-72 Okla Univ; MA 1970; Att'g E Ctrl St Univ; pa/Former Tchr; Shawnee Credit Bur; r/Prot; hon/Stories Pub'd in *Christian Record Braille Foun Inc*; Articles in *Seminole Collegian*, Seminole Jr Col.

RHEA, ELIZABETH DUNLAP oc/City Councilwoman; b/June 18, 1930; h/672 Sedgewood Dr, Rock Hill, SC 29730; ba/Same; m/James Copeland Jr; c/James Copeland III, Catherine Rhea Darby, John Dunlap; p/James O (dec) and Caroline Elizabeth Dunlap (dec); ed/Att'd Barry Col, Winthrop Col; cp/City Coun-wom; Jr Wel Leag, Sustaining Mem; Rock Hill Debutante Clb; Fine Arts Assn: Patrons Chm, Publicity Chm, Selection Com Chm; Rock Hill Arts Coun; Rock Hill Rec Comm; SC Pks & Rec Soc, Secy of Comm, Bd Mem; Nat Rec & Pks Assn; Municipal Leag of SC, Area VP; Come See Me; r/Epis; hon/JCs Wom of Yr 1979; Pres York Co Municipal Assn.

RHODES, CECIL B oc/Supervising Sanitarian; b/Sept 6, 1920; h/Rt 2 Box 298A, Brookhaven, MS 39601; b/Brookhaven; m/Olivia C; c/Sheila Marie Turnage, Byron C; p/Ben F (dec) and Cola Breland Rhodes (dec); ed/BA Miss Col 1946; mil/USAAF 1942-45; pa/Supvg Sanitarian for Dist VII, Miss St Bd Hlth; Miss Assn Sanitarians, Pres 1971-72; St Employees Assn of Miss; Miss St Bd of Registration for Sanitarians; cp/Brookhaven Evening Lions Clb, Pres 1977-78; r/Bapt; hon/Sanitarian of Yr 1980.

RHODES, JAMES O oc/Developer, Chief Executive Officer; b/May 7, 1935; h/Cleveland, TN; m/Pamela C; c/Deborah Carol, James Blake, Rondi Michelle; p/Ohlen A and Truma E Rhodes, Oolfewah, Tn; ed/BS Mus Ed So Missionary Col 1959; Masters Deg Univ So Calif 1967; pa/Develr Retirement Ctrs of Am Investors; Fdr & Opr Rhodes Ltd (Prods Custom-Made Mus); Tchr Band & Instruments: Lynwood Acad, Lynwood, Calif & Orangewood Acad, Gdn Grove, Calif; Perf'd for Faith for Today Telecasts & Evangelistic Crusades; Assoc'd w Adventist Across Am Film Present; r/7th Day Adventist; hon/15 Albums.

RHODES, JOHN R oc/Principal, Minister; b/Mar 30, 1932; h/1545 Birthnight St, Charleston, SC 29407; ba/C'ton; m/Betty W; c/Margaret Elizabeth, John Richard II, Thomas Patrick; p/John P Rhodes, Reynoldsville, PA; ed/BA 1956, MA 1973 Furman Univ; pa/Prin Harbor View Middle Sch; Pastor Meml Bapt Ch; SC Middle Sch Assn; Nat Middle Sch Assn; r/Bapt.

RHODES, PAMELA C oc/Recording Artist; h/Cleveland, TN; m/James O; c/Deborah Carol, James Blake, Rondi Michelle; p/G Blake and June L Chanslor, Albuquerque, NM; ed/BS Loma Linda Univ 1974; pa/Retirement Ctrs of Am Investors; Traveled in Europe & Scandanavia w Chamber Singers; Evangelistic Crusades & Campmeetings; r/7th Day Adventist; hon/2 Stereo Albums.

RICE, ALICE MARIE oc/Office Manager; b/Sept 15, 1942; h/2265 Westmeade Dr SW, Decatur, AL35603; ba/Decatur; m/Charles Aubrey; c/David Timothy Howell, Tammy Marie Howell; p/Joseph C and Opal H Lane, Cullman, AL; ed/Anderson's Bus Col 1962; Cert Profl Secy Rating 1971; pa/Secy, Exec Secy, Ofc Mgr, Compton Construction Co 1962-; Nat Secys Assn; cp/Prog Dir Ala Heart Fund Assn; r/Bapt; hon/CPS Rating 1971; Secy of Yr, Decatur Chapt 1973, Outstg Cit, Heart Fund 1973; W/W Am Wom; Personalities of Am 1982.

RICE, CLYDE C JR oc/Chief Executive Officer; b/Jul 31, 1942; ba/Rehab Specialists, PO Box 437, Fern Park, FL 32730; m/Nancy Jo; c/Claudia Anne, Andrea Louise; p/Frances B Rice, Chesapeake, VA;

ed/CLU Am Col of Life Underwriters 1976; BS Univ of SC 1965; pa/Chief Exec Ofcr, Water & Sewer Rehab Firm; Bd Dirs, Seminole Co Fraud & Worthless Check Assn; Nat Assn Life Underwriters; Seminole Co Assn Life Underwriters; cp/Gtr Seminole Co C of C: Pres, 1/VP, Chm Bus Ed Com, Chm Prog Com, Bd Dirs, Exec Com, Public Relats Com, Others; Seminole Co Ad Hoc Jail Com; Ctl Fla Estate Planning Coun; Coach & Sponsor of Little League Teams; Precinct Chm; Chm Lincoln Day Dinner; Treas, Seminole Co Repub Party; Others; r/Luth-Wisconsin Synod: Pres Ch Congreg, Ch Coun, Bd Elders, Bd Ed, Fin Secy, Lay Del for 5 States to Wis Evangelical Luth Synod; hon/Helen Keyser Dist'd Citizen Awd for Outstg Commun Ser.

RICE, LOUISE oc/Associate Professor, Coordinator of Reading; b/Nov 21, 1940; h/3016 Bramblewood Trail, Augusta, GA 30909; ba/Augusta; m/Wilson L; c/Wilson L Jr, Robert Christopher; p/dec; ed/BS Tuskegee Inst 1963; MA Tchrs Col, Columbia Univ 1969; PhD Univ Ga 1979; pa/Tchr Eng Wash HS, Cairo, Ga 1963-66; Tchr Eng & Rdg, Lucy Laney HS, Augusta, Ga 1966-68; Instr Eng & Rdg 1968-71, 1972-79; Assoc Prof & Coor Rdg, Paine Col; Intl Rdg Assn; Ga Coun Intl Rdg Assn; Phi Delta Kappa; cp/Delta Sigma Theta, Pres Augusta Alumnae Chapt; Jack & Jill Am Inc; NAACP; Links Inc; r/Bapt.

RICE, MARTHA B oc/Insurance Executive; b/Sept 15, 1942; h/431 Springvale Rd, Great Falls, VA 22066; ba/Great Falls; m/Earl D; c/Jennifer Lynn; p/C D Boyd, Annapolis, MD; Marjorie D Boyd, Vienna, VA; ed/Att'd So Meth Univ & N Tex St Univ; pa/Lic'd Ins Reg & Real Est Agt; Owner Ins Agcy; Nationwide Ins Indep Contractors Assn; Nationwide Agts Coop Assn; Nat Assn Life Underwriters; Wom's Life Underwriters Cong; Am Soc Profl & Exec Wom; cp/Gt Falls Citizens Assn; Village Ctr Merchants Assn, Secy; r/Epis; hon/W/W Am Wom; Challenger Clb 1977 & 79; Exec Clb 1977.

RICE, MICHAEL oc/Minister; b/July 25, 1942; h/2210 29th St, Ashland, KY 41101; ba/Ashland; m/Alice; c/Ronald Wayne, Joan Kathleen, Rebecca Lynn; p/Ben H Jr and Lorene Rice, Tollesboro, KY; ed/AB Asbury Col; MDiv Asbury Theol Sem; DMin Louisville Presb Theol Sem; pa/Min U Meth Ch; Bd Ordained Min, Ch Ext Com; r/U Meth.

RICE, MURIEL A DUNPHY oc/Artist, Librarian, Teacher; b/Mar 28, 1916; h/1818 Elizabeth Ave, Winston-Salem, NC 27103; m/Ronald Earl; c/Darlene R Guerry, Judith R Owen, Ronald E III; p/Bernard J and Luella P Dunphy, Canton, MI; ed/Att'd No Bapt Thoel Sem, Nat Bible Inst; pa/Artist; Assoc Artist, Winston-Salem; NC Watercolor Soc; High Point Art Guild; Intl Soc Artists; Libn Asst, Forsyth Co, NC; r/Bapt; hon/1 Wom Show W-S; 1st Prize Assoc'd Artist Show W-S.

RICE, WILLIAM Y oc/Investments; b/June 22, 1930; h/Longview, TX; m/Rachel Gallenkamp; c/William III, John Robin, Drew; p/John Herbert (dec) and Lucille Horton Rice, Longview, TX; ed/BBA Baylor Univ 1951; pa/Ptnr Magnum Corp; Chm Bd Town N Nat Bank; Dir Southland Savings Assn; Tex Oil Mktrs Assn; cp/Dir E Tex C of C & Longview C of C; Dir Sabine River Auth of Tex; 11 Yrs City Coun-man; 2 Terms Mayor Longview; r/Bapt.

RICHARD, RAYMOND JOSEPH JR oc/Vacuum Forming; b/July 9, 1941; h/706 60th Ave, Terr W, Bradenton, FL 33507; m/Virginia Mae Cromwell; c/Amber Lynn, Jeannine Marie, Todd Allen; p/Raymond Richard Sr, Skowhegan, ME; Doris Richard, Bradenton, FL; mil/NG; AUS; r/Cath; hon/Sev Ribbons for Oil Painting; Trophy Scuba Diving.

RICHARDSON, ALBERT CLEVELAND oc/Artist; b/Jan 29, 1938; h/808 N Second, Bellaire, TX 77401; ba/Bellaire; m/JoAnne K; c/Rickey Lee, Randall Scott, Lonnie Dee, Debra Jo, Albert Floyd, Robert Lewis; p/Floyd H and Ollie I Richardson, Wickes, AR; pa/Artist, Oil Indust & Nostalgic Scenes; Watercolor Art Soc Houston; Exhib'd in Many Invitational Art Shows; cp/Past Cub Master & Boy Scout Ldr; Little Leag Coach; Jr Fball Coach; r/Nazarene; hon/1st Pl Watercolor Div, Amarillo Tex Regional Show; Other Show Awds.

RICHARDSON, FRANCIS JOSEPH III oc/Investment Counsel, Banker, Financial Analyst; b/Mar 22, 1943; h/PO Drawer 52768, New Orleans, LA 70152; m/Carolyn Mary Bienvenu; ed/BBA Tulane Univ 1965, Law 1970; MBA Loyola Univ 1970; Investment Adv Tng & Bank Cert 1972-76; Fin Analysts Tng & CFA Studies 1973; NYSE Lic Brokerage Tng 1978-80; mil/NROTC 1961; AF Aux CAP 1958; pa/Michoud Launch Sys Br, Boeing Aerospace 1964-66; Data Procesing Div, IBM Corp 1966-71; VP & Trust Mgr, First Nat Bank of Commerce of New Orleans 1971-76; Investment Res William O'Neil & Co 1978-79; Bache, Halsey, Stuart, Shields Investments 1979-80; Fellow Fin Analysts Fed; Phi Delta Phi; Am Ec Assn; Creole Ec Coun, Fellow, Fin Analysts Fed; Fdg Mem La Engrg Soc Student Chapt Tulane; cp/New Orleans C of C; So Yacht Clb; New Orleans Country Clb; New Orleans Ath Clb; Celtic Clb; Le Debut de

Jeunnes Filles Novelle Orleans; Soc of the War of 1812 in New Orleans; Mil Order of Fgn Wars; Mil & Hospitaller Order of St Lazarus of Jerusalem: Mem & So Del Editor; hon/William C Kraus Awd; Yng Men's Bus Clb of New Orleans 1968; Nom'd for White House Fellows Prog by Cong-man F Edward Hebert & Mayor Moon Landrieu; Cert of Merit, Phi Delta Phi; Author Tutorial Level MBA Res, "Management Development Techniques of IBM, Xerox & NCR", "Taxable Estate Planning, Management Information & Control Systems."

RICHARDSON, HERBERT WAYNE oc/Maintenance Manager; b/Oct 16, 1946; h/2406 Reever Ave, Arlington, TX 76010; ba/Arlington; m/Victoria Anna Bielawski; c/Richard Wayne; p/George Richardson, W Elizabeth, PA; Lois Dietz Richardson (dec); ed/BA Humanities; MA Commun; mil/USN; pa/Wayn Co Writing; Commercial & Fiction Writer; cp/Optimist Intl; Lions Intl; PTA; IRA; Coach Yth Baseball & Fball; Metro GT Assn; r/Christian; hon/Pi Delta Epsilon; Stella Woodall Intl Poetry Soc; W/W Am Fin & Indust.

RICHARDSON, TAMMY U'LIN oc/Student; b/Oct 24, 1963; h/Alice, TX; p/Irvin Colonial and Eva Sams Richardson, Alice, TX; ed/Student Alice HS; cp/Beverly Miller Dance Studio; TAGS; Muscular Dystrophy Telethon Wkr; Alice Civic Ballet; Am Cancer Soc; r/Bapt; hon/Merit Awd, VFW Alice; Treas Math-Sci Clb; Nat Hon Soc; Treas Student Coun; Outstg Student in Hist & Eng; Vol Over 250 Hrs: Mus S Tex, Alice Public Lib, Alice Vet Clin, Alice C of C.

RICHARDSON, WILLIE oc/Director of Law Enforcement; b/Nov 17, 1939; ba/St Tax Commission, 1413 W Main St, Tupelo, MS 38801; m/Earline; c/Sonji, Willie III, Shawn; p/Alice Richardson, Greenville, MS; ed/BS Jackson St Univ; mil/Md ANG 1963-69; pa/Balto Colts Fball Team 1963-71; Dir Law Enforcement, Miss St Tax Comm; NFL Players Assn; cp/Jackson Touchdown Clb; r/Bapt; hon/All Pro Balto Colts, Pro Bowl 1967 & 68; Hall of Fame, Jackson St Univ 1978; Miss Sports Hall of Fame 1979.

RICHEY, LeNORA DELL oc/Teacher; b/July 31, 1924; h/1004 E Inez, Beeville, TX 78102; m/Walter E; c/Mussette, Mechelle; p/Fredrick O Duncan (dec); Mary E Arthurs (dec); ed/BS Lamar Univ; MEd Tex A&I Univ; pa/Tchr EMR Clrm & Homebound; cp/Ch Choir; Tops; AAUW; r/Christian.

RICHEY, WILLIAM C oc/Executive; b/Mar 29, 1925; h/5147 S Angela Rd, Memphis, TN 38117; ba/Memphis; c/W R, R C; p/W C (dec) and M V Richey (dec); ed/Att'd Univ Ark, Syracuse Univ, Univ Houston, NY Univ, Intl Schs Dartnell, USAF Pilot Trg; Mktg & Franchising Spec Grad; mil/USAAF WWII 1st Lt; pa/Pres & Fdr Mktg Conslts of Am Corp; Pres ITMA; AMA; ASE; Am Sems Assn; cp/Repub Party; Polit Conslt; Num Civic Orgs; r/Meth; hon/Num Awds; Author Num Books, Movies, Video Shows & Editorials on Franchising.

RICHIE, MOZELL GILBERT oc/Homemaker; b/Dec 24, 1936; h/702 Garraty Rd, San Antonio, TX 78209; m/William Clay Jr; c/Clay, Ross; p/Bud and Frances Gilbert; ed/BS Elem Ed; pa/Former Elem Tchr; cp/Vol Work w Schs, Ch, Symph & Art; r/Bapt; hon/Art Shows.

RICKENBACKER, JOHN H oc/Health Administrator; b/July 20, 1951; h/692 Crawford St NE, Orangebrug, SC 29115; ba/O'burg; m/Hazel Armstrong; p/John Jefferson and Maggie Whaley Rickenbacker; ed/BS 1973, MS 1975 SC St Col; pa/Tchr Felton Lab Sch 1973-74; Commun Coor, O'burg Co Consumer Hlth Coun 1974-78; Hlth Admr, O'burg Co Consumer Hlth Coun 1979-; SCEA 1973-74; Palmetto Low Country Hlth Sys Agcy; cp/Pres O'burg Co Yng Dems; Pres O'burg Chapt NAACP; r/CBapt; hon/Hd Start Ser Awd 1976; O'burg Co Yng Dems Ser Awd 1979.

RICKETSON, REATHA PAULINE oc/Homemaker; b/Aug 24, 1939; h/Rt 2 Box 137A, Alice, TX 78332; m/Duane; c/Dale, Darrell, Donald, p/Lonzo Victor Gray, Harlingen, TX; Nancy Ann Gray (dec); cp/PTA, Pres Dubose Sec'dy & Schallert; VP Alice City Coun PTA; Dist 16 PTA; Cub Scout Ldr; Mar of Dimes; Am Cancer Crusade Ldr; Ctrl Power & Light Co Wom's Clb Pres; Commun Ed Bd Dirs; Alice Teen Clb Bd Dirs; r/7th Day Adventist; hon/Silver Tray, Dubose Sch; Wall Plaque Outstg Work w PTA; Drum Awd, Most Outstg Mbrship Chm in Dist 16; Tex Life Mbrship; Ser Pins & Charms Tex PTA.

RIDDLE, LOU WEAVER oc/Instructor; h/6044 Northridge Rd, Columbia, SC 29206; m/Robert Marion; ed/Att'd Converse Col, Winthrop Col, Univ SC; pa/Tchr Adult Ed, Fairfield Co, SC; Tchr Color & Flower Arranging, Commun Col; Tchg Design, Univ SC; Nat Coun Instr Design, Flower Show Procedure & Symposiums; cp/Past Pres & Life Mem Gdn Clb of SC; Parliamentn & Past Pres Nationally Accred'd Judges Clb of SC; 6 Yrs on Nat Coun Bd, Nom'g Com, Flower Show Accred'd Chm; Charter Mem 2 Gdn Clbs; Hon Mem Columbia Gdn Clb; Am Guild

Flower Arrangers; Y'Hona Gdn Clb; hon/Outstg Wom of Yr, Up-to-Date Lit Clb; 1 of 10 Flower Arrangers to Exhibit Colored Pictures for 1st Colored Calendar Sponsored by Gdn Clb of SC; Margaret Moore Awd for Most Outstg Exhibit in Judges Class, Piedmont St Flower Show.

RIEL, ELOISE GREEN oc/Secretary, Computer Operator, Comptroller, Estimator; b/Oct 28, 1916; h/607 Wren St, Sumter, SC 29150; ba/Sumter; m/James Daniel II; c/Susan Riel Murphy, Deborah Riel Nix; p/William Wherry and Meta Elizabeth Green; pa/Pres Details Bi-Riel (Estimating Firm); cp/GSA Ldr 15 Yrs; r/Meth; hon/1st Wom Estimator of Gen Construction in SC.

RIGGS, BARRY LYNN oc/Administrator; b/Feb 27, 1953; h/3200 J Tanners Way, Richmond, VA 23224; ba/Richmond; p/John C and Ruth B Riggs, Staunton, VA; ed/BS VPI & St Univ 1975; MBA Va Commonwlth Univ 1981; pa/Va Elec & Power Co: Asst Engr 1975-77, Assoc Engr 1977-78, Inventory Analyst 1978-79, Sr Analyst Develr & Implement, Mats Mgmt Sys 1979-80, Supvr Inventory Control 1980-; Nat Soc Profl Engrs; Am Inst Indust Engrs; r/Bapt.

RIGGS, CECIL GRAHAM oc/Executive; b/Aug 23, 1935; h/207 Wheeler Rd, Seffner, FL 33584; ba/Tampa; m/Carolyn Jean Wilson; c/Sabrina, Janita; p/Otho Graham and Mildred Louise Massey Riggs; ed/Grad Cleveland Inst Elecs 1962; Grad Adv'd Mgmt Prog Harvard 1973; pa/Elec Tech, Automatic Elec Co 1956-69; Continental Communs Constrn Co: VP 1969-70, Pres, Exec Dir 1971-73; Pres Concomco Can Ltd, Montreal 1971-; Operating VP Arcata Installation Co 1972-73; VP Telephone Plant Constrn Corp 1972-; Pres Continental Communs Ser Corp 1973-; Concomco Corp, Tampa 1973-; Omega Intl Corp 1974-; Asst Dir Tampa Concentrated Employment Prog 1970-; Indust Rep Nat Alliance Bus-men Prog 1973-; Indust Telephone Pioneers Assn, Dir 1970-; Fla Telephone Assn; Intl Platform Assn; cp/Tampa C of C; Tower Clb; Buckhorn Golf & Country Clb; Harvard Bus Sch, Fla W Coast, Dir 1977-78.

RILEY, ENOS EDWARD oc/Proprietor; b/Oct 27, 1932; h/Rt 4 Box 406, Enterprise, Al; ba/Anniston, AL; m/Myra N; c/Cassandra R Hobson, Teresa M; Leslie; p/Enos E Sr (dec) and Elizabeth Riley (dec); ed/Grad Bus Course 1962; mil/AUS 1953-59; pa/Pres & Contractor AUS, Ft McClellan, Ala, Riley Support Ser 1972-74; Contract, AUS Superior Janitorial Ser 1976-80; Contract St Ala Custodial Sers 1978-80; Pres: Riley Support Sers Inc, Superior Janitorial Sers Inc, Custodial Sers Inc; cp/Mason; r/Meth.

RIMEL, GEORGE WILLIAM oc/Executive Editor, General Manager; b/Oct 5, 1944; h/285 W 56 St, Hialeah, FL 33012; ba/Miami; m/Helen Charlene Redford; c/George Jarrett, Christine Kimber; p/Barbara Rimel, Opa-Locka, FL; ed/Assoc Deg Miami Dade Col 1964; AUS Intell Sch 1966; USAF Data Handling 1966; mil/AUS Intell Analyst; pa/Acct Exec *Miami Herald* 1964-66, 1969-74; Sales Mgr *North Dade Journal* 1974-75; *Bradenton Herald*: Display Advtg Mgr 1975-76, Circulation Dir 1976-77; Gen Mgr-Exec Editor *The Community Reporter*; Savings & Loan Mktg Soc, Assoc Mem; Fla Magazine Assn; Profl Karate Assn; Pres Fed Credit Union; SCMA; INAE; Sertoma; cp/Cand Hialeah City Coun 1979; Loan Exec U Fund; Toastmasters; PTA; Pst Cub Scout Master; r/Meth; hon/W/W S 1980; Addy Billboard Awd 1977; INAE Idea Book 1976; Future Secys 1976; Kroehler Furniture Ad Awd 1970; Jt Accomodation Medal 1969; Nat Defense 1969; Good Conduct 1979; Eagle Scout 1956; God & Country 1956; Author All Lead Stories & Editorials 2 Yrs, *Community Reporter.*

RINEHART, LEILA MAE oc/Businesswoman; b/July 16, 1938; h/Apt 110, Club House Cove, 1100 Crystal Lake Dr, Pompano Bch, FL 33064; ba/Pompano Bch; p/Chester G and Elsie A Dahms Kirkhoff, Glenmoore, PA; pa/Owner Bus Sers Co; Ofcr of Plumbing Contracting Firm; Life Mem Nat Rifle Assn; Affil Mem Nat Water Ski Assn; cp/Local Civic Assns; r/Meth; hon/Excell in Eng.

RINEHART, RICHARD DUANE oc/Assistant Vice President; b/Apr 24,1947; h/5015 21st St W, Bradenton, FL 33507; ba/B'ton; c/Duane Eugene; p/H R and Mary S Rinehart, B'ton, FL; ed/AA Manatee Jr Col; AIB Standard Cert; pa/Inter City Nat Bank Asst VP; First Fla Banks Inc; Fla Bnkrs; cp/F&AM #31; Elks Lodge #1853; 3 Galloneer Manatee Co Blood Bank; r/Meth.

RIPPER, CHARLES LEWIS oc/Wildlife Illustrator-Author; b/Oct 28, 1929; h/3525 Brandon Rd, Huntington, WV 25704; ba/Same; m/Virginia Ogle; c/Elisabeth Anne, Janet Gail, Joy Lee; p/Arthur Daniel (dec) and Hazel Porter Ripper, Ft Myers, FL; ed/Grad Art Inst of Pgh 1949; mil/US Corps of Engrg 1951-53; pa/Lectr & Wkshop Ldr Cols, Civic Grps on Art & Conserv; Art for Nat Wildlife Fed, Audubon & Pubs; Illust'd 16 Books, Author 11 Books; r/Presb; hon/Winning Design, Nat Wild Turkey Fed Stamp & Print 1977.

PERSONALITIES OF THE SOUTH

RITSON, RINA oc/Golf Professional; b/May 31, 1939; h/Orlando, FL; ba/Lake Buena Vista Clb, PO Box 40, Lake Buena Vista, FL 32830; m/Philip Vassie; c/Mark McCann, Clive McCann, Ronald McCann; p/Jozef and Hester Vermaak, Transvaal, S Africa; ed/Grad Col w Dips in Art, Mus, Commercial Subjs; pa/Hd Golf Profl, Lake Buena Vista, Walt Disney World; LPGA Tchg Div; Conslt for Sports Intl; Tchr on S Africa Jr Golf Assn Prog; Tchr Clemson Univ Team; r/Meth; hon/Articles in *Golf Magazine* 1980.

RIZZO, MARY JOANNA oc/Professor; b/Dec 5, 1910; h/7214 St Charles Ave, New Orleans, LA 70118; ba/Same; p/BS St Mary's Dominican Col 1931; MA La St Univ 1945; PhD Univ Wis 1954; pa/Prof Speech, Drama, Communs, St Mary's Dominican Col; Dominican Nun, Order of St Dominic, Congreg of St Mary; Speech Commun Assn; So Speech Commun Assn; La Speech Commun Assn; Am Theatre Assn; Delta Epsilon Sigma; Phi Beta, Univ Wis Chapt; r/Cath; hon/W/W: Am Wom, S&SW; World W/W Wom; Dic Am Schlrs; Dominican Col: Best Dir & Prodr Awds, Best Speech Prof Awd; Interpretative Rdg Awds, New Orleans Sch Speech & Dramatic Art; Fdr Speech & Drama Dept St Mary's Dominican Col; Fdr Dominican Col Players; Fdr Speech Pathol Dept, St Mary's Dominican; Recip All Am Awd, All Cath Awd, All Columbian Medalist Awd; Author Num Rel Plays & Progs; Editor *Centennial of Dominican Sisters*.

RO, COLLA MAE oc/Homemaker; b/Feb 7, 1933; h/Rt 2 Box 200, Kindred Ave, Paducah, KY 42001; m/Chun Whang; c/Terry Wayne, Janet Lynn, Randall Chun; p/Woodrow Eason (dec); Harriett Rallens, Murphysboro, IL; ed/Att'd So Ill Univ 1963-65; pa/Optician: Conrad Optical 1963-65, Kee Optical 1965-67; cp/Den Ldr, Cub Scouts; Cnslr Boy Scouts; Delphic Study Grp 1977-; Univ Ky Homemkr: McCracken Co Public Relats Intl Chm, Area Homemkrs Intl Chm; McCracken Co Homemkrs, Chm Intl Day, May 1977; Paducah Commun Col: Pres Wom's Clb 1977-78, Chm Beautification 1977-, Commun Chorus 1973-; W Union Bapt Assn, Mission Friends Dir 1978-79; Heath Mid Sch Band Boosters, Chm Celebrity Auction 1980; r/Olivet Bapt Ch: SS Tchr, VBS Ldr; hon/Paducah, Ky Duchess Awd 1978; Univ Ky Ext Homemkrs Assn Purchase Area Winning Essay "My Desire for Am in 1976", Mar 24, 1974 & "Pathways to a Better America", Apr 9, 1975; Finalist in Bon Appetit for the Holidays Contest, Nov 1980; Article Pub'd in *The Paducah Sun*.

ROACH, DIANE F oc/Civic Worker, Secretary; b/Dec 24, 1938; h/707 Oakwood Tr, Ft Worth, TX 76112; m/Herman B; c/Kimberly Ann; p/Charles R Forsythe, St Charles, MO; Bernadette Forsythe (dec); ed/Att'd Wichita St Univ 1957-69; pa/Bkkpr 4th Nat Bank, Wichita, KS 1959-60; Rest Mgr, Townhouse Motor Hotel 1961-62; Asst Mgr Hiway Inn Motel 1962-64; Secy Ctrl Typewriter Co 1968-70; cp/Ponca City Wom's Clb: Exec Bd Mem 1974-79, Pres 1977-78, VP 1976-77, Public Affairs Chm 1974-76, Parliamentn 1978-79, Past Pres's Luncheon Chm 1978, Yrbook Chm 1976-78, Prog Chm 1976-77, Num Other Ofcs; Jr Dept Benefit Dance Chm, Kay Co Yth Shelter 1977; Camp Fire Ldr 1970-76; PTA; Bd Ed Citizens; Adv Coun 1975-76; Bd Ed City-wide Sch Census Chm 1976; E Jr HS Parent's Adv Coun Secy 1977-78; Ponca City Tennis Clb, Bd Dirs 1977-79, Publicity Chm 1977-78; Panhellenic 1968-78; Delta Delta Delta; Repub Party Precinct Chm 1975-78; Marland Mansion Tour Guide 1975-77; U Way, Wom's Div Capt 1975-77; Area Chm for Cancer, Heart, Multiple Scolorsis 1974-78; En Hill's PTA VP 1979-80; Fort Worth Wom's Clb: Hospitality 1979-80, Clb Affiliation 93 Clb, Social Com 1979-80; Woodhaven Country Clb; r/Cath.

ROATH, GLENNEN DEAN (SLIM) oc/Chief of Police; b/July 27, 1922; ba/Vallaint, OK; c/Lessie E, Tommy Virgel, Patsy Louise, Rusty Lane, Wally D, Yonna Uvana, Dawen Caranela, Keno Nerveo, Kathy Jean; p/Lessie A (dec) and Perl Roath (dec); ed/USN SCS CCC 1939; Okla Univ; mil/USN 1941; pa/Chief of Police, Valliant, Okla.

ROBB, ROY KENT oc/Chief Probation Officer; b/Aug 19, 1943; h/Gatesville, TX; ba/G'ville; m/Kay; c/James Kent, Joel Glenn; p/Roy E and Virginia J Robb, Bluffton, TX; ed/BS Howard Payne Univ 1968; Master Corrects, Am Technol Univ 1976; pa/Chief Probation Ofcr, 52nd Judicial Dist of Tex; Tex Corrects Assn, Chm Probation Div 1976-79; Tex Probation Assn, Pres 1979-; cp/G'ville C of C, Bd Dirs 1977-78; r/Bapt.

ROBBINS, JAMES MARTIN oc/Company Vice President; b/Feb 24, 1948; h/2521 3rd St NE, B'ham, AL 35215; ba/B'ham; m/Joyce Conn; c/Lloyd E (dec) and Lora C Robbins, Paris, TN; ed/BSEE Univ Tenn 1970; pa/VP Engrg & Construction Activs; Instrucment Soc Am, Treas; cp/B'ham Amateur Radio Clb, VP; r/Meth; hon/Nat Hon Soc 1965; Golden Scroll 1966; 4-H Clb Ldrship S'ship 1966.

ROBBINS, VIOLA MAE oc/Associate Professor; b/Jan 14, 1914; h/666 College Dr, Abilene, TX 79601; ba/Abilene; m/Woodard; p/Kenneth, Gail Walker; p/O O (dec) and Alta West (dec); ed/BS 1954, MS 1960, MBA 1980 Abilene Christian Univ; pa/Ofc Mgr & Exec Acct,

Furr Food Stores, Lubbock, Tex 1934-36; Asst to Fiscal Agt, Abilene Christian Univ 1954-60; Assoc Prof Bus Abilene Christian Univ 1960-; AAUW, Treas 1964-70, Pres 1970-72; Am Acctg Assn; Am Bus Law Assn; Delta Kappa Gamma; r/Ch of Christ; hon/Grad summa cum laude 1954; F'ship Honoree, AAUW 1974.

ROBBINS, WAYNE LINDSEY oc/College Vice President; b/Jan 8, 1936; h/500 Plantation Ct V-2, Nashville, TN 37221; ba/Nashville; m/Faye Elaine Wellborn; c/Wayne L Jr; pa/J L and Arlena Wortham Robbins, Covington, TN; ed/BS Miss St Univ 1958; BD SWn Bapt Theol Sem 1963; MEd Univ Ark 1967; MDiv SWn Bapt Theol Sem 1973; EdD Univ Ark 1975; mil/AUS Capt; pa/VP Belmont Col 1976-; Dean Students, Chattanooga St Commun Col 1975-76; Dir Fed Progs, Tenn Dept Ed 1974-75; Press Rep to US Sen Bill Brock 1973-74; Staff Asst US Cong-man John Paul Hammerschmidt 1972-73; Press Secy US Sen Strom Thurmond of SC 1970-72; Asst to Dean, Col Arts & Scis & Hd Baseball Coach Univ Ark 1965-70; Dean Men, Bluefield Col 1963-65; Instr Riverside Mil Acad 1959-60; Profl Baseball Player, Balto Orioles 1958-59; AAUA; Phi Delta Kappa; cp/Lions Clb; Repub Party; r/Bapt; hon/W/W: S&SW 1980-81, Students in Am Cols & Univs 1956-57; Many Articles in Rel & Ednl Pubs.

ROBBINS, YVONNE O'FERRALL oc/Veteran Service Officer; b/July 22, 1924; h/Natchez, MS; m/Oliver L (dec); c/Oliver L Jr, Jacqueline Y; p/Laurence C (dec) and Marie J O'Ferrall, Natchez, MS; mil/USN WAVES; pa/Vet Ser Ofcr, Natchez/Adams Co; Adm Asst, Peace Corps, Thailand; Dpty City Clerk, Natchez; Dpty City Clerk, Williamsburg, Va; Municipal Clerks Assn of Miss; Miss Hlth Sys Assn; SW Adv Coun; Exec Com Inner Agcy Coun; cp/Ser Ofcr Am Legion Post #4; r/Cath.

ROBERSON, FRED MARSHALL oc/Maintenance Engineering; b/Sept 28, 1921; m/Mary Ella Apple; c/Marshall C, Kathy V R Stiles; ed/Var Voc Trg: Air Cond'g, Heating, GE Appliances, Bell & Gossett Pumps; mil/AUS; cp/Civitan; Moose; r/Luth.

ROBERTS, CHARLES VERNON oc/Soil Conservationist; b/Feb 25, 1950; h/1000 University Blvd, Apt B-5, Kingsport, TN 37660; ba/Blountville, TN; m/Brenda; c/TaJuan; p/Ray Roberts (dec); Frances Roberts Wilson, Nashville, TN; ed/BS Tenn St Univ 1972; pa/Soil Conserv Soc Am; cp/Lions Clb; Ky Col; JCs; r/St John AME Ch; hon/Lion of Yr; Beta Kappa Chi; 100% Secy Lions Dist 120.

ROBERTS, DONALD RAY oc/Public Printer; b/Sept 165, 1922; h/5710 Clark Circle, Mechanicsville, VA 23111; ba/Richmond, VA; m/Lucy Claire; c/Connie Rhea, Michael Allen, Kennith Reginald; p/Harper Basil (dec) and Birdella Rhea Roberts, M'ville, VA; ed/BS Md Univ; mil/Staff Sgt; pa/Public Printer, Commonwlth of Va; VAGP; CAPA; PIV; NIGP; r/Bapt; hon/Purple Heart; Bronze Star; 5 Major Battle Stars; Outstg Ser Awd, Fed Ser; Cert of Apprec, Pres Truman.

ROBERTS, EDWARD CLAIBORNE oc/Pastor, Business Insurance Executive, School Teacher, Evangelist; b/Mar 10, 1939; h/Charlotte, NC; ba/Calvary Apostolic Ch, 7501 Grier Rd, Charlotte, NC; m/Betty Jean; c/Atleatha, David, Debra, Lori; p/James F (dec) and Leatha Roberts, Flint, MI; ed/AB Univ Mich 1967; Dip Flint Bible Inst 1976; mil/USAF 1960-64; pa/Sch Tchr; Ins Exec; Pastor Calvary Apostolic Ch; Mich & Nat Ed Assns; r/Pentecostal; hon/Dist'd Salesman Awd, St Farm Ins 1972-74, 76-77; Life Ins Millionaire Clb 1977-78; Edward C Roberts Day Proclamation, City of Flint 1981.

ROBERTS, JAMES DEOTIS oc/Professor; b/July 12, 1927; m/Elizabeth Caldwell; ba/Atlanta, GA; c/Edin Charmaine, Carlita Rose, Kristina LaFerne; ed/AB magna cum laude Johnson C Smith Univ 1947; BD Shaw Univ 1950; BD Hartford Sem Foun 1951; STM Hartford Sem 1952; PhD Univ Edinburgh 1957; pa/Pastor, Union Bapt Ch, Tarboro, NC 1948-50; Min to Migrants: Conn 1951-52, Del & NY 1960-61; Asst Pastor, Union Bapt Ch, Hartford, Conn 1950-52; Dean Rel, Ga Bapt Col 1952-53; Asst Prof Phil & Rel, Dir Rel Life & Activs, Shaw Univ 1953-55; Pastor-ad-Interim, Radnor Pk Congreg Ch, Glasgow, Scotland 1956-57; Assoc Prof Phil & Rel, Col Min, Shaw Univ 1957-58; Instr-Prof, Hist & Phil of Rel & Christian Theol, Howard Univ Sch of Rel 1958-73; Dean Sch Theol, Va Union Univ 1973-74; Prof Theol & Editor *The Journal of Religious Thought* Howard Univ Sch of Rel 1974-; Co-Dir Annual Conf of Black Theol, Collegeville, Minn; Vis Prog Theol, So Bapt Sem 1976; Vis Prof Theol Sch Theol, Claremont, Calif 1978; Am Acad Rel; Biblical Theologians; Hon Regent & Life Fellow, Intl Sociol Res Inst; Cont'g Com on World Rels, Temple of Understanding, Theol Comm, Nat Com of Black Ch-men; Intl Neo-Platonic Assn 1974; Am Soc Christian Ethics 1976; Conslt on Black/African Sources for *Religious Studies Review* 1974-; Editorial Bd *Insight: A Journal of World Religions*; Bd Dirs Inst for Ecumenical & Cultural Res; Steering Com of the Liberation Theol Grp, Am Acad Rel; Bd Dirs Assn Case Tchrs in Rel/Theol; Am Theol Soc; Intl Soc Polit Psych; hon/Author Num Books, Essays & Articles.

ROBERTS, JOE DeKALB oc/Interior Designer; b/Nov 28, 1923; h/24 Northgate, Laurel, MS 39440; ba/Laurel; m/Joy Beard; c/Russell D, Joe M; p/S D (dec) and Josie T Roberts (dec); ed/Doct Cand; mil/AUS; pa/Insterior Desginer; Communs Conslt; Profl Mem ASID; Speech Commun Assn; cp/Rotarian; Shriner; r/Prot; hon/W/W Am Cols & Univs; Phi Kappa Phi.

ROBERTS, JOYCE ELAINE oc/Nurse; b/Jan 9, 1949; h/Rt 2 Box 101A, Morton, MS 39117; ba/Morton; m/Don; c/Don Jr; p/William C and Travis Elizabeth Kennedy, Morton, MS; ed/Dip Prac Nsg 1973; AA Meridian Jr Col 1976; Post Grad Hinds Jr Col 1975; Critical Care Nsg 1979; pa/Scott Co Hosp: Vol 1964, Nurses's Aid 1965, LPN 1973, RN 1976; Meridian Jr Col Alumni; r/Bapt; hon/W/W Am Wom 1979-80.

ROBERTS, MARY BELLE oc/Social Worker; b/Sept 27, 1923; h/PO Box 340955, Coral Gables, FL 33114; ba/Miami; p/Joseph Gill (dec) and Inez G Roberts, Silver Springs, MD; ed/BS, MSW Univ Mich; Att'd NY Sch Social Work; c/Cert'd Social Wkr, St Md; Clin Reg NASW; Life Fellow Royal Soc Hlth; NASW; ACSW; NCSW; cp/Immed Past Pres Altrusa Clb of Miami; Chm Combined Classified Wom's Ser Clbs of Dade Co; Gift of F'ship Fund, AAUW; DAR; USD of 1812; r/Christian; hon/Nat Hon Soc; Phi Kappa Phi; W/W Am Wom 1979-80; Yng Adult Ser Comm, NCF of Fla; Persistance Awd, Yng Adults of S Fla.

ROBERTS, MARY DIANE oc/Associate Professor; b/Jan 24, 1942; h/1101 Locust Ave SE, Huntsville, AL 35801; ba/H'ville; p/W M and Susan Johnson Roberts, Selmer, TN; ed/BS, MS Miss St Univ; DPH Univ Tex Hlth Sci Ctr; pa/Assoc Prof, Sch Primary Med Care, Univ Ala-H'ville; Am Soc Allied Hlth Profs; Am Public Hlth Assn; Soc Tchrs of Fam Med; Assn Tchrs Preventive Med; cp/VChm Madison Co CRD Hlth Coun; Pres N Ala Hlth Ed Coun; r/Epis; hon/W/W: Hlth Care 1978, Am Wom 1979.

ROBERTS, MARY POPE oc/Homemaker; b/Dec 25, 1893; h/703 W Third St, Radford, VA 24141; m/Henry T; c/Thomas Walker; p/Leonard Miles (dec) and Diana Pope (dec); ed/Tchrs Dip James Madison Col, Radford Univ 1913; cp/Wom's Clb of Radford, Pres 2 Yrs; Charter Mem DAR; Radford Gdn Clb, Charter Mem; r/Presb.

ROBERTS, NOBLE LEE (CORKY) oc/Paramedic, Nursing Student; b/June 9, 1949; h/PO Box 220, Gainesville, TX 76240; ba/G'ville; m/Leticia Laura; p/Noble Lee Hawkes Sr (dec); Dorothy Jean Roberts, Dallas, TX; ed/AS; mil/AUS; USAF; pa/Student Cooke Co Col; Skydiving & Scuba Diving Instr; VP CCC Student Nurse Assn; cp/Pres CCC Skydiving Clb; Secy VFW Post; r/Bapt; hon/Sonny Burdell Meml #28; Instr & Jumpmaster Ratings; 12 Hr Freefall Badge.

ROBERTS, ROBERT JOSPEH oc/Insurance Agent; b/Oct 8, 1948; h/105 Deepwood, Richmond, KY 40475; ba/Richmond; m/Katherine Cox; c/Joseph Phillip, John Hargrave; p/Joseph Hacker Roberts (dec); Lou Ellen Roberts Craft, Manchester, KY; ed/BS En Ky Univ; pa/Million Dollar Round Table; Nat Assn Life Underwriters; cp/Sponsor Spec Olympics for Retard'd Citizens; r/Epis; hon/Nat Quality Awd; Nat Sales Achmt Awd; Million Dollar Round Table; Fidelity Union Hall of Fame.

ROBERTS, SUSAN C oc/Associate Professor; b/June 6, 1945; h/Key Biscayne, FL; ba/Barry Col, 11300 NE 2nd Ave, Miami Shores, FL 33161; m/Norman T; p/dec; ed/BA Rollins Col 1966; MA Univ S Fla 1969; PhD Unvi Fla 1972; pa/Assoc Prof Ed, Barry Col; Coun Excptl Chd; cp/Key Biscayne Wom's Clb; Nat Coun Jewish Wom, Bd Mem; r/Jewish; hon/Nom'd W/W S&SW 1979-80; Nom'd Outstg Wom of Yr, Barry Col 1977; Author Num Profl Articles Incl'g "Helping the Emotionally Disturbed Child Feel Secure in the Classroom."

ROBERTS, TERRY WILLIAM oc/Executive; b/July 30, 1950; h/3800 Spring Val Rd #153, Addison, TX 75234; ba/Dallas; m/Vicki Ann; c/Amy Elizbeth, Ashley William Nash; p/William P and Bettye Marie Roberts, Whitewright, TX; ed/AA Richland Col 1977; mil/USMC 1967-69; pa/Advtg Acct Exec, WFAA Radio; cp/Addison City Coun-man 1976-; Addison Bus-man's Assn 1976-; Human Resources Coun; N Tex Coun Govt 1978-; Am Heart Assn, Bd Dirs 1978-; NW Dallas Co C of C 1975-; r/Presb; hon/Mayor Pro-tem 1977-78; Hon Life Mem C of C.

ROBERTS, WILLIA DEAN oc/Retired Teacher; b/Sept 17, 1907; h/1202 Wiley Ave, Marshall, TX 75670; p/Mr and Mrs William Kelly (dec); pa/Ret'd Am Hist Tchr; TSTA; NRTA; cp/Zeta Phi Beta; r/Bapt; hon/Author "The Attitude of Texas Toward Secession from 1845 to 1861."

ROBERTSON, DuBOSE oc/Concert Singer, Teacher, Pianist; b/Jan 7, 1920; h/N Charleston, SC; c/Edward, Phyllias; p/Olive Delk, Hilda, SC; ed/Spec Student, Peabody Conservatory of Mus 1945-49; Am Theatre Wing 1950-51; BA Bapt Col 1971; mil/1940-45; pa/Tchr Mus, Piano & Voice; Presently Touring w Mus of MacDowell & Foster, "DuBose Robertson's Musical Portrait of Victorian America"; hon/Recording w Allegro Records, Approx 40 Songs; One of 1st Singers in US to Concertize as Solo Singer w String Group 1976.

ROBERTSON, FRANK BARRY III oc/Trust Officer; b/Oct 3, 1951; h/Rt 1 Box 34A, Waynesboro, VA 22980; ba/Staunton; p/F Barry Robertson Jr, Deerfield Bch, FL; Mrs Raymond D Zelek, Huntington, NY; ed/BA Univ Va; pa/Trust Ofcr, First & Merchants Nat Bank; Est Plan'g Coun; cp/Va Student Aid Foun; Repub Party; r/Epis; hon/1st Team All-Am Lacrosse, Univ Va, MVP 1974.

ROBERTSON, HOWARD NORMAN oc/Factory Representative; b/Oct 6, 1922; h/146 Beechwood Dr, Hattiesburg, MS 39401; m/Marjorie; c/Diane R Murphy, Sheryl Leigh Glausier; p/Philip O and Ada Robertson; ed/BS Bus, Masters Public Adm, Univ Okla; mis/USAF Ret'd; pa/Commercial Pilot; Real Est Lic; cp/Mason; VFW; Ret'd Ofcrs Assn; DAV; GOP; Westlake Homeowners Assn; r/Presb; hon/Air Medal 2 OLC; Commend Medal 1 OLC; EAME Ser Medal; 3 Battle Stars; Vietnam Ser Medal.

ROBINETTE, BETTY L oc/Nurse Epidemiologist; b/Nov 24, 1941; h/750 Country Club Dr, Wytheville, VA 24382; ba/W'ville; m/Daniel G; c/Daniel Jr, Brian Louis, Lisa Diane; p/John H (dec) and Eva Crawford Brown (dec); ed/RN Va Bapt Hosp Sch Nsg; pa/Assn Practitioners in Infection Control, Nat, St, Local Grps; cp/Red Cross Bloodmobile Vol; PTA; OES; r/So Bapt; hon/W/W Am Wom 1979-80.

ROBINSON, ALFRED BARNETTE oc/Brick Mason; b/Feb 7, 1934; h/115-A College St, Holly Springs, MS 38635; ba/Holly Springs; c/Denise R Adams, Donna K, Christopher T, Lorette Young, Jeryl Denise, Alfred B Jr; p/dec; pa/Carpenter & Brick Mason.

ROBINSON, B LYNN oc/Author, Executive; b/Sept 16, 1951; h/255 SW 7th St #2, Boca Raton, FL 33432; ba/E Lansing, MI; m/Kenneth H; c/Joseph Paul, Sharon Sue; p/Lennart U and Louise U Gennerfeldt, Lansing, MI; ed/BMus Mich St Univ 1975; MEd 1976, EdS 1980, EdD 1981 Fla Atlantic Univ; pa/Editor's Asst, Mich St Univ 1969-70; Flute Instr, Lansing Conservatory of Mus 1970-73; Instrl Tchr, Mus for Am Inc 1974; Res Asst, Editor of Mnthly Newslttr, Ctr for Ec Ed, Fla Atlantic Univ 1976-77; Fdr, Pres Lynnco Pubs 1978-; Nat Assn Female Execs; Phi Delta Kappa; MENSA; r/Luth; hon/W/W Am Wom; Personalities of Am; Author: *Guidebook to Happiness* 1978; *Living with the Unknown: A Guide to Coping with Multiple Sclerosis* 1978; *The Art of Talking* 1979.

ROBINSON, BARBARA GENEVA BATTLE oc/Retired Dietitian; b/Dec 1, 1923; h/Tuskegee Inst, AL; m/Wilbur Ronald; c/Wilbur Jr, John Preston, Alfonso Gomez; p/Charles Tecumseh (dec) and Leana Johnnie Peters Battle (dec); ed/BS Howard Univ 1943; Cert Dietetic Internship Howard Univ Hosp 1945; pa/Dietitian, VA Hosp 1945-79; Chm Ed Com Ala Dietetic Assn; Tuskegee Dist Dietetic Assn, Pres 1976 & 80; cp/Delta Sigma Theta, Chapt Pres 1974; hon/Mother of Yr, Wash Chapel AME Ch 1976; Hon'd As First Outstg Internship Dir, Tuskegee Dietetic Internship Alumni 1976.

ROBINSON, DEBBIE JEAN oc/Medical Service Director; b/Jan 16, 1955; h/Gainesville, FL; ba/Univ Fla, Vet Med Tchg Hosp, Dir Med Record Services, Box J-105, G'ville, FL 32610; p/Robert W (dec) and Angela E Robinson, Casselberry, FL; ed/BS Univ Ctrl Fla 1978; pa/RRA, Med Record Sers Dir, Univ Fla Vet Med Tchg Hosp; Former Med Care Evaluation Com Asst & Med Record Analyst; Sunshine Med Records Assn, Archivist, Arrangements Com Chm 1980; cp/Zeta Tau Alpha Alumni, Pres 1980-81, VP 1978-79; Vol Pink Lady, Alachua Gen Hosp, G'ville, Fla; Vol Pink Lady, Winter Pk Meml Hosp, Orlando; r/Epis; hon/RRA 1980.

ROBINSON, EMMA LOU oc/Retired Businesswoman; b/May 23, 1925; h/PO Box 158, Falkville, AL 35622; m/James H (Buck); c/Martha Humphrey, Jimmy Barber, Kay Saint; p/Emmett W (dec) and Dollie B McNutt, Falkville, AL; pa/Ret'd Rest Owner; cp/1 of First Coun-wom of Falkville; Campaigned in Var St & Local Elecs; r/Bapt; hon/Hon JC; Pres Clb of Ala.

ROBINSON, FELIX D oc/Mayor; b/Nov 11, 1911; h/PO Box 510, Whitewright, TX 75491; m/Catherine M; c/Jimmy, Felix Delano, Peggy Jean Holmes; p/dec; ed/Tex Lic'd Funeral Dir 1945; Lib Sch Claims Investigation 1962; Universal Sch Claims Adjusting 1962; E Tex St Univ, Div Cont'g Ed; pa/Mayor, City of Whitewright; cp/Pres Garland, Tex Area Dem Clb 1962-72; Whitewright Rotary Clb 1978-; Whitewright C of C 1978-; r/Bapt; hon/Awd'd Plaque, Whitewright C of C for Outstg Citizen of Yr 1979-80; Awd'd Plaque, Garland Dem Clb for Sers Rendered 1962-72.

ROBINSON, MARION EVERETT oc/Brick Mason; b/July 12, 1922; h/Rt 1 Box 75, Jackson Gap, Al 36861; m/Virginia L; c/Deirtra, Valerie;

p/John Milton (dec) and Evelyna Hubbard Robinson (dec); mil/USN WWII; pa/Pastor Flint Hill Bapt Ch, Alexander City, Ala; Dean The Early Rose Dist SS & BTU Cong of Christian Ed; Dir Talla-Coosa Yth Conf; cp/Pres Alexander Chapt Ala Vols in Correction; r/Prot.

ROBINSON, RALPH EUGENE oc/Administrator; b/Aug 10, 1937; h/Rt 2 Midway Sch Rd, Silver Creek, GA 30173; ba/Rome, GA; m/Margaret; c/Stephen Christopher, Cynthia Anne; p/Charles V Robinson (dec); Dorothy Hawley, Erie, PA; ed/BA Geo Wash Univ 1973; MBA Berry Col 1980; mil/LCDR MSC USN Ret'd; pa/Admr, Floyd Home Hlth Agcy; Ret'd Ofcrs Assn; Ga Assn Home Hlth Agcys; r/Prot.

ROBINSON, RALPH ROLLIN oc/Gynecologist; b/July 7, 1913; h/322 Englewood Rd, Middlesboro, KY 40965; ba/M'boro; c/Mart Stuart, Kim Ella, Nanch Harriett, Ralph R Jr, Rachel Catherine; p/Walter S Robinson Sr (dec); Mary Emma Inslee; ed/Engrg Deg Okla St Univ 1935; MD Univ Wash Sch Med 1951; Univ Okla: Internship 1951-52, Resident Ob-Gyn 1952-55; Cert'd Am Bd Ob-Gyn 1962; pa/Miners Meml Hosp, M'boro 1955-59; Swedish Hosp, Seattle, Wash 1959-63; Pineville Commun Hosp, Pineville, KY 1963-75; M'boro Commun Hosp 1963-, Chief Staff 1974-75; Claiborne Co Hosp, Tazewell, Tenn 1963-; Gyn Med Clins: B'ham Wom's Med Clin, Mobile Wom's Med Clin, Vol Med Clin, Tenn, Jackson Wom's Med Clin, Miss; Conslt: Battelle Pacific NW Labs, Wyeth Labs, World Population Coun, Abbott Labs, Julius Schmid Inc; Maternal & Infant Care Proj, Bell Co, Ky; Diplomate Am Bd Ob-Gyn; Am Col Surgs; Am Col Ob-Gyn; Wash St Med Soc; Seattle Profl Engrs Soc; Seattle Gyn Soc; Pan-Pacific Surg Assn; Pan-Am Med Assn; So Med Assn; Am Soc Abdominal Surgs; Bell Co Med Soc; Inventor Intra-Uterine Birth Control Device, Saf-T-Coil; Num Other Inventions; Part in Sci Session, Fifth Nat Cong Iranian Gyns & Obs, Tehran, Iran 1967; Att'd First Intl Cong Gyn Laparoscopy 1973; r/Presb; Deacon; hon/W/W S; Intl Men Achmt; Royal Blue Book; Notable Ams; Intl W/W Commun Ser; Others.

ROBINSON, RONNY EARL oc/Pastor, Correctional Officer; b/May 26, 1946; h/Rt 2, Bogue Chitto, MS 39629; ba/Brookhaven; m/Gay Case; c/Kelly, Chris, Ken; p/Kenneth and Modena Robinson, Morgan City, LA; ed/BA Miss Col 1968; Grad Delinquency Control Inst 1971; pa/Pastor Mt Moriah Bapt Ch; Pre-Sentence Investigator, 14th Dist, Miss Dept Corrections; Past Chaplain & Pres Miss Juvenile Correctl Ofcrs Assn; r/So Bapt; hon/Law Day Awd for Outstg Commun Ser, Hinds Co Bar Assn 1973.

ROCKEFELLER, JOHN D IV oc/Governor of West Virginia; m/Sharon Percy; c/Jamie, Valerie, Charles, Justin; ed/Grad Phillips Exeter Acad; Att'd Intl Christian Univ, Tokyo, Japan 1957-60; BA Harvard 1961; Att'd Yale Univ; pa/Appt'd by Pres John F Kennedy to Nat Adv Coun of Peace Corps 1961; Spec Asst to Peace Corps Dir R Sargent Shriver 1962; St Dept Bur of Far En Affairs, Desk Ofcr Indonesian Affairs & Spec Asst to Asst to Secy of St for Far En Affairs; Pres's Comm on Juvenile Delinquency & Yth Crime 1964; Action for Appalachian Yth; Pres WV Wesleyan Col 1972; WV Ho of Dels 1966: Coms on Fin, Ed & Agric & Natural Resources; Elect'd Secy of St 1968; Chm White Ho Conf on Balanced Nat Growth & Ec Devel 1978; Hd Pres's Comm on Coal Indust 1978; Chm So Regional Ed Bd 1979; Elect'd Gov WV 1976-; cp/Past Bd Mem Com of 100; Trustee Univ Notre Dame & Univ Chgo; Past Bd Mem Rockefellor Foun; Visiting Com on E Asian Studies, Harvard Univ; r/Presb; hon/1st WVn Chosen by US JCs as 1 of 10 Outstg Yng Men Am; 1 of 12 Col & Univ Pres Chosen to Rep US in Visit to People's Repub of China 1974; Incl'd in *Time* Magazine's List of "New Generation of Ldrs"; Hon Degs: WVU; Marshall Univ, Univ Cinci, Univ Ala, Davis & Elkins Col, Salem Col, WV Inst Technol, Dickinson Col, Bethany Col, WV St Col; Father of Yr, Nat Father's Day Com.

ROCKWELL, STANLEY BALDWIN JR oc/Counselor; b/May 18, 1954; h/PO Box 2022, Williamsburg, VA 23185; ba/W'burg; m/Shelley Rae Rubenking; p/Stanley Baldwin Rockwell Sr; Marion Ann Martin; ed/BA 1976, MEd 1977, William & Mary; pa/Cnslr, Substance Abuse Unit, En St Hosp; Am Psych Assn; APGA; Assn Specs in Grp Work 1979-; Psych Res Asst, Dept Trg & Res, En St Hosp 1978-80; Res Asst, Social Skills Trg Proj, En St Hosp 1978, 79; Tutor, Adult Skills Trg Proj, Col William & Mary 1978; Tech, Ctr for Excell Inc 1977-78; Student Asst, TV Sers, Col William & Mary 1975-77; cp/Va Museum; Nat Wildlife Assn; r/Meth; hon/Vol Ser Awd, En St Hosp 1980; Author & Co-Author Num Pubs.

RODES, GEORGE RONALD JR oc/Program Director; b/Feb 16, 1956; h/12420 Sawmill Rd #82, The Woodlands, TX 27380; ba/Conroe, TX; p/George (dec) and Shirley Rodes, Houston, TX; ed/AA; BBA; pa/Prog Dir YMCA; Sigma Phi Epsilon; Sam Houston St Univ Skydivers; SHSU Rodeo Clb; cp/Blinn Col Student Body Pres; Circle K; r/Bapt; hon/Eagle Scout; Blinn Band S'ship; Blinn & SHSU Dorm Pres.

RODGER, PATRICIA J oc/Management Consultant; b/July 30, 1939;

h/Corpus Christi, TX; c/Kathryn Margaret, Elizabeth Ann; ed/BA Denison Univ 1961; MBA Cand Corpus Christi St Univ; p/Mgmt Cnslt, Pat Rodger Assocs; Am Mgmt Assn; Nat Assn Female Execs; cp/Pres Money Mgmt Cnslg & Sers; U Way, Plan'g Coun; r/Presb; hon/YWCA Nom Career Wom of Yr.

RODGERS, ERIC DONELL oc/Student; b/Aug 30, 1959; h/813 Glenrose Ave, Cookeville, TN 38501; p/T D and Wanda Faye Rodgers; ed/BS Univ Tenn-Knoxville 1981; mil/USAR 2nd Lt; pa/Grad Student; USAR Ofcr; Phi Delta Theta: VP, Warden, House Mgr; Gamma Beta Phi; ROTC Cadet Brigade Staff; cp/Vol: YMCA, Heart Fund; r/So Bapt; hon/Grad w Hons; Most Outstg Sr in Phi Delta Theta; Phi Deta Theta Ath of Yr.

RODGERS, JOHN H JR oc/Research Scientist, Assistant Professor; b/Feb 1, 1950; h/2524 Freedom, Denton, TX 76201; ba/Denton; m/Martha R; c/Daniel Joseph; p/John H and Connie T Rodgers, Clemson, SC; ed/BS 1972, MS 1974 Clemson Univ; PhD VPI & SU 1977; mil/USAFR Capt; pa/Clemson Univ, Botany Dept: Res Asst, Water Resources Inst 1972-74, Lab Tchg Assn, Phycology, Plant Ecology, Biol Oceanology, Botany 1972-74; Biol Dept, Ctr for Envirl Studies, VPI & SU: Res Asst, Am Elec Pwr Corp 1974-75, Res Asst Energy Res & Devel Adm 1975-77, Res Assoc 1977-78; Dept Envirl Scis, Aquatic Ecol Sect, E Tenn St Univ: Asst Prof 1978-79; N Tex St Univ, Inst Applied Scis, Biol Dept: Adj Asst Prof & Res Scist II 1979-; Cnsltg Aquatic Ecologist to Sch Public Hlth, Univ Tex 1977-; Grant Proposal Review for Div Envirl Biol of Nat Sci Foun 1978-; Cnsltg Aquatic Ecologist, Ctr for Envirl Studies, VPI & SU 1978-; NTU Rep to Tex Sys Natural Labs 1980-; Cnsltg Aquatic Ecologist to Victor Equip Co 1980-; Am Soc Limnology & Oceanography; Ecological Soc Am; Am Water Resources Assn; N Am Benthological Soc; Water Pollution Control Fed; Assn SEn Biol; Phi Sigma Soc, Alpha Psi Chapt; Sigma Xi; Am Inst Biol Scis; AAAS; hon/Num Res Asst'ships; Phi Sigma Doct Res Awd 1977; Sigma Xi Doct Res Awd 1978; W/W S&SW 1979; Author/Co-Author Num Profl Pubs.

RODGERS, KATHERINE VIRGINIA oc/Chemist; b/June 16, 1937; h/351 Lakeside Ln, Houston, TX 77058; ba/Houston; p/R D (dec) and Laurie Rodgers, Arkadelphia, AR; ed/BS; pa/Chemist NASA; Am Chem Soc; cp/Repub Party; hon/NASA Grp Achmt Awd; Outstg Yng Wom Am 1966.

RODGERS, LILLIAN SCOTTIE oc/Retired Postmaster; b/Oct 3, 1917; h/307 S Henderson St, Donalsonville, GA 31745; ba/Bascom, FL; c/Rodney Mike and Ronny Mack; p/Samuel M (dec) and Nellie Carolyn Cantrell Womack (dec); r/Free Will Bapt; hon/Hon'd by Bascom City Town Coun Upon Retirement.

RODRIGUEZ, CAROLYNE B oc/Program Specialist; b/Jan 9, 1947; h/PO Box 33131, San Antonio, TX 78233; ba/Austin; m/Homero; p/William B and Doreen Barton, Cocoa Bch, FL; ed/BA Univ Tex-Austin 1969; pa/Prog Spec, Tex Dept Human Resources, Ofc of Policy Plan'g & Evaluation 1980-; Social Sers Prog Conslt, Tex Dept Human Resources, Protect Sers for Chd Br 1979-80; Coor Support Sers, Ctr Battered Wom, 1978-79; Supvr Foster Home Devel, Tex Dept Human Resources 1974-78; Foster Home Devel Wkr, Travis Co Child Wel Unit 1970-74; Day Care Lic'g Wkr, Tex Dept Human Resources 1970; Social Sers Wkr 1969-70; Regional Advr, Nat Foster Parents Assn 1980-; Tex St Foster Parents Inc; cp/Adv Com, Austin Ctr for Battered Wom 1980-; Alpha Phi; r/Prot; hon/Commend for Recog of Outstg Ser to Chd of Tex 1978; Awd for Outstg Contbn to Commun 1979; Author Handbook for Vols, Ctr for Battered Wom 1978; Dir Devel of Foster Home Recruitment Brochures & Guidebook.

ROEVER, FREDERICK H oc/Physician; b/June 9, 1940; ba/1 E Valencia Dr, Newport Richey, FL 33552; m/Patricia Anne; c/Christopher Paul; p/Henry F and Irma S Roever, Holiday, FL; ed/BS Haverford Col 1962; MD Hahnemann Med Col 1968; mil/AUS Capt; pa/Chief, Dept Med, Tarpon Springs Hosp; Fellow Am Col Phys; AMA; Fla Med Soc; Christian Med Soc; Am Soc Internal Med; Undersea Med Soc; cp/VFW; Am Legion; Assn AUS; Mil Order World Wars; r/Luth; hon/Bronze Star; Air Medal; Combat Med Badge 1969; Vietnamese Hon Med 1969; Tchg Awd, Student Am Med Soc; Diplomat Am Bd Internal Med.

ROGERS, AUDREY LEA oc/Businesswoman; b/Nov 8, 1920; h/Rt 1 Box 179E, Oakland Acres, Somerville, TN 38068; ba/Oakland; m/James Presley; c/Jerry Leland Ryan; p/James Ronald (dec) and Eula M Ray, Somerville, TN; ed/Electrology Deg, Hoffmans; mil/WAC 4 Yrs; pa/Co-Owner Rogers Auto Sales; Cosmetologist; Notary Public; cp/Hist Soc; Dem Clb; Nat Radio CB Posse; OES; Cancer Soc; Past Pres Holland Kennel Clb; Past Pres W Mich Pet Assn; VP VFW Aux; hon/E Awd, Oakridge Atomic Indust; Hon Life Mem Air & Defense Team; Am Campaign Awd; WWII Awd.

PERSONALITIES OF THE SOUTH

ROGERS, GAINES MADISON oc/Dean; b/June 11, 1918; h/112 Grand Ridge Dr, Starkville, MS 39759; ba/Miss St; m/Betty Pollay; c/Cita R Pickett, Liza R Killough; p/James Duckworth (dec) and Alice Gaines Rogers (dec); ed/BS Clemson Univ; MA, PhD Univ Va; mil/1st Lt Signal Corps; pa/Prof Fin & Dean Col Bus & Indust, Miss St Univ 1968-; Prof Fin & Dean Sch Bus, Wake Forest Univ 1948-68; Bd Dirs Depositors Savings Assn; Past Mem Exec Com Am Assem Col Schs of Bus; Chm Constitution & By-Laws Com, AACSH; cp/Bd Dirs Miss Ec Coun; Rotarian; Past Pres So Bus Assn; r/Presb; hon/Beta Gamma Sigma; Phi Kappa Phi; W/W: Am, Am Col & Univ Admrs; Blue Book.

ROGERS, JAN FAULK oc/Library Coordinator; b/Feb 8, 1946; h/3028 Ga Hwy 16 W, Griffin, GA 30223; ba/Griffin; m/Robert L; c/Jana Lyn, Rebecca Lee; p/John Hughey Faulk Jr (dec); Edwina Faulk Cox, Chgo, IL; ed/BA, MS Fla St Univ; pa/Lib Coor, Bd Ed; ALA; GLA; GAE; cp/Girl Scout Ldr; Pres PTO; LWV; r/Presb; hon/Beta Phi Mu; Author *Georgia: Home of President Jimmy Carter & First Lady: Rosalynn Carter.*

ROGERS, KEITH RODNEY oc/Teacher; b/Sept 19, 1945; h/3907 N Pottenger, Shawnee, OK 74801; ba/Shawnee; m/Judith; c/Keith Ray, Karl; p/Otis R and Hazel K Rogers, Littleton, CO; ed/AA Casper Col; BA Idaho St Univ; BA Univ Okla; pa/Okla Dist Chm Nat Forensic Leag 1978-79, 79-80; NEA; OEA; cp/Layreader; Vestry; Shawnee Little Theatre; Okla Commun Theatre Assn; Dem Party; r/Epis; hon/Outstg Edr 1972-73; NFL Okla Dist Chm; Okla Speech Adv Bd; Coach of NFL Nat Boy's Ext Winner 1979.

ROGERS, LEWIS FRANK oc/Professor and Department Head; b/May 31, 1939; h/Rt 9 Box 286-A, Gainesville, GA 30501; ba/G'ville; m/Betty Carlisle; c/Kellie Elizabeth, Sean Lewis; p/Marion Dewitt (dec) and Birdie Mae Dement Rogers, Meridian, MS; ed/BS Univ So Miss; PhD Univ Ga; mil/USMC Lt Col; pa/Prof & Hd Geol & Physics Dept, G'ville Col; Chm Ga Regents Com on Geol; Pres G'ville Col Fac Senate; Phi Kappa Phi; Phi Delta Kappa; r/Meth; hon/Nat Sci Foun Grant for Adv'd Study, Univ Miss.

ROGERS, PAUL A'COURT oc/Senior Program Manager; b/Oct 12, 1939; h/6412 Forest Mill, Laurel, MD 20810; ba/Riverdale, MD; m/Cathy Green; p/Noel and Jessie Rogers, Santa Maria, CA; ed/BS Syracuse Univ; mil/USN; pa/Publicity Chm ASNE; AMA; NL & NI; cp/Bd Dirs MHC; r/Prot; on/W/W Fin & Indust.

ROGERS, REBECCA LAINE oc/Administrator; b/Sept 2, 1952; h/2200 Henry Rd, Anniston, AL 36201; ba/Anniston; p/W L and Myrthel Hill Rogers, Anniston, AL; ed/BS Jacksonville St Univ 1973; Adm for Nsg Home Admrs, Geo Wash Univ 1976; pa/Admr Golden Springs Nsg Fac; Ala Nsg Home Assn, Secy 1977-79, Peer Review Chm 1980, Conv Com & Ed Com 1980; Am Col Nsg Home Admrs; Nat Coun Hlth Care Assn; Am Acad Hlth Adm; cp/C of C; Chm Ala's Rock 'n Roll-A-Thon, Am Heart Assn; r/Bapt; hon/W/W: Hlth Care 1978, Am Wom 1979-80.

ROGERS, SHELBY M oc/Headmistress; b/Aug 17, 1937; h/Rt 7, Statesboro, GA 30458; m/Harold E Sr; c/Harold E Jr; p/Mr and Mrs D C Mixon (dec); ed/BS Ga So Col; Adv'd Study Univ Fla, Fla St Univ, Univ So Fla; pa/Public Sch Tchr, Ga & Fla; Hdmistress Pathway Day Sch 4 Yrs; Lwr Sch Dir, Bulloch Acad 1 Yr; Hdmistress Bulloch Acad 1980-; r/Prot.

ROLLO, F DAVID oc/Professor, Executive; b/Apr 15, 1939; h/Louisville, KY; ba/Humana, 1800 First Nat Tower, PO Box 1438, L'ville, KY 40201; m/Deane; c/Mindee; p/Frank C and Augustine Rollo, Endwell, NY; ed/BS Harper Col 1959; MS Univ Miam 1965; PhD Johns Hopkins Univ 1968; MD Update St Med Ctr 1972; mil/USARNG Capt; pa/Prof Radiology, Vanderbilt Univ Med Ctr 1977-; Spec Nuclear Med & Ultrasound; VP Adv'd Med Technol & Med Affairs; Res Conslt, Johns Hopkins Univ, Applied Physics Lab 1969-; Res Conslt, Univ Tex Med Br 1972-; Conslt: Searle Radiographics Inc 1974-, Picker Corp, Nuclear Med Div 1975-, Union Carbide Med Diagnostics Div 1975-, Letterman Army Med Ctr 1974-; Dir Nuclear Med Div 1977-; Assoc Dir Radiological Scis 1977-; Dir Med Sers, VA Hosp Nashville 1979-; Prof Radiology & Radiological Scis, VA Hosp Nashville 1979-; Am Math Soc; Assn Physicists in Med & Biol; Hlth Physics Soc; Soc Nuclear Med; Students of AMA; Nat Assn Residents & Interns; Am Col Nuclear Phys; Assn Univ Radiologists; Am Col Radiologists; Radiological Soc N Am; Quality Assurance Com, Am Col Nuclear Phys; Manuscript Reviewer: *Am Jour Radiology, Journal Nuclear Med, Jour Physics in Med & Biol*; Chm Quality Control Com Instrumentation, Soc Nuclear Med 1977-; Vanderbilt Univ: Radiolgy Resident Select Com, Hosp Med Bd, Chm Radioisotope Com, Radiology Res Com, Lib & Tchg Com, Grad Ed Com, Radiolgy Speace Com, Handicap Adv Com, Chm Clin Res & Drug Com, Clin Res Ctr Adv Com, Clin Res Ctr Adv Com, Med Sch Admissions Com, Chm Clin Radioisotope Com, MIS Com; Prog Chm SEn Chapt Soc of Nuclear Med; Num Other Orgs & Coms; cp/St Bernerd Sch Bd; Chm L'ville Gymnastics Assn; r/Rom Cath; hon/ACS Awd in Chem, Broome

Tech Commun Col 1957; Am Math Soc Awd, Harper Col 1958; Phi Theta Kappa; F'ship Univ Miami & Johns Hopkins Univ; Outstg Yng Men Am 1971; Am Men & Wom in Sci 1972; W/W Calif 1974; Bronze Med Sci Awd, Soc Nuclear Med 1975; Num Res Grants; Dist'd Alumnus Awd, Broome Tech Commun Col 1976; Outstg Tchr Awd in Radiology, UCSF 1974-75, 75-76; Num Other Hons; Author/Co-Author Num Profl Pubs.

ROMERO, DUDLEY M oc/Executive; b/Nov 26, 1942; h/332 Wentworth Blvd, Lafayette, LA 70508; ba/Lafayette; m/Rexine B; c/Stephen, Stephanie, Sharon; p/Ophe Romero, Abbeville, LA; Ada M Griffin (dec); ed/BA; MBA; pa/Hosp Assoc Exec VP; ACHA; Yng Admrs LHA; Pers Socs; cp/Past Pres Pius Ath Assn; PTA; Booster Clb; r/Cath; hon/COE Boss of Yr 197273; Fire & Safety Awds.

RONE, DENNIS B oc/Evangelist; b/Nov 30, 1954; h/PO Box 586, Raleigh, MS 39153; ba/Raleigh; p/R G and Betty Rone, Somerville, TN; ed/Grad Memphis Sch Preaching; pa/Radio Spkr for "The King is Coming"; r/Ch of Christ.

RORSCHACH, MARTHA KAY KING oc/Instructor, Horse Breeder; b/July 14, 1938; h/Kilgore, TX; m/Richard G; c/Stepch: Richard H, ReaganC, Andrew M; p/Issac Monroe Jr and Jessie Faye Latham King, Trinity, TX; ed/Att'd Baylor Univ 1956-58; BA SMU 1961; MA Stephen F Austin St Univ 1972; pa/Fashion Designer, Higginbotham-Bailey Mfg Co; Lang Arts Tchr, Groveton HS; Instr Art & Fashion Mdsg, Kilgore Col; Oper Shadowbrook Farm, Arabian Horse Breeding; Arabian Horse Clb of Tex, VP & Dir; E Tex Fine Arts Assn, Pres; Tex Jr Col Tchrs Assn; Tex Jr Col Mgmt Edrs Assn; Dir City Nat Bank of Kilgore; VP & Dir Little River Drilling Co; cp/Beta Sigma Phi City Coun, Pres; Vol Am Cancer Soc; Mar of Dimes; Commun Concerts Assn; r/Presb; hon/Nat Hon Soc 1956; Miss Waco 1957; 2nd Place Miss Tex Finals; Kappa Pi 1971; Outstg Yng Wom Am 1972; Ky Col 1978.

ROSADO, ELMA B oc/Technical Consultant; b/Jan 31, 1954; h/Box 1020, Vaga Baja, PR 00764; ba/Hato Rey, PR; m/Pedro J Panzardi; p/Rafael and Maria Barbosa Rosado, Arecibo, PR; ed/BS Univ PR 1976; pa/Tech Conslt, Fernando L Rodriguez & Assocs 1981-; Chem Roche Prods Inc 1976-80; Res Asst PR Nuclear Ctr 1976; Res Asst Univ PR 1973-75; AIChE; AWIS; AAUW; hon/W/W Am Wom 1981-82.

ROSE, CLARENCE C oc/Assistant Professor; b/Nov 5, 1948; h/40 Washington Ave, Radford, VA 24141; ba/Radford; m/Jean H; c/Jennifer, Donald; p/Clarence C (dec) and Rita T Rose, New Haven, MI; ed/BS Ferris St Col 1972; MBA Ctrl Mich Univ 1974; PhD Cand Va Tech; mil/USN 1966-69; pa/Asst Prof, Dept Bus, Radford Univ 1977-; Instr, Dept Mgmt, Ferris St Col 1974-77; Spec Agt & Agcy Mgr, NWn Mutual Life Ins Co 1972-74; Am Soc Public Adm; cp/Big Rapids Little Leag, Pres, VP, Team Mgr 1970-77; Big Rapids JCs 1975-77; r/Cath; hon/Ferris St Col Vet's Scholastic Hon Soc 1970-72; Author "Bureaucracy Expresses Itself" *Social Science Quarterly* 1981.

ROSE, MARY ANN McCARTHY oc/Teacher; b/Jan 16, 1942; h/Greenville, NC; m/Walter J Pories; c/Susan Pories, Mary Jane Pories, Carolyn Pories, Kathleen Pories, Lisa Pories, Michael Pories; p/John F and Margaret Heckel McCarthy, Rocky River, OH; ed/BSN Georgetown Univ 1963; MSN Case Wn Reserve Univ 1974; EdD NC St Univ 1981; pa/Tchr Grad Studies in Nsg, ECU; Assoc Dir The Cancer Ctr, Cleveland, OH; NLN; Soc Sigma Xi; Sigma Theta Tau; Phi Kappa Phi; Am Soc Clin Oncology; Oncology Nsg Soc; Am Public Hlth Assn; hon/Helen Lathrop Bunge Awd 1974; Num Contbns to Profl Jours.

ROSENBAUM, BILLY WAYNE oc/Chief Deputy Sheriff; b/Sept 21, 1949; h/Brenham, TX; ba/PO Box 786, Brenham, TX 77833; p/Lee Roy and Bernice H Rosenbaum, Brenham, TX; ed/AA Blinn Jr Col 1970; BS Sam Houston St Univ 1972; Cert Law Enforcement, HSU 1972; Adv'd Cert, Tex Comm on Law Enforcement, Ofcr Standards & Ed 1977; pa/Chif Dpty Sheriff, Wash Co Sheriff's Dept 1971-; Dpty Sheriff, Wash Co 1972-76; Charter Mem Wash Co Peace Ofcrs Assn, Pres 1978; Nat Sheriff's Assn; Sheriff's Assn of Tex; cp/Brenham Vol Fire Dept; Wash Co Child Wel Bd; Wash Co Softball Assn, Past VP & Dir; SHSU Alumni Assn; r/Luth; hon/Law Ofcr of Yr 1978, Brenham JCs.

ROSS, BERNEATHA DANTZLER oc/Educational Director; b/Nov 2, 1928; h/925 W 1st N St, Summerville, SC 29483; ba/Ridgeville, SC; m/Arnold M Dantzler; c/Jade D Fisher, Barbara R Baylock; p/Simuel T (dec) and Annie G Ross (dec); pa/Ednl Dir, Child Devel Resource Conslt, Co of Dorchester Child Devel Ctr; r/Prot; hon/Trophy for Tchr-Made Tchg Mats; Silver Plate Awd for Most Supportive Trainee; Silver Plate Awd for Most Congenial Trainee; Rec'd Best All-Round Trophy of Trainees of 3 Cycles of Proj Task 1978-80.

ROSS, EDWIN STUART oc/Hospital Administrator; b/Apr 22, 1943; m/Pamela Lee Snyder; c/Edwin Stuart, Stephen Eric, Sarah Johanna; p/Edwin Stuart and Mary Christine Hickey Ross, New Hyde Pk, NY;

PERSONALITIES OF THE SOUTH

ed/EdB Univ Dayton 1965; MEd Univ So Calif 1976; mil/AUS 1965-77 Maj; pa/Med Adm Ofcr, Med Ser Corps, Atlanta, Ga 1965-66; Asst Chief Med Supply & Ser, Darnall Army Hosp, Ft Hood, Tex 1969-72; Procurement Ofcr Fitzsimmons Gen Hosp, Denver, Colo 1972-73; Chief Med Supply AUS Hosp, Okinawa, Japan 1973-76; Asst Dir Logistics, Acad Hlth Scis, San Antonio, Tex 1976-77; Dir Ctrl & Unit Supply, Univ Tex Med Br; Chm Indust Liaison Com & Bd Dirs Am Hosp Assn's Soc for Hosp Ctrl Ser Pers; Bd Dirs Tex Hosp Assn's Soc for Ctrl Ser Pers; Bd Govs Mats Mgmt Assn of Hlth Care Facilities, Chm 1979; Nat Hosp Purchasing Mgmt/Mats Mgmt; Houston Soc for Ctrl Ser Pers, Chm Bd Govs 1979; Cert'd Profl in Hlth Care Mats Mgmt, Intl Mats Mgmt Soc; Conslt & Lectr on Mats Mgmt, Surg Case Cart Sys, Quality Assurance & Records Keeping; Reserve Instr Mid-Mgmt, Galveston Col; Reserve Instr, Sch Allied Hlth Scis, Univ Tex Med Br; cp/Reg'd Referee, US Soccer Fed; hon/W/W S&SW 1980; Bronze Star, Merit Ser Medal; Humanitarian Ser Medal; Army Commend Medal; Parachutist Badge; Author Num Profl & Mil Pubs.

ROSS, ERNIE oc/Artist, Manager; b/Feb 21, 1947; h/Pulaski, VA; m/Mary W; c/Loren Faith; p/Arland (dec) and Mary Frances Ross (dec); mil/USN; pa/Mgr Medicine Man Jeans; hon/Scholastic Gold Key Arts Awd; Best in Show for Art, Pulaski, Va; Best In Show Dublin, Va; Best Artist in Narrows, Va; Peoples Choice Awd SW Va 1979; Painting Owned by Ted Kennedy.

ROSS, HEZEKIAH oc/Pastor, Fireman; b/Mar 10, 1929; m/Lelia Mae; c/Rosalyn Elaine; p/George (dec) and Ella Ophelia Ross (dec); ed/Bethune Cookman Col; mil/AUS; pa/Pastor W Sanford Free Will Holiness Ch; Exec VP Good Samaritan Home Inc; Bd Dirs U Way Seminole Co; cp/Chm Black Div U Way of Seminole Co; Chm Black Div Am Cancer Soc; Grievance Com Sanford Housing Auth; r/Prot; hon/Cert of Recog for Commun Ser, Alpha Kappa Alpha.

ROSS, JEFFREY KEITH oc/Minister of Youth; b/Jan 28, 1957; h/4853-T Homestead Terr, Kansas City, MO 64151; ba/Kan City; m/Linda Sue; p/Roy Jack and Virginia Ross, Winchester, KY; ed/BA William Jewell Col; MDiv Cand Mid-Wn Bapt Theol Sem; pa/Campus Christian Mins; Ch Yth Mins; r/So Bapt; hon/H I Hester Awd William Jewell Col.

ROSS, KENNETH oc/Attorney; b/July 26, 1945; h/Longview, TX; ba/Box 3106, Longview, TX 75605; c/Jennifer, Marian, Justin; p/Finley and Mary Ross, Joinerville, TX; ed/BS 1967, JD 1969 Baylor Univ; pa/Sharp, Ward, Ross, McDaniel & Starr, Attys; Gregg Co Bar Assn, Pres 1973; cp/LeTourneau Col Trustee; Dir E Tex Treatment Ctr; Baylor Univ Devel Coun; Kiwanis Clb of Longview, Pres 1974-75; r/Bapt.

ROSS, NELL TRIPLETT oc/Teacher, Businesswoman; b/Feb 14, 1922; h/2738 McConnell Dr, Baton Rouge, LA 70809; ba/Baton Rouge; m/William Dee Jr; c/William Dee III; p/Ethel Earl (dec) and Myrtie Harrison Triplett, Mentone Plantation, MS; ed/BA, Dip Public Sch Mus Millsaps Col; pa/Secy, Ptnr Mentone Plantation Partnership; Co-Owner Financial Cnsltg Sers Inc; Elem & HS Tchr; cp/Patron Delta Debutante Clb; Wom's Aux Baton Rouge Symph; Campus Clb, La St Univ, Past Pres; Chi Omega Alumnae Assn of Baton Rouge, Past Pres; La Arts & Sci Ctr Guild; Friends of Anglo Am Art Mus; Bd Mem YWCA; Foun Hist La; Kappa Alpha Dames Clb; PTA; Cub Scout Den Mother; Rotary Ann; Baton Rouge Country Clb; Camelot Clb; Former Mem: Piedmont Clb, Bocage Clb, Knife & Fork Clb; r/Meth; hon/Commun Ldrs & Noteworthy Ams, World W/W Wom; DIB; Nat Soc Dir 1974-79.

ROSS, SANDRA LYNN oc/Coronary Care Supervisor; b/July 18, 1950; h/502 Denim Dr, Erwin, NC 28339; ba/Erwin; c/Christie Ann; p/Floyd Carpenter, Havre de Grace, MD; Bonnie Larche, Buies Creek, NC; ed/Dip St Agnes Sch Nsg; pa/RN; Mobile Intensive Care Nurse; Coronary Care Supvr; Coor-Dir Hosp Co Adv'd Life Support Prog; Instr EMT & Intermediate Paramedic Progs; ARC Bd Mem; Spec Olympics Bd Mem; cp/Assn Retard'd Citizens; JCettes; r/Cath; hon/Spec Olympics Vol Awd 1979-80; ARC Outstg Citizen Awd 1981; Erwin C of C Wom of Yr 1980-81.

ROSS, WILLIE HERMAN SR oc/Minister; b/June 15, 1934; m/Edith Altanease Lane; c/Teresia, Eleanor, Willie H Jr, Christopher, Sterlin, Sanita, Gary, Rhoda, Hilda; p/Jesse J Ross Sr, Houston, TX; Ellen Marie Legington (dec); ed/USAF Non-Comm'd Ofcrs Ldrship Acad 1959; Valdosta Tech Sch 1973-75; Ga Mil Col 1976-77; Bryany's Theol Sem 1977-78; mil/USAF 1952-72 Ret'd; pa/Fire Suppression Engr; Rescue & EMT; Bapt Min; Pres 11th Dist Conv of Gen Missionary Bapt Conv of Ga Inc; VP Thomasville Bapt Assn; Pres Lowndes Co Mtl Hlth Assn; cp/Public Relats Ofcr for Local Chapt NAACP; VChm Local Chapt SCLC; Cand Mayor Valdosta 1980; r/Bapt; hon/Plaque for Outstg Support in Singing, New Hope Bapt Ch Male Chorus 1979; Plaque Providence Bapt Ch Yths for Outstg Ldrship 1973; Awd, Camp Relitso for Christian Ed; 3rd Pl Trophy DECA, St of Ga 1975.

ROTH, WILLIAM STANLEY oc/Executive Vice President; b/Jan 12, 1929; h/341 Laredo Dr, B'ham, AL 35226; ba/B'ham; m/Hazel Adcock; c/R Charles, W Stanley; p/Sam Irving (dec) and Louise Caroline Martin Roth (dec); ed/AA Asheville-Biltmore Jr Col 1948; BS UNC 1950; mil/USNR 1947-52; pa/Dpty Regional Exec Nat Coun BSA 1953-65; Exec VP Am Humanics 1965-67; Dir Devel, Bethany Med Ctr, Kansas City, Kan 1967-74; Exec VP Geisinger Med Ctr Foun, Danville, Penn 1974-78; Exec VP Foun, Bapt Med Ctrs 1978-; Nat Assn Hosp Devel, Past Nat Pres; Nat Soc Fund Raising Execs, KC Area Chapt Pres, Ala Chapt Pres; Am Soc Hosp Public Relats Dirs, Regional Dir & Nat Nom'g Com; Am Acad Hosp Public Relats; Kan City Area Soc Hosp Public Relats Dirs, Past Pres; Kan City Area Hosp Assn, Public Relats Chm 5 Yrs; Mid-W Hlth Cong, Public Relats Chm 3 Yrs; Mid-Am Hosp Devel Dirs, Past Pres; Hosp Assn Penn, Polit Action Adv Com; NAHD Ednl Trust, Pres; cp/Alpha Phi Omega, Nat Pres 4 Yrs, Nat Exec Bd 1950-80; Rotary Clb, Danville, Penn, Pres; Am Red Cross, Bd Dirs; YMCA, Bd Dirs; U Fund, Civic, Hlth & Wel Chm; BSA, St Chm of Ldrship Devel, Mem Coun Exec Bd, Regional Com & Nat Coun; Delta Upsilon Frat, Chapt Pres & NC Alumni Pres; r/Presb; hon/Nat Dist'd Ser Awd, Order of Arrow; Nat Dist'd Ser Awd, Alpha Phi Omega; Dpty Chief Intl Gilwell Woodbadge Trg; Order of Golden Fleece; Order of Holy Grail; Nom US Jr C of C, Nat's 10 Outstg Yng Men; Fellow Nat Assn Hosp Devel; 1972 Nat Public Relats Awd Hlth & Wel Mins; 15 Other Nat & Regional Awds Devel & Public Relats; W/W: Hlth Care, S&SW; Editor *Torch and Trefoil* 1960-61.

ROTHENBERG, IRWIN Z oc/Laboratory Manager; b/Feb 17, 1944; h/Memphis, TN; ba/Crittenden Meml Hosp, 200 Tyler St, W Memphis, AR 72301; p/Alex and Tillie Rothenberg, Hollywood, FL; ed/BS Brooklyn Col, CUNY 1965; MS Colo St Univ 1969; MT Good Samaritan Sch Med Tech 1974; pa/Staff Tech, Carl Hayden Commun Hosp 1974; Adm Technol, McKee Med Ctr 1974-79; Lab Mgr Crittenden Meml Hosp 1979-; Colo Soc Med Technols, Pres Elect Denver Chapt 1978; Colo Med Tech Rep to St PSRO 1977-78; ASMT; Phi Kappa Phi; Sigma Xi; ASC; Clin Lab Mgrs Assn; cp/Larimer Co Voc-Tech Sch Adv Bd 1976-78; r/Jewish; hon/W/W S&SW 1980-81; Author "Summary of Microbial Research in Antarctic" *Antarctic Journal* 1968.

ROTHGEB, RICHARD PRICE oc/Personnel Administrator; b/Nov 21, 1941; h/1710 Winfore Ct, Miolothian, VA; m/Susan McCarn; c/Joseph Wall, Michael Price; p/Clark Martin and Jenetta Price Rothgeb, Richmond, VA; ed/Assoc Commerce 1973; Bach Commerce 1974; MBA Univ Richmond 1977; mil/Va ANG 1964-70; pa/Pers Admr, Retreat Hosp 1973-; Am Soc Pers Admrs; Am Soc Hosp Pers Admrs; Va Assn Hosp Pers Admrs, Treas 1978, Secy 1979, VP 1980; cp/Charter Mem Miolothian JCs, Treas 1975; r/Meth; hon/Shotzberger S'ship 1973; Nat Evening Sch S'ship 1974.

ROUSE, BISHOP C JR oc/Process Engineer; b/Dec 4, 1948; h/Rt 1 Box 230-A, Shelby, NC 28150; ba/Shelby; m/Minnie L; c/Claudia, Bishop III, Kafi; p/B C Sr and Lula W Rouse, Bamberg, SC; ed/BS Allen Univ 1971; pa/Fiber Industs Inc 1973-; cp/Waco Elem Sch PTO, Pres 1980-81; Burns Jr HS PTO, VP 1981-82; Wash Elem Sch Cub Scouts, Cub Master 1979-81; Cleveland Co Sch Adv Coun 1980-82; Cleveland Co Comm for Wom 1980-82; Fiber Industs Basketball Team, Coach 1980-81; Wash Bapt Ch Softball Team, Coach 1979-81; Wash Bapt Ch Trustee 1981-83; r/Bapt; hon/Citizenship Awd for Outstg Sers to Waco Sch Commun 1981; Cert of Apprec, Outstg Ser to Boyhood, Cub Scouts 1981; W/W Black Ams 1981; Outstg Yng Men Am 1980; PTO Awd for Outstg Ser as Waco Schs PTO Pres 1981; Greatest Coach Awd, Ch Softball Team 1979; Tchg Associateships, Ohio St Univ, VPI, Howard Univ; Karate Tourn Winner, Charlotte, NC 1977; Missionary, Honolulu, HI 1968; CSUI-ANL Hons Prog, Argonne Nat Lab 1971; Highest Awd of Achmt, Dale Carnegie 1977.

ROWE, WILLIE LUCILLE REED oc/Painter; Teacher; b/Sept 12, 1914; h/Box 1473, Ft Stockton, TX 79735; ba/Ft Stockton; M/Henry Hilliard; c/John Hilliard, Mary Sue R Miller Lowe; p/William Austin (dec) and Lucille Lincecum Reed, Goliad, TX; mil/Editor "Film News", New Orleans Port of Embarkation; pa/Painter; Etcher, Tchr, Restorer of Paintings, Riggs Meml Mus; Former Asst Curator of Art, The Cabildo; cp/Ft Stockton C of C; r/Epis; hon/W/W Am Art 1962; W Tex C of C Art Achmt Awd.

ROY, ELSIJANE TRIMBLE oc/District Judge; b/Apr 2, 1916; h/Riviere Apts, Little Rock, AR 72203; ba/Little Rock; m/James M; c/James Morrison; p/Thomas Clark and Elsie Jane Walls Trimble; ed/JD Univ Ark 1939; pa/Admitted to Ark Bar 1939; Atty Ark Revenue Dept, Little Rock 1939-64; Mem Firm Reid, Evrard & Roy, Blytheville, Ark 1947-54; Roy & Roy, Blytheville 1954-63; Law Clk Ark Supreme Ct, Little Rock 1963-65; Assoc Justice 1975-77; US Dist Judge, E&W Dist of Ark 1977-; Judge Pulaski Co Circuit Ct 1966; Asst Atty Gen Ark 1967; Sr Law Clb US Dist Ct, Little Rock & Ft Smith 1968-73; Ark Bar Assn; AAUW: Pres Little Rock Chapt 1939, 42; Nat Assn Wom Lwyrs; Ark Wom Lwyrs, Pres 1940-41; Mortar Bd; PEO; Chi Omega; cp/Med Adv Com Univ Ark

262

Med Ctr 1952-54; Com-Wom Dem Party 16th Jud Dist 1940-42; V-Chm Ark Dem St Com 1946-48; Chm Com Ark Constitl Comm 1967-68.

ROY, JOHNNY BERNARD oc/Urologist; b/Jan 21, 1938; h/11400 N Barnes, Okla City, OK 73120; ba/Okla City; m/Sandy; c/Jennifer Anne; p/Bernard B and Regina V Saka Roy, Okla City, OK; ed/Dip Baghdad Col 1956; MD Univ Baghdad Col Med 1962; pa/Asst Prof Univ Okla Col Med; Chief Urology, VA Med Ctr, Okla City; Former Chief Urology Kaiser Foun Hosps of Hawaii; Former NIH Res Fellow, Univ Okla Med Ctr 1970-71; Pres Okla Urol Assn; Am Urol Assn; AMA; So Med Assn; Am Col of Surgs; Intl Col Surgs; Soc Univ Urols; Am Fertility Soc; Okla St Med Assn; Okla Co Med Soc, Editorial Bd; cp/Pres Nat Kidney Foun of Okla; Repub Party; r/Roman Cath; hon/AMA Phys Recog Awd 1969; W/W S&SW 1980; 20 Articles in Med Jours; 6 Exhibs Presented to Med Convs.

ROYALL, JAMES LEE JR oc/Eductional Administrator; b/Feb 11, 1944; h/Gatesville, NC; m/Valerie Virginia; c/Malita B; p/James L Sr and Helen Royall, Portsmouth, VA; ed/BS Norfolk St Univ 1970; MA Hampton Inst 1972; Adv'd Study Old Dominion Univ 1974; EdD Col William & Mary 1978; mil/Army ROTC Norfolk St Univ 1964-66; pa/Ednl Admr: Va Bch City Schs, Norfolk St Univ, Paige Day Care & Child Devel Ctr of Gtr Tidewater, Child & Fam Sers, Adj Asst Prof, Tidewater Commun Col, Jones Col, Roanoke Chowan Tech Col, Gates Co Public Schs; Nat Assn Ed of Yng Chm; NC Assn Supervision & Curric Devel; cp/Caliver Manor Civic Leag; Dem Party; r/Bapt; hon/Awds: Miss NC Teen 1980, City of Norfolk Public Schs 1977, Rainbow Ed Sch 1978, Paige Day Care & Child Devel Ctr of Gtr Tidewater 1978, Spec Olympics Prog 1979-80, Tidewater Chapt Am Red Cross 1979, Public Sch Gates Co 1980; Author Wkly Column in *Journal and Guide* Newspaper "Parent's Survival/Raising Your Kinds Without Losing Your Kool!"; Author Sev Handbooks and Guides for Tchrs & Parents.

RUBIN, MARVIN ALEXANDER oc/Engineer; b/Oct 17, 1921; h/1321 Grey Oak, San Antonio, TX 78213; ba/San Antonio; m/Edith; c/Glenda R Kane, Jan R Newland; p/Frank Rubin (dec); Gussie Finesilver Bryant, San Antonio, TX; ed/Tex Mil Inst 1939; BS Mich St Univ 1942; BS Ind Ist Technol 1956; mil/USMC 1942-45, 50-51; pa/Pres Marvin A Rubin & Co Proj Devel Conslts; VP Proj Devel La Quinta Motor Inns Inc; VP, Prin Ptnr Travis Braun & Assoc Conslltg Engrs; Asst to VP, Engrg, Mo, Kan & Tex RR Co; Am Assn Cost Engrs; Construction Specification Inst; Tex Soc Solar Engrs; Intl Soc Solar Engrs; Precast Concrete Inst; r/Jewish; hon/Paper in 'The Revised Proceedings of the Dept of Energy's Solar Update" 1978; Prepared & Presented Paper PCI Conv 1977 & DOE Sponsored Sems 1978.

RUBY, RALPH JR oc/Professor; b/Apr 11, 1944; h/Jonesboro, AR; ba/Box 2534, St Univ, AR 72467; p/Ralph (dec) and Justine Ruby (dec); ed/BS 1969, MS 1972 Univ Tenn; EdD Univ Mo 1975; mil/USNR 1961-67; pa/Prof Ark St Univ; Am Voc Assn, Life Mem; Delta Pi Epsilon; Kappa Delta Pi; Phi Delta Kappa, Life Mem; Nat Bus Ed Assn; So Bus Ed Assn; Ark Bus Ed Assn; Ark Voc Bus Ed Assn; Phi Beta Lambda; Nat Assn Tchr Ed for Bus & Ofc Ed, Life Mem; r/Bapt; hon/EPDA Awd 1973-74, 74-75; Author Sev Books & Contbr to Profl Jours.

RUCINSKI, CAROLE ANN BROWN oc/Zone Licensing Manager; b/Sept 6, 1942; h/Marietta, GA; m/Kenneth J; p/Harold William Brown (dec); Ann Theiss, Middleburgh Hgts, OH; ed/Capitol Univ w/out Walls 1978-79; pa/Zone Lic'g Mgr, Franchise Sales, McDonald's Corp 1972-; Owner Big Red Q Quickprinter Ctr 1979-; Nat Assn Female Execs; Am Soc Profl & Exec Wom; cp/Cobb Co C of C; Providence Corners Civic Assn; r/Cath; hon/W/W: Am Wm, S&SW; Career Wom of Wk, Charleston, WV 1970.

RUDLER, GARRY WILLIAM oc/City Manager; b/Sept 28, 1945; h/504 R N St Benadict, Stanton, TX 79782; ba/Stanton; m/Marie; c/Sherri Hylene, Krysti Lynelle, Beth Nicole, Bradley Essex, Kimberly Dyonne Angelina Maria; p/dec; ed/Maple Woods Col 1973, 76; Flo Val Col 1978-79; mil/1963-70; pa/Asst Dir Public Works, N Kan City, Mo 1972, 76; Dir Public Works, Wapato, Wash 1977; City Mgr, Stanton, Tex 1977; Am Public Works Assn Tex City Mgmt Assn; r/Bapt; hon/Resolution of Apprec, Mayor & City Coun of N Kan City, Mo 1977.

RUETER, W G (BILL) oc/Executive; b/Nov 21, 1936; h/1101 Genimi Dr, Austin, TX 78758; ba/Austin; m/Patricia A; c/John David, William Matthew Franklin; p/John W (dec) and Geraldine Rueter, Waco, TX; ed/AS San Antonio Col 1957; BS Univ Tex Austin 1959; MS New Mex Highlands Univ 1965; PhD Tex A&M Univ 1976; pa/Math Instr Tex Public Sch; Chm Math Dept, Proj Dir Tex St Tech Inst; Dir Occupl Progs & Dean Instr, Austin Commun Col; Pres Systematic Sers Inc; Math Conslt; Tex Tech Soc, Bd Dirs; Phi Delta Kappa; Tex Jr Col Tchrs Assn; Am Tech Edrs Assn; cp/Sch Bd Connally Public Schs; Pflugerville Ath Booster Clb, Pres; PTA; r/Assem of God; hon/Nat Sci Foun Grant 1964; Outstg Edrs of Am 1970; Var Articles in Profl Jours.

RUMMEL, LeVERA YVONNE oc/Student; b/Mar 10, 1960; h/PO Box 147, Copperas Cove, TX 76522; ba/Blue Mountain, MS; p/Gus and Audrey Evans Rummel, Copperas Cove, TX; ed/BS Cand Blue Mtn Col 1982; pa/Key Punch Oper, Ctrl Tex Col Summer 1979; Proofer Gateway Graphics Inc Summer 1980; Future Bus Ldrs of Am 1974-78, VP, Hist; FHA 1975-77, Secy; FTA 1975-78; Am Home Ec Assn 1979-80; r/Bapt; hon/W/W Voc & Tech Students in Am 1977; Grad Top 15 % of Class 1978; 4 First Pl Awds in Art & FHA Shows; Over All Best of Show, Art 1980; Grand Prize in FHA Show 1978.

RUPNICK, WALTER J oc/Executive; b/Nov 30, 1921; h/2037½ Garnet Ave, San Diego, CA 92109; c/Carol Dian, Walter Jr; p/dec; mil/USN; pa/Chm of Bd & Pres; cp/Lions Clb; San Diego C of C; r/Cath; hon/W/W.

RUSCH, HERMANN GREGORY oc/Chairman, Chef; b/Sept 26, 1907; h/13 Colman Dr, Louisburg, WV; m/Violet; c/Gregory, Ronald (dec), Preston, Christopher; p/Arnold and Emilia Rusch; pa/The Greenbriar: Exec Chef Steward 1955, Exec Food Dir 1957-78, Chm Greenbrier Culinary Prog 1978-; Profl Career Europe: Hotel D'Espagne St Croix, Vaud; Jungfrau & Victoria, Interlaken, Switz; Bauer au Lac, Zurich, Switz; Kulm Hotel, St Moritz, Switz; Casino, Bale, Switz; Kulm Hotel, Arosa, Switz; Semiramis in Cairo, Egypt; Palace Hotel Lausanne, Switz; Mena House, Pyramid, Egypt; Exhib in Stockholm, Sweden; Meurice in Paris, France; Appt'd Chef Steward for Swiss Pavillon, World's Fair, NY 1939-40 by Swiss Govt; Chef Steward USA: Selmonico Hotel, NYC 1940; Villa Margherita, Charleston, SC 1941; Whitman Hotel, Miami Bch, Fl 1942; Belmont Plaza Hotel, NY 1942-47; Lexington Hotel, NY 1947-55; The Greenbrier, White Sulphur Springs, WV 1955-; Supvg Chef, USA Olympic Com: Melbourne, Australia 1955; Pan Am Games, Chgo, Ill 1959; Winter Olympic Games, Squaw Val, Calif 1960; Olympic Games, Rome, Italy 1960; Pan Am Games, Sao Paulo, Brazil 1963; Winter Olympics, Innsbruck, Autria 1964; Olympic Games, Tokyo, Japan 1964; Chm Food & Housing: Pan Am Games, Winnipeg, Can 1967; Winter Games, Grenoble, France 1968; Olympic Games, Mexico City 1968; Dir Food Sers Num Olympic Games 1971-80; Ofcr of Les Amis D'Escoffier; Bd Govs Am Culinary Fed; Corres Mem Culinary Acad France; Chm Chef de Cuisine Assn of Am; Hon Mem: Epicurian Clb, London, Circle de Chef de Cuisine, Bern, Switz, Intl Chef's Assn, Vatel Clb, NY, Brit Culinary Assn, Oesterreichischer Kochverbank; French Culinary Acad; Am Nat Coun on Hotel & Rest Ed; Num Other Profl Orgs; hon/Gold Medal: ZIKA Intl Exhib, Zurich 1930 & Expostione de Albergheiri, Rome, Italy 1932; 5 Times Winner Grand Prix, Nat Hotel Expostion, NY; 2 Times Winner Prize of Hon, Nat Hotel Exposition; Winner DeBand Awd 1956; Recip First Otto Gentsch Gold Medal 1959; Ky Col 1958; Rec'd First Caesar Ritz Awd, Soc Bacchus 1966; Winner Grand Prix for The Greenbrier; Hon Citizen of WV 1971; Cit from US Olympic Com for Dist'd Ser Rendered to 5 Olympiads 1973; Recip Diplome d'Honneur 1973; Num Other Awds & Hons; Author Num Cookbooks.

RUSHING, IRVIN WILLIAM JR oc/Director; b/Oct 26, 1930; h/Corsicana, TX; ba/Navarro Col, Div Sci & Math, Corsicana, TX 75110; m/Maude A; c/John Mayfield, Abigail Lucille; p/Irvin W and Lucile B Rushing, Corsicana, TX; ed/BA 1951, MA 1953 E Tex St Univ; Grad Study Univ Okla, Penn St Univ, Colo St Univ, Baylor Univ, Stephen F Austin St Univ; pa/Dir Div Sci & Math, Navarro Col; Sci Edr: Talco HS, Plainview HS, Athens HS, Navarro Col; CUEBS, St Pres 1976; NSPI, Pres Elect Tex Chapt; Tex Jr & Commun Col Tchrs Assn; Editorial Bd Am Inst Bio Sci Ednl Jour 1977 & 78; Intl Cong Indiv Instr; r/Christian; hon/Poster Presentation at Windsor, Can Meeting of Intl Cong for Indiv Instr; Prod'd 78 Video Tapes in Biol, Chem & Human Anatomy 1976-80.

RUSHTON, JAMES DENNIS oc/Consulting Engineer; b/Mar 5, 1941; h/201 Tanner Rd, Taylors, SC 29687; ba/Greenville, SC; m/Judith E; c/Ellison Elaine, Angela Claire, James Dennis Jr; p/Dennis F and Clara F Rushton, Greenwood, SC; ed/BS Clemson Univ 1963; MBA Furman Univ 1972; Master Engrg Clemson Univ 1977; PhD Univ Idaho 1980; pa/Staff Engr, J E Sirrine Co 1979-; Indep Conslt 1976-78; J E Sirrine Co: Chem Dept Proj Engr & Asst Hd Chem Sect 1969-74, Process Staff Engr 1975-76; Sr Process Engr, Suntide Refining Co 1969; Dept Proj Engr, Chem Sect of Process Dept, J E Sirrine Co 1965-68; Process Engr, Olin Corp 1963-65; AIChE; Tech Assn Pulp & Paper Indust; Nat Assn Corrosion Engrs; cp/Sertoma Intl; r/So Bapt; hon/Author/Co-Author Num Profl Pubs.

RUSNAK, SHARON DALE SMITH oc/Program Assistant; b/Oct 12, 1949; h/965 N Patrick Henry Dr, Arlinton, VA 22205; ba/Reston, VA; m/Stefan Lee; p/Randolph Brooking and Mary Lou Beavan Smith, Pikeville, KY; ed/BA Berea Col 1971; MA Geo Wash Univ 1980; pa/Congman Carl D Perkins, US Ho of Reps: Ofc Mgr 1977-80, Secy 1971-76, Summer Employee 1967-70; Prog Asst to Exec Dir Nat Dance Assn, Conslt for Elem Ed, AAPHERD 1980-; Metro Dance Assn; Nat Dance Assn AAHPERD; Sacred Dance Guild; r/Meth; hon/Ky Col 1974.

PERSONALITIES OF THE SOUTH

RUSS, BLANCHE AUDREY oc/Executive Director; b/Nov 21, 1931; h/7374 Timberbreek, San Antonio, TX 78227; ba/San Antonio; m/Linwood F; c/Audrey Irene Dove, Linwood C; p/Edward (dec) and Irene Jones, Scotland Neck, NC; ed/BA; MA; pa/Exec Dir; r/Bapt.

RUSSELL, DORIS SUE oc/Homemaker; b/Dec 24, 1934; h/8600 Hickory Hill Ln SE, Huntsville, AL 35802; m/James W; c/Susan Ann Hajarizadah, Linda Carol, Sherri Diane; p/Bruce E and Thelma Whitley McAlpin, Heflin, AL; ed/BS Jacksonville St Univ 1957; cp/Magna Charta Dames; Col Dames XVII Century, Treas, Col Walter Aston Chapt; DAR, H'ville Chapt; Tenn Val Geneal Soc; Am Red Cross; PTA; Madison Co Chapt Jacksonville St Univ Alumni Assn, Past VP, Secy-Treas; Kappa Delta Pi; r/Calvery Bible Ch; hon/Danford Foun Awd 1953; Ala St 4-H Achmt Awd 1950; Hereditary Reg of USA 1977, 78; Contbr to *The George Whitley Family 1974, Abbeville County Family History 1979.*

RUSSELL, GAIL YVONNE oc/Instructor; b/June 5, 1955; h/Morehead, KY; ba/Univ Breckinridge Sch, Univ Blvd-MSU; Morehead, KY 40351; m/Donald F; p/F Howard Wright, Louisville, KY; Shirley N Klotz, Guston, KY; ed/BS Morehead St Univ 1977; pa/Instr Ed, Morehead St Univ, Tchr Univ's Model Sch; NSTA; cp/Advr Delta Gamma; Phi Kappa Phi; Harvest Fest Beauty Pageant Prodr; r/Prot; hon/CWENS Hon Sorority; Outstg Teenager of Am 1973.

RUSSELL, GRACE JARRELL WILLIAMS oc/Writer, Artist; b/July 4, 1924; h/709 Wade Hampton Rd, Dyersburg, TN 38024; ba/D'burg; m/Henry E; c/Margaret Lill Rudolph, Rose Ellen Weiner, Henry E III, Stephen A, Betty Grace Houser; p/Aubrey H Williams, Memphis, TN; Lill Jarrell Williams (dec); ed/BA Lambuth Col, SMU 1946; pa/Writer; Artist; Tour Host to Europe & Mid East; Pres Nat Leag Am Pen Wom, St of Tenn 1980-82; Pres SEn Jurisdiction Dist Supts Wives 1966-67; Conf Susanna Pres 1972; cp/Wom's Clb; Ch Wom U; PTA; Delta Delta Delta; r/U Meth; hon/NLAPW Chd's Story Prize 1978; World Meth Conf Fam Min Exch 1963; Del to Reopening of City Road Chapel, London 1978; Observer World Meth Conf 1981; Author *Rings and Things* 1971; *Hope in My Heart* 1978; *Lets Look at Love, Explore* 1979; Newspaper Column in Sev Papers.

RUSSELL, JIMMIE DANIEL oc/Director of Bands; b/May 27, 1943; h/1307 Crow, Waco, TX 76705; ba/Waco; m/Margaret Sowell; c/Andrea Lynn, Jonathan David; p/Jesse D Russell (dec); Celia John Boles Russell Wood, Weslaco, TX; ed/BMus N Tex St Univ 1969; MMus Tex A&I Univ 1973; mil/USN 1960-64; pa/Tex Mus Edrs Assn; Tex Bandmasters Assn; NAJA; NARD; cp/Lions Clb; Masonic Lodge; Karem Shrine Temple, Dir Shrine Band; r/Ch of Christ; b/Outstg Tchr, La Vega HS 1978-79.

RUSSELL, JUDY oc/Computer Programmer; b/Oct 3, 1946; h/Jasper, AL; ba/Drummond Coal Co, 101 Walston Br Rd, Jasper, AL; m/Phillip; c/Jerry, Scott; p/George (dec) and Ruby Burton (dec); ed/Att'g Jefferson St Col; pa/Computer Programmer Drummond Coal Co; Corresp Secy NSA; Secy Sardis Ch of Nazarene; cp/NSA; DPMA; PTA; r/Prot; hon/Secy of Yr 1980.

RUSSELL, MARY LOUISE oc/Retired Nurse; b/Dec 20, 1916; h/107 E Shandon, Midland, TX 79701; m/Joe T; c/Shirely Todd, Richard V, Joann, Mary Lou, Joe T Jr, Esther Diane; ed/RN 1937; pa/Ret'd Nurse in Fields of Indust, Ofc, Surg, Sch, Public Hlth, Red Cross; Am Red Cross;

Tex Public Hlth Assn; ANA; r/Cath; hon/Commun Nurse of Yr 1980; 35 Yr Pin, Am Red Cross 1979.

RUSSOM, JAMES RAYFORD oc/Minister; b/Dec 9, 1949; h/Bethany, OK; ba/4501 N Meridian, Okla City, OK 73112; m/Susan Theresa Smith; c/Mark Stephen; p/Rayford Pinkney and Leola Jane Briley Russom, Memphis, TN; ed/Att'd Trevecca Nazarene Col 1967-68; AA Nazarene Bible Col; Cert'd Nat Bible Col Am; Further Study Glendale Grad Sch Theol 1974, Wn Grad Sch of Ch of Growth; Att'g Bethany Nazarene Col; mil/Cadet USAF-CAP 1964-67; 1st Lt USAF; pa/Pastor Ch of the Nazarene 1971-; NW Okla Dist Ch of Nazarene, Dist Pres Nazarene Yth Intl; Regional Coun SW Region Nazarene Yth Intl, Dist Ch Growth Com, Dist Christian Life Bd, Chm Nazarene Fam Nite at Six Flags Steering Com; cp/Spec Mayor's Com 1975; W Long Bch Comun Action Comm 1974-76; r/Prot; hon/St Rep for St Tenn USAF-CAP Cadet Div; Fed Aviation Orientation; Billy Mitchell Achmt Awd 1967; Ch Growth Awds: So Calif Dist Ch of Nazarene 1975, NW Okla Dist Ch of Nazarene 1979-80; Author Yth Musical "A Reason to Sing" 1971; Spec Wkshop Pub "Drama Puppetry and Ventriloquism in the Local Church" 1978; "Spiritual Gifts Wkshop" 1979.

RYAN, ALICE LEE oc/Director Physical Therapy; b/Aug 14, 1943; ba/St Vincent's Infirmary, Phys Therapy Dept, W Markham & Univ Ave, Little Rock, AR 72204; m/James A; c/John Patrick; p/Leo F and Alice M Farney, Little Rock, AR; ed/BS Nazareth Col 1965; Cert Phys Therapy, Army Med Field Ser Sch 1965; pa/Phys Therapist, AMSC USA 1966-67; Staff Phys Therapist St Vincent Infirm 1967-68; Dir Phys Therapy, St Vincent Infirm 1968-; Ark Chapt Am Phys Therapy Assn: Pres, VP, Secy-Treas; cp/Secy Sch Bd; St Vincent's Ladies Aux, Secy-Treas, VP, Pres; r/Rom Cath; hon/W/W Cols & Univs 1965.

RYAN, BARBARA JEAN oc/University Administrator; b/Dec 16, 1934; h/Rt 5 Box 378, Guthrie, OK 73044; ba/Edmond; p/L J and Edith B Ryan, Broken Arrow, OK; ed/BS; MS; EdD; pa/Univ Admr, Inst Res; Assn Inst Res; Am Coun Ed; Am Assn Higher Ed; AAHPE; NEA; Am Ednl Res Assn; AMA; Am Assn Sports Med; Nat Ctr for Higher Ed Mgmt Sys; N Ctrl Assn Schs & Cols; AAUP; Pres's Coun Yth Fitness; Delta Psi Kappa; Ctrl St Cols & Univs Coop Res Grp; So Dist Assn Hlth & PE; Okla Assn Hlth & PE; OEA; Higher Ed Alumni Coun Okla; Okla Heart Assn; Okla Assn Col & Univ Bus Ofcrs; Home Ec Assn St Conv; Okla Ext Homemakers Coun; Changing Role of Wom Conf, Okla St Univ; Okla Assn Affirmative Action Ofcrs; Okla Pers Assn; cp/C of C; Higher Ed Alumni Coun of Okla; hon/W/W: Am Wom, Am Wom of S; Heart Assn Merit Awd; Recip Ser Grant, Cardiovascular Physiology Inst.

RYMER, BOBBIE NELL oc/Nurse; b/Mar 10, 1931; h/Rt 3 Box 560-6, Granbury, TX 76048; m/William Norman; c/Janice Lanelle Ray, Floyd Daniel, William Frank, Gilbert Daryl; p/Elbert Daniel Sowell, Granbury, TX; Lola Myrtis Wellborn Sowell (dec); ed/RN; pa/TNA; ANA; NLN; cp/Govtl Affairs Com, Chm for Dist 37 TNA; r/Bapt; hon/W/W Am Wom.

RYMER, WILMA oc/Businesswoman; b/May 16, 1928; h/Cleveland, TN; m/Hubert; c/Sherry Lynn Scoggins, Kimberly R Solomon, Hubert; /Leroy Stiles, Chattanooga, TN; Ethel Partin Stiles (dec); pa/Owner Rymer Handbags 1969-; r/Holiness; hon/Chosen for Story Pub in *Life Styles* Thanksgiving Edition 1980.

PERSONALITIES OF THE SOUTH

S

SABAINI, DAVID DARRELL oc/Director of Radio; b/Mar 3, 1954; h/Radford, VA; ba/WVRU Radio, Box 5794, Radford Univ, Radford, VA 24142; m/Kathleen; c/Angela; p/Silvio J Sabaini, Oak Brook Terr, IL; ed/BS 1976, MS 1979 Ill St Univ; pa/Radio/TV Critic *Decatur Herald & Review;* Station Mgr, Instr, WJMU, Millikin Univ; News Reporter WSOY-AM/FM, Decatur, Ill; Dir Radio, Radford Univ; Am Bus Commun Assn; Speech Commun Assn; cp/Former Speech Writer for St Atty's Cand; r/So Bapt; hon/Outstg Yng Men Am 1980; S'ship for MS Deg.

SAENZ, JOSE RAYMUNDO oc/Educator; b/May 6, 1948; h/4214 Patrick, Corpus Christi, TX 78413; ba/Corpus Christi; c/Kara Christine; p/Felix C and Maria Del Carmen Larrasquitu De Saenz, Brownsville, TX; ed/BA Tex A&I Univ 1971; MA Univ Chgo 1975; pa/Dir Outreach & Mobilization, Nueles Co MH-MR Commun Ctr 1971-73; Therapist, Fam Cnslg Ser 1976-77; Fac Del Mar Col 1977-; Pvt Prac, Clin Social Wkr, Psychotherapy Conslt 1975-; Del Mar Ed Assn, Chm Leg Com 1979-80; Tex Jr Col Tchrs Assn; NASW; Tex Chapt NASW; Corpus Christi Grp Psychotherapy Soc; Am Grp Psychotherapy Assn; cp/Vol Action Ctr, VP of Bd, Exec Com, Ex Dir Search Com; Instituto De Cultura Hispanica Bd, Chm Cultural Progs Com; r/Cath; hon/W/W S&SW 1979; Intl Men Achmt 1980; Cert Outstg Contbn to Public Ed 1979; Dir Dist'd Ams.

SAENZ, ROGER oc/Bank Vice President; b/Apr 18, 1952; h/1422 Virginia, Kingsville, TX 78363; ba/Alice, TX; m/Velma L; c/Roger Damian, Edward Daniel; p/Daniel and Lydia G Saenz, Alice, TX; ed/BS Indust Engrg; MBA; pa/VP Alice Nat Bnk; Am Inst Indust Engrs; Am Assn MBA Execs; cp/K of C.

SAFFELS, MICHAEL AARON oc/Minister, Social Worker; b/Oct 26, 1953; h/Box 322, 2825 Lexington Rd, Louisville, KY 40206; m/Catherine Angelyn Jones; p/George Aaron and Anna Wayne Saffels, Attalla, AL; ed/BS Univ Ala 1974; MDiv So Bapt Theol Sem 1980; pa/Social Wkr I, Commonwlth Ky, Dept Human Resources, Bur Hlth Sers 1979-; Min Mus, Parkwood Bapt Ch 1978-79; Satellite Coor, DeKalb Ctr, Cherokee-Etowah-DeKalb Mtl Hlth Ctr 1975-76; Mlt Hlth Wkr, Aftercare, Cherokee-Etowah-DeKalb Mtl Hlth Ctr 1974-75; cp/Ft Payne JCs, Chap 1975-76; Indep Voter; r/So Bapt; hon/Nat Merit Finalist 1971; Alumni Hons S'ship, Univ Ala 1971-74.

SAFLEY, JOHN WILEY JR (SKIP) oc/Artist; b/1549 NW 37th, Okla City, OK 73118; ba/Same; m/Kara Burney; p/John Wiley and Betty Sue Safley, Rocky Mt, NC; ed/BA Duke Univ 1975; MEd Univ Tex 1976; pa/Owner & Oper Prismatic Reflections Glass Studio; Am Craft Coun; Stained Glass Assn Am; r/Presb; hon/Num Showings Incl'g 1-Man 3 Mo Show at Okla Hist Soc Mus 1980-81.

SAHAI, HARDEO oc/Statistician, Educator; b/Jan 19, 1942; h/Calle I, D-25, Ciudad Universitaria, San Juan, PR 00931; ba/Mayaguez, PR; m/Lillian; c/Amogh; p/Sukhdeo Prasad and Roopwati Srivastava, India; ed/BS Lucknow Univ 1962; MS Banaras Hindu Univ 1964; MS Univ Chgo 1968; PhD Univ Ky 1971; pa/Assoc Prof, Dept Math, Univ PR 1976-; Vis Res Prof, Dept Statistics & Applied Math, Fed Univ Ceara (Brazil) 1978-79; Conslt PR Univ Conslt Corp 1977; Res Investigator, Water Resources Res Inst, Univ PR 1975-76; Statistical Conslt, PR Driving Safety Evaluation Proj 1973; Asst Prof, Dept Math, Univ PR 1972-76; Mgmt Scist, Mgmt Sys Devel Dept, Burroughs Corp, Detroit, Mich 1972; Res Asst, Dept Statistics, Univ Ky 1969-71; Tchg Asst, Dept Statistics, Univ Ky 1968-69; Statistical Programmer, Chgo Hlth Res Foun, Chgo Civic Ctr 1968; Statistical Programmer for Cleft Palate Ctr, Univ Ill 1967; Statistician for Res & Plan'g Div, Blue Cross Assn 1966; Asst Statistical Ofcr, Durgapur Steel Plant (India) 1965; Lectr Math & Statistics, Banaras Hindu Univ 1964-65; Inst Math Statistics; Bernoulli Soc Math Statistic & Probability; Biometrics Soc, En N Am Region; Indian Statistical Assn; Am Statistical Assn; hon/Govt of India Merit S'ship; Univ of India Merit S'ship; Banaras Hindu Univ Medal; Univ Chgo F'ship; Am Men & Wom Sci; W/W S&SW; Num Contbns to Profl Jours.

ST CLAIR, HELEN ALLISON oc/Executive Director; b/July 23, 1932; h/102 Meadowlane, Rt 3, Lake Cavalier, Jackson, MS 39213; ba/Jackson; m/Fred Weems Sr; c/Loyce Anne, Fred Weems Jr, Thomas Reid; p/Mrs George M Allison, Stevenson, AL; ed/Univ Ala, Univ Va; pa/Supvr Camp Lejeune Ofcrs Wives Sitting Ser; Tchr Prince William Co Schs, Va; Exec Dir Miss Optometric Assn; Intl Assn Optometric Execs, VP, Pres-Elect, Pres, Past Pres 1981; Am Soc Assn Execs; Am Public Hlth Assn; cp/Ctrl Miss Chapt Bd Dirs Am Red Cross; Miss Coun on Aging 1976-80, VChm; Ctrl Miss Sub Area Coun; Miss Hlth Sys Agcy; Hlth Ed Promo, Grp Mbrship Chm; r/Meth; hon/Bd Dirs So Col Optometry 1979; Author "Life is Worth Seeing" 1979; Contbg Editor *Southern Journal of Optometry* & *Mississippi Optometrist* 1976-.

ST CYR, CORDELL JOSEPH oc/Staff Engineer; b/Aug 22, 1939; h/11518 Mullins Dr, Houston, TX 77035; ba/Houston; m/Lora A Lefler; c/Cynthia, Jacqueline, Christopher, Randall, Brian; p/Harold J and Jennie Lee Richard Devillier; ed/Att'd La St Univ; mil/AUS 1961-64; pa/Pipeline Sys Analyst, Monterey Pipeline Co 1967-71; Sys Analysis, Design & Energy Conservaton Spec, Ofc Bldgs Arch & Engrg, Exxon Co 1971-; Assn Energy Engrs, Pres Houston Chapt; Am Soc Heating, Ventilating & Air Cond'g Engrs; cp/Repub Party; r/Cath; hon/Outstg Grad'g Mus Student 1957; Outstg Grad'g Student Cartographic Drafting, AUS Engrs Sch; Outstg Grad'g Sr, La St Univ; Am Soc Civil Engrs Annual Awd, St of La.

SALE, TOM S III oc/Professor and Administrator; b/July 27, 1942; h/PO Box 1365, Ruston, LA 71270; ba/Ruston; m/Liza; c/Thomas, Jennifer, Sarah; p/Thomas S Jr and Mary Belle Sale, Haynesville, LA; ed/BA Tulane Univ 1964; MA Duke Univ 1966; PhD LSU 1972; pa/Prof Investments & Bank Mgmt & Admr, Dept Ecs & Fin, La Tech Univ; Dallas Assn Investment Analysts; So Ec Assn; r/Epis; hon/Omicron Delta Kappa; Beta Gamma Sigma; Author Num Profl Articles.

SALYER, KENNETH EVERETT oc/Plastic Surgeon; b/Aug 18, 1936; h/3600 Gaston Ave, Suite 1157, Dallas, TX 75246; m/Shaaron Kaye Steeby; c/Kenneth Everett Jr, Amy Leigh; ed/BS Univ Mo-KC 1958; MD Univ Kan Sch Med 1962; Parkland Meml Hosp: Intern 1962-63, Gen Surg Residency 1963-66, Sr & Chief Resident Gen Surg 1966-67; Surg Fellow, Univ Tex, SWn Med Sch 1965-67; Plastic Surg Residency, Univ Kan Sch Med 1967-68; Chief Resident in Plastic Surg, Univ Kan Sch Med 1968-69; pa/Univ Tex SWn Med Sch: Asst Prof Surg & Chm Div Plastic Surg 1969-73, Assoc Prof Surg & Chm Div Plastic Surg 1973-78, Prof Surg & Chm Div Plastic Surg 1978; Pvt Pract, Kenneth E Salyer MD & Assocs PA 1978-; Active Att'g Staff, Chd's Med Ctr, Dallas, Tex; Active Att'g Staff, Baylor Univ Med Ctr, Dallas; Att'g Staff Oncology, Charles A Sammons Cancer Ctr, Dallas; Conslt in Plastic Surg, Presb Hosp, Dallas; Conslt Plastic Surg, John Peter Smith Hosp, Ft Worth; Conslt Plastic Surg Scottish Rite Hosp Crippled Chd, Dallas; Am Soc Plastic & Reconstructive Surgs; Ednl Foun of Am Soc Plastic & Reconstructive Surgs; Am Assn Plastic Surgs; Fellow Am Col Surgs; Soc Hd & Neck Surgs; Plastic Surg Res Coun; Craniofacial Biol Grp, Am Assn Dent Res; Intl Assn Dent Res; Am Soc Maxillofacial Surgs; Am Cleft Palate Assn; Ednl Foun Am Cleft Palate Assn; Am Burn Assn; Am Soc Aesthetic Plastic Surg; Intl Soc Aesthetic Plastic Surg; Pan Pacific Surg Assn; Phys Art Assn; AMA; Tex St Med Assn; Tex Soc Plastic Surgs; Dallas Co Med Assn; Dallas Soc Plastic Surgs; Kan St Med Assn; Wyandotte Co Med Assn; cp/Intl Craniofacial Travel Clb 1973-; McKorkle Soc 1974-; Exhibs Com, Ednl Foun of Am Soc Plastic & Reconstructive Surg 1976-; r/Meth; hon/Nat Inst Hlth Awd, Public Hlth Ser, Sr Clin Traineeship, Cancer Control Prog 1967-69; Plastic Surg Resident Prog Part Awd, 2nd Pl 1969; Hon Mention, S'ship Competition 1972; Res Grant Awd 1975, 1976; Hektoen Gold Medal for Original Investigation Awd'd to "Spectrum of Research and Clinical Management of Craniofacial Anomalies" 1977; Author/Co-Author Num Profl Pubs.

SALYER, PAULINE ALICE oc/Executive, Artist, Real Estate Broker; b/Sept 30, 1912; h/3111 NW 19, Okla City, OK 73107; m/B M Jr; c/Jerry Joe, Mona Sue S Lambird, Christopher Montgomery; p/Leslie Ewen (dec) and Nora Dell Thompson Johnson (dec); ed/Bus Col; pa/VP Salyer Refining Co 1948-57; Secy-Treas Salyer Stay Ready Filter Co 1957-69; Pres Salyer Pub'g Co 1964-; Reasl Est Broker Pauline Salyer Realty 1964-; Fdr World Org China Painters 1967, Pres 1967-77, Chm Bd Dirs 1977-, Life Trustee; Juried Show Art Gal, Calif St Univ 1977; Fdr & Life Mem Olka St Fed China Decorators; Intl Procelain Art Tchrs; Okla Art Leag; r/Meth; hon/1-Man Show; Author *Great Artists of China Decoration* 1964.

SAMFORD, WILLIAM JAMES JR oc/Attorney; h/575 Cloverdale Rd, Montgomery, AL; ba/Mont; p/Mrs William J Samford, Opelika, AL; ed/BA Auburn Univ 1972; JD Univ Ala Sch Law 1978; mil/USAF 1972-75; pa/Legal Advr to Gov of Ala; Litigation Atty, Fed Deposit Ins Corp, Wash DC; Pres Ala Public Ser Commn; Ala Trial Lwyrs Assn; Am Trial Lwyrs Assn; Am Bar Assn; Ala Bar Assn; Am Adjudicature Assn; Nat Assn Regulatory Utility Commrs; cp/U Way Fund Dr; Dem Party; hon/Outstg Regulatory Utility Commr, Ben & Bar Hon Soc.

SAMPLE, CAROL BERNIECE KVINGE oc/Professor; b/Aug 2, 1924; h/Box 167, Keene, TX 76059; ba/Keene; c/Terry Lee, Robert Lynn; p/Carl (dec) and Gertie Kringe, Keene, TX; ed/BA Union Col; MA E Tenn St; PhD Tex Christian Univ; pa/Prof Eng, SWn Adventist Col; VP Assn of Adventist Forums, Keene Chapt; cp/Supt Keene SDA Sabbath Sch, Sr Div; r/Seventh Day Adventist; hon/W/W Am Wom.

SAMPSON, LARRY LeROY oc/Director of Physical Therapy; b/Jan 13, 1941; h/4748 Wine Ridge Ln, B'ham, AL 35244; ba/B'ham; m/Marie A Weaver; c/Ian Ezekiel; p/Emory Sampson, Balto, MD; Agnes Mearilla Lam (dec); ed/BA Univ Va 1963; Cert Phys Therapy Univ Penn 1964; M Med Sci Emory Univ 1972; mil/AUS 1965-67; pa/Phys Therapist, Univ Va

265

Hosp 1964; Pvt Pract Phys Therapy 1976-70; Asst Prof, Clin Coor, Univ Vt 1972-77; Dir Phys Therapy, Univ Ala 1977-; Leg Chm St APTA Chapts, Ga 1971, Vt 1972; Am Phys Therapy Assn; NE Clin Coors 1972-76; cp/Nat Rifle Assn; Am Bowling Assn; Univ Va Basketball Mgr 4 Yrs; Pres UAB Bowling Leag 1979-81; r/Meth; hon/Dupont Regional S'ship 1959; Elks St Ldrship Awd 1959; Var Indiv & Team Nat Rifle Records 1967-70; W/W S&SW.

SAMPSON, MAY DOROTHY oc/Teacher; b/May 23, 1946; ba/Griffin, GA; ed/BS Albany St Col 1968; MEd W Ga Col 1974; Study No Ill Univ; pa/Eng Tech Spalding Jr HS; Griffin-Spalding Co Assn Edrs, Correcp Secy & Fac Rep; cp/Girl Scout Ldr Troop 112; r/Bapt.

SAMS, ALICE ELIZABETH CATON oc/Instructor; b/Mar 10, 1934; h/503 Oak Wood Dr, Enterprise, AL 36330; ba/Enterprise; m/Warren Newton Jr; c/Devon Elizabeth, Catherine Anne, Alice Pendleton, Warren Newton; p/Frederic Ingram and Dorothy V Caton Epley, Bellaire Bluff, FL; ed/BMus UNC-Greensboro 1956; pa/Instr Voice, Enterprise St Jr Col; Pvt Instr Voice & Piano; Coffee Co Arts Alliance; Metro Opera Guild; Soloist Enterprise Commun Chorus; cp/Patron Enterprise Chapt Nat Fed Mus Clb; Sponsor Jr Mus Clb; r/Epis; hon/Perf'd for Prince Charles 1972; Contbr to, Compiled, Edited "Booklet for Air Force Academy Brides" 1969 & 70.

SAMS, GLORIA V oc/Regional Health Coordinator; b/May 15, 1951; h/206 Mimosa St, Somerset, KY 42501; ba/Somerset; m/Robert W; p/Glenn Rice (dec) and Edna VanBever, Somerset, KY; ed/BS Psych; pa/Ky Cancer Comm; Ky Hospice Assn; cp/U Way Bd Dirs; Ky Ed Tele Mini Bd; Lake Cumberland Perf'g Arts Bd; Somerset Gdn Clb; r/Meth; hon/W/W Am Cols; Wom of Yr 1979; Col Pentacle Psi Chi.

SAMUEL, DOROTHY IONE JOHNSON oc/Professor; b/Jan 16, 1917; h/921-A 24 Ave N, Nashville, TN 37208; ba/N'ville; m/William Archie; p/Joseph Spurgeon (dec) and Pearl Bland Johnson (dec); ed/BS; MA; Study Abroad, Univ Leiden, Holland 1961; Post Grad Studies Ohio St Univ, Univ Penn, Vanderbilt Univ; pa/Prof French & Eng, Tenn St Univ; Assoc Editor *The Faculty Journal*; cp/Nat Trust for Hist Preservs; UN Assn; U Givers Fund; US China Peoples Friendship Assn; r/Christian; hon/Alpha Kappa Mu; Ford Foun Grant; Valedictorian & Sev S'ships; Pi Delta Phi; Am Studies S'ship; Author Novelette, Short Stories, Poems.

SANCHEZ, DIANNA GAYLE oc/Public Administrator; b/Sept 25, 1942; h/617-A Belltower Ave, Deltona, FL 32725; ba/Deland; m/Daniel P; c/Gabriella M, Meshell M; p/James D and Mary Carver Parks, Olympia, WA; ed/BA Sacramento St Univ; Post Grad Americana Ldrship Col; pa/Former St Yng Dem, Secy; Former St Dem Secy, Wash St; r/New Horizons Ch, Pres Bd; hon/Nat Student Register 1971-72; Bus Mgr, Wash Assn Com Col Student Govts.

SANCHEZ, MARIA ANNA oc/Nursing Service Supervisor; b/Sept 22, 1934; h/1726 Tarlton, Corpus Christi, TX 78415; ba/Corpus Christi; m/Farron; c/John David, Rose, Sharon, Cynthia, Michael; p/Antonio Ruil (dec) and Angelina; ed/Assoc Nsg; pa/BORN; Rep TNA; cp/THA; AHA BORN; r/Meth; hon/Outstg Nurse 1971; W/W Am Wom 1979-80.

SANCHEZ-CIFUENTES, ZOILA oc/Principal; b/June 26, 1930; h/1433 NW 33 Ct, Miami, FL 33125; ba/Miami; m/Lazaro; c/Jose Ramon, Jose Antonio; p/Eusebio Fernandez (dec); Librada Guillermo, Miami, FL; ed/MEd; pa/Prin & Owner Sunny Day Nursery Sch; Latin Bus & Profl Wom's Clb; Cuban Wom's Clb; Bilingual Pvt Schs Assn; cp/Miami-Cuban Lions Clb Lady Aux, Pres Social Asst; r/Cath; hon/Hon Mem Nat Sch Edrs From Cuba 1971; Med Ednl Merit 1973; Awd of Hon 1971; Hon Mention on Radio WQBA 1973; Citizen Merit for Outstg Labor in Favor of Commun 1974; Cert Apprec, Miami Cuban Lions Clb 1975; Commend, Metro Dade Co 1976; Cit of Merit, Nat Multiple Sclerosis Soc 1976; Acknowledgement of Merit, Lions Intl 1977; Cert Apprec, City of Miami 1977; Awd Luis Perez Espinos 1977; Recog of Merit, Miami Cuban Lions Clb 1978; Cert Miami Cuban Lions Clb 1978; Awd of Recog Lincoln-Marti Schs; Awd of Recog, Biprisa 1978; Cert Apprec Cuban Unit Commun Mtl Hlth Prog 1979.

SANDEL, BETTY SUE HICKS oc/Assistant Director; b/Sept 13, 1929; h/Snyder, TX; c/Pamela Joy Piedfort, Harold Richard, Paula Joe (dec); p/Travis B Hicks, Ruidoso, NM; Clara Parker Hicks (dec); ed/AA Midland Col 1974; BS Angelo St Univ 1977; pa/Asst Dir Adult Voc Ed, Cont'g Ed & Mid-Mgmt Instr 1979-; AVA; TVTA; TJCTA; TJCMEA, Treas 1979-80; Jr Col DECA, Profl Mem; Col DECA 1974-77, Treas 1975, Pres 1974; Jr Col DECA Midland Col; r/Prot; hon/ABWA S'ship 1975-76, 76-77; 2nd Public Relats Problem Solving, Jr Col DECA Ldrship Conf 1974 & 2nd Pers Mgmt 1974; W/W Am Cols & Univs 1975.

SANDERS, TERRY L oc/Branch Manager; b/Apr 11, 1956; h/Dunnellon, FL; ba/Fidelity Fed Savings & Loan, 1643 N US Hwy 41, PO Box 1249, Dunnellon, FL 32630; p/Ira Lee and Cleo E Sanders, Dunnellon, FL; ed/AA Ctrl Fla Commun Col 1976; pa/Dunnellon Ofc Br Mgr, Fidelity Fed S&L; cp/Bd Dirs Dunnellon C of C; r/Bapt; hon/W/W Am HS Students 1974; Outstg Am HS Student 1974; Phi Theta Kappa 1976.

SANDERS, VIRGINIA FRALEY oc/Nurse; b/Jan 10, 1916; h/1701 25th Ave, Meridian, MS 39301; ba/Meridian; m/Henry G; c/Faye Price; p/G E Sr and Gertrude Stutts Fraley, Macon, MS; pa/RPN; Owner Sanders Guest Home; cp/ABWA, Pres, Past Treas & Enrollment Tea Chm; Magnolia BPW Clb, Past Pres; Grover Burnett Chapt OES, Past Worthy Matron; Rebekah Lodge, Past Noble Grand; Rose Gdn Clb, Past Pres; Lauderdale Co Assn of Retard'd Chd; Sr Citizens; Am Legion Aux; Pythian Sisters; r/Bapt; hon/Wom of Yr, ABWA.

SANDFORD, JUANITA M DADISMAN oc/Assistant Professor, Coordinator; b/Arkadelphia, AR; ba/Box 322, HSU, Arkadelphia, AR 71923; m/Herman P; c/Susan Jane Wooderson, Linda Ann Wells; Mary K; p/Carl O Dadisman, Wichita, KS; Mabel Stearman Dadisman (dec); ed/BA 1947, MA 1948 Baylor Univ; pa/Asst Prof Sociol & Coor Wom's Studies, Henderson St Univ; Wayland Bapt Col; Ft Smith Jr Col; Ouachita Bapt Univ; Ark, SWn & Am Sociol Assns; Mid-S & So Sociol Assns; Ark Coun Wom in Higher Ed; cp/NOW; Nat Wom's Polit Caucus; Gov's Comm on Status of Wom; Atty Gen Adv Bd Mem; r/Christian; hon/W/W Am Wom; W/W & Where in Wom's Studies; Author *I Didn't Get a Lot Done Today* 1974 & *Poverty in the Land of Opportunity* 1978; Contbg Author *Images of Women in Bible* 1977.

SANDIFER, VELDA RAE oc/Realtor; b/Feb 14, 1934; h/226 Fairway Ct, Hopkinsville, KY 42240; ba/H'ville; m/Earl E; c/Debbie S Dunn, Donna S Cooksey, William G, Clifton R; p/Nettie R Richey, H'ville, KY; Grad Rltrs Inst; pa/Real Est Broker, Property Mgmt; H'ville Bd Rltrs, Pres 1970; 2 3-Yr Terms Dir Ky Assn Rltrs; cp/VP H'ville Christian Co C of C; r/Bapt; hon/Rltr of Yr 1970.

SANDOVAL, MERCEDES CROS oc/Professor, Unit Director; b/Nov 12, 1933; h/1120 NE 80th St, Miami, FL 33138; ba/Miami; c/Carlos Juan, Lydia Teresa, Ricardo Miguel, Mercedes Caridad; p/Juan and Elena Cros; ed/Dr SS Univ Havana; M Anthrop, Fla St Univ; PhD Univ Madrid; pa/Pres Anthrop, Dir Mtl Hlth Unit; Res on Afro Culture & Rel; cp/Past Chm Allepaltah Neighborhood for Commun Devel Prog; r/Cath; hon/Grad cum laude Univ Madrid; Outstg Fac Awd 1972, 79; Apple Awd 1974.

SANFORD, EDGAR EARL oc/Ambulance Service Director; b/Sept 23, 1943; h/1946 Bayview Dr, Madisonville, KY 42431; ba/M'ville; m/Georgia; c/Earl Jr, Rebecca Lee, Steven Ray, (Stepch:) John Camp; p/L E and Dorothy Wilkerson, Newton, TX; ed/ALS Wn Ky Univ; mil/USAF 8 Yrs; pa/Dir Med Ctr Ambulance Ser; Soc for Public Hlth Edrs; Ky Public Hlth Assn; EMT; cp/Masonic Lodge; r/Bapt; hon/Ky Col.

SANTA-MARIA, YVONNE Z oc/Administrator; b/Oct 10, 1928; h/4761 SW 4th St, Miami, FL 33134; p/Raul (dec) and Yvonne Giberga Santa-Maria (dec); ed/Dominican Acad, Havana, Cuba & Miami, Fla; Ruston Acad, Havana, Cuba; Linden Hall Jr Col, Lititz, Penn; cp/St, Dist 11, Local BPW Clb; Herstory of Fla Inc, By-Laws Chp 1976-; Cuban Wom's Clb 1974-; Hlth Plan'g Coun S Fla, Exec Com 1977-, Nom'g Com 1978-; FIU, Inst for Wom Adv Bd 1975-; Cuban Mus of Arts & Culture Inc 1977-; Wom's Ec Devel Coor Task Force, Dade Co Comm on Status of Wom 1977-; Hemispheric Cong for Wom, Bd Mem 1977-; Nat Assn Cuban-Am Wom Inc 1977-; Inter-Am Comm of Wom, Mem US Com of Coop 1977-; FIU Affirmative Action Assocs 1978-; IPMA, So Fla Chapt 1978-, Nat Mem 1979-; Dade Co Assn Retard'd Citizens 1978-; Dept Commun Affairs, Comm on Human Relats Long Term Employment Proj, Miami Adv Bd Mem 1979-; Fla Comm of Human Relats, Adv Com on Cert of Regulatory Bds, 1979-; Havana Yacht Clb; Havana Biltmore Yacht & Country Clb; Past Mem Num Others Orgs & Coms; r/Cath; hon/Recip Bobbie Plager Meml Trophy, Latin BPW 1971-72; Recip Plaque, Latin BPW for Outstg Sers as Pres of Clb 1972; Recip The Gran Orden Martiana Del Merito Ciudadano, Liceo Clb 1974; Cert of Apprec, Dist 11 PBW 1975; The Gran Orden Del Bicentenario, Liceo Cubano 1976; 1 of the Most Dynamic Wom Dade Co, *Miami Magazine* 1976; 1 of 10 Most Outstg Mems Commun, Cuban Wom's Clb 1977; Cert Apprec, Latin BPS 1977; Nom'd for 30th Annual Dade Co Outstg Citizen Awd 1977; 1 of 100 Cuban-Ams of Recog'd Ldrship in Commun 1977; Cert Apprec, Comite de Damas Leonas 1977; Cert Apprec, Mins-Laymen Voter Registration Com of Dade Co 1977; Part in Num Lectures, Panel Discussions, Interviews & Wkshops.

SANTELLANA, RICHARD S oc/Assistant City Manager; b/Nov 29, 1949; h/1641 Hamilton, Harlingen, TX 78550; ba/Harlingen; m/Rosabel E; c/Richard Anthony; p/Rodney C and Victoria S Lentz, Austin, TX; ed/BBA SW Tex St Univ 1972; pa/Dir Fin, Urban Renewal Agcy 1972-74;

PERSONALITIES OF THE SOUTH

Grants Acct, St Bar Tex 1974-76; City Treas, City of San Marco, Tex 1976-78; Asst City Mgr, City of Harlingen 1978-; Municipal Fin Ofcrs Assn of US & Can; Tex City Mgrs Assn; Charter Mem Tex Assn Govtl Data Processing Mgrs; cp/Harlingen JCs; r/Cath; hon/Awd of Fin Reporting Achmt, Municipal Fin Ofcrs Assn 1980.

SARAFIAN, SYLVIA ANNETTE oc/Computer Scientist; b/June 16, 1931; h/13856 Bora Bora Way, #105C, Marina Del Rey, CA 90291; ba/Marina Del Rey; p/Antranig Arakel (dec) and Elizabeth Zorian Sarafian, Newton Highlands, MA; ed/BA Mt Holyoke Col; pa/Author Compufarm, Time-Shared Payroll/Cost Acctg Sys for Agric Cost Control & Maximized Wkr Utilizathion Sys; Author Aurora, Agric Acctg Sys; Co-Author Safe Unemployment Ins; cp/Assoc Mem Repub St Ctrl Com 1975, 76,78, 79; 27th Confl Dist Adv Coun; r/Armenian Apostolic Ch; hon/W/W W; DIB.

SARGENT, WILLIAM EARL oc/Teacher, Assistant to Director; b/Aug 2, 1919; h/902 Myers Circle SW, Vienna, MA 22180; ba/Arlington, VA; p/Edward Brwon Sr (dec) and Lucy Edna Simms Sargent (dec); ed/BA The Am Univ 1953; MEd 1963; Postgrad Studies VPI & SU 1976-; mil/USN 1942-46; pa/Dir Burgundy Farm Country Day Sch 1960-63; Elem Clrm Tchr, Arlington Co 1954-60, 67-70, 77-78; Tchr Sem for Gifted Elem Students 1963-67; Sch Social Wkr 1970-72; Child Devel Conslt 1972-76; Elem Sci Tchr 1976-77; Tchr Eng as 2nd Lang 1978-79; Team Ldr, Asst Dir Arlington-Trinity Tchr Corps Proj in Bilingual & Multicultural Ed; Am Orthopsychi Assn; Am Sch Cnslrs; APGA; Nat Assn Biling Ed; U Tchg Prof; Assn for Tchr Ed; cp/Fairfax Co Dem Com 1970; Greenbelt Consumer Sers Inc; Clan Fraser Soc of N Am; Clan Stewart Soc Am; Sims-Simms Fam Geneal & Meml Soc, Fdr & Trustee; Irish-Am Cultural Assn; Friends of St Andrew, Scotworld, Leabhar, Communn na Canain Albannaich; r/Unitarian; hon/W/W: Am Ed 1965, S&SW 1980-81.

SASSIN, CAROL ANN oc/Counselor, Business Consultant, Teacher; b/Oct 28, 1942; h/1601 Schley St, Wharton, TX 77488; ba/Same; p/Victor John and Judith Marie Manofsky Sassin, Wharton, TX; ed/BBA; MBA; pa/Tex Bus Ed Assn; TPGA; APGA; AAUW; Tex Career & Guid Assn; Delta Sigma Pi; r/Cath; hon/W/W Am Wom; World W/W Wom in Ed; Personalites of Am; World W/W Wom; Intl W/W Ed; Book of Hon.

SATYU, NUGGEHALLI NEIL oc/Family Physician; b/Jan 8, 1947; h/Terrell, TX; ba/Terrell; m/Revathi; c/Anjali, Arpana; p/N R and Sharada Narayan, Bangalore, India; ed/BS 1970; MRCP 1971; LRCS 1971; CCFP; pa/Fam Pract; Can Med Assn; Kaufman Co Med Soc; Tex Med Assn; Am Acad Fam Phys; cp/Am Heart Assn, Kaufman Co Div; Med Advr; r/Hindu.

SAUCEMAN, FRED WILLIAM JR oc/Community Relations Officer; b/June 19, 1956; h/515 Winchester St, Rockwood, TN 37854; ba/Harriman, TN; m/Jill D; p/Fred W Sr (dec) and Wanda R Sauceman, Greeneville, TN; ed/BA 1978, MA 1980 E Tenn St Univ; pa/Announcer WGRV Radio 1972-74; Announcer WSMG Radio 1974-78; Reporter WKPT-TV 1978-79; Instr Eng, E Tenn St Univ 1978-80; Copywriter, Plus Mark Inc 1979-80; Commun Relats Ofcr, Roane St Commun Col; Phi Kappa Phi; ETSU Pres's Pride; ETSU Nat Alumni Assn; r/Meth; hon/Outstg Student Fgn Langs; ETSU 1978; Dean's Awd, ETSU 1978; Frank Freimann S'ship Recip 1974-78.

SAUNDERS, ANNETTE G oc/Educator; b/Sept 24, 1930; h/6987 J Roswell Rd, Atlanta, GA 30328; ba/Roswell; m/William J (dec); c/Amanda Lou, Michael William; p/William Van (dec) and Cora Y Gunter (dec); ed/B Bus Ed 1971, M Bus Ed 1978 Ga St Univ; pa/Fulton Co Sch Sys Voc Ofc Trg Coor, Coor'g Work-Experience Prog for Voc Students 1971-; ISBE; NBEA; GBEA; AVA; GBA; Am Soc Tng & Devel; Am Coun Consumer Interests; cp/Exec Bd N Springs U Meth Ch 1979; N Fulton Co C; r/Prot; hon/Recip Edr of Yr Awd, 5th Cong Dist, Ga Voc Assn 1977; Outstg Ser Awd, Ga Dept Ed, Bus & Ofc Ed 1979; Outstg Bus Edr, 5th Cong Dist, Ga Bus Ed Assn 1981.

SAUNDERS, LENWOOD O DANIEL oc/Minister; b/Mar 21, 1927; ba/Morganton, NC; m/Lena Davis; c/Alinda M Gatson, Gwendolyn A Flood, Louis O, Frank W, Wayman Lee; p/dec; ed/BTheol Kittrell Col 1956; Att'd The Urban Tng Ctr for Christian Mission 1966; Master Barber Cert, Modern Barber Col 1946-47; mil/AUS 1945-46; pa/Master Barber Kinston, NC 1947-53, Warrenton, NC 1953-60, Wilimington, NC 1960-66; Carpenter & Painter 1953-60; Min African Meth Ch, Morganton, NC; Former Chm Northampton Co Human Relats Comm; cp/Org'd & Elec'd Pres Black Min Conf; Chm Ch Work Com, NC Br NAACP; 1st VP Burke Co NAACP; Burke Co Commerce; VChm Blue Ridge Commun Action Bd of Dirs; Bd Dirs Burke Co Status of Wom; Appt'd by Gov James Hunt to NC Yth Adv Coun; r/AME Ch; hon/Recip NC Commun Ldrship Awd for Outstg Ser in Field of Human Rights & Social Just 1979; Outstg Min City of Hickory 1973; Outstg Min, Wn NC Conf AME Ch 1973; Min Yr Black

Commun for Outstg Ldrship in Ch & Hickory Commun 1973; Min of Yr for Outstg Commun Ser, NAACP 174; Invited to White House by Pres Jimmy Carter as Black Ldr of S 1979; Min of Yr, Burke Co NAACP 1978.

SAUNDERS, WILLIAM oc/Executive Director; b/Feb 14, 1935; h/PO Box 36, Johns Island, SC 29455; ba/Charleston, SC; m/Henrietta J; c/William, Sharon, Loretta, Kathleen, Byron, Gary, Myra, Alpheia, Clinton; ed/Drug Ed Tng, SE Regional Drug Ed Tng & Resources Ctr of Univ Miami 1972; mil/AUS 1951-54 Staff Sgt; pa/Exec Dir Com on Better Racial Assurance; VP Brothers Broadcasting Corp, Owners of WPAL & WXVI; 1 of Orgrs of U Citizens Party, St SC 1970; 1 of Develrs of Black Land Sers, Beaufort, SC 1972; cp/Charleston Area Commun Relats Com; Trident U Way Inc; U Way of SC Exec Com; Penn Commun Ctr Inc; VP Sea Island Comprehensive Hlth Care Corp; Chm SC St Adv Bd Sickle Cell Anemia; St Johns Epis Mission Ctr; Trident C of C; C'ton B&P Assn; C'ton Co Am Cancer Soc; C'ton Co Hlth Care Adv Coun; Human Sers Coun, Tri-Co; Trident 2000 Crime Commr; C'ton Co Ec Oppor Comm; St Johns HS Adv Bd; Rural Missions Inc; Comm to Study Public Sch Sys of C'ton Co; Trident 2000 Bd Dirs; Comprehensive Hlth Care Plan'g, Tri-Co Area; r/Meth; hon/Cert of Recog for Outstg Contbns in Field Commun & Public Affairs, SC Leg, Ho of Res 1972; Citizen of Yr, Alpha Chapt Omega Psi Phi 1972; Commun Ldrship, Shaw Univ w/out Walls 1976; Outstg Ldrship, C'ton Co Substance Abuse Comm 1976; Author Sev Pubs; Editor "Low Country Newslttr" 1966-69.

SAUTER, MARY S oc/Artist; b/Mar 12, 1903; h/Sarasota, FL; c/Edwin C Jr; p/Major Schuessler (dec); Leila Dobbins (dec); ed/Att'd Va Col 1922; Art Students Leag, NY; Other Studies NY & Europe; pa/Painting Portraits in Watercolors & Oils; Am Soc Miniature Painters; Pres Little Clb; Chm Fine Arts Com, Fed Wom's Clbs of Conn 1945-50; hon/Exhibs Yrly, NY, Phila, Wash DC 1930-64; Perm Colect Smithsonian Inst.

SAVOY, VIVIAN C oc/Teacher; b/Oct 11, 1921; h/8651 Othello, Houston, TX 77029; ba/Houston; m/John I; c/George Leslie Kennard; p/George W (dec) and Margery Willis McGowan (dec); ed/BA; MEd; pa/NEA; Tex St Tchrs Assn; Tex Clrm Tchrs Assn; Houston Coun Ed; Tex So Rdg Coun; Zeta Phi Beta; Houston Tchrs Assn; Assn Supervision & Curric Devel; cp/YWCA; Houston C of C, Pleasantville Civic Leag; r/Meth; hon/Grad Col w Dist; Winner Delta S'ship; Eng Prize; Grad F'ship; Miss Homecoming; 1st Pl Winner in St Essay-Writing Contest; 1st Pl Winner Co Queen Contest; Hon'd w Savoy Day; Hon Awds from Scout Work & Ser to Ed & Tchg Prof.

SAWYER, AUBREY MACK JR oc/Department Chairman, Professional Photographer; b/Oct 27, 1945; h/206 Park Ave, Smithfield, NC 27577; m/Faye Berry; c/Chadwick, Brantley; p/Aubrey M Sr and Maybelle K Sawyer, Elizabeth City, NC; ed/Att'd Chowan Col 1964-66; BS Atlantic Christian Col 1970-72; pa/Profl Photog; Commercial Artist; Owner Mack Art Designs & Gals; Owner A Mack Sawyer Photo; Chm Art Dept, Johnston Tech Inst; Profl Photgs of NC; cp/Sudan Temple Shrine; r/Meth; hon/Num Exhibs & 1-Man Shows.

SAXTON, WILLIAM oc/Executive Director; b/Oct 30, 1942; h/Midland, TX; ba/Midland; m/Linda L; c/Jamie, Michael; p/Wesley Saxton; Agnes Saxton (dec); ed/BS Midland Luth Col 1967; MS N Tex St Univ 1972; pa/Exec Dir Bivens Homes for the Aging, Amarillo, Tex 1972-80; Exec Dir Trinity Towers 1980-; Tex Assn Homes for the Aging; Chm 1981-82, Chm Public Polity 1980-81, Chapt Chp 1977-80, Dir 1976-79; Am Assn Homes for the Aging: Ho Dels 1981, Public Policy Com 1981; Gerontological Soc 1973-; Am Assn Nsg Homes Admrs; cp/Amarillo Sr Citizens Assn, Pres 1973-75; Amarillo Multiser Ctr, Pres 1979-80, Bd Dirs 1978-79; r/Epis; hon/Chevalier Deg 1963; Pres Emeritus Amarillo Sr Citizens Assn 1975; Pres's Awd, Tex Assn Homes for the Aging 1979.

SAYERS, IRIS WEBB oc/Payroll; b/July 6; h/603 12th St, Radford, VA 24141; ba/Radford; m/H D; c/H D Jr, Gary M, Judy R; p/Toney W and Dora S Webb, Allisonia, VA; ed/Grad Perry Bus Sch 1943; Att'd New River Commun Col 1972-73, Radford Col 1961; pa/Payroll Dept, Lynchburg Foundry; Past Pres Radford BPW Clb; cp/Radford City Coun; Radford Plan'g Comm; Past Pres Kuhn Barnett PTA; Past Secy McHarg PTA; Past Secy Sunset Vil Wom's Clb; r/First Christian Ch.

SAYERS, WILLIAM EARL oc/Assistant Branch Manager; b/May 17, 1934; h/E Tallassee, AL; m/Anne R; c/Mark E, Rhonda S Robertson; p/John W Sayers, E Tallassee, AL; ed/BBA Col William & Mary 1961; mil/USMC 1953-56; pa/Asst Br Mgr, HHS Audit Agcy; Cert'd Internal Auditor; Alpha Kappa Psi; Assn Govt Accts; cp/City Coun-man, City of Tallassee; r/Bapt.

SCHAAK, ANNA MARIE oc/Supplies Attendant; b/July 4, 1934; h/Box 465, Comanche, OK 73529; ba/Lawton, OK: p/Ed (dec) and Bertha

267

PERSONALITIES OF THE SOUTH

Schaak (dec); ed/Att'd Univ Okla & Cameron Univ; pa/Supplies Attendant, SWn Bell Telephone Co; cp/Mayor & Mem City Coun of Comanche; Co-Chm Stephens Co Dem Party 1975-76, Chm 1977-78; Comanche BPW Clb; r/Bapt.

SCHACHAR, RONALD oc/Ophthalmology; b/Dec 28, 1941; ba/1020 N Hwy 75, Denison, TX a75020; ed/BS 1963, MD 1967; PhD 1974; pa/Ophthalmology; ·Secy Keratorefracture Soc; hon/Phi Beta Kappa; Author 3 Books & Num Profl Articles.

SCHAEFER, FRANCIS (FRANK) JOSEPH oc/Teacher, Coach, Minister; b/Sept 18, 1947; h/Harker Hghts, TX; ba/Fairway Middle Sch, Killeen Indep Sch Dist, Whitlow & Farth, Killeen, TX 76541; m/Helen Maria Quick; c/James Byron, Joy Christine, Jennifer Hope; p/Mrs James L Sangster, Houston, TX; ed/BA Stephen F Austin St Univ 1970; MDiv SWn Bapt Theol Sem 1974; Tchr Cert Mary Hardin Baylor Univ 1978; Mid-Mgmt Cert Tarelton St Univ 1980; DMin Cand SWn Bapt Theol Sem; pa/Old N Bapt Ch, Nacogdoches, Tex 1969-70; First Bapt Ch, Dallas, 1970-74; Asst Mission Pastor Geo W Taueet Chapel, Mission Pastor Meadow Gdns Chapel; Pastor Trinity Bapt Ch/Evangelisch Freikirclich Gemide, Metterich, W Germany 1974-77; Pastor First Bapt Ch, Nolanville, Tex 1977-78; Fairway Middle Sch, Killeen Indep Sch Dist 1978-: Tchr Speech, Drama, Tex Hist, Hd Fball Coach, KISD Citizenship Com; Shelby-Doches Bapt Assn, Yth & Resolutions Com; European Bapt Assn, Missions Com, Theol Ed by Ext Com, Budget & Fin Com; TSTA, Fac Rep 1980-81; Tex HS Coaching Assn 1978-; cp/Killeen Evening Lions Clb, Budget & Fin Com, Civic Affairs Com, Crippled Chd Com; r/So Bapt; hon/Outstg Yng Men Am 1978; OES Rel S'ship 1970; Num HS & Col Awds; Curric Guide for Killeen Indep Sch Dist, Middle Sch Level.

SCHAFFER, RONALD LEE oc/Minister; b/Aug 8, 1937; h/5305 Rosecrest Circle, Tampa, FL 33617; ba/Tampa; m/Martha Ann; c/Daniel, Jesse, Alfred, Rebecca; p/Roland Doyle Schaffer (dec); Ethel Eckoff Rivers, Jacksonville, FL; ed/ThG; BA; MA; PhD; mil/USN; pa/Fdr & Pres Fla Chds Home Inc, Faith Chds Home; Pres Temple Hgts Chridtian Schs Inc; r/Indep Bapt; hon/Temple Terrace JC 1972; Hon DDiv Hyles Anderson Col 1973; Hon LLD Bapt Christian Univ 1977.

SCHEINER, JAMES JOSEPH oc/Orthopedic Surgeon; b/May 4, 1936; m/Marcia; c/Marc, Michael, David, Alan; p/Norman and Lillian Scheiner, LA, CA; ed/BS; MD Univ Cinci; mil/USAF Capt; pa/Pvt Prac Orthopedic Surg; AMA; Va Med Soc; Am Acad Ortho Surg; Va Ortho Soc; Mil Med Soc; So Med Soc; PAMS; Intl Soc CV Surg; Arlington Med Soc; cp/Dir Wom's Nat Bank; r/Jewish; hon/Phi Beta Kappa; Dir Ortho Surg Jefferson Meml Hosp; Alpha Omega Alpha; MSD Lecture Series; Num Med Res.

SCHERMERHORN, WILLIAM LYNN oc/Executive; b/June 28, 1942; h/Dallas, TX; m/Lynda R Cowley; c/Jonathan Tyler; p/Irma G (dec) and Lynn George Schermerhorn, Sioux Falls, SD; ed/BA Univ SD 1966; mil/AUS 1966-68 1st Lt; pa/Assoc Prog Mgr, AE Stalen Mfg Co, Decatur, Ill 1968-72; Prod Mgr Gen Foods Corp, White Plains, NY 1972-74; Sr Prod Mgr, Brown & Williamson Tobacco Corp, Louisville, KY; Nat Advtg Mgr, Dir of Advtg & Brand Mgmt, Dr Pepper Co, Dallas, Tex; Am Mktg Assn; Assn Nat Advtrs; Delta Tau Delta; cp/Repub Party; r/Rom Cath.

SCHEXNAYDER, GLENN D oc/Physician; b/Dec 6, 1950; h/107 Belle Alliance Dr, Donaldsonville, LA 70346; ba/D'ville; m/Shirley Hebert; c/Glenn David Jr, Brett Robert; p/Earl A and Vera Derbes Schexnayder, D'ville, LA; ed/BS LSU-BR 1972; MD LSU-NO 1975; Bd Cert, Am Bd Fam Med 1978; F'ship Am Acad Fam Phys 1979; pa/Fam Med; Chief of Staff, Prevost Meml Hosp; cp/Bd Dirs D'ville C of C; r/Rom Cath; hon/Alpha Omicron Alpha; Nat Hon Soc; Upjohn Achmt Awd 1975; W/W 1980-81.

SCHLAM, EDWARD H oc/Dermatologist; b/May 9, 1944; ba/2500 University Dr, Sunrise, FL 33322; m/Hollis; c/Myles, Evan; p/Rae Schlam, Sunrise, FL; ed/BS cum laude Brooklyn Col 1965; MD St Univ NY, Downst Med Ctr 1979; Intern Maimonides Med Ctr, Brooklyn 1969-70; Resident Dermatology 1970-72, Chief Resident Derm 1972-73, St Univ NY, Downst Med Cr, Kings Co Hosp; pa/Clin Instr, Dept Derm, St Univ NY, Downst Med Ctr, Kings Co Hosp 1973; Clin Instr, Dept Derm, Univ Miami Med Sch, Jackson Meml Hosp 1973-; Hosp Att'g Staff: Jackson Meml Hosp, Fla Med Ctr Lauderdale Lakes; Univ Commun Hosp Tamarae, Margate Gen Hosp, Bennett Commun Hosp, Plantation Gen Hosp; AMA; FMA; Broward Co Med Assn; Broward Co Dermatologic Assn; Diplomate Am Acad Derm; r/Jewish; hon/Dip Am Bd Derm 1974.

SCHLUSEMEYER, CHRISTINA SCHILLER oc/Horse Trainer, Instructor; b/Apr 26, 1942; h/Rt 9 Box 88, Ocala, FL 32670; m/Leigh Barton; c/Hilary Clarie; p/Paul Harka Schiller (dec); Mrs Karl S Lashley; ed/BA Smith Col; p/Christina S Schlusemeyer Tng Stables, Ocala, Fla 1979-; Am Horse Show Assn; Bd Mem N Fla Hunter & Jumper Assn;

r/Rom Cath; hon/Trained AHSA Nat High Score Horses of Yr 1975; Author Sev Articles for *Practical Horseman* & *Chronicle of the Horse*.

SCHMIDGALL, ROBERT LEE oc/Professor; b/Mar 28, 1943; h/324 S 23rd St, Arkadelphia, AR 71923; ba/Arkadelphia; p/William Henry (dec) and Cleona Elizabeth Ackerly Schmidgall (dec); ed/BA Bradley Univ 1965; PhD Ind Univ 1969; pa/Chem, No Regional Lab USDA 1969-70; Instr Chem Univ Ark 1969-70; Prof Chem Henderston St Univ 1970-; Ctrl Ark Sect, Am Chem Soc; Sigma Xi; r/Prot; hon/Outstg Edr of Am 1975; W/W S&SW 1980-81.

SCHMIDT, MIRIAM KIRBYE oc/Volunteer Worker; b/Feb 24, 1905; m/Ira Burdsell; c/James Kirbye, Mary Kay; p/J Edward Kirbye, Raleigh, NC; Isabelle Clark Kirbye (dec); ed/Master Cert Univ Des Moines 1969; Nat Coun St Gdn Clbs Schs for Judging; cp/Commr GSA 1946-49; Regent Stephens Chapt DAR 1960-62; Kappa Alpha Theta; Pres Wom's C of C, Decatur, Ala 1956-57; Judges Coun #7, Huntsville, Ala; Judges Coun Gdn Clbs of Ala, VP Dist 1 1970-72; r/Chrsitian Sci; hon/Gdn Clb Movement & Standard Flower Show Awds; Judge Nat Coun Flower Shows.

SCHNEIDER, KATHARINE CURTIS oc/Financial Analyst; b/June 21, 1949; h/McLean, VA; ba/1101 17th St NW, Wash DC 20036; m/Lloyd R; c/Jeremy Scott; p/Frank L Curtis; Mary F Sacklin; ed/BA Univ Neb 1971; MBA Univ So Calif 1977; pa/CPA; Fin Analyst, Ec Cnsltg Firm; Assn MBA Execs; DC Inst CPAs; Am Woms Soc CPA; Am Inst CPAs; cp/NOW; Am Civil Liberties Union; Nat Trust for Hist Preserv; New England Hist & Geneal Soc; Smithsinoan Inst; hon/Prix D'Honneur 1966, 67; Nat Hon Soc 1967; Pi Mu Epsilon 1970; Beta Gamma Sigma 1977; Beta Alpha Psi 1977.

SCHNEIDER, LLOYD RHYNEHART oc/Attorney, Editor; b/July 25, 1949; h/1903 Woodgate Ln, McLean, VA 22101; ba/Wash DC; m/Katharine Mary Curtis; c/Jeremy Scott; p/Lloyd William and Mary Ellen Schneider, Omaha, NE; ed/BS w Dist; JD w Hons; mil/USAF 1971-Capt; pa/Editor AF JAG Reporter; ABA; ATLA; AFA; FBA; PAD; ASME; cp/AF Yng Lwyr Del to ABA; Bd Dirs Westgate Chd Care Ctr; hon/Order of the Coif; S Calif Law Review; Am Legion Awds for Scholastic & Mil Excell.

SCHOFIELD, PAUL oc/Agent; b/Dec 21, 1954; h/PO Box 147, Ellaville, GA 31806; ba/Americus; m/Brenda B; c/Paul Anthony; p/David B and Peggy Schofield, Junction City, GA; ed/Life Underwriter Grad; mil/USN 3 Yrs; pa/Agt Life of Ga; cp/JCs; Boys Fball Coach; r/Bapt; hon/Sales of Mo, July 1978; Spkr Annual Pacesetters Clb.

SCHUCK, MARJORIE MASSEY oc/Publisher, Editor, Author, Poet, Lecturer; b/Oct 9, 1921; h/8245 26th Ave N, St Petersburg, FL 33710; ba/St Petersburg; m/Franz (dec); p/Carl Frederick Massey (dec); Margaret Harriet Parmele Eastman, St Petersburg, FL; ed/Att'd Univ Minn & NYU; pa/Co-Fdr Intl Poetry Jour *Poetry Venture* 1968, Editor, Pubr 1968-; Co-Editor, Pubr *The Poetry Venture Quarterly Essays* 1968-71; Est'd Own Pub'g House & Commercial Printing Firm: Valkyrie Press Inc, St Petersburg 1972; Fdr, Estblr MS Records Inc & Majorie Schuck (Mus) Pub'g Inc 1974; Fdr Valkyrie Press Round Table 1975; Opened Valkyrie Press Ref Lib 1976; Lectr; Radio & TV Appearances; Judge of Poetry & Speech Contests; Helped Est Fla Suncoast Writers' Conf: Co-Dir, Poetry Chm, Lectr; Author Num Articles & Poems; Mem: Acad Am Poets, Nat Soc of Lit & the Arts, Com of Small Mag Editors & Pubrs, Pinellas Arts Coun (Chm), Nat Fed Press Wom Inc; Others; cp/Pinellas Suncoast C of C; hon/Num Hons & Awds; W/W: Am Wom, Fin & Indust, S&SW; World W/W of Wom; Intl W/W in Poetry; DIB; Intl Register of Profiles; Selected as 1 of 76 Fla Patriots, Bicent Comm of St of Fla 1976, Rec'd Cit for Contbns to Lit, Art & Bus.

SCHULER, BETH ANN oc/District Conservationist; b/Aug 2, 1954; h/PO Box 413, Benton, KY 42025; ba/Benton; p/James K and Dorothy A Schuler, Sandusky, OH; ed/BA, MS Murray St Univ; pa/USDA Soil Conser Ser, Dist Conservationist; Soil Conserv Soc Am; Am Soc Agronomy; hon/Gamma Beta Phi; Dean's List.

SCHULTE, JOSEPHINE HELEN oc/Professor; b/May 9, 1929; h/5523 Callaghan Rd, 1703, San Antonio, TX 78229; ba/San Antonio; p/Mathias and Theresa Schulte (dec); ed/AA Sacred Heart Jr Col 1949; BS Spring Hill Col 1957; MA Univ So Miss 1961; MA Trinity Univ 1976; PhD Loyola Univ 1969; Att'd: Schiller Col, Bonnigheim, Germany, Summer 1972; St Mary's Univ 1971-72, Universidad de las Americas, Mexico City 1968-69; El Colegio de Mexico 1967; Instituto Mexicano-Norteamericano 1966; La Universidad Nacional de Mexico 1966; La Universidad de La Habana, Cuba, Summer 1950; pa/St Mary's Univ 1970-; Prof Hist, Assoc Prof Hist, Dir Latin Am Studies Prog, Grad Advr in Hist, Grad Coun; Asst Prof Hist, Univ of the Ams, Mexico City 1967-70; Tchg Fellow Hist, Loyola Univ 1962-66; Tchr Prichard Jr HS, Mobile 1962; Instr Am Hist & Eng Comp, Spring Hill Col 1960-62 & Summer 1963; Tchr German, Brookley Field

AFB, Mobile 1951-62; German-Spanish Translator 1949-62; Res Assoc & Adm Asst, So Inst Mgmt 1959-60; cp/Judge for La Bahia Awd; Bd Dirs SWn Conf Latin Am Studies; Annual Judge Social Sci Projs in Public Schs; Pres S Ala & W Fla Br Sacred Heart Col Alumnae Assn; r/Rom Cath; hon/Newberry Lib F'ship Awd 1978; Plaque for Twice Judging a Social Sci Proj in San Antonio HS 1978; Tchr of Wk, San Antonio *Express* 1974; A Yr and Seven Mos Org of Am Sts F'ship Awd in Mexico; 4-Yr Tchg F'ship Loyola Univ; 2-Yr Tuition Remission S'ship Sacred Heart Jr Col; 1st Prize for Speech "The Consitution: Temple of Liberty" 1946; Translated Dr Leopoldo Zea's Book *El Positivismo en Mexico* 1974; World W/W Wom; W/W Am Wom; Directory Am Schrls.

SCHULTE, LINDA oc/Director Public Information; b/Oct 8, 1946; h/9544 Canterbury Riding, Laurel, MD 20810; ba/Balto; p/Charles S C Sullivan; Dorothy F Sullivan (dec); ed/BA Wn Md Col; pa/Dir Public Info, Md Dept Human Resources 1975-; Dir Public Info Md St Energy Policy Ofc 1973-75; Dir Public Info, Univ Balto 1972-73; Asst Dir Commun Relats, Balto Chapt Am Red Cross 1970-72; Dir Col Relats, Balto Chapt Am Red Cross 1969-70; Prog Dir Supplemental Activs Overseas, Am Nat Red Cross, Saigon 1968-69; Md, Del, DC Press Assn; Md Press Clb; AAUW; Assoc'd Photogs Intl; Wn Md Alumni Assn; Nat Assn Govt Communrs; cp/Celebrities Com, WNVT Public TV Auction-on-the-Air 1975; Mayor's Adv Com on Municipal Problems & Solutions 1973-74; Communs Com, Wn Md Col 1972-73; Bd Dirs Balto City's House of Ruth 1978-; hon/Wn Md Hon Wom's Soc; Wn Md Alumni Citizenship Awd.

SCHULTZ, ROBERT MELVIN JR oc/Staff Arranger; b/Sept 29, 1948; h/6526 SW 114 Ave, Miami, FL 33173; ba/Hialeah, FL; m/Pamela B; p/Robert M Schultz, Beckley, WV; Barbara Burwell, Greensburg, PA; ed/BM 1974, MM 1977 WVU; mil/USN 4 Yrs; pa/Composer & Pianist; Staff Arranger Columbia Screen Gems Pubs.

SCHURR, SANDRA LEE oc/Principal, Writer, Consultant; b/Oct 28, 1938; h/Sarasota, FL; ba/Vencie Elem Sch, Bahama St, Venice, FL 33595; m/Donald K; c/Donald K Jr, Peter S; p/Victor B (dec) and Geraldine S Seaman, Saginaw, MI; ed/BA 1970, MA 1976 Oakland Univ; pa/Prin Venice Elem Sch; Writer, Conslt, Pubr of Tchr Ed Mats; Fla Assn Sch Admrs; Nat Assn Elem Sch Prins; r/Prot; hon/Little Red Sch-house Awd 1980.

SCHWARTZ, MARK E oc/Division Manager; b/May 9, 1953; h/Ft Worth, TX; ba/7725 Sand, Ft Worth,TX 76118; p/Dr and Mrs E W Schwartz, Dodge City, KS; ed/BA Univ Kan 1971; MBA So Meth Univ 1976; pa/Ft Worth Nat Bank: Fin Analyst 1976-77, Sr Fin Analyst 1977, Corresp Bank Rep 1977-78, Corresp Bnk Ofcr 1978; Mgr Wire Rope Corp of Am, Synthetic Web Sling Div 1979-; Am Inst Bnkg; cp/Bd Dirs Ft Worth W-side YMCA, Tchr Proj Bus 1977, Tchr Fin Plan'g for Small Bus 1978; YMCA Basketball Coach 1978-79; r/Cath; hon/Recip Victor Awd, Sales-Mktg Execs of Ft Worth 1979; W/W S&SW 1980.

SCHWEITZER, GERTRUDE oc/Artist; h/Stone Hill Farm, Colts Neck, NJ 07722; pa/Painter; Sculptor; Num 1-Man Shows: Montclair Art Mus NJ, Washington Water Color Clb, Currier Gal of Art, Manchester, NH, Erie Public Mus, Penn, Galleria Charpentier, Paris, France, Galleria Al Cavallino, Venice, Italy, Galleria Il Naviglio, Milan, Italy, Witte Meml Mus, San Antonio, Tex, Others; Exhib'd At: Corcoran Gal, Wash DC, Art Inst of Chgo, Rhode Isl Sch of Design, Mus Art, Sante Fe, NM, Others; Rep'd in Mus Collects: The Brooklyn Mus, NY, Toledo Mus Art, Ohio, Atlanta Art Assn Gals, Ga, Mus Modern Art, Paris, France, The Nat Acad of Design, Soc of the Four Arts, Palm Bch, Fla, Others; hon/Elected to Nat Acad of Design; 1st Am to Have 1-Man Show at Gallerie Charpentier, Paris; 1st Am to be Rep'd in Albi Mus Contemporary Collect, France; Pratt Inst Alumni Medal; Am Water Color Soc Medal; Num 1st Prizes; Grumbacher Awd, Audubon 27th Annual Exhib, NYC; Num Others; Author Book: *Peintures et Dessins*; W/W Art & Antiques, DIB, Notable Ams, W/W: Am Wom, Am, World, S&SW, E.

SCIACCA, WILLIAM WAYNE SR oc/Food Service Administrator; b/June 20, 1945; h/4236 Walmsley Ave, New Orleans, LA 70125; ba/New Orleans; m/Priscilla Dianne Neal; c/William Jr, Deborah, Mark; p/Thomas John and Pauline Louise Sciacca; ed/BA LSU 1967; mil/AUS Capt; pa/Dir Food Ser Tulane Med Ctr Hosp & Clin; Conslt Hosp Affil Mgmt Corp, Ad Hoc; Am Soc Hosp Food Ser Admrs, Pres SE Bayou Chapt La; La Ret Assn; cp/Lions; Assn Reserve Ofcrs; Am Heart Assn; Dem Party; Theta Xi; r/Rom Cath; hon/3 Star Rating, Washington Post; Bronze Star; Cross of Gallantry; Combat Infantry Badge.

SCOGGIN, BOBBIE JO oc/Executive; b/Dec 6, 1929; h/3407 37th St, Lubbock, TX 79413; ba/Lubbock; m/James Vance; c/James Stephen; p/W R (dec) and Maggie Stockton Gentry (dec); pa/VP Am St Bank; Nat Assn Bank Wom Inc; Soroptomist Intl; Lubbock Advtg Fed; cp/Bus Chm, Am Cancer Soc; Maid of Cotton Com, Lubbock Arts Fest 1979; r/Meth; hon/Nom Profl Wom of Lubbock 1979.

SCOTT, BECKY W oc/Teacher; b/June 2, 1947; h/701 W 26th St, Tifton, GA 31794; m/James William; c/James Austin, Becky Michele, William Curtis; p/Curtis and Hazel Wells, Sycamore, GA; ed/BA Univ Ga; r/Meth.

SCOTT, CHARLES ORLEN JR oc/Executive; b/May 11, 1934; h/PO Box 1348, Natchez, MS 39120; m/Betty P; c/Michael Gregory, Lola Lee S Redwine, Angela Suzette Floyd; p/Charles Orlen (dec) and Lola Fuller Scott, Mobile, AL; ed/Att'd Miss St Univ Sch Forestry 1960; mil/USN; pa/Pres Mullins Pulpwood Inc; Exec VP & Gen Mgr Ricks Lumber Co, Ricks Chips & Adams Co Lumber Sales; Bd Dirs Am Pulpwood Assn; Bd Dirs SW Hardwood Lumber Mfg Clb; Past Pres W-side Hardwood Clb; cp/Natchez, Miss C of C; r/Presb.

SCOTT, EDWIN JEROME oc/Assistant to Director; b/July 6, 1954; h/1006 Lloyd St, Morristown, TN 37814; ba/M'town; m/Gaynell S; c/Sherrye LaShay, Dewayne Lamonte; p/Ambrose and Emma B Scott, Shelby, NC; ed/AA, BSBA; pa/Asst to Dir of Prog & Human Resource Devel; cp/JCs; r/Bapt; hon/W/W Am Jr Col; Men Achmt; JC of Qtr.

SCOTT, IRENE FEAGIN oc/Judge; b/Oct 6, 1912; h/4815 25th Rd, N, Arlington, VA 22207; ba/Wash DC; m/Thomas Jefferson; c/Thomas Jefferson Jr, Irene Scott Carroll; p/Arthur Henry and Irene Peach Feagin (dec); ed/AB 1932, LLB 1936 Univ Ala; LLM Cath Univ; Hon LLD Univ Ala 1978; pa/Judge US Tax Ct; Ala Bar Assn; Am Bar Assn, Secy of Taxation; Fed Bar Assn; Nat Assn Wom Lwyrs; Bar Assn of DC (Hon); Inter-Am Bar Assn; cp/PTA; Girl Scout Ldr; Bd Dirs Mt Olivet Foun, Arlington; Com to Set Curric for Masters of Law in Tax, Univ Ala Law Sch; r/Meth: Adm Bd; hon/Hon LLD Univ Ala 1978.

SCOTT, JAMES BENARD oc/Teacher; b/Feb 10, 1920; ba/Terrell, TX; m/Merlene Davis; c/Bernadette L Threets, Paulette S Bunton, Sheri S Snell; p/Peter (dec) and Amanda Scott (dec); ed/BS, MS Prairie View A&M; mil/AUS 1942-46; pa/Voc Agric Tchr; Tex Voc Tech Assn; Tex St Tchrs Assn; Nat Voc Agric Tchrs Assn; Am Voc Assn; Voc Agric Tchrs Assn of Tex; cp/Selective Ser Bd Mem; Kaufman Co Plan'g Com, Secy; Kaufman Co Livestock Com; r/Ch of Christ; hon/Ser Awds: 5, 10, 15, 20, 25, 30, 35 Yr; Dist'd Ser Awd, VATAT 1975 & 80; Hon St Farmer.

SCOTT, JERRY DEAMUS oc/Educational Director; b/June 20, 1936; h/7801 Cranley Rd, Powell, TN 37840; ba/Oak Ridge; c/Eric, Karla, Stephanie; p/Deamus Elmus and Della Sue Campbell Scott, Greeneville, TN; ed/BS Univ Tenn 1958; MEd Miss St Univ 1970; MS 1975, EdD 1977 Univ Tenn; Cert'd Instr Personal Dynamics Inst Progs: Adventures in Attitudes & Personal Profile Sys & Job Factor Analysis; mil/AUS 1958-60; pa/Tchr Vol Agric, Greene Co Schs, Greeneville, Tenn 1961-69; Curric Conslt, Ga St Dept Ed 1970-72; Dir Voc Ed, Unicoi Co Schs, Erwin, Tenn 1972-74; Dir Career & Voc Ed, Oak Ridge City Schs 1975-; Oak Ridge Ed Assn; E Tenn Ed Assn: Tenn Ed Assn; NEA; Tenn Voc Assn, Co-Chm Leg Com; Am Voc Assn; Tenn Voc Agric Tchrs Assn, Bd Dirs; Tenn Assn Supervision & Curric Devel; So Assn Cnslr Ed & Supervision; Tenn Coun Local Dirs of Voc-Tech Ed, VP, Chm Leg Com; Nat Coun Local Admrs; Am Soc Tng & Devel; Phi Kappa Phi; Phi Delta Kappa; Iota Lambda Sigma; Omicron Tau Theta, Secy, Treas, VP, Pres; cp/Oak Ridge Century Lions Clb, Secy, VP, Pres; r/Bapt; hon/Ed Profl Devel F'ship, Univ Tenn 1974-75; Experienced Tchr F'ship, Miss St Univ 1969-70; Outstg Sec'dy Edr 1974; W/W S&SW 1980; Author "The Role of Business and Industry in Vocational Eduction in th Public Schools in Tennessee."

SCOTT, LINDA PRESTON oc/Psychologist; b/Feb 20, 1941; h/239 Westover Rd, Frankfort, KY 40601; ba/Johnson City; m/Brett Dorse; c/Brett Preston; p/E Jay and Grayce Mollette Preston, Paintsville, KY; ed/BS Pikeville Col 1962; MA En Ky Univ 1968; PhD Univ Ky-Lexington 1972; Visited Univs in Japan, Korea, Thailand & Hong Kong, Summer 1975; Mthly Sems in Psychotherapy, S Bch Psychi Ctr, Staten Isl, NY 1975-76; Other Sems & Wkshops; pa/Claims Rep, Social Security 1962-67; Tchg Fellow, Sch of Hlth, Phys Ed & Rec, En Ky Univ 1967-68; Instr, Dept Hlth, Phys Ed & Rec, Univ Ky 1969-70; Tchg Asst-Instr, Dept Social & Philos Studies, Col of Ed, Univ Ky 1970-72; Visiting Asst Prof, Grad Sch of Ed, Univ Louisville 1972; Asst-Assoc Prof, Dept Ed/Psych, Ky St Univ 1972-78; Dir Res in Ed & Psych, Prin Investigator of Ctrl Sts Res Ser Proj 1973-78; Tchr Classes in Psych for Evening Sch & Ext Prog 1974-78; Dir Inst for Appalachian Affairs, E Tenn St Univ 1978-; Rural Am Wom; Ctrl Sts Res Ser, Exec Com; Ohio Val Philos of Ed Soc, Prog Com Chm; AAUP, Acad Freedom & Tenure Com; Nat Philos of Ed Soc; Assn Correctional Psychs; Am Correctional Assn, Pres Wom's Grp; MENSA; Piaget Soc; Ky Coun on Crime & Delinquency; Nat Coun Crime & Delinquency; Coun on Appalachian Wom, Bd Mem; Rural Regional Ed Assn; Tenn Co Hist Series, Adv Bd Mem; Tenn Com for the Humanities, Bd Mem; SEn Wom's Studies Assn, Editor Newslttr; Appalachian Commun Arts, Bd Mem; Comm on Status of Wom, Adv Com; r/Presb; hon/W/W Am Cols & Univs; Outstg Edrs Am; Edr's Biog; W/W Ky; World W/W Wom; Intl Biogs; Men & Wom of Sci; Personalities of Am;

Notable Ams; Men & Wom Dist; Commun Ldrs & Noteworthy Ams; Num Presentations Incl'g Keynote Speech to Annual Meeting of Tenn Folklore Soc: "What Say Ye Hillbilly: Toward a New Folklore of Appalachia"; Num Articles to Profl Jours Incl'g "The Influence of Country Music on Sex Roles in Rural America" *Human Services in the Rural Environment* & "Any Help From Philosophy" *Insights* Dec 1974.

SCOTT, MADISON MYERS oc/Supvervisor; b/Jan 13, 1949; p/N Philip Scott and Anne M Scott, Lexington, KY; ed/BA Bard Col; Att'd Grad Sch Columbia Univ; pa/Supvr Lexington Mus, Lexington St Pk & Other Intlly Famous Attractions; Land & Nature Trust of the Bluegrass & the Mayor Lexington; cp/Bd Dirs Lexington Repertory Theatre Co; Chm Dem Voter Registration, Fayette Co, Ky 1970 & 80; r/Presb; hon/Ky Col 1979; Mayoral Commend 1979; Author Num Articles for Newspapers; Num TV Interviews 1976-80.

SCOTT, NANCY SUE oc/Teacher; b/Dec 25, 1946; h/Denison, TX; ba/800 W Florence, Denison, TX 75202; p/J L (dec) and Marguerite Scott, Denison, TX; ed/ALS Grayson Co Jr Col 1967; BS 1969, MLS 1972 ETSU; pa/Elem Tchr 12 Yrs; Tex Clrm Tchrs Assn, St Dist X Dir; Chm Profession Excell Com; Denison CTA, Fac Rep; Tex St Tchrs Assn; Denison Ed Assn; NEA; Tex Lib Assn; cp/Alpha Chi; Delta Gamma, Psi Chapt; OES; Rainbow Adv Bd; Life Mem Tex PTA; r/Meth.

SCOTT, PATRICIA ANNE oc/Educational Administrator; b/July 3, 1938; h/Admiral Bristol Hosp, Sch of Nsg, Nisantas, Istanbul, Turkey; ba/Same; c/David Marc Freedman, Lesli Anne Freedman; p/Francis R and Catherine Delores Dunham Scott; ed/BS Columbia Union Col 1961; MSN Univ Pa 1970; pa/Ednl Admr, Admiral Bristol Hosp Sch of Nsg 1979-; Asst Prof, Coor Madison Campus, Madison Ext Campus, Div of Nsg, So Missionary Col 1975-79; Dir Nsg Sers, Seventh Day Adventist Hosp, Pakistan 1973-75; Asst Prof, Loma Linda Univ Sch of Nsg 1972-73; Asst Prof Physical & Mtl Illness, Wesley Col Dept Nsg 1970-72; Relief Charge Nurse, VA Hosp, Summer 1969; Red Cross Instr, School Nurse, S Ruislip AFB, England 1966-68; Clin Instr, Oper'g & Recovery Room, Anatomy Lab Assn, Surg Nsg, Capital City Sch of Nsg, DC Gen Hosp 1964-66; Pvt Duty Nsg, Med, Surg & Psychi Patients, Wash DC RN Registry, Suburban Nurses Registry, Holy Cross Hosp, George Wash Univ Hosp, Wash Adventist Hosp 1963-64; Staff Nurse Emer Room, Relief Charge ICU, Wash Adventist Hosp 1961-62; Staff Nurse Labor & Delivery, Wash Adventist Hosp 1961; Dental Assn, Anesthesia Asst, Harold H Connor DDS 1960; ANA; TSNA, Dist 3; Assn Seventh Day Adventist Nurses; Am Heart Assn; Nashville Mtl Hlth Assn; Am Red Cross; Profl Traveling Nurses Assn; cp/Editor *The Roundabout* 1965-66; Editor *The Highlighter* 1970-71; Tchr Adult Sabbath Sch Class 1977-; r/Seventh Day Adventist; hon/Student Pilot; Author "Search for Sacrifice" & "Going to College Is..." 1957; W/W Am Wom; Sigma Theta Tau.

SCOTT, ROBERT L JR oc/Training Officer; b/Dec 15, 1944; h/13808 Sutters Mill Rd, Midlothian, VA 23113; ba/Richmond; m/Delores Dean Rich; c/Kimberly Dean; p/Robert L Scott Sr, Norfolk, VA; Miriam Ivey Scott, Midlothian, VA; ed/BS 1970, AS 1980, MA 1981, MEd Cand 1982; mil/AUS 1965-67; pa/Tng Ofcr; ASTD; Bellwood Mgmt Assn; cp/Brandermill Homeowners Assn; r/Ch of God; hon/Hon Grad; Outstg Yng Men Am 1974; Outstg Perf Appraisal 1977; Cert Achmt 1978.

SCOTT, THOMAS ALLEN oc/Postmaster; b/Apr 22, 1939; h/310 Schilling St, Athens, AL 35611; ba/Athens; m/Faye; c/Perry, Matthew; p/John and Lucille Scott, Athens, AL; ed/BS Athens St Col; mil/AUS 1963-65; pa/Postmaster; cp/Athens-Limestone Co C of C; r/Ch of Christ.

SCOTT, WILTON C oc/Retired Dean; b/Aug 29, 1921; h/1520 Chevy Chase Rd, Savannah, GA 31301; m/Lillian Shank; c/Teresa L Cutter, Cheryl Lucas; p/Curtis (dec) and Mary Scott (dec); ed/Grad Xavier Univ 1940; MA NYU 1953; 6th Yr Spec Dip NYU 1956; Further Study Columbia Univ, Duquesne Univ, No Ill Univ; mil/AUS; pa/Ret'd Dean Extended Sers, Savannah St Col; Nat Coun of Public Relats Assn; Adult Ed Assn of USA; cp/Bd Dirs YMCA; hon/Merit Ser Awd in Communs, So Regional Pres Inst; Local & Nat YMCA Awds; Columbia Univ Golden Crown Cert; Outstg Edr of Yr 1974-75; Dist'd Magazine Advr Awd; Dip of Hon for Commun Ser; Silver Jubilee Alumnus Awd, Xavier Univ; Columbia Univ Gold Key in Jour; Cert of Merit for Dist'd Ser in Communs & Human Relats, Intl Biogl Assn; So Univs Student Govt Assn's Cert of Apprec as Pubs Advr; Fellow IBA; Intl W/W; Commun Ldrs & Noteworthy Ams; Cited for Accomps by Sen Herman Talmadge; 100% Right Clb's Recog, Dignity & Worthy Among All Men 1967.

SCROGGIE, WARREN GENE oc/Farmer, Real Estate Broker; b/Oct 27, 1943; h/PO Box 1357, Belleview, FL 32620; m/Donna J; c/Jud, Josh, Jeremy; p/Ralph and Norma Scroggie; ed/Grad Rltr Inst; pa/Reg'd Real Est Broker, Scroggie Rlty Inc; Contractor Scroggie Construction; Nat Assn Rltrs; cp/S Marion C of C; Former Mem S Marion JCs; r/Bapt; hon/5 Gallon Donor Awd, Blood Bank; Go-Getter Awd, JCs; Spark Plug Awd,

JCs; Apprec Awd, C of C; Coaches Awd, Indep Fball Leag; Recog Awd 7th Dist Fla JCs.

SCROGGINS, FERMIN DALE oc/Vocational Administrator; b/May 30, 1922; h/PO Box 366, DeSoto, TX 75115; ba/DeSoto; m/Emerine Mary; p/Floyd and Maud Scroggins, Bowie, TX; pa/Voc Admr, DeSoto ISD.

SCRUGGS, ROBERT G oc/Housing Officer; b/Aug 7, 1947; h/PO Box 18626, Raleigh, NC 27619; ba/Raleigh; p/Robert Wade and Sue Belle Scruggs, Horse Shoe, NC; ed/BS Mars Hill Col 1974; AAS Asheville-Buncombe Tech Col 1972; AF NCO Ldrship Sch 1969; Mgmt Analysis Sch 1968; mil/AUS 1966-70; pa/ARC Housing Ofcr, Appalachian Housing Prog; Loan Asst w Farmers Home Adm; Rehab Placement Spec w NC Employment Security Comm; Am Mgmt Assn; Nat Assn DVOPS; cp/Life Mem & Past Dist Comdr Am Legion, Disabled Am Vets, VFW; Pres Pisgah Chapt Trout Unltd; CCDB of Mil Order of the Cooties; Wake Co YDC; SCV; NC St Employees Assn; NC St Wildlife Fed; Wake Co Wildlife Clb; Life Mem: Air Force Assn, Air Force Sgts Assn, AMVETS, BASS, Fed Fly Fisherman, Intl Backpackers Assn, Issiac Walton Leag, Nat Geog Soc, Nat Muzzleloaders Assn, Nat Order Trench Rats, Nat Rifle Assn, Nat Wildlife Fed, NC Geneal Soc, NC Rifle & Pistol Assn, Non-Com Ofcrs Assn, Trout Unltd, r/So Bapt; hon/Am Legion Nat Achmt Awd 1977; W/W Am Jr Cols 1972; W/W S&SW 1980; Disabled Am Vets Dept Outstg Dist Comdr Awd 1980; VAVS Vol Pin & Cert: 100 Hr, 300 Hr; Am Legion Dept Vets Org Rep Vol Cert; Am Legion, DAV & VFW Mbrhsip Recruitement Awd; Disabled Am Vets Dept Outstg Dist Comdr Awd.

SEABOCK, GLENN LEWIS oc/Principal; b/May 27, 1933; h/Rt 5 Box 1321, Hickory, NC 28610; ba/Granite Falls; m/Lila F; c/Elizabeth Lynn, Sarah Lee; p/Hershel J (dec) and Zora Y Seabock, Hickory, NC; ed/BA; MA; EdS; pa/Elem Sch Prin; NCASA; Caldwell Co Prin's Assn; NCA/AP; cp/Granite Falls Rotary Clb; r/Luth; hon/Prin of Yr 1978-79; Pres Granite Falls Rotary Clb 1978-79.

SEAGEARS, MARGARET JACQUELINE oc/Chairman; h/1512 S Arlington Ridge Rd, Arlington, VA 22202; ba/Wash DC; m/Malcolm Thomas; c/George J Ward, Gary K Ward; p/Robert (dec) and Louise West Oliver (dec); ed/AMS Montessori Tchr Tng Cert, Cornell Univ; BS William Patterson St Tchrs Col; MS Univ PR 1967; MA cum laude Columbia Univ 1953; PhD Cand Univ So Calif; pa/Chair, Pres Task Force on Sex Discrimination, Dept of Interior 1978-; Conslt to Fed Wom's Prog, Ofc of Secy, Dept HEW 1976-77; Conslt to US Commr of Ed on Minority Affairs and Spec Projs Relating to Ed; DC Dept Manpwr 1976: YACC, CETA WOW, Job Corps, DC Comm of Arts; Prin/Dir Escuela las Nereidas, The Montessori Center of PR 1973-77; Fdr & Pres First Montessori Tchr Tng Col in Caribbean; Nat Assn Indep Schs; Am Montessori Soc; Nat Assn Univ Wom; NEA; Am Montessori Intl; Nat Assn Child Devel; Nat Assn Sec'dy Prins; Intl Sch Assn; PR Bicent Comm, Chp for Pvt & Public Ed; Past Chp CARE in Caribbean; Conslt to Penn Pvt Sch Accreditation Assn; Conslt to Univ Sagrado Corazon in PR; Conslt to PR Dept Ed; cp/Fdr PR Chd's Theatre; Fdr Fest Arts, San Juan 1968; r/Epis; hon/1 of 10 Outstg Career Wom 1978, Wash Star; W/W Am Wom 1979; F'sip Rutgers Univ 1951, Glassboro St Tchrs Col 1952; Civic Awd Commun Ser, St Thomas, VI 1960; Girl Scout Awd of Excell 1965; Dist'd Ser Awd for Handicapped 1965; Kiwanis Awd for Outstg Citizen 1972; Outstg Ser Awd, Soc Mtl Retard PR 1973; CARE Awd for Outstg Ser 1974; Wom of Yr, Intl Yr of Wom 1975.

SEALE, EDYTHE WHITTINGTON oc/Retired Dairy Farmer; b/Sept 14, 1914; h/Rt 1 Box 66, Meadville, MS; m/Charlie Norman; c/Charlie Norman Jr, Curtis Maxwell; p/Julius Jerome and Effie Jones Whittington; ed/Att'd Copial Lincoln Jr Col 1934; Att'g Art Classes at Brookhaven and McComb, Woodwkg Class Meadville; pa/Franklin Wom's Clb; Pres Bude Home Demo Clb; cp/VP Franklin Fair Assn; Pres VMC of Concord Bapt Ch; r/Bapt; hon/Num Blue Ribbons for Quilts, Canning & Painting; Art Show Meadville Lib 1980.

SEALE, MARGARET RUTH LAMB oc/Music Publisher, Composer, Teacher; b/Apr 20, 1915; h/4674 Franklin Ave, New Orleans, LA 70122; ba/Same; m/Clifton C (dec); c/Clifton C III, Joy Ruth, Robert; p/James Lamb (dec); Edna L Phillips (dec); ed/B Ch Mus, M Ch Mus New Orleans Bapt Theol Sem; pa/Prod of Mus Show "Li'l Ol' Looziana"; Pub'g Mus; cp/ABWA; Alliance for Good Govt; C of C Aux; r/Bapt; hon/ABWA Wom of Yr 1978; Boss of Yr 1979.

SEARS, SARAH ANN oc/Office Nurse; b/June 11, 1929; h/510 Olive Ave, Box 425, Dalhart, TX 79022; ba/Dalhart; m/Marvin G; c/Jimmie Leslie, Kenneth Eugene, Jack Weslie, Joe Alan, Randall Anthony, William Martin; p/William Amos (dec) and Blanche Estelle Douthirt Raines (dec); ed/LVN; RN; pa/Am Assn Med Assts; cp/Am Heart Assn; Pilots Intl; Elkettes; VFW Aux; r/Rom Cath; hon/W/W Am Wom 1979-80.

SEATON, CHRISTINE WHEELER oc/Teacher; b/Sept 25, 1926; h/Rt 3 Box 408, Dyersburg, TN 38024; m/Vernon Leon; c/David Lynn; p/George Washington and Tilda Wheeler; ed/BS Ed; pa/Life Mem NEA; Delta Kappa Gamma; Pres D'burg Ed Assn; Del to NEA Conv 1969; cp/Dir D'burg Wom's Clb; Four Seasons Gdn Clb; Finley Home Demo Clb; Past Chm Dyer Co Wom in 1962; Dem Party; r/Bapt; hon/Awd of Merit 1978-79, Dyer Co Fair; Floral Awd Horticultural Excell 1979; Rosette for Best of Show in Related Arts & Crafts 1979; Cert Apprec, Gov 1975.

SEATON, MARY NOLAN oc/Treasurer; b/May 10, 1914; h/1509 Decatur Pike, Athens, TN 37303; m/dec; c/Paul Ray, John Nolan; p/Charles Lee (dec) and Mary Susan Nolan (dec); ed/Bus Col 1953; pa/Elem Tchr 6 Yrs; Treas Seaton Iron & Metal Co Inc; cp/Nat Rep WOW 1977-80; Rep'd E Tenn at San Diego, Calif Nat Conv WOW; r/Meth; hon/Wom of Woodcraft 1971, Woodmen of World; Plaque, Spec Recog WOW 1972; Hon Plaque 1979 WOW.

SEAWOOD, JAMES RUSSELL oc/Associate Professor; b/May 16, 1923; h/Pine Bluff, AR; ba/UA-PB, Box 74, Pine Bluff, AR 71601; m/Martha Vata; c/James L, M Leona, Gordan R, Jane Russell; p/Leona Nesbitt, St Louis, MO; ed/BA Univ Ark 1947; MA Tchrs Col Columbia Univ 1948; PhD Kan St Univ 1979; mil/AUS 1943-45; pa/Assoc Prof Indust Technol, Univ Ark & Chm Review of Indust Technol Progs; Chm Tool & Equip Inventories; Proposal Writing Com; Com on New Progs; S'ship Com; Homecoming Com; AAUP; Ark Chapt AAUP; Am Voc Assn; NEA; AEA; Ark Assn Public Cont'g & Adult Ed; New Tradesmen of Ark; Am Coun Indust Arts Tchrs Ed; Omega Psi Phi; cp/Hon Dpty Sheriff 1974-76; Spec Dpty Sheriff 1976-78, 78-; r/Bapt; hon/25 yr Pin UAPB 1973; Awd Cert, 25 Yrs Merit Ser to Higher Ed in Ark 1978.

SEAY, MIRIAM TYE oc/Retired; b/Oct 31, 1918; m/Mathew B; c/Carol Tye S Nichols, Raymond M; p/Thomas O (dec) and Leta Cowart Tye (dec); ed/AA Abraham Baldwin Agric Col 1938; BSHE Univ Ga 1940; pa/Farm & Home Adm 1940-44; St Fla Social Wkr 1945-80; Social Dir Lakeland Convalescent Ctr; Commun Ser Coun, Secy; Am Red Cross, Local Disaster Team; cp/AAUW; r/Meth; hon/AM Flag Flown Over US Capital in Hon of Long Yrs Ser; 2 Hlth & Rehab Ser Merit Awds 1973 & 80; W/W Am Wom 1980.

SEDGWICK, BILL oc/Realtor; b/Nov 20, 1945; h/Rt 1, 240 Glenwood Tr, Forney, TX 75126; m/Dianne; c/Tracy, Carrie, Suzie; p/Don W and Mary M Sedgwick, Pt Lavaca, TX; ed/BS SWTSU 1970; mil/USAR & NG 6 Yrs; pa/Owner Real Est & Hme Bldg Co; Kaufman-Van Zandt Bd Rltrs 1973-, Pres 1979, VP 1978; cp/Forney ISD Sch Bd 1976-82, Pres 1980; Forney Kiwanis 1980; Bd Dirs Forney Bank & Trust 1977-; r/Cath.

SEGRE, BERYL GAY oc/Assistant Professor; b/Feb 15, 1943; h/New Orleans, LA; ba/Hlth Ed Prog, Dillard Univ, 2601 Gentilly Blvd, New Orleans, LA 70122; p/Wesley N Segre, New Orleans, LA; E Lucile Segre (dec); ed/AB Fisk Univ 1966; MSW Tulane Univ Sch of Social Work 1971; MPH Tulane Univ Sch of Public Hlth & Tropical Med 1975; pa/Asst Prof Hlth Ed, Coor Hlth Ed Prog, Dillard Univ 1979-; Social Wkr, Dept Pediatrics, Yale-New Haven Hosp 1971-74; Social Ser & Rehab Supvr, New Orleans Hlth Dept Methodone Clin 1971-; Social Wkr, Fam Plan'g Inc 1969; Casewkr, Phila Co Bd Asst 1966-68; NASW; APHA; cp/New Orleans Chapt Links Inc: Corresp Secy 1976-80, Pres 1980-82; Dillard Aux, Pres 1980-82; Alpha Kappa Alpha 1971-; Am Lung Assn of La 1981-; NAACP; r/Prot; hon/YWCA Bicent Achmt Awd 1976.

SEIDEL, MARIANNE oc/Psychiatrist; b/Feb 2, 1943; h/6651 Lakeridge Dr, Texarkana, TX 75503; ba/Texarkana; p/Karl A and Annemarie K Seidel, Hendersonville, NC; ed/BS; MP; pa/AMA; Am Psychi Assn; hon/Phi Beta Kappa.

SEIKEL, ROBERT EUGENE oc/Branch Manager; b/Feb 23, 1933; h/Rt 5 Box 300, Shawnee, OK 74801; ba/Shawnee; m/Charlotte Joan; c/Jay, Terri, Craig, David; p/Leo V and Opal Seikel; ed/BBA Univ Okla; mil/AUS 1953-55; pa/Br Mgr Social Security Adm; Mayor's Coun on Aging; Past Pres The Commun Ser Coun; cp/Clerk on Sch Bd D-32; Scout Master Boy Scout Troop 443; Shawnee Lions Clb; r/Ch of Christ; hon/JC Ser to Humanity Awd; 2 Spec Achmt Awds, Social Security Adm.

SEIZ, ALICE J oc/Store Supervisor; b/Jan 8, 1954; h/Dallas, TX; ba/Exxon Co USA, 1201 E Airport Frwy, Irving, TX 75062; ed/BA 1976, MBA 1980 Rutgers Univ; pa/Sr Ofc Admr, Siemens Corp 1976-78; Tng Analyst, Equitable Life 1978-79; Mktg Analyst, Exxon Co, Dallas, Tex 1980-81; Store Supvr, Exxon Co, Irving, Tex 1981-; AMBA; NAFE; cp/Jr Achmt Advr 1981; hon/W/W Am Wom 1980-81.

SELF, CLARK JR oc/Businessman; b/July 10, 1933; h/5527 79th St, Lubbock, TX 79424; ba/Slaton, TX; m/Jean Sargent; c/Leslie Ann, Todd Alan, Charles, Michael, Juli; p/Clark Sr and Irene Self, Slaton, TX;

ed/BBA Tex Tech Univ; pa/Owner-Mgr Self Furniture Co; Co-Owner Century Developments; Past Dist Dir SW Home Furnishings Assn; cp/Rotary Clb; Past Pres Slaton C of C & BCD; r/Ch of Christ; hon/Trustee Lubbock Christian Col & Lubbock Christian Schs.

SELLERS, FRED COURT oc/Certified Public Accountant; b/Jan 19, 1924; h/11601 Green Oaks St, Houston, TX 77024; ba/Houston; m/Ray Vina Aucoin; c/Fred Court, Sharon Ann; p/James Henry & Etta Court Sellers; ed/Univ Houston 1940-43; mil/USAAF 1943-46; pa/Sr Acct U Gas Corp, Houston 1941-59; Self-Employed, Houston 1969-; Corporate Secy: Postive Feed Inc, Sealy, Tex; Corporate Secy: Northwest Assocs, Houston, Tex; Pre Harris Co Yth S'ship Fund; Am Inst CPAs; Tex Soc CPAs; Houston Chapt Tex Soc CPAs; cp/Optimist Clb, Past VP; Rotary Clb; r/Bapt; Deacon; hon/Key Man Awd, Jr C of C 1948.

SELLERS, JOSEPH AMOS oc/Tire Center Executive; b/Aug 27, 1927; ba/2802 Johnston St, Lafayette, LA 70503; m/Irene Dugas; c/Karl Steven, Janet Claire; p/Emile (dec) and Ematile Lemaire Sellers, Lafayette, LA; mil/USAF 1945-47; Rice Farmer, 1947-48; Asst Party Chief US Coast & Geodetic Surveys 1948-53; High Presssure Pump Oper, Freeport Sulphur Co 1953-54; Owner Sellers Texaco Ser 1954-66; Mgr Tire Ctr, BF Goodrich Tire Co; cp/Gtr Lafayette C of C; Dem Party; r/Cath.

SELLS, HARLON DEE oc/Laborer; b/Feb 26, 1918; h/Alpine, TN; c/David, Linda, Danny, Juanita, Barbara, Billie, Mike; p/Alvin and Ellen Sells; mil/AUS 4½ Yrs; pa/Hydraulic Ram.

SENA, DEAN R oc/Business Consultant; b/June 15, 1945; h/9516 S Dixie Hwy, Miami, FL 33156; m/Sherrill Barfield; c/Derek; p/D Richard and Dorothy Parsons Sena, Coral Gables, FL; ed/BA Univ Miami; pa/Reg'd Real Est Broker; Acquisition & Mergers Spec; Am Mktg Assn; Nat Assn Bus Brokers; cp/Country Clb of Coral Gables; r/Cath; hon/Civitan Clb Outstg Salesmanship Awd; Author "Buying and Selling a Business."

SENESAC, RAY oc/Administrator; ba/Montgomery County Courthouse, Conroe, TX 77301; m/Married; pa/Worked w US Coast & Geodetic Survey, took part in producing 1st radio beam maps for commercial aviation; Worked w Tenn Valley Auth; Topographic Draftsman, US Army Corps of Engrs; Flood Plain Admr for Montgomery Co; Profl Singing Perfs w LA Civic Light Opera Assn, Hollywood Bowl Choir (perf'd w Frank Sinatra, Judy Garland, Lena Horne, Nelson Eddy, Others); Major Prodns incl: *The Vagabond King, Carmen, The Merry Widow,* Others; Recording Artist.

SENG, MINNIE A oc/Librarian, Editor; b/Nov 30, 1909; p/Edward (dec) and Ella Pattie Seng (dec); ed/AB Univ Mich 1932; ABLS 1935; MALS 1943; pa/Asst Med Libn, Univ Iowa; Order Libn, Mich Technol Univ; Hd Cataloger, Calif St Univ; Editor Ed Index, H W Wilson Co; Hd Cataloger, St Ambrose Col; Frostburg St Col; Am Horticultural Soc; AAUW, Corresp Secy 1978-; cp/House & Gdn Clb; r/Prot; hon/Editor Ed Index 1959-66.

SENNETT, CHARLES EDWARD oc/Minister; b/Oct 23, 1942; h/606 W G St, Elizabethton, TN 37643; ba/E'ton; m/Elizabeth Dorlene Thorne; c/Charles Dwayne, Michael Edward; p/R E and Belvia Sennett, Seffner, FL; ed/BDiv, MMin; DMin; pa/Coor Fgn & US Mission Work; Cert'd to Tch Ldrship Classes; Radio & TV Work; Bus Dir; Spkr Wkshops & Lectures; cp/Scout Master; Pres Fire Dept; r/Ch of Christ.

SENTELL, SUZANNE HARRISON oc/Administrative Head, Corporate Secretary; b/Oct 17, 1946; m/Gilbert L; c/Christopher Gilbert; p/Benjamin Franklin Sr (dec) and Susie Williams Harrison, Eufaula, AL; ed/BS Univ Ala 1968; pa/Sentell Engrg Inc 1981-; Sentell, Morin & Bass Inc 1977-81; Almon & Assocs Inc 1973-77; Tuscaloosa Homebldrs Aux, Treas 1981, Corres Secy 1979, Telephone Com, Leg Com, Chm Budget & Auditing, Hist 1978; r/Bapt; hon/Nat Merit Awd, Scrapbook, Tuscaloosa Homebldrs Aux 1978.

SEPULVEDA, JUANITA (JANIE) oc/Manager; b/Mar 27, 1940; h/709 Alpine, Palestine, TX 75801; ba/Palestine; m/Arturo; c/Arturo Reynaldo, Carlos Aaron, Marcos Adrian; p/Geronimo S Gonzales, Luling, TX; Nicolasa M Gonzales, San Antonio, TX; ed/Secy Sch 1 Yr; Jr Col 2 Yrs; pa/Mgr Little Mexico Rest; TSTA; Adv Coun HECE; Assoc'd Clarities; cp/PCCW; SHIYO Advr; Cancer Crusader; Title I Adv Coun; r/Cath; SS Tchr; hon/Chili Cook Off Winner.

SETTELL, ANGELA A LOYOLA oc/Key District Manager; b/Sept 4, 1944; h/8656 Totempole Dr, Cinci, OH 45242; ba/Cinci; m/Bruce Allen; c/Sommer Hunt; p/Angel Mina and Carmelite Richter Loyola, New Orleans, LA; ed/BS La St Univ 1966; pa/Key Dist Mgr, Intl Examrs & Computer Audit Specs, IRS; Phi Chi Theta, Nat Pres 1974-78; Profl Frat Assn, Nat VP 1980-81; r/Cath; hon/Phi Chi Theta Key Awd 1966; Outstg Yng Wom Am 1976; W/W Am 1980.

SEVER, ZIYA oc/Department Chairman; b/July 14, 1935; ba/Alvin, TX; m/Suzanne; c/Rashid, Timor, Cindy; p/Mehmed Nuri (dec) and Bilkis Sever (dec); ed/BA 1959, MA 1964 Univ Tulsa; Post Grad Work Univ Houston 1977-80; pa/Chm Art Dept, Alvin Commun Col; Num Exhibs; Clear Lake Art Leag; Tex Jr Col Tchrs Assn; Alvin Art Leag; r/Moslem; hon/Hon Mention, Drawing, Brockton Art Assn 7th Nat Exhib 1964; Gold Medal of Hon, Watercolor, Nat Exhib Low Ruins Gal 1965; Hon Mention, Oil, Carlsbad Area Art Assn Spring Exhib 1965; Hon Mention, Oil, 10th Annual Nat Exhib Sun Carnival 1965; Hon Mention, Oil, 11th Annual Nat Exhib 1966; Silver Awd, Watercolor, Fourth Dorchester Nat Exhib 1967; Cash Awd of Merit, Mus of Fine Arts, Shreveport, La 1967; City of Baytown XIII Annual Nat Art Exhib 1979; Tulsa St Fair: 3rd Pl Oil 1959, 2nd Pl Oil 1961, 1st Pl Oil 1962; Best in Show, Spring Fest Tyler, Tex 1963; Cash Awd of Merit, Regional Juried Art Exhib, Newport News, Va 1969; Top Awd, Regional Mercury Mall Jury & Exhib, Hampton, Va 1974; Other Awds for Art; Author Textbook *Drawing* 1979.

SEWELL, ELOISE BUSH oc/Principal; b/Aug 11, 1931; m/Freddie H; c/Freddie Jr, Reginald, Charles; p/Sam Bush, Marshall, TX; ed/BA Bishop Col 1952; MEd Prairie View A&M Univ 1971; Adm Cert, Prairie View 1975; pa/Prin San Antonio Indep Sch Dist, Pauline Nelson Elem Sch; Tex Elem Prins & Supvrs Assn; NEA; TSTA; San Antonio Admrs Assn; Phi Delta Kappa; Alamo Rdg Coun; cp/Nat Coun Negro Wom Inc; Top Ladies Dist, Corres Secy; r/Epis; hon/Plaque for Outstg Achmts in Ed, Gamma Tau Chapt Phi Delta Kappa 1980; Mem Proj Com Pub "Education for Responsible Citizenship" 1977.

SEWELL, LEON O oc/Coordinator; b/May 5, 1930; h/Box 25824, Okla City, OK 73125; ba/Okla City; m/Lucille; c/Redina, Lenora, Charles, (Stepch:) Cathy, Daniel; p/Bailey O Sewell (dec); Ruby Evans, Okla City, OK; ed/BA Okla Bapt Univ; pa/Coor'g Chaplain & Cnslg Sers for St Insts; cp/Rotary Intl, Past Pres Weatherford, Okla Clb; r/Bapt; hon/Chapt for Okla St Senate 1970, 72, 74.

SEXAUER, ARWIN F B GARELLICK oc/Retired Head Librarian, Poet-Lyricist-Composer; b/Aug 18, 1921; h/Cherry Tree Hill, E Montpelier, VT 05651, or Idle Tide Cottage, Box 303, Sanibel, FL 33957; m/Howard T; c/Dawn-Linnie Bashaw Mennucci, Alson C Bashaw; p/Alson B and Linnie A Fletcher (dec); ed/Hon D Litt World Univ; Hon Dip Athens, Greece; Diploma di benemerenza, Accademia Leonardo da Vinci; pa/Co-Fdr Mus Mission Inc; Hd Libn, Kellogg-Hubbard Lib 1974-76, Asst Libn 1966-73; Editor Vt Odd Fellow Mag 1959-70; Staff Reporter *Times-Argus Daily* 1964-65; Radio/Theatre Monologist 1939-53; Free-lance Writer 1936-; Hon Fellow Anglo-Am Acad; Life Fellow Intl Acad Poets; Dist'd Fellow ABI; World Poetry Soc Intercontl; Dr Stella Woodall Poetry Soc Intl; ASCAP; Gospel Mus Assn; Intl Platform Assn, Vt Lib Assn; Centro Studi E Scambi Internationali, Accademia Leonardo da Vinci of Rome; Assoc Mem Acad Am Poets; NY Poetry Forum; IPA Poets Acad; Intl Press Assn; IOOF; Works Placed in 20 Archival Depostis Inclg: Palace of Monaco, Israel Inst Sacred Mus, Kennedy Meml in Jerusalem, USN Band Mus Lib; cp/4-H Ldr 21 Yrs; r/U Meth; hon/4-H: Diamond Awd, Merit Plaque; Poet Laureate Awd, Accademia Leonardo da Vinci; First Wom Editor Vt Odd Fellow Mag; 133 Awds & Hons; Recip; 27 Intl Mus Instruments in Apprec of Mus Mission; 31 Intl & Am Biogl Listings; Richard Rodgers Mus Foun Awd; Grand Ole Opry Trust Fund Mus Awd; Dist'd Ser Cit for Poetry, World Bd Regents of World Poetry Soc Intercontl; Author Sev Profl Pubs Inclg *Remembered Winds*, Book of Poetry; *Music Mission Songs from La Casa de Paz* 1981.

SEXTON, FRANCES CROSS oc/Accountant; b/Aug 23, 1935; h/Rt 2 Box 26, Denison, TX 75020; ba/Denison; m/Bobby J; c/Rebecca Jo, Mary Frances; p/Odes and Agnes Cross, Durant, OK; ed/Att'd SEn Univ & Grayson Co Col; pa/Proprietor Sexton Tax Ser; Pres Sexton Elec Inc; Nat Elec Contractors Assn; BPW Clb; Nat Assn Tax Consltrs; r/Cath; hon/Caught Trophy Barracuda, Miami, FL.

SEXTON, JAMES DAVID oc/Assistant Professor; b/May 20, 1948; h/1139 Rudd Ave, Auburn, AL 36830; ba/Auburn; p/James E Sexton, Morristown, TN; Mary N Sexton, Lenoir City, TN; ed/BS 1970, MS 1974, PhD 1980 Univ Tenn; mil/AUS 1970-72; pa/Tchr-Dir Early Childhood Ed & Acting Dir Ednl Sers, SC Dept Mtl Retard, Whitten Ctr 1974-80; Asst Prof Rehab & Spec Ed, Auburn Univ, 1980-; Am Assn Mtl Deficiency; Am Home Ec Assn; cp/Assn Retard'd Citizens; hon/Piedmont Employee of Yr 1976; Author "Involving Families in an Eductional Program for Institutionalized Multihandicapped Children" 1976; "Waterplay for Multihandicapped Children" 1975.

SGROI, MICK oc/Free-lance Pantomimist; b/Apr 7, 1946; ba/Louisville, KY; c/Marceline Etienete, Andre Lloyd, Lance Eric; p/Mick Sgroi; Carol Thompson, Belleville, IL; ed/Studied w Etienne Decroux 1969, Marcel Marceau 1969; MFA So Ill Univ 1980; pa/Free-lance Pantomimist; Intl Mimes & Pantomimists; r/Universalist; hon/Co Judge

Declared Mar 21 "Mick Sgroi Day" Hancock Co; Artist-in-Residence, Ky Arts Comm 1981; Artist-in-Residence, Spec Arts Proj, Jefferson Co 1977-81.

SHADDOCK, JOANNA RUTH oc/Assistant Supervisor; b/Feb 19, 1935; h/2804 Winter Park Dr, Lexington, KY 40502; ba/Frankfort, KY; p/Estes (dec) and Ethelleen Shaddock (dec); pa/Asst Supvr; r/Bapt.

SHAFFER, LAWRENCE BLAINE III oc/Assistant Professor; b/Aug 14, 1950; h/10129 Finky Rd, Apt G, Okla City, OK 73120; ba/Okla City; p/L B Jr and Frances Shaffer, Duncan, OK; ed/BS Tulane Univ 1972; MD Univ Okla 1976; pa/Asst Prof, Univ Okla Col Med, Dept Psychi & Behavioral Scis; r/Prot; hon/Laughlin Fellow 1979, Am Col Psychi.

SHAFRAN, GEORGE PETER oc/Executive; b/May 4, 1926; h/4026 41st St, N, Arlington, VA 22207; ba/Arlington; m/Angela D; c/Thomas G, James B, Jack D, Jane M; p/dec; ed/Patterson St Tchrs Col 1944; mil/USN 1944-47, 48-51 Lt; pa/Fdr & Owner Better Homes Rlty; Pres & Owner Homes for Living Inc, Rlty Prog'g Corp; Nat Assn Rltrs; No Va Bd of Rltrs, Past Pres; Va Assn Rltrs, Past Dir; Omega Tau Rho; VP Harrison & Shafran Inc; Dir Better Homes Mortgage Corp; Dir First & Merchants Nat Bank; Dir No Va Savings & Loan Assn; Dir Rel Heritage of Am; cp/Va Gen Assem 1970-71; Bd Mem Dept Conserv & Ec Devel; Dir Am Coun Capital Formation; r/Epis; hon/Rltr of Yr 1965; Ethics Awd 1967; Bus-man of Yr 1976; Sev Articles to Real Est Pubs.

SHANBOUR, LINDA LIVINGSTON oc/Physiologist; b/Mar 15, 1942; h/Cape Royale, 14 Imperial Cir, Coldspring, TX 77331; ba/Houston; c/Richard Livingston, Kamal Anthony, Brian Michael; p/Charles Lee and Ada Patricia Livingston, Okla City, OK; ed/BS Ctrl St Univ; MS Univ Okla; PhD Univ Ala; pa/Fdg & Charter Mem Tex Res Soc on Alcoholism; Physiologist, Univ Tex Med Sch at Houston; cp/Adv Bd Vols of Am; r/Epis; hon/BS summa cum laude 1963; NIH Predoct F'ship 1965-68; NIH Res Scist Devel Awd 1972-77.

SHANE, ALAN RICHARD oc/Attorney, Executive; b/Feb 29, 1948; h/4174 Inverrary Dr, Lauderhill, FL 33319; ba/Miami; p/Raymond and Francine Shane, Tamarac, FL; ed/BS Univ Ill 1969; JD Loyola Univ 1972; pa/VP, Secy, Gen Counsel Royal Trust Bank Corp; Admitted to US Supreme Ct 1977; Fla, Ill & DC Bars; Am Bar Assn; Ill St Bar Assn; Decalogue Soc; Corp Counsel Assn of Dade Co; r/Jewish; hon/Apprec Awd for Cont Support of the Goals of AWRT 1979; Author Num Profl Articles.

SHANE, DEBORAH LYNNE oc/Executive; b/Mar 24, 1950; ba/4699 N St Rd 7, Ft Lauderdale, FL 33319; p/Raymond and Francine Shane; ed/BA 1971, PhD 1977 Univ Miami-Coral Gables; pa/VP & Dir: Assoc Leasing Intl Corp & Assoc Fin Instl Corp; Gold Coast Chapt, Am Wom in Radio & TV Inc, Pres 1978-79, 79-80; Wom's Fla Assn of Broadcasters Inc, Pres 1978-; Spec Advr, US Inst of Theatre Technol, So Fla Area; Recording Secy, Bd Dirs & St Com Chm (1978), Fla Motion Picture & TV Assn, S Chapt; Nat Acad of TV Arts & Scis, Miami Chapt; Wom in Communs, Miami Chapt; Soc of Motion Picture & TV Engrs, Miami Chapt; Chgo Wom in Broadcasting; Playwrights Ctr, Chgo; Am Fed TV & Radio Artists, Miami; Guest Author *Lighting Dimensions Magazine* Oct 1977; Guest Author *Backstage Magazine* May 1978; Life Mem Nat Thespians Soc, Troupe 113; Fla Assn Broadcasters; cp/Delta Zeta, Gold Coast Alumnae Chapt, Recommendations Chm 1978, 79; Gtr Ft Lauderdale Panhellenic; Chaverim Chapt B'nai B'rith Wom; Press Coor, Gov Reuben Askew, St of Fla Sunshine Amendment Day, Dade Co, Mar 1976; Sigma Phi Epsilon, Pres Little Sisters & Sweetheart 1970; Ednl Foun Am Wom in Radio & TV Inc; Univ Miami Alumni Assn; AWRT Spkrs Bur; Liaison Advr, Col Communrs in Broadcasting, Univ Miami; r/Jewish; hon/W/W Am Wom; St Bd Com Chm FMPTA 1978, 79; Delta Zeta Outstg Alumnae Recog Awd for Achmts in Broadcasting Career 1977; B'nai B'rith Wom of Yr for Public Ser to Commun 1974; Judge, News & Documentaries, 17th Annual Chgo Emmy Awds; Chgo Wom in Broadcasting Spec Awd for Promoting Better Chd's Prog'g 1974; Public Relats Coun, Fla Hosp Assn, Judge for 11th Annual Awds Comp 1978; Am Wom in Radio & TV Apprec Awd 1978, 79; Key to City of Miami Bch & AWRT Day Proclaimed in Hon, May 30, 1979; 1st Annual Gold Coaster Outstg TV Talent.

SHANKLE, MILLICENT HISLOP oc/Businesswoman; b/Sept 14, 1942; h/405 Fairhope, Fairhope, AL 36532; m/Damon Lewis; c/Martha Elaine, Dana Elizabeth; p/Ed Jr (dec) and Alice Elaine Faust Hislop, W Monroe, LA; ed/BBA Baylor Univ 1965; Reg'd Bridal Conslt, Nat Bridal Ser; pa/Sch Tchr 5 Yrs; Owner Thoroughly Modern Millie Bridal Shop; Fairhope Retail Mchts Assn, Bd Dirs; r/Bapt.

SHARMA, SUNIL K oc/Industrial Engineer; b/Mar 14, 1946; h/15331 E Westwood, Houston, TX 77071; ba/Houston; m/Rashmi; c/Sanjay; p/M L and Shanta Sharma, Jaipur, India; ed/BE Univ Indore, India 1969; MS Miss St Univ 1974; MBA Univ Houston 1978; pa/Dir Mgmt Engrg, St

PERSONALITIES OF THE SOUTH

Luke's Epis & Tex Chd's Hosps 1978-; Sr Mgmt Engr, St Joseph Hosp 1976-78; Sales Mgr Thomas Nelson Co 1972-76; Machine Shop Supvr, Indian Smeltings & Refining Co 1969-70; AIIE; Hosp Mgmt Sys Soc; Gtr Houston Hosp Mgmt Sys Soc, Secy 1980, Treas 1979, Dir & Mbrship Chm 1976-78; cp/Pres & Social Chm Intl Clb MSU; VP India Assn of MSU; Rep'd S Region, Nat Assn Fgn Students Affairs Annual Conf; r/Hindu; hon/Hon Citizen Awd; W/W S&SW 1980-81; Alpha Pi Mu; Author Sev Profl Pubs.

SHARP, OPAL M oc/Affiliate Broker; b/Feb 13, 1912; h/1750 Ocoee St NE, Cleveland, TN 37311; m/James G (dec); c/Francine S Buchanan; p/Edgar Owen (dec) and Electa R McNabb (dec); ed/Nat Sch Bus Grad; Att'd Univ Chattanooga & Cleveland St Commun Col; pa/Real Est; Farming; C'land Bd Rltrs, Ed & Civic Com; Wom's Coun Bd Rltrs, Treas; cp/C'land/Bradley C of C; Secy Operation Commun Beautiful of C of C; r/U Meth; hon/Winner Num Ribbons, C'land Gdn Clb; Pres C'land Wom's Clb.

SHARPE, KENNETH RICHARD oc/Evangelist; b/Mar 31, 1957; h/Rt 3 Box 97, Leicester, NC 28748; m/Nancy; p/James Wilson and Dorothy Lee Sharpe, Leicester, NC; ed/BA Gardner-Webb Col 1979; Att'g SWn Bapt Theol Sem; pa/NC St Bapt Conv; r/So Bapt.

SHARWELL, GEORGE ROBERT oc/Professor; b/Jan 2, 1937; h/3523 Wilmot St, Columbia, SC 29205; ba/Columbia; c/Brad Alan, Erin Elizabeth; p/Truman Parker and Agnes May Sharwell, Trenton, NJ; ed/BA Allegheny Col 1960; MS Va Commonwlth Univ 1964; JD Univ SC 1974; ml/USAF 1955-59; pa/Prof, Col Social Work, Univ SC; Admitted to SC St Bar 1975, Cont'g Legal Ed Com 1975-76, Fam Law Com 1976-77, Lwyrs Asst Com 1979-80; Am Bar Assn 1975-; AAUP 1970-; Coun on Social Work Ed 1969-; Nat Coun Fam Relats 1974-; Fam Law Sect, Am Bar Assn 1974-; Acad of Cert'd Social Wkrs 1971-; NASW 1962-; Reg'd Social Wkr, St of SC; SC Social Wel Forum: Mem 1969-, Chm Leg Com 1977-78, Dir 1978-80, Chm Hist Com 1979-80; SC St Chapt NASW: Mem 1969-, VP 1977-78, Pres 1979-81; Univ Press of Univ of SC: Press Com 1975-, Conslr on Social Wel Matters 1975-, Chm Press Com 1978-80; Mng Ed, *Arete* 1970-; Editorial Bd *Social Work* 1976-78; Conslg Editor *Social Work* 1978-80; Manuscript Reviewer: *Jour of Sex Res, Jour of Social Wel, Chd & Yth Sers Review, Social Devel Issues*; Mem Review Panel for Juvenile Just Standards, Jt Com of Am Bar Assn 1975-76; cp/Coord for Sch Bd, Richland Sch Dist 2, Dem Primary 1976; SC Child Protect Adv Com: Chm Com on Leg 1977-79; Optimist Clb, Pres 1979-80; Palmetto Place Child Care Shelter, Dir 1977-80; Contact HELP Ser Hotline, Dir 1977-80; U Way of Midlands, SC: Info & Referral Adv Bd 1975-76, Resource Info Com 1976-77; Commun Care Inc, Dir 1969-71; Bosom Drug Cnslg Ctr, Dir 1971-72; r/Meth; hon/W/W S&SW; Optimist Awd for Yth Ser 1979; Pub'd Num Articles & Book Reviews in Profl Jours; Pub'd Chapt in *Toward Human Dignity: Social Work in Practice* 1979.

SHATTUCK, JUDITH JOYCE oc/Businesswoman; b/June 6, 1946; h/16110 Harpoon Ct, Crosby, TX 77532; ba/Crosby; m/Vernon Cecil; c/Pamela Rae, John Baillio; p/John (dec) and Evelyn Civeroio (dec); ed/Att'd Univ Tex, Univ NM, Univ Albuquerque; pa/Data Processing; Art Shows; cp/Girashy Sch Vol Prog; Registration of Voters; Vol in Polit & Sch Campaigns; Cystic Fibrosis Campaign Mgr 1978; r/Cath; hon/Art Awds; Vol Awds; Citizens Adv Com, Crosby Sch Com.

SHAUGHNESSY, MARY ETHEL oc/Director of Dietetics; b/Feb 6, 1916; h/St Mary's Medical Center, Oakhill Ave, Knoxville, TN; p/Edward Michael Shaughnessy (dec); Charolyn Jecker (dec); ed/BS Edgecliff Col 1946, Grad Study Univ Cinci 1946; Internship & Grad Study St Louis Univ 1946-47; Spec Study, Tchr Col, Cinci 1943-44; pa/Dir Dietary Sers, St Mary's Med Ctr 1965-; Dir Dietetics, Mercy Hosp 1955-65; Dir Dietetics, Our Lady of Mercy Hosp 1948-55; Chm & Editor of Dietary Ser Sect, *Hospital Progress Journal*, Catholic Hosp Assn 1952-53; Treas, Food Ser Assn, Hamilton, Ohio 1960-61; Co-Chm Food Adm Sect, Ohio Dietetic Assn 1963, Chm 1964-65; Knoxville Dist Dietetic Assn, Pres 1969-70; Other Spec Appts; Am Soc Hosp Food Ser Admrs, Am Hosp Assn; Am Dietetic Assn; Tenn Dietetic Assn; Knoxville Dist Dietetic Assn; Mem Task Force for St Tenn For Surveying St Food Sers of 31 St Insts 1974; r/Rom Cath; hon/Outstg Dietitian for St of Tenn 1971; Rec'd Voc Ed Awd, Knoxville City Sch Bd 1975; Cert of Apprec, Univ Tenn, Col Home Ec 1973-80; Ky Col 1968; W/W S&SW 1980-81; Am Soc Hosp Food Ser Admrs, Dist'd Hlth Care Amdr; Author Sev Profl Articles.

SHAW, ALENE SHEARER oc/Retired Teacher; b/Jan 26, 1909; h/Box 504, Pembroke, GA 31321; m/James Tennant (dec); c/Shearer Shaw Rogers; p/Oscar French and Rosa Elliott Shearer; ed/BS Ga So Col 1954; Att'd Young Harris Col 1928; pa/Elem Tchr 31 Yrs; Piano Instr; pa/Pres Bryan Unit Ga Ed Assn; Pres Ga Ret'd Tchrs Assn 1980-81; cp/Past Pres Pembroke Garden Clb; Beta Theta Chapt Delta Kappa Gamma; r/U Meth; Organist.

SHAW, CASWELL EURE oc/Minister; b/July 10, 1939; h/210 Brandon Ave, Tarboro, NC 27886; ba/Tarboro; m/Patricia Bissette; c/William Glenn, David Allen; p/Naomi Dickens Shaw, Halifax, NC; ed/AB Atlantic Christian Col 1963; BD SEn Theol Sem 1966; pa/U Meth Min 19 Yrs; Mem Bd of Ch & Soc; Bd of Min; r/Meth; hon/"This is Your Life, Caswell Shaw", by Ch.

SHAW, JESSIE IRENE oc/Bookkeeper; b/Mar 6, 1905; h/Ponca City, OK; m/Arthur; c/Clarence R, Doris Maxine Lewis; p/George Nelson (dec) and Margret Elizabeth Rice (dec); ed/Ponce City Bus Col 1945; pa/Bkkpr & Ofc Mgr, Shaw's Auto Parts & Machine; cp/Kay Co Repub Wom, Pres 2 Yrs; Ponca City Wom's Clb, Pres & Treas; Okla Fed BPW Clbs, St Treas 2 Yrs & Leg, Fin, Pers Devel Ch-wom 1 Yr; r/First Ch of God; hon/Wom of Yr, BPW Clb 1962-63.

SHAW, LARRY DON oc/State Representative; Rancher; b/Jan 29, 1953; h/1307 Barnes, Big Spring, TX 79720; ba/Austin, TX; p/Larry and Bertie Shaw, Knott, TX; ed/BS Tex Tech Univ 1975; pa/Cotton Farmer; Partner in Lazy S Cattle Co (w family); Tex Farm Bur; Tex Farmers Union; Spokesman for Am Agri Movement in W Tex; cp/Mem Tex St Ho of Reps 1980-; Rep of 63rd Dist, Chm Environmental Affairs Com, Chm Elections Com, Steering Com of House Dem Caucus, Steering Com of House Study Group; Regional Coor of 60-county area for Tex Yg Dems; Elected to St Yg Dems Exec Com 1975; C of C; hon/Outstg Yg Man of Am; Only Freshman to Ser on Steering Com of House Study Group & House Dem Caucus.

SHEARER, CHARLES EDWARD JR oc/Lawyer, Financial Planner; b/Sept 2, 1922; h/4839 Yorktown Blvd, Arlington, VA 22207; ba/Wash DC & Sprinfield, VA; m/Ruth M Nicholson; c/Kay Ellen Gardiner, Beth Ann; p/Charles E and Helen L Shearer; ed/AS; AB; JD; CLU; mil/AUS 1942-46; USAR 1946-53; pa/Nat Assn Life Underwriters; DC Bar Assn; cp/VP Metro YMCA; Chm Bd Trustees US JC Foun; Repub Party; r/Epis; hon/Outstg Yng Man Ind 1956.

SHEATS, MORRIS oc/Speaker; b/June 9, 1940; h/12002 Saddlehorn Ln, Mansfield, TX 76063; m/Janet; c/Shanda, Morris II; p/Mr and Mrs HM Sheats, Lubbock, TX; ed/BA Tex Tech Univ 1962; MDiv SWn Theol Sem 19654; pa/Pres Ldrship Tng Inc; cp/Mansfield City Coun 1980; r/So Bapt; hon/Author *You Can Be Emotionally Healed* 1977 & *You Can Have a Happy Family* 1978.

SHELL, VICKI E oc/Coordinator of Special Activities; b/July 4, 1947; h/Murray, KY; ba/Dept Indust Ed, Murray St Univ, Murray, KY 42071; m/Jack H; c/Brian Douglas; p/Harvey and Nelle Ellis, Murray, KY; ed/BS cum laude 1968, MA 1969, MA +30 1972 Murray St Univ; PhD Ohio St Univ 1979; pa/Coor Spec Activs, Dept Indust Ed, Murray St Univ 1978-; Res Assoc, Ohio St Univ 1976-78; Dist Ed Coor & DECA Advr, Murray Area Voc Ed Ctr 1972-76; Dist Ed Coor & DECA Advr, N Marshall HS 1969-71; Tchg Asst, Murray St Univ 1968-69; Am Indust Arts Assn; Am Coun Indust Arts Tchr Ed; Am Vocat Ind Ed Assn; Epsilon Pi Tau; NADET; AVA; KVA; DECA; CDTE; KADET; Phi Delta Kappa; Am Voc Ed Res Assn; Am Ednl Res Assn; PTA, Pres; cp/Murray Wom's Clb; Murray Swim Team, Swim Meet Timer & Line Judge; Charity Ball; Murray Country Clb; Chd's Hosp Fund Dir, Vol for Muirfield Golf Tourn; r/U Meth; hon/Outstg Yng Wom Ky 1980; Appt'd Mem Adv Com to Area Voc Ed, Ky Bd Occupl Ed; Selected Mem Adv Com on Eligibility & Accred for US Dept HEW 1975-78; Outstg Dist Ed Tchr of Ky 1975; Outstg Yng Wom Am 1972; Fav Tchr N Marshall HS 1971; W/W Students in Am Cols & Univs 1968; Author Num Reports & Profl Pubs.

SHELLEY, DAVID AUSTIN oc/Retired; b/Mar 2, 1914; h/2012 Galilee Rd, Barnwell, SC 29812; m/Lease Forrest; c/Frances S Hill; p/David Archie and Frances Elizabeth Shelley; ed/BS Clemson Univ 1936; Grad Work Univ Ark 1954, Colo A&M Col 1956, Univ Wis 1959; mil/AUS 1941-45; pa/Ret'd after 35 Yrs w Clemson Univ Ext Ser: Asst Co Agt, Co Agt, Dist Agt, Coor Recruitment, Tng & Devel; cp/Lions Clb; Clemson Alumni Assn; Past Chm Hosp Bd; r/Bapt; Deacon, SS Tchr; hon/Lion of Yr 1964-65; Dist'd Ser Awd, Nat Assn Co Agric Agts 1956.

SHELLY, RICHARD W oc/Assistant Professor; b/July 7, 1945; h/1710 Vermira Pl, Charlottesville, VA 22901; ba/C'ville; m/Vicki; c/Kellie, Sara; p/Earl W and Catherine P Shelly, Alexandria, VA; ed/BS Col William & Mary; MEd, EdD Univ Va; pa/Asst Prof, Gen Med Fac, Univ Va Sch Med; Coor Postgrad Internship in Respiratory Therapy; VP Nat Bd Respiratory Therapy; cp/Bd Dirs/Capt; Seminole Trail VFD; r/Bapt; hon/Pub'd in *Research in Education; Fire Engineering; Respiratory Care*.

SHELTON, BESSIE ELIZABETH oc/Educator, Musician, Research Specialist; b/Jan 25; h/Cumberland, MD; p/Robert (dec) and Bessie P Shelton, Lynchburg, VA; ed/BA WV St Col 1958; MS St Univ NY 1960; Dip Universal Schs 1971; Dip NAm Sch Travel 1972; Dip Nashville Sch Songwriting 1975; Add'l Study NWn Univ, Univ Va, Va Wn Col; ;

273

mil/USN 1951-55; pa/Edr, Ednl Media Spec, Bd Ed of Allegany Co, Cumberland, MD 1977-; Ednl Res Spec 1974-77; Instrl Media Spec, Lynchburg Bd Ed 1966-74; Mus Conslt 1972-; Travel Conslt 1972-; Asst Hd Ctrl Ref Div, Circulation Libn, Art & Mus Libn, Queens Borough Public Lib, Jamaica, NY 1962-65; Yng Adult Libn, Brooklyn Public Lib 1960-62; NEA; Md St Tchrs Assn; Allegany Co Tchrs Assn; Life Damae Mem Clover Intl Poetry Assn; Life Mem Vocal Artists of Am; Intercontl Biogl Assn; Intl Entertainers Guild; Achievers Intl; cp/Tri-St Commun Concert Assn; Dem Party; r/Bapt; hon/Cert of Merit, Ser as Choir Soloist, USN Tng Ctr, Great Lakes, Ill 1951; S'ship Awd 1957; Pi Delta Phi 1957; Sigma Delta Pi 1958; Cert Merit, Ser to WV St Col Band 1958; BA w Hons, WV St Col 1958; Talent Awd 1969; Sweetheart of Day, Radio St WVLA 1973; Achievers Intl Merit Awd 1980; Contbr of Poems to *Clover Collection of Verse* 1974; *Great Contemporary Poems* 1978 & Var Other Pubs.

SHELTON, GAYLE COCHRANE JR oc/Government Official; b/Aug 11, 1918; h/Birmingham, AL; ba/B'ham; p/Gayle Cochrane Shelton, Jackson, MS; Marguerite Perryman Brown (dec); ed/BA LSU 1940; LLB Georgetown Univ 1942; FBI Acad 1942; mil/FBI 1940-47; pa/Intl Trade, Mgmt/Adm; Pres & COE, Pacific Wholesalers, Inc 1947-62; Pres & COE Am Overseas Sales Corp 1957-62; Dist Dir US Dept Commerce 1962-; Area Dir Intl Trade Adm, US Dept Commerce 1978-; Ala World Trade Assn, Fdr, Dir 1967-, Pres 1974-77; Bd Advrs, Intl Trade Ctr, Univ Ala 1979-; Internationale des Etudiants de Sciences Economique et Commerciales; Chm Ala Intl Bus Forum, Univ Ala 1966-; Exec Secy Ala Export Coun 1964-; cp/Pres Guam C of C 1955-57; Rotary Intl 1950-57; Chm Bd Tax Appeals, Govt Guam 1952-56; Chm Bd Equalization, Govt Guam 1952-56; VP B'ham Fest Arts 1973-74; r/Epis; hon/Spec Achmt Awds, US Dept Commerce 1971-80; Bronze Medal Awd, US Dept Commerce 1967; Ala World Trade Man of Yr, Ala World Trade Assn 1972; Silver Medal Awd, US Dept Commerce 1973; Awd Merit, Nat Defense Exec Reserve, US Dept Commerce 1974; Lectr & Contbr to Trade & Profl Jours.

SHELTON, JIMMIE RUTH oc/Technical Secretary; b/Sept 1, 1937; h/1304 Golf Dr, SW, Cleveland, TN 37311; ba/Charleston, TN; m/C L; c/Teresa Ann S Swafford; p/Jimmy and Ruth Haven, C'land, TN; pa/Secy to Mgr, Specialty Chems, SE Regional Process Technol Dept, Olin Corp; Cherokee Chapt Profl Secys Intl 1968-, Past Treas, Advr, Recording Secy, VP; hon/Achmt Awds, Cherokee Chapt Profl Secys Intl 1976 & 78; Secy of Yr 1980.

SHELTON, ORESS ORLANDO oc/Professional Barber; b/July 4, 1944; h/Alexander City, AL; m/Bethra; p/Abraham Sr (dec) and Laura Lowe Shelton (dec); ed/Att'd Ala & A&M Col 1960-63; Grad Profl Investigator Sch 1969; ADC Tractor Trailer Sch 1970; pa/La-Do-Tam Hair Ctr; cp/Imperial Lodge #312, Treas; NAACP & SCLC; r/Bapt.

SHELTON, WILLIAM BERNARD oc/Credit Adjuster; b/Dec 7, 1956; h/128½ Carroll St, Somerset, KY 42501; m/Kathy; c/Kyle; p/Bernard and Patricia Shelton, Somerset, KY; ed/City Col of Chgo 1974-76; Univ Ky 1976-78; mil/AUS 1974-76 E-4; pa/Credit Adjuster, 1st & Farmers Nat Bank; cp/Somerset-Pulaski Co JCs; Ky Yng Dems, 5th Dist Chm; r/Meth; hon/Outstg Yng Dem of 5th Dist, 1978 & 79.

SHEPARD, CHARLES VIRGIL oc/Personnel Executive; b/Nov 14, 1940; h/101 Shadow Ridge Dr, Fox Chapel, PA 15238; ba/Pgh, PA; m/Judy Ann Wells; c/Cynthia Lynn; p/Charles Woodrow (dec) and Catherine Elizabeth Shepard, Springfield, IL; ed/BA; MBA; pa/Pers Exec, Rockwell Intl; Aerspace Industs Assn, Indust Relats Coun; cp/Bd Dirs Pgh Public Theatre; r/Meth.

SHEPHERD, MYRTLE BARNETT MacDONALD oc/Retired Educator; b/Jan 28, 1898; h/1515 Community Ln, Midland, TX 79701; m/John E MacDonald; 2nd Walter F Shepherd; c/John E Macdonald Jr, Doris Evelyn M Dodd, Leland Lloyd MacDonald; p/Judge Rial (dec) and Mary Tate Matthew S Barnett (dec); ed/BA 1949, MEd 1951 Sul Ross St Univ; Other Study: Tex Univ-Austin, SW St Univ, Our Lady of Lake Univ; pa/Ret'd Dean; Pres 2 Yrs Presidio Co Unit TSTA; Bexar Co Unit TSTA, Pres 2 Yrs; NEA; TRTA; MRTA, Past VP; Delta Kappa Gamma; Epsilon Baeta; Tex Alpha Alumnus Chapt Alpha Chi; cp/OES; Pilot Clb; Midland Wom's Clb; Midland Porcelain Art Clb, 1st VP; Lt William Brewer Chapt DAR, Chaplain; Midland Soc Parliamtns, Treas; Midland Aux Mid Med Soc, Past Treas & S'ship Chm; r/Bapt; hon/Hon Admissions Ofcr, Acad W Point 1969; Cert US Mil; Writing Autobiography, Book of Poems, Book of Prayers & Devotionals.

SHEPPARD, DANA MARIE BOOTHE opc/Executive; b/Feb 17, 1950; h/Christiansburg, VA; ba/1055 W Main St, C'burg, VA; m/Jerry Wayne; c/Tony Wayne; p/Earnest Draper and Elizabeth Ann Boothe, C'burg, VA; ed/Sch of: Credit, Adv'd Telephone Collection, Pers Mgmt, Telephone Skiptracing, Indep Bus Owners, Sales; Dale Carnegie Course; pa/Pres Credit Bur of New River Val; Va Collectors Assn, Secy; cp/Repub

Nat Com; C of C; r/Bapt; hon/Awd for Bd Mem, C'burg C of C; Cert Apprec, Kiwanis Clb, C'burg 1981.

SHERIDAN, SUSAN JANE WARNER oc/Consultant; b/Dec 6, 1941; h/2736 Quenby, Houston, TX 77005; ba/Houston; m/Jack M; c/Jane Margaret, Lisl Warner, Scott Michael; p/William J and Mathilda B Warner, Placentia, CA; ed/BS 1963, MEd 1964 Univ Org; Att'd San Jose St Col, Ctrl Wash St Col, Univ Houston-Clear Lake City; EdD Univ Houston 1974; pa/Tchr Pearl Buck Sch; Fdr & Tchr Nellie Burke Sch; Tchr, Supvr Harris Co Ctr for Retard'd Inc; Supvr of Spec Ed, Galena Pk Indep Sch Dist; Asst Prof Univ Houston at Clear Lake City; Adj, Asst Prof, Univ Houston; Conslt in Spec Ed & Early Childhood Ed, Harris Co Dept Ed; Am Assn Mtl Deficiency; Coun Excptl Chd, Higher Ed Rep; Houston/Metro Ednl Diagnosticians, Advr; Tex Ednl Diagnosticians, Journ Editor; Phi Delta Kappa; cp/Bd Mem Magnificat Half-way Houses Inc; Adv Bd Sepc Ed, LaPorte ISD; r/Prot; hon/Recip Spec Recog Awd, Kiwanis Clb 1966; Outstg Yng Wom Am Awd 1966; Univ Houston Clear Lake City Grantee 1977-78; W/W S&SW 1980-81; Author Sev Curric Manuals & Num Profl Articles.

SHERMAN, EDWIN BERNARD oc/Manufacturers Representative; b/Aug 18, 1938; h/9037 SW 62nd Terr, Miami, FL 33173; ba/Miami; c/Montelle, Allen; p/Al A Sherman (dec); Montelle Epstein (dec); ed/BS 1961; Student Law 1961; pa/Gen Devel Corp 1961-62; Pillsburg Co 1962-65; Thomas Industs 1965-67; Pres E B Sherman Co 1967-; Pres The Glass Menagerie 1980-; cp/Pres Golden Shones Condominium Assn; Illuminating Engrg Soc; Nat Elec Mfrs Rep Assn; Am Home Lighting Reps Assn; Am Pottery Assn, Fdg Dir; Alpha Epsilon Pi; Dem Party; Elks; Miami Ski Clb; r/Jewish; hon/Recip Sales Awds; 1st Pl Lighting Competition 1967, 2nd Pl SE Regional Lighting Competition 1967, Illuminating Engrg Soc.

SHERRILL, DONALD G oc/Researcher; b/May 22, 1944; h/Stone Mtn, GA; ba/Engineering Experiment Station, Georgia Inst of Technol, Atlanta, GA 30332; m/Brenda H; c/David A; p/G D and Caroline Sherrill, St Lucie, FL; ed/MCP Ga Inst Technol 73; BA Mankato St Univ 1967; mil/USNR Flight Ofcr; pa/Res Scist, Ga Inst Technol, Engrg Expt Sta 1979-; Battelle So Opers 1973-79; Am Plan'g Assn, Del to Plan'g Confs 1976-77; Am Inst Cert'd Planners; World Future Soc, VP Ga Chapt, Prog Chm, Budget Com, Spec Projs Com; r/U Ch of Christ; hon/W/W S&SW.

SHERROD, MICHAEL COURTNEY oc/Banker; b/Oct 3, 1947; h/Midland, TX; ba/PO Box 1599, MIdland, TX 79702; m/Joann N; p/L W and Margaret A Sherrod, El Paso, TX; ed/BBA Univ Tex-El Paso 1973; mil/USMC 1966-69; pa/Asst VP FIrst Nat Bank of Midland; Am Inst Bnkg; Am Bnkrs Assn; cp/Commandant, Dept Tex Marine Corps Leag; r/Cath; hon/Dist'd Citizens Medal 1980, MC Leag; 5 Dist'd Ser Awds, MC Leag.

SHIFFLETT, PEARL BURKETT oc/Postal Clerk; b/Apr 13, 1927; h/I 20 E, Rt 1 Box 133, Big Spring, TX 99720; ba/Big Spring; m/Herman Wesley; c/Frances Lynn Nogue, Sammie Jo Sullivan, Dorothy Gayle Reynolds, Pamela; p/Joe B (dec) and Exa Logan Burkett (dec); pa/Secy Local Postal Wkrs Union; Secy Am Postal Wkrs Union; r/Bapt; hon/Wom of Yr, Tex Delta Delta Chapt Phi Sigma Alpha 1975; Retail Sales of Mo, W Tex Dist USPS.

SHIFLET, JOHN COLEMAN JR oc/Superintendent; b/Oct 1, 1946; ba/John De La Howe Sch, McCormick, SC 29835; m/Deborah Gentry; c/Kelly Aiton; p/John Coleman and Lucy Holbrook Shiflet, Ninety Six, SC; ed/AA Anderson Col; AB Univ Ga; MEd Clemson Univ; pa/Supt John De La Howe Sch; Ofcr SEn Grp Child Care Assn & SC Child Care Assn; cp/Lions Clb; r/Bapt.

SHIPLEY, REIGN HUGH oc/Band Director; b/Dec 20, 1928; h/PO Box 148, Vernon, FL 32462; ba/Vernon; m/O Lenore; c/Mary Jo Watlington, William J, Carol Margaret; p/William H (dec) and Geraldine I Shipley (dec); ed/AB, MA Morehead Univ; pa/Band Dir, Tchr, Vernon HS; FTP; NEA; Fla Bandmasters; r/Disciples of Christ; hon/W/W Am Ed; Hon Order Ky Cols.

SHIPP, VICTOR R oc/Retired; b/Nov 22, 1921; h/615 NW 19th St, Okla City, OK 73103; m/Wilma F; c/Douna Ann Kratschmann, Linda Lou Butler, Donald Ray; p/Ray Shipp (dec); Pauline Ballensky (dec); mil/AUS Capt; USAFR 2nd Lt; pa/Ret'd Corp Exec; Devel'd & Owned Star Printing Co until 1942; Fdr Victor R Shipp Co, Printers of Dist 1945-49; Sales Engr, Am Type Fdrs Inc 1949; Prod Engr, So Calif Newspaper Prod Com; Gen Mgr SWn Press 1954-59; Mgmt Cnsltg Engr, Greenville, SC & Wichita Falls, Tex; Fdr Vic Shipp Typography Inc 1961-73; Ret'd 1973; Modeled Profl for Newspapers, Mags & TV; Capt Charter Airline; Former Mem: Ctrl Okla Indust Editors, Intl Assn Bus Commrs; cp/Mem Okla City Advtg Clb, Okla Clty Art Dirs Clb; Am Legion; Reserve Ofcrs Assn; Okla City BBB; Am Advtg Fed; Okla City C

PERSONALITIES OF THE SOUTH

of C; Printing Indust of Am; Past Secy Creative Printers of Am; Pubr *Ad Galley* 10 Yrs; US Senatorial Clb; Nat Adv Bd Am Security Coun; hon/Awds from Regional & Nat Orgs in Advtg & Communs; Air Medal; Dist'd Flying Cross; WWII Victory Medal.

SHIRK, PERRY WILLIAM oc/Analyst; b/Aug 21, 1930; h/8944 Centerway Rd, Gaithersburg, MD 20706; ba/Arlington, VA; m/Jean M Wentsel; c/Steven Michael, Glenn David; p/John I (dec) and Alice R Shirk, Clark, SD; ed/BS Ariz St Univ; MS Geo Wash Univ; mil/USAF 1951-73 Ret'd Lt Col; pa/Analyst, Logistic Mgmt; Soc Logistic Engrs; Am Defense Preparedness Assn; cp/Shrine; World Vision Supporter; r/Presb; hon/Merit Ser Medal 1973; Air Medal w 9 OLC; W/W Fin & Indust 1979-80.

SHIRLEY, GEORGE oc/Director of Personnel; b/July 3, 1939; h/8901 Placid Dr, Okla City, OK 73111; m/Della; c/Elender, LaShanda; p/Wick and Olene Shirley, Indianapolis, IN; ed/BA Okla Christian Col 1966; MA Okla Univ 1980; pa/IPMA; NPELR; r/Ch of Christ.

SHOCK, JAMES RICHARD oc/Manufacturing Manager; b/Sept 8, 1945; h/Rt 6 Box 17, Cookeville, TN 38501; ba/C'ville; m/Anna; c/Jimmy, Joan Marie; p/Fred H and Oleatha J Smith, Trotwood, OH; ed/BSIM Univ Cinci 1969; pa/Indust Engrg Supvr, Duriron Co, Dayton, OH; Mfg Mgr, Duriron Co Inc, C'ville; AIIE; NMA; cp/Rotary Clb; C'ville Chapt Nat Exch Clb, Pres 1981; U Way Dr Chm 1980; U Way Pres 1981; YMCA, Exec Bd; Friends of the Ct; T-Ball Baseball Coach; Spec Olympics Vol; Advr to Proj SSAVE, Tenn Tech; Beta Omicron Chapt, Theta Chi; Jr Achmt, Advr; r/Meth; hon/Eagle Scout 1958.

SHOCKLEE, JOHN WARREN oc/Funeral Service Educator; b/Jan 13, 1932; h/3660 Applewood Rd, Richmnd, VA 23234; ba/Chester, VA; m/Shirley; c/J Mark, David R, Brian C; p/D U and M Alice Shocklee, Coleman, TX; ed/Dip Funeral Ser, Dallas Inst; BS Bethany Nazarene Col; MEd Va St Univ; mil/USMC 1951-54; pa/Fun Ser Edr, John Tyler Commun Col; Am Bd Funeral Ser Ed: Standards & Criteria Com, Accred Com; cp/Curric Com on Funeral Mgmt; r/Prot.

SHOCKLEY, STEVEN BRUCE oc/Administrator; b/Apr 18, 1949; ba/Johnson City, TN; m/Nancy T; c/Steven B Jr, Allison K; p/G W and Helen I Shockley, Montgomery, AL; ed/BS Univ Ala 1971; pa/Sears, Roebuck & Co 1971-75; Asst Dir Alumni Affairs & Dir Chapter Devel, Univ Ala 1976-80; Dir Alumni Affairs, E Tenn St Univ 1980-; CASE; cp/U Fund 1972-79; JCs 1972-75; r/Cath.

SHOOK, HAROLD GRAHAM oc/Consultant; b/Apr 25, 1920; h/McLean House, Apt 1020, 6800 Fleetwood Rd, McLean, VA 22101; m/Rae B Mayfield (dec); 2nd Marilyn J Berger; c/Stephen J, Michael G, Diavid C, Wiliam M; p/Harold Edgar (dec) and Nellie Blanche Graham Shook (dec); ed/AA San Fran Jr Col 1940; BA Univ Calif Berkeley 1955; Nat War Col 1961; MA Geo Wash Univ 1967; mil/USAF 1941-68; pa/Pres Life Mgmt Serv Inc; Am Soc Tng & Devel; Am Mgmt Assn; APGA; World Futures Soc; Co-Chm Regional ASTD Conf, Wash DC; cp/Repub Nat & St Coms; Masons; r/Epis; hon/Legion of Merit; DFC; Air Medal; 18 OLCs; Fouragierre; Croix de Guerre.

SHOPE, MARK L oc/Director; b/Nov 4, 1952; h/2123 Aberdeen Rd, Dothan, AL 36301; ba/Dothan; m/Kay D; c/Virginia Shay; p/T M and E Laneive Shope, Bessemer, AL; ed/BS 1974, MS 1976, EdS 1981 Troy St Univ; pa/Dir Student Affairs, Troy St Univ 1975-80; Dir Career Devel Ctr & HS Relats, Geo C Wallace St Commun Col 1981-; Phi Delta Kappa: Newlttr Editor 1977-81, Treas 1980-81, Pres 1981-82; APGA 1977-79; cp/Citizens Adv Com, Wireglass Mtl Hlth Ctr: VChm 1979-80, Chm 1980-81; Dothan Lions Clb, Tailtwister 1980-81, Lion Tamer 1981-82; Parents Anonymous, Publicity Chm, Bd Dirsa 1981-82; hon/Gamma Beta Phi 1977; Outstg Kappan 1980; Outstg Yng Man Am 1979.

SHORT, CHARLES ERNEST oc/Repairman; b/Sept 22, 1924; m/Margaret V; c/David A (dec), Anne Marie; p/Chester Ernest Croston Short, Groveland, MA; Florence Maude Merrill, Groveland, MS; mil/USNR 1942-45; pa/Repairman So Bell Telephone Co 32 Yrs; cp/Scoutmaster Troop 590 Lake Helen, Fla; Comdr Am Legion Post 127 Lake Helen-Cassandaga; r/Mormon; hon/Vigil Awd in Order of Arrow 1978; Scouters Tng Awd 1975; Dist Awd of Merit 1979; Scouters Key 1976.

SHORT, DOROTHY LOUISE BISHOP oc/Arranger; b/June 20, 1921; h/13314 Moran Dr, Tampa, FL 33618; m/Robert Henry van Voorhis (dec); 2nd Roland Thomas; c/Kenneth Robert Van Voorhis, David Curtis Van Voorhis, Patricia V Tarlton; p/Robert Curtis and Marguerite Wells Bishop; ed/BA magna cum laude Duke Univ 1942; pa/Arranger 700+ Songs for Barbershop Quartets & Choruses; Tchr Mus, Var Sweet Adeline Intl Mus Schs; Mem Sweet Adeline Assn Cert'd Arrangers; cp/Am Contract Bridge Leag, Pres Gainesville Unit 1976-77; Phi Beta Kappa; Repub Party; r/Presb; hon/Life Master Am Contract Bridge Leag.

SHOUSE, THOMAS FRANKLIN III oc/Park Ranger; b/Apr 21, 1941; h/Cleveland, TN; m/Paula Kay; c/Johnny James, Patricia Leann; p/Thomas Franklin Jr and Ruby Dunn Shouse; mil/USAF 8 Yrs; pa/Ranger II, Tenn St Parks; cp/Bd Mem Red Clay Theatre; Tenn Rangers Assn; Scoutmaster 27 Yrs; r/Prot.

SHUE, BARBARA P oc/Director; b/Oct 19, 1952; h/Rt 2 Box 138B, Staunton, VA 24401; ba/Staunton; m/David M; p/John J (dec) and Gladys R Parente, Barre, PA; ed/BA Moravian Col; MSW Univ Minn-Duluth; pa/Mtl Retard Dir, Val Commun Mtl Retard Sers; NASW; AAMD; hon/Dean's List in Col.

SHULL, VALDAREE WHITE oc/Director; b/May 9, 1930; h/1312 Wesson Rd, Shelby, NC; ba/Shelby; m/Jack; c/Pamela, Jerry; p/Tilden Sherman (dec) and Leonia Heafner White (dec); ed/Grad Howard Bus Col 1954; Chgo Sch Nsg 1946; AA Gardner-Webb Col; BA Limestone Col 1962; Med Duke Univ 1971; Curric, Supervision & Adm Spec WCU 1977; Edl Spec & PhD SEn Univ 1979; pa/Promo Asst Missions & Rel Ed & Yth Dir in Bapt Ch; Tchr Public Schs 14 Yrs; Tchr Pvt Piano 15 Yrs; Dir Ldrship Progs in Pers & Profl Devel & Cnslg & Guid Assocs; Am Psych Assn; APGA; Mtl Hlth Cnslrs & Therapists Assn; NC Ed Res in Ed; NEA; NCEA; Pres CC Clrm Tchrs Assn; Pres Shelby Br AAUW; Pres Alpha Delta Kappa; Pres Phi Delta Kappa; cp/C of C; Christian Wom's Clbs; BPW Clbs; r/Bapt; hon/Jour Awd 1958; Gov Apprec Cert as Spec Vol in St, Nat, Commun; Author Articles on Cnslg for Newspapers; Book *Today's Women* 1979.

SHUMATE, RONALD EARL oc/Coach; b/Sept 21, 1939; m/Peggy W; c/Laura A, Ronald Jr, Lisa M; p/Earl E and Thelma L Shumate; ed/BS 1961, MA 1969 Tenn Tech Univ; mil/AUS 1962-64; pa/Hd Basketball Coach, SE Mo St; Nat Assn Basketball Coaches; cp/Shrine; r/Bapt; hon/Nat Coach of Yr 1977.

SIDDONS, JAMES DeWITT oc/Associate Professor; b/Nov 1, 1948; h/Lynchburg, VA; ba/Div of Mus, Liberty Bapt Col, Lynchburg, VA 24506; m/Joy; p/James Claudius Siddons Jr (dec); Belle Cox, Lake Dallas, TX; ed/BMus 1970 N Tex St Univ; MMus Univ London 1971; Mombusho Res Schlr, Tokyo Univ of Arts 1972-74; PhD Cand N Tex St Univ; pa/Assoc Prof Mus, Liberty Bapt Col; Am Mus Soc; Intl Mus Soc; Mus Lib Assn Hymn Soc of Am; Soc Asian Mus; r/Bapt; hon/Pi Kappa Lambda 1970; Author "Japan Section" *Directory of Music Research Libraries* 1979, "Libraries and Collections - Japan" *The New Grove's Dictionary of Music* 1980; "Librarians Guide to Musical Japan" *Fontes Artis Musical* 1977; Editor *Musical Analysis* 1972-74.

SIGLER, JAMES MARTIN oc/US Army Officer; b/Apr 15, 1936; h/Qtrs 114 Ft Corckett, Galveston, TX 77550; ba/Galveston; m/Marilyn Carole McKibbin; c/James Martin Jr, Cynthia Jean, Robert Scott; p/Byron E Sigler Jr (dec); Pauline Kubiak (dec); ed/BS US Mil Acad, W Point 1958; MS Univ Ill 1962; AUS Command & Gen Staff Col 1970; AUS War Col 1979; mil/AUS Col; pa/Dist Engr, Galveston Dist Army Corps of Engrs; Soc Am Mil Engrs; r/Prot; hon/Legion of Merit; Defense Merit Ser Medal; Army Merit Ser Medal.

SIKES, LAWRENCE C oc/Golf Professional; b/June 7, 1947; h/607 Shady Grove, Springdale, AR 72764; ba/Fayetteville, AR; p/Jewell Sikes, Springdale, AR; ed/BA Ark Tech; mil/USANG; pa/Golf Coach Univ Ark; Golf Profl; PGA; r/Bapt.

SILK, DOLORES HAM oc/Executive; b/Dec 4, 1943; h/5587 Gates Cove, Memphis, TN 38115; ba/Memphis; m/A Evans; p/Mable T Ham, Bartlett, TN; ed/Att'd Univ Tenn 1961-62, Memphis St Univ 1965-66; Univ Ga, SEn Regional Credit Union Sch 1974-76; pa/Mgr Memphis Plant DuPont Employees Credit Union 1971-; Treas Memphis Area Chapt of Credit Unions 1978-80; Coor Memphis Area Credit Union Mgrs Assn 1976-78; r/Bapt.

SILLERS, MARJORIE JOYCE oc/Teacher; b/June 28, 1931; h/439 Aruba Ct, Satellite Bch, FL 32937; c/Christine S Davidson, Wiliam, Ann Maurine, Matthew B; p/Harry and Ethel Ackroyd, Satellite Bch, FL; ed/BA Salve Regina Col 1952; MEd Univ Ctrl Fla 1975; pa/Tchr Sea Pk Elem Sch, Satellite Bch; Nat Coun Social Studies; r/Rom Cath; hon/Cervantes Medal 1951; Sarah Brown Sullivan Eng Awd 1952; Sedes Sapeintiae Gold Key 1952; F'ship Japan Inst for Social & Ec Affairs 1981; Nom Brevard Co Tchr of Yr 1973.

SILLS, MICHAEL CLARK oc/Telecommunicator; b/July 6, 1961; h/Rt 5, Dunn, NC 28334; p/Milton and Brenda Bass, Dunn, NC; ed/Police Info Network Sch 1979; NC Patrol Telecommunrs Sch 1981; pa/Telecommunr, NC St Hwy Patrol; cp/Spivey's Corner Fire Dept; r/Bapt; hon/Dist'd Ser Awd, Spivey's Corner Fire Dept 1979.

SILVA, SARAH FRANCES SEXTON oc/Nurse Supervisor; b/Aug

14; h/Stantonville, TN; m/Harry L (dec); c/Lloyd Ernest, Larry Joe; p/W E (dec) and Madie Sarah Sexton, Gunter, TX; ed/RN Bapt Meml Hosp Sch Nsg 1943; AA Freed Hardeman Col 1973; BSN Murray St Univ 1974; pa/Public Hlth Nurse Supvr; ANA; TNA; Tenn Public Hlth Assn, Nurses Sect, Chm & Secy; Tenn St Employees Assn, Secy Region of East McNairy, Hardemann, Fayette Cos, Secy; cp/PTA Pres; Repub Wom's Clb; r/Ch of Christ; SS Tchr; hon/Sigma Theta Tau, Delta Epsilon Chapt; 15 Yrs Ser McNairy Co Public Hlth Dept.

SILVER, JACQUELYN TIMMES oc/Data Processing; b/Dec 28, 1945; h/15914 Club Crest Dr #1114, Dallas, TX 75248; ba/Dallas; p/Francis Xavier Timmes (dec); Dorothy Anne Wellington (dec); ed/BA; MA; pa/NRMA; cp/Univ Calif Alumni Assn; r/Cath; hon/Phi Beta Kappa; Grad summa cum laude; W/W Fin & Indust 1979-80.

SILVERMAN, FAYE-ELLEN oc/Professor, Composer; b/Oct 2, 1947; h/1000 E Soppa Rd, Balto, MD 21204; ba/Townswon; p/Paula Silverman, Mt Vernon, NY; ed/BA cum laude Barnard Col; MA Harvard Univ; DMA Columbia Univ; pa/Prof, Mus Dept, Goucher Col; 18 Pub'd Compositions; 3 Pub'd Articles & Performances; Concerts in US & Abroad; hon/Stokowski Composition Contest (Age 13); Many Other Hons.

SILVERS, MORGAN DOUGHERTY oc/Podiatrist; b/Mar 29, 1942; h/RR #1, Box 511, Gadsden, AL 35901; ba/Anniston, AL; m/Karen; c/Kara, Morgan; p/Florent Morgan and Evelyn Mae Silvers, Piqua, OH; ed/BS Ohio No Univ 1965; DPM Ohio Col Podiatric Med 1977; Surg Residency Wom's Gen Hosp, Cleveland, Ohio 1978; Min Studies Berean Sch Bible 1979; pa/Podiatrist; Ala Podiatry Assn, VP 1979-80; Am Podiatry Assn; cp/Talladega Rotary Clb; r/Full Gospel Christian; hon/Salutatorian, Class of 1977, Ohio Podiatry Col; Pi Delta 1977; JCs Outstg Yng Man Am Awd 1977; Author Articles to Am Podiatry Assn Jour 1976.

SILVIN, RICHARD RENE oc/Hospital Consultant; b/May 16, 1948; h/280 New Mex Ave NW, Wash DC 20007; ba/Wash Dc; p/John L and Nancy T Silvin, Vichy, France; ed/BS Georgetown Univ; MBA Cornell Univ; pa/VP Intl Devel, Am Med Intl Inc; Am Col Hosp Admrs; Intl Hosp Fed; Dir Faith & Hope; Dir Acad Hosp Conslts; hon/Author Num Articles to Profl Jours; W/W: Fin & Indust, Hlth Care.

SIMMONS, ANNE B oc/Retired Teacher; b/Aug 12, 1915; h/Rt 2 Box 228, McComb, MS 39648; m/Ewell J; c/Mary Anne Rinkle; p/Frederic E (dec) and Urla B Dennard (dec); ed/AA Copaih-Lincoln Jr Col 1936; BS 1958, MEd 1964 Univ So Miss; pa/Bkkpr & Cashier 7 Yrs; Tchr Elem Sch 9 Yrs; Tchr Maths, HS & Elem 11 Yrs; St Bernard Tchrs Assn; La Tchrs Assn; St Bernard Ret'd Tchrs Assn; La Ret'd Tchrs Assn; Nat Ret'd Tchrs Assn; cp/BPW Clb, Past Treas; AAUW; UDC, Secy; Holmesville Homemkrs Clb, Public Relats Chm; r/Epis; hon/Outstg Tchr, Gauthier Sch, St Bernard Parish 1976.

SIMMONS, GEORGE MILLS oc/Geologist, Exploration Manager; b/May 9, 1943; h/Midland, TX; ba/Coquina Oil Corp, 400 N Marienfeld, Midland, TX 79702; m/Victoria; c/Kelly, Kristen, Geoffrey, Curtis; p/Paul C and Ann H Simmons, Creve Coeur, MO; ed/BA Monmouth Col 1967; MS Univ Iowa 1969; pa/Oil & Gas Exploration; AAPG; AIPG; AIME; cp/Trustee Camping & Ed Foun; Dir Camp Kooch-I-Ching, Boys Camp Intl, Falls, Minn; r/Presb; hon/Author "Geology of a Portion of the Hope Bay Greenstone Belt, Northwest Territories, Canada."

SIMMONS, PATRICK oc/Attorney; b/Dec 11, 1954; h/Mexia, TX; ba/Groesbeck, TX; m/Wendy; p/Roy and Virginia Simmons, Mexia, TX; ed/BBA Univ Tex 1976; JD Baylor Sch Law 1979; pa/Atty w Simmons & Simmons 1979-81; Asst Co Aty, Limestone Co, 1980-81; Assoc Editor Baylor Law Review; Tex Bar Assn; Tex Dist & Co Attys Assn; Nat Col Dist Attys; Tex Trial Lwyrs Assn; cp/Secy Mexia JCs; r/Cath.

SIMMONS, ROBERT ROY oc/Affirmative Action Officer; b/Mar 20, 1937; h/322 Sequoyah Trail, Norman, OK 73069; ba/Tinker AFB, OK; m/Mendell; c/Brynda, Audrey, Michelle, Bobby; p/Ruby L Snow, Columbus, OH; ed/BS Langston Univ; MA Okla Univ; pa/ASPA; cp/Norman Human Rights Comm; Sooner Toastmasters; r/Bapt.

SIMMS, ST ELMO oc/Ticket Agent; b/Nov 14, 1920; h/97 Gordon St, Charleston, SC 29403; ba/C'ton; m/Mildred C; c/Carmen S Gaston; p/Jasper S (dec) and Anna I Simms (dec); ed/Nat Radio Inst; mil/1942-46 Staff Sgt; pa/Ticket Agt, Greyhound Lines Inc 48 yrs; r/Presb; hon/Awd'd for Outstg Contbn & Merit Sers as Vol to Commun 1972; Blacks & Revolution 1976 Awd, Bicent Com for Ednl Projs; Plaque for Becoming 33° Mason 1976; Awd for Outstg Ser as Chm Petition Com of Arabian Temple #139, AEAONMS; Plaque for Dist'd Noble for Outstg Contbns to Spirit & Ideals of Imperial Coun 1980; 40 Yr Ser Awd, Greyhound Lines Inc.

SIMON, GARY ALAN oc/Real Estate Broker; b/Oct 9, 1956; h/Chapel Hil, NC; ba/1801 E Franklin St, Suite 101, Chapel Hill, NC 27514; p/Jerry Simon, Norfolk, VA; Lois Simon, Chapel Hill, NC; ed/BA UNV 1980; pa/Owner Simon & Assocs; Chapel Hill Bd Rltrs; Chapel Hill Multiple Listing Ser; cp/Chapel Hill C of C; r/Judea Reform Congreg; hon/Outstg Yng Men Am 1979.

SIMON, GLORIA ODI oc/Nurse Epidemiologist, Flight Nurse; b/July 9, 1939; h/415 NE 46th St, Lawton, OK 73501; ba/Sheppard AFB, TX; m/Donald T; c/Christina Maria, Angela Maria, Julienne Marie, Donald Thomas; p/dec; ed/Dip Nurse, St Luke's Hosp 1962; BA 1975, MA 1976 Univ Philippines; BSN Cameron Univ 1979; mil/USAF 1962-; pa/OR Nurse Monterey Co Hosp, Salinas, Calif 1962-65; OR Nurse 861st Med Grp, Glasgow AFB, Mont 1965-67; OB Nurse St Joseph's Hosp, Minot, NC 1968-70; Clin Instr, Col of Nsg, Angeles Univ, Angeles City, Philippines; Nurse Epidemiolist, USAF Regional Hosp, Sheppard AFB, Tex 1980-; NLN; Assn Practitioners in Infection Control; AF Assn; Reserve Ofcrs Assn US; Assn Mil Surgs of US; Clark Air Base Nurses Org, VP 1972-73; cp/Am Red Cross, Nurse 1965-; Nurse Conslt, USAF Med Civic Action Prog, Philippines 1973-76; r/Epis; hon/Cert Oper Baby Life, Vietnam Chd's Airlift 1975, Am Red Cross, Clark Air Base, Philippines; Nat Deans List 1979; Univ Philippines Dean's List 1972-76.

SIMON, LILLIE BELLE oc/Assistant Administrator; b/Feb 28, 1916; h/120 Edmund Dr, Long Bch, MS 39560; ba/Gulfport; p/Joseph Ceily Simon (dec); Nannie Mae Huckinson (dec); ed/RN 1938 Bapt Meml; BS Siena Col 1959; pa/ANA; Soc Nsg Ser Admrs; Am Mgmt Assn; cp/Metro Dinner Clb; Altrusa Clb of Gulfport, Pres; r/Meth; hon/Nurse of Yr 1962, Memphis, Tenn; W/W Am Wom 1979-80; Personalities of S 1967.

SIMPKINS, HUBERT WILLIE oc/Farmer; b/June 6, 1933; h/Rt 1 Box 159, Hiwassee, VA 24347; m/Hazel; c/Wanda, Debra; p/Reupard and Stella Simpkins, Hiwassee, VA; mil/AUS; pa/Dairy Farmer.

SIMPKINS, NAT STONE III oc/Tree Surgeon; b/Apr 16, 1912; h/908 E 6th St, Stuart, FL 33494; m/Carmen; c/Natascha, Nina, Nat, Alex; p/Nat (dec) and Olivia Simpkins; pa/Tree Surg; Ret'd Pres Horticultural Sers; cp/Repub Party; r/Epis.

SIMPSON, CHARLIE WAYNE oc/Minister, Student; b/Jan 23, 1946; h/PO Box 67, Como, NC 27818; m/Charlotte; c/Denise, Craig, Chad; p/Mr and Mrs Alfred Simpson, Tifton, GA; pa/Min; r/So Bapt.

SIMPSON, DANIEL L JR oc/Clown; b/Aug 6, 1952; h/825 Lee, Kerrville, TX 78028; m/Christine E Dugosh; c/Matthew Martin; p/Daniel Lee and Mary Ann Simpson, Olmitz, KS; ed/Col 1 Yr; mil/AUS 1971-76; pa/Self-Employed Clown; Clowns of Am Inc; Father Kempers Klowns; cp/K of C, Chancellor; Disabled Am Vets; r/Cath; hon/Army Commend Medal 1976; Plaque from K of C for Outstg Chancellor & Yth Dir 1979.

SIMPSON, JACK BENJAMIN oc/Executive; b/Oct 30, 1937; h/68 Isla Bahia Dr, Ft Lauderdale, FL 33316; m/Winona Clara Walden; c/Janet Lazann, Richard Benjamin, Randall Walden, Angela Elizabeth; p/Benjamin Harrison and Verda Mae Woods Simpson; ed/Att'd Wn Ky Univ, Ind Univ, Norton Sch Med Technol; pa/Asst Chief Med Technol, Jackson Co Hosp, Seymour, Ind 1958-61; Chief Med Technol & Bus Mgr, Mershon Med Labs, Indpls 1962-66; Mng Ptnr, 106th St Assocs, Indpls 1969-72; Mng Ptnr Delray Rd Assocs Ltd, Indpls 1970-71; Fdr, Ofcr & Dir Am Monitor Corp 1966-; Mng Ptnr Astroland Enterprises, Indpls 1968-; Dir Indpls Broadcasting Inc 1969-; Mng Ptnr Allisonville Assocs Ltd & Keystone Assocs Ltd, Indpls 1970-; Pres & Dir Topps Constrn Co, Brandenton, Fla 1973-; Mng Ptnr Rucker Assocs Ltd, Indpls 1974-; Mng Ptnr Grandview Assocs Ltd, Indpls 1977-; Mng Ptnr Westgate Assocs Ltd & Raintree Assocs Ltd, Indpls 1978-; Am & Ind Socs Med Technols; Am Soc Clin Pathols; Indpls Soc Med Technol; Royal Soc Hlth, London; hon/Ky Col; W/W S&SW; Notable Ams; Book of Hon; Personalities of Am; DIB; Commun Ldrs & Noteworthy Ams; LFABI; Men of Achmt; Men & Wom Dist; Am Registry Series; Ernest Kay Pers Hall of Fam; Reg of Med Technols, ASCP.

SIMPSON, JAMES HARRISON oc/Social Worker; b/June 14, 1934; h/Lexington, KY; ba/Dept Human Resources, Bur for Social Sers, 275 W Sixth Floor, Frankfort, KY 40602; p/William B Simpson (dec); Anna M Logan, Stanford, KY; ed/BA Ky St Univ 1960; MSSW Univ Louisville; mil/AUS 1954-56; USAR 1956-60; pa/Mgr Juvenile Sers Br, Ky St Social Works; Coor Bur Equal Employment Opptor; Child Wel Leag Am; Pres Ky Coun Crime & Delinquency; Ky Human Sers Assn; Nat Org Crime & Delinquency; Am Correctional Assn; cp/Dem Party; r/Bapt; hon/W/W S&SW 1980; Ky Coun on Crime & Delinquency Awd 1980.

SIMPSON, JAMES KENNETH oc/Department Chairman; b/Sept 25, 1940; h/Florence, AL; ba/Mus Dept, Univ N Ala, Box 5183, Florence, Al 55630; m/Gloria McMullan; c/Lynn Renee, Leslie Faye; p/Asa Salathiel and Verna Pritchett Simpson, Montgomery, AL; ed/BME, Univ So Miss 1962; MMus 1971, DA 1973 Univ Miss; mil/NG 6 Yrs; pa/Solo Clarinetist, Tupelo Symph Orch; Prof & Chm, Dept Mus, Univ N Ala; Phi Beta Mu, Secy-Treas; Assn of Ala Col Mus Admrs, Secy-Treas; Phi Kappa Phi; Phi Mu Alpha Sinfonia; Mem Big Band, Quad Cities Commun Jazz Band; hon/Outstg Edrs of Am 1975.

SIMPSON, JAMES MATTHEW oc/US Army Officer; b/July 7, 1946; h/97 5th Artillery Rd, Ft Leavenworth, KS 66027; ba/Ft Leavenworth; m/Janita Ahn; c/John Cabot; p/James H and Agnes R Simpson, Morehead City, NC; ed/BA Ec; BABA; MA Ec; MMAS; PhD; Grad AUS Command & Gen Staff Col; mil/AUS Major; pa/AUS Command & Gen Staff Col; Assn AUS; VFW; Embassy Assn; cp/Phi Sigma Alpha; Korean-Am Assn; r/Bapt; hon/Grad summa cum laude, BA & MA; Bronze Star w/V; Merit Ser Medal; 2 Army Commend Medals; 2 Purple Hearts; Armed Forces Expeditionary Medal.

SIMS, ALVIN LAMAR oc/Clinic Administrator; b/May 29, 1946; h/Armuchec, GA; ba/10 Hospital Cir, Rome, GA 30161; m/Dot; c/Christy; p/Alvin and Dorothy Sims, Lanett, AL; ed/BS Auburn Univ 1968; pa/Staff Acct, VanLandingham & Whittington CPA; Controller, Pharr Yarns of Ga; Clin Admr, Robert F Norton Wom's Clin; Ga Med Grp Admrs, Pres; Med Grp Mgmt Assn; cp/Rome Lions Clb, Chm Budget Com; Exch Clb of Rome; Jr Achievement of Rome, Past Steering Com Chm; Past Mem Rome JCs, Treas; r/Bapt; hon/Lanett HS Beta Clb 1963-64; 5 Cits for Work w Jr Achievement 1969-72; JC of Mo 1971; JC Key Man Awd 1972; Pres GMGA 1980.

SIMS, NELDA F oc/Musician, Business Manager, Real Estate Investor; b/Nov 30, 1924; h/#4 Valley Forge Dr, Houston, TX 77024; ba/Houston; m/James N; c/Gail S Shipley, Howard James; p/dec; ed/Att'd Tex Applied Mus, Massey's Bus Col, Univ Houston, W Tex St Univ; pa/Perfr, Jazz Combo; cp/Kiwanis Pianist; r/U Meth; hon/Intl W/W Mus; W/W Am Wom; Nom'd World W/W Wom.

SIMS, RUSSELL ADRON oc/Associate Professor; b/July 2, 1933; ba/Bowling Green, KY; c/Lisa S Vickers, Russell Scott; p/Adron A (dec) and Mattie Sims, Batesville, AR; ed/AA So Bapt Col 1953; BA Ouachita Bapt Col 1956; MEd 1971, EdD 1974 Univ Ark; pa/Assoc Prof, Wn Ky Univ 1980-; Rec Spec, Bechtel Inc, Saudi Arabia 1979; Asst Prof, Ark Tech Univ 1973-79; Rec Dir, Fairfield Commun Land Co 1972-73; Ath Dir-Coach, Mich, Tenn, Ark 1956-69; AAHPER; Ark AHPER, Dist I Pres, VP Rec Div; Ky AHPER; Nat Rec & Pks Assn; Ky Rec & Pks Soc; Ark & Ky Ofcls Assn; Am Assn Leisure & Rec; Assn Res, Adm, Profl Couns & Socs; cp/Optimist Clb, Pres 1964; r/Bapt; hon/Ark Coach of Yr, Dist II 1964-65; W/W S&SW 1980-81; Author Sev Articles & Recommends.

SIMSTEIN, NEIL LELAND oc/Surgeon; b/Nov 16, 1942; h/Winston-Salem, NC; ba/474 Forsyth Med Pk, W-S, NC 27103; m/Beverly; c/Jessica, Julia, Rebecca; p/Irving J (dec) and Rose S Simstein, Perth Amboy, NJ; ed/BS Wake Forest Univ 1964; MD NY Med Col 1970; mil/USN 1971-78; pa/Gen & Vascular Surg, Pvt Prac; Clin Instr Bowman Gray Sch Med; Fellow Intl Col Surgs; Fellow SEn Surg Soc; Michael E DeBakey Surg Soc; cp/Forsyth Co Repub Party, Exec Bd; r/Hebrew; hon/Many Contbns to Med Lit.

SINGER, RAYMOND oc/Restauranteur; b/Sept 16, 1936; m/June; c/Debrah, Katherine, (Stepch:) Steven, James; p/Richard and Herta Wilhelmina Manske Singer, Bonita Springs, FL; ed/Deg Fla St Univ 1962; mil/AUS; pa/Mgr Morrisons Cafeterias, Greenville, SC 1961-62, Spartanburg, SC 1962-63, Jacksonville, Fla 1963-66; Owner Flaming Fountain Rest, Naples, Fla 1966-76; Conslt Food Ser 1976-77; Gen Ptnr & Mgr Captains Table Resort, Everglades City, Fla 1977-; Bd Food Rev, Colleier Co, Pres Coller Co Chapt 1971, 1972; Treas FRA 1970, VP 1971-72, Pres 1973; cp/US Ski Assn; Mtl Hlth Bd; Naples C of C; Naples Bath & Tennis Clb; Pres Naples Snow Seekers Ski Clb; r/Prot; hon/Outstg Restauranteur, St of Fla 1973.

SINGH, RAJENDRA P oc/Surgeon, Assistant Clinical Professor; b/Sept 16, 1939; ba/Woodland Meml Pk, 300 Stanaford Rd, Beckley, WV 25801; m/Sushma; c/Sonia, Jay Pal; p/Akbal Bahadur and Kamala Singh; ed/MD 1963, MS 1966, Agra, India; FRCS (Edin) 1968; FRCS (Eng) 1978; MAMS (Delhi) 1971; FACS 1980; pa/Asst Clin Prof Surg, Marshall Univ; Att'g Surg: Raleigh Gen Hosp, Appalachian Regional Hosp, Beckley Hosp, Beckley, WV; Fellow Am Col Surgs; Fellow Royal Col Surgs; r/Hindu; hon/Cert of Hon in Pathol; Res S'ship Min of Hlth, India 1964-66; 2nd Prize for Paper Read before WV Chapt Am Col Surgs 1976; Author Num Profl Articles Incl'g "Lymphangiosarcoma in Postmastectomy Lymphoedema" 1971 & "Clinical Experience with Granulomatous Ileocolitis" 1979.

SINGLETON, NAN CHACHERE oc/Associate Dean and Professor; b/July 2, 1930; h/Baton Rogue, LA; ba/Sch of Home Econ, La St Univ,

Baton Rogue, LA 70803; m/Howard; c/Larry Ike Chachere (dec), Barbara C Martin (dec), Jon Scott Chachere; p/Otis A (dec) and Olivia D Wells (dec); ed/BS La Tech Univ 1950; MA Univ SWn La 1962; PhD La St Univ 1974; pa/Assoc Dean, Div Gen Studies & Commun Ed, Assoc Prof, Sch Home Ec, LSU; La Home Ec Assn, Pres 1980-81; Baton Rouge Dist Dietetic Assn, Pres 1980-81; AHEA; ADA; Phi Delta Kappa; Delta Kappa Gamma; Gamma Sigma Delta; Omicron Nu; Soc for Nutrition Ed; Inst Food Technols; cp/BPW Clb; r/Epis; hon/W/W: Am Wom 1980, S&SW 1980; Author/Co-Author Num Books & Articles.

SINGLETON, RAYMOND LeVON oc/Executive, Realtor; b/Oct 26, 1927; h/2115 Atlanta Ave NW, Lawton, OK 73505; ba/Lawton; m/Anna Lou Bates; c/Sherrie, Gayla; p/James William and Ruby Mae Singleton, Shawnee, OK; ed/Att'd Okla A&M Col 1945-46; mil/USN 1946-47; pa/VP SWn Stationery & Bank Supply; Rltr Century 21, Scoggins Rltr; Nat Assn Rltrs; Nat Ofc Products Assn; cp/VFW; Am Legion; C of Co; Pres Lawton Country Clb; r/Ch of Christ; hon/W/W: Okla 1975, S&SW 1980-81.

SINGTON, FRED W oc/Retailer; b/Feb 24, 1910; h/Birmingham, AL; ba/2017 5th Ave N, B'ham, AL 35203; m/Nancy Napier; c/Fred Jr, David, Leonard; p/Max (dec) and Hallye Spiro Sington (dec); ed/AB 1931, Hon LHD 1955 Univ Ala; mil/USNR 1942-46; pa/Coach Duke Univ 1931-34; Profl Baseball, Atlanta 1931, Washington 1934, Chattanooga 1936, Brooklyn 1937-38; Ala-Jefferson Co Products Mart Auth; Past Pres & Treas Nat Sporting Goods Assn; cp/Past Pres SEn Fball Ofcls Assn; Past Pres B'ham Kiwanis Clb; Past Capt Monday Morning Qtrback Clb; Mem "A" Clb; Grand Order of Krewe; Masons; Shriners; Past Pres Bd, Ala St Fair Auth; Past Chm Downtown B'ham YMCA; Chm B'ham C of C Ath Affairs Com; Ath Dir Downtown Action Com; Jr Achievement Bd; Boy Scout Coun; Civic Ctr Plan'g Com; Coach for Ala Spec Mtlly Retard'd Olympics; Past Lt Gov Ala Kiwanis; Bd Dirs City Federal Savings & Loan; Bd Dirs Vuleau Life Ins Co; Bd B'ham Mdse Mart; Chm Legion Field Traffic Com; Co-Chm Wom's Intercol Aths, Univ Ala;r/Presb; hon/Phi Beta Kappa; Winner Porter Cup for Best Ath; Pan Hellenic Best Student Awd 1931; Elec'd to Fball Hall of Fame 1955; Ala Sports Hall of Fame; B'hams Man of Yr 1970; Pres Univ Ala Nat Alumni 1959-60; Dist'd Alumnus Awd, Univ Ala 1967; Pat Trammell Awd, Univ Ala 1970; Eskine Ramsay Awd 1972; City of Hope Humanitarian Awd; Denver Nat Hosp, Man of Yr 1978; Ala Cable TV Man of Yr 1978; Sertoma Clb Humanitarian Awd 1978.

SIQUEIROS, KATY oc/Real Estate; b/Dec 2, 1930; h/8244 Strickland Dr, El Paso, TX 79907; ba/El Paso; c/Randy, Elizabeth Cecilia, David Michael; p/D R (dec) and Guadalupe Soto Saucedo (dec); pa/Violinist; Real Est Salesperson; cp/ABWA; Intl City Chapt; BPW; AFM; TAR; NAREB; Nothnagle Round Table; r/Cath; hon/Salesman of Yr 1972; #1 Hovious Gal of Homes, 6 Yrs.

SIRIANNI, ANTHONY GIRARD oc/Pianist, Teacher; b/Feb 1, 1953; h/Brevard, NC; ba/Brevard Col, Dept Mus, Brevard, NC 28712; p/Fred and Jean Sirianni, Eau Claire, WI; ed/BMus Univ Wis 1975; MMus Mich St Univ 1978; pa/Artist in Residence (Piano), Brevard Col; Pi Kappa Lambda; Mus Tchrs Nat Assn; hon/1st Prize, 1980 Gershwin Piano Competition; Touring Artist w SC Arts Comm.

SIROIS, GERALD F oc/Priest; b/Apr 3, 1932; ba/Cookeville, TN; p/Leon V (dec) and Hermance Gagnon Sirois, Madawaska, ME; ed/BA Cath Univ 1957; MA Rivier Col 1972; pa/Tchr Sec'dy Ed 1962-76; Parish Work, Diocese of Nashville, Tenn 1976-; Soc Of Divine Savior; r/Cath.

SIROTE, JEROME DAVID JR oc/US Air Force; b/Mar 15, 1958; h/Huntsville, AL; p/Jerome David Sr and Emma Jean Sirote; ed/BS USAF Acad 1980; mil/USAF; pa/Lt USAF; r/Meth; hon/Gen's Color Bearer, USAF Acad 1977; Flight Comdr 1980.

SISK, DONALD RAY oc/Far Eastern Director; b/May 30, 1933; h/2905 Westside Dr, Chattanooga, TN 37404; ba/Chat; m/Virginia Ruth; c/Timothy Ray, Angela Renee Border; p/Earl Bryan (dec) and Beulah Gertrude Sisk (dec); ed/AA Bethel Col; BA Mrray State Univ; DD; pa/Pastor 8 Yrs; Missionary in Japan 8 Yrs; Far En Dir Bapt Intl Missions Inc; r/So Bapt; hon/Pres Bible Col in Japan; 2nd VP Southwide Bapt F'ship.

SISSOM, EVELYN JANELLE LEE oc/Artist; b/Feb 11, 1934; h/Box 5014 TTV, Cookeville, TN 38501; m/Leighton E; c/Terry, Denny; p/Thurman and Janelle Lee, Manchester, TN; pa/Tenn Art Leag; Cumberland Art Soc; Intl Soc Artists; r/Ch of Christ; hon/Ctrl S Art Exhib Grand Awd; Tenn All-St Show 3rd Awd; Paintings Selected for Nat Exhib; Nat Acad Gals; Salmatgundi Clb.

SISSON, HOWARD MILES SR oc/Mechanic; b/Feb 8, 1904; h/810 Pendleton St, Radford, VA; m/Jeanette Boyer; c/Howard Miles Jr, Lucy

PERSONALITIES OF THE SOUTH

Anne S Sproul; p/Thomas Shelton (dec) and Mary Damaris Miles Sisson; ed/Hemphill Diesel Engrg Sch; pa/Mechanic; r/Meth; hon/Howard M Sisson Playground, Dedicated by Radford Rec Comm 1975.

SIZER, PHILLIP SPELMAN oc/Executive; b/Apr 11, 1926; h/14127 Tanglewood Dr, Dallas, TX 75234; ba/Dallas; m/Evelyn Sue; c/Phillip S Jr, Ves; p/Frank (dec) and Helen S Sizer, Walnut Creek, CA; ed/BSME, So Meth Univ; mil/USN; pa/Otis Engrg Corp 1948-; Chief Engr 1962-70, Elected Ofcr 1970, Bd Dirs 1974, Sr VP & Tech Dir; Tau Beta Pi; Kappa Mu Epsilon; Reg'd Profl Engr: Tex, Okla & Alberta, Can; ASME: Chm, V-Chm, Dir Var Coms, Local & St Levels; SPPE & SCCA Coms, ANSI/ASME SPPE-1; ASME Codes & Standards Com; Past Pres Assn of Wellhead Equip Mfrs; Offshore Technol Conf Exec Com 1977-79; SPE; NOMADS; Author & Co-Author Sev Papers; Holder Over 50 Oilfield Related Patents; hon/Engr of Yr, N Tex Sect ASME 1971; Fellow ASME 1972; W/W: Engrg, S&SW, Fin & Indust.

SKALAK, CONSTANCE HAVIRD oc/Associate Professor; b/Aug 24, 1934; h/3543 Bellerive Cir, Martinez, GA 30907; ba/Augusta; m/Robert Claiborne; c/Victor Roule, Carl Meyer; p/Oliver John and Kate Bradley Havird; ed/BSN; MN; pa/Assoc Prof Nsg, Augusta Col; ANA; NLN; cp/Secy Repub Party 1971; r/Presb; SS Tchr; hon/Sigma Theta Tau; Outstg Nsg Tchr 1979, Secy Alumni Assn Augusta Col (First Time Awd Given).

SKELTON, JAMES ALONZO oc/Businessman; b/Apr 14, 1920; h/1832 38th St, Meridian, MS 39301; ba/Meridian; m/Gertrude Olivia; c/James Charles, Michael Shafe; p/William Shafe (dec) and Neacy Cornelia Skelton (dec); mil/AUS 1942-46; pa/Co-Owner & Exec VP Fam Budget Ser; VP Imperial Fin Corp; Past Pres Meridian Loan Exch; cp/Enterprise Lodge 1951; Sts Johns Lodge 618, Meridian, MS 1954, Master Mason; Scottish Rite 1958; York Rite; Life Mem Hamasa Shrine Temple, Potentate 1972; Oriental Guide; Pres Meridian Shrine Clb 1961-62; Pres Hamasa Uniform Bodies Assn 1963-65; Pres Dixie Shrine Assn 1971-72, Secy 1972-; Life Mem Shriner's Hosp for Crippled Chd; 100 Million Dollar Clb; Meridian Chapt #11 OES; Rep to Imperial Coun 9 Yrs; Pres Hamasa Widow's Fund; Chm Hamasa Spec Activs Fund & Hosp Prog; Royal Order of Jesters; Jimmie Rodgers Meml Fest, Pres 1976-79; Pres Meridian Area Navy Leag 1978-79; Chm Miss Parks Comm 1977-79; Col on Miss Gov's Staff; C of C Mil Liason Com; Vol Wkr GLOW Fund 25 Yrs; Past Cmdr Am Legion Post 21 & Post 79; Former Cub Scout Master, Oakland Heights Sch; r/Meth; Adm Bd; hon/Recip Freedom Foun Awd 1954.

SKIDMORE, LAWRENCE M oc/Criminal Justice Coordinator; b/Jan 9, 1946; h/Lakeland, FL; ba/PO Box 60, Bartow, FL 33830; p/Joseph S and Helen Skidmore, Holmes Bch, FL; ed/AA Manatee Jr Col 1970; BS Fla St Univ 1972; MS Rollins Col 1977; mil/USAF Sgt; pa/Pt-time Adj Prof, Fla So Col; Crim Just Coor, Dept Crim Just, Polk Co Bd Co Commrs 1978-; Crim Just Planner, Ctrl Fla Regional Plan'g Coun 1974-78; Juvenile Probation Ofcr, St Fla Div Yth Sers 1972-74; Pol Co Crim Just Task Force; Pres Imperial Radio Control Flying Clb; Fla Coun Crime & Delinquency; Fla St Alumni Assn; cp/Bartow Lions Clb; Bd Dirs Polk Co Coalition for Chd & Yth; Past Mem Bd Dirs Prog to Aid Drug Abusers 1977-78; Past Mem Bd Dirs Mlt Hlth Assn 1979-80; Past Mem Alcohol Prevention Task Force 1979; Past Mem Nat Assn Crim Just Planners 1979; r/Assem of God; hon/W/W S&SW 1980-81; Cert of Apprec, Fla Coun Crime & Delinquency 1980; Cert of Apprec, Ctlr Fla Regional Plan'g Coun, Crim Just Adv Com 1980; Cert of Apprec, First Step, Inc of Lakeland 1977; Cert of Apprec, Rollins Col for Appellate Jurisprudence & Legal Reasoning 1977; Awd for Outstg Part w MD Assn 1979; W/W Students in Am Jr Cols.

SKINNER, JAMES V oc/Athletic Director; b/July 20, 1946; h/Brenham, TX; ba/1200 Carlee Dr, Brenham, TX 77833; m/Dianne Skelton; c/Steven, Brad; p/Dick and Dorothy Skinner, Corrigan, TX; ed/Att'd Blinn Jr Col 1965-66; BS Ed Stephen F Austin St Univ; pa/Hd Fball Coach & Ath Dir, Brenham HS; pa/Dist Chm TCIL 1978; Bd Dirs Tex Assn Pvt Schs 1979; Tex HS Coaches Assn 1974-; r/Bapt; hon/St Finalist, Fball, TCIL 1977; St Champ, Track, TCIL 1978; TCIL Coach of Yr, Track 1978; St Champ, Fball, TAPS 1979; TAPS Coach of Yr, Fball 1979; St Finalist, Girls Basketball, TAPS 1980.

SKINNER, ROBERT EARL oc/Farmer; b/June 23, 1943; h/Rt 1, Hartford, AL 36344; m/Robin; c/Charles Robert, Jarvis Edward; p/A L and Ora B Skinner, Hartford, AL; pa/Farmer; r/Meth; hon/Ala Peanut Farmer 1979.

SKIPPER, ROBERT VERNON oc/Retailer; b/Mar 26, 1948; h/1504 Old Memphis Pike, Tuscumbia, AL 35674; ba/Tuscumbia; m/Jo Ann Walker; c/Lani, Suzy, Tracy; p/Norman Edwin and Anne Margret Phillips Skipper, Bells, TN; ed/AA Freed-Hardeman Col 1972; BA David Lipscomb Col 1974; MA Univ N Ala 1977; pa/Psychi Tech, Ctrl St Psychi

Hosp 1972-74; Dir Easter Seal Ctr for Handicapped Chd 1974-75; Dir Opers Goodwill Industs 1975-76; Dir Patient Activs, Eliza Coffee Meml Hosp, Florence, Ala 1979-79; Self-Employed Retail Sales; APGA; Phi Chi; cp/Dem Party; BOPE (Elks Clb); r/Ch of Christ; hon/W/W S&SW 1981.

SLAATTE, HOWARD ALEXANDER oc/Clergyman, Professor; b/Oct 18, 1919; h/407 Grand Blvd, Huntington, WV 25705; ba/H'ton; m/Mildred; c/Elaine Tran, Mark Edwin, Paul Andrew; p/Iver T (dec) and Esther'Slaatte (dec); ed/AA; BA cum laude; BD cum laude; PhD; pa/Prof & Chm, Dept Philos, Marshall Univ; Pres WV Philos Soc 1967-68; Coms at Marshall Univ; Author 7 Profl Books; cp/Bd Mem Optimist Clb Intl of H'ton; r/U Meth Min; hon/Pilling F'ship, Drew Univ to Oxford 1949-50; Alumni Awd, Kendall Col 1964.

SLAGLE, PATTI LYNN oc/Director of Continuity, Receptionist; b/June 5, 1959; h/PO Box 575, Harlan, KY 40831; ba/Harlan; p/Vernon Slagle (dec); Ruby Howard, Harlan, KY; ed/Att'd Cumberland Col 1976; SE Commun Col 1977; Morehead St Univ 1978-79; pa/Legal Secy, Rice & Huff Attys at Law 1978; Dir Continuity & Wom's Progs, WHLN Radio 1979-80; Adm Secy Univ Ky Med Ctr, Phys Therapy 1980; Dir of Continuity & Wom's Progs, WHLN Radio 1980-; cp/Dir Kings Kids Choral Grp 1976-81; r/So Bapt; hon/W/W: Am Wom 1981, Am HS Students 1976, 77; Bauch & Laumb Sci Awd 1977.

SLAGLE, WILLIAM LEE oc/Director of Intercollegiate Debate; b/Mar 8, 1947; h/Macon, GA; ba/Dept Speech & Drama, Mercer Univ, Macon, GA 31207; p/William Robert and Sylva Frances Stanford Slagle, Amarillo, TX; ed/BS W Tex St Univ 1969; MA Tex Tech Univ 1976; pa/Tchr Dalhart HS, Dalhart, Tex 1969-75; Assoc Dir Debate, Tex Tech Univ 1976-77; Dir Debate, Mercer Univ 1977-; Delta Sigma Rho, Tau Kappa Alpha; Am Forensic Assn, Public Relats Com; Speech Commun Assn; Ga Speech Commun Assn; Dist VI Nat Debate Tourn Com; Nat Forensic Leag; r/Epis; hon/Dist'd Tchr Awd, Dalhart Indep Sch Dist 1970, 72, 75; Author *Affirmative Approaches to Foreign Trade Policy 1979*, *Affirmative Approaches to Consumer Product Safety 1980*; "A Study of Cross Examination Debate Styles" 1977.

SLATER, BETTY CARL MONTGOMERY oc/Coordinator for Psychiatric Services; b/Sept 13, 1934; h/9231 Garland Dr, Savannah, GA 31406; ba/Savannah; m/Jack D; c/Tracy Allen, Sandra Carol, William Dudley; p/W D (dec) and Peachie Mae Montgomery, Danville, KY; ed/Nsg Dip; BS Cand; pa/Coor Psychi Sers; RN; GNA, First Dist Pres 1979-81; Coun of Assocs, Am Soc Nsg Ser Adm; ANA; SE Ga Hlth Sys Agcy; cp/Wom's Aux of Ritualistic Divan & Alee Temple Shrine; Patron Little Theatre of Savannah; hon/W/W Am Wom.

SLATER, CONSTANCE FINCH oc/Special Educator; b/Sept 13, 1931; h/6221 NW 17th St, Ft Lauderdale, FL; ba/Ft Lauderdale; m/Fred C; c/Steven, Scott, Stacey S Owens, Sherrill S Barb; p/George and Dorothy M Finch, Plymouth, MA; ed/AA Broward Commun Col 1968-73; BA Shaw Univ 1975; Post Grad Fla Atlantic Univ 1976-77; pa/Ofc Mgr, Commercial Union Assurance Co 1950; Fam & Child Ser Agcy, San Bernardino, Calif 1951; Gate City Sash & Door Co 1952-54; Tchr Wingate Oaks Ctr, Ft Lauderdale; Owner-Dir Tall Pine Camp for Excptl Citizens, Coker Creek, Tenn; Coun for Excptl Chd; Am Assn Mtl Deficiency; Nat Assn Retard'd Citizens; cp/Secy Parents & Friends Sunland Tng Ctr; VChm Dist 10, Fla Human Rights Advocacy Com Mtl Retard; Rep N Ctlr Adv Com, Supt Schs Dist Adv Voc Ed for Handicapped; Fellow Fla Intl Univ; Past Grad Symposium on Mtl Retard, Elwyn Insts; r/Prot; hn/Nom'd Tchr of Yr 1980; Spec Olympic Vol 1979; Cert of Recog for Outstg Determination in Achieving Ednl Goals 1975.

SLAUGHTER, JANE MUNDY oc/Author, Retired Nurse; b/Oct 2, 1905; h/Jacksonville, FL; m/Frank; c/Frank G Jr, Randolph M; p/Luther Thomas (dec) and Pearl K Mundy (dec); ed/RN Jefferson Hosp, Roanoke, Va 1926; pa/RN, Oper'g Room Supvr, Jefferson Hosp; Author Fiction; Va Nsg Assn; cp/Chm Dem for Eisenhower, Nixon 1952, 60; r/Riverside Presb Ch; hon/Top Grade Va St Bd Nsg 1926; Author *Espy and the Catnappers; Pepsy Le Chat; Tess of the Shenandoah.*

SLEDGE, ROBERT OWEN oc/Businessman; b/Aug 4, 1929; h/202 Sunf Ave, Sunflower, MS 38778; ba/Sunflower; m/June Thompson; c/Carolyn Ann, Robert Owen Jr; p/Willie C Sledge, Sunflower, MS; mil/USN Submarine Ser; pa/Co-Owner Sledge Telephone Co; Ala Miss Indep Telephone Assn, Bd Dirs; cp/Rotary Clb, Past Pres; Mason Lodge, Past Master; Moorhead Hunting Clb, Bd Dirs; Sunflower Meth Ch SS Supt; r/Prot.

SLESINSKI, THERESA oc/Consultant; b/Oct 7, 1944; h/April Pt S 95, Montgomery, TX 77356; ba/Houston; p/Anthony R and Antonina Wnorowski Slesinski, Mont, TX; ed/BA 1973, MS 1976; pa/Org Devel, Conslt, Exxon Co USA; Am Soc Tnrs & Develrs; APGA; r/Cath; hon/W/W S&SW 1980-81; Alpha Kappa Delta; Sigma Tau Delta; Author

278

"Analysis of the Effects of a Preretirement Program on a Group Employed in Private Industry."

SLIFER, KENNETH BENJAMIN oc/Professor; b/Apr 5, 1915; h/3239 Doverside Dr, Nashville, TN 37207; ba/Nashville; m/Thelma Richards; c/Marita Sue Smith; p/dec; ed/AB Trevecca Col 1950; MDiv Vanderbilt Univ 1953; MA Austin Peay St Univ 1965; EdD Auburn Univ 1973; pa/Min 18 Yrs; Tchr; Former Dean Instrn, Motlow St Commun Col; Prof Psych, Trevecca Col, Nashville; Tenn Psych Assn; Middle Tenn Psych Assn; AAUP; r/Ch of the Nazarene; hon/W/W Am Cols & Univs.

SLIMOVITZ, MORRIS L oc/Businessman; b/July 18, 1904; h/Jefferson St, Newbern, TN 38059; ba/Same; p/Aaron and Sarah Slimovitz, Haifa, Israel; mil/AUS WWII; pa/Owner Glove Factory; Dir Glove Inst Am; cp/32° Mason; Shriner; Rotarian; C of C; r/Jewish; hon/Americanism Awd, DAR; Man of Yr, Newbern Indust Co.

SLOAN, JUANITA GILLEN oc/Teacher; b/Sept 11, 1928; h/4501 Clearwater Dr, Corpus Christi, TX 78413; ba/Corpus Christi; m/Robert S; c/Norman Kent Gillen Jr, Kyle David Gillen, (Stepchd:) Suzanne S Lewis, Carol E, Rebecca L; p/S J and Nettie Beulah Wilson Greenwood, Tyler, TX; ed/BBA w hons; MBE; pa/Assoc Prof Bus Adm, Dept Bus & Ecs, Del Mar Col; ISBE; NBEA; M-PBEA; TSTA; TJCTA; TBEA; DMEA; Delta Pi Epsilon; r/Meth; hon/Tex Bus Tchr of Yr 1978; Dist Bus Tchr of Yr 1971 & 78; Piper Prof Nom 1967-69; NBEA Profl Ser Awd in Bus Ed 1968; NBEA Merit Awd 1959; W/W Students in Am Univs & Cols 1958-59.

SLOAT, LOU WALLIN oc/Educator; b/Oct 28, 1943; h/PO Box 93, Lufkin, TX 75901; ba/Lufkin; m/Karen Marie McDowell; c/Bryan Houston, Heather Ann, Joanna Marie, Shannon Lea; p/Robert Louis (dec) and Elvira Wallin Sloat, Detroit, MI; ed/BSF Stephen F Austin St Univ; mil/USN 4 Yrs; pa/Area Edr, Tex Forest Ser; Editor Tex Chapt SAF Newslttr; Chm Public Info Com, Soc Am Foresters, Tex Chapt; cp/Disaster & Emergency Sers Chm, Am Red Cross; Public Info Ofcr, Angelina Co Fire Fighters Assn; r/Epis; hon/Tex Forest Ser Outstg Ser Awd 1978-79; Pub'd Over 250 Articles & Stories in St, Nat & Local Pubs.

SLONIM, ROBERTA RAYMOND oc/Physician; b/Mar 4, 1933; ba/Miami, FL; m/Ralph J; c/Suzanne M; p/Gabriel and Bahita Daoud Hanna Raymond; ed/BS cum laude 1953, MD 1957 Geo Wash Univ; Col of Mt St Mincent 1949-52, Scranton Univ 1953; Nat Inst Hlth, F'ship in Rheumatic Disease; pa/Intern Jackson Meml Hosp 1957; Res Fellow Nat Inst Hlth in Rheumatology 1958-60; Res in Infectious Disease, Univ Miami 1960-61; Dept Internal Med VA Hosp, Coral Gables, Fla 1961-62; Clin Instr Arthritis, Univ Miami Med Sch 1962-64; Pvt Prac of Rheumatology 1963-72; Nutritional Cnslg & Nutrition-Internal Med, Pvt Pract 1972-; Dade Co Med Assn; Arthritis Foun; Geriatrics Assn; So Fla Psychi Assn; Res Grants Com, Arthritis Foun; cp/Nat China Painting; Intl China Painting Tchrs Org; Orchid Growers Assn; So Fla Avocado & Lime Growers Assn; Nutrition Today Soc; Sports Med; r/Cath; hon/Sev Res Pubs on Arthritis & on Treatment of Gout; Letter Commend, White House 1962; Cert for Adv'd Med Hypnotherapy 1963.

SMALLEY, RALPH LEROY oc/Truck Driver; b/Nov 14, 1931; h/Rt 3, Bessemer City, NC 28016; ba/Belmont, NC; m/Eula Marie; c/James Frank; p/Don and Violet Smalley, Chesnee, SC; mil/NG; pa/Long Haul Truck Driver, Burlington Industs Inc; r/Bapt; hon/NC Driver of Mo Awd, Dec 1978.

SMILEY, JANE P oc/Executive; b/Nov 11, 1942; h/Radford, VA; ba/PO Box 5550, Radford Univ, Radford, VA 24142; c/Thomas Bradley, John Russell; p/Homer and Mary B Purtle, Prescott, AR; ed/BA Univ Ark-Little Rock 1969; MA VPI & SU 1976; pa/Radford Univ: Acting VP Bus Affairs, Asst to VP for Bus Affairs, Asst Prof Bus; Am Soc Public Adm, Com for Wom in Public Adm w/in SW Va Chapt; r/Prot; hon/Nom'd for Excell in Tchg Awd 1978, 79, 80.

SMITH, A REGINALD oc/Executive; b/July 4, 1942; ba/5457 Monroe Rd, Charlotte, NC 28212; m/Judy Beal; c/Artie, Allison; p/Arthur and Dorothy Byers; ed/Att'd NCSU 1960-62; Grad w Hons CPCC; pa/VP Arthur Smith Studios 1963-69; Acct Exec, Mission Broadcasting Co 1969-71; VP Ralph Squires Co, Sales & Mktg 1971-75; Pres Smith-Allen Co, 1975; Pres Devel Mktg Enterprises Inc 1976; Pres Ash Devel Co Inc 1978; Dir Clay Mus Corp 1964; Pres NC Home Bldrs Sales & Mktg Coun 1979-80; Nat Assn Home Bldrs; NC Home Bldrs Assn; Home Bldrs Assn of Charlotte; NAHB Sales & Mktg Coun; NAHB Land Devel Com; NAHB Sales & Mktg Com; NAHB Spike Clb; Carmel Country Clb; Myrtle Bch Tennis Clb; r/Calvery Ch; hon/W/W S&SW; NAHB Life Spike; NAHB Life Mem Million Dollar Cir; Author *Power of Love, Your Are the One* 1959.

SMITH, ADA McNEAL oc/Teacher; b/Sept 23, 1925; h/Kinston, NC; m/Leamon O; c/Thelmasenia Leanee; p/dec; ed/BS WSSU 1947; MEd NCCU 1958; pa/Sci Tchr, Woodington Jr HS; Person Co Bd Ed 1947-54; Lenoir Co Bd Ed 1954-81; NCAE; NEA; Nat Sci Foun; cp/Dem Party; NAACP; PTSA; Amez Missionary Soc; Kinston High Band Boosters; r/Meth; hon/Hon Grad HS & Col; Med in Math; Winner in Local & St Sci Fairs.

SMITH, ANDREW WALLIN oc/Ranger, Commentator; b/Jan 11, 1919; h/Rt 1 Box 310, Giddings, TX 78942; ba/Same; m/Elizabeth; c/Andrea Elizabeth Oden, Patrick Wallin; p/Raymond Harold (dec) and Nannie Elizabeth Wallin Smith (dec); ed/Sam Houston St Univ 1939; Lamar Tech Voc Sch 1941-42; mil/AUS Paratroopers; pa/Tchr Blue Print Rdg & Shipbldg, Brown & Root Constr Co 1942-43; Agric Prodr 1947-65; Rancher & Heavy Equip Opers Instr 1966-73; Rancher & Agric Radio Writer-Commentator 1974-; cp/Lee Co Cattlemen's Assn, Pres 1978; Tex Farm Bur, Bd Dir, Chm Beef Commodity Div 1976-80; Indep Cattlemen's Assn, Dist Councilor 1974-75; Dist Chm Nat Beeferendum Promo 1979-80; Tex & SWn Cattlemen's Assn; Nat Cattlemen's Assn; Dime Box Yth Rodeo Assn, Rodeo Chm 1964; Lee Co Sheriff's Posse, Rodeo Chm 1965; Giddings Rotary Clb, Bd Dirs & Pres Elec 1981-82; r/Presb; hn/Outstg Agric Radio Pers, Wash Co Soil & Water Conserv Dist 1977; Dist'd Ser-Public News Media, Burleson & Lee Soil & Water Conserv Dist 1979; Soil & Water Conserv Dists of Tex Region III Public Media Awd 1979; Giddings, Tex C of C Voice of Agric Awd 1981.

SMITH, ANNINIAS CORNELIUS oc/Teacher; b/Nov 9, 1944; h/1300 Ward St, Greenville, NC 27834; p/Hulbert Hooker, Grifton, NC; Martha Smith (dec); ed/BS A&T St Univ; Grad Study Univ Md, E Carolina Univ; mil/AUS; pa/Tchr Mtlly Handicapped Chd, Pitt Co Schs; Pt-time Farmville Rec Dept; NCAE; ACT; NEA; cp/Prince Hall Shriner; 33° Mason; Royal Arch Mason; Grand Secy St of NC Odd Fellow; NAACP; Vol Sr Citizens Work; r/Little Creek FWB Ch; hon/W/W S&SW 1980; Awd'd Sev Plaques for Outstg Ldrship; News Editor, *Ayden Newsleader*; Col Newspaper Reporter.

SMITH, ARTHUR CLOYD oc/Retired; b/June 22, 1895; m/Maybelle; c/William Callen; p/dec; mil/AUS 1917-19; pa/RR Brakeman & Conductor 1919-59; Del to Nat Convs of Brotherhood of RR Trainmen 1931 & 39; cp/Pres Unit #62, Nat Assn Ret'd & Vet Railway Employees Inc, Former Grand VP, Att'd 6 Bianniel Convs, Chm By-Laws & Constitution Com, Elec'd Grand Dir, Dist 1, Wichita, Kan Conv; 10th Dist Ser Ofcr, VFW; Comdr Trailer Est Barracks, 2398, Vets of WWI; Over 200 Hrs As Vol at Vet Hosp, Bay Pines, Fla.

SMITH, B J oc/Pastor; b/June 28, 1939; h/Texarkana, TX; m/Joyce; c/Michael, Bryan; p/John and Modean Smith, Greenville, TX; pa/Fdr & Pastor Northside Assem of God Ch; r/Assem of God.

SMITH, BETTYE JANE oc/Dean; b/Apr 7, 1926; h/408 Springdale Dr, Columbus, MS 39701; ba/Columbus; p/Jesse Doswell and Ethel McCarthy Smith, Columbus, MS; ed/BS; MA; EdD; pa/Dean, Sch Nsg, Miss Univ for Wom; Chp Miss Coun of Deans & Dirs 1977-79; NLN; ANA; Am Public Hlth Assn; Am Assn Polit & Social Sci; cp/Adm Bd & Recording Steward, Wesley U Meth Ch; Hlth & Ed Com, Lowndes C of C; r/Meth; hon/Nurse of Yr, Pike Co, Ala & Dist V Ala St Nurses Assn; W/W Am Wom 1979-80; Outstg Edrs of Am 1974-75; Alpha Epsilon Chapt Pi Lambda Theta 1958; Kappa Chapt Kappa Delta Pi 1958.

SMITH, BOBBY EARL oc/Salesman; b/Dec 13, 1942; h/Bellville, TX; ba/Brenham, TX; m/Paula Jo Renfro; c/Shon Eric, Randi Sheree, Wendy, Scott, Rebecca Shannon, Robert Shane; p/A C and Mary Helen Smith, Jacksonville, TX; ed/Att'd Stephen F Austin Col, Jacksonville Bapt Col; mil/Tex NG; pa/Bob Smith Mobil Consignee & TBA Dist; Rodger Paxton Pout, Olds, Buick & GMC Inc, Brenham, Tex; Evening Optimist; Tex Ser Station Assn; Am Qtr Hose Assn; Nat Rltrs Assn; cp/Oldsmobile Vanguard 1976, 78, 79, 80; r/Meth; hon/Buick Sales Mgr Object Awd 199-80; Top Sales, Mobile Oil SW Div; Greatest Obj St of Tex, Buick Sales Mgr in Run Through Warehouse Contest.

SMITH, BOYCE MILES oc/Stockbroker; b/Apr 3, 1924; h/4120 Morning Trail, College Pk, GA 30349; ba/Atlanta; m/Helen M Snavely; c/Sherry A De Los Santos, Stanley M, Sally Anne, Scott Anthony; p/William Pinkston (dec) and Alice Vivian Smith (dec); ed/BS Univ Ark 1950; Meteorology Univ Tex 1961; MS Colo St Univ 1965; mil/AUS; pa/Chief Forecaster USAF, Athens, Greece 1961-64; Dir Geophys Dept, Technol Div, Wright-Patterson AFB 1965-69; Staff Meteorologist, Taiwan Defense Command, USN, Taipei, Taiwan 1969-71; Vice Cmdr 1st Weather Grp, USAF, Saigon, Vietnam 1971-72; Mem Spl Staff AUS, Europe, 1972-75; Condr 5th Wea Sqdn USAF, Ft McPherson, Ga 1975-79; Stockbroker, Daley & Co 1980-; Envir Conslt, Repub China AF, Taipei 1969-71; Am Meteorological Soc; Am Geophys Union; Alpha Chi Sigma; cp/BSA; Soc Security Analyst; Am Assn Indev Investors; r/Meth; hon/Legion of Merit; Merit Ser Medal w OLC; Air Med w 4 OLC; Author Classified Articles & Reviews 1965-69.

PERSONALITIES OF THE SOUTH

SMITH, CHARLES LARRY (The Country Mouse) oc/Entertainer; b/July 4, 1952; h/Hartselle, AL; c/Dorthy Jean and Grace Ann; p/Roy E and Harley Faye Smith, Hartselle, AL; ed/EMT; mil/USN; pa/Country Mus Performer; Writer of Over 200 Songs; Country Mus Assn; Nashville Song Writers Assn.

SMITH, DALE HOWARD oc/Trainer; b/Mar 28, 1950; h/Seminole, FL; m/Glennalee Gail; c/Christina, Lynda; p/Donald L Smith, Chgo, IL; Doris E Pulley, Marion, IL; mil/USN 1968-72; pa/Owner & Tnr Mantrackers; Ponca City Policeman; r/Bapt.

SMITH, DAVID LEE oc/Director; b/Jan 4, 1940; h/532 Washington St NW, Camden, AR 71701; ba/E Camden; m/Patsy Jean; c/Dawn Elizabeth, Janell Lisa; p/Floyd J Smith, Jonesville, MI; ed/BA Univ Md 1972; MS Univ Ark 1973; PhD Clayton Univ 1980; mil/USAF 1959-72; AUS 1976-80; pa/Dir Bus Mgmt Div So Ark Univ, Tech Br; So Bus Ed Assn; Nat Assn Accts; Ark 2 Yr Col Tchrs Assn; cp/Am Legion; r/Meth; hon/Author Num Profl Articles.

SMITH, DAVID RAY oc/Home Instruction Teacher; b/Feb 15, 1952; h/Box 224, Pikeville, KY 41501; p/Randolph B and Mary Lou Beavan Smith, Pikeville, KY; ed/BUS Morehead St Univ 1975; Att'd Asbury Col 1970-74, Freewill Bapt Bible Col 1970-71; pa/Home Instrn Tchr, Pike Co Bd Ed 1981; Actor The King's Players; Cadet Bell-Ringer for Salvation Army; Speech & Drama Tourn Coor, Pike & Knott Cos; Alpha Psi Omega; La Tertulia, Pres Spanish Soc Asbury; Am Theatre Assn; Christian Theatre Artists Guild; Radius; Speech Commun Assn; cp/Rep Toastmasters Intl Clb; Local Bd Dirs Goodwill Inc; Polit Cand, Bd Mem Pike Co Ed 1980; r/Meth; hon/1 of 70 Ky Students to Study Spanish on Pioneer Expedition to Guatemala & Mexico 1968; Awd'd 2 S'ships from Asbury Col 1971-72.

SMITH, DELPHIA FRAZIER oc/Writer, Poet, Painter, Sculptress, Wood Carver, Musician, Singer, Exhibitor, Speaker; b/Apr 24, 1921; h/202 9th St, Mammoth Spring, AR 72554; m/Clyde L; ed/Many Courses in Nsg, Self-Help, Art Apprec, Art & Bus & Langs; DLitt, World Univ 1979; pa/TV Appearances; Exhib: Templari Gal, San Felice Ciroco, Italy; Pub'd in Most of World in Anthols, Mags, Books, Papers; Pub'd 35 Books; World Poetry Soc; Nat Carvers Mus: Patron, Exhib, Rep Staff Writer; Life Mem Soc of Lit Designators; Nat Trust for Hist Preserv; Crest Clb; Fdr, Fellow Intl Poetry Soc; Inter-Cont Biog Assn; Collectors Guild; Poets Cong; Sculptress Collectors Ltd; SW Mo Mus Inc; World of Creative Thinkers; Smithsonian Assocs Intl; Am F'ship Soc; Citizens for Decent Lit; Kindness Clb; Major Poets; Japan Forum; Leonardo Di Vinci Acad; Centro Studi E Scambi Intl; Adv Bd: Am Security Coun, ABI, Others; hon/Silver Pin & Bronze Medal, Am Security Coun; Large Plaque ABI; Gold Pin Intl Platform Assn; 2 Dist'd Ser Cit Awds, World Poetry Soc 1971 & 79; Gold Loving Cup & Oil Portrait, Japan Forum; 3 Gold Medals, Di Vinci Acad; Gold Medal, CSSI; 3 Silver Medals, Centro Di Cultura SS Crose UK; 2 Intl Awds, Clover Poetry Comp; Many Other Awds, Dips, Cits, Ribbons; Bronze Plaque W/W in Poetry; DIB; Cert Inter-Cont Biog Assn; W/W Am Wom; Commun Ldrs & Noteworthy Ams; Intl Register of Profiles; Notable Ams of Bicent Era; World W/W Intells; Writers Directory; Other Biog Listings.

SMITH, DONALD ALAN oc/Artist, Businessman; b/Dec 4, 1934; h/4 Tanglewood Ct, Athens, GA 30606; ba/Athens; c/Kirk Martin, Angela; p/Brooks and Ella Jaeger Smith, Florence, SC; ed/BFA Univ Ga 1956; mil/USAR; pa/Artist; Owner The Adsmith, Advtg Agcy; Advtg Fed Am; Atlanta Advtg Clb; Athens Ad Clb, Bd Dirs; cp/Bd Dirs Am Cancer Soc; Athens Area C of C; r/Presb; hon/Phi Eta Sigma; Phi Kappa Phi; Phi Beta Kappa; Athens Yng Man Yr 1966; Outstg Ser Awd, Athens Area C of C 1966; Outstg Yng Man Am 1967; Outstg Personalities of S 1967; W/W S&SW 1980; Art Dirs Clb of Atlanta Gold Awd 1960, Silver Awd 1961; Commun Art Awd of Excell 1961; Advtg Fed Am 7th Dist Silver Awd 1964, Gold Awd 1968 & 71; Art Dirs Clb Atlanta Silver Awd 1966; Inst Outdor Advtg: 3 Gold Awds 1965, Awd of Excell 1965, 3 Gold Awds 1966, 3 Awds Excell 1966; Milk Indust Foun Adv Awd 1969; Intl Paper Co Packaging Design Awd 1970; 4 Atlanta Advtg Clb Phoenix Awds 1970; Mid-S Advtg Show Awd of Excell 1971, 72; So Creativity Show: 2 Awds Excell 1973, 2 Gold Awds 1979, 7 Awds Excell 1979, 5 Awds Excell 1980; Ga-Ala Newspaper Assn Gold Awd 1972; Ga Press Assn Awd of Excell 1977; So Classified Ad Mgrs Best Ad Campaign Awd 1979; Ga Press Assn Awd 1980; Danda Awd Hon Mention 1979; Am Cancer Soc Outstg Ser Awd (St) 1980; Illustrator Num Book; Author Num Articles.

SMITH, DOROTHY B oc/Executive; b/Jan 24, 1920; h/Charlotte, NC; m/Arthur; c/Arthur Reginald, Constance Brown, Robert Clayton; p/R H (dec) and Dovie Rains Byars (dec); ed/Tchr Dip in Japanese Flower Arrangements, Ikenobo Inst 1968; pa/VP Arthur Smith Studios; VP Clay Mus Corp; China Painter; cp/Chm Christian Wom's Clb, Advr & Area Rep; Charlotte City Clb; Life Mem Gdn Clb of NC; Pres Sardiswood Gdn Clb; Mint Mus Art; Charlotte Symph Patron; Hon Chm Charlotte Emer Yth Care Ctr; Bd Dirs NC Bapt Chds Homes; r/Bapt; hon/Mother of Yr 1960; Winner Over 100 Blue Ribbons for Flower Arranging & Horticulture.

SMITH, EDMOND M oc/Bank Officer; b/Apr 14, 1942; m/Ann; c/Mary Alice, Edmond M III; p/Mr and Mrs E M Smith Sr; ed/BA Vanderbilt Univ 1964; MBA Univ So Calif 1971; ABA Grad Commercial Lending Sch 1975; pa/Sr VP Bristol Region, First Nat Bank of Sullivan Co; Beta Gamma Sigma; cp/Repub; Robert Morris Assn; r/Bapt/Presb.

SMITH, EDWIN oc/Executive; b/May 9, 1941; h/4927 Thunder Rd, Dallas, TX 75234; ba/Dallas; m/Alicia; c/Steven, Stacey; p/Wilbur H E (dec) and Ethel Lucille Smith (dec); ed/Cert of Design, Parsons Sch Design 1963; mil/USANG 1963-69 Staff Sgt; pa/SWn Bell Telephone Co, Acct Exec 1976-; Am Soc Tnrs & Develrs; Assn of Profl Color Labs; Profl Photogs Assn; Photo Mktg Assn; Sales & Mktg Assn of Dallas; Staff Assocs, Foun for Metaphys Studies; cp/Dallas Black C of C; Variety Clb of Tex; r/Ecumenical Metaphysical; hon/W/W S&SW 19810-81; SWn Bell Outstg Sales Achmt 1978, 79.

SMITH, ERNEST LESTER oc/Superintendent; b/Dec 20, 1926; h/Rt 1 Box 216-B, Geneva, AL 36340; m/Ruth; c/Ernest L Jr; p/Mack (dec) and Dora Smith (dec); ed/BS 1952; M Deg 1965; mil/1945-47; pa/PE Tchr & HS Coach, Asst Prin Riverside HS 6 Yrs; Prin E J Lewis HS 5 Yrs; Asst Prin Samson HS 5 Yrs; Dir ESAA Prog; Supt Ed Geneva Co; Pres Geneva Co Tchrs Assn; Treas Dist 7 Assn; cp/ADC Co Coor; SEA Region Plan'g Comm; 2nd VP Lodge #379; Secy NAACP; Phi Delta Kappa; r/Bapt; Deacon.

SMITH, EVA D oc/Nursing Faculty and Administrator; b/Aug 14, 1938; h/Natchez, MS; ba/Alcorn St Univ, PO Box 1830, Natchez, MS 39120; p/Cary J and Estella D Smith, Scotland Neck, NC; ed/BS Winston-Salem St Univ 1959; MS DePaul Univ 1965; Post Master Study Univ Chgo 1974-75; PhD Kan St Univ 1978; pa/Chp Dept BS Nsg, Alcorn St Univ 1978-; Nsg Instr, Michael Reese Sch Nsg 1965-75; Staff & Hd Nurse, Hines VA Hosp 1961-63, 64-65; Staff Nurse, Bertie Meml Hosp 1959-61; ANA, Prog & Nom'g Coms; NLN, Prog Com; Adult Ed Assn USA; Phi Delta Kappa; Phi Delta Gamma; Zeta Phi Beta, Local Pres & VP, St Dir; cp/NAACP; Girl Scout Ldr; r/U Ch of Christ; hon/Humanitarian Awd, Zeta Phi Beta 1980; Wom of Yr 1973, Pk Manor U Ch of Christ; Author "Non-Clinical Practice of Continuing Education - Meets the Needs of the Demanding Nursing Profession" 1979.

SMITH, FRANCES S THORNTON oc/Retired Teacher; b/Jan 22, 1916; h/704 Berkshire Dr, Hattiesburg, MS; m/J P Maxwell; c/Frances Gale Saenz, Lee Gibson, David M; p/Tom Mabe and Dee Elizabeth Lovett Thornton; ed/BS Univ So Miss 1940; pa/Tchr: Brooklyn, Miss 1938-39; Waynesboro, Miss 1941-42; Pascagoula City Schs 1963-76; cp/Universal Clb; Gdn Craft Clb; Thursday Home & Gdn Clb; UDC; Kings Daughs & Sons; Ann Deavours Cir; r/U Meth; hon/W/W Am Wom 1958-59; Life Mem PTA 1955; Life Mem Wom's Soc Christian Ser 1958; Author *The Faith That Compelled Us* 1979; Article "A Perfectly Thrilling Adventure" in PTA Mag.

SMITH, FRANK T oc/Retired; b/Oct 29, 1911; h/703 W Grove, Terrell, TX 75160; m/Mable Augusta; c/Ferman R, Angela D Neasley; p/Chalrie (dec) and Angie Smith (dec); mil/WWII; pa/Ret'd from Atlantic Richfield Oil Co; Terrell City Coun; cp/Renaissance Civic Clb; r/Bapt.

SMITH, GEORGIA ELIZABETH oc/Counselor, Administrator; b/Nov 28, 1954; h/Box 2934 Station B, Nashville, TN 37235; ba/N'ville; p/Mr and Mrs John F Smith, Colo Springs, CO; ed/BA Colo St Univ 1975; BS Wn Ill Univ 1978; pa/Col Student Pers Admr-Cnslr, Vanderbilt Univ; Nat Assn Student Pers Admrs; APGA; Am Col Pers Assn; r/Christian; hon/W/W S&SW 1980; Grad Asst 1976-78, Wn Ill Univ; Author 'The Effectiveness of a Career Guidance Class: An Organizational Comparison" *Journal of College Student Personnel* 1981.

SMITH, GERALDINE MARIE oc/Teacher; b/Apr 5, 1943; h/319 E 24th St, Tyler, TX 75702; m/William Earl; c/Arlisa Marie, William LaMarquis; p/Alvin Sr and Effie L Nobles, Mt Enterprise, TX; ed/Assoc Deg; BS; MEd; pa/Elem Tchr, Chapel Hill Elem, Tyler; PTA; TSTA; TCTA; NEA; Zeta Phi Beta; cp/Mar of Dimes; Lib Clb; Lit Book Clb; YMCA; r/Ch of God in Christ; hon/Zeta of Yr 1979; Hon Student; Yth Dir; Best Dressed 1960-64.

SMITH, HARRISON HARVEY oc/Consultant; b/Oct 24, 1915; h/177 Ocean Ln Dr, Key Biscayne, FL 33149; ba/Same; m/Margaret Simons (dec); c/Barbara, Marjorie, Susan, Rosanne, Elizabeth; p/Ernest Gray Smith (dec); Marjorie Harvey (dec); ed/PG Work Medill Sch Jour, NWn Univ 1936-37; mil/1945-46; pa/Pres Wilkes-Barre Pub Co 1946-79; Editor *Wilkes-Barre Record* 1962-72; Newspaper Columnist 1954-78; Conslt

Newspaper Pub'g; Am Soc Newspaper Editors; Nat Conf Editorial Writers; Pa Newspaper Pubrs Assn, Exec Com 1954-62; Penn Assn Press, Pres 1953; Sigma Delta Chi; cp/Wyoming Hist Soc, Pres 1971-74; Wilkes-Barre Gen Hosp, VP 1954-76; Dir First En Bank 1946-; Wy Val Chapt ARC, Chm 1954-55; NE Pa Blood Ctr, Chm 1955-56; r/Presb; hon/Recip Dist'd Ser Awd, US Jr C of C 1979; Commend Awd, AUS 1946; 33° Mason; Contbr to Hist Pubs, Penn Poetry Collect, Bicent Editions.

SMITH, HENRY L oc/Assistant Superintendent; b/July 25, 1931; h/1526 Kenilworth Pkwy, Baton Rouge, LA 70808; m/LaVonne Elaine; cp/Preston Browning, Robin Elaine; p/Henry Leroy Smith (dec); Jennie May Hill (dec); ed/AB Lenoir Rhyne Col 1955; MEd Univ Va 1962; EdD Univ Va 1967; mil/USN 1947-49; pa/Asst St Supt, Div Spec Ednl Sers, La St Dept Ed 1976-; Assoc Prof & Chm, Spec Ed Progs, Auburn Univ 1973-75; Sr St Plan Ofcr, Aid to Sts Br, Bur of Ed for Handicapped, US Ofc Ed 1969-73; Dir Spec Ed, Charlotte-Mecklenburg Public Schs, NC 1967-69; Dir Spec Ed, Lynchburg Public Schs 1962-67; USOE F'ship 1960-62; Instr, Grad Studies in Mtl Retard, Univ Va 1961-70; Instr Spec Ed, Lynchburg Col 1962-64; Tchr EMR's & Phy Ed for Handicapped, Hd Basketball Coach & Asst Fball Coach: Flint Grove Public Schs (Gastonia, NC), Rosman HS (Rosman, NC), Brevard Sr HS, Clarke Jr HS (Charlottesville, Va) 1955-60; Life Mem Coun for Excptl Chd; 1st VP Intl Coun Excptl Chd 1980-81; Prog Adv Com of World Cong on Future Spec Ed; Am Assn Mtl Deficiency; Orthopsychi Assn; Kappa Delta Pi; Phi Delta Kappa; Assn Chd w Lrng Disabilities; Assn Retard'd Citizens; Coun for Adm of Spec Ed; Nat Assn St Dirs of Spec Ed; La Tchrs Assn; AAMD; Other Profl Orgs; hon/Man of Yr Awd, Va 1965; Edr of Yr Awd, Lynchburg, Va 1965; Recip Spoke Awd as Outstg JC in NC; Recip Outstg Public Servant of La 1978, La Assn Retard'd Citizens; Recip Pres Cup, La Assn Retard'd Cltizens 1979; Recip Dist'd Ser Awd, La Assn Gifted & Talented 1979; Recip Outstg Edr of Yr Awd 1979, Phi Delta Kappa Chapt La St Univ.

SMITH, HULET oc/Minister; b/Aug 11, 1950; h/1308 Green View Dr, Griffin, GA 30223; m/Peggy L; c/Robbie, Peter Gregory, George Thomas; p/Willie Thomas (dec) and Ruby Estelle Smith, Thomaston, GA; pa/Ordained Min, Ch of God: Evangelist 8 Yrs, Pastor 4 Yrs; hon/Dist Yth Dir 1977-79; Pres Gtr Griffin Area Min Assn 1979-80.

SMITH, IVORY oc/Retired Teacher, Businessman; b/Aug 20, 1899; h/Laurinburg, NC; ba/L'burg; m/Isabelle T; c/Ivory H Jr, John T; p/Henry A (dec) and Mary B Smith (dec); ed/Dip Tuskegee Inst 1929; pa/Vol Agric Tchr: Grambling, La 1929-31, L'burg Inst 1931-53, Scotland Co 1953-64; Dir Wash Pk Low Rent Housing 1964-66; Proprietor I H Smith Ser 1966-; City & St Tchrs Assn; NEA; Am Tchrs Assn; Dist, St & Nat Voc Agric Tchrs Assn; Farmer's Clb; NFA; cp/Home & Gdn Clbs; Vet's Orgs; Boy's Clb; Boy Scouts; Masons; Shriners; Consistory; C of C; r/Presb; hon/Silver Beaver 1965; 33° Mason 1966; Shriners Annual Awd 1969; Oak Hill Commun Awd 1975; 20 Yr Ser Key, Plant Food Inst of NC & Va; Cit for 25 Yrs, Nat Voc Agric Tchrs Assn; Author/Co-Author; Shriner of Yr 1963.

SMITH, J T oc/Preacher; b/June 24, 1933; h/855 Crawford St, Dyersburg, TN 38024; ba/D'burg; m/Geneva (Brownie); c/Judy, Joy, Pattie, Debra; p/Gillis B (dec) and Lucile Smith (dec); ed/Att'd Fla Christian Col; pa/Preacher 28 Yrs, Evangelist Work in 22 Sts, the Panama Canal Zone & Philippine Islands; r/Ch of Christ.

SMITH, JERRY KENT oc/Sportswriter; b/July 29, 1947; h/2304 Terrace, Copperas Cove, TX 76522; ba/Killeen; c/Matthew David; p/Kenneth N and Marjorie L Smith, Gdn City, KS; ed/BA 1970, MA 1972 Kan St Tchrs Col; Studies at Gdn City Jr Col, Ft Hays Ks St Col, Am Technol Univ; pa/Sportswriter *Killeen Daily Herald*; Tex Sports Writers Assn; r/Prot; hon/Author *Copperas Cove: City of Five Hills. A Centennial History.*

SMITH, JIMMY HAROLD oc/Businessman; b/Oct 2, 1933; h/301 Heather Dr, Bristol, VA 24201; ba/Bristol; m/Carol Jayne; c/Jimmy H Jr, William Blanton, Elizabeth Adams; p/Roy and Golden Smith Rutherford, Halifax, VA; ed/Lic'd Funeral Dir & Embalmer; mil/AUS; pa/Owner High Pt Grocery; cp/Chm Tri-City ARE Ind Comm, VChm; Wash Co Bd Supv; r/Bapt; hon/Good Conduct Medal; Korea Defense Medal.

SMITH, JULIUS MICHAEL oc/Executive; b/June 6, 1951; h/310 S Smylie, Brookhaven, MS 39601; ba/B'haven; p/Julius W and Mildred L Smith, B'haven, MS; ed/AA Copial-Lincoln Jr Col; BBA Univ Miss; Basic & Standard Certs Am Inst Bnkg; pa/VP Data Processing B'haven Bank; cp/Past Treas B'haven JCs; Lincoln Co U Givers Fund; Lions Clb; B'haven-Lincoln Co C of C; r/Ch of Christ.

SMITH, KATHERINE de DORY oc/Librarian; h/6833 Pacific Ln, Annandale, VA 22033; m/C Rodney; ed/BA 1950; MS 1962; pa/Serial Libn, Univ Ky 1959-62; Adult Sers, Bklyn Public Lib, NY 1962-64; Ref Libn, US Mil Acad, W Pt 1964-67, 1968-69; Chief Libn, Bien Hoa Base Lib,

Vietnam 1967-68; Army Map Ser, Topographical Cmd 1969-70; Supvry Libn , Ft Belvoir AUS Engr Ctr Mil Acad Prep Sch Lib, Ft Belvoir, Va 1970-77; Assn of Asian Studies; Am Acad Fac Polit & Social Sci; Spec Libs Assn; Smithsonian Inst; NY Lib Clb; Fac Instr Univ Va, Lib Sci; Assn AUS; r/Cath; hon/Vietnam Ser Medal; Cert Apprec 1968; Lttr of Commend, US St Dept.

SMITH, LANDER ARTHUR oc/General Practitioner; b/Apr 1, 1953; h/17 Forest Ln, Conway, AR 72032; ba/Conway; p/Mack R and Myra L Smith, Fordyce, AR; ed/BS; MD; pa/Gen Practitioner; r/Bapt; hon/Grad w Hons, So Ark Univ.

SMITH, LEE oc/Artist; b/May 26, 1931; h/515 Skyline Dr, Fayetteville, AR 72701; m/Roy C; c/Denise Anne S Rice, Charles Edward, James William; p/Dorothy Williams, Lincoln, AR; ed/Att'd West Ark & Univ Ark; pa/Portrait Painting; NLAPW; cp/JCettes, Pres; BPW; 4-H Ldr; Girl Scout Asst Ldr; Band Parents; Swim Boosters, Publicity Dir; hon/Num Prizes in Juried Shows Throughout S.

SMITH, LELA JO ANN oc/Nurse; b/Aug 8, 1941; h/910 W Fischer, Sherman, TX 75090; ba/Sherman; m/Jerry Mack; p/Joe Aston (dec) and Foye Virginia Jennings, Sherman, TX; ed/ADN 1975; LVN 1965; pa/RN; St & Nat Infection Control Orgs; cp/Yng Dems; St Sch for Retard'd Chd; Am Heart Assn; r/Meth; hon/Life Mem Susannah Wisley Cir.

SMITH, MARSHALL WAYNE oc/Dean; b/Feb 22, 1946; h/2307 Greenwood Dr SE, Decatur, AL 35601; ba/Decatur; m/Sheila Bonham; c/Heather, Matthew; p/Marshall Lee and Velma Letson Smith, Hueytown, AL; ed/BA Univ Ala; MEd W Ga Col; PhD Univ Ala; mil/USAFR; pa/Dean Col, Calhoun Commun Col; Dean Students & Asst Prof Ed, So Ga Col; Dir Residence Halls, Univ Ala; Pres Elec, Ala Jr & Commun Col Assn; Kappa Delta Pi; Phi Theta Kappa; Phi Delta Kappa; cp/Kiwanis Clb, Bd Dirs; N Ala Fball Ofcls Assn; r/Presb; hon/Ofcl of Yr; Outstg Yng Man Am 1973; Author "Help for TAG Progs" 1979.

SMITH, MARY ELIZABETH oc/Homemaker; b/Dec 16, 1962; h/816 Hwy 30 E, Selma, AL 36701; p/Herman and Charlie Mae Smith, Selma, Al; cp/Ala Girl's St; r/Bapt.

SMITH, MARY ISABELLE oc/Retired Teacher, Property Manager; b/Oct 5, 1905; h/310 High St, Trenton, TN 38382; ba/Same; p/Leslie Warren (dec) and Mary Davis Smith (dec); ed/BS Peabody Col; pa/Ret'd Tchr, Public Schs & Mus; Mgr Low Rental Property; Past Pres Mus Lovers Clb; cp/Fund Raising Com, Co Lib & Chm Annex; r/Presb: Hon Life Mem Wom of Ch; hon/Nat Guild Myth Hall of Fame; W/W World of Wom; Notable Ams; Intl W/W Mus; Pres-Elect UDCs.

SMITH, MARY MADESTA oc/Retired Educator; b/Feb 1, 1915; m/Elley W (dec); p/Frank W Greene (dec); Addie Lemox Greene Sexton (dec); ed/BA Bishop Col 1937; Att'd Univ Colo, Univ Tex, UCLA, Texarkana Col, Univ Wyo, Univ Ark; pa/Ret'd Edr, Sch Admr; Ret'd Ark Tchr Assn; Ret'd Tex Tchr Assn; Ark Tchr Assn; NEA; Nat Coun Tchrs of Eng & Span; PTA, Publicity Chm 20 Yrs; Nat PTA; AAUW; cp/Olivia Williams Dist of Fed Wom's Clb; Queen Mary of Heroines of Jericho Palace; Past Pres Semper Fidelis Social & Civic Clb, VP & Prog Chp; Gen Chp Ebony Fashion Fair; Black Hook-Up; Past Basilius Phi Delta Kappa, Fdr Beta Rho Chapt; Zeta Phi Beta; Bd Dirs Texarkana Commun Concert Assn; John T Felt Am Legion Aux #45, Prog Chp Am Ed Wk; Jr High Essay & Rdg Contest, Hist of Aux; Hist Soc of Texarkana & Clarksville; C of C Clarksville; Little Iota Com; Friends of Lib, C'ville; r/Bapt; hon/Life Mem Col Hill Jr High PTA; Nat Life Mem Cong of PTA; Plaque for 41 Yrs Tchr, Texarkana, Ark Classroom Tchrs 1976; Silver Tray & Cert for 45 Yrs Tchg, Clrm Tchr Texarkana 1979; Spec Cert for Part in Texarkana Centennial Celebration, Hist Soc 1976; 3 Plaques for Faithful Ser As Fdr, Beta Rho Chapt Phi Delta Kappa; Cert of Merit, Texarkana Lending Top Lib; Spec Reception Plaque On Retirement from Semper Fidelis Social & Civic Clb; W/W Tex Ed 1976.

SMITH, MARY WILMOUS oc/Cosmotologist; b/Apr 13, 1924; h/1703 W 13th, Sanford, Fl 32771; m/James (dec); c/Marian Evette; p/John King (dec); Eva Jones (dec); pa/Cosmotologist; Rental Leasing; Trustee of OBCA 18 yrs; cp/Sanford C of C; Voter Leag; NAACP; Sanford Housing Auth; City of Sanford Code Enforcement; r/Holiness; hon/OBCA Awd 1959; Ser Awd 1967; Humanitarian Awd 1978; Commun Awd 1979; Concern'd Citizen Awd 1980; Humanitarian Awd 1981.

SMITH, NANCY IRLENE oc/Director of Cardiology; b/Feb 8, 1947; h/2122 Greenway Dr NW, Winter Haven, FL 33880; ba/Lake Charles, LA; c/Gregory Richard; p/Robert G and Bessie M Wagner, Winter Haven, FL; ed/AS Polk Jr Col 1970; St Mary's Col 1980; pa/Critical Care Nurse; RN; Dir Cardiology, Lake Charles Meml Hosp; ANA; FNA; r/Luth; hon/W/W Am Wom.

PERSONALITIES OF THE SOUTH

SMITH, NANCY VERONICA oc/Counselor; b/Nov 8, 1950; h/Rt 2 Box 365, Perkinston, MS; ba/Pass Christian, MS; m/Doyle Grant; c/Leah, Jay, Ray; p/Ray and Alicia Necaise Favre, Kiln, Ms; ed/AA Pearl River Jr Col 1970; BS 1971, MEd 1974 Univ So Miss; pa/Sch Cnslr, Hancock N Ctrl Sch; Miss PGA; r/Cath; hon/W/W S&SW 1980.

SMITH, NORA SMITH oc/Teacher; b/Mar 8, 1910; h/104 Evergreen, Jackson, TN 38301; ba/Same; m/James Elbert (dec); p/James Thomas (dec) and Betsy Richardson Smith (dec); ed/BA Union Univ; MA Memphis St Univ; pa/Ret'd Edr; Life Mem NEA; Past Pres Henderson Co Tchrs Assn; Past Pres Jackson City Tchrs Assn; cp/W Tenn Hist Soc; Hon Mem Postal Clerks Aux; Past Pres (Local & St) Delta Kappa Gamma; BPW Clb; Org'd 1st Future Tchrs Am Chapt in Henderson Co; r/Bapt; hon/Jackson PBW Wom of Yr; Wom of Achmt 1955.

SMITH, OLIVER A JR oc/Realtor; b/June 24, 1915; h/Knoxville, TN; m/Evelyn Dooley; c/Oliver III, Diana, Carrol S Tombras; p/Oliver A (dec) and Alva Seaton Smith, Concord, TN; ed/BS Univ Tenn 1939; pa/Real Est; Real Est Auctioneer; Appraiser; Investment Csnlr; Nat Auctioneer Assn; Nat Review Appraiser Assn; Rltr Assn; Nat Farm Equip Assn; Nat Farmers Loan Assn; cp/Fdr W Town Optimist Clb; Fdr Farragut Civic Clb; Lions Clb; Wise Mens Clb; Nat Platform Assn; r/Presb; hon/Optimist of Yr; Bd Dirs Covenant Col, Chattanooga, Tenn.

SMITH, ROBERT OWEN oc/Golf Professional; b/Dec 3, 1940; h/813 Schulze, Norman, OK 73069; ba/Norman; m/Judy; c/Sherry Dee, Robert Owen IV; p/dec; ed/BS Univ Okla; mil/AUS; pa/GOLF Profl; S Ctrl PGA Jr Golf Chm 1976, 77, 79; Pres Okla Turfgrass Res Foun 1977; Co-Sponsor Sooner Golf Camp 175-76; Rules of Golf Instrn, LPGA Tchg Sem 1977 & 79; r/Epis; hon/Horton Smith Awd 1978.

SMITH, RUPERT LYNDON oc/Executive; b/Feb 5, 1947; h/3001 Marywood Dr, Durham, NC 27712; ba/Durham; m/Sharon Lynn; c/Rupert Chandler, Robert Trent; p/George Robert and Virginia Mott Smith, Arcadia, FL; ed/BS Univ Fla 1969; mil/AUS 1970-72; pa/GTSE: VP Public Affairs 1979-, Communs Mgr 1976-79, External Communs Mgr 1975-76, Public Info Admr 1974-75, Div Public Affairs Admr 1973-74, Public Affairs Asst 1972-73; Past Pres Durham Public Relats Soc; cp/NC Mus Life & Sci, Pres; Durham Co Red Cross, Dir; Durham JCs, Former Dir; Drug Rehab Ser, Former Dir; Durham Co C of C, Former Com Chm; Durham Co U Way, Past VP Public Relats; r/Prot; hon/W/W S&SW 1980; Outstg Yng Men Am 1980; Army Commend Medal 1972; Carnegie Nat Awd for Heroism 1965.

SMITH, SUSAN LOUISE oc/Occupational Therapist; b/Feb 19, 1935; h/816 Orleans St, New Orleans, LA 70116; ba/Metairie, LA; p/J Raymond (dec) and Edna L Smith, Rockport, MA; ed/BS Ed; MA Occup Therapy; JD Cand; pa/Am Occup Therapy Assn, Accred Com; Intl Chp La Occup Therapy Assn; hon/Life Mem La Occup Therapy Assn; Fellow Am Occup Therapy Assn.

SMITH, THOMAS LEE oc/Consultant; b/Aug 8, 1949; h/Rt 7 Box 377, Murfreesboro, TN 37130; ba/Nashville; m/Patricia Ann; c/Robert, Charlie, Jonathan; p/Jesse and Margie Smith, Jacksonville, FL; ed/BS 1971, MEd 1973 Tenn Temple Univ; EdD Freedom Univ 1978; pa/Mktg & Ednl Conslt; Thomas Nelson Pubrs; Am Mgmt Assn; Phi Delta Kappa; Co-Fdr & Secy Tenn Assn Christian Schs; cp/Rotary Clb; JCs; Repub Concord Grp; Repub Cand for St Sen 1980; Murfreesboro C of C; r/Bapt; hon/Hon Asst to Gov George Wallace 1976; Hon Col, Gov Lamar Alexander Staff 1980; Million Dollar Sales Clb, Thomas Nelson Pubrs 1979; Author *What Every Parent Should Know About Education* 1976; *Parent-Teacher Cooperation* 1976; *Are Your Children Being Sheltered?* 1977.

SMITH, WILLIE A oc/Transportation and Property Officer; b/June 26, 1927; h/18 James St, Statesboro, GA 30453; m/Grace Donaldson; c/Willie A Jr, Eric G; p/Sidney C Smith, Detroit, MI; Annie Laura Smith, Statesboro, GA; ed/Att'd Ga So Col 1975-79; mil/USAF M Sgt Ret'd; pa/Prog Dir Ec Devel; Ga Commun Action Assn, Bd Dirs; cp/SE Ga Hlth Sys Agcy; Exec Bd Bulloch Co Plan'g Comm; Chm Sta-Buc Inc; Pres U Citizens Fed Credit Union; Bulloch Co Bd Ed; r/U Meth; hon/Sta-Buc Inc Man of Yr 1973.

SMITH, ZELFRED CLYDE JR oc/Pastor; b/Dec 18, 1931; h/PO Box 1515, Corinth, MS 38834; ba/Corinth; m/Jean D; c/Donna S Lowery, Zelfred III, Stephen, Timothy; p/Zelfred C Sr and Mary E Smith, Corinth, MS; ed/BA; DD; pa/Pastor Grace Bible Bapt Ch; cp/Pres Magnolia St Assn Christian Schs; hon/DD Bob Jones Univ 1979.

SMITHEY, KAREN BIGGS b/July 14, 1941; h/Box 545, Boling, TX 77420; ba/Boling; m/William L Jr; c/Audra Karen; p/Robert Oscar and Mittie Pugh Biggs, Wharton, TX; ed/BS SW Tex St Univ 1962, MEd Sam Houston St Univ 1978; pa/Tchr-Dir Westgate Nursery Sch 1972-74; Voc

Homemaking Ed: Wharton HS 1962-64, Bay City HS 1969-71, Boling HS 1975-; Co Ext Agt, Tex A&M Univ 1964-67, Ft Bend Co, Tex Agric Ext Ser; Voc Homemaking Tcrs Assn of Tex; Am Home Ec Assn; Assn Childhood Ed Intl; cp/E Wharton Co Unit Am Cancer Soc, Bd Dirs; Mtl Hlth Assn; Mar of Dimes, Mother's Mar Chp; Lioness Intl, Local Chapt Pres; r/Ch of Christ; hon/Outstg Home Ec Student 1962; Phi Theta Kappa; Delta Kappa Gamma; W/W S&SW 1980.

SNIDER, JOHN ALLEN oc/Funeral Director; b/Jan 15, 1941; ba/307 W Franklin, Waxahachie, TX 75165; m/Jacquelyn Sue; c/Dana Sue, Shane Alan, JoAnna Lyn; p/John R and Helen Snider, Bourbonnais, IL; ed/Att'd Trevecca Nazarene Col 1965; Mesa Col 1972-74, Dallas Inst Mortuary Sci 1971-72; pa/Funeral Dir, Val Funeral Home 1972-75; Owner-Funeral Dir Rudolph-Snider Funeral Home 1975-; Nat Funeral Dirs Assn; Tex Funeral Dirs Assn; N Tex Funeral Dirs Assn, Bd Dirs 1976-79; cp/City Coun-man, City of Waxahachie 1980-; Chm Sustentation Dr, SWn Assems of God Col 1980; Waxahachie C of C, Past Mem Bd Dirs; Waxahachie Rotary Clb; Waxahachie Country Clb; YMCA, Bd Mgmt; Waxahachie Sr Citizens Ctr, Chm Bd Dirs; Ellis Co Coun Govts, Com on Aging; Salvation Army Ext Ser of Waxahachie, Past Chm; U Fund; Ellis Co Com on Aging, VChm Bd; N Ctrl Tex Coun Govts, City Of Waxahachie Rep; r/Nazarene; hon/Grad w Hons Dallas Inst Mortuary Sci; Boss of Yr, ABWA 1981.

SNUGGS, ANN oc/Media Relations; b/Nov 18, 1947; h/1906 W 24tt, Pine Bluff, AR 71603; ba/Hot Springs, AR; p/Grover E Jr and Sara Russell Snuggs, Pine Bluff, AR; ed/BS Ed, MS Ed Henderson St Univ; pa/Publicity, Oaklawn Jockey Clb; r/U Meth; hon/Theta Alpha Phi; Kappa Delta Pi; Alpha Chi.

SNYDER, GENE oc/Congressman; b/Jan 26, 1928; m/Patricia Creighton Robertson; c/Mark; p/M G and Lois E Snyder; ed/Att'd Univ Louisville; Grad cum laude Jefferson Sch of Law; mil/CAP Lt Col; pa/Elected to Cong 1962, 1966-; Appt'd to Public Wks Com 90th Cong; Appt'd Merchant Marine & Fisheries Com 91st Cong; Elected to 2 Terms Magistrate of Jefferson Co's First Dist (First Repub Elected to Dist); Past Pres Lincoln Clb of Ky; Past Pres First Magisterial Dist Repub Clb; Mem Var Repub Clbs; Pract'g Atty w Ofcs in St Matthews, Ky; Lic'd Rltr w Ofcs in St Matthews & Covington, Ky; Ky, L'ville & DC Bar Assns; Nat Assn Real Est Fliers; Nat Inst Real Est Boards; Past VP Ky Magistrates & Commrs Assn; Former Jeffersontown City Atty; cp/Past Pres: Jeffersontown Optimists Clb, Jeffersontown Civic Ctr, Jeffersontown Commun Coun; Mem Ky Farm Bur.

SNYDER, JAMES RICHARD oc/Division Chairman; b/Oct 14, 1946; h/206 Cherry Rd, Enterprise, AL 36330; ba/Enterprise; m/Judy L; c/James Matthew, Benjamin Thomas; p/Harry M (dec) and Mary Nealey Snyder, Panama City, FL; ed/B Mus Ed Troy St Univ 1968; MA 1971, EdD 1977 Univ Ala; pa/Instr & Chm Div Fine Arts, Enterprise St Jr Col 1978-; Dir/Orgr Enterprise Commun Chorus 1978-; Clinician & Adjudicator, Fla Vocal Assn Dist & St Fests, Ala Vocal Assn Dist Contests & Ch Mus Fests; Phi Mu Alpha Sinfonia; Pi Kappa Lambda; Phi Delta Kappa; Kappa Delta Pi; Ala Vocal Assn; Ala Mus Edrs Assn; Ala Ed Assn; NEA; Mus Edrs Nat Conf; Am Choral Dirs Assn; Assn Ala Col Mus Admrs; r/So Bapt; hon/Appeared in: "The Boyfriend"; "Comedy on the Bridge"; "Ahmal and the Night Visitors"; "Marriage of Figaro"; "Don Pasquale"; Guest Soloist at Num Civic & Ch Activs; Concerts Throughout SE & in Austria, Germany & Italy; Author Num Profl Pubs.

SNYDER, JOHN WILLIAM oc/Accountant; b/Oct 3, 1944; h/Harker Hgts, TX; m/Lois Marie; c/John Jr, James; p/Christina Warren, New Albany, IN; mil/AUS 1962-72 Capt; pa/Owner Hgts Bkkp'g Ser 1971-; cp/JCs; Kiwanis; Harker Hgts Rec Assn; Harker Hgts Bus Assn; r/Bapt; hon/W/W Am Univ & Cols 1974-75; Outstg Yng Man Am 1976; W/W PhI Beta Lambda for St Tex 1975; 1st Pl Extemporaneous Spkg Awd 1974; Runner-Up Mr Future Bus Exec, Tex St Phi Beta Lambda 1975; Co-Author Mil Pubs.

SOEFJE, ALAN ERNST oc/Management Consultant; b/Apr 29, 1933; h/16404 Ledge Pk, San Antonio, TX 78232; ba/Same; m/Lois Tate; c/Eddie; p/Erwin W and Linda Soefje; ed/BBA Tex A&M Univ 1954; JD St Mary's Univ Law Sch 1970; MA Univ No Colo 1977; mil/1949-80; pa/Mgmt Conslt Indust & Govt; Lectr Incarnate Word Col & San Antonio Col in Mgmt & Bus Law Courses; Real Est Broker & Advr; Sem Dir for San Antonio Area for Nat Defense Univ Nat Security Mgmt Sem Prog; Mil Order of World Wars, Jr Vice Cmdr, Adjutant & Treas; Charter Pres Leon Val Lions Clb; Troop Com Chp of BS Troop 484; Dir Leon Val Pageant Assn; cp/Reserve Ofcrs Assn; AF Assn; Daedalians; 36th Inf Div; Delta Theta Phi; San Antonio Bd Rltrs; Nat Assn Rltrs; r/Cath; Rel Tchr; hon/W/W S&SW; KBAT Tex Star Awd for Commun Ser; Lions Intl Commun Ser Awd; Mil Order of World Wars Outstg Ser Awd.

SOHL, ROBERT CHARLES oc/Marketing Operations; b/Nov 6, 1943; h/3806 Brewster Circle, Waldorf, MD 20601; ba/Rockville, MD;

m/Margaret Clark; c/Catherine Mary; Robert Charles Jr; p/Richard (dec) and Jeanette Nixon, Dunedin, FL; ed/BS Hartwick Col; Bus Cert LaSalle Univ; Cert Wharton Sch; pa/Mktg Opers, C&P Telephone Co; cp/Pres SMCC; Fdg Dir Pinetialo Civic Assn; Steering Com Mattawoman Watershed Proj; r/Luth; hon/W/W Fin & Indust 1979-80; 101% Sales Clb, C&P Telephone.

SOLLENBERGER, ARLENE LUCILLE oc/Musician; b/Nov 19, 1920; h/Ft Worth, TX; ba/Tex Christian Univ, Landreth #232, Ft Worth, TX 76129; p/Jesse Clarence (dec) and Versa Elvira Dorr Sollenberger (dec); ed/B Mus Ed Bethany Col 1938-42; MMus Ed Univ Mich 1947, MMus Voice 1948; pa/Assoc Prof Voice, Tex Christian Univ 1959-; Instr, Pvt Voice Lessons, Univ Mich 1950-59; Mus Supvr Public Sch Sys, Stafford, Kan 1944-46; Mus Supvr Rural Consolidated Schs, Garfield, Kan 1943-44; Delta Kappa Gamma, S'ship Fund Chm; Pi Kappa Lambda, Nat Bd Regents; Sigma Alpha Iota; Nat Assn Tchrs of Singing, Regional Gov, Singer at Nat Conv; Nat Fed Mus Clbs; Pi Lambda Theta; Tex Fed Mus Clbs; AAUW; Profl Wom at Tex Christian Univ; cp/Woms Clb of Ft Worth; Euterpean Clb, Chm Twilight Musicale Series; TCU Fine Arts Guild; TCU Fac Wom's Clb; Altrusa Intl Clb of Ft Worth; r/Meth; hon/Fulbright Grant, Germany 1956; Sigma Alpha Iota Sword of Hon 1955; Nat Fed Mus Clb Life Mem; Hon Mem Tau Beta Sigma; Author Book Review "The Singing Voice" 1971.

SOLOMON, HOWARD DAVID oc/Urologist; b/July 3, 1945; h/306 Coventry Cir, Seguia, TX 78155; ba/Seguia; m/Lyndell E; c/Norman E, David I; p/Sam and Ethel Solomon, Burlington, VT; ed/BA 1967, MD 1971 Univ Vt; Intern Tripler Army Med Ctr, Honolulu 1971-72; Residency Brooke Army Med Ctr, Ft Sam Houston 1972-76; mil/USAR 1967-79 Lt Col; pa/Pvt Prac Urologist; Conslt Urology, VA Hosp, Kerrville, Tex 1977-79; Asst Chief Urology Ser, Brooke Army Med Ctr 1977-79; Diplomate Am Bd Med Examrs; Fellow Am Col Surgs; Diplomate Am Bd Urology; Assn Mil Surgs of US; Tex Med Assn; San Antonio Urological Soc; Soc Govt Ser Urologists; S Ctrl Sect Am Urological Assn; Am Urological Assn; r/Jewish; hon/Author Num Profl Pubs.

SOMMER, PATRICIA ANN oc/Dean; b/Apr 2, 1938; ba/Tenn Tech Univ, Sch Nsg, Cookeville, TN 38501; c/Marleny Baquero, Mariam Ramirez, Campo Elias Garzon, Martha Ruth, Dolly Riano; p/dec; ed/BS Tex Christian Univ 1969; MS Tex Wom's Univ 1972; Grad Study Tex Christian Univ 1973-76; PhD Tex Wom's Univ 1979; pa/Assoc Prof & Dean Sch Nsg, Tenn Tech Univ 1980-; Asst Prof, Pediatric Nsg, Univ Tex-Arlington 1973-76; Asst Prof, Maternity Nsg, Univ Tex-Arlington 1973-79; ANA; TNA; St Tex Nurses Assn, Profl Sers Com 1979-80; Dist 3 Nurses Assn, Chp Leg Com, Pres 1977, Bd Mem 1978-80; Nurses Assn of Am Col of OB-Gyn, Local VP 1974-; NLN; Sigma Theta Tau; Phi Lambda Theta; cp/Camp Fire Ldr 1973-75, Assoc Ldr 1976; Stephen F Austin Elem Sch, PTA Pres 1974-75; Vol Am Red Cross; Westside YMCA Bd Dirs 1975-76; City Disaster Plan'g Com 1976-; Secy Ridglea Swimming Pool Bd Dirs 1976-77; Chp Missions Com Wn Hills Bapt Ch; Proj Dir Aux Multiple Sclerosis Assn of Tarrant Co 1980; r/Bapt; hon/Cert & 5 Yr Pin Am Red Cross; Nom'd Tchr of Yr Univ Tex-Arlington 1976; Plaque for Ser, Tarrant Bapt Conv 1977; ANA Pin for Outstg Ser as Pres, Tex Nurses Assn Dist 3 1978; Plaque for Outstg Ser in Org Sers of TNA Dist 3, Tex Nurses Assn, St Level 1978; Nom'd Outstg Student of Yr Tex Wom's Univ 1979; Nom'd Fac & Students Piper Awd, Univ Tex-Arlington 1980; AMOCO Outstg Tchr of Yr Awd Univ Tex-Arlington 1980; Cert of Recog, Hlth Sys Agcy Area 5, Tex 1979-80; Outstg Nurse 20 Yrs Ser, Jackson Meml Hosp Alumni Reunion 1980; Author "Touch Can Make a Difference in Patient Care" in Texas Nurse.

SOOCH, KEWAL SINGH oc/Chemist; b/Feb 1, 1941; h/314 Tennessee St, Forrest City, AR 72335; ba/Forrest City, AR; p/Malook Singh and Ishar Kaur Dhaliwal Sooch, Punjab, India; ed/BS w Hons 1967, MS w Hons 1968 Panjab Univ Chanigarh; Fac Sci, Govt Col, Hoshiarpur, India 1962; E Ark Commun Col 1975-76; pa/Chemist & Quality Assurance Supvr, Na-Churs Plant Food Co; Fellow Am Chem Soc; Fellow Am Soc Quality Control; r/Nirankari Mission; hon/W/W Am 1980-81.

SORENSEN, GAIL A oc/Assistant Professor; b/July 23, 1948; h/Arcata, CA; ba/Dept Speech Commun, Humboldt St Univ, Arcata, CA 95521; p/Earl Richard and Phyllis McMurdo Sorensen, Fennville, MI; ed/BA Mich St Univ 1969; MS Ill St Univ 1972; EdD WVU 1980; pa/Asst Prof Humboldt St Univ; Lectr WV Univ; Instr Salisbury St Col; Howell HS, Howell, Mich; Intl Commun Assn; Speech Commun Assn; En Commun Assn; Wn Speech Commun Assn; Mich St Alumni Assn; Ill St Alumni Assn; WVU Alumni Assn; Assn St Col & Univ Profs; hon/Author Sev Profl Pubs.

SOTTILE, JAMES III oc/Executive; b/Aug 3, 1940; h/846 Malibu Ln, Indialantic, FL 32903; ba/Melbourne, FL; m/Judith H; c/James IV, John Michael, Scott Joseph, Thomas Lawrence, Jennifer Lynn; p/James and Ethel Hooks Sottile, Coral Gables, FL; ed/BS cum laude Univ Fla; pa/Mining Co Exec; Yng Pres's Org; r/Rom Cath.

SOUBLET, PAUL JOSEPH LOUIS oc/Retired Military, Taxidermist, Rancher, Student; b/May 18, 1930; h/Cameron, NC; ba/PO Box 174, Olivia, NC 28368; p/Louis B (dec) and Emma G Saulny, New Orleans, LA; ed/Cert Wash Sch Art 1973; Att'd Campbell Col 1972; Att'g Meth Col 1979-; Mil/Ret'd US Spec Forces 1972; pa/Opers & Intell, AUS; Firefighter NC Forest Ser; Taxidermist; Cattle & Horse Ranching; Nat Taxidermist Assn; Appaloosa Horse Clb; cp/Harnett Co Arts Coun, Bd Dirs 1979-; Sustaining Mem Repub Nat Com; Fayetteville Mus Art; r/Rom Cath; hon/Gov's Spec Ser Awd 1976; 1st Pl Creative Skill SE Fair, Ga 1967; 1st Pl All Army Watercolors 1959; 1st Pl All Army Watercolors/Drawing 1961; Illustrated Book *September Dead and Other Poems* 1953.

SOUSA, REBECCA ORRENDER oc/Homemaker; b/May 22, 1927; h/2360 Little John Tr SE, Marietta, GA 30067; m/Rudy E (dec); c/Tori, Drew, Pam Anderson; p/Charles B (dec) and Elsie Orrender; cp/Square Dancer; r/Bapt.

SOUTHWELL, ALETHA GRACE VINSON oc/Personnel Officer; b/May 6, 1927; h/2506 Wyckford Way, Louisville, KY 40219; ba/L'ville; m/Raleigh Duane; c/Susan Patrice Hauser, Stephen Duane; p/Thomas C Vinson (dec); Exer E Fincher Vinson Pendergraft (dec); ed/BS Am Technol Univ; pa/Pers Ofcr, VA Regional Ofcr; Fed Exec Assn; Fed Pers Coun; cp/ABWA; Waco Legal Secys Assn; r/Presb; hon/World W/W 1978-79.

SOUZA, ANTHONY R oc/Developer; b/Mar 9, 1948; h/6240 Plaited Reed, Columbia, MD 21044; ba/Columbia; p/Roseanne S; c/Anthony II, Dominic J; p/Raymond W and Matilda J Souza, Provincetown, MA; ed/BS US Coast Guard Acad; mil/USCG 1970-76; pa/Fin Sers; Ins; Million Dollar Round Table 1977-80; Columbia Bus Exch 1977-80; Life Underwriters Assn, Nat & Local 1976-80; Pres Webb's Study Grp 1978-79; Past Mem Reserve Ofcrs Assn 1976-79; cp/LUPAC 1978-80; Past Mem Fin Com, St John the Evangelist Roman Cath Ch 1977-79; Chm Bond Com 1977-78; Past Mem Nat Exch Clb 1978-79; r/Cath; hon/W/W Fin & Indust 1978-80; 3 Nat Quality Awds 1978-80; 2 Nat Sales Achmt Awds 1977-80; Spec Session Spkr, Million Dollar Round Table Meeting 1979; Wallace Assocs Most Outstg Achmt Ever by New Assoc 1976.

SOWELL, GENEVA WENTZ oc/Sales Clerk; b/Nov 7, 1926; h/808 W Suwanee St, Fitzgerald, GA 31750; m/James Newton Jr; c/James N III, Marilyn Alicia White, Valla Regina Walker; p/Herman Ralph (dec) and Marietta Bennett Wentz (dec); pa/Sales Clerk, Drug Store; cp/Wom's Clb: Secy-Treas, VP, Pres; Ladies of Nasah, Corres Secy 1980-81; Conductress OES: Former Sta of Ruth, Sta of Marshall, Sta of Esther, Assoc Matron, Worthy Matron; Am Leagion Aux: Sgt-at-Arms, 2nd VP, 1st VP, Pres; r/U Meth.

SPACH, JULE CHRISTIAN oc/Executive Director; b/Dec 21, 1923; h/444 Anita Dr, Winston-Salem, NC; ba/W-S; m/Nancy Clendenin; c/Lynn Davis, Margaret Creech, Ann Thomerson, Cecilia, Robert; p/dec; ed/VMI 1942; B Che Ga Tech 1979; Duke Univ 1955; M Adm UNC-Goldsboro 1976; Hon LHD Stillman Col 1977; Litt D Bellhaven Col 1977; LLD King Col 1977; mil/USAF Pilot; pa/Missionary, Presb Ch, USA; Moderator, 118th Gen Assem, Presb Ch; Exec Dir Triad U Meth Home; AAHA; cp/Lions Clb; Rotary, Chm Commun & Intl Ser; r/Prot; hon/Author Profl Article.

SPANN, BONNIE CRAFT oc/Cosmetologist; b/Apr 4, 1936; h/2907 B 45th, Lubbock, TX 79413; ba/Lubbock; c/Vickie Sue; p/Walter Leslie Craft, Roaring Springs, TX; Ruby Knight Craft (dec); ed/Draughon's Bus Col 1955; Isbell's Univ Beauty Culture 1961; Okla St Univ 1970; Contemporary Hair Styling 1972; mil/Dept Army Civilian Tchr, Dept Defense Overseas Schs 1975-81; pa/Lic'd Cosmetology Instr & Cosmetologist; Tex Voc Tng Instr; Voc Tng Instr, Dept of Defense Overseas Schs, Europe 1979-80, 80-81; Chp Career Voc Ed Div, DODDSEUR 1977-78; Tex Tchrs Assn; Okla Tchrs Assn; Am Voc Tchrs Assn; Am Esthetician Assn; Tex Cosmetologist/Hairdressers Affil; cp/Good Grooming Instr, Am Red Cross, European Region Mil; r/Assem of God; hon/Valedictorian in HS 1954; Merit Awd, Isbell's Univ of Beauty Culture 1961; Sustained Superior Awd for Tchg DODDSEUR 1980; Red Cross Apprec Awd 1981; Author Cosmetology Course Outline; Music "Psalm 21" 1979 & "Thou Art Worthy" 1980.

SPANN, DAN HENRY oc/Social Worker; b/Feb 15, 1953; h/Columbus, MS; p/Eddie Spann (dec); Travis Jr and Ella M Hairston Sturdivant; ed/BA Rust Col 1976 Att'd Miss St Univ, Univ Graz, Columbia So Sch of Law, Cornell Col; Att'g Miss St Univ; pa/Dir Special Sers, Lowndes Co Hd Start; Social Ser Asst, Lowndes Co Hd Start, Columbus; Rust Col Public Relats Ofc; Plant Mgrs Ofc, Columbus AFB Hosp; Student Asst to Dr Robert Hannon, Chm Social Sci Dept, Rust Col; Ofc of Lt Gov Jim Hunt, Raleigh, NC; Ofc of St Senator John W Winters, Raleigh, NC; Asst Campaign Mgr, Dr Robert Hannon For US Senate, St of NC; Work in Num Other Campaigns; cp/Yth Motivation Task Force, Nat Alliance Bus-men; Bd Dirs Prairie Opport Inc, Chm Pers Com; Chm Spec

PERSONALITIES OF THE SOUTH

Sers Assn, Commun Ed Ext Mary Holmes Col; Bd Dirs Sims Scott YMCA; Minority Peoples Coun; Bd Dirs Commun Ed Ctr; VP & Mem Exec Bd of Columbus-Lowndes Co Voters Leag; Phi Alpha Theta; Alpha Phi Alpha, Past Pres Iota Gamma Chapt; Dem Party, St of Miss; r/Mt Zion Bapt Ch: Yth Dir, Former SS Tchr; hon/Outstg Hi-Y Advr Awd 1979; Alpha Man of Yr, Iota Gamma Chapt; Good Housekeeping Awd, Rust Col; Lb Ser Awd, S D Lee HS.

SPEAKMAN, SHELBIE JEAN oc/Manager; b/Sept 23, 1937; h/Rt 2 Lakewood Ests, Richmond, KY 40475; ba/Richmond; m/Amos N; c/Linda J, Brenda C; p/Eugene B and Lena F Sears, Richmond, KY; pa/Mgr Hager Cabinets; cp/OES, Past Matron; r/Christian.

SPEAR, AUTUMN NAIDENE oc/Secretary and Partner; b/Nov 12, 1933; h/7224 Canongate Dr, Dallas, TX 75248; ba/Same; m/Donald David; c/Kenneth R Golie, Peter W Howes, Robin Dawn; p/Edward S (dec) and Emma Amanda Boyce White, Portland, OR: pa/Ptnr & Secy Agape Fin; Spkr: Convs, Ladies F'ships, Retreats; cp/Pres Wom's Aglow F'ship, Cinci, Oh 1974-75, St Treas 1975; Ed Bd Billy Graham Crusade, Cinci, Oh 1975; r/Christian; hon/Nom'd Wom of Yr 1975, Cinci, Oh.

SPEARS, CHARLOTTE R oc/Executive; b/Aug 26, 1923; m/Charles A; c/John Alexander, Bradford Fee, Betsy S Voiles, Russell Charles; p/J W (dec) and Elizabeth H Russell, Sherman, TX; ed/AA Stephens Col 1942; BS Univ Tex 1945; pa/Bd Dirs Texoma Savings & Loan Assn, Sherman, Tex; cp/Indep Dem, St Conv 1972; Bd Trustees, Sherman Indep Sch Dist; Charter Mem & Bd Sherman LWV; Past Chm Sherman Housing 1970; r/Trinity Presb; hon/Wom of Achmt Awd 1976, AAUW; Apprec Awd, STEP 1968.

SPEARS, CONWAY EDWARD oc/Pastor; Director Learning Center; b/July 3, 1942; h/4334 Oak St, Montgomery, AL 36105; ba/Mont; m/Eleanita F; c/Eric Edward, Leonard Lewis; p/Leon Conway (dec) and Dorothy T Spears, B'ham, AL; ed/BS Miles Col 1976; MDiv Interdenom Theol Ctr 1978; Hon Doc Deg Sociol, Payne Sem 1978; DDiv Interdenom Theol Ctr 1978; mil/USAF Asst Surg & Cnslr to Yth; pa/Job Develr/Cnslr; Tchr; Asst Prin; Coor Manpwr Devel Tng Prog; Hd Cnlsr Opport Indust Ctr; Ednl Poverty Program Div; Pastor First Christian Meth Epis Ch; Dir Lrng Ctr; CME Rep on Nat Impact Com; Chief Orderly CME Ch; Coor & Cnslr Manpwr Consortium; Bd Jefferson Co Com of Equal Opport; Accred Com B'ham Public Schs; cp/NAACP; Pres Yth Devel; Elk Lodge; Omega Psi Phi; Advr Intl Interracial Org at ITC; Bd Hlth Clins in B'ham; Elec'd First Black Pres of No Hlth Clins of B'ham; r/Meth; hon/Coach of Yr ITC 1976 & 77; Prison Min Awd 1977; Kappa Phi Man of Yr 1974; Min of Yr, B'ham 1975; Anniston Dist, B'ham Conf Ser Awd 1976; Outstg & Dedicated Ser Awd of Interdenom Theol Ctr 1977 & 78; Miles Col Humanitarian Awd 1974-75; Humanitarian Awd, Nurses Assn B'ham 1975; Dedicated Citizenship Ser Awd, Atlanta, Ga 1977; Hon Doc Deg in Sociol, Payne Sem; Author "The Atonement of God"; "God is Still on the Throne"; "Grace of God."

SPECTOR, DANIEL EARL oc/Supervisory Education Specialist; b/Dec 19, 1942; h/1615 Fairway Cir, Jacksonville, AL 36265; ba/Ft McClellan, AL; m/Esta Gelda Rappaport; c/Warren Leigh, Susan Artemis; p/Rabbi Joseph and Dorothy Margaret Spector, New Castle, PA; ed/AB Geo Wash Univ 1963; Att'd Univ Fla Grad Sch 1963-1964; MA 1972, PhD 1975 Univ Tex-Austin; Att'd J'ville St Univ 1976, 78; mil/USAFR 1964-70; pa/AUS 1965-80, Civilian Pers Spec, Mgmt Analyst, Ed Spec; Am Hist Assn; Mil Testing Assn; cp/Hiram Lodge 42; B'nai B'rith; MENSA; r/Jewish; hon/Alumni S'ship; NDEA F'ship; NDFL F'ship; Lebanon-Am Soc Awd for Excell in Arab Lang Studies; Author Num Book Reviews & Articles on Hist & Ednl Subjs in Sev Jours.

SPEIGHT, DAVID LARRY oc/Associate Professor; b/July 28, 1943; h/4527 Lee Dr NW, Cleveland, TN 37311; ba/C'land; m/Joyce Tallent; c/David Henry, Jonathan Mark; p/David Ernest and Frances Wilma Speight, Lexington, TN; ed/BS Univ Tenn-Martin 1965; MS Univ Tenn-Knoxville 1967; Add'l Grad Work NCSU 1969, Ariz St Univ 1971, Univ Kan 1967-68; pa/Assoc Prof Biol, C'land St Commun Col 1968-; NEA; TEA; ETEA; C'land St Commun Col Ed Assn, Secy-Treas 1980-81; Tenn Acad Sci; r/Ctrl Ch of Christ, Deacon; hon/Outstg Edr of Am 1971; Outstg Yng Men Am 1973; W/W S&SW 1980; NSE Grantee 1969-73.

SPELL, GEORGE ROBERT oc/Assistant Professor; b/Aug 29, 1937; h/Atlanta, GA; ba/Dept of Speech & Drama, Ga St Univ, Univ Plaza, Atlanta, GA 30303; p/Harvey Spell (dec); Sarah P Townsend, Augusta, GA; ed/BS 1959; MEd 1964; MFA 1967; PhD 1976; pa/Speech & Drama: Sec'dy Sch Tchr, Sr Col Prof, Univ Prof; Ga Speech Commun, Past Pres; So Speech Commun, Past Mem Exec Bd; Speech Commun Assn; Phi Kappa Phi, Past Treas Valdosta Chapt; r/Prot; hon/Outstg Edrs Am 1975; Pres's Awd for Outstg Ldrship in Ga Speech 1970.

SPENCER, CYNTHIA GAYLE oc/Educator; Department Chairman;

b/Aug 14, 1947; h/100 Dovershire Rd, Matthews, NC 28105; m/William G; p/Harry J and Adois Baker, Charlotte, NC; ed/BA, MAT Univ Sc; pa/Phys Ed Dept Chm, Providence Day Sch; Nat Volleyball Coaches Assn; USTA; r/Meth.

SPILLER, ELLEN BRUBAKER oc/Instructor; b/July 17, 1932; h/211 Rue Orleans, Baytown,TX 77520; ba/B'town; m/Sam C; c/Katherine Quesney, Georgianne; p/George Nunley (dec) and Lou Greathouse Brubaker, San Marcos, TX; ed/BJ Univ Tex; MA Univ Houston; pa/Instr Eng, Lee Col; Var Profl Orgs & Coms; cp/Altar Guild, All Sts Epis Ch; r/Epis; hon/Wom in Communs; TR Largen S'ship.

SPINKS, DOROTHY MATTHEWS oc/Personnel Management; b/Sept 9,1916; h/4415 19th Rd N, Arlington, VA 22207; ba/Arlington; m/Eugene C; c/Roger A, Brian E, Kerry E, Sharon I Pack; p/Stanely G Matthews (dec); Minnie Bowers, Olney, MD; ed/BSS Am Inst Bus; Att'd Geo Wash Univ; Univ Va; pa/Civilian Pers Mgmt-EEO Spec, Hqs USN Civilian Pers 1968-; Admr Ofcr, Peace Corps 1961-68; Hemispheric Cong of BPW of Am 1975; Nat Fed BPW Clbs Inc, Nat Steering Com on Leg Proposals 1978-, Nat Leg Platform Com 1977; Va Fed BPW Clbs Inc, Leg Chm 1977-78, Leg Com Mem 1975-77, Dist Leg Chm 1978-79, By-Laws Com Chm 1979; Rosslyn BPW Clb, Pres 1976-77, Leg Chm 1974-76, 1979-; Arlington Co Com on Status of Wom, Chp 1978-, Mem 1976-; Federally Employed Wom Inc, Regional Coor on Leg Matters 1978-; Cong of Wom's Orgs in Va 1975; WEAL, St VP 1977-; cp/Scouting: Cadettes & Cubs 14 Yrs, Ldr & Den Mother; U Meth Epis Ch: Com on Socil Concerns 1978-, Chancel Choir, SS Tchr, Var Coms 1972-; r/Meth; hon/Wom of Yr, Rosslyn BPW Lucheon Clb 1978; Spkr of Yr Awd, Va Fed BPW Clbs 1978; 2nd Pl Winner Nat BPW Conv 1978; Ideal Secy, Alpha Iota 1942; Occup Commends & Related Recogs.

SPITZER, RUTH BALDWIN oc/Organist; b/Oct 27, 1914; h/486 W Market St, Harrisonburg, VA 22801; p/Perry Franklin (dec) and Mabel Baldwin Spitzer (dec); ed/BS James Madison Univ 1937 BME Shenandoah Conservatory of Mus 1941; pa/Organist, Harrisonburg Ch of the Brethren 1938-68; Piano Tchr, H'burg 1941-44; Organist: Lindsey Funeral Home 1949-, Temple Beth El 1950-, Christian Sci Informal Grp 1967-, Dayton U Meth Ch 1968-69, 1976-, Trinity U Ch of Christ 1968-75; Accompanist for Soloists, Ch & SS Grps, Sch Grps, Spec Meetings & Weddings; Hd, Picture Framing Dept, Glen's Gift Ctr 1959-77; cp/Am Guild Organists, H'burg-Rockingham Chapt, Secy & Publicity Chm 1955-59; Life Mem Shenandoah Col Alumni Assn; Life Mem James Madison Univ Alumni Assn; Class Agt, 1941 Class of Shenandoah Conservatory Alumni; Orgr & Secy H'burg HS Class of 1933 Reunion, 1976; r/Presb; hon/Hon w Luncheon, H'burg Ch of the Brethren 1963; Hon by Temple Beth El 1962 & 1974; W/W: Am Wom, S&SW; Va Lives by Morton; 2000 Wom Achmt; Nat Social Dir; World W/W Wom; DIB; Personalities of Am; Intl W/W Commun Ser; Commun Ldrs Va; Commun Ldrs & Noteworthy Ams; Notable Ams; Life Patroness Sigma Alpha Iota, James Madison Univ Chapt.

SPIVEY, PAMELA ANN MAYS oc/Certified Professional Secretary; b/Dec 6, 1951; h/Radford, VA; ba/Inland Motor-SPD, 501 First St, Radford, VA 24141; m/V Ray; p/Benjamin Newton (dec) and Doris Belle Sutherland Mays (dec); ed/Dip Nat Bus Col, Roanoke, Va; Cert'd Profl Secy, Inst for Certifying Secys 1979; Att'd Radford Univ, New River Commun Col, Wytheville Commun Col; pa/Exec Secy to VP Mktg & Mktg Mgr, Inland Motor Spec Prods Div; Past Confidential Secy to Lt Gov of Va, John Dalton; Charter Mem & Fdr New River Val Chapt Nat Secys Assn Intl, Past Pres 1977-78; Nat Secys Assn Instl; Cert'd Profl Secys Assn 1979-; cp/Pulaski Co Repub Wom's Clb, Pres 1976-79; Va Fed Repub Wom, Bd Mem 1976-; Radford City Repub Com 1975-; Va Repub St Ctrl Com 1979-81; BPW Clb 1971-74; Treas Galax BPW Clb 1972; r/Meth; hon/App'd By Gov John Dalton to Serve on Va Comm on Status of Wom 1979-81; Mem Va Comm on Status of Wom's Task Force on Wom Offenders; Yng Career Wom of Radford 1980-81; Dist Yng Career Wom 1980-81; Att'd Pres's White House Conf on Wom at White House 1980.

SPOHN, PEGGY WEEKS oc/Director Program Division; b/Aug 23, 1944; h/1741 Harvard St NW, Wash DC 20009; ba/Wash DC; p/Edwin R and Maudie H Weeks, N Rose, NY; ed/BA Le Moyne Col; MA Fordham Univ; pa/Dir Prog Div Ofc Commun Investment; Nat Assn Housing & Redevel Ofcls; Nat Housing Conf; cp/Vol w Hope Vil, A Coop Commun; Trainee/Vol w Cayuga Co Commun Coun; r/Cath; hon/Outstg Yng Wom Am 1978, 79; W/W Fin & Indust 1979; Alpha Al Awd, Fed Home Loan Bank Bd 1979.

SPRAY, ROBERT L JR oc/Clinical Psychologist; b/Feb 18, 1948; h/1525 Case, Batesville, AR 72501; ba/B'ville; p/Mr and Mrs Robert L Spray Sr, Ponca City, Ok; ed/BA Univ Okla; MA, PhD Univ Ark; pa/Psychotherapy w Adults, Chd, Fams, Grps; Supervision of Other Profls; r/So Bapt.

284

SPRAYBERRY, MARY EVELYN oc/Nurse; b/July 7, 1938; h/Box 6911, Nettleton, MS 38858; ba/Amory, MS; m/Clovis Leon; c/Michael David; p/V T and Ruby C Harris, Nettleton, MS; ed/Dip Grad Univ Hosp Sch Nsg 1960; pa/RN; Pres Dist 25 Nurses Assn 1978-79; Instr Prepared Child Birth Classes; r/Bapt; hon/W/W Am Wom 1979-80.

SPRINGS, PATRICIA McCLOSKEY oc/Teacher; b/Sept 4, 1941; h/PO Box 85, Taft, OK 74463; m/Alexander; c/Alex Romell, LaShon Blanchette, Patricia Elizabeth; p/William R and Elizabeth E McCloskey, Sapulpa, OK; ed/BA Langston Univ; MEd NEOSU-Tahlequah; pa/Tchr; Mus K-12, Band 3-12, Jr & Sr HS Chorus; cp/Ch Choir Sponsor, Chp Bldg Fund; r/Cole Chapel CME Ch.

SPRUCE, FRANCES BLYTHE oc/Manager; b/May 4, 1927; h/PO Box 9882, Chevy Chase, MD 20015; ba/Wash DC; p/Samuel Steward and Nell Trabue Anderson Spruce, Chevy Chase, MD; ed/AA Mt Vernon Jr Col 1947; BA Geo Wash Univ 1950; Grad Work Cath Univ; Studied Painting Corcoran Gal of Art; pa/Mgr Mktg Ser, Blue Cross; cp/Montgomery Players; Arts Clb of Wash; Kensington Players; Players Intl; British Embassy Players; Brit Commonwlth Soc N Am; Past Judge No Va One Act Play Tourn, Mont Teen Contest, Forensic Contest; Paintings Exhib'd & Sold; Past Pres Wash Theatre Alliance, Chm Ruby Griffith Adm'g Com of Awd Comp 1968-71; Pi Beta Phi; Pres DC Alumnae Clb; r/Prot; hon/Silver Tray, Brit Embassy Players 1971; Author & Illustrator 2 Chds Books.

SPRUILL, OSCAR JR oc/Bus Operator; b/Nov 23, 1931; ba/B'ham, Al; m/Josie M; p/Oscar Sr (dec) and Josie R Spruill (dec); ed/Sc Engrg, Water Purification 1952; Radio & TV Rapair 1961; B'ham Police Acad 1967; Mondy Bible Col 1966; ThB B'ham Bible Col 1963; mil/AUS 1951-73 Sgt; pa/Pastor First Bapt Ch, Harriman Pk, B'ham, Ala; Ordained 1969; B'ham Police Dept; Jeffco Transit Bus Oper; cp/Mayor Coun, Jacco Coun B'ham Action Team; r/Bapt; hon/Spec Invetigator Treas Dept 1971; Tng in Passenger Relats 1980; Outstg Law Enforcement Ofcr 1975; Fav Citizen 1979; W/W 1981; Author Num Profl Pubs.

SQUATRIGLIA, ROBERT WILLIAM oc/Educator, Psychologist, Associate Chancellor and Dean; b/Nov 23, 1937; h/Conway, SC; ba/USC-Coastal Carlina Col, Col Rd, Conway, SC 29526; m/Betty P; c/Robert Jr, Elizabeth Lee, Katherine Anne, Stephen Karl; p/P William (dec) and Mary E Ogenskis Squatriglia, Naugatuck, CT; ed/AB 1960, MA 1965 Col William & Mary; PhD Univ SC 1970; mil/AUS Capt; pa/Assoc Chancellor, Dean Student Devel, Assoc Prof USC-Coastal Carolina Col 1977-; Assoc Dean Student Affairs, Psych, SUNY-Albany 1972-77; VP Student Affairs, Dean Student Ser, SUNY-Brockport 1970-72; Dir VA Cnslg, Univ SC 1967-70; Asst Dean Men, Col William & Mary 1963-67; AAHE; ACPA; APGA; AAUP; NASPA; SCPA; SC Dir, NASPA 1980-81; cp/Horry Co Commun Ed Adv Coun, Chm 1979-81; Phi Delta Kappa, VP; Conway Rotary Clb, Bd Dirs 1980-83; K of C; r/Rom Cath; hon/Omicron Delta Kappa; SUNY Chancellor's Res Awd 1975-77; ACE-NASPA Ldrship Inst 1979; Blue Key; Contbr, Presenter, Spkr, Nat Profl Jours & Confs.

STACKLER, LOUIS MICHAEL oc/Planner; b/June 28, 1948; h/405 N 19th, Enid, OK 73701; ba/Enid; m/Susan; c/Elizabeth Anne; p/Louis and Margaret Stackler, Wilmington, DE; ed/AB King's Col 1970; MA Okla St Univ 1974; mil/USNR; pa/Urban & Regional Planner; Hlth Planner; Am Soc Public Adm; Am Hlth Plan'g Assn; Okla Hlth & Wel Soc; Okla Public Hlth Assn; cp/K of C; Am Heart Assn; Okla Affil; Ret'd Sr Vol Prog Bd; Foster Grandparent Prog Bd; YMCA; U Way Bd of Enid; r/Rom Cath; hon/Outstg Vol of Yr, Heart Assn 1978.

STADSKLEV, JOAN BYLSMA oc/Musician; b/Oct 26, 1944; h/Rt 1 Box 585, Marianna, FL 32446; ba/Marianna; m/Thomas D; p/Frank Sr and Wilma F Bylsma, Lynn Haven, FL; ed/BMus Fla St Univ 1963-67; pa/Sigma Alpha Iota; Nat Assn Mus Therapy 1967-; Voice Instr Chipola Jr Col; cp/Pilot Clb Intl 1971, Local, St & Intl Coms; r/Presb; Mus Dir 1969-; hon/Outstg Yng Wom Am 1978; Garnet Key FSU; Outstg Farm Fam 1977; Pilot Clb Outstg Clb & Commun Ser Awd 1978; Aspen Mus Fest 1979.

STAFFORD, ANITA FAYE RUTHERFORD oc/Department Chairman, Child Therapist; b/Oct 6, 1946; m/Jessie L; c/David Wayne, Steve Lee; p/Sidney Friend and Nina Johnson Rutherford, Midwest City, OK; ed/BS 1979, MS 1971 Ctrl St Univ; EdD Okla St Univ 1975; pa/Chm Dept Child Devel & Fam Living, Assoc Prof, Tex Wom's Univ 1976-; Child Therapist; Asst Prof Oscar Rose Jr Col 1975-76; Asst Prof Okla Christian Col 1973-75; Lectr Ctrl St Univ 1970-73; Charter Mem Okla Assn Ed of Yng Chd, Secy 1973; Nat Coun Fam Relats; AAUP; Tex Assn Univ Profs; Soc Child Devel Res; cp/Repub Party; Altrusa Intl; r/Bapt; hon/Phi Delta Gamma; Phi Delta Kappa; Effective Tchg Awd; W/W Am Wom; Author Num Profl Pubs Incl'g "Low Income Parents Perception of Early Childhood Education" & "Profile of the Creative Family" 1981.

STAFFORD, THOMAS JOHN oc/Contracting Officer; b/Jan 28, 1940; h/4242 E-W Hwy, Chevy Chase, MD 20015; ba/Wash DC; p/Thomas J (dec) and Ruth Virginia Koerber Stafford, Sharon, PA; ed/BS; MBA; mil/USAF Capt; pa/Contracting Ofcr, US Fish & Wildlife Ser; Nat Contract Mgmt Assn; cp/Bd Dirs JCs; r/Presb; hon/W/W Am; Outstg Procurement Ofcr, AF 1969; 2 AF Commend Medals.

STAGGS, JAMES R oc/Counselor; b/June 14, 1927; h/PO Box 247, McNeil, AR 71752; ba/Stephens, AR; p/dec; ed/BBA; M Guid & Cnslg; mil/AUS 2 Yrs; pa/HS Cnslr; AEA; NEA; Probation Cnslg; Pvt Cnslg; cp/Directs Pageants: Judges, Emcee, Entertains; r/Bapt; Dir & Pianist of Men of Calvary, Gospel Singing Evangelism; hon/W/W Am Univs & Cols.

STALLINGS, JESSE DANIEL oc/Provisioning Manager; b/Apr 20, 1915; h/Buda, TX; ba/6500 Tracor Ln, Austin, TX 78721; m/Toinette Marie Heffington; c/Sharon Sue, Michael Daniel, Melissa Marie, Robin Joseph; p/William Thomas and Katherine Lee Hall Stallings; ed/Cert SW Photo Arts Inst, Intl Inst Photo Arts 1950; Cert Inst Cert'd Profl Mgrs 1977; Cert Sr Mem Soc Logisitcs Engrs; Cert Ofcrs Refresher Course, The Calvary Sch 1940; Cert Supvr Mgmt Course, Am Mgmt Assn 1973; mil/Tex NG 112th Cavalry 1930-40, 112th Cavalry AUS 1940-43; 112th Spec Combat Team 1942-45; Ret'd Capt; pa/Stunt Man & Actor 1930-40; Construction Supt, Henderson Lee & Storage 1948; Field Supt, Municipal Ser Co 1939; Construction Mgr, Gulf S Utilities 1949-50; Mgr Myris Photo Labs 1950-51; Art Editor & Public Relats Dir, SWn Square Dancer Mag 1951-52; Supvr St Farm Ins Co 1952-62; Mgr Provisioning Dept, Collins Radio Div, Rockwell Inst, Logistcs/Provisioning Conslt, Garland & Austin, Tex 1977-; Provisioning Mgr & Sr Logistics Engr, Tracor Inc 1978-; Nat Mgmt Assn; Soc Logistics Engrs; Elec Industs Assn; Am Mgmt Assn; cp/112th Cavalry Assn, Dallas; 1st Cav Assn, Ft Hood, Tex; Horse Cavalry Assn, Ft Bliss, Tex; Ret'd Ofcrs Assn; VFW; Team Ldr, US Savings Bond Dr 1975; Loan Exec, U Way Fund Dr 1976; Orgr & Curator, 112 Cavalry Assn Mus 1960-; Orgr, Pres & Bd Mem 112th Cavalry Assn 1956-; hon/Lttr of Apprec, Bicent Mus Comm of Irving, Tex 1976; Ldrship Awd, N Tex Chapt Soc Logistics Engrs; Patriotic Ser Awd, US Treas Dept 1975; Lttr Commend, Pres of Rockwell Intl 1976; Purple Heart; Bronze Star; Combat Infantry Badge.

STALLWORTH, EDWARD oc/Retired Army; b/Feb 27, 1918; h/Tuskegee Inst, AL; ba/PO Box 91, Tuskegee Inst, AL 36088; m/Claudia B; c/Jacqueline S Montgomery, Cynthia S Player, Arlene K; p/dec; mil/AUS Ret'd; pa/Formerly Dir JROTC, Macon Co Sch Sys; Ret'd Tchr Macon Co, Ala; Pres-Elec Tuskegee Optimist Clb Intl; cp/Pres's Clb of Ala; Coun-man City of Tuskegee; Indust Devel Bd; Election Law Commr for St Ala; r/Meth; hon/Dist'd Ser Awd, City of Tuskegee 1977 & 79; Outstg Ser Awd, Macon Co JROTC 1967-76; Apprec Awd, Tuskegee Optimist Clb Intl; Cert Achmt, AUS 1960, 1961; Cert Apprec AUS 1964.

STAMMER, KATHRYN A GROEBE oc/Accounting Clerk, Student; b/May 26, 1953; h/PO Box 85, Oswego, KS; ba/Oswego; m/Keith E; c/Karyn Dawn; p/John L (dec) and Lucille M Groebe, Bartlesville, OK; ed/BCE Ozark Bible Col 1976; Att'g Labette Commun Col; pa/Acctg Clerk, Stamco Inc; cp/5th Dist Repub Wom; r/First Christian Ch: Cantata Choir Dir, Worship Ser Pianist, Past Pres Ladies Ser Grp 1980; hon/Okla Girls St Del 1970; Outstg Vocal Awd, Col HS 1971; Elks Clb S'ship 1971; Soroptimist Clb's Tng Awd 1981.

STAMPA, JULIAN CLAUDE oc/Radiological Technologist; b/May 18, 1942; h/Brandenton, AL; m/Michele; p/Julian M (dec) and Ericka I Stampa (dec); ed/Radiological Technol, Manatee Meml Hosp 1974; mil/AUS 1960-63, 1965-72 Staff Sgt; AUS Instr 1969; pa/Chief Technol, L W Blake Meml Hosp 1974-78; Chief Computorized Tomographer, Out-Patient Radiology Sers; Am Registry of Radiol Technol 1974-; cp/Manatee Yth Soccer Assn, Pres 1980-; US Soccer Fed Referee 1979-; USCG Aux, Flotilla 81; r/Presb; hon/Grad w Hons NCO Acad & IMJIN Scout Acad; Commend USCG; All-Co Soccer Midfielder, W Chester Co 1959; Class Validictorian, Manatee Meml Hosp.

STANBERRY, JAMES PHILLIP oc/Educator, Clergyman, Psychotherapist; b/Apr 19, 1930; h/Baton Rouge, LA; ba/9755 Goodwood Blvd, Baton Rouge, LA 70815; m/Frances Joyce Robinson; c/Melanie; p/J Roy (dec) and Eula Irene Stanberry Fugate (dec); ed/BA Okla Bapt Univ 1965; MRE Mid-Wn Bapt Theol Sem 1970; EdD Sch Ed SWn Bapt Sem 1976; mil/USAF 1951-53; pa/Min Christian Ed, Broadmoor Bapt Ch; Conslt to Chs & Insts in Fam Therapy & Psych of Human Relats; Clin Mem Am Assn Marraige & Fam Therapists; Am Psych Assn; Rel Ed Assn; r/Bapt; Author Sev Articles & Essays.

STANFILL, DOROTHY oc/Freelance Writer; b/Dec 22, 1911; h/1 Mimosa Dr, Jackson, TN 38301; m/Charles T; c/Arthur Hall; p/William Scott McMahen, Stanton, TN; Irma Josephine Galloway, Trezevant, TN; ed/BA Lambuth Col 1962; pa/Pvt Secy; Ins Co Exec; Advtg Sales Work;

Tchr 7 Yrs; Tenn Poetry Soc; Chickasaw Chapt NAPW; Jackson Writers Grp; Tenn Press & Author Clb; cp/Dem Wom's Org; r/Meth; hon/Deep S Conf 1st Prize 1971, 1973, 2nd Prize 1969; Nat Press & Authors Clb, 3rd Prize for Nat 1976; Num Prizes in NLWV Fiction Contests; 1st 1976, 1978, 2nd Juvenile Fiction 1980, Hon Men 1980, Many Others; Fiction Editor *Old Hickory Review;* Author *Katharine and the Quarter-Mile Drag and Other Stories* 1st edition 1978, 2nd edition 1979; Over 100 Stories in Var Pubs.

STANFILL, YVONNE ANNETTE oc/Deputy District Clerk; b/Oct 27, 1958; h/402 E Walnut, Grandview, TX 76050; ba/Cleburne, TX; p/Devon Stanfill, San Antonio, TX; Emma Jean Lowe, Grandview, TX; ed/AA Hill Jr Col; pa/Dpty Dist Clerk, Johnson Co, Tex; r/Bapt; hon/HJC Cheerleader 1977 & 78; Most Beautiful Girl of HJC.

STANLEY, LUCY REDUS oc/Retired Principal; b/Jan 2, 1908; h/321 Hine St, Athens, AL 35611; m/William L Sr; c/William L Jr, David L Sr; p/Luther (dec) and Bessie Redus (dec); ed/BS cum laude A&M Univ; pa/Ret'd Prin; AEA; NEA; ARTA; Ret'd Tchrs Assn; cp/Grand Worthy Matron, OES; Matrons Cultural Clb; Secy Comm Ofcl Jefferson Co Progressive Dem Coun; r/Congregational; hon/Hon Staff Atty Bill Baxley; Cert of Merit Matrons Cultural Clb.

STANLEY, MONTY RAY oc/Police Officer; b/Oct 28, 1951; h/1805 N Place, Plano, TX 75074; ba/Carrollton; m/Susan Loree Hall; c/Angela Christine; Aileen Dawn; p/W R and Faye Stanley, Sulpher Springs, TX; ed/BBA N Tex St Univ 1974; Att'g Abilene Christian Univ, Dallas; pa/Police Ofcr; r/Ch of Christ; hon/Carrollton Police Dept Ofcr of Yr 1978; Sev Tennis Awds in HS & Col.

STARK, NORMAN oc/Actor, Writer, Musician; b/Sept 15, 1940; h/391 NE 175th St, N Miami Bch, FL 33162; c/Michelle Allison; p/Martin Stark, Sunrise, FL; Margaret Stark (dec); ed/Newark St Col 1963-69; mil/AUS 1963-69; pa/Acad Mus Sers - Pres Mus Ednl Ser 1975-77; Owner Acad of Mus 1975-77; Actor/Asst Dir, Miami Film Sers 1979-80; PWP Playhouse, Dir; Fla Motion Picture & TV Assn; cp/BEST Grp, Pres; r/Jewish; hon/W/W SE 1980; Editor "Night Owl" Newark St Col 1967-69; Editor NY Col of Mus Newslttr; Columnist Coral Springs Forum Newslttr; Reporter Commun Newspapers; Editor Photo News 1977.

STARLING, HARVEY MILTON oc/Evangelist, Bible Instructor; b/Oct 29, 1932; h/Florence, AL; ba/PO Box BE, Florence, AL 35630; m/Patsy Elkins; c/Machelle, Milton, Vernon, Alan; p/Mr and Mrs J V Starling, Pocahontas, AR; ed/Att'd Harding Univ 1950-54; pa/Evangelist, Darby Dr Ch of Christ; Bible Instr Intl Bible Col; Conducted Over 700 Revivals; Crusades in 38 Sts & 40 Nations; Author Num Tracts & Articles.

STARNES, RUTH STARNES oc/Accountant; b/Apr 21, 1929; h/507 Westover Dr, Monroe, NC 28110; ba/Monroe; m/C Dudley (dec); c/Carol S Hess, Joan; p/Thomas H Starnes; Ruby Stewart; ed/BA Pfeiffer Col; AA Wingate Col; pa/Nat Soc Accts; NC Soc Accts; cp/Dem Wom of NC, Pres 1978-80; r/Presb; hon/BPW's Langy-Williams Awd.

STATON, JAMES LORIN SR oc/Nurse Educator; b/Feb 3, 1936; h/706 E 11th St, Russellville, AR 72801; ba/R'ville; c/James L Jr; p/Shirley Stafford Staton, Hardy, KY; ed/RN; CRNA; AS; BA; MA; MSN; ABD; mil/AUS Nurse Corps; pa/Nurse Edr, Ark Tech Univ; r/Prot; hon/Cert of Achmt, Ireland Army Hosp, Ft Knox, Ky 1969.

STATON, L COLLEEN oc/Executive Director; b/Apr 1, 1925; h/2325 Carolinda Dr, Waco TX 76720; ba/Waco; m/Robert L; c/Judy Gent; p/A S (dec) and E Pearl Hamilton, Waco, TX; pa/Exec Dir YWCA; Mid-Sts Staff Assn YWCA; Indian Springs Chapt ABWA; r/Bapt; hon/Tex Sen Resolution 1971; Better Am Awd, Waco Bd Rltrs 1979.

STAUBLIN, JUDITH A oc/Financial District Manager; b/Jan 17, 1936; h/3640 Peachtree Crns W #1303, Norcross, GA 30092; ba/Norcross; c/Juli Jackson, Scott Jackson; p/L Fred and E Virginia Wiley, Anderson, IN; pa/Fin Dist Mgr, NCR Corp; Fin Mgrs Soc; cp/C of C; U Fund; hon/W/W Am Wom 1979-80.

STEELMAN, DON LOUIS oc/Attorney at Law, Justice of the Peace; h/Marshall, TX; ba/PO Box 1582, 100 E Burleson, Marshall, TX 75670; p/J W (dec) and Nettie Steelman, Marshall, TX; ed/BA Univ Tex-Austin 1970; JD Univ Tex Sch Law 1973; pa/Atty at Law; Just of Peace; Tex Bar Assn; Harrison Co Bar Assn; Tex Just of Peace & Constable Assn; Tex Assn Wkr's for the Blind, Bd Dirs; Pres's White House Lib Conf, Del; cp/Concerned Homeowners of Marshall, Tex, Atty & Bd Mem; r/Bapt; hon/Phi Eta Sigma 1966; Phi Beta Kappa 1969.

STEIN, DAVID ERIC oc/US Air Force Officer; b/Jan 13, 1950; h/4331 S Bend Cir E, Jacksonville, FL 32207; ba/Griffiss AFB, NY; p/Stanley W and Dorothy J Lilley Stein, J'ville, FL; ed/BS High Hons 1971, MS 1977

Univ Fla; mil/AUS 1977-79 1st Lt; USAF 1979- Capt; pa/Physics Instr, Ford Fellow & Res Asst 1971-76; Am Phy Soc; Am Assn Physics Tchrs; AF Assn; Intl Platform Assn; Optical Soc Am; r/Nondenom; hon/Phi Beta Kappa; Omicron Delta Kappa; Phi Kappa Phi; Fla Blue Key.

STEINHOFF, DAVID oc/Student; b/Oct 30, 1962; ba/Manning, SC; p/Doris Steinhoff, Manning, SC; ed/Student Manning HS; pa/FBLA; 4-H; Jr Sci Clb; Lib Clb; Drama Clb; r/Bapt; hon/3rd Pl Nat Winner, 4-H Egg & Poultry Conf 1979, 80; Intl Yth in Achmt 1981; W/W Am HS Students 1971; Nat 4-H Winner Wood Sci, Nat 4-H Cong 1980.

STEMPER, WILLIAM JR oc/Clergyman, Chairman of the Board; b/Dec 24, 1947; h/1354 First Ave, NYC, NY 10021; p/William Sr and Mildred Wells Stemper, Sanford, FL; ed/BA Stetson Univ 1969; MA Emory Univ 1972; MDiv Union Theol Sem 1974; pa/Chm Bd, Forum Corp Responsibility Inc; Epis Clergyman, Lectr; Epis Soc for Min in Higher Ed; Omicron Delta Kappa; cp/Ripon Soc; Shriner; 32° Mason; Union Leag Clb of NY; Metro Opera Clb; r/Epis; hon/Algernon Sydney Sullivan 1969; Head Student Govt, Union Theol Sem 1974; Author *Approaching the Narrows;* Articles Pub'd in Num Masonic Pubs, *Wall Street Journal, New York Times, The Corporate Examiner.*

STENHOLM, CHARLES W oc/Congressman; b/Oct 26, 1938; ba/Ho of Reps, 1610 Longworth Bldg, Wash DC 20515; m/Cynthia Ann Watson; c/Chris, Cary, Courtney Ann; p/Lambert and Irene Stenholm (dec); ed/Att'd Tarleton St Jr Col 1959; BS 1961, MS 1962 Tex Tech Univ; pa/Farmer, Pres Double S Farms Inc; Elected to 96th Cong, 1978; Com on Agric w Subcom Assignments to Cotton, Dairy & Poultry, Livestock & Grains, Oilseeds & Rice; Small Bus Com w Subcom Assignment to Spec Small Bus Probs; Tex Voc Agric 1962-64; Exec VP Rolling Plains Cotton Growers 1964-67; Gen Mgr Stamford Elect Coop 1967-76; Adv Dir, First Nat Bank Stamford; r/Luth; hon/Am Farmer Deg, Hon Am Farmer, Hon St Farmer, FFA; Charter Trustee Cotton Inc; Pres Rolling Plains Cotton Growers; Pres Tex Elect Coops; Pres Stamford C of C; St Dem Exec Com; Tex St ASC Com; Gerald W Thomas Awd, Outstg Agriculturalist, Tex Tech Univ; Dist'd Alumnus Awd, Tarleton St Univ.

STEPHENS, BARBARA ANNETTE MOSSE oc/Medical Technologist, Medical Hematologist; b/Feb 8, 1944; h/Howe, TX; ba/Med Plaza Hosp, 1111 Gallagher Rd, Sherman, TX 75020; m/Paul W; c/Paul Richard, Phillip Ray, Penny Renea; p/Arthur Mason and Sara Elizabeth Traylor Mosse, Pottsboro, TX; ed/AS Grayson Co Jr Col 1969; BS 1971, Grad Study 1971-72 Tex Wom's Univ; pa/Lab Tech, Med Plaza Hosp; Supvr Spec Chems & Hematology; Am Soc Clin Pathols; Woodmen of World; Am Heart Assn; TWU Alumnae; Tri Beta Clb, Sponsor 1971-72; MT (ASCP); H (ASEP); cp/Am Heart Assn, CPR Instr; Chm & CPR Task Force Chm, CPR Coor MPH; r/Meth; hon/Cert of Merit, AHA 1980; All Am Citizen 1980; Presentation of Paper, Conf on Citizen CPR; Co-Author E-Z CPR Song.

STEPHENS, JOHN UTLEY oc/Businessman; b/Sept 22, 1915; h/4804 Cypress, N Little Rock, AR 72116; ba/N Little Rock; m/Sarah Louise Wood; c/John Robert, Ronald Eugene; ed/Draughton Bus Col; mil/Aviation Engrs 3 Yrs; pa/Grocer; r/Presb.

STEPHENSON, MARY LYNN oc/Pathologist, Psychologist; b/Sept 18, 1943; h/Garland, TX; c/Richard William; p/John Bryden, Depew, OK; Jewell Bryden, W Columbia, TX; ed/BS SW Tex Univ 1965; MA Wichita St Univ 1972; Cert'd Graphoanalyst 1978; Graphoanalytical Psych 1979; pa/Speech & Lang Pathol, Richardson Indep Sch Dist, Sec'dy Level; Graphoanalytical Psych; Am Speech & Hearing Assn; Am Graphotherapy Assn; r/Ch of Higher Consciousness; hon/Author *The KI Technique: A Self Improvement Prog for Students, A Self Improvement Prog for Teens & Adults, A Self Improvement Prog for Salesmen, Businessmen, Executives.*

STEPHENSON, MILDRED oc/Homemaker; b/Dec 21, 1912; h/Hartselle, AL; c/Jimmy F, Janie L Nolen; p/Henry (dec) and Rebecca Morris (dec); ed/Att'd Auburn Univ Ext Ser; cp/Morgan Co Homemkrs Coun, Treas 1979-81, Secy-Reporter; Hopewell Homemkrs Clb, Co Intl Chm; Homebound Tchr SS; Asst Libn W Hartselle Bapt Ch; Vol Work Summerford & Falkville Nsg Homes; Morgan Co Ext Coun, Secy-Treas; r/Bapt; hon/Recip Ldrship Awd, Morgan Co, Ala 1979; 1st Pl St Feature Article Contest 1979.

STEPP, FLORENCE DAVIS oc/Teacher; b/Jan 6, 1929; h/Box 1041, Fitzgerald, GA 31750; ba/Fitzgerald; m/William Thomas Jr; c/Wiliam Thomas III, Katherine Davis; p/Withers and Annie Davis, Garner, NC; ed/BS; pa/Tchr Fitzgerald Jr HS; Pres FAE; Advr PATL; Data Collector; GAE; NEA; cp/DAR; Red Cross Bloodmobile Vol; r/Epis; hon/Fitzgerald Tchr of Yr 1979; Outstg Elem Tchr 1974; W/W.

STERNLIEB, ANTONIA oc/Physician; b/June 10, 1912; h/7414 Pine

Pk Dr, S Lake Worth, FL 33463; p/Samuel and Dora Sternlieb, Vienna, Austria; ed/MD, Dpty Med Supt, Dept Hosps; pa/Gen Med Pract, NY Dept Med Supt, Dept Hosps; Asst Clin Psychi, Mtl Hygiene Clin; cp/Bd Govs Nat Bus & Profl Coun; r/Jewish; hon/Fordham Hosp Alumni Assn, Cert Hon; US Treas Dept Awd; W/W Am Wom.

STEVENS, ARTHUR oc/Retired; h/601 Albert Pike, Hot Springs Nat Pk, AR 71901; cp/Charter Mem Melting Pot Geneal Soc; SAR; Nat Geneal Soc; Garland Co Hist Soc; Assoc Nat Archives; Ark St Hist Soc; Ark Geneal Soc; Disciples of Christ Hist Soc; St Louis Geneal Soc; Jackson Co, Ark Geneal Soc.

STEVENS, GRACE MAE oc/Teacher; b/Aug 16, 1920; m/James R (dec); c/James Allen, Vera Kathryn; p/Joseph and Ollie Mae Hilton, Stillwater, OK; ed/BS; pa/Public Sch Tchr; r/Bapt.

STEVENS, NORMA YOUNG oc/Professor; b/Oct 23, 1927; h/Nashville, TN; m/Howard L; c/Catherine S Self, Karen S Cantrell, Kristen Leslie; p/S Taylor Young, Canton, GA; Cora Stephens Young (dec); ed/BFA Univ Ga 1949; MRE New Orleans Bapt Theol Sem 1956; EdD Univ Ga 1970; Dip Span, Escuela de Idiomas, San Jose, CR 1961; pa/Landscape Arch 1950-54; Co-Dir Dept Testing & Cnslg, Mex Bapt Sem 1962-74; Prof Ed, Belmont Col 1974-; Am Psych Assn; Tenn Psych Assn; Kappa Delta Pi; r/So Bapt; hon/W/W S&SW 1980-81; Author *Go Out With Joy* 1966; Contbr to *Everyday Five Minutes with God*; Co-Author *The Christian and Divorce* 1980; Var Articles & Short Stories.

STEVENSON, DRUCILLA PACE oc/Homemaker; b/Feb 21, 1918; h/1303 Phillips St, Corinth, MS 38834; m/Robert C; c/Glenda S Tennyson, Robert C Jr, Albert Pace; p/Albert D Sr (dec) and Emmie Long Pace (dec); cp/Past Matron Corinth Chapt #27 OES; Pres Firefighters Aux; r/Bapt; hon/St Mrs Firefighter 1979.

STEVENSON, JOE L oc/Associate Professor, Accountant; b/Jan 13, 1930; h/Rt 3 Box 135, Bluefield, VA 24605; ba/Richlands, VA; m/Wanda Bailey; c/Melody; p/James Melvin (dec) and Virginia Lockhart Stevenson (dec); ed/Cert McLains Bus Col 1952; BS Concord Col 1962; ME VPI & SU 1968; mil/AUS 1952-54; pa/Assoc Prof SW Va Commun Col; Adj Prof Bluefield St Col; CPA; Delta Pi Epsilon; Blue Key Nat Hon Frat; cp/Steering Com, Mtn-Dominion Resource & Conservation Com; Adm Bd Va Ave U Meth Ch; r/Meth; hon/NBEA Merit Awd 1962; W/W S&SW 1980.

STEWARD, JAMES KAYLOR JR oc/Curriculum Specialist; b/Sept 28, 1943; h/Stillwater, OK; ba/CIMC, St Dept Voc-Tech Ed, 1515 W 6th St, Stillwater, OK 74074; m/Diane Jean; c/Jimmy, Wendy, David; p/Jeames K and Geraldine F Steward, Shawnee, OK; ed/BS Okla St Univ 1966; pa/Voc Agric Tchr 10 Yrs; Farm Bus Mgmt Instr, Wn Okla Area Vo-Tech 3 Yrs; Farm Bus Mgmt Curric Spec, St Dept Voc-Tech; OVATA, PI Grp Pres; OVA; AVA; NVATA; OEA; cp/Charter Mem McLoud Lions Clb; Pottawatomie Co Fair Bd Mem 5 Yrs; Dem Party; Okla Yng Farmers Assn; hon/Hon St Farmer Deg, Okla FFA 1976; Hon'd by Pottawatomie Co 4-H 1977; Spec Recog OVATA 1978; Okla Extern Ldrship Prog 1979; Contbr to Devel of Okla Voc-Tech Curric for Farm Bus Mgmt 1977-.

STEWART, BONNIE PHA FURY oc/Nurse; b/June 30, 1934; h/7105 Mandarin Dr, Biloxi, MS 39532; ba/Biloxi; m/Wayne Edward; c/Bonnie Sue Creel, Deborah Pha Fields, Ginger Kae Camp, Barry Wayne; p/Nick Sr and Maxwell Spence Fury, New Orleans, LA; ed/ADN; BSN Cand Univ So Miss; pa/ANA; MNA; Dist 5 Nurses Assn; Assn Critical Care Nurses; Assn Evening & Night Supvrs; Instr & Initiator of Intern Prog for Grad Nurses 1979; Instr & Lectr Nsg Ed; Ec & Gen Wel Com, Dist 5 Nurses Assn, Chm 1975-77; Bd Dirs 1979; cp/Girl Scouts 12 Yrs; Boy Scouts 10 Yrs; 1st Cnslr to Pres, Relief Soc, Biloxi Ward; r/Mormon; hon/Grad w Hons Nsg Sch; W/W Am Wom.

STEWART, CATHERINE SUE FLANIGAN oc/Former Government Worker; b/Jan 21, 1935; ba/Sue's Travel, 10400 Dixie Hwy, Suite 207, Val Station, KY 40272; m/dec; c/Kenneth W Gilkie, Sandra D; p/Johnnie W (dec) and Scottie Mae Perry (dec); ed/Grad Herron Beauty Sch 1961; Airline Travel Sch 1980; cp/AFGE; hon/Awd for Over 200 Hrs in Med Records, AUS Hosp 1972; Govt Awd 1973; Red Cross Awd 1972; AUS Awd 1973.

STEWART, FRED oc/Retired; b/Oct 31, 1895; h/806 S Broad St, Scottsboro, AL 35768; m/Malda Ruty; c/Freda (dec), Estelle, Bobby, Horace, Ollie, Walter; p/dec; mil/AUS 1918-19; pa/Farmer; Preacher; r/Primitive Bapt; hon/Author *The Second Coming of Christ and the Thousand Year Reign* 1980.

STEWART, HAZEL BLACKLEDGE oc/Executive; b/May 3; h/2276 Napoleon Ave, Pearl, MS 39208; ba/Jackson; c/William Clay; p/Charles W (dec) and W A Blackledge, Laurel, MS; ed/Ole Miss Sch Bnkg; pa/VP

Bus Devel, Fidelity Bank; Written & Conducted Human Relats & Motiv Sems; cp/Pres Jackson Sales Clb; Bd Dirs Mtl Hlth for St Miss; Nat Bank Woms Assn; Zonta Intl; Desk & Derrick; Gtr Jackson Apt Assn; r/Bapt; hon/Dist'd Sales Awd 1976.

STEWART, LOUIS ALVIN oc/Superintendent; b/Feb 28, 1928; h/2515 S Congress Ave, Austin, TX 78704; ba/Same; m/Della Polly; c/Debra Gayle, Louis Alvin Jr; p/George A and Albina Elizabeth Stewart, Flatonia, TX; ed/BS Tex A&M Univ 1953; MA Sam Houston St Univ 1971; mil/USAF 1946-47; pa/Supt Travis Co Juvenile Ct; Pres Tex Juvenile Detention Assn; Pres Tex Inst Chd & Yth; Regional Chm Tex Probation & Parole Assn; Instl Div Chm Tex Probation & Parole Assn; Prog Com & Elec Code Chm, Tex Corrects Assn; Bd Dirs Nat Juvenile Detention Assn; cp/Pres PTA, St Ignatius Sch & Holy Cross HS; VP, Bd Dirs, Bluebonnet Yth Ranch; r/Cath; hon/Halls of Detention Awd; 20 Yr Ser Awd, Travis Co Juvenile Ct.

STEWART, WILBURN I (dec) oc/Shoe Repairman; b/Feb 13, 1931; h/Yukon, OK; m/Betty L; c/Terrie S Taylor; p/A D (dec) and Eva Stewart, Woodward, OK; mil/AUS; pa/Shoe Repairman; cp/JCs; Rotary Clb, Woodward & Yukon Charter Mem; r/U Meth.

STIFF, DELORES MATLEN oc/Director of Research; b/June 27, 1945; h/2114 Woodbine Ave, Fayetteville, NC 28303; ba/F'ville; p/Walter Stiff, Va Bch, VA; Juanita Stiff, Norfolk, VA; ed/BS; MS; PhD; pa/Dir Instl Res, F'ville St Univ; Assn Instl Res; NC Assn Instl Res; So Assn Instl Res; AAHPER; cp/Tchr Nat Lit Adv Rdg Prog; r/Epis; hon/Outstg Yng Wom Am 1979; Kappa Delta Pi.

STILES, SUZANNE STONE oc/Singer, Voice Teacher, Manager; h/11440 St Michaels Dr, Dallas, TX 75230; m/Robert D; c/Sarah Charlotte, Robert D Jr, William George; p/Sarah Snook Lundgren, Paducah, KY; ed/AB Geo Wash Univ; Tchr Cert, Voice, Peabody Conserv Mus; pa/Fdr & Gen Mgr Dallas Chamber Opera Soc 1977-; Voice Tchr 1971-; Sung w Opera Cos in Balto, Wash DC, Minn & Dallas; Dallas Mus Tchrs Assn; Nat Assn Tchrs Singing; r/Luth.

STILLER, GLORIA oc/Teacher; b/July 15, 1948; h/Rt 1 Box 353, Rockwell, NC 28138; ba/Faith, NC; m/Walter R; c/William Brandond, Andrea Christina; p/Joel Worth Sr and Chloia Parrish Sexton, Salisbury, NC; ed/BS cum laude Appalachian St Univ 1970; MEd cum laude UNCC 1975; pa/Elem Tchr: Randolph Co 1970-72, Rowan Co 1972-; Steering Com for Accred, So Assn Cols & Schs; NCAE; NEA: Past Fac Rep NCAE; Past Testing Coor, Annual Testing Prog, Faith Sch; Past Sch Base Com; Resource Progs; cp/Pilot Clb Intl; r/U Ch of Christ; Ch Wom's Org; Past Jr Class Tchr; hon/Nom'd Outstg Yng Edr 1970-71, 1971-72; Nom'd Tchr of Yr 1977-78, 80-81.

STILLS, CHARLES D oc/General Manager; b/May 19, 1934; h/Dallas, TX; ba/Am Petrofina Inc, PO Box 2159, Dallas, TX 75221; m/Ruth E; c/Beverly Anne, David Alexander, Lauren Annette; ed/B Che Univ Penn 1964; pa/Res Chemist, Rohm & Haas Co 1954-63; Organic Chem, US Dept Agric 1963-66; Mgr Prods Supply, Atlantic Richfield 1966-72; Gen Mgr, Supply & Transp, Am Petrofina Inc; Am Chem Soc; Spkrs Bur, Atlantic Richfield; cp/Pres Bd Mgrs Christ's Home; Pres Alumni Assn, Christ's Home; r/Presb; hon/Exch Clb Awd; S'ship to Univ Penn; Latin Prize; Patent 1965; Co-Author Sev Profl Articles.

STIMPSON, KATHY G oc/Social Worker; b/Apr 3, 1914; h/Rt 3 Box 348, Laurel Rd, Clinton, TN 37716; m/Edward J; c/Peter Gagnon, p/Henry and Anna Messner Gagnon, Rockland, MI; mil/AUS 1944-45; pa/Dir Chd's Wel & Distressed Fams Agcy; cp/Local Pres Ch Wom U; Holston Conf Bd, Wom's Soc of Christian Ser; Pres Clinton Dist WSCS; Conf Com, Ecumenical Affairs; Christian Unity & Interrel Concerns; St Bd Ch Wom U, Pres, VP; VP Tenn Assn Chs; Chm E Tenn Region TAC; Pres YWCA; r/U Meth; hon/W/W Am Wom 1964-65; Rec'd Columbus Awd 1976, K of C; Eagles Lodge Mother of Yr 1959.

STIPE, JOHN R oc/Executive; b/Oct 12, 1930; h/140 Virginia Cir, Forrest City, AR 72335; ba/Forrest City; m/Mary Ann C; c/Richard M, Roger W; p/R I (dec) and Ethel Marie Stipe (dec); ed/BS Univ Ark; mil/Ark ANG Ret'd Capt; pa/Pres Forrest City Production Credit Assn; cp/Secy & Dir St Francis Co Fair Assn; Past Pres Ark Assn PIA; Dir Rotary Clb; Dir C of C; Farm Bur; Riceland Foods; Past Pres, Past Nat Dir JCs; Past Mem 6th Farm Credit Dist Adv Comm; Adv Coun GT Chd, St Dept Ed; r/Bapt; hon/Key Man, FC JCs; Outstg Ark JC VP.

STIRGUS, JAMES oc/Assistant Superintendent; b/June 2, 1930; ba/Vicksburg Public Schs, Vicksburg, MS 39180; m/Annie A; c/Connie Ann, Wayne Anthony, Michael J, James Jr; p/Wilie Stirgus, New Orleans, LA; Carrie S Tolliver (dec); ed/BS Alcorn St Univ 1958; MS Jackson St Univ 1960; mil/AUS 1951-55; pa/Asst Supt, V'burg Public Schs; AASA; ASCD; VAE; NEA; Phi Delta Kappa; cp/Port City Kiwanis, Pres; Am

Legion; Elk's; Alpha Phi Alpha; C of C; r/U Meth; hon/Nat Defense Ribbon; Good Conduct Medal.

STOCKS, DAVID ALAN oc/Broker Services Representative; b/May 17, 1940; h/Box 32, Wilson Pike, Arrington, TN 37014; m/Linda Mitchell; c/Elizabeth Claire, Melissa Maria, Bradley David; p/Gifford Bonds (dec); Clarice M Stocks, Arrington, TN; ed/BS Univ N Ala 1962; MBA Univ Tenn 1978; mil/ROTC Florence St Col 1959-61; AUS S/Sgt; pa/Indep Contractor, Century 21 Franchises 1971-; Dir Tenn Real Est Comm 1976-79; Mfrs Rep, The Lovable Co Intl 1971-76; David A Stocks & Assocs 1968-71; Grp Ins Conslt, Metro Life Ins Co 1965-68; Life & Qualifying Mem Million Dollar Roundtable; cp/US JCs; Exch Clb; Mooreland Est Homeowners Assn, Dir; r/Ch of Christ; hon/Soc of Pershing Rifles.

STOCKSTILL, DAVID A oc/Artist; b/Nov 5, 1951; h/PO Box 1043, Picayune, MS 39466; p/Alvin (dec) and Ethel M Stockstill, Nicholson, MS; pa/Artist; cp/Pearl River Art Leag, Pres 1978-79; Pearl River Assn for Chd w Lrng Disabilities, VP 1979; Friends of the Margaret Reid Crosby Meml Lib, Bd Dirs; Bd Dirs U Way; Bd Dirs Pearl River Co Heart Fund; Pearl River Assn Retard'd Citizens; Chp Mtl Hlth For Pearl River, Co of Nicholson; r/Bapt; hon/Outstg Ser Awd, U Way; Silver Tray for Work as Pres, Pearl River Art Leag; Outstg Yng Man of Yr, JCs; 2nd & 3rd Pl, Pearl River Art Leag Spring Show; 6 2nd Pl & 1 3rd Pl, Pearl River Co Fair.

STODDARD, DONNA MELISSA oc/Professor and Department Coordinator; b/July 1, 1916; h/925 E Lexington St, Lakeland, FL 33801; ba/Lakeland; p/Franklin George and Olive Livingstone Stoddard; ed/BS Fla So Col 1937; MEd Penn St 1941; Further Study NY Sch of Interior Design, Univ Fla, Univ Tampa, Art Inst Pgh; pa/Art Prof & Coor Art Dept, Fla So Col; FFA; AFA; LAG; RAA; SEAA; SECAC; FEA; FAEA; NEA; FWC; AAUP; Charter Mem, Alpha Omicrom Pi, Kappa Gamma Chapt; Beta Sigma Phi, Intl Hon Mem; Pan Hellenic Assn; Fellow Royal Soc Art; Kappa Pi, 2nd VP; Assoc Mem AID; Intl Platform Assn; cp/OES; Art Chm Polk Co WEDU (Ednl TV Sta in Tampa) for Art Auction; Co-Chm Re-Elect Pres, Polk Co; Pres Polk Co Chapt Leukemia Assn; Bd Girls Clbs Am; Bd *Design Magazine*; Nat Accredited Flower Show Judge 1947-; Dir 99 Print Clb 1948; Dir Intl Art Exhib in Fla & Intl Art Exhib at Fla So Col 1952; hon/Am Artist's Profl Leag; AAUW, Lakeland Br; Chm Am Culture, FSC; FSC Cit; Grumbacher Awd; Miami Wom's Clb Gold Medal Awd; Yr Book Dedication, FSC *Interlachen* 1954; Cert of Merit for Dist'd Ser to Art & Ed, DIB.

STOKELY, JAMES ROYAL SR oc/Salesman; b/June 24, 1919; h/PO Box 1102, Thomson, GA 30824; m/Wanda M; c/James Jr, David, Michael, Margie; p/Marion Clark Sr (dec) and Johnnie Farr Stokely (dec); mil/AUS WWII Supply Clerk; pa/Salesman; cp/Secy Winchester Gun Clb; r/U Meth.

STOKES, JOHN LAFAYETTE oc/Assistant Curator; b/Apr 6, 1956; h/175 Williford, Memphis, TN 38112; ba/Memphis; p/Gilbert Harold and Maria Lopez Stokes, Brandon, MS; ed/Att'g Memphis St Univ; pa/Asst Curator of Birds, Supvr Bird Sect, Memphis Zoo & Aquarium; Coor Rehab Prog; Am Assn Zookeepers; r/Rom Cath; hon/1 of Top 5 Zookprs in Nation 1979; Cert of Excell in Zookpg.

STOLTE, KAREN MARIE oc/Nurse Educator, Mid-wife; b/Dec 14,1941; h/3105 Orlando Rd, Okla Clty, OK 73120; ba/Okla City; p/Thomas Fariss and Lucille E Stolte, McLouth, KS; ed/BSN Univ Kan 1962; MSN Yale Univ 1965; PhD Univ Kan 1976; pa/Staff Nurse, Univ Kan Med Ctr 1962-63; Instr, Asst Prof, Univ Iowa Col of Nsg 1966-71; Instr in Nurse-Midwifery, Yale Univ Summers 1966, 67, 70; Assoc Prof, Univ Okla Col Nsg 1976-; ANA; Intl Commun Assn; Am Col Nurse-Midwives, Nom'g Com, Ed Com, FSQ Com; cp/Ctrl Okla Childbirth Ed Assn, 2nd VP, Dir Sers 1976-78; r/So Bapt; hon/Spec Nurse Res Fellow, USPHS, DHEW 1971-74; Sigma Theta Tau; BSN w Dist; Co-Author "Patients Perceptions of the Touch They Received During Labor" 1980; "Postpartum Perceptions of Touch Received During Labor" 1979.

STONE, DAVID GRAHAM oc/Investment Broker, Account Executive; b/May 5, 1948; h/2316 N Lockhart, Sherman, TX 75090; ba/Sherman; m/Carleen Wilson; c/Nora Elizabeth, Raymond Alexander; p/Raymond Jr and Louise Beal Stone, La Jolla, CA; ed/Austin Col 1971-75; mil/AUS 1968-71 Staff Sgt; pa/Texoma Regional Plan'g Comm, Manpwr Planner, Manpwr Coor 1974-77; Eppler, Guerin & Turner, Inc, Investment Broker, Acct Exec 1977-; cp/Repub Party; Sherman Noon Lion's Clb, Mbrship Chm & Dir; Salvation Army, Sherman Dir; Jr Achmt of Grayson Co, Pres; Sherman C of C, Ed Com Chm; BSA, Past Explorer Advr; r/Epis; Acolyte Dir, Past Vestryman; hon/Gov's Public Ser Intern 1973; Vietnam Campaign Medal 1969-70; Bronze Star Medal 1970; Wall St Jour Student Awd 1974; Pi Gamma Mu 1974; Author Texoma Regional Selected Hlth Resources Survey 1973; Texoma Regional Manpwr Plans 1974-77.

STONE, RICHARD DARIUS oc/Deputy General Counsel; b/June 8, 1953; h/Austin, TX; ba/Gov's Ofc, St Capitol Bldg, Austin, TX 78711; p/Irving and Barbara Stone, Dallas, TX; ed/Undergrad Baylor Univ 1975; JD Baylor Univ Sch Law 1977; pa/Atty; Dpty Gen Counsel to Gov Clements; St Bar of Tex; Dallas Bar Assn; cp/Repub Party of Tex; r/Bapt; hon/Baylor Law Sch, Order of the Barrister 1977; Personal Asst to Gov Clements, Campaign 1978; Phi Delta Theta; Top 5 Most Eligible Bachelors in Austin 1979; Outstg Yng Men Am 1979; Author "Scientific Evidence in Criminal Rape Cases" *Texas Bar Journal* July 1977.

STONE, RUBY ELIZABETH BROWN oc/Retired; b/Dec 30, 1915; m/Chancellor Hines (dec); p/William Albert (dec) and Mattie Catherine Heard Brown (dec); ed/Henderson St Col, Univ Ark; pa/Elem Tchr 1936-41; Pers Asst, Ark St Hwy Dept 1941-44; War Dept Pers 1945-47; Ret'd Pers Asst & Secy to Pers Dir, Asst Pers Admr 1947-; Am Soc Pers Admrs, Bd Dirs 1973-76; Ark Pers Assn; Ask Assn Hosp Pers Dirs; cp/Life Mem Chi Sigma; Notary Public; Chm Credit Com 1953-; First Fed Savers Clb Am; Lady of Dec Noble, Scimitar Temple of Little Rock, Ark; r/Meth; hon/U Way Campaigns; Author St Ark Pers Policy Manual; Dept Policy & Procedure Manual.

STORY, W W oc/Pastor; b/Dec 20, 1934; h/PO Box 55, Garber, OK 73738; ba/Garber; m/Patsy Sue; c/Larry Michael; p/Hazel Story, Tulsa, OK; ed/Undergrad Sem; mil/USMC; pa/Meth Min; Conrad Evangelistic Assn; cp/VP Lions Clb; Dir Sr Citizen Ctr; Garfield Co Hlth Dept; r/U Meth: Ordained Elder.

STOUFFER, JOYCE K oc/Deputy Chief; h/1015 Gallatin Dr, San Antonio, TX 78245; p/John B Stouffer, Mercersburg, PA; ed/BS York Col of Penn 1973; M Guid & Cnslg, Phillips Univ 1978; mil/USAF 1974-; pa/Asst Chief Protocol, HQs AF Logistcs Command, Wright-Patterson AFB 1977-79; Gen Elec 1980; Contract Negotiator, Directorate of Contracting & Mfg, Kelly AFB 1981; Life Mem AF Assn; cp/4-H Dairy Clb 1960-68; Garfield Co Yth Ctr, Mil Activs Coor & Advr; Pres & Fdr Gallatin Action Com; SA-ALC/PM Briefing Team; Aerospace Ed Foun; Miss Contracting Coor; Nat Contracting Mgmt Assn; Commun Ed Com; Combined Fed Campaign Vol; Vol AF Asst Campaign; Vol AF Assn Dir; Vol Mem Cinci Art Mus 1979-80; Vol Mem Cinci Symph 1979-80; Green Co Mtl Hlth Advr 1978-79; r/U Ch of Christ; hon/Gen Elec Mgmt Awd for Outstg Perf 1980; AF Commend Medal; Merit Ser Medal; Jimmy Doolittle Awd, Aerospace Ed Foun 1980; Outstg Yng Wom Am 1980; Commun Ldrs Am 1981; Pres Gallatin Actions Com.

STOVALL, JEAN BURCH oc/Associate Realtor; b/Dec 16, 1945; h/Henderson, NC; m/Charles W; c/Shannon Burch, Kendall Shay, Charles Wayne III; p/Dennis Hampton and Ruth Douglas Burch, Lumberton, NC; ed/Coker Col 1962-64; BS Pembroke St Univ 1966; MA Cand Ctrl Mich Univ; pa/Country Knolls Rlty; Col of Albemarle 1974-80; Wayne Commun Col 1972-74; Nat Rltrs Assn; cp/Pres Elizabeth JCettes; External VP NC JCettes; Regional Dir NC JCettes; VP Jr Wom's Clb; r/Presb; hon/Juanita Bryant Citizenship Awd 1978; Pasquotank Co Five Outstg Yng Wom 1979; First Runner-Up Lit Div NC Jr Wom's Clb 1979.

STOWE, JAMES oc/Novelist, Teacher; b/Aug 25, 1950; h/411 E NY Ave #12, El Paso, TX 79902; m/Diane; c/Natalie; p/Jesson L and Bernice Stowe, El Paso, TX; ed/BA 1973, MA 1978 Univ Tex-El Paso; pa/Tchr Eng; Novelist; Mystery Writers of Am; hon/Film Rights to *Winter Stalk* Purchased by Universal Studios; Author *Winter Stalk* 1979.

STOWHAS, MARGARITA CLARA oc/Executive Director; b/Nov 18, 1937; h/7733 Dentcrest, Dallas, TX 75240; ba/Dallas; c/Chris M Cantin; p/A Raul and Graciela S de Stowhas, Santiago, Chile; ed/PhD; pa/Exec Dir Dallas Intl Lang Ctr; r/Mormon.

STRAKA, DAVID EUGENE oc/Director of Music; b/May 19, 1948; h/33 W Elm St, Fayetteville, AR 72701; ba/F'ville; m/Jane Norwood; c/David Matthew, Andrew Norwood, Rebecca Jane; p/Ernest L and Margaret E Straka, Clifton, CO; ed/BA Adams St Col 1973; MMus Cand Univ Kan; pa/Dir Mus, Ctrl U Meth Ch; Am Guild Organists; Presb Assn of Mus; F'ship of U Meth Mus; Guild of English Handbell Ringers; Choristers Guild; hon/Perf'd w Kan Univ Symph (Piano); Studied w Sequeira Costa; Played in Master Classes w Leon Fleisher.

STRANGE, KAREN SUE TAYLOR oc/Records Analyst; b/Apr 6, 1948; h/Rt 5 Box 159, Kingston, TN 37763; ba/Oak Ridge; m/Everette R; c/Brian Everette, Joseph Taylor; p/Clarence V (dec) and Colleen Maggard Taylor, Kingston, TN; ed/Att'd Carson-Newman Col 1966-67, E Tenn St Univ 1967-68; pa/Records Analyst, Records Mgmt Prog, Union Carbide Corp, Nuclear Div, Dept Energy; Indep Recording Artist; cp/Roane Choral Soc; Parent's Adv Coun Kingston Elem Sch, Secy; r/Bapt; hon/Tenn's Outstg Achmt Awd 1980; Tenn Col, Aide de Camp, Gov's Staff 1980; 2 Single Recordings Released.

STRATHMANN, PHYLLIS ANN oc/Businesswoman; b/Mar 24, 1941; h/117 Vista Del Rey, El Paso, TX 79912; ba/El Paso; m/James J; c/Mark R, Laura K; p/Ralph L Meeds, Edinburgh, IN; pa/Owner Great Western Properties; Pres El Paso Apt Assn; Tex Apt Assn; Cert'd Property Mgr; Rltr; Inst Real Est Mgmt; hon/Only Wom Cert'd Property Mgr in El Paso; First Wom Pres El Paso Apt Assn.

STRAUSS, ANNETTE GREENFIELD oc/Executive; b/Jan 26, 1924; h/Dallas, TX; m/Theodore H; c/Nancy Jaeger, Janie McGarr; p/Edith Greenfield, Houston, TX; ed/Att'd Rice Univ 1940-41; BA Univ Tex-Austin 1944; MA summa cum laude Columbia Univ 1945; pa/VP Public Affairs, Bozell & Jacobs Advtg & Public Relats Firm; Dir Richardson Savings & Loan Assn; cp/Univ Tex-Dallas, Devel Bd; Univ Tex-Austin Adv Coun of Col of Liberal Arts Foun; Dallas Pks & Rec Bd, Spec Assignment, Chm of Cultural Com; Chm Bd TACA; CBDA, Exec Com; Chm Cultural Achmt Task Force, Goals for Dallas; Dallas C of C, Steering Com & Adv Coun Ldrship Dallas, Cultural Com; Dallas Metro Opera Hospitality Bd, Co-Chm; Bd Dirs or Bd Trustees: Kennedy Ctr for Performing Arts, Nat Wom's Assn of Symph Orchs, Dallas Symph Assn, Dallas Theater Ctr, Dallas Civic Ballet, Dallas Metro Opera Assn, Dallas Civic Leag, Baylor Dental Col, St Paul Hosp, Nat Jewish Hosp, Chd's Med Ctr, Nat Coun Am Jewish Com, Dallas Vol Action Ctr, Dallas UN Assn Ednl Opports Inc, Creative Lrng Ctr of Dallas, Foun of Jewish Fed, Commun Chest Trust Fund (Adv Bd), Tex Hist Foun, Timberlawn Foun; Former Ofcr & Bd Dirs Num Other Coms & Orgs; hon/*Town & Country* Magazine Hon Roll of Vol Wom in US 1979; Nat Jewish Hosp Humanitarian Awd 1978; Linz Awd for Commun Ser 1975; Conf of Christians & Jews Brotherhood Awd 1972; Human Relats Awd, Am Jewish Com 1971; Zonta Awd for Commun Ser 1968; Arete Awd for Commun Ser 1967; Nat Jewish Hosp Wom of Yr 1965.

STRECKFUS, BARBARA ANN oc/Photo Artist; b/Jan 23, 1935; h/7913 Parke W Dr, Glen Burnie, MD 21061; ba/Same; m/John Charles; c/Dana Lynn, Eric Vaughn; p/Dana B and Margaret E Morgan Nelson, Dundalk, MD; pa/Photo Artist & Restorer, Retouch Spec Inc; APAG; PP of A; PP of M; cp/GSA; Pres Tops Clb; Treas Essex Rec Coun; r/Meth; hon/Wom of Yr Awd, Keith Cole Labs; W/W Am Wom.

STREED, WILLIAM ERIC oc/Manager; b/May 23, 1944; h/1709 Burce Dr, E Bch, St Simons Isl, GA 31522; p/William R Streed, Savannah, GA; Juanita W Streed, St Simons Isl, GA; ed/BSME Univ Miss; pa/Reinforced Plastics Mfg Mgr; ASME; Soc Plastics Engrs; cp/St Bd Trustees Yth Est, Secy Exec Com; Past Pres St Simons Isl Exch Clb; r/Luth; hon/St Alumni Dir & Past St Dir Alpha Tau Omega.

STREETER, BETTIE C oc/Retired; b/June 20, 1941; h/Greenville, NC; p/Geraldine C Woods, Rochester, NY; ed/BS NC Ctrl Univ 1963; pa/Ret'd Tchr Pitt Co & Beaufort Co Schs; NC Ctrl Alumni Assn; cp/NAACP; Black Assem; Greenville Indust C M Eppes High Alumni Assn; Lilies of Calvary, Mt Calvary FWB Ch; r/Mt Calvary FWB Ch; hon/Outstg Work in Greenville Indust Alumni Assn.

STRICKLAND, GLEN JR oc/Professor, Director; b/Jan 3, 1943; h/1103 S Terrace Blvd, Muskogee, OK 74401; ba/Tahlequah; p/Glen Strickland Sr, Muskogee, OK; Faye Bilman, Denver CO; ed/BA 1965, MA 1976 NEn St Univ; pa/Instr Speech & Debate, Free Lance Radio Announcer 1965-67, Baylor Univ Debate Coach; Instr Univ Denver 1967-71; Dir Pubs OCDE Pubrs 1971-74; News Dir KOGA Radio, Ogallala, Neb 1974-75; News Dir KMUS Radio 1975-76; Dir Upward Bound, Connors Col 1976-78; Prof Speech, Dir Debate & Forensics, NEn St Univ 1978-; Am Forensic Assn; Asian Speech Assn; Nat Forensic Leag; AAUP; cp/Bd Dirs Muskogee Dugout Clb; Ogallala JCs; Co Dem Chm, Arapahoe Co, Colo; Bd Dirs Muskogee Knothole Assn 1966; r/Presb; hon/JC of Mo 1968; W/W Wn US 1968; Outstg Yng Man Am 1979; 2nd Nat Debate Tourn 1975; W/W AM Cols & Univs 1964, 65; Author Sev Ref Books Incl'g *Reforming the Penal System & Revising Foreign Commitments*.

STRICKLAND, JESSIE HAZEL oc/Language Arts Specialist; b/Nov 30, 1948; h/PO Box 2361, Rt 6 King Springs Pike, Johnson City, TN 37601; ba/Johnson City; m/Robert Alvin; p/Samuel H (dec) and Lena Pearman Shields, Elizabethton, TN; ed/BS; MA; EdS Cand E Tenn St Univ; pa/Tenn St Lang Arts Spec, Dept Ed; Alpha Delta Kappa, Alpha Nu Chapt; TASCD; ASEARS; First Tenn Dist Supvrs Study Coun; NACE; Judge Regional Tenn Ofc Occups Clbs Public Spkg Contest 1978-79; Judge Regional & St Voc Indust Clbs of Am Public Spkg Contest 1979; St of Tenn Evaluation Team for Col Site Visits of Tchr Preparation Insts 1977-80; Curric Com, St of Tenn's Basic Skills & Proficiency Testing Prog 1979-80; Field Evaluator Spec Courses, St of Tenn, First Tenn Dist 1979-80; cp/Past Pres Dem Com of Roan Mtn, Tenn; Past Mem Dem Steering & Wom's Com for Elizabethton; Past Chm Dem Yth for E'ton; Part in E'ton's Closed Tennis Tourn; Am Red Cross Vol; Past Chm VFW's "Voice of Democracy" Oratorical Contest at Roan Mtn; Past Chm Optimist Clb Oratorical Contest;

STRICKLAND, ROBERT MADISON oc/Army Officer; b/June 25, 1943; h/2887 Cela, Memphis, TN 38128; ba/Ft Rucker, AL; m/Linda Lee; c/Robert Madison Jr, James Douglas; p/James Monroe (dec) and Lenora May Strickland, Trout Run, PA; ed/BA Nyack Col 1966; mil/AUS 1967-; pa/Aviator, Ofcr AUS; Assn AUS; US Armor Assn; Army Aviation Assn Am; cp/Hon Order Ky Cols; r/Meth; hon/Dist'd Flying Cross 2 OLC 1970; Bronze Star 1970; Air Medal w V 17 OLC 1969-70; Author "A Captain's View of Decentralized Training" 1975.

STRICKS, RICHARD BERT oc/Attorney at Law; b/June 12, 1951; h/#28 Chatham Dr, New Orleans, LA 70122; ba/New Orleans; m/Rosemary Grenier; p/William and Eva Lesser Stricks, Cinci, OH; ed/Att'd Inter-Am Univ of PR 1969-70; BA Univ Cinci 1973; JD Tulane Univ Sch Law 1976; pa/Admitted to Prac LA 1976; US Dist Ct 1976; US 5th Circuit Ct of Appeals 1978; US Supreme Ct 1980; Am Bar Assn; La St Bar Assn; Assn Trial Lwyrs Am; La Trial Lwyrs Assn; Nat Assn Crim Defense Lwyrs; Nat Assn Social Security; cp/B'nai B'rith; r/Jewish; hon/Guest Lectr, Loyola Univ of New Orleans.

STRINGER, HERMAN E oc/Personnel Manager; b/Aug 22, 1937; h/Cullman, AL; m/Betty Sue Dawson; c/Paul, Suellan, Scott; p/Herman O (dec) and Ester Stringer (dec); ed/Carolina Commun Col; Univ Wis; Wallace St Commun Col; Univ Ala; mil/Ret'd USMC 1954-76 Top Sgt; pa/Pers Mgr; cp/Chm Cullman Dist Job Ser Improvement Prog; Bd Mem Ala St JSIP; Chm Local Commun Relats Org; Comdr Am Legion Post #4, Cullman, Ala; N Ctrl Ala Geneal Soc; Past Mem Cullman Lions Clb; Loyal Order of the Moose; Wallace St Indust Com; ASPA, Decatur Chapt; Cullman Indust Relats Clb; Little Leag Fball & Baseball Coach 15 Yrs; Dist Mbrship Chm BSA; r/St John's U Meth Ch; hon/W/W: Am Jr Col, S&SW; DECCA; 3rd in St of Ala Col Comp for Indust Decision Making.

STRINGFELLOW, MARY ELIZABETH oc/Retired; b/Dec 18, 1912; h/117 Fairlane Cir, Alexande City, AL 35010; m/Louie Damon (dec); p/Lewis Elmer Ellison (dec); Ruth Harris Harshbarger (dec); cp/Red Cross; Heart Assn; Cancer Soc; Commun Chest; Mar of Dimes; Ala Lung Assn; Chm Commun Concerts 1958-59; VP, Recording Secy, Treas, Publicity Chm Xi Xi Chapt Beta Sigma Phi; Publicity Chm, Pres of Preceptor Epsilon Chapt Beta Sigma Phi; RSVP Wkr; Treas Tallapoosa Co Mtl Hlth Chapt 22 Yrs; r/Meth; hon/1 of 25 Outstg Bus Wom, Alexander City Outlook 1974; Miss BPW, BPW Clb 1964-65; Placque for Ser Rendered to St Pres of Ala JCettes 1974-75; Cert of Apprec, Alexander City JCettes 1974-75.

STRIPLING, JOHNNIE RUTH ERVIN oc/Teacher; b/Aug 14, 1944; h/3005 N Whitten Ave, Tyler, TX 75702; m/Aaron J; p/John Henry Ervin, Gilmer, TX; Lela Belle Granville Ervin (dec); ed/BA Tex Col Tyler 1966; MEd N Tex St Univ 1970; Profl Supvrs Cert, N Tex St Univ 1970; pa/Tchr: Goldsberry Elem Sch, Joinerville, Tex 1966-69; Lincoln HS, LaMarque, Tex 1969-70; Boulter Jr HS, Tyler, Tex 1970-72; Part-Time Cnslr, Tyler Jr Col 1978-79; Elem Tchr Whitehouse ISD, Whitehouse, Tex 1972-; NEA; Tex St Tchrs Assn; Smith Co Tchrs Assn; AAUW; Delta Sigma Theta; E Tex Coun Rdg; Intl Rdg Assn; cp/E Tex Chapt Links Inc, Secy; Tyler Org Wom, Pres; N Tyler Br YMCA, Secy; Penny Scramble for Yng Chd Nat Security Bank, Origional Org; Exec Adv Bd Mem Nat Security Bank Tyler; Whitehouse Intermediate PTA, Treas; Tex Col Explorers Clb; N Tex St Univ Alumni Assn; Heroines of Jerico Lodge; r/Bapt; hon/Solfeggio Mus Awd 1965; W/W Tex Ed 1975-76; Outstg Sers to Yth Awd, YMCA 1978-80; Spec Contbr YMCA Awd 1978; Local Tchr of Yr Awd 1969; YMCA 1978-80; Spec Contbr YMCA Awd 1978; Local Tchr of Yr Awd 1969; W/W Outstg Wom Am 1981; Friends of Tex Col Awd 1980.

STROBLE, ROSALIE TIGER oc/Administrative Assistant; b/Feb 12, 1951; h/513 Balto, Muskogee, OK 74401; ba/Muskogee; m/Vernon L Jr; c/Alicia LeAnne, Angela Denise; p/John M and Lucinda L Tiger, Muskogee, OK; ed/BA BA; pa/Acting Dir & Adm Asst, Adm for Native Ams Progs; Okla ANA Dirs Assn; r/Prot; hon/W/W Am Univs & Cols 1977; Alpha Chi; Am Indian Merit Awd 1977; Pi Gamma Mu; Nat Hon Soc, NEn St Univ.

STROBUSH, EARL MORRIS oc/Air Force; b/July 30, 1944; h/40 Brabham Dr, Dalzell, SC 29040; ba/APO NY, NY; m/Pauline Patricia Lee Wallace; p/Russell James Strobush, Racine, WI; Ruby Christine Boyd, Murfreesboro, TN; ed/BS William Carey Col 1978; Non-Com Ofcr Acad 1977; mil/USAF 1963-; pa/Grad Assn Non-Com Ofcr Acad, Shaw Chapt Publicity Chm, Rheinland P Falz Chapt VP; AF Sgts Assn, Life Mem; r/Luth.

STROM, JAMES LEE oc/University Administrator; b/Dec 13, 1933;

PERSONALITIES OF THE SOUTH

h/102 Winchester Ct, Clemson, SC 29631; ba/Clemson; m/Margaret Faye Adams; c/Mark, Stephen, Nancy, Sharon; p/Charles Lee Strom, Charleston, SC; Ruby Jernigan Strom (dec); ed/BSEE Clemson Univ 1956; BBA Augusta Col 1970; PhD Clemson Univ 1975; mil/AUS Signal Corps 1957-59; pa/Aircraft Engr, Lockheed Aircraft Co 1956-57, 59-61; Supvr, Polaris Fire Control, Missile Guidance & Computer Sys, Dept of Navy 1961-64; Sr Res Engr, Contl Grps Inc 1964-67, Mgr Process Control 1967-71; Dir Plan'g & Corp Relats, Ofc of Devel, Clemson Univ 1971-80, Dir Devel 1980-; Exec Dir Clemson Univ Foun 1980-; Editorial Com of Col & Univ Sys Exch 1978-, Chm 1979-; Col & Univ Machine Records 1977-; Col & Univ Sys Exch 1975- Coun Adv & Support of Ed 1973-; Soc for Col & Univ Plan'g 1972-80; Vol Support Com, Nat Assn St Univs & Land Grant Cols 1980-; Nat Assn St Univs & Land Grant Cols 1980-; Prof Mgmt Tri-Co Tech Col 1978-; cp/Great Towns Prog, City of Clemson 1980-, Chm Industs Com 1980-, Sales Team 1980-; Bd Dirs Gtr Clemson Inc 1980-; Bd Dirs Pickens Co U Way 1977-, Budget Com 1977-79; Fin Com Blue Ridge Dist Boy Scouts 1976-79; Bd Dirs Clemson YMCA 1976-, Chm 1976-; Clemson YMCA Prog Com 1975-76; Adv Com of Outdoor Ed-Rec Lab 1978-; SC Appalachian Coun Govts Manpwr Study Com 1973-75; r/Bapt; VChm Bd Deacons, SS Tchr; hon/Grad summa cum laude 1970; W/W S&SW 1980; Num Profl Pubs.

STROUD, JOSEPH CLEVELAND oc/Police Sergeant; b/July 30, 1953; h/3407-H Arnold Ave, Opelika, AL 36801; ba/Auburn, AL; m/Karen A; p/Betty G Stroud, Opelika, AL; ed/Att'g Auburn Univ-Mont; Grad SW Ala Police Acad 1977; Grad Photo-Elec Intoximeter Sch, Dept Public Hlth 1978; pa/Auburn Police Dept, Sgt Uniform Patrol Div; FOP; r/Ch of Christ.

STROUD, STEPHEN DWIGHT oc/Dental Lab Technician; b/Feb 2, 1951; h/LaGrange, NC; ba/LaGrange; m/Janet Herring; c/Stephen Dwight Jr, Amy Nicole; p/Emily Stroud, LaGrange, NC; ed/Att'd Lanier Oral Arts Dental Studio, NC Apprenticeship Coun 1970-75; pa/Proprietor & Oper Quality Ceramic's Dental Lab; Nat Dental Lab Assn; Nat Dental Techs Assn; cp/Master Mason, Lenoir Lodge 233; LaGrange JCs, Treas 1977; LaGrange Rotary Clb; Advtmt Chm Lenoir Co Jr Miss 1979, Chm BSA Troop 114; Lenoir Co Babe Ruth Bd Dirs 1980-83; LaGrange C of C, Bd Dirs; LaGrange Little Leag Baseball, Coach, Dir & Pres 1976-80; La Grange Fball Leag, Fin Chm, Fball Coach 1972, 73; LaGrange Basketball Little Leag Coach 1973, Dir 1980; U Way Campaign for Mosley Hall Twp, Lt 1979; Dir Am Cancer Soc in Mosely Hall Twp 1978, 79; Boy Scout Coor 1970; LaGrange Yth Com 1980-81; r/Meth; hon/Little Brown Jug Awd, Rotarian to Yr 1979; C Kersey Smith Awd, Lenoir Co Unit Am Cancer Soc 1980.

STUBBS, GORDON EUGENE oc/Management Analyst; b/July 21, 1926; h/5414 Juliet St, Springfield, VA 22151; ba/Rockville, MD; m/Ruby Mae Durham; c/Lester Eugene, Gordon William; p/Homer Albert Stubbs (dec); Emily Violet Armstrong (dec); ed/BGS Chaminade Col; MS, PhD Univ Hawaii; MA Ctrl Mich Univ; mil/USAF 1943-46, 51-69; pa/Perf Engr, Adm Mgr, PHS Forms Mgmt Ofcr; Mgmt Analyst, Ofc of Asst Secy for Hlth; cp/Dem Party; r/Bapt; hon/AF Commend Medal; Outstg Achmt Awd; Flying Awd.

STUDSTILL, OWEN LAMAR JR oc/School Psychologist, Teacher, Coach; b/Oct 20, 1955; h/2811 Vineville Ave, Macon, GA 31204; ba/Barnesville, GA; p/Owen L Sr and Doris A Studstill, Macon, GA; pa/Sch Psych, Tchr, Coach, Barnesville Acad; r/Meth; hon/All St, All-Star HS Basketball; Phi Kappa Phi; Col Lttrman Basketball.

STUMP, ROBERT RAY oc/Social Worker; b/Jan 26, 1938; h/400 Biggs Ave, Thomasville, NC 27360; ba/T'ville; m/Phyllis Darlene; c/Gregory, Melissa, Terri; p/Raymond W (dec) and Bernice Stump, Harrisburg, IL; ed/BS Georgetown Col 1960; MRE So Bapt Theol Sem 1964; MSW UNC 1968; pa/Bapt Chd's Homes of NC 17 Yrs; NASW; ACSW; Bd Dirs NC Conf Social Sers; Pres NC Child Care Assn; cp/Lions Clb; Scout Master; rBapt; hon/Columnist for *Charity and Children.*

SUÁREZ, CESÁR-ANTONIO oc/Opera and Concert Artist; b/June 2, 1952; h/811 NW 92nd Ave, Pembroke Pines, FL 33024; ba/Same; m/Geraldine Elizabeth Novack; c/Germaine, Lola-Charmaine, Gina-Lilia; p/Jose M and Dolores Couto Suarez; ed/Cinci Conserv Mus; Temple Univ Col Mus; Brevard Mus Ctr; Grad Giuseppe Verdi Conservatorio Di Milano; Juilliard Sch; pa/Debut L'Elisir D'Amore, Ronizaetti, Hartford, Conn; Operatic Bel Canto Tenor & Concert Artist; Am Guild Mus Artists; hon/S'ship to Univ Cinci Col Conserv of Mus 1968; Local Winner Nat Piano Playing Auditions, Miami, Fla 1969; S'ship Miami Mus Clb 1968-69, 69-70, 70-71, 71-72; S'ship Miami Bch Mus & Arts Leag 1972; Nom'd Cuban Student of Yr 1969; Winner 3rd & 4th Annual Awd, Soc of Yng Perfrs 1969; Mrs Arthur E Burke S'ship 1969 & 70; Cert of Merit for Outstg Accomp 1970; Cert of Merit, Nat Intersch Mus Activs Comm 1969; Metro Opera Auditions, Finalist 1971; Metro Opera Auditions Winner 1972 & 73; Irving Berlin S'ship 1974-75; Rockefeller Foun S'ship 1976; Lila Acheson

Wallace S'ship 1975-76; Am Opera Ctr S'ship 1976-77, 77-78; Nat Opera Inst Grant 1977-78; XIX Concorso Internazionale Giovani Cantanti Lirici 1976.

SUAREZ-DEL CAMPO, RAUL A oc/Architect; h/Mar 3, 1947; h/6950 W 6thSt, Hialeah, FL 33014; ba/Same; m/Lourdes Amparo; c/Raul Antonio, Michael Alexander, Jeannette Marie, Lisa Ann; p/Ramon and Sayda Suarez-Del Campo, Brandon, FL; ed/BA, MArch Wash Univ; pa/Arch Fla & PR 1969-74; Proprietor Raul A Suarez-Del Campo Arch, Miami 1974-; Inspecting Arch Bank of Miami; Pres CONSTAD Corp; Instr Commun Design Wkshop Wash Univ; r/Cath; hon/Cert Nat Coun Arch Reg Bds; W/W Fin & Indust.

SUDDUTH, BETTY JANE oc/Vocational Evaluator; b/June 15, 1930; h/908 Cokesbury Dr, Columbia, SC 29203; ba/Columbia; p/Fred Harold (dec) and Elsie Campbell Sudduth (dec); ed/AA N Greenville Col 1950; BS 1952, MA 1978 Winthrop Col; pa/Tchr Westminster, SC 12 Yrs; Asst Home Demo Agt, Lee Co, SC 3 Yrs; SCSH Evaluator w Voc Rehab 14 Yrs; SC Assn Voc Home Ec Tchrs, Secy 2 Yrs; Columbia Home Ec, Pres 1 Yr; Am Home Ec Assn; SC Home Ec Ass; Nat Rehab Assn; cp/Pilot Clb of Columbia 1967-, SC Dist Lt Gov & Gov; r/Bapt; hon/Nom'd for Spec Awd in Dist Pilot Clb of Columbia; 25 Yr Awd for Tchg SC.

SUGARMAN, BETTY A oc/Social Worker; b/Apr 8, 1945; h/202 NW 26th St, Gainesville, FL 32607; ba/G'ville; p/Seymour and Gladys Packer Sugarman, Fall River, MA; ed/AB Connechut Col; MS Columbia Univ Sch Social Work; pa/Clin Social Wkr, Univ Fla Med Sch, Dept Psychi; Chp Univ Fla Med Sch Interdept Social Work Fac; Conslt Mlt Hlth; Co Appt'd Mem Bd Review Crime Victim Relief Fund; r/Jewish; hon/Fellow Columbia Univ; Author Articles & Pamphlets.

SUITER, LEO FRANK oc/Entertainer; b/Sept 18, 1925; h/27 Andrews Dr, Daleville, AL 36322; m/Alice G; c/Eddie F, Noah M, Robert J; p/Noah Madison Suiter (dec); Myrtle Simpson Suiter Brown (dec); mil/AUS 20 Yrs; pa/Pilot, Fixed & Rotary Wing; Instrm Flight Instr; AUSA; cp/Lions Clb, Secy-Treas, Pres; r/Bapt.

SUITER, ROBERT JAMES oc/Multi-Service Engineer; b/Dec 30, 1958; h/Daleville, AL; c/Maurice E McCollum, John B Bivins; p/Leo F Suiter, Dalesville, AL; Polly M Hardman, Fayetteville, GA; ed/Geo C Wallace Commun Col 1979-81; pa/Multi-Ser Engrg.

SULLIVAN, MARGURETTE oc/Restauranteur; b/May 14, 1932; h/2402 Adams Ct, Samford, FL 32771; m/Robert G; c/Craig Scott, Carla Griffin, G Scott, Pam; p/Allen E Smith; Susie Spivey; pa/Pres & VP Rest Corp; Nat Res Assn; Rltr; r/Bapt; hon/Top 20 Vol Awds, Famous Recipe Last 7 Yrs.

SULLIVAN, ROBERT G (JERRY) oc/Restauranteur; b/Jan 12, 1925; h/2402 Adams Ct, Samford, FL 32771; ba/3 Locations; m/Margurette; c/Craig Scott, Carla Griffin, G Scott, Pam; p/W H Sullivan, Dayton, OH; ed/BS Miami Univ; mil/USN Ret'D Fighter Pilot; pa/Owner & Oper Rest Corp; Nat Rest Assn; Ret'd Ofcrs Assn; cp/C of C; Active Pilot; r/Bapt; hon/Top 20 Vol Awds, Famous Recipe Last 7 Yrs; Var Mil Awds & Medals.

SUMMERS, SALLY WILLIAMS oc/Teacher; b/June 6, 1915; h/157 Combs St, Hazard, KY 41701; ba/AvaWam, KY; m/James B (dec); c/James Lewis, John Hunter, Janet Irene, Margaret Jean; p/Granville Wiliams (dec); Mary Patterson (dec); ed/BA; pa/Elem Sch Tchr; KEA; NEA; Pres Elect PCEA; Bldg Rep Concerns Com; cp/VP Alcoholic Adv Coun; r/Bapt; hon/Outstg Elem Tchr 1974; Personalities of Am.

SUNDERLAND, ZELL ELIZABETH oc/Certified Public Accountant; b/Apr 13, 1941; h/1724 Crestmont Dr, Huntington, WV 25701; ba/H'ton; p/Ernest L (dec) and Anna Elizabeth Billups Sunderland (dec); ed/Marshall Univ; pa/Ptnr Diamond, Sunderland & Co CPAs; Past Pres H'ton Chapt Am Soc Wom Accts; Am Inst CPAs; WV Soc CPAs; Am Woms Soc CPAs; cp/Pilot Clb of H'ton; H'ton Chpat Nat Fed Blind; hon/Lucy E Prichard Awd, Pilot Clb of H'ton 1973.

SURBECK, ELAINE oc/Assistant Professor; b/Dec 30, 1943; h/259 Oak St, Auburn, AL 36830; ba/Auburn; p/Marion and Camilla Moore Surbeck, Cheney, WA; ed/BA Univ Wash 1966; MEd 1971, EdD 1974 Univ Ga; pa/Asst Prof Early Childhood Ed, Auburn Univ 1979-; Tng Coor, Day Care Proj, Dept Human Resources Grant, Univ Ga 1978-79; Vis Asst Prof, Early Childhood Ed, Univ Ga 1977-79; Asst Prof, Child Devel, Dept Home Ec, Ariz St Univ 1975-78; Coor, Child Devel Lab, Asst Prof Child Devel, Dept Home Ec, Ariz St Univ 1975-78; Tchg Asst to Dr Keith Osborn, Univ Ga 1972-73; NAEYC Annual Conf Discussion Ldr 1972; Tchg Asst, Early Childhood Ed, Univ Ga 1971-72; Student Tchr Supvr, Early Childhood Level, Univ Ga 1971-73; Conslt to Hd Start Ctr, Athens, Ga 1971-72; Discussion Ldr, Hd St Wkshops 1971-72; Kindergarten Tchr,

PERSONALITIES OF THE SOUTH

Edmonds Sch Dist 1966-69; Conslt: Toledo & Ga "Learning to Learn" Tchr Ed Proj 1977-79; Manuscript Reviewer, Wadsworth Pub Co, Infancy & Early Childhood Devel 1977-; Book Reviewer for Childhood Ed 1976-; Colloquium Mem, "Learning to Learn" Inc 1974-; Soc for Res in Child Devel; Val of Sun Assn for Ed of Yng Chd; Phi Delta Kappa; Phi Kappa Phi; Kappa Delta Pi; Nat Assn Ed of Yng Chd; Assn Childhood Ed Intl; r/Luth; hon/Phi Kappa Phi; W/W Am Wom; Author/Co-Author Num Profl Pubs.

SUTHERLAND, PEARL ROSE RADICE oc/Human Resources Officer; b/Apr 4, 1935; m/Alex T; c/Helen Marie Dube, Patricia Anne Petersen, Gerard Allen; p/Gerald and Ida Gloria Rose, NY, NY; ed/AS 1975; BS 1977; MBA 1979; pa/Purchasing Mgr 1974-77, Pers Mgr 1977-; Am Soc Pers Admrs; Am Bus Woms Assn; cp/Holy Fam Cath Sch Bd 1977-78; Secy Latin Affairs Com N Miami Bch; Am Red Cross Vol; Heart Sun Vol; Holy Fam Stewardship Com, Co-Chm; Comm Outreach; r/Cath; hon/Cert of Apprec, City of N Miami Bch; Article Pub'd 1977; Fla Soc Pub'd Poets 1978.

SUTTON, BOBBY GENE oc/Detective; b/Aug 3, 1950; h/Woodward, OK; ba/1220-9th, Woodward, OK 73801; m/Susan R; p/Carl A (dec) and Georgia R Sutton; ed/BS NWn Okla St Univ 1976; Num Law Enforcement Tng Dips; mil/AUS 1970-72; Okla ANG 1974-76; pa/Woodward Police Dept: Patrolman 1976-80, Detective 1980-; r/Prot.

SUTTON, DORIS GREENE oc/Associate Professor; b/June 11, 1935; h/5 Governor's Manor, Richmond, KY 40475; ba/Richmond; c/Charles William; p/Kenneth Clarence Greene, Orange Pk, FL; Jamie Stacey Miller, Lexington, KY; ed/AB Georgetown Col 1956; MA 1966, PhD 1973, Post Doct Study 1977 Univ Ky; pa/Assoc Prof Eng, En Ky Univ; Exec Com Conf on Col Composition & Commun; Chm Nat Task Force on Testing in Eng; NCTE; Pres EKU Fac Clb; EKU Ath Com; cp/Commun Vol, US Bur Prisons; r/Prot; hon/Ky Col 1980; W/W S&SW 1980; Author 12 Profl Jour Articles 1973-79.

SUTTON, NEEL MURRAY oc/Beauty Consultant; b/June 25, 1939; h/14551F Old Courthouse Way, Newport News, VA 23602; ba/Same; m/Donald Vaughan; c/Andrew Meserve Rankin, Christopher Murray Rankin; p/William Benton and Marie Neel Murray, Bridgeport, CT; ed/Am Airlines Stewardess Col 1959-60; Att'd Univ Bridgeport 1957-59; Dale Carnegie Course 1976; pa/Sales & Bus Owner, Spic & Span Sers Inc 1975-80; Profl Beauty Conslt, Mary Kay Cosmetics; Reach for Recovery; hon/Future Dir Mary Kay Cosmetics 1981; Semi-Annual Unit Queen of Sales, Mary Kay Cosmetics 1980.

SWAGGERTY, GLENN O oc/Pastor, College President; b/May 7, 1940; h/Rossville, GA; m/Geneva; c/Steven Glenn, Kimberly Ann, Randall Wade; p/Henry M and Evelyn E Swaggerty, Ross, GA; ed/ThB; ThM; DDiv; pa/Pres Bible Col & Sem; Pastor; Nat Clergy Assn; Chattanooga Area Coun; Rossville Area Coun; cp/C of C; Rossville C of Coun; r/Full Gospel; hon/Hon Awd for Writing; Author 4 Unpub'd Books.

SWAIM, GARY D oc/Communications Chairman; b/Nov 17, 1934; h/524 Campana G, Irving, TX 75061; ba/Irving; m/Mary L; c/Don, Steve; p/Glyn D and Juanita J Swaim, San Bernardino, CA; ed/BA Univ Calif-Riverside 1966; PhD Univ Redlands 1971; pa/Acad Admr, Prof, Univ Redlands 1966-69; Asst Dean - Dean of Undergrad Studies, Univ Redlands 1973-79; Div Chm Communs & Humanites, N Lake Col 1979-; Conf on Christianity & Lit; MLA; cp/Dem Party; US Tennis Assn; Bd Mem Cultural Affairs Coun; Irving Symph Assn; r/Ch of Christ; Elder; hon/Outstg Edr Am 1975; W/W S&SW 1980.

SWANSON, DAVID ALLEN oc/Attorney; b/Aug 28, 1954; h/Raleigh, NC; ba/325 N Salisbury St, Raleigh, NC 27611; p/J Howard and Eva Blair Swanson, Lenoir, NC; ed/AB UNC-CH 1977; JD Campbell Univ Sch of Law 1980; Admitted to NC Bar 1980; pa/Atty w NC Dept Human Resources; Counsel to Gov's Task Force on Waste Mgmt; NC Bar Assn; Am Bar Assn; cp/UNC Gen Alumni Assn; Delta Upsilon; Delta Theta Phi; 2nd VP Wake Co Yng Dems; Pres UNC Yng Dems; Pres Campbell Yng Dems; Secy NC Col Dems; NC Dem St Exec Com; hon/Outstg Yng Men Am 1979; Order of the Old Well; Gov's Crime Preven & Public Info Com; 1 of 5 Most Outstg Col Dems in NC 1976; Outstg Col Dem in NC 1978; Author 1981 Yng Dem NC Org Handbook; Author Org Handbook for NC Col Dems 1977; Author 1980 Yng Dem NC Leg Issues Package.

SWANSON, J HOWARD oc/Accountant; b/1937 Swan Dr SW, Lenoir, NC 28645; ba/Lenoir; m/Eva Blair; c/David A, Gary L, Mary Ann; p/John Newland Swanson (dec); Ella Deal Ferguson (dec); ed/Att'd Lenoir-Rhyne Col 19450-41; pa/Treas & Dir Appalachian Poster Advtg Co Inc; NC Soc Accts; cp/Hibriten Masonic Lodge; Mem & Secy Caldwell Co Bd Ed; Former Mem Caldwell Co Dem Exec Com; r/Bapt; hon/Past Pres NC Region Antique Auto Clb of Am; Past Pres & Present Dir NC Region Horseless Carriage Clb of Am; Pres NC Folk & Square Dance Fed NC.

SWEARENGEN, GEARETHA PEARL oc/Teacher; b/Nov 22, 1951; h/Oakland, MS; m/Jimmie Lee Sr; c/Romericus Taylor, Jimmitte and Gearetha, Jimmie Lee Jr; p/William and Jessie Mae Swain Pearl, Natchez, MS; ed/BS Alcorn St Univ 1972; pa/Spec Ed Tchr, Oakland Elem Sch; r/Bapt; hon/Sch Awds.

SWEENEY, JAMES EDWARD oc/Air Force Officer; b/July 6, 1950; h/Clearfield, UT; p/Howard and Margie Mae Swain Sweeney, Detroit, MI; ed/BS En Mich Univ 1975; MA Univ No Colo 1979; Grad USAF Ofcrs Tng Sch 1977; pa/USAF Commun-Elec Ofcr; Armed Forces Communs & Elecs Assn; Captians & Lts Coun, Recorder; r/Prot; hon/Am Legion Sch Awd 1965; Charles Palmer Davis Current Events Awd 1965; Highest Hon Grad Cass Tech HS 1969; Hon Grad Chanute Tech Tng Ctr 1969; Hon Student En Mich Univ 1973-75; Air Force Commend Medal 1979.

SWEET, WORTH ALFRED SR oc/Clergyman; b/June 26, 1914; h/263 Kerr St NW, Concord, NC 28025; ba/Concord; m/Rachel W; c/Worth Alfred Jr, Charlie S, Edward F; p/George Edward (dec) and Julia Westmoreland Sweet (dec); ed/Pfeiffer Jr Col 1942; Appalachian St Univ 1946; Candler Sch Theol, Emory Univ 1952; pa/Clergyman U Meth Ch, Wn NC Conf; Pres WNCC Meth Credit Union 1949-; Secy Meth Rural F'ship 1948; Pres Meth Rural F'ship 1952-53; Pres Concord Min Assn 1955; Pres Salisbury Min Assn 1957; Pres Ramseur Min Assn 1961; Pres Salisbury Brotherhood Coun 1958; Secy WNCC Bd Christian Social Concerns 1964; Treas WNCC Bd Christian Social Concerns 1965-72; Mem of Exec Com WNCC Bd Pensions 1972-80; Pres Hudson Commun Devel Assn 1969-71; cp/Pres Elect Jefferson Rotary Clb 1980; r/Meth.

SWEETEN, JESS oc/Sheriff, Special Investigator; b/May 7, 1905; h/Caldwell, TX; m/Hazel; c/Jessie Nell, Peggy Ann Durham; p/John and Nellie Davis Sweeten; pa/Sheriff Henderson Co, Tex 20 Yrs; Spec Investigator, Mobil Oil Co 15 Yrs; r/Bapt.

SWINDALL, MARGARET LEE oc/Teacher; b/Aug 20, 1927; h/PO Box 27, Goodwater, AL 35072; m/John L; c/Laura Lee S West, Margie; p/P N and Robbie Hardy Davis; ed/BS Auburn Univ 1953; Masters Univ Ala-B'ham 1980; pa/Elem Sch Tchr, Goodwater Elem Sch; pa/AEA; Coosa Co Ed Assn; NEA; cp/Ala Cowbell Assn; Pres Coosa Co Cowbells; Delta Kappa Gamma, VP & Chm Num Coms; r/Presb; Chm Presb Cir; hon/Kappa Delta Pi.

SWOFFORD, JOHN DOUGLAS oc/Director of Athletics; b/Dec 6, 1948; h/Chapel Hill, NC; ba/PO Box 3000, Carmichael Auditorium, Chapel Hill, NC 27514; m/Rebecca; c/Autumn, Chad; p/Helen Swofford, N Wilkesboro, NC; ed/AB UNC-CH 1971; MEd Ohio Univ 1973; pa/UNC-CH: Dir Aths 1980-, Asst Dir Aths 1976-80; Ath Ticket Mgr, Univ Va 1973-76; Nat Assn Col Dirs Aths; Nat Assn Ath Fundraisers; Col Ath Bus Mgrs Assn, Bd Dirs; Ohio Univ Ath Adm Masters Deg Prog Exec Bd; US Intercol Lacrosse Assn; cp/E Chapel Hill Rotary Clb, Treas & Prog Com Mem; Adm Bd Univ U Meth Ch; Div Chm Chapel Hill U Way 1978; r/Prot; hon/W/W Col Aths 1970; Phi Delta Theta; Pres F'ship Christian Aths; Guest Lectr, Col Ath Bus Mgrs Assn Nat Conv 1978.

SWYGERT, ANNIE LEE oc/Plumber; b/Oct 14, 1911; h/Rt 1 Box 144, Prosperity, SC 29127; ba/Prosperity; m/William Kenneth (dec); p/Bunard Leroy (dec) and Annie Maude Shealy (dec); pa/St Lic'd Plumbing Contractor; Co-Ptnr & Mgr: Swaggert's Plumbing & Swaggert's Florist; Nat Assn PHCC; Nat Wom's Aux Profl Dealers Assn; cp/Write Your Cong-man Clb; Right to Work Com; Nat Trust for Hist Preserv; Cancer Vol; Newberry Co Beautification Com; Recording Secy Newberry BPW Clb; Azalea Gdn Clb; r/Luth; SS Tchr, Chp Cir #2 LCW; hon/Career Wom 1978; 30 Yr LCW Pin; W/W SC 1974; Outstg Am in S 1975; Personalities of the S 1976-77; Intl W/W Commun Ser 1979.

291

PERSONALITIES OF THE SOUTH

T

TABER, WILLIAM RHETT JR oc/Trust Banking; b/Mar 18, 1947; h/1515 Nuuanu Ave, Queen Tower #100, Honolulu, HI 96817; ba/Honolulu; m/Linda E; p/William Rhett and Margaret M Taber, Bradenton, FL; ed/BA The Citadel; Att'd Univ Fla Trust Sch & NWn Univ Trust Sch; MBA Pepperdine Univ; mil/USAR Capt; pa/Bishop Trust Co; Hawaii Est Plan'g Coun; Command & Gen Staff Col, AUS; Fla Real Est Lic; cp/Pvt Pilot's Lic; Past Boy Scout Master; r/Epis; hon/Pres Awd; Army Commend Medal; Pub of NWn Univ Thesis by Am Bankers Assn.

TABOR, ALFRED DONALD oc/Insurance Salesman; b/Mar 6, 1929; h/Sanford, FL; ba/PO Box 994, Sanford, FL 32771; m/Eula L; c/Ivan P; p/dec; ed/Att'd Rollins Col 1977, Ctrl Fla Bible Col 1978; mil/USN 1950-54; pa/Profl Fund Raising for Cols 1954-61; Life Ins Salesman, NY Life 1961-; Seminole Co Life Ins Assn, Pres 1970-71; cp/Rotary Clb; r/Christian Ch; hon/Ky Col 1973; Million Dollar Round Table.

TAFFEE, WILLIAM FRANCES JR oc/Engineering Specialist; b/May 22, 1922; h/Anniston, AL; m/Lois Luedders; c/Kathleen, Patricia, Mary, Beth; p/William F Taffee Sr (dec); Pearl L Wildt (dec); ed/BS 1948, MS 1948 Mich St Univ; mil/USAF Air Transp Command 3 Yrs; pa/Engrg Spec Monsanto Co; cp/Anniston Commun Theater Bd of Dirs; Civitan Bd; K of C, Ala St Dpty; r/Cath; Ordained Perm Deacon for Diocese of B'ham, Ala.

TAGLIARINI, JOHN ALDEN oc/Teacher; b/Aug 28, 1952; h/5928 E Hilltop Ln, Lakeland, FL 33801; ba/L'land; m/Patricia Rose; c/Jennifer Michele, Gianna Paige; p/Salvatore and Mary I Tagliarini, Tampa, FL; ed/BA Vocal Mus Ed; MMus Choral Conducting; pa/Vocal Mus Tchr; Dist V Fla Vocal Assn; Adjudicator Hillsborough Co Jr High Fests 1978, 79; cp/Mus Dir Webster Meml Bapt Ch; r/Bapt; hon/Nancy Mayo Awd, Univ So Fla 1974; Pres Upsilon Psi Chapt Phi Mu Alpha; Pres Student MENC Chapt.

TALBOT, FREDERICK HILBORN oc/Bishop; b/Oct 13, 1927; h/Atlanta, GA; ba/208 Auburn Ave, Atlanta, GA 30303; m/Sylvia Ross; p/(dec); ed/BA cum laude Allen Univ; MDiv Yale Univ Div Sch; STM Pacific Sch of Rel; DHum Wilberforce Univ, Allen Univ, Morris Brown Col; pa/Presidig Bishop, AME Ch, Ga; cp/NAACP; r/AME Ch.

TALBOT, GWENDOLYN EDITH oc/Pathologist; Executive; b/Oct 6, 1946; h/8222 Wycliffe Ct, Manassas, VA 22110; ba/Manassas; p/Charles Robert II and Eleanor Marion Morse Talbot, Chelmsford, MA; ed/BA 1969, MA 1971 Univ Ariz; Post Grad Study Pima Col 1971; Cert Clin Competence in Speech-Lang Pathol 1972, Am Speech-Lang-Hearing Assn; pa/Pres Speech Pathol Conslt Sers 1976-; Conslt Speech-Lang Pathol: Prince William Hosp, Manassas, Va 1973-; Potomac Hosp, Woodbridge, Va 1974-; Prince William Co Hlth Dept 1975-; Fdr, Pres Chronic Pain Outreach 1976-; Conslt Speech-Lang Pathol: Mt Vernon Nsg Ctr, Alexandria, Va 1978-; Manassas Manor Nsg & Convalescent Ctr 1973-; Iliff Nsg Ctr, Fairfax, Va 1980-; Mar-Salle Nsg Ctr, Inc, Wash DC 1980-; Upper Rappahanock Area Hlth Dept, Fredericksburg, Va 1976-; Bur of Crippled Chd & Adults 1976-; Chief Exec Ofcr, Incorporator, Rehab Day Ctrs Inc 1980-; Am Speech-Lang-Hearing Assn; Intl Assn Logopedics & Phoniatrics; Speech & Hearing Assn of Va; Sigma Alpha Eta, Pres 1969; cp/Prince William Co Child Abuse Steering Com 1976-78; Manassas Pk Sch Sys Spec Ed Adv Bd 1977-; Bd Dirs Am Cancer Soc 1975-; Speech Pathol, New Voice Clb of No Va of ACS 1973-77; Bd Dirs Manassas Area Assn Retard'd Citizens 1976-; Pres Wheelchair Sports Devel Progs for No Va 1979-; Instr in CPR, Water Safety & First Aid, Am Red Cross; EMT 1971-; Chapt Hd, Prince William Co Nat Jr Tennis Leag 1976-77, Fin Chm 1977-79; Soroptimist Intl Clb of Manassas 1974-; Treas, Mbrship Chm 1974-; Jr Wom's Clb of Manassas, Mbrship Chm, Mtl Hlth & Mtl Retard Del, Hlth Fair Chm, Public Affairs Dept Chm; DAR 1965-; r/Meth; hon/Recip Dist'd Ser Commend Tucson-Pima Co Civil Defense Comm for Search & Rescue Opers 1973; First Major, Lowell HS Regiment of Girl Ofcrs, Comm'd 1963; Sigma Alpha Eta, Key Mbrship 1969; Cert of Clin Competence, Am Speech-Lang-Hearing Assn 1972; WW S&SW 1980-81; Ofcr of Ed Grant, Univ Ariz 1969; Contbr to The Politics of Pain 1978.

TALIAFERRO, WILLIAM oc/Professor; b/Aug 16, 1933; h/227 W Castle Harbour, Friendswood, TX 77546; ba/Alvin; m/Pamela Sue Bryen; c/Beth, Dan, Rose, Ben; p/Ben Seaborn and Willie Mae Sasser Taliaferro, Arlington, GA; ed/AA Chipola Jr Col 1951; BA Univ Fla 1953; MS Fla St Univ 1968; EdD Univ Houston 1979; mil/USAF 1953-75 Ret'd Col; pa/Mil Ofcr; Prof of Polit Sci; Am Ed Res Assn; Tex Jr Col Tchrs Assn; Alvin Commun Col Tchrs Assn; cp/Kiwanis; Scottish Rite of Freemasonry; 32° Mason; Lion; Arnold Air Soc; r/Bapt; hon/Air Force Commend Medal 1968 & 68; Arnold Air Soc Gold Medal 1968; Dist'd Flying Cross 1969; Air Medal w 6 OLC 1969; S Vietnam Cross of Gallentry 1970; AF Merit Ser

Medal 1975; 14 Other Mil Medals & Awds 1953-75; Recog'd by Gov Dale Bumpers of Ark for Outstg Ser to St 1970; Awd'd Hon Ark Traveller 1971; Author Num Profl Articles; Book *A Historical Study of Campus Governance, Tenure and Salaries in Public Two-Year Colleges in Texas* 1979.

TALLANT, BILLY FRANK oc/Welder; b/Feb 5, 1933; h/Pursley, TX; ba/Rt 1, Purdon, TX 76679; m/Louise Murchison; c/Billy Jr, Jimmy, Mary, David; p/James Frank (dec) and Annie Eula Ray Tallant, Corsicana, TX; pa/Artifact Soc; Navarro Co Hist Soc; cp/Navarro Co Geneal Soc; r/Ch of Christ.

TALLEY, WALTER REED oc/Attorney at Law; b/Mar 3, 1925; h/Bradenton, FL; ba/410 12th St W, Bradenton, FL 33505; m/Donna Lee; c/Walter R Jr, Alex R, Daniel Lee; p/Walter Russell (dec) and Ruth R Talley, Bradenton, FL; ed/BA Univ NC 1949; Att'd Univ Fla 1967; Acad Fla Trial Lwyrs 1963; mil/USMC 1942-46, 1950-52 Capt; pa/Trial Lwyr; Manatee Co Bar Assn; Fla Bar Assn; St of Fla Public Defenders Assn, Past Pres; Manatee Co Prosecuting Atty 1956-60; Public Defender, 12th Judicial Circuit of Fla 1964-70; Former City Judge for Anna Maria, Holmes Bch & Bradenton Bch 1960-70; cp/Bradenton Kiwanis Clb, Dir; Manatee Co Bar Assn, Past Pres; r/Epis.

TALLEY, WILLIAM WOODROW II oc/Energy Management Consultant; b/Aug 17, 1942; h/1701 Huntingtn, Okla City, OK 73116; ba/Okla City; m/Sandra S; c/Britani Suzanne, Kimberly V; p/William Woodrow and Jacquita Elizabeth Talley, Hobart, OK; ed/BS 1964, MS 1971, PhD 1973 Univ Okla; mil/USN Nuclear Sub Ofcr; pa/Mng Ptnr, Resource Analysis & Mgmt Grp 1976-; Co-Chm Okla Adv Coun on Energy 1975-; Energy Mgmt & Fuels Technol to Sev Cos & Govt Agcys 1969-; Am Chem Soc; AIChE; Am Nuclear Soc; Fdg Mem Am Nuclear Soc, Nuclear Process Heat Application Com; Inst Nuclear Mats Mgmt; cp/Bd Dirs Allied Arts Foun; Bd Dirs Frontiers of Sci Foun; Bd Dirs Okla Symph Orch; r/Epis; hon/Author Num Profl Pubs.

TAN, BILLY TOO SENG oc/Instructor, Accountant; b/July 22, 1954; h/3238 Carlotta St, Baton Rouge, LA 70802; ba/Baton Rouge; p/Hong San Tan and Siew Huay Khoo, Johor, Malaysia; ed/BS magna cum laude So Univ 1976; MBA La St Univ 1978; pa/Instr So Univ; Acct Harris & Harrisson CPAs; Mgr E St Rental; Nat Acctg Assn; hon/W/W Students in Am Univs & Cols 1975-76; Tough Minded Bus Awd 1974, Gold Awd 1975, SWn Co.

TANNER, GLORIA ANN oc/Professor of Nursing, Acting Dean; b/Dec 18, 1931; h/Seneca, SC; ba/532 Col of Nsg Bldg, Clemson Univ, Clemson, SC 29631; p/Hillman B and Gladys McK Tanner, Seneca, SC; ed/Dip St Joseph's Infirm 1952; BSN Mt St Agnes Col 1956; MS Univ Md 1964; EdD Tchrs Col, Columbia Univ 1974; pa/Clemson Univ: Acting Dean Col of Nsg 1980-, Dir Nsg Res 1979-, Asst to Dean for Res Devel, Col of Nsg 1977-79, Assoc Prof Col of Nsg 1974-75, Asst Prof Col of Nsg 1952-71; ANA; ANA Coun of Nurse Resrs; NLN; AAUP; Am Heart Assn; Hlth Care Adv Bd of SC Dept Hlth & Envirl Control; St-wide Master Plan'g Com on Nsg Ed; SC Comm on Higher Ed 1980-81; Cont'g Ed & Recog Prog Com SCNA 1974-78; Nsg Ed Com, SC Heart Assn 1974-77; So Regional Ed Bd, Liaison Com, Demo Projs in Grad Ed 1978-79; Coun on Col Ed for Nsg 1980; r/Cath; hn/Phi Lambda Theta; Sigma Theta Tau; Fac Res Grant 1978-79; W/W S&SW 1980-81; USPHS Profl Nurse Traineeship 1962, 71; Author Sev Articles in Profl Jours.

TANNER, WALLACE DEWEY oc/Retired; b/Aug 22, 1898; h/Athens, TX; m/May Sue Stout; c/Margie Ethalee T Smith, Daluh Dean T Wyrick, Douglas Woodrow, Mary Doyle T Houston; p/John Monroe (dec) and Mollie Mary Freshour Tanner (dec); pa/Ret'd Auto Salesman & Cattle Trader; cp/Pres E Tex Singers 11 Yrs; Pres Athens Courthouse Singing Class; r/First Christian Ch; hon/Outstg Truck Salesman for Chevrolet 1961.

TATRO, ETHEL HELEN oc/Educator; b/Sept 14, 1933; h/3058 Westwood Ct, Augusta, GA 30909; ba/Augusta; m/Jack C; c/Audrey, David, Jack; p/Carl (dec) and Florence Rang, W Palm Bch, FL; ed/RN; PhD; pa/Nurse Edr, Med Col of Ga; Chm Adult Nsg; r/Luth; hon/Sigma Theta Tau; Phi Beta Kappa; Sigma Xi; Kappa Delta Pi.

TAYLOR, BETTY ANN oc/Nurse; b/Oct 4, 1940; h/Rt 1 Box 55, Independence, VA 24348; ba/Galax; m/Ray; c/James Edward, John Wesley; p/Clarence James and Dorothy Turner Cobb, Franklin, VA; pa/RN; Supvr Post Anesthesia Recovery Unit, Twin Co Commun Hosp 1979-; Dir Nurses, Twin Co Commun Hosp 1975-78; Mem AORN; Past Mem: VNA, ANA, Coun of Nsg Ser Facilitators; cp/Cert'd CPR Instr, Am Heart Assn 1974-81; r/Bapt; hon/W/W Am Wom 1978-79; Plaque in Recog of Contbns to LPN Progs in Area 1978.

TAYLOR, BOBBY R oc/Minister; b/Aug 9, 1947; h/Rt 6 Box 147-A,

292

Greenville, NC 27834; m/Audrey Brewington; c/Stephen Ray; p/Monford Taylor, Columbia, NC; Sylvia Hollis Taylor (dec); ed/AS Mt Olive Col; BA Atlantic Christian Col; mil/USN 1968; pa/Min; Pres NC St Leag Conv; Dir Christian Cadet Conf; Pres Free Will Bapt F'ship; cp/Chm Pitt Co Dinner, Mt Olive Col 1979, 80; r/Free Will Bapt; hon/Outstg Yng Men Am 1979.

TAYLOR, BOBBY RAY oc/Personnel Supervisor; b/Aug 3, 1933; h/PO Box 455, Pikeville, NC 27863; m/Hortense Boutwell; p/John David Taylor, McComb, MS; Cora Hale Taylor (dec); ed/AA Copiah-Lincoln Jr Col 1954; BS Univ So Miss 1956; mil/USNR 1956-62; pa/Pers Supvr, MacMillan Bloedel Containers; Mem & Past Pres SW Miss Mgmt Assn; cp/Past Mem: Summit Rotary Clb (Past Pres), McComb C of C, JSIP (Past Dist Rep), Pacesetter Div U Way (Past Chm), SW Miss Jr Col Voc Improvement Com (V-Chm); r/Bapt; hon/Voted Most Versatile HS Class of 1952; Mgr of Mfg Fac Receiving Sears Symbol of Excell Awd 1973, 74, 75; Ser Above Self Awd, Summit Rotary 1977; Paul Harris Fellow Awd, Rotary Intl 1980.

TAYLOR, C PAT oc/Associate Academic Dean; b/Dec 10, 1945; h/27 Windale, Jackson, TN 38301; ba/Jackson; m/Judith C; c/Marijo, Charla; p/Charles A and Georgia Taylor, Salem, KY; ed/BS Univ Tenn-Martin 1968; MA Wn Ky Univ 1971; EdD Memphis St Univ 1975; pa/Assoc Adac Dean, Union Univ; Assn Tchr Edrs; Kappa Delta Pi; Tenn Coun SS; cp/Dem Party; r/So Bapt; Deacon, SS Tchr; hon/Outstg Prof of Yr Awd, Belmont Col 1977-78; W/W S 1979.

TAYLOR, DORIS WRIGHT-HARRIS oc/Resource Specialist/Diagnostician; b/Jan 7, 1923; h/614 Sligo Ave #201, Silver Spring, MD 20910; ba/Wash DC; p/Ernest Wright (dec); Delilah M Cook, Wash DC; ed/BS Miner Tchrs Col 1946; MS Gallaudet Col 1961; Further Study: Univ Redlands, Univ Calif, Univ Neb, Geo Wash Univ, DC Tchr Col; pa/Spec Ed Tchr, Garrison Elem Sch, DC Public Schs 1976-; Asst Prof Ed, Bowie St Col 1971-75; cp/Mem Conf of Execs of Am Schs for the Deaf Inc; Past Pres, Secy, Dean of Pledges, Phi Sigma Phi; Assn Chd w Lrng Disabilities, Wash DC Chapt; Nat Coun Adm Wom in Ed; Nat Coun Negro Wom; First Anti-Basileus, Phi Delta Kappa, Beta Chapt 1971-72; Former Mem Num Orgs & Coms; hon/Cert of Apprec for Vol Sers, 12th St YMCA 1949; Hon Student Atlantic Bus Col 1951; Intl Coop Adm Ser Awd, US Govt 1959; Govt Grant to Attend Univ Neb 1966; Cert of Apprec, DC Assn Deaf 1967; Cert for Part, Phi Delta Kappa Wkshop "Spec Ed" 1973; Cert Apprec, Vol Corps, Prince Georges Co Schs 1973; Cert for Part, Phi Delta Kappa Wk "Think Metric" 1974; Personalities of S 1974; Cert for Part Phi Delta Kappa Wkship "Making Social Studies Come Alive" 1975; Personalities of the S, Bicent Ed 1975-76; Cert for Part, Phi Delta Kappa Wkshop "Better Ideas in Ed" 1977; Author Sev Profl Articles.

TAYLOR, ELLEN BORDEN BROADHURST oc/Volunteer Worker in Preservation and Beautification Projects; b/Jan 18, 1913; h/616 Hancock St, Smithfield, NC 27577; m/Marvin E; c/Marvin E Jr, Jack Borden, William L; p/Jack Johnson Broadhurst (dec); Mabel Moran Borden (dec); ed/Converse Col; cp/Past Mem Govs Adv Com on Beautification; Dir "Keep NC Beautiful Inc"; Past Mem Bd Govs Elizabethan Gdn, Manteo, NC; Life Mem: Gdn Clb of NC Inc, Nat Coun of St Gdn Clbs Inc, NC Art Soc, Soc of Mayflower Descs in St of NC; Nat Soc Colonial Dames of Am in St of NC; Nat Coun St Gdn Clb Inc; Reg Roadsides Rep, Action Com for Envir, Judge of Flower Shows; Past Mem Steering Com to Form Jt Lib for Town of Smithfield & Johnston Co, Later Mem Bldg Com; Past Chm Lib Bd Trustees; Charter Mem: Smithfield Gdn Clb, Johnston Co Hist Soc, Johnston Co Geneal Soc, NC Geneal Soc; Past Pres Smithfield Gdn Clb; Steering Com for Smithfield's Bicent; Charter Mem & VRegent Smith-Bryan Chapt, Nat Soc DAR, Org'd as Bicent Proj in 1976; r/Smithfield St Paul's Epis Ch; Former SS Tchr; hon/Chm Local Com that Pub'd Jtly w NC Dept Cultural Resources "An Inventory of Historic Architecture, Smithfield, NC" 1977.

TAYLOR, GEORGE ARTHUR oc/Economist; b/May 6, 1942; h/Lake of the Woods, Box 318, Locust Grove, VA 22508; ba/Wash DC; m/Cynthia Caren; p/Raymond and Dorthy Taylor, Cinci, OH; ed/BA, MA, PhD Ohio St Univ; mil/USAF 1960-63, 1967-68 Major; pa/Am Mktg Assn; So Ec Assn; Nat Assn Bus Ed; cp/Repub Party; r/Epis; hon/Silver Star; Purple Heart.

TAYLOR, JoANN GILBERT oc/Home Economist; b/Nov 5, 1938; h/2703 Hundred Oaks, Ruston, LA 71270; ba/Ruston; m/Richard Earl; c/Linda Gray T Wilson; p/Arvel and Nellie R Gilbert, Marion, LA; ed/BS NE La St Univ 1959; MS La Tech Univ 1966; pa/La St Univ Ext Ser: Asst Home Ec, W Carroll Parish 1961-62, Asst-Assoc Home Ec, Lincoln Parish 1962-69, Area Clothing Agt, Lincoln & Jackson Parishes 1979-; Am Home Ec Assn; La Home Ec Assn; Nat Asn Ext Home Ecs; Regional Dir La Assn Ext Home Ecs; Epsilon Sigma Phi; cp/Pres Ruston Quota Clb 1976-77, 77-78; Dist Gov Quota Intl Inc 1978-79; r/Bapt; hon/Comm'd as Col on Staff of La Gov Edwards 1979; W/W Am Wom 1981-82.

TAYLOR, JOHN MICHAEL oc/Director of Public Utilities, City Engineer; b/Aug 25, 1950; h/Henderson, NC; ba/City of Henderson, PO Box 1434, Henderson, NC 27536; m/Judy Ann; p/June Mason and Kathleen W Taylor, High Point, NC; ed/AAS Guilford Tech Inst 1971; pa/City Engr, City of Henderson; New Hanover Co 1978-80; PJ Coble Construction Co 1977-78; Construction Supt, Broad St Mini-Mall, Beaman's Projs Inc 1977; SB Simmons Grading & Construction Co 1976-77; Davis-Martin & Assocs 1972-76; Civil Engrg Tech, NC Dept Transp 1970-72; R D Tillson & Assocs 1969-70; Am Water Works Assn; NC Water Works Opers Assn; r/Meth; hon/Accepted to Study & Acquire Degrees after Intensive Consultation.

TAYLOR, KENNETH BYRON oc/Dean; b/Aug 22, 1927; h/Phil Campbell AL; ba/NW Ala St Jr Col; Rt w Box 48, Phil Campbell, AL; m/Willene; c/Kenneth B Jr, Patrick Randall, Ronald Dale (dec); p/H B and Lottie Mae Taylor, Phil Campbell, AL; ed/BS 1952, MA 1955, EdS 1971 Univ Ala; mil/Field Artillery 1945-46; pa/Dean NW Ala St Jr Col 1965-; Trustee Walker Co Tchrs Assn 1964-65; Pres NW Ala St Jr Col 1969-; Winston Co Tchrs Assn 1955-56; cp/Lions Clb; Intl Relation Clb, Pres Local Chapt; r/Bapt; hon/W/W Am Cols & Univ Adm 1970-71; Author Ednl Prog at NW Ala St Jr Col 1970-71.

TAYLOR, LAUREN ALLANA HOLLEY oc/Social Service Director, Consultant; b/Sept 10, 1948; h/Balto, MD; m/Wayman Woodland; c/Stephanie Lynn Coleman, Amber Danette; p/Winston Willouby Holley, Norfolk, VA; Mary E Shaw, Balto, MD; ed/BS Morgan St Univ 1976; MA Antioch Univ 1978; pa/Mgmt Tnr & Conslts Inc: Dir, Conslt in Mtl Hlth, Fam Cnslr; Supvr, Am Red Cross, Balto Chapt; cp/Asst Coor Min for Aged New Life Missionary Bapt; r/Bapt; hon/W/W Am Wom 1981-82; Mbrship Dr Awd, NAACP 1980; Awd of Merit NAACP 1980.

TAYLOR, MARGIE ARNSDORFF oc/Businesswoman; b/Aug 17, 1924; h/Ridgeland, SC; m/James F; c/Celeste T Lucas, Franklin A, Robyn T Wood; p/Lawrence Arnsdorff (dec); Kate A Reeves, Ridgeland, SC; ed/Deg Ryans Bus Col 1942; pa/Motel Owner & Oper 1955-; Secy-Treas JFT Enterprises Inc; cp/Jasper Co C of C; Gdn Clb; r/Bapt; hon/W/W Am Wom 1980.

TAYLOR, MAX RUSSELL oc/Businessman, Tennis Coach; b/July 7, 1955; h/3522 King Cir, Corsicana, TX 75110; ba/Same; m/Debra Jane; c/Amy Beth; p/Maxie Bell (dec) and Faye Alien Taylor, Palestine, TX; ed/BS; MEd; pa/Tennis Coach/Phy Ed Instr; Owner Topspin Racquet Shop; Tex Tennis Coaches Assn; AAHPER; TSTA; r/Disciple of Christ; hon/W/W Am HS; Grad F'ship to Stephen F Austin Univ.

TAYLOR, NANCY JANE oc/Hospital Administrator; b/Feb 17, 1941; h/PO Box 688, Leesburg, FL 32748; ba/L'burg; m/Olman P Jr; p/Bedford and Helen Pickup, Hamburg, NY; ed/Masters Hlth Care Adm; pa/Am Acad Hosp Admrs; Am Hosp Assn; Fla Leag Hosps; cp/BPW; Local & Co C of C; Elks Aux; r/Meth; hon/VP C of C; PSRO.

TAYLOR, RICHARD oc/Agency Manager; b/June 29, 1933; h/112 Guadalupe, Athens, TX 75751; ba/Athens; m/Jonell W; c/Pam, Patsy; p/Edward A Taylor, Liberal, KS; Golda J Taylor, Winfield, KS; mil/USAF 4 Yrs; pa/Life Underwriter; The Gideons Intl, Pres, Secy; Treas Athens Camp, Farm Bur Million Dollar Round Table; Pres's Clb; r/Meth.

TAYLOR, ROBERT JR oc/Section Leader; b/Nov 22, 1947; h/Ocala, Fl; m/Doris J; c/Robert III, Tarvis J, Terenah R; p/Robert and Julia Taylor, Ocala, FL; mil/AUS 1967-; pa/81 MM Mortar, Sect Ldr, Sgt; r/Bapt; hon/NDSM 1968; VSM 1969; RVNCM 1969; Prcht Badge 1968; CIB 1968; EIB 1975; Drill Sgt Badge 1970; GCMDL 4th Awd 1979; Army Commend Medal 1979; Campaign Stars: VN Counteroffensive Phase V; VN Counteroffensive Phase VI; TeT 69 Counteroffensive.

TAYLOR, RON J oc/Distributor; b/Apr 14, 1945; h/700 N 26th St, Corsicana, TX 75110; m/Betty Jane; c/Sabra Marie; p/Floyd and Bertie Taylor, Weatherford, TX; mil/AUS 6 Yrs Radio, Telephone & Carrier Oper; pa/Amway Distrbr; Tom's Peanut, Shipping; cp/REACT, Navarro Co; Tex St Guard; r/Bapt; hon/Adj Gen's Indiv Awd.

TAYLOR, RONALD DALE oc/Chemical Engineer, Educator; b/Oct 25, 1949; h/3911 Elaine Dr, Bryan, TX 77801; p/Joe Lee and Floyie LaVania Wilcox Taylor, Bryan, TX; ed/BS Tex Tech Univ 1973; MA Univ Houston 1978; pa/AIChE, SW Tex; Res, Plastics & Corrosion; Matrix Games; cp/Houston Crisis Hotline; ACS; TSTA; Houston Commun Action; r/Ch of Christ; hon/500 Hr Lttr, Crisis Hotline 1979; DIB 1979; W/W S&SW 1978-79.

TAYLOR, SHAHANE RICHARDSON JR oc/Ophthalmologist; b/Sept 5, 1928; h/Greensboro, NC; ba/348 N Elm St, Greensboro, NC 27401; m/Betty Teague; c/Shahane R III, Anne Teague, Mary Hooker; p/Shahane R Taylor Sr, G'boro, NC; Mary Hooker Taylor (dec); ed/AB

PERSONALITIES OF THE SOUTH

1955, MD 1959 UNC-CH; mil/AUS Signal Corps 1951-53; USAR Capt; pa/Phys & SUrg, Mng Ptnr Taylor Clin; Guilford Co Med Soc, Pres 1977; G'boro Acad Med; NC Med Soc, Exec Coun 1980; AMA; SMA; Am Acad Oph; Soc Eye Surgs; Pan Am Soc; cp/G'boro Country Clb; G'boro City Clb, Bd Dirs; G'boro Whist Clb; Merchants & Mfrs Clb; ARRL; Mensa Intl; r/Epis; hon/W/W S&SW 1979-81; Qtr Century Wireless Assn 1979; Ch Sect on Ophthal Med Soc 1969; Chm Com on Eye Care 1969-73; Pres Elect Med Alumni UNC 1980; Chm Ser Wesley Long Hosp 1973-.

TAYLOR, THELMA oc/Writer; b/June 18, 1924; h/Rt 5, Cynthiana, KY 41031; m/Norman; c/David, Judy T Martin; p/Thomas and Lucy Kate Henson; pa/KPW; NPW; KPA; BPW; cp/Iris Soc; r/Christian; hon/4-H Soil Conserv.

TAYLOR, THEMAN RAY oc/Educator; b/May 14, 1941; h/1808 Clara Dr, Conway, AR 72032; ba/Conway; m/Jackie Faye; c/Donobbra, Theman, Nena, Deirdra; p/James Leon (dec) and Lillie Mae Taylor, Dallas, TX; ed/AA; BA; MA; PhD; pa/Asst Prof Hist, Univ Ctrl Ark; Bd Mem: NAACP; Self Care Foun, Channel Coast Ofcls Assn; cp/Chm Geo Wash Carver S'ship Clb Com; hon/Nat Fellow Awd (Ford); Dissertation Fellow Awd for Res (UCSB).

TAYLOR, THOMAS ALLEN oc/Leatherworker; b/Sept 28, 1946; h/Rt 5 Box 542, S Hillsborough, Arcadia, FL; m/Sharon; c/Mark Allen, Tammy Ann; p/Garnett S and Thelma Taylor, Arcadia, FL; mil/Fla NG E-4; pa/Profl Alligator Wrestler 1964-75; Saddle Maker & Custom Leather Work 1975-; Owner T-Tay Leathercraft; cp/F&AM Masonic Lodge, Master Mason; Elks Clb; r/Bapt; hon/Author Num Newspaper Articles.

TEAFORD, RUTH ROMINE oc/Teacher; b/Aug 7, 1927; h/PO Drawer E, Townley, AL 35587; ba/Townley; m/Paul W; c/James Cecil Files; p/Luther N Romine (dec); Mary Atkins (dec); ed/ABS 1966; BS 1968; MA 1975, 78; AA Cert in Ed 1979; pa/Eng Tchr, Chm Walker Co Eng Tchrs; Kappa Delta Pi; Chi Delta Pi; Phi Theta; Delta Kappa Gamma, S'ship Chm, Creative Person, Secy; AEA; NEA; WCTA; WCCT; A-Vote; cp/Walker Co Heritage Assn, Secy-Treas, Bd Dirs; PTA, Pres, Prog Chm; r/Ch of God; hon/Nom'd Wom of Achmt Walker Co 1979; Fav Tchr of Ala 1980; Author Wkly Featured Article on Hist & Folklore *Daily Mountain Eagle*; Author Book of Folklore *Southern Homespun* 1980.

TEAGUE, WILLIAM JOSEPH oc/Writer, Historian; b/Sept 2, 1941; h/3914 Hawthorne Ave, Dallas, TX 75219; ba/Dallas; m/Byrd Fuertes; p/Henry J Teague, Odessa, TX; Ruth Cody Teague (dec); ed/BA Univ Tex-Austin 1963; MA So Meth Univ 1971; PhD N Tex St Univ 1977; Post Doct Study Univ Wis 1978-79; mil/USN 1963-65; pa/Communs/Tech Writer, Univ Computing Co, Dallas; Adj Prof of Hist, Richland Col, Dallas; Reg Book Review Columnist, *Dallas Morning News*; Am Hist Assn; Am Polit Assn; So Hist Assn; AAUP; r/Epis; hon/Post-Doct F'ship, Nat Endowment for the Humanities 1978; Post-Doct F'ship Nat Hist Pubs & Records Comm 1979; Post-Doct F'ship Lyndon B Johnson Foun 1979; Post-Doct F'ship, So F'ship 1980; W/W S&SW 1981; Pub'd Author.

TEAL, JACQUELYNE SUE oc/Executive; b/Nov 1, 1946; h/Metairie, LA; ba/Professional Consultants, 419 Carondelet, 4th Floor, New Orleans, LA 70130; p/Benjamin Robert and Beatrice Cole Teal, St Cloud, FL; pa/Pres Corporate Consults Inc 1980-; Nat Assn Female Execs; Am Soc Profl & Exec Wom; Nat Assn Pers Consults; La Assn Pers Consults; Cert'd Pers Consult Soc La; cp/C of C-New Orleans & River Region; Coun of Indep Businesses, Adv Bd Mem; Ambassadors Clb; MENSA; r/Prot; hon/Cert'd Pers Consult 1980.

TELFORD, DONALD M oc/Teacher; b/June 22; h/Largo, FL; m/Nelle Y; c/Janet, Dianne T Biscoglia; p/dec; ed/BS Kan St Univ 1930; MS E Tenn St Univ 1971; mil/AUS 1918-19, 1942-61 Ret'd Lt Col; pa/Fball Coach; Prof Baseball Umpire; Col Math Tchr; Resolution Com, Reserve Ofcr Assn; NEA; Disabled Am Vets; r/Cath; hon/Approx 18 Commend Awds, AUS 1943-61; Cit by Gordon Mil Col 1966; Univ Md Math Awd 1955; Author Sev Articles Incl'g "The Effect of Tobacco Smoke on the Non-Smoker" 1968.

TERRELL, JERRY DAY oc/Educator; b/May 3, 1941; h/702 Wilson Pike, Brentwood, TN 37027; ba/Nashville; m/Mary Dykes; c/Rex Edward, Jeffery Newton, Timothy Alan; p/William N Sr and Thelma Day Terrell, McComb, MS; ed/BS Univ So Miss; MRE SWn Bapt Theol Sem; pa/NAEYC; SACUS; TACUS; Intl Platform Assn; cp/Exch Clb; Carondelet Civic Assn; r/Bapt.

TERRELL, S PATRICIA oc/Assistant Professor; b/Sept 17, 1945; h/213 S Library St, Greenville, NC 27834; ba/G'ville; c/Wendi Loren; p/A L and Sybil Colby, Hattiesburg, MS; ed/BS; MEd; PhD; pa/Asst Prof, Dept Elem Ed, ECU; Col Rdg Assn; Intl Rdg Assn; Kappa Delta Pi; Phi Delta Kappa; AAUW; r/Bapt; hon/Outstg Yng Wom Am; Outstg Instr.

TERRY, DONNA JEAN oc/Teacher, Coach; b/June 25, 1947; h/Denton, TX; ba/Tex Wom's Univ, PO Box 22133, TWU Station, Denton, TX 76204; p/F M Terry, Memphis, TN; Vivian Terry, Memphis, TN; ed/BS Memphis St Univ 1970; M Exercise Physiology Tex Wom's Univ 1981; pa/Coach Softball Team, Tex Wom's Univ; Profl Softball Player; AAHPER; Assn Inter Aths for Wom; r/Bapt; hon/MVP in Volleyball, Softball, Basketball; Chosen for Nat Swimming Team; Trip to China to Rep USA in Sport of Softball; Contbr to *Coaching Women's Athletics*.

TERRY, FRANK WOMACK oc/District Supervisor; b/Apr 21, 1924; h/42 Monument Ave, Harrisonburg, VA 22801; m/Kathleen Coleman; p/Charlie L (dec) and Maggie L Terry (dec); ed/LaSalle Univ; mil/USAF 106th Inf Div; pa/St Tax Dist Supvr; Hotel Mgmt; VGEA; Hotel Greeters of Am; r/Bapt; hon/2 Battle Stars; Top Awd Dale Carnegie Class.

TERRY, HARRY REGINALD oc/Associate Realtor; b/Aug 27, 1907; h/389 W Wilbur Ave, Lake Mary, FL 32746; ba/Lake Mary; m/Mary S; c/Jan Louise (dec); p/Fred Wiliam (dec) and Leona Cornish Terry (dec); ed/Rochester Polytech Inst 1927-28; Syracuse Univ 1929; pa/Ret'd Ofc Engr & Chief of Contract Adm, Corps Engrs, AUS Installations; Soc Am Mil Engrs; N Seminole Regional Sewer Com; cp/Lake Mary Rotary Clb, Tres; Sanford Optimist Clb, Pres, Secy; Seminole Country Dem Exec Com; Lake Mary C of C, Dir; Lake Mary City Coun-man; r/Presb; Elder; hon/Life Mem Optimist Intl 1971; Outstg Secy, Optimist Intl 1972; Dedicated Ser on Inc Com by Lake Mary C of C 1973; Outstg Ser to Water Dept as City Coun-man 1980.

TERRY, W CLAUDE JR oc/Automobile Dealer; b/Feb 4, 1929; h/Oneida, TN; ba/Oneida; m/Fay Rene Sexton; c/Gail, Patricia, Wilda, William Claude III; p/W Claude (dec) and Paralee Cowan Terry (dec); ed/BS Univ Tenn 1950; Att'd Columbia Mil Acad 1944-46; mil/AUS 1951-53 1st Lt; pa/Self-Employed Auto Dlr; Tenn Auto Dlrs Assn; cp/Kiwanis Clb; Repub: Del, 2nd Cong Dist to Repub Nat Conv 1964; Am Legion; Conservation Comm 1981-83; r/Ch of Christ; hon/JCs Outstg Yng Man of Yr 1963.

TERRY, WARREN BERGEN oc/Entrepreneur; b/Aug 11, 1918; h/Oak Hill, Domino Stud Farm, PO Box 11761, Lexington, KY 40577; ba/L'ton; m/Frances S; c/Warren B Jr, William Michael, Sumner Patrick, Timothy Edward Nicholas; p/William Bergen (dec) and Clester Hopkins Terry, Vandalia, IL; pa/Chm of Bd, Blue Grass Coca-Cola Bottling Co; Pres & Chm of Bd Coca-Cola Bottling Co of So Ill; Pres Renwar Corp; Pres & Owner Terry Properties Inc; Owner Lexington Hilton Inn & Howard Johnson's Motor Lodge, N L'ton; 70% Owner Hyatt Regency Hotel, L'ton; Owner Domino Stud Farm & Poplar Hill Farms (Thoroughbred Horses); Owner Griffin Gate Farm; cp/Univ Ky: Bd Trustees, Fellow, Devel Coun, Bd Advrs for Patterson Sch Diplomacy; Transylvania Univ: Bd Curators, Exec Com; Ky C of C, Bd Dirs; L'ton Jr Leag Horse Show Adv Bd; r/Meth; hon/1 of Pgh 100, 1954, *Time Magazine*.

TERRY, WILLIAM RAY oc/Executive; b/June 29, 1949; h/927 South St, Roanoke, AL 36274; ba/Roanoke; c/Tamara; p/Jesse A and Velma G Terry, Roanoke, AL; ed/Morehouse Col 1971; Weaver Sch of Real Est 1974; pa/VP Hillcrest Corp 1973-; Secy Terry Properties 1972-; VP Terry Constrn 1973-; VP Terry Mfg Co 1971-; Owner Terry Upholstery Shop 1980-; Lic'd Real Est Broker; Notary Public; r/Bapt; Deacon 1979-, Supt SS 1980-, VP SWn Union Dist SS & BTU Cong; hon/W/W S&SW 1980-81.

TETLIE, HAROLD MAULAND oc/Pastor, Missionary; b/Aug 24, 1926; h/Box 1607, Alice, TX 78332; ba/Same; p/Harold B (dec) and Anna M Tetlie (dec); ed/BA St Olaf Col 1951; MBA Univ Denver 1956; BD Luther Theol Sem 1965; Doct Study Cornell Univ; mil/WWII; pa/Tchr HS & Univ; Missionary in Mex 11 Yrs; cp/Secy Proj Area Com, Urban Renewal; Coor JACS; r/Indep Luth; hon/Ser to Mankind Awd, Setoma Clb of Corpus Christi.

TEW, E JAMES JR oc/Quality Assurance Manager; b/July 7, 1933; h/Dallas, TX; m/Barbara D Evans; c/Teresa Annette, Linda Diane, Brian James; p/Elmer James Tew Sr (dec); Bessie Fay Bennet (dec); ed/Arlington St Jr Col 1955-57; BBA So Meth Univ 1969; MBA 1975, MS 1972 Univ Dallas; mil/AUS 1953-55; USAR 1955- Chief Warrant Ofcr; pa/Mgr Quality Assurance Opers & Corp Ref Standard Lab, Tex Instruments Inc; Equip Grp 1957-; Am Soc Quality Control, Chm Dallas-Ft Worth Sect; Am Nat Metric Coun; Optical Soc Tex; US Metric Assn; Tex Metric Coun, Dallas Regional Dir; cp/Dallas C of C Career Ed Adv Bd: Chm World Mfg Com 1974-77, Elec Judge & Precinct Chm 1961-64, Del to Co & St Convs; Advr to Richland & Mt View Cols; Texins Assn Bd Dirs, VP; r/Bapt; hon/Fellow Am Soc QC 1975; Am MENSA; W/W S&SW; Cert'd Adv'd Metrication Spec, US Metric Assn; Profl Quality Engr, St Calif; Author Num Pubs & Profl Papers.

294

PERSONALITIES OF THE SOUTH

TEW, SUZETTE PETTIS oc/Controller; b/Sept 17, 1953; h/Meridian, Ms; ba/PO Box 5355, Meridian, MS 39301; m/Philip Rush; c/Kenneth; p/Tollie Calvin and Joyce McDevitt Pettis, Shubuta, MS; ed/Att'g Miss St Univ; Hon Grad Sch for Bank Adm, Univ Wis 1980; BS Univ So Miss 1975; pa/Peoples Bank of Miss, NA: Controller 1980-, Secy to Bd Dirs, Acctg Ofcr 1976-79, Asst Auditor 1975-76; Univ So Miss Alumni Assn; Am Soc Wom Accts; Univ So Miss Alumni Assn; BPW Clb; Phi Chi Theta, Alumni Mem; cp/Meridian Area Navy Leag, Treas 1980; r/Bapt; hon/Meridian Yng Career Wom, BPW 1978.

THAXTON, MARVIN DELL oc/Attorney at Law; b/June 1, 1925; h/12 Lakeside Ln, Newport, AR 72112; ba/Newport; m/Carolyn Alexander; c/Rebecca T Henderson, Gail T Fogleman, Marvin D Jr; p/Montgomery Dell Thaxton, Little Rock, AR; Ida Scheurer Thaxton (dec); ed/JD Univ Ark 1949; mil/USMM S Pacific Theater; pa/Am, Ark, Jackson Co Bar Assns; Am Judicature Soc; Chm Ark Bar Assn; Com Unauthorized Pract; Real Est; Probate; cp/Pres Newport Rotary Clb; Pres, Bd Dirs Newport Sch; Pres En Ark Yng Mens Clbs; Pres Newport C of C; r/U Meth: Past Chm Ofcl Bd, Dist Lay Ldr; hon/Spec Assoc Justice, Ark Supreme Ct 1978.

THERRIEN, FRANCOIS XAVIER JR oc/Business and Tax Consultant; b/June 6, 1928; h/1492 Canterbury Cir, Casselberry, FL 32707; ba/Winter Park, FL; m/Yoshiko Kashima; c/Francois Xavier III, Norman, Sakura, Izumi; p/Francis Xavier and Doris Alma Cote Therrien, Amesbury, MA: ed/BS US Mil Acad, West Point 1950; MS Univ Ariz 1962; mil/AUS 1950-70 Ret'd Lt Col; pa/Dist Dir R J Carroll Asscs 1970-; Instr Seminole Commun Col 1974-; Secy Buck Enterprises, Orlando 1978-; Secy Cosmic Corp, Orlando, 1978-; Dir E J Air Sers Inc 1978-; Dir Art Works Inc 1972-; Dir Arabian Express Inc 1979-; Nat Assn Enrolled Agts; Nat Fed Indep Bus; r/Cath; hon/W/W S&SW 1980-81; Croix de Guerre w Palm; Silver Star; Bronze Star; Air Medal; Army Commend Medal.

THOMAS, BILLY RAY oc/Teacher and Coach; b/Aug 18, 1932; h/Elk City, OK; m/Eileen Verkler; c/James, Billy, Elizabeth; p/Lola Thomas, Willow, OK; ed/BA SWn St Univ 1958; Grad Studies W Tex St Univ; MEd SWn St 1975; mil/USAF 4 Yrs; pa/Coach Miami, Tex & Clarendon, Tex; Tchr Elk City Public Schs 8 Yrs; Phi Delta Kappa; St Umpiring Staff for ASA; r/Bapt; hon/Author Curric Guide for Understanding St, Co, Municipal Govt in Okla.

THOMAS, BRENDA SUE oc/Medical Technician; b/July 6, 1947; h/1211 Moss Ave, Union City, TN 38261; ba/Union City; m/Richard E; c/Kenneth Stephen; p/Henry E and Ruby Brasure Morrow, Fulton, KY; ed/AS; pa/Med Tech (ASCP), Obion Co Gen Hosp; ASCP; NCA; ASMT; W Tenn Soc Med Technol; r/Bapt; hon/Grad summa cum laude; Phi Theta Kappa; Chem Awd 1979; Capt Winning Team MLT Student Col Bowl, St Tenn 1979.

THOMAS, DAVID L oc/Attorney at Law; b/Feb 26, 1937; h/2470 Old Monrovia Rd, Huntsville, AL 35806; ba/H'ville; m/e'Claire David; c/David Jr, Jeffrey; p/Dea Theodore (dec) and Mary Lee Thomas, H'ville, AL; ed/AB 1958, LLB 1961, JD 1961 Univ Ala; pa/Asst Dist Atty, 23rd Judicial Circuit 1961-65; Dist Atty 1965-69; Indiv Prac Law 1969-; cp/Pres H'ville JCs 1963; Bd Dirs H'ville Indust Expansion Com 1963-64; Bd Dirs C of C 1963-64; Bd Dirs Sertoma Clb 1965; Madison Co Dem Exec Com 1964-68; Am & Madison Co Bar Assn; Am & Ala Trial Lwyrs Assns; Am Judicature Soc; Ala Crim Defense Lwyrs Assn; r/Prot; hon/Senatorship JCs Intl 1975; Mr Lawman Awd 1965.

THOMAS, DAVID RAYMOND oc/Physician; b/Apr 26, 1946; h/Tucker, GA; ba/4484 N Shallowford Rd, Atlanta, GA 30338; m/Janice N; c/Beth, Heather, Michael; p/Raymond P (dec) and Dot Thomas, Madison, MS; ed/BS 1968, MD 1971, Post Doct Study 1971-75 Univ Miss; pa/Perimeter Med Grp 1980; Pvt Pract, Internal Med 1975-80; Clin Instr Med, Univ Miss 1975-80, Adj Prof Microbiol 1975-80, Miss St Univ; Diplomate Am Bd Internal Med 1975; Am Col Phys; Am Soc Internal Med; Am Heart Assn; Am Cancer Soc; Miss Div Am Cancer Soc, Bd Dirs; Miss Med Assn; Prairie Med Soc 1975-80, Bd Censors; NE Miss Acad Med 1980; Bd Incrs, Hlth Care; Med Staff Shallowford Hosp, St Joseph Hosp; cp/Bd Dirs Optimist Clb 1979-80; r/Ch of Christ; hon/Alpha Epsilon Delta; Gamma Beta Phi; Univ Schlr, Unv Miss; Nat Merit Lttr of Commend; W/W 17th Ed.

THOMAS, DIAHANN WYKE oc/Manufacturing Company Executive; b/Sept 25, 1951; h/3001 7th St Unit D, Metairie, LA 70002; ba/New Orleans, LA; p/Christopher J Wyke (dec); Audrey L Suhr; ed/AA Fla St Jr Col 1973; BS Fla St Univ 1976; MBA Univ N Fla 1977; pa/Western Electric Co Inc: Staff Assoc (NO) 1977, ESS Installation Supvr (NO) 1978-79, Account Analyst (Birmingham, Ala) 1979-80, Dept Chief Customer Ser 1980-; Instr Univ of New Orleans 1978-79; Grad Asst, Univ of N Fla 1976-77; Other Former Positions; Assn of MBA Execs; Am Mgmt Assn; Nat Assn Female Execs; IPA; Am Soc Profl & Exec Wom; Author,

"The Economic Impact of the Univ of N Fla on Duval County" (1978); cp/Wom's Polit Caucus; hon/Beta Gamma Sigma; Sigma Iota Epsilon.

THOMAS, DOUGALD ROBERT (TOMMY) oc/Construction; b/Mar 26, 1930; h/306 E E St, Erwin, NC 28339; ba/Erwin; m/Ruby Denning; c/Bunny Currin, John Denning; p/Dougald Robert Thomas (dec); Ethel Reeves Wood, Dunn, NC; pa/D R Thomas Construction Co Inc; cp/Rotary Clb of Erwin; r/Bapt: Layman w NC Bapt Brotherhood.

THOMAS, GARY CECIL oc/Copy Machine Dealer; b/Feb 6, 1944; h/Rt 2, Naples, TX 75568; ba/Tyler, TX; m/Mary Kay; c/Kellie Rae and Matthew Allen; p/Cecil and Claudine Thomas, Naples, TX; ed/Am Inst Bnkg; pa/Copy Machine Dlr; r/Meth; hon/Savin Salesman of Yr 1977 & 78.

THOMAS, GEORGE oc/Physician; b/June 8, 1944; h/Brandenton, FL; ba/124 Manatee Ave E, Bradenton, FL 33508; m/Mariamma; c/George Jr, Joseph, Mathew; p/Thomas and Mary George; ed/Pre-Med St Thomas Col, Palai, India; MD Kottayam Med Col, Kenala Univ, India 1970; Residency S Balto Gen Hosp 1973-76; F'ship in Cardiology, NJ Med Col 1976-78; pa/Pvt Pract, Cardiology & Internal Med; Fellow FACC; Am Col Phys; Manatee Med Soc; Fla W Coast Acad Cardiology; Fla Med Assn; r/Rom Cath; hon/Yng Investigators Awd 1978, Am Col Cardiology; Author Sev Res Papers.

THOMAS, JULIA MAE oc/Reading Specialist; b/May 10, 1928; h/PO Box 52484, New Orleans, LA 70152; ba/New Orlean; c/Clyde L; p/Posey Stewart (dec); Mary Gardette, LA, CA; ed/BA So Univ; MA DePaul Univ; pa/Resolution Com IRA; Spkr Atlanta, Ga IRA 1979; Exhibr AASA; ASCD; cp/Eta Phi Beta; Phi Delta Kappa; LWV; hon/Nom'd "Those Who Excel" of Springfield, Ill 1977; Kappa Delta Pi.

THOMAS, MARY LOUISE oc/County Extension Agent; b/June 17, 1926; h/804 Rockwall St, Terrell, TX 75160; ba/Kaufman; m/Bismarck Jr; c/Bismarck III, Von Carl; p/Charles J Greenwood, Berkeley, CA; Lillian Moore Greenwood (dec); ed/BS Bishop Col 1958; Grad Study Prairie View A&M Univ, Colo St Univ, Tex A&M Univ, Merritt Bus Col; pa/Co Home Demo Agt, Tex Agric Ext Ser, Kaufman Co 1949-53; CHDA Hopkins Co 1954-58; Elem Sch Tchr, Kaufman Co 1958-59; Co Ext Agt, Home Ec, Kaufman Co 1959-; Tex Assn Ext Home Ecs, Treas 1971-73, 2nd VP 1980-81; Recruitment Com Nat Assn Ext Home Ecs 1973; Asst Dir Dist 4 Tex Assn Ext Home Ecs 1971-73; cp/Pres Pilot Clb of Kaufman 1980-81; Hist 22 Marechal Niel Clb of Terrell; Ed Com Indep Funeral Dirs Assn of Tex; r/Bapt: Ednl Dir, Ldr Yth Dept of Ch Tng; hon/Dist'd Ser Plaque, Tex Assn Ext Home Ecs & Nat Assn Ext Home Ecs 1980; Cert for Merit Ser, Epsilon Sigma Phi 1980; 10 & 20 Yr Certs of Ser USDA 1962, 1972; 20 Yr Cert Recog, Epsilon Sigma Phi 1972; Dist'd Ser Awd, Kaufman Indep Sch Dist for Coop Ed 1980; Nom'd W/W Am Wom 1981-82; Grad summa cum laude Bishop Col 1948; Valedictorian Ctrl HS, Jefferson, Tex 1944.

THOMAS, NELDA JO HALL oc/Registered Nurse; b/Dec 21, 1923; h/Rt 2 Box 196, Vernon, TX 76384; ba/Vernon; m/Charles S; c/Sylvia, Randy, Greg, Scott, Gordon; p/J L (dec) and Sallie Bolton Hall (dec); ed/Assoc Deg Nsg, Mid-Wn St Univ 1976; pa/Secy 1940-41; SSS Employee 1941-42; Hostess Canton Cafe 1972-73; Spec 1, Mtl Hlth-Mtl Retard Ctr 1976-78; Nurse Supvr, Chillicothe Hosp 1976-78; Charge Nurse Wilbarger Gen Hosp 1978-; cp/Bd Dirs Campfire Girls 1956-59; N-side Booster Clb; Red Cross Blood Mobile Vol; Den Mother Boy Scouts 1970-72; r/U Meth; hon/Valedictorian Vernon HS 1940; W/W Am HS & Cols 1940; Recip Ser Awd, BSA 1971; W/W Am Wom 1979-80; Selected for AJN Panel 1978.

THOMAS, NOEL HOWARD oc/Police Psychologist; b/Oct 25, 1949; h/517 Via Sevilla, Mesquite, TX 75150; ba/Dallas; m/Donna Marie Kontovich; c/Pamela Ann; p/Frank Jr and Peggy A Roderman Thomas, Dallas, TX; ed/BS, MS Abilene Christian Univ; mil/USAR 1st Lt; pa/Charter Mem Am Assn Biofeedback Clins; Fellow, Soc of Investigative & Forensic Hypnosis; AACI; So Police & Crim Psychs; Tex Psych Assn; r/Ch of Christ; hon/Cert of Completion, Dallas Police Acad 1969; Hostage Negotiation, FBI 1975; Psych Assoc Tex St Bd Exmrs of Psych 1977; Cert of Completion, Law Enforcement Hypnosis Inst 1977; Cert of Merit, Dallas Police Dept 1978.

THOMAS, PHILIP ROBINSON oc/Executive; b/Dec 9, 1934; h/Hwy 956, Ethel, LA 70730; ba/Ethel; m/Wayne Heirtzler; c/Martin N R, Stephen D R; p/Leslie R and Margaret L Thomas, Nelson, NZ; ed/BS 1959, MS 1961 Univ London; Post Grad Work 1961-64 Univ London; pa/Pres Mgmt Cnsltg Co; IEEE; Brit Inst Radio & Elec Engrs.

THOMAS, SARAH LOUVENIA oc/Executive; b/Feb 6, 1935; h/PO Box 71, Salem, AL 36874; m/Benny Jr; c/Gregory Anthony, Ronald McArthur, Maggie Lorelda; p/Arthur Ward Sr, Salem, AL; Maggie Mae Ward (dec); ed/PN, Booker T Wash Sch Pract Nsg 1953; Dip Auburn Univ

PERSONALITIES OF THE SOUTH

& Univ Ala 1980; pa/St Francis Hosp, OR Nurse; Ctrl Supply Supvr Lee Co Hosp; Hlth Edr, E Ala Mtl Hlth; Fdr & Exec Dir SE Ctlr Ala Sickle Cell Clin Assn Inc; ANA; cp/Lee Co Br Chapt NAACP, Secy; Ala Dem Conf for Lee Co, Registrar; LWV; r/Bapt; hon/OES of Yr 1971; St Grand Matron, Modern F&AM of World 1972; Awd'd So Regional Coun Ldrship Devel Prog for Outstg Ldrship in Commun & St 1976-77; Dist'd Ser Awd, Mayor of Tuskegee 1980; Gold Plaque for Untiring Hours Devoted to E Ala Sickle Cell Assn Inc.

THOMPSON, ALFRED ALEXANDER oc/Businessman; b/Feb 21, 1889; h/Melbourne, FL; m/Effie C; c/James Alfred, Mary L, Peter L, Shirley Kay; p/Alexander Thompson (dec); Amanda M Clinger (dec); ed/Tchr Tng; pa/Bdr & Develr of Homes in Fla; Garment Mfr; Appliance Store Owner; Mayor of Manchester, Ohio; r/Prot; hon/Awd'd Gifts & Hons for Being Oldest & Longest Married Couple in Orange & Seminole Cos 1979 (Married 69 Yrs).

THOMPSON, ANDREW BOYD JR oc/Executive; b/Mar 30, 1930; h/4353 Amherst Rd, Montgomery, AL 36116; ba/Mont; m/Laura June Guy; c/Guy Bradly, Eric Kiepp; p/Andrew B Sr and Frieda Jaqueline Smith Thompson, Mont, AL; ed/Att'd Auburn Univ 1948-49; mil/AUS 1951-54; pa/Mats Engr Asst, Ala Hwy Dept 1949-51, 1954-55; Lab Mgr, Tech Mont Br So Testing Labs 1955; Salesman & Store Mgr, Mel's Photo Shop 21 1955-57, 1958-66; Ins Agt, Prudential Ins Co of Am 1957-58; Furniture Salesman, Sears, Roebuck Co 1966; VP & Gen Mgr, Editor Nat Photo Pricing Ser Inc 1966-81, Pres 1981-; Photo Mktg Assn, Intl; Photo Mfrs & Distbrs Assn; Reserve Ofcrs Assn; cp/Mont C of C; Intl Platform Assn; Epilepsy Chapt of Mont Area, Past Pres, Past VP, Past & Pres Secy, Bd Dirs; 3/200/31st Dixie Div Clb, Secy; Fellow ABI Res Assn; Fellow IBA; Pi Kappa Alpha; Past Mem Am Legion & VFW; r/Meth; hon/Am Legion Med for Outstg Platoon Ldr in HS Reserve Ofcrs Tng Corps 1948; Competed for Gen Gorgas Sci S'ship (Awd'd Money & Title Gen Gorgas Schlr 1948); Army Commend Medal; Good Conduct Medal; Nat Defense Ser Medal; Korean Ser Medal w 2 Campaign Stars; Army Reserve Components Achmt Medal w 2 Bronze OLC; Armed Forces Reserve Medal w 10 Yr Device; UN Ser Medal; Merit Unit Cit w Bronze OLC; 2 Korean Pres Unit Cits; Expert Badge for Pistol; Sharpshooter Badges for Rifle & Carbine; DIB; Men of Achmt; Intl W/W: Commun Ser, Intells; Men & Wom Dist; Intl Reg of Profiles; W/W S&SW; Other Biogl Listings.

THOMPSON, ARLENA IMOGENE oc/Teacher; b/Aug 13, 1927; h/1520 30th Ave, Meridian, MS 39301; ba/Meridian; m/Marcellous C Sr; c/Gail Patrice, Marcellous c Jr; p/Andrew Jr and Mary Jane Kendrick, Stonewal, MS; ed/BS Jackson St Univ; MS Univ Wis; pa/Pres Meridian Assn Edrs; Lay Adv Com Supt; Secy Miss Cong Parents & Tchrs; Pres Elect Dist II Bd Dirs, Outgoing Bd Mem, Miss Assn Edrs; Pres St Mins Wives Alliance; Nat Assn Mins Wives USA Inc; Nat Coun SS; Assn for Supervision & Curric Devel; cp/Ed Com Meridian C of C; M-Pact Coun; OES Chapt #2; Sys-Wide Improvement Coun, Meridian Public Schs; r/Bapt; hon/Yrbook Dedication 1977; Human Relats & Profl Ldrship.

THOMPSON, BERT oc/Professor; b/June 28, 1949; h/Rt 10, Box 266-J, Cookeville, TN 38501; ba/C'ville; m/Rhonda; c/Chad Aric, Cody Alex; p/C A and Mary Ruth Thompson, Dalhart, TX; ed/BS; MS; PhD pa/Am Soc Microbiol; Inst Food Technol; r/Ch of Christ; hon/Am Man of Sci; Intl Yth Achmt.

THOMPSON, BOBBY W oc/Executive; b/Oct 25, 1945; h/112 Liles, Searcy, AR 72143; ba/Searcy; m/Nancy Jo Dacus; c/Tiffeny, Heather, Dacus; p/James A and Etta M Thompson, Searcy, AR; pa/Pres Thompson Indust Prods Inc; ISSA; cp/BD Dirs Optimist Clb; r/Ch of Christ; hon/Pres Harding Acad Alumni Assn.

THOMPSON, DEBORAH oc/Executive Director; b/Mar 3, 1947; h/Jacksonville, FL; ba/333 Laura St, Suite 500, J'ville, FL 32202; m/Joseph P; c/Michelle Rae, Luveidya Ayesha; p/Hattie R Kemp, Rochester, MN; ed/AA Mobile St Jr Col 1967; BA Univ Minn 1970; pa/Exec Dir J'ville Neighborhood Resource Ctr 1980-; Dir Housing Cnslg Prog, J'ville Urban Leag 1975-80; Dir Yth Employment, NAACP 1971; Chm Bd of Consumer Credit Cnslg Sers of J'ville; Chm Regional Energy Action Com, St of Fla; Nat Assn Female Execs, J'ville Network Dir; cp/NE Fla Plan'g & Zoning Assn, Bd Mem; J'ville Urban Leag; Nat & Fla Assns of Parliamtns; hon/Certs from US Dept Housing & Urban Devel, Naval Air Sta J'ville Wom's Ctr, Fla Jr Col; Awd from Wom Involved in Commun Action 1980.

THOMPSON, EFFIE CLARK oc/Homemaker; b/Aug 29, 1891; h/425 Willow Tree Dr, Melbourne, FL 32935; m/Alfred Alexander; c/James Alfred, Mary L, Peter L, Shirley Kay; p/Sherman and Mary Humphrey Clark (dec); r/Prot; hon/Awd'd Gifts & Hons for Being Oldest & Longest Married Couple in Orange & Seminole Cos 1979.

THOMPSON, GEORGE WESLEY oc/Chairman of the Board; b/Mar 15, 1915; h/109 E William David Pkwy, Metairie, LA 70005; ba/New

Orleans; m/Margaret Doyle; c/Sue T Guenther; p/Talmadge D and Ruth A Thompson, Spokane, WA; pa/Chm of Bd Altamil Corp; Dir: Am Box Co, Aluminum Forge Co, Fontaine Truck Equip Co; cp/Repub Party; r/Presb; hon/Past Pres Wirebound Box Mfrs Assn.

THOMPSON, HUGH ARTHUR oc/Dentist; b/Jan 1, 1954; h/101 Upperman Ln, Baxter, TN 38544; m/Debra J; p/Arthur Jr and Wallene B Thompson, Baxter, TN; ed/BS 1976, DDS Univ Tenn Ctr for Hlth Scis 1979; pa/Pvt Prac Dentist; Am Dental Assn; cp/Alpha Tau Omega; r/Bapt.

THOMPSON, JAMES C oc/Director of Human Resources; b/June 28, 1944; h/16207 Shrewsbury Cir, Spring, TX 77373; ba/Houston; m/Mary Kathleen; c/Michael Paige, Matthew Pryce; p/Marvin R and Myrtle Thompson, Albuquerque, NM; ed/BA 1970, MBA 1975 Univ NM; pa/Dir Human Resources, Touche Ross & Co 1978-; Sr VP & Dir, Human Resources Div, Bank of the SW, Houston 1977-78; Dir-Corp Pers, Affil Bankshares of Colo 1975-77; VP & Dir Pers, First Nat Bank Albuquerque 1970-75; Chm Univ Houston Exec Prog Adv Com; Rice Univ Exec Prog Adv Com; Tex A&M Adv Coun; Chm SW Regional Employers Coun; Regional VP Am Mgmt Assn; Regional VP Am Soc Pers Admrs; Past Pres Houston Pers Assn; Exec Adv Com, Am Bnkg Assn; Past Pres Univ NM Alumni Assn; cp/C of C; Chm Klein Sch Bd; Houston F'ship of Christian Aths; Key Exec Commun Fund Campaign; Houston Symph; VChm Am Heart Assn; r/Christian.

THOMPSON, JAMES E oc/Chancellor; b/Feb 27, 1950; h/4 Oakley Dr, Rt 5, Crossville, TN 38555; ba/C'ville; m/Linda Wheeler; c/Virgil W; p/Carl A and Ola Dell Thompson; ed/BS Middle Tenn St Univ 1972; JD Memphis St Univ Sch Law 1975; pa/Chancellor, 4th Chancery Div of Tenn; cp/Pres Yng Repubs, Cumberland Co 1972-73; Cumberland Co Campaign Coor, Pres Gerald Ford 1976, Senator Howard Baker 1978; Am, Tenn Bar Assn; Am, Tenn Trial Lwyrs Assn; Tenn Crim Defense Lwyrs Assn; 3° Mason; 32° Mason, Scottish Rite; r/Calvary Temple Ch; hon/Memphis St Law Review; Highest Average in Crim Law; AM Juror; Awd for Agcy; Grad in Top 10 from Law Sch; 3 Yr Winner in Fball, Mid Tenn St Univ.

THOMPSON, JESSE oc/Minister; b/Jan 26, 1948; h/514 Duncan St, Orangeburg, SC 29115; m/Corlette; p/Essie Mae Thompson, Orangeburg, Sc; ed/BA Benedict Col; MRE SEn Bapt Sem; pa/Min; cp/NAACP; Intl Min Alliance; Capital City 47 Masonic Lodge; r/Bapt.

THOMPSON, KENNETH HERMAN oc/Dean of Instruction; b/Feb 18, 1909; h/106 Van Winkle Grove, Berea, KY 40403; m/Verna C; c/Kenneth H Jr, Veree Woodbridge; p/dec; ed/AB Chadron St Col 1930; MA No Colo Univ 1934; PhD Univ Neb 1946; Post Doct Study Univ Mich-Ann Arbor 1956; mil/USNR; pa/Dean Instrn, Berea Col 1946-75; Ednl Work India 1938-42, Pakistan 1955-56, Australia 1966, Rhodesia 1963, Taiwan 1979; Life Mem NEA; Nat Assn Fgn Student Affairs, Pres Region VI; Phi Kappa Phi; Psi Chi; Pi Delta Kappa; Phi Delta Kappa; cp/Exec Secy VS Ednl Foun in Pakistan 1955-56; Pres Blue Grass Coun BSA 1954-55; Adv Coun Ky Auth for Ednl TV 1959-84; r/Presb; hon/Dist'd Alumnus Awd 1958, Dist'd Ser Awd 1980, Chadron St Col; Hon Alumnus, Berea Col 1979; Author "Finding Friends in Latin Lands"; Contbr to Profl Jours in USA, India, Australia, Taiwan.

THOMPSON, L DEAN oc/Minister; b/June 17, 1946; h/207 High St, Eufaula, OK 74432; ba/Eufaula; m/Norma J; c/Jim, Janie, Tara Leigh; p/Ivan L Thompson, Grand, KS; Eva E Thompson (dec); ed/BA Bethany Nazarene Col 1968; MM Pgh St Univ 1975; PhD Studies Univ Kan 1976; pa/Min First Ch of the Nazarene: Columbus, Kan; Rolla, Mo; Eufaula, Okla; Mo Dist Yth Intl Coun; SE Okla Nazarene Yth Intl Coun Secy; Secy Eufaula Area Min Alliance; Bd Dirs Lake Eufaula U Mins; cp/Repub Cand Co Treas 1974; Energy Steering Com, City of Rolla 1979; Chm Rolla Nutrition Site Adv Coun 1979; Gov's Coun on Aging 1979; r/Ch of the Nazarene; hon/Yng Artists Awd, Pgh St Univ 1975.

THOMPSON, MARVIN CULLUM oc/Executive; b/May 11, 1924; h/3512 Beverly Dr, Dallas, TX 75205; ba/Dallas; m/Elizabeth; c/Barbara, Lynda, Cullum Jr, Elizabeth, Robert Cedric; p/Robert William (dec) and Llora Cullum Thompson, Dallas, TX; ed/BS Wharton Sch, Univ Penn; pa/U Fidelity Ins Co: Pres 1961-, Exec VP 1960-61, Exec Com 1958-60, VP 1958, Bd Dirs 1958, Secy 1957-58; Dir, Mem Exec Com Citizens Nat Bank 1973; Dir Lofe Ofc Mgmt Assn 1979; cp/Bd Dirs Trinity Christian Acad; Dir Metro YMCA of Dallas, Nat Core Com; Dir Dallas Coun on World Affairs; Dir Dallas Zoological Soc; Dir Citizens Traffic Com; Dir Ctrl Bus Dist Assn; Dallas Assem; Dallas Citizens Coun; Salesmanship Clb of Dallas; NTSU Ins Adv Coun; Newcomen Soc of NA; Cotton Bowl Coun; Idlewild Clb; Dallas Country Clb; City Clb; r/Presb; Elder.

THOMPSON, PATRICIA W oc/Concert Pianist, Author; h/8719 Bold Forest, Houston, TX 77088; m/Thomas S; c/Stephanie Ann, Hilary

296

Faith; p/W R and Florence Williamson, El Paso, TX; pa/Concert Pianist; Author; Profl Model; r/Bapt; hon/W/W Am HS 1967.

THOMPSON, TINA MARCELLA oc/Speech and Language Pathologist; b/Aug 8, 1958; h/Rt 1 Box 1063, Orangeburg, SC 29115; p/Willie J and Pearl Thompson, O'burg, SC; ed/BA SC St Col 1979; Att'g Grad Sch, SC St Col; pa/SRA w 1890 Res Proj: An Investigation of Communication Behavior in Rural Chd; Nat Student Speech, Lang & Hearing Assn; Secy O'burg Chapt NSSLHA; cp/Am Red Cross; r/Cath; hon/Pres Schlr Silver Medallion 1976-77, 77-78, 78-79, 79-80; Alpha Kappa Alpha Awd 1978; Mobile Oil Contest Winner 1978; Jr Traineeship in Speech Pathol 1978-79; Nat Dean's List 1978-79; Sr Traineeship in Speech Pathol 1979; RSA S'ship 1980; Outstg Yng Wom Am 1979-80; Commun Ldrs of Am 1980; DIB 1980; Alpha Kappa Mu; Sigma Alpha Eta; Alpha Kappa Alpha.

THOMPSON, VIVIAN OPAL oc/Nurse; b/Nov 30, 1925; h/205 Penn Ave, Richlands, VA 24641; p/Luther Smith (dec) and Cora Bell Baugh Thompson (dec); ed/Dip Knoxville Gen Hosp Sch of Nsg 1947; Att'd Classes & Sems in Nsg, SW Commun Col 1973-81; pa/Reg'd Nurse VA, Tenn, WV; OB Supvr, Gen Hosp, Knoxville, Tenn 1947-48; Gen Duty, Clinch Valley Clin Hosp, Richlands, VA 1958-52; Ind Nsg, Morocco, Africa 1952-56; Supvr C V C Hosp, Richlands, VA 1957-61; Charge Nurse, Bluefield Sanitarium, Bluefield, WV 1961-65; Charge Nurse, Rochingham Meml Hosp, harrisonburg, Va 1965-68; Supvr C V C Hosp, Richlands, Va 1968-79; Charge Nurse OB Dept, CVCH 1979-; Past Mem Am Assn Indust Nurses; NLN; VLN; cp/Dem Party; r/Presb; hon/W/W Am Wom 1979-80; 11 Yr Cert of Achmt CVCH; DIB; Book of Hon; Men & Wom of Dist; World W/W Wom; Other Biogl Listings.

THORNTON, HOWARD L oc/Executive; b/July 14, 1934; h/Columbus, GA; ba/Plas-Tech Pers Inc, 3228 Cody Rd, Suite 107, Columbus, GA 31907; m/Sandra L; c/Tali Jay, Danielle Lee; p/Edith C Krause, Hartville, MO; mil/AUS 1954-74 Sgt; pa/Pres Plas-Tech Pers Inc 1976-; Mgr Dunhill of Columbus 1975-76; Mgr Wn Temporary Sers, Indust Div 1974; Nat Pers Assocs; Nat Fed Indep Bus; BBB; Hon Mem Ga Sheriff's Assn; cp/C of C; r/Prot; hon/W/W S&SW; Merit Ser Medal 1974; Bronze Star Medal 1971; 2 Army Commend Medals; Vietnam Ser Medal; Over 30 Certs of Achmt; Lttrs of Commend.

THORNTON, MARTHA KATHERINE (KITTY) oc/Writer, Lecturer, Historian; b/May 10, 1913; h/268 Hillsboro Ave, L'ton, KY 40505; m/James Winstead Sr; c/James Winstead Jr, Mary Gray Kelleher; p/Henry Daab; Mary Gray Daab (dec); ed/Att'd Univ Ky; Grad Fugazzi Bus Col; cp/Pres Wom's Clb of Ctrl Ky; Pres Fayette Co Homemkrs Assn; Secy Ky Br of NLAPW; Bd Govs Citizens Assn for Plan'g; Bd Dirs: Fam Cnslg Ser, Blue Cross/Blue Shield Consumers, Metro Envirl Improvement Comm; r/Cath; Pres St Peter Altar Soc; Dir Devel Lex Cath HS; hon/Ky Merit Mother 1979; Feature Article Winner, Ky Ext Homemkrs Assn 1974; W/W World of Wom; Author Num Articles.

THORNTON, NANCY RUMSEY oc/City Clerk; b/Aug 10, 1955; h/Rt 6 Box 657, Sylacauga, AL 35150; ba/Sylacauga; m/Steven; c/Raven Michelle; p/Emmett and Christine Rumsey, Sylacauga, AL; pa/City Clerk, Oak Grove, Ala; r/Bapt.

THOTA, VYKUNTAPATHI oc/Teacher, Researcher; b/Nov 3, 1940; h/Petersburg, Va; ba/Va St Univ, Box 5002-N, Petersburg, VA 23803; m/Ratnagirikumari; c/Srilakshmi; p/Seshadri and Lakshmamma; ed/BS Osmania Univ 1961; MS Kan St Univ 1962; PhD Mich St Univ 1966; pa/Va St Univ: Prof, Dept Lib Info Scis & Instrl Media, Sch Ed 1979-, Assoc Prof 1976-79, Asst Prof 1972-76; Asst Prof, Dept Instrl Tech, Sch Ed, So Ill Univ 1967-72; Mich St Univ: Res Assoc & Adm Asst, Nat Spec Media Insts, Instrl Media Ctr 1965-67, Res Asst 1965-65, Grad Asst, AV Ctr 1963-64; Assn for Ednl Communs & Tech; Phi Delta Kappa, VSU Chapt VP; Kappa Delta Pi; Beta Kappa Chi; ASCD; Dept of Higher Ed of VEA; VEMA; Intl AV Soc; HEMA; hon/W/W S&SW 1980; Intl AV Soc 1980; Am Film Inst 1980; Beta Kappa Chi 1978; Kappa Delta Pi 1976; Prof of Yr VSU 1974-75; Inst of Intl Ed F'ship Holder 1965; Phi Delta Kappa 1964; Grad Asst MSU 1963-64; Gold Medalist (summa cum laude) Osmania Univ 1961; Num Books & Papers Pub'd.

THRASH, SARA ARLINE oc/Educator; b/Mar 14, 1928; h/4200 14th Way NE, St Petersburg, FL 33703; ba/St Leo, FL; m/Willard; c/Douglas, Diane, Mark, David; p/Arlie E (dec) and Leola McDonald Cate (dec); ed/BA; MA; EdS; PhD; Post Doct Studies; pa/Prof Spec Ed; LD Conslt; Parent Therapist; Nat Lectr; cp/Jackson Co Fam Steering Com; Repub Task Force Com; Hd St Conslt; r/Bapt; SS Tchr Couples Class; Fam Living Wkshops; hon/Pres Cit; 2 Papers at First World Cong on Future Spec Ed, Scotland 1978; W/W: Ed, Am Wom; Author *Little Things That Keep Families Together & God, Go With Me Through My Detour*.

THRIFT, RALPH EVANS oc/Letter Carrier; b/Dec 31, 1934; h/Rt 4

Box 223, Rock Hill, SC 29730; ba/Rock Hill; m/Josephine G; c/Pamela, Amelia; p/Burt A Sr (dec) and Sally C Thrift, Rock Hill, SC; mil/AUS; pa/Postal Ser; Host Wkly TV Show; Cntry Wn Singer; Wn Sqare Dance Instr & Caller, Cert'd by Callerlab; Co-Prodr Carolina Cntry; SC Callers Assn, Pres 1978-79; Intl Callers Assn; cp/Am Legion; Mason; Shriner; r/Bapt; hon/Awd of Apprec for Sers, Gov of SC Robert West 1968.

THURMAN, MORTIMER JEFFERSON SR oc/Facility Director; b/Nov 15, 1937; h/Rt 1 Box 113T, Jackson's Gap, AL 36861; ba/Alex City, AL; m/Joyce Amelia Templeton; c/Mortimer Jefferson Jr, Margaret Alma, Sarah Louise; p/Marion Augustus and Alma Baldwin Thurman, Sylacauga, AL; ed/BS 1960, MEd 1977 Auburn Univ; pa/Commun Based Facility Dir, St of Ala Dept Corrections; Ala Chief Probation Ofcrs Assn, Secy; FOP Lodge #23, Chaplain; Am Assn Correctional Assn; E Ala Peace Ofcrs Assn, Pres & Secy; Ala Peace Ofcrs Assn; Ala Law Enforcement Plan'g Agcy; cp/Lions Clb, Tail Twister; Bethel Vol Fire Dept, Chief; E Tallapoosa Emer Med Ser, Pres; EMT Assn, Coosa-Tallapoosa, Pres; Ala Forestry Comm Rural Commun Fire Protec Steering Com, Chm; r/Meth; ho/Authro "Alternatives to Detention" for 17th Annual Conf on Corrections; "Convict Labor in the Southeastern United States."

THURMAN, NANCY LEE oc/Homemaker; b/Aug 1, 1924; h/3238 Circle Dr, Hopkinsville, KY 42240; m/Duard N; c/D Niven, John Lochry; p/Jess (dec) and Eddie Bates Lochry (dec); ed/BS w High Dist Univ Ky; pa/Former Tchr Home Ec & Eng; cp/Pres Ch Wom U in Ky 1977-80; Pres Wom's Clb, Univ of Ky Commun Col; Pres Assn for SPMD; Ofcr LWV; r/Meth; Ofcr in Local, Dist Conf UMW; Lay Leader; U Meth Conf Bds; hon/Valiant Wom 1979; Wom of Yr 1976.

THURMAN, VIVIAN LOUISE ANDERS oc/Associate Geophysical Technician; b/Dec 2, 1944; h/310 E Wadley, Midland, TX 79701; ba/Midland; m/Curtis L; c/Tyrone, Kirk; p/John and Lucille Jane Anders, Midland, TX; ed/Att'd Prairie View A&M Col 1961-65; pa/Assoc Geophys Tech, Exxon Co USA; r/Bapt.

TICE, JESSICA IRENE SPRUILL oc/Extension Home Economist; b/Mar 21, 1952; h/Rt 2 Box 60, Moyock, NC 27958; ba/Currituck; m/Roger Jeffrey; p/William Edward and Erma Irene Phelps Spruill; ed/AA Col of the Albemarle 1973; BS ECU 1975; Att'g NCSU; pa/Assoc Home Ec Ext Agt, NC Agric Ext Ser, NCSU 1977-; Am Home Ec Assn; Nat Assn Ext Home Ecists; NC Assn Ext Home Ecists, NE Dist Secy 1978, 2nd VP 1979, 1st VP 1980; Pres-Elect 1981; cp/Currituck Coun on the Status of Wom; Currituck Hist Soc; Currituck Friends of the Lib; Currituck Ski & Outing Clb, Secy-Treas 1979; Moyock Wom's Clb; hon/Yng Agts Ser Awd 1980; Phi Upsilon Omicron 1974; W/W Am Wom 1981-82; Notable Personalities of Am 1981.

TIDWELL, MARY ALICE oc/Executive; Certified Public Accountant; b/Apr 16, 1924; h/2216 Wn Dr, Midland, TX 79701; ba/Midland; p/M Anthony (dec) and Ella Lenora Taylor Tidwell (dec); ed/AAS Abilene Christian Univ & Odessa Col; pa/CPA; VP Fin, Knox Industs Inc; Am Inst CPAs; Tex Soc CPAs; Permian Basin Petro Assn; cp/Immed Past Pres Altrusa Clb of Midland; Treas Dist 9 Altrusa Intl Inc 1978-80; US Senatorial Clb; r/Ch of Christ; hon/Awd as Outst Com Chm, Permian Basin Chapt TSCPAs 1971-72.

TIDWELL, NORMAN OLEN oc/Electronic Technician; b/May 21, 1927; m/Mary Ann Benson; c/Byron Otis, James Robert; p/Shuford Bascom (dec) and Lillie Estelle Tidwell, Texarkana, TX; mil/Naval Constr Batt 144; pa/Elec Tech, NASA; cp/Huntsville Obediance Tng Clb, Past Pres & Tng Dir.

TIETKE, WILHELM oc/Gastroenterologist; b/Oct 15, 1938; h/2707 Westminster Way, Huntsville, AL 35801; ba/H'ville; m/Imme; c/Cornelia, Claudia, Isabel; p/Frieda Tietke, W Germany; ed/MD Univ Goettingen 1968; Internship Sparrow Hosp 1970; Resident 1971-73, F'ship Gastroenterology 1973-75 Henry Ford Hosp; pa/Internal Med/Gastro-enterology; AMA; ACP; ASGE; r/Luth.

TILLETT, VIRGINIA SIMMONS oc/Coordinator; b/May 22, 1941; h/Manteo, NC; m/William Leo Sr; c/Johnny Lugo, Michael Anthony; p/William Seward and Earlene Simmons, Manteo, NC; ed/Att'd Elizabeth City St Univ 1959-60, 1975; Col of the Albemarle, Div of Cont'g Ed; pa/Coor Off-Campus Col Courses & Adult Cont'g Ed Courses; CETA Cnslr, Ec Improvement Coun Inc 1979-80; Libn Dare Co Public Lib 1974-79; Hd Tchr Ec Improvement Coun Inc 1965-74; NC Lib Assn; Employment & Tng Assn; NC Sch Bd Assn; cp/NC Marine Fsheries Comm; Dare Co Bd Ed, VChm; Den Mother Dare Co Boy Scouts; Chp PTA Prog Com; Circus Tent Min Vols; Grand Jury; Dem Party; Bd Mem Ec Improvement Coun; Roanoke Commun Orgs; Home Hlth Org; VChp Dare Co Cancer Soc; Fin Secy U Order of Tent #269; NC LWV; Leg Com Chp, NC BPW; r/Bapt; SS Tchr, Fin Secy.

TILLMAN, CELESTINE oc/Teacher; b/Dec 12, 1933; h/10761 S Gibbens Dr, Baton Rouge, LA 70807; ba/Baton Rouge; p/Elbert Lee Tillman Sr, LA, CA; Lillie May Tillman (dec); ed/BS So Univ 1955; MS Howard Univ 1957; Post Grad Study Penn St Univ, La St Univ; pa/So Univ: Analytical & Inorganic Chem Instr 1957-63, Asst Prof 1963-80, Assoc Prof 1980-; Res Chem, Atlantic Richfield Hanford Co, Summer 1973, 77; Res Fellow Penn St Univ 1958-60; NSF Chem Fac Fellow, La St Univ, Summers 1968, 69, 71; Am Chem Soc; Nat Org for Profl Advmt of Black Chems & Chem Engrs; AAAS; Iota Sigma Pi; SDE/GWIS; Phi Delta Kappa; Assn for Wom in Sci; La Acad of Sci; Baton Rouge Anal Instr Discussion Grp; Kappa Delta Pi; Alpha Kappa Mu; Beta Kappa Chi; cp/Delta Sigma Theta; LVW; YWCA; NAACP; La Coun on Human Relats; Audubon Coun GSA; Nat Coun Negro Wom; r/Christian; hon/Chem Tchr of Yr, So Univ 1979-80.

TILLY, LOIS AMELIA oc/Teacher, Organist; b/Jan 27; h/PO Box 3442, New Orleans, AL 70177; ba/New Orleans; p/Rev and Mrs Andrew T Tilly, Chgo, IL; ed/BA So Univ; MA Xavier Univ; Further Studies Loyola Univ, Univ So Miss; pa/Vocal Mus Tchr, PA Capdau Jr HS; Min Mus Ctrl Missionary Bapt Ch; Secy Bethlehem Bapt Ch; Guest Organist Mt Zion Bapt Ch, Grace Chapel, St James Meth Ch La, New Olivet, Ebenezer, Stronger Hope Bapt Ch; Mus Edrs Nat Conf; F'ship of Christian Mus; Am Choral Dirs Assn; Middle Sch Assn; Choiristers Guild; r/Ctrl Missionary Bapt Ch: Min Mus, Bkkpr, Exec Secy, Chancel Choir, Willing Wkrs, Jr Mission, Dir Piano Ed, Asst BTU Tchr, Dir VBS, Co-Organist, Nat Bapt Conv 1977; Nat Bapt St Conv 1980; hon/W/W 17th Ed; Author *Music in the Middle Schools;* Accompanist to Brenda L Cooper on Album "His Eye is on the Sparrow" & to Willa Mae Brown on 45 "A Charge to Keep I Have."

TIMBERLAKE, ROBERTS EDGAR oc/Artist; b/Jan 22, 1937; h/621 Rosewood Dr, Lexington, NC 27292; ba/L'ton; m/Kay Musgrave; c/Robin Kelly, Roberts Edgar Jr, Daniel Lee; p/Casper H Sr and Ella Raper Timberlake, Lexington, NC; ed/BS Univ NC-Chapel Hill; mil/NROTC Univ NC; pa/VP Past Owner Piedmont Gas Ser Co, Piedmont Funeral Home Inc & The Land Co; Pres & Owner The Heritage Gal; NC Arts Coun, Bd Dirs; NC Sch of the Arts, Adv Bd; High Pt Col, Bd Visitors; Wake Forest Univ, Chm of Parents Coun; cp/Ofcl Bd 1st U Meth Ch; Sigma Chi; JCs; Order of Gimghoul; Kiwanis; Bd Dirs Uwhammie Coun of BSA; r/Meth; hon/Ofcl Artist of Keep Am Beautiful Inc; Designed & Painted US PS Christmas Stamp 1980; Public Ser Awd, NC 1979; Author *The Bob Timberlake Collection* 1977 & *The World of Bob Timberlake* 1979; Pub'd in Num Periodicals.

TINDOL, LAYMON HAYES oc/Salesman; b/June 25, 1949; h/533 N John St, N Brockton, AL 36351; m/Edith Marler; c/Lance; p/Walter Ray and Annie Lee Willis Tindol, N Brockton, AL; pa/Rt Salesman, Propane Gas & Appliance Co; cp/Past Dir N Brockton JCs; Capt New Brockton Rescue Squad, 1st Lt 8 Mos; Ala Assn Rescue Squads; St Lic'd EMT; Appt'd to City Coun Mar; Elect'd City Coun-man July 1980; r/Ch of God.

TINKER, J TROY oc/Student, Continuity Director; b/Sept 23, 1957; h/Rt 5, Box 221 LL, Conway, AR 72032; ba/Conway; m/Margaret Anne Gunderman; p/Herman L Tinker (dec); Jesse Tinker Snow, Vilonia, AR; ed/BA Cand; pa/Advtg Copywriter; Broadcaster; cp/Conway Commun Arts; K of C; r/Cath; hon/Nat Pi Kappa Delta Champ Oral Interpretation 1977; 2 Pi Kappa Gold Medals 1979.

TINKEY, TED D oc/Manager; b/Feb 11, 1937; h/1522 Zebulon Dr, Griffin, GA 30223; ba/Griffin; m/Jane Shipp; c/Michelle; p/Mildred Tinkey, Pierceton, IN; ed/BS Purdue Univ; mil/AUS; pa/Mgr Centeral Plan'g, Basics Div; cp/Moose Clb; Lions Clb; r/Meth; hon/Ser Awd Moose; Sales Awd Century 21.

TIPPIT, CLIFFORD BRUCE oc/Pastor; b/Jan 9, 1954; h/PO Box 97, Lewisville, AR 71845; m/Kathy Joan Marable; p/Von and Jean Tippit, Hot Springs, AR; ed/BA Ouachita Bapt Univ 1976; MDiv SWn Bapt Theol Sem 1979; pa/Pastor; cp/Rotary Clb; r/Bapt; hon/W/W Am Cols & Univs 1976.

TISDALE, VERLIE ANN oc/Teacher; b/Dec 17, 1948; h/5035 Riverdale Rd N-16, College Pk, GA 30337; ba/Atlanta; m/Lamar; c/Dedric Durell; p/Joseph and Comuel Jackson, Englewood, NJ; ed/BS; MS; PhD; pa/Biol Tchr, Spelman Col; SEn Am So Microbiol; SEn Cancer Res Assn; SEn Cell & Devel Biol; r/U Meth.

TITUS, PHYLLIS oc/Radiation Therapy Technologist; b/July 9, 1949; h/3095 Peacock Ln, Mulberry, FL 33869; ba/Lakeland; m/Lon; c/Bryan; p/Charles and Aline West, Dunn, NC; ed/Grad Radiologic Technol Sch 1969; Grad Univ Ctrl Fla Sch Radiation Therapy 1980; pa/Chief Technol in Radiation Therapy, Lakeland Gen Hosp, Dept Radiation Therapy; r/Bapt; hon/Grad 1st in Class in RT Sch & RTT Sch.

TOBAL, MARCOS ANDRES oc/Electrical Engineer, Land Developer; b/Sept 19, 1952; h/Hollywood, FL; ba/Harbour Terrace Inc, 1160 Kane Concourse, Bay Harbor Islands, FL 33154; m/Jane Mae; c/Rachel, Joseph Eli; p/Jose and Joyce Tobal, Surfside, FL; ed/BS Univ Miami 1975; pa/Elec Engr Nat Elecs, Mexico City 1975; Engr-Owner Studio Ctr Sound Recordings Inc 1976-79; Pres, Land Develr, Harbour Terrace Inc 1979-; Pres, Elec Res, Overtone Inc 1976-; Audio Engrg Soc; Nat Space Inst; IEEE; cp/Solar Lobby; Intl Aquanaut Foun; hon/Gold Record Awds: "Do You Wanna Get Funky with Me?" 1977, "Fantasy Love Affair" 1978, "Dance With Me" 1978 (by Peter Brown); "Get Off" (Single & LP by Foxy); W/W S&SW 1980.

TOBEY, HELEN MARGARETHA oc/Civic Worker; b/Apr 6, 1938; h/1730 Fla Ave, Woodbridge, VA 22191; ba/Woodbridge; m/Orn H; c/Melissa, Donnamarie, Rex, Kristina; p/Daniel H and Helen Kirk Pleitner; ed/Wash Missionary Col; pa/Att'd Acting Dir, Prince William Co Mtl Hlth, Mtl Retard Ser Bd 1976-77; Appt'd to Direct 2 Non-Profit Co Funded Spec Ed Facs into Prince William Co Sch Sys 1975; Appt'd to Form & Chair Multiple Disciplinary Team to Staff Spec Needs at Indep Hill Sch for Excptl Chd 1974-76; Urban Redevel Ofcl, St Paul, Minn 1971-72; cp/Prince William Co Dem Com 1973-; Chm Dumfries Dist Dem Com 1977-79; Prince William Co Mtl Hlth & Mtl Retard Ser Bd: VChm 1974-75, Chm 1975-; Dumfries Hist Soc; VFW Aux; OES; Order of White Shrine of Jerusalem; UDC; Prince William Co Rep Hlth Sys Agcy No Va; No Va Substance Abuse Coun to No Va Plan'g Dist Comm; No Va Mtl Hlth & Retard Sers Bd; Former Mem Comprehensive Hlth Plan'g Coun No Va; Bd Dirs & Exec Com Prince William Co Chapt Am Red Cross; Chm Woodbridge Nsg Home Citizen's Bd Dirs; Chm Woodbridge Nsg Home Citizens Bd Dirs; r/En Orthodox; hon/Citizen of Yr, Wash Star Prince William Co 1976; Recip 2 Gubernatorial Awds for Outstg Humanitarian Ser.

TODD, BETTY MAE oc/Retired; b/Feb 6, 1927; h/PO Box 1410, Altamonte Springs, FL 32701; m/Byron Eugene; c/Dale Patricia; p/Walter Lewis Brown (dec); Ethel L Hughes (dec); ed/Alexandria Sch Nsg; pa/Pediactric Affil, Chd's Hosp, Wash DC; Psychi Affil, St Elizabeth's Psychi Hosp, Wash DC; Public Hlth Affil, Alexandria, Va Out-Patient Clin & In-Home; Pvt Duty Nurse 1950-51; Recovery Room, Walter Reed Army Med Ctr 1951-71; Pt-time Winter Pk & Fla S in ER, Seminole Meml Hosp Utilization Review Coor Infection Control Nurse, Orlando Gen Hosp Charge Nurse 1973-78; hon/W/W Am 1979-80; Awd for Invention of Cardiac Cath Machine Lock; Awd for Invention of Bugi Case Used for Urethral Dilation.

TODD, LEE BARNHARDT oc/Physician; b/Mar 13, 1905; h/Quinwood, WV; m/Daisy Burns; c/Jane T Young, John R, Ann T Jones; ed/BS Col of William and Mary 1927; MD Med Col Va 1932; Internship Med Col of Va 1932-34; pa/GP of Med 1934-43, Quinwood, WV; Med Dept AUS 1943-46; Dir Hlth Dept, Newport News, VA 1946-51; GP of Med, Quinwood, WV 1951-; Chapt Am Acad Pediatrics; Assn Am Phys & Surgs; Am Heart Assn; WV Heart Assn; Greenbrier Med Assn; AMA; Pi Kappa Alpha; ODK; AOA; AAPS; Chi Beta Phi; Theta Chi Delta; cp/Super Chiefs Clb, William & Mary Col; Col of William & Mary Ednl Foun; Greenbrier Golf & Tennis Clb; Rainelle Golf Clb; Co-Fdr Order of the White Jackets; Nat Mussle Loading Rifle Assn; Nat Trust for Hist Preserv; Smithsonian Assocs; Shriners; Grand Capt Royal Arch Masons; Grand Commandery of Knights Temple of the St of WV; Pres's Coun of the Col of William & Mary 1973-78; Pres Order of the White Jacket; William & Mary Hall of Fame; hon/Commun Ldrs Am; 2000 Men Achmt; W/W E; Commun Ldrs S; AMA; Am Thoracic Soc; DIB; English Blue Book; Personalities of WV; Wisdom Awd of Hon; Man of Yr Wn Greenbrier Area C of C 1976; Intl Reg of Profile; Fellow Royal Soc Hlth; WV Heritage Ency; Nat Social Reg; Intl Platform Assn; W/W Am; Nat Audubon Soc.

TODD, PARRISH oc/Producer; b/June 15, 1956; h/Shelby, NC; pa/PO Box 2119, Shelby, NC 28150; p/William Scott and Miriam Fincher Todd, Shelby, NC; ed/Att'd Univ SC; pa/Prodr: Films, Commercials, TV, Features, Industs, Documentaries.

TOLAND, MARY BERNADETTE oc/Social Worker; b/Aug 7, 1941; h/3412 Garrison St NW, Wash DC 20008; ba/Wheaton, MD; p/Edmund Michael (dec) and Lenora Sheehan Toland (dec); pa/NASW; Reg Clin Social Wkrs; Acad Cert'd Social Wkrs; Gtr Wash Soc Clin Social Work; cp/Mlt Hlth Adv Com, Bd Ed, Mtgy City, Md; r/Cath; hon/Recog & Apprec Awd, Am Assn Chd w Lrng Disabilities; W/W Am Wom 1979-80; Nat Inst of Mtl Hlth Trainee 1978-79; Treas Doc Students Assn, Cath Univ Am.

TOLLESON, TOMMY KEITH oc/Social Worker; b/Feb 18, 1951; h/Sherman, TX; m/Martha Freeman; c/Keith Freeman; p/Victor S and Virginia Tolleson, Greenville, TX; ed/BS E Tex St Univ 1975; pa/Social Wkr, Tex Dept Human Resources; Grayson Co Social Sers Assn; r/Prot; hon/Social Sers Wkr of Yr 1980.

TOLLISON, ROBERT HORACE oc/Chief Administrator; b/Nov 24, 1933; h/Sherman, TX; m/Virginia Adell; c/Robert H Jr, Danny; p/Clarence and Namoi Tollison, Denison, TX; ed/Certs Univ Tex-Austin, Lamar Univ, Univ Tex-Arlington; mil/USAF 1952-56; pa/Chief Admr & Chief Appraiser, Grayson Co Single Appraisal Dist; Tex Assn Assessing Ofcrs; NE Chapt Assessing Ofcrs; r/Bapt.

TOMASSI, THERESA CECILIA oc/Executive Secretary; b/Dec 13, 1959; h/153 NW 3rd Ave, Florida City, FL 33034; ba/Homestead, FL; p/Joseph Frank and Adriana Tecla Tomassi; pa/Exec Secy, Gen Supt DCA Housing; cp/Campaigning Senatorial Elec 1978; r/Cath; hon/Pres's Hon Roll; Deans List.

TOMLIN, ALTRAC RUTH oc/Counselor; b/Aug 9, 1932; h/Killeen, TX; ba/Killeen HS, 500 N 38 St, Killeen, TX 76541; m/Shafter; c/Deborah, Craig, Sheryl, Cristel; p/Henry and Blanche Speight, Mt Vernon, NY; ed/BS 1967; MEd 1974; EdD Cand; pa/Cnslr, Killeen HS; Killeen Clrm Tchrs Assn, Pres 1978-79, Pres Elec 1977-78, Human Relats Chm, Mbrship Chm, Tchr Pers Sers Chm, Retirement Chm; TSTA; TCTA; NEA; TPGA; cp/Mu Theta Omega Chapt, Alpha Kappa Alpha, Pres; Tex Black Dem Caucus; NAACP; Public Relats Chp for Cand for City Coun; r/Bapt; hon/Human Relats Awd, Dist XII TSTA; Human Relats Awd TCTA 1977; Best Spkr Awd, Twin Lakes Toastmistress Clb 1976.

TOMLIN, HYRICE oc/Admission Counselor and Recruiter; b/Dec 15, 1952; h/Langston, OK; ba/Langston Univ, Langston, OK 73050; m/Vickey Ann; c/Lakisha, Hyrice; p/Elwood and Thelma Tomlin, Boley, OK; ed/BA Langston Univ 1977; mil/AUS 1972-74; pa/HS & Col Relation Ofcr, Langston Univ; 3rd Class Broadcasters Lic; cp/Alpha Phi Alpha; NAACP; r/Bapt.

TOMPKINS, ROBERT THOMAS oc/Teacher, Painter; b/June 2, 1943; h/1253 Cottage Dr, Greenville, MS; m/Nadene Parham; c/Michael Jay, Allyson Carol; p/William Charles and Sarah Brown Tompkins, Greenville, MS; ed/BS 1965, MEd 1973 Delta St Univ; pa/Art Tchr: Jacksonville, Fla 1967-68, Solomon JR HS, Greenville, MS 1966-67; Greenville HS 1968-; Wildlife Painter; Portrait & Still-life Painter; Miss Art Ed Assn; G'ville Clrm Tchr Assn; cp/G'ville Art Assn Bd 1969; r/Bapt; hon/Grand Awd, SEn Art Awd, Panama City, Fla 1974; Winner 1980 Miss Duck Stamp Contest; 2nd Pl Crosstie Fest, Cleveland, Miss 1975; Pi Kappa Alpha, Pledge Master 1964; Inner Circle, Delta St Univ; Secy Freshman Class, DSU 1961-62; Portarit Dr Henry Jacobs, Dean of Ed DSU.

TOPPIN, GWENDOLYN LILA oc/Teacher; b/Oct 3, 1921; h/7918 Rodeo, El Paso, TX 79915; m/Cyril F; p/Raliegh (dec) and Mollie Westfield (dec); ed/Att'd: Ala A&M Col; Ala St Tchrs Col; BA Tex Wn Col; MA Univ Tex-El Paso; Cert Spec Ed & Supvrn UTEP; Booker T Wash Bus Col; Intl Bus Col; pa/Asst Libn Ala A&M Col; Tchr Anniston Public Schs; Oper Benham Beauty Shop; Tchr: Fort Knox Day Care Care Nursery & Kindergarten, El Paso Indep Sch Dist; CEC Hosp; NEA; TSTA; Tex Clrm Tchrs Assn, Del to Conv; El Pso Tchrs Assn, Fac Rep; Rep for Henderson Jr High, Tchrs Hon Soc; Delta Kappa Gamma, Photog, S'ship Chm; Kappa Delta Pi, Hist & Photog, Decorations Chm; Alpha Psi Omega; cp/Asst Girl Scout Ldr, Troop 66, Cotolquilla Coun; Den Mother, Cub Scouts; Jr Hostess USO, Anniston, Ala; Fest Theater Part, El Paso "Miracle Worker"; "The Crucible"; "MacBeth"; Downtown Theater Part, El Paso "Street Car Named Desire"; OES; Daughs of Isis: Illus Commandress, 1st Lt Commandress, 2nd Lt Commandress, 1st Ceremonial Daugh; Henderson PTA; El Paso Br AAUW; Wom's Aux Univ Tex, Communs Com; Delta Sigma Theta; Nat Leag Am Pen Wom Inc, El Paso Br; Wom's Dept El Paso C of C; El Paso Ballet Guild; Links Inc; El Paso Edrs Polit Com; Nat Coun Negro Wom; r/Meth; hon/Tchr of Yr Henderson Inter Sch 1963; Nom'd Best Actress, Fest Theater; Chosen Best Crew Mem, Col Players, Tex Wn Col; First Black to Appear in Theatrical Prod on Stage at Tex Wn Col; First Black to Receive Deg at Tex Wn Col 1957; SW Cultural Aw 1979; Delta Wom of Yr 1979.

TOPSY, AZEAL oc/Homemaker; b/Aug 13, 1906; h/522 E Shepherd St, Denison, TX 75020; m/William; c/George Washington, Dorothy Nell, Washie Nell Dehorney; p/Morris (dec) and Alice White (dec); pa/Ret'd Missionary, Evangelist; r/Bapt.

TORCZYNSKI, ELISE oc/Physician; b/July 2, 1933; h/13631 Twin Lake Ln, Tampa, FL 33624; ba/Tampa; p/Vincent Francis and Helen Anne Torczynski, Chgo, IL; ed/BS; MD; pa/Dir Eye Pathol Lab, Univ S Fla; Chief of Ophthalmology Ser, Haley VAH, Tampa; r/Cath; hoh/NIH-HEED F'ships 1973-75.

TOUTEN, LINDA A oc/Teacher; b/July 15, 1952; h/Daytona Bch, FL; ba/Mainland Sr HS, 125 S Clyde Morris Blvd, Daytona Bch, FL 32015; p/Nicolena C Touten, Daytona Bch, FL; ed/AA Daytona Bch Commun Col 1972; BA Univ S Fla 1974; pa/Tchr Speech/Debate & Eng: Seabreeze

Sr HS 1 Yr, Mainland Sr HS 6 Yrs; Volusia Co Edrs Assn; Fla & Nat Speech Commun Assns; NCTE; cp/Reg'd Dem; r/Cath; hon/Outstg Non-Tenure Tchr of Yr, Mainland Sr HS 1977; Fla Speech Conv Panel Spkr 1978 & 79.

TOWNES, WILLA MAE CRAWFORD oc/Retired Librarian; b/Nov 25, 1897; h/Van Dr, Seminole, OK 74868; m/John Bibb (dec); c/Ann; p/Charles and Elmira Crawford (dec); ed/BS; MLS; pa/Ret'd Home Ec Instr & Libn Seminole Jr Col; Former Owner, Mgr The Townes Newcomer Ser; cp/Okla Arts & Humanities Coun; Dir Seminole Hist Soc; r/Meth; hon/Awds from St & Seminole Arts Coun; Awds from Seminole Hist Soc.

TRAMMEL, DOROTHY JEAN oc/Teacher Assistant; b/Jan 24, 1928; h/Rt 3 Box 455, Portland, TN 37148; m/Harold L Sr; c/Harold L Jr, Blenda Jean; p/Carlin and Estelle Vaughn, Portland, TN; pa/Title I Rdg Tchr Assn, Sumner Co Bd Ed, Gallatin, TN; PTA, Pres Elem & HS; Treas Sumner Co Coun of PTAs; r/Ch of Christ; hon/Life Mem PTA 1966.

TRAMMELL, ALSIE oc/Retired; b/Dec 12, 1909; h/3176 Valleydale Dr SW, Atlanta, GA 30311; p/Townsend Jackson (dec) and Alzadie Davidson Trammell (dec); ed/BA Bennett Col 1937; BSN Dillard Univ 1947; mil/US Cadet Nurse Corp 1944-47; pa/Dir Student Hlth Sers, Bennett Col 1947-80; Dir Student Hlth Sers, Nat Sci Foun Progs 1960-77; Am Col Hlth Assocs; Am Nat Red Corss; r/Meth; hon/Placcue, Bennett Col Fam 1980; Placque Bennett Col Nat Alumnus Assn Spec Ser Awd 1980.

TRANQUILLO, MARY DORA oc/Program Coordinator; b/Apr 14, 1943; h/34 Turnstone Dr, Clearwater, FL 33519; ba/C'water; m/Joseph A; c/Maria; p/Guy and Dora Caranfa, St Petersburg, FL; ed/BFA Pratt Inst 1965; MA NYU 1971; Further Study: Fashion Inst of Technol, Univ S Fla, Univ Bridgeport, Sacred Heart Univ; pa/Instr St Petersburg Jr Col; Home Ec Tchr: Plant City HS, Brandon Jr HS, & Derby HS; Art Tchr St Joseph's HS, Christ the King HS; Asst Buyer Frederick Atkins; Koscot Distbr; Freelance Designer; Prog Coor Fashion Mdsg; AHEA, Mbrship Chm; FVA; AVA; FACC; ACPTC; cp/Kiwanis Aux; r/Rom Cath; hon/Student Govt Silver Awd 1965; W/W S&SW 1980-81; DECA Outstg Sers Awd 1979.

TREADWAY, JAMES L oc/Postmaster; b/Sept 9, 1930; h/Rt 3 Box 108, Timberidge Rd, Erwin, TN 37650; ba/Flag Pond; m/Ora Dean; c/James Douglas, Charles Duane, Timothy Darian; p/Arthur and Mary Lee Treadway, Brookneal, VA; mil/USAF Ret'd; cp/Pres HS Band Boosters Assn; VP HS PTA; Co Tax Equalization Bd; r/Bapt: Deacon, SS Dir; hon/Sev Mil Awds & Decorations Incl'g 2 Bronze Stars.

TREEN, DAVID C oc/Governor of Louisiana; b/July 16, 1928; h/Gov's Mansion, Baton Rouge, LA; ba/Baton Rouge; m/Dolores Brisbi; c/Jennifer Neville, David Conner Jr, Cynthia Lunceford; p/Joseph Paul and Elizabeth Spier Treen; ed/BA Tulane Univ 1948; LLB Tulane Univ Law Sch 1950; mil/USAF 1950-52; pa/Assoc Atty, Deutsch, Kerrigan & Stiles 1950-51; VP & Legal Counsel, Simplex Mfg Corp 1952-57; Assoc Atty, Beard, Blue & Schmitt (Later Ptnr Beard, Blue, Schmitt & Treen) 1957-72; Congressman, 3rd Dist of La 1973-80; Gov, St of La 1980-; Mem Num Repub Coms Throughout Career; hon/Recip Dist'd Ser Awd, Nat Yng Repub Fed 1968; Hon Grad Tulane Univ Law Sch.

TRENT, KENNETH EUGENE oc/Farmer, Rancher; b/Dec 9, 1940; h/Dumont Rt, Paducah, TX 79248; ba/Same; m/Jane R; c/Kerry; p/EL and Thelma Trent, Lufkin, TX; ed/BBA W Tex St Univ; mil/AUS 1964-70; cp/Bd Dirs King-Cottle Water Corp; Airport Bd; r/Disciples of Christ; hon/Dist'd Flying Cross; Outstg Yng Men Am 1976.

TRENT, ROSE MARIE oc/Financial Executive, Taxidermist; b/Oct 7, 1943; h/Rt 2 Box 125A, Yukon, OK 73099; ba/Yukon; m/Jeffrey C; c/Anna Marie, Tracy Neal (Buddy), Jeffrey Earl, Stoney Alexander, Sunny Eric; p/Alex and Mary Lou Hooyman, Grand Marais, MI; ed/Att'd La Salle Univ 1968-72; BS Ctrl St Univ 1981; pa/Owner J&R Ranch-Acctg Ser 1968-78; Pres J&R Ranch Inc 1978-; Secy & Fin Advr, Jeffrey C Trent, CPA Inc; Clifton Oil & Gas Inc; Gold Crown Res Inc 1979; Dir & Fin Advr Southside Auto Body Inc 1978-; ARC & SPARC Inc 1979-; VP & Dir Hillman's Taxidermy Studio Inc 1980-; Nat Taxidermy Assn; Okla Taxidermist Assn, Secy-Treas 1980; ABWA, Treas Yukon Chapt; Ducks Unltd; Bass Anglers Assn; Nat Rifle Assn; Smithsonian Inst; Nat Wildlife Fed; cp/Ldr Campfire Girls: Yukon 1972-74, Dist Ldr 1972-74; r/Cath; hon/W/W Am Wom 1980.

TRENTHAM, HAROLD LEE oc/Executive; b/Nov 3, 1923; m/Marjorie Valentine; c/Marsha Lee, Harold Lee Jr, Gary Lee; p/Shannon Otis and Ina Davis Rankin Trentham; ed/AA Mars Hill Col; BChe NC St Univ; pa/Pres CEO Trentham Corp/Graff Engrg Corp 1960-; VP Engrg Delta Engrg Corp 1955-60; Process Engr, VP Opers, Fish Engrg Corp 1948-58; Res Engr, Celanese Corp/Tenn Eastman Co 1943-48; Tex Profl Engr #10,571; Intl Platform Assn; Univ Clb; Tex Soc Profl Engrs; AIChE;

PERSONALITIES OF THE SOUTH

ACS; AAAS; SAR; cp/Houston C of C; US C of C; Galveston Hist Foun VP; Tex Law Enforcement Ofcrs Assn; U Fed of Doll Clbs; Sminthsonian Assocs; r/Bapt; hon/Sev US, Can & Brit Patents in Field; Author Sev Articles in Jours Relat'd to Petrochems, Sulfur, Chem.

TREUTING, EDNA GANNON oc/Director Nursing Section; b/Dec 16, 1925; h/8040 Morrison Rd, New Orleans, LA 70126; ba/New Orleans; m/August Raymond; c/Keith, Karen, Madeline, Jaime, Jay; p/Alphonse Joseph (dec) and Clara David Gannon (dec); ed/DPH; MPH; BSN Ed; RN; FNP; pa/Dir Nsg Sect Tulane SPH & TM; Nsg Ed Dir Commun Hlth Nsg; Fam Nurse Pract; Nsg Adm & Occupl Hlth Nsg; r/Cath; hon/Outstg Wom of Day 1960-61; Pres Opti-Mrs Intl Ldrship Awd 1961; Nom'd Nat Delta Omega Merit Awd 1978; W/W Hlth Care 1977; Delta Omega, Eta Chapt 1976; W/W Am Wom 1978.

TREVINO, FERNANDO MANUEL oc/Health Services Researcher; b/Aug 20, 1949; h/10427 Tullymore Dr, Adelphi, MD 20783; ba/Hyattsville, MD; m/Dorothy Bullock; p/Manuel Emilio and Consuelo Galindo Trevino, Eagle Pass, TX; ed/BS Univ Houston 1971; MPH 1975, PhD 1979 Univ Tex; mil/AUS Med Ser Corps Capt; pa/Asst Prof Fam Med, Univ Tex Med Br 1980-; Social Sci Analyst, Nat Ctr for Hlth Statistics 1980-; Coor Spec Progs, Univ Tex Med Br-Galveston 1974-80; Instr Allied Hlth Scis, Univ Tex Med Br 1973-74; Am Public Hlth Assn; Am Acad Hlth Adm; Sigma Xi; r/Cath; hon/Outstg Yng Men Am 1978; Men of Achmt 1980; W/W S&SW 1980; Num Pubs in Med, Psychi, & Behavioral Sci Jours.

TREVINO, RAMIRO R oc/Retired; b/Nov 20, 1921; h/PO Box 662, 1234 Easterling, Alice, TX 78332; m/Ercilia G; c/Maria I, Rosalinda, Luis C, Elddy C; p/Jose E (dec) and Frances R Trevino; mil/1942-46; pa/Ret'd Postal Employee; Mgr Security Agcy; Pres Postal Union 2 Terms; cp/PTA, Pres 3 Yrs; City Coun PTA, VP 1 Yr; r/Cath; hon/Hon Awds for Part in Commun Sports for Yth 1976-78; BSA 1950-68.

TREW, REBA CLAIR oc/Homemaker; b/Dec 4, 1925; h/Greenville, KY; m/Buford O; c/Leland Jiles; p/Gideon Morgan (dec) and Harriet Jane Jiles (dec); ed/Att'g Ky Wesleyan Col; cp/Muhlenberg Co Art Guild; G'ville Wom's Clb; r/Meth; hon/Best of Show, Annual Juried Spring Art Comp, Ky Wesleyan Col 1980.

TRICKEL, JOHN oc/Professor; b/Aug 25, 1942; h/Richardson, TX; ba/Richland Col, 12800 Abrams Rd, Dallas, TX 75243; m/Irita K; c/Erik Ernest, Brooke Rene; p/Ernest S and Lillian C Trickel, Wagoner, OK; ed/BA 1964, MA 1966 Univ Tulsa; Att'd Clark Univ 1969-72; EdD N Tex St Univ 1980; pa/Hist Instr Westark Commun Col 1967-69; Ednl Sales Control Data Corp 1972-73; Hist Prof Richland Col 1973-; Tex Jr Col Tchrs Assn; Org of Am Hists; Dallas Co Commun Col Fac Assn; Phi Alpha Theta, VP 1965-66; cp/Hamilton Pk PTA; r/Meth; hon/Grad Asst Awd, Univ Tulsa 1965-66; NDEA Title IV Schlr 1969-70; Grad Tchr Asst, Clark Univ 1970-71; Author Sev Ednl Guides.

TRIMBLE, BOBBY JACK oc/Oil Scout; b/Apr 6, 1930; h/1419 Sparks, Midland, TX 79701; m/Shirley; c/Tracya, Sherry; mil/AUS 1948-51; pa/Oil Scout, No Natural Gas Co; Pres Christmas-in-April Bd Dirs; r/Bapt; hon/Tex Gov's Awd for Outstg Vol 1981.

TROBAUGH, ALLEN KIEFFER oc/Independent Oil Producer; b/Oct 20, 1919; h/Midland, TX; ba/1405 First National Bank Bldg, Midland, TX 79701; m/Melba Yearian; c/Georgia Kay, Sidney Virginia, Susan Ann, Thomas Allen; p/Henry Earl (dec) and Georgia Kieffer Trobaugh (dec); ed/Att'd Clemson Univ 1937-39; BE Univ So Calif 1948; mil/USAC 1941-46; pa/Reg'd Profl Petro Engr (Self-Employed); Dir First Nat Bank of Midland; Dir Magnatex Industs; Pres, Dir & CEO, PBCP Sers Inc; AIME; SPE; cp/Past Pres Bd: High Sky Girls Ranch, Metro YMCA, Human Relats Coun, U Way; Exec Com: C of C, U Way, YMCA; r/First Christian Ch; Past Pres Bd Elders; hon/Optimist Clb Commun Ser Awd 1979; YMCA Vol of Yr 1980.

TROLINGER, PATRICIA JANE oc/Historian, Genealogist; b/Mar 17, 1930; h/Ottawa Hill Rt 1 Box 226A, Miami, OK; ba/Miami; m/Donald C; c/Richard James, Jill Elaine Prator, Betty Ann Gifthorn, Matthew Swift; p/David Richard and Frances Roberta Smith Scruggs (dec); ed/Okla Col for Wom 1948-49; pa/Tribal Hist, Modoc Tribe of Okla; cp/Regent, Asa Alexander Chapt, Nat Soc DAR; Hist Okla Soc NSDAR; Okla Hist Soc; Okla Heritage Assn; Tulsa Geneal Soc; Ottawa Co Hist Soc; E Tenn Hist Soc; Colonial Dames of XVII Century; DAC; US Daughs of 1812; UDC; r/Presb.

TROTTER, SUE ELDREDGE oc/Homemaker; b/Feb 2, 1928; h/1208 Woodacres Dr, Athens, TN 37303; m/Robert William; c/Patricia Sue, Jane Ida, Robert W Jr, Nancy Carol; p/Mr and Mrs LeRoy Johnson Rldredge Sr (dec); ed/BMus Univ Chattanooga 1950; pa/Mus Ed Tchr 1950-56; cp/Athens Area Coun for the Arts, Exec Dir 1979-80; YMCA Bd

Dirs 1971-73; U Fund, Bd Dirs 1979-81; C of C Bd Dirs 1980-83; Sr Citizens Bd Dirs 1981; Tenn Alliance of the Arts Communs, Bd Dirs 1980-81; Residency Dir CART; r/Meth; hon/Best Residency Dir CART SE.

TRUNDLE, LINDA IRENE oc/Nursing Supervisor; b/Dec 25, 1947; h/19601 Beallsville Rd, Beallsville, MD 20704; ba/Cheverly, MD; p/Gordon G and Vera Baker Reed, Cameron,WV; ed/Dip Ohio Val Gen Hosp Sch Nsg; Enrolled in Univ of St of NY Regents Ext Deg Prog for BSN; pa/Nsg Supvr, PGGH & MC; ANA; MNA: AACN; cp/Repub Party; r/Ch of Christ; hon/W/W Am Wom 1979-80.

TSAO, MING-JYI oc/Anesthesiologist; b/Jan 16, 1944; h/Ocala, FL; ba/131 SW 15th St, Ocala, FL 32670; m/Yieh-Ying; c/Alice S, Benjamin E; p/Ho-Song and Wu-How Tsao, Taiwan; ed/MD Kaohsiung Med Col, Taiwan 1970; mil/Chinese Navy Med Ofcr 1971; pa/Dir Dept Anesthesiol, Munroe Regional Med Ctr; Intl Anesthesia Res Soc; Fla Med Assn; r/Buddhism; hon/Phys Recog Awd, AMA 1976; Fellow Am Col Anesthesiol 1976; Diplomate Am Bd Anesthesiol 1977.

TUBERVILLE, ROBERT SHELTON oc/Letter Carrier; b/Aug 29, 1932; h/Rt 2 Box 251, Sparkman, AR 71763; m/Betty Lou Posey; c/Ronald, Benjamin, Cheryl Kay; p/Mrs C R Tuberville Sr, Camden, AR; mil/AUS; pa/Rural Lttr Carrier; cp/Bd Dirs Ouachita Elec Coop, Past VP; Former Mem Bd Dirs Ark Elec Coops Inc; Charter Mem Sparkman Lions Clb, Past VP; r/Bapt; hon/Hon Mem FFA 1971.

TUCK, LEONORE DOROMAL oc/Teacher, Dietitian; b/Oct 30, 1933; h/Camelot Subdivision, Buies Creek, NC 27506; ba/Buies Creek; m/William P; c/Paul Doromal; p/Emilio and Carmen Doromal, Iloilo City, Philippines; ed/BE Radford Col 1954; MS Univ Tenn 1955; MPH UNC-CH 1967; pa/Chm Home Dec Dept Campbell Univ; Dietary Conslt, Golden Yrs Nsg Home & Parrish Meml Nsg Home; Pres Campbell Univ AAUp; Chm Fac Senate Campbell Univ; Ed Chm NC Dietetic Assn; AHEA; APHA; Food & Nutrition Coun; cp/Commr Harnett City Metro Water Sys 1978-82; NC Fams Task Force; 1st VP Harnett City Dem Wom Org; 14th Dist ERA Coor 1978-79; r/Bapt; hon/Tandang Sora Awd to Study in USA 1953; Grad Fellow, Univ Tenn 1954; HEW Chd's Fellow UNC-CH 1966-67; Burrough Wellcome Schlr 1978; Recip AHEA/Calif Grantsmanship Ctr S'ship 1979; *News and Observer* Tar Heel of Week 1979.

TUCK, N BARTON oc/Executive; b/Jan 3, 1938; h/4 Brookside Way, Greenville, SC 29605; ba/G'ville; m/Linda A; c/Katherine, Emily, Linda, Noel; p/Noel B Tuck Sr, Henderson, NC; Emily Barnette Tuck (dec); ed/BA Univ NC 1960; pa/Corp Pres US Shelter Corp; Am Inst CPAs; SC Assn CPAs; NC Assn CPAs; cp/G'ville C of C, Bd Dirs; r/Bapt.

TUCKER, DAVID oc/Pastor, Supervisor; b/Feb 1, 1952; m/Synthia Marie; c/Synethia Lamia; p/Allen Tucker (dec); Jimie D Sutton, Alex City, AL; pa/Dept Supvr; cp/Masonic Lodge 956; r/Meth; hon/Plaque of Apprec, Haven U Meth Ch.

TUCKER, GEORGE RICKY oc/Police Chief; b/Feb 9, 1956; h/Spring Hope, NC; ba/PO Box 40, Bailey, NC; m/Dianne Grimes; p/George Kent and Jensey Boykin Tucker, Spring Hope, NC; ed/Grad Coastal Plains Police Acad 1977; pa/Police Chief, Town of Bailey; Defensive Tactics Instr for Coastal Plains Police Acad; cp/EMT w Mt Pleasant Rescue Squad; r/Meth.

TUCKER, SHARON M oc/General Office Clerk; b/Nov 2, 1959; h/Petersburg, VA; p/Madison A and Willie Anna Tucker, Petersburg, VA; ed/Att'g Va St Univ; pa/Gen Ofc Clerk, VSU; Phi Beta Lambda 1979-; Future Bus Ldrs Am 1977-78; r/Bapt; hon/Letter of Dedication from Summer Job at Ft Lee, P'burg 1978; Dean's List Student 1978-80; Outstg Future Bus Ldrs Am Student 1977-78; Cert of Awd FBLA 1977-78.

TUGGLE-TURK, GLORIA MARIA oc/Media Specialist; b/Sept 1, 1936; h/3238 Imperial Dr, Macon, GA 31211; ba/Macon; c/Tanya Marchanda, Charles Melvin; p/Aurelia Barrow Turk (dec); ed/BS 1957; pa/Media Specialist, Bibb Co Bd of Ed, Hall Sch Media Ctr; GAE; BAE; GLMD; NEA; Nat Afro-Am; Mo Chm, Hall Sch; cp/Dem Campaign Wkr; r/Bapt; hon/W/W Am Wom 1981-82; Den Mother Awd 1973; St Storytelling Awd 1975; St Read-a-Thon Winner, Macon Assn for Retard'd Citizens 1978 & 81.

TURNBOW, CYNTHIA ANN WILLIAMS oc/Student; b/Mar 25, 1952; h/1623 Olive St, Murray, KY 42071; m/Oscar D; c/Aaron Seth, Anne-Elizabethe; p/Willard C (dec) and Margie H Williams, Newbern, TN; ed/BS; Grad Student Murray St Univ; pa/Profl Christian Min in Song; Author *Readers Theatre on Poetry of Jesse Stuart*; cp/Yng Repubs; UD of C; Calloway Co Commun Theatre; r/So Bapt; hon/Jesse Stuart F'ship, Murray St Univ; Hist of Dyer Co, Tenn; Independence Hall of Chgo Essay Winner; MSU Choir.

TURNER, DAVID MERWYN oc/Student; b/Feb 12, 1958; h/3000 Murworth Apt 1908, Houston, TX 77025; ba/Houston; m/Pamela Marie Miller; p/Howard E and Norma Lee Turner, Edmond, OK; ed/BS Okla Christian Col; PhD Cand Rice Univ; cp/Social Ser Clbs; Alpha Lambda Omega; OCC; r/Ch of Christ; hon/Valedictorian, Edmond HS; Grad summa cum laude, Okla Christian Col; Pres Am Chem Soc; Alpha Chi Omega; Act S'ship; Nat Merit Commend Student 1974; W/W Am HS 1975.

TURNER, DONALD EDWIN oc/Missionary; b/Dec 23, 1932; h/212 E May, DeLand, FL 32720; ba/Maitland, Fl; m/Donna B Fletcher; c/Roger, Joy, Russell, Rollin; p/Rollin Edward and Ella Almeta Childs Turner, Arcadia, FL; ed/BA Carson-Newman Col 1957; MDiv New Orleans Bapt Theol Sem 1961; DMin So Bapt Theol Sem 1978; mil/USNR 1951-55; pa/Pastor: Pine Orchard Bapt Ch, Oakdale, Tenn 1955-58, First Bapt Ch, Raceland, La 1959-62, Truett Meml Bapt Ch, Hayesville, NC; Missionary to Brazil 1965-; Exec Secy St Bapt Conv, Aracaju, Sergipe; Chaplain of Friendship House, Christian Social Min, Ricife, PE, Brazil; Min Assns; cp/Lions Clb NC; r/Bapt.

TURNER, ELNORA K oc/Homemaker; b/Sept 15, 1931; h/Rt 3 Box 61, Lawndale, NC 28090; m/Boyce C Jr; c/Barbara T Morrison, Boyce C III, David Wayne, Michael B; p/David Jr and Hazel M Ketchum, Balto, MD; cp/Chp CF, NC Foun; Treas Pleasant Hill Meth Ch; Secy Belwood Rec; Pres Belwood Commun Pk; Secy Belwood Commun Watch; Ofcr Fallston OES #282; r/Meth.

TURNER, JOE VERNON JR oc/Executive; b/Oct 22, 1944; h/Monroe, LA; m/Elizabeth Anne; c/Mary; p/Joe V Turner, Temple, TX; Estelle Turner, Phoenix, AR; ed/Att'd Tex Tech Univ; pa/VP Softlines, Howard Brandiscount Stores Inc; cp/Substaining Mem Nat Repub Com; r/Presb; hon/W/W S&SW.

TURNER, JOSEPH JACKSON JR oc/Executive Director; b/July 28, 1949; h/304 Augusta Rd, Clemson, SC 29631; ba/Clemson; m/Cathy Campbell; c/J Jackson III, Anne C; p/J J Turner, Spartanburg, SC; Jeane W Turner, (dec); ed/BS 1971; MS 1977; mil/USAR 1971-77; pa/Exec Dir Iptay Ath Assn; CASE; cp/Pres Elect Clemson Rotary; VP BSA; r/So Bapt; hon/Eagle Scout.

TURNER, JOSEPHINE oc/Management Specialist; b/July 2, 1939; h/881 Cherokee Rd, Auburn, AL 36830; ba/Auburn; p/L O (dec) and Ethel May Turner, Somerville, AL; ed/BS 1966, MS 1968 Univ Ala; PhD Purdue Univ 1975; pa/Fam Resource Mgmt Spec, Ala Coop Ext Ser; cp/LWV; AAUW; Dist St & Nat Home Ec Assns; ACCI; r/Ch of God; hon/ACCI Dissertation Awd 1977; Home Ec Hon Assns.

TURNER, KAY HOMESLEY oc/Nurse; b/Nov 5, 1944; h/Rt 2 Box 392, Cherryville, NC 28021; m/Lawrence David; c/Elizabeth, David, Millicent; p/A P Homesley, C'ville, NC; ed/AAS; pa/RN; NCNA; r/So Bapt; hon/Mother of Yr 1976.

TURNER, LEONARD PHILIP oc/Entertainer, Producer; b/Dec 11, 1932; h/1275 Sun Circle W, Melbourne, FL 32935; ba/Melbourne; m/Rosanne; c/Andrea, Denise, Beverly; p/William Arthur (dec) and Mary Letterina Pace Turner (dec); ed/London Tech, Royal Acad London; mil/RAF; pa/Pres Brit-Am Mus Prods Inc; Prodr Num SHows Incl'g "Dimensions in Sound" & "The Cascading Strings"; Am Fed Mus; Orch Ldrs Assn; cp/Rotary Intl; r/Rom Cath; hon/Winner Universal-Intl Glenn Miller Awd.

TURNER, MECHELL ROBERTS oc/Teacher, Student; b/Aug 24, 1959; h/PO Box 506, Buies Creek, NC 27506; m/Stephen Mark; c/Wade Benton; p/Carl Wade and Mary Lou Roberts, St Petersburg, FL; ed/BA Campbell Univ 1981; pa/Eng Tchr; NCTE; SNEA; cp/Mabel Powell Eng Clb, Pres; Pershing Rifles, Secy; Campbell Univ Wom's Clb; r/So Bapt.

TURNER, R H (BO) oc/Police Chief; b/Aug 28, 1930; h/637 Cedar Bayou Rd, Baytown, TX 77520; ba/Baytown; m/D'Eva; c/Susie Allen; p/W C (dec) and Ethel Louise Turner (dec); ed/Grad SWn Police Acad; Adv'd Cert Tex Comm on Law Enforcement Standards & Ed; Att'd Tex A&M Univ, Stephen F Austin St Univ, Lee Col; pa/Baytown Police Chief; Admr & Fiscal Mgr, Harris Co Org'd Crime Unit; Chm Bd of Govs, Harris Co Org'd Crime Unit; Chm Law Enforcement Div, Harris Co Minorities & Law Enforcement Coalition; Tex Police Assn; Tex Municipal Police Assn; Intl Chiefs of Police Assn; Baytown Police Assn; Houston-Galveston Area Coun of Govt's Criminal Just Adv Bd, Police Tng Subcom; cp/W Baytown Kiwanis Clb, VP; Baytown C of C; Baytown Odd Fellows Lodge #960; Baytown Masonic Lodge #1357; r/Bapt; hon/Baytown Optimist Clb's Policeman of Yr 1968; 1 of Few Selected from Tex Law Enforcement Ofcrs to Attend US Just Dept Sponsored Meeting on Minority Police Problems in St.

TURNER, RANDY WARREN oc/Minister; b/Nov 16, 1953; h/Rt 2 Box 33E4, Jackson, MS 39209; ba/Same; m/Sharon Price; p/L W and Millie Cohea Turner, Senatobia, MS; ed/BS Miss Col 1976 MDiv New Orleans Bapt Theol Sem 1980; pa/Pastor Pocahontas Bapt Ch; Exec Com Hinds-Madison Bapt Assn; r/So Bapt; hon/Outstg Yng Men Am 1980.

TURNER, REBECCA PATRICIA PADILLA oc/Student; b/Jan 25, 1954; h/416 Lookout Pl, Fayetteville, NC 28301; ba/Greenville; m/Mark Lee; c/Kristofer Daniel; p/Frank Gus and Patricia Hoctor Padilla, F'ville, NC; ed/BA ECU 1981; mil/AUS 1974-75; AFROTC 2nd; pa/USAF 2nd Lt; r/Rom Cath; hon/Nat Sojourners Awd, AFROTC 1980; Nat Hon Soc; 1971.

TURNER, VANGIE LUELLA oc/Executive; b/June 26, 1920; h/600 Glenthorne Rd, Columbia, SC 29203; ba/Columbia; p/Lawrence Thomas Turner, Lawndale, NC; Lillie Mae Norman Turner (dec); ed/Att'd Blantons Bus Col 1940-41; Univ SC Ext Studies 1960; La Salle Ext Univ 1967-70; SC Sch of Real Est 1977; pa/Elec Wholesale & Lighting Co Exec: Secy & Treas; Corp Acct; Dir Trustee Retirement Plans; SC St & Nat BPW Clb; cp/Treas Eau Claire BPW Clb 1978-79; Trustee Col Pl U Meth Ch 1976-78; Fin Com Col Place U Meth Ch 1973-75; r/Meth; hon/Cert Hon Soc of Accts; Cert Acctg Proficiency; Cert SC Sch Real Est; Trophy Best All Round Student; Salutatorian HS; W/W Am Wom 1979-80.

TURNER, WILLIE oc/Businessman; b/July 6, 1925; h/Corbin, KY; m/Frances Marshall; c/Lynda Lois, R Steven; p/Mary Barton Turner, Rockhold, KY: ed/Att'd Union Col 1978-79; B Mktg 1965, Col of Rt Mgr of Mktg, NYC; mil/Civil Air Patrol; pa/Purchasing Agt, Corbin's Pepsi Cola & Dr Pepper Bottling Co; cp/Flag Day Chm, Lion Clb Radion & TV Auctioneer; Corbin Lions Clb, 3rd VP 1978-79, 2nd VP 1979-80, 1st VP 1980-81, Pres 1981-82; hon/Lion of Yr 1974-75; Ky Col 1969; Pepsi Cola Bottling Co Inc Dist'd Ser 34 Yrs 1976, 35 Yrs 1977, 36 Yrs 1978, 37 Yrs 1979; Pepsi-Cola Sales Wkshop Awd of Achmt 1960; Outstg Accomp Cert Dale Carnegie Course 1971; Cert of Apprec, Nat Sfety Coun Defensive Driving Campaign 1971; Cit of Merit, MD Assns Am.

TURPIN, ANNIE MAE LOVE oc/Retired; b/Nov 22, 1905; h/24 Morton Rd, Harriman, TN 27748; m/Roy H; p/Charles Thedore Love; Mollie Poole Love Morgan; ed/Grad Hiawassee Col; r/Bapt; hon/Salutatorian Hiwassee Col; Good Housekeeping Awd Hiwassee Col; 13 Blue, 20 Red, 9 Other Ribbons Roane Co Fair.

TWINING, HENRIETTA S oc/Professor; b/Feb 25, 1931; h/1213 Willowbrook Dr SE, Apt 7, Huntsville, AL 35802; ba/Normal; c/Patricia Marlene Rioux, Donald Eugene; p/Leonard E and Olga Wolf Stover, Enid, OK; ed/BS 1962; MS 1967; pa/Instr Eng, Dept Eng & Fgn Lang; Prof Eng Ala A&M Univ, Advr to Freshmen, Mem Basic Skills Com, Chm Textbook Selection; NEA: AEA; ACETA; ACTC; ATCE; cp/Hon America Day Com 1979; r/Presb; hon/Kappa Delta Pi; Alpha Chi; Most Outstg Female Intr, Student Govt Assn Ala A&M Univ 1979-80; Plaque for Dedicated Ser to St Cumberland Presb Ch 1979; Personalities of S 1978-79.

TYNES, KATHERINE M (KATY) oc/Director and Consultant; b/Dec 6, 1951; h/New Orleans, LA; p/Mrs Walker A Tynes, Springfield, MO; ed/AA 1971, BA 1972 Stephens; Sec'dy Tchr Cert, Drury Col 1974; MSW Tulane Univ 175; pa/Psychi Social Work; Dir Social Ser, Milve Residential Treatment Ctr; Conslt Mtl Hlth Agcys; NASW; La Assn Clin Social Wkrs; La Mtl Hlth Assn; NEA; La Assn Juvenile Wkrs; Am Correctional Assns; Commun Food Distbn Bank; cp/New Orleans Jr Leag; ACSW; r/Epis; hon/Outstg Yng Wom Am 1980; W/W Am Wom 1981; Personalities of Am 1981.

TYSON, HELEN FLYNN oc/Retired Budget Analyst/US Government Career Employee; b/Feb 17, 1913; h/4900 N Old Dominion Dr, Arlington, VA 22207; m/James Franklin (dec); p/Walter Thomas Flynn (dec); Frances Elizabeth Smith (dec); ed/Pineland Jr Col; Guilford Col; Am Univ; Num Specialized Courses in Mgmt & Assoc'd Fields; Related Sems & Insts; pa/Budget Analyst, HQs USAF, Wash DC 1957-74 (Ret'd); Supvry Budget Ofcr, HQs USAF Mil Transport Command 1955-56; Asst Budget & Acctg Ofcr, Pope AFB, NC 1949-54; Chief Clerical Asst, Disbursing Ofc, Pope AFB, NC 1946-48; Chief Supvry Legal Asst, Vets Adm, NC Reg Ofc, Fayetteville/Winston-Salem, NC 1941-45; Auditor/Disbursing Spec, Disbursing Ofc, AUS, Ft Bragg, NC 1935-40; Am Soc Mil Comptrollers, Wash DC Chapt; Am Inst Parliamentns; Ofcrs Clb, Mil Dist of Wash; cp/NC St Soc in Wash DC; Guilford Col Alumni Assn, Class Rep 1975-; Altrusa Intl: Pres No Va Clb 1974-75, Dir 1975-77; Nat Fdn BPW Clbs: Spec Coms Nat Fdn, Past Leg Chm Va Fdn, Past Parliamentn Dist IX Va Fdn, Histn 1975-76, Former Pres Fairfax Co, Va & Fayetteville, NC Clbs; Co-Fdr Forrestal Clb Wash DC, Toastmistress Intl; Inter-Ser Clb Coun of Arlington, Va: VP 1976, Pres 1977; Ft Belvoir Civilian-Mil Adv Coun: Steering Com 1975-, VP 1977; Cong of Woms Orgs in Va, Past Leg Chm; Arlington Co Salvation Army Wom's Aux; Arlington Com of 100; Former

Dir PAID; Ptnrs of the Alliance, Agcy for Intl Devel: Past Mem Co-Orgr Alliances Between Capital of US & Capital of Brazil & Between St of Va & Santa Cantarina; r/U Meth; hon/US Treas Awd for Patriotic Coop in Behalf of War Bond Effort 1945 & 46; US St Dept Awd for Contbns to Citizen Effort in Hemispheric Ptnrship 1970; Inter-Ser Clb Coun of Arlington, Va Wom of Yr 1975; Ft Belvoir Civilian-Mil Adv Coun "Good Neighbor" Awd for Ldrship in Promotion of Commun Relat'ship 1978; Fellow ABI 1978; Num Occupl Related Commends & Recogs; Pub'd "Nat Bus Wom" 1971 & 72, "Altrusa Intl Bultn" 1975.

TYSON, JOHN ETHREDGE oc/Mathematician; b/Sept 12, 1941; h/Huntsville, AL; m/Brenda Marie Brady; c/Robert Hess Garlough III, Kara Dianne, Rebecca Christine, p/Howard Lamar and Ossie Lou Griffin Tyson; ed/BS Univ Montevallo 1964; Adv'd Studies Univ Ala; pa/Computer Sys Analyst/Sci Application, Boeing Aerospace Co; Past Mem: Nat Mgmt Assn & Data Processing Mgmt Assn; IEEE Computer Soc; cp/Assoc Mem H'ville JCs; Prin Fdr & Mem Exhaulted Rooster Clb; Bd of Control of H'ville Hist Constitution Hall Pk; r/Presb; hon/Pres Awds of Hon, JCs 1974, 76; Outstg Assoc JC 1979.

PERSONALITIES OF THE SOUTH

U

UNDERWOOD, JOHNNIE CARL oc/District Executive; b/May 27, 1957; h/PO Box 804, Wynne, AR 72396; ba/Jonesboro; p/Robert and Carrie Yarborough, Boise City, OK; ed/BS Panhandle St Univ; pa/Dist Exec BSA; cp/Kiwanis Clb; r/Ch of Christ; hon/Valedictorian; W/W Am HS; Eagle Scout; Nat Dean's List; Dean's Hon Roll; Pres's Hon Roll.

UNDERWOOD, RICHARD LOYD oc/Farmer; b/Aug 30, 1940; h/Big Spring, TX; m/Patricia E; c/Scott, Dawn, Tessa, Cassie; p/Louis and Ida Underwood, Big Spring, TX; ed/BS Tex Tech Univ 1963; mil/NG 6 Yrs; pa/Owner-Oper Farm; Howard Co ASCS VChm; Howard Co Farm Bur Bd Dirs; cp/Howard Co Fair Bd, Past Pres; W Tex Telephone Bd Dir, VP; r/Bapt; hon/Gov's Com to Make Agric #1.

UNGER, PAUL TEMPLE oc/Executive; b/June 9, 1942; h/2000 Huntington Ave, Alexandria, VA 22303; b/Wash DC; c/Kimberly Anne, David Temple; p/Samuel Unger (dec); Estelle Slater, Palm Bch, FL; ed/BA; MBA; pa/Ptnr, Exec Search Firm Grady-Unger & Co AFCEA; ASPA; ASBMC; Dir Temple, Henry & Roberts; cp/Dir Wash Scenes; George Bush for Pres; r/Jewish.

UNSELL, LAVONNE DALBY oc/Investments; b/Sept 9, 1923; h/3009 Maple Ave #212, Dallas, TX 75201; m/(dec); c/Rhona S; p/James Grover and Denise Trice Dalby, Daingerfield, TX; ed/BS, Grad Courses, Tex Woms Univ; pa/Tex Nsg Home Assn; cp/Tex SHCC; Bd Regents Tex Wom's Univ; Alternate Del, Dem Nat Conv; Co-Chm, First Cong Dist "Johnson for Pres" Campaign; Def Adv Comm on Wom in the Sers, Wash DC; Co-Chm Sen Bentsen's Campaign; Coor Gov Briscoe's Campaign; Mem Cong-man Robert's Steering Com; Mem Denton Co Dem Woms Assn; Dist Prs, Jr Clbs Tex Fed Wom; Tex Am Cancer Soc Bd; Mem Tex Comm on Status of Wom; Others; r/Meth; hon/Dist Clbwom of Yr & Third in St, Tex Fed Woms Clbs; Pres Merit Ser Awd, Tex Woms Univ; W/W Am Polits.

UPHAM, JOHN EXLEY JR oc/Organist, Student; b/Feb 18, 1959; h/715 Rogers Ln, Raliegh, NC 27610; ba/Buies Creek; p/John E Sr (dec) and Carol R Upham, Raleigh, NC; ed/Att'g Campbell Univ, BMus Cand 1982; pa/Student; Organist St Stephen's Epis Ch; Am Guild Organists; Am Choral Dirs Assn; Mus Edrs Nat Conf; Metro Opera Guild; Cape Fear Chorale; r/Epis; hon/Vivian Dawson Massey Mus Awd 1980; Yth of Mo Awd, Dec 1976; Betty Byrd Green Mus S'ship 1979; Outstg Perf Awd, Sen Robert Morgan 1976.

UPTON, CARROLL MARVIN oc/Minister, District Superintendent; b/June 7, 1932; h/High Pt, NC; ba/PO Box 1111, Kernersville, NC 27284; m/Carolyn Richardson; c/Phillip Wayne, Nathan Carroll, Donald Marvin; p/Marvin U Upton, Salisbury, NC; Ethel A Upton (dec); ed/ThB So Pilgrim Col; pa/Pastor: St Paul Wesleyan, Gold Hill, NC; First Wesleyan, Milwaukee, Wis; First Wesleyan, Robbins, NC; N Kannapolis Wesleyan, Kannapolis, NC; Mt Zion Wesleyan, Thomasville, NC; Asst Dist Supt & Chm Dist Bd Min Standing; Thomasville Min Assn, Secy, Pres; cp/Lions Clb; r/Wesleyan Ch: Dist Supt of NC E Dist.

USREY, CLAUDINE C oc/Nurse, Counselor; b/Jan 8, 1945; h/710 Kings Way, Americus, GA 31709; ba/Americus; m/Samuel Raymond; c/Michael Raymond, John Christopher; p/Cecil (dec) and Carrie Elizabeth Colburn, DuPont, GA; ed/LPN; pa/Dept of Human Resources, Mtl Hlth Clin; cp/Beta Sigma Phi; r/Bapt; hon/Girl of Yr 1975-76, 78-79; Perfect Attendance Beta Sigma Phi 6 Yrs.

PERSONALITIES OF THE SOUTH

V

VACHER, CAROLE DOUGHTON oc/Clinical Psychologist; b/Dec 31, 1937; h/Knoxville, TN; m/A Ray Mayberry; c/Elizabeth M; p/John Harold and Mamie Frith Doughton; ed/BA WV Wesleyan Col 1960; MA Ohio Univ 1962; Clin Intern in Psych Vanderbilt Univ Sch Med 1972-73; PhD NC St Univ 1973; pa/Birth Defects Coor, WV Univ Med Sch 1962-63; Res Assoc, UNC Med Sch 1965-70; Res Psych, NC Dept Mtl Hlth 1973-75; Asst Prof Psych, Fam Pract Res Prog, E Tenn Univ Sch Med 1975-77; Prevention Coor, Overlook Mtl Hlth Ctr 1977-; Pvt Pract of Clin Psych, Maryville Psychi Sers 1974-; Am Psych Assn 1975-; Div 29 1979-, Div 27 1979-; Tenn Psych Assn 19175-; Knoxville Area Psych Assn 1977-; cp/Psych Res Conslt NC Dept Mtl Hlth 1971-73; Conslt to Knox Co Child Abuse Review Team 1977-; Mtl Hlth Assn of Knox Co, Spkrs Bur 1979-; Contact Telphone Mins 1980-; Knoxville Med Assn Aux, Bd Mem & Mtl Hlth Chm 1980-; Tenn Med Assn Aux, Bd Mem & St Mtl Hlth Chm 1981-82; Org'd "Worry Clinic" on Pre-Teen & Teenage Alcohol & Drug Problems for Knox Co & Surrounding Cos 1981; r/Meth; hon/Mtl Hlth S'ship Recip NC Dept Mtl Hlth 1970-71; Cert'd Lic'd PhD Clin Psych in Tenn 1975-; Outstg Vol Ser to Tenn Dept Human Sers 1978; Phi Kappa Phi; Psi Chi; Alpha Psi Omega, Pres 1959-60; Haught Lit Soc 1959; Wesleyan Key Awd 1960; Author *Consultation Education: Development and Evaluation* & Num Profl Jour Articles.

VAETH, AGATHA MIN-CHUN FANG oc/Nurse; b/Feb 19, 1935; h/855 Flannery Rd Apt 721, Baton Rouge, LA 70815; ba/Carville; m/Randy H; c/David, Phillip, Elizabeth; p/Yung-Cheng and Wen-Pu Cheng Fang, Taipei, Taiwan; ed/RN; pa/Nurse USPHS Hosp; Am Red Cross Vol Nurse; Translated from Eng to Chinese, Recorded onto Video Cassette Tape "Diagnosis of Hanslen's Disease" 1978; r/Confucious; hon/Recip Apprec Awd Otoe Missouria Tribal Coun 1974; Awd for High Quality Perf USPHS, HEW 1978.

VALLELY, CHERYL CLEMENTS oc/Teacher; b/Oct 13, 1957; h/PO Box 3051, Opelika, AL 36801; m/John Joseph; p/William and Carole Clements, Auburn, AL; ed/BA Art Ed; pa/Art Tchr; r/Bapt; hon/Miss Ala World; Ala Textile Queen; Miss Lake Martin; Miss SE Ala; Lee Co Maid of Cotton; Lee Co Farm Bur Queen; Lee Co Fair Queen; Ala Miss US Teen; Nat Miss Teenage Ldrship in Nat Miss Teenage Am Comp; Outstg Yng Ams.

VALRIE, GEORGIA SHARPE oc/Assistant to Director; b/Mar 1, 1949; h/3709 Fox Trail Cir, Huntsville, AL; ba/Normal; m/Erskine L; c/Kreslyon Lynette; p/Elmore and Myrtle Sharp, Prichard, AL: ed/BS Adult & Cont'g Ed; BA Sociol; pa/Asst to Dir, Adult & Cont'g Ed; Adult Ed Assn; Kappa Delta Phi; cp/Alpha Kappa Alpha; H'ville Hosp Vol; r/Bapt; hon/Marching Maroon & White Band Ser Awd 1975.

VAN AUKEN, ROBERT DANFORTH oc/Professor; b/Oct 31, 1915; h/420 Highland Rd, Midwest City, OK 73110; ba/Norman; m/Ruth C; c/Robert Hanlon, Joseph Marshall, David Danforth, Howard Evans, Jonathan Lewis; p/Howard Robert (dec) and Mable Hanlon Van Auken (dec); ed/Att'd Guilford Col 1933-35; Gen Motors Inst Technol 1936-38; USAAC Flying Sch 1938-39; Grad Armed Forces Staff Col 1950; Univ Pgh 1953-54; BS Univ Dayton 1958; MA Univ Okla 1967; mil/1938-61 Ret'd Lt Col; pa/Univ Okla: Pers Ofcr 1962-65, Fac Mem 1965-75, Dir Student Progs & Career Devel Col of Bus Adm 1975-79, Fac Mem Mgmt Div Col of Bus Adm 1979-, Acting Dir Mgmt Div 1980-; Mgmt Conslt 1963-; ASPA; Acad Mgmt; Ret'd Ofcrs Assn; Mil Order of World Wars; Delta Sigma Pi; cp/32° Mason; Lions Clb; Repub Party; r/Prot; hon/Silver Star; Purple Heart; Beta Gamma Sigma; Textbook Reviewer for Houghton, Mifflin Co 1973 & W B Saundes 1978; Author "How Much Should You Pay Your Employees" *Oklahoma Business Bulletin* 1972.

VANCE, JOHN S oc/Businessman; b/May 9, 1949; h/100½ N 9th St, Opelika, AL 36801; ba/Opelika; m/Judy Daniel; p/Kenneth Coleman and Rebecca Roberts Vance, Opelika, AL; ed/Att'd Ga Mil Col 1968-70; Columbus Col; pa/Owner Opelika-Auburn Comm Inc & Opelika Answering Ser; RCC Mobile Telephone Pagers; Advtg Mgr Opelika Coca-Cola Co 1974, Rt Salesman 1975; Salesman Bence-Morris Mtrs 1975-77; VP Ala Assn Radio Utilites; cp/3rd VP, Pres & Depty Dist Gov Ala Lions Clb; Assoc Mem Nat & Ala Homebldrs Assn; r/Bapt; hon/Winner Sales Contest, Buick Motor Div 1977.

VANDERWORK, CAROL oc/Instructor; b/Dec 31, 1945; h/Rt 2, Taloga, OK 73667; ba/Taloga; m/Mickey M; c/Lee Allen, Dell Marvin, Leslie Ann; p/Manford and Margaret Davis Jenkinson, Burlington, OK; ed/BE Okla St Univ 1968; ME SWn Okla St Univ 1972; pa/Eng/Speech Instr, Taloga HS; Am Fidelity Life Ins Co, Pensacola, Fla; OEA, Co Secy; Okla Coun Tchrs Eng; NCTE; cp/Fed Clb; Repub Party; r/Christian; hon/Outstg Yng Wom Am 1974; W/W Am Wom 1980.

VANDIVER, RAYMOND FRANKLIN JR oc/Farmer; b/Mar 3, 1930; h/2600 Sutcliff Dr NE, Huntsville, AL 35811; ba/New Market; m/Martha McCown; c/Mary Lynn Carlton, Frank, Iris Ann; p/Raymond Franklin and Annie Mae Vandiver, New Market, AL; ed/Att'd Auburn Univ; pa/Farmer; St Agric & Indust Bd; Former Mem & Pres St Soil & Water Com; Bd Mem So Cotton Growers; City Bd of Ed; St Plan'g Comm under CETA; cp/Former Mem Rural YMCA Bd; Huntsville-Madison Co C of C; H'ville-Madison Co Indust Devel Assn; Kiwanis Clb; H'ville Art Mus; Former Mem H'ville Acme Clb; r/Presb; hon/Yng Farmer of Yr 1959.

VAN FOSSEN, HELEN KEY oc/Physician; b/May 19, 1926; h/4317 Burgundy Rd, Memphis, TN 38111; ba/Memphis; p/Harry Thomas (dec) and Maude Olivia McPhate Van Fossen, Oak Grove, LA; ed/BS 1948, MD 1955 La St Univ; pa/Prac'g Pvt Phys in Gastroenterology & Internal Med 1962-; Am Gastroenterol Assn; Am Col Gastroenterol, Fellow; Am Soc Gastrointestinal Endoscopy; Am Soc Internal Med; AMA; Am Med Wom's Assn; Memphis Acad Internal Med; Memphis & Shelby Med Soc; So Med Assn; Tenn Med Assn; Tenn Soc Gastrointestinal Endoscopy; Tenn Soc Internal Med; cp/Bd Dirs Memphis Ballet Soc; VP Ballet S 1970-; Guarantor of Metro Opera 1970-; Fellow Metro Opera 1978-; r/Epis; hon/Certs Am Bd Internal Med 1978 & Subspec Bd in Gastroenterology 1979; Author & Co-Author.

VAN HOOK, WANDA M oc/Assistant Director; b/Aug 19, 1926; h/524 Skyline Ln, Stillwater, OK 74074; ba/Stillwater; m/Victor L; c/Vicki Lynne, Donna Carol; p/Charles C and Elsa E Murphy, New Bloomfield, MO; ed/BS Ed; pa/Asst Dir Admissions, Okla St Univ; AAUW; Nat Secy Assn Intl; Okla Assn Col Registrars & Adm Ofcrs; Alpha Xi Delta, Pres Corp Bd; r/Bapt; hon/Recip Cert AF Inst of Technol.

VANN, MAMIE GODWIN oc/Retired Teacher; b/Nov 6, 1908; h/Dunn, NC; m/Earl G; c/Virginia V King; p/Archie Bryant (dec) and Addie Byrd Godwin (dec); ed/Att'd ECU 1927-29, Wake Forest Col, Atlantic Christian Col, NC St Univ; pa/Elem Tchr, NC Public Schs 36 yrs; NCEA; Pres Sampson Co Ed Assn; cp/Harnett Co Arts Coun; Dunn Wom's Clb; Harnett Co Dem Wom; Citizens Com for Better Govt; NEA; Charter Mem Dunn Chapt OES; r/Meth; hon/Articles Pub'd In NC Ed Assn Jour 1935.

van RIJN, RITA PRICE oc/Director; b/Nov 29, 1943; h/Dickey Woods, Adamsville, TN 38310; ba/Selmer, TN; m/Peter; c/Alexandria; p/Watson and Josephine Stewart Price, Adamsville, TN; ed/BS Psych; pa/Dir McNairy Co Adult Activ Ctr; W Tenn Dirs for Developmentlly Disabled; Nat Assn Retard'd Citizens; Am Assn Mtl Deficiency; Region IIX Title XX Adv Coun; r/Bapt.

VARNADORE, BEVERLY SWEEDEN oc/Executive Secretary; b/Feb 11, 1944; h/Clinton, TN; ba/Oak Ridge Nat Lab, PO Box X, Oak Ridge, TN 37830; c/C Alan; p/Jack Sweeden, Gonzales, LA; Mary B Bedell, Oak Ridge, TN; ed/Att'd Roan St Commun Col; pa/Exec Secy, Chem Technol, Oak Ridge Nat lab 1962-; BPW Clb, Past Secy, Past Newslttr Editor; Former Mem Nat Secy Assn; cp/Pilot Clb, Past Chaplain, Past Secy; Parents w/out Partners, Pres Local Chapt, Past Secy; Past Secy E Tenn Val Region; r/Bapt.

VARNER, BARBARA JEAN oc/Teacher; b/Dec 25, 1927; h/Rt 8 Box 286, Asheboro, NC 27203; m/Robert Roe Jr; c/Michael Wyatt, Phillip Lee, Beth Ann V Barton, Sarah Jean V Gordon, Joel Robert; p/Jesse Sylvester (dec) and Burnetta Dick Pace, Palm Bch, FL; pa/Pt-time Tatting Tchr, Randolph Tech Col; Guild of Piedmont Handicrafters; r/Meth.

VAUGHAN, ELIZABETH R oc/Ophthalmologist; b/July 28, 1940; h/10562 Silverock, Dallas, TX 75218; ba/Dallas c/Mark Charles, Amy Elizabeth; p/Julius Charels and Martha Stradley Robertson, El Paso, TX; ed/BA Univ Tex 1962; MD Univ Tex SWn Med Sch 1966; Intern Chd's Med Ctr, Dallas; Resident Ophthalmology, Parkland Meml Hosp 1967-70; Spec Courses: Harvard Med Sch 1968, Armed Forces Inst of Pathol 1970, Phacoemulsification Course 1973, Intra-Ocular Lens Implantation Tng 1973; pa/Ophthalmologist; Christian Med Soc; Life Mem Univ Tex Alumni Assn; AMA; Dallas Co Med Soc; Tex Med Assn; Am Assn Ophthalmology; Dallas Acad Ophthalmology; Am Acad Ophthalmology; Dallas Acad Ophthalmol; Contact Lens Assn of Ophthalmol; Intl Eye Foun Soc of Eye Surgs; Tex Soc for Preven of Blindness; Clin Instr Ophthalmol, Univ Tex SWn Med Sch; Staff Mem: Parkland Meml Hosp, Presb Hosp, Baylor Univ Med Ctr, Mary Shields Hosp, VA Hosp; r/Christian: Ordained Min 1978; Pres Elizabeth Vaughan Mins Inc.

VAUGHAN, EMORY ABNER oc/Retired; b/July 16, 1914; h/Rt 3 Box 621, Roanoke Rapids, NC 27870; m/Maggie Blow; c/Lezia V Rose; p/John Robert (dec) and Bessie Parker Vaughan (dec); ed/Med & Surg Tech Dip, O'Riley Gen Hosp; Cert in Life Saving & Water Safety, Am Red Cross; Num Certs Resque Col; mil/AUS 1940-45 Staff Sgt; pa/Life Ins Underwriter, Durham Life Ins Co 19 Yrs; Ret'd Chief Jailor, Halifax Co

Sheriff's Dept; cp/Roanoke Val Rescue Squad; r/Meth; hon/This Weeks Citizen, Halifax Co Newspaper 1978; Cert of Apprec 1981, Roanoke Val Rescue Squad; Squadsman of Yr Awd; Rec'd Num Certs BSA; Eamet Campaign Medal w 5 Bronze Ser Stars; Good Conduct Medal; Am Defense Ser Medal; Merit Ser Unit Insignia.

VAUGHAN, RICHARD IRVIN oc/General Contractor; b/Jan 23, 1913; h/611 E Winder St, Henderson, NC 27536; m/Tessie Bobbitt; c/Gertrude, Frances, Barbara, Richard, David, Samuel, Linda; p/John D (dec) and Gertrude Cooke Vaughan (dec); ed/Att'd Shaw Univ; pa/Self-Employed Painter; cp/Pres Vance Co NAACP; VP Dem Clb; Chm City of Henderson E Precinct #1; r/Bapt; Chm & VChm Deacon Bd; hon/Cert of Apprec, Vance Co Chapt NAACP 1978; Cert of Recog, Vance Co Bapt SS Conv 1980; Plaque 20 Yrs SS Supt 1964; Fball Recog 1930-34.

VAUGHN, ADRIAN EUGENE oc/Material Handler; b/July 12, 1947; h/601 So Robinson, Cleburne, TX 76031; p/Murray L Vaughn, Cleburne, TX; Mildred Hutchison Vaughn, Cleburne, TX; pa/Material Handler, Customer Ser Dept, Rangaire Corp; r/Meth.

VAUGHN, FRANCES AGATHA oc/Library Director; b/Aug 10, 1929; h/20 Casa de Amigos, Brownsville, TX 78521; ba/B'ville; m/William J; p/Carmela Nazzaro, N Miami Bch, FL; ed/BS Univ Tex-Austin 1962; MLS N Tex St Univ 1969; MBA Pan Am Univ 1979; pa/Lib Adm, Arnulfo Oliveira Meml Lib; Beta Phi Mu; Alpha Lambda Sigma, Treas 1969-72; AAUW, Histn, Exec Bd; NTSU-Lib Staff Assn, Secy-Treas, Chm Mbrship Com; TSC-Fac Assn, Secy-Treas; ALA; TLA; Am Mgmt Assn; cp/TSC Voc Tenical Coun, Secy; r/Epis; hon/Augustus St Sauden's Medal ;1946; Author Book of Poetry 1963; Editor MBA Res Proj 1978.

VAUGHN, GEORGE PARKER oc/Architect; b/May 12, 1949; h/San Antonio, TX; ba/San Antonio; m/Carol Jean; c/Greg, Shelly; p/Carroll Lee and Florine Parker Vaughn, El Paso, TX; ed/BArch w Hons Tex Tech Univ 1972; p/Ken Rehler & Assocs Inc, Archs 1972-76; Rehler, Vaughn, Beaty & Koone Inc, Archs 1976–; Nat Coun Arch Registration Bds; Am Inst Archs; Tex Soc Archs; San Antonio Chapt Construction Specifications Inst, Pres 1979-80, Treas 1978-79; cp/Alamo Hghts Rotary Clb, Sgt-at-Arms 1979-80, VP 1980-81; r/Ch of Christ; Deacon 1976–; hon/Waid Ed Fund S'ship 1971; Tau Sigma Delta 1971; Reynolds Aluminum Design Awd 1971; W/W S&SW 1980; Outstg Yng Man Am 1979; Featherlite Design Comp 1971.

.**VEALS, ELNORA** oc/Teacher; b/Apr 14, 1943; h/Woodville, MS; c/Kenyatta Michelle; p/Mary B Veals, Woodville, MS; ed/BS 1966, ME 1972; pa/Tchr Wilkinson Co Sch Bd; Wilkinson Co Tchrs Assn; Miss Tchrs Assn, Polit Action Chm; Miss Coun SS; r/Bapt; hon/Dist'd Am HS Tchr 1976-79.

VEERKAMP, MARK ALAN oc/Store Manager; b/Jan 10, 1957; h/2433 Whitmire #78, Midland, TX 79701; ba/Midland; m/Patricia; c/Gregory; p/Walter and Ruth Veerkamp, Ft Wayne, IN; ed/BS Ind Univ 1979; AS Purdue Univ 1979; pa/Store Mgr, OG Wilson Catalog Showroom 1974–; Am Mktg Assn; r/Cath.

VELA, REBECCA HILDA ESCAMILLA oc/Interviewer; b/Dec 5, 1934; h/Mission, TX; ba/15 S 15th St, McAllen, TX; c/Elizabeth V Huerta, Humberto Jr, Cynthia V Lerma; p/Patricio Escamilla Sr, Brownsville, TX; Aurora S Escamilla, Morris, IL; ed/BS Pan Am Univ 1974; pa/Receptionist & Dental Asst, Hugo Dominguez DDS 1952-54; Tchr Aide, Mission Indep Sch Dist 1965-68, 1968-69; Tchr Ofc of Ec Opport Day Care Ctr 1968; Clerk Tex Employment Comm 1968; Commun Ser Aide 1969; Tex Employment Comm: Employment Interviewer I 1976, Interviewer II 1979, Interviewer III 1980; TPEA; IAPES; cp/Jr Girl Scout Ldr 1966-67; Ad-Hoc Adv Com 1966-67; VP PTA 1967; Mission Band Boosters 1969-80, VP 1976-77, Pres 1977-79, Exec Bd 1979-80; r/Meth; hon/High Hons in Spanish 1942; Homemaking Awd 1952; Tex Employment Comm 5 & 10 Yrs Pins; E Wayland Krisan Grants; W/W Am Wom 1981-82.

VENDITTO, JAMES JOSEPH oc/Engineer; b/Nov 13, 1951; ba/1220 Bank & Trust Tower, Corpus Christi, TX 78477; m/Ann R Carson; c/Vincent James, Joseph Ryan; p/Vincenzio R and Maria N Cassetti Venditto, Irvington, NY; ed/BS Univ Okla 1973; pa/Regional Ser Sales Engr; AIChE; API; SPE; NSPE; TSPE; Intl Platform Assn; cp/Repub Party; r/Cath; hon/Reg'd Profl Engr in Tex PE #42776.

VESTAL, DAN ALBERT oc/Evangelist; b/June 29, 1918; h/5100 Cockrell Ave, Ft Worth, TX 76133; ba/Ft Worth; m/Lindle Marie; c/Daniel, James, Ruth V Mills, Martha V Asebedo; p/George Albert (dec) and Eula Vestal (dec); ed/Att'd Baylor Univ & SWn Bapt Theol Sem; Hon Dip Dallas Bapt Col; pa/Evangelist; r/Bapt.

VESTER, AGNES PEELE oc/Instructor; b/June 16, 1921; h/1210 S Tarboro St, Wilson, NC 27893; ba/Wilson; m/Al A; c/Mary Alane, Franklin Peele; p/Robert Louis (dec) and Vanie Bailey Peele (dec); ed/Dip Nsg (RN) Carolina Gen Hosp, Wilson 1942; BA cum laude Atlantic Christian Col 1972; MEd NC St Univ 1974; pa/Inser Ed Instr, Wilson Meml Hosp; ANA; NCNA; Nat & St Leag Nsg; cp/Red Cross; Heart Assn; Arthritis Foun; r/Free Will Bapt; hon/Alpha Chi; W/W Students of Am Cols & Univs; World W/W Wom in Ed.

VESTGARD, ESTELLE BURNHAM oc/Retired Teacher; b/May 21, 1914; h/321 Wildwood Dr, Anniston, AL 36201; m/Vincent (dec); p/Horace (dec) and Annie Cheatwood Burnham (dec); ed/BS; MA; pa/Ret'd Tchr; Alpha Delta Kappa; AAUW; r/Bapt.

VICKERS, EDWARD DAVIN oc/Senior Programmer/Analyst; b/Jan 10, 1945; h/1217 E Rock Springs Rd NE, Atlanta, GA 30306; ba/Atlanta, GA; p/Eldridge M Vickers, Whigham, GA; Eula B Miller, Cairo, GA; ed/BS Valdosta St Col; pa/EDP Sr Progr/Analyst; So Co Sers Profl Devel Assn; cp/Pres Atlanta Writers Clb 1978-79; hon/Author Echo in the Woods (Book of Poetry).

VICKREY, JAMES F JR oc/College President; b/Feb 6, 1942; c/John; p/James F Vickrey (dec); Mildred K Murray, Montgomery, AL; ed/AB 1964, MA 1965 Auburn Univ; PhD Fla St Univ 1972; Postgrad Study Harvard Bus Sch 1974; pa/Instr Speech & Forensics, Auburn Univ 1965-68; Asst Debate Coach, Univ Ala 1968-69; Fla St Univ: Instr Bus Commun 1969-70, Adm Asst to Exec VP 1970-71; Dir Univ Relats, Univ of So Fla 1971-75; Asst to Pres & Dir Public Affairs, Univ Sys of Fla 1975-77; Pres Univ Montevallo 1977–; Mem Ed Com, Fine Arts Coun, Tampa 1973-75; Bd Dirs U Way 1979–; Ala Film Comm; S Allen Edgar Fellow; Am Assn St Col & Univs; Am Coun Ed; Pres Ala Alpha Chapt of Am Assn Univ Admrs; Pres Ala Assn Cols & Univs; Assn Col Admrs; Phi Eta Sigma; Phi Kappa Phi; Omicron Delta Kappa; cp/Kiwanis; Dem Party; Rotary Clb; r/Meth; hon/Recip Algernon Sidney Sullivan Awd 1964; Recip of S Allen Edgar F'ship Awd 1965; Phi Eta Sigma Nat S'ship Awd 1964; Phi Delta Phi Awd, Most Outstg First Yr Student, Law Sch Univ Ala 1969; Excptl Achmt Awd, CASE 1976; Grand Awd CASE 1977; 1 of 100 Outstg Yng Ldrs Am; Contbr Articles on Speech Commun to Schlrly Jours & Movie Related Mats to Pop Mags & Newspapers.

VIERA, CRISTOBAL EUGENIO oc/Surgeon; b/Sept 6, 1941; ba/Miami, FL; m/Estela; c/Estelle Marie, Christopher; p/Cristobal and Luz Marina Garcia Viera, Havana, Cuba; ed/BS Univ Miami Sch of Med 1966; MD Univ Miami Sch Med 1970; Am Bd Surg 1977; FACS 1978; FACG 1980; mil/AUS pa/Gen & Vascular Surg; Univ Miami Sch Med: Clin Instr, Dept Surg 1976; Part-Time Clin Instr, Dept Surg 1975-76; Chief Resident, Dept Surg 1974-75; Sr Res, Dept Surg 1973-74; Resident Dept Surg 1972-73; Dade Co Med Soc; Fla Med Assn; AMA; Am Col Surgs; Phi Chi; So Med Assn; Active Mem Am Cancer Soc; r/Cath; hon/Student Res Day, Hon Mention 1968; Most Effective & Popular Housestaff Tchr 1974-75; Author Num Profl Res Papers.

VIGIL, JOE GABRIEL oc/General Manager; b/Oct 24, 1939; m/Linda A; c/Joe G II; p/Tony and Isabel Contreras, Moab, UT; ed/Att'd Univ NM; mil/82nd Airborn; pa/Pres Vigil Frozen Foods Co Inc; cp/Exec Bd W Tenn Coun, BSA; Dist Commnr & Dist Chm Bedford Forrest Dist; r/Rom Cath; hon/Bronze Star; Purple Heart; Combat Inf-man Bage; Eagle Scout; Dist'd Awd of Merit; Wood Badge Beads; Silver Beaver.

VINCENT, BRUCE HAVIRD oc/Executive; b/Nov 7, 1947; h/200 Atlantic, Corpus Christi, TX 78404; ba/Corpus Christi; m/Pamela Jean Benson; c/Jennifer Jean, Bryce Havird; p/Dales Leon and Mildred Sara Vincent, Clifton, VA; ed/AB Duke Univ 1969; MBA Univ Houston 1976; mil/USN 1969-73 Lt JG; pa/Exec VP, Chief Oper'g Ofcr & Dir, Peninsula Resources Corp, (Indep Oil & Gas Co); Indep Petro Assn Am; Tex Mid-Cont Oil & Gas Assn; Intl Assn Drilling Contractors; cp/Corpus Christi C of C; S Tex C of C; r/Epis.

VINCENT, ROBBIE ANN oc/Secretary, Reserve Policewoman; b/Aug 5, 1943; h/PO Box 67, Hanceville, AL 35077; ba/H'ville; m/James Ronald; c/Morgan Ann Ballard, Nickolas Shon Ballard, Belinda Gayle; p/Robert L and Hazel I Crumbley; ed/AA Wallace St Commun Col; pa/Secy; Reser Policewom; r/Bapt.

VINE, LOUIS LLOYD oc/Veterinarian; b/May 19, 1922; h/120 Meadowbrook Dr, Chapel Hill, NC 27514; ba/Chapel Hill; m/Florence; c/Joan, James, Sandra; p/Paul and Belle Vine, Paramus, NJ; ed/DVM; pa/Vet; Author; r/Jewish; hon/Best Dog of Yr; Cat Book, Guild Selection.

VINING, JEAN WINGATE oc/Associate Professor; b/Aug 1, 1938; h/1800 Harvard Ave, Metairie, LA 70001; ba/New Orleans; m/William S Jr; c/Ashley Jeannine; p/Wiley Oscar (dec) and Mildred Rowland Wingate, Hinesville, GA; ed/BS cum laude Univ Ga; MEd Ga So Col; EdD Univ New Orleans; pa/Assoc Prof Ofc Adm, Conslt in Ofc Tng & Devel,

Univ New Orleans; Author & Book Reviewer; AAUW; So Bus Ed Assn; Nat Bus Ed Assn; ABCA; Kappa Delta Pi; Phi Delta Kappa; UNO Spkrs Bur; cp/Am Cancer Soc, Sect Ldr; Repub Party; r/Meth; hon/W/W Am Wom; Grad Res F'ship, UNO 1975-76; Fac S'ship, Armstrong St Col.

VINYARD, REBECCA CORNELIUS oc/Underwriter; b/Jan 3, 1926; h/3503 Lake St, Gadsden, AL 35901; ba/Gadsden; m/William Terry; p/Zion Alvie (dec) and Fannie Gibson Cornelius, Oneonta, AL; ed/Att'd Athens Col; Life Ofc Mgmt Assn; Inst Home Ofc Underwriting; pa/Home Ofc Underwriter; Past Pres Ala Home Ofc Underwriting Assn; SE Region Underwriters Assn; Inst Home Ofc Underwriters Assn; cp/Past Pres Gadsden-Etowah Co YMCA Bd Dirs; SE Region YMCA Bd Dirs; SE Region Intl Com SER; Life Mem Gadsden Metro C of C; Goodwill Ambassador Gadsden Metro C of C; Past Pres Altrusa Clb of Gadsden; r/U Meth; hon/Dist'd Ser Awd, John H Forney Hist Soc; Dist'd Ser Awd Gadsden-Etosah Co YMCA; Outstg Sales & Ser, Gadsden Metro C of C; 2 Pres Sports Awds for Swimming, 1 Signed By Pres Jerry Ford & 1 Signed by Jimmy Carter.

VINSON, CLARENCE DAVID JR oc/Educator; b/June 23, 1933; h/Anniston, AL; ba/Gen Sci Dept, Jacksonville St Univ, J'ville, AL 36265; p/Clarence David Vinson, Anniston, AL; Vera Pearl Vinson (dec); ed/BS 1954, MS 1959 J'ville St Univ; PhD Univ Ala 1977; Further Study Univ No Colo & Univ Wyo; mil/AUS 1955-57; pa/Assoc Prof Sci, J'ville St Univ; NEA; AEA; Local Ed Assn; Assoc Cnslr Ala Jr Assn Sci; cp/Am Numismatic Assn; Bd Dirs Anniston Bowling Assn; Dem Party; r/Eulation First Bapt Ch: Deacon; hon/W/W S&SW 1980-81; Kappa Delta Pi 1954; Kappa Phi Kappa 1969.

VINSON, MILDRED GALLMAN oc/Teacher-Coordinator; b/Oct 18, 1928; h/2204 Woodrow Ave, Waycross, GA 31501; ba/Waycross; m/Clinton Douglas; c/Douglas Allen; p/Ashland Edward (dec) and Irene Richardson Gallman, Raymond, MS; ed/BS Miss St Univ; MEd Valdosta St Col; pa/Bus Tchr-Coor; WEA; GEA; NEA; GBEA; NBEA; BOE; GVAE; AVA; cp/OES, Worthy Matron; Mar of Dimes; Heart Fund; MD Dr; Cancer Soc; r/Bapt; hon/Ga FBLA Region VII Advr of Yr; Phi Kappa Phi; Outstg Dist Bus Tchr; Ware Co Bus Tchr of Yr; Typing & Shorthand Awds; Ware Co Wom of Yr Nom.

VINYARD, REBECCA CORNELIUS oc/Underwriter; b/Jan 3, 1926; h/3503 Lake St, Gadsden, AL 35901; ba/Gadsden; m/William Terry; p/Zion Alvie (dec) and Fannie Gibson Cornelius, Oneonta, AL; ed/Att'd Athens Col; Life Ofc Mgmt Assn; Inst Home Ofc Underwriting; pa/Home Ofc Underwriter; Past Pres Ala Home Ofc Underwriting Assn; SE Region Underwriters Assn; Inst Home Ofc Underwriters Assn; cp/Past Pres Gadsden-Etowah Co YMCA Bd Dirs; SE Region YMCA Bd Dirs; SE Region Intl Com SER; Life Mem Gadsden Metro C of C; Goodwill Ambassador Gadsden Metro C of C; Past Pres Altrusa Clb of Gadsden;

r/U Meth; hon/Dist'd Ser Awd, John H Forney Hist Soc; Dist'd Ser Awd Gadsden-Etosah Co YMCA; Outstg Sales & Ser, Gadsden Metro C of C; 2 Pres Sports Awds for Swimming, 1 Signed By Pres Jerry Ford & 1 Signed by Jimmy Carter.

VIOHL, FREDERICK ALBERT oc/Assistant Professor; b/May 25, 1941; h/3413 Woodhill Rd, Montgomery, AL 36109; ba/Troy; m/Marti L; c/Lisa, Andrew; p/Fred W and Margarete Viohl, Nokomis, FL; ed/BS 1966, MBA 1968 NYU; EdD Univ Ga 1979; mil/USAF 1967-76 Major; pa/Mktg Mgr, Trane Corp, Transp Div 1976-77; Zone Mgr, Kelly Hlth Care, Kelly Sers Inc 1977-79; Asst Prof Mktg & Mgmt, Troy St Univ 1979-; AF Assn; AAUP; NEA; Am Mgmt Assn; cp/Pres's Clb, Troy St Univ; Ed Com Maxwell-Gunter Credit Union; hon/Soc Logistics Engrs Awd 1980; W/W S 1980-81; Author *Leadership Laboratory* 1976.

VOLLBEER, FRED H oc/Business Manager and CEO; b/Jan 3, 1944; h/Miami Lakes, FL; ba/Miami; m/Bonnie D; c/Robert Scott; p/Walter H Vollbeer (dec); Fern J Skelley, Davenport, IA; ed/BBA Univ Iowa 1966; MA Univ Va 1971; mil/USAF Pentagon 1967-71; pa/VP Fin, LA Clarke & Son Inc 1972-76; CFO Williams Limber Co Inc 1976-78; CEO Carver Enterprises 1978-; Bus Mgr Roy J Carver; Alpha Kappa Psi, Life Mem; r/Luth.

VON KUTZLEBEN, BERND EBERHARD oc/Nuclear Engineer; b/May 23, 1950; h/Huntingtown, MD; ba/Combustion Engrg Inc, 1000 Prospect Hill Rd, Windsor, CT 06096; p/Siegfried Edwin Wolfgang Erich and Ursula Herta von Kutzleben, Wyckoff, NJ; ed/BS Univ Hamburg, Germany 1974; BS 1976, MS 1979 Fahhochschule Wedel, Wedel, Germany; pa/Nuclear Engr, Combustion Engrg Inc; r/Prot.

VOWELS, ELEANOR ELAINE oc/Director of Handicapped Programs; b/Oct 3, 1937; h/7718 Jaffrey Rd, Oxon Hill, MD; ba/Wash DC; m/Theodore Roosevelt Jr; c/David Scott p/Amanda Wooding, Carnegie, PA; ed/BS Howard Univ; MA Cath Univ Am; pa/Proj Dir for Handicapped, DC Gen Hosp, Dept Pediatrics; DC Consortium of Handicapped Programs, Pres 1979-81; DC Assn for Retard'd Citizens: Bd Dirs 1972-79, Exec Bd 1977-79, Secy 1978-79; r/Bapt; hon/W/W Wom 1980; World W/W Wom 1981.

VROOM, JAMES RANDALL oc/Health Administrator; b/Sept 12, 1954; h/Apt I-8 Boone Hall Dr, Charleston, SC 29407; ba/C'ton; p/Henry Joseph and Janet Louise Vroom, E Patchogue, NY; ed/BA cum laude 1976, MHA 1978 Duke Univ; mil/USNR Med Ser Corps Lt; pa/Hlth Admr, Asst Chief, Fin & Mat Mgmt Ser; CPA Cand; Part-time Staff Acct Dennis P Baars CPA; Am Col Hosp Admrs; NC Assn CPAs; Am Hosp Assn; Hosp Fin Mgmt Assn; r/Cath.

W

WADDELL, GENEVIEVE JOHNSON oc/Office Director; b/July 4, 1941; h/7520 Whites Creek Pike, Joelton, TN 37080; ba/Nashville; m/R Eugene; c/Michael, John; Stepchd: Rhonda Sagraves, Robert, Paul, Marcia; p/Isaac E Johnson (dec); Rosa Davis J Flora (dec); ed/Att'd Free Will Bapt Bible Col & Fresno St Univ; pa/Dir Mayor's Ofc for Handicapped Persons; Scribblers; Spkr 31st Conf Nat Assn Human Rights Wkrs; Spkr Nat Leag Cities' Prog on 504 1978; Appt'd by Mayor to Serve on Spec Task Force on Pedestrian Safety 1979; Prog Com Ldrship Nashville; Publicist for Neighborhood Watch Prog, Designed Logo & Slogan for Prog; cp/Bd Mem Nashville Leag for Hard of Hearing; Joelton Wom's Clb; Davidson Co Dem Wom's Clb; Intl Yr of Child Com; Wom's Polit Caucus; Dem Polit Campaigns; r/Free Will Bapt; hon/Nat Assn Human Rights Wkrs Awd for Significant Contbns to Cause of Human Rights in Am; Gov's Cit for Outstg Ser in Best Interests of St of Tenn; 1 of 19 Tenn Dels to 1977 White House Conf on Handicapped Indivs; Author Book *Djoro!* 1972.

WADDELL, WILLIAM KENNETH oc/Businessman; b/Oct 11, 1938; ba/1501 S Sterling, Morganton, NC; m/Jo Ann T; c/David Kenneth; p/Steve Waddell; Bertha Almeta Henrick; ed/Att'd Gaston Commun Col 1969-70; BA Univ NC 1962; pa/Owner Ins Agcy 1970-; Pers Dept Nationwide Ins Co 1967-70; Textile Engr, Chatham Mfg Co 1960-67; Nat Assn Small Bus-man; Nat Assn Life Underwriters; Wn Carolina Life Underwriters Assn; cp/NC Masonic Frat, Catawba Val Lodge #207; Secy 1974-78, Jr Warden 1979, Sr Warden 1980, Master 1981; r/Bapt; hon/Num Hons & Awds.

WADE, B F oc/Texas Highway Patrol; b/Aug 21, 1927; h/2906 Wydewood Dr, Midland, TX 79701; m/Marie; c/Jimmie Lee, Pamela, Cynthia Dianne, Treasa; p/W L (dec) and Della Wade, Savoy, TX; ed/Att'd Pan-Am Univ, Sam Houston Univ, Lamar Univ, Univ Louisville; Grad So Police Inst, Univ Louisville; mil/USN 1945-46; pa/Capt Tex Hwy Patrol; Dist Comdr, Midland Hwy Patrol Dist; Univ L'ville Alumni Assn; Tex Police Assn; cp/Mason; r/Bapt.

WADE, GLENDA oc/Regional Coordinator; b/May 22, 1950; h/652 S Kentucky, Madisonville, KY 42431; ba/M'ville; m/Clark; c/Clark Jr, Tiffany; p/Sargent and Lorene Hendrix Peppers, Earlington, KY; ed/BA Ky St Univ 1972; MA Morehead St Univ 1974; pa/Commun Ed Spec Wn Ky Legal Sers; Regional Coor Ky Bapt Chil Care; VP Br NAACP; Chp ACTO Prog; Area Dir 9 Co Area Ky Human Rights/NAACP Comm; r/Bapt; hon/Pres's S'ship for Acads 1968; First Rdg Is Fundamental Dir Awd 1979; Del to White House Conf on Fams 1980; Ky Col 1974.

WADE, MARIE oc/Nurse; b/June 7, 1929; h/2906 Wydewood Dr, Midland, TX 79701; m/B F; c/Jimmie Lee, Pamela Marie, Cynthia Diane, Treasa Renee; p/Clarence and Lois Lee Begner, Princeville, IL; ed/LVN Sch, Sherman, Tex; pa/Lic'd Voc Nurse; Pt-Time Nurse in Charge; r/Meth.

WADE, THOMAS EDWARD oc/Professor; b/Sept 14, 1943; h/707 Old West Point Rd, Starkville, MS 39759; ba/Miss St; m/Ann Elizabeth Chitty; c/Amy Renee, Nathan Thomas; p/Wilton Fred (dec) and Alice Lucyle Hedge Wade, Jacksonville, FL; ed/BSEE 1966, MSEE 1969, PhD 1974 Univ Fla; pa/Illumination Engr, Reynolds, Smith & Hills Arch & Engrg Firm 1964; TV Studio Engr, Univ Fla GENESIS Sys 1966-68; Int Asst Prof Electl Engrg, Univ Fla 1975; Admr Electron Divice Res Ctr, Univ Fla 1976; Asst Prof Electl Engr, Miss St Univ 1976-79; Assoc Prof Electl Engrg MSU 1980-; Sigma Xi; Tau Beta Pi; Eta Kappa Nu; Sigma Tau; IEEE; Am Assn Engrg Ed; Am Sci Affil; AAAS; Miss Engrg Soc; Electronics Intl Adv Comm; Miss Acad Sci; Intl Soc Hybrid Microelectronics; cp/Rotary Intl; Fla Blue Key, VP 1974; Omicron Delta Kappa; Epsilon Lambda Chi, Pres 1970; Alpha Phi Omega, Pres 1969, VP 1968; r/Bapt: Bd Deacons, Fin Com, Chancel Choir; hon/Rec'd Outstg Undergrad Engrg Tchr Awd, Univ of Fla 1979; Ldrship Cert, Fla Engrg Soc 1972; Ldrship Key, Benton Engrg Soc 1970; Pub'd Over 20 Articles in Ref Jours; Presented Over 10 Papers at Tech Confs; Prin Investigator for Govt Res Contracts.

WAGERS, JAMES RALPH oc/Retired; b/Dec 9, 1916; h/112 Pearl St, PO Box 105, Berea, KY 40403; m/Dorothy Powell; c/James Robert, Wiliam Haden; p/Jim (dec) and Hannah Wagers (dec); pa/Ret'd US Postal Ser: Postal Clerk/Carrier 1937-50, Asst Post Master 1950-78; cp/Zoning Adjustment Com, City of Berea 1978; Charter Mem Lions Clb; Berea City Coun, Coun-man Elect'd 1979; r/Disciples of Christ; Treas of Ch 32 Yrs; hon/Ser Awd for 41 Yrs w Postal Ser 1979; Cert of Tng in Delivery Sers Mgmt 1977; Job Perf Improvement Tng 1977; Var Other Hon in Course of Job Promo.

WAGNER, CLARENCE MADISON oc/Pastor; b/Dec 11, 1934; ba/PO Box 2283, Gainesville, GA 30503; m/Bettye Jemison; c/Clarence Madison Jr, Dionne Celes; p/Louis Otis Wagner (dec); Dovie Whiteside Peavy (dec); ed/BS Univ Kan City; BBE Carver Bible Col; mil/USAF 1952-56; pa/Pastor First Bapt Ch G'ville; Bd Dirs Nat Bapt Cong; Bd Dirs Morehouse Sch Rel; Pres Interdenom Black Min's Assn; r/Bapt; hon/Contb'g Writer *National Baptist Voice* & *The Georgia Baptist Paper*; Mem Curric Writing Staff of SS Pub'g Bd Nat Bapt Conv; Author *Seeds of Faith, Profiles of Black Georgia Baptists, The Same Jesus*; Dedicated Ser Awd, Gen Missionary Bapt Conv of Ga Inc 1979; Ga Dept Public Safety 1978; VIP Awd, Radio Sta WGGA 1979; Green Hunter Scribe Awd, Zeta Phi Lambda 1979; Jubilee Commend, City of G'ville 1980; Key to City of Savannah 1980.

WAGONER, BETTIE RODERMUND oc/Administrative Officer; b/May 29, 1923; h/142 Miot St, Columbia, SC 29204; ba/Columbia, SC; m/Donald W (dec); p/C W and Vina Powell Rodermund, Quincey, FL; ed/Commercial Cert, Anderson Col; pa/Admr Ofcr, DPCA-Ft Jackson; cp/Am Race Soc; Nat Trust for Hist Preserv; Smithsonian Assoc; Am Horticultural Soc; Zool Soc; r/Presb.

WAGONER, LOU ANN HAGAN oc/Teacher; b/Aug 8, 1947; h/101 Nottingham Dr, Alexander City, Al 35010; ba/Alex City; m/Marvin A; c/T Bryan, M Hagan, C Burke; p/Thomas L and Christine C Hagan; ed/BS Sec'dy Ed 1971, BS Elem Ed 1973 MEd 1975 Auburn Univ; pa/Clrm Tchr Math, Sci, Hlth, William L Radney Elem Sch; NCTM; ACTM; AEA; cp/GFWC Alex City Jr Se Leag, Home Life Dept Chm & VP/Pres Elect; r/Bapt; hon/Outstg Clbwom of Yr, GFWC Alex City Jr Ser Leag; Jeanine Morrow Outstg Clbwom of Yr for Ala.

WAHEED, LEAH CARMEN oc/Student; b/Aug 30, 1965; h/1110 Searcy Dr, Killeen, TX; p/Kamal S (dec) and Namat S Waheed, Killeen, TX; ed/HS Student; cp/Worthy Advr, Killeen Assem 1976, Order of the Rainbow Girls; r/Meth; hon/Nat Jr Hon Soc; TMEA Freshman Region Choir, Div I Rating on Solos; Hon Roll, Region & Dist.

WAKEFIELD, GEORGE NORTON SR oc/Retired; b/Feb 28, 1899; h/Hawthorne, FL; m/Helen Draper; c/Barbara Gene W Wainwright, George Norton Jr; p/Francis Bryan and Ethel Kilbourn Wakefield (dec); ed/BS 1925; MA 1932; mil/US Student Army Tng Corps; pa/Voc Agric Instr 35½ Yrs; Agric Ed Advr, Inst Inter-Am Affairs 10 Yrs; Pres Fla Assn Voc Agric Tchrs 1933-34; Hon Advr Fla Assn FFA; cp/Pres Homestead Rotary Clb; Dem Party; r/Epis; hon/Master Tchr of Fla 1936; Master Tchr of So Region 1936; Author Handbook for Mems of Fla Assn FFA.

WALDEN, MATTIE M oc/Minister, Instructor, News Columnist, Radio Announcer; b/June 26, 1924; h/Rt 2 Box 492, Siler City, NC 27344; m/Willie Ralph Sr; c/Willie II; p/Calvin Marshall (dec) and Laura Brooks Matthews (dec); ed/Att'd Shaw Univ; BD 1972, ThB 1974 Teamers Col; pa/Pastor Johnsonville AME Zion Ch, Pineview, NC; Arts & Craft, Bible Instr, Ctrl Carolina Tech Col, Sanford, NC; Indep Order of St Luke, Grand Outside Centanal; Gen Mgr Dixie Jubilees; cp/Energy Conserv Com, Commun Action Prog, Wn Chatham Min Assn; r/Meth; hon/Wom of Yr 1973; Poems & Sermonettes Pub'd in Chatham Newspaper.

WALDO, JOEL WILLIAM oc/District Executive; b/Sept 27, 1957; h/1129 N Greenwich, Russellville, AR 72801; ba/Alexandria, LA; p/Lola Waldo, R'ville, AR; ed/BS ATU; pa/Dist Exec, Attakapas Coun BSA; Prog Dir Summer Camp; r/Cumberland Presb.

WALDROP, WILLIAM ALLEN JR oc/Chief of Classification; b/May 31, 1951; m/Debra Ann; c/Patrick Alan, Jason Craig; p/William A Sr and Susan Waldrop, Marietta, GA; ed/BBA W Ga Col 1974; Further Study Ga St Univ 1975; pa/Chief of Classification, SE Region EPA; Class & Compensation Soc, Pres Atlanta Chapt 1979; Intl Pers Mgmt Assn; cp/Peachtree Ctr Toastmasters Clb, Pres 1976; Dist 14, St of Ga, Toastmasters: N Ga Lt Gov 1977, Adm Lt Gov 1978, Dist Gov 1979; r/Bapt; hon/Superior Perf Awd EPA 1976; CTM Awd 1976, 78; Dist'd Toastmaster Awd 1980, Area Gov of Yr 1977; Lttrs of Commend EPA 1976-79.

WALKER, ALMENA NORRIS oc/Librarian, Counselor; b/Sept 13, 1935; h/1308 N Mangum St, Durham, NC 27701; c/Aljoesan, Alvernon, Alvin; p/Alvis Sr and Almena N Walker, Durham, NC; ed/BA 1976, MA 1978 NC Ctrl Univ; Postgrad Prog UNC-CH; pa/Asst Dir Rec, DC Rec Dept 1958-61; Asst Dir NC Deaf & Blind Sch 1963-64; Dir Adult Prog, YWCA, Durham 1965-66; Spec Rec, Murdock Ctr, Butner 1966-68; Asst Dir After-Sch Care, Durham Co 1979; Res Supvr NCCU; Libn Durham Co; Pres Carr Jr HS PTA 1978; Exec Com Durham Dem Party 1974-76; Durham Com Wom in Action; Recip Cert Pan Hellenic Coun 1978-79; APGA; NCPGA; Advr Sigma Gamma Rho; Beta Lambda; r/Bapt; hon/Salvation Army Awd 1979; W/W S&SW 1979; Top Adv'g Ser 1978.

WALKER, ARA BELLE oc/Assistant Executive Director; b/Aug 4,

PERSONALITIES OF THE SOUTH

1916; h/PO Box 245, Smiths, AL 36877; m/J G (dec); c/Barbara W East, Shirley W Williams; p/B F (dec) and Carrie L House (dec); ed/Grad Truman-Smith Bus Inst 1935; Mgmt Sems Auburn Univ 1969 & 1973-74; Cont'g Ed Classes, Columbus Col 1970; pa/Asst Exec Dir Phenix City Housing Auth; cp/Charter Mem ABWA, Indian Val Chapt Recording Sech, VP, Pres, SE Dist VP; Phenix City Lioness Clb; Friendship Fire Dept Bd of Dirs, Treas, Pres Aux; Russell Co Cancer Soc; Conchafty Coun of Girl Scouts; r/Primitive Bapt; hon/Wom of Yr ABWA 1971-72, 79-80; Mardi Gras Queen 1978, Wom of the Moose; Cert of Merit, Phenix City JCettes; Nom for Outstg Wom Helping Wom 1980; Personalities of the S 1971.

WALKER, CHARLES A oc/Educator; b/Dec 14, 1935; h/3113 Shamrock S, Tallahassee, FL 32308; ba/Tallahassee; m/Barbara; c/Pamela, Juan, Kim; ed/BS Ark AM&N Col 1957; MS Wash St Univ 1959; PhD Loyola Univ of Chgo Med Sch 1969; pa/Dean & Prof Pharm, Sch of Pharm, Fla A&M Univ 1974-; Res Investigator, Life Sci Inst-NASA 1975 & 76; Res Investigator Neurochem, Marine Biol Lab 1972; Prof & Chm, Dept Physiol & Pharm, Sch of Vet Med, Tuskegee Inst 1971-74; Pharm Conslt, VA Hosp, Tuskegee, AL 1970-; Res Assoc, Univ Calif, Lawrence Radiation Lab, Summer 1970; Assoc Prof Pharm, Sch of Vet Med, Tuskegee Inst 1969-71; Asst Prof Pharm, Sch of Vet Med, Tuskegee Inst 1963-65; Asst Prof Biol, Ft Val St Col 1959-63; Sigma Xi; AAAS; NY Acad Scis; Intl Soc Chronobiol; Am Inst Chem Fellow; Phi Zeta; Am Soc Pharm & Expmtl Therapeutics; Neurosci Soc; Am Inst Biol Scis; Fed Am Soc for Expmtl Biol; APhA; Acad Pharm Scis; Fla Pharm Assn Kappa Psi; Hon Life Mem Fla Soc Hosp Pharm; Am Assn Cols of Pharm; Am Soc Hosp Pharms; Conslt: Hypertension Screening Prog by Tallahassee Urban Leag, Minority Ctr for Grad Ed of Purdue Univ, Reviewer for Sci Proposals of EPA, Reviewer for Sci Manuscripts for Sci on Biorhythms, Reviewer for Sci Manuscripts for Intl Jour of Chronobiol, The Macy Foun Black Schlrs Prog at Woods Hole, MA; cp/Adv Coun, Prog in Med Scis, Fla A&M Univ, Fla St Univ & Univ Fla; Chm Fla A&M Univ Hlth Sci Adv Com; So Assn Cols & Schs, Fla A&M Univ Self-Study Steering Com; Adv Coun Minority Biomed Support Prog; William Gunn St, Pharm, Med & Dental Soc; Chm St of Fla Hlth & Rehab Sers Drug Formulary Com 1975-; Co-Chm Dist III AACP-NABP 1977-78; Nat Urban Leag; Woods Hole Marine Biol Lab Corp; Co-Chm Prog Com AACP Annual Meeting 1978; Chm Steering Com Intl Symposium on Chronopharm & Chronotherapeutics 1978; Black Caucus Brain Trust on Hlth Probs; hon/1 of 15 Grad Students Chosen for an Awd by Am Soc Pharm & Expmtl Therapeutics for Res 1968; Co-Prin Investigator, NSF Grant, "Studies on the Pathogenesis of Listeria Infections" 1969-71; AEC "Q" Clearance, File #CA-37711 1970; Dist'd Tchr of Yr Awd, Sch of Vet Med & Norden Labs 1970; Prin Investigator, Convulsants & Biogenic Amines in the CNS, PMAF 1973-75; Prin Investigator, Circadian Rhythms in the Toxicity of CNS Drugs, Ofc of Naval Res 1973-; Prin Investigator: NIH 1973-75, NASA 1974-, NIH 1975-78; Dir Grants to Support Intl Symposium on Chronopharmacology by NASA & ONR; Boss of Yr 1976, Silver Dome Chapt Am Bus Wom's Assn; Key Note Spkr Num Sems & Meetings; Author Num Profl Pubs Incl'g "Sleep Aids, Sedatives and Stimulant Products" 1979 & "The Effects of Ethanol on Twenty-Four Hour Glycine Rhythms in Rodents" 1979.

WALKER, CHARLOTTE ESTHER oc/Clinical Social Worker; b/Apr 16, 1949; h/25 Skyland Dr, Greenville, SC 29607; ba/G'ville; m/Obie Walker, Newark, NJ; Ozella Walker, G'ville, SC; ed/AB Johnson C Smith Univ; MA Univ Chgo; pa/Clin Social Wkr & Coor Spec'd Mtl Hlth Sers; NASW; Reg of Interpreters for Deaf; Crisis Intervention Adv Bd; cp/Ldrship G'ville Grad; Past Pres YWCA Bd Dirs 1978; Citizen Crime Comm; r/Bapt; hon/Outstg Yng Wom Am 1976 & 77; W/W Am Wom 1979; Cluster Coor's Awd, Alpha Kappa Alpha 1979.

WALKER, DAVID LERON oc/Professor; b/Sept 7, 1955; h/Ormond Bch, FL; ba/Area of Mus, Bethune-Cookman Col, Daytona Bch, FL 32015; m/Deborah W; p/James and Susie Walker, Memphis, TN; ed/BS Univ Ark-Pine Bluff 1976; MA Univ No Iowa 1977; PhD George Peabody Col of Vanderbilt Univ 1980; pa/Asst Prof Voice/Mus Ed, Bethune-Cookman Col; Dir Meharry Med Col Singers; Instr Voice Class/Mus Apprec, Tenn St Men's & Wom's Prisons; Mus Spec, Waterloo, Iowa Rec & Arts Comm; Instr Social Psych of Mus, Am Bapt Theol Sem; Vocal Mus Tchr, Logan Jr HS, Waterloo, Iowa; Artist-in-Residencies & Recitals/Concerts; Mus Edrs Nat Conf; Am Choral Dirs Assn; ASCD; Mu Alpha Nu, Co-Fdr; Alpha Kappa Mu; cp/Alpha Phi Alpha; r/Bapt; hon/Winthrop Rockefeller Foun Schlr 1975-76; Author Music Education in Community Development Continuing Education and Correctional Programming 1980; Co-Author Tennessee Artist in Schools Evaluation Instrument; Picture Theory of Role Perception, & Design of Musical Auditory Recall Tool.

WALKER, DONNA KAY WOODS oc/Educator; b/Aug 25, 1946; h/PO Box 6583, Marietta, GA 30065; ba/Atlanta; m/R W; p/R E and E E Prather Woods, Austin, TX; ed/BA; BS; MEd; pa/NEA; FCTA; FLAG; AATF; r/Rom Cath; hon/MENSA; W/W Am Wom; 1979-80 Rep from Heard's Ferry Tchr of Yr.

WALKER, EDNA GROVEY oc/Businesswoman, Teacher; b/July 5, 1923; h/5027 Briscoe St, Houston, TX 77033; ba/Houston; m/James S; c/Godwyn R, Stepchd: Deborah W Bibbs, Donn Royce; p/George W (dec) and Margery Willis McGowan (dec); ed/BS Houston Col for Negroes; MA TSU; Cert of Grad Nat Tax Tng Sch; Cert of Course Completion, Sch of Philosophy, Univ Brazil; pa/Owner & Asst Mgr Roy's Bar-B-Q; NEA; TSTA; HTA; Zeta Phi Beta; Assn of Am Oversees Edrs; cp/YWCA; Houston Citizens C of C; r/Prot; hon/Outstg Ser Awd, Harris Co TB Assn 1962; Fulbright Grant to Univ Brazil 1962; Ser Awd, 10th Epis Dist YPD of AME 1976; World W/W Wom.

WALKER, HENRY NELL oc/Retired; b/July 7, 1918; h/Manchester Rd, Jasper, AL; p/Columbus Henry (dec) and Lummie Smith Walker (dec); ed/Att'd Univ Ala & Walker Jr Col; pa/Ret'd Plant Assigner, S Ctrl Bell Telephone Co; Tuscaloosa Coun of Telephone Pioneers, Pres; Jasper Clb of Telephone Pioneers, Pres; cp/OES, Worthy Matron; VFW Aux VP; r/Ch of Christ; hon/Outstg Spkr Dale Carnegie Course 1952; Pres Parrish HS Student Body 1936; Asst Ldr Adventures in Christian Living Course 1972.

WALKER, JOHN W oc/Attorney; b/Jun 3, 1937; ba/Little Rock, AR; m/Gloria; c/John Jr, Murray, Pamela, Patricia, Ester; ed/BA Pine Bluff Ark 1958; MA NYU 1961; LLB Yale Univ 1964; pa/Admitted to Ark Bar 1964; US Supreme Ct Bar 1973; Staff Atty, NAACP Legal Defense & Ednl Fund (NYC) 1964-65; Individ Pract of Law 1965-68; Partner w firm of Walker, Kaplan & Mays (Little Rock), now Sr Partner; cp/Ark Constit Revision Study Comm; So Growth Policies Bd; Chm, Opport Indust Comm; So Regional Coun; Am Nat Bar Assn; Bd Dirs, NAACP Legal Def & Ednl Fund; hon/Recip of Mrs David D Terry Awd; Pres of Ldrship Roundtable.

WALKER, LUCILE HILL oc/Lecturer; b/Feb 2, 1900; h/704 W 11th St, Plainview, TX 79072; ba/Same; m/Julius Waring (dec); c/Julius Waring Jr; p/Daniel Chapman (dec) and Alma Amerial Hill (dec); ed/BS Tex Wom's Univ 1921; mil/Dollar-a-Yr Wom for Treas USA WWII; pa/Tchr Sci, Memphis HS 1920-24; Choral Dir, Presb Ch 1943-58; Editor Texas Clubwoman 1949-54; Lectr & Book Reviewer 1942-; cp/Past Pres Caprock; Local Orgr, DAR, Mary McCoy Baines Chapt; Woman's Clbs of P'view; AAUW; P'view Br, Hale Co Hist Comm; Org'g Mem Grace Presb Ch; Chm U Fund Dr for P'view 1958, 60; Chm Dem Party of Hale Co 1958-60; St Dem Party Exec Com 1948-52; Del Nat Dem Party Conv 1960; Tex War Bonds Com 1941-42; r/Presb; hon/Outstg Alumnus Tex Wom's Univ 1947; Citizen of Yr 1960, P'view; Tex Hist Comm Dist'd Ser Awd 1974-77; Bicent Dist'd Hons Awd, Wayland Bapt Col; Dist'd Area Ser Awd, W Tex St Univ 1976; Llano Estacado Mus Ser Awd 1979; US Treas Silver Ser Awd 1946; Many Other Awds & Hons.

WALKER, PAMELA MARIE DOTSON oc/Intensive Care Unit Supervisor; b/June 9, 1952; h/Rt 3 Box 277Z12, Fitzgerald, GA 31750; ba/Fitzgerald; m/James Franklyn; c/David Franklyn; p/J Eugene Sr and Margaret Martin Dotson, Savannah, GA; ed/BSN Med Col of Ga; MS Ga St Univ; pa/RN; ICU Supvr; Am Assn Critical Care Nurses; Ga Heart Assn; r/Cath; hon/W/W Am Wom 1979-80.

WALKER, ROBERTA RUTH oc/Assistant Professor; b/May 7, 1914; h/224 Paso Noble, El Paso, TX 79912; ba/El Paso; m/George Frank (dec); c/Robert Michael; p/L D William (dec) and Kathleen Grey Squires Potts (dec); ed/AA San Bernardino Val Col 1934; Att'd UCLA 1934-36; BA Tex Col Mines & Metall 1948; MA Tex Wn Col 1953; pa/Asst Prof Eng, Univ Tex-El Paso (Staff Mem 1948-); Tex Assn Col Tchrs, VP 1976-77; Rhetoric Soc Am; Rocky Mt MLA; Nat Conf Tchrs Engl; cp/El Paso C of C; UTEP Alumni Assn; DAR; Magna Charta Dames; Pi Lambda Theta; Kappa Delta Pi; Sigma Delta Pi; hon/Excell in Tchg Awd, UTEP 1968.

WALKER, SANDRA LOUISE oc/Student; b/Mar 17, 1961; h/1002 Park, Little Rock, AR 72203; ba/Ft Worth, TX; p/Sylvester Walker, San Diego, CA; Mary Jean Brown, Little Rock, AR; ed/Student; pa/Del Taco Employee; r/Bapt.

WALKER, WALLACE WELDON oc/Fireman; b/May 10, 1929; h/904 E Centennial, Sherman, TX 75090; m/Dorla Eudy; c/Glenda, Duke, Mike, Barry; p/William H Walker, Sherman, TX; ed/Tex A&M Firefighting Sch; EMT Grayson Co Col; mil/AUS 1951-52; pa/Lt Sherman, Tex Fire Dept; cp/Noon Optimist Clb, VP; Pres Little Leag; Comdr Am Legion Post 29; r/Bapt.

WALKER, WILLARD WILLIAM oc/Chief Deputy Sheriff; b/Jan 13, 1946; Porter, TX; ba/300 Main St, Conroe, TX 77301; m/Linda Karen; c/Michelle Rae; p/Willard William Sr (dec) and Genevieve E Walker, Houston, TX; mil/USMC 1964-66; pa/Harris Co Sheriff's Dept 1967-74; Harris Co Med Examiner 1974-76; Montgomery Co Sheriff's Dept 1976-; Nat Sheriff's Assn; Nat VP Nat Assn Chiefs of Police; Criminal Just Adv

308

Com, Mont Co; Pres Mont Co Law Enforcement Assn; Tex Narcotics Ofcrs Assn; cp/Am Legion; Ducks Unltd; Nat Rifle Assn; Lions Clb; Mont Co Fair Assn; r/Bapt; hon/100 Clb Awd; Nat Awd Police Ofcr of Yr 1975; Outstg Instr Tex A&M Univ 1979.

WALLACE, FOY C oc/Businessman and Executive; b/May 5, 1914; h/107 E Main St, Gunter, TX 75058; m/Mary Jennie C Robinson; c/Barbara Ann Moses, Don Thomas; p/Don Carlos Wallace (dec); Hattie Mae Young (dec); ed/Att'd Tyler Commercial Col & N Tex St Tchrs Col; pa/Gunter Drug Store; D C Wallace Gin & Elevator; Est'd Gunter Lumber Co; N Tex Construction Co 1957-; Twin Cities Construction Co & Indust Installations Inc; cp/Orig Bd Dirs Hilltop Haven; Mayor Gunter 1976; Est'd Goodwill Industs of Grayson Co, Mem Bd Dirs; Pres Texoma Regional Plan'g Comm 1979-; Dir Howe St Bank; Rotary Clb; r/Ch of Christ; Elder; Paul Harris Fellow, Rotary Clb 1980.

WALLACE, JOYCE COTTER oc/Real Estate Broker; b/Mar 16, 1932; h/2305 Riverhill Dr, Valdosta, GA 31601; ba/Valdosta; c/R Michael, Russell Cotter, Megan Marie; p/Gerald John (dec) and Alta Dettling Cotter (dec); ed/BS Marygrove Col; Grad Studies Ctrl Mich Univ; pa/Home Ec Tchr 5 Yrs, Mich & Mont; Real Est Salesp & Broker, Mike Bajalia Inc 6 Yrs; Valdosta Bd of Rltrs, Exec Secy; AAUW; r/Cath; hon/Ga Chicken Cooking Queen 1964; Ark Chicken Cooking Queen 1967.

WALLACE, SAM FRANKLIN oc/Pastor; b/July 28, 1938; h/Rt 1 Box 168, Trinity, AL 35673; m/Brenda; c/Michael Lee, Dwight Franklin, Samuel Marc; p/John F and Bessie Wallace; ed/Att'd Sanford Univ; pa/Pastor Mt View Bapt Ch; Secy-Treas Muscle Shoals Bapt Assn Pastor's Conf; Bible Class Ldr, Muscle Shoals Bapt Assn Yth Coun; cp/VP PTO; VP Ath Booster Clb; r/Bapt; hon/Min of Wk, Nov 24, 1978.

WALLER, GENE oc/Executive Director; b/Sept 1, 1912; h/1329 Lindale, Norman, OK 73069; ba/Norman; m/Sally L; c/Linda Lee, Michael; p/Bert (dec) and Rose Waller (dec); pa/Exec Dir Action Inc (CETA); Cleveland Co Fed Progs Dir; cp/Dem Party; r/Epis; hon/Nat Commun Action Honoree 1979; Bldg Named in Hon of Work.

WALLER, HARRY EDWARD oc/Telecommunications Engineer; b/May 26, 1922; ba/Bruce Telephone Co, Bruce, MS; m/Bernice Connely; c/Shellye W White, Connie W Allen; p/Charles Marvin Waller (dec); Mary Alexander (dec); ed/BS Univ Ky 1949; mil/AUS Signal Corps WWII; pa/Pres & Mgr Bruce Telephone Co Inc; Nat Soc Cable TV Engrs; Indep Telephone Pioneer Assn, Nat Pres 1978-79; Nat Cable TV Assn; Ala-Miss Telephne, Past Pres; cp/Lions Clb, Charter Pres; Miss Ec Coun; r/Bapt.

WALLER, ROBERT EDWARD oc/Coach; b/Aug 1, 1950; h/123 Sherwood Ave, Washington, GA 30673; ba/Augusta; m/Catherine Reese; c/Jeremy Reese; p/James E Waller, Danielsville, GA; Margret T Waller (dec); ed/BS Univ Ga; pa/Hd Fball & Wrestling Coach; Ga HS Coaches Assn; r/Christian.

WALSH, RUTH HAMILL MURPHY oc/Associate Professor; h/14814 Daisy Ln, Tampa, FL 33612; ba/Tampa; m/John K; c/Joyce G, Gregory S, Kyle Ann Pierson, Connie M; p/Edward S (dec) and Elizabeth Stack Murphy, Williamsville, NY; ed/AB Barnard Col, Columbia Univ 1947; MA SUNY-Buffalo 1964; PhD Univ S Fla 1976; pa/Assoc Prof Mgmt, Col Bus Adm, Univ S Fla; Author 2 Books & Num Jour Articles; hon/Beta Gamma Sigma; Phi Kappa Phi; Sigma Tau Delta.

WALTERS, STANLEY CRAIG oc/Executive Vice President; b/Sept 26, 1921; h/Greenville, MS; ba/Lake Ferguson, Greenville, MS; m/Sarah; c/Mary Elizabeth, Peggy Craig; p/L M (dec) and Elizabeth Craig Walters (dec); ed/AA Jones Co Jr Col 1940; BS Univ Ala 1942; mil/USMC 1941-45; USN 1958; pa/Hd Labor Relats, Exec VP Mainstream Shipyards & Supply Inc 1973-; Industs Relats Nicholson File Co 1966-73; Dir of Pers US Plywood & Mengel Co 1957-66; Am Soc Pers Admrs; Pres G'ville Pers Coun; Nat VP The Propeller Clb of US; Chm Employee Relats Miss Mfrs Assn; cp/Dir G'ville C of C; Past Pres Exch Clb; Lions Clb; Secy G'ville Propeller 7 Yrs; r/Meth; hon/W/W S&SW 1980; Accred'd Exec Pers 1976-.

WALTON, CAROLE oc/Clinical Social Worker; b/Oct 20, 1949; h/5555 Roswell Rd NE, Apt K-2, Atlanta, GA 30342; ba/Douglasville, GA; p/Leo Walton, Harison, AR; Arlette Armstrong, Cape Girardeau, MO; ed/BA Lambuth Col 1971; MA Univ Chgo 1974; pa/Coor Fam Sers, Anneewakee Treatment Ctr 1976-; Clin Social Worker, Proviso Mtl Hlth Ctr, Westchester, Ill 1974-76; Dir Self-Travel Prog, Chgo Assn for Retard'd Citizens 1973; Social Wkr, Genesee Co Mtl Hlth Sers, Flint, Mich 1971-72; NASW; ACSW; NASW Register of Clin Social Wkrs; Ga Soc Clin Social Wkrs, Mbrship Chp 1981; Pres 1982; cp/Sierra Clb; r/Epis; hon/W/W Am Wom 1981.

WALTON, NEAL OWEN oc/Student; b/Sept 14, 1961; h/10 Linwood Dr, Marshall, TX 75670; p/Seth Roe Jr and Vera Elizabeth Bellew Walton, Marshall, TX; ed/Att'g E Tex Bapt Col; cp/Key Clb; Yng Texans for Connally; r/So Bapt; hon/VP Mod Mus Masters; Pres Nat Hon Soc; Att'd Tex Boys St; All Region Band; Quiz Bowl Team; Danforth Willard Coker Awd; Am Legion Awd; Kiwanis Awd; Soroptimist Awd; W/W Am HS Students; Intl Yth Achmt.

WAN, RICHARD T C oc/Physician; b/Apr 3, 1936; h/Thomas St, Morgantown, KY 42261; ba/M'town; c/Julia, Everett; p/Henry and Doris Wan; ed/Rotating Internship 1960-61; Internal Med Residency 1961-62; Sr Intern 1962-63; Residency & F'ship of Pediatrics 1963-66; pa/KMA; AMA; Tri-Co Med Soc; Butler Co Hlth Dept; cp/Lions Clb; Repub Party; r/Bapt.

WANDERMAN, RICHARD G oc/Physician; b/Apr 17, 1943; h/2536 Ashburton Pl N, Cordova, TN 38018; c/Richard G Jr, Gregory Lloyd; p/Herman L Wanderman (dec); Helen W Schneider, NY, NY; ed/BA; MD; FAAP; pa/Pediatrician; Clin Assoc Prof Ped, Univ Tenn; Soc Adol Med; cp/Swim Coach MJCC; MENSA; r/Jewish; hon/Num Biogl Listings.

WARD, CARL ALLAN oc/Clinical Psychologist; b/July 6, 1945; h/8616 NW Plaza Dr, Suite 210, Dallas, TX 75225; p/James N and Francis L Ward, Dallas; ed/BS N Tex St Univ 1971; PhD Fla Inst Tech 1980; mil/Former Green Beret, Psych-War Officer; pa/Clin Dir, Behavioral Medicine Ctr of Dallas; Am, SW, Dallas & Tex Psych Assns; Am Assn of Marriage and Fam Therapists; Tex Marriage & Fam Therapy Assn; cp/American Security Coun; r/Christian; hon/Diplomate Am Academy of Behavioral Med.

WARD, JOSEPH OFFIE oc/Assistant Public Works Superintendent; b/June 13, 1943; h/201 Tracey Circle, Enterprise, AL; ba/Enterprise; m/Joyce Faye Erickson; c/Joseph Martin, Jason Eric, Jennifer Ashley; p/Offie Elijah and Elsie Iveynez Ward, Coffee Springs, AL; ed/Att'd Shelton St Tech Col 1972-75, Brewer St Jr Col 1975-77; mil/USN 1965-67; pa/Asst Public Works Supt 1978-; Ala St Hwy Dept 1968-76, 1961-65; r/Prot; hon/Cit, Secy of Navy; Lttr Recog for Outstg Ser in Vietnam.

WARD, LEW O oc/Oil Producer; b/July 24, 1930; h/900 Brookside Dr, Enid, OK 73701; ba/Enid; c/Casidy Ann, William Carlton; p/L O II (dec) and Addie Ward, Enid, OK; ed/BS Univ Okla; mil/Corps of Engrg 1st Lt 1953-55; pa/Indep Oil Prodr; Pres Okla Indep Petro Assn; Dir Indep Petro Assn of Am; cp/Rotary; Ambucs Bus Clb; C of C; Fin Chm Okla Repub Party; r/Meth; hon/Dist'd Ser Awd 1977, Okla Petro Coun.

WARD, MORRIS C oc/Regional Office Manager; b/June 13, 1931; h/2932 Col Cir, Corsicana, TX 75110; ba/Corsicana; m/Margaret M; c/Linda Sue Burpo, Peggy Ann Faichtinger, Carolyn Kay Conn; p/Clem (dec) and Anna Laura Ward (dec); mil/USN 1951-55; pa/Regional Ofc Mgr, Lone Star Gas Co; cp/Bd Dirs Tex Chd Camp; Lions Clb Intl, Dist Gov; r/Bapt; hon/Outstg Com Chm C of C; JC of Yr; Lion of Yr; Gov's Awd of Merit; Mbrship Advmt Awd; Mbrship Key Awd; Mbrship Advmt Key Awd.

WARD, REBECCA S oc/Teacher; b/Aug 11, 1946; h/234 St John, Dyersburg, TN; m/J Randy; c/Edie; p/Kenneth and Ruth Stevens, Bolivar, TN; ed/BS 1967, MEd 1976 Memphis St Univ; pa/Rdg Tchr, Dyersburg City Schs, Jennie Bell Elem; NEA; TEA; PTA Hardin Co Ed Assn: Secy, Chm Profl Rights-Responsiblity Com; Tchr Recruitment Com, Ins Com, Salary Com; D'burg Ed Assn: Tchr Wel Com, Sunshine Com; W Tenn Ed Assn; Delta Kappa Gamma: 2nd VP, Mbrship Com, Pers Growth & Sers Com; cp/Chm Heart Fund 1971; r/First Bapt Ch: Primary SS Tchr; VBS Tchr; Yth II SS Co-Dir; Couples Class Christian Tng Co-Ldr; Wom's Missionary Union Coun; Career Bapt Yng Wom, Pres, Mission-Action Chm; Girls Aux Ldr; Girls Aux Dir; Couples SS Class Secy; hon/Outstg Yng Edr of Yr, Hardin Co JCs; Tchr of Yr, Adamsville JCs; Outstg Yng Wom of Am 1971, 80; Gov's Ldrship Chain of Back to Basics Com 1979.

WARD, SAMUEL JOSEPH JR oc/Executive; b/Jan 7, 1928; h/2635 Radstock Rd, Midlothian, VA 23113; ba/Richmond; m/Sue McDuffee; c/Samuel Joseph III, Raymond Curtis, Dana Reginald, James Grady, Robert Edwin, Glenn William; p/Samuel Joseph (dec) and Frankie Lee Inez, Savannah, GA; ed/AS Armstrong Col 1949; BS Ga Inst Tech 1951; Indust Col of the Armed Forces 1975; mil/AUS Paratroopers; USAFR Col; pa/VP & Public Relats Dir, Bank of Va; First Nat Bank of Atlanta; Savannah Gas Co; Savannah Area C of C; Chm Public Relats Coun, Bank Mktg Assn; Chm Public Relats & Mktg Com, Va Bnkrs Assn; cp/VP Robert E Lee Coun BSA; Communs Com, Richmond C of C; Ed Com Va St C of C; r/Presb; Past Chm Bd of Deacons; hon/Outstg Yng Man Yr 1962; Golden Deeds, Lions Clb 1967; Bank Mktg Awd 1969; Annual Report Awd 1969, 72, 74, 76, 79; Author "Issues in Communications: The Changing World of Bank Public Relations Developing a Marketing Plan" 1976.

WARD, SHIRLEY ANN oc/Research Director; b/Jan 27, 1933; h/Dallas, TX; c/Lisa Lynn; p/George W Martin, Dallas, TX; ed/BA Austin Col 1955; MA 1963, Cnslg Certf 1974, So Meth Univ; PhD N Tex St Univ 1979; pa/Public Sch Tchr 1955-73; Lang Tnr, Ctr for Behavioral Studies, Denton, Tex 1975-77; Psych, Pupil Appraisal Ctr, N Tex St Univ 1976-77; Psych Tchr, Richland Col 1976-79; Cnlsr, Fin Sers Network, Dallas 1976-80; Cnslr, Pvt Pract 1980-; Res Dir Total Life Care 1980-; cp/Repub Party; r/Presb; hon/Author Num Profl Pubs.

WARDEN, LEWIS CHRISTOPHER oc/Lawyer, Author; b/Aug 26, 1913; h/1903 NE 15th St, Gainesville, FL 32601; ba/Same; m/Emma Elizabeth Wallace; c/Rebecca Louise W Bowman, Deborah Lou; p/Christopher M (dec) and Alice Lewis Warden (dec); ed/AB Ohio St Univ 1934; LLB 1937, JD 1969 Harvard Univ; mil/AUS Field Artillery 1942; pa/Pract Law 1937-42, Ohio; Common Pleas Judge 1945-50, Ohio; The Lwyrs Coop Pub Co: Editor 1950-78, Supvg Editor 1961-68, Proj Editor 1968-78; r/Meth; hon/Author Sev Books Incl'g *The Life of Blackstone* & *Torrent of the Willows*; Incl'd in Num Biogl Works.

WARDERS, JESSE PUCKETT oc/Instructor, Real Estate and Insurance Broker; b/July 13, 1917; h/2524 W Chestnut St, Louisville, KY 40211; m/Lena Woods; c/William L; p/Pearl Lena Jackson, L'ville, KY; ed/BS 1952, MS 1960 Ind Univ; mil/AUS 1941-45 1st Sgt; pa/US Dept HUD; Real Est & Ins Broker; Ecs Instr, Univ Ill; L'ville Real Est Brokers Assn, Pres; Nat Assn Real Est Brokers, VP; L'ville Urban Renewal & Commun Devel Agcy, Commr; St Joseph's Infirmary, Modr of Bd Trustees; Commun Action Comm, Commr; cp/Ky St Rep 1966; Plymouth Settlement House, Pres Bd of Dirs 1967-69; Life Mem NAACP; r/U Ch of Christ: Chm Bd Trustees 1970-71, Deacon Bd 1980-; hon/Fair Housing Awd, US Dept HUD 1981; Ky Col 1979; Captain of Belle of L'ville 1979; 25 Yr Ser Awd, L'ville Real Est Bd 1973; Plymouth Congreg U Ch of Christ Centennial Awd 1977; Dist'd Citizen, City of L'ville 1979; Cert of Apprec, US Dept Housing & Devel; St Joseph Infirm Salutes Jesse P Warders, Bd Trustees 1970-76; Brooklawn, In Apprec of Ser & Dedication 1980; Salt River Navy Rear Admiral 1979.

WARNER, PATRICIA DAVIS oc/Consultant; b/Jan 25, 1949; h/3850 Antoinette Dr, Montgomery, AL 36111; ba/Mont; m/Anthony H III; p/Billy M and Mary Gay Davis, Mont, AL; ed/BA Huntingdon Col 1970; MA Univ Ala 1971; pa/Public Relats Dir, Ala St Dept Ed, Adult Ed Sect; Proj Editor, Fuller & Dees Div, *Times Mirror*; Public Relats Conslt, Ala Public Lib Ser; Bd Dirs Wom in Communs Inc; IABC/Mont; SEn Lib Assn; Ala Lib Assn; Bd Dirs Inst of Rel Drama, Huntingdon Col; cp/Jr Wom's Clb of Mont Inc; VP Ctrl Ala Regional Coun on Alcoholism; Bd Advrs Ala Hist Comm; Ctlr Ala Mar of Dimes; Chm of Bd Ala Outdoor Drama Coun; r/Meth; hon/Gov's Envirl Quality Awd 1978; Pub of Yr, IABC/Mont for 4-Color Brochure Design 1979.

WARREN, ELEANOR RUTH oc/Executive; b/Oct 19, 1946; h/201 W Ch, Morrilton, AR; ba/M'ton; p/Lillie Belle Watson Warren, Morrilton, AR; ed/Att'd Univ Ctrl Ark & Univ Ark 1964-66; pa/VP & Gen Mgr Warren Enterprises Inc 1966-; Eleanor's Discount Fashion; M'ton Retail Merchants Assn; Ark Retail Merchants; US Nat Retail Merchants; M'ton Downtown Revitalization Com; Small Bus Assn Ark; Nat Bus Assn; Nat C of C; cp/Latin Clb; Del from Ark, Nat Latin Conv 1963; Pres Conway Co Hist Preserv Assn; Preserv of Downtown M'ton Bus Dist; r/Presb; hon/Selected to Rep Ark at Inaugural of Pres Lyndon Johnson 1965; Miss Congeniality, Miss M'ton Pageant 1965; W/W Ark 1974.

WARREN, LILLIE BELLE WATSON oc/Executive; b/Feb 24, 1909; h/201 W Ch St, Morrilton, AR 72110; ba/M'ton; m/Truman John Sr (dec); c/Mary Louise Wilson, Truman John Jr; Eleanor Ruth; p/Finis Bascum and Maude Eleanor Ashe Watson, Ico, AR; ed/Monticello Agric-Mech Acad 1924-27; Ark St Tchrs Col 1927-33; pa/Pres Warren Enterprises 1964-; Home Ec Tchr, Mabelvale, HS 1929-33; M'ton Retail Merchants Assn; Ark Retail Merchants; US Nat Retail Merchants; M'ton Downtown Revitalization Com; M'ton C of C; Nat C of C; Small Bus Assn of Ark; Nat Bus Assn; cp/Conserv of Hist Places Wild Life, Gdn Clb Pres 1940-42; Pathfinder Clb 1939-43; Cub Scout Ldr 1952-60; Girl Scout Ldr 1951-62; 10 Co Girl Scout Coun 1952-62; Bldg Com Chwom, Nat Hist Places in Conway Co, Ark, Ark Arts Ctr 1973-; r/Presb; hon/Outstg Homemkr Student in Monticello Agric-Mech Acad 1927; W/W: S&SW 1980, Am 1980.

WARREN, LYNWOOD oc/Farmer; b/Aug 7, 1931; h/Rt 1 Box 163, Tifton, GA 31794; m/Myrtle C; c/Carolyn, Tony, Regina, Danny; p/G W and Claudia Mae Warren; p/Farm Owner & Oper; Tift Co Commr; Agric Prodrs Inc, Chm of Bd; Farm Bur; cp/Public Sch Trustee; Bd of Selective Sers; Exch Clb of Tifton, Treas; r/Bapt; hon/Tift Co Man of Yr in Soil Conserv 1962; Outstg Yng Farmer of Yr 1965; Farmer of Yr, Kiwanis Clb 1965; Ga's FHA Farmer of Yr 1970; Contbr to Num Farming Jours & Newspapers.

WARREN, MARY DENNY oc/Director Nursing Services; b/June 13, 1919; h/Rt 1 Box 44, Baxter, TN 38544; m/Chesley W; c/Lenda Barksdale, Micki Knott; p/Effie Denny, Oak Ridge, TN; ed/RN Sch of Nsg 1946; Baccalaureate Deg 1950; MSN 1963; pa/Nsg Adm; Sigma Theta Tau; Am Red Cross; Nat Soc Nsg Admrs; Am Hosp Assn; Tenn Hosp Assn; Fac Mem Tenn Tech Univ; Nat Leag Nsg; cp/Civil Defense Chm; Pres Stroke Clb; r/Ch of Christ; hon/Nurse of Yr, Md 1963; W/W S&SW 1980-81; Life Mem Sigma Theta Tau.

WASHINGTON, CHARLES A oc/Chemist; b/July 4, 1936; h/118 Decatur Rd, Oak Ridge, TN 37830; ba/Oak Ridge; m/Eva G; c/Charles A Jr, Samuel Henry; p/Earnest and Lillie B Washington, Attapulgus, GA; ed/MS; mil/USAF; pa/Chemist, Union Carbide; cp/US Comm on Civil Rights, Adv Bd for St Tenn; Anderson Co Exec Bd; Charter Mem & VP Downtown Optimist Clb; Mem Expo-82 Com; Past Pres Atomic City Sportmen Clb; Trustee Atomic City Elk's Lodge 1301; Past Bd Mem ACLU; Pres Oak Ridge Human Resources Bd; r/Presb; Elder; hon/Col Aide-de-Camp Cert, Gov Blanton.

WASHINGTON, DONALD RAY oc/Deputy Sheriff; b/June 13, 1955; ba/Orange Co Sheriff's Dept, Orange, TX 77630; m/Barbara; c/Amanda, Donald Jr; p/Thomas Washington Sr, Orange, TX; Virgie Washington (dec); ed/Law Enforcement Cert, Lamar Univ; pa/Dpty Sheriff; r/Cath.

WASHINGTON, GEORGE BERNETT oc/Postal Clerk, Real Estate Salesman; b/Mar 19, 1910; h/838 Beckwith St SW, Atlanta, GA; ba/Forest Pk, GA; m/Daisy Lovett; c/Carrie W Smith, Henri W Robinson; p/dec; ed/Morehouse Col 1936-38; Acctg Dip Blayton Sch Acctg 1950; Dip Ga Rlty Bd; mil/AUS 1943-45; pa/US Postal Clerk; Real Est Salesman; Nat Alliance of Postal Employees, Past Treas; Ga Rltrs Assn; AFL; cp/NAACP; UNCF, Grp Ldr for PO Dept; Shriner; Mason; Meal-on-Wheels Vol, DeKalb Co; r/Bapt; Deacon, Supt SS; hon/Brotherhood Awd 1979, Providence Bapt Ch; Wkly Contbr to Rel Newslttr Pub'd by Ch.

WASHINGTON, JOE IVA JR oc/Teacher and Coach; b/May 16, 1951; h/Louisville, KY; ba/MacDonald Middle Sch, Phys Ed Dept, 7729 McCracken St, Ft Knox, KY 40121; m/Youlanda Cumings; p/Joe Iva Sr and Reedius Mae Washington; ed/AA 1971, BS 1973 En Ky Univ; Masters Cand; pa/Phys Ed Tchr-Coach, MacDonald Middle Sch; Ky Trackers Fball Team, Am Fball Assn 1979; Career Day Prog 1979; Clin for Gov's Coun on Phys Fitness & Sports 1978-79; Hd Basketball Coach, Ft Knox 1978-79; Active Clin for Pres's Coun on Phys Fitness & Sports 1977-79; Dir Fitness Mobile for Mayor's Summer Prog 1977-78; Conducted Nutrition & Hlth Fitness Wkship in Somerset, Ky Public Hlth Assn & Ky Heart Assn 1977; Clin for Rubberband Man Fitness Wkship 1977; Asst HS Fball Coach, Ft Knox 1973; Middle Sch Gymnastic Coach 1973; JV Coach 1973; Cert'd Correction Therapist 1973; Wkshop w Sr Citizens 1975-80; Inser Day Wkshops for Tchrs 1978-80; KAHPER; PEPI Chp for Phys Ed Public Info; Kappa Alpha Psi; FCA; r/Christian; hon/Ky's Tchr of Yr 1980; Nom'd Nat Tchr of Yr 1980; Ky Col; Other Awds & Hons.

WATERMAN, CAROLYN LANPHER oc/Professor; b/Nov 23, 1939; ba/Bethany Nazarene Col, Bethany, OK; m/Darwin Earle; c/Stephen, Paula; p/Gertrude Whitehead, Bethany, OK; ed/BA cum laude En Nazarene Col 1961; MA Bethany Nazarene Col 1976; pa/Prof Speech Communs, Bethany Nazarene Col 1976-; Calif Public Schs 1964-68; Ctrl Sts Speech Assn; Speech Commun Assn; r/Nazarene; hon/W/W Am Cols & Univs 1961; Article Pub'd in ERIC Reports 1980 "The Chicana: Traditional Values in Transition."

WATERS, HENRIETTA E oc/Social Work Educator; b/July 4, 1927; h/Miami, FL; ba/Barry Col, 11300 NE 2nd Ave, Miami, FL 33161; m/Robert H Sr; c/Robert H Jr; p/Hazel Robinson, Rockford, ILL; ed/BS Ctrl St Univ 1949; MSW Univ Kan 1961; pa/Child Welfare Supvr, Chgo Wel Dept; Child Welfare Dist Ofc Supvr & Conslt, Kan Dept Social Welfare; Asst Prof Univ Kan Sch of Social Welfare; Assoc Prof, Barry Col Sch of Social Work; Conslt Dade Co Commun Action Agcy; NASW; ACSW; Coun on Social Work Ed, House of Dels; Nat Assn Black Social Wkrs; Behavioral Sci Inst; cp/VP Urban Leag of Gtr Miami; Trustee Bd of Public Hlth Trust; Exec Com, Chd's Psychi Ctr; Former VP YWCA of Dade Co; Adv Com Human Resources Child Devel; r/Meth; hon/Barry Col Profl Achmt Awd 1979.

WATERS, RUTH ANN oc/Homemouth; b/Sept 10, 1932; h/1171 W Pace Ferry Rd NW, Atlanta, GA 30327; Milton B Satcher Jr; c/David Anthony, Milton B III, James Kerr; p/Loy Anthony and Ruth Coleman Waters; ed/BS Univ Ga 1953; pa/Exec Secy Alpha Delta Pi; Exec Secy Allied Hlth Careers Ofc, Med Assn of Ga Hdqtrs; cp/Pres Aux to Med Assn of Ga; Past Pres Interns & Residents Wives Clb; Chm AMAG Achmt Awd; Chm Res & Romance of Med, Hist, Mbrship Chm, Area VP Allied Hlth Careers Ofc, MAG Hdqtrs; Jr Dir Huguenot Soc; Cherokee Chapt

DAR; Atlanta Symph Assn; Mus of Art; Atlanta Hist Soc; Yng Wom of Arts; Camellia Garden Clb; r/Presb; hon/Outstg Alumnae, Alpha Delta Pi 1970; Cert of Hon Fulton Co Med Soc 1970.

WATKINS, EDWIN R oc/Retired; b/Mar 19, 1911; h/102 Wiliams Ave, Corbin, KY 40701; m/Renia Holt; c/Ronnie; p/James T (dec) and Elizabeth Baird Watkins (dec); ed/Bunnell's Corbin Bus Col 1929; mil/WWII; pa/Civil Ser: Dept of Army 1959-66; USDA-FNS 1966-80; Dist Mgr Regional Ofc Amdrs, Ggcy Supvrs; cp/US Civil Ser Retirement Sys; Fed Ser Credit Union; r/Bapt; hon/Cert of Awd, USDA-FNS 1974; Cert of Apprec-Recog of 24 Yrs Fed Ser, USDA-FNS.

WATKINS, LYNETTE LEONE oc/Professional Artist; b/Oct 20, 1949; h/313 Cherry, Levelland, TX 79336; m/Dan; c/Patterson Blake, Stephen Barrett; p/Steve and Rosemary Hezmall, Rudoso, NM; ed/BA Ft Lewis Col 1970; pa/Sec'dy Public Sch Choral Tchr; Pvt Mus & Art Tchr; Art Tchr So Plains Col; Profl Artist; L'land Piano Tchrs Assn, Pres; Progressive Jr Wom's Clb, Progs Chm; NEA; Nat Org Mus Ed; L'land Art Assn; r/Nazarene; hon/Sev Hons in Art, Juried Art Shows; Outstg Yng Wom Am; Dean's List, Ft Lewis Col.

WATROUS, ELEANOR BURNS oc/Executive; b/Nov 9, 1914; ba/New Orleans, LA: m/Herbert L; p/John T and Ellen Lacey Burns; ed/Grad Soule Bus Col 1931; pa/Secy-Treas, Chm of Bd Long Elec Supply Co Inc; Pres Eleanor B Long Realty Co; Watrous Tree Farm; Watrous Willie Rd Nursery; cp/Nat Assn Elect Distrs; Pano; Optimist Clb; r/Cath; hon/Humanitarian Awd, NAED 1966.

WATSON, FLOYD T oc/Minister; b/May 19, 1945; h/417 Edgefield Hwy, Belvedere, SC 29841; ba/N Augusta; m/Cheryl JoAnne; c/James Ryan, Wendy Christine; p/D W and Margaret S Watson, Langley, SC; ed/BMin; pa/Pastor Ridgeview Bapt Ch; cp/PTA; Mason; r/So Bapt; hon/Taught New Testament Survey.

WATSON, GREGORY HARRISS oc/Defense Systems Analyst; b/July 16, 1948; h/4754 Tapestry Dr, Fairfax, VA 22032; ba/Wash DC; m/Cynthia Sue Sandberg; c/Andrew Daniel; p/Robert John and Anne Bellotte Watson, Tenafly, NJ; ed/BA cum laude Taylor Univ 1970; MS USC 1975; Dip Indust Col of Armed Forces 1980; mil/USN 1971-77 Flight Ofcr; pa/Regional Mgr, Sr Analyst, Atlantic Analysis Corp 1977-78; Mem of Profl Staff, Ctr for Naval Analysis 1978-80; Dpty Dir for Signal Processing, Sensors Div, APW Sys Proj Ofc 1980-; Opers Res Soc of Am; Mil Opers Res Soc, Chm, Test & Evaluation Wkg Grp 1980; Ofcrs Christian F'ship, Local Rep in Fairfax; cp/Repub Party; r/Prot; hon/Grad F'ship, Am Univ 1970-71; Navy Achmt Medal 1977; Author Num Classified Tech Reports; Contbr to Chief of Naval Mat Software Symposium 1980.

WATSON, JOHNIE BUTLER oc/Artist; b/Oct 18, 1925; h/4055 Dement St, New Orleans, LA 70127; ba/Picayune, MS; m/Stanley J; c/Stanley J Jr, John Mark, David Lee, Anne Gaye; p/John S (dec) and Lillie Eakies Butler, Warner, OK; pa/Artist: Porcelain & Ceramics; Nat Ceramics Assn & Guild of Picayune; cp/Teach Porcelain & Ceramic Art; r/So Bapt.

WATSON, MARIETTA GATES oc/Banker; b/May 25, 1930; ba/Carolina Bank, 145 W Main St, Sanford, NC 27330; m/George W; c/G Worth III; p/Lucille P Gates, Sanford, NC; ed/AA Campbell Col 1951; Cert NC Sch Bnkg 1975; Cert BAI Sch of Bnkg 1979; pa/Peoples Bank & Trust Co, Mullens, WV 1951-54; Carolina Bank, Sanford 1954-; AIB Instr; Nat Assn Bank Wom Inc, Grp Chm Region Com Chm, Regional VP; Sanford BPW Clb, 2nd VP, 1st VP, Pres; cp/Lee Co Rec Comm; NC Rec Foun Bd Trustees; r/U Ch of Christ; hon/Dist'd Alumnus, Campbell Col 1977.

WATSON, MONTE oc/Carpenter, Breeder; b/Oct 30, 1959; h/Rt 1 Box 187, Mooreland, OK 73852; p/Dale and Lucile Watson, Mooreland, OK; pa/Breeder & Exhibr of Poultry; Cert'd Flock Selector & Testor; cp/Pres Woodward Co Poultry Fed; Okla St Dir Belgian Booted & d'Uccle Bantam Clb; Okla St Dir Wyandotte Bantam Clb of Am; hon/13 Awds, Amarillo, Tex, Mar 20, 1980; 65 Awds Amarillo Sept 19 & 20, 1980; 47 Awds, Wichita, Kan Oct 18 & 19, 1980; Appears in Nat Poultry Improvement Plan Booklet 1981; Am Poultry Assn Yrbook 1980-81; Am Bantam Assn Yrbook 1981; Poultry Press 1980-81.

WATTS, ALMA GERTRUDE oc/Teacher, Coordinator; b/May 25, 1926; h/Low Moor, VA; p/Harry Leibig Watts, Covingtn, VA; Helen Hull Watts (dec); pa/Tchr Hlth, Phy Ed, Driver Ed; Coor Commun Ed, City of Clifton Forge & Supvr Adult Ed; VEA; NEA; VADETS; r/Presb; SS Tchr, Adult Bible Class; hon/Driver Ed Tchr of Yr, St of Va.

WATTS, JOHN DANIEL Executive; b/Sept 29, 1942; h/648 W Beam Ave, Yukon, OK 73099; p/Daniel Monroe and Bernice Creel Watts;

ed/Att'd Univ Alaska 1962-63; mil/USAF 1960-64; pa/Police Ofcr Dallas, Tex 1965-66; Supvr J & R Map Co, Van Buren, AR 1967-70; Exec Security Fin Co, Spartanburg, SC 1971-73; Exec BP Industs, Midland, Tex 1974-75; Pres & Chief Exec Ofcr Impact Map Co, Lubbock, Tex 1975-; cp/Profl Photogs Of Tex; Nat Free Lance Photogs Assn; Assoc's Photogs Intl; Printing Industs of Am; C of C of US; Repub Party; r/Meth; hon/Recip Pres Unit Cit Awd, USAF 1963; Ednl Achmt Awd USAF 1963; Awd of Merit USAF 1964; Photo Excell Awd, Photo Five Photo Soc 6 Times 1968-74; Mgr of Yr, Security Fin Co 1973; Cert'd Fin Analyst, Dun & Bradstreet 1980.

WATTS, JOYCE M oc/Realtor Associate; b/Mar 13, 1948; h/310 W Minnesota Ave, DeLand, FL 32720; ba/DeLand; m/C Allen; c/Kristin E, Mark A; p/Richard J and Grace C McDeavitt, Lake Helen, FL; ed/Fla Real Est Lic 1979; BBA Campbell Univ 1978; pa/Rltr-Assoc Loconte Real Est & Investment Co; DeLand & W Volusia Bd Rltrs; cp/Secy Bd Trustees Trinity U Meth Ch; Appt'd Mem Vision 80 Task Force, City of DeLand; Zeta Theta Chapt Epsilon Sigma Alphs, Publicity Chm; r/Meth.

WATTS, PHILIP LLEWELLYN oc/Bank Executive Trainee; b/Nov 10, 1955; h/Jellico, TN; ba/Union Bank, PO Drawer 120, Jellico, TN 37762; m/Teresa A; p/Ned C and Joanne Watts, Jellico, TN; ed/BS Cumberland Col 1978; Dip Yng Bankers Div Tenn Bnkrs Assn 1979-80; pa/Bank Exec Trainee; cp/JC, Jellico Chapt Secy-Treas; Jellico Civic Clb, Secy-Treas; Blue Devil Sports Broadcasting Corp, Prodr-Treas; r/First Bapt Ch; hon/Hon Page Ho of Rep, St of Ky; W/W Am HS Students 1972-73.

WEATHERHOLTZ, JOAN H oc/Supervisor; b/Nov 10, 1933; h/10184 Owen Brown Rd, Columbia , MD 21044; ba/Balto, MD; m/Clyde M; p/A G and Velma Hutter; ed/AA Potomac St Col 1954; BS WVU 1956; MEd Univ Md 1966; pa/Tchr Hawanko HS 1956-62; Supvr Howard Co Bd Ed 1962-74; Chief Food & Nutrition Br, Md St Dept Ed 1978-; Delta Kappa Gamma; Am Sch Food Ser Assn; Md Sch Food Ser Assn, Advr; Am Home Ec Assn, Nom'g Com; Md Home Ec Assn, Pres, Secy; Am Voc Assn; Md Voc Assn, Pres, Sect Ldr; Home Ec Ed Assn of NEA; r/Presb; hon/Author Article for Delta Kappa Gamme Bltn & Var Sch Lunch Bltns in Md.

WEATHERS, WALTER FRIDGE oc/Regional Director; b/Nov 21, 1950; h/222 E Blalock Cir, Liberty, MS 39645; m/Patricia Ilene Blalock; c/Kimberly, Max, Ashley, Brad; p/Milton W (dec) and Jewell O Weathers, Liberty, MS; ed/BA Univ So Miss 1976; pa/St Dept Public Welfare 1975-; Spec Rep of Ch of Jesus Christ of Latter Day Saints, Fukuoka, Japan 1970-72; Am Public Wel Assn; St Employees Assn of Miss; Miss Conf in Social Wel; cp/Chm Amite Co Chapt Miss Lung Assn; r/Mormon; hon/Outstg Yng Men Am 1977.

WEATHERSPOON, TOMMYE LEE oc/Relay Engineer; b/Feb 6, 1951; h/2101 NW 178 St, Opa-Locka, FL 33056; ba/Miami; p/Donnie and Kathryn Weatherspoon, Delray Bch, FL; ed/BSEE Fla A&M Univ; MBA Barry Col; pa/Relay Engr, Fla Power & Light Co; Fla Engrg Soc; IEEE; Black Engrg Soc; Nat Soc Profl Engrs; cp/Big Brother Prog; NAACP; SCLC; r/Bapt; hon/W/W Am 1981-82; Star Student Awds 1978; Dade Co Man of Yr 1979; Author "Solid St Relaying in the Future" for Fla Engrg Soc Jour.

WEAVER, JACQUELINE LANG oc/Professor, Associate Director; b/Jan 18, 1947; h/Houston, TX; ba/Univ Houston, Col of Law, Houston, TX 77004; m/Kirk K; c/Kyle, Kenyon; p/Hans J and Ruth Crowl Lang, LI, NY; ed/BA Harvard Col 1968; PHC UCLA 1971; JD Univ Houston Law Sch; pa/Prof & Assoc Dir Energy Studies, Univ Houston Col of Law; Economist; Lwyr; pa/ABA; St Bar of Tex; cp/Radcliffe Clb; hon/Author Num Profl Pubs.

WEAVER, LARRY J oc/Administrator, Physician Assistant, Chief X-Ray Technologist; b/July 26, 1941; h/220 Plaza Dr, Daleville, AL 36322; ba/D'ville; m/Judy N; c/Christopher A, Sandra K; p/Lonnie Weaver, Highland Home, AL; Mavis Gipsons, Luverne, AL; ed/BS Bus Adm; mil/AUS Chief Warrant Ofcr; pa/Am Reg of Radiologial Technols; r/Meth.

WEAVER, MACON MOORE oc/Assistant Professor; b/Nov 7, 1935; h/Jackson, MS; ba/Dept Anatomy, Univ Miss Med Ctr, 2500 N St Street, Jackson, MS 39216; m/Evelyn Knisely; c/Macon Moore Jr; p/William Blackwell Sr (dec) and Beulah Rebecca Weaver (dec); ed/BA 1967; MSPH 1962 UNC-CH; PhD Univ Miss 1972; mil/AUS 1957-59; pa/Asst Prof Anatomy, Univ Miss Med Ctr; Miss Heart Assn; So Soc Anatomists; Am Heart Assn, Coun Mem; Am Assn Anatomy; Miss Acad Sci; Sigma Xi; AAAS; cp/Dem Party; hon/Miss Heart Assn F'ship 1974 & Grant 1975; Contbr Articles to Profl Jours.

WEAVER, PRESTON DOUGLAS THOMAS oc/Administrator;

b/Apr 8, 1940; h/4570 St Andrews Dr, SW, Atlanta, GA 30331; c/Derrick Rudolph; p/Richard Edward Weaver, Balto, MD; Alma Bass Weaver (dec); ed/BA 1962, MA 1963 NC Ctrl Univ; Att'd Va St Univ NDEA Guid & Cnslg Inst Summer Prog 1964; pa/Dir Exodus Right-to-Read Acad/Adm Asst to Exodus-Cities-In-Schs Pres 1980-; Exec Dir Region IV Citizens Coun Inc 1971-79; Model Cities Liaison Spec, NC Dept Natural & Ec Resources 1970-71; Voc Cnslr, Jt Orange Chatham Commun Action Prog 1969-70; Proj Dir GROW Inc 1967-68; Adm Asst/Progr, Oper Breakthrough Inc 1965-67; Guid Cnslr, CE Perry HS 1963-64; Am Soc Public Adm; APGA; cp/Fulton Co Yng Dems; Parents for Action; Ga PTSA; VP Therrell HS PTSA 1977-; r/Bapt; hon/W/W S&SW 1980.

WEBB, ANNE KAVANAUGH oc/Supervisor of Instruction; b/June 26, 1937; h/Rt 1 Box 8, Spring Oaks Ests, Shelbyville, KY 40065; ba/S'ville; m/Robert R; c/Allen Randolph; p/William Lackey (dec) and Mary Ann Kavanaugh, Danville, KY; ed/BA; MS; EdS; pa/KEA; NEA: KASCD; ASCD; KAES; Delta Kappa Gamma; Pi Lambda Theta; r/Epis.

WEBB, LARRY WAYNE oc/Employment Counselor; b/Apr 3, 1948; h/Colonial Acres Apt #68, Anne Ave SW, Leeds, AL 35094; ba/Anniston; p/Chester Lee Sr and Essie Martin Webb, Leeds, AL; ed/BS 1974, MA 1979 Univ Ala; Dip Crim Investigation Course, AUS Mil Police Sch 1977; mil/USAF 1966-70; AUS 1975-78; pa/Social Wkr, Ala Dept Pensions & Security 1974-75; Yth Ser Cnslr, Ala Dept Yth Sers 1979-80; Employment Cnslr, Ala Dept Indust Relats 1980-; ALPGA; cp/MENSA; Xi Chapt Kappa Delta Pi; Bicolani Martial Arts Fed; Kenshihkan Karrie and Kobudo Assn; Intl Kuntaw Fed; r/Buddhism; hon/Ford Foun CEEB Upper Div Schlr 1972-74; W/W Students in Jr Cols 1971-72; W/W S&SW 1980-81; Recip Yth Devel Ednl Achmt Awd, Jefferson Co Com for Ec Opport.

WEBB, MABEL LUCILE oc/Retired; b/Oct 13, 1907; h/Bonham, TX; pa/Ret'd Sch Tchr, Chem Lab Tech, Social Wkr 24 Yrs; cp/George Blakely Chapt Nat Soc DAR: Regent, V-Regent, Registrar, Public Relats; Nat Defense; Gdn Clb; Friends of Sam Rayburn; UDC; r/Congreg Meth; hon/Geneal Contbns to Fannin Co Folks & Facts & Grayson Co Frontier Village.

WEBB, McKINLEY JR oc/Senior Youth Development Worker; b/Jan 21, 1926; h/Albany, GA; m/Azzie S; p/McKinley Sr and Josephine Webb, Arlington, GA; ed/Att'd Savannah St Col 1947-50; mil/AUS 1944-46, 51-69 Ret'd; pa/Sr Yth Devel Wkr, Albany Regional Yth Devel Ctr; r/Bapt; hon/Employee of Yr 1977, 79, Albany RYDC.

WEBB, PERCY EUGENE oc/Retired; b/Sept 24, 1887; h/420 Agee Ave NW, Camden, AR 71701; m/Kate Alicia Wooten; c/Kathryn Craig Snyder, Florra Gene Thomas; p/William Smar (dec) and Ida Alicia Taylor Webb (dec); mil/WWI 2nd Lt; pa/Ret'd Power Plant Supt; r/U Meth.

WEBB, TOMMY B oc/Teacher; b/Dec 9, 1947; h/Rt 1 Box 52, Cleburne, TX 76031; ba/Cleburne; m/Dianne; c/Troy, Kenneth; p/Clyde and Julie Webb, Cleburne, TX; ed/BS, MS Tarleton St Univ; mil/NG 6 Yrs; pa/Voc Agric Tchr; St, Local Ed Assns; Tex St Clrm Assn; NVAT; AVA; Dir Tex FFA; Johnson Co Jr Livestock Assn; cp/Little Leag Baseball; r/Bapt; Deacon & Dir 11-12 Grad Dept; hon/Pres Lake Whitney Dist Agric Tchr Assn.

WEBSTER, TERRY L oc/Student; b/Feb 19, 1957; h/Rt 4 Box 88E, Norman, OK 73071; p/Albert J and Jonni Webster, Norman, OK; ed/BA Univ Okla 1980; pa/Lic'd Min 1975; r/So Bapt; hon/Assoc Summer Missionary 1976; BSU Missionary Summer 1979; Deans Hon, Okla Bapt Univ 1977.

WEBSTER, VERA DARE ROUSE oc/Writer, Editor, Publisher, Executive; b/Dec 15, 1918; h/230 E 48th St, NY, NY 10017; 403 Main St, Winterville, NC 28590; ba/Winterville, NC; m/James William; c/Jenifer W Avina, Lynn W Hunsucker; p/George L (dec) and Malissa L Rouse, Winterville, NC; ed/AB ECU 1940; MA Univ Va 1958; Post Grad Study UNC, Univ Colo, USC, Ill Inst Tech; pa/Author & Conslt, Ednl Div Prentice-Hall Inc 1977-79; Pres Advances in Instrn, Harcourt Brace Jovanovich 1976-77; Mgr Juvenile & Spec Progs, David McKay Co 1975-76; Mgr Sci Pubs, Golden Press, Wn Pub'g Co 1968-75; Hd Elem Sect & Nat Sci Conslt, Harcourt Brace Jovanovich 1961-68; Sci Tchr 1941-61; Nat Sci Tchr Assn, Life Mem; AAAS; cp/Coached Tennis YMCA 10 Yrs; Helped Devel Local Chapt Boys Clb of Am; Dir Little Theater Prods; Designed Stage Settings & Floats for Commun Projs; hon/W/W Am; Author *From One Seed* 1976; *What is a Bird?; What is a Mammal?; What is an Insect?; What is a Tree?; What is a Flower?; & What is a Fruit?* 1976.

WEDDLE, LEO FRANKLIN oc/Professor; b/June 4, 1929; h/Prestonsburg, KY; ba/Prestonsburg Commun Col, P'burg, KY 41653; m/Laura T; c/Laura Lynn, Leo Jeffrey; p/Leo F Sr and Bessie Weddle, Somerset, KY; ed/BA 1959, MA 1960 Univ Ky; Add'l Study Morehead St Univ, En St Univ, Univ Ky; mil/USMC 1950-53; pa/Campbellsville Col

1961-65: Dean of Men, Dean of Students, Prof Psych, Dorm Hd Resident; Somerset Commun Col 1965-66, Prof Psych, Coor of Convocation-Dedication Ceremonies; Prestonsburg Commun Col, Prof Psych 1966-; Am Assn Jr Cols; Ky Assn Jr Cols; Ky Assn Communs Technol; Assn Commun Col Profs; Ky Sociol Assn; Ky Gerontol Assn; Nat Folk Sch Assn, Secy; cp/P'burh, Ky Plan'g Comm; Exec Com Big Sandy AreaCommun Action Prog; Bd Dirs David Alternate Sch; Bd Dirs Jenny Wiley Drama Assn; Bd Dirs Nat Folk Sch Assn, Secy; Lions Clb, VP; r/Bapt; hon/Recip Most Pop Prof Awd, Campbellsville Col 1966; Phi Delta Kappa; Kappa Delta Pi 1961-62; Recip Yrbook Dedication C'ville Col 1966; Recip Outstg Lion, Somerset Lions Clb 1961; W/W S&SW 1980-81.

WEDIG, FRANK ELLIOTT oc/Attorney at Law; b/Dec 17, 1950; h/1004 N Benavides, Pt Lavaca, TX 77979; ba/Pt Lavaca; m/Cheryl Ann Standlee; p/Frank (dec) and Eula Grace Wedig, Lavaca, TX; ed/BBA SW Tex St Univ; JD Univ Tex; pa/Calhoun Co Bar Assn, VP; cp/Pt Lavaca Rotary Clb, Secy; C of C; Am Cancer Soc, Pres; SW Tex St Univ Alumni Bd of Dirs; r/Epis.

WEED, JACQUELINE CHRISTINE oc/Teacher; b/Nov 9, 1952; h/1319 Laclede Ave 217, Jacksonville, FL 32205; ba/J'ville; m/David Preston; p/Elmer and Christine Brown, Orlando, FL; ed/BS 1974 Univ So Fla; MS Univ Ctrl Fla 1978; pa/Tchr Biol & Chem, Ed White Sch; Nat Assn Sci Tchr; Fla Assn Sci Tchrs; Duval Assn; Sci Tchrs; Phi Kappa Phi; Kappa Delta Pi; Kappa Delta; cp/Chd's Coor Ofcl Bd Mem Yth Advr, First U Meth Ch Winter Pk; r/U Meth; hon/Outstg Yng Wom of Am 1977; W/W Cols & Univs 1974; Pres Mortar Bd & Panhellenic Coun 1974; Resident Hall Coun, Pres's Hon Coun 1974.

WEIL, FERD F SR oc/Marketing Consultant; ba/Nat Bank of Commerce, 20 S 20th St, B'ham, AL 35233; pa/Nat Bank of Commerce: Bd Dirs 1969-79, Exec Com 8 Yrs, Mktg Conslt 1974-; Pres Weil Furs Inc, Consolidare Enterprises Inc; cp/VP Jefferson-Shelby Lung Assn; Chm B'ham Pkg Auth; Chm Downtown Action Com; Chm Jefferson Co Trade Mart; Secy-Treas B'ham Fball Foun; Pres Oper New B'ham; Treas Jefferson Co Com for Ec Opport; Treas Local Devel Corp of B'ham; Treas Muscular Dystrophy Assn; Bd Mem: B'ham Area C of C, Congreg of Temple Emanu-El, Coun of Clbs, Jewish Commun Ctr, Bapt Foun Bd, Sertoma Bd, Jefferson Co Arthritis Foun, N Southland Ins Co (Tuscaloosa, Ala), So Security Life Ins Co (Orlando, Fla); Com Mem: Mayor's Adv Com, Jewish Commun Com, Commun Affairs Com of B'ham; Mem Rotary Clb; Mem Civil Defense Corp; hon/June 3, 1975 Proclaimed Ferd F Weil Day, B'ham; Man of Yr, Yng Men's Bus Clb 1967; US PO Public Ser Awd; Lawson St Commun Col Citizen Awd 1974; B'ham Civic Salesman of Yr; B'ham Bar Assn's Liberty Bell Awd 1972; City of Hope Humanitarian Awd 1977.

WEINMAN, PHYLLIS EVELYN HOPKINS oc/Director of Volunteer Services; b/Jan 22, 1932; h/San Antonio, TX; ba/SW Tex Meth Hosp, 7700 Floyd Curl Dr, San Antonio, TX 78229; c/Phillip David, Russell Martin, Raymond Scott, Bruce Howard, James William; p/John Philip Hopkins (dec); Ruby Stewart Nicholson, Ft Pierce, FL; ed/Grad Incarnate Word 1948; Att'd Univ Fla 1950; pa/SW Tex Meth Hosp: Editorial Asst, Public Relats Dept 1966-70, Dir Public Relats 1970-76, Coor Commun Relats 1976-77, Dir Vol Sers 1977-; Am Hosp Assn; Am Soc Dirs of Vol Sers; Tex Hosp Assn; Tex Soc Hosp Public Relats, St Awds Ct Chm 1971-72, St Dir 1972-73, St Nom'g Ct Chm 1973-74, Pres San Antonio Chapt 1971; Tex Assn Dirs of Vol Sers; cp/Bd Dirs Blue Bird Aux to SW Tex Meth Hosp 1963-, 3rd VP 1965; r/Prot; hon/W/W S&SW; Author Patient Handbooks, Annual Reports, Patient Brochures & Newslttrs.

WEIR, ANN EPPS oc/Dean of Women; b/Aug 9, 1936; h/Brenham, TX; ba/902 Col Ave, Brenham, TX 77833; m/Jerrell; c/David, Don; p/Richard E (dec) and Mae H Epps (dec); ed/BA 1957; MEd 1960; pa/HS Tchr, Pasadena Indep Sch Dist & Lufkin Indep Sch Dist; Dean of Wom, Blinn Col; Tex Assn Eng Tchrs; Tex Assn Wom Deans, Admrs, Cnslrs; Tex Jr Col Tchrs Assn; cp/Pilot Clb; r/Bapt.

WEIR, RONALD LEE oc/Associate Professor; b/Apr 13, 1943; h/1304 Beechwood Dr, Johnson City, TN 37601; ba/Johnson City; m/Mary Hannah Ware; c/John Edward, Ronald Jason, James Austin; p/John A and Geneva Weir, Monroe, LA; ed/BS 1965, MBA 1967 NE La Univ; DBA Miss St Univ 1977; pa/NWn La Univ 1967-68; Miss St Univ 1970-71; Assoc Prof Mktg E Tenn St Univ 1971-; So Mktg Assn; Am Advtg Assn; cp/Johnson City C of C; Directions 2000; Tenn St-wide Consumer Ed Prog; Fac Senate, E Tenn St Univ; r/Ch of Christ; hon/Wall St Jour Student Achmt Awd 1965; W/W: Students in Am Univs & Cols 1964-65, S&SW 1980; Omicron Delta Kappa; Outstg Fac Mem, E Tenn St Univ 1976; Proj Horizon Awd Winning Team, Dept HEW, Tenn St-wide Consumer Ed Prog 1976; Outstg Yng Men Am 1975; Beta Gamma Sigma; Author "The Misidentification Problem: An Exploratory Study of the Relative Communication Effectiveness of Comparative and

Noncomparative Television Commercials"; Sev Articles & Num Cnsltg Reports.

WEISENSEL, MARY ELISE oc/Social Worker; b/Dec 11, 1950; h/2542 Cox Mill Rd, Hopkinsville, KY 42240; ba/H'ville; p/Fred and Lucile Weisensel, Atkinson, WI; ed/BS Univ Wis-Oshkosh; MSSW Univ Tenn-Knoxville; pa/Dir of Social Sers, H'ville; Tenn Conf on Social Wel; NASW; Tenn Chapt NASW; cp/Task Force on Child Abuse; Am Kidney Foun; H'ville Inter-Agcy Coun; r/Cath.

WEISS, DAVIDA S oc/Educator; b/Nov 11, 1939; h/7605 Pennyburn Dr, Dallas, TX 75248; ba/Plano, TX; m/George B; c/Bill, Debbie; p/Jacob and Estelle Solomon, Plainfield, NJ; ed/BA George Peabody Col for Tchrs, Vanderbilt Univ; MA Univ Tex-Dallas; pa/Team Ldr SS Dept, Haggard Middle Sch; Tex Coun SS; Tex Tchrs Assn; NEA; Plano Ed Assn; Fac Rep Plano Ed Assn; Fac Coun Rep w Supt; cp/Pres Richmond Jewish Commun Ctr Nursery Sch 1968; Pres Prestonwood Elem Sch PTA 1971-72; Va Commonwlth Univ Fellow 1968-70.

WELCH, JIMMY GALE oc/Executive; b/May 1, 1946; h/140 Fairfield Dr, Dyersburg, TN 38024; ba/D'burg; m/Linda Bargery; c/Amy Carol, James Ryan; p/Herbert S and Magalene Welch, Bogota, TN; ed/BS, MS Univ Tenn-Martin; mil/AUS 1968-71 Lt; NG Capt; pa/Prod Credit Assn: Field Rep 1971, Co Mgr 1972, VP 1975, Sr VP 1979-; r/Rotary Clb; Fund Raiser BSA; Red Cross; UT Alumni Assn; Am Cancer Soc; r/Bapt; hon/Bronze Star; Outstg Yng Men Am 1975; Hon Chapt Farmer, D'burg FFA 1975-79; Cert of Merit, Vietnam Vets.

WELSH, JACQUELINE ADELE oc/Personnel Officer; b/Jan 16, 1933; h/El Paso, TX; m/Gary P; c/Nicole, Debra, Gary Jr, James, John; p/Everett Chief (dec) and Willa Broadwater Nicholson, El Paso, TX; ed/Att'd Okla St Univ 1951-52, Univ Tex-El Paso 1955-57, Univ Md; pa/Bank of El Paso: Pers Ofcr 1980-, Mgr Mkt Sers 1979-80, Credit Mgr 1978-79; Tchr Mod Dance, Jefferson HS 1955-58; Chm Nat Assn Bank Wom; El Paso Assn Pers Adm; Am Soc Pers Adm; cp/Ldrship El Paso 1980-81; r/Meth; hon/Cert for Recog Achmt in Bus Commun, Bank of El Paso & El Paso YWCA 1981.

WENZLAU, JOHN NORBERT HANS oc/Executive; b/Aug 20, 1946; h/4409 Woodland Pk Blvd, Arlington, TX 76013; m/Katherine Kickliter; c/Matthew Brian; p/Otto and Ursula Wenzlau, BC, Can; ed/BA 1968, MA 1970 Univ Ore; MDiv SWn Bapt Sem 1980; pa/Pres MLE Inc 1976-; VP Maple Leaf Enterprises 1976-; Regional Sales Mgr, Rentway Canada Ltd 1974-76; Mktg Spec Xerox Corp 1970-74; cp/Repub Nat Com; r/So Bapt.

WERBLO, DOROTHY FUNK oc/Child Advocate; b/Aug 8; h/Houston, TX; p/Adam and Emma Gust Funk; ed/BS Ind St Univ; MA Univ Minn; EdD Univ Ga; pa/Child Advocate, Pvt Pract; Am Psych Assn; MENSA: Gifted Child Coor, St of Tex; Houston Area Assn GT, Intergrp Liaison Ofcr; Kappa Delta Phi; Phi Kappa Phi; hon/Dr Dot Day May 27, 1981; Author Num Articles in Profl Jours; Columnist IPSA Dixit - Chime & Informensa.

WERLIN, ROSELLA HARWOOD oc/Freelance Journalist; b/Sept 17, 1912; h/Houston, TX; m/Joseph S (dec); c/Herbert Holland, Joella W Autrey, Ernest Pyle; p/Henry J Harwood (dec); Celia Horowitz (dec); pa/Vol Public Relats Dir AWVS; Freelance Jour Accepted by *Reader's Digest, Houston Post, Dallas News, Chicago Tribune*; Intl Traveler; cp/Former Publicity Dir Am Wom's Vol Sers, WWII; Publicity Com War Bond Drs, Commun Chest Promo & Other Wel Progs; r/Temple Emanu El; hon/Nat Assn Press Wom, Wom of Achmt 1979.

WESLEY, ESTHER BESSIE oc/Executive Secretary-Director; b/Sept 16, 1920; h/Brevard, NC; ba/Brevard C of C, PO Box 589, Brevard, NC 29712; m/Paul; c/Paula Berglund, David Paul, Deborah Jane, Samantha Jane; p/Samuel (dec) and JoAnna Stephane Pasquarella, Bath, PA; pa/Supvr/Instr NJ Bell Telephone; Vol Art/Craft Tchr, NY City Schs 1951-53; Exec Secy/Dir Brevard C of C 1977-; cp/VP Brevard BPW Clb; NC Assn C of C Execs; Wn NC Assoc'd Communs; r/Presb; hon/W/W Am Wom 1981.

WESLEY, GARLIN SR oc/Retired; b/Aug 15, 1926; h/Rt 2 Box 352, Diana, TX 75640; c/Shirley Jean, Garlin Jr, Waymon, Alva Nell, Carl, Monte, Jeaneete, Thomas, Don, Debra, Gerald Dewayne; p/Willis Wesley Jr, Diana, TX; ed/Dip Booker T Washington Trade Sch 1948; mil/AUS Sgt; pa/Machine Oper, Lone St Steel Co 22 Yrs; cp/Am Legion; Notary Public; r/Meth; hon/Am Defense Ser Medal; Am Theater Campaign Medal; Asiatic Pacific Campaign Medal w 2 Bronze Stars; Good Conduct Medal, Victory Medal.

WESLEY, STEVEN LYNN oc/Sales Manager; b/Sept 5, 1948; h/304 Pinehaardt Dr, Selma, AL 36701; ba/Selma; m/Donna G; c/Melanie

---

Lynn, Stephanie Gayle; p/Roy E Sr and Rubye C Wesley, Midfield, AL; pa/Sales Mgr, Metro Life; cp/Selma-Dallas Co C of C; Asst Treas Lions Clb; r/Meth; hon/Pres Nat Hon Soc 1966; Merit S'ship; Samford Univ S'ship Awd 1966.

WESLEY, THERESSA GUNNELS oc/Writer; b/Feb 9, 1945; h/Little Rock, AR; m/John W; c/Dwayne, Rashida, Kameelah, Jameel; p/Fred and Florence Gunnels, Morrilton, AR; ed/BA Philander Smith Col 1967; MA Kent St Univ; pa/Eng Tchr, Springfield, Mo Public Schs 1967-70 & Pulaski Co Public Schs, Little Rock, Ark 1970-71; Eng Instr Univ Wis-Eau Claire 1972-74; Rdg Spec & Eng Tchr Mpls Public Schs 1974-75; Eng Prof & Career Cnslg & Placement Dir, Philander Smith Col 1975-78; hon/Author *Black American Writers, Past and Present* 1975.

WEST, EDWIN DAVID oc/Commercial Loan Officer; b/Feb 1, 1956; h/907 N Lafayette St, Apt #20, Shelby, NC 28160; ba/Shelby; p/Fred B and Margaret A West, Raleigh, NC; ed/BS UNC; pa/Am Inst Bnkrs; cp/Shelby JCs; UNC Gen Alumni Assn; r/Bapt.

WEST, HELEN LOIS oc/Postmaster; b/Aug 11, 1934; h/1019 E Washington St, Sentinel, OK 73664; ba/Sentinel; c/Michael Douglas, Pamela Diane Farris, Terri Lynn; p/Leslie A (dec) and Viola Irene House, Lookeba, OK; ed/Cert Dale Carnegie Course; pa/Postmaster, US Postal Ser; Agt Am Trustee Life Corp; Secy Sentinel HS; Secy Lookeba Farmers Coop Gin; Nat Postmasters Assn, Dist Pres; Nat Leag Postmasters, Secy & St Editor; cp/C of C, Bd Mem, Secy; Vol Ambulance Ser; Coor Local Beauty Pageant; Am Red Cross; r/First Bapt Ch: Choir, SS Tchr, Camp Cnslr, WMU, Secy; hon/Apprec Awd, C of C; Carnegie Hero Fund Comm Awd 1969.

WEST, PATRICIA A oc/Deputy Director; b/July 14, 1941; h/1900 W Markham #6, Little Rock, AR 72205; ba/Little Rock; p/Eugene West, Forrest City, AR; Margie Combs, Flint, MI; pa/Dpty Dir, Labor Standards, Ark Dept Labor; r/Forrest City Christ Ch: Secy-Treas Epis Ch-wom; hon/Nat NAACP's Thalheimer Awd 1979.

WEST, ROSS ANTHONY oc/Instructor; b/Dec 13, 1954; h/1602 Vaugine Ave, Pine Bluff, AR 71601; ba/Itta Bena, MS; p/Gladys R West, Pine Bluff, AR; ed/BME cum laude Univ Ark-Pine Bluff 1976; MA Ohio St Univ 1977; pa/Prin Oboist, Greenville, Miss Symph Orch; Cnslr & Dir Mus Activs, Ark Bapt St Conv Summer Camp, Paron, Ark; Instr Miss Valley St Univ, Itta Bena, Miss; Alpha Kappa Mu; Intl Double-Reed Soc; Col Mus Soc; r/Bapt; hon/Outstg Univ Student in Mus 1976; W/W Students in Am Cols & Univs.

WESTBROOK, DOUGLAS CALVIN oc/Professor; b/Aug 21, 1927; h/2201 Georgetown, Denton, TX 76201; ba/Denton; m/Audrey M; c/Melody Ann W Curtis, Douglas Lane, Cindy W Dooley; p/Mrs B F Westbrook Sr, Natchitoches, LA; ed/BS NSC of La 1949; MA CSCE of Greeley, Colo 1953; EdD LSU-Baton Rouge 1970; pa/Dir Student Sers, Tchr Sec'dy Ed, NTSU 1970-; Mus Edrs Supvr, LSU Lab Sch 1954-67; Mus Tchr Caddo Parish Schs, Vivian, La 1950-54; Mus Tchr Natchitoches Parish Sch, Natchitoches, La 1949-50; Nat Assn Acad Affairs Adm; Phi Delta Kappa; Tex Assn Col Tchrs; Assn Tchr Edrs; Fac Sponsor Student Ed Assn; Tex Ed Agcy; Acad Affairs Adm; Profl Devel Coun; Mid-Cities Tchr Ctr, Arlington; E Tex Tchr Ctr, Richardson Assn; Ft Worth Tchr Edrs Ctr; cp/Dir "Improving Tchg Effectiveness" 1978, Ft Worth, Tex; Fac Rep Student Govt Assn; Mem Pers Affairs Com; Sec'dy Div Curric Com; Fac Senate's Hons Com; r/Meth; hon/Author/Co-Author Num Pubs.

WESTBROOK, EUNICE oc/Retired; b/Sept 1, 1906; h/411 St Roud Rd, Shelby, NC 28150; p/Mr and Mrs W H Westbrook (dec); ed/Bus Schs; mil/WAC 4½ Yrs; pa/BPW Clb, Pres Local Clb, Dist Dir; cp/Heart Assn; Red Cross; Co Dem Clb; r/Bapt; hon/Lung Assn, Easter Seal, Red Cross, Am Legion Awds.

WESTERHOUSE, LEON MARTIN oc/Music Evangelist; b/Dec 23, 1934; h/#8 12th Ct NW, Birmingham, AL 35215; ba/Same; m/Patsy Nabors; c/Wendy Patricia, Wayne Martin, Warren Leon; p/Jessie Johnson and Lovis Martin Westerhouse; ed/BMus Univ Ala 1959; mil/AUS 1957-63; pa/Mus Dir So Bapt Evangelists 1977-78; cp/Mus Evangelism 15 Yrs; r/So Bapt; hon/TV Singer, B'ham; 9 Record Albums; Sang at Over 450 Revivals.

WESTMORELAND, THOMAS D JR oc/Chemist; b/June 2, 1940; h/9319 Midvale Dr, Shreveport, LA 71118; ba/S'port; m/Martha Beard; c/Anne Laura, Kyle Thomas; p/Thomas Delbert and Marguerite Beatrice Westmoreland, Longview, TX; ed/BS 1963, MS 1965 N Tex St Univ; PhD La St Univ 1971; pa/Postdoct Fellow LSU 1971-72; Sr Expmtl/Analytical Chem, U Technologies 1972-76; Sr Res Chemist, Pennzoil Prods Co 1976-; Am Chem Soc: Local Chm, Chm-Elect, Treas; Sigma Xi, Secy; Phi Eta Sigma, Pres; Alpha Xi Sigma; Kappa Mu Epsilon; cp/Manchester, Conn JCs, St Dir; Masons; r/Bapt; hon/W/W S&SW 1980-81; Gov's Civic

Ldrship Awd, Conn 1975-76; 1 of 12 Outstg JCs in Conn 1975-76; C William Brownfield Meml Awd, Conn 1976; E I DuPont Tchg Awd, LSU 1968-69; Outstg AFROTC Cadet, N Tex St Univ 1958-59; Valedictorian, Judson Grove HS 1958; Author Sci Articles in Num Profl Jours Incl'g *Journal of the American Chemical Society* & *Journal of Solution Chemistry.*

WHACK, PAULINE oc/Administrative Assistant; b/Feb 17, 1951; h/Manning, SC; m/Willie; c/Lisa, Willie, Johnny; p/Hayward and Dorothy Johnson, Kingstree, SC; ed/Certs in Bible Study; Var Sems on Purchasing Mgmt & Supvn; pa/Adm Asst, Clarendon Co; SC Assn Cos; SC Assn Purchasing Ofcls; r/Ch of Christ; hon/Waitress of Mo 1973; Hon Student 1962; Notary Public; Var Awds for Completion of Purchasing Sems.

WHALEY, DENNIS WAYNE oc/Minister, Professor; b/July 21, 1952; h/Spring, TX; m/Kristeena Ruth; p/Rush Jr and Ruth Whaley, Houston, TX; ed/AA SWn Col 1972; BS Evangel Col 1974; Grad Study TWU, Sam Houston St Univ; pa/Min Assems of God Ch; Prof Communs; Tex Jr Col Speech & Theatre Assn, Exec Ofcr; Speech Commun Assn; TSCA; cp/Dem Party Precinct Chm 1980; r/Assems of God; hon/W/W SW 1980; Outstg Yng Men Am 1976; SWn Col Alumni of Yr 1975.

WHALEY, VERNON M oc/Minister; b/Oct 6, 1949; h/Nashville, TN; ba/3606 W End Ave, Nashville, TN 37205; m/Elizabeth Nelle Smith; c/Laurie Elizabeth, Jeremy Joel; p/D L and Eunice Pike Whaley, Kinston, NC; ed/BA Free Will Bapt Bible Col 1972; MCM 1978, DMin 1979 Luther Rice Sem; pa/Prof Mus, Free Will Bapt Bible Col 1979-; Min Mus First Free Will Bapt Ch, Albany, Ga 1972-78; Min Mus Cufer's Chapel Free Will Bapt Ch, Nashville 1970-72; Free Will Bapt Mus Mins, Pres 1973-77; Am Choral Dirs Assn; Nat Assn Tchrs of Singing; Hymn Soc of Am; r/Free Will Bapt; hon/Leigh Waddell Meml S'ship 1969; Author Sev Articles.

WHARTON, EDWARD CALVIN oc/Evangelist, Educator; b/Feb 1, 1931; h/Lubbock, TX; ba/Sunset Sch of Preaching, 3723 34th St, Lubbock, TX 79410; m/Martha; c/Edward Jr, Michael, Pamela, Teresa; p/Lois Wharton Routh, Arlington, TX; mil/USAF; pa/Prof Hist Christian Evidences, Sunset Sch of Preaching; r/Ch of Christ; Author Num Rel Books & Tracts Incl'g *The Scheme of Redemption 1971 & The Case for Historic Christianity* 1976; Contbr Articles to Star Bible Pubs & Firm Foun.

WHEELER, LARRY EDWARD oc/Supervisor; b/July 18, 1933; h/Harriman, TN; ba/Oak Ridge, TN; m/Nancy Branam; p/Earldon Lester (dec) and Venus Wheeler, Chevy Chase, MD; ed/AB Concord Col 1960; Grad Study Univ Tenn-Knoxville; mil/AUS; pa/Supvr Uranium Acctg & Control Sect, Union Carbide, Oak Ridge Gaseous Diffusion Plant; Nat Assn Accts, Nat Com on Socio-Ecs, Past Pres Knoxville Chapt; Inst of Nuclear Mats Mgmt, Nat Registration Com; cp/Dem Party Precinct Chm Roane Co; Cand Tenn St Rep; Elected Chm Adv Com for Acctg Curric Knoxville St Tech Inst; r/Meth.

WHEELER, TONY LADELL oc/Lab Technician; b/Sept 16, 1956; h/C-11 Chateau Apts, Rome, GA 30161; ba/Cartersville, GA; p/J W Wheeler, Acworth, GA; Elsie L Wooten, Cedar Bluff, AL; ed/Att'd Maryville Col 1976-77; pa/Lab Tech, Thompson, Weinman & Co; cp/Yng Dems of Floyd Co, Bd Dirs; Dem Assn Floyd Co; r/So Bapt; hon/Wkg on Book on Polits of Floyd Co.

WHEELER, WILLIAM BRYAN III oc/Project Manager, Author; b/June 21, 1940; h/160 King Cir, Athens, GA 30606; m/Mary Sue Lewis; c/Alicia Nanette, William Bryan IV; p/William Bryan and Olive Mae Criner Wheeler; ed/AAS Capital Inst Technol 1966; BLA Univ Ga 1975; ND 1978, PhD 1980 Bangor Inst; mil/USMC 1958-61; pa/Proj Mgr, Loef Co Inc 1981-; Plan'g Dir, NE Ga Area Plan'g & Devel Comm 1978-81; Regional Planner, Mid Flint Area Plan'g & Devel Comm 1975-78; Plan'g Dir, E Coast Stainless Steel 1970-71; Sys Plan'g Engr, Bendix Corp, Goddand Space Flight Ctr 1966-70; Sr Field Engr, Fed Elect Corp 1965-66; Tech Supvr, Xerox Corp 1964-65; Transp Planner, Fla St Road Dept 1963-64; Meteorological Tech Rep 1962-63; Elects Field Engr, Radiation Inc 1961-62; Am Soc Landscape Archs, Am Soc Plan'g Ofcls; MENSA; Am Plan'g Assn; r/Celtic; hon/Six Apollo Mission Awds, NASA/Bendix; W/W S&SW 1980-81; Author *The Quest* (Novel); "Oconee County - A Land Use Analysis"; "Waycross Housing Project - An Ecological Statement"; Var NASA Tech Papers & Mid Flint APDC Plan'g Pubs.

WHEELES, ANITA HARRIS oc/Teacher and Coach; b/Feb 9, 1954; h/Rt 1 Box 205, Auburn, AL 36830; ba/Notasulga, AL; m/Donny Hush; p/Orby T Harris, Lineville, AL; Audrey Heath, Ashland, AL; ed/BS, MA Auburn Univ; pa/Phy Ed Tchr, Ath Tnr, Coach; Nat Ath Tnrs Assn; Ala Ed Assn; cp/Vol Fire Dept, SW Lee Co; r/Bapt; hon/Kappa Delta Pi.

WHETSELL, DOUGLAS WAYNE oc/Physician; b/July 2, 1943;

h/911 Middleton, NE Orangeburg, SC 29115; ba/NE O'burg; m/Lynne; c/Doug Jr; p/Joseph E Whetsell (dec); Louise Dantzler Shuler, Bowman, SC; ed/BS Wofford Col; MD Med Col SC; mil/USAF 1967-77 Lt Col; pa/Phys Internal Med & Pulmonary Disorders; AMA; Am Thoracic Soc; ACP; SC Thoracic Soc; FACCP; cp/Med Dir O-C Tech Col Respiratory Therapy Sch; Dist TB Conslt, SC St Hlth Dept; r/Meth; hon/Diplomate Am Bd Internal Med in Pulmonary Diseases.

WHILLOCK, CARL S oc/Executive; b/May 7, 1926; m/Margaret Moore; c/10 Chd; ed/BS 1948, MA 1951 Univ Ark; JD George Washington Univ 1960; mil/USN 1943-46; pa/HS Tchr 1946-47; Pvt Bus, Livestock Feeds/Wholesale Petro 1949-55; Exec Asst to US Rep J W Trimble 1955-63; Pvt Law Pract 1963-66; Prosecuting Atty, 14th Judicial Dist of Ark 1965-66; Asst to Pres, Univ Ark-Fayetteville 1966-71; Pt-Time Instr Polit Sci, Univ Ark-F'ville 1967, 69, 73; Dir Univ Relats, Univ Ark-F'ville 1971-74; Campaign Mgr, David Pryor's Campaign for Gov Ark 1974-75; Exec Secy, Gov David Pryor 1975; VP Govtl Relats/Public Affairs, Univ Ark-F'ville 1975-78; Pres Ark St Univ 1978-80; Gen Mgr Ark Elect Coops Inc & Ark Elect Coop Corp 1980-; cp/Bd Dirs Commercial Nat Bank, Little Rock; St Vincent Infirmary Foun Bd; Univ Ark Indust Adv Coun, Col of Engrg; Exec Com Univ Ark at Little Rock, Adv Coun for Col of Bus Adm; Bd Dirs Gtr Little Rock C of C; Ark Gen Assem 1953 & 55, Rep Van Buren Co; Chm Fayetteville Housing Auth; Pres Clinton Sch Bd; 2nd VP F'ville C of C; Chm Clinton Water & Sewer Comm; Dir Van Buren Co Hosp, Clinton; Exec Com So Growth Policies Bd.

WHISENANT, MARY SUE oc/Homemaker, Genealogist; b/July 26, 1930; h/1297 Lancelot Rd, Abilene, TX 79602; m/Kenneth Groves; c/Mary Patrice W McIntyre, Gary Russell; p/dec; ed/BBA Hardin Simmons Univ 1951; pa/K W Well Ser Ofc Mgr 8 Yrs, VP; Geneal; cp/Abigail Ann Berry Chesley Chapt DAR, Org'g Registrar, Regent, Registrar; George Cogdell Chapt DAC: Org'g Corresp Secy, Regent; Tex DAC, Tex St Public Relats Chm; Org'g Recording Secy, Recording Secy; Huguenot Soc of the Fdrs of Manakin in the Colony of Va; John Hudnall Chapt US Daughs of 1812; W Tex Colony Magna Charta Dames, Libn; Gen Tom Green Chapt UDC, Recording Secy; Benjamin Blackburn Chapt Colonial Dames of XVII Century; W Tex Geneal Soc; r/So Bapt; hon/Ldrship & Outstg Ser, Tex DAR 1977 & 78; 2nd Pl Nat DAC Awd Pressbook 1980; Contbr to: *Early Families of the North Carolina Counties of Rockingham and Stokes with Revolutionary Service.*

WHITAKER, CAROLYN VIRGINIA oc/Assistant Professor, Adult Family Nurse Practitioner; b/Apr 26, 1937; h/PO Box 208, Red Boiling Springs, TN 37150; ba/Cookeville; p/Charles S and Margaret Lorene Whitaker, Nashville, TN; ed/BSN 1962, MSN 1972 Vanderbilt Univ; pa/Jt Fam Pract w William R Bushong MD 1973-80; Asst Prof Sch of Nsg, Tenn Tech Univ 1980-; Exec Com Div Commun Hlth Nsg, Cong for Nsg Pract; ANA 1976-80; Cert Bd, Div Commun Hlth Nsg, ANA 1980-82; cp/Altrusa Intl; N-CAP; TN-CAP; hon/Fellow Am Acad Nsg; Sigma Theta Tau; Contbr *Independent Nursing Practice* 1976.

WHITCOMB, PATRICIA SCATCHARD oc/Downtown Revitalization Director; b/July 24, 1953; h/Salisbury, NC; ba/City of Salisbury, PO Box 479, Salisbury, NC 28144; p/LeRoy G Scatchard, Allentown, PA; ed/BA Cedar Crest Col 1975; pa/Proj Mgr, Nat Main St Ctr Prog, Salisbury 1980-; Ctrl City Revitalization Corp, Rocky Mt, NC: Exec Dir 1979-80, Adm Asst 1977-79; Asst News Dir WRMT Radio Sta 1976-77; Asst Dean Adms, Manhattanville Col, Purchase, NY 1976; Asst Dir Admissions, Wells Col, Aurora, NY 1975-76; Bd Dirs NC Downtown Devel Assn; Intl Downtown Execs Assn; cp/AAUW; Nat Fed BPW Clbs, Rocky Mt Pres 1979; Beta Sigma Phi; Pres & Recording Secy Rocky Mt Eta Kappa; r/Epis; hon/Rocky Mt BPW Clb Yng Careerist of Yr 1978; Wom of Yr Rocky Mt BPW 1980; Rocky Mt JCettes Outstg Yng Wom of Yr 1980.

WHITE, BARBARA WILLIAMS oc/Instructor; b/Feb 26, 1943; h/1213 Devils Dip, Tallahassee, FL 32308; ba/Tallahassee; m/Julian E; c/Tonja Victoria, Phaedra Aurelia; p/Ernestine Austin, Jacksonville, FL; ed/BS Fla A&M Univ 1964; BS 1974, MSW 1975 Fla St Univ; PhD Cand Fla St Univ; pa/Dir Leon Co 4-C Coun Inc; Asst Prof Fla A&M Univ; Instr Sch of Social Work, Fla St Univ; Pres Fla Chapt NASW; Nat Com on Minority Affairs, NASW; cp/Alpha Kappa Alpha; Links Inc; Wom's Polit Caucus; r/Epis; hon/Tchr of Yr, Dept of Sociol, Fla A&M Univ 1979; Acad of Cert'd Social Wkrs.

WHITE, CARRIE BARRAN oc/Teacher; b/May 8, 1909; h/Rt 10, Box 306, Cullman, AL 35055; m/J B; c/Manis W McHenry; p/Edgar (dec) and Ida Barran (dec); ed/BS Florence St Col; MA Peabody; pa/Elem Tchr; r/Bapt; hon/BS w Hons.

WHITE, DAVID ELLISON oc/Professor; b/July 2, 1947; h/PO Box 37, Gilsum, NH 03448; ba/Keene, NH; m/Beth Carrington; c/Adam Carrington, Noah Ellison; p/Charles Goodwin (dec) and Gertrude E

White, Camden, AR; ed/BA 1969, MEd 1973, EdD 1975 Univ Va; pa/Elem & Spec Ed Tchr, Va Public Schs 1969-72; Prof Keene St Col 1975-; Chd's Lit Assn; Soc Chd's Book Writers; NCTE; Phi Delta Kappa; hon/Nat Tchg Fellow, Keene St Col 1979-80; Spaulding-Potter Grant to Devel Annual Chd's Lit Fest 1977; Outstg Elem Tchr Am 1971-72; Author "A Conversation with Maurice Sendak" 1980.

WHITE, E V (PLUG) oc/County Commissioner; b/Oct 1, 1932; h/Rt 2 Box 536, Decatur, AL 35603; m/Frances A; c/Renee, Vann, Jim, Alodie, Irvin; p/dec; ed/Att'd Univ N Ala 1950-53; pa/Co Commr; Pt-time Farmer; cp/Decatur JCs, Bd Dirs; Assn Co Comms of Ala, Pres St Assn 1976-77; Nat Assn Comms; r/Bapt: Deacon, SS Tchr, Tng Union Dir, Treas; hon/Outstg Yng Farmer, Farm Bur 1963; Decatur JCs Outstg Yng Farmer 1964; Past Pres St Assn Co Comms of Ala.

WHITE, ETHYLE HERMAN oc/Artist; b/Apr 19, 1904; h/PO Box 1976, Anahuac, TX 77514; m/S Roy; c/De Lois Eileen Mohrie, Patsyruth Wheeler; p/Ferdinand and Minnie Simmang Herman; pa/Exhib'd Num 1-Man & Grp Shows, Tex; Rep'd Public Collects in US; Pvt Collects in Switzerland, Germany, Sweden; Del Intl Com Centro Studi E Scambi Internationali; Anahuac Fine Arts Grp, San Antonio, Beaumont, Galveston; Houston Art Leag; cp/Daughs Repub Tex; UDC; Watercolor Soc; NLAPW; OES; Fine Arts Clb Anahuac; r/Epis; hon/Author, Illustrator *Arabella*; Author *Poet's Hour*.

WHITE, GAYLE FARMER oc/Business Manager, Assistant Professor, Executive; b/Dec 30, 1943; h/114 Lightfoot, Enterprise, AL; ba/Dothan, AL; p/A O and Doris B Farmer, Elba, AL; ed/BS 1971, MBA 1974 Troy St Univ; pa/Bus Mgr TSU 1979-; Asst Prof, Sch of Bus, TSU 1974-79; Pres Transition Sers 1979-; Data Processing System Analyst 1962-74; NEA; AEA; Gamma Beta Phi; Am Mktg Assn; So Mgmt Assn; Wireglass Data Processing Assn; cp/BPW: Dist Dir 1978-; Co-Dir Dist 1977-78; Pres Elba BPW 1977; Pilot Clb, Public Relats Chm; MS Vol; Girls Ranch of Ala Vol; TSU Guest Lectr; Polit Campaign Vol Wkr; Alumni Assn; Fed Wom Sem Rep; r/Bapt; hon/Pilot Clb Wom of Yr 1978; Outstg Yng Wom of Am 1976, 77, 78; Gamma Delta Phi Hon Grad 1971.

WHITE, GLORIA MEYER oc/Nurse; b/May 12, 1936; h/7 Riverlyn Terr, Ft Smith, AR 72903; ba/Ft Smith; m/Jefferson Earle III; c/Julia Frances, Lisa Doris; p/William G (dec) and Doris Meyer, Ft Smith, AR; ed/RN; BSN; pa/Fdr & Exec VP Proj Compassion Inc (Care of Dying); cp/Sebastian Co Med Aux; PEO Chapt BD; Heritage Foun; Retirement Homes of Ft Smith Inc; r/Luth; hon/Wom Achiever of Yr, *SW Times Record* 1972; Golden Deeds Awd, Ft Smith Exch Clb 1974; Gov's Outstg Vol Awd 1976; Vol Activist Awd, Ft Smith Salvation Army 1979.

WHITE, JO ANN oc/Manager; b/Apr 20, 1949; ba/210 W 10th, Greenville, NC 27834; m/James E Jr; p/Dan and Elma Wethington, Vanceboro, NC; ed/Hardbarger Bus Col; Dale Carnegie; pa/Regional Mgr, CBI Collections; Sponsor Credit Women; Assn Credit Burs; Am Collectors Assn; cp/C of C; So Mgmt Inst; Collects Mgmt Devel Sch 1978; hon/Boss of Yr.

WHITE, JOHN L oc/Chief Deputy Jailer; b/Jan 4, 1938; h/Richmond, KY; ba/Madison Co Jail, 141 N 2nd St, Richmond, KY 40475; m/Ellen Marie; c/John N, Karen M; p/Chenault Sr and Minnie White, Richmond, KY; mil/USN; ed/Chief Dpty Jailer, Madison Co Jail; r/Bapt.

WHITE, MARVIN R oc/College President; b/Aug 6, 1921; h/Station A, Poplarville, MS 39470; ba/Same; m/Marjorie Lee; c/Cavlin R, Lyda Sue Winegarden; ed/BS; MEd; EdD; mil/WWII, Korea; pa/Pres Pearl River Jr Col; Red Red Rose; Phi Theta Kappa; cp/Past Pres Rotary Clb; Past Pres Lions Clb; r/Meth; hon/Past Pres Miss Jr Col Assn; Mem Jr Col Comm; Miss Elem & Sec'dy Accred'g Comm; Rotary Clb Paul Harris Fellow.

WHITE, OCTURUS IVAN JR oc/Associate Warden; b/June 23, 1949; h/Lake Placid, NY; ba/Fed Correctional Inst-Ray Brook, Ray Brook, NY; m/L Dawn K; c/Robert; p/W Ivan Sr and J M White, Marshall, TX; ed/BA Wiley Col 1971; MSW magna cum laude Washington Univ 1972; pa/Social Worker, Malcolm Bliss Mtl Hlth Ctr; Instr Tarrant Co Jr Col, Ft Worth, Tex; Recognizance Investigator, St Louise Dept Corrects, Neighborhood Yth Corps; Fed Bus Prisons: Case Mgr, Unit Mgr, Camp Supt, Assoc Warden Progs; NASW; Nat Assn Black Social Wkrs; Am Correct Assn; cp/NAACP; r/Bapt; hon/Alpha Awd 1971; Omega Psi Phi Awd 1968; Recip Inst of Intl Ed S'ship 1969-70; W/W 1969-70, 1970-71.

WHITE, PATRICIA LEE QUARLES (PAT) oc/Pageant Director; b/May 16, 1940; h/Rt 1, Celina, TN 38551; ba/Celina; m/James A; c/Donna; p/Juanita Quarles, Louisville, KY; pa/St Dir, Teenworld Pageant: Ky, Ind, Ohio, WV, Va, Miss, NY, Calif, SD, Wash, Ore, Ariz, Colo, NM & St Coor Tenn; cp/Civitan Clb.

WHITE, PATRICIA SMITH oc/Extension Agent; b/Dec 18, 1928; h/Rt 5 Box 82A, Mechanicsville, MD 20659; ba/Leonardtown; c/Cynthia E W Cartwright, Brian W; p/Ernest L and Ruth A L Smith, Esmond, RI; ed/BS Univ Rhode Island 1950; MS Commun Devel 1972; PhD Cand; pa/Commun Resource Devel Area Ext Agt; Commun Devel Soc Am; Epsilon Sigma Phi; Md Coop Ext Ser CRD; cp/LWV, St Mary's Co; Potomac River Assn; r/Unitarian; hon/Notable Ams 1976-77; Hon'd by Montgomery Co C of C as Outstg Commun Ldr; Listed in 12 Biogl Pubs.

WHITE, RONALD oc/Fireman; b/Aug 3, 1955; h/1305S 23rd St, Copperas Cove, TX; ba/Copperas Cove; p/Joe and Shirley White; ed/Fire Dept Cert Prog 1979; pa/Fireman, Copperas Cove FD; cp/Copperas Cove JCs; Loyal Order of Moose; r/Luth; hon/Fireman of Qtr, Exch Clb; Cert of Apprec, Fire Preven Wk & Miss Flame Contest.

WHITE, ROTHA MURRAY oc/Retired Teacher; b/Nov 25, 1911; h/PO Box 472, Spring Hope, NC 27882; m/Robert Bruce; p/W O (dec) and Melissa Baines Murray (dec); ed/AB Elem Ed; pa/Tchr 41 Yrs; Delta Kappa Gamma; NEA; NCAE; cp/Vol Libn; r/Bapt: Deacon, Ch Clerk, SS Class Pres; hon/Jefferson Davis Awd, UDC; Dist 6 Dir UDC & Local Chapt Pres.

WHITE, RUTH EVELYN oc/Evangelist; b/Nov 6, 1941; h/613 Vine St, Carthage, TX 75633; m/John Jr; c/John III; p/Lonnie B and Ruth Faye Chimney, Garrison, TX; ed/BS Tex Col 1964; Further Study Stephen F Austin St Univ & Wiley Col; pa/Sci & Math Instr 14 Yrs; Nat Evangelist; NEA; TSTA; Carthage Clrm Assn; Zeta Phi Beta; cp/Voter Leag, Tyler Br; Naacp, Tyler Br Pres; PTA; r/Ch of God in Christ: Yth for Christ & Prison Min; Fdr 3 Chs; hon/Tchr of Yr, Carthage HS 1978; Yth for Christ Hon as Local Fdr 1978; Phi Delta Psi; NAACP Ser Awd 1965.

WHITEFIELD, CAROLYN LEE oc/Attorney; b/May 1, 1946; h/Rt 4 Box 632-X, Texarkana, AR 75502; ba/Texarkana; m/Jerry Allen McDowell; p/William Parker and Julia Arabella Whitefield, Texarkana, AR; ed/BS So St Col; JD Univ Ark; pa/Ark Bar Assn; Tex Bar Assn; Am Bar Assn; cp/Dem Party; r/Bapt.

WHITESIDES, GLENN EDWARD oc/College President; b/Dec 23, 1935; h/2104 Luther St, Newberry, SC 29108; ba/Newberry; m/Jeris Anne; c/Jane Elizabeth, Anna Catherine, John Hampton; p/Wright Melvin and Elma Worthy Whitesides, Chester, SC; ed/AB Erskine Col; MA, PhD Fla St Univ; Post-Doct Harvard Univ; pa/Pres Newberry Col; Exec Com Conf of Small Pvt Cols; Pres's Adv Bd NAIA; cp/SC Nat Bank Bd Dirs; Kiwanis Clb; U Way of Midlands Bd Dirs; r/Luth; hon/Outstg Yng Men Am 1972; Var W/W Listings.

WHITFIELD, CAROL J oc/Beauty Consultant; b/Sept 16, 1944; h/8208 Westmoreland Dr, Sarasota, FL 33580; m/H Leland Jr; c/Denise; p/Mrs Robert Hepler, Media, PA; ed/BS Susquehanna Univ 1966; pa/Sr Beauty Conslt, Mary Kay Cosmetics Inc; cp/Beta Sigma Phi; r/Luth; hon/Unit Queen of Sales 1979; Future Dir Designation 1980.

WHITFIELD, STEPHEN KENNETH oc/Training Administrator; b/June 22, 1948; h/Lynchburg, VA; ba/PO Box 1330, Salisbury, NC 28144; m/Nancy O; c/Stephen Kenneth Jr; p/Robert C Jr and Rosemary Whitfield, Durham, NC; ed/BS UNC-CH 1970; pa/Tchr E C Glass HS, Lynchburg 1971-74; Salesman: Real Est 1974-78, Life Ins 1978-80; Tng Admr 1980-; Am Soc Tng & Devel; Past Mem Am Speech & Hearing Assn; cp/Va JCs, Past Dir, VP, Past St Proj Dir for Mobile Neo-Natal Unit Proj; K of C 3°, Past Dir Yth Activs for Local Chapt; Repub Party; r/Cath.

WHITLOCK, QUENTON H JR oc/Minister; b/Nov 5, 1948; h/718 Delverton Rd, Columbia, SC 29203; ba/Columbia; m/Tarlena B; c/Tara Tamekia; p/Q H and Pearley Whitlock, Holly Springs, MS; ed/BS Miss Indust Col; MDiv Interdenom Theol Ctr; pa/Min; cp/NAACP; Columbia Christian Action Coun.

WHITLOW, TED WILSON oc/Construction Executive; b/Dec 15, 1930; h/124 Lakeland, Rt 4, Lewisville, TX 75067; ba/Dallas; m/Sherry M; p/Ted (dec) and Merle L Whitlow, Belton, TX; ed/BBA Tex A&M Univ 1956; mil/USMC 1951-52; pa/Constrn Supt, So Bldg & Investment Corp 1956-65; Property Mgr, Huie Properties 1965-68; Pres Whitlow Constrn 1968-77; Constrn Exec Mahaffey Constrn 1977-; Conslt Sch of Constrn, Tex Christian Univ 1965-66 & Tex Tech Inst 1975-77; cp/Hunting Hall of Fame Foun; Life Mem Nat Rifle Assn; Life Mem Tex Rifle Assn; Safari Intl; Ducks Unltd; Dallas Woods & Waters, Boone & Crockett; r/Meth.

WHITMAN, JAMES MADISON oc/Special Assistant to Plant Director; b/Aug 12, 1911; h/Auburn, AL; m/Olliem; p/dec; ed/Dip Frigidaire Ser Sch; pa/Spec Asst to Dir, Phys Plant Div, Auburn Univ; Refrig Ser Engrs Soc: Pres St Assn 1964-65, Bd Dirs 2 Yrs, Pres Local Chapt 3 Terms, Secy-Treas 2 Yrs; cp/Pres Auburn Outing Clb 1977, Bd Dirs 3

Yrs; r/Bapt; hon/Sporlan Valve Co Man of Yr Awd, RSES 1970; Valedictorian HS Class 1931.

WHITTEN, NEOLA LORENE oc/Naturalist Artist; b/Nov 21, 1922; h/Box 665, Hooks, TX 75561; ba/Hooks; m/Bob Bill; c/Robert A, William E, Elaine Sparks; p/John Douglas Jr (dec) and Bessie Bond Barnett (dec); ed/Grad McKensie Baldwin Bus Col 1941; Basic Drawing & Comp 1974, Adv'd Art, Painting in Oil 1976, Watercolor, Pastel & Acrylic Courses 1978, Hanson's Conservatory of Arts; Texarkana Arts & Humanities Coun, Yrly Plan'g Com; Charter Mem & Secy Four Sts Regional Art Clb; Mt Pleasant Art Soc; SWn Watercolor Soc; cp/Bd Dirs Hooks Am Cancer Soc; r/Bapt; hon/3rd Pl Four St Regional Annual Show 1977.

WHITTEN, SARA oc/Training Director and Special Events Coordinator; b/Oct 21, 1931; h/Tupelo, MS; ba/McRae's Dept Store, 139 Tupelo Mall, Tupelo, MS 38801; m/Bobby L; c/Robert Brit, Mary Eugenia; p/O B (dec) and Mary Lou Rogers (dec); ed/Att'd Univ Miss 1950; Mich St Univ, Mall Promo Inst 1977; Bus Devel Inst 1976; Certs Am Inst Bnkg 1970-75; pa/First Bank Tupelo; Bank of Miss; Tupelo Mall Mgr; McRae's Tng & Spec Events Coor; cp/Past Treas, Co Chm & Pres Heart Assn; Lee U Neighbors; Tupelo Clean & Beautiful; Commun Devel Foun; Red Cross Instr; BPW, Charter Mem; Retail Trade Coun; r/Bapt; hon/Heart Assn Awd of Dist 1977; Cert of Achmt in Retail Mktg, Nat Res Bur 1979; Author Case Hist & Success Story in Shopping Ctr Newslttr.

WHITTENTON, DAVID OSCAR JR oc/Staff Manager; b/Mar 12, 1955; h/Rt 3 Box 124, Dunn, NC 28334; ba/Dunn; m/Jennifer Hamilton; p/David O and Jean N Whittenton, Dunn, NC; pa/Staff Mgr Durham Life Ins Co; cp/Lions Clb; r/Assem of God.

WHITTLE, JOE BOB oc/Home Builder; b/Apr 26, 1936; h/2814 Andover, Midland, TX; m/Faye; c/Marcus, Larry, Shawn, Danette; p/Edgar and Beola Whittle, Midland, TX; mil/AUS Airborne; pa/Home Bldr; Midland Home Bldrs Assn, Pres; Tex Assn Bldrs Inc; Nat Home Bldrs Assn; cp/S-side Lions Clb, Pres; r/Bapt; hon/Outstg Ser & Contbn to Home Bldg Indust 1980.

WHITTON, THOMAS RICHARD oc/Management Consultant, Entrepreneur, Investor, Merger Specialist; b/June 14, 1940; h/4017 Valley Rd, Paducah, KY 42001; ba/Paducah; m/Geri A; c/Thomas Jr, Melinda Leigh; p/Richard L and Lillian R Whitton, Indpls, IN; ed/BS Murray St Col 1963; pa/Mgmt Trainee, Salesman, Dist Mgr Morse Div Borg Warner 1963-69; Formed & Oper'd 3 Indust Wholesale Supply Cos in Ky 1968-76; Mgmt Conslt 1977-; Dir Corp Fin Assocs; Dir & Conslt Var Pvt Firms; r/Bapt; hon/Man of Yr, Corp Fin Assn 1980; Murray St Univ S'ship Est'd for Grads of Paducah Tilghman HS by Mr Whitton.

WICKES, JEANNIE KIM oc/Evangelistic Concert Singer, Author; b/May 27, 1947; h/PO Box 1370, W Memphis, AR 72301; ba/W Memphis; p/George and Eva Wickes, Dayton, IN; ed/MMus Ind Univ; pa/Chm Kim's Mins Inc; Billy Graham Mus Team; cp/Sings for Polit Rallies & God & Country Days; hon/Fulbright Schlr Vienna Inst Mus & Dramatic Arts.

WIERNIK, PETER H oc/Director, Professor; b/June 16, 1939; h/5026 Round Tower Pl, Columbia, MD 21044; ba/Balto; m/Roberta Fuller; c/Julie Anne, Lisa Britt, Peter Harrison; p/Harris and Mollie Emmerman Wiernik, Waco, TX; ed/BA 1961, MD 1965 Univ Va; mil/US Public Hlth Ser; pa/Dir Balto Cancer Res Prog; Prof Med Univ Md Hosp; Am Soc Clin Investigation; Am Assn Cancer Res; Am Soc Clin Oncology; r/Jewish; hon/Phi Beta Kappa; Alpha Omega Alpha; Sigma Xi.

WIGGINS, NELL oc/Merchant, Fashion Coordinator; b/Oct 11, 1935; h/Rt 3 Box 1076, Henderson, NC 27536; ba/Henderson; m/Jospeh F; c/Dean Marvin and Dennis Martin Hodge; p/Mrs Abner Cobb, Henderson, NC; ed/Carolina Col Beauty Culture 1954; pa/Merchant; Cosmetologist; Henderson Mall Mchts Assn, Treas 2 Yrs, Pres 2 Yrs; Henderson-Vance C of C, Pres 2 Yrs, Dir 3 Yrs; cp/Dir NC St Optometric Aux; Vance-Granville Commun Col Fashion Adv Bd; Adv Bd Vance Co Schs; Bd Dirs NCNB; hon/Citizen of Yr, Vance Co 1980.

WILBUR, WARREN WILSON oc/Rancher; b/Mar 15, 1913; h/RR 2, Twin Ranches, Miami, OK 74354; ba/Same; m/Allene; c/Warren Lee, De Maris Lau; p/Avery Lee and Margaret Hartley Wilbur, Baxter Springs, KS; ed/Spec Student Okla St Univ 1931-32; pa/Cattle Rancher; r/Bapt; hon/Boy Scout Silver Beaver 1950; St of Okla Bapt Brotherhood Pres 1951; Masonic Post Master of Lodge 493 1949; Hon Life Mem Lions, Columbus, Kan; Currently Writing *Hunting Around the World with Warren Wilbur.*

WILDER, RUTH STEWART oc/Director of Nursing Services; b/May 27, 1921; h/2219 Matthews St, Huntsville, AL 35801; ba/Madison;

m/Archie De Masters; p/John (dec) and Nellie W Stewart (dec); ed/BS; RN; pa/Dir Nsg Sers, Madison Nsg Home; ANA; Sigma Theta Tau; cp/BPW; Am Heart Assn; Coms w U Way; r/Luth; hon/Ala Nurse of Yr; St & Nat Awds, Civil Defense as Vol Tchr; W/W Am Wom; Heart Assn Awds; U Way Plaque.

WILKERSON, SHIRLEY ELIZABETH oc/Senior Citizens Coordinator; b/June 13, 1934; h/121 E Crawford St, Salisbury, NC 28144; ba/Salisbury; m/Robert Boyden Sr; c/Elizabeth Ann Leichman, Robert Boyden Jr, James Arthur; p/Lee Eston (dec) and Olene Heilig Copley, Salisbury, NC; ed/Var Courses Rowan Tech Inst, Catawba Col, NC St Univ; pa/Sr Citizens Coor, Salisbury Rec Dept; NC Rec & Pk Soc; Chm Sr Citizen Com; St Advr to NC Assn of Sr Citizens Clbs; Dist Advr NC Assn Sr Citizen Clbs; Adv Bd Rowan Co Coun on Aging; cp/Girl Scout Ldr; Cub Scout Den Mother; r/Luth; hon/Tarheel Girls' St 1951; Outstg Yng Wom Am 1969; NC Assn Sr Citizens Clbs St Advr 1981.

WILKINSON, ANCIL CLIFTON oc/Retired; h/Box 577, Monticello, KY 42533; m/Barbara McIntosh; c/Susan Carol, Barbara Jo, William Mason; p/Joseph T and Ada True Wilkinson, Liberty, KY; ed/Att'd Wn Ky St Col & Univ Ky; mil/USN 1944-46 Radio Opers; pa/Co Supvr & Dist Supvr USDA-FMHA; Pt-Time Public Relats, Monticello Bnkg Co; Chm Wayne Co Dem Fin Com, Ky Gov John Y Brown; cp/Kiwanis; Sportsman Clb, Secy-Treas; Unit Commr Boy Scouts & Cub Scouts; Former Mason; r/Christian; hon/Superior Ser Awd, USDA; Medal, Secy Agric Orville Freeman 1967; Plaque for Scouting.

WILKINSON, BRUCE H oc/Educator; b/Sept 4, 1947; ba/Atlanta, GA; m/Darlene M; c/David, Jennifer; p/James S and Joan M Wilkinson, Marietta, GA; ed/BA 1969, ThB 1970 NEn Bible Col; ThM Dallas Theol Sem 1974; pa/Editorial Asst, Dallas Theol Sem; Prof Multnomah Sch of the Bible; Pres & Fdr Walk Thru the Bible Min 1974; Sem Instr 1974; Pres & Dir Christian Growth 1980; Exec Editor *Daily Walk* 1978; Pres Christian Growth Clb 1980-; Pres Assn; Am Mgmt Assn; Bd Dirs Nat Inst Biblical Studies; Adv Bd Intl Coun Biblical Inerrancy; Bd Dirs F'ship of Cos for Christ; cp/Atlanta C of Cong 1979-; r/Prot; hon/Alumni of Yr, NEn Bible Col; W/W S&SW 1980; Author *Walk Thru the Old Testament* 1974 & *Walk Thru the New Testament* 1975; Co-Author *Walk Thru Personal Bible Study Methods* 1978.

WILLARD, NEAL JR oc/Interior Designer; b/Apr 13, 1937; h/411 Abbott St, Greenwood, SC 29646; ba/Greenwood; p/Neal Jr and Sue R Willard, Greenwood, SC; ed/Att'd NY Sch Interior Design 1968; mil/AUS 2 Yrs; pa/Interior Designer, Bus Mgr, VP, R J Sprott's Inc; ASID; r/Bapt.

WILLEFORD, CATHERINE PROCTOR oc/Civic Leader; h/PO Box 2, Kannapolis, NC 28081; m/Brice I Jr; c/Brice J III, Catherine Elizabeth; p/Catherine Folk, Edgefield, SC; ed/BS Winthrop Col 1957; MS LSU 1959; cp/Bd Dirs: Old Courthouse Theater, Am Red Cross, VP U Way, Chm Gov's Plan'g Bd, V-Chm Precinct Wom 1968, S Piedmont Hlth Assn; Girl Scout & Cub Scout Ldr; Pres Tchr Parent Coun, A L Brown HS 1979; Pres Gdn Clb Coun 1969; Chm ECW 1982; r/Epis; hon/W/W Am Wom 1981; Sr Order Winthrop.

WILLIAMS, ANNIE JOHN oc/Retired Teacher, Historical Researcher; b/Aug 26, 1913; h/2021 Sprunt Ave, Durham, NC 27705; ba/Same; p/John Wesley and Martha Anne Walker Williams; ed/AB Greensboro Col 1933; MA UNC-CH 1939; pa/NCCTM; NCTM, Life Mem; Delta Kappa Gamma, Eta Chapt; cp/Pierian Lit Clb; Assn for Preserv of Eno River Val; Rockingham Co Hist Soc; r/Meth; hon/W W Rankin Meml Awd for Excell in Math Ed 1975; Hon Mem Mu Alpha Theta 1978; NC St Univ, Dept of Math & Sci Ed, Cert of Recog of Contbns to Excell in Math & Sci Ed 1979.

WILLIAMS, ARMSTRONG oc/Student; b/Feb 5, 1959; h/Rt 4 Box 256, Marion, SC 29571; ba/Orangeburg, SC; p/James and Thelma Williams, Marion, SC; mil/ROTC; pa/Student; cp/NAACP; Yng Dems; Polit Sci Clb; r/Prot; hon/ROTC 2 Yr S'ship; Pres Schlr; ROTC Sojourner Aw; Phi Beta Sigma; SGA Pres; Outstg Achmt Orangeburg Boys Attention Home.

WILLIAMS, ARTHUR LEE III oc/Funeral Business; b/Jan 12, 1950; h/PO Box 119, Chipley, FL 32428; ba/Chipley; m/Renae W; c/Jason Brian; p/Arthur Lee Jr and Otha Louise Williams, Graceville, FL; ed/AA Chipola Jr Col; pa/Funeral Bus; cp/Past Pres Chipley JCs; r/U Meth.

WILLIAMS, B STEVEN oc/Minister Music and Youth; b/Aug 22, 1948; h/Enterprise, AL; ba/Hillcrest Bapt Ch, 500 Alberta St, Enterprise, AL 36330; m/M Joyce Wade; c/Vicki, Tammi, Jonathan; p/Billie F and Mary Ellen Napier Williams, Graniteville, SC; ed/MCM New Orleans Bapt Theol Sem 1979; BS Univ SC 1975; mil/USAF 1968-72; pa/Min Mus & Yth, Hillcrest Bapt Ch; r/Bapt; hon/Pi Kappa Lambda.

WILLIAMS, BARBARA KAY oc/Student; b/July 23, 1959; h/Rt 5 Box 41, Athens, TN 37303; p/Luther Francis and Barbara Ann Gibson Williams, Athens, TN; ed/BS Cand David Lipscomb Col; pa/Col Student; r/Ch of Christ; hon/HS Math Awd 1974, 75; French Awd 1976; Kiwanis Awds 1974-76; HS Valedictorian 1977; Nat Hon Soc 1976-77; Valedictorian S'ship to David Lipscomb Col 1977; Deans List & Hon Roll, David Lipscomb Col.

WILLIAMS, CAROLYN ANTONIDES oc/Professor; b/Oct 27, 1939; h/Laurel Hill Rd, Chapel Hill, NC 27514; ba/Chapel Hill; m/Frank Canon; p/John Dwight (dec) and Dorothy Hoffman Antonides, Louisville, KY; ed/BS; MS; PhD; pa/Prof Sch of Public Hlth, UNC-CH; Chm Res Adv Com, Am Nurses Found; Pubs Bd, Am Public Hlth Assn; V-Chm on Res, ANA; Conslt Nat Ctr for Hlth Sers Res, HEW; hon/Grad w Hons, Tex Wom's Univ 1961; F'ship Am Public Hlth Assn 1969; F'ship Am Acad Nsg 1975; World Hlth Org Travel F'ship 1978.

WILLIAMS, CHARLES DEAN oc/Emergency Medical Services Chief; b/Aug 20, 1930; h/Midland, TX; m/Martha Ann; c/Charles Wayne, Tracy Kevin, Dana Kim; p/J T Williams, Hobbs, NM; Mrs M L Buhn, Odessa, TX; ed/Att'd Odessa Col & Midland Col; pa/Dir City of Midland Fire Dept EMS Div 1980-; Dir EMS, Permian Basin Regional Plan'g Comm 1975-80; City of Odessa Fire Dept: Tng Chief 1970-75, Station Capt 1956-70, Equip Oper 1953-56, Firefighter 1951-53; Intl Soc Fire Ser Instrs; Tex Soc Fire Ser Instrs; Tex Soc EMTs; cp/Ofcr & Bd Dirs Hi-Noon Optimist Clb; Masonic Lodge #955; Odessa Scottish Rite Assn; Frat Order of Eagles; r/Luth; hon/Certs for Pers Mgmt, Public Relats & Equip Opers.

WILLIAMS, CHARLES DONALD oc/Educator; b/Aug 16, 1944; h/218 Laurel St, C-12, Hartford, CT 06105; ba/Hartford; p/Macy (dec) and Carolyn M Williams, Walterboro, SC; ed/BS Claflin Col; pa/Hd Tchr Conn Child & Fam Sers, Chd's Village; Hartford Fed Tchrs; cp/NAACP; Elk, Chapt Oak Lodge #67, IBPOE of W; First Deg Mason, Excelsior Lodge #167; Sang w Hartford Symph Chorale; r/Meth; hon/Tchr of Yr 1975; "Sphinx Man" of Alpha Phi Alpha; Commend from Asst Supt, Hartford Public Schs; Commend from Supt, Hartford Public Schs.

WILLIAMS, DAVID CARL oc/Banker, Manager; b/May 24, 1950; h/503 Louis Circle SE, Huntsville, AL 35803; ba/H'ville; m/Patsy; c/David Carl Jr; p/Walter A Sr and Elaine D Williams, Gadsden, AL; ed/BA Univ Ala 1972; Certs Am Inst Bnkg; AUS Ofcr Sch 1973; mil/Ala ANG Capt; pa/Mgr Ctrl Bank of Ala; AYB, Area Coor; AIB, Past Local Pres, Past Bd Govs; cp/Huntsville JCs: VP, Past Dir, Past VP; 32° Mason; Shriner; Past Chm Heart Assn, Free Enterprise Com; r/Bapt; hon/John H Armbruster Meml Awd 1980 (Outstg JC Am); St of Ala Outstg JC; Outstg JC Dir, H'ville JCs.

WILLIAMS, DORIS E oc/Payroll Director, Chief of Naval Reserve; b/Mar 12, 1931; h/PO Box 26622, New Orleans, LA 70186; ba/New Orleans; p/Neely Carder (dec) and Eva C Stewart Williams (dec); ed/Cert Acctg, Univ Tenn 1971; pa/Chief Naval Reserve; Nat Assn Female Execs; Am Soc Mil Comptrollers; Am Soc Profl & Exec Wom; cp/Dems for Progress; Wom's Org, N Miss; r/Assem of God; hon/Outstg Employee, USN 1978, 79, 80, 81; Author Payroll Ser Guide 1979.

WILLIAMS, EDWIN RUSSELL oc/Executive; b/Aug 4, 1946; h/McComb, MS; ba/N Blvd at State St, PO Box 667, McComb, MS 39648; m/Vickie Parker; c/Lorna Price, Angela Russell; p/Williams Atkins Williams Jr (dec); Lorna Russell Williams Cole, McComb, MS; ed/BBA Univ Miss 1968; Pastoral Mins Dip, Nashville 1975; MDiv 1979, ThD 1980 New Orleans Bapt Theol Sem; RPG II Programming Sch, IBM 1980; mil/AUS 1968-70; Miss NG 1971-75; USAR Capt; pa/Pres Williams Wholesale Grocery Co Inc; Miss Wholesale Grocers Assn, Past Mem Bd Dirs, Chm Resolution Com; Nat Assn Wholesale Grocers; cp/Am Legion; Mason; C of C; Rotarian; r/So Bapt; Deacon; hon/Phi Kappa Psi; VP Soc Advmt Mgmt 1967; Scabbard & Blade Mil Assn; Dist'd Mil Student 1967-68; Dist'd Mil Grad 1968; Army Commend Medal 1970; Lic'd to Gospel Mins 1978.

WILLIAMS, ELLIS oc/Associate Minister, Police Lieutenant; b/Oct 27, 1931; h/3108 Metropolitan St, New Orleans, LA 70126; ba/New Orleans; m/Priscilla Norman; c/Debra, Rita, Claude, Lathan, Glen, Zelia; p/Elise McDowell, Greenwood, MS; ed/BA 1972, MEd 1974, MCJ 1980 Loyola Univ of S; pa/New Orleans Police Ofcr 1964, Police Sgt 197, Police Lt 1979; Fingerprint Ident Tech & Cert'd Polographist; La & Intl Assns of Ident; La & Am Polygraph Assns; FOP; Am Law Enforcement Ofcrs Assn; cp/Dem Party; Past Master Masonic Order; r/Bapt; hon/Cross Keys, Nat Hon & Ser Frat; Kappa Delta Pi.

WILLIAMS, FREDDIE SR oc/Assistant Principal; b/June 8, 1938; m/Millie Marie; c/Freddie Jr, Tirzah N, Maurice A; p/Volover W Sr (dec) and Fannie Williams, DeRidder, LA; ed/BS 1961, MEd 1971, Grad Study 1973 So Univ; Cert of Part, NDEA Inst, So Univ 1967; pa/Asst Prin, Baton Rouge High Magnet Sch; LAE; LAP; NEA; Nat Assn Sec'dy Sch Prins; Phi Delta Kappa: Corresp Secy, 1st VP of Mbrship; Voting Mem Pupil Sers Com, E Baton Rouge Parish Sch Bd; Com on Curric Devel for GT Students, E Baton Rouge Parish Schs; cp/YMCA; Prince Hall Masonic Order; Commun Assn for Wel of Sch Chd; Layman Org, Bethel AME Ch; Heritage (Non-Profit Singing Grp); r/AME Ch; hon/Kappan of Yr, So Univ Chapt Phi Delta Kappa 1981; Author "A Study of Dialectical Differences Between White and Black Students in East Baton Rouge Parish" 1966.

WILLIAMS, GLENWOOD CREIGHTON oc/Accountant; b/June 19, 1920; h/1103 Beth Ct, Old Armstrong Pl, Georgetown, KY 40324; ba/Frankfort, KY; m/James M (dec); c/Ann W Eades, Emily Jane Rankin, Glenn Marvin, Gerald Lynn; p/Sterling (dec) and Elizabeth Creighton (dec); pa/Acct Commonwlth of Ky; cp/PTO; Gov's Conf on Energy; Bd Dirs Ctrl Ky Mtl Hlth Assn; r/Bapt; hon/St & Nat Life Mbrships PTA.

WILLIAMS, HELEN McMULLEN oc/Teacher, Real Estate Manager, Politician; b/Oct 2, 1926; h/Jackson, MS; ba/Same; m/X Reuben; c/Susan Diane, Ronald Marx; p/Leland (dec) and Lida Bell McMullen (dec); ed/BS 1948, Cert in Speech 1961 Univ Iowa; MS Jackson St Univ 1976; pa/Real Est Mgmt; Fed'd Tchrs of Phila, Pa; Jackson Tchrs Assn, VP; MEA; Am Fed Tchrs; cp/Cand: City Commr 1973, US Ho of Reps 1974, St Ho of Reps 1975, Mayor 1977, US Senate 1978; Dem Party; Jacksonians for Helen Williams Clb, Fin Secy; Nat Wom's Leag, Past VP; JPS Adv Coun, Rep; Dramatic Wkshop, Pres; r/Bapt; hon/Hon DH 1974; YMCA Ser Cert; Girl Scout Ldr Ser Awd; Alpha Kappa Alpha Hon Recog for Polit Ldrship as Cand for City Commr 1973; Author "A Comparative Study of the Philadelphia School System and the Jackson Public Schools" 1978, 79, 80-81.

WILLIAMS, HUGH EVANS oc/Grocer; b/Jan 30, 1921; h/Rt 3 Box 568, Granite Falls, NC 28630; m/Pauline Bingham; p/Robert W and Edna Evans Williams; ed/HS Grad; pa/Grocery Bus, Thomas & Howard Co 20 Yrs; r/Grace Chapel U Meth Ch: SS Tchr, Bd Mem, Ch Treas 5 Yrs; hon/5 Yr, 10 Yr & 20 Yr Ser Pins; Author Hist of Grace Chapel for Anniv Celebration.

WILLIAMS, ISAAC EDWARD oc/Pastor; b/July 2, 1924; m/Alma O; c/Isaac Jr; p/Addie Williams, Chesapeake, VA; ed/AB Va Union Univ; MA Hampton Inst; MDiv SE Bapt Theol Sem; DD Va Sem; mil/USAF; pa/Tchr; Pastor First Bapt Ch, Suffolk.

WILLIAMS, JACOB LORY III oc/Geologist; b/Nov 7, 1920; h/1502 Princeton, Midland, TX 79701; ba/Midland; m/Angela; c/Stephen, Kathryn, Mary Annette, Jacob; p/Jacob Lory Jr (dec) and Opal Williams, Lancaster, PA; ed/BS Iowa St Col; mil/WWII; pa/Geol, Tex Pacific Oil Co; Am Assn Petro Geols; W Tex Geol Soc; cp/Midland Geneal Soc.

WILLIAMS, JOHNNIE BEATRICE oc/Assistant Professor; b/Feb 15, 1943; h/3441 Sunset Dr, Shreveport, LA 71109; ba/S'port; m/Edward L; p/John Benjamin and Maggie Mae Flucas Bursey; ed/BS Grambling Univ 1965; MS Ind Univ 1969; Post Grad Studies: La Tech Univ 1974, Univ Santa Clara 1974, So Univ 1974; pa/Chm Bus Dept, DeSoto HS 1964-69; Asst Prof, Dept Ofc Adm, So Univ 1969-; Dir Coop Ed 1976-; Am Fed Tchrs; Grambling Alumni Assn; Nat Bus Ed Assn; cp/Secy David Raines Commun Coun, David Raines Commun Ctr 1972-73, Receptionist 1971-72; Campaign Asst, Rep Alphonse Jackson 1974-75; Vol Asst to Satelite Prog, Drug Abuse Shire House 1973-74; Relief Ofc Asst, La Bank & Trust Co 1978; Beaird-Poulan Div, Emerson Elec Co 1978; Vol Campaign Asst, Buddy Roemer 1978, June Phillips 1979; Commun Adv Coun for Gen Motors 1978-79; Secy Queensborough in Action 1980; Secy to Security Nat Bank; Ind Univ Alumni Assn; r/Bapt; hon/Delta Sigma Theta; Outstg Yng Wom Am 1970; W/W S&SW 1980-81.

WILLIAMS, JULIUS JR oc/Coach; b/May 8, 1943; h/McComb, MS; m/Shirley Ann; c/Ursula Patrice, Julius III, Jarrod Jamiel; p/Louella Williams, McComb, MS; ed/BS Alcorn St Univ 1965; MS Jackson St Univ 1979; Further Study Univ So Miss, Alcorn St Univ; pa/Tchr-Coach, Wilkinson Co Tng Sch, Woodville, Miss 1965-66; Hd Coach Basketball & Track, Asst Varsity Fball, Eva Gordon Attendance Ctr 1967-73; Hd Fball & Hd Varsity Track Coach, So Pike Jr HS 1973-; Miss Coaching Assn; Miss Assn Edrs; NEA; AAPHER; r/Jehovah Witness; hon/Pike Co Alcornite of Yr 1980.

WILLIAMS, LATIMER FREEMAN oc/Warehouseman; b/Nov 18, 1911; h/Jacksonville, FL; m/Annie R; c/Brenda Ann; p/Jewell Lee (dec) and Emma L Williams (dec); ed/Fred Douglas Bus & Voc Sch 1949; Att'd Edward Waters Col; mil/AUS 1942-46; pa/Warehouseman, NAS; cp/Chaplain Johnson Br YMCA & Am Legion Post 197; Bd Mgmt YMCA; r/U Meth; hon/Post Ofc Dept Cert Tng 1965; Cert Apprec, USN 1970-73; Cert for Active Part in Am Legion Post 197; Cert'd Lay Spkr, Fla Annual Conf U Meth Ch 1978; Cert Apprec as Div Ldr YMCA 1963; Cert Apprec,

St Stephen AME Ch for Merit & Dedicated Ser to City of Jacksonville 1969; Plaques from YMCA 1963, 67, 74, 79; Plaque Alpha Kappa Alpha for Outstg Ser 1977-78; Cert of Awd in Recog of Commun Ser, Green Pasture Guild 1962.

WILLIAMS, LUTHER FRANCIS oc/Educator; b/May 14, 1932; h/Rt 5 Box 41, Athens, TN 37303; ba/Cleveland, TN; m/Barbara; c/Carol Ann, Patricia Lynn, Barbara Kay; p/Frelon Charles (dec) and Mattie Lee Williams, Athens, TN; ed/AS Freed Hardeman Col 1957; BS Tenn Wesleyan Col 1964; MMath Univ SC 1967; EdD Univ Tenn 1977; pa/Tchr Math: Meigs HS, Decatur, Tenn 1961-66; McMinn HS, Athens, Tenn 1967-68; Cleveland St Commun Col 1968-74, 75-77; Dir Inst Res, Cleveland St Commun Col 1977-; Min: Etowah Ch of Christ, Etowah, Tenn 1951-54, 61-66, 76-; Dublin Ch of Christ, Dublin, Ga 1957-61; Ctrl Ch of Christ, Athens, Tenn 1969-72; Calhoun Ch of Christ, Calhoun, Tenn 1972-76; NEA; Nat Coun Res & Plan'g; Phi Delta Kappa; U Tchg Prof; cp/Repub Party; Bd Dirs Richmond-Tatum Schs; Bd Dirs Christian Student Ctr; r/Ch of Christ; hon/Fac S'ship Ldrship Awd, Freed Hardeman Col; W/W S&SW 1980-81; NSF Grant 1966-67; NSF Fac F'ship 1974-75.

WILLIAMS, MARVIN EUGENE oc/Fire Captain; b/Nov 15, 1935; h/2977 Osage, Camden, AR 71701; ba/Camden; m/Mary; p/Altha Williams, Camden, AR; pa/Capt Camden Fire Dept; cp/VP Camden Evening Lions Clb; Pres Ark St Firefighters; r/Bapt; hon/Outstg Lion 1978.

WILLIAMS, MELVA JEAN oc/Executive; b/June 11, 1935; h/6150 Indigo Ct, Ft Worth, TX 76112; ba/Ft Worth; m/J B; c/Mark, Doris, Robin, Jeannie; p/Wayne Mulholland; Mildred E Graham Bailey, Ft Worth, TX; ed/Grad Roberta's Finishing Sch 1950; Grad Charron-Williams Commercial Col 1954; pa/Pres & Dir SEn Resources Corp; VP & Dir SERPCO Inc; Secy-Treas & Dir J J & L Drilling Co Inc; Ptnr: Laser Drilling, Magnafrac, Tenabo Venture & B&W Real Est Investments; cp/Repub Party; r/Meth; hon/W/W Am Wom 1981-82.

WILLIAMS, MIKE oc/Consultant, Executive; b/Feb 23, 1952; ba/Oklahoma City, OK; m/C J Murphy; p/John G and Roberta Williams, Woodward, OK; pa/Advtg & Polit Consltg; Pres At Your Ser Inc; Pres Panhandle Communs Inc; Bd Dirs Okla City Press Clb; Bd Dirs Okla Leag for Blind; Sigma Delta Chi; cp/Okla City C of C; S Okla City C of C; r/Bapt; hon/Outstg Yng Men Am 1977 & 80; Okla Guardsman Awd 1973; UPI Outstg News Report 1972; AP Outstg News Report 1976.

WILLIAMS, MIRIAM LYERLY oc/Homemaker; b/Jan 27, 1918; h/Woodleaf, NC; m/Neal (dec); c/Juanita W Wine, Edith W Martin; p/Walter Lee (dec) and Beulah Correll Lyerly, Woodleaf, NC; ed/Att'd Mitchell Jr Col 1936, Univ Va; cp/Worthy Matron, Queen Esther Chapt #14 OES; Charter Mem Order of White Shrine; Cnslr Jobs Daughs; Girls Scout Troop Ldr; Pres PTA Red Hill Sch; Chaplain Mollie Southerland Clb; Circle Bible Moderator & Var Ofcr, Wom of Ch, Reid Meml Presb Ch; Vol Work Talmadge Hosp; r/Presb; hon/Love Quilt from Session House SS Class 1980.

WILLIAMS, PAULINE BINGHAM oc/Hosery Mill; b/Sept 25, 1918; h/Rt 3 Box 568, Granite Falls, NC; m/Hugh E; p/Joseph William and Essie Mae Sain Bingham, Morganton, NC; pa/Hosery Mill 18 Yrs; Waitress & Cook, Woolworths 21 yrs; r/Meth; hon/Life Mem Wom's Soc Christian Ser 1956; 15 Yr Ser Pin, Morganton Full Fashion Hosery Mill; Cit of Ser Awd, Woolworth 1980.

WILLIAMS, REUBEN oc/Instructor, Postal Mail Carrier, Income Tax Computer; b/June 5, 1922; h/Jackson, MS; m/Helen M; c/Ronald Marx, Susan Diane; p/Sinclair (dec) and Catherine Williams (dec); ed/BS Jackson St Univ 1953; mil/AUS; pa/Tchr Sec'dy Sci & Math; Computing Income Tax; Dist'g Mail as Mail Carrier; MTA; MEA; JTA; cp/NAPE, Fin Secy; VFW; YMCA; BSA, Com Chm; Dem Party; r/Bapt; hon/AUS Hon Discharge 1946; NAPE Recog Awd; Father of Yr 1973; Boy Scout Ser Cert 1973.

WILLIAMS, ROBERT FRANKLIN JR oc/Minister; b/June 7, 1942; h/Rt 1 Box 65, Columbia, MS 39429; ba/Same; m/Rosalind D; c/Carol Maria, Bryan Davis; p/Robert Franklin Sr and Lessie Vinson Williams; ed/BS Troy St Univ; MDiv New Orleans Bapt Theol Sem; pa/So Bapt Min; Secy-Treas Marion Co Min Assn; cp/Charter Mem Marion Assn Retard'd Citizens; r/So Bapt; hon/Phi Theta Kappa.

WILLIAMS, RONALD MARX oc/Telephone Repairman/Lineman; b/Aug 5, 1949; h/Jackson, MS; m/Wanda Davis; c/Shaladia Davis; p/Reuben and Helen M Williams, Jackson, MS; ed/BA Jackson St Univ; BS Wiley Col; mil/USNG; USAR Mil Police; pa/So Ctrl Bell Telephone Co, Engrg Dept, Telephone Repairman/Lineman; CWA; cp/YMCA; BSA; Com Chm Dem Party; r/Bapt; hon/Personalities of S 1975-76; Good

Conduct Medal; Sharp Shooter Medal; Nat Defense Ser Medal; Scout Ldr Awd; Hon AUS Discharge 1972; Author "What America Means to Me" 1964.

WILLIAMS, RUBY C oc/Homemaker; b/Nov 23, 1911; h/Rt 9, Hillcrest, Richmond, KY 40475; ba/Same; m/Winston (dec); p/Madison J (dec) and Lillie Mae Carrier (dec); pa/Sch Tchr; Cake Decorator; Bakery Owner; Farmer; cp/Fair Bd; St Homemakers Bd; Fund Raiser; r/Bapt: SS Tchr, Dir Ch Tng; hon/Duchess of Paducah Awd.

WILLIAMS, RUBY JO SMITH oc/Teacher; b/Sept 26, 1936; h/2015 E Alma Ave, Sherman, TX 75090; ba/Sherman; m/Q D; p/Henry C Sr and Luberta Smith, Ft Worth, TX; ed/BA Wiley Col 1959; MEd N Tex St Univ 1972; Post Grad Studies E Tex St Univ; pa/Tchr Elem Sch Art & SS: Gainesville ISD 7 Yrs, Sherman ISD 11 Yrs; Sherman Ed Assn, Secy, Mbrship Chm, Dist Del; Tex Clrm Tchrs Assn, Dist Mbrship Chm, St Del; NEA; Tex St Tchrs Assn, Dist Human Relats Chm; Sherman Clrm Tchrs Assn; cp/AAUW, Pres; Delta Kappa Gamma; Sherman Neighborhood Involvement Com, Chm; Heart Fund Bd; Texoma Regional Blood Bank Bd; Girls Clb Bd; Altrusa Ser Clb; r/Ch of Christ; hon/Salutatorian, I M Terrell HS 1956; Sherman Citizen of Yr 1978; AAUW Outstg Wom Edr 1978-79; All Am City Hon 1980.

WILLIAMS, SUSAN DIANE oc/Medical Technologist; b/Oct 12, 1956; h/Jackson, MS & Phila, PA; p/Reuben and Helen M Williams, Jackson, MS; ed/BA 1979; BS Univ Penn 1979; pa/Med Technol, Bacteriology & Microbiol Lab, Univ Pa Hosp; Assn of Med Technols; Nat Hon Soc, Secy; Biracial Com Chm, Univ Pa; cp/Mu Alpha Theta; Nat Thespian Soc; Pre-Med Clb; Dem Party; r/Bapt; hon/HS Valedictorian, Grad w Hons Univ Pa 1979; Alpha Kappa Alpha Hons Awd; Bausch-Lomb Awd; Eng Awd; DAR Math Awd 1979; Nat Postal Alliance Awd 1974; W/W Am HS Students 1973; Personalities of S 1975-76; Outstg Univ Student 1978-79.

WILLIAMS, VENORA A oc/Assistant to Director; b/Apr 8, 1910; h/Big Spring, TX; p/James Arthur and Ethel Flowers, San Antonio, TX; ed/BA 1948, MEd 1957; pa/Sch Tchr 40 Yrs; Asst to Dir Sr Citizen Ctr; TSTA; NEA; r/AME Ch.

WILLIAMS, WILLIE LETHAIT oc/Assistant Director of Financial Aid; b/Mar 26, 1946; h/101 Monteigo St, Centerville, GA 31028; ba/Ft Valley; m/Mary Jean Moore; c/Keary Deron, LaTonya Meandrea; p/Willie (dec) and Ethel Bynum Williams, Percy, GA; ed/BS 1973; MS 1974; mil/AUS; pa/Asst Dir Fin Aid; APGA; So Assn Student Fin Aid; cp/Kappa Alpha Psi, Treas; Sr Warden F&AM; r/Bapt; hon/Outstg Yng Man Am; DIB; Notable Am Awd; W/W S&SW; Army Commend Medal; Air Medal; Vietnam Campaign & Ser Medal; Good Conduct Medal.

WILLIAMS, WYNN DIXON JR oc/Retired; b/Nov 3, 1895; h/309 S Fourth St, Union City, TN 38261; p/Wynn D Sr (dec) and Caroline Bourne Williams (dec); mil/US Inf Sgt Maj 1918; pa/Bank Cashier 23 yrs; Ofc Mgr 37 Yrs; cp/V-Mayor 8 Yrs; Chm Ration Bd BWII; r/So Bapt; hon/Comdr Am Legion; Pres Rotary Clb; Master Mason.

WILLIAMSON, LON EUGENE oc/Coal Miner and Advisor; b/Apr 22, 1951; h/Main St, Inez, KY 41224; p/Eugene and Ruth Ann Williamson, Inez, KY; ed/En Ky Univ 1969-73; pa/Small Bus Owner; cp/El Hasa Temple AAONMS; 32° York Rite Mason; Past Master Mason Hale #672; Ky JC; BPOE Lodge 1408; Alpha Theta Chi Alumni; r/Prot; hon/Master Mason Hale Lodge 672 1979-81; Wkly Column *Martin County Mercury* 1979-81.

WILLIAMSON, MARTI oc/Folksinger, Composer; b/Nov 10, 1927; h/Harrodsburg, KY; m/Forrest Jr; c/Gary N, Charles W; p/Virgil and Esther Gaynor, Hawesville, KY; ed/Bus Ed 1947; pa/Folksinger, Composer, Folk Harpist; r/U Meth.

WILLIAMSON, ROBERT oc/Student, Businessman; b/Nov 5, 1952; h/Rt 5 Box 224A, Chatham, VA 24531; ba/Radford; p/Robert M Sr and Hope T Williamson, Chatham, VA; ed/AAS Sullivan Co Commun Col; Att'g Radford Univ; pa/Owner First Flight Rest & Lounge; cp/Radford Univ Tartan Clb; Delta Phi Chapt Pi Kappa Phi, Social Chm 1978-79, Pres 1979-80; hon/Student Govt, Non-Acad Affairs Chp 1978-79; VP Student Govt Radford Univ 1979-80.

WILLIAMSON, T J oc/Teacher and Principal; b/Sept 14, 1926; h/Marshall, TX; ba/Wm B Travis Sch, 200 W Carolanne, Marshall, TX 75670; m/Joyce; c/Doug; p/J Henry (dec) and Lucy Williamson (dec); ed/BS 1950, MEd 1952 Stephen F Austin St Univ; PhD Work E Tex St Univ 1965-68; mil/USNR 1944-46; pa/Tchr Blooming Grove, Tex 1950; Elem & Jr HS Prin 1950-56; Prin William B Travis Sch 1956-; Life Mem TSTA & NEA; Marshall Ed Assn; PTA; Life Mem & Dist Pres TEPSA, Dist & St Comm; cp/Lions Clb; JCs; Optimists Clb, Pres; r/Bapt; Deacon; hon/Optimist of Yr 1970-71.

WILLIS, FLAY ALEXANDER oc/Merchant; b/Nov 22, 1914; h/Box 72, Belwood, NC 28090; m/Edna Wright; c/Margaret W Dalton, Grace W Simpson, David Alexander; p/dec; pa/Self-Employed Merchant; cp/Past Scout Master; Past Master Fallston Masonic Lodge #356 AF&AM; Treas & Chm Bldg Com Fallston Lodge #356; Past Dist Dpty Grand Master of 56 Masonic Dist of NC; 3 Times Worthy Patron OES of Fallston Chapt #282; 32nd Scottish Rite Bodies of Charlotte; S Mtn Shrine Clb; Shrine Oasis Temple of Charlotte; Upper Cleveland C of C, Pres 3 Yrs; Belwood Town Coun-man & Mayor Pro-Tem; r/U Meth; SS Tchr; SS Supt; hon/Merit Ser Awd, Fallston Masonic Lodge; Elected by Supreme Coun 33rd to Rec Knight Comdr of Ct of Hon 1979; 25 Yr Mbrship Pin, Fallston Lodge #356 1980.

WILLIS, MARTHA ELAINE ROGERS oc/Director of Teacher Education, Educational Psychologist, Assistant Professor; b/Mar 7, 1946; h/4 Merriman Ave, Inman, SC 29349; ba/Spartanburg; m/William David Jr; p/Rodeheaver Homer and Pauline Cook Rogers, Moore, SC; ed/BS 1968, MA 1969 Furman Univ; PhD Univ SC 1976; pa/Dir Tchr Ed, Assoc Dir Grad Prog in Ed, Asst Prof Ed, Converse Col 1980-; Asst Prof Psych & Ed, Shenandoah Col 1976-80; Dir Social Sers, Warren Meml Hosp 1975-78; Tchg Asst, Univ SC 1973-75; Tchr Public Schs Greenville, SC & Winchester, VA 1967-73; Delta Kappa Gamma; Soc for Hosp Social Work Dirs; AHA; hon/Furman Schlr S'ship Awd 1964-68; Co-Author *Human Behavior Reconsidered*.

WILLIS, WILLIE oc/Education Guidance Counselor; h/APO, NY; m/Rosie M; c/Willie J Jr, Timothy Wayne, Gregory Antonio, Sherita Devone, Frederick Alan; p/Oliver Sr (dec) and Annie B Willis (dec); ed/AA Daniel Payne Jr Col 1960; AB Rust Col 1965; MS Kan St Tchrs Col 1970; Work Toward PhD Columbia Pacific Univ; mil/USAF 1961-62; pa/Osceola Public Sch Sys 1965-69; Rust Col 1970-73; DOD Blytheville AFB 1973-76; DOD AF 1976-78; RAF Mildenhall, England; DOD USA 1979-80; RAF Bentwaters AFB 1980-. Instr Univ Nebraska Overseas Prog; APGA; cp/Phi Beta Sigma; VP Rust Col Alumni Assn for SW Region; hon/W/W SW Region 1980-81; Contbr to Devel of Interdisciplinary Explorations Prog for Freshman at Rust Col.

WILLISTON, FREDERICK FRANCIS oc/Senior Account Manager; b/Apr 24, 1945; h/5047 Watergate Dr, Myrtle Bch, SC 29577; ba/Myrtle Bch; m/Carol Ann Greaser; c/Matthew Charles, Samuel James, Theresa Marie; p/John D and Evelyn E Borgman Williston, Kingwood, WV; ed/BS WVU 1968; 1st Class Radio 1975; Commercial & Instrument Flying Ratings; MAI Webster Col 1980; mil/USAF 1968-73 Capt; USAFR 1975-Major; pa/AVX: Sr Acct Mgr, Prod Supvr; Sales Mgr Ocean One Sales Inc; Salesman Mutual of Omaha; Arnold Air Soc, Past Comdr; Reserve Ofcrs Assn; VFW; Air Force Assn; cp/SWITCH, Spokesman; Grand Strand Amateur Radio Clb; Repub; Adoption Assistance; r/Rom Cath: Eucharistic & Lay Ldr; hon/Dist'd Flying Cross w 2 OLCs; Air Medal 26 Clusters; Vietnam Cross of Gallantry w Palm; Others; Mem MENZA.

WILLMON, JESSE CONRAD oc/Minister, Educator, Consultant; b/Feb 13, 1931; h/1307 Patton Creek Dr, Birmingham, L 35226; m/Patricia Yvon Alexander; c/David Randolph, Stephen Douglas, Walter Jonathan, Richard Mark; p/Otto Clifford (dec) and Lura Mae Willmon, Northport, AL; ed/BS 1957, MA 1970, PhD 1975 Univ Ala; MMin So Bapt Theol Sem 1960; mil/USAF 1951-55; pa/Missionary Edr to Middle East; Ednl Conslt to Govts of Libya, Jordan, Egypt, Lebanon & Syria & to USAF in Turkey; Prof Higher Ed Adm, Univ Ala; Min U Meth Ch; Conslt Middle E; Phi Delta Kappa; Kappa Delta Pi; Middle East Studies Assn of N Am; r/U Meth; hon/Hon Charter Mem Arab Mus Coun, Leag of Arab Sts; Author Num Profl Articles.

WILLS, SHIRLEY ANN oc/Director of News and Information; b/Sept 22, 1950; h/San Antonio, TX; ba/Univ Tex-San Antonio; News and Info Ofc, San Antonio, TX 78285; p/Mary Rose Wills, San Antonio, TX; ed/BA w Hons Trinity Univ 1973; pa/Dir News & Info, Univ Tex-San Antonio 1978-; Info Writer Univ Tex-San Antonio 1976-78; Mktg Coor, Frost Nat Bank 1974-76; Spec Events Coor, Joske's 1973-76; San Antonio Chapt Wom in Communs Inc, Pres, VP, Secy; San Antonio Chapt Intl Assn Bus Communs Inc, VP; Tex Public Relats Assn, Conf Co-Chm; cp/San Antonio Area Coun Girl Scouts Inc, Public Relats Com; San Antonio Conserv Soc; U Way, Allocation Panel Mem; hon/Awds from Intl Assn Bus Commrs, San Antonio Chapt 1978-80; Outstg Yng Wom Am 1978; Wom in Communs Hdliner 1981; Yng Careerist, San Antonio BPW Clb 1981; Ldrship San Antonio.

WILSON, ANDGELIA PROCTOR oc/Businesswoman; b/Oct 7, 1946; h/1209 Normandy Rd, Macon, GA 31210; ba/Macon; m/Robert L; c/Lori Leigh; p/H A and Minnie Proctor, Macon, GA; ed/BA Wesleyan Col; pa/Co-Owner Brown's Bookstore; ABA; cp/Gdn Clb Hist; Lic'd Real Est Agt; Active in Sch & Ch Work; r/Meth.

WILSON, BOYD CECIL SR oc/Retail Hardware; b/Mar 26, 1920; h/Hudson, NC; m/June Virginia Abernathy; c/Boyd Cecil Jr, Bennie Cynthia W Carpenter; p/Marvin A (dec) and Ethel M Wilson (dec); ed/Att'd Clevenger Bus Col 1949; mil/WWII; pa/Mgr & Co-Owner Wilson & Abernathy Hardware Co & Hudson Hardware & Supply; Dir Granite Savings & Loan; cp/Chm Caldwell Solid Conserv; Hudson Plan'g Bd; Hudson Lions Clb, Past Pres, Past Zone Chm, Past Dpty Dist Gov; r/U Meth; hon/Lion of Yr 1973-74, 69; Fdrs Day PTA Hudson Elem, Hudson Man of Yr 1972; L A Sysart Citizenship Awd.

WILSON, D TERRY oc/Pastor; b/July 28, 1946; h/2704 Cindy, Big Spring, TX 79720; ba/Big Spring; m/Linda; c/Kimberly Kay; p/Leroy and Eunice Wilson, Midland, TX; ed/BS SWn Assems of God Col 1968; pa/Pastor Evangel Temple Assem of God Ch; Former Pastor First Assem of God, Bluejacket, Okla; Pers Mgr N Park Joske's Store; Employment Recruiter, Collins Radio; r/Assem of God.

WILSON, DAROTHY LOUYSE oc/Property Officer; b/Feb 25, 1918; h/3845 Nichols Blvd, Jackson, MS 39212; ba/Jackson; p/Joe C (dec) and Annie Wilson (dec); pa/Property Ofcr; cp/Mus Natural Sci Foun; r/Bapt; hon/W/W Am Wom.

WILSON, DURWARD EARL (WILL) oc/Executive; b/Sept 23, 1925; h/Rt Worth, TX; ba/3901 Hemphill St, Ft Worth, TX 76110; m/Sara Ann; p/Sam and Eunice Scoggins Wilson; ed/BS Ga Inst Technol 1950; mil/USAC 1943-46; pa/I E DuPont Co Chattanooga, Tenn 1950-54, Div Prodn Assit, Wilmington, Del 1954-56; Sr Mgmt Conslt, John M Avent & Assn 1956-58; Tex Steel Co: Plan'g Mgmt 1958-59, Asst VP 1959-66, VP 1966-72, Exec VP 1972-75, Pres 1975-; Chm of Bd & Pres Tex Steel Co of Can Ltd; Pres, Dir: L & M Mfg Co, Steel Casting Machine Co, SW Steel Casting Co, Bus Commun Inc; Dir Liberty Mfg Co, Tex & Armstrong Oil & Land Co, Natchez, Miss; Bd Dirs: Steel Fdrs Soc Am, Cast Metals Fed, Nat Foundrymen Assn; Pres SFSA; Chm Tex Govt Affairs of Cast Metals Fed; Chm Envirl Com CMF; r/Epis.

WILSON, EUNICE IDELLA oc/Funeral Director; b/June 28, 1920; h/1110 Pine Ave, Sanford, FL 32771; p/Thomas Sr (dec) and Gussie L Wilson, Sanford, FL; ed/Deg Mortuary Sci, NY Sch Embalming & Restorative Arts 1939; Embalmer's Lic 1943; Funeral Dir's Lic 1944; pa/Owner, Mortician/Funeral Dir Wilson-Eichelberger Mortuary; Exec Bd Fla Morticians Assn; Past Pres Orange, Osceola & Seminole Co Funeral Dir's Assn; Treas 4th Regional Dist Fla Morticians Assn; cp/Sanford C of C; Alpha, Gamma, Epsilon Nu Delta; Nat Funeral Dirs Assn; NAACP, Seminole Co Chapt; Adv Coun Seminole Commun Col; Devel Div Daughs of Elks; OES; r/Allen Chapel AME Ch; hon/Mortician of Yr.

WILSON, GINNY oc/Teacher; b/Jan 26, 1951; h/Rt 1, Highland Home, Al 36041; ba/Highland Home; p/Charlie (dec) and Florelle Wilson, Highland Home, AL; ed/BS Troy St Univ 1972; MEd Auburn Univ 1976; Sixth Yr Cert Auburn Univ 1978; Psychometrist Lic 1978; pa/Elem Tchr 1972-80; Student Cnslr, Neuropsychi Unit, Farview Med Ctr 1978; Student Cnslr, Div of Cont'g Ed, Auburn Univ 1979; Student Cnslr Pre-Trial Diversion Prog, Montgomery DA Ofc 1979-80; NEA; AEA; Crenshaw Co Ed Assn; APGA; Col Student Pers Assn; ALPGA; Ala Sch Cnslrs Assn; Fac Rep AEA; Alpha Delta Kappa; cp/Dem Party; Highland Home PTO; r/Ch of Christ; hon/W/W S&SW 1980-81.

WILSON, GREGORY BRUCE oc/Associate Professor; b/Oct 15, 1948; h/2706 Cameron Blvd, Isle of Palms, SC 29451; ba/Charleston, SC; p/Bruce Norman and Miriam Joyce Wilson, Santa Ana, CA; ed/BA 1971, PhD 1974 UCLA; pa/Res Asst Dept Biol, UCLA 1972; Res Asst, Dept Microbiol & Immunol, Sch of Med UCLA 1973-75; Res Asst, Dept Biol, UCLA 1973-74; Nat Cystic Fibrosis Res Foun Res Fellow 1974; NCFRF Res Fellow & Postdoct Schlr, Sect of Immunol, Dept Med, UCSF 1974-75; Dept Basic & Clin Immunol & Microbiol, Cols of Med & Dental Med, Med Univ SC: Assoc 1975-76, Asst Prof 1976-79, Assoc Prof 1979-; Med Adv Bd Nat Foun Mar of Dimes 1977-; Med Adv Bd Cystic Fibrosis Foun, Chm 1979-80, V-Chm 1980-; Bd Dirs Cystic Fibrosis Foun 1979-; Exec Bd Mem SC Coun of Indep Hlth Orgs 1980-; Mem Molecular, Cellular Biol Patholbiol Fac 1979-; AAAS; Sigma Xi; Soc Exptml Biol & Med; Reticuloendothelial Soc; NY Acad Scis; Am Fed Clin Res; hon/Res Fellow Nat Cystic Fibrosis Foun 1974-76; Basil O'Connor Grant Awdee, Nat Foun Mar of Dimes 1976-79; W/W S&SW 1980; Author Num Profl Publs.

WILSON, HOWARD ALEXANDER oc/Automobile Dealer; b/Feb 10, 1927; h/5154 Sunnyvale Dr, Jackson, MS 39211; ba/Jackson; m/Joy; c/Phillip Russell, Joy Kathryn, Howard Alan, Charles Douglas; p/George A (dec) and Katie V Wilson, Jackson, MS; ed/BS Univ So Miss; mil/AUS 1944-46; pa/Mgr Used Car Dept 1953-57, Fowler Buick Co; VP Fowler Buick Co 1962-79; Pres Howard Wilson Chrysler-Plymouth 1979-; Pres 4 Auto Auction 1957-62; Pres Howard Wilson Motor Co 1957-62; Pres Big V Used Car Sales Mgrs Assn; VP-Dir Jackson Sales & Mktg Execs; Dir Jackson Apt Owners Assn; Miss Auto Dlrs Assn; cp/Tchr Proj Bus,

Jackson Public Schs 1975-76; Jackson C of C; BBB; Bd Dirs Pitt-Greenville C of C; Treas Pitt Co Dem Party; Pitt Co-City of Greenville Plan'g & Zoning Comm; r/Bapt; hon/Appt'd by Gov James B Hunt Jr to Gov's Adv Com on Agric, Forestry & Seafood Indust; Outstg Mem Jackson S&ME 1975; W/W Fin & Indust; Most Outstg Vol 1980, Pitt-Greenville C of C.

WILSON, HOWARD NELSON oc/Retired Manager; b/Jan 14, 1919; h/Greenville, NC; ba/PO Box 505, Greenville, NC 27834; m/Frances Corley; c/Mrs Eugene W Moore; Mrs Michael McDaniel; p/Mrs Harry E Wilson, Athens, GA; ed/BSAE Univ Ga 1949; BA Univ Balto 1951; mil/USAF 6 Yrs; Ret'd USAFR 1969 Col; pa/SEn Sales Mgr, Intl Minerals & Chem Sorp; Am Soc Agric Engrs; cp/Pres Exch Clb of Greenville; V-Chm Coastal Plains Chapt Ser Corps of Ret'd Execs; Bd Dirs So Flue-Cured Tobacco; G'ville Area C of C: Cong Action Com, St Concerns Com, Local Concerns Com, Agri-Bus Com, Mbrship Com, ECU-City of G'ville Com; Active in St & Local Dem Party; Spec Gifts Chm Pitt Co U Way; ECU Pirate Clb; Brook Val Golf & Country Clb; Mason; Sudan Temple Shrine; r/Bapt.

WILSON, JACQUES MARCEL PATRICK oc/Executive Director; b/Aug 4, 1920; h/5533 Alhambra Cir, Coral Gables, FL 33146; ba/Miami; m/Clotilde Tavares de Lima; c/Jacqueline M W Martin, James F T, Alfred R T, John P T, Gregory B T, Guy M T; p/James F T (dec) and Simone M E Wilson, Miami, FL; ed/AB 1952, MEd 1960 Univ Miami; PD Univ Tex 1966; mil/USAAC & USAF 1942-57 Capt; pa/Exec Dir, Miami Intl Inst Technol Transfer 1980-; Dir & Conslt on Biling Ed, Curric Design & Intl Ed, Jacaranda Enterprises 1977-; Conslt Fgn Lang & Biling Ed, St of Fla 1975-77; Asst Dir Admissions for Latin Ams, Univ Miami 1977-80; Asst Prov for Intl Progs, Univ W Fla 1972-75; Chm Fgn Lang, Univ W Fla 1970-72; Asst Dir Inst Inter-Am Studies, Univ Miami 1967-70; Chm Fgn Langs, Our Lady of the Lake Col; So Conf on Lang Tchg; MLA; Am Assn Tchrs of Span & Portuguese; Fla Fgn Lang Assn; r/Cath; hon/W/W Am Ed; DIB; Intl Schlrs Dir; W/W Fla 1974; Commun Ldrs & Noteworthy Ams; Contemporary Author 1975; Men of Achmt; Author Num Profl Pubs; Iron Arrow, Univ Miami 1941; 4 Fulbright Comm Vis'g Prof'ships.

WILSON, JUANITA MARIE SANDGREN oc/Teacher; b/Sept 10, 1950; h/830 Ventnor Dr, Newport News, VA 23602; ba/Hampton; m/Thomas Edwin; p/Walter Harold and Gertrude Brunner Sandgren, New Hyde Pk, NY; ed/BS SUNY-Cortland; MS Univ Okla; pa/Tchr of Hearing Inpaired Chd, Hampton; Dept Chm Prog for Hearing Impaired; cp/Former Girl Scout Ldr; r/Luth; hon/Hampton Rd JCs Tchr of Yr Finalist 1978; Fed Stipend Grant to Lexington Sch for Deaf Infant Tng Prog; W/W Child Devel Profls.

WILSON, LINDA C oc/Director; b/June 7, 1949; h/805 S Ouida St, Enterprise, AL 35330; ba/Enterprise; m/Roger; p/Mervis D Coon, Opp, Al; ed/MS 1972, BS 1970, AA 1969; pa/Dir Career Devel Ctr & Job Placement, Enterprise St Jr Col; Proj Dir, Displaced Homemaker Resource Ctr, Enterprise St Jr Col 1979-; Coor Coop Ed & Bus Instr, Enterprise St Jr Col 1973-76; Ednl Cnslr, Army Ed Ctr 1973; Eng Tchr, Enterprise Jr HS 1971-73; Elem Sch Tchr, New Brockton, AL 1970-71; Am Voc Assn; Ala Assn Wom in Commun & Jr Cols; Ala Jr & Commun Col Assn; VP/Pres Elect New & Related Sers Sect Ala Voc Assn; cp/Chp Enterprise HS Voc Ed Coun; r/Bapt; hon/Grad magna cum laude Troy St Univ 1970; W/W Students in Am Jr Cols 1969; Co-Author Opers Manual 1979.

WILSON, LOUISE LOEFFLER oc/Senior Economist; b/May 15, 1931; h/704 S Pitt St, Alexandria, VA 22314; ba/Wash DC; c/Kenneth Taft, Lesley Louise; p/Emil F (dec) and Hilda Beck Loeffler; ed/BA Chatham Col 1952; pa/Actuary, Marsh & McLennan, Boston & Pgh 1952-53, 57-58; Freelance Writer 1953-54, 58-59; Asst Dir, Acting Dir Public Relats, Chatham Col 1955-57; Budget Analyst, Allstate Ins 1960-61; Dir Pubs & Res Assn Foun for Study Cycles 1961-66; Info Retrieval Spec, Univ Pgh 1967; Coor Info Ctr Alcoa 1967-76, Intl Forecaster 1969-76, Fin Analyst 169-76, Assoc Economist 1976-; Nat Ec Clb; Soc of Gut Ecs; Coun of Ams; Nat Assn Mfrs; Bus Roundtable; Nat Assn Bus Ecs; US C of C; Am Coun for Capital Formation; Fed Statistics Users Conf; Nat Acad Arts & Scis; cp/Chatham Col Bd Trustees 1975-78; Chatham Col Alumnae Assn, Exec Coun; Exec Woms Coun of Gtr Pgh, Fdg Mem; r/Presb; hon/Contbr to Profl Jours.

WILSON, MARY ROSS oc/Nurse; b/Feb 18, 1932; h/2339 Kensington Rd, Macon, GA 31211; ba/Macon; m/Carl T; c/Stephen Ross, David Carl; p/Ottis Holt (dec) and Litsey Isley Ross, Burlington, NC; ed/RN Macon Hosp Sch Nsg 1953; Cert'd OR Nurse 1980; pa/Macon Hosp: Staff Nurse OR 1953-56, Hd Nurse OR 1956-70, Supvr OR 1970-; Coliseum Park Hosp: Supvr Surg Dept 1970-79, Dir Surg Dept 1979-;

Macon Hosp Alumni Assn, Pres 1967-71; Adj Instr, Ga Col 1975-76; Mem Panels OR Assn OR Nurses, Pres Middle Ga Chapt 1978; OR Buying Ser; SEn Surg Nurse Assn; Profl Advr Mid Ga Chapt Assn OR Techs 1971-78; Del to AORN Cong 1975, 76, 78; cp/Riverside Golf & Country Clb; DAR; r/Meth; hon/Coliseum Park Hosp Employee of Yr 1972; W/W S&SW 1980.

WILSON, NANCY CAROL oc/Associate Professor; b/July 11, 1940; h/Univ Hgts, Apt #8, Talbert Dr, Hopkinsville, KY 42240; ba/H'ville; p/John C and Lille C Wilson, Atoka, TN; ed/BBA, MEd Memphis St Univ; pa/Assoc Prof & Coor Secy Adm Prog, Univ Ky-H'ville Commun Col; Intl Soc Bus Ed; Nat Bus Ed Assn, Ky St Mbrship Dir 1974-76; So Bus Ed Assn: Exec Bd, Basic Bus Sect, Commun Col Div, Secy Sect; Ky Bus Ed Assn, Exec Bd 1973-76; Delta Pi Epsilon; Nat Col Assn for Secys, Nat 1st VP 1978-80; Nat Secys Assn Intl, Admr of Cert'd Profl Secy Exam; r/Presb; hon/Outstg Yng Wom Am 1974; World W/W Wom in Ed 1977; W/W Wom in World; F'ship of Intl Biogs 1979; Great Tchr Awd, Univ of Ky-H'ville Commun Col 1977.

WILSON, NANCY FAUCETTE oc/Office Manager; b/Nov 6; h/1740 Maynard St, Henderson, NC 27536; ba/Henderson; m/Charles D; p/H B and Estelle M Faucette, Henderson, NC; ed/Att'g Univ NC; pa/Nat Fed BPW Clb, Leg Chm 4 Yrs, St Leg Com, VP 1977; Am Auto Racers, Writers & Broadcasters Assn 1974-78; Sports Staff *Auto Sports Weekly* 1970-77; Drove Race Car 1964-73; cp/Org'd Coun on Status of Wom, Vance Co 1977; Org'd Rape Crisis Grp, Vance Co 1977; St Sexual Assault Com; Org'd Animal Shelter Com; Org'd Vance Co Humane Soc, Bd Mem & Publicity Chm; Animal Control Adv Com, Vance Co; Precinct Chm 7 Yrs; Del to Dist & St Dem Convs; Co Nom'g Com Chm Dem Party 1977; Co-Chm Congressman L H Fountain in Co 3 Terms; Chm Vance Co Dem Party; Co Co-Chm Carter-Mondale Re-Elect Com; Org'd Vance Co Dem Woms Clb; Get Out the Vote Supvr 1980; St Dem Exec Com; r/Meth; hon/Wom of Yr 1977, Henderson BPW Clb.

WILSON, ONIE MAE oc/Teacher; b/Sept 8, 1930; h/Rt 1 Box 786, Washington, TX 77880; m/Earl; c/Donald Kirk and Dennis Craig; p/Ed (dec) and Ola Mae Ewing, Washington, TX; ed/BS 1952, MEd 1957 Prairie View Univ; Add'l Studies Tex So Univ, Univ Houston, Col of the Mainland, Tex A&M Univ; pa/Tchr Brenham Elem Sch 26 Yrs; Tchr Adult & GED Classes, Brenham St Sch 14 Yrs; NEA; Tex St Tchrs Assn, Life Mem; Tex Clrm Assn; Brenham Clrm Assn; Local Pres TSTA, Secy, Treas, Del to Nat, St Dist 15 Yrs; Chm to Dist TSTA Audit Com; Local Leg Chp 1980; cp/Brenham Civic Clb; Am Legion; Sigma Chi Chi; Washington Co 4-H Coun; r/AME; hon/Certs of Hon 1972-80; Convocation Dir Paul Quinn Col 1972-80; Instr Chd's Min 1972-80; Cert Merit 8th Quadrennial Conv Wkshops 1975; Cert Merits for Tchg Techniques of Adults 1972; Many Certs & Awds for Commun Projs; Tchr of Yr, Brenham Indep Sch Dist 1975; Outstg Citizen Awd, Black Hist Mo 1981; Noted Spkr & Lectr 1972-81.

WILSON, PAUL E oc/Osteopathic Physician; ba/19 SE Wenona Ave, Ocala, FL 32670; m/Elta F Metcalfe; c/Paul E Jr; ed/Grad KCOS 1935; Intern Laughlin & KCOS Hosps; pa/Pract Bartow, Fla 1935-42 & Ocala, Fla 1942-; FOMA, Pres 1954-55; AOA: Pres 1974-75, Ho of Dels 1954-71, 2nd & 3rd VP, Bd Trustees 1968-77; Past Pres KCOS Alumni Assn; KCOM Bd Trustees 1964-73, V-Chm 1973; Past Chm Fla Am Acad Osteopathy; Past Pres Am Acad Osteopathy; cp/Charter Mem Silver Springs Lions Clb: Past Pres, Zone Chm, Dpty Dist Gov; FAA Examr 1964-80; Masonic Lodge; Elks Lodge; Golden Hills Golf & Turf Clb; r/U Meth; hon/Am Acad Osteopathy Andrew Taylor Still Medallion of Hon 1980; Am Osteopathic Assn Dist'd Ser Cert 1979; FOMA Dist'd Ser Awd 1965; FOMA Gen Pract of Yr Awd 1968.

WILSON, PAULETTA M oc/Instructor; b/June 14, 1949; h/Rt 2 Box 289, Catlettsburg, KY 41129; ba/Huntington, WV; m/Gene A; c/Mark W; p/Paul Matovich, Prichard, WV; Mary Stafford, Ashland, KY; ed/AB, MBA Marshall Univ; pa/Instr Marshall Univ; Coor Wom in Bus Sem 1978 & 79; r/Prot; hon/Most Outstg Student Tchr 1974-75; W/W Am Wom 1979-80.

WILSON, SANDRA JEAN oc/Educational Parent Coordinator; b/May 3, 1950; h/1304 Marlin Ct, Bay City, TX 77414; ba/Bay City; m/William Garfield; c/Holly Ann; p/Clarence L and Ann I McClain, Cleveland, OH; ed/EdB Ohio Univ 1972; MEd Cleveland St Univ 1979; pa/Title I Parent Coor, Bay City Indep Sch Dist 1979-; Rdg Tchr, Proj CARE Title VII, Warrensville Hghts Bd Ed 1978-79; Spec Emphasis Proj, Rdg Spec, Cleveland Bd Ed 1976-78; Lang Arts Conslt, J B Lippincott Co 1974-76; Elem Tchr, Cleveland Bd Ed 1972-74; Assn Compensatory Edrs of Tex; Delta Kappa Gamma; Phi Delta Kappa; r/Meth.

WILSON, SANDRA SCOTT oc/Genealogist; b/Apr 30, 1943; h/Rt 6 Box 10, Arrowhead Rd, Indian Hills Sub-Div, Alex City, AL 35010; m/Robert Earl; c/William Gregory, Robert Glen, Susanne Alayne;

PERSONALITIES OF THE SOUTH

p/William Emmitt and Mary A Harris Scott, Alex City, AL; ed/Grad Patricia Stevens Bus & Fashion Col 1961; LaSalle Ext Univ; pa/Former Exec Secy; Geneal; Tallapoosa Co Hist Soc; Geneal Soc of E Ala; cp/Former BPW Clb; Former Cub Scout Ldr & Camp Fire Ldr; Bd Dirs BSA; Vol Heart Fund Assn; Bd Dirs First Presb Day Sch; r/Presb: Former Yth Dir, SS Tchr, Choir.

WILSON, SHARON C oc/Executive; b/Feb 24, 1946; h/215 Phoenetia Ave, Coral Gables, FL 33134; ba/Miami; m/John Victor; p/John R and Ruth Joan Sweeney Hendrie, Long Branch, NJ; ed/BA Fla Intl Univ 1979; pa/Exec Eastern Airlines; Miami Mgmt Coun; cp/Egyptology Soc; Inst Maya Studies; Arch Soc; Mus Sci, Miami; hon/Nat Hon Soc 1965; Ruth Kaplan Meml S'ship 1965-66; NJ St S'ship.

WILSON, SHIRLEY S oc/Football Coach; b/Sept 26, 1926; h/3309 Medford Dr, Durham, NC 27705; ba/Durham; m/Katie; c/John, Cathy, Steve; p/(dec); ed/BS Davidson Col; MEd UNC; mil/USN; pa/Hd Fball Coach, Duke Univ 1978-; Hd Recruiter & Chief Adm Asst, Hd JV Coach, Qtrback Coach, Duke Univ 1977-78; Dir Aths & Hd Fball Coach, Elon Col 1967-77; Prep Coach 1950-66; Am Fball Coaches Assn; Nat Chm Kodak Coach of Yr Awds Banquet, Am Fball Coaches Assn, 1978; Past Pres Carolinas Conf Ath Dirs & Fball Coaches; cp/Nat Dir Pop Warner Jr Leag Fball; Exec Bd BSA, Cherokee Coun; SS Tchr; F'ship Christian Aths, Pres Alamance-Burlington Chapt; Burlington Rotary Clb, Bd Dirs; U Fund Campaign Ldr; C of C "Minute Men"; YMCA Yth Basketball Coach; Co-Chm 1976 & Chm 1977 Boy Scouts "Scout-O-Rama"; r/Presb; hon/Conf Coach of Yr 1969, 71, 72, 73; Dist Coach of Yr 1971, 72, 73, 76; NC Coach of Yr 1973; Nom Nat Coach of Yr 1971, 72, 73, 76; Nat Runner-Up Coach of Yr 1973; Twice had only Undefeated Col Fball Team in NC; Kodak Coach of Yr 3 Times; Pub'd in Num Profl Jours; Hon Chm Spec Olympics.

WILSON, WILLIAM FEATHERGAIL oc/Executive; b/Dec 25, 1934; h/422 Fantasia, San Antonio, TX 78216; ba/San Antonio; m/Elizabeth Gail Harmison; c/Douglas Hord, Clayton Hill, Wendy Elanore; p/Glenn Caldwell and Marion Hord Wilson; ed/BA 1957, BS w Hons 1960, MA 1962 Univ Tex-Austin; pa/Dept Geol, Univ Tex 1958-61; Texaco Inc 1961-65; El Paso Natural Gas Co 1965-66; Indep Petro Geologist, Rancher, Real Est Exec 1966-70; Envirl Geologist, Alamo Area Coun Govts 1970; Acct Exec, Merrill Lynch Fenner & Smith 1970-74; Sr Exploration Geologist, Tesoro Petro Corp 1974; Exploration Mgr, Placid Oil Co 1978-; Instr, Geol, Univ Tex 1976-; Am Assn Petro Geologists; Geological Soc Am; Assn Profl Geological Scists; S Tex Geol Soc, Pres & Editor Bltn 1976-; AAAS; Sigma Gamma Epsilon.

WIMBERLY, C W JR oc/Physician; b/Oct 12, 1943; h/119 President Cir, Summerville, SC 29483; ba/S'ville; m/Patricia; c/Christopher William, Jason Andrew, Mark Patrick; p/Clarence and Alma Wimberly, St George, SC; ed/BS Wofford Col; MD 1969, Fam Pract Res 1969-72, Med Univ SC; mil/USAF 1972-74; pa/Pres Summerville Fam Pract; AMA; Am Acad Fam Phys; cp/Sertoma Clb; Mason; r/Meth; hon/W/W 1980; C of C Bd 1979; Author "Comparative Profiles of Residency Training and Family Practice" 1974.

WIMBERLY, GEORGE TERRANCE oc/Security, Cattleman; b/Feb 23, 1930; h/Rt 5 Box 227, Marianna, FL 32460; ba/Sneads, FL; m/Zacqueline E; c/Stepchd: Bill Wester, Tamaria Joyner; p/J E (dec) and Edna Ball Wimberly (dec); mil/USAF 4 Yrs; pa/Security Dept, St of Fla; Cattleman; Pt-time Farmer; cp/Deacon, E-side Bapt Ch; Am-Intl Charolais Assn; Fla-Ga Charolais Assn; NW Fla Charolais Assn; Fla Cattlemen; r/Bapt; Ordained Deacon 1955.

WINDHAM, MAUD BYRD oc/Retired Teacher; b/Dec 20, 1906; h/231 Forrest Ave, Enterprise, AL 36330; m/Ben K (dec); p/Ed (dec) and Erie Hildreth Byrd (dec); ed/BS Troy St Tchrs Col; pa/Ret'd Tchr Jr HS Math; Del NEA Conv, La 1960; NEA; AEA; Pres Dale Co Tchrs Assn 1960-61; cp/Nat Defense Chm, DAR, Ozark Chapt 1976-79; Sponsor Hist Marker in Daleville 1958; Charter Mem: Dale Co Hist Soc, Pea River Hist & Geneal Soc, Ft Rucker Hist Soc; Ala Hist Assn; Widows of WWI Vets; DAR; Public Spkr on Local Hist & Bible; r/Meth; Cert'd Lay Spkr; hon/Best Wom Citizen of Daleville 1955; Author Hist Daleville, Ala 1957; New Math S'ship SW Mo St Col 1959; Incl'd in *Our Yester Years*, Bicent of Ret'd Tchrs of Ala 1976.

WINGATE, MARTHA LLOYCE MASTERS oc/Supervisor Nursing Service; b/Nov 12, 1937; h/PO Box 283, Gatesville, TX 76528; ba/Waco; m/Vernon Whedbee; c/Regena, Yana S; p/T H and Naomi Kelly Masters, Anadarko, OK; ed/AAS Ctrl Tex Col 1974; pa/RN, Supvr Nsg Ser Hillcrest Bapt Meml Hosp; Am Soc Evening & Night Supvrs, Charter Mem; cp/Charter Mem Caryall Co Child Wel Bd; Fdr & Conslt Parents Anonymous, Copperas Co, Tex; r/Bapt; hon/Hon Grad,

WINKLER, PHILLIP BLAIR oc/Assistant Professor; b/Mar 17, 1940; h/2122 Starlight Dr, Dyersburg, TN 38024; ba/D'burg; m/Mary Linda; c/Linda Adrienne; p/Clemens Winkler (dec); Lily Nash, Belleville, IL; ed/BS So Ill Univ; MA NE Mo Univ; Att'g Middle Tenn St Univ; pa/Asst Prof Hist; Chm Fac Assem 1977-79; Fac Rep to St Bd Regents; Bicent Com

for D'burg St Commun Col; Chm SS Div 1971-72; cp/Lions Clb Intl; W Tenn Amateur Retrievers Clb; r/Ch of Jesus Christ of Latter Day Saints; hon/Outstg Fac-Staff Mem of Yr 1978-79; Kappa Delta Pi; Phi Alpha Theta.

WINNINGHAM, ROBERT CARL oc/Counselor; b/Mar 1, 1948; h/Goldsboro, NC 27530; ba/G'boro; p/Ann Winningham, Colo Springs, CO; ed/AAS El Paso Commun Col 1971; Cont'g Ed Pikes Peak Col, Colo Univ, ECU; pa/Cnslr Wayne Commun Col; Hist Res; Smithsonian Inst Res Assoc; Lic'd Nat Archives; cp/Wayne Co Hist Soc; Sons of Confed; Mayflower Descs; Yng Dems; BSA; r/Rom Cath; hon/Contbr to *North South Trader; Civil War Times Illus'd*.

WINSTEAD, MELINDA RUTH KEYES oc/Teacher; b/Oct 6, 1952; h/220 E Ch St, Quitman, MS 39355; ba/Q'man; m/Ricky Norman; p/Robert Webber Sr (dec) and Peggy H Keyes, Hattiesburg, MD; ed/BA William Carey Col 1973; MS Univ So Miss 1975; pa/Eng Tchr; MCTE; cp/Lambda Iota Tau; Mar of Dimes & Heart Fund Campaigns; r/Bapt; hon/Pres Alpha Lambda; Alpha Chi; Lambda Iota Tau; SMEA; Danforth Foun S'ship Nom; Grad magna cum laude William Carey Col 1973.

WINTER, KATIE MARILYN CALDWELL oc/Attorney, Teacher; b/Apr 18, 1940; h/2811 Dunnwood Ln, Acworth, GA 30101; ba/Marietta; c/Joseph Clayton McDaniel Jr, James Caldwell McDaniel; p/Jacob J Sr and Kathryn Winter Caldwell; ed/BS Livingston Univ 1962; JD Woodrow Wilson Col 1974; pa/NEA; GEA; NCTE; Am Bar Assn, Energy Resource Law Com: V-Chm 1978-79, Chm 1979-80; cp/Bd Dirs Roger Ascham Acad; BSA Troop 637: Bd Dirs, Secy-Treas; r/Presb; hon/Outstg Alumni Assn Awd 1976, Woodrow Wilson Col Law; Outstg Yng Wom Am 1977; W/W: Am Wom 1979, Am Law 1979; Recip Golden Key Awd, Livingston Univ 1979.

WINTERS, JAMES MICHAEL oc/Pastor; b/Oct 24, 1979; h/Rt 5 Box 390, Somerset, KY 42501; ba/Same; m/Kathy Ann Ball; c/Melissa Ann, Rebecca Michelle; p/James Mermon and Elizabeth Willie Wilson Winters, Gainesville, GA; ed/Cert Achmt in Bible; mil/USANG; r/So Bapt.

WIRTZ, ADELE WATSON oc/Retired; b/Sept 15, 1893; h/1801 Lavaca St, Austin, TX 78701; m/L M (dec); c/Virginie W Shepperd; p/David Hughes (dec) and Nona Watson (dec); ed/BA Univ Tex; Further Study Univ Houston, Univ NH; pa/Tchr 4 Yrs; City Sales Desk, Maxwell House Coffee, Houston; r/Epis; hon/Var Prizes for Poetry.

WISEMAN, BERNARD oc/Illustrator, Author, Cartoonist; b/Aug 26, 1922; h/Melbourne, FL; m/Susan Nadine; c/Andrew Lee, Michael Avrom, Peter Franklin; p/Abraham Zalman (dec) and Yetta Leah Wiseman (dec); ed/Art Sch 1946-48; New Sch for Social Res 1946-48; mil/USCG WWII; pa/Author-Illustr Chd's Books; Cartoonist; r/Hebrew; hon/Cartoons for *New Yorker, Punch* & Other Major Pubs; Author for *Boy's Life* 1947-59.

WISHARD, BETTY J oc/Executive; b/Oct 12, 1948; h/New Orleans, LA; ba/New Orleans; p/George L and Helen Pijut, Southfield, MI; ed/BS Mich St Univ 1971; pa/Asst VP & Dir Tng & Devel, Hibernia Nat Bank, New Orleans 1978-; Conslt: Am Soc Tng & Devel, Assn of Multi-Image, Nat Assn Bank Wom & Am Mgmt Assn; Mktg Rep, Venez Regardez; Nat Sem Ldr, Nat Assn Bank Wom, Ednl Foun 1977-; Bank Ednl Advr, NABW Deg Prog for Wom, LSU 1978-; Mgr Sales, Commun & Human Relats Tng, No Trust Bank, Chgo, Ill 1975-78; Tng Dir Charles A Stevens Stores, Chgo 1971-75; Nat Assn Bank Wom; Am Inst Bnkg; Bank Adm Inst; Am Soc Tng & Devel; Assn Multi-Image; Intl Platform Assn; Am Soc Profl & Exec Wom; Bankers Spec Interest Grp ASTD Nat Conv: Nat Co-Chp 1979, Nat Chp 1980; cp/Bd Dirs Local Chapt Am Soc Tng & Devel: Chp Local Job & Talent Inventory Com, Co-Chp Affirmative Action Com; Bd Dirs Martha Washington Home for Dependent Crippled Chd, Chd's Hosp, Chgo 1977-78; Judge, Cook Co, Chgo 1972; hon/W/W: Am Wom, S&SW; Hon Chp Mason Dorm, Mich St Univ 1970; Ofcr Retailing Clb 1970-71; Author.

WISSEL, MARK EDWARD oc/Business Manager; b/Aug 23, 1952; h/F-S Rock Creek Apts, Dothan, AL 36303; ba/Dothan; p/Joseph and Mary C Wissell, Daleville, AL; ed/BS Bus Ed/Computer Sci; pa/Bus Mgr; Ala Voc Assn; Am Voc Assn; Ala Manpower Tng Assn; Phi Beta Lambda; Nat Employment Tng Assn; cp/Jr C of C; Conslt Dothan Adult & Commun Ed; Indust Relats Adv Com; r/Cath; hon/SE Ala Employee of Yr; VFW Essay Winner; Hon Mem Quill & Scroll; Nat Hon Soc; W/W Am Col Students.

WITHERSPOON, EVERETTE LEVON oc/Administrator and Professor; b/Feb 8, 1941; h/146 Oak Pk Dr, Nashville, TN 37207; ba/Nashville; m/Ida; c/Everette Jr, Chris; p/Johnny and Mary Witherspoon, Durham, NC; ed/BS; MS; EdD; pa/Prof Ed, Admr, Tenn St Univ; TEA; Phi Delta Kappa; NEA; ASCD; TASCD; TAMS; Ednl Conslt; cp/Former Pres Nashville Clb of Frontier Intl; r/Congreg Ch; hon/External Ser Awd for Dist'd Commun Ser; Outstg Ser Awd, Frontier Intl.

PERSONALITIES OF THE SOUTH

WITTMER, JAMES FREDERICK oc/Administrator, Executive; b/Dec 30, 1932; h/2304 Woodthrush, Ponca City, OK 74601; ba/Ponca City; m/Juanita; c/Ellen, Carol, Nancy; p/Eva C Wittmer, Bowling Green, KY; ed/Pre-Med Mich Technol Univ 1950-51 & Wash Univ 1951-53; MD cum laude Wash Univ Sch Med 1957; Internship Univ Va Hosp 1957-78; Res Fellow, Wash Univ Sch Med 1954-56; MPH Harvard Sch Public Hlth 1961; Primary Course in Aviation Med, Randolph AFB 1958; Aerospace Med Spec Tng Prog, USAF Sch of Aerospace Med 1960-63; Grad USAF Squadron Ofcrs Sch 1963; Grad Air Command & Staff Sch 1968; Att'd Num Short Courses & Symposia; mil/USAF 1958-70 Col; pa/USAF Aerospace Med Spec & Admr 1958-79; Dean Sch of Allied Hlth Scis, Univ Tex Hlth Scis Ctr, San Antonio 1979-80; Asst Med Dir, Conoco Inc 1980-81; Mobil Oil Corp, Med Dept 1981-; Diplomate, Am Bd Preventive Med, Aerospace Med 1965; Alpha Omega Alpha; Am Col Phys; Am Col Preven Med; Delta Omega; Fellow Aerospace Med Assn: Ed & Tng Com, Constitution & By-Laws Com; AMA: Com on Allied Hlth Ed & Accred, Chm Mil Subcom; TMA; Bexas Co Med Soc; Am Soc Allied Hlth Professions 1979; Aerospace Med Assn, San Antonio Chapt Secy 1964-65; r/Prot; hon/C V Mosby Scholastic Excell Awd, Class of 1957, Wash Univ Sch Med; Alpha Omega Alpha; Delta Omega; Fellow Am Col Preven Med; FACP; Fellow Aerospace Med Assn; AMA Cont'g Ed Awds 1969, 72, 75, 78; W/W S&SW 1975-; Author Sev Profl Articles Incl'g "Definition of Space Flight Medical Kits: A Rationale" *Aerospace Medical Division* 1967 & "Flying Mission of FACAF Physiology Unit" *USAF Medical Service Digest*, 1973.

WITTNER, TED PHILIP oc/General Agent, Chairman of the Board; b/Sept 17, 1928; h/PO Box 13029, St Petersburg, FL 33733; ba/St P'burg; m/Sylvia Heller (dec), 2nd Jean Giles; c/Sharyn W Jacobson, Pamela Anne; p/(dec); ed/BS Univ Fla 1950; mil/USAF 1950-53 2nd Lt; pa/Mgr Bell Luggage Co 1953-54; Pvt Life Ins Agt 1955-56; Gen Agt Crown Life Ins Co 1956-64; Pres Ted P Wittner & Assocs, St P'burg 1964-67; Chm of Bd & Pres, Wittner & Co 1968-; Mng Gen Agt, Crown Life Ins Co 1964-; Profl Ofc Ctr Develr 1966-; Chm Profit Progs Co, St P'burg 1969-76; Dir Para-Med Enterprises Inc, St P'burg 1971-74; Chm of Bd (1974-75), Dir Nat Trust Bank of St P'burg 1970-75; Chm of Bd, Pinellas Bank, St P'burg 1976-; Fdg Mem & Past Pres St P'burg Gen Agts & Mgrs Assn; Nat Assn Life Underwriters; Qualifying & Life Mem Million Dollar Round Table; Mem & Past Pres Crown Life Brokerage Gen Agts Assn; Assoc Mem Urban Land Inst, Wash DC; Fla Ins Exch Devel Com 1979; Bd Govs Ins Exch of Ams; cp/Dir & Past Pres Commerce Clb of Pinellas Co; Dir & Past VP St P'burg Area C of C; Dir Com of 100 of Pinellas Co; Past Mem St P'burg Civic Adv Bd; Past Mem, Bd Dirs, Pinellas Assn for Retard'd Chd; Secy-Treas, Dir, Menorah Ctr Inc, HUD 199 Unit, Moderate Income Housing; Fla Blue Key; Tau Epsilon, Tau Alpha Chapt, Univ Fla; St P'burg Intl Folk Fair Soc; Suncoast Tiger Bay Clb; Museum of Fine Arts of St P'burg; Suncoasters, St P'burg Fest of Sts; Golden Triangle Clb; St P'burg Yacht Clb; Mem & Past Pres, Chm of Bd (1964-66) Congreg B'nai Israel; B'nai B'rith Intl, Pres's Clb; r/Jewish; hon/#1 in Co Awd, Crown Life Ins Co 1971; Agcy Persistency Awd, Crown Life 1971; Nat Assn Life Underwriters, Nat Quality Awd; Mbrship to Millionaires Clb, Wash Nat Ins Co 1974; Beautification Awds for Properties: Wittner Ctr E 1978, Wittner Ctr W 1979, Wittner Med Pk 1975; First Spec Awd for City of St P'burg for Design Excell 1977; Man of Yr Awd, B'nai B'rith 1971; Mr Sugardaddy, Diabetic Assn of Pinellas Co 1980; W/W: Fin & Indust, S&SW, Hon Soc Am; Men of Achmt.

WOHLFORD, CATHERINE oc/Realtor Associate; b/Jan 21, 1937; h/406 Wood Fern Cir, Anderson, SC 29621; m/Lowell C; c/Regina, Renee, Randall; p/Hubert M and Toye M Bishop, Christiansburg, VA; ed/Grad Phillips Bus Col 1970; pa/Real Est; Anderson Bd Rltrs; Wom's Coun Rltrs; r/Prot; hon/Miss Blacksburg, Va 1956; Miss VPI Engrg Dept 1957; Anderson Co Sales Assoc of Yr 1979 & 80; Million Dollar Clb 1978-80.

WOLF, JAMES GARY oc/Professor, Professional Pianist; b/June 28, 1933; h/2142 Chinook Trail, Maitland, FL 32751; ba/Orlando; m/Carolyn Ann Lygrisse; c/Derek James, Margery Dawn; p/James C and Viva Marie Wolf, Wichita, KS; ed/BME Wichita St Univ 1955; MMus 1960, DMA 1964 Eastman Sch Mus; mil/USMA Band 1955-58; pa/Instr of Mus, Univ Denver 1962-64; Asst Prof & Assoc Prof Mus, Univ S Fla 1964-72; Prof Mus, Chm Mus Dept, Univ Ctrl Fla 1972-; Mus Tchrs Nat Assn; Fla St Mus Thcrs Assn, Pres-Elect; Ctrl Fla MTN; Tampa MTA; MENC; Fla Col Mus Edrs Assn, VP; Am Mattbray Assn, VP; Phi Mu Alpha Sinfonia; Fla Fed Mus Clbs; r/Presb; hon/Naztzger Yng Artist Awd, Wichita Symph Orch; Alumni S'ship Wichita St Univ; Fulbright Schrl, Mozarteum, Salzburg, Austria 1960-61; Univ Excell Awd, Tchr of Yr, Univ Ctrl Fla 1980.

WOLF, KENNETH MARK oc/Executive; b/Oct 8, 1948; h/7315 Domonique, Dallas, TX 75214; ba/Dallas; m/Gayla M; c/Lee, Fanncy, Jared; p/Frank A Wolf (dec); Ursula Wolf Millers, Dallas, TX; ed/BA; MBA; pa/Co VP & Co-Owner; Owner WMK Investments Inc; cp/Jr JCs; hon/W/W Tex 1975.

WOLFE, CAROLYN R oc/Writer, Poet; b/Dec 29, 1943; h/Rt 12 Box 48, Davidson Hgts Dr, Winston-Salem, NC 27107; ba/W-S; m/David E; c/Debbie, Mark; p/Laurel and Ruby Robbins, W-S, NC; pa/Author *Shadows*; r/Epis; hon/Pub'd in Nat Soc Pub'd Poets 1976.

WOLFE, DENNY T JR oc/Associate Professor; b/Jan 18, 1943; h/4603 Southampton Arch, Portsmouth, VA 23703; ba/Norfolk; m/Celia O; c/Cary, Ashley; p/Carmen Wolfe, Morehead City, NC; ed/AA Lees-McRae Col 1963; BS 1965, MS 1970 Appalachian St Univ; PhD Duke Univ 1974; pa/Tchr: W Lincoln HS, Lincolnton, NC 1965-66 & F L Ashley HS, Gastonia, NC 1966-70; Dir of Admissions, Lees-McRae Col 1970-74; Dir Div of Lang, St Dept Public Instrn 1974-79; Assoc Prof Ed, Sch Ed, Old Dominion Univ 1979-; NCTE; ASCD; r/Meth; hon/Outstg Yng Men Am 1970; Outstg Edrs Am 1971; Notable Ams of Bicent Era 1976; DIB; Author Num Profl Articles Inclg "Thinking Through Film" 1979 & "What the Beginning English Teacher Should Know About Language" 1979.

WOLFE, MICHAEL JOSEPH oc/Radio and Television Sports Personality; b/Feb 23, 1938; h/1017 Honeycreek Ct, Lexington, KY; m/Dolores; c/Michael C; p/Oliver J (dec) and Irene K Wolfe (dec); mil/USMC 1959-61; pa/News & Sports Dir KHOW Radio, Denver, Colo; Sports Dir WTOP TV, Wash DC; Sports Dir WKQQ Radio, Lexington, Ky; r/Cath; hon/Awds From: Am Cancer Soc, Epilepsy Foun, Mar of Dimes, MDA, MS Soc, Lions Clb, Kiwanis Clb, Optimist Clb, JCs 1970-79.

WOLLSTEIN, DONALD GUSTAV oc/Management Consultant, Public Accountant, Tax Specialist; b/May 28, 1923; h/PO Box 1977, Sanford, FL 32771; m/Florence Edith Ellis; p/Gustav Herman Henry (dec) and Anna Millicent Hoffmann Wollstein (dec); ed/Grad NWn Univ 1953; Att'd Univ Wis; Inst Natural Therapy: Master of Herbalism 1957, Dip Applied Psych, Dip Phys Therapy & Massage; Grad Intl Graphoanalysis Soc; Doctor Naturopathy, Bernadian Univ 1974; pa/Field Rep for Mortgage Closing, Hammond Mortgage Co 1941-44; Cashiers Dept, Paul H Davis & Co 1945-48; Supvr Cashiers Dept, Kleins Sporting Goods Co 1948-51; Statis Staff, Millar Coffee Co 1951-54; Owner & Oper Donald Woostein Enterprises 1954-79; Res Spec in Biblical, Parapsych & Reincarnation Field, 1961-; Intl Graphoanalysis Soc; Assn Res & Enlightenment; cp/Allemande Square Dance Clb, Kenosha; Adult Adv Coun YMCA; US Power Squadron; Andean Explorers Clb; hon/W/W Midwest 1978-79; DIB 1979-80; Cert for Spec Sers, Amazon El Dorado Expedition 1971; Alpha Psi Omega; Composer "My God, My God"; "Victory March" & "My Elusive Angel."

WONG, VIVIAN A oc/Executive; b/Oct 21, 1940; m/Thomas K F; c/Madeline, Madina, Michele, Anita; p/Kenny Lai-Hang (dec) and Suk-Yin Sin Swan, Greenville, SC; ed/Grad KCC Eng Col 1958; Eton Col 1959-60; Furman Univ 1972-74; pa/Owner Dagon Den Rest Chain; Exec VP Wong Enterprises Inc (Import/Export); Intl Food Ser; Secy-Treas Greenville Rest Assn; Nat Rest Assn; r/Epis; hon/W/W SE US.

WOOD, ANNETTE VARNER oc/Artist; b/Nov 17, 1946; h/Rt 1 Box 72, Churchville, VA 24421; m/David Calvin; c/Cheryl Lanette, David Dwayne, Christine Ann; p/William Oaklyn Varner, Staunton, VA; Anna Sayre Varner (dec); ed/Val Voc Tech Col; pa/Work w LD Chd in Public Sch Sys; cp/Staunton Fine Arts Assn; Yng Homemakers of Va; r/Presb (Mem 1 of Oldest Presb Chs in Shenandoah Val); hon/Sev Awds for Oil & Pastel Paintings.

WOOD, JAMES H oc/Accountant; b/Sept 9, 1947; h/PO Box 2102, Castalian Springs, TN; ba/Hartsville; m/Thelma L; c/Villa, Olivia, Jennifer; p/Jay and Betty Wood, Dayton, TN; ed/Cert Accts Receivabe/Payable, St Area Voc-Tech; Grad Vol St Commun Col 1979; mil/USN 1966-70 3rd Class Petty Ofcr; pa/Cost Acctg Ofcr, TVA; cp/Disabled Am Vets; Hartsville JCs; r/Bapt; hon/W/W S&SW.

WOOD, JOLEAN MORTON oc/Equal Opportunity Officer; b/June 23, 1929; h/128 Old Georgia Rd, Spartanburg, SC 29302; ba/S'burg; m/Walter E Jr; c/Phillip Lester and Thomas Ryan, Karen Michele; p/Joe Roland and Pecolia Smith Morton, S'burg, SC; ed/Torrington Bus Sch 1950; Cont'g Ed Univ SC & Tri-Co Tech Coll; pa/Equal Opport Ofcr, Piedmont Commun Actions Inc 1967-; SC Equal Opport Ofcrs Assn, Pres 1978-80; SC Chapt Nat Assn Human Rights Wkrs, Secy 1979; SC Assn Human Ser Agcys Inc, Secy 1980; cp/Charter Mem Spartan Chapt ABWA; r/Presb; Pres CWU of SC 1981; hon/Nom Jefferson Awd 1981; Outstg Ldrship in Human Rights, SE Assn EOO 1979; Dept of Commerce Awd of Apprec for Outstg Contbn to 1980 Census; Wom of Yr, ABWA 1981.

WOOD, KAREN McMAHON oc/Office Manager; b/Sept 29, 1944; h/4015 Piedmont Dr SE, Huntsville, GA 35802; ba/Same; m/W Graham; p/V Lee and Annetta Louise McMahon, St Louis, MO; ed/BS Elem Ed; MS Spec Ed; mil/DOD Japan 2 Yrs; pa/Tchr 5 Yrs; Real Est Brokr 8 Yrs; Med

Ofc Mgr 5 Yrs; cp/AAUW; Alpha Chi Omega, Local Pres; r/Epis; hon/Outstg Wom Am 1976, 77; Personalities of S 1976-77.

WOOD, LAWRENCE JACKSON JR oc/Missionary; b/Dec 13, 1946; h/PO Box 11272, Carrefour Rd, Pont-au-Prince, Haiti, WI; ba/Cleveland, TN; m/Peggy Jean Kirkland; c/Gregory Scott, Gary Lee, Kimberly; p/Lawrence J Sr and Martha Louise Eddy Wood, Gadsden, AL; ed/GED 1965; mil/USAR; pa/Missionary, Ch of God; Gen Overseer, Ch Preserv Endeavor; r/Ch of God; hon/Writer for *The Vision Speaks*, Mthly Paper of Ch of God.

WOOD, LOREN EDWIN oc/Engineering Manager; b/Dec 25, 1927; h/905 Coward Creek Dr, Friendswood, TX 77546; ba/Houston; m/Ann H; c/Joan, Alice, Scott, Carol; p/Elmer Roe (dec) and Alice Eleanor Philbrick Wood (dec); ed/BS magna cum laude Brown Univ 1949; MS Cornell Univ 1950; Grad Engrg & Engrg Mgmt Progs MIT 1954, Univ Fla 1955, UCLA 1958; mil/USAF 1961-68 Capt; pa/Mgr Tech Plan'g & Var Projs Supporting NASA/JSC, TRW Defense & Space Sys Grp 1966-; Keyrole in Selection of Mission Model & Vehicles for Manned Lunar Landing Mission 1961, Mgr *Gemini* Flight Testing 1962-66; Head Test Plan'g for Atlas-Thor-Minuteman ICBM Progs 1956-61; Engr, Army Ordn, USAF Armaments 1950-56; AIAA, Chm Houston Sect 1975-76, Chm Technol Applications Com 1971-75; cp/City Coun-man & Mayor Pro-Tem, Friendswood 1977-; City Charter Comm 1971; Sch Plan'g Bd 1973-74; r/Commun Bible Ch; hon/W/W: Engrg, S&SW; Phi Beta Kappa; Sigma Xi; Nat Awds AIAA Ldrship & Radio-TV Work for Space Prog; Author Num Tech Documents & Articles.

WOOD, LUCILLE oc/Instructor and Coach; b/Sept 1, 1931; h/Rt 2 Box 303, Louisville, MS 39339; ba/Decatur, MS; p/George S (dec) and Edna Myres Wood (dec); ed/AA E Ctrl Jr Col 1951; BS 1953, MA 1955 Univ So Miss; pa/Hlth, Phys Ed & Rec Instr & Wom's Basketball Coach, E Ctrl Jr Col 1956-; Phys Ed Instr, Tennis & Basketball Coach, Copial-Lincoln Jr Col 1953-56; Miss Assn Edrs; Nat Jr Col Coaches Assn; Miss Jr Col Coaches Assn, Pres; Miss Jr Col Fac Assn; Delta Kappa Gamma; Selection Com Nat Jr Col Coach of Yr 1980-; r/Bapt; hon/E Ctrl Jr Col Alumnus of Yr 1964; Coached St Jr Col Champs 1970, 73, 76, 79 & Div Champs 1976, 79, 80; Team in Regional Tourn 1973, 77, 78, 79, 80; All-Star Jr Col Coach 1978; Miss Assn Coach of Yr 1979; Miss Jr Col Coach of Yr 1979; W/W S&SW 1980.

WOODALL, RONALD STEVEN oc/Executive; b/Sept 19, 1953; h/3303 Rolling Green Ln, Missouri City, TX 77459; ba/Houston; m/Rebecca K Waldrep; c/Ronald Steven, Jennifer Noel, Amy Michelle, Robert Brandon; p/Ronald Grady and Mary Ellen Woodall, Houston, TX; ed/BA Houston Bapt Univ 1975; pa/Exec VP, Ron's Krispy Fried Chicken Inc; Nat Rest Assn; Tex Rest Assn; Gtr Houston Conv Coun; Intl Franchise Assn; cp/Life Mem Repub Party; Conf Air Force; Former Pres Thunderbird N Homeowners Assn; Mktg & Distb Ednl Adv Bd Houston ISD; Adv Com PACE, Mo City; Chancellors Racquet Clb; Quail Val Cntry Clb; r/Bapt.

WOODALL, STELLA oc/Poet, Editor, Publisher, Writer; b/Jan 15, 1899; h/PO Box 253, Junction, TX 76849; m/(dec); c/Ruth James, Anna Frsot, Clara Beth Urban; p/(dec); ed/BLitt; Dr Lttrs & Humanites; mil/Civilian Ser 20 Yrs; Ret'd AF Hist-Writer; pa/Writer for AF; Editor-Pubr *Adventures in Poetry* Magazine; Free-Lance Writer; Pres Intl for Life, Stella Woodall Poetry Soc Int; Nat Pres Am Poetry Leag; Intl Pres, Patriotic Poetry Sem; Orgr & Charter Pres Nat Leag Am Pen Wom, San Antonio Chapt; Pres La Junta Study Clb; Nat Co-Chm Promote Poetry in Am; Nat Liaison Ofcr World Poetry Soc; Public Relats Dir U Poets Laureate Intl; Editorial & Adv Bd Intl W/W Poetry; Judge on Editorial & Adv Bd, Hon Mem Commun Ldrs & Noteworthy Ams; cp/Past Pres Armed Forces Writers Leag; Centro Studi e Scambi Internacionali; Tex Sen Adv Coun on Leg Affairs; Tex Comm on Arts & Humanities; Dir Beautify San Antonio Assn; Nat Assn Ret'd Fed Employees; Past Pres Sr Citizens Clb; Past 1st VP Nat Soc Arts & Lttrs, San Antonio Chapt; r/Meth; hon/Gold Awd for *Anthology Of Tex Poets*; Gold Awd, Nom'd For Pulitzer Prize, Best Book of Yr 1977 *Stella Woodall's Collected Poems*; Intl Wom 1975 & 76; Cit which now Hangs on Wall of Intl Hall of Fame for Wom of Dist; 2 Gold Laurel Leaf Crowns, U Poets Laureate Intl; Silver Bowl for Sers to Strategy Bd Round Table, San Antonio Wom's Clb; Gold Plaque, 3rd World Congress of Poets, Balto; "Mrs Uncle Sam" Bicent Rep 1976; Ambassador of Good Will for City & St; Biog Listed in Commun Ldrs & Noteworthy Ams, Am Soc Dist'd Citizens; Nat Social Register; W/W Tex; Intl W/W Poetry; Book of Honor; Writer's Directory; Intl W/W Commun Ser; World W/W Wom; DIB; W/W Am Wom; and Many More.

WOODARD, BLONDENA oc/Tax Accountant, Business Consultant; b/Apr 23, 1940; h/1202 Oak St, Richmond, VA 23222; p/Jesse B and Pauline H Woodard, Newport News, VA; ed/BS Va St Univ 1966; Att'd So Conn St 1967; MA Va St Univ 1980; pa/Owner Tico & Co (Tax & Bus

Mgmt Sers); Nat Assn Rltrs; Nat Bus Wom Assn; Yng Profls of Tidewater; Nat Assn Black Accts; Va Assn Rltrs; cp/NAACP; Va Black Caucus; r/Bapt; hon/Dist'd Ser Awd, Yng Profls of Tri-Cities; W/W S&SW 1980.

WOODING, NATHANIEL HENRY oc/Physician; b/Mar 7, 1909; h/67 Cary St, Halifax, VA 24558; ba/Halifax; m/Anne Elizabeth Shillady; c/Nathaniel Henry, West Gilliam; p/Robert Henry and Elizabeth Carter Wooding; ed/Att'd Hampden-Sydney Col 1927-28; Dip Sch Nsg, Bloomingdale Hosp 1933; BA NYU 1938; MD LI Col Med 1942; mil/AUS WWII; pa/Staff Nurse Payne Whitney Clin, NYC 1933-34, NY St Psychi Inst & Hosp, Bellevue Hosp, LI Col Hosp 1939-43; Intern Med Col Va Hosps 1943; Pract Med Spec'g in Anesthesiology, Halifax, Va 1946-; Med Examiner, Halifax Co 1946; Staff Halifax Commun Hosp, South Boston Hosp, Commun Meml Hosp, S Hill Meml Coun 1954-56, 1960-; Supvr Banister Dist, Halifax Co 1968-; AMA; Halifax Co & Va Med Socs; Med Soc Va; S Piedmont Med Soc; Am Acad Gen Pract; AAAS; cp/Va Archeol Soc; Va Hist Soc; Halifax Co Min Assn; r/Epis; hon/Contbr Articles to Med Pubs.

WOODRUFF, GEORGIA DELORES WILBUR oc/Inservice Director; b/Mar 31, 1926; h/511 Mays St, Jasper, TX 75951; ba/Jasper; m/James Calvin (dec); c/James Calvin Jr, Barbara Jean, Jesse J; p/Clarence Nelson (dec) and Gertrude Alice Sewell Wilbur, Jasper, TX; ed/Dip Nsg; AA Lamar Col; pa/RN & Inser Dir, Mary Dickerson Meml Hosp; ANA; NLN; cp/Dem Party; Pres's Com; r/Pentecostal; hon/W/W Am Wom 1979.

WOODRUFF, JEAN LEIGH oc/Instructor, Assistant Editor; b/Sept 19, 1950; h/PO Box 561, Clemson, SC 29631; ba/Clemson; p/Alton L Woodruff, Fayetteville, NC; Jean W Tulli, Clemson, SC; ed/BA Univ NC-Greensboro 1972; MBA Emory Univ 1974; Att'd Clemson Univ 1974-79; PhD Cand Univ Ga; Att'd Univ Oslo (Norway) Summer 1979; pa/Instr Mktg, Clemson Univ 1974-; Asst Editor *Textile Marketing Letter* 1975-; So Mktg Assn; Am Mktg Assn; Mid-Atlantic Mktg Assn, 1980 Proceedings Editor; Inst Mgmt Sci; cp/Ldr Girl Scout Cadette Troop 30; Advr Clemson Collegiate Civitan; Advr Phi Gmma Nu; LWV; AAUW; Univ Wom's Clbs; r/Bapt; hon/Yng Careerist of Yr 1977 Anderson, SC BPW Clb; Yng Careerist of Yr 1st Runner Up 1977 St of SC; Regent's Schlr Univ of Ga 1977-78; Res Grant, Clemson Univ 1977; Outstg Yng Wom of Am 1978; W/W S&SW 1980; Dist'd Ser Awd, SC Civitan 1980; Author *Handbook of Textile Marketing* 1981; Num Profl Reports & Articles.

WOODRUFF, NANCY MORRIS oc/Director of Early Childhood Education; b/Dec 27, 1948; h/Hattiesburg, MS; ba/Box 148, Child Devel Ctr, William Carey Col, H'burg, MS 39401; m/Homer Franklin III; p/Joel Kirk and Ruble McMillin Morris; ed/BA Miss Univ for Wom 1970; MEd Delta St Univ 1971; Post Grad Study Delta St 1972, Univ So Miss 1978-80, William Carey Col 1977-; pa/Psychometrist, Region I Mtl Hlth Ctr, Clarksdale, Miss 1971-73; Dir Deinstitutionalization, Ellisville St Sch, Ellisville, Miss 1973-76; Dir Univ Yr for Action, William Carey Col 1976-78; Dir Early Childhood Ed, William Carey Col 1978-; Pi Gamma Mu, Pres; AMEG; Delta Kappa Gamma; MAACUS; HAACUS; SACUS; Miss Assn Grp Homes, Secy; cp/Hattiesburg Needlepoint Guild; Civic Leag Chm; MUW; Began 1st Pre-Sch Prog for GT Chd in Miss (GATE); r/Meth; hon/Outstg Yng Wom Am 1980; Winner Mid-S Jr Authors Contest 1965; Dean's List; Pres's List 1966-70; Mortar Board 1976; Lantern Acad Hons Soc 1974; Phi Kappa Phi 1970; Author "The Effect of Token Reinforcement on Verbal Concept Learning with Trainable Mentally Retarded Children."

WOODS, PHILLIP J oc/Minister; b/Nov 11, 1932; h/Rt 9 Box 200, Burlington, NC 27215; m/Claudia B; c/Phyllis A Cutts, Vivian V, Spencer E, Phillip D, Claudia A, Esther M; p/Spencer E and Georgia A Woods, Leasburg, NC; ed/ThB UCBI of Durhanm 1969; pa/Min; V-Moderator Cedar Grove Missionary Bapt Assn; cp/Dem Party; NAACP; Past Master Allen's Masonic Lodge; Jamet Digg's Consistory 308; Eljebel Temple #95.

WOODWARD, HENRY ELIHUE (WOODY) oc/Sales Manager; b/July 16, 1934; h/831 Flicker Dr, Dyersburg, TN 38024; ba/D'burg; m/Faye W; c/Henry C, Richard, Angela; p/Stanley E Woodward, Sedalia, MO; mil/AUS Ret'd Sgt Maj; pa/Life Ins Sales Mgr; cp/Gideons Intl; Am Legion; VFW; Shriner; Nat Assn Life Underwriters; r/Bapt; hon/Bronze Star; Legion of Merit w OLC; Army Commend Medal; AF Commend Medal; Other Hons & Awds.

WOOLARD, PAT oc/Executive; b/Nov 2, 1942; h/Midland, Tx; ba/PO Box 8103, Midland, TX 79703; m/Jimmie Dale; c/Laura Lee, Susan Ann, Darren Milton; p/Lloyd and Eloise Pittman, Midland, TX; ed/Att'd Lubbock Christian Col 1961-62; pa/VP, Secy-Treas Woolard Elect; r/Ch of Christ.

WOOTEN, WILLARD (BILL) M oc/Retired Musician; b/July 29, 1912; h/1003 N Magnolia Ave, Dunn, NC 29334; m/Kathlene Marshall; c/Willard, James, Charles, Kathy; p/Charlie M (dec) and Florence H

PERSONALITIES OF THE SOUTH

Wooten (dec); ed/AA; BA; pa/Entertainer; Performer; Jr & Sr Bands; Jazz Pianist; cp/YMCA; Scouts; Phi Beta Sigma; NEA; Notary; Var Sports Activs; r/Bapt; hon/Tchr of Yr; Orig Piano Stylist; St Pk Wkr.

WORDEN, LUCILLE W oc/Instructor; b/July 4, 1920; h/Rt 2 Box 636, Crystal River, FL 32629; m/T R Sparkman (dec), Remarried; c/Elizabeth Rae Leavell, Thomas Ray Sparkman Jr; p/James G (dec) and Hattie E Wall, Crystal River, FL; ed/BS harding Col 1947; BAEED Univ Fla 1970; pa/Home Ec Instr, Crystal River HS 1947-61; Basketball Coach 1947-52; Mid Sch Instr 1965-80; FTA; NEA; Bldg Rep, Nat Sci Assn; cp/Co Red Cross, W-side Chm 1961; Mar of Dimes Chm 1962; Charter Mem Jr Wom's Clb, 1st VP; Charter Mem Gdn Clb: Pres, Secy, Treas; Am Legion Aux, Secy 5 Yrs; r/Ch of Christ; hon/Hon Student 1947, 70; Tchr of Yr 1972 & 78; Basketball Plays Pub'd in Conf Booklet 1951; Ser of Excell in Safety & Inspection, Redstone Arsonel 1946; Others.

WORKMAN, VIRGINIA W oc/Free-Lance Writer, Teacher; b/Sept 16, 1921; h/2902 Rexwood Dr, Tallahassee, FL 32304; m/Ernest R; c/Nancy Johnston, Deborah; p/William Harvey (dec) and Savella Weaver; ed/Toledo Col & Sem, Off-Campus Div; BS Sanford Univ 1950; MA Univ Ala 1960; mil/WAVES; pa/Span & Eng Tchr 20 Yrs; Author *The Lord is My Strength*; Bd Dirs Capitol Christian Acad 1963-69; Num Ed Assns; Span Clb of Sanford; Mission Clb; r/Bapt; hon/Num Stories Pub'd in Regular Bapt Pres & Other Rel Pubs.

WORLEY, NANCY LILLIAN oc/Teacher; b/Nov 7, 1951; h/622 Seventh Ave SW, Decatur, AL 35601; ba/Decatur; p/Leonard O (dec) and Lillian S Worley, New Hope, AL; ed/BA Univ Montevallo 1973; MA Jacksonville St Univ 1974; Att'd Univ London, Birkbeck Col 1972, Univ Edinburgh & Univ Ala 1975; pa/Tchr, Latin, Speech, Cheerldg, Decatur HS 1973-; Tchr Eng, NE St Jr Col 1975-; Calhoun Commun Sch 1976-80; Nat Jr Classical Leag: SE Mbrship Chm, Dramatic Rdg Chm; Ala Jr Classical Leag, St Chm 1979-; Am Classical Leag, Promo Com; Classical Assn of Middle W & S, Mbrship Com; Ala Classical Assn, Pres 1979-80, VP 1978-79; Decatur Ed Assn: Pres 1979-80, VP 1978-79, Bd Dirs 1980-81, Secy 1977-78, Leg Chm, A-Vote Chm, Fac Rep, Del to St Assem; UTP Uniserv Coun V, Pres 1979-80; Ala Ed Assn: Bd Dirs 1979-82, Leg Comm, Public Relats Comm, Negotiations Team; NEA, Resolutions Com Alternate, Del to Rep Assem; Ala Clrm Tchrs Assn, VP 1980-81; Decatur Clrm Tchrs Assn: Pres 1980-81, Bd Dirs 1977-80, Secy 1978; Opport Toastmistress Clb: VP, Secy, Parliamentn, Speech Contest Chm; Delta Kappa Gamma, Gamma Beta Chapt, VP 1980-81; Va Soc of Eng & US; Ala Fgn Lang Tchrs Assn; Nat/Ala Coun of Tchrs of Eng; Ala Speech & Theatre Assn; Huntsville Lit Assn; Intl Assn Human Relats Lab Tng; cp/AAUW: Div Commun Area Rep, Decatur 1st VP, Decatur Secy-Treas, S'ship Com, Creative Writing Com, Art Fair Com; Morgan Co LWV; Am Field Ser, Student Sponsor; Ala/Madison Co Yng Dems; Ala Wom's Campaign Orgs; Phi Mu Alumnae of NE Ala, Secy; Huntsville Broadway Theatre Leag, Fac Sponsor; Huntsville Little Theatre; Ala Shakespeare Fest, Patron; Univ Montevallo Alumni Assn, S'ship Com; Town & Gown Theatre of B'ham; Ala Cystic Fibrosis Foun, Morgan Co Chm 2 Yrs; Wheeler Basin Lib Rdg for Blind; Morgan Co Mtl Hlth Assn; Decatur Concert Assn, Mbrship Wkr; Intl Bus Stop, Publicity Chm; r/Bapt; hon/Ala's Outstg Yng Edr 1980; Morgan Co Outstg Yng Edr 1979; Outstg Yng Wom Am 1977; W/W Am Cols & Univs 1973; Latin S'ship 1970, 71; Phi Mu S'ship Awd 1970-72; Acad Hons S'ship 1969; Highest Hons S'ship 1970-72; Sigma Tau Delta; Kappa Delta Pi; Lambda Sigma Chi; Eta Sigma Phi; Dean's List 1969; Pres's List 1970-72; Grad magna cum laude 1973; 20 Yng Ldrs Decatur 1980.

WORRELL, YVONNE MARGARET oc/Dental Hygienist; b/Aug 7, 1944; h/5111 8th Rd S, Arlington, VA 22204; ba/Arlington; m/Peter Eric Skardon Pover; c/Evi-Luise, Steven E (dec), (Stepson) Ashley Christian; p/Ray R and Trudi W Worrell, Fairfax, VA; ed/RDH Marquette Univ 1963; Cert Lnag Inst, Minerva, Switz; pa/Reg'd Dental Hygienist; ADHA; DCDMA; Wash Area Writers; Sigma Phi Alpha; cp/Vol Chd's Hosp; r/Epis; hon/W/W Am Wom 1979; Winner Westinghouse Sci Talent 1961.

WORTHAM, ROBERT JOHN oc/Judge, Attorney; b/Sept 8, 1947; h/Beaumont, TX; ba/Beaumont; m/Linda Fitzgerald; c/R J Jr; p/Lauretta Wortham; ed/BA Lamar Univ 1971; JD Baylor Law Sch 1974; pa/Jefferson Co Dist Atty's Ofc 1974-75; Waldman & Smallwood 1975-78; Ptnr Waldman & Smallwood 1979-80; Tchr Paralegal Classes Lamar Univ; Past Secy-Treas Jr Bar Assn, Jefferson Co; Judge 60th Judicial Dist Ct, Jefferson Co, Tex 1980; Vis'g Judge, 58th Judicial Dist Ct 1981-; Lic'd to Pract Supreme Ct Tex; US Dist Ct, En Dist Tex; US Dist Ct, So Dist Tex; Jefferson Co Bar Assn; Pt Arthur Bar Assn; Jefferson Co Jr Bar Assn; cp/SW Fball Ofcls Assn; Bd of Firemen's Pension Fund; Dir Cerebral Palsy Foun; Dir Baylor Law Sch Alumni Assn; Wkd Repub Elect Ballot Security 1974 & 76; Wkd for Gov Clements Campaign 1978; Repub Precinct Chm; Sustaining Mem Gov Clements Com; r/Epis; hon/Delta Theta Phi.

WREN, DONALD GREGORY oc/Physical Therapist; b/May 1, 1947;

h/4 Oakdale Cir, Conway, AR 72032; ba/Conway; m/Pam; c/Amber Lea; p/W Donald and Jeanne Wren, Little Rock, AR; ed/BS Univ Ctrl Ark 1969; Baylor Med Ctr Sch of Phys Therapy 1970; pa/Pres Ark Chapt Am Phys Therapy Assn; St Exam Bd for Phys Therapist Ark; Nat Ath Tnrs Assn; Am Col Sports Med; r/Meth.

WREN, RUTH MARIE oc/Education-Epidemiology Supervisor; b/July 17, 1930; h/5809 Tautoga, El Paso, TX 79924; m/Bobby Joe; c/Robert Allen, Melvin Russell, Lee Roy, Marilyn Marie; p/Marshall Edward and Flora Lee Lindley Brown, Big Spring, TX; pa/Asst Kitchen Mgr, Providence Meml Hosp; Asst Therapeutic Dietitian, SWn Gen Hosp; Inspector Consumer Hlth Protection, City of El Paso; Instr-Supvr Consumer Hlth Protect, City of El Paso; Ed/Epidemiology Supvr, El Paso City Co Hlth Unit; Bd Mem: Adv Coun Tech Voc Ed in Tex; Infectious Disease Control Practitioners Coun, Trans Pecos Hlth Career Exec Com, Ed Reporter Pan Am Hlth Org; Tex Public Hlth Assn; Nutrition & Food Safety Resources Com; Nutrition & Food Protection Coalition of El Paso; Nat Assn Female Execs; r/Meth; hon/W/W S&SW 1980.

WRENN, BESSIE MAE NOBLE oc/Field Inspector; b/June 21; h/B'ham, AL; ba/Suite 301, Bagby Dr, B'ham, AL 35209; p/Sam (dec) and Eula M Noble, B'ham, AL; ed/BS Ala A&M Univ; BSW 1975, MSW 1976 Univ Ala; Cert Mgmt, Mgmt Inst, Univ Ala 1979; pa/Caseworker 1967-70; St of Ala, Jefferson Co Dept Pensions & Security 1970-76; Casework Reviewer, Casework Supvr 1976-77; Wel Dist Field Supvr 1977-79; Wel Field Supvr, Ofc of Inspector, Gen Dept of Pensions & Security, St of Ala 1979-; NASW; Ala Conf Social Work; Jefferson Co Human Sers Clb; r/Meth; hon/W/W Am Wom 1981-82; Personalities of Am 1982.

WRIGHT, DANA LAWRENCE oc/Homemaker; b/Sept 29, 1925; h/1610 Primrose Ln, Borger, TX 79007; m/Lewis Clavin; c/Lewis Calvin Jr, Cecilia Anne W Seitz; p/Amon Philpot and Jessica Parson Lawrence (dec); ed/UNC; pa/Tex Panhandle Heritage Foun; Nat Trust Hist Preserv, Fine Arts, W Tex Univ; cp/Commun Concert Assn, Bd Mem; Borger Mus Clb; Wom Div C of C: Bd Mem, VP, Charter Mem; VP 20th Cent Clb; Forum Clb; VP Commun Forum; Nat Audubon Soc; Phillips Gdn Clb; Am Cancer Soc, Hutchinson Co: Bd Dirs, Pres; BSA; GSA; Bd Mem ARC; Beta Sigma Phi: Past Pres, Mem-at-Large; r/1st U Meth Ch: Am Bible Soc; Bible-A-Mo Clb; Meth Ch Sch, Asheville, NC 1953-57.

WRIGHT, DIANNE HAMBY oc/Librarian; b/May 4, 1941; h/103 Starmount Dr, Valdosta, GA 31601; ba/Valdosta; m/Fred A; p/Alvin D and Kathryn Morris Hamby, Valdosta, GA; ed/BS Valdosta St Col 1966; MSLS Fla St Univ 1970; pa/Libn Valdosta St Col 1970-; Lib Asst, Valdosta St Col 1968-69; Tchr Valdosta Jr HS 1967-68; Lib Asst, Ariz St Univ Lib 1967; ALA; SEn Lib Assn; GLA, Sect Chm 1975-77; Beta Phi Mu; Org'd & 1st Pres Valdosta & Lowndes Lib Assn; r/Prot; hon/Ofcl Del Ga Gov's Conf on Lib & Info Sci 1977; Editor SGAL-CGAL Union List of Serials 1979.

WRIGHT, EUGENE BOX oc/Lawyer; b/Feb 21, 1943; h/3607 Highgreen Dr, Kingwood, TX 77339; ba/Cleveland, TX; m/Linda G; c/Laura Elizabeth, Alan Fulton, Julia Anne; p/Hugh Franch and Madaline Box Wright; ed/BA So Meth Univ 1965; JD Univ Houston 1968; pa/City Atty, City of Cleveland 1969-72; Pvt Pract Law, Cleveland; Pres Wright Energy Corp; Atty: US Life Title Ins Co, SW Title Ins Co, Title Ins Co of Minnesota, Pioneer Nat Title Ins Co, Lwyrs Title Ins Corp, Chgo Title Ins Co & Stewart Title Guaranty Co; Dir & Secy: Splendora Lumber Co, C'land Pub'g Co Inc, Triangle Press Inc, Gtr Beaumont Pub'g Co, Olympic Inc; Tex Bar Assn; US Supreme Ct Bar; US Ct of Appeals; 5th Circuit; US Dist Ct; En Dist of Tex; Am Judicature Soc; Am Trial Lwyrs Assn; Phi Mu Alpha Sinfonia; Delta Sigma Pi; Beta Gamma Sigma; Phi Delta Phi; Pres Chambers-Liberty Cos Bar Assn; Chm Bicent Com, City of C'land; cp/UN Day Chm City of C'land 1977 & 78; Pres C'land Rotary Clb; Dir Gtr C'land C or C; Dir W Liberty Co Indust Foun; Secy C'land Country Clb; hon/Ky Col 1971; W/W Tex 1973; Outstg Yng Men Am 1975, 77; W/W Am Law; DIB; Personalities of Am; Intl W/W Intells.

WRIGHT, EVELYN JEAN oc/Corporate Service Representative; b/Feb 13, 1951; p/Warren G and Bertha E Neeper Wright, Wapakoneta, OH; ed/BA Ohio St Univ 1973; pa/Corp Ser Rep, Crown Life Ins; Ohio St Alumni Assn; ABWA; Soc for Tech Commun; cp/Repub Wom's Clb; OES; r/Prot; hon/W/W Am Wom.

WRIGHT, JAMES EDWARD oc/Agricultural Extension Agent; h/PO Box 215, Winton, NC 27986; ba/Winton; m/Ann Davis; c/Diana W James, James E Jr; p/Alner William and Lillie Bannerman Wright; ed/BS; Post Grad Studies; mil/USAR 1st Lt; pa/Co Agric Ext Agt; NACAA; NCACAA; 1st VP CADA; cp/RC Drug Ed Team; Exalted Ruler Home Base Elks Lodge; Dean of Pledges, Kappa Alpha Psi; Hertford Co OSHA Com; r/Willow Oak AME Ch: Steward; hon/DSA 1972; Outstg Ldrship Awd in Commun Devel, Cofield, NC 1968; Outstg & Valuable Commun Ser Awd, Rich Square BPW Clb 1977; Cit of Wk, Hertford Co, Aug 1978; NACAA Commun Awd.

PERSONALITIES OF THE SOUTH

WRIGHT, LAURA FRANCES oc/Professor; b/July 3, 1906; h/Montevallo, AL; p/Elliott D (dec) and Frances Burns Wright (dec); ed/BA Col of St Teresa 1926; MA Marquette Univ 1947; PhD Univ Wis-Madison 1952; Dip Dramatic Art, Conservatory, Col of St Teresa 1926; Nat Sch Elocution 1926; pa/Fdr, Dir Waukesha, Wis Little Theatre 1938-42; Fdr, Dir Waukesha Yng Peoples Theatre 1939-47; Tchr, Speech, Theatre, Forensics, Waukesha HS 1929-47; Instr, Speech-Theatre Dept, Clarke Col 1947; Asst Prof, Dir Clin Speech, Univ ND 1952-54; Prof, Chm Dept Speech, Univ Montevallo 1954-73; Wis Speech Assn; Wis Drama Guild; Ctrl Sts Speech Assn; Speech Commun Assn of Am; So Speech Assn; Ala Speech Assn; Chm Div of Speech Pathol; Speech & Hearing of Ala; Speech, Hearing, Lang Assn Am; Phi Beta; Delta Kappa Gamma; BPW; Quota Clb; Bd Mem Montevallo Area Commun Sers; r/Cath; hon/Hon Soc Col of St Teresa 1926; Duffey Awd, Outstg Alumnus, Sch of Speech, Marquette Univ 1968; Fellow Speech, Hearing, Lang Assn Am 1968; Hons of Assn, Speech & Hearing Assn Ala 1976; Laura F Wright Speech-Theatre Res Lib Dedicated 1975; Laura F Wright Commun Diagnostic Ctr Dedicated 1978; W/W: Mid-W, Am Wom; DIB; Author *Hearing Services: A Community Evaluation* 1952.

WRIGHT, MARIE RUNYAN oc/Teacher; b/Oct 6, 1919; h/Rt 1 Box 7, Bonnerdale, AR 71933; m/Verbie V; c/Barbara W Gillespie, Roberta W Turner; ed/BSE 1960, MSE 1964 Henderson St Univ; Post Grad Work Univ Ark; pa/Public Sch Tchr, Glenwood, AR; cp/OES: Worthy Matron 1962, Dpty Grand Lectr 1963, 64 & Grand Adah, Golden Rule Session, Grand Chapt of St Ark 1968; PTA; r/Meth; hon/Author *Tracking Barefoot Runyan* 1980.

WRIGHT, RUTHMARY R oc/Consultant and Psychotherapist; b/Jan 20, 1934; h/1117 Briarcliff Rd, Burlington, NC 27215; ba/B'ton; m/Roderick L Reinecke; c/Paul David, John Christopher, Leslie Sue, Laura Claire; p/Warner B and Claribel Kemp Ragsdale, Silver Spring, MD; ed/BA Bucknell Univ 1955; Post Grad Work LSU; MA Hood Col 1975; Cert Inst of Pastoral Psychtherapy 1975; pa/Dir Conslt, Ed & Prevention, Alamance-Caswell Area Mtl Hlth/Mlt Retard Prog; Controd Assocs; Am Assn Marriage & Fam Therapy, Clin Mem; NC Grp Behavior Soc; r/Epis.

WULLENWABER, FRANK C oc/Sales Manager; b/Oct 29, 1954; h/Dunn, NC; ba/PO Box 7, Dunn, NC 28334; p/Mr (dec) and Mrs Al Wullenwaber, Dunn, NC; ed/BA UNC-Wilmington 1978; pa/Sales Mgr,

Tomahawk Farms Inc; cp/St Dir Dunn JCs; r/U Meth; hon/Grandman Awd, Intl Telephone & Telegraph for Outstg Perf in Sales; Mil Order of World Wars for Outstg Perf in Field of Academics & Sports.

WYATT, JOHN DOUGLAS oc/Director; b/May 5, 1903; h/132 N 3rd, Selmer, TN 38375; ba/Selmer; p/John David (dec) and Irene Leeth Wyatt (dec); ed/Att'd Union Univ, Univ Tenn-Knoxville, Memphis St Univ; Grad John B Rogers Sch of Producing; mil/USCG; pa/Dir Selmer Sr Citizens Inc; cp/Pres PTA; Arts Assn; Stephen Foster Mus Clb; r/Meth; Choir Dir 20 Yrs; hon/Commun Betterment Awd, C of C; Dedicated Ser Awd, Mus Min.

WYCKOFF, JEAN ELLEN oc/Director Health Center; b/Oct 30, 1921; h/Dallas, TX; m/Michael Joel; c/Stuart M, Craig L, Arthur L, Karen Sue; p/Arthur A L (dec) and Ida S Boocheroff (dec); ed/BS, ML Univ Pgh; PhD Tex Wom's Univ 1980; mil/Flight Nurse; pa/Dir Hlth Ctr, El Centro Col; Cert'd Alcohol Cnslr; Marriage & Fam Therapist; TEP of Am Soc Grp Psychotherapy & Psychodrama; Bd Dirs Dallas Coun on Alcoholism; TAMFT; ARC; Coun of Dels, Am Col Hlth Assn; ASGPP; cp/Wkshop Ldr, St White House Conf on Aging; r/Jewish; hon/Air Medal; Fellow Am Col Hlth Assn; Fellow Am Soc Grp Psychotherapy & Psychodrama.

WYNN, PRINCE F oc/Teacher; b/Oct 19, 1935; h/Frederick, MD; c/Francine; p/Frank (dec) and Viola Wynn (dec); ed/BA Savannah St Col; MA Wayne St Univ; Adv Study Hood Col; pa/Spec Ed Indust Arts Tchr; Blanchard HS, Appling, Ga 1957-68; Brunswich HS, Brunswich, Md 1969-71; Rock Creek Sch, Frederick, Md 1971-; FCIA; MSTA; NEA; AIAA; MIAA; cp/Civitan Clb; Bd Dirs Frederick Co Assn Retard'd Citizens; r/Bapt; hon/Cert of Apprec, Frederick Co Spec Olympic Com.

WYRICK, MARY K (CATHERINE) oc/Free-Lance Public Relations Advertising; h/1706 Foster, Magnolia, AR 71753; ba/Magnolia; m/Tullie Mooney; c/Mary T Critcher, Walter Kelvin; p/W O (dec) and Willie Merritt Williamson (dec); ed/Att'd Jr Col; pa/Free-lance Public Relats Advtg; Local "News and Views" Radio Prog KVMA 1954-; BPW; Am Wom Radio & TV; cp/Sponsor Magnolia Newcomers Clb 25 Yrs; Good Neighbors Inc; Pilot Clb; LWV; Rec Comm; City Plan'g Comm; r/U Meth; hon/Cited by *Look* 1956; Ofcl City Hostess 1954; Ark Mother 1966; Top 10 Wom in Ark 1966.

Y

YANT, ROBERTA oc/Retired Teacher; b/Jan 28, 1910; h/320 Olive, Texarkana, TX 75501; p/H S (dec) and Edna McKee Yant (dec); ed/BA; MEd; Post Grad Study E Carolina Univ; SMU; Intl Acad of Spanish; pa/HS Span Tchr 39 Yrs; cp/Vol Ser Bur; Texarkana BPW Clb; r/Presb; hon/Commr to Gen Assem; Synod Presb Bd; Hon Mem Prog Agcy of U Presb Ch.

YARBOROUGH, ROBERT EARL oc/Manager; b/Jan 22, 1946; h/Lot 23, Stage Creek Trailer Pk, Marianna, FL 32446; ba/Marianna; m/Ruth Ann; c/Christine Ann; p/Mrs E W Yarborough, Ochlocknee, GA; mil/AUS; pa/Mgr Dixie Fin Corp; Nat Consumer Fin Assn; cp/Lions Clb; r/Cath.

YARBRO, MARY RUTH oc/Housewife; b/Dec 24, 1938; h/PO Box 172, Dyersburg, TN 38024; m/M Ross; c/Danny, Gayle, Guy David, Dudley Ross; p/Guy Daniel and Clatie Elizabeth Craft Yarbro; r/Meth.

YASNYI, LINDA F oc/Advertising, Public Relations, Marketing Consultant, Entrepreneur; b/Feb 27, 1951; h/1636 Amelia St, New Orleans, LA 70115; p/Ben (dec) and Bertha M Yasnyi, New Orleans, LA; ed/Communs of Arts & Scis, Univ New Orleans 1974; pa/Traffic Sales Ser Mgr, New Orleans ABC-TV Affil, WVUE-TV 1974-78, Dir Public Relats & Advtg 1978-80; Hyatt Regency, New Orleans: Advtg, Mktg & Public Relats Conslt 1980-; cp/Nat LWV; Leag Jewish Wom; Advtg Clb of New Orleans; Am Advtg Fd: Bd Mem, Secy, Editor of Newsletter, VP 1981-82; r/Jewish; hon/Silver Medal Awd for Consumer Mag, Advtg Clb of New Orleans 1978; 1st Pl Employee Relats, Public Relats Achmts, Am Hotel & Motel Assn 1979; Outstg Yng Wom Am 1980; Awd for Dir of Media Auction, Advtg Clb of New Orleans 1980.

YATES, BILLY SUMMERS oc/Executive; b/Dec 7, 1925; h/Dyersburg, TN; ba/213-219 W Ct, D'burg, TN; m/Mary Emmalene Eidson; c/William Mark, Laura Y Emerson, Mary Jane, Joseph Stephen; p/Arthur P and Nettie Summers Yates; ed/Att'd Murray St Univ 1946-48; mil/USN 1943-46; pa/Fdr, Owner, Mgr: Gen Appliance & Furniture Co 1948-; Dir First Citizens Nat Bank 1973-; Mem Fin & Trust Com 1977-; Tenn Retail Merchants Assn, Pres 1980-81; Nat Assn Retail Dlrs of Am, Exec Com 1965-; cp/D'burg Co of C, Dir 1964-68, VP 1968-70; Pres Dyer Co Fair Assn 1965-66; Chm Reelfoot Regional Lib Bd 1967-68; Meth Hosp, Memphis, Tenn Bd Mgrs 1980-; r/Meth; hon/Outstg Yng Man Am, Jr C of C 1951; Creative Salesman of Yr, Ladies Home Jour-NARDA 1959; Tenn Retailer of Yr 1974; Outstg Bus Man of Yr, Dyer Co, D'burg C of C 1979.

YATES, SANDRA KAYE CAIN oc/Administrative Assistant; b/June 26, 1952; h/1601 Blackhawk Dr, Opelika, AL 36801; ba/Opelika; m/James S; c/James S II, Wendy Michele, Jamye Rene; p/Horace E and Onzell V Cain, Childersburg, AL; ed/Alverson-Droughn Col 1971; Nat Col DA 1978-80; Paralegal Inst; pa/Adm Asst, Dist Atty's Ofc; Owner Girl Friday Unltd Employment Agcy; Co-Owner Hlth Resorts of Ala Inc; Pres Lee Co Legal Secy Assn; Pres Ala Dist Atty's Secy Assn; Ala Assn Legal Secys; Nat Assn Legal Secys; cp/Pres Demolay Mothers Clb; Lee Co Coun for Neglected & Dependent Chd; r/Bapt.

YATES, VICTORIA b/July 24, 1922; h/Salisbury, NC; ba/Livingston Col, Salisbury, NC 28144; m/Walter L; c/W Ladell Jr; p/Rufus Wesley Prince (dec); Dolores Prince Cortijo, Rio Piedras, Puerto Rico; ed/Oakwood Col 1944-46; Hunter Col 1946-47; AB Oakwood Col 1978; MA Columbia Univ 1950; Summer: Col Univ, Union Sem, Univ PR, Universidad Nacional, Mexico, Univ NC-CH, Madrid Univ, UNC, Univ Andes; pa/Oakwood Col Acad 1948-49; Livingston Col 1950-; Asst Secy, MLA 1968-70; Secy AAUW 1973-75; Area Rep Intl Relats AAUW 1975-78; r/Meth; hon/Fulbright Schlr to Colombia, S Am 1961; Phelp Stokes Fund, Caribbean Am Schlrs Exch Prog 1978; Phelp Stokes Fund Recip 1978; Ethnic Heritage Sem Part to Ivory Coast, Upper Volta, Sierra Leone, W Africa.

YEARGAN, JAMES EDWARD oc/Store Manager; b/Jan 22, 1953; h/LaFayette, AL; ba/4 First St, LaFayette, AL 36862; p/James C and Catherine C Yeargan, LaFayette, AL; ed/BS Samford Univ 1975; pa/Mgr Yeargan's Clothing Stor; Assoc Bd Ala Retail Assn; LaFayette Indust Devel Bd, Pres 1977-80; LaFayette Bus & Merchants Assn; cp/Chambers Co Rural Devel Com; Chambers Co Cattlemen Assn; Chambers Co Mus, Treas; r/Bapt; hon/Outstg Yng Men Am 1980.

YEATTS, PEARLINE oc/Associate Professor; b/Mar 16, 1932; h/Athens, GA; m/Charles B Thomas; c/Steve; p/dec; ed/BS Fla St Univ 1953; MEd 1957, PhD 1966 Univ Fla; pa/Assoc Prof Ednl Psych, Univ Ga; Pi Lambda Theta; Phi Delta Kappa; Kappa Delta Pi; Am Res Assn; cp/Pres Med Aux; Pres Hosp Aux; Adv Bd Mtl Hlth Assn; VP Symph Bd; hon/Conslt in Area of Spousing & Parenting & Child & Yth Mgmt.

YELTON, NOEL GRAY oc/Agriculture; b/June 12, 1937; h/Rt 5 Box 1977, Lebanon, TN 37087; m/Johnnie Mae Wright; c/Allen Gray, Angela Renee; p/Clarence Gray and Mary Irene Hays Yelton, Lebanon, TN; mil/AUS 1957-59 PFC; pa/FFA Alumni Assn; Wilson Co Farmers Coop; r/Presb; Elder; hon/Outstg Yng Farmer 1961; Outstg Dist Conserv Farmer 1979; Goodyear Tire & Rubber Conserv Merit Awd 1979; Am Farmer Deg 1957; St Farmer Deg 1955.

YELVERTON, STEVEN HAROLD oc/Soil Conservationist; b/Apr 30, 1957; h/Rt 2 Box 222, Daleville, AL 36322; ba/Troy; p/James H and Dorothy J Yelverton, Daleville, AL; ed/Att'g Auburn Univ; pa/Soil Conserv Ser; r/Bapt.

YETTER, TINA MARIE oc/Advertising Administrator; b/Nov 18, 1955; h/5124 Raymond Jays, El Paso, TX 79903; ba/El Paso; p/Richard and Lollie Yetter, El Paso, TX; ed/Att'd Tex Tech Univ; Att'g Univ Tex-El Paso; pa/Advtg Admr, Cummins Rio Grande Diesel; Acct Exec, Harris & Harris Public Relats 3 Yrs; El Paso Press Clb; Tex Press Wom Dist I, Corresp Secy; Advtg Fed Am, El Paso Chapt; Public Relats Soc Am, Rio Grande Chapt; Tex Intercol Press Assn; cp/Recording Secy El Paso BPW Clb; r/Meth; hn/Yng Career Wom of Yr, El Paso BPW Clb; Delta Delta Delta S'ship; SWn Sun Carnival Princess 1974; Finalist Miss La Placita 1975; 1st Pl Awd, Mag Illustration, Tex Intercol Press Assn.

YIANTSOU, CHRIS G oc/Physician; b/Oct 23, 1947; h/2525 Lakeview Dr, Bedford, TX 76021; m/Barbara Tibbets; p/Athanasios Moutzakas and Pinelopi Trigoni Yiantsou, Athens, Greece; ed/AA Frank Phillips Jr Col 1969; BS cum laude Univ Houston 1972; MD Tex Tech Univ 1975; St Paul Hosp, Dallas: Intern 1975-76, Res Med 1976-78, Res Gastroenterology 1978-79; Res Gastroenterology VA Hosp, Dallas 1979; pa/Med Pract Spec'g in Gastroenterology, Bedford, Tex 1979-; AMA; ACP; cp/Rotary Clb; Sotogrande Tennis Ctr; Hurst-Euless-Bedford C of C; r/Greek Orthodox; hon/Rho Chi; Phi Kappa Phi; Phi Theta Kappa; Bristol Awd 1972; W/W S&SW.

YOCOM, GWEN NICHOLS oc/Teacher, Composer-Musician; b/July 16, 1922; h/215 Citation St, Texarkana, TX 75501; m/John William Jr; c/Billie Gwen Womack, John William III, Kathie Jo Miot; p/Lewis Webber Nichols, Houston, TX; Mary Jo Britt Nichols (dec); ed/BSE So Ark Univ 1962; ME E Tex St Univ 1976; pa/Elem Tchr; Ch Organist; Piano Tchr; TSTA; NEA; TCTA, Sch Rep; Tex PTA Hon Life Mem; Delta Kappa Gamma, Local Mus Chm & Tex St Mus Com Mem; AAUW, 2nd VP; Tex Conf U Meth Wom, Organist at Meeting; r/Meth; hon/Composer "Top of the Mountain" *Intl Delta Kappa Gamma Prog Manual* 1978-79, 80; St Level Delta Kappa Gamma Hons 1979, 80; DAR Hons 1979, 80; Hon'd as Outstg Am Composer, Wednesday Mus Clb of Texarkana; Perf'd for Num Profl Orgs; Wrote & Perf'd Jingle for Texarkana Clean Commun Assn; Wrote & Perf'd Production Num for Miss Texarkana Pageant 1980; St, Nat, Intl Hons by Winning Top Hons in Contest of Orig Sacred Mus Progs Comp; 1 of 3 Am Composers to be Studied & Hon'd by Ga Delta Kappa Gamma Soc.

YORK, DON E oc/Executive; b/Sept 28, 1943; h/917 Althea St, Johnson City, TN 37601; ba/Johnson City; m/Parolea McCampbell; p/Dewey A (dec) and Bernice Ward York, Johnson City, TN; ed/BS E Tenn St Univ 1967; mil/USN; pa/Asst VP, First Tenn Bank; E Tenn St Univ Nat Alumni Assn, Treas; cp/Appalachian Chapt Mar of Dimes, Treas; U Way of Johnson City, Chm 1979; 1st VP John Sevier Chapt Am Ins Bnkg; r/Bapt: SS Tchr, Deacon; hon/E Tenn St Univ Outstg Ldrship Awd 1978, 79.

YOUNG, BARRON oc/Lifeguard, Pool Manager; b/Feb 15, 1952; m/Azaletha; c/Nathan Paul, Eric Barron; p/Paul and Lucy Young, College Pk, GA; ed/Att'd Acad of Prof Drafting pa/Lifeguard; Swimming Tchr; Pool Mgr; r/Bapt; hon/10 Yr Ser Pin 1980; Water Safety Ser Awd 1981.

YOUNG, ELEANOR ANNE oc/Associate Professor and Co-Director; b/Oct 8, 1925; h/1701 Alametos, San Antonio, TX 78201; ba/San Antonio; p/Carl B (dec) and Eleanor H Young (dec); ed/BA; MEd; PhD; RD Cert in Human Nutrition; Am Bd Nutrition; pa/Assoc Prof Med & Co-Dir Div of Human Nutrition; Am Gastroenterological Assn; Am Soc Clin Nutrition; Am Dietetic Assn; Am Soc Parenteral & Enteral Nutrition; Am Public Hlth Assn; cp/Am Heart Assn; Camino Real Hlth Sys Agcy; S Tex Hlth Ed Ctr; r/Active Mem Sisters of the Incarnate Word; hon/Sigma Xi; Assoc of Am Wom in Sci; W/W: Am Wom, S&SW; World W/W Wom; Personalities of Am.

YOUNG, EVELYN ELIZABETH oc/Director; b/Oct 31, 1919; h/3001 La Vista, Bay City, TX 77414; ba/Bay City; m/Jack Wesley Jr; c/Jack Wesley III, Clark Hopkins; p/William Bond (dec) and Dora Lynn George Harris (dec); ed/BA Tex Wom's Univ; MLS N Tex St Univ; pa/Dir Lrng Resources Ctr, Bay City ISD; TLA; ALA; Tex Assn Sch Libns; Tex St

Tchrs Assn; Delta Kappa Gamma; cp/Bd Dirs: Bay City Public Lib, Friends of Lib, Matagorda Co Mus, Pilot Intl; C of C; r/Presb: Ruling Elder; hon/St Bds: Tex Cong Parents & Tchrs, Tex Lib Assn, TASL; Delta Kappa Gamma; Pilot Intl 1st Lt Gov/Gov Elect, Tex Dist; Life Mem PTA; Pilot of Yr 1978.

YOUNG, HENRY ARCHIE oc/Associate Professor and Director Communication Skills; h/1187 Bayberry Ave, Baton Rouge, LA 70807; ba/Baton Rouge; m/Evelyn Stamper; c/Ronald Paul, Darryl Wayne, Ericka Arniece; p/Eddie Young Sr (dec); Arniece Gordon Young Horton (dec); ed/BA So Univ 1955; MA La ST Univ 1963; PhD Kan St Univ 1973; mil/AUS 1955-57; pa/So Univ: Dir Commun Skills Ctr & Assoc Prof 1977-, Dir Speech & Theatre Ed 1970-77, Supvg Tchr Speech & Theatre 1961-70; Public Sch Speech Correctionist, Iberville Parish Sch Bd 1957-61; Phi Delta Kappa; Kappa Phi Kappa; Nat Regional Dir, Alpha Psi Omega; Nat Assn Dramatic & Speech Arts; cp/Dem Party; Park Vista Assn; r/Bapt; hon/St's Best Actor 1951; Valedictorian 1951; T H Harris S'ship 1951; W/W Students 1955; Best Dir 1963, 68-70; W/W S 1980.

YOUNG, HENRY GRADY oc/Veterinary Acupuncturist; h/Thomasville, GA; m/Alma Pace; c/G Leon; p/Henry J Young; ed/Ga St Col for Men 1931-33; Univ Ga 1937; DVM Auburn Univ 1941; pa/Small Animal & Equine Pract, Ret'd 1978; Lectr Acupuncture; Org'd Intl Vet Acupuncture Soc; St Bd Vet Examrs; AVMA; GVMA; SGVMA, Exec 7 Yrs; Big Ben VMA; cp/Rotary Clb; Elks Clb; Farm Bur; Livestock Assn; r/Meth; hon/Cit of Apprec 1966; Vet of Yr, Ga 1974; Author "Atlas of Veterinary Acupuncture Charts" & "Basic Manual of Veterinary Acupuncture."

YOUNG, JAMES D oc/Special Agent; b/June 9, 1943; h/3606 47 St, Meridian, MS 39301; ba/Meridian; m/Gloria Sue; c/Brad, Gloria Holly; p/Hazel and Tom Young, Quitman, MS; mil/USN 4 Yrs; pa/Meridian Life Underwriters Assn; cp/Downtown Meridian Optimist Clb; r/Ch of Christ: Deacon; hon/Million Dollar Roundtable; Rookie of Yr in Miss 1976; Miss Agcy Bldr Awd; Nat Quality Awd.

YOUNG, JAMES HARVEY oc/Pharmacist, USAF Officer; b/July 27, 1948; h/607 A Seventh St, Maxwsell AFB, AL 36113; ba/Maxwell AFB; m/Nancy G; c/Dawn Renee, Kimberly Elizabeth; p/James L and Alice Young, Manor, GA; ed/AS S Ga Col 1968; BS Mercer Univ So Sch Pharm 1971; Dip Air Univ Squadron Ofcr Sch 1979; mil/USAF; pa/Pharm, Eckerd Drugs 1972-74; Owner-Oper Economy Drugs 1974-78; USAF Capt, Pharm Ofcr, Chief Outpatient Pharm 1978-; Tri-Co Pharm Assn, Pres; Ga Pharm Assn, VP 8th Dist; cp/Bd Dirs Loundes Chapt Kidney Foun 1977; Chm Bd of Dirs, Chm Steering Com, Pres Loundes Diabetes Assn 1976-77; Bd Dir Am Diabetes Assn, Ga Affil 1977-78; r/Bapt; hon/W/W: Students in Am Jr Cols 1967-68, S&SW 1980-81.

YOUNG, JAMES HILLIARD oc/Director of Institutional Development; b/Jan 29, 1946; h/1900 E 6th St, Greenville, NC 27834; ba/G'ville; m/Rebecca Barrow; c/Laura, Lisa; p/J W Jr and Lois S Young, Ahoskie, NC; ed/BS 1968, MA 1973 ECU; EdD NC St Univ 1977; pa/Dir Inst Devel, Pitt Commun Col 1977-; Asst to Pres, Pitt Tech Inst 1972-75; Dir Sports Info, ECU 1971-72; Dir Farmville Br, Pitt Tech Inst 1969-71; Acting Asst Dean of Men, ECU 1968-69; NC Commun Col Adult Ed Assn; NC Assn Res in Ed; Nat Coun for Resource Devel of Am Assn Commun & Jr Cols; Bd Dirs Nat Coun Resource Devel/AACJC; Nat Chm Com on St Couns, Nat Coun Resource Devel/AACJC; Past Pres Coun Ofcrs for Resource Devel; Region IV Coor, Nat Coun Resource Devel/AACJC; Editorial Asst *The Community College Review*; Adj Grad Prof of Higher & Adult Ed, George Wash Univ; Adj Grad Prof Adult & Commun Col Ed, NC St Univ; Nat Coun for Staff, Prog & Org Devel/AACJC; hon/W/W:

S&SW 1980-81, Students in Am Cols & Univs 1968; Most Outstg Student Legr 1978; ECU Pubs Bd Awd 1967; Author Num Profl Pubs & Papers.

YOUNG, JEWEL ANDREWS oc/Principal; b/Sept 16, 1915; ba/Marshall, TX; m/(dec); p/R T Andrews Sr, Indpls, IN; J Augusta Andrews, Wash DC; pa/Prin G W Carver Elem Sch; NEA; TSTA; Marshall Ed Assn; Phi Delta Kappa; E Tex Ed Res Coun Inc; Tex Elem Prin Assn; Nat Elem Prin Assn; cp/Secy Marshall Civic Ctr Adv Bd; U Way Bd; VP Cancer Bd; Trustee Bd Wiley Col; r/U Meth; hon/Profl Devel & Achmt Awd 1978; Ed Awd 1979; Outstg Ser Awd 1971; Outstg Achmt Awd 1971; Wom of Yr ABWA 1980.

YOUNG, NELDA JEAN oc/Pharmacist; b/June 18, 1956; h/RR 2 Box 74, Selmer, TN 38375; ba/Brownsville, TN; p/Gene and Lavada Young, Selmer, TN; ed/BS Pharm; pa/Pharm, Haywood Pk Hosp; Am Pharm Assn; r/Ch of Christ; hon/Outstg Ser to Am Pharm Assn; Secy Lambda Kappa Sigma; Mbrship Coor Am Pharm Assn.

YOUNG, PATRICK J H oc/Architect; b/Mar 17, 1930; h/PO Box 2396, Jackson, MS 39205; m/Hildegard Luise Vassmer; p/Andrew A J (dec) and Helen Loh Young, Scarsdale, NY; ed/Diplom-Ingenieur, Architekt (Germany); pa/AIA; Am Inst Physics; Acoustical Soc of Am; r/Prot; hon/Fellow ABI.

YOUNT, WILLIAM RICHARD oc/Minister of Education; b/July 8, 1948; h/6644 Fisher Ave, Falls Ch, VA 22046; ba/Falls Ch; m/Barbara Parish; c/Barbara Leanne, William Christian; p/William Lee and Audrey Shalley Yount, Clearwater, FL; ed/BS Univ Md 1973; MRE 1975, EdD 1978 SWn Bapt Theol Sem; mil/USAR SP4; pa/Pastor to Deaf, First Bapt Ch, Irving, Tex 1973-76; Min Ed, Columbia Bapt Ch 1976-; Registry of Interpreters for the Deaf; CSC; r/So Bapt; hon/J M Price S'ship Awd, SWn Bapt Theol Sem 1974; J P Price Meml Awd 1975; W/W Students Am Cols & Univs 1975 & 76; Albert Marsh Meml Awd 1976; Outstg Yng Men Am 1977; Author Num Profl Pubs.

YOUNTS, MILLARD STEPHEN (MITT) oc/Executive; b/May 9, 1950; h/Box 265, So Pines, NC 28387; ba/So Pines; p/Jack Spurgeon and Elizabeth Mendenhall Younts; ed/BA Wash & Lee Univ 1972; MA UNC-CH 1978; pa/Sta WEEB, So Pines 1973-: Sta Mgr 1974-79; Sandhill Commun Broadcasters Inc: VP 1974-79, Pres & Gen Mgr 1979-; Nat Assn Broadcasters; Daytime Broadcasters Assn: VP, Dir; Sigma Delta Chi; Sigma Nu; cp/C of C; Ducks Unltd; Overseas Press; Country Clb of NC; Elks; Kiwanis; r/Presb.

YOUNTS, WILLIE ANTOINETTE CAMP oc/Housewife; b/Sept 28, 1892; h/Atlanta, GA; m/Charles R; p/Paul Douglas (dec) and Ella Virginia Cobb Camp (dec); ed/BS, BMus Hollins Col; r/Bapt hon/Algernon Sydney Sullivan Awd, Hollins Col 1965; Hollins Medal 1967; LHD Deg, Erskine Col 1980; Chm Awd, Erskine Bd Cnslrs.

YOUSEF, YOUSEF A oc/Professor; b/Mar 27, 1930; h/Orlando, FL; m/Shirley J; c/Mike, Tim; p/Aziz Yousef and Mofida Yacoub, Alexandria, Egypt; ed/BSCE Alexandria Univ 1952; MSSE 1962, PhD 1965 Univ Tex-Austin; mil/Egyptian Army 1953-54; pa/Prof Engrg, Univ Ctrl Fla; Gordon J Barnett Prof of Envirl Sys Mgmt; Dir Envirl Sys Inst, Univ Ctrl Fla; Res Scist Assoc, Univ Tex-Austin; AEEP; WPCF; AWWA; ASCE; ASEE; NSPE; FES; FW&FPCOA; Profl Engr Fla & Tex; Chm Student Activs Com FSIAWWA, FPCA, FW&FPCOA; cp/PTA; BSA; Reg'd Voter; r/Coptic Orthodox; hon/Univ Awd for Excell in Res 1980; Walt Disney World Commun Ser Awd 1976; Sigma Xi; Chi Epsilon; Tau Beta Pi; Author Over 35 Articles in Tech Jours; Reports & Chapts in Var Books Relat'd to Envirl Engrg.

Z

ZADROZNA, DON J oc/Program Operations and Contracts Manager; b/Dec 21, 1934; h/Rt 4 Box 102 B, Elizabethton, TN 37643; ba/Johnson City; m/Mickey; c/Donna, Donald, David; p/Walter and Jean Zadrozna, Bergenfield, NJ; ed/BSME Univ Bridgeport 1957; pa/U Aircraft Res 1957; Worthington Corp 1958-62; Tex Instrs Inc 1962-; Nat Contracts Mgmt Assn; Am Soc Mech Engrs; Am Soc Indust Engrs; cp/Carter Co C of C, Bd Dirs; VP Jr C of C, Irving, Tex; Alpha Phi Ommega, Treas; r/Cath.

ZAFIRUDDIN, MOHAMMAD oc/Family Medicine; b/Jan 1, 1933; h/3113 Chelsea Dr, Augusta, GA 30909; ba/Augusta; m/Barira Khatoon; c/Anwer Rasheed, Qaise Rasheed, Qurratulain Tabassum, Farhatulain Tasneem, Nikhat Sima, Sarwer Rasheed; p/Nabi Akhtar and Hajra Khatoon, India; ed/Darbhanga Med Col Bihar Univ: MB, BS; Bd Cert'd & Dip Fam Pract Am Bd Fam Pract 1978; FAAFP 1979; FLEX Exam Med Lic USA; pa/Bihar St Med Ser 1959-65; Res House Ofcr, Darbhanga Med Col Hosp 1957-59; Res Med & Pediatrics, Brit Nat Hlth Ser, England 1965-70; Pvt Pract Med, India 1970-72; Phys Morganton, NC 1972-73; Res Michel Reese Med Ctr 1973-74; Phy Pownal, ME 1974-75; Phys Weston Hosp, Weston, WV 1975-77; Pvt Pract, Augusta, GA 1978-; Med Staff: St Joseph Hosp & Univ Hosp; So Med Assn; Am Acad Fam Pract, Am Geriatrics Soc; r/Islam.

ZAGURSKY, GEORGE PALMER oc/Supervising Engineer; b/Dec 14, 1943; h/9041 SW 140th St, Miami, FL 33176; ba/Miami; m/Jacquelyn Hayden; c/Adam Hayden; p/George and Kathryn Hreneczko Zagursky, Yonkers, NY; ed/BS Miss St Univ 1968; MBA 1975; Doct Cand Nova Univ; pa/Supvg Engr, Power Plant Engr Dept, Fla Power & Light; Am Soc Mech Engrs; Am Nuclear Soc; cp/Good Govt Mgmt Assn; r/Luth; hon/Miss Acad Sci Schlr.

ZASTOUPIL, MARK A oc/Corporate Industrial Engineer; b/Aug 29, 1951; h/PO Box 1184, Mt Dora, FL 32757; ba/Mt Dora; c/Jeanna Kay; p/Arthur John and Ruth June Grimm Zastoupil, Janesville, WI; ed/BSIE Univ Wis 1973; Bus Mgmt Dip, LaSalle Univ 1976; pa/Corp Indust Engr, Doric Foods Corp 1978-; Green Giant Co 1973-78; AACE; AIIE; cp/Rotary Clb of Mt Dora, Bd Dirs 1980-81; Wis Alumni Assn; Mt Dora C of C; Adv Com Bd, Bus Dept Mt Dora HS; r/Meth; hon/W/W S&SW.

ZETLIN, THALIA oc/Marketing and Product Development; b/Mar 18, 1952; ba/Hallandale, FL; p/Lev and Eve Zetlin, Manhasset, NY; ed/BA NYU 1974; PAS Univ Miami Sch Bus 1975; MBA Fla Atlantic Univ 1980; pa/Pres Zetlin-Beer-Liu Inc; VP, Dir Zetlin-Argo Liaison & Guidance Corp; Dir Thalia B Linen Boutique; Export Conslt, Polar Chips Intl; Computer Programmer Lev Zetlin Assocs Inc 1972-73, Mktg Coor 1973-75; Acct Exec, Whittelsey Woods 1975-76; Mensa; Intertel; Am Mgmt Assn; cp/Fla Team Intl Challange Cup; r/Jewish; hon/Phi Kappa Phi 1977.

ZIMMERLY, ARTHUR W oc/Director of Engineering; b/June 6, 1918; ba/Dir of Engrg, Wadley Hosp, 1000 Pine St, Texarkana, TX 75507; m/Cleo Johnson; c/Delbert, Mary Z May; p/Charles P (dec) and Louisa F Zimmerly (dec); ed/Col of the Mines; Intl Corresp Sch; Tex A&M Col; Univ Tex; pa/Elec Apprenticeship 1933-37; Plumbing Apprenticeship 1937-41; Supt Mech Construction on Hosps 13 Yrs; Dir Engrg, Wadley Hosp 21+ Yrs; Past Pres Tex Assn Hosp Engrs; Ark Assn Hosp Engrs: 1st Pres, Fellow 1974-; Ark Hosp Assn, Personal Mem; Am Soc Hosp Engrs: Bd Dirs 4 Yrs, Chm Bylaws Com, Ad Hoc Com on Equip Standards; Tex Hosp Rep to Am Soc Hosp Engrs 6 Yrs; cp/U Way Budget & Fin Com; Bd Dirs, Tri-St Chapt, Am Red Cross; Bd Dirs & Past Pres Boy's Clb; Bldg Com, Texarkana Hist Soc & Mus; Noon Optimist Clb; r/Bapt: Deacon; hon/W/W SW 1980; Robert C Paul Awd 1980; Author AHA Engrg Handbook, Chapt 11 1974.

ZIMMERMAN, LARRY WAYNE oc/Executive; b/Aug 28, 1948; h/Highland, MD; ba/6900 Wis Ave, Chevy Chase, MD 20015; m/Susan Carol Heitmuller; p/Bernard William and Mary Louise Zimmerman, Lanham, MD; ed/BSCE Valparaiso Univ 1970; pa/VP Arthur Beard Engrg Inc; Reg'd Civil Engr & Cert'd Value Spec; Am Mgmt Assn; Soc Am Value Engrs, Dir DC Chapt; Water Pollution Control Fed; Am Water Works Assn; r/Luth; hon/W/W Bus & Fin; Co-Author Value Engineering 1980.

ZIMMERMAN, RAYMOND ERNEST oc/Consulting Engineer; b/Oct 19, 1903; h/4803 Sunset Cts #502, Cape Coral, FL 33904; m/Loretta Francis Markle; c/Robert, David, Patricia, Barbara, Gail; p/Corwin (dec) and Katherine Zimmerman (dec); ed/BS 1926, MS 1927, EM 1930 Penn St Univ; mil/AUS Ret'd Lt Col; pa/World-Wide Coal Spec; Past Prof & Hd Dept, Col of Mineral Sci, Penn St Univ; Dir of Res & Mgr Coal Processing for Var Cos; VP Paul Weir Co, World-Wide Mining Conslts; AIME; CIM (Can); IM&ME (UK), Fellow; Profl Engr USA & Can; Fellow Min Processing Soc (UK); cp/Masonic Orders, 32°; Pi Kappa Phi; r/Prot; hon/Phi Lambda Upsilon; Sigma Xi; Sigma Gamma Epsilon; Author Coking Properties of Coal 1979; Contbg Author Coal Preparation 1980; Assoc Editor World Coal; Author Many Tech Articles in Sci Jours.

ZINN, ELIAS PAUL oc/Executive; b/July 11, 1954; h/Houston, TX; m/Janis Turboff; p/Julius and Harriett Dubinski Zinn, Sugarland, TX; ed/Att'd Univ Tex; pa/Pres, Chief Exec, Chief Oper Ofcr Custom H F; BBB; cp/Contbr WA & Var Other Orgs; C of C: Houston, Dallas, Okla City, Phoenix; r/Jewish.

ZIPPERER, JOHN KYLE oc/Farmer; b/Feb 28, 1919; h/Valdosta, GA; m/Mary H; c/John K Jr, Mary Sue Z McLane; p/John H and Thelma C Zipperer, Valdosta, GA; ed/Att'd Abraham Baldwin Agric Col; mil/USAAC; US Inf NG; pa/Ret'd Asst Dir Commodities Promo Div, Ga Dept Agric; Lowndes Co Farm Bur, Pres; Nat Soy Bean Com, Am Farm Bur; cp/Lowndes Co Bd Commrs; Valdosta-Lowndes Co C of C, Bd Dirs, Chm Agric Com; r/Bapt; hon/Dist'd Flying Cross, USAC; Air Medal w 2 Silver OLCs.

ZOHDI, MAGD ELDIN oc/Professor; b/Apr 18, 1933; h/5050 S Chalet Ct, Baton Rouge, LA 70808; m/Omnia; c/Tarek, Mona; p/Ismail and Nemat Zohdi, Cairo, Egypt; ed/Dip Engrg 1954; BS 1962; MS 1965; PhD 1969; pa/Maintenance Engrg, Design Engrg 1954-60; Instr 1962-64; Okla St Univ 1966-68; Assoc Prof, La St Univ 1969-75; Prof, Indust Engrg, LSU 1975-; Coor Engrg Mgmt Prog, LSU 1977-80; Dir Machining Tng Inst 1978-80; SME; AIIE; Alpha Pi Mu; Sigma Xi; Tau Beta Pi, Grad Fac Mem; cp/Chm Bd Am Contracting & Trading Corp; r/Muslim; hon/W/W Am 1980; Outstg Edrs Am 1972; Standard Oil Excell in Undergrad Tchg Awd 1971; Fav Prof, Student Vote 1970-71; Pres Hon Awd, OKU 1968; Fulbright S'ship 1964; Pub'd Author Num Profl Jours.

ZORRILLA, LEOPOLDO oc/Surgeon; b/June 29, 1941; h/312 Ivy Ln, San Antonio, TX 78209; ba/San Antonio; m/Esther; c/Aida, Monica, Miguel; p/Leopoldo and Stella Zorrilla; ed/BS Escuela Nacional Preporatoria, Universidad Nacional Autonoma de Mexico 1957; MD Escuela Nacional de Medicina, Universidad Nacional Autonoma de Mexico; Intern Univ Tex, S Tex Med Sch & Bexar Co Hosp Dist 1963-64; Res Gen Surg, Univ Tex, Med Sch San Antonio & Bexar Co Hosp Dist 1965-69; Res Thoracic & Cardiovascular Surg, Univ Tex, Med Sch of San Antonio & Bexar Co Hosp Dist 1969-71; pa/Cardiovascular & Thoracic Surg; Instr Microbiol & Parasitol, Univ Tex Med Sch 1962-63; Asst Experimental Lab of Biol, Secy of Ed 162-63; Clin Assoc Prof, Thoracic & Cardiovascular Surg, Univ Tex Med Sch; Pres Denton A Cooley Cardiovascular Surg Soc 1978-79; Bexar Co Med Soc; Tex Med Assn; AMA; San Antonio Med Assn; San Antonio Surg Soc; Soc Thoracic Surgs; So Thoracic Surg Assn; FACC; FACS; FACCP; FACA; FICS; Fellow Cardiovascular Surg, Tex Heart Inst 1971-72; hon/Dip for Top Med Student, Nat Univ Mex Med Sch 1960; Highest Average Grade Among Cands Taking Profl Exams to Obtain MD; Phys Recog Awd, AMA 1969, 72; Author Num Profl Articles.

ZSCHAU, JULIUS JAMES oc/Executive; b/Apr 1, 1940; ba/2515 Countryside Blvd, Suite A, Clearwater, FL 33515; m/Leila Joan Krueger; c/Kristen Elisabeth, Kimberly Erna, Kira Jamie; p/Raymond Johann Ernst (dec) and Rosamond Lillian Malicoat Zschau, Phoenix, AZ; ed/BS 1962, JD 1966 Univ Ill; LLM John Marshall Law Sch 1978; mil/USNR (Active) 1962-64; (Inactive) 1964- Comdr; pa/Atty Ill Ctrl RR Co; Assoc Coin & Sheerin; Assoc Snyder, Clarke, Dalziel, Holmquist & Johnson; Counsel Ill Ctr Corp; VP Gen Counsel; Secy Am Agronomics Corp; Pres Sorota & Zschau; ABA; Chgo Bar Assn; Clearwater Bar Assn; Fla Bar; Ill St Bar Assn; Land Trust Com Fla Bar; cp/Kiwanis Clb, Clearwater E, Dir; Clearwater C of C; Chm Govtl Affairs Coun; Cand Repub Nom Ill St Const Conv; r/Ch of Christ; hon/Author "Preservation of Wetlands."

The Governing Board of Editors, Board of Directors and Staff of *The American Biographical Institute* wish to congratulate the preceding biographees on their

leadership, dedication and achievements.

Appendix I

State-Locator Index

ALABAMA

Abercrombie, Betty Webber
Acevedo-Akin, Angela Rosa
Adair, Lillian Duffee
Adams, Terry Wayne
Adkison, Charla F. S.
Adrian, John L.
Agan, Verlon Otho
Anderson, Thomas Wayne
Andrews, David Kirkland
Armstrong, Anita Gay
Armstrong, Lucile W.
Bagby, William Woodrow
Baines, Donald Dean
Baker, Mabel Louise
Balentine, Robert Chapman
Ballard, Betty Ruth
Barfield, Kenny Dale
Battles, Wilfred Clay
Bauer, Kathy Kirk
Baugh, Jimmy Dale
Baxter, Cheryl Harbin
Beaube, Albert Vardaman
Beck, Lee Randolph
Bekurs, William McDonough
Benefield, Larry David
Bentley, Frank H.
Berry, Julia Elizabeth
Bevill, Tom
Bishop, William Lee
Blackmon, Jo Ann
Blake, Jr., John Everett
Blankenship, Rodney Wayne
Blanton, Jr., Fred
Bliesener, Ada Michelmann
Bolton, Euri Belle
Bounds, Sarah Etheline
Bourgeois, Linda R. R.
Boyd, Lillie A.
Bracewell, Thomas Frederick
Braswell, Ethel Lanier
Brewer, David Curtis
Brokaw, Jr., Marvin J.
Browder, Johnie Mae
Brown, Sandra Loy
Bryant, Anita Jane
Brymer, Mariah Bradford
Buegler, Brian Joseph
Burks, Gilbert Denson
Butler, Raymond Preston
Bynum, Jodie
Calhoun, James Walter
Campbell, Carolyn Holcombe
Campbell, III, Robert Craig
Campbell-Goymer, Nancy Ruth
Capleton, Eddie Lee

Capps, Bruce J.
Carmichael, Dorothy S.
Chambless, Jr., Ralph Proctor
Christian, Samuel Terry
Clark, Willard
Clayton, Jerry Mack
Coker, Lillian Johnson
Coleman, Claudette Tonia
Colle, Barbara W.
Collins, Clarence Cecil
Combs, Sonya Rea H.
Cooper, Warren
Covin, Theron Michael
Creek, Joseph William
Cross, Edna Morris
Crownover, Kenneth Andrew
Crump, Freida
Crumpton, Marilyn Elizabeth
Cruse, Irma Russell
Cushing, Harrell Rich
Dodd, Teddy
Daniels, Tonja Anne
David, Andrew Ganes
Davis, Jr., Henry
Davis, Jr., John Alton
Davis, Jr., Roger Warren
Davis, W. Hubert
Dedmon, Bobby Gene
Denis, Sandra Smith
Dennis, Paul T.
Denny, Jr., William Aloysius
DeRusso, Mitchell Lance
Dewberry, Inez Stephens
Dial, John Halvin
Donnelly, Bradford Hilton
Donnelly, Daniel Herring
Donnelly, Edward Daniel
Douglas, Janice Hendon
Drummond, Garry Neil
Dunn, Edra Norris
Dunn, Ernestine Long
Dyer, Carolyn Elizabeth
Eaker, Sylvia Britton
Eason, Sharon E. H.
Earnest, James Ezra
Edmonson, Mary Louise Baird
Edwards, Joe E.
Elkins, Russell Keith
Ellison, Dorothy S.
Essenwanger, Oskar M. K.
Farmer, Wade Odice
Farr, Roy H.
Felts, James Donivan
Fincher, Freeman O.
Fitzgerald, Albert Joseph
Flack, Wilma Lee
Flegle, Larry Vernon
Fletcher, Dixie Chafin
Foster, Caroline Robinson

Foster, Eva Gargus
Fowler, Bruce Wayne
Fowler, E. Bert
Freeman, Katherine
Friedman, Barbara Baxter
Fucci, Linda Dean
Fuller, Gary Lee
Furr, Frank
Furr, Ray A.
Gardner, Herbert F.
Garner, James
Garrison, Lawrence
Garth, Gwendolyn Sharpley
Gaston, Jr., Charles L.
Geer, George H.
Gibson, Edward L.
Gillion, Marguerite Copeland
Glover, Kenneth S.
Goff, Kenneth Dale
Gonce, Marion Wilson
Grant, Ike
Grant, Jr., William Alexander
Gunn, George Robert
Gunter, Aubrey Murray
Haley, Jess Lee
Hall, IV, Samuel Jonathan
Hall, Jr., Thomas Francis
Harris, Jane Maddox
Harris, Mildred Marshall
Harrison, Henry Ford
Hassell, Dorothy Howard
Heatherly, Jerry Ronald
Henderson, Carol Morner
Hermann, Brenda Louise Ann
Higginbotham, Sara
Higgs, William Robert
Hill, Laura Freeman
Hixon, Christine P.
Holly, Lewis Reynolds
Holston, Jr., James
Hoover, Miriam Jackson
Hope, David Lee
Howard, Leonard Ambers
Howard, Marjorie Elaine
Howell, Winston C.
Hoyle, Emma Jean
Hubbard, Edward Sims
Huttenstine, Marian Louise
Inman, Imogene J.
Irby, Paul Daniel
Jenkins, Gelah Evelyn
Jennings, Brenda M.
Jinks, Sr., Kenneth Allen
Johnson, E. C.
Johnson, Odie Quitman
Jones, Annie Ruth
Jones, Bettye G.
Jones, Mildred Josephine
Jones, Paul O.

Kelley, Carlton William
Kelley, Michael Francis
King, Lynn Hawkins
Kirby, Mayme Clark
Knaub, Donald E.
Knight, Eugene
Knopp, William Earl
Koplon, Maneul
Kranert, Veda Proctor
Kutzman, Sondra Klementis
Langford, Mabel Hayes
Larkin, Barbara Shores
Lasseter, David F.
Lawson, Archie David
Lawson, Inez, G.
Layton, T. Ethel
Lazenby, William Douglas
Lee, David Lennox
Lemley, Barbara F.
Lester, Edgel C.
Liu, Y. A.
Locklar, Wayne Everett
Lovelace, Katie W.
Lowder, Edward Lewis
Lowery, Dwight Nelson
Luccasen, Jr., Rapheal Andrew
Luce, Dwain Gregory
Lyman, Ruth Ann
Lyon, Rebecca Saxon
Maddox, Joe Wayne
Mandrell, Regina Moreno
Marbury, Larry A.
Marsh, Randall Conway
Martin, Dolores Leonard
Martin, Patty L. A.
Martin, Sherrill Virginia
Mashburn, Charles Leonard
Mathews, Allen McLeod
Maxwell, Louis
Maynor, III, Hal Wharton
Meigs, Walter R.
Merriweather, Betty Rose Atmore
Miller, Lloyd Jackson
Mills, Dolories Miles
Milton, Jerry Martin
Miranda, Osmundo Afonso
Mitchell, Kelly Karnale
Mitchell, William Eason
Montgomery, Joseph Horace
Montgomery, Lucretia Brown
Morrissette, Hattie Mae
Moss, Dike Lee
Murphree, William R.
Myles, Patricia Glass
McAlister, Thomas Edward
McIntyre, Michael Todd
Neighbors, Jr., Joe Larson
Novell, Earl Kenyon
Nunnelley, Kenneth Sloan
Owen, Ross C.
Parker, Melissa Anne
Patterson, Earline C.
Pauley, Alta L.
Phillips, Regina Kay
Pickens, Willodine Robbins
Pilgrim, Raymond W.
Poitevint, Katherine Brown
Prestridge, Clara Ann
Purnell, Frank Delano
Rabin, Jack
Randall, James Allen
Rankin, Julius Earle
Ray, Jr., Michael Thomas
Reid, Jr., Richard Stetson
Reynolds, Mildred Dawn
Rice, Alice Marie
Riley, Enos Edward
Robbins, James Martin
Roberts, Mary Diane

Robinson, Barbara Geneva
Robinson, Emma Lou
Robinson, Marion, Everett
Rogers, Rebecca Laine
Roth, William Stanley
Russell, Doris Sue
Russell, Judy
Samford, Jr., William James
Sampson, Larry Le Roy
Sams, Alice Elizabeth
Sayers, William Earl
Schmidt, Miriam Kirbye
Scott, Thomas Allen
Sentell, Suzanne Harrison
Sexton, James David
Shankle, Millicent Hislop
Shelton, Jr., Gayle Cochrane
Shelton, Oress Orlando
Shope, Mark L.
Silvers, Morgan Dougherty
Simpson, James Kenneth
Sington, Fred W.
Sirote, Jr., Jerome David
Skinner, Robert Earl
Skipper, Robert Vernon
Smith, Charles Larry
Smith, Ernest Lester
Smith, Marshall Wayne
Smith, Mary Elizabeth
Snyder, James Richard
Spector, Daniel Earl
Spruill, Jr., Oscar
Stallworth, Edward
Stanley, Lucy Redus
Starling, Harvey Milton
Stewart, Fred
Stringer, Herman E.
Stringfellow, Mary Elizabeth
Stroud, Joseph Cleveland
Suiter, Leo Frank
Suiter, Robert James
Surbeck, Elaine
Swindall, Margaret Lee
Taffee, Jr., William Francis
Taylor, Kenneth Byron
Teaford, Ruth Romine
Terry, William Ray
Thomas, David L.
Thomas, Sarah Ward
Thompson, Jr., Andrew Boyd
Thornton, Nancy Rumsey
Thurman, Sr., Mortimer Jefferson
Tidwell, Norman Olen
Tietke, Wilhelm
Tindol, Laymon Hayes
Tucker, David
Turner, Josephine
Twining, Henrietta S.
Tyson, John Ethredge
Vallely, Cheryl Clements
Valrie, Georgia Sharpe
Vance, John S.
Vandiver, Jr., Raymond Franklin
Vestgard, Estelle Burnham
Vickrey, Jr., James F.
Vincent, Robbie Ann
Vinyard, Rebecca Cornelius
Vinson, Jr, Clarence David
Viohl, Frederick Albert
Wagoner, Lou Ann Hagan
Walker, Ara Belle
Walker, Henry Nell
Wallace, Sam Franklin
Ward, Joseph Offie
Warner, Patricia Davis
Weaver, Larry J.
Webb, Larry Wayne
Wesley, Steven Lynn
Westerhouse, Leon Martin

Wheeles, Anita Harris
White, Carrie Barran
White, E. V.
White, Gayle Farmer
Whitman, James Madison
Wilder, Ruth Stewart
Williams, David Carl
Williams, B. Steven
Willmon, Jesse Conrad
Wilson, Ginny
Wilson, Linda C.
Wilson, Sandra Scott
Windham, Maud Byrd
Wissel, Mark Edward
Wood, Karen McMahon
Worley, Nancy Lillian
Wrenn, Bessie Mae
Wright, Laura Frances
Yates, Sandra Cain
Yeargan, James Edward
Young, James Harvey

ARKANSAS

Adcox, II, James Murray
Aeilts, Michael Edward
Baker, Garland Ray
Baker, Gilbert Ray
Banks, Marlon Chandler
Benson, John Bernard
Bidewell, Charles Robert
Bobo, Eugenia Annette
Boden, Lily Wright
Breckenridge, Marilyn Grace
Brewer, Orpha Roseta
Brittain, Kathy H.
Brown, Charles Howard
Brown, Richard
Bryant, Howell Dee
Bumpers, Dale
Burks, Jimmy L.
Burris, Frances
Burrow, T. Bruce
Calvert, Richard L.
Carson, Sonja Yvonne
Case, Jack W.
Cheatham, Joel W.
Clinton, Bill
Cook, Doris Marie
Cook, Shirley
Cooley, Carolyn Ann
Cooley, James Frances
Creggett, Carutha Earnestyne
Cumbie, Michael Howard
Cunningham, Bethel Payton
Daves, Doryes
Deatherage, Octavia Hudson
Dillon, Terry Lynn
Di Massimo, E. Faye
Driftwood, Jimmy
Eaton, James Woodford
Eckert, Elaine Berg
Edwards, Richmond Summers
Faulk, Lillian T.
Flanzer, Jerry Philip
Foster, Robert J.
Frueauff, Sue Adcock
Garner, C. Wayne
Gentry, William Norton
Giles, Stephen Richmond
Glover, Marion Sue
Goldsby, Wilmer Dean
Gregson, Thomas Larry
Gronwald, Viola Hill
Hale, Norman Fisher
Harris, Virginia D.
Hartsfield, Betty T.

Hartsfield, Wayland Marshall
Hayles, Jasper A.
Haynes, Mary Margaret
Hildebrand, Jr., George
Hindmarsh, James Wesley
Holder, Clinton L.
Hood, Susan Diane
Hooker, Billie J.
Huffman, Donald R.
Hughes, Edwin McCulloc
Jenkins, Jr., Will M.
Johnson, Beverly Kim
Johnson, Geraldine Meador
Johnson, Rufus Winfield
Jones, Floyd Leon
Kahler, Taibi
Kaundart, Wes
Keaton, Edwin Alexander
King, Calvin Richard
Konert, Ann Marie
Kunkel, Mary Elizabeth
Laird, Robert Donald
Landtroop, Michael Eugene
Larey, Bert B.
Lawson, Carrie O.
Lawson, Samuel David
Lewis, Bessie David
Lewins, IV, Thomas M.
Lyles, Yvonne Brigman
Mack, Janis C.
Martz, Irene
Miller, Gregg Edward
Miller, Marilyn Eve
Miller, Maxine
Minton, Hubert Lee
Moore, Bettye Jo Read
Morris, Delovis A.
Morsani, Al
Mosby, Jr, Robert Scott
Myers, Cecil Everett
Nayles, Lee C.
Nester, Ruel Paullus
New, Michael W.
Nichols, Gregory D.
Nichols, Marguerite
Niemiec, Jerome Peter
Nokes, Georgina Woodruff
Pallone, Sharon Raney
Parrish, Wilma King
Patangia, Hirak C.
Paul, Patsy L. Wittenauer
Phillips, Alvon Wayne
Pillert, Pat Akers
Plummer, Jack Moore
Qualls, Patricia Stella
Ramsey, Thomas Harrison
Redmond, Stanley Edward
Reeves, Annie Laura
Roy, Elsijane Trimble
Ruby, Jr., Ralph
Ryan, Alice Lee
Sandford, Juanita M. Dadisman
Schmidgall, Robert Lee
Seawood, James Russell
Sikes, Lawrence C.
Smith, David Lee
Smith, Delphia Frazier
Smith, Lander Arthur
Smith, Lee
Snuggs, Ann
Sooch, Kewal Singh
Spray, Jr., Robert L.
Staffs, James R.
Stark, Jr., Bert
Staton, Sr., James Lorin
Stephens, John Utley
Stevens, Arthur
Stipe, John R.
Stone, Ruby Elizabeth

Straka, David Eugene
Taylor, Theman Ray
Thaxton, Marvin Dell
Thompson, Bobby W.
Tinker, J. Troy
Tippit, Clifford Bruce
Tuberville, Robert Shelton
Underwood, Johnnie Carl
Waldo, Joel William
Walker, Sandra Louise
Warren, Eleanor Ruth
Warren, Lillie Bell
Webb, Percy Eugene
Wesley, Theressa Gunnels
West, Ross Anthony
West, Patricia A.
Whillock, Carl S.
White, Gloria
Whitefield, Carolyn Lee
Wickes, Jeannie Kim
Williams, Marvin Eugene
Wren, Donald Gregory
Wright, Marie Runyan
Wyrick, Mary K.

DISTRICT OF COLUMBIA

Ainslie, Michael Lewis
Bemley, Jesse L.
Brown, Mildred Johnson
Harper, III, James Weldon
Jackson, Anthony D.
Keating, William F.
Kelly, Eric Leroi
Kraetsch, Gayla Anne
Moore, Julia Shirley
Pannell, Rinaldo Dimitri
Rahall, II, Nick Joe
Ramseur, Alviadean
Silvin, Richard Rene
Spohn, Peggy Weeks
Toland, Mary Bernadette

FLORIDA

Abel, Florine
Acker, Louise Ida
Ackerman, Lois
Adamson, William E.
Allen-Jones, Pamela
Altman, Steven
Amodio, Joseph John
Anderson, Jim
Anderson, Victoria Elaine
Antonova, Elizabeth
Arango, Abelardo de Jesus
Arndt, Pauline B.
Arthur, Bradley
Arthur, Jeffrey Michael
Askew, Reubin O'Donovan
Axton, Araminta Elizabeth Akin
Ayers, James Lee
Bagwell, Gerald E.
Baker, Earl B.
Balladares, Mario Perez
Barbo, Anita Gail
Barfield, Eddie E.
Barnes, Annette Casey
Barnes, Linward Irvin
Barrowman, Kino Sakuma
Bayless, Dan J.
Baynard, Mildred Moyer
Bays, Hattie
Beall, Sr., Roy Burns
Beasley, Edwin Lee

Bell, Blanche Kelley
Bendell, Leonard
Bennett, Charles E.
Birdsong, Gloria J.
Bishop, Katherine Elizabeth
Blackburn, Jr., James Ross
Blackman, Betty Lou
Blakeley, Polly Figg
Blevins, Dallas Ray
Bliss, Mary Ann
Bloom, Harold Edward
Bochman, William Charles
Bolesky, Karen Luise
Bonds, Virginia W.
Bokhardt, Edward Lee
Boozer, John Elbert
Borkan, William Noah
Bowman, Robert D
Boyce, Jeddiah Monroe
Boydston, Carol Ann
Bradbury, Rosanne B.
Braiman, Dale Edward
Brassell, Carl Steve
Bratt, James Howard
Bruck, Charlotte Marie
Bryan, II, Jacob Franklin
Bucher, Francois
Buck, Vivian Louise
Buehring, Mary Ellen
Bugg, Charles
Burris, John Louis
Busek, Bernice A. W.
Buslig, Bela Stephen
Butcher, Lois M.
Butler, Michael Bernard
Campbell, L. Adonis
Cann, Marjorie Mitchell
Cardoso, Anthony A.
Carlton, Fran
Carnevale, Dario
Carrabba, Michael Paul
Carter, Harriet Vanessa
Castro, Theresa
Caturano, Carlo
Chacko, John K. Y.
Chambers, Michael Lee
Chastain, Cecil P.
Cheng, Bin-Luh
Clark, Marie Tramontana
Clarkson, Charles Andrew
Clarkson, Lawrence William
Clontz, Jean Toney
Clunn, Patricia Ann
Cohen, Sheryl E.
Collins, Ada Latrelle
Collins, Jacquelyn E.
Conard, Richard T.
Corbitt, Sarah Caruthers
Corsello, Lily Joann
Costello, Paul A.
Crews, Harold Richardson
Croft, H. Colbert
Croft, Joyce
Cromwell, Cheryl Dorsey
Crossley, Jr., George Leslie
Crowther, John Belcher
Cushman, Laura
Dabney, Hubert O'Donald
Davidson, Joy A.
Davis, Sr., John Clement
Davis, Samuel Adams
Davis, Sara Jewell
Davis, Pamela Jo
DeLattibeaudiere, Alfred George
Della Valle, Dorothy Muir
DeMaio, Anthony Francis
De Sear, Jr., Vernon L.
De Villar, Delia Diaz
Dinculeanu, Nicolae

Douglas, Sr., Robert Walter
Drake, Paul David
Drake, Robert Eldon
Duffee, Betty Brown
Duffer, Michael Irad
Dummer, Dyeann Reddig
Dunn, Elsie Hyder
Dunn, Richard Van
Dykes, Margaret Himmel
Earwood, Margaret Ogden
Edwards, Elwyn Gerald
Edwards, Martha Lo Green
Elmore, Ponce Leroy
Embree, Thomas E.
Evans, Marilyn Bailey
Fair, Matthew Dewey
Farber, Erich Alexander
Farmer, George
Farr, David T.
Faulk, Wayne Stephen
Fedor, Sharon Jeanne
Fernandez, Eric
Fess, Richard Allen
Field, Elizabeth Ashlock
Figuerdo, Nancy
Fish, William Sterling
Flake, Janice Louise
Fleming, Lacie Theresa
Fordyce, Michael W.
Fortune, Hilda Orr
Foster, Anne S.
Fox, Paul John
Fragale, Anthony Francis
Franklin, Jr., Sylvester
French, John H.
Friedman, Richard Nathan
Fuller, James Walker
Fulton, Michael Nelson
Gaines, Ruth Carpenter
Gainous, Jr., Rabie J.
Garland, Ruth Taylor
Gasperoni, Emil
Gay, Marjorie Anderson
Gaynor, Leah
Geldart, Donald Blair
Geltz, Charles Gottlieb
Gerstung, Katherine
Gerato, Erasmo Gabriele
Gibbs, Jr., George Fort
Gilbert, Leonard H.
Gildred, Victoria
Gilhooley, George
Gittner, Cory Hugh
Glenn, Carolyn Love
Goff, Doyle Roger
Gomez, Jorge
Gottschalk, Constance
Graham, Bob
Greene, Ray Joseph
Griffiths, Muriel Anne
Grimm, Betty Jane
Gutowski, Edward Paul
Habal, Mutaz B.
Hamrock, Marilyn Angela
Harbert, Barbara Koch
Harbert, Jason Talmage
Hardman, Patricia Kirven
Harris, James Robert
Harris, Maude Edwards
Harte, Eva Mary
Hassell, Herman
Hastings, Peter Coleman
Haviland, Leona
Haws, Ronald William
Hayes, Betty Jo Bates
Hayter, Darlene C. Holland
Head, Marilyn Eleanor
Heald, Tee Davis
Heavner, Jr., John Milton

Heidrich, Herman J.
Heltsley, Thomas Allan
Hernandez, Maria C.
Herndon, Betty Lou
Herold, Crystal Lee
Hester, James Timothy
Hester, Ruthia Riggins
Hickey, Elizabeth Grandoff
Hickon, Frances Aspinwall
Hiller, Jr., E. A. Sturgis
Hobby, Nellie Leilla
Holcomb, Mildred
Holland, Hal Derrington
Hooper, Marjorie Seaton
Horgan, Michael Cornelius
Hornsby, J. Russell
Houck, II, Edward B.
Hough, Margaret Lee
Hubbard, Frank Muldrow
Humphries, Joan
Hunsaker, Edwin Luaine
Huth, Douglas Werner
Imparato, Edward Thomas
Jarkowski, Boleslaw Zenon
Jeffret, Mary Madelin
Jenks, Sallie Ann
Johns, Randall L.
Johnson, Joyce K.
Johnston, Ada Clara
Johnston, James E.
Jones, Miriam Esther C.
Khuen-Kryk, Barbara Cottom
Kimber, Alice Mae
Kimber, Victor Daniel
King, Bonnie Ezzell
Kiser, S. Craig
Kish, Lawana Frey
Klein, Bernard
Klopfenstein, Connie Becker
Kokenzie, Henry Fayette
Krider, John Samuel
Kuzbyt, Raymond
LaBarbera, Frank Thomas
Lammerding, John Jude
Lancaster, James Franklin
Lang, Franz
Langley, Sr., Wilbur H.
La Rowe, Georgia Ann
Larsson, Donald Eric
Lawson, Kenneth Ray
Lawandales, Rochelle W.
Lee, Joseph R.
Leetzow, Jr., Leonard Ermond
Lefevre, Margaret Clark
Leonhart, William Harold
Levine, Jack H.
Liesen, Dorothy Ann Thiel
Ligon, Janice Maiden
Loper, Marilyn Sue
Luckey, Diane V. M.
MacKinnon, F. T.
Manning, Altha
Marmo, Franklin Christopher
Marshall, Kathryn Amy
Martinez, Milton E.
Martinez, Sergio Ernesto
Mathews, Wanda Phillips
Matyi, Marie Friedley
Meeks, Sr., Philip
Meetz, Janette Jackson
Mendell, Jay Stanley
Meryman, Charles Dale
Meyer, Grace Bernstein
Mezian, William Sarkis
Mikronis, Christos Edgar
Minshew, C. Genece
Miranda, Mercedes Diaz-Cuervo
Moore, Vivian Myers
Moos, Joy

Morris, Julia Rith
Morris, Ruth Falls
Morton, Christine Rita
Moss, Mike
Mount, Margaret Elizabeth
Mowbray, James Arthur
Munro, Nancy James
Murray, Janet Baum
Myers, Robert Lawrence
McClure, George Gillen
Nakashima, Tadayoshi
Nelson, Lawrence R.
Nelson, Ralph Erwin
Nelson, William Roy
Newman, Willie B.
Nies, Jr., Robert John
Nill, Carl Jonathan
Niver, Pruella Cromartie
Noble, Frances Elizabeth
Oates, Grady Rembert
Oldham, Dorothy A. Cloudman
Oliver, Sheryl Lynn
Osborne, Basil Royston
Osborne, Karen
Oswald, William Jack
Parker, Herbert Gerald
Parker, Joanna Jayne
Parker, Loislee M.
Parrish, Margie Embs Wood
Penaroque, Ernest
Perez, Josephine
Perlman, Eileen Eleanor
Petterson, Sylvia Roysene
Phillips, Eleanor Z.
Phillips, Margarita Gomez
Pickel, Conrad L.
Pielago, Brunilda Nunez
Pirnat, Janet Wenger
Pittman, Sidney E.
Pitts, Keeffee L.
Platt, Jan Kaminis
Plivka, Andres Daniel
Polopolus, Jean Calton
Ponds, Jr., Otis D.
Porter, Darwin F.
Porter, Henry L.
Powell, Iris Burnette
Proctor, Howard Blake
Pyle, Jr., Raymond James
Randolph, Lester
Rappaport, Harold
Ratliff, Dale H.
Raval, Pinakin M.
Recio, Francisco Hernandez
Reed, Carol Ann
Reeves, Samuel Dwain
Richard, Jr., Raymond Joseph
Riggs, Cecil Graham
Rimel, George William
Rinehart, Leila Mae
Rinehart, Richard Duane
Ritson, Rina
Roberts, Mary Belle
Roberts, Susan C.
Robinson, B. Lynn
Robinson, Debbie Jean
Roever, Frederick H.
Ross, Hezekiah
Sanchez, Dianna Gayle
Sanchez-Cifuentes, Zoila
Sanders, Terry L.
Sandoval, Mercedes Cros
Santa-Maria, Yvonne Z.
Sauter, Mary s.
Schaffer, Ronald Lee
Schlam, Edward H.
Schlusemeyer, Christina Schiller
Schuck, Marorie M.
Schultz, Jr., Robert Melvin

Schurr, Sandra Lee
Scroggie, Warren Gene
Seay, Miriam Tye
Sena, Dean R.
Shane, Alan Richard
Shane, Deborah
Sherman, Edwin Bernard
Shipley, Reign Hugh
Short, Charles Ernest
Short, Dorothy B.
Sillers, Marjorie Joyce
Simpkins, III, Nat Stone
Singer, Raymond
Skidmore, Lawrence M.
Slater, Constance Finch
Slaughter, Jane Mundy
Slonim, Roberta Raymond
Smith, Arthur Cloyd
Smith, Dale Howard
Smith, Harrison Harvey
Smith, Mary Wilmous
Smith, Nancy Irlene
Smith, Thomas L.
Scottile, III, James
Stadsklev, Joan Bylsma
Stampa, Julian Claude
Stark, Norman
Stein, David Eric
Sternlieb, Antonia
Stewart, Jeannette Morency
Stoddard, Donna Melissa
Suarez, Ceasr Antonio
Suarez-Del-Campo, Raul A.
Sugarman, Betty A.
Sullivan, Margurette
Sullivan, Robert G.
Tabor, Alfred Donald
Tagliarini, John Alden
Talley, Walter Reed
Taylor, Nancy Jane
Taylor, Jr., Robert
Taylor, Thomas Allen
Telford, Donald McCrea
Terry, Harry Reginald
Therrien, Jr., Francois Xavier
Thomas, George
Thompson, Alfred Alexander
Thompson, Deborah
Thompson, Effie Clark
Thrash, Sara Arline
Titus, Phyllis
Tobal, Marcos Andres
Todd, Betty Mae
Tomassi, Theresa Cecilia
Torczynski, Elise
Touton, Linda A.
Tranquillo, Mary Dora
Tsao, Ming-Jyi
Turner, Donald Edwin
Turner, Leonard Philip
Viera, Christobal Eugenio
Vollber, Fred H.
Wakefield, Sr., George Norton
Walker, Charles A.
Walker, David Le'ron
Wallace, Alfreda J.
Walsh, Ruth Hammill Murphy
Warden, Lewis Christopher
White, Barbara Williams
Whitfield, Carol J.
Williams, III, Arthur Lee
Williams, Latimer Freeman
Wilson, Jacques M. P.
Wilson, Paul E.
Wilson, Sharon C.
Wimberly, George Terrance
Wiseman, Bernard
Wolf, James Gary
Wollstein, Donald Gustav

Worden, Lucille W.
Workman, Virginia W.
Wright, Evelyn Jean
Yarborough, Robert Earl
Yousef, Yousef A.
Zagursky, George Palmer
Zastoupil, Mark A.
Zetlin, Thalia
Zimmerman, Raymond Ernest
Zschau, Julius James

GEORGIA

Abbott, Sr., Gary Louis
Abernathy, Ralph David
Abrams, Bobby
Acton, William Carroll
Alderman, Jr., Louis Cleveland
Allison, William W.
Anderson, James Otis
Bagen, Sara Jacobs
Baker, Willie Gaskin
Barfield, Virginia Grant
Barnes, Marylou Riddleberger
Barron, Bobby Curtis
Baxley, Eugene L.
Belcher, William Oyd
Bell, Getha Gina
Bennett, Jr., Willam N.
Benton, Delmus Cecil
Beverly, W. Ronald
Blanchard, Patrick G.
Blayton, Doris Ada
Blicksilver, Edith
Bodnar, Donald George
Boe, Gerard Patrick
Bolen, William Harold
Bond, H. Julian
Borowsky, Jane Barrow
Bowers, Linda Kay
Bradley, John D.
Brightwell, Juanita S.
Brinson, Valera
Brooks, Owen Wayne
Brown, Amanda J.
Brown, Billy Joe
Brown, J. Billy
Brumeloe, Thomas Ezra
Bryant, Jimmy Carl
Buckins, Hattie F.
Buice, Patterson N.
Burchfield, Jewel Calvin
Burris, Maureen Smith
Byers, Kathleen L.
Cahoon, John Tillman
Cargile, Mary Chasteen
Carithers, Helen
Cavanagh, Harrison Dwight
Chambers, Louise Pierce
Charleston, Ollie Peters
Childers, Terry Oliver
Chitwood, Lorene McDaniel
Clayton, Robert L.
Clements, Mason Carter
Coffee, Mack
Coggins, Patrick Churchill
Collin, Mary A.
Collins, Jr., C. D.
Collins, Jr., Raymond L.
Collins, Ruth Harvey
Collins, Sadie Bell
Connor, Jerry
Constant, Clinton
Copeland, Mary L. Jones
Costa, Manuel A.
Coston, Robert Donald
Cousins, Sharon Daves

Crockett, Delores Loraine
Crump, Mary Quinn
Dabney, Sr., Joseph Earl
Daniel, Eunice Bacon
Dasher, Charlotte Ann
Davenport, Evelyn Cora
Dayhuff, III, Charles Hal
Delves, John Alistair
Dewberry, Jr., Marvin Larry
Dickerson, Adolphus Sumner
Dinning, Ada Rozell
Donahue, Katherine C. C.
Drinnon, Doris Jean
Drury, John Terry
Duke, Alvan Eugene
Duke, Julie Anne
Duke, R. L.
Eaves, A. Reginald
Edgens, Dana Byington
Edwards, Willie George
Eidson, John Olin
Elkins, Jr., James Andrew
Ellison, Darrell F.
Engerrand, Doris A. Dieskow
Fannings, Shirley McGee
Farmer, Jay Pratt
Fendley, Charles Robert
Findley, Bowden
Fiorentino, Carmine
Forsyth, Prescott
Fortson, Jr., Benjamin Wynn
Fox, Sandra Elaine
Freeman, Mary Bertha
Gentry, T. Rudene
Gore, III, Dean Franklin
Goss, Eunice, R. A.
Graham, Susann Burford
Grant, Monroe Cleveland
Green, Ruth Goswick
Greene, Randall Allan
Griffin, Dorothy Roper
Griffin, Larry Don
Gruber, Ellen Joan
Hall, Sue Hammack
Ham, Robert Ellis
Hammond, William Jackie
Hand, G. Othell
Harris, Pamella D.
Hart, Eloise
Hartline, Jeff
Harvard, Beverly Joyce
Harvey, Gerald
Hayes, Oscar Lawrence
Hazel, Delores Simmons
Hazel, James Andrew
Hibbs, Betty Ellis
Hobby, Jr., Robert Donald
Holley, Anna Marie
Hollingsworth, Denver
Holyoak, Hugh Kenneth
Honeycutt, Jerry Randall
Hopkins, George M. M.
Horton, Willie Mae
Houser, Louise Kelley
Howe, Sr., Courtney Everett
Hulvey, Larry William
Hutchins, Myldred Flanigan
Jackson, Jr., Maynard Holbrook
Jennings, Thomas Harold
Johnson, Agata Palmisano
Johnson, Carlene Franklin
Johnson, Dorothy Purnell
Johnson, Frank J.
Johnson, Peter Michael
Johnston, James Franklin
Jones, Annie Gay
Jones, Betty V. B.
Jones, Evelyn Lee
Jones, Maggie O'Neal

Joyner, Delores
Kauffman, Glenn Edward
Kidd, Virginia Steadman
King, Ralph Donald
Kinney, Mary Alice
Knowles, Faye Bottoms
Korduba-Underwood, Olga Maria
Ladson, Lucia Zaehert
Laerm, Joshua
Lamb, Jr., Fred F.
Lathem, Betty Brooks
Lawson, Marshall Lee
Lewis, Rosa Mae
Liner, Olga L.
Lipscomb, Buford Milton
Littlefield, Jr., Richard Wells
Longmire, Siothia R.
Lowry, Vinie Langley
Lynn, Byron Stephen
MacMillan, Judith Ruth
Marsden, Ruth Elizabeth
Martin, Clifford W.
Mason, Marjorie Smith
Massell, Sam
Mathis, Gwendolyn Ann
Maxey, Joe O.
Maxwell, Ruth Ledbetter
Maynard, Kenneth Delano
Mealing, Esther Morrison
Millwood, Jr., Clayton Lamar
Moore, Jon Milton
Morgan, Jr., Branch
Morgan, Karl Ziegler
Moseley, Nancy Lea
Murdoch, Helen Hembree
Murphy, Mary K. C.
Murphy, Michael Conlon
McClain, Ruth Brantley
Nox, Gordon Hilliary
Ogletree, David Lawrence
Ogunsusi, Patricia A.
Olinger, Ralph Harvard
Ong, Antonio Lim
Osborne, James Sanford
Pafford, Gladys Lucile
Parker, Jr., Bill C.
Payne, Grace Lillian
Pendergrass, Suzane Shingler
Pendleton, Inez M.
Pesto, John Lawrence
Peters, Kathleen Joy
Pitts, Sr., Roy L.
Poe, Booker
Polatty, Rose Jackson
Polstra, Larry John
Pope, Douglas Lee
Pope, III, George Washington
Pryor, Wallace C.
Ray, Eliza Owen Britt
Rice, Louise
Roberts, James Deotis
Robinson, Ralph Eugene
Rodgers, Lillian Scottie
Rogers, Jan Faulk
Rogers, Lewis Frank
Rogers, Shelby M.
Ross, Sr., Willie Herman
Rucinski, Carole Ann
Sampson, May Dorothy
Saunders, Annette G.
Schofield, Paul
Scott, Becky W.
Scott, Wilton C.
Sherrill, Donald G.
Sims, Alvin Lamar
Skalak, Constance Havird
Slagle, William Lee
Slater, Betty C.M.
Smith, Boyce Miles

Smith, Donald Alan
Smith, Sr., Hulet
Smith, Willie A.
Sowell, Geneva Wentz
Sousa, George Robert
Staublin, Judith A.
Stepp, Florence Davis
Stokely, Sr., James Royal
Streed, William Eric
Studstill, Jr., Owen Lamar
Swaggerty, Glenn O.
Tatro, Ethel Helen
Thomas, David Raymond
Thornton, Howard L.
Tinkey, Ted D.
Tisdale, Verlie Ann
Trammell, Alsie
Usrey, Claudine C.
Vickers, Edwad Davin
Vinson, Mildred Gallman
Wagner, Clarence, Madison
Waldrop, Jr., William Allen
Walker, Donna Kay Woods
Walker, Pamela Dotson
Wallace, Joyce Cotter
Waller, Robert Edward
Walton, Carole
Warren, Lynwood
Washington, George Bernett
Waters, Ruth Ann
Weaver, Preston D. T.
Webb, Jr., McKinley
Wheeler, Tony Ladell
Wheeler, III, William Bryan
Wilkinson, Bruce H.
Williams, WIllie Lethait
Wilson, Andgelia Proctor
Wilson, Mary Ross
Winter, Katie Marilyn C.
Wright, Dianne Hamby
Yeatts, Pearline
Young, Henry Grady
Younts, Willie Antoinette
Zafiruddin, Mohammad
Zipperer, John Kyle

KENTUCKY

Abbott, Lester B.
Abner, Orville
Adams, David
Adams, Herbert Hall
Agee, Nell V.
Alexander, Robert William
Anderson, Evelyn Pearl
Ashby, Barbara B.
Bailey, Margaret W.
Baker, Alma Watkins
Baker, Eric White
Barnett, Ronald Harold
Belcher, Edith Faye
Bergeron, Maurice L.
Bernard, Delmar George
Blevins, Mary Frances Dobbs
Blevins, Phillip K.
Blythe, Lenamae
Bogie, Nora A. Brock
Book, John Kenneth
Boone, Emily C. K.
Bowling, Lowell O.
Bradley, Joseph Edward
Breckenridge, Jr., Howard
Brown, Billie Gordon
Brown, Kenneth Alden
Browne, William Joseph
Brumfield, Don

Buchanan, Sue Broadrick
Burgess, Sr., Blair Davis
Butler, Charles E.
Butts, Michele Tucker
Byers, David Wilburn
Callen, Jeffrey P.
Carr, David Shpeherd
Carrington, Sharon Reid
Carson, Sylvia
Carter, Mack King
Catron, Jennie Rachel
Catron, William Richard
Churchwell, John Richard
Civey, III, George Arnott
Clark, Charles Douglas
Clayton, DeWayne Lamont
Click, Paula Tammie
Coldiron, Fannie Lee
Coldiron, Pearl McHargue
Colmer, Neil Alan
Conley, Lois Jean
Cooper, Bennis L.
Cooper, James Ivin
Coots, Herman Woodrow
Correll, Charles E.
Cox, Coy Gene
Crafton, Paula Marita
Daniels, Carol Dean
Davis, Edward Waller
Davis, Ruth Rogers
Dennison, Jerry Lee
Denton, Thomas Stewart
Dix, Barbara Louise
Dobbs, Virginia Elizabeth
Dorn, William Denton
Doyle, Elizabeth Ann Lewis
Dragoo, Barbara Ellen
Drummond, Kathleen
Dunn, Michael Ratliff
Earles, Pat S.
Eilerman, Charles Bernard
England, James Calvin
England, Perry Lewis
Engle, Edgar V.
Feathers, Cheryl Ann Wright
Ford, Jr., Gordon Buell
Ford, Jr., William Edwin
Foster, Maurae H.
Fox, Lucy Reed
Franklin, Herbert
Gabbard, Ralph W.
Garland, Virinda Lee
Garrison, Juanita
Gevedon, Millard Lee
Gibson, Beatrice
Gibson, Ray Allen
Goff, Eris Hughs
Graddy, IV, William Henry
Gray, Gwendolyn E. W.
Greathouse, Gladys Millard
Green, Joe Ralph
Gregory, Yvonne Belmont
Gresham, Jr., Roy Milton
Gunn, Danny E.
Gwaltney, Mildred B.
Hamra, Armel Jean
Hancock, Joyce Ann
Hansford, Willard
Hays, Edwin Keith
Hopewell, Paul Dennis
Hopkins, Larry J.
Howard, Curtis Damone
Huddleston, Frank Henry
Huffman, Dixie Matherly
Hyden, Jerry W.
Ikerd, Jr., Frank Heller
Ireland, Kate
Isenberg, Charles Clayton
Jackson, Earl Junior

Jasper, Danny
Jessie, Paula Blanton
Johnson, Mary Ann
Johnson, Mary Louise
Johnson, Norma W.
Jones, Elsie Williams
Keene, Susie
Kelley, Duane Neil
Kim, Suk Ki
Kirkland, William Minor
Kirkwood, El Wanda J. Shields
Knight, Richard Gene
Kruse, Richard Harry
Lacy, Elsie H.
Lake, Wendell Wilkie
Lamb, Mary Kay
Lawrence, IV, Robert Landy
Lawson, Dorothy Mae
Lee, Steven Michael
Lester, Deborah Moore
Locke, John P.
Lockwood, David M.
Logue, Bruce Wayne
Long, Elsie S.
Lowery, Michael Douglas
Major, Florence Ruby
Malone, Nancy Cameron
Marcum, Hilda Berniece
Marks, John Courtney
Martin, Melvin D.
Martin, Terry Joe
Mercer, Sharon Eli
Milburn, Theresa Holtzclaw
Milburn, William Isaac
Milby, Ruth Kittrell
Mills, Wanda Lee
Mitchusson, Stella Hudson
Moore, David Eugene
Morris, Cecil Arthur
Morris, Harry Lee
Muntz, Charles Edward
Myers, Helen Mack
Nelson, Thomas Dwight
Nicely, Gary L.
Noah, Shirley Jean
Ogden, Frederic, Dorrance
Oliphant, Sonny
Outland, Charles Michael
Parsley, Brantley Hamilton
Patrick, Jean Fraser
Phillips, Donald Eugene
Pickering, Martha Elizabeth
Pierson, Jane Wilhelmina
Pollio, Michael A.
Porter, Stephen Michael
Proffitt, Thomas William
Pullum, Jr., George William
Reece, Donnie Richard
Rice, Michael
Roberts, Robert Joseph
Robinson, Ralph R.
Rollo, F. David
Russell, Gail Yvonne
Saffels, Michael Aaron
Sams, Glria V.
Sandifer, Velda Rae
Sanford, Edgar Earl
Schuler, Beth Ann
Scott, Linda Preston
Scott, Madison Myers
Sgroi, Mick
Shaddock, Joanna Ruth
Shell, Vicki E.
Shelton, William Bernard
Simpson, James Harrison
Sims, Russell Adron
Slagle, Patti Lynn
Smith, David Ray
Snyder, Gene

Southwell, Aletha Vinson
Speakman, Shelbie Jean
Stewart, Catherine Sue
Summer, Sally Williams
Sutton, Doris Greene
Taylor, Thelma
Terry, Warren Bergen
Thompson, Kenneth Herman
Thorton, Martha Katherine
Thurman, Nancy Lee
Trew, Reba Clair
Turnbow, Cynthia Ann Williams
Turner, Willie
Wade, Glenda
Wagers, James Ralph
Wan, Richard T. C.
Washington, Jr., Joe Iva
Watkins, Edwin R.
Webb, Anne Kavanaugh
Weddle, Leo Franklin
Weinsensel, Mary Elsie
White, John L.
Whitton, Thomas Richard
Wilkinson, Ancil Clifton
Williams, Glenwood Creighton
Williams, Ruby C.
Williamson, Lou Eugene
Williamson, Marti
Wilson, Nancy Carol
Wilson, Pauletta M.
Winters, James Michael
Wolfe, Michael Joseph
Yost, Frank A.

LOUISIANA

Allen, Elbert E.
Babineaux, Linda Randall
Baharloo, Carla Ruzic
Baker, Helen V. B.
Ballard, John Wayne
Barnett, Rosemarie Long
Bello, Jan R.
Berger, George Donald
Berry, Kathrlyn Ballard
Bevins, II, Thomas Peter
Blaise, Phynye L. G.
Boggs, Corinne Claiborne
Booth, Mary Jean Young
Bracewell, Mervell Winzer
Braxda, Frederick Wicks
Brecheen, Doris Wilkinson
Brian, Jr., Alexis Morgan
Brooks, Frederic Lenox
Brooks, James Wright
Brumfield, Shannon Maureen
Bynum, Jack L.
Caldwell-Burke, Maxine
Carbon, Jr., Frank Henry
Carey, Harvey L.
Cazalas, Mary Williams
Christian, Linda Kay
Cooper, Michele Abington
Cox, Hollis Utah
Cunningham, Sandra
Danner, Carolyn Davidson
Davis, Ouida Sue Ristom
Dennison, Kathleen Mulvey
Deutsch, Eberhard Paul
Dodson, Margaret
Edwards, Ella Chandler
England, Lynne L.
Finch, Thomas W.
Fisher, Elizabeth C. B.
Fitzsimons, Agnes Marie
Flannery, Gerald V.
Fuller, Claude Conyer

Gibson, Jon Lee
Hall, Celie Williams
Halperin, Sanford B.
Harris, Sharah Renea
Harston, Hazel Toler
Hebert, Carolyn Mae St. Amant
Helm, Boyd Edward
Hewitt, Helen Smith
Higgins, James Watson
Hindsman, Billie Faye
Hood, Edwin Cornell
Huckabay, Georgia Anne
Jackson, Shirley Johnson
Kedia, Prahlad Ray
Kern, Blaine S.
Kidd, Catherine June
Kinchen, Thomas Alexander
Knight, Karen Linda
Langley, Janie S.
Lee, La Juana Williams
Lin, Chiang
Lipstate, Eugene J.
Little, Florence E. H.
Long, Russell B.
Loyola, Andrea A.
Manson, Frederick Lee
Markham, William Hubert
Massett, William August
Matheny, Tom Harrell
Maund, Linda Kay
Michaelis, Carol Tingey
Miller, Preston Joseph
Miller, Sr., Richard L.
Moore, Frederick Alvin
Neef, Hazel E. Mouton
Patrick, Victor Eugene
Pearce, Charles Wellington
Pearce, Dorothey DeL.
Pitts, Emma Thomas
Popadic, Joseph Stephen
Pugh, Sr., Charles Wernis
Purtle, Virginia
Rathmell, Aretta Jennings
Register, Milton Dean
Richardson, III, Francis Joseph
Rizzo, Mary Joanna
Romera, Dudley M.
Ross, Nell Triplett
Sale, III, Tom S.
Schexnayder, Glenn D.
Sciacca, Sr., William Wayne
Seale, Ruth Lamb
Sellers, Joseph Amos
Singleton, Nan Chachere
Smith, Henry L.
Smith, Susan Louise
Spillers, Jr., Lloyd S.
Stanberry, James Phillip
Stricks, Richard Bert
Tan, Billy Too Seng
Taylor, JoAnn Gilbert
Teal, Jacquelyne Sue
Thomas, Julia Mae
Thomas, Philip Robinson
Thompson, George Wesley
Tillman, Celestine
Tilly, Lois Amelia
Treen, DAvid C.
Treuting, Edna Gannon
Turner, Jr., Joe Vernon
Tynes, Katherine M.
Vaeth, Aatha Min-Chun Fang
Vining, Jean Wingate
Watrous, Eleanor Burns
Watson, Johnie Butler
Westmoreland, Jr., Thomas D.
Williams, Doris E.
Williams, Ellis
Williams, Sr., Freddie

Williams, Johnnie Beatrice
Wishard, Betty J.
Yasnyi, Linda F.
Yelverton, Steven Harold
Young, Henry Archie
Zohdi, Magd Eldin

MARYLAND

Ahalt, Mary J.
Andrews, James David
Armstrong, Ernest W.
Barfield, Rufus Lenro
Bishop, James Edward
Botts, Mercedes Blow
Braddy, Johnny Ell
Brandt, III, Edward William
Bridges, Leon
Bush, Esther Lorean
Cameron, Jr., Don Davis
Carpenter, Norma Rowe
Clemons, Claire Nell
Colbe, Bonnie Lee
Coyne, Margaret Purcell
Dean, Vallie Loleta
Donlon, Michele Lynn
Drach, Marian Capozzi
Ehrlich, Bernard Herbert
Fox, Roaxanne Elaine
Gershowitz, Sonya
Goldstein, J. Jeffrey
Greentree, Eleanor M.
Hahn, Alan Theodore
Harper, Bernice Catherine
Harris, Florence Catherine
Hawkins, Sarah Margarett
Henschel, Beverly Jean
Horner, Patricia Irene
Houck, Jr., Lewis Daniel
Housewright, Riley Dee
Howard, Barbara Burrow
Hug, Richard E.
James, David P.
Jeffries, William Worthington
Jenkins, Andrea Sharon
Keel, Jr., Alton Gold
Kohler, Helen Rosalie
Kronk, Annie King
Li, Choh-Luh
Marsicovete, Joseph Charles
Martin, Linda Reid
Matthews, D. Ernest
Miller, George Crawford
Mumby, William
Myers, Samuel Lloyd
Nee, Linda Elizabeth
Nemesh, Anna
Orwig, Anne Louise
Ourednik, John Matthew
Pearman, Sr., Reginald A.
Peterson, Donald M.
Potts, Bernard
Proctor, Ruth Alice
Rao, Mamidanna Seshagiri
Rea, Hazel White
Reed, Jr., Proctor
Rogers, Paul A'Court
Schulte, Linda Sullivan
Seng, Minnie A.
Shelton, Bessie Elizabeth
Shirk, Perry William
Silverman, Faye-Ellen
Souza, Anthony R.
Sohl, Robert Charles
Spruce, Frances Blythe
Stafford, Thomas John
Streckfus, Barbara Ann

Taylor, Doris, Wright-Harris
Trundle, Linda Irene
von Kutzleben, Bernd Eberhard
Weatherholtz, Joan H.
White, Patricia Smith
Wiernik, Peter H.
Wynn, Prince F.

MISSISSIPPI

Abadie, Jr., Charles F.
Ables, Clyde Rayford
Abraham, II, George Ellis
Adams, Jr., John Melvin
Adams, Larry Edward
Allen, Pauline Virginia
Allred, Judy A.
Anderson, Harold A.
Anderson, Herbert R.
Balmat, Cora Suits
Barnes, Bernard
Batson, Blanche Desmond
Battle, Minnie
Beck, James Keith
Bennett, E. Ray
Betterton, Robert Jerry
Biggers, Jane Richardson
Black, Barbara Joyce
Bole, Robert H.
Bounds, Iduma P.
Boyd, Fay Merrill
Boyd, Otis
Boyles, Mary Lou Massey
Braddock, Paul Frank
Branch, Joe L.
Brantley, Sylvia Luzette
Breazeale, Marvin E.
Brewer, Betty Ann
Broadway, Ronald Rex
Browder, Milford O.
Brown, Billy Gunn
Brown, Bina Ruth
Brown, Jether Lee Walker
Brown, Patsy Sue
Brown, Sr., Richard Jess
Browning, William C.
Brumfield, Robert Edsel
Bullock, Robert Edward
Burge, Jerry C.
Burnett, Nellie Lee
Bush, Miller Wayne
Butcher, Vera Robinson
Butler, Shirley Gee
Butler, William Cuttiss
Bynum, L. S.
Byrd, Marquita Lavon
Cain, Murray Leland
Calvery, Sr., Thomas Cleaton
Carter, Jr., Charles F.
Carter, Jr., John A. P.
Case, Eugene Cliff
Casey, Offa Lunsford
Cocilova, Norma Jane
Cooper, Bobby G.
Cotten, Frances Louise
Cox, Alma E. Van Hook
Cox, John Wesley
Cranston, John W.
Crapo, Dorothy S.
Crowe, Richard A.
Daniels, Douglas Bryan
Davis, Jr., Sidney D.
Davis, William Ralph
Deese, Rutha Merle
Dick, Sr., W. Arsene
Dilworth, Derbert L.

Dixon, Peggy Lee
Dorman, Roy Loil
Dorsey, Leonia Collins
Dye, Brad
Eckhardt, Ruth H. F.
Ellzey, Francis Lindsey
Emanuel, Alice Harriet
Farmer, Charles Richard
Floyd, Lewis Earl
Fulton, Virginia
Furr, Elizabeth Sugg
Garrett, Mary Laura
Gatlin, Walton Eugene
Gentry, Jr., Charles Melvin
Ginn, Doris
Golden, Jr., Woodrow Wilson
Goodwin, Frances Elizabeth
Gordy, Joe C.
Gore, Billy Mac
Gough, Helen
Grayson, Jacob Henry
Greer, Patricia Fay
Griffin, Daniel Watson
Halbert, Jean F.
Hall, Charles Worth Leo
Hammer, Michael Wallace
Haralson, Linda
Harrell, Roxann
Haris, Eva Hall
Harris, Henry Lee
Harris, Versie H.
Harrison, Albert Curtis
Hayes, Maxine Delores
Hayes, Phyllis
Hazard, Florence McLeod
Heath, Bobby Jerrell
Higginbotham, Katie Sowell
Hinton, Betty B.
Holloway, Carl Dewitt
Hopper, Eugene
Hughes, Edith M.
Hughes, Robert B.
Irvin, Christine Frelix
Jackson, Marjorette
Jackson, Martha S.
Jacobs, Keith William
Johnson, Charles Elbert
Johnson, Michael Roy
Johnson, Nellie
Johnson, Richard Alvin
Johnston, Ricky E.
Jones, Donald Reginald
Jones, Dorothy Dix
Jordan, III, Samuel
Kenmar, Daniel Joe
Kennedy, Sherron Mae
Kinder, Jr., Frederick Earl
Knight, Mary L.
Ledbetter, Jeannette Given
Leonhard, Sr., John R.
Lewis, Charles B.
Lewis, Emma Goldman
Lilly, Thomas Gerald
Lindsey, Charles Albert
Louis, Helen Louise
Lucas, Aubrey Keith
Lucius, Dennis Joe
Lynch, Mary Lynn
Magee, Sadie E.
Marantz, Bart
Marks, Alphonse Michael
Mattox, Johnny Lynn
Maxwell, Frances Marion
Melchor, Ollie Mae
Middleton, Maria Dickerson
Minton, Marvel Sue
Mitchell, Janet White
Mize, Mark
Mohr, Gordon Jack

Moize, Jerry Dee
Morris, Cynthia Elizabeth
Mott, Jerry
Murray, Hal J.
McHenry, William Earl
McNabb, Martha Sue
Nix, James Carroll
Norman, Wallace
Paden, Curtis W.
Papasan, Mavour Ruth
Parker, Sr., Amos Philip
Patrick, Gracie M. Bonner
Patterson, Suzannah Annette
Pelton,.R., William Allen
Pendleton, Joyce Sharp
Phillips, George Landon
Pigott, Helen Sue
Pirkle, Estus Washington
Pitchford, David W.
Pitts, Ben Ellis
Reynolds, Evelyn C.
Rhodes, Cecil B.
Richardson, Willie
Robbins, Yvonne O'Ferrall
Roberts, Joe DeKalb
Roberts, Joyce Elaine
Robertson, Howard Norman
Robinson, Alfred Barnette
Robinson, Ronny Earl
Rogers, Gaines Madison
Rone, Dennis B.
Ross, Jeffrey Keith
St. Clair, Helen Allison
Sanders, Virginia Fraley
Scorr, Jr., Charles Orlen
Seale, Edythe Whittington
Simmons, Anne B.
simon, Lillie Belle
Skelton, James Alonzo
Sledge, Robert Owen
Smith, Bettye Jane
Smith, Eva D.
Smith, Frances S. Thornton
Smith, Julius Michael
Smith, Nancy Veronica
Smith, Jr., Zelfred Clyde
Sprayberry, Mary Evelyn
Stevenson, Drucilla Pace
Stewart, Bonnie Pha Fury
Stewart, Hazel Blackledge
Stirgus, James
Stockstill, David A.
Swearengen, Gearetha Pearl
Tew, Suzette Pettis
Thompson, Arlene Imogene
Tompkins, Robert Thomas
Turner, Randy Warren
Veals, Elnora
Wade, Thomas Edward
Waller, Harry Edward
Walters, Stanley Craig
Weathers, Walter Fridge
Weaver, Macon Moore
White, Marvin R.
Whitten, Sara
Williams, Edwin Russell
Williams, Jr., Julius
Williams, Jr., Robert Franklin
Williams, Ronald Marx
Wilson, Darothy Louyse
Wilson, Howard Alexander
Winstead, Melinda R. K.
Wood, Lucille
Woodruff, Nancy Morris
Young, James D.
Young, Patrick J.H.

NORTH CAROLINA

Abernathy, James Ralph
Abrahamson, Carol A.
Adams, George Emery
Adams, Helena Bradley
Adams, Raythell Greene
Affeldt, Harley Paul
Ahmad, Nasiha
Ahuja, Vijay
Aldridge, Marvin Warren
Alexander, Ellis Turner
Alexander, Joseph Vance
Alexander, Randall Lee
Allen, Ethelene M.
Allen, Frances
Allen, James E.
Allen, Jerry Arthur
Allen, Jerry Young
Alley, Faye Greene
Alston, McCarroll
Andrews, Hazel P.
Andrews, Ike F.
Arrington, Christine
Attayek, Jr., Joseph Edward
Austin, Jo Anne
Austin, Judie P. M.
Avery, Mary Page
Ayscue, Alfred Thomas
Baker, Linda Faye
Ballou, Leonard Ross
Barbour, Mary Cecil M.
Barden, III, Charles
Barnes, Mary W.
Barnes, Melver Raymond
Bass, Eunice
Batten, James William
Beasley, Tony Eugene
Becton, Charles L.
Bell, Martha
Benson, Jr., A. D.
Berger, Gary Sterling
Best, Madeline
Blackmon, Danny Robert
Bolton, Rhonda Joanne
Bowles, Jay Clyde
Bretto, Chalotte Christine
Brewer, Eula Withrow
Brewington, David Ross
Bridges, S. Evelyn
Brinson, Davie Gray
Britton, Jackie Peele
Broadway, Benjamin Fayette
Broadway, Christiana Ruth Johnson
Broome, Sadie Allran
Brown, Earle Porter
Brown, Jr., Willex
Bryant,Jr., R. Kelly
Bryant, Sue Medlin
Buckner, James Russell
Bunce, Louise Longnecker
Burns, Barbara Reid
Burton, Lucille Pearson
Byrd, Ida Fay
Camp, Tonyia Marie
Cannon, Isabella Walton
Carver, J. A.
Cesar, Thomas Eugene
Chalker, Jess Frank
Chambliss, Marvin Henry
Chatman, Jerry Matthew
Childers, Bill Sanford
Clapp, John Van
Clapp, Lawrence Everett
Clark, Elizabeth Adams
Clary, John Paul
Cline, Ernestine Wolfe
Cline, Jeanie M.
Coats, Wayne Alfred
Coker, Roy Akinyele
Cole, Mary Elizabeth F.

Collins, Linda G.
Conklin, Deborah Jeanne
Connell, Suzanne S. M.
Cook, James Columbus
Cooper, Donald Paul
Cox, Brenda D.
Creech, L. T
Creech, Roger Aron
Croxton, Jr., Thomas Clyburn
Cunningham, Patricia Jenkins
Dallaire, Andrew R.
Daubenspeck, Wayne Martel
Daughtridge, Partha Council
Davis, Ruth Esther
Deal, Lillie Mae T.
Deitz, Eddie James
Dietz, Guenther
Dingfelder, James Ray
Drake, Suzanne Lee
Draughon, Johnnie Earl
Earley, Debra Georgette
Eason, Frances Rogers
Edwards, Jim
El-Bayadi, Nagui Rizk
Elliott, Frank Dwight
Ellis, William L.
Epps, William Saxe
Fischer, Dominic Peter
Fitzgerald, Mary Ellen
Flaherty, Jr., David Thomas
Fleetwood, Caroline Land
Foley, Charles Bradford
Forgy, Byron Keith
Foster, Albert Lawing
Foster, Jr., Spurgeon Holmes
Foster, Willi Krapels
Fountain, L. H.
Fox, Charles Leigh
Frazier, III, Thomas W.
Freeman, Ronald Bruce
Freeze, Elizabeth B.
Gantt, Charles David
Gauthier, Thomas Rugg
German, Finley LaFayette
Gholston, Betty Jean
Gibson, Randy A.
Giddens, Beulah
Gillespie, Vic
Gilman, III, Albert Franklin
Glover, Ralph
Godley, Jr., William Larry
Godwin, Frances Mae
Goins, Louise Copening
Gooch, Jr., Hubert Lee
Gower, Douglas
Grantham, Kelly Rose
Green, G. Carl
Green, James H.
Green, Martha Grace
Grissom, Maurice Warren
Hall, Michael T.
Hampton, Carolyn Hutchins
Harb, Mitchell A.
Haritun, Rosalie Ann
Harley, Josephine Anne
Harrell, Rosalind Knott
Harris, Keith Corley
Harrison, Jr., Henry Milton
Hause, III, Robert Luke
heath, William Henry
Hedgepeth, Luther Lawrence
Helms, John Benjamin
Henderson, Richard Delano
Hensley, Jeanette Catherine
Hill, Rosemary Augusta
Hinson, Joy Lou E.
Hitchcock, Jr., Walter LeVanois
Hidge, Louise
Hogan, Cleo Greer

Holmes, Jeffrey L.
Homes, Roy Anderson
Holt, Florence S.
Horne, Annie Pearl
Hostetter, Carlisle
Houge, Trina Mossete
Hudson, Marian S. P.
Hyder, Brian Douglas
Inman, Lucy Daniels
Isenhour, Jr., Grady Eugene
Jackson, Jr., Colon Stonewall
Jackson, Daniel H.
Jackson, Jr., Samuel Watson
Jackson, Velma Alston
Jackson, Vida Kay
Jayson, Joseph Morton
Johns, Glenn Max
Johnson, Ruby E.
Johnson, Jr., Walter Thaniel
Jones, Harry Edward
Jones, Jessie Mae
Jones, Mary Whitley
Jones, Reba A.
Jones, Ruby Williamson
Jones Jr., Thomas M.
Jones, Walter Beaman
Jones Jr., Walter s.
Jonnalagadda, Murali Mohan Rao
Jordan, Jr., John R.
Kenan, Sebastian Reginald
Kendrick, Boyce Abner
Kennedy, Sr., Paul Jennings
Kirksey, Floyd Thomas
Knowles, Mark Andrew
Lambeth, James Erwin
Lavender, Eula Mae Taylor
Lawson, Sophia Gregson
Levine, Leon
Lewis, Romeo
Locke, Don C.
Logan, Frenise Avedis
Loman, James Harold
Long, Inez Henderson
Long, Sarah
Long, Shirley Dobbins
Long, Thurman Baxter
Lovell, Clayton C.
Luter, Jr., Raleigh Owen
Mahaffey, Charles Edward
Mangieri, Teresa Ann
Manning, David A.
Manning, Leah V.
Marchmand, Jr., James Franklin
Marsh, Joseph Virgil
Martin, Doris-Marie Constable
Martinez, Inez N.
Mathews, Richard Lee
Medlin, Cathleen Lewis
Meyer, Louis B.
Mieir, Charles Edward
Miller, Jr., Gilbert Carl
Miller, James Vernon
Mintz, Ronald Lee
Moore, Herbert Moffett
Moore, Mary Bulluck
Moseley, Michael
Moses, Fred
Moss, Faye K.
Mtangi, Stanlake Anesu
Murphy, Mohn Francis
Murray, Percy Edward
McElmon, Albert Noble
McNeeley, Jr., Cyrus Carmi
Nakarai, Charles F. T.
Naples, Robert Francis
Nesbitt, Vanda Whicker
Newton, Eleanor Runell
Oglesby, Helen Agnew
O'Neal, Robert P.

Orr, Rachel Leona
Ostrom, Alice Koonts
Owensby, Earl
Palmer, Patricia G.
Parker, III, Elmer Blaney
Parker, Joseph Chapman
Parker, Milton Bickley
Parrish, Judith Belche
Parsons, William Douglas
Patrick, Lynne Parker
Patterson, Jerry Lee
Peacock, Sherrill Edwin
Perry, Sr., Glenn Huylett
Perry, Marcus Wooten
Peterson, Robert Glen
Peterson, Sherry C.
Phifer, Rebecca Roll
Pittman, Rachel Newbern
Pittman, Sandra Lowry
Presnell, Jr., Jesse Guy
Prince, Elizabeth Collins
Pulley, Jr., William Paul
Purdy, Edith C. W.
Rader, Eugene Blackwell
Radford, Ann Gurley
Rash, Lloyd Monroe
Raynor, III, George Marion
Reeve, Joan Price
Reeves, Earl Lamar
Rice, Muriel A. Dunphy
Roberts, Edward Claiborn
Rose, Mary Ann
Ross, Sandra Lynn
Rouse, Jr., Bishop C.
Royall, Jr., James Lee
Saunders, Lenwood O. Daniel
Sawyer, Jr., Aubrey Mack
Scruggs, Robert G.
Seabock, Glenn Lewis
Sharpe, Kennth Richard
Shaw, Caswell Eure
Shull, Valdaree White
Sills, Michael Clark
Simon, Gary Alan
Simpson, Charlie Wayne
Sinstein, Neil Leland
Smalley, Ralph Leroy
Smith, A. Reginald
Smith, Ada McNeal
Smith, Anninias Cornelius
Smith, Dorothy B.
Smith Ivory H.
Smith, Rupert Lyndon
Soublet, Paul, J. L.
Spach, Jule Christian
Starnes, Ruth S.
Stiff, Delores Matlen
Stiller,Gloria
Stovall, Jean Burch
Streeter, Bettie C.
Stroud, Stephen Dwight
Stump, Robert Ray
Swanson, J. Howard
Sweet, Sr., Worth Alfred
Swofford, John Douglas
Taylor, Bobby R.
Taylor, Ellen B.B.
Taylor, John Michael
Taylor, Jr., Shahane Richardson
Terrell, S. Patricia
Thomas, Dougald Robert
Tice, Jessica I.S.
Tillett, Virginia Simmons
Timberlake, Roberts Edgar
Todd, Parrish
Tuck, Leonore Doromal
Tucker, George Rickey
Turner, Elnora K.
Turner, Kay Homesley

Turner, Mechell Roberts
Turner, Rebecca P. P.
Upham, Jr., John Exley
Upton, Carroll Marvin
Vann, Mamie Godwin
Varner, Barbara Jean
Vaughan, Emory Abner
Vaughan, Richard Irvin
Vester, Agnes Peele
Vine, Louis Lloyd
Waddell, William Kenneth
Walden, Mattie M.
Walker, Almena Norris
Watson, Marietta Gates
Webster, Vera D. R.
West, Edwin David
Westbrook, Eunice
Whitcomb, Patricia Scatchard
White, Jo-Ann
White, Rotha Murray
Whittenton, Jr., David Oscar
Wiggins, Nell
Willeford, Catherine Proctor
Williams, Annie John
Williams, Carolyn Antonides
Williams, Hugh Evans
Williams, Miriam Lyerly
Williams, Pauline Bingham
Willis, Flay Alexander
Wilson, Sr., Boyd Cecil
Wilson, Howard Nelson
Wilson, Nancy Faucette
Wilson, Shirley S.
Wolfe, Carolyn R.
Woods, Phillip J.
Wooten, Willard M.
Wright, James Edward
Wright, Ruthmary R.
Wullenwaber, Frank C.
Yates, Victoria
Young, James Hilliard
Younts, Millard Stephen

OKLAHOMA

Adams, Leonard W.
Andrews, M. DeWayne
Anthony, Christine
Anthony, Robert Holland
Appling, Raymond Holland
Bachi, Naomi Mabel
Bailey, Bob G.
Baker, Gladys Melissa
Barnes, Velma Ardell
Beck, James Pierce
Becquart, Betty Louise
Beltz, LaVerna Louise
Benton, Andrew Keith
Beutler, Randy Leon
Bicek, Jeannette L.
Blair, Bobby Charles
Bolton, Synia Christian
Bowen, Richard Dale
Bowers, Carol Ann
Boyd, Tom W.
Bradley, Leon
Brady, Bryan Virgil
Breece, Shirley Looper
Brisard, Yvonne Stephanie
Britton, Barbara Ann
Britton, Michael Linn
Brochu, Sr., Robert Henry
Brown, Alfred William
Buchanac, Gwendolyn Ann
Buckner, Robert
Burris, Wilford C.

Campbell, David Gwynne
Chamberlin, Linda Gregg
Chappell, Claudia B.
Cockrell, Patricia Keron
Cole, Jr., Robert A.
Conoghan, Dorothy Dell
Corbett, William Paul
Cowen, Dora Revell
Craighead, Cecelia Jo
Cronkhite, Pat A.
Daugherty, Fred
Davis, Lourie Bell
Davis, Sr., Roy Lavelle
Davis, Violet Amy
Decker, Josephine
Dell, Annie White
Dennis, C. Wendyl
Dennis, Cherre Nixon
Dentici, Patricia Diane
deSteiguer, John Rodolph
Dickerson, Dorothy M.
Draper, Mary Wanda
Eck, Kenneth Frank
Edmondson, Jeannete B.
Elias, Karen Lynn
Epps, Mieke N.
Everett, Jr., Karl Menoher
Fields, Betty Jo
Fields, Gladys Dolores
Fink, Kenneth Ernest
Fleming, Richard M.
Foster, Cary Don
Fank, Kate
Frevele, Janice M. C.
Frye, Mary Lois
Fuqua, William Andrew
Garretson, Casey Charlene
Giberson, Mickie Lynn
Gilmore, Joan Elizabeth
Graham, Rebekah Newman
Gray, Minnie Dell Cromwell
Gregg, Alice Joan
Hadley, Jimmy R.
Hale, James Ray
Hampton, Carol C. M.
Hampton, Gene Edward
Hanna, Donna F.
Hard, Gordon Wayne
Hardeman, Carole Hall
Harrell, James Alfred
Harris, Imogene Harrell
Hayes, Deanne
Hembree, Beverly Kate
Herring, Clyde Lee
Hiebert, Cheryle Jeanne
Hildabrand, Herbert Logan
Hollrah, Grace French
Holmes, Elizabeth Ann
Hoover, Eva V.
Houston, Olivia Nash
Huey, Adrienne Cochran
Hull, Donna Jean
Hynum, Ben F.
Jackson, Berenice Lloyd
James, Nona Faye
Johnson, Gladys R.
Johnson, Hugh Christopher
Jones, Lora Lee
Kelly, Jr., Ernest E.
Kilgore, Donna Sue
King, Daniel Gray
Kittleman, Martha A. H.
Koeninger, Jimmy Glen
Kuykendall, Mack Lawrence
Lambert, Doris Lynn
Laughlin, Ray E.
Lawter, J. Mike
Lee, Samuel C.
Lewis, Gladys Sherman

Lokey, Esther Geneva
Long, Charles Alexander
Long, Kathleen E.
LoVecchio, Joseph Victor
Loving, Garvis Inez
Lowry, Lester Lee
Marker, Dan E.
Marlin, Jeff Thomas
Martinez, Betty Elnora
Matthews, Elsie C. Spears
Mathews, Jr., Wilford Dale
Maxwell, Leona V. McWilliams
May, Sue Louise
Meibuhr, Arthur C.
Merrill, Fran J.
Merrill, Maurice Hitchcock
Minor, Jim D.
Morgan, Michael L.
Moyer, Robert Alexander
Neal, Vina Eldora
Nichols, Sarah Letha
Norvell, III, John Edmondson
Nottingham, Harmon Allen
Odom, Leon David
Oliphant, Thomas A.
Parham. Inez Myers McCollum
Parker, eudine Marie
Patterson, Susan Pierce
Pegues, Wennette Osceola West
Penner, Lettie Lou
Perkins, Arland Vincent
Perry, Marguerite Freeman
Pledger, S., Edward Lewis
Primeaux-Smith, Valentine Joy
Ray, Alice Louise Holly
Reneau, Beatrice Dennis
Resley, George Boulter
Reynolds, Wanetta
Roath, Glennen Dean
Rogers, Keith Rodney
Roy, Johnny Bernard
Russom, James Rayford
Ryan, Barbara Jean
Stafley, Jr., John Wiley
Salyer, Pauline Alice
Schaak, Anna Marie
Seikel, Robert Eugene
Sewell, Leon O.
Shaffer, III, Lawrence Blaine
Shaw, Jessie Irene
Shipp, Victoria R.
Shirley, George
Simmons, Robert Roy
Simon, Gloria Odi
Singleton, Raymond LeVon
Smith, Robert Owen
Springs, Patricia McCloskey
Stackler, Louis Michael
Stevens, Grace Mae
Steward, Jr., James Kaylor
Stewart, Wilburn I.
Stolte, Karen Marie
Story, W. W.
Strickland, Jr., Glen
Stroble, Rosalie Tiger
Sutton, Bobby Gene
Talley, II, William Woodrow
Thomas, Billy Ray
Thompson, L. Dean
Tomlin, Hyrice
Townes, Willa Mae
Trolinger, Patricia Jane
Van Auken, Robert Danforth
Vanderwork, Carol
Van Hook, Wanda M.
Waller, Gene
Ward, Lew O.
Waterman, Carolyn Lanpher
Watson,Monte

Watts, John Daniel
Webster, Terry L.
West, Helen Lois
Wilbur, Warren Wikon
Williams, Mike

PUERTO RICO

Aranda, Juan M.
Carattini, Cesar
Cintron, Emma V.
Del-Rosario, Ernesto
Garcia-Palmieri, Mario R.
Gomez, Nelida
Hernandez, Migdalia A.
Landron Villamil, Jose M.
Larde, Enrique Roberto
Morales-Nieva, Ignacio
Ortabasi, Ugur
Ortiz, Araceli
Quinones, Gilda
Rosado, Elma B.
Sahai, Hardeo

SOUTH CAROLINA

Adams, George Randall
Altman, Jean Drennon
Anderson, Clyde
Anderson, Dolores Femer
Andrews, Vera J.
Arnett, Jerry Lorris
Arnett, Penelope Susan
Ash, Thomas Grey
Atchley, Bill L.
Bailey, Donald Lincoln
Barnett, Luther Zedic
Baron, Mark
Bender, Margaret Krivonak
Berry, Lou H.
Blasius, Jack Michael
Bonds, John Bledsoe
Bosier, Betty Brown
Boucher, Carter
Bradley, Steven Russell
Breeze, Edwin Carter
Brown, David Michael
Brown, Linda Jo
Brown, William Ray
Bryant, Elizabeth Noe
Buck, Edgar Alton
Buist, Sam Izlar
Cargill, Paula Marie
Chance, Elizabeth Moore
Chandler, Barbara Etta
Chishom, Andrew James
Chitty, Jr., James R.
Clark, Alphonso H.
Clark, Annie Frances
Clark, Jr., Niles Craig
Clement, Janye Mattison
Coker, Theodore James
Connelly, Susan Jones
Cooper, Celestine Juliet
Cornwell, Ruby Pendergrass
Cox, Bettie L. K.
Dennis, Linda H.
Dent, Woody G.
Derrick, Mary V. D.
De Shields, Linda J.
de Treville, Ruth S.
Douglas, Rosslee Green
Drake, Anne Billingslea
Drucker, Meyer

Ducworth, George Marion
Eaddy, Betsy Jo
Faggett, Harry Lee
Faglie, Kay M. R.
Ferrell, Norma Ann
Finney, Ernest A.
Fludd, Willie Edward
Forrester, Joyce Duncan
Franklin, Douglass Everette
Freeman, Judy Delk
Gardner, Donald Angus
Garvin, Barney Willard
Gaunce, James Richard
Gordon, Carson A.
Grigsby, Jr., Robert Lee
Guthrie, Sylvia Eugene
Haddon, John Herbert
Hallinan, Linda D.
Hardee, Hoyt James
Harris, Vander E.
Hollings, Ernest Frederick
Howard, Harry L.
Hucks, Larry A.
James, Florine Deloris
Jenkins, Edward E.
Jenkins, Warren Marion
Johnson, Guerry Wayne
Johnson, Rebecca Corley
Jones, II, Clarence Eugene
Kelley, John H.
Kerr, Andre Fielding
Kizer, Charles Raymond
Ladson, Barbara M. R.
Langley, Lucille Tolbert
LaPrince, Kenneth R.
Lewis, Anna Elizabeth
Lewis, Elizabeth Johnson
Lewis, Erv
Lewis, Pauline Evans
Lister, Doris Watford
Lowery, Hattie Perry
Mackey, II, Dan B.
Matthews, James A.
Moon, Elvin D.
Mott, Bobby Ricshan
Murray, Charles Edward
Nelson, George Agle
Odom, Jr., Stephen
Orloff, Susan Nessa
Pate, Alethea Fennell
Payne, G. Frederick
Powell, Jr., Andrew Jefferson
Powers, Johnny Don
Reed, Clarence Alexander
Revisky, Charles Wayne
Rhea, Elizabeth Dunlap
Rhodes, John R.
Rickenbacker, John H.
Riddle, Robert Marion
Riel, Eloise Green
Robertson, DuBose
Ross, Berneatha Dantzler
Rushton, James Dennis
Saunders, William
Shelley, David Austin
Shiflet, Jr., John Coleman
Simms, St. Elmo
Squatriglia, Robert William
Steinhoss, David
Strobush, Earl Morris
Strom, James Lee
Sudduth, Betty Jane
Swygert, Annie Lee
Tanner, Gloria Ann
Taylor, Margie Ainsdorff
Thompson, Tina Marcella
Thrift, Ralph Evans
Tuck, N. Bartin
Turner, Jr., Joseph Jackson

Turner, Vangie Luella
Vroom, James Randall
Wagoner, Bettie Rodermund
Walker, Charlotte Esther
Watson, Floyd T.
Whack, Pauline J.
Whetsell, Douglas Wayne
Whitesides, Glenn Edward
Whitlock, Jr., Quenton H.
Willard, Jr., Neal
Williams, Armstrong
Willis, Martha E. R.
Wilson, Gregory Bruce
Wimberly, Jr., C. W.
Wong, Vivian A.
Wood, Jolean Morton
Woodruff, Jean Leigh

TENNESSEE

Acres, Norman Clifton
Adams, George Douglas
Adams, Lucy Neeley
Adkins, Bobby Joe
Aldrich, Betty B.
Alexander, Lamar
Allen, Hazel
Allman, Martha Kinzer
Anderson, Edwin Glenn
Anderson, Joe Lashlee
Anderson, Margaret Anna
Anderson, Vivian M.
Angel, Clyde Thomas
Atchley, Bobbie Joyce
Atkins, Mittie
Atkinson, Carl P.
Bailey, Jr., Malcolm Lee
Baldree, Mary Oneida
Ball, Jr., Louis Oliver
Bamman, Betty Mae
Bandy, Edna Brashears
Barber, Melba Maylene
Barham, Betty Hays
Barker, J. Byron
Barkley, Paul Hubbard
Barrett, Barbara Taylor
Battle, Jr., Frank
Bay, Charles Howard
Beard, Gary Alan
Beasley, Herman
Bell, William
Bennett, Donald Garry
Bhatia, Dil Mohan Singh
Blanton, Ernestine Mynard
Blevins, Melvin Eugene
Booher, Charles B.
Boucher, Betty Jane
Bowen, Matilda R.
Bowman, Thelma Shanks
Bratton, Thomas William
Brown, Kenneth Neil
Brown, Rickey
Brzezicki, Michael Joseph
Burdette, Theodore Allen
Burts, Frieda Culberson
Bush, Danny Elward
Bussard, Dennis R.
Byrd, Joe W.
Cabage, Grayce M. H.
Cagle, Charles Wayne
Calloway, William
Campbell, Agnes Knight
Carpenter, Susan
Chisamore, Ruth M. T.
Chrietzberg, Bertha Clark
Cissell, William Bernard
Clark, Cydne Ericca

Clift, Annie Sue
Clift, Michael E.
Climer, Terry
Cobb, James Thomas
Cochran, Mary Jo
Cockrell, Jr., Claude O.
Cole, Judy B. Shell
Collier, Gary Samuel
Comer, Harold Dee
Conlon, Kathleen Parker
Conner, Jr., Lewis H.
Cooper, Agnes Pearson
Cooper, Ellis Ewen
Cooper, Mary Berry
Cothran, Glenda Marie
Crawford, John A.
Crawford, Margaret Watkins
Crews, Thelma Ayn
Crisp, Harold
Cronan, Harvey Bert
Culbertson, Katheryn C.
Cumbee, Jr., Johnnie Glenn
Davis, Fred P.
Davis, Jr., John Clarence
Davis, Margaret Frances
Day, Jr., James Terry
Day, Maggie Lee
Deere, Edward
DeHoff, George W.
Deison, Harriet Schoellkopf
DeMere, McCarthy
Dettwiller, George Frederick
Dickey, Ronald Neal
Diggs, Steven Franklin
Dobson, Thomas Ray
Dodds, Naomi Jean C.
Dozier, Carroll T.
Drum, Emily A.
Duke, Donald Edward
Dunn, Floyd
Durr, Sheila Avery
Dwyer, Leona DeMere
Edrington, George Elden
Elliott, Shirley Rae
Ellis, Roy Frazier
Fant, III, Charles W.
Farmer, Mildred LaVerne
Farmer, William Alton
Fields, June Nash
Fleischer, Arthur Carroll
Flowers, John T.
Fogleman, Billye Sherman
Fogleman, Stella
Foster, Thomas Lane
Fox, Irene Leinart
Fox, Portland Porter
Freeman, Betty Delaine
Freeman, Sr., James Drew
Fulton, Jr., Roy
Galle, Jr., William Preston
Gallimore, Tellus M.
Ganaway, Bettye Jean
Gannon, Jr., Leroy Columbus
Garbiras, Susan E.
Geho, Claudia G. Waldrep
Gibson, Roxie E.
Gooch, Patricia Carolyn
Goode, Wade Calvin
Gooding, Erle Stanley
Graves, Edward Shannon
Green, Jr., Hugh Edward
Gregg, Willie Ruth
Gude, William D.
Guettner, Patrick David
Guillen, Wanda Vaughn
Hairell, William Blagovest
Hamilton, Robert Lee
Hampton, Ophina R.
Hanlon, Freda Andrea

Hardin, Margaret G.
Harris, Gladys B.
Harrison, Jr., Ircel Columbus
Harrison, Yewell
Hawkins, Sr., Jimmy W.
Hayre, Richard William
Herr, Arba Owen
Hill, Jr., Arnold P.
Hill, Lucille Miller
Hobbs, Judy Lee
Hobbs, Sonia Akol Blanco
Hodges, Joseph Edward
Holt, Douglas Eugene
Holtman, Darlington Frank
Howard, Karan Anica
Hubbard, Billie Yvonne
Hubbard, Marquetta Lynn
Hunter, Patricia Finn
Hunter, Reuben Andrew
Inman, Sr., Larry Joe
Irland, Marquita L.
Jamison, Christine Morris
Jensen, Jacksie Ann
Joe, Young-Choon Charles
Johnson, Anne Curtis
Johnson, Jr., James Franklin
Johnson, Mark O.
Jones, Ed
Jones, Hutton Reese
Jones, Janet Hair
Judd, Jean T.
Kasperbauer, James Clemens
Kelly, Stanley Durham
Kerr, Douglas, Moseley
Kindall, Luther Martin
Kingdon, Douglas Ernest
Krashney, Pat Jett
Kroeger, Carroll Vincent
Lambert, Jr., Martin Lee
Lavely, Philip Elson
Lawson, Gale Leland
Leonard, Clarence Leo
Leslie, Joe Newland
Lewis, Olee
Liles, Donald Melvin
Lindsey, Evelyn G.
Littlefield, Camillia Hughes
Littrell, Terrill Donald
Lockwood, Bobby
Long, Bernice H.
Lott, Nancy Brasher
Luster, Ronnie Lee
Maness, Betty
Marquiss, Jane Chatten
Marrs, William L.
Marshall, Arthur Glenn
Marshall, David
Martin, Frank Michael
Mathews, Walter Mason
Matthews, Paul Thomas
Mays, Rita Diane
Maze, Martha Malone
Miller, Jewell H.
Miller, Loren G.
Milligan, Jr., Thomas Braden
Mines, Eras Anthony
Moore, Ronald Dean
Morgan, III, Julian Earl
Morman, Square
Morris, Gladys H.
Mosier, Ronald Ray
Mueller, Roy Clement
Murray, Crosby L.
McCarty, Raymond M.
McNally, James Rand
Nakarai, Toyozo W.
Napier, Shirley Rita
Neumann, Idabelle Marie
Newman, Bobbie Sue

Nolan, Ollie Jean
Norman, Ronald Lee
Ogg, Sr., E. Jerald
Oliver, Robert Thomas
Osburn, Carroll Duane
Patterson, James K.
Peterson, Dorothy Burnett
Peterson, Patricia Grier
Peterson, Robert Elmer
Pflasterer, Louise Wood
Pogue, Susan Small
Pope, Grover C. Allen
Price, Jr., Alva Jackson
Price, Henry Lee
Proud, Johnny D.
Ramsey, Gary Robert
Randolph, Margaret Ann
Ratcliffe, Shelia Pannell
Ray, Lexie B.
Rayburn, Dennis Harold
Read, William David
Redwine, Angie
Reed, Monika Bexten
Rhodes, James O.
Rhodes, Pamela C.
Richey, William C.
Robbins, Wayne Lindsey
Roberts, Charles Vernon
Rogers, Audrey Lea
Rothenberg, Irwin Z.
Russell, Grace J. W.
Rymer, Wilma
Samuel, Dorothy Ione Johnson
Sauceman, Jr., Fred William
Scott, Edwin Jerome
Scott, Jerry Deamus
Scott, Patricia Anne
Seaton, Christine Wheeler
Seaton, Mary Nolan
Sells, Harlon Dee
Sennett, Charles Edward
Sharp, Opal M.
Shaughnessy, Mary Ethel
Shelton, Jimmie Ruth
Shock, James Richard
Shockley, Steven Bruce
Shouse, III, Thomas Franklin
Silk, Dolores Ham
Silva, Sarah Frances S.
Sirois, Gerald F.
Sisk, Donald Ray
Slifer, Kenneth Benjamin
Slimovitz, Morris L.
Smith, Edmond M.
Smith, Georgia Elizabeth
Smith, J. T.
Smith, Mary Isabelle
Smith, Nora Smith
Smith, Jr., Olver A.
Smith, Thomas Lee
Sommer, Patricia Ann
Speight, David Larry
Stanfill, Dorothy
Stevens, Norma Young
Stimpson, Kathy G.
Stocks, David A.
Stokes, John Lafayette
Strange, Karen Sue Taylor
Strickland, Jessie Hazel
Strickland, Robert Madison
Taylor, C. Pat
Terrell, Jerry Day
Thomas, Brenda Sue
Thompson, Bert
Thompson, Hugh Arthur
Thompson, James E.
Trammel, Dorothy Jean
Treadway, james L.
Trotter, Sue Eldredge

Turpin, Annie Mae
Vacher, Carole Doughton
Van Fossen, Helen Key
van Rijn, Rita Price
Varnadore, Beverly Sweeden
Vigil, Joe Gabriel
Waddell, Genevieve Johnson
Wanderman, Richard G.
Ward, Rebecca S.
Warren, Mary Denny
Washington, Charles A.
Watts, Philip Llewellyn
Weir, Ronald Lee
Welch, Jimmy Gale
Whaley, Vernon M.
Wheeler, Larry Edward
Whitaker, Carolyn Virginia
White, Patricia Lee Quarles
Williams, Barbara Kay
Williams, Luther Francis
Williams, Jr., Wynn Dixon
Winkler, Phillip Blair
Witherspoon, Everette Levon
Wood, James H.
Woodward, Henry Elihne
Wyatt, John Douglas
Yarbro, Mary Ruth
Yates, Billy Summers
Yelton, Noel Gray
York, Don E.
Young, Nelda Jean
Zadrozna, Don J.

TEXAS

Abrams, Loyd Glenn
Acker, W. L.
Adams, Lillian Loyce
Adams, Troy
Adamson, N. A.
Addington, William Hubert
Aderhold, Josephine Elizabeth
Ahrens, Sandra G
Aiken, Bruce Tansill
Albrecht, Jr., Marvin
Alderman, III, Louis Cleveland
Alexander, Louis
Alexander, Roy L.
Allen, George Calvin
Allred, Phillip Lance
Alluisi, Earl Arthur
Almarez, Jr., Felix D.
Alsup, Reba
Altchuler, Steven Ira
Alvarado, Juanita
Amir-Moez, Ali Reza
Anderson, Doris Ehlinger
Anderson, Owanah Pickens
Anderson, Ronnie J.
Anderson, Jr., Roy Leonard
Arce, Raul
Arsen, Leo
Asher, Vernon
Ashworth, Charles Clayton
Atchley, Vivian M.
Aultman, Larry L.
Aurispa, Eddie
Avera, Carl Lee
Baker, Charles Franklin
Baker, William Duncan
Balcolm, Karen Suzanne
Barnes, Lavonia J. B.
Barnes, Nelda
Barriss, Kathleen Colelia
Bass, William Michael
Bates, Jr., John Paul
Bautsch, Virginia Belle

Beaman, Margarine G.
Beatty, Carolyn Ann
Beckham, William Bradley
Beckstrom, Harriett Perry
Bell, Billie Jean
Bell, Bob J.
Bell, Julian Augustus
Bengtson, Edythe B.
Benson, Melba Woosley
Berkey, Jr., Maurice Edward
Bernal, Jesus R.
Bertrand, Russell Earl
Bickerstaff, Wanna Ruth
Bilbrey, Stan C.
Billeiter, David John
Biskamp, Mona Spencer
Blair, Major Elliot
Blakeney, Roger Neal
Blevins, E. Edward
Blomstedt, Robert Kent
Boeckman, Charles
Boler, Danny
Bolner, Clifton Joseph
Boltz, Clara Belle
Bonock, Dorothy Louise
Boren, Molly Sarver
Bourland, Vergal H.
Boyd, Jimmy Wayne
Boyer, Viola Lillie
Brady, Laura E.
Brasfield, Carolyn Allen
Bratcher, Margie Nan
Brereton, Thomas Francis
Bridges, Howard Sneed
Bridges Ronald Clayton
Broadhurst, Norman Neil
Brooks, James L.
Brooks, John D.
Brooks, Velma Lotrice
Brown, Carol Wynn
Brown, Cleta Jean
Brown, Gwendolyn Ruth
Brown, Lee Elliott
Brown, Randall Allen
Brown, Ray
Brownlee, Mary Catherine
Bruff, Beverly Olive
Buck, Carolyn Felter
Bunting, John James
Bures, Jr., Paul Leslie
Burkhardt, Mary Elizabeth
Burleson, Noyce M.
Burns, Frances W. H.
Burrell, Lafayette
Burt, Marvin V.
Butler, Kelley W.
Butts, Kenneth Olin
Calendar, A. D.
Call, Charles Altman
Canales, Modesto
Cantrell, Truett Vaughn
Cantu, Anna Maria
Cantu, Rodolfo
Capen, Edgar A.
Caras, Robert Lawrence
Carmody, Seamus
Carmon, Barbara A.
Carter, Freddye Jo
Carter, Mary M. H.
Carter, Nancy Lucretia
Carter, Virginia Nell
Catechis, Spyros
Cates, Stella Oates
Cavil, Willi Mae
Cavin, Bruce Wayne
Chambers, Margaret Mathilde
Chandler, Bob J.
Chaudler, Guy Edward
Chicca, Vivian Theresa

Childress, Graham Hugh
Chlapek, Calvin Joe
Christopher, Charles Augustus
Clar, Barry David
Clark, Doris Jean
Clayton, Billy Wayne
Cleveland, Lynda Gail
Closser, Patrick D.
Cloud, John Worth
Cobb, Jack LeRoy
Cochran, Iva Dell
Coffman, Jerry Raymond
Colburn, Kathleen Graham
Cole, Randy D.
Coleman, Carobel Blair
Coligado, Eduardo
Colson, Sharon K. T.
Colvin, Jr., George Ray
Conner, Jerry H.
Conway, Martha Ann
Cook, Deborah Sue
Cooke, Don Emmett
Cooley, Jane F.
Cooper, Charlotte Hervey
Cooper, Kenneth Dean
Copron, Carlotta M.
Corum, B. H.
Cotton, Eleanor L. G.
Cox, Arthur Boyce
Cox, Davis Griffith
Cox, Gail Willbern
Cox, Glenda
Cox, Morgan Samuel
Cox, William Andrew
Cozad, John Erving
Crawford, Larry Gene
Creek, John Dennis
Criswell, Leonard L.
Cromer, Charles Marion
Cross, Virginia Rose
Cruz, Gilbert Ralph
Culbertson, Richard Donnell
Cullum, Robert Francis
Cunningham, Karon Lynette
Cyphers, Carrol Kerlick
Dabney, William Robert
Dale, Russel
Darnell, David R.
Davis, Joy Durham
Davis, Paul Lavere
Davis, Rosie Lee
Dawson, Jr., F. D.
Dean, Anne Frey
Dean, Peter W.
Dearman, Deborah Kay
Deason, Daniel Arthur
DeBakey, Lois
DeBakey, Michael E.
de la Cruz, Hugo Luis
de la Garza, Jr., S. M.
De La Vina, Robert
Delco, Wilhelmina Ruth
Delgado, George Henry
Dempsey, III, Neal
Dengler, John Charles
Denn, Donald Eugene
Dennis, Robert Howard
Denton, Betty A. Grant
Diamond, Faye
Dickey, Lynn Carter
Diggs, Christine Heath
Dockery, Orville Don
Donohue, Jr., John W.
Dougherty, Francis Kelly
Dow, Charles David
Dow, Norman G.
Dugan, Mildred C.
Duncan, Sylvia Anna
Dunn, Norma

Dupree, Maxine Nelson
Eades. Bascomb Galloway
Eads, Sherry Lynn
East, Loyd Eddie
Eastmen, Walter Dale
Eaton, Frank Hollis
Ebert, Reva Janette
Echols, Michael Wayne
Edwards, Del M.
Edwards, Thelma Cliett
Elbjorn, Charles David
Elizondo, Alfredo Gerusa
Elliott, J. Robert
Elliott, William Wayne
Ellis, Bonnie Lee
Ellis, Verne R.
Emmons, Judith Florence
Emmons, Tetta Wanda
Emory, Emerson
English, Robert James
Enriquez, Gaudalupe
Fain, Annie Love
Fant, Elena B.
Farley, Grace Louise
Farquhar, Betty Murphy
Farrar, Beverly Jayne
Farris, Terrell Eleanor
Feeney, Kevin
Felty, Ronald Gene
Fez-Barringten, Barie
Fields, Dearie White
Fifer, Jr., Clifton
Fillyaw, Harold
Finnell, Scott
Fitzgerald, Dixie
Flint, Charles R.
Flood, Joan Moore
Flournoy, Richard Lynn
Flury Scott L.
Ford, Allene May
Forsgard, Eddie Camille
Fosdick, Franklin Lawrence
Fox, Edgar Leroy
Fox, Mary Elizabeth
Fox, Vivian Scrutchin
Foy, Ronald Thomas
Francis, Paulette Kropp
Francovilla, Mary Ann
Fank, Luanne Thornton
Fraze, Denny T.
Freeman, Joe Phillip
Froehlich, Sue Ann
Frost, Jr., Elton
Galiga, Glenn Edwin
Garcia, Jr., Lino
Garrett, James Herschel
Garza, David Champlon
Garza, Juan
Garza, Noe Eliberto
Gates, Betty Russell
Gavora, Betty J.
Gawlik, Pauline Green
Gentry, Marlene Ann
Georg, Terry Alice
George, Jr., Louie B.
Giles, Althea
Gilliland, Claudia Jo
Ginzel, Franklin L.
Gipson, Thomas Allen
Girgus, Samuel D.
Glick, Perry Aaron
Godfrey, Horace Chilton
Goff, Jacqueline Ann
Gonzalez, Antonio
Good, Elizabeth Leatherwood
Goodlett, Annie Beth
Goodson, Shannon L.
Gordon, Jerry L.
Gossett, John Sartain

Gould, Lynda Gay
Gramm, Phil
Grams, II, Irving John
Grappa, Gerald Peter
Graves, June
Green, Robert Leo
Greenwell, Lula May Smith
Greenwood, Pat Minter
Griffin, Betty Don
Griffin, James Oliver
Griffin, Rodney Leverett
Griffith, Thomas E.
Guajardo, Derly
Guelker, Nora Lee
Gumer, Inderpal Singh
Gunkel, Frances Marie
Haberecht, Rolf R.
Haire, Carol Diane
Hall, William Clifton
Hanford, Patrick Joseph
Harbison, Margaret A.W.W.
Hardy, Joyce Pounds
Hardy, Lane Henry
Harlow, Freeda
Harlow, Joyce M.S.B.
Harrell, Barbara Ellen
Harris, David
Harris, Pat
Hartley, Herbert Clifton
Hartsell, Sr., Donald Wayne
Harvel, Ross
Harville, Jean Ellen
Havens, Delores D.
Hawkins, Herman Herbert
Hay, Betty Jo
Hayes, Marlena Nelson
Hayes, Rayburn Paul
Hazlewood, Hope
Heatherley, Elinor Elizabeth
Hefley, Pauline M.
Henderson, Dennis S.
Henderson, Marylea
Henderson, Wanda Marie
Hendrick, Leonard Earl
Henry, Dellie Mae
Henry, Johnnie
Hensley, Jr., R. E.
Henson, Bernice A.
Hernandez, Ramon Francisco
Hernandez, Tanila Tanis
Herndon, Charles Presley
Hester, Ellen Nora
Hicks, Gus
Hicks, Robert Stephen
Hicks, Selma Louise
High, Robert Edward
Hildebrand, Joyce Bruff
Hill, Joe Dennis
Hill, Paul Anthony
Hill, Thomas Norman
Hillis, Shelby Ross
Hillman, Jon G.
Hindman, Janet Lanell
Hinojosa, Jr., Louis
Ho, Minh Vuong
Hobbs, Ben T.
Hobbs, Carole Cornell
Hodge, Joanna Kirk
Hoffman, Elise
Hogan, Susan Wilson
Holder, Adolphus Doyle
Hollin, Shelby W.
Hollman, Robert Emmett
Holmes, Jr., William Walker
Hoover, Mary Alice
Hopkins, George Bernard
Horn, Hazel
Horne, Pamela Swan
Horton, Amos L.

Horton, Robert G.
Houe, Erana Nash
House, Jerry Brent
Houston, Lawrence J.
Howington, Lew Haywood
Hrdlicka, Robert James
Huantes, Margarita Rivas
Hudson, Mary G. C.
Hudson, Shirley
Huffman, George E.
Hughes, Mike
Hunt, Koleta Glover
Hunter, Cannie Mae
Hurt, Allie Teague
Hutton, Scott
Hynds, Tohnie E.
Igbokwe, Emmanuel Chukwuemeka
Irwin, Johnie Dee
Jackson, Betty Ruth
Jackson, Henry Holman
Jackson, Ruby McNeely
Jackson, Vader L.
Jaffe, Herman
Jaggers, Zack
Jaksha, John Timothy
James, Jr., Advergus Dell
James, Earl Edward
Jameson, Will Allen
Jamieson, Frank Martin
Jary, Roland Saunders
Jeter, Larry Joe
Johnson, Bessie Mae
Johnson, Dorothy Louise
Johnson, Donald Mark
Johnson, Nancy Carol
Johnson, Patricia Ann
Johnson, Robert Clifford
Johnston, Betty Jo
Jones, Christine A. Hatch
Jones, Johnnye Mae
Jones, Margaret O.
Jones, Mildred Lucille
Jones, Neal T.
Kaerwer, Bobby Newton
Karels, James D.
Kee, Joyce Marie
Keel, H. Wayne
Kenney, Gilbert
Ketchum, Charles Raymond
Killian, Michael Gene
King, Jr., Isaac Monroe
Klein, Melvyn Norman
Kleinhaus, John James
Kliewer, William Philip
Knori, Betty Joyce
Knudson, Helon
Koock, Mary Faulk
Kreder, Catherine Jean
Laing, Betty Jean
Lambert, Aurora Blanche
Lambert, Russell R.
Landers, Jr., James Walter
Lankford, Joe Ann
Larimer, Gregg
Lary, Gene
Lashare, Caroline Ann
Latham, Jr., Frank W.
Leeper, Linda Gayle
LeMaster, David R.
Lerma, Everardo C.
Lewis, Callie Ann Daniels
Lewis, John Oliver
Lewis, Orval L.
Licholat, Ruth Taylor
Lillard, Ronald Kim
Lindley, Ruth Alexander
Lindsey, Jr., Hiram Edward
Linebaugh, Jr., Nathaniel Lee
Lintzen, Wilbert

Lipton, Kenneth Albert
Liska, Darin Vladimir
Lloyd, Eva Jo
Long, Jr., Richard L.
Lopez, Nicolasa
Lorey, II, Willis Edward
Lowrie, Bonita Ann
Lowry, K. Patricia
Lummus, Eileen Davis
Lutes, Candida J.
Lynch, Jr., William Wright
Lynn, Jr., James William
Lyons, Kirk David
Maberry, Louise Jones
Macik, Helen Marie
Maddox, Nova C.
Madrigal, Roberto
Mahaffey, Margaret Michele
Manery, Carol Sue
Manfull, Daniel Malcolm
Mangold, Lana Carole
Mann, Charles Kenneth
Manning, Beth Shelton
Mansfield, Asa
Marrero, Frank
Marrera, Ruby M.
Martin, Robert R.
Martin, Thomas Howard
Martin, William E.
Martinez, Joel
Martinez, Ricardo Arguijo
Martinez, Robert
Martinez, Roberto Gutierrez
Mayfield, Mary Sue
Mays, Benita Banister
Melgar, Julio
Merian, Audrey
Metzgar, Robert Douglas
Meystedt, Lucille E.
Michael, Marbeth Gail
Miesse, Mary Elizabeth
Milholland, Thomas Alva
Miller, Janel Howell
Miller, Patsy
Miller, Rebecca Ellisa
Miller, Robert Gregory
Miller, Thelma Clay
Miller, Thomas Allen
Milstead, Eldon Andrew
Minor, David Michael
Miracle, Jerene
Mischen, Bettye Ann
Mitchell, Edgar Elliott
Mitchell, Joseph Clovis
Mitchell, Ruth May
Miolina, Agustina R.
Moore, Ercylene E.
Moore, Iona June
Moore, James Turner
Moore, Patricia Ann
Mora, Zeke R.
Morgan, Maxie Dell
Morrison, Grace Blanch
Morse, Eugenia Maude
Morse, Samuel A.
Mosley, III, William F.
Moss, Jerry Pat
Mouton, Jane Srygley
Munter, Paul H.
Myers, Marceau Chevalier
Myers, Virginia Hunter
McCrary, Guy Richard
McKinley, Frank Arnold
Nacol, Mae
Naua, Robert
Navarro, Alfred
Neal, II, Frank Albert
Needham, Allyn Bryant
Needham, Jr., James Ray

Wallace, Foy C.
Ward, Morris C.
Washington, Donald Ray
Watkins, Lynette Leone
Weaver, Jacqueline Lang
Webb, Mabel Lucile
Webb, Tommy B.
Wedig, Frank Elliott
Weinman, Phyllis Evelyn
Weir, Ann Epps
Weiss, Davida S.
Welsh, jacqueline Adele
Wenzlau, John Norbert Hans
Werlin, Rosella Harwood
Wesley, Sr., Garlin
West, Syntha Jane
Westbrook, Douglas Calvin
Whaley, Dennis Wayne
Wharton, Edward Calvin
Whisenant, Mary Sue
White, Ethyle Herman
White, Ronald
White, Ruth Evelyn
Whitlow, Ted Wilson
Whitten, Neola Lorene
Whittle, Joe Bob
Williams, Charles Dean
Williams, III, Jacob Lory
Williams, Ruby Jo
Williams, Venora A.
Williamson, T. J.
Wills, Shirley Ann
Wilson, D. Terry
Wilson, Durward Earl
Wilson, Onie Mae
Wilson, Sandra Jean
Wilson, William Feathergail
Wingate, Martha L.M.
Wirtz, Adele Watson
Wolf, Kennth Mark
Wood, Loren Edwin
Woodall, Ronald Steven
Woodall, Stella
Woodruff, Georgia Wilbur
Woolard, Mrs. Jimmie
Wortham, Robert John
Wren, Ruth Marie
Wright, Eugene Box
Wyckoff, Jean Ellen
Yant, Roberta
Yetter, Tina Marie
Yiantsou, Chris G.
Yocom, Gwen Nichols
Young, Eleanor Anne
Young, Evelyn Elizabeth
Young, Jewel Andrews
Zimmerly, Arthur W.
Zinn, Elias Paul
Zorilla, Leopoldo

VIRGINIA

Adams, II, James Carlie
Akers, James E.
Alderman, Joyce A. S.
Aldredge, Jr., James Henry
Allaire, Paul E.
Almond, Jr., James Lindsay
Almond, Jr., Joseph C.
Alvey, Jr., Edward
Angell, Sue Eakin
Ayers, Stephen Curtis
Baird, David C.
Baltimore, Sr., Carroll A.
Bandy, Herman Mosby
Bankit, Judith Irene
Barton, Alexander James

Batts, Lana Richards
Beheshti, Hooshang M.
Belcher, Julie A. M.
Bell, Jr., Franklin Arthur
Benn, Herman Thomas
Bennett, James Paul
Bich, Nguyen Ngoc
Bill, Carol E.
Bing, Richard McPhail
Binns, Floyd Thomas
Birch, Robert Louis
Blackburn, Laura Beth
Blood, Ingrid Maria
Blumberg, Michael Z.
Board, Sally Ann
Bolton, William B.
Booker, Doris E. W.
Boone, Jr., Harry Lindsay
Boucher, Frederick Carlyle
Bourque, Robert Martin
Bradshaw, Harry W.
Brenner, JoAnn Fishman
Brinkley, Mark Kenton
Brohard, Ellen·B.
Brooks, Garland Odell
Bryant, Sylvia Leigh
Bueker, Kathleen Ann
Burton, Cleland Patricia
Butler, Manley Caldwell
Calatayud, Juan Bautista
Caldwell, Willia, Thomas
Calloway, William Bennett
Campbell, Virginia Patrice
Caroon, Edna Earl Whitley
Carrell, Charlotte Peterson
Carrell, Finis Dixon
Carter, Charles Finley
Carvalho, Julie Ann
Chappell, Jr., Eugene Watson
Chaudhuri, Tapan K.
Childress, Thomas Burns
Clothier, Juliette Croxton
Clower, William Dewey
Coburn, David Thayer
Coleman, Janette Shaw
Coll, Alberto Raoul
Collier, Jr., Judson Waverly
Collins, Clinton
Corprew, Annette M.
Cox, Mark Stephen
Crafton-Masterson, Adrienne
Daniell, Vance Lyndall
Dechart, Daniel Stratton
Derrick, Homer
d'Evengnee, Charles Paul
Dhillon, Harpal Singh
Dod, Steve Bare
Dorman, Jr., Jack Eubank
Dorman, Pamela Ann
Douthat, Jr., Thomas Alexander
Driscoll, John Albert
Easter, Martha Corbin
Edgerton, Wilbert Delano
Edmonds, Donald Ray
Ellinger, Richard Alvin
Emden, Karen Anne
Engels, Janice Jeanne
England, Dickie West
Fairchild, James D.
Feagans, Robert Ryan
Fernstrom, Meredith Mitchum
Fields, Robert I.
Freeman, Frank Ray
Freund, Emma Frances
Friend, Edith Overton
Gade, Clifford W.
Garland, Jack Richard
Garner, Geraldine M. O.
Gimenez, John

Girard, Charles M.
Godsmand, Mitchell Sidney
Gimenez, John
Goodson, Annie Harris
Guerrant, Doris Jeanne
Hall, Robert Evans
Hancock, Samuel Lee
Hanks, Joanna Emily
Haren, James Harrison
Harman, Jr., Cody
Harville, Sr., Leonard Barrington
Havar, Vaschahar
Havelos, Sam George
Herron, Jr., Edwin Hunter
Hewett, Sr., Robert Joseph
Hill, Richard Lee
Hillier, George Thomas
Hindson, Edward E.
Hiner, Louis Chase
Hobson, Kate Evangeline
Hofmaster, Richard Namon
Holt, Frances Goodwin
Hooker, Holly Duane
Huebner, Richard Allen
Huffer, David Stone
Hunt, Elizabeth S.
Hunt, Susanne Carol
Hurt, Nellie Gray
Hutto, Bette Braswell
Jonosky, Thomas Alan
Johnson, Glen Eric
Johnson, Joyce Dundalow
Jones, Ernest Lee
Jones, Herb
Jones, Nicholas
Jones, Virgil Carrington
Justice, Charles Chappell
Kale, Jr., W. Wilford
Kandil, Osama A.
Kaufman, Irene Mathias
Kelly, Barbara Ann
Kennedy, Susan Estabrook
Kerns, Edith Bailey
Kincaid, Betsy Strause
Kirvin, Jr., Leo E.
Knox, Jane Weatherly M.
Kohler, Karl Eugene
Kolendrianos, Carol Ann
Kranowski, Nathan
Kupper, Marjorie Lakin
Largen, Mary Ann
Layman, Joyce Ann
Leary, Wilbur Talmadge
Lester, Shirley Rife
Lewis, Dale Paul
Lochridge, IV, Willard Fiske
Locy, Jr., Wade Dallis
Manuel, Paul Neal
Martin, Deborah L. M.
Maska, Edwin
May, Juanita W.
Meister, Peter William
Meredith, Jr., Douglas Raymond
Miller, Bruce Richard
Miller, Judith A.
Milne, Nancy Hoback
Moore, Frances Smith
Morley, Ronald David
Morris, Mary Lee
Morrison, Dorothy Perry
Mow, Anna Beahm
Neeper, Ralph Arnold
Nelson, Bryant McNeill
Nelson, Elizabeth
Newton, Lillian Hinson
Nichols, Christine Lynn
Obermayer, Herman Joseph
Olson, James Robert
Pascoe, Jr., Charles Thomas

Plitt, Jeanne Given
Poage, Cynthia Jean
Porter, Michael Leroy
Poster, Carol
Protopapas, Panayotis
Quarles, Charles Ellis
Rainey, Loyd Daniel
Rmey, Harold Thomas
Ray, Newton Hardman
Reed, Jummy B.
Reynolds, Thomas William
Rice, Martha B.
Riggs, Barry Lynn
Roberts, Donald Ray
Roberts, Mary Pope
Robertson, III, Frank Barry
Robinette, Betty L.
Rockwell, Jr., Stanley Baldwin
Rose, Clarence C.
Ross, Ernice
Rothgeb, Richard Price
Rusnak, Sharon Dale Smith
Sabaini, David Darrell
Sargent, William Earl
Sayers, Iris Webb
Scheiner, James Joseph
Schneider, Katherine Curtis
Schneider, Lloyd Rhynehart
Scott, Irene Feagin
Scott, Jr., Robert L.
Seagears, Margaret Jacqueline
Shafran, George Peter
Shearer, Jr., Charles Edward
Shelly, Richard W.
Sheppard, Dana Marie Boothe
Schocklee, John Warren
Shook, Harold Graham
Simpkins, Hubert Willie
Sisson, Sr., Howard Miles
Smiley, Jane P.
Smith, Jimmy Harold

Spinks, Dorothy Matthews
Spitzer, Ruth Baldwin
Spivey, Pamelia Ann Mays
Stevenson, Joe L.
Stubbs, Gordon Eugene
Talbot, Gwendolyn Edith
Taylor, Betty Ann
Taylor, George Arthur
Terry, Frank Womack
Thompson, Vivian Opal
Thota, Vykuntapathi
Tobey, Helen M.
Tucker, Sharon M.
Tyson, Helen Flynn
Unger, Paul Temple
Ward, Jr., Samuel Joseph
Watson, Gregory Harriss
Watts, Alma Gertrude
Whitfield, Stephen Kenneth
Williams, Isaac Edward
Williamson, Robert
Wilson, Juanita M.S.
Wilson, Louise Loeffler
Wolfe, Denny T.
Wood, Annette Varner
Woodard, Blondena
Wooding, Nathaniel H.
Worrell, Yvonne Margaret
Yount, William Richard

VIRGIN ISLANDS

Ellison, Robert Alexander

WEST VIRGINIA

Akers, David Jackson

Amjad, Hassan
Anderson, Opal Haynes
Bell, Shirley Kay
Cessna, Phyllis K.
Chapman, Elma Sines
Chiodo, Vincent M. P.
Collins, Lou Ann
Crutchfield, Carolyn Ann
DeHaven, Sandra Mae
Deitz, Jr., Robert Lee
De La Pena, Cordell Amado
Fawley, Jr., Okey Brown
Frantz, Ann Browning
Freyler, William John
Gardner, Lela M.
Garton, Charles E.
George, Raymond Charles
Gore, John Howard
Hairston, Irene Jeanette
Hoffman, Leah Jane
Hyre, Charles Steven
Johnson, James Arthur
Kelley, Judy Rae
Kinder, Eugene Harrill
Ledwell, Jo Starnes
Leonard, Jr., Nels
Ludwig, Ray Woodrow
Marshall, Jr., H. Richard
Martin, Wilma Jean
Moore, Gibbs Berry
Naviaux, LaRee DeVee
Oni, Claudius Adesina
Peck, Betty Lee
Reese, Virginia Denyer
Ripper, Charles Lewis
Rockefeller. IV, John D.
Rusch, Hermann Gregory
Singh, Rajendra Pratap
Slaatte, Howard Alexander
Sunderland, Zell Elizabeth
Todd, Lee, B.

During editorial scheduling, the following listees have recently relocated outside the geographical scope of this publication. All have contributed more than a majority of dedicated efforts to the South, either through professional or personal involvements.

CALIFORNIA

Altamura, Michael Victor
Bishop, Virgil Merrell
Gilbert, Adam Hill
Greer, Wesley Dwaine
Hahn, Lorena Grace
Harrison, David Francis
Libblick, Marvin Max
McDonald, Mori, Marianne
Munson, Wanda M.
Sarafian, Sylvia Annette
Sorensen, Gail A.

COLORADO

Conway, Colleen

CONNECTICUT

Austad, Arnold David
Williams, Charles Donald

HAWAII

Daschke, Carl Edward
Taber, Jr., William Rhett

IDAHO

Hambleton, Berniece Campbell

ILLINOIS

Akins, Clinton Miles
Coffey, Thomas Henderson
Frank, Ruby Merinda
Lasater, John Porter
Ovassapian, Andranik

INDIANA

Bales, Hazel
Fontana, Paul Andre
Gray, Jonnie E.

IOWA

Foster, Betty V.
Laposky, Ben Francis

JAPAN

Nozaki, Masako

MAINE

Hasty, Richard Spencer

MASSACHUSETTS

Anderson, Margaret Louise

MEXICO

Elliott, Simon
Osborn, II, Thomas Noel

MICHIGAN

Bhugra, Satnam, Singh
Brown, John W.
Carter, Thomas Aubrey
Igbokwe, Gwendolyn M. C.
Kozlowski, Theodore James

MISSOURI

Limpus, Pat Longino
Lockard, Betty Pine

NEW HAMPSHIRE

White, David Ellison

NEW JERSEY

Hanns, Christian Alexander
Schweitzer, Gertrude

NEW MEXICO

Begaye, Andrew F.
Jordan, Peggy
Kerr, Catherine Earl
Lowrance, Muriel Edwards

NEW YORK

Abrahamson, Bergljot
Beckworth, Deborah Jean
Emmick, Sr., Roger
Harris Gilmann, Ruth N.
Johns, Jr., Clarence Benjamin
Stemper, Jr., William
White, Jr., Octurus Ivan
Willis, Willie

OHIO

Andrew, Ron D.
Blood, Gordon W.
Carter, Lillie Mae Bland
Clayton, Boyd Lee
Donnelly, Phyllis Beswick

Neal, Montford Lee
Settell, Angela A. Loyola

OREGON

Pinkerton, Glen Irvin

PENNSYLVANIA

Bryant, Le Earl Ann
Edmunds, Edward Wayne
Eichenlaub, Richard Jeffrey
Lawson, Barbara A.
Lawson, John E.
Love, Louise Gardner
Shepard, Charles Virgil
Williams, Susan Diane

UTAH

Autrey, C. E.
Bye, Raymond Sigurd
Sweeney, James Edward

VERMONT

Sexauer, Arwin F.B.G.

WYOMING

Colburn, Bettye Vaughn

The **State-Locator Index** is one of the Institute's newest and most functional publication innovations. This **Index** guarantees easy accessibility of all individuals listed in this publication, presented according to alphabetical positions by separate states.

Appendix II

Honorary Editorial Advisory Board
American Biographical Institute

Laura Elizabeth Beverly, F.A.B.I.
Hempstead, New York

Professor of Special Education, Board of Cooperative Educational Services,
Nassau County, New York
Researcher, Educator, Consultant

B. Everard Blanchard, Ph.D., D.D.
Villa Park, Illinois

President, Villa Educational Research Associates
Researcher, Educational Administrator, Author

Louise Boggess
San Mateo, California

Free-Lance Writer, Lecturer, Educator

Irving Brazinsky, D.S., F.A.B.I.
Matawan, New Jersey

Senior Research and Development Engineer, Halcon ROD Corporation
Researcher, Educator, Author

Arnold Brekke, Ph.D., F.A.B.I.
St. Paul, Minnesota

Consultant and Proprietor, Brekke Knowledge-Resources Creation-
Production Enterprises
Researcher, Scientist, Educator, Lecturer, Consultant, Inventor

Charlotte Mae Brett, M.A., F.A.B.I., L.F.A.B.I.
Spencer, Iowa

Retired Educator, Family Genealogist

Juanita Sumner Brightwell, F.A.B.I.
Americus, Georgia

Retired Director of Library Services, Lake Blackshear Regional Library,
Americus; Former President, Georgia Library Association
Researcher, Administrator, Librarian

Sylvia Leigh Bryant, F.I.B.A., L.A.A.B.I.
Madison Heights, Virginia

Editor-Publisher, *The Anthology Society*
Poet, Free-Lance Writer, Editor

Frederick D. Byington, Ed.D., F.A.B.I.
Philadelphia, Pennsylvania

Director, Byton Private School, Philadelphia
Administrator, Educator, Consultant

Laura Elizabeth Beverly, F.A.B.I.
Hempstead, New York

Professor of Special Education, Board of Cooperative Educational Services, Nassau County, New York
Researcher, Educator, Consultant

B. Everard Blanchard, Ph.D., D.D.
Villa Park, Illinois

President, Villa Educational Research Associates
Researcher, Educational Administrator, Author

Louise Boggess
San Mateo, California

Free-Lance Writer, Lecturer, Educator

Irving Brazinsky, D.S., F.A.B.I.
Matawan, New Jersey

Senior Research and Development Engineer, Halcon ROD Corporation
Researcher, Educator, Author

Arnold Brekke, Ph.D., F.A.B.I.
St. Paul, Minnesota

Consultant and Proprietor, Brekke Knowledge-Resources Creation-Production Enterprises
Researcher, Scientist, Educator, Lecturer, Consultant, Inventor

Charlotte Mae Brett, M.A., F.A.B.I., L.F.A.B.I.
Spencer, Iowa

Retired Educator, Family Genealogist

Juanita Sumner Brightwell, F.A.B.I.
Americus, Georgia

Retired Director ot Library Services, Lake Blackshear Regional Library, Americus; Former President, Georgia Library Association
Researcher, Administrator, Librarian

Sylvia Leigh Bryant, F.I.B.A., L.A.A.B.I.
Madison Heights, Virginia

Editor-Publisher, *The Anthology Society*
Poet, Free-Lance Writer, Editor

Frederick D. Byington, Ed.D., F.A.B.I.
Philadelphia, Pennsylvania

Director, Byton Private School, Philadelphia
Administrator, Educator, Consultant

Juan B. Calatayud, M.D., F.A.C.A.
Washington, D.C.

Professor, George Washington University School of Medicine;
Private Physician

Joseph Peter Cangemi, M.D., F.A.C.A.
Bowling Green, Kentucky

Professor of Psychology, Western Kentucky University
Management Consultant, Researcher, Educator

Avery G. Church, F.A.A.A., F.A.B.I., F.I.A.P.
Mobile, Alabama

Research Staff and Board of Directors, The Sociological and Anthropological
Services Institute, Inc.; Lecturer in Anthropology, University of Southern
Alabama
Educator, Scientist, Poet

C. Eugene Coke, Ph.D.
F.R.S.C., F.A.B.I., F.S.D.C., F.T.I., F.C.I.C.
Ormond Beach, Florida

President, Coke and Associate Consultants
Researcher, Author, Scientist, International Authority on Man-Made Fibers

James F. L. Connell, Ph.D., C.P.G.
Montevallo, Alabama

Professor of Geology and Geography; Independent Consulting Geologist

Grover F. Daussman, Ph.D.
Huntsville, Alabama

Engineering Consultant; Former United States Government Engineer

Elias D. Dekazos, Ph.D.
Athens, Georgia

Plant Physiologist, R. Russell Agriculture Research Center

Veena B. Desai, M.D.
M.R.C.O.G., F.A.C.O.G., F.A.C.S., F.I.C.S.
Portsmouth, New Hampshire

Private Practice of Obstetrics and Gynecology

The Prince Vladimir E. Doggett-Eletsky
Riverside, California

President, Doggett and Doggett Enterprises
Business Executive

Mildred C. Dugan, M.D.
Fort Worth, Texas
Physician

James Don Edwards, Ph.D.
Athens, Georgia
J. M. Tull Professor of Accounting, University of Georgia
Researcher, Educator

Henri C. Flesher, Ph.D., D.D., F.A.B.I.
Eloy, Arizona
Retired Publisher and Journalist

Sandra Fowler, F.A.B.I., L.A.A.B.I.
West Columbia, West Virginia
Associate Editor, *Ocarina* and *The Album*
Editor, Publisher

Lorraine S. Gall, Ph.D., F.A.B.I.
Houston, Texas
Senior Microbiological Consultant, Private Business
Researcher, Space Scientist, Educator

Carrie Leigh George, Ph.D., M.Div., Ed.S., D.Rel.
Atlanta, Georgia
Senior Counselor and Assistant Professor of Curriculum and Instruction,
Georgia State University; Ordained Clergywoman
Researcher, Consultant, Educator

Vivian W. Giles
Danville, Virginia
Owner-Manager, Vivian Giles Business Services

Antonio Giraudier, F.A.B.I., L.P.A.B.I.
New York City, New York
Writer, Author, Poet, Artist

Admiral A. B. Hammett
Fort Lauderdale, Florida
Retired United States Naval Reserve Commander

Marjorie S. Hooper, L.H.D., L.F.A.B.I.
Dunedin, Florida
Retired Research Associate for Visual Disabilities Track of the College of
Education, Florida State University; Former Editor, American Printing House
for the Blind
Researcher, Editor/Publisher Management and Production

Lewis Daniel Houck, Jr., Ph.D., L.F.I.B.A., F.A.B.I.
Kensington, Maryland

Project Leader for Economic Research Service,
United States Department of Agriculture
Economic Researcher and Consultant, Author, Educator, Businessman

Edwin M. Hughes, Ed.D., F.I.B.A., F.A.B.I.
Searcy, Arkansas

Private Psychology Practice; Executive Secretary, Arkansas Board of
Examiners in Psychology
Researcher, Educator

Geraldine Grosvenor Hunnewell,
F.I.B.A., F.A.B.I., A.F.S., F.T.L.A., F.I.P.A.
Sunland, California

Researcher, Naturalist, Author, Scholar

Anna M. Jackson, Ph.D., A.B.P.P., F.A.B.I.
Lakewood, Colorado

Director of Medical Student Advisory Office and Associate Professor of
Psychiatry, University of Colorado; Clinical Psychologist
Researcher, Educator

Myrtle J. Jones, L.A.A.B.I.
Rome, Georgia

Retired Assistant Professor of English, Floyd Junior College
Researcher, Educator

Greta Kempton, F.A.B.I.
New York City, New York

National Portrait Artist

Catherine Earl Bailey Kerr, L.P.A.B.I.
Roswell, New Mexico

Owner-Manager, Kerr International School of Art
International Artist

Mozelle Bigelow Kraus, Ed.D., L.A.A.B.I.
Washington, D.C.

Private Psychology Practice

Rev. Dr. Violet Joan Krech-Cisowski
Chicago, Illinois

Consultant, Educator, Prophetess

Barbara Lacy
Barstow, California
Librarian, U.S. Army

Enrique Roberto Larde, M.G.A., F.A.B.I.
Old San Juan, Puerto Rico

Director and Treasurer, South Continental Insurance Agency, Inc.; Director
and Executive Vice President, Corporacion Insular de Seguros; Director and
First Vice President, Asociacion de Companias de Seguros Incorporadas en
Puerto Rico, Inc.
Researcher, Business Executive

Shu-Tien Li, Ph.D., P.E., Eng.D.
F.A.S.C.E., F.A.A.A.S., F.A.C.I.
Orange, California

Founder and President, Li Institution of Science and Technology; President,
World Open University
Researcher, Educator, Administrator, Consultant

Florence E. H. Little, F.I.B.A, F.A.B.I., L.F.A.B.I.
La Place, Louisiana

Genealogist, Educator, Musician

Ruby E. Stutts Lyells, L.H.D.
Jackson, Mississippi

Federal Jury Commissioner, United States District Court, Southern District of
Mississippi; Trustee, Prentiss Institute
Researcher, Writer, Librarian

Krishna Shankar Manudhane, Ph.D., F.A.B.I.
Cincinnati, Ohio

Director of Product Development Department, ICN Pharmaceuticals, Inc.
Researcher

Robert C. McGee, Jr., F.A.B.I.
Richmond, Virginia

President, Swan, Inc.
Business Executive, Aeronautical Engineer, Consultant, Administrator

Rod McKuen
Beverly Hills, California

Poet, Composer-Lyricist, Author, Performer
President: Stanyan Records, Discus New Gramophone Society, Mr. Kelly
Productions, Montcalm Productions, Stanyan Books, Cheval Books, Biplane
Books, Rod McKuen Enterprises

1

M. S. Megahed, M.D., F.R.C.P., F.A.B.I.
North Tonawanda, New York

Private Neurological Practive; Former Physician to King Saud of Saudi Arabia
Researcher, Professional Authorships

Mildred M. Milazzo, F.A.B.I.
Vienna, Virginia

Research Analyst, Author, Former Fiscal Analyst, United States Department
of Health, Education, and Welfare

Martha Joy Mitchell, F.A.B.I.
Nashville, Tennessee

Head Librarian, Franklin High School, Nashville
Researcher

Herbert B. Mobley, D.D., L.P.A.B.I.
Summit Station, Pennsylvania

President and Editor-in-Chief, Jan-Bert Press, Inc.; Emeritus Pastor, St.
Mark's (Brown's) United Church of Christ, Summit Station

Irving Morris, M.L.S., F.A.B.I.
Long Island City, New York

Educator and Library Media Specialist, L. D. Brandeis High School Annex,
New York City

Makio Murayama, Ph.D.
Bethesda, Maryland

Research Biochemist, National Institute of Health

Virginia Simmons Nyabongo, Ph.D.
Nashville, Tennessee

Professor of French, Tennessee State University
Researcher, Author, Educator

George Robert Overby, Ph.D., F.A.B.I., L.P.A.B.I.
Orlando, Florida

Chancellor, Freedom University; Founder, President, The International
Association of Christian Education
Author, Lecturer, Consultant, Educator

D. C. Parks, F.A.B.I.
Bakersfield, California

Founder, President, Addictive Drugs Educational Foundation
Consultant, Counselor, Analyst

Elizabeth Marie Polley, L.F.I.B.A., L.F.A.B.I.
Vallejo, California
Art Consultant, Journalist, Artist

Sartell Prentice, Jr.
Pasadena, California
Independent Lecturer and Consultant on Incentive Employee Profit Sharing
Plans

Jarnagin Bernard Ricks, F.A.B.I.
Shreveport, Louisiana
Writer, Composer, Professional Astrologer, International Clairvoyant

Roland B. Scott, M.D.
Washington, D.C.
Professor of Pediatrics and Child Health and Director Sickle Cell Center,
Howard University
Educator, Administrator

Vera Estelle Sellars-Colyer
Grandfield, Oklahoma
President-Agent, Colyer Insurance Agency, Inc.

Delphia Frazier Smith, F.I.P.S.
Mammoth Spring, Arkansas
Writer, Poet, Artist, Musician

Herbert H. Tarson, Ph.D., F.A.B.I.
La Mesa, California
Vice President for Academic Affairs, National University, San Diego
Researcher, Educator

General Wayne C. Temple, Ph.D.
Springfield, Illinois
Deputy Director, Illinois State Archives; Lt. General in Illinois State Militia
Researcher, Author, Archivist

Andrew B. Thompson, Jr., F.I.B.A., L.A.A.B.I.
Montgomery, Alabama
Vice President, General Manager, Editor, National Photo Pricing Service,
Inc.

Basil P. Toutorsky, D.Mus., L.P.A.B.I., F.A.B.I., L.F.I.B.A.
Washington, D.C.
Director, Toutorsky Academy of Music
Professor, Composer, Pianist

Aliyah W. M. von Nussbaumer, Ph.D., D.Th.
Houston, Texas
Research Librarian, Published Author, Educator

Marian Williams, L.F.A.B.I.
Lakewood, Ohio
Free-Lance Writer and Poet, Researcher

Roger Lodge Wolcott
Atwater, Ohio
Former Specialist in Aeromechanical Research and Development,
Engineering Department, Goodyear Aerospace Corporation, Akron;
Secretary, The Lighter Than Air Society
Aviation Pioneer, Inventor, Association Executive

Stella Woodall, D.Lit., F.A.B.I.
Junction, Texas
President-Director, Stella Woodall Poetry Society International; Editor-
Publisher, *Adventures in Poetry Magazine*
Author, Editor, Publisher, Poet

Dr. Howard John Zitko
Tucson, Arizona
President and Chairman of the Board, World University